SALARY FACTS

FACTS

Handbook

The Definitive Source of Pay Information on 800 Jobs

The Editors @ JIST

JIST Works
America's Career Publisher

Salary Facts Handbook
The Definitive Source of Pay Information on 800 Jobs

© 2008 by JIST Publishing

Published by JIST Works, an imprint of JIST Publishing
7321 Shadeland Station, Suite 200
Indianapolis, Indiana 46256-3923

Phone: 800-648-JIST   Fax: 877-454-7839
E-mail: info@jist.com   Web site: www.jist.com

Some Other Books by the Editors at JIST

EZ Occupational Outlook Handbook
Health-Care CareerVision Book and DVD
200 Best Jobs for Introverts

150 Best Jobs for a Better World
Enhanced Occupational Outlook Handbook
Guide to America's Federal Jobs

Quantity discounts are available for JIST products. Have future editions of JIST books automatically delivered to you on publication through our convenient standing order program. Please call 800-648-JIST or visit www.jist.com for a free catalog and more information.

Visit www.jist.com for information on JIST, free job search information, tables of contents and sample pages, and ordering information on our many products.

Acquisitions Editor: Susan Pines
Writer and Database Work: Laurence Shatkin, Ph.D.
Development Editor: Stephanie Koutek
Cover and Interior Designer: Marie Kristine Parial-Leonardo
Cover Photo Credits: Adam Gault/Digital Vision/Getty Images; Jack Hollingsworth/redchopsticks/Getty Images
Interior Layout: Marie Kristine Parial-Leonardo
Proofreaders: Paula Lowell, Jeanne Clark

Printed in the United States of America

12 11 10 09 08 07   9 8 7 6 5 4 3 2 1

Library of Congress Cataloging-in-Publication Data
Salary facts handbook : the definitive source of pay information on 800 jobs / The Editors at JIST.
    p. cm.
Includes index.
ISBN 978-1-59357-515-1 (softcover : alk. paper) -- ISBN 978-1-59357-516-8 (hardcover : alk. paper)
1. Wages--United States--Handbooks, manuals, etc. 2. Professional employees--Salaries, etc.--United States--Handbooks, manuals, etc. 3. Occupations--United States--Handbooks, manuals, etc. 4. Vocational guidance--United States--Handbooks, manuals, etc. I. JIST Works, Inc.
HD4975.S253 2008
331.2'8--dc22

                                                    2007043023

ISBN 978-1-59357-515-1 softcover
ISBN 978-1-59357-516-8 hardcover

Earn the Pay You Deserve

What level of pay do you deserve? Like everything else in economics, it depends on the market, but many workers have only a vague idea of what similar workers are being paid. This book can give you detailed information about what people are being paid for the kind of work you do.

You'll find authoritative wage figures from the U.S. Department of Labor and the Census Bureau for 800 occupations based on a survey of 1.2 million businesses: Not just national averages, but also figures for states, major metropolitan areas, and different industries. Not just one-size-fits-all figures, but also adjustment factors you can use to help fit your salary expectations to your actual situation. See the earnings effect of your level of education, gender, or veteran status. See what beginning workers are earning and what the best-paid 10 percent bring home.

This book will give you ideas about how to improve your earnings by getting further education, moving to a new location, or shifting to a higher-powered industry. If you're still planning your career, you will find lists that compare jobs, industries, and locations by salaries so you can target the most promising choices.

Ultimately, your pay depends on an agreement between you and your employer. Use this book to learn specific strategies and tips to help you negotiate the best possible salary. Avoid the traps that let interviewers screen you out of a job and use techniques that can persuade employers to pay you more than they may have intended.

Unless you're planning to work as a volunteer, you need this book to be sure you're getting the best possible wage.

Some Things You Can Do with This Book

- Develop long-term career plans for a good-paying job.
- Identify jobs, industries, or locations where you can earn better wages than you're getting now.
- Develop plans to improve your earnings by getting additional education or training.
- Ask for a raise based on the average salary for your job in your metropolitan area.
- Prepare for interviews and salary negotiations by learning strategies for handling discussions of salary.

These are a few of the many ways you can use this book. We hope you find it as interesting to browse as we did to put together. We have tried to make it easy to use and as interesting as occupational information can be.

When you are done with this book, pass it along or tell someone else about it. We wish you well in your career and in your life.

Credits and Acknowledgments

While the authors created this book, it is based on the work of many others. The occupational information is based on data obtained from the U.S. Department of Labor and the U.S. Census Bureau. These sources provide the most authoritative occupational information available. The job titles and their related descriptions are from the Standard Occupational Classification taxonomy, which was developed by researchers and developers under the direction of the U.S. Department of Labor. They, in turn, were assisted by thousands of employers who provided details on the nature of work in the many thousands of job samplings used in the taxonomy's development.

Table of Contents

Summary of Major Sections

Introduction. A short overview to help you better understand and use the book. *Starts on page 1.*

Part I. Tips for the Best Salary. Learn how to boost your earnings. Identifies the factors that affect earnings: education, location, industry, labor unions, veteran status, gender, and work hours. Explains how to leverage your knowledge and skills for better pay in your present job or in a new occupation. Gives specific tips for negotiating your pay, including the overall strategy, useful information to have for the interview, negotiating during the interview, and responding to a job offer. *Starts on page 9.*

Part II. Pay Rankings of Jobs, Industries, and Locations. Compares jobs by ranking them according to their earnings. Lists are organized in several useful ways, such as the highest-paying jobs at each level of education or training and the highest-paying jobs in each industry. Also ranks industries, states, and metropolitan areas by their average pay. From these lists you may get ideas about jobs or industries to consider or places where you might relocate. *Starts on page 17.*

Part III. Salary Facts. Provides detailed salary facts about 800 occupations: national wages at several different levels; best-paying industries; wages in the 50 states and the 30 metropolitan areas with the biggest workforces; and income effects of personal factors such as level of education, gender, and veteran status. Information is based on authoritative government surveys. *Starts on page 67.*

Part IV. Frequently Asked Questions About Salary. Answers many common questions about pay, such as who does and does not qualify for minimum wage or overtime pay, how much of your pay can be based on commissions, and what severance pay and hazard pay are. *Starts on page 869*

Appendix A. Resources for Further Exploration. Lists several helpful resources for researching the facts about pay and jobs and for learning how to conduct a successful job hunt. *Starts on page 873.*

Appendix B. Salary Adjustment Percentages for All Metropolitan Areas. Provides percentages that you can use to adjust national average income figures upward or downward to match local income levels. *Starts on page 875.*

Appendix C. Names of Metropolitan Areas Used in This Book. Provides the official names for the metropolitan areas referred to in Part III. *Starts on page 879.*

Index. *Starts on page 880.*

Detailed Table of Contents

Introduction

It's only fair that you should get the pay you deserve, but there's no simple way to determine what your pay should be. Employers make pay decisions based on many factors, including your skills, your experience, your formal credentials, and your attitude toward the job.

But above all, employers need to consider what other employers are paying. Just like motorists filling up at the gas station, shoppers buying fruit at the grocery store, or people renting an apartment, employers must pay roughly the same price for the same kind of merchandise. Unless there's nobody else who can do your job, your labor is offered in the context of a labor market, so employers who are buying your labor need to pay a price reasonably close to the going rate.

This book can help you learn what employers are paying people working in jobs like yours—or in jobs you're considering. And it can give you useful strategies for boosting your pay.

How Much Are Other People Earning?

Of all the working people in the United States, about 7.5 percent are self-employed and roughly 4.5 percent are unemployed. The remaining workers—almost 90 percent—are wage earners or salary earners. There are about 130 million of these paid workers, and they are the focus of this book.

In this book we use the terms "wage" and "salary" interchangeably, but labor laws make a distinction. Wage earners are paid by the amount of time (hours or days) they work, and they may get paid at a higher rate for any overtime hours they work. Tips may be an important part of their income. Salary earners, on the other hand, are paid a regular annual sum and do not get overtime pay for putting in extra hours to handle heavy workloads that may develop from time to time. However, they may earn bonuses or commissions on top of their base salary rate.

Almost all workers get additional compensation known as fringe benefits—for example, health care insurance, retirement funds, vacation time, a uniform to wear at work, or use of a company car. These benefits vary widely depending on employers, and sometimes they are hard to measure in dollar terms, so figures on the fringe benefits of various occupations are not readily available.

However, the U.S. Department of Labor provides extensive reports on the dollar figures for earnings in various occupations and industries. For all paid workers, the median earning figure in 2006—meaning that half earned more, half less—was $30,400. The 25th percentile was $20,270 and the 75th percentile was $47,820; 50 percent of workers fall between these two wage figures. Looking at the low and high ends of the distribution, we find that only 10 percent of workers earned less than $15,500 (the 10th percentile figure), and only 10 percent of workers earned more than $72,960 (the 90th percentile figure). See Figure 1 for a graphic representation of the distribution of wages.

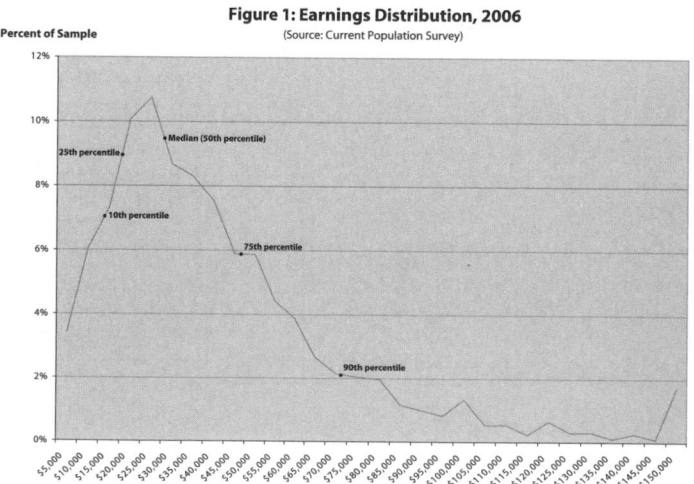

Figure 1: Earnings Distribution, 2006
(Source: Current Population Survey)

Percent of Sample

25th percentile
Median (50th percentile)
10th percentile
75th percentile
90th percentile

1

The general trend in wage and salary earnings is a modest increase—a little more than three percent increase each year in the average for all workers. In fact, this increase is so modest that it is not keeping up with increases in the cost of living. For example, between December 2006 and the previous December, wages for all civilian workers increased by only 3.4 percent, whereas the price of residential electric power increased by 5.8 percent and the price of gasoline increased by 7.0 percent. That means that, unless your pay increases are doing better than average, you are losing ground.

Some people boost their wages at a better rate than the average by acquiring new skills and getting promoted. Others work harder at their job and have a work arrangement, such as being paid on commission, that rewards their increased productivity. Perhaps the most dramatic way to increase your pay is to move into a better-paying occupation—and this book may give you some ideas about what occupations to consider. (The lists in Part II are especially relevant.) Of course, you can also find ways to earn extra cash outside your regular job, such as taking on a second job part time; making smart investments; or starting a small home-based business, such as trading collectibles on eBay.

How Can I Use the Information in This Book?

Did you ever fill up your car with gasoline and then feel regret when you spotted another gas station selling at a lower price per gallon? Although gas prices in any market are roughly the same, price differences can always be found. As you drive around your own town each day, you learn the current average price of gas and which gas stations tend to charge more or less than the average. When you're in an unfamiliar town, however, you don't have that knowledge of the gasoline market.

The salary market can be even harder to figure out. Unlike the prices posted prominently at filling stations, pay figures may be jealously guarded by employers. Classified ads or job postings on the Internet often use unenlightening phrases such as "Salary commensurate with experience" rather than useful figures. And if employers are reluctant to divulge wage figures, workers are even more closemouthed. It's considered bad manners to ask people how much they're earning—or to brag about how much you're earning.

That's why the facts in this book can be particularly useful. You can use them for several different purposes.

What Pay Is Appropriate for What I'm Now Doing?

If you know what other people are earning for what you're now doing, you'll be better able to negotiate your pay with your current boss or with a new employer for the same kind of work. So look up what Part III of this book says about the

job that is closest to your present position. Find your job title in the index or in the table of contents, which groups similar jobs together.

In Part III you'll find several figures that can help you decide on an appropriate wage: average figures, the range of the wages most commonly paid, and figures near the lower and upper extremes. You also can find the going rates for the industry where you're working, for your state, and for your metropolitan area. (If you don't live in or near one of the 30 metro areas shown there, turn to Appendix B, find your metro area, and use the accompanying percentage figure to adjust the national average figures upward or downward to reflect wage trends where you live.) Finally, you can see how earnings are affected by several other factors, such as your level of education, your sex, and your veteran status. (Later in this introduction you'll see a sample Part III entry for an occupation and an explanation of how to interpret the various data elements.)

Once you've considered where you are in your career, where you are geographically, and several other aspects of your situation, you can use the relevant figures in Part III to adjust your earnings expectations upward or downward from the averages. You may find that you're not earning as much as comparable workers—or conversely, that you're being paid well compared to the going rate. Either finding is good to know. With this knowledge, you can work out a strategy for getting the highest wage that's reasonably possible for someone in your circumstances, or you can decide how to change your circumstances to improve your earnings.

In Part I you'll find useful tips for how to negotiate your salary. Together with the facts from Part III, these strategies may help you convince your boss that you deserve a raise. Or they may convince you that your present pay is as high as you can expect in your present position and that to improve your pay you'll need to move on—to another job, another location, another industry, or even another occupation.

If you do decide to move on, or if you're *already* thinking that way, or if you're young and still planning your career, the lists in Part II can inform you about the comparative pay in various jobs, locations, and industries.

What Pay Might I Expect If I Changed Location or Industry?

If you're willing to consider relocation but want to remain in your present occupation, the wage figures in Part III for states and metropolitan areas—and the percentage figures for metropolitan areas in Appendix B—may indicate where the pay is better than in your present community. Compare the average wage figures for your state and for other states where you'd consider relocating. Do the same for metropolitan areas. If you're not yet in college but have a definite career goal, use this information to help you decide which colleges to apply for. Even colleges with a national reputation usually have the best hiring connections with employers in their geographical area.

Keep in mind that geographical areas that offer higher salaries often have higher costs of living. Before deciding to relocate, you'll want to investigate how costs compare, especially rental rates or home prices, so you can judge whether moving will actually improve your standard of living.

Part III also shows the 10 best-paying industries for each of the 800 jobs listed there. If you have flexible skills, you may consider looking for work with an employer in a better-paying field. Or if you're still in school, you might use this information to help you plan a concentration within your major.

What Pay Might I Expect in Various Careers?

Maybe you're considering pay as part of a career decision. Whether you're a young person planning your education, a person considering a career change in your middle years, or an older person planning for work in retirement, potential pay is probably an important factor in your career choice.

This book can be useful because it covers such a broad range of occupations. By browsing the lists in Part II and comparing jobs in terms of their average earnings, you can identify career goals that offer the level of pay you want. You can look at the list of all occupations or the more-specialized lists. For example, if you are planning to get a bachelor's degree, you may want to look at the list of the jobs for which that is the normal educational requirement; the list is ordered with the best-paying jobs at the top. If you are nearing retirement and are considering part-time work, you will be interested in the list of the 20 best-paying jobs held by part-time workers.

If you already have an occupation in mind, or if Part II inspires you to explore one in greater depth, it's time to look at the detailed earnings figures in Part III. Find the job in the index or in the table of contents, which is ordered into easy-to-understand groups such as management jobs, business jobs, health-care jobs, and construction jobs. Then turn to the appropriate page in Part III and browse the wealth of salary facts—average earnings, high and low earning ranges, earnings in various geographical locations and industries, and the effects on earnings of various factors such as level of education. (The next section of this introduction describes the Part III information topics in detail and shows a sample entry.)

Of course, when you make a career choice you need to consider more than just the earnings. This book does not have room for in-depth job descriptions, but for every job Part III includes a brief definition, a statement of the level of education or training required, and figures that indicate the rate of job growth and the number of annual job openings. These facts can help you make a preliminary decision about whether the job is worth investigating further. If it is worth exploring, see Appendix A for suggested resources to use.

What Information Does This Book Contain?

Part I discusses the factors that affect your earnings and outlines some strategies for boosting your income, including tips for negotiating your salary. Part IV answers some frequently asked questions about salary.

But what makes this book unique is the wealth of information in Parts II and III on the earnings in various jobs, industries, and locations. The information is developed from the most recent statistics compiled by the Bureau of Labor Statistics (U.S. Department of Labor) and by the Bureau of the Census (U.S. Department of Commerce).

The information in Part II consists of lists—for example, the 15 best-paying jobs in each state. Each list or set of lists begins with an introduction that explains the contents that follow, and all lists are ordered from highest-paying to lowest-paying.

Salary Facts in Part III

Part III consists of 800 entries with salary facts about individual occupations. This list and the sample entry from Part III on the next page explain the topics we cover for each of the 800 jobs:

- **Job Number and Title.** This is the information for the job used in the Standard Occupational Classification, the scheme that all branches of the federal government use for naming and classifying jobs.

- **Definition.** This summary of job duties is also derived from the SOC taxonomy. Because you may know (or hold) the job under a different name, the definition can help you decide whether the job featured in this entry is the one you have in mind.

- **Education or Training Required.** This is the level of education most commonly required for the job, as determined by the Bureau of Labor Statistics (BLS). In some cases, licensing requirements set this level by law. In other cases, the level reflects the current preference of employers. If you are making a career decision, this information can help you decide whether this job appeals to you. It also may help differentiate the job from a similar job that requires a different level of preparation.

- **Job Growth.** This figure represents how much the workforce for the occupation will grow between 2004 and 2014, according to the projections of the BLS. The average (mean) growth projected for all occupations is 13.0 percent.

- **Annual Openings.** This figure is the estimated number of annual job openings, again for the decade between 2004 and 2014, as projected by the BLS. The average for all occupations is about 35,000 job openings per year.

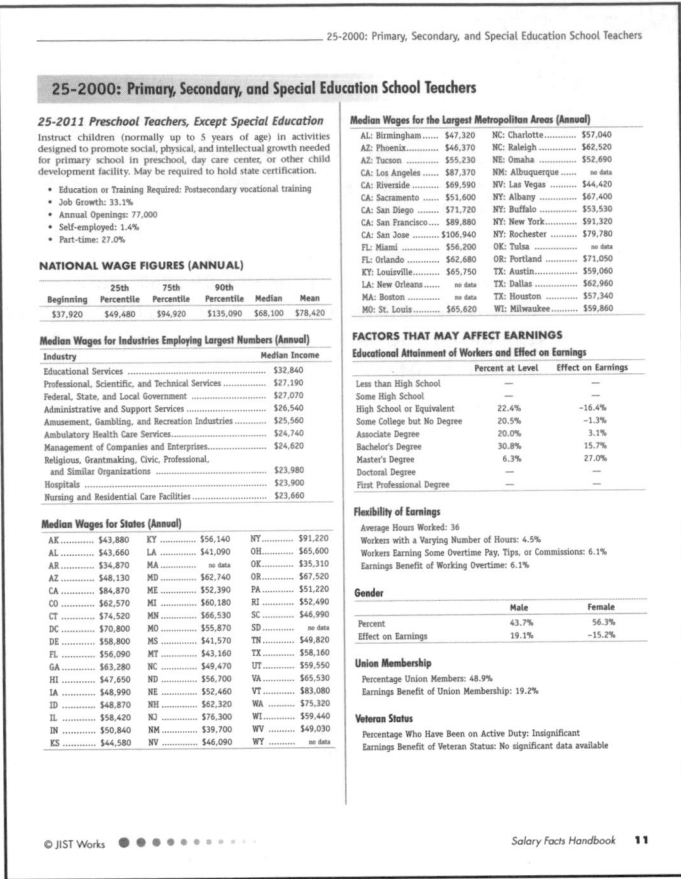

25-2000: Primary, Secondary, and Special Education School Teachers

25-2011 Preschool Teachers, Except Special Education
Instruct children (normally up to 5 years of age) in activities designed to promote social, physical, and intellectual growth needed for primary school in preschool, day care center, or other child development facility. May be required to hold state certification.

- Education or Training Required: Postsecondary vocational training
- Job Growth: 33.1%
- Annual Openings: 77,000
- Self-employed: 1.4%
- Part-time: 27.0%

NATIONAL WAGE FIGURES (ANNUAL)

Beginning	25th Percentile	75th Percentile	90th Percentile	Median	Mean
$37,920	$49,480	$94,920	$135,090	$68,100	$78,420

Median Wages for Industries Employing Largest Numbers (Annual)

Industry	Median Income
Educational Services	$32,840
Professional, Scientific, and Technical Services	$27,190
Federal, State, and Local Government	$27,070
Administrative and Support Services	$26,540
Amusement, Gambling, and Recreation Industries	$25,560
Ambulatory Health Care Services	$24,740
Management of Companies and Enterprises	$24,620
Religious, Grantmaking, Civic, Professional, and Similar Organizations	$23,980
Hospitals	$23,900
Nursing and Residential Care Facilities	$23,660

Median Wages for States (Annual)

AK	$43,880	KY	$56,140	NY	$91,220
AL	$43,660	LA	$41,090	OH	$65,600
AR	$34,870	MA	no data	OK	$35,310
AZ	$48,130	MD	$62,740	OR	$67,520
CA	$84,870	ME	$52,390	PA	$51,220
CO	$62,570	MI	$60,180	RI	$52,490
CT	$74,520	MN	$66,530	SC	$46,990
DC	$70,800	MO	$55,870	SD	no data
DE	$58,800	MS	$41,570	TN	$49,820
FL	$56,090	MT	$43,160	TX	$58,160
GA	$63,280	NC	$49,470	UT	$59,550
HI	$47,650	ND	$56,700	VA	$65,530
IA	$48,990	NE	$52,460	VT	$83,080
ID	$48,870	NH	$62,320	WA	$75,320
IL	$58,420	NJ	$76,300	WI	$59,440
IN	$50,840	NM	$39,700	WV	$49,030
KS	$44,580	NV	$46,090	WY	no data

Median Wages for the Largest Metropolitan Areas (Annual)

AL: Birmingham	$47,320	NC: Charlotte	$57,040
AZ: Phoenix	$46,370	NC: Raleigh	$62,520
AZ: Tucson	$55,230	NE: Omaha	$52,690
CA: Los Angeles	$87,370	NM: Albuquerque	no data
CA: Riverside	$69,590	NV: Las Vegas	$44,420
CA: Sacramento	$51,600	NY: Albany	$67,400
CA: San Diego	$71,720	NY: Buffalo	$53,530
CA: San Francisco	$89,880	NY: New York	$91,320
CA: San Jose	$106,940	NY: Rochester	$79,780
FL: Miami	$56,200	OK: Tulsa	no data
FL: Orlando	$62,680	OR: Portland	$71,050
KY: Louisville	$65,750	TX: Austin	$59,060
LA: New Orleans	no data	TX: Dallas	$62,960
MA: Boston	no data	TX: Houston	$57,340
MO: St. Louis	$65,620	WI: Milwaukee	$59,860

FACTORS THAT MAY AFFECT EARNINGS

Educational Attainment of Workers and Effect on Earnings

	Percent at Level	Effect on Earnings
Less than High School	—	—
Some High School	—	—
High School or Equivalent	22.4%	-16.4%
Some College but No Degree	20.5%	-1.3%
Associate Degree	20.0%	3.1%
Bachelor's Degree	30.8%	15.7%
Master's Degree	6.3%	27.0%
Doctoral Degree	—	—
First Professional Degree	—	—

Flexibility of Earnings
Average Hours Worked: 36
Workers with a Varying Number of Hours: 4.5%
Workers Earning Some Overtime Pay, Tips, or Commissions: 6.1%
Earnings Benefit of Working Overtime: 6.1%

Gender

	Male	Female
Percent	43.7%	56.3%
Effect on Earnings	19.1%	-15.2%

Union Membership
Percentage Union Members: 48.9%
Earnings Benefit of Union Membership: 19.2%

Veteran Status
Percentage Who Have Been on Active Duty: Insignificant
Earnings Benefit of Veteran Status: No significant data available

---

- **Self-Employed.** This figure shows the portion of the workforce that is self-employed, according to the BLS. For all occupations, the average is a bit more than 10 percent. If this figure is more than 30 percent, you'll find a note to remind you that the earnings figures reported in this book do not reflect self-employed workers. In many cases, however, this note provides an estimate of average self-employment earnings for the occupation, based on the Current Population Survey. The CPS is a survey program that the BLS conducts on behalf of the Bureau of the Census; its methods are described in greater detail later in this introduction.

- **Part-Time.** This figure shows the percentage of part-time workers in the occupation, according to the Current Population Survey. About 27 percent of all workers are part time.

- **National Wage Figures.** The dollar figures under this heading, like all dollar figures in this book, are wage estimates for May 2006. (This is the most recent data that was available at the time this book was written.) A later section of this introduction, called "Where Does the Information Come From?," discusses how these estimates are compiled and what kinds of pay they include and do not include. The heading indicates whether these figures represent annual or hourly pay. Hourly pay is reported for only a few occupations, such as Actors and Dancers, in which workers rarely can expect to work every week.

- **Beginning.** This figure represents the level of pay that exceeds the earnings of the lowest-paid 10 percent of workers (the tenth percentile). This serves as a rough estimate of what beginning workers may be paid. It is possible that a beginning worker with unusual credentials or skills may be paid a higher wage. For example, some beginning workers may have relevant experience in a related occupation that boosts their earnings. On the other hand, if this figure is close to the minimum wage (currently a little below $11,000 under federal law), it is also possible that low-skilled workers may be stuck at a wage close to this figure for several years and may have few chances to improve their earnings other than leaving the occupation for a better-paying one.

- **25th Percentile.** One-quarter of all workers earn less than this amount. (Figure 1, earlier in this introduction, illustrates the distribution of earnings in 2006 and shows the percentile levels that are used in this book.)

- **Median and Mean.** These figures are commonly used as indications of the "average" earnings in the job. They are discussed in greater detail in the next section of this introduction.

- **75th Percentile.** One-quarter of all workers earn more than this amount. The 25th percentile and the 75th percentile are useful for giving a sense of the range of income levels because half of all workers have earnings that fall between these two levels. Most workers who have some years of experience in the occupation but no outstanding skills or other powerful wage-boosting factors have earnings that fall within this range.

- **90th Percentile.** This figure indicates the level of pay that exceeds what 90 percent of workers are paid. Although only a small number of workers reach this level of pay, it gives you an idea of the wage potential of the job. A few workers may earn much more.

- **Median Wages for Industries Employing Largest Numbers.** The industries referred to here are derived from the North American Industry Classification System (NAICS), which divides the economy into 89 industries. To create this list, we identified the 25 industries that employ the largest number of workers for the occupation; then we listed the 10 highest-paying of these industries. In cases where workers are highly concentrated in a small number of industries, fewer than 10 may be listed. The industries included are ordered from highest- to lowest-paying. It is possible that an industry employing a very small number of workers may offer a higher wage, but that usually happens when those workers have exceptional skills that are suited for that niche. For example, the lawyers who defend the Beverage and Tobacco Product Manufacturing industry against lawsuits have a median salary of $145,190, but there are only 50 of them, so this industry was not one of the 25 largest for lawyers and therefore is not listed for this occupation.

- **Median Wages for States.** The median wages for the occupation in each of the 50 states, plus the District of Columbia, are listed here. States are ordered alphabetically by their two-letter postal abbreviation, so your state's median wage appears in the same place for every job.

- **Median Wages for the Largest Metropolitan Areas.** This table lists the median wages for the occupation in the 30 metropolitan areas with the largest number of paid workers in all occupations (not necessarily the largest populations). Metro areas are ordered alphabetically by the names of the primary state and city included, although in some cases they include portions of one or more adjacent states. Most of the names of the metro areas are abbreviated; for example, the official name for the Philadelphia metro area is Philadelphia–Camden–Wilmington, PA–NJ–DE–MD. The full names of the 30 metro areas are listed in Appendix C. If you do not live in one of these metro areas, turn to Appendix B, which lists all other metro areas. Find your metro area (or the one nearest you) and make a note of the positive or negative percentage figure for local wage trends. Multiply the national wage figures by this percentage to determine roughly how much to add to or subtract from the national averages in order to compute realistic wage figures for your community.

- **Factors That May Affect Earnings.** The dollar figures given for the job are averages, but nobody is precisely average. Being a man or a woman may increase the likelihood that you'll be paid more or less than the average; so can having a certain level of education or veteran status. The topics under this heading provide percentage figures that can help you adjust average earnings figures upward or downward to reflect your situation. The information for all of these topics is derived from CPS data.

- **Educational Attainment of Workers and Effect on Earnings.** Very few occupations have ironclad educational requirements, but people who have less than the recommended amount of education tend to be paid less than better-educated workers. In addition, having more education than is normally required can boost your earnings. This table shows the percentage of workers at various levels of education and how their pay differs from the overall average by either a positive or negative percentage. These figures may inspire you to get more education or at least indicate the advantage or disadvantage of your current educational status. (The figures showing percentages of workers at each educational level may not add up to 100% because we don't report figures for levels with a very small sample size.)

- **Flexibility of Earnings.** Earnings in some jobs are highly flexible because workers' hours tend to vary from one week to the next or the workers receive tips or commissions. Under this heading you can see workers' average hours per week; the percentage of workers who report that their weekly work hours vary; the percentage of workers whose pay includes overtime pay, tips, or commissions; and a percentage figure that indicates how working longer than the average amount affects *total hourly* earnings. This last figure deserves additional explanation. Some workers have contracts that require them to be paid "time and a half" for overtime work, so putting in extra hours can boost their total hourly earnings considerably. Some other workers are paid a fixed salary no matter how many hours they work, so putting in extra hours actually *lowers* their total hourly earnings. Sometimes these uncompensated overtime workers are already earning at a lower rate. For example, new teachers are usually the lowest paid, yet they need to work the longest hours (with no extra compensation) because of their inexperience with lesson preparation; their per-hour pay thus is quite a bit lower than that of more experienced teachers.

- **Gender.** This topic shows the percentage of male and female workers in the occupation and the effect of their gender on their earnings. For most occupations female workers earn less, but this is not always the result of discrimination in the way wages are determined. In some cases the disparity results from choices female employees make about their work arrangements. For example, some women leave the workforce or work part-time hours for some years while their children are very young. In other cases comparable male and female workers may be earning similar pay, but in the past male workers have greatly outnumbered female workers; therefore, female workers are more likely to be relative newcomers who are earning less.

- **Union Membership.** Union members usually earn higher wages than nonmembers in the same occupation. This topic shows the percentage of union members in the occupation and what effect union membership has on earnings. If the number of union members is less than four percent, the percentage is given as "insignificant" and no effect on earnings is reported.

- **Veteran Status.** This topic shows the percentage of workers who have been on active duty in the military and what effect this status has on earnings. Note that people who have served in the reserves or National Guard and who have never been called up for active duty may consider themselves veterans but are not counted in this group. If the number of veterans is less than four percent, the percentage is given as "insignificant" and no effect on earnings is reported.

Why Does the Book Focus on Median Wage Figures Instead of the Mean?

No single figure can sum up all the variation of wages in an occupation. But most people want to know an "average" wage that represents the wage level for a large number of people in the occupation. It's helpful to remember that the distribution of earnings figures for most occupations follows a bell-shaped curve, and the largest concentration of workers in such a curve is near the center. In other words, the odds are greatest that your wage will come close to the wage figure at or near the center of the bell-shaped curve—the figure at the location where half earn more, half earn less. That figure is the median.

By comparison, the mean figure (the algebraic average) does not tell you as much about the wage you're likely to earn. However, *comparing* the mean to the median can be useful, because when the two figures differ significantly the distribution of wages is not typical, not bell-shaped. In such cases, the average is being thrown off by an excess of star earners or of pitifully low earners.

Here is an example that explains what can cause a big difference between median and mean. Let's say we're looking at an occupation with only seven workers, and this is how their earnings are distributed:

Worker	Annual Earnings
A	$10,000
B	$20,000
C	$30,000
D	$40,000 (median: half earn more than D, half less)
E	$50,000
F	$60,000
G	$70,000

The median wage is $40,000, and if you do the math you'll find that $40,000 is also the mean (average) wage. That makes sense because the wages are distributed very evenly here.

But let's say that worker G suddenly becomes a star and earns $400,000. The median does not change, but the mean now soars to $87,143. Having a star earner in the mix of workers creates a big gap between the median and the mean. But if you had to choose *which* figure to use to represent the income in this occupation, you'd be wise to continue to use D's earnings—the median—because most of the workers' earnings are still closer to D's level than they are to $87,143.

A real-life example is Real Estate Sales Agents. It is easy to get into this occupation but hard to be very successful. Many workers drop out after a few low-earning years or stay in the job on only a part-time basis. Only a few workers have the drive, persistence, and luck to become the outstanding sales agents in their communities, but these few earn really high incomes. Therefore, although the median wage is $39,760, the star earners pull the mean up to $54,350. Several other examples of occupations with star earners may be drawn from the media and show business: Broadcast News Analysts, Radio and Television Announcers, and Athletes and Sports Competitors.

Because a large difference between mean and median is useful to know about, this book includes a note whenever the difference is greater than 20 percent.

It's also helpful to look at the difference between the 25th and 75th percentiles—the figures that bracket the middle 50 percent—because this spread also reveals something about the distribution of earnings within the occupation. For the 800 jobs included in this book, the 75th percentile is greater than the 25th percentile by a bit more than half, on average. But for Athletes and Sports Competitors, an occupation with great variation of salaries, the 75th percentile is more than four times as high: $94,040 compared to $22,770. By contrast, several very low-paying jobs such as Dishwashers or Shampooers have narrow brackets because workers are paid at the minimum wage (or lower) and few ever get raises; people who want to earn more find a different type of work.

Where Does the Information Come From?

The earnings data for this book comes from the most authoritative source available: the Occupational Employment Statistics (OES) survey of the U.S. Department of Labor. Annually in May, the OES program releases earnings data representing the previous May. This book is based on the figures released in May 2007 and represents May 2006, the most recent figures available at press time.

The Department of Labor creates the OES survey materials, provides technical support, and determines the sample of establishments (businesses and organizations that employ people). The actual data collection is done by state workforce agencies in the 50 states, plus the District of Columbia and U.S. territories. The states analyze the data and create wage estimates at the state and local level, and the U.S. Department of Labor uses the states' analyses to create national estimates. OES surveys about 1.2 million establishments over a three-year cycle, rotating among different sets of establishments to avoid placing an undue burden on the people who respond to the survey.

What Earnings Does the OES Cover?

The OES survey covers all full-time and part-time wage and salary workers in nonfarm industries. The survey does not cover self-employed workers, owners and partners in unincorporated firms, household workers, or unpaid family workers. This means that although it can be considered a good resource for most occupations, for a few occupations it is not as accurate: for example, occupations with a large fraction of self-employed workers or occupations concentrated in agriculture.

The dollar figures reported by OES represent straight-time gross pay exclusive of premium pay. More specifically, the OES earnings include the job's base rate; cost-of-living allowances; guaranteed pay; hazardous-duty pay; incentive pay, including commissions and production bonuses; on-call pay; and tips but do not include back pay, jury duty pay, overtime pay, severance pay, shift differentials, nonproduction bonuses, or tuition reimbursements.

For a few occupations—for example, Actors and Dancers—earnings vary so much from week to week that an annual figure cannot be estimated. OES reports only an hourly wage for these occupations, and that is the figure we use in this book.

When the wages of an occupation are greater than $70.00 per hour or $145,600 per year, OES does not report a figure, so this book reports "More than $145,600 per year." This is the case for the median earnings figures of only 11 of the 800 jobs covered by this book.

What About the "Factors That May Affect Earnings"?

The percentage figures used in this section of salary facts were derived from data gathered in 2006 for the Current Population Survey. The figure for percentage of part-time workers also comes from this source. The CPS is a monthly survey of about 50,000 households conducted by the Bureau of the Census for the Bureau of Labor Statistics. It is the primary source of information on the labor force characteristics of the U.S. population. The sample is scientifically selected to represent the civilian noninstitutional population.

Sometimes, for certain occupations and certain topics, the number of people surveyed by CPS was too low for a reliable estimate, and it was necessary instead to base the estimate on a small family of occupations. For example, the number of female Physicists was so low that it was necessary to combine it with at least one other occupation to produce an estimate of male–female earning differences. In such cases, we followed the Standard Occupational Classification—the scheme of job titles that all agencies of the government use—to find the lowest-level grouping with a reasonable number of survey respondents. In this case, the lowest-level useful group was Physicists and Astronomers, and therefore for this topic you will find the same percentage figures listed for Physicists and for Astronomers. In other cases we needed to base the estimates on a larger group of occupations. For example, the number of veterans among Physicists and Astronomers was very low, so to estimate the effect of veteran status it was necessary to combine these two occupations with seven others in the larger occupational group called Physical Scientists. Thus, for this topic you will find the same percentage figure listed for Physicists, Astronomers, Chemists, Materials Scientists, and five other occupations.

Is There a Way to Calculate More Up-to-Date Earnings Figures?

The OES wage figures used in this book were released in May 2007 and represent May 2006. They are the most recent figures available from the Department of Labor when this book was written, but you can adjust them to match wage levels for a later date. At www.bls.gov/ect, find the tables for the Employment Cost Index (ECI). Then use the ECI tables for different industries and for different three-month intervals to inflate historic earnings figures and thus estimate earnings for a more current date.

But it is hardly necessary to update the figures in this book unless you are reading a copy that has been on the shelf for many years. We live in a time of low inflation. In fact, as noted earlier in this introduction, wages are growing more slowly than most living costs. The rate of wage inflation has stayed roughly the same for several years, so if you don't mind doing the math, you can use 3 percent as a rough annual inflation factor. For certain occupations, industries, and regions of the nation the rate of inflation may be higher or lower.

What About Other Sources of Pay Figures?

Your state's workforce agency uses the OES methodology to gather earnings data at the state and regional level. Their information may be a useful addition to the figures in this book, especially for regions that are not covered by this book. See Appendix A for information about how to access earnings figures at the state and regional levels.

A number of for-profit Web sites also have information about earnings, but quality varies greatly. One site gathers information from people who come to the site seeking salary information. These people's input can be misleading because they are not a scientifically selected sample and they may be misinformed about commissions and bonuses they are actually getting. Another site scans job listings to determine the going rate for various occupations, but this method also can be misleading because so many jobs are filled without being advertised and many job postings do not list a salary. Still another site provides reports on occupational earnings for a metropolitan area you specify, but the figures in their free reports are not based on occupation-specific data from that metro area; instead, they use data from a national sample and inflate it or deflate it according to local wage trends for all occupations. This is the same method you can apply by using Appendix B and is not as accurate as the occupation-specific metro wage figures you'll find in Part III.

Some companies are in the business of doing salary surveys and charge a fee for reports. Some of these companies, such as the Hay Group, provide salary survey reports for human resource departments of corporations. Personnel managers subscribe to these reports to learn the current market rates—in other words, the salaries they need to pay their employees to stay competitive.

Other companies, such as Salary.com, work the other side of the street: For a fee, they provide reports that enable job-seekers to know what level of pay they should be demanding from employers. If you are about to enter salary negotiations for a job in a city where there are enough similar jobs to provide a decent survey sample, a report of this kind can be useful. However, if you want to compare salaries of several kinds of jobs or several locations, the costs of multiple reports can add up quickly. In addition, if the job is not a common one in the location you're considering, a report of this kind will not have much more specific data than is available to the OES survey that is the basis of the metro-area salary figure in this book. Before you pay for a salary survey report, investigate what sample it is based on and make sure the sample is local, specific to your occupation, and recent.

PART I

Tips for the Best Salary

Everybody wants more pay. In this part of the book, you can learn how to boost your earnings.

More Education Equals Higher Salary

One of the best ways to get a better salary is to become better educated. Education really does pay. Yes, Bill Gates made his billions after dropping out of college. But on average, the more years of schooling you get, the better your earning potential. Training and work experience also tend to boost your earnings.

We analyzed 2006 data from the Current Population Survey to determine the average earnings of people at various levels of education. Note that these figures are not based on the level of education typically required by the job in which the people are working or the average earnings of people in that job. These figures represent the *actual* levels of education attained by the survey respondents and their actual earnings:

Some high school	$18,506
High school or equivalent	$30,986
Some college but no degree	$32,264
Associate degree	$37,685
Bachelor's degree	$52,018
Master's degree	$61,852
Doctoral degree	$77,325
First professional degree	$81,427

The advantage of education has been growing in recent years. In these 2006 figures, bachelor's degree holders have a 68 percent earnings advantage over high school grads; in 1992, the difference was 64 percent.

You may not have the interest, ability, or resources to get a bachelor's degree, but getting an associate degree, certification, informal training, or just some years of work experience can help you qualify for a higher-paying job than you may be qualified for now. As you look over the salary facts in Part III of this book, pay attention to the figures that show how the educational attainment of workers affects their incomes. You'll see that workers with college or graduate degrees often have an earnings advantage of several percentage points. So try not to rule out jobs that require more education or training than you have now. Instead, let them inspire you to set your goals higher.

Other Factors That Affect Earnings

There's an old sarcastic saying that goes, "If you're so smart, why aren't you rich?" It's true that getting one more academic degree is not the only way to fatten your paycheck. When you look at the salary facts in Part II, you'll notice some other factors that can affect your level of income.

Location

If you look at this book's wage figures for states and metropolitan areas, you will notice that earnings are much higher in some locations than in others. You may be considering boosting your pay by pulling up stakes and moving to a region of the country where wages are higher. To be sure, high-wage localities sometimes also have a high cost of living, meaning that your improved earnings will put you into a higher tax bracket without buying you a more comfortable lifestyle. In the new community you may face keener competition for jobs. Also, for a few jobs, different communities have different licensing requirements.

But in other cases you can genuinely improve your circumstances by relocating. For example, for industries that involve a lot of collaborative work, businesses tend to cluster in certain geographical areas (think of Hollywood for the movies, Nashville for music, or Silicon Valley for high-tech). Workers who live in such hubs of collaborative activity often can be more productive and thus more able to achieve an affluent standard of living than workers who are located elsewhere. On the other hand, for jobs where people tend to work solo (think of Dentists or Massage Therapists), the reverse is often true—workers can earn more if they move to a region where there are few colleagues and therefore little competition.

If you are thinking of relocating to improve your earnings, some other factors you should consider are the amount and cost of the commuting you may have to do in your new location. The time and expense of commuting can effectively erode your earning power. For example, let's say you're earning $800 per week for 40 hours of work, which equals $20 per hour. If your daily commute to and from work takes an hour each way, you're actually devoting 50 hours per week to your work, which means you are effectively earning $16 per hour. After you also subtract your costs for gasoline, tolls, and the wear and tear on your vehicle, your job in your new location actually may be paying you less than your old job in your old location. So the relationship between the location of your job and your earnings can be a complex matter.

Industry

People in the same occupation often earn very different amounts in different industries. For example, Database Administrators working in the Securities, Commodity Contracts, and Other Financial Investments and Related Activities industry earn an average of $78,510, whereas those working in Educational Services earn an average of only $53,160. Most educational institutions pay less than private industry, especially an industry in which the ability to manipulate financial databases in useful ways leads directly to higher profits.

Whatever the reasons, wage differences between industries can be large, so if income is your primary goal, you should target the best-paying industries. This usually is easiest to do while you are preparing to enter the occupation—that is, while you're getting your education or training. You can select a college, a college major, a concentration within a major, an internship, or a training program that aims for the industry you have as your target. After you have been in the workforce for many years, you may find it difficult to move to a very different industry because your work experience is not particularly relevant, even when the occupational title is the same. You may need to take classes or get informal training to learn the skills required in the better-paying industry.

You also need to consider whether work conditions in the new industry will be to your liking; for example, longer work hours or more frequent travel may be expected. Also, competition is likely to be greater where the salaries are higher.

Most occupations have a professional association that can inform you of the different requirements and conditions across the nation and in various industries. With this information, you can make an informed choice about whether aspiring towards a particular industry would be a good opportunity for you.

Union Membership

Wages tend to be higher for unionized jobs. The U.S. Department of Labor reports that, in 2006, full-time wage and salary workers who were union members had median usual weekly earnings of $833, compared with a median of $642 for wage and salary workers who were not represented by unions—an advantage of almost 38 percent. The advantage varies from one occupation to another, and in Part II of this book you can see the percentage difference for individual occupations that have significant union membership.

Unionized jobs often may be found in locations where an industry is well established, so the advantages of unionization may be combined with other regional advantages. For example, aircraft mechanics and service technicians in the Detroit–Warren–Livonia, Michigan, metropolitan area have median earnings of $73,070, probably because Northwest Airlines has its hub at Detroit and their mechanics are unionized. By comparison, the New Haven, Connecticut, metropolitan area has no major airline hub and only a small aircraft service facility with nonunionized workers; aircraft mechanics and service technicians there earn a median of only $26,280.

Veteran Status

In Part III you can see, for each occupation, the earnings difference for those who have served on active duty. When earnings of veterans are compared to earnings of nonveterans in the same occupation, the average advantage comes to an impressive 14.6 percent, based on 2006 data.

The difference in pay is not hard to understand when you view military service as a form of training and work experience. Military training and service can teach you occupation-specific skills such as electronics, bookkeeping, food preparation, or vehicle repair. It also teaches teamwork, a positive attitude toward authority, tolerance of diversity, global awareness, and other skills and work habits that are useful in almost any career. Compared to private industry, the military has an excellent track record of encouraging the achievement of women and minority-group recruits. In addition, the educational benefits of the G.I. Bill help many veterans improve their credentials, and military experience may help with networking efforts that are so crucial to getting a job interview. You can read more about these advantages and about specific occupations linked to military training in *150 Best Jobs Through Military Training* (JIST). People who have served in the reserves or National Guard may share some of these advantages even if they are never called up for active duty.

Of course, military service has its disadvantages, such as loss of independence and risks to personal safety. It also has benefits that have nothing to do with your career development, such as the satisfaction of serving your country. Like college, it may or may not suit you, and you have to meet certain entry requirements. Unlike college, it is no longer an option after you exceed certain age limits.

Gender

In 2006 women earned about 75 percent of what men working in the same occupation earned. As the introduction notes, this disparity is not always the result of discrimination. But it probably still is in many cases.

If you're a woman, there are strategies you can use to try to maximize your chances of receiving a fair wage. Some occupations have a better ratio of female-to-male wages, as you can see when you look at the salary facts in Part II. Some employers have programs in place to recruit women for positions where they have been underrepresented. In other cases, a manager who is a determined and inspiring mentor can accomplish as much for your career as a formal program might. When you research possible employers, try to find out whether they have a record of such efforts. Sometimes they do not publicize these efforts, but you may learn about their reputation for fairness by speaking with women who work for the employer. Also remember to consider the availability of female-friendly fringe benefits, such as paid maternity leave.

If you think you may be getting lower pay because of discrimination, turn to Part IV and read the discussion of the laws that apply to this situation.

Work Hours

Some jobs offer opportunities for you to earn extra income by working longer or unusual hours. If you are investigating jobs that are paid by the hour, you should find out whether workers receive extra pay (such as time-and-a-half) for overtime work or for work on the nighttime or weekend shift. Note that the earnings figures reported in this book do not reflect these differences, but you may get a rough idea of their impact by looking at the "Average Hours Worked," the percentage figure for "Workers with a Varying Number of Hours," and the percentage figure for the "Earnings Benefit of Working Overtime."

A policy of extra pay for overtime or shift work does not guarantee that these work hours will be available to you. Businesses that are prospering or that experience busy seasons (for example, vacation resorts or tax-preparation services) are more likely to offer overtime work.

Of course, many jobs are not paid by the hour. For some jobs, especially in sales, commissions can be a big part of the pay package and can produce great rewards for extra hours of work. These dollars do figure into the earnings reported in this book. On the other hand, the bonuses that employers sometimes bestow to compensate for grueling work schedules are not reflected here, nor can you always count on receiving such compensation. As a result, working overtime may actually cause you to earn less per hour, producing a *negative* percentage for the "Earnings Benefit of Working Overtime," although in the long run your dedication to your work may result in a promotion.

In sum, overtime or shift work may be very lucrative or may go unrewarded, so as you investigate jobs you should find out what to expect. Some rewards will be spelled out in your employment contract, but some may result from bonuses or promotions. The best way to learn about the likelihood of the latter is by talking to current or former employees.

If you're considering working only part time, look at the salary facts for the occupation to see what percentage of workers have this arrangement. (About 27 percent of all workers do.) Part-time work may suit your lifestyle, but you are likely to pay a price for your extra hours of freedom: Part-time workers earn on average 11.1% less per hour than do full-time workers in the same occupation, and most of them also lack important fringe benefits that full-time employees enjoy. There are exceptions: Registered Nurses and several other health-care workers actually earn at a *higher* hourly rate when they work part-time, probably because most of them are working on the night or weekend shift or in private-duty home-care situations. Also, some employers who rely heavily on part-time workers (for example, Starbucks) offer fringe benefits for a work week of less than 40 hours.

Earning More by Leveraging Your Knowledge and Skills

Your pay depends most of all on your knowledge and skills: They're what you bring to the employment market, what you supply in exchange for the employer's demands. Your educational and training credentials and your veteran status are only stand-ins for your knowledge and skills. Your slick resume and the glowing recommendations of your former employers are only promises that you can deliver the goods.

Leveraging Knowledge and Skills in Your Job

To earn the highest pay in your occupation, you need to have the particular package of knowledge and skills that are needed in the best-paying industry and in the best-paying specialization within that industry. For example, if you're an accountant, you would earn big bucks by being proficient at accounting for stocks and bonds, because the best-paying industry is Securities, Commodity Contracts, and Other Financial Investments and Related Activities. You could earn even bigger bucks if you had expert knowledge of some specialization within that industry, such as taxation or computer applications. With mastery of more obscure knowledge, you might do still better—say, if you were thoroughly familiar with the accounting methods appropriate for international investments, spoke a Middle Eastern language fluently, and worked for a company that frequently dealt with a stock exchange in that part of the world. Of course, with such specialized knowledge, you would be able to find work in only a limited number of companies. And if business relations with your country of expertise were cut off because of a political crisis, your high-paying job might come to a sudden end.

So remember that flexibility, just like specialized knowledge, is also a useful skill. As work tasks change, or as the work environment undergoes changes, you need to be able to adapt to the new realities. This is especially true for technology, which affects so many work tasks and is constantly evolving, but it also applies to the regulatory environment, fickle popular tastes, foreign competition, and countless other fluid factors that can affect the way your job gets done and therefore your income—and ultimately your ability to stay employed.

Flexibility is partly a matter of self-confidence; if you believe in yourself, you can bounce back from setbacks and convince employers that you are just the person they need for a new job. But even more important is the ability to learn. As your job changes, you need to be able to learn the newly required knowledges and skills. This is sometimes a matter of getting academic credentials, but more often it means informal learning. For the cutting-edge skills that command the best incomes (say, adapting accounting software to account for foreign stock transactions in Arabic), classes have not yet been developed and you have to create your own curriculum, perhaps a combination of reading articles and manuals, scouring the Web, picking people's brains, and trial-and-error experimentation. If you're lucky, your employer will support your program of formal or informal learning, but in some work situations you may have to devote your spare time and your own funds. Consider this an investment in future earnings.

Leveraging Your Knowledge and Skills in a New Occupation

If you are very flexible, you may seek to earn a higher salary by changing your occupation. Or you may be forced into such a change because opportunities in your present occupation are drying up. You should be using this book not only to look at the salary facts for your present occupation or for the occupation you presently aspire to, but also to look for opportunities in jobs that you might later grow into. Transition into a new occupation does not always mean acquiring a new degree, passing a certification exam, or meeting some other formal requirement. Often it's simply a matter of taking stock of your existing knowledge and skills, learning some new tricks informally, and then packaging yourself in a new way.

You may not realize how many skills and insights you have learned on the job. When you work in an occupation for many years, you acquire a broad knowledge of your industry and probably some expertise in your particular specialization. You know common problems that workers deal with, shortcuts and resources that help get the job done, important markets, how the cycle of seasons affects business, the regulatory or infrastructure environment, major competitors, and emerging issues. You also acquire personal contacts in the industry, in the businesses and industries that buy from and sell to your industry, and perhaps in the schools that train tomorrow's workforce. You can "speak the language" that all of these contacts understand.

So consider several ways that you might leverage this knowledge and these contacts in new occupations. Here are just a few, starting with the most obvious and moving toward some you may not have thought about:

- Instead of being a "doer," you can become a *manager*. With the right organizational and people skills, you can coordinate people and resources in your field. You may need to get some additional education to prepare for this transition, or you may be able to get your employer to give you a trial assignment with a managerial task so you can demonstrate that you already have the skills.

- Instead of being on your employer's payroll, you can become a *consultant* or *freelance worker*. This work arrangement can give you more flexible hours, more variety, more opportunities to travel, more opportunities to work at home, and more recognition. Of course, your income may lose some predictability, and you will need many of the same organizational skills as a manager, plus marketing skills to acquire clients.

- You can *teach* the subject. If you relate well to young people, you may consider teaching in high school or even lower grades. Of course, a teaching license requires a college degree with certain coursework and often passing an exam. Teaching the subject in college usually requires a master's degree, but to teach a vocational subject at the postsecondary level you may need no more than extensive work experience. You may also find work as a *trainer* in a business setting.

- Every industry needs skilled workers, so you can *recruit* workers for your field. As a recruiter, you can leverage your knowledge of job requirements in the industry and perhaps your contacts in "feeder" schools or other established sources of new hires.

- You can work in *sales*. For example, if you have been a teacher and know the education market well, your expertise can help you land a job selling textbooks or other educational resources.

- You can work as a *buyer* in your industry, either of raw materials, finished goods, or services. This job allows you to use knowledge about matters such as who the sellers are, what forces affect the market, and what contributes to quality in goods and services.

- You can work as a *broker* or *agent* who brings the buyers and sellers together. This applies to a lot more than just real estate. For example, consider the agents who work in show business. Some of them are former actors who leverage their knowledge of who does the hiring and what the employers are looking for. What business deals might you arrange in your industry?

- You can work as an *investment analyst* in the industry and leverage your knowledge of which companies or commodities are likely to gain or lose value.

- Because you know what determines quality or value in your field, and perhaps legal requirements for work outputs, you can become an *inspector* or *appraiser*. For example, after experience as a construction worker, you may be able to become a building inspector. Work in the arts may qualify you to become an art appraiser.

- If you have a flair for words, you can work as a *writer* about the industry. Every industry has trade publications and technical manuals. Assemble a portfolio of your best writing to show employers or consulting clients what you know and can do.

- You may become a *representative* or *advocate* for the workers in your industry. In some unionized trades, the union officials often rise from the rank and file. Professional associations, including lobbying groups, sometimes fill

vacancies in their paid staff with members who have been active volunteers.

- In many of the work roles listed here, you can function as an *entrepreneur* rather than try to get hired by an existing business. For example, to become a broker of some kind, you may create your own brokerage business. To teach an occupation, you may set up your own school (or, in the arts, a studio). You may set up a business that buys, sells, or repairs a type of product that you're familiar with.

Of course, if your industry is shrinking fast, this approach may not work well for you. After people stopped driving buggies, there wasn't much point in trying to sell buggies, repair them, write about them, or teach people how to drive them. On the other hand, even though the shoe manufacturing industry in the United States is only a tiny fraction of what it once was, there is still a need for buyers and sellers of shoes, managers of shoe stores, repairers of high-priced shoes, and technicians to fashion orthotic inserts for shoes. And a few specialty shoe manufacturers are still in business on these shores.

So be creative in your thinking about how you might parlay your skills and knowledge into a better-paying job. Keep in mind that these alternative occupations do not pay equally well. For example, training workers typically pays less than managing the same workers.

Negotiating Your Pay When You're Hired

Academic degrees, exceptional skills, living in a high-wage area, finding a high-paying job specialization—none of these factors will result in earnings until an employer *makes a salary offer*. In most cases the employer will have a salary figure in mind but also will have some freedom to offer more or less, so to get the best possible salary offer you need a strategy for negotiating your pay. Keep in mind that the following suggestions cover only salary-related issues; this book does not have room to cover other issues related to interviewing successfully and evaluating a job offer wisely.

Your Strategy: Save Salary for Last

The most important principle to remember is to save discussion of salary for the very end of the interview and hiring-decision process. Employers often ask for your salary expectations (or perhaps your salary history) very early, perhaps even as part of the job application form or letter. This makes it easy for them to screen out a large number of applicants who don't match the salary figure they have in mind.

Don't screen yourself out by giving this information. Tell them that your salary expectations depend on the specific features of the job, and you need to know more about this job to decide what a reasonable salary figure would be. If there's a blank on the job application demanding a figure, write "Negotiable." As for your salary history, say that the job in question may not be totally comparable to your past jobs, and you need to discuss the similarities and differences so that both you and the employer can decide what pay is appropriate. Note that these arguments contribute to your pitch for why they should interview you. If the employer refuses to interview you unless you indicate your salary expectations, give only a large ballpark estimate and make clear that you expect both parties will be flexible as you learn more about each other.

Useful Information to Have at the Interview

At the interview, information is your strongest weapon. Some of the information that can boost your pay has to do with your own background: your skills, your demonstrated work ethic, and ideally your specific contribution to your former employers' earnings. ("I developed a method to cut costs by 5 percent and brought in 50 new clients, thus boosting annual earnings by 10 percent.") Show-and-tell can be very helpful; you don't have to be an artist to have a portfolio. Any tangible representation of your work output will be useful. If it's too big to bring along, bring photographs; if it can't be photographed, use testimonial letters, news clippings, or excerpts from business reports.

Another important kind of information is your knowledge about the business that has the job opening. The more you know about your prospective employer, the better you'll be able to show how your skills match the company's needs. If you know they're prosperous, you can expect to have less difficulty asking for a high salary. If you know they're going through hard times, you can argue that they need you to change their fortunes and can ask that your starting salary be reviewed once you start contributing to their success.

The third kind of information you need is about the labor market. All decisions about pay are made in the context of a market in which employers make offers and workers make demands. You need to know the going rate for this occupation in this industry, in this location, in this kind of business, and for a person with your kind of skills as indicated by your background. This book is designed to provide salary facts that can help you. Through personal contacts in your targeted business (or one similar to it) you may even be able to learn the earnings of workers like you. It is not considered polite to ask people what they're earning, but you may specify a pay figure and ask your contacts whether they think the figure is too high or low.

Negotiating During the Interview

The purpose of the job interview is to allow you and the employer to gather enough information to decide whether you're a good fit. Only *after* that decision is made—when they're offering you the job—should the issue of salary come up or get specific.

While the interviewer is gathering information about your background and skills, you need to use every opportunity to explain how you can improve the organization's bottom line, because that is what justifies better pay. You may even be able to point out ways in which you can do a bigger job than what the employer originally had in mind. For example, because of your background you may be able to take on technical duties, design tasks, or managerial roles not normally associated with the job. If you and the interviewer agree on pay early in the interview, all of this discussion will be wasted. By postponing talk about pay, you allow this information to influence the salary offer.

The interviewer may steer the conversation toward pay early in the interview, not so much to lock you into a certain level of pay as to simplify the interviewer's task of screening you out of the job. Be prepared with some responses that can shift the conversation back to your qualifications for the job. For example, if the interviewer asks what pay you expect, you might answer, "I'm sure you pay your employees fairly, and I expect you to pay me a fair wage for a person with my background. So let's discuss my background and what I can do for your business." Or you might say, "Let's save that discussion for when we're ready to close the deal. If you're ready to offer me the job now, okay, but I think you need to know more about me and what I can do for your organization." Still another tactic is to throw the question back at the interviewer: "Why don't you tell me what range of salaries you pay for this position?" Ask a friend to sit down for a practice interview and try out responses similar to these so you can get comfortable with this strategy and achieve a tone that is not evasive or off-putting.

If this strategy does not work and you feel you must specify your salary expectation early in the interview, give a rather broad range, make clear that it is based on research rather than on wishful thinking, and suggest that its relevance to your case depends on further discussion. For example, in an interview for an accounting job you might say, "I've investigated what accountants are earning in this area. The average is about $55,000, but of course many of them don't have a master's in this field, as I do, and that can make a 10 percent difference in earnings. That would put the figure in the low 60s, but then again, it's going to depend on what I'll be doing for you. With my background in computer applications and taxation, I think I can do more for you than most other applicants you're going to interview." Then you would discuss how your skills match the company's needs as you understand them. You might also mention that your salary expectations depend on the overall compensation package.

Although you should try to avoid discussing salary, it's a good idea to ask the interviewer what fringe benefits are typical at the company. Usually there's a standard set of benefits, and the interviewer may even offer you a printed summary. This is not the time to negotiate these benefits, but you may want to do so later, so it is helpful to learn in advance what the baseline benefits are. Find out whether any benefits require you to pay part of the costs.

You also need to understand other factors that may affect your paycheck. Is the pay rate determined by a union contract? (If so, you will not be able to negotiate your pay or benefits, but both probably will be better than they would be otherwise.) Does the company pay commissions or performance-related bonuses? Are you eligible for overtime pay and, if so, what work hours can you expect?

Negotiating After the Job Offer

You may be offered the job at the interview, but more likely the offer will come afterward. Let's assume that you want the job if it pays well enough. Based on your research, you should have a figure in mind that you consider fair.

Ideally, the employer will make you a salary offer, and you can decide how to react. If it's more than you expected, congratulations! But if it's less than the figure you had in mind, remember that you don't have to decide right away whether or not to accept it. Ask for time to think it over, and use that time to plan your negotiating strategy.

Some of the following strategies may help you build a case for a better salary when you call back with a counteroffer. You also may choose to mention some of them when they make their initial offer, giving them something to think about at the same time that you're considering their offer:

- If another employer has made a better offer, that's the most powerful argument you can use.

- If you have no other offers, but your research tells you the going rate is higher than what they're offering, tell them so. Keep in mind that they probably also have researched the employment market, so be sure you have very good sources to point to.

- If they won't raise their offer enough to suit your expectations, ask them to agree to review your salary sooner than they normally would.

- Employers who won't budge on salary offers sometimes are willing to make concessions on benefits or perks that you want. Maybe you can get extra vacation, use of a company car, or the ability to work at home part of the week. Sometimes you can argue that you both will gain from the benefit; for example, if the company pays your tuition expenses for night classes they will profit from your improved skills.

- You may also be able to get concessions on certain work responsibilities you either want or want to avoid. For example, you might ask to be given a managerial task that's not normally part of the job, and this eventually could lead to a higher-paying position. Any tasks you ask to avoid should be lower-level so that ruling them out would not interfere with your growth in the job.

It's possible that the employer, when offering you the job, may ask *you* to specify the level of pay you expect. The arguments you might have used during the interview are no longer relevant, so you'll need to quote a figure—or, better, a range—based on your understanding of the going rate. If the employer makes a lower counteroffer, use some of the preceding arguments to try to sweeten the deal.

Negotiating a Raise

Getting a raise is different from negotiating starting pay and therefore calls for different strategies. Negotiations for a raise are easier on all parties concerned. You are more of a known quantity (or should be) than when you were hired, you have become familiar with your boss, and you now have inside knowledge of the business. You also have more control over the timing of the negotiations, and it's important that you choose a time when the business is not in trouble, when your boss's budget for the coming year is still fluid, and when you have some recent accomplishments you can point to. Set up a meeting specifically for this purpose (you might say the topic is "my compensation"). If you have a regularly scheduled annual performance-appraisal meeting, you might use that occasion if you are very confident that the appraisal will be positive, but you should alert your boss ahead of time that you intend to include compensation in the discussion. You should have a specific figure in mind, but you must be prepared to be flexible about it.

Most important of all, be prepared to justify your request for a raise with something more relevant than your desires or your needs. The cost of living may be going up, but everyone else in the company is equally affected by that. You need to be able to argue that you are worth more to the business than your current rate of pay.

The *fairness strategy* is to point out that other workers like you, with a similar level of skill and productivity, are being paid more than you are. To make this argument, you need to prepare for the interview by researching the going rate of pay for workers in your position, in your industry, in your area, and with your credentials and skills. That's where this book can be extremely useful. You also should find out as much as you can about pay for comparable employees in your organization—although that information may be difficult to obtain. As in a hiring interview, the strongest card you can hold is a salary offer from another employer (or another department in your company), but good knowledge of the going rates inside and outside your business is the next best card to hold.

The *merit strategy* is to point out that you are working at a higher level than when your pay was last set; you now perform what is in effect a new job but are being paid at the rate of your old job. If you can point to a matching job description for a higher-paid job, you may want to argue for a promotion rather than a raise. But even if you're not asking for a change of job title, you may be able to point to specific work tasks and indicators of skill and productivity that put you at a higher level than you were before. If you can take credit for cost savings, new revenue streams, faster or better output, or higher profit margins, you will have a strong case, especially if you can point to specific achievements. A newly acquired degree or certification may serve as an indication of improved skills; indeed, in some work situations it automatically produces a raise. With most employers mere seniority does not merit a raise; if you are simply doing your job as required, you deserve continued employment but no raise.

Have a response prepared in case your boss turns you down. Your boss may concede your arguments based on fairness or merit but still be unable to grant you a raise because of a tight budget or concerns about the future. In that case, it is fair for you to ask when you can bring up the issue again and what the chances are that you will get a positive answer at that time. A good general response to a rejection is to say, "I understand your position." This implies that your boss wants to give you a raise but is unable to, and thus both you and your boss save face. It also leaves open your subsequent course of action. By contrast, a response such as "That's not fair" or "I deserve better" amounts to a criticism of your boss and implies that you're going to look for work elsewhere or scale back your work effort. Unless you are ready to quit or be fired, that is not a helpful strategy.

As with negotiations for starting salary, if your boss cannot offer your desired level of pay, you may ask for extra fringe benefits or perks instead. Still another recourse is to ask to be paid a commission or bonus for the new business or savings you generate; this pay arrangement is feasible only if you can quantify exactly how much revenue you bring in or save.

Money Is Only One Consideration

Not every workday is payday. Holding a job means putting in the required hours, doing the required tasks, being exposed to a particular work setting and to co-workers, and experiencing all the many other aspects of work. Therefore, when you evaluate a job offer, you need to consider all its potential rewards, as well as its possible drawbacks.

Following are some nonmonetary factors that may influence your decision. Investigate these before the interview and use the interview to fill in any gaps in your knowledge.

- Does the organization's business or activity match your own interests and beliefs? It is easier to apply yourself if you are enthusiastic about what the organization does.

- How will the size of the organization affect you? Large firms generally offer a greater variety of training programs and career paths, more levels for advancement, and better benefits than do small firms. Large employers also may have more advanced technologies. However, many jobs in large firms tend to be highly specialized. Jobs in small firms may offer broader authority and responsibility, a closer working relationship with top management, and a chance to see your contribution to the success of the organization.

- Is the organization relatively new or well established? New businesses have a high failure rate, but for many people the excitement of helping to create a company and the potential for sharing in its success more than offset the risk of job loss.

- Is the company private or public? An individual or a family may control a privately owned company, and key jobs may be reserved for relatives and friends. A board of directors controls a publicly owned company, and key jobs usually are open to anyone.

- Are you comfortable with the location of the job? If the job is in another section of the country, you need to consider the cost of living, the availability of housing and transportation, and the quality of educational and recreational facilities in that section of the country. Even if the job location is in your area, you should consider the burdens of commuting.

- Does the work match your interests and make use of your skills? The responsibilities of the job should be explained in enough detail to answer this question.

- How important is the job in this company? An explanation of where you fit in the organization and how you are supposed to contribute to its overall objectives should give you an idea of the job's importance.

- Does the job routinely require overtime to meet deadlines, achieve goals for sales or production, or better serve customers? If so, consider the effect that the work hours will have on your personal life.

- How long do most people who enter this job stay with the company? High turnover can mean dissatisfaction with the work or something else about the job.

- What opportunities come with the job? Besides good earnings, a good job offers you opportunities to learn new skills and rise to positions of greater authority, responsibility, and prestige. A lack of opportunities can dampen interest in the work and result in frustration and boredom. Does the company have a training plan for you? What is the next step on the career ladder? If you have to wait for a job to become vacant before you can be promoted, how long does this usually take?

If all of these considerations seem daunting, remember that you're not making a lifetime decision. If the job does not work out, you may be able to negotiate changes in your work arrangement or find a job elsewhere.

Pay Rankings of Jobs, Industries, and Locations

In this part of the book you can see interesting sets of jobs ranked by their pay. For example, you can see jobs at different levels of required education or training and jobs held by men and women, by people in various age brackets, by veterans, and by part-time workers. You can also see lists of industries, states, and metropolitan areas ranked by their average pay. All of these lists are ranked by descending level of earnings, with the best-paying items in each list (jobs, industries, and so forth) listed at the top. Items with equal earnings are ordered alphabetically.

Earnings figures for men and women, age brackets, veterans, and part-time workers are derived from the Current Population Survey. All other figures are based on the Occupational Employment Survey.

All Jobs Ranked by Median Earnings

This list ranks all the occupations for which we could obtain data on median annual earnings. (Five of the 800 occupations in this book are missing because their earnings data is available only for hourly wages.) Keep in mind that workers in several of the lowest-ranked jobs customarily receive a portion of their income as tips. Although earnings from tips are supposed to be included in the figures that the Department of Labor obtains in its OES survey, it is possible that some workers are concealing part of their tip-derived income and that their actual income is somewhat higher.

All Jobs Ranked by Median Earnings

Rank	Title	Median Earnings
1.	Anesthesiologists	more than $145,600
2.	Chief Executives	more than $145,600
3.	Family and General Practitioners	more than $145,600
4.	Internists, General	more than $145,600
5.	Obstetricians and Gynecologists	more than $145,600
6.	Oral and Maxillofacial Surgeons	more than $145,600
7.	Orthodontists	more than $145,600
8.	Physicians and Surgeons, All Other	more than $145,600
9.	Prosthodontists	more than $145,600
10.	Psychiatrists	more than $145,600
11.	Surgeons	more than $145,600
12.	Airline Pilots, Copilots, and Flight Engineers	$141,090
13.	Pediatricians, General	$138,130
14.	Dentists, General	$132,140
15.	Air Traffic Controllers	$117,240
16.	Podiatrists	$108,220
17.	Engineering Managers	$105,430
18.	Lawyers	$102,470
19.	Judges, Magistrate Judges, and Magistrates	$101,690
20.	Computer and Information Systems Managers	$101,580
21.	Natural Sciences Managers	$100,080
22.	Marketing Managers	$98,720
23.	Petroleum Engineers	$98,380
24.	Astronomers	$95,740
25.	Pharmacists	$94,520
26.	Physicists	$94,240
27.	Computer and Information Scientists, Research	$93,950
28.	Sales Managers	$91,560
29.	Dentists, All Other Specialists	$91,200
30.	Optometrists	$91,040
31.	Financial Managers	$90,970
32.	Nuclear Engineers	$90,220
33.	Political Scientists	$90,140
34.	Human Resources Managers, All Other	$88,510
35.	Computer Hardware Engineers	$88,470
36.	Aerospace Engineers	$87,610
37.	Law Teachers, Postsecondary	$87,240
38.	Mathematicians	$86,930
39.	Industrial-Organizational Psychologists	$86,420
40.	Computer Software Engineers, Systems Software	$85,370
41.	General and Operations Managers	$85,230
42.	Physical Scientists, All Other	$83,450
43.	Actuaries	$82,800
44.	Managers, All Other	$82,490
45.	Public Relations Managers	$82,180
46.	Engineers, All Other	$81,660
47.	Purchasing Managers	$81,570
48.	Electronics Engineers, Except Computer	$81,050
49.	Training and Development Managers	$80,250
50.	Computer Software Engineers, Applications	$79,780
51.	Chemical Engineers	$78,860
52.	Education Administrators, Elementary and Secondary School	$77,740
53.	Sales Engineers	$77,720
54.	Industrial Production Managers	$77,670
55.	Health Specialties Teachers, Postsecondary	$77,190
56.	Atmospheric and Space Scientists	$77,150
57.	Economists	$77,010
58.	Engineering Teachers, Postsecondary	$76,670
59.	Biochemists and Biophysicists	$76,320
60.	Psychologists, All Other	$76,310
61.	Electrical Engineers	$75,930
62.	Agricultural Sciences Teachers, Postsecondary	$75,140
63.	Physician Assistants	$74,980
64.	Compensation and Benefits Managers	$74,750
65.	Materials Scientists	$74,610
66.	Education Administrators, Postsecondary	$73,990
67.	Materials Engineers	$73,990
68.	Biomedical Engineers	$73,930
69.	Construction Managers	$73,700
70.	Medical and Health Services Managers	$73,340
71.	Transportation, Storage, and Distribution Managers	$73,080
72.	Advertising and Promotions Managers	$73,060
73.	Marine Engineers and Naval Architects	$72,990
74.	Geoscientists, Except Hydrologists and Geographers	$72,660
75.	Administrative Law Judges, Adjudicators, and Hearing Officers	$72,600
76.	Mining and Geological Engineers, Including Mining Safety Engineers	$72,160
77.	Veterinarians	$71,990
78.	Economics Teachers, Postsecondary	$71,850
79.	Environmental Engineers	$69,940
80.	Mechanical Engineers	$69,850
81.	Computer Systems Analysts	$69,760
82.	Nuclear Power Reactor Operators	$69,370
83.	First-Line Supervisors/Managers of Police and Detectives	$69,310
84.	Atmospheric, Earth, Marine, and Space Sciences Teachers, Postsecondary	$69,300
85.	Biological Science Teachers, Postsecondary	$69,210
86.	Industrial Engineers	$68,620
87.	Civil Engineers	$68,600
88.	Computer Specialists, All Other	$68,570
89.	Securities, Commodities, and Financial Services Sales Agents	$68,500
90.	Physics Teachers, Postsecondary	$68,170

Rank	Title	Median Earnings
91.	Art Directors	$68,100
92.	Management Analysts	$68,050
93.	Administrative Services Managers	$67,690
94.	Education Administrators, All Other	$66,620
95.	Financial Analysts	$66,590
96.	Health and Safety Engineers, Except Mining Safety Engineers and Inspectors	$66,290
97.	Hydrologists	$66,260
98.	Physical Therapists	$66,200
99.	Radiation Therapists	$66,170
100.	Personal Financial Advisors	$66,120
101.	Agricultural Engineers	$66,030
102.	Statisticians	$65,720
103.	Computer Programmers	$65,510
104.	First-Line Supervisors/Managers of Non-Retail Sales Workers	$65,510
105.	Nuclear Technicians	$65,500
106.	Financial Examiners	$65,370
107.	Chiropractors	$65,220
108.	Social Scientists and Related Workers, All Other	$64,920
109.	Environmental Science Teachers, Postsecondary	$64,780
110.	Database Administrators	$64,670
111.	Operations Research Analysts	$64,650
112.	Architecture Teachers, Postsecondary	$64,620
113.	Network Systems and Data Communications Analysts	$64,600
114.	Agents and Business Managers of Artists, Performers, and Athletes	$64,500
115.	Sales Representatives, Wholesale and Manufacturing, Technical and Scientific Products	$64,440
116.	Forestry and Conservation Science Teachers, Postsecondary	$64,430
117.	Architects, Except Landscape and Naval	$64,150
118.	Postsecondary Teachers, All Other	$63,930
119.	Elevator Installers and Repairers	$63,620
120.	Mathematical Scientists, All Other	$63,570
121.	Logisticians	$63,430
122.	Geographers	$62,990
123.	First-Line Supervisors/Managers of Fire Fighting and Prevention Workers	$62,900
124.	Anthropology and Archeology Teachers, Postsecondary	$62,820
125.	Gaming Managers	$62,820
126.	Dental Hygienists	$62,800
127.	Fashion Designers	$62,610
128.	Power Distributors and Dispatchers	$62,590
129.	Nuclear Medicine Technologists	$62,300
130.	Network and Computer Systems Administrators	$62,130
131.	Business Teachers, Postsecondary	$62,040
132.	Political Science Teachers, Postsecondary	$61,820
133.	Medical Scientists, Except Epidemiologists	$61,680
134.	Health Diagnosing and Treating Practitioners, All Other	$61,570
135.	Budget Analysts	$61,430
136.	Chemistry Teachers, Postsecondary	$61,220
137.	Social Sciences Teachers, Postsecondary, All Other	$61,210
138.	Biological Scientists, All Other	$60,940
139.	Real Estate Brokers	$60,790
140.	Occupational Therapists	$60,470
141.	Sociologists	$60,290
142.	Chemists	$59,870
143.	Clinical, Counseling, and School Psychologists	$59,440
144.	Geography Teachers, Postsecondary	$59,000
145.	Orthotists and Prosthetists	$58,980
146.	Market Research Analysts	$58,820
147.	Psychology Teachers, Postsecondary	$58,670
148.	Detectives and Criminal Investigators	$58,260
149.	Technical Writers	$58,050
150.	Occupational Health and Safety Specialists	$58,030
151.	Locomotive Engineers	$57,990
152.	Microbiologists	$57,980
153.	Speech-Language Pathologists	$57,710
154.	Computer Science Teachers, Postsecondary	$57,620
155.	Commercial Pilots	$57,480
156.	Electrical and Electronics Repairers, Powerhouse, Substation, and Relay	$57,400
157.	History Teachers, Postsecondary	$57,390
158.	Registered Nurses	$57,280
159.	Diagnostic Medical Sonographers	$57,160
160.	Audiologists	$57,120
161.	Life Scientists, All Other	$56,970
162.	Epidemiologists	$56,670
163.	Urban and Regional Planners	$56,630
164.	Sociology Teachers, Postsecondary	$56,620
165.	Mathematical Science Teachers, Postsecondary	$56,420
166.	Area, Ethnic, and Cultural Studies Teachers, Postsecondary	$56,380
167.	Producers and Directors	$56,310
168.	Environmental Scientists and Specialists, Including Health	$56,100
169.	Soil and Plant Scientists	$56,080
170.	Postmasters and Mail Superintendents	$55,790
171.	Business Operations Specialists, All Other	$55,650
172.	Railroad Conductors and Yardmasters	$55,530
173.	Home Economics Teachers, Postsecondary	$55,310
174.	Nursing Instructors and Teachers, Postsecondary	$55,280
175.	Landscape Architects	$55,140
176.	Power Plant Operators	$55,000
177.	Conservation Scientists	$54,970
178.	Philosophy and Religion Teachers, Postsecondary	$54,880
179.	Ship Engineers	$54,820
180.	Accountants and Auditors	$54,630
181.	Library Science Teachers, Postsecondary	$54,570
182.	Commercial and Industrial Designers	$54,560
183.	Social Work Teachers, Postsecondary	$54,340
184.	Engineering Technicians, Except Drafters, All Other	$54,250
185.	First-Line Supervisors/Managers of Mechanics, Installers, and Repairers	$53,890
186.	First-Line Supervisors/Managers of Construction Trades and Extraction Workers	$53,850
187.	Food Scientists and Technologists	$53,810
188.	Flight Attendants	$53,780
189.	Financial Specialists, All Other	$53,680
190.	Gas Plant Operators	$53,670

(continued)

(continued)

Rank	Title	Median Earnings
191.	Captains, Mates, and Pilots of Water Vessels	$53,430
192.	Aerospace Engineering and Operations Technicians	$53,300
193.	Zoologists and Wildlife Biologists	$53,300
194.	Art, Drama, and Music Teachers, Postsecondary	$53,160
195.	Communications Teachers, Postsecondary	$53,110
196.	Cost Estimators	$52,940
197.	Education Teachers, Postsecondary	$52,800
198.	Instructional Coordinators	$52,790
199.	First-Line Supervisors/Managers of Correctional Officers	$52,580
200.	Telecommunications Equipment Installers and Repairers, Except Line Installers	$52,430
201.	Petroleum Pump System Operators, Refinery Operators, and Gaugers	$52,380
202.	Credit Analysts	$52,350
203.	Insurance Underwriters	$52,350
204.	Human Resources, Training, and Labor Relations Specialists, All Other	$52,270
205.	Farm, Ranch, and Other Agricultural Managers	$52,070
206.	Media and Communication Equipment Workers, All Other	$52,070
207.	Social and Community Service Managers	$52,070
208.	Foreign Language and Literature Teachers, Postsecondary	$51,900
209.	Loan Officers	$51,760
210.	English Language and Literature Teachers, Postsecondary	$51,730
211.	Multi-Media Artists and Animators	$51,350
212.	Foresters	$51,190
213.	Electrical Power-Line Installers and Repairers	$50,780
214.	Purchasing Agents, Except Wholesale, Retail, and Farm Products	$50,730
215.	Claims Adjusters, Examiners, and Investigators	$50,660
216.	Electrical and Electronic Engineering Technicians	$50,660
217.	Transportation Inspectors	$50,390
218.	Compensation, Benefits, and Job Analysis Specialists	$50,230
219.	Signal and Track Switch Repairers	$50,150
220.	Anthropologists and Archeologists	$49,930
221.	Criminal Justice and Law Enforcement Teachers, Postsecondary	$49,730
222.	Medical and Clinical Laboratory Technologists	$49,700
223.	Funeral Directors	$49,620
224.	Sales Representatives, Wholesale and Manufacturing, Except Technical and Scientific Products	$49,610
225.	Arbitrators, Mediators, and Conciliators	$49,490
226.	Recreation and Fitness Studies Teachers, Postsecondary	$49,270
227.	Insurance Appraisers, Auto Damage	$49,180
228.	Chemical Plant and System Operators	$49,080
229.	Librarians	$49,060
230.	Subway and Streetcar Operators	$48,980
231.	Railroad Brake, Signal, and Switch Operators	$48,860
232.	Vocational Education Teachers, Secondary School	$48,690
233.	Writers and Authors	$48,640
234.	Historians	$48,520
235.	First-Line Supervisors/Managers of Transportation and Material-Moving Machine and Vehicle Operators	$48,330

Rank	Title	Median Earnings
236.	Special Education Teachers, Secondary School	$48,330
237.	Surveyors	$48,290
238.	Cartographers and Photogrammetrists	$48,240
239.	Radiologic Technologists and Technicians	$48,170
240.	Sales Representatives, Services, All Other	$48,100
241.	Fire Inspectors and Investigators	$48,050
242.	Training and Development Specialists	$47,830
243.	Animal Scientists	$47,800
244.	Aircraft Mechanics and Service Technicians	$47,740
245.	Secondary School Teachers, Except Special and Vocational Education	$47,740
246.	Special Education Teachers, Middle School	$47,650
247.	Educational, Vocational, and School Counselors	$47,530
248.	Police and Sheriff's Patrol Officers	$47,460
249.	Respiratory Therapists	$47,420
250.	Emergency Management Specialists	$47,410
251.	Public Relations Specialists	$47,350
252.	First-Line Supervisors/Managers of Production and Operating Workers	$47,300
253.	Transit and Railroad Police	$47,080
254.	Compliance Officers, Except Agriculture, Construction, Health and Safety, and Transportation	$47,050
255.	Editors	$46,990
256.	Dietitians and Nutritionists	$46,980
257.	Boilermakers	$46,960
258.	Avionics Technicians	$46,950
259.	Electrical and Electronics Drafters	$46,830
260.	Industrial Engineering Technicians	$46,810
261.	Purchasing Agents and Buyers, Farm Products	$46,770
262.	Broadcast News Analysts	$46,710
263.	Film and Video Editors	$46,670
264.	Construction and Building Inspectors	$46,570
265.	Special Education Teachers, Preschool, Kindergarten, and Elementary School	$46,360
266.	Curators	$46,300
267.	Middle School Teachers, Except Special and Vocational Education	$46,300
268.	Telecommunications Line Installers and Repairers	$46,280
269.	Plant and System Operators, All Other	$46,270
270.	Precision Instrument and Equipment Repairers, All Other	$46,250
271.	Pile-Driver Operators	$46,180
272.	Geological and Petroleum Technicians	$46,160
273.	Stationary Engineers and Boiler Operators	$46,040
274.	Mechanical Engineering Technicians	$45,850
275.	Millwrights	$45,630
276.	Tax Examiners, Collectors, and Revenue Agents	$45,620
277.	Court Reporters	$45,610
278.	Elementary School Teachers, Except Special Education	$45,570
279.	Control and Valve Installers and Repairers, Except Mechanical Door	$45,440
280.	Aircraft Structure, Surfaces, Rigging, and Systems Assemblers	$45,410
281.	Gas Compressor and Gas Pumping Station Operators	$45,400
282.	Forensic Science Technicians	$45,330
283.	Electrical and Electronics Repairers, Commercial and Industrial Equipment	$45,180

Rank	Title	Median Earnings
284.	Legal Support Workers, All Other	$45,140
285.	Postal Service Clerks	$44,800
286.	Electro-Mechanical Technicians	$44,720
287.	Wholesale and Retail Buyers, Except Farm Products	$44,640
288.	Appraisers and Assessors of Real Estate	$44,460
289.	Postal Service Mail Carriers	$44,350
290.	Tool and Die Makers	$44,290
291.	Vocational Education Teachers, Middle School	$44,240
292.	Adult Literacy, Remedial Education, and GED Teachers and Instructors	$43,910
293.	Postal Service Mail Sorters, Processors, and Processing Machine Operators	$43,900
294.	Vocational Education Teachers, Postsecondary	$43,900
295.	Designers, All Other	$43,870
296.	Insurance Sales Agents	$43,870
297.	Fish and Game Wardens	$43,700
298.	Mechanical Drafters	$43,700
299.	Electricians	$43,610
300.	Kindergarten Teachers, Except Special Education	$43,580
301.	Social Workers, All Other	$43,580
302.	First-Line Supervisors/Managers of Office and Administrative Support Workers	$43,510
303.	Rail Car Repairers	$43,320
304.	Marriage and Family Therapists	$43,210
305.	Electrical and Electronics Installers and Repairers, Transportation Equipment	$43,110
306.	Property, Real Estate, and Community Association Managers	$43,070
307.	Drafters, All Other	$43,060
308.	Medical and Public Health Social Workers	$43,040
309.	Paralegals and Legal Assistants	$43,040
310.	Food Service Managers	$43,020
311.	Sound Engineering Technicians	$43,010
312.	Brickmasons and Blockmasons	$42,980
313.	Plumbers, Pipefitters, and Steamfitters	$42,770
314.	Advertising Sales Agents	$42,750
315.	Media and Communication Workers, All Other	$42,570
316.	Probation Officers and Correctional Treatment Specialists	$42,500
317.	Numerical Tool and Process Control Programmers	$42,480
318.	Employment, Recruitment, and Placement Specialists	$42,420
319.	Lodging Managers	$42,320
320.	Cardiovascular Technologists and Technicians	$42,300
321.	Interior Designers	$42,260
322.	Therapists, All Other	$42,250
323.	Meeting and Convention Planners	$42,180
324.	Occupational Health and Safety Technicians	$42,160
325.	Occupational Therapist Assistants	$42,060
326.	Model Makers, Metal and Plastic	$42,050
327.	Artists and Related Workers, All Other	$41,990
328.	Fine Artists, Including Painters, Sculptors, and Illustrators	$41,970
329.	Architectural and Civil Drafters	$41,960
330.	Set and Exhibit Designers	$41,820
331.	Farm and Home Management Advisors	$41,710
332.	First-Line Supervisors/Managers, Protective Service Workers, All Other	$41,570
333.	Computer Support Specialists	$41,470
334.	Physical Therapist Assistants	$41,360
335.	Health Educators	$41,330
336.	Locomotive Firers	$41,290
337.	Tapers	$41,280
338.	Roof Bolters, Mining	$41,250
339.	Fire Fighters	$41,190
340.	Gaming Supervisors	$41,160
341.	Athletes and Sports Competitors	$41,060
342.	Industrial Machinery Mechanics	$41,050
343.	Refractory Materials Repairers, Except Brickmasons	$40,780
344.	Archivists	$40,730
345.	Medical Equipment Repairers	$40,580
346.	Civil Engineering Technicians	$40,560
347.	Environmental Engineering Technicians	$40,560
348.	Audio-Visual Collections Specialists	$40,530
349.	Structural Iron and Steel Workers	$40,480
350.	Mobile Heavy Equipment Mechanics, Except Engines	$40,440
351.	Continuous Mining Machine Operators	$40,430
352.	Chemical Equipment Operators and Tenders	$40,290
353.	Camera Operators, Television, Video, and Motion Picture	$40,060
354.	Rail-Track Laying and Maintenance Equipment Operators	$40,000
355.	Mine Cutting and Channeling Machine Operators	$39,990
356.	Graphic Designers	$39,900
357.	Explosives Workers, Ordnance Handling Experts, and Blasters	$39,890
358.	Aircraft Cargo Handling Supervisors	$39,840
359.	Pump Operators, Except Wellhead Pumpers	$39,800
360.	Real Estate Sales Agents	$39,760
361.	Music Directors and Composers	$39,750
362.	Clergy	$39,680
363.	Commercial Divers	$39,590
364.	First-Line Supervisors/Managers of Helpers, Laborers, and Material Movers, Hand	$39,570
365.	Chemical Technicians	$39,240
366.	Riggers	$39,220
367.	Rail Transportation Workers, All Other	$39,150
368.	Respiratory Therapy Technicians	$39,120
369.	Shuttle Car Operators	$39,060
370.	Crane and Tower Operators	$39,040
371.	Bridge and Lock Tenders	$39,010
372.	Production, Planning, and Expediting Clerks	$38,620
373.	Rotary Drill Operators, Oil and Gas	$38,460
374.	Reinforcing Iron and Rebar Workers	$38,220
375.	Counselors, All Other	$38,210
376.	Legal Secretaries	$38,190
377.	Tire Builders	$38,120
378.	Agricultural Inspectors	$38,100
379.	Environmental Science and Protection Technicians, Including Health	$38,090
380.	Life, Physical, and Social Science Technicians, All Other	$37,920
381.	Radio Operators	$37,890
382.	Mathematical Technicians	$37,880
383.	Rail Yard Engineers, Dinkey Operators, and Hostlers	$37,880

(continued)

(continued)

Rank	Title	Median Earnings
384.	Embalmers	$37,840
385.	First-Line Supervisors/Managers of Farming, Fishing, and Forestry Workers	$37,750
386.	Education Administrators, Preschool and Child Care Center/Program	$37,740
387.	Radio Mechanics	$37,690
388.	Bus and Truck Mechanics and Diesel Engine Specialists	$37,660
389.	Heating, Air Conditioning, and Refrigeration Mechanics and Installers	$37,660
390.	Airfield Operations Specialists	$37,630
391.	Eligibility Interviewers, Government Programs	$37,540
392.	Child, Family, and School Social Workers	$37,480
393.	Mining Machine Operators, All Other	$37,370
394.	Sheet Metal Workers	$37,360
395.	First-Line Supervisors/Managers of Landscaping, Lawn Service, and Groundskeeping Workers	$37,300
396.	Loading Machine Operators, Underground Mining	$37,250
397.	Executive Secretaries and Administrative Assistants	$37,240
398.	Healthcare Practitioners and Technical Workers, All Other	$37,200
399.	Traffic Technicians	$37,140
400.	Farmers and Ranchers	$37,130
401.	Cargo and Freight Agents	$37,110
402.	Insulation Workers, Mechanical	$36,900
403.	Operating Engineers and Other Construction Equipment Operators	$36,890
404.	Tile and Marble Setters	$36,590
405.	Athletic Trainers	$36,560
406.	Carpenters	$36,550
407.	Licensed Practical and Licensed Vocational Nurses	$36,550
408.	Computer, Automated Teller, and Office Machine Repairers	$36,480
409.	Brokerage Clerks	$36,390
410.	Law Clerks	$36,360
411.	Derrick Operators, Oil and Gas	$36,240
412.	Wellhead Pumpers	$36,150
413.	Drywall and Ceiling Tile Installers	$36,140
414.	Surgical Technologists	$36,080
415.	Water and Liquid Waste Treatment Plant and System Operators	$36,070
416.	Title Examiners, Abstractors, and Searchers	$36,020
417.	Stonemasons	$35,960
418.	Loan Counselors	$35,790
419.	Correctional Officers and Jailers	$35,760
420.	Biological Technicians	$35,710
421.	Painters, Transportation Equipment	$35,680
422.	Interpreters and Translators	$35,560
423.	Extraction Workers, All Other	$35,450
424.	Hazardous Materials Removal Workers	$35,450
425.	Mental Health and Substance Abuse Social Workers	$35,410
426.	Patternmakers, Metal and Plastic	$35,380
427.	Community and Social Service Specialists, All Other	$35,210
428.	Automotive Body and Related Repairers	$35,180
429.	Health Technologists and Technicians, All Other	$35,140
430.	Truck Drivers, Heavy and Tractor-Trailer	$35,040

Rank	Title	Median Earnings
431.	Recreational Therapists	$34,990
432.	Separating, Filtering, Clarifying, Precipitating, and Still Machine Setters, Operators, and Tenders	$34,970
433.	Camera and Photographic Equipment Repairers	$34,850
434.	Audio and Video Equipment Technicians	$34,840
435.	Security and Fire Alarm Systems Installers	$34,810
436.	Machinists	$34,770
437.	Metal Workers and Plastic Workers, All Other	$34,710
438.	Plasterers and Stucco Masons	$34,700
439.	Choreographers	$34,660
440.	Glaziers	$34,610
441.	Carpet Installers	$34,560
442.	Maintenance Workers, Machinery	$34,550
443.	Earth Drillers, Except Oil and Gas	$34,500
444.	Mental Health Counselors	$34,380
445.	Chefs and Head Cooks	$34,370
446.	Museum Technicians and Conservators	$34,340
447.	Directors, Religious Activities and Education	$34,260
448.	Sales and Related Workers, All Other	$34,250
449.	Bailiffs	$34,210
450.	Floor Layers, Except Carpet, Wood, and Hard Tiles	$34,190
451.	Telephone Operators	$34,140
452.	Desktop Publishers	$34,130
453.	Substance Abuse and Behavioral Disorder Counselors	$34,040
454.	First-Line Supervisors/Managers of Retail Sales Workers	$33,960
455.	Home Appliance Repairers	$33,860
456.	Social Science Research Assistants	$33,860
457.	Dredge Operators	$33,820
458.	Automotive Service Technicians and Mechanics	$33,780
459.	Human Resources Assistants, Except Payroll and Timekeeping	$33,750
460.	Private Detectives and Investigators	$33,750
461.	Paperhangers	$33,710
462.	Hoist and Winch Operators	$33,620
463.	Lay-Out Workers, Metal and Plastic	$33,600
464.	Computer Operators	$33,560
465.	Reporters and Correspondents	$33,470
466.	Self-Enrichment Education Teachers	$33,440
467.	Massage Therapists	$33,400
468.	Survey Researchers	$33,360
469.	Prepress Technicians and Workers	$33,310
470.	Engine and Other Machine Assemblers	$33,250
471.	Motorboat Mechanics	$33,210
472.	Procurement Clerks	$33,100
473.	Forest Fire Inspectors and Prevention Specialists	$32,940
474.	Installation, Maintenance, and Repair Workers, All Other	$32,940
475.	Excavating and Loading Machine and Dragline Operators	$32,930
476.	Service Unit Operators, Oil, Gas, and Mining	$32,910
477.	Electric Motor, Power Tool, and Related Repairers	$32,860
478.	Semiconductor Processors	$32,860
479.	Medical and Clinical Laboratory Technicians	$32,840
480.	First-Line Supervisors/Managers of Personal Service Workers	$32,800
481.	Fabric and Apparel Patternmakers	$32,730

Rank	Title	Median Earnings
482.	Cement Masons and Concrete Finishers	$32,650
483.	Metal-Refining Furnace Operators and Tenders	$32,640
484.	Dental Laboratory Technicians	$32,580
485.	Job Printers	$32,410
486.	Payroll and Timekeeping Clerks	$32,400
487.	Motorboat Operators	$32,350
488.	Surveying and Mapping Technicians	$32,340
489.	Roofers	$32,260
490.	Dispatchers, Except Police, Fire, and Ambulance	$32,190
491.	Education, Training, and Library Workers, All Other	$32,160
492.	Lathe and Turning Machine Tool Setters, Operators, and Tenders, Metal and Plastic	$32,160
493.	Bus Drivers, Transit and Intercity	$32,090
494.	Locksmiths and Safe Repairers	$32,020
495.	Tank Car, Truck, and Ship Loaders	$31,970
496.	Maintenance and Repair Workers, General	$31,910
497.	Logging Workers, All Other	$31,870
498.	Makeup Artists, Theatrical and Performance	$31,820
499.	Agricultural and Food Science Technicians	$31,730
500.	Communications Equipment Operators, All Other	$31,680
501.	Computer-Controlled Machine Tool Operators, Metal and Plastic	$31,670
502.	Terrazzo Workers and Finishers	$31,630
503.	Mechanical Door Repairers	$31,610
504.	Milling and Planing Machine Setters, Operators, and Tenders, Metal and Plastic	$31,570
505.	Highway Maintenance Workers	$31,540
506.	Patternmakers, Wood	$31,510
507.	Recreational Vehicle Service Technicians	$31,510
508.	Paper Goods Machine Setters, Operators, and Tenders	$31,490
509.	Police, Fire, and Ambulance Dispatchers	$31,470
510.	Septic Tank Servicers and Sewer Pipe Cleaners	$31,430
511.	Welders, Cutters, Solderers, and Brazers	$31,400
512.	Paving, Surfacing, and Tamping Equipment Operators	$31,300
513.	First-Line Supervisors/Managers of Housekeeping and Janitorial Workers	$31,290
514.	Statistical Assistants	$31,250
515.	Painters, Construction and Maintenance	$31,190
516.	Medical Appliance Technicians	$31,180
517.	Information and Record Clerks, All Other	$31,150
518.	Insurance Claims and Policy Processing Clerks	$31,120
519.	Rolling Machine Setters, Operators, and Tenders, Metal and Plastic	$31,050
520.	Printing Machine Operators	$30,990
521.	Court, Municipal, and License Clerks	$30,980
522.	Welding, Soldering, and Brazing Machine Setters, Operators, and Tenders	$30,980
523.	Loan Interviewers and Clerks	$30,970
524.	Watch Repairers	$30,900
525.	Forest and Conservation Technicians	$30,880
526.	Heat Treating Equipment Setters, Operators, and Tenders, Metal and Plastic	$30,850
527.	Automotive Glass Installers and Repairers	$30,720
528.	Broadcast Technicians	$30,690
529.	Tool Grinders, Filers, and Sharpeners	$30,640
530.	Sailors and Marine Oilers	$30,630
531.	Bookkeeping, Accounting, and Auditing Clerks	$30,560
532.	Multiple Machine Tool Setters, Operators, and Tenders, Metal and Plastic	$30,530
533.	Insulation Workers, Floor, Ceiling, and Wall	$30,510
534.	Construction and Related Workers, All Other	$30,470
535.	Meter Readers, Utilities	$30,330
536.	Pipelayers	$30,330
537.	Furnace, Kiln, Oven, Drier, and Kettle Operators and Tenders	$30,320
538.	Opticians, Dispensing	$30,300
539.	Structural Metal Fabricators and Fitters	$30,290
540.	Material Moving Workers, All Other	$30,270
541.	Bookbinders	$30,260
542.	Dental Assistants	$30,220
543.	Transportation Workers, All Other	$30,180
544.	Parking Enforcement Workers	$30,160
545.	Motorcycle Mechanics	$30,050
546.	Electronic Home Entertainment Equipment Installers and Repairers	$29,980
547.	Credit Authorizers, Checkers, and Clerks	$29,970
548.	Medical Transcriptionists	$29,950
549.	Drilling and Boring Machine Tool Setters, Operators, and Tenders, Metal and Plastic	$29,870
550.	Jewelers and Precious Stone and Metal Workers	$29,750
551.	Logging Equipment Operators	$29,700
552.	Pourers and Casters, Metal	$29,570
553.	Farm Equipment Mechanics	$29,460
554.	Word Processors and Typists	$29,430
555.	Inspectors, Testers, Sorters, Samplers, and Weighers	$29,420
556.	Mixing and Blending Machine Setters, Operators, and Tenders	$29,330
557.	Log Graders and Scalers	$29,240
558.	Travel Agents	$29,210
559.	Musical Instrument Repairers and Tuners	$29,200
560.	Rehabilitation Counselors	$29,200
561.	Bill and Account Collectors	$29,050
562.	Forging Machine Setters, Operators, and Tenders, Metal and Plastic	$28,980
563.	Refuse and Recyclable Material Collectors	$28,970
564.	Floor Sanders and Finishers	$28,890
565.	Billing and Posting Clerks and Machine Operators	$28,850
566.	Timing Device Assemblers, Adjusters, and Calibrators	$28,830
567.	Foundry Mold and Coremakers	$28,740
568.	Coin, Vending, and Amusement Machine Servicers and Repairers	$28,710
569.	Fallers	$28,710
570.	Correspondence Clerks	$28,700
571.	Segmental Pavers	$28,700
572.	Helpers—Extraction Workers	$28,680
573.	Extruding and Forming Machine Setters, Operators, and Tenders, Synthetic and Glass Fibers	$28,670
574.	Teachers and Instructors, All Other	$28,660
575.	Reservation and Transportation Ticket Agents and Travel Clerks	$28,540
576.	Model Makers, Wood	$28,470
577.	Travel Guides	$28,460
578.	New Accounts Clerks	$28,390
579.	Fabric Menders, Except Garment	$28,370

(continued)

(continued)

Rank	Title	Median Earnings
580.	Customer Service Representatives	$28,330
581.	Extruding and Drawing Machine Setters, Operators, and Tenders, Metal and Plastic	$28,250
582.	Tree Trimmers and Pruners	$28,250
583.	Electronic Equipment Installers and Repairers, Motor Vehicles	$28,220
584.	Medical Secretaries	$28,090
585.	Crushing, Grinding, and Polishing Machine Setters, Operators, and Tenders	$28,080
586.	Grinding, Lapping, Polishing, and Buffing Machine Tool Setters, Operators, and Tenders, Metal and Plastic	$28,080
587.	Medical Records and Health Information Technicians	$28,030
588.	Cutting and Slicing Machine Setters, Operators, and Tenders	$27,930
589.	Animal Control Workers	$27,910
590.	Pest Control Workers	$27,880
591.	Graduate Teaching Assistants	$27,840
592.	Psychiatric Technicians	$27,780
593.	Extruding, Forming, Pressing, and Compacting Machine Setters, Operators, and Tenders	$27,710
594.	Electromechanical Equipment Assemblers	$27,560
595.	Plating and Coating Machine Setters, Operators, and Tenders, Metal and Plastic	$27,470
596.	Proofreaders and Copy Markers	$27,450
597.	Secretaries, Except Legal, Medical, and Executive	$27,450
598.	Parts Salespersons	$27,430
599.	Tax Preparers	$27,360
600.	Industrial Truck and Tractor Operators	$27,270
601.	Fishers and Related Fishing Workers	$27,250
602.	Upholsterers	$27,230
603.	Conveyor Operators and Tenders	$27,220
604.	Office and Administrative Support Workers, All Other	$27,200
605.	Gaming Surveillance Officers and Gaming Investigators	$27,130
606.	Rock Splitters, Quarry	$27,130
607.	Animal Breeders	$27,090
608.	Emergency Medical Technicians and Paramedics	$27,070
609.	Cabinetmakers and Bench Carpenters	$27,010
610.	Healthcare Support Workers, All Other	$26,990
611.	First-Line Supervisors/Managers of Food Preparation and Serving Workers	$26,980
612.	Coaches and Scouts	$26,950
613.	Butchers and Meat Cutters	$26,930
614.	Protective Service Workers, All Other	$26,920
615.	Outdoor Power Equipment and Other Small Engine Mechanics	$26,910
616.	Coating, Painting, and Spraying Machine Setters, Operators, and Tenders	$26,830
617.	Veterinary Technologists and Technicians	$26,780
618.	Assemblers and Fabricators, All Other	$26,730
619.	Pesticide Handlers, Sprayers, and Applicators, Vegetation	$26,700
620.	Library Technicians	$26,560
621.	Fence Erectors	$26,400
622.	Cutting, Punching, and Press Machine Setters, Operators, and Tenders, Metal and Plastic	$26,340
623.	Order Clerks	$26,340

Rank	Title	Median Earnings
624.	Construction Laborers	$26,320
625.	Animal Trainers	$26,310
626.	Coil Winders, Tapers, and Finishers	$26,300
627.	Interviewers, Except Eligibility and Loan	$26,290
628.	Medical Assistants	$26,290
629.	Photographers	$26,170
630.	Skin Care Specialists	$26,170
631.	Shipping, Receiving, and Traffic Clerks	$26,070
632.	Fiberglass Laminators and Fabricators	$25,980
633.	Medical Equipment Preparers	$25,950
634.	Fitness Trainers and Aerobics Instructors	$25,910
635.	Costume Attendants	$25,740
636.	Roustabouts, Oil and Gas	$25,700
637.	Pharmacy Technicians	$25,630
638.	Etchers and Engravers	$25,590
639.	Social and Human Service Assistants	$25,580
640.	Bindery Workers	$25,570
641.	Electrical and Electronic Equipment Assemblers	$25,560
642.	Molding, Coremaking, and Casting Machine Setters, Operators, and Tenders, Metal and Plastic	$25,560
643.	Ophthalmic Laboratory Technicians	$25,460
644.	Weighers, Measurers, Checkers, and Samplers, Recordkeeping	$25,370
645.	Helpers—Brickmasons, Blockmasons, Stonemasons, and Tile and Marble Setters	$25,350
646.	Truck Drivers, Light or Delivery Services	$25,300
647.	Cementing and Gluing Machine Operators and Tenders	$25,170
648.	Building Cleaning Workers, All Other	$25,090
649.	Manufactured Building and Mobile Home Installers	$25,080
650.	Occupational Therapist Aides	$25,020
651.	Furniture Finishers	$25,010
652.	Molders, Shapers, and Casters, Except Metal and Plastic	$25,010
653.	Public Address System and Other Announcers	$24,990
654.	Production Workers, All Other	$24,890
655.	Bus Drivers, School	$24,820
656.	Data Entry Keyers	$24,690
657.	Concierges	$24,600
658.	Office Machine Operators, Except Computer	$24,540
659.	Religious Workers, All Other	$24,330
660.	Radio and Television Announcers	$24,310
661.	Textile Knitting and Weaving Machine Setters, Operators, and Tenders	$24,290
662.	Sawing Machine Setters, Operators, and Tenders, Wood	$24,280
663.	Team Assemblers	$24,190
664.	Craft Artists	$24,090
665.	Dietetic Technicians	$24,040
666.	Woodworking Machine Setters, Operators, and Tenders, Except Sawing	$23,940
667.	Helpers—Pipelayers, Plumbers, Pipefitters, and Steamfitters	$23,910
668.	Psychiatric Aides	$23,900
669.	Cooling and Freezing Equipment Operators and Tenders	$23,880
670.	Grinding and Polishing Workers, Hand	$23,880
671.	Merchandise Displayers and Window Trimmers	$23,820

Rank	Title	Median Earnings
672.	Mail Clerks and Mail Machine Operators, Except Postal Service	$23,810
673.	Helpers—Electricians	$23,760
674.	Office Clerks, General	$23,710
675.	Farm Labor Contractors	$23,550
676.	Food and Tobacco Roasting, Baking, and Drying Machine Operators and Tenders	$23,510
677.	Models	$23,340
678.	Textile Bleaching and Dyeing Machine Operators and Tenders	$23,290
679.	Photographic Process Workers	$23,280
680.	Barbers	$23,150
681.	Gaming Cage Workers	$23,150
682.	Food Batchmakers	$23,100
683.	Helpers—Carpenters	$23,060
684.	Textile Winding, Twisting, and Drawing Out Machine Setters, Operators, and Tenders	$23,050
685.	Packaging and Filling Machine Operators and Tenders	$22,990
686.	Painting, Coating, and Decorating Workers	$22,970
687.	Textile, Apparel, and Furnishings Workers, All Other	$22,950
688.	Tailors, Dressmakers, and Custom Sewers	$22,910
689.	Receptionists and Information Clerks	$22,900
690.	Umpires, Referees, and Other Sports Officials	$22,880
691.	Cooks, Private Household	$22,870
692.	Cleaning, Washing, and Metal Pickling Equipment Operators and Tenders	$22,850
693.	Helpers, Construction Trades, All Other	$22,760
694.	Slot Key Persons	$22,720
695.	Motor Vehicle Operators, All Other	$22,710
696.	Preschool Teachers, Except Special Education	$22,680
697.	Residential Advisors	$22,670
698.	Machine Feeders and Offbearers	$22,640
699.	Switchboard Operators, Including Answering Service	$22,640
700.	Woodworkers, All Other	$22,580
701.	Agricultural Workers, All Other	$22,470
702.	Cutters and Trimmers, Hand	$22,330
703.	Helpers—Installation, Maintenance, and Repair Workers	$22,270
704.	Nursing Aides, Orderlies, and Attendants	$22,180
705.	Demonstrators and Product Promoters	$22,150
706.	Tellers	$22,140
707.	File Clerks	$22,090
708.	Physical Therapist Aides	$22,060
709.	Bakers	$22,030
710.	Shoe Machine Operators and Tenders	$21,910
711.	Gaming Service Workers, All Other	$21,890
712.	Bicycle Repairers	$21,790
713.	Helpers—Roofers	$21,760
714.	Floral Designers	$21,700
715.	Slaughterers and Meat Packers	$21,690
716.	Library Assistants, Clerical	$21,640
717.	Textile Cutting Machine Setters, Operators, and Tenders	$21,620
718.	Cooks, All Other	$21,610
719.	Couriers and Messengers	$21,540
720.	Security Guards	$21,530
721.	Tire Repairers and Changers	$21,340
722.	Helpers—Painters, Paperhangers, Plasterers, and Stucco Masons	$21,330
723.	Hairdressers, Hairstylists, and Cosmetologists	$21,320
724.	Food Cooking Machine Operators and Tenders	$21,280
725.	Landscaping and Groundskeeping Workers	$21,260
726.	Laborers and Freight, Stock, and Material Movers, Hand	$21,220
727.	Crossing Guards	$21,060
728.	Telemarketers	$20,990
729.	Forest and Conservation Workers	$20,810
730.	Driver/Sales Workers	$20,770
731.	Helpers—Production Workers	$20,740
732.	Teacher Assistants	$20,740
733.	Gaming Change Persons and Booth Cashiers	$20,680
734.	Recreation Workers	$20,470
735.	Shoe and Leather Workers and Repairers	$20,450
736.	Stock Clerks and Order Fillers	$20,440
737.	Grounds Maintenance Workers, All Other	$20,420
738.	Tour Guides and Escorts	$20,420
739.	Cooks, Institution and Cafeteria	$20,410
740.	Ambulance Drivers and Attendants, Except Emergency Medical Technicians	$20,370
741.	Meat, Poultry, and Fish Cutters and Trimmers	$20,370
742.	Sewers, Hand	$20,370
743.	Funeral Attendants	$20,350
744.	Taxi Drivers and Chauffeurs	$20,350
745.	Cooks, Restaurant	$20,340
746.	Agricultural Equipment Operators	$20,230
747.	Door-To-Door Sales Workers, News and Street Vendors, and Related Workers	$20,190
748.	Transportation Attendants, Except Flight Attendants and Baggage Porters	$20,070
749.	Veterinary Assistants and Laboratory Animal Caretakers	$19,960
750.	Janitors and Cleaners, Except Maids and Housekeeping Cleaners	$19,930
751.	Retail Salespersons	$19,760
752.	Counter and Rental Clerks	$19,570
753.	Photographic Processing Machine Operators	$19,500
754.	Pharmacy Aides	$19,440
755.	Home Health Aides	$19,420
756.	Manicurists and Pedicurists	$19,190
757.	Farmworkers, Farm and Ranch Animals	$19,060
758.	Personal Care and Service Workers, All Other	$18,970
759.	Sewing Machine Operators	$18,810
760.	Gaming and Sports Book Writers and Runners	$18,800
761.	Locker Room, Coatroom, and Dressing Room Attendants	$18,610
762.	Hotel, Motel, and Resort Desk Clerks	$18,460
763.	Baggage Porters and Bellhops	$18,360
764.	Nonfarm Animal Caretakers	$18,140
765.	Food Servers, Nonrestaurant	$18,090
766.	Cleaners of Vehicles and Equipment	$18,060
767.	Cooks, Short Order	$17,880
768.	Laundry and Dry-Cleaning Workers	$17,850
769.	Pressers, Textile, Garment, and Related Materials	$17,800

(continued)

(continued)

Rank	Title	Median Earnings
770.	Food Preparation and Serving Related Workers, All Other	$17,780
771.	Personal and Home Care Aides	$17,770
772.	Service Station Attendants	$17,750
773.	Packers and Packagers, Hand	$17,650
774.	Child Care Workers	$17,630
775.	Maids and Housekeeping Cleaners	$17,580
776.	Motion Picture Projectionists	$17,450
777.	Food Preparation Workers	$17,410
778.	Parking Lot Attendants	$17,320
779.	Graders and Sorters, Agricultural Products	$17,200
780.	Lifeguards, Ski Patrol, and Other Recreational Protective Service Workers	$17,160
781.	Cashiers	$16,810
782.	Farmworkers and Laborers, Crop, Nursery, and Greenhouse	$16,540
783.	Bartenders	$16,350
784.	Amusement and Recreation Attendants	$16,290
785.	Hosts and Hostesses, Restaurant, Lounge, and Coffee Shop	$16,170
786.	Shampooers	$16,170
787.	Counter Attendants, Cafeteria, Food Concession, and Coffee Shop	$16,130
788.	Ushers, Lobby Attendants, and Ticket Takers	$15,880
789.	Dishwashers	$15,750
790.	Legislators	$15,660
791.	Cooks, Fast Food	$15,410
792.	Dining Room and Cafeteria Attendants and Bartender Helpers	$15,310
793.	Combined Food Preparation and Serving Workers, Including Fast Food	$15,050
794.	Waiters and Waitresses	$14,850
795.	Gaming Dealers	$14,730

Jobs Ranked by Earnings Within Education and Training Levels

The lists in this section organize jobs into groups based on the education or training typically required for entry.

Jobs in these lists are assigned to the level where the Department of Labor assigns them. Keep in mind that in many jobs educational or training requirements are flexible and people may be hired despite having somewhat different credentials. The dollar figures show the median annual earnings for *all* workers in the occupation, regardless of how much education or training they actually have. In Part III you can see the actual educational attainments of the workers in each occupation.

Jobs That Require Short-Term On-the-Job Training

Average for all jobs at this level: $20,297

Occupation	Median Earnings
1. Postal Service Clerks	$44,800
2. Postal Service Mail Carriers	$44,350

Occupation	Median Earnings
3. Postal Service Mail Sorters, Processors, and Processing Machine Operators	$43,900
4. Riggers	$39,220
5. Shuttle Car Operators	$39,060
6. Bridge and Lock Tenders	$39,010
7. Production, Planning, and Expediting Clerks	$38,620
8. Traffic Technicians	$37,140
9. Maintenance Workers, Machinery	$34,550
10. Telephone Operators	$34,140
11. Human Resources Assistants, Except Payroll and Timekeeping	$33,750
12. Engine and Other Machine Assemblers	$33,250
13. Procurement Clerks	$33,100
14. Communications Equipment Operators, All Other	$31,680
15. Information and Record Clerks, All Other	$31,150
16. Court, Municipal, and License Clerks	$30,980
17. Loan Interviewers and Clerks	$30,970
18. Sailors and Marine Oilers	$30,630
19. Meter Readers, Utilities	$30,330
20. Transportation Workers, All Other	$30,180
21. Parking Enforcement Workers	$30,160
22. Credit Authorizers, Checkers, and Clerks	$29,970
23. Bill and Account Collectors	$29,050
24. Refuse and Recyclable Material Collectors	$28,970
25. Correspondence Clerks	$28,700
26. Helpers—Extraction Workers	$28,680
27. Reservation and Transportation Ticket Agents and Travel Clerks	$28,540
28. Tree Trimmers and Pruners	$28,250
29. Electromechanical Equipment Assemblers	$27,560
30. Proofreaders and Copy Markers	$27,450
31. Industrial Truck and Tractor Operators	$27,270
32. Conveyor Operators and Tenders	$27,220
33. Office and Administrative Support Workers, All Other	$27,200
34. Animal Breeders	$27,090
35. Healthcare Support Workers, All Other	$26,990
36. Protective Service Workers, All Other	$26,920
37. Order Clerks	$26,340
38. Coil Winders, Tapers, and Finishers	$26,300
39. Interviewers, Except Eligibility and Loan	$26,290
40. Shipping, Receiving, and Traffic Clerks	$26,070
41. Medical Equipment Preparers	$25,950
42. Costume Attendants	$25,740
43. Bindery Workers	$25,570
44. Electrical and Electronic Equipment Assemblers	$25,560
45. Weighers, Measurers, Checkers, and Samplers, Recordkeeping	$25,370
46. Helpers—Brickmasons, Blockmasons, Stonemasons, and Tile and Marble Setters	$25,350
47. Truck Drivers, Light or Delivery Services	$25,300
48. Building Cleaning Workers, All Other	$25,090
49. Occupational Therapist Aides	$25,020
50. Bus Drivers, School	$24,820
51. Office Machine Operators, Except Computer	$24,540
52. Helpers—Pipelayers, Plumbers, Pipefitters, and Steamfitters	$23,910

Occupation	Median Earnings
53. Psychiatric Aides	$23,900
54. Mail Clerks and Mail Machine Operators, Except Postal Service	$23,810
55. Helpers—Electricians	$23,760
56. Office Clerks, General	$23,710
57. Food and Tobacco Roasting, Baking, and Drying Machine Operators and Tenders	$23,510
58. Gaming Cage Workers	$23,150
59. Food Batchmakers	$23,100
60. Helpers—Carpenters	$23,060
61. Packaging and Filling Machine Operators and Tenders	$22,990
62. Painting, Coating, and Decorating Workers	$22,970
63. Textile, Apparel, and Furnishings Workers, All Other	$22,950
64. Receptionists and Information Clerks	$22,900
65. Helpers, Construction Trades, All Other	$22,760
66. Motor Vehicle Operators, All Other	$22,710
67. Machine Feeders and Offbearers	$22,640
68. Switchboard Operators, Including Answering Service	$22,640
69. Agricultural Workers, All Other	$22,470
70. Cutters and Trimmers, Hand	$22,330
71. Helpers—Installation, Maintenance, and Repair Workers	$22,270
72. Tellers	$22,140
73. File Clerks	$22,090
74. Physical Therapist Aides	$22,060
75. Helpers—Roofers	$21,760
76. Library Assistants, Clerical	$21,640
77. Couriers and Messengers	$21,540
78. Security Guards	$21,530
79. Tire Repairers and Changers	$21,340
80. Helpers—Painters, Paperhangers, Plasterers, and Stucco Masons	$21,330
81. Food Cooking Machine Operators and Tenders	$21,280
82. Landscaping and Groundskeeping Workers	$21,260
83. Laborers and Freight, Stock, and Material Movers, Hand	$21,220
84. Crossing Guards	$21,060
85. Telemarketers	$20,990
86. Driver/Sales Workers	$20,770
87. Helpers—Production Workers	$20,740
88. Teacher Assistants	$20,740
89. Gaming Change Persons and Booth Cashiers	$20,680
90. Recreation Workers	$20,470
91. Stock Clerks and Order Fillers	$20,440
92. Grounds Maintenance Workers, All Other	$20,420
93. Meat, Poultry, and Fish Cutters and Trimmers	$20,370
94. Sewers, Hand	$20,370
95. Funeral Attendants	$20,350
96. Taxi Drivers and Chauffeurs	$20,350
97. Door-To-Door Sales Workers, News and Street Vendors, and Related Workers	$20,190
98. Transportation Attendants, Except Flight Attendants and Baggage Porters	$20,070
99. Veterinary Assistants and Laboratory Animal Caretakers	$19,960
100. Janitors and Cleaners, Except Maids and Housekeeping Cleaners	$19,930

Occupation	Median Earnings
101. Retail Salespersons	$19,760
102. Counter and Rental Clerks	$19,570
103. Photographic Processing Machine Operators	$19,500
104. Pharmacy Aides	$19,440
105. Home Health Aides	$19,420
106. Farmworkers, Farm and Ranch Animals	$19,060
107. Personal Care and Service Workers, All Other	$18,970
108. Gaming and Sports Book Writers and Runners	$18,800
109. Locker Room, Coatroom, and Dressing Room Attendants	$18,610
110. Hotel, Motel, and Resort Desk Clerks	$18,460
111. Baggage Porters and Bellhops	$18,360
112. Nonfarm Animal Caretakers	$18,140
113. Food Servers, Nonrestaurant	$18,090
114. Cleaners of Vehicles and Equipment	$18,060
115. Cooks, Short Order	$17,880
116. Pressers, Textile, Garment, and Related Materials	$17,800
117. Food Preparation and Serving Related Workers, All Other	$17,780
118. Personal and Home Care Aides	$17,770
119. Service Station Attendants	$17,750
120. Packers and Packagers, Hand	$17,650
121. Child Care Workers	$17,630
122. Maids and Housekeeping Cleaners	$17,580
123. Motion Picture Projectionists	$17,450
124. Food Preparation Workers	$17,410
125. Parking Lot Attendants	$17,320
126. Lifeguards, Ski Patrol, and Other Recreational Protective Service Workers	$17,160
127. Cashiers	$16,810
128. Farmworkers and Laborers, Crop, Nursery, and Greenhouse	$16,540
129. Bartenders	$16,350
130. Amusement and Recreation Attendants	$16,290
131. Hosts and Hostesses, Restaurant, Lounge, and Coffee Shop	$16,170
132. Shampooers	$16,170
133. Counter Attendants, Cafeteria, Food Concession, and Coffee Shop	$16,130
134. Ushers, Lobby Attendants, and Ticket Takers	$15,880
135. Dishwashers	$15,750
136. Cooks, Fast Food	$15,410
137. Dining Room and Cafeteria Attendants and Bartender Helpers	$15,310
138. Combined Food Preparation and Serving Workers, Including Fast Food	$15,050
139. Waiters and Waitresses	$14,850

Jobs That Require Moderate-Term On-the-Job Training

Average for all jobs at this level: $30,813

Occupation	Median Earnings
1. Sales Representatives, Wholesale and Manufacturing, Technical and Scientific Products	$64,440
2. Locomotive Engineers	$57,990
3. Railroad Conductors and Yardmasters	$55,530

(continued)

(continued)

	Occupation	Median Earnings
4.	Media and Communication Equipment Workers, All Other	$52,070
5.	Signal and Track Switch Repairers	$50,150
6.	Sales Representatives, Wholesale and Manufacturing, Except Technical and Scientific Products	$49,610
7.	Subway and Streetcar Operators	$48,980
8.	Railroad Brake, Signal, and Switch Operators	$48,860
9.	Sales Representatives, Services, All Other	$48,100
10.	Precision Instrument and Equipment Repairers, All Other	$46,250
11.	Pile-Driver Operators	$46,180
12.	Control and Valve Installers and Repairers, Except Mechanical Door	$45,440
13.	Gas Compressor and Gas Pumping Station Operators	$45,400
14.	Advertising Sales Agents	$42,750
15.	Model Makers, Metal and Plastic	$42,050
16.	Locomotive Firers	$41,290
17.	Tapers	$41,280
18.	Roof Bolters, Mining	$41,250
19.	Refractory Materials Repairers, Except Brickmasons	$40,780
20.	Audio-Visual Collections Specialists	$40,530
21.	Continuous Mining Machine Operators	$40,430
22.	Chemical Equipment Operators and Tenders	$40,290
23.	Camera Operators, Television, Video, and Motion Picture	$40,060
24.	Rail-Track Laying and Maintenance Equipment Operators	$40,000
25.	Mine Cutting and Channeling Machine Operators	$39,990
26.	Explosives Workers, Ordnance Handling Experts, and Blasters	$39,890
27.	Pump Operators, Except Wellhead Pumpers	$39,800
28.	Commercial Divers	$39,590
29.	Rail Transportation Workers, All Other	$39,150
30.	Rotary Drill Operators, Oil and Gas	$38,460
31.	Tire Builders	$38,120
32.	Radio Operators	$37,890
33.	Rail Yard Engineers, Dinkey Operators, and Hostlers	$37,880
34.	Eligibility Interviewers, Government Programs	$37,540
35.	Mining Machine Operators, All Other	$37,370
36.	Loading Machine Operators, Underground Mining	$37,250
37.	Executive Secretaries and Administrative Assistants	$37,240
38.	Cargo and Freight Agents	$37,110
39.	Insulation Workers, Mechanical	$36,900
40.	Operating Engineers and Other Construction Equipment Operators	$36,890
41.	Brokerage Clerks	$36,390
42.	Derrick Operators, Oil and Gas	$36,240
43.	Wellhead Pumpers	$36,150
44.	Drywall and Ceiling Tile Installers	$36,140
45.	Title Examiners, Abstractors, and Searchers	$36,020
46.	Correctional Officers and Jailers	$35,760
47.	Extraction Workers, All Other	$35,450
48.	Hazardous Materials Removal Workers	$35,450
49.	Patternmakers, Metal and Plastic	$35,380
50.	Truck Drivers, Heavy and Tractor-Trailer	$35,040
51.	Separating, Filtering, Clarifying, Precipitating, and Still Machine Setters, Operators, and Tenders	$34,970

	Occupation	Median Earnings
52.	Camera and Photographic Equipment Repairers	$34,850
53.	Metal Workers and Plastic Workers, All Other	$34,710
54.	Carpet Installers	$34,560
55.	Earth Drillers, Except Oil and Gas	$34,500
56.	Sales and Related Workers, All Other	$34,250
57.	Bailiffs	$34,210
58.	Floor Layers, Except Carpet, Wood, and Hard Tiles	$34,190
59.	Dredge Operators	$33,820
60.	Paperhangers	$33,710
61.	Hoist and Winch Operators	$33,620
62.	Lay-Out Workers, Metal and Plastic	$33,600
63.	Computer Operators	$33,560
64.	Installation, Maintenance, and Repair Workers, All Other	$32,940
65.	Excavating and Loading Machine and Dragline Operators	$32,930
66.	Service Unit Operators, Oil, Gas, and Mining	$32,910
67.	Cement Masons and Concrete Finishers	$32,650
68.	Metal-Refining Furnace Operators and Tenders	$32,640
69.	Payroll and Timekeeping Clerks	$32,400
70.	Motorboat Operators	$32,350
71.	Surveying and Mapping Technicians	$32,340
72.	Roofers	$32,260
73.	Dispatchers, Except Police, Fire, and Ambulance	$32,190
74.	Lathe and Turning Machine Tool Setters, Operators, and Tenders, Metal and Plastic	$32,160
75.	Bus Drivers, Transit and Intercity	$32,090
76.	Locksmiths and Safe Repairers	$32,020
77.	Tank Car, Truck, and Ship Loaders	$31,970
78.	Maintenance and Repair Workers, General	$31,910
79.	Logging Workers, All Other	$31,870
80.	Computer-Controlled Machine Tool Operators, Metal and Plastic	$31,670
81.	Mechanical Door Repairers	$31,610
82.	Milling and Planing Machine Setters, Operators, and Tenders, Metal and Plastic	$31,570
83.	Highway Maintenance Workers	$31,540
84.	Paper Goods Machine Setters, Operators, and Tenders	$31,490
85.	Police, Fire, and Ambulance Dispatchers	$31,470
86.	Septic Tank Servicers and Sewer Pipe Cleaners	$31,430
87.	Paving, Surfacing, and Tamping Equipment Operators	$31,300
88.	Statistical Assistants	$31,250
89.	Painters, Construction and Maintenance	$31,190
90.	Insurance Claims and Policy Processing Clerks	$31,120
91.	Rolling Machine Setters, Operators, and Tenders, Metal and Plastic	$31,050
92.	Printing Machine Operators	$30,990
93.	Welding, Soldering, and Brazing Machine Setters, Operators, and Tenders	$30,980
94.	Heat Treating Equipment Setters, Operators, and Tenders, Metal and Plastic	$30,850
95.	Tool Grinders, Filers, and Sharpeners	$30,640
96.	Bookkeeping, Accounting, and Auditing Clerks	$30,560
97.	Multiple Machine Tool Setters, Operators, and Tenders, Metal and Plastic	$30,530
98.	Insulation Workers, Floor, Ceiling, and Wall	$30,510
99.	Construction and Related Workers, All Other	$30,470

Occupation	Median Earnings
100. Pipelayers	$30,330
101. Furnace, Kiln, Oven, Drier, and Kettle Operators and Tenders	$30,320
102. Structural Metal Fabricators and Fitters	$30,290
103. Material Moving Workers, All Other	$30,270
104. Bookbinders	$30,260
105. Dental Assistants	$30,220
106. Drilling and Boring Machine Tool Setters, Operators, and Tenders, Metal and Plastic	$29,870
107. Logging Equipment Operators	$29,700
108. Pourers and Casters, Metal	$29,570
109. Word Processors and Typists	$29,430
110. Inspectors, Testers, Sorters, Samplers, and Weighers	$29,420
111. Mixing and Blending Machine Setters, Operators, and Tenders	$29,330
112. Log Graders and Scalers	$29,240
113. Forging Machine Setters, Operators, and Tenders, Metal and Plastic	$28,980
114. Floor Sanders and Finishers	$28,890
115. Billing and Posting Clerks and Machine Operators	$28,850
116. Timing Device Assemblers, Adjusters, and Calibrators	$28,830
117. Foundry Mold and Coremakers	$28,740
118. Coin, Vending, and Amusement Machine Servicers and Repairers	$28,710
119. Fallers	$28,710
120. Segmental Pavers	$28,700
121. Extruding and Forming Machine Setters, Operators, and Tenders, Synthetic and Glass Fibers	$28,670
122. Travel Guides	$28,460
123. Fabric Menders, Except Garment	$28,370
124. Customer Service Representatives	$28,330
125. Extruding and Drawing Machine Setters, Operators, and Tenders, Metal and Plastic	$28,250
126. Crushing, Grinding, and Polishing Machine Setters, Operators, and Tenders	$28,080
127. Grinding, Lapping, Polishing, and Buffing Machine Tool Setters, Operators, and Tenders, Metal and Plastic	$28,080
128. Cutting and Slicing Machine Setters, Operators, and Tenders	$27,930
129. Animal Control Workers	$27,910
130. Pest Control Workers	$27,880
131. Psychiatric Technicians	$27,780
132. Extruding, Forming, Pressing, and Compacting Machine Setters, Operators, and Tenders	$27,710
133. Plating and Coating Machine Setters, Operators, and Tenders, Metal and Plastic	$27,470
134. Secretaries, Except Legal, Medical, and Executive	$27,450
135. Parts Salespersons	$27,430
136. Tax Preparers	$27,360
137. Fishers and Related Fishing Workers	$27,250
138. Gaming Surveillance Officers and Gaming Investigators	$27,130
139. Rock Splitters, Quarry	$27,130
140. Outdoor Power Equipment and Other Small Engine Mechanics	$26,910
141. Coating, Painting, and Spraying Machine Setters, Operators, and Tenders	$26,830
142. Assemblers and Fabricators, All Other	$26,730

Occupation	Median Earnings
143. Pesticide Handlers, Sprayers, and Applicators, Vegetation	$26,700
144. Fence Erectors	$26,400
145. Cutting, Punching, and Press Machine Setters, Operators, and Tenders, Metal and Plastic	$26,340
146. Construction Laborers	$26,320
147. Animal Trainers	$26,310
148. Medical Assistants	$26,290
149. Fiberglass Laminators and Fabricators	$25,980
150. Roustabouts, Oil and Gas	$25,700
151. Pharmacy Technicians	$25,630
152. Social and Human Service Assistants	$25,580
153. Molding, Coremaking, and Casting Machine Setters, Operators, and Tenders, Metal and Plastic	$25,560
154. Ophthalmic Laboratory Technicians	$25,460
155. Cementing and Gluing Machine Operators and Tenders	$25,170
156. Manufactured Building and Mobile Home Installers	$25,080
157. Molders, Shapers, and Casters, Except Metal and Plastic	$25,010
158. Production Workers, All Other	$24,890
159. Data Entry Keyers	$24,690
160. Concierges	$24,600
161. Sawing Machine Setters, Operators, and Tenders, Wood	$24,280
162. Team Assemblers	$24,190
163. Dietetic Technicians	$24,040
164. Woodworking Machine Setters, Operators, and Tenders, Except Sawing	$23,940
165. Cooling and Freezing Equipment Operators and Tenders	$23,880
166. Grinding and Polishing Workers, Hand	$23,880
167. Merchandise Displayers and Window Trimmers	$23,820
168. Models	$23,340
169. Textile Bleaching and Dyeing Machine Operators and Tenders	$23,290
170. Photographic Process Workers	$23,280
171. Textile Winding, Twisting, and Drawing Out Machine Setters, Operators, and Tenders	$23,050
172. Cleaning, Washing, and Metal Pickling Equipment Operators and Tenders	$22,850
173. Residential Advisors	$22,670
174. Woodworkers, All Other	$22,580
175. Demonstrators and Product Promoters	$22,150
176. Shoe Machine Operators and Tenders	$21,910
177. Gaming Service Workers, All Other	$21,890
178. Bicycle Repairers	$21,790
179. Floral Designers	$21,700
180. Slaughterers and Meat Packers	$21,690
181. Textile Cutting Machine Setters, Operators, and Tenders	$21,620
182. Cooks, All Other	$21,610
183. Forest and Conservation Workers	$20,810
184. Tour Guides and Escorts	$20,420
185. Cooks, Institution and Cafeteria	$20,410
186. Ambulance Drivers and Attendants, Except Emergency Medical Technicians	$20,370
187. Agricultural Equipment Operators	$20,230

(continued)

(continued)

Occupation	Median Earnings
188. Sewing Machine Operators	$18,810
189. Laundry and Dry-Cleaning Workers	$17,850

Jobs That Require Long-Term On-the-Job Training
Average for all jobs at this level: $36,023

Occupation	Median Earnings
1. Air Traffic Controllers	$117,240
2. Nuclear Power Reactor Operators	$69,370
3. Elevator Installers and Repairers	$63,620
4. Power Distributors and Dispatchers	$62,590
5. Power Plant Operators	$55,000
6. Flight Attendants	$53,780
7. Gas Plant Operators	$53,670
8. Telecommunications Equipment Installers and Repairers, Except Line Installers	$52,430
9. Petroleum Pump System Operators, Refinery Operators, and Gaugers	$52,380
10. Electrical Power-Line Installers and Repairers	$50,780
11. Claims Adjusters, Examiners, and Investigators	$50,660
12. Insurance Appraisers, Auto Damage	$49,180
13. Chemical Plant and System Operators	$49,080
14. Police and Sheriff's Patrol Officers	$47,460
15. Transit and Railroad Police	$47,080
16. Compliance Officers, Except Agriculture, Construction, Health and Safety, and Transportation	$47,050
17. Boilermakers	$46,960
18. Telecommunications Line Installers and Repairers	$46,280
19. Plant and System Operators, All Other	$46,270
20. Stationary Engineers and Boiler Operators	$46,040
21. Millwrights	$45,630
22. Aircraft Structure, Surfaces, Rigging, and Systems Assemblers	$45,410
23. Tool and Die Makers	$44,290
24. Electricians	$43,610
25. Rail Car Repairers	$43,320
26. Brickmasons and Blockmasons	$42,980
27. Plumbers, Pipefitters, and Steamfitters	$42,770
28. Media and Communication Workers, All Other	$42,570
29. Numerical Tool and Process Control Programmers	$42,480
30. Artists and Related Workers, All Other	$41,990
31. Fine Artists, Including Painters, Sculptors, and Illustrators	$41,970
32. Fire Fighters	$41,190
33. Athletes and Sports Competitors	$41,060
34. Industrial Machinery Mechanics	$41,050
35. Structural Iron and Steel Workers	$40,480
36. Crane and Tower Operators	$39,040
37. Reinforcing Iron and Rebar Workers	$38,220
38. Heating, Air Conditioning, and Refrigeration Mechanics and Installers	$37,660
39. Airfield Operations Specialists	$37,630
40. Sheet Metal Workers	$37,360
41. Farmers and Ranchers	$37,130
42. Tile and Marble Setters	$36,590
43. Carpenters	$36,550

Occupation	Median Earnings
44. Water and Liquid Waste Treatment Plant and System Operators	$36,070
45. Stonemasons	$35,960
46. Painters, Transportation Equipment	$35,680
47. Interpreters and Translators	$35,560
48. Automotive Body and Related Repairers	$35,180
49. Audio and Video Equipment Technicians	$34,840
50. Machinists	$34,770
51. Plasterers and Stucco Masons	$34,700
52. Glaziers	$34,610
53. Home Appliance Repairers	$33,860
54. Motorboat Mechanics	$33,210
55. Fabric and Apparel Patternmakers	$32,730
56. Dental Laboratory Technicians	$32,580
57. Job Printers	$32,410
58. Terrazzo Workers and Finishers	$31,630
59. Patternmakers, Wood	$31,510
60. Recreational Vehicle Service Technicians	$31,510
61. Welders, Cutters, Solderers, and Brazers	$31,400
62. Medical Appliance Technicians	$31,180
63. Watch Repairers	$30,900
64. Automotive Glass Installers and Repairers	$30,720
65. Opticians, Dispensing	$30,300
66. Motorcycle Mechanics	$30,050
67. Musical Instrument Repairers and Tuners	$29,200
68. Model Makers, Wood	$28,470
69. Upholsterers	$27,230
70. Cabinetmakers and Bench Carpenters	$27,010
71. Coaches and Scouts	$26,950
72. Butchers and Meat Cutters	$26,930
73. Photographers	$26,170
74. Etchers and Engravers	$25,590
75. Furniture Finishers	$25,010
76. Public Address System and Other Announcers	$24,990
77. Radio and Television Announcers	$24,310
78. Textile Knitting and Weaving Machine Setters, Operators, and Tenders	$24,290
79. Craft Artists	$24,090
80. Tailors, Dressmakers, and Custom Sewers	$22,910
81. Umpires, Referees, and Other Sports Officials	$22,880
82. Cooks, Private Household	$22,870
83. Bakers	$22,030
84. Shoe and Leather Workers and Repairers	$20,450
85. Cooks, Restaurant	$20,340

Jobs That Require Work Experience in a Related Occupation
Average for all jobs at this level: $44,185

Occupation	Median Earnings
1. Managers, All Other	$82,490
2. Industrial Production Managers	$77,670
3. Transportation, Storage, and Distribution Managers	$73,080
4. First-Line Supervisors/Managers of Police and Detectives	$69,310
5. First-Line Supervisors/Managers of Non-Retail Sales Workers	$65,510

Occupation	Median Earnings
6. First-Line Supervisors/Managers of Fire Fighting and Prevention Workers	$62,900
7. Gaming Managers	$62,820
8. Real Estate Brokers	$60,790
9. Detectives and Criminal Investigators	$58,260
10. Postmasters and Mail Superintendents	$55,790
11. First-Line Supervisors/Managers of Mechanics, Installers, and Repairers	$53,890
12. First-Line Supervisors/Managers of Construction Trades and Extraction Workers	$53,850
13. Captains, Mates, and Pilots of Water Vessels	$53,430
14. Cost Estimators	$52,940
15. First-Line Supervisors/Managers of Correctional Officers	$52,580
16. Purchasing Agents, Except Wholesale, Retail, and Farm Products	$50,730
17. Transportation Inspectors	$50,390
18. First-Line Supervisors/Managers of Transportation and Material-Moving Machine and Vehicle Operators	$48,330
19. Fire Inspectors and Investigators	$48,050
20. Emergency Management Specialists	$47,410
21. First-Line Supervisors/Managers of Production and Operating Workers	$47,300
22. Purchasing Agents and Buyers, Farm Products	$46,770
23. Construction and Building Inspectors	$46,570
24. Wholesale and Retail Buyers, Except Farm Products	$44,640
25. Vocational Education Teachers, Postsecondary	$43,900
26. First-Line Supervisors/Managers of Office and Administrative Support Workers	$43,510
27. Food Service Managers	$43,020
28. Lodging Managers	$42,320
29. First-Line Supervisors/Managers, Protective Service Workers, All Other	$41,570
30. Gaming Supervisors	$41,160
31. Aircraft Cargo Handling Supervisors	$39,840
32. First-Line Supervisors/Managers of Helpers, Laborers, and Material Movers, Hand	$39,570
33. Agricultural Inspectors	$38,100
34. First-Line Supervisors/Managers of Farming, Fishing, and Forestry Workers	$37,750
35. First-Line Supervisors/Managers of Landscaping, Lawn Service, and Groundskeeping Workers	$37,300
36. Choreographers	$34,660
37. Chefs and Head Cooks	$34,370
38. First-Line Supervisors/Managers of Retail Sales Workers	$33,960
39. Private Detectives and Investigators	$33,750
40. Self-Enrichment Education Teachers	$33,440
41. Forest Fire Inspectors and Prevention Specialists	$32,940
42. First-Line Supervisors/Managers of Personal Service Workers	$32,800
43. First-Line Supervisors/Managers of Housekeeping and Janitorial Workers	$31,290
44. New Accounts Clerks	$28,390
45. First-Line Supervisors/Managers of Food Preparation and Serving Workers	$26,980
46. Farm Labor Contractors	$23,550
47. Graders and Sorters, Agricultural Products	$17,200

Jobs That Require Postsecondary Vocational Training

Average for all jobs at this level: $30,004

Occupation	Median Earnings
1. Commercial Pilots	$57,480
2. Electrical and Electronics Repairers, Powerhouse, Substation, and Relay	$57,400
3. Ship Engineers	$54,820
4. Aircraft Mechanics and Service Technicians	$47,740
5. Avionics Technicians	$46,950
6. Electrical and Electronics Drafters	$46,830
7. Court Reporters	$45,610
8. Electrical and Electronics Repairers, Commercial and Industrial Equipment	$45,180
9. Appraisers and Assessors of Real Estate	$44,460
10. Mechanical Drafters	$43,700
11. Electrical and Electronics Installers and Repairers, Transportation Equipment	$43,110
12. Drafters, All Other	$43,060
13. Sound Engineering Technicians	$43,010
14. Occupational Health and Safety Technicians	$42,160
15. Architectural and Civil Drafters	$41,960
16. Mobile Heavy Equipment Mechanics, Except Engines	$40,440
17. Real Estate Sales Agents	$39,760
18. Legal Secretaries	$38,190
19. Embalmers	$37,840
20. Radio Mechanics	$37,690
21. Bus and Truck Mechanics and Diesel Engine Specialists	$37,660
22. Healthcare Practitioners and Technical Workers, All Other	$37,200
23. Licensed Practical and Licensed Vocational Nurses	$36,550
24. Computer, Automated Teller, and Office Machine Repairers	$36,480
25. Surgical Technologists	$36,080
26. Health Technologists and Technicians, All Other	$35,140
27. Security and Fire Alarm Systems Installers	$34,810
28. Desktop Publishers	$34,130
29. Automotive Service Technicians and Mechanics	$33,780
30. Massage Therapists	$33,400
31. Prepress Technicians and Workers	$33,310
32. Electric Motor, Power Tool, and Related Repairers	$32,860
33. Makeup Artists, Theatrical and Performance	$31,820
34. Electronic Home Entertainment Equipment Installers and Repairers	$29,980
35. Medical Transcriptionists	$29,950
36. Jewelers and Precious Stone and Metal Workers	$29,750
37. Farm Equipment Mechanics	$29,460
38. Travel Agents	$29,210
39. Electronic Equipment Installers and Repairers, Motor Vehicles	$28,220
40. Medical Secretaries	$28,090
41. Emergency Medical Technicians and Paramedics	$27,070
42. Library Technicians	$26,560
43. Skin Care Specialists	$26,170
44. Fitness Trainers and Aerobics Instructors	$25,910
45. Barbers	$23,150
46. Slot Key Persons	$22,720
47. Preschool Teachers, Except Special Education	$22,680

(continued)

Occupation	Median Earnings
48. Nursing Aides, Orderlies, and Attendants	$22,180
49. Hairdressers, Hairstylists, and Cosmetologists	$21,320
50. Manicurists and Pedicurists	$19,190
51. Gaming Dealers	$14,730

Jobs That Require an Associate Degree

Average for all jobs at this level: $47,896

Occupation	Median Earnings
1. Computer Specialists, All Other	$68,570
2. Radiation Therapists	$66,170
3. Nuclear Technicians	$65,500
4. Dental Hygienists	$62,800
5. Fashion Designers	$62,610
6. Nuclear Medicine Technologists	$62,300
7. Registered Nurses	$57,280
8. Diagnostic Medical Sonographers	$57,160
9. Engineering Technicians, Except Drafters, All Other	$54,250
10. Aerospace Engineering and Operations Technicians	$53,300
11. Electrical and Electronic Engineering Technicians	$50,660
12. Funeral Directors	$49,620
13. Radiologic Technologists and Technicians	$48,170
14. Respiratory Therapists	$47,420
15. Industrial Engineering Technicians	$46,810
16. Geological and Petroleum Technicians	$46,160
17. Mechanical Engineering Technicians	$45,850
18. Forensic Science Technicians	$45,330
19. Electro-Mechanical Technicians	$44,720
20. Fish and Game Wardens	$43,700
21. Paralegals and Legal Assistants	$43,040
22. Cardiovascular Technologists and Technicians	$42,300
23. Interior Designers	$42,260
24. Occupational Therapist Assistants	$42,060
25. Computer Support Specialists	$41,470
26. Physical Therapist Assistants	$41,360
27. Medical Equipment Repairers	$40,580
28. Civil Engineering Technicians	$40,560
29. Environmental Engineering Technicians	$40,560
30. Chemical Technicians	$39,240
31. Respiratory Therapy Technicians	$39,120
32. Environmental Science and Protection Technicians, Including Health	$38,090
33. Life, Physical, and Social Science Technicians, All Other	$37,920
34. Biological Technicians	$35,710
35. Social Science Research Assistants	$33,860
36. Semiconductor Processors	$32,860
37. Medical and Clinical Laboratory Technicians	$32,840
38. Agricultural and Food Science Technicians	$31,730
39. Forest and Conservation Technicians	$30,880
40. Broadcast Technicians	$30,690
41. Medical Records and Health Information Technicians	$28,030
42. Veterinary Technologists and Technicians	$26,780

Jobs That Require a Bachelor's Degree

Average for all jobs at this level: $53,503

Occupation	Median Earnings
1. Airline Pilots, Copilots, and Flight Engineers	$141,090
2. Petroleum Engineers	$98,380
3. Nuclear Engineers	$90,220
4. Computer Hardware Engineers	$88,470
5. Aerospace Engineers	$87,610
6. Computer Software Engineers, Systems Software	$85,370
7. Physical Scientists, All Other	$83,450
8. Engineers, All Other	$81,660
9. Electronics Engineers, Except Computer	$81,050
10. Computer Software Engineers, Applications	$79,780
11. Chemical Engineers	$78,860
12. Sales Engineers	$77,720
13. Atmospheric and Space Scientists	$77,150
14. Electrical Engineers	$75,930
15. Physician Assistants	$74,980
16. Materials Scientists	$74,610
17. Materials Engineers	$73,990
18. Biomedical Engineers	$73,930
19. Construction Managers	$73,700
20. Marine Engineers and Naval Architects	$72,990
21. Mining and Geological Engineers, Including Mining Safety Engineers	$72,160
22. Environmental Engineers	$69,940
23. Mechanical Engineers	$69,850
24. Computer Systems Analysts	$69,760
25. Industrial Engineers	$68,620
26. Civil Engineers	$68,600
27. Securities, Commodities, and Financial Services Sales Agents	$68,500
28. Financial Analysts	$66,590
29. Health and Safety Engineers, Except Mining Safety Engineers and Inspectors	$66,290
30. Personal Financial Advisors	$66,120
31. Agricultural Engineers	$66,030
32. Computer Programmers	$65,510
33. Financial Examiners	$65,370
34. Database Administrators	$64,670
35. Network Systems and Data Communications Analysts	$64,600
36. Architects, Except Landscape and Naval	$64,150
37. Logisticians	$63,430
38. Network and Computer Systems Administrators	$62,130
39. Health Diagnosing and Treating Practitioners, All Other	$61,570
40. Budget Analysts	$61,430
41. Biological Scientists, All Other	$60,940
42. Chemists	$59,870
43. Orthotists and Prosthetists	$58,980
44. Market Research Analysts	$58,820
45. Technical Writers	$58,050
46. Occupational Health and Safety Specialists	$58,030
47. Life Scientists, All Other	$56,970
48. Soil and Plant Scientists	$56,080
49. Business Operations Specialists, All Other	$55,650
50. Landscape Architects	$55,140
51. Conservation Scientists	$54,970

Occupation	Median Earnings
52. Accountants and Auditors	$54,630
53. Commercial and Industrial Designers	$54,560
54. Food Scientists and Technologists	$53,810
55. Financial Specialists, All Other	$53,680
56. Zoologists and Wildlife Biologists	$53,300
57. Credit Analysts	$52,350
58. Insurance Underwriters	$52,350
59. Human Resources, Training, and Labor Relations Specialists, All Other	$52,270
60. Social and Community Service Managers	$52,070
61. Loan Officers	$51,760
62. Multi-Media Artists and Animators	$51,350
63. Foresters	$51,190
64. Compensation, Benefits, and Job Analysis Specialists	$50,230
65. Medical and Clinical Laboratory Technologists	$49,700
66. Writers and Authors	$48,640
67. Special Education Teachers, Secondary School	$48,330
68. Surveyors	$48,290
69. Cartographers and Photogrammetrists	$48,240
70. Training and Development Specialists	$47,830
71. Animal Scientists	$47,800
72. Secondary School Teachers, Except Special and Vocational Education	$47,740
73. Special Education Teachers, Middle School	$47,650
74. Public Relations Specialists	$47,350
75. Editors	$46,990
76. Dietitians and Nutritionists	$46,980
77. Film and Video Editors	$46,670
78. Special Education Teachers, Preschool, Kindergarten, and Elementary School	$46,360
79. Middle School Teachers, Except Special and Vocational Education	$46,300
80. Tax Examiners, Collectors, and Revenue Agents	$45,620
81. Elementary School Teachers, Except Special Education	$45,570
82. Legal Support Workers, All Other	$45,140
83. Adult Literacy, Remedial Education, and GED Teachers and Instructors	$43,910
84. Designers, All Other	$43,870
85. Insurance Sales Agents	$43,870
86. Kindergarten Teachers, Except Special Education	$43,580
87. Social Workers, All Other	$43,580
88. Property, Real Estate, and Community Association Managers	$43,070
89. Medical and Public Health Social Workers	$43,040
90. Probation Officers and Correctional Treatment Specialists	$42,500
91. Employment, Recruitment, and Placement Specialists	$42,420
92. Therapists, All Other	$42,250
93. Meeting and Convention Planners	$42,180
94. Set and Exhibit Designers	$41,820
95. Farm and Home Management Advisors	$41,710
96. Graphic Designers	$39,900
97. Child, Family, and School Social Workers	$37,480
98. Athletic Trainers	$36,560
99. Law Clerks	$36,360

Occupation	Median Earnings
100. Loan Counselors	$35,790
101. Community and Social Service Specialists, All Other	$35,210
102. Recreational Therapists	$34,990
103. Museum Technicians and Conservators	$34,340
104. Directors, Religious Activities and Education	$34,260
105. Survey Researchers	$33,360
106. Education, Training, and Library Workers, All Other	$32,160
107. Teachers and Instructors, All Other	$28,660
108. Religious Workers, All Other	$24,330

Jobs That Require Work Experience Plus Degree

Average for all jobs at this level: $81,410

Occupation	Median Earnings
1. Chief Executives	more than $145,600
2. Engineering Managers	$105,430
3. Judges, Magistrate Judges, and Magistrates	$101,690
4. Computer and Information Systems Managers	$101,580
5. Natural Sciences Managers	$100,080
6. Marketing Managers	$98,720
7. Sales Managers	$91,560
8. Financial Managers	$90,970
9. Human Resources Managers, All Other	$88,510
10. General and Operations Managers	$85,230
11. Actuaries	$82,800
12. Public Relations Managers	$82,180
13. Purchasing Managers	$81,570
14. Training and Development Managers	$80,250
15. Education Administrators, Elementary and Secondary School	$77,740
16. Compensation and Benefits Managers	$74,750
17. Education Administrators, Postsecondary	$73,990
18. Medical and Health Services Managers	$73,340
19. Advertising and Promotions Managers	$73,060
20. Administrative Law Judges, Adjudicators, and Hearing Officers	$72,600
21. Art Directors	$68,100
22. Management Analysts	$68,050
23. Administrative Services Managers	$67,690
24. Education Administrators, All Other	$66,620
25. Agents and Business Managers of Artists, Performers, and Athletes	$64,500
26. Producers and Directors	$56,310
27. Farm, Ranch, and Other Agricultural Managers	$52,070
28. Arbitrators, Mediators, and Conciliators	$49,490
29. Vocational Education Teachers, Secondary School	$48,690
30. Broadcast News Analysts	$46,710
31. Vocational Education Teachers, Middle School	$44,240
32. Music Directors and Composers	$39,750
33. Education Administrators, Preschool and Child Care Center/Program	$37,740
34. Reporters and Correspondents	$33,470
35. Legislators	$15,660

Jobs That Require a Master's Degree

Average for all jobs at this level: $51,309

Occupation	Median Earnings
1. Political Scientists	$90,140
2. Industrial-Organizational Psychologists	$86,420
3. Health Specialties Teachers, Postsecondary	$77,190
4. Economists	$77,010
5. Engineering Teachers, Postsecondary	$76,670
6. Psychologists, All Other	$76,310
7. Agricultural Sciences Teachers, Postsecondary	$75,140
8. Geoscientists, Except Hydrologists and Geographers	$72,660
9. Economics Teachers, Postsecondary	$71,850
10. Atmospheric, Earth, Marine, and Space Sciences Teachers, Postsecondary	$69,300
11. Biological Science Teachers, Postsecondary	$69,210
12. Physics Teachers, Postsecondary	$68,170
13. Hydrologists	$66,260
14. Physical Therapists	$66,200
15. Statisticians	$65,720
16. Social Scientists and Related Workers, All Other	$64,920
17. Environmental Science Teachers, Postsecondary	$64,780
18. Operations Research Analysts	$64,650
19. Architecture Teachers, Postsecondary	$64,620
20. Forestry and Conservation Science Teachers, Postsecondary	$64,430
21. Postsecondary Teachers, All Other	$63,930
22. Mathematical Scientists, All Other	$63,570
23. Geographers	$62,990
24. Anthropology and Archeology Teachers, Postsecondary	$62,820
25. Business Teachers, Postsecondary	$62,040
26. Political Science Teachers, Postsecondary	$61,820
27. Chemistry Teachers, Postsecondary	$61,220
28. Social Sciences Teachers, Postsecondary, All Other	$61,210
29. Occupational Therapists	$60,470
30. Sociologists	$60,290
31. Geography Teachers, Postsecondary	$59,000
32. Psychology Teachers, Postsecondary	$58,670
33. Speech-Language Pathologists	$57,710
34. Computer Science Teachers, Postsecondary	$57,620
35. History Teachers, Postsecondary	$57,390
36. Epidemiologists	$56,670
37. Urban and Regional Planners	$56,630
38. Sociology Teachers, Postsecondary	$56,620
39. Mathematical Science Teachers, Postsecondary	$56,420
40. Area, Ethnic, and Cultural Studies Teachers, Postsecondary	$56,380
41. Environmental Scientists and Specialists, Including Health	$56,100
42. Home Economics Teachers, Postsecondary	$55,310
43. Nursing Instructors and Teachers, Postsecondary	$55,280
44. Philosophy and Religion Teachers, Postsecondary	$54,880
45. Library Science Teachers, Postsecondary	$54,570
46. Social Work Teachers, Postsecondary	$54,340
47. Art, Drama, and Music Teachers, Postsecondary	$53,160
48. Communications Teachers, Postsecondary	$53,110
49. Education Teachers, Postsecondary	$52,800

Occupation	Median Earnings
50. Instructional Coordinators	$52,790
51. Foreign Language and Literature Teachers, Postsecondary	$51,900
52. English Language and Literature Teachers, Postsecondary	$51,730
53. Anthropologists and Archeologists	$49,930
54. Criminal Justice and Law Enforcement Teachers, Postsecondary	$49,730
55. Recreation and Fitness Studies Teachers, Postsecondary	$49,270
56. Librarians	$49,060
57. Historians	$48,520
58. Educational, Vocational, and School Counselors	$47,530
59. Curators	$46,300
60. Marriage and Family Therapists	$43,210
61. Health Educators	$41,330
62. Archivists	$40,730
63. Clergy	$39,680
64. Counselors, All Other	$38,210
65. Mathematical Technicians	$37,880
66. Mental Health and Substance Abuse Social Workers	$35,410
67. Mental Health Counselors	$34,380
68. Substance Abuse and Behavioral Disorder Counselors	$34,040
69. Rehabilitation Counselors	$29,200
70. Graduate Teaching Assistants	$27,840

Jobs That Require a Doctoral Degree

Average for all jobs at this level: $65,431

Occupation	Median Earnings
1. Astronomers	$95,740
2. Physicists	$94,240
3. Computer and Information Scientists, Research	$93,950
4. Mathematicians	$86,930
5. Biochemists and Biophysicists	$76,320
6. Medical Scientists, Except Epidemiologists	$61,680
7. Clinical, Counseling, and School Psychologists	$59,440
8. Microbiologists	$57,980

Jobs That Require a First Professional Degree

Average for all jobs at this level: $93,861

Occupation	Median Earnings
1. Anesthesiologists	more than $145,600
2. Family and General Practitioners	more than $145,600
3. Internists, General	more than $145,600
4. Obstetricians and Gynecologists	more than $145,600
5. Oral and Maxillofacial Surgeons	more than $145,600
6. Orthodontists	more than $145,600
7. Physicians and Surgeons, All Other	more than $145,600
8. Prosthodontists	more than $145,600
9. Psychiatrists	more than $145,600
10. Surgeons	more than $145,600
11. Pediatricians, General	$138,130
12. Dentists, General	$132,140
13. Podiatrists	$108,220
14. Lawyers	$102,470

Occupation	Median Earnings
15. Pharmacists	$94,520
16. Dentists, All Other Specialists	$91,200
17. Optometrists	$91,040
18. Law Teachers, Postsecondary	$87,240
19. Veterinarians	$71,990
20. Chiropractors	$65,220
21. Audiologists	$57,120

Industries Ranked by Median Pay

This list ranks 89 industries by their median earnings for workers in all occupations.

Industry	Median Earnings
1. Securities, Commodity Contracts, and Other Financial Investments and Related Activities	$56,710
2. Utilities	$53,240
3. Oil and Gas Extraction	$53,150
4. Internet Publishing and Broadcasting	$53,070
5. Pipeline Transportation	$52,610
6. Internet Service Providers, Web Search Portals, and Data Processing Service	$50,690
7. Telecommunications	$49,860
8. Computer and Electronic Product Manufacturing	$48,880
9. Rail Transportation	$48,820
10. Professional, Scientific, and Technical Services	$48,750
11. Petroleum and Coal Products Manufacturing	$48,680
12. Management of Companies and Enterprises	$47,450
13. Postal Service	$45,070
14. Funds, Trusts, and Other Financial Vehicles	$44,490
15. Air Transportation	$44,470
16. Monetary Authorities—Central Bank	$42,990
17. Transportation Equipment Manufacturing	$42,230
18. Publishing Industries (Except Internet)	$42,210
19. Chemical Manufacturing	$41,160
20. Hospitals	$40,850
21. Lessors of Nonfinancial Intangible Assets (Except Copyrighted Works)	$40,840
22. Federal, State, and Local Government	$40,510
23. Insurance Carriers and Related Activities	$40,190
24. Water Transportation	$40,160
25. Wholesale Electronic Markets and Agents and Brokers	$39,830
26. Educational Services	$38,250
27. Mining (Except Oil and Gas)	$37,860
28. Broadcasting (Except Internet)	$37,780
29. Construction of Buildings	$37,430
30. Heavy and Civil Engineering Construction	$35,890
31. Machinery Manufacturing	$35,570
32. Specialty Trade Contractors	$35,400
33. Merchant Wholesalers, Durable Goods	$35,340
34. Truck Transportation	$35,260
35. Paper Manufacturing	$35,100
36. Primary Metal Manufacturing	$34,520
37. Support Activities for Mining	$34,340
38. Waste Management and Remediation Services	$33,550

Industry	Median Earnings
39. Support Activities for Transportation	$33,300
40. Credit Intermediation and Related Activities	$33,180
41. Beverage and Tobacco Product Manufacturing	$33,000
42. Ambulatory Health Care Services	$32,850
43. Electrical Equipment, Appliance, and Component Manufacturing	$32,500
44. Other Information Services	$31,890
45. Fabricated Metal Product Manufacturing	$31,810
46. Merchant Wholesalers, Nondurable Goods	$31,570
47. Printing and Related Support Activities	$31,440
48. Couriers and Messengers	$31,300
49. Nonmetallic Mineral Product Manufacturing	$30,890
50. Miscellaneous Manufacturing	$30,590
51. Forestry and Logging	$30,380
52. Motor Vehicle and Parts Dealers	$30,100
53. Real Estate	$28,820
54. Repair and Maintenance	$28,680
55. Plastics and Rubber Products Manufacturing	$28,540
56. Warehousing and Storage	$28,510
57. Motion Picture and Sound Recording Industries	$28,380
58. Performing Arts, Spectator Sports, and Related Industries	$28,060
59. Religious, Grantmaking, Civic, Professional, and Similar Organizations	$27,940
60. Furniture and Related Product Manufacturing	$27,310
61. Nonstore Retailers	$27,290
62. Wood Product Manufacturing	$26,360
63. Electronics and Appliance Stores	$25,630
64. Museums, Historical Sites, and Similar Institutions	$25,460
65. Transit and Ground Passenger Transportation	$25,420
66. Textile Mills	$25,250
67. Furniture and Home Furnishings Stores	$25,180
68. Scenic and Sightseeing Transportation	$25,100
69. Food Manufacturing	$24,850
70. Building Material and Garden Equipment and Supplies Dealers	$24,680
71. Rental and Leasing Services	$24,490
72. Textile Product Mills	$24,120
73. Leather and Allied Product Manufacturing	$23,130
74. Nursing and Residential Care Facilities	$23,100
75. Administrative and Support Services	$23,010
76. Health and Personal Care Stores	$22,590
77. Social Assistance	$22,110
78. Personal and Laundry Services	$20,420
79. Apparel Manufacturing	$20,320
80. Amusement, Gambling, and Recreation Industries	$19,740
81. Accommodation	$19,680
82. Miscellaneous Store Retailers	$19,670
83. General Merchandise Stores	$19,050
84. Clothing and Clothing Accessories Stores	$18,950
85. Food and Beverage Stores	$18,910
86. Sporting Goods, Hobby, Book, and Music Stores	$18,640
87. Support Activities for Agriculture and Forestry	$17,140
88. Gasoline Stations	$17,020
89. Food Services and Drinking Places	$16,150

The 10 Best-Paying Jobs in Each Industry

The following lists cover 89 industries and show their 10 highest-paid occupations. The occupations are selected from the 50 with the biggest workforces within the industry and are included only if the workforce for the occupation consists of more than 300 workers. Earnings figures indicate the median wage workers are paid *in this industry*.

The 10 Best-Paying Jobs in the Accommodation Industry

Occupation	Median Earnings
1. General and Operations Managers	$63,330
2. Food Service Managers	$48,670
3. First-Line Supervisors/Managers of Mechanics, Installers, and Repairers	$43,820
4. Gaming Supervisors	$43,450
5. Lodging Managers	$41,830
6. Sales Representatives, Services, All Other	$41,620
7. Accountants and Auditors	$41,620
8. Chefs and Head Cooks	$39,830
9. Meeting and Convention Planners	$38,220
10. First-Line Supervisors/Managers of Office and Administrative Support Workers	$33,160

The 10 Best-Paying Jobs in the Administrative and Support Services Industry

Occupation	Median Earnings
1. General and Operations Managers	$76,090
2. Registered Nurses	$63,960
3. Business Operations Specialists, All Other	$52,380
4. Accountants and Auditors	$51,150
5. Sales Representatives, Services, All Other	$43,640
6. Sales Representatives, Wholesale and Manufacturing, Except Technical and Scientific Products	$42,710
7. Licensed Practical and Licensed Vocational Nurses	$41,910
8. First-Line Supervisors/Managers of Office and Administrative Support Workers	$40,530
9. Employment, Recruitment, and Placement Specialists	$39,440
10. First-Line Supervisors/Managers of Landscaping, Lawn Service, and Groundskeeping Workers	$35,900

The 10 Best-Paying Jobs in the Air Transportation Industry

Occupation	Median Earnings
1. Airline Pilots, Copilots, and Flight Engineers	more than $145,600
2. Financial Managers	$95,390
3. Managers, All Other	$86,570
4. Transportation, Storage, and Distribution Managers	$78,950
5. General and Operations Managers	$77,910
6. Sales Managers	$75,320
7. Administrative Services Managers	$72,080
8. Engineers, All Other	$70,960
9. Network and Computer Systems Administrators	$68,260
10. Computer Programmers	$67,670

The 10 Best-Paying Jobs in the Ambulatory Health Care Services Industry

Occupation	Median Earnings
1. Physicians and Surgeons, All Other	more than $145,600
2. Family and General Practitioners	more than $145,600
3. Surgeons	more than $145,600
4. Internists, General	more than $145,600
5. Anesthesiologists	more than $145,600
6. Pediatricians, General	$140,520
7. Dentists, General	$135,470
8. Optometrists	$90,050
9. General and Operations Managers	$74,600
10. Physician Assistants	$74,490

The 10 Best-Paying Jobs in the Amusement, Gambling, and Recreation Industries

Occupation	Median Earnings
1. General and Operations Managers	$62,750
2. Accountants and Auditors	$47,910
3. Gaming Supervisors	$41,260
4. Chefs and Head Cooks	$41,150
5. First-Line Supervisors/Managers of Landscaping, Lawn Service, and Groundskeeping Workers	$40,370
6. First-Line Supervisors/Managers of Office and Administrative Support Workers	$37,690
7. Executive Secretaries and Administrative Assistants	$33,600
8. First-Line Supervisors/Managers of Retail Sales Workers	$32,960
9. First-Line Supervisors/Managers of Personal Service Workers	$31,830
10. First-Line Supervisors/Managers of Food Preparation and Serving Workers	$31,310

The 10 Best-Paying Jobs in the Apparel Manufacturing Industry

Occupation	Median Earnings
1. Chief Executives	more than $145,600
2. General and Operations Managers	$95,220
3. Sales Managers	$89,740
4. Industrial Production Managers	$70,590
5. Fashion Designers	$67,320
6. Computer Programmers	$60,020
7. Accountants and Auditors	$57,170
8. Sales Representatives, Wholesale and Manufacturing, Except Technical and Scientific Products	$51,870
9. Fabric and Apparel Patternmakers	$45,080
10. Purchasing Agents, Except Wholesale, Retail, and Farm Products	$44,790

The 10 Best-Paying Jobs in the Beverage and Tobacco Product Manufacturing Industry

Occupation	Median Earnings
1. General and Operations Managers	$97,100
2. Sales Managers	$82,680
3. Industrial Production Managers	$80,960
4. Transportation, Storage, and Distribution Managers	$69,450
5. Accountants and Auditors	$57,880

Occupation	Median Earnings
6. First-Line Supervisors/Managers of Mechanics, Installers, and Repairers	$57,120
7. First-Line Supervisors/Managers of Non-Retail Sales Workers	$56,890
8. First-Line Supervisors/Managers of Production and Operating Workers	$50,430
9. First-Line Supervisors/Managers of Transportation and Material-Moving Machine and Vehicle Operators	$48,430
10. First-Line Supervisors/Managers of Office and Administrative Support Workers	$46,640

The 10 Best-Paying Jobs in the Broadcasting Industry (Except Internet)

Occupation	Median Earnings
1. Sales Managers	$108,070
2. Marketing Managers	$100,880
3. General and Operations Managers	$92,860
4. Financial Managers	$92,480
5. Managers, All Other	$84,570
6. First-Line Supervisors/Managers of Non-Retail Sales Workers	$74,900
7. Advertising and Promotions Managers	$71,120
8. Electronics Engineers, Except Computer	$67,150
9. First-Line Supervisors/Managers of Mechanics, Installers, and Repairers	$59,970
10. Network and Computer Systems Administrators	$59,380

The 10 Best-Paying Jobs in the Building Material and Garden Equipment and Supplies Dealers Industry

Occupation	Median Earnings
1. Sales Managers	$71,600
2. General and Operations Managers	$64,420
3. First-Line Supervisors/Managers of Non-Retail Sales Workers	$56,430
4. Accountants and Auditors	$51,680
5. Human Resources, Training, and Labor Relations Specialists, All Other	$50,340
6. Business Operations Specialists, All Other	$45,810
7. Sales Representatives, Wholesale and Manufacturing, Technical and Scientific Products	$45,490
8. First-Line Supervisors/Managers of Mechanics, Installers, and Repairers	$44,140
9. Sales Representatives, Wholesale and Manufacturing, Except Technical and Scientific Products	$44,000
10. First-Line Supervisors/Managers of Office and Administrative Support Workers	$42,350

The 10 Best-Paying Jobs in the Chemical Manufacturing Industry

Occupation	Median Earnings
1. General and Operations Managers	$115,450
2. Natural Sciences Managers	$109,390
3. Financial Managers	$97,010
4. Biochemists and Biophysicists	$85,730
5. Industrial Production Managers	$84,520
6. Medical Scientists, Except Epidemiologists	$82,590
7. Managers, All Other	$80,480
8. Chemical Engineers	$80,180

Occupation	Median Earnings
9. Industrial Engineers	$69,130
10. Sales Representatives, Wholesale and Manufacturing, Technical and Scientific Products	$67,450

The 10 Best-Paying Jobs in the Clothing and Clothing Accessories Stores Industry

Occupation	Median Earnings
1. Chief Executives	more than $145,600
2. Financial Managers	$87,810
3. Purchasing Managers	$71,080
4. Accountants and Auditors	$60,000
5. Sales Managers	$57,070
6. General and Operations Managers	$56,490
7. Business Operations Specialists, All Other	$53,460
8. Fashion Designers	$53,170
9. Wholesale and Retail Buyers, Except Farm Products	$43,700
10. First-Line Supervisors/Managers of Production and Operating Workers	$39,270

The 10 Best-Paying Jobs in the Computer and Electronic Product Manufacturing Industry

Occupation	Median Earnings
1. General and Operations Managers	$122,020
2. Engineering Managers	$118,720
3. Marketing Managers	$115,580
4. Computer and Information Systems Managers	$112,710
5. Financial Managers	$104,630
6. Managers, All Other	$102,360
7. Aerospace Engineers	$91,370
8. Computer Hardware Engineers	$90,990
9. Computer Software Engineers, Systems Software	$90,120
10. Computer Software Engineers, Applications	$89,780

The 10 Best-Paying Jobs in the Construction of Buildings Industry

Occupation	Median Earnings
1. Chief Executives	more than $145,600
2. General and Operations Managers	$96,710
3. Financial Managers	$82,780
4. Construction Managers	$71,940
5. Civil Engineers	$67,000
6. Architects, Except Landscape and Naval	$64,100
7. Property, Real Estate, and Community Association Managers	$59,830
8. Business Operations Specialists, All Other	$57,850
9. Cost Estimators	$56,570
10. Accountants and Auditors	$56,050

The 10 Best-Paying Jobs in the Couriers and Messengers Industry

Occupation	Median Earnings
1. Managers, All Other	$90,460
2. Engineers, All Other	$83,570
3. General and Operations Managers	$80,550
4. Transportation, Storage, and Distribution Managers	$78,760
5. Airline Pilots, Copilots, and Flight Engineers	$69,900

(continued)

(continued)

Occupation	Median Earnings
6. First-Line Supervisors/Managers of Mechanics, Installers, and Repairers	$68,860
7. Business Operations Specialists, All Other	$68,770
8. Aircraft Mechanics and Service Technicians	$67,430
9. Human Resources, Training, and Labor Relations Specialists, All Other	$61,360
10. First-Line Supervisors/Managers of Transportation and Material-Moving Machine and Vehicle Operators	$55,960

The 10 Best-Paying Jobs in the Credit Intermediation and Related Activities Industry

Occupation	Median Earnings
1. Chief Executives	more than $145,600
2. Computer and Information Systems Managers	$103,810
3. Sales Managers	$103,690
4. Marketing Managers	$97,590
5. General and Operations Managers	$91,250
6. Computer Software Engineers, Systems Software	$84,790
7. Computer Software Engineers, Applications	$78,880
8. Financial Managers	$76,530
9. Computer Programmers	$73,340
10. Administrative Services Managers	$72,670

The 10 Best-Paying Jobs in the Educational Services Industry

Occupation	Median Earnings
1. Health Specialties Teachers, Postsecondary	$77,930
2. Education Administrators, Elementary and Secondary School	$77,790
3. Education Administrators, Postsecondary	$73,900
4. Biological Science Teachers, Postsecondary	$69,200
5. Postsecondary Teachers, All Other	$63,950
6. Business Teachers, Postsecondary	$62,050
7. Clinical, Counseling, and School Psychologists	$59,820
8. Instructional Coordinators	$54,320
9. Art, Drama, and Music Teachers, Postsecondary	$53,090
10. Speech-Language Pathologists	$52,850

The 10 Best-Paying Jobs in the Electrical Equipment, Appliance, and Component Manufacturing Industry

Occupation	Median Earnings
1. General and Operations Managers	$105,170
2. Engineering Managers	$95,580
3. Industrial Production Managers	$78,780
4. Electronics Engineers, Except Computer	$70,130
5. Electrical Engineers	$67,680
6. Mechanical Engineers	$65,910
7. Industrial Engineers	$64,450
8. Sales Representatives, Wholesale and Manufacturing, Technical and Scientific Products	$62,160
9. Sales Representatives, Wholesale and Manufacturing, Except Technical and Scientific Products	$56,620
10. Accountants and Auditors	$54,990

The 10 Best-Paying Jobs in the Electronics and Appliance Stores Industry

Occupation	Median Earnings
1. Computer and Information Systems Managers	$90,930
2. Sales Engineers	$79,450
3. Computer Software Engineers, Applications	$77,470
4. General and Operations Managers	$76,540
5. Computer Software Engineers, Systems Software	$75,100
6. Sales Managers	$72,280
7. Computer Systems Analysts	$66,490
8. Computer Programmers	$65,140
9. Network and Computer Systems Administrators	$57,500
10. Sales Representatives, Wholesale and Manufacturing, Technical and Scientific Products	$54,690

The 10 Best-Paying Jobs in the Fabricated Metal Product Manufacturing Industry

Occupation	Median Earnings
1. General and Operations Managers	$91,300
2. Industrial Production Managers	$70,830
3. Industrial Engineers	$61,240
4. Mechanical Engineers	$59,920
5. Accountants and Auditors	$55,090
6. Sales Representatives, Wholesale and Manufacturing, Except Technical and Scientific Products	$54,480
7. Cost Estimators	$49,370
8. First-Line Supervisors/Managers of Production and Operating Workers	$47,850
9. Purchasing Agents, Except Wholesale, Retail, and Farm Products	$45,040
10. Mechanical Drafters	$41,770

The 10 Best-Paying Jobs in the Federal, State, and Local Government

Occupation	Median Earnings
1. Lawyers	$87,730
2. General and Operations Managers	$82,340
3. Managers, All Other	$81,230
4. Computer Specialists, All Other	$75,550
5. First-Line Supervisors/Managers of Police and Detectives	$69,510
6. Civil Engineers	$67,640
7. First-Line Supervisors/Managers of Fire Fighting and Prevention Workers	$63,050
8. Management Analysts	$62,840
9. Business Operations Specialists, All Other	$59,980
10. Claims Adjusters, Examiners, and Investigators	$59,960

The 10 Best-Paying Jobs in the Food and Beverage Stores Industry

Occupation	Median Earnings
1. Pharmacists	$95,600
2. General and Operations Managers	$61,760
3. Sales Managers	$56,390
4. Sales Representatives, Wholesale and Manufacturing, Except Technical and Scientific Products	$47,040
5. Food Service Managers	$40,120
6. First-Line Supervisors/Managers of Production and Operating Workers	$39,250

Occupation	Median Earnings
7. First-Line Supervisors/Managers of Office and Administrative Support Workers	$36,530
8. Truck Drivers, Heavy and Tractor-Trailer	$35,680
9. Wholesale and Retail Buyers, Except Farm Products	$35,500
10. First-Line Supervisors/Managers of Helpers, Laborers, and Material Movers, Hand	$33,400

The 10 Best-Paying Jobs in the Food Manufacturing Industry

Occupation	Median Earnings
1. General and Operations Managers	$86,800
2. Industrial Production Managers	$69,660
3. First-Line Supervisors/Managers of Mechanics, Installers, and Repairers	$55,080
4. Accountants and Auditors	$53,720
5. Sales Representatives, Wholesale and Manufacturing, Except Technical and Scientific Products	$50,970
6. First-Line Supervisors/Managers of Production and Operating Workers	$43,800
7. Industrial Machinery Mechanics	$37,760
8. Maintenance and Repair Workers, General	$35,160
9. Production, Planning, and Expediting Clerks	$34,990
10. Truck Drivers, Heavy and Tractor-Trailer	$33,900

The 10 Best-Paying Jobs in the Food Services and Drinking Places Industry

Occupation	Median Earnings
1. Chief Executives	$110,440
2. General and Operations Managers	$54,680
3. Accountants and Auditors	$45,860
4. Sales Representatives, Services, All Other	$43,320
5. Food Service Managers	$42,360
6. First-Line Supervisors/Managers of Office and Administrative Support Workers	$38,500
7. Executive Secretaries and Administrative Assistants	$33,730
8. Training and Development Specialists	$32,510
9. Chefs and Head Cooks	$32,140
10. First-Line Supervisors/Managers of Housekeeping and Janitorial Workers	$30,180

The 10 Best-Paying Jobs in the Forestry and Logging Industry

Occupation	Median Earnings
1. General and Operations Managers	$64,290
2. Foresters	$60,730
3. First-Line Supervisors/Managers of Farming, Fishing, and Forestry Workers	$46,910
4. Mobile Heavy Equipment Mechanics, Except Engines	$35,730
5. Bus and Truck Mechanics and Diesel Engine Specialists	$34,410
6. Logging Workers, All Other	$32,230
7. Operating Engineers and Other Construction Equipment Operators	$31,090
8. Truck Drivers, Heavy and Tractor-Trailer	$30,590
9. Logging Equipment Operators	$30,240
10. Maintenance and Repair Workers, General	$29,170

The 10 Best-Paying Jobs in the Funds, Trusts, and Other Financial Vehicles Industry

Occupation	Median Earnings
1. Chief Executives	more than $145,600
2. Real Estate Brokers	more than $145,600
3. Lawyers	$115,520
4. Financial Managers	$106,680
5. General and Operations Managers	$105,420
6. Computer and Information Systems Managers	$104,450
7. Marketing Managers	$95,880
8. Actuaries	$85,530
9. Computer Software Engineers, Applications	$81,720
10. Administrative Services Managers	$79,270

The 10 Best-Paying Jobs in the Furniture and Home Furnishings Stores Industry

Occupation	Median Earnings
1. Chief Executives	$130,630
2. Sales Managers	$79,990
3. General and Operations Managers	$68,830
4. Business Operations Specialists, All Other	$64,840
5. First-Line Supervisors/Managers of Construction Trades and Extraction Workers	$53,470
6. Accountants and Auditors	$51,590
7. Cost Estimators	$46,640
8. Sales Representatives, Wholesale and Manufacturing, Except Technical and Scientific Products	$46,010
9. First-Line Supervisors/Managers of Retail Sales Workers	$42,940
10. Wholesale and Retail Buyers, Except Farm Products	$41,820

The 10 Best-Paying Jobs in the Furniture and Related Product Manufacturing Industry

Occupation	Median Earnings
1. General and Operations Managers	$83,610
2. Industrial Production Managers	$66,330
3. Industrial Engineers	$58,360
4. Sales Representatives, Wholesale and Manufacturing, Except Technical and Scientific Products	$51,720
5. Accountants and Auditors	$50,840
6. Cost Estimators	$45,990
7. First-Line Supervisors/Managers of Office and Administrative Support Workers	$43,210
8. First-Line Supervisors/Managers of Production and Operating Workers	$42,770
9. Purchasing Agents, Except Wholesale, Retail, and Farm Products	$42,090
10. Executive Secretaries and Administrative Assistants	$34,040

The 10 Best-Paying Jobs in the Gasoline Stations Industry

Occupation	Median Earnings
1. Chief Executives	$90,470
2. Sales Managers	$54,010
3. General and Operations Managers	$51,400
4. Accountants and Auditors	$45,160

(continued)

(continued)

Occupation	Median Earnings
5. First-Line Supervisors/Managers of Mechanics, Installers, and Repairers	$44,000
6. First-Line Supervisors/Managers of Transportation and Material-Moving Machine and Vehicle Operators	$35,970
7. Wholesale and Retail Buyers, Except Farm Products	$34,860
8. Food Service Managers	$34,350
9. First-Line Supervisors/Managers of Office and Administrative Support Workers	$33,640
10. First-Line Supervisors/Managers of Helpers, Laborers, and Material Movers, Hand	$32,590

The 10 Best-Paying Jobs in the General Merchandise Stores Industry

Occupation	Median Earnings
1. Pharmacists	$100,050
2. General and Operations Managers	$66,340
3. Managers, All Other	$53,010
4. Sales Managers	$50,920
5. Human Resources, Training, and Labor Relations Specialists, All Other	$40,320
6. Wholesale and Retail Buyers, Except Farm Products	$39,190
7. Industrial Truck and Tractor Operators	$39,150
8. Payroll and Timekeeping Clerks	$38,390
9. First-Line Supervisors/Managers, Protective Service Workers, All Other	$38,130
10. First-Line Supervisors/Managers of Production and Operating Workers	$37,330

The 10 Best-Paying Jobs in the Health and Personal Care Stores Industry

Occupation	Median Earnings
1. Chief Executives	more than $145,600
2. Optometrists	$101,700
3. Pharmacists	$94,610
4. Sales Managers	$67,170
5. Orthotists and Prosthetists	$61,830
6. Sales Representatives, Wholesale and Manufacturing, Technical and Scientific Products	$56,490
7. Accountants and Auditors	$55,750
8. Audiologists	$55,210
9. Registered Nurses	$50,390
10. Sales Representatives, Wholesale and Manufacturing, Except Technical and Scientific Products	$47,800

The 10 Best-Paying Jobs in the Heavy and Civil Engineering Construction Industry

Occupation	Median Earnings
1. Chief Executives	more than $145,600
2. General and Operations Managers	$95,640
3. Financial Managers	$88,730
4. Property, Real Estate, and Community Association Managers	$77,470
5. Construction Managers	$76,760
6. Civil Engineers	$69,690
7. Cost Estimators	$59,330
8. Accountants and Auditors	$57,480

Occupation	Median Earnings
9. First-Line Supervisors/Managers of Construction Trades and Extraction Workers	$54,000
10. First-Line Supervisors/Managers of Mechanics, Installers, and Repairers	$53,100

The 10 Best-Paying Jobs in the Hospitals Industry

Occupation	Median Earnings
1. Pharmacists	$93,370
2. Medical and Health Services Managers	$78,370
3. Physicians and Surgeons, All Other	$77,020
4. Physical Therapists	$66,210
5. Occupational Therapists	$61,250
6. Registered Nurses	$58,500
7. Diagnostic Medical Sonographers	$56,860
8. Business Operations Specialists, All Other	$51,950
9. Medical and Clinical Laboratory Technologists	$49,910
10. Radiologic Technologists and Technicians	$48,830

The 10 Best-Paying Jobs in the Insurance Carriers and Related Activities Industry

Occupation	Median Earnings
1. Chief Executives	more than $145,600
2. General and Operations Managers	$110,280
3. Financial Managers	$103,160
4. Sales Managers	$102,370
5. Computer and Information Systems Managers	$101,290
6. Lawyers	$100,910
7. Marketing Managers	$93,500
8. Managers, All Other	$89,150
9. Actuaries	$82,170
10. Administrative Services Managers	$76,800

The 10 Best-Paying Jobs in the Internet Publishing and Broadcasting Industry

Occupation	Median Earnings
1. General and Operations Managers	$122,270
2. Computer and Information Systems Managers	$113,050
3. Managers, All Other	$103,340
4. Computer Software Engineers, Systems Software	$84,370
5. Computer Software Engineers, Applications	$82,810
6. First-Line Supervisors/Managers of Non-Retail Sales Workers	$78,090
7. Computer Systems Analysts	$76,450
8. Management Analysts	$71,160
9. Sales Representatives, Wholesale and Manufacturing, Technical and Scientific Products	$66,780
10. Market Research Analysts	$65,500

The 10 Best-Paying Jobs in the Internet Service Providers, Web Search Portals, and Data-Processing Services Industry

Occupation	Median Earnings
1. Chief Executives	more than $145,600
2. Marketing Managers	$117,040
3. Sales Managers	$115,350
4. General and Operations Managers	$110,890

Occupation	Median Earnings
5. Computer and Information Systems Managers	$106,650
6. Financial Managers	$106,020
7. Managers, All Other	$103,500
8. Computer Software Engineers, Systems Software	$82,940
9. Computer Software Engineers, Applications	$78,740
10. Administrative Services Managers	$77,210

The 10 Best-Paying Jobs in the Leasing and Licensing Firms Industry

Occupation	Median Earnings
1. Lawyers	$141,020
2. General and Operations Managers	$101,340
3. Sales Managers	$58,430
4. Compliance Officers, Except Agriculture, Construction, Health and Safety, and Transportation	$56,350
5. Management Analysts	$55,760
6. Business Operations Specialists, All Other	$53,760
7. Accountants and Auditors	$52,490
8. Public Relations Specialists	$51,420
9. Market Research Analysts	$50,920
10. First-Line Supervisors/Managers of Office and Administrative Support Workers	$48,580

The 10 Best-Paying Jobs in the Leather and Allied Product Manufacturing Industry

Occupation	Median Earnings
1. General and Operations Managers	$82,370
2. Sales Representatives, Wholesale and Manufacturing, Except Technical and Scientific Products	$45,030
3. First-Line Supervisors/Managers of Production and Operating Workers	$37,500
4. Bookkeeping, Accounting, and Auditing Clerks	$30,100
5. Textile Bleaching and Dyeing Machine Operators and Tenders	$27,810
6. Customer Service Representatives	$27,230
7. Textile, Apparel, and Furnishings Workers, All Other	$25,570
8. Production Workers, All Other	$25,100
9. Laborers and Freight, Stock, and Material Movers, Hand	$24,600
10. Machine Feeders and Offbearers	$24,270

The 10 Best-Paying Jobs in the Machinery Manufacturing Industry

Occupation	Median Earnings
1. General and Operations Managers	$100,380
2. Engineering Managers	$93,360
3. Industrial Production Managers	$78,040
4. Sales Engineers	$68,950
5. Electrical Engineers	$67,950
6. Industrial Engineers	$64,340
7. Mechanical Engineers	$63,180
8. Sales Representatives, Wholesale and Manufacturing, Technical and Scientific Products	$62,530
9. Sales Representatives, Wholesale and Manufacturing, Except Technical and Scientific Products	$55,440
10. Accountants and Auditors	$54,400

The 10 Best-Paying Jobs in the Management of Companies and Enterprises Industry

Occupation	Median Earnings
1. Chief Executives	more than $145,600
2. Lawyers	$128,610
3. Computer and Information Systems Managers	$105,980
4. Financial Managers	$105,410
5. General and Operations Managers	$105,130
6. Marketing Managers	$103,070
7. Sales Managers	$98,240
8. Managers, All Other	$92,930
9. Computer Software Engineers, Systems Software	$83,080
10. Computer Software Engineers, Applications	$78,580

The 10 Best-Paying Jobs in the Merchant Wholesalers, Durable Goods Industry

Occupation	Median Earnings
1. Sales Managers	$101,540
2. General and Operations Managers	$94,930
3. Computer Software Engineers, Systems Software	$88,980
4. Computer Software Engineers, Applications	$84,410
5. Computer Systems Analysts	$78,720
6. Computer Programmers	$72,210
7. Sales Engineers	$71,340
8. First-Line Supervisors/Managers of Non-Retail Sales Workers	$70,860
9. Business Operations Specialists, All Other	$62,590
10. Sales Representatives, Wholesale and Manufacturing, Technical and Scientific Products	$61,730

The 10 Best-Paying Jobs in the Merchant Wholesalers, Nondurable Goods Industry

Occupation	Median Earnings
1. Chief Executives	more than $145,600
2. General and Operations Managers	$94,000
3. Sales Managers	$93,680
4. Financial Managers	$92,330
5. First-Line Supervisors/Managers of Non-Retail Sales Workers	$66,130
6. Transportation, Storage, and Distribution Managers	$65,160
7. Sales Representatives, Wholesale and Manufacturing, Technical and Scientific Products	$64,600
8. Accountants and Auditors	$56,680
9. Business Operations Specialists, All Other	$56,240
10. First-Line Supervisors/Managers of Transportation and Material-Moving Machine and Vehicle Operators	$46,940

The 10 Best-Paying Jobs in the Mining Industry (Except Oil and Gas)

Occupation	Median Earnings
1. General and Operations Managers	$83,000
2. Industrial Production Managers	$79,940
3. Mining and Geological Engineers, Including Mining Safety Engineers	$68,730
4. First-Line Supervisors/Managers of Mechanics, Installers, and Repairers	$64,770

(continued)

(continued)

Occupation	Median Earnings
5. First-Line Supervisors/Managers of Construction Trades and Extraction Workers	$62,580
6. Accountants and Auditors	$56,050
7. First-Line Supervisors/Managers of Production and Operating Workers	$55,330
8. Sales Representatives, Wholesale and Manufacturing, Except Technical and Scientific Products	$53,150
9. First-Line Supervisors/Managers of Transportation and Material-Moving Machine and Vehicle Operators	$51,240
10. Installation, Maintenance, and Repair Workers, All Other	$49,480

The 10 Best-Paying Jobs in the Miscellaneous Manufacturing Industry

Occupation	Median Earnings
1. General and Operations Managers	$96,370
2. Industrial Production Managers	$78,350
3. Mechanical Engineers	$66,880
4. Sales Representatives, Wholesale and Manufacturing, Technical and Scientific Products	$66,070
5. Industrial Engineers	$64,980
6. Accountants and Auditors	$55,470
7. Sales Representatives, Wholesale and Manufacturing, Except Technical and Scientific Products	$51,080
8. First-Line Supervisors/Managers of Office and Administrative Support Workers	$47,310
9. Purchasing Agents, Except Wholesale, Retail, and Farm Products	$46,710
10. First-Line Supervisors/Managers of Production and Operating Workers	$46,680

The 10 Best-Paying Jobs in the Miscellaneous Store Retailers Industry

Occupation	Median Earnings
1. Sales Managers	$62,300
2. General and Operations Managers	$61,370
3. First-Line Supervisors/Managers of Non-Retail Sales Workers	$53,510
4. Accountants and Auditors	$49,710
5. First-Line Supervisors/Managers of Mechanics, Installers, and Repairers	$45,090
6. Sales Representatives, Wholesale and Manufacturing, Except Technical and Scientific Products	$43,650
7. Business Operations Specialists, All Other	$42,640
8. Wholesale and Retail Buyers, Except Farm Products	$39,980
9. First-Line Supervisors/Managers of Office and Administrative Support Workers	$36,770
10. Sales Representatives, Services, All Other	$36,700

The 10 Best-Paying Jobs in the Monetary Authorities—Central Bank Industry

Occupation	Median Earnings
1. General and Operations Managers	$115,680
2. Financial Managers	$111,280
3. Computer Software Engineers, Applications	$83,170
4. Financial Examiners	$76,630
5. Computer Systems Analysts	$72,420

Occupation	Median Earnings
6. Network Systems and Data Communications Analysts	$67,630
7. Management Analysts	$65,420
8. Accountants and Auditors	$62,450
9. Financial Analysts	$61,720
10. Computer Support Specialists	$51,900

The 10 Best-Paying Jobs in the Motion Picture and Sound Recording Industries

Occupation	Median Earnings
1. Chief Executives	more than $145,600
2. Sales Managers	$113,450
3. Financial Managers	$105,970
4. General and Operations Managers	$94,400
5. First-Line Supervisors/Managers of Non-Retail Sales Workers	$84,680
6. Producers and Directors	$71,030
7. Art Directors	$70,050
8. Computer Programmers	$65,730
9. Writers and Authors	$65,590
10. Network and Computer Systems Administrators	$64,680

The 10 Best-Paying Jobs in the Motor Vehicle and Parts Dealers Industry

Occupation	Median Earnings
1. Chief Executives	more than $145,600
2. Sales Managers	$97,850
3. General and Operations Managers	$92,560
4. Financial Managers	$85,890
5. Credit Analysts	$67,620
6. Accountants and Auditors	$56,730
7. Wholesale and Retail Buyers, Except Farm Products	$53,130
8. First-Line Supervisors/Managers of Retail Sales Workers	$52,280
9. First-Line Supervisors/Managers of Mechanics, Installers, and Repairers	$51,710
10. Sales Representatives, Services, All Other	$51,530

The 10 Best-Paying Jobs in the Museums, Historical Sites, and Similar Institutions Industry

Occupation	Median Earnings
1. Chief Executives	$141,290
2. General and Operations Managers	$74,020
3. Managers, All Other	$66,690
4. Public Relations Managers	$63,880
5. Accountants and Auditors	$50,110
6. Curators	$43,670
7. Business Operations Specialists, All Other	$42,240
8. Computer Support Specialists	$41,260
9. Librarians	$40,720
10. First-Line Supervisors/Managers of Office and Administrative Support Workers	$40,090

The 10 Best-Paying Jobs in the Nonmetallic Mineral Product Manufacturing Industry

Occupation	Median Earnings
1. General and Operations Managers	$87,600
2. Industrial Production Managers	$70,230
3. Industrial Engineers	$60,820
4. First-Line Supervisors/Managers of Mechanics, Installers, and Repairers	$55,280
5. Accountants and Auditors	$52,920
6. Sales Representatives, Wholesale and Manufacturing, Except Technical and Scientific Products	$51,530
7. First-Line Supervisors/Managers of Transportation and Material-Moving Machine and Vehicle Operators	$47,370
8. First-Line Supervisors/Managers of Production and Operating Workers	$46,850
9. First-Line Supervisors/Managers of Office and Administrative Support Workers	$46,450
10. Industrial Machinery Mechanics	$39,930

The 10 Best-Paying Jobs in the Nonstore Retailers Industry

Occupation	Median Earnings
1. Pharmacists	$88,190
2. General and Operations Managers	$76,150
3. Sales Managers	$74,290
4. Computer Programmers	$58,060
5. First-Line Supervisors/Managers of Non-Retail Sales Workers	$53,960
6. First-Line Supervisors/Managers of Mechanics, Installers, and Repairers	$50,500
7. Accountants and Auditors	$49,600
8. Sales Representatives, Wholesale and Manufacturing, Technical and Scientific Products	$48,230
9. First-Line Supervisors/Managers of Transportation and Material-Moving Machine and Vehicle Operators	$46,210
10. Sales Representatives, Wholesale and Manufacturing, Except Technical and Scientific Products	$45,600

The 10 Best-Paying Jobs in the Nursing and Residential Care Facilities Industry

Occupation	Median Earnings
1. Physical Therapists	$68,590
2. General and Operations Managers	$67,720
3. Occupational Therapists	$63,740
4. Medical and Health Services Managers	$62,600
5. Registered Nurses	$52,070
6. Accountants and Auditors	$49,700
7. Social and Community Service Managers	$46,290
8. Physical Therapist Assistants	$44,400
9. First-Line Supervisors/Managers of Office and Administrative Support Workers	$40,570
10. Licensed Practical and Licensed Vocational Nurses	$38,180

The 10 Best-Paying Jobs in the Oil and Gas Extraction Industry

Occupation	Median Earnings
1. Chief Executives	more than $145,600
2. Lawyers	$134,760
3. Engineering Managers	$123,400
4. Petroleum Engineers	$110,240
5. General and Operations Managers	$106,440
6. Financial Managers	$106,200
7. Geoscientists, Except Hydrologists and Geographers	$106,060
8. Industrial Production Managers	$105,870
9. Managers, All Other	$103,030
10. Mining and Geological Engineers, Including Mining Safety Engineers	$90,990

The 10 Best-Paying Jobs in the Other Information Services Industry

Occupation	Median Earnings
1. General and Operations Managers	$100,470
2. Computer Software Engineers, Applications	$88,470
3. Computer Systems Analysts	$75,440
4. Managers, All Other	$72,260
5. Sales Representatives, Services, All Other	$67,250
6. Computer Programmers	$61,050
7. Accountants and Auditors	$57,360
8. Business Operations Specialists, All Other	$56,300
9. Sales Representatives, Wholesale and Manufacturing, Except Technical and Scientific Products	$55,580
10. Reporters and Correspondents	$51,850

The 10 Best-Paying Jobs in the Paper Manufacturing Industry

Occupation	Median Earnings
1. General and Operations Managers	$110,080
2. Sales Managers	$100,400
3. Industrial Production Managers	$80,840
4. Industrial Engineers	$71,600
5. First-Line Supervisors/Managers of Mechanics, Installers, and Repairers	$64,220
6. Sales Representatives, Wholesale and Manufacturing, Except Technical and Scientific Products	$63,780
7. Accountants and Auditors	$55,920
8. First-Line Supervisors/Managers of Production and Operating Workers	$53,570
9. Millwrights	$52,190
10. Electricians	$51,260

The 10 Best-Paying Jobs in the Performing Arts, Spectator Sports, and Related Industries

Occupation	Median Earnings
1. General and Operations Managers	$82,480
2. Agents and Business Managers of Artists, Performers, and Athletes	$69,250
3. Accountants and Auditors	$54,180
4. Music Directors and Composers	$50,570
5. Automotive Service Technicians and Mechanics	$48,810
6. Producers and Directors	$47,560
7. Athletes and Sports Competitors	$45,880
8. Business Operations Specialists, All Other	$45,750
9. Carpenters	$42,720
10. First-Line Supervisors/Managers of Office and Administrative Support Workers	$42,040

The 10 Best-Paying Jobs in the Personal and Laundry Services Industry

Occupation	Median Earnings
1. General and Operations Managers	$65,950
2. Funeral Directors	$49,130
3. Sales Representatives, Wholesale and Manufacturing, Except Technical and Scientific Products	$44,660
4. First-Line Supervisors/Managers of Office and Administrative Support Workers	$39,080
5. Sales Representatives, Services, All Other	$38,570
6. Embalmers	$37,860
7. First-Line Supervisors/Managers of Transportation and Material-Moving Machine and Vehicle Operators	$36,630
8. First-Line Supervisors/Managers of Production and Operating Workers	$35,300
9. First-Line Supervisors/Managers of Personal Service Workers	$34,420
10. Sales and Related Workers, All Other	$33,640

The 10 Best-Paying Jobs in the Petroleum and Coal Products Manufacturing Industry

Occupation	Median Earnings
1. Engineering Managers	$116,990
2. General and Operations Managers	$108,190
3. Petroleum Engineers	$95,630
4. Industrial Production Managers	$88,810
5. Chemical Engineers	$85,030
6. Industrial Engineers	$79,760
7. Mechanical Engineers	$75,190
8. First-Line Supervisors/Managers of Mechanics, Installers, and Repairers	$69,540
9. Chemists	$63,870
10. Sales Representatives, Wholesale and Manufacturing, Except Technical and Scientific Products	$63,000

The 10 Best-Paying Jobs in the Pipeline Transportation Industry

Occupation	Median Earnings
1. General and Operations Managers	$97,650
2. Engineers, All Other	$90,750
3. Petroleum Engineers	$85,980
4. Business Operations Specialists, All Other	$69,370
5. First-Line Supervisors/Managers of Production and Operating Workers	$65,090
6. First-Line Supervisors/Managers of Mechanics, Installers, and Repairers	$64,360
7. Computer Systems Analysts	$63,260
8. Purchasing Agents, Except Wholesale, Retail, and Farm Products	$58,220
9. Accountants and Auditors	$56,640
10. Engineering Technicians, Except Drafters, All Other	$56,220

The 10 Best-Paying Jobs in the Plastics and Rubber Products Manufacturing Industry

Occupation	Median Earnings
1. General and Operations Managers	$95,240
2. Industrial Production Managers	$70,010
3. Mechanical Engineers	$63,590
4. Industrial Engineers	$60,980

Occupation	Median Earnings
5. Sales Representatives, Wholesale and Manufacturing, Except Technical and Scientific Products	$57,060
6. Accountants and Auditors	$53,220
7. First-Line Supervisors/Managers of Office and Administrative Support Workers	$46,340
8. Purchasing Agents, Except Wholesale, Retail, and Farm Products	$45,110
9. First-Line Supervisors/Managers of Production and Operating Workers	$43,800
10. Tool and Die Makers	$43,220

The 10 Best-Paying Jobs in the Postal Service Industry

Occupation	Median Earnings
1. Transportation, Storage, and Distribution Managers	$79,450
2. Administrative Services Managers	$77,970
3. Detectives and Criminal Investigators	$76,920
4. Compliance Officers, Except Agriculture, Construction, Health and Safety, and Transportation	$73,450
5. Network Systems and Data Communications Analysts	$72,590
6. Computer Systems Analysts	$72,390
7. Management Analysts	$72,340
8. Operations Research Analysts	$70,430
9. Sales and Related Workers, All Other	$66,970
10. Accountants and Auditors	$66,850

The 10 Best-Paying Jobs in the Primary Metal Manufacturing Industry

Occupation	Median Earnings
1. General and Operations Managers	$98,780
2. Industrial Production Managers	$76,520
3. Industrial Engineers	$63,330
4. Mechanical Engineers	$61,710
5. First-Line Supervisors/Managers of Mechanics, Installers, and Repairers	$59,300
6. Sales Representatives, Wholesale and Manufacturing, Except Technical and Scientific Products	$55,260
7. Accountants and Auditors	$54,470
8. Assemblers and Fabricators, All Other	$52,240
9. First-Line Supervisors/Managers of Production and Operating Workers	$50,010
10. Electricians	$47,160

The 10 Best-Paying Jobs in the Printing and Related Support Activities Industry

Occupation	Median Earnings
1. General and Operations Managers	$96,610
2. Industrial Production Managers	$73,350
3. Accountants and Auditors	$54,690
4. Sales Representatives, Wholesale and Manufacturing, Except Technical and Scientific Products	$53,660
5. First-Line Supervisors/Managers of Production and Operating Workers	$49,580
6. Sales Representatives, Services, All Other	$48,460
7. First-Line Supervisors/Managers of Office and Administrative Support Workers	$46,980
8. Cost Estimators	$46,010

Occupation	Median Earnings
9. Purchasing Agents, Except Wholesale, Retail, and Farm Products	$43,660
10. Industrial Machinery Mechanics	$41,940

The 10 Best-Paying Jobs in the Professional, Scientific, and Technical Services Industry

Occupation	Median Earnings
1. General and Operations Managers	$117,010
2. Engineering Managers	$108,260
3. Lawyers	$108,070
4. Computer and Information Systems Managers	$106,990
5. Financial Managers	$101,600
6. Computer Software Engineers, Systems Software	$86,420
7. Engineers, All Other	$80,840
8. Computer Software Engineers, Applications	$79,510
9. Electrical Engineers	$78,120
10. Management Analysts	$76,130

The 10 Best-Paying Jobs in the Publishing Industries (Except Internet)

Occupation	Median Earnings
1. General and Operations Managers	$111,260
2. Computer and Information Systems Managers	$110,020
3. Marketing Managers	$105,670
4. Sales Managers	$100,220
5. Managers, All Other	$91,340
6. Computer Software Engineers, Systems Software	$87,180
7. Computer Software Engineers, Applications	$83,360
8. Computer Programmers	$76,740
9. Management Analysts	$75,140
10. Computer Systems Analysts	$72,500

The 10 Best-Paying Jobs in the Rail Transportation Industry

Occupation	Median Earnings
1. General and Operations Managers	$99,580
2. Managers, All Other	$90,240
3. Transportation, Storage, and Distribution Managers	$87,880
4. Computer Programmers	$75,850
5. Management Analysts	$71,580
6. Accountants and Auditors	$65,360
7. Business Operations Specialists, All Other	$61,880
8. First-Line Supervisors/Managers of Transportation and Material-Moving Machine and Vehicle Operators	$60,640
9. Human Resources, Training, and Labor Relations Specialists, All Other	$59,480
10. Locomotive Engineers	$58,740

The 10 Best-Paying Jobs in the Real Estate Industry

Occupation	Median Earnings
1. Chief Executives	more than $145,600
2. Financial Managers	$102,380
3. General and Operations Managers	$92,130
4. Construction Managers	$83,410
5. Financial Analysts	$62,730
6. Real Estate Brokers	$61,160
7. Loan Officers	$56,890

Occupation	Median Earnings
8. Accountants and Auditors	$56,300
9. First-Line Supervisors/Managers of Non-Retail Sales Workers	$54,600
10. Appraisers and Assessors of Real Estate	$44,460

The 10 Best-Paying Jobs in the Religious, Grantmaking, Civic, Professional, and Similar Organizations Industry

Occupation	Median Earnings
1. Chief Executives	$132,690
2. General and Operations Managers	$83,040
3. Financial Managers	$79,110
4. Public Relations Managers	$74,040
5. Managers, All Other	$69,460
6. Administrative Services Managers	$62,710
7. Accountants and Auditors	$53,280
8. Training and Development Specialists	$49,610
9. Social and Community Service Managers	$49,510
10. Editors	$48,090

The 10 Best-Paying Jobs in the Rental and Leasing Services Industry

Occupation	Median Earnings
1. General and Operations Managers	$72,950
2. Sales Managers	$67,020
3. Accountants and Auditors	$53,450
4. Sales Representatives, Wholesale and Manufacturing, Except Technical and Scientific Products	$49,690
5. First-Line Supervisors/Managers of Mechanics, Installers, and Repairers	$49,480
6. Sales Representatives, Services, All Other	$49,260
7. Business Operations Specialists, All Other	$48,450
8. Sales Representatives, Wholesale and Manufacturing, Technical and Scientific Products	$46,100
9. First-Line Supervisors/Managers of Non-Retail Sales Workers	$45,570
10. First-Line Supervisors/Managers of Transportation and Material-Moving Machine and Vehicle Operators	$44,160

The 10 Best-Paying Jobs in the Repair and Maintenance Industry

Occupation	Median Earnings
1. General and Operations Managers	$71,910
2. First-Line Supervisors/Managers of Mechanics, Installers, and Repairers	$49,700
3. Sales Representatives, Wholesale and Manufacturing, Except Technical and Scientific Products	$47,220
4. Sales Representatives, Services, All Other	$45,910
5. Cost Estimators	$44,930
6. First-Line Supervisors/Managers of Production and Operating Workers	$44,030
7. Medical Equipment Repairers	$42,280
8. First-Line Supervisors/Managers of Office and Administrative Support Workers	$41,630
9. Electrical and Electronics Repairers, Commercial and Industrial Equipment	$40,100
10. Heating, Air Conditioning, and Refrigeration Mechanics and Installers	$39,970

The 10 Best-Paying Jobs in the Scenic and Sightseeing Transportation Industry

Occupation	Median Earnings
1. General and Operations Managers	$67,200
2. Commercial Pilots	$52,560
3. Captains, Mates, and Pilots of Water Vessels	$36,400
4. Maintenance and Repair Workers, General	$29,740
5. Transportation Workers, All Other	$27,390
6. Motorboat Operators	$25,790
7. Reservation and Transportation Ticket Agents and Travel Clerks	$24,800
8. Bus Drivers, Transit and Intercity	$24,370
9. Tour Guides and Escorts	$22,240
10. Sailors and Marine Oilers	$21,620

The 10 Best-Paying Jobs in the Securities, Commodity Contracts, and Other Financial Investments and Related Activities Industry

Occupation	Median Earnings
1. Chief Executives	more than $145,600
2. General and Operations Managers	$138,840
3. Lawyers	$136,470
4. Sales Managers	$134,160
5. Financial Managers	$132,110
6. Marketing Managers	$124,000
7. Computer and Information Systems Managers	$120,340
8. Managers, All Other	$94,920
9. Computer Software Engineers, Systems Software	$88,660
10. Administrative Services Managers	$86,510

The 10 Best-Paying Jobs in the Social Assistance Industry

Occupation	Median Earnings
1. General and Operations Managers	$62,710
2. Registered Nurses	$50,180
3. Clinical, Counseling, and School Psychologists	$49,590
4. Social and Community Service Managers	$48,170
5. Accountants and Auditors	$46,100
6. Business Operations Specialists, All Other	$40,390
7. First-Line Supervisors/Managers of Office and Administrative Support Workers	$38,010
8. Instructional Coordinators	$36,550
9. Marriage and Family Therapists	$36,010
10. Education Administrators, Preschool and Child Care Center/Program	$35,670

The 10 Best-Paying Jobs in the Specialty Trade Contractors Industry

Occupation	Median Earnings
1. General and Operations Managers	$83,650
2. Construction Managers	$73,920
3. Elevator Installers and Repairers	$63,870
4. First-Line Supervisors/Managers of Mechanics, Installers, and Repairers	$54,600
5. Cost Estimators	$53,880
6. First-Line Supervisors/Managers of Construction Trades and Extraction Workers	$53,600
7. Sales Representatives, Services, All Other	$51,210

Occupation	Median Earnings
8. Sales Representatives, Wholesale and Manufacturing, Except Technical and Scientific Products	$50,140
9. Brickmasons and Blockmasons	$42,760
10. Structural Iron and Steel Workers	$42,640

The 10 Best-Paying Jobs in the Sporting Goods, Hobby, Book, and Music Stores Industry

Occupation	Median Earnings
1. Chief Executives	$105,160
2. General and Operations Managers	$60,040
3. Sales Managers	$55,210
4. Accountants and Auditors	$49,050
5. Sales Representatives, Wholesale and Manufacturing, Except Technical and Scientific Products	$42,890
6. Business Operations Specialists, All Other	$39,340
7. First-Line Supervisors/Managers of Mechanics, Installers, and Repairers	$38,780
8. Wholesale and Retail Buyers, Except Farm Products	$35,250
9. First-Line Supervisors/Managers of Office and Administrative Support Workers	$33,630
10. First-Line Supervisors/Managers of Retail Sales Workers	$32,370

The 10 Best-Paying Jobs in the Support Activities for Agriculture and Forestry Industry

Occupation	Median Earnings
1. General and Operations Managers	$70,980
2. Commercial Pilots	$55,170
3. Accountants and Auditors	$54,620
4. Farm, Ranch, and Other Agricultural Managers	$52,310
5. Sales Representatives, Wholesale and Manufacturing, Except Technical and Scientific Products	$48,070
6. First-Line Supervisors/Managers of Mechanics, Installers, and Repairers	$47,830
7. First-Line Supervisors/Managers of Production and Operating Workers	$40,740
8. First-Line Supervisors/Managers of Office and Administrative Support Workers	$37,460
9. First-Line Supervisors/Managers of Helpers, Laborers, and Material Movers, Hand	$34,880
10. Executive Secretaries and Administrative Assistants	$34,520

The 10 Best-Paying Jobs in the Support Activities for Mining Industry

Occupation	Median Earnings
1. Geoscientists, Except Hydrologists and Geographers	$95,370
2. Petroleum Engineers	$81,120
3. General and Operations Managers	$80,720
4. Computer Systems Analysts	$64,160
5. Sales Representatives, Wholesale and Manufacturing, Technical and Scientific Products	$60,530
6. Ship Engineers	$57,070
7. Sales Representatives, Services, All Other	$56,850
8. First-Line Supervisors/Managers of Construction Trades and Extraction Workers	$56,230

Occupation	Median Earnings
9. First-Line Supervisors/Managers of Production and Operating Workers	$55,520
10. Electrical and Electronic Engineering Technicians	$55,170

The 10 Best-Paying Jobs in the Support Activities for Transportation Industry

Occupation	Median Earnings
1. General and Operations Managers	$82,510
2. Transportation, Storage, and Distribution Managers	$73,650
3. Crane and Tower Operators	$58,440
4. Ship Engineers	$57,870
5. Captains, Mates, and Pilots of Water Vessels	$57,140
6. Business Operations Specialists, All Other	$55,980
7. Sales Representatives, Services, All Other	$54,200
8. First-Line Supervisors/Managers of Mechanics, Installers, and Repairers	$54,180
9. First-Line Supervisors/Managers of Transportation and Material-Moving Machine and Vehicle Operators	$52,370
10. Commercial Pilots	$52,250

The 10 Best-Paying Jobs in the Telecommunications Industry

Occupation	Median Earnings
1. Computer and Information Systems Managers	$110,610
2. General and Operations Managers	$105,200
3. Sales Managers	$99,510
4. Financial Managers	$98,460
5. Managers, All Other	$89,920
6. Computer Software Engineers, Applications	$83,490
7. Computer Software Engineers, Systems Software	$83,370
8. Sales Engineers	$82,440
9. First-Line Supervisors/Managers of Non-Retail Sales Workers	$79,120
10. Market Research Analysts	$74,730

The 10 Best-Paying Jobs in the Textile Mills Industry

Occupation	Median Earnings
1. General and Operations Managers	$94,370
2. Industrial Production Managers	$69,010
3. Industrial Engineers	$61,860
4. Sales Representatives, Wholesale and Manufacturing, Except Technical and Scientific Products	$55,970
5. Accountants and Auditors	$53,450
6. First-Line Supervisors/Managers of Mechanics, Installers, and Repairers	$48,550
7. First-Line Supervisors/Managers of Office and Administrative Support Workers	$43,960
8. First-Line Supervisors/Managers of Production and Operating Workers	$42,510
9. Graphic Designers	$38,340
10. Executive Secretaries and Administrative Assistants	$37,430

The 10 Best-Paying Jobs in the Textile Product Mills Industry

Occupation	Median Earnings
1. General and Operations Managers	$85,650
2. Industrial Production Managers	$64,420

Occupation	Median Earnings
3. Industrial Engineers	$59,710
4. Accountants and Auditors	$53,890
5. Sales Representatives, Wholesale and Manufacturing, Except Technical and Scientific Products	$47,160
6. Purchasing Agents, Except Wholesale, Retail, and Farm Products	$43,010
7. First-Line Supervisors/Managers of Office and Administrative Support Workers	$42,330
8. First-Line Supervisors/Managers of Production and Operating Workers	$40,990
9. Graphic Designers	$35,480
10. Executive Secretaries and Administrative Assistants	$35,110

The 10 Best-Paying Jobs in the Transit and Ground Passenger Transportation Industry

Occupation	Median Earnings
1. Chief Executives	$112,710
2. General and Operations Managers	$67,770
3. Transportation, Storage, and Distribution Managers	$63,390
4. Accountants and Auditors	$51,700
5. First-Line Supervisors/Managers of Mechanics, Installers, and Repairers	$51,650
6. Business Operations Specialists, All Other	$47,550
7. Sales Representatives, Services, All Other	$44,080
8. First-Line Supervisors/Managers of Transportation and Material-Moving Machine and Vehicle Operators	$41,880
9. First-Line Supervisors/Managers of Office and Administrative Support Workers	$40,350
10. First-Line Supervisors/Managers of Helpers, Laborers, and Material Movers, Hand	$38,750

The 10 Best-Paying Jobs in the Transportation Equipment Manufacturing Industry

Occupation	Median Earnings
1. Engineering Managers	$106,870
2. General and Operations Managers	$97,470
3. Computer Software Engineers, Applications	$84,100
4. Aerospace Engineers	$82,990
5. Industrial Production Managers	$82,310
6. Business Operations Specialists, All Other	$70,910
7. Mechanical Engineers	$70,390
8. Industrial Engineers	$69,070
9. Management Analysts	$67,960
10. Electricians	$61,510

The 10 Best-Paying Jobs in the Truck Transportation Industry

Occupation	Median Earnings
1. Chief Executives	$118,560
2. Sales Managers	$75,550
3. Financial Managers	$73,760
4. General and Operations Managers	$71,440
5. Transportation, Storage, and Distribution Managers	$68,110
6. Sales Representatives, Services, All Other	$55,740
7. First-Line Supervisors/Managers of Mechanics, Installers, and Repairers	$50,280

(continued)

(continued)

Occupation	Median Earnings
8. First-Line Supervisors/Managers of Transportation and Material-Moving Machine and Vehicle Operators	$49,840
9. Sales Representatives, Wholesale and Manufacturing, Except Technical and Scientific Products	$49,510
10. Accountants and Auditors	$48,350

The 10 Best-Paying Jobs in the Utilities Industry

Occupation	Median Earnings
1. Managers, All Other..	$105,660
2. Engineering Managers	$97,730
3. General and Operations Managers	$94,750
4. Nuclear Engineers	$90,380
5. Engineers, All Other	$82,010
6. Electrical Engineers	$77,870
7. Computer Systems Analysts	$75,950
8. Nuclear Power Reactor Operators..............................	$69,590
9. Nuclear Technicians...	$69,580
10. First-Line Supervisors/Managers of Production and Operating Workers...	$69,260

The 10 Best-Paying Jobs in the Warehousing and Storage Industry

Occupation	Median Earnings
1. General and Operations Managers	$79,490
2. Transportation, Storage, and Distribution Managers	$69,120
3. First-Line Supervisors/Managers of Mechanics, Installers, and Repairers	$52,310
4. Business Operations Specialists, All Other	$50,880
5. Sales Representatives, Wholesale and Manufacturing, Except Technical and Scientific Products	$50,120
6. Accountants and Auditors	$49,840
7. First-Line Supervisors/Managers of Transportation and Material-Moving Machine and Vehicle Operators	$47,880
8. Logisticians	$45,600
9. First-Line Supervisors/Managers of Office and Administrative Support Workers	$44,600
10. First-Line Supervisors/Managers of Production and Operating Workers...	$44,320

The 10 Best-Paying Jobs in the Waste Management and Remediation Services Industry

Occupation	Median Earnings
1. General and Operations Managers	$81,210
2. Environmental Engineers	$72,240
3. Construction Managers	$71,600
4. Transportation, Storage, and Distribution Managers	$71,460
5. Health and Safety Engineers, Except Mining Safety Engineers and Inspectors	$67,440
6. Accountants and Auditors	$57,050
7. Cost Estimators...	$56,920
8. First-Line Supervisors/Managers of Production and Operating Workers...	$56,630
9. First-Line Supervisors/Managers of Mechanics, Installers, and Repairers	$56,430
10. Business Operations Specialists, All Other	$55,970

The 10 Best-Paying Jobs in the Water Transportation Industry

Occupation	Median Earnings
1. Financial Managers	$95,880
2. General and Operations Managers	$92,370
3. Transportation, Storage, and Distribution Managers	$86,880
4. Marine Engineers and Naval Architects	$82,780
5. Sales Representatives, Services, All Other	$66,020
6. Captains, Mates, and Pilots of Water Vessels................	$56,300
7. Ship Engineers	$54,490
8. First-Line Supervisors/Managers of Transportation and Material-Moving Machine and Vehicle Operators	$54,080
9. Accountants and Auditors	$53,620
10. First-Line Supervisors/Managers of Office and Administrative Support Workers	$44,920

The 10 Best-Paying Jobs in the Wholesale Electronic Markets and Agents and Brokers Industry

Occupation	Median Earnings
1. Sales Managers	$107,420
2. General and Operations Managers	$104,720
3. Marketing Managers	$96,630
4. Financial Managers	$91,690
5. Sales Engineers..	$81,580
6. Computer Software Engineers, Applications	$79,890
7. First-Line Supervisors/Managers of Non-Retail Sales Workers	$78,260
8. Sales Representatives, Wholesale and Manufacturing, Technical and Scientific Products	$69,510
9. Computer Programmers	$66,320
10. Market Research Analysts	$60,540

The 10 Best-Paying Jobs in the Wood Product Manufacturing Industry

Occupation	Median Earnings
1. General and Operations Managers	$82,220
2. Industrial Production Managers	$65,320
3. Industrial Engineers	$55,670
4. Accountants and Auditors	$51,170
5. Sales Representatives, Wholesale and Manufacturing, Except Technical and Scientific Products	$49,330
6. Purchasing Agents, Except Wholesale, Retail, and Farm Products	$44,300
7. First-Line Supervisors/Managers of Production and Operating Workers...	$42,480
8. First-Line Supervisors/Managers of Office and Administrative Support Workers	$42,330
9. Electricians	$38,410
10. Industrial Machinery Mechanics	$37,910

States Ranked by Median Earnings

This list ranks the 50 states, plus the District of Columbia, by their median earnings for workers in all occupations. When you compare states, keep in mind that earnings vary in different parts of a state and the cost of living also varies across states, so being in a low-paying state does not necessarily mean having a low standard of living.

State	Median Earnings
1. District of Columbia	$49,810
2. Massachusetts	$37,350
3. Connecticut	$36,940
4. Alaska	$36,810
5. New Jersey	$35,840
6. New York	$35,170
7. Washington	$34,970
8. Maryland	$34,810
9. California	$34,040
10. Minnesota	$33,560
11. Michigan	$32,990
12. Colorado	$32,910
13. Delaware	$32,910
14. Rhode Island	$32,430
15. Illinois	$31,650
16. Virginia	$31,610
17. New Hampshire	$31,440
18. Hawaii	$31,130
19. Oregon	$31,020
20. Wisconsin	$30,130
21. Ohio	$30,100
22. Pennsylvania	$29,800
23. Vermont	$29,510
24. Nevada	$28,750
25. Georgia	$28,660
26. Arizona	$28,650
27. Wyoming	$28,650
28. Maine	$28,630
29. Indiana	$28,500
30. Idaho	$28,020
31. Kansas	$28,010
32. Utah	$28,000
33. North Carolina	$27,980
34. Missouri	$27,950
35. Nebraska	$27,080
36. Florida	$27,670
37. Texas	$27,570
38. Iowa	$27,520
39. Tennessee	$27,280
40. Kentucky	$27,270
41. New Mexico	$26,730
42. South Carolina	$26,730
43. North Dakota	$26,570
44. Louisiana	$26,420
45. Alabama	$25,980
46. Oklahoma	$25,840
47. Montana	$25,670
48. South Dakota	$24,870
49. Arkansas	$24,810
50. West Virginia	$24,770
51. Mississippi	$24,300

The 15 Best-Paying Jobs in Each State

For each of the 50 states, plus the District of Columbia, you can see the 15 jobs with the highest median earnings.

You can see the median earnings for all of these states for each job in Part III.

Alabama

Occupation	Median Earnings
1. Anesthesiologists	more than $145,600
2. Family and General Practitioners	more than $145,600
3. Internists, General	more than $145,600
4. Obstetricians and Gynecologists	more than $145,600
5. Oral and Maxillofacial Surgeons	more than $145,600
6. Orthodontists	more than $145,600
7. Psychiatrists	more than $145,600
8. Surgeons	more than $145,600
9. Chiropractors	$145,010
10. Chief Executives	$142,170
11. Pediatricians, General	$136,610
12. Physicians and Surgeons, All Other	$127,120
13. Dentists, General	$121,620
14. Administrative Law Judges, Adjudicators, and Hearing Officers	$119,320
15. Law Teachers, Postsecondary	$107,180

Alaska

Occupation	Median Earnings
1. Anesthesiologists	more than $145,600
2. Dentists, General	more than $145,600
3. Obstetricians and Gynecologists	more than $145,600
4. Pediatricians, General	more than $145,600
5. Physicians and Surgeons, All Other	more than $145,600
6. Surgeons	more than $145,600
7. Family and General Practitioners	$144,650
8. Airline Pilots, Copilots, and Flight Engineers	$141,780
9. Optometrists	$137,730
10. Chief Executives	$106,330
11. Pharmacists	$105,610
12. Petroleum Engineers	$104,360
13. Engineering Managers	$99,440
14. Atmospheric and Space Scientists	$93,110
15. Lawyers	$89,210

Arizona

Occupation	Median Earnings
1. Anesthesiologists	more than $145,600
2. Internists, General	more than $145,600
3. Obstetricians and Gynecologists	more than $145,600
4. Oral and Maxillofacial Surgeons	more than $145,600
5. Orthodontists	more than $145,600
6. Pediatricians, General	more than $145,600
7. Psychiatrists	more than $145,600
8. Surgeons	more than $145,600

(continued)

(continued)

Occupation	Median Earnings
9. Chief Executives	$137,130
10. Physicians and Surgeons, All Other	$135,670
11. Family and General Practitioners	$131,340
12. Dentists, General	$119,820
13. Podiatrists	$111,390
14. Engineering Managers	$108,220
15. Lawyers	$98,060

Arkansas

Occupation	Median Earnings
1. Anesthesiologists	more than $145,600
2. Family and General Practitioners	more than $145,600
3. Internists, General	more than $145,600
4. Obstetricians and Gynecologists	more than $145,600
5. Orthodontists	more than $145,600
6. Surgeons	more than $145,600
7. Psychiatrists	$138,190
8. Health Diagnosing and Treating Practitioners, All Other	$115,110
9. Chief Executives	$107,210
10. Pediatricians, General	$99,160
11. Aerospace Engineers	$93,910
12. Optometrists	$91,860
13. Pharmacists	$90,570
14. Air Traffic Controllers	$89,820
15. Computer Hardware Engineers	$85,650

California

Occupation	Median Earnings
1. Airline Pilots, Copilots, and Flight Engineers	more than $145,600
2. Anesthesiologists	more than $145,600
3. Chief Executives	more than $145,600
4. Internists, General	more than $145,600
5. Judges, Magistrate Judges, and Magistrates	more than $145,600
6. Obstetricians and Gynecologists	more than $145,600
7. Orthodontists	more than $145,600
8. Physicians and Surgeons, All Other	more than $145,600
9. Psychiatrists	more than $145,600
10. Surgeons	more than $145,600
11. Pediatricians, General	$141,680
12. Family and General Practitioners	$138,840
13. Dentists, General	$129,020
14. Lawyers	$124,830
15. Air Traffic Controllers	$123,310

Colorado

Occupation	Median Earnings
1. Anesthesiologists	more than $145,600
2. Chief Executives	more than $145,600
3. Dentists, General	more than $145,600
4. Internists, General	more than $145,600
5. Nuclear Engineers	more than $145,600
6. Obstetricians and Gynecologists	more than $145,600
7. Orthodontists	more than $145,600

Occupation	Median Earnings
8. Pediatricians, General	more than $145,600
9. Psychiatrists	more than $145,600
10. Surgeons	more than $145,600
11. Physicians and Surgeons, All Other	$128,340
12. Air Traffic Controllers	$127,880
13. Family and General Practitioners	$121,240
14. Airline Pilots, Copilots, and Flight Engineers	$111,640
15. Industrial-Organizational Psychologists	$110,520

Connecticut

Occupation	Median Earnings
1. Anesthesiologists	more than $145,600
2. Chief Executives	more than $145,600
3. Dentists, General	more than $145,600
4. Internists, General	more than $145,600
5. Judges, Magistrate Judges, and Magistrates	more than $145,600
6. Obstetricians and Gynecologists	more than $145,600
7. Oral and Maxillofacial Surgeons	more than $145,600
8. Orthodontists	more than $145,600
9. Psychiatrists	more than $145,600
10. Surgeons	more than $145,600
11. Family and General Practitioners	$144,950
12. Securities, Commodities, and Financial Services Sales Agents	$130,120
13. Pediatricians, General	$126,810
14. Physicians and Surgeons, All Other	$126,720
15. Podiatrists	$113,300

Delaware

Occupation	Median Earnings
1. Anesthesiologists	more than $145,600
2. Chief Executives	more than $145,600
3. Dentists, General	more than $145,600
4. Health Diagnosing and Treating Practitioners, All Other	more than $145,600
5. Internists, General	more than $145,600
6. Obstetricians and Gynecologists	more than $145,600
7. Optometrists	more than $145,600
8. Physicians and Surgeons, All Other	more than $145,600
9. Surgeons	more than $145,600
10. Family and General Practitioners	$141,130
11. Marketing Managers	$125,560
12. Lawyers	$124,470
13. Engineering Managers	$113,480
14. Biochemists and Biophysicists	$110,110
15. Psychiatrists	$109,760

District of Columbia

Occupation	Median Earnings
1. Chief Executives	more than $145,600
2. Lawyers	$134,860
3. Internists, General	$128,880
4. Psychiatrists	$127,990
5. Nuclear Engineers	$125,610
6. Public Relations Managers	$122,220

Occupation	Median Earnings
7. Human Resources Managers, All Other	$118,630
8. Engineering Managers	$116,450
9. Computer and Information Systems Managers	$113,890
10. Engineers, All Other	$113,880
11. General and Operations Managers	$113,800
12. Dentists, General	$113,130
13. Managers, All Other	$112,550
14. Veterinarians	$111,870
15. Natural Sciences Managers	$111,710

Florida

Occupation	Median Earnings
1. Airline Pilots, Copilots, and Flight Engineers	more than $145,600
2. Anesthesiologists	more than $145,600
3. Chief Executives	more than $145,600
4. Family and General Practitioners	more than $145,600
5. Internists, General	more than $145,600
6. Obstetricians and Gynecologists	more than $145,600
7. Oral and Maxillofacial Surgeons	more than $145,600
8. Orthodontists	more than $145,600
9. Pediatricians, General	more than $145,600
10. Physicians and Surgeons, All Other	more than $145,600
11. Surgeons	more than $145,600
12. Psychiatrists	$142,680
13. Judges, Magistrate Judges, and Magistrates	$139,750
14. Air Traffic Controllers	$122,900
15. Dentists, General	$120,960

Georgia

Occupation	Median Earnings
1. Anesthesiologists	more than $145,600
2. Athletes and Sports Competitors	more than $145,600
3. Chief Executives	more than $145,600
4. Dentists, All Other Specialists	more than $145,600
5. Dentists, General	more than $145,600
6. Family and General Practitioners	more than $145,600
7. Internists, General	more than $145,600
8. Obstetricians and Gynecologists	more than $145,600
9. Oral and Maxillofacial Surgeons	more than $145,600
10. Orthodontists	more than $145,600
11. Physicians and Surgeons, All Other	more than $145,600
12. Podiatrists	more than $145,600
13. Psychiatrists	more than $145,600
14. Surgeons	more than $145,600
15. Optometrists	$137,150

Hawaii

Occupation	Median Earnings
1. Dentists, General	more than $145,600
2. Family and General Practitioners	more than $145,600
3. Internists, General	more than $145,600
4. Physicians and Surgeons, All Other	more than $145,600
5. Psychiatrists	$140,550
6. Obstetricians and Gynecologists	$139,800
7. Pediatricians, General	$132,430

Occupation	Median Earnings
8. Chief Executives	$125,360
9. Engineering Managers	$101,930
10. Air Traffic Controllers	$99,320
11. Natural Sciences Managers	$95,930
12. Construction Managers	$92,310
13. Training and Development Managers	$92,240
14. Pharmacists	$90,620
15. Atmospheric and Space Scientists	$90,200

Idaho

Occupation	Median Earnings
1. Anesthesiologists	more than $145,600
2. Dentists, General	more than $145,600
3. Family and General Practitioners	more than $145,600
4. Internists, General	more than $145,600
5. Judges, Magistrate Judges, and Magistrates	more than $145,600
6. Obstetricians and Gynecologists	more than $145,600
7. Physicians and Surgeons, All Other	more than $145,600
8. Psychiatrists	more than $145,600
9. Surgeons	more than $145,600
10. Pediatricians, General	$137,590
11. Actuaries	$109,780
12. Nuclear Engineers	$100,990
13. Chemical Engineers	$100,070
14. Engineering Managers	$98,370
15. Physicists	$92,660

Illinois

Occupation	Median Earnings
1. Airline Pilots, Copilots, and Flight Engineers	more than $145,600
2. Anesthesiologists	more than $145,600
3. Chief Executives	more than $145,600
4. Family and General Practitioners	more than $145,600
5. Internists, General	more than $145,600
6. Judges, Magistrate Judges, and Magistrates	more than $145,600
7. Obstetricians and Gynecologists	more than $145,600
8. Oral and Maxillofacial Surgeons	more than $145,600
9. Orthodontists	more than $145,600
10. Physicians and Surgeons, All Other	more than $145,600
11. Surgeons	more than $145,600
12. Air Traffic Controllers	$134,650
13. Podiatrists	$127,530
14. Lawyers	$120,760
15. Pediatricians, General	$116,660

Indiana

Occupation	Median Earnings
1. Anesthesiologists	more than $145,600
2. Family and General Practitioners	more than $145,600
3. Internists, General	more than $145,600
4. Obstetricians and Gynecologists	more than $145,600
5. Oral and Maxillofacial Surgeons	more than $145,600
6. Orthodontists	more than $145,600
7. Physicians and Surgeons, All Other	more than $145,600
8. Psychiatrists	more than $145,600

(continued)

(continued)

Occupation	Median Earnings
9. Surgeons	more than $145,600
10. Chief Executives	$133,450
11. Air Traffic Controllers	$127,340
12. Dentists, General	$125,340
13. Podiatrists	$114,850
14. Atmospheric and Space Scientists	$109,700
15. Biochemists and Biophysicists	$107,940

Iowa

Occupation	Median Earnings
1. Anesthesiologists	more than $145,600
2. Dentists, General	more than $145,600
3. Family and General Practitioners	more than $145,600
4. Internists, General	more than $145,600
5. Obstetricians and Gynecologists	more than $145,600
6. Oral and Maxillofacial Surgeons	more than $145,600
7. Pediatricians, General	more than $145,600
8. Psychiatrists	more than $145,600
9. Surgeons	more than $145,600
10. Physicians and Surgeons, All Other	$144,020
11. Chief Executives	$117,110
12. Podiatrists	$111,320
13. Economics Teachers, Postsecondary	$92,660
14. Natural Sciences Managers	$92,270
15. Judges, Magistrate Judges, and Magistrates	$89,610

Kansas

Occupation	Median Earnings
1. Anesthesiologists	more than $145,600
2. Family and General Practitioners	more than $145,600
3. Internists, General	more than $145,600
4. Obstetricians and Gynecologists	more than $145,600
5. Oral and Maxillofacial Surgeons	more than $145,600
6. Orthodontists	more than $145,600
7. Physicians and Surgeons, All Other	more than $145,600
8. Podiatrists	more than $145,600
9. Psychiatrists	more than $145,600
10. Surgeons	more than $145,600
11. Pediatricians, General	$128,380
12. Air Traffic Controllers	$126,210
13. Dentists, General	$119,520
14. Chief Executives	$112,340
15. Judges, Magistrate Judges, and Magistrates	$112,230

Kentucky

Occupation	Median Earnings
1. Anesthesiologists	more than $145,600
2. Family and General Practitioners	more than $145,600
3. Obstetricians and Gynecologists	more than $145,600
4. Oral and Maxillofacial Surgeons	more than $145,600
5. Orthodontists	more than $145,600
6. Pediatricians, General	more than $145,600
7. Physicians and Surgeons, All Other	more than $145,600
8. Podiatrists	more than $145,600

Occupation	Median Earnings
9. Psychiatrists	more than $145,600
10. Surgeons	more than $145,600
11. Internists, General	$141,900
12. Chief Executives	$122,500
13. Air Traffic Controllers	$115,450
14. Pharmacists	$99,050
15. Dentists, General	$97,480

Louisiana

Occupation	Median Earnings
1. Anesthesiologists	more than $145,600
2. Family and General Practitioners	more than $145,600
3. Internists, General	more than $145,600
4. Obstetricians and Gynecologists	more than $145,600
5. Oral and Maxillofacial Surgeons	more than $145,600
6. Orthodontists	more than $145,600
7. Pediatricians, General	more than $145,600
8. Physicians and Surgeons, All Other	more than $145,600
9. Surgeons	more than $145,600
10. Chief Executives	$132,720
11. Engineering Managers	$105,100
12. Physicists	$102,850
13. Health Diagnosing and Treating Practitioners, All Other	$91,750
14. Dentists, General	$90,860
15. Optometrists	$90,170

Maine

Occupation	Median Earnings
1. Anesthesiologists	more than $145,600
2. Audiologists	more than $145,600
3. Dentists, All Other Specialists	more than $145,600
4. Dentists, General	more than $145,600
5. Obstetricians and Gynecologists	more than $145,600
6. Physicians and Surgeons, All Other	more than $145,600
7. Surgeons	more than $145,600
8. Internists, General	$143,460
9. Psychiatrists	$141,320
10. Pediatricians, General	$138,840
11. Family and General Practitioners	$130,300
12. Judges, Magistrate Judges, and Magistrates	$115,070
13. Pharmacists	$103,570
14. Chief Executives	$98,250
15. Optometrists	$94,770

Maryland

Occupation	Median Earnings
1. Anesthesiologists	more than $145,600
2. Chief Executives	more than $145,600
3. Family and General Practitioners	more than $145,600
4. Obstetricians and Gynecologists	more than $145,600
5. Oral and Maxillofacial Surgeons	more than $145,600
6. Orthodontists	more than $145,600
7. Surgeons	more than $145,600
8. Internists, General	$145,520

Occupation	Median Earnings
9. Nuclear Engineers	$119,930
10. Dentists, General	$119,720
11. Physicians and Surgeons, All Other	$117,960
12. Pediatricians, General	$116,630
13. Air Traffic Controllers	$114,500
14. Computer and Information Systems Managers	$111,440
15. Health Specialties Teachers, Postsecondary	$111,110

Massachusetts

Occupation	Median Earnings
1. Airline Pilots, Copilots, and Flight Engineers	more than $145,600
2. Chief Executives	more than $145,600
3. Family and General Practitioners	more than $145,600
4. Internists, General	more than $145,600
5. Obstetricians and Gynecologists	more than $145,600
6. Oral and Maxillofacial Surgeons	more than $145,600
7. Orthodontists	more than $145,600
8. Psychiatrists	more than $145,600
9. Surgeons	more than $145,600
10. Pediatricians, General	$145,100
11. Physicians and Surgeons, All Other	$136,510
12. Dentists, General	$136,360
13. Natural Sciences Managers	$130,710
14. Astronomers	$118,350
15. Engineering Managers	$118,120

Michigan

Occupation	Median Earnings
1. Anesthesiologists	more than $145,600
2. Dentists, General	more than $145,600
3. Family and General Practitioners	more than $145,600
4. Obstetricians and Gynecologists	more than $145,600
5. Oral and Maxillofacial Surgeons	more than $145,600
6. Psychiatrists	more than $145,600
7. Surgeons	more than $145,600
8. Physicians and Surgeons, All Other	$143,800
9. Internists, General	$142,070
10. Chief Executives	$136,490
11. Pediatricians, General	$132,720
12. Air Traffic Controllers	$103,160
13. Engineering Managers	$102,730
14. Optometrists	$99,680
15. Dentists, All Other Specialists	$99,040

Minnesota

Occupation	Median Earnings
1. Anesthesiologists	more than $145,600
2. Chief Executives	more than $145,600
3. Dentists, All Other Specialists	more than $145,600
4. Internists, General	more than $145,600
5. Obstetricians and Gynecologists	more than $145,600
6. Oral and Maxillofacial Surgeons	more than $145,600
7. Orthodontists	more than $145,600
8. Pediatricians, General	more than $145,600
9. Physicians and Surgeons, All Other	more than $145,600

Occupation	Median Earnings
10. Podiatrists	more than $145,600
11. Psychiatrists	more than $145,600
12. Surgeons	more than $145,600
13. Family and General Practitioners	$145,450
14. Dentists, General	$138,690
15. Air Traffic Controllers	$137,220

Mississippi

Occupation	Median Earnings
1. Family and General Practitioners	more than $145,600
2. Internists, General	more than $145,600
3. Obstetricians and Gynecologists	more than $145,600
4. Pediatricians, General	more than $145,600
5. Surgeons	more than $145,600
6. Anesthesiologists	$140,100
7. Psychiatrists	$136,470
8. Dentists, General	$124,880
9. Engineering Managers	$105,340
10. Physicians and Surgeons, All Other	$103,860
11. Nuclear Engineers	$101,310
12. Chief Executives	$96,840
13. Pharmacists	$89,030
14. Physicists	$87,010
15. Natural Sciences Managers	$86,450

Missouri

Occupation	Median Earnings
1. Anesthesiologists	more than $145,600
2. Athletes and Sports Competitors	more than $145,600
3. Dentists, General	more than $145,600
4. Family and General Practitioners	more than $145,600
5. Internists, General	more than $145,600
6. Obstetricians and Gynecologists	more than $145,600
7. Oral and Maxillofacial Surgeons	more than $145,600
8. Orthodontists	more than $145,600
9. Physicians and Surgeons, All Other	more than $145,600
10. Psychiatrists	more than $145,600
11. Surgeons	more than $145,600
12. Judges, Magistrate Judges, and Magistrates	$142,340
13. Pediatricians, General	$138,120
14. Chief Executives	$136,870
15. Podiatrists	$129,400

Montana

Occupation	Median Earnings
1. Internists, General	more than $145,600
2. Obstetricians and Gynecologists	more than $145,600
3. Psychiatrists	more than $145,600
4. Surgeons	more than $145,600
5. Family and General Practitioners	$129,780
6. Dentists, General	$113,190
7. Physicians and Surgeons, All Other	$113,030
8. Air Traffic Controllers	$92,900
9. Petroleum Engineers	$86,130
10. Pharmacists	$84,950

(continued)

(continued)

Occupation	Median Earnings
11. Atmospheric and Space Scientists	$79,010
12. Chemical Engineers	$75,880
13. Natural Sciences Managers	$75,470
14. Engineering Managers	$72,920
15. Psychologists, All Other	$70,810

Nebraska

Occupation	Median Earnings
1. Anesthesiologists	more than $145,600
2. Family and General Practitioners	more than $145,600
3. Internists, General	more than $145,600
4. Obstetricians and Gynecologists	more than $145,600
5. Orthodontists	more than $145,600
6. Physicians and Surgeons, All Other	more than $145,600
7. Surgeons	more than $145,600
8. Pediatricians, General	$137,310
9. Dentists, General	$136,220
10. Psychiatrists	$132,540
11. Chief Executives	$130,330
12. Air Traffic Controllers	$93,400
13. Engineering Managers	$91,970
14. Optometrists	$90,030
15. Marketing Managers	$89,320

Nevada

Occupation	Median Earnings
1. Chief Executives	more than $145,600
2. Family and General Practitioners	more than $145,600
3. Health Diagnosing and Treating Practitioners, All Other	more than $145,600
4. Internists, General	more than $145,600
5. Obstetricians and Gynecologists	more than $145,600
6. Physicians and Surgeons, All Other	more than $145,600
7. Psychiatrists	more than $145,600
8. Real Estate Brokers	more than $145,600
9. Surgeons	more than $145,600
10. Judges, Magistrate Judges, and Magistrates	$132,090
11. Nuclear Engineers	$131,960
12. Dentists, General	$129,470
13. Chiropractors	$121,320
14. Podiatrists	$114,970
15. Lawyers	$106,950

New Hampshire

Occupation	Median Earnings
1. Anesthesiologists	more than $145,600
2. Dentists, General	more than $145,600
3. Internists, General	more than $145,600
4. Obstetricians and Gynecologists	more than $145,600
5. Pediatricians, General	more than $145,600
6. Physicians and Surgeons, All Other	more than $145,600
7. Podiatrists	more than $145,600
8. Surgeons	more than $145,600
9. Air Traffic Controllers	$140,950

Occupation	Median Earnings
10. Family and General Practitioners	$131,350
11. Psychiatrists	$128,600
12. Chief Executives	$126,220
13. Engineering Managers	$104,620
14. Engineering Teachers, Postsecondary	$101,550
15. Optometrists	$96,300

New Jersey

Occupation	Median Earnings
1. Anesthesiologists	more than $145,600
2. Chief Executives	more than $145,600
3. Dentists, All Other Specialists	more than $145,600
4. Internists, General	more than $145,600
5. Obstetricians and Gynecologists	more than $145,600
6. Orthodontists	more than $145,600
7. Physicians and Surgeons, All Other	more than $145,600
8. Prosthodontists	more than $145,600
9. Psychiatrists	more than $145,600
10. Surgeons	more than $145,600
11. Family and General Practitioners	$141,150
12. Judges, Magistrate Judges, and Magistrates	$141,120
13. Pediatricians, General	$132,800
14. General and Operations Managers	$131,760
15. Natural Sciences Managers	$127,310

New Mexico

Occupation	Median Earnings
1. Family and General Practitioners	more than $145,600
2. Internists, General	more than $145,600
3. Life Scientists, All Other	more than $145,600
4. Obstetricians and Gynecologists	more than $145,600
5. Orthodontists	more than $145,600
6. Psychiatrists	more than $145,600
7. Surgeons	more than $145,600
8. Anesthesiologists	$134,420
9. Dentists, General	$122,640
10. Pediatricians, General	$121,280
11. Physicians and Surgeons, All Other	$120,020
12. Air Traffic Controllers	$117,870
13. Actuaries	$116,270
14. Engineering Managers	$116,050
15. Aerospace Engineers	$99,990

New York

Occupation	Median Earnings
1. Airline Pilots, Copilots, and Flight Engineers	more than $145,600
2. Anesthesiologists	more than $145,600
3. Chief Executives	more than $145,600
4. Family and General Practitioners	more than $145,600
5. Internists, General	more than $145,600
6. Obstetricians and Gynecologists	more than $145,600
7. Oral and Maxillofacial Surgeons	more than $145,600
8. Orthodontists	more than $145,600
9. Surgeons	more than $145,600
10. Psychiatrists	$135,700

Occupation	Median Earnings
11. Sales Managers	$134,680
12. Pediatricians, General	$134,370
13. Air Traffic Controllers	$133,350
14. Physicians and Surgeons, All Other	$132,840
15. Marketing Managers	$129,420

North Carolina

Occupation	Median Earnings
1. Anesthesiologists	more than $145,600
2. Chief Executives	more than $145,600
3. Dentists, General	more than $145,600
4. Family and General Practitioners	more than $145,600
5. Internists, General	more than $145,600
6. Obstetricians and Gynecologists	more than $145,600
7. Oral and Maxillofacial Surgeons	more than $145,600
8. Orthodontists	more than $145,600
9. Pediatricians, General	more than $145,600
10. Podiatrists	more than $145,600
11. Surgeons	more than $145,600
12. Psychiatrists	$141,880
13. Physicians and Surgeons, All Other	$131,180
14. Optometrists	$121,090
15. Natural Sciences Managers	$104,840

North Dakota

Occupation	Median Earnings
1. Dentists, General	more than $145,600
2. Family and General Practitioners	more than $145,600
3. Internists, General	more than $145,600
4. Psychiatrists	more than $145,600
5. Surgeons	$127,060
6. Chief Executives	$123,290
7. Physicians and Surgeons, All Other	$120,600
8. Judges, Magistrate Judges, and Magistrates	$114,760
9. Engineering Managers	$85,120
10. Administrative Law Judges, Adjudicators, and Hearing Officers	$83,370
11. Pharmacists	$80,580
12. Optometrists	$79,520
13. Air Traffic Controllers	$78,150
14. Natural Sciences Managers	$76,620
15. Agricultural Sciences Teachers, Postsecondary	$76,010

Ohio

Occupation	Median Earnings
1. Anesthesiologists	more than $145,600
2. Dentists, General	more than $145,600
3. Family and General Practitioners	more than $145,600
4. Internists, General	more than $145,600
5. Obstetricians and Gynecologists	more than $145,600
6. Oral and Maxillofacial Surgeons	more than $145,600
7. Orthodontists	more than $145,600
8. Physicians and Surgeons, All Other	more than $145,600
9. Psychiatrists	more than $145,600
10. Surgeons	more than $145,600

Occupation	Median Earnings
11. Pediatricians, General	$144,390
12. Chief Executives	$139,450
13. Air Traffic Controllers	$128,800
14. Petroleum Engineers	$111,890
15. Dentists, All Other Specialists	$109,750

Oklahoma

Occupation	Median Earnings
1. Internists, General	more than $145,600
2. Obstetricians and Gynecologists	more than $145,600
3. Pediatricians, General	more than $145,600
4. Podiatrists	more than $145,600
5. Psychiatrists	more than $145,600
6. Surgeons	more than $145,600
7. Anesthesiologists	$145,120
8. Family and General Practitioners	$144,990
9. Dentists, General	$116,840
10. Physicists	$107,620
11. Geoscientists, Except Hydrologists and Geographers	$103,130
12. Air Traffic Controllers	$101,090
13. Physicians and Surgeons, All Other	$92,350
14. Airline Pilots, Copilots, and Flight Engineers	$91,050
15. Judges, Magistrate Judges, and Magistrates	$89,490

Oregon

Occupation	Median Earnings
1. Airline Pilots, Copilots, and Flight Engineers	more than $145,600
2. Anesthesiologists	more than $145,600
3. Dentists, All Other Specialists	more than $145,600
4. Internists, General	more than $145,600
5. Obstetricians and Gynecologists	more than $145,600
6. Oral and Maxillofacial Surgeons	more than $145,600
7. Orthodontists	more than $145,600
8. Pediatricians, General	more than $145,600
9. Physicians and Surgeons, All Other	more than $145,600
10. Podiatrists	more than $145,600
11. Surgeons	more than $145,600
12. Family and General Practitioners	$138,510
13. Dentists, General	$135,130
14. Chief Executives	$121,020
15. Physicists	$117,140

Pennsylvania

Occupation	Median Earnings
1. Anesthesiologists	more than $145,600
2. Dentists, All Other Specialists	more than $145,600
3. Internists, General	more than $145,600
4. Obstetricians and Gynecologists	more than $145,600
5. Oral and Maxillofacial Surgeons	more than $145,600
6. Orthodontists	more than $145,600
7. Surgeons	more than $145,600
8. Psychiatrists	$136,980
9. Chief Executives	$135,460
10. Family and General Practitioners	$135,200
11. Pediatricians, General	$128,090

(continued)

(continued)

	Occupation	Median Earnings
12.	Physicians and Surgeons, All Other	$123,900
13.	Podiatrists	$110,880
14.	Dentists, General	$110,050
15.	Natural Sciences Managers	$105,160

Rhode Island

	Occupation	Median Earnings
1.	Chief Executives	more than $145,600
2.	Family and General Practitioners	more than $145,600
3.	Internists, General	more than $145,600
4.	Judges, Magistrate Judges, and Magistrates	more than $145,600
5.	Obstetricians and Gynecologists	more than $145,600
6.	Oral and Maxillofacial Surgeons	more than $145,600
7.	Psychiatrists	more than $145,600
8.	Surgeons	more than $145,600
9.	Pediatricians, General	$128,780
10.	Dentists, General	$128,260
11.	Air Traffic Controllers	$111,250
12.	Human Resources Managers, All Other	$101,110
13.	Engineering Managers	$99,120
14.	Computer and Information Systems Managers	$96,380
15.	Optometrists	$96,230

South Carolina

	Occupation	Median Earnings
1.	Anesthesiologists	more than $145,600
2.	Family and General Practitioners	more than $145,600
3.	Internists, General	more than $145,600
4.	Obstetricians and Gynecologists	more than $145,600
5.	Oral and Maxillofacial Surgeons	more than $145,600
6.	Orthodontists	more than $145,600
7.	Surgeons	more than $145,600
8.	Physicians and Surgeons, All Other	$143,670
9.	Pediatricians, General	$132,350
10.	Chief Executives	$131,910
11.	Dentists, General	$119,660
12.	Podiatrists	$104,350
13.	Dentists, All Other Specialists	$99,150
14.	Pharmacists	$94,910
15.	Physical Scientists, All Other	$93,040

South Dakota

	Occupation	Median Earnings
1.	Dentists, General	more than $145,600
2.	Family and General Practitioners	more than $145,600
3.	Internists, General	more than $145,600
4.	Obstetricians and Gynecologists	more than $145,600
5.	Pediatricians, General	more than $145,600
6.	Surgeons	more than $145,600
7.	Anesthesiologists	$144,240
8.	Securities, Commodities, and Financial Services Sales Agents	$128,600
9.	Physicians and Surgeons, All Other	$121,540
10.	Judges, Magistrate Judges, and Magistrates	$110,140

	Occupation	Median Earnings
11.	Physical Scientists, All Other	$101,920
12.	Chief Executives	$94,850
13.	Engineering Managers	$92,320
14.	Optometrists	$91,620
15.	Computer and Information Systems Managers	$89,640

Tennessee

	Occupation	Median Earnings
1.	Anesthesiologists	more than $145,600
2.	Dentists, General	more than $145,600
3.	Internists, General	more than $145,600
4.	Obstetricians and Gynecologists	more than $145,600
5.	Oral and Maxillofacial Surgeons	more than $145,600
6.	Orthodontists	more than $145,600
7.	Pediatricians, General	more than $145,600
8.	Psychiatrists	more than $145,600
9.	Surgeons	more than $145,600
10.	Podiatrists	$139,550
11.	Family and General Practitioners	$136,760
12.	Physicians and Surgeons, All Other	$124,230
13.	Air Traffic Controllers	$121,230
14.	Chief Executives	$118,950
15.	Dentists, All Other Specialists	$104,700

Texas

	Occupation	Median Earnings
1.	Anesthesiologists	more than $145,600
2.	Chief Executives	more than $145,600
3.	Dentists, General	more than $145,600
4.	Internists, General	more than $145,600
5.	Obstetricians and Gynecologists	more than $145,600
6.	Orthodontists	more than $145,600
7.	Pediatricians, General	more than $145,600
8.	Physicians and Surgeons, All Other	more than $145,600
9.	Surgeons	more than $145,600
10.	Airline Pilots, Copilots, and Flight Engineers	$144,980
11.	Family and General Practitioners	$141,730
12.	Psychiatrists	$141,680
13.	Air Traffic Controllers	$115,830
14.	Podiatrists	$115,040
15.	Engineering Managers	$113,210

Utah

	Occupation	Median Earnings
1.	Anesthesiologists	more than $145,600
2.	Family and General Practitioners	more than $145,600
3.	Internists, General	more than $145,600
4.	Obstetricians and Gynecologists	more than $145,600
5.	Oral and Maxillofacial Surgeons	more than $145,600
6.	Pediatricians, General	more than $145,600
7.	Physicians and Surgeons, All Other	more than $145,600
8.	Chief Executives	$143,490
9.	Dentists, General	$139,210
10.	Psychiatrists	$130,800
11.	Pharmacists	$94,850

Occupation	Median Earnings
12. Engineering Managers	$94,210
13. Engineering Teachers, Postsecondary	$89,370
14. Lawyers	$89,260
15. Optometrists	$87,430

Vermont

Occupation	Median Earnings
1. Obstetricians and Gynecologists	more than $145,600
2. Optometrists	more than $145,600
3. Physicians and Surgeons, All Other	$142,240
4. Psychiatrists	$132,080
5. Chief Executives	$127,660
6. Engineering Managers	$124,210
7. Family and General Practitioners	$121,420
8. Dentists, General	$118,640
9. Pharmacists	$95,150
10. Computer and Information Systems Managers	$91,510
11. Sales Managers	$90,540
12. Industrial Production Managers	$85,260
13. General and Operations Managers	$85,080
14. Natural Sciences Managers	$83,930
15. Art Directors	$83,080

Virginia

Occupation	Median Earnings
1. Airline Pilots, Copilots, and Flight Engineers	more than $145,600
2. Anesthesiologists	more than $145,600
3. Chief Executives	more than $145,600
4. Dentists, General	more than $145,600
5. Family and General Practitioners	more than $145,600
6. Internists, General	more than $145,600
7. Obstetricians and Gynecologists	more than $145,600
8. Oral and Maxillofacial Surgeons	more than $145,600
9. Orthodontists	more than $145,600
10. Prosthodontists	more than $145,600
11. Psychiatrists	more than $145,600
12. Surgeons	more than $145,600
13. Air Traffic Controllers	$134,970
14. Podiatrists	$130,600
15. Pediatricians, General	$125,260

Washington

Occupation	Median Earnings
1. Anesthesiologists	more than $145,600
2. Chief Executives	more than $145,600
3. Dentists, General	more than $145,600
4. Internists, General	more than $145,600
5. Obstetricians and Gynecologists	more than $145,600
6. Oral and Maxillofacial Surgeons	more than $145,600
7. Orthodontists	more than $145,600
8. Physicians and Surgeons, All Other	more than $145,600
9. Podiatrists	more than $145,600
10. Surgeons	more than $145,600
11. Psychiatrists	$142,900
12. Family and General Practitioners	$139,890

Occupation	Median Earnings
13. Pediatricians, General	$130,360
14. Engineering Managers	$116,690
15. Optometrists	$112,980

West Virginia

Occupation	Median Earnings
1. Anesthesiologists	more than $145,600
2. Family and General Practitioners	more than $145,600
3. Internists, General	more than $145,600
4. Obstetricians and Gynecologists	more than $145,600
5. Physicians and Surgeons, All Other	more than $145,600
6. Psychiatrists	more than $145,600
7. Surgeons	more than $145,600
8. Dentists, General	$143,720
9. Pediatricians, General	$135,030
10. Administrative Law Judges, Adjudicators, and Hearing Officers	$99,380
11. Pharmacists	$94,220
12. Engineering Managers	$92,850
13. Physical Scientists, All Other	$90,380
14. Natural Sciences Managers	$87,190
15. Aerospace Engineers	$86,940

Wisconsin

Occupation	Median Earnings
1. Anesthesiologists	more than $145,600
2. Chief Executives	more than $145,600
3. Family and General Practitioners	more than $145,600
4. Internists, General	more than $145,600
5. Obstetricians and Gynecologists	more than $145,600
6. Oral and Maxillofacial Surgeons	more than $145,600
7. Orthodontists	more than $145,600
8. Pediatricians, General	more than $145,600
9. Physicians and Surgeons, All Other	more than $145,600
10. Psychiatrists	more than $145,600
11. Surgeons	more than $145,600
12. Dentists, All Other Specialists	$129,920
13. Dentists, General	$127,330
14. Air Traffic Controllers	$101,750
15. Pharmacists	$101,050

Wyoming

Occupation	Median Earnings
1. Anesthesiologists	more than $145,600
2. Family and General Practitioners	more than $145,600
3. Internists, General	more than $145,600
4. Obstetricians and Gynecologists	more than $145,600
5. Surgeons	more than $145,600
6. Dentists, General	$110,410
7. Pediatricians, General	$106,630
8. Chief Executives	$99,820
9. Pharmacists	$87,710
10. Petroleum Engineers	$87,410
11. Industrial Production Managers	$86,740
12. Optometrists	$86,420

(continued)

(continued)

Occupation	Median Earnings
13. Engineering Managers	$80,870
14. Education Administrators, Postsecondary.....................	$77,140
15. Mining and Geological Engineers, Including Mining Safety Engineers	$73,740

The 10 Best-Paying Jobs in Each Metropolitan Area

For each of the 30 metropolitan areas with the biggest paid working populations you can see the 10 jobs with the highest median earnings.

(You can see the median earnings for all 30 of these metropolitan areas for each job in Part III.)

Atlanta–Sandy Springs–Marietta, GA

Occupation	Median Earnings
1. Anesthesiologists	more than $145,600
2. Athletes and Sports Competitors....................	more than $145,600
3. Chief Executives	more than $145,600
4. Dentists, All Other Specialists........................	more than $145,600
5. Dentists, General..................................	more than $145,600
6. Family and General Practitioners....................	more than $145,600
7. Internists, General	more than $145,600
8. Obstetricians and Gynecologists	more than $145,600
9. Optometrists......................................	more than $145,600
10. Oral and Maxillofacial Surgeons	more than $145,600

Baltimore–Towson, MD

Occupation	Median Earnings
1. Anesthesiologists	more than $145,600
2. Chief Executives	more than $145,600
3. Family and General Practitioners....................	more than $145,600
4. Obstetricians and Gynecologists	more than $145,600
5. Orthodontists	more than $145,600
6. Surgeons	more than $145,600
7. Internists, General	$141,850
8. Health Specialties Teachers, Postsecondary	$117,420
9. Dentists, General..................................	$117,060
10. Psychiatrists....................................	$111,910

Boston–Cambridge–Quincy, MA–NH

Occupation	Median Earnings
1. Anesthesiologists	more than $145,600
2. Chief Executives	more than $145,600
3. Family and General Practitioners....................	more than $145,600
4. Internists, General	more than $145,600
5. Obstetricians and Gynecologists	more than $145,600
6. Oral and Maxillofacial Surgeons	more than $145,600
7. Orthodontists	more than $145,600
8. Pediatricians, General	more than $145,600
9. Podiatrists	more than $145,600
10. Psychiatrists....................................	more than $145,600

Chicago–Naperville–Joilet, IL–IN–WI

Occupation	Median Earnings
1. Airline Pilots, Copilots, and Flight Engineers ..	more than $145,600
2. Anesthesiologists	more than $145,600
3. Chief Executives	more than $145,600
4. Dentists, All Other Specialists........................	more than $145,600
5. Obstetricians and Gynecologists	more than $145,600
6. Oral and Maxillofacial Surgeons	more than $145,600
7. Physicians and Surgeons, All Other	more than $145,600
8. Surgeons	more than $145,600
9. Judges, Magistrate Judges, and Magistrates	$144,440
10. Internists, General	$142,150

Cincinnati–Middletown, OH–KY–IN

Occupation	Median Earnings
1. Anesthesiologists	more than $145,600
2. Dentists, General..................................	more than $145,600
3. Obstetricians and Gynecologists	more than $145,600
4. Orthodontists	more than $145,600
5. Pediatricians, General	more than $145,600
6. Physicians and Surgeons, All Other	more than $145,600
7. Surgeons	more than $145,600
8. Chief Executives	$143,570
9. Internists, General	$138,840
10. Psychiatrists....................................	$136,550

Cleveland–Elyria–Mentor, OH

Occupation	Median Earnings
1. Chief Executives	more than $145,600
2. Dentists, General..................................	more than $145,600
3. Family and General Practitioners....................	more than $145,600
4. Obstetricians and Gynecologists	more than $145,600
5. Orthodontists	more than $145,600
6. Surgeons	more than $145,600
7. Psychiatrists....................................	$144,140
8. Pediatricians, General	$141,790
9. Physicians and Surgeons, All Other	$137,480
10. Internists, General	$136,170

Columbus, OH

Occupation	Median Earnings
1. Anesthesiologists	more than $145,600
2. Chief Executives	more than $145,600
3. Dentists, General..................................	more than $145,600
4. Family and General Practitioners....................	more than $145,600
5. Internists, General	more than $145,600
6. Obstetricians and Gynecologists	more than $145,600
7. Oral and Maxillofacial Surgeons	more than $145,600
8. Orthodontists	more than $145,600
9. Physicians and Surgeons, All Other	more than $145,600
10. Psychiatrists....................................	more than $145,600

Dallas–Fort Worth–Arlington, TX

Occupation	Median Earnings
1. Anesthesiologists	more than $145,600
2. Chief Executives	more than $145,600
3. Dentists, General	more than $145,600
4. Family and General Practitioners	more than $145,600
5. Internists, General	more than $145,600
6. Obstetricians and Gynecologists	more than $145,600
7. Orthodontists	more than $145,600
8. Pediatricians, General	more than $145,600
9. Physicians and Surgeons, All Other	more than $145,600
10. Psychiatrists	more than $145,600

Denver–Aurora, CO

Occupation	Median Earnings
1. Anesthesiologists	more than $145,600
2. Chief Executives	more than $145,600
3. Health Diagnosing and Treating Practitioners, All Other	more than $145,600
4. Internists, General	more than $145,600
5. Obstetricians and Gynecologists	more than $145,600
6. Pediatricians, General	more than $145,600
7. Psychiatrists	more than $145,600
8. Surgeons	more than $145,600
9. Air Traffic Controllers	$136,410
10. Dentists, General	$128,010

Detroit–Warren–Livonia, MI

Occupation	Median Earnings
1. Anesthesiologists	more than $145,600
2. Captains, Mates, and Pilots of Water Vessels	more than $145,600
3. Chief Executives	more than $145,600
4. Dentists, General	more than $145,600
5. Family and General Practitioners	more than $145,600
6. Obstetricians and Gynecologists	more than $145,600
7. Orthodontists	more than $145,600
8. Psychiatrists	more than $145,600
9. Surgeons	more than $145,600
10. Physicians and Surgeons, All Other	$139,000

Houston–Sugar Land–Baytown, TX

Occupation	Median Earnings
1. Anesthesiologists	more than $145,600
2. Athletes and Sports Competitors	more than $145,600
3. Chief Executives	more than $145,600
4. Dentists, General	more than $145,600
5. Internists, General	more than $145,600
6. Obstetricians and Gynecologists	more than $145,600
7. Orthodontists	more than $145,600
8. Surgeons	more than $145,600
9. Physicians and Surgeons, All Other	$135,170
10. Air Traffic Controllers	$134,480

Kansas City, MO–KS

Occupation	Median Earnings
1. Anesthesiologists	more than $145,600
2. Family and General Practitioners	more than $145,600
3. Internists, General	more than $145,600
4. Obstetricians and Gynecologists	more than $145,600
5. Orthodontists	more than $145,600
6. Physicians and Surgeons, All Other	more than $145,600
7. Psychiatrists	more than $145,600
8. Surgeons	more than $145,600
9. Chief Executives	$143,040
10. Air Traffic Controllers	$128,510

Las Vegas–Paradise, NV

Occupation	Median Earnings
1. Chief Executives	more than $145,600
2. Family and General Practitioners	more than $145,600
3. Internists, General	more than $145,600
4. Obstetricians and Gynecologists	more than $145,600
5. Physicians and Surgeons, All Other	more than $145,600
6. Psychiatrists	more than $145,600
7. Real Estate Brokers	more than $145,600
8. Surgeons	more than $145,600
9. Judges, Magistrate Judges, and Magistrates	$136,630
10. Nuclear Engineers	$132,300

Los Angeles–Long Beach–Santa Ana, CA

Occupation	Median Earnings
1. Airline Pilots, Copilots, and Flight Engineers	more than $145,600
2. Anesthesiologists	more than $145,600
3. Chief Executives	more than $145,600
4. Internists, General	more than $145,600
5. Obstetricians and Gynecologists	more than $145,600
6. Oral and Maxillofacial Surgeons	more than $145,600
7. Orthodontists	more than $145,600
8. Physicians and Surgeons, All Other	more than $145,600
9. Psychiatrists	more than $145,600
10. Surgeons	more than $145,600

Miami–Fort Lauderdale–Miami Beach, FL

Occupation	Median Earnings
1. Anesthesiologists	more than $145,600
2. Chief Executives	more than $145,600
3. Family and General Practitioners	more than $145,600
4. Internists, General	more than $145,600
5. Obstetricians and Gynecologists	more than $145,600
6. Orthodontists	more than $145,600
7. Surgeons	$144,520
8. Judges, Magistrate Judges, and Magistrates	$139,690
9. Psychiatrists	$139,060
10. Air Traffic Controllers	$134,500

Minneapolis–St. Paul–Bloomington, MN–WI

Occupation	Median Earnings
1. Anesthesiologists	more than $145,600
2. Chief Executives	more than $145,600
3. Internists, General	more than $145,600
4. Obstetricians and Gynecologists	more than $145,600
5. Oral and Maxillofacial Surgeons	more than $145,600
6. Orthodontists	more than $145,600
7. Pediatricians, General	more than $145,600
8. Physicians and Surgeons, All Other	more than $145,600
9. Podiatrists	more than $145,600
10. Psychiatrists	more than $145,600

New York–Northern New Jersey–Long Island, NY–NJ–PA

Occupation	Median Earnings
1. Airline Pilots, Copilots, and Flight Engineers	more than $145,600
2. Athletes and Sports Competitors	more than $145,600
3. Chief Executives	more than $145,600
4. Orthodontists	more than $145,600
5. Psychiatrists	$138,880
6. Air Traffic Controllers	$138,170
7. Judges, Magistrate Judges, and Magistrates	$137,210
8. Physicians and Surgeons, All Other	$135,660
9. Marketing Managers	$130,580
10. Pediatricians, General	$130,370

Orlando–Kissimmee, FL

Occupation	Median Earnings
1. Anesthesiologists	more than $145,600
2. Chief Executives	more than $145,600
3. Dentists, General	more than $145,600
4. Obstetricians and Gynecologists	more than $145,600
5. Pediatricians, General	more than $145,600
6. Physicians and Surgeons, All Other	more than $145,600
7. Podiatrists	more than $145,600
8. Surgeons	more than $145,600
9. Judges, Magistrate Judges, and Magistrates	$140,410
10. Agents and Business Managers of Artists, Performers, and Athletes	$126,900

Philadelphia–Camden–Wilmington, PA–NJ–DE–MD

Occupation	Median Earnings
1. Anesthesiologists	more than $145,600
2. Chief Executives	more than $145,600
3. Dentists, All Other Specialists	more than $145,600
4. Obstetricians and Gynecologists	more than $145,600
5. Orthodontists	more than $145,600
6. Physicians and Surgeons, All Other	more than $145,600
7. Psychiatrists	more than $145,600
8. Surgeons	more than $145,600
9. Internists, General	$140,660
10. Judges, Magistrate Judges, and Magistrates	$139,800

Phoenix–Mesa–Scottsdale, AZ

Occupation	Median Earnings
1. Anesthesiologists	more than $145,600
2. Internists, General	more than $145,600
3. Obstetricians and Gynecologists	more than $145,600
4. Oral and Maxillofacial Surgeons	more than $145,600
5. Orthodontists	more than $145,600
6. Pediatricians, General	more than $145,600
7. Psychiatrists	more than $145,600
8. Surgeons	more than $145,600
9. Psychologists, All Other	$145,480
10. Chief Executives	$143,900

Pittsburgh, PA

Occupation	Median Earnings
1. Family and General Practitioners	more than $145,600
2. Internists, General	more than $145,600
3. Obstetricians and Gynecologists	more than $145,600
4. Surgeons	more than $145,600
5. Pediatricians, General	$143,670
6. Psychiatrists	$143,410
7. Anesthesiologists	$136,940
8. Chief Executives	$127,640
9. Air Traffic Controllers	$125,600
10. Podiatrists	$123,790

Portland–Vancouver–Beaverton, OR–WA

Occupation	Median Earnings
1. Anesthesiologists	more than $145,600
2. Chief Executives	more than $145,600
3. Family and General Practitioners	more than $145,600
4. Internists, General	more than $145,600
5. Obstetricians and Gynecologists	more than $145,600
6. Pediatricians, General	more than $145,600
7. Physicists	more than $145,600
8. Psychiatrists	more than $145,600
9. Surgeons	more than $145,600
10. Physicians and Surgeons, All Other	$132,370

Riverside–San Bernardino–Ontario, CA

Occupation	Median Earnings
1. Anesthesiologists	more than $145,600
2. Chief Executives	more than $145,600
3. Dentists, General	more than $145,600
4. Obstetricians and Gynecologists	more than $145,600
5. Physicians and Surgeons, All Other	more than $145,600
6. Psychiatrists	more than $145,600
7. Surgeons	more than $145,600
8. Family and General Practitioners	$145,210
9. Internists, General	$139,990
10. Pediatricians, General	$133,530

Sacramento–Arden-Arcade–Roseville, CA

Occupation	Median Earnings
1. Psychiatrists	more than $145,600
2. Surgeons	more than $145,600
3. Internists, General	$144,160
4. Pediatricians, General	$141,610
5. Air Traffic Controllers	$133,670
6. Dentists, General	$133,210
7. Family and General Practitioners	$133,150
8. Chief Executives	$121,860
9. Physicians and Surgeons, All Other	$120,190
10. Engineering Managers	$112,330

St. Louis, MO–IL

Occupation	Median Earnings
1. Anesthesiologists	more than $145,600
2. Athletes and Sports Competitors	more than $145,600
3. Chief Executives	more than $145,600
4. Dentists, General	more than $145,600
5. Internists, General	more than $145,600
6. Obstetricians and Gynecologists	more than $145,600
7. Orthodontists	more than $145,600
8. Pediatricians, General	more than $145,600
9. Physicians and Surgeons, All Other	more than $145,600
10. Surgeons	more than $145,600

San Diego–Carlsbad–San Marcos, CA

Occupation	Median Earnings
1. Athletes and Sports Competitors	more than $145,600
2. Chief Executives	more than $145,600
3. Family and General Practitioners	more than $145,600
4. Obstetricians and Gynecologists	more than $145,600
5. Pediatricians, General	more than $145,600
6. Physicians and Surgeons, All Other	more than $145,600
7. Surgeons	more than $145,600
8. Internists, General	$139,620
9. Air Traffic Controllers	$135,380
10. Physical Scientists, All Other	$134,860

San Francisco–Oakland–Fremont, CA

Occupation	Median Earnings
1. Anesthesiologists	more than $145,600
2. Chief Executives	more than $145,600
3. Dentists, General	more than $145,600
4. Family and General Practitioners	more than $145,600
5. Internists, General	more than $145,600
6. Obstetricians and Gynecologists	more than $145,600
7. Orthodontists	more than $145,600
8. Psychiatrists	more than $145,600
9. Surgeons	more than $145,600
10. Podiatrists	$140,630

Seattle–Tacoma–Bellevue, WA

Occupation	Median Earnings
1. Anesthesiologists	more than $145,600
2. Athletes and Sports Competitors	more than $145,600
3. Chief Executives	more than $145,600
4. Dentists, General	more than $145,600
5. Internists, General	more than $145,600
6. Obstetricians and Gynecologists	more than $145,600
7. Physicians and Surgeons, All Other	more than $145,600
8. Psychiatrists	more than $145,600
9. Surgeons	more than $145,600
10. Family and General Practitioners	$137,500

Tampa–St. Petersburg–Clearwater, FL

Occupation	Median Earnings
1. Anesthesiologists	more than $145,600
2. Chief Executives	more than $145,600
3. Internists, General	more than $145,600
4. Law Teachers, Postsecondary	more than $145,600
5. Obstetricians and Gynecologists	more than $145,600
6. Psychiatrists	more than $145,600
7. Surgeons	more than $145,600
8. Physicians and Surgeons, All Other	$139,900
9. Judges, Magistrate Judges, and Magistrates	$139,840
10. Air Traffic Controllers	$135,100

Washington–Arlington–Alexandria, DC–VA–MD–WV

Occupation	Median Earnings
1. Airline Pilots, Copilots, and Flight Engineers	more than $145,600
2. Anesthesiologists	more than $145,600
3. Chief Executives	more than $145,600
4. Dentists, General	more than $145,600
5. Internists, General	more than $145,600
6. Orthodontists	more than $145,600
7. Prosthodontists	more than $145,600
8. Family and General Practitioners	$138,760
9. Psychiatrists	$137,090
10. Air Traffic Controllers	$135,040

The 20 Best-Paying Jobs for Men and Women

These lists show the 20 jobs with the best pay for men and women. The earnings figures are not the average earnings for *all* workers in the occupation, but the average of the actual earnings of *men* or *women* in the occupation. The lists are limited to occupations for which data is available from the Current Population Survey in 2006. Some high-paying jobs may be missing because of insufficient data.

You can see the percentage of men and women working and the percentage by which their sex raises or lowers their earnings compared to the average for both sexes for each job in Part III.

The 20 Best-Paying Jobs for Men

Average pay for all men: $44,452

Occupation	Average Earnings
1. Optometrists	$107,975
2. Actuaries	$105,045
3. Economists	$103,254
4. Natural Sciences Managers	$98,943
5. Chief Executives	$98,492
6. Lawyers	$97,123
7. Physicians and Surgeons	$96,752
8. Engineering Managers	$92,880
9. Petroleum Engineers	$90,882
10. Astronomers and Physicists	$90,583
11. Market and Survey Researchers	$87,156
12. Chiropractors	$85,793
13. Veterinarians	$83,563
14. Aerospace Engineers	$83,152
15. Physical Scientists, All Other	$81,583
16. Personal Financial Advisors	$81,321
17. Marine Engineers and Naval Architects	$81,005
18. Marketing and Sales Managers	$80,442
19. Sales Engineers	$80,436
20. Computer and Information Systems Managers	$79,926

Note: The Current Population Survey does not provide separate earnings figures for the specific jobs represented by jobs 7, 10, 11, and 18. In Part III, job 7 is represented by Anesthesiologists; Family and General Practitioners; Internists, General; Obstetricians and Gynecologists; Pediatricians, General; Psychiatrists; Surgeons; and Physicians and Surgeons, All Other. Job 10 is represented by the separate jobs Astronomers and Physicists. Job 11 is represented by Market Research Analysts and Survey Researchers. Job 18 is represented by Marketing Managers and Sales Managers.

The 20 Best-Paying Jobs for Women

Average pay for all women: $31,824

Occupation	Average Earnings
1. Economists	$88,406
2. Physicians and Surgeons	$80,685
3. Lawyers	$78,852
4. Chief Executives	$76,886
5. Aerospace Engineers	$76,206
6. Computer and Information Systems Managers	$69,361
7. Chemical Engineers	$68,598
8. Computer Software Engineers	$67,324
9. Electrical and Electronics Engineers	$67,113
10. Environmental Engineers	$65,783
11. Pharmacists	$65,613
12. Civil Engineers	$65,230
13. Engineers, All Other	$65,112
14. Chemists and Materials Scientists	$64,853
15. Dentists	$64,569
16. Air Traffic Controllers and Airfield Operations Specialists	$61,841
17. Industrial Engineers, Including Health and Safety	$61,067
18. Budget Analysts	$60,904
19. Mechanical Engineers	$59,881
20. Physical Scientists, All Other	$59,672

Note: The Current Population Survey does not provide separate earnings figures for the specific jobs represented by jobs 2, 8, 9, 14, 15, 16, and 17. In Part III, job 2 is represented by Anesthesiologists; Family and General Practitioners; Internists, General; Obstetricians and Gynecologists; Pediatricians, General; Psychiatrists; Surgeons; and Physicians and Surgeons, All Other. Job 8 is represented by Computer Software Engineers, Applications; and Computer Software Engineers, Systems Software. Job 9 is represented by Electrical Engineers and Electronics Engineers, Except Computer. Job 14 is represented by the separate jobs Chemists and Materials Scientists. Job 15 is represented by Dentists, General; Oral and Maxillofacial Surgeons; Orthodontists; Prosthodontists; and Dentists, All Other. Job 16 is represented by Air Traffic Controllers and Airfield Operations Specialists. Job 17 is represented by Health and Safety Engineers, Except Mining Safety Engineers and Inspectors and Industrial Engineers.

The 20 Best-Paying Jobs by Age

These lists show the 20 best-paying jobs for people in various age brackets. Like the earnings figures for men and women, the figures here are the averages of the actual earnings of the identified group of people, not an average of all workers in the occupation.

The 20 Best-Paying Jobs Held by People Age 16–24

Average pay for all workers in this age bracket: $17,764

Occupation	Average Earnings
1. Derrick, Rotary Drill, and Service Unit Operators, Oil, Gas, and Mining	$60,945
2. Railroad Conductors and Yardmasters	$54,398
3. Ship and Boat Captains and Operators	$50,310
4. Environmental Scientists and Geoscientists	$49,878
5. Computer Software Engineers	$47,886
6. Engineers, All Other	$47,562
7. Industrial Engineers, Including Health and Safety	$46,020
8. Mining Machine Operators	$44,953
9. Architects, Except Naval	$43,775
10. Aerospace Engineers	$43,658
11. Financial Analysts	$43,325
12. Mechanical Engineers	$41,369
13. Market and Survey Researchers	$41,275
14. Electrical and Electronics Engineers	$40,737
15. Management Analysts	$40,048
16. Dental Hygienists	$39,842
17. Chief Executives	$39,112
18. Construction Managers	$38,402
19. Physical Scientists, All Other	$38,052
20. Civil Engineers	$37,868

Note: The Current Population Survey does not provide separate earnings figures for the specific jobs represented by jobs 1, 3, 4, 5, 7, 8, 9, 13, and 14. In Part III, job 1 is represented by Derrick Operators, Oil and Gas; Rotary Drill Operators, Oil and Gas; and Service Unit Operators, Oil, Gas, and Mining. Job 3 is represented by Captains, Mates, and Pilots of Water Vessels and Motorboat Operators. Job 4 is represented by Environmental Scientists and Specialists, Including Health; Geoscientists, Except Hydrologists and Geographers; and Hydrologists. Job 5 is represented by Computer Software Engineers, Applications and Computer Software Engineers, Systems Software. Job 7 is represented by Health and Safety Engineers, Except Mining Safety Engineers and Inspectors and Industrial Engineers. Job 8 is represented by Continuous Mining Machine Operators; Mine Cutting and Channeling Machine Operators; and Mining Machine Operators, All Other. Job 9 is represented by Architects, Except Landscape and Naval and Landscape Architects. Job

13 is represented by Market Research Analysts and Survey Researchers. Job 14 is represented by Electrical Engineers and Electronics Engineers, Except Computer.

The 20 Best-Paying Jobs Held by People Age 25–34

Average pay for all workers in this age bracket: $35,125

Occupation	Average Earnings
1. Sales Engineers	$78,683
2. Economists	$77,996
3. Lawyers	$75,261
4. Optometrists	$74,615
5. Chief Executives	$73,781
6. Engineering Managers	$73,339
7. Derrick, Rotary Drill, and Service Unit Operators, Oil, Gas, and Mining	$72,129
8. Aerospace Engineers	$68,202
9. Fire Inspectors	$67,843
10. Dentists	$67,718
11. Personal Finance Advisors	$67,532
12. Pharmacists	$66,840
13. Electrical and Electronics Engineers	$66,779
14. Power Plant Operators	$66,475
15. Actuaries	$66,268
16. Computer Software Engineers	$65,235
17. Computer and Information Systems Managers	$64,269
18. Physicians and Surgeons	$64,110
19. Earth Drillers, Except Oil and Gas	$62,534
20. Management Analysts	$62,105

Note: The Current Population Survey does not provide separate earnings figures for the specific jobs represented by jobs 10, 13, 16, and 18. In Part III, job 10 is represented by Dentists, General; Oral and Maxillofacial Surgeons; Orthodontists; Prosthodontists; and Dentists, All Other Specialists. Job 13 is represented by Electrical Engineers and Electronics Engineers, Except Computer. Job 16 is represented by Computer Software Engineers, Applications and Computer Software Engineers, Systems Software. Job 18 is represented by Anesthesiologists; Family and General Practitioners; Internists, General; Obstetricians and Gynecologists; Pediatricians, General; Psychiatrists; Surgeons; and Physicians and Surgeons, All Other.

The 20 Best-Paying Jobs Held by People Age 35–44

Average pay for all workers in this age bracket: $41,720

Occupation	Average Earnings
1. Actuaries	$111,870
2. Economists	$105,465
3. Physicians and Surgeons	$99,208
4. Chief Executives	$99,104
5. Engineering Managers	$96,900
6. Lawyers	$95,277
7. Air Traffic Controllers and Airfield Operations Specialists	$84,132
8. Marketing and Sales Managers	$82,596
9. Aerospace Engineers	$82,245
10. Computer and Information Systems Managers	$82,081
11. Sales Engineers	$81,693
12. Chemical Engineers	$80,410
13. Computer Hardware Engineers	$79,926
14. Electrical and Electronics Engineers	$79,521
15. Pharmacists	$79,024
16. Computer Software Engineers	$77,980

Occupation	Average Earnings
17. Dentists	$77,586
18. Materials Engineers	$77,094
19. Personal Finance Advisors	$76,938
20. Environmental Engineers	$76,220

Note: The Current Population Survey does not provide separate earnings figures for the specific jobs represented by jobs 3, 7, 8, 14, 16, and 17. In Part III, job 3 is represented by Anesthesiologists; Family and General Practitioners; Internists, General; Obstetricians and Gynecologists; Pediatricians, General; Psychiatrists; Surgeons; and Physicians and Surgeons, All Other. Job 7 is represented by Air Traffic Controllers and Airfield Operations Specialists. Job 8 is represented by Marketing Managers and Sales Managers. Job 14 is represented by Electrical Engineers and Electronics Engineers, Except Computer. Job 16 is represented by Computer Software Engineers, Applications and Computer Software Engineers, Systems Software. Job 17 is represented by Dentists, General; Oral and Maxillofacial Surgeons; Orthodontists; Prosthodontists; and Dentists, All Other Specialists.

The 20 Best-Paying Jobs Held by People Age 45–54

Average pay for all workers in this age bracket: $43,146

Occupation	Average Earnings
1. Chiropractors	$127,426
2. Economists	$124,775
3. Actuaries	$115,294
4. Astronomers and Physicists	$108,711
5. Physicians and Surgeons	$104,759
6. Natural Sciences Managers	$104,533
7. Chief Executives	$96,936
8. Lawyers	$96,371
9. Petroleum Engineers	$95,030
10. Airline Pilots, Copilots, and Flight Engineers	$93,053
11. Sales Engineers	$92,777
12. Engineering Managers	$91,718
13. Aerospace Engineers	$90,701
14. Physical Scientists, All Other	$85,902
15. Computer Software Engineers	$84,314
16. Computer and Information Systems Managers	$81,961
17. Personal Finance Advisors	$81,898
18. Air Traffic Controllers and Airfield Operations Specialists	$81,694
19. Dentists	$80,775
20. Environmental Engineers	$80,166

Note: The Current Population Survey does not provide separate earnings figures for the specific jobs represented by jobs 4, 5, 10, 15, 18, and 19. In Part III, job 4 is represented by the separate jobs Astronomers and Physicists. Job 5 is represented by Anesthesiologists; Family and General Practitioners; Internists, General; Obstetricians and Gynecologists; Pediatricians, General; Psychiatrists; Surgeons; and Physicians and Surgeons, All Other. Job 10 is represented by Airline Pilots, Copilots, and Flight Engineers and Commercial Pilots. Job 15 is represented by Computer Software Engineers, Applications and Computer Software Engineers, Systems Software. Job 18 is represented by Air Traffic Controllers and Airfield Operations Specialists. Job 19 is represented by Dentists, General; Oral and Maxillofacial Surgeons; Orthodontists; Prosthodontists; and Dentists, All Other Specialists.

The 20 Best-Paying Jobs Held by People Age 55–64

Average pay for all workers in this age bracket: $41,784

Occupation	Average Earnings
1. Dentists	$102,143
2. Physicians and Surgeons	$99,353

(continued)

(continued)

Occupation	Average Earnings
3. Astronomers and Physicists	$99,110
4. Physical Scientists, All Other	$97,078
5. Lawyers	$95,889
6. Economists	$95,671
7. Chief Executives	$94,813
8. Engineering Managers	$94,266
9. Aerospace Engineers	$92,421
10. Veterinarians	$90,973
11. Environmental Engineers	$90,146
12. Psychologists	$82,161
13. Miscellaneous Social Scientists and Related Workers	$81,547
14. Pumping Station Operators	$79,968
15. Pharmacists	$79,786
16. Urban and Regional Planners	$79,589
17. Medical Scientists	$79,454
18. Architects, Except Naval	$79,345
19. Computer Software Engineers	$78,553
20. Electrical and Electronics Engineers	$77,881

Note: The Current Population Survey does not provide separate earnings figures for the specific jobs represented by jobs 1, 2, 3, 12, 13, 14, 17, 18, 19, and 20. In Part III, job 1 is represented by Dentists, General; Oral and Maxillofacial Surgeons; Orthodontists; Prosthodontists; and Dentists, All Other Specialists. Job 2 is represented by Anesthesiologists; Family and General Practitioners; Internists, General; Obstetricians and Gynecologists; Pediatricians, General; Psychiatrists; Surgeons; and Physicians and Surgeons, All Other. Job 3 is represented by the separate jobs Astronomers and Physicists. Job 12 is represented by Clinical, Counseling, and School Psychologists; Industrial-Organizational Psychologists; and Psychologists, All Other. Job 13 is represented by Anthropologists and Archeologists; Geographers; Historians; Political Scientists; and Social Scientists and Related Workers, All Other. Job 14 is represented by Gas Compressor and Gas Pumping Station Operators; Pump Operators, Except Wellhead Pumpers; and Wellhead Pumpers. Job 17 is represented by Epidemiologists; Medical Scientists, Except Epidemiologists; and Life Scientists, All Other. Job 18 is represented by Architects, Except Landscape and Naval and Landscape Architects. Job 19 is represented by Computer Software Engineers, Applications and Computer Software Engineers, Systems Software. Job 20 is represented by Electrical Engineers and Electronics Engineers, Except Computer.

The 20 Best-Paying Jobs Held by People 65 or Older

Average pay for all workers in this age bracket: $27,669

Occupation	Average Earnings
1. Securities, Commodities, and Financial Services Sales Agents	$94,057
2. Electrical and Electronics Engineers	$88,623
3. Physicians and Surgeons	$87,270
4. Computer Software Engineers	$86,962
5. Engineering Managers	$83,333
6. Computer and Information Systems Managers	$80,873
7. Lawyers	$79,745
8. Engineers, All Other	$76,909
9. Mechanical Engineers	$76,394
10. Civil Engineers	$73,207
11. Industrial Engineers, Including Health and Safety	$71,498
12. Construction Managers	$69,102
13. Psychologists	$66,464
14. Chief Executives	$65,965
15. Loan Counselors and Officers	$65,453
16. Purchasing Managers	$64,718

Occupation	Average Earnings
17. Medical Scientists	$63,662
18. Postsecondary Teachers	$62,498
19. Architects, Except Naval	$58,565
20. Personal Finance Advisors	$56,199

Note: The Current Population Survey does not provide separate earnings figures for the specific jobs represented by jobs 2, 3, 4, 11, 13, 15, 17, 18, and 19. In Part III, job 2 is represented by Electrical Engineers and Electronics Engineers, Except Computer. Job 3 is represented by Anesthesiologists; Family and General Practitioners; Internists, General; Obstetricians and Gynecologists; Pediatricians, General; Psychiatrists; Surgeons; and Physicians and Surgeons, All Other. Job 4 is represented by Computer Software Engineers, Applications and Computer Software Engineers, Systems Software. Job 11 is represented by Health and Safety Engineers, Except Mining Safety Engineers and Inspectors and Industrial Engineers. Job 13 is represented by Clinical, Counseling, and School Psychologists; Industrial-Organizational Psychologists; and Psychologists, All Other. Job 15 is represented by Loan Counselors and Loan Officers. Job 17 is represented by Epidemiologists; Medical Scientists, Except Epidemiologists; and Life Scientists, All Other. Job 18 is represented by 38 postsecondary teaching jobs, beginning with Business Teachers, Postsecondary. Job 19 is represented by Architects, Except Landscape and Naval and Landscape Architects.

The 20 Best-Paying Jobs Held by Military Veterans

This list shows the 20 best-paying jobs for people who have been on active duty in the military. The earnings figures are the averages of veterans in these occupations.

The 20 Best-Paying Jobs Held by Military Veterans

Average pay for veterans in all jobs: $49,304

Occupation	Average Earnings
1. Physicians and Surgeons	$97,003
2. Aerospace Engineers	$92,519
3. Lawyers	$92,348
4. Chief Executives	$92,254
5. Engineering Managers	$92,058
6. Human Resources Managers	$82,965
7. Architects, Except Naval	$81,062
8. Psychologists	$80,904
9. Airline Pilots and Flight Engineers	$80,608
10. Computer and Information Systems Managers	$80,310
11. Sales Engineers	$78,337
12. Computer Software Engineers	$77,280
13. Budget Analysts	$75,135
14. Operations Research Analysts	$74,847
15. Education Administrators	$74,611
16. Physician Assistants	$73,796
17. Ship and Boat Captains and Operators	$73,772
18. Environmental Scientists and Geoscientists	$72,925
19. Electrical and Electronics Engineers	$72,900
20. Marketing and Sales Managers	$72,632

Note: The Current Population Survey does not provide separate earnings figures for the specific jobs represented by jobs 1, 6, 7, 8, 9, 12, 15, 17, 18, 19, and 20. In Part III, job 1 is represented by Anesthesiologists; Family and General Practitioners; Internists, General; Obstetricians and Gynecologists; Pediatricians, General; Psychiatrists; Surgeons; and Physicians and Surgeons, All Other. Job 6 is represented by Compensation and Benefits Managers; Training and Development Managers; and Human Resources Managers, All Other. Job 7 is represented by Architects, Except Landscape and Naval and Landscape Architects. Job 8 is represented by Clinical, Counseling, and School Psychologists; Industrial-Organizational Psychologists; and Psychologists, All Other. Job 9 is represented by Airline Pilots, Copilots, and Flight Engineers and Commercial Pilots. Job 12 is represented by Computer Software Engineers, Applications and Computer Software Engineers, Systems Software. Job 15 is represented by Education Administrators, Preschool and Child Care Center/Program; Education Administrators, Elementary and Secondary School; Education Administrators, Postsecondary; and Education Administrators, All Other. Job 17 is represented by Captains, Mates, and Pilots of Water Vessels and Motorboat Operators. Job 18 is represented by Environmental Scientists and Specialists, Including Health; Geoscientists, Except Hydrologists and Geographers; and Hydrologists. Job 19 is represented by Electrical Engineers and Electronics Engineers, Except Computer. Job 20 is represented by Marketing Managers and Sales Managers.

The 20 Best-Paying Jobs Held by Part-Time Workers

This list shows the 20 best-paying jobs for people who are working part time. The earnings figures are the averages of part-time workers in these occupations; full-time workers earn more.

You can see the percentage of part-time workers and the average hours worked per week for each job in Part III.

The 20 Best-Paying Jobs Held by Part-Time Workers

Average pay for part-time workers in all jobs: $13,644

Occupation	Average Earnings
1. Managers, All Other	$32,920
2. Registered Nurses	$30,680
3. Property, Real Estate, and Community Association Managers	$29,525
4. Transportation Attendants	$23,008

Occupation	Average Earnings
5. Education Administrators	$22,863
6. Lawyers	$20,700
7. Real Estate Brokers and Sales Agents	$20,214
8. Licensed Practical and Licensed Vocational Nurses	$19,256
9. Hairdressers, Hairstylists, and Cosmetologists	$19,183
10. Counselors	$19,033
11. Teachers, Postsecondary	$16,902
12. Designers	$16,709
13. Preschool and Kindergarten Teachers	$16,592
14. Recreation and Fitness Workers	$16,421
15. Bartenders	$16,382
16. Accountants and Auditors	$15,624
17. Painters, Construction and Maintenance	$15,564
18. Dental Assistants	$14,456
19. Driver/Sales Workers and Truck Drivers	$14,332
20. First-Line Supervisors/Managers of Food Preparation and Serving Workers	$14,285

Note: The Current Population Survey does not provide separate earnings figures for the specific jobs represented by jobs 4, 5, 7, 10, 11, 12, 13, 14, and 19. In Part III, job 4 is represented by Flight Attendants and Transportation Attendants, Except Flight Attendants and Baggage Porters. Job 5 is represented by Education Administrators, Preschool and Child Care Center/Program; Education Administrators, Elementary and Secondary School; Education Administrators, Postsecondary; and Education Administrators, All Other. Job 7 is represented by Real Estate Brokers and Real Estate Sales Agents. Job 10 is represented by Substance Abuse and Behavioral Disorder Counselors; Educational, Vocational, and School Counselors; Marriage and Family Therapists; Mental Health Counselors; Rehabilitation Counselors; and Counselors, All Other. Job 11 is represented by 38 postsecondary teaching jobs, beginning with Business Teachers, Postsecondary. Job 12 is represented by Commercial and Industrial Designers; Fashion Designers; Floral Designers; Graphic Designers; Interior Designers; Merchandise Displayers and Window Trimmers; Set and Exhibit Designers; and Designers, All Other. Job 13 is represented by Preschool Teachers, Except Special Education and Kindergarten Teachers, Except Special Education. Job 14 is represented by Fitness Trainers and Aerobics Instructors and Recreation Workers. Job 19 is represented by Driver/Sales Workers; Truck Drivers, Heavy and Tractor-Trailer; and Truck Drivers, Light or Delivery Services.

PART III

Salary Facts

This part of the book presents the salary facts for 800 occupations. They are ordered according to the Standard Occupational Classification (SOC), the system that the federal government uses to group similar jobs together. One way to find an occupation you're looking for is to look for a group that seems appropriate. For example, if you were looking for Accountants and Auditors you might look in the table of contents under the major group heading "13-0000 Business and Financial Operations Occupations" or the minor group heading "13-2000 Financial Specialists." Alternatively, you can look up the occupational title in the alphabetical index beginning on p. 880.

The information that follows is based on the best and most recent sources available. The introduction to this book identifies the sources and explains how to interpret each information topic. If you find a job that interests you and want to explore it in greater depth, you can find useful resources identified in Appendix A.

11-0000 Management Occupations

11-1000 Top Executives

11-1011 Chief Executives

Determine and formulate policies and provide the overall direction of companies or private- and public-sector organizations within the guidelines set up by a board of directors or similar governing body. Plan, direct, or coordinate operational activities at the highest level of management with the help of subordinate executives and staff managers.

- Education or Training Required: Work experience plus degree
- Job Growth: 14.9%
- Annual Openings: 38,000
- Self-Employed: 16.2%
- Part-Time: 13.8%

NATIONAL WAGE FIGURES (ANNUAL)

Beginning	25th Percentile	Median	Mean	75th Percentile	90th Percentile
$61,970	$94,870	more than $145,600	$144,600	more than $145,600	more than $145,600

Median Wages for Industries Employing Largest Numbers (Annual)

Industry	Median Income
Computer and Electronic Product Manufacturing........	more than $145,600
Construction of Buildings...	more than $145,600
Credit Intermediation and Related Activities	more than $145,600
Heavy and Civil Engineering Construction	more than $145,600
Hospitals	more than $145,600
Insurance Carriers and Related Activities	more than $145,600
Machinery Manufacturing..	more than $145,600
Management of Companies and Enterprises	more than $145,600
Merchant Wholesalers, Durable Goods	more than $145,600
Merchant Wholesalers, Nondurable Goods.................	more than $145,600

Median Wages for States (Annual)

AK............$106,330	KY $122,500	NY .. more than $145,600
AL $142,170	LA $132,720	OH $139,450
AR...........$107,210	MA .. more than $145,600	OK $89,170
AZ $137,130	MD .. more than $145,600	OR $121,020
CA.. more than $145,600	ME $98,250	PA $135,460
CO.. more than $145,600	MI $136,490	RI .. more than $145,600
CT.. more than $145,600	MN .. more than $145,600	SC..............$131,910
DC.. more than $145,600	MO $136,870	SD $94,850
DE.. more than $145,600	MS $96,840	TN $118,950
FL .. more than $145,600	MT .... no data	TX .. more than $145,600
GA.. more than $145,600	NC.... more than $145,600	UT $143,490
HI $125,360	ND $123,290	VA .. more than $145,600
IA $117,110	NE $130,330	VT $127,660
ID $84,790	NH $126,220	WA.. more than $145,600
IL .. more than $145,600	NJ.... more than $145,600	WI .. more than $145,600
IN $133,450	NM $90,010	WV $83,200
KS $112,340	NV.... more than $145,600	WY $99,820

Median Wages for the Largest Metropolitan Areas (Annual)

AZ: Phoenix $143,900	MI: Detroit .... more than $145,600
CA: Los Angeles .... more than $145,600	MN: Minneapolis.. more than $145,600
CA: Riverside .... more than $145,600	MO: Kansas City $143,040
CA: Sacramento $121,860	MO: St. Louis...... more than $145,600
CA: San Diego .... more than $145,600	NV: Las Vegas...... more than $145,600
CA: San Francisco more than $145,600	NY: New York ...... more than $145,600
CO: Denver .... more than $145,600	OH: Cincinnati $143,570
DC: Washington .... more than $145,600	OH: Cleveland .... more than $145,600
FL: Miami .... more than $145,600	OH: Columbus .... more than $145,600
FL: Orlando .... more than $145,600	OR: Portland ...... more than $145,600
FL: Tampa .... more than $145,600	PA: Philadelphia.. more than $145,600
GA: Atlanta.......... more than $145,600	PA: Pittsburgh $127,640
IL: Chicago .... more than $145,600	TX: Dallas .... more than $145,600
MA: Boston .... more than $145,600	TX: Houston........ more than $145,600
MD: Baltimore ...... more than $145,600	WA: Seattle .... more than $145,600

FACTORS THAT MAY AFFECT EARNINGS

Educational Attainment of Workers and Effect on Earnings

	Percent at Level	Effect on Earnings
Less than High School	—	—
Some High School	1.5%	−33.0%
High School or Equivalent	14.4%	−17.4%
Some College but No Degree	14.4%	−12.0%
Associate Degree	9.0%	−10.4%
Bachelor's Degree	31.3%	3.1%
Master's Degree	19.2%	12.1%
Doctoral Degree	4.4%	29.1%
First Professional Degree	5.3%	26.0%

Flexibility of Earnings

Average Hours Worked: 41
Workers with a Varying Number of Hours: 10.9%
Workers Earning Some Overtime Pay, Tips, or Commissions: 8.5%
Earnings Benefit of Working Overtime: −21.4%

Gender

	Male	Female
Percent	76.6%	23.4%
Effect on Earnings	1.7%	−24.2%

Union Membership

Percentage Union Members: Insignificant
Earnings Benefit of Union Membership: No significant data available

Veteran Status

Percentage Who Have Been on Active Duty: 11.8%
Earnings Benefit of Veteran Status: −1.4%

11-1021 General and Operations Managers

Plan, direct, or coordinate the operations of companies or public- and private-sector organizations. Duties and responsibilities include formulating policies, managing daily operations, and planning the use of materials and human resources, but are too diverse and general in nature to be classified in any one functional area of management or administration, such as personnel, purchasing, or administrative services. Includes owners and managers who head small business establishments whose duties are primarily managerial.

- Education or Training Required: Work experience plus degree
- Job Growth: 17.0%
- Annual Openings: 208,000
- Self-Employed: 0.6%
- Part-Time: 4.4%

NATIONAL WAGE FIGURES (ANNUAL)

Beginning	25th Percentile	Median	Mean	75th Percentile	90th Percentile
					more than
$42,210	$58,230	$85,230	$99,280	$128,580	$145,600

Median Wages for Industries Employing Largest Numbers (Annual)

Industry	Median Income
Professional, Scientific, and Technical Services	$117,010
Insurance Carriers and Related Activities	$110,280
Management of Companies and Enterprises	$105,130
Construction of Buildings	$96,710
Merchant Wholesalers, Durable Goods	$94,930
Merchant Wholesalers, Nondurable Goods	$94,000
Motor Vehicle and Parts Dealers	$92,560
Real Estate	$92,130
Fabricated Metal Product Manufacturing	$91,300
Credit Intermediation and Related Activities	$91,250

Median Wages for States (Annual)

AK $64,720	KY $67,160	NY $106,620
AL $74,940	LA $67,500	OH $82,930
AR $73,760	MA $93,260	OK $59,390
AZ $79,360	MD $95,230	OR $81,390
CA $99,960	ME $72,700	PA $85,430
CO $82,580	MI $81,970	RI.............. $89,790
CT $104,920	MN $84,690	SC.............. $72,880
DC $113,800	MO $84,510	SD $86,500
DE $90,910	MS $64,020	TN $68,240
FL $86,480	MT $56,160	TX $81,270
GA $71,780	NC $88,100	UT $73,990
HI $83,650	ND $73,950	VA $109,230
IA $77,320	NE $80,100	VT $85,080
ID $53,320	NH $77,730	WA $107,920
IL $88,440	NJ $131,760	WI $85,610
IN $80,520	NM $66,710	WV $64,210
KS $69,240	NV $86,000	WY $62,070

Median Wages for the Largest Metropolitan Areas (Annual)

AZ: Phoenix............ $83,680	MI: Detroit $90,430
CA: Los Angeles $104,110	MN: Minneapolis $94,000
CA: Riverside $90,070	MO: Kansas City........ $85,480
CA: Sacramento $93,040	MO: St. Louis............ $91,350
CA: San Diego $100,320	NV: Las Vegas $88,410
CA: San Francisco.... $110,990	NY: New York...........$126,750
CO: Denver $91,190	OH: Cincinnati.......... $84,720
DC: Washington $113,970	OH: Cleveland $90,230
FL: Miami $92,990	OH: Columbus $86,970
FL: Orlando $83,000	OR: Portland $90,040
FL: Tampa $87,650	PA: Philadelphia $102,810
GA: Atlanta $77,180	PA: Pittsburgh $82,740
IL: Chicago $93,670	TX: Dallas $91,460
MA: Boston $98,290	TX: Houston $92,860
MD: Baltimore $93,990	WA: Seattle $118,050

FACTORS THAT MAY AFFECT EARNINGS

Educational Attainment of Workers and Effect on Earnings

	Percent at Level	Effect on Earnings
Less than High School	—	—
Some High School	3.2%	−23.9%
High School or Equivalent	21.1%	−11.0%
Some College but No Degree	20.4%	−6.7%
Associate Degree	12.5%	−13.3%
Bachelor's Degree	25.5%	7.7%
Master's Degree	13.1%	23.3%
Doctoral Degree	2.5%	17.4%
First Professional Degree	1.6%	44.7%

Flexibility of Earnings

Average Hours Worked: 43
Workers with a Varying Number of Hours: 6.5%
Workers Earning Some Overtime Pay, Tips, or Commissions: 9.0%
Earnings Benefit of Working Overtime: −12.7%

Gender

	Male	Female
Percent	70.9%	29.1%
Effect on Earnings	7.8%	−17.9%

Union Membership

Percentage Union Members: Insignificant
Earnings Benefit of Union Membership: No significant data available

Veteran Status

Percentage Who Have Been on Active Duty: 11.8%
Earnings Benefit of Veteran Status: −1.4%

11-1031 Legislators

Develop laws and statutes at the federal, state, or local level.

- Education or Training Required: Work experience plus degree
- Job Growth: 2.0%
- Annual Openings: 3,000
- Self-Employed: 0.0%
- Part-Time: 11.3%

NATIONAL WAGE FIGURES (ANNUAL)

Beginning	25th Percentile	Median	Mean	75th Percentile	90th Percentile
$12,190	$13,530	$15,660	$32,730	$38,690	$75,270

Note: The mean is significantly higher than the median because of the presence of a few star earners.

Median Wages for Industries Employing Largest Numbers (Annual)

Industry	Median Income
Federal, State, and Local Government	$15,660

Median Wages for States (Annual)

AK	no data	KY	no data	NY	$74,420
AL	$13,370	LA	$13,580	OH	$14,240
AR	$14,130	MA	no data	OK	$14,610
AZ	$25,420	MD	$14,520	OR	$19,110
CA	$37,170	ME	$14,640	PA	$13,510
CO	no data	MI	$25,400	RI	no data
CT	$31,180	MN	$14,220	SC	$13,470
DC	no data	MO	$32,190	SD	$30,260
DE	no data	MS	$21,050	TN	$13,250
FL	$27,860	MT	no data	TX	$13,770
GA	$14,190	NC	no data	UT	$16,700
HI	$38,190	ND	no data	VA	$13,700
IA	$23,890	NE	$14,200	VT	no data
ID	no data	NH	$13,000	WA	$52,300
IL	$14,600	NJ	$15,750	WI	$13,940
IN	$22,350	NM	$14,530	WV	$14,120
KS	$26,380	NV	$36,270	WY	no data

Median Wages for the Largest Metropolitan Areas (Annual)

AZ: Phoenix	$25,630	MI: Detroit	$35,130
CA: Los Angeles	$45,720	MN: Minneapolis	$14,010
CA: Riverside	$37,600	MO: Kansas City	$29,240
CA: Sacramento	$36,620	MO: St. Louis	$14,640
CA: San Diego	$35,570	NV: Las Vegas	$38,590
CA: San Francisco	$46,490	NY: New York	$38,720
CO: Denver	no data	OH: Cincinnati	$14,800
DC: Washington	$15,100	OH: Cleveland	$14,160
FL: Miami	$28,530	OH: Columbus	$13,670
FL: Orlando	$34,530	OR: Portland	$53,510
FL: Tampa	$27,340	PA: Philadelphia	$14,500
GA: Atlanta	$16,940	PA: Pittsburgh	$13,710
IL: Chicago	$15,270	TX: Dallas	$13,850
MA: Boston	no data	TX: Houston	$13,770
MD: Baltimore	$34,340	WA: Seattle	$88,210

FACTORS THAT MAY AFFECT EARNINGS

Educational Attainment of Workers and Effect on Earnings

Figures are based on a group of occupations: Top Executives

	Percent at Level	Effect on Earnings
Less than High School	—	—
Some High School	2.7%	−25.3%
High School or Equivalent	17.6%	−15.4%
Some College but No Degree	17.1%	−9.0%
Associate Degree	11.4%	−12.1%
Bachelor's Degree	27.5%	5.3%
Master's Degree	15.6%	17.4%
Doctoral Degree	3.8%	25.3%
First Professional Degree	3.8%	35.2%

Flexibility of Earnings

Average Hours Worked: 41
Workers with a Varying Number of Hours: 9.3%
Workers Earning Some Overtime Pay, Tips, or Commissions: 8.7%
Earnings Benefit of Working Overtime: −20.2%

Gender

	Male	Female
Percent	73.6%	26.4%
Effect on Earnings	32.2%	−8.1%

Union Membership

Percentage Union Members: Insignificant
Earnings Benefit of Union Membership: No significant data available

Veteran Status

Percentage Who Have Been on Active Duty: 11.8%
Earnings Benefit of Veteran Status: −1.4%

11-2000 Advertising, Marketing, Promotions, Public Relations, and Sales Managers

11-2011 Advertising and Promotions Managers

Plan and direct advertising policies and programs or produce collateral materials, such as posters, contests, coupons, or giveaways, to create extra interest in the purchase of a product or service for a department, for an entire organization, or on an account basis.

- Education or Training Required: Work experience plus degree
- Job Growth: 20.3%
- Annual Openings: 9,000
- Self-Employed: 6.7%
- Part-Time: 13.9%

NATIONAL WAGE FIGURES (ANNUAL)

Beginning	25th Percentile	Median	Mean	75th Percentile	90th Percentile
$36,230	$48,870	$73,060	$85,140	$109,030	more than $145,600

Median Wages for Industries Employing Largest Numbers (Annual)

Industry	Median Income
Professional, Scientific, and Technical Services	$93,860
Securities, Commodity Contracts, and Other Financial Investments and Related Activities	$92,980
Motion Picture and Sound Recording Industries	$91,060
Telecommunications	$84,060
Management of Companies and Enterprises	$79,930
Merchant Wholesalers, Durable Goods	$78,570
Insurance Carriers and Related Activities	$76,000
Publishing Industries (Except Internet)	$74,940
Administrative and Support Services	$72,320
Merchant Wholesalers, Nondurable Goods	$71,950

Median Wages for States (Annual)

State	Wage	State	Wage	State	Wage
AK	$56,210	KY	$49,830	NY	$109,120
AL	$53,140	LA	$52,520	OH	$69,570
AR	$54,270	MA	$83,440	OK	$52,940
AZ	$60,220	MD	$75,040	OR	$61,530
CA	$77,090	ME	$52,010	PA	$68,220
CO	$58,120	MI	$93,600	RI	$68,820
CT	$76,910	MN	$94,890	SC	$50,460
DC	$73,900	MO	$78,550	SD	no data
DE	$85,080	MS	$50,800	TN	$46,310
FL	$80,150	MT	$34,530	TX	$71,370
GA	$65,470	NC	$61,560	UT	$55,620
HI	$66,810	ND	$44,550	VA	$67,760
IA	$52,400	NE	$77,610	VT	$70,110
ID	$39,800	NH	$61,900	WA	$94,310
IL	$67,850	NJ	$104,830	WI	$67,780
IN	$62,220	NM	$46,190	WV	$46,940
KS	$55,620	NV	$61,170	WY	no data

Median Wages for the Largest Metropolitan Areas (Annual)

Area	Wage	Area	Wage
AZ: Phoenix	$64,300	MI: Detroit	$95,540
CA: Los Angeles	$80,890	MN: Minneapolis	$100,480
CA: Riverside	$59,930	MO: Kansas City	$75,040
CA: Sacramento	$59,610	MO: St. Louis	$84,360
CA: San Diego	$66,020	NV: Las Vegas	$64,220
CA: San Francisco	$81,880	NY: New York	$114,530
CO: Denver	$71,660	OH: Cincinnati	$63,700
DC: Washington	$67,560	OH: Cleveland	$84,920
FL: Miami	$87,100	OH: Columbus	$74,520
FL: Orlando	$65,120	OR: Portland	$80,530
FL: Tampa	$88,910	PA: Philadelphia	$89,330
GA: Atlanta	$68,330	PA: Pittsburgh	$50,150
IL: Chicago	$67,990	TX: Dallas	$85,580
MA: Boston	$87,100	TX: Houston	$59,070
MD: Baltimore	$93,370	WA: Seattle	$94,070

FACTORS THAT MAY AFFECT EARNINGS

Educational Attainment of Workers and Effect on Earnings

	Percent at Level	Effect on Earnings
Less than High School	—	—
Some High School	—	—
High School or Equivalent	—	—
Some College but No Degree	17.1%	−14.1%
Associate Degree	—	—
Bachelor's Degree	59.8%	10.6%
Master's Degree	9.8%	25.8%
Doctoral Degree	—	—
First Professional Degree	—	—

Figures do not total 100% because some levels have a very small sample size.

Flexibility of Earnings

Average Hours Worked: 39
Workers with a Varying Number of Hours: 8.7%
Workers Earning Some Overtime Pay, Tips, or Commissions: 17.0%
Earnings Benefit of Working Overtime: −3.2%

Gender

	Male	Female
Percent	47.5%	52.5%
Effect on Earnings	12.2%	−17.8%

Union Membership

Percentage Union Members: Insignificant
Earnings Benefit of Union Membership: No significant data available

Veteran Status

Percentage Who Have Been on Active Duty: 7.5%
Earnings Benefit of Veteran Status: −0.6%

11-2021 Marketing Managers

Determine the demand for products and services offered by a firm and its competitors and identify potential customers. Develop pricing strategies with the goal of maximizing the firm's profits or share of the market while ensuring that the firm's customers are satisfied. Oversee product development or monitor trends that indicate the need for new products and services.

- Education or Training Required: Work experience plus degree
- Job Growth: 20.8%
- Annual Openings: 23,000
- Self-Employed: 3.6%
- Part-Time: 8.8%

NATIONAL WAGE FIGURES (ANNUAL)

Beginning	25th Percentile	Median	Mean	75th Percentile	90th Percentile
$51,160	$70,080	$98,720	$107,610	$136,710	more than $145,600

Median Wages for Industries Employing Largest Numbers (Annual)

Industry	Median Income
Securities, Commodity Contracts, and Other Financial Investments and Related Activities	$124,000
Internet Service Providers, Web Search Portals, and Data-Processing Services	$117,040
Computer and Electronic Product Manufacturing	$115,580
Chemical Manufacturing	$106,680
Professional, Scientific, and Technical Services	$105,970
Publishing Industries (Except Internet)	$105,670
Merchant Wholesalers, Durable Goods	$105,510
Merchant Wholesalers, Nondurable Goods	$104,500
Management of Companies and Enterprises	$103,070
Miscellaneous Manufacturing	$101,970

Median Wages for States (Annual)

AK	$67,100	KY	$76,870	NY	$129,420
AL	$76,480	LA	$61,550	OH	$90,540
AR	$69,680	MA	$113,050	OK	$76,080
AZ	$67,570	MD	$88,260	OR	$84,100
CA	$115,620	ME	$69,730	PA	$91,760
CO	$85,850	MI	$85,570	RI	$72,210
CT	$103,850	MN	$108,360	SC	$72,160
DC	$96,210	MO	$91,120	SD	$85,090
DE	$125,560	MS	$56,630	TN	$69,030
FL	$92,380	MT	$57,450	TX	$100,080
GA	$89,360	NC	$92,110	UT	$78,930
HI	$73,050	ND	$68,640	VA	$117,750
IA	$71,300	NE	$89,320	VT	$79,330
ID	$75,500	NH	$81,730	WA	$112,310
IL	$89,860	NJ	$116,890	WI	$88,110
IN	$77,100	NM	$56,760	WV	$62,020
KS	$80,600	NV	$76,940	WY	$71,890

Median Wages for the Largest Metropolitan Areas (Annual)

AZ: Phoenix	$71,410	MI: Detroit	$91,800
CA: Los Angeles	$105,850	MN: Minneapolis	$109,960
CA: Riverside	$92,930	MO: Kansas City	$86,930
CA: Sacramento	$95,010	MO: St. Louis	$99,050
CA: San Diego	$106,300	NV: Las Vegas	$82,710
CA: San Francisco	$127,510	NY: New York	$130,580
CO: Denver	$86,930	OH: Cincinnati	$89,470
DC: Washington	$102,610	OH: Cleveland	$94,680
FL: Miami	$95,480	OH: Columbus	$88,090
FL: Orlando	$95,690	OR: Portland	$92,210
FL: Tampa	$97,340	PA: Philadelphia	$109,470
GA: Atlanta	$93,190	PA: Pittsburgh	$98,480
IL: Chicago	$91,760	TX: Dallas	$99,910
MA: Boston	$114,540	TX: Houston	$109,300
MD: Baltimore	$92,610	WA: Seattle	$119,240

FACTORS THAT MAY AFFECT EARNINGS

Educational Attainment of Workers and Effect on Earnings

Figures are based on a group of occupations: Advertising, Marketing, Promotions, Public Relations, and Sales Managers

	Percent at Level	Effect on Earnings
Less than High School	—	—
Some High School	—	—
High School or Equivalent	16.8%	−16.7%
Some College but No Degree	16.0%	−12.8%
Associate Degree	12.6%	−6.6%
Bachelor's Degree	36.4%	7.1%
Master's Degree	14.6%	22.9%
Doctoral Degree	—	—
First Professional Degree	—	—

Flexibility of Earnings

Average Hours Worked: 40
Workers with a Varying Number of Hours: 5.6%
Workers Earning Some Overtime Pay, Tips, or Commissions: 18.5%
Earnings Benefit of Working Overtime: −0.9%

Gender

	Male	Female
Percent	59.8%	40.2%
Effect on Earnings	12.6%	−25.2%

Union Membership

Percentage Union Members: Insignificant
Earnings Benefit of Union Membership: No significant data available

Veteran Status

Percentage Who Have Been on Active Duty: 7.5%
Earnings Benefit of Veteran Status: −0.6%

11-2022 Sales Managers

Direct the actual distribution or movement of a product or service to the customer. Coordinate sales distribution by establishing sales territories, quotas, and goals and establish training programs for sales representatives. Analyze sales statistics gathered by staff to determine sales potential and inventory requirements and monitor the preferences of customers.

- Education or Training Required: Work experience plus degree
- Job Growth: 19.7%
- Annual Openings: 40,000
- Self-Employed: 3.5%
- Part-Time: 8.8%

NATIONAL WAGE FIGURES (ANNUAL)

Beginning	25th Percentile	Median	Mean	75th Percentile	90th Percentile
$45,140	$62,140	$91,560	$102,730	$132,910	more than $145,600

Median Wages for Industries Employing Largest Numbers (Annual)

Industry	Median Income
Securities, Commodity Contracts, and Other Financial Investments and Related Activities	$134,160
Professional, Scientific, and Technical Services	$116,930
Computer and Electronic Product Manufacturing	$114,070
Broadcasting (Except Internet)	$108,070
Wholesale Electronic Markets and Agents and Brokers	$107,420
Chemical Manufacturing	$105,310
Credit Intermediation and Related Activities	$103,690
Insurance Carriers and Related Activities	$102,370
Merchant Wholesalers, Durable Goods	$101,540
Publishing Industries (Except Internet)	$100,220

Median Wages for States (Annual)

State	Wage	State	Wage	State	Wage
AK	$54,490	KY	$77,430	NY	$134,680
AL	$79,610	LA	$67,070	OH	$89,290
AR	$75,590	MA	$104,380	OK	$63,650
AZ	$73,440	MD	$99,290	OR	$90,150
CA	$104,160	ME	$69,590	PA	$87,450
CO	$96,300	MI	$85,000	RI	$87,240
CT	$100,920	MN	$102,870	SC	$78,130
DC	$74,740	MO	$93,450	SD	$87,360
DE	$104,070	MS	$65,600	TN	$68,100
FL	$104,310	MT	$52,060	TX	$88,190
GA	$90,060	NC	$84,140	UT	$79,030
HI	$65,030	ND	$65,530	VA	$98,890
IA	$80,250	NE	$83,500	VT	$90,540
ID	$56,780	NH	$93,740	WA	$110,660
IL	$92,720	NJ	$107,610	WI	$90,680
IN	$82,430	NM	$64,950	WV	$69,200
KS	$80,720	NV	$65,280	WY	$52,680

Median Wages for the Largest Metropolitan Areas (Annual)

Area	Wage	Area	Wage
AZ: Phoenix	$75,980	MI: Detroit	$94,220
CA: Los Angeles	$105,580	MN: Minneapolis	$107,470
CA: Riverside	$95,430	MO: Kansas City	$92,260
CA: Sacramento	$88,000	MO: St. Louis	$97,930
CA: San Diego	$100,890	NV: Las Vegas	$67,010
CA: San Francisco	$109,200	NY: New York	$129,310
CO: Denver	$98,400	OH: Cincinnati	$96,270
DC: Washington	$98,570	OH: Cleveland	$97,830
FL: Miami	$109,690	OH: Columbus	$90,920
FL: Orlando	$91,530	OR: Portland	$97,460
FL: Tampa	$109,070	PA: Philadelphia	$99,940
GA: Atlanta	$95,440	PA: Pittsburgh	$81,300
IL: Chicago	$96,220	TX: Dallas	$95,040
MA: Boston	$109,000	TX: Houston	$94,400
MD: Baltimore	$106,260	WA: Seattle	$116,560

FACTORS THAT MAY AFFECT EARNINGS

Educational Attainment of Workers and Effect on Earnings

Figures are based on a group of occupations: Advertising, Marketing, Promotions, Public Relations, and Sales Managers

	Percent at Level	Effect on Earnings
Less than High School	—	—
Some High School	—	—
High School or Equivalent	16.8%	−16.7%
Some College but No Degree	16.0%	−12.8%
Associate Degree	12.6%	−6.6%
Bachelor's Degree	36.4%	7.1%
Master's Degree	14.6%	22.9%
Doctoral Degree	—	—
First Professional Degree	—	—

Flexibility of Earnings

Average Hours Worked: 40
Workers with a Varying Number of Hours: 5.6%
Workers Earning Some Overtime Pay, Tips, or Commissions: 18.5%
Earnings Benefit of Working Overtime: −0.9%

Gender

	Male	Female
Percent	59.8%	40.2%
Effect on Earnings	12.6%	−25.2%

Union Membership

Percentage Union Members: Insignificant
Earnings Benefit of Union Membership: No significant data available

Veteran Status

Percentage Who Have Been on Active Duty: 7.5%
Earnings Benefit of Veteran Status: −0.6%

11-2031 Public Relations Managers

Plan and direct public relations programs designed to create and maintain a favorable public image for employer or client or, if engaged in fundraising, plan and direct activities to solicit and maintain funds for special projects and nonprofit organizations.

- Education or Training Required: Work experience plus degree
- Job Growth: 21.7%
- Annual Openings: 5,000
- Self-Employed: 1.6%
- Part-Time: 10.0%

NATIONAL WAGE FIGURES (ANNUAL)

Beginning	25th Percentile	Median	Mean	75th Percentile	90th Percentile
$42,980	$58,590	$82,180	$92,250	$115,030	more than $145,600

Median Wages for Industries Employing Largest Numbers (Annual)

Industry	Median Income
Telecommunications	$116,450
Merchant Wholesalers, Nondurable Goods	$113,710
Securities, Commodity Contracts, and Other Financial Investments and Related Activities	$111,690
Computer and Electronic Product Manufacturing	$108,580
Publishing Industries (Except Internet)	$101,440
Motion Picture and Sound Recording Industries	$100,210
Internet Service Providers, Web Search Portals, and Data-Processing Services	$99,770
Utilities	$99,500
Professional, Scientific, and Technical Services	$98,900
Management of Companies and Enterprises	$94,970

Median Wages for States (Annual)

AK	$54,290	KY	$63,150	NY	$106,460
AL	$66,760	LA	$45,420	OH	$78,650
AR	$64,550	MA	$97,880	OK	$57,370
AZ	$62,920	MD	$82,100	OR	$57,750
CA	$94,600	ME	$58,660	PA	$69,930
CO	$84,290	MI	$78,540	RI	$87,800
CT	$80,130	MN	$89,680	SC	$56,130
DC	$122,220	MO	$76,360	SD	$71,700
DE	$96,580	MS	$43,970	TN	$54,370
FL	$87,020	MT	$43,520	TX	$78,350
GA	$68,020	NC	$65,400	UT	$70,900
HI	$64,230	ND	$53,840	VA	$111,760
IA	$59,920	NE	$80,450	VT	$76,550
ID	$47,630	NH	$75,850	WA	$91,280
IL	$73,030	NJ	$107,800	WI	$71,040
IN	$63,350	NM	$52,440	WV	$53,800
KS	$81,950	NV	$87,690	WY	$50,810

Median Wages for the Largest Metropolitan Areas (Annual)

AZ: Phoenix	$68,290	MI: Detroit	$82,250
CA: Los Angeles	$96,620	MN: Minneapolis	$91,030
CA: Riverside	$86,600	MO: Kansas City	$88,390
CA: Sacramento	$94,770	MO: St. Louis	$80,250
CA: San Diego	$83,300	NV: Las Vegas	$88,640
CA: San Francisco	$100,240	NY: New York	$112,310
CO: Denver	$90,230	OH: Cincinnati	$71,180
DC: Washington	$118,810	OH: Cleveland	$86,280
FL: Miami	$94,630	OH: Columbus	$79,880
FL: Orlando	$77,870	OR: Portland	$61,730
FL: Tampa	$80,490	PA: Philadelphia	$83,520
GA: Atlanta	$72,760	PA: Pittsburgh	$70,920
IL: Chicago	$75,320	TX: Dallas	$88,050
MA: Boston	$100,050	TX: Houston	$80,250
MD: Baltimore	$83,510	WA: Seattle	$95,530

FACTORS THAT MAY AFFECT EARNINGS

Educational Attainment of Workers and Effect on Earnings

	Percent at Level	Effect on Earnings
Less than High School	—	—
Some High School	—	—
High School or Equivalent	—	—
Some College but No Degree	—	—
Associate Degree	15.5%	−16.2%
Bachelor's Degree	50.7%	6.9%
Master's Degree	19.7%	23.0%
Doctoral Degree	—	—
First Professional Degree	—	—

Figures do not total 100% because some levels have a very small sample size.

Flexibility of Earnings

Average Hours Worked: 40
Workers with a Varying Number of Hours: 2.3%
Workers Earning Some Overtime Pay, Tips, or Commissions: 5.8%
Earnings Benefit of Working Overtime: −7.9%

Gender

	Male	Female
Percent	59.8%	40.2%
Effect on Earnings	12.6%	−25.2%

Union Membership

Percentage Union Members: 4.7%
Earnings Benefit of Union Membership: −10.8%

Veteran Status

Percentage Who Have Been on Active Duty: 7.5%
Earnings Benefit of Veteran Status: −0.6%

11-3000 Operations Specialties Managers

11-3011 Administrative Services Managers

Plan, direct, or coordinate supportive services of an organization, such as recordkeeping, mail distribution, telephone operator/receptionist, and other office support services. May oversee facilities planning and maintenance and custodial operations.

- Education or Training Required: Work experience plus degree
- Job Growth: 16.9%
- Annual Openings: 25,000
- Self-Employed: 0.2%
- Part-Time: 6.4%

NATIONAL WAGE FIGURES (ANNUAL)

Beginning	25th Percentile	Median	Mean	75th Percentile	90th Percentile
$34,970	$48,200	$67,690	$72,840	$90,350	$117,610

Median Wages for Industries Employing Largest Numbers (Annual)

Industry	Median Income
Telecommunications	$87,670
Securities, Commodity Contracts, and Other Financial Investments and Related Activities	$86,510
Computer and Electronic Product Manufacturing	$84,310
Utilities	$84,130
Publishing Industries (Except Internet)	$80,020
Management of Companies and Enterprises	$77,040
Insurance Carriers and Related Activities	$76,800
Professional, Scientific, and Technical Services	$75,620
Credit Intermediation and Related Activities	$72,670
Hospitals	$71,620

Median Wages for States (Annual)

State	Wage	State	Wage	State	Wage
AK	$62,120	KY	$55,430	NY	$85,680
AL	$58,360	LA	$49,910	OH	$67,950
AR	$55,240	MA	$71,740	OK	$46,450
AZ	$49,080	MD	$64,780	OR	$64,410
CA	$77,880	ME	$53,230	PA	$62,000
CO	$67,470	MI	$66,080	RI	$77,540
CT	$74,950	MN	$74,290	SC	$50,520
DC	$71,080	MO	$66,440	SD	$64,760
DE	$70,470	MS	$39,250	TN	$45,930
FL	$76,350	MT	$51,040	TX	$72,830
GA	$60,560	NC	$61,270	UT	$59,040
HI	$60,620	ND	$54,460	VA	$76,510
IA	$66,340	NE	$60,360	VT	$64,910
ID	$44,670	NH	$64,740	WA	$81,450
IL	$52,740	NJ	$85,640	WI	$68,980
IN	$57,290	NM	$50,900	WV	$52,790
KS	$56,860	NV	$60,080	WY	$51,950

Median Wages for the Largest Metropolitan Areas (Annual)

Area	Wage	Area	Wage
AZ: Phoenix	$49,300	MI: Detroit	$75,000
CA: Los Angeles	$78,720	MN: Minneapolis	$76,180
CA: Riverside	$67,290	MO: Kansas City	$68,230
CA: Sacramento	$70,080	MO: St. Louis	$63,270
CA: San Diego	$77,980	NV: Las Vegas	$58,270
CA: San Francisco	$87,290	NY: New York	$88,860
CO: Denver	$69,480	OH: Cincinnati	$70,230
DC: Washington	$74,410	OH: Cleveland	$65,400
FL: Miami	$82,420	OH: Columbus	$72,350
FL: Orlando	$72,140	OR: Portland	$69,450
FL: Tampa	$71,630	PA: Philadelphia	$75,690
GA: Atlanta	$63,980	PA: Pittsburgh	$48,390
IL: Chicago	$56,700	TX: Dallas	$73,400
MA: Boston	$73,230	TX: Houston	$78,530
MD: Baltimore	$61,500	WA: Seattle	$83,710

FACTORS THAT MAY AFFECT EARNINGS

Educational Attainment of Workers and Effect on Earnings

	Percent at Level	Effect on Earnings
Less than High School	—	—
Some High School	—	—
High School or Equivalent	21.6%	−21.3%
Some College but No Degree	29.7%	−4.2%
Associate Degree	17.1%	10.3%
Bachelor's Degree	18.9%	8.3%
Master's Degree	11.7%	26.7%
Doctoral Degree	—	—
First Professional Degree	—	—

Flexibility of Earnings

Average Hours Worked: 41
Workers with a Varying Number of Hours: 3.2%
Workers Earning Some Overtime Pay, Tips, or Commissions: 7.2%
Earnings Benefit of Working Overtime: −4.9%

Gender

	Male	Female
Percent	75.6%	24.4%
Effect on Earnings	−0.8%	—

Union Membership

Percentage Union Members: 8.0%
Earnings Benefit of Union Membership: −11.3%

Veteran Status

Percentage Who Have Been on Active Duty: 9.5%
Earnings Benefit of Veteran Status: 7.6%

11-3021 Computer and Information Systems Managers

Plan, direct, or coordinate activities in such fields as electronic data processing, information systems, systems analysis, and computer programming.

- Education or Training Required: Work experience plus degree
- Job Growth: 25.9%
- Annual Openings: 25,000
- Self-Employed: 1.2%
- Part-Time: 2.6%

NATIONAL WAGE FIGURES (ANNUAL)

Beginning	25th Percentile	Median	Mean	75th Percentile	90th Percentile
$60,800	$79,240	$101,580	$107,250	$129,250	more than $145,600

Median Wages for Industries Employing Largest Numbers (Annual)

Industry	Median Income
Securities, Commodity Contracts, and Other Financial Investments and Related Activities	$120,340
Computer and Electronic Product Manufacturing	$112,710
Telecommunications	$110,610
Publishing Industries (Except Internet)	$110,020
Professional, Scientific, and Technical Services	$106,990
Internet Service Providers, Web Search Portals, and Data-Processing Services	$106,650
Merchant Wholesalers, Durable Goods	$106,060
Management of Companies and Enterprises	$105,980
Transportation Equipment Manufacturing	$105,010
Credit Intermediation and Related Activities	$103,810

Median Wages for States (Annual)

State	Wage	State	Wage	State	Wage
AK	$78,680	KY	$78,760	NY	$117,990
AL	$88,210	LA	$76,470	OH	$97,690
AR	$74,950	MA	$110,920	OK	$80,100
AZ	$89,530	MD	$111,440	OR	$92,810
CA	$114,460	ME	$76,350	PA	$100,970
CO	$105,430	MI	$95,290	RI	$96,380
CT	$101,460	MN	$103,470	SC	$80,610
DC	$113,890	MO	$92,800	SD	$89,640
DE	$109,580	MS	$67,780	TN	$74,650
FL	$95,900	MT	$67,380	TX	$101,290
GA	$95,090	NC	$99,450	UT	$83,720
HI	$88,030	ND	$74,090	VA	$117,920
IA	$84,430	NE	$88,080	VT	$91,510
ID	$74,640	NH	$95,230	WA	$103,420
IL	$92,090	NJ	$119,040	WI	$89,670
IN	$80,660	NM	$80,820	WV	$75,210
KS	$84,080	NV	$88,300	WY	$61,580

Median Wages for the Largest Metropolitan Areas (Annual)

Area	Wage	Area	Wage
AZ: Phoenix	$91,650	MI: Detroit	$102,410
CA: Los Angeles	$110,610	MN: Minneapolis	$104,800
CA: Riverside	$89,940	MO: Kansas City	$93,590
CA: Sacramento	$97,050	MO: St. Louis	$94,650
CA: San Diego	$101,690	NV: Las Vegas	$89,050
CA: San Francisco	$124,600	NY: New York	$124,970
CO: Denver	$107,220	OH: Cincinnati	$97,420
DC: Washington	$118,730	OH: Cleveland	$100,390
FL: Miami	$97,240	OH: Columbus	$103,370
FL: Orlando	$100,740	OR: Portland	$98,880
FL: Tampa	$93,600	PA: Philadelphia	$113,920
GA: Atlanta	$99,150	PA: Pittsburgh	$89,730
IL: Chicago	$94,930	TX: Dallas	$105,950
MA: Boston	$112,020	TX: Houston	$105,080
MD: Baltimore	$108,630	WA: Seattle	$107,230

FACTORS THAT MAY AFFECT EARNINGS

Educational Attainment of Workers and Effect on Earnings

	Percent at Level	Effect on Earnings
Less than High School	—	—
Some High School	—	—
High School or Equivalent	10.5%	−13.4%
Some College but No Degree	19.5%	−10.9%
Associate Degree	12.2%	−6.3%
Bachelor's Degree	34.1%	4.8%
Master's Degree	19.8%	10.5%
Doctoral Degree	1.7%	7.1%
First Professional Degree	—	—

Flexibility of Earnings

Average Hours Worked: 40
Workers with a Varying Number of Hours: 5.9%
Workers Earning Some Overtime Pay, Tips, or Commissions: 7.3%
Earnings Benefit of Working Overtime: −5.2%

Gender

	Male	Female
Percent	72.8%	27.2%
Effect on Earnings	4.0%	−9.4%

Union Membership

Percentage Union Members: Insignificant
Earnings Benefit of Union Membership: No significant data available

Veteran Status

Percentage Who Have Been on Active Duty: 9.5%
Earnings Benefit of Veteran Status: 7.6%

11-3031 Financial Managers

Plan, direct, and coordinate accounting, investing, banking, insurance, securities, and other financial activities of a branch, office, or department of an establishment.

- Education or Training Required: Work experience plus degree
- Job Growth: 14.8%
- Annual Openings: 63,000
- Self-Employed: 3.2%
- Part-Time: 9.9%

NATIONAL WAGE FIGURES (ANNUAL)

Beginning	25th Percentile	Median	Mean	75th Percentile	90th Percentile
$50,290	$66,690	$90,970	$101,450	$125,180	more than $145,600

Median Wages for Industries Employing Largest Numbers (Annual)

Industry	Median Income
Securities, Commodity Contracts, and Other Financial Investments and Related Activities	$132,110
Internet Service Providers, Web Search Portals, and Data-Processing Services	$106,020
Management of Companies and Enterprises	$105,410
Computer and Electronic Product Manufacturing	$104,630
Insurance Carriers and Related Activities	$103,160
Real Estate	$102,380
Professional, Scientific, and Technical Services	$101,600
Publishing Industries (Except Internet)	$100,760
Telecommunications	$98,460
Chemical Manufacturing	$97,010

Median Wages for States (Annual)

State	Wage	State	Wage	State	Wage
AK	$70,860	KY	$74,240	NY	$126,490
AL	$75,810	LA	$66,160	OH	$88,880
AR	$69,510	MA	$96,380	OK	$65,280
AZ	$77,440	MD	$92,300	OR	$88,640
CA	$97,970	ME	$64,790	PA	$86,960
CO	$93,610	MI	$86,700	RI	$90,030
CT	$97,620	MN	$99,010	SC	$76,100
DC	$110,620	MO	$90,900	SD	$85,280
DE	$100,810	MS	$61,480	TN	$63,680
FL	$88,570	MT	$58,390	TX	$90,900
GA	$84,590	NC	$80,160	UT	$74,900
HI	$76,550	ND	$71,400	VA	$100,750
IA	$78,310	NE	$83,930	VT	$79,600
ID	$61,500	NH	$75,070	WA	$93,780
IL	$93,370	NJ	$112,330	WI	$90,600
IN	$82,440	NM	$66,920	WV	$61,560
KS	$74,590	NV	$80,380	WY	$65,300

Median Wages for the Largest Metropolitan Areas (Annual)

Metro Area	Wage	Metro Area	Wage
AZ: Phoenix	$81,120	MI: Detroit	$94,900
CA: Los Angeles	$99,040	MN: Minneapolis	$103,110
CA: Riverside	$85,860	MO: Kansas City	$85,280
CA: Sacramento	$83,320	MO: St. Louis	$93,660
CA: San Diego	$92,840	NV: Las Vegas	$82,870
CA: San Francisco	$110,630	NY: New York	$130,300
CO: Denver	$97,290	OH: Cincinnati	$93,260
DC: Washington	$107,780	OH: Cleveland	$93,810
FL: Miami	$92,310	OH: Columbus	$89,220
FL: Orlando	$83,260	OR: Portland	$93,440
FL: Tampa	$92,500	PA: Philadelphia	$101,600
GA: Atlanta	$89,810	PA: Pittsburgh	$81,260
IL: Chicago	$96,250	TX: Dallas	$95,330
MA: Boston	$100,240	TX: Houston	$102,670
MD: Baltimore	$90,970	WA: Seattle	$99,570

FACTORS THAT MAY AFFECT EARNINGS

Educational Attainment of Workers and Effect on Earnings

	Percent at Level	Effect on Earnings
Less than High School	—	—
Some High School	1.2%	−29.2%
High School or Equivalent	17.4%	−24.7%
Some College but No Degree	20.6%	−18.4%
Associate Degree	10.9%	−13.7%
Bachelor's Degree	32.0%	11.9%
Master's Degree	16.0%	33.0%
Doctoral Degree	1.1%	23.9%
First Professional Degree	0.8%	75.4%

Flexibility of Earnings

Average Hours Worked: 40
Workers with a Varying Number of Hours: 4.4%
Workers Earning Some Overtime Pay, Tips, or Commissions: 9.9%
Earnings Benefit of Working Overtime: 7.2%

Gender

	Male	Female
Percent	45.0%	55.0%
Effect on Earnings	30.7%	−17.8%

Union Membership

Percentage Union Members: Insignificant
Earnings Benefit of Union Membership: No significant data available

Veteran Status

Percentage Who Have Been on Active Duty: 9.5%
Earnings Benefit of Veteran Status: 7.6%

11-3041 Compensation and Benefits Managers

Plan, direct, or coordinate compensation and benefits activities and staff of an organization.

- Education or Training Required: Work experience plus degree
- Job Growth: 21.5%
- Annual Openings: 4,000
- Self-Employed: 1.2%
- Part-Time: 6.4%

NATIONAL WAGE FIGURES (ANNUAL)

Beginning	25th Percentile	Median	Mean	75th Percentile	90th Percentile
$42,750	$55,370	$74,750	$82,010	$99,690	$132,820

Median Wages for Industries Employing Largest Numbers (Annual)

Industry	Median Income
Securities, Commodity Contracts, and Other Financial Investments and Related Activities	$93,900
Computer and Electronic Product Manufacturing	$89,940
Publishing Industries (Except Internet)	$86,050
Management of Companies and Enterprises	$85,330
Insurance Carriers and Related Activities	$83,840
Professional, Scientific, and Technical Services	$81,790
Chemical Manufacturing	$79,560
Credit Intermediation and Related Activities	$79,040
Transportation Equipment Manufacturing	$76,390
Real Estate	$74,830

Median Wages for States (Annual)

AK	$66,350	KY	$62,500	NY	$93,080
AL	$66,780	LA	$58,010	OH	$80,520
AR	$62,570	MA	$94,820	OK	$59,250
AZ	$55,320	MD	$73,030	OR	$79,850
CA	$82,110	ME	$64,640	PA	$68,320
CO	$68,520	MI	$70,290	RI	$69,460
CT	$76,910	MN	$100,990	SC	$63,100
DC	$72,520	MO	$74,320	SD	$70,960
DE	$92,340	MS	$54,860	TN	$55,950
FL	$84,330	MT	$51,960	TX	$83,200
GA	$71,670	NC	$72,090	UT	$69,860
HI	$65,290	ND	$57,820	VA	$81,850
IA	$64,250	NE	$70,060	VT	$73,360
ID	$56,540	NH	$63,700	WA	$84,280
IL	$67,670	NJ	$102,340	WI	$71,190
IN	$60,270	NM	$54,300	WV	$55,950
KS	$68,120	NV	$57,470	WY	$61,670

Median Wages for the Largest Metropolitan Areas (Annual)

AZ: Phoenix	$55,130	MI: Detroit	$76,640
CA: Los Angeles	$77,440	MN: Minneapolis	$101,270
CA: Riverside	$61,370	MO: Kansas City	$70,830
CA: Sacramento	$76,980	MO: St. Louis	$76,420
CA: San Diego	$86,310	NV: Las Vegas	$57,010
CA: San Francisco	$96,370	NY: New York	$101,700
CO: Denver	$71,880	OH: Cincinnati	$83,610
DC: Washington	$77,230	OH: Cleveland	$89,080
FL: Miami	$86,940	OH: Columbus	$90,200
FL: Orlando	$82,820	OR: Portland	$82,980
FL: Tampa	$86,970	PA: Philadelphia	$79,190
GA: Atlanta	$74,390	PA: Pittsburgh	$63,180
IL: Chicago	$70,330	TX: Dallas	$90,140
MA: Boston	$96,410	TX: Houston	$86,430
MD: Baltimore	$66,580	WA: Seattle	$85,460

FACTORS THAT MAY AFFECT EARNINGS

Educational Attainment of Workers and Effect on Earnings

Figures are based on a group of occupations: Operations Specialties Managers

	Percent at Level	Effect on Earnings
Less than High School	—	—
Some High School	2.7%	−30.4%
High School or Equivalent	20.9%	−15.1%
Some College but No Degree	20.4%	−13.2%
Associate Degree	11.5%	−6.5%
Bachelor's Degree	26.2%	8.9%
Master's Degree	15.4%	25.5%
Doctoral Degree	1.3%	40.4%
First Professional Degree	1.3%	59.4%

Flexibility of Earnings

Average Hours Worked: 40
Workers with a Varying Number of Hours: 4.6%
Workers Earning Some Overtime Pay, Tips, or Commissions: 9.5%
Earnings Benefit of Working Overtime: −2.3%

Gender

	Male	Female
Percent	34.2%	65.8%
Effect on Earnings	32.2%	−8.1%

Union Membership

Percentage Union Members: Insignificant
Earnings Benefit of Union Membership: No significant data available

Veteran Status

Percentage Who Have Been on Active Duty: 9.5%
Earnings Benefit of Veteran Status: 7.6%

11-3042 Training and Development Managers

Plan, direct, or coordinate the training and development activities and staff of an organization.

- Education or Training Required: Work experience plus degree
- Job Growth: 25.9%
- Annual Openings: 3,000
- Self-Employed: 1.3%
- Part-Time: 6.4%

NATIONAL WAGE FIGURES (ANNUAL)

Beginning	25th Percentile	Median	Mean	75th Percentile	90th Percentile
$43,530	$58,770	$80,250	$86,670	$107,450	$141,140

Median Wages for Industries Employing Largest Numbers (Annual)

Industry	Median Income
Securities, Commodity Contracts, and Other Financial Investments and Related Activities	$113,290
Internet Service Providers, Web Search Portals, and Data-Processing Services	$101,910
Computer and Electronic Product Manufacturing	$98,030
Publishing Industries (Except Internet)	$97,880
Utilities	$97,090
Telecommunications	$93,840
Professional, Scientific, and Technical Services	$90,330
Merchant Wholesalers, Durable Goods	$89,860
Merchant Wholesalers, Nondurable Goods	$87,750
Chemical Manufacturing	$87,730

Median Wages for States (Annual)

State	Wage	State	Wage	State	Wage
AK	$73,540	KY	$61,590	NY	$100,430
AL	$61,040	LA	$45,590	OH	$80,960
AR	$70,090	MA	$104,740	OK	$51,610
AZ	$63,730	MD	$81,460	OR	$76,930
CA	$90,150	ME	$64,790	PA	$74,000
CO	$73,750	MI	$74,640	RI	$63,920
CT	$79,380	MN	$99,500	SC	$67,910
DC	$104,660	MO	$71,360	SD	no data
DE	$107,610	MS	$55,770	TN	$58,480
FL	$83,680	MT	$46,220	TX	$81,600
GA	$80,030	NC	$81,370	UT	$73,470
HI	$92,240	ND	$60,320	VA	$89,690
IA	$72,580	NE	$69,290	VT	no data
ID	$49,080	NH	$77,750	WA	$88,670
IL	$67,830	NJ	$106,510	WI	$71,940
IN	$59,460	NM	$53,750	WV	$57,130
KS	$73,950	NV	$63,270	WY	no data

Median Wages for the Largest Metropolitan Areas (Annual)

Metro	Wage	Metro	Wage
AZ: Phoenix	$64,570	MI: Detroit	$79,400
CA: Los Angeles	$93,250	MN: Minneapolis	$99,760
CA: Riverside	$75,660	MO: Kansas City	$67,770
CA: Sacramento	$84,430	MO: St. Louis	$77,260
CA: San Diego	$85,090	NV: Las Vegas	$62,280
CA: San Francisco	$102,990	NY: New York	$108,540
CO: Denver	$74,680	OH: Cincinnati	$78,630
DC: Washington	$97,850	OH: Cleveland	$82,010
FL: Miami	$86,780	OH: Columbus	$92,990
FL: Orlando	$74,890	OR: Portland	$80,070
FL: Tampa	$90,680	PA: Philadelphia	$92,550
GA: Atlanta	$81,930	PA: Pittsburgh	$70,890
IL: Chicago	$70,180	TX: Dallas	$85,970
MA: Boston	$105,410	TX: Houston	$84,360
MD: Baltimore	$85,970	WA: Seattle	$91,810

FACTORS THAT MAY AFFECT EARNINGS

Educational Attainment of Workers and Effect on Earnings

Figures are based on a group of occupations: Operations Specialties Managers

	Percent at Level	Effect on Earnings
Less than High School	—	—
Some High School	2.7%	−30.4%
High School or Equivalent	20.9%	−15.1%
Some College but No Degree	20.4%	−13.2%
Associate Degree	11.5%	−6.5%
Bachelor's Degree	26.2%	8.9%
Master's Degree	15.4%	25.5%
Doctoral Degree	1.3%	40.4%
First Professional Degree	1.3%	59.4%

Flexibility of Earnings

Average Hours Worked: 40
Workers with a Varying Number of Hours: 4.6%
Workers Earning Some Overtime Pay, Tips, or Commissions: 9.5%
Earnings Benefit of Working Overtime: −2.3%

Gender

	Male	Female
Percent	34.2%	65.8%
Effect on Earnings	32.2%	−8.1%

Union Membership

Percentage Union Members: Insignificant
Earnings Benefit of Union Membership: No significant data available

Veteran Status

Percentage Who Have Been on Active Duty: 9.5%
Earnings Benefit of Veteran Status: 7.6%

11-3049 Human Resources Managers, All Other

All Human Resources Managers not listed separately.

- Education or Training Required: Work experience plus degree
- Job Growth: 15.9%
- Annual Openings: 4,000
- Self-Employed: 1.3%
- Part-Time: 6.4%

NATIONAL WAGE FIGURES (ANNUAL)

Beginning	25th Percentile	Median	Mean	75th Percentile	90th Percentile
$51,810	$67,710	$88,510	$94,910	$114,860	more than $145,600

Median Wages for Industries Employing Largest Numbers (Annual)

Industry	Median Income
Computer and Electronic Product Manufacturing	$106,620
Publishing Industries (Except Internet)	$104,600
Telecommunications	$102,450
Securities, Commodity Contracts, and Other Financial Investments and Related Activities	$99,770
Professional, Scientific, and Technical Services	$99,280
Management of Companies and Enterprises	$98,400
Chemical Manufacturing	$97,260
Miscellaneous Manufacturing	$95,560
Credit Intermediation and Related Activities	$91,770
Insurance Carriers and Related Activities	$90,010

Median Wages for States (Annual)

AK	$71,230	KY	$73,210	NY	$91,700
AL	$73,270	LA	$58,500	OH	$87,290
AR	$68,050	MA	$102,570	OK	$48,690
AZ	$65,610	MD	$94,530	OR	$82,270
CA	$102,250	ME	$66,130	PA	$90,120
CO	$88,090	MI	$87,270	RI	$101,110
CT	$92,840	MN	$91,590	SC	$67,900
DC	$118,630	MO	$81,630	SD	$71,250
DE	$103,510	MS	$64,250	TN	$72,510
FL	$83,450	MT	$57,320	TX	$91,880
GA	$85,470	NC	$78,740	UT	$81,990
HI	$73,130	ND	$67,170	VA	$106,630
IA	$72,610	NE	$85,780	VT	$77,310
ID	$72,060	NH	$82,880	WA	$94,560
IL	$82,050	NJ	$104,660	WI	$85,410
IN	$70,630	NM	$53,080	WV	$61,680
KS	$82,460	NV	$74,250	WY	$59,250

Median Wages for the Largest Metropolitan Areas (Annual)

AZ: Phoenix	$64,210	MI: Detroit	$94,450
CA: Los Angeles	$102,870	MN: Minneapolis	$93,620
CA: Riverside	$86,530	MO: Kansas City	$86,800
CA: Sacramento	$83,050	MO: St. Louis	$87,300
CA: San Diego	$89,590	NV: Las Vegas	$72,880
CA: San Francisco	$112,250	NY: New York	$98,260
CO: Denver	$93,530	OH: Cincinnati	$83,090
DC: Washington	$114,060	OH: Cleveland	$94,470
FL: Miami	$88,290	OH: Columbus	$91,520
FL: Orlando	$81,530	OR: Portland	$85,020
FL: Tampa	$85,280	PA: Philadelphia	$97,100
GA: Atlanta	$89,310	PA: Pittsburgh	$88,790
IL: Chicago	$83,680	TX: Dallas	$102,210
MA: Boston	$104,780	TX: Houston	$89,090
MD: Baltimore	$91,580	WA: Seattle	$96,800

FACTORS THAT MAY AFFECT EARNINGS

Educational Attainment of Workers and Effect on Earnings

Figures are based on a group of occupations: Operations Specialties Managers

	Percent at Level	Effect on Earnings
Less than High School	—	—
Some High School	2.7%	−30.4%
High School or Equivalent	20.9%	−15.1%
Some College but No Degree	20.4%	−13.2%
Associate Degree	11.5%	−6.5%
Bachelor's Degree	26.2%	8.9%
Master's Degree	15.4%	25.5%
Doctoral Degree	1.3%	40.4%
First Professional Degree	1.3%	59.4%

Flexibility of Earnings

Average Hours Worked: 40
Workers with a Varying Number of Hours: 4.6%
Workers Earning Some Overtime Pay, Tips, or Commissions: 9.5%
Earnings Benefit of Working Overtime: −2.3%

Gender

	Male	Female
Percent	34.2%	65.8%
Effect on Earnings	32.2%	−8.1%

Union Membership

Percentage Union Members: Insignificant
Earnings Benefit of Union Membership: No significant data available

Veteran Status

Percentage Who Have Been on Active Duty: 9.5%
Earnings Benefit of Veteran Status: 7.6%

11-3051 Industrial Production Managers

Plan, direct, or coordinate the work activities and resources necessary for manufacturing products in accordance with cost, quality, and quantity specifications.

- Education or Training Required: Work experience in a related occupation
- Job Growth: 0.8%
- Annual Openings: 13,000
- Self-Employed: 1.7%
- Part-Time: 5.0%

NATIONAL WAGE FIGURES (ANNUAL)

Beginning	25th Percentile	Median	Mean	75th Percentile	90th Percentile
$47,230	$59,650	$77,670	$83,970	$100,810	$130,680

Median Wages for Industries Employing Largest Numbers (Annual)

Industry	Median Income
Professional, Scientific, and Technical Services	$92,280
Computer and Electronic Product Manufacturing	$89,160
Management of Companies and Enterprises	$88,820
Petroleum and Coal Products Manufacturing	$88,810
Publishing Industries (Except Internet)	$87,590
Chemical Manufacturing	$84,520
Merchant Wholesalers, Nondurable Goods	$82,720
Transportation Equipment Manufacturing	$82,310
Administrative and Support Services	$82,010
Beverage and Tobacco Product Manufacturing	$80,960

Median Wages for States (Annual)

State	Wage	State	Wage	State	Wage
AK	$63,420	KY	$70,230	NY	$85,420
AL	$67,560	LA	$69,070	OH	$72,680
AR	$69,460	MA	$86,120	OK	$63,340
AZ	$70,330	MD	$82,020	OR	$75,000
CA	$82,140	ME	$65,120	PA	$77,110
CO	$71,210	MI	$83,420	RI	$81,510
CT	$85,330	MN	$78,840	SC	$76,750
DC	$88,780	MO	$72,560	SD	$68,480
DE	$91,270	MS	$65,470	TN	$64,390
FL	$77,750	MT	$64,410	TX	$88,050
GA	$74,250	NC	$73,540	UT	$74,200
HI	$61,350	ND	$62,840	VA	$78,910
IA	$69,910	NE	$70,020	VT	$85,260
ID	$64,220	NH	$79,800	WA	$86,380
IL	$76,320	NJ	$87,410	WI	$74,080
IN	$70,630	NM	$61,590	WV	$62,480
KS	$78,750	NV	$72,280	WY	$86,740

Median Wages for the Largest Metropolitan Areas (Annual)

Area	Wage	Area	Wage
AZ: Phoenix	$81,260	MI: Detroit	$90,980
CA: Los Angeles	$78,230	MN: Minneapolis	$85,630
CA: Riverside	$71,280	MO: Kansas City	$77,620
CA: Sacramento	$74,400	MO: St. Louis	$75,290
CA: San Diego	$85,270	NV: Las Vegas	$83,300
CA: San Francisco	$91,230	NY: New York	$91,130
CO: Denver	$69,890	OH: Cincinnati	$77,900
DC: Washington	$88,050	OH: Cleveland	$76,340
FL: Miami	$77,000	OH: Columbus	$70,730
FL: Orlando	$78,010	OR: Portland	$80,240
FL: Tampa	$85,450	PA: Philadelphia	$85,360
GA: Atlanta	$77,030	PA: Pittsburgh	$73,760
IL: Chicago	$77,900	TX: Dallas	$88,730
MA: Boston	$89,790	TX: Houston	$96,360
MD: Baltimore	$84,180	WA: Seattle	$88,220

FACTORS THAT MAY AFFECT EARNINGS

Educational Attainment of Workers and Effect on Earnings

	Percent at Level	Effect on Earnings
Less than High School	—	—
Some High School	2.8%	−30.7%
High School or Equivalent	29.9%	−16.5%
Some College but No Degree	18.0%	−6.7%
Associate Degree	9.5%	−7.9%
Bachelor's Degree	26.8%	15.8%
Master's Degree	10.9%	22.9%
Doctoral Degree	—	—
First Professional Degree	—	—

Flexibility of Earnings

Average Hours Worked: 42
Workers with a Varying Number of Hours: 5.4%
Workers Earning Some Overtime Pay, Tips, or Commissions: 9.4%
Earnings Benefit of Working Overtime: −2.6%

Gender

	Male	Female
Percent	83.6%	16.4%
Effect on Earnings	1.6%	—

Union Membership

Percentage Union Members: Insignificant
Earnings Benefit of Union Membership: No significant data available

Veteran Status

Percentage Who Have Been on Active Duty: 9.5%
Earnings Benefit of Veteran Status: 7.6%

11-3061 Purchasing Managers

Plan, direct, or coordinate the activities of buyers, purchasing officers, and related workers involved in purchasing materials, products, and services.

- Education or Training Required: Work experience plus degree
- Job Growth: 7.0%
- Annual Openings: 8,000
- Self-Employed: 0.3%
- Part-Time: 2.2%

NATIONAL WAGE FIGURES (ANNUAL)

Beginning	25th Percentile	Median	Mean	75th Percentile	90th Percentile
$46,540	$60,890	$81,570	$86,020	$105,780	$132,040

Median Wages for Industries Employing Largest Numbers (Annual)

Industry	Median Income
Professional, Scientific, and Technical Services	$95,270
Management of Companies and Enterprises	$93,510
Federal, State, and Local Government	$92,890
Computer and Electronic Product Manufacturing	$89,980
Chemical Manufacturing	$86,540
Administrative and Support Services	$84,140
Transportation Equipment Manufacturing	$83,350
Electrical Equipment, Appliance, and Component Manufacturing	$79,370
Construction of Buildings	$79,300
Paper Manufacturing	$78,450

Median Wages for States (Annual)

State	Wage	State	Wage	State	Wage
AK	$72,780	KY	$68,640	NY	$88,590
AL	$79,780	LA	$55,690	OH	$76,680
AR	$69,530	MA	$85,560	OK	$60,600
AZ	$71,180	MD	$100,420	OR	$76,350
CA	$86,500	ME	$71,020	PA	$78,650
CO	$86,180	MI	$83,300	RI	$79,990
CT	$84,460	MN	$88,860	SC	$67,320
DC	$111,670	MO	$80,230	SD	$69,130
DE	$104,800	MS	$56,910	TN	$59,430
FL	$85,010	MT	$56,210	TX	$88,270
GA	$73,200	NC	$76,760	UT	$74,850
HI	$58,880	ND	$67,600	VA	$102,950
IA	$70,690	NE	$83,850	VT	$78,490
ID	$68,930	NH	$79,320	WA	$89,240
IL	$74,850	NJ	$104,690	WI	$75,190
IN	$72,220	NM	$74,980	WV	$63,780
KS	$71,200	NV	$69,100	WY	$60,420

Median Wages for the Largest Metropolitan Areas (Annual)

Area	Wage	Area	Wage
AZ: Phoenix	$70,590	MI: Detroit	$89,150
CA: Los Angeles	$83,650	MN: Minneapolis	$92,410
CA: Riverside	$72,120	MO: Kansas City	$78,740
CA: Sacramento	$84,440	MO: St. Louis	$86,280
CA: San Diego	$84,110	NV: Las Vegas	$69,790
CA: San Francisco	$94,250	NY: New York	$97,350
CO: Denver	$86,310	OH: Cincinnati	$81,920
DC: Washington	$110,200	OH: Cleveland	$79,740
FL: Miami	$87,910	OH: Columbus	$71,790
FL: Orlando	$82,510	OR: Portland	$81,610
FL: Tampa	$89,820	PA: Philadelphia	$90,670
GA: Atlanta	$75,820	PA: Pittsburgh	$72,820
IL: Chicago	$75,620	TX: Dallas	$92,540
MA: Boston	$89,700	TX: Houston	$92,430
MD: Baltimore	$92,160	WA: Seattle	$90,010

FACTORS THAT MAY AFFECT EARNINGS

Educational Attainment of Workers and Effect on Earnings

	Percent at Level	Effect on Earnings
Less than High School	—	—
Some High School	—	—
High School or Equivalent	19.0%	−11.9%
Some College but No Degree	19.0%	−19.8%
Associate Degree	10.6%	−18.7%
Bachelor's Degree	33.9%	4.8%
Master's Degree	14.3%	48.8%
Doctoral Degree	—	—
First Professional Degree	—	—

Flexibility of Earnings

Average Hours Worked: 39
Workers with a Varying Number of Hours: 4.1%
Workers Earning Some Overtime Pay, Tips, or Commissions: 8.2%
Earnings Benefit of Working Overtime: −3.5%

Gender

	Male	Female
Percent	59.3%	40.7%
Effect on Earnings	10.8%	−13.6%

Union Membership

Percentage Union Members: 5.2%
Earnings Benefit of Union Membership: −5.1%

Veteran Status

Percentage Who Have Been on Active Duty: 9.5%
Earnings Benefit of Veteran Status: 7.6%

11-3071 Transportation, Storage, and Distribution Managers

Plan, direct, or coordinate transportation, storage, or distribution activities in accordance with governmental policies and regulations. Includes logistics managers.

- Education or Training Required: Work experience in a related occupation
- Job Growth: 12.7%
- Annual Openings: 15,000
- Self-Employed: 2.8%
- Part-Time: 6.5%

NATIONAL WAGE FIGURES (ANNUAL)

Beginning	25th Percentile	Median	Mean	75th Percentile	90th Percentile
$43,180	$55,910	$73,080	$78,560	$93,820	$120,470

Median Wages for Industries Employing Largest Numbers (Annual)

Industry	Median Income
Computer and Electronic Product Manufacturing	$98,530
Rail Transportation	$87,880
Professional, Scientific, and Technical Services	$86,890
Utilities	$85,290
Management of Companies and Enterprises	$84,270
Federal, State, and Local Government	$83,910
Postal Service	$79,450
Air Transportation	$78,950
Couriers and Messengers	$78,760
Chemical Manufacturing	$73,880

Median Wages for States (Annual)

AK $67,730	KY $65,840	NY $86,010
AL $63,840	LA $57,380	OH $74,310
AR $70,000	MA $71,580	OK $48,460
AZ $59,430	MD $76,730	OR $69,120
CA $75,520	ME $59,860	PA $77,100
CO $72,370	MI $74,310	RI $71,320
CT $75,000	MN $80,050	SC........... $57,870
DC $106,160	MO $73,270	SD $72,460
DE $86,060	MS $53,910	TN $61,960
FL $82,280	MT $66,190	TX $68,280
GA $67,440	NC $65,800	UT $64,150
HI $73,170	ND $65,580	VA $81,570
IA $70,650	NE $74,360	VT $73,730
ID $49,820	NH $81,170	WA $82,940
IL $75,080	NJ $88,330	WI $70,180
IN $69,300	NM $69,340	WV $58,710
KS $75,440	NV $65,450	WY $72,920

Median Wages for the Largest Metropolitan Areas (Annual)

AZ: Phoenix $56,480	MI: Detroit $75,690
CA: Los Angeles $74,440	MN: Minneapolis $82,930
CA: Riverside $70,290	MO: Kansas City $79,390
CA: Sacramento $74,300	MO: St. Louis............. $75,350
CA: San Diego $74,730	NV: Las Vegas $61,820
CA: San Francisco.... $83,050	NY: New York............ $89,710
CO: Denver $73,280	OH: Cincinnati.......... $74,770
DC: Washington $90,820	OH: Cleveland $83,700
FL: Miami $81,120	OH: Columbus $72,130
FL: Orlando $86,710	OR: Portland $72,470
FL: Tampa $85,500	PA: Philadelphia $83,920
GA: Atlanta $69,600	PA: Pittsburgh $77,100
IL: Chicago $75,580	TX: Dallas $69,740
MA: Boston $72,270	TX: Houston $69,600
MD: Baltimore $76,570	WA: Seattle $86,750

FACTORS THAT MAY AFFECT EARNINGS

Educational Attainment of Workers and Effect on Earnings

	Percent at Level	Effect on Earnings
Less than High School	—	—
Some High School	5.9%	−21.2%
High School or Equivalent	37.6%	−4.1%
Some College but No Degree	23.5%	−7.3%
Associate Degree	8.2%	−6.1%
Bachelor's Degree	20.8%	21.6%
Master's Degree	3.5%	18.6%
Doctoral Degree	—	—
First Professional Degree	—	—

Flexibility of Earnings

Average Hours Worked: 41
Workers with a Varying Number of Hours: 3.8%
Workers Earning Some Overtime Pay, Tips, or Commissions: 14.8%
Earnings Benefit of Working Overtime: −5.3%

Gender

	Male	Female
Percent	85.4%	14.6%
Effect on Earnings	1.0%	—

Union Membership

Percentage Union Members: 5.7%
Earnings Benefit of Union Membership: 6.3%

Veteran Status

Percentage Who Have Been on Active Duty: 9.5%
Earnings Benefit of Veteran Status: 7.6%

11-9000 Other Management Occupations

11-9011 Farm, Ranch, and Other Agricultural Managers

On a paid basis, manage farms, ranches, aquacultural operations, greenhouses, nurseries, timber tracts, cotton gins, packing houses, or other agricultural establishments for employers. Carry out production, financial, and marketing decisions relating to the managed operations following guidelines from the owner. May contract tenant farmers or producers to carry out the day-to-day activities of the managed operation. May supervise planting, cultivating, harvesting, and marketing activities. May prepare cost, production, and other records. May perform physical work and operate machinery.

- Education or Training Required: Work experience plus degree
- Job Growth: 4.0%
- Annual Openings: 20,000
- Self-Employed: 0.0%
- Part-Time: 12.1%

NATIONAL WAGE FIGURES (ANNUAL)

Beginning	25th Percentile	Median	Mean	75th Percentile	90th Percentile
$29,760	$39,840	$52,070	$58,550	$71,840	$100,050

Median Wages for Industries Employing Largest Numbers (Annual)

Industry	Median Income
Forestry and Logging	$77,150
Beverage and Tobacco Product Manufacturing	$77,070
Management of Companies and Enterprises	$58,770
Food Manufacturing	$58,520
Federal, State, and Local Government	$56,470
Merchant Wholesalers, Nondurable Goods	$56,100
Administrative and Support Services	$52,910
Educational Services	$52,390
Support Activities for Agriculture and Forestry	$52,310
Amusement, Gambling, and Recreation Industries	$46,960

Median Wages for States (Annual)

State	Wage	State	Wage	State	Wage
AK	no data	KY	$47,920	NY	$67,540
AL	$45,280	LA	$56,680	OH	$49,640
AR	$60,220	MA	$37,140	OK	no data
AZ	$73,500	MD	no data	OR	$47,480
CA	$56,730	ME	no data	PA	$49,920
CO	$43,210	MI	no data	RI	no data
CT	$59,520	MN	no data	SC	no data
DC	no data	MO	$56,320	SD	$37,890
DE	no data	MS	$51,570	TN	no data
FL	$101,450	MT	no data	TX	$41,520
GA	no data	NC	$39,650	UT	$62,550
HI	no data	ND	no data	VA	no data
IA	$49,070	NE	$43,560	VT	no data
ID	$51,710	NH	no data	WA	$81,420
IL	$42,920	NJ	$71,660	WI	$61,120
IN	$43,960	NM	$46,520	WV	$36,480
KS	$57,780	NV	no data	WY	no data

Median Wages for the Largest Metropolitan Areas (Annual)

Area	Wage	Area	Wage
AZ: Phoenix	no data	MI: Detroit	no data
CA: Los Angeles	no data	MN: Minneapolis	no data
CA: Riverside	no data	MO: Kansas City	no data
CA: Sacramento	$59,940	MO: St. Louis	no data
CA: San Diego	no data	NV: Las Vegas	no data
CA: San Francisco	no data	NY: New York	$74,960
CO: Denver	no data	OH: Cincinnati	no data
DC: Washington	no data	OH: Cleveland	no data
FL: Miami	no data	OH: Columbus	no data
FL: Orlando	no data	OR: Portland	no data
FL: Tampa	no data	PA: Philadelphia	$50,090
GA: Atlanta	no data	PA: Pittsburgh	no data
IL: Chicago	$46,760	TX: Dallas	no data
MA: Boston	$37,110	TX: Houston	no data
MD: Baltimore	no data	WA: Seattle	no data

FACTORS THAT MAY AFFECT EARNINGS

Educational Attainment of Workers and Effect on Earnings

	Percent at Level	Effect on Earnings
Less than High School	5.6%	−1.3%
Some High School	14.4%	−24.6%
High School or Equivalent	30.0%	−1.4%
Some College but No Degree	20.0%	−3.8%
Associate Degree	14.4%	6.7%
Bachelor's Degree	13.1%	15.3%
Master's Degree	—	—
Doctoral Degree	—	—
First Professional Degree	—	—

Flexibility of Earnings

Average Hours Worked: 36
Workers with a Varying Number of Hours: 23.6%
Workers Earning Some Overtime Pay, Tips, or Commissions: 7.5%
Earnings Benefit of Working Overtime: −13.6%

Gender

	Male	Female
Percent	78.2%	21.8%
Effect on Earnings	3.6%	—

Union Membership

Percentage Union Members: Insignificant
Earnings Benefit of Union Membership: No significant data available

Veteran Status

Percentage Who Have Been on Active Duty: 10.2%
Earnings Benefit of Veteran Status: 14.9%

11-9012 Farmers and Ranchers

On an ownership or rental basis, operate farms, ranches, greenhouses, nurseries, timber tracts, or other agricultural production establishments that produce crops, horticultural specialties, livestock, poultry, finfish, shellfish, or animal specialties. May plant, cultivate, harvest, perform post-harvest activities on, and market crops and livestock; may hire, train, and supervise farm workers or supervise a farm labor contractor; may prepare cost, production, and other records. May maintain and operate machinery and perform physical work.

- Education or Training Required: Long-term on-the-job training
- Job Growth: –14.5%
- Annual Openings: 96,000
- Self-Employed: 100.0%
- Part-Time: 18.2%

Note: Earnings figures do not reflect self-employed workers, who make up virtually all of the workforce for this occupation.

NATIONAL WAGE FIGURES (ANNUAL)

Beginning	25th Percentile	Median	Mean	75th Percentile	90th Percentile
$22,750	$29,550	$37,130	$43,520	$47,600	$76,030

Median Wages for Industries Employing Largest Numbers (Annual)

Industry	Median Income
Support Activities for Agriculture and Forestry	$40,580

Median Wages for States (Annual)

AK	no data	KY	no data	NY	no data
AL	no data	LA	no data	OH	no data
AR	no data	MA	no data	OK	no data
AZ	no data	MD	no data	OR	no data
CA	no data	ME	no data	PA	no data
CO	no data	MI	no data	RI	no data
CT	no data	MN	no data	SC	no data
DC	no data	MO	no data	SD	no data
DE	no data	MS	no data	TN	no data
FL	no data	MT	no data	TX	no data
GA	no data	NC	no data	UT	no data
HI	no data	ND	no data	VA	no data
IA	no data	NE	no data	VT	no data
ID	no data	NH	no data	WA	no data
IL	no data	NJ	no data	WI	no data
IN	no data	NM	$38,520	WV	no data
KS	no data	NV	no data	WY	no data

Median Wages for the Largest Metropolitan Areas (Annual)

AZ: Phoenix	no data	MI: Detroit	no data
CA: Los Angeles	no data	MN: Minneapolis	no data
CA: Riverside	no data	MO: Kansas City	no data
CA: Sacramento	no data	MO: St. Louis	no data
CA: San Diego	no data	NV: Las Vegas	no data
CA: San Francisco	no data	NY: New York	no data
CO: Denver	no data	OH: Cincinnati	no data
DC: Washington	no data	OH: Cleveland	no data
FL: Miami	no data	OH: Columbus	no data
FL: Orlando	no data	OR: Portland	no data
FL: Tampa	no data	PA: Philadelphia	no data
GA: Atlanta	no data	PA: Pittsburgh	no data
IL: Chicago	no data	TX: Dallas	no data
MA: Boston	no data	TX: Houston	no data
MD: Baltimore	no data	WA: Seattle	no data

FACTORS THAT MAY AFFECT EARNINGS

Educational Attainment of Workers and Effect on Earnings

Figures are based on a group of occupations: Other Management Occupations

	Percent at Level	Effect on Earnings
Less than High School	1.6%	–39.8%
Some High School	4.8%	–34.7%
High School or Equivalent	18.8%	–16.4%
Some College but No Degree	18.1%	–13.0%
Associate Degree	12.6%	–8.5%
Bachelor's Degree	22.0%	8.5%
Master's Degree	14.9%	26.1%
Doctoral Degree	4.0%	47.7%
First Professional Degree	3.1%	37.6%

Flexibility of Earnings

Average Hours Worked: 28
Workers with a Varying Number of Hours: 35.3%
Workers Earning Some Overtime Pay, Tips, or Commissions: 8.9%
Earnings Benefit of Working Overtime: –8.3%

Gender

	Male	Female
Percent	75.0%	25.0%
Effect on Earnings	3.6%	—

Union Membership

Percentage Union Members: 5.1%
Earnings Benefit of Union Membership: 5.4%

Veteran Status

Percentage Who Have Been on Active Duty: 10.2%
Earnings Benefit of Veteran Status: 14.9%

11-9021 Construction Managers

Plan, direct, coordinate, or budget, usually through subordinate supervisory personnel, activities concerned with the construction and maintenance of structures, facilities, and systems. Participate in the conceptual development of a construction project and oversee its organization, scheduling, and implementation.

- Education or Training Required: Bachelor's degree
- Job Growth: 10.4%
- Annual Openings: 28,000
- Self-Employed: 54.2%
- Part-Time: 11.6%

Note: A large fraction of the workforce for this occupation is self-employed and earns an average of $57,180. All other earnings figures for this occupation are based on workers who are paid a wage or salary.

NATIONAL WAGE FIGURES (ANNUAL)

Beginning	25th Percentile	Median	Mean	75th Percentile	90th Percentile
$43,210	$56,090	$73,700	$82,760	$98,350	$135,780

Median Wages for Industries Employing Largest Numbers (Annual)

Industry	Median Income
Food Services and Drinking Places	$94,210
Utilities	$88,960
Telecommunications	$87,500
Rail Transportation	$84,540
Mining (Except Oil and Gas)	$83,660
Real Estate	$83,410
Oil and Gas Extraction	$82,110
Management of Companies and Enterprises	$81,890
Hospitals	$81,210
Professional, Scientific, and Technical Services	$79,470

Median Wages for States (Annual)

AK	$79,900	KY	$58,490	NY	$99,430
AL	$59,210	LA	$58,740	OH	$80,060
AR	$49,450	MA	$87,880	OK	$55,500
AZ	$73,200	MD	$79,950	OR	$75,910
CA	$87,890	ME	$67,300	PA	$73,370
CO	$71,040	MI	$81,730	RI	$74,520
CT	$80,790	MN	$79,760	SC	$67,470
DC	$76,920	MO	$63,310	SD	$66,310
DE	$74,960	MS	$49,410	TN	$55,430
FL	$73,910	MT	$54,600	TX	$59,120
GA	$66,390	NC	$68,470	UT	$70,350
HI	$92,310	ND	$60,140	VA	$88,760
IA	$64,180	NE	$62,440	VT	$76,840
ID	$58,830	NH	$71,480	WA	$96,250
IL	$81,480	NJ	$95,170	WI	$77,010
IN	$72,250	NM	$59,120	WV	$61,900
KS	$66,060	NV	$80,600	WY	$62,730

Median Wages for the Largest Metropolitan Areas (Annual)

AZ: Phoenix	$73,730	MI: Detroit	$93,650
CA: Los Angeles	$86,680	MN: Minneapolis	$86,550
CA: Riverside	$86,430	MO: Kansas City	$69,770
CA: Sacramento	$85,620	MO: St. Louis	$66,040
CA: San Diego	$88,260	NV: Las Vegas	$81,710
CA: San Francisco	$97,570	NY: New York	$105,690
CO: Denver	$70,600	OH: Cincinnati	$80,110
DC: Washington	$89,700	OH: Cleveland	$81,840
FL: Miami	$80,120	OH: Columbus	$77,350
FL: Orlando	$77,140	OR: Portland	$74,890
FL: Tampa	$71,450	PA: Philadelphia	$82,720
GA: Atlanta	$68,430	PA: Pittsburgh	$67,610
IL: Chicago	$84,570	TX: Dallas	$60,930
MA: Boston	$91,480	TX: Houston	$62,820
MD: Baltimore	$81,430	WA: Seattle	$101,280

FACTORS THAT MAY AFFECT EARNINGS

Educational Attainment of Workers and Effect on Earnings

	Percent at Level	Effect on Earnings
Less than High School	1.4%	−59.9%
Some High School	6.9%	−21.0%
High School or Equivalent	29.4%	−0.8%
Some College but No Degree	19.1%	−1.8%
Associate Degree	14.3%	−8.6%
Bachelor's Degree	22.1%	11.1%
Master's Degree	6.4%	22.4%
Doctoral Degree	—	—
First Professional Degree	—	—

Flexibility of Earnings

Average Hours Worked: 37
Workers with a Varying Number of Hours: 14.3%
Workers Earning Some Overtime Pay, Tips, or Commissions: 13.0%
Earnings Benefit of Working Overtime: −11.0%

Gender

	Male	Female
Percent	92.2%	7.8%
Effect on Earnings	0.9%	—

Union Membership

Percentage Union Members: 7.4%
Earnings Benefit of Union Membership: 10.8%

Veteran Status

Percentage Who Have Been on Active Duty: 10.2%
Earnings Benefit of Veteran Status: 14.9%

11-9031 Education Administrators, Preschool and Child Care Center/Program

Plan, direct, or coordinate the academic and nonacademic activities of preschool and child care centers or programs.

- Education or Training Required: Work experience plus degree
- Job Growth: 27.9%
- Annual Openings: 9,000
- Self-Employed: 3.2%
- Part-Time: 16.9%

NATIONAL WAGE FIGURES (ANNUAL)

Beginning	25th Percentile	Median	Mean	75th Percentile	90th Percentile
$24,470	$29,690	$37,740	$43,430	$51,300	$70,360

Median Wages for Industries Employing Largest Numbers (Annual)

Industry	Median Income
Professional, Scientific, and Technical Services	$59,850
Educational Services	$52,940
Nursing and Residential Care Facilities	$46,360
Hospitals	$45,500
Federal, State, and Local Government	$45,450
Management of Companies and Enterprises	$45,150
Ambulatory Health Care Services	$44,790
Religious, Grantmaking, Civic, Professional, and Similar Organizations	$37,060
Social Assistance	$35,670

Median Wages for States (Annual)

AK	$39,580	KY	$31,190	NY	$51,690
AL	$36,260	LA	$35,960	OH	$33,260
AR	$35,600	MA	$45,010	OK	$27,120
AZ	$33,170	MD	$40,260	OR	$34,880
CA	$43,560	ME	$36,540	PA	$37,390
CO	$35,360	MI	$40,830	RI	$44,920
CT	$41,950	MN	$39,730	SC	$30,900
DC	$37,710	MO	$41,160	SD	$41,720
DE	$38,300	MS	$34,930	TN	$28,770
FL	$45,410	MT	$27,940	TX	$32,640
GA	$32,350	NC	$34,560	UT	$31,430
HI	$38,700	ND	$32,080	VA	$38,460
IA	$28,930	NE	$34,930	VT	$34,860
ID	$48,220	NH	$36,200	WA	$47,760
IL	$42,260	NJ	$45,040	WI	$37,060
IN	$32,590	NM	$35,460	WV	$33,600
KS	$39,750	NV	$32,550	WY	$32,290

Median Wages for the Largest Metropolitan Areas (Annual)

AZ: Phoenix	$32,360	MI: Detroit	$44,960
CA: Los Angeles	$42,460	MN: Minneapolis	$40,040
CA: Riverside	$38,720	MO: Kansas City	$42,530
CA: Sacramento	$38,680	MO: St. Louis	$43,590
CA: San Diego	$40,200	NV: Las Vegas	$35,560
CA: San Francisco	$49,770	NY: New York	$52,900
CO: Denver	$32,590	OH: Cincinnati	$29,770
DC: Washington	$40,270	OH: Cleveland	$32,100
FL: Miami	$49,460	OH: Columbus	$39,480
FL: Orlando	$35,980	OR: Portland	$35,140
FL: Tampa	$44,320	PA: Philadelphia	$43,380
GA: Atlanta	$32,560	PA: Pittsburgh	$30,690
IL: Chicago	$44,140	TX: Dallas	$33,470
MA: Boston	$45,600	TX: Houston	$34,120
MD: Baltimore	$40,740	WA: Seattle	$49,110

FACTORS THAT MAY AFFECT EARNINGS

Educational Attainment of Workers and Effect on Earnings

Figures are based on a group of occupations: Other Management Occupations

	Percent at Level	Effect on Earnings
Less than High School	1.6%	−39.8%
Some High School	4.8%	−34.7%
High School or Equivalent	18.8%	−16.4%
Some College but No Degree	18.1%	−13.0%
Associate Degree	12.6%	−8.5%
Bachelor's Degree	22.0%	8.5%
Master's Degree	14.9%	26.1%
Doctoral Degree	4.0%	47.7%
First Professional Degree	3.1%	37.6%

Flexibility of Earnings

Average Hours Worked: 37
Workers with a Varying Number of Hours: 14.3%
Workers Earning Some Overtime Pay, Tips, or Commissions: 8.9%
Earnings Benefit of Working Overtime: −0.6%

Gender

	Male	Female
Percent	36.1%	63.9%
Effect on Earnings	13.3%	−9.6%

Union Membership

Percentage Union Members: 5.1%
Earnings Benefit of Union Membership: 5.4%

Veteran Status

Percentage Who Have Been on Active Duty: 10.2%
Earnings Benefit of Veteran Status: 14.9%

11-9032 Education Administrators, Elementary and Secondary School

Plan, direct, or coordinate the academic, clerical, or auxiliary activities of public or private elementary or secondary-level schools.

- Education or Training Required: Work experience plus degree
- Job Growth: 10.4%
- Annual Openings: 27,000
- Self-Employed: 3.6%
- Part-Time: 16.9%

NATIONAL WAGE FIGURES (ANNUAL)

Beginning	25th Percentile	Median	Mean	75th Percentile	90th Percentile
$51,320	$63,010	$77,740	$79,200	$94,420	$112,990

Median Wages for Industries Employing Largest Numbers (Annual)

Industry	Median Income
Professional, Scientific, and Technical Services	$135,170
Administrative and Support Services	$86,850
Federal, State, and Local Government	$79,410
Educational Services	$77,790
Hospitals	$70,290
Nursing and Residential Care Facilities	$65,330
Religious, Grantmaking, Civic, Professional, and Similar Organizations	$60,530
Social Assistance	$50,400

Median Wages for States (Annual)

AK	$84,770	KY	$66,810	NY	$94,860
AL	$65,490	LA	$57,600	OH	$84,370
AR	$65,180	MA	$85,200	OK	$56,440
AZ	$67,400	MD	$79,320	OR	$80,130
CA	$94,180	ME	$65,210	PA	$82,880
CO	$75,910	MI	$86,450	RI	$83,650
CT	$102,660	MN	$85,290	SC	$68,440
DC	no data	MO	$69,930	SD	$57,290
DE	$96,730	MS	$65,290	TN	$64,910
FL	$74,120	MT	$60,330	TX	$65,110
GA	$76,670	NC	$62,270	UT	$71,780
HI	$66,870	ND	$63,490	VA	$76,010
IA	$71,040	NE	$72,540	VT	$67,560
ID	$72,210	NH	$71,240	WA	$85,740
IL	$87,750	NJ	$101,080	WI	$79,240
IN	$73,490	NM	$66,450	WV	$57,690
KS	$65,710	NV	$75,250	WY	$67,820

Median Wages for the Largest Metropolitan Areas (Annual)

AZ: Phoenix	$70,310	MI: Detroit	$97,600
CA: Los Angeles	$101,170	MN: Minneapolis	$90,520
CA: Riverside	$94,640	MO: Kansas City	$73,370
CA: Sacramento	$87,630	MO: St. Louis	$78,930
CA: San Diego	$100,920	NV: Las Vegas	$77,380
CA: San Francisco	$96,350	NY: New York	$103,090
CO: Denver	$81,040	OH: Cincinnati	$83,430
DC: Washington	$89,200	OH: Cleveland	$95,170
FL: Miami	$81,580	OH: Columbus	$87,430
FL: Orlando	$72,830	OR: Portland	$83,840
FL: Tampa	$77,900	PA: Philadelphia	$96,560
GA: Atlanta	$78,910	PA: Pittsburgh	$87,650
IL: Chicago	$94,730	TX: Dallas	$67,790
MA: Boston	$86,330	TX: Houston	$68,680
MD: Baltimore	$77,600	WA: Seattle	$88,880

FACTORS THAT MAY AFFECT EARNINGS

Educational Attainment of Workers and Effect on Earnings

Figures are based on a group of occupations: Other Management Occupations

	Percent at Level	Effect on Earnings
Less than High School	1.6%	−39.8%
Some High School	4.8%	−34.7%
High School or Equivalent	18.8%	−16.4%
Some College but No Degree	18.1%	−13.0%
Associate Degree	12.6%	−8.5%
Bachelor's Degree	22.0%	8.5%
Master's Degree	14.9%	26.1%
Doctoral Degree	4.0%	47.7%
First Professional Degree	3.1%	37.6%

Flexibility of Earnings

Average Hours Worked: 37
Workers with a Varying Number of Hours: 14.3%
Workers Earning Some Overtime Pay, Tips, or Commissions: 8.9%
Earnings Benefit of Working Overtime: −0.6%

Gender

	Male	Female
Percent	36.1%	63.9%
Effect on Earnings	13.3%	−9.6%

Union Membership

Percentage Union Members: 5.1%
Earnings Benefit of Union Membership: 5.4%

Veteran Status

Percentage Who Have Been on Active Duty: 10.2%
Earnings Benefit of Veteran Status: 14.9%

11-9033 Education Administrators, Postsecondary

Plan, direct, or coordinate research, instructional, student administration and services, and other educational activities at postsecondary institutions, including universities, colleges, and junior and community colleges.

- Education or Training Required: Work experience plus degree
- Job Growth: 21.3%
- Annual Openings: 18,000
- Self-Employed: 3.3%
- Part-Time: 16.9%

NATIONAL WAGE FIGURES (ANNUAL)

Beginning	25th Percentile	Median	Mean	75th Percentile	90th Percentile
$41,120	$53,800	$73,990	$82,820	$101,950	$137,900

Median Wages for Industries Employing Largest Numbers (Annual)

Industry	Median Income
Hospitals	$87,500
Professional, Scientific, and Technical Services	$86,600
Religious, Grantmaking, Civic, Professional, and Similar Organizations	$84,290
Federal, State, and Local Government	$79,060
Educational Services	$73,900
Management of Companies and Enterprises	$70,390

Median Wages for States (Annual)

State	Wage	State	Wage	State	Wage
AK	no data	KY	$65,070	NY	$86,900
AL	$65,120	LA	$64,630	OH	$81,150
AR	$69,250	MA	$82,190	OK	$56,470
AZ	$84,030	MD	$82,110	OR	$73,260
CA	$83,260	ME	$54,940	PA	$71,790
CO	$71,870	MI	$78,070	RI	$83,030
CT	$91,030	MN	$74,190	SC	$63,720
DC	$66,200	MO	$69,660	SD	$72,500
DE	$77,820	MS	$73,710	TN	$65,740
FL	$73,000	MT	no data	TX	$75,490
GA	$69,570	NC	$64,590	UT	$70,790
HI	$84,680	ND	$59,320	VA	$76,840
IA	$62,730	NE	$56,130	VT	$74,180
ID	$71,860	NH	$65,680	WA	$72,940
IL	$61,770	NJ	$83,610	WI	$64,100
IN	$57,120	NM	$71,040	WV	$60,010
KS	$77,200	NV	$85,850	WY	$77,140

Median Wages for the Largest Metropolitan Areas (Annual)

Area	Wage	Area	Wage
AZ: Phoenix	$93,730	MI: Detroit	$83,350
CA: Los Angeles	$82,160	MN: Minneapolis	$73,550
CA: Riverside	$85,600	MO: Kansas City	$77,760
CA: Sacramento	$95,420	MO: St. Louis	$63,390
CA: San Diego	$59,100	NV: Las Vegas	$68,810
CA: San Francisco	$85,950	NY: New York	$87,640
CO: Denver	$72,140	OH: Cincinnati	$85,500
DC: Washington	$81,270	OH: Cleveland	$80,350
FL: Miami	$78,460	OH: Columbus	$97,290
FL: Orlando	$72,110	OR: Portland	$69,660
FL: Tampa	$77,530	PA: Philadelphia	$81,080
GA: Atlanta	$69,930	PA: Pittsburgh	$60,480
IL: Chicago	$64,400	TX: Dallas	$79,090
MA: Boston	$85,130	TX: Houston	$86,290
MD: Baltimore	$78,780	WA: Seattle	$74,100

FACTORS THAT MAY AFFECT EARNINGS

Educational Attainment of Workers and Effect on Earnings

Figures are based on a group of occupations: Other Management Occupations

	Percent at Level	Effect on Earnings
Less than High School	1.6%	−39.8%
Some High School	4.8%	−34.7%
High School or Equivalent	18.8%	−16.4%
Some College but No Degree	18.1%	−13.0%
Associate Degree	12.6%	−8.5%
Bachelor's Degree	22.0%	8.5%
Master's Degree	14.9%	26.1%
Doctoral Degree	4.0%	47.7%
First Professional Degree	3.1%	37.6%

Flexibility of Earnings

Average Hours Worked: 37

Workers with a Varying Number of Hours: 14.3%

Workers Earning Some Overtime Pay, Tips, or Commissions: 8.9%

Earnings Benefit of Working Overtime: −0.6%

Gender

	Male	Female
Percent	36.1%	63.9%
Effect on Earnings	13.3%	−9.6%

Union Membership

Percentage Union Members: 5.1%

Earnings Benefit of Union Membership: 5.4%

Veteran Status

Percentage Who Have Been on Active Duty: 10.2%

Earnings Benefit of Veteran Status: 14.9%

11-9039 Education Administrators, All Other

All education administrators not listed separately.

- Education or Training Required: Work experience plus degree
- Job Growth: 20.3%
- Annual Openings: 4,000
- Self-Employed: 3.3%
- Part-Time: 16.9%

NATIONAL WAGE FIGURES (ANNUAL)

Beginning	25th Percentile	Median	Mean	75th Percentile	90th Percentile
$36,580	$49,520	$66,620	$71,520	$88,590	$114,500

Median Wages for Industries Employing Largest Numbers (Annual)

Industry	Median Income
Ambulatory Health Care Services	$89,540
Professional, Scientific, and Technical Services	$87,650
Hospitals	$78,310
Religious, Grantmaking, Civic, Professional, and Similar Organizations	$73,820
Federal, State, and Local Government	$72,630
Amusement, Gambling, and Recreation Industries	$67,760
Management of Companies and Enterprises	$67,280
Administrative and Support Services	$65,750
Educational Services	$63,620
Museums, Historical Sites, and Similar Institutions	$60,410

Median Wages for States (Annual)

AK	$57,370	KY	$55,670	NY	$84,300
AL	$64,440	LA	no data	OH	$73,500
AR	$68,690	MA	$71,910	OK	$58,470
AZ	$59,200	MD	$87,040	OR	$55,080
CA	$69,840	ME	$39,060	PA	$60,410
CO	$65,530	MI	$72,410	RI	$78,900
CT	$72,470	MN	$60,900	SC	$57,540
DC	$96,040	MO	$61,630	SD	$60,600
DE	$67,260	MS	$72,780	TN	$52,900
FL	$70,810	MT	$52,170	TX	$50,380
GA	$72,560	NC	$53,410	UT	$63,590
HI	$65,890	ND	$56,450	VA	$87,070
IA	$55,460	NE	$44,340	VT	$52,560
ID	$68,090	NH	$62,250	WA	$52,400
IL	$71,610	NJ	$56,020	WI	$59,920
IN	$54,800	NM	$56,980	WV	$77,270
KS	$73,350	NV	$71,560	WY	no data

Median Wages for the Largest Metropolitan Areas (Annual)

AZ: Phoenix	$68,120	MI: Detroit	$95,040
CA: Los Angeles	$69,480	MN: Minneapolis	$66,240
CA: Riverside	$53,280	MO: Kansas City	$69,550
CA: Sacramento	$75,850	MO: St. Louis	$66,060
CA: San Diego	$57,680	NV: Las Vegas	$70,940
CA: San Francisco	$79,840	NY: New York	$76,770
CO: Denver	$56,010	OH: Cincinnati	$43,910
DC: Washington	$91,150	OH: Cleveland	$79,000
FL: Miami	$67,660	OH: Columbus	$80,690
FL: Orlando	$69,230	OR: Portland	$68,780
FL: Tampa	$73,040	PA: Philadelphia	$66,390
GA: Atlanta	$83,640	PA: Pittsburgh	$55,100
IL: Chicago	$69,260	TX: Dallas	$46,750
MA: Boston	$79,080	TX: Houston	$60,540
MD: Baltimore	$84,990	WA: Seattle	$51,930

FACTORS THAT MAY AFFECT EARNINGS

Educational Attainment of Workers and Effect on Earnings

Figures are based on a group of occupations: Other Management Occupations

	Percent at Level	Effect on Earnings
Less than High School	1.6%	–39.8%
Some High School	4.8%	–34.7%
High School or Equivalent	18.8%	–16.4%
Some College but No Degree	18.1%	–13.0%
Associate Degree	12.6%	–8.5%
Bachelor's Degree	22.0%	8.5%
Master's Degree	14.9%	26.1%
Doctoral Degree	4.0%	47.7%
First Professional Degree	3.1%	37.6%

Flexibility of Earnings

Average Hours Worked: 37
Workers with a Varying Number of Hours: 14.3%
Workers Earning Some Overtime Pay, Tips, or Commissions: 8.9%
Earnings Benefit of Working Overtime: –0.6%

Gender

	Male	Female
Percent	36.1%	63.9%
Effect on Earnings	13.3%	–9.6%

Union Membership

Percentage Union Members: 5.1%
Earnings Benefit of Union Membership: 5.4%

Veteran Status

Percentage Who Have Been on Active Duty: 10.2%
Earnings Benefit of Veteran Status: 14.9%

11-9041 Engineering Managers

Plan, direct, or coordinate activities in such fields as architecture and engineering or research and development in these fields.

- Education or Training Required: Work experience plus degree
- Job Growth: 13.0%
- Annual Openings: 15,000
- Self-Employed: 0.5%
- Part-Time: 2.9%

NATIONAL WAGE FIGURES (ANNUAL)

Beginning	25th Percentile	Median	Mean	75th Percentile	90th Percentile
$67,470	$84,090	$105,430	$110,030	$130,170	more than $145,600

Median Wages for Industries Employing Largest Numbers (Annual)

Industry	Median Income
Oil and Gas Extraction	$123,400
Computer and Electronic Product Manufacturing	$118,720
Petroleum and Coal Products Manufacturing	$116,990
Merchant Wholesalers, Durable Goods	$109,850
Management of Companies and Enterprises	$109,420
Professional, Scientific, and Technical Services	$108,260
Transportation Equipment Manufacturing	$106,870
Federal, State, and Local Government	$104,460
Telecommunications	$103,470
Administrative and Support Services	$103,000

Median Wages for States (Annual)

AK	$99,440	KY	$88,190	NY	$112,360
AL	$93,750	LA	$105,100	OH	$92,760
AR	$85,510	MA	$118,120	OK	$88,300
AZ	$108,220	MD	$110,470	OR	no data
CA	$118,490	ME	$90,390	PA	$96,090
CO	$109,780	MI	$102,730	RI	$99,120
CT	$102,850	MN	$101,350	SC	$92,070
DC	$116,450	MO	$92,950	SD	$92,320
DE	$113,480	MS	$105,340	TN	$79,820
FL	$100,350	MT	$72,920	TX	$113,210
GA	$91,150	NC	$95,090	UT	$94,210
HI	$101,930	ND	$85,120	VA	$113,750
IA	$84,790	NE	$91,970	VT	$124,210
ID	$98,370	NH	$104,620	WA	$116,690
IL	$93,300	NJ	$118,550	WI	$90,260
IN	$85,060	NM	$116,050	WV	$92,850
KS	$97,250	NV	$103,280	WY	$80,870

Median Wages for the Largest Metropolitan Areas (Annual)

AZ: Phoenix	$109,410	MI: Detroit	$109,140
CA: Los Angeles	$111,760	MN: Minneapolis	$104,470
CA: Riverside	$96,020	MO: Kansas City	$98,700
CA: Sacramento	$112,330	MO: St. Louis	no data
CA: San Diego	$111,840	NV: Las Vegas	$114,030
CA: San Francisco	$120,710	NY: New York	$119,620
CO: Denver	$109,980	OH: Cincinnati	$103,690
DC: Washington	$120,410	OH: Cleveland	$94,420
FL: Miami	$101,910	OH: Columbus	$85,700
FL: Orlando	$93,760	OR: Portland	no data
FL: Tampa	$99,100	PA: Philadelphia	$111,800
GA: Atlanta	$92,540	PA: Pittsburgh	$89,950
IL: Chicago	$95,630	TX: Dallas	$114,710
MA: Boston	$121,460	TX: Houston	$117,330
MD: Baltimore	$105,370	WA: Seattle	$120,630

FACTORS THAT MAY AFFECT EARNINGS

Educational Attainment of Workers and Effect on Earnings

	Percent at Level	Effect on Earnings
Less than High School	—	—
Some High School	—	—
High School or Equivalent	10.2%	−24.2%
Some College but No Degree	11.2%	−9.9%
Associate Degree	—	—
Bachelor's Degree	41.8%	2.9%
Master's Degree	27.6%	9.6%
Doctoral Degree	—	—
First Professional Degree	—	—

Figures do not total 100% because some levels have a very small sample size.

Flexibility of Earnings

Average Hours Worked: 42
Workers with a Varying Number of Hours: 5.7%
Workers Earning Some Overtime Pay, Tips, or Commissions: 6.3%
Earnings Benefit of Working Overtime: −23.4%

Gender

	Male	Female
Percent	92.7%	7.3%
Effect on Earnings	2.6%	—

Union Membership

Percentage Union Members: Insignificant
Earnings Benefit of Union Membership: No significant data available

Veteran Status

Percentage Who Have Been on Active Duty: 10.2%
Earnings Benefit of Veteran Status: 14.9%

11-9051 Food Service Managers

Plan, direct, or coordinate activities of an organization or department that serves food and beverages.

- Education or Training Required: Work experience in a related occupation
- Job Growth: 11.5%
- Annual Openings: 61,000
- Self-Employed: 40.5%
- Part-Time: 11.4%

Note: A large fraction of the workforce for this occupation is self-employed and earns an average of $50,200. All other earnings figures for this occupation are based on workers who are paid a wage or salary.

NATIONAL WAGE FIGURES (ANNUAL)

Beginning	25th Percentile	Median	Mean	75th Percentile	90th Percentile
$27,400	$34,210	$43,020	$46,780	$55,100	$70,810

Median Wages for Industries Employing Largest Numbers (Annual)

Industry	Median Income
Air Transportation	$72,840
Ambulatory Health Care Services	$63,660
Hospitals	$58,830
Food Manufacturing	$55,460
Management of Companies and Enterprises	$52,850
Religious, Grantmaking, Civic, Professional, and Similar Organizations	$52,820
Professional, Scientific, and Technical Services	$51,980
Nonstore Retailers	$49,240
Museums, Historical Sites, and Similar Institutions	$49,210
Real Estate	$49,150

Median Wages for States (Annual)

State	Wage	State	Wage	State	Wage
AK	$30,590	KY	$35,890	NY	$46,210
AL	$38,080	LA	$37,610	OH	$40,390
AR	$36,810	MA	$46,310	OK	$32,510
AZ	$40,560	MD	$46,680	OR	$43,100
CA	$43,600	ME	$40,490	PA	$46,360
CO	$44,330	MI	$41,040	RI	$54,690
CT	$47,590	MN	$38,600	SC	$40,560
DC	$43,670	MO	$52,310	SD	$41,670
DE	$59,990	MS	$36,550	TN	$32,970
FL	$50,860	MT	$30,780	TX	$46,760
GA	$45,600	NC	$44,280	UT	$43,080
HI	$43,990	ND	$45,320	VA	$44,960
IA	$39,090	NE	$40,460	VT	$49,120
ID	$29,440	NH	$43,700	WA	$67,270
IL	$39,270	NJ	$58,840	WI	$38,190
IN	$39,020	NM	$40,560	WV	$34,570
KS	$38,590	NV	$47,090	WY	$36,510

Median Wages for the Largest Metropolitan Areas (Annual)

Area	Wage	Area	Wage
AZ: Phoenix	$41,430	MI: Detroit	$45,090
CA: Los Angeles	$43,790	MN: Minneapolis	$40,450
CA: Riverside	$43,070	MO: Kansas City	$49,640
CA: Sacramento	$42,280	MO: St. Louis	$47,240
CA: San Diego	$43,700	NV: Las Vegas	$47,060
CA: San Francisco	$46,210	NY: New York	$53,870
CO: Denver	$47,450	OH: Cincinnati	$41,290
DC: Washington	$47,390	OH: Cleveland	$39,450
FL: Miami	$52,130	OH: Columbus	$44,200
FL: Orlando	$48,890	OR: Portland	$44,260
FL: Tampa	$53,930	PA: Philadelphia	$58,030
GA: Atlanta	$47,130	PA: Pittsburgh	$46,090
IL: Chicago	$43,080	TX: Dallas	$50,010
MA: Boston	$48,230	TX: Houston	$49,140
MD: Baltimore	$49,040	WA: Seattle	$72,120

FACTORS THAT MAY AFFECT EARNINGS

Educational Attainment of Workers and Effect on Earnings

	Percent at Level	Effect on Earnings
Less than High School	2.2%	−4.0%
Some High School	9.5%	−36.1%
High School or Equivalent	31.8%	−6.4%
Some College but No Degree	23.0%	−2.3%
Associate Degree	12.5%	−4.1%
Bachelor's Degree	17.2%	29.9%
Master's Degree	3.4%	27.0%
Doctoral Degree	—	—
First Professional Degree	—	—

Flexibility of Earnings

Average Hours Worked: 39
Workers with a Varying Number of Hours: 11.4%
Workers Earning Some Overtime Pay, Tips, or Commissions: 13.7%
Earnings Benefit of Working Overtime: −0.3%

Gender

	Male	Female
Percent	56.8%	43.2%
Effect on Earnings	15.0%	−14.1%

Union Membership

Percentage Union Members: Insignificant
Earnings Benefit of Union Membership: No significant data available

Veteran Status

Percentage Who Have Been on Active Duty: 10.2%
Earnings Benefit of Veteran Status: 14.9%

11-9061 Funeral Directors

Perform various tasks to arrange and direct funeral services, such as coordinating transportation of body to mortuary for embalming, interviewing family or other authorized person to arrange details, selecting pallbearers, procuring official for religious rites, and providing transportation for mourners.

- Education or Training Required: Associate degree
- Job Growth: 6.7%
- Annual Openings: 3,000
- Self-Employed: 19.7%
- Part-Time: 7.1%

NATIONAL WAGE FIGURES (ANNUAL)

Beginning	25th Percentile	Median	Mean	75th Percentile	90th Percentile
$28,410	$37,200	$49,620	$57,250	$65,260	$91,800

Median Wages for Industries Employing Largest Numbers (Annual)

Industry	Median Income
Federal, State, and Local Government	$60,250
Personal and Laundry Services	$49,130

Median Wages for States (Annual)

AK	no data	KY	$43,140	NY	$59,070
AL	$37,620	LA	$36,290	OH	$54,140
AR	$33,980	MA	no data	OK	$47,560
AZ	$39,820	MD	$57,850	OR	$49,800
CA	$52,170	ME	$41,830	PA	$53,430
CO	$45,720	MI	$55,310	RI	$65,710
CT	$65,840	MN	$52,440	SC	$44,720
DC	$57,660	MO	$43,770	SD	$50,520
DE	$67,240	MS	$28,490	TN	$32,450
FL	$45,580	MT	$44,400	TX	$39,490
GA	$54,030	NC	$45,550	UT	$59,990
HI	no data	ND	$60,650	VA	$69,340
IA	$53,870	NE	$48,210	VT	$52,190
ID	$45,240	NH	$47,890	WA	$60,330
IL	$57,960	NJ	$64,830	WI	$49,100
IN	$45,780	NM	$43,200	WV	$51,240
KS	$44,420	NV	$60,180	WY	$43,130

Median Wages for the Largest Metropolitan Areas (Annual)

AZ: Phoenix	$43,490	MI: Detroit	$56,590
CA: Los Angeles	$49,310	MN: Minneapolis	$54,460
CA: Riverside	$52,200	MO: Kansas City	$54,170
CA: Sacramento	no data	MO: St. Louis	$50,350
CA: San Diego	$44,660	NV: Las Vegas	$62,030
CA: San Francisco	$63,180	NY: New York	$60,210
CO: Denver	$42,960	OH: Cincinnati	$49,970
DC: Washington	$57,330	OH: Cleveland	$55,890
FL: Miami	$44,480	OH: Columbus	$38,410
FL: Orlando	$48,390	OR: Portland	$51,600
FL: Tampa	$47,840	PA: Philadelphia	$57,900
GA: Atlanta	$49,960	PA: Pittsburgh	$46,990
IL: Chicago	$58,930	TX: Dallas	$41,490
MA: Boston	$64,220	TX: Houston	$37,740
MD: Baltimore	$61,500	WA: Seattle	no data

FACTORS THAT MAY AFFECT EARNINGS

Educational Attainment of Workers and Effect on Earnings

	Percent at Level	Effect on Earnings
Less than High School	—	—
Some High School	—	—
High School or Equivalent	—	—
Some College but No Degree	18.9%	−12.6%
Associate Degree	29.7%	−18.3%
Bachelor's Degree	35.1%	19.0%
Master's Degree	—	—
Doctoral Degree	—	—
First Professional Degree	—	—

Figures do not total 100% because some levels have a very small sample size.

Flexibility of Earnings

Average Hours Worked: 37
Workers with a Varying Number of Hours: 15.7%
Workers Earning Some Overtime Pay, Tips, or Commissions: 9.3%
Earnings Benefit of Working Overtime: −8.3%

Gender

	Male	Female
Percent	83.5%	16.5%
Effect on Earnings	12.2%	−17.8%

Union Membership

Percentage Union Members: Insignificant
Earnings Benefit of Union Membership: No significant data available

Veteran Status

Percentage Who Have Been on Active Duty: 10.2%
Earnings Benefit of Veteran Status: 14.9%

11-9071 Gaming Managers

Plan, organize, direct, control, or coordinate gaming operations in a casino. Formulate gaming policies for their area of responsibility.

- Education or Training Required: Work experience in a related occupation
- Job Growth: 22.6%
- Annual Openings: 1,000
- Self-Employed: 4.0%
- Part-Time: 14.3%

NATIONAL WAGE FIGURES (ANNUAL)

Beginning	25th Percentile	Median	Mean	75th Percentile	90th Percentile
$35,100	$46,520	$62,820	$67,340	$81,770	$104,070

Median Wages for Industries Employing Largest Numbers (Annual)

Industry	Median Income
Accommodation	$74,140
Federal, State, and Local Government	$62,250
Amusement, Gambling, and Recreation Industries	$57,500
Performing Arts, Spectator Sports, and Related Industries	$57,280

Median Wages for States (Annual)

State		State		State	
AK	no data	KY	no data	NY	no data
AL	no data	LA	$66,450	OH	no data
AR	no data	MA	no data	OK	$36,970
AZ	$64,900	MD	no data	OR	$52,710
CA	$71,670	ME	no data	PA	no data
CO	no data	MI	no data	RI	no data
CT	no data	MN	$58,740	SC	no data
DC	no data	MO	$53,600	SD	$56,620
DE	no data	MS	$70,300	TN	no data
FL	no data	MT	$33,340	TX	no data
GA	no data	NC	no data	UT	no data
HI	no data	ND	no data	VA	no data
IA	$56,080	NE	no data	VT	no data
ID	$44,890	NH	no data	WA	$70,870
IL	$64,110	NJ	$74,140	WI	no data
IN	$63,950	NM	$55,010	WV	no data
KS	no data	NV	$70,880	WY	no data

Median Wages for the Largest Metropolitan Areas (Annual)

Area		Area	
AZ: Phoenix	$69,630	MI: Detroit	no data
CA: Los Angeles	$82,750	MN: Minneapolis	no data
CA: Riverside	$68,700	MO: Kansas City	$55,000
CA: Sacramento	no data	MO: St. Louis	$49,900
CA: San Diego	$79,520	NV: Las Vegas	$75,300
CA: San Francisco	$47,670	NY: New York	no data
CO: Denver	no data	OH: Cincinnati	no data
DC: Washington	no data	OH: Cleveland	no data
FL: Miami	no data	OH: Columbus	no data
FL: Orlando	no data	OR: Portland	no data
FL: Tampa	no data	PA: Philadelphia	no data
GA: Atlanta	no data	PA: Pittsburgh	no data
IL: Chicago	$65,360	TX: Dallas	no data
MA: Boston	no data	TX: Houston	no data
MD: Baltimore	no data	WA: Seattle	$76,050

FACTORS THAT MAY AFFECT EARNINGS

Educational Attainment of Workers and Effect on Earnings

	Percent at Level	Effect on Earnings
Less than High School	—	—
Some High School	—	—
High School or Equivalent	27.3%	−24.7%
Some College but No Degree	40.9%	−8.6%
Associate Degree	—	—
Bachelor's Degree	—	—
Master's Degree	—	—
Doctoral Degree	—	—
First Professional Degree	—	—

Figures do not total 100% because some levels have a very small sample size.

Flexibility of Earnings

Average Hours Worked: 32
Workers with a Varying Number of Hours: 14.6%
Workers Earning Some Overtime Pay, Tips, or Commissions: 8.7%
Earnings Benefit of Working Overtime: −8.3%

Gender

	Male	Female
Percent	58.6%	41.4%
Effect on Earnings	12.2%	−17.8%

Union Membership

Percentage Union Members: 5.1%
Earnings Benefit of Union Membership: 5.4%

Veteran Status

Percentage Who Have Been on Active Duty: 10.2%
Earnings Benefit of Veteran Status: 14.9%

11-9081 Lodging Managers

Plan, direct, or coordinate activities of an organization or department that provides lodging and other accommodations.

- Education or Training Required: Work experience in a related occupation
- Job Growth: 16.6%
- Annual Openings: 10,000
- Self-Employed: 40.2%
- Part-Time: 19.2%

Note: A large fraction of the workforce for this occupation is self-employed and earns an average of $52,840. All other earnings figures for this occupation are based on workers who are paid a wage or salary.

NATIONAL WAGE FIGURES (ANNUAL)

Beginning	25th Percentile	Median	Mean	75th Percentile	90th Percentile
$25,120	$31,870	$42,320	$49,560	$58,380	$82,510

Median Wages for Industries Employing Largest Numbers (Annual)

Industry	Median Income
Management of Companies and Enterprises	$71,710
Hospitals	$55,180
Heavy and Civil Engineering Construction	$50,410
Amusement, Gambling, and Recreation Industries	$50,030
Food Services and Drinking Places	$49,810
Social Assistance	$48,540
Federal, State, and Local Government	$47,810
Educational Services	$47,780
Nursing and Residential Care Facilities	$42,720
Accommodation	$41,830

Median Wages for States (Annual)

State	Wage	State	Wage	State	Wage
AK	$38,350	KY	$38,700	NY	$56,090
AL	$33,750	LA	$32,820	OH	$41,590
AR	$31,210	MA	$46,550	OK	no data
AZ	$37,710	MD	$42,850	OR	$38,540
CA	$43,720	ME	$43,400	PA	$43,610
CO	$42,730	MI	$45,880	RI	$53,050
CT	$51,930	MN	$38,840	SC	$36,980
DC	$63,910	MO	$44,070	SD	$40,530
DE	$48,360	MS	$36,280	TN	$34,000
FL	$49,260	MT	$31,230	TX	$47,710
GA	$46,810	NC	$38,470	UT	$46,380
HI	$46,960	ND	$40,410	VA	$50,160
IA	$33,270	NE	$33,700	VT	$62,180
ID	$27,530	NH	$43,220	WA	$76,090
IL	$47,290	NJ	$60,210	WI	$39,820
IN	$37,400	NM	$35,130	WV	$33,660
KS	$39,100	NV	$48,480	WY	$34,350

Median Wages for the Largest Metropolitan Areas (Annual)

Area	Wage	Area	Wage
AZ: Phoenix	$47,000	MI: Detroit	$48,750
CA: Los Angeles	$45,090	MN: Minneapolis	$42,010
CA: Riverside	$37,960	MO: Kansas City	$46,360
CA: Sacramento	$45,030	MO: St. Louis	$49,190
CA: San Diego	$46,170	NV: Las Vegas	$51,440
CA: San Francisco	$45,490	NY: New York	$68,410
CO: Denver	$53,150	OH: Cincinnati	$43,720
DC: Washington	$60,220	OH: Cleveland	$48,690
FL: Miami	$49,690	OH: Columbus	$46,300
FL: Orlando	$53,870	OR: Portland	$42,960
FL: Tampa	$46,530	PA: Philadelphia	$54,690
GA: Atlanta	$56,550	PA: Pittsburgh	$39,090
IL: Chicago	$50,670	TX: Dallas	$48,590
MA: Boston	$50,720	TX: Houston	$52,740
MD: Baltimore	$38,890	WA: Seattle	$77,550

FACTORS THAT MAY AFFECT EARNINGS

Educational Attainment of Workers and Effect on Earnings

	Percent at Level	Effect on Earnings
Less than High School	—	—
Some High School	4.1%	−48.1%
High School or Equivalent	27.2%	−9.7%
Some College but No Degree	22.4%	−7.0%
Associate Degree	6.1%	−6.9%
Bachelor's Degree	27.2%	18.8%
Master's Degree	9.5%	11.7%
Doctoral Degree	—	—
First Professional Degree	—	—

Flexibility of Earnings

Average Hours Worked: 38
Workers with a Varying Number of Hours: 15.3%
Workers Earning Some Overtime Pay, Tips, or Commissions: 9.9%
Earnings Benefit of Working Overtime: 4.6%

Gender

	Male	Female
Percent	49.0%	51.0%
Effect on Earnings	3.2%	−7.8%

Union Membership

Percentage Union Members: Insignificant
Earnings Benefit of Union Membership: No significant data available

Veteran Status

Percentage Who Have Been on Active Duty: 10.2%
Earnings Benefit of Veteran Status: 14.9%

11-9111 Medical and Health Services Managers

Plan, direct, or coordinate medicine and health services in hospitals, clinics, managed care organizations, public health agencies, or similar organizations.

- Education or Training Required: Work experience plus degree
- Job Growth: 22.8%
- Annual Openings: 33,000
- Self-Employed: 5.7%
- Part-Time: 11.4%

NATIONAL WAGE FIGURES (ANNUAL)

Beginning	25th Percentile	Median	Mean	75th Percentile	90th Percentile
$45,050	$57,240	$73,340	$81,160	$94,780	$127,830

Median Wages for Industries Employing Largest Numbers (Annual)

Industry	Median Income
Transportation Equipment Manufacturing	$117,940
Food and Beverage Stores	$105,590
Computer and Electronic Product Manufacturing	$98,710
Wholesale Electronic Markets and Agents and Brokers	$94,590
Professional, Scientific, and Technical Services	$93,250
Miscellaneous Manufacturing	$92,580
Nonstore Retailers	$90,960
Funds, Trusts, and Other Financial Vehicles	$89,170
Merchant Wholesalers, Nondurable Goods	$87,780
Health and Personal Care Stores	$86,570

Median Wages for States (Annual)

State	Wage	State	Wage	State	Wage
AK	$78,320	KY	$66,590	NY	$85,130
AL	$70,530	LA	$59,110	OH	$68,870
AR	$62,190	MA	$86,210	OK	$60,730
AZ	$62,740	MD	$79,260	OR	$76,290
CA	$88,610	ME	$65,780	PA	$67,900
CO	$75,030	MI	$72,170	RI	$80,850
CT	$83,270	MN	$78,320	SC	$63,270
DC	$74,600	MO	$68,790	SD	$66,540
DE	$72,110	MS	$62,940	TN	$64,450
FL	$78,050	MT	$64,400	TX	$68,720
GA	$67,190	NC	$70,080	UT	$71,700
HI	$84,480	ND	$61,140	VA	$74,570
IA	$59,790	NE	$65,320	VT	$76,630
ID	$62,280	NH	$75,790	WA	$97,710
IL	$67,460	NJ	$90,360	WI	$74,100
IN	$65,490	NM	$67,330	WV	$58,900
KS	$62,180	NV	$75,000	WY	$66,060

Median Wages for the Largest Metropolitan Areas (Annual)

Area	Wage	Area	Wage
AZ: Phoenix	$61,570	MI: Detroit	$74,960
CA: Los Angeles	$90,430	MN: Minneapolis	$82,630
CA: Riverside	$81,630	MO: Kansas City	$68,850
CA: Sacramento	$94,990	MO: St. Louis	$71,620
CA: San Diego	$87,270	NV: Las Vegas	$73,010
CA: San Francisco	$100,150	NY: New York	$91,300
CO: Denver	$79,740	OH: Cincinnati	$69,870
DC: Washington	$82,220	OH: Cleveland	$71,080
FL: Miami	$81,950	OH: Columbus	$70,390
FL: Orlando	$76,000	OR: Portland	$84,120
FL: Tampa	$78,080	PA: Philadelphia	$76,040
GA: Atlanta	$67,650	PA: Pittsburgh	$68,990
IL: Chicago	$71,550	TX: Dallas	$67,410
MA: Boston	$89,730	TX: Houston	$77,120
MD: Baltimore	$75,500	WA: Seattle	$99,710

FACTORS THAT MAY AFFECT EARNINGS

Educational Attainment of Workers and Effect on Earnings

	Percent at Level	Effect on Earnings
Less than High School	—	—
Some High School	—	—
High School or Equivalent	11.7%	−28.7%
Some College but No Degree	15.1%	−20.8%
Associate Degree	17.4%	−21.7%
Bachelor's Degree	27.2%	9.5%
Master's Degree	21.4%	23.9%
Doctoral Degree	4.2%	47.9%
First Professional Degree	3.0%	18.4%

Flexibility of Earnings

Average Hours Worked: 40
Workers with a Varying Number of Hours: 6.0%
Workers Earning Some Overtime Pay, Tips, or Commissions: 8.8%
Earnings Benefit of Working Overtime: −0.7%

Gender

	Male	Female
Percent	31.7%	68.3%
Effect on Earnings	24.4%	−7.3%

Union Membership

Percentage Union Members: Insignificant
Earnings Benefit of Union Membership: No significant data available

Veteran Status

Percentage Who Have Been on Active Duty: 10.2%
Earnings Benefit of Veteran Status: 14.9%

11-9121 Natural Sciences Managers

Plan, direct, or coordinate activities in such fields as life sciences, physical sciences, mathematics, and statistics and research and development in these fields.

- Education or Training Required: Work experience plus degree
- Job Growth: 13.6%
- Annual Openings: 5,000
- Self-Employed: 0.0%
- Part-Time: 16.9%

NATIONAL WAGE FIGURES (ANNUAL)

Beginning	25th Percentile	Median	Mean	75th Percentile	90th Percentile
$60,300	$77,320	$100,080	$107,970	$130,900	more than $145,600

Median Wages for Industries Employing Largest Numbers (Annual)

Industry	Median Income
Merchant Wholesalers, Nondurable Goods	$125,620
Insurance Carriers and Related Activities	$124,440
Management of Companies and Enterprises	$121,500
Internet Service Providers, Web Search Portals, and Data-Processing Services	$120,380
Oil and Gas Extraction	$113,580
Computer and Electronic Product Manufacturing	$113,130
Professional, Scientific, and Technical Services	$112,550
Chemical Manufacturing	$109,390
Food Manufacturing	$107,060
Miscellaneous Manufacturing	$106,440

Median Wages for States (Annual)

State	Wage	State	Wage	State	Wage
AK	$85,140	KY	$75,630	NY	$106,120
AL	$96,270	LA	$80,170	OH	$87,230
AR	$84,700	MA	$130,710	OK	$85,360
AZ	$79,420	MD	$104,170	OR	$90,050
CA	$119,050	ME	$74,410	PA	$105,160
CO	$104,960	MI	$90,120	RI	no data
CT	$93,790	MN	$99,030	SC	$90,750
DC	$111,710	MO	$91,090	SD	$81,670
DE	no data	MS	$86,450	TN	$79,710
FL	$86,570	MT	$75,470	TX	$100,280
GA	$92,360	NC	$104,840	UT	$80,770
HI	$95,930	ND	$76,620	VA	$110,980
IA	$92,270	NE	$88,780	VT	$83,930
ID	$80,750	NH	$82,020	WA	$106,980
IL	$89,030	NJ	$127,310	WI	$86,530
IN	no data	NM	$73,920	WV	$87,190
KS	$92,210	NV	$71,790	WY	$67,990

Median Wages for the Largest Metropolitan Areas (Annual)

Area	Wage	Area	Wage
AZ: Phoenix	$75,020	MI: Detroit	$108,660
CA: Los Angeles	$107,820	MN: Minneapolis	$102,310
CA: Riverside	$95,800	MO: Kansas City	$94,900
CA: Sacramento	$94,170	MO: St. Louis	$101,120
CA: San Diego	$130,780	NV: Las Vegas	$73,890
CA: San Francisco	$132,260	NY: New York	$130,090
CO: Denver	$102,130	OH: Cincinnati	$97,550
DC: Washington	$110,870	OH: Cleveland	$81,000
FL: Miami	$93,730	OH: Columbus	$93,720
FL: Orlando	$107,010	OR: Portland	$94,780
FL: Tampa	$75,300	PA: Philadelphia	$118,890
GA: Atlanta	$94,810	PA: Pittsburgh	$97,360
IL: Chicago	$89,240	TX: Dallas	$105,180
MA: Boston	$137,250	TX: Houston	$101,590
MD: Baltimore	$89,370	WA: Seattle	$113,630

FACTORS THAT MAY AFFECT EARNINGS

Educational Attainment of Workers and Effect on Earnings

	Percent at Level	Effect on Earnings
Less than High School	—	—
Some High School	—	—
High School or Equivalent	—	—
Some College but No Degree	—	—
Associate Degree	—	—
Bachelor's Degree	—	—
Master's Degree	56.3%	16.8%
Doctoral Degree	—	—
First Professional Degree	—	—

Figures do not total 100% because some levels have a very small sample size.

Flexibility of Earnings

Average Hours Worked: 41
Workers with a Varying Number of Hours: 14.3%
Workers Earning Some Overtime Pay, Tips, or Commissions: 5.3%
Earnings Benefit of Working Overtime: –8.3%

Gender

	Male	Female
Percent	61.3%	38.7%
Effect on Earnings	12.2%	–17.8%

Union Membership

Percentage Union Members: 10.5%
Earnings Benefit of Union Membership: 5.4%

Veteran Status

Percentage Who Have Been on Active Duty: 10.2%
Earnings Benefit of Veteran Status: 14.9%

11-9131 Postmasters and Mail Superintendents

Direct and coordinate operational, administrative, management, and supportive services of a U.S. post office or coordinate activities of workers engaged in postal and related work in assigned post office.

- Education or Training Required: Work experience in a related occupation
- Job Growth: 0.0%
- Annual Openings: 2,000
- Self-Employed: 0.0%
- Part-Time: 16.9%

NATIONAL WAGE FIGURES (ANNUAL)

Beginning	25th Percentile	Median	Mean	75th Percentile	90th Percentile
$38,230	$46,160	$55,790	$55,630	$64,230	$76,590

Median Wages for Industries Employing Largest Numbers (Annual)

Industry	Median Income
Postal Service	$55,790

Median Wages for States (Annual)

AK ... $43,060	KY ... $51,600	NY ... $57,200
AL ... $56,740	LA ... $57,340	OH ... $56,740
AR ... $51,590	MA ... $64,000	OK ... $53,530
AZ ... $58,030	MD ... $58,220	OR ... $55,800
CA ... $61,890	ME ... $53,940	PA ... $55,550
CO ... $54,290	MI ... $58,770	RI ... $61,380
CT ... $62,730	MN ... $55,510	SC ... $57,720
DC ... no data	MO ... $52,910	SD ... $48,950
DE ... $65,550	MS ... $56,490	TN ... $58,990
FL ... $65,140	MT ... $47,860	TX ... $56,640
GA ... $59,270	NC ... $57,950	UT ... $56,030
HI ... $61,730	ND ... $45,600	VA ... $54,940
IA ... $53,300	NE ... $52,360	VT ... $51,280
ID ... $54,100	NH ... $58,460	WA ... $57,160
IL ... $55,270	NJ ... $68,130	WI ... $57,290
IN ... $55,170	NM ... $47,260	WV ... $48,180
KS ... $51,950	NV ... $53,310	WY ... $49,280

Median Wages for the Largest Metropolitan Areas (Annual)

AZ: Phoenix	$66,460	MI: Detroit	$70,690
CA: Los Angeles	$82,020	MN: Minneapolis	$63,190
CA: Riverside	$67,910	MO: Kansas City	$56,770
CA: Sacramento	$62,590	MO: St. Louis	$57,640
CA: San Diego	$72,610	NV: Las Vegas	no data
CA: San Francisco	$69,380	NY: New York	$69,790
CO: Denver	$61,440	OH: Cincinnati	$60,270
DC: Washington	$60,270	OH: Cleveland	$62,790
FL: Miami	no data	OH: Columbus	$59,790
FL: Orlando	$68,290	OR: Portland	$65,910
FL: Tampa	$73,060	PA: Philadelphia	$62,640
GA: Atlanta	$67,720	PA: Pittsburgh	$56,350
IL: Chicago	$67,190	TX: Dallas	$66,880
MA: Boston	$67,770	TX: Houston	$66,060
MD: Baltimore	$63,690	WA: Seattle	$67,120

FACTORS THAT MAY AFFECT EARNINGS

Educational Attainment of Workers and Effect on Earnings

Figures are based on a group of occupations: Other Management Occupations

	Percent at Level	Effect on Earnings
Less than High School	1.6%	−39.8%
Some High School	4.8%	−34.7%
High School or Equivalent	18.8%	−16.4%
Some College but No Degree	18.1%	−13.0%
Associate Degree	12.6%	−8.5%
Bachelor's Degree	22.0%	8.5%
Master's Degree	14.9%	26.1%
Doctoral Degree	4.0%	47.7%
First Professional Degree	3.1%	37.6%

Flexibility of Earnings

Average Hours Worked: 37
Workers with a Varying Number of Hours: 14.3%
Workers Earning Some Overtime Pay, Tips, or Commissions: 8.9%
Earnings Benefit of Working Overtime: −8.3%

Gender

	Male	Female
Percent	61.3%	38.7%
Effect on Earnings	12.2%	−17.8%

Union Membership

Percentage Union Members: 5.1%
Earnings Benefit of Union Membership: 5.4%

Veteran Status

Percentage Who Have Been on Active Duty: 10.2%
Earnings Benefit of Veteran Status: 14.9%

11-9141 Property, Real Estate, and Community Association Managers

Plan, direct, or coordinate selling, buying, leasing, or governance activities of commercial, industrial, or residential real estate properties.

- Education or Training Required: Bachelor's degree
- Job Growth: 15.3%
- Annual Openings: 58,000
- Self-Employed: 48.2%
- Part-Time: 36.1%

Note: A large fraction of the workforce for this occupation is self-employed and earns an average of $88,850. All other earnings figures for this occupation are based on workers who are paid a wage or salary.

NATIONAL WAGE FIGURES (ANNUAL)

Beginning	25th Percentile	Median	Mean	75th Percentile	90th Percentile
$20,140	$28,700	$43,070	$52,290	$64,200	$95,170

Note: The mean is significantly higher than the median because of the presence of a few star earners.

Median Wages for Industries Employing Largest Numbers (Annual)

Industry	Median Income
Telecommunications	$82,870
Computer and Electronic Product Manufacturing	$79,040
Heavy and Civil Engineering Construction	$77,470
Utilities	$75,680
Management of Companies and Enterprises	$73,230
Hospitals	$72,750
Educational Services	$70,730
Support Activities for Mining	$69,130
Insurance Carriers and Related Activities	$66,850
Credit Intermediation and Related Activities	$65,910

Median Wages for States (Annual)

AK	$54,370	KY	$35,680	NY	$71,570
AL	$56,120	LA	$31,630	OH	$59,480
AR	$25,900	MA	$57,240	OK	$30,570
AZ	$45,710	MD	$61,290	OR	$36,590
CA	$34,660	ME	$45,960	PA	$48,790
CO	$48,650	MI	$47,100	RI	$46,630
CT	$52,340	MN	$45,880	SC	$42,980
DC	$69,600	MO	$56,910	SD	$27,560
DE	$62,650	MS	$29,060	TN	$36,880
FL	$49,860	MT	$25,860	TX	$34,150
GA	$48,560	NC	$55,240	UT	$46,610
HI	$38,040	ND	$41,030	VA	$70,560
IA	$39,740	NE	$55,600	VT	$36,600
ID	$23,210	NH	$49,850	WA	$51,710
IL	$51,070	NJ	$58,550	WI	no data
IN	$47,250	NM	$39,990	WV	$31,120
KS	$49,600	NV	$36,600	WY	$32,740

Median Wages for the Largest Metropolitan Areas (Annual)

AZ: Phoenix	$49,770	MI: Detroit	$50,440
CA: Los Angeles	$32,930	MN: Minneapolis	$48,660
CA: Riverside	$26,890	MO: Kansas City	$57,600
CA: Sacramento	$32,860	MO: St. Louis	$52,660
CA: San Diego	$37,990	NV: Las Vegas	$37,650
CA: San Francisco	$45,090	NY: New York	$70,190
CO: Denver	$58,310	OH: Cincinnati	$45,990
DC: Washington	$64,720	OH: Cleveland	$60,350
FL: Miami	$49,110	OH: Columbus	$63,640
FL: Orlando	$40,280	OR: Portland	$42,110
FL: Tampa	$49,980	PA: Philadelphia	$56,640
GA: Atlanta	$49,440	PA: Pittsburgh	$42,440
IL: Chicago	$52,170	TX: Dallas	$38,430
MA: Boston	$58,050	TX: Houston	$30,500
MD: Baltimore	$68,880	WA: Seattle	$52,450

FACTORS THAT MAY AFFECT EARNINGS

Educational Attainment of Workers and Effect on Earnings

	Percent at Level	Effect on Earnings
Less than High School	—	—
Some High School	6.6%	−31.7%
High School or Equivalent	23.3%	−21.0%
Some College but No Degree	24.9%	−4.7%
Associate Degree	8.0%	−16.8%
Bachelor's Degree	27.9%	21.8%
Master's Degree	7.2%	36.7%
Doctoral Degree	—	—
First Professional Degree	—	—

Flexibility of Earnings

Average Hours Worked: 32
Workers with a Varying Number of Hours: 15.3%
Workers Earning Some Overtime Pay, Tips, or Commissions: 9.5%
Earnings Benefit of Working Overtime: 16.4%

Gender

	Male	Female
Percent	48.7%	51.3%
Effect on Earnings	22.0%	−8.1%

Union Membership

Percentage Union Members: Insignificant
Earnings Benefit of Union Membership: No significant data available

Veteran Status

Percentage Who Have Been on Active Duty: 10.2%
Earnings Benefit of Veteran Status: 14.9%

11-9151 Social and Community Service Managers

Plan, organize, or coordinate the activities of a social service program or community outreach organization. Oversee the program or organization's budget and policies regarding participant involvement, program requirements, and benefits. Work may involve directing social workers, counselors, or probation officers.

- Education or Training Required: Bachelor's degree
- Job Growth: 25.5%
- Annual Openings: 17,000
- Self-Employed: 2.2%
- Part-Time: 19.2%

NATIONAL WAGE FIGURES (ANNUAL)

Beginning	25th Percentile	Median	Mean	75th Percentile	90th Percentile
$31,050	$39,240	$52,070	$56,090	$67,540	$88,600

Median Wages for Industries Employing Largest Numbers (Annual)

Industry	Median Income
Heavy and Civil Engineering Construction	$70,490
Insurance Carriers and Related Activities	$69,370
Hospitals	$59,840
Federal, State, and Local Government	$59,070
Educational Services	$58,570
Securities, Commodity Contracts, and Other Financial Investments and Related Activities	$57,470
Management of Companies and Enterprises	$54,160
Administrative and Support Services	$53,320
Professional, Scientific, and Technical Services	$52,310
Ambulatory Health Care Services	$51,610

Median Wages for States (Annual)

AK	$45,300	KY	$44,860	NY	$61,760
AL	$44,510	LA	$47,580	OH	$51,600
AR	$37,960	MA	$52,180	OK	$34,680
AZ	$45,220	MD	$56,630	OR	$49,830
CA	$56,520	ME	$47,700	PA	$55,850
CO	$51,190	MI	$51,230	RI	$54,900
CT	$53,710	MN	$56,710	SC	$38,950
DC	$60,570	MO	$38,910	SD	$52,100
DE	$59,040	MS	$32,500	TN	$41,990
FL	$56,710	MT	$35,620	TX	$43,720
GA	$53,440	NC	$46,360	UT	$50,380
HI	$52,550	ND	$48,170	VA	$66,120
IA	$42,970	NE	$47,530	VT	$55,360
ID	$41,530	NH	$49,970	WA	$79,650
IL	$43,010	NJ	$69,020	WI	$49,540
IN	$41,150	NM	$43,110	WV	$42,360
KS	$43,680	NV	$52,900	WY	$40,310

Median Wages for the Largest Metropolitan Areas (Annual)

AZ: Phoenix	$47,780	MI: Detroit	$53,580
CA: Los Angeles	$58,270	MN: Minneapolis	$58,170
CA: Riverside	$64,490	MO: Kansas City	$40,710
CA: Sacramento	$53,210	MO: St. Louis	$40,080
CA: San Diego	$56,440	NV: Las Vegas	$49,300
CA: San Francisco	$56,090	NY: New York	$68,490
CO: Denver	$52,970	OH: Cincinnati	$55,060
DC: Washington	$63,760	OH: Cleveland	$52,520
FL: Miami	$63,380	OH: Columbus	$52,440
FL: Orlando	$50,330	OR: Portland	$51,940
FL: Tampa	$54,020	PA: Philadelphia	no data
GA: Atlanta	$54,740	PA: Pittsburgh	$46,890
IL: Chicago	$45,750	TX: Dallas	$51,000
MA: Boston	$54,480	TX: Houston	$46,320
MD: Baltimore	$56,640	WA: Seattle	$85,430

FACTORS THAT MAY AFFECT EARNINGS

Educational Attainment of Workers and Effect on Earnings

	Percent at Level	Effect on Earnings
Less than High School	—	—
Some High School	2.1%	−49.4%
High School or Equivalent	11.1%	−23.6%
Some College but No Degree	15.0%	−17.1%
Associate Degree	7.4%	−6.5%
Bachelor's Degree	35.0%	0.0%
Master's Degree	22.9%	20.4%
Doctoral Degree	4.2%	58.0%
First Professional Degree	1.8%	2.6%

Flexibility of Earnings

Average Hours Worked: 37
Workers with a Varying Number of Hours: 6.1%
Workers Earning Some Overtime Pay, Tips, or Commissions: 4.0%
Earnings Benefit of Working Overtime: −3.9%

Gender

	Male	Female
Percent	34.0%	66.0%
Effect on Earnings	17.2%	−8.1%

Union Membership

Percentage Union Members: Insignificant
Earnings Benefit of Union Membership: No significant data available

Veteran Status

Percentage Who Have Been on Active Duty: 10.2%
Earnings Benefit of Veteran Status: 14.9%

11-9199 Managers, All Other

All managers not listed separately.

- Education or Training Required: Work experience in a related occupation
- Job Growth: 7.8%
- Annual Openings: 105,000
- Self-Employed: 59.0%
- Part-Time: 16.0%

Note: A large fraction of the workforce for this occupation is self-employed and earns an average of $65,990. All other earnings figures for this occupation are based on workers who are paid a wage or salary.

NATIONAL WAGE FIGURES (ANNUAL)

Beginning	25th Percentile	Median	Mean	75th Percentile	90th Percentile
$43,190	$59,100	$82,490	$87,250	$109,720	$138,170

Median Wages for Industries Employing Largest Numbers (Annual)

Industry	Median Income
Utilities	$105,660
Internet Service Providers, Web Search Portals, and Data-Processing Services	$103,500
Computer and Electronic Product Manufacturing	$102,360
Transportation Equipment Manufacturing	$98,950
Professional, Scientific, and Technical Services	$95,050
Securities, Commodity Contracts, and Other Financial Investments and Related Activities	$94,920
Merchant Wholesalers, Durable Goods	$93,130
Management of Companies and Enterprises	$92,930
Publishing Industries (Except Internet)	$91,340
Rail Transportation	$90,240

Median Wages for States (Annual)

State	Wage	State	Wage	State	Wage
AK	$62,890	KY	$71,810	NY	$77,440
AL	$80,970	LA	$59,000	OH	$86,540
AR	$69,500	MA	$87,370	OK	$71,220
AZ	$66,580	MD	$105,110	OR	$68,450
CA	$94,870	ME	$65,250	PA	$71,300
CO	$92,970	MI	$86,930	RI	$76,160
CT	$88,400	MN	$90,410	SC	$61,820
DC	$112,550	MO	$58,490	SD	$67,780
DE	$99,100	MS	$74,770	TN	$66,240
FL	$76,320	MT	$56,780	TX	$86,220
GA	$86,580	NC	$77,010	UT	$67,190
HI	$72,610	ND	$65,070	VA	$99,900
IA	$58,850	NE	$69,500	VT	$70,110
ID	$61,660	NH	$81,580	WA	$95,390
IL	$72,750	NJ	$92,700	WI	$78,410
IN	$51,550	NM	$66,760	WV	$58,080
KS	$68,710	NV	$75,170	WY	$51,440

Median Wages for the Largest Metropolitan Areas (Annual)

Area	Wage	Area	Wage
AZ: Phoenix	$65,580	MI: Detroit	no data
CA: Los Angeles	$90,740	MN: Minneapolis	$93,880
CA: Riverside	$82,860	MO: Kansas City	$79,180
CA: Sacramento	$98,650	MO: St. Louis	$47,210
CA: San Diego	$92,780	NV: Las Vegas	$74,440
CA: San Francisco	$103,410	NY: New York	$91,040
CO: Denver	$99,680	OH: Cincinnati	$98,640
DC: Washington	$110,350	OH: Cleveland	$85,310
FL: Miami	$80,230	OH: Columbus	$85,290
FL: Orlando	$72,820	OR: Portland	$77,600
FL: Tampa	$76,500	PA: Philadelphia	$81,220
GA: Atlanta	$89,190	PA: Pittsburgh	$77,300
IL: Chicago	$75,200	TX: Dallas	$87,860
MA: Boston	$92,070	TX: Houston	$88,610
MD: Baltimore	$99,930	WA: Seattle	$97,800

FACTORS THAT MAY AFFECT EARNINGS

Educational Attainment of Workers and Effect on Earnings

	Percent at Level	Effect on Earnings
Less than High School	0.9%	−49.3%
Some High School	2.7%	−32.3%
High School or Equivalent	19.6%	−19.4%
Some College but No Degree	20.1%	−12.9%
Associate Degree	12.1%	−5.9%
Bachelor's Degree	25.6%	10.9%
Master's Degree	14.3%	25.0%
Doctoral Degree	2.3%	46.3%
First Professional Degree	2.5%	42.9%

Flexibility of Earnings

Average Hours Worked: 38
Workers with a Varying Number of Hours: 9.3%
Workers Earning Some Overtime Pay, Tips, or Commissions: 8.5%
Earnings Benefit of Working Overtime: −4.3%

Gender

	Male	Female
Percent	63.2%	36.8%
Effect on Earnings	12.2%	−17.8%

Union Membership

Percentage Union Members: 5.1%
Earnings Benefit of Union Membership: −13.8%

Veteran Status

Percentage Who Have Been on Active Duty: 10.2%
Earnings Benefit of Veteran Status: 14.9%

13-0000: Business and Financial Operations Occupations

13-1000 Business Operations Specialists

13-1011 Agents and Business Managers of Artists, Performers, and Athletes

Represent and promote artists, performers, and athletes to prospective employers. May handle contract negotiation and other business matters for clients.

- Education or Training Required: Work experience plus degree
- Job Growth: 11.8%
- Annual Openings: 2,000
- Self-Employed: 39.3%
- Part-Time: 26.2%

Note: Earnings figures do not reflect self-employed workers, who make up a large fraction of the workforce for this occupation.

NATIONAL WAGE FIGURES (ANNUAL)

Beginning	25th Percentile	Median	Mean	75th Percentile	90th Percentile
$28,870	$37,640	$64,500	$84,070	$114,400	more than $145,600

Note: The mean is significantly higher than the median because of the presence of a few star earners.

Median Wages for Industries Employing Largest Numbers (Annual)

Industry	Median Income
Broadcasting (Except Internet)	$71,030
Performing Arts, Spectator Sports, and Related Industries	$69,250
Management of Companies and Enterprises	$61,470
Religious, Grantmaking, Civic, Professional, and Similar Organizations	$59,090
Educational Services	$43,540
Motion Picture and Sound Recording Industries	$31,280

Median Wages for States (Annual)

AK	no data	KY	no data	NY	$92,110
AL	no data	LA	no data	OH	$58,640
AR	no data	MA	no data	OK	no data
AZ	$37,190	MD	$37,210	OR	no data
CA	$81,580	ME	no data	PA	$43,630
CO	$35,500	MI	$36,030	RI	no data
CT	$30,920	MN	$35,130	SC	no data
DC	no data	MO	$41,590	SD	no data
DE	no data	MS	no data	TN	no data
FL	$56,330	MT	no data	TX	$34,050
GA	$38,670	NC	$57,560	UT	$41,050
HI	$59,010	ND	no data	VA	$67,890
IA	no data	NE	no data	VT	$33,950
ID	no data	NH	no data	WA	no data
IL	$61,100	NJ	$74,270	WI	$36,710
IN	$40,700	NM	$42,280	WV	no data
KS	$26,780	NV	$77,060	WY	no data

Median Wages for the Largest Metropolitan Areas (Annual)

AZ: Phoenix	$39,100	MI: Detroit	$35,760
CA: Los Angeles	$87,950	MN: Minneapolis	$34,730
CA: Riverside	$33,720	MO: Kansas City	$30,560
CA: Sacramento	no data	MO: St. Louis	$51,470
CA: San Diego	$87,090	NV: Las Vegas	$78,420
CA: San Francisco	$46,340	NY: New York	$90,760
CO: Denver	$34,630	OH: Cincinnati	$78,820
DC: Washington	$69,830	OH: Cleveland	$53,390
FL: Miami	$52,190	OH: Columbus	no data
FL: Orlando	$126,900	OR: Portland	no data
FL: Tampa	no data	PA: Philadelphia	$40,500
GA: Atlanta	$38,780	PA: Pittsburgh	no data
IL: Chicago	$61,540	TX: Dallas	$28,610
MA: Boston	no data	TX: Houston	$50,100
MD: Baltimore	no data	WA: Seattle	$84,150

FACTORS THAT MAY AFFECT EARNINGS

Educational Attainment of Workers and Effect on Earnings

	Percent at Level	Effect on Earnings
Less than High School	—	—
Some High School	—	—
High School or Equivalent	—	—
Some College but No Degree	25.0%	−30.8%
Associate Degree	—	—
Bachelor's Degree	41.7%	17.7%
Master's Degree	—	—
Doctoral Degree	—	—
First Professional Degree	—	—

Figures do not total 100% because some levels have a very small sample size.

Flexibility of Earnings

Average Hours Worked: 31
Workers with a Varying Number of Hours: 14.9%
Workers Earning Some Overtime Pay, Tips, or Commissions: 17.9%
Earnings Benefit of Working Overtime: 6.6%

Gender

	Male	Female
Percent	53.8%	46.2%
Effect on Earnings	12.2%	−17.8%

Union Membership

Percentage Union Members: Insignificant
Earnings Benefit of Union Membership: No significant data available

Veteran Status

Percentage Who Have Been on Active Duty: 8.8%
Earnings Benefit of Veteran Status: 13.8%

13-1021 Purchasing Agents and Buyers, Farm Products

Purchase farm products for further processing or resale.

- Education or Training Required: Work experience in a related occupation
- Job Growth: 7.0%
- Annual Openings: 2,000
- Self-Employed: 8.5%
- Part-Time: 25.0%

NATIONAL WAGE FIGURES (ANNUAL)

Beginning	25th Percentile	Median	Mean	75th Percentile	90th Percentile
$26,520	$34,770	$46,770	$53,730	$64,100	$88,650

Median Wages for Industries Employing Largest Numbers (Annual)

Industry	Median Income
Beverage and Tobacco Product Manufacturing	$60,580
Professional, Scientific, and Technical Services	$57,790
Support Activities for Agriculture and Forestry	$57,620
Warehousing and Storage	$57,170
Chemical Manufacturing	$56,970
Management of Companies and Enterprises	$56,460
Fabricated Metal Product Manufacturing	$52,590
Machinery Manufacturing	$51,690
Insurance Carriers and Related Activities	$50,870
Merchant Wholesalers, Nondurable Goods	$48,730

Median Wages for States (Annual)

State	Wage	State	Wage	State	Wage
AK	no data	KY	no data	NY	$73,210
AL	$47,990	LA	$35,490	OH	$45,970
AR	$44,840	MA	no data	OK	$36,920
AZ	$42,680	MD	$40,910	OR	$51,100
CA	$51,890	ME	$40,940	PA	$40,640
CO	$31,010	MI	$46,250	RI	no data
CT	$45,260	MN	$55,050	SC	$44,180
DC	no data	MO	$42,870	SD	$43,880
DE	no data	MS	$28,510	TN	$41,810
FL	$53,610	MT	$40,030	TX	$49,010
GA	$38,360	NC	$48,430	UT	$39,470
HI	$38,330	ND	$53,010	VA	$49,420
IA	$49,130	NE	$47,680	VT	no data
ID	$50,820	NH	no data	WA	$55,810
IL	$47,610	NJ	$50,810	WI	$36,710
IN	$50,840	NM	no data	WV	$26,520
KS	$45,730	NV	$44,320	WY	no data

Median Wages for the Largest Metropolitan Areas (Annual)

Area	Wage	Area	Wage
AZ: Phoenix	$49,270	MI: Detroit	$46,630
CA: Los Angeles	$54,420	MN: Minneapolis	$60,550
CA: Riverside	$64,170	MO: Kansas City	$57,070
CA: Sacramento	no data	MO: St. Louis	$49,260
CA: San Diego	no data	NV: Las Vegas	$40,910
CA: San Francisco	$59,830	NY: New York	$74,830
CO: Denver	$63,390	OH: Cincinnati	$50,680
DC: Washington	$55,480	OH: Cleveland	$35,690
FL: Miami	$54,670	OH: Columbus	$61,710
FL: Orlando	$53,880	OR: Portland	no data
FL: Tampa	no data	PA: Philadelphia	$43,850
GA: Atlanta	$32,030	PA: Pittsburgh	$27,370
IL: Chicago	$50,230	TX: Dallas	$63,050
MA: Boston	no data	TX: Houston	$47,740
MD: Baltimore	$41,160	WA: Seattle	$58,800

FACTORS THAT MAY AFFECT EARNINGS

Educational Attainment of Workers and Effect on Earnings

Figures are based on a group of occupations: Business Operations Specialists

	Percent at Level	Effect on Earnings
Less than High School	—	—
Some High School	2.3%	−37.9%
High School or Equivalent	19.6%	−14.2%
Some College but No Degree	21.9%	−10.8%
Associate Degree	13.8%	−7.9%
Bachelor's Degree	26.8%	7.3%
Master's Degree	12.5%	30.9%
Doctoral Degree	1.2%	43.9%
First Professional Degree	1.3%	61.6%

Flexibility of Earnings

Average Hours Worked: 40
Workers with a Varying Number of Hours: 6.0%
Workers Earning Some Overtime Pay, Tips, or Commissions: 20.0%
Earnings Benefit of Working Overtime: 6.6%

Gender

	Male	Female
Percent	48.9%	51.1%
Effect on Earnings	12.2%	−17.8%

Union Membership

Percentage Union Members: 10.0%
Earnings Benefit of Union Membership: −7.2%

Veteran Status

Percentage Who Have Been on Active Duty: 8.8%
Earnings Benefit of Veteran Status: 13.8%

13-1022 Wholesale and Retail Buyers, Except Farm Products

Buy merchandise or commodities, other than farm products, for resale to consumers at the wholesale or retail level, including both durable and nondurable goods. Analyze past buying trends, sales records, price, and quality of merchandise to determine value and yield. Select, order, and authorize payment for merchandise according to contractual agreements. May conduct meetings with sales personnel and introduce new products.

- Education or Training Required: Work experience in a related occupation
- Job Growth: 8.4%
- Annual Openings: 20,000
- Self-Employed: 10.9%
- Part-Time: 33.3%

NATIONAL WAGE FIGURES (ANNUAL)

Beginning	25th Percentile	Median	Mean	75th Percentile	90th Percentile
$26,270	$33,640	$44,640	$51,010	$60,590	$83,080

Median Wages for Industries Employing Largest Numbers (Annual)

Industry	Median Income
Utilities	$56,850
Management of Companies and Enterprises	$54,390
Motor Vehicle and Parts Dealers	$53,130
Telecommunications	$50,070
Machinery Manufacturing	$49,720
Warehousing and Storage	$49,370
Federal, State, and Local Government	$46,180
Specialty Trade Contractors	$45,750
Merchant Wholesalers, Nondurable Goods	$45,390
Wholesale Electronic Markets and Agents and Brokers	$45,020

Median Wages for States (Annual)

State	Wage	State	Wage	State	Wage
AK	$40,810	KY	$36,340	NY	$52,540
AL	$38,140	LA	$36,390	OH	$41,090
AR	$40,220	MA	$47,370	OK	$36,970
AZ	$40,390	MD	$46,360	OR	$41,490
CA	$46,550	ME	$36,720	PA	$44,410
CO	$40,830	MI	$48,310	RI	no data
CT	$51,330	MN	$50,970	SC	$43,600
DC	$48,260	MO	$40,730	SD	$40,150
DE	$49,250	MS	$38,960	TN	$38,860
FL	$41,780	MT	$37,520	TX	$46,350
GA	$40,670	NC	$41,010	UT	$41,960
HI	$40,670	ND	$44,620	VA	$46,170
IA	$38,070	NE	$39,850	VT	$35,950
ID	$27,870	NH	$45,880	WA	$44,630
IL	$44,120	NJ	$56,120	WI	$40,430
IN	$39,980	NM	$39,210	WV	$32,790
KS	$37,860	NV	$48,710	WY	$29,500

Median Wages for the Largest Metropolitan Areas (Annual)

Area	Wage	Area	Wage
AZ: Phoenix	$42,540	MI: Detroit	$53,170
CA: Los Angeles	$47,110	MN: Minneapolis	$52,970
CA: Riverside	$42,210	MO: Kansas City	$45,140
CA: Sacramento	$51,540	MO: St. Louis	$42,990
CA: San Diego	$46,940	NV: Las Vegas	$50,910
CA: San Francisco	$47,720	NY: New York	$57,030
CO: Denver	$43,760	OH: Cincinnati	$45,960
DC: Washington	$48,680	OH: Cleveland	$43,880
FL: Miami	$42,280	OH: Columbus	$43,220
FL: Orlando	$44,230	OR: Portland	$42,990
FL: Tampa	$39,020	PA: Philadelphia	$49,270
GA: Atlanta	$41,350	PA: Pittsburgh	$41,710
IL: Chicago	$45,760	TX: Dallas	$51,170
MA: Boston	$49,290	TX: Houston	$46,310
MD: Baltimore	$45,390	WA: Seattle	$44,540

FACTORS THAT MAY AFFECT EARNINGS

Educational Attainment of Workers and Effect on Earnings

	Percent at Level	Effect on Earnings
Less than High School	—	—
Some High School	3.5%	−5.4%
High School or Equivalent	26.5%	−17.7%
Some College but No Degree	26.1%	−3.0%
Associate Degree	11.3%	1.0%
Bachelor's Degree	29.1%	18.2%
Master's Degree	—	—
Doctoral Degree	—	—
First Professional Degree	—	—

Flexibility of Earnings

Average Hours Worked: 34
Workers with a Varying Number of Hours: 8.4%
Workers Earning Some Overtime Pay, Tips, or Commissions: 12.8%
Earnings Benefit of Working Overtime: 2.9%

Gender

	Male	Female
Percent	44.2%	55.8%
Effect on Earnings	12.2%	−17.8%

Union Membership

Percentage Union Members: Insignificant
Earnings Benefit of Union Membership: No significant data available

Veteran Status

Percentage Who Have Been on Active Duty: 8.8%
Earnings Benefit of Veteran Status: 13.8%

13-1023 Purchasing Agents, Except Wholesale, Retail, and Farm Products

Purchase machinery, equipment, tools, parts, supplies, or services necessary for the operation of an establishment. Purchase raw or semi-finished materials for manufacturing.

- Education or Training Required: Work experience in a related occupation
- Job Growth: 8.1%
- Annual Openings: 19,000
- Self-Employed: 3.5%
- Part-Time: 13.6%

NATIONAL WAGE FIGURES (ANNUAL)

Beginning	25th Percentile	Median	Mean	75th Percentile	90th Percentile
$31,350	$39,000	$50,730	$54,160	$66,730	$83,900

Median Wages for Industries Employing Largest Numbers (Annual)

Industry	Median Income
Telecommunications	$63,680
Federal, State, and Local Government	$60,150
Utilities	$57,310
Professional, Scientific, and Technical Services	$56,620
Management of Companies and Enterprises	$54,820
Transportation Equipment Manufacturing	$54,720
Computer and Electronic Product Manufacturing	$54,020
Insurance Carriers and Related Activities	$51,560
Chemical Manufacturing	$51,190
Construction of Buildings	$48,880

Median Wages for States (Annual)

State		State		State	
AK	$56,560	KY	$44,140	NY	$53,950
AL	$50,540	LA	$40,840	OH	$49,990
AR	$40,530	MA	$57,920	OK	$45,720
AZ	$45,840	MD	$60,250	OR	$45,470
CA	$54,930	ME	$42,460	PA	$50,510
CO	$52,970	MI	$55,290	RI	$51,950
CT	$56,820	MN	$51,490	SC	$46,150
DC	$73,960	MO	$45,630	SD	$40,740
DE	$54,400	MS	$37,410	TN	$43,490
FL	$44,940	MT	$40,950	TX	$47,470
GA	$49,590	NC	$46,770	UT	$47,480
HI	$53,020	ND	$45,660	VA	$58,280
IA	$41,830	NE	$48,500	VT	$45,100
ID	$43,150	NH	$49,800	WA	$56,550
IL	$51,660	NJ	$58,790	WI	$45,620
IN	$44,740	NM	$50,420	WV	$41,030
KS	$46,910	NV	$46,300	WY	$44,400

Median Wages for the Largest Metropolitan Areas (Annual)

Area		Area	
AZ: Phoenix	$45,570	MI: Detroit	$63,300
CA: Los Angeles	$53,910	MN: Minneapolis	$53,500
CA: Riverside	$47,390	MO: Kansas City	$51,000
CA: Sacramento	$50,360	MO: St. Louis	$50,930
CA: San Diego	$54,310	NV: Las Vegas	$46,710
CA: San Francisco	$61,390	NY: New York	$59,610
CO: Denver	$54,120	OH: Cincinnati	$51,060
DC: Washington	$68,030	OH: Cleveland	$49,480
FL: Miami	$45,070	OH: Columbus	$54,780
FL: Orlando	$44,360	OR: Portland	$50,480
FL: Tampa	$45,920	PA: Philadelphia	$56,790
GA: Atlanta	$50,760	PA: Pittsburgh	$48,710
IL: Chicago	$52,240	TX: Dallas	$50,010
MA: Boston	$60,260	TX: Houston	$48,870
MD: Baltimore	$56,760	WA: Seattle	$58,060

FACTORS THAT MAY AFFECT EARNINGS

Educational Attainment of Workers and Effect on Earnings

	Percent at Level	Effect on Earnings
Less than High School	—	—
Some High School	—	—
High School or Equivalent	25.3%	−25.6%
Some College but No Degree	25.0%	−3.9%
Associate Degree	14.0%	7.0%
Bachelor's Degree	26.2%	16.3%
Master's Degree	7.9%	33.2%
Doctoral Degree	—	—
First Professional Degree	—	—

Flexibility of Earnings

Average Hours Worked: 38
Workers with a Varying Number of Hours: 4.5%
Workers Earning Some Overtime Pay, Tips, or Commissions: 10.5%
Earnings Benefit of Working Overtime: −2.2%

Gender

	Male	Female
Percent	48.0%	52.0%
Effect on Earnings	18.9%	−15.6%

Union Membership

Percentage Union Members: 5.4%
Earnings Benefit of Union Membership: 8.3%

Veteran Status

Percentage Who Have Been on Active Duty: 8.8%
Earnings Benefit of Veteran Status: 13.8%

13-1031 Claims Adjusters, Examiners, and Investigators

Review settled claims to determine that payments and settlements have been made in accordance with company practices and procedures, ensuring that proper methods have been followed. Report overpayments, underpayments, and other irregularities. Confer with legal counsel on claims requiring litigation.

- Education or Training Required: Long-term on-the-job training
- Job Growth: 15.1%
- Annual Openings: 28,000
- Self-Employed: 2.5%
- Part-Time: 25.7%

NATIONAL WAGE FIGURES (ANNUAL)

Beginning	25th Percentile	Median	Mean	75th Percentile	90th Percentile
$30,890	$38,520	$50,660	$52,750	$65,210	$79,170

Median Wages for Industries Employing Largest Numbers (Annual)

Industry	Median Income
Rail Transportation	$62,770
Utilities	$60,410
Federal, State, and Local Government	$59,960
Securities, Commodity Contracts, and Other Financial Investments and Related Activities	$55,620
Merchant Wholesalers, Nondurable Goods	$53,250
Rental and Leasing Services	$50,120
Insurance Carriers and Related Activities	$48,710
Repair and Maintenance	$48,170
Real Estate	$48,150
Management of Companies and Enterprises	$46,630

Median Wages for States (Annual)

State	Wage	State	Wage	State	Wage
AK	$59,770	KY	$49,120	NY	$55,400
AL	$53,560	LA	$54,840	OH	$53,270
AR	$52,070	MA	$50,110	OK	$42,360
AZ	$46,820	MD	$52,280	OR	$49,560
CA	$55,820	ME	$48,320	PA	$48,120
CO	$50,070	MI	$56,610	RI	$48,730
CT	$55,020	MN	$43,210	SC	no data
DC	$58,080	MO	$47,850	SD	$48,340
DE	$42,720	MS	$53,520	TN	$47,530
FL	$46,100	MT	$37,060	TX	$48,860
GA	$48,490	NC	$47,240	UT	$45,560
HI	$60,010	ND	$39,200	VA	$51,330
IA	$42,380	NE	$40,860	VT	$53,460
ID	$49,010	NH	$54,760	WA	$53,530
IL	$51,320	NJ	$56,850	WI	$47,910
IN	$46,380	NM	$53,090	WV	$51,000
KS	$46,780	NV	$45,390	WY	$43,880

Median Wages for the Largest Metropolitan Areas (Annual)

Area	Wage	Area	Wage
AZ: Phoenix	$46,630	MI: Detroit	$57,120
CA: Los Angeles	$54,130	MN: Minneapolis	$43,370
CA: Riverside	$57,100	MO: Kansas City	$52,180
CA: Sacramento	$55,240	MO: St. Louis	$46,570
CA: San Diego	$55,980	NV: Las Vegas	$45,060
CA: San Francisco	$59,690	NY: New York	$58,220
CO: Denver	$53,810	OH: Cincinnati	$52,580
DC: Washington	$49,890	OH: Cleveland	$53,530
FL: Miami	$45,730	OH: Columbus	$51,390
FL: Orlando	$46,370	OR: Portland	$49,260
FL: Tampa	$46,370	PA: Philadelphia	$49,430
GA: Atlanta	$48,590	PA: Pittsburgh	$50,650
IL: Chicago	$52,310	TX: Dallas	$51,260
MA: Boston	$52,660	TX: Houston	$52,960
MD: Baltimore	$53,580	WA: Seattle	$55,160

FACTORS THAT MAY AFFECT EARNINGS

Educational Attainment of Workers and Effect on Earnings

Figures are based on a group of occupations: Business Operations Specialists

	Percent at Level	Effect on Earnings
Less than High School	—	—
Some High School	2.3%	−37.9%
High School or Equivalent	19.6%	−14.2%
Some College but No Degree	21.9%	−10.8%
Associate Degree	13.8%	−7.9%
Bachelor's Degree	26.8%	7.3%
Master's Degree	12.5%	30.9%
Doctoral Degree	1.2%	43.9%
First Professional Degree	1.3%	61.6%

Flexibility of Earnings

Average Hours Worked: 36
Workers with a Varying Number of Hours: 8.0%
Workers Earning Some Overtime Pay, Tips, or Commissions: 11.3%
Earnings Benefit of Working Overtime: 0.9%

Gender

	Male	Female
Percent	41.8%	58.2%
Effect on Earnings	15.8%	−6.6%

Union Membership

Percentage Union Members: 7.6%
Earnings Benefit of Union Membership: −7.2%

Veteran Status

Percentage Who Have Been on Active Duty: 8.8%
Earnings Benefit of Veteran Status: 13.8%

13-1032 Insurance Appraisers, Auto Damage

Appraise automobile or other vehicle damage to determine cost of repair for insurance claim settlement and seek agreement with automotive repair shop on cost of repair. Prepare insurance forms to indicate repair cost or cost estimates and recommendations.

- Education or Training Required: Long-term on-the-job training
- Job Growth: 16.6%
- Annual Openings: 2,000
- Self-Employed: 2.9%
- Part-Time: 25.7%

NATIONAL WAGE FIGURES (ANNUAL)

Beginning	25th Percentile	Median	Mean	75th Percentile	90th Percentile
$34,220	$40,870	$49,180	$49,980	$57,830	$68,420

Median Wages for Industries Employing Largest Numbers (Annual)

Industry	Median Income
Management of Companies and Enterprises......................	$52,080
Insurance Carriers and Related Activities	$49,510
Rental and Leasing Services	$49,320
Administrative and Support Services	$45,250
Motor Vehicle and Parts Dealers.....................................	$44,890
Professional, Scientific, and Technical Services	$44,180
Repair and Maintenance...	$43,970

Median Wages for States (Annual)

AK	no data	KY	$47,350	NY	$51,800
AL	$48,180	LA	$51,030	OH	$48,620
AR	$37,180	MA	$53,870	OK	$44,970
AZ	$50,620	MD	$50,160	OR	no data
CA	$51,560	ME	$48,260	PA	$49,360
CO	$51,110	MI	$48,970	RI	no data
CT	$51,160	MN	$51,640	SC	$43,040
DC	no data	MO	$46,840	SD	no data
DE	no data	MS	$48,100	TN	$50,580
FL	$45,480	MT	$43,250	TX	$47,870
GA	$48,670	NC	$47,280	UT	$51,190
HI	$54,070	ND	no data	VA	$49,790
IA	$40,540	NE	$57,340	VT	no data
ID	$49,470	NH	$46,730	WA	$54,260
IL	$48,270	NJ	$48,530	WI	$42,900
IN	$48,070	NM	no data	WV	no data
KS	$45,880	NV	$48,810	WY	no data

Median Wages for the Largest Metropolitan Areas (Annual)

AZ: Phoenix............	$50,850	MI: Detroit	no data
CA: Los Angeles	$50,210	MN: Minneapolis	$52,070
CA: Riverside	no data	MO: Kansas City........	$46,460
CA: Sacramento	$52,220	MO: St. Louis............	$47,790
CA: San Diego	$40,130	NV: Las Vegas	$48,810
CA: San Francisco....	$49,850	NY: New York............	$50,460
CO: Denver	$52,940	OH: Cincinnati..........	no data
DC: Washington	$50,700	OH: Cleveland	$53,400
FL: Miami	$49,600	OH: Columbus	no data
FL: Orlando	$46,930	OR: Portland	no data
FL: Tampa	$40,830	PA: Philadelphia	$51,070
GA: Atlanta	$48,130	PA: Pittsburgh	$48,410
IL: Chicago	$48,420	TX: Dallas	$46,690
MA: Boston	$55,650	TX: Houston	$51,820
MD: Baltimore	$49,680	WA: Seattle	$53,070

FACTORS THAT MAY AFFECT EARNINGS

Educational Attainment of Workers and Effect on Earnings

Figures are based on a group of occupations: Business Operations Specialists

	Percent at Level	Effect on Earnings
Less than High School	—	—
Some High School	2.3%	−37.9%
High School or Equivalent	19.6%	−14.2%
Some College but No Degree	21.9%	−10.8%
Associate Degree	13.8%	−7.9%
Bachelor's Degree	26.8%	7.3%
Master's Degree	12.5%	30.9%
Doctoral Degree	1.2%	43.9%
First Professional Degree	1.3%	61.6%

Flexibility of Earnings

Average Hours Worked: 36

Workers with a Varying Number of Hours: 8.0%

Workers Earning Some Overtime Pay, Tips, or Commissions: 11.3%

Earnings Benefit of Working Overtime: 0.9%

Gender

	Male	Female
Percent	46.8%	53.2%
Effect on Earnings	15.8%	−6.6%

Union Membership

Percentage Union Members: 7.6%

Earnings Benefit of Union Membership: −7.2%

Veteran Status

Percentage Who Have Been on Active Duty: 8.8%

Earnings Benefit of Veteran Status: 13.8%

13-1041 Compliance Officers, Except Agriculture, Construction, Health and Safety, and Transportation

Examine, evaluate, and investigate eligibility for or conformity with laws and regulations governing contract compliance of licenses and permits and other compliance and enforcement inspection activities not classified elsewhere.

- Education or Training Required: Long-term on-the-job training
- Job Growth: 11.6%
- Annual Openings: 17,000
- Self-Employed: 0.0%
- Part-Time: 7.0%

NATIONAL WAGE FIGURES (ANNUAL)

Beginning	25th Percentile	Median	Mean	75th Percentile	90th Percentile
$27,860	$33,920	$47,050	$50,890	$62,760	$80,380

Median Wages for Industries Employing Largest Numbers (Annual)

Industry	Median Income
Postal Service	$73,450
Utilities	$70,550
Securities, Commodity Contracts, and Other Financial Investments and Related Activities	$65,210
Computer and Electronic Product Manufacturing	$64,440
Telecommunications	$60,870
Management of Companies and Enterprises	$56,970
Miscellaneous Manufacturing	$56,900
Chemical Manufacturing	$56,800
Publishing Industries (Except Internet)	$56,420
Professional, Scientific, and Technical Services	$56,380

Median Wages for States (Annual)

AK	$43,590	KY	$39,370	NY	$51,660
AL	$45,340	LA	$38,290	OH	$49,520
AR	$39,180	MA	$59,510	OK	$36,800
AZ	$45,790	MD	$51,740	OR	$44,450
CA	$53,900	ME	$42,590	PA	$41,750
CO	$48,500	MI	$48,170	RI	$45,090
CT	$56,980	MN	$52,430	SC	$38,550
DC	$68,130	MO	$45,530	SD	$39,850
DE	$48,180	MS	$34,000	TN	$40,980
FL	$38,080	MT	$38,210	TX	$48,790
GA	$43,610	NC	$40,290	UT	$35,300
HI	$40,240	ND	$48,970	VA	$46,490
IA	$43,900	NE	$43,720	VT	$51,110
ID	$40,270	NH	$40,990	WA	$52,380
IL	$45,910	NJ	$52,130	WI	$45,620
IN	$40,210	NM	$50,690	WV	$36,180
KS	$44,620	NV	$37,260	WY	$44,680

Median Wages for the Largest Metropolitan Areas (Annual)

AZ: Phoenix	$42,290	MI: Detroit	$51,350
CA: Los Angeles	$53,240	MN: Minneapolis	$52,450
CA: Riverside	$48,250	MO: Kansas City	$49,970
CA: Sacramento	$51,160	MO: St. Louis	$46,980
CA: San Diego	$53,290	NV: Las Vegas	$34,720
CA: San Francisco	$60,780	NY: New York	$52,660
CO: Denver	$50,370	OH: Cincinnati	$47,610
DC: Washington	$61,830	OH: Cleveland	$44,540
FL: Miami	$40,430	OH: Columbus	$57,420
FL: Orlando	$34,490	OR: Portland	$44,420
FL: Tampa	$40,860	PA: Philadelphia	$46,150
GA: Atlanta	$42,350	PA: Pittsburgh	$40,990
IL: Chicago	$47,700	TX: Dallas	$45,980
MA: Boston	$59,970	TX: Houston	$46,730
MD: Baltimore	$46,130	WA: Seattle	$50,130

FACTORS THAT MAY AFFECT EARNINGS

Educational Attainment of Workers and Effect on Earnings

	Percent at Level	Effect on Earnings
Less than High School	—	—
Some High School	—	—
High School or Equivalent	18.3%	−13.1%
Some College but No Degree	22.0%	−21.3%
Associate Degree	13.4%	−12.5%
Bachelor's Degree	32.8%	5.4%
Master's Degree	9.7%	44.9%
Doctoral Degree	—	—
First Professional Degree	—	—

Flexibility of Earnings

Average Hours Worked: 39
Workers with a Varying Number of Hours: 3.5%
Workers Earning Some Overtime Pay, Tips, or Commissions: 10.4%
Earnings Benefit of Working Overtime: 24.0%

Gender

	Male	Female
Percent	46.0%	54.0%
Effect on Earnings	5.6%	−4.0%

Union Membership

Percentage Union Members: 19.8%
Earnings Benefit of Union Membership: −14.5%

Veteran Status

Percentage Who Have Been on Active Duty: 8.8%
Earnings Benefit of Veteran Status: 13.8%

13-1051 Cost Estimators

Prepare cost estimates for product manufacturing, construction projects, or services to aid management in bidding on or determining price of product or service. May specialize according to particular service performed or type of product manufactured.

- Education or Training Required: Work experience in a related occupation
- Job Growth: 18.2%
- Annual Openings: 15,000
- Self-Employed: 2.2%
- Part-Time: 21.6%

NATIONAL WAGE FIGURES (ANNUAL)

Beginning	25th Percentile	Median	Mean	75th Percentile	90th Percentile
$31,600	$40,320	$52,940	$56,820	$69,460	$88,310

Median Wages for Industries Employing Largest Numbers (Annual)

Industry	Median Income
Computer and Electronic Product Manufacturing	$60,710
Transportation Equipment Manufacturing	$60,600
Heavy and Civil Engineering Construction	$59,330
Professional, Scientific, and Technical Services	$58,500
Management of Companies and Enterprises	$58,490
Waste Management and Remediation Services	$56,920
Construction of Buildings	$56,570
Specialty Trade Contractors	$53,880
Machinery Manufacturing	$53,180
Insurance Carriers and Related Activities	$52,640

Median Wages for States (Annual)

State	Wage	State	Wage	State	Wage
AK	$57,660	KY	$46,170	NY	$59,690
AL	$45,410	LA	$48,380	OH	$51,230
AR	$47,240	MA	$66,130	OK	$48,630
AZ	$49,100	MD	$54,380	OR	$50,950
CA	$58,690	ME	$44,210	PA	$48,300
CO	$54,100	MI	$58,000	RI	$56,290
CT	$57,010	MN	$55,390	SC	$47,210
DC	$75,740	MO	$52,130	SD	$40,870
DE	$54,190	MS	$45,870	TN	$46,340
FL	$48,420	MT	$46,610	TX	$51,300
GA	$49,050	NC	$49,990	UT	$50,060
HI	$59,920	ND	$41,300	VA	$53,250
IA	$46,100	NE	$44,080	VT	$52,880
ID	$41,670	NH	$51,700	WA	$57,070
IL	$59,880	NJ	$62,010	WI	$50,090
IN	$48,770	NM	$43,270	WV	$41,330
KS	$45,880	NV	$57,530	WY	$54,740

Median Wages for the Largest Metropolitan Areas (Annual)

Area	Wage	Area	Wage
AZ: Phoenix	$52,030	MI: Detroit	$64,870
CA: Los Angeles	$58,100	MN: Minneapolis	$57,370
CA: Riverside	$54,300	MO: Kansas City	$54,030
CA: Sacramento	$62,860	MO: St. Louis	$55,970
CA: San Diego	$57,050	NV: Las Vegas	$56,990
CA: San Francisco	$68,640	NY: New York	$66,950
CO: Denver	$56,050	OH: Cincinnati	$49,720
DC: Washington	$58,340	OH: Cleveland	$53,420
FL: Miami	$55,650	OH: Columbus	$52,830
FL: Orlando	$45,780	OR: Portland	$53,370
FL: Tampa	$45,880	PA: Philadelphia	$55,920
GA: Atlanta	$50,610	PA: Pittsburgh	$45,000
IL: Chicago	$61,840	TX: Dallas	$53,010
MA: Boston	$68,760	TX: Houston	$58,760
MD: Baltimore	$55,290	WA: Seattle	$59,810

FACTORS THAT MAY AFFECT EARNINGS

Educational Attainment of Workers and Effect on Earnings

	Percent at Level	Effect on Earnings
Less than High School	—	—
Some High School	—	—
High School or Equivalent	25.0%	−14.5%
Some College but No Degree	25.8%	7.8%
Associate Degree	15.2%	−17.0%
Bachelor's Degree	26.5%	14.5%
Master's Degree	5.3%	9.0%
Doctoral Degree	—	—
First Professional Degree	—	—

Flexibility of Earnings

Average Hours Worked: 39
Workers with a Varying Number of Hours: 5.3%
Workers Earning Some Overtime Pay, Tips, or Commissions: 15.4%
Earnings Benefit of Working Overtime: 9.8%

Gender

	Male	Female
Percent	87.3%	12.7%
Effect on Earnings	3.1%	—

Union Membership

Percentage Union Members: Insignificant
Earnings Benefit of Union Membership: No significant data available

Veteran Status

Percentage Who Have Been on Active Duty: 8.8%
Earnings Benefit of Veteran Status: 13.8%

13-1061 Emergency Management Specialists

Coordinate disaster response or crisis management activities, provide disaster-preparedness training, and prepare emergency plans and procedures for natural (e.g., hurricanes, floods, earthquakes), wartime, or technological (e.g., nuclear power plant emergencies, hazardous materials spills) disasters or hostage situations.

- Education or Training Required: Work experience in a related occupation
- Job Growth: 22.8%
- Annual Openings: 2,000
- Self-Employed: 0.0%
- Part-Time: 25.7%

NATIONAL WAGE FIGURES (ANNUAL)

Beginning	25th Percentile	Median	Mean	75th Percentile	90th Percentile
$25,690	$35,200	$47,410	$50,450	$63,010	$80,850

Median Wages for Industries Employing Largest Numbers (Annual)

Industry	Median Income
Waste Management and Remediation Services	$67,180
Professional, Scientific, and Technical Services	$62,250
Management of Companies and Enterprises	$60,410
Air Transportation	$58,390
Utilities	$58,020
Fabricated Metal Product Manufacturing	$55,730
Hospitals	$54,020
Petroleum and Coal Products Manufacturing	$51,750
Insurance Carriers and Related Activities	$51,220
Educational Services	$50,120

Median Wages for States (Annual)

AK	$51,470	KY	$37,220	NY	$51,350
AL	$35,810	LA	$47,490	OH	$56,950
AR	$36,100	MA	$49,620	OK	$32,810
AZ	$50,920	MD	$54,610	OR	$48,630
CA	$68,490	ME	$37,390	PA	$43,380
CO	$63,540	MI	$50,570	RI	$54,940
CT	$61,910	MN	$54,800	SC	$48,030
DC	$54,820	MO	$42,150	SD	$30,450
DE	no data	MS	$31,720	TN	$40,230
FL	$54,290	MT	$33,560	TX	$44,500
GA	$40,940	NC	$42,180	UT	$44,600
HI	no data	ND	$42,440	VA	$57,230
IA	$37,890	NE	$36,620	VT	$49,450
ID	$53,390	NH	$40,470	WA	$56,900
IL	$34,610	NJ	$48,290	WI	$50,180
IN	$33,700	NM	$38,600	WV	$31,540
KS	$37,170	NV	$56,200	WY	$40,670

Median Wages for the Largest Metropolitan Areas (Annual)

AZ: Phoenix	$53,660	MI: Detroit	$55,610
CA: Los Angeles	$71,130	MN: Minneapolis	$64,950
CA: Riverside	$60,150	MO: Kansas City	$54,300
CA: Sacramento	$59,790	MO: St. Louis	$49,050
CA: San Diego	$70,310	NV: Las Vegas	$46,760
CA: San Francisco	$78,510	NY: New York	$49,860
CO: Denver	$67,620	OH: Cincinnati	$42,800
DC: Washington	$57,050	OH: Cleveland	$68,360
FL: Miami	$55,840	OH: Columbus	no data
FL: Orlando	$63,740	OR: Portland	$65,380
FL: Tampa	no data	PA: Philadelphia	$45,990
GA: Atlanta	$56,130	PA: Pittsburgh	no data
IL: Chicago	$35,900	TX: Dallas	$57,590
MA: Boston	$53,740	TX: Houston	$50,590
MD: Baltimore	$53,830	WA: Seattle	$55,650

FACTORS THAT MAY AFFECT EARNINGS

Educational Attainment of Workers and Effect on Earnings

Figures are based on a group of occupations: Business Operations Specialists

	Percent at Level	Effect on Earnings
Less than High School	—	—
Some High School	2.3%	−37.9%
High School or Equivalent	19.6%	−14.2%
Some College but No Degree	21.9%	−10.8%
Associate Degree	13.8%	−7.9%
Bachelor's Degree	26.8%	7.3%
Master's Degree	12.5%	30.9%
Doctoral Degree	1.2%	43.9%
First Professional Degree	1.3%	61.6%

Flexibility of Earnings

Average Hours Worked: 36
Workers with a Varying Number of Hours: 8.0%
Workers Earning Some Overtime Pay, Tips, or Commissions: 11.3%
Earnings Benefit of Working Overtime: 23.8%

Gender

	Male	Female
Percent	28.5%	71.5%
Effect on Earnings	21.9%	−11.0%

Union Membership

Percentage Union Members: 7.6%
Earnings Benefit of Union Membership: −7.2%

Veteran Status

Percentage Who Have Been on Active Duty: 8.8%
Earnings Benefit of Veteran Status: 13.8%

13-1071 Employment, Recruitment, and Placement Specialists

Recruit and place workers.

- Education or Training Required: Bachelor's degree
- Job Growth: 30.5%
- Annual Openings: 30,000
- Self-Employed: 2.5%
- Part-Time: 25.7%

NATIONAL WAGE FIGURES (ANNUAL)

Beginning	25th Percentile	Median	Mean	75th Percentile	90th Percentile
$26,590	$32,770	$42,420	$50,070	$58,320	$81,680

Median Wages for Industries Employing Largest Numbers (Annual)

Industry	Median Income
Utilities	$62,260
Computer and Electronic Product Manufacturing	$61,520
Publishing Industries (Except Internet)	$59,210
Telecommunications	$56,370
Internet Service Providers, Web Search Portals, and Data-Processing Services	$56,120
Professional, Scientific, and Technical Services	$52,990
Securities, Commodity Contracts, and Other Financial Investments and Related Activities	$50,980
Merchant Wholesalers, Durable Goods	$49,920
Construction of Buildings	$49,540
Credit Intermediation and Related Activities	$49,090

Median Wages for States (Annual)

AK	$43,430	KY	$31,290	NY	$47,070
AL	$34,570	LA	$33,110	OH	$41,960
AR	$31,010	MA	$51,050	OK	$33,330
AZ	$36,760	MD	$50,760	OR	$39,230
CA	$51,800	ME	$43,730	PA	$40,910
CO	$42,910	MI	$47,160	RI	$44,190
CT	$53,380	MN	$45,020	SC	$33,820
DC	$48,070	MO	$37,460	SD	$37,920
DE	$48,330	MS	$31,020	TN	$39,640
FL	$35,550	MT	$33,730	TX	$39,110
GA	$44,020	NC	$39,500	UT	$38,120
HI	$42,740	ND	$37,740	VA	$44,430
IA	$43,030	NE	$43,580	VT	$38,550
ID	$42,400	NH	$42,510	WA	$52,680
IL	$39,800	NJ	$50,610	WI	no data
IN	$37,050	NM	$33,770	WV	$35,590
KS	$38,500	NV	$37,670	WY	$32,030

Median Wages for the Largest Metropolitan Areas (Annual)

AZ: Phoenix	$36,940	MI: Detroit	$47,710
CA: Los Angeles	$49,070	MN: Minneapolis	$45,840
CA: Riverside	$40,090	MO: Kansas City	$40,710
CA: Sacramento	$54,800	MO: St. Louis	$41,790
CA: San Diego	$47,950	NV: Las Vegas	$36,740
CA: San Francisco	$56,490	NY: New York	$49,630
CO: Denver	$43,660	OH: Cincinnati	$46,590
DC: Washington	$52,150	OH: Cleveland	$44,640
FL: Miami	$38,620	OH: Columbus	$40,660
FL: Orlando	$35,020	OR: Portland	$40,860
FL: Tampa	$33,910	PA: Philadelphia	$44,150
GA: Atlanta	$46,750	PA: Pittsburgh	$43,010
IL: Chicago	$40,090	TX: Dallas	$41,180
MA: Boston	$51,600	TX: Houston	$46,550
MD: Baltimore	$52,760	WA: Seattle	$57,410

FACTORS THAT MAY AFFECT EARNINGS

Educational Attainment of Workers and Effect on Earnings

Figures are based on a group of occupations: Business Operations Specialists

	Percent at Level	Effect on Earnings
Less than High School	—	—
Some High School	2.3%	−37.9%
High School or Equivalent	19.6%	−14.2%
Some College but No Degree	21.9%	−10.8%
Associate Degree	13.8%	−7.9%
Bachelor's Degree	26.8%	7.3%
Master's Degree	12.5%	30.9%
Doctoral Degree	1.2%	43.9%
First Professional Degree	1.3%	61.6%

Flexibility of Earnings

Average Hours Worked: 36
Workers with a Varying Number of Hours: 8.0%
Workers Earning Some Overtime Pay, Tips, or Commissions: 11.3%
Earnings Benefit of Working Overtime: 10.3%

Gender

	Male	Female
Percent	28.5%	71.5%
Effect on Earnings	15.3%	−6.4%

Union Membership

Percentage Union Members: 7.6%
Earnings Benefit of Union Membership: −7.2%

Veteran Status

Percentage Who Have Been on Active Duty: 8.8%
Earnings Benefit of Veteran Status: 13.8%

13-1072 Compensation, Benefits, and Job Analysis Specialists

Conduct programs of compensation and benefits and job analysis for employer. May specialize in specific areas, such as position classification and pension programs.

- Education or Training Required: Bachelor's degree
- Job Growth: 20.4%
- Annual Openings: 15,000
- Self-Employed: 2.7%
- Part-Time: 25.7%

NATIONAL WAGE FIGURES (ANNUAL)

Beginning	25th Percentile	Median	Mean	75th Percentile	90th Percentile
$32,180	$39,400	$50,230	$53,500	$63,800	$80,150

Median Wages for Industries Employing Largest Numbers (Annual)

Industry	Median Income
Telecommunications	$59,830
Computer and Electronic Product Manufacturing	$58,380
Publishing Industries (Except Internet)	$58,070
Professional, Scientific, and Technical Services	$55,700
Transportation Equipment Manufacturing	$55,430
Management of Companies and Enterprises	$52,960
Real Estate	$52,950
Chemical Manufacturing	$52,030
Merchant Wholesalers, Durable Goods	$51,670
Merchant Wholesalers, Nondurable Goods	$51,220

Median Wages for States (Annual)

AK	$48,380	KY	$40,650	NY	$57,810
AL	$42,700	LA	$37,240	OH	$48,290
AR	$39,940	MA	$56,460	OK	$38,890
AZ	$44,990	MD	$54,220	OR	$43,910
CA	$55,880	ME	$43,370	PA	$47,500
CO	$53,160	MI	$53,550	RI	$48,260
CT	$57,900	MN	$47,850	SC	$40,220
DC	$62,640	MO	$43,580	SD	$39,440
DE	$53,680	MS	$37,590	TN	$42,120
FL	$45,140	MT	$38,820	TX	$48,220
GA	$45,100	NC	$47,280	UT	$44,380
HI	$44,210	ND	$47,310	VA	$49,280
IA	$39,190	NE	$48,180	VT	$45,270
ID	$48,000	NH	$44,450	WA	$52,840
IL	$52,460	NJ	$57,180	WI	$46,620
IN	$45,570	NM	$45,370	WV	$37,730
KS	$47,360	NV	$52,080	WY	$44,260

Median Wages for the Largest Metropolitan Areas (Annual)

AZ: Phoenix	$45,940	MI: Detroit	$56,970
CA: Los Angeles	$55,050	MN: Minneapolis	$48,780
CA: Riverside	$47,260	MO: Kansas City	$46,800
CA: Sacramento	$57,330	MO: St. Louis	$45,790
CA: San Diego	$53,110	NV: Las Vegas	$50,410
CA: San Francisco	$58,820	NY: New York	$59,330
CO: Denver	$55,590	OH: Cincinnati	$48,390
DC: Washington	$58,960	OH: Cleveland	$47,950
FL: Miami	$49,070	OH: Columbus	$51,580
FL: Orlando	$45,030	OR: Portland	$45,250
FL: Tampa	$43,090	PA: Philadelphia	$52,200
GA: Atlanta	$46,870	PA: Pittsburgh	$44,690
IL: Chicago	$52,870	TX: Dallas	$51,380
MA: Boston	$56,920	TX: Houston	$50,600
MD: Baltimore	$52,780	WA: Seattle	$54,870

FACTORS THAT MAY AFFECT EARNINGS

Educational Attainment of Workers and Effect on Earnings

Figures are based on a group of occupations: Business Operations Specialists

	Percent at Level	Effect on Earnings
Less than High School	—	—
Some High School	2.3%	−37.9%
High School or Equivalent	19.6%	−14.2%
Some College but No Degree	21.9%	−10.8%
Associate Degree	13.8%	−7.9%
Bachelor's Degree	26.8%	7.3%
Master's Degree	12.5%	30.9%
Doctoral Degree	1.2%	43.9%
First Professional Degree	1.3%	61.6%

Flexibility of Earnings

Average Hours Worked: 36
Workers with a Varying Number of Hours: 8.0%
Workers Earning Some Overtime Pay, Tips, or Commissions: 11.3%
Earnings Benefit of Working Overtime: 10.3%

Gender

	Male	Female
Percent	28.5%	71.5%
Effect on Earnings	15.3%	−6.4%

Union Membership

Percentage Union Members: 7.6%
Earnings Benefit of Union Membership: −7.2%

Veteran Status

Percentage Who Have Been on Active Duty: 8.8%
Earnings Benefit of Veteran Status: 13.8%

13-1073 Training and Development Specialists

Conduct training and development programs for employees.

- Education or Training Required: Bachelor's degree
- Job Growth: 20.8%
- Annual Openings: 32,000
- Self-Employed: 2.8%
- Part-Time: 25.7%

NATIONAL WAGE FIGURES (ANNUAL)

Beginning	25th Percentile	Median	Mean	75th Percentile	90th Percentile
$27,450	$35,980	$47,830	$51,100	$63,200	$80,630

Median Wages for Industries Employing Largest Numbers (Annual)

Industry	Median Income
Utilities	$68,850
Computer and Electronic Product Manufacturing	$58,790
Securities, Commodity Contracts, and Other Financial Investments and Related Activities	$56,280
Telecommunications	$56,210
Merchant Wholesalers, Durable Goods	$56,140
Air Transportation	$55,810
Professional, Scientific, and Technical Services	$55,700
Internet Service Providers, Web Search Portals, and Data-Processing Services	$54,200
Publishing Industries (Except Internet)	$53,550
Chemical Manufacturing	$53,440

Median Wages for States (Annual)

State	Wage	State	Wage	State	Wage
AK	$48,590	KY	$42,100	NY	$51,620
AL	$41,510	LA	$39,680	OH	$47,020
AR	$36,880	MA	$56,480	OK	$36,740
AZ	$41,840	MD	$44,830	OR	$45,620
CA	$55,150	ME	$41,150	PA	$45,940
CO	$48,050	MI	$50,340	RI	$49,050
CT	$55,140	MN	$53,880	SC	$44,920
DC	$69,930	MO	$44,230	SD	$34,460
DE	$55,510	MS	$37,500	TN	$42,290
FL	$45,150	MT	$39,190	TX	$47,330
GA	$51,640	NC	$45,570	UT	$40,020
HI	$47,470	ND	$38,470	VA	$51,870
IA	$38,830	NE	$41,390	VT	$45,850
ID	$43,050	NH	$49,800	WA	$53,760
IL	$47,990	NJ	$57,580	WI	$43,690
IN	$42,660	NM	$38,010	WV	$41,740
KS	$47,350	NV	$40,030	WY	$39,240

Median Wages for the Largest Metropolitan Areas (Annual)

Area	Wage	Area	Wage
AZ: Phoenix	$43,040	MI: Detroit	$51,390
CA: Los Angeles	$54,530	MN: Minneapolis	$56,140
CA: Riverside	$44,600	MO: Kansas City	$51,100
CA: Sacramento	$50,470	MO: St. Louis	$46,220
CA: San Diego	$62,560	NV: Las Vegas	$45,790
CA: San Francisco	$65,400	NY: New York	$56,790
CO: Denver	$49,200	OH: Cincinnati	$47,550
DC: Washington	$55,970	OH: Cleveland	$46,680
FL: Miami	$48,990	OH: Columbus	$50,690
FL: Orlando	$41,120	OR: Portland	$49,220
FL: Tampa	$44,710	PA: Philadelphia	$51,610
GA: Atlanta	$56,230	PA: Pittsburgh	$43,000
IL: Chicago	$49,260	TX: Dallas	$49,150
MA: Boston	$58,160	TX: Houston	$51,480
MD: Baltimore	$45,790	WA: Seattle	$55,370

FACTORS THAT MAY AFFECT EARNINGS

Educational Attainment of Workers and Effect on Earnings

Figures are based on a group of occupations: Business Operations Specialists

	Percent at Level	Effect on Earnings
Less than High School	—	—
Some High School	2.3%	−37.9%
High School or Equivalent	19.6%	−14.2%
Some College but No Degree	21.9%	−10.8%
Associate Degree	13.8%	−7.9%
Bachelor's Degree	26.8%	7.3%
Master's Degree	12.5%	30.9%
Doctoral Degree	1.2%	43.9%
First Professional Degree	1.3%	61.6%

Flexibility of Earnings

Average Hours Worked: 36
Workers with a Varying Number of Hours: 8.0%
Workers Earning Some Overtime Pay, Tips, or Commissions: 11.3%
Earnings Benefit of Working Overtime: 10.3%

Gender

	Male	Female
Percent	28.5%	71.5%
Effect on Earnings	15.3%	−6.4%

Union Membership

Percentage Union Members: 7.6%
Earnings Benefit of Union Membership: −7.2%

Veteran Status

Percentage Who Have Been on Active Duty: 8.8%
Earnings Benefit of Veteran Status: 13.8%

13-1079 Human Resources, Training, and Labor Relations Specialists, All Other

All human resources, training, and labor relations specialists not listed separately.

- Education or Training Required: Bachelor's degree
- Job Growth: 24.1%
- Annual Openings: 26,000
- Self-Employed: 1.8%
- Part-Time: 25.7%

NATIONAL WAGE FIGURES (ANNUAL)

Beginning	25th Percentile	Median	Mean	75th Percentile	90th Percentile
$26,000	$38,980	$52,270	$54,700	$69,450	$88,630

Median Wages for Industries Employing Largest Numbers (Annual)

Industry	Median Income
Utilities	$68,180
Transportation Equipment Manufacturing	$63,420
Computer and Electronic Product Manufacturing	$63,250
Postal Service	$62,630
Federal, State, and Local Government	$62,310
Telecommunications	$61,940
Publishing Industries (Except Internet)	$60,310
Professional, Scientific, and Technical Services	$57,280
Chemical Manufacturing	$56,730
Management of Companies and Enterprises	$56,590

Median Wages for States (Annual)

AK $57,890	KY $44,560	NY $47,770
AL $45,240	LA $44,170	OH $46,810
AR $43,580	MA $57,430	OK $49,290
AZ $42,020	MD $62,740	OR $52,870
CA $59,110	ME $44,380	PA $44,640
CO $55,030	MI $54,750	RI $46,790
CT $61,170	MN $50,800	SC $48,510
DC $83,720	MO $51,100	SD $60,990
DE $52,210	MS $57,280	TN $50,790
FL $48,580	MT $47,730	TX $50,780
GA $56,190	NC $51,080	UT $49,110
HI $60,100	ND $47,040	VA $59,930
IA $40,210	NE $50,190	VT $55,250
ID $49,400	NH $47,760	WA $57,510
IL $47,290	NJ $58,400	WI $39,790
IN $40,890	NM $50,070	WV $47,830
KS $52,630	NV $52,420	WY $46,500

Median Wages for the Largest Metropolitan Areas (Annual)

AZ: Phoenix $39,710	MI: Detroit $58,220
CA: Los Angeles $58,540	MN: Minneapolis $52,540
CA: Riverside $58,560	MO: Kansas City $56,160
CA: Sacramento $58,490	MO: St. Louis............ $45,070
CA: San Diego $47,160	NV: Las Vegas $52,050
CA: San Francisco.... $70,630	NY: New York............ $54,670
CO: Denver $57,140	OH: Cincinnati.......... $46,730
DC: Washington $73,820	OH: Cleveland $49,380
FL: Miami $50,710	OH: Columbus $50,120
FL: Orlando $47,580	OR: Portland $56,420
FL: Tampa $47,350	PA: Philadelphia $53,990
GA: Atlanta $58,950	PA: Pittsburgh $21,140
IL: Chicago $52,490	TX: Dallas $53,210
MA: Boston $58,910	TX: Houston $52,940
MD: Baltimore $62,740	WA: Seattle $59,070

FACTORS THAT MAY AFFECT EARNINGS

Educational Attainment of Workers and Effect on Earnings

Figures are based on a group of occupations: Business Operations Specialists

	Percent at Level	Effect on Earnings
Less than High School	—	—
Some High School	2.3%	−37.9%
High School or Equivalent	19.6%	−14.2%
Some College but No Degree	21.9%	−10.8%
Associate Degree	13.8%	−7.9%
Bachelor's Degree	26.8%	7.3%
Master's Degree	12.5%	30.9%
Doctoral Degree	1.2%	43.9%
First Professional Degree	1.3%	61.6%

Flexibility of Earnings

Average Hours Worked: 36

Workers with a Varying Number of Hours: 8.0%

Workers Earning Some Overtime Pay, Tips, or Commissions: 11.3%

Earnings Benefit of Working Overtime: 10.3%

Gender

	Male	Female
Percent	28.5%	71.5%
Effect on Earnings	15.3%	−6.4%

Union Membership

Percentage Union Members: 7.6%

Earnings Benefit of Union Membership: −7.2%

Veteran Status

Percentage Who Have Been on Active Duty: 8.8%

Earnings Benefit of Veteran Status: 13.8%

13-1081 Logisticians

Analyze and coordinate the logistical functions of a firm or organization. Responsible for the entire life cycle of a product, including acquisition, distribution, internal allocation, delivery, and final disposal of resources.

- Education or Training Required: Bachelor's degree
- Job Growth: 13.2%
- Annual Openings: 7,000
- Self-Employed: 0.7%
- Part-Time: 25.7%

NATIONAL WAGE FIGURES (ANNUAL)

Beginning	25th Percentile	Median	Mean	75th Percentile	90th Percentile
$39,410	$50,000	$63,430	$65,640	$79,150	$97,020

Median Wages for Industries Employing Largest Numbers (Annual)

Industry	Median Income
Telecommunications	$70,150
Federal, State, and Local Government	$68,510
Computer and Electronic Product Manufacturing	$68,170
Utilities	$67,430
Wholesale Electronic Markets and Agents and Brokers	$66,210
Publishing Industries (Except Internet)	$65,450
Management of Companies and Enterprises	$63,510
Professional, Scientific, and Technical Services	$62,420
Transportation Equipment Manufacturing	$61,940
Postal Service	$60,690

Median Wages for States (Annual)

AK $62,690	KY $56,850	NY $67,440
AL $72,080	LA $57,730	OH $62,980
AR $60,860	MA $66,510	OK $60,200
AZ $64,510	MD $72,620	OR $57,870
CA $67,570	ME $59,350	PA $63,790
CO $69,380	MI $65,120	RI $61,620
CT $61,960	MN $62,180	SC $58,320
DC $77,820	MO $53,930	SD $57,440
DE $61,150	MS $50,260	TN $57,440
FL $56,940	MT $54,420	TX $55,300
GA $60,650	NC $57,500	UT $59,640
HI $72,050	ND $57,790	VA $67,650
IA $58,140	NE $55,820	VT .... no data
ID $47,870	NH $56,580	WA $63,760
IL $63,250	NJ $74,470	WI $57,960
IN $60,430	NM $88,610	WV $52,810
KS $61,840	NV $57,220	WY .... no data

Median Wages for the Largest Metropolitan Areas (Annual)

AZ: Phoenix	$67,350	MI: Detroit	$70,870
CA: Los Angeles	$66,010	MN: Minneapolis	no data
CA: Riverside	$62,460	MO: Kansas City	$52,340
CA: Sacramento	$66,310	MO: St. Louis	$62,930
CA: San Diego	$65,100	NV: Las Vegas	$58,310
CA: San Francisco	$70,260	NY: New York	$74,300
CO: Denver	$68,890	OH: Cincinnati	$62,110
DC: Washington	$73,940	OH: Cleveland	$58,640
FL: Miami	$50,940	OH: Columbus	$62,650
FL: Orlando	$66,130	OR: Portland	$59,140
FL: Tampa	$57,920	PA: Philadelphia	$64,320
GA: Atlanta	$59,490	PA: Pittsburgh	$59,070
IL: Chicago	$59,190	TX: Dallas	$55,480
MA: Boston	$67,530	TX: Houston	$59,540
MD: Baltimore	$68,870	WA: Seattle	$63,400

FACTORS THAT MAY AFFECT EARNINGS

Educational Attainment of Workers and Effect on Earnings

	Percent at Level	Effect on Earnings
Less than High School	—	—
Some High School	—	—
High School or Equivalent	23.2%	−18.2%
Some College but No Degree	21.4%	−8.3%
Associate Degree	10.7%	−4.5%
Bachelor's Degree	32.1%	12.8%
Master's Degree	10.7%	20.7%
Doctoral Degree	—	—
First Professional Degree	—	—

Flexibility of Earnings

Average Hours Worked: 39
Workers with a Varying Number of Hours: 3.3%
Workers Earning Some Overtime Pay, Tips, or Commissions: 20.7%
Earnings Benefit of Working Overtime: 6.6%

Gender

	Male	Female
Percent	67.3%	32.7%
Effect on Earnings	21.9%	−11.0%

Union Membership

Percentage Union Members: Insignificant
Earnings Benefit of Union Membership: No significant data available

Veteran Status

Percentage Who Have Been on Active Duty: 8.8%
Earnings Benefit of Veteran Status: 13.8%

13-1111 *Management Analysts*

Conduct organizational studies and evaluations, design systems and procedures, conduct work simplifications and measurement studies, and prepare operations and procedures manuals to assist management in operating more efficiently and effectively. Includes program analysts and management consultants.

- Education or Training Required: Work experience plus degree
- Job Growth: 20.1%
- Annual Openings: 82,000
- Self-Employed: 24.7%
- Part-Time: 33.6%

NATIONAL WAGE FIGURES (ANNUAL)

Beginning	25th Percentile	Median	Mean	75th Percentile	90th Percentile
$39,840	$50,860	$68,050	$77,270	$92,390	$128,330

Median Wages for Industries Employing Largest Numbers (Annual)

Industry	Median Income
Merchant Wholesalers, Durable Goods	$90,440
Real Estate	$77,210
Professional, Scientific, and Technical Services	$76,130
Publishing Industries (Except Internet)	$75,140
Securities, Commodity Contracts, and Other Financial Investments and Related Activities	$73,160
Postal Service	$72,340
Computer and Electronic Product Manufacturing	$72,040
Management of Companies and Enterprises	$68,660
Utilities	$67,980
Transportation Equipment Manufacturing	$67,960

Median Wages for States (Annual)

State	Wage	State	Wage	State	Wage
AK	$68,330	KY	$62,230	NY	$70,480
AL	$66,140	LA	$55,800	OH	$65,620
AR	$48,540	MA	$80,830	OK	$55,140
AZ	$60,590	MD	$71,170	OR	$56,260
CA	$71,320	ME	$56,580	PA	$71,560
CO	$73,910	MI	$73,050	RI	$61,340
CT	$73,910	MN	$70,720	SC	$60,020
DC	$76,040	MO	$63,880	SD	$55,780
DE	$83,280	MS	$55,350	TN	$54,760
FL	$58,950	MT	$53,440	TX	$54,280
GA	$71,440	NC	$69,460	UT	$68,450
HI	$68,160	ND	$55,680	VA	$76,490
IA	$57,300	NE	$57,690	VT	$70,150
ID	$70,370	NH	$74,060	WA	$70,190
IL	$71,120	NJ	$81,220	WI	$55,000
IN	$56,290	NM	$57,750	WV	$59,370
KS	$60,410	NV	$66,970	WY	$48,390

Median Wages for the Largest Metropolitan Areas (Annual)

Area	Wage	Area	Wage
AZ: Phoenix	$62,640	MI: Detroit	$81,460
CA: Los Angeles	$69,450	MN: Minneapolis	$71,710
CA: Riverside	$59,210	MO: Kansas City	$66,910
CA: Sacramento	$62,760	MO: St. Louis	$65,120
CA: San Diego	$73,950	NV: Las Vegas	$67,200
CA: San Francisco	$78,200	NY: New York	$78,510
CO: Denver	$74,440	OH: Cincinnati	$69,530
DC: Washington	$78,710	OH: Cleveland	$66,290
FL: Miami	$63,090	OH: Columbus	$62,410
FL: Orlando	$63,590	OR: Portland	$63,240
FL: Tampa	$65,940	PA: Philadelphia	$76,950
GA: Atlanta	$74,150	PA: Pittsburgh	$76,180
IL: Chicago	$71,680	TX: Dallas	$66,410
MA: Boston	$82,560	TX: Houston	$55,990
MD: Baltimore	$69,820	WA: Seattle	$71,670

FACTORS THAT MAY AFFECT EARNINGS

Educational Attainment of Workers and Effect on Earnings

	Percent at Level	Effect on Earnings
Less than High School	—	—
Some High School	—	—
High School or Equivalent	10.8%	−29.0%
Some College but No Degree	11.7%	−13.4%
Associate Degree	9.3%	−23.1%
Bachelor's Degree	38.6%	0.4%
Master's Degree	24.4%	22.8%
Doctoral Degree	2.4%	21.1%
First Professional Degree	1.8%	41.0%

Flexibility of Earnings

Average Hours Worked: 34
Workers with a Varying Number of Hours: 12.5%
Workers Earning Some Overtime Pay, Tips, or Commissions: 11.6%
Earnings Benefit of Working Overtime: 2.8%

Gender

	Male	Female
Percent	57.8%	42.2%
Effect on Earnings	13.1%	−14.7%

Union Membership

Percentage Union Members: Insignificant
Earnings Benefit of Union Membership: No significant data available

Veteran Status

Percentage Who Have Been on Active Duty: 8.8%
Earnings Benefit of Veteran Status: 13.8%

13-1121 Meeting and Convention Planners

Coordinate activities of staff and convention personnel to make arrangements for group meetings and conventions.

- Education or Training Required: Bachelor's degree
- Job Growth: 22.2%
- Annual Openings: 4,000
- Self-Employed: 5.1%
- Part-Time: 31.3%

NATIONAL WAGE FIGURES (ANNUAL)

Beginning	25th Percentile	Median	Mean	75th Percentile	90th Percentile
$25,880	$32,840	$42,180	$45,580	$55,040	$70,950

Median Wages for Industries Employing Largest Numbers (Annual)

Industry	Median Income
Credit Intermediation and Related Activities	$54,150
Computer and Electronic Product Manufacturing	$51,270
Publishing Industries (Except Internet)	$50,670
Motion Picture and Sound Recording Industries	$50,440
Securities, Commodity Contracts, and Other Financial Investments and Related Activities	$50,210
Internet Service Providers, Web Search Portals, and Data-Processing Services	$49,430
Insurance Carriers and Related Activities	$49,360
Professional, Scientific, and Technical Services	$47,490
Management of Companies and Enterprises	$46,170
Merchant Wholesalers, Durable Goods	$45,590

Median Wages for States (Annual)

AK .... no data	KY $36,230	NY $51,020
AL $32,780	LA $35,250	OH $38,230
AR $28,260	MA $47,730	OK $29,270
AZ $39,990	MD $42,900	OR $36,040
CA $43,880	ME $33,120	PA $41,270
CO $39,340	MI $38,620	RI $43,490
CT $53,300	MN $42,150	SC $34,220
DC $47,990	MO $37,670	SD $27,240
DE $42,240	MS $29,480	TN $38,200
FL $39,500	MT $28,510	TX $41,370
GA $41,020	NC $36,580	UT $39,300
HI $45,270	ND .... no data	VA $45,350
IA $32,510	NE $35,710	VT $35,000
ID $42,740	NH $37,490	WA $42,300
IL $49,810	NJ $43,750	WI $36,500
IN $36,370	NM $34,410	WV $38,370
KS $35,340	NV $43,210	WY $28,150

Median Wages for the Largest Metropolitan Areas (Annual)

AZ: Phoenix $41,270	MI: Detroit $40,450
CA: Los Angeles $45,820	MN: Minneapolis $43,480
CA: Riverside $37,790	MO: Kansas City $40,400
CA: Sacramento $41,740	MO: St. Louis $39,820
CA: San Diego $40,210	NV: Las Vegas $35,270
CA: San Francisco $46,460	NY: New York $51,460
CO: Denver $43,680	OH: Cincinnati $40,120
DC: Washington $47,460	OH: Cleveland $39,450
FL: Miami $48,440	OH: Columbus $38,450
FL: Orlando $35,510	OR: Portland $38,600
FL: Tampa $34,410	PA: Philadelphia $47,100
GA: Atlanta $42,080	PA: Pittsburgh $34,170
IL: Chicago $51,170	TX: Dallas $44,500
MA: Boston $49,040	TX: Houston $40,050
MD: Baltimore $43,320	WA: Seattle $42,690

FACTORS THAT MAY AFFECT EARNINGS

Educational Attainment of Workers and Effect on Earnings

	Percent at Level	Effect on Earnings
Less than High School	—	—
Some High School	—	—
High School or Equivalent	14.9%	−24.0%
Some College but No Degree	17.0%	−35.4%
Associate Degree	14.9%	−6.2%
Bachelor's Degree	36.2%	21.2%
Master's Degree	17.0%	16.7%
Doctoral Degree	—	—
First Professional Degree	—	—

Flexibility of Earnings

Average Hours Worked: 35
Workers with a Varying Number of Hours: 6.5%
Workers Earning Some Overtime Pay, Tips, or Commissions: 14.0%
Earnings Benefit of Working Overtime: 6.6%

Gender

	Male	Female
Percent	29.9%	70.1%
Effect on Earnings	21.9%	−11.0%

Union Membership

Percentage Union Members: 6.0%
Earnings Benefit of Union Membership: −7.2%

Veteran Status

Percentage Who Have Been on Active Duty: 8.8%
Earnings Benefit of Veteran Status: 13.8%

13-1199 Business Operations Specialists, All Other

All business operations specialists not listed separately.

- Education or Training Required: Bachelor's degree
- Job Growth: 27.0%
- Annual Openings: 193,000
- Self-Employed: 0.0%
- Part-Time: 24.3%

NATIONAL WAGE FIGURES (ANNUAL)

Beginning	25th Percentile	Median	Mean	75th Percentile	90th Percentile
$30,070	$40,680	$55,650	$60,240	$74,700	$96,590

Median Wages for Industries Employing Largest Numbers (Annual)

Industry	Median Income
Transportation Equipment Manufacturing	$70,910
Couriers and Messengers	$68,770
Utilities	$67,500
Telecommunications	$67,150
Computer and Electronic Product Manufacturing	$66,550
Merchant Wholesalers, Durable Goods	$62,590
Professional, Scientific, and Technical Services	$62,160
Publishing Industries (Except Internet)	$61,890
Federal, State, and Local Government	$59,980
Management of Companies and Enterprises	$59,000

Median Wages for States (Annual)

AK $63,940	KY $50,010	NY $62,940
AL $59,360	LA $43,570	OH $47,070
AR $42,310	MA $61,350	OK $55,180
AZ $49,420	MD $61,270	OR $46,220
CA $56,520	ME $50,800	PA $59,580
CO $63,370	MI $65,090	RI $58,010
CT $63,080	MN $46,250	SC $48,650
DC $76,230	MO $50,930	SD $51,880
DE $61,130	MS $42,730	TN $62,350
FL $53,590	MT $45,670	TX $56,640
GA $57,260	NC $51,070	UT $52,550
HI $55,940	ND $48,410	VA $64,150
IA $42,950	NE $49,410	VT $57,060
ID $45,800	NH $45,890	WA $61,710
IL $55,340	NJ $61,130	WI $49,580
IN $51,040	NM $51,880	WV $50,030
KS $51,690	NV $55,240	WY $46,870

Median Wages for the Largest Metropolitan Areas (Annual)

AZ: Phoenix	$48,310	MI: Detroit	$77,130
CA: Los Angeles	$56,440	MN: Minneapolis	$49,190
CA: Riverside	$56,340	MO: Kansas City	$61,430
CA: Sacramento	$51,900	MO: St. Louis	$50,830
CA: San Diego	$53,390	NV: Las Vegas	$55,510
CA: San Francisco	$64,480	NY: New York	$63,130
CO: Denver	$64,290	OH: Cincinnati	$50,360
DC: Washington	$72,850	OH: Cleveland	$49,690
FL: Miami	$56,140	OH: Columbus	$49,100
FL: Orlando	$53,230	OR: Portland	$47,680
FL: Tampa	$53,240	PA: Philadelphia	$62,440
GA: Atlanta	$58,260	PA: Pittsburgh	$54,880
IL: Chicago	$56,750	TX: Dallas	$58,350
MA: Boston	$60,970	TX: Houston	$60,890
MD: Baltimore	$59,340	WA: Seattle	$63,930

FACTORS THAT MAY AFFECT EARNINGS

Educational Attainment of Workers and Effect on Earnings

	Percent at Level	Effect on Earnings
Less than High School	—	—
Some High School	—	—
High School or Equivalent	16.2%	−20.7%
Some College but No Degree	28.1%	−15.6%
Associate Degree	9.1%	−22.8%
Bachelor's Degree	30.0%	13.7%
Master's Degree	12.6%	34.5%
Doctoral Degree	—	—
First Professional Degree	—	—

Flexibility of Earnings

Average Hours Worked: 36
Workers with a Varying Number of Hours: 4.8%
Workers Earning Some Overtime Pay, Tips, or Commissions: 8.4%
Earnings Benefit of Working Overtime: 23.8%

Gender

	Male	Female
Percent	28.0%	72.0%
Effect on Earnings	21.9%	−11.0%

Union Membership

Percentage Union Members: 9.5%
Earnings Benefit of Union Membership: 6.7%

Veteran Status

Percentage Who Have Been on Active Duty: 8.8%
Earnings Benefit of Veteran Status: 13.8%

13-0000: Business and Financial Operations Occupations

13-2000 Financial Specialists

13-2011 Accountants and Auditors

Examine, analyze, and interpret accounting records for the purpose of giving advice or preparing statements. Install or advise on systems of recording costs or other financial and budgetary data.

- Education or Training Required: Bachelor's degree
- Job Growth: 22.4%
- Annual Openings: 157,000
- Self-Employed: 10.9%
- Part-Time: 22.2%

NATIONAL WAGE FIGURES (ANNUAL)

Beginning	25th Percentile	Median	Mean	75th Percentile	90th Percentile
$34,470	$42,520	$54,630	$60,670	$71,960	$94,050

Median Wages for Industries Employing Largest Numbers (Annual)

Industry	Median Income
Securities, Commodity Contracts, and Other Financial Investments and Related Activities	$61,670
Telecommunications	$59,800
Computer and Electronic Product Manufacturing	$58,850
Chemical Manufacturing	$57,910
Publishing Industries (Except Internet)	$57,770
Specialty Trade Contractors	$57,120
Merchant Wholesalers, Durable Goods	$57,000
Professional, Scientific, and Technical Services	$56,950
Motor Vehicle and Parts Dealers	$56,730
Merchant Wholesalers, Nondurable Goods	$56,680

Median Wages for States (Annual)

State	Wage	State	Wage	State	Wage
AK	$54,100	KY	$45,950	NY	$64,810
AL	$48,510	LA	$45,550	OH	$53,210
AR	$44,420	MA	$57,760	OK	$44,590
AZ	$48,370	MD	$58,430	OR	$51,890
CA	$57,820	ME	$45,980	PA	$53,110
CO	$54,970	MI	$54,210	RI	$57,420
CT	$62,840	MN	$53,510	SC	$47,590
DC	$63,360	MO	$50,080	SD	$43,930
DE	$53,670	MS	$45,850	TN	$47,120
FL	$50,660	MT	$44,600	TX	$52,580
GA	$53,340	NC	$51,720	UT	$50,010
HI	$47,390	ND	$40,990	VA	$58,630
IA	$48,170	NE	$51,730	VT	$53,790
ID	$42,930	NH	$49,360	WA	$55,520
IL	$57,330	NJ	$65,010	WI	$53,560
IN	$51,320	NM	$46,950	WV	$41,980
KS	$48,750	NV	$49,120	WY	$41,180

Median Wages for the Largest Metropolitan Areas (Annual)

Area	Wage	Area	Wage
AZ: Phoenix	$48,910	MI: Detroit	$56,380
CA: Los Angeles	$56,680	MN: Minneapolis	$55,080
CA: Riverside	$53,660	MO: Kansas City	$50,810
CA: Sacramento	$56,070	MO: St. Louis	$53,690
CA: San Diego	$56,660	NV: Las Vegas	$49,610
CA: San Francisco	$63,150	NY: New York	$67,880
CO: Denver	$56,590	OH: Cincinnati	$54,370
DC: Washington	$64,380	OH: Cleveland	$52,720
FL: Miami	$53,960	OH: Columbus	$53,910
FL: Orlando	$49,820	OR: Portland	$54,490
FL: Tampa	$49,370	PA: Philadelphia	$59,590
GA: Atlanta	$55,330	PA: Pittsburgh	$48,040
IL: Chicago	$58,860	TX: Dallas	$55,740
MA: Boston	$58,590	TX: Houston	$56,050
MD: Baltimore	$57,160	WA: Seattle	$56,700

FACTORS THAT MAY AFFECT EARNINGS

Educational Attainment of Workers and Effect on Earnings

	Percent at Level	Effect on Earnings
Less than High School	—	—
Some High School	0.6%	−45.1%
High School or Equivalent	9.7%	−21.2%
Some College but No Degree	15.7%	−23.5%
Associate Degree	16.3%	−15.7%
Bachelor's Degree	39.4%	10.9%
Master's Degree	16.3%	24.1%
Doctoral Degree	0.6%	−6.4%
First Professional Degree	1.0%	41.6%

Flexibility of Earnings

Average Hours Worked: 37
Workers with a Varying Number of Hours: 5.5%
Workers Earning Some Overtime Pay, Tips, or Commissions: 8.8%
Earnings Benefit of Working Overtime: 8.8%

Gender

	Male	Female
Percent	39.8%	60.2%
Effect on Earnings	23.4%	−10.2%

Union Membership

Percentage Union Members: 4.7%
Earnings Benefit of Union Membership: −3.8%

Veteran Status

Percentage Who Have Been on Active Duty: 6.5%
Earnings Benefit of Veteran Status: 13.5%

© JIST Works   Salary Facts Handbook 119

13-2021 Appraisers and Assessors of Real Estate

Appraise real property to determine its fair value. May assess taxes in accordance with prescribed schedules.

- Education or Training Required: Postsecondary vocational training
- Job Growth: 22.8%
- Annual Openings: 9,000
- Self-Employed: 37.2%
- Part-Time: 24.5%

Note: Earnings figures do not reflect self-employed workers, who make up a large fraction of the workforce for this occupation.

NATIONAL WAGE FIGURES (ANNUAL)

Beginning	25th Percentile	Median	Mean	75th Percentile	90th Percentile
$24,000	$32,080	$44,460	$51,110	$64,460	$86,140

Median Wages for Industries Employing Largest Numbers (Annual)

Industry	Median Income
Postal Service	$87,210
Funds, Trusts, and Other Financial Vehicles	$78,720
Utilities	$74,130
Construction of Buildings	$73,800
Management of Companies and Enterprises	$71,450
Securities, Commodity Contracts, and Other Financial Investments and Related Activities	$67,230
Heavy and Civil Engineering Construction	$67,110
Credit Intermediation and Related Activities	$60,350
Insurance Carriers and Related Activities	$49,690
Internet Service Providers, Web Search Portals, and Data-Processing Services	$46,310

Median Wages for States (Annual)

AK	no data	KY	no data	NY	$46,010
AL	$42,700	LA	$37,140	OH	$38,650
AR	$30,910	MA	$55,920	OK	$27,300
AZ	$40,110	MD	$46,030	OR	$48,230
CA	$66,990	ME	$41,630	PA	$39,660
CO	$44,750	MI	$50,530	RI	$45,220
CT	$56,360	MN	$46,780	SC	$36,450
DC	$60,450	MO	$33,310	SD	$34,030
DE	$45,020	MS	$38,630	TN	$34,540
FL	$45,330	MT	$37,150	TX	$45,970
GA	$36,810	NC	$40,260	UT	$41,200
HI	$54,210	ND	$34,650	VA	$46,400
IA	$42,300	NE	$36,610	VT	$47,230
ID	$36,950	NH	$53,670	WA	$51,020
IL	$37,710	NJ	$64,270	WI	$43,100
IN	$30,120	NM	$38,060	WV	$30,190
KS	$38,300	NV	$59,870	WY	$45,060

Median Wages for the Largest Metropolitan Areas (Annual)

AZ: Phoenix	$43,240	MI: Detroit	$57,490
CA: Los Angeles	$71,030	MN: Minneapolis	$48,080
CA: Riverside	$57,510	MO: Kansas City	$39,570
CA: Sacramento	$56,960	MO: St. Louis	$29,050
CA: San Diego	$59,320	NV: Las Vegas	$60,780
CA: San Francisco	$79,310	NY: New York	$62,010
CO: Denver	$49,130	OH: Cincinnati	$44,340
DC: Washington	$60,560	OH: Cleveland	$40,220
FL: Miami	$54,700	OH: Columbus	$44,210
FL: Orlando	$36,160	OR: Portland	$48,980
FL: Tampa	$62,990	PA: Philadelphia	$61,670
GA: Atlanta	$41,030	PA: Pittsburgh	$33,780
IL: Chicago	$44,210	TX: Dallas	$68,060
MA: Boston	$70,820	TX: Houston	$42,210
MD: Baltimore	$42,230	WA: Seattle	$52,670

FACTORS THAT MAY AFFECT EARNINGS

Educational Attainment of Workers and Effect on Earnings

	Percent at Level	Effect on Earnings
Less than High School	—	—
Some High School	—	—
High School or Equivalent	16.0%	−16.9%
Some College but No Degree	24.0%	−26.7%
Associate Degree	13.0%	−2.3%
Bachelor's Degree	37.0%	19.8%
Master's Degree	9.0%	9.1%
Doctoral Degree	—	—
First Professional Degree	—	—

Flexibility of Earnings

Average Hours Worked: 35
Workers with a Varying Number of Hours: 12.8%
Workers Earning Some Overtime Pay, Tips, or Commissions: 18.8%
Earnings Benefit of Working Overtime: 6.4%

Gender

	Male	Female
Percent	64.3%	35.7%
Effect on Earnings	21.9%	−11.0%

Union Membership

Percentage Union Members: 10.7%
Earnings Benefit of Union Membership: 16.9%

Veteran Status

Percentage Who Have Been on Active Duty: 6.5%
Earnings Benefit of Veteran Status: 13.5%

13-2031 Budget Analysts

Examine budget estimates for completeness, accuracy, and conformance with procedures and regulations. Analyze budgeting and accounting reports for the purpose of maintaining expenditure controls.

- Education or Training Required: Bachelor's degree
- Job Growth: 13.5%
- Annual Openings: 6,000
- Self-Employed: 2.0%
- Part-Time: 21.8%

NATIONAL WAGE FIGURES (ANNUAL)

Beginning	25th Percentile	Median	Mean	75th Percentile	90th Percentile
$40,070	$49,070	$61,430	$63,920	$77,000	$93,080

Median Wages for Industries Employing Largest Numbers (Annual)

Industry	Median Income
Internet Service Providers, Web Search Portals, and Data-Processing Services	$88,450
Real Estate	$84,490
Computer and Electronic Product Manufacturing	$74,790
Postal Service	$73,820
Construction of Buildings	$72,690
Oil and Gas Extraction	$70,030
Rail Transportation	$68,990
Professional, Scientific, and Technical Services	$67,910
Chemical Manufacturing	$67,270
Transportation Equipment Manufacturing	$66,990

Median Wages for States (Annual)

AK	$63,010	KY	no data	NY	$59,480
AL	$59,630	LA	$45,430	OH	$59,660
AR	$51,050	MA	$65,860	OK	$53,600
AZ	$57,080	MD	$66,590	OR	$54,740
CA	$68,870	ME	$54,690	PA	$58,970
CO	$62,070	MI	no data	RI	$62,100
CT	$63,060	MN	$54,810	SC	$49,860
DC	$74,010	MO	no data	SD	$45,090
DE	$56,700	MS	$51,350	TN	$54,050
FL	$51,740	MT	$48,650	TX	$57,960
GA	$58,210	NC	$56,090	UT	$58,860
HI	$62,790	ND	$53,850	VA	$68,950
IA	$54,640	NE	$54,020	VT	$54,810
ID	$49,920	NH	$57,060	WA	$64,480
IL	$67,620	NJ	$71,240	WI	$57,220
IN	$57,360	NM	$57,250	WV	$52,250
KS	$51,960	NV	$59,530	WY	$56,170

Median Wages for the Largest Metropolitan Areas (Annual)

AZ: Phoenix	$57,120	MI: Detroit	no data
CA: Los Angeles	$70,030	MN: Minneapolis	$54,800
CA: Riverside	$57,080	MO: Kansas City	$54,370
CA: Sacramento	$59,520	MO: St. Louis	no data
CA: San Diego	$64,430	NV: Las Vegas	$57,450
CA: San Francisco	$79,260	NY: New York	$68,480
CO: Denver	$65,020	OH: Cincinnati	$57,110
DC: Washington	$75,210	OH: Cleveland	$57,770
FL: Miami	$50,720	OH: Columbus	no data
FL: Orlando	$52,070	OR: Portland	$58,020
FL: Tampa	$54,620	PA: Philadelphia	$61,480
GA: Atlanta	$60,490	PA: Pittsburgh	$53,540
IL: Chicago	$70,660	TX: Dallas	$59,230
MA: Boston	$67,440	TX: Houston	$65,210
MD: Baltimore	$57,310	WA: Seattle	$64,990

FACTORS THAT MAY AFFECT EARNINGS

Educational Attainment of Workers and Effect on Earnings

	Percent at Level	Effect on Earnings
Less than High School	—	—
Some High School	—	—
High School or Equivalent	13.6%	0.6%
Some College but No Degree	13.6%	−31.6%
Associate Degree	—	—
Bachelor's Degree	42.4%	3.5%
Master's Degree	19.7%	21.5%
Doctoral Degree	—	—
First Professional Degree	—	—

Figures do not total 100% because some levels have a very small sample size.

Flexibility of Earnings

Average Hours Worked: 39
Workers with a Varying Number of Hours: 3.1%
Workers Earning Some Overtime Pay, Tips, or Commissions: 5.5%
Earnings Benefit of Working Overtime: 6.1%

Gender

	Male	Female
Percent	44.3%	55.7%
Effect on Earnings	21.9%	−11.0%

Union Membership

Percentage Union Members: 8.2%
Earnings Benefit of Union Membership: −3.0%

Veteran Status

Percentage Who Have Been on Active Duty: 6.5%
Earnings Benefit of Veteran Status: 13.5%

13-2041 Credit Analysts

Analyze current credit data and financial statements of individuals or firms to determine the degree of risk involved in extending credit or lending money. Prepare reports with this credit information for use in decision-making.

- Education or Training Required: Bachelor's degree
- Job Growth: 3.6%
- Annual Openings: 3,000
- Self-Employed: 0.0%
- Part-Time: 21.8%

NATIONAL WAGE FIGURES (ANNUAL)

Beginning	25th Percentile	Median	Mean	75th Percentile	90th Percentile
$30,620	$38,480	$52,350	$60,190	$73,150	$100,280

Median Wages for Industries Employing Largest Numbers (Annual)

Industry	Median Income
Publishing Industries (Except Internet)	$71,010
Motor Vehicle and Parts Dealers	$67,620
Securities, Commodity Contracts, and Other Financial Investments and Related Activities	$66,320
Utilities	$65,750
Professional, Scientific, and Technical Services	$58,850
Telecommunications	$56,790
Merchant Wholesalers, Durable Goods	$54,700
Computer and Electronic Product Manufacturing	$54,250
Internet Service Providers, Web Search Portals, and Data-Processing Services	$53,490
Management of Companies and Enterprises	$51,830

Median Wages for States (Annual)

AK	no data	KY	$53,750	NY	$73,710
AL	$45,800	LA	$42,210	OH	$48,420
AR	$46,210	MA	$53,120	OK	$42,510
AZ	$32,310	MD	$53,300	OR	$51,170
CA	$62,080	ME	$37,030	PA	$43,570
CO	$63,770	MI	$46,030	RI	$58,260
CT	$60,310	MN	$53,130	SC	$48,730
DC	$70,490	MO	$46,610	SD	$46,110
DE	no data	MS	$43,200	TN	$42,880
FL	$51,310	MT	$38,140	TX	$53,580
GA	$57,480	NC	$55,650	UT	$44,390
HI	$45,430	ND	$58,050	VA	$56,010
IA	$44,460	NE	$38,110	VT	$50,340
ID	$58,270	NH	$45,210	WA	$48,700
IL	$53,510	NJ	$55,810	WI	$41,530
IN	$50,450	NM	$44,800	WV	$41,690
KS	$43,450	NV	$54,430	WY	$35,070

Median Wages for the Largest Metropolitan Areas (Annual)

AZ: Phoenix	$31,670	MI: Detroit	$52,960
CA: Los Angeles	$59,890	MN: Minneapolis	$53,830
CA: Riverside	$57,680	MO: Kansas City	$45,420
CA: Sacramento	$67,100	MO: St. Louis	$46,750
CA: San Diego	$58,650	NV: Las Vegas	$55,940
CA: San Francisco	$72,110	NY: New York	$70,170
CO: Denver	$67,390	OH: Cincinnati	$51,110
DC: Washington	$58,950	OH: Cleveland	$52,320
FL: Miami	$50,170	OH: Columbus	$43,960
FL: Orlando	$54,240	OR: Portland	$52,470
FL: Tampa	$48,850	PA: Philadelphia	$45,620
GA: Atlanta	$62,610	PA: Pittsburgh	$38,020
IL: Chicago	$54,340	TX: Dallas	$53,490
MA: Boston	$53,780	TX: Houston	$56,490
MD: Baltimore	$54,330	WA: Seattle	$49,710

FACTORS THAT MAY AFFECT EARNINGS

Educational Attainment of Workers and Effect on Earnings

	Percent at Level	Effect on Earnings
Less than High School	—	—
Some High School	—	—
High School or Equivalent	—	—
Some College but No Degree	18.4%	−29.1%
Associate Degree	—	—
Bachelor's Degree	46.9%	3.9%
Master's Degree	18.4%	42.0%
Doctoral Degree	—	—
First Professional Degree	—	—

Figures do not total 100% because some levels have a very small sample size.

Flexibility of Earnings

Average Hours Worked: 38
Workers with a Varying Number of Hours: 2.9%
Workers Earning Some Overtime Pay, Tips, or Commissions: 6.0%
Earnings Benefit of Working Overtime: 6.1%

Gender

	Male	Female
Percent	35.7%	64.3%
Effect on Earnings	21.9%	−11.0%

Union Membership

Percentage Union Members: 5.1%
Earnings Benefit of Union Membership: −3.0%

Veteran Status

Percentage Who Have Been on Active Duty: 6.5%
Earnings Benefit of Veteran Status: 13.5%

13-2051 Financial Analysts

Conduct quantitative analyses of information affecting investment programs of public or private institutions.

- Education or Training Required: Bachelor's degree
- Job Growth: 17.3%
- Annual Openings: 28,000
- Self-Employed: 6.7%
- Part-Time: 30.5%

NATIONAL WAGE FIGURES (ANNUAL)

Beginning	25th Percentile	Median	Mean	75th Percentile	90th Percentile
$40,340	$50,700	$66,590	$77,280	$90,690	$130,130

Median Wages for Industries Employing Largest Numbers (Annual)

Industry	Median Income
Securities, Commodity Contracts, and Other Financial Investments and Related Activities	$81,060
Computer and Electronic Product Manufacturing	$70,030
Merchant Wholesalers, Durable Goods	$69,950
Oil and Gas Extraction	$69,820
Publishing Industries (Except Internet)	$69,420
Administrative and Support Services	$68,590
Utilities	$68,470
Transportation Equipment Manufacturing	$68,230
Professional, Scientific, and Technical Services	$65,530
Machinery Manufacturing	$65,340

Median Wages for States (Annual)

State	Wage	State	Wage	State	Wage
AK	$70,620	KY	$52,880	NY	$77,700
AL	$59,700	LA	$54,810	OH	$59,570
AR	$54,320	MA	$72,630	OK	$53,210
AZ	$55,520	MD	$62,580	OR	$65,000
CA	$74,430	ME	$61,490	PA	$56,820
CO	$60,660	MI	$67,790	RI	$57,690
CT	$77,390	MN	$65,950	SC	$48,690
DC	$66,040	MO	$58,370	SD	$46,430
DE	$69,650	MS	$56,200	TN	$53,570
FL	$56,880	MT	$65,750	TX	$62,790
GA	$62,760	NC	$62,290	UT	$56,320
HI	$58,010	ND	$63,980	VA	$69,550
IA	$56,350	NE	$53,230	VT	$66,990
ID	$57,820	NH	$65,050	WA	$74,580
IL	$67,550	NJ	$75,790	WI	$56,150
IN	$52,350	NM	$50,960	WV	$47,440
KS	$59,260	NV	$69,200	WY	$52,460

Median Wages for the Largest Metropolitan Areas (Annual)

Metro	Wage	Metro	Wage
AZ: Phoenix	$55,430	MI: Detroit	$74,480
CA: Los Angeles	$73,570	MN: Minneapolis	$66,020
CA: Riverside	$61,230	MO: Kansas City	$59,150
CA: Sacramento	$68,040	MO: St. Louis	$59,360
CA: San Diego	$61,170	NV: Las Vegas	$64,890
CA: San Francisco	$88,810	NY: New York	$80,870
CO: Denver	$61,640	OH: Cincinnati	$63,130
DC: Washington	$71,350	OH: Cleveland	$57,540
FL: Miami	$60,240	OH: Columbus	$59,630
FL: Orlando	$55,450	OR: Portland	$65,130
FL: Tampa	$51,700	PA: Philadelphia	$63,360
GA: Atlanta	$63,630	PA: Pittsburgh	$54,740
IL: Chicago	$68,440	TX: Dallas	$64,690
MA: Boston	$73,030	TX: Houston	$62,760
MD: Baltimore	$61,560	WA: Seattle	$75,920

FACTORS THAT MAY AFFECT EARNINGS

Educational Attainment of Workers and Effect on Earnings

	Percent at Level	Effect on Earnings
Less than High School	—	—
Some High School	—	—
High School or Equivalent	—	—
Some College but No Degree	—	—
Associate Degree	—	—
Bachelor's Degree	47.8%	−1.4%
Master's Degree	30.4%	26.2%
Doctoral Degree	—	—
First Professional Degree	—	—

Figures do not total 100% because some levels have a very small sample size.

Flexibility of Earnings

Average Hours Worked: 35
Workers with a Varying Number of Hours: 10.8%
Workers Earning Some Overtime Pay, Tips, or Commissions: 11.4%
Earnings Benefit of Working Overtime: 24.1%

Gender

	Male	Female
Percent	61.6%	38.4%
Effect on Earnings	21.9%	−11.0%

Union Membership

Percentage Union Members: 5.1%
Earnings Benefit of Union Membership: −3.0%

Veteran Status

Percentage Who Have Been on Active Duty: 6.5%
Earnings Benefit of Veteran Status: 13.5%

13-2052 Personal Financial Advisors

Advise clients on financial plans, utilizing knowledge of tax and investment strategies, securities, insurance, pension plans, and real estate. Duties include assessing clients' assets, liabilities, cash flow, insurance coverage, tax status, and financial objectives to establish investment strategies.

- Education or Training Required: Bachelor's degree
- Job Growth: 25.9%
- Annual Openings: 17,000
- Self-Employed: 38.9%
- Part-Time: 15.4%

Note: A large fraction of the workforce for this occupation is self-employed and earns an average of $75,700. All other earnings figures for this occupation are based on workers who are paid a wage or salary.

NATIONAL WAGE FIGURES (ANNUAL)

Beginning	25th Percentile	Median	Mean	75th Percentile	90th Percentile
$32,340	$44,130	$66,120	$86,730	$114,260	more than $145,600

Note: The mean is significantly higher than the median because of the presence of a few star earners.

Median Wages for Industries Employing Largest Numbers (Annual)

Industry	Median Income
Heavy and Civil Engineering Construction	$102,850
Securities, Commodity Contracts, and Other Financial Investments and Related Activities	$72,570
Personal and Laundry Services	$68,680
Management of Companies and Enterprises	$66,250
Motor Vehicle and Parts Dealers	$63,700
Real Estate	$62,970
Religious, Grantmaking, Civic, Professional, and Similar Organizations	$62,460
Administrative and Support Services	$61,460
Credit Intermediation and Related Activities	$61,260
Professional, Scientific, and Technical Services	$59,800

Median Wages for States (Annual)

AK	$44,530	KY	$39,970	NY	$90,640
AL	$72,670	LA	$51,580	OH	$67,900
AR	$50,600	MA	no data	OK	$58,470
AZ	$57,580	MD	$59,480	OR	$51,900
CA	$70,810	ME	$91,180	PA	$61,870
CO	no data	MI	$75,570	RI	$57,450
CT	$75,430	MN	$60,560	SC	$48,200
DC	$48,480	MO	$49,980	SD	$54,230
DE	$69,120	MS	$58,360	TN	$60,290
FL	$52,840	MT	$50,400	TX	$66,690
GA	$61,960	NC	$57,670	UT	$53,300
HI	$73,670	ND	$38,630	VA	$71,530
IA	$67,420	NE	$43,580	VT	$67,150
ID	$39,080	NH	$59,520	WA	$59,350
IL	$66,330	NJ	$74,850	WI	$57,210
IN	$57,490	NM	$51,180	WV	$35,960
KS	$84,840	NV	$46,030	WY	no data

Median Wages for the Largest Metropolitan Areas (Annual)

AZ: Phoenix	$64,250	MI: Detroit	$84,270
CA: Los Angeles	$72,680	MN: Minneapolis	$61,410
CA: Riverside	$67,060	MO: Kansas City	$61,890
CA: Sacramento	$44,270	MO: St. Louis	$50,760
CA: San Diego	$72,410	NV: Las Vegas	$44,990
CA: San Francisco	$77,030	NY: New York	$91,770
CO: Denver	no data	OH: Cincinnati	$68,190
DC: Washington	$58,080	OH: Cleveland	$88,230
FL: Miami	$50,590	OH: Columbus	$62,900
FL: Orlando	$44,970	OR: Portland	$50,710
FL: Tampa	$61,950	PA: Philadelphia	$62,970
GA: Atlanta	$63,050	PA: Pittsburgh	$69,010
IL: Chicago	$69,690	TX: Dallas	$69,630
MA: Boston	no data	TX: Houston	$64,450
MD: Baltimore	$65,670	WA: Seattle	$60,580

FACTORS THAT MAY AFFECT EARNINGS

Educational Attainment of Workers and Effect on Earnings

	Percent at Level	Effect on Earnings
Less than High School	—	—
Some High School	—	—
High School or Equivalent	8.5%	−24.9%
Some College but No Degree	12.6%	−25.2%
Associate Degree	10.1%	−30.6%
Bachelor's Degree	42.9%	−0.1%
Master's Degree	20.6%	29.8%
Doctoral Degree	2.4%	53.7%
First Professional Degree	2.4%	52.1%

Flexibility of Earnings

Average Hours Worked: 38
Workers with a Varying Number of Hours: 8.9%
Workers Earning Some Overtime Pay, Tips, or Commissions: 26.0%
Earnings Benefit of Working Overtime: 0.4%

Gender

	Male	Female
Percent	65.6%	34.4%
Effect on Earnings	25.9%	−32.4%

Union Membership

Percentage Union Members: Insignificant
Earnings Benefit of Union Membership: No significant data available

Veteran Status

Percentage Who Have Been on Active Duty: 6.5%
Earnings Benefit of Veteran Status: 13.5%

13-2053 Insurance Underwriters

Review individual applications for insurance to evaluate degree of risk involved and determine acceptance of applications.

- Education or Training Required: Bachelor's degree
- Job Growth: 8.0%
- Annual Openings: 13,000
- Self-Employed: 1.0%
- Part-Time: 16.7%

NATIONAL WAGE FIGURES (ANNUAL)

Beginning	25th Percentile	Median	Mean	75th Percentile	90th Percentile
$32,270	$40,000	$52,350	$57,960	$71,070	$92,240

Median Wages for Industries Employing Largest Numbers (Annual)

Industry	Median Income
Real Estate	$83,140
Securities, Commodity Contracts, and Other Financial Investments and Related Activities	$58,080
Hospitals	$55,820
Insurance Carriers and Related Activities	$52,600
Credit Intermediation and Related Activities	$51,950
Management of Companies and Enterprises	$50,870
Professional, Scientific, and Technical Services	$50,810
Funds, Trusts, and Other Financial Vehicles	$48,850
Religious, Grantmaking, Civic, Professional, and Similar Organizations	$48,610
Federal, State, and Local Government	$47,450

Median Wages for States (Annual)

AK	$65,420	KY	$43,360	NY	$61,890
AL	$43,490	LA	$42,280	OH	$52,130
AR	$46,160	MA	$63,360	OK	$39,510
AZ	$43,250	MD	$52,490	OR	$55,240
CA	$57,870	ME	$49,480	PA	$53,830
CO	$60,190	MI	$52,260	RI	$42,830
CT	$63,170	MN	$52,890	SC	$36,270
DC	$54,120	MO	$45,540	SD	$51,730
DE	$59,430	MS	$43,430	TN	$53,640
FL	$45,630	MT	$35,490	TX	$50,360
GA	$55,020	NC	$48,040	UT	$49,640
HI	$47,730	ND	$44,110	VA	$48,030
IA	$44,810	NE	$48,510	VT	$50,000
ID	$49,620	NH	$55,190	WA	$56,340
IL	$52,440	NJ	$63,650	WI	$47,400
IN	$50,810	NM	$48,340	WV	$39,110
KS	$48,430	NV	$55,110	WY	$35,080

Median Wages for the Largest Metropolitan Areas (Annual)

AZ: Phoenix	$43,220	MI: Detroit	$51,660
CA: Los Angeles	$57,570	MN: Minneapolis	$55,100
CA: Riverside	$49,530	MO: Kansas City	$52,000
CA: Sacramento	$62,100	MO: St. Louis	$45,310
CA: San Diego	$50,970	NV: Las Vegas	$53,570
CA: San Francisco	$61,440	NY: New York	$66,340
CO: Denver	$62,460	OH: Cincinnati	$52,290
DC: Washington	$50,620	OH: Cleveland	$53,950
FL: Miami	$45,130	OH: Columbus	$52,010
FL: Orlando	$44,040	OR: Portland	$56,080
FL: Tampa	$49,850	PA: Philadelphia	$56,130
GA: Atlanta	$56,860	PA: Pittsburgh	$48,990
IL: Chicago	$51,920	TX: Dallas	$51,370
MA: Boston	$66,550	TX: Houston	$53,860
MD: Baltimore	$54,720	WA: Seattle	$58,120

FACTORS THAT MAY AFFECT EARNINGS

Educational Attainment of Workers and Effect on Earnings

	Percent at Level	Effect on Earnings
Less than High School	—	—
Some High School	—	—
High School or Equivalent	17.4%	−26.4%
Some College but No Degree	19.8%	−19.7%
Associate Degree	10.7%	20.2%
Bachelor's Degree	41.3%	8.8%
Master's Degree	7.4%	36.0%
Doctoral Degree	—	—
First Professional Degree	—	—

Flexibility of Earnings

Average Hours Worked: 39
Workers with a Varying Number of Hours: 0.4%
Workers Earning Some Overtime Pay, Tips, or Commissions: 8.8%
Earnings Benefit of Working Overtime: 21.5%

Gender

	Male	Female
Percent	30.8%	69.2%
Effect on Earnings	—	−8.9%

Union Membership

Percentage Union Members: 5.1%
Earnings Benefit of Union Membership: −3.0%

Veteran Status

Percentage Who Have Been on Active Duty: 6.5%
Earnings Benefit of Veteran Status: 13.5%

13-2061 Financial Examiners

Enforce or ensure compliance with laws and regulations governing financial and securities institutions and financial and real estate transactions. May examine, verify correctness of, or establish authenticity of records.

- Education or Training Required: Bachelor's degree
- Job Growth: 9.5%
- Annual Openings: 3,000
- Self-Employed: 0.0%
- Part-Time: 21.8%

NATIONAL WAGE FIGURES (ANNUAL)

Beginning	25th Percentile	Median	Mean	75th Percentile	90th Percentile
$34,790	$46,510	$65,370	$71,240	$91,380	$118,000

Median Wages for Industries Employing Largest Numbers (Annual)

Industry	Median Income
Administrative and Support Services	$82,070
Federal, State, and Local Government	$76,920
Monetary Authorities—Central Bank	$76,630
Management of Companies and Enterprises	$73,910
Internet Service Providers, Web Search Portals, and Data-Processing Services	$67,800
Religious, Grantmaking, Civic, Professional, and Similar Organizations	$64,760
Securities, Commodity Contracts, and Other Financial Investments and Related Activities	$64,330
Ambulatory Health Care Services	$57,720
Credit Intermediation and Related Activities	$56,000
Insurance Carriers and Related Activities	$56,000

Median Wages for States (Annual)

State	Wage	State	Wage	State	Wage
AK	no data	KY	$54,630	NY	$69,010
AL	$52,040	LA	$70,800	OH	$65,330
AR	$66,550	MA	$63,740	OK	$61,540
AZ	no data	MD	$57,110	OR	$55,900
CA	$73,550	ME	$55,770	PA	$73,100
CO	$63,850	MI	$66,140	RI	no data
CT	$77,460	MN	$63,420	SC	$45,420
DC	$105,640	MO	$84,090	SD	$60,490
DE	$72,690	MS	$54,540	TN	$68,570
FL	$61,190	MT	$44,170	TX	$73,500
GA	$58,720	NC	$71,340	UT	$59,090
HI	$55,470	ND	$66,390	VA	$73,780
IA	$65,140	NE	$65,270	VT	$50,680
ID	$49,970	NH	$67,400	WA	$69,930
IL	$71,330	NJ	$69,270	WI	$56,380
IN	$54,190	NM	$67,840	WV	$62,020
KS	$64,650	NV	$56,380	WY	no data

Median Wages for the Largest Metropolitan Areas (Annual)

Area	Wage	Area	Wage
AZ: Phoenix	no data	MI: Detroit	$72,240
CA: Los Angeles	$72,440	MN: Minneapolis	$66,730
CA: Riverside	$58,730	MO: Kansas City	$98,190
CA: Sacramento	$68,330	MO: St. Louis	$74,460
CA: San Diego	$71,070	NV: Las Vegas	$55,620
CA: San Francisco	$95,140	NY: New York	$73,780
CO: Denver	$63,990	OH: Cincinnati	$70,270
DC: Washington	$92,390	OH: Cleveland	$64,000
FL: Miami	$55,980	OH: Columbus	$68,670
FL: Orlando	$56,060	OR: Portland	$65,600
FL: Tampa	$85,250	PA: Philadelphia	$71,080
GA: Atlanta	$57,840	PA: Pittsburgh	$82,880
IL: Chicago	$69,370	TX: Dallas	$80,150
MA: Boston	$62,930	TX: Houston	$81,440
MD: Baltimore	$57,810	WA: Seattle	$74,800

FACTORS THAT MAY AFFECT EARNINGS

Educational Attainment of Workers and Effect on Earnings

	Percent at Level	Effect on Earnings
Less than High School	—	—
Some High School	—	—
High School or Equivalent	—	—
Some College but No Degree	—	—
Associate Degree	—	—
Bachelor's Degree	50.0%	13.9%
Master's Degree	—	—
Doctoral Degree	—	—
First Professional Degree	—	—

Figures do not total 100% because some levels have a very small sample size.

Flexibility of Earnings

Average Hours Worked: 40
Workers with a Varying Number of Hours: 1.9%
Workers Earning Some Overtime Pay, Tips, or Commissions: 12.0%
Earnings Benefit of Working Overtime: 6.1%

Gender

	Male	Female
Percent	67.9%	32.1%
Effect on Earnings	21.9%	−11.0%

Union Membership

Percentage Union Members: 66.7%
Earnings Benefit of Union Membership: −3.0%

Veteran Status

Percentage Who Have Been on Active Duty: 6.5%
Earnings Benefit of Veteran Status: 13.5%

13-2071 Loan Counselors

Provide guidance to prospective loan applicants who have problems qualifying for traditional loans. Guidance may include determining the best type of loan and explaining loan requirements or restrictions.

- Education or Training Required: Bachelor's degree
- Job Growth: 17.7%
- Annual Openings: 5,000
- Self-Employed: 2.8%
- Part-Time: 21.8%

NATIONAL WAGE FIGURES (ANNUAL)

Beginning	25th Percentile	Median	Mean	75th Percentile	90th Percentile
$24,990	$29,150	$35,790	$41,840	$47,040	$65,370

Median Wages for Industries Employing Largest Numbers (Annual)

Industry	Median Income
Motor Vehicle and Parts Dealers	$61,850
Federal, State, and Local Government	$44,550
Management of Companies and Enterprises	$39,870
Construction of Buildings	$39,380
Insurance Carriers and Related Activities	$39,080
Administrative and Support Services	$38,080
Securities, Commodity Contracts, and Other Financial Investments and Related Activities	$37,860
Credit Intermediation and Related Activities	$37,150
Real Estate	$36,280
Educational Services	$35,680

Median Wages for States (Annual)

AK	no data	KY	$38,230	NY	$35,840
AL	$30,750	LA	$36,560	OH	$35,680
AR	$37,200	MA	no data	OK	$30,990
AZ	$36,170	MD	$36,560	OR	$34,670
CA	$37,710	ME	$34,860	PA	$37,840
CO	$45,200	MI	$38,450	RI	$34,360
CT	$42,870	MN	$43,230	SC	$30,590
DC	$54,960	MO	$35,850	SD	no data
DE	$36,200	MS	$40,200	TN	$38,730
FL	$31,630	MT	$27,430	TX	$32,620
GA	$35,160	NC	$31,200	UT	$32,410
HI	$34,630	ND	no data	VA	$39,670
IA	$30,940	NE	$29,800	VT	$36,620
ID	$33,920	NH	$36,800	WA	$39,590
IL	$42,430	NJ	$37,620	WI	$35,810
IN	$31,000	NM	$29,750	WV	$34,470
KS	$33,450	NV	$45,870	WY	no data

Median Wages for the Largest Metropolitan Areas (Annual)

AZ: Phoenix	$36,790	MI: Detroit	$36,200
CA: Los Angeles	$39,250	MN: Minneapolis	$48,890
CA: Riverside	$35,520	MO: Kansas City	$38,750
CA: Sacramento	$38,170	MO: St. Louis	$33,720
CA: San Diego	$32,420	NV: Las Vegas	$47,480
CA: San Francisco	$45,200	NY: New York	$35,650
CO: Denver	$47,890	OH: Cincinnati	$36,260
DC: Washington	$38,730	OH: Cleveland	$35,370
FL: Miami	$30,530	OH: Columbus	$37,700
FL: Orlando	$28,920	OR: Portland	$36,070
FL: Tampa	$35,300	PA: Philadelphia	$39,470
GA: Atlanta	$37,110	PA: Pittsburgh	$34,250
IL: Chicago	$42,830	TX: Dallas	$33,480
MA: Boston	no data	TX: Houston	$33,830
MD: Baltimore	$39,430	WA: Seattle	$38,430

FACTORS THAT MAY AFFECT EARNINGS

Educational Attainment of Workers and Effect on Earnings

Figures are based on a group of occupations: Financial Specialists

	Percent at Level	Effect on Earnings
Less than High School	—	—
Some High School	0.9%	−48.6%
High School or Equivalent	15.3%	−14.9%
Some College but No Degree	17.8%	−20.2%
Associate Degree	15.3%	−13.4%
Bachelor's Degree	34.0%	10.8%
Master's Degree	13.8%	28.2%
Doctoral Degree	1.3%	11.8%
First Professional Degree	1.3%	51.1%

Flexibility of Earnings

Average Hours Worked: 37
Workers with a Varying Number of Hours: 6.8%
Workers Earning Some Overtime Pay, Tips, or Commissions: 12.0%
Earnings Benefit of Working Overtime: 13.2%

Gender

	Male	Female
Percent	47.3%	52.7%
Effect on Earnings	25.7%	−15.6%

Union Membership

Percentage Union Members: 5.1%
Earnings Benefit of Union Membership: −3.0%

Veteran Status

Percentage Who Have Been on Active Duty: 6.5%
Earnings Benefit of Veteran Status: 13.5%

13-2072 Loan Officers

Evaluate, authorize, or recommend approval of commercial, real estate, or credit loans. Advise borrowers on financial status and methods of payments. Includes mortgage loan officers and agents, collection analysts, loan servicing officers, and loan underwriters.

- Education or Training Required: Bachelor's degree
- Job Growth: 8.3%
- Annual Openings: 38,000
- Self-Employed: 2.7%
- Part-Time: 21.8%

NATIONAL WAGE FIGURES (ANNUAL)

Beginning	25th Percentile	Median	Mean	75th Percentile	90th Percentile
$29,590	$37,590	$51,760	$61,930	$73,630	$107,040

Median Wages for Industries Employing Largest Numbers (Annual)

Industry	Median Income
Federal, State, and Local Government	$60,690
Internet Service Providers, Web Search Portals, and Data-Processing Services	$60,680
Securities, Commodity Contracts, and Other Financial Investments and Related Activities	$58,270
Motor Vehicle and Parts Dealers	$58,230
Real Estate	$56,890
Rental and Leasing Services	$56,830
Management of Companies and Enterprises	$55,090
Religious, Grantmaking, Civic, Professional, and Similar Organizations	$55,010
Funds, Trusts, and Other Financial Vehicles	$53,920
Insurance Carriers and Related Activities	$53,350

Median Wages for States (Annual)

State	Wage	State	Wage	State	Wage
AK	$64,870	KY	$40,630	NY	$63,280
AL	$55,170	LA	$37,550	OH	$46,730
AR	$50,280	MA	$71,050	OK	$43,850
AZ	$58,070	MD	$51,940	OR	$51,410
CA	$60,820	ME	$49,240	PA	$42,890
CO	$52,170	MI	$45,770	RI	$64,840
CT	$68,300	MN	$57,500	SC	$45,840
DC	$54,000	MO	$47,920	SD	$43,250
DE	$48,480	MS	$44,140	TN	$40,800
FL	$48,580	MT	$41,220	TX	$54,490
GA	$53,450	NC	$45,560	UT	$45,120
HI	$61,230	ND	$50,420	VA	$50,690
IA	$44,400	NE	$51,320	VT	$50,570
ID	$45,810	NH	$53,360	WA	$52,800
IL	$55,590	NJ	$54,190	WI	$48,400
IN	$44,290	NM	$43,590	WV	$42,460
KS	$49,110	NV	$46,710	WY	$42,240

Median Wages for the Largest Metropolitan Areas (Annual)

Area	Wage	Area	Wage
AZ: Phoenix	$60,250	MI: Detroit	$45,830
CA: Los Angeles	$59,450	MN: Minneapolis	$62,020
CA: Riverside	$65,630	MO: Kansas City	$47,360
CA: Sacramento	$60,550	MO: St. Louis	$46,280
CA: San Diego	$62,610	NV: Las Vegas	$47,050
CA: San Francisco	$68,040	NY: New York	$60,000
CO: Denver	$51,580	OH: Cincinnati	$50,560
DC: Washington	$52,270	OH: Cleveland	$42,240
FL: Miami	$50,790	OH: Columbus	$45,790
FL: Orlando	$43,720	OR: Portland	$53,370
FL: Tampa	$48,880	PA: Philadelphia	$46,160
GA: Atlanta	$53,800	PA: Pittsburgh	$44,260
IL: Chicago	$57,240	TX: Dallas	$58,960
MA: Boston	$72,410	TX: Houston	$54,750
MD: Baltimore	$56,560	WA: Seattle	$52,850

FACTORS THAT MAY AFFECT EARNINGS

Educational Attainment of Workers and Effect on Earnings

Figures are based on a group of occupations: Financial Specialists

	Percent at Level	Effect on Earnings
Less than High School	—	—
Some High School	0.9%	−48.6%
High School or Equivalent	15.3%	−14.9%
Some College but No Degree	17.8%	−20.2%
Associate Degree	15.3%	−13.4%
Bachelor's Degree	34.0%	10.8%
Master's Degree	13.8%	28.2%
Doctoral Degree	1.3%	11.8%
First Professional Degree	1.3%	51.1%

Flexibility of Earnings

Average Hours Worked: 37
Workers with a Varying Number of Hours: 6.8%
Workers Earning Some Overtime Pay, Tips, or Commissions: 12.0%
Earnings Benefit of Working Overtime: 13.2%

Gender

	Male	Female
Percent	47.3%	52.7%
Effect on Earnings	25.7%	−15.6%

Union Membership

Percentage Union Members: 5.1%
Earnings Benefit of Union Membership: −3.0%

Veteran Status

Percentage Who Have Been on Active Duty: 6.5%
Earnings Benefit of Veteran Status: 13.5%

13-2081 Tax Examiners, Collectors, and Revenue Agents

Determine tax liability or collect taxes from individuals or business firms according to prescribed laws and regulations.

- Education or Training Required: Bachelor's degree
- Job Growth: 5.1%
- Annual Openings: 4,000
- Self-Employed: 0.0%
- Part-Time: 20.0%

NATIONAL WAGE FIGURES (ANNUAL)

Beginning	25th Percentile	Median	Mean	75th Percentile	90th Percentile
$27,290	$34,840	$45,620	$49,690	$62,530	$81,890

Median Wages for Industries Employing Largest Numbers (Annual)

Industry	Median Income
Federal, State, and Local Government	$45,620

Median Wages for States (Annual)

State	Wage	State	Wage	State	Wage
AK	$63,460	KY	$39,910	NY	$50,730
AL	$40,500	LA	$43,380	OH	$54,680
AR	$29,800	MA	$56,560	OK	$32,770
AZ	$45,870	MD	$50,420	OR	$39,810
CA	$53,640	ME	$35,520	PA	no data
CO	$54,100	MI	$60,410	RI	$55,200
CT	$68,950	MN	no data	SC	$37,770
DC	no data	MO	$38,270	SD	$36,180
DE	$55,580	MS	$28,410	TN	$40,870
FL	$35,300	MT	$39,550	TX	$44,340
GA	$39,530	NC	$38,660	UT	$38,730
HI	$66,070	ND	$59,010	VA	$44,830
IA	$51,660	NE	$45,610	VT	$48,340
ID	$49,110	NH	$38,610	WA	$49,690
IL	$59,060	NJ	$62,520	WI	$54,670
IN	$31,970	NM	$46,200	WV	$24,800
KS	$43,460	NV	$56,570	WY	$53,560

Median Wages for the Largest Metropolitan Areas (Annual)

Area	Wage	Area	Wage
AZ: Phoenix	$46,780	MI: Detroit	$61,270
CA: Los Angeles	$72,590	MN: Minneapolis	no data
CA: Riverside	$57,050	MO: Kansas City	$40,180
CA: Sacramento	$52,360	MO: St. Louis	$58,500
CA: San Diego	$65,870	NV: Las Vegas	$62,490
CA: San Francisco	$70,360	NY: New York	$56,950
CO: Denver	$54,280	OH: Cincinnati	$42,160
DC: Washington	$58,830	OH: Cleveland	$59,410
FL: Miami	$49,150	OH: Columbus	no data
FL: Orlando	$34,670	OR: Portland	$50,150
FL: Tampa	$39,290	PA: Philadelphia	$42,830
GA: Atlanta	$40,760	PA: Pittsburgh	no data
IL: Chicago	$63,410	TX: Dallas	$60,290
MA: Boston	$55,260	TX: Houston	$66,800
MD: Baltimore	$48,770	WA: Seattle	$52,680

FACTORS THAT MAY AFFECT EARNINGS

Educational Attainment of Workers and Effect on Earnings

	Percent at Level	Effect on Earnings
Less than High School	—	—
Some High School	—	—
High School or Equivalent	25.0%	−17.2%
Some College but No Degree	21.7%	−0.1%
Associate Degree	12.0%	−9.5%
Bachelor's Degree	34.8%	17.0%
Master's Degree	—	—
Doctoral Degree	—	—
First Professional Degree	—	—

Figures do not total 100% because some levels have a very small sample size.

Flexibility of Earnings

Average Hours Worked: 38

Workers with a Varying Number of Hours: 2.8%

Workers Earning Some Overtime Pay, Tips, or Commissions: 6.1%

Earnings Benefit of Working Overtime: 6.1%

Gender

	Male	Female
Percent	43.3%	56.7%
Effect on Earnings	21.9%	−11.0%

Union Membership

Percentage Union Members: 36.4%

Earnings Benefit of Union Membership: 11.6%

Veteran Status

Percentage Who Have Been on Active Duty: 6.5%

Earnings Benefit of Veteran Status: 13.5%

13-2082 Tax Preparers

Prepare tax returns for individuals or small businesses, but do not have the background or responsibilities of an accredited or certified public accountant.

- Education or Training Required: Moderate-term on-the-job training
- Job Growth: 10.6%
- Annual Openings: 11,000
- Self-Employed: 35.6%
- Part-Time: 40.9%

Note: A large fraction of the workforce for this occupation is self-employed and earns an average of $39,130. All other earnings figures for this occupation are based on workers who are paid a wage or salary.

NATIONAL WAGE FIGURES (ANNUAL)

Beginning	25th Percentile	Median	Mean	75th Percentile	90th Percentile
$16,080	$20,380	$27,360	$33,160	$39,830	$56,640

Note: The mean is significantly higher than the median because of the presence of a few star earners.

Median Wages for Industries Employing Largest Numbers (Annual)

Industry	Median Income
Merchant Wholesalers, Durable Goods	$45,890
Insurance Carriers and Related Activities	$42,320
Credit Intermediation and Related Activities	$42,270
Management of Companies and Enterprises	$40,450
Professional, Scientific, and Technical Services	$27,150
Administrative and Support Services	$26,910

Median Wages for States (Annual)

AK	no data	KY	$29,990	NY	$25,980
AL	$22,030	LA	$20,590	OH	$22,160
AR	$19,500	MA	$58,080	OK	$21,700
AZ	$38,230	MD	$31,550	OR	$28,200
CA	$40,700	ME	$26,270	PA	$21,700
CO	$28,740	MI	no data	RI	$23,480
CT	$30,110	MN	$28,720	SC	$25,930
DC	$42,610	MO	$25,100	SD	$25,290
DE	$28,940	MS	$21,270	TN	$26,050
FL	$23,500	MT	$29,260	TX	$24,440
GA	$31,030	NC	$32,370	UT	$27,250
HI	$39,710	ND	$30,130	VA	$23,320
IA	$25,630	NE	$24,320	VT	$35,570
ID	$33,590	NH	$35,220	WA	$27,980
IL	$25,130	NJ	$38,270	WI	$30,830
IN	$22,140	NM	$23,460	WV	$20,710
KS	$36,110	NV	no data	WY	no data

Median Wages for the Largest Metropolitan Areas (Annual)

AZ: Phoenix	$38,630	MI: Detroit	$70,380
CA: Los Angeles	$42,040	MN: Minneapolis	$31,020
CA: Riverside	$32,310	MO: Kansas City	$28,020
CA: Sacramento	$34,270	MO: St. Louis	$22,910
CA: San Diego	$44,480	NV: Las Vegas	no data
CA: San Francisco	no data	NY: New York	$28,310
CO: Denver	$23,600	OH: Cincinnati	$26,440
DC: Washington	$29,990	OH: Cleveland	$31,280
FL: Miami	$24,110	OH: Columbus	$20,430
FL: Orlando	$25,600	OR: Portland	$39,850
FL: Tampa	$25,880	PA: Philadelphia	$25,420
GA: Atlanta	$32,740	PA: Pittsburgh	$23,910
IL: Chicago	$27,820	TX: Dallas	$24,980
MA: Boston	$60,260	TX: Houston	$25,030
MD: Baltimore	$30,860	WA: Seattle	$28,560

FACTORS THAT MAY AFFECT EARNINGS

Educational Attainment of Workers and Effect on Earnings

	Percent at Level	Effect on Earnings
Less than High School	—	—
Some High School	—	—
High School or Equivalent	18.9%	−39.6%
Some College but No Degree	24.3%	−49.2%
Associate Degree	10.8%	−24.5%
Bachelor's Degree	36.5%	27.1%
Master's Degree	8.1%	103.2%
Doctoral Degree	—	—
First Professional Degree	—	—

Flexibility of Earnings

Average Hours Worked: 24
Workers with a Varying Number of Hours: 19.9%
Workers Earning Some Overtime Pay, Tips, or Commissions: 10.7%
Earnings Benefit of Working Overtime: 6.1%

Gender

	Male	Female
Percent	40.4%	59.6%
Effect on Earnings	21.9%	−11.0%

Union Membership

Percentage Union Members: 4.0%
Earnings Benefit of Union Membership: −3.0%

Veteran Status

Percentage Who Have Been on Active Duty: 6.5%
Earnings Benefit of Veteran Status: 13.5%

13-2099 Financial Specialists, All Other

All financial specialists not listed separately.

- Education or Training Required: Bachelor's degree
- Job Growth: 14.4%
- Annual Openings: 14,000
- Self-Employed: 1.0%
- Part-Time: 14.7%

NATIONAL WAGE FIGURES (ANNUAL)

Beginning	25th Percentile	Median	Mean	75th Percentile	90th Percentile
$30,720	$39,470	$53,680	$59,600	$72,780	$94,600

Median Wages for Industries Employing Largest Numbers (Annual)

Industry	Median Income
Couriers and Messengers	$77,270
Utilities	$72,290
Transportation Equipment Manufacturing	$67,440
Computer and Electronic Product Manufacturing	$64,640
Merchant Wholesalers, Durable Goods	$64,160
Real Estate	$62,440
Professional, Scientific, and Technical Services	$61,030
Telecommunications	$60,680
Motor Vehicle and Parts Dealers	$58,650
Management of Companies and Enterprises	$58,070

Median Wages for States (Annual)

State	Wage	State	Wage	State	Wage
AK	$50,370	KY	$43,820	NY	$57,190
AL	$50,570	LA	$41,490	OH	$56,000
AR	$34,380	MA	$58,380	OK	$54,040
AZ	$54,290	MD	$45,440	OR	$49,660
CA	$53,790	ME	$46,470	PA	$54,980
CO	$56,850	MI	$52,790	RI	$45,510
CT	$51,470	MN	$53,200	SC	no data
DC	$77,770	MO	$54,000	SD	no data
DE	$38,700	MS	$55,400	TN	$61,920
FL	$48,420	MT	$43,020	TX	$50,300
GA	$46,150	NC	$53,870	UT	$50,270
HI	$55,140	ND	$48,760	VA	$65,260
IA	$36,210	NE	$44,440	VT	$55,170
ID	$49,490	NH	$61,350	WA	$54,720
IL	$56,630	NJ	$63,610	WI	$45,880
IN	$52,020	NM	$49,300	WV	$47,450
KS	$52,390	NV	$40,900	WY	$33,890

Median Wages for the Largest Metropolitan Areas (Annual)

Area	Wage	Area	Wage
AZ: Phoenix	$53,450	MI: Detroit	$63,950
CA: Los Angeles	$50,370	MN: Minneapolis	$54,930
CA: Riverside	$37,220	MO: Kansas City	$57,490
CA: Sacramento	$54,660	MO: St. Louis	$51,810
CA: San Diego	$55,850	NV: Las Vegas	$42,860
CA: San Francisco	$68,710	NY: New York	$60,450
CO: Denver	$60,500	OH: Cincinnati	$55,710
DC: Washington	$74,210	OH: Cleveland	$56,480
FL: Miami	$51,240	OH: Columbus	$60,600
FL: Orlando	$46,050	OR: Portland	$51,840
FL: Tampa	$46,260	PA: Philadelphia	$53,140
GA: Atlanta	$48,390	PA: Pittsburgh	$44,330
IL: Chicago	$58,510	TX: Dallas	$52,030
MA: Boston	$59,890	TX: Houston	$68,030
MD: Baltimore	$39,360	WA: Seattle	$57,560

FACTORS THAT MAY AFFECT EARNINGS

Educational Attainment of Workers and Effect on Earnings

	Percent at Level	Effect on Earnings
Less than High School	—	—
Some High School	—	—
High School or Equivalent	14.3%	31.4%
Some College but No Degree	33.3%	−44.4%
Associate Degree	—	—
Bachelor's Degree	33.3%	17.5%
Master's Degree	—	—
Doctoral Degree	—	—
First Professional Degree	—	—

Figures do not total 100% because some levels have a very small sample size.

Flexibility of Earnings

Average Hours Worked: 33
Workers with a Varying Number of Hours: 15.3%
Workers Earning Some Overtime Pay, Tips, or Commissions: 14.0%
Earnings Benefit of Working Overtime: 6.1%

Gender

	Male	Female
Percent	43.6%	56.4%
Effect on Earnings	21.9%	−11.0%

Union Membership

Percentage Union Members: 7.0%
Earnings Benefit of Union Membership: −3.0%

Veteran Status

Percentage Who Have Been on Active Duty: 6.5%
Earnings Benefit of Veteran Status: 13.5%

15-0000: Computer and Mathematical Occupations

15-1000 Computer Specialists

15-1011 Computer and Information Scientists, Research

Conduct research into fundamental computer and information science as theorists, designers, or inventors. Solve or develop solutions to problems in the field of computer hardware and software.

- Education or Training Required: Doctoral degree
- Job Growth: 25.6%
- Annual Openings: 2,000
- Self-Employed: 5.1%
- Part-Time: 13.0%

NATIONAL WAGE FIGURES (ANNUAL)

Beginning	25th Percentile	Median	Mean	75th Percentile	90th Percentile
$53,590	$71,930	$93,950	$96,440	$118,100	$144,880

Median Wages for Industries Employing Largest Numbers (Annual)

Industry	Median Income
Internet Publishing and Broadcasting	$118,610
Publishing Industries (Except Internet)	$115,660
Computer and Electronic Product Manufacturing	$115,210
Broadcasting (Except Internet)	$112,630
Internet Service Providers, Web Search Portals, and Data-Processing Services	$99,560
Professional, Scientific, and Technical Services	$94,590
Motion Picture and Sound Recording Industries	$88,810
Management of Companies and Enterprises	$88,700
Federal, State, and Local Government	$87,580
Machinery Manufacturing	$86,000

Median Wages for States (Annual)

State	Wage	State	Wage	State	Wage
AK	no data	KY	$71,850	NY	$102,780
AL	$90,330	LA	no data	OH	$86,780
AR	$43,420	MA	$114,190	OK	$73,590
AZ	$81,980	MD	$94,550	OR	no data
CA	$112,770	ME	no data	PA	$67,640
CO	$88,320	MI	$86,480	RI	$90,240
CT	$105,290	MN	$109,700	SC	$74,810
DC	$95,150	MO	$88,660	SD	no data
DE	$91,230	MS	$72,550	TN	$80,540
FL	$86,880	MT	no data	TX	$81,580
GA	$80,590	NC	$87,460	UT	$74,990
HI	no data	ND	no data	VA	$94,990
IA	$72,800	NE	$52,850	VT	no data
ID	no data	NH	$94,830	WA	$99,090
IL	$88,200	NJ	$92,550	WI	$76,090
IN	$90,030	NM	no data	WV	$84,350
KS	$81,520	NV	$99,330	WY	no data

Median Wages for the Largest Metropolitan Areas (Annual)

Area	Wage	Area	Wage
AZ: Phoenix	$78,310	MI: Detroit	no data
CA: Los Angeles	$109,960	MN: Minneapolis	$110,620
CA: Riverside	no data	MO: Kansas City	$89,460
CA: Sacramento	no data	MO: St. Louis	$91,860
CA: San Diego	$90,750	NV: Las Vegas	no data
CA: San Francisco	$120,300	NY: New York	$102,600
CO: Denver	$85,490	OH: Cincinnati	$91,060
DC: Washington	$101,130	OH: Cleveland	no data
FL: Miami	$92,800	OH: Columbus	$83,410
FL: Orlando	$96,690	OR: Portland	no data
FL: Tampa	$76,440	PA: Philadelphia	$97,560
GA: Atlanta	$89,180	PA: Pittsburgh	no data
IL: Chicago	$87,890	TX: Dallas	$71,380
MA: Boston	$113,220	TX: Houston	$66,930
MD: Baltimore	$87,060	WA: Seattle	$113,680

FACTORS THAT MAY AFFECT EARNINGS

Educational Attainment of Workers and Effect on Earnings

	Percent at Level	Effect on Earnings
Less than High School	—	—
Some High School	—	—
High School or Equivalent	10.1%	−17.0%
Some College but No Degree	19.2%	−19.5%
Associate Degree	13.2%	−15.9%
Bachelor's Degree	36.6%	5.8%
Master's Degree	16.2%	22.4%
Doctoral Degree	3.0%	62.6%
First Professional Degree	—	—

Flexibility of Earnings

Average Hours Worked: 38
Workers with a Varying Number of Hours: 4.5%
Workers Earning Some Overtime Pay, Tips, or Commissions: 9.2%
Earnings Benefit of Working Overtime: 1.4%

Gender

	Male	Female
Percent	68.1%	31.9%
Effect on Earnings	5.8%	−10.1%

Union Membership

Percentage Union Members: 6.3%
Earnings Benefit of Union Membership: −10.7%

Veteran Status

Percentage Who Have Been on Active Duty: 11.0%
Earnings Benefit of Veteran Status: 7.0%

15-1021 Computer Programmers

Convert project specifications and statements of problems and procedures to detailed logical flow charts for coding into computer language. Develop and write computer programs to store, locate, and retrieve specific documents, data, and information. May program Web sites.

- Education or Training Required: Bachelor's degree
- Job Growth: 2.0%
- Annual Openings: 28,000
- Self-Employed: 4.5%
- Part-Time: 11.5%

NATIONAL WAGE FIGURES (ANNUAL)

Beginning	25th Percentile	Median	Mean	75th Percentile	90th Percentile
$38,460	$49,580	$65,510	$69,500	$85,080	$106,610

Median Wages for Industries Employing Largest Numbers (Annual)

Industry	Median Income
Publishing Industries (Except Internet)	$76,740
Securities, Commodity Contracts, and Other Financial Investments and Related Activities	$76,650
Credit Intermediation and Related Activities	$73,340
Merchant Wholesalers, Durable Goods	$72,210
Computer and Electronic Product Manufacturing	$70,550
Chemical Manufacturing	$70,070
Utilities	$69,150
Telecommunications	$67,490
Professional, Scientific, and Technical Services	$67,190
Management of Companies and Enterprises	$67,170

Median Wages for States (Annual)

State	Wage	State	Wage	State	Wage
AK	$61,810	KY	$56,060	NY	$65,960
AL	$58,740	LA	$52,150	OH	$59,440
AR	$55,940	MA	$73,590	OK	$53,580
AZ	$58,940	MD	$69,010	OR	$63,880
CA	$73,610	ME	$53,560	PA	$61,650
CO	$70,340	MI	$64,300	RI	$62,360
CT	$70,170	MN	$63,310	SC	$55,780
DC	$68,230	MO	$60,650	SD	$43,590
DE	$75,220	MS	$52,250	TN	$58,820
FL	$62,050	MT	$47,590	TX	$69,870
GA	$67,920	NC	$66,940	UT	$61,670
HI	$57,090	ND	$41,600	VA	$72,820
IA	$53,990	NE	$55,700	VT	$54,800
ID	$56,620	NH	$49,600	WA	$84,310
IL	$65,770	NJ	$76,730	WI	$55,970
IN	$56,110	NM	$58,300	WV	$42,300
KS	$61,480	NV	$60,830	WY	$37,450

Median Wages for the Largest Metropolitan Areas (Annual)

Area	Wage	Area	Wage
AZ: Phoenix	$61,270	MI: Detroit	$67,050
CA: Los Angeles	$71,270	MN: Minneapolis	$64,390
CA: Riverside	$50,020	MO: Kansas City	$67,040
CA: Sacramento	$66,430	MO: St. Louis	$65,170
CA: San Diego	$72,500	NV: Las Vegas	$60,060
CA: San Francisco	$79,080	NY: New York	$73,580
CO: Denver	$70,900	OH: Cincinnati	$59,070
DC: Washington	$75,490	OH: Cleveland	$64,110
FL: Miami	$64,070	OH: Columbus	$63,030
FL: Orlando	$66,380	OR: Portland	$66,820
FL: Tampa	$60,230	PA: Philadelphia	$65,980
GA: Atlanta	$69,640	PA: Pittsburgh	$64,810
IL: Chicago	$66,970	TX: Dallas	$73,580
MA: Boston	$73,070	TX: Houston	$75,060
MD: Baltimore	$69,360	WA: Seattle	$88,580

FACTORS THAT MAY AFFECT EARNINGS

Educational Attainment of Workers and Effect on Earnings

	Percent at Level	Effect on Earnings
Less than High School	—	—
Some High School	—	—
High School or Equivalent	9.0%	−15.3%
Some College but No Degree	18.6%	−15.5%
Associate Degree	12.9%	−10.5%
Bachelor's Degree	38.9%	3.6%
Master's Degree	16.0%	15.1%
Doctoral Degree	3.1%	63.4%
First Professional Degree	—	—

Flexibility of Earnings

Average Hours Worked: 38
Workers with a Varying Number of Hours: 3.6%
Workers Earning Some Overtime Pay, Tips, or Commissions: 7.0%
Earnings Benefit of Working Overtime: −4.4%

Gender

	Male	Female
Percent	74.7%	25.3%
Effect on Earnings	7.1%	−9.9%

Union Membership

Percentage Union Members: 4.7%
Earnings Benefit of Union Membership: −7.7%

Veteran Status

Percentage Who Have Been on Active Duty: 11.0%
Earnings Benefit of Veteran Status: 7.0%

15-1031 Computer Software Engineers, Applications

Develop, create, and modify general computer applications software or specialized utility programs. Analyze user needs and develop software solutions. Design software or customize software for client use with the aim of optimizing operational efficiency. May analyze and design databases within an application area, working individually or coordinating database development as part of a team.

- Education or Training Required: Bachelor's degree
- Job Growth: 48.4%
- Annual Openings: 54,000
- Self-Employed: 2.4%
- Part-Time: 13.1%

NATIONAL WAGE FIGURES (ANNUAL)

Beginning	25th Percentile	Median	Mean	75th Percentile	90th Percentile
$49,350	$62,830	$79,780	$82,000	$98,470	$119,770

Median Wages for Industries Employing Largest Numbers (Annual)

Industry	Median Income
Computer and Electronic Product Manufacturing	$89,780
Merchant Wholesalers, Durable Goods	$84,410
Transportation Equipment Manufacturing	$84,100
Telecommunications	$83,490
Publishing Industries (Except Internet)	$83,360
Internet Publishing and Broadcasting	$82,810
Chemical Manufacturing	$82,110
Funds, Trusts, and Other Financial Vehicles	$81,720
Machinery Manufacturing	$81,700
Miscellaneous Manufacturing	$79,990

Median Wages for States (Annual)

AK $70,080	KY $60,520	NY $83,010
AL $71,390	LA $59,460	OH $72,750
AR $60,840	MA $88,140	OK $61,940
AZ $71,330	MD $83,140	OR $82,180
CA $90,140	ME $64,200	PA $76,910
CO $82,210	MI $75,170	RI $82,070
CT $80,010	MN $77,260	SC $68,500
DC $76,730	MO $73,600	SD $67,060
DE $80,360	MS $56,140	TN $65,580
FL $69,860	MT $52,900	TX $78,120
GA $78,590	NC $81,610	UT $67,240
HI $71,200	ND $52,700	VA $84,450
IA $69,700	NE $67,020	VT $61,470
ID $73,330	NH $77,500	WA $79,920
IL $75,630	NJ $83,720	WI $67,130
IN $66,320	NM $69,240	WV $63,200
KS $75,200	NV $73,310	WY $53,440

Median Wages for the Largest Metropolitan Areas (Annual)

AZ: Phoenix $70,480	MI: Detroit $76,780
CA: Los Angeles $84,890	MN: Minneapolis $77,880
CA: Riverside $77,620	MO: Kansas City $74,820
CA: Sacramento $81,960	MO: St. Louis $76,540
CA: San Diego $86,160	NV: Las Vegas $73,600
CA: San Francisco $93,860	NY: New York $87,190
CO: Denver $81,960	OH: Cincinnati $72,620
DC: Washington $86,870	OH: Cleveland $70,040
FL: Miami $65,600	OH: Columbus $74,280
FL: Orlando $70,980	OR: Portland $85,970
FL: Tampa $64,530	PA: Philadelphia $80,440
GA: Atlanta $81,670	PA: Pittsburgh $73,600
IL: Chicago $77,270	TX: Dallas $77,620
MA: Boston $88,220	TX: Houston $83,100
MD: Baltimore $84,550	WA: Seattle $82,510

FACTORS THAT MAY AFFECT EARNINGS

Educational Attainment of Workers and Effect on Earnings

Figures are based on a group of occupations: Computer Specialists

	Percent at Level	Effect on Earnings
Less than High School	—	—
Some High School	1.7%	−47.4%
High School or Equivalent	11.5%	−13.3%
Some College but No Degree	20.0%	−16.7%
Associate Degree	14.6%	−10.4%
Bachelor's Degree	31.8%	6.6%
Master's Degree	16.0%	19.3%
Doctoral Degree	3.1%	50.5%
First Professional Degree	1.3%	35.3%

Flexibility of Earnings

Average Hours Worked: 38
Workers with a Varying Number of Hours: 4.5%
Workers Earning Some Overtime Pay, Tips, or Commissions: 8.9%
Earnings Benefit of Working Overtime: −11.2%

Gender

	Male	Female
Percent	78.2%	21.8%
Effect on Earnings	2.8%	−7.2%

Union Membership

Percentage Union Members: 5.5%
Earnings Benefit of Union Membership: −9.6%

Veteran Status

Percentage Who Have Been on Active Duty: 11.0%
Earnings Benefit of Veteran Status: 7.0%

15-1032 Computer Software Engineers, Systems Software

Research, design, develop, and test operating systems-level software, compilers, and network distribution software for medical, industrial, military, communications, aerospace, business, scientific, and general computing applications. Set operational specifications and formulate and analyze software requirements. Apply principles and techniques of computer science, engineering, and mathematical analysis.

- Education or Training Required: Bachelor's degree
- Job Growth: 43.0%
- Annual Openings: 37,000
- Self-Employed: 2.4%
- Part-Time: 13.1%

NATIONAL WAGE FIGURES (ANNUAL)

Beginning	25th Percentile	Median	Mean	75th Percentile	90th Percentile
$53,580	$67,620	$85,370	$87,250	$105,330	$125,750

Median Wages for Industries Employing Largest Numbers (Annual)

Industry	Median Income
Computer and Electronic Product Manufacturing	$90,120
Merchant Wholesalers, Durable Goods	$88,980
Securities, Commodity Contracts, and Other Financial Investments and Related Activities	$88,660
Wholesale Electronic Markets and Agents and Brokers	$88,410
Repair and Maintenance	$88,070
Chemical Manufacturing	$87,920
Publishing Industries (Except Internet)	$87,180
Professional, Scientific, and Technical Services	$86,420
Credit Intermediation and Related Activities	$84,790
Internet Publishing and Broadcasting	$84,370

Median Wages for States (Annual)

AK	no data	KY	$68,270	NY	$88,090
AL	$79,880	LA	$65,050	OH	$78,030
AR	$68,820	MA	$90,520	OK	$67,240
AZ	$78,570	MD	$91,820	OR	$91,360
CA	$93,970	ME	$69,810	PA	$80,420
CO	$83,270	MI	$74,420	RI	$84,190
CT	$83,570	MN	$84,340	SC	$69,280
DC	$79,740	MO	$74,430	SD	$67,710
DE	$84,880	MS	$61,130	TN	$67,070
FL	$75,980	MT	$60,910	TX	$86,410
GA	$76,150	NC	$85,050	UT	$75,080
HI	$78,540	ND	$64,440	VA	$93,700
IA	$67,260	NE	$75,270	VT	$81,040
ID	$77,150	NH	$85,690	WA	no data
IL	$85,130	NJ	$95,900	WI	$74,660
IN	$69,290	NM	$90,920	WV	$60,680
KS	$74,880	NV	$75,110	WY	$59,460

Median Wages for the Largest Metropolitan Areas (Annual)

AZ: Phoenix	$79,980	MI: Detroit	$74,780
CA: Los Angeles	$87,040	MN: Minneapolis	$83,710
CA: Riverside	$73,780	MO: Kansas City	$74,820
CA: Sacramento	$78,820	MO: St. Louis	$76,400
CA: San Diego	$89,840	NV: Las Vegas	$83,190
CA: San Francisco	$96,860	NY: New York	$94,720
CO: Denver	$82,500	OH: Cincinnati	$79,250
DC: Washington	$94,420	OH: Cleveland	$73,680
FL: Miami	$76,120	OH: Columbus	$82,160
FL: Orlando	$77,710	OR: Portland	$90,720
FL: Tampa	$73,080	PA: Philadelphia	$83,680
GA: Atlanta	$78,720	PA: Pittsburgh	$73,100
IL: Chicago	$87,340	TX: Dallas	$87,830
MA: Boston	$90,770	TX: Houston	$87,910
MD: Baltimore	$94,870	WA: Seattle	no data

FACTORS THAT MAY AFFECT EARNINGS

Educational Attainment of Workers and Effect on Earnings

Figures are based on a group of occupations: Computer Specialists

	Percent at Level	Effect on Earnings
Less than High School	—	—
Some High School	1.7%	−47.4%
High School or Equivalent	11.5%	−13.3%
Some College but No Degree	20.0%	−16.7%
Associate Degree	14.6%	−10.4%
Bachelor's Degree	31.8%	6.6%
Master's Degree	16.0%	19.3%
Doctoral Degree	3.1%	50.5%
First Professional Degree	1.3%	35.3%

Flexibility of Earnings

Average Hours Worked: 38
Workers with a Varying Number of Hours: 4.5%
Workers Earning Some Overtime Pay, Tips, or Commissions: 8.9%
Earnings Benefit of Working Overtime: −11.2%

Gender

	Male	Female
Percent	78.2%	21.8%
Effect on Earnings	2.8%	−7.2%

Union Membership

Percentage Union Members: 5.5%
Earnings Benefit of Union Membership: −9.6%

Veteran Status

Percentage Who Have Been on Active Duty: 11.0%
Earnings Benefit of Veteran Status: 7.0%

15-1041 Computer Support Specialists

Provide technical assistance to computer system users. Answer questions or resolve computer problems for clients in person, via telephone, or from remote location. May provide assistance concerning the use of computer hardware and software, including printing, installation, word processing, electronic mail, and operating systems.

- Education or Training Required: Associate degree
- Job Growth: 23.0%
- Annual Openings: 87,000
- Self-Employed: 0.9%
- Part-Time: 18.3%

NATIONAL WAGE FIGURES (ANNUAL)

Beginning	25th Percentile	Median	Mean	75th Percentile	90th Percentile
$25,290	$32,110	$41,470	$44,350	$53,640	$68,540

Median Wages for Industries Employing Largest Numbers (Annual)

Industry	Median Income
Transportation Equipment Manufacturing	$53,080
Computer and Electronic Product Manufacturing	$49,450
Securities, Commodity Contracts, and Other Financial Investments and Related Activities	$48,960
Publishing Industries (Except Internet)	$45,810
Chemical Manufacturing	$45,060
Machinery Manufacturing	$44,590
Merchant Wholesalers, Durable Goods	$43,230
Insurance Carriers and Related Activities	$43,090
Telecommunications	$42,970
Professional, Scientific, and Technical Services	$42,940

Median Wages for States (Annual)

AK	$45,960	KY	$35,330	NY	$46,090
AL	$34,840	LA	$39,400	OH	$40,060
AR	$33,540	MA	$50,880	OK	$32,350
AZ	$43,480	MD	$44,850	OR	$39,870
CA	$46,640	ME	$37,270	PA	$37,900
CO	$45,820	MI	$41,100	RI	$40,480
CT	$48,020	MN	$43,480	SC	$36,760
DC	$48,570	MO	$38,190	SD	$32,440
DE	$50,710	MS	$33,660	TN	$40,540
FL	$35,500	MT	$32,210	TX	$38,890
GA	$37,120	NC	$40,770	UT	$34,890
HI	$38,870	ND	$30,530	VA	$44,890
IA	$38,940	NE	$37,100	VT	$38,290
ID	$35,490	NH	$41,290	WA	$45,840
IL	$43,220	NJ	$46,270	WI	$38,630
IN	$35,370	NM	$38,550	WV	$30,820
KS	$37,610	NV	$34,510	WY	$35,470

Median Wages for the Largest Metropolitan Areas (Annual)

AZ: Phoenix	$44,090	MI: Detroit	$43,440
CA: Los Angeles	$43,840	MN: Minneapolis	$44,740
CA: Riverside	$43,210	MO: Kansas City	$40,540
CA: Sacramento	$46,300	MO: St. Louis	$38,720
CA: San Diego	$43,830	NV: Las Vegas	$33,970
CA: San Francisco	$54,270	NY: New York	$48,830
CO: Denver	$48,360	OH: Cincinnati	$40,420
DC: Washington	$48,340	OH: Cleveland	$39,210
FL: Miami	$36,110	OH: Columbus	$42,900
FL: Orlando	$35,790	OR: Portland	$42,590
FL: Tampa	$34,400	PA: Philadelphia	$42,150
GA: Atlanta	$39,640	PA: Pittsburgh	$36,520
IL: Chicago	$44,300	TX: Dallas	$41,590
MA: Boston	$52,520	TX: Houston	$40,730
MD: Baltimore	$44,460	WA: Seattle	$50,070

FACTORS THAT MAY AFFECT EARNINGS

Educational Attainment of Workers and Effect on Earnings

	Percent at Level	Effect on Earnings
Less than High School	—	—
Some High School	2.0%	−63.3%
High School or Equivalent	15.6%	−8.5%
Some College but No Degree	26.3%	−11.2%
Associate Degree	15.3%	−8.9%
Bachelor's Degree	32.7%	16.4%
Master's Degree	7.2%	22.7%
Doctoral Degree	—	—
First Professional Degree	—	—

Flexibility of Earnings

Average Hours Worked: 37
Workers with a Varying Number of Hours: 3.1%
Workers Earning Some Overtime Pay, Tips, or Commissions: 10.2%
Earnings Benefit of Working Overtime: 6.1%

Gender

	Male	Female
Percent	71.1%	28.9%
Effect on Earnings	5.3%	−9.5%

Union Membership

Percentage Union Members: 4.5%
Earnings Benefit of Union Membership: 3.7%

Veteran Status

Percentage Who Have Been on Active Duty: 11.0%
Earnings Benefit of Veteran Status: 7.0%

15-1051 Computer Systems Analysts

Analyze science, engineering, business, and all other data-processing problems for application to electronic data processing systems. Analyze user requirements, procedures, and problems to automate or improve existing systems and review computer system capabilities, workflow, and scheduling limitations. May analyze or recommend commercially available software. May supervise computer programmers.

- Education or Training Required: Bachelor's degree
- Job Growth: 31.4%
- Annual Openings: 56,000
- Self-Employed: 5.0%
- Part-Time: 13.0%

NATIONAL WAGE FIGURES (ANNUAL)

Beginning	25th Percentile	Median	Mean	75th Percentile	90th Percentile
$42,780	$54,320	$69,760	$72,230	$87,600	$106,820

Median Wages for Industries Employing Largest Numbers (Annual)

Industry	Median Income
Securities, Commodity Contracts, and Other Financial Investments and Related Activities	$79,910
Merchant Wholesalers, Durable Goods	$78,720
Computer and Electronic Product Manufacturing	$76,150
Utilities	$75,950
Telecommunications	$73,580
Chemical Manufacturing	$72,720
Publishing Industries (Except Internet)	$72,500
Transportation Equipment Manufacturing	$71,970
Professional, Scientific, and Technical Services	$71,690
Administrative and Support Services	$71,640

Median Wages for States (Annual)

AK	$72,650	KY	$62,190	NY	$76,790
AL	$64,110	LA	$55,020	OH	$67,320
AR	$56,490	MA	$77,050	OK	$60,210
AZ	$65,220	MD	$77,030	OR	$66,060
CA	$74,260	ME	$65,990	PA	$63,360
CO	$72,400	MI	$72,180	RI	$69,700
CT	$75,680	MN	$68,470	SC	$61,740
DC	$74,690	MO	$66,760	SD	$59,140
DE	$73,550	MS	$53,260	TN	$59,750
FL	$59,820	MT	$55,830	TX	$68,450
GA	$72,270	NC	$68,480	UT	$62,850
HI	$64,050	ND	$47,790	VA	$74,520
IA	$62,650	NE	$62,800	VT	$61,390
ID	$61,900	NH	$66,980	WA	$72,520
IL	$73,350	NJ	$79,420	WI	$62,150
IN	$61,980	NM	$52,570	WV	$59,220
KS	$62,120	NV	$68,650	WY	$44,760

Median Wages for the Largest Metropolitan Areas (Annual)

AZ: Phoenix	$67,920	MI: Detroit	$76,340
CA: Los Angeles	$73,220	MN: Minneapolis	$69,630
CA: Riverside	$63,220	MO: Kansas City	$63,300
CA: Sacramento	$70,810	MO: St. Louis	$69,300
CA: San Diego	$71,010	NV: Las Vegas	$71,430
CA: San Francisco	$82,410	NY: New York	$81,850
CO: Denver	$71,600	OH: Cincinnati	$70,970
DC: Washington	$77,860	OH: Cleveland	$65,640
FL: Miami	$59,690	OH: Columbus	$70,310
FL: Orlando	$61,800	OR: Portland	$69,390
FL: Tampa	$64,360	PA: Philadelphia	$67,850
GA: Atlanta	$74,420	PA: Pittsburgh	$59,720
IL: Chicago	$75,350	TX: Dallas	$75,390
MA: Boston	$77,620	TX: Houston	$69,170
MD: Baltimore	$75,700	WA: Seattle	$74,610

FACTORS THAT MAY AFFECT EARNINGS

Educational Attainment of Workers and Effect on Earnings

	Percent at Level	Effect on Earnings
Less than High School	—	—
Some High School	—	—
High School or Equivalent	10.1%	−17.0%
Some College but No Degree	19.2%	−19.5%
Associate Degree	13.2%	−15.9%
Bachelor's Degree	36.6%	5.8%
Master's Degree	16.2%	22.4%
Doctoral Degree	3.0%	62.6%
First Professional Degree	—	—

Flexibility of Earnings

Average Hours Worked: 38
Workers with a Varying Number of Hours: 4.5%
Workers Earning Some Overtime Pay, Tips, or Commissions: 9.2%
Earnings Benefit of Working Overtime: 1.4%

Gender

	Male	Female
Percent	68.1%	31.9%
Effect on Earnings	3.8%	−6.7%

Union Membership

Percentage Union Members: 6.3%
Earnings Benefit of Union Membership: −10.7%

Veteran Status

Percentage Who Have Been on Active Duty: 11.0%
Earnings Benefit of Veteran Status: 7.0%

15-1061 Database Administrators

Coordinate changes to computer databases; test and implement the database, applying knowledge of database management systems. May plan, coordinate, and implement security measures to safeguard computer databases.

- Education or Training Required: Bachelor's degree
- Job Growth: 38.2%
- Annual Openings: 9,000
- Self-Employed: 0.5%
- Part-Time: 12.3%

NATIONAL WAGE FIGURES (ANNUAL)

Beginning	25th Percentile	Median	Mean	75th Percentile	90th Percentile
$37,350	$48,560	$64,670	$67,460	$84,830	$103,010

Median Wages for Industries Employing Largest Numbers (Annual)

Industry	Median Income
Securities, Commodity Contracts, and Other Financial Investments and Related Activities	$79,130
Utilities	$77,460
Transportation Equipment Manufacturing	$74,420
Computer and Electronic Product Manufacturing	$74,010
Professional, Scientific, and Technical Services	$68,950
Insurance Carriers and Related Activities	$68,930
Management of Companies and Enterprises	$67,680
Credit Intermediation and Related Activities	$66,300
Merchant Wholesalers, Nondurable Goods	$66,100
Publishing Industries (Except Internet)	$64,480

Median Wages for States (Annual)

AK	$70,470	KY	$57,740
AL	$56,130	LA	$60,410
AR	$55,910	MA	$72,570
AZ	$55,620	MD	$70,290
CA	$72,680	ME	$56,410
CO	$69,910	MI	$61,490
CT	$72,230	MN	$67,020
DC	$59,880	MO	$55,680
DE	$65,840	MS	$54,590
FL	$57,510	MT	$40,020
GA	$68,530	NC	$63,860
HI	$57,480	ND	$45,770
IA	$57,430	NE	$63,850
ID	$58,270	NH	$71,360
IL	$63,850	NJ	$72,980
IN	$54,670	NM	$51,080
KS	$54,960	NV	$57,680

NY	$70,940
OH	$65,920
OK	$52,960
OR	$67,460
PA	$59,950
RI	$69,540
SC	$56,420
SD	$49,300
TN	$62,910
TX	$63,040
UT	$63,370
VA	$72,570
VT	$55,570
WA	$73,040
WI	$63,400
WV	$35,820
WY	$41,340

Median Wages for the Largest Metropolitan Areas (Annual)

AZ: Phoenix	$54,710	MI: Detroit	$65,690
CA: Los Angeles	$70,940	MN: Minneapolis	$68,820
CA: Riverside	$61,770	MO: Kansas City	$55,330
CA: Sacramento	$65,040	MO: St. Louis	$59,810
CA: San Diego	$66,110	NV: Las Vegas	$65,960
CA: San Francisco	$85,390	NY: New York	$75,030
CO: Denver	$68,270	OH: Cincinnati	$70,750
DC: Washington	$70,250	OH: Cleveland	$63,590
FL: Miami	$58,870	OH: Columbus	$68,610
FL: Orlando	$64,180	OR: Portland	$69,260
FL: Tampa	$55,210	PA: Philadelphia	$64,210
GA: Atlanta	$70,660	PA: Pittsburgh	$56,410
IL: Chicago	$64,430	TX: Dallas	$68,750
MA: Boston	$74,700	TX: Houston	$62,230
MD: Baltimore	$73,900	WA: Seattle	$76,320

FACTORS THAT MAY AFFECT EARNINGS

Educational Attainment of Workers and Effect on Earnings

	Percent at Level	Effect on Earnings
Less than High School	—	—
Some High School	—	—
High School or Equivalent	10.2%	−15.1%
Some College but No Degree	18.6%	−19.3%
Associate Degree	13.7%	−15.4%
Bachelor's Degree	36.5%	5.9%
Master's Degree	16.6%	21.0%
Doctoral Degree	2.7%	64.5%
First Professional Degree	—	—

Flexibility of Earnings

Average Hours Worked: 39
Workers with a Varying Number of Hours: 4.3%
Workers Earning Some Overtime Pay, Tips, or Commissions: 8.7%
Earnings Benefit of Working Overtime: −22.0%

Gender

	Male	Female
Percent	63.0%	37.0%
Effect on Earnings	7.5%	—

Union Membership

Percentage Union Members: 6.3%
Earnings Benefit of Union Membership: −10.3%

Veteran Status

Percentage Who Have Been on Active Duty: 11.0%
Earnings Benefit of Veteran Status: 7.0%

15-1071 Network and Computer Systems Administrators

Install, configure, and support an organization's local area network (LAN), wide area network (WAN), and Internet system or a segment of a network system. Maintain network hardware and software. Monitor network to ensure network availability to all system users and perform necessary maintenance to support network availability. May supervise other network support and client server specialists and plan, coordinate, and implement network security measures.

- Education or Training Required: Bachelor's degree
- Job Growth: 38.4%
- Annual Openings: 34,000
- Self-Employed: 0.6%
- Part-Time: 12.7%

NATIONAL WAGE FIGURES (ANNUAL)

Beginning	25th Percentile	Median	Mean	75th Percentile	90th Percentile
$38,610	$48,520	$62,130	$65,260	$79,160	$97,080

Median Wages for Industries Employing Largest Numbers (Annual)

Industry	Median Income
Securities, Commodity Contracts, and Other Financial Investments and Related Activities	$72,290
Telecommunications	$69,140
Computer and Electronic Product Manufacturing	$68,590
Transportation Equipment Manufacturing	$66,750
Publishing Industries (Except Internet)	$66,690
Utilities	$66,280
Management of Companies and Enterprises	$66,020
Merchant Wholesalers, Nondurable Goods	$65,500
Professional, Scientific, and Technical Services	$65,330
Internet Service Providers, Web Search Portals, and Data-Processing Services	$62,910

Median Wages for States (Annual)

AK	$62,750	KY	$49,780	NY	$72,340
AL	$54,430	LA	$52,190	OH	$58,710
AR	$48,690	MA	$71,850	OK	$50,990
AZ	$56,030	MD	$68,690	OR	$57,890
CA	$70,240	ME	$53,220	PA	$61,380
CO	$66,670	MI	$55,820	RI	$59,850
CT	$64,310	MN	$61,720	SC	$51,630
DC	$64,560	MO	$57,950	SD	$46,850
DE	$69,910	MS	$46,890	TN	$57,660
FL	$59,630	MT	no data	TX	$58,840
GA	$62,970	NC	$59,420	UT	$56,460
HI	$56,210	ND	$44,860	VA	$69,920
IA	$54,620	NE	$56,550	VT	$55,000
ID	$45,780	NH	$58,780	WA	$66,260
IL	$60,270	NJ	$71,350	WI	$56,520
IN	$52,360	NM	$50,570	WV	$49,530
KS	$56,130	NV	$61,620	WY	$44,210

Median Wages for the Largest Metropolitan Areas (Annual)

AZ: Phoenix	$58,380	MI: Detroit	$58,850
CA: Los Angeles	$66,630	MN: Minneapolis	$65,060
CA: Riverside	$64,490	MO: Kansas City	$61,880
CA: Sacramento	$63,460	MO: St. Louis	$60,760
CA: San Diego	$66,320	NV: Las Vegas	$66,790
CA: San Francisco	$78,120	NY: New York	$76,790
CO: Denver	$70,610	OH: Cincinnati	$60,010
DC: Washington	$71,990	OH: Cleveland	$60,060
FL: Miami	$61,610	OH: Columbus	$62,510
FL: Orlando	$60,900	OR: Portland	$60,670
FL: Tampa	$59,740	PA: Philadelphia	$67,300
GA: Atlanta	$66,560	PA: Pittsburgh	$59,420
IL: Chicago	$61,630	TX: Dallas	$63,810
MA: Boston	$72,710	TX: Houston	$63,500
MD: Baltimore	$68,600	WA: Seattle	$68,690

FACTORS THAT MAY AFFECT EARNINGS

Educational Attainment of Workers and Effect on Earnings

	Percent at Level	Effect on Earnings
Less than High School	—	—
Some High School	1.2%	−48.5%
High School or Equivalent	11.4%	−14.4%
Some College but No Degree	20.9%	−18.4%
Associate Degree	14.2%	−13.9%
Bachelor's Degree	33.5%	6.8%
Master's Degree	15.5%	22.2%
Doctoral Degree	2.4%	65.6%
First Professional Degree	—	—

Flexibility of Earnings

Average Hours Worked: 38
Workers with a Varying Number of Hours: 5.5%
Workers Earning Some Overtime Pay, Tips, or Commissions: 8.9%
Earnings Benefit of Working Overtime: −6.3%

Gender

	Male	Female
Percent	83.4%	16.6%
Effect on Earnings	3.3%	—

Union Membership

Percentage Union Members: 5.6%
Earnings Benefit of Union Membership: −7.0%

Veteran Status

Percentage Who Have Been on Active Duty: 11.0%
Earnings Benefit of Veteran Status: 7.0%

15-1081 Network Systems and Data Communications Analysts

Analyze, design, test, and evaluate network systems, such as local area networks (LAN); wide area networks (WAN); and Internet, intranet, and other data communications systems. Perform network modeling, analysis, and planning. Research and recommend network and data communications hardware and software. Includes telecommunications specialists who deal with the interfacing of computer and communications equipment. May supervise computer programmers.

- Education or Training Required: Bachelor's degree
- Job Growth: 54.6%
- Annual Openings: 43,000
- Self-Employed: 19.9%
- Part-Time: 14.7%

NATIONAL WAGE FIGURES (ANNUAL)

Beginning	25th Percentile	Median	Mean	75th Percentile	90th Percentile
$38,410	$49,510	$64,600	$67,460	$82,630	$101,740

Median Wages for Industries Employing Largest Numbers (Annual)

Industry	Median Income
Computer and Electronic Product Manufacturing	$76,200
Securities, Commodity Contracts, and Other Financial Investments and Related Activities	$75,890
Transportation Equipment Manufacturing	$73,240
Telecommunications	$70,940
Management of Companies and Enterprises	$68,490
Credit Intermediation and Related Activities	$67,920
Professional, Scientific, and Technical Services	$67,070
Utilities	$66,710
Publishing Industries (Except Internet)	$66,140
Insurance Carriers and Related Activities	$65,620

Median Wages for States (Annual)

State	Wage	State	Wage	State	Wage
AK	$57,780	KY	$54,590	NY	$72,290
AL	$59,630	LA	$46,210	OH	$66,270
AR	$53,950	MA	$76,330	OK	$50,620
AZ	$57,540	MD	$70,310	OR	$59,580
CA	$69,060	ME	$64,920	PA	$64,730
CO	$66,120	MI	$63,730	RI	$65,860
CT	$67,280	MN	$71,090	SC	$55,120
DC	$68,150	MO	$60,450	SD	$45,460
DE	$60,590	MS	$45,670	TN	$56,590
FL	$54,200	MT	$45,040	TX	$60,160
GA	$58,860	NC	$62,980	UT	$53,960
HI	$59,560	ND	$44,140	VA	$73,520
IA	$59,700	NE	$56,370	VT	$58,890
ID	$39,320	NH	$58,820	WA	$71,990
IL	$64,040	NJ	$76,870	WI	$56,550
IN	$61,350	NM	$59,890	WV	$37,550
KS	$55,830	NV	$61,570	WY	$46,730

Median Wages for the Largest Metropolitan Areas (Annual)

Area	Wage	Area	Wage
AZ: Phoenix	$57,960	MI: Detroit	$64,950
CA: Los Angeles	$65,350	MN: Minneapolis	$72,110
CA: Riverside	$58,040	MO: Kansas City	$58,260
CA: Sacramento	$64,200	MO: St. Louis	$66,550
CA: San Diego	$67,130	NV: Las Vegas	$63,640
CA: San Francisco	$77,540	NY: New York	$76,800
CO: Denver	$73,150	OH: Cincinnati	$66,210
DC: Washington	$76,150	OH: Cleveland	$67,200
FL: Miami	$55,340	OH: Columbus	$68,320
FL: Orlando	$55,720	OR: Portland	$62,120
FL: Tampa	$59,960	PA: Philadelphia	$67,980
GA: Atlanta	$60,220	PA: Pittsburgh	$59,920
IL: Chicago	$65,060	TX: Dallas	$67,810
MA: Boston	$77,070	TX: Houston	$64,130
MD: Baltimore	$65,680	WA: Seattle	$75,450

FACTORS THAT MAY AFFECT EARNINGS

Educational Attainment of Workers and Effect on Earnings

	Percent at Level	Effect on Earnings
Less than High School	—	—
Some High School	1.1%	−65.7%
High School or Equivalent	10.9%	−13.2%
Some College but No Degree	21.6%	−20.1%
Associate Degree	15.1%	−12.8%
Bachelor's Degree	33.4%	8.9%
Master's Degree	14.4%	21.3%
Doctoral Degree	2.5%	72.2%
First Professional Degree	1.0%	60.5%

Flexibility of Earnings

Average Hours Worked: 37
Workers with a Varying Number of Hours: 6.9%
Workers Earning Some Overtime Pay, Tips, or Commissions: 9.3%
Earnings Benefit of Working Overtime: 11.1%

Gender

	Male	Female
Percent	74.5%	25.5%
Effect on Earnings	2.7%	−12.9%

Union Membership

Percentage Union Members: 5.7%
Earnings Benefit of Union Membership: −8.6%

Veteran Status

Percentage Who Have Been on Active Duty: 11.0%
Earnings Benefit of Veteran Status: 7.0%

15-1099 Computer Specialists, All Other

All computer specialists not listed separately.

- Education or Training Required: Associate degree
- Job Growth: 19.0%
- Annual Openings: 15,000
- Self-Employed: 6.7%
- Part-Time: 13.1%

NATIONAL WAGE FIGURES (ANNUAL)

Beginning	25th Percentile	Median	Mean	75th Percentile	90th Percentile
$35,500	$50,950	$68,570	$69,370	$87,120	$103,270

Median Wages for Industries Employing Largest Numbers (Annual)

Industry	Median Income
Federal, State, and Local Government	$75,550
Chemical Manufacturing	$73,760
Transportation Equipment Manufacturing	$71,120
Computer and Electronic Product Manufacturing	$70,900
Professional, Scientific, and Technical Services	$67,070
Utilities	$67,050
Credit Intermediation and Related Activities	$66,530
Securities, Commodity Contracts, and Other Financial Investments and Related Activities	$65,890
Merchant Wholesalers, Durable Goods	$65,730
Merchant Wholesalers, Nondurable Goods	$64,890

Median Wages for States (Annual)

AK	$74,860	KY	$55,440	NY	$67,040
AL	$70,840	LA	$51,010	OH	$60,750
AR	$55,600	MA	$70,670	OK	$65,620
AZ	$60,270	MD	$83,140	OR	$58,730
CA	$70,080	ME	$60,610	PA	$66,940
CO	$69,550	MI	$58,860	RI	$65,660
CT	$65,120	MN	$62,990	SC	$58,990
DC	$91,020	MO	$69,060	SD	$64,890
DE	$63,560	MS	$66,050	TN	$60,110
FL	$63,990	MT	$57,670	TX	$65,900
GA	$65,450	NC	$68,570	UT	$57,480
HI	$77,150	ND	$55,730	VA	$83,760
IA	$50,050	NE	$62,400	VT	$66,770
ID	$51,800	NH	$60,810	WA	$68,440
IL	$69,430	NJ	$63,890	WI	$51,230
IN	$66,540	NM	$68,550	WV	$74,170
KS	$65,420	NV	$55,310	WY	$55,780

Median Wages for the Largest Metropolitan Areas (Annual)

AZ: Phoenix	$59,010	MI: Detroit	$64,160
CA: Los Angeles	$64,610	MN: Minneapolis	$64,780
CA: Riverside	$61,570	MO: Kansas City	$73,390
CA: Sacramento	$60,880	MO: St. Louis	$67,150
CA: San Diego	$66,290	NV: Las Vegas	$54,350
CA: San Francisco	$79,810	NY: New York	$66,470
CO: Denver	$71,410	OH: Cincinnati	$58,700
DC: Washington	$88,210	OH: Cleveland	$65,650
FL: Miami	$60,060	OH: Columbus	$64,330
FL: Orlando	$37,570	OR: Portland	$65,530
FL: Tampa	$68,150	PA: Philadelphia	$63,320
GA: Atlanta	$67,090	PA: Pittsburgh	$62,940
IL: Chicago	$71,330	TX: Dallas	$59,090
MA: Boston	$70,400	TX: Houston	$66,030
MD: Baltimore	$82,480	WA: Seattle	$68,640

FACTORS THAT MAY AFFECT EARNINGS

Educational Attainment of Workers and Effect on Earnings

Figures are based on a group of occupations: Computer Specialists

	Percent at Level	Effect on Earnings
Less than High School	—	—
Some High School	1.7%	−47.4%
High School or Equivalent	11.5%	−13.3%
Some College but No Degree	20.0%	−16.7%
Associate Degree	14.6%	−10.4%
Bachelor's Degree	31.8%	6.6%
Master's Degree	16.0%	19.3%
Doctoral Degree	3.1%	50.5%
First Professional Degree	1.3%	35.3%

Flexibility of Earnings

Average Hours Worked: 38
Workers with a Varying Number of Hours: 4.5%
Workers Earning Some Overtime Pay, Tips, or Commissions: 8.9%
Earnings Benefit of Working Overtime: 1.4%

Gender

	Male	Female
Percent	74.3%	25.7%
Effect on Earnings	5.6%	−10.5%

Union Membership

Percentage Union Members: 5.5%
Earnings Benefit of Union Membership: −9.6%

Veteran Status

Percentage Who Have Been on Active Duty: 11.0%
Earnings Benefit of Veteran Status: 7.0%

15-2000 Mathematical Science Occupations

15-2011 Actuaries

Analyze statistical data, such as mortality, accident, sickness, disability, and retirement rates, and construct probability tables to forecast risk and liability for payment of future benefits. May ascertain premium rates required and cash reserves necessary to ensure payment of future benefits.

- Education or Training Required: Work experience plus degree
- Job Growth: 23.2%
- Annual Openings: 3,000
- Self-Employed: 0.0%
- Part-Time: 2.3%

NATIONAL WAGE FIGURES (ANNUAL)

Beginning	25th Percentile	Median	Mean	75th Percentile	90th Percentile
$46,470	$58,710	$82,800	$91,810	$114,570	more than $145,600

Median Wages for Industries Employing Largest Numbers (Annual)

Industry	Median Income
Professional, Scientific, and Technical Services	$92,660
Funds, Trusts, and Other Financial Vehicles	$85,530
Securities, Commodity Contracts, and Other Financial Investments and Related Activities	$83,130
Insurance Carriers and Related Activities	$82,170
Federal, State, and Local Government	$79,780
Management of Companies and Enterprises	$77,840
Internet Service Providers, Web Search Portals, and Data-Processing Services	$74,030
Hospitals	$68,090
Administrative and Support Services	$62,100
Credit Intermediation and Related Activities	$57,970

Median Wages for States (Annual)

AK	no data	KY	$81,720	NY	$99,460
AL	$48,100	LA	$85,990	OH	$71,820
AR	no data	MA	$80,950	OK	$53,130
AZ	$64,620	MD	$95,080	OR	$94,270
CA	$85,480	ME	no data	PA	$85,640
CO	$90,770	MI	$58,800	RI	no data
CT	$88,320	MN	$86,470	SC	$68,210
DC	$83,920	MO	$94,180	SD	no data
DE	no data	MS	no data	TN	$69,100
FL	$79,870	MT	no data	TX	$89,840
GA	$78,260	NC	$79,960	UT	$71,800
HI	no data	ND	no data	VA	$70,450
IA	$81,700	NE	$76,110	VT	$58,540
ID	$109,780	NH	$84,070	WA	$75,820
IL	$85,160	NJ	$83,140	WI	$79,370
IN	$79,600	NM	$116,270	WV	no data
KS	$88,810	NV	no data	WY	no data

Median Wages for the Largest Metropolitan Areas (Annual)

AZ: Phoenix	$65,900	MI: Detroit	$49,690
CA: Los Angeles	$87,310	MN: Minneapolis	$86,710
CA: Riverside	no data	MO: Kansas City	$93,800
CA: Sacramento	$79,880	MO: St. Louis	$101,530
CA: San Diego	$78,710	NV: Las Vegas	no data
CA: San Francisco	$88,450	NY: New York	$97,280
CO: Denver	$91,380	OH: Cincinnati	$76,330
DC: Washington	$78,180	OH: Cleveland	$64,410
FL: Miami	$71,490	OH: Columbus	$61,890
FL: Orlando	no data	OR: Portland	$92,200
FL: Tampa	$82,660	PA: Philadelphia	$91,880
GA: Atlanta	$78,260	PA: Pittsburgh	$80,280
IL: Chicago	$84,130	TX: Dallas	$94,130
MA: Boston	$79,950	TX: Houston	$74,420
MD: Baltimore	$98,570	WA: Seattle	$75,020

FACTORS THAT MAY AFFECT EARNINGS

Educational Attainment of Workers and Effect on Earnings

	Percent at Level	Effect on Earnings
Less than High School	—	—
Some High School	—	—
High School or Equivalent	—	—
Some College but No Degree	—	—
Associate Degree	—	—
Bachelor's Degree	69.6%	−8.5%
Master's Degree	26.1%	12.9%
Doctoral Degree	—	—
First Professional Degree	—	—

Flexibility of Earnings

Average Hours Worked: 40

Workers with a Varying Number of Hours: 6.0%

Workers Earning Some Overtime Pay, Tips, or Commissions: 7.1%

Earnings Benefit of Working Overtime: 2.3%

Gender

	Male	Female
Percent	71.6%	28.4%
Effect on Earnings	5.6%	−10.5%

Union Membership

Percentage Union Members: 5.9%

Earnings Benefit of Union Membership: −11.2%

Veteran Status

Percentage Who Have Been on Active Duty: 13.0%

Earnings Benefit of Veteran Status: 9.0%

15-2021 Mathematicians

Conduct research in fundamental mathematics or in application of mathematical techniques to science, management, and other fields. Solve or direct solutions to problems in various fields by mathematical methods.

- Education or Training Required: Doctoral degree
- Job Growth: –1.3%
- Annual Openings: Fewer than 500
- Self-Employed: 0.0%
- Part-Time: 2.3%

NATIONAL WAGE FIGURES (ANNUAL)

Beginning	25th Percentile	Median	Mean	75th Percentile	90th Percentile
$43,500	$62,970	$86,930	$86,780	$106,250	$132,190

Median Wages for Industries Employing Largest Numbers (Annual)

Industry	Median Income
Professional, Scientific, and Technical Services	$93,650
Federal, State, and Local Government	$89,170
Publishing Industries (Except Internet)	$58,940
Educational Services	$52,270

Median Wages for States (Annual)

State	Wage	State	Wage	State	Wage
AK	no data	KY	no data	NY	$81,530
AL	$92,100	LA	no data	OH	$76,490
AR	no data	MA	no data	OK	no data
AZ	no data	MD	$96,090	OR	no data
CA	$96,550	ME	no data	PA	$45,840
CO	$93,970	MI	no data	RI	no data
CT	$87,140	MN	no data	SC	no data
DC	$104,560	MO	no data	SD	no data
DE	no data	MS	no data	TN	no data
FL	$70,440	MT	no data	TX	$65,730
GA	no data	NC	$60,570	UT	no data
HI	no data	ND	no data	VA	$92,330
IA	no data	NE	no data	VT	no data
ID	no data	NH	no data	WA	$90,360
IL	$79,780	NJ	$110,480	WI	$51,270
IN	no data	NM	no data	WV	no data
KS	no data	NV	no data	WY	no data

Median Wages for the Largest Metropolitan Areas (Annual)

Metro	Wage	Metro	Wage
AZ: Phoenix	no data	MI: Detroit	no data
CA: Los Angeles	no data	MN: Minneapolis	no data
CA: Riverside	no data	MO: Kansas City	no data
CA: Sacramento	no data	MO: St. Louis	no data
CA: San Diego	$102,090	NV: Las Vegas	no data
CA: San Francisco	$93,530	NY: New York	no data
CO: Denver	no data	OH: Cincinnati	no data
DC: Washington	$99,740	OH: Cleveland	no data
FL: Miami	no data	OH: Columbus	no data
FL: Orlando	no data	OR: Portland	no data
FL: Tampa	no data	PA: Philadelphia	no data
GA: Atlanta	no data	PA: Pittsburgh	no data
IL: Chicago	$86,780	TX: Dallas	no data
MA: Boston	no data	TX: Houston	no data
MD: Baltimore	$90,860	WA: Seattle	no data

FACTORS THAT MAY AFFECT EARNINGS

Educational Attainment of Workers and Effect on Earnings

Figures are based on a group of occupations: Mathematical Science Occupations

	Percent at Level	Effect on Earnings
Less than High School	—	—
Some High School	—	—
High School or Equivalent	6.3%	–24.4%
Some College but No Degree	10.6%	–15.5%
Associate Degree	7.9%	–14.5%
Bachelor's Degree	37.0%	0.0%
Master's Degree	28.0%	7.5%
Doctoral Degree	7.4%	26.2%
First Professional Degree	—	—

Flexibility of Earnings

Average Hours Worked: 36
Workers with a Varying Number of Hours: 13.0%
Workers Earning Some Overtime Pay, Tips, or Commissions: 6.8%
Earnings Benefit of Working Overtime: 2.3%

Gender

	Male	Female
Percent	82.6%	17.4%
Effect on Earnings	5.6%	–10.5%

Union Membership

Percentage Union Members: 14.3%
Earnings Benefit of Union Membership: –11.2%

Veteran Status

Percentage Who Have Been on Active Duty: 13.0%
Earnings Benefit of Veteran Status: 9.0%

15-2031 Operations Research Analysts

Formulate and apply mathematical modeling and other optimizing methods, using a computer to develop and interpret information that assists management with decision making, policy formulation, or other managerial functions. May develop related software, service, or products. Frequently concentrates on collecting and analyzing data and developing decision support software. May develop and supply optimal time, cost, or logistics networks for program evaluation, review, or implementation.

- Education or Training Required: Master's degree
- Job Growth: 8.4%
- Annual Openings: 7,000
- Self-Employed: 1.2%
- Part-Time: 2.3%

NATIONAL WAGE FIGURES (ANNUAL)

Beginning	25th Percentile	Median	Mean	75th Percentile	90th Percentile
$38,760	$48,820	$64,650	$69,100	$85,760	$108,290

Median Wages for Industries Employing Largest Numbers (Annual)

Industry	Median Income
Computer and Electronic Product Manufacturing	$74,810
Chemical Manufacturing	$71,080
Postal Service	$70,430
Professional, Scientific, and Technical Services	$70,350
Merchant Wholesalers, Durable Goods	$69,670
Federal, State, and Local Government	$68,470
Couriers and Messengers	$68,010
Management of Companies and Enterprises	$67,710
Internet Service Providers, Web Search Portals, and Data-Processing Services	$67,090
Telecommunications	$66,550

Median Wages for States (Annual)

State	Wage	State	Wage	State	Wage
AK	$50,140	KY	$56,670	NY	$67,160
AL	$74,510	LA	$43,400	OH	$64,830
AR	$46,600	MA	$72,220	OK	$71,540
AZ	$54,540	MD	$82,050	OR	$62,240
CA	$67,480	ME	$64,050	PA	$62,200
CO	$62,620	MI	$65,000	RI	$85,260
CT	$69,300	MN	$58,400	SC	$54,080
DC	$84,380	MO	$59,970	SD	$42,400
DE	$70,860	MS	$64,320	TN	$56,070
FL	$49,520	MT	$53,190	TX	$68,480
GA	$54,270	NC	$62,890	UT	$49,080
HI	$68,970	ND	no data	VA	$84,620
IA	$48,830	NE	$54,380	VT	no data
ID	$58,080	NH	$57,410	WA	$71,580
IL	$68,150	NJ	$85,550	WI	$55,010
IN	$61,190	NM	$77,810	WV	$57,180
KS	$69,610	NV	$64,540	WY	no data

Median Wages for the Largest Metropolitan Areas (Annual)

Metro	Wage	Metro	Wage
AZ: Phoenix	$55,550	MI: Detroit	$64,240
CA: Los Angeles	$64,450	MN: Minneapolis	$57,450
CA: Riverside	$59,890	MO: Kansas City	$63,420
CA: Sacramento	$63,100	MO: St. Louis	$64,140
CA: San Diego	$77,250	NV: Las Vegas	$61,830
CA: San Francisco	$71,050	NY: New York	$78,810
CO: Denver	$59,610	OH: Cincinnati	no data
DC: Washington	$87,690	OH: Cleveland	$62,460
FL: Miami	$50,690	OH: Columbus	$71,080
FL: Orlando	$48,060	OR: Portland	$61,850
FL: Tampa	$47,410	PA: Philadelphia	$69,870
GA: Atlanta	$56,170	PA: Pittsburgh	$47,510
IL: Chicago	$67,540	TX: Dallas	$62,150
MA: Boston	$72,250	TX: Houston	$74,000
MD: Baltimore	$87,730	WA: Seattle	$74,610

FACTORS THAT MAY AFFECT EARNINGS

Educational Attainment of Workers and Effect on Earnings

	Percent at Level	Effect on Earnings
Less than High School	—	—
Some High School	—	—
High School or Equivalent	7.9%	−19.4%
Some College but No Degree	12.7%	−13.8%
Associate Degree	10.3%	−11.2%
Bachelor's Degree	38.1%	0.1%
Master's Degree	27.0%	11.1%
Doctoral Degree	—	—
First Professional Degree	—	—

Flexibility of Earnings

Average Hours Worked: 39
Workers with a Varying Number of Hours: 3.0%
Workers Earning Some Overtime Pay, Tips, or Commissions: 8.6%
Earnings Benefit of Working Overtime: −7.6%

Gender

	Male	Female
Percent	59.7%	40.3%
Effect on Earnings	12.3%	—

Union Membership

Percentage Union Members: 7.9%
Earnings Benefit of Union Membership: −4.3%

Veteran Status

Percentage Who Have Been on Active Duty: 13.0%
Earnings Benefit of Veteran Status: 9.0%

15-2041 Statisticians

Engage in the development of mathematical theory or apply statistical theory and methods to collect, organize, interpret, and summarize numerical data to provide usable information. May specialize in fields such as bio-statistics, agricultural statistics, business statistics, economic statistics, or other fields.

- Education or Training Required: Master's degree
- Job Growth: 4.6%
- Annual Openings: 2,000
- Self-Employed: 3.6%
- Part-Time: 11.1%

NATIONAL WAGE FIGURES (ANNUAL)

Beginning	25th Percentile	Median	Mean	75th Percentile	90th Percentile
$37,010	$48,480	$65,720	$69,080	$87,850	$108,630

Median Wages for Industries Employing Largest Numbers (Annual)

Industry	Median Income
Chemical Manufacturing	$83,560
Securities, Commodity Contracts, and Other Financial Investments and Related Activities	$81,370
Computer and Electronic Product Manufacturing	$78,560
Miscellaneous Manufacturing	$77,150
Transportation Equipment Manufacturing	$75,200
Professional, Scientific, and Technical Services	$72,200
Federal, State, and Local Government	$71,600
Internet Service Providers, Web Search Portals, and Data-Processing Services	$71,060
Management of Companies and Enterprises	$69,620
Credit Intermediation and Related Activities	$65,740

Median Wages for States (Annual)

State	Wage	State	Wage	State	Wage
AK	$69,620	KY	$57,310	NY	$56,690
AL	$54,630	LA	$50,470	OH	$56,850
AR	no data	MA	$73,610	OK	$38,660
AZ	$63,680	MD	$84,620	OR	$53,530
CA	$75,730	ME	$56,680	PA	$61,210
CO	$63,380	MI	$63,480	RI	no data
CT	$78,340	MN	$61,700	SC	$42,210
DC	$92,240	MO	$55,480	SD	no data
DE	no data	MS	no data	TN	$46,220
FL	$52,120	MT	$47,630	TX	$68,070
GA	$67,790	NC	$60,530	UT	$54,750
HI	$55,690	ND	$45,640	VA	$72,300
IA	$55,790	NE	$52,550	VT	$49,280
ID	no data	NH	$55,880	WA	$63,010
IL	$66,670	NJ	$68,550	WI	$63,120
IN	$44,530	NM	$52,510	WV	$80,480
KS	$46,170	NV	no data	WY	no data

Median Wages for the Largest Metropolitan Areas (Annual)

Area	Wage	Area	Wage
AZ: Phoenix	$68,370	MI: Detroit	$68,890
CA: Los Angeles	$72,750	MN: Minneapolis	$61,640
CA: Riverside	no data	MO: Kansas City	$66,430
CA: Sacramento	$60,800	MO: St. Louis	$68,930
CA: San Diego	$74,180	NV: Las Vegas	no data
CA: San Francisco	$76,570	NY: New York	$64,850
CO: Denver	$62,500	OH: Cincinnati	$61,350
DC: Washington	$87,080	OH: Cleveland	$57,670
FL: Miami	$57,530	OH: Columbus	$57,640
FL: Orlando	$50,480	OR: Portland	$56,690
FL: Tampa	$49,200	PA: Philadelphia	$71,280
GA: Atlanta	$74,230	PA: Pittsburgh	$46,840
IL: Chicago	$67,750	TX: Dallas	$82,490
MA: Boston	$74,670	TX: Houston	$69,640
MD: Baltimore	$74,820	WA: Seattle	$62,230

FACTORS THAT MAY AFFECT EARNINGS

Educational Attainment of Workers and Effect on Earnings

	Percent at Level	Effect on Earnings
Less than High School	—	—
Some High School	—	—
High School or Equivalent	—	—
Some College but No Degree	—	—
Associate Degree	—	—
Bachelor's Degree	25.0%	−10.6%
Master's Degree	40.0%	−2.4%
Doctoral Degree	15.0%	49.9%
First Professional Degree	—	—

Figures do not total 100% because some levels have a very small sample size.

Flexibility of Earnings

Average Hours Worked: 37
Workers with a Varying Number of Hours: 1.8%
Workers Earning Some Overtime Pay, Tips, or Commissions: 4.9%
Earnings Benefit of Working Overtime: 2.3%

Gender

	Male	Female
Percent	54.8%	45.2%
Effect on Earnings	5.6%	−10.5%

Union Membership

Percentage Union Members: 4.9%
Earnings Benefit of Union Membership: −11.2%

Veteran Status

Percentage Who Have Been on Active Duty: 13.0%
Earnings Benefit of Veteran Status: 9.0%

15-2091 Mathematical Technicians

Apply standardized mathematical formulas, principles, and methodology to technological problems in engineering and physical sciences in relation to specific industrial and research objectives, processes, equipment, and products.

- Education or Training Required: Master's degree
- Job Growth: 3.4%
- Annual Openings: Fewer than 500
- Self-Employed: 0.0%
- Part-Time: 2.3%

NATIONAL WAGE FIGURES (ANNUAL)

Beginning	25th Percentile	Median	Mean	75th Percentile	90th Percentile
$25,860	$29,990	$37,880	$46,010	$51,890	$72,040

Note: The mean is significantly higher than the median because of the presence of a few star earners.

Median Wages for Industries Employing Largest Numbers (Annual)

Industry	Median Income
Professional, Scientific, and Technical Services	$52,860
Computer and Electronic Product Manufacturing	$44,240
Management of Companies and Enterprises	$37,910
Insurance Carriers and Related Activities	$36,670
Educational Services	$36,140
Federal, State, and Local Government	$31,510

Median Wages for States (Annual)

State	Wage	State	Wage	State	Wage
AK	no data	KY	no data	NY	$39,920
AL	no data	LA	no data	OH	$36,800
AR	no data	MA	no data	OK	no data
AZ	no data	MD	no data	OR	no data
CA	$35,020	ME	no data	PA	no data
CO	no data	MI	no data	RI	no data
CT	no data	MN	$41,500	SC	no data
DC	no data	MO	no data	SD	no data
DE	no data	MS	no data	TN	no data
FL	$31,920	MT	no data	TX	no data
GA	$34,280	NC	no data	UT	no data
HI	no data	ND	no data	VA	$47,020
IA	no data	NE	no data	VT	no data
ID	no data	NH	no data	WA	$39,420
IL	no data	NJ	$122,480	WI	no data
IN	no data	NM	no data	WV	no data
KS	no data	NV	no data	WY	no data

Median Wages for the Largest Metropolitan Areas (Annual)

Area	Wage	Area	Wage
AZ: Phoenix	no data	MI: Detroit	no data
CA: Los Angeles	no data	MN: Minneapolis	$42,850
CA: Riverside	no data	MO: Kansas City	no data
CA: Sacramento	no data	MO: St. Louis	no data
CA: San Diego	$29,360	NV: Las Vegas	no data
CA: San Francisco	no data	NY: New York	no data
CO: Denver	no data	OH: Cincinnati	no data
DC: Washington	no data	OH: Cleveland	no data
FL: Miami	no data	OH: Columbus	no data
FL: Orlando	no data	OR: Portland	no data
FL: Tampa	no data	PA: Philadelphia	no data
GA: Atlanta	$37,500	PA: Pittsburgh	no data
IL: Chicago	no data	TX: Dallas	no data
MA: Boston	no data	TX: Houston	no data
MD: Baltimore	no data	WA: Seattle	no data

FACTORS THAT MAY AFFECT EARNINGS

Educational Attainment of Workers and Effect on Earnings

Figures are based on a group of occupations: Miscellaneous Mathematical Scientists

	Percent at Level	Effect on Earnings
Less than High School	—	—
Some High School	—	—
High School or Equivalent	—	—
Some College but No Degree	—	—
Associate Degree	—	—
Bachelor's Degree	—	—
Master's Degree	—	—
Doctoral Degree	37.5%	2.1%
First Professional Degree	—	—

Figures do not total 100% because some levels have a very small sample size.

Flexibility of Earnings

Average Hours Worked: 39
Workers with a Varying Number of Hours: 3.5%
Workers Earning Some Overtime Pay, Tips, or Commissions: 6.8%
Earnings Benefit of Working Overtime: 2.3%

Gender

	Male	Female
Percent	59.2%	40.8%
Effect on Earnings	5.6%	−10.5%

Union Membership

Percentage Union Members: 5.9%
Earnings Benefit of Union Membership: −11.2%

Veteran Status

Percentage Who Have Been on Active Duty: 13.0%
Earnings Benefit of Veteran Status: 9.0%

15-2099 Mathematical Scientists, All Other

All mathematical scientists not listed separately.

- Education or Training Required: Master's degree
- Job Growth: 6.2%
- Annual Openings: 1,000
- Self-Employed: 0.0%
- Part-Time: 2.3%

NATIONAL WAGE FIGURES (ANNUAL)

Beginning	25th Percentile	Median	Mean	75th Percentile	90th Percentile
$35,480	$48,420	$63,570	$64,920	$77,540	$93,210

Median Wages for Industries Employing Largest Numbers (Annual)

Industry	Median Income
Credit Intermediation and Related Activities	$70,770
Management of Companies and Enterprises	$67,850
Insurance Carriers and Related Activities	$61,110
Professional, Scientific, and Technical Services	$61,050
Real Estate	$55,110
Educational Services	$43,090
Hospitals	$37,550
Federal, State, and Local Government	$35,520

Median Wages for States (Annual)

AK	no data	KY	no data
AL	no data	LA	no data
AR	no data	MA	$50,180
AZ	no data	MD	$31,860
CA	$61,680	ME	no data
CO	no data	MI	$63,770
CT	$53,260	MN	$59,480
DC	no data	MO	no data
DE	no data	MS	no data
FL	$37,400	MT	no data
GA	no data	NC	no data
HI	no data	ND	no data
IA	no data	NE	no data
ID	no data	NH	no data
IL	$67,100	NJ	$36,200
IN	no data	NM	no data
KS	no data	NV	no data

NY	$77,200
OH	$67,420
OK	no data
OR	no data
PA	$54,870
RI	no data
SC	no data
SD	no data
TN	no data
TX	$44,930
UT	no data
VA	$30,200
VT	no data
WA	$50,230
WI	$47,340
WV	no data
WY	no data

Median Wages for the Largest Metropolitan Areas (Annual)

AZ: Phoenix	no data	MI: Detroit	$57,690
CA: Los Angeles	$58,350	MN: Minneapolis	no data
CA: Riverside	$54,700	MO: Kansas City	no data
CA: Sacramento	$53,210	MO: St. Louis	no data
CA: San Diego	$58,290	NV: Las Vegas	no data
CA: San Francisco	$65,880	NY: New York	no data
CO: Denver	no data	OH: Cincinnati	no data
DC: Washington	$31,570	OH: Cleveland	no data
FL: Miami	no data	OH: Columbus	no data
FL: Orlando	no data	OR: Portland	no data
FL: Tampa	no data	PA: Philadelphia	$58,460
GA: Atlanta	no data	PA: Pittsburgh	no data
IL: Chicago	no data	TX: Dallas	no data
MA: Boston	no data	TX: Houston	no data
MD: Baltimore	no data	WA: Seattle	$51,830

FACTORS THAT MAY AFFECT EARNINGS

Educational Attainment of Workers and Effect on Earnings

Figures are based on a group of occupations: Miscellaneous Mathematical Scientists

	Percent at Level	Effect on Earnings
Less than High School	—	—
Some High School	—	—
High School or Equivalent	—	—
Some College but No Degree	—	—
Associate Degree	—	—
Bachelor's Degree	—	—
Master's Degree	—	—
Doctoral Degree	37.5%	2.1%
First Professional Degree	—	—

Figures do not total 100% because some levels have a very small sample size.

Flexibility of Earnings

Average Hours Worked: 39
Workers with a Varying Number of Hours: 3.5%
Workers Earning Some Overtime Pay, Tips, or Commissions: 6.8%
Earnings Benefit of Working Overtime: 2.3%

Gender

	Male	Female
Percent	59.2%	40.8%
Effect on Earnings	5.6%	−10.5%

Union Membership

Percentage Union Members: 5.9%
Earnings Benefit of Union Membership: −11.2%

Veteran Status

Percentage Who Have Been on Active Duty: 13.0%
Earnings Benefit of Veteran Status: 9.0%

17-0000: Architecture and Engineering Occupations

17-1000 Architects, Surveyors, and Cartographers

17-1011 Architects, Except Landscape and Naval

Plan and design structures, such as private residences, office buildings, theaters, factories, and other structural property.

- Education or Training Required: Bachelor's degree
- Job Growth: 17.3%
- Annual Openings: 7,000
- Self-Employed: 20.1%
- Part-Time: 22.1%

NATIONAL WAGE FIGURES (ANNUAL)

Beginning	25th Percentile	Median	Mean	75th Percentile	90th Percentile
$39,420	$49,780	$64,150	$69,760	$83,450	$104,970

Median Wages for Industries Employing Largest Numbers (Annual)

Industry	Median Income
Credit Intermediation and Related Activities	$95,670
Insurance Carriers and Related Activities	$89,450
Postal Service	$77,730
Federal, State, and Local Government	$74,090
Management of Companies and Enterprises	$73,020
Hospitals	$72,680
Heavy and Civil Engineering Construction	$70,050
Nonmetallic Mineral Product Manufacturing	$66,570
Educational Services	$66,100
Specialty Trade Contractors	$65,190

Median Wages for States (Annual)

State	Wage	State	Wage	State	Wage
AK	$75,440	KY	$57,600	NY	$68,350
AL	$66,650	LA	$56,640	OH	$65,400
AR	no data	MA	$73,120	OK	$58,920
AZ	$60,790	MD	$66,060	OR	$53,440
CA	$72,030	ME	$56,230	PA	$68,240
CO	$54,110	MI	$66,070	RI	$63,410
CT	$70,720	MN	$63,810	SC	$69,300
DC	$62,980	MO	$60,990	SD	$61,790
DE	$68,650	MS	$52,900	TN	$59,620
FL	$58,530	MT	$48,500	TX	$62,720
GA	$64,680	NC	$59,610	UT	$61,610
HI	$56,200	ND	$47,970	VA	$66,430
IA	$60,270	NE	$65,410	VT	$62,720
ID	$62,670	NH	$62,380	WA	$64,330
IL	$61,550	NJ	$72,710	WI	$58,110
IN	$56,010	NM	$60,380	WV	$67,210
KS	$60,680	NV	$60,090	WY	$53,370

Median Wages for the Largest Metropolitan Areas (Annual)

Area	Wage	Area	Wage
AZ: Phoenix	$62,420	MI: Detroit	$69,170
CA: Los Angeles	$69,890	MN: Minneapolis	$64,250
CA: Riverside	$59,540	MO: Kansas City	$65,720
CA: Sacramento	$75,280	MO: St. Louis	$59,480
CA: San Diego	$77,590	NV: Las Vegas	$59,840
CA: San Francisco	$75,070	NY: New York	$69,980
CO: Denver	$53,470	OH: Cincinnati	$66,730
DC: Washington	$67,390	OH: Cleveland	$66,880
FL: Miami	$59,810	OH: Columbus	$65,670
FL: Orlando	$56,110	OR: Portland	$56,260
FL: Tampa	$55,230	PA: Philadelphia	$70,450
GA: Atlanta	$63,940	PA: Pittsburgh	$62,530
IL: Chicago	$61,430	TX: Dallas	$65,700
MA: Boston	$72,580	TX: Houston	$66,030
MD: Baltimore	$64,740	WA: Seattle	$66,270

FACTORS THAT MAY AFFECT EARNINGS

Educational Attainment of Workers and Effect on Earnings

Figures are based on a group of occupations: Architects, Surveyors, and Cartographers

	Percent at Level	Effect on Earnings
Less than High School	—	—
Some High School	—	—
High School or Equivalent	7.3%	−28.7%
Some College but No Degree	6.9%	−43.9%
Associate Degree	6.0%	2.4%
Bachelor's Degree	50.5%	5.4%
Master's Degree	25.7%	3.7%
Doctoral Degree	—	—
First Professional Degree	—	—

Flexibility of Earnings

Average Hours Worked: 40
Workers with a Varying Number of Hours: 6.5%
Workers Earning Some Overtime Pay, Tips, or Commissions: 10.8%
Earnings Benefit of Working Overtime: −2.5%

Gender

	Male	Female
Percent	77.8%	22.2%
Effect on Earnings	11.5%	—

Union Membership

Percentage Union Members: Insignificant
Earnings Benefit of Union Membership: No significant data available

Veteran Status

Percentage Who Have Been on Active Duty: 5.4%
Earnings Benefit of Veteran Status: 12.9%

17-1012 Landscape Architects

Plan and design land areas for such projects as parks and other recreational facilities; airports; highways; hospitals; schools; land subdivisions; and commercial, industrial, and residential sites.

- Education or Training Required: Bachelor's degree
- Job Growth: 19.4%
- Annual Openings: 1,000
- Self-Employed: 23.7%
- Part-Time: 22.1%

NATIONAL WAGE FIGURES (ANNUAL)

Beginning	25th Percentile	Median	Mean	75th Percentile	90th Percentile
$34,230	$42,720	$55,140	$60,480	$73,240	$95,420

Median Wages for Industries Employing Largest Numbers (Annual)

Industry	Median Income
Utilities	$83,140
Real Estate	$63,190
Amusement, Gambling, and Recreation Industries	$62,800
Construction of Buildings	$61,530
Federal, State, and Local Government	$59,890
Management of Companies and Enterprises	$57,980
Educational Services	$57,420
Professional, Scientific, and Technical Services	$56,360
Heavy and Civil Engineering Construction	$55,500
Specialty Trade Contractors	$49,470

Median Wages for States (Annual)

State	Wage	State	Wage	State	Wage
AK	$71,390	KY	$43,110	NY	$64,880
AL	$64,220	LA	$44,830	OH	$46,610
AR	$50,860	MA	$58,620	OK	$47,510
AZ	$57,470	MD	$55,740	OR	$51,670
CA	$64,710	ME	$56,660	PA	$47,510
CO	$53,640	MI	$55,010	RI	no data
CT	$56,010	MN	$55,230	SC	$49,220
DC	$76,780	MO	$44,190	SD	no data
DE	$52,990	MS	$53,110	TN	$50,790
FL	$50,350	MT	$35,290	TX	$54,050
GA	$60,100	NC	$53,010	UT	$55,540
HI	$60,940	ND	no data	VA	$50,590
IA	$36,970	NE	$52,970	VT	$37,570
ID	$55,060	NH	$67,370	WA	$54,770
IL	$54,180	NJ	$65,700	WI	$49,090
IN	$42,300	NM	$61,460	WV	$56,380
KS	$46,430	NV	$44,300	WY	$58,420

Median Wages for the Largest Metropolitan Areas (Annual)

Area	Wage	Area	Wage
AZ: Phoenix	$58,580	MI: Detroit	$59,300
CA: Los Angeles	$71,480	MN: Minneapolis	$55,470
CA: Riverside	$42,640	MO: Kansas City	$42,840
CA: Sacramento	$69,970	MO: St. Louis	$45,830
CA: San Diego	$71,750	NV: Las Vegas	$42,090
CA: San Francisco	$59,180	NY: New York	$66,610
CO: Denver	$53,380	OH: Cincinnati	$47,240
DC: Washington	$56,790	OH: Cleveland	$45,640
FL: Miami	$47,900	OH: Columbus	$52,090
FL: Orlando	$53,630	OR: Portland	$56,430
FL: Tampa	$50,260	PA: Philadelphia	$51,140
GA: Atlanta	$65,500	PA: Pittsburgh	$57,100
IL: Chicago	$53,860	TX: Dallas	no data
MA: Boston	$59,430	TX: Houston	$53,300
MD: Baltimore	$56,610	WA: Seattle	$53,800

FACTORS THAT MAY AFFECT EARNINGS

Educational Attainment of Workers and Effect on Earnings

Figures are based on a group of occupations: Architects, Surveyors, and Cartographers

	Percent at Level	Effect on Earnings
Less than High School	—	—
Some High School	—	—
High School or Equivalent	7.3%	−28.7%
Some College but No Degree	6.9%	−43.9%
Associate Degree	6.0%	2.4%
Bachelor's Degree	50.5%	5.4%
Master's Degree	25.7%	3.7%
Doctoral Degree	—	—
First Professional Degree	—	—

Flexibility of Earnings

Average Hours Worked: 40
Workers with a Varying Number of Hours: 6.5%
Workers Earning Some Overtime Pay, Tips, or Commissions: 10.8%
Earnings Benefit of Working Overtime: −2.5%

Gender

	Male	Female
Percent	77.8%	22.2%
Effect on Earnings	11.5%	—

Union Membership

Percentage Union Members: Insignificant
Earnings Benefit of Union Membership: No significant data available

Veteran Status

Percentage Who Have Been on Active Duty: 5.4%
Earnings Benefit of Veteran Status: 12.9%

17-1021 Cartographers and Photogrammetrists

Collect, analyze, and interpret geographic information provided by geodetic surveys, aerial photographs, and satellite data. Research, study, and prepare maps and other spatial data in digital or graphic form for legal, social, political, educational, and design purposes. May work with Geographic Information Systems (GIS). May design and evaluate algorithms, data structures, and user interfaces for GIS and mapping systems.

- Education or Training Required: Bachelor's degree
- Job Growth: 15.2%
- Annual Openings: 1,000
- Self-Employed: 2.9%
- Part-Time: 22.1%

NATIONAL WAGE FIGURES (ANNUAL)

Beginning	25th Percentile	Median	Mean	75th Percentile	90th Percentile
$30,910	$37,480	$48,240	$52,600	$65,240	$80,520

Median Wages for Industries Employing Largest Numbers (Annual)

Industry	Median Income
Telecommunications	$65,770
Utilities	$56,210
Management of Companies and Enterprises	$54,740
Oil and Gas Extraction	$53,820
Federal, State, and Local Government	$53,210
Administrative and Support Services	$49,570
Support Activities for Mining	$48,250
Professional, Scientific, and Technical Services	$45,440
Internet Service Providers, Web Search Portals, and Data-Processing Services	$44,720
Educational Services	$42,500

Median Wages for States (Annual)

State	Wage	State	Wage	State	Wage
AK	$51,850	KY	$37,850	NY	$52,720
AL	$39,460	LA	$57,420	OH	$46,430
AR	$51,090	MA	$47,730	OK	$36,900
AZ	$44,660	MD	$67,730	OR	$46,730
CA	$55,990	ME	$41,170	PA	$39,880
CO	$57,790	MI	$58,220	RI	no data
CT	no data	MN	$49,210	SC	$42,780
DC	no data	MO	$45,310	SD	$38,450
DE	no data	MS	$39,830	TN	$37,780
FL	no data	MT	$38,490	TX	$57,980
GA	$46,280	NC	$44,590	UT	$48,760
HI	$44,950	ND	$28,330	VA	$65,630
IA	$38,170	NE	$44,380	VT	$33,580
ID	$43,430	NH	$36,500	WA	$58,200
IL	$41,930	NJ	$60,060	WI	$46,000
IN	$39,120	NM	$42,890	WV	no data
KS	$40,800	NV	$62,130	WY	$40,700

Median Wages for the Largest Metropolitan Areas (Annual)

Area	Wage	Area	Wage
AZ: Phoenix	$46,230	MI: Detroit	no data
CA: Los Angeles	$55,150	MN: Minneapolis	$56,450
CA: Riverside	$54,170	MO: Kansas City	$41,690
CA: Sacramento	$62,600	MO: St. Louis	$42,590
CA: San Diego	$54,270	NV: Las Vegas	$66,080
CA: San Francisco	$64,240	NY: New York	$54,480
CO: Denver	$65,710	OH: Cincinnati	no data
DC: Washington	$74,100	OH: Cleveland	$46,450
FL: Miami	no data	OH: Columbus	$47,500
FL: Orlando	no data	OR: Portland	$51,180
FL: Tampa	$37,700	PA: Philadelphia	$49,160
GA: Atlanta	$50,280	PA: Pittsburgh	$42,010
IL: Chicago	$48,840	TX: Dallas	$56,530
MA: Boston	$53,640	TX: Houston	$75,250
MD: Baltimore	$50,270	WA: Seattle	$59,310

FACTORS THAT MAY AFFECT EARNINGS

Educational Attainment of Workers and Effect on Earnings

Figures are based on a group of occupations: Architects, Surveyors, and Cartographers

	Percent at Level	Effect on Earnings
Less than High School	—	—
Some High School	—	—
High School or Equivalent	7.3%	−28.7%
Some College but No Degree	6.9%	−43.9%
Associate Degree	6.0%	2.4%
Bachelor's Degree	50.5%	5.4%
Master's Degree	25.7%	3.7%
Doctoral Degree	—	—
First Professional Degree	—	—

Flexibility of Earnings

Average Hours Worked: 40
Workers with a Varying Number of Hours: 5.6%
Workers Earning Some Overtime Pay, Tips, or Commissions: 10.8%
Earnings Benefit of Working Overtime: −1.7%

Gender

	Male	Female
Percent	77.8%	22.2%
Effect on Earnings	2.3%	−15.8%

Union Membership

Percentage Union Members: Insignificant
Earnings Benefit of Union Membership: No significant data available

Veteran Status

Percentage Who Have Been on Active Duty: 5.4%
Earnings Benefit of Veteran Status: 12.9%

17-1022 Surveyors

Make exact measurements and determine property boundaries. Provide data relevant to the shape, contour, gravitation, location, elevation, or dimension of land or land features on or near the earth's surface for engineering, mapmaking, mining, land evaluation, construction, and other purposes.

- Education or Training Required: Bachelor's degree
- Job Growth: 15.9%
- Annual Openings: 4,000
- Self-Employed: 3.7%
- Part-Time: 22.1%

NATIONAL WAGE FIGURES (ANNUAL)

Beginning	25th Percentile	Median	Mean	75th Percentile	90th Percentile
$26,690	$35,720	$48,290	$51,390	$63,990	$79,910

Median Wages for Industries Employing Largest Numbers (Annual)

Industry	Median Income
Religious, Grantmaking, Civic, Professional, and Similar Organizations	$74,070
Management of Companies and Enterprises	$65,860
Support Activities for Mining	$58,370
Utilities	$54,180
Federal, State, and Local Government	$52,900
Specialty Trade Contractors	$49,490
Heavy and Civil Engineering Construction	$47,880
Professional, Scientific, and Technical Services	$47,730
Construction of Buildings	$47,190
Support Activities for Transportation	$46,230

Median Wages for States (Annual)

AK	$56,160	KY	$40,110	NY	$53,730
AL	$35,710	LA	$39,260	OH	$50,050
AR	$33,720	MA	$50,710	OK	$36,490
AZ	$44,500	MD	$50,070	OR	$58,870
CA	$68,260	ME	$45,170	PA	$46,610
CO	$47,530	MI	$50,210	RI:	$51,790
CT	$49,510	MN	$56,630	SC	$36,460
DC	$71,080	MO	$41,610	SD	$41,970
DE	$44,850	MS	$31,490	TN	$36,290
FL	$46,330	MT	$35,980	TX	$52,870
GA	$39,280	NC	$48,230	UT	$43,250
HI	$46,780	ND	$43,920	VA	$40,810
IA	$39,050	NE	$40,860	VT	$40,360
ID	$47,750	NH	$46,850	WA	$60,340
IL	$53,960	NJ	$57,600	WI	$46,630
IN	$40,620	NM	$48,250	WV	$38,770
KS	$38,320	NV	$59,720	WY	$47,870

Median Wages for the Largest Metropolitan Areas (Annual)

AZ: Phoenix	$43,990	MI: Detroit	$53,960
CA: Los Angeles	$71,890	MN: Minneapolis	$57,000
CA: Riverside	$64,330	MO: Kansas City	$41,580
CA: Sacramento	$74,510	MO: St. Louis	$51,930
CA: San Diego	$66,790	NV: Las Vegas	$59,180
CA: San Francisco	$69,470	NY: New York	$57,670
CO: Denver	$48,120	OH: Cincinnati	$45,270
DC: Washington	$47,650	OH: Cleveland	$57,110
FL: Miami	$51,390	OH: Columbus	$44,980
FL: Orlando	$42,480	OR: Portland	$69,270
FL: Tampa	$44,450	PA: Philadelphia	$48,230
GA: Atlanta	$39,670	PA: Pittsburgh	$45,330
IL: Chicago	$56,390	TX: Dallas	no data
MA: Boston	$52,220	TX: Houston	$61,310
MD: Baltimore	$51,520	WA: Seattle	$60,470

FACTORS THAT MAY AFFECT EARNINGS

Educational Attainment of Workers and Effect on Earnings

Figures are based on a group of occupations: Architects, Surveyors, and Cartographers

	Percent at Level	Effect on Earnings
Less than High School	—	—
Some High School	—	—
High School or Equivalent	7.3%	−28.7%
Some College but No Degree	6.9%	−43.9%
Associate Degree	6.0%	2.4%
Bachelor's Degree	50.5%	5.4%
Master's Degree	25.7%	3.7%
Doctoral Degree	—	—
First Professional Degree	—	—

Flexibility of Earnings

Average Hours Worked: 40
Workers with a Varying Number of Hours: 5.6%
Workers Earning Some Overtime Pay, Tips, or Commissions: 10.8%
Earnings Benefit of Working Overtime: −1.7%

Gender

	Male	Female
Percent	77.8%	22.2%
Effect on Earnings	2.3%	−15.8%

Union Membership

Percentage Union Members: Insignificant
Earnings Benefit of Union Membership: No significant data available

Veteran Status

Percentage Who Have Been on Active Duty: 5.4%
Earnings Benefit of Veteran Status: 12.9%

17-2000 Engineers

17-2011 Aerospace Engineers

Perform a variety of engineering work in designing, constructing, and testing aircraft, missiles, and spacecraft. May conduct basic and applied research to evaluate adaptability of materials and equipment to aircraft design and manufacture. May recommend improvements in testing equipment and techniques.

- Education or Training Required: Bachelor's degree
- Job Growth: 8.3%
- Annual Openings: 6,000
- Self-Employed: 0.0%
- Part-Time: 20.6%

NATIONAL WAGE FIGURES (ANNUAL)

Beginning	25th Percentile	Median	Mean	75th Percentile	90th Percentile
$59,610	$71,360	$87,610	$89,260	$106,450	$124,550

Median Wages for Industries Employing Largest Numbers (Annual)

Industry	Median Income
Federal, State, and Local Government	$97,740
Professional, Scientific, and Technical Services	$93,590
Administrative and Support Services	$92,990
Computer and Electronic Product Manufacturing	$91,370
Merchant Wholesalers, Durable Goods	$90,800
Transportation Equipment Manufacturing	$82,990
Management of Companies and Enterprises	$81,620
Electrical Equipment, Appliance, and Component Manufacturing	$81,530
Couriers and Messengers	$79,460
Machinery Manufacturing	$79,120

Median Wages for States (Annual)

AK	no data	KY	no data	NY	no data
AL	$90,920	LA	no data	OH	$83,590
AR	$93,910	MA	no data	OK	$79,000
AZ	$78,760	MD	$88,770	OR	no data
CA	$94,950	ME	$86,670	PA	no data
CO	$85,860	MI	$58,120	RI	no data
CT	$72,840	MN	$69,110	SC	$74,930
DC	$109,530	MO	no data	SD	no data
DE	no data	MS	$79,700	TN	$83,360
FL	$73,380	MT	no data	TX	$88,210
GA	no data	NC	$71,970	UT	no data
HI	no data	ND	no data	VA	$101,580
IA	no data	NE	no data	VT	no data
ID	no data	NH	no data	WA	no data
IL	$74,340	NJ	$87,810	WI	no data
IN	$68,720	NM	$99,990	WV	$86,940
KS	$81,520	NV	$104,470	WY	no data

Median Wages for the Largest Metropolitan Areas (Annual)

AZ: Phoenix	$73,260	MI: Detroit	no data
CA: Los Angeles	$95,580	MN: Minneapolis	$76,250
CA: Riverside	$70,570	MO: Kansas City	$108,340
CA: Sacramento	no data	MO: St. Louis	no data
CA: San Diego	$85,510	NV: Las Vegas	$106,840
CA: San Francisco	no data	NY: New York	$89,670
CO: Denver	$83,190	OH: Cincinnati	no data
DC: Washington	$105,270	OH: Cleveland	$100,140
FL: Miami	$73,130	OH: Columbus	$73,270
FL: Orlando	$68,940	OR: Portland	$72,210
FL: Tampa	$68,430	PA: Philadelphia	no data
GA: Atlanta	no data	PA: Pittsburgh	no data
IL: Chicago	$96,930	TX: Dallas	$88,690
MA: Boston	no data	TX: Houston	no data
MD: Baltimore	$85,520	WA: Seattle	no data

FACTORS THAT MAY AFFECT EARNINGS

Educational Attainment of Workers and Effect on Earnings

	Percent at Level	Effect on Earnings
Less than High School	—	—
Some High School	—	—
High School or Equivalent	9.8%	−26.2%
Some College but No Degree	9.8%	−31.3%
Associate Degree	5.9%	−30.0%
Bachelor's Degree	46.1%	3.8%
Master's Degree	18.6%	15.1%
Doctoral Degree	9.8%	29.1%
First Professional Degree	—	—

Flexibility of Earnings

Average Hours Worked: 39
Workers with a Varying Number of Hours: 5.5%
Workers Earning Some Overtime Pay, Tips, or Commissions: 16.8%
Earnings Benefit of Working Overtime: −16.4%

Gender

	Male	Female
Percent	86.9%	13.1%
Effect on Earnings	4.9%	—

Union Membership

Percentage Union Members: 6.4%
Earnings Benefit of Union Membership: −7.1%

Veteran Status

Percentage Who Have Been on Active Duty: 13.5%
Earnings Benefit of Veteran Status: −0.6%

17-2021 Agricultural Engineers

Apply knowledge of engineering technology and biological science to agricultural problems concerned with power and machinery, electrification, structures, soil and water conservation, and processing of agricultural products.

- Education or Training Required: Bachelor's degree
- Job Growth: 12.0%
- Annual Openings: Fewer than 500
- Self-Employed: 0.0%
- Part-Time: 14.3%

NATIONAL WAGE FIGURES (ANNUAL)

Beginning	25th Percentile	Median	Mean	75th Percentile	90th Percentile
$42,390	$53,040	$66,030	$67,810	$80,370	$96,270

Median Wages for Industries Employing Largest Numbers (Annual)

Industry	Median Income
Management of Companies and Enterprises	$72,610
Beverage and Tobacco Product Manufacturing	$70,800
Support Activities for Agriculture and Forestry	$70,470
Merchant Wholesalers, Nondurable Goods	$69,470
Professional, Scientific, and Technical Services	$68,110
Food Manufacturing	$66,970
Federal, State, and Local Government	$65,350
Machinery Manufacturing	$63,430
Educational Services	$49,900

Median Wages for States (Annual)

State	Wage	State	Wage	State	Wage
AK	no data	KY	$54,800	NY	$80,930
AL	$42,700	LA	$66,290	OH	$74,300
AR	no data	MA	no data	OK	no data
AZ	$72,550	MD	$78,030	OR	no data
CA	$68,120	ME	no data	PA	$54,700
CO	$66,350	MI	$58,610	RI	no data
CT	no data	MN	$54,790	SC	$67,120
DC	no data	MO	$70,150	SD	no data
DE	no data	MS	no data	TN	$65,790
FL	$67,000	MT	no data	TX	$60,790
GA	$68,990	NC	$83,150	UT	no data
HI	no data	ND	$65,690	VA	$58,580
IA	$59,560	NE	$66,420	VT	no data
ID	$52,060	NH	no data	WA	$62,880
IL	$69,060	NJ	$64,580	WI	$64,610
IN	$53,850	NM	no data	WV	no data
KS	$71,430	NV	no data	WY	no data

Median Wages for the Largest Metropolitan Areas (Annual)

Area	Wage	Area	Wage
AZ: Phoenix	no data	MI: Detroit	no data
CA: Los Angeles	$73,140	MN: Minneapolis	no data
CA: Riverside	no data	MO: Kansas City	no data
CA: Sacramento	no data	MO: St. Louis	no data
CA: San Diego	no data	NV: Las Vegas	no data
CA: San Francisco	no data	NY: New York	$78,360
CO: Denver	no data	OH: Cincinnati	$76,370
DC: Washington	$81,210	OH: Cleveland	no data
FL: Miami	no data	OH: Columbus	no data
FL: Orlando	no data	OR: Portland	no data
FL: Tampa	no data	PA: Philadelphia	no data
GA: Atlanta	no data	PA: Pittsburgh	no data
IL: Chicago	$63,220	TX: Dallas	no data
MA: Boston	no data	TX: Houston	no data
MD: Baltimore	no data	WA: Seattle	no data

FACTORS THAT MAY AFFECT EARNINGS

Educational Attainment of Workers and Effect on Earnings

Figures are based on a group of occupations: Engineers

	Percent at Level	Effect on Earnings
Less than High School	—	—
Some High School	—	—
High School or Equivalent	9.5%	−21.3%
Some College but No Degree	14.4%	−14.5%
Associate Degree	12.8%	−9.0%
Bachelor's Degree	36.6%	3.6%
Master's Degree	20.2%	12.1%
Doctoral Degree	4.5%	37.4%
First Professional Degree	1.1%	20.8%

Flexibility of Earnings

Average Hours Worked: 45
Workers with a Varying Number of Hours: 5.4%
Workers Earning Some Overtime Pay, Tips, or Commissions: 11.4%
Earnings Benefit of Working Overtime: −10.2%

Gender

	Male	Female
Percent	88.2%	11.8%
Effect on Earnings	2.3%	−15.8%

Union Membership

Percentage Union Members: 6.0%
Earnings Benefit of Union Membership: −7.1%

Veteran Status

Percentage Who Have Been on Active Duty: 13.5%
Earnings Benefit of Veteran Status: −0.6%

17-2031 Biomedical Engineers

Apply knowledge of engineering, biology, and biomechanical principles to the design, development, and evaluation of biological and health systems and products, such as artificial organs, prostheses, instrumentation, medical information systems, and health management and care delivery systems.

- Education or Training Required: Bachelor's degree
- Job Growth: 30.7%
- Annual Openings: 1,000
- Self-Employed: 7.2%
- Part-Time: 14.3%

NATIONAL WAGE FIGURES (ANNUAL)

Beginning	25th Percentile	Median	Mean	75th Percentile	90th Percentile
$44,930	$56,420	$73,930	$78,030	$93,420	$116,330

Median Wages for Industries Employing Largest Numbers (Annual)

Industry	Median Income
Wholesale Electronic Markets and Agents and Brokers	$84,940
Professional, Scientific, and Technical Services	$82,270
Federal, State, and Local Government	$77,390
Computer and Electronic Product Manufacturing	$77,300
Chemical Manufacturing	$77,150
Management of Companies and Enterprises......................	$76,500
Miscellaneous Manufacturing	$76,470
Merchant Wholesalers, Durable Goods	$76,440
Ambulatory Health Care Services...................................	$71,130
Merchant Wholesalers, Nondurable Goods	$66,520

Median Wages for States (Annual)

AK	no data	KY	$53,530	NY	$73,660
AL	$62,470	LA	$53,280	OH	$62,340
AR	$44,030	MA	no data	OK	$53,080
AZ	$48,480	MD	$77,460	OR	$56,490
CA	$84,820	ME	no data	PA	$68,380
CO	$77,670	MI	$56,680	RI	$72,420
CT	$80,520	MN	$74,790	SC.............	no data
DC	$56,020	MO	$70,570	SD	no data
DE	no data	MS	$51,510	TN	$63,490
FL	$63,020	MT	no data	TX	$61,160
GA	$58,490	NC	$68,600	UT	$70,880
HI	no data	ND	no data	VA	$96,320
IA	no data	NE	$54,450	VT	no data
ID	no data	NH	$44,430	WA	$79,680
IL	no data	NJ	$72,340	WI	$78,620
IN	$67,720	NM	$44,960	WV	no data
KS	no data	NV	no data	WY	no data

Median Wages for the Largest Metropolitan Areas (Annual)

AZ: Phoenix............	$50,260	MI: Detroit	$81,730
CA: Los Angeles	$85,480	MN: Minneapolis	$75,030
CA: Riverside	no data	MO: Kansas City	$64,990
CA: Sacramento	no data	MO: St. Louis............	$71,180
CA: San Diego	$80,300	NV: Las Vegas	no data
CA: San Francisco....	$84,590	NY: New York............	$76,710
CO: Denver	$77,550	OH: Cincinnati..........	$71,490
DC: Washington	$77,770	OH: Cleveland	$61,640
FL: Miami	no data	OH: Columbus	no data
FL: Orlando	no data	OR: Portland	$65,540
FL: Tampa	no data	PA: Philadelphia	$74,240
GA: Atlanta	$62,150	PA: Pittsburgh	$70,500
IL: Chicago	$66,230	TX: Dallas	$64,980
MA: Boston	no data	TX: Houston	$51,560
MD: Baltimore	$73,710	WA: Seattle	$80,300

FACTORS THAT MAY AFFECT EARNINGS

Educational Attainment of Workers and Effect on Earnings

Figures are based on a group of occupations: Engineers

	Percent at Level	Effect on Earnings
Less than High School	—	—
Some High School	—	—
High School or Equivalent	9.5%	−21.3%
Some College but No Degree	14.4%	−14.5%
Associate Degree	12.8%	−9.0%
Bachelor's Degree	36.6%	3.6%
Master's Degree	20.2%	12.1%
Doctoral Degree	4.5%	37.4%
First Professional Degree	1.1%	20.8%

Flexibility of Earnings

Average Hours Worked: 38
Workers with a Varying Number of Hours: 11.8%
Workers Earning Some Overtime Pay, Tips, or Commissions: 12.5%
Earnings Benefit of Working Overtime: −10.2%

Gender

	Male	Female
Percent	60.0%	40.0%
Effect on Earnings	2.3%	−15.8%

Union Membership

Percentage Union Members: 12.5%
Earnings Benefit of Union Membership: −7.1%

Veteran Status

Percentage Who Have Been on Active Duty: 13.5%
Earnings Benefit of Veteran Status: −0.6%

17-2041 Chemical Engineers

Design chemical plant equipment and devise processes for manufacturing chemicals and products, such as gasoline, synthetic rubber, plastics, detergents, cement, paper, and pulp, by applying principles and technology of chemistry, physics, and engineering.

- Education or Training Required: Bachelor's degree
- Job Growth: 10.6%
- Annual Openings: 3,000
- Self-Employed: 0.0%
- Part-Time: 4.8%

NATIONAL WAGE FIGURES (ANNUAL)

Beginning	25th Percentile	Median	Mean	75th Percentile	90th Percentile
$50,060	$62,410	$78,860	$81,600	$98,100	$118,670

Median Wages for Industries Employing Largest Numbers (Annual)

Industry	Median Income
Petroleum and Coal Products Manufacturing	$85,030
Pipeline Transportation	$84,420
Management of Companies and Enterprises	$83,910
Federal, State, and Local Government	$83,580
Professional, Scientific, and Technical Services	$82,030
Chemical Manufacturing	$80,180
Transportation Equipment Manufacturing	$78,340
Computer and Electronic Product Manufacturing	$77,020
Merchant Wholesalers, Durable Goods	$76,830
Paper Manufacturing	$75,530

Median Wages for States (Annual)

State	Wage	State	Wage	State	Wage
AK	$88,970	KY	$80,300	NY	$77,000
AL	$79,150	LA	$85,480	OH	$76,300
AR	$75,240	MA	$81,330	OK	$63,780
AZ	$63,800	MD	$79,700	OR	no data
CA	$86,260	ME	$75,590	PA	$73,080
CO	$86,670	MI	$66,760	RI	no data
CT	$79,680	MN	$70,530	SC	$74,170
DC	$99,680	MO	$71,970	SD	no data
DE	$90,690	MS	$74,300	TN	$72,580
FL	$76,030	MT	$75,880	TX	$81,570
GA	$73,030	NC	$76,840	UT	$82,840
HI	no data	ND	$74,730	VA	$86,280
IA	$67,650	NE	$58,960	VT	no data
ID	$100,070	NH	$73,580	WA	$84,960
IL	$74,180	NJ	$84,420	WI	$76,130
IN	$82,900	NM	no data	WV	$84,040
KS	$75,450	NV	no data	WY	$58,360

Median Wages for the Largest Metropolitan Areas (Annual)

Area	Wage	Area	Wage
AZ: Phoenix	$59,730	MI: Detroit	$69,640
CA: Los Angeles	$79,230	MN: Minneapolis	$73,020
CA: Riverside	$64,460	MO: Kansas City	$71,170
CA: Sacramento	$82,050	MO: St. Louis	$79,860
CA: San Diego	$88,930	NV: Las Vegas	no data
CA: San Francisco	$90,310	NY: New York	$80,400
CO: Denver	$77,780	OH: Cincinnati	$88,570
DC: Washington	$88,920	OH: Cleveland	$78,710
FL: Miami	$68,500	OH: Columbus	$70,570
FL: Orlando	no data	OR: Portland	no data
FL: Tampa	$81,030	PA: Philadelphia	$82,080
GA: Atlanta	$64,920	PA: Pittsburgh	$79,130
IL: Chicago	$74,920	TX: Dallas	$62,420
MA: Boston	$81,580	TX: Houston	$89,090
MD: Baltimore	$79,610	WA: Seattle	$78,820

FACTORS THAT MAY AFFECT EARNINGS

Educational Attainment of Workers and Effect on Earnings

	Percent at Level	Effect on Earnings
Less than High School	—	—
Some High School	—	—
High School or Equivalent	—	—
Some College but No Degree	—	—
Associate Degree	—	—
Bachelor's Degree	49.4%	−2.7%
Master's Degree	27.2%	11.1%
Doctoral Degree	8.6%	24.2%
First Professional Degree	—	—

Figures do not total 100% because some levels have a very small sample size.

Flexibility of Earnings

Average Hours Worked: 41
Workers with a Varying Number of Hours: 5.0%
Workers Earning Some Overtime Pay, Tips, or Commissions: 9.0%
Earnings Benefit of Working Overtime: −7.8%

Gender

	Male	Female
Percent	82.9%	17.1%
Effect on Earnings	1.3%	—

Union Membership

Percentage Union Members: 4.5%
Earnings Benefit of Union Membership: −7.1%

Veteran Status

Percentage Who Have Been on Active Duty: 13.5%
Earnings Benefit of Veteran Status: −0.6%

17-2051 Civil Engineers

Perform engineering duties in planning, designing, and overseeing construction and maintenance of building structures and facilities, such as roads, railroads, airports, bridges, harbors, channels, dams, irrigation projects, pipelines, power plants, water and sewage systems, and waste disposal units. Includes architectural, structural, traffic, ocean, and geo-technical engineers.

- Education or Training Required: Bachelor's degree
- Job Growth: 16.5%
- Annual Openings: 19,000
- Self-Employed: 4.9%
- Part-Time: 13.3%

NATIONAL WAGE FIGURES (ANNUAL)

Beginning	25th Percentile	Median	Mean	75th Percentile	90th Percentile
$44,810	$54,520	$68,600	$72,120	$86,260	$104,420

Median Wages for Industries Employing Largest Numbers (Annual)

Industry	Median Income
Oil and Gas Extraction	$87,700
Computer and Electronic Product Manufacturing	$82,830
Pipeline Transportation	$79,140
Chemical Manufacturing	$76,280
Management of Companies and Enterprises	$74,560
Rail Transportation	$73,010
Transportation Equipment Manufacturing	$71,230
Waste Management and Remediation Services	$70,810
Utilities	$70,730
Merchant Wholesalers, Durable Goods	$70,520

Median Wages for States (Annual)

AK $75,620	KY $65,630	NY $70,400
AL $62,760	LA $70,200	OH $65,160
AR $60,550	MA $72,880	OK $66,150
AZ $64,220	MD $68,650	OR $65,100
CA $77,250	ME $58,630	PA $63,630
CO $70,220	MI $61,050	RI.............. $68,710
CT $73,450	MN $68,130	SC.............. $62,690
DC $79,770	MO $62,710	SD $60,290
DE $71,570	MS $68,260	TN $67,180
FL $69,380	MT $56,250	TX $69,740
GA............ $64,700	NC $62,080	UT $59,650
HI $68,950	ND $57,290	VA $72,080
IA $66,310	NE $64,470	VT $63,990
ID $63,160	NH $61,750	WA............ $69,510
IL $68,390	NJ $75,130	WI $60,970
IN $59,250	NM $64,700	WV $56,380
KS $65,440	NV $73,660	WY $53,890

Median Wages for the Largest Metropolitan Areas (Annual)

AZ: Phoenix............ $65,620	MI: Detroit $60,730
CA: Los Angeles $77,030	MN: Minneapolis $69,190
CA: Riverside $73,490	MO: Kansas City........ $67,810
CA: Sacramento $77,380	MO: St. Louis............ $65,230
CA: San Diego $71,480	NV: Las Vegas $76,950
CA: San Francisco.... $83,340	NY: New York............ $76,260
CO: Denver $73,270	OH: Cincinnati.......... $63,220
DC: Washington $78,500	OH: Cleveland $64,690
FL: Miami $70,150	OH: Columbus $65,400
FL: Orlando $68,580	OR: Portland $67,030
FL: Tampa $71,370	PA: Philadelphia $67,400
GA: Atlanta $66,940	PA: Pittsburgh $64,550
IL: Chicago $70,200	TX: Dallas $66,200
MA: Boston $74,620	TX: Houston $79,480
MD: Baltimore $62,490	WA: Seattle $70,830

FACTORS THAT MAY AFFECT EARNINGS

Educational Attainment of Workers and Effect on Earnings

	Percent at Level	Effect on Earnings
Less than High School	—	—
Some High School	—	—
High School or Equivalent	5.4%	−35.2%
Some College but No Degree	8.7%	−25.3%
Associate Degree	8.0%	−6.2%
Bachelor's Degree	46.7%	0.8%
Master's Degree	25.7%	9.5%
Doctoral Degree	3.3%	41.9%
First Professional Degree	—	—

Flexibility of Earnings

Average Hours Worked: 40
Workers with a Varying Number of Hours: 4.6%
Workers Earning Some Overtime Pay, Tips, or Commissions: 11.7%
Earnings Benefit of Working Overtime: −6.8%

Gender

	Male	Female
Percent	88.1%	11.9%
Effect on Earnings	1.2%	—

Union Membership

Percentage Union Members: 8.2%
Earnings Benefit of Union Membership: −4.0%

Veteran Status

Percentage Who Have Been on Active Duty: 13.5%
Earnings Benefit of Veteran Status: −0.6%

17-2061 Computer Hardware Engineers

Research, design, develop, and test computer or computer-related equipment for commercial, industrial, military, or scientific use. May supervise the manufacturing and installation of computer or computer-related equipment and components.

- Education or Training Required: Bachelor's degree
- Job Growth: 10.1%
- Annual Openings: 5,000
- Self-Employed: 0.8%
- Part-Time: 25.0%

NATIONAL WAGE FIGURES (ANNUAL)

Beginning	25th Percentile	Median	Mean	75th Percentile	90th Percentile
$53,910	$69,500	$88,470	$91,280	$111,030	$135,260

Median Wages for Industries Employing Largest Numbers (Annual)

Industry	Median Income
Internet Service Providers, Web Search Portals, and Data-Processing Services	$95,940
Miscellaneous Manufacturing	$93,770
Publishing Industries (Except Internet)	$93,630
Computer and Electronic Product Manufacturing	$90,990
Utilities	$90,610
Machinery Manufacturing	$90,470
Federal, State, and Local Government	$87,860
Professional, Scientific, and Technical Services	$87,570
Merchant Wholesalers, Durable Goods	$87,010
Credit Intermediation and Related Activities	$86,010

Median Wages for States (Annual)

AK	no data	KY	no data	NY	$88,590
AL	$77,870	LA	$46,770	OH	$77,960
AR	$85,650	MA	$94,780	OK	$84,490
AZ	$78,620	MD	$89,820	OR	no data
CA	$94,530	ME	no data	PA	$88,360
CO	$97,890	MI	$70,690	RI	$82,170
CT	$74,110	MN	$85,310	SC	$62,870
DC	$89,800	MO	no data	SD	$63,900
DE	$74,670	MS	$73,920	TN	$50,160
FL	$86,790	MT	$46,230	TX	$92,750
GA	$87,380	NC	$84,330	UT	no data
HI	$68,960	ND	no data	VA	$92,130
IA	$69,080	NE	$70,480	VT	no data
ID	no data	NH	no data	WA	no data
IL	$79,910	NJ	$88,360	WI	$71,670
IN	$56,960	NM	no data	WV	$73,880
KS	$77,620	NV	$71,320	WY	no data

Median Wages for the Largest Metropolitan Areas (Annual)

AZ: Phoenix	$77,790	MI: Detroit	$69,300
CA: Los Angeles	$84,290	MN: Minneapolis	$81,390
CA: Riverside	$76,620	MO: Kansas City	$88,550
CA: Sacramento	$88,750	MO: St. Louis	$88,470
CA: San Diego	$85,480	NV: Las Vegas	$73,910
CA: San Francisco	$91,130	NY: New York	$90,910
CO: Denver	$83,170	OH: Cincinnati	$64,730
DC: Washington	$93,760	OH: Cleveland	$71,830
FL: Miami	$82,660	OH: Columbus	no data
FL: Orlando	$84,430	OR: Portland	no data
FL: Tampa	$86,750	PA: Philadelphia	$84,260
GA: Atlanta	$91,960	PA: Pittsburgh	$87,130
IL: Chicago	$79,520	TX: Dallas	$98,440
MA: Boston	$95,930	TX: Houston	$93,980
MD: Baltimore	$88,060	WA: Seattle	no data

FACTORS THAT MAY AFFECT EARNINGS

Educational Attainment of Workers and Effect on Earnings

	Percent at Level	Effect on Earnings
Less than High School	—	—
Some High School	—	—
High School or Equivalent	—	—
Some College but No Degree	22.6%	−37.6%
Associate Degree	—	—
Bachelor's Degree	41.7%	8.3%
Master's Degree	25.0%	20.4%
Doctoral Degree	—	—
First Professional Degree	—	—

Figures do not total 100% because some levels have a very small sample size.

Flexibility of Earnings

Average Hours Worked: 39
Workers with a Varying Number of Hours: 3.7%
Workers Earning Some Overtime Pay, Tips, or Commissions: 4.0%
Earnings Benefit of Working Overtime: −11.6%

Gender

	Male	Female
Percent	83.8%	16.2%
Effect on Earnings	3.0%	—

Union Membership

Percentage Union Members: Insignificant
Earnings Benefit of Union Membership: No significant data available

Veteran Status

Percentage Who Have Been on Active Duty: 13.5%
Earnings Benefit of Veteran Status: −0.6%

17-2071 Electrical Engineers

Design, develop, test, or supervise the manufacturing and installation of electrical equipment, components, or systems for commercial, industrial, military, or scientific use.

- Education or Training Required: Bachelor's degree
- Job Growth: 11.8%
- Annual Openings: 12,000
- Self-Employed: 3.3%
- Part-Time: 14.3%

NATIONAL WAGE FIGURES (ANNUAL)

Beginning	25th Percentile	Median	Mean	75th Percentile	90th Percentile
$49,120	$60,640	$75,930	$78,900	$94,050	$115,240

Median Wages for Industries Employing Largest Numbers (Annual)

Industry	Median Income
Motion Picture and Sound Recording Industries	$97,420
Construction of Buildings	$82,600
Computer and Electronic Product Manufacturing	$80,150
Wholesale Electronic Markets and Agents and Brokers	$79,530
Fabricated Metal Product Manufacturing	$78,280
Professional, Scientific, and Technical Services	$78,120
Publishing Industries (Except Internet)	$78,080
Internet Service Providers, Web Search Portals, and Data-Processing Services	$78,040
Utilities	$77,870
Heavy and Civil Engineering Construction	$77,350

Median Wages for States (Annual)

AK	$88,100	KY	$67,290	NY	$77,720
AL	$74,590	LA	$69,550	OH	$64,700
AR	$65,180	MA	$87,680	OK	$69,650
AZ	$75,820	MD	$84,100	OR	$77,950
CA	$84,670	ME	$68,410	PA	$71,980
CO	$77,090	MI	$72,720	RI	$76,280
CT	$75,020	MN	$74,860	SC	$76,210
DC	$85,290	MO	$72,200	SD	$63,100
DE	$82,760	MS	$63,890	TN	$72,450
FL	$73,500	MT	$62,100	TX	$84,020
GA	$71,820	NC	$68,850	UT	$74,330
HI	$73,550	ND	$73,800	VA	$75,270
IA	$72,600	NE	$73,390	VT	$71,400
ID	$74,170	NH	$75,860	WA	$75,240
IL	$70,620	NJ	$77,600	WI	$70,850
IN	$66,510	NM	$74,360	WV	$73,350
KS	$65,900	NV	$74,490	WY	$68,520

Median Wages for the Largest Metropolitan Areas (Annual)

AZ: Phoenix	$75,620	MI: Detroit	$76,960
CA: Los Angeles	$81,200	MN: Minneapolis	$75,970
CA: Riverside	$81,690	MO: Kansas City	$77,650
CA: Sacramento	$77,230	MO: St. Louis	$68,370
CA: San Diego	$80,750	NV: Las Vegas	$75,050
CA: San Francisco	$87,600	NY: New York	$85,370
CO: Denver	$76,600	OH: Cincinnati	$64,170
DC: Washington	$83,920	OH: Cleveland	$70,970
FL: Miami	$72,790	OH: Columbus	$68,070
FL: Orlando	$71,530	OR: Portland	$79,360
FL: Tampa	$74,000	PA: Philadelphia	$78,890
GA: Atlanta	$74,410	PA: Pittsburgh	$72,260
IL: Chicago	$72,580	TX: Dallas	$82,880
MA: Boston	$88,510	TX: Houston	$92,350
MD: Baltimore	$82,290	WA: Seattle	$74,930

FACTORS THAT MAY AFFECT EARNINGS

Educational Attainment of Workers and Effect on Earnings

Figures are based on a group of occupations: Engineers

	Percent at Level	Effect on Earnings
Less than High School	—	—
Some High School	—	—
High School or Equivalent	9.5%	−21.3%
Some College but No Degree	14.4%	−14.5%
Associate Degree	12.8%	−9.0%
Bachelor's Degree	36.6%	3.6%
Master's Degree	20.2%	12.1%
Doctoral Degree	4.5%	37.4%
First Professional Degree	1.1%	20.8%

Flexibility of Earnings

Average Hours Worked: 40
Workers with a Varying Number of Hours: 5.4%
Workers Earning Some Overtime Pay, Tips, or Commissions: 11.4%
Earnings Benefit of Working Overtime: −5.4%

Gender

	Male	Female
Percent	92.3%	7.7%
Effect on Earnings	1.7%	—

Union Membership

Percentage Union Members: 6.0%
Earnings Benefit of Union Membership: −7.1%

Veteran Status

Percentage Who Have Been on Active Duty: 13.5%
Earnings Benefit of Veteran Status: −0.6%

17-2072 Electronics Engineers, Except Computer

Research, design, develop, and test electronic components and systems for commercial, industrial, military, or scientific use, utilizing knowledge of electronic theory and materials properties. Design electronic circuits and components for use in fields such as telecommunications, aerospace guidance and propulsion control, acoustics, or instruments and controls.

- Education or Training Required: Bachelor's degree
- Job Growth: 9.7%
- Annual Openings: 11,000
- Self-Employed: 3.2%
- Part-Time: 14.3%

NATIONAL WAGE FIGURES (ANNUAL)

Beginning	25th Percentile	Median	Mean	75th Percentile	90th Percentile
$52,050	$64,440	$81,050	$82,820	$99,630	$119,900

Median Wages for Industries Employing Largest Numbers (Annual)

Industry	Median Income
Federal, State, and Local Government	$88,890
Securities, Commodity Contracts, and Other Financial Investments and Related Activities	$87,530
Professional, Scientific, and Technical Services	$87,420
Publishing Industries (Except Internet)	$87,350
Transportation Equipment Manufacturing	$86,030
Management of Companies and Enterprises	$85,700
Computer and Electronic Product Manufacturing	$81,600
Machinery Manufacturing	$79,850
Miscellaneous Manufacturing	$79,360
Merchant Wholesalers, Durable Goods	$77,740

Median Wages for States (Annual)

AK	$74,380	KY	$67,550	NY	$80,320
AL	$86,450	LA	$75,940	OH	$75,020
AR	$65,820	MA	$83,740	OK	$75,180
AZ	$76,000	MD	$88,960	OR	$73,450
CA	$90,740	ME	$78,090	PA	$83,260
CO	$80,020	MI	$72,280	RI	$92,120
CT	$73,530	MN	$72,360	SC	$69,060
DC	$95,070	MO	$70,660	SD	$61,280
DE	$64,860	MS	$77,170	TN	$68,920
FL	$76,180	MT	$62,640	TX	$78,530
GA	$71,480	NC	$73,870	UT	$73,410
HI	$80,420	ND	$73,170	VA	$85,660
IA	$63,060	NE	$64,460	VT	$81,940
ID	$72,130	NH	$95,850	WA	$76,180
IL	$72,130	NJ	$96,220	WI	$66,840
IN	$75,130	NM	$89,160	WV	$59,870
KS	no data	NV	$72,050	WY	$60,510

Median Wages for the Largest Metropolitan Areas (Annual)

AZ: Phoenix	$73,860	MI: Detroit	$73,980
CA: Los Angeles	$85,850	MN: Minneapolis	$75,400
CA: Riverside	$83,540	MO: Kansas City	no data
CA: Sacramento	no data	MO: St. Louis	$79,220
CA: San Diego	$90,140	NV: Las Vegas	$68,800
CA: San Francisco	$89,160	NY: New York	$95,630
CO: Denver	$78,440	OH: Cincinnati	$67,150
DC: Washington	$89,210	OH: Cleveland	$71,730
FL: Miami	$71,700	OH: Columbus	$67,600
FL: Orlando	$81,990	OR: Portland	$77,130
FL: Tampa	$74,530	PA: Philadelphia	$87,670
GA: Atlanta	$73,140	PA: Pittsburgh	$77,170
IL: Chicago	$72,060	TX: Dallas	$85,200
MA: Boston	$87,740	TX: Houston	$73,240
MD: Baltimore	$85,020	WA: Seattle	$76,730

FACTORS THAT MAY AFFECT EARNINGS

Educational Attainment of Workers and Effect on Earnings

Figures are based on a group of occupations: Engineers

	Percent at Level	Effect on Earnings
Less than High School	—	—
Some High School	—	—
High School or Equivalent	9.5%	−21.3%
Some College but No Degree	14.4%	−14.5%
Associate Degree	12.8%	−9.0%
Bachelor's Degree	36.6%	3.6%
Master's Degree	20.2%	12.1%
Doctoral Degree	4.5%	37.4%
First Professional Degree	1.1%	20.8%

Flexibility of Earnings

Average Hours Worked: 40
Workers with a Varying Number of Hours: 5.4%
Workers Earning Some Overtime Pay, Tips, or Commissions: 11.4%
Earnings Benefit of Working Overtime: −5.4%

Gender

	Male	Female
Percent	92.3%	7.7%
Effect on Earnings	1.7%	—

Union Membership

Percentage Union Members: 6.0%
Earnings Benefit of Union Membership: −7.1%

Veteran Status

Percentage Who Have Been on Active Duty: 13.5%
Earnings Benefit of Veteran Status: −0.6%

17-2081 Environmental Engineers

Design, plan, or perform engineering duties in the prevention, control, and remediation of environmental health hazards, utilizing various engineering disciplines. Work may include waste treatment, site remediation, or pollution control technology.

- Education or Training Required: Bachelor's degree
- Job Growth: 30.0%
- Annual Openings: 5,000
- Self-Employed: 0.3%
- Part-Time: 13.3%

NATIONAL WAGE FIGURES (ANNUAL)

Beginning	25th Percentile	Median	Mean	75th Percentile	90th Percentile
$43,180	$54,150	$69,940	$72,590	$88,480	$106,230

Median Wages for Industries Employing Largest Numbers (Annual)

Industry	Median Income
Pipeline Transportation	$85,710
Rail Transportation	$85,180
Oil and Gas Extraction	$80,470
Petroleum and Coal Products Manufacturing	$79,870
Transportation Equipment Manufacturing	$79,250
Computer and Electronic Product Manufacturing	$77,180
Utilities	$76,020
Plastics and Rubber Products Manufacturing	$74,410
Chemical Manufacturing	$74,120
Administrative and Support Services	$73,510

Median Wages for States (Annual)

AK	$74,430	KY	$60,130	NY	$70,220
AL	$64,900	LA	$65,860	OH	$70,040
AR	$57,130	MA	$74,160	OK	$70,160
AZ	$58,280	MD	$76,980	OR	$70,140
CA	$77,290	ME	$66,040	PA	$69,430
CO	$69,450	MI	$75,770	RI	$65,930
CT	$73,590	MN	$70,520	SC	$61,640
DC	$92,300	MO	$63,260	SD	$59,430
DE	$59,960	MS	$54,910	TN	$75,800
FL	$61,490	MT	$54,470	TX	$68,580
GA	$62,290	NC	$66,760	UT	$68,640
HI	$77,750	ND	$52,480	VA	$66,850
IA	$62,550	NE	$68,110	VT	$61,830
ID	$61,370	NH	$58,230	WA	$74,680
IL	$69,410	NJ	$78,690	WI	$64,190
IN	$64,080	NM	$65,070	WV	$66,730
KS	$80,620	NV	$71,910	WY	$57,830

Median Wages for the Largest Metropolitan Areas (Annual)

AZ: Phoenix	$66,260	MI: Detroit	$81,860
CA: Los Angeles	$78,130	MN: Minneapolis	$72,900
CA: Riverside	$83,260	MO: Kansas City	$74,480
CA: Sacramento	$72,490	MO: St. Louis	$61,130
CA: San Diego	$70,040	NV: Las Vegas	$75,290
CA: San Francisco	$84,350	NY: New York	$78,060
CO: Denver	$73,580	OH: Cincinnati	$68,950
DC: Washington	$86,350	OH: Cleveland	$80,930
FL: Miami	no data	OH: Columbus	$73,810
FL: Orlando	$56,740	OR: Portland	$62,930
FL: Tampa	$55,990	PA: Philadelphia	$75,460
GA: Atlanta	$62,180	PA: Pittsburgh	$70,550
IL: Chicago	$71,690	TX: Dallas	$76,960
MA: Boston	$74,380	TX: Houston	$72,740
MD: Baltimore	$73,070	WA: Seattle	$76,940

FACTORS THAT MAY AFFECT EARNINGS

Educational Attainment of Workers and Effect on Earnings

	Percent at Level	Effect on Earnings
Less than High School	—	—
Some High School	—	—
High School or Equivalent	—	—
Some College but No Degree	—	—
Associate Degree	—	—
Bachelor's Degree	54.2%	2.3%
Master's Degree	33.3%	8.0%
Doctoral Degree	—	—
First Professional Degree	—	—

Figures do not total 100% because some levels have a very small sample size.

Flexibility of Earnings

Average Hours Worked: 39
Workers with a Varying Number of Hours: 5.0%
Workers Earning Some Overtime Pay, Tips, or Commissions: 11.1%
Earnings Benefit of Working Overtime: –10.2%

Gender

	Male	Female
Percent	77.3%	22.7%
Effect on Earnings	2.3%	–15.8%

Union Membership

Percentage Union Members: 16.7%
Earnings Benefit of Union Membership: –7.1%

Veteran Status

Percentage Who Have Been on Active Duty: 13.5%
Earnings Benefit of Veteran Status: –0.6%

17-2111 Health and Safety Engineers, Except Mining Safety Engineers and Inspectors

Promote worksite or product safety by applying knowledge of industrial processes, mechanics, chemistry, psychology, and industrial health and safety laws.

- Education or Training Required: Bachelor's degree
- Job Growth: 13.4%
- Annual Openings: 2,000
- Self-Employed: 0.5%
- Part-Time: 14.3%

NATIONAL WAGE FIGURES (ANNUAL)

Beginning	25th Percentile	Median	Mean	75th Percentile	90th Percentile
$41,050	$51,630	$66,290	$68,400	$83,240	$100,160

Median Wages for Industries Employing Largest Numbers (Annual)

Industry	Median Income
Petroleum and Coal Products Manufacturing	$77,990
Utilities	$75,830
Computer and Electronic Product Manufacturing	$73,730
Transportation Equipment Manufacturing	$73,350
Support Activities for Mining	$72,780
Professional, Scientific, and Technical Services	$72,400
Management of Companies and Enterprises	$71,620
Merchant Wholesalers, Nondurable Goods	$70,480
Merchant Wholesalers, Durable Goods	$69,460
Machinery Manufacturing	$68,710

Median Wages for States (Annual)

State	Wage	State	Wage	State	Wage
AK	no data	KY	$57,830	NY	$70,750
AL	$65,740	LA	$59,230	OH	$67,300
AR	$63,420	MA	$78,820	OK	$44,600
AZ	$66,270	MD	$65,620	OR	$68,370
CA	$74,330	ME	$47,300	PA	$58,910
CO	$76,880	MI	$71,470	RI	$67,490
CT	$68,490	MN	$70,490	SC	$73,410
DC	$84,000	MO	$62,030	SD	$58,410
DE	$71,720	MS	$56,630	TN	$64,560
FL	$57,240	MT	$55,290	TX	$65,730
GA	$58,090	NC	$59,890	UT	$61,140
HI	$63,670	ND	no data	VA	$62,510
IA	$62,890	NE	$70,510	VT	$66,740
ID	$72,250	NH	$61,710	WA	$74,000
IL	$63,940	NJ	$81,100	WI	$62,940
IN	$55,170	NM	$52,600	WV	$48,660
KS	$58,360	NV	$60,540	WY	$52,570

Median Wages for the Largest Metropolitan Areas (Annual)

Metro	Wage	Metro	Wage
AZ: Phoenix	$69,690	MI: Detroit	$73,540
CA: Los Angeles	$74,460	MN: Minneapolis	$71,420
CA: Riverside	$66,670	MO: Kansas City	$62,800
CA: Sacramento	$76,050	MO: St. Louis	$67,540
CA: San Diego	$73,220	NV: Las Vegas	$61,400
CA: San Francisco	$84,290	NY: New York	$77,060
CO: Denver	$68,670	OH: Cincinnati	$70,170
DC: Washington	$74,480	OH: Cleveland	$66,180
FL: Miami	$54,110	OH: Columbus	$65,620
FL: Orlando	$52,280	OR: Portland	no data
FL: Tampa	$61,560	PA: Philadelphia	$64,150
GA: Atlanta	$60,840	PA: Pittsburgh	$68,860
IL: Chicago	$65,730	TX: Dallas	$62,320
MA: Boston	$79,080	TX: Houston	$64,850
MD: Baltimore	$59,310	WA: Seattle	$69,720

FACTORS THAT MAY AFFECT EARNINGS

Educational Attainment of Workers and Effect on Earnings

Figures are based on a group of occupations: Engineers

	Percent at Level	Effect on Earnings
Less than High School	—	—
Some High School	—	—
High School or Equivalent	9.5%	−21.3%
Some College but No Degree	14.4%	−14.5%
Associate Degree	12.8%	−9.0%
Bachelor's Degree	36.6%	3.6%
Master's Degree	20.2%	12.1%
Doctoral Degree	4.5%	37.4%
First Professional Degree	1.1%	20.8%

Flexibility of Earnings

Average Hours Worked: 40
Workers with a Varying Number of Hours: 5.4%
Workers Earning Some Overtime Pay, Tips, or Commissions: 11.4%
Earnings Benefit of Working Overtime: 2.6%

Gender

	Male	Female
Percent	88.2%	11.8%
Effect on Earnings	2.3%	−15.8%

Union Membership

Percentage Union Members: 6.0%
Earnings Benefit of Union Membership: −7.1%

Veteran Status

Percentage Who Have Been on Active Duty: 13.5%
Earnings Benefit of Veteran Status: −0.6%

17-2112 Industrial Engineers

Design, develop, test, and evaluate integrated systems for managing industrial production processes, including human work factors, quality control, inventory control, logistics and material flow, cost analysis, and production coordination.

- Education or Training Required: Bachelor's degree
- Job Growth: 16.0%
- Annual Openings: 13,000
- Self-Employed: 0.4%
- Part-Time: 14.3%

NATIONAL WAGE FIGURES (ANNUAL)

Beginning	25th Percentile	Median	Mean	75th Percentile	90th Percentile
$44,790	$55,060	$68,620	$70,630	$84,850	$100,980

Median Wages for Industries Employing Largest Numbers (Annual)

Industry	Median Income
Oil and Gas Extraction	$81,150
Petroleum and Coal Products Manufacturing	$79,760
Professional, Scientific, and Technical Services	$75,870
Computer and Electronic Product Manufacturing	$74,590
Management of Companies and Enterprises	$73,820
Telecommunications	$73,720
Wholesale Electronic Markets and Agents and Brokers	$72,440
Federal, State, and Local Government	$72,400
Utilities	$72,360
Paper Manufacturing	$71,600

Median Wages for States (Annual)

AK	$85,820	KY	$59,860	NY	$68,320
AL	$62,980	LA	$55,760	OH	$65,530
AR	$57,960	MA	$76,920	OK	$66,150
AZ	$64,880	MD	$72,960	OR	no data
CA	$78,970	ME	$67,410	PA	$66,930
CO	$72,730	MI	$73,240	RI	$68,050
CT	$72,120	MN	$70,190	SC	$64,750
DC	$79,860	MO	$65,850	SD	$56,950
DE	$75,430	MS	$58,490	TN	$61,270
FL	$60,740	MT	$61,650	TX	$73,440
GA	$64,540	NC	$64,430	UT	$69,200
HI	$79,310	ND	$62,440	VA	$66,650
IA	$58,870	NE	$61,130	VT	$70,410
ID	no data	NH	$70,210	WA	$69,660
IL	$63,310	NJ	$72,980	WI	$62,240
IN	$63,280	NM	$78,260	WV	$60,630
KS	$62,960	NV	$56,640	WY	$60,010

Median Wages for the Largest Metropolitan Areas (Annual)

AZ: Phoenix	$63,510	MI: Detroit	$77,440
CA: Los Angeles	$73,620	MN: Minneapolis	$73,210
CA: Riverside	$63,140	MO: Kansas City	$65,220
CA: Sacramento	$71,080	MO: St. Louis	$70,480
CA: San Diego	$75,780	NV: Las Vegas	$55,780
CA: San Francisco	$86,340	NY: New York	$76,540
CO: Denver	$74,230	OH: Cincinnati	$70,360
DC: Washington	$80,040	OH: Cleveland	$65,560
FL: Miami	$57,590	OH: Columbus	$63,260
FL: Orlando	$65,190	OR: Portland	no data
FL: Tampa	$59,250	PA: Philadelphia	$73,850
GA: Atlanta	$66,690	PA: Pittsburgh	$70,400
IL: Chicago	$65,780	TX: Dallas	$71,740
MA: Boston	$79,260	TX: Houston	$83,380
MD: Baltimore	$73,930	WA: Seattle	$69,200

FACTORS THAT MAY AFFECT EARNINGS

Educational Attainment of Workers and Effect on Earnings

Figures are based on a group of occupations: Engineers

	Percent at Level	Effect on Earnings
Less than High School	—	—
Some High School	—	—
High School or Equivalent	9.5%	−21.3%
Some College but No Degree	14.4%	−14.5%
Associate Degree	12.8%	−9.0%
Bachelor's Degree	36.6%	3.6%
Master's Degree	20.2%	12.1%
Doctoral Degree	4.5%	37.4%
First Professional Degree	1.1%	20.8%

Flexibility of Earnings

Average Hours Worked: 40
Workers with a Varying Number of Hours: 5.4%
Workers Earning Some Overtime Pay, Tips, or Commissions: 11.4%
Earnings Benefit of Working Overtime: 2.6%

Gender

	Male	Female
Percent	77.4%	22.6%
Effect on Earnings	2.3%	−15.8%

Union Membership

Percentage Union Members: 6.0%
Earnings Benefit of Union Membership: −7.1%

Veteran Status

Percentage Who Have Been on Active Duty: 13.5%
Earnings Benefit of Veteran Status: −0.6%

17-2121 Marine Engineers and Naval Architects

Design, develop, and evaluate the operation of marine vessels, ship machinery, and related equipment, such as power supply and propulsion systems.

- Education or Training Required: Bachelor's degree
- Job Growth: 8.5%
- Annual Openings: Fewer than 500
- Self-Employed: 0.0%
- Part-Time: 25.0%

NATIONAL WAGE FIGURES (ANNUAL)

Beginning	25th Percentile	Median	Mean	75th Percentile	90th Percentile
$45,200	$56,280	$72,990	$75,400	$90,790	$113,320

Median Wages for Industries Employing Largest Numbers (Annual)

Industry	Median Income
Federal, State, and Local Government	$88,940
Oil and Gas Extraction	$87,910
Water Transportation	$82,780
Transportation Equipment Manufacturing	$75,340
Machinery Manufacturing	$66,870
Professional, Scientific, and Technical Services	$66,180
Educational Services	$64,100
Support Activities for Transportation	$58,630

Median Wages for States (Annual)

AK	no data	KY	no data	NY	no data
AL	$71,650	LA	$55,030	OH	$78,250
AR	no data	MA	$67,370	OK	no data
AZ	no data	MD	$72,720	OR	no data
CA	$71,490	ME	$73,400	PA	$78,350
CO	no data	MI	$70,320	RI	no data
CT	no data	MN	no data	SC	$79,170
DC	$104,950	MO	no data	SD	no data
DE	no data	MS	$75,750	TN	no data
FL	$63,570	MT	no data	TX	$87,360
GA	no data	NC	no data	UT	no data
HI	$77,640	ND	no data	VA	$71,090
IA	no data	NE	no data	VT	no data
ID	no data	NH	no data	WA	$73,290
IL	no data	NJ	no data	WI	no data
IN	no data	NM	no data	WV	no data
KS	no data	NV	no data	WY	no data

Median Wages for the Largest Metropolitan Areas (Annual)

AZ: Phoenix	no data	MI: Detroit	no data
CA: Los Angeles	no data	MN: Minneapolis	no data
CA: Riverside	no data	MO: Kansas City	no data
CA: Sacramento	no data	MO: St. Louis	no data
CA: San Diego	$66,900	NV: Las Vegas	no data
CA: San Francisco	$94,630	NY: New York	$62,050
CO: Denver	no data	OH: Cincinnati	no data
DC: Washington	$93,070	OH: Cleveland	no data
FL: Miami	$61,640	OH: Columbus	no data
FL: Orlando	no data	OR: Portland	no data
FL: Tampa	$87,750	PA: Philadelphia	$56,370
GA: Atlanta	no data	PA: Pittsburgh	no data
IL: Chicago	no data	TX: Dallas	no data
MA: Boston	$68,990	TX: Houston	$89,140
MD: Baltimore	$60,170	WA: Seattle	$68,970

FACTORS THAT MAY AFFECT EARNINGS

Educational Attainment of Workers and Effect on Earnings

Figures are based on a group of occupations: Engineers

	Percent at Level	Effect on Earnings
Less than High School	—	—
Some High School	—	—
High School or Equivalent	9.5%	−21.3%
Some College but No Degree	14.4%	−14.5%
Associate Degree	12.8%	−9.0%
Bachelor's Degree	36.6%	3.6%
Master's Degree	20.2%	12.1%
Doctoral Degree	4.5%	37.4%
First Professional Degree	1.1%	20.8%

Flexibility of Earnings

Average Hours Worked: 37
Workers with a Varying Number of Hours: 13.8%
Workers Earning Some Overtime Pay, Tips, or Commissions: 9.1%
Earnings Benefit of Working Overtime: −10.2%

Gender

	Male	Female
Percent	80.6%	19.4%
Effect on Earnings	2.3%	−15.8%

Union Membership

Percentage Union Members: 36.4%
Earnings Benefit of Union Membership: −7.1%

Veteran Status

Percentage Who Have Been on Active Duty: 13.5%
Earnings Benefit of Veteran Status: −0.6%

17-2131 Materials Engineers

Evaluate materials and develop machinery and processes to manufacture materials for use in products that must meet specialized design and performance specifications. Develop new uses for known materials. Includes those working with composite materials or specializing in one type of material, such as graphite, metal and metal alloys, ceramics and glass, plastics and polymers, and naturally occurring materials.

- Education or Training Required: Bachelor's degree
- Job Growth: 12.2%
- Annual Openings: 2,000
- Self-Employed: 0.0%
- Part-Time: 14.3%

NATIONAL WAGE FIGURES (ANNUAL)

Beginning	25th Percentile	Median	Mean	75th Percentile	90th Percentile
$46,120	$57,850	$73,990	$75,960	$92,210	$112,140

Median Wages for Industries Employing Largest Numbers (Annual)

Industry	Median Income
Federal, State, and Local Government	$90,290
Transportation Equipment Manufacturing	$80,830
Management of Companies and Enterprises	$79,900
Professional, Scientific, and Technical Services	$77,190
Paper Manufacturing	$75,190
Machinery Manufacturing	$74,800
Petroleum and Coal Products Manufacturing	$74,250
Utilities	$73,820
Computer and Electronic Product Manufacturing	$72,710
Educational Services	$71,620

Median Wages for States (Annual)

AK	no data	KY	$76,830	NY	$65,960
AL	$70,290	LA	$73,050	OH	$75,030
AR	$67,690	MA	$82,530	OK	$60,040
AZ	$64,780	MD	$91,750	OR	$74,000
CA	$80,540	ME	$73,400	PA	$68,740
CO	$95,560	MI	$72,020	RI	$69,100
CT	$79,940	MN	$70,820	SC	$78,320
DC	no data	MO	$58,390	SD	no data
DE	no data	MS	$66,650	TN	$84,120
FL	$62,990	MT	$41,560	TX	$75,910
GA	$65,670	NC	$69,750	UT	$69,140
HI	no data	ND	no data	VA	$91,210
IA	$66,920	NE	$69,730	VT	$63,940
ID	$63,490	NH	$68,800	WA	$70,600
IL	$68,700	NJ	$71,920	WI	$66,190
IN	$70,510	NM	no data	WV	$64,660
KS	$87,070	NV	$66,090	WY	no data

Median Wages for the Largest Metropolitan Areas (Annual)

AZ: Phoenix	$65,160	MI: Detroit	$74,330
CA: Los Angeles	$77,790	MN: Minneapolis	$73,340
CA: Riverside	$68,430	MO: Kansas City	$45,140
CA: Sacramento	$78,760	MO: St. Louis	$71,490
CA: San Diego	$81,500	NV: Las Vegas	$68,920
CA: San Francisco	$74,900	NY: New York	$67,110
CO: Denver	$92,550	OH: Cincinnati	$55,040
DC: Washington	$97,920	OH: Cleveland	$83,110
FL: Miami	$51,640	OH: Columbus	$61,620
FL: Orlando	no data	OR: Portland	no data
FL: Tampa	$90,920	PA: Philadelphia	$76,320
GA: Atlanta	$66,360	PA: Pittsburgh	$72,740
IL: Chicago	$71,090	TX: Dallas	$81,150
MA: Boston	$86,220	TX: Houston	$75,860
MD: Baltimore	$88,760	WA: Seattle	$68,440

FACTORS THAT MAY AFFECT EARNINGS

Educational Attainment of Workers and Effect on Earnings

	Percent at Level	Effect on Earnings
Less than High School	—	—
Some High School	—	—
High School or Equivalent	—	—
Some College but No Degree	—	—
Associate Degree	—	—
Bachelor's Degree	57.9%	−3.7%
Master's Degree	15.8%	26.4%
Doctoral Degree	—	—
First Professional Degree	—	—

Figures do not total 100% because some levels have a very small sample size.

Flexibility of Earnings

Average Hours Worked: 39
Workers with a Varying Number of Hours: 5.8%
Workers Earning Some Overtime Pay, Tips, or Commissions: 14.3%
Earnings Benefit of Working Overtime: −10.2%

Gender

	Male	Female
Percent	94.4%	5.6%
Effect on Earnings	2.3%	−15.8%

Union Membership

Percentage Union Members: Insignificant
Earnings Benefit of Union Membership: No significant data available

Veteran Status

Percentage Who Have Been on Active Duty: 13.5%
Earnings Benefit of Veteran Status: −0.6%

17-2141 Mechanical Engineers

Perform engineering duties in planning and designing tools, engines, machines, and other mechanically functioning equipment. Oversee installation, operation, maintenance, and repair of such equipment as centralized heat, gas, water, and steam systems.

- Education or Training Required: Bachelor's degree
- Job Growth: 11.1%
- Annual Openings: 11,000
- Self-Employed: 2.5%
- Part-Time: 11.3%

NATIONAL WAGE FIGURES (ANNUAL)

Beginning	25th Percentile	Median	Mean	75th Percentile	90th Percentile
$45,170	$55,420	$69,850	$72,580	$87,550	$104,900

Median Wages for Industries Employing Largest Numbers (Annual)

Industry	Median Income
Federal, State, and Local Government	$81,670
Petroleum and Coal Products Manufacturing	$75,190
Computer and Electronic Product Manufacturing	$74,970
Management of Companies and Enterprises	$74,480
Professional, Scientific, and Technical Services	$73,920
Paper Manufacturing	$73,890
Chemical Manufacturing	$71,700
Construction of Buildings	$71,580
Utilities	$71,450
Transportation Equipment Manufacturing	$70,390

Median Wages for States (Annual)

State	Wage	State	Wage	State	Wage
AK	$86,160	KY	$59,170	NY	$67,890
AL	$71,250	LA	$63,440	OH	$62,970
AR	$57,730	MA	$79,000	OK	$67,510
AZ	$73,430	MD	$77,960	OR	$68,400
CA	$79,660	ME	$68,470	PA	$66,830
CO	$74,710	MI	$72,340	RI	$80,410
CT	$68,090	MN	$64,860	SC	$66,240
DC	$91,110	MO	$62,350	SD	$58,980
DE	$77,560	MS	$60,620	TN	$63,060
FL	$65,500	MT	$53,600	TX	$75,380
GA	$67,630	NC	$65,480	UT	$72,160
HI	$77,850	ND	$61,170	VA	$72,890
IA	$61,940	NE	$65,160	VT	$60,770
ID	no data	NH	$66,060	WA	$76,720
IL	$65,050	NJ	$78,080	WI	$63,300
IN	$65,050	NM	$79,860	WV	$64,100
KS	$67,890	NV	$70,150	WY	$67,470

Median Wages for the Largest Metropolitan Areas (Annual)

Area	Wage	Area	Wage
AZ: Phoenix	$68,020	MI: Detroit	$75,910
CA: Los Angeles	$76,740	MN: Minneapolis	$66,610
CA: Riverside	$68,850	MO: Kansas City	$64,980
CA: Sacramento	$79,330	MO: St. Louis	$66,100
CA: San Diego	$77,420	NV: Las Vegas	$74,410
CA: San Francisco	$83,080	NY: New York	$76,910
CO: Denver	$75,710	OH: Cincinnati	$69,070
DC: Washington	$83,950	OH: Cleveland	$62,700
FL: Miami	$58,480	OH: Columbus	$65,070
FL: Orlando	$64,270	OR: Portland	$69,620
FL: Tampa	$65,430	PA: Philadelphia	$74,440
GA: Atlanta	$69,800	PA: Pittsburgh	$66,150
IL: Chicago	$67,290	TX: Dallas	$77,810
MA: Boston	$81,340	TX: Houston	$79,980
MD: Baltimore	$74,170	WA: Seattle	$78,190

FACTORS THAT MAY AFFECT EARNINGS

Educational Attainment of Workers and Effect on Earnings

	Percent at Level	Effect on Earnings
Less than High School	—	—
Some High School	—	—
High School or Equivalent	7.5%	−20.1%
Some College but No Degree	14.2%	−11.2%
Associate Degree	14.2%	−4.5%
Bachelor's Degree	41.4%	−0.4%
Master's Degree	18.7%	20.8%
Doctoral Degree	3.0%	6.4%
First Professional Degree	—	—

Flexibility of Earnings

Average Hours Worked: 41
Workers with a Varying Number of Hours: 4.1%
Workers Earning Some Overtime Pay, Tips, or Commissions: 13.5%
Earnings Benefit of Working Overtime: −7.8%

Gender

	Male	Female
Percent	94.2%	5.8%
Effect on Earnings	0.1%	—

Union Membership

Percentage Union Members: 5.1%
Earnings Benefit of Union Membership: 2.6%

Veteran Status

Percentage Who Have Been on Active Duty: 13.5%
Earnings Benefit of Veteran Status: −0.6%

17-2151 Mining and Geological Engineers, Including Mining Safety Engineers

Determine the location and plan the extraction of coal, metallic ores, nonmetallic minerals, and building materials such as stone and gravel. Work involves conducting preliminary surveys of deposits or undeveloped mines and planning their development; examining deposits or mines to determine whether they can be worked at a profit; making geological and topographical surveys; evolving methods of mining best suited to character, type, and size of deposits; and supervising mining operations.

- Education or Training Required: Bachelor's degree
- Job Growth: –1.5%
- Annual Openings: Fewer than 500
- Self-Employed: 0.0%
- Part-Time: 14.3%

NATIONAL WAGE FIGURES (ANNUAL)

Beginning	25th Percentile	Median	Mean	75th Percentile	90th Percentile
$42,040	$54,390	$72,160	$77,620	$94,110	$128,410

Median Wages for Industries Employing Largest Numbers (Annual)

Industry	Median Income
Specialty Trade Contractors	$91,460
Oil and Gas Extraction	$90,990
Management of Companies and Enterprises	$86,070
Federal, State, and Local Government	$72,440
Mining (Except Oil and Gas)	$68,730
Chemical Manufacturing	$67,460
Professional, Scientific, and Technical Services	$63,700
Support Activities for Mining	$59,230
Utilities	$57,710

Median Wages for States (Annual)

State	Wage	State	Wage	State	Wage
AK	$80,820	KY	$69,010	NY	$56,530
AL	$78,790	LA	$74,610	OH	$66,360
AR	no data	MA	no data	OK	no data
AZ	$53,540	MD	no data	OR	no data
CA	$84,450	ME	no data	PA	$56,920
CO	$84,840	MI	$69,290	RI	no data
CT	no data	MN	$71,530	SC	no data
DC	no data	MO	$78,140	SD	no data
DE	no data	MS	no data	TN	$54,010
FL	$64,720	MT	no data	TX	$80,750
GA	$73,700	NC	$51,970	UT	$86,030
HI	no data	ND	no data	VA	$80,580
IA	no data	NE	no data	VT	no data
ID	$75,810	NH	no data	WA	$64,570
IL	$75,970	NJ	no data	WI	no data
IN	$70,970	NM	$65,200	WV	$60,020
KS	no data	NV	$70,050	WY	$73,740

Median Wages for the Largest Metropolitan Areas (Annual)

Area	Wage	Area	Wage
AZ: Phoenix	$55,330	MI: Detroit	no data
CA: Los Angeles	$79,350	MN: Minneapolis	no data
CA: Riverside	$50,920	MO: Kansas City	no data
CA: Sacramento	no data	MO: St. Louis	$80,870
CA: San Diego	no data	NV: Las Vegas	no data
CA: San Francisco	no data	NY: New York	no data
CO: Denver	$87,720	OH: Cincinnati	no data
DC: Washington	$85,860	OH: Cleveland	no data
FL: Miami	no data	OH: Columbus	no data
FL: Orlando	no data	OR: Portland	no data
FL: Tampa	no data	PA: Philadelphia	$58,580
GA: Atlanta	$74,800	PA: Pittsburgh	$57,400
IL: Chicago	$104,930	TX: Dallas	$70,810
MA: Boston	no data	TX: Houston	$96,630
MD: Baltimore	no data	WA: Seattle	$64,460

FACTORS THAT MAY AFFECT EARNINGS

Educational Attainment of Workers and Effect on Earnings

	Percent at Level	Effect on Earnings
Less than High School	—	—
Some High School	—	—
High School or Equivalent	—	—
Some College but No Degree	—	—
Associate Degree	—	—
Bachelor's Degree	58.8%	15.6%
Master's Degree	—	—
Doctoral Degree	—	—
First Professional Degree	—	—

Figures do not total 100% because some levels have a very small sample size.

Flexibility of Earnings

Average Hours Worked: 36
Workers with a Varying Number of Hours: 11.8%
Workers Earning Some Overtime Pay, Tips, or Commissions: 17.6%
Earnings Benefit of Working Overtime: –10.2%

Gender

	Male	Female
Percent	90.4%	9.6%
Effect on Earnings	2.3%	–15.8%

Union Membership

Percentage Union Members: 6.0%
Earnings Benefit of Union Membership: –7.1%

Veteran Status

Percentage Who Have Been on Active Duty: 13.5%
Earnings Benefit of Veteran Status: –0.6%

17-2161 Nuclear Engineers

Conduct research on nuclear engineering problems or apply principles and theory of nuclear science to problems concerned with release, control, and utilization of nuclear energy and nuclear waste disposal.

- Education or Training Required: Bachelor's degree
- Job Growth: 7.3%
- Annual Openings: 1,000
- Self-Employed: 0.0%
- Part-Time: 14.3%

NATIONAL WAGE FIGURES (ANNUAL)

Beginning	25th Percentile	Median	Mean	75th Percentile	90th Percentile
$65,220	$77,920	$90,220	$92,040	$105,710	$124,510

Median Wages for Industries Employing Largest Numbers (Annual)

Industry	Median Income
Administrative and Support Services	$104,130
Professional, Scientific, and Technical Services	$92,600
Utilities	$90,380
Fabricated Metal Product Manufacturing	$85,150
Federal, State, and Local Government	$84,250
Educational Services	$67,660

Median Wages for States (Annual)

State		State		State	
AK	no data	KY	no data	NY	$93,730
AL	no data	LA	$86,970	OH	$106,550
AR	no data	MA	$87,500	OK	no data
AZ	no data	MD	$119,930	OR	no data
CA	$89,610	ME	no data	PA	$89,040
CO	more than $145,600	MI	no data	RI	no data
CT	$94,150	MN	no data	SC	$90,190
DC	$125,610	MO	$87,310	SD	no data
DE	no data	MS	$101,310	TN	no data
FL	$89,320	MT	no data	TX	$92,290
GA	$106,910	NC	no data	UT	no data
HI	no data	ND	no data	VA	$78,830
IA	no data	NE	no data	VT	no data
ID	$100,990	NH	no data	WA	$78,760
IL	$101,010	NJ	$83,200	WI	$68,890
IN	no data	NM	no data	WV	no data
KS	no data	NV	$131,960	WY	no data

Median Wages for the Largest Metropolitan Areas (Annual)

AZ: Phoenix	no data	MI: Detroit	no data
CA: Los Angeles	$89,180	MN: Minneapolis	$75,510
CA: Riverside	no data	MO: Kansas City	$83,040
CA: Sacramento	no data	MO: St. Louis	no data
CA: San Diego	no data	NV: Las Vegas	$132,300
CA: San Francisco	$88,620	NY: New York	no data
CO: Denver	no data	OH: Cincinnati	no data
DC: Washington	$109,890	OH: Cleveland	no data
FL: Miami	no data	OH: Columbus	$111,150
FL: Orlando	no data	OR: Portland	no data
FL: Tampa	no data	PA: Philadelphia	$92,250
GA: Atlanta	no data	PA: Pittsburgh	no data
IL: Chicago	$101,560	TX: Dallas	no data
MA: Boston	no data	TX: Houston	no data
MD: Baltimore	no data	WA: Seattle	$117,480

FACTORS THAT MAY AFFECT EARNINGS

Educational Attainment of Workers and Effect on Earnings

Figures are based on a group of occupations: Engineers

	Percent at Level	Effect on Earnings
Less than High School	—	—
Some High School	—	—
High School or Equivalent	9.5%	−21.3%
Some College but No Degree	14.4%	−14.5%
Associate Degree	12.8%	−9.0%
Bachelor's Degree	36.6%	3.6%
Master's Degree	20.2%	12.1%
Doctoral Degree	4.5%	37.4%
First Professional Degree	1.1%	20.8%

Flexibility of Earnings

Average Hours Worked: 41
Workers with a Varying Number of Hours: 5.4%
Workers Earning Some Overtime Pay, Tips, or Commissions: 12.5%
Earnings Benefit of Working Overtime: −10.2%

Gender

	Male	Female
Percent	66.7%	33.3%
Effect on Earnings	2.3%	−15.8%

Union Membership

Percentage Union Members: 12.5%
Earnings Benefit of Union Membership: −7.1%

Veteran Status

Percentage Who Have Been on Active Duty: 13.5%
Earnings Benefit of Veteran Status: −0.6%

17-2171 Petroleum Engineers

Devise methods to improve oil and gas well production and determine the need for new or modified tool designs. Oversee drilling and offer technical advice to achieve economical and satisfactory progress.

- Education or Training Required: Bachelor's degree
- Job Growth: –0.1%
- Annual Openings: 1,000
- Self-Employed: 7.2%
- Part-Time: 4.5%

NATIONAL WAGE FIGURES (ANNUAL)

Beginning	25th Percentile	Median	Mean	75th Percentile	90th Percentile
$57,960	$75,880	$98,380	$101,620	$123,130	more than $145,600

Median Wages for Industries Employing Largest Numbers (Annual)

Industry	Median Income
Oil and Gas Extraction	$110,240
Securities, Commodity Contracts, and Other Financial Investments and Related Activities	$96,390
Petroleum and Coal Products Manufacturing	$95,630
Heavy and Civil Engineering Construction	$92,690
Professional, Scientific, and Technical Services	$92,430
Administrative and Support Services	$91,740
Pipeline Transportation	$85,980
Federal, State, and Local Government	$85,150
Utilities	$84,190
Merchant Wholesalers, Nondurable Goods	$82,830

Median Wages for States (Annual)

AK	$104,360	KY	$77,690	NY	$91,120
AL	$72,930	LA	$88,000	OH	$111,890
AR	$84,260	MA	no data	OK	$86,730
AZ	no data	MD	no data	OR	no data
CA	$99,030	ME	no data	PA	$56,350
CO	$94,080	MI	$72,550	RI	no data
CT	no data	MN	no data	SC	no data
DC	no data	MO	$92,070	SD	no data
DE	no data	MS	$65,680	TN	no data
FL	no data	MT	$86,130	TX	$108,610
GA	no data	NC	no data	UT	$84,080
HI	no data	ND	no data	VA	no data
IA	no data	NE	no data	VT	no data
ID	no data	NH	no data	WA	$92,480
IL	$75,280	NJ	no data	WI	no data
IN	no data	NM	$80,980	WV	$78,830
KS	$57,790	NV	no data	WY	$87,410

Median Wages for the Largest Metropolitan Areas (Annual)

AZ: Phoenix	no data	MI: Detroit	no data
CA: Los Angeles	$92,270	MN: Minneapolis	no data
CA: Riverside	no data	MO: Kansas City	no data
CA: Sacramento	no data	MO: St. Louis	no data
CA: San Diego	no data	NV: Las Vegas	no data
CA: San Francisco	no data	NY: New York	$90,750
CO: Denver	$100,280	OH: Cincinnati	no data
DC: Washington	$98,260	OH: Cleveland	no data
FL: Miami	no data	OH: Columbus	no data
FL: Orlando	no data	OR: Portland	no data
FL: Tampa	no data	PA: Philadelphia	$85,210
GA: Atlanta	no data	PA: Pittsburgh	$80,570
IL: Chicago	no data	TX: Dallas	$102,710
MA: Boston	no data	TX: Houston	$112,970
MD: Baltimore	no data	WA: Seattle	no data

FACTORS THAT MAY AFFECT EARNINGS

Educational Attainment of Workers and Effect on Earnings

	Percent at Level	Effect on Earnings
Less than High School	—	—
Some High School	—	—
High School or Equivalent	—	—
Some College but No Degree	—	—
Associate Degree	—	—
Bachelor's Degree	53.6%	–0.5%
Master's Degree	—	—
Doctoral Degree	—	—
First Professional Degree	—	—

Figures do not total 100% because some levels have a very small sample size.

Flexibility of Earnings

Average Hours Worked: 41
Workers with a Varying Number of Hours: 14.5%
Workers Earning Some Overtime Pay, Tips, or Commissions: 6.5%
Earnings Benefit of Working Overtime: –10.2%

Gender

	Male	Female
Percent	92.2%	7.8%
Effect on Earnings	2.3%	–15.8%

Union Membership

Percentage Union Members: Insignificant
Earnings Benefit of Union Membership: No significant data available

Veteran Status

Percentage Who Have Been on Active Duty: 13.5%
Earnings Benefit of Veteran Status: –0.6%

17-2199 Engineers, All Other

All engineers not listed separately.

- Education or Training Required: Bachelor's degree
- Job Growth: 15.4%
- Annual Openings: 19,000
- Self-Employed: 4.7%
- Part-Time: 25.2%

NATIONAL WAGE FIGURES (ANNUAL)

Beginning	25th Percentile	Median	Mean	75th Percentile	90th Percentile
$46,080	$62,710	$81,660	$81,750	$100,320	$120,610

Median Wages for Industries Employing Largest Numbers (Annual)

Industry	Median Income
Federal, State, and Local Government	$92,470
Pipeline Transportation	$90,750
Computer and Electronic Product Manufacturing	$86,650
Couriers and Messengers	$83,570
Utilities	$82,010
Professional, Scientific, and Technical Services	$80,840
Chemical Manufacturing	$80,450
Management of Companies and Enterprises	$79,520
Wholesale Electronic Markets and Agents and Brokers	$78,490
Paper Manufacturing	$77,630

Median Wages for States (Annual)

AK	$82,450	KY	$66,190	NY	$76,840
AL	$91,900	LA	$58,260	OH	$77,310
AR	$69,430	MA	$87,990	OK	$60,360
AZ	$78,070	MD	$93,090	OR	$74,310
CA	$87,600	ME	$84,980	PA	$73,600
CO	$82,440	MI	no data	RI	$91,990
CT	$76,660	MN	no data	SC	$68,940
DC	$113,880	MO	$71,180	SD	$77,540
DE	$74,220	MS	$85,370	TN	$76,560
FL	$71,240	MT	$51,370	TX	$86,570
GA	$71,530	NC	$71,620	UT	$67,830
HI	$88,690	ND	no data	VA	$97,930
IA	$59,620	NE	$61,130	VT	$80,350
ID	$60,710	NH	$74,220	WA	$82,740
IL	$71,780	NJ	$87,060	WI	$68,080
IN	$75,140	NM	$92,560	WV	$74,280
KS	$69,470	NV	$61,430	WY	$64,470

Median Wages for the Largest Metropolitan Areas (Annual)

AZ: Phoenix	$74,010	MI: Detroit	no data
CA: Los Angeles	$92,460	MN: Minneapolis	no data
CA: Riverside	$75,620	MO: Kansas City	$85,600
CA: Sacramento	$83,860	MO: St. Louis	$63,710
CA: San Diego	$74,450	NV: Las Vegas	$60,100
CA: San Francisco	$90,700	NY: New York	$89,160
CO: Denver	$85,310	OH: Cincinnati	$72,260
DC: Washington	$109,150	OH: Cleveland	$80,400
FL: Miami	$69,980	OH: Columbus	$63,940
FL: Orlando	no data	OR: Portland	$77,630
FL: Tampa	$61,780	PA: Philadelphia	$69,790
GA: Atlanta	$74,610	PA: Pittsburgh	$79,770
IL: Chicago	$73,800	TX: Dallas	$84,580
MA: Boston	$88,570	TX: Houston	$91,550
MD: Baltimore	$85,120	WA: Seattle	no data

FACTORS THAT MAY AFFECT EARNINGS

Educational Attainment of Workers and Effect on Earnings

	Percent at Level	Effect on Earnings
Less than High School	—	—
Some High School	—	—
High School or Equivalent	6.8%	−10.7%
Some College but No Degree	9.9%	−9.6%
Associate Degree	16.0%	−8.0%
Bachelor's Degree	39.5%	0.8%
Master's Degree	22.4%	8.9%
Doctoral Degree	3.4%	33.6%
First Professional Degree	—	—

Flexibility of Earnings

Average Hours Worked: 39
Workers with a Varying Number of Hours: 6.5%
Workers Earning Some Overtime Pay, Tips, or Commissions: 10.9%
Earnings Benefit of Working Overtime: −2.8%

Gender

	Male	Female
Percent	86.5%	13.5%
Effect on Earnings	2.3%	−15.8%

Union Membership

Percentage Union Members: 4.9%
Earnings Benefit of Union Membership: −5.9%

Veteran Status

Percentage Who Have Been on Active Duty: 13.5%
Earnings Benefit of Veteran Status: −0.6%

17-3000 Drafters, Engineering, and Mapping Technicians

17-3011 Architectural and Civil Drafters

Prepare detailed drawings of architectural and structural features of buildings or drawings and topographical relief maps used in civil engineering projects, such as highways, bridges, and public works. Utilize knowledge of building materials, engineering practices, and mathematics to complete drawings.

- Education or Training Required: Postsecondary vocational training
- Job Growth: 4.6%
- Annual Openings: 9,000
- Self-Employed: 6.1%
- Part-Time: 20.9%

NATIONAL WAGE FIGURES (ANNUAL)

Beginning	25th Percentile	Median	Mean	75th Percentile	90th Percentile
$27,010	$33,550	$41,960	$43,900	$52,220	$63,310

Median Wages for Industries Employing Largest Numbers (Annual)

Industry	Median Income
Wholesale Electronic Markets and Agents and Brokers	$63,930
Waste Management and Remediation Services	$53,920
Computer and Electronic Product Manufacturing	$52,300
Utilities	$50,680
Management of Companies and Enterprises	$47,810
Administrative and Support Services	$47,500
Real Estate	$46,940
Heavy and Civil Engineering Construction	$45,630
Federal, State, and Local Government	$44,630
Primary Metal Manufacturing	$44,100

Median Wages for States (Annual)

State	Wage	State	Wage	State	Wage
AK	$45,300	KY	$36,680	NY	$45,520
AL	$39,200	LA	$40,040	OH	$40,720
AR	$33,720	MA	$45,240	OK	$37,670
AZ	$42,970	MD	$38,500	OR	$39,370
CA	$47,130	ME	$36,990	PA	$39,410
CO	$46,350	MI	$40,180	RI	$43,960
CT	$44,860	MN	$45,490	SC	$42,780
DC	$41,470	MO	$38,050	SD	$30,970
DE	$41,300	MS	$35,060	TN	$37,520
FL	$40,000	MT	$33,190	TX	$40,990
GA	$40,360	NC	$41,020	UT	$38,220
HI	$38,100	ND	$34,000	VA	$41,230
IA	$39,980	NE	$39,740	VT	$42,070
ID	$35,770	NH	$41,990	WA	$44,740
IL	$39,130	NJ	$47,510	WI	$39,700
IN	$39,240	NM	$36,340	WV	$38,030
KS	$36,620	NV	$49,330	WY	$35,040

Median Wages for the Largest Metropolitan Areas (Annual)

Area	Wage	Area	Wage
AZ: Phoenix	$43,960	MI: Detroit	$40,460
CA: Los Angeles	$46,610	MN: Minneapolis	$47,870
CA: Riverside	$44,210	MO: Kansas City	$39,430
CA: Sacramento	$42,420	MO: St. Louis	$38,880
CA: San Diego	$47,310	NV: Las Vegas	$46,910
CA: San Francisco	$51,830	NY: New York	$47,720
CO: Denver	$48,150	OH: Cincinnati	$40,450
DC: Washington	$41,670	OH: Cleveland	$42,900
FL: Miami	$40,920	OH: Columbus	$40,000
FL: Orlando	$40,940	OR: Portland	$40,010
FL: Tampa	$40,550	PA: Philadelphia	$40,980
GA: Atlanta	$41,560	PA: Pittsburgh	$39,020
IL: Chicago	$38,310	TX: Dallas	$44,550
MA: Boston	$44,870	TX: Houston	$47,170
MD: Baltimore	$39,480	WA: Seattle	$46,270

FACTORS THAT MAY AFFECT EARNINGS

Educational Attainment of Workers and Effect on Earnings

Figures are based on a group of occupations: Drafters, Engineering, and Mapping Technicians

	Percent at Level	Effect on Earnings
Less than High School	—	—
Some High School	3.4%	−41.5%
High School or Equivalent	22.2%	−1.9%
Some College but No Degree	27.6%	−5.2%
Associate Degree	25.4%	4.6%
Bachelor's Degree	17.3%	11.8%
Master's Degree	3.4%	1.0%
Doctoral Degree	—	—
First Professional Degree	—	—

Flexibility of Earnings

Average Hours Worked: 36
Workers with a Varying Number of Hours: 9.3%
Workers Earning Some Overtime Pay, Tips, or Commissions: 21.8%
Earnings Benefit of Working Overtime: 0.9%

Gender

	Male	Female
Percent	78.2%	21.8%
Effect on Earnings	6.4%	—

Union Membership

Percentage Union Members: 11.1%
Earnings Benefit of Union Membership: 24.1%

Veteran Status

Percentage Who Have Been on Active Duty: 18.7%
Earnings Benefit of Veteran Status: 14.1%

17-3012 Electrical and Electronics Drafters

Prepare wiring diagrams, circuit board assembly diagrams, and layout drawings used for manufacture, installation, and repair of electrical equipment in factories, power plants, and buildings.

- Education or Training Required: Postsecondary vocational training
- Job Growth: 1.2%
- Annual Openings: 3,000
- Self-Employed: 6.4%
- Part-Time: 20.9%

NATIONAL WAGE FIGURES (ANNUAL)

Beginning	25th Percentile	Median	Mean	75th Percentile	90th Percentile
$29,290	$36,660	$46,830	$49,610	$60,160	$74,490

Median Wages for Industries Employing Largest Numbers (Annual)

Industry	Median Income
Pipeline Transportation	$57,010
Utilities	$56,110
Wholesale Electronic Markets and Agents and Brokers	$55,520
Primary Metal Manufacturing	$52,380
Heavy and Civil Engineering Construction	$50,710
Management of Companies and Enterprises	$50,710
Computer and Electronic Product Manufacturing	$48,950
Merchant Wholesalers, Durable Goods	$48,140
Specialty Trade Contractors	$47,900
Federal, State, and Local Government	$47,360

Median Wages for States (Annual)

State	Wage	State	Wage	State	Wage
AK	no data	KY	$37,620	NY	$60,820
AL	$47,960	LA	$43,360	OH	$40,380
AR	$43,260	MA	$53,000	OK	$41,940
AZ	$49,900	MD	$53,060	OR	$41,710
CA	$49,560	ME	$42,860	PA	$47,600
CO	$52,990	MI	$44,540	RI	$49,270
CT	$48,710	MN	$47,140	SC	$45,060
DC	no data	MO	$45,500	SD	$36,040
DE	$59,240	MS	$38,220	TN	$40,660
FL	$43,140	MT	$39,370	TX	$46,810
GA	$51,090	NC	$44,850	UT	$40,660
HI	$38,180	ND	$34,270	VA	$41,980
IA	$53,790	NE	$46,360	VT	$38,310
ID	$42,070	NH	$52,300	WA	$45,750
IL	$47,090	NJ	$50,060	WI	$43,190
IN	$44,480	NM	no data	WV	$40,510
KS	$45,280	NV	$46,360	WY	$32,070

Median Wages for the Largest Metropolitan Areas (Annual)

Area	Wage	Area	Wage
AZ: Phoenix	$52,520	MI: Detroit	$44,540
CA: Los Angeles	$45,280	MN: Minneapolis	$48,700
CA: Riverside	$41,560	MO: Kansas City	$50,260
CA: Sacramento	$48,850	MO: St. Louis	$43,720
CA: San Diego	$51,260	NV: Las Vegas	$48,630
CA: San Francisco	$54,730	NY: New York	$61,360
CO: Denver	$52,880	OH: Cincinnati	$50,940
DC: Washington	$46,520	OH: Cleveland	$40,710
FL: Miami	$41,050	OH: Columbus	$31,710
FL: Orlando	$40,400	OR: Portland	$44,600
FL: Tampa	$48,460	PA: Philadelphia	$51,830
GA: Atlanta	$52,150	PA: Pittsburgh	no data
IL: Chicago	$46,820	TX: Dallas	$48,850
MA: Boston	$54,510	TX: Houston	$56,710
MD: Baltimore	$53,080	WA: Seattle	$47,860

FACTORS THAT MAY AFFECT EARNINGS

Educational Attainment of Workers and Effect on Earnings

Figures are based on a group of occupations: Drafters, Engineering, and Mapping Technicians

	Percent at Level	Effect on Earnings
Less than High School	—	—
Some High School	3.4%	−41.5%
High School or Equivalent	22.2%	−1.9%
Some College but No Degree	27.6%	−5.2%
Associate Degree	25.4%	4.6%
Bachelor's Degree	17.3%	11.8%
Master's Degree	3.4%	1.0%
Doctoral Degree	—	—
First Professional Degree	—	—

Flexibility of Earnings

Average Hours Worked: 36
Workers with a Varying Number of Hours: 9.3%
Workers Earning Some Overtime Pay, Tips, or Commissions: 21.8%
Earnings Benefit of Working Overtime: 0.9%

Gender

	Male	Female
Percent	78.2%	21.8%
Effect on Earnings	6.4%	—

Union Membership

Percentage Union Members: 11.1%
Earnings Benefit of Union Membership: 24.1%

Veteran Status

Percentage Who Have Been on Active Duty: 18.7%
Earnings Benefit of Veteran Status: 14.1%

17-3013 Mechanical Drafters

Prepare detailed working diagrams of machinery and mechanical devices, including dimensions, fastening methods, and other engineering information.

- Education or Training Required: Postsecondary vocational training
- Job Growth: 5.5%
- Annual Openings: 7,000
- Self-Employed: 5.5%
- Part-Time: 20.9%

NATIONAL WAGE FIGURES (ANNUAL)

Beginning	25th Percentile	Median	Mean	75th Percentile	90th Percentile
$28,230	$34,680	$43,700	$45,960	$55,130	$67,860

Median Wages for Industries Employing Largest Numbers (Annual)

Industry	Median Income
Pipeline Transportation	$53,760
Chemical Manufacturing	$50,360
Management of Companies and Enterprises	$48,310
Administrative and Support Services	$48,030
Utilities	$46,680
Specialty Trade Contractors	$46,020
Primary Metal Manufacturing	$45,290
Computer and Electronic Product Manufacturing	$44,660
Professional, Scientific, and Technical Services	$44,340
Federal, State, and Local Government	$44,320

Median Wages for States (Annual)

State	Wage	State	Wage	State	Wage
AK	no data	KY	$40,670	NY	$49,050
AL	$40,090	LA	$35,750	OH	$40,330
AR	$35,470	MA	$55,750	OK	$41,940
AZ	$38,700	MD	$42,330	OR	$45,500
CA	$45,710	ME	no data	PA	$42,830
CO	$44,410	MI	$51,200	RI	$43,060
CT	$47,390	MN	$45,920	SC	$47,850
DC	no data	MO	$43,230	SD	$31,380
DE	$62,040	MS	$29,640	TN	$42,060
FL	$40,570	MT	$36,750	TX	$45,580
GA	$43,860	NC	$44,330	UT	$38,660
HI	no data	ND	$36,840	VA	no data
IA	$38,290	NE	$32,970	VT	$44,710
ID	$34,560	NH	$41,790	WA	$50,410
IL	$42,530	NJ	$49,340	WI	$42,970
IN	$42,810	NM	$43,180	WV	$33,000
KS	$38,990	NV	$44,090	WY	$36,630

Median Wages for the Largest Metropolitan Areas (Annual)

Area	Wage	Area	Wage
AZ: Phoenix	$37,790	MI: Detroit	$55,460
CA: Los Angeles	$44,540	MN: Minneapolis	$49,150
CA: Riverside	$40,100	MO: Kansas City	$43,320
CA: Sacramento	$34,950	MO: St. Louis	$48,060
CA: San Diego	$50,830	NV: Las Vegas	$45,870
CA: San Francisco	$54,310	NY: New York	$53,400
CO: Denver	$46,430	OH: Cincinnati	$41,150
DC: Washington	$43,270	OH: Cleveland	$40,390
FL: Miami	$41,960	OH: Columbus	$39,790
FL: Orlando	$41,910	OR: Portland	$48,390
FL: Tampa	$40,410	PA: Philadelphia	$47,880
GA: Atlanta	$44,870	PA: Pittsburgh	$44,200
IL: Chicago	$43,010	TX: Dallas	$44,180
MA: Boston	no data	TX: Houston	$50,490
MD: Baltimore	$38,310	WA: Seattle	$57,850

FACTORS THAT MAY AFFECT EARNINGS

Educational Attainment of Workers and Effect on Earnings

Figures are based on a group of occupations: Drafters, Engineering, and Mapping Technicians

	Percent at Level	Effect on Earnings
Less than High School	—	—
Some High School	3.4%	−41.5%
High School or Equivalent	22.2%	−1.9%
Some College but No Degree	27.6%	−5.2%
Associate Degree	25.4%	4.6%
Bachelor's Degree	17.3%	11.8%
Master's Degree	3.4%	1.0%
Doctoral Degree	—	—
First Professional Degree	—	—

Flexibility of Earnings

Average Hours Worked: 36
Workers with a Varying Number of Hours: 9.3%
Workers Earning Some Overtime Pay, Tips, or Commissions: 21.8%
Earnings Benefit of Working Overtime: 0.9%

Gender

	Male	Female
Percent	78.2%	21.8%
Effect on Earnings	6.4%	—

Union Membership

Percentage Union Members: 11.1%
Earnings Benefit of Union Membership: 24.1%

Veteran Status

Percentage Who Have Been on Active Duty: 18.7%
Earnings Benefit of Veteran Status: 14.1%

17-3019 Drafters, All Other

All drafters not listed separately.

- Education or Training Required: Postsecondary vocational training
- Job Growth: 14.0%
- Annual Openings: 2,000
- Self-Employed: 3.3%
- Part-Time: 20.9%

NATIONAL WAGE FIGURES (ANNUAL)

Beginning	25th Percentile	Median	Mean	75th Percentile	90th Percentile
$26,340	$33,340	$43,060	$45,480	$55,920	$69,810

Median Wages for Industries Employing Largest Numbers (Annual)

Industry	Median Income
Transportation Equipment Manufacturing	$57,430
Oil and Gas Extraction	$53,300
Computer and Electronic Product Manufacturing	$48,850
Telecommunications	$48,050
Chemical Manufacturing	$47,710
Utilities	$47,140
Heavy and Civil Engineering Construction	$44,260
Management of Companies and Enterprises	$44,120
Specialty Trade Contractors	$43,390
Miscellaneous Manufacturing	$41,490

Median Wages for States (Annual)

AK	no data	KY	$32,130	NY	$49,170
AL	$41,580	LA	$35,840	OH	$38,850
AR	$42,830	MA	$55,530	OK	$38,440
AZ	$41,170	MD	$36,690	OR	$41,760
CA	$45,100	ME	$37,130	PA	$45,230
CO	$50,660	MI	no data	RI	$42,140
CT	$43,210	MN	$43,200	SC	$35,690
DC	no data	MO	$43,930	SD	no data
DE	no data	MS	$40,900	TN	no data
FL	$36,710	MT	no data	TX	$42,350
GA	$35,690	NC	no data	UT	$43,490
HI	$39,920	ND	no data	VA	no data
IA	$31,910	NE	$36,730	VT	no data
ID	$44,790	NH	$38,440	WA	no data
IL	$40,160	NJ	$46,830	WI	$34,690
IN	$38,460	NM	no data	WV	no data
KS	$44,020	NV	$46,190	WY	$47,970

Median Wages for the Largest Metropolitan Areas (Annual)

AZ: Phoenix	$43,750	MI: Detroit	no data
CA: Los Angeles	$46,620	MN: Minneapolis	$46,600
CA: Riverside	$42,190	MO: Kansas City	$44,110
CA: Sacramento	$52,820	MO: St. Louis	$43,760
CA: San Diego	$23,350	NV: Las Vegas	$48,580
CA: San Francisco	$62,030	NY: New York	$50,560
CO: Denver	$58,750	OH: Cincinnati	$38,180
DC: Washington	$42,440	OH: Cleveland	$37,440
FL: Miami	$37,230	OH: Columbus	$41,330
FL: Orlando	$33,210	OR: Portland	$41,790
FL: Tampa	$40,100	PA: Philadelphia	$47,380
GA: Atlanta	$44,720	PA: Pittsburgh	no data
IL: Chicago	$40,990	TX: Dallas	$45,330
MA: Boston	$56,170	TX: Houston	$42,450
MD: Baltimore	$38,540	WA: Seattle	no data

FACTORS THAT MAY AFFECT EARNINGS

Educational Attainment of Workers and Effect on Earnings

Figures are based on a group of occupations: Drafters, Engineering, and Mapping Technicians

	Percent at Level	Effect on Earnings
Less than High School	—	—
Some High School	3.4%	−41.5%
High School or Equivalent	22.2%	−1.9%
Some College but No Degree	27.6%	−5.2%
Associate Degree	25.4%	4.6%
Bachelor's Degree	17.3%	11.8%
Master's Degree	3.4%	1.0%
Doctoral Degree	—	—
First Professional Degree	—	—

Flexibility of Earnings

Average Hours Worked: 36
Workers with a Varying Number of Hours: 9.3%
Workers Earning Some Overtime Pay, Tips, or Commissions: 21.8%
Earnings Benefit of Working Overtime: 0.9%

Gender

	Male	Female
Percent	78.2%	21.8%
Effect on Earnings	6.4%	—

Union Membership

Percentage Union Members: 11.1%
Earnings Benefit of Union Membership: 24.1%

Veteran Status

Percentage Who Have Been on Active Duty: 18.7%
Earnings Benefit of Veteran Status: 14.1%

17-3021 Aerospace Engineering and Operations Technicians

Operate, install, calibrate, and maintain integrated computer/communications systems consoles; simulators; and other data acquisition, test, and measurement instruments and equipment to launch, track, position, and evaluate air and space vehicles. May record and interpret test data.

- Education or Training Required: Associate degree
- Job Growth: 8.5%
- Annual Openings: 1,000
- Self-Employed: 0.5%
- Part-Time: 20.9%

NATIONAL WAGE FIGURES (ANNUAL)

Beginning	25th Percentile	Median	Mean	75th Percentile	90th Percentile
$34,570	$43,440	$53,300	$54,480	$63,900	$74,860

Median Wages for Industries Employing Largest Numbers (Annual)

Industry	Median Income
Air Transportation	$65,570
Professional, Scientific, and Technical Services	$59,540
Management of Companies and Enterprises	$55,710
Transportation Equipment Manufacturing	$51,860
Computer and Electronic Product Manufacturing	$48,910
Educational Services	$43,470
Miscellaneous Manufacturing	$42,360

Median Wages for States (Annual)

AK	no data	KY	no data	NY	$50,760
AL	$47,570	LA	no data	OH	$47,210
AR	no data	MA	$49,880	OK	$56,930
AZ	$54,580	MD	$45,210	OR	no data
CA	$54,360	ME	no data	PA	no data
CO	$62,750	MI	$48,310	RI	no data
CT	$49,370	MN	no data	SC	no data
DC	no data	MO	$33,840	SD	no data
DE	no data	MS	no data	TN	$66,340
FL	$53,610	MT	no data	TX	$57,140
GA	no data	NC	no data	UT	no data
HI	no data	ND	no data	VA	$65,320
IA	no data	NE	no data	VT	no data
ID	no data	NH	no data	WA	$49,860
IL	no data	NJ	$49,780	WI	no data
IN	$40,180	NM	no data	WV	no data
KS	$49,080	NV	$67,770	WY	no data

Median Wages for the Largest Metropolitan Areas (Annual)

AZ: Phoenix	$54,910	MI: Detroit	$46,390
CA: Los Angeles	$55,460	MN: Minneapolis	no data
CA: Riverside	no data	MO: Kansas City	no data
CA: Sacramento	no data	MO: St. Louis	$33,840
CA: San Diego	no data	NV: Las Vegas	no data
CA: San Francisco	$45,480	NY: New York	$54,680
CO: Denver	no data	OH: Cincinnati	no data
DC: Washington	$69,130	OH: Cleveland	$41,140
FL: Miami	$54,750	OH: Columbus	no data
FL: Orlando	$55,940	OR: Portland	no data
FL: Tampa	$50,810	PA: Philadelphia	no data
GA: Atlanta	no data	PA: Pittsburgh	no data
IL: Chicago	$42,450	TX: Dallas	$59,300
MA: Boston	no data	TX: Houston	no data
MD: Baltimore	$45,000	WA: Seattle	$50,400

FACTORS THAT MAY AFFECT EARNINGS

Educational Attainment of Workers and Effect on Earnings

Figures are based on a group of occupations: Drafters, Engineering, and Mapping Technicians

	Percent at Level	Effect on Earnings
Less than High School	—	—
Some High School	3.4%	−41.5%
High School or Equivalent	22.2%	−1.9%
Some College but No Degree	27.6%	−5.2%
Associate Degree	25.4%	4.6%
Bachelor's Degree	17.3%	11.8%
Master's Degree	3.4%	1.0%
Doctoral Degree	—	—
First Professional Degree	—	—

Flexibility of Earnings

Average Hours Worked: 36
Workers with a Varying Number of Hours: 9.3%
Workers Earning Some Overtime Pay, Tips, or Commissions: 21.8%
Earnings Benefit of Working Overtime: −2.8%

Gender

	Male	Female
Percent	79.4%	20.6%
Effect on Earnings	3.7%	−12.3%

Union Membership

Percentage Union Members: 11.1%
Earnings Benefit of Union Membership: 24.1%

Veteran Status

Percentage Who Have Been on Active Duty: 18.7%
Earnings Benefit of Veteran Status: 14.1%

17-3022 Civil Engineering Technicians

Apply theory and principles of civil engineering in planning, designing, and overseeing construction and maintenance of structures and facilities under the direction of engineering staff or physical scientists.

- Education or Training Required: Associate degree
- Job Growth: 14.1%
- Annual Openings: 10,000
- Self-Employed: 0.3%
- Part-Time: 20.9%

NATIONAL WAGE FIGURES (ANNUAL)

Beginning	25th Percentile	Median	Mean	75th Percentile	90th Percentile
$25,250	$31,310	$40,560	$42,380	$51,230	$62,920

Median Wages for Industries Employing Largest Numbers (Annual)

Industry	Median Income
Telecommunications	$67,980
Utilities	$55,070
Mining (Except Oil and Gas)	$52,160
Management of Companies and Enterprises	$50,910
Real Estate	$50,790
Fabricated Metal Product Manufacturing	$47,280
Heavy and Civil Engineering Construction	$45,330
Publishing Industries (Except Internet)	$44,400
Construction of Buildings	$41,490
Professional, Scientific, and Technical Services	$40,510

Median Wages for States (Annual)

AK	$55,400	KY	no data	NY	$47,320
AL	$30,350	LA	$39,370	OH	$41,710
AR	$32,480	MA	$45,690	OK	$40,670
AZ	$42,740	MD	$44,970	OR	$47,340
CA	$53,400	ME	$40,530	PA	$37,080
CO	$45,150	MI	$41,790	RI	$41,970
CT	$56,680	MN	$47,860	SC	$35,730
DC	no data	MO	$37,430	SD	$33,060
DE	$38,800	MS	$30,320	TN	$41,980
FL	$40,840	MT	$39,100	TX	$31,750
GA	$33,560	NC	$38,620	UT	$36,100
HI	$40,510	ND	$38,430	VA	$43,120
IA	$39,570	NE	$34,150	VT	$45,080
ID	$43,330	NH	$42,250	WA	$48,000
IL	$42,710	NJ	$42,820	WI	$41,080
IN	$36,380	NM	$40,850	WV	$34,670
KS	$39,260	NV	$45,300	WY	$37,400

Median Wages for the Largest Metropolitan Areas (Annual)

AZ: Phoenix	$43,190	MI: Detroit	$42,560
CA: Los Angeles	$55,280	MN: Minneapolis	$49,630
CA: Riverside	$56,280	MO: Kansas City	$44,550
CA: Sacramento	$52,470	MO: St. Louis	$39,760
CA: San Diego	$52,870	NV: Las Vegas	$48,230
CA: San Francisco	$56,390	NY: New York	$45,250
CO: Denver	$44,250	OH: Cincinnati	$43,860
DC: Washington	$47,880	OH: Cleveland	$42,360
FL: Miami	$45,230	OH: Columbus	$42,060
FL: Orlando	$39,240	OR: Portland	$49,470
FL: Tampa	$38,960	PA: Philadelphia	$35,630
GA: Atlanta	$33,430	PA: Pittsburgh	$39,390
IL: Chicago	$42,680	TX: Dallas	$35,590
MA: Boston	$46,310	TX: Houston	$36,130
MD: Baltimore	$43,430	WA: Seattle	$49,500

FACTORS THAT MAY AFFECT EARNINGS

Educational Attainment of Workers and Effect on Earnings

Figures are based on a group of occupations: Drafters, Engineering, and Mapping Technicians

	Percent at Level	Effect on Earnings
Less than High School	—	—
Some High School	3.4%	−41.5%
High School or Equivalent	22.2%	−1.9%
Some College but No Degree	27.6%	−5.2%
Associate Degree	25.4%	4.6%
Bachelor's Degree	17.3%	11.8%
Master's Degree	3.4%	1.0%
Doctoral Degree	—	—
First Professional Degree	—	—

Flexibility of Earnings

Average Hours Worked: 36
Workers with a Varying Number of Hours: 9.3%
Workers Earning Some Overtime Pay, Tips, or Commissions: 21.8%
Earnings Benefit of Working Overtime: −2.8%

Gender

	Male	Female
Percent	79.4%	20.6%
Effect on Earnings	3.7%	−12.3%

Union Membership

Percentage Union Members: 11.1%
Earnings Benefit of Union Membership: 24.1%

Veteran Status

Percentage Who Have Been on Active Duty: 18.7%
Earnings Benefit of Veteran Status: 14.1%

17-3023 Electrical and Electronic Engineering Technicians

Apply electrical and electronic theory and related knowledge, usually under the direction of engineering staff, to design, build, repair, calibrate, and modify electrical components, circuitry, controls, and machinery for subsequent evaluation and use by engineering staff in making engineering design decisions.

- Education or Training Required: Associate degree
- Job Growth: 9.8%
- Annual Openings: 18,000
- Self-Employed: 0.4%
- Part-Time: 20.9%

NATIONAL WAGE FIGURES (ANNUAL)

Beginning	25th Percentile	Median	Mean	75th Percentile	90th Percentile
$30,120	$39,270	$50,660	$50,840	$60,470	$73,200

Median Wages for Industries Employing Largest Numbers (Annual)

Industry	Median Income
Motion Picture and Sound Recording Industries	$64,000
Federal, State, and Local Government	$63,100
Utilities	$57,500
Postal Service	$57,240
Support Activities for Mining	$55,170
Chemical Manufacturing	$53,870
Transportation Equipment Manufacturing	$53,860
Telecommunications	$53,820
Hospitals	$53,690
Internet Service Providers, Web Search Portals, and Data-Processing Services	$52,990

Median Wages for States (Annual)

State	Wage	State	Wage	State	Wage
AK	$63,680	KY	$44,850	NY	$55,290
AL	$48,360	LA	$50,090	OH	$48,000
AR	$41,040	MA	$49,630	OK	$49,700
AZ	$48,630	MD	$54,490	OR	$44,750
CA	$54,640	ME	$45,420	PA	$47,610
CO	$49,820	MI	$50,840	RI	$53,050
CT	$51,300	MN	$45,710	SC	$47,440
DC	$61,190	MO	$50,660	SD	$36,460
DE	$50,210	MS	$50,730	TN	$49,720
FL	$49,020	MT	$52,050	TX	$52,070
GA	$51,900	NC	$47,850	UT	$46,880
HI	$58,480	ND	$47,310	VA	$52,420
IA	$44,490	NE	$47,130	VT	$44,570
ID	$46,670	NH	$45,470	WA	$54,790
IL	$51,920	NJ	$53,890	WI	$44,360
IN	$50,690	NM	$54,560	WV	$50,550
KS	$47,300	NV	$49,500	WY	$51,580

Median Wages for the Largest Metropolitan Areas (Annual)

Area	Wage	Area	Wage
AZ: Phoenix	$48,570	MI: Detroit	$50,710
CA: Los Angeles	$51,510	MN: Minneapolis	$47,590
CA: Riverside	$56,240	MO: Kansas City	$51,250
CA: Sacramento	$48,940	MO: St. Louis	$52,760
CA: San Diego	$54,510	NV: Las Vegas	$49,500
CA: San Francisco	$59,220	NY: New York	$60,050
CO: Denver	$53,220	OH: Cincinnati	$46,560
DC: Washington	$54,410	OH: Cleveland	$49,570
FL: Miami	$49,950	OH: Columbus	$46,720
FL: Orlando	$46,340	OR: Portland	$44,150
FL: Tampa	$43,460	PA: Philadelphia	$50,890
GA: Atlanta	$52,100	PA: Pittsburgh	$44,650
IL: Chicago	$51,770	TX: Dallas	$54,700
MA: Boston	$49,850	TX: Houston	$52,590
MD: Baltimore	$52,910	WA: Seattle	$53,150

FACTORS THAT MAY AFFECT EARNINGS

Educational Attainment of Workers and Effect on Earnings

Figures are based on a group of occupations: Drafters, Engineering, and Mapping Technicians

	Percent at Level	Effect on Earnings
Less than High School	—	—
Some High School	3.4%	−41.5%
High School or Equivalent	22.2%	−1.9%
Some College but No Degree	27.6%	−5.2%
Associate Degree	25.4%	4.6%
Bachelor's Degree	17.3%	11.8%
Master's Degree	3.4%	1.0%
Doctoral Degree	—	—
First Professional Degree	—	—

Flexibility of Earnings

Average Hours Worked: 36
Workers with a Varying Number of Hours: 9.3%
Workers Earning Some Overtime Pay, Tips, or Commissions: 21.8%
Earnings Benefit of Working Overtime: −2.8%

Gender

	Male	Female
Percent	79.4%	20.6%
Effect on Earnings	3.7%	−12.3%

Union Membership

Percentage Union Members: 11.1%
Earnings Benefit of Union Membership: 24.1%

Veteran Status

Percentage Who Have Been on Active Duty: 18.7%
Earnings Benefit of Veteran Status: 14.1%

17-3024 *Electro-Mechanical Technicians*

Operate, test, and maintain unmanned, automated, servo-mechanical, or electromechanical equipment. May operate unmanned submarines, aircraft, or other equipment at worksites, such as oil rigs, deep ocean exploration, or hazardous waste removal. May assist engineers in testing and designing robotics equipment.

- Education or Training Required: Associate degree
- Job Growth: 9.7%
- Annual Openings: 2,000
- Self-Employed: 0.5%
- Part-Time: 20.9%

NATIONAL WAGE FIGURES (ANNUAL)

Beginning	25th Percentile	Median	Mean	75th Percentile	90th Percentile
$29,830	$35,730	$44,720	$46,540	$56,360	$68,700

Median Wages for Industries Employing Largest Numbers (Annual)

Industry	Median Income
Management of Companies and Enterprises	$57,150
Heavy and Civil Engineering Construction	$56,890
Professional, Scientific, and Technical Services	$54,030
Utilities	$51,110
Fabricated Metal Product Manufacturing	$47,440
Transportation Equipment Manufacturing	$47,390
Educational Services	$45,500
Plastics and Rubber Products Manufacturing	$42,860
Merchant Wholesalers, Durable Goods	$42,670
Miscellaneous Manufacturing	$42,470

Median Wages for States (Annual)

AK	no data	KY	$49,300	NY	$43,280
AL	$55,470	LA	$49,210	OH	$42,370
AR	no data	MA	$42,790	OK	$37,410
AZ	$40,320	MD	$42,440	OR	$42,080
CA	$45,640	ME	$48,630	PA	$40,730
CO	$49,820	MI	$62,570	RI	$35,380
CT	$44,980	MN	$45,410	SC	$37,380
DC	no data	MO	$42,900	SD	no data
DE	$33,340	MS	$36,800	TN	$48,980
FL	$34,380	MT	no data	TX	$46,910
GA	$44,930	NC	$41,760	UT	$45,990
HI	no data	ND	no data	VA	$46,750
IA	no data	NE	no data	VT	no data
ID	$37,830	NH	$42,100	WA	$46,980
IL	$44,110	NJ	$43,090	WI	$41,740
IN	$45,560	NM	$53,120	WV	$37,540
KS	no data	NV	no data	WY	no data

Median Wages for the Largest Metropolitan Areas (Annual)

AZ: Phoenix	$39,380	MI: Detroit	$58,090
CA: Los Angeles	$45,210	MN: Minneapolis	$46,940
CA: Riverside	$36,420	MO: Kansas City	no data
CA: Sacramento	$32,750	MO: St. Louis	no data
CA: San Diego	$42,580	NV: Las Vegas	no data
CA: San Francisco	$45,710	NY: New York	$48,110
CO: Denver	$43,690	OH: Cincinnati	$34,960
DC: Washington	$49,300	OH: Cleveland	$43,800
FL: Miami	$36,440	OH: Columbus	$59,120
FL: Orlando	$34,770	OR: Portland	$44,910
FL: Tampa	$34,590	PA: Philadelphia	$37,390
GA: Atlanta	no data	PA: Pittsburgh	no data
IL: Chicago	$45,080	TX: Dallas	$46,810
MA: Boston	$42,500	TX: Houston	$52,300
MD: Baltimore	$41,580	WA: Seattle	$43,810

FACTORS THAT MAY AFFECT EARNINGS

Educational Attainment of Workers and Effect on Earnings

Figures are based on a group of occupations: Drafters, Engineering, and Mapping Technicians

	Percent at Level	Effect on Earnings
Less than High School	—	—
Some High School	3.4%	−41.5%
High School or Equivalent	22.2%	−1.9%
Some College but No Degree	27.6%	−5.2%
Associate Degree	25.4%	4.6%
Bachelor's Degree	17.3%	11.8%
Master's Degree	3.4%	1.0%
Doctoral Degree	—	—
First Professional Degree	—	—

Flexibility of Earnings

Average Hours Worked: 36
Workers with a Varying Number of Hours: 9.3%
Workers Earning Some Overtime Pay, Tips, or Commissions: 21.8%
Earnings Benefit of Working Overtime: −2.8%

Gender

	Male	Female
Percent	79.4%	20.6%
Effect on Earnings	3.7%	−12.3%

Union Membership

Percentage Union Members: 11.1%
Earnings Benefit of Union Membership: 24.1%

Veteran Status

Percentage Who Have Been on Active Duty: 18.7%
Earnings Benefit of Veteran Status: 14.1%

17-3025 Environmental Engineering Technicians

Apply theory and principles of environmental engineering to modify, test, and operate equipment and devices used in the prevention, control, and remediation of environmental pollution, including waste treatment and site remediation. May assist in the development of environmental pollution remediation devices under direction of engineer.

- Education or Training Required: Associate degree
- Job Growth: 24.4%
- Annual Openings: 2,000
- Self-Employed: 0.3%
- Part-Time: 20.9%

NATIONAL WAGE FIGURES (ANNUAL)

Beginning	25th Percentile	Median	Mean	75th Percentile	90th Percentile
$25,110	$30,920	$40,560	$43,100	$53,250	$66,120

Median Wages for Industries Employing Largest Numbers (Annual)

Industry	Median Income
Machinery Manufacturing	$62,130
Utilities	$58,930
Food Manufacturing	$52,870
Petroleum and Coal Products Manufacturing	$52,180
Chemical Manufacturing	$51,780
Computer and Electronic Product Manufacturing	$49,690
Fabricated Metal Product Manufacturing	$47,810
Nonmetallic Mineral Product Manufacturing	$47,310
Construction of Buildings	$45,900
Mining (Except Oil and Gas)	$44,180

Median Wages for States (Annual)

AK	no data	KY	$38,790	NY	$38,360
AL	$32,510	LA	$36,390	OH	$44,780
AR	$35,870	MA	$43,060	OK	$39,060
AZ	$40,850	MD	$31,810	OR	$43,720
CA	$47,100	ME	$40,590	PA	$36,710
CO	$40,510	MI	$46,220	RI	no data
CT	$40,390	MN	$48,970	SC	$44,770
DC	$59,180	MO	$50,980	SD	no data
DE	$40,340	MS	$35,180	TN	$52,370
FL	$31,280	MT	$38,400	TX	$38,490
GA	$33,160	NC	$38,110	UT	$28,540
HI	no data	ND	$41,420	VA	$39,020
IA	$39,770	NE	$32,670	VT	$36,330
ID	$49,290	NH	$44,070	WA	$42,880
IL	$44,300	NJ	$41,170	WI	$42,940
IN	$38,390	NM	$35,480	WV	$37,180
KS	$43,980	NV	$45,060	WY	$39,670

Median Wages for the Largest Metropolitan Areas (Annual)

AZ: Phoenix	$36,150	MI: Detroit	$43,750
CA: Los Angeles	$53,120	MN: Minneapolis	$52,900
CA: Riverside	$32,190	MO: Kansas City	$46,180
CA: Sacramento	$43,560	MO: St. Louis	$49,250
CA: San Diego	$52,880	NV: Las Vegas	no data
CA: San Francisco	$52,780	NY: New York	$41,480
CO: Denver	$42,380	OH: Cincinnati	$31,340
DC: Washington	$37,310	OH: Cleveland	$50,340
FL: Miami	$33,940	OH: Columbus	$50,590
FL: Orlando	$29,980	OR: Portland	$47,180
FL: Tampa	$31,490	PA: Philadelphia	$36,640
GA: Atlanta	$33,060	PA: Pittsburgh	$28,970
IL: Chicago	$44,060	TX: Dallas	$37,500
MA: Boston	$43,330	TX: Houston	$37,500
MD: Baltimore	$43,040	WA: Seattle	$43,710

FACTORS THAT MAY AFFECT EARNINGS

Educational Attainment of Workers and Effect on Earnings

Figures are based on a group of occupations: Drafters, Engineering, and Mapping Technicians

	Percent at Level	Effect on Earnings
Less than High School	—	—
Some High School	3.4%	−41.5%
High School or Equivalent	22.2%	−1.9%
Some College but No Degree	27.6%	−5.2%
Associate Degree	25.4%	4.6%
Bachelor's Degree	17.3%	11.8%
Master's Degree	3.4%	1.0%
Doctoral Degree	—	—
First Professional Degree	—	—

Flexibility of Earnings

Average Hours Worked: 36
Workers with a Varying Number of Hours: 9.3%
Workers Earning Some Overtime Pay, Tips, or Commissions: 21.8%
Earnings Benefit of Working Overtime: −2.8%

Gender

	Male	Female
Percent	79.4%	20.6%
Effect on Earnings	3.7%	−12.3%

Union Membership

Percentage Union Members: 11.1%
Earnings Benefit of Union Membership: 24.1%

Veteran Status

Percentage Who Have Been on Active Duty: 18.7%
Earnings Benefit of Veteran Status: 14.1%

17-3026 Industrial Engineering Technicians

Apply engineering theory and principles to problems of industrial layout or manufacturing production, usually under the direction of engineering staff. May study and record time, motion, method, and speed involved in performance of production, maintenance, clerical, and other worker operations for such purposes as establishing standard production rates or improving efficiency.

- Education or Training Required: Associate degree
- Job Growth: 10.5%
- Annual Openings: 7,000
- Self-Employed: 0.3%
- Part-Time: 20.9%

NATIONAL WAGE FIGURES (ANNUAL)

Beginning	25th Percentile	Median	Mean	75th Percentile	90th Percentile
$30,190	$37,040	$46,810	$50,920	$60,860	$79,180

Median Wages for Industries Employing Largest Numbers (Annual)

Industry	Median Income
Internet Service Providers, Web Search Portals, and Data-Processing Services	$75,520
Insurance Carriers and Related Activities	$74,900
Professional, Scientific, and Technical Services	$60,420
Federal, State, and Local Government	$57,930
Utilities	$53,830
Transportation Equipment Manufacturing	$49,980
Beverage and Tobacco Product Manufacturing	$49,130
Management of Companies and Enterprises	$47,320
Merchant Wholesalers, Durable Goods	$47,020
Chemical Manufacturing	$45,310

Median Wages for States (Annual)

State	Wage	State	Wage	State	Wage
AK	no data	KY	$41,590	NY	$46,390
AL	$38,740	LA	$41,280	OH	$45,280
AR	$37,450	MA	$48,320	OK	no data
AZ	$39,680	MD	$52,210	OR	no data
CA	$53,950	ME	$46,910	PA	$45,940
CO	$51,910	MI	$45,580	RI	$38,660
CT	$52,370	MN	$43,680	SC	$43,850
DC	$51,570	MO	$41,700	SD	$36,090
DE	$52,970	MS	$45,350	TN	$45,020
FL	$41,090	MT	no data	TX	$57,110
GA	$46,380	NC	$45,740	UT	$51,330
HI	no data	ND	$39,350	VA	$48,440
IA	$39,640	NE	$56,280	VT	$41,920
ID	$45,670	NH	$43,540	WA	no data
IL	$43,980	NJ	$50,310	WI	$41,020
IN	$43,020	NM	no data	WV	no data
KS	$42,280	NV	no data	WY	no data

Median Wages for the Largest Metropolitan Areas (Annual)

Area	Wage	Area	Wage
AZ: Phoenix	$37,800	MI: Detroit	$46,400
CA: Los Angeles	$50,230	MN: Minneapolis	$46,620
CA: Riverside	$44,720	MO: Kansas City	$55,320
CA: Sacramento	no data	MO: St. Louis	$45,640
CA: San Diego	$56,060	NV: Las Vegas	no data
CA: San Francisco	$56,100	NY: New York	$49,330
CO: Denver	$49,540	OH: Cincinnati	$48,150
DC: Washington	$58,860	OH: Cleveland	$46,910
FL: Miami	$43,190	OH: Columbus	$44,410
FL: Orlando	$47,660	OR: Portland	no data
FL: Tampa	$34,980	PA: Philadelphia	$54,180
GA: Atlanta	$46,800	PA: Pittsburgh	$44,290
IL: Chicago	$45,000	TX: Dallas	$64,510
MA: Boston	$49,650	TX: Houston	$57,830
MD: Baltimore	$48,630	WA: Seattle	no data

FACTORS THAT MAY AFFECT EARNINGS

Educational Attainment of Workers and Effect on Earnings

Figures are based on a group of occupations: Drafters, Engineering, and Mapping Technicians

	Percent at Level	Effect on Earnings
Less than High School	—	—
Some High School	3.4%	−41.5%
High School or Equivalent	22.2%	−1.9%
Some College but No Degree	27.6%	−5.2%
Associate Degree	25.4%	4.6%
Bachelor's Degree	17.3%	11.8%
Master's Degree	3.4%	1.0%
Doctoral Degree	—	—
First Professional Degree	—	—

Flexibility of Earnings

Average Hours Worked: 36
Workers with a Varying Number of Hours: 9.3%
Workers Earning Some Overtime Pay, Tips, or Commissions: 21.8%
Earnings Benefit of Working Overtime: −2.8%

Gender

	Male	Female
Percent	79.4%	20.6%
Effect on Earnings	3.7%	−12.3%

Union Membership

Percentage Union Members: 11.1%
Earnings Benefit of Union Membership: 24.1%

Veteran Status

Percentage Who Have Been on Active Duty: 18.7%
Earnings Benefit of Veteran Status: 14.1%

17-3027 Mechanical Engineering Technicians

Apply theory and principles of mechanical engineering to modify, develop, and test machinery and equipment under direction of engineering staff or physical scientists.

- Education or Training Required: Associate degree
- Job Growth: 12.3%
- Annual Openings: 5,000
- Self-Employed: 0.4%
- Part-Time: 20.9%

NATIONAL WAGE FIGURES (ANNUAL)

Beginning	25th Percentile	Median	Mean	75th Percentile	90th Percentile
$29,770	$36,770	$45,850	$47,710	$57,310	$70,090

Median Wages for Industries Employing Largest Numbers (Annual)

Industry	Median Income
Pipeline Transportation	$54,630
Oil and Gas Extraction	$52,730
Utilities	$50,500
Specialty Trade Contractors	$50,180
Miscellaneous Manufacturing	$49,520
Management of Companies and Enterprises	$48,950
Computer and Electronic Product Manufacturing	$48,680
Transportation Equipment Manufacturing	$48,660
Primary Metal Manufacturing	$47,740
Federal, State, and Local Government	$46,790

Median Wages for States (Annual)

AK	$57,760	KY	$42,040	NY	$47,470
AL	$41,110	LA	$38,820	OH	$43,030
AR	$34,120	MA	$49,130	OK	$39,220
AZ	$44,030	MD	$51,050	OR	$52,580
CA	$50,830	ME	$40,320	PA	$43,610
CO	$45,610	MI	$45,640	RI	$43,590
CT	$46,140	MN	$47,280	SC	$43,410
DC	no data	MO	$43,360	SD	$38,110
DE	$54,720	MS	$42,950	TN	$41,380
FL	$43,180	MT	$51,280	TX	$51,420
GA	$42,590	NC	$43,920	UT	$42,410
HI	no data	ND	$42,000	VA	$43,860
IA	$38,520	NE	$47,460	VT	$41,320
ID	$32,250	NH	$43,520	WA	$54,580
IL	$46,860	NJ	$45,620	WI	$45,130
IN	$48,180	NM	$46,730	WV	$34,390
KS	$42,680	NV	$44,030	WY	no data

Median Wages for the Largest Metropolitan Areas (Annual)

AZ: Phoenix	$43,350	MI: Detroit	$44,280
CA: Los Angeles	$44,800	MN: Minneapolis	$49,430
CA: Riverside	$44,420	MO: Kansas City	$45,550
CA: Sacramento	$43,320	MO: St. Louis	$47,850
CA: San Diego	$45,510	NV: Las Vegas	$46,800
CA: San Francisco	$60,660	NY: New York	$48,800
CO: Denver	$48,370	OH: Cincinnati	$37,640
DC: Washington	$46,750	OH: Cleveland	$45,980
FL: Miami	$46,860	OH: Columbus	$44,000
FL: Orlando	$34,130	OR: Portland	$52,050
FL: Tampa	$45,940	PA: Philadelphia	$43,310
GA: Atlanta	$43,880	PA: Pittsburgh	$47,770
IL: Chicago	$53,390	TX: Dallas	$60,140
MA: Boston	$49,510	TX: Houston	$49,870
MD: Baltimore	$53,050	WA: Seattle	$55,530

FACTORS THAT MAY AFFECT EARNINGS

Educational Attainment of Workers and Effect on Earnings

Figures are based on a group of occupations: Drafters, Engineering, and Mapping Technicians

	Percent at Level	Effect on Earnings
Less than High School	—	—
Some High School	3.4%	−41.5%
High School or Equivalent	22.2%	−1.9%
Some College but No Degree	27.6%	−5.2%
Associate Degree	25.4%	4.6%
Bachelor's Degree	17.3%	11.8%
Master's Degree	3.4%	1.0%
Doctoral Degree	—	—
First Professional Degree	—	—

Flexibility of Earnings

Average Hours Worked: 36
Workers with a Varying Number of Hours: 9.3%
Workers Earning Some Overtime Pay, Tips, or Commissions: 21.8%
Earnings Benefit of Working Overtime: −2.8%

Gender

	Male	Female
Percent	79.4%	20.6%
Effect on Earnings	3.7%	−12.3%

Union Membership

Percentage Union Members: 11.1%
Earnings Benefit of Union Membership: 24.1%

Veteran Status

Percentage Who Have Been on Active Duty: 18.7%
Earnings Benefit of Veteran Status: 14.1%

17-3029 Engineering Technicians, Except Drafters, All Other

All engineering technicians, except drafters, not listed separately.

- Education or Training Required: Associate degree
- Job Growth: 12.3%
- Annual Openings: 10,000
- Self-Employed: 0.2%
- Part-Time: 20.9%

NATIONAL WAGE FIGURES (ANNUAL)

Beginning	25th Percentile	Median	Mean	75th Percentile	90th Percentile
$30,530	$41,900	$54,250	$53,850	$66,070	$77,080

Median Wages for Industries Employing Largest Numbers (Annual)

Industry	Median Income
Telecommunications	$64,410
Oil and Gas Extraction	$59,760
Utilities	$58,890
Federal, State, and Local Government	$58,820
Transportation Equipment Manufacturing	$56,740
Pipeline Transportation	$56,220
Chemical Manufacturing	$55,500
Paper Manufacturing	$55,420
Merchant Wholesalers, Nondurable Goods	$54,360
Support Activities for Transportation	$54,070

Median Wages for States (Annual)

State	Wage	State	Wage	State	Wage
AK	$52,760	KY	$42,620	NY	$46,130
AL	$54,570	LA	$52,120	OH	$55,640
AR	$48,260	MA	$48,600	OK	$55,850
AZ	$52,110	MD	$65,030	OR	$45,510
CA	$53,200	ME	$68,360	PA	$56,460
CO	$52,850	MI	no data	RI	$57,220
CT	$53,930	MN	$52,020	SC	$54,290
DC	$71,710	MO	$48,920	SD	$52,960
DE	no data	MS	$59,310	TN	$51,880
FL	$50,710	MT	$49,150	TX	$51,570
GA	$45,760	NC	$45,440	UT	$55,060
HI	$69,590	ND	$41,970	VA	$65,890
IA	$47,280	NE	$48,680	VT	no data
ID	$49,960	NH	$41,170	WA	$64,960
IL	$55,510	NJ	$61,790	WI	$51,620
IN	$54,440	NM	$51,130	WV	$56,060
KS	$53,100	NV	$51,120	WY	$46,470

Median Wages for the Largest Metropolitan Areas (Annual)

Area	Wage	Area	Wage
AZ: Phoenix	$54,320	MI: Detroit	no data
CA: Los Angeles	$44,820	MN: Minneapolis	$54,560
CA: Riverside	$55,100	MO: Kansas City	$61,890
CA: Sacramento	$51,460	MO: St. Louis	$40,480
CA: San Diego	$55,890	NV: Las Vegas	$48,560
CA: San Francisco	$65,130	NY: New York	$52,790
CO: Denver	$55,390	OH: Cincinnati	no data
DC: Washington	$65,300	OH: Cleveland	$61,450
FL: Miami	$46,700	OH: Columbus	$44,530
FL: Orlando	$45,010	OR: Portland	$46,130
FL: Tampa	$49,240	PA: Philadelphia	$63,810
GA: Atlanta	$41,560	PA: Pittsburgh	$51,900
IL: Chicago	$56,080	TX: Dallas	$44,460
MA: Boston	$47,780	TX: Houston	$52,340
MD: Baltimore	$65,000	WA: Seattle	no data

FACTORS THAT MAY AFFECT EARNINGS

Educational Attainment of Workers and Effect on Earnings

Figures are based on a group of occupations: Drafters, Engineering, and Mapping Technicians

	Percent at Level	Effect on Earnings
Less than High School	—	—
Some High School	3.4%	−41.5%
High School or Equivalent	22.2%	−1.9%
Some College but No Degree	27.6%	−5.2%
Associate Degree	25.4%	4.6%
Bachelor's Degree	17.3%	11.8%
Master's Degree	3.4%	1.0%
Doctoral Degree	—	—
First Professional Degree	—	—

Flexibility of Earnings

Average Hours Worked: 36
Workers with a Varying Number of Hours: 9.3%
Workers Earning Some Overtime Pay, Tips, or Commissions: 21.8%
Earnings Benefit of Working Overtime: −2.8%

Gender

	Male	Female
Percent	79.4%	20.6%
Effect on Earnings	3.7%	−12.3%

Union Membership

Percentage Union Members: 11.1%
Earnings Benefit of Union Membership: 24.1%

Veteran Status

Percentage Who Have Been on Active Duty: 18.7%
Earnings Benefit of Veteran Status: 14.1%

17-3031 Surveying and Mapping Technicians

Perform surveying and mapping duties, usually under the direction of a surveyor, cartographer, or photogrammetrist, to obtain data used for construction, mapmaking, boundary location, mining, or other purposes. May calculate mapmaking information and create maps from source data such as surveying notes, aerial photography, satellite data, or other maps to show topographical features, political boundaries, and other features. May verify accuracy and completeness of topographical maps.

- Education or Training Required: Moderate-term on-the-job training
- Job Growth: 9.6%
- Annual Openings: 9,000
- Self-Employed: 4.3%
- Part-Time: 29.5%

NATIONAL WAGE FIGURES (ANNUAL)

Beginning	25th Percentile	Median	Mean	75th Percentile	90th Percentile
$20,020	$25,070	$32,340	$34,590	$42,230	$53,310

Median Wages for Industries Employing Largest Numbers (Annual)

Industry	Median Income
Utilities	$45,390
Management of Companies and Enterprises	$44,360
Religious, Grantmaking, Civic, Professional, and Similar Organizations	$42,610
Pipeline Transportation	$39,660
Oil and Gas Extraction	$39,270
Educational Services	$39,110
Federal, State, and Local Government	$38,510
Mining (Except Oil and Gas)	$34,810
Support Activities for Mining	$34,790
Construction of Buildings	$34,170

Median Wages for States (Annual)

AK	$44,480	KY	$27,420	NY	$36,230
AL	$24,630	LA	$27,200	OH	$32,240
AR	$26,510	MA	$42,560	OK	$31,760
AZ	$36,350	MD	$34,730	OR	$36,960
CA	$50,520	ME	$31,300	PA	$29,290
CO	$38,750	MI	$34,620	RI	no data
CT	$40,180	MN	$44,250	SC	$28,040
DC	no data	MO	$32,670	SD	$28,610
DE	$31,450	MS	$25,570	TN	$29,730
FL	$28,690	MT	$29,060	TX	$28,630
GA	$28,460	NC	$30,730	UT	$27,510
HI	$35,630	ND	$37,180	VA	$32,950
IA	$30,390	NE	$30,030	VT	$34,190
ID	$31,240	NH	$31,380	WA	$40,070
IL	$38,330	NJ	$36,780	WI	$33,600
IN	$31,950	NM	$33,790	WV	$26,550
KS	$30,220	NV	$45,900	WY	$32,300

Median Wages for the Largest Metropolitan Areas (Annual)

AZ: Phoenix	$36,460	MI: Detroit	$36,230
CA: Los Angeles	$50,480	MN: Minneapolis	$45,390
CA: Riverside	$57,060	MO: Kansas City	$35,820
CA: Sacramento	$54,220	MO: St. Louis	$33,980
CA: San Diego	$48,070	NV: Las Vegas	$50,280
CA: San Francisco	$54,920	NY: New York	$38,570
CO: Denver	$41,910	OH: Cincinnati	$32,660
DC: Washington	$42,170	OH: Cleveland	$35,160
FL: Miami	$28,370	OH: Columbus	$29,640
FL: Orlando	$31,760	OR: Portland	$39,130
FL: Tampa	$26,920	PA: Philadelphia	$36,520
GA: Atlanta	$30,780	PA: Pittsburgh	$23,850
IL: Chicago	$40,760	TX: Dallas	$30,800
MA: Boston	$45,410	TX: Houston	$31,430
MD: Baltimore	$32,280	WA: Seattle	$42,510

FACTORS THAT MAY AFFECT EARNINGS

Educational Attainment of Workers and Effect on Earnings

	Percent at Level	Effect on Earnings
Less than High School	—	—
Some High School	—	—
High School or Equivalent	33.3%	−2.3%
Some College but No Degree	33.3%	0.5%
Associate Degree	16.7%	16.4%
Bachelor's Degree	8.8%	4.7%
Master's Degree	—	—
Doctoral Degree	—	—
First Professional Degree	—	—

Figures do not total 100% because some levels have a very small sample size.

Flexibility of Earnings

Average Hours Worked: 34
Workers with a Varying Number of Hours: 9.3%
Workers Earning Some Overtime Pay, Tips, or Commissions: 19.7%
Earnings Benefit of Working Overtime: 9.3%

Gender

	Male	Female
Percent	90.1%	9.9%
Effect on Earnings	0.7%	—

Union Membership

Percentage Union Members: 6.6%
Earnings Benefit of Union Membership: 24.1%

Veteran Status

Percentage Who Have Been on Active Duty: 18.7%
Earnings Benefit of Veteran Status: 14.1%

19-0000: Life, Physical, and Social Science Occupations

19-1000 Life Scientists

19-1011 Animal Scientists

Conduct research in the genetics, nutrition, reproduction, growth, and development of domestic farm animals.

- Education or Training Required: Bachelor's degree
- Job Growth: 12.9%
- Annual Openings: Fewer than 500
- Self-Employed: 31.3%
- Part-Time: 12.3%

Note: Earnings figures do not reflect self-employed workers, who make up a large fraction of the workforce for this occupation.

NATIONAL WAGE FIGURES (ANNUAL)

Beginning	25th Percentile	Median	Mean	75th Percentile	90th Percentile
$31,540	$37,930	$47,800	$53,230	$62,950	$81,430

Median Wages for Industries Employing Largest Numbers (Annual)

Industry	Median Income
Federal, State, and Local Government	$69,090
Professional, Scientific, and Technical Services	$54,210
Religious, Grantmaking, Civic, Professional, and Similar Organizations	$46,490
Support Activities for Agriculture and Forestry	$45,550
Educational Services	$43,430
Food Manufacturing	$40,350

Median Wages for States (Annual)

AK	no data	KY	no data	NY	no data
AL	no data	LA	no data	OH	no data
AR	no data	MA	no data	OK	no data
AZ	no data	MD	no data	OR	no data
CA	$61,590	ME	no data	PA	no data
CO	no data	MI	no data	RI	no data
CT	no data	MN	$48,070	SC	no data
DC	no data	MO	$73,480	SD	no data
DE	no data	MS	$34,150	TN	no data
FL	no data	MT	no data	TX	$41,430
GA	no data	NC	no data	UT	no data
HI	no data	ND	no data	VA	no data
IA	$44,330	NE	$46,600	VT	no data
ID	no data	NH	no data	WA	no data
IL	no data	NJ	$71,020	WI	$45,830
IN	no data	NM	no data	WV	no data
KS	$54,170	NV	no data	WY	no data

Median Wages for the Largest Metropolitan Areas (Annual)

AZ: Phoenix	no data	MI: Detroit	no data
CA: Los Angeles	no data	MN: Minneapolis	no data
CA: Riverside	no data	MO: Kansas City	no data
CA: Sacramento	no data	MO: St. Louis	no data
CA: San Diego	no data	NV: Las Vegas	no data
CA: San Francisco	$60,280	NY: New York	$61,750
CO: Denver	no data	OH: Cincinnati	no data
DC: Washington	$93,010	OH: Cleveland	no data
FL: Miami	no data	OH: Columbus	no data
FL: Orlando	no data	OR: Portland	no data
FL: Tampa	no data	PA: Philadelphia	no data
GA: Atlanta	no data	PA: Pittsburgh	no data
IL: Chicago	no data	TX: Dallas	$40,280
MA: Boston	no data	TX: Houston	$42,620
MD: Baltimore	no data	WA: Seattle	no data

FACTORS THAT MAY AFFECT EARNINGS

Educational Attainment of Workers and Effect on Earnings

Figures are based on a group of occupations: Life Scientists

	Percent at Level	Effect on Earnings
Less than High School	—	—
Some High School	—	—
High School or Equivalent	3.9%	−32.4%
Some College but No Degree	3.4%	−40.6%
Associate Degree	5.3%	−28.2%
Bachelor's Degree	35.0%	−13.7%
Master's Degree	21.0%	0.5%
Doctoral Degree	23.5%	29.2%
First Professional Degree	6.4%	36.0%

Flexibility of Earnings

Average Hours Worked: 39
Workers with a Varying Number of Hours: 8.0%
Workers Earning Some Overtime Pay, Tips, or Commissions: 4.8%
Earnings Benefit of Working Overtime: 5.3%

Gender

	Male	Female
Percent	53.4%	46.6%
Effect on Earnings	3.4%	−1.4%

Union Membership

Percentage Union Members: 8.3%
Earnings Benefit of Union Membership: −10.7%

Veteran Status

Percentage Who Have Been on Active Duty: 4.9%
Earnings Benefit of Veteran Status: 9.6%

19-1012 Food Scientists and Technologists

Use chemistry, microbiology, engineering, and other sciences to study the principles underlying the processing and deterioration of foods; analyze food content to determine levels of vitamins, fat, sugar, and protein; discover new food sources; research ways to make processed foods safe, palatable, and healthful; and apply food science knowledge to determine the best ways to process, package, preserve, store, and distribute food.

- Education or Training Required: Bachelor's degree
- Job Growth: 10.9%
- Annual Openings: 1,000
- Self-Employed: 28.8%
- Part-Time: 12.3%

NATIONAL WAGE FIGURES (ANNUAL)

Beginning	25th Percentile	Median	Mean	75th Percentile	90th Percentile
$29,620	$37,740	$53,810	$59,260	$76,960	$97,350

Median Wages for Industries Employing Largest Numbers (Annual)

Industry	Median Income
Professional, Scientific, and Technical Services	$68,900
Management of Companies and Enterprises	$68,620
Merchant Wholesalers, Nondurable Goods	$67,750
Wholesale Electronic Markets and Agents and Brokers	$61,080
Federal, State, and Local Government	$59,070
Support Activities for Agriculture and Forestry	$53,520
Beverage and Tobacco Product Manufacturing	$49,350
Food Manufacturing	$49,140
Chemical Manufacturing	$46,760
Educational Services	$43,200

Median Wages for States (Annual)

AK	no data	KY	$61,330	NY	$50,600
AL	$40,510	LA	no data	OH	$64,270
AR	$31,520	MA	$57,310	OK	$41,750
AZ	$35,400	MD	$57,650	OR	$38,490
CA	$53,690	ME	no data	PA	$60,130
CO	$56,580	MI	no data	RI	no data
CT	$35,280	MN	$69,050	SC	$43,580
DC	no data	MO	$53,330	SD	$43,130
DE	no data	MS	$43,840	TN	$32,030
FL	$38,760	MT	no data	TX	$57,640
GA	$44,060	NC	$51,020	UT	$47,050
HI	$70,480	ND	$48,270	VA	$39,770
IA	$49,780	NE	$29,850	VT	$41,640
ID	$46,540	NH	no data	WA	$55,190
IL	$65,750	NJ	$66,510	WI	$47,250
IN	$43,450	NM	no data	WV	no data
KS	$57,850	NV	no data	WY	no data

Median Wages for the Largest Metropolitan Areas (Annual)

AZ: Phoenix	no data	MI: Detroit	no data
CA: Los Angeles	$54,020	MN: Minneapolis	$72,670
CA: Riverside	no data	MO: Kansas City	$48,080
CA: Sacramento	no data	MO: St. Louis	$58,410
CA: San Diego	no data	NV: Las Vegas	no data
CA: San Francisco	$69,420	NY: New York	$69,730
CO: Denver	$59,290	OH: Cincinnati	$70,760
DC: Washington	$86,140	OH: Cleveland	no data
FL: Miami	$45,880	OH: Columbus	$72,540
FL: Orlando	$26,240	OR: Portland	$40,020
FL: Tampa	$38,360	PA: Philadelphia	$60,470
GA: Atlanta	$42,470	PA: Pittsburgh	$70,220
IL: Chicago	$69,600	TX: Dallas	$69,170
MA: Boston	$59,860	TX: Houston	no data
MD: Baltimore	$55,570	WA: Seattle	$60,820

FACTORS THAT MAY AFFECT EARNINGS

Educational Attainment of Workers and Effect on Earnings

Figures are based on a group of occupations: Life Scientists

	Percent at Level	Effect on Earnings
Less than High School	—	—
Some High School	—	—
High School or Equivalent	3.9%	−32.4%
Some College but No Degree	3.4%	−40.6%
Associate Degree	5.3%	−28.2%
Bachelor's Degree	35.0%	−13.7%
Master's Degree	21.0%	0.5%
Doctoral Degree	23.5%	29.2%
First Professional Degree	6.4%	36.0%

Flexibility of Earnings

Average Hours Worked: 39
Workers with a Varying Number of Hours: 8.0%
Workers Earning Some Overtime Pay, Tips, or Commissions: 4.8%
Earnings Benefit of Working Overtime: 5.3%

Gender

	Male	Female
Percent	53.4%	46.6%
Effect on Earnings	3.4%	−1.4%

Union Membership

Percentage Union Members: 8.3%
Earnings Benefit of Union Membership: −10.7%

Veteran Status

Percentage Who Have Been on Active Duty: 4.9%
Earnings Benefit of Veteran Status: 9.6%

19-1013 Soil and Plant Scientists

Conduct research in breeding, physiology, production, yield, and management of crops and agricultural plants; their growth in soils; and control of pests or study the chemical, physical, biological, and mineralogical composition of soils as they relate to plant or crop growth. May classify and map soils and investigate effects of alternative practices on soil and crop productivity.

- Education or Training Required: Bachelor's degree
- Job Growth: 13.9%
- Annual Openings: 1,000
- Self-Employed: 35.9%
- Part-Time: 12.3%

Note: Earnings figures do not reflect self-employed workers, who make up a large fraction of the workforce for this occupation.

NATIONAL WAGE FIGURES (ANNUAL)

Beginning	25th Percentile	Median	Mean	75th Percentile	90th Percentile
$33,650	$42,410	$56,080	$59,330	$72,020	$93,460

Median Wages for Industries Employing Largest Numbers (Annual)

Industry	Median Income
Administrative and Support Services	$69,290
Food Manufacturing	$68,330
Merchant Wholesalers, Nondurable Goods	$61,090
Management of Companies and Enterprises	$60,200
Federal, State, and Local Government	$59,690
Professional, Scientific, and Technical Services	$55,710
Building Material and Garden Equipment and Supplies Dealers	$54,590
Support Activities for Agriculture and Forestry	$53,060
Educational Services	$43,540
Museums, Historical Sites, and Similar Institutions	$36,470

Median Wages for States (Annual)

State	Wage	State	Wage	State	Wage
AK	no data	KY	$41,140	NY	no data
AL	$57,400	LA	$57,710	OH	$48,620
AR	$44,130	MA	no data	OK	$69,160
AZ	$59,480	MD	$72,230	OR	$60,890
CA	$65,420	ME	$54,360	PA	$59,430
CO	$55,220	MI	$58,830	RI	no data
CT	$62,750	MN	$45,840	SC	$55,720
DC	$77,770	MO	$44,150	SD	$46,930
DE	$40,380	MS	$51,860	TN	$59,230
FL	$61,060	MT	$51,340	TX	$58,170
GA	$54,670	NC	$52,470	UT	$51,680
HI	$61,060	ND	$50,090	VA	$58,030
IA	$54,830	NE	$44,650	VT	no data
ID	$66,730	NH	no data	WA	$60,390
IL	$53,610	NJ	$52,300	WI	$44,120
IN	$34,600	NM	$61,690	WV	$62,230
KS	$59,950	NV	no data	WY	$46,480

Median Wages for the Largest Metropolitan Areas (Annual)

Area	Wage	Area	Wage
AZ: Phoenix	no data	MI: Detroit	no data
CA: Los Angeles	$52,810	MN: Minneapolis	no data
CA: Riverside	$68,250	MO: Kansas City	$65,800
CA: Sacramento	$70,940	MO: St. Louis	$44,110
CA: San Diego	$64,360	NV: Las Vegas	no data
CA: San Francisco	$79,050	NY: New York	$55,510
CO: Denver	no data	OH: Cincinnati	no data
DC: Washington	$77,300	OH: Cleveland	no data
FL: Miami	$60,530	OH: Columbus	no data
FL: Orlando	no data	OR: Portland	$58,890
FL: Tampa	no data	PA: Philadelphia	$40,230
GA: Atlanta	$67,470	PA: Pittsburgh	no data
IL: Chicago	$52,740	TX: Dallas	no data
MA: Boston	no data	TX: Houston	no data
MD: Baltimore	no data	WA: Seattle	$67,540

FACTORS THAT MAY AFFECT EARNINGS

Educational Attainment of Workers and Effect on Earnings

Figures are based on a group of occupations: Life Scientists

	Percent at Level	Effect on Earnings
Less than High School	—	—
Some High School	—	—
High School or Equivalent	3.9%	−32.4%
Some College but No Degree	3.4%	−40.6%
Associate Degree	5.3%	−28.2%
Bachelor's Degree	35.0%	−13.7%
Master's Degree	21.0%	0.5%
Doctoral Degree	23.5%	29.2%
First Professional Degree	6.4%	36.0%

Flexibility of Earnings

Average Hours Worked: 39
Workers with a Varying Number of Hours: 8.0%
Workers Earning Some Overtime Pay, Tips, or Commissions: 4.8%
Earnings Benefit of Working Overtime: 5.3%

Gender

	Male	Female
Percent	53.4%	46.6%
Effect on Earnings	3.4%	−1.4%

Union Membership

Percentage Union Members: 8.3%
Earnings Benefit of Union Membership: −10.7%

Veteran Status

Percentage Who Have Been on Active Duty: 4.9%
Earnings Benefit of Veteran Status: 9.6%

19-1021 Biochemists and Biophysicists

Study the chemical composition and physical principles of living cells and organisms, their electrical and mechanical energy, and related phenomena. May conduct research to further understanding of the complex chemical combinations and reactions involved in metabolism, reproduction, growth, and heredity. May determine the effects of foods, drugs, serums, hormones, and other substances on tissues and vital processes of living organisms.

- Education or Training Required: Doctoral degree
- Job Growth: 21.0%
- Annual Openings: 1,000
- Self-Employed: 2.7%
- Part-Time: 12.3%

NATIONAL WAGE FIGURES (ANNUAL)

Beginning	25th Percentile	Median	Mean	75th Percentile	90th Percentile
$40,820	$53,390	$76,320	$80,900	$100,060	$129,510

Median Wages for Industries Employing Largest Numbers (Annual)

Industry	Median Income
Chemical Manufacturing	$85,730
Miscellaneous Manufacturing	$85,340
Professional, Scientific, and Technical Services	$79,210
Merchant Wholesalers, Nondurable Goods	$76,420
Management of Companies and Enterprises	$75,880
Hospitals	$71,790
Computer and Electronic Product Manufacturing	$70,060
Ambulatory Health Care Services	$64,840
Administrative and Support Services	$55,370
Food Manufacturing	$50,810

Median Wages for States (Annual)

State	Wage	State	Wage	State	Wage
AK	no data	KY	$44,020	NY	$71,570
AL	no data	LA	$37,850	OH	$53,470
AR	$68,990	MA	$86,450	OK	$39,130
AZ	no data	MD	$51,620	OR	no data
CA	$78,950	ME	$60,780	PA	$84,570
CO	$76,920	MI	$54,170	RI	$71,360
CT	$83,270	MN	no data	SC	$60,280
DC	$64,850	MO	$69,930	SD	no data
DE	$110,110	MS	no data	TN	$44,280
FL	$64,500	MT	no data	TX	$50,010
GA	$103,880	NC	$69,750	UT	no data
HI	no data	ND	no data	VA	$60,030
IA	no data	NE	no data	VT	no data
ID	no data	NH	no data	WA	$56,920
IL	$68,250	NJ	no data	WI	$44,660
IN	$107,940	NM	no data	WV	no data
KS	no data	NV	no data	WY	no data

Median Wages for the Largest Metropolitan Areas (Annual)

Area	Wage	Area	Wage
AZ: Phoenix	no data	MI: Detroit	no data
CA: Los Angeles	$58,430	MN: Minneapolis	no data
CA: Riverside	no data	MO: Kansas City	no data
CA: Sacramento	$80,390	MO: St. Louis	$73,700
CA: San Diego	$77,750	NV: Las Vegas	no data
CA: San Francisco	$83,370	NY: New York	$85,110
CO: Denver	$67,860	OH: Cincinnati	$47,420
DC: Washington	$59,230	OH: Cleveland	$67,320
FL: Miami	no data	OH: Columbus	no data
FL: Orlando	no data	OR: Portland	no data
FL: Tampa	no data	PA: Philadelphia	$99,380
GA: Atlanta	$103,950	PA: Pittsburgh	$81,700
IL: Chicago	no data	TX: Dallas	$76,550
MA: Boston	$87,520	TX: Houston	no data
MD: Baltimore	$49,830	WA: Seattle	$60,510

FACTORS THAT MAY AFFECT EARNINGS

Educational Attainment of Workers and Effect on Earnings

Figures are based on a group of occupations: Life Scientists

	Percent at Level	Effect on Earnings
Less than High School	—	—
Some High School	—	—
High School or Equivalent	3.9%	−32.4%
Some College but No Degree	3.4%	−40.6%
Associate Degree	5.3%	−28.2%
Bachelor's Degree	35.0%	−13.7%
Master's Degree	21.0%	0.5%
Doctoral Degree	23.5%	29.2%
First Professional Degree	6.4%	36.0%

Flexibility of Earnings

Average Hours Worked: 39
Workers with a Varying Number of Hours: 2.3%
Workers Earning Some Overtime Pay, Tips, or Commissions: 4.8%
Earnings Benefit of Working Overtime: 5.3%

Gender

	Male	Female
Percent	53.4%	46.6%
Effect on Earnings	3.4%	−1.4%

Union Membership

Percentage Union Members: 8.3%
Earnings Benefit of Union Membership: −10.7%

Veteran Status

Percentage Who Have Been on Active Duty: 4.9%
Earnings Benefit of Veteran Status: 9.6%

19-1022 Microbiologists

Investigate the growth, structure, development, and other characteristics of microscopic organisms such as bacteria, algae, or fungi. Includes medical microbiologists who study the relationship between organisms and disease or the effects of antibiotics on microorganisms.

- Education or Training Required: Doctoral degree
- Job Growth: 17.2%
- Annual Openings: 1,000
- Self-Employed: 2.9%
- Part-Time: 12.3%

NATIONAL WAGE FIGURES (ANNUAL)

Beginning	25th Percentile	Median	Mean	75th Percentile	90th Percentile
$35,460	$43,850	$57,980	$65,200	$80,550	$108,270

Median Wages for Industries Employing Largest Numbers (Annual)

Industry	Median Income
Computer and Electronic Product Manufacturing	$67,930
Management of Companies and Enterprises	$65,180
Federal, State, and Local Government	$64,460
Miscellaneous Manufacturing	$61,880
Professional, Scientific, and Technical Services	$59,910
Hospitals	$58,350
Chemical Manufacturing	$55,910
Merchant Wholesalers, Nondurable Goods	$53,120
Food Manufacturing	$49,740
Administrative and Support Services	$47,190

Median Wages for States (Annual)

AK	no data	KY	$43,350	NY	$61,460
AL	$52,630	LA	$66,730	OH	$54,460
AR	$52,330	MA	$51,480	OK	$43,380
AZ	$65,550	MD	$90,500	OR	$46,920
CA	$69,840	ME	$52,780	PA	no data
CO	$52,500	MI	$53,010	RI	no data
CT	$52,710	MN	$49,760	SC	$47,410
DC	$80,970	MO	$54,800	SD	no data
DE	$54,190	MS	$51,610	TN	$48,510
FL	$49,660	MT	$52,510	TX	$43,300
GA	$74,680	NC	$51,860	UT	$45,910
HI	$51,580	ND	no data	VA	$46,420
IA	$58,630	NE	$55,210	VT	no data
ID	$45,980	NH	$65,250	WA	$53,780
IL	$62,000	NJ	$55,890	WI	$47,300
IN	$45,980	NM	no data	WV	$35,770
KS	$40,440	NV	$54,860	WY	no data

Median Wages for the Largest Metropolitan Areas (Annual)

AZ: Phoenix	$62,070	MI: Detroit	$54,080
CA: Los Angeles	$64,950	MN: Minneapolis	$49,750
CA: Riverside	$64,090	MO: Kansas City	$44,890
CA: Sacramento	$56,650	MO: St. Louis	$54,160
CA: San Diego	$73,360	NV: Las Vegas	no data
CA: San Francisco	$77,040	NY: New York	$57,600
CO: Denver	$59,830	OH: Cincinnati	$76,120
DC: Washington	$84,600	OH: Cleveland	no data
FL: Miami	$52,000	OH: Columbus	$54,670
FL: Orlando	no data	OR: Portland	$47,000
FL: Tampa	no data	PA: Philadelphia	no data
GA: Atlanta	$75,340	PA: Pittsburgh	$58,630
IL: Chicago	$62,740	TX: Dallas	$45,510
MA: Boston	$50,710	TX: Houston	$42,230
MD: Baltimore	$95,990	WA: Seattle	$54,580

FACTORS THAT MAY AFFECT EARNINGS

Educational Attainment of Workers and Effect on Earnings

Figures are based on a group of occupations: Life Scientists

	Percent at Level	Effect on Earnings
Less than High School	—	—
Some High School	—	—
High School or Equivalent	3.9%	−32.4%
Some College but No Degree	3.4%	−40.6%
Associate Degree	5.3%	−28.2%
Bachelor's Degree	35.0%	−13.7%
Master's Degree	21.0%	0.5%
Doctoral Degree	23.5%	29.2%
First Professional Degree	6.4%	36.0%

Flexibility of Earnings

Average Hours Worked: 39
Workers with a Varying Number of Hours: 2.3%
Workers Earning Some Overtime Pay, Tips, or Commissions: 4.8%
Earnings Benefit of Working Overtime: 5.3%

Gender

	Male	Female
Percent	53.4%	46.6%
Effect on Earnings	3.4%	−1.4%

Union Membership

Percentage Union Members: 8.3%
Earnings Benefit of Union Membership: −10.7%

Veteran Status

Percentage Who Have Been on Active Duty: 4.9%
Earnings Benefit of Veteran Status: 9.6%

19-1023 Zoologists and Wildlife Biologists

Study the origins, behavior, diseases, genetics, and life processes of animals and wildlife. May specialize in wildlife research and management, including the collection and analysis of biological data to determine the environmental effects of present and potential use of land and water areas.

- Education or Training Required: Bachelor's degree
- Job Growth: 13.0%
- Annual Openings: 1,000
- Self-Employed: 2.5%
- Part-Time: 12.3%

NATIONAL WAGE FIGURES (ANNUAL)

Beginning	25th Percentile	Median	Mean	75th Percentile	90th Percentile
$32,800	$41,400	$53,300	$56,120	$67,200	$84,580

Median Wages for Industries Employing Largest Numbers (Annual)

Industry	Median Income
Professional, Scientific, and Technical Services	$57,980
Federal, State, and Local Government	$53,850
Educational Services	$44,120
Religious, Grantmaking, Civic, Professional, and Similar Organizations	$42,900
Museums, Historical Sites, and Similar Institutions	$36,510

Median Wages for States (Annual)

State	Wage	State	Wage	State	Wage
AK	$55,270	KY	no data	NY	$54,510
AL	$49,340	LA	$53,690	OH	$45,020
AR	$52,100	MA	$75,770	OK	$45,360
AZ	$58,240	MD	$80,330	OR	$53,690
CA	$59,350	ME	$48,810	PA	$37,340
CO	$52,030	MI	$56,090	RI	$61,280
CT	$68,420	MN	no data	SC	$47,690
DC	$90,890	MO	$43,530	SD	$53,880
DE	no data	MS	$54,930	TN	$53,350
FL	$45,550	MT	$47,890	TX	$54,810
GA	$42,570	NC	$48,660	UT	$45,780
HI	$58,130	ND	$53,870	VA	$47,940
IA	$55,360	NE	$43,540	VT	$54,140
ID	$47,850	NH	$45,920	WA	$56,900
IL	$51,330	NJ	$48,650	WI	$46,620
IN	$59,900	NM	$52,830	WV	$42,270
KS	no data	NV	$55,270	WY	$45,370

Median Wages for the Largest Metropolitan Areas (Annual)

Area	Wage	Area	Wage
AZ: Phoenix	$63,310	MI: Detroit	$45,020
CA: Los Angeles	$49,490	MN: Minneapolis	$43,830
CA: Riverside	$60,520	MO: Kansas City	$44,360
CA: Sacramento	$57,330	MO: St. Louis	$41,390
CA: San Diego	$58,830	NV: Las Vegas	$54,610
CA: San Francisco	$60,670	NY: New York	$45,500
CO: Denver	$54,040	OH: Cincinnati	no data
DC: Washington	$80,510	OH: Cleveland	no data
FL: Miami	$51,650	OH: Columbus	no data
FL: Orlando	$52,080	OR: Portland	$57,690
FL: Tampa	$45,560	PA: Philadelphia	$30,740
GA: Atlanta	$34,950	PA: Pittsburgh	no data
IL: Chicago	no data	TX: Dallas	$50,790
MA: Boston	$77,410	TX: Houston	$60,320
MD: Baltimore	$73,850	WA: Seattle	$57,310

FACTORS THAT MAY AFFECT EARNINGS

Educational Attainment of Workers and Effect on Earnings

Figures are based on a group of occupations: Life Scientists

	Percent at Level	Effect on Earnings
Less than High School	—	—
Some High School	—	—
High School or Equivalent	3.9%	−32.4%
Some College but No Degree	3.4%	−40.6%
Associate Degree	5.3%	−28.2%
Bachelor's Degree	35.0%	−13.7%
Master's Degree	21.0%	0.5%
Doctoral Degree	23.5%	29.2%
First Professional Degree	6.4%	36.0%

Flexibility of Earnings

Average Hours Worked: 39
Workers with a Varying Number of Hours: 2.3%
Workers Earning Some Overtime Pay, Tips, or Commissions: 4.8%
Earnings Benefit of Working Overtime: 5.3%

Gender

	Male	Female
Percent	53.4%	46.6%
Effect on Earnings	3.4%	−1.4%

Union Membership

Percentage Union Members: 8.3%
Earnings Benefit of Union Membership: −10.7%

Veteran Status

Percentage Who Have Been on Active Duty: 4.9%
Earnings Benefit of Veteran Status: 9.6%

19-1029 Biological Scientists, All Other

All biological scientists not listed separately.

- Education or Training Required: Bachelor's degree
- Job Growth: 17.0%
- Annual Openings: 3,000
- Self-Employed: 2.6%
- Part-Time: 12.3%

NATIONAL WAGE FIGURES (ANNUAL)

Beginning	25th Percentile	Median	Mean	75th Percentile	90th Percentile
$34,300	$46,920	$60,940	$63,560	$75,810	$95,130

Median Wages for Industries Employing Largest Numbers (Annual)

Industry	Median Income
Computer and Electronic Product Manufacturing	$79,180
Professional, Scientific, and Technical Services	$68,370
Chemical Manufacturing	$63,650
Federal, State, and Local Government	$62,320
Ambulatory Health Care Services	$58,960
Hospitals	$57,820
Miscellaneous Manufacturing	$54,310
Educational Services	$43,590
Religious, Grantmaking, Civic, Professional, and Similar Organizations	$38,490
Museums, Historical Sites, and Similar Institutions	$37,990

Median Wages for States (Annual)

AK	$67,480	KY	$55,090	NY	$61,460
AL	$58,420	LA	$61,020	OH	$58,250
AR	$62,170	MA	$73,100	OK	$60,630
AZ	$59,250	MD	$73,840	OR	$59,450
CA	$59,200	ME	no data	PA	$62,010
CO	$60,890	MI	$56,840	RI	$65,650
CT	no data	MN	$60,490	SC	$58,150
DC	no data	MO	$57,240	SD	$51,120
DE	$52,650	MS	$65,430	TN	$62,510
FL	$44,630	MT	$56,630	TX	$58,520
GA	$57,010	NC	$65,120	UT	$57,900
HI	$65,130	ND	$55,260	VA	$61,220
IA	$58,840	NE	$64,830	VT	$57,200
ID	$60,090	NH	$65,330	WA	$65,840
IL	$64,950	NJ	$74,140	WI	$45,320
IN	$60,980	NM	$60,420	WV	$61,600
KS	$57,400	NV	$57,680	WY	$58,590

Median Wages for the Largest Metropolitan Areas (Annual)

AZ: Phoenix	no data	MI: Detroit	$55,900
CA: Los Angeles	$60,390	MN: Minneapolis	$70,300
CA: Riverside	$58,200	MO: Kansas City	$60,360
CA: Sacramento	$64,770	MO: St. Louis	$59,310
CA: San Diego	$60,610	NV: Las Vegas	$58,710
CA: San Francisco	$66,980	NY: New York	$63,870
CO: Denver	$69,200	OH: Cincinnati	$57,820
DC: Washington	$74,690	OH: Cleveland	no data
FL: Miami	$52,570	OH: Columbus	$49,880
FL: Orlando	$45,150	OR: Portland	$67,810
FL: Tampa	$42,540	PA: Philadelphia	$64,570
GA: Atlanta	$56,790	PA: Pittsburgh	$58,920
IL: Chicago	$61,670	TX: Dallas	$61,990
MA: Boston	$74,760	TX: Houston	$62,180
MD: Baltimore	$71,980	WA: Seattle	$72,420

FACTORS THAT MAY AFFECT EARNINGS

Educational Attainment of Workers and Effect on Earnings

Figures are based on a group of occupations: Life Scientists

	Percent at Level	Effect on Earnings
Less than High School	—	—
Some High School	—	—
High School or Equivalent	3.9%	−32.4%
Some College but No Degree	3.4%	−40.6%
Associate Degree	5.3%	−28.2%
Bachelor's Degree	35.0%	−13.7%
Master's Degree	21.0%	0.5%
Doctoral Degree	23.5%	29.2%
First Professional Degree	6.4%	36.0%

Flexibility of Earnings

Average Hours Worked: 39
Workers with a Varying Number of Hours: 2.3%
Workers Earning Some Overtime Pay, Tips, or Commissions: 4.8%
Earnings Benefit of Working Overtime: 5.3%

Gender

	Male	Female
Percent	53.4%	46.6%
Effect on Earnings	3.4%	−1.4%

Union Membership

Percentage Union Members: 8.3%
Earnings Benefit of Union Membership: −10.7%

Veteran Status

Percentage Who Have Been on Active Duty: 4.9%
Earnings Benefit of Veteran Status: 9.6%

19-1031 Conservation Scientists

Manage, improve, and protect natural resources to maximize their use without damaging the environment. May conduct soil surveys and develop plans to eliminate soil erosion or to protect rangelands from fire and rodent damage. May instruct farmers, agricultural production managers, or ranchers in best ways to use crop rotation, contour plowing, or terracing to conserve soil and water; in the number and kind of livestock and forage plants best suited to particular ranges; and in range and farm improvements, such as fencing and reservoirs for stock watering.

- Education or Training Required: Bachelor's degree
- Job Growth: 6.3%
- Annual Openings: 2,000
- Self-Employed: 9.0%
- Part-Time: 12.3%

NATIONAL WAGE FIGURES (ANNUAL)

Beginning	25th Percentile	Median	Mean	75th Percentile	90th Percentile
$29,860	$40,950	$54,970	$55,410	$68,460	$80,260

Median Wages for Industries Employing Largest Numbers (Annual)

Industry	Median Income
Management of Companies and Enterprises	$67,140
Federal, State, and Local Government	$55,490
Professional, Scientific, and Technical Services	$53,550
Religious, Grantmaking, Civic, Professional, and Similar Organizations	$51,490
Educational Services	$50,140
Museums, Historical Sites, and Similar Institutions	$38,410

Median Wages for States (Annual)

AK $64,730	KY $60,550	NY $52,130
AL $63,100	LA $60,480	OH $54,040
AR $65,290	MA $56,740	OK $50,360
AZ $57,250	MD .... no data	OR $55,370
CA $62,350	ME $54,860	PA $34,550
CO $56,150	MI $61,880	RI.............. no data
CT $66,860	MN $54,960	SC............ $59,140
DC $106,760	MO $23,260	SD $51,180
DE .... no data	MS $38,290	TN $60,110
FL $63,010	MT $53,530	TX $54,980
GA $59,900	NC $47,870	UT $59,480
HI $59,720	ND $56,930	VA $66,890
IA $50,830	NE $52,480	VT $54,080
ID $58,640	NH $50,340	WA $61,260
IL $59,230	NJ $65,290	WI $56,490
IN $61,360	NM $55,840	WV $60,760
KS $62,600	NV $58,900	WY $58,200

Median Wages for the Largest Metropolitan Areas (Annual)

AZ: Phoenix $58,460	MI: Detroit $67,030
CA: Los Angeles $75,370	MN: Minneapolis $54,500
CA: Riverside $71,630	MO: Kansas City $41,940
CA: Sacramento $61,640	MO: St. Louis $34,790
CA: San Diego .... no data	NV: Las Vegas .... no data
CA: San Francisco $62,770	NY: New York $57,720
CO: Denver $52,660	OH: Cincinnati .... no data
DC: Washington $87,950	OH: Cleveland .... no data
FL: Miami $66,710	OH: Columbus .... no data
FL: Orlando .... no data	OR: Portland $64,850
FL: Tampa $76,320	PA: Philadelphia $45,550
GA: Atlanta $66,530	PA: Pittsburgh .... no data
IL: Chicago $59,240	TX: Dallas $57,690
MA: Boston $55,540	TX: Houston .... no data
MD: Baltimore .... no data	WA: Seattle $74,700

FACTORS THAT MAY AFFECT EARNINGS

Educational Attainment of Workers and Effect on Earnings

Figures are based on a group of occupations: Life Scientists

	Percent at Level	Effect on Earnings
Less than High School	—	—
Some High School	—	—
High School or Equivalent	3.9%	–32.4%
Some College but No Degree	3.4%	–40.6%
Associate Degree	5.3%	–28.2%
Bachelor's Degree	35.0%	–13.7%
Master's Degree	21.0%	0.5%
Doctoral Degree	23.5%	29.2%
First Professional Degree	6.4%	36.0%

Flexibility of Earnings

Average Hours Worked: 39
Workers with a Varying Number of Hours: 8.3%
Workers Earning Some Overtime Pay, Tips, or Commissions: 4.8%
Earnings Benefit of Working Overtime: 5.3%

Gender

	Male	Female
Percent	53.4%	46.6%
Effect on Earnings	3.4%	–1.4%

Union Membership

Percentage Union Members: 8.3%
Earnings Benefit of Union Membership: –10.7%

Veteran Status

Percentage Who Have Been on Active Duty: 4.9%
Earnings Benefit of Veteran Status: 9.6%

19-1032 Foresters

Manage forested lands for economic, recreational, and conservation purposes. May inventory the type, amount, and location of standing timber; appraise the timber's worth; negotiate the purchase; and draw up contracts for procurement. May determine how to conserve wildlife habitats, creek beds, water quality, and soil stability and how best to comply with environmental regulations. May devise plans for planting and growing new trees, monitor trees for healthy growth, and determine the best time for harvesting. Develop forest management plans for public and privately owned forested lands.

- Education or Training Required: Bachelor's degree
- Job Growth: 6.7%
- Annual Openings: 1,000
- Self-Employed: 9.1%
- Part-Time: 12.3%

NATIONAL WAGE FIGURES (ANNUAL)

Beginning	25th Percentile	Median	Mean	75th Percentile	90th Percentile
$33,490	$40,870	$51,190	$52,450	$62,290	$74,570

Median Wages for Industries Employing Largest Numbers (Annual)

Industry	Median Income
Utilities	$62,480
Forestry and Logging	$60,730
Administrative and Support Services	$59,960
Paper Manufacturing	$59,140
Management of Companies and Enterprises	$58,210
Merchant Wholesalers, Durable Goods	$57,000
Wood Product Manufacturing	$54,170
Wholesale Electronic Markets and Agents and Brokers	$54,020
Federal, State, and Local Government	$49,880
Educational Services	$45,340

Median Wages for States (Annual)

State	Wage	State	Wage	State	Wage
AK	$57,270	KY	no data	NY	$48,310
AL	$54,720	LA	$59,270	OH	$48,690
AR	$50,020	MA	$53,840	OK	$41,470
AZ	$44,260	MD	$53,290	OR	$58,300
CA	$56,180	ME	$46,310	PA	$47,410
CO	$55,190	MI	$57,680	RI	no data
CT	no data	MN	$52,770	SC	$53,180
DC	no data	MO	$44,620	SD	$47,090
DE	no data	MS	$46,920	TN	$42,000
FL	$40,520	MT	$49,590	TX	$56,010
GA	$56,010	NC	$51,850	UT	$48,400
HI	no data	ND	no data	VA	$57,020
IA	$34,860	NE	$46,070	VT	$52,610
ID	$56,350	NH	$45,270	WA	$51,580
IL	$52,080	NJ	$48,750	WI	$46,650
IN	$44,000	NM	$54,410	WV	$40,020
KS	no data	NV	$54,910	WY	$54,750

Median Wages for the Largest Metropolitan Areas (Annual)

Area	Wage	Area	Wage
AZ: Phoenix	no data	MI: Detroit	no data
CA: Los Angeles	no data	MN: Minneapolis	$53,780
CA: Riverside	$70,840	MO: Kansas City	no data
CA: Sacramento	$70,350	MO: St. Louis	$43,150
CA: San Diego	no data	NV: Las Vegas	no data
CA: San Francisco	no data	NY: New York	$46,020
CO: Denver	no data	OH: Cincinnati	no data
DC: Washington	$74,220	OH: Cleveland	no data
FL: Miami	no data	OH: Columbus	no data
FL: Orlando	no data	OR: Portland	$61,240
FL: Tampa	$47,260	PA: Philadelphia	$56,640
GA: Atlanta	no data	PA: Pittsburgh	$51,980
IL: Chicago	$57,950	TX: Dallas	no data
MA: Boston	$53,000	TX: Houston	no data
MD: Baltimore	no data	WA: Seattle	$50,740

FACTORS THAT MAY AFFECT EARNINGS

Educational Attainment of Workers and Effect on Earnings

Figures are based on a group of occupations: Life Scientists

	Percent at Level	Effect on Earnings
Less than High School	—	—
Some High School	—	—
High School or Equivalent	3.9%	−32.4%
Some College but No Degree	3.4%	−40.6%
Associate Degree	5.3%	−28.2%
Bachelor's Degree	35.0%	−13.7%
Master's Degree	21.0%	0.5%
Doctoral Degree	23.5%	29.2%
First Professional Degree	6.4%	36.0%

Flexibility of Earnings

Average Hours Worked: 39
Workers with a Varying Number of Hours: 8.3%
Workers Earning Some Overtime Pay, Tips, or Commissions: 4.8%
Earnings Benefit of Working Overtime: 5.3%

Gender

	Male	Female
Percent	53.4%	46.6%
Effect on Earnings	3.4%	−1.4%

Union Membership

Percentage Union Members: 8.3%
Earnings Benefit of Union Membership: −10.7%

Veteran Status

Percentage Who Have Been on Active Duty: 4.9%
Earnings Benefit of Veteran Status: 9.6%

19-1041 Epidemiologists

Investigate and describe the determinants and distribution of disease, disability, and other health outcomes and develop the means for prevention and control.

- Education or Training Required: Master's degree
- Job Growth: 26.2%
- Annual Openings: 1,000
- Self-Employed: 0.4%
- Part-Time: 12.3%

NATIONAL WAGE FIGURES (ANNUAL)

Beginning	25th Percentile	Median	Mean	75th Percentile	90th Percentile
$36,920	$45,220	$56,670	$60,290	$71,080	$87,300

Median Wages for Industries Employing Largest Numbers (Annual)

Industry	Median Income
Ambulatory Health Care Services	$73,090
Professional, Scientific, and Technical Services	$69,050
Hospitals	$62,380
Federal, State, and Local Government	$52,990
Educational Services	$46,530

Median Wages for States (Annual)

AK	no data	KY	$44,910	NY	no data
AL	$57,000	LA	$45,030	OH	$54,010
AR	$48,180	MA	$60,840	OK	$57,180
AZ	$43,750	MD	$58,930	OR	$58,130
CA	$69,930	ME	no data	PA	$62,730
CO	$63,050	MI	$57,550	RI	no data
CT	$67,940	MN	no data	SC	no data
DC	$64,640	MO	$44,480	SD	no data
DE	no data	MS	$30,160	TN	$60,320
FL	$54,210	MT	no data	TX	$43,610
GA	$58,480	NC	$59,170	UT	$49,170
HI	no data	ND	no data	VA	$60,090
IA	no data	NE	$51,730	VT	no data
ID	no data	NH	no data	WA	$63,350
IL	no data	NJ	$58,850	WI	$58,410
IN	no data	NM	$47,450	WV	no data
KS	$57,590	NV	no data	WY	no data

Median Wages for the Largest Metropolitan Areas (Annual)

AZ: Phoenix	no data	MI: Detroit	$57,290
CA: Los Angeles	$70,570	MN: Minneapolis	no data
CA: Riverside	no data	MO: Kansas City	$70,640
CA: Sacramento	no data	MO: St. Louis	$54,820
CA: San Diego	no data	NV: Las Vegas	no data
CA: San Francisco	$85,170	NY: New York	$71,150
CO: Denver	no data	OH: Cincinnati	no data
DC: Washington	$65,410	OH: Cleveland	no data
FL: Miami	no data	OH: Columbus	no data
FL: Orlando	no data	OR: Portland	$59,220
FL: Tampa	no data	PA: Philadelphia	$59,510
GA: Atlanta	$58,710	PA: Pittsburgh	no data
IL: Chicago	no data	TX: Dallas	$45,690
MA: Boston	$61,160	TX: Houston	no data
MD: Baltimore	$58,560	WA: Seattle	$59,240

FACTORS THAT MAY AFFECT EARNINGS

Educational Attainment of Workers and Effect on Earnings

Figures are based on a group of occupations: Life Scientists

	Percent at Level	Effect on Earnings
Less than High School	—	—
Some High School	—	—
High School or Equivalent	3.9%	−32.4%
Some College but No Degree	3.4%	−40.6%
Associate Degree	5.3%	−28.2%
Bachelor's Degree	35.0%	−13.7%
Master's Degree	21.0%	0.5%
Doctoral Degree	23.5%	29.2%
First Professional Degree	6.4%	36.0%

Flexibility of Earnings

Average Hours Worked: 39
Workers with a Varying Number of Hours: 4.2%
Workers Earning Some Overtime Pay, Tips, or Commissions: 4.8%
Earnings Benefit of Working Overtime: 8.4%

Gender

	Male	Female
Percent	54.6%	45.4%
Effect on Earnings	21.9%	−13.4%

Union Membership

Percentage Union Members: 8.3%
Earnings Benefit of Union Membership: −10.7%

Veteran Status

Percentage Who Have Been on Active Duty: 4.9%
Earnings Benefit of Veteran Status: 9.6%

19-1042 Medical Scientists, Except Epidemiologists

Conduct research dealing with the understanding of human diseases and the improvement of human health. Engage in clinical investigation or other research, production, technical writing, or related activities.

- Education or Training Required: Doctoral degree
- Job Growth: 34.1%
- Annual Openings: 15,000
- Self-Employed: 0.4%
- Part-Time: 12.3%

NATIONAL WAGE FIGURES (ANNUAL)

Beginning	25th Percentile	Median	Mean	75th Percentile	90th Percentile
$35,490	$44,830	$61,680	$70,350	$88,130	$117,520

Median Wages for Industries Employing Largest Numbers (Annual)

Industry	Median Income
Wholesale Electronic Markets and Agents and Brokers	$92,680
Federal, State, and Local Government	$87,190
Merchant Wholesalers, Nondurable Goods	$82,810
Chemical Manufacturing	$82,590
Computer and Electronic Product Manufacturing	$78,900
Miscellaneous Manufacturing	$73,520
Professional, Scientific, and Technical Services	$70,490
Ambulatory Health Care Services	$68,400
Management of Companies and Enterprises	$64,820
Administrative and Support Services	$62,340

Median Wages for States (Annual)

State	Wage	State	Wage	State	Wage
AK	no data	KY	no data	NY	$59,840
AL	$46,610	LA	$56,170	OH	$52,670
AR	$64,950	MA	$76,770	OK	$42,480
AZ	$60,860	MD	$76,770	OR	no data
CA	$73,770	ME	no data	PA	$60,320
CO	$71,740	MI	$51,950	RI	$49,980
CT	$80,950	MN	$54,740	SC	$56,530
DC	$68,530	MO	$58,190	SD	$50,860
DE	no data	MS	no data	TN	$58,300
FL	$65,500	MT	no data	TX	$44,120
GA	$76,900	NC	no data	UT	$55,010
HI	$58,360	ND	no data	VA	$61,600
IA	no data	NE	$37,590	VT	$74,080
ID	$35,580	NH	no data	WA	$60,570
IL	$56,590	NJ	$81,060	WI	$46,270
IN	no data	NM	no data	WV	$83,710
KS	$50,480	NV	$83,380	WY	no data

Median Wages for the Largest Metropolitan Areas (Annual)

Area	Wage	Area	Wage
AZ: Phoenix	$63,130	MI: Detroit	$60,750
CA: Los Angeles	$66,580	MN: Minneapolis	$54,490
CA: Riverside	$71,480	MO: Kansas City	no data
CA: Sacramento	$77,360	MO: St. Louis	$58,890
CA: San Diego	$57,370	NV: Las Vegas	$74,170
CA: San Francisco	$82,440	NY: New York	$73,680
CO: Denver	$63,070	OH: Cincinnati	$60,210
DC: Washington	$84,540	OH: Cleveland	$60,910
FL: Miami	$64,330	OH: Columbus	no data
FL: Orlando	$81,230	OR: Portland	no data
FL: Tampa	$53,670	PA: Philadelphia	$78,630
GA: Atlanta	$65,180	PA: Pittsburgh	no data
IL: Chicago	$59,430	TX: Dallas	no data
MA: Boston	no data	TX: Houston	no data
MD: Baltimore	$46,340	WA: Seattle	$56,960

FACTORS THAT MAY AFFECT EARNINGS

Educational Attainment of Workers and Effect on Earnings

Figures are based on a group of occupations: Life Scientists

	Percent at Level	Effect on Earnings
Less than High School	—	—
Some High School	—	—
High School or Equivalent	3.9%	−32.4%
Some College but No Degree	3.4%	−40.6%
Associate Degree	5.3%	−28.2%
Bachelor's Degree	35.0%	−13.7%
Master's Degree	21.0%	0.5%
Doctoral Degree	23.5%	29.2%
First Professional Degree	6.4%	36.0%

Flexibility of Earnings

Average Hours Worked: 39
Workers with a Varying Number of Hours: 4.2%
Workers Earning Some Overtime Pay, Tips, or Commissions: 4.8%
Earnings Benefit of Working Overtime: 8.4%

Gender

	Male	Female
Percent	54.6%	45.4%
Effect on Earnings	21.9%	−13.4%

Union Membership

Percentage Union Members: 8.3%
Earnings Benefit of Union Membership: −10.7%

Veteran Status

Percentage Who Have Been on Active Duty: 4.9%
Earnings Benefit of Veteran Status: 9.6%

19-1099 Life Scientists, All Other

All life scientists not listed separately.

- Education or Training Required: Bachelor's degree
- Job Growth: 20.6%
- Annual Openings: 3,000
- Self-Employed: 0.9%
- Part-Time: 12.3%

NATIONAL WAGE FIGURES (ANNUAL)

Beginning	25th Percentile	Median	Mean	75th Percentile	90th Percentile
$32,950	$41,820	$56,970	$64,480	$79,160	$104,780

Median Wages for Industries Employing Largest Numbers (Annual)

Industry	Median Income
Merchant Wholesalers, Durable Goods	$69,410
Professional, Scientific, and Technical Services	$66,330
Merchant Wholesalers, Nondurable Goods	$66,320
Federal, State, and Local Government	$62,360
Hospitals	$57,220
Chemical Manufacturing	$56,900
Amusement, Gambling, and Recreation Industries	$51,210
Educational Services	$46,570
Ambulatory Health Care Services	$46,100
Administrative and Support Services	$44,660

Median Wages for States (Annual)

AK	no data	KY	$47,040	NY	$53,250
AL	$46,480	LA	no data	OH	$63,230
AR	no data	MA	$69,140	OK	no data
AZ	$66,930	MD	$65,380	OR	$59,110
CA	$67,120	ME	no data	PA	$46,130
CO	no data	MI	$58,790	RI	$46,300
CT	$65,630	MN	$48,900	SC	$44,420
DC	$67,700	MO	$54,600	SD	no data
DE	no data	MS	no data	TN	$60,400
FL	$50,500	MT	no data	TX	$39,970
GA	$80,300	NC	$65,270	UT	no data
HI	$50,820	ND	no data	VA	$62,700
IA	$43,560	NE	$60,810	VT	no data
ID	$42,780	NH	$51,590	WA	$56,550
IL	$55,640	NJ	$67,820	WI	$45,990
IN	$54,980	NM	more than $145,600	WV	no data
KS	$30,300	NV	$54,170	WY	no data

Median Wages for the Largest Metropolitan Areas (Annual)

AZ: Phoenix	$65,850	MI: Detroit	$44,190
CA: Los Angeles	$58,100	MN: Minneapolis	$62,150
CA: Riverside	$59,350	MO: Kansas City	no data
CA: Sacramento	$84,140	MO: St. Louis	$55,060
CA: San Diego	$72,280	NV: Las Vegas	no data
CA: San Francisco	$66,610	NY: New York	$65,070
CO: Denver	no data	OH: Cincinnati	$63,810
DC: Washington	$65,890	OH: Cleveland	no data
FL: Miami	$54,190	OH: Columbus	no data
FL: Orlando	$47,520	OR: Portland	$61,760
FL: Tampa	$51,140	PA: Philadelphia	$52,140
GA: Atlanta	$75,450	PA: Pittsburgh	$41,200
IL: Chicago	$55,600	TX: Dallas	$39,210
MA: Boston	no data	TX: Houston	no data
MD: Baltimore	$68,470	WA: Seattle	no data

FACTORS THAT MAY AFFECT EARNINGS

Educational Attainment of Workers and Effect on Earnings

Figures are based on a group of occupations: Life Scientists

	Percent at Level	Effect on Earnings
Less than High School	—	—
Some High School	—	—
High School or Equivalent	3.9%	−32.4%
Some College but No Degree	3.4%	−40.6%
Associate Degree	5.3%	−28.2%
Bachelor's Degree	35.0%	−13.7%
Master's Degree	21.0%	0.5%
Doctoral Degree	23.5%	29.2%
First Professional Degree	6.4%	36.0%

Flexibility of Earnings

Average Hours Worked: 39
Workers with a Varying Number of Hours: 4.2%
Workers Earning Some Overtime Pay, Tips, or Commissions: 4.8%
Earnings Benefit of Working Overtime: 5.3%

Gender

	Male	Female
Percent	60.9%	39.1%
Effect on Earnings	3.4%	−1.4%

Union Membership

Percentage Union Members: 8.3%
Earnings Benefit of Union Membership: −10.7%

Veteran Status

Percentage Who Have Been on Active Duty: 4.9%
Earnings Benefit of Veteran Status: 9.6%

19-2000 Physical Scientists

19-2011 Astronomers

Observe, research, and interpret celestial and astronomical phenomena to increase basic knowledge and apply such information to practical problems.

- Education or Training Required: Doctoral degree
- Job Growth: 10.5%
- Annual Openings: Fewer than 500
- Self-Employed: 0.0%
- Part-Time: 12.4%

NATIONAL WAGE FIGURES (ANNUAL)

Beginning	25th Percentile	Median	Mean	75th Percentile	90th Percentile
$44,590	$62,050	$95,740	$95,000	$125,420	more than $145,600

Median Wages for Industries Employing Largest Numbers (Annual)

Industry	Median Income
Federal, State, and Local Government	$118,810
Professional, Scientific, and Technical Services	$95,620
Educational Services	$68,390

Median Wages for States (Annual)

AK	no data	KY	no data	NY	no data
AL	no data	LA	no data	OH	no data
AR	no data	MA	$118,350	OK	no data
AZ	no data	MD	no data	OR	no data
CA	no data	ME	no data	PA	no data
CO	$92,080	MI	no data	RI	no data
CT	no data	MN	no data	SC	no data
DC	no data	MO	no data	SD	no data
DE	no data	MS	no data	TN	no data
FL	no data	MT	no data	TX	$71,060
GA	no data	NC	no data	UT	no data
HI	$80,590	ND	no data	VA	$121,880
IA	no data	NE	no data	VT	no data
ID	no data	NH	no data	WA	no data
IL	no data	NJ	no data	WI	no data
IN	no data	NM	no data	WV	no data
KS	no data	NV	no data	WY	no data

Median Wages for the Largest Metropolitan Areas (Annual)

AZ: Phoenix	no data	MI: Detroit	no data
CA: Los Angeles	no data	MN: Minneapolis	no data
CA: Riverside	no data	MO: Kansas City	no data
CA: Sacramento	no data	MO: St. Louis	no data
CA: San Diego	no data	NV: Las Vegas	no data
CA: San Francisco	no data	NY: New York	no data
CO: Denver	no data	OH: Cincinnati	no data
DC: Washington	$120,020	OH: Cleveland	no data
FL: Miami	no data	OH: Columbus	no data
FL: Orlando	no data	OR: Portland	no data
FL: Tampa	no data	PA: Philadelphia	no data
GA: Atlanta	no data	PA: Pittsburgh	no data
IL: Chicago	no data	TX: Dallas	no data
MA: Boston	$119,720	TX: Houston	no data
MD: Baltimore	no data	WA: Seattle	no data

FACTORS THAT MAY AFFECT EARNINGS

Educational Attainment of Workers and Effect on Earnings

Figures are based on a group of occupations: Physical Scientists

	Percent at Level	Effect on Earnings
Less than High School	—	—
Some High School	—	—
High School or Equivalent	—	—
Some College but No Degree	3.3%	−23.5%
Associate Degree	3.9%	−40.9%
Bachelor's Degree	38.9%	−8.1%
Master's Degree	23.6%	2.6%
Doctoral Degree	23.6%	19.8%
First Professional Degree	3.9%	19.9%

Flexibility of Earnings

Average Hours Worked: 39
Workers with a Varying Number of Hours: 4.2%
Workers Earning Some Overtime Pay, Tips, or Commissions: 6.8%
Earnings Benefit of Working Overtime: −6.9%

Gender

	Male	Female
Percent	66.6%	33.4%
Effect on Earnings	5.1%	−8.4%

Union Membership

Percentage Union Members: 8.2%
Earnings Benefit of Union Membership: −16.7%

Veteran Status

Percentage Who Have Been on Active Duty: 8.8%
Earnings Benefit of Veteran Status: 14.3%

19-2012 Physicists

Conduct research into the phases of physical phenomena, develop theories and laws on the basis of observation and experiments, and devise methods to apply laws and theories to industry and other fields.

- Education or Training Required: Doctoral degree
- Job Growth: 7.0%
- Annual Openings: 1,000
- Self-Employed: 0.0%
- Part-Time: 12.4%

NATIONAL WAGE FIGURES (ANNUAL)

Beginning	25th Percentile	Median	Mean	75th Percentile	90th Percentile
$52,070	$72,910	$94,240	$95,580	$117,080	$143,570

Median Wages for Industries Employing Largest Numbers (Annual)

Industry	Median Income
Ambulatory Health Care Services	$122,660
Hospitals	$120,020
Chemical Manufacturing	$98,390
Miscellaneous Manufacturing	$98,320
Professional, Scientific, and Technical Services	$97,380
Federal, State, and Local Government	$97,090
Computer and Electronic Product Manufacturing	$95,510
Utilities	$81,790
Fabricated Metal Product Manufacturing	$64,920
Educational Services	$58,350

Median Wages for States (Annual)

AK	no data	KY	$89,310	NY	$94,000
AL	$100,710	LA	$102,850	OH	$89,720
AR	$45,950	MA	$100,180	OK	$107,620
AZ	$80,610	MD	$108,450	OR	$117,140
CA	$95,140	ME	$90,520	PA	$98,620
CO	$86,050	MI	$71,380	RI	$95,470
CT	$59,360	MN	$94,400	SC	$69,640
DC	$109,780	MO	$86,260	SD	no data
DE	$69,930	MS	$87,010	TN	$82,670
FL	$93,370	MT	no data	TX	$83,910
GA	$93,230	NC	no data	UT	no data
HI	$87,140	ND	no data	VA	$94,360
IA	$81,820	NE	$84,400	VT	no data
ID	$92,660	NH	$89,220	WA	$78,100
IL	$97,270	NJ	$103,450	WI	$45,850
IN	$96,810	NM	no data	WV	no data
KS	$53,810	NV	$82,720	WY	no data

Median Wages for the Largest Metropolitan Areas (Annual)

AZ: Phoenix	no data	MI: Detroit	$100,890
CA: Los Angeles	$103,110	MN: Minneapolis	$90,530
CA: Riverside	$96,150	MO: Kansas City	no data
CA: Sacramento	$84,670	MO: St. Louis	$84,650
CA: San Diego	$85,760	NV: Las Vegas	$94,050
CA: San Francisco	$99,040	NY: New York	$100,110
CO: Denver	no data	OH: Cincinnati	$84,120
DC: Washington	$112,130	OH: Cleveland	$98,440
FL: Miami	$95,510	OH: Columbus	$91,470
FL: Orlando	no data	OR: Portland	more than $145,600
FL: Tampa	$89,370	PA: Philadelphia	$91,720
GA: Atlanta	no data	PA: Pittsburgh	no data
IL: Chicago	$98,070	TX: Dallas	$101,480
MA: Boston	$99,700	TX: Houston	$89,420
MD: Baltimore	$100,340	WA: Seattle	no data

FACTORS THAT MAY AFFECT EARNINGS

Educational Attainment of Workers and Effect on Earnings

Figures are based on a group of occupations: Physical Scientists

	Percent at Level	Effect on Earnings
Less than High School	—	—
Some High School	—	—
High School or Equivalent	—	—
Some College but No Degree	3.3%	−23.5%
Associate Degree	3.9%	−40.9%
Bachelor's Degree	38.9%	−8.1%
Master's Degree	23.6%	2.6%
Doctoral Degree	23.6%	19.8%
First Professional Degree	3.9%	19.9%

Flexibility of Earnings

Average Hours Worked: 39
Workers with a Varying Number of Hours: 4.2%
Workers Earning Some Overtime Pay, Tips, or Commissions: 6.8%
Earnings Benefit of Working Overtime: −6.9%

Gender

	Male	Female
Percent	66.6%	33.4%
Effect on Earnings	5.1%	−8.4%

Union Membership

Percentage Union Members: 8.2%
Earnings Benefit of Union Membership: −16.7%

Veteran Status

Percentage Who Have Been on Active Duty: 8.8%
Earnings Benefit of Veteran Status: 14.3%

19-2021 Atmospheric and Space Scientists

Investigate atmospheric phenomena and interpret meteorological data gathered by surface and air stations, satellites, and radar to prepare reports and forecasts for public and other uses.

- Education or Training Required: Bachelor's degree
- Job Growth: 16.5%
- Annual Openings: 1,000
- Self-Employed: 0.0%
- Part-Time: 66.7%

NATIONAL WAGE FIGURES (ANNUAL)

Beginning	25th Percentile	Median	Mean	75th Percentile	90th Percentile
$39,090	$55,530	$77,150	$77,810	$96,490	$119,700

Median Wages for Industries Employing Largest Numbers (Annual)

Industry	Median Income
Computer and Electronic Product Manufacturing	$99,860
Federal, State, and Local Government	$85,100
Professional, Scientific, and Technical Services	$70,900
Broadcasting (Except Internet)	$65,900
Educational Services	$64,570

Median Wages for States (Annual)

State	Wage	State	Wage	State	Wage
AK	$93,110	KY	$78,460	NY	$67,580
AL	$72,930	LA	$76,760	OH	$80,220
AR	no data	MA	$57,820	OK	$67,990
AZ	$78,970	MD	$91,300	OR	$84,140
CA	$91,750	ME	no data	PA	$78,270
CO	$77,480	MI	$73,430	RI	no data
CT	$68,830	MN	$56,060	SC	$73,710
DC	no data	MO	$82,300	SD	$63,940
DE	no data	MS	$66,970	TN	$73,840
FL	$84,930	MT	$79,010	TX	$75,650
GA	$67,630	NC	$85,620	UT	$76,220
HI	$90,200	ND	$68,390	VA	$80,560
IA	$68,750	NE	$75,640	VT	no data
ID	$80,080	NH	$53,560	WA	$70,840
IL	$40,560	NJ	$92,270	WI	$61,180
IN	$109,700	NM	no data	WV	no data
KS	$74,840	NV	$74,920	WY	no data

Median Wages for the Largest Metropolitan Areas (Annual)

Area	Wage	Area	Wage
AZ: Phoenix	no data	MI: Detroit	no data
CA: Los Angeles	no data	MN: Minneapolis	$54,050
CA: Riverside	no data	MO: Kansas City	$87,450
CA: Sacramento	$78,240	MO: St. Louis	no data
CA: San Diego	$73,270	NV: Las Vegas	no data
CA: San Francisco	$78,700	NY: New York	$91,660
CO: Denver	$71,630	OH: Cincinnati	no data
DC: Washington	$93,070	OH: Cleveland	no data
FL: Miami	$89,170	OH: Columbus	no data
FL: Orlando	no data	OR: Portland	$88,120
FL: Tampa	$79,030	PA: Philadelphia	no data
GA: Atlanta	$66,700	PA: Pittsburgh	no data
IL: Chicago	$40,430	TX: Dallas	$79,330
MA: Boston	$56,940	TX: Houston	no data
MD: Baltimore	$83,720	WA: Seattle	$69,620

FACTORS THAT MAY AFFECT EARNINGS

Educational Attainment of Workers and Effect on Earnings

	Percent at Level	Effect on Earnings
Less than High School	—	—
Some High School	—	—
High School or Equivalent	—	—
Some College but No Degree	—	—
Associate Degree	—	—
Bachelor's Degree	46.2%	21.3%
Master's Degree	—	—
Doctoral Degree	—	—
First Professional Degree	—	—

Figures do not total 100% because some levels have a very small sample size.

Flexibility of Earnings

Average Hours Worked: 33
Workers with a Varying Number of Hours: 9.8%
Workers Earning Some Overtime Pay, Tips, or Commissions: 7.7%
Earnings Benefit of Working Overtime: −6.9%

Gender

	Male	Female
Percent	80.0%	20.0%
Effect on Earnings	6.1%	−24.4%

Union Membership

Percentage Union Members: 15.4%
Earnings Benefit of Union Membership: −16.7%

Veteran Status

Percentage Who Have Been on Active Duty: 8.8%
Earnings Benefit of Veteran Status: 14.3%

19-2031 Chemists

Conduct qualitative and quantitative chemical analyses or chemical experiments in laboratories for quality or process control or to develop new products or knowledge.

- Education or Training Required: Bachelor's degree
- Job Growth: 7.3%
- Annual Openings: 5,000
- Self-Employed: 0.4%
- Part-Time: 12.4%

NATIONAL WAGE FIGURES (ANNUAL)

Beginning	25th Percentile	Median	Mean	75th Percentile	90th Percentile
$35,480	$44,780	$59,870	$66,040	$82,610	$106,310

Median Wages for Industries Employing Largest Numbers (Annual)

Industry	Median Income
Federal, State, and Local Government	$72,530
Management of Companies and Enterprises	$68,330
Paper Manufacturing	$64,500
Merchant Wholesalers, Nondurable Goods	$64,430
Utilities	$64,200
Petroleum and Coal Products Manufacturing	$63,870
Plastics and Rubber Products Manufacturing	$62,840
Computer and Electronic Product Manufacturing	$62,190
Miscellaneous Manufacturing	$60,360
Chemical Manufacturing	$59,980

Median Wages for States (Annual)

AK $70,230	KY $51,010	NY $61,770
AL $51,930	LA $63,540	OH $57,390
AR $61,020	MA $73,020	OK $53,950
AZ $52,560	MD $85,290	OR $48,510
CA $68,780	ME $47,040	PA $55,550
CO $60,200	MI $53,890	RI $68,880
CT $64,580	MN $59,980	SC $60,860
DC $87,190	MO $56,070	SD $44,530
DE $72,440	MS $53,420	TN $51,840
FL $48,310	MT $39,060	TX $52,260
GA $59,290	NC $55,510	UT $54,410
HI $54,900	ND $52,920	VA $67,650
IA $51,030	NE $46,110	VT $49,180
ID $82,080	NH $58,700	WA $65,290
IL $56,300	NJ $62,000	WI $47,120
IN $72,810	NM $48,000	WV $55,090
KS $52,990	NV $58,280	WY $46,210

Median Wages for the Largest Metropolitan Areas (Annual)

AZ: Phoenix $52,280	MI: Detroit $51,580
CA: Los Angeles $66,380	MN: Minneapolis $60,660
CA: Riverside $62,100	MO: Kansas City $60,220
CA: Sacramento $67,980	MO: St. Louis $57,030
CA: San Diego $75,870	NV: Las Vegas $63,380
CA: San Francisco $66,470	NY: New York $62,730
CO: Denver $58,640	OH: Cincinnati $63,300
DC: Washington $91,770	OH: Cleveland $55,860
FL: Miami $48,360	OH: Columbus $59,050
FL: Orlando $49,380	OR: Portland $50,360
FL: Tampa $52,280	PA: Philadelphia $62,690
GA: Atlanta $59,110	PA: Pittsburgh $65,200
IL: Chicago $56,610	TX: Dallas $56,170
MA: Boston $74,110	TX: Houston $56,160
MD: Baltimore $67,100	WA: Seattle $58,160

FACTORS THAT MAY AFFECT EARNINGS

Educational Attainment of Workers and Effect on Earnings

Figures are based on a group of occupations: Physical Scientists

	Percent at Level	Effect on Earnings
Less than High School	—	—
Some High School	—	—
High School or Equivalent	—	—
Some College but No Degree	3.3%	−23.5%
Associate Degree	3.9%	−40.9%
Bachelor's Degree	38.9%	−8.1%
Master's Degree	23.6%	2.6%
Doctoral Degree	23.6%	19.8%
First Professional Degree	3.9%	19.9%

Flexibility of Earnings

Average Hours Worked: 39
Workers with a Varying Number of Hours: 4.2%
Workers Earning Some Overtime Pay, Tips, or Commissions: 6.8%
Earnings Benefit of Working Overtime: 2.4%

Gender

	Male	Female
Percent	65.9%	34.1%
Effect on Earnings	0.1%	—

Union Membership

Percentage Union Members: 8.2%
Earnings Benefit of Union Membership: −16.7%

Veteran Status

Percentage Who Have Been on Active Duty: 8.8%
Earnings Benefit of Veteran Status: 14.3%

19-2032 Materials Scientists

Research and study the structures and chemical properties of various natural and manmade materials, including metals, alloys, rubber, ceramics, semiconductors, polymers, and glass. Determine ways to strengthen or combine materials or develop new materials with new or specific properties for use in a variety of products and applications.

- Education or Training Required: Bachelor's degree
- Job Growth: 8.0%
- Annual Openings: Fewer than 500
- Self-Employed: 0.4%
- Part-Time: 12.4%

NATIONAL WAGE FIGURES (ANNUAL)

Beginning	25th Percentile	Median	Mean	75th Percentile	90th Percentile
$41,810	$55,170	$74,610	$77,010	$96,800	$118,670

Median Wages for Industries Employing Largest Numbers (Annual)

Industry	Median Income
Federal, State, and Local Government	$98,140
Miscellaneous Manufacturing	$94,030
Computer and Electronic Product Manufacturing	$87,450
Food Manufacturing	$86,630
Plastics and Rubber Products Manufacturing	$80,470
Management of Companies and Enterprises	$80,110
Professional, Scientific, and Technical Services	$80,040
Machinery Manufacturing	$73,160
Nonmetallic Mineral Product Manufacturing	$69,250
Chemical Manufacturing	$69,050

Median Wages for States (Annual)

State	Wage	State	Wage	State	Wage
AK	no data	KY	$69,200	NY	$62,800
AL	$83,800	LA	no data	OH	$78,150
AR	no data	MA	$91,650	OK	no data
AZ	$61,340	MD	$97,470	OR	$54,580
CA	$84,030	ME	no data	PA	$83,270
CO	$71,550	MI	$53,850	RI	no data
CT	$70,960	MN	$81,300	SC	no data
DC	no data	MO	$64,050	SD	no data
DE	$50,390	MS	$31,280	TN	$54,620
FL	$70,100	MT	no data	TX	$71,450
GA	$66,230	NC	$81,340	UT	no data
HI	no data	ND	no data	VA	$95,900
IA	$66,800	NE	no data	VT	no data
ID	no data	NH	$81,010	WA	$79,690
IL	$84,620	NJ	$94,110	WI	$76,290
IN	$61,160	NM	no data	WV	no data
KS	no data	NV	$68,090	WY	no data

Median Wages for the Largest Metropolitan Areas (Annual)

Area	Wage	Area	Wage
AZ: Phoenix	$55,020	MI: Detroit	$55,990
CA: Los Angeles	$90,010	MN: Minneapolis	$82,220
CA: Riverside	$67,590	MO: Kansas City	no data
CA: Sacramento	no data	MO: St. Louis	$64,730
CA: San Diego	$70,370	NV: Las Vegas	no data
CA: San Francisco	$96,030	NY: New York	$66,830
CO: Denver	$78,060	OH: Cincinnati	$55,410
DC: Washington	$94,970	OH: Cleveland	$78,630
FL: Miami	no data	OH: Columbus	$88,150
FL: Orlando	no data	OR: Portland	$53,440
FL: Tampa	no data	PA: Philadelphia	$76,770
GA: Atlanta	$64,930	PA: Pittsburgh	no data
IL: Chicago	$86,670	TX: Dallas	$73,070
MA: Boston	$90,540	TX: Houston	$75,140
MD: Baltimore	$91,940	WA: Seattle	no data

FACTORS THAT MAY AFFECT EARNINGS

Educational Attainment of Workers and Effect on Earnings

Figures are based on a group of occupations: Physical Scientists

	Percent at Level	Effect on Earnings
Less than High School	—	—
Some High School	—	—
High School or Equivalent	—	—
Some College but No Degree	3.3%	−23.5%
Associate Degree	3.9%	−40.9%
Bachelor's Degree	38.9%	−8.1%
Master's Degree	23.6%	2.6%
Doctoral Degree	23.6%	19.8%
First Professional Degree	3.9%	19.9%

Flexibility of Earnings

Average Hours Worked: 39
Workers with a Varying Number of Hours: 4.2%
Workers Earning Some Overtime Pay, Tips, or Commissions: 6.8%
Earnings Benefit of Working Overtime: 2.4%

Gender

	Male	Female
Percent	65.9%	34.1%
Effect on Earnings	0.1%	—

Union Membership

Percentage Union Members: 8.2%
Earnings Benefit of Union Membership: −16.7%

Veteran Status

Percentage Who Have Been on Active Duty: 8.8%
Earnings Benefit of Veteran Status: 14.3%

19-2041 Environmental Scientists and Specialists, Including Health

Conduct research or perform investigation for the purpose of identifying, abating, or eliminating sources of pollutants or hazards that affect either the environment or the health of the population. Utilizing knowledge of various scientific disciplines, may collect, synthesize, study, report, and take action based on data derived from measurements or observations of air, food, soil, water, and other sources.

- Education or Training Required: Master's degree
- Job Growth: 17.1%
- Annual Openings: 8,000
- Self-Employed: 4.2%
- Part-Time: 12.4%

NATIONAL WAGE FIGURES (ANNUAL)

Beginning	25th Percentile	Median	Mean	75th Percentile	90th Percentile
$34,590	$42,840	$56,100	$61,120	$74,480	$94,670

Median Wages for Industries Employing Largest Numbers (Annual)

Industry	Median Income
Pipeline Transportation	$77,790
Utilities	$71,900
Oil and Gas Extraction	$68,840
Management of Companies and Enterprises	$66,970
Rail Transportation	$64,180
Computer and Electronic Product Manufacturing	$63,160
Machinery Manufacturing	$61,790
Petroleum and Coal Products Manufacturing	$61,150
Chemical Manufacturing	$60,190
Transportation Equipment Manufacturing	$59,570

Median Wages for States (Annual)

AK	$59,590	KY	$47,370	NY	$61,080
AL	$48,160	LA	$51,690	OH	$57,250
AR	$47,490	MA	$74,030	OK	$39,510
AZ	$48,250	MD	$60,530	OR	$58,220
CA	$64,650	ME	$45,550	PA	$59,400
CO	$67,740	MI	$57,180	RI	$61,310
CT	$61,120	MN	$54,950	SC	$45,480
DC	$91,640	MO	$40,240	SD	$45,650
DE	$52,150	MS	$35,810	TN	$45,310
FL	$46,810	MT	$39,310	TX	$48,000
GA	$54,590	NC	$45,960	UT	$61,780
HI	$56,550	ND	$51,440	VA	$73,960
IA	no data	NE	$42,750	VT	$49,460
ID	$56,030	NH	$53,150	WA	$60,580
IL	$62,830	NJ	$63,080	WI	$52,000
IN	$46,640	NM	$54,360	WV	$41,770
KS	$53,790	NV	$69,980	WY	$47,730

Median Wages for the Largest Metropolitan Areas (Annual)

AZ: Phoenix	$47,830	MI: Detroit	$56,070
CA: Los Angeles	$60,610	MN: Minneapolis	$55,290
CA: Riverside	$58,140	MO: Kansas City	$52,700
CA: Sacramento	$67,940	MO: St. Louis	$46,880
CA: San Diego	$56,470	NV: Las Vegas	$76,910
CA: San Francisco	$72,470	NY: New York	$63,240
CO: Denver	$71,420	OH: Cincinnati	$59,130
DC: Washington	$84,210	OH: Cleveland	$48,720
FL: Miami	$50,680	OH: Columbus	no data
FL: Orlando	$44,830	OR: Portland	$59,420
FL: Tampa	$45,350	PA: Philadelphia	$64,530
GA: Atlanta	$55,950	PA: Pittsburgh	$47,570
IL: Chicago	$63,930	TX: Dallas	$63,700
MA: Boston	$78,230	TX: Houston	$46,970
MD: Baltimore	$57,930	WA: Seattle	$63,500

FACTORS THAT MAY AFFECT EARNINGS

Educational Attainment of Workers and Effect on Earnings

Figures are based on a group of occupations: Physical Scientists

	Percent at Level	Effect on Earnings
Less than High School	—	—
Some High School	—	—
High School or Equivalent	—	—
Some College but No Degree	3.3%	−23.5%
Associate Degree	3.9%	−40.9%
Bachelor's Degree	38.9%	−8.1%
Master's Degree	23.6%	2.6%
Doctoral Degree	23.6%	19.8%
First Professional Degree	3.9%	19.9%

Flexibility of Earnings

Average Hours Worked: 39
Workers with a Varying Number of Hours: 4.2%
Workers Earning Some Overtime Pay, Tips, or Commissions: 6.8%
Earnings Benefit of Working Overtime: −2.9%

Gender

	Male	Female
Percent	78.0%	22.0%
Effect on Earnings	3.4%	—

Union Membership

Percentage Union Members: 8.2%
Earnings Benefit of Union Membership: −16.7%

Veteran Status

Percentage Who Have Been on Active Duty: 8.8%
Earnings Benefit of Veteran Status: 14.3%

19-2042 Geoscientists, Except Hydrologists and Geographers

Study the composition, structure, and other physical aspects of the earth. May use geological, physics, and mathematics knowledge in exploration for oil, gas, minerals, or underground water or in waste disposal, land reclamation, or other environmental problems. May study the earth's internal composition, atmospheres, and oceans and its magnetic, electrical, and gravitational forces. Includes mineralogists, crystallographers, paleontologists, stratigraphers, geodesists, and seismologists.

- Education or Training Required: Master's degree
- Job Growth: 8.3%
- Annual Openings: 2,000
- Self-Employed: 5.1%
- Part-Time: 12.4%

NATIONAL WAGE FIGURES (ANNUAL)

Beginning	25th Percentile	Median	Mean	75th Percentile	90th Percentile
$39,740	$51,860	$72,660	$79,890	$100,650	$135,950

Median Wages for Industries Employing Largest Numbers (Annual)

Industry	Median Income
Utilities	$108,220
Management of Companies and Enterprises	$106,100
Oil and Gas Extraction	$106,060
Support Activities for Mining	$95,370
Publishing Industries (Except Internet)	$78,120
Securities, Commodity Contracts, and Other Financial Investments and Related Activities	$73,160
Mining (Except Oil and Gas)	$72,570
Federal, State, and Local Government	$65,910
Waste Management and Remediation Services	$65,110
Professional, Scientific, and Technical Services	$64,260

Median Wages for States (Annual)

AK $83,780	KY $55,720	NY $56,440
AL $50,930	LA $75,120	OH $66,490
AR $58,250	MA no data	OK $103,130
AZ $56,620	MD $82,100	OR $73,640
CA $73,600	ME $47,620	PA $63,360
CO $79,880	MI $61,810	RI no data
CT no data	MN $55,270	SC $33,420
DC $87,890	MO $65,230	SD $55,130
DE $60,420	MS $77,120	TN $49,140
FL $51,670	MT $70,520	TX $93,340
GA $59,380	NC $64,230	UT $55,790
HI $77,210	ND no data	VA $75,010
IA $62,210	NE $61,340	VT $76,890
ID $61,670	NH $55,120	WA $65,320
IL $67,790	NJ $73,560	WI $64,010
IN $48,900	NM $66,360	WV $43,320
KS $55,070	NV $68,900	WY $63,160

Median Wages for the Largest Metropolitan Areas (Annual)

AZ: Phoenix $53,320	MI: Detroit $59,080
CA: Los Angeles $68,500	MN: Minneapolis $56,170
CA: Riverside $54,450	MO: Kansas City $58,290
CA: Sacramento $73,830	MO: St. Louis $66,970
CA: San Diego $75,120	NV: Las Vegas $76,190
CA: San Francisco $82,680	NY: New York no data
CO: Denver $95,180	OH: Cincinnati no data
DC: Washington $93,410	OH: Cleveland no data
FL: Miami $58,290	OH: Columbus $58,500
FL: Orlando $55,330	OR: Portland $68,430
FL: Tampa $57,130	PA: Philadelphia $69,390
GA: Atlanta $58,860	PA: Pittsburgh $65,060
IL: Chicago $70,100	TX: Dallas $85,230
MA: Boston no data	TX: Houston $103,320
MD: Baltimore $54,860	WA: Seattle $70,510

FACTORS THAT MAY AFFECT EARNINGS

Educational Attainment of Workers and Effect on Earnings

Figures are based on a group of occupations: Physical Scientists

	Percent at Level	Effect on Earnings
Less than High School	—	—
Some High School	—	—
High School or Equivalent	—	—
Some College but No Degree	3.3%	−23.5%
Associate Degree	3.9%	−40.9%
Bachelor's Degree	38.9%	−8.1%
Master's Degree	23.6%	2.6%
Doctoral Degree	23.6%	19.8%
First Professional Degree	3.9%	19.9%

Flexibility of Earnings

Average Hours Worked: 39
Workers with a Varying Number of Hours: 4.2%
Workers Earning Some Overtime Pay, Tips, or Commissions: 6.8%
Earnings Benefit of Working Overtime: −2.9%

Gender

	Male	Female
Percent	78.0%	22.0%
Effect on Earnings	3.4%	—

Union Membership

Percentage Union Members: 8.2%
Earnings Benefit of Union Membership: −16.7%

Veteran Status

Percentage Who Have Been on Active Duty: 8.8%
Earnings Benefit of Veteran Status: 14.3%

19-2043 Hydrologists

Research the distribution, circulation, and physical properties of underground and surface waters; study the form and intensity of precipitation, its rate of infiltration into the soil, its movement through the earth, and its return to the ocean and atmosphere.

- Education or Training Required: Master's degree
- Job Growth: 31.6%
- Annual Openings: 1,000
- Self-Employed: 4.3%
- Part-Time: 12.4%

NATIONAL WAGE FIGURES (ANNUAL)

Beginning	25th Percentile	Median	Mean	75th Percentile	90th Percentile
$42,080	$51,370	$66,260	$68,230	$82,140	$98,320

Median Wages for Industries Employing Largest Numbers (Annual)

Industry	Median Income
Utilities	$75,070
Professional, Scientific, and Technical Services	$66,300
Federal, State, and Local Government	$66,220
Educational Services	$50,640

Median Wages for States (Annual)

AK $73,880	KY no data	NY $49,650
AL $73,620	LA $69,940	OH $67,610
AR $60,410	MA $76,610	OK $75,620
AZ $54,750	MD $74,610	OR $72,100
CA $76,800	ME $68,840	PA $80,110
CO $72,430	MI $67,540	RI no data
CT $52,750	MN no data	SC $51,170
DC no data	MO $66,340	SD $60,770
DE no data	MS no data	TN $69,300
FL $67,860	MT $63,730	TX $60,430
GA $77,670	NC $50,710	UT $63,910
HI no data	ND no data	VA $80,840
IA no data	NE $51,510	VT no data
ID $59,050	NH $62,540	WA $71,500
IL $69,810	NJ $68,380	WI $54,990
IN $66,250	NM $59,170	WV no data
KS $56,740	NV $72,020	WY $51,240

Median Wages for the Largest Metropolitan Areas (Annual)

AZ: Phoenix	$51,270	MI: Detroit	no data
CA: Los Angeles	$85,420	MN: Minneapolis	no data
CA: Riverside	$82,060	MO: Kansas City	$57,520
CA: Sacramento	$76,760	MO: St. Louis	no data
CA: San Diego	$68,580	NV: Las Vegas	$80,840
CA: San Francisco	$84,740	NY: New York	no data
CO: Denver	$74,940	OH: Cincinnati	$71,340
DC: Washington	$87,020	OH: Cleveland	no data
FL: Miami	$69,130	OH: Columbus	$65,250
FL: Orlando	no data	OR: Portland	$77,930
FL: Tampa	$57,310	PA: Philadelphia	$76,040
GA: Atlanta	$77,950	PA: Pittsburgh	no data
IL: Chicago	no data	TX: Dallas	$56,460
MA: Boston	$81,010	TX: Houston	$62,850
MD: Baltimore	$66,220	WA: Seattle	$70,520

FACTORS THAT MAY AFFECT EARNINGS

Educational Attainment of Workers and Effect on Earnings

Figures are based on a group of occupations: Physical Scientists

	Percent at Level	Effect on Earnings
Less than High School	—	—
Some High School	—	—
High School or Equivalent	—	—
Some College but No Degree	3.3%	−23.5%
Associate Degree	3.9%	−40.9%
Bachelor's Degree	38.9%	−8.1%
Master's Degree	23.6%	2.6%
Doctoral Degree	23.6%	19.8%
First Professional Degree	3.9%	19.9%

Flexibility of Earnings

Average Hours Worked: 39
Workers with a Varying Number of Hours: 4.2%
Workers Earning Some Overtime Pay, Tips, or Commissions: 6.8%
Earnings Benefit of Working Overtime: −2.9%

Gender

	Male	Female
Percent	78.0%	22.0%
Effect on Earnings	3.4%	—

Union Membership

Percentage Union Members: 8.2%
Earnings Benefit of Union Membership: −16.7%

Veteran Status

Percentage Who Have Been on Active Duty: 8.8%
Earnings Benefit of Veteran Status: 14.3%

© JIST Works

19-2099 Physical Scientists, All Other

All physical scientists not listed separately.

- Education or Training Required: Bachelor's degree
- Job Growth: 14.6%
- Annual Openings: 2,000
- Self-Employed: 2.7%
- Part-Time: 6.7%

NATIONAL WAGE FIGURES (ANNUAL)

Beginning	25th Percentile	Median	Mean	75th Percentile	90th Percentile
$41,440	$59,210	$83,450	$85,310	$109,430	$136,130

Median Wages for Industries Employing Largest Numbers (Annual)

Industry	Median Income
Machinery Manufacturing	$106,920
Computer and Electronic Product Manufacturing	$104,470
Federal, State, and Local Government	$88,870
Professional, Scientific, and Technical Services	$86,780
Transportation Equipment Manufacturing	$85,730
Merchant Wholesalers, Nondurable Goods	$80,730
Administrative and Support Services	$74,020
Utilities	$73,000
Ambulatory Health Care Services	$67,240
Merchant Wholesalers, Durable Goods	$64,670

Median Wages for States (Annual)

State	Wage	State	Wage	State	Wage
AK	$79,030	KY	$63,790	NY	$79,180
AL	$91,890	LA	$55,980	OH	$83,640
AR	$55,700	MA	$88,180	OK	$74,970
AZ	$59,990	MD	$101,880	OR	$73,440
CA	$108,480	ME	no data	PA	$89,050
CO	$70,740	MI	$68,550	RI	$82,340
CT	$78,280	MN	no data	SC	$93,040
DC	$109,830	MO	no data	SD	$101,920
DE	no data	MS	$76,510	TN	$46,280
FL	$64,770	MT	$60,220	TX	$85,810
GA	$87,290	NC	$55,390	UT	$73,410
HI	$65,040	ND	no data	VA	$103,920
IA	no data	NE	$37,280	VT	no data
ID	$85,990	NH	$56,680	WA	$83,110
IL	$82,870	NJ	$94,790	WI	$43,480
IN	$66,870	NM	$94,950	WV	$90,380
KS	$84,500	NV	$88,180	WY	no data

Median Wages for the Largest Metropolitan Areas (Annual)

Area	Wage	Area	Wage
AZ: Phoenix	no data	MI: Detroit	$86,670
CA: Los Angeles	$85,480	MN: Minneapolis	no data
CA: Riverside	no data	MO: Kansas City	$84,300
CA: Sacramento	$69,660	MO: St. Louis	$70,190
CA: San Diego	$134,860	NV: Las Vegas	$93,690
CA: San Francisco	$79,880	NY: New York	$96,250
CO: Denver	$82,710	OH: Cincinnati	$75,600
DC: Washington	$109,280	OH: Cleveland	$83,920
FL: Miami	$61,370	OH: Columbus	$92,220
FL: Orlando	$84,450	OR: Portland	$70,900
FL: Tampa	$49,760	PA: Philadelphia	$89,890
GA: Atlanta	$87,910	PA: Pittsburgh	$97,330
IL: Chicago	$83,610	TX: Dallas	$88,030
MA: Boston	$89,500	TX: Houston	no data
MD: Baltimore	$92,220	WA: Seattle	$80,870

FACTORS THAT MAY AFFECT EARNINGS

Educational Attainment of Workers and Effect on Earnings

	Percent at Level	Effect on Earnings
Less than High School	—	—
Some High School	—	—
High School or Equivalent	—	—
Some College but No Degree	—	—
Associate Degree	—	—
Bachelor's Degree	32.8%	−15.4%
Master's Degree	20.6%	−5.8%
Doctoral Degree	37.4%	15.6%
First Professional Degree	6.9%	21.9%

Flexibility of Earnings

Average Hours Worked: 40
Workers with a Varying Number of Hours: 3.8%
Workers Earning Some Overtime Pay, Tips, or Commissions: 3.7%
Earnings Benefit of Working Overtime: −5.5%

Gender

	Male	Female
Percent	58.1%	41.9%
Effect on Earnings	13.9%	−11.4%

Union Membership

Percentage Union Members: 4.9%
Earnings Benefit of Union Membership: −16.7%

Veteran Status

Percentage Who Have Been on Active Duty: 8.8%
Earnings Benefit of Veteran Status: 14.3%

19-3000 Social Scientists and Related Workers

19-3011 Economists

Conduct research, prepare reports, or formulate plans to aid in solution of economic problems arising from production and distribution of goods and services. May collect and process economic and statistical data, using econometric and sampling techniques.

- Education or Training Required: Master's degree
- Job Growth: 5.6%
- Annual Openings: 1,000
- Self-Employed: 0.0%
- Part-Time: 21.4%

NATIONAL WAGE FIGURES (ANNUAL)

Beginning	25th Percentile	Median	Mean	75th Percentile	90th Percentile
$42,280	$55,740	$77,010	$83,500	$103,500	$136,550

Median Wages for Industries Employing Largest Numbers (Annual)

Industry	Median Income
Utilities	$90,950
Postal Service	$90,740
Securities, Commodity Contracts, and Other Financial Investments and Related Activities	$90,080
Monetary Authorities—Central Bank	$82,930
Management of Companies and Enterprises	$81,200
Professional, Scientific, and Technical Services	$80,350
Federal, State, and Local Government	$77,010
Merchant Wholesalers, Durable Goods	$76,360
Religious, Grantmaking, Civic, Professional, and Similar Organizations	$74,770
Credit Intermediation and Related Activities	$74,300

Median Wages for States (Annual)

AK	$69,140	KY	$56,110	NY	$84,320
AL	$66,590	LA	$75,920	OH	$70,710
AR	$44,120	MA	$60,660	OK	$47,400
AZ	$65,890	MD	$100,780	OR	$70,440
CA	$79,780	ME	$47,970	PA	$79,930
CO	$86,310	MI	$69,650	RI	no data
CT	$70,370	MN	no data	SC	$55,580
DC	$95,200	MO	$67,160	SD	no data
DE	$76,330	MS	$63,470	TN	$70,970
FL	$72,510	MT	$42,330	TX	$74,210
GA	$75,870	NC	no data	UT	$60,230
HI	no data	ND	no data	VA	$77,770
IA	no data	NE	$81,390	VT	$69,480
ID	$52,910	NH	$51,490	WA	$68,410
IL	$78,130	NJ	$84,470	WI	$63,920
IN	$57,150	NM	$50,190	WV	$32,300
KS	no data	NV	$72,910	WY	$49,370

Median Wages for the Largest Metropolitan Areas (Annual)

AZ: Phoenix	$69,100	MI: Detroit	$64,950
CA: Los Angeles	$81,900	MN: Minneapolis	no data
CA: Riverside	$96,140	MO: Kansas City	$75,060
CA: Sacramento	$71,750	MO: St. Louis	$66,420
CA: San Diego	$38,250	NV: Las Vegas	no data
CA: San Francisco	$86,280	NY: New York	$95,200
CO: Denver	$83,410	OH: Cincinnati	no data
DC: Washington	$95,310	OH: Cleveland	$78,580
FL: Miami	$72,250	OH: Columbus	$71,620
FL: Orlando	$74,300	OR: Portland	$71,830
FL: Tampa	no data	PA: Philadelphia	$83,390
GA: Atlanta	$78,230	PA: Pittsburgh	$80,100
IL: Chicago	$77,070	TX: Dallas	$81,210
MA: Boston	$61,240	TX: Houston	$79,580
MD: Baltimore	$92,470	WA: Seattle	$79,740

FACTORS THAT MAY AFFECT EARNINGS

Educational Attainment of Workers and Effect on Earnings

	Percent at Level	Effect on Earnings
Less than High School	—	—
Some High School	—	—
High School or Equivalent	—	—
Some College but No Degree	—	—
Associate Degree	—	—
Bachelor's Degree	15.9%	−16.4%
Master's Degree	50.0%	−7.7%
Doctoral Degree	22.7%	18.7%
First Professional Degree	—	—

Figures do not total 100% because some levels have a very small sample size.

Flexibility of Earnings

Average Hours Worked: 43
Workers with a Varying Number of Hours: 4.1%
Workers Earning Some Overtime Pay, Tips, or Commissions: 9.5%
Earnings Benefit of Working Overtime: 3.3%

Gender

	Male	Female
Percent	65.7%	34.3%
Effect on Earnings	13.9%	−11.4%

Union Membership

Percentage Union Members: 11.1%
Earnings Benefit of Union Membership: −6.5%

Veteran Status

Percentage Who Have Been on Active Duty: 6.0%
Earnings Benefit of Veteran Status: 9.4%

19-3021 Market Research Analysts

Research market conditions in local, regional, or national areas to determine potential sales of a product or service. May gather information on competitors, prices, sales, and methods of marketing and distribution. May use survey results to create a marketing campaign based on regional preferences and buying habits.

- Education or Training Required: Bachelor's degree
- Job Growth: 19.6%
- Annual Openings: 20,000
- Self-Employed: 7.2%
- Part-Time: 25.0%

NATIONAL WAGE FIGURES (ANNUAL)

Beginning	25th Percentile	Median	Mean	75th Percentile	90th Percentile
$32,250	$42,190	$58,820	$65,930	$84,070	$112,510

Median Wages for Industries Employing Largest Numbers (Annual)

Industry	Median Income
Transportation Equipment Manufacturing	$81,480
Computer and Electronic Product Manufacturing	$79,660
Telecommunications	$74,730
Publishing Industries (Except Internet)	$70,970
Internet Service Providers, Web Search Portals, and Data-Processing Services	$70,100
Securities, Commodity Contracts, and Other Financial Investments and Related Activities	$68,190
Internet Publishing and Broadcasting	$65,500
Chemical Manufacturing	$65,150
Merchant Wholesalers, Durable Goods	$64,370
Management of Companies and Enterprises	$62,680

Median Wages for States (Annual)

State	Wage	State	Wage	State	Wage
AK	no data	KY	$52,570	NY	$59,920
AL	$46,570	LA	$37,000	OH	$57,800
AR	$51,480	MA	$63,350	OK	$45,260
AZ	$47,910	MD	$62,720	OR	no data
CA	$62,340	ME	$51,770	PA	$50,270
CO	$65,540	MI	$63,310	RI	$47,990
CT	$63,000	MN	$61,990	SC	$47,280
DC	$63,110	MO	$51,600	SD	$36,500
DE	$73,170	MS	$42,970	TN	$44,890
FL	$50,150	MT	$43,000	TX	$58,790
GA	$55,300	NC	$60,320	UT	$49,360
HI	$61,930	ND	$46,510	VA	$71,570
IA	$42,510	NE	$52,070	VT	$45,980
ID	$46,850	NH	$59,880	WA	$79,450
IL	$52,740	NJ	$67,480	WI	$56,310
IN	$47,190	NM	$61,160	WV	$43,040
KS	$51,090	NV	$49,050	WY	$40,670

Median Wages for the Largest Metropolitan Areas (Annual)

Area	Wage	Area	Wage
AZ: Phoenix	$51,830	MI: Detroit	$67,010
CA: Los Angeles	$58,090	MN: Minneapolis	$63,760
CA: Riverside	$45,660	MO: Kansas City	$55,310
CA: Sacramento	$49,100	MO: St. Louis	$51,880
CA: San Diego	$57,620	NV: Las Vegas	$46,210
CA: San Francisco	$71,240	NY: New York	$65,300
CO: Denver	$67,340	OH: Cincinnati	$56,860
DC: Washington	$73,070	OH: Cleveland	$58,210
FL: Miami	$52,060	OH: Columbus	$58,370
FL: Orlando	$49,550	OR: Portland	no data
FL: Tampa	$46,200	PA: Philadelphia	$65,530
GA: Atlanta	$57,400	PA: Pittsburgh	$39,880
IL: Chicago	$54,470	TX: Dallas	$60,010
MA: Boston	$64,740	TX: Houston	$61,160
MD: Baltimore	$61,850	WA: Seattle	$84,070

FACTORS THAT MAY AFFECT EARNINGS

Educational Attainment of Workers and Effect on Earnings

Figures are based on a group of occupations: Social Scientists and Related Workers

	Percent at Level	Effect on Earnings
Less than High School	—	—
Some High School	—	—
High School or Equivalent	5.1%	−26.3%
Some College but No Degree	7.5%	−36.0%
Associate Degree	3.6%	−26.8%
Bachelor's Degree	24.8%	−3.1%
Master's Degree	38.2%	2.1%
Doctoral Degree	16.4%	22.5%
First Professional Degree	4.2%	33.8%

Flexibility of Earnings

Average Hours Worked: 37
Workers with a Varying Number of Hours: 3.4%
Workers Earning Some Overtime Pay, Tips, or Commissions: 7.6%
Earnings Benefit of Working Overtime: 18.1%

Gender

	Male	Female
Percent	38.7%	61.3%
Effect on Earnings	—	−14.3%

Union Membership

Percentage Union Members: 13.7%
Earnings Benefit of Union Membership: −6.5%

Veteran Status

Percentage Who Have Been on Active Duty: 6.0%
Earnings Benefit of Veteran Status: 9.4%

19-3022 Survey Researchers

Design or conduct surveys. May supervise interviewers who conduct the survey in person or over the telephone. May present survey results to client.

- Education or Training Required: Bachelor's degree
- Job Growth: 25.9%
- Annual Openings: 3,000
- Self-Employed: 7.8%
- Part-Time: 25.0%

NATIONAL WAGE FIGURES (ANNUAL)

Beginning	25th Percentile	Median	Mean	75th Percentile	90th Percentile
$16,720	$22,150	$33,360	$39,680	$50,960	$73,630

Median Wages for Industries Employing Largest Numbers (Annual)

Industry	Median Income
Federal, State, and Local Government	$54,570
Educational Services	$45,320
Management of Companies and Enterprises	$40,310
Religious, Grantmaking, Civic, Professional, and Similar Organizations	$32,220
Publishing Industries (Except Internet)	$32,160
Professional, Scientific, and Technical Services	$31,050
Insurance Carriers and Related Activities	$28,610
Social Assistance	$27,290
Administrative and Support Services	$19,390

Median Wages for States (Annual)

State	Wage	State	Wage	State	Wage
AK	no data	KY	$36,260	NY	$54,010
AL	$26,360	LA	no data	OH	$28,740
AR	$28,830	MA	$31,780	OK	$27,020
AZ	$27,970	MD	no data	OR	$33,240
CA	$49,170	ME	$48,050	PA	$22,840
CO	$25,010	MI	$47,830	RI	$47,070
CT	no data	MN	$41,810	SC	$21,940
DC	$41,250	MO	$32,910	SD	no data
DE	no data	MS	no data	TN	$21,890
FL	$27,810	MT	$13,470	TX	$24,340
GA	$24,090	NC	$40,720	UT	$17,400
HI	$32,050	ND	no data	VA	$46,300
IA	$33,310	NE	$29,030	VT	$40,170
ID	$17,750	NH	no data	WA	$44,900
IL	$28,270	NJ	$37,250	WI	$69,750
IN	$39,150	NM	no data	WV	no data
KS	$36,570	NV	no data	WY	no data

Median Wages for the Largest Metropolitan Areas (Annual)

Area	Wage	Area	Wage
AZ: Phoenix	$28,870	MI: Detroit	$83,090
CA: Los Angeles	$47,570	MN: Minneapolis	$41,920
CA: Riverside	no data	MO: Kansas City	$31,170
CA: Sacramento	$40,470	MO: St. Louis	$35,390
CA: San Diego	$56,540	NV: Las Vegas	no data
CA: San Francisco	$53,870	NY: New York	$49,530
CO: Denver	$26,820	OH: Cincinnati	$32,630
DC: Washington	$51,000	OH: Cleveland	$21,430
FL: Miami	$26,820	OH: Columbus	no data
FL: Orlando	no data	OR: Portland	$33,170
FL: Tampa	$27,840	PA: Philadelphia	$23,030
GA: Atlanta	$23,480	PA: Pittsburgh	no data
IL: Chicago	$27,950	TX: Dallas	$38,040
MA: Boston	$31,540	TX: Houston	$21,760
MD: Baltimore	$19,940	WA: Seattle	$46,640

FACTORS THAT MAY AFFECT EARNINGS

Educational Attainment of Workers and Effect on Earnings

Figures are based on a group of occupations: Social Scientists and Related Workers

	Percent at Level	Effect on Earnings
Less than High School	—	—
Some High School	—	—
High School or Equivalent	5.1%	−26.3%
Some College but No Degree	7.5%	−36.0%
Associate Degree	3.6%	−26.8%
Bachelor's Degree	24.8%	−3.1%
Master's Degree	38.2%	2.1%
Doctoral Degree	16.4%	22.5%
First Professional Degree	4.2%	33.8%

Flexibility of Earnings

Average Hours Worked: 37
Workers with a Varying Number of Hours: 3.4%
Workers Earning Some Overtime Pay, Tips, or Commissions: 7.6%
Earnings Benefit of Working Overtime: 18.1%

Gender

	Male	Female
Percent	38.7%	61.3%
Effect on Earnings	—	−14.3%

Union Membership

Percentage Union Members: 13.7%
Earnings Benefit of Union Membership: −6.5%

Veteran Status

Percentage Who Have Been on Active Duty: 6.0%
Earnings Benefit of Veteran Status: 9.4%

19-3031 Clinical, Counseling, and School Psychologists

Diagnose and treat mental disorders; learning disabilities; and cognitive, behavioral, and emotional problems, using individual, child, family, and group therapies. May design and implement behavior modification programs.

- Education or Training Required: Doctoral degree
- Job Growth: 19.1%
- Annual Openings: 10,000
- Self-Employed: 38.2%
- Part-Time: 25.0%

Note: Earnings figures do not reflect self-employed workers, who make up a large fraction of the workforce for this occupation.

NATIONAL WAGE FIGURES (ANNUAL)

Beginning	25th Percentile	Median	Mean	75th Percentile	90th Percentile
$35,280	$45,300	$59,440	$66,110	$77,750	$102,730

Median Wages for Industries Employing Largest Numbers (Annual)

Industry	Median Income
Professional, Scientific, and Technical Services	$114,920
Administrative and Support Services	$76,250
Religious, Grantmaking, Civic, Professional, and Similar Organizations	$72,290
Hospitals	$64,990
Ambulatory Health Care Services	$63,590
Federal, State, and Local Government	$59,880
Educational Services	$59,820
Management of Companies and Enterprises	$54,760
Funds, Trusts, and Other Financial Vehicles	$54,320
Social Assistance	$49,590

Median Wages for States (Annual)

State	Wage	State	Wage	State	Wage
AK	$57,900	KY	$48,980	NY	$69,850
AL	$51,440	LA	$46,420	OH	$74,010
AR	$51,760	MA	$59,980	OK	$42,570
AZ	$45,230	MD	$62,060	OR	$59,030
CA	$72,260	ME	$53,500	PA	$57,840
CO	$60,940	MI	$61,080	RI	$65,910
CT	$67,840	MN	$59,620	SC	$50,790
DC	$57,800	MO	$47,090	SD	$56,400
DE	$60,250	MS	$42,500	TN	$50,410
FL	$56,660	MT	$42,760	TX	$51,860
GA	$59,960	NC	$50,560	UT	$55,930
HI	$58,400	ND	$53,570	VA	$63,970
IA	$50,580	NE	$52,000	VT	$51,250
ID	$52,880	NH	$51,350	WA	$57,450
IL	$54,290	NJ	$76,870	WI	$56,200
IN	$53,720	NM	$46,070	WV	$42,720
KS	$47,070	NV	$60,940	WY	$52,880

Median Wages for the Largest Metropolitan Areas (Annual)

Area	Wage	Area	Wage
AZ: Phoenix	$45,200	MI: Detroit	$61,230
CA: Los Angeles	$75,490	MN: Minneapolis	$60,910
CA: Riverside	$71,520	MO: Kansas City	$43,990
CA: Sacramento	$63,310	MO: St. Louis	$51,910
CA: San Diego	$68,480	NV: Las Vegas	$56,870
CA: San Francisco	$76,260	NY: New York	$76,510
CO: Denver	$59,600	OH: Cincinnati	$60,370
DC: Washington	$67,550	OH: Cleveland	$78,410
FL: Miami	$55,040	OH: Columbus	$75,390
FL: Orlando	$51,510	OR: Portland	$63,660
FL: Tampa	$56,530	PA: Philadelphia	$63,910
GA: Atlanta	$60,760	PA: Pittsburgh	$58,070
IL: Chicago	$54,550	TX: Dallas	$52,180
MA: Boston	$58,260	TX: Houston	$55,610
MD: Baltimore	$60,050	WA: Seattle	$60,120

FACTORS THAT MAY AFFECT EARNINGS

Educational Attainment of Workers and Effect on Earnings

Figures are based on a group of occupations: Social Scientists and Related Workers

	Percent at Level	Effect on Earnings
Less than High School	—	—
Some High School	—	—
High School or Equivalent	5.1%	−26.3%
Some College but No Degree	7.5%	−36.0%
Associate Degree	3.6%	−26.8%
Bachelor's Degree	24.8%	−3.1%
Master's Degree	38.2%	2.1%
Doctoral Degree	16.4%	22.5%
First Professional Degree	4.2%	33.8%

Flexibility of Earnings

Average Hours Worked: 37
Workers with a Varying Number of Hours: 3.4%
Workers Earning Some Overtime Pay, Tips, or Commissions: 7.6%
Earnings Benefit of Working Overtime: 1.1%

Gender

	Male	Female
Percent	32.3%	67.7%
Effect on Earnings	—	−5.9%

Union Membership

Percentage Union Members: 13.7%
Earnings Benefit of Union Membership: −6.5%

Veteran Status

Percentage Who Have Been on Active Duty: 6.0%
Earnings Benefit of Veteran Status: 9.4%

19-3032 Industrial-Organizational Psychologists

Apply principles of psychology to personnel, administration, management, sales, and marketing problems. Activities may include policy planning; employee screening, training, and development; and organizational development and analysis. May work with management to reorganize the work setting to improve worker productivity.

- Education or Training Required: Master's degree
- Job Growth: 20.4%
- Annual Openings: Fewer than 500
- Self-Employed: 37.6%
- Part-Time: 25.0%

Note: Earnings figures do not reflect self-employed workers, who make up a large fraction of the workforce for this occupation.

NATIONAL WAGE FIGURES (ANNUAL)

Beginning	25th Percentile	Median	Mean	75th Percentile	90th Percentile
$48,380	$66,310	$86,420	$89,920	$115,000	$139,620

Median Wages for Industries Employing Largest Numbers (Annual)

Industry	Median Income
Professional, Scientific, and Technical Services	$105,760
Ambulatory Health Care Services	$81,480
Management of Companies and Enterprises	$80,090
Educational Services	$62,400
Federal, State, and Local Government	$49,590

Median Wages for States (Annual)

AK	no data	KY	no data	NY	no data
AL	no data	LA	no data	OH	$68,050
AR	no data	MA	$65,250	OK	no data
AZ	no data	MD	no data	OR	no data
CA	no data	ME	no data	PA	$81,360
CO	$110,520	MI	no data	RI	no data
CT	no data	MN	no data	SC	no data
DC	$71,280	MO	no data	SD	no data
DE	no data	MS	no data	TN	no data
FL	no data	MT	no data	TX	no data
GA	$80,700	NC	no data	UT	no data
HI	no data	ND	no data	VA	$91,090
IA	no data	NE	no data	VT	no data
ID	no data	NH	no data	WA	no data
IL	no data	NJ	no data	WI	no data
IN	no data	NM	$82,010	WV	no data
KS	no data	NV	no data	WY	no data

Median Wages for the Largest Metropolitan Areas (Annual)

AZ: Phoenix	no data	MI: Detroit	no data
CA: Los Angeles	no data	MN: Minneapolis	no data
CA: Riverside	no data	MO: Kansas City	no data
CA: Sacramento	no data	MO: St. Louis	$138,380
CA: San Diego	no data	NV: Las Vegas	no data
CA: San Francisco	no data	NY: New York	$96,170
CO: Denver	no data	OH: Cincinnati	no data
DC: Washington	$79,930	OH: Cleveland	no data
FL: Miami	no data	OH: Columbus	no data
FL: Orlando	no data	OR: Portland	no data
FL: Tampa	no data	PA: Philadelphia	no data
GA: Atlanta	no data	PA: Pittsburgh	no data
IL: Chicago	no data	TX: Dallas	no data
MA: Boston	$67,900	TX: Houston	no data
MD: Baltimore	no data	WA: Seattle	no data

FACTORS THAT MAY AFFECT EARNINGS

Educational Attainment of Workers and Effect on Earnings

Figures are based on a group of occupations: Social Scientists and Related Workers

	Percent at Level	Effect on Earnings
Less than High School	—	—
Some High School	—	—
High School or Equivalent	5.1%	−26.3%
Some College but No Degree	7.5%	−36.0%
Associate Degree	3.6%	−26.8%
Bachelor's Degree	24.8%	−3.1%
Master's Degree	38.2%	2.1%
Doctoral Degree	16.4%	22.5%
First Professional Degree	4.2%	33.8%

Flexibility of Earnings

Average Hours Worked: 37
Workers with a Varying Number of Hours: 3.4%
Workers Earning Some Overtime Pay, Tips, or Commissions: 7.6%
Earnings Benefit of Working Overtime: 1.1%

Gender

	Male	Female
Percent	32.3%	67.7%
Effect on Earnings	—	−5.9%

Union Membership

Percentage Union Members: 13.7%
Earnings Benefit of Union Membership: −6.5%

Veteran Status

Percentage Who Have Been on Active Duty: 6.0%
Earnings Benefit of Veteran Status: 9.4%

19-3039 Psychologists, All Other

All psychologists not listed separately.

- Education or Training Required: Master's degree
- Job Growth: 9.9%
- Annual Openings: 1,000
- Self-Employed: 27.4%
- Part-Time: 25.0%

NATIONAL WAGE FIGURES (ANNUAL)

Beginning	25th Percentile	Median	Mean	75th Percentile	90th Percentile
$33,220	$53,820	$76,310	$80,360	$95,820	$123,840

Median Wages for Industries Employing Largest Numbers (Annual)

Industry	Median Income
Social Assistance	$94,310
Professional, Scientific, and Technical Services	$84,040
Federal, State, and Local Government	$82,520
Management of Companies and Enterprises	$79,340
Hospitals	$74,290
Ambulatory Health Care Services	$69,530
Educational Services	$57,010
Nursing and Residential Care Facilities	$49,240

Median Wages for States (Annual)

AK	no data	KY	$57,710	NY	$69,570
AL	$84,300	LA	$73,150	OH	$72,600
AR	$79,930	MA	$71,740	OK	$73,840
AZ	no data	MD	$83,830	OR	$84,440
CA	$85,070	ME	no data	PA	$73,310
CO	$65,190	MI	$58,120	RI	$71,540
CT	$78,880	MN	$69,370	SC	$73,820
DC	no data	MO	$69,260	SD	$77,350
DE	no data	MS	no data	TN	$76,040
FL	$82,170	MT	$70,810	TX	$84,510
GA	$74,200	NC	$65,360	UT	no data
HI	no data	ND	no data	VA	$84,260
IA	no data	NE	no data	VT	no data
ID	no data	NH	$83,810	WA	$57,280
IL	$82,390	NJ	$90,690	WI	$81,740
IN	$69,480	NM	$55,580	WV	$65,590
KS	no data	NV	no data	WY	no data

Median Wages for the Largest Metropolitan Areas (Annual)

AZ: Phoenix	$145,480	MI: Detroit	$49,630
CA: Los Angeles	$92,490	MN: Minneapolis	$82,290
CA: Riverside	$32,230	MO: Kansas City	$76,160
CA: Sacramento	$94,150	MO: St. Louis	$66,790
CA: San Diego	$59,040	NV: Las Vegas	no data
CA: San Francisco	$84,500	NY: New York	$69,980
CO: Denver	$64,170	OH: Cincinnati	$71,810
DC: Washington	$85,310	OH: Cleveland	$71,840
FL: Miami	$89,240	OH: Columbus	no data
FL: Orlando	no data	OR: Portland	$82,310
FL: Tampa	$76,640	PA: Philadelphia	$84,220
GA: Atlanta	$76,290	PA: Pittsburgh	$79,040
IL: Chicago	$88,030	TX: Dallas	$85,320
MA: Boston	$75,210	TX: Houston	$82,530
MD: Baltimore	$79,260	WA: Seattle	$55,670

FACTORS THAT MAY AFFECT EARNINGS

Educational Attainment of Workers and Effect on Earnings

Figures are based on a group of occupations: Social Scientists and Related Workers

	Percent at Level	Effect on Earnings
Less than High School	—	—
Some High School	—	—
High School or Equivalent	5.1%	−26.3%
Some College but No Degree	7.5%	−36.0%
Associate Degree	3.6%	−26.8%
Bachelor's Degree	24.8%	−3.1%
Master's Degree	38.2%	2.1%
Doctoral Degree	16.4%	22.5%
First Professional Degree	4.2%	33.8%

Flexibility of Earnings

Average Hours Worked: 37
Workers with a Varying Number of Hours: 3.4%
Workers Earning Some Overtime Pay, Tips, or Commissions: 7.6%
Earnings Benefit of Working Overtime: 1.1%

Gender

	Male	Female
Percent	32.3%	67.7%
Effect on Earnings	—	−5.9%

Union Membership

Percentage Union Members: 13.7%
Earnings Benefit of Union Membership: −6.5%

Veteran Status

Percentage Who Have Been on Active Duty: 6.0%
Earnings Benefit of Veteran Status: 9.4%

19-3041 Sociologists

Study human society and social behavior by examining the groups and social institutions that people form, as well as various social, religious, political, and business organizations. May study the behavior and interaction of groups, trace their origin and growth, and analyze the influence of group activities on individual members.

- Education or Training Required: Master's degree
- Job Growth: 4.7%
- Annual Openings: Fewer than 500
- Self-Employed: 11.7%
- Part-Time: 25.0%

NATIONAL WAGE FIGURES (ANNUAL)

Beginning	25th Percentile	Median	Mean	75th Percentile	90th Percentile
$36,790	$44,610	$60,290	$68,300	$88,240	$115,770

Median Wages for Industries Employing Largest Numbers (Annual)

Industry	Median Income
Religious, Grantmaking, Civic, Professional, and Similar Organizations	$89,860
Nursing and Residential Care Facilities	$70,140
Professional, Scientific, and Technical Services	$67,060
Federal, State, and Local Government	$56,090
Educational Services	$46,380

Median Wages for States (Annual)

State	Wage	State	Wage	State	Wage
AK	no data	KY	no data	NY	$57,120
AL	no data	LA	no data	OH	$61,220
AR	no data	MA	$64,900	OK	no data
AZ	$60,590	MD	no data	OR	no data
CA	$60,780	ME	no data	PA	$58,200
CO	no data	MI	no data	RI	no data
CT	no data	MN	no data	SC	no data
DC	$90,380	MO	no data	SD	no data
DE	no data	MS	no data	TN	no data
FL	$84,310	MT	no data	TX	$40,490
GA	no data	NC	no data	UT	$52,710
HI	no data	ND	no data	VA	$83,320
IA	no data	NE	no data	VT	no data
ID	$53,630	NH	no data	WA	no data
IL	$71,650	NJ	no data	WI	$46,310
IN	no data	NM	no data	WV	no data
KS	no data	NV	no data	WY	no data

Median Wages for the Largest Metropolitan Areas (Annual)

Metro	Wage	Metro	Wage
AZ: Phoenix	$64,690	MI: Detroit	no data
CA: Los Angeles	no data	MN: Minneapolis	no data
CA: Riverside	no data	MO: Kansas City	no data
CA: Sacramento	$67,360	MO: St. Louis	no data
CA: San Diego	no data	NV: Las Vegas	no data
CA: San Francisco	no data	NY: New York	$62,120
CO: Denver	no data	OH: Cincinnati	no data
DC: Washington	$90,510	OH: Cleveland	no data
FL: Miami	$74,410	OH: Columbus	no data
FL: Orlando	no data	OR: Portland	no data
FL: Tampa	no data	PA: Philadelphia	$56,810
GA: Atlanta	$37,980	PA: Pittsburgh	no data
IL: Chicago	$67,830	TX: Dallas	no data
MA: Boston	$67,100	TX: Houston	no data
MD: Baltimore	$35,530	WA: Seattle	no data

FACTORS THAT MAY AFFECT EARNINGS

Educational Attainment of Workers and Effect on Earnings

Figures are based on a group of occupations: Social Scientists and Related Workers

	Percent at Level	Effect on Earnings
Less than High School	—	—
Some High School	—	—
High School or Equivalent	5.1%	−26.3%
Some College but No Degree	7.5%	−36.0%
Associate Degree	3.6%	−26.8%
Bachelor's Degree	24.8%	−3.1%
Master's Degree	38.2%	2.1%
Doctoral Degree	16.4%	22.5%
First Professional Degree	4.2%	33.8%

Flexibility of Earnings

Average Hours Worked: 37
Workers with a Varying Number of Hours: 3.4%
Workers Earning Some Overtime Pay, Tips, or Commissions: 7.6%
Earnings Benefit of Working Overtime: 9.5%

Gender

	Male	Female
Percent	46.7%	53.3%
Effect on Earnings	13.9%	−11.4%

Union Membership

Percentage Union Members: 50.0%
Earnings Benefit of Union Membership: −6.5%

Veteran Status

Percentage Who Have Been on Active Duty: 6.0%
Earnings Benefit of Veteran Status: 9.4%

19-3051 Urban and Regional Planners

Develop comprehensive plans and programs for use of land and physical facilities of local jurisdictions such as towns, cities, counties, and metropolitan areas.

- Education or Training Required: Master's degree
- Job Growth: 15.2%
- Annual Openings: 3,000
- Self-Employed: 0.0%
- Part-Time: 16.7%

NATIONAL WAGE FIGURES (ANNUAL)

Beginning	25th Percentile	Median	Mean	75th Percentile	90th Percentile
$35,610	$44,480	$56,630	$58,940	$71,390	$86,880

Median Wages for Industries Employing Largest Numbers (Annual)

Industry	Median Income
Real Estate	$72,690
Management of Companies and Enterprises	$67,450
Utilities	$63,800
Professional, Scientific, and Technical Services	$62,710
Construction of Buildings	$61,340
Educational Services	$59,710
Religious, Grantmaking, Civic, Professional, and Similar Organizations	$58,480
Federal, State, and Local Government	$55,410
Social Assistance	$52,230

Median Wages for States (Annual)

State	Wage	State	Wage	State	Wage
AK	$58,210	KY	$42,430	NY	$58,930
AL	$52,540	LA	$39,890	OH	$52,820
AR	$41,330	MA	$65,620	OK	$57,200
AZ	$53,850	MD	$56,170	OR	$59,870
CA	$68,210	ME	$52,560	PA	$45,340
CO	$60,450	MI	$55,950	RI	$61,970
CT	$67,060	MN	$56,990	SC	$44,610
DC	$82,340	MO	$50,610	SD	$38,980
DE	$58,120	MS	$37,060	TN	$45,880
FL	$56,770	MT	$43,100	TX	$47,930
GA	$51,420	NC	$47,490	UT	$52,980
HI	$58,730	ND	$51,660	VA	$54,860
IA	$48,020	NE	$53,030	VT	$51,620
ID	$49,920	NH	$47,820	WA	$62,440
IL	$56,510	NJ	$62,120	WI	$47,170
IN	$43,610	NM	$42,780	WV	$48,520
KS	$51,890	NV	$67,880	WY	$50,000

Median Wages for the Largest Metropolitan Areas (Annual)

Area	Wage	Area	Wage
AZ: Phoenix	$56,290	MI: Detroit	$54,950
CA: Los Angeles	$67,210	MN: Minneapolis	$59,270
CA: Riverside	$66,340	MO: Kansas City	$51,950
CA: Sacramento	$67,510	MO: St. Louis	$54,470
CA: San Diego	$65,590	NV: Las Vegas	$71,680
CA: San Francisco	$78,970	NY: New York	$62,980
CO: Denver	$63,540	OH: Cincinnati	$55,130
DC: Washington	$66,780	OH: Cleveland	$50,160
FL: Miami	$66,270	OH: Columbus	$53,180
FL: Orlando	$52,230	OR: Portland	$63,290
FL: Tampa	$58,600	PA: Philadelphia	$58,740
GA: Atlanta	$53,620	PA: Pittsburgh	$47,220
IL: Chicago	$51,070	TX: Dallas	$51,590
MA: Boston	$69,440	TX: Houston	$54,660
MD: Baltimore	$55,710	WA: Seattle	$65,490

FACTORS THAT MAY AFFECT EARNINGS

Educational Attainment of Workers and Effect on Earnings

	Percent at Level	Effect on Earnings
Less than High School	—	—
Some High School	—	—
High School or Equivalent	—	—
Some College but No Degree	—	—
Associate Degree	—	—
Bachelor's Degree	42.1%	−2.0%
Master's Degree	47.4%	2.8%
Doctoral Degree	—	—
First Professional Degree	—	—

Figures do not total 100% because some levels have a very small sample size.

Flexibility of Earnings

Average Hours Worked: 39
Workers with a Varying Number of Hours: 2.4%
Workers Earning Some Overtime Pay, Tips, or Commissions: 7.1%
Earnings Benefit of Working Overtime: 9.5%

Gender

	Male	Female
Percent	73.7%	26.3%
Effect on Earnings	13.9%	−11.4%

Union Membership

Percentage Union Members: 16.7%
Earnings Benefit of Union Membership: −6.5%

Veteran Status

Percentage Who Have Been on Active Duty: 6.0%
Earnings Benefit of Veteran Status: 9.4%

19-3091 Anthropologists and Archeologists

Study the origin, development, and behavior of humans. May study the way of life, language, or physical characteristics of existing people in various parts of the world. May engage in systematic recovery and examination of material evidence, such as tools or pottery remaining from past human cultures, to determine the history, customs, and living habits of earlier civilizations.

- Education or Training Required: Master's degree
- Job Growth: 17.0%
- Annual Openings: Fewer than 500
- Self-Employed: 3.8%
- Part-Time: 25.0%

NATIONAL WAGE FIGURES (ANNUAL)

Beginning	25th Percentile	Median	Mean	75th Percentile	90th Percentile
$28,940	$36,150	$49,930	$52,900	$66,610	$81,490

Median Wages for Industries Employing Largest Numbers (Annual)

Industry	Median Income
Federal, State, and Local Government	$59,560
Professional, Scientific, and Technical Services	$45,010
Museums, Historical Sites, and Similar Institutions	$40,820
Educational Services	$40,750

Median Wages for States (Annual)

AK	$60,440	KY	$51,740	NY	$56,450
AL	no data	LA	$37,150	OH	no data
AR	no data	MA	no data	OK	no data
AZ	$51,040	MD	$32,270	OR	$53,850
CA	$55,300	ME	no data	PA	$45,790
CO	$40,920	MI	$56,020	RI	no data
CT	no data	MN	$59,820	SC	$43,140
DC	$38,490	MO	$42,260	SD	$43,740
DE	no data	MS	$34,470	TN	$42,950
FL	$51,840	MT	$58,110	TX	$46,000
GA	no data	NC	$46,840	UT	$59,090
HI	$56,660	ND	no data	VA	$40,370
IA	no data	NE	no data	VT	no data
ID	$52,060	NH	no data	WA	$44,530
IL	no data	NJ	$45,170	WI	$49,380
IN	no data	NM	$48,550	WV	$40,030
KS	no data	NV	$59,380	WY	$42,230

Median Wages for the Largest Metropolitan Areas (Annual)

AZ: Phoenix	$57,980	MI: Detroit	no data
CA: Los Angeles	$48,920	MN: Minneapolis	$61,030
CA: Riverside	$53,710	MO: Kansas City	no data
CA: Sacramento	$54,930	MO: St. Louis	no data
CA: San Diego	$67,240	NV: Las Vegas	$59,770
CA: San Francisco	$53,670	NY: New York	$47,150
CO: Denver	no data	OH: Cincinnati	no data
DC: Washington	$38,940	OH: Cleveland	no data
FL: Miami	no data	OH: Columbus	no data
FL: Orlando	no data	OR: Portland	$44,180
FL: Tampa	no data	PA: Philadelphia	no data
GA: Atlanta	no data	PA: Pittsburgh	no data
IL: Chicago	no data	TX: Dallas	no data
MA: Boston	no data	TX: Houston	no data
MD: Baltimore	no data	WA: Seattle	$42,610

FACTORS THAT MAY AFFECT EARNINGS

Educational Attainment of Workers and Effect on Earnings

Figures are based on a group of occupations: Social Scientists and Related Workers

	Percent at Level	Effect on Earnings
Less than High School	—	—
Some High School	—	—
High School or Equivalent	5.1%	−26.3%
Some College but No Degree	7.5%	−36.0%
Associate Degree	3.6%	−26.8%
Bachelor's Degree	24.8%	−3.1%
Master's Degree	38.2%	2.1%
Doctoral Degree	16.4%	22.5%
First Professional Degree	4.2%	33.8%

Flexibility of Earnings

Average Hours Worked: 37
Workers with a Varying Number of Hours: 3.4%
Workers Earning Some Overtime Pay, Tips, or Commissions: 7.6%
Earnings Benefit of Working Overtime: 9.5%

Gender

	Male	Female
Percent	46.7%	53.3%
Effect on Earnings	13.9%	−11.4%

Union Membership

Percentage Union Members: 13.7%
Earnings Benefit of Union Membership: −6.5%

Veteran Status

Percentage Who Have Been on Active Duty: 6.0%
Earnings Benefit of Veteran Status: 9.4%

19-3092 Geographers

Study nature and use of areas of earth's surface, relating and inter-preting interactions of physical and cultural phenomena. Conduct research on physical aspects of a region, including land forms, cli-mates, soils, plants, and animals, and conduct research on the spatial implications of human activities within a given area, including social characteristics, economic activities, and political organiza-tion, as well as researching interdependence between regions at scales ranging from local to global.

- Education or Training Required: Master's degree
- Job Growth: 6.8%
- Annual Openings: Fewer than 500
- Self-Employed: 4.2%
- Part-Time: 25.0%

NATIONAL WAGE FIGURES (ANNUAL)

Beginning	25th Percentile	Median	Mean	75th Percentile	90th Percentile
$37,530	$50,120	$62,990	$63,720	$77,770	$93,930

Median Wages for Industries Employing Largest Numbers (Annual)

Industry	Median Income
Federal, State, and Local Government	$66,500
Professional, Scientific, and Technical Services	$51,550
Educational Services	$40,770

Median Wages for States (Annual)

AK	no data	KY	no data	NY	$64,600
AL	no data	LA	no data	OH	no data
AR	no data	MA	no data	OK	no data
AZ	no data	MD	$71,800	OR	$62,470
CA	$60,780	ME	no data	PA	$46,850
CO	$66,370	MI	no data	RI	no data
CT	no data	MN	no data	SC	no data
DC	no data	MO	no data	SD	no data
DE	no data	MS	$43,540	TN	no data
FL	$61,650	MT	no data	TX	no data
GA	no data	NC	no data	UT	no data
HI	no data	ND	no data	VA	$82,400
IA	no data	NE	no data	VT	no data
ID	no data	NH	no data	WA	no data
IL	no data	NJ	no data	WI	no data
IN	no data	NM	no data	WV	no data
KS	no data	NV	no data	WY	no data

Median Wages for the Largest Metropolitan Areas (Annual)

AZ: Phoenix	no data	MI: Detroit	no data
CA: Los Angeles	no data	MN: Minneapolis	no data
CA: Riverside	no data	MO: Kansas City	no data
CA: Sacramento	no data	MO: St. Louis	no data
CA: San Diego	no data	NV: Las Vegas	no data
CA: San Francisco	no data	NY: New York	no data
CO: Denver	no data	OH: Cincinnati	no data
DC: Washington	$74,560	OH: Cleveland	no data
FL: Miami	no data	OH: Columbus	no data
FL: Orlando	no data	OR: Portland	no data
FL: Tampa	no data	PA: Philadelphia	no data
GA: Atlanta	no data	PA: Pittsburgh	no data
IL: Chicago	no data	TX: Dallas	no data
MA: Boston	no data	TX: Houston	no data
MD: Baltimore	no data	WA: Seattle	no data

FACTORS THAT MAY AFFECT EARNINGS

Educational Attainment of Workers and Effect on Earnings

Figures are based on a group of occupations: Social Scientists and Related Workers

	Percent at Level	Effect on Earnings
Less than High School	—	—
Some High School	—	—
High School or Equivalent	5.1%	−26.3%
Some College but No Degree	7.5%	−36.0%
Associate Degree	3.6%	−26.8%
Bachelor's Degree	24.8%	−3.1%
Master's Degree	38.2%	2.1%
Doctoral Degree	16.4%	22.5%
First Professional Degree	4.2%	33.8%

Flexibility of Earnings

Average Hours Worked: 37
Workers with a Varying Number of Hours: 3.4%
Workers Earning Some Overtime Pay, Tips, or Commissions: 7.6%
Earnings Benefit of Working Overtime: 9.5%

Gender

	Male	Female
Percent	46.7%	53.3%
Effect on Earnings	13.9%	−11.4%

Union Membership

Percentage Union Members: 13.7%
Earnings Benefit of Union Membership: −6.5%

Veteran Status

Percentage Who Have Been on Active Duty: 6.0%
Earnings Benefit of Veteran Status: 9.4%

19-3093 Historians

Research, analyze, record, and interpret the past as recorded in sources such as government and institutional records; newspapers and other periodicals; photographs; interviews; films; and unpublished manuscripts, such as personal diaries and letters.

- Education or Training Required: Master's degree
- Job Growth: 4.3%
- Annual Openings: Fewer than 500
- Self-Employed: 3.6%
- Part-Time: 25.0%

NATIONAL WAGE FIGURES (ANNUAL)

Beginning	25th Percentile	Median	Mean	75th Percentile	90th Percentile
$23,450	$33,550	$48,520	$52,750	$69,320	$89,940

Median Wages for Industries Employing Largest Numbers (Annual)

Industry	Median Income
Professional, Scientific, and Technical Services	$52,830
Federal, State, and Local Government	$48,180
Religious, Grantmaking, Civic, Professional, and Similar Organizations	$46,950
Educational Services	$43,480
Museums, Historical Sites, and Similar Institutions	$43,390

Median Wages for States (Annual)

AK	$51,600	KY	no data	NY	$26,110
AL	$48,330	LA	$33,400	OH	no data
AR	no data	MA	$53,610	OK	$31,010
AZ	$46,640	MD	$56,170	OR	no data
CA	$53,880	ME	no data	PA	$52,580
CO	$58,230	MI	$45,830	RI	no data
CT	no data	MN	no data	SC	no data
DC	$82,300	MO	no data	SD	no data
DE	$37,460	MS	$30,020	TN	no data
FL	$51,630	MT	no data	TX	$44,560
GA	$49,630	NC	$43,830	UT	$45,150
HI	no data	ND	no data	VA	$78,140
IA	no data	NE	no data	VT	no data
ID	no data	NH	no data	WA	$47,100
IL	$40,690	NJ	$57,930	WI	$43,490
IN	no data	NM	no data	WV	no data
KS	$40,050	NV	no data	WY	no data

Median Wages for the Largest Metropolitan Areas (Annual)

AZ: Phoenix	no data	MI: Detroit	no data
CA: Los Angeles	no data	MN: Minneapolis	no data
CA: Riverside	no data	MO: Kansas City	$59,480
CA: Sacramento	$46,460	MO: St. Louis	no data
CA: San Diego	no data	NV: Las Vegas	no data
CA: San Francisco	$65,510	NY: New York	$46,400
CO: Denver	no data	OH: Cincinnati	no data
DC: Washington	$80,050	OH: Cleveland	no data
FL: Miami	no data	OH: Columbus	no data
FL: Orlando	no data	OR: Portland	no data
FL: Tampa	no data	PA: Philadelphia	$65,690
GA: Atlanta	$48,890	PA: Pittsburgh	no data
IL: Chicago	$39,130	TX: Dallas	no data
MA: Boston	$60,110	TX: Houston	no data
MD: Baltimore	no data	WA: Seattle	$46,910

FACTORS THAT MAY AFFECT EARNINGS

Educational Attainment of Workers and Effect on Earnings

Figures are based on a group of occupations: Social Scientists and Related Workers

	Percent at Level	Effect on Earnings
Less than High School	—	—
Some High School	—	—
High School or Equivalent	5.1%	−26.3%
Some College but No Degree	7.5%	−36.0%
Associate Degree	3.6%	−26.8%
Bachelor's Degree	24.8%	−3.1%
Master's Degree	38.2%	2.1%
Doctoral Degree	16.4%	22.5%
First Professional Degree	4.2%	33.8%

Flexibility of Earnings

Average Hours Worked: 37
Workers with a Varying Number of Hours: 3.4%
Workers Earning Some Overtime Pay, Tips, or Commissions: 7.6%
Earnings Benefit of Working Overtime: 9.5%

Gender

	Male	Female
Percent	46.7%	53.3%
Effect on Earnings	13.9%	−11.4%

Union Membership

Percentage Union Members: 13.7%
Earnings Benefit of Union Membership: −6.5%

Veteran Status

Percentage Who Have Been on Active Duty: 6.0%
Earnings Benefit of Veteran Status: 9.4%

19-3094 Political Scientists

Study the origin, development, and operation of political systems. Research a wide range of subjects, such as relations between the United States and foreign countries, the beliefs and institutions of foreign nations, or the politics of small towns or a major metropolis. May study topics such as public opinion, political decision making, and ideology. May analyze the structure and operation of governments, as well as various political entities. May conduct public opinion surveys, analyze election results, or analyze public documents.

- Education or Training Required: Master's degree
- Job Growth: 7.3%
- Annual Openings: Fewer than 500
- Self-Employed: 4.7%
- Part-Time: 25.0%

NATIONAL WAGE FIGURES (ANNUAL)

Beginning	25th Percentile	Median	Mean	75th Percentile	90th Percentile
$36,730	$56,100	$90,140	$86,370	$115,750	$133,120

Median Wages for Industries Employing Largest Numbers (Annual)

Industry	Median Income
Federal, State, and Local Government	$101,570
Religious, Grantmaking, Civic, Professional, and Similar Organizations	$69,860
Professional, Scientific, and Technical Services	$57,070
Educational Services	$43,570

Median Wages for States (Annual)

State		State		State	
AK	no data	KY	no data	NY	no data
AL	no data	LA	no data	OH	no data
AR	no data	MA	no data	OK	no data
AZ	no data	MD	$90,400	OR	no data
CA	$87,730	ME	no data	PA	$67,410
CO	no data	MI	no data	RI	no data
CT	no data	MN	no data	SC	no data
DC	$100,010	MO	no data	SD	no data
DE	no data	MS	no data	TN	no data
FL	no data	MT	no data	TX	$30,880
GA	no data	NC	no data	UT	no data
HI	no data	ND	no data	VA	$106,570
IA	no data	NE	no data	VT	no data
ID	no data	NH	no data	WA	$70,580
IL	no data	NJ	no data	WI	no data
IN	no data	NM	no data	WV	no data
KS	no data	NV	no data	WY	no data

Median Wages for the Largest Metropolitan Areas (Annual)

Metro		Metro	
AZ: Phoenix	no data	MI: Detroit	no data
CA: Los Angeles	no data	MN: Minneapolis	no data
CA: Riverside	no data	MO: Kansas City	no data
CA: Sacramento	no data	MO: St. Louis	no data
CA: San Diego	no data	NV: Las Vegas	no data
CA: San Francisco	no data	NY: New York	$69,660
CO: Denver	no data	OH: Cincinnati	no data
DC: Washington	$100,620	OH: Cleveland	no data
FL: Miami	no data	OH: Columbus	no data
FL: Orlando	no data	OR: Portland	no data
FL: Tampa	no data	PA: Philadelphia	no data
GA: Atlanta	no data	PA: Pittsburgh	no data
IL: Chicago	no data	TX: Dallas	no data
MA: Boston	no data	TX: Houston	no data
MD: Baltimore	no data	WA: Seattle	$68,400

FACTORS THAT MAY AFFECT EARNINGS

Educational Attainment of Workers and Effect on Earnings

Figures are based on a group of occupations: Social Scientists and Related Workers

	Percent at Level	Effect on Earnings
Less than High School	—	—
Some High School	—	—
High School or Equivalent	5.1%	−26.3%
Some College but No Degree	7.5%	−36.0%
Associate Degree	3.6%	−26.8%
Bachelor's Degree	24.8%	−3.1%
Master's Degree	38.2%	2.1%
Doctoral Degree	16.4%	22.5%
First Professional Degree	4.2%	33.8%

Flexibility of Earnings

Average Hours Worked: 37
Workers with a Varying Number of Hours: 3.4%
Workers Earning Some Overtime Pay, Tips, or Commissions: 7.6%
Earnings Benefit of Working Overtime: 9.5%

Gender

	Male	Female
Percent	46.7%	53.3%
Effect on Earnings	13.9%	−11.4%

Union Membership

Percentage Union Members: 13.7%
Earnings Benefit of Union Membership: −6.5%

Veteran Status

Percentage Who Have Been on Active Duty: 6.0%
Earnings Benefit of Veteran Status: 9.4%

19-3099 Social Scientists and Related Workers, All Other

All social scientists and related workers not listed separately.

- Education or Training Required: Master's degree
- Job Growth: 12.3%
- Annual Openings: 3,000
- Self-Employed: 7.5%
- Part-Time: 25.0%

NATIONAL WAGE FIGURES (ANNUAL)

Beginning	25th Percentile	Median	Mean	75th Percentile	90th Percentile
$38,230	$49,860	$64,920	$67,720	$81,610	$103,390

Median Wages for Industries Employing Largest Numbers (Annual)

Industry	Median Income
Miscellaneous Manufacturing	$75,620
Postal Service	$71,220
Nursing and Residential Care Facilities	$69,810
Religious, Grantmaking, Civic, Professional, and Similar Organizations	$69,650
Publishing Industries (Except Internet)	$69,580
Professional, Scientific, and Technical Services	$67,800
Internet Service Providers, Web Search Portals, and Data-Processing Services	$67,740
Federal, State, and Local Government	$66,950
Administrative and Support Services	$63,420
Management of Companies and Enterprises	$57,150

Median Wages for States (Annual)

AK	no data	KY	$55,810	NY	$54,310
AL	$66,420	LA	$55,900	OH	$66,450
AR	$55,640	MA	$60,620	OK	$57,010
AZ	$59,260	MD	$84,020	OR	$62,060
CA	$63,930	ME	$39,830	PA	$67,300
CO	$66,530	MI	$61,490	RI	$56,900
CT	$66,310	MN	$59,120	SC	$59,750
DC	$74,450	MO	$47,300	SD	$56,930
DE	$67,420	MS	$46,600	TN	$60,800
FL	$65,710	MT	$57,400	TX	$66,000
GA	$63,450	NC	$58,850	UT	$56,890
HI	$67,850	ND	$57,320	VA	$91,230
IA	$58,190	NE	$65,540	VT	$64,190
ID	$34,700	NH	$57,390	WA	$58,560
IL	$58,370	NJ	$68,560	WI	$51,060
IN	$51,760	NM	$60,470	WV	$35,980
KS	$66,090	NV	$59,050	WY	$48,120

Median Wages for the Largest Metropolitan Areas (Annual)

AZ: Phoenix	$52,730	MI: Detroit	$70,550
CA: Los Angeles	$64,070	MN: Minneapolis	$58,660
CA: Riverside	$63,710	MO: Kansas City	$73,740
CA: Sacramento	$61,780	MO: St. Louis	$66,050
CA: San Diego	$65,920	NV: Las Vegas	$61,430
CA: San Francisco	$67,900	NY: New York	$56,490
CO: Denver	$68,950	OH: Cincinnati	$60,400
DC: Washington	$86,240	OH: Cleveland	$67,830
FL: Miami	$71,930	OH: Columbus	$59,160
FL: Orlando	$69,380	OR: Portland	$62,970
FL: Tampa	$65,890	PA: Philadelphia	$65,980
GA: Atlanta	$63,940	PA: Pittsburgh	$63,230
IL: Chicago	$56,100	TX: Dallas	$69,830
MA: Boston	$60,360	TX: Houston	$68,070
MD: Baltimore	$79,710	WA: Seattle	$55,220

FACTORS THAT MAY AFFECT EARNINGS

Educational Attainment of Workers and Effect on Earnings

Figures are based on a group of occupations: Social Scientists and Related Workers

	Percent at Level	Effect on Earnings
Less than High School	—	—
Some High School	—	—
High School or Equivalent	5.1%	−26.3%
Some College but No Degree	7.5%	−36.0%
Associate Degree	3.6%	−26.8%
Bachelor's Degree	24.8%	−3.1%
Master's Degree	38.2%	2.1%
Doctoral Degree	16.4%	22.5%
First Professional Degree	4.2%	33.8%

Flexibility of Earnings

Average Hours Worked: 37
Workers with a Varying Number of Hours: 3.4%
Workers Earning Some Overtime Pay, Tips, or Commissions: 7.6%
Earnings Benefit of Working Overtime: 9.5%

Gender

	Male	Female
Percent	46.7%	53.3%
Effect on Earnings	13.9%	−11.4%

Union Membership

Percentage Union Members: 13.7%
Earnings Benefit of Union Membership: −6.5%

Veteran Status

Percentage Who Have Been on Active Duty: 6.0%
Earnings Benefit of Veteran Status: 9.4%

19-4000 Life, Physical, and Social Science Technicians

19-4011 Agricultural and Food Science Technicians

Work with agricultural scientists in food, fiber, and animal research, production, and processing; assist with animal breeding and nutrition work; under supervision, conduct tests and experiments to improve yield and quality of crops or to increase the resistance of plants and animals to disease or insects. Includes technicians who assist food scientists or food technologists in the research, development, production technology, quality control, packaging, processing, and use of foods.

- Education or Training Required: Associate degree
- Job Growth: 13.4%
- Annual Openings: 1,000
- Self-Employed: 0.0%
- Part-Time: 11.1%

NATIONAL WAGE FIGURES (ANNUAL)

Beginning	25th Percentile	Median	Mean	75th Percentile	90th Percentile
$20,850	$25,640	$31,730	$33,700	$39,870	$49,270

Median Wages for Industries Employing Largest Numbers (Annual)

Industry	Median Income
Management of Companies and Enterprises	$35,410
Chemical Manufacturing	$33,630
Beverage and Tobacco Product Manufacturing	$33,430
Food Manufacturing	$32,700
Educational Services	$32,660
Professional, Scientific, and Technical Services	$31,440
Building Material and Garden Equipment and Supplies Dealers	$31,240
Merchant Wholesalers, Nondurable Goods	$29,680
Federal, State, and Local Government	$28,330
Administrative and Support Services	$28,220

Median Wages for States (Annual)

State	Wage	State	Wage	State	Wage
AK	no data	KY	$31,110	NY	$34,970
AL	$27,910	LA	$37,810	OH	$33,460
AR	$31,560	MA	$34,440	OK	$38,670
AZ	$55,620	MD	$40,120	OR	$28,690
CA	$32,370	ME	no data	PA	$30,790
CO	no data	MI	$30,010	RI	no data
CT	$40,790	MN	$35,700	SC	$31,980
DC	no data	MO	no data	SD	$24,740
DE	no data	MS	$27,100	TN	$36,280
FL	$32,990	MT	no data	TX	$28,260
GA	no data	NC	$31,420	UT	$33,320
HI	$35,030	ND	$32,980	VA	$27,190
IA	$31,240	NE	$32,870	VT	no data
ID	$39,240	NH	$33,470	WA	$29,480
IL	$33,920	NJ	$43,700	WI	$30,680
IN	$32,570	NM	$23,810	WV	no data
KS	$32,460	NV	no data	WY	no data

Median Wages for the Largest Metropolitan Areas (Annual)

Area	Wage	Area	Wage
AZ: Phoenix	$53,200	MI: Detroit	no data
CA: Los Angeles	$32,790	MN: Minneapolis	no data
CA: Riverside	$37,290	MO: Kansas City	$35,800
CA: Sacramento	$26,370	MO: St. Louis	$37,290
CA: San Diego	$25,370	NV: Las Vegas	no data
CA: San Francisco	$41,350	NY: New York	$36,660
CO: Denver	no data	OH: Cincinnati	$38,760
DC: Washington	$44,210	OH: Cleveland	$44,170
FL: Miami	$35,020	OH: Columbus	$35,000
FL: Orlando	$33,630	OR: Portland	$23,400
FL: Tampa	$30,830	PA: Philadelphia	$35,690
GA: Atlanta	$28,110	PA: Pittsburgh	$34,610
IL: Chicago	$33,100	TX: Dallas	$31,230
MA: Boston	$34,650	TX: Houston	$30,570
MD: Baltimore	no data	WA: Seattle	$38,090

FACTORS THAT MAY AFFECT EARNINGS

Educational Attainment of Workers and Effect on Earnings

	Percent at Level	Effect on Earnings
Less than High School	—	—
Some High School	—	—
High School or Equivalent	33.3%	−26.1%
Some College but No Degree	23.3%	14.1%
Associate Degree	20.0%	9.0%
Bachelor's Degree	—	—
Master's Degree	—	—
Doctoral Degree	—	—
First Professional Degree	—	—

Figures do not total 100% because some levels have a very small sample size.

Flexibility of Earnings

Average Hours Worked: 35
Workers with a Varying Number of Hours: 6.8%
Workers Earning Some Overtime Pay, Tips, or Commissions: 16.1%
Earnings Benefit of Working Overtime: 9.4%

Gender

	Male	Female
Percent	57.4%	42.6%
Effect on Earnings	13.9%	−11.4%

Union Membership

Percentage Union Members: 10.6%
Earnings Benefit of Union Membership: 33.7%

Veteran Status

Percentage Who Have Been on Active Duty: 7.4%
Earnings Benefit of Veteran Status: 26.6%

19-4021 Biological Technicians

Assist biological and medical scientists in laboratories. Set up, operate, and maintain laboratory instruments and equipment; monitor experiments; make observations; and calculate and record results. May analyze organic substances, such as blood, food, and drugs.

- Education or Training Required: Associate degree
- Job Growth: 17.2%
- Annual Openings: 8,000
- Self-Employed: 0.0%
- Part-Time: 25.2%

NATIONAL WAGE FIGURES (ANNUAL)

Beginning	25th Percentile	Median	Mean	75th Percentile	90th Percentile
$23,670	$28,580	$35,710	$38,240	$45,770	$57,890

Median Wages for Industries Employing Largest Numbers (Annual)

Industry	Median Income
Miscellaneous Manufacturing	$45,570
Computer and Electronic Product Manufacturing	$43,040
Chemical Manufacturing	$39,310
Professional, Scientific, and Technical Services	$38,240
Administrative and Support Services	$38,090
Management of Companies and Enterprises	$37,350
Hospitals	$36,050
Ambulatory Health Care Services	$35,640
Wholesale Electronic Markets and Agents and Brokers	$35,590
Educational Services	$34,950

Median Wages for States (Annual)

AK	$31,410	KY	$28,690	NY	$34,830
AL	$29,170	LA	$28,160	OH	$34,180
AR	$31,280	MA	$44,470	OK	$24,220
AZ	$30,060	MD	$37,350	OR	$31,090
CA	$40,380	ME	no data	PA	$34,840
CO	$37,140	MI	$31,630	RI	no data
CT	$44,560	MN	$42,110	SC	$31,800
DC	$40,940	MO	$32,670	SD	$27,790
DE	no data	MS	$30,510	TN	$30,760
FL	$31,890	MT	$29,190	TX	$34,140
GA	$33,040	NC	$35,970	UT	$28,040
HI	$28,800	ND	$26,510	VA	$33,780
IA	$33,580	NE	$30,190	VT	$31,110
ID	$30,410	NH	$37,110	WA	$35,880
IL	$30,600	NJ	$42,370	WI	$33,410
IN	$37,640	NM	$29,910	WV	$29,590
KS	$31,540	NV	$30,090	WY	$30,670

Median Wages for the Largest Metropolitan Areas (Annual)

AZ: Phoenix	$34,670	MI: Detroit	$31,450
CA: Los Angeles	$37,240	MN: Minneapolis	$35,790
CA: Riverside	$33,550	MO: Kansas City	$34,920
CA: Sacramento	$41,480	MO: St. Louis	no data
CA: San Diego	$39,430	NV: Las Vegas	$35,970
CA: San Francisco	$42,720	NY: New York	$40,160
CO: Denver	no data	OH: Cincinnati	$34,080
DC: Washington	$41,220	OH: Cleveland	$37,010
FL: Miami	$32,740	OH: Columbus	$32,590
FL: Orlando	$28,960	OR: Portland	$33,600
FL: Tampa	$34,690	PA: Philadelphia	$38,430
GA: Atlanta	$28,810	PA: Pittsburgh	$31,080
IL: Chicago	$29,850	TX: Dallas	$41,360
MA: Boston	$46,440	TX: Houston	no data
MD: Baltimore	$35,400	WA: Seattle	$37,510

FACTORS THAT MAY AFFECT EARNINGS

Educational Attainment of Workers and Effect on Earnings

	Percent at Level	Effect on Earnings
Less than High School	—	—
Some High School	—	—
High School or Equivalent	20.0%	–18.7%
Some College but No Degree	—	—
Associate Degree	—	—
Bachelor's Degree	40.0%	0.4%
Master's Degree	—	—
Doctoral Degree	—	—
First Professional Degree	—	—

Figures do not total 100% because some levels have a very small sample size.

Flexibility of Earnings

Average Hours Worked: 37
Workers with a Varying Number of Hours: 7.4%
Workers Earning Some Overtime Pay, Tips, or Commissions: 13.3%
Earnings Benefit of Working Overtime: 9.4%

Gender

	Male	Female
Percent	45.4%	54.6%
Effect on Earnings	13.9%	–11.4%

Union Membership

Percentage Union Members: 10.0%
Earnings Benefit of Union Membership: 33.7%

Veteran Status

Percentage Who Have Been on Active Duty: 7.4%
Earnings Benefit of Veteran Status: 26.6%

19-4031 Chemical Technicians

Conduct chemical and physical laboratory tests to assist scientists in making qualitative and quantitative analyses of solids, liquids, and gaseous materials for purposes such as research and development of new products or processes; quality control; maintenance of environmental standards; and other work involving experimental, theoretical, or practical application of chemistry and related sciences.

- Education or Training Required: Associate degree
- Job Growth: 4.4%
- Annual Openings: 7,000
- Self-Employed: 0.0%
- Part-Time: 3.8%

NATIONAL WAGE FIGURES (ANNUAL)

Beginning	25th Percentile	Median	Mean	75th Percentile	90th Percentile
$24,560	$30,640	$39,240	$40,970	$49,870	$60,120

Median Wages for Industries Employing Largest Numbers (Annual)

Industry	Median Income
Utilities	$57,420
Petroleum and Coal Products Manufacturing	$47,160
Merchant Wholesalers, Nondurable Goods	$45,120
Waste Management and Remediation Services	$43,220
Machinery Manufacturing	$42,640
Chemical Manufacturing	$42,260
Plastics and Rubber Products Manufacturing	$41,740
Mining (Except Oil and Gas)	$41,100
Primary Metal Manufacturing	$39,720
Federal, State, and Local Government	$39,710

Median Wages for States (Annual)

State	Wage	State	Wage	State	Wage
AK	$38,340	KY	$37,450	NY	$37,130
AL	$40,070	LA	$47,810	OH	$39,480
AR	$30,690	MA	$41,390	OK	$36,410
AZ	$34,030	MD	$42,600	OR	$36,500
CA	$39,270	ME	$33,100	PA	$38,170
CO	$40,540	MI	$35,560	RI	$34,800
CT	$40,460	MN	$38,930	SC	$41,580
DC	no data	MO	$42,210	SD	$27,190
DE	$57,210	MS	$32,720	TN	$38,580
FL	$34,110	MT	$27,560	TX	$45,940
GA	$34,600	NC	$36,180	UT	$33,100
HI	no data	ND	$23,720	VA	$44,540
IA	$38,760	NE	$35,310	VT	$32,050
ID	$33,930	NH	$41,350	WA	$39,310
IL	$38,560	NJ	$40,690	WI	$35,770
IN	$37,660	NM	no data	WV	$39,250
KS	$38,240	NV	$43,630	WY	$29,520

Median Wages for the Largest Metropolitan Areas (Annual)

Area	Wage	Area	Wage
AZ: Phoenix	$35,220	MI: Detroit	$39,590
CA: Los Angeles	$37,950	MN: Minneapolis	$40,840
CA: Riverside	$34,890	MO: Kansas City	$40,070
CA: Sacramento	$34,730	MO: St. Louis	$43,690
CA: San Diego	$41,510	NV: Las Vegas	$46,580
CA: San Francisco	$39,830	NY: New York	$38,700
CO: Denver	$37,280	OH: Cincinnati	$40,070
DC: Washington	$48,650	OH: Cleveland	$40,040
FL: Miami	$33,780	OH: Columbus	$38,460
FL: Orlando	$33,650	OR: Portland	$35,660
FL: Tampa	$30,150	PA: Philadelphia	$44,680
GA: Atlanta	$31,650	PA: Pittsburgh	$36,740
IL: Chicago	$40,480	TX: Dallas	$38,910
MA: Boston	$42,980	TX: Houston	$50,540
MD: Baltimore	$38,980	WA: Seattle	$39,970

FACTORS THAT MAY AFFECT EARNINGS

Educational Attainment of Workers and Effect on Earnings

	Percent at Level	Effect on Earnings
Less than High School	—	—
Some High School	—	—
High School or Equivalent	31.0%	−5.1%
Some College but No Degree	23.0%	−3.2%
Associate Degree	20.7%	−5.6%
Bachelor's Degree	20.7%	24.3%
Master's Degree	—	—
Doctoral Degree	—	—
First Professional Degree	—	—

Flexibility of Earnings

Average Hours Worked: 37
Workers with a Varying Number of Hours: 5.6%
Workers Earning Some Overtime Pay, Tips, or Commissions: 25.8%
Earnings Benefit of Working Overtime: 9.4%

Gender

	Male	Female
Percent	64.1%	35.9%
Effect on Earnings	13.9%	−11.4%

Union Membership

Percentage Union Members: 19.6%
Earnings Benefit of Union Membership: 17.3%

Veteran Status

Percentage Who Have Been on Active Duty: 7.4%
Earnings Benefit of Veteran Status: 26.6%

19-4041 Geological and Petroleum Technicians

Assist scientists in the use of electrical, sonic, or nuclear measuring instruments in both laboratory and production activities to obtain data indicating potential sources of metallic ore, gas, or petroleum. Analyze mud and drill cuttings. Chart pressure, temperature, and other characteristics of wells or bore holes. Investigate and collect information leading to the possible discovery of new oil fields.

- Education or Training Required: Associate degree
- Job Growth: 6.5%
- Annual Openings: 1,000
- Self-Employed: 1.6%
- Part-Time: 25.2%

NATIONAL WAGE FIGURES (ANNUAL)

Beginning	25th Percentile	Median	Mean	75th Percentile	90th Percentile
$22,020	$31,560	$46,160	$51,490	$63,740	$88,150

Median Wages for Industries Employing Largest Numbers (Annual)

Industry	Median Income
Utilities	$60,410
Oil and Gas Extraction	$57,760
Management of Companies and Enterprises	$57,500
Merchant Wholesalers, Nondurable Goods	$54,440
Pipeline Transportation	$43,860
Mining (Except Oil and Gas)	$41,280
Federal, State, and Local Government	$38,050
Support Activities for Mining	$38,020
Educational Services	$35,820
Professional, Scientific, and Technical Services	$34,080

Median Wages for States (Annual)

State	Wage	State	Wage	State	Wage
AK	$50,970	KY	no data	NY	no data
AL	$34,560	LA	$52,180	OH	$42,210
AR	no data	MA	$39,580	OK	$45,670
AZ	no data	MD	$42,680	OR	no data
CA	$68,080	ME	no data	PA	$39,730
CO	$55,620	MI	$27,750	RI	no data
CT	no data	MN	$40,410	SC	$33,540
DC	no data	MO	$28,980	SD	no data
DE	no data	MS	no data	TN	$34,740
FL	$40,480	MT	no data	TX	$41,530
GA	$39,870	NC	no data	UT	$39,740
HI	no data	ND	no data	VA	$28,660
IA	no data	NE	no data	VT	no data
ID	$31,340	NH	no data	WA	no data
IL	no data	NJ	$50,030	WI	no data
IN	$62,640	NM	$34,300	WV	$31,320
KS	no data	NV	$45,880	WY	$45,770

Median Wages for the Largest Metropolitan Areas (Annual)

Metro	Wage	Metro	Wage
AZ: Phoenix	no data	MI: Detroit	no data
CA: Los Angeles	$69,600	MN: Minneapolis	no data
CA: Riverside	no data	MO: Kansas City	no data
CA: Sacramento	no data	MO: St. Louis	$30,490
CA: San Diego	$47,790	NV: Las Vegas	no data
CA: San Francisco	no data	NY: New York	$48,130
CO: Denver	$57,560	OH: Cincinnati	no data
DC: Washington	$28,340	OH: Cleveland	no data
FL: Miami	no data	OH: Columbus	no data
FL: Orlando	no data	OR: Portland	no data
FL: Tampa	no data	PA: Philadelphia	$41,010
GA: Atlanta	no data	PA: Pittsburgh	$45,440
IL: Chicago	no data	TX: Dallas	$40,690
MA: Boston	$36,920	TX: Houston	$46,910
MD: Baltimore	$42,680	WA: Seattle	no data

FACTORS THAT MAY AFFECT EARNINGS

Educational Attainment of Workers and Effect on Earnings

	Percent at Level	Effect on Earnings
Less than High School	—	—
Some High School	—	—
High School or Equivalent	—	—
Some College but No Degree	28.6%	14.2%
Associate Degree	—	—
Bachelor's Degree	—	—
Master's Degree	—	—
Doctoral Degree	—	—
First Professional Degree	—	—

Figures do not total 100% because some levels have a very small sample size.

Flexibility of Earnings

Average Hours Worked: 40

Workers with a Varying Number of Hours: 4.0%

Workers Earning Some Overtime Pay, Tips, or Commissions: 23.8%

Earnings Benefit of Working Overtime: 9.4%

Gender

	Male	Female
Percent	67.1%	32.9%
Effect on Earnings	13.9%	–11.4%

Union Membership

Percentage Union Members: 4.8%

Earnings Benefit of Union Membership: 33.7%

Veteran Status

Percentage Who Have Been on Active Duty: 7.4%

Earnings Benefit of Veteran Status: 26.6%

19-4051 Nuclear Technicians

Assist scientists in both laboratory and production activities by performing technical tasks involving nuclear physics, primarily in operation, maintenance, production, and quality control support activities.

- Education or Training Required: Associate degree
- Job Growth: 13.7%
- Annual Openings: 1,000
- Self-Employed: 0.0%
- Part-Time: 25.2%

NATIONAL WAGE FIGURES (ANNUAL)

Beginning	25th Percentile	Median	Mean	75th Percentile	90th Percentile
$42,550	$54,240	$65,500	$64,760	$76,570	$89,240

Median Wages for Industries Employing Largest Numbers (Annual)

Industry	Median Income
Utilities	$69,580
Educational Services	$65,730
Professional, Scientific, and Technical Services	$60,660
Fabricated Metal Product Manufacturing	$60,140
Hospitals	$55,760
Ambulatory Health Care Services	$54,710
Administrative and Support Services	$54,150

Median Wages for States (Annual)

AK	no data	KY	no data	NY	no data
AL	no data	LA	$57,760	OH	$58,280
AR	no data	MA	$65,070	OK	no data
AZ	no data	MD	no data	OR	no data
CA	no data	ME	no data	PA	$71,930
CO	no data	MI	$74,430	RI	no data
CT	no data	MN	no data	SC	$56,810
DC	no data	MO	no data	SD	no data
DE	no data	MS	no data	TN	$59,840
FL	$59,920	MT	no data	TX	no data
GA	no data	NC	no data	UT	no data
HI	no data	ND	no data	VA	no data
IA	no data	NE	no data	VT	no data
ID	no data	NH	no data	WA	no data
IL	$67,660	NJ	no data	WI	no data
IN	no data	NM	no data	WV	no data
KS	no data	NV	no data	WY	no data

Median Wages for the Largest Metropolitan Areas (Annual)

AZ: Phoenix	no data	MI: Detroit	no data
CA: Los Angeles	no data	MN: Minneapolis	no data
CA: Riverside	no data	MO: Kansas City	no data
CA: Sacramento	no data	MO: St. Louis	no data
CA: San Diego	no data	NV: Las Vegas	no data
CA: San Francisco	no data	NY: New York	no data
CO: Denver	no data	OH: Cincinnati	no data
DC: Washington	no data	OH: Cleveland	no data
FL: Miami	no data	OH: Columbus	no data
FL: Orlando	no data	OR: Portland	no data
FL: Tampa	no data	PA: Philadelphia	$68,870
GA: Atlanta	no data	PA: Pittsburgh	no data
IL: Chicago	$69,050	TX: Dallas	no data
MA: Boston	$65,630	TX: Houston	no data
MD: Baltimore	no data	WA: Seattle	no data

FACTORS THAT MAY AFFECT EARNINGS

Educational Attainment of Workers and Effect on Earnings

Figures are based on a group of occupations: Life, Physical, and Social Science Technicians

	Percent at Level	Effect on Earnings
Less than High School	—	—
Some High School	3.1%	−39.3%
High School or Equivalent	22.3%	2.7%
Some College but No Degree	27.9%	−13.9%
Associate Degree	14.8%	−7.8%
Bachelor's Degree	20.9%	23.2%
Master's Degree	7.0%	−6.6%
Doctoral Degree	—	—
First Professional Degree	—	—

Flexibility of Earnings

Average Hours Worked: 35
Workers with a Varying Number of Hours: 5.6%
Workers Earning Some Overtime Pay, Tips, or Commissions: 37.5%
Earnings Benefit of Working Overtime: 9.4%

Gender

	Male	Female
Percent	64.1%	35.9%
Effect on Earnings	13.9%	−11.4%

Union Membership

Percentage Union Members: 12.5%
Earnings Benefit of Union Membership: 33.7%

Veteran Status

Percentage Who Have Been on Active Duty: 7.4%
Earnings Benefit of Veteran Status: 26.6%

19-4061 Social Science Research Assistants

Assist social scientists in laboratory, survey, and other social research. May perform publication activities, laboratory analysis, quality control, or data management. Normally these individuals work under the direct supervision of a social scientist and assist in those activities that are more routine.

- Education or Training Required: Associate degree
- Job Growth: 17.4%
- Annual Openings: 4,000
- Self-Employed: 1.2%
- Part-Time: 28.9%

NATIONAL WAGE FIGURES (ANNUAL)

Beginning	25th Percentile	Median	Mean	75th Percentile	90th Percentile
$20,500	$26,270	$33,860	$35,840	$43,310	$54,930

Median Wages for Industries Employing Largest Numbers (Annual)

Industry	Median Income
Management of Companies and Enterprises	$41,470
Federal, State, and Local Government	$40,690
Religious, Grantmaking, Civic, Professional, and Similar Organizations	$39,160
Computer and Electronic Product Manufacturing	$37,640
Publishing Industries (Except Internet)	$36,620
Internet Service Providers, Web Search Portals, and Data-Processing Services	$34,320
Ambulatory Health Care Services	$34,110
Educational Services	$33,060
Professional, Scientific, and Technical Services	$33,060
Hospitals	$31,540

Median Wages for States (Annual)

AK	no data	KY	$26,170	NY	no data
AL	no data	LA	no data	OH	$36,990
AR	$34,440	MA	$43,030	OK	$32,920
AZ	$32,560	MD	$38,970	OR	$35,470
CA	$38,150	ME	$31,110	PA	no data
CO	$32,990	MI	$36,080	RI	no data
CT	$39,410	MN	no data	SC	$28,120
DC	$34,260	MO	$37,200	SD	no data
DE	no data	MS	no data	TN	no data
FL	$37,840	MT	$27,300	TX	$39,140
GA	$51,680	NC	$33,950	UT	$21,980
HI	$37,900	ND	no data	VA	$38,930
IA	no data	NE	$27,870	VT	no data
ID	no data	NH	no data	WA	$34,820
IL	no data	NJ	$30,910	WI	$33,000
IN	$33,230	NM	no data	WV	$34,060
KS	no data	NV	no data	WY	no data

Median Wages for the Largest Metropolitan Areas (Annual)

AZ: Phoenix	no data	MI: Detroit	$35,020
CA: Los Angeles	$34,120	MN: Minneapolis	no data
CA: Riverside	$45,690	MO: Kansas City	$38,440
CA: Sacramento	$32,050	MO: St. Louis	no data
CA: San Diego	$25,710	NV: Las Vegas	no data
CA: San Francisco	$37,240	NY: New York	no data
CO: Denver	$31,490	OH: Cincinnati	$29,160
DC: Washington	$37,020	OH: Cleveland	$40,570
FL: Miami	$27,210	OH: Columbus	$36,300
FL: Orlando	$41,510	OR: Portland	$31,870
FL: Tampa	$29,700	PA: Philadelphia	no data
GA: Atlanta	$53,940	PA: Pittsburgh	$42,530
IL: Chicago	$41,330	TX: Dallas	$38,160
MA: Boston	$43,140	TX: Houston	no data
MD: Baltimore	$36,590	WA: Seattle	$33,270

FACTORS THAT MAY AFFECT EARNINGS

Educational Attainment of Workers and Effect on Earnings

Figures are based on a group of occupations: Other Life, Physical, and Social Science Technicians

	Percent at Level	Effect on Earnings
Less than High School	—	—
Some High School	3.2%	−25.9%
High School or Equivalent	18.4%	19.5%
Some College but No Degree	31.8%	−21.4%
Associate Degree	11.5%	−10.8%
Bachelor's Degree	20.3%	21.7%
Master's Degree	9.7%	1.6%
Doctoral Degree	2.8%	74.4%
First Professional Degree	—	—

Flexibility of Earnings

Average Hours Worked: 35
Workers with a Varying Number of Hours: 6.1%
Workers Earning Some Overtime Pay, Tips, or Commissions: 15.7%
Earnings Benefit of Working Overtime: 10.0%

Gender

	Male	Female
Percent	59.1%	40.9%
Effect on Earnings	13.9%	−11.4%

Union Membership

Percentage Union Members: 10.0%
Earnings Benefit of Union Membership: 37.6%

Veteran Status

Percentage Who Have Been on Active Duty: 7.4%
Earnings Benefit of Veteran Status: 26.6%

19-4091 Environmental Science and Protection Technicians, Including Health

Perform laboratory and field tests to monitor the environment and investigate sources of pollution, including those that affect health. Under direction of an environmental scientist or specialist, may collect samples of gases, soil, water, and other materials for testing and take corrective actions as assigned.

- Education or Training Required: Associate degree
- Job Growth: 16.3%
- Annual Openings: 6,000
- Self-Employed: 1.4%
- Part-Time: 28.9%

NATIONAL WAGE FIGURES (ANNUAL)

Beginning	25th Percentile	Median	Mean	75th Percentile	90th Percentile
$23,600	$29,450	$38,090	$40,260	$49,340	$60,700

Median Wages for Industries Employing Largest Numbers (Annual)

Industry	Median Income
Utilities	$61,430
Petroleum and Coal Products Manufacturing	$51,180
Chemical Manufacturing	$47,810
Paper Manufacturing	$46,990
Waste Management and Remediation Services	$44,910
Computer and Electronic Product Manufacturing	$43,580
Merchant Wholesalers, Nondurable Goods	$42,460
Federal, State, and Local Government	$41,910
Mining (Except Oil and Gas)	$38,790
Educational Services	$37,780

Median Wages for States (Annual)

State	Wage	State	Wage	State	Wage
AK	$36,590	KY	$37,190	NY	$36,930
AL	$32,910	LA	$33,340	OH	$31,400
AR	$32,490	MA	$40,920	OK	$26,670
AZ	no data	MD	$44,990	OR	$41,890
CA	$43,460	ME	$30,230	PA	$33,250
CO	$45,430	MI	$38,300	RI	$39,260
CT	$47,960	MN	$40,720	SC	no data
DC	$54,500	MO	$35,010	SD	$22,250
DE	$32,090	MS	$27,290	TN	$45,580
FL	$33,330	MT	$35,330	TX	$37,660
GA	$32,230	NC	$33,900	UT	$40,140
HI	$38,230	ND	no data	VA	$38,150
IA	$41,380	NE	$38,340	VT	$31,160
ID	$41,980	NH	$35,010	WA	$48,840
IL	$48,120	NJ	$38,430	WI	$37,770
IN	$34,020	NM	$38,510	WV	$26,570
KS	$35,040	NV	$38,540	WY	$32,260

Median Wages for the Largest Metropolitan Areas (Annual)

Metro	Wage	Metro	Wage
AZ: Phoenix	$43,840	MI: Detroit	$39,850
CA: Los Angeles	$44,040	MN: Minneapolis	$41,290
CA: Riverside	$54,870	MO: Kansas City	$34,090
CA: Sacramento	$43,220	MO: St. Louis	$42,840
CA: San Diego	$46,840	NV: Las Vegas	$38,190
CA: San Francisco	$54,110	NY: New York	$37,630
CO: Denver	$46,100	OH: Cincinnati	$35,560
DC: Washington	$48,950	OH: Cleveland	$34,330
FL: Miami	$34,690	OH: Columbus	$31,670
FL: Orlando	$34,540	OR: Portland	$43,250
FL: Tampa	$31,350	PA: Philadelphia	$36,000
GA: Atlanta	$33,760	PA: Pittsburgh	$24,040
IL: Chicago	$45,520	TX: Dallas	$46,160
MA: Boston	$42,070	TX: Houston	$33,210
MD: Baltimore	$43,350	WA: Seattle	$39,300

FACTORS THAT MAY AFFECT EARNINGS

Educational Attainment of Workers and Effect on Earnings

Figures are based on a group of occupations: Other Life, Physical, and Social Science Technicians

	Percent at Level	Effect on Earnings
Less than High School	—	—
Some High School	3.2%	−25.9%
High School or Equivalent	18.4%	19.5%
Some College but No Degree	31.8%	−21.4%
Associate Degree	11.5%	−10.8%
Bachelor's Degree	20.3%	21.7%
Master's Degree	9.7%	1.6%
Doctoral Degree	2.8%	74.4%
First Professional Degree	—	—

Flexibility of Earnings

Average Hours Worked: 33
Workers with a Varying Number of Hours: 6.2%
Workers Earning Some Overtime Pay, Tips, or Commissions: 15.7%
Earnings Benefit of Working Overtime: 10.0%

Gender

	Male	Female
Percent	59.1%	40.9%
Effect on Earnings	13.9%	−11.4%

Union Membership

Percentage Union Members: 10.0%
Earnings Benefit of Union Membership: 37.6%

Veteran Status

Percentage Who Have Been on Active Duty: 7.4%
Earnings Benefit of Veteran Status: 26.6%

19-4092 Forensic Science Technicians

Collect, identify, classify, and analyze physical evidence related to criminal investigations. Perform tests on weapons or substances such as fiber, hair, and tissue to determine significance to investigation. May testify as expert witnesses on evidence or crime laboratory techniques. May serve as specialists in area of expertise, such as ballistics, fingerprinting, handwriting, or biochemistry.

- Education or Training Required: Associate degree
- Job Growth: 36.4%
- Annual Openings: 2,000
- Self-Employed: 1.5%
- Part-Time: 28.9%

NATIONAL WAGE FIGURES (ANNUAL)

Beginning	25th Percentile	Median	Mean	75th Percentile	90th Percentile
$27,530	$34,640	$45,330	$48,130	$58,380	$73,100

Median Wages for Industries Employing Largest Numbers (Annual)

Industry	Median Income
Professional, Scientific, and Technical Services	$50,010
Federal, State, and Local Government	$45,980
Hospitals	$41,980
Ambulatory Health Care Services	$38,760
Educational Services	$26,700

Median Wages for States (Annual)

State	Wage	State	Wage	State	Wage
AK	$54,360	KY	$32,710	NY	no data
AL	$41,850	LA	$40,490	OH	$44,740
AR	$31,720	MA	$51,940	OK	$46,470
AZ	$46,850	MD	$57,690	OR	$54,100
CA	$58,480	ME	no data	PA	$47,720
CO	$49,110	MI	$46,130	RI	no data
CT	$66,020	MN	no data	SC	$38,680
DC	$49,660	MO	$43,960	SD	no data
DE	$52,270	MS	$46,040	TN	$43,540
FL	$39,470	MT	no data	TX	$38,390
GA	$29,890	NC	$33,970	UT	$36,790
HI	$43,650	ND	no data	VA	$51,140
IA	no data	NE	$33,710	VT	no data
ID	$44,330	NH	$49,930	WA	$53,510
IL	$54,160	NJ	$34,740	WI	no data
IN	no data	NM	$48,920	WV	$30,210
KS	$54,170	NV	no data	WY	no data

Median Wages for the Largest Metropolitan Areas (Annual)

Area	Wage	Area	Wage
AZ: Phoenix	$47,100	MI: Detroit	$45,930
CA: Los Angeles	$63,180	MN: Minneapolis	no data
CA: Riverside	no data	MO: Kansas City	no data
CA: Sacramento	$54,490	MO: St. Louis	$58,230
CA: San Diego	no data	NV: Las Vegas	no data
CA: San Francisco	$64,950	NY: New York	$50,270
CO: Denver	$51,750	OH: Cincinnati	no data
DC: Washington	$54,110	OH: Cleveland	no data
FL: Miami	$44,380	OH: Columbus	no data
FL: Orlando	$39,030	OR: Portland	$57,760
FL: Tampa	$42,800	PA: Philadelphia	no data
GA: Atlanta	$33,330	PA: Pittsburgh	no data
IL: Chicago	$50,810	TX: Dallas	$42,750
MA: Boston	no data	TX: Houston	$43,410
MD: Baltimore	no data	WA: Seattle	no data

FACTORS THAT MAY AFFECT EARNINGS

Educational Attainment of Workers and Effect on Earnings

Figures are based on a group of occupations: Other Life, Physical, and Social Science Technicians

	Percent at Level	Effect on Earnings
Less than High School	—	—
Some High School	3.2%	−25.9%
High School or Equivalent	18.4%	19.5%
Some College but No Degree	31.8%	−21.4%
Associate Degree	11.5%	−10.8%
Bachelor's Degree	20.3%	21.7%
Master's Degree	9.7%	1.6%
Doctoral Degree	2.8%	74.4%
First Professional Degree	—	—

Flexibility of Earnings

Average Hours Worked: 33
Workers with a Varying Number of Hours: 6.2%
Workers Earning Some Overtime Pay, Tips, or Commissions: 15.7%
Earnings Benefit of Working Overtime: 10.0%

Gender

	Male	Female
Percent	59.1%	40.9%
Effect on Earnings	13.9%	−11.4%

Union Membership

Percentage Union Members: 10.0%
Earnings Benefit of Union Membership: 37.6%

Veteran Status

Percentage Who Have Been on Active Duty: 7.4%
Earnings Benefit of Veteran Status: 26.6%

19-4093 Forest and Conservation Technicians

Compile data pertaining to size, content, condition, and other characteristics of forest tracts under direction of foresters; train and lead forest workers in forest propagation and fire prevention and suppression. May assist conservation scientists in managing, improving, and protecting rangelands and wildlife habitats and help provide technical assistance regarding the conservation of soil, water, and related natural resources.

- Education or Training Required: Associate degree
- Job Growth: 6.6%
- Annual Openings: 6,000
- Self-Employed: 1.1%
- Part-Time: 28.9%

NATIONAL WAGE FIGURES (ANNUAL)

Beginning	25th Percentile	Median	Mean	75th Percentile	90th Percentile
$22,450	$26,270	$30,880	$33,780	$40,030	$49,380

Median Wages for Industries Employing Largest Numbers (Annual)

Industry	Median Income
Management of Companies and Enterprises	$46,420
Religious, Grantmaking, Civic, Professional, and Similar Organizations	$35,140
Educational Services	$34,380
Professional, Scientific, and Technical Services	$31,580
Federal, State, and Local Government	$30,680
Museums, Historical Sites, and Similar Institutions	$30,300

Median Wages for States (Annual)

AK	$35,080	KY	$31,780	NY	$34,630
AL	$34,960	LA	$39,010	OH	$36,110
AR	$36,030	MA	$38,050	OK	$35,020
AZ	$29,520	MD	no data	OR	$30,980
CA	$31,290	ME	$27,940	PA	$32,290
CO	$29,360	MI	$38,320	RI	no data
CT	$68,180	MN	$33,870	SC	$33,390
DC	no data	MO	$27,410	SD	$28,780
DE	no data	MS	$35,580	TN	$29,910
FL	$36,900	MT	$29,070	TX	$35,230
GA	$36,500	NC	$34,620	UT	$27,990
HI	$34,360	ND	$32,480	VA	$32,640
IA	$36,160	NE	$22,570	VT	$29,430
ID	$29,410	NH	$30,090	WA	$31,410
IL	$35,130	NJ	$43,280	WI	$34,380
IN	$30,210	NM	$29,500	WV	$30,760
KS	$36,710	NV	$30,440	WY	$28,640

Median Wages for the Largest Metropolitan Areas (Annual)

AZ: Phoenix	$29,860	MI: Detroit	no data
CA: Los Angeles	$30,700	MN: Minneapolis	$31,080
CA: Riverside	$35,450	MO: Kansas City	no data
CA: Sacramento	$31,950	MO: St. Louis	$27,840
CA: San Diego	$35,690	NV: Las Vegas	$33,440
CA: San Francisco	$30,730	NY: New York	$44,520
CO: Denver	$30,650	OH: Cincinnati	no data
DC: Washington	$43,130	OH: Cleveland	no data
FL: Miami	$34,910	OH: Columbus	no data
FL: Orlando	no data	OR: Portland	$33,220
FL: Tampa	no data	PA: Philadelphia	$43,020
GA: Atlanta	no data	PA: Pittsburgh	no data
IL: Chicago	$36,440	TX: Dallas	no data
MA: Boston	no data	TX: Houston	no data
MD: Baltimore	no data	WA: Seattle	$37,190

FACTORS THAT MAY AFFECT EARNINGS

Educational Attainment of Workers and Effect on Earnings

Figures are based on a group of occupations: Other Life, Physical, and Social Science Technicians

	Percent at Level	Effect on Earnings
Less than High School	—	—
Some High School	3.2%	−25.9%
High School or Equivalent	18.4%	19.5%
Some College but No Degree	31.8%	−21.4%
Associate Degree	11.5%	−10.8%
Bachelor's Degree	20.3%	21.7%
Master's Degree	9.7%	1.6%
Doctoral Degree	2.8%	74.4%
First Professional Degree	—	—

Flexibility of Earnings

Average Hours Worked: 33
Workers with a Varying Number of Hours: 6.2%
Workers Earning Some Overtime Pay, Tips, or Commissions: 15.7%
Earnings Benefit of Working Overtime: 10.0%

Gender

	Male	Female
Percent	59.1%	40.9%
Effect on Earnings	11.0%	−14.6%

Union Membership

Percentage Union Members: 10.0%
Earnings Benefit of Union Membership: 37.6%

Veteran Status

Percentage Who Have Been on Active Duty: 7.4%
Earnings Benefit of Veteran Status: 26.6%

19-4099 Life, Physical, and Social Science Technicians, All Other

All life, physical, and social science technicians not listed separately.

- Education or Training Required: Associate degree
- Job Growth: 20.0%
- Annual Openings: 18,000
- Self-Employed: 2.7%
- Part-Time: 28.9%

NATIONAL WAGE FIGURES (ANNUAL)

Beginning	25th Percentile	Median	Mean	75th Percentile	90th Percentile
$21,890	$28,740	$37,920	$40,870	$50,790	$64,060

Median Wages for Industries Employing Largest Numbers (Annual)

Industry	Median Income
Petroleum and Coal Products Manufacturing	$60,890
Nonmetallic Mineral Product Manufacturing	$54,580
Transportation Equipment Manufacturing	$53,580
Publishing Industries (Except Internet)	$49,820
Support Activities for Transportation	$49,030
Pipeline Transportation	$47,730
Primary Metal Manufacturing	$46,490
Chemical Manufacturing	$44,970
Miscellaneous Manufacturing	$43,460
Paper Manufacturing	$43,410

Median Wages for States (Annual)

AK	$45,890	KY	$29,630	NY	$39,900
AL	$39,740	LA	$39,240	OH	$37,620
AR	no data	MA	$46,760	OK	$52,780
AZ	$36,500	MD	$46,870	OR	no data
CA	$44,110	ME	$53,720	PA	$41,930
CO	$41,590	MI	$40,560	RI	$38,930
CT	$44,240	MN	no data	SC	$37,390
DC	$40,440	MO	$30,390	SD	$37,180
DE	$43,150	MS	$39,570	TN	$44,960
FL	$33,940	MT	$37,460	TX	$28,770
GA	$28,750	NC	no data	UT	$33,300
HI	$43,980	ND	$42,340	VA	$40,720
IA	$33,840	NE	no data	VT	no data
ID	$31,500	NH	$37,460	WA	$50,570
IL	$40,480	NJ	$41,730	WI	$34,400
IN	no data	NM	$36,350	WV	$31,350
KS	$43,950	NV	$41,080	WY	$38,730

Median Wages for the Largest Metropolitan Areas (Annual)

AZ: Phoenix	$34,310	MI: Detroit	$44,620
CA: Los Angeles	$40,800	MN: Minneapolis	no data
CA: Riverside	$35,930	MO: Kansas City	$48,120
CA: Sacramento	$43,300	MO: St. Louis	$37,690
CA: San Diego	$30,920	NV: Las Vegas	$54,360
CA: San Francisco	$42,700	NY: New York	$41,080
CO: Denver	$41,890	OH: Cincinnati	$45,810
DC: Washington	$47,280	OH: Cleveland	$37,940
FL: Miami	$32,090	OH: Columbus	$36,870
FL: Orlando	$33,910	OR: Portland	no data
FL: Tampa	$35,500	PA: Philadelphia	$45,960
GA: Atlanta	$32,830	PA: Pittsburgh	no data
IL: Chicago	$42,310	TX: Dallas	$29,540
MA: Boston	$46,500	TX: Houston	$33,830
MD: Baltimore	$42,550	WA: Seattle	$50,250

FACTORS THAT MAY AFFECT EARNINGS

Educational Attainment of Workers and Effect on Earnings

Figures are based on a group of occupations: Other Life, Physical, and Social Science Technicians

	Percent at Level	Effect on Earnings
Less than High School	—	—
Some High School	3.2%	−25.9%
High School or Equivalent	18.4%	19.5%
Some College but No Degree	31.8%	−21.4%
Associate Degree	11.5%	−10.8%
Bachelor's Degree	20.3%	21.7%
Master's Degree	9.7%	1.6%
Doctoral Degree	2.8%	74.4%
First Professional Degree	—	—

Flexibility of Earnings

Average Hours Worked: 33
Workers with a Varying Number of Hours: 6.2%
Workers Earning Some Overtime Pay, Tips, or Commissions: 15.7%
Earnings Benefit of Working Overtime: 10.0%

Gender

	Male	Female
Percent	57.5%	42.5%
Effect on Earnings	13.9%	−11.4%

Union Membership

Percentage Union Members: 10.0%
Earnings Benefit of Union Membership: 37.6%

Veteran Status

Percentage Who Have Been on Active Duty: 7.4%
Earnings Benefit of Veteran Status: 26.6%

21-0000: Community and Social Services Occupations

21-1000 Counselors, Social Workers, and Other Community and Social Service Specialists

21-1011 Substance Abuse and Behavioral Disorder Counselors

Counsel and advise individuals with alcohol; tobacco; drug; or other problems, such as gambling and eating disorders. May counsel individuals, families, or groups or engage in prevention programs.

- Education or Training Required: Master's degree
- Job Growth: 28.7%
- Annual Openings: 11,000
- Self-Employed: 5.0%
- Part-Time: 22.6%

NATIONAL WAGE FIGURES (ANNUAL)

Beginning	25th Percentile	Median	Mean	75th Percentile	90th Percentile
$22,600	$27,330	$34,040	$35,950	$42,650	$52,340

Median Wages for Industries Employing Largest Numbers (Annual)

Industry	Median Income
Insurance Carriers and Related Activities	$54,980
Educational Services	$42,060
Hospitals	$38,560
Professional, Scientific, and Technical Services	$37,930
Federal, State, and Local Government	$37,910
Management of Companies and Enterprises	$36,780
Ambulatory Health Care Services	$34,000
Religious, Grantmaking, Civic, Professional, and Similar Organizations	$33,210
Social Assistance	$32,960
Administrative and Support Services	$32,920

Median Wages for States (Annual)

AK $41,770	KY $32,690	NY $38,440
AL $31,540	LA $27,300	OH $35,490
AR $24,120	MA $38,360	OK $28,370
AZ $41,520	MD $37,040	OR $33,380
CA $31,460	ME $35,640	PA $32,640
CO $31,630	MI $36,880	RI $35,710
CT $36,940	MN $39,500	SC $36,850
DC $38,790	MO $32,640	SD $30,850
DE $33,410	MS $24,440	TN $30,690
FL $33,270	MT $34,440	TX $31,370
GA $34,880	NC $35,250	UT $36,380
HI $40,000	ND $40,750	VA $39,430
IA $31,860	NE $31,850	VT $39,790
ID $31,110	NH $33,410	WA $33,930
IL $30,430	NJ $36,220	WI $37,170
IN $30,780	NM $33,090	WV $31,940
KS $31,260	NV $37,780	WY $37,450

Median Wages for the Largest Metropolitan Areas (Annual)

AZ: Phoenix $44,330	MI: Detroit $35,360
CA: Los Angeles $28,960	MN: Minneapolis $39,860
CA: Riverside $29,930	MO: Kansas City $33,170
CA: Sacramento $33,100	MO: St. Louis $33,700
CA: San Diego $34,740	NV: Las Vegas $40,190
CA: San Francisco $33,730	NY: New York $40,090
CO: Denver $30,890	OH: Cincinnati $37,480
DC: Washington $42,230	OH: Cleveland $36,280
FL: Miami $35,350	OH: Columbus $37,370
FL: Orlando $34,230	OR: Portland $35,110
FL: Tampa $28,870	PA: Philadelphia $32,120
GA: Atlanta $35,860	PA: Pittsburgh $29,290
IL: Chicago $30,590	TX: Dallas $33,480
MA: Boston $37,560	TX: Houston $31,870
MD: Baltimore $36,240	WA: Seattle $34,700

FACTORS THAT MAY AFFECT EARNINGS

Educational Attainment of Workers and Effect on Earnings

Figures are based on a group of occupations: Counselors, Social Workers, and Other Community and Social Service Specialists

	Percent at Level	Effect on Earnings
Less than High School	—	—
Some High School	1.7%	−43.8%
High School or Equivalent	12.1%	−22.5%
Some College but No Degree	15.8%	−24.0%
Associate Degree	10.3%	−12.0%
Bachelor's Degree	30.5%	3.0%
Master's Degree	25.8%	25.7%
Doctoral Degree	1.6%	26.6%
First Professional Degree	1.9%	36.6%

Flexibility of Earnings

Average Hours Worked: 35
Workers with a Varying Number of Hours: 6.6%
Workers Earning Some Overtime Pay, Tips, or Commissions: 6.1%
Earnings Benefit of Working Overtime: 5.1%

Gender

	Male	Female
Percent	33.2%	66.8%
Effect on Earnings	3.8%	−2.3%

Union Membership

Percentage Union Members: 21.2%
Earnings Benefit of Union Membership: 23.3%

Veteran Status

Percentage Who Have Been on Active Duty: 5.5%
Earnings Benefit of Veteran Status: 7.4%

21-1012 Educational, Vocational, and School Counselors

Counsel individuals and provide group educational and vocational guidance services.

- Education or Training Required: Master's degree
- Job Growth: 14.8%
- Annual Openings: 32,000
- Self-Employed: 5.8%
- Part-Time: 22.6%

NATIONAL WAGE FIGURES (ANNUAL)

Beginning	25th Percentile	Median	Mean	75th Percentile	90th Percentile
$27,240	$36,120	$47,530	$49,760	$60,990	$75,920

Median Wages for Industries Employing Largest Numbers (Annual)

Industry	Median Income
Insurance Carriers and Related Activities	$53,170
Educational Services	$50,710
Federal, State, and Local Government	$46,500
Hospitals	$42,770
Credit Intermediation and Related Activities	$41,860
Professional, Scientific, and Technical Services	$39,810
Management of Companies and Enterprises	$37,390
Ambulatory Health Care Services	$35,150
Religious, Grantmaking, Civic, Professional, and Similar Organizations	$34,860
Social Assistance	$31,630

Median Wages for States (Annual)

AK	$45,900	KY	$49,780	NY	$52,720
AL	$45,080	LA	$44,650	OH	$58,180
AR	$49,050	MA	$50,350	OK	$36,750
AZ	$39,780	MD	$47,710	OR	$46,660
CA	$49,880	ME	$42,060	PA	$44,630
CO	$44,960	MI	$53,660	RI	$56,770
CT	$52,570	MN	$41,090	SC	$44,480
DC	$43,970	MO	$41,530	SD	$34,750
DE	$45,930	MS	$45,610	TN	$41,210
FL	$48,480	MT	$38,310	TX	$50,180
GA	$52,030	NC	$42,200	UT	$43,690
HI	$48,360	ND	$41,350	VA	$53,740
IA	$40,700	NE	$41,690	VT	$45,190
ID	$46,470	NH	$47,360	WA	$49,140
IL	$55,570	NJ	$62,490	WI	$45,730
IN	no data	NM	$44,210	WV	$39,380
KS	$44,380	NV	$46,600	WY	$42,050

Median Wages for the Largest Metropolitan Areas (Annual)

AZ: Phoenix	$38,380	MI: Detroit	$62,000
CA: Los Angeles	$45,350	MN: Minneapolis	$41,260
CA: Riverside	$53,860	MO: Kansas City	$46,700
CA: Sacramento	$54,290	MO: St. Louis	$46,620
CA: San Diego	$48,830	NV: Las Vegas	$46,670
CA: San Francisco	$55,310	NY: New York	$59,640
CO: Denver	$47,810	OH: Cincinnati	$60,560
DC: Washington	$61,230	OH: Cleveland	$66,750
FL: Miami	$46,960	OH: Columbus	$57,880
FL: Orlando	$47,480	OR: Portland	$47,110
FL: Tampa	$53,240	PA: Philadelphia	$47,760
GA: Atlanta	$54,580	PA: Pittsburgh	$46,610
IL: Chicago	$62,420	TX: Dallas	$52,010
MA: Boston	$51,170	TX: Houston	$52,910
MD: Baltimore	$40,020	WA: Seattle	$49,700

FACTORS THAT MAY AFFECT EARNINGS

Educational Attainment of Workers and Effect on Earnings

Figures are based on a group of occupations: Counselors, Social Workers, and Other Community and Social Service Specialists

	Percent at Level	Effect on Earnings
Less than High School	—	—
Some High School	1.7%	−43.8%
High School or Equivalent	12.1%	−22.5%
Some College but No Degree	15.8%	−24.0%
Associate Degree	10.3%	−12.0%
Bachelor's Degree	30.5%	3.0%
Master's Degree	25.8%	25.7%
Doctoral Degree	1.6%	26.6%
First Professional Degree	1.9%	36.6%

Flexibility of Earnings

Average Hours Worked: 35
Workers with a Varying Number of Hours: 6.6%
Workers Earning Some Overtime Pay, Tips, or Commissions: 6.1%
Earnings Benefit of Working Overtime: 5.1%

Gender

	Male	Female
Percent	33.2%	66.8%
Effect on Earnings	3.8%	−2.3%

Union Membership

Percentage Union Members: 21.2%
Earnings Benefit of Union Membership: 23.3%

Veteran Status

Percentage Who Have Been on Active Duty: 5.5%
Earnings Benefit of Veteran Status: 7.4%

21-1013 Marriage and Family Therapists

Diagnose and treat mental and emotional disorders, whether cognitive, affective, or behavioral, within the context of marriage and family systems. Apply psychotherapeutic and family systems theories and techniques in the delivery of professional services to individuals, couples, and families for the purpose of treating such diagnosed nervous and mental disorders.

- Education or Training Required: Master's degree
- Job Growth: 25.4%
- Annual Openings: 3,000
- Self-Employed: 5.5%
- Part-Time: 22.6%

NATIONAL WAGE FIGURES (ANNUAL)

Beginning	25th Percentile	Median	Mean	75th Percentile	90th Percentile
$25,280	$32,950	$43,210	$44,700	$54,150	$69,050

Median Wages for Industries Employing Largest Numbers (Annual)

Industry	Median Income
Federal, State, and Local Government	$48,890
Hospitals	$46,660
Ambulatory Health Care Services	$44,630
Professional, Scientific, and Technical Services	$44,540
Management of Companies and Enterprises	$43,040
Religious, Grantmaking, Civic, Professional, and Similar Organizations	$40,600
Social Assistance	$36,010
Nursing and Residential Care Facilities	$33,420

Median Wages for States (Annual)

AK	$39,500	KY	no data	NY	$35,880
AL	no data	LA	$49,990	OH	$46,510
AR	no data	MA	no data	OK	$50,420
AZ	$45,540	MD	$41,840	OR	$48,610
CA	$41,390	ME	$31,850	PA	$37,360
CO	no data	MI	no data	RI	no data
CT	$45,830	MN	$48,220	SC	no data
DC	no data	MO	no data	SD	$34,620
DE	no data	MS	no data	TN	no data
FL	$39,820	MT	no data	TX	no data
GA	$44,760	NC	$46,210	UT	$44,160
HI	$46,770	ND	no data	VA	$37,310
IA	$31,230	NE	$36,380	VT	$47,400
ID	$45,640	NH	$38,180	WA	$42,040
IL	$35,170	NJ	$51,190	WI	$46,440
IN	$37,910	NM	$41,060	WV	$42,390
KS	no data	NV	$50,430	WY	no data

Median Wages for the Largest Metropolitan Areas (Annual)

AZ: Phoenix	$47,400	MI: Detroit	no data
CA: Los Angeles	$45,420	MN: Minneapolis	$47,850
CA: Riverside	$40,700	MO: Kansas City	$45,650
CA: Sacramento	$50,540	MO: St. Louis	$37,600
CA: San Diego	$44,180	NV: Las Vegas	no data
CA: San Francisco	no data	NY: New York	$49,540
CO: Denver	no data	OH: Cincinnati	$41,380
DC: Washington	$48,270	OH: Cleveland	no data
FL: Miami	$42,330	OH: Columbus	no data
FL: Orlando	$32,400	OR: Portland	$53,500
FL: Tampa	$38,820	PA: Philadelphia	$48,790
GA: Atlanta	$44,870	PA: Pittsburgh	$30,790
IL: Chicago	$37,790	TX: Dallas	no data
MA: Boston	$59,700	TX: Houston	$36,740
MD: Baltimore	$41,710	WA: Seattle	$45,560

FACTORS THAT MAY AFFECT EARNINGS

Educational Attainment of Workers and Effect on Earnings

Figures are based on a group of occupations: Counselors, Social Workers, and Other Community and Social Service Specialists

	Percent at Level	Effect on Earnings
Less than High School	—	—
Some High School	1.7%	−43.8%
High School or Equivalent	12.1%	−22.5%
Some College but No Degree	15.8%	−24.0%
Associate Degree	10.3%	−12.0%
Bachelor's Degree	30.5%	3.0%
Master's Degree	25.8%	25.7%
Doctoral Degree	1.6%	26.6%
First Professional Degree	1.9%	36.6%

Flexibility of Earnings

Average Hours Worked: 35
Workers with a Varying Number of Hours: 6.6%
Workers Earning Some Overtime Pay, Tips, or Commissions: 6.1%
Earnings Benefit of Working Overtime: 5.1%

Gender

	Male	Female
Percent	33.2%	66.8%
Effect on Earnings	3.8%	−2.3%

Union Membership

Percentage Union Members: 21.2%
Earnings Benefit of Union Membership: 23.3%

Veteran Status

Percentage Who Have Been on Active Duty: 5.5%
Earnings Benefit of Veteran Status: 7.4%

21-1014 Mental Health Counselors

Counsel with emphasis on prevention. Work with individuals and groups to promote optimum mental health. May help individuals deal with addictions and substance abuse; family, parenting, and marital problems; suicide; stress management; problems with self-esteem; and issues associated with aging and mental and emotional health.

- Education or Training Required: Master's degree
- Job Growth: 27.2%
- Annual Openings: 14,000
- Self-Employed: 5.0%
- Part-Time: 22.6%

NATIONAL WAGE FIGURES (ANNUAL)

Beginning	25th Percentile	Median	Mean	75th Percentile	90th Percentile
$21,890	$26,780	$34,380	$37,840	$45,610	$59,700

Median Wages for Industries Employing Largest Numbers (Annual)

Industry	Median Income
Federal, State, and Local Government	$44,560
Management of Companies and Enterprises	$40,100
Educational Services	$38,880
Hospitals	$38,060
Ambulatory Health Care Services	$36,080
Social Assistance	$33,710
Religious, Grantmaking, Civic, Professional, and Similar Organizations	$31,400
Administrative and Support Services	$28,940
Nursing and Residential Care Facilities	$27,280

Median Wages for States (Annual)

AK	$38,970	KY	$32,220	NY	$29,830
AL	$31,240	LA	$28,090	OH	$38,600
AR	$39,450	MA	$32,770	OK	$33,010
AZ	$35,020	MD	$31,240	OR	$44,740
CA	$36,350	ME	$40,150	PA	$29,720
CO	$32,940	MI	$38,020	RI	$36,640
CT	$34,320	MN	$37,880	SC	no data
DC	$24,020	MO	$40,890	SD	$34,590
DE	$31,860	MS	$33,870	TN	$27,070
FL	$35,130	MT	no data	TX	no data
GA	$35,540	NC	$33,630	UT	$33,650
HI	no data	ND	$37,790	VA	$39,100
IA	$30,990	NE	$33,370	VT	$45,650
ID	$37,710	NH	$39,110	WA	$39,050
IL	$32,630	NJ	$35,850	WI	$40,560
IN	$32,630	NM	$40,600	WV	$34,890
KS	$31,620	NV	$47,490	WY	$36,930

Median Wages for the Largest Metropolitan Areas (Annual)

AZ: Phoenix	$33,280	MI: Detroit	$35,720
CA: Los Angeles	$31,250	MN: Minneapolis	$39,990
CA: Riverside	$59,810	MO: Kansas City	$41,750
CA: Sacramento	$45,710	MO: St. Louis	$39,640
CA: San Diego	$30,850	NV: Las Vegas	$46,800
CA: San Francisco	$46,410	NY: New York	$32,050
CO: Denver	$31,120	OH: Cincinnati	$36,650
DC: Washington	$39,020	OH: Cleveland	$35,730
FL: Miami	$40,020	OH: Columbus	$39,510
FL: Orlando	$39,640	OR: Portland	$43,590
FL: Tampa	$30,900	PA: Philadelphia	$34,810
GA: Atlanta	$34,830	PA: Pittsburgh	$26,940
IL: Chicago	$33,560	TX: Dallas	$36,120
MA: Boston	$33,420	TX: Houston	$37,510
MD: Baltimore	$33,220	WA: Seattle	$39,500

FACTORS THAT MAY AFFECT EARNINGS

Educational Attainment of Workers and Effect on Earnings

Figures are based on a group of occupations: Counselors, Social Workers, and Other Community and Social Service Specialists

	Percent at Level	Effect on Earnings
Less than High School	—	—
Some High School	1.7%	−43.8%
High School or Equivalent	12.1%	−22.5%
Some College but No Degree	15.8%	−24.0%
Associate Degree	10.3%	−12.0%
Bachelor's Degree	30.5%	3.0%
Master's Degree	25.8%	25.7%
Doctoral Degree	1.6%	26.6%
First Professional Degree	1.9%	36.6%

Flexibility of Earnings

Average Hours Worked: 35
Workers with a Varying Number of Hours: 6.6%
Workers Earning Some Overtime Pay, Tips, or Commissions: 6.1%
Earnings Benefit of Working Overtime: 5.1%

Gender

	Male	Female
Percent	33.2%	66.8%
Effect on Earnings	3.8%	−2.3%

Union Membership

Percentage Union Members: 21.2%
Earnings Benefit of Union Membership: 23.3%

Veteran Status

Percentage Who Have Been on Active Duty: 5.5%
Earnings Benefit of Veteran Status: 7.4%

21-1015 Rehabilitation Counselors

Counsel individuals to maximize the independence and employability of persons coping with personal, social, and vocational difficulties that result from birth defects, illness, disease, accidents, or the stress of daily life. Coordinate activities for residents of care and treatment facilities. Assess client needs and design and implement rehabilitation programs that may include personal and vocational counseling, training, and job placement.

- Education or Training Required: Master's degree
- Job Growth: 23.9%
- Annual Openings: 19,000
- Self-Employed: 5.5%
- Part-Time: 22.6%

NATIONAL WAGE FIGURES (ANNUAL)

Beginning	25th Percentile	Median	Mean	75th Percentile	90th Percentile
$19,260	$22,980	$29,200	$32,870	$39,000	$53,170

Median Wages for Industries Employing Largest Numbers (Annual)

Industry	Median Income
Insurance Carriers and Related Activities	$45,520
Hospitals	$40,170
Federal, State, and Local Government	$39,810
Real Estate	$39,800
Educational Services	$36,560
Miscellaneous Store Retailers	$35,580
Management of Companies and Enterprises	$32,010
Professional, Scientific, and Technical Services	$31,960
Ambulatory Health Care Services	$29,700
Religious, Grantmaking, Civic, Professional, and Similar Organizations	$29,700

Median Wages for States (Annual)

State	Wage	State	Wage	State	Wage
AK	$31,900	KY	$30,780	NY	$23,940
AL	$32,520	LA	$30,630	OH	$37,280
AR	$31,540	MA	$29,780	OK	$20,940
AZ	$26,990	MD	$28,090	OR	$26,450
CA	$35,180	ME	no data	PA	$29,930
CO	$28,540	MI	$40,600	RI	no data
CT	$31,910	MN	$34,880	SC	$31,790
DC	$34,820	MO	$29,540	SD	$29,560
DE	$33,160	MS	$32,520	TN	$19,330
FL	$29,080	MT	$29,440	TX	$32,460
GA	$37,060	NC	$29,230	UT	no data
HI	no data	ND	no data	VA	$28,110
IA	$23,710	NE	$29,780	VT	$46,620
ID	$33,700	NH	$27,450	WA	$32,260
IL	$29,570	NJ	$32,020	WI	$33,060
IN	$27,160	NM	$27,320	WV	$30,400
KS	$24,840	NV	$28,850	WY	$34,590

Median Wages for the Largest Metropolitan Areas (Annual)

Area	Wage	Area	Wage
AZ: Phoenix	$24,430	MI: Detroit	$33,900
CA: Los Angeles	$42,560	MN: Minneapolis	$34,630
CA: Riverside	$28,430	MO: Kansas City	$29,850
CA: Sacramento	$39,790	MO: St. Louis	$30,070
CA: San Diego	$30,050	NV: Las Vegas	$26,380
CA: San Francisco	$35,960	NY: New York	$26,530
CO: Denver	$28,650	OH: Cincinnati	$35,360
DC: Washington	$31,020	OH: Cleveland	$39,740
FL: Miami	$28,840	OH: Columbus	$46,260
FL: Orlando	$28,010	OR: Portland	$28,870
FL: Tampa	$30,400	PA: Philadelphia	$29,870
GA: Atlanta	$39,670	PA: Pittsburgh	$31,740
IL: Chicago	$29,860	TX: Dallas	$33,180
MA: Boston	$29,630	TX: Houston	$34,140
MD: Baltimore	$29,690	WA: Seattle	$31,450

FACTORS THAT MAY AFFECT EARNINGS

Educational Attainment of Workers and Effect on Earnings

Figures are based on a group of occupations: Counselors, Social Workers, and Other Community and Social Service Specialists

	Percent at Level	Effect on Earnings
Less than High School	—	—
Some High School	1.7%	−43.8%
High School or Equivalent	12.1%	−22.5%
Some College but No Degree	15.8%	−24.0%
Associate Degree	10.3%	−12.0%
Bachelor's Degree	30.5%	3.0%
Master's Degree	25.8%	25.7%
Doctoral Degree	1.6%	26.6%
First Professional Degree	1.9%	36.6%

Flexibility of Earnings

Average Hours Worked: 35
Workers with a Varying Number of Hours: 6.6%
Workers Earning Some Overtime Pay, Tips, or Commissions: 6.1%
Earnings Benefit of Working Overtime: 5.1%

Gender

	Male	Female
Percent	33.2%	66.8%
Effect on Earnings	3.8%	−2.3%

Union Membership

Percentage Union Members: 21.2%
Earnings Benefit of Union Membership: 23.3%

Veteran Status

Percentage Who Have Been on Active Duty: 5.5%
Earnings Benefit of Veteran Status: 7.4%

21-1019 Counselors, All Other

All counselors not listed separately.

- Education or Training Required: Master's degree
- Job Growth: 23.1%
- Annual Openings: 4,000
- Self-Employed: 3.1%
- Part-Time: 22.6%

NATIONAL WAGE FIGURES (ANNUAL)

Beginning	25th Percentile	Median	Mean	75th Percentile	90th Percentile
$21,880	$28,950	$38,210	$40,280	$49,700	$60,600

Median Wages for Industries Employing Largest Numbers (Annual)

Industry	Median Income
Educational Services	$50,620
Professional, Scientific, and Technical Services	$48,380
Hospitals	$40,560
Federal, State, and Local Government	$37,870
Ambulatory Health Care Services	$37,470
Management of Companies and Enterprises	$34,660
Administrative and Support Services	$34,180
Real Estate	$34,040
Social Assistance	$31,880
Religious, Grantmaking, Civic, Professional, and Similar Organizations	$29,990

Median Wages for States (Annual)

AK	$38,760	KY	no data	NY	$40,360
AL	$33,130	LA	$31,460	OH	$38,000
AR	no data	MA	$30,930	OK	no data
AZ	$36,650	MD	$42,380	OR	$41,080
CA	$39,060	ME	no data	PA	$43,190
CO	no data	MI	$38,210	RI	$24,290
CT	no data	MN	$35,310	SC	no data
DC	no data	MO	$23,620	SD	no data
DE	no data	MS	no data	TN	$24,290
FL	$32,910	MT	no data	TX	$52,140
GA	$38,470	NC	$28,980	UT	no data
HI	$39,450	ND	$43,550	VA	$36,080
IA	$27,700	NE	no data	VT	no data
ID	$17,560	NH	$32,800	WA	$46,020
IL	$32,050	NJ	$35,320	WI	$37,940
IN	$27,560	NM	no data	WV	no data
KS	$38,460	NV	$36,480	WY	$39,240

Median Wages for the Largest Metropolitan Areas (Annual)

AZ: Phoenix	$36,040	MI: Detroit	$40,530
CA: Los Angeles	$34,410	MN: Minneapolis	$39,850
CA: Riverside	no data	MO: Kansas City	$37,810
CA: Sacramento	$31,760	MO: St. Louis	$29,100
CA: San Diego	$43,040	NV: Las Vegas	$39,290
CA: San Francisco	$46,390	NY: New York	$38,590
CO: Denver	no data	OH: Cincinnati	no data
DC: Washington	$37,570	OH: Cleveland	no data
FL: Miami	$34,930	OH: Columbus	no data
FL: Orlando	$34,590	OR: Portland	$51,610
FL: Tampa	$28,900	PA: Philadelphia	$40,780
GA: Atlanta	$38,590	PA: Pittsburgh	$42,660
IL: Chicago	$29,630	TX: Dallas	$54,920
MA: Boston	$31,160	TX: Houston	$53,900
MD: Baltimore	$43,340	WA: Seattle	$46,630

FACTORS THAT MAY AFFECT EARNINGS

Educational Attainment of Workers and Effect on Earnings

Figures are based on a group of occupations: Counselors, Social Workers, and Other Community and Social Service Specialists

	Percent at Level	Effect on Earnings
Less than High School	—	—
Some High School	1.7%	−43.8%
High School or Equivalent	12.1%	−22.5%
Some College but No Degree	15.8%	−24.0%
Associate Degree	10.3%	−12.0%
Bachelor's Degree	30.5%	3.0%
Master's Degree	25.8%	25.7%
Doctoral Degree	1.6%	26.6%
First Professional Degree	1.9%	36.6%

Flexibility of Earnings

Average Hours Worked: 35
Workers with a Varying Number of Hours: 6.6%
Workers Earning Some Overtime Pay, Tips, or Commissions: 6.1%
Earnings Benefit of Working Overtime: 5.1%

Gender

	Male	Female
Percent	33.2%	66.8%
Effect on Earnings	3.8%	−2.3%

Union Membership

Percentage Union Members: 21.2%
Earnings Benefit of Union Membership: 23.3%

Veteran Status

Percentage Who Have Been on Active Duty: 5.5%
Earnings Benefit of Veteran Status: 7.4%

21-1021 Child, Family, and School Social Workers

Provide social services and assistance to improve the social and psychological functioning of children and their families and to maximize the family well-being and the academic functioning of children. May assist single parents, arrange adoptions, and find foster homes for abandoned or abused children. In schools, they address such problems as teenage pregnancy, misbehavior, and truancy. May also advise teachers on how to deal with problem children.

- Education or Training Required: Bachelor's degree
- Job Growth: 19.0%
- Annual Openings: 31,000
- Self-Employed: 3.3%
- Part-Time: 22.6%

NATIONAL WAGE FIGURES (ANNUAL)

Beginning	25th Percentile	Median	Mean	75th Percentile	90th Percentile
$24,480	$29,590	$37,480	$40,640	$49,060	$62,530

Median Wages for Industries Employing Largest Numbers (Annual)

Industry	Median Income
Educational Services	$47,730
Hospitals	$40,930
Federal, State, and Local Government	$40,590
Professional, Scientific, and Technical Services	$37,370
Real Estate	$35,620
Ambulatory Health Care Services	$34,240
Management of Companies and Enterprises	$33,430
Administrative and Support Services	$33,300
Nursing and Residential Care Facilities	$32,190
Social Assistance	$31,940

Median Wages for States (Annual)

State	Wage	State	Wage	State	Wage
AK	$36,460	KY	no data	NY	$42,540
AL	$33,600	LA	$39,500	OH	$33,520
AR	$29,780	MA	$47,830	OK	$29,150
AZ	$33,960	MD	$45,490	OR	$36,380
CA	$45,460	ME	$36,100	PA	$30,220
CO	$42,600	MI	$45,620	RI	$52,190
CT	$56,910	MN	$47,880	SC	$29,400
DC	$46,600	MO	$30,730	SD	$30,760
DE	$42,960	MS	$29,380	TN	$33,250
FL	$32,520	MT	$32,450	TX	$32,970
GA	$36,400	NC	$37,440	UT	$31,430
HI	$45,850	ND	$37,130	VA	$37,250
IA	$35,530	NE	$30,280	VT	$36,730
ID	$34,250	NH	$38,910	WA	$36,990
IL	$48,730	NJ	$49,490	WI	$42,780
IN	$30,910	NM	$28,970	WV	$26,800
KS	$33,010	NV	$44,520	WY	$34,560

Median Wages for the Largest Metropolitan Areas (Annual)

Area	Wage	Area	Wage
AZ: Phoenix	$34,200	MI: Detroit	$46,370
CA: Los Angeles	$48,820	MN: Minneapolis	$51,020
CA: Riverside	$45,430	MO: Kansas City	$32,210
CA: Sacramento	$40,440	MO: St. Louis	$34,710
CA: San Diego	no data	NV: Las Vegas	$44,920
CA: San Francisco	$50,060	NY: New York	$44,980
CO: Denver	$44,960	OH: Cincinnati	$34,600
DC: Washington	$49,540	OH: Cleveland	$34,730
FL: Miami	$32,970	OH: Columbus	$35,530
FL: Orlando	$33,520	OR: Portland	$36,600
FL: Tampa	$37,250	PA: Philadelphia	$34,400
GA: Atlanta	$36,480	PA: Pittsburgh	$29,860
IL: Chicago	$48,070	TX: Dallas	$35,300
MA: Boston	$46,610	TX: Houston	$33,050
MD: Baltimore	$45,030	WA: Seattle	$37,380

FACTORS THAT MAY AFFECT EARNINGS

Educational Attainment of Workers and Effect on Earnings

Figures are based on a group of occupations: Counselors, Social Workers, and Other Community and Social Service Specialists

	Percent at Level	Effect on Earnings
Less than High School	—	—
Some High School	1.7%	−43.8%
High School or Equivalent	12.1%	−22.5%
Some College but No Degree	15.8%	−24.0%
Associate Degree	10.3%	−12.0%
Bachelor's Degree	30.5%	3.0%
Master's Degree	25.8%	25.7%
Doctoral Degree	1.6%	26.6%
First Professional Degree	1.9%	36.6%

Flexibility of Earnings

Average Hours Worked: 35
Workers with a Varying Number of Hours: 3.8%
Workers Earning Some Overtime Pay, Tips, or Commissions: 6.1%
Earnings Benefit of Working Overtime: −15.3%

Gender

	Male	Female
Percent	17.4%	82.6%
Effect on Earnings	2.3%	−0.5%

Union Membership

Percentage Union Members: 21.2%
Earnings Benefit of Union Membership: 23.3%

Veteran Status

Percentage Who Have Been on Active Duty: 5.5%
Earnings Benefit of Veteran Status: 7.4%

21-1022 Medical and Public Health Social Workers

Provide persons, families, or vulnerable populations with the psychosocial support needed to cope with chronic, acute, or terminal illnesses, such as Alzheimer's, cancer, or AIDS. Services include advising family caregivers, providing patient education and counseling, and making necessary referrals for other social services.

- Education or Training Required: Bachelor's degree
- Job Growth: 25.9%
- Annual Openings: 14,000
- Self-Employed: 3.0%
- Part-Time: 22.6%

NATIONAL WAGE FIGURES (ANNUAL)

Beginning	25th Percentile	Median	Mean	75th Percentile	90th Percentile
$27,280	$34,110	$43,040	$44,690	$53,740	$64,070

Median Wages for Industries Employing Largest Numbers (Annual)

Industry	Median Income
Insurance Carriers and Related Activities	$49,900
Hospitals	$48,560
Educational Services	$45,780
Professional, Scientific, and Technical Services	$45,250
Ambulatory Health Care Services	$44,230
Federal, State, and Local Government	$42,310
Administrative and Support Services	$41,500
Management of Companies and Enterprises	$41,350
Personal and Laundry Services	$38,240
Nursing and Residential Care Facilities	$37,690

Median Wages for States (Annual)

AK $48,500	KY $37,330	NY $46,160
AL $36,760	LA $39,740	OH $40,820
AR $37,360	MA $48,030	OK $39,330
AZ $41,890	MD $50,010	OR $46,770
CA $55,500	ME $37,190	PA $40,350
CO $41,460	MI $43,160	RI $45,340
CT $49,550	MN $44,950	SC $34,550
DC $56,770	MO $38,210	SD $33,800
DE $50,460	MS $33,050	TN $41,600
FL $39,930	MT $33,550	TX $41,920
GA $42,390	NC $39,090	UT $44,290
HI $51,280	ND $34,600	VA $41,630
IA $36,900	NE $36,110	VT $41,430
ID $39,340	NH $45,300	WA $49,040
IL $42,770	NJ $49,350	WI $43,080
IN $40,270	NM $37,530	WV $31,900
KS $41,150	NV $52,020	WY $35,190

Median Wages for the Largest Metropolitan Areas (Annual)

AZ: Phoenix $42,400	MI: Detroit $43,820
CA: Los Angeles $54,060	MN: Minneapolis $46,560
CA: Riverside $54,180	MO: Kansas City $40,400
CA: Sacramento $56,580	MO: St. Louis $39,700
CA: San Diego $54,160	NV: Las Vegas $50,690
CA: San Francisco $60,070	NY: New York $50,650
CO: Denver $41,710	OH: Cincinnati $39,350
DC: Washington $53,960	OH: Cleveland $43,600
FL: Miami $44,150	OH: Columbus $40,240
FL: Orlando $38,020	OR: Portland $51,250
FL: Tampa $36,570	PA: Philadelphia $44,610
GA: Atlanta $43,790	PA: Pittsburgh $40,590
IL: Chicago $44,620	TX: Dallas $42,320
MA: Boston $51,610	TX: Houston $46,120
MD: Baltimore $50,210	WA: Seattle $51,340

FACTORS THAT MAY AFFECT EARNINGS

Educational Attainment of Workers and Effect on Earnings

Figures are based on a group of occupations: Counselors, Social Workers, and Other Community and Social Service Specialists

	Percent at Level	Effect on Earnings
Less than High School	—	—
Some High School	1.7%	−43.8%
High School or Equivalent	12.1%	−22.5%
Some College but No Degree	15.8%	−24.0%
Associate Degree	10.3%	−12.0%
Bachelor's Degree	30.5%	3.0%
Master's Degree	25.8%	25.7%
Doctoral Degree	1.6%	26.6%
First Professional Degree	1.9%	36.6%

Flexibility of Earnings

Average Hours Worked: 35
Workers with a Varying Number of Hours: 3.8%
Workers Earning Some Overtime Pay, Tips, or Commissions: 6.1%
Earnings Benefit of Working Overtime: −15.3%

Gender

	Male	Female
Percent	17.4%	82.6%
Effect on Earnings	2.3%	−0.5%

Union Membership

Percentage Union Members: 21.2%
Earnings Benefit of Union Membership: 23.3%

Veteran Status

Percentage Who Have Been on Active Duty: 5.5%
Earnings Benefit of Veteran Status: 7.4%

21-1023 Mental Health and Substance Abuse Social Workers

Assess and treat individuals with mental, emotional, or substance abuse problems, including abuse of alcohol, tobacco, and/or other drugs. Activities may include individual and group therapy, crisis intervention, case management, client advocacy, prevention, and education.

- Education or Training Required: Master's degree
- Job Growth: 26.7%
- Annual Openings: 15,000
- Self-Employed: 2.5%
- Part-Time: 22.6%

NATIONAL WAGE FIGURES (ANNUAL)

Beginning	25th Percentile	Median	Mean	75th Percentile	90th Percentile
$22,490	$27,940	$35,410	$37,980	$45,720	$57,630

Median Wages for Industries Employing Largest Numbers (Annual)

Industry	Median Income
Professional, Scientific, and Technical Services	$40,540
Hospitals	$39,760
Federal, State, and Local Government	$39,630
Insurance Carriers and Related Activities	$37,160
Educational Services	$36,910
Ambulatory Health Care Services	$35,650
Administrative and Support Services	$34,910
Social Assistance	$34,370
Management of Companies and Enterprises	$33,890
Religious, Grantmaking, Civic, Professional, and Similar Organizations	$32,770

Median Wages for States (Annual)

State	Wage	State	Wage	State	Wage
AK	$34,950	KY	$34,410	NY	$40,020
AL	$27,340	LA	$39,800	OH	$33,740
AR	$35,760	MA	$39,340	OK	$25,620
AZ	$35,530	MD	$46,230	OR	$29,340
CA	$35,910	ME	$38,930	PA	$32,060
CO	$30,410	MI	$39,360	RI	$40,500
CT	$43,570	MN	$47,100	SC	$23,780
DC	$45,090	MO	$30,050	SD	$31,380
DE	$41,680	MS	$28,850	TN	$26,970
FL	$31,330	MT	$29,710	TX	$30,840
GA	$30,290	NC	$36,930	UT	$35,110
HI	$47,020	ND	$35,770	VA	$42,510
IA	$32,560	NE	$30,520	VT	$39,220
ID	$30,870	NH	$34,620	WA	$35,880
IL	$30,750	NJ	$47,500	WI	$41,580
IN	$36,570	NM	$33,440	WV	$21,760
KS	$34,700	NV	no data	WY	$25,920

Median Wages for the Largest Metropolitan Areas (Annual)

Area	Wage	Area	Wage
AZ: Phoenix	$36,140	MI: Detroit	$37,550
CA: Los Angeles	$34,190	MN: Minneapolis	$46,420
CA: Riverside	$35,840	MO: Kansas City	$35,580
CA: Sacramento	$35,900	MO: St. Louis	$31,660
CA: San Diego	$36,800	NV: Las Vegas	$54,780
CA: San Francisco	$39,230	NY: New York	$42,800
CO: Denver	$30,720	OH: Cincinnati	$32,110
DC: Washington	$48,640	OH: Cleveland	$37,960
FL: Miami	$35,270	OH: Columbus	$35,720
FL: Orlando	$28,460	OR: Portland	$27,190
FL: Tampa	$28,780	PA: Philadelphia	$32,240
GA: Atlanta	$30,670	PA: Pittsburgh	$35,370
IL: Chicago	$31,630	TX: Dallas	$29,380
MA: Boston	$42,560	TX: Houston	$34,390
MD: Baltimore	$47,880	WA: Seattle	$35,790

FACTORS THAT MAY AFFECT EARNINGS

Educational Attainment of Workers and Effect on Earnings

Figures are based on a group of occupations: Counselors, Social Workers, and Other Community and Social Service Specialists

	Percent at Level	Effect on Earnings
Less than High School	—	—
Some High School	1.7%	−43.8%
High School or Equivalent	12.1%	−22.5%
Some College but No Degree	15.8%	−24.0%
Associate Degree	10.3%	−12.0%
Bachelor's Degree	30.5%	3.0%
Master's Degree	25.8%	25.7%
Doctoral Degree	1.6%	26.6%
First Professional Degree	1.9%	36.6%

Flexibility of Earnings

Average Hours Worked: 35
Workers with a Varying Number of Hours: 3.8%
Workers Earning Some Overtime Pay, Tips, or Commissions: 6.1%
Earnings Benefit of Working Overtime: −15.3%

Gender

	Male	Female
Percent	17.4%	82.6%
Effect on Earnings	2.3%	−0.5%

Union Membership

Percentage Union Members: 21.2%
Earnings Benefit of Union Membership: 23.3%

Veteran Status

Percentage Who Have Been on Active Duty: 5.5%
Earnings Benefit of Veteran Status: 7.4%

21-1029 Social Workers, All Other

All social workers not listed separately.

- Education or Training Required: Bachelor's degree
- Job Growth: 19.6%
- Annual Openings: 7,000
- Self-Employed: 2.0%
- Part-Time: 22.6%

NATIONAL WAGE FIGURES (ANNUAL)

Beginning	25th Percentile	Median	Mean	75th Percentile	90th Percentile
$25,540	$32,530	$43,580	$44,950	$56,420	$68,500

Median Wages for Industries Employing Largest Numbers (Annual)

Industry	Median Income
Insurance Carriers and Related Activities	$54,290
Hospitals	$51,680
Federal, State, and Local Government	$49,130
Educational Services	$45,280
Real Estate	$41,280
Professional, Scientific, and Technical Services	$40,290
Religious, Grantmaking, Civic, Professional, and Similar Organizations	$37,730
Administrative and Support Services	$37,550
Ambulatory Health Care Services	$36,520
Nursing and Residential Care Facilities	$34,820

Median Wages for States (Annual)

State	Wage	State	Wage	State	Wage
AK	$43,260	KY	$24,440	NY	$48,080
AL	$44,980	LA	$41,520	OH	$39,110
AR	$35,100	MA	$43,470	OK	$31,610
AZ	$51,940	MD	$45,670	OR	$41,770
CA	$45,310	ME	$48,830	PA	$37,200
CO	$37,700	MI	$57,350	RI	$50,310
CT	$50,380	MN	$46,140	SC	$38,010
DC	$60,930	MO	$36,630	SD	$64,480
DE	no data	MS	$61,320	TN	$45,800
FL	$35,350	MT	$41,930	TX	$31,240
GA	$38,250	NC	$55,480	UT	$54,880
HI	$59,320	ND	$54,700	VA	$49,650
IA	$35,110	NE	$43,060	VT	no data
ID	$58,860	NH	$40,420	WA	$47,640
IL	$37,940	NJ	no data	WI	$53,220
IN	$33,700	NM	$24,400	WV	$57,960
KS	$41,290	NV	$54,500	WY	$31,590

Median Wages for the Largest Metropolitan Areas (Annual)

Area	Wage	Area	Wage
AZ: Phoenix	no data	MI: Detroit	$62,650
CA: Los Angeles	$40,190	MN: Minneapolis	$45,640
CA: Riverside	$46,650	MO: Kansas City	$40,710
CA: Sacramento	no data	MO: St. Louis	$41,890
CA: San Diego	$39,500	NV: Las Vegas	no data
CA: San Francisco	$48,400	NY: New York	$49,680
CO: Denver	$38,990	OH: Cincinnati	$41,520
DC: Washington	$55,500	OH: Cleveland	$37,970
FL: Miami	$36,610	OH: Columbus	$41,330
FL: Orlando	$29,180	OR: Portland	$44,140
FL: Tampa	$41,090	PA: Philadelphia	$41,820
GA: Atlanta	$40,660	PA: Pittsburgh	$51,280
IL: Chicago	$37,730	TX: Dallas	$30,220
MA: Boston	$45,670	TX: Houston	$31,190
MD: Baltimore	$48,000	WA: Seattle	$47,760

FACTORS THAT MAY AFFECT EARNINGS

Educational Attainment of Workers and Effect on Earnings

Figures are based on a group of occupations: Counselors, Social Workers, and Other Community and Social Service Specialists

	Percent at Level	Effect on Earnings
Less than High School	—	—
Some High School	1.7%	−43.8%
High School or Equivalent	12.1%	−22.5%
Some College but No Degree	15.8%	−24.0%
Associate Degree	10.3%	−12.0%
Bachelor's Degree	30.5%	3.0%
Master's Degree	25.8%	25.7%
Doctoral Degree	1.6%	26.6%
First Professional Degree	1.9%	36.6%

Flexibility of Earnings

Average Hours Worked: 35
Workers with a Varying Number of Hours: 3.8%
Workers Earning Some Overtime Pay, Tips, or Commissions: 6.1%
Earnings Benefit of Working Overtime: −15.3%

Gender

	Male	Female
Percent	17.4%	82.6%
Effect on Earnings	2.3%	−0.5%

Union Membership

Percentage Union Members: 21.2%
Earnings Benefit of Union Membership: 23.3%

Veteran Status

Percentage Who Have Been on Active Duty: 5.5%
Earnings Benefit of Veteran Status: 7.4%

21-1091 Health Educators

Promote, maintain, and improve individual and community health by helping individuals and communities to adopt healthy behaviors. Collect and analyze data to identify community needs prior to planning, implementing, monitoring, and evaluating programs designed to encourage healthy lifestyles, policies, and environments. May also serve as a resource to assist individuals, other professionals, or the community and may administer fiscal resources for health education programs.

- Education or Training Required: Master's degree
- Job Growth: 22.5%
- Annual Openings: 8,000
- Self-Employed: 0.1%
- Part-Time: 22.6%

NATIONAL WAGE FIGURES (ANNUAL)

Beginning	25th Percentile	Median	Mean	75th Percentile	90th Percentile
$24,750	$31,300	$41,330	$45,370	$56,580	$72,500

Median Wages for Industries Employing Largest Numbers (Annual)

Industry	Median Income
Hospitals	$52,170
Administrative and Support Services	$50,640
Management of Companies and Enterprises	$46,790
Insurance Carriers and Related Activities	$46,480
Federal, State, and Local Government	$44,550
Educational Services	$44,350
Professional, Scientific, and Technical Services	$39,130
Religious, Grantmaking, Civic, Professional, and Similar Organizations	$38,490
Ambulatory Health Care Services	$36,840
Nursing and Residential Care Facilities	$34,480

Median Wages for States (Annual)

State	Wage	State	Wage	State	Wage
AK	$38,330	KY	$38,710	NY	$39,450
AL	$40,280	LA	$48,520	OH	$41,880
AR	$46,780	MA	$42,730	OK	$39,330
AZ	$37,570	MD	$71,680	OR	$45,220
CA	$37,950	ME	$35,480	PA	$38,690
CO	$45,400	MI	$47,400	RI	no data
CT	$51,350	MN	$42,990	SC	$37,120
DC	$58,230	MO	$36,900	SD	$39,400
DE	$46,930	MS	$31,490	TN	$34,290
FL	$43,780	MT	$33,720	TX	$35,200
GA	$52,880	NC	$42,030	UT	$42,060
HI	$44,290	ND	$30,480	VA	$39,110
IA	$35,820	NE	$36,760	VT	$43,930
ID	$42,310	NH	$41,640	WA	$48,760
IL	$41,120	NJ	$44,010	WI	$41,770
IN	$33,710	NM	$36,040	WV	$26,690
KS	$42,810	NV	$49,000	WY	$40,640

Median Wages for the Largest Metropolitan Areas (Annual)

Area	Wage	Area	Wage
AZ: Phoenix	$41,850	MI: Detroit	$48,490
CA: Los Angeles	$34,220	MN: Minneapolis	$45,780
CA: Riverside	$31,110	MO: Kansas City	$47,630
CA: Sacramento	$59,430	MO: St. Louis	$36,160
CA: San Diego	$34,700	NV: Las Vegas	$61,730
CA: San Francisco	$47,890	NY: New York	$41,930
CO: Denver	$43,240	OH: Cincinnati	$43,820
DC: Washington	$69,600	OH: Cleveland	$49,850
FL: Miami	$46,170	OH: Columbus	$37,650
FL: Orlando	$34,770	OR: Portland	$51,120
FL: Tampa	$49,590	PA: Philadelphia	$37,470
GA: Atlanta	$60,140	PA: Pittsburgh	$47,900
IL: Chicago	$43,370	TX: Dallas	$41,660
MA: Boston	$44,980	TX: Houston	$38,320
MD: Baltimore	$52,630	WA: Seattle	$51,760

FACTORS THAT MAY AFFECT EARNINGS

Educational Attainment of Workers and Effect on Earnings

Figures are based on a group of occupations: Counselors, Social Workers, and Other Community and Social Service Specialists

	Percent at Level	Effect on Earnings
Less than High School	—	—
Some High School	1.7%	−43.8%
High School or Equivalent	12.1%	−22.5%
Some College but No Degree	15.8%	−24.0%
Associate Degree	10.3%	−12.0%
Bachelor's Degree	30.5%	3.0%
Master's Degree	25.8%	25.7%
Doctoral Degree	1.6%	26.6%
First Professional Degree	1.9%	36.6%

Flexibility of Earnings

Average Hours Worked: 35
Workers with a Varying Number of Hours: 3.6%
Workers Earning Some Overtime Pay, Tips, or Commissions: 6.1%
Earnings Benefit of Working Overtime: −17.3%

Gender

	Male	Female
Percent	24.9%	75.1%
Effect on Earnings	31.2%	−9.5%

Union Membership

Percentage Union Members: 21.2%
Earnings Benefit of Union Membership: 23.3%

Veteran Status

Percentage Who Have Been on Active Duty: 5.5%
Earnings Benefit of Veteran Status: 7.4%

21-1092 Probation Officers and Correctional Treatment Specialists

Provide social services to assist in rehabilitation of law offenders in custody or on probation or parole. Make recommendations for actions involving formulation of rehabilitation plan and treatment of offender, including conditional release and education and employment stipulations.

- Education or Training Required: Bachelor's degree
- Job Growth: 12.8%
- Annual Openings: 14,000
- Self-Employed: 0.1%
- Part-Time: 22.6%

NATIONAL WAGE FIGURES (ANNUAL)

Beginning	25th Percentile	Median	Mean	75th Percentile	90th Percentile
$28,000	$33,880	$42,500	$46,130	$56,280	$71,160

Median Wages for Industries Employing Largest Numbers (Annual)

Industry	Median Income
Educational Services	$43,260
Federal, State, and Local Government	$43,030
Hospitals	$35,150
Administrative and Support Services	$33,040
Religious, Grantmaking, Civic, Professional, and Similar Organizations	$32,910
Professional, Scientific, and Technical Services	$30,990
Ambulatory Health Care Services	$30,590
Social Assistance	$28,130
Nursing and Residential Care Facilities	$27,070

Median Wages for States (Annual)

AK	$49,930	KY	no data	NY	$55,470
AL	$37,170	LA	$37,200	OH	$41,920
AR	$29,710	MA	$59,790	OK	$29,140
AZ	$37,910	MD	$50,510	OR	$44,690
CA	$70,280	ME	no data	PA	$41,860
CO	$50,860	MI	no data	RI	no data
CT	$56,860	MN	$56,980	SC	$32,540
DC	no data	MO	$33,380	SD	$33,940
DE	no data	MS	$24,120	TN	$31,500
FL	$36,480	MT	$35,910	TX	$34,000
GA	$36,080	NC	$34,510	UT	$35,960
HI	$48,660	ND	$39,950	VA	$40,700
IA	$53,080	NE	$34,260	VT	$47,290
ID	$35,130	NH	$45,700	WA	$47,170
IL	$49,690	NJ	$53,920	WI	$43,030
IN	$31,950	NM	$34,830	WV	$25,370
KS	$36,610	NV	$55,100	WY	$39,310

Median Wages for the Largest Metropolitan Areas (Annual)

AZ: Phoenix	no data	MI: Detroit	no data
CA: Los Angeles	no data	MN: Minneapolis	$60,740
CA: Riverside	$78,000	MO: Kansas City	$33,540
CA: Sacramento	no data	MO: St. Louis	$35,160
CA: San Diego	no data	NV: Las Vegas	no data
CA: San Francisco	$77,080	NY: New York	$55,480
CO: Denver	$49,480	OH: Cincinnati	no data
DC: Washington	$45,630	OH: Cleveland	$45,590
FL: Miami	$36,600	OH: Columbus	no data
FL: Orlando	$36,440	OR: Portland	$49,860
FL: Tampa	$37,210	PA: Philadelphia	$47,290
GA: Atlanta	$36,470	PA: Pittsburgh	$41,550
IL: Chicago	$47,000	TX: Dallas	$33,320
MA: Boston	$59,370	TX: Houston	$36,220
MD: Baltimore	$50,830	WA: Seattle	$47,290

FACTORS THAT MAY AFFECT EARNINGS

Educational Attainment of Workers and Effect on Earnings

Figures are based on a group of occupations: Counselors, Social Workers, and Other Community and Social Service Specialists

	Percent at Level	Effect on Earnings
Less than High School	—	—
Some High School	1.7%	−43.8%
High School or Equivalent	12.1%	−22.5%
Some College but No Degree	15.8%	−24.0%
Associate Degree	10.3%	−12.0%
Bachelor's Degree	30.5%	3.0%
Master's Degree	25.8%	25.7%
Doctoral Degree	1.6%	26.6%
First Professional Degree	1.9%	36.6%

Flexibility of Earnings

Average Hours Worked: 35
Workers with a Varying Number of Hours: 3.6%
Workers Earning Some Overtime Pay, Tips, or Commissions: 6.1%
Earnings Benefit of Working Overtime: −17.3%

Gender

	Male	Female
Percent	29.5%	70.5%
Effect on Earnings	31.2%	−9.5%

Union Membership

Percentage Union Members: 21.2%
Earnings Benefit of Union Membership: 23.3%

Veteran Status

Percentage Who Have Been on Active Duty: 5.5%
Earnings Benefit of Veteran Status: 7.4%

21-1093 Social and Human Service Assistants

Assist professionals from a wide variety of fields, such as psychology, rehabilitation, or social work, to provide client services, as well as support for families. May assist clients in identifying available benefits and social and community services and help clients obtain them. May assist social workers with developing, organizing, and conducting programs to prevent and resolve problems relevant to substance abuse, human relationships, rehabilitation, or adult daycare.

- Education or Training Required: Moderate-term on-the-job training
- Job Growth: 29.7%
- Annual Openings: 61,000
- Self-Employed: 0.1%
- Part-Time: 22.6%

NATIONAL WAGE FIGURES (ANNUAL)

Beginning	25th Percentile	Median	Mean	75th Percentile	90th Percentile
$16,180	$20,350	$25,580	$27,200	$32,440	$40,780

Median Wages for Industries Employing Largest Numbers (Annual)

Industry	Median Income
Professional, Scientific, and Technical Services	$33,670
Federal, State, and Local Government	$30,320
Insurance Carriers and Related Activities	$28,870
Real Estate	$28,870
Hospitals	$28,730
Miscellaneous Store Retailers	$28,060
Educational Services	$26,700
Administrative and Support Services	$26,600
Management of Companies and Enterprises	$25,450
Ambulatory Health Care Services	$25,400

Median Wages for States (Annual)

AK	$30,950	KY	$22,000	NY	$26,700
AL	$25,950	LA	$28,980	OH	$24,990
AR	$21,140	MA	$27,820	OK	$25,380
AZ	$27,270	MD	$30,280	OR	$26,620
CA	$29,030	ME	$22,880	PA	$24,140
CO	$27,700	MI	$27,210	RI	$26,360
CT	$37,500	MN	$25,610	SC	$22,960
DC	$36,630	MO	$23,310	SD	$21,390
DE	$28,690	MS	$20,190	TN	$23,480
FL	$27,550	MT	$21,310	TX	$15,410
GA	$25,290	NC	$24,560	UT	$20,950
HI	$27,640	ND	$21,530	VA	$25,500
IA	$25,630	NE	$22,990	VT	$27,430
ID	$19,740	NH	$24,510	WA	$23,720
IL	$26,090	NJ	$28,890	WI	$28,660
IN	$24,260	NM	$25,110	WV	$15,750
KS	$23,790	NV	$24,210	WY	$21,290

Median Wages for the Largest Metropolitan Areas (Annual)

AZ: Phoenix	$29,490	MI: Detroit	$27,190
CA: Los Angeles	$28,990	MN: Minneapolis	$26,710
CA: Riverside	$26,810	MO: Kansas City	$25,460
CA: Sacramento	$32,260	MO: St. Louis	$24,480
CA: San Diego	$27,920	NV: Las Vegas	no data
CA: San Francisco	no data	NY: New York	$27,350
CO: Denver	$29,520	OH: Cincinnati	$26,820
DC: Washington	$34,590	OH: Cleveland	$24,700
FL: Miami	$28,320	OH: Columbus	$24,560
FL: Orlando	$27,200	OR: Portland	$25,720
FL: Tampa	$27,170	PA: Philadelphia	$26,630
GA: Atlanta	$27,220	PA: Pittsburgh	$22,500
IL: Chicago	$26,480	TX: Dallas	$15,600
MA: Boston	$29,450	TX: Houston	$21,780
MD: Baltimore	$30,670	WA: Seattle	$25,370

FACTORS THAT MAY AFFECT EARNINGS

Educational Attainment of Workers and Effect on Earnings

Figures are based on a group of occupations: Counselors, Social Workers, and Other Community and Social Service Specialists

	Percent at Level	Effect on Earnings
Less than High School	—	—
Some High School	1.7%	−43.8%
High School or Equivalent	12.1%	−22.5%
Some College but No Degree	15.8%	−24.0%
Associate Degree	10.3%	−12.0%
Bachelor's Degree	30.5%	3.0%
Master's Degree	25.8%	25.7%
Doctoral Degree	1.6%	26.6%
First Professional Degree	1.9%	36.6%

Flexibility of Earnings

Average Hours Worked: 35
Workers with a Varying Number of Hours: 3.6%
Workers Earning Some Overtime Pay, Tips, or Commissions: 6.1%
Earnings Benefit of Working Overtime: −17.3%

Gender

	Male	Female
Percent	29.5%	70.5%
Effect on Earnings	31.2%	−9.5%

Union Membership

Percentage Union Members: 21.2%
Earnings Benefit of Union Membership: 23.3%

Veteran Status

Percentage Who Have Been on Active Duty: 5.5%
Earnings Benefit of Veteran Status: 7.4%

21-1099 Community and Social Service Specialists, All Other

All community and social service specialists not listed separately.

- Education or Training Required: Bachelor's degree
- Job Growth: 32.0%
- Annual Openings: 17,000
- Self-Employed: 0.0%
- Part-Time: 22.6%

NATIONAL WAGE FIGURES (ANNUAL)

Beginning	25th Percentile	Median	Mean	75th Percentile	90th Percentile
$21,120	$27,550	$35,210	$37,410	$45,400	$57,790

Median Wages for Industries Employing Largest Numbers (Annual)

Industry	Median Income
Insurance Carriers and Related Activities	$47,290
Construction of Buildings	$40,310
Hospitals	$39,460
Real Estate	$39,300
Federal, State, and Local Government	$39,040
Publishing Industries (Except Internet)	$37,270
Educational Services	$35,020
Professional, Scientific, and Technical Services	$34,490
Museums, Historical Sites, and Similar Institutions	$34,160
Management of Companies and Enterprises	$33,230

Median Wages for States (Annual)

AK	$37,640	KY	$29,660	NY	$38,140
AL	no data	LA	$28,610	OH	$33,490
AR	$26,780	MA	$34,160	OK	$28,530
AZ	$36,740	MD	$35,120	OR	$33,330
CA	$41,260	ME	$26,980	PA	$31,060
CO	$35,230	MI	$42,620	RI	$33,550
CT	$41,930	MN	$36,420	SC	$28,730
DC	$43,370	MO	$29,450	SD	no data
DE	$32,870	MS	no data	TN	$33,380
FL	$35,010	MT	$29,240	TX	$32,870
GA	$32,200	NC	$36,160	UT	$30,620
HI	$43,980	ND	$29,670	VA	$43,890
IA	$26,320	NE	$34,110	VT	$27,630
ID	$37,890	NH	$30,170	WA	$37,530
IL	$31,230	NJ	$42,220	WI	$31,670
IN	$27,480	NM	$34,660	WV	$24,790
KS	$27,920	NV	$37,140	WY	$22,900

Median Wages for the Largest Metropolitan Areas (Annual)

AZ: Phoenix	$35,990	MI: Detroit	$43,200
CA: Los Angeles	$43,560	MN: Minneapolis	$37,060
CA: Riverside	no data	MO: Kansas City	$29,530
CA: Sacramento	$39,930	MO: St. Louis	$28,340
CA: San Diego	$41,050	NV: Las Vegas	$37,850
CA: San Francisco	$40,820	NY: New York	$38,360
CO: Denver	$36,560	OH: Cincinnati	$34,550
DC: Washington	$41,670	OH: Cleveland	$35,270
FL: Miami	$32,560	OH: Columbus	$40,670
FL: Orlando	$35,480	OR: Portland	$33,520
FL: Tampa	$36,670	PA: Philadelphia	$34,520
GA: Atlanta	$33,590	PA: Pittsburgh	$29,190
IL: Chicago	$32,690	TX: Dallas	$42,070
MA: Boston	$34,090	TX: Houston	$32,130
MD: Baltimore	$33,110	WA: Seattle	$38,370

FACTORS THAT MAY AFFECT EARNINGS

Educational Attainment of Workers and Effect on Earnings

Figures are based on a group of occupations: Counselors, Social Workers, and Other Community and Social Service Specialists

	Percent at Level	Effect on Earnings
Less than High School	—	—
Some High School	1.7%	−43.8%
High School or Equivalent	12.1%	−22.5%
Some College but No Degree	15.8%	−24.0%
Associate Degree	10.3%	−12.0%
Bachelor's Degree	30.5%	3.0%
Master's Degree	25.8%	25.7%
Doctoral Degree	1.6%	26.6%
First Professional Degree	1.9%	36.6%

Flexibility of Earnings

Average Hours Worked: 35
Workers with a Varying Number of Hours: 3.6%
Workers Earning Some Overtime Pay, Tips, or Commissions: 6.1%
Earnings Benefit of Working Overtime: −17.3%

Gender

	Male	Female
Percent	29.5%	70.5%
Effect on Earnings	31.2%	−9.5%

Union Membership

Percentage Union Members: 21.2%
Earnings Benefit of Union Membership: 23.3%

Veteran Status

Percentage Who Have Been on Active Duty: 5.5%
Earnings Benefit of Veteran Status: 7.4%

21-2000 Religious Workers

21-2011 Clergy

Conduct religious worship and perform other spiritual functions associated with beliefs and practices of religious faith or denomination. Provide spiritual and moral guidance and assistance to members.

- Education or Training Required: Master's degree
- Job Growth: 12.4%
- Annual Openings: 26,000
- Self-Employed: 0.3%
- Part-Time: 12.9%

NATIONAL WAGE FIGURES (ANNUAL)

Beginning	25th Percentile	Median	Mean	75th Percentile	90th Percentile
$20,730	$28,280	$39,680	$43,060	$53,200	$69,720

Median Wages for Industries Employing Largest Numbers (Annual)

Industry	Median Income
Personal and Laundry Services	$53,640
Federal, State, and Local Government	$53,590
Hospitals	$42,940
Administrative and Support Services	$41,950
Ambulatory Health Care Services	$40,680
Professional, Scientific, and Technical Services	$40,480
Management of Companies and Enterprises	$39,220
Religious, Grantmaking, Civic, Professional, and Similar Organizations	$37,220
Nursing and Residential Care Facilities	$36,700
Real Estate	$36,460

Median Wages for States (Annual)

State	Wage	State	Wage	State	Wage
AK	$35,580	KY	$39,190	NY	$42,400
AL	$35,640	LA	$39,370	OH	$33,800
AR	$33,340	MA	$45,100	OK	$33,250
AZ	$36,890	MD	$37,730	OR	$43,290
CA	$48,850	ME	$48,890	PA	$30,520
CO	$44,210	MI	$29,590	RI	$37,250
CT	$54,240	MN	$36,580	SC	$40,560
DC	no data	MO	$37,860	SD	$35,360
DE	no data	MS	$30,110	TN	$40,660
FL	$32,570	MT	$30,750	TX	$38,010
GA	$35,110	NC	$43,020	UT	no data
HI	$36,490	ND	$38,620	VA	$34,230
IA	$39,040	NE	$41,850	VT	$34,730
ID	$36,380	NH	$44,860	WA	$45,920
IL	$35,790	NJ	$45,760	WI	$43,330
IN	$36,580	NM	$36,040	WV	$21,970
KS	$36,310	NV	$54,650	WY	no data

Median Wages for the Largest Metropolitan Areas (Annual)

Area	Wage	Area	Wage
AZ: Phoenix	$35,450	MI: Detroit	$31,970
CA: Los Angeles	$52,700	MN: Minneapolis	$44,820
CA: Riverside	$37,170	MO: Kansas City	$36,770
CA: Sacramento	$53,850	MO: St. Louis	$40,990
CA: San Diego	$41,680	NV: Las Vegas	$54,200
CA: San Francisco	$55,590	NY: New York	$46,280
CO: Denver	$45,390	OH: Cincinnati	$32,320
DC: Washington	$39,280	OH: Cleveland	$41,330
FL: Miami	$35,290	OH: Columbus	$42,000
FL: Orlando	$33,000	OR: Portland	$42,550
FL: Tampa	$30,700	PA: Philadelphia	$36,360
GA: Atlanta	$32,060	PA: Pittsburgh	$32,800
IL: Chicago	$35,060	TX: Dallas	$39,040
MA: Boston	$43,810	TX: Houston	$38,500
MD: Baltimore	$36,540	WA: Seattle	$50,130

FACTORS THAT MAY AFFECT EARNINGS

Educational Attainment of Workers and Effect on Earnings

	Percent at Level	Effect on Earnings
Less than High School	1.9%	−47.1%
Some High School	1.9%	−35.9%
High School or Equivalent	7.8%	−32.4%
Some College but No Degree	11.8%	−13.8%
Associate Degree	5.9%	−19.8%
Bachelor's Degree	20.1%	−8.7%
Master's Degree	33.9%	11.0%
Doctoral Degree	10.2%	22.4%
First Professional Degree	6.4%	41.4%

Flexibility of Earnings

Average Hours Worked: 34
Workers with a Varying Number of Hours: 20.6%
Workers Earning Some Overtime Pay, Tips, or Commissions: 2.2%
Earnings Benefit of Working Overtime: −13.0%

Gender

	Male	Female
Percent	87.2%	12.8%
Effect on Earnings	2.4%	—

Union Membership

Percentage Union Members: Insignificant
Earnings Benefit of Union Membership: No significant data available

Veteran Status

Percentage Who Have Been on Active Duty: 11.3%
Earnings Benefit of Veteran Status: 0.1%

21-2021 Directors, Religious Activities and Education

Direct and coordinate activities of a denominational group to meet religious needs of students. Plan, direct, or coordinate church school programs designed to promote religious education among church membership. May provide counseling and guidance relative to marital, health, financial, and religious problems.

- Education or Training Required: Bachelor's degree
- Job Growth: 18.5%
- Annual Openings: 10,000
- Self-Employed: 0.0%
- Part-Time: 22.2%

NATIONAL WAGE FIGURES (ANNUAL)

Beginning	25th Percentile	Median	Mean	75th Percentile	90th Percentile
$18,860	$25,700	$34,260	$37,570	$45,340	$61,040

Median Wages for Industries Employing Largest Numbers (Annual)

Industry	Median Income
Federal, State, and Local Government	$83,210
Hospitals	$60,510
Management of Companies and Enterprises	$54,750
Professional, Scientific, and Technical Services	$44,660
Educational Services	$34,910
Nursing and Residential Care Facilities	$34,310
Religious, Grantmaking, Civic, Professional, and Similar Organizations	$33,660
Social Assistance	$33,390

Median Wages for States (Annual)

State	Wage	State	Wage	State	Wage
AK	no data	KY	no data	NY	$32,580
AL	no data	LA	no data	OH	$32,960
AR	no data	MA	$33,550	OK	$24,240
AZ	$33,970	MD	no data	OR	$32,050
CA	$35,780	ME	no data	PA	$36,950
CO	$40,360	MI	$30,830	RI	$35,150
CT	no data	MN	$44,910	SC	$43,600
DC	no data	MO	no data	SD	no data
DE	no data	MS	$32,300	TN	no data
FL	$31,200	MT	$24,530	TX	$37,430
GA	$37,330	NC	$46,240	UT	no data
HI	$29,100	ND	no data	VA	$37,350
IA	$27,970	NE	no data	VT	no data
ID	no data	NH	no data	WA	$39,900
IL	$34,930	NJ	$48,940	WI	$33,060
IN	$25,940	NM	no data	WV	no data
KS	no data	NV	no data	WY	no data

Median Wages for the Largest Metropolitan Areas (Annual)

Area	Wage	Area	Wage
AZ: Phoenix	$35,350	MI: Detroit	$30,170
CA: Los Angeles	$36,190	MN: Minneapolis	$48,730
CA: Riverside	$30,110	MO: Kansas City	no data
CA: Sacramento	$34,180	MO: St. Louis	no data
CA: San Diego	$31,370	NV: Las Vegas	no data
CA: San Francisco	$42,390	NY: New York	$40,270
CO: Denver	$39,960	OH: Cincinnati	$33,000
DC: Washington	$31,080	OH: Cleveland	$39,360
FL: Miami	$31,820	OH: Columbus	no data
FL: Orlando	$35,380	OR: Portland	$32,670
FL: Tampa	$30,460	PA: Philadelphia	no data
GA: Atlanta	$30,310	PA: Pittsburgh	$26,640
IL: Chicago	$34,990	TX: Dallas	$27,400
MA: Boston	$34,590	TX: Houston	$52,720
MD: Baltimore	$37,970	WA: Seattle	$38,450

FACTORS THAT MAY AFFECT EARNINGS

Educational Attainment of Workers and Effect on Earnings

	Percent at Level	Effect on Earnings
Less than High School	—	—
Some High School	—	—
High School or Equivalent	—	—
Some College but No Degree	15.9%	−37.9%
Associate Degree	—	—
Bachelor's Degree	47.8%	−14.4%
Master's Degree	20.3%	65.7%
Doctoral Degree	—	—
First Professional Degree	—	—

Figures do not total 100% because some levels have a very small sample size.

Flexibility of Earnings

Average Hours Worked: 32
Workers with a Varying Number of Hours: 8.3%
Workers Earning Some Overtime Pay, Tips, or Commissions: 1.4%
Earnings Benefit of Working Overtime: −11.6%

Gender

	Male	Female
Percent	39.9%	60.1%
Effect on Earnings	38.3%	−25.4%

Union Membership

Percentage Union Members: Insignificant
Earnings Benefit of Union Membership: No significant data available

Veteran Status

Percentage Who Have Been on Active Duty: 11.3%
Earnings Benefit of Veteran Status: 0.1%

21-2099 Religious Workers, All Other

All religious workers not listed separately.

- Education or Training Required: Bachelor's degree
- Job Growth: 7.4%
- Annual Openings: 9,000
- Self-Employed: 0.1%
- Part-Time: 41.3%

NATIONAL WAGE FIGURES (ANNUAL)

Beginning	25th Percentile	Median	Mean	75th Percentile	90th Percentile
$14,210	$16,140	$24,330	$29,350	$36,180	$52,940

Note: The mean is significantly higher than the median because of the presence of a few star earners.

Median Wages for Industries Employing Largest Numbers (Annual)

Industry	Median Income
Federal, State, and Local Government	$39,280
Nursing and Residential Care Facilities	$36,020
Ambulatory Health Care Services	$32,890
Hospitals	$28,660
Educational Services	$27,980
Religious, Grantmaking, Civic, Professional, and Similar Organizations	$23,560
Social Assistance	$22,900

Median Wages for States (Annual)

State	Wage	State	Wage	State	Wage
AK	no data	KY	no data	NY	no data
AL	no data	LA	no data	OH	$20,490
AR	$15,260	MA	$31,840	OK	no data
AZ	$21,330	MD	$27,380	OR	$28,500
CA	$24,290	ME	no data	PA	$19,760
CO	$24,370	MI	$26,130	RI	no data
CT	no data	MN	$29,740	SC	no data
DC	no data	MO	no data	SD	no data
DE	no data	MS	no data	TN	no data
FL	$23,560	MT	no data	TX	no data
GA	$17,420	NC	$25,160	UT	no data
HI	$18,260	ND	no data	VA	no data
IA	$24,730	NE	no data	VT	no data
ID	no data	NH	no data	WA	$41,120
IL	no data	NJ	no data	WI	no data
IN	$22,980	NM	no data	WV	no data
KS	no data	NV	no data	WY	no data

Median Wages for the Largest Metropolitan Areas (Annual)

Area	Wage	Area	Wage
AZ: Phoenix	no data	MI: Detroit	$23,690
CA: Los Angeles	$23,200	MN: Minneapolis	$30,180
CA: Riverside	no data	MO: Kansas City	no data
CA: Sacramento	no data	MO: St. Louis	no data
CA: San Diego	$24,870	NV: Las Vegas	no data
CA: San Francisco	no data	NY: New York	$22,530
CO: Denver	no data	OH: Cincinnati	$13,760
DC: Washington	$23,630	OH: Cleveland	no data
FL: Miami	$23,210	OH: Columbus	no data
FL: Orlando	$24,620	OR: Portland	$28,250
FL: Tampa	$27,810	PA: Philadelphia	$17,800
GA: Atlanta	$18,650	PA: Pittsburgh	no data
IL: Chicago	no data	TX: Dallas	no data
MA: Boston	no data	TX: Houston	no data
MD: Baltimore	$25,150	WA: Seattle	$42,610

FACTORS THAT MAY AFFECT EARNINGS

Educational Attainment of Workers and Effect on Earnings

	Percent at Level	Effect on Earnings
Less than High School	—	—
Some High School	5.8%	−86.6%
High School or Equivalent	15.5%	−16.0%
Some College but No Degree	18.4%	2.2%
Associate Degree	12.6%	6.0%
Bachelor's Degree	26.2%	6.1%
Master's Degree	15.5%	1.0%
Doctoral Degree	—	—
First Professional Degree	—	—

Figures do not total 100% because some levels have a very small sample size.

Flexibility of Earnings

Average Hours Worked: 27
Workers with a Varying Number of Hours: 9.2%
Workers Earning Some Overtime Pay, Tips, or Commissions: 2.7%
Earnings Benefit of Working Overtime: −11.6%

Gender

	Male	Female
Percent	36.2%	63.8%
Effect on Earnings	7.0%	−5.0%

Union Membership

Percentage Union Members: Insignificant
Earnings Benefit of Union Membership: No significant data available

Veteran Status

Percentage Who Have Been on Active Duty: 11.3%
Earnings Benefit of Veteran Status: 0.1%

23-0000: Legal Occupations

23-1000 Lawyers, Judges, and Related Workers

23-1011 Lawyers

Represent clients in criminal and civil litigation and other legal proceedings, draw up legal documents, and manage or advise clients on legal transactions. May specialize in a single area or may practice broadly in many areas of law.

- Education or Training Required: First professional degree
- Job Growth: 15.0%
- Annual Openings: 40,000
- Self-Employed: 24.1%
- Part-Time: 14.2%

NATIONAL WAGE FIGURES (ANNUAL)

Beginning	25th Percentile	Median	Mean	75th Percentile	90th Percentile
$50,580	$69,910	$102,470	$113,660	more than $145,600	more than $145,600

Median Wages for Industries Employing Largest Numbers (Annual)

Industry	Median Income
Computer and Electronic Product Manufacturing	$144,850
Internet Service Providers, Web Search Portals, and Data-Processing Services	$143,820
Lessors of Nonfinancial Intangible Assets (Except Copyrighted Works)	$141,020
Telecommunications	$140,030
Publishing Industries (Except Internet)	$136,750
Securities, Commodity Contracts, and Other Financial Investments and Related Activities	$136,470
Oil and Gas Extraction	$134,760
Merchant Wholesalers, Nondurable Goods	$133,570
Utilities	$130,440
Chemical Manufacturing	$129,030

Median Wages for States (Annual)

AK	$89,210	KY	$80,600	NY	$113,600
AL	$91,750	LA	$83,030	OH	$90,240
AR	$60,700	MA	$110,490	OK	$75,430
AZ	$98,060	MD	$99,870	OR	$85,490
CA	$124,830	ME	$78,760	PA	$92,750
CO	$89,880	MI	$92,960	RI	$81,810
CT	$103,490	MN	$101,240	SC	$85,400
DC	$134,860	MO	$91,720	SD	$62,620
DE	$124,470	MS	$70,920	TN	$92,230
FL	$89,110	MT	$53,320	TX	$105,370
GA	$103,460	NC	$92,900	UT	$89,260
HI	$82,840	ND	$68,620	VA	$108,650
IA	$81,090	NE	$78,340	VT	$71,820
ID	$84,100	NH	$81,990	WA	$78,350
IL	$120,760	NJ	$106,080	WI	$90,180
IN	$72,320	NM	$76,860	WV	$70,980
KS	$65,490	NV	$106,950	WY	$61,960

Median Wages for the Largest Metropolitan Areas (Annual)

AZ: Phoenix	$104,180	MI: Detroit	$97,830
CA: Los Angeles	$131,000	MN: Minneapolis	$108,450
CA: Riverside	$107,440	MO: Kansas City	$89,180
CA: Sacramento	$98,860	MO: St. Louis	$98,320
CA: San Diego	$115,560	NV: Las Vegas	$105,480
CA: San Francisco	$131,690	NY: New York	$118,020
CO: Denver	$95,020	OH: Cincinnati	$93,210
DC: Washington	$129,320	OH: Cleveland	$102,330
FL: Miami	$93,960	OH: Columbus	$86,430
FL: Orlando	$108,450	OR: Portland	$93,550
FL: Tampa	$91,610	PA: Philadelphia	$102,510
GA: Atlanta	$112,640	PA: Pittsburgh	$93,860
IL: Chicago	$124,480	TX: Dallas	$116,250
MA: Boston	$112,780	TX: Houston	$124,620
MD: Baltimore	$102,290	WA: Seattle	$82,500

FACTORS THAT MAY AFFECT EARNINGS

Educational Attainment of Workers and Effect on Earnings

	Percent at Level	Effect on Earnings
Less than High School	—	—
Some High School	—	—
High School or Equivalent	—	—
Some College but No Degree	—	—
Associate Degree	—	—
Bachelor's Degree	—	—
Master's Degree	—	—
Doctoral Degree	23.3%	2.0%
First Professional Degree	52.1%	3.8%

Figures do not total 100% because some levels have a very small sample size.

Flexibility of Earnings

Average Hours Worked: 41
Workers with a Varying Number of Hours: 8.8%
Workers Earning Some Overtime Pay, Tips, or Commissions: 5.6%
Earnings Benefit of Working Overtime: −14.7%

Gender

	Male	Female
Percent	67.4%	32.6%
Effect on Earnings	7.0%	−5.0%

Union Membership

Percentage Union Members: 5.7%
Earnings Benefit of Union Membership: −8.0%

Veteran Status

Percentage Who Have Been on Active Duty: 9.1%
Earnings Benefit of Veteran Status: 3.4%

23-1021 Administrative Law Judges, Adjudicators, and Hearing Officers

Conduct hearings to decide or recommend decisions on claims concerning government programs or other government-related matters and prepare decisions. Determine penalties or the existence and the amount of liability or recommend the acceptance or rejection of claims or compromise settlements.

- Education or Training Required: Work experience plus degree
- Job Growth: 10.1%
- Annual Openings: 1,000
- Self-Employed: 0.0%
- Part-Time: 14.2%

NATIONAL WAGE FIGURES (ANNUAL)

Beginning	25th Percentile	Median	Mean	75th Percentile	90th Percentile
$36,190	$49,540	$72,600	$77,730	$102,210	$133,850

Median Wages for Industries Employing Largest Numbers (Annual)

Industry	Median Income
Federal, State, and Local Government	$72,590

Median Wages for States (Annual)

AK $64,910	KY .... no data	NY $76,490
AL $119,320	LA $52,420	OH .... no data
AR $38,590	MA $64,780	OK $57,180
AZ $61,780	MD .... no data	OR $55,290
CA $112,210	ME $45,570	PA .... no data
CO $81,100	MI $91,560	RI $74,280
CT $77,640	MN .... no data	SC $48,470
DC .... no data	MO $63,110	SD .... no data
DE $51,880	MS $37,980	TN $49,830
FL $83,250	MT $51,380	TX $66,720
GA $57,060	NC $49,230	UT $59,700
HI .... no data	ND $83,370	VA $64,850
IA .... no data	NE .... no data	VT .... no data
ID $51,620	NH $46,110	WA $76,290
IL $57,990	NJ $89,270	WI $93,380
IN $88,890	NM $56,560	WV $99,380
KS $84,650	NV $57,150	WY .... no data

Median Wages for the Largest Metropolitan Areas (Annual)

AZ: Phoenix $62,360	MI: Detroit $98,050
CA: Los Angeles $110,510	MN: Minneapolis ...... no data
CA: Riverside $116,970	MO: Kansas City $94,730
CA: Sacramento $108,070	MO: St. Louis $95,650
CA: San Diego $115,710	NV: Las Vegas .... no data
CA: San Francisco $118,720	NY: New York $77,260
CO: Denver $81,390	OH: Cincinnati $62,020
DC: Washington $107,680	OH: Cleveland $78,700
FL: Miami $83,460	OH: Columbus .... no data
FL: Orlando $111,680	OR: Portland $57,680
FL: Tampa $83,200	PA: Philadelphia $80,230
GA: Atlanta $55,500	PA: Pittsburgh .... no data
IL: Chicago $62,050	TX: Dallas $95,490
MA: Boston .... no data	TX: Houston $86,270
MD: Baltimore .... no data	WA: Seattle $75,530

FACTORS THAT MAY AFFECT EARNINGS

Educational Attainment of Workers and Effect on Earnings

Figures are based on a group of occupations: Lawyers, Judges, and Related Workers

	Percent at Level	Effect on Earnings
Less than High School	—	—
Some High School	—	—
High School or Equivalent	—	—
Some College but No Degree	—	—
Associate Degree	—	—
Bachelor's Degree	9.2%	−10.0%
Master's Degree	9.4%	2.3%
Doctoral Degree	23.3%	2.0%
First Professional Degree	52.1%	3.8%

Figures do not total 100% because some levels have a very small sample size.

Flexibility of Earnings

Average Hours Worked: 41
Workers with a Varying Number of Hours: 8.8%
Workers Earning Some Overtime Pay, Tips, or Commissions: 5.6%
Earnings Benefit of Working Overtime: −14.7%

Gender

	Male	Female
Percent	64.5%	35.5%
Effect on Earnings	51.6%	−21.2%

Union Membership

Percentage Union Members: 5.7%
Earnings Benefit of Union Membership: −8.0%

Veteran Status

Percentage Who Have Been on Active Duty: 9.1%
Earnings Benefit of Veteran Status: 3.4%

23-1022 Arbitrators, Mediators, and Conciliators

Facilitate negotiation and conflict resolution through dialogue. Resolve conflicts outside of the court system by mutual consent of parties involved.

- Education or Training Required: Work experience plus degree
- Job Growth: 15.5%
- Annual Openings: Fewer than 500
- Self-Employed: 0.0%
- Part-Time: 14.2%

NATIONAL WAGE FIGURES (ANNUAL)

Beginning	25th Percentile	Median	Mean	75th Percentile	90th Percentile
$28,090	$36,070	$49,490	$58,790	$73,670	$102,020

Median Wages for Industries Employing Largest Numbers (Annual)

Industry	Median Income
Management of Companies and Enterprises	$76,360
Educational Services	$61,190
Hospitals	$55,820
Federal, State, and Local Government	$54,320
Merchant Wholesalers, Durable Goods	$53,910
Religious, Grantmaking, Civic, Professional, and Similar Organizations	$51,770
Professional, Scientific, and Technical Services	$49,290
Administrative and Support Services	$47,080

Median Wages for States (Annual)

AK	no data	KY	$55,990	NY	no data
AL	no data	LA	no data	OH	$55,720
AR	$64,980	MA	$62,650	OK	no data
AZ	$50,510	MD	no data	OR	$70,910
CA	$62,810	ME	$52,020	PA	$38,310
CO	no data	MI	$86,850	RI	$57,990
CT	$74,370	MN	no data	SC	$40,620
DC	$60,340	MO	$51,020	SD	no data
DE	no data	MS	$24,270	TN	$71,940
FL	no data	MT	$48,430	TX	$46,860
GA	$38,970	NC	$44,510	UT	$35,280
HI	no data	ND	no data	VA	$82,350
IA	$75,640	NE	no data	VT	no data
ID	$41,650	NH	no data	WA	$72,240
IL	$86,840	NJ	$83,260	WI	$53,170
IN	$45,610	NM	$49,010	WV	$30,030
KS	$36,010	NV	$61,870	WY	no data

Median Wages for the Largest Metropolitan Areas (Annual)

AZ: Phoenix	$51,530	MI: Detroit	$94,100
CA: Los Angeles	$77,160	MN: Minneapolis	no data
CA: Riverside	$66,230	MO: Kansas City	$51,070
CA: Sacramento	no data	MO: St. Louis	$54,790
CA: San Diego	no data	NV: Las Vegas	no data
CA: San Francisco	$57,360	NY: New York	no data
CO: Denver	no data	OH: Cincinnati	$48,190
DC: Washington	$84,040	OH: Cleveland	$59,810
FL: Miami	$118,040	OH: Columbus	no data
FL: Orlando	$51,630	OR: Portland	$75,860
FL: Tampa	no data	PA: Philadelphia	$36,790
GA: Atlanta	$38,050	PA: Pittsburgh	$57,070
IL: Chicago	$70,030	TX: Dallas	$42,960
MA: Boston	$60,740	TX: Houston	no data
MD: Baltimore	$36,140	WA: Seattle	$74,740

FACTORS THAT MAY AFFECT EARNINGS

Educational Attainment of Workers and Effect on Earnings

Figures are based on a group of occupations: Lawyers, Judges, and Related Workers

	Percent at Level	Effect on Earnings
Less than High School	—	—
Some High School	—	—
High School or Equivalent	—	—
Some College but No Degree	—	—
Associate Degree	—	—
Bachelor's Degree	9.2%	–10.0%
Master's Degree	9.4%	2.3%
Doctoral Degree	23.3%	2.0%
First Professional Degree	52.1%	3.8%

Figures do not total 100% because some levels have a very small sample size.

Flexibility of Earnings

Average Hours Worked: 41
Workers with a Varying Number of Hours: 8.8%
Workers Earning Some Overtime Pay, Tips, or Commissions: 5.6%
Earnings Benefit of Working Overtime: –14.7%

Gender

	Male	Female
Percent	64.5%	35.5%
Effect on Earnings	51.6%	–21.2%

Union Membership

Percentage Union Members: 5.7%
Earnings Benefit of Union Membership: –8.0%

Veteran Status

Percentage Who Have Been on Active Duty: 9.1%
Earnings Benefit of Veteran Status: 3.4%

23-1023 Judges, Magistrate Judges, and Magistrates

Arbitrate, advise, adjudicate, or administer justice in a court of law. May sentence defendant in criminal cases according to government statutes. May determine liability of defendant in civil cases. May issue marriage licenses and perform wedding ceremonies.

- Education or Training Required: Work experience plus degree
- Job Growth: 6.9%
- Annual Openings: 1,000
- Self-Employed: 0.0%
- Part-Time: 14.2%

NATIONAL WAGE FIGURES (ANNUAL)

Beginning	25th Percentile	Median	Mean	75th Percentile	90th Percentile
$29,540	$53,920	$101,690	$95,640	$135,010	more than $145,600

Median Wages for Industries Employing Largest Numbers (Annual)

Industry	Median Income
Federal, State, and Local Government	$101,690

Median Wages for States (Annual)

AK	no data	KY	no data	NY	$121,310
AL	$54,650	LA	$15,380	OH	$59,650
AR	$28,920	MA	$103,560	OK	$89,490
AZ	$66,110	MD	$52,920	OR	$97,210
CA	more than $145,600	ME	$115,070	PA	$60,320
CO	$106,380	MI	$97,690	RI	more than $145,600
CT	more than $145,600	MN	no data	SC	$55,130
DC	no data	MO	$142,340	SD	$110,140
DE	$103,470	MS	$27,920	TN	$59,500
FL	$139,750	MT	$36,330	TX	$74,760
GA	$71,860	NC	$46,030	UT	$44,340
HI	no data	ND	$114,760	VA	no data
IA	$89,610	NE	no data	VT	no data
ID	more than $145,600	NH	no data	WA	$91,440
IL	more than $145,600	NJ	$141,120	WI	$99,880
IN	no data	NM	$40,610	WV	$35,460
KS	$112,230	NV	$132,090	WY	no data

Median Wages for the Largest Metropolitan Areas (Annual)

AZ: Phoenix	$65,700	MI: Detroit	$103,590
CA: Los Angeles	no data	MN: Minneapolis	no data
CA: Riverside	no data	MO: Kansas City	$127,370
CA: Sacramento	no data	MO: St. Louis	$144,820
CA: San Diego	no data	NV: Las Vegas	$136,630
CA: San Francisco	no data	NY: New York	$137,210
CO: Denver	$106,950	OH: Cincinnati	no data
DC: Washington	no data	OH: Cleveland	$71,180
FL: Miami	$139,690	OH: Columbus	no data
FL: Orlando	$140,410	OR: Portland	$100,460
FL: Tampa	$139,840	PA: Philadelphia	$139,800
GA: Atlanta	$109,200	PA: Pittsburgh	no data
IL: Chicago	$144,440	TX: Dallas	$90,220
MA: Boston	$105,340	TX: Houston	$64,720
MD: Baltimore	$54,320	WA: Seattle	no data

FACTORS THAT MAY AFFECT EARNINGS

Educational Attainment of Workers and Effect on Earnings

Figures are based on a group of occupations: Lawyers, Judges, and Related Workers

	Percent at Level	Effect on Earnings
Less than High School	—	—
Some High School	—	—
High School or Equivalent	—	—
Some College but No Degree	—	—
Associate Degree	—	—
Bachelor's Degree	9.2%	−10.0%
Master's Degree	9.4%	2.3%
Doctoral Degree	23.3%	2.0%
First Professional Degree	52.1%	3.8%

Figures do not total 100% because some levels have a very small sample size.

Flexibility of Earnings

Average Hours Worked: 41
Workers with a Varying Number of Hours: 8.8%
Workers Earning Some Overtime Pay, Tips, or Commissions: 5.6%
Earnings Benefit of Working Overtime: −14.7%

Gender

	Male	Female
Percent	64.5%	35.5%
Effect on Earnings	51.6%	−21.2%

Union Membership

Percentage Union Members: 5.7%
Earnings Benefit of Union Membership: −8.0%

Veteran Status

Percentage Who Have Been on Active Duty: 9.1%
Earnings Benefit of Veteran Status: 3.4%

23-2000 Legal Support Workers

23-2011 Paralegals and Legal Assistants

Assist lawyers by researching legal precedent, investigating facts, or preparing legal documents. Conduct research to support a legal proceeding, to formulate a defense, or to initiate legal action.

- Education or Training Required: Associate degree
- Job Growth: 29.7%
- Annual Openings: 28,000
- Self-Employed: 4.2%
- Part-Time: 17.3%

NATIONAL WAGE FIGURES (ANNUAL)

Beginning	25th Percentile	Median	Mean	75th Percentile	90th Percentile
$27,450	$33,920	$43,040	$45,460	$54,690	$67,540

Median Wages for Industries Employing Largest Numbers (Annual)

Industry	Median Income
Publishing Industries (Except Internet)	$63,610
Telecommunications	$57,910
Internet Service Providers, Web Search Portals, and Data-Processing Services	$57,330
Computer and Electronic Product Manufacturing	$56,970
Lessors of Nonfinancial Intangible Assets (Except Copyrighted Works)	$56,050
Merchant Wholesalers, Nondurable Goods	$53,900
Merchant Wholesalers, Durable Goods	$53,630
Oil and Gas Extraction	$53,550
Construction of Buildings	$53,180
Chemical Manufacturing	$52,810

Median Wages for States (Annual)

State	Wage	State	Wage	State	Wage
AK	$44,440	KY	$32,390	NY	$48,430
AL	$41,070	LA	$35,680	OH	$41,260
AR	$38,150	MA	$46,990	OK	$36,490
AZ	$45,030	MD	$45,270	OR	$39,410
CA	$50,870	ME	$40,750	PA	$40,560
CO	$43,140	MI	$45,360	RI	$42,850
CT	$44,460	MN	$46,520	SC	$36,060
DC	$49,460	MO	$38,720	SD	$42,480
DE	$45,850	MS	$31,830	TN	$35,610
FL	$40,740	MT	$27,670	TX	$42,340
GA	$42,260	NC	$34,390	UT	$39,800
HI	$42,540	ND	$37,460	VA	$42,060
IA	$37,140	NE	$37,850	VT	$42,200
ID	$40,560	NH	$41,340	WA	$45,970
IL	$43,910	NJ	$48,120	WI	$41,110
IN	$36,960	NM	$37,640	WV	$31,840
KS	$34,350	NV	$43,830	WY	$28,110

Median Wages for the Largest Metropolitan Areas (Annual)

Area	Wage	Area	Wage
AZ: Phoenix	$46,240	MI: Detroit	$46,850
CA: Los Angeles	$51,140	MN: Minneapolis	$49,120
CA: Riverside	$47,400	MO: Kansas City	$38,940
CA: Sacramento	$45,900	MO: St. Louis	$39,360
CA: San Diego	$52,590	NV: Las Vegas	$43,400
CA: San Francisco	$54,150	NY: New York	$50,350
CO: Denver	$45,410	OH: Cincinnati	$36,650
DC: Washington	$49,010	OH: Cleveland	$45,890
FL: Miami	$45,640	OH: Columbus	$43,220
FL: Orlando	$43,170	OR: Portland	$44,030
FL: Tampa	$41,610	PA: Philadelphia	$44,530
GA: Atlanta	$44,000	PA: Pittsburgh	$40,980
IL: Chicago	$44,750	TX: Dallas	$44,080
MA: Boston	$47,700	TX: Houston	$47,020
MD: Baltimore	$47,180	WA: Seattle	$50,690

FACTORS THAT MAY AFFECT EARNINGS

Educational Attainment of Workers and Effect on Earnings

	Percent at Level	Effect on Earnings
Less than High School	—	—
Some High School	—	—
High School or Equivalent	16.0%	−3.5%
Some College but No Degree	21.0%	−11.3%
Associate Degree	23.4%	−8.6%
Bachelor's Degree	31.1%	13.2%
Master's Degree	4.0%	13.2%
Doctoral Degree	—	—
First Professional Degree	2.9%	29.6%

Flexibility of Earnings

Average Hours Worked: 36
Workers with a Varying Number of Hours: 3.3%
Workers Earning Some Overtime Pay, Tips, or Commissions: 11.0%
Earnings Benefit of Working Overtime: 10.9%

Gender

	Male	Female
Percent	10.9%	89.1%
Effect on Earnings	—	−1.9%

Union Membership

Percentage Union Members: Insignificant
Earnings Benefit of Union Membership: No significant data available

Veteran Status

Percentage Who Have Been on Active Duty: 4.2%
Earnings Benefit of Veteran Status: −8.7%

23-2091 Court Reporters

Use verbatim methods and equipment to capture, store, retrieve, and transcribe pretrial and trial proceedings or other information. Includes stenocaptioners who operate computerized stenographic captioning equipment to provide captions of live or prerecorded broadcasts for hearing-impaired viewers.

- Education or Training Required: Postsecondary vocational training
- Job Growth: 14.8%
- Annual Openings: 3,000
- Self-Employed: 10.9%
- Part-Time: 23.6%

NATIONAL WAGE FIGURES (ANNUAL)

Beginning	25th Percentile	Median	Mean	75th Percentile	90th Percentile
$23,430	$33,160	$45,610	$48,370	$61,530	$77,770

Median Wages for Industries Employing Largest Numbers (Annual)

Industry	Median Income
Federal, State, and Local Government	$49,320
Administrative and Support Services	$41,770

Median Wages for States (Annual)

AK	no data	KY	$33,360	NY	$69,120
AL	$15,680	LA	$32,060	OH	$40,460
AR	no data	MA	$62,520	OK	$41,430
AZ	$49,820	MD	$32,910	OR	no data
CA	$69,470	ME	$51,950	PA	$39,630
CO	$51,430	MI	$43,680	RI	$60,430
CT	no data	MN	no data	SC	$35,400
DC	$42,760	MO	no data	SD	$56,570
DE	no data	MS	$31,140	TN	$42,800
FL	$38,360	MT	$33,390	TX	$48,470
GA	$43,270	NC	$36,250	UT	$46,670
HI	no data	ND	$49,580	VA	$52,100
IA	$55,290	NE	no data	VT	no data
ID	no data	NH	no data	WA	$63,120
IL	$43,480	NJ	$38,990	WI	$37,320
IN	$29,860	NM	no data	WV	$42,930
KS	$52,900	NV	$43,050	WY	no data

Median Wages for the Largest Metropolitan Areas (Annual)

AZ: Phoenix	no data	MI: Detroit	$50,940
CA: Los Angeles	no data	MN: Minneapolis	no data
CA: Riverside	no data	MO: Kansas City	$49,340
CA: Sacramento	$51,940	MO: St. Louis	no data
CA: San Diego	no data	NV: Las Vegas	no data
CA: San Francisco	$77,650	NY: New York	no data
CO: Denver	$52,800	OH: Cincinnati	no data
DC: Washington	$43,120	OH: Cleveland	$25,230
FL: Miami	$40,320	OH: Columbus	$47,090
FL: Orlando	$37,160	OR: Portland	no data
FL: Tampa	$23,360	PA: Philadelphia	$39,770
GA: Atlanta	$54,640	PA: Pittsburgh	$41,540
IL: Chicago	$42,510	TX: Dallas	$58,330
MA: Boston	$63,030	TX: Houston	$55,200
MD: Baltimore	$30,060	WA: Seattle	no data

FACTORS THAT MAY AFFECT EARNINGS

Educational Attainment of Workers and Effect on Earnings

Figures are based on a group of occupations: Legal Support Workers

	Percent at Level	Effect on Earnings
Less than High School	—	—
Some High School	2.1%	−57.4%
High School or Equivalent	18.6%	−6.3%
Some College but No Degree	22.5%	−12.4%
Associate Degree	19.5%	−5.5%
Bachelor's Degree	28.0%	12.2%
Master's Degree	6.1%	36.2%
Doctoral Degree	—	—
First Professional Degree	2.4%	29.3%

Flexibility of Earnings

Average Hours Worked: 35
Workers with a Varying Number of Hours: 3.3%
Workers Earning Some Overtime Pay, Tips, or Commissions: 11.3%
Earnings Benefit of Working Overtime: 3.9%

Gender

	Male	Female
Percent	23.2%	76.8%
Effect on Earnings	—	−5.2%

Union Membership

Percentage Union Members: Insignificant
Earnings Benefit of Union Membership: No significant data available

Veteran Status

Percentage Who Have Been on Active Duty: 4.2%
Earnings Benefit of Veteran Status: −8.7%

23-2092 Law Clerks

Assist lawyers or judges by researching or preparing legal documents. May meet with clients or assist lawyers and judges in court.

- Education or Training Required: Bachelor's degree
- Job Growth: 7.7%
- Annual Openings: 7,000
- Self-Employed: 11.5%
- Part-Time: 23.6%

NATIONAL WAGE FIGURES (ANNUAL)

Beginning	25th Percentile	Median	Mean	75th Percentile	90th Percentile
$21,870	$28,560	$36,360	$39,210	$46,490	$59,240

Median Wages for Industries Employing Largest Numbers (Annual)

Industry	Median Income
Insurance Carriers and Related Activities	$42,440
Administrative and Support Services	$41,900
Federal, State, and Local Government	$38,710
Credit Intermediation and Related Activities	$37,840
Educational Services	$37,840
Management of Companies and Enterprises	$35,220
Professional, Scientific, and Technical Services	$34,460
Religious, Grantmaking, Civic, Professional, and Similar Organizations	$23,280

Median Wages for States (Annual)

AK	no data	KY	$27,390	NY	$37,730
AL	$29,020	LA	$33,210	OH	$29,480
AR	$22,690	MA	$44,450	OK	$33,390
AZ	$36,950	MD	$49,230	OR	$40,420
CA	$36,900	ME	$45,340	PA	$36,260
CO	$35,170	MI	$37,260	RI	$51,280
CT	$39,640	MN	no data	SC	$45,620
DC	$47,110	MO	$23,280	SD	no data
DE	$41,790	MS	$25,770	TN	$30,870
FL	$34,560	MT	$34,950	TX	$33,240
GA	$41,660	NC	$25,290	UT	$32,670
HI	$45,450	ND	$36,410	VA	$32,210
IA	$26,560	NE	$35,800	VT	no data
ID	$35,630	NH	no data	WA	$39,380
IL	$41,480	NJ	$38,110	WI	$36,280
IN	$31,850	NM	$45,430	WV	$28,610
KS	$26,930	NV	$45,130	WY	$23,830

Median Wages for the Largest Metropolitan Areas (Annual)

AZ: Phoenix	no data	MI: Detroit	$37,750
CA: Los Angeles	$37,790	MN: Minneapolis	$42,110
CA: Riverside	no data	MO: Kansas City	$28,970
CA: Sacramento	$34,860	MO: St. Louis	$29,260
CA: San Diego	$33,220	NV: Las Vegas	$44,270
CA: San Francisco	$46,580	NY: New York	$38,510
CO: Denver	$36,700	OH: Cincinnati	$28,340
DC: Washington	$40,940	OH: Cleveland	$34,680
FL: Miami	$34,790	OH: Columbus	$24,070
FL: Orlando	$22,810	OR: Portland	$38,450
FL: Tampa	$44,540	PA: Philadelphia	$42,080
GA: Atlanta	$47,320	PA: Pittsburgh	no data
IL: Chicago	$41,530	TX: Dallas	$30,850
MA: Boston	$45,260	TX: Houston	$39,270
MD: Baltimore	$52,400	WA: Seattle	$43,110

FACTORS THAT MAY AFFECT EARNINGS

Educational Attainment of Workers and Effect on Earnings

Figures are based on a group of occupations: Legal Support Workers

	Percent at Level	Effect on Earnings
Less than High School	—	—
Some High School	2.1%	−57.4%
High School or Equivalent	18.6%	−6.3%
Some College but No Degree	22.5%	−12.4%
Associate Degree	19.5%	−5.5%
Bachelor's Degree	28.0%	12.2%
Master's Degree	6.1%	36.2%
Doctoral Degree	—	—
First Professional Degree	2.4%	29.3%

Flexibility of Earnings

Average Hours Worked: 35
Workers with a Varying Number of Hours: 3.3%
Workers Earning Some Overtime Pay, Tips, or Commissions: 11.3%
Earnings Benefit of Working Overtime: 3.9%

Gender

	Male	Female
Percent	23.2%	76.8%
Effect on Earnings	—	−5.2%

Union Membership

Percentage Union Members: Insignificant
Earnings Benefit of Union Membership: No significant data available

Veteran Status

Percentage Who Have Been on Active Duty: 4.2%
Earnings Benefit of Veteran Status: −8.7%

23-2093 Title Examiners, Abstractors, and Searchers

Search real estate records, examine titles, or summarize pertinent legal or insurance details for a variety of purposes. May compile lists of mortgages, contracts, and other instruments pertaining to titles by searching public and private records for law firms, real estate agencies, or title insurance companies.

- Education or Training Required: Moderate-term on-the-job training
- Job Growth: 0.9%
- Annual Openings: 8,000
- Self-Employed: 10.7%
- Part-Time: 23.6%

NATIONAL WAGE FIGURES (ANNUAL)

Beginning	25th Percentile	Median	Mean	75th Percentile	90th Percentile
$21,970	$27,790	$36,020	$40,660	$47,320	$63,650

Median Wages for Industries Employing Largest Numbers (Annual)

Industry	Median Income
Heavy and Civil Engineering Construction	$51,280
Construction of Buildings	$42,800
Oil and Gas Extraction	$41,910
Real Estate	$41,790
Securities, Commodity Contracts, and Other Financial Investments and Related Activities	$41,430
Federal, State, and Local Government	$39,700
Support Activities for Mining	$38,140
Management of Companies and Enterprises	$37,610
Insurance Carriers and Related Activities	$37,530
Hospitals	$37,080

Median Wages for States (Annual)

State	Wage	State	Wage	State	Wage
AK	$46,460	KY	$30,510	NY	$38,070
AL	$32,730	LA	$30,590	OH	$36,080
AR	$26,030	MA	$47,740	OK	$32,530
AZ	$38,370	MD	$34,850	OR	$46,980
CA	$51,480	ME	$33,220	PA	$29,930
CO	$41,370	MI	$36,100	RI	no data
CT	$52,650	MN	$40,510	SC	$32,120
DC	$50,590	MO	$28,960	SD	$30,100
DE	$34,270	MS	$25,290	TN	$32,750
FL	$36,370	MT	$34,540	TX	$34,600
GA	$33,280	NC	$40,510	UT	$42,090
HI	$37,290	ND	$28,690	VA	$31,490
IA	$26,060	NE	$30,740	VT	$69,810
ID	$34,740	NH	$33,130	WA	$38,320
IL	$28,060	NJ	$38,970	WI	$32,810
IN	$31,310	NM	$34,840	WV	$28,530
KS	$25,380	NV	$40,480	WY	$28,750

Median Wages for the Largest Metropolitan Areas (Annual)

Area	Wage	Area	Wage
AZ: Phoenix	$39,100	MI: Detroit	$37,170
CA: Los Angeles	$49,330	MN: Minneapolis	$45,380
CA: Riverside	$50,720	MO: Kansas City	$33,150
CA: Sacramento	$46,930	MO: St. Louis	$31,520
CA: San Diego	$63,700	NV: Las Vegas	$39,680
CA: San Francisco	$51,920	NY: New York	$40,100
CO: Denver	$44,830	OH: Cincinnati	$35,860
DC: Washington	$35,680	OH: Cleveland	$40,890
FL: Miami	$37,430	OH: Columbus	$38,580
FL: Orlando	$35,040	OR: Portland	$56,610
FL: Tampa	$39,750	PA: Philadelphia	$36,600
GA: Atlanta	$38,890	PA: Pittsburgh	$25,440
IL: Chicago	$28,220	TX: Dallas	$38,310
MA: Boston	$48,250	TX: Houston	$29,580
MD: Baltimore	$37,390	WA: Seattle	$39,500

FACTORS THAT MAY AFFECT EARNINGS

Educational Attainment of Workers and Effect on Earnings

Figures are based on a group of occupations: Legal Support Workers

	Percent at Level	Effect on Earnings
Less than High School	—	—
Some High School	2.1%	−57.4%
High School or Equivalent	18.6%	−6.3%
Some College but No Degree	22.5%	−12.4%
Associate Degree	19.5%	−5.5%
Bachelor's Degree	28.0%	12.2%
Master's Degree	6.1%	36.2%
Doctoral Degree	—	—
First Professional Degree	2.4%	29.3%

Flexibility of Earnings

Average Hours Worked: 35

Workers with a Varying Number of Hours: 3.3%

Workers Earning Some Overtime Pay, Tips, or Commissions: 11.3%

Earnings Benefit of Working Overtime: 3.9%

Gender

	Male	Female
Percent	23.2%	76.8%
Effect on Earnings	—	−5.2%

Union Membership

Percentage Union Members: Insignificant

Earnings Benefit of Union Membership: No significant data available

Veteran Status

Percentage Who Have Been on Active Duty: 4.2%

Earnings Benefit of Veteran Status: −8.7%

23-2099 Legal Support Workers, All Other

All legal support workers not listed separately.

- Education or Training Required: Bachelor's degree
- Job Growth: 7.1%
- Annual Openings: 12,000
- Self-Employed: 10.0%
- Part-Time: 23.6%

NATIONAL WAGE FIGURES (ANNUAL)

Beginning	25th Percentile	Median	Mean	75th Percentile	90th Percentile
$27,220	$35,270	$45,140	$50,520	$59,410	$84,840

Median Wages for Industries Employing Largest Numbers (Annual)

Industry	Median Income
Machinery Manufacturing	$60,310
Computer and Electronic Product Manufacturing	$55,410
Miscellaneous Manufacturing	$54,170
Chemical Manufacturing	$53,470
Telecommunications	$53,150
Management of Companies and Enterprises	$52,710
Lessors of Nonfinancial Intangible Assets (Except Copyrighted Works)	$50,080
Support Activities for Mining	$48,610
Ambulatory Health Care Services	$48,140
Federal, State, and Local Government	$46,790

Median Wages for States (Annual)

AK	$46,730	KY	$37,690	NY	$42,240
AL	$41,880	LA	$36,600	OH	$39,630
AR	$43,080	MA	$41,570	OK	$38,570
AZ	$43,530	MD	$42,850	OR	$43,060
CA	$45,630	ME	$41,370	PA	$42,860
CO	$41,470	MI	$38,390	RI	$36,680
CT	$50,590	MN	$47,150	SC	no data
DC	$47,620	MO	$37,050	SD	no data
DE	$47,730	MS	$38,990	TN	$41,750
FL	$36,620	MT	$37,600	TX	$41,460
GA	$47,030	NC	$29,250	UT	$42,010
HI	$40,690	ND	no data	VA	$78,320
IA	$37,080	NE	$42,860	VT	$35,800
ID	$30,690	NH	$40,020	WA	$52,620
IL	$42,080	NJ	$50,860	WI	$41,620
IN	no data	NM	$36,610	WV	$38,700
KS	$45,630	NV	no data	WY	$32,160

Median Wages for the Largest Metropolitan Areas (Annual)

AZ: Phoenix	$44,170	MI: Detroit	$37,510
CA: Los Angeles	$43,030	MN: Minneapolis	$46,720
CA: Riverside	$42,240	MO: Kansas City	$44,530
CA: Sacramento	$51,700	MO: St. Louis	$43,630
CA: San Diego	$49,040	NV: Las Vegas	no data
CA: San Francisco	$53,200	NY: New York	$45,860
CO: Denver	$41,390	OH: Cincinnati	$39,110
DC: Washington	$73,740	OH: Cleveland	$43,240
FL: Miami	$37,970	OH: Columbus	no data
FL: Orlando	$38,070	OR: Portland	$48,170
FL: Tampa	$37,280	PA: Philadelphia	$48,220
GA: Atlanta	$50,370	PA: Pittsburgh	$41,420
IL: Chicago	$43,090	TX: Dallas	$37,740
MA: Boston	$42,320	TX: Houston	$47,750
MD: Baltimore	$42,780	WA: Seattle	$52,490

FACTORS THAT MAY AFFECT EARNINGS

Educational Attainment of Workers and Effect on Earnings

Figures are based on a group of occupations: Legal Support Workers

	Percent at Level	Effect on Earnings
Less than High School	—	—
Some High School	2.1%	−57.4%
High School or Equivalent	18.6%	−6.3%
Some College but No Degree	22.5%	−12.4%
Associate Degree	19.5%	−5.5%
Bachelor's Degree	28.0%	12.2%
Master's Degree	6.1%	36.2%
Doctoral Degree	—	—
First Professional Degree	2.4%	29.3%

Flexibility of Earnings

Average Hours Worked: 35
Workers with a Varying Number of Hours: 3.3%
Workers Earning Some Overtime Pay, Tips, or Commissions: 11.3%
Earnings Benefit of Working Overtime: 3.9%

Gender

	Male	Female
Percent	23.2%	76.8%
Effect on Earnings	—	−5.2%

Union Membership

Percentage Union Members: Insignificant
Earnings Benefit of Union Membership: No significant data available

Veteran Status

Percentage Who Have Been on Active Duty: 4.2%
Earnings Benefit of Veteran Status: −8.7%

25-0000 Education, Training, and Library Occupations

25-1000 Postsecondary Teachers

25-1011 Business Teachers, Postsecondary

Teach courses in business administration and management, such as accounting, finance, human resources, labor relations, marketing, and operations research. Includes both teachers primarily engaged in teaching and those who do a combination of both teaching and research.

- Education or Training Required: Master's degree
- Job Growth: 32.2% (for all postsecondary teaching occupations)
- Annual Openings: 329,000 (for all postsecondary teaching occupations)
- Self-Employed: 0.4%
- Part-Time: 24.8%

NATIONAL WAGE FIGURES (ANNUAL)

Beginning	25th Percentile	Median	Mean	75th Percentile	90th Percentile
$31,780	$43,180	$62,040	$70,220	$89,230	$120,620

Median Wages for Industries Employing Largest Numbers (Annual)

Industry	Median Income
Educational Services	$62,050
Professional, Scientific, and Technical Services	$45,620

Median Wages for States (Annual)

AK........... $48,410	KY $59,330	NY .... no data
AL $59,440	LA .... no data	OH $50,820
AR........... no data	MA............. $80,930	OK $41,100
AZ $55,900	MD............. $72,320	OR $75,000
CA .... no data	ME $46,690	PA $67,030
CO $56,990	MI $66,860	RI.............. $83,650
CT $73,980	MN............. $49,690	SC............. $58,150
DC $67,090	MO............. $65,110	SD $52,570
DE $83,880	MS $53,370	TN $49,030
FL $69,220	MT $40,710	TX $56,850
GA........... $64,770	NC $56,910	UT $64,900
HI $78,700	ND $55,220	VA $73,700
IA $57,140	NE $53,650	VT $53,800
ID .... no data	NH $67,360	WA $56,800
IL $67,690	NJ $68,970	WI $65,340
IN $53,930	NM............. $63,210	WV $50,500
KS $58,430	NV $42,800	WY $60,970

Median Wages for the Largest Metropolitan Areas (Annual)

AZ: Phoenix............ $57,690	MI: Detroit $39,410
CA: Los Angeles $74,250	MN: Minneapolis $48,770
CA: Riverside $74,130	MO: Kansas City........ $60,370
CA: Sacramento $79,710	MO: St. Louis............. $65,250
CA: San Diego $79,630	NV: Las Vegas .... no data
CA: San Francisco.... $74,740	NY: New York............ $66,060
CO: Denver $50,710	OH: Cincinnati.......... $48,740
DC: Washington $74,740	OH: Cleveland $67,830
FL: Miami $69,490	OH: Columbus $59,670
FL: Orlando $70,680	OR: Portland $78,760
FL: Tampa $67,240	PA: Philadelphia $70,670
GA: Atlanta $74,280	PA: Pittsburgh.......... $65,130
IL: Chicago $72,020	TX: Dallas $52,930
MA: Boston $87,220	TX: Houston .... no data
MD: Baltimore $68,690	WA: Seattle $55,280

FACTORS THAT MAY AFFECT EARNINGS

Educational Attainment of Workers and Effect on Earnings

Figures are based on a group of occupations: Postsecondary Teachers

	Percent at Level	Effect on Earnings
Less than High School	—	—
Some High School	—	—
High School or Equivalent	2.2%	−40.5%
Some College but No Degree	6.6%	−53.9%
Associate Degree	4.4%	−14.3%
Bachelor's Degree	20.2%	−33.1%
Master's Degree	29.9%	−8.9%
Doctoral Degree	28.3%	42.5%
First Professional Degree	8.1%	28.8%

Flexibility of Earnings

Average Hours Worked: 32
Workers with a Varying Number of Hours: 9.5%
Workers Earning Some Overtime Pay, Tips, or Commissions: 2.1%
Earnings Benefit of Working Overtime: −4.1%

Gender

	Male	Female
Percent	53.7%	46.3%
Effect on Earnings	16.1%	−13.5%

Union Membership

Percentage Union Members: 18.9%
Earnings Benefit of Union Membership: 12.1%

Veteran Status

Percentage Who Have Been on Active Duty: 7.4%
Earnings Benefit of Veteran Status: 20.1%

25-1021 Computer Science Teachers, Postsecondary

Teach courses in computer science. May specialize in a field of computer science, such as the design and function of computers or operations and research analysis. Includes both teachers primarily engaged in teaching and those who do a combination of both teaching and research.

- Education or Training Required: Master's degree
- Job Growth: 32.2% (for all postsecondary teaching occupations)
- Annual Openings: 329,000 (for all postsecondary teaching occupations)
- Self-Employed: 0.4%
- Part-Time: 24.8%

NATIONAL WAGE FIGURES (ANNUAL)

Beginning	25th Percentile	Median	Mean	75th Percentile	90th Percentile
$32,130	$42,710	$57,620	$65,000	$81,900	$108,780

Median Wages for Industries Employing Largest Numbers (Annual)

Industry	Median Income
Educational Services	$57,630
Professional, Scientific, and Technical Services	$42,400

Median Wages for States (Annual)

AK	no data	KY	$52,210	NY	no data
AL	$54,340	LA	no data	OH	$45,120
AR	no data	MA	$81,430	OK	$32,980
AZ	$53,750	MD	$54,280	OR	$86,750
CA	no data	ME	$47,070	PA	$67,510
CO	$50,320	MI	$65,860	RI	$81,820
CT	$60,350	MN	$54,600	SC	$56,090
DC	$48,790	MO	$60,290	SD	$47,280
DE	$72,210	MS	$53,210	TN	$56,910
FL	$64,020	MT	$39,700	TX	$54,480
GA	$54,070	NC	$49,830	UT	$67,850
HI	$62,430	ND	$50,570	VA	$68,970
IA	$53,540	NE	$45,300	VT	$52,290
ID	no data	NH	$52,970	WA	$57,650
IL	$64,520	NJ	$68,700	WI	$63,730
IN	$49,380	NM	$55,990	WV	$46,560
KS	$56,530	NV	$36,430	WY	$53,760

Median Wages for the Largest Metropolitan Areas (Annual)

AZ: Phoenix	$54,440	MI: Detroit	$59,730
CA: Los Angeles	$73,330	MN: Minneapolis	$54,770
CA: Riverside	$79,920	MO: Kansas City	$56,140
CA: Sacramento	$82,580	MO: St. Louis	$61,950
CA: San Diego	$58,620	NV: Las Vegas	no data
CA: San Francisco	$77,370	NY: New York	$71,360
CO: Denver	$46,580	OH: Cincinnati	$49,280
DC: Washington	$71,200	OH: Cleveland	$47,310
FL: Miami	$68,800	OH: Columbus	$44,980
FL: Orlando	$65,890	OR: Portland	$92,230
FL: Tampa	$57,220	PA: Philadelphia	$58,400
GA: Atlanta	$56,010	PA: Pittsburgh	$77,330
IL: Chicago	$67,380	TX: Dallas	$49,520
MA: Boston	$80,920	TX: Houston	$57,580
MD: Baltimore	$51,720	WA: Seattle	$57,210

FACTORS THAT MAY AFFECT EARNINGS

Educational Attainment of Workers and Effect on Earnings

Figures are based on a group of occupations: Postsecondary Teachers

	Percent at Level	Effect on Earnings
Less than High School	—	—
Some High School	—	—
High School or Equivalent	2.2%	−40.5%
Some College but No Degree	6.6%	−53.9%
Associate Degree	4.4%	−14.3%
Bachelor's Degree	20.2%	−33.1%
Master's Degree	29.9%	−8.9%
Doctoral Degree	28.3%	42.5%
First Professional Degree	8.1%	28.8%

Flexibility of Earnings

Average Hours Worked: 32
Workers with a Varying Number of Hours: 9.5%
Workers Earning Some Overtime Pay, Tips, or Commissions: 2.1%
Earnings Benefit of Working Overtime: −4.1%

Gender

	Male	Female
Percent	53.7%	46.3%
Effect on Earnings	16.1%	−13.5%

Union Membership

Percentage Union Members: 18.9%
Earnings Benefit of Union Membership: 12.1%

Veteran Status

Percentage Who Have Been on Active Duty: 7.4%
Earnings Benefit of Veteran Status: 20.1%

25-1022 Mathematical Science Teachers, Postsecondary

Teach courses pertaining to mathematical concepts, statistics, and actuarial science and to the application of original and standardized mathematical techniques in solving specific problems and situations.

- Education or Training Required: Master's degree
- Job Growth: 32.2% (for all postsecondary teaching occupations)
- Annual Openings: 329,000 (for all postsecondary teaching occupations)
- Self-Employed: 0.4%
- Part-Time: 24.8%

NATIONAL WAGE FIGURES (ANNUAL)

Beginning	25th Percentile	Median	Mean	75th Percentile	90th Percentile
$31,580	$41,830	$56,420	$62,790	$76,450	$103,330

Median Wages for Industries Employing Largest Numbers (Annual)

Industry	Median Income
Management of Companies and Enterprises	$82,310
Professional, Scientific, and Technical Services	$70,050
Educational Services	$56,390

Median Wages for States (Annual)

AK	$62,060	KY	$47,890	NY	no data
AL	$50,390	LA	no data	OH	$54,480
AR	no data	MA	$68,640	OK	$36,250
AZ	$45,260	MD	$59,220	OR	$71,930
CA	no data	ME	$49,060	PA	$61,670
CO	$54,290	MI	$62,050	RI	no data
CT	$56,030	MN	$50,840	SC	$54,120
DC	$62,100	MO	$57,060	SD	$49,420
DE	$63,340	MS	$50,580	TN	$48,330
FL	$54,720	MT	$42,070	TX	$47,310
GA	$50,940	NC	$51,140	UT	$55,010
HI	$63,110	ND	$43,950	VA	$48,540
IA	$61,020	NE	$50,670	VT	$53,850
ID	no data	NH	$55,780	WA	$52,400
IL	$57,580	NJ	$64,440	WI	$54,060
IN	$51,700	NM	$58,240	WV	$50,970
KS	$48,390	NV	$38,150	WY	$50,100

Median Wages for the Largest Metropolitan Areas (Annual)

AZ: Phoenix	$42,670	MI: Detroit	$60,190
CA: Los Angeles	no data	MN: Minneapolis	$51,120
CA: Riverside	$71,160	MO: Kansas City	$51,190
CA: Sacramento	$88,220	MO: St. Louis	$60,310
CA: San Diego	$92,670	NV: Las Vegas	no data
CA: San Francisco	$78,960	NY: New York	$68,270
CO: Denver	$47,600	OH: Cincinnati	$52,400
DC: Washington	$59,450	OH: Cleveland	$55,820
FL: Miami	no data	OH: Columbus	$61,750
FL: Orlando	$46,990	OR: Portland	$73,070
FL: Tampa	$48,260	PA: Philadelphia	$59,250
GA: Atlanta	$59,150	PA: Pittsburgh	$62,350
IL: Chicago	$61,960	TX: Dallas	$41,090
MA: Boston	$66,200	TX: Houston	no data
MD: Baltimore	$58,750	WA: Seattle	$58,130

FACTORS THAT MAY AFFECT EARNINGS

Educational Attainment of Workers and Effect on Earnings

Figures are based on a group of occupations: Postsecondary Teachers

	Percent at Level	Effect on Earnings
Less than High School	—	—
Some High School	—	—
High School or Equivalent	2.2%	−40.5%
Some College but No Degree	6.6%	−53.9%
Associate Degree	4.4%	−14.3%
Bachelor's Degree	20.2%	−33.1%
Master's Degree	29.9%	−8.9%
Doctoral Degree	28.3%	42.5%
First Professional Degree	8.1%	28.8%

Flexibility of Earnings

Average Hours Worked: 32
Workers with a Varying Number of Hours: 9.5%
Workers Earning Some Overtime Pay, Tips, or Commissions: 2.1%
Earnings Benefit of Working Overtime: −4.1%

Gender

	Male	Female
Percent	53.7%	46.3%
Effect on Earnings	16.1%	−13.5%

Union Membership

Percentage Union Members: 18.9%
Earnings Benefit of Union Membership: 12.1%

Veteran Status

Percentage Who Have Been on Active Duty: 7.4%
Earnings Benefit of Veteran Status: 20.1%

25-1031 Architecture Teachers, Postsecondary

Teach courses in architecture and architectural design, such as architectural environmental design, interior architecture/design, and landscape architecture. Includes both teachers primarily engaged in teaching and those who do a combination of both teaching and research.

- Education or Training Required: Master's degree
- Job Growth: 32.2% (for all postsecondary teaching occupations)
- Annual Openings: 329,000 (for all postsecondary teaching occupations)
- Self-Employed: 0.4%
- Part-Time: 24.8%

NATIONAL WAGE FIGURES (ANNUAL)

Beginning	25th Percentile	Median	Mean	75th Percentile	90th Percentile
$37,670	$50,250	$64,620	$67,390	$82,050	$101,700

Median Wages for Industries Employing Largest Numbers (Annual)

Industry	Median Income
Educational Services	$64,640

Median Wages for States (Annual)

AK	no data	KY	no data	NY	no data
AL	$57,570	LA	no data	OH	$71,240
AR	no data	MA	$77,370	OK	no data
AZ	no data	MD	no data	OR	$69,480
CA	no data	ME	no data	PA	$60,200
CO	no data	MI	$63,740	RI	$75,800
CT	no data	MN	no data	SC	$57,730
DC	no data	MO	$68,880	SD	no data
DE	no data	MS	no data	TN	no data
FL	$68,530	MT	no data	TX	$59,450
GA	no data	NC	$58,850	UT	$64,730
HI	no data	ND	no data	VA	$63,840
IA	no data	NE	$39,930	VT	no data
ID	no data	NH	no data	WA	no data
IL	$57,010	NJ	$59,930	WI	$64,990
IN	$50,860	NM	$56,440	WV	no data
KS	$69,460	NV	no data	WY	no data

Median Wages for the Largest Metropolitan Areas (Annual)

AZ: Phoenix	no data	MI: Detroit	no data
CA: Los Angeles	$60,280	MN: Minneapolis	no data
CA: Riverside	no data	MO: Kansas City	no data
CA: Sacramento	no data	MO: St. Louis	$69,370
CA: San Diego	$54,560	NV: Las Vegas	no data
CA: San Francisco	$69,440	NY: New York	$81,240
CO: Denver	no data	OH: Cincinnati	no data
DC: Washington	no data	OH: Cleveland	no data
FL: Miami	no data	OH: Columbus	no data
FL: Orlando	no data	OR: Portland	no data
FL: Tampa	$49,680	PA: Philadelphia	no data
GA: Atlanta	no data	PA: Pittsburgh	no data
IL: Chicago	$41,180	TX: Dallas	no data
MA: Boston	$77,930	TX: Houston	no data
MD: Baltimore	no data	WA: Seattle	no data

FACTORS THAT MAY AFFECT EARNINGS

Educational Attainment of Workers and Effect on Earnings

Figures are based on a group of occupations: Postsecondary Teachers

	Percent at Level	Effect on Earnings
Less than High School	—	—
Some High School	—	—
High School or Equivalent	2.2%	−40.5%
Some College but No Degree	6.6%	−53.9%
Associate Degree	4.4%	−14.3%
Bachelor's Degree	20.2%	−33.1%
Master's Degree	29.9%	−8.9%
Doctoral Degree	28.3%	42.5%
First Professional Degree	8.1%	28.8%

Flexibility of Earnings

Average Hours Worked: 32
Workers with a Varying Number of Hours: 9.5%
Workers Earning Some Overtime Pay, Tips, or Commissions: 2.1%
Earnings Benefit of Working Overtime: −4.1%

Gender

	Male	Female
Percent	53.7%	46.3%
Effect on Earnings	16.1%	−13.5%

Union Membership

Percentage Union Members: 18.9%
Earnings Benefit of Union Membership: 12.1%

Veteran Status

Percentage Who Have Been on Active Duty: 7.4%
Earnings Benefit of Veteran Status: 20.1%

25-1032 Engineering Teachers, Postsecondary

Teach courses pertaining to the application of physical laws and principles of engineering for the development of machines, materials, instruments, processes, and services. Includes teachers of subjects such as chemical, civil, electrical, industrial, mechanical, mineral, and petroleum engineering. Includes both teachers primarily engaged in teaching and those who do a combination of both teaching and research. Includes both teachers primarily engaged in teaching and those who do a combination of both teaching and research.

- Education or Training Required: Master's degree
- Job Growth: 32.2% (for all postsecondary teaching occupations)
- Annual Openings: 329,000 (for all postsecondary teaching occupations)
- Self-Employed: 0.4%
- Part-Time: 24.8%

NATIONAL WAGE FIGURES (ANNUAL)

Beginning	25th Percentile	Median	Mean	75th Percentile	90th Percentile
$41,880	$57,350	$76,670	$82,080	$101,510	$129,610

Median Wages for Industries Employing Largest Numbers (Annual)

Industry	Median Income
Educational Services	$76,540

Median Wages for States (Annual)

State	Wage	State	Wage	State	Wage
AK	no data	KY	no data	NY	no data
AL	$73,030	LA	no data	OH	$81,630
AR	no data	MA	$97,570	OK	$50,600
AZ	no data	MD	$87,820	OR	$97,580
CA	no data	ME	no data	PA	$80,670
CO	$83,330	MI	$71,870	RI	$88,740
CT	no data	MN	no data	SC	$53,810
DC	$67,940	MO	$74,950	SD	no data
DE	no data	MS	no data	TN	$69,260
FL	$77,320	MT	$59,760	TX	$81,640
GA	$68,000	NC	$73,050	UT	$89,370
HI	no data	ND	$62,940	VA	$70,970
IA	no data	NE	$50,060	VT	$59,720
ID	no data	NH	$101,550	WA	$93,700
IL	$74,260	NJ	$76,520	WI	$74,750
IN	$98,100	NM	no data	WV	no data
KS	$81,710	NV	no data	WY	no data

Median Wages for the Largest Metropolitan Areas (Annual)

Metro	Wage	Metro	Wage
AZ: Phoenix	no data	MI: Detroit	$68,580
CA: Los Angeles	no data	MN: Minneapolis	no data
CA: Riverside	$114,780	MO: Kansas City	$73,750
CA: Sacramento	no data	MO: St. Louis	$75,300
CA: San Diego	no data	NV: Las Vegas	no data
CA: San Francisco	$85,990	NY: New York	$72,600
CO: Denver	no data	OH: Cincinnati	no data
DC: Washington	$75,670	OH: Cleveland	$82,930
FL: Miami	$75,940	OH: Columbus	no data
FL: Orlando	$78,710	OR: Portland	$92,790
FL: Tampa	$78,920	PA: Philadelphia	$71,420
GA: Atlanta	no data	PA: Pittsburgh	$93,620
IL: Chicago	$74,700	TX: Dallas	$83,780
MA: Boston	$98,610	TX: Houston	no data
MD: Baltimore	no data	WA: Seattle	no data

FACTORS THAT MAY AFFECT EARNINGS

Educational Attainment of Workers and Effect on Earnings

Figures are based on a group of occupations: Postsecondary Teachers

	Percent at Level	Effect on Earnings
Less than High School	—	—
Some High School	—	—
High School or Equivalent	2.2%	−40.5%
Some College but No Degree	6.6%	−53.9%
Associate Degree	4.4%	−14.3%
Bachelor's Degree	20.2%	−33.1%
Master's Degree	29.9%	−8.9%
Doctoral Degree	28.3%	42.5%
First Professional Degree	8.1%	28.8%

Flexibility of Earnings

Average Hours Worked: 32
Workers with a Varying Number of Hours: 9.5%
Workers Earning Some Overtime Pay, Tips, or Commissions: 2.1%
Earnings Benefit of Working Overtime: −4.1%

Gender

	Male	Female
Percent	53.7%	46.3%
Effect on Earnings	16.1%	−13.5%

Union Membership

Percentage Union Members: 18.9%
Earnings Benefit of Union Membership: 12.1%

Veteran Status

Percentage Who Have Been on Active Duty: 7.4%
Earnings Benefit of Veteran Status: 20.1%

25-1041 Agricultural Sciences Teachers, Postsecondary

Teach courses in the agricultural sciences. Includes teachers of agronomy, dairy sciences, fisheries management, horticultural sciences, poultry sciences, range management, and agricultural soil conservation. Includes both teachers primarily engaged in teaching and those who do a combination of both teaching and research.

- Education or Training Required: Master's degree
- Job Growth: 32.2% (for all postsecondary teaching occupations)
- Annual Openings: 329,000 (for all postsecondary teaching occupations)
- Self-Employed: 0.4%
- Part-Time: 24.8%

NATIONAL WAGE FIGURES (ANNUAL)

Beginning	25th Percentile	Median	Mean	75th Percentile	90th Percentile
$41,440	$55,630	$75,140	$77,190	$94,150	$118,180

Median Wages for Industries Employing Largest Numbers (Annual)

Industry	Median Income
Educational Services	$75,150

Median Wages for States (Annual)

AK	no data	KY	no data	NY	no data
AL	$61,030	LA	no data	OH	no data
AR	no data	MA	no data	OK	no data
AZ	$72,040	MD	no data	OR	no data
CA	no data	ME	no data	PA	$83,320
CO	no data	MI	no data	RI	no data
CT	no data	MN	no data	SC	$51,430
DC	no data	MO	$64,060	SD	no data
DE	no data	MS	no data	TN	no data
FL	$80,960	MT	no data	TX	$84,740
GA	no data	NC	no data	UT	$59,300
HI	no data	ND	$76,010	VA	no data
IA	no data	NE	$61,950	VT	no data
ID	no data	NH	no data	WA	no data
IL	$63,200	NJ	$87,790	WI	$74,460
IN	no data	NM	no data	WV	no data
KS	$78,660	NV	no data	WY	no data

Median Wages for the Largest Metropolitan Areas (Annual)

AZ: Phoenix	no data	MI: Detroit	no data
CA: Los Angeles	no data	MN: Minneapolis	$68,330
CA: Riverside	$84,610	MO: Kansas City	no data
CA: Sacramento	no data	MO: St. Louis	$56,980
CA: San Diego	no data	NV: Las Vegas	no data
CA: San Francisco	$70,160	NY: New York	no data
CO: Denver	no data	OH: Cincinnati	no data
DC: Washington	$68,500	OH: Cleveland	no data
FL: Miami	$76,940	OH: Columbus	no data
FL: Orlando	$77,430	OR: Portland	no data
FL: Tampa	no data	PA: Philadelphia	no data
GA: Atlanta	no data	PA: Pittsburgh	no data
IL: Chicago	$53,090	TX: Dallas	no data
MA: Boston	no data	TX: Houston	$52,640
MD: Baltimore	no data	WA: Seattle	no data

FACTORS THAT MAY AFFECT EARNINGS

Educational Attainment of Workers and Effect on Earnings

Figures are based on a group of occupations: Postsecondary Teachers

	Percent at Level	Effect on Earnings
Less than High School	—	—
Some High School	—	—
High School or Equivalent	2.2%	−40.5%
Some College but No Degree	6.6%	−53.9%
Associate Degree	4.4%	−14.3%
Bachelor's Degree	20.2%	−33.1%
Master's Degree	29.9%	−8.9%
Doctoral Degree	28.3%	42.5%
First Professional Degree	8.1%	28.8%

Flexibility of Earnings

Average Hours Worked: 32
Workers with a Varying Number of Hours: 9.5%
Workers Earning Some Overtime Pay, Tips, or Commissions: 2.1%
Earnings Benefit of Working Overtime: −4.1%

Gender

	Male	Female
Percent	53.7%	46.3%
Effect on Earnings	16.1%	−13.5%

Union Membership

Percentage Union Members: 18.9%
Earnings Benefit of Union Membership: 12.1%

Veteran Status

Percentage Who Have Been on Active Duty: 7.4%
Earnings Benefit of Veteran Status: 20.1%

25-1042 Biological Science Teachers, Postsecondary

Teach courses in biological sciences. Includes both teachers primarily engaged in teaching and those who do a combination of both teaching and research.

- Education or Training Required: Master's degree
- Job Growth: 32.2% (for all postsecondary teaching occupations)
- Annual Openings: 329,000 (for all postsecondary teaching occupations)
- Self-Employed: 0.4%
- Part-Time: 24.8%

NATIONAL WAGE FIGURES (ANNUAL)

Beginning	25th Percentile	Median	Mean	75th Percentile	90th Percentile
$37,620	$49,420	$69,210	$82,110	$101,780	more than $145,600

Median Wages for Industries Employing Largest Numbers (Annual)

Industry	Median Income
Professional, Scientific, and Technical Services	$82,870
Educational Services	$69,200
Hospitals	$56,900

Median Wages for States (Annual)

State		State		State	
AK	no data	KY	$54,120	NY	no data
AL	no data	LA	no data	OH	$57,040
AR	no data	MA	$96,560	OK	$54,440
AZ	$62,220	MD	$72,650	OR	$75,450
CA	no data	ME	$58,810	PA	$64,250
CO	$61,250	MI	$64,260	RI	$68,420
CT	no data	MN	$48,690	SC	$56,470
DC	$61,920	MO	$60,220	SD	$62,710
DE	no data	MS	$52,900	TN	$53,060
FL	$61,420	MT	no data	TX	$90,470
GA	$67,400	NC	$60,720	UT	$66,410
HI	$87,580	ND	$50,500	VA	$66,980
IA	$57,840	NE	$53,550	VT	no data
ID	no data	NH	$67,790	WA	$60,900
IL	$78,690	NJ	$71,780	WI	$60,310
IN	$57,880	NM	$53,820	WV	$58,410
KS	$62,490	NV	no data	WY	$55,990

Median Wages for the Largest Metropolitan Areas (Annual)

Area		Area	
AZ: Phoenix	$62,890	MI: Detroit	$63,850
CA: Los Angeles	$76,870	MN: Minneapolis	$50,880
CA: Riverside	$84,710	MO: Kansas City	$59,430
CA: Sacramento	no data	MO: St. Louis	$58,840
CA: San Diego	no data	NV: Las Vegas	no data
CA: San Francisco	$93,540	NY: New York	$69,540
CO: Denver	$50,950	OH: Cincinnati	no data
DC: Washington	$67,440	OH: Cleveland	$52,260
FL: Miami	no data	OH: Columbus	no data
FL: Orlando	$52,430	OR: Portland	$75,410
FL: Tampa	$49,640	PA: Philadelphia	$63,990
GA: Atlanta	$76,500	PA: Pittsburgh	$61,690
IL: Chicago	$84,770	TX: Dallas	$62,390
MA: Boston	$104,840	TX: Houston	$102,320
MD: Baltimore	$77,960	WA: Seattle	no data

FACTORS THAT MAY AFFECT EARNINGS

Educational Attainment of Workers and Effect on Earnings

Figures are based on a group of occupations: Postsecondary Teachers

	Percent at Level	Effect on Earnings
Less than High School	—	—
Some High School	—	—
High School or Equivalent	2.2%	−40.5%
Some College but No Degree	6.6%	−53.9%
Associate Degree	4.4%	−14.3%
Bachelor's Degree	20.2%	−33.1%
Master's Degree	29.9%	−8.9%
Doctoral Degree	28.3%	42.5%
First Professional Degree	8.1%	28.8%

Flexibility of Earnings

Average Hours Worked: 32
Workers with a Varying Number of Hours: 9.5%
Workers Earning Some Overtime Pay, Tips, or Commissions: 2.1%
Earnings Benefit of Working Overtime: −4.1%

Gender

	Male	Female
Percent	53.7%	46.3%
Effect on Earnings	16.1%	−13.5%

Union Membership

Percentage Union Members: 18.9%
Earnings Benefit of Union Membership: 12.1%

Veteran Status

Percentage Who Have Been on Active Duty: 7.4%
Earnings Benefit of Veteran Status: 20.1%

25-1043 Forestry and Conservation Science Teachers, Postsecondary

Teach courses in environmental and conservation science. Includes both teachers primarily engaged in teaching and those who do a combination of both teaching and research.

- Education or Training Required: Master's degree
- Job Growth: 32.2% (for all postsecondary teaching occupations)
- Annual Openings: 329,000 (for all postsecondary teaching occupations)
- Self-Employed: 0.4%
- Part-Time: 24.8%

NATIONAL WAGE FIGURES (ANNUAL)

Beginning	25th Percentile	Median	Mean	75th Percentile	90th Percentile
$36,290	$46,900	$64,430	$66,970	$84,140	$102,630

Median Wages for Industries Employing Largest Numbers (Annual)

Industry	Median Income
Educational Services	$64,630

Median Wages for States (Annual)

AK	no data	KY	no data	NY	no data
AL	$69,430	LA	no data	OH	no data
AR	no data	MA	$51,760	OK	no data
AZ	$34,350	MD	no data	OR	no data
CA	no data	ME	no data	PA	$65,890
CO	no data	MI	no data	RI	no data
CT	no data	MN	no data	SC	no data
DC	no data	MO	no data	SD	no data
DE	no data	MS	no data	TN	no data
FL	$75,150	MT	no data	TX	no data
GA	no data	NC	$54,180	UT	no data
HI	no data	ND	no data	VA	no data
IA	no data	NE	no data	VT	no data
ID	no data	NH	no data	WA	no data
IL	no data	NJ	$63,230	WI	$66,990
IN	no data	NM	no data	WV	no data
KS	no data	NV	no data	WY	no data

Median Wages for the Largest Metropolitan Areas (Annual)

AZ: Phoenix............	no data	MI: Detroit	no data
CA: Los Angeles	no data	MN: Minneapolis	no data
CA: Riverside	no data	MO: Kansas City........	no data
CA: Sacramento	no data	MO: St. Louis............	no data
CA: San Diego	no data	NV: Las Vegas	no data
CA: San Francisco....	no data	NY: New York...........	no data
CO: Denver	no data	OH: Cincinnati..........	no data
DC: Washington	no data	OH: Cleveland	no data
FL: Miami	no data	OH: Columbus	no data
FL: Orlando	no data	OR: Portland	no data
FL: Tampa	no data	PA: Philadelphia	no data
GA: Atlanta	no data	PA: Pittsburgh	no data
IL: Chicago	no data	TX: Dallas	no data
MA: Boston	no data	TX: Houston	no data
MD: Baltimore	no data	WA: Seattle	no data

FACTORS THAT MAY AFFECT EARNINGS

Educational Attainment of Workers and Effect on Earnings

Figures are based on a group of occupations: Postsecondary Teachers

	Percent at Level	Effect on Earnings
Less than High School	—	—
Some High School	—	—
High School or Equivalent	2.2%	−40.5%
Some College but No Degree	6.6%	−53.9%
Associate Degree	4.4%	−14.3%
Bachelor's Degree	20.2%	−33.1%
Master's Degree	29.9%	−8.9%
Doctoral Degree	28.3%	42.5%
First Professional Degree	8.1%	28.8%

Flexibility of Earnings

Average Hours Worked: 32
Workers with a Varying Number of Hours: 9.5%
Workers Earning Some Overtime Pay, Tips, or Commissions: 2.1%
Earnings Benefit of Working Overtime: −4.1%

Gender

	Male	Female
Percent	53.7%	46.3%
Effect on Earnings	16.1%	−13.5%

Union Membership

Percentage Union Members: 18.9%
Earnings Benefit of Union Membership: 12.1%

Veteran Status

Percentage Who Have Been on Active Duty: 7.4%
Earnings Benefit of Veteran Status: 20.1%

25-1051 Atmospheric, Earth, Marine, and Space Sciences Teachers, Postsecondary

Teach courses in the physical sciences, except chemistry and physics. Includes both teachers primarily engaged in teaching and those who do a combination of both teaching and research.

- Education or Training Required: Master's degree
- Job Growth: 32.2% (for all postsecondary teaching occupations)
- Annual Openings: 329,000 (for all postsecondary teaching occupations)
- Self-Employed: 0.4%
- Part-Time: 24.8%

NATIONAL WAGE FIGURES (ANNUAL)

Beginning	25th Percentile	Median	Mean	75th Percentile	90th Percentile
$37,330	$50,390	$69,300	$74,880	$94,470	$121,500

Median Wages for Industries Employing Largest Numbers (Annual)

Industry	Median Income
Educational Services	$68,540

Median Wages for States (Annual)

AK .... no data	KY $57,130	NY .... no data
AL $57,740	LA .... no data	OH $70,560
AR .... no data	MA $79,930	OK $36,320
AZ $72,860	MD .... no data	OR .... no data
CA .... no data	ME .... no data	PA $69,630
CO $70,040	MI $69,600	RI .... no data
CT .... no data	MN $67,960	SC $51,450
DC $48,410	MO $63,570	SD .... no data
DE .... no data	MS .... no data	TN .... no data
FL $58,200	MT .... no data	TX $68,630
GA $45,910	NC $71,080	UT $71,390
HI $77,580	ND $59,670	VA $66,080
IA $67,300	NE $51,010	VT .... no data
ID .... no data	NH .... no data	WA $60,870
IL $64,580	NJ $74,090	WI $63,210
IN $59,970	NM $71,660	WV $42,260
KS $74,990	NV .... no data	WY .... no data

Median Wages for the Largest Metropolitan Areas (Annual)

AZ: Phoenix $52,180	MI: Detroit .... no data
CA: Los Angeles $95,650	MN: Minneapolis ...... no data
CA: Riverside $74,800	MO: Kansas City $65,180
CA: Sacramento ...... no data	MO: St. Louis $68,490
CA: San Diego .... no data	NV: Las Vegas .... no data
CA: San Francisco $74,320	NY: New York $76,040
CO: Denver $61,000	OH: Cincinnati $67,580
DC: Washington $72,670	OH: Cleveland .... no data
FL: Miami $64,690	OH: Columbus .... no data
FL: Orlando .... no data	OR: Portland $58,380
FL: Tampa $55,050	PA: Philadelphia $75,820
GA: Atlanta .... no data	PA: Pittsburgh .... no data
IL: Chicago $62,370	TX: Dallas $78,670
MA: Boston $89,630	TX: Houston .... no data
MD: Baltimore .... no data	WA: Seattle .... no data

FACTORS THAT MAY AFFECT EARNINGS

Educational Attainment of Workers and Effect on Earnings

Figures are based on a group of occupations: Postsecondary Teachers

	Percent at Level	Effect on Earnings
Less than High School	—	—
Some High School	—	—
High School or Equivalent	2.2%	−40.5%
Some College but No Degree	6.6%	−53.9%
Associate Degree	4.4%	−14.3%
Bachelor's Degree	20.2%	−33.1%
Master's Degree	29.9%	−8.9%
Doctoral Degree	28.3%	42.5%
First Professional Degree	8.1%	28.8%

Flexibility of Earnings

Average Hours Worked: 32
Workers with a Varying Number of Hours: 9.5%
Workers Earning Some Overtime Pay, Tips, or Commissions: 2.1%
Earnings Benefit of Working Overtime: −4.1%

Gender

	Male	Female
Percent	53.7%	46.3%
Effect on Earnings	16.1%	−13.5%

Union Membership

Percentage Union Members: 18.9%
Earnings Benefit of Union Membership: 12.1%

Veteran Status

Percentage Who Have Been on Active Duty: 7.4%
Earnings Benefit of Veteran Status: 20.1%

25-1052 Chemistry Teachers, Postsecondary

Teach courses pertaining to the chemical and physical properties and compositional changes of substances. Work may include instruction in the methods of qualitative and quantitative chemical analysis. Includes both teachers primarily engaged in teaching and those who do a combination of both teaching and research.

- Education or Training Required: Master's degree
- Job Growth: 32.2% (for all postsecondary teaching occupations)
- Annual Openings: 329,000 (for all postsecondary teaching occupations)
- Self-Employed: 0.4%
- Part-Time: 24.8%

NATIONAL WAGE FIGURES (ANNUAL)

Beginning	25th Percentile	Median	Mean	75th Percentile	90th Percentile
$36,160	$46,920	$61,220	$70,100	$85,550	$116,910

Median Wages for Industries Employing Largest Numbers (Annual)

Industry	Median Income
Professional, Scientific, and Technical Services	$62,110
Educational Services	$61,160

Median Wages for States (Annual)

AK	no data	KY	$56,370	NY	no data
AL	$52,830	LA	no data	OH	$60,860
AR	no data	MA	$74,470	OK	$41,730
AZ	$49,150	MD	$61,610	OR	$79,030
CA	no data	ME	$57,790	PA	$61,920
CO	$68,120	MI	$59,420	RI	$71,950
CT	$68,120	MN	$49,010	SC	$54,770
DC	$57,070	MO	$59,240	SD	$53,060
DE	no data	MS	$56,800	TN	no data
FL	$62,050	MT	no data	TX	$64,960
GA	$55,520	NC	$61,560	UT	$68,950
HI	$70,590	ND	$52,360	VA	$56,410
IA	$61,680	NE	$51,050	VT	$58,030
ID	no data	NH	$67,850	WA	$54,140
IL	$60,990	NJ	$69,400	WI	$56,350
IN	$60,160	NM	$53,980	WV	$58,540
KS	$57,960	NV	no data	WY	$61,040

Median Wages for the Largest Metropolitan Areas (Annual)

AZ: Phoenix	$43,380	MI: Detroit	$65,010
CA: Los Angeles	$67,690	MN: Minneapolis	$50,960
CA: Riverside	$78,020	MO: Kansas City	$57,640
CA: Sacramento	no data	MO: St. Louis	$60,740
CA: San Diego	no data	NV: Las Vegas	no data
CA: San Francisco	$78,360	NY: New York	$71,620
CO: Denver	$65,320	OH: Cincinnati	$59,100
DC: Washington	$60,830	OH: Cleveland	$62,690
FL: Miami	$67,970	OH: Columbus	$74,620
FL: Orlando	$64,290	OR: Portland	$72,370
FL: Tampa	$57,940	PA: Philadelphia	$62,040
GA: Atlanta	$57,130	PA: Pittsburgh	$58,630
IL: Chicago	$61,320	TX: Dallas	$66,220
MA: Boston	$73,560	TX: Houston	no data
MD: Baltimore	$61,030	WA: Seattle	$56,040

FACTORS THAT MAY AFFECT EARNINGS

Educational Attainment of Workers and Effect on Earnings

Figures are based on a group of occupations: Postsecondary Teachers

	Percent at Level	Effect on Earnings
Less than High School	—	—
Some High School	—	—
High School or Equivalent	2.2%	−40.5%
Some College but No Degree	6.6%	−53.9%
Associate Degree	4.4%	−14.3%
Bachelor's Degree	20.2%	−33.1%
Master's Degree	29.9%	−8.9%
Doctoral Degree	28.3%	42.5%
First Professional Degree	8.1%	28.8%

Flexibility of Earnings

Average Hours Worked: 32
Workers with a Varying Number of Hours: 9.5%
Workers Earning Some Overtime Pay, Tips, or Commissions: 2.1%
Earnings Benefit of Working Overtime: −4.1%

Gender

	Male	Female
Percent	53.7%	46.3%
Effect on Earnings	16.1%	−13.5%

Union Membership

Percentage Union Members: 18.9%
Earnings Benefit of Union Membership: 12.1%

Veteran Status

Percentage Who Have Been on Active Duty: 7.4%
Earnings Benefit of Veteran Status: 20.1%

25-1053 Environmental Science Teachers, Postsecondary

Teach courses in environmental science. Includes both teachers primarily engaged in teaching and those who do a combination of both teaching and research.

- Education or Training Required: Master's degree
- Job Growth: 32.2% (for all postsecondary teaching occupations)
- Annual Openings: 329,000 (for all postsecondary teaching occupations)
- Self-Employed: 0.4%
- Part-Time: 24.8%

NATIONAL WAGE FIGURES (ANNUAL)

Beginning	25th Percentile	Median	Mean	75th Percentile	90th Percentile
$32,890	$46,500	$64,780	$71,980	$89,680	$119,260

Median Wages for Industries Employing Largest Numbers (Annual)

Industry	Median Income
Educational Services	$64,530

Median Wages for States (Annual)

State	Wage	State	Wage	State	Wage
AK	no data	KY	no data	NY	no data
AL	no data	LA	no data	OH	$59,060
AR	no data	MA	$68,840	OK	no data
AZ	no data	MD	$73,830	OR	no data
CA	no data	ME	$53,580	PA	$60,860
CO	no data	MI	no data	RI	no data
CT	no data	MN	$51,500	SC	no data
DC	$57,290	MO	no data	SD	no data
DE	no data	MS	no data	TN	no data
FL	$53,770	MT	$47,700	TX	$67,440
GA	$52,220	NC	$72,180	UT	$63,560
HI	no data	ND	no data	VA	$62,860
IA	no data	NE	no data	VT	$48,370
ID	no data	NH	$59,370	WA	$59,220
IL	$73,080	NJ	$70,210	WI	$62,210
IN	no data	NM	no data	WV	no data
KS	no data	NV	no data	WY	no data

Median Wages for the Largest Metropolitan Areas (Annual)

Area	Wage	Area	Wage
AZ: Phoenix	no data	MI: Detroit	no data
CA: Los Angeles	$76,370	MN: Minneapolis	no data
CA: Riverside	$79,500	MO: Kansas City	no data
CA: Sacramento	no data	MO: St. Louis	no data
CA: San Diego	no data	NV: Las Vegas	no data
CA: San Francisco	$87,380	NY: New York	$68,920
CO: Denver	no data	OH: Cincinnati	no data
DC: Washington	$59,330	OH: Cleveland	no data
FL: Miami	no data	OH: Columbus	no data
FL: Orlando	no data	OR: Portland	no data
FL: Tampa	$50,420	PA: Philadelphia	$60,130
GA: Atlanta	no data	PA: Pittsburgh	$58,790
IL: Chicago	$76,050	TX: Dallas	no data
MA: Boston	$65,440	TX: Houston	no data
MD: Baltimore	no data	WA: Seattle	no data

FACTORS THAT MAY AFFECT EARNINGS

Educational Attainment of Workers and Effect on Earnings

Figures are based on a group of occupations: Postsecondary Teachers

	Percent at Level	Effect on Earnings
Less than High School	—	—
Some High School	—	—
High School or Equivalent	2.2%	−40.5%
Some College but No Degree	6.6%	−53.9%
Associate Degree	4.4%	−14.3%
Bachelor's Degree	20.2%	−33.1%
Master's Degree	29.9%	−8.9%
Doctoral Degree	28.3%	42.5%
First Professional Degree	8.1%	28.8%

Flexibility of Earnings

Average Hours Worked: 32
Workers with a Varying Number of Hours: 9.5%
Workers Earning Some Overtime Pay, Tips, or Commissions: 2.1%
Earnings Benefit of Working Overtime: −4.1%

Gender

	Male	Female
Percent	53.7%	46.3%
Effect on Earnings	16.1%	−13.5%

Union Membership

Percentage Union Members: 18.9%
Earnings Benefit of Union Membership: 12.1%

Veteran Status

Percentage Who Have Been on Active Duty: 7.4%
Earnings Benefit of Veteran Status: 20.1%

25-1054 Physics Teachers, Postsecondary

Teach courses pertaining to the laws of matter and energy. Includes both teachers primarily engaged in teaching and those who do a combination of both teaching and research.

- Education or Training Required: Master's degree
- Job Growth: 32.2% (for all postsecondary teaching occupations)
- Annual Openings: 329,000 (for all postsecondary teaching occupations)
- Self-Employed: 0.4%
- Part-Time: 24.8%

NATIONAL WAGE FIGURES (ANNUAL)

Beginning	25th Percentile	Median	Mean	75th Percentile	90th Percentile
$39,580	$50,870	$68,170	$74,650	$91,420	$120,210

Median Wages for Industries Employing Largest Numbers (Annual)

Industry	Median Income
Educational Services	$68,040

Median Wages for States (Annual)

AK	no data	KY	$60,010	NY	no data
AL	$72,400	LA	no data	OH	$73,250
AR	no data	MA	$81,910	OK	$44,220
AZ	$67,490	MD	$70,160	OR	$83,100
CA	no data	ME	$67,470	PA	$68,050
CO	$75,670	MI	$64,250	RI	$72,790
CT	no data	MN	$56,690	SC	$59,210
DC	$75,100	MO	$61,900	SD	$56,850
DE	no data	MS	$55,350	TN	$61,720
FL	$65,750	MT	no data	TX	$65,190
GA	$62,680	NC	$67,380	UT	$67,160
HI	$83,960	ND	no data	VA	$61,390
IA	$75,310	NE	$54,060	VT	$65,620
ID	no data	NH	$89,730	WA	$60,940
IL	$68,210	NJ	$83,100	WI	$64,590
IN	$72,100	NM	$70,070	WV	$61,520
KS	$60,280	NV	no data	WY	no data

Median Wages for the Largest Metropolitan Areas (Annual)

AZ: Phoenix	no data	MI: Detroit	$59,860
CA: Los Angeles	no data	MN: Minneapolis	$64,510
CA: Riverside	$72,130	MO: Kansas City	$56,990
CA: Sacramento	no data	MO: St. Louis	$69,670
CA: San Diego	no data	NV: Las Vegas	no data
CA: San Francisco	$77,050	NY: New York	$83,210
CO: Denver	$67,010	OH: Cincinnati	$70,320
DC: Washington	$75,730	OH: Cleveland	$72,620
FL: Miami	$65,130	OH: Columbus	no data
FL: Orlando	$62,340	OR: Portland	$75,000
FL: Tampa	$64,860	PA: Philadelphia	$67,280
GA: Atlanta	$70,090	PA: Pittsburgh	$69,320
IL: Chicago	$69,590	TX: Dallas	$65,190
MA: Boston	$83,670	TX: Houston	$78,930
MD: Baltimore	$65,200	WA: Seattle	no data

FACTORS THAT MAY AFFECT EARNINGS

Educational Attainment of Workers and Effect on Earnings

Figures are based on a group of occupations: Postsecondary Teachers

	Percent at Level	Effect on Earnings
Less than High School	—	—
Some High School	—	—
High School or Equivalent	2.2%	−40.5%
Some College but No Degree	6.6%	−53.9%
Associate Degree	4.4%	−14.3%
Bachelor's Degree	20.2%	−33.1%
Master's Degree	29.9%	−8.9%
Doctoral Degree	28.3%	42.5%
First Professional Degree	8.1%	28.8%

Flexibility of Earnings

Average Hours Worked: 32
Workers with a Varying Number of Hours: 9.5%
Workers Earning Some Overtime Pay, Tips, or Commissions: 2.1%
Earnings Benefit of Working Overtime: −4.1%

Gender

	Male	Female
Percent	53.7%	46.3%
Effect on Earnings	16.1%	−13.5%

Union Membership

Percentage Union Members: 18.9%
Earnings Benefit of Union Membership: 12.1%

Veteran Status

Percentage Who Have Been on Active Duty: 7.4%
Earnings Benefit of Veteran Status: 20.1%

25-1061 Anthropology and Archeology Teachers, Postsecondary

Teach courses in anthropology or archeology. Includes both teachers primarily engaged in teaching and those who do a combination of both teaching and research.

- Education or Training Required: Master's degree
- Job Growth: 32.2% (for all postsecondary teaching occupations)
- Annual Openings: 329,000 (for all postsecondary teaching occupations)
- Self-Employed: 0.4%
- Part-Time: 24.8%

NATIONAL WAGE FIGURES (ANNUAL)

Beginning	25th Percentile	Median	Mean	75th Percentile	90th Percentile
$37,590	$49,160	$62,820	$68,240	$83,760	$109,330

Median Wages for Industries Employing Largest Numbers (Annual)

Industry	Median Income
Educational Services	$62,870

Median Wages for States (Annual)

AK	no data	KY	$52,110	NY	no data
AL	no data	LA	no data	OH	$61,150
AR	no data	MA	$71,400	OK	no data
AZ	$55,860	MD	$67,320	OR	$76,010
CA	no data	ME	$70,170	PA	$69,180
CO	$56,270	MI	$67,360	RI	$77,450
CT	no data	MN	$52,710	SC	no data
DC	$52,620	MO	$62,250	SD	no data
DE	no data	MS	no data	TN	$56,910
FL	$63,740	MT	no data	TX	$66,980
GA	$61,970	NC	$63,240	UT	no data
HI	$71,180	ND	no data	VA	$55,180
IA	$57,480	NE	no data	VT	no data
ID	no data	NH	$54,600	WA	$56,110
IL	$67,350	NJ	$65,190	WI	$57,830
IN	no data	NM	$60,220	WV	no data
KS	$84,610	NV	$56,120	WY	no data

Median Wages for the Largest Metropolitan Areas (Annual)

AZ: Phoenix	no data	MI: Detroit	no data
CA: Los Angeles	$75,470	MN: Minneapolis	$56,500
CA: Riverside	$71,570	MO: Kansas City	no data
CA: Sacramento	no data	MO: St. Louis	$68,250
CA: San Diego	$70,170	NV: Las Vegas	no data
CA: San Francisco	$67,440	NY: New York	$70,120
CO: Denver	$55,280	OH: Cincinnati	$48,140
DC: Washington	$60,620	OH: Cleveland	no data
FL: Miami	$68,930	OH: Columbus	no data
FL: Orlando	no data	OR: Portland	$83,230
FL: Tampa	$64,820	PA: Philadelphia	$66,240
GA: Atlanta	$62,530	PA: Pittsburgh	no data
IL: Chicago	$69,760	TX: Dallas	no data
MA: Boston	$71,450	TX: Houston	no data
MD: Baltimore	$65,490	WA: Seattle	$59,170

FACTORS THAT MAY AFFECT EARNINGS

Educational Attainment of Workers and Effect on Earnings

Figures are based on a group of occupations: Postsecondary Teachers

	Percent at Level	Effect on Earnings
Less than High School	—	—
Some High School	—	—
High School or Equivalent	2.2%	−40.5%
Some College but No Degree	6.6%	−53.9%
Associate Degree	4.4%	−14.3%
Bachelor's Degree	20.2%	−33.1%
Master's Degree	29.9%	−8.9%
Doctoral Degree	28.3%	42.5%
First Professional Degree	8.1%	28.8%

Flexibility of Earnings

Average Hours Worked: 32
Workers with a Varying Number of Hours: 9.5%
Workers Earning Some Overtime Pay, Tips, or Commissions: 2.1%
Earnings Benefit of Working Overtime: −4.1%

Gender

	Male	Female
Percent	53.7%	46.3%
Effect on Earnings	16.1%	−13.5%

Union Membership

Percentage Union Members: 18.9%
Earnings Benefit of Union Membership: 12.1%

Veteran Status

Percentage Who Have Been on Active Duty: 7.4%
Earnings Benefit of Veteran Status: 20.1%

25-1062 Area, Ethnic, and Cultural Studies Teachers, Postsecondary

Teach courses pertaining to the culture and development of an area (e.g., Latin America), an ethnic group, or any other group (e.g., women's studies, urban affairs). Includes both teachers primarily engaged in teaching and those who do a combination of both teaching and research.

- Education or Training Required: Master's degree
- Job Growth: 32.2% (for all postsecondary teaching occupations)
- Annual Openings: 329,000 (for all postsecondary teaching occupations)
- Self-Employed: 0.4%
- Part-Time: 24.8%

NATIONAL WAGE FIGURES (ANNUAL)

Beginning	25th Percentile	Median	Mean	75th Percentile	90th Percentile
$31,770	$43,100	$56,380	$63,710	$77,890	$106,080

Median Wages for Industries Employing Largest Numbers (Annual)

Industry	Median Income
Educational Services	$56,600

Median Wages for States (Annual)

AK .... no data	KY $50,150	NY .... no data
AL .... no data	LA .... no data	OH $58,930
AR .... no data	MA $59,920	OK .... no data
AZ $54,680	MD $53,990	OR $66,170
CA .... no data	ME .... no data	PA $63,730
CO $54,510	MI $49,550	RI .... no data
CT $65,670	MN $53,890	SC .... no data
DC $53,100	MO $71,520	SD $36,030
DE .... no data	MS .... no data	TN $54,820
FL $58,000	MT .... no data	TX $43,680
GA $48,190	NC $51,230	UT .... no data
HI $57,650	ND .... no data	VA $48,250
IA .... no data	NE .... no data	VT $54,200
ID .... no data	NH $73,030	WA $58,940
IL $51,570	NJ $67,340	WI $56,640
IN .... no data	NM $50,480	WV .... no data
KS $43,640	NV .... no data	WY .... no data

Median Wages for the Largest Metropolitan Areas (Annual)

AZ: Phoenix............	$50,930	MI: Detroit	no data
CA: Los Angeles	$60,070	MN: Minneapolis	$55,450
CA: Riverside	$57,170	MO: Kansas City........	no data
CA: Sacramento	no data	MO: St. Louis............	$75,810
CA: San Diego	no data	NV: Las Vegas	no data
CA: San Francisco....	$60,780	NY: New York............	$58,020
CO: Denver	$51,590	OH: Cincinnati..........	$53,060
DC: Washington	$55,750	OH: Cleveland	no data
FL: Miami	$57,270	OH: Columbus	$75,270
FL: Orlando	no data	OR: Portland	no data
FL: Tampa	no data	PA: Philadelphia	$69,370
GA: Atlanta	no data	PA: Pittsburgh	$50,740
IL: Chicago	$50,980	TX: Dallas	no data
MA: Boston	$58,800	TX: Houston	no data
MD: Baltimore	no data	WA: Seattle	no data

FACTORS THAT MAY AFFECT EARNINGS

Educational Attainment of Workers and Effect on Earnings

Figures are based on a group of occupations: Postsecondary Teachers

	Percent at Level	Effect on Earnings
Less than High School	—	—
Some High School	—	—
High School or Equivalent	2.2%	−40.5%
Some College but No Degree	6.6%	−53.9%
Associate Degree	4.4%	−14.3%
Bachelor's Degree	20.2%	−33.1%
Master's Degree	29.9%	−8.9%
Doctoral Degree	28.3%	42.5%
First Professional Degree	8.1%	28.8%

Flexibility of Earnings

Average Hours Worked: 32
Workers with a Varying Number of Hours: 9.5%
Workers Earning Some Overtime Pay, Tips, or Commissions: 2.1%
Earnings Benefit of Working Overtime: −4.1%

Gender

	Male	Female
Percent	53.7%	46.3%
Effect on Earnings	16.1%	−13.5%

Union Membership

Percentage Union Members: 18.9%
Earnings Benefit of Union Membership: 12.1%

Veteran Status

Percentage Who Have Been on Active Duty: 7.4%
Earnings Benefit of Veteran Status: 20.1%

25-1063 Economics Teachers, Postsecondary

Teach courses in economics. Includes both teachers primarily engaged in teaching and those who do a combination of both teaching and research.

- Education or Training Required: Master's degree
- Job Growth: 32.2% (for all postsecondary teaching occupations)
- Annual Openings: 329,000 (for all postsecondary teaching occupations)
- Self-Employed: 0.4%
- Part-Time: 24.8%

NATIONAL WAGE FIGURES (ANNUAL)

Beginning	25th Percentile	Median	Mean	75th Percentile	90th Percentile
$38,630	$52,140	$71,850	$79,370	$96,230	$130,990

Median Wages for Industries Employing Largest Numbers (Annual)

Industry	Median Income
Educational Services	$71,860

Median Wages for States (Annual)

AK	no data	KY	$76,420	NY	no data
AL	$62,890	LA	no data	OH	$73,070
AR	no data	MA	$82,850	OK	$35,580
AZ	$88,510	MD	$66,860	OR	$90,180
CA	no data	ME	$66,400	PA	$78,160
CO	$68,010	MI	$71,310	RI	$90,240
CT	$79,960	MN	$66,210	SC	$62,620
DC	$57,540	MO	$71,370	SD	no data
DE	no data	MS	$61,550	TN	no data
FL	$70,160	MT	no data	TX	$69,610
GA	$70,980	NC	$74,780	UT	$74,340
HI	$76,150	ND	$61,840	VA	$65,080
IA	$92,660	NE	$74,080	VT	$58,400
ID	no data	NH	$88,290	WA	$64,280
IL	$69,320	NJ	$74,670	WI	$70,230
IN	$67,840	NM	$67,520	WV	no data
KS	$92,760	NV	$67,750	WY	no data

Median Wages for the Largest Metropolitan Areas (Annual)

AZ: Phoenix	no data	MI: Detroit	$68,580
CA: Los Angeles	$86,070	MN: Minneapolis	$75,080
CA: Riverside	$91,450	MO: Kansas City	$68,880
CA: Sacramento	no data	MO: St. Louis	$80,400
CA: San Diego	$98,970	NV: Las Vegas	no data
CA: San Francisco	$84,880	NY: New York	$76,460
CO: Denver	$70,800	OH: Cincinnati	$71,640
DC: Washington	$63,090	OH: Cleveland	$70,240
FL: Miami	$73,250	OH: Columbus	$80,370
FL: Orlando	$65,070	OR: Portland	$77,350
FL: Tampa	$70,350	PA: Philadelphia	$77,910
GA: Atlanta	$78,920	PA: Pittsburgh	$74,930
IL: Chicago	$71,960	TX: Dallas	$67,170
MA: Boston	$86,340	TX: Houston	no data
MD: Baltimore	$59,690	WA: Seattle	$62,590

FACTORS THAT MAY AFFECT EARNINGS

Educational Attainment of Workers and Effect on Earnings

Figures are based on a group of occupations: Postsecondary Teachers

	Percent at Level	Effect on Earnings
Less than High School	—	—
Some High School	—	—
High School or Equivalent	2.2%	−40.5%
Some College but No Degree	6.6%	−53.9%
Associate Degree	4.4%	−14.3%
Bachelor's Degree	20.2%	−33.1%
Master's Degree	29.9%	−8.9%
Doctoral Degree	28.3%	42.5%
First Professional Degree	8.1%	28.8%

Flexibility of Earnings

Average Hours Worked: 32
Workers with a Varying Number of Hours: 9.5%
Workers Earning Some Overtime Pay, Tips, or Commissions: 2.1%
Earnings Benefit of Working Overtime: −4.1%

Gender

	Male	Female
Percent	53.7%	46.3%
Effect on Earnings	16.1%	−13.5%

Union Membership

Percentage Union Members: 18.9%
Earnings Benefit of Union Membership: 12.1%

Veteran Status

Percentage Who Have Been on Active Duty: 7.4%
Earnings Benefit of Veteran Status: 20.1%

25-1064 Geography Teachers, Postsecondary

Teach courses in geography. Includes both teachers primarily engaged in teaching and those who do a combination of both teaching and research.

- Education or Training Required: Master's degree
- Job Growth: 32.2% (for all postsecondary teaching occupations)
- Annual Openings: 329,000 (for all postsecondary teaching occupations)
- Self-Employed: 0.4%
- Part-Time: 24.8%

NATIONAL WAGE FIGURES (ANNUAL)

Beginning	25th Percentile	Median	Mean	75th Percentile	90th Percentile
$34,300	$47,300	$59,000	$62,850	$76,630	$98,200

Median Wages for Industries Employing Largest Numbers (Annual)

Industry	Median Income
Educational Services	$59,000

Median Wages for States (Annual)

AK	no data	KY	$47,390	NY	no data
AL	$58,060	LA	no data	OH	$59,400
AR	no data	MA	$65,320	OK	no data
AZ	$65,080	MD	$60,760	OR	no data
CA	no data	ME	no data	PA	$66,410
CO	$60,430	MI	$57,400	RI	no data
CT	no data	MN	$55,980	SC	$58,010
DC	$52,370	MO	$49,310	SD	no data
DE	no data	MS	no data	TN	$50,420
FL	$61,940	MT	no data	TX	$55,500
GA	$66,150	NC	$58,930	UT	no data
HI	$70,360	ND	no data	VA	$53,430
IA	no data	NE	no data	VT	no data
ID	no data	NH	no data	WA	$48,670
IL	$58,330	NJ	$64,730	WI	$55,510
IN	$54,210	NM	$64,720	WV	no data
KS	$54,580	NV	no data	WY	no data

Median Wages for the Largest Metropolitan Areas (Annual)

AZ: Phoenix	no data	MI: Detroit	no data
CA: Los Angeles	$62,080	MN: Minneapolis	$56,970
CA: Riverside	no data	MO: Kansas City	no data
CA: Sacramento	no data	MO: St. Louis	$52,670
CA: San Diego	$62,760	NV: Las Vegas	no data
CA: San Francisco	$62,150	NY: New York	$63,970
CO: Denver	no data	OH: Cincinnati	$58,720
DC: Washington	$57,850	OH: Cleveland	no data
FL: Miami	$58,100	OH: Columbus	no data
FL: Orlando	no data	OR: Portland	no data
FL: Tampa	no data	PA: Philadelphia	$65,010
GA: Atlanta	no data	PA: Pittsburgh	no data
IL: Chicago	$58,370	TX: Dallas	no data
MA: Boston	$63,980	TX: Houston	no data
MD: Baltimore	$66,670	WA: Seattle	no data

FACTORS THAT MAY AFFECT EARNINGS

Educational Attainment of Workers and Effect on Earnings

Figures are based on a group of occupations: Postsecondary Teachers

	Percent at Level	Effect on Earnings
Less than High School	—	—
Some High School	—	—
High School or Equivalent	2.2%	−40.5%
Some College but No Degree	6.6%	−53.9%
Associate Degree	4.4%	−14.3%
Bachelor's Degree	20.2%	−33.1%
Master's Degree	29.9%	−8.9%
Doctoral Degree	28.3%	42.5%
First Professional Degree	8.1%	28.8%

Flexibility of Earnings

Average Hours Worked: 32

Workers with a Varying Number of Hours: 9.5%

Workers Earning Some Overtime Pay, Tips, or Commissions: 2.1%

Earnings Benefit of Working Overtime: −4.1%

Gender

	Male	Female
Percent	53.7%	46.3%
Effect on Earnings	16.1%	−13.5%

Union Membership

Percentage Union Members: 18.9%

Earnings Benefit of Union Membership: 12.1%

Veteran Status

Percentage Who Have Been on Active Duty: 7.4%

Earnings Benefit of Veteran Status: 20.1%

25-1065 Political Science Teachers, Postsecondary

Teach courses in political science, international affairs, and international relations. Includes both teachers primarily engaged in teaching and those who do a combination of both teaching and research.

- Education or Training Required: Master's degree
- Job Growth: 32.2% (for all postsecondary teaching occupations)
- Annual Openings: 329,000 (for all postsecondary teaching occupations)
- Self-Employed: 0.4%
- Part-Time: 24.8%

NATIONAL WAGE FIGURES (ANNUAL)

Beginning	25th Percentile	Median	Mean	75th Percentile	90th Percentile
$35,730	$47,340	$61,820	$69,040	$82,960	$113,480

Median Wages for Industries Employing Largest Numbers (Annual)

Industry	Median Income
Educational Services	$61,820

Median Wages for States (Annual)

AK	$59,080	KY	$48,350	NY	no data
AL	$56,080	LA	no data	OH	$65,010
AR	no data	MA	$75,640	OK	$38,440
AZ	$47,290	MD	$64,480	OR	$68,340
CA	no data	ME	no data	PA	$67,590
CO	$59,070	MI	$60,620	RI	$81,310
CT	$71,400	MN	$63,210	SC	$56,770
DC	$57,910	MO	$59,550	SD	$64,970
DE	no data	MS	$56,880	TN	$58,530
FL	$53,080	MT	no data	TX	$56,440
GA	$59,630	NC	$61,790	UT	$58,820
HI	$72,740	ND	$53,000	VA	$58,190
IA	$57,160	NE	no data	VT	$57,940
ID	no data	NH	$69,170	WA	$65,380
IL	$62,250	NJ	$70,240	WI	$57,930
IN	$62,440	NM	$68,120	WV	$50,240
KS	$66,340	NV	$50,380	WY	no data

Median Wages for the Largest Metropolitan Areas (Annual)

AZ: Phoenix	$43,910	MI: Detroit	$61,820
CA: Los Angeles	$79,270	MN: Minneapolis	$70,510
CA: Riverside	$73,060	MO: Kansas City	$62,280
CA: Sacramento	no data	MO: St. Louis	$65,060
CA: San Diego	no data	NV: Las Vegas	no data
CA: San Francisco	$70,080	NY: New York	$70,680
CO: Denver	$57,370	OH: Cincinnati	$54,550
DC: Washington	$61,480	OH: Cleveland	$51,230
FL: Miami	$65,390	OH: Columbus	$75,450
FL: Orlando	$46,440	OR: Portland	$62,090
FL: Tampa	$55,930	PA: Philadelphia	$65,600
GA: Atlanta	$64,910	PA: Pittsburgh	$72,060
IL: Chicago	$66,120	TX: Dallas	$49,770
MA: Boston	$75,190	TX: Houston	no data
MD: Baltimore	$58,750	WA: Seattle	no data

FACTORS THAT MAY AFFECT EARNINGS

Educational Attainment of Workers and Effect on Earnings

Figures are based on a group of occupations: Postsecondary Teachers

	Percent at Level	Effect on Earnings
Less than High School	—	—
Some High School	—	—
High School or Equivalent	2.2%	−40.5%
Some College but No Degree	6.6%	−53.9%
Associate Degree	4.4%	−14.3%
Bachelor's Degree	20.2%	−33.1%
Master's Degree	29.9%	−8.9%
Doctoral Degree	28.3%	42.5%
First Professional Degree	8.1%	28.8%

Flexibility of Earnings

Average Hours Worked: 32
Workers with a Varying Number of Hours: 9.5%
Workers Earning Some Overtime Pay, Tips, or Commissions: 2.1%
Earnings Benefit of Working Overtime: −4.1%

Gender

	Male	Female
Percent	53.7%	46.3%
Effect on Earnings	16.1%	−13.5%

Union Membership

Percentage Union Members: 18.9%
Earnings Benefit of Union Membership: 12.1%

Veteran Status

Percentage Who Have Been on Active Duty: 7.4%
Earnings Benefit of Veteran Status: 20.1%

25-1066 Psychology Teachers, Postsecondary

Teach courses in psychology, such as child, clinical, and developmental psychology, and psychological counseling. Includes both teachers primarily engaged in teaching and those who do a combination of both teaching and research.

- Education or Training Required: Master's degree
- Job Growth: 32.2% (for all postsecondary teaching occupations)
- Annual Openings: 329,000 (for all postsecondary teaching occupations)
- Self-Employed: 0.4%
- Part-Time: 24.8%

NATIONAL WAGE FIGURES (ANNUAL)

Beginning	25th Percentile	Median	Mean	75th Percentile	90th Percentile
$32,800	$44,150	$58,670	$64,580	$79,230	$104,390

Median Wages for Industries Employing Largest Numbers (Annual)

Industry	Median Income
Educational Services	$58,640

Median Wages for States (Annual)

AK	no data	KY	$52,020	NY	no data
AL	$51,120	LA	no data	OH	$54,650
AR	no data	MA	$68,380	OK	$49,950
AZ	$46,650	MD	$59,490	OR	$71,980
CA	no data	ME	$54,120	PA	$63,680
CO	$54,540	MI	$55,520	RI	$67,130
CT	$64,220	MN	$51,160	SC	$56,840
DC	$54,750	MO	$57,110	SD	$54,760
DE	$54,360	MS	$52,350	TN	$55,980
FL	$62,410	MT	no data	TX	$57,560
GA	$55,920	NC	$54,560	UT	$58,380
HI	$71,240	ND	$51,570	VA	$55,260
IA	$56,810	NE	$53,580	VT	$56,180
ID	no data	NH	$53,180	WA	$54,820
IL	$56,650	NJ	$71,090	WI	$52,210
IN	$55,430	NM	$56,420	WV	$53,200
KS	$58,710	NV	$53,110	WY	$55,450

Median Wages for the Largest Metropolitan Areas (Annual)

AZ: Phoenix	$43,660	MI: Detroit	$58,450
CA: Los Angeles	$72,820	MN: Minneapolis	$53,200
CA: Riverside	$69,180	MO: Kansas City	$57,460
CA: Sacramento	$83,820	MO: St. Louis	$59,230
CA: San Diego	$77,470	NV: Las Vegas	$51,080
CA: San Francisco	$71,430	NY: New York	$70,980
CO: Denver	$44,990	OH: Cincinnati	$51,930
DC: Washington	$58,540	OH: Cleveland	$55,340
FL: Miami	no data	OH: Columbus	$63,160
FL: Orlando	$54,430	OR: Portland	$69,540
FL: Tampa	$58,770	PA: Philadelphia	$63,360
GA: Atlanta	$58,280	PA: Pittsburgh	$63,110
IL: Chicago	$58,130	TX: Dallas	$54,550
MA: Boston	$66,020	TX: Houston	no data
MD: Baltimore	$54,740	WA: Seattle	$57,490

FACTORS THAT MAY AFFECT EARNINGS

Educational Attainment of Workers and Effect on Earnings

Figures are based on a group of occupations: Postsecondary Teachers

	Percent at Level	Effect on Earnings
Less than High School	—	—
Some High School	—	—
High School or Equivalent	2.2%	−40.5%
Some College but No Degree	6.6%	−53.9%
Associate Degree	4.4%	−14.3%
Bachelor's Degree	20.2%	−33.1%
Master's Degree	29.9%	−8.9%
Doctoral Degree	28.3%	42.5%
First Professional Degree	8.1%	28.8%

Flexibility of Earnings

Average Hours Worked: 32
Workers with a Varying Number of Hours: 9.5%
Workers Earning Some Overtime Pay, Tips, or Commissions: 2.1%
Earnings Benefit of Working Overtime: −4.1%

Gender

	Male	Female
Percent	53.7%	46.3%
Effect on Earnings	16.1%	−13.5%

Union Membership

Percentage Union Members: 18.9%
Earnings Benefit of Union Membership: 12.1%

Veteran Status

Percentage Who Have Been on Active Duty: 7.4%
Earnings Benefit of Veteran Status: 20.1%

25-1067 Sociology Teachers, Postsecondary

Teach courses in sociology. Includes both teachers primarily engaged in teaching and those who do a combination of both teaching and research.

- Education or Training Required: Master's degree
- Job Growth: 32.2% (for all postsecondary teaching occupations)
- Annual Openings: 329,000 (for all postsecondary teaching occupations)
- Self-Employed: 0.4%
- Part-Time: 24.8%

NATIONAL WAGE FIGURES (ANNUAL)

Beginning	25th Percentile	Median	Mean	75th Percentile	90th Percentile
$30,880	$42,280	$56,620	$63,160	$76,310	$104,820

Median Wages for Industries Employing Largest Numbers (Annual)

Industry	Median Income
Educational Services	$56,610

Median Wages for States (Annual)

AK	no data	KY	$51,870	NY	no data
AL	$47,640	LA	no data	OH	$56,510
AR	no data	MA	$63,610	OK	$38,520
AZ	$54,160	MD	$57,360	OR	$65,900
CA	no data	ME	$56,670	PA	$58,310
CO	$53,400	MI	$53,380	RI..............	$74,140
CT	$55,960	MN	$50,990	SC..............	$54,550
DC	$61,120	MO	$52,810	SD	$47,450
DE	no data	MS	$51,370	TN	no data
FL	$55,190	MT	$42,170	TX	$46,750
GA	$55,030	NC	$51,310	UT	$55,480
HI	$69,220	ND	$51,800	VA	$53,700
IA	$55,410	NE	$46,110	VT	$48,200
ID	no data	NH	$53,800	WA	$55,050
IL	$65,370	NJ	$60,260	WI	$55,400
IN	$53,790	NM	$60,650	WV	$52,220
KS	$52,100	NV	$41,340	WY	no data

Median Wages for the Largest Metropolitan Areas (Annual)

AZ: Phoenix............	no data	MI: Detroit	$55,250
CA: Los Angeles	$71,040	MN: Minneapolis	$52,580
CA: Riverside	$93,620	MO: Kansas City........	$48,300
CA: Sacramento	$91,810	MO: St. Louis............	$51,070
CA: San Diego	$84,290	NV: Las Vegas	no data
CA: San Francisco....	$73,720	NY: New York............	$63,700
CO: Denver	$53,600	OH: Cincinnati..........	$54,140
DC: Washington	$63,780	OH: Cleveland	$61,990
FL: Miami	$65,840	OH: Columbus	$65,470
FL: Orlando	$53,360	OR: Portland	$66,210
FL: Tampa	$59,060	PA: Philadelphia	$57,540
GA: Atlanta	$63,820	PA: Pittsburgh	$60,780
IL: Chicago	$68,630	TX: Dallas	$42,410
MA: Boston	$59,710	TX: Houston	$48,820
MD: Baltimore	no data	WA: Seattle	$57,880

FACTORS THAT MAY AFFECT EARNINGS

Educational Attainment of Workers and Effect on Earnings

Figures are based on a group of occupations: Postsecondary Teachers

	Percent at Level	Effect on Earnings
Less than High School	—	—
Some High School	—	—
High School or Equivalent	2.2%	−40.5%
Some College but No Degree	6.6%	−53.9%
Associate Degree	4.4%	−14.3%
Bachelor's Degree	20.2%	−33.1%
Master's Degree	29.9%	−8.9%
Doctoral Degree	28.3%	42.5%
First Professional Degree	8.1%	28.8%

Flexibility of Earnings

Average Hours Worked: 32
Workers with a Varying Number of Hours: 9.5%
Workers Earning Some Overtime Pay, Tips, or Commissions: 2.1%
Earnings Benefit of Working Overtime: −4.1%

Gender

	Male	Female
Percent	53.7%	46.3%
Effect on Earnings	16.1%	−13.5%

Union Membership

Percentage Union Members: 18.9%
Earnings Benefit of Union Membership: 12.1%

Veteran Status

Percentage Who Have Been on Active Duty: 7.4%
Earnings Benefit of Veteran Status: 20.1%

25-1069 Social Sciences Teachers, Postsecondary, All Other

All postsecondary social sciences teachers not listed separately.

- Education or Training Required: Master's degree
- Job Growth: 32.2% (for all postsecondary teaching occupations)
- Annual Openings: 329,000 (for all postsecondary teaching occupations)
- Self-Employed: 0.4%
- Part-Time: 24.8%

NATIONAL WAGE FIGURES (ANNUAL)

Beginning	25th Percentile	Median	Mean	75th Percentile	90th Percentile
$29,750	$45,270	$61,210	$69,640	$89,730	$123,180

Median Wages for Industries Employing Largest Numbers (Annual)

Industry	Median Income
Ambulatory Health Care Services	more than $145,600
Educational Services	$60,940

Median Wages for States (Annual)

AK	no data	KY	no data	NY	no data
AL	no data	LA	no data	OH	$58,020
AR	no data	MA	$97,630	OK	no data
AZ	no data	MD	$70,240	OR	no data
CA	no data	ME	no data	PA	no data
CO	no data	MI	$58,540	RI	no data
CT	no data	MN	no data	SC	no data
DC	no data	MO	no data	SD	no data
DE	no data	MS	no data	TN	no data
FL	$63,260	MT	no data	TX	no data
GA	$49,190	NC	$46,980	UT	no data
HI	no data	ND	no data	VA	$53,470
IA	$66,710	NE	$57,310	VT	no data
ID	no data	NH	$57,140	WA	$47,430
IL	$55,480	NJ	$54,410	WI	$69,540
IN	no data	NM	no data	WV	no data
KS	$57,480	NV	no data	WY	no data

Median Wages for the Largest Metropolitan Areas (Annual)

AZ: Phoenix	no data	MI: Detroit	$51,140
CA: Los Angeles	$79,790	MN: Minneapolis	no data
CA: Riverside	no data	MO: Kansas City	no data
CA: Sacramento	no data	MO: St. Louis	no data
CA: San Diego	no data	NV: Las Vegas	no data
CA: San Francisco	no data	NY: New York	$61,100
CO: Denver	no data	OH: Cincinnati	no data
DC: Washington	$65,760	OH: Cleveland	no data
FL: Miami	$64,550	OH: Columbus	no data
FL: Orlando	no data	OR: Portland	$57,040
FL: Tampa	no data	PA: Philadelphia	$58,770
GA: Atlanta	no data	PA: Pittsburgh	no data
IL: Chicago	$57,760	TX: Dallas	no data
MA: Boston	$70,150	TX: Houston	no data
MD: Baltimore	no data	WA: Seattle	$44,500

FACTORS THAT MAY AFFECT EARNINGS

Educational Attainment of Workers and Effect on Earnings

Figures are based on a group of occupations: Postsecondary Teachers

	Percent at Level	Effect on Earnings
Less than High School	—	—
Some High School	—	—
High School or Equivalent	2.2%	−40.5%
Some College but No Degree	6.6%	−53.9%
Associate Degree	4.4%	−14.3%
Bachelor's Degree	20.2%	−33.1%
Master's Degree	29.9%	−8.9%
Doctoral Degree	28.3%	42.5%
First Professional Degree	8.1%	28.8%

Flexibility of Earnings

Average Hours Worked: 32
Workers with a Varying Number of Hours: 9.5%
Workers Earning Some Overtime Pay, Tips, or Commissions: 2.1%
Earnings Benefit of Working Overtime: −4.1%

Gender

	Male	Female
Percent	53.7%	46.3%
Effect on Earnings	16.1%	−13.5%

Union Membership

Percentage Union Members: 18.9%
Earnings Benefit of Union Membership: 12.1%

Veteran Status

Percentage Who Have Been on Active Duty: 7.4%
Earnings Benefit of Veteran Status: 20.1%

25-1071 Health Specialties Teachers, Postsecondary

Teach courses in health specialties, such as veterinary medicine, dentistry, pharmacy, therapy, laboratory technology, and public health. Includes both teachers primarily engaged in teaching and those who do a combination of both teaching and research.

- Education or Training Required: Master's degree
- Job Growth: 32.2% (for all postsecondary teaching occupations)
- Annual Openings: 329,000 (for all postsecondary teaching occupations)
- Self-Employed: 0.4%
- Part-Time: 24.8%

NATIONAL WAGE FIGURES (ANNUAL)

Beginning	25th Percentile	Median	Mean	75th Percentile	90th Percentile
$36,990	$52,500	$77,190	$91,260	$118,020	more than $145,600

Median Wages for Industries Employing Largest Numbers (Annual)

Industry	Median Income
Educational Services	$77,930
Professional, Scientific, and Technical Services	$77,180
Ambulatory Health Care Services	$73,200
Hospitals	$68,950
Management of Companies and Enterprises	$57,390
Federal, State, and Local Government	$56,140
Nursing and Residential Care Facilities	$37,660
Social Assistance	$28,620

Median Wages for States (Annual)

AK	no data	KY	$88,670	NY	no data
AL	$74,420	LA	no data	OH	$57,130
AR	no data	MA	$85,670	OK	$72,130
AZ	$85,510	MD	$111,110	OR	no data
CA	no data	ME	$53,400	PA	$80,400
CO	no data	MI	$74,600	RI	$78,610
CT	no data	MN	$72,210	SC	$56,130
DC	$80,970	MO	$94,720	SD	$58,300
DE	$62,710	MS	no data	TN	no data
FL	$71,400	MT	no data	TX	$91,310
GA	no data	NC	$91,350	UT	$59,560
HI	$73,800	ND	$58,760	VA	$71,930
IA	no data	NE	$79,340	VT	no data
ID	no data	NH	no data	WA	no data
IL	$68,530	NJ	$62,340	WI	$61,410
IN	no data	NM	$54,380	WV	no data
KS	$63,020	NV	$50,720	WY	$57,460

Median Wages for the Largest Metropolitan Areas (Annual)

AZ: Phoenix	$62,790	MI: Detroit	no data
CA: Los Angeles	$77,890	MN: Minneapolis	no data
CA: Riverside	$116,490	MO: Kansas City	$85,750
CA: Sacramento	no data	MO: St. Louis	$98,730
CA: San Diego	$86,760	NV: Las Vegas	$41,390
CA: San Francisco	$77,150	NY: New York	$82,590
CO: Denver	no data	OH: Cincinnati	$59,780
DC: Washington	$75,440	OH: Cleveland	no data
FL: Miami	$53,050	OH: Columbus	no data
FL: Orlando	$57,380	OR: Portland	no data
FL: Tampa	$72,660	PA: Philadelphia	no data
GA: Atlanta	no data	PA: Pittsburgh	no data
IL: Chicago	$66,980	TX: Dallas	no data
MA: Boston	$85,830	TX: Houston	$97,920
MD: Baltimore	$117,420	WA: Seattle	no data

FACTORS THAT MAY AFFECT EARNINGS

Educational Attainment of Workers and Effect on Earnings

Figures are based on a group of occupations: Postsecondary Teachers

	Percent at Level	Effect on Earnings
Less than High School	—	—
Some High School	—	—
High School or Equivalent	2.2%	−40.5%
Some College but No Degree	6.6%	−53.9%
Associate Degree	4.4%	−14.3%
Bachelor's Degree	20.2%	−33.1%
Master's Degree	29.9%	−8.9%
Doctoral Degree	28.3%	42.5%
First Professional Degree	8.1%	28.8%

Flexibility of Earnings

Average Hours Worked: 32
Workers with a Varying Number of Hours: 9.5%
Workers Earning Some Overtime Pay, Tips, or Commissions: 2.1%
Earnings Benefit of Working Overtime: −4.1%

Gender

	Male	Female
Percent	53.7%	46.3%
Effect on Earnings	16.1%	−13.5%

Union Membership

Percentage Union Members: 18.9%
Earnings Benefit of Union Membership: 12.1%

Veteran Status

Percentage Who Have Been on Active Duty: 7.4%
Earnings Benefit of Veteran Status: 20.1%

25-1072 Nursing Instructors and Teachers, Postsecondary

Demonstrate and teach patient care in classroom and clinical units to nursing students. Includes both teachers primarily engaged in teaching and those who do a combination of both teaching and research.

- Education or Training Required: Master's degree
- Job Growth: 32.2% (for all postsecondary teaching occupations)
- Annual Openings: 329,000 (for all postsecondary teaching occupations)
- Self-Employed: 0.4%
- Part-Time: 24.8%

NATIONAL WAGE FIGURES (ANNUAL)

Beginning	25th Percentile	Median	Mean	75th Percentile	90th Percentile
$34,140	$43,750	$55,280	$58,690	$70,170	$88,640

Median Wages for Industries Employing Largest Numbers (Annual)

Industry	Median Income
Federal, State, and Local Government	$74,950
Ambulatory Health Care Services	$73,180
Professional, Scientific, and Technical Services	$73,080
Hospitals	$65,070
Educational Services	$54,160
Nursing and Residential Care Facilities	$50,800
Social Assistance	$43,430
Management of Companies and Enterprises	$35,630

Median Wages for States (Annual)

AK	no data	KY	$51,520	NY	no data
AL	$50,090	LA	no data	OH	$54,410
AR	no data	MA	$60,640	OK	$43,950
AZ	$42,610	MD	$64,830	OR	no data
CA	no data	ME	$51,750	PA	$57,890
CO	$61,710	MI	$62,900	RI	$55,700
CT	$65,770	MN	$58,310	SC	$56,230
DC	no data	MO	$58,050	SD	$45,760
DE	no data	MS	$44,490	TN	$49,500
FL	$57,740	MT	$40,450	TX	$52,360
GA	$53,200	NC	$53,090	UT	$47,750
HI	no data	ND	$45,040	VA	$56,600
IA	$49,510	NE	$48,560	VT	no data
ID	no data	NH	$49,530	WA	$54,550
IL	$53,600	NJ	$69,810	WI	$55,800
IN	$50,190	NM	$54,410	WV	$43,000
KS	$51,030	NV	no data	WY	$48,320

Median Wages for the Largest Metropolitan Areas (Annual)

AZ: Phoenix	$34,620	MI: Detroit	$59,390
CA: Los Angeles	$60,160	MN: Minneapolis	$63,500
CA: Riverside	$71,570	MO: Kansas City	$57,580
CA: Sacramento	$80,690	MO: St. Louis	$59,630
CA: San Diego	$64,210	NV: Las Vegas	no data
CA: San Francisco	$63,420	NY: New York	$67,240
CO: Denver	no data	OH: Cincinnati	$51,890
DC: Washington	$71,350	OH: Cleveland	$59,650
FL: Miami	$68,140	OH: Columbus	$53,790
FL: Orlando	$57,630	OR: Portland	no data
FL: Tampa	$55,140	PA: Philadelphia	$60,870
GA: Atlanta	$56,330	PA: Pittsburgh	$55,590
IL: Chicago	$54,930	TX: Dallas	$50,240
MA: Boston	$58,220	TX: Houston	$61,490
MD: Baltimore	$65,430	WA: Seattle	$59,550

FACTORS THAT MAY AFFECT EARNINGS

Educational Attainment of Workers and Effect on Earnings

Figures are based on a group of occupations: Postsecondary Teachers

	Percent at Level	Effect on Earnings
Less than High School	—	—
Some High School	—	—
High School or Equivalent	2.2%	−40.5%
Some College but No Degree	6.6%	−53.9%
Associate Degree	4.4%	−14.3%
Bachelor's Degree	20.2%	−33.1%
Master's Degree	29.9%	−8.9%
Doctoral Degree	28.3%	42.5%
First Professional Degree	8.1%	28.8%

Flexibility of Earnings

Average Hours Worked: 32
Workers with a Varying Number of Hours: 9.5%
Workers Earning Some Overtime Pay, Tips, or Commissions: 2.1%
Earnings Benefit of Working Overtime: −4.1%

Gender

	Male	Female
Percent	53.7%	46.3%
Effect on Earnings	16.1%	−13.5%

Union Membership

Percentage Union Members: 18.9%
Earnings Benefit of Union Membership: 12.1%

Veteran Status

Percentage Who Have Been on Active Duty: 7.4%
Earnings Benefit of Veteran Status: 20.1%

25-1081 Education Teachers, Postsecondary

Teach courses pertaining to education, such as counseling, curriculum, guidance, instruction, teacher education, and teaching English as a second language.

- Education or Training Required: Master's degree
- Job Growth: 32.2% (for all postsecondary teaching occupations)
- Annual Openings: 329,000 (for all postsecondary teaching occupations)
- Self-Employed: 0.4%
- Part-Time: 24.8%

NATIONAL WAGE FIGURES (ANNUAL)

Beginning	25th Percentile	Median	Mean	75th Percentile	90th Percentile
$29,900	$39,050	$52,800	$57,410	$69,840	$94,960

Median Wages for Industries Employing Largest Numbers (Annual)

Industry	Median Income
Educational Services	$52,830

Median Wages for States (Annual)

AK	$62,580	KY	$48,310	NY	no data
AL	$49,200	LA	no data	OH	$50,700
AR	no data	MA	$58,060	OK	no data
AZ	$43,950	MD	$59,270	OR	$58,530
CA	no data	ME	no data	PA	$55,760
CO	$51,410	MI	$44,720	RI	$55,110
CT	$55,040	MN	$52,860	SC	$50,830
DC	$47,890	MO	$48,570	SD	$50,760
DE	$54,710	MS	$46,900	TN	$53,070
FL	$56,800	MT	$30,180	TX	$48,030
GA	$54,630	NC	$49,300	UT	$43,960
HI	$56,810	ND	$50,370	VA	$54,410
IA	$50,680	NE	$50,370	VT	$50,450
ID	no data	NH	$50,930	WA	$53,390
IL	$50,740	NJ	$61,970	WI	$50,070
IN	$47,590	NM	$51,550	WV	$44,400
KS	$45,670	NV	no data	WY	$48,030

Median Wages for the Largest Metropolitan Areas (Annual)

AZ: Phoenix	$36,900	MI: Detroit	$42,960
CA: Los Angeles	$71,580	MN: Minneapolis	$54,970
CA: Riverside	$63,530	MO: Kansas City	$46,030
CA: Sacramento	$67,030	MO: St. Louis	$51,640
CA: San Diego	$94,290	NV: Las Vegas	no data
CA: San Francisco	$69,450	NY: New York	$62,480
CO: Denver	$51,590	OH: Cincinnati	$49,480
DC: Washington	$56,120	OH: Cleveland	$40,290
FL: Miami	$66,530	OH: Columbus	$59,880
FL: Orlando	$57,590	OR: Portland	$58,140
FL: Tampa	$58,820	PA: Philadelphia	$54,960
GA: Atlanta	$46,920	PA: Pittsburgh	$54,200
IL: Chicago	$50,270	TX: Dallas	$47,660
MA: Boston	$57,800	TX: Houston	$51,080
MD: Baltimore	$53,820	WA: Seattle	$56,700

FACTORS THAT MAY AFFECT EARNINGS

Educational Attainment of Workers and Effect on Earnings

Figures are based on a group of occupations: Postsecondary Teachers

	Percent at Level	Effect on Earnings
Less than High School	—	—
Some High School	—	—
High School or Equivalent	2.2%	-40.5%
Some College but No Degree	6.6%	-53.9%
Associate Degree	4.4%	-14.3%
Bachelor's Degree	20.2%	-33.1%
Master's Degree	29.9%	-8.9%
Doctoral Degree	28.3%	42.5%
First Professional Degree	8.1%	28.8%

Flexibility of Earnings

Average Hours Worked: 32
Workers with a Varying Number of Hours: 9.5%
Workers Earning Some Overtime Pay, Tips, or Commissions: 2.1%
Earnings Benefit of Working Overtime: -4.1%

Gender

	Male	Female
Percent	53.7%	46.3%
Effect on Earnings	16.1%	-13.5%

Union Membership

Percentage Union Members: 18.9%
Earnings Benefit of Union Membership: 12.1%

Veteran Status

Percentage Who Have Been on Active Duty: 7.4%
Earnings Benefit of Veteran Status: 20.1%

25-1082 Library Science Teachers, Postsecondary

Teach courses in library science.

- Education or Training Required: Master's degree
- Job Growth: 32.2% (for all postsecondary teaching occupations)
- Annual Openings: 329,000 (for all postsecondary teaching occupations)
- Self-Employed: 0.4%
- Part-Time: 24.8%

NATIONAL WAGE FIGURES (ANNUAL)

Beginning	25th Percentile	Median	Mean	75th Percentile	90th Percentile
$33,120	$42,620	$54,570	$57,550	$69,430	$87,430

Median Wages for Industries Employing Largest Numbers (Annual)

Industry	Median Income
Educational Services	$54,580

Median Wages for States (Annual)

AK	no data	KY	no data	NY	no data
AL	$48,990	LA	no data	OH	no data
AR	no data	MA	$38,770	OK	$40,140
AZ	no data	MD	$51,520	OR	$65,070
CA	no data	ME	no data	PA	$55,760
CO	no data	MI	$68,050	RI	no data
CT	no data	MN	no data	SC	$51,570
DC	$59,480	MO	$54,140	SD	no data
DE	no data	MS	$46,830	TN	no data
FL	$55,620	MT	no data	TX	$45,870
GA	$46,790	NC	$60,340	UT	no data
HI	no data	ND	no data	VA	no data
IA	$54,430	NE	$55,500	VT	no data
ID	no data	NH	no data	WA	$61,170
IL	$50,370	NJ	$67,980	WI	$54,900
IN	no data	NM	no data	WV	no data
KS	$54,690	NV	no data	WY	no data

Median Wages for the Largest Metropolitan Areas (Annual)

AZ: Phoenix	no data	MI: Detroit	no data
CA: Los Angeles	$77,230	MN: Minneapolis	no data
CA: Riverside	no data	MO: Kansas City	$73,100
CA: Sacramento	no data	MO: St. Louis	$54,550
CA: San Diego	no data	NV: Las Vegas	no data
CA: San Francisco	$79,390	NY: New York	$68,730
CO: Denver	no data	OH: Cincinnati	no data
DC: Washington	$53,660	OH: Cleveland	no data
FL: Miami	no data	OH: Columbus	no data
FL: Orlando	no data	OR: Portland	no data
FL: Tampa	$58,160	PA: Philadelphia	$57,450
GA: Atlanta	$45,190	PA: Pittsburgh	no data
IL: Chicago	$53,900	TX: Dallas	no data
MA: Boston	no data	TX: Houston	no data
MD: Baltimore	no data	WA: Seattle	no data

FACTORS THAT MAY AFFECT EARNINGS

Educational Attainment of Workers and Effect on Earnings

Figures are based on a group of occupations: Postsecondary Teachers

	Percent at Level	Effect on Earnings
Less than High School	—	—
Some High School	—	—
High School or Equivalent	2.2%	−40.5%
Some College but No Degree	6.6%	−53.9%
Associate Degree	4.4%	−14.3%
Bachelor's Degree	20.2%	−33.1%
Master's Degree	29.9%	−8.9%
Doctoral Degree	28.3%	42.5%
First Professional Degree	8.1%	28.8%

Flexibility of Earnings

Average Hours Worked: 32
Workers with a Varying Number of Hours: 9.5%
Workers Earning Some Overtime Pay, Tips, or Commissions: 2.1%
Earnings Benefit of Working Overtime: −4.1%

Gender

	Male	Female
Percent	53.7%	46.3%
Effect on Earnings	16.1%	−13.5%

Union Membership

Percentage Union Members: 18.9%
Earnings Benefit of Union Membership: 12.1%

Veteran Status

Percentage Who Have Been on Active Duty: 7.4%
Earnings Benefit of Veteran Status: 20.1%

25-1111 Criminal Justice and Law Enforcement Teachers, Postsecondary

Teach courses in criminal justice, corrections, and law enforcement administration.

- Education or Training Required: Master's degree
- Job Growth: 32.2% (for all postsecondary teaching occupations)
- Annual Openings: 329,000 (for all postsecondary teaching occupations)
- Self-Employed: 0.4%
- Part-Time: 24.8%

NATIONAL WAGE FIGURES (ANNUAL)

Beginning	25th Percentile	Median	Mean	75th Percentile	90th Percentile
$29,450	$38,770	$49,730	$55,310	$64,640	$89,850

Median Wages for Industries Employing Largest Numbers (Annual)

Industry	Median Income
Educational Services	$49,670

Median Wages for States (Annual)

AK	no data	KY	no data	NY	no data
AL	$39,340	LA	no data	OH	$48,670
AR	no data	MA	$54,270	OK	no data
AZ	$50,280	MD	$51,170	OR	$57,280
CA	no data	ME	$45,150	PA	$55,940
CO	$44,960	MI	$51,630	RI	no data
CT	$53,960	MN	$47,580	SC	$57,690
DC	$51,490	MO	$48,540	SD	no data
DE	no data	MS	$54,970	TN	$45,110
FL	$55,240	MT	no data	TX	$44,770
GA	$39,900	NC	$44,960	UT	$45,990
HI	no data	ND	no data	VA	$48,680
IA	$46,570	NE	no data	VT	$50,200
ID	no data	NH	no data	WA	$48,850
IL	$47,170	NJ	$57,450	WI	$57,300
IN	$42,380	NM	no data	WV	$61,020
KS	no data	NV	no data	WY	no data

Median Wages for the Largest Metropolitan Areas (Annual)

AZ: Phoenix	$43,780	MI: Detroit	$36,360
CA: Los Angeles	$77,720	MN: Minneapolis	$50,540
CA: Riverside	$62,570	MO: Kansas City	$48,500
CA: Sacramento	no data	MO: St. Louis	$57,540
CA: San Diego	no data	NV: Las Vegas	no data
CA: San Francisco	$55,120	NY: New York	$57,330
CO: Denver	no data	OH: Cincinnati	no data
DC: Washington	$51,190	OH: Cleveland	$57,090
FL: Miami	no data	OH: Columbus	$47,250
FL: Orlando	no data	OR: Portland	$62,080
FL: Tampa	no data	PA: Philadelphia	$53,450
GA: Atlanta	$56,890	PA: Pittsburgh	$57,380
IL: Chicago	$47,840	TX: Dallas	$53,770
MA: Boston	$54,660	TX: Houston	$51,960
MD: Baltimore	$55,320	WA: Seattle	$43,010

FACTORS THAT MAY AFFECT EARNINGS

Educational Attainment of Workers and Effect on Earnings

Figures are based on a group of occupations: Postsecondary Teachers

	Percent at Level	Effect on Earnings
Less than High School	—	—
Some High School	—	—
High School or Equivalent	2.2%	-40.5%
Some College but No Degree	6.6%	-53.9%
Associate Degree	4.4%	-14.3%
Bachelor's Degree	20.2%	-33.1%
Master's Degree	29.9%	-8.9%
Doctoral Degree	28.3%	42.5%
First Professional Degree	8.1%	28.8%

Flexibility of Earnings

Average Hours Worked: 32
Workers with a Varying Number of Hours: 9.5%
Workers Earning Some Overtime Pay, Tips, or Commissions: 2.1%
Earnings Benefit of Working Overtime: -4.1%

Gender

	Male	Female
Percent	53.7%	46.3%
Effect on Earnings	16.1%	-13.5%

Union Membership

Percentage Union Members: 18.9%
Earnings Benefit of Union Membership: 12.1%

Veteran Status

Percentage Who Have Been on Active Duty: 7.4%
Earnings Benefit of Veteran Status: 20.1%

25-1112 Law Teachers, Postsecondary

Teach courses in law.

- Education or Training Required: First professional degree
- Job Growth: 32.2% (for all postsecondary teaching occupations)
- Annual Openings: 329,000 (for all postsecondary teaching occupations)
- Self-Employed: 0.4%
- Part-Time: 24.8%

NATIONAL WAGE FIGURES (ANNUAL)

Beginning	25th Percentile	Median	Mean	75th Percentile	90th Percentile
$40,080	$57,650	$87,240	$94,290	$122,730	more than $145,600

Median Wages for Industries Employing Largest Numbers (Annual)

Industry	Median Income
Educational Services	$87,300

Median Wages for States (Annual)

AK ... no data	KY ... $87,000	NY ... no data
AL ... $107,180	LA ... no data	OH ... $90,550
AR ... no data	MA ... no data	OK ... $66,440
AZ ... no data	MD ... no data	OR ... no data
CA ... no data	ME ... no data	PA ... $69,340
CO ... no data	MI ... $96,840	RI ... no data
CT ... no data	MN ... $91,350	SC ... $46,710
DC ... $92,900	MO ... $91,250	SD ... no data
DE ... no data	MS ... $77,170	TN ... $95,460
FL ... $98,190	MT ... no data	TX ... $90,080
GA ... $108,420	NC ... $81,470	UT ... no data
HI ... no data	ND ... $64,060	VA ... $60,350
IA ... no data	NE ... $81,610	VT ... no data
ID ... no data	NH ... no data	WA ... $77,760
IL ... $92,670	NJ ... $94,100	WI ... $84,160
IN ... $90,700	NM ... no data	WV ... no data
KS ... no data	NV ... $82,780	WY ... no data

Median Wages for the Largest Metropolitan Areas (Annual)

AZ: Phoenix ... no data	MI: Detroit ... no data
CA: Los Angeles ... $90,620	MN: Minneapolis ... $91,210
CA: Riverside ... $65,890	MO: Kansas City ... no data
CA: Sacramento ... no data	MO: St. Louis ... $98,670
CA: San Diego ... $94,210	NV: Las Vegas ... no data
CA: San Francisco ... $101,240	NY: New York ... $103,560
CO: Denver ... no data	OH: Cincinnati ... $90,520
DC: Washington ... $91,430	OH: Cleveland ... no data
FL: Miami ... no data	OH: Columbus ... no data
FL: Orlando ... no data	OR: Portland ... no data
FL: Tampa ... more than $145,600	PA: Philadelphia ... no data
GA: Atlanta ... no data	PA: Pittsburgh ... no data
IL: Chicago ... $92,550	TX: Dallas ... no data
MA: Boston ... no data	TX: Houston ... no data
MD: Baltimore ... no data	WA: Seattle ... $87,050

FACTORS THAT MAY AFFECT EARNINGS

Educational Attainment of Workers and Effect on Earnings

Figures are based on a group of occupations: Postsecondary Teachers

	Percent at Level	Effect on Earnings
Less than High School	—	—
Some High School	—	—
High School or Equivalent	2.2%	−40.5%
Some College but No Degree	6.6%	−53.9%
Associate Degree	4.4%	−14.3%
Bachelor's Degree	20.2%	−33.1%
Master's Degree	29.9%	−8.9%
Doctoral Degree	28.3%	42.5%
First Professional Degree	8.1%	28.8%

Flexibility of Earnings

Average Hours Worked: 32
Workers with a Varying Number of Hours: 9.5%
Workers Earning Some Overtime Pay, Tips, or Commissions: 2.1%
Earnings Benefit of Working Overtime: −4.1%

Gender

	Male	Female
Percent	53.7%	46.3%
Effect on Earnings	16.1%	−13.5%

Union Membership

Percentage Union Members: 18.9%
Earnings Benefit of Union Membership: 12.1%

Veteran Status

Percentage Who Have Been on Active Duty: 7.4%
Earnings Benefit of Veteran Status: 20.1%

25-1113 Social Work Teachers, Postsecondary

Teach courses in social work.

- Education or Training Required: Master's degree
- Job Growth: 32.2% (for all postsecondary teaching occupations)
- Annual Openings: 329,000 (for all postsecondary teaching occupations)
- Self-Employed: 0.4%
- Part-Time: 24.8%

NATIONAL WAGE FIGURES (ANNUAL)

Beginning	25th Percentile	Median	Mean	75th Percentile	90th Percentile
$31,410	$41,930	$54,340	$57,990	$70,170	$91,610

Median Wages for Industries Employing Largest Numbers (Annual)

Industry	Median Income
Educational Services	$54,310

Median Wages for States (Annual)

AK	no data	KY	$48,970	NY	no data
AL	$47,200	LA	no data	OH	$56,580
AR	no data	MA	$61,110	OK	no data
AZ	no data	MD	no data	OR	$63,050
CA	no data	ME	no data	PA	$59,720
CO	no data	MI	$58,990	RI	$57,560
CT	no data	MN	$52,080	SC	$45,220
DC	$75,850	MO	$59,600	SD	no data
DE	no data	MS	$47,890	TN	no data
FL	$55,780	MT	no data	TX	$51,080
GA	$54,800	NC	$53,800	UT	no data
HI	no data	ND	$44,330	VA	$48,430
IA	$53,460	NE	no data	VT	$46,430
ID	no data	NH	no data	WA	no data
IL	$49,100	NJ	$54,890	WI	$54,940
IN	$46,500	NM	no data	WV	$52,140
KS	$54,830	NV	no data	WY	no data

Median Wages for the Largest Metropolitan Areas (Annual)

AZ: Phoenix	no data	MI: Detroit	$57,520
CA: Los Angeles	no data	MN: Minneapolis	$49,990
CA: Riverside	no data	MO: Kansas City	no data
CA: Sacramento	no data	MO: St. Louis	$70,250
CA: San Diego	no data	NV: Las Vegas	no data
CA: San Francisco	no data	NY: New York	$56,280
CO: Denver	no data	OH: Cincinnati	$54,950
DC: Washington	$73,080	OH: Cleveland	no data
FL: Miami	$53,370	OH: Columbus	no data
FL: Orlando	no data	OR: Portland	$64,470
FL: Tampa	$56,540	PA: Philadelphia	$58,720
GA: Atlanta	$57,800	PA: Pittsburgh	no data
IL: Chicago	$50,870	TX: Dallas	$52,090
MA: Boston	$59,020	TX: Houston	no data
MD: Baltimore	no data	WA: Seattle	no data

FACTORS THAT MAY AFFECT EARNINGS

Educational Attainment of Workers and Effect on Earnings

Figures are based on a group of occupations: Postsecondary Teachers

	Percent at Level	Effect on Earnings
Less than High School	—	—
Some High School	—	—
High School or Equivalent	2.2%	−40.5%
Some College but No Degree	6.6%	−53.9%
Associate Degree	4.4%	−14.3%
Bachelor's Degree	20.2%	−33.1%
Master's Degree	29.9%	−8.9%
Doctoral Degree	28.3%	42.5%
First Professional Degree	8.1%	28.8%

Flexibility of Earnings

Average Hours Worked: 32
Workers with a Varying Number of Hours: 9.5%
Workers Earning Some Overtime Pay, Tips, or Commissions: 2.1%
Earnings Benefit of Working Overtime: −4.1%

Gender

	Male	Female
Percent	53.7%	46.3%
Effect on Earnings	16.1%	−13.5%

Union Membership

Percentage Union Members: 18.9%
Earnings Benefit of Union Membership: 12.1%

Veteran Status

Percentage Who Have Been on Active Duty: 7.4%
Earnings Benefit of Veteran Status: 20.1%

25-1121 Art, Drama, and Music Teachers, Postsecondary

Teach courses in drama; music; and the arts, including fine and applied art, such as painting and sculpture, or design and crafts.

- Education or Training Required: Master's degree
- Job Growth: 32.2% (for all postsecondary teaching occupations)
- Annual Openings: 329,000 (for all postsecondary teaching occupations)
- Self-Employed: 0.4%
- Part-Time: 24.8%

NATIONAL WAGE FIGURES (ANNUAL)

Beginning	25th Percentile	Median	Mean	75th Percentile	90th Percentile
$29,290	$39,550	$53,160	$58,250	$71,540	$94,270

Median Wages for Industries Employing Largest Numbers (Annual)

Industry	Median Income
Performing Arts, Spectator Sports, and Related Industries	$65,640
Educational Services	$53,090
Sporting Goods, Hobby, Book, and Music Stores	$45,390

Median Wages for States (Annual)

AK .... no data	KY $49,730	NY .... no data
AL $48,920	LA .... no data	OH $47,340
AR .... no data	MA $61,670	OK $39,520
AZ $48,890	MD $44,890	OR $63,010
CA .... no data	ME .... no data	PA $50,800
CO $48,510	MI $45,710	RI $66,230
CT $57,610	MN $49,690	SC $50,420
DC $62,770	MO $53,490	SD $47,530
DE $55,610	MS $46,030	TN $48,270
FL $53,420	MT $47,680	TX $48,780
GA $49,830	NC $49,060	UT .... no data
HI $58,680	ND $42,160	VA $49,860
IA $50,500	NE $47,410	VT $48,720
ID .... no data	NH $54,600	WA $47,730
IL $58,460	NJ $57,380	WI $49,600
IN $47,260	NM $45,620	WV $50,410
KS $52,330	NV $38,110	WY $48,760

Median Wages for the Largest Metropolitan Areas (Annual)

AZ: Phoenix	$38,030	MI: Detroit	$31,160
CA: Los Angeles	$73,630	MN: Minneapolis	$51,730
CA: Riverside	$72,650	MO: Kansas City	$52,230
CA: Sacramento	$69,380	MO: St. Louis	$56,730
CA: San Diego	$80,170	NV: Las Vegas	$39,260
CA: San Francisco	$70,480	NY: New York	$63,000
CO: Denver	$47,570	OH: Cincinnati	$41,070
DC: Washington	$53,940	OH: Cleveland	$45,740
FL: Miami	$66,940	OH: Columbus	$50,550
FL: Orlando	$48,340	OR: Portland	$63,640
FL: Tampa	$52,010	PA: Philadelphia	$50,460
GA: Atlanta	$57,890	PA: Pittsburgh	$50,560
IL: Chicago	$64,310	TX: Dallas	$47,200
MA: Boston	$60,690	TX: Houston	no data
MD: Baltimore	$46,990	WA: Seattle	$48,160

FACTORS THAT MAY AFFECT EARNINGS

Educational Attainment of Workers and Effect on Earnings

Figures are based on a group of occupations: Postsecondary Teachers

	Percent at Level	Effect on Earnings
Less than High School	—	—
Some High School	—	—
High School or Equivalent	2.2%	−40.5%
Some College but No Degree	6.6%	−53.9%
Associate Degree	4.4%	−14.3%
Bachelor's Degree	20.2%	−33.1%
Master's Degree	29.9%	−8.9%
Doctoral Degree	28.3%	42.5%
First Professional Degree	8.1%	28.8%

Flexibility of Earnings

Average Hours Worked: 32
Workers with a Varying Number of Hours: 9.5%
Workers Earning Some Overtime Pay, Tips, or Commissions: 2.1%
Earnings Benefit of Working Overtime: −4.1%

Gender

	Male	Female
Percent	53.7%	46.3%
Effect on Earnings	16.1%	−13.5%

Union Membership

Percentage Union Members: 18.9%
Earnings Benefit of Union Membership: 12.1%

Veteran Status

Percentage Who Have Been on Active Duty: 7.4%
Earnings Benefit of Veteran Status: 20.1%

25-1122 Communications Teachers, Postsecondary

Teach courses in communications, such as organizational communications, public relations, radio/television broadcasting, and journalism. Includes both teachers primarily engaged in teaching and those who do a combination of both teaching and research.

- Education or Training Required: Master's degree
- Job Growth: 32.2% (for all postsecondary teaching occupations)
- Annual Openings: 329,000 (for all postsecondary teaching occupations)
- Self-Employed: 0.4%
- Part-Time: 24.8%

NATIONAL WAGE FIGURES (ANNUAL)

Beginning	25th Percentile	Median	Mean	75th Percentile	90th Percentile
$28,850	$39,470	$53,110	$56,600	$70,180	$90,710

Median Wages for Industries Employing Largest Numbers (Annual)

Industry	Median Income
Educational Services	$53,080

Median Wages for States (Annual)

AK	no data	KY	$48,270	NY	no data
AL	$51,950	LA	no data	OH	$49,160
AR	no data	MA	$61,250	OK	$39,710
AZ	$47,980	MD	$56,920	OR	$65,040
CA	no data	ME	no data	PA	$55,260
CO	$41,010	MI	$56,320	RI	no data
CT	$58,760	MN	$47,760	SC	$41,430
DC	$55,880	MO	$54,980	SD	$47,020
DE	no data	MS	$51,210	TN	$47,310
FL	$52,750	MT	no data	TX	$45,850
GA	$49,880	NC	$52,660	UT	$46,770
HI	$60,530	ND	$49,230	VA	$52,770
IA	$53,030	NE	$44,220	VT	$55,260
ID	no data	NH	$59,390	WA	$47,190
IL	$50,940	NJ	$55,470	WI	$54,630
IN	$54,160	NM	$48,100	WV	$50,870
KS	$56,460	NV	$44,990	WY	$45,550

Median Wages for the Largest Metropolitan Areas (Annual)

AZ: Phoenix	$47,300	MI: Detroit	$54,170
CA: Los Angeles	$76,300	MN: Minneapolis	$49,330
CA: Riverside	$69,520	MO: Kansas City	$63,310
CA: Sacramento	$73,060	MO: St. Louis	$58,190
CA: San Diego	$82,140	NV: Las Vegas	no data
CA: San Francisco	$61,620	NY: New York	$59,910
CO: Denver	$38,080	OH: Cincinnati	$49,300
DC: Washington	$55,070	OH: Cleveland	$47,360
FL: Miami	$62,260	OH: Columbus	$45,060
FL: Orlando	$48,090	OR: Portland	$62,520
FL: Tampa	$54,130	PA: Philadelphia	$53,870
GA: Atlanta	$53,530	PA: Pittsburgh	$51,500
IL: Chicago	$52,250	TX: Dallas	$45,110
MA: Boston	$62,880	TX: Houston	no data
MD: Baltimore	$60,660	WA: Seattle	$49,680

FACTORS THAT MAY AFFECT EARNINGS

Educational Attainment of Workers and Effect on Earnings

Figures are based on a group of occupations: Postsecondary Teachers

	Percent at Level	Effect on Earnings
Less than High School	—	—
Some High School	—	—
High School or Equivalent	2.2%	−40.5%
Some College but No Degree	6.6%	−53.9%
Associate Degree	4.4%	−14.3%
Bachelor's Degree	20.2%	−33.1%
Master's Degree	29.9%	−8.9%
Doctoral Degree	28.3%	42.5%
First Professional Degree	8.1%	28.8%

Flexibility of Earnings

Average Hours Worked: 32
Workers with a Varying Number of Hours: 9.5%
Workers Earning Some Overtime Pay, Tips, or Commissions: 2.1%
Earnings Benefit of Working Overtime: −4.1%

Gender

	Male	Female
Percent	53.7%	46.3%
Effect on Earnings	16.1%	−13.5%

Union Membership

Percentage Union Members: 18.9%
Earnings Benefit of Union Membership: 12.1%

Veteran Status

Percentage Who Have Been on Active Duty: 7.4%
Earnings Benefit of Veteran Status: 20.1%

25-1123 English Language and Literature Teachers, Postsecondary

Teach courses in English language and literature, including linguistics and comparative literature.

- Education or Training Required: Master's degree
- Job Growth: 32.2% (for all postsecondary teaching occupations)
- Annual Openings: 329,000 (for all postsecondary teaching occupations)
- Self-Employed: 0.4%
- Part-Time: 24.8%

NATIONAL WAGE FIGURES (ANNUAL)

Beginning	25th Percentile	Median	Mean	75th Percentile	90th Percentile
$28,880	$38,680	$51,730	$57,320	$70,400	$94,290

Median Wages for Industries Employing Largest Numbers (Annual)

Industry	Median Income
Educational Services	$51,770
Professional, Scientific, and Technical Services	$42,190

Median Wages for States (Annual)

AK .... no data	KY $45,380	NY .... no data
AL $39,580	LA .... no data	OH $50,100
AR .... no data	MA $57,850	OK $35,990
AZ $40,840	MD $55,460	OR $73,770
CA .... no data	ME $47,800	PA $57,200
CO $47,310	MI $58,520	RI .... no data
CT $55,960	MN $51,320	SC............. $48,010
DC $60,660	MO $55,600	SD $46,800
DE $62,160	MS $50,500	TN $43,990
FL $46,670	MT $42,380	TX $45,840
GA $49,210	NC $46,850	UT $49,820
HI $54,890	ND $39,640	VA $46,960
IA $54,360	NE $39,150	VT $53,910
ID .... no data	NH $54,630	WA $46,290
IL $49,770	NJ $65,190	WI $49,780
IN $50,340	NM $46,350	WV $50,700
KS $47,670	NV $38,080	WY $44,220

Median Wages for the Largest Metropolitan Areas (Annual)

AZ: Phoenix............	$36,440	MI: Detroit	$57,350
CA: Los Angeles	$80,160	MN: Minneapolis	$50,640
CA: Riverside	$67,770	MO: Kansas City........	$52,040
CA: Sacramento	$69,260	MO: St. Louis............	$59,960
CA: San Diego	$81,250	NV: Las Vegas	no data
CA: San Francisco....	$65,450	NY: New York............	$64,090
CO: Denver	$42,940	OH: Cincinnati..........	$46,910
DC: Washington	$57,110	OH: Cleveland	$56,430
FL: Miami	$50,830	OH: Columbus	$54,960
FL: Orlando	$45,740	OR: Portland	$76,700
FL: Tampa	$46,180	PA: Philadelphia	$54,880
GA: Atlanta	$55,800	PA: Pittsburgh	$66,280
IL: Chicago	$52,080	TX: Dallas	$40,290
MA: Boston	$55,270	TX: Houston	no data
MD: Baltimore	$55,650	WA: Seattle	$49,400

FACTORS THAT MAY AFFECT EARNINGS

Educational Attainment of Workers and Effect on Earnings

Figures are based on a group of occupations: Postsecondary Teachers

	Percent at Level	Effect on Earnings
Less than High School	—	—
Some High School	—	—
High School or Equivalent	2.2%	−40.5%
Some College but No Degree	6.6%	−53.9%
Associate Degree	4.4%	−14.3%
Bachelor's Degree	20.2%	−33.1%
Master's Degree	29.9%	−8.9%
Doctoral Degree	28.3%	42.5%
First Professional Degree	8.1%	28.8%

Flexibility of Earnings

Average Hours Worked: 32
Workers with a Varying Number of Hours: 9.5%
Workers Earning Some Overtime Pay, Tips, or Commissions: 2.1%
Earnings Benefit of Working Overtime: −4.1%

Gender

	Male	Female
Percent	53.7%	46.3%
Effect on Earnings	16.1%	−13.5%

Union Membership

Percentage Union Members: 18.9%
Earnings Benefit of Union Membership: 12.1%

Veteran Status

Percentage Who Have Been on Active Duty: 7.4%
Earnings Benefit of Veteran Status: 20.1%

25-1124 Foreign Language and Literature Teachers, Postsecondary

Teach courses in foreign (i.e., other than English) languages and literature.

- Education or Training Required: Master's degree
- Job Growth: 32.2% (for all postsecondary teaching occupations)
- Annual Openings: 329,000 (for all postsecondary teaching occupations)
- Self-Employed: 0.4%
- Part-Time: 24.8%

NATIONAL WAGE FIGURES (ANNUAL)

Beginning	25th Percentile	Median	Mean	75th Percentile	90th Percentile
$29,410	$38,780	$51,900	$60,050	$70,770	$100,790

Median Wages for Industries Employing Largest Numbers (Annual)

Industry	Median Income
Educational Services	$51,890

Median Wages for States (Annual)

State	Wage	State	Wage	State	Wage
AK	no data	KY	$44,400	NY	no data
AL	$43,930	LA	no data	OH	$54,020
AR	no data	MA	$63,670	OK	$34,500
AZ	$48,990	MD	$58,430	OR	$60,810
CA	no data	ME	$44,680	PA	$56,000
CO	$50,440	MI	$52,910	RI	$62,030
CT	no data	MN	$47,560	SC	$50,040
DC	$60,320	MO	$53,060	SD	$42,730
DE	$44,750	MS	$53,100	TN	$46,440
FL	$53,760	MT	no data	TX	$48,210
GA	$46,970	NC	$46,280	UT	$48,930
HI	$54,840	ND	$38,970	VA	$49,790
IA	$54,370	NE	$46,790	VT	$59,770
ID	no data	NH	$61,490	WA	$47,470
IL	$45,830	NJ	$56,960	WI	$50,320
IN	$49,160	NM	$52,260	WV	$49,620
KS	$46,550	NV	$35,660	WY	$43,960

Median Wages for the Largest Metropolitan Areas (Annual)

Area	Wage	Area	Wage
AZ: Phoenix	$46,120	MI: Detroit	$53,300
CA: Los Angeles	$81,860	MN: Minneapolis	$45,920
CA: Riverside	$75,470	MO: Kansas City	$53,430
CA: Sacramento	$79,750	MO: St. Louis	$55,010
CA: San Diego	$81,680	NV: Las Vegas	no data
CA: San Francisco	$44,210	NY: New York	$57,030
CO: Denver	$52,180	OH: Cincinnati	$38,640
DC: Washington	$55,680	OH: Cleveland	$55,660
FL: Miami	no data	OH: Columbus	$60,150
FL: Orlando	$43,810	OR: Portland	$62,020
FL: Tampa	$49,780	PA: Philadelphia	$53,770
GA: Atlanta	$46,490	PA: Pittsburgh	$50,890
IL: Chicago	$44,420	TX: Dallas	$55,640
MA: Boston	$61,910	TX: Houston	no data
MD: Baltimore	$60,510	WA: Seattle	$51,070

FACTORS THAT MAY AFFECT EARNINGS

Educational Attainment of Workers and Effect on Earnings

Figures are based on a group of occupations: Postsecondary Teachers

	Percent at Level	Effect on Earnings
Less than High School	—	—
Some High School	—	—
High School or Equivalent	2.2%	−40.5%
Some College but No Degree	6.6%	−53.9%
Associate Degree	4.4%	−14.3%
Bachelor's Degree	20.2%	−33.1%
Master's Degree	29.9%	−8.9%
Doctoral Degree	28.3%	42.5%
First Professional Degree	8.1%	28.8%

Flexibility of Earnings

Average Hours Worked: 32
Workers with a Varying Number of Hours: 9.5%
Workers Earning Some Overtime Pay, Tips, or Commissions: 2.1%
Earnings Benefit of Working Overtime: −4.1%

Gender

	Male	Female
Percent	53.7%	46.3%
Effect on Earnings	16.1%	−13.5%

Union Membership

Percentage Union Members: 18.9%
Earnings Benefit of Union Membership: 12.1%

Veteran Status

Percentage Who Have Been on Active Duty: 7.4%
Earnings Benefit of Veteran Status: 20.1%

25-1125 History Teachers, Postsecondary

Teach courses in human history and historiography.

- Education or Training Required: Master's degree
- Job Growth: 32.2% (for all postsecondary teaching occupations)
- Annual Openings: 329,000 (for all postsecondary teaching occupations)
- Self-Employed: 0.4%
- Part-Time: 24.8%

NATIONAL WAGE FIGURES (ANNUAL)

Beginning	25th Percentile	Median	Mean	75th Percentile	90th Percentile
$32,150	$43,360	$57,390	$63,200	$76,800	$101,530

Median Wages for Industries Employing Largest Numbers (Annual)

Industry	Median Income
Educational Services	$57,390

Median Wages for States (Annual)

AK .... no data	KY $48,070	NY .... no data
AL $46,570	LA .... no data	OH $57,030
AR .... no data	MA $69,910	OK $43,060
AZ $48,490	MD $63,850	OR $73,460
CA .... no data	ME $54,940	PA $61,500
CO $54,240	MI $54,840	RI .... no data
CT .... no data	MN $51,930	SC $54,520
DC $50,060	MO $53,600	SD $54,820
DE .... no data	MS $49,160	TN $49,570
FL $54,000	MT $49,180	TX $56,080
GA $53,040	NC $52,600	UT .... no data
HI $70,830	ND $47,060	VA $53,860
IA $56,350	NE $53,310	VT $56,350
ID .... no data	NH $58,360	WA $51,270
IL $54,370	NJ $65,130	WI $56,340
IN $57,250	NM $56,600	WV $55,700
KS $49,760	NV $43,650	WY .... no data

Median Wages for the Largest Metropolitan Areas (Annual)

AZ: Phoenix............ $45,460	MI: Detroit $53,330
CA: Los Angeles $73,910	MN: Minneapolis $54,300
CA: Riverside $67,890	MO: Kansas City........ $54,770
CA: Sacramento $72,530	MO: St. Louis............ $54,540
CA: San Diego $69,140	NV: Las Vegas .... no data
CA: San Francisco.... $70,160	NY: New York........... $65,830
CO: Denver $50,140	OH: Cincinnati.......... $53,370
DC: Washington $56,690	OH: Cleveland $54,710
FL: Miami $54,880	OH: Columbus $69,330
FL: Orlando $46,590	OR: Portland $67,120
FL: Tampa $55,470	PA: Philadelphia $60,400
GA: Atlanta $57,770	PA: Pittsburgh $68,670
IL: Chicago $56,110	TX: Dallas $45,460
MA: Boston $68,390	TX: Houston .... no data
MD: Baltimore $66,080	WA: Seattle $56,140

FACTORS THAT MAY AFFECT EARNINGS

Educational Attainment of Workers and Effect on Earnings

Figures are based on a group of occupations: Postsecondary Teachers

	Percent at Level	Effect on Earnings
Less than High School	—	—
Some High School	—	—
High School or Equivalent	2.2%	−40.5%
Some College but No Degree	6.6%	−53.9%
Associate Degree	4.4%	−14.3%
Bachelor's Degree	20.2%	−33.1%
Master's Degree	29.9%	−8.9%
Doctoral Degree	28.3%	42.5%
First Professional Degree	8.1%	28.8%

Flexibility of Earnings

Average Hours Worked: 32
Workers with a Varying Number of Hours: 9.5%
Workers Earning Some Overtime Pay, Tips, or Commissions: 2.1%
Earnings Benefit of Working Overtime: −4.1%

Gender

	Male	Female
Percent	53.7%	46.3%
Effect on Earnings	16.1%	−13.5%

Union Membership

Percentage Union Members: 18.9%
Earnings Benefit of Union Membership: 12.1%

Veteran Status

Percentage Who Have Been on Active Duty: 7.4%
Earnings Benefit of Veteran Status: 20.1%

25-1126 Philosophy and Religion Teachers, Postsecondary

Teach courses in philosophy, religion, and theology.

- Education or Training Required: Master's degree
- Job Growth: 32.2% (for all postsecondary teaching occupations)
- Annual Openings: 329,000 (for all postsecondary teaching occupations)
- Self-Employed: 0.4%
- Part-Time: 24.8%

NATIONAL WAGE FIGURES (ANNUAL)

Beginning	25th Percentile	Median	Mean	75th Percentile	90th Percentile
$31,660	$41,710	$54,880	$60,180	$73,260	$96,600

Median Wages for Industries Employing Largest Numbers (Annual)

Industry	Median Income
Educational Services	$55,290

Median Wages for States (Annual)

AK	no data	KY	$53,560	NY	no data
AL	$55,330	LA	no data	OH	$48,580
AR	no data	MA	$68,630	OK	$43,560
AZ	$51,310	MD	$65,820	OR	$47,990
CA	no data	ME	$43,260	PA	$59,490
CO	$52,260	MI	$57,270	RI	$67,750
CT	$65,780	MN	$49,000	SC	$45,700
DC	$56,170	MO	$51,150	SD	$41,500
DE	no data	MS	$55,580	TN	$49,130
FL	$51,240	MT	no data	TX	$52,960
GA	$54,800	NC	$54,590	UT	$48,830
HI	$63,280	ND	no data	VA	$48,340
IA	$54,410	NE	$43,330	VT	$55,620
ID	no data	NH	$59,590	WA	$55,270
IL	$55,180	NJ	$64,170	WI	$53,930
IN	$53,280	NM	$55,000	WV	$44,590
KS	$56,080	NV	$39,850	WY	no data

Median Wages for the Largest Metropolitan Areas (Annual)

AZ: Phoenix	$39,750	MI: Detroit	$53,260
CA: Los Angeles	$63,350	MN: Minneapolis	$52,670
CA: Riverside	$65,480	MO: Kansas City	$52,760
CA: Sacramento	$74,040	MO: St. Louis	$51,400
CA: San Diego	$60,180	NV: Las Vegas	no data
CA: San Francisco	$68,910	NY: New York	$63,590
CO: Denver	$45,500	OH: Cincinnati	$43,860
DC: Washington	$57,420	OH: Cleveland	$42,890
FL: Miami	$51,720	OH: Columbus	$67,930
FL: Orlando	$49,530	OR: Portland	$46,700
FL: Tampa	$54,260	PA: Philadelphia	$63,770
GA: Atlanta	$63,190	PA: Pittsburgh	$59,900
IL: Chicago	$56,610	TX: Dallas	$52,630
MA: Boston	$67,080	TX: Houston	$71,230
MD: Baltimore	$72,540	WA: Seattle	$56,870

FACTORS THAT MAY AFFECT EARNINGS

Educational Attainment of Workers and Effect on Earnings

Figures are based on a group of occupations: Postsecondary Teachers

	Percent at Level	Effect on Earnings
Less than High School	—	—
Some High School	—	—
High School or Equivalent	2.2%	−40.5%
Some College but No Degree	6.6%	−53.9%
Associate Degree	4.4%	−14.3%
Bachelor's Degree	20.2%	−33.1%
Master's Degree	29.9%	−8.9%
Doctoral Degree	28.3%	42.5%
First Professional Degree	8.1%	28.8%

Flexibility of Earnings

Average Hours Worked: 32
Workers with a Varying Number of Hours: 9.5%
Workers Earning Some Overtime Pay, Tips, or Commissions: 2.1%
Earnings Benefit of Working Overtime: −4.1%

Gender

	Male	Female
Percent	53.7%	46.3%
Effect on Earnings	16.1%	−13.5%

Union Membership

Percentage Union Members: 18.9%
Earnings Benefit of Union Membership: 12.1%

Veteran Status

Percentage Who Have Been on Active Duty: 7.4%
Earnings Benefit of Veteran Status: 20.1%

25-1191 Graduate Teaching Assistants

Assist department chairperson, faculty members, or other professional staff members in college or university by performing teaching or teaching-related duties, such as teaching lower-level courses, developing teaching materials, preparing and giving examinations, and grading examinations or papers. Graduate assistants must be enrolled in a graduate school program. Graduate assistants who primarily perform non-teaching duties, such as laboratory research, should be reported in the occupational category related to the work performed.

- Education or Training Required: Master's degree
- Job Growth: 32.2% (for all postsecondary teaching occupations)
- Annual Openings: 329,000 (for all postsecondary teaching occupations)
- Self-Employed: 0.4%
- Part-Time: 24.8%

NATIONAL WAGE FIGURES (ANNUAL)

Beginning	25th Percentile	Median	Mean	75th Percentile	90th Percentile
$15,830	$21,270	$27,840	$30,190	$37,250	$46,770

Median Wages for Industries Employing Largest Numbers (Annual)

Industry	Median Income
Administrative and Support Services	$29,610
Educational Services	$27,850
Religious, Grantmaking, Civic, Professional, and Similar Organizations	$26,620
Professional, Scientific, and Technical Services	$24,250

Median Wages for States (Annual)

State		State		State	
AK	no data	KY	no data	NY	no data
AL	$22,870	LA	no data	OH	$36,420
AR	no data	MA	$43,460	OK	$20,750
AZ	no data	MD	$35,900	OR	$34,840
CA	no data	ME	no data	PA	$25,690
CO	no data	MI	no data	RI	no data
CT	no data	MN	no data	SC	$28,330
DC	$30,860	MO	no data	SD	no data
DE	no data	MS	no data	TN	$15,020
FL	$36,730	MT	no data	TX	$26,120
GA	$15,690	NC	no data	UT	no data
HI	no data	ND	$27,790	VA	no data
IA	no data	NE	$33,060	VT	no data
ID	no data	NH	$27,570	WA	$35,310
IL	$21,030	NJ	$26,510	WI	$25,090
IN	no data	NM	no data	WV	no data
KS	$29,770	NV	no data	WY	no data

Median Wages for the Largest Metropolitan Areas (Annual)

AZ: Phoenix	no data	MI: Detroit	no data
CA: Los Angeles	$26,790	MN: Minneapolis	no data
CA: Riverside	$38,990	MO: Kansas City	$27,420
CA: Sacramento	no data	MO: St. Louis	no data
CA: San Diego	$22,910	NV: Las Vegas	no data
CA: San Francisco	$37,100	NY: New York	$25,740
CO: Denver	no data	OH: Cincinnati	no data
DC: Washington	$31,010	OH: Cleveland	no data
FL: Miami	$36,670	OH: Columbus	no data
FL: Orlando	no data	OR: Portland	no data
FL: Tampa	no data	PA: Philadelphia	$27,140
GA: Atlanta	$23,570	PA: Pittsburgh	no data
IL: Chicago	$20,970	TX: Dallas	$24,610
MA: Boston	$44,210	TX: Houston	no data
MD: Baltimore	$40,110	WA: Seattle	no data

FACTORS THAT MAY AFFECT EARNINGS

Educational Attainment of Workers and Effect on Earnings

Figures are based on a group of occupations: Postsecondary Teachers

	Percent at Level	Effect on Earnings
Less than High School	—	—
Some High School	—	—
High School or Equivalent	2.2%	−40.5%
Some College but No Degree	6.6%	−53.9%
Associate Degree	4.4%	−14.3%
Bachelor's Degree	20.2%	−33.1%
Master's Degree	29.9%	−8.9%
Doctoral Degree	28.3%	42.5%
First Professional Degree	8.1%	28.8%

Flexibility of Earnings

Average Hours Worked: 32
Workers with a Varying Number of Hours: 9.5%
Workers Earning Some Overtime Pay, Tips, or Commissions: 2.1%
Earnings Benefit of Working Overtime: −4.1%

Gender

	Male	Female
Percent	53.7%	46.3%
Effect on Earnings	16.1%	−13.5%

Union Membership

Percentage Union Members: 18.9%
Earnings Benefit of Union Membership: 12.1%

Veteran Status

Percentage Who Have Been on Active Duty: 7.4%
Earnings Benefit of Veteran Status: 20.1%

25-1192 Home Economics Teachers, Postsecondary

Teach courses in child care, family relations, finance, nutrition, and related subjects as pertaining to home management.

- Education or Training Required: Master's degree
- Job Growth: 32.2% (for all postsecondary teaching occupations)
- Annual Openings: 329,000 (for all postsecondary teaching occupations)
- Self-Employed: 0.4%
- Part-Time: 24.8%

NATIONAL WAGE FIGURES (ANNUAL)

Beginning	25th Percentile	Median	Mean	75th Percentile	90th Percentile
$27,090	$39,790	$55,310	$60,630	$74,580	$100,660

Median Wages for Industries Employing Largest Numbers (Annual)

Industry	Median Income
Educational Services	$55,700

Median Wages for States (Annual)

State		State		State	
AK	no data	KY	$40,820	NY	no data
AL	$51,740	LA	no data	OH	$59,270
AR	no data	MA	no data	OK	$22,750
AZ	$29,540	MD	no data	OR	no data
CA	no data	ME	no data	PA	$61,790
CO	no data	MI	$50,630	RI	no data
CT	no data	MN	no data	SC	no data
DC	no data	MO	$47,880	SD	no data
DE	no data	MS	$48,790	TN	no data
FL	no data	MT	no data	TX	$56,590
GA	$62,620	NC	$49,100	UT	no data
HI	no data	ND	no data	VA	$37,910
IA	no data	NE	$49,190	VT	no data
ID	no data	NH	no data	WA	$52,870
IL	$53,610	NJ	$63,890	WI	$51,360
IN	$44,830	NM	$53,680	WV	no data
KS	$56,900	NV	no data	WY	no data

Median Wages for the Largest Metropolitan Areas (Annual)

Area		Area	
AZ: Phoenix	no data	MI: Detroit	no data
CA: Los Angeles	$89,880	MN: Minneapolis	no data
CA: Riverside	$79,360	MO: Kansas City	no data
CA: Sacramento	no data	MO: St. Louis	$56,300
CA: San Diego	$79,280	NV: Las Vegas	no data
CA: San Francisco	$78,560	NY: New York	$63,240
CO: Denver	no data	OH: Cincinnati	no data
DC: Washington	no data	OH: Cleveland	no data
FL: Miami	no data	OH: Columbus	no data
FL: Orlando	no data	OR: Portland	no data
FL: Tampa	no data	PA: Philadelphia	no data
GA: Atlanta	no data	PA: Pittsburgh	no data
IL: Chicago	$54,540	TX: Dallas	$58,700
MA: Boston	no data	TX: Houston	no data
MD: Baltimore	no data	WA: Seattle	no data

FACTORS THAT MAY AFFECT EARNINGS

Educational Attainment of Workers and Effect on Earnings

Figures are based on a group of occupations: Postsecondary Teachers

	Percent at Level	Effect on Earnings
Less than High School	—	—
Some High School	—	—
High School or Equivalent	2.2%	−40.5%
Some College but No Degree	6.6%	−53.9%
Associate Degree	4.4%	−14.3%
Bachelor's Degree	20.2%	−33.1%
Master's Degree	29.9%	−8.9%
Doctoral Degree	28.3%	42.5%
First Professional Degree	8.1%	28.8%

Flexibility of Earnings

Average Hours Worked: 32
Workers with a Varying Number of Hours: 9.5%
Workers Earning Some Overtime Pay, Tips, or Commissions: 2.1%
Earnings Benefit of Working Overtime: −4.1%

Gender

	Male	Female
Percent	53.7%	46.3%
Effect on Earnings	16.1%	−13.5%

Union Membership

Percentage Union Members: 18.9%
Earnings Benefit of Union Membership: 12.1%

Veteran Status

Percentage Who Have Been on Active Duty: 7.4%
Earnings Benefit of Veteran Status: 20.1%

25-1193 Recreation and Fitness Studies Teachers, Postsecondary

Teach courses pertaining to recreation, leisure, and fitness studies, including exercise physiology and facilities management.

- Education or Training Required: Master's degree
- Job Growth: 32.2% (for all postsecondary teaching occupations)
- Annual Openings: 329,000 (for all postsecondary teaching occupations)
- Self-Employed: 0.4%
- Part-Time: 24.8%

NATIONAL WAGE FIGURES (ANNUAL)

Beginning	25th Percentile	Median	Mean	75th Percentile	90th Percentile
$25,140	$35,190	$49,270	$54,020	$67,510	$90,790

Median Wages for Industries Employing Largest Numbers (Annual)

Industry	Median Income
Educational Services	$50,260
Religious, Grantmaking, Civic, Professional, and Similar Organizations	$39,150
Federal, State, and Local Government	$30,730
Amusement, Gambling, and Recreation Industries	$27,830

Median Wages for States (Annual)

AK	no data	KY	$46,440	NY	no data
AL	$54,900	LA	no data	OH	$47,460
AR	no data	MA	$55,050	OK	$36,030
AZ	no data	MD	$60,280	OR	$61,280
CA	no data	ME	$51,310	PA	$48,180
CO	$39,940	MI	$51,350	RI	no data
CT	$55,790	MN	$48,810	SC	$50,170
DC	$61,020	MO	$50,330	SD	$44,320
DE	no data	MS	$49,370	TN	$39,570
FL	$48,520	MT	$17,730	TX	$44,980
GA	$43,170	NC	$48,700	UT	$48,280
HI	$48,690	ND	$44,700	VA	$43,310
IA	$39,570	NE	$42,310	VT	$44,500
ID	no data	NH	$58,630	WA	$40,100
IL	$49,500	NJ	$41,770	WI	$45,000
IN	$36,530	NM	$48,600	WV	$38,570
KS	$33,280	NV	no data	WY	no data

Median Wages for the Largest Metropolitan Areas (Annual)

AZ: Phoenix	no data	MI: Detroit	$46,270
CA: Los Angeles	$80,940	MN: Minneapolis	$49,700
CA: Riverside	$76,540	MO: Kansas City	$41,110
CA: Sacramento	$81,280	MO: St. Louis	no data
CA: San Diego	$90,180	NV: Las Vegas	no data
CA: San Francisco	$77,740	NY: New York	$55,030
CO: Denver	$35,440	OH: Cincinnati	$47,330
DC: Washington	$53,160	OH: Cleveland	$49,740
FL: Miami	$63,990	OH: Columbus	$49,180
FL: Orlando	no data	OR: Portland	$48,210
FL: Tampa	$49,530	PA: Philadelphia	$36,000
GA: Atlanta	$47,850	PA: Pittsburgh	$49,000
IL: Chicago	$48,260	TX: Dallas	$45,020
MA: Boston	$55,020	TX: Houston	$52,020
MD: Baltimore	$58,500	WA: Seattle	$40,010

FACTORS THAT MAY AFFECT EARNINGS

Educational Attainment of Workers and Effect on Earnings

Figures are based on a group of occupations: Postsecondary Teachers

	Percent at Level	Effect on Earnings
Less than High School	—	—
Some High School	—	—
High School or Equivalent	2.2%	−40.5%
Some College but No Degree	6.6%	−53.9%
Associate Degree	4.4%	−14.3%
Bachelor's Degree	20.2%	−33.1%
Master's Degree	29.9%	−8.9%
Doctoral Degree	28.3%	42.5%
First Professional Degree	8.1%	28.8%

Flexibility of Earnings

Average Hours Worked: 32
Workers with a Varying Number of Hours: 9.5%
Workers Earning Some Overtime Pay, Tips, or Commissions: 2.1%
Earnings Benefit of Working Overtime: −4.1%

Gender

	Male	Female
Percent	53.7%	46.3%
Effect on Earnings	16.1%	−13.5%

Union Membership

Percentage Union Members: 18.9%
Earnings Benefit of Union Membership: 12.1%

Veteran Status

Percentage Who Have Been on Active Duty: 7.4%
Earnings Benefit of Veteran Status: 20.1%

25-1194 Vocational Education Teachers, Postsecondary

Teach or instruct vocational or occupational subjects at the postsecondary level (but at less than the baccalaureate) to students who have graduated or left high school. Includes correspondence school instructors; industrial, commercial, and government training instructors; and adult education teachers and instructors who prepare persons to operate industrial machinery and equipment and transportation and communications equipment. Teaching may take place in public or private schools whose primary business is education or in a school associated with an organization whose primary business is other than education.

- Education or Training Required: Work experience in a related occupation
- Job Growth: 32.2% (for all postsecondary teaching occupations)
- Annual Openings: 329,000 (for all postsecondary teaching occupations)
- Self-Employed: 0.4%
- Part-Time: 24.8%

NATIONAL WAGE FIGURES (ANNUAL)

Beginning	25th Percentile	Median	Mean	75th Percentile	90th Percentile
$25,420	$32,920	$43,900	$47,110	$57,850	$73,610

Median Wages for Industries Employing Largest Numbers (Annual)

Industry	Median Income
Wholesale Electronic Markets and Agents and Brokers	$61,980
Religious, Grantmaking, Civic, Professional, and Similar Organizations	$57,700
Merchant Wholesalers, Durable Goods	$49,420
Hospitals	$48,020
Professional, Scientific, and Technical Services	$44,710
Management of Companies and Enterprises	$44,650
Federal, State, and Local Government	$44,630
Educational Services	$44,020
Insurance Carriers and Related Activities	$41,860
Administrative and Support Services	$41,020

Median Wages for States (Annual)

AK	no data	KY	$40,190	NY	no data
AL	$46,630	LA	no data	OH	$40,950
AR	no data	MA	$50,240	OK	$41,760
AZ	$43,660	MD	$33,270	OR	$48,650
CA	no data	ME	$43,600	PA	$40,340
CO	$36,810	MI	$52,750	RI	no data
CT	$42,850	MN	no data	SC	$36,860
DC	$51,180	MO	$42,040	SD	$43,350
DE	$56,890	MS	$47,030	TN	$40,140
FL	$47,470	MT	$32,200	TX	$37,880
GA	$42,990	NC	$41,840	UT	$39,490
HI	$49,150	ND	$40,080	VA	$40,240
IA	$42,870	NE	$45,130	VT	$34,990
ID	no data	NH	$40,680	WA	$45,990
IL	$46,380	NJ	$45,570	WI	$58,370
IN	$35,530	NM	$36,470	WV	$37,220
KS	$46,790	NV	$36,440	WY	no data

Median Wages for the Largest Metropolitan Areas (Annual)

AZ: Phoenix	$42,980	MI: Detroit	$37,040
CA: Los Angeles	$45,100	MN: Minneapolis	$51,550
CA: Riverside	$44,030	MO: Kansas City	$48,690
CA: Sacramento	$55,460	MO: St. Louis	$45,580
CA: San Diego	$66,970	NV: Las Vegas	$36,170
CA: San Francisco	$61,890	NY: New York	$46,990
CO: Denver	$37,120	OH: Cincinnati	$37,980
DC: Washington	$43,710	OH: Cleveland	$37,620
FL: Miami	$58,130	OH: Columbus	$38,860
FL: Orlando	$42,170	OR: Portland	$43,980
FL: Tampa	$39,550	PA: Philadelphia	$46,600
GA: Atlanta	$40,910	PA: Pittsburgh	$36,110
IL: Chicago	$47,590	TX: Dallas	$32,010
MA: Boston	$51,600	TX: Houston	no data
MD: Baltimore	$27,700	WA: Seattle	$48,790

FACTORS THAT MAY AFFECT EARNINGS

Educational Attainment of Workers and Effect on Earnings

Figures are based on a group of occupations: Postsecondary Teachers

	Percent at Level	Effect on Earnings
Less than High School	—	—
Some High School	—	—
High School or Equivalent	2.2%	−40.5%
Some College but No Degree	6.6%	−53.9%
Associate Degree	4.4%	−14.3%
Bachelor's Degree	20.2%	−33.1%
Master's Degree	29.9%	−8.9%
Doctoral Degree	28.3%	42.5%
First Professional Degree	8.1%	28.8%

Flexibility of Earnings

Average Hours Worked: 32
Workers with a Varying Number of Hours: 9.5%
Workers Earning Some Overtime Pay, Tips, or Commissions: 2.1%
Earnings Benefit of Working Overtime: −4.1%

Gender

	Male	Female
Percent	53.7%	46.3%
Effect on Earnings	16.1%	−13.5%

Union Membership

Percentage Union Members: 18.9%
Earnings Benefit of Union Membership: 12.1%

Veteran Status

Percentage Who Have Been on Active Duty: 7.4%
Earnings Benefit of Veteran Status: 20.1%

25-1199 Postsecondary Teachers, All Other

All postsecondary teachers not listed separately.

- Education or Training Required: Master's degree
- Job Growth: 32.2% (for all postsecondary teaching occupations)
- Annual Openings: 329,000 (for all postsecondary teaching occupations)
- Self-Employed: 0.4%
- Part-Time: 24.8%

NATIONAL WAGE FIGURES (ANNUAL)

Beginning	25th Percentile	Median	Mean	75th Percentile	90th Percentile
$33,590	$45,920	$63,930	$72,310	$92,330	$120,580

Median Wages for Industries Employing Largest Numbers (Annual)

Industry	Median Income
Professional, Scientific, and Technical Services	$65,480
Educational Services	$63,950
Religious, Grantmaking, Civic, Professional, and Similar Organizations	$61,160
Federal, State, and Local Government	$60,750
Management of Companies and Enterprises	$49,570
Personal and Laundry Services	$42,370

Median Wages for States (Annual)

AK .... no data	KY $37,460	NY .... no data
AL $45,910	LA .... no data	OH $57,200
AR .... no data	MA .... no data	OK $51,240
AZ $46,970	MD $50,480	OR .... no data
CA .... no data	ME .... no data	PA $54,770
CO $36,150	MI $65,850	RI $63,140
CT .... no data	MN $57,390	SC $52,260
DC $57,460	MO $57,620	SD .... no data
DE $67,400	MS $21,500	TN $48,270
FL $55,530	MT .... no data	TX $70,530
GA $38,640	NC $50,840	UT $52,220
HI $61,570	ND .... no data	VA $52,060
IA $38,430	NE $79,700	VT $48,300
ID .... no data	NH $46,510	WA $53,900
IL $64,680	NJ $65,050	WI $59,340
IN $55,380	NM .... no data	WV $55,950
KS $56,770	NV $38,360	WY $46,870

Median Wages for the Largest Metropolitan Areas (Annual)

AZ: Phoenix	no data	MI: Detroit	$45,810
CA: Los Angeles	$73,610	MN: Minneapolis	$55,170
CA: Riverside	$65,660	MO: Kansas City	no data
CA: Sacramento	$81,220	MO: St. Louis	$67,740
CA: San Diego	$51,920	NV: Las Vegas	no data
CA: San Francisco	$66,110	NY: New York	$78,100
CO: Denver	$38,550	OH: Cincinnati	$56,690
DC: Washington	$46,840	OH: Cleveland	$34,380
FL: Miami	$58,920	OH: Columbus	$57,110
FL: Orlando	$41,990	OR: Portland	no data
FL: Tampa	$63,630	PA: Philadelphia	$62,220
GA: Atlanta	no data	PA: Pittsburgh	$56,160
IL: Chicago	$67,460	TX: Dallas	no data
MA: Boston	$74,540	TX: Houston	$105,510
MD: Baltimore	$50,830	WA: Seattle	no data

FACTORS THAT MAY AFFECT EARNINGS

Educational Attainment of Workers and Effect on Earnings

Figures are based on a group of occupations: Postsecondary Teachers

	Percent at Level	Effect on Earnings
Less than High School	—	—
Some High School	—	—
High School or Equivalent	2.2%	−40.5%
Some College but No Degree	6.6%	−53.9%
Associate Degree	4.4%	−14.3%
Bachelor's Degree	20.2%	−33.1%
Master's Degree	29.9%	−8.9%
Doctoral Degree	28.3%	42.5%
First Professional Degree	8.1%	28.8%

Flexibility of Earnings

Average Hours Worked: 32
Workers with a Varying Number of Hours: 9.5%
Workers Earning Some Overtime Pay, Tips, or Commissions: 2.1%
Earnings Benefit of Working Overtime: −4.1%

Gender

	Male	Female
Percent	53.7%	46.3%
Effect on Earnings	16.1%	−13.5%

Union Membership

Percentage Union Members: 18.9%
Earnings Benefit of Union Membership: 12.1%

Veteran Status

Percentage Who Have Been on Active Duty: 7.4%
Earnings Benefit of Veteran Status: 20.1%

25-2000 Primary, Secondary, and Special Education School Teachers

25-2011 Preschool Teachers, Except Special Education

Instruct children (normally up to 5 years of age) in activities designed to promote social, physical, and intellectual growth needed for primary school in preschool, day care center, or other child development facility. May be required to hold state certification.

- Education or Training Required: Postsecondary vocational training
- Job Growth: 33.1%
- Annual Openings: 77,000
- Self-Employed: 1.4%
- Part-Time: 27.0%

NATIONAL WAGE FIGURES (ANNUAL)

Beginning	25th Percentile	Median	Mean	75th Percentile	90th Percentile
$14,870	$17,790	$22,680	$25,900	$29,720	$39,960

Median Wages for Industries Employing Largest Numbers (Annual)

Industry	Median Income
Educational Services	$32,840
Professional, Scientific, and Technical Services	$27,190
Federal, State, and Local Government	$27,070
Administrative and Support Services	$26,540
Amusement, Gambling, and Recreation Industries	$25,560
Ambulatory Health Care Services	$24,740
Management of Companies and Enterprises	$24,620
Religious, Grantmaking, Civic, Professional, and Similar Organizations	$23,980
Hospitals	$23,900
Nursing and Residential Care Facilities	$23,660

Median Wages for States (Annual)

State	Wage	State	Wage	State	Wage
AK	$25,250	KY	$21,270	NY	$28,170
AL	$19,940	LA	$17,760	OH	$20,570
AR	$17,330	MA	$27,050	OK	$18,670
AZ	$20,580	MD	$24,150	OR	$22,100
CA	$25,460	ME	$22,750	PA	$20,350
CO	$23,850	MI	$26,800	RI	$26,220
CT	$25,910	MN	$28,110	SC	$18,830
DC	$27,480	MO	$21,130	SD	$25,920
DE	$24,190	MS	$19,960	TN	$16,530
FL	$20,970	MT	$19,450	TX	$18,170
GA	$19,080	NC	$18,270	UT	$24,030
HI	$24,450	ND	$22,310	VA	$22,090
IA	$18,910	NE	$21,890	VT	$25,150
ID	$22,140	NH	$23,680	WA	$25,040
IL	$25,490	NJ	$29,270	WI	$20,970
IN	$20,560	NM	$20,260	WV	$20,800
KS	$22,710	NV	$21,870	WY	$20,180

Median Wages for the Largest Metropolitan Areas (Annual)

Area	Wage	Area	Wage
AZ: Phoenix	$20,330	MI: Detroit	$28,560
CA: Los Angeles	$25,020	MN: Minneapolis	$27,880
CA: Riverside	$20,750	MO: Kansas City	$21,670
CA: Sacramento	$23,180	MO: St. Louis	$22,070
CA: San Diego	$26,000	NV: Las Vegas	$21,530
CA: San Francisco	$28,940	NY: New York	$31,170
CO: Denver	$25,880	OH: Cincinnati	$21,420
DC: Washington	$26,290	OH: Cleveland	$22,400
FL: Miami	$20,930	OH: Columbus	$20,750
FL: Orlando	$21,620	OR: Portland	$22,840
FL: Tampa	$22,280	PA: Philadelphia	$23,070
GA: Atlanta	$19,350	PA: Pittsburgh	$17,450
IL: Chicago	$26,740	TX: Dallas	$18,560
MA: Boston	$27,440	TX: Houston	$17,070
MD: Baltimore	$22,930	WA: Seattle	$25,060

FACTORS THAT MAY AFFECT EARNINGS

Educational Attainment of Workers and Effect on Earnings

Figures are based on a group of occupations: Primary, Secondary, and Special Education School Teachers

	Percent at Level	Effect on Earnings
Less than High School	—	—
Some High School	1.4%	−55.5%
High School or Equivalent	7.0%	−46.0%
Some College but No Degree	9.1%	−39.9%
Associate Degree	8.1%	−39.9%
Bachelor's Degree	38.6%	1.2%
Master's Degree	30.6%	28.4%
Doctoral Degree	2.2%	26.1%
First Professional Degree	3.0%	40.6%

Flexibility of Earnings

Average Hours Worked: 36
Workers with a Varying Number of Hours: 4.5%
Workers Earning Some Overtime Pay, Tips, or Commissions: 2.2%
Earnings Benefit of Working Overtime: 6.1%

Gender

	Male	Female
Percent	2.3%	97.7%
Effect on Earnings	—	−2.3%

Union Membership

Percentage Union Members: 48.9%
Earnings Benefit of Union Membership: 19.2%

Veteran Status

Percentage Who Have Been on Active Duty: Insignificant
Earnings Benefit of Veteran Status: No significant data available

25-2012 Kindergarten Teachers, Except Special Education

Teach elemental natural and social science, personal hygiene, music, art, and literature to children from 4 to 6 years old. Promote physical, mental, and social development. May be required to hold state certification.

- Education or Training Required: Bachelor's degree
- Job Growth: 22.4%
- Annual Openings: 28,000
- Self-Employed: 1.5%
- Part-Time: 27.0%

NATIONAL WAGE FIGURES (ANNUAL)

Beginning	25th Percentile	Median	Mean	75th Percentile	90th Percentile
$28,590	$34,880	$43,580	$47,040	$56,370	$71,410

Median Wages for Industries Employing Largest Numbers (Annual)

Industry	Median Income
Educational Services	$44,250
Federal, State, and Local Government	$37,770
Hospitals	$33,140
Religious, Grantmaking, Civic, Professional, and Similar Organizations	$28,820
Social Assistance	$26,190

Median Wages for States (Annual)

AK	$52,020	KY	$42,310	NY	$68,390
AL	$39,400	LA	$38,360	OH	$45,860
AR	$38,130	MA	$50,790	OK	$33,030
AZ	$35,300	MD	$45,410	OR	$39,430
CA	$51,710	ME	$40,080	PA	$47,250
CO	$40,680	MI	$49,180	RI	$59,820
CT	$56,770	MN	$44,630	SC	$40,280
DC	$35,250	MO	$38,070	SD	$31,880
DE	$41,690	MS	$35,350	TN	$38,710
FL	$44,270	MT	$34,230	TX	$41,490
GA	$44,590	NC	$36,690	UT	$37,660
HI	$35,410	ND	$37,360	VA	$47,270
IA	$36,070	NE	$41,790	VT	$42,460
ID	$25,700	NH	$36,690	WA	$44,550
IL	$38,410	NJ	$49,500	WI	$43,060
IN	$44,310	NM	$40,110	WV	$41,480
KS	$38,190	NV	$33,050	WY	$40,690

Median Wages for the Largest Metropolitan Areas (Annual)

AZ: Phoenix	$37,370	MI: Detroit	$53,320
CA: Los Angeles	$47,980	MN: Minneapolis	$47,220
CA: Riverside	$55,450	MO: Kansas City	$39,390
CA: Sacramento	$48,970	MO: St. Louis	$41,450
CA: San Diego	$41,210	NV: Las Vegas	$32,430
CA: San Francisco	$51,240	NY: New York	$69,680
CO: Denver	$43,820	OH: Cincinnati	$45,810
DC: Washington	$51,800	OH: Cleveland	$56,250
FL: Miami	$44,950	OH: Columbus	$49,380
FL: Orlando	$38,100	OR: Portland	$40,150
FL: Tampa	$47,430	PA: Philadelphia	$48,030
GA: Atlanta	$44,640	PA: Pittsburgh	$52,350
IL: Chicago	$38,100	TX: Dallas	$43,040
MA: Boston	$48,690	TX: Houston	$43,070
MD: Baltimore	$43,530	WA: Seattle	$46,700

FACTORS THAT MAY AFFECT EARNINGS

Educational Attainment of Workers and Effect on Earnings

Figures are based on a group of occupations: Primary, Secondary, and Special Education School Teachers

	Percent at Level	Effect on Earnings
Less than High School	—	—
Some High School	1.4%	−55.5%
High School or Equivalent	7.0%	−46.0%
Some College but No Degree	9.1%	−39.9%
Associate Degree	8.1%	−39.9%
Bachelor's Degree	38.6%	1.2%
Master's Degree	30.6%	28.4%
Doctoral Degree	2.2%	26.1%
First Professional Degree	3.0%	40.6%

Flexibility of Earnings

Average Hours Worked: 36
Workers with a Varying Number of Hours: 4.5%
Workers Earning Some Overtime Pay, Tips, or Commissions: 2.2%
Earnings Benefit of Working Overtime: 6.1%

Gender

	Male	Female
Percent	2.3%	97.7%
Effect on Earnings	—	−2.3%

Union Membership

Percentage Union Members: 48.9%
Earnings Benefit of Union Membership: 19.2%

Veteran Status

Percentage Who Have Been on Active Duty: Insignificant
Earnings Benefit of Veteran Status: No significant data available

25-2021 Elementary School Teachers, Except Special Education

Teach pupils in public or private schools at the elementary level basic academic, social, and other formative skills.

- Education or Training Required: Bachelor's degree
- Job Growth: 18.2%
- Annual Openings: 203,000
- Self-Employed: 0.0%
- Part-Time: 27.0%

NATIONAL WAGE FIGURES (ANNUAL)

Beginning	25th Percentile	Median	Mean	75th Percentile	90th Percentile
$30,370	$36,680	$45,570	$48,700	$58,170	$72,720

Median Wages for Industries Employing Largest Numbers (Annual)

Industry	Median Income
Federal, State, and Local Government	$48,970
Educational Services	$45,610
Administrative and Support Services	$43,040
Nursing and Residential Care Facilities	$41,890
Religious, Grantmaking, Civic, Professional, and Similar Organizations	$37,650
Hospitals	$31,680
Social Assistance	$29,150

Median Wages for States (Annual)

State	Wage	State	Wage	State	Wage
AK	$55,500	KY	$41,620	NY	$66,300
AL	$39,950	LA	$38,300	OH	$49,850
AR	$38,260	MA	$56,310	OK	$34,430
AZ	$33,620	MD	$49,050	OR	$46,050
CA	$54,160	ME	$43,220	PA	$48,530
CO	$43,190	MI	$55,800	RI	$59,440
CT	$58,260	MN	$45,340	SC	$40,810
DC	no data	MO	$37,900	SD	$32,950
DE	$48,260	MS	$36,850	TN	$39,290
FL	$44,340	MT	$34,400	TX	$42,440
GA	$46,410	NC	$37,820	UT	$41,090
HI	$41,920	ND	$38,640	VA	$51,130
IA	$35,290	NE	$42,060	VT	$43,910
ID	$44,780	NH	$46,320	WA	$49,350
IL	$50,000	NJ	$51,630	WI	$45,110
IN	$46,060	NM	$40,230	WV	$40,300
KS	$36,950	NV	$35,390	WY	$44,570

Median Wages for the Largest Metropolitan Areas (Annual)

Area	Wage	Area	Wage
AZ: Phoenix	$32,680	MI: Detroit	$62,090
CA: Los Angeles	$52,600	MN: Minneapolis	$46,260
CA: Riverside	$57,010	MO: Kansas City	$39,490
CA: Sacramento	$53,210	MO: St. Louis	$43,780
CA: San Diego	$60,350	NV: Las Vegas	$33,570
CA: San Francisco	$54,580	NY: New York	$68,570
CO: Denver	$46,070	OH: Cincinnati	$47,560
DC: Washington	$58,490	OH: Cleveland	$58,920
FL: Miami	$46,510	OH: Columbus	$52,080
FL: Orlando	$39,870	OR: Portland	$46,430
FL: Tampa	$47,620	PA: Philadelphia	$49,360
GA: Atlanta	$47,140	PA: Pittsburgh	$49,480
IL: Chicago	$52,030	TX: Dallas	$44,040
MA: Boston	$56,150	TX: Houston	$44,120
MD: Baltimore	$48,600	WA: Seattle	$49,180

FACTORS THAT MAY AFFECT EARNINGS

Educational Attainment of Workers and Effect on Earnings

Figures are based on a group of occupations: Primary, Secondary, and Special Education School Teachers

	Percent at Level	Effect on Earnings
Less than High School	—	—
Some High School	1.4%	−55.5%
High School or Equivalent	7.0%	−46.0%
Some College but No Degree	9.1%	−39.9%
Associate Degree	8.1%	−39.9%
Bachelor's Degree	38.6%	1.2%
Master's Degree	30.6%	28.4%
Doctoral Degree	2.2%	26.1%
First Professional Degree	3.0%	40.6%

Flexibility of Earnings

Average Hours Worked: 36
Workers with a Varying Number of Hours: 8.8%
Workers Earning Some Overtime Pay, Tips, or Commissions: 2.2%
Earnings Benefit of Working Overtime: −16.0%

Gender

	Male	Female
Percent	17.8%	82.2%
Effect on Earnings	9.8%	−1.7%

Union Membership

Percentage Union Members: 48.9%
Earnings Benefit of Union Membership: 19.2%

Veteran Status

Percentage Who Have Been on Active Duty: Insignificant
Earnings Benefit of Veteran Status: No significant data available

25-2022 Middle School Teachers, Except Special and Vocational Education

Teach students in public or private schools in one or more subjects at the middle, intermediate, or junior high level, which falls between elementary and senior high school as defined by applicable state laws and regulations.

- Education or Training Required: Bachelor's degree
- Job Growth: 13.7%
- Annual Openings: 83,000
- Self-Employed: 0.0%
- Part-Time: 27.0%

NATIONAL WAGE FIGURES (ANNUAL)

Beginning	25th Percentile	Median	Mean	75th Percentile	90th Percentile
$31,450	$37,560	$46,300	$49,470	$58,730	$73,350

Median Wages for Industries Employing Largest Numbers (Annual)

Industry	Median Income
Educational Services	$46,340
Hospitals	$46,020
Federal, State, and Local Government	$44,430
Administrative and Support Services	$40,220
Religious, Grantmaking, Civic, Professional, and Similar Organizations	$36,660
Nursing and Residential Care Facilities	$36,440
Social Assistance	$33,480

Median Wages for States (Annual)

State	Wage	State	Wage	State	Wage
AK	$55,210	KY	$42,360	NY	$66,350
AL	$40,600	LA	$37,080	OH	$51,530
AR	$40,270	MA	$55,210	OK	$35,100
AZ	$36,360	MD	$47,360	OR	$46,340
CA	$57,630	ME	$42,420	PA	$51,300
CO	$43,290	MI	$56,350	RI	$56,330
CT	$59,140	MN	$44,030	SC	$41,370
DC	no data	MO	$40,230	SD	$34,870
DE	$47,220	MS	$37,470	TN	$40,070
FL	$45,280	MT	$34,550	TX	$43,100
GA	$46,500	NC	$36,750	UT	$44,620
HI	$42,230	ND	no data	VA	$47,040
IA	$38,130	NE	$42,630	VT	$43,890
ID	no data	NH	$44,800	WA	$49,340
IL	$46,240	NJ	$52,870	WI	$44,080
IN	$47,130	NM	$41,790	WV	$39,810
KS	$36,860	NV	$42,030	WY	$44,120

Median Wages for the Largest Metropolitan Areas (Annual)

Area	Wage	Area	Wage
AZ: Phoenix	$37,430	MI: Detroit	$59,300
CA: Los Angeles	$59,210	MN: Minneapolis	$45,470
CA: Riverside	$55,840	MO: Kansas City	$39,580
CA: Sacramento	$52,940	MO: St. Louis	$43,860
CA: San Diego	$66,990	NV: Las Vegas	$40,890
CA: San Francisco	$57,630	NY: New York	$67,360
CO: Denver	$47,040	OH: Cincinnati	$50,320
DC: Washington	$53,310	OH: Cleveland	$60,590
FL: Miami	$48,590	OH: Columbus	$53,040
FL: Orlando	$39,740	OR: Portland	$46,790
FL: Tampa	no data	PA: Philadelphia	$53,730
GA: Atlanta	$46,810	PA: Pittsburgh	$49,220
IL: Chicago	$48,530	TX: Dallas	$44,670
MA: Boston	$54,810	TX: Houston	$44,640
MD: Baltimore	$44,190	WA: Seattle	$49,000

FACTORS THAT MAY AFFECT EARNINGS

Educational Attainment of Workers and Effect on Earnings

Figures are based on a group of occupations: Primary, Secondary, and Special Education School Teachers

	Percent at Level	Effect on Earnings
Less than High School	—	—
Some High School	1.4%	−55.5%
High School or Equivalent	7.0%	−46.0%
Some College but No Degree	9.1%	−39.9%
Associate Degree	8.1%	−39.9%
Bachelor's Degree	38.6%	1.2%
Master's Degree	30.6%	28.4%
Doctoral Degree	2.2%	26.1%
First Professional Degree	3.0%	40.6%

Flexibility of Earnings

Average Hours Worked: 36
Workers with a Varying Number of Hours: 8.8%
Workers Earning Some Overtime Pay, Tips, or Commissions: 2.2%
Earnings Benefit of Working Overtime: −16.0%

Gender

	Male	Female
Percent	17.8%	82.2%
Effect on Earnings	9.8%	−1.7%

Union Membership

Percentage Union Members: 48.9%
Earnings Benefit of Union Membership: 19.2%

Veteran Status

Percentage Who Have Been on Active Duty: Insignificant
Earnings Benefit of Veteran Status: No significant data available

25-2023 Vocational Education Teachers, Middle School

Teach or instruct vocational or occupational subjects at the middle school level.

- Education or Training Required: Work experience plus degree
- Job Growth: –0.9%
- Annual Openings: 2,000
- Self-Employed: 0.0%
- Part-Time: 27.0%

NATIONAL WAGE FIGURES (ANNUAL)

Beginning	25th Percentile	Median	Mean	75th Percentile	90th Percentile
$31,420	$36,730	$44,240	$46,650	$54,810	$67,490

Median Wages for Industries Employing Largest Numbers (Annual)

Industry	Median Income
Educational Services	$44,240

Median Wages for States (Annual)

AK............ $48,050	KY $44,420	NY $49,090
AL $40,610	LA $39,290	OH $52,140
AR $40,110	MA $44,330	OK $35,780
AZ $34,340	MD $45,190	OR $48,170
CA $55,750	ME $46,800	PA $51,770
CO $41,510	MI $38,440	RI .... no data
CT $62,620	MN $49,480	SC.............. $41,410
DC .... no data	MO $41,650	SD .... no data
DE .... no data	MS $39,460	TN $41,050
FL $47,040	MT $37,350	TX $44,730
GA $48,360	NC $42,170	UT $40,680
HI .... no data	ND .... no data	VA $46,690
IA $37,740	NE $46,050	VT $43,900
ID .... no data	NH $44,040	WA $49,720
IL $44,280	NJ $59,320	WI $46,620
IN $51,370	NM $42,040	WV .... no data
KS $37,370	NV .... no data	WY .... no data

Median Wages for the Largest Metropolitan Areas (Annual)

AZ: Phoenix............ $36,640	MI: Detroit $60,180
CA: Los Angeles $61,790	MN: Minneapolis $48,190
CA: Riverside $49,830	MO: Kansas City $44,590
CA: Sacramento $53,720	MO: St. Louis............ $46,090
CA: San Diego .... no data	NV: Las Vegas .... no data
CA: San Francisco .... no data	NY: New York............ $57,930
CO: Denver .... no data	OH: Cincinnati.......... $54,060
DC: Washington $58,570	OH: Cleveland $66,470
FL: Miami $52,280	OH: Columbus $55,770
FL: Orlando $46,050	OR: Portland $46,640
FL: Tampa .... no data	PA: Philadelphia $51,280
GA: Atlanta $48,450	PA: Pittsburgh $54,680
IL: Chicago $48,800	TX: Dallas $45,540
MA: Boston $43,620	TX: Houston $47,350
MD: Baltimore $45,180	WA: Seattle $49,280

FACTORS THAT MAY AFFECT EARNINGS

Educational Attainment of Workers and Effect on Earnings

Figures are based on a group of occupations: Primary, Secondary, and Special Education School Teachers

	Percent at Level	Effect on Earnings
Less than High School	—	—
Some High School	1.4%	–55.5%
High School or Equivalent	7.0%	–46.0%
Some College but No Degree	9.1%	–39.9%
Associate Degree	8.1%	–39.9%
Bachelor's Degree	38.6%	1.2%
Master's Degree	30.6%	28.4%
Doctoral Degree	2.2%	26.1%
First Professional Degree	3.0%	40.6%

Flexibility of Earnings

Average Hours Worked: 36
Workers with a Varying Number of Hours: 8.8%
Workers Earning Some Overtime Pay, Tips, or Commissions: 2.2%
Earnings Benefit of Working Overtime: –16.0%

Gender

	Male	Female
Percent	21.5%	78.5%
Effect on Earnings	9.8%	–1.7%

Union Membership

Percentage Union Members: 48.9%
Earnings Benefit of Union Membership: 19.2%

Veteran Status

Percentage Who Have Been on Active Duty: Insignificant
Earnings Benefit of Veteran Status: No significant data available

25-2031 Secondary School Teachers, Except Special and Vocational Education

Instruct students in secondary public or private schools in one or more subjects at the secondary level, such as English, mathematics, or social studies. May be designated according to subject matter specialty, such as typing instructors, commercial teachers, or English teachers.

- Education or Training Required: Bachelor's degree
- Job Growth: 14.4%
- Annual Openings: 107,000
- Self-Employed: 0.0%
- Part-Time: 27.0%

NATIONAL WAGE FIGURES (ANNUAL)

Beginning	25th Percentile	Median	Mean	75th Percentile	90th Percentile
$31,760	$38,360	$47,740	$51,150	$61,090	$76,100

Median Wages for Industries Employing Largest Numbers (Annual)

Industry	Median Income
Educational Services	$47,780
Hospitals	$47,410
Federal, State, and Local Government	$42,240
Administrative and Support Services	$41,770
Nursing and Residential Care Facilities	$41,710
Social Assistance	$37,940
Religious, Grantmaking, Civic, Professional, and Similar Organizations	$36,960

Median Wages for States (Annual)

State	Wage	State	Wage	State	Wage
AK	$54,340	KY	$43,200	NY	$66,990
AL	$40,900	LA	$39,800	OH	$50,740
AR	$40,790	MA	$55,050	OK	$35,640
AZ	$36,150	MD	$52,100	OR	$46,580
CA	$56,930	ME	$41,430	PA	$48,270
CO	$44,130	MI	$56,160	RI	$59,320
CT	$60,200	MN	$45,090	SC	$42,880
DC	no data	MO	$39,340	SD	$33,850
DE	$52,400	MS	$38,090	TN	$41,500
FL	$46,950	MT	$36,800	TX	$44,160
GA	$47,990	NC	$39,220	UT	$45,140
HI	$49,440	ND	$36,870	VA	$51,170
IA	$35,260	NE	$41,120	VT	$45,310
ID	$45,240	NH	$47,330	WA	$51,090
IL	$55,210	NJ	$55,780	WI	$45,820
IN	$46,810	NM	$42,520	WV	$40,600
KS	$37,050	NV	$43,080	WY	$43,000

Median Wages for the Largest Metropolitan Areas (Annual)

Area	Wage	Area	Wage
AZ: Phoenix	$37,020	MI: Detroit	$62,820
CA: Los Angeles	$58,520	MN: Minneapolis	$46,410
CA: Riverside	$54,950	MO: Kansas City	$39,190
CA: Sacramento	$53,630	MO: St. Louis	$44,950
CA: San Diego	$58,090	NV: Las Vegas	$41,260
CA: San Francisco	$58,070	NY: New York	$70,830
CO: Denver	$47,990	OH: Cincinnati	$51,170
DC: Washington	$59,550	OH: Cleveland	$58,970
FL: Miami	$51,980	OH: Columbus	$51,280
FL: Orlando	$41,030	OR: Portland	$48,380
FL: Tampa	$49,940	PA: Philadelphia	$52,350
GA: Atlanta	$48,000	PA: Pittsburgh	$48,710
IL: Chicago	$59,370	TX: Dallas	$44,760
MA: Boston	$55,160	TX: Houston	$46,110
MD: Baltimore	$52,570	WA: Seattle	$51,150

FACTORS THAT MAY AFFECT EARNINGS

Educational Attainment of Workers and Effect on Earnings

Figures are based on a group of occupations: Primary, Secondary, and Special Education School Teachers

	Percent at Level	Effect on Earnings
Less than High School	—	—
Some High School	1.4%	−55.5%
High School or Equivalent	7.0%	−46.0%
Some College but No Degree	9.1%	−39.9%
Associate Degree	8.1%	−39.9%
Bachelor's Degree	38.6%	1.2%
Master's Degree	30.6%	28.4%
Doctoral Degree	2.2%	26.1%
First Professional Degree	3.0%	40.6%

Flexibility of Earnings

Average Hours Worked: 36
Workers with a Varying Number of Hours: 6.8%
Workers Earning Some Overtime Pay, Tips, or Commissions: 2.2%
Earnings Benefit of Working Overtime: −19.5%

Gender

	Male	Female
Percent	44.0%	56.0%
Effect on Earnings	3.4%	−3.2%

Union Membership

Percentage Union Members: 48.9%
Earnings Benefit of Union Membership: 19.2%

Veteran Status

Percentage Who Have Been on Active Duty: Insignificant
Earnings Benefit of Veteran Status: No significant data available

25-2032 Vocational Education Teachers, Secondary School

Teach or instruct vocational or occupational subjects at the secondary school level.

- Education or Training Required: Work experience plus degree
- Job Growth: 9.1%
- Annual Openings: 10,000
- Self-Employed: 0.0%
- Part-Time: 27.0%

NATIONAL WAGE FIGURES (ANNUAL)

Beginning	25th Percentile	Median	Mean	75th Percentile	90th Percentile
$33,070	$39,710	$48,690	$51,050	$60,190	$73,280

Median Wages for Industries Employing Largest Numbers (Annual)

Industry	Median Income
Educational Services	$48,820
Social Assistance	$38,370
Federal, State, and Local Government	$38,020
Nursing and Residential Care Facilities	$34,490

Median Wages for States (Annual)

State	Wage	State	Wage	State	Wage
AK	$58,310	KY	$46,310	NY	$65,590
AL	$45,690	LA	$41,570	OH	$55,470
AR	$41,950	MA	$60,310	OK	$39,790
AZ	$39,790	MD	$52,760	OR	$49,380
CA	$58,890	ME	$45,040	PA	$51,990
CO	$47,090	MI	$57,860	RI	no data
CT	$61,070	MN	$46,280	SC	$46,030
DC	no data	MO	$41,600	SD	$35,150
DE	$59,340	MS	$42,190	TN	$39,490
FL	$51,760	MT	$41,250	TX	$45,520
GA	$50,630	NC	$43,230	UT	$44,400
HI	$43,790	ND	$42,400	VA	$49,630
IA	$39,070	NE	$43,430	VT	$47,680
ID	$44,920	NH	$51,550	WA	$52,290
IL	$47,930	NJ	$55,760	WI	$44,530
IN	$50,460	NM	$42,990	WV	$41,870
KS	$41,650	NV	$47,710	WY	$44,910

Median Wages for the Largest Metropolitan Areas (Annual)

Area	Wage	Area	Wage
AZ: Phoenix	$43,990	MI: Detroit	$62,710
CA: Los Angeles	$64,240	MN: Minneapolis	$49,230
CA: Riverside	$56,470	MO: Kansas City	$45,700
CA: Sacramento	$51,260	MO: St. Louis	$46,620
CA: San Diego	$57,140	NV: Las Vegas	no data
CA: San Francisco	$60,310	NY: New York	$70,060
CO: Denver	$53,370	OH: Cincinnati	$57,840
DC: Washington	$61,000	OH: Cleveland	$63,770
FL: Miami	no data	OH: Columbus	$55,170
FL: Orlando	$46,050	OR: Portland	$53,080
FL: Tampa	no data	PA: Philadelphia	$55,170
GA: Atlanta	$50,910	PA: Pittsburgh	$48,130
IL: Chicago	$59,860	TX: Dallas	$47,690
MA: Boston	$60,310	TX: Houston	$48,930
MD: Baltimore	$51,780	WA: Seattle	$52,310

FACTORS THAT MAY AFFECT EARNINGS

Educational Attainment of Workers and Effect on Earnings

Figures are based on a group of occupations: Primary, Secondary, and Special Education School Teachers

	Percent at Level	Effect on Earnings
Less than High School	—	—
Some High School	1.4%	−55.5%
High School or Equivalent	7.0%	−46.0%
Some College but No Degree	9.1%	−39.9%
Associate Degree	8.1%	−39.9%
Bachelor's Degree	38.6%	1.2%
Master's Degree	30.6%	28.4%
Doctoral Degree	2.2%	26.1%
First Professional Degree	3.0%	40.6%

Flexibility of Earnings

Average Hours Worked: 36
Workers with a Varying Number of Hours: 6.8%
Workers Earning Some Overtime Pay, Tips, or Commissions: 2.2%
Earnings Benefit of Working Overtime: −19.5%

Gender

	Male	Female
Percent	21.5%	78.5%
Effect on Earnings	18.3%	−6.8%

Union Membership

Percentage Union Members: 48.9%
Earnings Benefit of Union Membership: 19.2%

Veteran Status

Percentage Who Have Been on Active Duty: Insignificant
Earnings Benefit of Veteran Status: No significant data available

25-2041 Special Education Teachers, Preschool, Kindergarten, and Elementary School

Teach elementary and preschool school subjects to educationally and physically handicapped students. Includes teachers who specialize and work with audibly and visually handicapped students and those who teach basic academic and life processes skills to the mentally impaired.

- Education or Training Required: Bachelor's degree
- Job Growth: 23.3%
- Annual Openings: 18,000
- Self-Employed: 0.5%
- Part-Time: 27.0%

NATIONAL WAGE FIGURES (ANNUAL)

Beginning	25th Percentile	Median	Mean	75th Percentile	90th Percentile
$31,320	$37,500	$46,360	$49,710	$59,320	$73,620

Median Wages for Industries Employing Largest Numbers (Annual)

Industry	Median Income
Management of Companies and Enterprises	$49,320
Educational Services	$46,900
Federal, State, and Local Government	$44,990
Ambulatory Health Care Services	$39,150
Nursing and Residential Care Facilities	$36,930
Social Assistance	$34,430
Hospitals	$33,850
Religious, Grantmaking, Civic, Professional, and Similar Organizations	$28,190

Median Wages for States (Annual)

AK $56,570	KY $41,050	NY $58,000
AL $40,430	LA $37,820	OH $48,040
AR $39,620	MA $51,370	OK $36,600
AZ $35,870	MD $49,690	OR $49,940
CA $58,420	ME $41,280	PA .... no data
CO $46,970	MI $56,990	RI $54,220
CT $60,050	MN $47,620	SC $43,060
DC $44,510	MO $39,340	SD $32,580
DE $53,300	MS $38,770	TN $38,030
FL $46,400	MT $32,360	TX $42,610
GA $45,560	NC $38,390	UT $39,540
HI $41,670	ND $38,050	VA $48,280
IA $37,180	NE $40,780	VT $44,400
ID $31,910	NH $45,340	WA $48,500
IL $49,420	NJ $52,090	WI $44,290
IN $44,690	NM $39,190	WV $39,160
KS $38,890	NV $42,620	WY $38,770

Median Wages for the Largest Metropolitan Areas (Annual)

AZ: Phoenix	$37,190	MI: Detroit	no data
CA: Los Angeles	$58,800	MN: Minneapolis	$49,820
CA: Riverside	$59,750	MO: Kansas City	$42,030
CA: Sacramento	$55,120	MO: St. Louis	$45,260
CA: San Diego	$65,240	NV: Las Vegas	$43,190
CA: San Francisco	$58,260	NY: New York	$63,250
CO: Denver	$51,730	OH: Cincinnati	$47,220
DC: Washington	$56,800	OH: Cleveland	$57,830
FL: Miami	$48,170	OH: Columbus	$47,070
FL: Orlando	$39,870	OR: Portland	$49,450
FL: Tampa	no data	PA: Philadelphia	no data
GA: Atlanta	$46,020	PA: Pittsburgh	$48,930
IL: Chicago	$52,400	TX: Dallas	$44,290
MA: Boston	$49,990	TX: Houston	$44,530
MD: Baltimore	$48,270	WA: Seattle	$49,810

FACTORS THAT MAY AFFECT EARNINGS

Educational Attainment of Workers and Effect on Earnings

Figures are based on a group of occupations: Primary, Secondary, and Special Education School Teachers

	Percent at Level	Effect on Earnings
Less than High School	—	—
Some High School	1.4%	−55.5%
High School or Equivalent	7.0%	−46.0%
Some College but No Degree	9.1%	−39.9%
Associate Degree	8.1%	−39.9%
Bachelor's Degree	38.6%	1.2%
Master's Degree	30.6%	28.4%
Doctoral Degree	2.2%	26.1%
First Professional Degree	3.0%	40.6%

Flexibility of Earnings

Average Hours Worked: 36
Workers with a Varying Number of Hours: 6.0%
Workers Earning Some Overtime Pay, Tips, or Commissions: 2.2%
Earnings Benefit of Working Overtime: −12.8%

Gender

	Male	Female
Percent	16.5%	83.5%
Effect on Earnings	10.5%	−2.3%

Union Membership

Percentage Union Members: 48.9%
Earnings Benefit of Union Membership: 19.2%

Veteran Status

Percentage Who Have Been on Active Duty: Insignificant
Earnings Benefit of Veteran Status: No significant data available

25-2042 Special Education Teachers, Middle School

Teach middle school subjects to educationally and physically handicapped students. Includes teachers who specialize and work with audibly and visually handicapped students and those who teach basic academic and life processes skills to the mentally impaired.

- Education or Training Required: Bachelor's degree
- Job Growth: 19.9%
- Annual Openings: 8,000
- Self-Employed: 0.5%
- Part-Time: 27.0%

NATIONAL WAGE FIGURES (ANNUAL)

Beginning	25th Percentile	Median	Mean	75th Percentile	90th Percentile
$32,420	$38,460	$47,650	$52,550	$61,530	$80,170

Median Wages for Industries Employing Largest Numbers (Annual)

Industry	Median Income
Educational Services	$47,760
Social Assistance	$45,950
Management of Companies and Enterprises	$45,210
Ambulatory Health Care Services	$41,500
Hospitals	$39,700
Nursing and Residential Care Facilities	$37,190
Federal, State, and Local Government	$36,760

Median Wages for States (Annual)

State	Wage	State	Wage	State	Wage
AK	$57,740	KY	$40,410	NY	no data
AL	$41,060	LA	$38,390	OH	$50,240
AR	$40,900	MA	$51,750	OK	$35,300
AZ	$36,580	MD	$53,060	OR	$47,770
CA	$58,440	ME	$40,720	PA	$49,500
CO	$45,470	MI	$55,490	RI	$54,610
CT	$61,590	MN	$47,550	SC	$42,380
DC	no data	MO	$39,950	SD	$33,430
DE	$50,960	MS	$39,100	TN	$38,660
FL	$44,990	MT	$39,310	TX	$42,370
GA	$46,010	NC	$38,510	UT	$36,240
HI	$43,790	ND	no data	VA	$46,490
IA	$38,700	NE	$39,160	VT	$44,660
ID	no data	NH	$44,770	WA	$48,820
IL	$50,730	NJ	$51,220	WI	$42,890
IN	$43,810	NM	$39,550	WV	$36,960
KS	$36,770	NV	$41,550	WY	$43,120

Median Wages for the Largest Metropolitan Areas (Annual)

Area	Wage	Area	Wage
AZ: Phoenix	$38,680	MI: Detroit	$59,410
CA: Los Angeles	$60,390	MN: Minneapolis	$48,260
CA: Riverside	$56,410	MO: Kansas City	$42,700
CA: Sacramento	$53,510	MO: St. Louis	$43,120
CA: San Diego	$68,610	NV: Las Vegas	no data
CA: San Francisco	$56,880	NY: New York	$81,150
CO: Denver	$48,840	OH: Cincinnati	$48,950
DC: Washington	$55,210	OH: Cleveland	$62,320
FL: Miami	no data	OH: Columbus	$49,210
FL: Orlando	$37,910	OR: Portland	$50,380
FL: Tampa	no data	PA: Philadelphia	$51,870
GA: Atlanta	$47,980	PA: Pittsburgh	$47,090
IL: Chicago	$54,360	TX: Dallas	$44,430
MA: Boston	$51,280	TX: Houston	$44,100
MD: Baltimore	$50,410	WA: Seattle	$48,620

FACTORS THAT MAY AFFECT EARNINGS

Educational Attainment of Workers and Effect on Earnings

Figures are based on a group of occupations: Primary, Secondary, and Special Education School Teachers

	Percent at Level	Effect on Earnings
Less than High School	—	—
Some High School	1.4%	−55.5%
High School or Equivalent	7.0%	−46.0%
Some College but No Degree	9.1%	−39.9%
Associate Degree	8.1%	−39.9%
Bachelor's Degree	38.6%	1.2%
Master's Degree	30.6%	28.4%
Doctoral Degree	2.2%	26.1%
First Professional Degree	3.0%	40.6%

Flexibility of Earnings

Average Hours Worked: 36
Workers with a Varying Number of Hours: 6.0%
Workers Earning Some Overtime Pay, Tips, or Commissions: 2.2%
Earnings Benefit of Working Overtime: −12.8%

Gender

	Male	Female
Percent	16.5%	83.5%
Effect on Earnings	10.5%	−2.3%

Union Membership

Percentage Union Members: 48.9%
Earnings Benefit of Union Membership: 19.2%

Veteran Status

Percentage Who Have Been on Active Duty: Insignificant
Earnings Benefit of Veteran Status: No significant data available

25-2043 Special Education Teachers, Secondary School

Teach secondary school subjects to educationally and physically handicapped students. Includes teachers who specialize and work with audibly and visually handicapped students and those who teach basic academic and life processes skills to the mentally impaired.

- Education or Training Required: Bachelor's degree
- Job Growth: 17.9%
- Annual Openings: 11,000
- Self-Employed: 0.5%
- Part-Time: 27.0%

NATIONAL WAGE FIGURES (ANNUAL)

Beginning	25th Percentile	Median	Mean	75th Percentile	90th Percentile
$32,760	$38,910	$48,330	$52,520	$62,640	$78,020

Median Wages for Industries Employing Largest Numbers (Annual)

Industry	Median Income
Educational Services	$48,550
Federal, State, and Local Government	$48,450
Ambulatory Health Care Services	$45,170
Hospitals	$44,580
Social Assistance	$41,350
Nursing and Residential Care Facilities	$35,520

Median Wages for States (Annual)

AK	$55,700	KY	$42,510	NY	$70,570
AL	$41,640	LA	$39,680	OH	$50,160
AR	$41,020	MA	$52,620	OK	$36,510
AZ	$39,540	MD	$54,980	OR	$49,190
CA	$59,140	ME	$41,110	PA	$51,210
CO	$46,670	MI	$57,990	RI	$59,790
CT	$62,550	MN	$49,210	SC	$42,600
DC	no data	MO	$38,990	SD	$33,520
DE	$54,590	MS	$40,300	TN	$39,920
FL	$44,910	MT	$36,290	TX	$42,900
GA	$47,120	NC	$38,340	UT	$39,190
HI	$44,360	ND	$40,830	VA	$54,750
IA	$38,270	NE	$40,210	VT	$46,640
ID	$42,830	NH	$44,530	WA	$49,780
IL	$49,870	NJ	$55,530	WI	$47,690
IN	$45,860	NM	$41,690	WV	$37,870
KS	$39,050	NV	$43,410	WY	$42,910

Median Wages for the Largest Metropolitan Areas (Annual)

AZ: Phoenix	$40,150	MI: Detroit	$66,590
CA: Los Angeles	$60,450	MN: Minneapolis	$52,290
CA: Riverside	$53,320	MO: Kansas City	$42,250
CA: Sacramento	$54,960	MO: St. Louis	$49,460
CA: San Diego	$67,940	NV: Las Vegas	$43,190
CA: San Francisco	$54,160	NY: New York	$75,250
CO: Denver	$49,490	OH: Cincinnati	$49,020
DC: Washington	$66,970	OH: Cleveland	$59,210
FL: Miami	no data	OH: Columbus	$50,160
FL: Orlando	$38,800	OR: Portland	$48,970
FL: Tampa	no data	PA: Philadelphia	$53,290
GA: Atlanta	$48,370	PA: Pittsburgh	$52,300
IL: Chicago	$55,650	TX: Dallas	$45,200
MA: Boston	$51,650	TX: Houston	$44,870
MD: Baltimore	$54,930	WA: Seattle	$50,860

FACTORS THAT MAY AFFECT EARNINGS

Educational Attainment of Workers and Effect on Earnings

Figures are based on a group of occupations: Primary, Secondary, and Special Education School Teachers

	Percent at Level	Effect on Earnings
Less than High School	—	—
Some High School	1.4%	−55.5%
High School or Equivalent	7.0%	−46.0%
Some College but No Degree	9.1%	−39.9%
Associate Degree	8.1%	−39.9%
Bachelor's Degree	38.6%	1.2%
Master's Degree	30.6%	28.4%
Doctoral Degree	2.2%	26.1%
First Professional Degree	3.0%	40.6%

Flexibility of Earnings

Average Hours Worked: 36
Workers with a Varying Number of Hours: 6.0%
Workers Earning Some Overtime Pay, Tips, or Commissions: 2.2%
Earnings Benefit of Working Overtime: −12.8%

Gender

	Male	Female
Percent	16.5%	83.5%
Effect on Earnings	10.5%	−2.3%

Union Membership

Percentage Union Members: 48.9%
Earnings Benefit of Union Membership: 19.2%

Veteran Status

Percentage Who Have Been on Active Duty: Insignificant
Earnings Benefit of Veteran Status: No significant data available

25-3000 Other Teachers and Instructors

25-3011 Adult Literacy, Remedial Education, and GED Teachers and Instructors

Teach or instruct out-of-school youths and adults in remedial education classes, preparatory classes for the General Educational Development test, literacy, or English as a Second Language. Teaching may or may not take place in a traditional educational institution.

- Education or Training Required: Bachelor's degree
- Job Growth: 15.6%
- Annual Openings: 27,000
- Self-Employed: 28.6%
- Part-Time: 53.6%

NATIONAL WAGE FIGURES (ANNUAL)

Beginning	25th Percentile	Median	Mean	75th Percentile	90th Percentile
$24,610	$32,660	$43,910	$46,690	$57,310	$75,680

Median Wages for Industries Employing Largest Numbers (Annual)

Industry	Median Income
Amusement, Gambling, and Recreation Industries	$49,370
Federal, State, and Local Government	$46,650
Educational Services	$45,240
Hospitals	$41,470
Nursing and Residential Care Facilities	$36,930
Religious, Grantmaking, Civic, Professional, and Similar Organizations	$35,920
Social Assistance	$35,180
Administrative and Support Services	$32,640

Median Wages for States (Annual)

AK	$35,740	KY	$30,760	NY	$53,010
AL	$41,300	LA	$31,810	OH	$44,340
AR	$40,720	MA	$43,630	OK	$36,350
AZ	$35,430	MD	$44,330	OR	$41,900
CA	$60,600	ME	$39,320	PA	$41,330
CO	$34,000	MI	$48,880	RI	$38,550
CT	$52,020	MN	$37,020	SC	$44,050
DC	$28,680	MO	$36,200	SD	$27,910
DE	$45,960	MS	$29,520	TN	$38,070
FL	$44,040	MT	$31,290	TX	$41,500
GA	$40,190	NC	$35,900	UT	$40,800
HI	$45,740	ND	$47,460	VA	$46,420
IA	$30,410	NE	$29,100	VT	$38,540
ID	$31,070	NH	$40,420	WA	$40,030
IL	$40,450	NJ	$55,960	WI	$45,220
IN	$32,860	NM	$26,470	WV	$31,410
KS	$33,950	NV	$41,720	WY	$37,300

Median Wages for the Largest Metropolitan Areas (Annual)

AZ: Phoenix	$35,640	MI: Detroit	$50,550
CA: Los Angeles	$75,510	MN: Minneapolis	$39,600
CA: Riverside	$62,500	MO: Kansas City	$33,800
CA: Sacramento	$40,590	MO: St. Louis	$40,070
CA: San Diego	$41,550	NV: Las Vegas	$41,600
CA: San Francisco	$50,860	NY: New York	$55,870
CO: Denver	$33,960	OH: Cincinnati	$35,700
DC: Washington	$43,660	OH: Cleveland	$64,720
FL: Miami	$46,400	OH: Columbus	$48,710
FL: Orlando	no data	OR: Portland	$34,850
FL: Tampa	no data	PA: Philadelphia	$45,450
GA: Atlanta	$40,560	PA: Pittsburgh	$32,550
IL: Chicago	$39,220	TX: Dallas	no data
MA: Boston	$45,830	TX: Houston	$44,380
MD: Baltimore	$42,080	WA: Seattle	$42,920

FACTORS THAT MAY AFFECT EARNINGS

Educational Attainment of Workers and Effect on Earnings

Figures are based on a group of occupations: Other Teachers and Instructors

	Percent at Level	Effect on Earnings
Less than High School	—	—
Some High School	4.8%	−73.5%
High School or Equivalent	17.2%	−14.8%
Some College but No Degree	21.5%	−13.7%
Associate Degree	10.0%	−3.2%
Bachelor's Degree	29.4%	17.5%
Master's Degree	14.0%	28.1%
Doctoral Degree	1.6%	29.9%
First Professional Degree	—	—

Flexibility of Earnings

Average Hours Worked: 25
Workers with a Varying Number of Hours: 11.9%
Workers Earning Some Overtime Pay, Tips, or Commissions: 5.8%
Earnings Benefit of Working Overtime: 2.9%

Gender

	Male	Female
Percent	35.1%	64.9%
Effect on Earnings	18.8%	−12.7%

Union Membership

Percentage Union Members: 8.7%
Earnings Benefit of Union Membership: 33.9%

Veteran Status

Percentage Who Have Been on Active Duty: 9.5%
Earnings Benefit of Veteran Status: 34.1%

25-3021 Self-Enrichment Education Teachers

Teach or instruct courses other than those that normally lead to an occupational objective or degree. Courses may include self-improvement, nonvocational, and nonacademic subjects. Teaching may or may not take place in a traditional educational institution.

- Education or Training Required: Work experience in a related occupation
- Job Growth: 25.3%
- Annual Openings: 74,000
- Self-Employed: 31.1%
- Part-Time: 53.6%

Note: A large fraction of the workforce for this occupation is self-employed and earns an average of $26,740. All other earnings figures for this occupation are based on workers who are paid a wage or salary.

NATIONAL WAGE FIGURES (ANNUAL)

Beginning	25th Percentile	Median	Mean	75th Percentile	90th Percentile
$17,740	$23,480	$33,440	$38,470	$48,000	$66,600

Median Wages for Industries Employing Largest Numbers (Annual)

Industry	Median Income
Funds, Trusts, and Other Financial Vehicles	$66,280
Real Estate	$48,700
Broadcasting (Except Internet)	$48,040
Air Transportation	$43,860
Support Activities for Transportation	$43,810
Merchant Wholesalers, Nondurable Goods	$38,200
Federal, State, and Local Government	$37,570
Hospitals	$36,120
Educational Services	$35,820
Administrative and Support Services	$35,790

Median Wages for States (Annual)

State	Wage	State	Wage	State	Wage
AK	$37,250	KY	$27,750	NY	$31,680
AL	$33,410	LA	$38,820	OH	$28,510
AR	$34,130	MA	$34,480	OK	$28,610
AZ	$27,280	MD	$31,920	OR	$29,530
CA	$37,250	ME	$30,830	PA	$34,580
CO	$31,210	MI	$35,590	RI	$33,540
CT	$44,620	MN	$38,890	SC	$33,880
DC	$36,260	MO	$26,520	SD	$24,350
DE	$34,920	MS	$29,840	TN	$31,770
FL	$30,150	MT	$21,710	TX	$29,490
GA	$30,330	NC	$31,600	UT	$23,030
HI	$34,400	ND	$14,770	VA	$42,400
IA	$28,830	NE	$22,470	VT	$40,980
ID	$33,910	NH	$46,990	WA	$36,570
IL	$37,220	NJ	$41,550	WI	$33,600
IN	$30,050	NM	$40,930	WV	$24,930
KS	$31,120	NV	$34,460	WY	$14,710

Median Wages for the Largest Metropolitan Areas (Annual)

Metro	Wage	Metro	Wage
AZ: Phoenix	$29,460	MI: Detroit	$37,920
CA: Los Angeles	$37,120	MN: Minneapolis	$38,310
CA: Riverside	$33,340	MO: Kansas City	$28,440
CA: Sacramento	$27,210	MO: St. Louis	$42,530
CA: San Diego	$46,420	NV: Las Vegas	$34,620
CA: San Francisco	$38,390	NY: New York	$35,560
CO: Denver	$35,590	OH: Cincinnati	$24,920
DC: Washington	$35,480	OH: Cleveland	$33,150
FL: Miami	$36,460	OH: Columbus	$40,790
FL: Orlando	$28,170	OR: Portland	$33,080
FL: Tampa	$30,180	PA: Philadelphia	$39,670
GA: Atlanta	$30,330	PA: Pittsburgh	$27,170
IL: Chicago	$40,490	TX: Dallas	$28,760
MA: Boston	$34,150	TX: Houston	$37,300
MD: Baltimore	$31,950	WA: Seattle	$37,840

FACTORS THAT MAY AFFECT EARNINGS

Educational Attainment of Workers and Effect on Earnings

Figures are based on a group of occupations: Other Teachers and Instructors

	Percent at Level	Effect on Earnings
Less than High School	—	—
Some High School	4.8%	−73.5%
High School or Equivalent	17.2%	−14.8%
Some College but No Degree	21.5%	−13.7%
Associate Degree	10.0%	−3.2%
Bachelor's Degree	29.4%	17.5%
Master's Degree	14.0%	28.1%
Doctoral Degree	1.6%	29.9%
First Professional Degree	—	—

Flexibility of Earnings

Average Hours Worked: 25
Workers with a Varying Number of Hours: 11.9%
Workers Earning Some Overtime Pay, Tips, or Commissions: 5.8%
Earnings Benefit of Working Overtime: 2.9%

Gender

	Male	Female
Percent	35.1%	64.9%
Effect on Earnings	18.8%	−12.7%

Union Membership

Percentage Union Members: 8.7%
Earnings Benefit of Union Membership: 33.9%

Veteran Status

Percentage Who Have Been on Active Duty: 9.5%
Earnings Benefit of Veteran Status: 34.1%

25-3099 Teachers and Instructors, All Other

All teachers and instructors not listed separately.

- Education or Training Required: Bachelor's degree
- Job Growth: 14.9%
- Annual Openings: 169,000
- Self-Employed: 17.2%
- Part-Time: 53.6%

NATIONAL WAGE FIGURES (ANNUAL)

Beginning	25th Percentile	Median	Mean	75th Percentile	90th Percentile
$16,210	$20,660	$28,660	$35,370	$44,320	$63,560

Note: The mean is significantly higher than the median because of the presence of a few star earners.

Median Wages for Industries Employing Largest Numbers (Annual)

Industry	Median Income
Motion Picture and Sound Recording Industries	$77,640
Computer and Electronic Product Manufacturing	$64,580
Publishing Industries (Except Internet)	$56,810
Merchant Wholesalers, Durable Goods	$55,790
Air Transportation	$54,380
Machinery Manufacturing	$52,530
Funds, Trusts, and Other Financial Vehicles	$51,520
Federal, State, and Local Government	$50,780
Merchant Wholesalers, Nondurable Goods	$45,870
Internet Service Providers, Web Search Portals, and Data-Processing Services	$45,100

Median Wages for States (Annual)

State	Wage	State	Wage	State	Wage
AK	$38,550	KY	$24,550	NY	$30,730
AL	$27,460	LA	$42,540	OH	$45,540
AR	$25,890	MA	$30,060	OK	$16,000
AZ	$28,880	MD	$49,850	OR	$36,950
CA	$41,550	ME	$20,800	PA	$35,770
CO	$36,140	MI	$51,790	RI	$30,800
CT	$47,990	MN	$37,010	SC	$20,450
DC	$34,690	MO	$23,690	SD	$41,110
DE	$52,570	MS	$21,390	TN	$31,640
FL	$25,000	MT	$17,880	TX	$17,920
GA	$18,990	NC	$20,710	UT	$19,260
HI	$43,450	ND	$42,790	VA	$26,230
IA	$29,590	NE	$37,970	VT	$21,350
ID	$36,230	NH	$25,470	WA	$31,540
IL	$35,350	NJ	$24,630	WI	$29,650
IN	$21,820	NM	$50,430	WV	$29,970
KS	$24,850	NV	$28,680	WY	$31,070

Median Wages for the Largest Metropolitan Areas (Annual)

Area	Wage	Area	Wage
AZ: Phoenix	$26,330	MI: Detroit	no data
CA: Los Angeles	$38,940	MN: Minneapolis	$34,850
CA: Riverside	$44,920	MO: Kansas City	$26,470
CA: Sacramento	$42,260	MO: St. Louis	$26,210
CA: San Diego	$35,100	NV: Las Vegas	$34,960
CA: San Francisco	$43,640	NY: New York	$31,810
CO: Denver	$39,690	OH: Cincinnati	$28,260
DC: Washington	$39,920	OH: Cleveland	$47,920
FL: Miami	$22,420	OH: Columbus	$51,510
FL: Orlando	$28,190	OR: Portland	$34,200
FL: Tampa	no data	PA: Philadelphia	$26,180
GA: Atlanta	$19,140	PA: Pittsburgh	$35,840
IL: Chicago	$31,620	TX: Dallas	$19,110
MA: Boston	$27,040	TX: Houston	$18,190
MD: Baltimore	$50,210	WA: Seattle	$32,880

FACTORS THAT MAY AFFECT EARNINGS

Educational Attainment of Workers and Effect on Earnings

Figures are based on a group of occupations: Other Teachers and Instructors

	Percent at Level	Effect on Earnings
Less than High School	—	—
Some High School	4.8%	−73.5%
High School or Equivalent	17.2%	−14.8%
Some College but No Degree	21.5%	−13.7%
Associate Degree	10.0%	−3.2%
Bachelor's Degree	29.4%	17.5%
Master's Degree	14.0%	28.1%
Doctoral Degree	1.6%	29.9%
First Professional Degree	—	—

Flexibility of Earnings

Average Hours Worked: 25
Workers with a Varying Number of Hours: 11.9%
Workers Earning Some Overtime Pay, Tips, or Commissions: 5.8%
Earnings Benefit of Working Overtime: 2.9%

Gender

	Male	Female
Percent	35.1%	64.9%
Effect on Earnings	18.8%	−12.7%

Union Membership

Percentage Union Members: 8.7%
Earnings Benefit of Union Membership: 33.9%

Veteran Status

Percentage Who Have Been on Active Duty: 9.5%
Earnings Benefit of Veteran Status: 34.1%

25-4000 Librarians, Curators, and Archivists

25-4011 Archivists

Appraise, edit, and direct safekeeping of permanent records and historically valuable documents. Participate in research activities based on archival materials.

- Education or Training Required: Master's degree
- Job Growth: 13.4%
- Annual Openings: 1,000
- Self-Employed: 6.5%
- Part-Time: 32.4%

NATIONAL WAGE FIGURES (ANNUAL)

Beginning	25th Percentile	Median	Mean	75th Percentile	90th Percentile
$23,890	$30,610	$40,730	$44,400	$53,990	$73,060

Median Wages for Industries Employing Largest Numbers (Annual)

Industry	Median Income
Management of Companies and Enterprises	$49,600
Publishing Industries (Except Internet)	$48,170
Federal, State, and Local Government	$46,830
Motion Picture and Sound Recording Industries	$43,560
Professional, Scientific, and Technical Services	$42,370
Performing Arts, Spectator Sports, and Related Industries	$42,230
Other Information Services	$41,280
Administrative and Support Services	$40,740
Educational Services	$40,690
Hospitals	$38,200

Median Wages for States (Annual)

AK	no data	KY	$36,470	NY	$41,480
AL	$49,330	LA	$36,760	OH	$31,180
AR	$40,540	MA	$45,670	OK	$31,530
AZ	$47,360	MD	$59,340	OR	$45,210
CA	$40,020	ME	no data	PA	$37,810
CO	$43,430	MI	$39,080	RI	$48,210
CT	$30,710	MN	$41,150	SC	$32,130
DC	$61,610	MO	$49,840	SD	no data
DE	$39,130	MS	$41,780	TN	$31,780
FL	$32,580	MT	no data	TX	$40,360
GA	$46,650	NC	$31,650	UT	$39,970
HI	$43,710	ND	no data	VA	$47,040
IA	no data	NE	no data	VT	no data
ID	no data	NH	no data	WA	$39,290
IL	$39,870	NJ	$28,990	WI	$46,090
IN	$27,790	NM	$39,330	WV	no data
KS	$27,580	NV	no data	WY	$34,690

Median Wages for the Largest Metropolitan Areas (Annual)

AZ: Phoenix	$46,380	MI: Detroit	$42,190
CA: Los Angeles	$36,880	MN: Minneapolis	$42,280
CA: Riverside	no data	MO: Kansas City	$37,340
CA: Sacramento	no data	MO: St. Louis	$52,510
CA: San Diego	no data	NV: Las Vegas	no data
CA: San Francisco	$43,300	NY: New York	$42,620
CO: Denver	$43,960	OH: Cincinnati	no data
DC: Washington	$66,400	OH: Cleveland	no data
FL: Miami	$30,160	OH: Columbus	no data
FL: Orlando	no data	OR: Portland	no data
FL: Tampa	$31,300	PA: Philadelphia	$39,620
GA: Atlanta	$51,580	PA: Pittsburgh	no data
IL: Chicago	$38,960	TX: Dallas	$37,940
MA: Boston	$48,330	TX: Houston	$43,130
MD: Baltimore	$41,650	WA: Seattle	$37,120

FACTORS THAT MAY AFFECT EARNINGS

Educational Attainment of Workers and Effect on Earnings

Figures are based on a group of occupations: Librarians, Curators, and Archivists

	Percent at Level	Effect on Earnings
Less than High School	—	—
Some High School	2.8%	−82.6%
High School or Equivalent	10.2%	−34.6%
Some College but No Degree	14.6%	−50.9%
Associate Degree	7.7%	−30.2%
Bachelor's Degree	24.6%	1.1%
Master's Degree	36.2%	33.2%
Doctoral Degree	—	—
First Professional Degree	—	—

Flexibility of Earnings

Average Hours Worked: 31
Workers with a Varying Number of Hours: 4.1%
Workers Earning Some Overtime Pay, Tips, or Commissions: 2.7%
Earnings Benefit of Working Overtime: 1.3%

Gender

	Male	Female
Percent	18.4%	81.6%
Effect on Earnings	18.3%	−6.8%

Union Membership

Percentage Union Members: 21.4%
Earnings Benefit of Union Membership: 33.0%

Veteran Status

Percentage Who Have Been on Active Duty: Insignificant
Earnings Benefit of Veteran Status: No significant data available

25-4012 Curators

Administer affairs of museum and conduct research programs. Direct instructional, research, and public service activities of institution.

- Education or Training Required: Master's degree
- Job Growth: 15.7%
- Annual Openings: 1,000
- Self-Employed: 6.4%
- Part-Time: 32.4%

NATIONAL WAGE FIGURES (ANNUAL)

Beginning	25th Percentile	Median	Mean	75th Percentile	90th Percentile
$26,320	$34,410	$46,300	$49,980	$61,740	$80,030

Median Wages for Industries Employing Largest Numbers (Annual)

Industry	Median Income
Other Information Services	$59,080
Amusement, Gambling, and Recreation Industries	$55,440
Professional, Scientific, and Technical Services	$52,800
Educational Services	$49,320
Federal, State, and Local Government	$48,450
Museums, Historical Sites, and Similar Institutions	$43,670
Performing Arts, Spectator Sports, and Related Industries	$43,570
Religious, Grantmaking, Civic, Professional, and Similar Organizations	$43,130

Median Wages for States (Annual)

AK	no data	KY	$39,840	NY	$56,060
AL	$38,510	LA	$30,210	OH	$38,290
AR	$29,770	MA	$54,050	OK	$36,690
AZ	$42,760	MD	$47,970	OR	$36,580
CA	$54,700	ME	$42,240	PA	$47,130
CO	$50,800	MI	$45,940	RI	$52,910
CT	$59,250	MN	$54,060	SC	$40,400
DC	$69,540	MO	$41,690	SD	$37,600
DE	$56,530	MS	$35,900	TN	$43,420
FL	$50,140	MT	$27,770	TX	$45,000
GA	$41,670	NC	$36,410	UT	$46,300
HI	no data	ND	no data	VA	$46,430
IA	$48,020	NE	$42,660	VT	no data
ID	no data	NH	$50,370	WA	$50,480
IL	$55,750	NJ	$39,950	WI	$44,410
IN	$40,230	NM	$45,260	WV	$79,670
KS	$32,430	NV	$47,150	WY	$25,960

Median Wages for the Largest Metropolitan Areas (Annual)

AZ: Phoenix	$36,180	MI: Detroit	$47,020
CA: Los Angeles	$55,650	MN: Minneapolis	$58,390
CA: Riverside	$58,750	MO: Kansas City	$50,090
CA: Sacramento	$39,270	MO: St. Louis	$49,000
CA: San Diego	$60,900	NV: Las Vegas	no data
CA: San Francisco	$61,080	NY: New York	$61,060
CO: Denver	no data	OH: Cincinnati	$18,580
DC: Washington	$56,520	OH: Cleveland	$41,840
FL: Miami	$52,110	OH: Columbus	$38,880
FL: Orlando	$53,420	OR: Portland	$42,290
FL: Tampa	no data	PA: Philadelphia	$53,910
GA: Atlanta	$52,090	PA: Pittsburgh	$47,510
IL: Chicago	$57,780	TX: Dallas	$46,370
MA: Boston	$58,590	TX: Houston	$43,730
MD: Baltimore	$59,100	WA: Seattle	$57,090

FACTORS THAT MAY AFFECT EARNINGS

Educational Attainment of Workers and Effect on Earnings

Figures are based on a group of occupations: Librarians, Curators, and Archivists

	Percent at Level	Effect on Earnings
Less than High School	—	—
Some High School	2.8%	−82.6%
High School or Equivalent	10.2%	−34.6%
Some College but No Degree	14.6%	−50.9%
Associate Degree	7.7%	−30.2%
Bachelor's Degree	24.6%	1.1%
Master's Degree	36.2%	33.2%
Doctoral Degree	—	—
First Professional Degree	—	—

Flexibility of Earnings

Average Hours Worked: 31
Workers with a Varying Number of Hours: 4.1%
Workers Earning Some Overtime Pay, Tips, or Commissions: 2.7%
Earnings Benefit of Working Overtime: 1.3%

Gender

	Male	Female
Percent	18.4%	81.6%
Effect on Earnings	18.3%	−6.8%

Union Membership

Percentage Union Members: 21.4%
Earnings Benefit of Union Membership: 33.0%

Veteran Status

Percentage Who Have Been on Active Duty: Insignificant
Earnings Benefit of Veteran Status: No significant data available

25-4013 Museum Technicians and Conservators

Prepare specimens, such as fossils, skeletal parts, lace, and textiles, for museum collection and exhibits. May restore documents or install, arrange, and exhibit materials.

- Education or Training Required: Bachelor's degree
- Job Growth: 14.1%
- Annual Openings: 2,000
- Self-Employed: 9.4%
- Part-Time: 32.4%

NATIONAL WAGE FIGURES (ANNUAL)

Beginning	25th Percentile	Median	Mean	75th Percentile	90th Percentile
$20,600	$26,360	$34,340	$38,060	$46,120	$61,270

Median Wages for Industries Employing Largest Numbers (Annual)

Industry	Median Income
Other Information Services	$42,100
Performing Arts, Spectator Sports, and Related Industries	$39,010
Professional, Scientific, and Technical Services	$37,780
Educational Services	$36,060
Federal, State, and Local Government	$35,540
Museums, Historical Sites, and Similar Institutions	$32,030
Religious, Grantmaking, Civic, Professional, and Similar Organizations	$28,290

Median Wages for States (Annual)

AK	no data	KY	$29,460	NY	$42,100
AL	$29,770	LA	$22,210	OH	$28,640
AR	$27,060	MA	$39,520	OK	$27,280
AZ	$30,650	MD	$43,580	OR	$28,600
CA	$37,710	ME	$28,010	PA	$35,070
CO	$35,920	MI	$24,960	RI	$28,970
CT	$40,320	MN	$35,720	SC	$27,770
DC	$53,270	MO	$30,580	SD	$25,510
DE	no data	MS	no data	TN	$28,940
FL	$33,640	MT	no data	TX	$32,900
GA	$32,400	NC	$33,500	UT	$29,550
HI	no data	ND	no data	VA	$33,070
IA	$32,230	NE	$24,880	VT	$30,480
ID	no data	NH	$41,340	WA	$31,280
IL	$33,490	NJ	$18,350	WI	$38,270
IN	$33,790	NM	$31,840	WV	$24,640
KS	$28,960	NV	no data	WY	no data

Median Wages for the Largest Metropolitan Areas (Annual)

AZ: Phoenix	$32,280	MI: Detroit	no data
CA: Los Angeles	$43,840	MN: Minneapolis	no data
CA: Riverside	$37,090	MO: Kansas City	$31,040
CA: Sacramento	no data	MO: St. Louis	$30,050
CA: San Diego	$30,520	NV: Las Vegas	no data
CA: San Francisco	$41,300	NY: New York	$42,310
CO: Denver	no data	OH: Cincinnati	no data
DC: Washington	$50,110	OH: Cleveland	no data
FL: Miami	$35,860	OH: Columbus	no data
FL: Orlando	no data	OR: Portland	$28,010
FL: Tampa	$26,570	PA: Philadelphia	$31,340
GA: Atlanta	$34,490	PA: Pittsburgh	$39,440
IL: Chicago	$33,220	TX: Dallas	$34,910
MA: Boston	$39,630	TX: Houston	$41,630
MD: Baltimore	$43,470	WA: Seattle	$31,990

FACTORS THAT MAY AFFECT EARNINGS

Educational Attainment of Workers and Effect on Earnings

Figures are based on a group of occupations: Librarians, Curators, and Archivists

	Percent at Level	Effect on Earnings
Less than High School	—	—
Some High School	2.8%	−82.6%
High School or Equivalent	10.2%	−34.6%
Some College but No Degree	14.6%	−50.9%
Associate Degree	7.7%	−30.2%
Bachelor's Degree	24.6%	1.1%
Master's Degree	36.2%	33.2%
Doctoral Degree	—	—
First Professional Degree	—	—

Flexibility of Earnings

Average Hours Worked: 31
Workers with a Varying Number of Hours: 4.1%
Workers Earning Some Overtime Pay, Tips, or Commissions: 2.7%
Earnings Benefit of Working Overtime: 1.3%

Gender

	Male	Female
Percent	18.4%	81.6%
Effect on Earnings	18.3%	−6.8%

Union Membership

Percentage Union Members: 21.4%
Earnings Benefit of Union Membership: 33.0%

Veteran Status

Percentage Who Have Been on Active Duty: Insignificant
Earnings Benefit of Veteran Status: No significant data available

25-4021 Librarians

Administer libraries and perform related library services. Work in a variety of settings, including public libraries, schools, colleges and universities, museums, corporations, government agencies, law firms, non-profit organizations, and health care providers. Tasks may include selecting, acquiring, cataloguing, classifying, circulating, and maintaining library materials and furnishing reference, bibliographical, and readers' advisory services. May perform in-depth, strategic research and synthesize, analyze, edit, and filter information. May set up or work with databases and information systems to catalogue and access information.

- Education or Training Required: Master's degree
- Job Growth: 4.9%
- Annual Openings: 8,000
- Self-Employed: 0.0%
- Part-Time: 27.3%

NATIONAL WAGE FIGURES (ANNUAL)

Beginning	25th Percentile	Median	Mean	75th Percentile	90th Percentile
$30,930	$39,250	$49,060	$50,860	$60,800	$74,670

Median Wages for Industries Employing Largest Numbers (Annual)

Industry	Median Income
Motion Picture and Sound Recording Industries	$61,470
Securities, Commodity Contracts, and Other Financial Investments and Related Activities	$57,530
Broadcasting (Except Internet)	$57,270
Monetary Authorities - —Central Bank	$56,990
Management of Companies and Enterprises	$56,870
Transportation Equipment Manufacturing	$56,520
Computer and Electronic Product Manufacturing	$56,420
Professional, Scientific, and Technical Services	$54,920
Credit Intermediation and Related Activities	$54,250
Chemical Manufacturing	$53,600

Median Wages for States (Annual)

State	Wage	State	Wage	State	Wage
AK	$53,960	KY	$47,000	NY	$52,690
AL	$42,600	LA	$42,580	OH	$51,010
AR	$44,280	MA	$55,270	OK	$36,750
AZ	$40,570	MD	$52,250	OR	$52,340
CA	$58,960	ME	$41,010	PA	$49,180
CO	$52,350	MI	$50,420	RI	$56,540
CT	$56,270	MN	$50,570	SC	$45,100
DC	$59,440	MO	$45,740	SD	$31,520
DE	$56,040	MS	$40,140	TN	$41,380
FL	$47,830	MT	$36,320	TX	$46,950
GA	$55,480	NC	$44,750	UT	$42,090
HI	$51,700	ND	$39,400	VA	$54,420
IA	$42,250	NE	$44,800	VT	$34,960
ID	$39,180	NH	$42,530	WA	$56,390
IL	$51,640	NJ	$57,520	WI	$47,330
IN	$44,880	NM	$42,170	WV	$41,340
KS	$41,490	NV	$55,300	WY	$40,280

Median Wages for the Largest Metropolitan Areas (Annual)

Area	Wage	Area	Wage
AZ: Phoenix	$41,620	MI: Detroit	$48,690
CA: Los Angeles	$61,060	MN: Minneapolis	$52,030
CA: Riverside	$53,990	MO: Kansas City	$46,650
CA: Sacramento	$54,130	MO: St. Louis	$47,770
CA: San Diego	$56,100	NV: Las Vegas	$55,270
CA: San Francisco	$61,630	NY: New York	$55,810
CO: Denver	$53,970	OH: Cincinnati	$49,900
DC: Washington	$60,580	OH: Cleveland	$48,070
FL: Miami	$49,490	OH: Columbus	$53,420
FL: Orlando	$47,170	OR: Portland	$54,480
FL: Tampa	$49,550	PA: Philadelphia	$52,260
GA: Atlanta	$57,610	PA: Pittsburgh	$44,910
IL: Chicago	$54,990	TX: Dallas	$47,660
MA: Boston	$56,350	TX: Houston	$48,260
MD: Baltimore	$48,380	WA: Seattle	$58,760

FACTORS THAT MAY AFFECT EARNINGS

Educational Attainment of Workers and Effect on Earnings

	Percent at Level	Effect on Earnings
Less than High School	—	—
Some High School	—	—
High School or Equivalent	8.7%	−25.8%
Some College but No Degree	10.2%	−42.7%
Associate Degree	7.2%	−34.7%
Bachelor's Degree	24.9%	−8.6%
Master's Degree	44.2%	22.4%
Doctoral Degree	—	—
First Professional Degree	2.3%	22.6%

Flexibility of Earnings

Average Hours Worked: 33
Workers with a Varying Number of Hours: 4.2%
Workers Earning Some Overtime Pay, Tips, or Commissions: 2.7%
Earnings Benefit of Working Overtime: 1.3%

Gender

	Male	Female
Percent	15.8%	84.2%
Effect on Earnings	—	−4.0%

Union Membership

Percentage Union Members: 24.5%
Earnings Benefit of Union Membership: 30.2%

Veteran Status

Percentage Who Have Been on Active Duty: Insignificant
Earnings Benefit of Veteran Status: No significant data available

25-4031 Library Technicians

Assist librarians by helping readers in the use of library catalogs, databases, and indexes to locate books and other materials and by answering questions that require only brief consultation of standard reference. Compile records; sort and shelve books; remove or repair damaged books; register patrons; check materials in and out of the circulation process. Replace materials in shelving area (stacks) or files. Includes bookmobile drivers who operate bookmobiles or light trucks that pull trailers to specific locations on a predetermined schedule and assist with providing services in mobile libraries.

- Education or Training Required: Postsecondary vocational training
- Job Growth: 13.4%
- Annual Openings: 25,000
- Self-Employed: 0.2%
- Part-Time: 58.3%

NATIONAL WAGE FIGURES (ANNUAL)

Beginning	25th Percentile	Median	Mean	75th Percentile	90th Percentile
$15,820	$20,220	$26,560	$27,910	$34,280	$42,850

Median Wages for Industries Employing Largest Numbers (Annual)

Industry	Median Income
Management of Companies and Enterprises	$37,970
Professional, Scientific, and Technical Services	$35,030
Broadcasting (Except Internet)	$32,610
Motion Picture and Sound Recording Industries	$32,020
Hospitals	$31,200
Religious, Grantmaking, Civic, Professional, and Similar Organizations	$30,540
Publishing Industries (Except Internet)	$28,630
Museums, Historical Sites, and Similar Institutions	$28,500
Administrative and Support Services	$27,880
Educational Services	$27,100

Median Wages for States (Annual)

State	Wage	State	Wage	State	Wage
AK	$36,550	KY	$23,370	NY	$26,160
AL	$19,930	LA	$24,270	OH	$27,790
AR	$22,690	MA	$32,650	OK	$17,110
AZ	$25,070	MD	$33,280	OR	$30,500
CA	$32,860	ME	$26,510	PA	$24,710
CO	$28,060	MI	$24,780	RI	$30,590
CT	$31,370	MN	$33,970	SC	$21,210
DC	$38,330	MO	$26,280	SD	$22,100
DE	$29,400	MS	$20,840	TN	$22,760
FL	$26,640	MT	$20,000	TX	$23,420
GA	$24,910	NC	$27,260	UT	$23,080
HI	$31,390	ND	$22,130	VA	$31,400
IA	$19,780	NE	$21,610	VT	$25,010
ID	$21,830	NH	$27,640	WA	$33,920
IL	$22,840	NJ	$28,730	WI	$24,470
IN	$22,850	NM	$21,070	WV	$23,690
KS	$22,050	NV	no data	WY	$19,090

Median Wages for the Largest Metropolitan Areas (Annual)

Area	Wage	Area	Wage
AZ: Phoenix	$25,010	MI: Detroit	$27,800
CA: Los Angeles	$33,710	MN: Minneapolis	$35,690
CA: Riverside	$31,720	MO: Kansas City	$26,730
CA: Sacramento	$33,040	MO: St. Louis	$26,880
CA: San Diego	$34,000	NV: Las Vegas	no data
CA: San Francisco	$37,810	NY: New York	$28,730
CO: Denver	$29,650	OH: Cincinnati	$26,120
DC: Washington	$38,020	OH: Cleveland	$32,480
FL: Miami	$29,850	OH: Columbus	$32,010
FL: Orlando	$27,570	OR: Portland	$34,800
FL: Tampa	$24,970	PA: Philadelphia	$27,150
GA: Atlanta	$26,700	PA: Pittsburgh	$20,720
IL: Chicago	$23,630	TX: Dallas	$25,910
MA: Boston	$34,680	TX: Houston	$25,900
MD: Baltimore	$32,860	WA: Seattle	$35,170

FACTORS THAT MAY AFFECT EARNINGS

Educational Attainment of Workers and Effect on Earnings

	Percent at Level	Effect on Earnings
Less than High School	—	—
Some High School	12.5%	−84.0%
High School or Equivalent	10.7%	−29.2%
Some College but No Degree	39.3%	−27.4%
Associate Degree	12.5%	−15.8%
Bachelor's Degree	12.5%	39.4%
Master's Degree	12.5%	171.4%
Doctoral Degree	—	—
First Professional Degree	—	—

Flexibility of Earnings

Average Hours Worked: 21
Workers with a Varying Number of Hours: 3.6%
Workers Earning Some Overtime Pay, Tips, or Commissions: 1.8%
Earnings Benefit of Working Overtime: 1.3%

Gender

	Male	Female
Percent	29.6%	70.4%
Effect on Earnings	18.3%	−6.8%

Union Membership

Percentage Union Members: 14.0%
Earnings Benefit of Union Membership: 33.0%

Veteran Status

Percentage Who Have Been on Active Duty: Insignificant
Earnings Benefit of Veteran Status: No significant data available

25-9000 Other Education, Training, and Library Occupations

25-9011 Audio-Visual Collections Specialists

Prepare, plan, and operate audiovisual teaching aids for use in education. May record, catalogue, and file audiovisual materials.

- Education or Training Required: Moderate-term on-the-job training
- Job Growth: 18.6%
- Annual Openings: 1,000
- Self-Employed: 3.8%
- Part-Time: 39.3%

NATIONAL WAGE FIGURES (ANNUAL)

Beginning	25th Percentile	Median	Mean	75th Percentile	90th Percentile
$22,170	$29,290	$40,530	$42,090	$54,190	$65,610

Median Wages for Industries Employing Largest Numbers (Annual)

Industry	Median Income
Educational Services	$40,940
Hospitals	$39,130
Museums, Historical Sites, and Similar Institutions	$36,850
Federal, State, and Local Government	$36,640
Social Assistance	$36,350
Merchant Wholesalers, Nondurable Goods	$29,270

Median Wages for States (Annual)

State	Wage	State	Wage	State	Wage
AK	no data	KY	no data	NY	$31,100
AL	$21,930	LA	no data	OH	$47,520
AR	no data	MA	$43,380	OK	$34,630
AZ	$28,060	MD	$35,490	OR	$26,370
CA	$38,260	ME	$29,160	PA	$32,580
CO	no data	MI	$35,240	RI	no data
CT	$55,100	MN	$54,030	SC	$23,160
DC	$32,910	MO	$30,760	SD	no data
DE	no data	MS	no data	TN	$37,920
FL	$40,120	MT	no data	TX	$44,750
GA	$35,160	NC	$31,780	UT	$29,180
HI	$34,490	ND	no data	VA	$34,770
IA	$32,260	NE	no data	VT	no data
ID	$50,500	NH	no data	WA	$38,250
IL	$32,030	NJ	$42,540	WI	$39,010
IN	$30,980	NM	no data	WV	no data
KS	no data	NV	no data	WY	no data

Median Wages for the Largest Metropolitan Areas (Annual)

Area	Wage	Area	Wage
AZ: Phoenix	$31,520	MI: Detroit	$27,790
CA: Los Angeles	$38,160	MN: Minneapolis	$56,090
CA: Riverside	$41,250	MO: Kansas City	no data
CA: Sacramento	$52,730	MO: St. Louis	$38,310
CA: San Diego	$36,610	NV: Las Vegas	no data
CA: San Francisco	$42,970	NY: New York	$39,180
CO: Denver	no data	OH: Cincinnati	$51,050
DC: Washington	$34,180	OH: Cleveland	$46,960
FL: Miami	no data	OH: Columbus	$49,860
FL: Orlando	no data	OR: Portland	$36,500
FL: Tampa	no data	PA: Philadelphia	$35,580
GA: Atlanta	$31,660	PA: Pittsburgh	no data
IL: Chicago	$33,110	TX: Dallas	$52,400
MA: Boston	$49,390	TX: Houston	$48,490
MD: Baltimore	no data	WA: Seattle	$37,360

FACTORS THAT MAY AFFECT EARNINGS

Educational Attainment of Workers and Effect on Earnings

	Percent at Level	Effect on Earnings
Less than High School	—	—
Some High School	—	—
High School or Equivalent	5.9%	−42.3%
Some College but No Degree	9.9%	−42.5%
Associate Degree	6.9%	9.5%
Bachelor's Degree	31.7%	−6.2%
Master's Degree	38.6%	12.4%
Doctoral Degree	—	—
First Professional Degree	—	—

Figures do not total 100% because some levels have a very small sample size.

Flexibility of Earnings

Average Hours Worked: 29
Workers with a Varying Number of Hours: 4.7%
Workers Earning Some Overtime Pay, Tips, or Commissions: 7.6%
Earnings Benefit of Working Overtime: 22.5%

Gender

	Male	Female
Percent	8.3%	91.7%
Effect on Earnings	18.3%	−6.8%

Union Membership

Percentage Union Members: 17.6%
Earnings Benefit of Union Membership: 15.8%

Veteran Status

Percentage Who Have Been on Active Duty: Insignificant
Earnings Benefit of Veteran Status: No significant data available

25-9021 Farm and Home Management Advisors

Advise, instruct, and assist individuals and families engaged in agriculture, agricultural-related processes, or home economics activities. Demonstrate procedures and apply research findings to solve problems; instruct and train in product development, sales, and the utilization of machinery and equipment to promote general welfare. Includes county agricultural agents, feed and farm management advisers, home economists, and extension service advisors.

- Education or Training Required: Bachelor's degree
- Job Growth: 7.7%
- Annual Openings: 2,000
- Self-Employed: 3.8%
- Part-Time: 39.3%

NATIONAL WAGE FIGURES (ANNUAL)

Beginning	25th Percentile	Median	Mean	75th Percentile	90th Percentile
$21,560	$30,750	$41,710	$46,990	$55,690	$73,520

Median Wages for Industries Employing Largest Numbers (Annual)

Industry	Median Income
Professional, Scientific, and Technical Services	$54,500
Food Manufacturing	$45,670
Educational Services	$45,050
Religious, Grantmaking, Civic, Professional, and Similar Organizations	$39,120
Management of Companies and Enterprises	$35,020
Social Assistance	$32,460
Federal, State, and Local Government	$24,120

Median Wages for States (Annual)

AK	no data	KY	no data	NY	$36,780
AL	$50,650	LA	no data	OH	$39,320
AR	no data	MA	no data	OK	$35,180
AZ	no data	MD	no data	OR	$53,970
CA	$53,420	ME	no data	PA	no data
CO	no data	MI	no data	RI	no data
CT	no data	MN	$37,760	SC	$34,510
DC	no data	MO	no data	SD	no data
DE	no data	MS	$25,970	TN	$18,550
FL	$39,320	MT	no data	TX	$25,800
GA	$21,530	NC	$43,650	UT	no data
HI	no data	ND	$40,120	VA	$44,680
IA	$35,210	NE	$47,510	VT	no data
ID	$34,010	NH	no data	WA	$36,730
IL	no data	NJ	$50,830	WI	$43,680
IN	no data	NM	no data	WV	$37,530
KS	$42,610	NV	no data	WY	$39,730

Median Wages for the Largest Metropolitan Areas (Annual)

AZ: Phoenix	no data	MI: Detroit	no data
CA: Los Angeles	$58,870	MN: Minneapolis	$38,500
CA: Riverside	no data	MO: Kansas City	no data
CA: Sacramento	no data	MO: St. Louis	no data
CA: San Diego	no data	NV: Las Vegas	no data
CA: San Francisco	$44,370	NY: New York	$60,340
CO: Denver	no data	OH: Cincinnati	no data
DC: Washington	$55,520	OH: Cleveland	no data
FL: Miami	$39,080	OH: Columbus	no data
FL: Orlando	$41,590	OR: Portland	$52,240
FL: Tampa	$44,740	PA: Philadelphia	no data
GA: Atlanta	$22,950	PA: Pittsburgh	no data
IL: Chicago	$60,240	TX: Dallas	$22,770
MA: Boston	no data	TX: Houston	$30,280
MD: Baltimore	no data	WA: Seattle	$33,100

FACTORS THAT MAY AFFECT EARNINGS

Educational Attainment of Workers and Effect on Earnings

	Percent at Level	Effect on Earnings
Less than High School	—	—
Some High School	—	—
High School or Equivalent	5.9%	−42.3%
Some College but No Degree	9.9%	−42.5%
Associate Degree	6.9%	9.5%
Bachelor's Degree	31.7%	−6.2%
Master's Degree	38.6%	12.4%
Doctoral Degree	—	—
First Professional Degree	—	—

Figures do not total 100% because some levels have a very small sample size.

Flexibility of Earnings

Average Hours Worked: 29
Workers with a Varying Number of Hours: 4.7%
Workers Earning Some Overtime Pay, Tips, or Commissions: 7.6%
Earnings Benefit of Working Overtime: 22.5%

Gender

	Male	Female
Percent	8.3%	91.7%
Effect on Earnings	18.3%	−6.8%

Union Membership

Percentage Union Members: 17.6%
Earnings Benefit of Union Membership: 15.8%

Veteran Status

Percentage Who Have Been on Active Duty: Insignificant
Earnings Benefit of Veteran Status: No significant data available

25-9031 Instructional Coordinators

Develop instructional material, coordinate educational content, and incorporate current technology in specialized fields that provide guidelines to educators and instructors for developing curricula and conducting courses.

- Education or Training Required: Master's degree
- Job Growth: 27.5%
- Annual Openings: 15,000
- Self-Employed: 3.1%
- Part-Time: 39.3%

NATIONAL WAGE FIGURES (ANNUAL)

Beginning	25th Percentile	Median	Mean	75th Percentile	90th Percentile
$29,040	$38,800	$52,790	$55,570	$70,320	$87,510

Median Wages for Industries Employing Largest Numbers (Annual)

Industry	Median Income
Machinery Manufacturing	$69,450
Merchant Wholesalers, Durable Goods	$68,830
Computer and Electronic Product Manufacturing	$65,000
Publishing Industries (Except Internet)	$61,290
Professional, Scientific, and Technical Services	$59,440
Internet Publishing and Broadcasting	$57,900
Federal, State, and Local Government	$57,050
Hospitals	$55,260
Insurance Carriers and Related Activities	$54,560
Educational Services	$54,320

Median Wages for States (Annual)

State	Wage	State	Wage	State	Wage
AK	$47,310	KY	$50,720	NY	$57,670
AL	$55,140	LA	$42,870	OH	$57,020
AR	$50,020	MA	$58,810	OK	$43,130
AZ	$40,650	MD	$50,420	OR	$56,150
CA	$60,010	ME	$47,800	PA	$49,840
CO	$58,810	MI	$58,370	RI	$56,360
CT	$73,700	MN	$58,530	SC	$57,630
DC	$65,860	MO	$47,810	SD	$44,900
DE	$53,010	MS	$47,350	TN	$46,000
FL	$46,320	MT	$37,340	TX	$55,940
GA	$43,650	NC	$48,090	UT	$45,890
HI	$44,530	ND	$52,170	VA	$62,640
IA	$50,210	NE	$51,930	VT	$51,330
ID	$33,870	NH	$53,910	WA	$59,360
IL	$46,850	NJ	$71,120	WI	$54,250
IN	$44,490	NM	$44,720	WV	$44,310
KS	$44,510	NV	$60,920	WY	$50,670

Median Wages for the Largest Metropolitan Areas (Annual)

Area	Wage	Area	Wage
AZ: Phoenix	$40,160	MI: Detroit	$60,180
CA: Los Angeles	$63,050	MN: Minneapolis	$61,540
CA: Riverside	$69,490	MO: Kansas City	$48,780
CA: Sacramento	$68,500	MO: St. Louis	$53,490
CA: San Diego	$46,070	NV: Las Vegas	$59,850
CA: San Francisco	$47,600	NY: New York	$64,020
CO: Denver	$59,190	OH: Cincinnati	$57,840
DC: Washington	$57,250	OH: Cleveland	$61,960
FL: Miami	$46,540	OH: Columbus	$56,130
FL: Orlando	$46,840	OR: Portland	$58,490
FL: Tampa	$51,370	PA: Philadelphia	$54,380
GA: Atlanta	$43,510	PA: Pittsburgh	$57,970
IL: Chicago	$47,230	TX: Dallas	$56,730
MA: Boston	$60,250	TX: Houston	$61,970
MD: Baltimore	$52,620	WA: Seattle	$59,070

FACTORS THAT MAY AFFECT EARNINGS

Educational Attainment of Workers and Effect on Earnings

	Percent at Level	Effect on Earnings
Less than High School	—	—
Some High School	—	—
High School or Equivalent	5.9%	−42.3%
Some College but No Degree	9.9%	−42.5%
Associate Degree	6.9%	9.5%
Bachelor's Degree	31.7%	−6.2%
Master's Degree	38.6%	12.4%
Doctoral Degree	—	—
First Professional Degree	—	—

Figures do not total 100% because some levels have a very small sample size.

Flexibility of Earnings

Average Hours Worked: 29
Workers with a Varying Number of Hours: 4.7%
Workers Earning Some Overtime Pay, Tips, or Commissions: 7.6%
Earnings Benefit of Working Overtime: 22.5%

Gender

	Male	Female
Percent	8.3%	91.7%
Effect on Earnings	18.3%	−6.8%

Union Membership

Percentage Union Members: 17.6%
Earnings Benefit of Union Membership: 15.8%

Veteran Status

Percentage Who Have Been on Active Duty: Insignificant
Earnings Benefit of Veteran Status: No significant data available

25-9041 Teacher Assistants

Perform duties that are instructional in nature or deliver direct services to students or parents. Serve in a position for which a teacher or another professional has ultimate responsibility for the design and implementation of educational programs and services.

- Education or Training Required: Short-term on-the-job training
- Job Growth: 14.1%
- Annual Openings: 252,000
- Self-Employed: 0.2%
- Part-Time: 39.5%

NATIONAL WAGE FIGURES (ANNUAL)

Beginning	25th Percentile	Median	Mean	75th Percentile	90th Percentile
$13,910	$16,430	$20,740	$21,860	$26,160	$31,610

Median Wages for Industries Employing Largest Numbers (Annual)

Industry	Median Income
Professional, Scientific, and Technical Services	$24,450
Management of Companies and Enterprises	$22,870
Nursing and Residential Care Facilities	$22,500
Hospitals	$22,330
Federal, State, and Local Government	$21,880
Educational Services	$21,110
Museums, Historical Sites, and Similar Institutions	$19,910
Ambulatory Health Care Services	$19,690
Religious, Grantmaking, Civic, Professional, and Similar Organizations	$18,760
Administrative and Support Services	$18,650

Median Wages for States (Annual)

AK	$30,270	KY	$19,750	NY	$21,740
AL	$15,740	LA	$14,790	OH	$23,580
AR	$14,680	MA	$23,350	OK	$14,360
AZ	$19,500	MD	$23,950	OR	$24,680
CA	$25,790	ME	$25,290	PA	$18,810
CO	$23,120	MI	$24,120	RI	$24,850
CT	$23,740	MN	$22,870	SC	$16,000
DC	$20,260	MO	$17,170	SD	$20,370
DE	$25,090	MS	$14,060	TN	$17,140
FL	$20,230	MT	$18,710	TX	$16,370
GA	$15,630	NC	$18,070	UT	$20,180
HI	$20,720	ND	$22,770	VA	$21,010
IA	$18,460	NE	$19,720	VT	$21,880
ID	$20,500	NH	$23,080	WA	$26,300
IL	$19,560	NJ	$21,890	WI	$23,860
IN	$19,930	NM	$14,600	WV	$20,670
KS	$18,140	NV	$24,470	WY	$20,400

Median Wages for the Largest Metropolitan Areas (Annual)

AZ: Phoenix	$19,720	MI: Detroit	$25,400
CA: Los Angeles	$25,710	MN: Minneapolis	$23,580
CA: Riverside	$26,370	MO: Kansas City	$17,910
CA: Sacramento	$23,120	MO: St. Louis	$19,230
CA: San Diego	$25,900	NV: Las Vegas	$24,350
CA: San Francisco	$28,970	NY: New York	$22,980
CO: Denver	$24,570	OH: Cincinnati	$22,680
DC: Washington	$26,170	OH: Cleveland	$27,120
FL: Miami	$19,100	OH: Columbus	$25,630
FL: Orlando	$20,550	OR: Portland	$25,800
FL: Tampa	$21,620	PA: Philadelphia	$19,970
GA: Atlanta	$16,470	PA: Pittsburgh	$18,310
IL: Chicago	$20,240	TX: Dallas	$17,270
MA: Boston	$23,680	TX: Houston	$17,120
MD: Baltimore	$22,590	WA: Seattle	$27,400

FACTORS THAT MAY AFFECT EARNINGS

Educational Attainment of Workers and Effect on Earnings

	Percent at Level	Effect on Earnings
Less than High School	—	—
Some High School	3.3%	−49.9%
High School or Equivalent	31.1%	−2.1%
Some College but No Degree	30.0%	−5.7%
Associate Degree	16.8%	−1.1%
Bachelor's Degree	16.4%	22.5%
Master's Degree	2.2%	28.5%
Doctoral Degree	—	—
First Professional Degree	—	—

Flexibility of Earnings

Average Hours Worked: 29
Workers with a Varying Number of Hours: 4.7%
Workers Earning Some Overtime Pay, Tips, or Commissions: 2.3%
Earnings Benefit of Working Overtime: 22.5%

Gender

	Male	Female
Percent	7.7%	92.3%
Effect on Earnings	—	−1.0%

Union Membership

Percentage Union Members: 29.7%
Earnings Benefit of Union Membership: 12.4%

Veteran Status

Percentage Who Have Been on Active Duty: Insignificant
Earnings Benefit of Veteran Status: No significant data available

25-9099 Education, Training, and Library Workers, All Other

All education, training, and library workers not listed separately.

- Education or Training Required: Bachelor's degree
- Job Growth: 20.5%
- Annual Openings: 9,000
- Self-Employed: 3.2%
- Part-Time: 39.5%

NATIONAL WAGE FIGURES (ANNUAL)

Beginning	25th Percentile	Median	Mean	75th Percentile	90th Percentile
$15,530	$21,090	$32,160	$35,640	$44,570	$61,950

Median Wages for Industries Employing Largest Numbers (Annual)

Industry	Median Income
Ambulatory Health Care Services	$52,950
Computer and Electronic Product Manufacturing	$49,690
Hospitals	$47,830
Publishing Industries (Except Internet)	$46,030
Other Information Services	$42,140
Management of Companies and Enterprises	$40,020
Performing Arts, Spectator Sports, and Related Industries	$36,900
Federal, State, and Local Government	$35,460
Merchant Wholesalers, Durable Goods	$33,930
Museums, Historical Sites, and Similar Institutions	$31,820

Median Wages for States (Annual)

State	Wage	State	Wage	State	Wage
AK	no data	KY	$36,280	NY	$45,790
AL	$25,520	LA	$36,370	OH	$28,670
AR	$35,080	MA	$41,250	OK	$15,940
AZ	$29,020	MD	$26,930	OR	$21,970
CA	$34,300	ME	$33,680	PA	$32,970
CO	$42,120	MI	$33,850	RI	$32,390
CT	$49,410	MN	$45,000	SC	$32,240
DC	$28,930	MO	$38,210	SD	$28,100
DE	$33,840	MS	$36,020	TN	$22,630
FL	$37,020	MT	no data	TX	$35,030
GA	$25,400	NC	$37,540	UT	$23,010
HI	$34,120	ND	$18,910	VA	$58,550
IA	$30,020	NE	$35,540	VT	no data
ID	$38,490	NH	$37,660	WA	$39,550
IL	$16,220	NJ	$53,470	WI	$29,600
IN	no data	NM	$28,380	WV	$23,040
KS	$35,160	NV	$42,870	WY	$30,510

Median Wages for the Largest Metropolitan Areas (Annual)

Area	Wage	Area	Wage
AZ: Phoenix	$40,820	MI: Detroit	$33,710
CA: Los Angeles	$31,580	MN: Minneapolis	$42,800
CA: Riverside	$35,970	MO: Kansas City	$40,610
CA: Sacramento	$39,720	MO: St. Louis	$34,400
CA: San Diego	$17,490	NV: Las Vegas	$39,260
CA: San Francisco	$43,590	NY: New York	$52,400
CO: Denver	$43,340	OH: Cincinnati	$28,800
DC: Washington	$34,990	OH: Cleveland	$32,730
FL: Miami	$35,540	OH: Columbus	$34,150
FL: Orlando	$37,860	OR: Portland	no data
FL: Tampa	$35,660	PA: Philadelphia	$37,410
GA: Atlanta	$40,510	PA: Pittsburgh	$33,120
IL: Chicago	$14,750	TX: Dallas	$41,560
MA: Boston	$41,870	TX: Houston	no data
MD: Baltimore	$28,730	WA: Seattle	no data

FACTORS THAT MAY AFFECT EARNINGS

Educational Attainment of Workers and Effect on Earnings

Figures are based on a group of occupations: Other Education, Training, and Library Occupations

	Percent at Level	Effect on Earnings
Less than High School	—	—
Some High School	3.1%	−53.6%
High School or Equivalent	29.1%	−9.1%
Some College but No Degree	28.6%	−12.3%
Associate Degree	15.9%	−4.9%
Bachelor's Degree	17.3%	21.6%
Master's Degree	5.2%	74.1%
Doctoral Degree	—	—
First Professional Degree	—	—

Flexibility of Earnings

Average Hours Worked: 29
Workers with a Varying Number of Hours: 4.7%
Workers Earning Some Overtime Pay, Tips, or Commissions: 3.4%
Earnings Benefit of Working Overtime: 22.5%

Gender

	Male	Female
Percent	8.3%	91.7%
Effect on Earnings	18.3%	−6.8%

Union Membership

Percentage Union Members: 27.3%
Earnings Benefit of Union Membership: 6.4%

Veteran Status

Percentage Who Have Been on Active Duty: Insignificant
Earnings Benefit of Veteran Status: No significant data available

27-0000: Arts, Design, Entertainment, Sports, and Media Occupations

27-1000 Art and Design Workers

27-1011 Art Directors

Formulate design concepts and presentation approaches and direct workers engaged in art work, layout design, and copy writing for visual communications media, such as magazines, books, newspapers, and packaging.

- Education or Training Required: Work experience plus degree
- Job Growth: 11.5%
- Annual Openings: 10,000
- Self-Employed: 55.8%
- Part-Time: 32.0%

Note: A large fraction of the workforce for this occupation is self-employed and earns an average of $33,220. All other earnings figures for this occupation are based on workers who are paid a wage or salary.

NATIONAL WAGE FIGURES (ANNUAL)

Beginning	25th Percentile	Median	Mean	75th Percentile	90th Percentile
$37,920	$49,480	$68,100	$78,420	$94,920	$135,090

Median Wages for Industries Employing Largest Numbers (Annual)

Industry	Median Income
Securities, Commodity Contracts, and Other Financial Investments and Related Activities	$96,380
Internet Service Providers, Web Search Portals, and Data-Processing Services	$90,350
Management of Companies and Enterprises	$82,460
Internet Publishing and Broadcasting	$80,660
Merchant Wholesalers, Nondurable Goods	$79,080
Transportation Equipment Manufacturing	$74,000
Administrative and Support Services	$73,910
Religious, Grantmaking, Civic, Professional, and Similar Organizations	$73,650
Merchant Wholesalers, Durable Goods	$73,340
Computer and Electronic Product Manufacturing	$73,020

Median Wages for States (Annual)

State	Wage	State	Wage	State	Wage
AK	$43,880	KY	$56,140	NY	$91,220
AL	$43,660	LA	$41,090	OH	$65,600
AR	$34,870	MA	no data	OK	$35,310
AZ	$48,130	MD	$62,740	OR	$67,520
CA	$84,870	ME	$52,390	PA	$51,220
CO	$62,570	MI	$60,180	RI	$52,490
CT	$74,520	MN	$66,530	SC	$46,990
DC	$70,800	MO	$55,870	SD	no data
DE	$58,800	MS	$41,570	TN	$49,820
FL	$56,090	MT	$43,160	TX	$58,160
GA	$63,280	NC	$49,470	UT	$59,550
HI	$47,650	ND	$56,700	VA	$65,530
IA	$48,990	NE	$52,460	VT	$83,080
ID	$48,870	NH	$62,320	WA	$75,320
IL	$58,420	NJ	$76,300	WI	$59,440
IN	$50,840	NM	$39,700	WV	$49,030
KS	$44,580	NV	$46,090	WY	no data

Median Wages for the Largest Metropolitan Areas (Annual)

Area	Wage	Area	Wage
AZ: Phoenix	$46,370	MI: Detroit	$64,910
CA: Los Angeles	$87,370	MN: Minneapolis	$69,800
CA: Riverside	$69,590	MO: Kansas City	$49,510
CA: Sacramento	$51,600	MO: St. Louis	$65,620
CA: San Diego	$71,720	NV: Las Vegas	$44,420
CA: San Francisco	$89,880	NY: New York	$91,320
CO: Denver	$70,590	OH: Cincinnati	$73,830
DC: Washington	$70,990	OH: Cleveland	$66,180
FL: Miami	$56,200	OH: Columbus	$54,830
FL: Orlando	$62,680	OR: Portland	$71,050
FL: Tampa	$60,530	PA: Philadelphia	$54,900
GA: Atlanta	$64,670	PA: Pittsburgh	$62,910
IL: Chicago	$59,460	TX: Dallas	$62,960
MA: Boston	no data	TX: Houston	$57,340
MD: Baltimore	$63,230	WA: Seattle	$76,710

FACTORS THAT MAY AFFECT EARNINGS

Educational Attainment of Workers and Effect on Earnings

Figures are based on a group of occupations: Art and Design Workers

	Percent at Level	Effect on Earnings
Less than High School	—	—
Some High School	2.8%	−56.6%
High School or Equivalent	21.1%	−18.4%
Some College but No Degree	19.3%	−3.6%
Associate Degree	18.8%	0.6%
Bachelor's Degree	29.1%	13.0%
Master's Degree	6.0%	23.9%
Doctoral Degree	—	—
First Professional Degree	—	—

Flexibility of Earnings

Average Hours Worked: 31
Workers with a Varying Number of Hours: 26.1%
Workers Earning Some Overtime Pay, Tips, or Commissions: 13.3%
Earnings Benefit of Working Overtime: −2.4%

Gender

	Male	Female
Percent	47.6%	52.4%
Effect on Earnings	12.0%	−12.8%

Union Membership

Percentage Union Members: Insignificant
Earnings Benefit of Union Membership: No significant data available

Veteran Status

Percentage Who Have Been on Active Duty: 4.6%
Earnings Benefit of Veteran Status: 22.0%

27-1012 Craft Artists

Create or reproduce hand-made objects for sale and exhibition, using a variety of techniques such as welding, weaving, pottery, and needlecraft.

- Education or Training Required: Long-term on-the-job training
- Job Growth: 10.6%
- Annual Openings: 1,000
- Self-Employed: 32.7%
- Part-Time: 32.0%

Note: A large fraction of the workforce for this occupation is self-employed and earns an average of $33,220. All other earnings figures for this occupation are based on workers who are paid a wage or salary.

NATIONAL WAGE FIGURES (ANNUAL)

Beginning	25th Percentile	Median	Mean	75th Percentile	90th Percentile
$14,130	$18,860	$24,090	$28,610	$35,840	$46,700

Median Wages for Industries Employing Largest Numbers (Annual)

Industry	Median Income
Motion Picture and Sound Recording Industries	$47,760
Educational Services	$42,300
Furniture and Home Furnishings Stores	$39,770
Federal, State, and Local Government	$34,710
Apparel Manufacturing	$33,620
Performing Arts, Spectator Sports, and Related Industries	$29,270
Professional, Scientific, and Technical Services	$29,110
Merchant Wholesalers, Nondurable Goods	$27,280
Clothing and Clothing Accessories Stores	$25,560
Merchant Wholesalers, Durable Goods	$25,010

Median Wages for States (Annual)

State		State		State	
AK	no data	KY	$14,340	NY	$36,960
AL	$20,440	LA	no data	OH	$19,400
AR	$17,320	MA	$28,520	OK	$16,490
AZ	no data	MD	no data	OR	$21,550
CA	$36,550	ME	$21,250	PA	$21,950
CO	$19,780	MI	$13,770	RI	no data
CT	no data	MN	$39,590	SC	$18,130
DC	no data	MO	$33,340	SD	$24,120
DE	no data	MS	no data	TN	no data
FL	$22,800	MT	$28,550	TX	$23,460
GA	$31,540	NC	$21,430	UT	$26,330
HI	no data	ND	no data	VA	$24,080
IA	no data	NE	$21,980	VT	no data
ID	no data	NH	no data	WA	$27,780
IL	$38,630	NJ	$24,110	WI	$20,700
IN	$22,440	NM	$17,260	WV	no data
KS	no data	NV	no data	WY	$22,810

Median Wages for the Largest Metropolitan Areas (Annual)

Area		Area	
AZ: Phoenix	no data	MI: Detroit	$18,860
CA: Los Angeles	$37,000	MN: Minneapolis	$21,240
CA: Riverside	no data	MO: Kansas City	no data
CA: Sacramento	no data	MO: St. Louis	$38,370
CA: San Diego	no data	NV: Las Vegas	no data
CA: San Francisco	no data	NY: New York	$42,410
CO: Denver	no data	OH: Cincinnati	no data
DC: Washington	no data	OH: Cleveland	$23,900
FL: Miami	no data	OH: Columbus	no data
FL: Orlando	no data	OR: Portland	$25,210
FL: Tampa	no data	PA: Philadelphia	no data
GA: Atlanta	$38,210	PA: Pittsburgh	no data
IL: Chicago	no data	TX: Dallas	no data
MA: Boston	$27,980	TX: Houston	no data
MD: Baltimore	no data	WA: Seattle	no data

FACTORS THAT MAY AFFECT EARNINGS

Educational Attainment of Workers and Effect on Earnings

Figures are based on a group of occupations: Art and Design Workers

	Percent at Level	Effect on Earnings
Less than High School	—	—
Some High School	2.8%	−56.6%
High School or Equivalent	21.1%	−18.4%
Some College but No Degree	19.3%	−3.6%
Associate Degree	18.8%	0.6%
Bachelor's Degree	29.1%	13.0%
Master's Degree	6.0%	23.9%
Doctoral Degree	—	—
First Professional Degree	—	—

Flexibility of Earnings

Average Hours Worked: 31
Workers with a Varying Number of Hours: 26.1%
Workers Earning Some Overtime Pay, Tips, or Commissions: 13.3%
Earnings Benefit of Working Overtime: −2.4%

Gender

	Male	Female
Percent	47.6%	52.4%
Effect on Earnings	12.0%	−12.8%

Union Membership

Percentage Union Members: Insignificant
Earnings Benefit of Union Membership: No significant data available

Veteran Status

Percentage Who Have Been on Active Duty: 4.6%
Earnings Benefit of Veteran Status: 22.0%

27-1013 Fine Artists, Including Painters, Sculptors, and Illustrators

Create original artwork, using any of a wide variety of mediums and techniques such as painting and sculpture.

- Education or Training Required: Long-term on-the-job training
- Job Growth: 10.2%
- Annual Openings: 4,000
- Self-Employed: 61.9%
- Part-Time: 32.0%

Note: A large fraction of the workforce for this occupation is self-employed and earns an average of $33,220. All other earnings figures for this occupation are based on workers who are paid a wage or salary.

NATIONAL WAGE FIGURES (ANNUAL)

Beginning	25th Percentile	Median	Mean	75th Percentile	90th Percentile
$18,350	$28,500	$41,970	$47,100	$58,550	$79,390

Median Wages for Industries Employing Largest Numbers (Annual)

Industry	Median Income
Motion Picture and Sound Recording Industries	$78,380
Federal, State, and Local Government	$52,300
Computer and Electronic Product Manufacturing	$51,430
Publishing Industries (Except Internet)	$46,610
Management of Companies and Enterprises	$44,750
Professional, Scientific, and Technical Services	$44,490
Ambulatory Health Care Services	$44,180
Miscellaneous Manufacturing	$40,880
Miscellaneous Store Retailers	$38,800
Administrative and Support Services	$38,790

Median Wages for States (Annual)

State		State		State	
AK	no data	KY	$25,120	NY	$50,930
AL	$47,720	LA	$22,510	OH	$28,620
AR	$17,730	MA	$46,510	OK	no data
AZ	$45,030	MD	$43,380	OR	$40,940
CA	$68,160	ME	$24,070	PA	$26,420
CO	$25,710	MI	$70,240	RI	$39,890
CT	$58,100	MN	$42,190	SC	no data
DC	no data	MO	$38,320	SD	no data
DE	no data	MS	no data	TN	$41,420
FL	$34,710	MT	$32,360	TX	$36,820
GA	$44,490	NC	$35,270	UT	$45,490
HI	no data	ND	no data	VA	$35,370
IA	$30,810	NE	$34,180	VT	$45,990
ID	no data	NH	no data	WA	$41,890
IL	$39,300	NJ	$42,780	WI	no data
IN	$41,590	NM	$17,860	WV	no data
KS	no data	NV	$26,860	WY	no data

Median Wages for the Largest Metropolitan Areas (Annual)

Area		Area	
AZ: Phoenix	$50,810	MI: Detroit	$73,630
CA: Los Angeles	$73,920	MN: Minneapolis	$42,910
CA: Riverside	no data	MO: Kansas City	$14,230
CA: Sacramento	$51,640	MO: St. Louis	$42,610
CA: San Diego	$57,190	NV: Las Vegas	$25,900
CA: San Francisco	no data	NY: New York	$50,780
CO: Denver	$28,420	OH: Cincinnati	no data
DC: Washington	$52,110	OH: Cleveland	$36,780
FL: Miami	$33,440	OH: Columbus	$24,210
FL: Orlando	$37,610	OR: Portland	$43,150
FL: Tampa	$26,820	PA: Philadelphia	$43,610
GA: Atlanta	$46,540	PA: Pittsburgh	$23,540
IL: Chicago	$50,280	TX: Dallas	$49,420
MA: Boston	$48,910	TX: Houston	$35,220
MD: Baltimore	$31,610	WA: Seattle	$42,740

FACTORS THAT MAY AFFECT EARNINGS

Educational Attainment of Workers and Effect on Earnings

Figures are based on a group of occupations: Art and Design Workers

	Percent at Level	Effect on Earnings
Less than High School	—	—
Some High School	2.8%	−56.6%
High School or Equivalent	21.1%	−18.4%
Some College but No Degree	19.3%	−3.6%
Associate Degree	18.8%	0.6%
Bachelor's Degree	29.1%	13.0%
Master's Degree	6.0%	23.9%
Doctoral Degree	—	—
First Professional Degree	—	—

Flexibility of Earnings

Average Hours Worked: 31
Workers with a Varying Number of Hours: 26.1%
Workers Earning Some Overtime Pay, Tips, or Commissions: 13.3%
Earnings Benefit of Working Overtime: −2.4%

Gender

	Male	Female
Percent	47.6%	52.4%
Effect on Earnings	12.0%	−12.8%

Union Membership

Percentage Union Members: Insignificant
Earnings Benefit of Union Membership: No significant data available

Veteran Status

Percentage Who Have Been on Active Duty: 4.6%
Earnings Benefit of Veteran Status: 22.0%

27-1014 Multi-Media Artists and Animators

Create special effects, animation, or other visual images, using film, video, computers, or other electronic tools and media, for use in products or creations such as computer games, movies, music videos, and commercials.

- Education or Training Required: Bachelor's degree
- Job Growth: 14.1%
- Annual Openings: 14,000
- Self-Employed: 60.8%
- Part-Time: 32.0%

Note: A large fraction of the workforce for this occupation is self-employed and earns an average of $33,220. All other earnings figures for this occupation are based on workers who are paid a wage or salary.

NATIONAL WAGE FIGURES (ANNUAL)

Beginning	25th Percentile	Median	Mean	75th Percentile	90th Percentile
$30,390	$38,980	$51,350	$58,030	$70,050	$92,720

Median Wages for Industries Employing Largest Numbers (Annual)

Industry	Median Income
Other Information Services	$65,760
Credit Intermediation and Related Activities	$58,600
Securities, Commodity Contracts, and Other Financial Investments and Related Activities	$58,600
Miscellaneous Store Retailers	$57,830
Motion Picture and Sound Recording Industries	$57,280
Administrative and Support Services	$55,900
Management of Companies and Enterprises	$54,360
Computer and Electronic Product Manufacturing	$52,810
Miscellaneous Manufacturing	$52,100
Internet Publishing and Broadcasting	$51,660

Median Wages for States (Annual)

State	Wage	State	Wage	State	Wage
AK	no data	KY	$43,780	NY	$56,520
AL	no data	LA	$28,680	OH	$44,080
AR	$36,710	MA	$45,420	OK	$38,930
AZ	$42,750	MD	$42,060	OR	$55,150
CA	$65,340	ME	$39,600	PA	$45,710
CO	$45,250	MI	$43,150	RI	$41,050
CT	$46,360	MN	$38,210	SC	$39,040
DC	no data	MO	$49,350	SD	$34,330
DE	no data	MS	no data	TN	$45,200
FL	$41,160	MT	no data	TX	$44,970
GA	$44,000	NC	$44,200	UT	$49,560
HI	$48,770	ND	no data	VA	$52,770
IA	$31,490	NE	$37,440	VT	$48,050
ID	no data	NH	$40,010	WA	$53,420
IL	$42,060	NJ	$52,550	WI	$44,300
IN	$51,850	NM	no data	WV	$32,960
KS	$33,890	NV	$45,050	WY	no data

Median Wages for the Largest Metropolitan Areas (Annual)

Area	Wage	Area	Wage
AZ: Phoenix	$41,720	MI: Detroit	$42,560
CA: Los Angeles	$65,400	MN: Minneapolis	$39,140
CA: Riverside	$53,700	MO: Kansas City	$36,570
CA: Sacramento	$61,150	MO: St. Louis	$60,340
CA: San Diego	$43,380	NV: Las Vegas	$43,930
CA: San Francisco	$72,060	NY: New York	$57,410
CO: Denver	$54,770	OH: Cincinnati	$42,520
DC: Washington	$56,750	OH: Cleveland	$46,300
FL: Miami	$40,990	OH: Columbus	$49,450
FL: Orlando	$41,150	OR: Portland	$66,540
FL: Tampa	$43,110	PA: Philadelphia	$48,860
GA: Atlanta	$46,910	PA: Pittsburgh	$40,410
IL: Chicago	$43,010	TX: Dallas	$47,200
MA: Boston	$45,430	TX: Houston	$45,240
MD: Baltimore	$40,260	WA: Seattle	$53,190

FACTORS THAT MAY AFFECT EARNINGS

Educational Attainment of Workers and Effect on Earnings

Figures are based on a group of occupations: Art and Design Workers

	Percent at Level	Effect on Earnings
Less than High School	—	—
Some High School	2.8%	−56.6%
High School or Equivalent	21.1%	−18.4%
Some College but No Degree	19.3%	−3.6%
Associate Degree	18.8%	0.6%
Bachelor's Degree	29.1%	13.0%
Master's Degree	6.0%	23.9%
Doctoral Degree	—	—
First Professional Degree	—	—

Flexibility of Earnings

Average Hours Worked: 31
Workers with a Varying Number of Hours: 26.1%
Workers Earning Some Overtime Pay, Tips, or Commissions: 13.3%
Earnings Benefit of Working Overtime: −2.4%

Gender

	Male	Female
Percent	47.6%	52.4%
Effect on Earnings	12.0%	−12.8%

Union Membership

Percentage Union Members: Insignificant
Earnings Benefit of Union Membership: No significant data available

Veteran Status

Percentage Who Have Been on Active Duty: 4.6%
Earnings Benefit of Veteran Status: 22.0%

27-1019 Artists and Related Workers, All Other

All artists and related workers not listed separately.

- Education or Training Required: Long-term on-the-job training
- Job Growth: 10.0%
- Annual Openings: 1,000
- Self-Employed: 31.7%
- Part-Time: 32.0%

Note: A large fraction of the workforce for this occupation is self-employed and earns an average of $33,220. All other earnings figures for this occupation are based on workers who are paid a wage or salary.

NATIONAL WAGE FIGURES (ANNUAL)

Beginning	25th Percentile	Median	Mean	75th Percentile	90th Percentile
$20,490	$28,880	$41,990	$48,890	$66,610	$88,430

Median Wages for Industries Employing Largest Numbers (Annual)

Industry	Median Income
Motion Picture and Sound Recording Industries	$88,730
Federal, State, and Local Government	$61,930
Accommodation	$44,240
Publishing Industries (Except Internet)	$42,390
Merchant Wholesalers, Nondurable Goods	$40,550
Educational Services	$39,150
Administrative and Support Services	$38,700
Merchant Wholesalers, Durable Goods	$37,690
Professional, Scientific, and Technical Services	$37,120
Management of Companies and Enterprises	$35,990

Median Wages for States (Annual)

State	Wage	State	Wage	State	Wage
AK	$35,880	KY	$43,290	NY	$52,130
AL	$44,750	LA	$31,930	OH	$29,500
AR	no data	MA	$40,210	OK	no data
AZ	$30,170	MD	$51,930	OR	$36,410
CA	$45,130	ME	$36,090	PA	$28,350
CO	$35,000	MI	$38,220	RI	no data
CT	$36,960	MN	$29,720	SC	$28,840
DC	$75,010	MO	$31,930	SD	no data
DE	no data	MS	no data	TN	$25,860
FL	$39,960	MT	$34,170	TX	$28,780
GA	$71,450	NC	$40,970	UT	$38,460
HI	no data	ND	no data	VA	$52,830
IA	$38,090	NE	$37,280	VT	no data
ID	$34,870	NH	$40,860	WA	$38,490
IL	$36,270	NJ	$40,930	WI	$30,100
IN	$31,280	NM	$41,270	WV	$62,980
KS	$38,570	NV	$39,430	WY	no data

Median Wages for the Largest Metropolitan Areas (Annual)

Metro	Wage	Metro	Wage
AZ: Phoenix	no data	MI: Detroit	$59,000
CA: Los Angeles	$47,820	MN: Minneapolis	$30,300
CA: Riverside	$65,480	MO: Kansas City	no data
CA: Sacramento	$31,260	MO: St. Louis	no data
CA: San Diego	$57,140	NV: Las Vegas	$40,680
CA: San Francisco	$57,840	NY: New York	$51,960
CO: Denver	$39,550	OH: Cincinnati	no data
DC: Washington	$72,570	OH: Cleveland	$30,790
FL: Miami	$39,100	OH: Columbus	no data
FL: Orlando	$42,760	OR: Portland	$45,500
FL: Tampa	no data	PA: Philadelphia	$29,830
GA: Atlanta	$81,950	PA: Pittsburgh	no data
IL: Chicago	$36,310	TX: Dallas	$44,460
MA: Boston	no data	TX: Houston	$28,230
MD: Baltimore	$34,120	WA: Seattle	$43,640

FACTORS THAT MAY AFFECT EARNINGS

Educational Attainment of Workers and Effect on Earnings

Figures are based on a group of occupations: Art and Design Workers

	Percent at Level	Effect on Earnings
Less than High School	—	—
Some High School	2.8%	−56.6%
High School or Equivalent	21.1%	−18.4%
Some College but No Degree	19.3%	−3.6%
Associate Degree	18.8%	0.6%
Bachelor's Degree	29.1%	13.0%
Master's Degree	6.0%	23.9%
Doctoral Degree	—	—
First Professional Degree	—	—

Flexibility of Earnings

Average Hours Worked: 31
Workers with a Varying Number of Hours: 26.1%
Workers Earning Some Overtime Pay, Tips, or Commissions: 13.3%
Earnings Benefit of Working Overtime: −2.4%

Gender

	Male	Female
Percent	47.6%	52.4%
Effect on Earnings	12.0%	−12.8%

Union Membership

Percentage Union Members: Insignificant
Earnings Benefit of Union Membership: No significant data available

Veteran Status

Percentage Who Have Been on Active Duty: 4.6%
Earnings Benefit of Veteran Status: 22.0%

27-1021 Commercial and Industrial Designers

Develop and design manufactured products, such as cars, home appliances, and children's toys. Combine artistic talent with research on product use, marketing, and materials to create the most functional and appealing product design.

- Education or Training Required: Bachelor's degree
- Job Growth: 10.8%
- Annual Openings: 7,000
- Self-Employed: 30.1%
- Part-Time: 32.0%

Note: A large fraction of the workforce for this occupation is self-employed and earns an average of $39,540. All other earnings figures for this occupation are based on workers who are paid a wage or salary.

NATIONAL WAGE FIGURES (ANNUAL)

Beginning	25th Percentile	Median	Mean	75th Percentile	90th Percentile
$31,510	$41,270	$54,560	$59,340	$72,610	$92,970

Median Wages for Industries Employing Largest Numbers (Annual)

Industry	Median Income
Transportation Equipment Manufacturing	$65,870
Administrative and Support Services	$65,400
Computer and Electronic Product Manufacturing	$64,890
Management of Companies and Enterprises	$64,700
Professional, Scientific, and Technical Services	$57,120
Fabricated Metal Product Manufacturing	$55,840
Publishing Industries (Except Internet)	$54,900
Merchant Wholesalers, Durable Goods	$53,450
Electrical Equipment, Appliance, and Component Manufacturing	$52,680
Paper Manufacturing	$50,730

Median Wages for States (Annual)

State	Wage	State	Wage	State	Wage
AK	no data	KY	$50,220	NY	$55,250
AL	$40,470	LA	$57,180	OH	$46,710
AR	$43,500	MA	$63,010	OK	$42,330
AZ	$50,580	MD	$52,760	OR	$41,710
CA	$59,800	ME	$44,200	PA	$51,230
CO	$49,810	MI	$69,090	RI	$51,020
CT	$53,490	MN	no data	SC	$35,510
DC	no data	MO	$46,880	SD	$29,770
DE	$46,020	MS	$42,580	TN	$43,530
FL	$38,900	MT	no data	TX	$48,790
GA	$45,900	NC	$48,090	UT	$54,620
HI	no data	ND	no data	VA	$56,720
IA	$46,020	NE	$34,050	VT	$39,560
ID	$36,080	NH	$45,390	WA	$51,060
IL	$55,630	NJ	$57,410	WI	$49,770
IN	$48,540	NM	$41,280	WV	no data
KS	$48,360	NV	$69,700	WY	no data

Median Wages for the Largest Metropolitan Areas (Annual)

Area	Wage	Area	Wage
AZ: Phoenix	$50,880	MI: Detroit	$72,190
CA: Los Angeles	$57,390	MN: Minneapolis	no data
CA: Riverside	$47,860	MO: Kansas City	$42,960
CA: Sacramento	$48,910	MO: St. Louis	$50,820
CA: San Diego	$49,540	NV: Las Vegas	$70,350
CA: San Francisco	$66,770	NY: New York	$55,110
CO: Denver	$49,880	OH: Cincinnati	$54,370
DC: Washington	$56,150	OH: Cleveland	$45,410
FL: Miami	$30,640	OH: Columbus	$46,300
FL: Orlando	$56,320	OR: Portland	$49,800
FL: Tampa	$38,060	PA: Philadelphia	$51,630
GA: Atlanta	$47,110	PA: Pittsburgh	$44,590
IL: Chicago	$55,870	TX: Dallas	$53,310
MA: Boston	$59,620	TX: Houston	$48,150
MD: Baltimore	$54,880	WA: Seattle	$51,690

FACTORS THAT MAY AFFECT EARNINGS

Educational Attainment of Workers and Effect on Earnings

Figures are based on a group of occupations: Art and Design Workers

	Percent at Level	Effect on Earnings
Less than High School	—	—
Some High School	2.8%	−56.6%
High School or Equivalent	21.1%	−18.4%
Some College but No Degree	19.3%	−3.6%
Associate Degree	18.8%	0.6%
Bachelor's Degree	29.1%	13.0%
Master's Degree	6.0%	23.9%
Doctoral Degree	—	—
First Professional Degree	—	—

Flexibility of Earnings

Average Hours Worked: 31
Workers with a Varying Number of Hours: 11.4%
Workers Earning Some Overtime Pay, Tips, or Commissions: 13.3%
Earnings Benefit of Working Overtime: 7.2%

Gender

	Male	Female
Percent	43.7%	56.3%
Effect on Earnings	11.6%	−8.2%

Union Membership

Percentage Union Members: Insignificant
Earnings Benefit of Union Membership: No significant data available

Veteran Status

Percentage Who Have Been on Active Duty: 4.6%
Earnings Benefit of Veteran Status: 22.0%

27-1022 Fashion Designers

Design clothing and accessories. Create original garments or design garments that follow well-established fashion trends. May develop the line of color and kinds of materials.

- Education or Training Required: Associate degree
- Job Growth: 8.4%
- Annual Openings: 2,000
- Self-Employed: 26.5%
- Part-Time: 32.0%

NATIONAL WAGE FIGURES (ANNUAL)

Beginning	25th Percentile	Median	Mean	75th Percentile	90th Percentile
$30,000	$42,140	$62,610	$69,270	$87,510	$117,120

Median Wages for Industries Employing Largest Numbers (Annual)

Industry	Median Income
Management of Companies and Enterprises	$70,570
Professional, Scientific, and Technical Services	$67,970
Apparel Manufacturing	$67,320
Merchant Wholesalers, Nondurable Goods	$62,760
Nonstore Retailers	$60,620
Leather and Allied Product Manufacturing	$57,350
Warehousing and Storage	$56,480
Clothing and Clothing Accessories Stores	$53,170
Performing Arts, Spectator Sports, and Related Industries	$52,650
Educational Services	$30,480

Median Wages for States (Annual)

AK	no data	KY	no data	NY	$72,700
AL	no data	LA	no data	OH	$54,690
AR	no data	MA	$51,880	OK	no data
AZ	$33,140	MD	$57,950	OR	$55,430
CA	$57,930	ME	no data	PA	$43,170
CO	$48,190	MI	$44,730	RI	$66,400
CT	$46,200	MN	$47,980	SC	no data
DC	no data	MO	$53,340	SD	no data
DE	no data	MS	no data	TN	$54,280
FL	$52,200	MT	no data	TX	$66,940
GA	$46,630	NC	$56,750	UT	$28,350
HI	no data	ND	no data	VA	$50,970
IA	no data	NE	no data	VT	no data
ID	no data	NH	$68,270	WA	$60,860
IL	no data	NJ	$62,350	WI	no data
IN	$36,160	NM	no data	WV	no data
KS	no data	NV	no data	WY	no data

Median Wages for the Largest Metropolitan Areas (Annual)

AZ: Phoenix	no data	MI: Detroit	no data
CA: Los Angeles	$58,500	MN: Minneapolis	$49,800
CA: Riverside	$55,750	MO: Kansas City	no data
CA: Sacramento	no data	MO: St. Louis	no data
CA: San Diego	$46,320	NV: Las Vegas	no data
CA: San Francisco	$70,360	NY: New York	$72,280
CO: Denver	no data	OH: Cincinnati	$49,240
DC: Washington	$55,040	OH: Cleveland	no data
FL: Miami	$48,110	OH: Columbus	no data
FL: Orlando	$86,330	OR: Portland	$58,770
FL: Tampa	no data	PA: Philadelphia	$60,500
GA: Atlanta	$46,380	PA: Pittsburgh	no data
IL: Chicago	no data	TX: Dallas	$71,640
MA: Boston	$60,490	TX: Houston	no data
MD: Baltimore	$58,610	WA: Seattle	$60,450

FACTORS THAT MAY AFFECT EARNINGS

Educational Attainment of Workers and Effect on Earnings

Figures are based on a group of occupations: Art and Design Workers

	Percent at Level	Effect on Earnings
Less than High School	—	—
Some High School	2.8%	−56.6%
High School or Equivalent	21.1%	−18.4%
Some College but No Degree	19.3%	−3.6%
Associate Degree	18.8%	0.6%
Bachelor's Degree	29.1%	13.0%
Master's Degree	6.0%	23.9%
Doctoral Degree	—	—
First Professional Degree	—	—

Flexibility of Earnings

Average Hours Worked: 31
Workers with a Varying Number of Hours: 11.4%
Workers Earning Some Overtime Pay, Tips, or Commissions: 13.3%
Earnings Benefit of Working Overtime: 7.2%

Gender

	Male	Female
Percent	44.5%	55.5%
Effect on Earnings	11.6%	−8.2%

Union Membership

Percentage Union Members: Insignificant
Earnings Benefit of Union Membership: No significant data available

Veteran Status

Percentage Who Have Been on Active Duty: 4.6%
Earnings Benefit of Veteran Status: 22.0%

27-1023 Floral Designers

Design, cut, and arrange live, dried, or artificial flowers and foliage.

- Education or Training Required: Moderate-term on-the-job training
- Job Growth: 10.3%
- Annual Openings: 14,000
- Self-Employed: 30.6%
- Part-Time: 32.0%

Note: A large fraction of the workforce for this occupation is self-employed and earns an average of $39,540. All other earnings figures for this occupation are based on workers who are paid a wage or salary.

NATIONAL WAGE FIGURES (ANNUAL)

Beginning	25th Percentile	Median	Mean	75th Percentile	90th Percentile
$15,040	$17,690	$21,700	$23,040	$27,330	$33,650

Median Wages for Industries Employing Largest Numbers (Annual)

Industry	Median Income
Merchant Wholesalers, Durable Goods	$33,510
Hospitals	$30,690
Food Services and Drinking Places	$27,150
Accommodation	$26,740
Professional, Scientific, and Technical Services	$25,520
Furniture and Home Furnishings Stores	$25,290
Rental and Leasing Services	$24,160
Food and Beverage Stores	$23,970
Administrative and Support Services	$23,750
Management of Companies and Enterprises	$23,620

Median Wages for States (Annual)

State	Wage	State	Wage	State	Wage
AK	$25,270	KY	$20,750	NY	$23,140
AL	$20,050	LA	$21,160	OH	$20,510
AR	$19,110	MA	$27,630	OK	$19,080
AZ	$23,300	MD	$25,380	OR	$21,610
CA	$23,690	ME	$21,370	PA	$21,440
CO	$22,900	MI	$22,180	RI	$23,290
CT	$26,320	MN	$22,520	SC	$19,780
DC	$28,170	MO	$18,530	SD	$20,460
DE	$23,590	MS	$17,380	TN	$20,590
FL	$22,200	MT	$18,380	TX	$19,780
GA	$21,120	NC	$22,480	UT	$18,980
HI	$21,480	ND	$18,420	VA	$22,270
IA	$19,060	NE	$20,200	VT	$24,310
ID	$18,490	NH	$23,620	WA	$25,920
IL	$21,630	NJ	$25,950	WI	$22,350
IN	$20,570	NM	$18,610	WV	$16,620
KS	$18,990	NV	$27,940	WY	$15,770

Median Wages for the Largest Metropolitan Areas (Annual)

Area	Wage	Area	Wage
AZ: Phoenix	$23,080	MI: Detroit	$23,350
CA: Los Angeles	$23,490	MN: Minneapolis	$25,270
CA: Riverside	$21,950	MO: Kansas City	$22,930
CA: Sacramento	$26,100	MO: St. Louis	$18,940
CA: San Diego	$20,990	NV: Las Vegas	$28,510
CA: San Francisco	$28,910	NY: New York	$28,030
CO: Denver	$22,600	OH: Cincinnati	$26,410
DC: Washington	$25,660	OH: Cleveland	$21,910
FL: Miami	$23,780	OH: Columbus	$26,330
FL: Orlando	$21,180	OR: Portland	$23,930
FL: Tampa	$23,340	PA: Philadelphia	$22,810
GA: Atlanta	$22,130	PA: Pittsburgh	$20,770
IL: Chicago	$22,660	TX: Dallas	$21,450
MA: Boston	$28,530	TX: Houston	$21,480
MD: Baltimore	$30,420	WA: Seattle	$28,650

FACTORS THAT MAY AFFECT EARNINGS

Educational Attainment of Workers and Effect on Earnings

Figures are based on a group of occupations: Art and Design Workers

	Percent at Level	Effect on Earnings
Less than High School	—	
Some High School	2.8%	−56.6%
High School or Equivalent	21.1%	−18.4%
Some College but No Degree	19.3%	−3.6%
Associate Degree	18.8%	0.6%
Bachelor's Degree	29.1%	13.0%
Master's Degree	6.0%	23.9%
Doctoral Degree	—	—
First Professional Degree	—	—

Flexibility of Earnings

Average Hours Worked: 31
Workers with a Varying Number of Hours: 11.4%
Workers Earning Some Overtime Pay, Tips, or Commissions: 13.3%
Earnings Benefit of Working Overtime: 7.2%

Gender

	Male	Female
Percent	44.5%	55.5%
Effect on Earnings	11.6%	−8.2%

Union Membership

Percentage Union Members: Insignificant
Earnings Benefit of Union Membership: No significant data available

Veteran Status

Percentage Who Have Been on Active Duty: 4.6%
Earnings Benefit of Veteran Status: 22.0%

27-1024 Graphic Designers

Design or create graphics to meet a client's specific commercial or promotional needs, such as packaging, displays, or logos. May use a variety of media to achieve artistic or decorative effects.

- Education or Training Required: Bachelor's degree
- Job Growth: 15.2%
- Annual Openings: 35,000
- Self-Employed: 25.6%
- Part-Time: 32.0%

NATIONAL WAGE FIGURES (ANNUAL)

Beginning	25th Percentile	Median	Mean	75th Percentile	90th Percentile
$24,120	$30,600	$39,900	$43,830	$53,310	$69,730

Median Wages for Industries Employing Largest Numbers (Annual)

Industry	Median Income
Federal, State, and Local Government	$51,530
Telecommunications	$47,720
Computer and Electronic Product Manufacturing	$47,110
Motion Picture and Sound Recording Industries	$47,080
Insurance Carriers and Related Activities	$45,640
Management of Companies and Enterprises	$45,620
Internet Service Providers, Web Search Portals, and Data-Processing Services	$44,440
Paper Manufacturing	$44,280
Professional, Scientific, and Technical Services	$43,620
Machinery Manufacturing	$42,990

Median Wages for States (Annual)

AK	$36,390	KY	$31,950	NY	$49,080
AL	$33,320	LA	$30,260	OH	$38,910
AR	$30,090	MA	$44,410	OK	$31,450
AZ	$38,530	MD	$43,030	OR	$37,670
CA	$46,560	ME	$31,930	PA	$36,210
CO	$37,310	MI	$42,220	RI	$42,580
CT	$43,590	MN	$39,230	SC	$32,770
DC	$55,370	MO	$34,790	SD	$30,200
DE	$39,880	MS	$32,990	TN	$33,650
FL	$35,430	MT	$24,130	TX	$38,140
GA	$41,110	NC	$35,880	UT	$34,400
HI	$38,660	ND	$27,870	VA	$43,320
IA	$32,550	NE	$31,880	VT	$36,010
ID	$36,450	NH	$37,530	WA	$41,120
IL	$40,420	NJ	$45,350	WI	$36,800
IN	$34,610	NM	$32,740	WV	$28,620
KS	$33,590	NV	$42,360	WY	$25,870

Median Wages for the Largest Metropolitan Areas (Annual)

AZ: Phoenix	$39,190	MI: Detroit	$49,030
CA: Los Angeles	$45,160	MN: Minneapolis	$41,730
CA: Riverside	$40,380	MO: Kansas City	$37,240
CA: Sacramento	$39,690	MO: St. Louis	$39,130
CA: San Diego	$43,470	NV: Las Vegas	$42,600
CA: San Francisco	$56,390	NY: New York	$50,550
CO: Denver	$39,030	OH: Cincinnati	$42,820
DC: Washington	$49,810	OH: Cleveland	$37,080
FL: Miami	$37,790	OH: Columbus	$47,010
FL: Orlando	$37,580	OR: Portland	$41,030
FL: Tampa	$33,040	PA: Philadelphia	$41,670
GA: Atlanta	$43,030	PA: Pittsburgh	$34,820
IL: Chicago	$41,620	TX: Dallas	$41,730
MA: Boston	$45,610	TX: Houston	$40,050
MD: Baltimore	$41,870	WA: Seattle	$45,720

FACTORS THAT MAY AFFECT EARNINGS

Educational Attainment of Workers and Effect on Earnings

Figures are based on a group of occupations: Art and Design Workers

	Percent at Level	Effect on Earnings
Less than High School	—	—
Some High School	2.8%	−56.6%
High School or Equivalent	21.1%	−18.4%
Some College but No Degree	19.3%	−3.6%
Associate Degree	18.8%	0.6%
Bachelor's Degree	29.1%	13.0%
Master's Degree	6.0%	23.9%
Doctoral Degree	—	—
First Professional Degree	—	—

Flexibility of Earnings

Average Hours Worked: 31
Workers with a Varying Number of Hours: 11.4%
Workers Earning Some Overtime Pay, Tips, or Commissions: 13.3%
Earnings Benefit of Working Overtime: 7.2%

Gender

	Male	Female
Percent	44.5%	55.5%
Effect on Earnings	11.6%	−8.2%

Union Membership

Percentage Union Members: Insignificant
Earnings Benefit of Union Membership: No significant data available

Veteran Status

Percentage Who Have Been on Active Duty: 4.6%
Earnings Benefit of Veteran Status: 22.0%

27-1025 Interior Designers

Plan, design, and furnish interiors of residential, commercial, or industrial buildings. Formulate design that is practical, aesthetic, and conducive to intended purposes, such as raising productivity, selling merchandise, or improving lifestyle. May specialize in a particular field, style, or phase of interior design.

- Education or Training Required: Associate degree
- Job Growth: 15.5%
- Annual Openings: 10,000
- Self-Employed: 25.3%
- Part-Time: 32.0%

NATIONAL WAGE FIGURES (ANNUAL)

Beginning	25th Percentile	Median	Mean	75th Percentile	90th Percentile
$24,270	$31,830	$42,260	$48,000	$57,230	$78,760

Median Wages for Industries Employing Largest Numbers (Annual)

Industry	Median Income
Federal, State, and Local Government	$65,590
Management of Companies and Enterprises	$51,280
Hospitals	$48,170
Wholesale Electronic Markets and Agents and Brokers	$47,680
Educational Services	$45,460
Clothing and Clothing Accessories Stores	$44,920
Merchant Wholesalers, Durable Goods	$44,650
Professional, Scientific, and Technical Services	$44,550
General Merchandise Stores	$44,060
Real Estate	$43,810

Median Wages for States (Annual)

State	Wage	State	Wage	State	Wage
AK	no data	KY	$32,590	NY	$52,070
AL	no data	LA	$32,570	OH	$38,180
AR	$29,740	MA	$50,190	OK	$35,210
AZ	$36,290	MD	$48,340	OR	$43,100
CA	$47,670	ME	$40,420	PA	$38,810
CO	$41,380	MI	$43,580	RI	no data
CT	$47,200	MN	$44,100	SC	$35,110
DC	$57,770	MO	$37,670	SD	$34,020
DE	$40,690	MS	$26,470	TN	$41,050
FL	$39,970	MT	$35,280	TX	$39,550
GA	$45,850	NC	$39,550	UT	$33,770
HI	$55,390	ND	$28,080	VA	$45,690
IA	$32,710	NE	$37,100	VT	$42,240
ID	$36,180	NH	$43,340	WA	$38,990
IL	$46,000	NJ	$54,070	WI	$37,600
IN	$33,140	NM	$35,070	WV	$25,310
KS	$34,780	NV	$44,210	WY	$38,940

Median Wages for the Largest Metropolitan Areas (Annual)

Area	Wage	Area	Wage
AZ: Phoenix	$36,300	MI: Detroit	$43,560
CA: Los Angeles	$48,080	MN: Minneapolis	$45,820
CA: Riverside	$46,530	MO: Kansas City	$38,470
CA: Sacramento	$42,880	MO: St. Louis	$40,290
CA: San Diego	$48,430	NV: Las Vegas	$45,230
CA: San Francisco	$49,400	NY: New York	$55,160
CO: Denver	$43,470	OH: Cincinnati	$37,050
DC: Washington	$53,120	OH: Cleveland	$42,150
FL: Miami	$43,070	OH: Columbus	$38,540
FL: Orlando	$37,520	OR: Portland	$43,110
FL: Tampa	$37,840	PA: Philadelphia	$41,880
GA: Atlanta	$47,550	PA: Pittsburgh	$49,530
IL: Chicago	$46,500	TX: Dallas	$40,590
MA: Boston	$50,650	TX: Houston	$41,790
MD: Baltimore	$52,820	WA: Seattle	$39,750

FACTORS THAT MAY AFFECT EARNINGS

Educational Attainment of Workers and Effect on Earnings

Figures are based on a group of occupations: Art and Design Workers

	Percent at Level	Effect on Earnings
Less than High School	—	—
Some High School	2.8%	−56.6%
High School or Equivalent	21.1%	−18.4%
Some College but No Degree	19.3%	−3.6%
Associate Degree	18.8%	0.6%
Bachelor's Degree	29.1%	13.0%
Master's Degree	6.0%	23.9%
Doctoral Degree	—	—
First Professional Degree	—	—

Flexibility of Earnings

Average Hours Worked: 31

Workers with a Varying Number of Hours: 11.4%

Workers Earning Some Overtime Pay, Tips, or Commissions: 13.3%

Earnings Benefit of Working Overtime: 7.2%

Gender

	Male	Female
Percent	44.5%	55.5%
Effect on Earnings	11.6%	−8.2%

Union Membership

Percentage Union Members: Insignificant

Earnings Benefit of Union Membership: No significant data available

Veteran Status

Percentage Who Have Been on Active Duty: 4.6%

Earnings Benefit of Veteran Status: 22.0%

27-1026 Merchandise Displayers and Window Trimmers

Plan and erect commercial displays, such as those in windows and interiors of retail stores and at trade exhibitions.

- Education or Training Required: Moderate-term on-the-job training
- Job Growth: 10.3%
- Annual Openings: 13,000
- Self-Employed: 25.9%
- Part-Time: 32.0%

NATIONAL WAGE FIGURES (ANNUAL)

Beginning	25th Percentile	Median	Mean	75th Percentile	90th Percentile
$15,630	$18,890	$23,820	$26,550	$31,000	$41,370

Median Wages for Industries Employing Largest Numbers (Annual)

Industry	Median Income
Management of Companies and Enterprises	$35,310
Furniture and Related Product Manufacturing	$35,300
Health and Personal Care Stores	$34,710
Electrical Equipment, Appliance, and Component Manufacturing	$33,180
Real Estate	$31,480
Clothing and Clothing Accessories Stores	$30,510
Food Manufacturing	$29,670
Miscellaneous Manufacturing	$28,480
Furniture and Home Furnishings Stores	$27,700
Beverage and Tobacco Product Manufacturing	$27,530

Median Wages for States (Annual)

AK	no data	KY	$20,940	NY	$31,760
AL	$19,390	LA	$18,520	OH	$21,820
AR	$22,080	MA	$30,900	OK	$20,520
AZ	$23,370	MD	$27,490	OR	$25,880
CA	$26,140	ME	$22,800	PA	$21,150
CO	$22,690	MI	$23,060	RI	$27,410
CT	$27,610	MN	$26,690	SC	$21,920
DC	$22,710	MO	$24,200	SD	$19,570
DE	$27,720	MS	$14,470	TN	$22,680
FL	$22,770	MT	$19,520	TX	$22,010
GA	$22,640	NC	$23,620	UT	$22,420
HI	$30,450	ND	$26,380	VA	$22,040
IA	$21,620	NE	$19,540	VT	$22,160
ID	$19,460	NH	$27,840	WA	$27,460
IL	$23,630	NJ	$28,020	WI	$24,680
IN	$20,120	NM	$23,670	WV	$17,280
KS	$21,940	NV	$20,800	WY	no data

Median Wages for the Largest Metropolitan Areas (Annual)

AZ: Phoenix	$23,420	MI: Detroit	$22,820
CA: Los Angeles	$26,450	MN: Minneapolis	$28,870
CA: Riverside	$24,020	MO: Kansas City	$24,430
CA: Sacramento	$22,780	MO: St. Louis	$23,830
CA: San Diego	$29,960	NV: Las Vegas	$21,060
CA: San Francisco	$27,750	NY: New York	$31,900
CO: Denver	$22,830	OH: Cincinnati	$19,910
DC: Washington	$21,870	OH: Cleveland	$22,300
FL: Miami	$24,300	OH: Columbus	$21,810
FL: Orlando	$23,170	OR: Portland	$26,200
FL: Tampa	$22,200	PA: Philadelphia	$27,870
GA: Atlanta	$21,760	PA: Pittsburgh	$27,280
IL: Chicago	$24,020	TX: Dallas	$22,860
MA: Boston	$31,920	TX: Houston	$21,480
MD: Baltimore	$28,020	WA: Seattle	$28,490

FACTORS THAT MAY AFFECT EARNINGS

Educational Attainment of Workers and Effect on Earnings

Figures are based on a group of occupations: Art and Design Workers

	Percent at Level	Effect on Earnings
Less than High School	—	—
Some High School	2.8%	−56.6%
High School or Equivalent	21.1%	−18.4%
Some College but No Degree	19.3%	−3.6%
Associate Degree	18.8%	0.6%
Bachelor's Degree	29.1%	13.0%
Master's Degree	6.0%	23.9%
Doctoral Degree	—	—
First Professional Degree	—	—

Flexibility of Earnings

Average Hours Worked: 31

Workers with a Varying Number of Hours: 11.4%

Workers Earning Some Overtime Pay, Tips, or Commissions: 13.3%

Earnings Benefit of Working Overtime: 7.2%

Gender

	Male	Female
Percent	44.5%	55.5%
Effect on Earnings	11.6%	−8.2%

Union Membership

Percentage Union Members: Insignificant

Earnings Benefit of Union Membership: No significant data available

Veteran Status

Percentage Who Have Been on Active Duty: 4.6%

Earnings Benefit of Veteran Status: 22.0%

27-1027 Set and Exhibit Designers

Design special exhibits and movie, television, and theater sets. May study scripts, confer with directors, and conduct research to determine appropriate architectural styles.

- Education or Training Required: Bachelor's degree
- Job Growth: 9.3%
- Annual Openings: 2,000
- Self-Employed: 27.6%
- Part-Time: 32.0%

NATIONAL WAGE FIGURES (ANNUAL)

Beginning	25th Percentile	Median	Mean	75th Percentile	90th Percentile
$21,990	$29,070	$41,820	$45,620	$58,600	$76,670

Median Wages for Industries Employing Largest Numbers (Annual)

Industry	Median Income
Specialty Trade Contractors	$76,470
Motion Picture and Sound Recording Industries	$65,410
Federal, State, and Local Government	$53,640
Publishing Industries (Except Internet)	$52,050
Broadcasting (Except Internet)	$50,900
Rental and Leasing Services	$45,690
Administrative and Support Services	$45,660
Museums, Historical Sites, and Similar Institutions	$39,750
Professional, Scientific, and Technical Services	$39,080
Performing Arts, Spectator Sports, and Related Industries	$37,560

Median Wages for States (Annual)

State	Wage	State	Wage	State	Wage
AK	no data	KY	$41,420	NY	$49,980
AL	no data	LA	$32,510	OH	$36,540
AR	no data	MA	$77,360	OK	$35,140
AZ	$31,300	MD	$53,020	OR	$51,410
CA	$57,870	ME	no data	PA	$41,850
CO	$26,380	MI	$44,940	RI	no data
CT	no data	MN	$42,290	SC	no data
DC	$64,780	MO	$32,970	SD	no data
DE	$40,580	MS	no data	TN	$35,400
FL	$34,000	MT	no data	TX	$33,260
GA	$36,850	NC	$32,660	UT	$39,970
HI	no data	ND	no data	VA	$36,080
IA	no data	NE	$26,220	VT	no data
ID	no data	NH	no data	WA	$44,850
IL	$46,230	NJ	$29,140	WI	$31,180
IN	$38,250	NM	$46,110	WV	no data
KS	$24,120	NV	$36,210	WY	no data

Median Wages for the Largest Metropolitan Areas (Annual)

Area	Wage	Area	Wage
AZ: Phoenix	$29,250	MI: Detroit	$46,000
CA: Los Angeles	$63,770	MN: Minneapolis	$41,660
CA: Riverside	$24,750	MO: Kansas City	no data
CA: Sacramento	no data	MO: St. Louis	$33,470
CA: San Diego	$40,250	NV: Las Vegas	$36,210
CA: San Francisco	$54,240	NY: New York	$49,120
CO: Denver	$43,380	OH: Cincinnati	$38,920
DC: Washington	$58,130	OH: Cleveland	no data
FL: Miami	$36,020	OH: Columbus	no data
FL: Orlando	$34,490	OR: Portland	$55,110
FL: Tampa	no data	PA: Philadelphia	$38,890
GA: Atlanta	$39,000	PA: Pittsburgh	$50,360
IL: Chicago	$47,350	TX: Dallas	$39,660
MA: Boston	no data	TX: Houston	$30,710
MD: Baltimore	$48,650	WA: Seattle	$47,870

FACTORS THAT MAY AFFECT EARNINGS

Educational Attainment of Workers and Effect on Earnings

Figures are based on a group of occupations: Art and Design Workers

	Percent at Level	Effect on Earnings
Less than High School	—	—
Some High School	2.8%	−56.6%
High School or Equivalent	21.1%	−18.4%
Some College but No Degree	19.3%	−3.6%
Associate Degree	18.8%	0.6%
Bachelor's Degree	29.1%	13.0%
Master's Degree	6.0%	23.9%
Doctoral Degree	—	—
First Professional Degree	—	—

Flexibility of Earnings

Average Hours Worked: 31
Workers with a Varying Number of Hours: 11.4%
Workers Earning Some Overtime Pay, Tips, or Commissions: 13.3%
Earnings Benefit of Working Overtime: 7.2%

Gender

	Male	Female
Percent	44.5%	55.5%
Effect on Earnings	11.6%	−8.2%

Union Membership

Percentage Union Members: Insignificant
Earnings Benefit of Union Membership: No significant data available

Veteran Status

Percentage Who Have Been on Active Duty: 4.6%
Earnings Benefit of Veteran Status: 22.0%

27-1029 Designers, All Other

All designers not listed separately.

- Education or Training Required: Bachelor's degree
- Job Growth: 13.6%
- Annual Openings: 2,000
- Self-Employed: 16.4%
- Part-Time: 32.0%

NATIONAL WAGE FIGURES (ANNUAL)

Beginning	25th Percentile	Median	Mean	75th Percentile	90th Percentile
$21,920	$31,210	$43,870	$48,890	$61,740	$80,180

Median Wages for Industries Employing Largest Numbers (Annual)

Industry	Median Income
Broadcasting (Except Internet)	$66,320
Publishing Industries (Except Internet)	$58,600
Federal, State, and Local Government	$58,030
Transportation Equipment Manufacturing	$57,290
Management of Companies and Enterprises	$55,260
Administrative and Support Services	$53,480
Paper Manufacturing	$52,400
Machinery Manufacturing	$47,270
Merchant Wholesalers, Nondurable Goods	$47,150
Amusement, Gambling, and Recreation Industries	$46,580

Median Wages for States (Annual)

State	Wage	State	Wage	State	Wage
AK	no data	KY	$25,600	NY	$43,370
AL	$64,200	LA	$50,820	OH	$40,780
AR	$24,760	MA	$63,850	OK	no data
AZ	$47,070	MD	$49,500	OR	no data
CA	$45,290	ME	$24,840	PA	$46,880
CO	$38,130	MI	$45,350	RI	$33,900
CT	$29,990	MN	$53,350	SC	no data
DC	$41,150	MO	$25,350	SD	no data
DE	no data	MS	no data	TN	$26,890
FL	$28,370	MT	no data	TX	$42,770
GA	$31,660	NC	$42,230	UT	$45,090
HI	no data	ND	no data	VA	$50,760
IA	no data	NE	$26,800	VT	no data
ID	$49,550	NH	$42,860	WA	$75,690
IL	$54,990	NJ	$45,000	WI	$44,170
IN	$33,280	NM	$48,410	WV	no data
KS	no data	NV	$44,240	WY	no data

Median Wages for the Largest Metropolitan Areas (Annual)

Area	Wage	Area	Wage
AZ: Phoenix	$47,420	MI: Detroit	$40,250
CA: Los Angeles	$42,360	MN: Minneapolis	$54,300
CA: Riverside	$42,870	MO: Kansas City	no data
CA: Sacramento	$57,540	MO: St. Louis	$24,030
CA: San Diego	no data	NV: Las Vegas	$43,750
CA: San Francisco	$43,240	NY: New York	$44,600
CO: Denver	no data	OH: Cincinnati	$40,260
DC: Washington	$39,750	OH: Cleveland	$41,570
FL: Miami	$28,080	OH: Columbus	$30,810
FL: Orlando	$24,230	OR: Portland	no data
FL: Tampa	$32,050	PA: Philadelphia	$44,450
GA: Atlanta	$30,850	PA: Pittsburgh	$45,340
IL: Chicago	$56,780	TX: Dallas	$48,790
MA: Boston	$62,940	TX: Houston	$36,540
MD: Baltimore	no data	WA: Seattle	no data

FACTORS THAT MAY AFFECT EARNINGS

Educational Attainment of Workers and Effect on Earnings

Figures are based on a group of occupations: Art and Design Workers

	Percent at Level	Effect on Earnings
Less than High School	—	—
Some High School	2.8%	−56.6%
High School or Equivalent	21.1%	−18.4%
Some College but No Degree	19.3%	−3.6%
Associate Degree	18.8%	0.6%
Bachelor's Degree	29.1%	13.0%
Master's Degree	6.0%	23.9%
Doctoral Degree	—	—
First Professional Degree	—	—

Flexibility of Earnings

Average Hours Worked: 31
Workers with a Varying Number of Hours: 11.4%
Workers Earning Some Overtime Pay, Tips, or Commissions: 13.3%
Earnings Benefit of Working Overtime: 7.2%

Gender

	Male	Female
Percent	44.5%	55.5%
Effect on Earnings	11.6%	−8.2%

Union Membership

Percentage Union Members: Insignificant
Earnings Benefit of Union Membership: No significant data available

Veteran Status

Percentage Who Have Been on Active Duty: 4.6%
Earnings Benefit of Veteran Status: 22.0%

27-2000 Entertainers and Performers, Sports and Related Workers

27-2011 Actors

Play parts in stage, television, radio, video, or motion picture productions for entertainment, information, or instruction. Interpret serious or comic role by speech, gesture, and body movement to entertain or inform audience. May dance and sing.

- Education or Training Required: Long-term on-the-job training
- Job Growth: 16.1%
- Annual Openings: 11,000
- Self-Employed: 17.1%
- Part-Time: 35.0%

NATIONAL WAGE FIGURES (HOURLY)

Beginning	25th Percentile	Median	Mean	75th Percentile	90th Percentile
$7.31	$8.47	$11.61	$21.84	$22.51	$51.02

Note: The mean is significantly higher than the median because of the presence of a few star earners.

Median Wages for Industries Employing Largest Numbers (Hourly)

Industry	Median Income
Amusement, Gambling, and Recreation Industries	$22.58
Performing Arts, Spectator Sports, and Related Industries...	$14.93
Hospitals	$12.53
Educational Services	$12.50
Motion Picture and Sound Recording Industries	$10.70

Median Wages for States (Hourly)

State	Wage	State	Wage	State	Wage
AK	no data	KY	$10.01	NY	$39.06
AL	$13.61	LA	no data	OH............	no data
AR	$6.57	MA	no data	OK	no data
AZ	no data	MD	$10.07	OR	$15.78
CA	$10.22	ME	$13.59	PA	no data
CO	$13.74	MI	no data	RI	no data
CT	no data	MN	$13.66	SC	$10.83
DC	$15.49	MO	$13.01	SD	no data
DE	no data	MS	no data	TN	no data
FL	$17.97	MT	no data	TX	no data
GA	$15.97	NC	no data	UT	no data
HI	no data	ND	no data	VA	no data
IA	$6.80	NE	$9.62	VT	no data
ID	$8.12	NH	no data	WA............	no data
IL	$16.47	NJ	no data	WI	$10.74
IN	$11.87	NM	$8.26	WV............	no data
KS	$6.92	NV	$21.23	WY............	no data

Median Wages for the Largest Metropolitan Areas (Hourly)

Area	Wage	Area	Wage
AZ: Phoenix............	no data	MI: Detroit	no data
CA: Los Angeles	$10.27	MN: Minneapolis	$12.96
CA: Riverside	$14.34	MO: Kansas City........	no data
CA: Sacramento	$10.00	MO: St. Louis............	$13.35
CA: San Diego	$14.27	NV: Las Vegas	$21.67
CA: San Francisco....	no data	NY: New York...........	$27.55
CO: Denver	$19.44	OH: Cincinnati..........	$8.81
DC: Washington	$11.42	OH: Cleveland	no data
FL: Miami	$23.82	OH: Columbus	no data
FL: Orlando	$25.21	OR: Portland	$10.66
FL: Tampa	$9.24	PA: Philadelphia	$13.72
GA: Atlanta	no data	PA: Pittsburgh	$18.89
IL: Chicago	$17.67	TX: Dallas	$7.55
MA: Boston	no data	TX: Houston	no data
MD: Baltimore	$9.56	WA: Seattle	no data

FACTORS THAT MAY AFFECT EARNINGS

Educational Attainment of Workers and Effect on Earnings

	Percent at Level	Effect on Earnings
Less than High School	—	—
Some High School	—	—
High School or Equivalent	—	—
Some College but No Degree	39.1%	9.4%
Associate Degree	—	—
Bachelor's Degree	—	—
Master's Degree	—	—
Doctoral Degree	—	—
First Professional Degree	—	—

Figures do not total 100% because some levels have a very small sample size.

Flexibility of Earnings

Average Hours Worked: 10
Workers with a Varying Number of Hours: 50.3%
Workers Earning Some Overtime Pay, Tips, or Commissions: 16.7%
Earnings Benefit of Working Overtime: 3.3%

Gender

	Male	Female
Percent	54.2%	45.8%
Effect on Earnings	2.4%	−2.9%

Union Membership

Percentage Union Members: 50.0%
Earnings Benefit of Union Membership: 31.5%

Veteran Status

Percentage Who Have Been on Active Duty: 6.0%
Earnings Benefit of Veteran Status: 7.3%

27-2012 Producers and Directors

Produce or direct stage, television, radio, video, or motion picture productions for entertainment, information, or instruction. Responsible for creative decisions, such as interpretation of script, choice of guests, set design, sound, special effects, and choreography.

- Education or Training Required: Work experience plus degree
- Job Growth: 16.6%
- Annual Openings: 11,000
- Self-Employed: 30.4%
- Part-Time: 23.3%

Note: A large fraction of the workforce for this occupation is self-employed and earns an average of $61,950. All other earnings figures for this occupation are based on workers who are paid a wage or salary.

NATIONAL WAGE FIGURES (ANNUAL)

Beginning	25th Percentile	Median	Mean	75th Percentile	90th Percentile
$27,980	$37,980	$56,310	$72,210	$88,700	more than $145,600

Note: The mean is significantly higher than the median because of the presence of a few star earners.

Median Wages for Industries Employing Largest Numbers (Annual)

Industry	Median Income
Lessors of Nonfinancial Intangible Assets (Except Copyrighted Works)	$89,010
Other Information Services	$79,640
Professional, Scientific, and Technical Services	$79,100
Rental and Leasing Services	$77,950
Internet Publishing and Broadcasting	$74,770
Motion Picture and Sound Recording Industries	$71,030
Internet Service Providers, Web Search Portals, and Data-Processing Services	$69,880
Administrative and Support Services	$62,660
Publishing Industries (Except Internet)	$61,370
Federal, State, and Local Government	$57,740

Median Wages for States (Annual)

AK	no data	KY	$35,450	NY	$84,930
AL	$37,320	LA	$36,310	OH	$47,000
AR	$36,900	MA	$48,740	OK	$40,760
AZ	$44,370	MD	$57,290	OR	$43,230
CA	$69,030	ME	$36,420	PA	$43,720
CO	$49,250	MI	$47,630	RI	$54,920
CT	$77,760	MN	$52,300	SC	$33,220
DC	$71,180	MO	$45,630	SD	$41,960
DE	no data	MS	$35,760	TN	no data
FL	$46,510	MT	$30,230	TX	$52,960
GA	$66,640	NC	$41,420	UT	$52,840
HI	$62,550	ND	$41,000	VA	$55,910
IA	$35,040	NE	$39,190	VT	$36,580
ID	$30,120	NH	$48,110	WA	$50,430
IL	$43,660	NJ	$67,610	WI	$48,540
IN	$44,500	NM	no data	WV	$33,740
KS	$41,930	NV	$46,940	WY	$40,870

Median Wages for the Largest Metropolitan Areas (Annual)

AZ: Phoenix	$47,560	MI: Detroit	$52,950
CA: Los Angeles	$77,920	MN: Minneapolis	$54,720
CA: Riverside	$51,310	MO: Kansas City	$48,510
CA: Sacramento	$52,420	MO: St. Louis	$57,830
CA: San Diego	$51,680	NV: Las Vegas	$47,320
CA: San Francisco	$67,840	NY: New York	$87,110
CO: Denver	$56,820	OH: Cincinnati	$44,030
DC: Washington	$64,930	OH: Cleveland	$57,850
FL: Miami	$49,280	OH: Columbus	$52,560
FL: Orlando	$59,820	OR: Portland	$45,430
FL: Tampa	$44,360	PA: Philadelphia	$39,140
GA: Atlanta	$68,780	PA: Pittsburgh	$54,660
IL: Chicago	$49,620	TX: Dallas	$59,440
MA: Boston	$50,720	TX: Houston	$67,400
MD: Baltimore	$53,070	WA: Seattle	$52,620

FACTORS THAT MAY AFFECT EARNINGS

Educational Attainment of Workers and Effect on Earnings

	Percent at Level	Effect on Earnings
Less than High School	—	—
Some High School	—	—
High School or Equivalent	13.4%	−20.7%
Some College but No Degree	6.3%	−3.2%
Associate Degree	9.8%	−14.4%
Bachelor's Degree	51.8%	8.8%
Master's Degree	14.3%	6.7%
Doctoral Degree	—	—
First Professional Degree	—	—

Flexibility of Earnings

Average Hours Worked: 34
Workers with a Varying Number of Hours: 17.1%
Workers Earning Some Overtime Pay, Tips, or Commissions: 13.7%
Earnings Benefit of Working Overtime: 6.5%

Gender

	Male	Female
Percent	60.0%	40.0%
Effect on Earnings	3.7%	—

Union Membership

Percentage Union Members: 9.2%
Earnings Benefit of Union Membership: 41.2%

Veteran Status

Percentage Who Have Been on Active Duty: 6.0%
Earnings Benefit of Veteran Status: 7.3%

27-2021 Athletes and Sports Competitors

Compete in athletic events.

- Education or Training Required: Long-term on-the-job training
- Job Growth: 21.1%
- Annual Openings: 6,000
- Self-Employed: 24.5%
- Part-Time: 35.0%

NATIONAL WAGE FIGURES (ANNUAL)

Beginning	25th Percentile	Median	Mean	75th Percentile	90th Percentile
$14,570	$22,770	$41,060	$74,440	$94,040	more than $145,600

Note: The mean is significantly higher than the median because of the presence of a few star earners.

Median Wages for Industries Employing Largest Numbers (Annual)

Industry	Median Income
Real Estate	$91,340
Sporting Goods, Hobby, Book, and Music Stores	$51,340
Performing Arts, Spectator Sports, and Related Industries	$45,880
Accommodation	$39,080
Federal, State, and Local Government	$36,270
Amusement, Gambling, and Recreation Industries	$33,720

Median Wages for States (Annual)

State	Wage	State	Wage	State	Wage
AK	no data	KY	$35,510	NY	no data
AL	$89,870	LA	$26,730	OH	$43,120
AR	no data	MA	no data	OK	$34,350
AZ	no data	MD	no data	OR	$52,100
CA	$38,010	ME	no data	PA	$32,680
CO	no data	MI	$34,730	RI	no data
CT	$29,630	MN	no data	SC	$27,160
DC	$65,570	MO	more than $145,600	SD	no data
DE	no data	MS	no data	TN	$33,440
FL	$37,470	MT	$31,100	TX	$38,960
GA	more than $145,600	NC	$43,570	UT	no data
HI	no data	ND	no data	VA	$34,100
IA	no data	NE	no data	VT	no data
ID	$39,800	NH	no data	WA	$47,050
IL	$15,560	NJ	$43,340	WI	$31,640
IN	$43,790	NM	no data	WV	$25,990
KS	$27,300	NV	$54,770	WY	no data

Median Wages for the Largest Metropolitan Areas (Annual)

Area	Wage	Area	Wage
AZ: Phoenix	no data	MI: Detroit	no data
CA: Los Angeles	$33,140	MN: Minneapolis	$95,430
CA: Riverside	$19,720	MO: Kansas City	no data
CA: Sacramento	no data	MO: St. Louis	more than $145,600
CA: San Diego	more than $145,600	NV: Las Vegas	$56,290
CA: San Francisco	no data	NY: New York	more than $145,600
CO: Denver	no data	OH: Cincinnati	$46,990
DC: Washington	$52,480	OH: Cleveland	no data
FL: Miami	$54,300	OH: Columbus	$42,330
FL: Orlando	no data	OR: Portland	no data
FL: Tampa	$32,680	PA: Philadelphia	$51,650
GA: Atlanta	more than $145,600	PA: Pittsburgh	no data
IL: Chicago	$16,600	TX: Dallas	$41,870
MA: Boston	no data	TX: Houston	more than $145,600
MD: Baltimore	no data	WA: Seattle	more than $145,600

FACTORS THAT MAY AFFECT EARNINGS

Educational Attainment of Workers and Effect on Earnings

Figures are based on a group of occupations: Entertainers and Performers, Sports and Related Workers

	Percent at Level	Effect on Earnings
Less than High School	—	—
Some High School	10.6%	−79.9%
High School or Equivalent	15.9%	−14.2%
Some College but No Degree	16.5%	−24.3%
Associate Degree	6.7%	−1.0%
Bachelor's Degree	31.8%	32.1%
Master's Degree	15.1%	31.2%
Doctoral Degree	—	—
First Professional Degree	—	—

Flexibility of Earnings

Average Hours Worked: 22
Workers with a Varying Number of Hours: 23.6%
Workers Earning Some Overtime Pay, Tips, or Commissions: 7.8%
Earnings Benefit of Working Overtime: −9.6%

Gender

	Male	Female
Percent	63.1%	36.9%
Effect on Earnings	16.7%	—

Union Membership

Percentage Union Members: 8.7%
Earnings Benefit of Union Membership: 76.0%

Veteran Status

Percentage Who Have Been on Active Duty: 6.0%
Earnings Benefit of Veteran Status: 7.3%

27-2022 Coaches and Scouts

Instruct or coach groups or individuals in the fundamentals of sports. Demonstrate techniques and methods of participation. May evaluate athletes' strengths and weaknesses as possible recruits or to improve the athletes' technique to prepare them for competition.

- Education or Training Required: Long-term on-the-job training
- Job Growth: 20.4%
- Annual Openings: 63,000
- Self-Employed: 21.5%
- Part-Time: 35.0%

NATIONAL WAGE FIGURES (ANNUAL)

	25th Percentile	Median	Mean	75th Percentile	90th Percentile
Beginning					
$13,990	$17,510	$26,950	$33,290	$40,850	$58,890

Note: The mean is significantly higher than the median because of the presence of a few star earners.

Median Wages for Industries Employing Largest Numbers (Annual)

Industry	Median Income
Performing Arts, Spectator Sports, and Related Industries	$41,540
Sporting Goods, Hobby, Book, and Music Stores	$37,000
Heavy and Civil Engineering Construction	$29,590
Federal, State, and Local Government	$28,130
Amusement, Gambling, and Recreation Industries	$27,210
Administrative and Support Services	$27,020
Educational Services	$26,930
Social Assistance	$26,150
Accommodation	$25,680
Religious, Grantmaking, Civic, Professional, and Similar Organizations	$21,660

Median Wages for States (Annual)

AK	$21,760	KY	$21,610	NY	$29,790
AL	$18,870	LA	$28,860	OH	$22,870
AR	$37,590	MA	$33,210	OK	$25,610
AZ	$25,570	MD	$35,960	OR	$29,160
CA	$29,650	ME	$14,710	PA	$16,170
CO	$27,730	MI	$22,340	RI	no data
CT	$24,740	MN	$23,200	SC	$34,200
DC	$43,950	MO	$36,900	SD	$26,560
DE	$25,810	MS	$40,930	TN	$24,460
FL	$32,440	MT	$14,730	TX	$26,900
GA	$35,260	NC	$28,660	UT	$23,910
HI	$28,730	ND	$18,530	VA	$28,490
IA	$16,360	NE	$24,160	VT	$26,170
ID	$23,300	NH	$41,370	WA	$32,030
IL	$16,110	NJ	$28,400	WI	$25,680
IN	$16,950	NM	$14,390	WV	$29,090
KS	$15,770	NV	$36,480	WY	$14,410

Median Wages for the Largest Metropolitan Areas (Annual)

AZ: Phoenix	$25,040	MI: Detroit	$22,330
CA: Los Angeles	no data	MN: Minneapolis	$24,460
CA: Riverside	$30,790	MO: Kansas City	$34,770
CA: Sacramento	$25,850	MO: St. Louis	$31,140
CA: San Diego	$25,600	NV: Las Vegas	$47,030
CA: San Francisco	$33,680	NY: New York	$29,550
CO: Denver	$25,940	OH: Cincinnati	$25,200
DC: Washington	$39,720	OH: Cleveland	$24,140
FL: Miami	$30,990	OH: Columbus	$27,370
FL: Orlando	$34,340	OR: Portland	$28,910
FL: Tampa	$36,400	PA: Philadelphia	$21,590
GA: Atlanta	$34,270	PA: Pittsburgh	$15,320
IL: Chicago	$18,610	TX: Dallas	$24,200
MA: Boston	$34,570	TX: Houston	$26,720
MD: Baltimore	$31,560	WA: Seattle	$33,460

FACTORS THAT MAY AFFECT EARNINGS

Educational Attainment of Workers and Effect on Earnings

Figures are based on a group of occupations: Entertainers and Performers, Sports and Related Workers

	Percent at Level	Effect on Earnings
Less than High School	—	—
Some High School	10.6%	−79.9%
High School or Equivalent	15.9%	−14.2%
Some College but No Degree	16.5%	−24.3%
Associate Degree	6.7%	−1.0%
Bachelor's Degree	31.8%	32.1%
Master's Degree	15.1%	31.2%
Doctoral Degree	—	—
First Professional Degree	—	—

Flexibility of Earnings

Average Hours Worked: 22
Workers with a Varying Number of Hours: 23.6%
Workers Earning Some Overtime Pay, Tips, or Commissions: 7.8%
Earnings Benefit of Working Overtime: −9.6%

Gender

	Male	Female
Percent	63.1%	36.9%
Effect on Earnings	16.7%	—

Union Membership

Percentage Union Members: 8.7%
Earnings Benefit of Union Membership: 76.0%

Veteran Status

Percentage Who Have Been on Active Duty: 6.0%
Earnings Benefit of Veteran Status: 7.3%

27-2023 Umpires, Referees, and Other Sports Officials

Officiate at competitive athletic or sporting events. Detect infractions of rules and decide penalties according to established regulations.

- Education or Training Required: Long-term on-the-job training
- Job Growth: 19.0%
- Annual Openings: 6,000
- Self-Employed: 24.8%
- Part-Time: 35.0%

NATIONAL WAGE FIGURES (ANNUAL)

Beginning	25th Percentile	Median	Mean	75th Percentile	90th Percentile
$14,120	$17,090	$22,880	$27,450	$33,840	$45,430

Median Wages for Industries Employing Largest Numbers (Annual)

Industry	Median Income
Professional, Scientific, and Technical Services	$28,920
Amusement, Gambling, and Recreation Industries	$24,750
Federal, State, and Local Government	$23,590
Educational Services	$22,620
Performing Arts, Spectator Sports, and Related Industries	$22,170
Religious, Grantmaking, Civic, Professional, and Similar Organizations	$19,980

Median Wages for States (Annual)

State	Wage	State	Wage	State	Wage
AK	no data	KY	$17,400	NY	no data
AL	no data	LA	no data	OH	$19,000
AR	no data	MA	no data	OK	no data
AZ	$25,100	MD	$29,050	OR	$23,420
CA	$26,600	ME	no data	PA	$19,310
CO	$17,850	MI	$29,300	RI	no data
CT	$18,460	MN	$29,730	SC	$31,240
DC	no data	MO	$26,940	SD	no data
DE	$14,930	MS	no data	TN	$29,530
FL	$27,160	MT	no data	TX	$24,160
GA	$22,550	NC	no data	UT	$15,800
HI	no data	ND	no data	VA	no data
IA	$19,570	NE	$13,330	VT	no data
ID	$13,420	NH	no data	WA	$38,980
IL	$18,890	NJ	$23,460	WI	$22,590
IN	$22,380	NM	no data	WV	$27,710
KS	$21,680	NV	no data	WY	no data

Median Wages for the Largest Metropolitan Areas (Annual)

Area	Wage	Area	Wage
AZ: Phoenix	$25,180	MI: Detroit	$32,690
CA: Los Angeles	$22,940	MN: Minneapolis	$23,390
CA: Riverside	$31,200	MO: Kansas City	$25,980
CA: Sacramento	$30,500	MO: St. Louis	$28,280
CA: San Diego	$26,660	NV: Las Vegas	no data
CA: San Francisco	$27,430	NY: New York	$30,590
CO: Denver	$18,950	OH: Cincinnati	$19,950
DC: Washington	$32,050	OH: Cleveland	$27,770
FL: Miami	$22,840	OH: Columbus	no data
FL: Orlando	no data	OR: Portland	$22,960
FL: Tampa	$28,560	PA: Philadelphia	$21,350
GA: Atlanta	$21,350	PA: Pittsburgh	$23,900
IL: Chicago	$19,700	TX: Dallas	$26,230
MA: Boston	no data	TX: Houston	$18,690
MD: Baltimore	$21,370	WA: Seattle	$40,460

FACTORS THAT MAY AFFECT EARNINGS

Educational Attainment of Workers and Effect on Earnings

Figures are based on a group of occupations: Entertainers and Performers, Sports and Related Workers

	Percent at Level	Effect on Earnings
Less than High School	—	—
Some High School	10.6%	−79.9%
High School or Equivalent	15.9%	−14.2%
Some College but No Degree	16.5%	−24.3%
Associate Degree	6.7%	−1.0%
Bachelor's Degree	31.8%	32.1%
Master's Degree	15.1%	31.2%
Doctoral Degree	—	—
First Professional Degree	—	—

Flexibility of Earnings

Average Hours Worked: 22
Workers with a Varying Number of Hours: 23.6%
Workers Earning Some Overtime Pay, Tips, or Commissions: 7.8%
Earnings Benefit of Working Overtime: −9.6%

Gender

	Male	Female
Percent	63.1%	36.9%
Effect on Earnings	16.7%	—

Union Membership

Percentage Union Members: 8.7%
Earnings Benefit of Union Membership: 76.0%

Veteran Status

Percentage Who Have Been on Active Duty: 6.0%
Earnings Benefit of Veteran Status: 7.3%

27-2031 Dancers

Perform dances. May also sing or act.

- Education or Training Required: Long-term on-the-job training
- Job Growth: 16.8%
- Annual Openings: 4,000
- Self-Employed: 20.3%
- Part-Time: 35.0%

NATIONAL WAGE FIGURES (HOURLY)

Beginning	25th Percentile	Median	Mean	75th Percentile	90th Percentile
$6.62	$7.31	$9.55	$13.86	$17.50	$25.75

Note: The mean is significantly higher than the median because of the presence of a few star earners.

Median Wages for Industries Employing Largest Numbers (Hourly)

Industry	Median Income
Performing Arts, Spectator Sports, and Related Industries	$15.29
Educational Services	$11.83
Amusement, Gambling, and Recreation Industries	$8.72
Food Services and Drinking Places	$7.52

Median Wages for States (Hourly)

AK	$12.65	KY	$8.91	NY	$18.79
AL	$9.06	LA	$7.88	OH	$11.76
AR	no data	MA	no data	OK	no data
AZ	no data	MD	no data	OR	$12.57
CA	$8.58	ME	no data	PA	$12.13
CO	$6.68	MI	$8.22	RI	$11.82
CT	$13.16	MN	$13.63	SC	$14.07
DC	no data	MO	$8.96	SD	no data
DE	no data	MS	no data	TN	$10.65
FL	$7.06	MT	$7.04	TX	$7.61
GA	$11.10	NC	$10.37	UT	$10.58
HI	$20.38	ND	no data	VA	$8.05
IA	$12.52	NE	no data	VT	no data
ID	no data	NH	no data	WA	$11.74
IL	$10.19	NJ	$11.56	WI	$8.54
IN	$7.27	NM	no data	WV	$10.46
KS	no data	NV	$21.02	WY	no data

Median Wages for the Largest Metropolitan Areas (Hourly)

AZ: Phoenix	no data	MI: Detroit	no data
CA: Los Angeles	$8.26	MN: Minneapolis	$13.63
CA: Riverside	no data	MO: Kansas City	$7.05
CA: Sacramento	no data	MO: St. Louis	no data
CA: San Diego	no data	NV: Las Vegas	$20.99
CA: San Francisco	$12.28	NY: New York	no data
CO: Denver	$6.44	OH: Cincinnati	no data
DC: Washington	$18.12	OH: Cleveland	$10.39
FL: Miami	$6.89	OH: Columbus	no data
FL: Orlando	$6.89	OR: Portland	no data
FL: Tampa	no data	PA: Philadelphia	$8.40
GA: Atlanta	$12.29	PA: Pittsburgh	no data
IL: Chicago	$9.43	TX: Dallas	$7.96
MA: Boston	no data	TX: Houston	$7.63
MD: Baltimore	no data	WA: Seattle	$11.80

FACTORS THAT MAY AFFECT EARNINGS

Educational Attainment of Workers and Effect on Earnings

Figures are based on a group of occupations: Entertainers and Performers, Sports and Related Workers

	Percent at Level	Effect on Earnings
Less than High School	—	—
Some High School	10.6%	−79.9%
High School or Equivalent	15.9%	−14.2%
Some College but No Degree	16.5%	−24.3%
Associate Degree	6.7%	−1.0%
Bachelor's Degree	31.8%	32.1%
Master's Degree	15.1%	31.2%
Doctoral Degree	—	—
First Professional Degree	—	—

Flexibility of Earnings

Average Hours Worked: 22
Workers with a Varying Number of Hours: 23.6%
Workers Earning Some Overtime Pay, Tips, or Commissions: 7.8%
Earnings Benefit of Working Overtime: 3.3%

Gender

	Male	Female
Percent	59.4%	40.6%
Effect on Earnings	12.0%	−12.8%

Union Membership

Percentage Union Members: 8.7%
Earnings Benefit of Union Membership: 76.0%

Veteran Status

Percentage Who Have Been on Active Duty: 6.0%
Earnings Benefit of Veteran Status: 7.3%

27-2032 Choreographers

Create and teach dance. May direct and stage presentations.

- Education or Training Required: Work experience in a related occupation
- Job Growth: 16.8%
- Annual Openings: 4,000
- Self-Employed: 17.7%
- Part-Time: 35.0%

NATIONAL WAGE FIGURES (ANNUAL)

Beginning	25th Percentile	Median	Mean	75th Percentile	90th Percentile
$15,710	$21,910	$34,660	$38,320	$49,810	$64,070

Median Wages for Industries Employing Largest Numbers (Annual)

Industry	Median Income
Social Assistance	$53,860
Performing Arts, Spectator Sports, and Related Industries	$38,750
Amusement, Gambling, and Recreation Industries	$38,480
Educational Services	$34,480
Administrative and Support Services	$30,490
Federal, State, and Local Government	$27,810
Religious, Grantmaking, Civic, Professional, and Similar Organizations	$26,270

Median Wages for States (Annual)

State	Wage	State	Wage	State	Wage
AK	no data	KY	$27,960	NY	$48,320
AL	$33,620	LA	$19,520	OH	$34,770
AR	no data	MA	$43,770	OK	no data
AZ	$39,740	MD	$61,690	OR	$40,110
CA	$38,950	ME	no data	PA	$26,490
CO	$44,570	MI	$35,120	RI	no data
CT	$35,510	MN	$33,210	SC	$37,750
DC	no data	MO	$52,190	SD	$21,570
DE	no data	MS	$21,850	TN	no data
FL	$52,770	MT	no data	TX	$28,210
GA	$76,820	NC	no data	UT	$32,000
HI	no data	ND	$33,460	VA	$44,360
IA	$31,840	NE	$23,630	VT	no data
ID	no data	NH	no data	WA	$47,000
IL	$28,190	NJ	$49,910	WI	$23,530
IN	$24,330	NM	$36,890	WV	no data
KS	$27,900	NV	$30,980	WY	$25,370

Median Wages for the Largest Metropolitan Areas (Annual)

Area	Wage	Area	Wage
AZ: Phoenix	$40,430	MI: Detroit	$31,060
CA: Los Angeles	$43,180	MN: Minneapolis	no data
CA: Riverside	$35,130	MO: Kansas City	$55,330
CA: Sacramento	no data	MO: St. Louis	no data
CA: San Diego	$40,610	NV: Las Vegas	$34,170
CA: San Francisco	$40,060	NY: New York	$51,470
CO: Denver	$46,180	OH: Cincinnati	$22,810
DC: Washington	$46,750	OH: Cleveland	no data
FL: Miami	no data	OH: Columbus	no data
FL: Orlando	no data	OR: Portland	$41,020
FL: Tampa	no data	PA: Philadelphia	$17,980
GA: Atlanta	$78,270	PA: Pittsburgh	$28,580
IL: Chicago	$40,020	TX: Dallas	$37,270
MA: Boston	$45,390	TX: Houston	$30,870
MD: Baltimore	$60,880	WA: Seattle	$47,880

FACTORS THAT MAY AFFECT EARNINGS

Educational Attainment of Workers and Effect on Earnings

Figures are based on a group of occupations: Entertainers and Performers, Sports and Related Workers

	Percent at Level	Effect on Earnings
Less than High School	—	—
Some High School	10.6%	−79.9%
High School or Equivalent	15.9%	−14.2%
Some College but No Degree	16.5%	−24.3%
Associate Degree	6.7%	−1.0%
Bachelor's Degree	31.8%	32.1%
Master's Degree	15.1%	31.2%
Doctoral Degree	—	—
First Professional Degree	—	—

Flexibility of Earnings

Average Hours Worked: 22
Workers with a Varying Number of Hours: 23.6%
Workers Earning Some Overtime Pay, Tips, or Commissions: 7.8%
Earnings Benefit of Working Overtime: 3.3%

Gender

	Male	Female
Percent	59.4%	40.6%
Effect on Earnings	12.0%	−12.8%

Union Membership

Percentage Union Members: 8.7%
Earnings Benefit of Union Membership: 76.0%

Veteran Status

Percentage Who Have Been on Active Duty: 6.0%
Earnings Benefit of Veteran Status: 7.3%

27-2041 Music Directors and Composers

Conduct, direct, plan, and lead instrumental or vocal performances by musical groups such as orchestras, choirs, and glee clubs. Includes arrangers, composers, choral directors, and orchestrators.

- Education or Training Required: Work experience plus degree
- Job Growth: 10.4%
- Annual Openings: 11,000
- Self-Employed: 44.8%
- Part-Time: 35.0%

Note: Earnings figures do not reflect self-employed workers, who make up a large fraction of the workforce for this occupation.

NATIONAL WAGE FIGURES (ANNUAL)

Beginning	25th Percentile	Median	Mean	75th Percentile	90th Percentile
$15,210	$23,660	$39,750	$53,320	$60,350	$110,850

Note: The mean is significantly higher than the median because of the presence of a few star earners.

Median Wages for Industries Employing Largest Numbers (Annual)

Industry	Median Income
Performing Arts, Spectator Sports, and Related Industries	$50,570
Motion Picture and Sound Recording Industries	$47,730
Educational Services	$46,270
Broadcasting (Except Internet)	$45,680
Social Assistance	$37,490
Religious, Grantmaking, Civic, Professional, and Similar Organizations	$34,560

Median Wages for States (Annual)

AK	no data	KY	$38,820	NY	$42,200
AL	no data	LA	no data	OH	no data
AR	no data	MA	$58,680	OK	no data
AZ	no data	MD	$46,920	OR	$41,630
CA	no data	ME	no data	PA	$27,960
CO	no data	MI	$32,800	RI	$28,730
CT	$53,240	MN	$53,230	SC	$25,800
DC	$47,560	MO	$53,000	SD	no data
DE	no data	MS	no data	TN	$29,930
FL	$36,860	MT	$15,260	TX	$34,100
GA	$55,160	NC	$60,330	UT	no data
HI	$34,800	ND	no data	VA	$34,500
IA	no data	NE	no data	VT	no data
ID	no data	NH	no data	WA	$56,940
IL	$38,100	NJ	$40,650	WI	$38,690
IN	$28,100	NM	$83,950	WV	no data
KS	no data	NV	no data	WY	no data

Median Wages for the Largest Metropolitan Areas (Annual)

AZ: Phoenix	no data	MI: Detroit	$43,320
CA: Los Angeles	no data	MN: Minneapolis	$53,700
CA: Riverside	$35,570	MO: Kansas City	no data
CA: Sacramento	$41,970	MO: St. Louis	no data
CA: San Diego	$72,790	NV: Las Vegas	$114,010
CA: San Francisco	$50,250	NY: New York	$46,310
CO: Denver	no data	OH: Cincinnati	$52,600
DC: Washington	$46,150	OH: Cleveland	no data
FL: Miami	$39,760	OH: Columbus	no data
FL: Orlando	$37,540	OR: Portland	$39,980
FL: Tampa	$31,810	PA: Philadelphia	$34,040
GA: Atlanta	no data	PA: Pittsburgh	$29,940
IL: Chicago	$37,810	TX: Dallas	$24,330
MA: Boston	$66,170	TX: Houston	no data
MD: Baltimore	$64,070	WA: Seattle	$59,390

FACTORS THAT MAY AFFECT EARNINGS

Educational Attainment of Workers and Effect on Earnings

Figures are based on a group of occupations: Entertainers and Performers, Sports and Related Workers

	Percent at Level	Effect on Earnings
Less than High School	—	—
Some High School	10.6%	−79.9%
High School or Equivalent	15.9%	−14.2%
Some College but No Degree	16.5%	−24.3%
Associate Degree	6.7%	−1.0%
Bachelor's Degree	31.8%	32.1%
Master's Degree	15.1%	31.2%
Doctoral Degree	—	—
First Professional Degree	—	—

Flexibility of Earnings

Average Hours Worked: 22
Workers with a Varying Number of Hours: 23.6%
Workers Earning Some Overtime Pay, Tips, or Commissions: 7.8%
Earnings Benefit of Working Overtime: 3.3%

Gender

	Male	Female
Percent	59.4%	40.6%
Effect on Earnings	12.0%	−12.8%

Union Membership

Percentage Union Members: 8.7%
Earnings Benefit of Union Membership: 76.0%

Veteran Status

Percentage Who Have Been on Active Duty: 6.0%
Earnings Benefit of Veteran Status: 7.3%

27-2042 Musicians and Singers

Play one or more musical instruments or entertain by singing songs in recital; in accompaniment; or as a member of an orchestra, band, or other musical group. Musical performers may entertain on stage, radio, TV, film, or video or record in studios.

- Education or Training Required: Long-term on-the-job training
- Job Growth: 14.0%
- Annual Openings: 37,000
- Self-Employed: 40.8%
- Part-Time: 35.0%

Note: Earnings figures do not reflect self-employed workers, who make up a large fraction of the workforce for this occupation.

NATIONAL WAGE FIGURES (HOURLY)

Beginning	25th Percentile	Median	Mean	75th Percentile	90th Percentile
$7.08	$10.81	$19.73	$27.51	$36.55	$57.37

Note: The mean is significantly higher than the median because of the presence of a few star earners.

Median Wages for Industries Employing Largest Numbers (Hourly)

Industry	Median Income
Accommodation	$35.92
Educational Services	$18.58
Amusement, Gambling, and Recreation Industries	$17.76
Food Services and Drinking Places	$14.72
Administrative and Support Services	$14.70

Median Wages for States (Hourly)

AK	no data	KY	$19.29	NY	$16.78
AL	$21.36	LA	no data	OH	$22.82
AR	no data	MA	no data	OK	$30.93
AZ	$13.79	MD	$34.24	OR	$25.15
CA	$32.52	ME	no data	PA	$14.29
CO	$19.63	MI	$17.67	RI	no data
CT	$22.69	MN	$21.74	SC	$23.45
DC	$14.62	MO	$22.54	SD	no data
DE	no data	MS	$26.68	TN	$14.89
FL	$13.75	MT	$6.73	TX	$13.11
GA	$14.58	NC	$14.16	UT	$17.17
HI	$25.21	ND	no data	VA	$15.39
IA	no data	NE	$16.36	VT	no data
ID	no data	NH	no data	WA	$28.67
IL	$16.65	NJ	$15.55	WI	$20.47
IN	$19.15	NM	$16.75	WV	no data
KS	$11.43	NV	$38.61	WY	no data

Median Wages for the Largest Metropolitan Areas (Hourly)

AZ: Phoenix	no data	MI: Detroit	$17.62
CA: Los Angeles	$34.38	MN: Minneapolis	$32.07
CA: Riverside	$21.58	MO: Kansas City	$18.44
CA: Sacramento	no data	MO: St. Louis	no data
CA: San Diego	$26.68	NV: Las Vegas	$40.21
CA: San Francisco	$34.45	NY: New York	$17.80
CO: Denver	no data	OH: Cincinnati	$21.57
DC: Washington	$17.32	OH: Cleveland	$15.72
FL: Miami	$12.15	OH: Columbus	no data
FL: Orlando	$10.60	OR: Portland	$21.96
FL: Tampa	$20.56	PA: Philadelphia	$12.81
GA: Atlanta	$12.45	PA: Pittsburgh	$32.51
IL: Chicago	$17.49	TX: Dallas	$14.09
MA: Boston	no data	TX: Houston	$8.75
MD: Baltimore	$38.15	WA: Seattle	$32.82

FACTORS THAT MAY AFFECT EARNINGS

Educational Attainment of Workers and Effect on Earnings

Figures are based on a group of occupations: Entertainers and Performers, Sports and Related Workers

	Percent at Level	Effect on Earnings
Less than High School	—	—
Some High School	10.6%	−79.9%
High School or Equivalent	15.9%	−14.2%
Some College but No Degree	16.5%	−24.3%
Associate Degree	6.7%	−1.0%
Bachelor's Degree	31.8%	32.1%
Master's Degree	15.1%	31.2%
Doctoral Degree	—	—
First Professional Degree	—	—

Flexibility of Earnings

Average Hours Worked: 22
Workers with a Varying Number of Hours: 23.6%
Workers Earning Some Overtime Pay, Tips, or Commissions: 7.8%
Earnings Benefit of Working Overtime: 3.3%

Gender

	Male	Female
Percent	66.5%	33.5%
Effect on Earnings	12.0%	−12.8%

Union Membership

Percentage Union Members: 8.7%
Earnings Benefit of Union Membership: 76.0%

Veteran Status

Percentage Who Have Been on Active Duty: 6.0%
Earnings Benefit of Veteran Status: 7.3%

27-2099 Entertainers and Performers, Sports and Related Workers, All Other

All entertainers and performers, sports and related workers not listed separately.

- Education or Training Required: Long-term on-the-job training
- Job Growth: 21.0%
- Annual Openings: 17,000
- Self-Employed: 23.9%
- Part-Time: 16.7%

NATIONAL WAGE FIGURES (HOURLY)

Beginning	25th Percentile	Median	Mean	75th Percentile	90th Percentile
$7.90	$10.33	$15.11	$16.84	$20.59	$27.34

Median Wages for Industries Employing Largest Numbers (Hourly)

Industry	Median Income
Hospitals	$18.41
Broadcasting (Except Internet)	$17.75
Motion Picture and Sound Recording Industries	$15.58
Accommodation	$14.68
Educational Services	$14.04
Federal, State, and Local Government	$13.95
Food Services and Drinking Places	$13.86
Amusement, Gambling, and Recreation Industries	$10.76
Administrative and Support Services	$8.69
Museums, Historical Sites, and Similar Institutions	$7.13

Median Wages for States (Hourly)

State	Wage	State	Wage	State	Wage
AK	no data	KY	$16.42	NY	no data
AL	$8.68	LA	no data	OH	$11.34
AR	$10.66	MA	no data	OK	no data
AZ	no data	MD	$13.27	OR	no data
CA	$15.03	ME	no data	PA	$9.38
CO	no data	MI	$18.45	RI	no data
CT	$22.71	MN	$10.93	SC	no data
DC	no data	MO	$16.52	SD	no data
DE	no data	MS	no data	TN	$25.23
FL	$16.44	MT	no data	TX	no data
GA	$11.04	NC	$6.82	UT	$10.95
HI	no data	ND	no data	VA	no data
IA	no data	NE	no data	VT	no data
ID	no data	NH	no data	WA	$22.65
IL	$10.13	NJ	$20.35	WI	$10.86
IN	$16.35	NM	no data	WV	no data
KS	no data	NV	$20.44	WY	no data

Median Wages for the Largest Metropolitan Areas (Hourly)

Area	Wage	Area	Wage
AZ: Phoenix	no data	MI: Detroit	$18.65
CA: Los Angeles	$15.16	MN: Minneapolis	$9.94
CA: Riverside	no data	MO: Kansas City	no data
CA: Sacramento	no data	MO: St. Louis	$10.56
CA: San Diego	$10.41	NV: Las Vegas	$21.02
CA: San Francisco	$12.75	NY: New York	$20.20
CO: Denver	no data	OH: Cincinnati	$8.36
DC: Washington	$12.84	OH: Cleveland	$11.25
FL: Miami	no data	OH: Columbus	no data
FL: Orlando	$15.43	OR: Portland	$21.71
FL: Tampa	$14.50	PA: Philadelphia	$9.17
GA: Atlanta	$9.26	PA: Pittsburgh	no data
IL: Chicago	$10.06	TX: Dallas	no data
MA: Boston	no data	TX: Houston	no data
MD: Baltimore	$13.44	WA: Seattle	$24.39

FACTORS THAT MAY AFFECT EARNINGS

Educational Attainment of Workers and Effect on Earnings

Figures are based on a group of occupations: Entertainers and Performers, Sports and Related Workers

	Percent at Level	Effect on Earnings
Less than High School	—	—
Some High School	10.6%	−79.9%
High School or Equivalent	15.9%	−14.2%
Some College but No Degree	16.5%	−24.3%
Associate Degree	6.7%	−1.0%
Bachelor's Degree	31.8%	32.1%
Master's Degree	15.1%	31.2%
Doctoral Degree	—	—
First Professional Degree	—	—

Flexibility of Earnings

Average Hours Worked: 24
Workers with a Varying Number of Hours: 26.8%
Workers Earning Some Overtime Pay, Tips, or Commissions: 8.3%
Earnings Benefit of Working Overtime: 3.3%

Gender

	Male	Female
Percent	52.0%	48.0%
Effect on Earnings	12.0%	−12.8%

Union Membership

Percentage Union Members: 8.7%
Earnings Benefit of Union Membership: 76.0%

Veteran Status

Percentage Who Have Been on Active Duty: 6.0%
Earnings Benefit of Veteran Status: 7.3%

27-3000 Media and Communication Workers

27-3011 Radio and Television Announcers

Talk on radio or television. May interview guests, act as master of ceremonies, read news flashes, identify station by giving call letters, or announce song title and artist.

- Education or Training Required: Long-term on-the-job training
- Job Growth: –6.5%
- Annual Openings: 8,000
- Self-Employed: 25.4%
- Part-Time: 32.0%

NATIONAL WAGE FIGURES (ANNUAL)

Beginning	25th Percentile	Median	Mean	75th Percentile	90th Percentile
$13,620	$16,850	$24,310	$36,120	$38,730	$68,600

Note: The mean is significantly higher than the median because of the presence of a few star earners.

Median Wages for Industries Employing Largest Numbers (Annual)

Industry	Median Income
Motion Picture and Sound Recording Industries	$54,280
Performing Arts, Spectator Sports, and Related Industries	$37,620
Federal, State, and Local Government	$37,470
Publishing Industries (Except Internet)	$28,670
Educational Services	$27,470
Religious, Grantmaking, Civic, Professional, and Similar Organizations	$27,310
Broadcasting (Except Internet)	$24,030
Food Services and Drinking Places	$21,330
Amusement, Gambling, and Recreation Industries	$20,210
Administrative and Support Services	$19,570

Median Wages for States (Annual)

AK	$32,810	KY	$17,740	NY	$46,240
AL	$18,580	LA	$22,560	OH	$20,520
AR	$21,970	MA	no data	OK	$17,080
AZ	$23,660	MD	$33,290	OR	$26,630
CA	$30,740	ME	$21,950	PA	$18,480
CO	$28,070	MI	$19,200	RI	$32,080
CT	$24,940	MN	$23,120	SC	$23,630
DC	no data	MO	$19,010	SD	$23,680
DE	$20,390	MS	$18,440	TN	$19,940
FL	$25,920	MT	$20,940	TX	$25,340
GA	$29,540	NC	$21,510	UT	$30,720
HI	$21,060	ND	$23,710	VA	$22,890
IA	$19,310	NE	$20,890	VT	$22,250
ID	$24,720	NH	$24,650	WA	$25,080
IL	$27,370	NJ	$39,410	WI	$22,630
IN	$19,720	NM	$16,450	WV	$21,400
KS	$25,360	NV	$34,690	WY	$23,210

Median Wages for the Largest Metropolitan Areas (Annual)

AZ: Phoenix	$25,520	MI: Detroit	no data
CA: Los Angeles	$33,950	MN: Minneapolis	$39,590
CA: Riverside	$23,030	MO: Kansas City	$24,950
CA: Sacramento	$29,960	MO: St. Louis	$22,110
CA: San Diego	$36,030	NV: Las Vegas	$39,610
CA: San Francisco	$35,080	NY: New York	$59,050
CO: Denver	$31,420	OH: Cincinnati	$22,240
DC: Washington	$38,240	OH: Cleveland	$20,390
FL: Miami	$26,530	OH: Columbus	$20,520
FL: Orlando	$51,570	OR: Portland	$43,820
FL: Tampa	$26,050	PA: Philadelphia	$37,850
GA: Atlanta	$30,190	PA: Pittsburgh	no data
IL: Chicago	$36,010	TX: Dallas	$28,350
MA: Boston	no data	TX: Houston	$27,020
MD: Baltimore	$36,810	WA: Seattle	$52,230

FACTORS THAT MAY AFFECT EARNINGS

Educational Attainment of Workers and Effect on Earnings

Figures are based on a group of occupations: Media and Communication Workers

	Percent at Level	Effect on Earnings
Less than High School	—	—
Some High School	1.9%	–68.6%
High School or Equivalent	8.3%	–15.4%
Some College but No Degree	16.6%	–27.2%
Associate Degree	8.7%	–13.5%
Bachelor's Degree	41.7%	5.9%
Master's Degree	17.0%	19.0%
Doctoral Degree	2.1%	32.6%
First Professional Degree	3.4%	64.9%

Flexibility of Earnings

Average Hours Worked: 33
Workers with a Varying Number of Hours: 9.1%
Workers Earning Some Overtime Pay, Tips, or Commissions: 8.2%
Earnings Benefit of Working Overtime: 8.9%

Gender

	Male	Female
Percent	69.2%	30.8%
Effect on Earnings	12.0%	–12.8%

Union Membership

Percentage Union Members: 6.0%
Earnings Benefit of Union Membership: 19.5%

Veteran Status

Percentage Who Have Been on Active Duty: 6.9%
Earnings Benefit of Veteran Status: 16.9%

27-3012 Public Address System and Other Announcers

Make announcements over loudspeaker at sporting or other public events. May act as master of ceremonies or disc jockey at weddings, parties, clubs, or other gathering places.

- Education or Training Required: Long-term on-the-job training
- Job Growth: 3.8%
- Annual Openings: 2,000
- Self-Employed: 26.2%
- Part-Time: 32.0%

NATIONAL WAGE FIGURES (ANNUAL)

Beginning	25th Percentile	Median	Mean	75th Percentile	90th Percentile
$14,000	$17,500	$24,990	$33,970	$40,310	$61,760

Note: The mean is significantly higher than the median because of the presence of a few star earners.

Median Wages for Industries Employing Largest Numbers (Annual)

Industry	Median Income
Performing Arts, Spectator Sports, and Related Industries	$34,600
Educational Services	$25,980
Motion Picture and Sound Recording Industries	$22,560
Food Services and Drinking Places	$21,190
Broadcasting (Except Internet)	$21,050
Amusement, Gambling, and Recreation Industries	$16,710

Median Wages for States (Annual)

State	Wage	State	Wage	State	Wage
AK	$22,940	KY	$17,200	NY	$27,120
AL	$26,440	LA	no data	OH	$29,230
AR	$17,240	MA	no data	OK	$14,040
AZ	$19,640	MD	$34,090	OR	no data
CA	$25,470	ME	no data	PA	$20,980
CO	$19,500	MI	$22,430	RI	no data
CT	$25,610	MN	$31,830	SC	$21,210
DC	no data	MO	$24,710	SD	$20,330
DE	no data	MS	no data	TN	$22,560
FL	$22,450	MT	$19,660	TX	$22,360
GA	$22,850	NC	$34,740	UT	$17,930
HI	no data	ND	$17,720	VA	no data
IA	$27,000	NE	$19,440	VT	$28,770
ID	$13,910	NH	no data	WA	$27,600
IL	$37,260	NJ	$14,920	WI	$33,620
IN	$18,680	NM	$14,030	WV	no data
KS	$26,410	NV	$29,020	WY	no data

Median Wages for the Largest Metropolitan Areas (Annual)

Area	Wage	Area	Wage
AZ: Phoenix	no data	MI: Detroit	$36,640
CA: Los Angeles	$24,550	MN: Minneapolis	$33,200
CA: Riverside	$35,440	MO: Kansas City	$25,880
CA: Sacramento	$20,710	MO: St. Louis	$23,840
CA: San Diego	no data	NV: Las Vegas	$28,710
CA: San Francisco	$25,420	NY: New York	$28,700
CO: Denver	$19,320	OH: Cincinnati	$40,430
DC: Washington	no data	OH: Cleveland	no data
FL: Miami	$31,620	OH: Columbus	$28,370
FL: Orlando	$25,220	OR: Portland	$21,860
FL: Tampa	$47,370	PA: Philadelphia	$20,050
GA: Atlanta	no data	PA: Pittsburgh	no data
IL: Chicago	$42,990	TX: Dallas	$19,030
MA: Boston	no data	TX: Houston	$21,730
MD: Baltimore	no data	WA: Seattle	$27,790

FACTORS THAT MAY AFFECT EARNINGS

Educational Attainment of Workers and Effect on Earnings

Figures are based on a group of occupations: Media and Communication Workers

	Percent at Level	Effect on Earnings
Less than High School	—	—
Some High School	1.9%	−68.6%
High School or Equivalent	8.3%	−15.4%
Some College but No Degree	16.6%	−27.2%
Associate Degree	8.7%	−13.5%
Bachelor's Degree	41.7%	5.9%
Master's Degree	17.0%	19.0%
Doctoral Degree	2.1%	32.6%
First Professional Degree	3.4%	64.9%

Flexibility of Earnings

Average Hours Worked: 33
Workers with a Varying Number of Hours: 9.1%
Workers Earning Some Overtime Pay, Tips, or Commissions: 8.2%
Earnings Benefit of Working Overtime: 8.9%

Gender

	Male	Female
Percent	69.2%	30.8%
Effect on Earnings	12.0%	−12.8%

Union Membership

Percentage Union Members: 6.0%
Earnings Benefit of Union Membership: 19.5%

Veteran Status

Percentage Who Have Been on Active Duty: 6.9%
Earnings Benefit of Veteran Status: 16.9%

27-3021 Broadcast News Analysts

Analyze, interpret, and broadcast news received from various sources.

- Education or Training Required: Work experience plus degree
- Job Growth: 4.3%
- Annual Openings: 1,000
- Self-Employed: 6.9%
- Part-Time: 32.0%

NATIONAL WAGE FIGURES (ANNUAL)

Beginning	25th Percentile	Median	Mean	75th Percentile	90th Percentile
$22,430	$30,080	$46,710	$66,910	$83,370	more than $145,600

Note: The mean is significantly higher than the median because of the presence of a few star earners.

Median Wages for Industries Employing Largest Numbers (Annual)

Industry	Median Income
Internet Publishing and Broadcasting	$54,390
Broadcasting (Except Internet)	$49,340
Educational Services	$42,300
Publishing Industries (Except Internet)	$32,060
Other Information Services	$21,290

Median Wages for States (Annual)

State	Wage	State	Wage	State	Wage
AK	no data	KY	$31,390	NY	$45,480
AL	$46,690	LA	$45,900	OH	$56,240
AR	$40,060	MA	no data	OK	$46,130
AZ	$49,760	MD	$59,010	OR	$51,210
CA	$73,940	ME	$18,970	PA	$30,630
CO	$45,520	MI	$56,380	RI	no data
CT	no data	MN	$42,940	SC	$36,180
DC	no data	MO	$52,770	SD	no data
DE	no data	MS	$28,490	TN	$56,660
FL	$72,150	MT	$17,650	TX	$42,510
GA	$43,130	NC	$50,100	UT	$40,610
HI	no data	ND	$24,650	VA	$46,760
IA	$33,690	NE	$30,840	VT	no data
ID	$32,230	NH	no data	WA	$60,800
IL	$50,860	NJ	$62,620	WI	$34,570
IN	$52,340	NM	no data	WV	no data
KS	no data	NV	$46,200	WY	no data

Median Wages for the Largest Metropolitan Areas (Annual)

Area	Wage	Area	Wage
AZ: Phoenix	$64,650	MI: Detroit	$57,900
CA: Los Angeles	$91,850	MN: Minneapolis	$51,960
CA: Riverside	$73,430	MO: Kansas City	$67,530
CA: Sacramento	no data	MO: St. Louis	no data
CA: San Diego	$78,980	NV: Las Vegas	$50,830
CA: San Francisco	no data	NY: New York	$57,760
CO: Denver	no data	OH: Cincinnati	$80,580
DC: Washington	no data	OH: Cleveland	$55,600
FL: Miami	$80,040	OH: Columbus	no data
FL: Orlando	$77,950	OR: Portland	no data
FL: Tampa	no data	PA: Philadelphia	$27,550
GA: Atlanta	$50,310	PA: Pittsburgh	no data
IL: Chicago	$66,130	TX: Dallas	$49,710
MA: Boston	no data	TX: Houston	no data
MD: Baltimore	$72,760	WA: Seattle	no data

FACTORS THAT MAY AFFECT EARNINGS

Educational Attainment of Workers and Effect on Earnings

Figures are based on a group of occupations: Media and Communication Workers

	Percent at Level	Effect on Earnings
Less than High School	—	—
Some High School	1.9%	−68.6%
High School or Equivalent	8.3%	−15.4%
Some College but No Degree	16.6%	−27.2%
Associate Degree	8.7%	−13.5%
Bachelor's Degree	41.7%	5.9%
Master's Degree	17.0%	19.0%
Doctoral Degree	2.1%	32.6%
First Professional Degree	3.4%	64.9%

Flexibility of Earnings

Average Hours Worked: 33
Workers with a Varying Number of Hours: 9.1%
Workers Earning Some Overtime Pay, Tips, or Commissions: 8.2%
Earnings Benefit of Working Overtime: 22.3%

Gender

	Male	Female
Percent	46.6%	53.4%
Effect on Earnings	12.0%	−12.8%

Union Membership

Percentage Union Members: 6.0%
Earnings Benefit of Union Membership: 19.5%

Veteran Status

Percentage Who Have Been on Active Duty: 6.9%
Earnings Benefit of Veteran Status: 16.9%

27-3022 Reporters and Correspondents

Collect and analyze facts about newsworthy events by interview, investigation, or observation. Report and write stories for newspaper, news magazine, radio, or television.

- Education or Training Required: Work experience plus degree
- Job Growth: 4.9%
- Annual Openings: 4,000
- Self-Employed: 6.8%
- Part-Time: 32.0%

NATIONAL WAGE FIGURES (ANNUAL)

Beginning	25th Percentile	Median	Mean	75th Percentile	90th Percentile
$19,180	$24,370	$33,470	$41,900	$51,700	$73,880

Note: The mean is significantly higher than the median because of the presence of a few star earners.

Median Wages for Industries Employing Largest Numbers (Annual)

Industry	Median Income
Telecommunications	$56,950
Other Information Services	$51,850
Federal, State, and Local Government	$40,640
Internet Publishing and Broadcasting	$38,510
Broadcasting (Except Internet)	$38,000
Publishing Industries (Except Internet)	$31,690
Educational Services	$28,940
Administrative and Support Services	$27,940
Religious, Grantmaking, Civic, Professional, and Similar Organizations	$25,120

Median Wages for States (Annual)

State	Wage	State	Wage	State	Wage
AK	$36,490	KY	$26,670	NY	$43,570
AL	$24,180	LA	$31,640	OH	$30,100
AR	$24,850	MA	no data	OK	$22,410
AZ	$28,860	MD	$39,610	OR	$30,620
CA	$42,090	ME	$31,550	PA	$33,180
CO	$33,850	MI	$29,660	RI	$60,110
CT	$36,600	MN	$35,560	SC	$30,950
DC	$52,080	MO	$25,050	SD	$24,930
DE	$29,020	MS	$28,510	TN	$34,470
FL	$38,010	MT	$26,390	TX	$29,640
GA	$30,100	NC	$29,610	UT	$35,780
HI	$64,670	ND	$25,260	VA	$31,940
IA	$27,830	NE	$27,740	VT	$30,510
ID	$29,190	NH	$33,880	WA	$44,410
IL	$27,020	NJ	$38,680	WI	$30,100
IN	$29,640	NM	$30,770	WV	$23,950
KS	$26,130	NV	$36,350	WY	$24,860

Median Wages for the Largest Metropolitan Areas (Annual)

Area	Wage	Area	Wage
AZ: Phoenix	$27,630	MI: Detroit	$29,210
CA: Los Angeles	$46,120	MN: Minneapolis	$62,480
CA: Riverside	$34,900	MO: Kansas City	$40,520
CA: Sacramento	$35,270	MO: St. Louis	$21,940
CA: San Diego	$43,340	NV: Las Vegas	$40,770
CA: San Francisco	$50,370	NY: New York	$45,960
CO: Denver	$58,690	OH: Cincinnati	$49,680
DC: Washington	$46,670	OH: Cleveland	$34,460
FL: Miami	$48,120	OH: Columbus	$29,190
FL: Orlando	no data	OR: Portland	$40,830
FL: Tampa	no data	PA: Philadelphia	$40,850
GA: Atlanta	no data	PA: Pittsburgh	$41,390
IL: Chicago	$28,740	TX: Dallas	$51,620
MA: Boston	no data	TX: Houston	$28,020
MD: Baltimore	$59,690	WA: Seattle	$55,900

FACTORS THAT MAY AFFECT EARNINGS

Educational Attainment of Workers and Effect on Earnings

Figures are based on a group of occupations: Media and Communication Workers

	Percent at Level	Effect on Earnings
Less than High School	—	—
Some High School	1.9%	−68.6%
High School or Equivalent	8.3%	−15.4%
Some College but No Degree	16.6%	−27.2%
Associate Degree	8.7%	−13.5%
Bachelor's Degree	41.7%	5.9%
Master's Degree	17.0%	19.0%
Doctoral Degree	2.1%	32.6%
First Professional Degree	3.4%	64.9%

Flexibility of Earnings

Average Hours Worked: 33
Workers with a Varying Number of Hours: 9.1%
Workers Earning Some Overtime Pay, Tips, or Commissions: 8.2%
Earnings Benefit of Working Overtime: 22.3%

Gender

	Male	Female
Percent	46.6%	53.4%
Effect on Earnings	12.0%	−12.8%

Union Membership

Percentage Union Members: 6.0%
Earnings Benefit of Union Membership: 19.5%

Veteran Status

Percentage Who Have Been on Active Duty: 6.9%
Earnings Benefit of Veteran Status: 16.9%

27-3031 Public Relations Specialists

Engage in promoting or creating good will for individuals, groups, or organizations by writing or selecting favorable publicity material and releasing it through various communications media. May prepare and arrange displays and make speeches.

- Education or Training Required: Bachelor's degree
- Job Growth: 22.9%
- Annual Openings: 38,000
- Self-Employed: 2.7%
- Part-Time: 23.0%

NATIONAL WAGE FIGURES (ANNUAL)

Beginning	25th Percentile	Median	Mean	75th Percentile	90th Percentile
$28,080	$35,600	$47,350	$53,760	$65,310	$89,220

Median Wages for Industries Employing Largest Numbers (Annual)

Industry	Median Income
Computer and Electronic Product Manufacturing	$66,360
Telecommunications	$58,010
Utilities	$57,210
Securities, Commodity Contracts, and Other Financial Investments and Related Activities	$54,630
Management of Companies and Enterprises	$52,940
Merchant Wholesalers, Durable Goods	$52,880
Federal, State, and Local Government	$52,150
Professional, Scientific, and Technical Services	$51,220
Publishing Industries (Except Internet)	$50,480
Merchant Wholesalers, Nondurable Goods	$49,410

Median Wages for States (Annual)

AK	$63,290	KY	$37,810	NY	$49,820
AL	$39,140	LA	$38,150	OH	$47,810
AR	$33,620	MA	$53,460	OK	$39,860
AZ	$39,590	MD	$51,420	OR	$46,670
CA	$52,020	ME	$42,950	PA	$45,980
CO	$47,270	MI	$48,170	RI	$48,470
CT	$52,160	MN	$49,260	SC	$38,150
DC	$73,150	MO	$43,060	SD	$35,010
DE	$47,380	MS	$34,100	TN	$39,640
FL	$44,650	MT	$40,010	TX	$46,550
GA	$43,840	NC	$44,310	UT	$43,610
HI	$44,900	ND	$37,820	VA	$54,740
IA	$42,130	NE	$37,500	VT	$43,580
ID	$48,630	NH	$43,110	WA	$53,680
IL	$44,000	NJ	$55,770	WI	$43,370
IN	$39,460	NM	$44,100	WV	$33,870
KS	$41,830	NV	$56,320	WY	$37,950

Median Wages for the Largest Metropolitan Areas (Annual)

AZ: Phoenix	$39,280	MI: Detroit	$53,010
CA: Los Angeles	$47,700	MN: Minneapolis	$49,540
CA: Riverside	$42,940	MO: Kansas City	$46,440
CA: Sacramento	$60,450	MO: St. Louis	$45,030
CA: San Diego	$48,090	NV: Las Vegas	$55,730
CA: San Francisco	$59,200	NY: New York	$52,950
CO: Denver	$51,100	OH: Cincinnati	$46,840
DC: Washington	$69,850	OH: Cleveland	$50,150
FL: Miami	$47,030	OH: Columbus	$50,790
FL: Orlando	$45,880	OR: Portland	$47,210
FL: Tampa	$43,990	PA: Philadelphia	$50,990
GA: Atlanta	$45,290	PA: Pittsburgh	$45,590
IL: Chicago	$43,910	TX: Dallas	$50,530
MA: Boston	$54,480	TX: Houston	$50,810
MD: Baltimore	$46,440	WA: Seattle	$54,730

FACTORS THAT MAY AFFECT EARNINGS

Educational Attainment of Workers and Effect on Earnings

	Percent at Level	Effect on Earnings
Less than High School	—	—
Some High School	—	—
High School or Equivalent	6.9%	−34.4%
Some College but No Degree	13.2%	−27.0%
Associate Degree	7.5%	−11.6%
Bachelor's Degree	48.4%	−1.3%
Master's Degree	17.6%	16.4%
Doctoral Degree	—	—
First Professional Degree	5.0%	76.1%

Flexibility of Earnings

Average Hours Worked: 37
Workers with a Varying Number of Hours: 5.7%
Workers Earning Some Overtime Pay, Tips, or Commissions: 9.5%
Earnings Benefit of Working Overtime: 3.5%

Gender

	Male	Female
Percent	35.4%	64.6%
Effect on Earnings	—	−8.0%

Union Membership

Percentage Union Members: 5.5%
Earnings Benefit of Union Membership: 4.0%

Veteran Status

Percentage Who Have Been on Active Duty: 6.9%
Earnings Benefit of Veteran Status: 16.9%

27-3041 Editors

Perform variety of editorial duties, such as laying out, indexing, and revising content of written materials, in preparation for final publication.

- Education or Training Required: Bachelor's degree
- Job Growth: 14.8%
- Annual Openings: 16,000
- Self-Employed: 14.8%
- Part-Time: 27.3%

NATIONAL WAGE FIGURES (ANNUAL)

Beginning	25th Percentile	Median	Mean	75th Percentile	90th Percentile
$27,340	$35,250	$46,990	$53,220	$64,140	$87,400

Median Wages for Industries Employing Largest Numbers (Annual)

Industry	Median Income
Securities, Commodity Contracts, and Other Financial Investments and Related Activities	$62,080
Transportation Equipment Manufacturing	$62,030
Merchant Wholesalers, Durable Goods	$59,650
Computer and Electronic Product Manufacturing	$57,760
Management of Companies and Enterprises	$57,000
Performing Arts, Spectator Sports, and Related Industries	$56,840
Professional, Scientific, and Technical Services	$52,730
Insurance Carriers and Related Activities	$50,330
Hospitals	$49,400
Telecommunications	$48,980

Median Wages for States (Annual)

State	Wage	State	Wage	State	Wage
AK	$57,910	KY	$37,060	NY	$57,470
AL	$43,030	LA	$40,370	OH	$45,550
AR	$38,820	MA	$54,150	OK	$40,050
AZ	$39,490	MD	$47,210	OR	$43,780
CA	$48,500	ME	$36,790	PA	$42,860
CO	$45,690	MI	$42,020	RI	$60,340
CT	$51,300	MN	$44,630	SC	no data
DC	$55,160	MO	$34,660	SD	$34,800
DE	$50,930	MS	$42,460	TN	$40,680
FL	$43,910	MT	$34,450	TX	$42,840
GA	$47,220	NC	$45,510	UT	$40,430
HI	$60,950	ND	$42,150	VA	$48,620
IA	$37,420	NE	$33,240	VT	$39,550
ID	$34,670	NH	$44,150	WA	$57,640
IL	$46,110	NJ	$51,640	WI	$41,760
IN	$39,300	NM	$41,510	WV	$30,650
KS	$34,630	NV	$43,600	WY	$37,460

Median Wages for the Largest Metropolitan Areas (Annual)

Area	Wage	Area	Wage
AZ: Phoenix	$41,850	MI: Detroit	$42,850
CA: Los Angeles	$46,790	MN: Minneapolis	$45,670
CA: Riverside	$49,760	MO: Kansas City	$34,760
CA: Sacramento	$46,900	MO: St. Louis	$45,940
CA: San Diego	$41,030	NV: Las Vegas	$46,270
CA: San Francisco	$55,390	NY: New York	$58,750
CO: Denver	$50,270	OH: Cincinnati	$40,590
DC: Washington	$54,640	OH: Cleveland	$48,810
FL: Miami	$45,660	OH: Columbus	$49,340
FL: Orlando	$42,640	OR: Portland	$46,760
FL: Tampa	$50,220	PA: Philadelphia	$46,510
GA: Atlanta	$49,510	PA: Pittsburgh	$53,160
IL: Chicago	$46,400	TX: Dallas	$52,280
MA: Boston	$54,860	TX: Houston	$43,900
MD: Baltimore	$46,080	WA: Seattle	$65,150

FACTORS THAT MAY AFFECT EARNINGS

Educational Attainment of Workers and Effect on Earnings

	Percent at Level	Effect on Earnings
Less than High School	—	—
Some High School	—	—
High School or Equivalent	5.0%	0.5%
Some College but No Degree	12.5%	−37.5%
Associate Degree	5.6%	−22.1%
Bachelor's Degree	56.9%	−0.7%
Master's Degree	15.6%	33.0%
Doctoral Degree	—	—
First Professional Degree	—	—

Flexibility of Earnings

Average Hours Worked: 34
Workers with a Varying Number of Hours: 7.4%
Workers Earning Some Overtime Pay, Tips, or Commissions: 9.4%
Earnings Benefit of Working Overtime: −4.4%

Gender

	Male	Female
Percent	46.3%	53.7%
Effect on Earnings	3.9%	−10.8%

Union Membership

Percentage Union Members: 4.5%
Earnings Benefit of Union Membership: 19.5%

Veteran Status

Percentage Who Have Been on Active Duty: 6.9%
Earnings Benefit of Veteran Status: 16.9%

27-3042 Technical Writers

Write technical materials, such as equipment manuals, appendices, or operating and maintenance instructions. May assist in layout work.

- Education or Training Required: Bachelor's degree
- Job Growth: 23.2%
- Annual Openings: 5,000
- Self-Employed: 7.3%
- Part-Time: 50.0%

NATIONAL WAGE FIGURES (ANNUAL)

Beginning	25th Percentile	Median	Mean	75th Percentile	90th Percentile
$35,520	$45,130	$58,050	$60,850	$73,750	$91,720

Median Wages for Industries Employing Largest Numbers (Annual)

Industry	Median Income
Securities, Commodity Contracts, and Other Financial Investments and Related Activities	$82,140
Utilities	$69,660
Telecommunications	$64,590
Chemical Manufacturing	$64,030
Religious, Grantmaking, Civic, Professional, and Similar Organizations	$63,960
Federal, State, and Local Government	$62,630
Computer and Electronic Product Manufacturing	$62,220
Wholesale Electronic Markets and Agents and Brokers	$61,170
Administrative and Support Services	$59,630
Publishing Industries (Except Internet)	$59,230

Median Wages for States (Annual)

State	Wage	State	Wage	State	Wage
AK	no data	KY	$46,720	NY	$59,820
AL	$51,790	LA	$47,320	OH	$49,970
AR	$41,260	MA	$68,640	OK	$39,630
AZ	$55,320	MD	$60,620	OR	$60,170
CA	$70,420	ME	$49,460	PA	$54,150
CO	$58,800	MI	$56,840	RI	no data
CT	$57,330	MN	$56,660	SC	$50,790
DC	$59,250	MO	$50,720	SD	$41,870
DE	$56,050	MS	$53,790	TN	$47,620
FL	$55,450	MT	$43,100	TX	$52,760
GA	$55,580	NC	$55,110	UT	$53,800
HI	$72,540	ND	$43,750	VA	$62,580
IA	$45,980	NE	$48,300	VT	$51,680
ID	$51,030	NH	$63,840	WA	$70,340
IL	$60,380	NJ	$63,710	WI	$50,090
IN	$50,260	NM	$48,760	WV	$40,700
KS	$46,410	NV	$53,770	WY	no data

Median Wages for the Largest Metropolitan Areas (Annual)

Area	Wage	Area	Wage
AZ: Phoenix	$55,280	MI: Detroit	$58,060
CA: Los Angeles	$65,310	MN: Minneapolis	$57,910
CA: Riverside	$57,530	MO: Kansas City	$51,360
CA: Sacramento	$56,280	MO: St. Louis	$50,320
CA: San Diego	$58,820	NV: Las Vegas	$52,590
CA: San Francisco	$82,890	NY: New York	$67,620
CO: Denver	$60,940	OH: Cincinnati	$55,710
DC: Washington	$63,420	OH: Cleveland	$41,500
FL: Miami	$53,200	OH: Columbus	$56,380
FL: Orlando	$56,340	OR: Portland	$66,300
FL: Tampa	$71,030	PA: Philadelphia	$58,160
GA: Atlanta	$59,020	PA: Pittsburgh	$50,330
IL: Chicago	$62,640	TX: Dallas	$57,670
MA: Boston	$69,460	TX: Houston	$49,140
MD: Baltimore	$57,880	WA: Seattle	$72,520

FACTORS THAT MAY AFFECT EARNINGS

Educational Attainment of Workers and Effect on Earnings

	Percent at Level	Effect on Earnings
Less than High School	—	—
Some High School	—	—
High School or Equivalent	8.7%	−7.9%
Some College but No Degree	15.9%	−19.2%
Associate Degree	15.9%	−17.2%
Bachelor's Degree	43.5%	7.9%
Master's Degree	13.0%	22.5%
Doctoral Degree	—	—
First Professional Degree	—	—

Flexibility of Earnings

Average Hours Worked: 37
Workers with a Varying Number of Hours: 2.6%
Workers Earning Some Overtime Pay, Tips, or Commissions: 6.7%
Earnings Benefit of Working Overtime: 8.9%

Gender

	Male	Female
Percent	50.5%	49.5%
Effect on Earnings	12.0%	−12.8%

Union Membership

Percentage Union Members: Insignificant
Earnings Benefit of Union Membership: No significant data available

Veteran Status

Percentage Who Have Been on Active Duty: 6.9%
Earnings Benefit of Veteran Status: 16.9%

27-3043 Writers and Authors

Originate and prepare written material, such as scripts, stories, advertisements, and other material.

- Education or Training Required: Bachelor's degree
- Job Growth: 17.7%
- Annual Openings: 14,000
- Self-Employed: 67.7%
- Part-Time: 33.2%

Note: A large fraction of the workforce for this occupation is self-employed and earns an average of $60,640. All other earnings figures for this occupation are based on workers who are paid a wage or salary.

NATIONAL WAGE FIGURES (ANNUAL)

Beginning	25th Percentile	Median	Mean	75th Percentile	90th Percentile
$25,430	$34,850	$48,640	$58,080	$67,820	$97,700

Median Wages for Industries Employing Largest Numbers (Annual)

Industry	Median Income
Motion Picture and Sound Recording Industries	$65,590
Federal, State, and Local Government	$64,930
Computer and Electronic Product Manufacturing	$62,310
Securities, Commodity Contracts, and Other Financial Investments and Related Activities	$60,410
Internet Service Providers, Web Search Portals, and Data-Processing Services	$56,800
Insurance Carriers and Related Activities	$53,260
Administrative and Support Services	$52,800
Professional, Scientific, and Technical Services	$52,770
Hospitals	$51,460
Management of Companies and Enterprises	$50,320

Median Wages for States (Annual)

State	Wage	State	Wage	State	Wage
AK	$49,270	KY	$40,460	NY	$54,690
AL	$40,840	LA	$40,410	OH	$41,640
AR	$41,260	MA	$48,590	OK	$44,740
AZ	$34,620	MD	$54,460	OR	$48,210
CA	$67,450	ME	$44,100	PA	$44,190
CO	$52,220	MI	$47,290	RI	$49,200
CT	$55,070	MN	$46,930	SC	$32,340
DC	$57,140	MO	$42,380	SD	$37,020
DE	$53,970	MS	$37,330	TN	$39,280
FL	$44,290	MT	$44,720	TX	$47,130
GA	$47,200	NC	$47,890	UT	no data
HI	$37,640	ND	$36,500	VA	$48,920
IA	$38,630	NE	$33,030	VT	$35,560
ID	$51,280	NH	$45,710	WA	$56,840
IL	$44,620	NJ	$51,570	WI	$35,760
IN	$37,380	NM	$39,940	WV	$31,180
KS	$41,980	NV	$42,480	WY	$35,100

Median Wages for the Largest Metropolitan Areas (Annual)

Area	Wage	Area	Wage
AZ: Phoenix	$33,940	MI: Detroit	$63,250
CA: Los Angeles	$74,870	MN: Minneapolis	$49,320
CA: Riverside	$56,030	MO: Kansas City	$49,310
CA: Sacramento	$46,680	MO: St. Louis	$40,390
CA: San Diego	no data	NV: Las Vegas	$42,740
CA: San Francisco	$64,530	NY: New York	$55,730
CO: Denver	$52,140	OH: Cincinnati	$39,040
DC: Washington	$57,200	OH: Cleveland	$53,150
FL: Miami	$48,700	OH: Columbus	$40,570
FL: Orlando	$36,000	OR: Portland	$50,550
FL: Tampa	$40,050	PA: Philadelphia	$45,510
GA: Atlanta	$50,730	PA: Pittsburgh	$42,570
IL: Chicago	$45,310	TX: Dallas	$55,880
MA: Boston	$49,450	TX: Houston	$42,910
MD: Baltimore	$44,940	WA: Seattle	$59,580

FACTORS THAT MAY AFFECT EARNINGS

Educational Attainment of Workers and Effect on Earnings

	Percent at Level	Effect on Earnings
Less than High School	—	—
Some High School	—	—
High School or Equivalent	—	—
Some College but No Degree	10.6%	−29.4%
Associate Degree	5.7%	−36.2%
Bachelor's Degree	51.2%	1.6%
Master's Degree	23.6%	9.2%
Doctoral Degree	—	—
First Professional Degree	—	—

Figures do not total 100% because some levels have a very small sample size.

Flexibility of Earnings

Average Hours Worked: 29
Workers with a Varying Number of Hours: 15.2%
Workers Earning Some Overtime Pay, Tips, or Commissions: 5.6%
Earnings Benefit of Working Overtime: 34.8%

Gender

	Male	Female
Percent	41.5%	58.5%
Effect on Earnings	12.0%	−12.8%

Union Membership

Percentage Union Members: 8.5%
Earnings Benefit of Union Membership: 36.6%

Veteran Status

Percentage Who Have Been on Active Duty: 6.9%
Earnings Benefit of Veteran Status: 16.9%

27-3091 Interpreters and Translators

Translate or interpret written, oral, or sign language text into another language for others.

- Education or Training Required: Long-term on-the-job training
- Job Growth: 19.9%
- Annual Openings: 4,000
- Self-Employed: 13.5%
- Part-Time: 32.0%

NATIONAL WAGE FIGURES (ANNUAL)

Beginning	25th Percentile	Median	Mean	75th Percentile	90th Percentile
$20,550	$26,920	$35,560	$39,750	$47,010	$64,290

Median Wages for Industries Employing Largest Numbers (Annual)

Industry	Median Income
Merchant Wholesalers, Durable Goods	$44,500
Telecommunications	$43,060
Accommodation	$41,960
Administrative and Support Services	$41,090
Transportation Equipment Manufacturing	$39,140
Professional, Scientific, and Technical Services	$37,860
Publishing Industries (Except Internet)	$37,790
Management of Companies and Enterprises	$37,700
Federal, State, and Local Government	$37,390
Nursing and Residential Care Facilities	$36,810

Median Wages for States (Annual)

AK	$43,650	KY	$34,780	NY	$40,360
AL	$29,690	LA	$33,330	OH	$36,680
AR	$19,830	MA	$36,540	OK	$20,370
AZ	$28,600	MD	$49,640	OR	$38,070
CA	$37,910	ME	$32,530	PA	$29,990
CO	$44,140	MI	$36,740	RI	$35,420
CT	$51,160	MN	$40,270	SC	$33,380
DC	$55,960	MO	$34,460	SD	$36,040
DE	no data	MS	$22,370	TN	$28,080
FL	$30,560	MT	no data	TX	$34,130
GA	$31,190	NC	$28,030	UT	$26,670
HI	$42,340	ND	no data	VA	$42,900
IA	$27,670	NE	$34,900	VT	$35,790
ID	$22,220	NH	$36,740	WA	$42,130
IL	$30,950	NJ	$41,070	WI	$38,190
IN	$30,120	NM	$36,770	WV	$21,190
KS	$28,500	NV	$34,430	WY	$28,950

Median Wages for the Largest Metropolitan Areas (Annual)

AZ: Phoenix	$31,760	MI: Detroit	$33,610
CA: Los Angeles	$38,640	MN: Minneapolis	$41,440
CA: Riverside	$39,390	MO: Kansas City	$34,570
CA: Sacramento	$36,650	MO: St. Louis	$34,350
CA: San Diego	$36,940	NV: Las Vegas	$35,290
CA: San Francisco	$62,380	NY: New York	$42,750
CO: Denver	$43,170	OH: Cincinnati	$33,310
DC: Washington	$51,790	OH: Cleveland	$37,780
FL: Miami	$29,760	OH: Columbus	$38,230
FL: Orlando	$30,230	OR: Portland	$45,050
FL: Tampa	no data	PA: Philadelphia	$38,240
GA: Atlanta	$33,320	PA: Pittsburgh	$28,660
IL: Chicago	$31,660	TX: Dallas	$32,510
MA: Boston	$38,090	TX: Houston	$37,900
MD: Baltimore	no data	WA: Seattle	no data

FACTORS THAT MAY AFFECT EARNINGS

Educational Attainment of Workers and Effect on Earnings

Figures are based on a group of occupations: Media and Communication Workers

	Percent at Level	Effect on Earnings
Less than High School	—	—
Some High School	1.9%	−68.6%
High School or Equivalent	8.3%	−15.4%
Some College but No Degree	16.6%	−27.2%
Associate Degree	8.7%	−13.5%
Bachelor's Degree	41.7%	5.9%
Master's Degree	17.0%	19.0%
Doctoral Degree	2.1%	32.6%
First Professional Degree	3.4%	64.9%

Flexibility of Earnings

Average Hours Worked: 33
Workers with a Varying Number of Hours: 9.1%
Workers Earning Some Overtime Pay, Tips, or Commissions: 8.2%
Earnings Benefit of Working Overtime: 8.9%

Gender

	Male	Female
Percent	30.7%	69.3%
Effect on Earnings	12.0%	−12.8%

Union Membership

Percentage Union Members: 6.0%
Earnings Benefit of Union Membership: 19.5%

Veteran Status

Percentage Who Have Been on Active Duty: 6.9%
Earnings Benefit of Veteran Status: 16.9%

27-3099 Media and Communication Workers, All Other

All media and communication workers not listed separately.

- Education or Training Required: Long-term on-the-job training
- Job Growth: 15.7%
- Annual Openings: 5,000
- Self-Employed: 24.9%
- Part-Time: 32.0%

NATIONAL WAGE FIGURES (ANNUAL)

Beginning	25th Percentile	Median	Mean	75th Percentile	90th Percentile
$22,580	$31,030	$42,570	$46,310	$56,780	$76,270

Median Wages for Industries Employing Largest Numbers (Annual)

Industry	Median Income
Transportation Equipment Manufacturing	$54,500
Merchant Wholesalers, Durable Goods	$53,610
Printing and Related Support Activities	$52,110
Internet Service Providers, Web Search Portals, and Data-Processing Services	$51,850
Publishing Industries (Except Internet)	$50,920
Administrative and Support Services	$50,630
Real Estate	$50,140
Management of Companies and Enterprises	$48,550
Museums, Historical Sites, and Similar Institutions	$46,080
Professional, Scientific, and Technical Services	$44,310

Median Wages for States (Annual)

State	Wage	State	Wage	State	Wage
AK	$41,630	KY	$38,630	NY	$48,860
AL	$27,480	LA	$28,560	OH	$39,130
AR	$20,290	MA	$38,870	OK	$25,730
AZ	$36,330	MD	$40,510	OR	$34,560
CA	$45,770	ME	$48,110	PA	$37,280
CO	$48,710	MI	$44,140	RI	$34,040
CT	$42,780	MN	$41,780	SC	$34,430
DC	$73,890	MO	$43,500	SD	no data
DE	$22,620	MS	no data	TN	$30,140
FL	$35,220	MT	no data	TX	$54,960
GA	$44,980	NC	$33,990	UT	$41,880
HI	$37,980	ND	no data	VA	$57,220
IA	no data	NE	$36,010	VT	no data
ID	$31,810	NH	$36,830	WA	$46,780
IL	$47,960	NJ	$43,310	WI	$52,890
IN	$41,630	NM	no data	WV	no data
KS	$56,590	NV	$44,940	WY	no data

Median Wages for the Largest Metropolitan Areas (Annual)

Area	Wage	Area	Wage
AZ: Phoenix	$36,210	MI: Detroit	$41,550
CA: Los Angeles	$43,700	MN: Minneapolis	$42,930
CA: Riverside	$37,890	MO: Kansas City	no data
CA: Sacramento	no data	MO: St. Louis	no data
CA: San Diego	$39,510	NV: Las Vegas	$46,280
CA: San Francisco	$55,140	NY: New York	$47,190
CO: Denver	$52,790	OH: Cincinnati	$34,550
DC: Washington	$48,890	OH: Cleveland	$39,760
FL: Miami	$33,260	OH: Columbus	$42,900
FL: Orlando	$36,880	OR: Portland	$36,480
FL: Tampa	no data	PA: Philadelphia	$43,630
GA: Atlanta	$49,510	PA: Pittsburgh	$40,110
IL: Chicago	$48,160	TX: Dallas	no data
MA: Boston	$42,450	TX: Houston	no data
MD: Baltimore	$41,730	WA: Seattle	$49,540

FACTORS THAT MAY AFFECT EARNINGS

Educational Attainment of Workers and Effect on Earnings

Figures are based on a group of occupations: Media and Communication Workers

	Percent at Level	Effect on Earnings
Less than High School	—	—
Some High School	1.9%	−68.6%
High School or Equivalent	8.3%	−15.4%
Some College but No Degree	16.6%	−27.2%
Associate Degree	8.7%	−13.5%
Bachelor's Degree	41.7%	5.9%
Master's Degree	17.0%	19.0%
Doctoral Degree	2.1%	32.6%
First Professional Degree	3.4%	64.9%

Flexibility of Earnings

Average Hours Worked: 33
Workers with a Varying Number of Hours: 9.1%
Workers Earning Some Overtime Pay, Tips, or Commissions: 8.2%
Earnings Benefit of Working Overtime: 8.9%

Gender

	Male	Female
Percent	30.7%	69.3%
Effect on Earnings	12.0%	−12.8%

Union Membership

Percentage Union Members: 6.0%
Earnings Benefit of Union Membership: 19.5%

Veteran Status

Percentage Who Have Been on Active Duty: 6.9%
Earnings Benefit of Veteran Status: 16.9%

27-4000 Media and Communication Equipment Workers

27-4011 Audio and Video Equipment Technicians

Set up or set up and operate audio and video equipment, including microphones, sound speakers, video screens, projectors, video monitors, recording equipment, connecting wires and cables, sound and mixing boards, and related electronic equipment for concerts, sports events, meetings and conventions, presentations, and news conferences. May also set up and operate associated spotlights and other custom lighting systems.

- Education or Training Required: Long-term on-the-job training
- Job Growth: 18.1%
- Annual Openings: 5,000
- Self-Employed: 5.9%
- Part-Time: 30.8%

NATIONAL WAGE FIGURES (ANNUAL)

Beginning	25th Percentile	Median	Mean	75th Percentile	90th Percentile
$19,980	$26,090	$34,840	$38,710	$46,320	$62,550

Median Wages for Industries Employing Largest Numbers (Annual)

Industry	Median Income
Social Assistance	$47,300
Credit Intermediation and Related Activities	$46,610
Repair and Maintenance	$45,820
Insurance Carriers and Related Activities	$44,170
Specialty Trade Contractors	$42,610
Management of Companies and Enterprises	$42,330
Professional, Scientific, and Technical Services	$41,670
Merchant Wholesalers, Durable Goods	$38,950
Electronics and Appliance Stores	$38,210
Federal, State, and Local Government	$37,790

Median Wages for States (Annual)

AK	no data	KY	$31,830	NY	$35,670
AL	$22,770	LA	no data	OH	$35,630
AR	$27,970	MA	$39,340	OK	$25,700
AZ	$26,070	MD	$41,780	OR	$35,290
CA	$37,850	ME	$34,110	PA	$36,650
CO	$34,890	MI	$31,180	RI	$34,670
CT	$40,150	MN	$34,530	SC	$30,110
DC	$37,310	MO	$33,270	SD	no data
DE	$35,580	MS	$26,440	TN	$29,910
FL	$33,920	MT	$25,590	TX	$28,100
GA	$35,510	NC	$32,220	UT	$30,340
HI	$35,670	ND	$32,540	VA	$30,330
IA	$35,060	NE	$27,100	VT	$28,180
ID	$41,600	NH	$39,390	WA	$33,340
IL	$33,600	NJ	$42,530	WI	$32,470
IN	$31,560	NM	$29,340	WV	$21,530
KS	$28,890	NV	$51,380	WY	$29,440

Median Wages for the Largest Metropolitan Areas (Annual)

AZ: Phoenix	$25,520	MI: Detroit	$32,520
CA: Los Angeles	$39,450	MN: Minneapolis	$35,040
CA: Riverside	$33,400	MO: Kansas City	$34,200
CA: Sacramento	$39,590	MO: St. Louis	$35,720
CA: San Diego	$35,500	NV: Las Vegas	$52,010
CA: San Francisco	$38,190	NY: New York	$36,650
CO: Denver	$36,100	OH: Cincinnati	$37,080
DC: Washington	$40,170	OH: Cleveland	$36,360
FL: Miami	$33,440	OH: Columbus	$30,100
FL: Orlando	$40,930	OR: Portland	$36,920
FL: Tampa	$32,910	PA: Philadelphia	$40,240
GA: Atlanta	$36,630	PA: Pittsburgh	$28,470
IL: Chicago	$34,550	TX: Dallas	$33,530
MA: Boston	$40,780	TX: Houston	$27,500
MD: Baltimore	$42,120	WA: Seattle	$36,500

FACTORS THAT MAY AFFECT EARNINGS

Educational Attainment of Workers and Effect on Earnings

Figures are based on a group of occupations: Media and Communication Equipment Workers

	Percent at Level	Effect on Earnings
Less than High School	—	—
Some High School	5.9%	−34.3%
High School or Equivalent	22.5%	−27.4%
Some College but No Degree	26.7%	−9.0%
Associate Degree	14.4%	20.8%
Bachelor's Degree	25.1%	19.0%
Master's Degree	—	—
Doctoral Degree	—	—
First Professional Degree	—	—

Flexibility of Earnings

Average Hours Worked: 29
Workers with a Varying Number of Hours: 17.9%
Workers Earning Some Overtime Pay, Tips, or Commissions: 16.6%
Earnings Benefit of Working Overtime: 14.3%

Gender

	Male	Female
Percent	64.7%	35.3%
Effect on Earnings	4.5%	—

Union Membership

Percentage Union Members: 7.1%
Earnings Benefit of Union Membership: 58.6%

Veteran Status

Percentage Who Have Been on Active Duty: 10.6%
Earnings Benefit of Veteran Status: 22.5%

27-4012 Broadcast Technicians

Set up, operate, and maintain the electronic equipment used to transmit radio and television programs. Control audio equipment to regulate volume level and quality of sound during radio and television broadcasts. Operate radio transmitter to broadcast radio and television programs.

- Education or Training Required: Associate degree
- Job Growth: 9.8%
- Annual Openings: 4,000
- Self-Employed: 7.4%
- Part-Time: 30.8%

NATIONAL WAGE FIGURES (ANNUAL)

Beginning	25th Percentile	Median	Mean	75th Percentile	90th Percentile
$15,680	$20,880	$30,690	$35,540	$45,310	$64,860

Median Wages for Industries Employing Largest Numbers (Annual)

Industry	Median Income
Performing Arts, Spectator Sports, and Related Industries	$46,450
Federal, State, and Local Government	$41,810
Motion Picture and Sound Recording Industries	$40,140
Telecommunications	$39,280
Professional, Scientific, and Technical Services	$38,610
Educational Services	$37,820
Publishing Industries (Except Internet)	$36,270
Rental and Leasing Services	$34,920
Nonstore Retailers	$34,310
Religious, Grantmaking, Civic, Professional, and Similar Organizations	$32,110

Median Wages for States (Annual)

AK	$32,890	KY	$27,490	NY	$40,790
AL	$24,930	LA	$20,850	OH	$34,800
AR	$22,320	MA	$32,280	OK	$28,500
AZ	$31,120	MD	$27,170	OR	$24,890
CA	$33,290	ME	$23,740	PA	$27,250
CO	$31,990	MI	$40,130	RI	$27,650
CT	$35,390	MN	$32,760	SC	$21,080
DC	$49,340	MO	$29,260	SD	$23,810
DE	$38,480	MS	$23,250	TN	$33,220
FL	$34,190	MT	$16,420	TX	$19,610
GA	$26,610	NC	$28,610	UT	$28,020
HI	$29,090	ND	$20,710	VA	$31,040
IA	$27,220	NE	$31,100	VT	$20,510
ID	$19,990	NH	$26,000	WA	$33,410
IL	$37,000	NJ	$53,780	WI	$27,070
IN	$25,060	NM	$25,270	WV	$17,970
KS	$26,830	NV	$27,610	WY	$23,350

Median Wages for the Largest Metropolitan Areas (Annual)

AZ: Phoenix	$32,060	MI: Detroit	$45,620
CA: Los Angeles	$34,030	MN: Minneapolis	$34,290
CA: Riverside	$23,090	MO: Kansas City	$33,910
CA: Sacramento	$43,350	MO: St. Louis	$25,340
CA: San Diego	$28,530	NV: Las Vegas	$33,260
CA: San Francisco	$46,070	NY: New York	$42,730
CO: Denver	$40,080	OH: Cincinnati	$35,800
DC: Washington	$43,770	OH: Cleveland	$39,900
FL: Miami	$36,130	OH: Columbus	$36,550
FL: Orlando	$40,270	OR: Portland	$26,290
FL: Tampa	$31,760	PA: Philadelphia	$34,290
GA: Atlanta	$29,630	PA: Pittsburgh	$25,310
IL: Chicago	$39,950	TX: Dallas	$23,350
MA: Boston	$31,100	TX: Houston	$23,360
MD: Baltimore	$30,620	WA: Seattle	$34,390

FACTORS THAT MAY AFFECT EARNINGS

Educational Attainment of Workers and Effect on Earnings

Figures are based on a group of occupations: Media and Communication Equipment Workers

	Percent at Level	Effect on Earnings
Less than High School	—	—
Some High School	5.9%	−34.3%
High School or Equivalent	22.5%	−27.4%
Some College but No Degree	26.7%	−9.0%
Associate Degree	14.4%	20.8%
Bachelor's Degree	25.1%	19.0%
Master's Degree	—	—
Doctoral Degree	—	—
First Professional Degree	—	—

Flexibility of Earnings

Average Hours Worked: 29
Workers with a Varying Number of Hours: 17.9%
Workers Earning Some Overtime Pay, Tips, or Commissions: 16.6%
Earnings Benefit of Working Overtime: 14.3%

Gender

	Male	Female
Percent	84.4%	15.6%
Effect on Earnings	4.5%	—

Union Membership

Percentage Union Members: 7.1%
Earnings Benefit of Union Membership: 58.6%

Veteran Status

Percentage Who Have Been on Active Duty: 10.6%
Earnings Benefit of Veteran Status: 22.5%

27-4013 Radio Operators

Receive and transmit communications, using radiotelegraph or radiotelephone equipment in accordance with government regulations. May repair equipment.

- Education or Training Required: Moderate-term on-the-job training
- Job Growth: –12.9%
- Annual Openings: Fewer than 500
- Self-Employed: 10.7%
- Part-Time: 30.8%

NATIONAL WAGE FIGURES (ANNUAL)

Beginning	25th Percentile	Median	Mean	75th Percentile	90th Percentile
$20,790	$28,860	$37,890	$38,870	$48,280	$57,920

Median Wages for Industries Employing Largest Numbers (Annual)

Industry	Median Income
Mining (Except Oil and Gas)	$61,460
Broadcasting (Except Internet)	$42,100
Federal, State, and Local Government	$38,750
Educational Services	$32,900
Transit and Ground Passenger Transportation	$25,170
Air Transportation	$23,660

Median Wages for States (Annual)

AK	no data	KY	no data	NY	no data
AL	$27,460	LA	$22,090	OH	no data
AR	no data	MA	no data	OK	no data
AZ	no data	MD	no data	OR	no data
CA	$36,000	ME	no data	PA	$34,440
CO	no data	MI	$50,030	RI	no data
CT	no data	MN	no data	SC	no data
DC	no data	MO	no data	SD	no data
DE	no data	MS	no data	TN	no data
FL	no data	MT	no data	TX	no data
GA	no data	NC	$34,640	UT	$40,820
HI	no data	ND	no data	VA	no data
IA	no data	NE	no data	VT	no data
ID	no data	NH	no data	WA	no data
IL	$42,830	NJ	no data	WI	no data
IN	no data	NM	no data	WV	no data
KS	no data	NV	no data	WY	no data

Median Wages for the Largest Metropolitan Areas (Annual)

AZ: Phoenix	no data	MI: Detroit	no data
CA: Los Angeles	no data	MN: Minneapolis	no data
CA: Riverside	no data	MO: Kansas City	no data
CA: Sacramento	no data	MO: St. Louis	no data
CA: San Diego	no data	NV: Las Vegas	no data
CA: San Francisco	no data	NY: New York	no data
CO: Denver	no data	OH: Cincinnati	no data
DC: Washington	no data	OH: Cleveland	no data
FL: Miami	no data	OH: Columbus	no data
FL: Orlando	no data	OR: Portland	no data
FL: Tampa	no data	PA: Philadelphia	$35,360
GA: Atlanta	no data	PA: Pittsburgh	no data
IL: Chicago	$45,890	TX: Dallas	no data
MA: Boston	no data	TX: Houston	no data
MD: Baltimore	no data	WA: Seattle	no data

FACTORS THAT MAY AFFECT EARNINGS

Educational Attainment of Workers and Effect on Earnings

Figures are based on a group of occupations: Media and Communication Equipment Workers

	Percent at Level	Effect on Earnings
Less than High School	—	—
Some High School	5.9%	–34.3%
High School or Equivalent	22.5%	–27.4%
Some College but No Degree	26.7%	–9.0%
Associate Degree	14.4%	20.8%
Bachelor's Degree	25.1%	19.0%
Master's Degree	—	—
Doctoral Degree	—	—
First Professional Degree	—	—

Flexibility of Earnings

Average Hours Worked: 29
Workers with a Varying Number of Hours: 17.9%
Workers Earning Some Overtime Pay, Tips, or Commissions: 16.6%
Earnings Benefit of Working Overtime: 14.3%

Gender

	Male	Female
Percent	84.4%	15.6%
Effect on Earnings	4.5%	—

Union Membership

Percentage Union Members: 7.1%
Earnings Benefit of Union Membership: 58.6%

Veteran Status

Percentage Who Have Been on Active Duty: 10.6%
Earnings Benefit of Veteran Status: 22.5%

27-4014 Sound Engineering Technicians

Operate machines and equipment to record, synchronize, mix, or reproduce music, voices, or sound effects in sporting arenas, theater productions, recording studios, or movie and video productions.

- Education or Training Required: Postsecondary vocational training
- Job Growth: 18.4%
- Annual Openings: 2,000
- Self-Employed: 6.5%
- Part-Time: 30.8%

NATIONAL WAGE FIGURES (ANNUAL)

Beginning	25th Percentile	Median	Mean	75th Percentile	90th Percentile
$21,050	$29,270	$43,010	$50,260	$65,590	$90,770

Median Wages for Industries Employing Largest Numbers (Annual)

Industry	Median Income
Publishing Industries (Except Internet)	$65,030
Accommodation	$47,680
Motion Picture and Sound Recording Industries	$47,420
Merchant Wholesalers, Durable Goods	$45,330
Professional, Scientific, and Technical Services	$44,430
Computer and Electronic Product Manufacturing	$43,500
Broadcasting (Except Internet)	$40,220
Educational Services	$39,190
Federal, State, and Local Government	$37,760
Administrative and Support Services	$36,870

Median Wages for States (Annual)

AK	no data	KY	no data	NY	$47,000
AL	$20,590	LA	$30,820	OH	$38,500
AR	$35,150	MA	$36,940	OK	$32,870
AZ	$19,280	MD	$42,800	OR	$45,440
CA	$61,210	ME	no data	PA	$32,600
CO	$31,610	MI	$32,800	RI	$30,770
CT	$38,220	MN	$43,590	SC	$23,900
DC	$43,400	MO	$35,990	SD	no data
DE	no data	MS	$32,220	TN	$34,930
FL	$30,720	MT	no data	TX	$34,410
GA	$33,350	NC	$36,310	UT	no data
HI	no data	ND	no data	VA	$40,460
IA	no data	NE	$36,080	VT	no data
ID	$24,600	NH	no data	WA	$33,890
IL	$34,090	NJ	$48,940	WI	$27,900
IN	$31,760	NM	$45,080	WV	no data
KS	no data	NV	$46,580	WY	no data

Median Wages for the Largest Metropolitan Areas (Annual)

AZ: Phoenix	$19,030	MI: Detroit	$16,210
CA: Los Angeles	$61,990	MN: Minneapolis	$46,050
CA: Riverside	no data	MO: Kansas City	$33,700
CA: Sacramento	$41,020	MO: St. Louis	$38,500
CA: San Diego	$56,760	NV: Las Vegas	$52,330
CA: San Francisco	no data	NY: New York	$47,900
CO: Denver	$34,800	OH: Cincinnati	no data
DC: Washington	$40,760	OH: Cleveland	no data
FL: Miami	$34,620	OH: Columbus	no data
FL: Orlando	$23,680	OR: Portland	$46,720
FL: Tampa	$31,550	PA: Philadelphia	$34,170
GA: Atlanta	$34,820	PA: Pittsburgh	no data
IL: Chicago	$34,040	TX: Dallas	$33,760
MA: Boston	$37,920	TX: Houston	$20,250
MD: Baltimore	$47,370	WA: Seattle	$32,970

FACTORS THAT MAY AFFECT EARNINGS

Educational Attainment of Workers and Effect on Earnings

Figures are based on a group of occupations: Media and Communication Equipment Workers

	Percent at Level	Effect on Earnings
Less than High School	—	—
Some High School	5.9%	−34.3%
High School or Equivalent	22.5%	−27.4%
Some College but No Degree	26.7%	−9.0%
Associate Degree	14.4%	20.8%
Bachelor's Degree	25.1%	19.0%
Master's Degree	—	—
Doctoral Degree	—	—
First Professional Degree	—	—

Flexibility of Earnings

Average Hours Worked: 29
Workers with a Varying Number of Hours: 17.9%
Workers Earning Some Overtime Pay, Tips, or Commissions: 16.6%
Earnings Benefit of Working Overtime: 14.3%

Gender

	Male	Female
Percent	84.4%	15.6%
Effect on Earnings	4.5%	—

Union Membership

Percentage Union Members: 7.1%
Earnings Benefit of Union Membership: 58.6%

Veteran Status

Percentage Who Have Been on Active Duty: 10.6%
Earnings Benefit of Veteran Status: 22.5%

27-4021 Photographers

Photograph persons, subjects, merchandise, or other commercial products. May develop negatives and produce finished prints.

- Education or Training Required: Long-term on-the-job training
- Job Growth: 12.3%
- Annual Openings: 23,000
- Self-Employed: 58.8%
- Part-Time: 32.7%

Note: A large fraction of the workforce for this occupation is self-employed and earns an average of $82,030. All other earnings figures for this occupation are based on workers who are paid a wage or salary.

NATIONAL WAGE FIGURES (ANNUAL)

Beginning	25th Percentile	Median	Mean	75th Percentile	90th Percentile
$15,540	$18,680	$26,170	$31,830	$38,730	$56,640

Note: The mean is significantly higher than the median because of the presence of a few star earners.

Median Wages for Industries Employing Largest Numbers (Annual)

Industry	Median Income
Other Information Services	$61,870
Transportation Equipment Manufacturing	$58,040
Internet Publishing and Broadcasting	$50,800
Management of Companies and Enterprises	$45,340
Computer and Electronic Product Manufacturing	$44,900
Ambulatory Health Care Services	$43,720
Hospitals	$42,600
Federal, State, and Local Government	$41,240
Educational Services	$38,770
Museums, Historical Sites, and Similar Institutions	$38,510

Median Wages for States (Annual)

State	Wage	State	Wage	State	Wage
AK	$38,540	KY	$24,790	NY	$30,760
AL	$20,630	LA	$22,790	OH	$20,470
AR	$24,420	MA	$33,810	OK	$20,840
AZ	$29,160	MD	$25,260	OR	$24,320
CA	$28,710	ME	$24,580	PA	$27,620
CO	$29,630	MI	$27,710	RI	$41,930
CT	no data	MN	$39,270	SC	$24,580
DC	$46,470	MO	$22,940	SD	$24,540
DE	$29,090	MS	$23,590	TN	$22,000
FL	$26,480	MT	$20,350	TX	$20,620
GA	$16,940	NC	$26,380	UT	$25,420
HI	$28,390	ND	$30,680	VA	$27,840
IA	$21,030	NE	$19,350	VT	$29,980
ID	$24,460	NH	$20,820	WA	$35,050
IL	$27,660	NJ	$27,780	WI	$31,190
IN	$26,300	NM	$25,950	WV	$23,030
KS	$20,010	NV	$31,740	WY	$30,880

Median Wages for the Largest Metropolitan Areas (Annual)

Area	Wage	Area	Wage
AZ: Phoenix	$30,570	MI: Detroit	$27,840
CA: Los Angeles	$27,670	MN: Minneapolis	$45,080
CA: Riverside	$30,200	MO: Kansas City	$27,650
CA: Sacramento	$23,390	MO: St. Louis	$26,120
CA: San Diego	$28,910	NV: Las Vegas	$31,950
CA: San Francisco	$43,510	NY: New York	$32,080
CO: Denver	$31,400	OH: Cincinnati	$17,720
DC: Washington	$29,930	OH: Cleveland	$21,380
FL: Miami	$27,110	OH: Columbus	$31,840
FL: Orlando	$28,180	OR: Portland	$24,060
FL: Tampa	$32,410	PA: Philadelphia	$30,000
GA: Atlanta	$14,790	PA: Pittsburgh	$22,630
IL: Chicago	$29,180	TX: Dallas	$18,820
MA: Boston	$31,540	TX: Houston	$21,990
MD: Baltimore	$26,530	WA: Seattle	$41,730

FACTORS THAT MAY AFFECT EARNINGS

Educational Attainment of Workers and Effect on Earnings

	Percent at Level	Effect on Earnings
Less than High School	—	—
Some High School	—	—
High School or Equivalent	17.8%	−46.2%
Some College but No Degree	30.0%	−17.9%
Associate Degree	12.2%	31.2%
Bachelor's Degree	27.8%	17.5%
Master's Degree	6.7%	111.1%
Doctoral Degree	—	—
First Professional Degree	—	—

Flexibility of Earnings

Average Hours Worked: 28
Workers with a Varying Number of Hours: 17.9%
Workers Earning Some Overtime Pay, Tips, or Commissions: 18.8%
Earnings Benefit of Working Overtime: 14.3%

Gender

	Male	Female
Percent	56.7%	43.3%
Effect on Earnings	12.0%	−12.8%

Union Membership

Percentage Union Members: 8.3%
Earnings Benefit of Union Membership: 58.6%

Veteran Status

Percentage Who Have Been on Active Duty: 10.6%
Earnings Benefit of Veteran Status: 22.5%

27-4031 Camera Operators, Television, Video, and Motion Picture

Operate television, video, or motion picture camera to photograph images or scenes for various purposes, such as TV broadcasts, advertising, video production, or motion pictures.

- Education or Training Required: Moderate-term on-the-job training
- Job Growth: 14.2%
- Annual Openings: 4,000
- Self-Employed: 21.1%
- Part-Time: 30.8%

NATIONAL WAGE FIGURES (ANNUAL)

Beginning	25th Percentile	Median	Mean	75th Percentile	90th Percentile
$18,810	$26,930	$40,060	$46,150	$59,440	$84,500

Median Wages for Industries Employing Largest Numbers (Annual)

Industry	Median Income
Management of Companies and Enterprises	$64,400
Federal, State, and Local Government	$51,880
Performing Arts, Spectator Sports, and Related Industries	$45,210
Motion Picture and Sound Recording Industries	$44,370
Religious, Grantmaking, Civic, Professional, and Similar Organizations	$43,990
Amusement, Gambling, and Recreation Industries	$43,050
Professional, Scientific, and Technical Services	$39,300
Publishing Industries (Except Internet)	$38,160
Administrative and Support Services	$38,080
Other Information Services	$35,040

Median Wages for States (Annual)

State	Wage	State	Wage	State	Wage
AK	no data	KY	$40,070	NY	$40,070
AL	$27,860	LA	no data	OH	$41,980
AR	$26,830	MA	$50,040	OK	$39,850
AZ	$41,530	MD	$53,970	OR	no data
CA	$65,640	ME	$27,370	PA	$33,100
CO	$34,340	MI	no data	RI	no data
CT	$41,150	MN	$26,360	SC	no data
DC	$58,570	MO	$28,430	SD	$19,070
DE	no data	MS	$29,570	TN	$43,440
FL	$34,120	MT	$27,710	TX	$26,550
GA	$22,430	NC	$37,320	UT	$51,180
HI	$25,800	ND	$17,750	VA	$44,930
IA	$26,890	NE	$33,810	VT	$23,440
ID	$17,630	NH	$32,590	WA	$47,940
IL	$39,330	NJ	$59,240	WI	$32,170
IN	$28,210	NM	$41,630	WV	$20,910
KS	$25,710	NV	$35,500	WY	no data

Median Wages for the Largest Metropolitan Areas (Annual)

Area	Wage	Area	Wage
AZ: Phoenix	$41,820	MI: Detroit	no data
CA: Los Angeles	$74,730	MN: Minneapolis	$29,300
CA: Riverside	no data	MO: Kansas City	$29,820
CA: Sacramento	$33,380	MO: St. Louis	$37,810
CA: San Diego	$50,540	NV: Las Vegas	$38,330
CA: San Francisco	$66,010	NY: New York	$41,510
CO: Denver	$37,580	OH: Cincinnati	$52,570
DC: Washington	$58,030	OH: Cleveland	$43,520
FL: Miami	$34,840	OH: Columbus	$40,750
FL: Orlando	$44,180	OR: Portland	$52,410
FL: Tampa	$39,510	PA: Philadelphia	$47,060
GA: Atlanta	$22,400	PA: Pittsburgh	$26,240
IL: Chicago	$42,740	TX: Dallas	$28,920
MA: Boston	$49,160	TX: Houston	$33,640
MD: Baltimore	$54,650	WA: Seattle	$52,560

FACTORS THAT MAY AFFECT EARNINGS

Educational Attainment of Workers and Effect on Earnings

Figures are based on a group of occupations: Media and Communication Equipment Workers

	Percent at Level	Effect on Earnings
Less than High School	—	—
Some High School	5.9%	−34.3%
High School or Equivalent	22.5%	−27.4%
Some College but No Degree	26.7%	−9.0%
Associate Degree	14.4%	20.8%
Bachelor's Degree	25.1%	19.0%
Master's Degree	—	—
Doctoral Degree	—	—
First Professional Degree	—	—

Flexibility of Earnings

Average Hours Worked: 29
Workers with a Varying Number of Hours: 17.9%
Workers Earning Some Overtime Pay, Tips, or Commissions: 16.6%
Earnings Benefit of Working Overtime: 14.3%

Gender

	Male	Female
Percent	64.7%	35.3%
Effect on Earnings	12.0%	−12.8%

Union Membership

Percentage Union Members: 7.1%
Earnings Benefit of Union Membership: 58.6%

Veteran Status

Percentage Who Have Been on Active Duty: 10.6%
Earnings Benefit of Veteran Status: 22.5%

27-4032 Film and Video Editors

Edit motion picture soundtracks, film, and video.

- Education or Training Required: Bachelor's degree
- Job Growth: 18.6%
- Annual Openings: 3,000
- Self-Employed: 18.2%
- Part-Time: 30.8%

NATIONAL WAGE FIGURES (ANNUAL)

Beginning	25th Percentile	Median	Mean	75th Percentile	90th Percentile
$22,710	$30,610	$46,670	$58,100	$74,650	$110,720

Note: The mean is significantly higher than the median because of the presence of a few star earners.

Median Wages for Industries Employing Largest Numbers (Annual)

Industry	Median Income
Motion Picture and Sound Recording Industries	$53,440
Publishing Industries (Except Internet)	$44,680
Management of Companies and Enterprises	$42,890
Professional, Scientific, and Technical Services	$40,270
Educational Services	$39,100
Performing Arts, Spectator Sports, and Related Industries	$38,860
Federal, State, and Local Government	$37,080
Amusement, Gambling, and Recreation Industries	$37,010
Broadcasting (Except Internet)	$36,800
Merchant Wholesalers, Durable Goods	$34,150

Median Wages for States (Annual)

State	Wage	State	Wage	State	Wage
AK	$38,470	KY	$35,720	NY	$56,770
AL	$27,940	LA	$26,050	OH	$35,370
AR	$25,420	MA	$42,740	OK	$40,410
AZ	$36,700	MD	$44,560	OR	$44,360
CA	$59,700	ME	$38,880	PA	$40,410
CO	$42,570	MI	$41,470	RI	no data
CT	no data	MN	$37,170	SC	$32,500
DC	no data	MO	$39,860	SD	no data
DE	no data	MS	no data	TN	$47,580
FL	$30,970	MT	no data	TX	$43,110
GA	$56,580	NC	$36,380	UT	no data
HI	$41,760	ND	no data	VA	$32,590
IA	$27,420	NE	no data	VT	no data
ID	no data	NH	no data	WA	$39,070
IL	$60,320	NJ	$41,880	WI	$34,780
IN	$29,160	NM	no data	WV	no data
KS	$29,650	NV	no data	WY	no data

Median Wages for the Largest Metropolitan Areas (Annual)

Area	Wage	Area	Wage
AZ: Phoenix	$35,760	MI: Detroit	$45,480
CA: Los Angeles	$65,410	MN: Minneapolis	$37,120
CA: Riverside	no data	MO: Kansas City	$40,570
CA: Sacramento	$23,880	MO: St. Louis	$33,740
CA: San Diego	$36,940	NV: Las Vegas	no data
CA: San Francisco	$43,750	NY: New York	$54,920
CO: Denver	$54,580	OH: Cincinnati	$32,010
DC: Washington	$32,480	OH: Cleveland	$45,800
FL: Miami	$31,080	OH: Columbus	$40,370
FL: Orlando	$23,230	OR: Portland	$46,150
FL: Tampa	$33,470	PA: Philadelphia	$46,040
GA: Atlanta	$65,870	PA: Pittsburgh	no data
IL: Chicago	$62,600	TX: Dallas	$51,220
MA: Boston	no data	TX: Houston	no data
MD: Baltimore	$47,830	WA: Seattle	$40,160

FACTORS THAT MAY AFFECT EARNINGS

Educational Attainment of Workers and Effect on Earnings

Figures are based on a group of occupations: Media and Communication Equipment Workers

	Percent at Level	Effect on Earnings
Less than High School	—	—
Some High School	5.9%	−34.3%
High School or Equivalent	22.5%	−27.4%
Some College but No Degree	26.7%	−9.0%
Associate Degree	14.4%	20.8%
Bachelor's Degree	25.1%	19.0%
Master's Degree	—	—
Doctoral Degree	—	—
First Professional Degree	—	—

Flexibility of Earnings

Average Hours Worked: 29
Workers with a Varying Number of Hours: 17.9%
Workers Earning Some Overtime Pay, Tips, or Commissions: 16.6%
Earnings Benefit of Working Overtime: 14.3%

Gender

	Male	Female
Percent	64.7%	35.3%
Effect on Earnings	12.0%	−12.8%

Union Membership

Percentage Union Members: 7.1%
Earnings Benefit of Union Membership: 58.6%

Veteran Status

Percentage Who Have Been on Active Duty: 10.6%
Earnings Benefit of Veteran Status: 22.5%

27-4099 Media and Communication Equipment Workers, All Other

All media and communication equipment workers not listed separately.

- Education or Training Required: Moderate-term on-the-job training
- Job Growth: 17.0%
- Annual Openings: 3,000
- Self-Employed: 0.0%
- Part-Time: 30.8%

NATIONAL WAGE FIGURES (ANNUAL)

Beginning	25th Percentile	Median	Mean	75th Percentile	90th Percentile
$21,630	$33,140	$52,070	$53,230	$71,640	$89,690

Median Wages for Industries Employing Largest Numbers (Annual)

Industry	Median Income
Federal, State, and Local Government	$67,380
Religious, Grantmaking, Civic, Professional, and Similar Organizations	$57,270
Rental and Leasing Services	$56,410
Publishing Industries (Except Internet)	$53,240
Management of Companies and Enterprises	$49,630
Electrical Equipment, Appliance, and Component Manufacturing	$48,580
Broadcasting (Except Internet)	$47,540
Motion Picture and Sound Recording Industries	$45,420
Food Services and Drinking Places	$43,600
Accommodation	$42,850

Median Wages for States (Annual)

State	Wage	State	Wage	State	Wage
AK	no data	KY	$33,270	NY	$58,230
AL	$53,920	LA	$67,590	OH	$42,180
AR	$30,920	MA	no data	OK	$59,970
AZ	$61,540	MD	$76,460	OR	$43,110
CA	$43,560	ME	$53,970	PA	no data
CO	$45,300	MI	$31,230	RI	no data
CT	$52,500	MN	$35,190	SC	$37,300
DC	$78,270	MO	$59,610	SD	no data
DE	no data	MS	$50,330	TN	$28,870
FL	$51,290	MT	no data	TX	$61,980
GA	$60,090	NC	$39,800	UT	$56,490
HI	$66,730	ND	no data	VA	$77,820
IA	$41,530	NE	$64,300	VT	no data
ID	$61,190	NH	no data	WA	$43,890
IL	$49,900	NJ	$66,880	WI	$46,530
IN	$61,840	NM	$61,590	WV	$59,550
KS	$58,220	NV	$44,210	WY	no data

Median Wages for the Largest Metropolitan Areas (Annual)

Area	Wage	Area	Wage
AZ: Phoenix	$54,730	MI: Detroit	$32,190
CA: Los Angeles	$38,150	MN: Minneapolis	$36,820
CA: Riverside	$41,120	MO: Kansas City	$67,650
CA: Sacramento	$48,360	MO: St. Louis	$62,400
CA: San Diego	$60,570	NV: Las Vegas	$46,920
CA: San Francisco	$55,320	NY: New York	$67,500
CO: Denver	$44,980	OH: Cincinnati	no data
DC: Washington	$81,580	OH: Cleveland	$40,960
FL: Miami	$39,990	OH: Columbus	$28,870
FL: Orlando	$47,700	OR: Portland	$47,200
FL: Tampa	$66,780	PA: Philadelphia	$59,130
GA: Atlanta	$59,000	PA: Pittsburgh	no data
IL: Chicago	$50,380	TX: Dallas	$70,470
MA: Boston	no data	TX: Houston	no data
MD: Baltimore	$78,170	WA: Seattle	$48,310

FACTORS THAT MAY AFFECT EARNINGS

Educational Attainment of Workers and Effect on Earnings

Figures are based on a group of occupations: Media and Communication Equipment Workers

	Percent at Level	Effect on Earnings
Less than High School	—	—
Some High School	5.9%	−34.3%
High School or Equivalent	22.5%	−27.4%
Some College but No Degree	26.7%	−9.0%
Associate Degree	14.4%	20.8%
Bachelor's Degree	25.1%	19.0%
Master's Degree	—	—
Doctoral Degree	—	—
First Professional Degree	—	—

Flexibility of Earnings

Average Hours Worked: 29
Workers with a Varying Number of Hours: 17.9%
Workers Earning Some Overtime Pay, Tips, or Commissions: 16.6%
Earnings Benefit of Working Overtime: 14.3%

Gender

	Male	Female
Percent	64.7%	35.3%
Effect on Earnings	12.0%	−12.8%

Union Membership

Percentage Union Members: 7.1%
Earnings Benefit of Union Membership: 58.6%

Veteran Status

Percentage Who Have Been on Active Duty: 10.6%
Earnings Benefit of Veteran Status: 22.5%

29-0000: Healthcare Practitioners and Technical Occupations

29-1000 Health Diagnosing and Treating Practitioners

29-1011 Chiropractors

Adjust spinal column and other articulations of the body to correct abnormalities of the human body believed to be caused by interference with the nervous system. Examine patient to determine nature and extent of disorder. Manipulate spine or other involved area. May utilize supplementary measures, such as exercise, rest, water, light, heat, and nutritional therapy.

- Education or Training Required: First professional degree
- Job Growth: 22.4%
- Annual Openings: 4,000
- Self-Employed: 49.2%
- Part-Time: 22.6%

Note: A large fraction of the workforce for this occupation is self-employed and earns an average of $88,100. All other earnings figures for this occupation are based on workers who are paid a wage or salary.

NATIONAL WAGE FIGURES (ANNUAL)

Beginning	25th Percentile	Median	Mean	75th Percentile	90th Percentile
$32,670	$45,710	$65,220	$81,070	$96,500	more than $145,600

Note: The mean is significantly higher than the median because of the presence of a few star earners.

Median Wages for Industries Employing Largest Numbers (Annual)

Industry	Median Income
Educational Services	$82,850
Administrative and Support Services	$73,130
Ambulatory Health Care Services	$65,200
Hospitals	$58,920
Nursing and Residential Care Facilities	$46,850

Median Wages for States (Annual)

State	Wage	State	Wage	State	Wage
AK	no data	KY	$83,230	NY	$74,520
AL	$145,010	LA	$51,420	OH	$84,820
AR	$71,840	MA	$77,320	OK	$57,680
AZ	$83,340	MD	$78,960	OR	$37,920
CA	$54,050	ME	$59,150	PA	$64,480
CO	no data	MI	$62,710	RI	$71,240
CT	$78,660	MN	$75,210	SC	$63,620
DC	no data	MO	$67,800	SD	$68,530
DE	$61,670	MS	$58,080	TN	$75,580
FL	$54,330	MT	$45,130	TX	$46,400
GA	$48,420	NC	$87,460	UT	$55,950
HI	$38,350	ND	$52,740	VA	$59,140
IA	$60,130	NE	$59,020	VT	$54,420
ID	$51,500	NH	$58,250	WA	$87,580
IL	$70,390	NJ	$72,170	WI	$82,010
IN	$70,010	NM	$51,820	WV	$57,070
KS	$73,560	NV	$121,320	WY	$55,560

Median Wages for the Largest Metropolitan Areas (Annual)

Area	Wage	Area	Wage
AZ: Phoenix	$87,880	MI: Detroit	$64,080
CA: Los Angeles	$46,170	MN: Minneapolis	$75,670
CA: Riverside	$76,730	MO: Kansas City	$55,270
CA: Sacramento	$47,450	MO: St. Louis	$72,530
CA: San Diego	$43,260	NV: Las Vegas	$122,400
CA: San Francisco	$83,000	NY: New York	$74,470
CO: Denver	no data	OH: Cincinnati	$81,140
DC: Washington	$112,420	OH: Cleveland	$95,490
FL: Miami	$48,540	OH: Columbus	$75,150
FL: Orlando	$104,660	OR: Portland	$48,160
FL: Tampa	$53,790	PA: Philadelphia	$62,740
GA: Atlanta	$47,530	PA: Pittsburgh	$62,500
IL: Chicago	$70,890	TX: Dallas	$41,950
MA: Boston	$72,290	TX: Houston	$47,750
MD: Baltimore	$59,200	WA: Seattle	$89,730

FACTORS THAT MAY AFFECT EARNINGS

Educational Attainment of Workers and Effect on Earnings

	Percent at Level	Effect on Earnings
Less than High School	—	—
Some High School	—	—
High School or Equivalent	—	—
Some College but No Degree	—	—
Associate Degree	—	—
Bachelor's Degree	—	—
Master's Degree	—	—
Doctoral Degree	45.5%	8.4%
First Professional Degree	27.3%	16.1%

Figures do not total 100% because some levels have a very small sample size.

Flexibility of Earnings

Average Hours Worked: 36
Workers with a Varying Number of Hours: 7.4%
Workers Earning Some Overtime Pay, Tips, or Commissions: 3.8%
Earnings Benefit of Working Overtime: –11.4%

Gender

	Male	Female
Percent	76.9%	23.1%
Effect on Earnings	21.3%	–5.0%

Union Membership

Percentage Union Members: 14.1%
Earnings Benefit of Union Membership: 4.8%

Veteran Status

Percentage Who Have Been on Active Duty: 5.9%
Earnings Benefit of Veteran Status: 28.6%

29-1021 Dentists, General

Diagnose and treat diseases, injuries, and malformations of teeth and gums and related oral structures. May treat diseases of nerve, pulp, and other dental tissues affecting vitality of teeth.

- Education or Training Required: First professional degree
- Job Growth: 13.5%
- Annual Openings: 7,000
- Self-Employed: 30.7%
- Part-Time: 25.6%

Note: Earnings figures do not reflect self-employed workers, who make up a large fraction of the workforce for this occupation.

NATIONAL WAGE FIGURES (ANNUAL)

Beginning	25th Percentile	Median	Mean	75th Percentile	90th Percentile
$68,990	$95,780	$132,140	$140,950	more than $145,600	more than $145,600

Median Wages for Industries Employing Largest Numbers (Annual)

Industry	Median Income
Ambulatory Health Care Services	$135,470
Professional, Scientific, and Technical Services	$123,000
Social Assistance	$109,050
Hospitals	$106,550
Federal, State, and Local Government	$103,660
Administrative and Support Services	$103,480
Nursing and Residential Care Facilities	$92,770
Educational Services	$91,150

Median Wages for States (Annual)

AK..more than $145,600	KY $97,480	NY $129,350
AL $121,620	LA $90,860	OH ..more than $145,600
AR............ $84,180	MA $136,360	OK $116,840
AZ $119,820	MD $119,720	OR $135,130
CA $129,020	ME ....more than $145,600	PA $110,050
CO ..more than $145,600	MI ....more than $145,600	RI.............$128,260
CT ..more than $145,600	MN $138,690	SC.............$119,660
DC $113,130	MO ....more than $145,600	SD....more than $145,600
DE ..more than $145,600	MS $124,880	TN....more than $145,600
FL $120,960	MT $113,190	TX....more than $145,600
GA..more than $145,600	NC ....more than $145,600	UT $139,210
HI ..more than $145,600	ND ....more than $145,600	VA....more than $145,600
IA ..more than $145,600	NE $136,220	VT $118,640
ID ..more than $145,600	NH ....more than $145,600	WA ..more than $145,600
IL $76,030	NJ $121,380	WI $127,330
IN $125,340	NM $122,640	WV $143,720
KS $119,520	NV $129,470	WY $110,410

Median Wages for the Largest Metropolitan Areas (Annual)

AZ: Phoenix	$115,280	MI: Detroit	more than $145,600
CA: Los Angeles	$112,430	MN: Minneapolis	$134,480
CA: Riverside	more than $145,600	MO: Kansas City	$95,890
CA: Sacramento	$133,210	MO: St. Louis	more than $145,600
CA: San Diego	$123,120	NV: Las Vegas	$121,670
CA: San Francisco	more than $145,600	NY: New York	$125,880
CO: Denver	$128,010	OH: Cincinnati	more than $145,600
DC: Washington	more than $145,600	OH: Cleveland	more than $145,600
FL: Miami	$114,460	OH: Columbus	more than $145,600
FL: Orlando	more than $145,600	OR: Portland	$131,210
FL: Tampa	$98,480	PA: Philadelphia	$131,180
GA: Atlanta	more than $145,600	PA: Pittsburgh	$94,760
IL: Chicago	$74,810	TX: Dallas	more than $145,600
MA: Boston	$137,440	TX: Houston	more than $145,600
MD: Baltimore	$117,060	WA: Seattle	more than $145,600

FACTORS THAT MAY AFFECT EARNINGS

Educational Attainment of Workers and Effect on Earnings

Figures are based on a group of occupations: Health Diagnosing and Treating Practitioners

	Percent at Level	Effect on Earnings
Less than High School	—	—
Some High School	0.5%	−51.9%
High School or Equivalent	3.7%	−35.9%
Some College but No Degree	6.1%	−22.2%
Associate Degree	25.7%	−14.6%
Bachelor's Degree	31.5%	1.4%
Master's Degree	14.5%	11.8%
Doctoral Degree	7.4%	30.3%
First Professional Degree	10.4%	22.8%

Flexibility of Earnings

Average Hours Worked: 35
Workers with a Varying Number of Hours: 6.8%
Workers Earning Some Overtime Pay, Tips, or Commissions: 13.6%
Earnings Benefit of Working Overtime: −11.4%

Gender

	Male	Female
Percent	77.4%	22.6%
Effect on Earnings	21.3%	−5.0%

Union Membership

Percentage Union Members: 14.1%
Earnings Benefit of Union Membership: 4.8%

Veteran Status

Percentage Who Have Been on Active Duty: 5.9%
Earnings Benefit of Veteran Status: 28.6%

29-1022 Oral and Maxillofacial Surgeons

Perform surgery on mouth, jaws, and related head and neck structure to execute difficult and multiple extractions of teeth, to remove tumors and other abnormal growths, to correct abnormal jaw relations by mandibular or maxillary revision, to prepare mouth for insertion of dental prosthesis, or to treat fractured jaws.

- Education or Training Required: First professional degree
- Job Growth: 16.2%
- Annual Openings: Fewer than 500
- Self-Employed: 15.7%
- Part-Time: 25.6%

NATIONAL WAGE FIGURES (ANNUAL)

Beginning	25th Percentile	Median	Mean	75th Percentile	90th Percentile
$60,550	$104,650	more than $145,600	$164,760	more than $145,600	more than $145,600

Median Wages for Industries Employing Largest Numbers (Annual)

Industry	Median Income
Ambulatory Health Care Services	more than $145,600
Nursing and Residential Care Facilities	$61,720
Hospitals	$57,100

Median Wages for States (Annual)

AK .... no data	KY ......more than $145,600	NY ....more than $145,600
AL ..more than $145,600	LA ......more than $145,600	OH ..more than $145,600
AR .... no data	MA......more than $145,600	OK .... no data
AZ ..more than $145,600	MD......more than $145,600	OR ....more than $145,600
CA $107,780	ME .... no data	PA ....more than $145,600
CO $103,620	MI .....more than $145,600	RI ....more than $145,600
CT ..more than $145,600	MN......more than $145,600	SC ....more than $145,600
DC .... no data	MO......more than $145,600	SD .... no data
DE .... no data	MS .... no data	TN ....more than $145,600
FL ..more than $145,600	MT .... no data	TX .... no data
GA ..more than $145,600	NC ......more than $145,600	UT ....more than $145,600
HI .... no data	ND .... no data	VA ....more than $145,600
IA ..more than $145,600	NE .... no data	VT .... no data
ID .... no data	NH .... no data	WA ..more than $145,600
IL ..more than $145,600	NJ $92,980	WI ....more than $145,600
IN .. more than $145,600	NM .... no data	WV .... no data

Median Wages for the Largest Metropolitan Areas (Annual)

AZ: Phoenix .... more than $145,600		MI: Detroit .... no data
CA: Los Angeles .... more than $145,600		MN: Minneapolis .. more than $145,600
CA: Riverside .... no data		MO: Kansas City .... no data
CA: Sacramento................... no data		MO: St. Louis .... no data
CA: San Diego..................... no data		NV: Las Vegas .... no data
CA: San Francisco .... no data		NY: New York................. $104,270
CO: Denver .... no data		OH: Cincinnati .... no data
DC: Washington .... no data		OH: Cleveland .... no data
FL: Miami........................... no data		OH: Columbus ...... more than $145,600
FL: Orlando .... no data		OR: Portland...................... no data
FL: Tampa .... no data		PA: Philadelphia $68,470
GA: Atlanta .... more than $145,600		PA: Pittsburgh .... no data
IL: Chicago .... more than $145,600		TX: Dallas .... no data
MA: Boston .... more than $145,600		TX: Houston .... no data
MD: Baltimore .... no data		WA: Seattle .... no data

FACTORS THAT MAY AFFECT EARNINGS

Educational Attainment of Workers and Effect on Earnings

Figures are based on a group of occupations: Health Diagnosing and Treating Practitioners

	Percent at Level	Effect on Earnings
Less than High School	—	—
Some High School	0.5%	−51.9%
High School or Equivalent	3.7%	−35.9%
Some College but No Degree	6.1%	−22.2%
Associate Degree	25.7%	−14.6%
Bachelor's Degree	31.5%	1.4%
Master's Degree	14.5%	11.8%
Doctoral Degree	7.4%	30.3%
First Professional Degree	10.4%	22.8%

Flexibility of Earnings

Average Hours Worked: 35
Workers with a Varying Number of Hours: 6.8%
Workers Earning Some Overtime Pay, Tips, or Commissions: 13.6%
Earnings Benefit of Working Overtime: −11.4%

Gender

	Male	Female
Percent	77.4%	22.6%
Effect on Earnings	21.3%	−5.0%

Union Membership

Percentage Union Members: 14.1%
Earnings Benefit of Union Membership: 4.8%

Veteran Status

Percentage Who Have Been on Active Duty: 5.9%
Earnings Benefit of Veteran Status: 28.6%

29-1023 Orthodontists

Examine, diagnose, and treat dental malocclusions and oral cavity anomalies. Design and fabricate appliances to realign teeth and jaws to produce and maintain normal function and to improve appearance.

- Education or Training Required: First professional degree
- Job Growth: 12.8%
- Annual Openings: 1,000
- Self-Employed: 35.9%
- Part-Time: 25.6%

Note: Earnings figures do not reflect self-employed workers, who make up a large fraction of the workforce for this occupation.

NATIONAL WAGE FIGURES (ANNUAL)

Beginning	25th Percentile	Median	Mean	75th Percentile	90th Percentile
$81,720	more than $145,600	more than $145,600	$176,900	more than $145,600	more than $145,600

Median Wages for Industries Employing Largest Numbers (Annual)

Industry	Median Income
Ambulatory Health Care Services	more than $145,600
Hospitals	$66,290

Median Wages for States (Annual)

AK .... no data	KY ......more than $145,600	NY....more than $145,600
AL ..more than $145,600	LA ......more than $145,600	OH ..more than $145,600
AR ..more than $145,600	MA......more than $145,600	OK .... no data
AZ ..more than $145,600	MD......more than $145,600	OR....more than $145,600
CA ..more than $145,600	ME .... no data	PA ....more than $145,600
CO ..more than $145,600	MI .... no data	RI.............. no data
CT ..more than $145,600	MN......more than $145,600	SC ....more than $145,600
DC .... no data	MO......more than $145,600	SD .... no data
DE .... no data	MS .... no data	TN....more than $145,600
FL ..more than $145,600	MT .... no data	TX....more than $145,600
GA ..more than $145,600	NC ......more than $145,600	UT $60,890
HI .... no data	ND .... no data	VA....more than $145,600
IA .... no data	NE ......more than $145,600	VT .... no data
ID $76,460	NH .... no data	WA ..more than $145,600
IL ..more than $145,600	NJ ......more than $145,600	WI....more than $145,600
IN ..more than $145,600	NM......more than $145,600	WV .... no data
KS ..more than $145,600	NV .... no data	WY .... no data

Median Wages for the Largest Metropolitan Areas (Annual)

AZ: Phoenix ....more than $145,600	MI: Detroit............more than $145,600
CA: Los Angeles ..more than $145,600	MN: Minneapolis....more than $145,600
CA: Riverside ...... no data	MO: Kansas City ....more than $145,600
CA: Sacramento.... no data	MO: St. Louis ....more than $145,600
CA: San Diego...... no data	NV: Las Vegas........ no data
CA: San Francisco more than $145,600	NY: New York ....more than $145,600
CO: Denver .... no data	OH: Cincinnati ......more than $145,600
DC: Washington....more than $145,600	OH: Cleveland........more than $145,600
FL: Miami............more than $145,600	OH: Columbus ......more than $145,600
FL: Orlando.......... no data	OR: Portland .... no data
FL: Tampa .... no data	PA: Philadelphia ....more than $145,600
GA: Atlanta ....more than $145,600	PA: Pittsburgh ...... no data
IL: Chicago .... no data	TX: Dallas ....more than $145,600
MA: Boston ....more than $145,600	TX: Houston..........more than $145,600
MD: Baltimore......more than $145,600	WA: Seattle .... no data

FACTORS THAT MAY AFFECT EARNINGS

Educational Attainment of Workers and Effect on Earnings

Figures are based on a group of occupations: Health Diagnosing and Treating Practitioners

	Percent at Level	Effect on Earnings
Less than High School	—	—
Some High School	0.5%	−51.9%
High School or Equivalent	3.7%	−35.9%
Some College but No Degree	6.1%	−22.2%
Associate Degree	25.7%	−14.6%
Bachelor's Degree	31.5%	1.4%
Master's Degree	14.5%	11.8%
Doctoral Degree	7.4%	30.3%
First Professional Degree	10.4%	22.8%

Flexibility of Earnings

Average Hours Worked: 35
Workers with a Varying Number of Hours: 6.8%
Workers Earning Some Overtime Pay, Tips, or Commissions: 13.6%
Earnings Benefit of Working Overtime: −11.4%

Gender

	Male	Female
Percent	77.4%	22.6%
Effect on Earnings	21.3%	−5.0%

Union Membership

Percentage Union Members: 14.1%
Earnings Benefit of Union Membership: 4.8%

Veteran Status

Percentage Who Have Been on Active Duty: 5.9%
Earnings Benefit of Veteran Status: 28.6%

29-1024 Prosthodontists

Construct oral prostheses to replace missing teeth and other oral structures to correct natural and acquired deformation of mouth and jaws; to restore and maintain oral function, such as chewing and speaking; and to improve appearance.

- Education or Training Required: First professional degree
- Job Growth: 13.6%
- Annual Openings: Fewer than 500
- Self-Employed: 38.2%
- Part-Time: 25.6%

Note: Earnings figures do not reflect self-employed workers, who make up a large fraction of the workforce for this occupation.

NATIONAL WAGE FIGURES (ANNUAL)

Beginning	25th Percentile	Median	Mean	75th Percentile	90th Percentile
$55,650	$103,500	more than $145,600	$158,940	more than $145,600	more than $145,600

Median Wages for Industries Employing Largest Numbers (Annual)

Industry	Median Income
Ambulatory Health Care Services	more than $145,600
Miscellaneous Manufacturing	$66,020

Median Wages for States (Annual)

AK	no data	KY	no data	NY	no data
AL	no data	LA	no data	OH	no data
AR	no data	MA	$81,300	OK	no data
AZ	no data	MD	no data	OR	no data
CA	no data	ME	no data	PA	no data
CO	no data	MI	no data	RI	no data
CT	no data	MN	no data	SC	no data
DC	no data	MO	no data	SD	no data
DE	no data	MS	no data	TN	no data
FL	no data	MT	no data	TX	no data
GA	no data	NC	no data	UT	no data
HI	no data	ND	no data	VA	more than $145,600
IA	no data	NE	no data	VT	no data
ID	no data	NH	no data	WA	no data
IL	no data	NJ	more than $145,600	WI	no data
IN	no data	NM	no data	WV	no data
KS	no data	NV	no data	WY	no data

Median Wages for the Largest Metropolitan Areas (Annual)

AZ: Phoenix	no data	MI: Detroit	no data
CA: Los Angeles	no data	MN: Minneapolis	no data
CA: Riverside	no data	MO: Kansas City	no data
CA: Sacramento	no data	MO: St. Louis	no data
CA: San Diego	no data	NV: Las Vegas	no data
CA: San Francisco	no data	NY: New York	no data
CO: Denver	no data	OH: Cincinnati	no data
DC: Washington	more than $145,600	OH: Cleveland	no data
FL: Miami	no data	OH: Columbus	no data
FL: Orlando	no data	OR: Portland	no data
FL: Tampa	no data	PA: Philadelphia	no data
GA: Atlanta	no data	PA: Pittsburgh	no data
IL: Chicago	no data	TX: Dallas	no data
MA: Boston	no data	TX: Houston	no data
MD: Baltimore	no data	WA: Seattle	no data

FACTORS THAT MAY AFFECT EARNINGS

Educational Attainment of Workers and Effect on Earnings

Figures are based on a group of occupations: Health Diagnosing and Treating Practitioners

	Percent at Level	Effect on Earnings
Less than High School	—	—
Some High School	0.5%	−51.9%
High School or Equivalent	3.7%	−35.9%
Some College but No Degree	6.1%	−22.2%
Associate Degree	25.7%	−14.6%
Bachelor's Degree	31.5%	1.4%
Master's Degree	14.5%	11.8%
Doctoral Degree	7.4%	30.3%
First Professional Degree	10.4%	22.8%

Flexibility of Earnings

Average Hours Worked: 35
Workers with a Varying Number of Hours: 6.8%
Workers Earning Some Overtime Pay, Tips, or Commissions: 13.6%
Earnings Benefit of Working Overtime: −11.4%

Gender

	Male	Female
Percent	77.4%	22.6%
Effect on Earnings	21.3%	−5.0%

Union Membership

Percentage Union Members: 14.1%
Earnings Benefit of Union Membership: 4.8%

Veteran Status

Percentage Who Have Been on Active Duty: 5.9%
Earnings Benefit of Veteran Status: 28.6%

29-1029 Dentists, All Other Specialists

All dentists not listed separately.

- Education or Training Required: First professional degree
- Job Growth: 12.2%
- Annual Openings: Fewer than 500
- Self-Employed: 43.2%
- Part-Time: 25.6%

Note: Earnings figures do not reflect self-employed workers, who make up a large fraction of the workforce for this occupation.

NATIONAL WAGE FIGURES (ANNUAL)

Beginning	25th Percentile	Median	Mean	75th Percentile	90th Percentile
$40,830	$52,160	$91,200	$108,340	more than $145,600	more than $145,600

Median Wages for Industries Employing Largest Numbers (Annual)

Industry	Median Income
Ambulatory Health Care Services	more than $145,600
Federal, State, and Local Government	$83,040
Hospitals	$80,590
Educational Services	$43,160
Social Assistance	$40,410

Median Wages for States (Annual)

AK	no data	KY	$35,770	NY	$54,760
AL	no data	LA	no data	OH	$109,750
AR	no data	MA	$115,450	OK	no data
AZ	$96,090	MD	$88,120	OR	more than $145,600
CA	$99,290	ME	more than $145,600	PA	more than $145,600
CO	$86,610	MI	$99,040	RI	no data
CT	no data	MN	more than $145,600	SC	$99,150
DC	no data	MO	$100,810	SD	no data
DE	no data	MS	no data	TN	$104,700
FL	$87,700	MT	no data	TX	$94,850
GA	more than $145,600	NC	$98,620	UT	no data
HI	no data	ND	no data	VA	$117,360
IA	no data	NE	no data	VT	no data
ID	no data	NH	no data	WA	$59,540
IL	no data	NJ	more than $145,600	WI	$129,920
IN	$100,930	NM	no data	WV	$78,030
KS	no data	NV	no data	WY	no data

Median Wages for the Largest Metropolitan Areas (Annual)

AZ: Phoenix	$112,860	MI: Detroit	no data
CA: Los Angeles	$93,880	MN: Minneapolis	no data
CA: Riverside	no data	MO: Kansas City	no data
CA: Sacramento	no data	MO: St. Louis	no data
CA: San Diego	no data	NV: Las Vegas	no data
CA: San Francisco	$92,890	NY: New York	$103,920
CO: Denver	no data	OH: Cincinnati	no data
DC: Washington	$105,620	OH: Cleveland	no data
FL: Miami	no data	OH: Columbus	no data
FL: Orlando	no data	OR: Portland	no data
FL: Tampa	no data	PA: Philadelphia	more than $145,600
GA: Atlanta	more than $145,600	PA: Pittsburgh	no data
IL: Chicago	more than $145,600	TX: Dallas	no data
MA: Boston	$104,380	TX: Houston	no data
MD: Baltimore	$100,490	WA: Seattle	no data

FACTORS THAT MAY AFFECT EARNINGS

Educational Attainment of Workers and Effect on Earnings

Figures are based on a group of occupations: Health Diagnosing and Treating Practitioners

	Percent at Level	Effect on Earnings
Less than High School	—	—
Some High School	0.5%	−51.9%
High School or Equivalent	3.7%	−35.9%
Some College but No Degree	6.1%	−22.2%
Associate Degree	25.7%	−14.6%
Bachelor's Degree	31.5%	1.4%
Master's Degree	14.5%	11.8%
Doctoral Degree	7.4%	30.3%
First Professional Degree	10.4%	22.8%

Flexibility of Earnings

Average Hours Worked: 35
Workers with a Varying Number of Hours: 6.8%
Workers Earning Some Overtime Pay, Tips, or Commissions: 13.6%
Earnings Benefit of Working Overtime: −11.4%

Gender

	Male	Female
Percent	77.4%	22.6%
Effect on Earnings	21.3%	−5.0%

Union Membership

Percentage Union Members: 14.1%
Earnings Benefit of Union Membership: 4.8%

Veteran Status

Percentage Who Have Been on Active Duty: 5.9%
Earnings Benefit of Veteran Status: 28.6%

29-1031 Dietitians and Nutritionists

Plan and conduct food service or nutritional programs to assist in the promotion of health and control of disease. May supervise activities of a department providing quantity food services, counsel individuals, or conduct nutritional research.

- Education or Training Required: Bachelor's degree
- Job Growth: 18.3%
- Annual Openings: 4,000
- Self-Employed: 3.6%
- Part-Time: 40.6%

NATIONAL WAGE FIGURES (ANNUAL)

Beginning	25th Percentile	Median	Mean	75th Percentile	90th Percentile
$29,860	$38,430	$46,980	$47,890	$57,090	$68,330

Median Wages for Industries Employing Largest Numbers (Annual)

Industry	Median Income
Professional, Scientific, and Technical Services	$56,800
Administrative and Support Services	$52,060
Ambulatory Health Care Services	$49,820
Wholesale Electronic Markets and Agents and Brokers	$48,940
Federal, State, and Local Government	$47,950
Hospitals	$47,470
Management of Companies and Enterprises	$47,110
Merchant Wholesalers, Nondurable Goods	$47,050
Health and Personal Care Stores	$45,850
Nursing and Residential Care Facilities	$45,840

Median Wages for States (Annual)

State	Wage	State	Wage	State	Wage
AK	$55,430	KY	$45,240	NY	$51,400
AL	$43,830	LA	$40,270	OH	$47,090
AR	$39,540	MA	$48,270	OK	$38,050
AZ	$41,670	MD	$53,610	OR	$52,010
CA	$56,680	ME	$43,440	PA	$43,320
CO	$36,900	MI	$45,400	RI	$52,500
CT	$58,070	MN	$49,920	SC	$38,320
DC	$54,080	MO	$38,640	SD	$41,520
DE	$48,350	MS	$38,830	TN	$41,620
FL	$45,690	MT	$44,970	TX	$46,450
GA	$43,130	NC	$44,230	UT	$44,040
HI	$53,150	ND	$42,160	VA	$46,250
IA	$42,640	NE	$43,930	VT	$44,910
ID	$41,130	NH	$47,860	WA	$53,310
IL	$42,100	NJ	$55,650	WI	$49,010
IN	$43,840	NM	$47,300	WV	$42,780
KS	$51,650	NV	$49,740	WY	$44,920

Median Wages for the Largest Metropolitan Areas (Annual)

Area	Wage	Area	Wage
AZ: Phoenix	$42,060	MI: Detroit	$45,140
CA: Los Angeles	$52,080	MN: Minneapolis	$50,730
CA: Riverside	$57,750	MO: Kansas City	$49,390
CA: Sacramento	$62,300	MO: St. Louis	$42,120
CA: San Diego	$49,240	NV: Las Vegas	$48,400
CA: San Francisco	$67,570	NY: New York	$53,750
CO: Denver	$35,380	OH: Cincinnati	$50,030
DC: Washington	$54,270	OH: Cleveland	$47,620
FL: Miami	$49,090	OH: Columbus	$45,550
FL: Orlando	$44,180	OR: Portland	$51,550
FL: Tampa	$43,690	PA: Philadelphia	$49,930
GA: Atlanta	$41,710	PA: Pittsburgh	$42,110
IL: Chicago	$44,380	TX: Dallas	$47,640
MA: Boston	$48,790	TX: Houston	$46,200
MD: Baltimore	$53,260	WA: Seattle	$54,980

FACTORS THAT MAY AFFECT EARNINGS

Educational Attainment of Workers and Effect on Earnings

	Percent at Level	Effect on Earnings
Less than High School	—	—
Some High School	—	—
High School or Equivalent	22.1%	−22.5%
Some College but No Degree	9.7%	−43.0%
Associate Degree	—	—
Bachelor's Degree	46.9%	11.9%
Master's Degree	11.5%	34.3%
Doctoral Degree	—	—
First Professional Degree	—	—

Figures do not total 100% because some levels have a very small sample size.

Flexibility of Earnings

Average Hours Worked: 32
Workers with a Varying Number of Hours: 4.1%
Workers Earning Some Overtime Pay, Tips, or Commissions: 5.7%
Earnings Benefit of Working Overtime: −11.4%

Gender

	Male	Female
Percent	9.0%	91.0%
Effect on Earnings	—	−1.3%

Union Membership

Percentage Union Members: 14.6%
Earnings Benefit of Union Membership: 26.8%

Veteran Status

Percentage Who Have Been on Active Duty: 5.9%
Earnings Benefit of Veteran Status: 28.6%

29-1041 Optometrists

Diagnose, manage, and treat conditions and diseases of the human eye and visual system. Examine eyes and visual system, diagnose problems or impairments, prescribe corrective lenses, and provide treatment. May prescribe therapeutic drugs to treat specific eye conditions.

- Education or Training Required: First professional degree
- Job Growth: 19.7%
- Annual Openings: 2,000
- Self-Employed: 27.4%
- Part-Time: 33.3%

NATIONAL WAGE FIGURES (ANNUAL)

Beginning	25th Percentile	Median	Mean	75th Percentile	90th Percentile
$45,030	$66,530	$91,040	$98,550	$118,490	more than $145,600

Median Wages for Industries Employing Largest Numbers (Annual)

Industry	Median Income
Management of Companies and Enterprises	$104,910
Health and Personal Care Stores	$101,700
Hospitals	$98,210
Miscellaneous Manufacturing	$96,130
Ambulatory Health Care Services	$90,050
Administrative and Support Services	$88,830
General Merchandise Stores	$86,540
Educational Services	$77,090
Federal, State, and Local Government	$65,360

Median Wages for States (Annual)

AK	$137,730	KY	$92,640	NY	$104,750
AL	$80,660	LA	$90,170	OH	$94,190
AR	$91,860	MA	$66,020	OK	$68,660
AZ	$84,360	MD	$97,500	OR	$82,740
CA	$92,580	ME	$94,770	PA	$82,900
CO	$63,490	MI	$99,680	RI	$96,230
CT	$98,350	MN	$108,810	SC	$76,450
DC	$72,490	MO	$83,250	SD	$91,620
DE	more than $145,600	MS	$83,290	TN	$74,960
FL	$91,220	MT	$58,790	TX	$79,590
GA	$137,150	NC	$121,090	UT	$87,430
HI	$79,600	ND	$79,520	VA	$95,230
IA	$86,010	NE	$90,030	VT	more than $145,600
ID	$47,390	NH	$96,300	WA	$112,980
IL	$89,190	NJ	$88,630	WI	$86,570
IN	$72,110	NM	$84,900	WV	$80,110
KS	$88,480	NV	$103,220	WY	$86,420

Median Wages for the Largest Metropolitan Areas (Annual)

AZ: Phoenix	$79,250	MI: Detroit	$101,890
CA: Los Angeles	$73,960	MN: Minneapolis	$109,960
CA: Riverside	$117,300	MO: Kansas City	$81,290
CA: Sacramento	$94,540	MO: St. Louis	$86,760
CA: San Diego	$85,520	NV: Las Vegas	$101,850
CA: San Francisco	$118,710	NY: New York	$99,020
CO: Denver	no data	OH: Cincinnati	$115,880
DC: Washington	$93,060	OH: Cleveland	$62,690
FL: Miami	$91,480	OH: Columbus	$87,050
FL: Orlando	$121,350	OR: Portland	$84,700
FL: Tampa	$42,760	PA: Philadelphia	$86,520
GA: Atlanta	more than $145,600	PA: Pittsburgh	no data
IL: Chicago	$89,660	TX: Dallas	$72,980
MA: Boston	$68,470	TX: Houston	$70,960
MD: Baltimore	$99,710	WA: Seattle	$111,220

FACTORS THAT MAY AFFECT EARNINGS

Educational Attainment of Workers and Effect on Earnings

	Percent at Level	Effect on Earnings
Less than High School	—	—
Some High School	—	—
High School or Equivalent	—	—
Some College but No Degree	—	—
Associate Degree	—	—
Bachelor's Degree	—	—
Master's Degree	—	—
Doctoral Degree	52.2%	25.2%
First Professional Degree	34.8%	−15.7%

Figures do not total 100% because some levels have a very small sample size.

Flexibility of Earnings

Average Hours Worked: 36
Workers with a Varying Number of Hours: 6.3%
Workers Earning Some Overtime Pay, Tips, or Commissions: 4.0%
Earnings Benefit of Working Overtime: −11.4%

Gender

	Male	Female
Percent	60.9%	39.1%
Effect on Earnings	21.3%	−5.0%

Union Membership

Percentage Union Members: 14.1%
Earnings Benefit of Union Membership: 4.8%

Veteran Status

Percentage Who Have Been on Active Duty: 5.9%
Earnings Benefit of Veteran Status: 28.6%

29-1051 Pharmacists

Compound and dispense medications, following prescriptions issued by physicians, dentists, or other authorized medical practitioners.

- Education or Training Required: First professional degree
- Job Growth: 24.6%
- Annual Openings: 16,000
- Self-Employed: 1.7%
- Part-Time: 29.9%

NATIONAL WAGE FIGURES (ANNUAL)

Beginning	25th Percentile	Median	Mean	75th Percentile	90th Percentile
$67,860	$83,180	$94,520	$93,500	$108,140	$119,480

Median Wages for Industries Employing Largest Numbers (Annual)

Industry	Median Income
Management of Companies and Enterprises	$102,010
General Merchandise Stores	$100,050
Merchant Wholesalers, Durable Goods	$100,010
Chemical Manufacturing	$98,270
Internet Service Providers, Web Search Portals, and Data-Processing Services	$98,160
Administrative and Support Services	$97,370
Warehousing and Storage	$96,050
Food and Beverage Stores	$95,600
Ambulatory Health Care Services	$95,440
Miscellaneous Store Retailers	$95,260

Median Wages for States (Annual)

AK $105,610	KY $99,050	NY $91,420
AL $91,570	LA $87,610	OH $92,750
AR $90,570	MA $87,500	OK $87,550
AZ $94,310	MD $90,530	OR $95,540
CA $110,310	ME $103,570	PA $87,460
CO $95,000	MI $95,230	RI $88,720
CT $94,580	MN $103,210	SC $94,910
DC $83,750	MO $90,970	SD $83,790
DE $93,770	MS $89,030	TN $100,910
FL $93,730	MT $84,950	TX $97,970
GA $94,540	NC $95,260	UT $94,850
HI $90,620	ND $80,580	VA $93,350
IA $88,400	NE $85,180	VT $95,150
ID $91,280	NH $94,350	WA $92,080
IL $94,210	NJ $92,680	WI $101,050
IN $91,280	NM $90,590	WV $94,220
KS $86,820	NV $97,180	WY $87,710

Median Wages for the Largest Metropolitan Areas (Annual)

AZ: Phoenix $95,010	MI: Detroit $94,760
CA: Los Angeles $108,560	MN: Minneapolis $103,880
CA: Riverside $109,740	MO: Kansas City $86,540
CA: Sacramento $111,290	MO: St. Louis $89,760
CA: San Diego $110,430	NV: Las Vegas $94,310
CA: San Francisco $111,880	NY: New York $91,550
CO: Denver $95,640	OH: Cincinnati $94,410
DC: Washington $90,560	OH: Cleveland $94,430
FL: Miami $95,360	OH: Columbus $88,190
FL: Orlando $93,450	OR: Portland $97,540
FL: Tampa $90,790	PA: Philadelphia $89,500
GA: Atlanta $94,990	PA: Pittsburgh $87,010
IL: Chicago $94,390	TX: Dallas $102,110
MA: Boston $86,890	TX: Houston $95,470
MD: Baltimore $90,180	WA: Seattle $92,030

FACTORS THAT MAY AFFECT EARNINGS

Educational Attainment of Workers and Effect on Earnings

	Percent at Level	Effect on Earnings
Less than High School	—	—
Some High School	—	—
High School or Equivalent	—	—
Some College but No Degree	—	—
Associate Degree	2.3%	−65.0%
Bachelor's Degree	41.6%	1.2%
Master's Degree	12.8%	14.2%
Doctoral Degree	21.8%	0.6%
First Professional Degree	18.7%	6.3%

Flexibility of Earnings

Average Hours Worked: 35
Workers with a Varying Number of Hours: 5.4%
Workers Earning Some Overtime Pay, Tips, or Commissions: 10.8%
Earnings Benefit of Working Overtime: −8.0%

Gender

	Male	Female
Percent	51.1%	48.9%
Effect on Earnings	5.2%	−4.6%

Union Membership

Percentage Union Members: 6.5%
Earnings Benefit of Union Membership: 23.7%

Veteran Status

Percentage Who Have Been on Active Duty: 5.9%
Earnings Benefit of Veteran Status: 28.6%

29-1061 Anesthesiologists

Administer anesthetics during surgery or other medical procedures.

- Education or Training Required: First professional degree
- Job Growth: 24.0%
- Annual Openings: 41,000
- Self-Employed: 11.5%
- Part-Time: 25.6%

NATIONAL WAGE FIGURES (ANNUAL)

Beginning	25th Percentile	Median	Mean	75th Percentile	90th Percentile
$114,200	more than $145,600	more than $145,600	$184,340	more than $145,600	more than $145,600

Median Wages for Industries Employing Largest Numbers (Annual)

Industry	Median Income
Administrative and Support Services	more than $145,600
Ambulatory Health Care Services	more than $145,600
Hospitals	more than $145,600
Educational Services	$80,190

Median Wages for States (Annual)

AK.. more than $145,600	KY ......more than $145,600	NY....more than $145,600
AL .. more than $145,600	LA ......more than $145,600	OH ..more than $145,600
AR.. more than $145,600	MA .... no data	OK $145,120
AZ .. more than $145,600	MD.....more than $145,600	OR....more than $145,600
CA .. more than $145,600	ME .....more than $145,600	PA....more than $145,600
CO .. more than $145,600	MI .....more than $145,600	RI.............. no data
CT .. more than $145,600	MN.....more than $145,600	SC ....more than $145,600
DC .... no data	MO......more than $145,600	SD $144,240
DE.. more than $145,600	MS $140,100	TN....more than $145,600
FL .. more than $145,600	MT .... no data	TX ....more than $145,600
GA.. more than $145,600	NC .....more than $145,600	UT....more than $145,600
HI .... no data	ND .... no data	VA ....more than $145,600
IA .. more than $145,600	NE .....more than $145,600	VT.............. no data
ID .. more than $145,600	NH .....more than $145,600	WA ..more than $145,600
IL .. more than $145,600	NJ ......more than $145,600	WI....more than $145,600
IN .. more than $145,600	NM $134,420	WV ..more than $145,600
KS.. more than $145,600	NV .... no data	WY ..more than $145,600

Median Wages for the Largest Metropolitan Areas (Annual)

AZ: Phoenix........ more than $145,600	MI: Detroit ....more than $145,600
CA: Los Angeles .. more than $145,600	MN: Minneapolis..more than $145,600
CA: Riverside ...... more than $145,600	MO: Kansas City ..more than $145,600
CA: Sacramento .... no data	MO: St. Louis ......more than $145,600
CA: San Diego .... no data	NV: Las Vegas .... no data
CA: San Francisco.. more than $145,600	NY: New York .... no data
CO: Denver .... more than $145,600	OH: Cincinnati ....more than $145,600
DC: Washington .. more than $145,600	OH: Cleveland .... no data
FL: Miami .... more than $145,600	OH: Columbus ....more than $145,600
FL: Orlando .... more than $145,600	OR: Portland ......more than $145,600
FL: Tampa .... more than $145,600	PA: Philadelphia..more than $145,600
GA: Atlanta .... more than $145,600	PA: Pittsburgh.......... $136,940
IL: Chicago .... more than $145,600	TX: Dallas ....more than $145,600
MA: Boston .... more than $145,600	TX: Houston........more than $145,600
MD: Baltimore .... more than $145,600	WA: Seattle ....more than $145,600

FACTORS THAT MAY AFFECT EARNINGS

Educational Attainment of Workers and Effect on Earnings

Figures are based on a group of occupations: Health Diagnosing and Treating Practitioners

	Percent at Level	Effect on Earnings
Less than High School	—	—
Some High School	0.5%	−51.9%
High School or Equivalent	3.7%	−35.9%
Some College but No Degree	6.1%	−22.2%
Associate Degree	25.7%	−14.6%
Bachelor's Degree	31.5%	1.4%
Master's Degree	14.5%	11.8%
Doctoral Degree	7.4%	30.3%
First Professional Degree	10.4%	22.8%

Flexibility of Earnings

Average Hours Worked: 35
Workers with a Varying Number of Hours: 6.8%
Workers Earning Some Overtime Pay, Tips, or Commissions: 13.6%
Earnings Benefit of Working Overtime: −41.2%

Gender

	Male	Female
Percent	67.8%	32.2%
Effect on Earnings	15.3%	−17.0%

Union Membership

Percentage Union Members: 14.1%
Earnings Benefit of Union Membership: 4.8%

Veteran Status

Percentage Who Have Been on Active Duty: 5.9%
Earnings Benefit of Veteran Status: 28.6%

29-1062 Family and General Practitioners

Diagnose, treat, and help prevent diseases and injuries that commonly occur in the general population.

- Education or Training Required: First professional degree
- Job Growth: 24.0%
- Annual Openings: 41,000
- Self-Employed: 11.5%
- Part-Time: 25.6%

NATIONAL WAGE FIGURES (ANNUAL)

Beginning	25th Percentile	Median	Mean	75th Percentile	90th Percentile
$69,990	$112,600	more than $145,600	$149,850	more than $145,600	more than $145,600

Median Wages for Industries Employing Largest Numbers (Annual)

Industry	Median Income
Administrative and Support Services	more than $145,600
Ambulatory Health Care Services	more than $145,600
Nursing and Residential Care Facilities	more than $145,600
Religious, Grantmaking, Civic, Professional, and Similar Organizations	more than $145,600
Hospitals	$144,730
Management of Companies and Enterprises	$142,720
Insurance Carriers and Related Activities	$141,880
Professional, Scientific, and Technical Services	$139,830
Social Assistance	$130,140
Federal, State, and Local Government	$112,560

Median Wages for States (Annual)

AK $144,650	KY ......more than $145,600	NY....more than $145,600
AL ..more than $145,600	LA .....more than $145,600	OH ..more than $145,600
AR..more than $145,600	MA.....more than $145,600	OK $144,990
AZ $131,340	MD.....more than $145,600	OR $138,510
CA $138,840	ME $130,300	PA $135,200
CO $121,240	MI ......more than $145,600	RI ....more than $145,600
CT $144,950	MN $145,450	SC ....more than $145,600
DC .... no data	MO.....more than $145,600	SD ....more than $145,600
DE $141,130	MS ......more than $145,600	TN $136,760
FL ..more than $145,600	MT $129,780	TX $141,730
GA..more than $145,600	NC .....more than $145,600	UT....more than $145,600
HI ..more than $145,600	ND .....more than $145,600	VA ....more than $145,600
IA ..more than $145,600	NE .....more than $145,600	VT $121,420
ID ..more than $145,600	NH $131,350	WA $139,890
IL ..more than $145,600	NJ $141,150	WI....more than $145,600
IN ..more than $145,600	NM.....more than $145,600	WV ..more than $145,600
KS ..more than $145,600	NV .....more than $145,600	WY ..more than $145,600

Median Wages for the Largest Metropolitan Areas (Annual)

AZ: Phoenix	$130,090	MI: Detroit	more than $145,600
CA: Los Angeles	$112,540	MN: Minneapolis	$142,850
CA: Riverside	$145,210	MO: Kansas City	more than $145,600
CA: Sacramento	$133,150	MO: St. Louis	$143,790
CA: San Diego	more than $145,600	NV: Las Vegas	more than $145,600
CA: San Francisco	more than $145,600	NY: New York	no data
CO: Denver	$118,440	OH: Cincinnati	$132,000
DC: Washington	$138,760	OH: Cleveland	more than $145,600
FL: Miami	more than $145,600	OH: Columbus	more than $145,600
FL: Orlando	$99,470	OR: Portland	more than $145,600
FL: Tampa	$133,920	PA: Philadelphia	$132,210
GA: Atlanta	more than $145,600	PA: Pittsburgh	more than $145,600
IL: Chicago	$138,300	TX: Dallas	more than $145,600
MA: Boston	more than $145,600	TX: Houston	$119,740
MD: Baltimore	more than $145,600	WA: Seattle	$137,500

FACTORS THAT MAY AFFECT EARNINGS

Educational Attainment of Workers and Effect on Earnings

Figures are based on a group of occupations: Health Diagnosing and Treating Practitioners

	Percent at Level	Effect on Earnings
Less than High School	—	—
Some High School	0.5%	−51.9%
High School or Equivalent	3.7%	−35.9%
Some College but No Degree	6.1%	−22.2%
Associate Degree	25.7%	−14.6%
Bachelor's Degree	31.5%	1.4%
Master's Degree	14.5%	11.8%
Doctoral Degree	7.4%	30.3%
First Professional Degree	10.4%	22.8%

Flexibility of Earnings

Average Hours Worked: 35
Workers with a Varying Number of Hours: 6.8%
Workers Earning Some Overtime Pay, Tips, or Commissions: 13.6%
Earnings Benefit of Working Overtime: −41.2%

Gender

	Male	Female
Percent	67.8%	32.2%
Effect on Earnings	15.3%	−17.0%

Union Membership

Percentage Union Members: 14.1%
Earnings Benefit of Union Membership: 4.8%

Veteran Status

Percentage Who Have Been on Active Duty: 5.9%
Earnings Benefit of Veteran Status: 28.6%

29-1063 Internists, General

Diagnose and provide non-surgical treatment of diseases and injuries of internal organ systems. Provide care mainly for adults who have a wide range of problems associated with the internal organs.

- Education or Training Required: First professional degree
- Job Growth: 24.0%
- Annual Openings: 41,000
- Self-Employed: 11.5%
- Part-Time: 25.6%

NATIONAL WAGE FIGURES (ANNUAL)

Beginning	25th Percentile	Median	Mean	75th Percentile	90th Percentile
$87,070	$128,250	more than $145,600	$160,860	more than $145,600	more than $145,600

Median Wages for Industries Employing Largest Numbers (Annual)

Industry	Median Income
Administrative and Support Services...................	more than $145,600
Ambulatory Health Care Services	more than $145,600
Nursing and Residential Care Facilities	more than $145,600
Federal, State, and Local Government	$144,310
Hospitals	$141,180
Management of Companies and Enterprises......................	$133,480
Educational Services	$47,430

Median Wages for States (Annual)

AK............ no data	KY $141,900	NY....more than $145,600
AL ..more than $145,600	LA ......more than $145,600	OH ..more than $145,600
AR ..more than $145,600	MA......more than $145,600	OK....more than $145,600
AZ ..more than $145,600	MD $145,520	OR....more than $145,600
CA ..more than $145,600	ME $143,460	PA....more than $145,600
CO ..more than $145,600	MI $142,070	RI ....more than $145,600
CT ..more than $145,600	MN......more than $145,600	SC ....more than $145,600
DC $128,880	MO......more than $145,600	SD ....more than $145,600
DE ..more than $145,600	MS ......more than $145,600	TN ....more than $145,600
FL ..more than $145,600	MT ......more than $145,600	TX ....more than $145,600
GA ..more than $145,600	NC ......more than $145,600	UT....more than $145,600
HI ..more than $145,600	ND ......more than $145,600	VA ....more than $145,600
IA ..more than $145,600	NE ......more than $145,600	VT .... no data
ID ..more than $145,600	NH......more than $145,600	WA ..more than $145,600
IL ..more than $145,600	NJ ......more than $145,600	WI....more than $145,600
IN ..more than $145,600	NM......more than $145,600	WV ..more than $145,600
KS ..more than $145,600	NV ......more than $145,600	WY ..more than $145,600

Median Wages for the Largest Metropolitan Areas (Annual)

AZ: Phoenix .... more than $145,600	MI: Detroit $135,980
CA: Los Angeles .... more than $145,600	MN: Minneapolis..more than $145,600
CA: Riverside $139,990	MO: Kansas City ..more than $145,600
CA: Sacramento $144,160	MO: St. Louis ......more than $145,600
CA: San Diego $139,620	NV: Las Vegas......more than $145,600
CA: San Francisco.. more than $145,600	NY: New York............. no data
CO: Denver .... more than $145,600	OH: Cincinnati $138,840
DC: Washington .... more than $145,600	OH: Cleveland $136,170
FL: Miami .... more than $145,600	OH: Columbus ....more than $145,600
FL: Orlando $117,850	OR: Portland ......more than $145,600
FL: Tampa .... more than $145,600	PA: Philadelphia $140,660
GA: Atlanta.......... more than $145,600	PA: Pittsburgh ....more than $145,600
IL: Chicago $142,150	TX: Dallas ....more than $145,600
MA: Boston .... more than $145,600	TX: Houston........more than $145,600
MD: Baltimore $141,850	WA: Seattle ....more than $145,600

FACTORS THAT MAY AFFECT EARNINGS

Educational Attainment of Workers and Effect on Earnings

Figures are based on a group of occupations: Health Diagnosing and Treating Practitioners

	Percent at Level	Effect on Earnings
Less than High School	—	—
Some High School	0.5%	−51.9%
High School or Equivalent	3.7%	−35.9%
Some College but No Degree	6.1%	−22.2%
Associate Degree	25.7%	−14.6%
Bachelor's Degree	31.5%	1.4%
Master's Degree	14.5%	11.8%
Doctoral Degree	7.4%	30.3%
First Professional Degree	10.4%	22.8%

Flexibility of Earnings

Average Hours Worked: 35
Workers with a Varying Number of Hours: 6.8%
Workers Earning Some Overtime Pay, Tips, or Commissions: 13.6%
Earnings Benefit of Working Overtime: −41.2%

Gender

	Male	Female
Percent	67.8%	32.2%
Effect on Earnings	15.3%	−17.0%

Union Membership

Percentage Union Members: 14.1%
Earnings Benefit of Union Membership: 4.8%

Veteran Status

Percentage Who Have Been on Active Duty: 5.9%
Earnings Benefit of Veteran Status: 28.6%

29-1064 Obstetricians and Gynecologists

Diagnose, treat, and help prevent diseases of women, especially those affecting the reproductive system and the process of childbirth.

- Education or Training Required: First professional degree
- Job Growth: 24.0%
- Annual Openings: 41,000
- Self-Employed: 11.5%
- Part-Time: 25.6%

NATIONAL WAGE FIGURES (ANNUAL)

Beginning	25th Percentile	Median	Mean	75th Percentile	90th Percentile
$103,070	more than $145,600	more than $145,600	$178,040	more than $145,600	more than $145,600

Median Wages for Industries Employing Largest Numbers (Annual)

Industry	Median Income
Ambulatory Health Care Services	more than $145,600
Hospitals	more than $145,600
Educational Services	$60,770

Median Wages for States (Annual)

AK ..more than $145,600	KY ......more than $145,600	NY ....more than $145,600
AL ..more than $145,600	LA ......more than $145,600	OH ..more than $145,600
AR ..more than $145,600	MA......more than $145,600	OK....more than $145,600
AZ ..more than $145,600	MD.....more than $145,600	OR....more than $145,600
CA ..more than $145,600	ME ......more than $145,600	PA ....more than $145,600
CO ..more than $145,600	MI ......more than $145,600	RI ....more than $145,600
CT ..more than $145,600	MN......more than $145,600	SC ....more than $145,600
DC .... no data	MO ......more than $145,600	SD ....more than $145,600
DE ..more than $145,600	MS ......more than $145,600	TN ....more than $145,600
FL ..more than $145,600	MT ......more than $145,600	TX ....more than $145,600
GA ..more than $145,600	NC ......more than $145,600	UT ....more than $145,600
HI $139,800	ND .... no data	VA ....more than $145,600
IA ..more than $145,600	NE ......more than $145,600	VT ....more than $145,600
ID ..more than $145,600	NH ......more than $145,600	WA ..more than $145,600
IL ..more than $145,600	NJ ......more than $145,600	WI ....more than $145,600
IN ..more than $145,600	NM......more than $145,600	WV ..more than $145,600
KS ..more than $145,600	NV ......more than $145,600	WY ..more than $145,600

Median Wages for the Largest Metropolitan Areas (Annual)

AZ: Phoenix .... more than $145,600	MI: Detroit .... more than $145,600
CA: Los Angeles .. more than $145,600	MN: Minneapolis more than $145,600
CA: Riverside ...... more than $145,600	MO: Kansas City.. more than $145,600
CA: Sacramento .... no data	MO: St. Louis .... more than $145,600
CA: San Diego...... more than $145,600	NV: Las Vegas .... more than $145,600
CA: San Francisco more than $145,600	NY: New York .... no data
CO: Denver .... more than $145,600	OH: Cincinnati.... more than $145,600
DC: Washington $115,920	OH: Cleveland .... more than $145,600
FL: Miami............ more than $145,600	OH: Columbus .... more than $145,600
FL: Orlando .... more than $145,600	OR: Portland ...... more than $145,600
FL: Tampa .... more than $145,600	PA: Philadelphia more than $145,600
GA: Atlanta .... more than $145,600	PA: Pittsburgh.... more than $145,600
IL: Chicago.......... more than $145,600	TX: Dallas .... more than $145,600
MA: Boston .... more than $145,600	TX: Houston ...... more than $145,600
MD: Baltimore .... more than $145,600	WA: Seattle........ more than $145,600

FACTORS THAT MAY AFFECT EARNINGS

Educational Attainment of Workers and Effect on Earnings

Figures are based on a group of occupations: Health Diagnosing and Treating Practitioners

	Percent at Level	Effect on Earnings
Less than High School	—	—
Some High School	0.5%	−51.9%
High School or Equivalent	3.7%	−35.9%
Some College but No Degree	6.1%	−22.2%
Associate Degree	25.7%	−14.6%
Bachelor's Degree	31.5%	1.4%
Master's Degree	14.5%	11.8%
Doctoral Degree	7.4%	30.3%
First Professional Degree	10.4%	22.8%

Flexibility of Earnings

Average Hours Worked: 35
Workers with a Varying Number of Hours: 6.8%
Workers Earning Some Overtime Pay, Tips, or Commissions: 13.6%
Earnings Benefit of Working Overtime: −41.2%

Gender

	Male	Female
Percent	67.8%	32.2%
Effect on Earnings	15.3%	−17.0%

Union Membership

Percentage Union Members: 14.1%
Earnings Benefit of Union Membership: 4.8%

Veteran Status

Percentage Who Have Been on Active Duty: 5.9%
Earnings Benefit of Veteran Status: 28.6%

29-1065 Pediatricians, General

Diagnose, treat, and help prevent children's diseases and injuries.

- Education or Training Required: First professional degree
- Job Growth: 24.0%
- Annual Openings: 41,000
- Self-Employed: 11.5%
- Part-Time: 25.6%

NATIONAL WAGE FIGURES (ANNUAL)

Beginning	25th Percentile	Median	Mean	75th Percentile	90th Percentile
$66,480	$103,230	$138,130	$141,440	more than $145,600	more than $145,600

Median Wages for Industries Employing Largest Numbers (Annual)

Industry	Median Income
Administrative and Support Services	$141,060
Ambulatory Health Care Services	$140,520
Hospitals	$133,030
Federal, State, and Local Government	$132,500
Educational Services	$89,850

Median Wages for States (Annual)

AK ..more than $145,600	KY .... more than $145,600	NY $134,370
AL $136,610	LA .... more than $145,600	OH $144,390
AR........... $99,160	MA $145,100	OK....more than $145,600
AZ ..more than $145,600	MD $116,630	OR....more than $145,600
CA $141,680	ME $138,840	PA $128,090
CO ..more than $145,600	MI $132,720	RI.............$128,780
CT $126,810	MN.... more than $145,600	SC.............$132,350
DC .... no data	MO $138,120	SD....more than $145,600
DE .... no data	MS .... more than $145,600	TN....more than $145,600
FL ..more than $145,600	MT $51,530	TX....more than $145,600
GA............ no data	NC ....more than $145,600	UT....more than $145,600
HI $132,430	ND .... no data	VA $125,260
IA ..more than $145,600	NE $137,310	VT .... no data
ID $137,590	NH ....more than $145,600	WA $130,360
IL $116,660	NJ $132,800	WI....more than $145,600
IN .... no data	NM $121,280	WV $135,030
KS $128,380	NV .... no data	WY $106,630

Median Wages for the Largest Metropolitan Areas (Annual)

AZ: Phoenix .... more than $145,600	MI: Detroit $132,880
CA: Los Angeles $140,210	MN: Minneapolis ..more than $145,600
CA: Riverside $133,530	MO: Kansas City $58,850
CA: Sacramento............ $141,610	MO: St. Louis .... more than $145,600
CA: San Diego ...... more than $145,600	NV: Las Vegas............ no data
CA: San Francisco $140,390	NY: New York $130,370
CO: Denver .... more than $145,600	OH: Cincinnati .. more than $145,600
DC: Washington............ $85,460	OH: Cleveland $141,790
FL: Miami.................... $116,020	OH: Columbus $113,060
FL: Orlando.......... more than $145,600	OR: Portland ...... more than $145,600
FL: Tampa .... no data	PA: Philadelphia........ $108,380
GA: Atlanta $45,410	PA: Pittsburgh $143,670
IL: Chicago $113,090	TX: Dallas.......... more than $145,600
MA: Boston.......... more than $145,600	TX: Houston.............. $106,840
MD: Baltimore.............. $108,440	WA: Seattle $126,680

FACTORS THAT MAY AFFECT EARNINGS

Educational Attainment of Workers and Effect on Earnings

Figures are based on a group of occupations: Health Diagnosing and Treating Practitioners

	Percent at Level	Effect on Earnings
Less than High School	—	—
Some High School	0.5%	−51.9%
High School or Equivalent	3.7%	−35.9%
Some College but No Degree	6.1%	−22.2%
Associate Degree	25.7%	−14.6%
Bachelor's Degree	31.5%	1.4%
Master's Degree	14.5%	11.8%
Doctoral Degree	7.4%	30.3%
First Professional Degree	10.4%	22.8%

Flexibility of Earnings

Average Hours Worked: 35
Workers with a Varying Number of Hours: 6.8%
Workers Earning Some Overtime Pay, Tips, or Commissions: 13.6%
Earnings Benefit of Working Overtime: −41.2%

Gender

	Male	Female
Percent	67.8%	32.2%
Effect on Earnings	15.3%	−17.0%

Union Membership

Percentage Union Members: 14.1%
Earnings Benefit of Union Membership: 4.8%

Veteran Status

Percentage Who Have Been on Active Duty: 5.9%
Earnings Benefit of Veteran Status: 28.6%

29-1066 Psychiatrists

Diagnose, treat, and help prevent disorders of the mind.

- Education or Training Required: First professional degree
- Job Growth: 24.0%
- Annual Openings: 41,000
- Self-Employed: 11.5%
- Part-Time: 25.6%

NATIONAL WAGE FIGURES (ANNUAL)

Beginning	25th Percentile	Median	Mean	75th Percentile	90th Percentile
$60,900	$118,450	more than $145,600	$149,990	more than $145,600	more than $145,600

Median Wages for Industries Employing Largest Numbers (Annual)

Industry	Median Income
Ambulatory Health Care Services	more than $145,600
Federal, State, and Local Government	more than $145,600
Management of Companies and Enterprises	more than $145,600
Nursing and Residential Care Facilities	more than $145,600
Social Assistance	more than $145,600
Hospitals	$140,210
Administrative and Support Services	$136,430
Educational Services	$114,620
Insurance Carriers and Related Activities	$110,180

Median Wages for States (Annual)

AK .... no data	KY ....more than $145,600	NY $135,700
AL ..more than $145,600	LA .... no data	OH ..more than $145,600
AR $138,190	MA....more than $145,600	OK....more than $145,600
AZ ..more than $145,600	MD .... no data	OR .... no data
CA ..more than $145,600	ME $141,320	PA $136,980
CO ..more than $145,600	MI ....more than $145,600	RI ....more than $145,600
CT ..more than $145,600	MN ....more than $145,600	SC............. no data
DC $127,990	MO ....more than $145,600	SD .... no data
DE $109,760	MS $136,470	TN....more than $145,600
FL $142,680	MT ....more than $145,600	TX $141,680
GA ..more than $145,600	NC $141,880	UT $130,800
HI $140,550	ND ....more than $145,600	VA ....more than $145,600
IA ..more than $145,600	NE $132,540	VT $132,080
ID ..more than $145,600	NH $128,600	WA $142,900
IL $73,420	NJ ....more than $145,600	WI....more than $145,600
IN ..more than $145,600	NM ....more than $145,600	WV ..more than $145,600
KS ..more than $145,600	NV ....more than $145,600	WY .... no data

Median Wages for the Largest Metropolitan Areas (Annual)

AZ: Phoenix ....more than $145,600	MI: Detroit ....more than $145,600
CA: Los Angeles ....more than $145,600	MN: Minneapolis..more than $145,600
CA: Riverside ....more than $145,600	MO: Kansas City ..more than $145,600
CA: Sacramento......more than $145,600	MO: St. Louis.............. $130,590
CA: San Diego $95,420	NV: Las Vegas......more than $145,600
CA: San Francisco ..more than $145,600	NY: New York.............. $138,880
CO: Denver ....more than $145,600	OH: Cincinnati $136,550
DC: Washington $137,090	OH: Cleveland $144,140
FL: Miami $139,060	OH: Columbus ....more than $145,600
FL: Orlando .... no data	OR: Portland ......more than $145,600
FL: Tampa ....more than $145,600	PA: Philadelphia..more than $145,600
GA: Atlanta ....more than $145,600	PA: Pittsburgh $143,410
IL: Chicago $116,820	TX: Dallas ....more than $145,600
MA: Boston ....more than $145,600	TX: Houston $75,670
MD: Baltimore $111,910	WA: Seattle ....more than $145,600

FACTORS THAT MAY AFFECT EARNINGS

Educational Attainment of Workers and Effect on Earnings

Figures are based on a group of occupations: Health Diagnosing and Treating Practitioners

	Percent at Level	Effect on Earnings
Less than High School	—	—
Some High School	0.5%	−51.9%
High School or Equivalent	3.7%	−35.9%
Some College but No Degree	6.1%	−22.2%
Associate Degree	25.7%	−14.6%
Bachelor's Degree	31.5%	1.4%
Master's Degree	14.5%	11.8%
Doctoral Degree	7.4%	30.3%
First Professional Degree	10.4%	22.8%

Flexibility of Earnings

Average Hours Worked: 35
Workers with a Varying Number of Hours: 6.8%
Workers Earning Some Overtime Pay, Tips, or Commissions: 13.6%
Earnings Benefit of Working Overtime: −41.2%

Gender

	Male	Female
Percent	67.8%	32.2%
Effect on Earnings	15.3%	−17.0%

Union Membership

Percentage Union Members: 14.1%
Earnings Benefit of Union Membership: 4.8%

Veteran Status

Percentage Who Have Been on Active Duty: 5.9%
Earnings Benefit of Veteran Status: 28.6%

29-1067 Surgeons

Treat diseases, injuries, and deformities by invasive methods, such as manual manipulation, or by using instruments and appliances.

- Education or Training Required: First professional degree
- Job Growth: 24.0%
- Annual Openings: 41,000
- Self-Employed: 11.5%
- Part-Time: 25.6%

NATIONAL WAGE FIGURES (ANNUAL)

Beginning	25th Percentile	Median	Mean	75th Percentile	90th Percentile
$116,850	more than $145,600	more than $145,600	$184,150	more than $145,600	more than $145,600

Median Wages for Industries Employing Largest Numbers (Annual)

Industry	Median Income
Ambulatory Health Care Services	more than $145,600
Federal, State, and Local Government	more than $145,600
Hospitals	more than $145,600
Educational Services	$126,780

Median Wages for States (Annual)

AK ..more than $145,600	KY ......more than $145,600	NY....more than $145,600
AL ..more than $145,600	LA ......more than $145,600	OH ..more than $145,600
AR ..more than $145,600	MA.....more than $145,600	OK....more than $145,600
AZ ..more than $145,600	MD.....more than $145,600	OR....more than $145,600
CA ..more than $145,600	ME......more than $145,600	PA....more than $145,600
CO ..more than $145,600	MI ......more than $145,600	RI ....more than $145,600
CT ..more than $145,600	MN.....more than $145,600	SC ....more than $145,600
DC .... no data	MO......more than $145,600	SD....more than $145,600
DE ..more than $145,600	MS ......more than $145,600	TN ....more than $145,600
FL ..more than $145,600	MT ......more than $145,600	TX ....more than $145,600
GA..more than $145,600	NC ......more than $145,600	UT .... no data
HI .... no data	ND $127,060	VA....more than $145,600
IA ..more than $145,600	NE ......more than $145,600	VT .... no data
ID ..more than $145,600	NH .....more than $145,600	WA ..more than $145,600
IL ..more than $145,600	NJ ......more than $145,600	WI....more than $145,600
IN ..more than $145,600	NM......more than $145,600	WV ..more than $145,600
KS ..more than $145,600	NV ......more than $145,600	WY ..more than $145,600

Median Wages for the Largest Metropolitan Areas (Annual)

AZ: Phoenix .... more than $145,600	MI: Detroit ....more than $145,600
CA: Los Angeles .... more than $145,600	MN: Minneapolis..more than $145,600
CA: Riverside .... more than $145,600	MO: Kansas City ..more than $145,600
CA: Sacramento .... more than $145,600	MO: St. Louis ......more than $145,600
CA: San Diego ...... more than $145,600	NV: Las Vegas......more than $145,600
CA: San Francisco .. more than $145,600	NY: New York.............. no data
CO: Denver............ more than $145,600	OH: Cincinnati ....more than $145,600
DC: Washington............ $123,790	OH: Cleveland ....more than $145,600
FL: Miami $144,520	OH: Columbus ....more than $145,600
FL: Orlando .... more than $145,600	OR: Portland ......more than $145,600
FL: Tampa .... more than $145,600	PA: Philadelphia..more than $145,600
GA: Atlanta .... more than $145,600	PA: Pittsburgh ....more than $145,600
IL: Chicago............ more than $145,600	TX: Dallas ....more than $145,600
MA: Boston .... more than $145,600	TX: Houston........more than $145,600
MD: Baltimore ...... more than $145,600	WA: Seattle ....more than $145,600

FACTORS THAT MAY AFFECT EARNINGS

Educational Attainment of Workers and Effect on Earnings

Figures are based on a group of occupations: Health Diagnosing and Treating Practitioners

	Percent at Level	Effect on Earnings
Less than High School	—	—
Some High School	0.5%	−51.9%
High School or Equivalent	3.7%	−35.9%
Some College but No Degree	6.1%	−22.2%
Associate Degree	25.7%	−14.6%
Bachelor's Degree	31.5%	1.4%
Master's Degree	14.5%	11.8%
Doctoral Degree	7.4%	30.3%
First Professional Degree	10.4%	22.8%

Flexibility of Earnings

Average Hours Worked: 35
Workers with a Varying Number of Hours: 6.8%
Workers Earning Some Overtime Pay, Tips, or Commissions: 13.6%
Earnings Benefit of Working Overtime: −41.2%

Gender

	Male	Female
Percent	67.8%	32.2%
Effect on Earnings	15.3%	−17.0%

Union Membership

Percentage Union Members: 14.1%
Earnings Benefit of Union Membership: 4.8%

Veteran Status

Percentage Who Have Been on Active Duty: 5.9%
Earnings Benefit of Veteran Status: 28.6%

29-1069 Physicians and Surgeons, All Other

All physicians and surgeons not listed separately.

- Education or Training Required: First professional degree
- Job Growth: 24.0%
- Annual Openings: 41,000
- Self-Employed: 11.5%
- Part-Time: 25.6%

NATIONAL WAGE FIGURES (ANNUAL)

Beginning	25th Percentile	Median	Mean	75th Percentile	90th Percentile
$45,160	$84,630	more than $145,600	$142,220	more than $145,600	more than $145,600

Median Wages for Industries Employing Largest Numbers (Annual)

Industry	Median Income
Administrative and Support Services	more than $145,600
Ambulatory Health Care Services	more than $145,600
Management of Companies and Enterprises	more than $145,600
Religious, Grantmaking, Civic, Professional, and Similar Organizations	more than $145,600
Social Assistance	more than $145,600
Insurance Carriers and Related Activities	$127,510
Nursing and Residential Care Facilities	$124,240
Professional, Scientific, and Technical Services	$120,010
Health and Personal Care Stores	$118,320
Merchant Wholesalers, Nondurable Goods	$117,110

Median Wages for States (Annual)

AK ..more than $145,600	KY ....more than $145,600	NY $132,840
AL $127,120	LA ....more than $145,600	OH ..more than $145,600
AR........... $77,870	MA $136,510	OK $92,350
AZ...........$135,670	MD $117,960	OR....more than $145,600
CA ..more than $145,600	ME ....more than $145,600	PA $123,900
CO $128,340	MI $143,800	RI.............. no data
CT $126,720	MN ...more than $145,600	SC.............$143,670
DC .... no data	MO ...more than $145,600	SD $121,540
DE ..more than $145,600	MS $103,860	TN $124,230
FL ..more than $145,600	MT $113,030	TX....more than $145,600
GA ..more than $145,600	NC $131,180	UT....more than $145,600
HI ..more than $145,600	ND $120,600	VA.... $116,830
IA $144,020	NE ...more than $145,600	VT $142,240
ID ..more than $145,600	NH ...more than $145,600	WA ..more than $145,600
IL ..more than $145,600	NJ ....more than $145,600	WI....more than $145,600
IN ..more than $145,600	NM $120,020	WV ..more than $145,600
KS ..more than $145,600	NV ....more than $145,600	WY .... no data

Median Wages for the Largest Metropolitan Areas (Annual)

AZ: Phoenix $131,620	MI: Detroit $139,000
CA: Los Angeles ....more than $145,600	MN: Minneapolis .. more than $145,600
CA: Riverside ....more than $145,600	MO: Kansas City.... more than $145,600
CA: Sacramento $120,190	MO: St. Louis ...... more than $145,600
CA: San Diego ......more than $145,600	NV: Las Vegas ...... more than $145,600
CA: San Francisco $123,910	NY: New York.................. $135,660
CO: Denver.................... no data	OH: Cincinnati...... more than $145,600
DC: Washington $119,990	OH: Cleveland $137,480
FL: Miami $121,200	OH: Columbus ...... more than $145,600
FL: Orlando ....more than $145,600	OR: Portland $132,370
FL: Tampa $139,900	PA: Philadelphia .. more than $145,600
GA: Atlanta ....more than $145,600	PA: Pittsburgh $115,960
IL: Chicago ....more than $145,600	TX: Dallas .... more than $145,600
MA: Boston $128,270	TX: Houston $135,170
MD: Baltimore $80,700	WA: Seattle .... more than $145,600

FACTORS THAT MAY AFFECT EARNINGS

Educational Attainment of Workers and Effect on Earnings

Figures are based on a group of occupations: Health Diagnosing and Treating Practitioners

	Percent at Level	Effect on Earnings
Less than High School	—	—
Some High School	0.5%	−51.9%
High School or Equivalent	3.7%	−35.9%
Some College but No Degree	6.1%	−22.2%
Associate Degree	25.7%	−14.6%
Bachelor's Degree	31.5%	1.4%
Master's Degree	14.5%	11.8%
Doctoral Degree	7.4%	30.3%
First Professional Degree	10.4%	22.8%

Flexibility of Earnings

Average Hours Worked: 35
Workers with a Varying Number of Hours: 6.8%
Workers Earning Some Overtime Pay, Tips, or Commissions: 13.6%
Earnings Benefit of Working Overtime: −41.2%

Gender

	Male	Female
Percent	67.8%	32.2%
Effect on Earnings	15.3%	−17.0%

Union Membership

Percentage Union Members: 14.1%
Earnings Benefit of Union Membership: 4.8%

Veteran Status

Percentage Who Have Been on Active Duty: 5.9%
Earnings Benefit of Veteran Status: 28.6%

29-1071 Physician Assistants

Under the supervision of a physician, provide health-care services typically performed by a physician. Conduct complete physicals, provide treatment, and counsel patients. May, in some cases, prescribe medication. Must graduate from an accredited educational program for physician assistants.

- Education or Training Required: Bachelor's degree
- Job Growth: 49.6%
- Annual Openings: 10,000
- Self-Employed: 1.3%
- Part-Time: 23.1%

NATIONAL WAGE FIGURES (ANNUAL)

Beginning	25th Percentile	Median	Mean	75th Percentile	90th Percentile
$43,100	$62,430	$74,980	$74,270	$89,220	$102,230

Median Wages for Industries Employing Largest Numbers (Annual)

Industry	Median Income
Professional, Scientific, and Technical Services	$83,440
Administrative and Support Services	$80,960
Hospitals	$76,890
Ambulatory Health Care Services	$74,490
Federal, State, and Local Government	$72,630
Educational Services	$72,120
Social Assistance	$55,950
Management of Companies and Enterprises	$46,890

Median Wages for States (Annual)

AK	$86,130	KY	$68,340	NY	$79,590
AL	$57,010	LA	$47,610	OH	$73,090
AR	$68,390	MA	$77,940	OK	$75,060
AZ	$73,550	MD	$87,040	OR	$75,990
CA	$83,870	ME	$78,570	PA	$64,400
CO	$73,430	MI	$74,640	RI	$71,520
CT	$83,370	MN	$79,140	SC	$75,110
DC	$66,910	MO	$65,200	SD	$75,370
DE	$77,680	MS	$35,810	TN	$64,890
FL	$77,720	MT	no data	TX	$81,180
GA	$72,220	NC	$73,910	UT	$72,270
HI	$68,530	ND	$66,860	VA	$59,420
IA	$73,600	NE	$73,850	VT	$77,080
ID	$72,080	NH	$75,660	WA	$78,690
IL	$63,660	NJ	$80,660	WI	$78,590
IN	$70,250	NM	$45,720	WV	$70,760
KS	$72,510	NV	$68,340	WY	$56,690

Median Wages for the Largest Metropolitan Areas (Annual)

AZ: Phoenix	$73,090	MI: Detroit	$74,200
CA: Los Angeles	$86,070	MN: Minneapolis	$78,390
CA: Riverside	$79,220	MO: Kansas City	$74,430
CA: Sacramento	$79,780	MO: St. Louis	$64,920
CA: San Diego	$73,300	NV: Las Vegas	$69,370
CA: San Francisco	$86,830	NY: New York	$83,630
CO: Denver	$74,010	OH: Cincinnati	$77,150
DC: Washington	$82,190	OH: Cleveland	$72,700
FL: Miami	$71,380	OH: Columbus	$76,080
FL: Orlando	$84,180	OR: Portland	$78,000
FL: Tampa	$80,740	PA: Philadelphia	$68,870
GA: Atlanta	$75,100	PA: Pittsburgh	$62,090
IL: Chicago	$55,690	TX: Dallas	$84,770
MA: Boston	$78,200	TX: Houston	$79,890
MD: Baltimore	$76,480	WA: Seattle	$80,090

FACTORS THAT MAY AFFECT EARNINGS

Educational Attainment of Workers and Effect on Earnings

	Percent at Level	Effect on Earnings
Less than High School	—	—
Some High School	—	—
High School or Equivalent	7.2%	−49.9%
Some College but No Degree	7.2%	−49.4%
Associate Degree	18.9%	−30.2%
Bachelor's Degree	25.2%	20.5%
Master's Degree	27.9%	14.5%
Doctoral Degree	—	—
First Professional Degree	10.8%	36.3%

Flexibility of Earnings

Average Hours Worked: 36
Workers with a Varying Number of Hours: 6.7%
Workers Earning Some Overtime Pay, Tips, or Commissions: 7.8%
Earnings Benefit of Working Overtime: 24.7%

Gender

	Male	Female
Percent	28.3%	71.7%
Effect on Earnings	21.3%	−5.0%

Union Membership

Percentage Union Members: 7.8%
Earnings Benefit of Union Membership: 4.8%

Veteran Status

Percentage Who Have Been on Active Duty: 5.9%
Earnings Benefit of Veteran Status: 28.6%

29-1081 Podiatrists

Diagnose and treat diseases and deformities of the human foot.

- Education or Training Required: First professional degree
- Job Growth: 16.2%
- Annual Openings: 1,000
- Self-Employed: 19.8%
- Part-Time: 25.6%

NATIONAL WAGE FIGURES (ANNUAL)

Beginning	25th Percentile	Median	Mean	75th Percentile	90th Percentile
$44,500	$68,890	$108,220	$118,500	more than $145,600	more than $145,600

Median Wages for Industries Employing Largest Numbers (Annual)

Industry	Median Income
Ambulatory Health Care Services	$111,050
Federal, State, and Local Government	$94,150
Hospitals	$86,910

Median Wages for States (Annual)

AK	no data	KY	more than $145,600	NY	$117,650
AL	$99,090	LA	no data	OH	$101,960
AR	no data	MA	$99,690	OK	more than $145,600
AZ	$111,390	MD	$101,550	OR	more than $145,600
CA	$64,560	ME	$92,530	PA	$110,880
CO	$108,380	MI	no data	RI	no data
CT	$113,300	MN	more than $145,600	SC	$104,350
DC	no data	MO	$129,400	SD	no data
DE	$91,090	MS	no data	TN	$139,550
FL	$108,570	MT	no data	TX	$115,040
GA	more than $145,600	NC	more than $145,600	UT	$44,930
HI	no data	ND	no data	VA	$130,600
IA	$111,320	NE	$78,540	VT	no data
ID	no data	NH	more than $145,600	WA	more than $145,600
IL	$127,530	NJ	$87,920	WI	$99,690
IN	$114,850	NM	no data	WV	no data
KS	more than $145,600	NV	$114,970	WY	no data

Median Wages for the Largest Metropolitan Areas (Annual)

AZ: Phoenix	$112,940	MI: Detroit	no data
CA: Los Angeles	$58,220	MN: Minneapolis	more than $145,600
CA: Riverside	no data	MO: Kansas City	no data
CA: Sacramento	no data	MO: St. Louis	$100,800
CA: San Diego	$134,570	NV: Las Vegas	$122,140
CA: San Francisco	$140,630	NY: New York	$110,880
CO: Denver	no data	OH: Cincinnati	$115,880
DC: Washington	$104,200	OH: Cleveland	$104,200
FL: Miami	$114,650	OH: Columbus	no data
FL: Orlando	more than $145,600	OR: Portland	no data
FL: Tampa	$104,980	PA: Philadelphia	$96,630
GA: Atlanta	no data	PA: Pittsburgh	$123,790
IL: Chicago	$128,590	TX: Dallas	$145,290
MA: Boston	more than $145,600	TX: Houston	$112,600
MD: Baltimore	$102,520	WA: Seattle	$134,910

FACTORS THAT MAY AFFECT EARNINGS

Educational Attainment of Workers and Effect on Earnings

Figures are based on a group of occupations: Health Diagnosing and Treating Practitioners

	Percent at Level	Effect on Earnings
Less than High School	—	—
Some High School	0.5%	−51.9%
High School or Equivalent	3.7%	−35.9%
Some College but No Degree	6.1%	−22.2%
Associate Degree	25.7%	−14.6%
Bachelor's Degree	31.5%	1.4%
Master's Degree	14.5%	11.8%
Doctoral Degree	7.4%	30.3%
First Professional Degree	10.4%	22.8%

Flexibility of Earnings

Average Hours Worked: 34
Workers with a Varying Number of Hours: 20.0%
Workers Earning Some Overtime Pay, Tips, or Commissions: 20.0%
Earnings Benefit of Working Overtime: −11.4%

Gender

	Male	Female
Percent	63.6%	36.4%
Effect on Earnings	21.3%	−5.0%

Union Membership

Percentage Union Members: 14.1%
Earnings Benefit of Union Membership: 4.8%

Veteran Status

Percentage Who Have Been on Active Duty: 5.9%
Earnings Benefit of Veteran Status: 28.6%

29-1111 Registered Nurses

Assess patient health problems and needs, develop and implement nursing care plans, and maintain medical records. Administer nursing care to ill, injured, convalescent, or disabled patients. May advise patients on health maintenance and disease prevention or provide case management. Licensing or registration required. Includes advance practice nurses, such as nurse practitioners, clinical nurse specialists, certified nurse midwives, and certified registered nurse anesthetists. Advanced practice nursing is practiced by RNs who have specialized formal, post-basic education and who function in highly autonomous and specialized roles.

- Education or Training Required: Associate degree
- Job Growth: 29.4%
- Annual Openings: 229,000
- Self-Employed: 0.7%
- Part-Time: 30.1%

NATIONAL WAGE FIGURES (ANNUAL)

Beginning	25th Percentile	Median	Mean	75th Percentile	90th Percentile
$40,250	$47,710	$57,280	$59,730	$69,850	$83,440

Median Wages for Industries Employing Largest Numbers (Annual)

Industry	Median Income
Administrative and Support Services	$63,960
Computer and Electronic Product Manufacturing	$63,820
Nonstore Retailers	$63,060
Funds, Trusts, and Other Financial Vehicles	$61,410
Chemical Manufacturing	$59,650
Federal, State, and Local Government	$59,270
Merchant Wholesalers, Nondurable Goods	$59,180
Management of Companies and Enterprises	$58,670
Hospitals	$58,500
Insurance Carriers and Related Activities	$57,600

Median Wages for States (Annual)

AK	$63,260	KY	$50,400	NY	$64,070
AL	$48,920	LA	$50,840	OH	$53,860
AR	$49,130	MA	$68,380	OK	$47,730
AZ	$58,360	MD	$67,870	OR	$64,060
CA	$73,280	ME	$53,550	PA	$55,800
CO	$58,560	MI	$57,850	RI	$60,290
CT	$63,490	MN	$62,980	SC	$51,800
DC	$62,140	MO	$51,280	SD	$47,240
DE	$60,650	MS	$48,180	TN	$51,390
FL	$54,730	MT	$51,060	TX	$55,440
GA	$54,480	NC	$51,860	UT	$53,690
HI	$69,000	ND	$48,490	VA	$54,590
IA	$46,010	NE	$49,560	VT	$51,830
ID	$50,060	NH	$54,440	WA	$64,140
IL	$55,180	NJ	$66,010	WI	$56,090
IN	$51,800	NM	$57,120	WV	$46,520
KS	$47,760	NV	$63,210	WY	$48,170

Median Wages for the Largest Metropolitan Areas (Annual)

AZ: Phoenix	$59,140	MI: Detroit	$61,590
CA: Los Angeles	$71,410	MN: Minneapolis	$65,040
CA: Riverside	$68,170	MO: Kansas City	$54,670
CA: Sacramento	$77,620	MO: St. Louis	$52,630
CA: San Diego	$69,890	NV: Las Vegas	$63,220
CA: San Francisco	$87,570	NY: New York	$70,740
CO: Denver	$61,690	OH: Cincinnati	$54,570
DC: Washington	$66,780	OH: Cleveland	$56,950
FL: Miami	$60,350	OH: Columbus	$53,790
FL: Orlando	$51,960	OR: Portland	$65,480
FL: Tampa	$54,460	PA: Philadelphia	$62,910
GA: Atlanta	$55,910	PA: Pittsburgh	$53,060
IL: Chicago	$57,940	TX: Dallas	$57,120
MA: Boston	$70,340	TX: Houston	$61,030
MD: Baltimore	$68,860	WA: Seattle	$69,130

FACTORS THAT MAY AFFECT EARNINGS

Educational Attainment of Workers and Effect on Earnings

	Percent at Level	Effect on Earnings
Less than High School	—	—
Some High School	0.4%	−31.0%
High School or Equivalent	2.8%	−25.6%
Some College but No Degree	6.7%	−8.0%
Associate Degree	35.6%	−10.0%
Bachelor's Degree	39.3%	4.7%
Master's Degree	11.2%	25.4%
Doctoral Degree	0.6%	23.1%
First Professional Degree	3.3%	3.3%

Flexibility of Earnings

Average Hours Worked: 33
Workers with a Varying Number of Hours: 7.1%
Workers Earning Some Overtime Pay, Tips, or Commissions: 16.4%
Earnings Benefit of Working Overtime: −6.0%

Gender

	Male	Female
Percent	8.7%	91.3%
Effect on Earnings	9.8%	−0.7%

Union Membership

Percentage Union Members: 16.5%
Earnings Benefit of Union Membership: 13.3%

Veteran Status

Percentage Who Have Been on Active Duty: 5.9%
Earnings Benefit of Veteran Status: 28.6%

29-1121 Audiologists

Assess and treat persons with hearing and related disorders. May fit hearing aids and provide auditory training. May perform research related to hearing problems.

- Education or Training Required: First professional degree
- Job Growth: 9.1%
- Annual Openings: Fewer than 500
- Self-Employed: 1.4%
- Part-Time: 66.7%

NATIONAL WAGE FIGURES (ANNUAL)

Beginning	25th Percentile	Median	Mean	75th Percentile	90th Percentile
$38,370	$47,220	$57,120	$61,110	$70,940	$89,160

Median Wages for Industries Employing Largest Numbers (Annual)

Industry	Median Income
Computer and Electronic Product Manufacturing	$63,470
Hospitals	$59,360
Ambulatory Health Care Services	$58,100
Social Assistance	$56,760
Nursing and Residential Care Facilities	$55,870
Administrative and Support Services	$55,500
Educational Services	$55,330
Health and Personal Care Stores	$55,210
Federal, State, and Local Government	$52,550
Professional, Scientific, and Technical Services	$52,210

Median Wages for States (Annual)

AK	no data	KY	$48,250	NY	$62,150
AL	$49,720	LA	$52,480	OH	$51,010
AR	$50,530	MA	$58,980	OK	$48,210
AZ	$38,480	MD	$61,060	OR	$62,640
CA	$61,800	ME	more than $145,600	PA	$50,490
CO	$57,340	MI	$58,080	RI	$59,840
CT	$61,280	MN	$58,660	SC	$59,070
DC	$70,100	MO	$52,980	SD	$50,050
DE	no data	MS	$42,770	TN	no data
FL	$67,180	MT	no data	TX	$53,980
GA	$59,660	NC	$54,660	UT	$53,270
HI	$60,430	ND	$59,210	VA	$59,860
IA	$49,160	NE	$44,820	VT	no data
ID	$56,040	NH	no data	WA	$57,220
IL	$52,480	NJ	$67,030	WI	$56,880
IN	$53,390	NM	no data	WV	$47,470
KS	$46,740	NV	no data	WY	no data

Median Wages for the Largest Metropolitan Areas (Annual)

AZ: Phoenix	$53,560	MI: Detroit	$61,930
CA: Los Angeles	$65,770	MN: Minneapolis	$57,720
CA: Riverside	$59,270	MO: Kansas City	$44,740
CA: Sacramento	$59,710	MO: St. Louis	$55,020
CA: San Diego	$56,590	NV: Las Vegas	no data
CA: San Francisco	$57,990	NY: New York	$66,810
CO: Denver	$60,450	OH: Cincinnati	no data
DC: Washington	$71,600	OH: Cleveland	$56,170
FL: Miami	$93,010	OH: Columbus	$49,420
FL: Orlando	no data	OR: Portland	$66,260
FL: Tampa	$76,850	PA: Philadelphia	$55,770
GA: Atlanta	$62,700	PA: Pittsburgh	$45,800
IL: Chicago	$53,340	TX: Dallas	$58,090
MA: Boston	$60,090	TX: Houston	$56,820
MD: Baltimore	$51,910	WA: Seattle	$67,350

FACTORS THAT MAY AFFECT EARNINGS

Educational Attainment of Workers and Effect on Earnings

	Percent at Level	Effect on Earnings
Less than High School	—	—
Some High School	—	—
High School or Equivalent	—	—
Some College but No Degree	—	—
Associate Degree	—	—
Bachelor's Degree	—	—
Master's Degree	53.8%	17.1%
Doctoral Degree	—	—
First Professional Degree	—	—

Figures do not total 100% because some levels have a very small sample size.

Flexibility of Earnings

Average Hours Worked: 34
Workers with a Varying Number of Hours: 5.3%
Workers Earning Some Overtime Pay, Tips, or Commissions: 22.2%
Earnings Benefit of Working Overtime: –11.4%

Gender

	Male	Female
Percent	20.4%	79.6%
Effect on Earnings	21.3%	–5.0%

Union Membership

Percentage Union Members: 14.8%
Earnings Benefit of Union Membership: 4.8%

Veteran Status

Percentage Who Have Been on Active Duty: 5.9%
Earnings Benefit of Veteran Status: 28.6%

29-1122 Occupational Therapists

Assess, plan, organize, and participate in rehabilitative programs that help restore vocational, homemaking, and daily living skills, as well as general independence, to disabled persons.

- Education or Training Required: Master's degree
- Job Growth: 33.6%
- Annual Openings: 7,000
- Self-Employed: 6.0%
- Part-Time: 39.4%

NATIONAL WAGE FIGURES (ANNUAL)

Beginning	25th Percentile	Median	Mean	75th Percentile	90th Percentile
$40,840	$50,450	$60,470	$62,510	$73,710	$89,450

Median Wages for Industries Employing Largest Numbers (Annual)

Industry	Median Income
Nursing and Residential Care Facilities	$63,740
Ambulatory Health Care Services	$63,020
Insurance Carriers and Related Activities	$61,780
Hospitals	$61,250
Administrative and Support Services	$60,510
Professional, Scientific, and Technical Services	$59,600
Federal, State, and Local Government	$58,410
Religious, Grantmaking, Civic, Professional, and Similar Organizations	$56,460
Management of Companies and Enterprises	$54,380
Educational Services	$54,370

Median Wages for States (Annual)

AK	no data	KY	$61,130	NY	$58,170
AL	$59,780	LA	$65,190	OH	$64,020
AR	$61,890	MA	$60,160	OK	$56,760
AZ	$45,530	MD	$67,900	OR	$60,820
CA	$73,660	ME	$51,690	PA	$58,560
CO	$55,010	MI	$55,330	RI	$57,050
CT	$64,830	MN	$55,920	SC	$58,940
DC	$53,250	MO	$55,850	SD	$51,520
DE	$40,250	MS	$63,230	TN	$62,300
FL	$65,740	MT	$54,010	TX	$63,140
GA	$62,930	NC	$60,580	UT	$57,360
HI	$55,320	ND	$50,560	VA	$61,330
IA	$54,450	NE	$51,240	VT	$54,510
ID	$49,650	NH	$52,690	WA	$59,680
IL	$63,940	NJ	$66,860	WI	$53,660
IN	$60,010	NM	$50,560	WV	$56,000
KS	$57,290	NV	$65,080	WY	$51,680

Median Wages for the Largest Metropolitan Areas (Annual)

AZ: Phoenix	$42,470	MI: Detroit	$56,490
CA: Los Angeles	$72,660	MN: Minneapolis	$56,410
CA: Riverside	$75,000	MO: Kansas City	$54,190
CA: Sacramento	$72,740	MO: St. Louis	$57,470
CA: San Diego	$75,170	NV: Las Vegas	$61,710
CA: San Francisco	$78,580	NY: New York	$63,360
CO: Denver	$54,410	OH: Cincinnati	$60,850
DC: Washington	$64,600	OH: Cleveland	$67,090
FL: Miami	$68,400	OH: Columbus	$69,150
FL: Orlando	$60,340	OR: Portland	$59,180
FL: Tampa	$69,800	PA: Philadelphia	$61,380
GA: Atlanta	$64,950	PA: Pittsburgh	$57,480
IL: Chicago	$64,090	TX: Dallas	$66,520
MA: Boston	$59,590	TX: Houston	$63,280
MD: Baltimore	$68,160	WA: Seattle	$59,870

FACTORS THAT MAY AFFECT EARNINGS

Educational Attainment of Workers and Effect on Earnings

	Percent at Level	Effect on Earnings
Less than High School	—	—
Some High School	—	—
High School or Equivalent	—	—
Some College but No Degree	—	—
Associate Degree	9.1%	−20.8%
Bachelor's Degree	59.6%	9.9%
Master's Degree	26.3%	−7.1%
Doctoral Degree	—	—
First Professional Degree	—	—

Flexibility of Earnings

Average Hours Worked: 31
Workers with a Varying Number of Hours: 6.1%
Workers Earning Some Overtime Pay, Tips, or Commissions: 5.7%
Earnings Benefit of Working Overtime: −11.4%

Gender

	Male	Female
Percent	9.7%	90.3%
Effect on Earnings	21.3%	−5.0%

Union Membership

Percentage Union Members: 15.2%
Earnings Benefit of Union Membership: 10.0%

Veteran Status

Percentage Who Have Been on Active Duty: 5.9%
Earnings Benefit of Veteran Status: 28.6%

29-1123 Physical Therapists

Assess, plan, organize, and participate in rehabilitative programs that improve mobility, relieve pain, increase strength, and decrease or prevent deformity of patients suffering from disease or injury.

- Education or Training Required: Master's degree
- Job Growth: 36.7%
- Annual Openings: 13,000
- Self-Employed: 4.5%
- Part-Time: 21.4%

NATIONAL WAGE FIGURES (ANNUAL)

Beginning	25th Percentile	Median	Mean	75th Percentile	90th Percentile
$46,510	$55,030	$66,200	$68,050	$78,080	$94,810

Median Wages for Industries Employing Largest Numbers (Annual)

Industry	Median Income
Amusement, Gambling, and Recreation Industries	$70,290
Administrative and Support Services	$68,860
Nursing and Residential Care Facilities	$68,590
Insurance Carriers and Related Activities	$68,570
Management of Companies and Enterprises	$66,910
Federal, State, and Local Government	$66,810
Ambulatory Health Care Services	$66,340
Hospitals	$66,210
Social Assistance	$61,580
Religious, Grantmaking, Civic, Professional, and Similar Organizations	$59,660

Median Wages for States (Annual)

State		State		State	
AK	no data	KY	$63,950	NY	$62,490
AL	$68,020	LA	$70,740	OH	$67,450
AR	$59,020	MA	$64,440	OK	$67,810
AZ	$62,860	MD	$68,940	OR	$63,220
CA	$73,940	ME	$57,500	PA	$65,640
CO	$59,050	MI	$65,980	RI	$66,040
CT	$69,150	MN	$62,100	SC	$62,530
DC	$61,330	MO	$61,810	SD	$58,170
DE	$64,110	MS	$68,910	TN	$68,950
FL	$67,480	MT	$56,520	TX	$70,800
GA	$67,270	NC	$64,240	UT	$63,820
HI	$61,340	ND	$59,440	VA	$65,790
IA	$60,310	NE	$62,860	VT	$55,740
ID	$61,980	NH	$59,010	WA	$66,780
IL	$64,580	NJ	$72,490	WI	$64,410
IN	$64,600	NM	$59,400	WV	$66,170
KS	$61,040	NV	$71,340	WY	$60,180

Median Wages for the Largest Metropolitan Areas (Annual)

Area		Area	
AZ: Phoenix	$61,660	MI: Detroit	$69,070
CA: Los Angeles	$72,360	MN: Minneapolis	$62,420
CA: Riverside	$75,610	MO: Kansas City	$60,870
CA: Sacramento	no data	MO: St. Louis	$60,060
CA: San Diego	$72,420	NV: Las Vegas	$72,690
CA: San Francisco	$79,510	NY: New York	$69,220
CO: Denver	$59,190	OH: Cincinnati	$68,010
DC: Washington	$68,590	OH: Cleveland	$66,490
FL: Miami	$68,620	OH: Columbus	$66,840
FL: Orlando	$63,490	OR: Portland	$63,490
FL: Tampa	$68,940	PA: Philadelphia	$66,740
GA: Atlanta	$69,630	PA: Pittsburgh	$63,710
IL: Chicago	$65,750	TX: Dallas	$72,990
MA: Boston	$64,240	TX: Houston	$70,770
MD: Baltimore	$67,950	WA: Seattle	$67,470

FACTORS THAT MAY AFFECT EARNINGS

Educational Attainment of Workers and Effect on Earnings

	Percent at Level	Effect on Earnings
Less than High School	—	—
Some High School	—	—
High School or Equivalent	2.8%	−44.4%
Some College but No Degree	2.8%	−56.5%
Associate Degree	9.0%	−14.4%
Bachelor's Degree	38.4%	3.7%
Master's Degree	36.0%	9.3%
Doctoral Degree	7.6%	−6.1%
First Professional Degree	3.3%	−3.5%

Flexibility of Earnings

Average Hours Worked: 34
Workers with a Varying Number of Hours: 6.7%
Workers Earning Some Overtime Pay, Tips, or Commissions: 8.1%
Earnings Benefit of Working Overtime: −19.2%

Gender

	Male	Female
Percent	37.3%	62.7%
Effect on Earnings	1.2%	−1.5%

Union Membership

Percentage Union Members: 7.7%
Earnings Benefit of Union Membership: 10.4%

Veteran Status

Percentage Who Have Been on Active Duty: 5.9%
Earnings Benefit of Veteran Status: 28.6%

29-1124 Radiation Therapists

Provide radiation therapy to patients as prescribed by a radiologist according to established practices and standards. Duties may include reviewing prescription and diagnosis; acting as liaison with physician and supportive care personnel; preparing equipment, such as immobilization, treatment, and protection devices; and maintaining records, reports, and files. May assist in dosimetry procedures and tumor localization.

- Education or Training Required: Associate degree
- Job Growth: 26.3%
- Annual Openings: 1,000
- Self-Employed: 0.0%
- Part-Time: 25.6%

NATIONAL WAGE FIGURES (ANNUAL)

Beginning	25th Percentile	Median	Mean	75th Percentile	90th Percentile
$44,840	$54,170	$66,170	$67,580	$78,550	$92,110

Median Wages for Industries Employing Largest Numbers (Annual)

Industry	Median Income
Administrative and Support Services	$75,320
Ambulatory Health Care Services	$69,990
Educational Services	$65,590
Hospitals	$63,910

Median Wages for States (Annual)

AK	no data	KY	$59,220	NY	$76,550
AL	$59,760	LA	$57,250	OH	$57,970
AR	$58,990	MA	$73,530	OK	$56,540
AZ	$72,630	MD	$66,170	OR	$74,180
CA	$79,080	ME	$57,760	PA	$64,120
CO	$72,180	MI	$56,430	RI	no data
CT	$77,150	MN	$63,940	SC	$60,120
DC	$54,100	MO	$61,260	SD	$50,720
DE	no data	MS	$66,080	TN	no data
FL	$65,500	MT	$65,380	TX	$72,750
GA	$57,090	NC	$63,620	UT	$61,350
HI	no data	ND	$62,220	VA	$59,230
IA	$55,140	NE	$59,280	VT	$55,880
ID	$55,850	NH	$73,050	WA	$80,110
IL	$62,260	NJ	$81,950	WI	$68,650
IN	$58,290	NM	$71,520	WV	$57,350
KS	$58,230	NV	$71,010	WY	$59,100

Median Wages for the Largest Metropolitan Areas (Annual)

AZ: Phoenix	$72,490	MI: Detroit	$63,350
CA: Los Angeles	$78,380	MN: Minneapolis	$62,440
CA: Riverside	$78,100	MO: Kansas City	$61,040
CA: Sacramento	no data	MO: St. Louis	$63,720
CA: San Diego	no data	NV: Las Vegas	$70,880
CA: San Francisco	$81,630	NY: New York	$79,310
CO: Denver	$70,530	OH: Cincinnati	$61,510
DC: Washington	$58,890	OH: Cleveland	no data
FL: Miami	$67,390	OH: Columbus	$61,780
FL: Orlando	$61,400	OR: Portland	$74,030
FL: Tampa	$63,740	PA: Philadelphia	$69,050
GA: Atlanta	$58,630	PA: Pittsburgh	$56,430
IL: Chicago	$60,020	TX: Dallas	$69,960
MA: Boston	$71,750	TX: Houston	$77,240
MD: Baltimore	$63,050	WA: Seattle	$83,230

FACTORS THAT MAY AFFECT EARNINGS

Educational Attainment of Workers and Effect on Earnings

	Percent at Level	Effect on Earnings
Less than High School	—	—
Some High School	—	—
High School or Equivalent	—	—
Some College but No Degree	—	—
Associate Degree	33.3%	–9.1%
Bachelor's Degree	55.6%	10.7%
Master's Degree	—	—
Doctoral Degree	—	—
First Professional Degree	—	—

Figures do not total 100% because some levels have a very small sample size.

Flexibility of Earnings

Average Hours Worked: 38
Workers with a Varying Number of Hours: 5.6%
Workers Earning Some Overtime Pay, Tips, or Commissions: 13.6%
Earnings Benefit of Working Overtime: –11.4%

Gender

	Male	Female
Percent	25.9%	74.1%
Effect on Earnings	21.3%	–5.0%

Union Membership

Percentage Union Members: 14.1%
Earnings Benefit of Union Membership: 4.8%

Veteran Status

Percentage Who Have Been on Active Duty: 5.9%
Earnings Benefit of Veteran Status: 28.6%

29-1125 Recreational Therapists

Plan, direct, or coordinate medically approved recreation programs for patients in hospitals, nursing homes, or other institutions. Activities include sports, trips, dramatics, social activities, and arts and crafts. May assess a patient condition and recommend appropriate recreational activity.

- Education or Training Required: Bachelor's degree
- Job Growth: 5.7%
- Annual Openings: 3,000
- Self-Employed: 0.0%
- Part-Time: 25.6%

NATIONAL WAGE FIGURES (ANNUAL)

Beginning	25th Percentile	Median	Mean	75th Percentile	90th Percentile
$20,880	$26,780	$34,990	$36,510	$44,850	$55,530

Median Wages for Industries Employing Largest Numbers (Annual)

Industry	Median Income
Federal, State, and Local Government	$40,690
Educational Services	$40,590
Management of Companies and Enterprises	$40,450
Hospitals	$38,910
Religious, Grantmaking, Civic, Professional, and Similar Organizations	$35,190
Ambulatory Health Care Services	$35,160
Amusement, Gambling, and Recreation Industries	$34,150
Professional, Scientific, and Technical Services	$33,450
Administrative and Support Services	$32,300
Nursing and Residential Care Facilities	$30,320

Median Wages for States (Annual)

State	Wage	State	Wage	State	Wage
AK	no data	KY	$31,730	NY	$42,670
AL	$29,930	LA	$30,810	OH	$37,530
AR	$34,180	MA	$34,230	OK	$32,270
AZ	$35,750	MD	$33,900	OR	$38,240
CA	$45,400	ME	$35,050	PA	$33,120
CO	$37,360	MI	$39,530	RI	$31,730
CT	$37,340	MN	$37,050	SC	$25,110
DC	$43,890	MO	$30,390	SD	$34,730
DE	$35,640	MS	$27,910	TN	$32,700
FL	$35,750	MT	$27,180	TX	$35,180
GA	$32,580	NC	$33,770	UT	$32,320
HI	$43,570	ND	$33,670	VA	$32,940
IA	$29,590	NE	$28,140	VT	$33,310
ID	$38,840	NH	$38,600	WA	$45,680
IL	$25,430	NJ	$37,790	WI	$35,050
IN	$29,850	NM	$29,840	WV	$26,510
KS	$27,730	NV	$30,460	WY	$36,010

Median Wages for the Largest Metropolitan Areas (Annual)

Area	Wage	Area	Wage
AZ: Phoenix	$35,960	MI: Detroit	$42,230
CA: Los Angeles	$44,630	MN: Minneapolis	$37,100
CA: Riverside	$36,450	MO: Kansas City	$33,070
CA: Sacramento	$42,760	MO: St. Louis	$29,880
CA: San Diego	$41,290	NV: Las Vegas	$30,480
CA: San Francisco	$52,430	NY: New York	$43,000
CO: Denver	$41,830	OH: Cincinnati	$37,070
DC: Washington	$40,420	OH: Cleveland	$37,240
FL: Miami	$39,080	OH: Columbus	no data
FL: Orlando	$28,650	OR: Portland	$38,540
FL: Tampa	$35,150	PA: Philadelphia	$35,870
GA: Atlanta	$33,510	PA: Pittsburgh	$33,810
IL: Chicago	$32,250	TX: Dallas	$39,240
MA: Boston	$34,760	TX: Houston	$39,070
MD: Baltimore	$32,860	WA: Seattle	$47,000

FACTORS THAT MAY AFFECT EARNINGS

Educational Attainment of Workers and Effect on Earnings

	Percent at Level	Effect on Earnings
Less than High School	—	—
Some High School	—	—
High School or Equivalent	—	—
Some College but No Degree	—	—
Associate Degree	—	—
Bachelor's Degree	61.5%	−3.2%
Master's Degree	—	—
Doctoral Degree	—	—
First Professional Degree	—	—

Figures do not total 100% because some levels have a very small sample size.

Flexibility of Earnings

Average Hours Worked: 33
Workers with a Varying Number of Hours: 4.5%
Workers Earning Some Overtime Pay, Tips, or Commissions: 3.7%
Earnings Benefit of Working Overtime: −11.4%

Gender

	Male	Female
Percent	17.9%	82.1%
Effect on Earnings	21.3%	−5.0%

Union Membership

Percentage Union Members: 11.1%
Earnings Benefit of Union Membership: 4.8%

Veteran Status

Percentage Who Have Been on Active Duty: 5.9%
Earnings Benefit of Veteran Status: 28.6%

29-1126 Respiratory Therapists

Assess, treat, and care for patients with breathing disorders. Assume primary responsibility for all respiratory care modalities, including the supervision of respiratory therapy technicians. Initiate and conduct therapeutic procedures; maintain patient records; and select, assemble, check, and operate equipment.

- Education or Training Required: Associate degree
- Job Growth: 28.4%
- Annual Openings: 7,000
- Self-Employed: 0.4%
- Part-Time: 6.5%

NATIONAL WAGE FIGURES (ANNUAL)

Beginning	25th Percentile	Median	Mean	75th Percentile	90th Percentile
$35,200	$40,840	$47,420	$48,610	$56,160	$64,190

Median Wages for Industries Employing Largest Numbers (Annual)

Industry	Median Income
Administrative and Support Services	$56,010
Professional, Scientific, and Technical Services	$53,540
Educational Services	$49,230
Wholesale Electronic Markets and Agents and Brokers	$48,700
Ambulatory Health Care Services	$48,110
Hospitals	$47,420
Merchant Wholesalers, Durable Goods	$46,910
Nursing and Residential Care Facilities	$46,530
Federal, State, and Local Government	$46,440
Health and Personal Care Stores	$43,800

Median Wages for States (Annual)

AK	$57,310	KY	$41,180	NY	$57,730
AL	$41,240	LA	$43,040	OH	$44,810
AR	$41,470	MA	$54,700	OK	$42,940
AZ	$43,870	MD	$57,490	OR	$50,020
CA	$58,310	ME	$47,870	PA	$46,900
CO	$47,190	MI	$46,470	RI	$51,470
CT	$54,240	MN	$53,670	SC	$43,000
DC	$45,840	MO	$42,910	SD	$45,990
DE	$53,150	MS	$39,520	TN	$43,760
FL	$43,440	MT	$43,750	TX	$44,690
GA	$44,410	NC	$45,050	UT	no data
HI	$56,830	ND	$38,730	VA	$49,860
IA	$42,540	NE	$46,310	VT	$44,850
ID	$44,310	NH	$51,230	WA	$54,160
IL	$45,350	NJ	$56,590	WI	$48,980
IN	$45,550	NM	$38,130	WV	$41,240
KS	$43,730	NV	$57,210	WY	$42,620

Median Wages for the Largest Metropolitan Areas (Annual)

AZ: Phoenix	$44,870	MI: Detroit	$46,900
CA: Los Angeles	$57,260	MN: Minneapolis	$54,210
CA: Riverside	$54,060	MO: Kansas City	$44,680
CA: Sacramento	$62,540	MO: St. Louis	$44,260
CA: San Diego	$57,580	NV: Las Vegas	$59,510
CA: San Francisco	$66,300	NY: New York	$59,790
CO: Denver	$47,650	OH: Cincinnati	$45,550
DC: Washington	$55,770	OH: Cleveland	$47,950
FL: Miami	$44,750	OH: Columbus	$45,200
FL: Orlando	$44,540	OR: Portland	$53,200
FL: Tampa	$41,900	PA: Philadelphia	$53,770
GA: Atlanta	$45,970	PA: Pittsburgh	$44,060
IL: Chicago	$47,520	TX: Dallas	$46,300
MA: Boston	$55,220	TX: Houston	$45,530
MD: Baltimore	$56,470	WA: Seattle	$55,400

FACTORS THAT MAY AFFECT EARNINGS

Educational Attainment of Workers and Effect on Earnings

	Percent at Level	Effect on Earnings
Less than High School	—	—
Some High School	—	—
High School or Equivalent	—	—
Some College but No Degree	10.8%	-17.6%
Associate Degree	52.3%	-4.8%
Bachelor's Degree	28.8%	12.8%
Master's Degree	—	—
Doctoral Degree	—	—
First Professional Degree	—	—

Figures do not total 100% because some levels have a very small sample size.

Flexibility of Earnings

Average Hours Worked: 35
Workers with a Varying Number of Hours: 4.3%
Workers Earning Some Overtime Pay, Tips, or Commissions: 11.7%
Earnings Benefit of Working Overtime: -11.4%

Gender

	Male	Female
Percent	34.0%	66.0%
Effect on Earnings	21.3%	-5.0%

Union Membership

Percentage Union Members: 7.5%
Earnings Benefit of Union Membership: 4.8%

Veteran Status

Percentage Who Have Been on Active Duty: 5.9%
Earnings Benefit of Veteran Status: 28.6%

29-1127 Speech-Language Pathologists

Assess and treat persons with speech, language, voice, and fluency disorders. May select alternative communication systems and teach their use. May perform research related to speech and language problems.

- Education or Training Required: Master's degree
- Job Growth: 14.6%
- Annual Openings: 5,000
- Self-Employed: 6.0%
- Part-Time: 29.4%

NATIONAL WAGE FIGURES (ANNUAL)

Beginning	25th Percentile	Median	Mean	75th Percentile	90th Percentile
$37,970	$46,360	$57,710	$60,840	$72,410	$90,400

Median Wages for Industries Employing Largest Numbers (Annual)

Industry	Median Income
Nursing and Residential Care Facilities	$69,540
Ambulatory Health Care Services	$64,210
Management of Companies and Enterprises	$62,180
Hospitals	$61,780
Federal, State, and Local Government	$61,130
Administrative and Support Services	$60,700
Social Assistance	$60,190
Religious, Grantmaking, Civic, Professional, and Similar Organizations	$54,820
Educational Services	$52,850

Median Wages for States (Annual)

State	Wage	State	Wage	State	Wage
AK	$67,130	KY	$52,200	NY	$60,980
AL	$48,010	LA	$57,280	OH	$65,000
AR	$47,100	MA	$60,730	OK	$45,320
AZ	$46,360	MD	$65,920	OR	$62,650
CA	$69,020	ME	$48,660	PA	$58,810
CO	$60,740	MI	$63,210	RI	$62,660
CT	$68,200	MN	$52,730	SC	$49,040
DC	$67,530	MO	$50,540	SD	$39,420
DE	$67,410	MS	$48,110	TN	$52,980
FL	$58,600	MT	$51,190	TX	$51,890
GA	$55,430	NC	$55,450	UT	$55,490
HI	$56,410	ND	$44,160	VA	$63,310
IA	$51,220	NE	$49,390	VT	$53,620
ID	$57,600	NH	$53,570	WA	$57,410
IL	$57,940	NJ	$69,580	WI	$54,100
IN	$57,610	NM	$54,530	WV	$43,670
KS	$49,520	NV	$76,270	WY	$50,390

Median Wages for the Largest Metropolitan Areas (Annual)

Area	Wage	Area	Wage
AZ: Phoenix	$46,040	MI: Detroit	$64,480
CA: Los Angeles	$69,300	MN: Minneapolis	$53,880
CA: Riverside	$72,610	MO: Kansas City	$52,090
CA: Sacramento	$60,850	MO: St. Louis	$55,310
CA: San Diego	$76,890	NV: Las Vegas	no data
CA: San Francisco	$72,930	NY: New York	$71,810
CO: Denver	$60,720	OH: Cincinnati	$65,220
DC: Washington	$68,380	OH: Cleveland	$67,840
FL: Miami	$64,990	OH: Columbus	$68,290
FL: Orlando	$49,090	OR: Portland	$61,980
FL: Tampa	$60,750	PA: Philadelphia	$64,350
GA: Atlanta	$59,990	PA: Pittsburgh	$51,080
IL: Chicago	$60,130	TX: Dallas	$52,720
MA: Boston	$59,570	TX: Houston	$54,390
MD: Baltimore	$67,120	WA: Seattle	$59,590

FACTORS THAT MAY AFFECT EARNINGS

Educational Attainment of Workers and Effect on Earnings

	Percent at Level	Effect on Earnings
Less than High School	—	—
Some High School	—	—
High School or Equivalent	—	—
Some College but No Degree	—	—
Associate Degree	—	—
Bachelor's Degree	10.4%	−6.4%
Master's Degree	83.2%	0.9%
Doctoral Degree	—	—
First Professional Degree	—	—

Figures do not total 100% because some levels have a very small sample size.

Flexibility of Earnings

Average Hours Worked: 34
Workers with a Varying Number of Hours: 3.1%
Workers Earning Some Overtime Pay, Tips, or Commissions: 4.4%
Earnings Benefit of Working Overtime: −11.4%

Gender

	Male	Female
Percent	4.7%	95.3%
Effect on Earnings	—	−0.2%

Union Membership

Percentage Union Members: 45.0%
Earnings Benefit of Union Membership: 19.6%

Veteran Status

Percentage Who Have Been on Active Duty: 5.9%
Earnings Benefit of Veteran Status: 28.6%

29-1129 Therapists, All Other

All therapists not listed separately.

- Education or Training Required: Bachelor's degree
- Job Growth: 15.0%
- Annual Openings: 2,000
- Self-Employed: 61.5%
- Part-Time: 28.8%

Note: Earnings figures do not reflect self-employed workers, who make up a large fraction of the workforce for this occupation.

NATIONAL WAGE FIGURES (ANNUAL)

Beginning	25th Percentile	Median	Mean	75th Percentile	90th Percentile
$20,880	$25,800	$42,250	$45,070	$56,940	$72,640

Median Wages for Industries Employing Largest Numbers (Annual)

Industry	Median Income
Administrative and Support Services	$62,150
Federal, State, and Local Government	$55,570
Hospitals	$48,330
Amusement, Gambling, and Recreation Industries	$48,020
Educational Services	$47,550
Religious, Grantmaking, Civic, Professional, and Similar Organizations	$46,280
Nursing and Residential Care Facilities	$41,400
Social Assistance	$40,800
Management of Companies and Enterprises	$40,740
Ambulatory Health Care Services	$27,420

Median Wages for States (Annual)

AK	no data	KY	$57,310	NY	$48,700
AL	$21,540	LA	$41,600	OH	$47,270
AR	no data	MA	$48,680	OK	no data
AZ	$28,950	MD	$49,040	OR	$49,270
CA	$55,000	ME	no data	PA	$49,410
CO	$50,430	MI	$44,220	RI	$49,480
CT	$65,890	MN	$57,250	SC	no data
DC	no data	MO	$36,070	SD	no data
DE	no data	MS	no data	TN	$35,600
FL	$51,710	MT	no data	TX	$46,230
GA	$39,300	NC	$55,570	UT	no data
HI	no data	ND	no data	VA	$54,760
IA	$47,270	NE	no data	VT	no data
ID	$30,670	NH	$52,400	WA	$65,210
IL	$41,080	NJ	$41,650	WI	no data
IN	$28,170	NM	$46,760	WV	no data
KS	no data	NV	$68,960	WY	no data

Median Wages for the Largest Metropolitan Areas (Annual)

AZ: Phoenix	$24,840	MI: Detroit	$49,090
CA: Los Angeles	$56,790	MN: Minneapolis	$56,740
CA: Riverside	no data	MO: Kansas City	no data
CA: Sacramento	no data	MO: St. Louis	$50,970
CA: San Diego	no data	NV: Las Vegas	no data
CA: San Francisco	no data	NY: New York	$49,310
CO: Denver	$53,700	OH: Cincinnati	$65,540
DC: Washington	no data	OH: Cleveland	$46,540
FL: Miami	$50,830	OH: Columbus	$39,580
FL: Orlando	$35,720	OR: Portland	no data
FL: Tampa	$51,080	PA: Philadelphia	$57,100
GA: Atlanta	$39,920	PA: Pittsburgh	$50,530
IL: Chicago	$41,650	TX: Dallas	$48,030
MA: Boston	$51,970	TX: Houston	$63,760
MD: Baltimore	$53,550	WA: Seattle	$61,740

FACTORS THAT MAY AFFECT EARNINGS

Educational Attainment of Workers and Effect on Earnings

	Percent at Level	Effect on Earnings
Less than High School	—	—
Some High School	—	—
High School or Equivalent	7.7%	−22.1%
Some College but No Degree	9.6%	−28.8%
Associate Degree	7.7%	−37.1%
Bachelor's Degree	29.8%	10.2%
Master's Degree	42.3%	9.8%
Doctoral Degree	—	—
First Professional Degree	—	—

Flexibility of Earnings

Average Hours Worked: 30
Workers with a Varying Number of Hours: 8.0%
Workers Earning Some Overtime Pay, Tips, or Commissions: 5.3%
Earnings Benefit of Working Overtime: −11.4%

Gender

	Male	Female
Percent	26.9%	73.1%
Effect on Earnings	21.3%	−5.0%

Union Membership

Percentage Union Members: 12.4%
Earnings Benefit of Union Membership: 49.1%

Veteran Status

Percentage Who Have Been on Active Duty: 5.9%
Earnings Benefit of Veteran Status: 28.6%

29-1131 Veterinarians

Diagnose and treat diseases and dysfunctions of animals. May engage in a particular function, such as research and development, consultation, administration, technical writing, sale or production of commercial products, or rendering of technical services to commercial firms or other organizations. Includes veterinarians who inspect livestock.

- Education or Training Required: First professional degree
- Job Growth: 17.4%
- Annual Openings: 8,000
- Self-Employed: 20.7%
- Part-Time: 10.3%

NATIONAL WAGE FIGURES (ANNUAL)

Beginning	25th Percentile	Median	Mean	75th Percentile	90th Percentile
$43,530	$56,450	$71,990	$81,490	$94,880	$133,150

Median Wages for Industries Employing Largest Numbers (Annual)

Industry	Median Income
Performing Arts, Spectator Sports, and Related Industries	$115,420
Administrative and Support Services	$80,590
Chemical Manufacturing	$78,550
Merchant Wholesalers, Nondurable Goods	$75,560
Personal and Laundry Services	$73,430
Museums, Historical Sites, and Similar Institutions	$72,530
Professional, Scientific, and Technical Services	$72,180
Federal, State, and Local Government	$70,490
Religious, Grantmaking, Civic, Professional, and Similar Organizations	$67,030
Educational Services	$62,830

Median Wages for States (Annual)

State	Wage	State	Wage	State	Wage
AK	$80,040	KY	$59,410	NY	$83,640
AL	$66,710	LA	$63,600	OH	$72,160
AR	$71,870	MA	$73,320	OK	$60,680
AZ	$72,420	MD	$83,670	OR	$66,380
CA	$87,350	ME	$67,730	PA	$79,980
CO	$63,010	MI	$71,590	RI	$74,310
CT	$93,730	MN	$69,120	SC	$64,290
DC	$111,870	MO	$64,300	SD	$57,090
DE	$84,670	MS	$57,480	TN	$64,140
FL	$69,900	MT	$53,980	TX	$74,060
GA	$65,650	NC	$72,320	UT	$70,430
HI	$71,900	ND	$58,770	VA	$79,080
IA	no data	NE	$58,450	VT	$65,740
ID	$60,190	NH	$78,180	WA	$73,440
IL	$68,130	NJ	$95,190	WI	$65,780
IN	$70,120	NM	$62,340	WV	$70,150
KS	$62,380	NV	$83,270	WY	$50,310

Median Wages for the Largest Metropolitan Areas (Annual)

Area	Wage	Area	Wage
AZ: Phoenix	$72,760	MI: Detroit	$85,160
CA: Los Angeles	$93,030	MN: Minneapolis	$69,980
CA: Riverside	$76,790	MO: Kansas City	$72,580
CA: Sacramento	$78,950	MO: St. Louis	$71,970
CA: San Diego	$90,840	NV: Las Vegas	$82,480
CA: San Francisco	$86,650	NY: New York	$98,140
CO: Denver	$63,570	OH: Cincinnati	$67,560
DC: Washington	$93,670	OH: Cleveland	$84,090
FL: Miami	$78,080	OH: Columbus	$76,240
FL: Orlando	$57,610	OR: Portland	$72,500
FL: Tampa	$67,070	PA: Philadelphia	$84,940
GA: Atlanta	$67,020	PA: Pittsburgh	$88,070
IL: Chicago	$69,370	TX: Dallas	$72,230
MA: Boston	$76,930	TX: Houston	$84,790
MD: Baltimore	$85,850	WA: Seattle	$81,520

FACTORS THAT MAY AFFECT EARNINGS

Educational Attainment of Workers and Effect on Earnings

	Percent at Level	Effect on Earnings
Less than High School	—	—
Some High School	—	—
High School or Equivalent	—	—
Some College but No Degree	—	—
Associate Degree	—	—
Bachelor's Degree	—	—
Master's Degree	—	—
Doctoral Degree	43.6%	1.0%
First Professional Degree	43.6%	4.7%

Figures do not total 100% because some levels have a very small sample size.

Flexibility of Earnings

Average Hours Worked: 39
Workers with a Varying Number of Hours: 10.8%
Workers Earning Some Overtime Pay, Tips, or Commissions: 10.4%
Earnings Benefit of Working Overtime: –38.8%

Gender

	Male	Female
Percent	49.6%	50.4%
Effect on Earnings	21.3%	–5.0%

Union Membership

Percentage Union Members: 14.1%
Earnings Benefit of Union Membership: 4.8%

Veteran Status

Percentage Who Have Been on Active Duty: 5.9%
Earnings Benefit of Veteran Status: 28.6%

29-1199 Health Diagnosing and Treating Practitioners, All Other

All health diagnosing and treating practitioners not listed separately.

- Education or Training Required: Bachelor's degree
- Job Growth: 22.5%
- Annual Openings: 6,000
- Self-Employed: 15.8%
- Part-Time: 11.8%

NATIONAL WAGE FIGURES (ANNUAL)

Beginning	25th Percentile	Median	Mean	75th Percentile	90th Percentile
$33,500	$43,520	$61,570	$83,110	$106,920	more than $145,600

Note: The mean is significantly higher than the median because of the presence of a few star earners.

Median Wages for Industries Employing Largest Numbers (Annual)

Industry	Median Income
Ambulatory Health Care Services	$99,430
Health and Personal Care Stores	$97,320
Transportation Equipment Manufacturing	$74,110
Federal, State, and Local Government	$72,510
Management of Companies and Enterprises	$65,580
Professional, Scientific, and Technical Services	$61,180
Insurance Carriers and Related Activities	$60,550
Miscellaneous Manufacturing	$56,820
Religious, Grantmaking, Civic, Professional, and Similar Organizations	$49,850
Hospitals	$48,290

Median Wages for States (Annual)

AK $68,670	KY .... no data	NY $101,040
AL $45,930	LA $91,750	OH $67,570
AR $115,110	MA $57,450	OK $49,020
AZ $79,280	MD $104,820	OR $63,960
CA $62,200	ME $72,720	PA $48,470
CO $73,550	MI $60,630	RI $50,640
CT $74,610	MN $64,460	SC .... no data
DC $94,040	MO $46,950	SD .... no data
DE .. more than $145,600	MS $65,380	TN $66,120
FL $63,170	MT .... no data	TX $52,920
GA $53,160	NC $62,700	UT $41,980
HI $64,040	ND .... no data	VA $119,450
IA $57,400	NE .... no data	VT .... no data
ID $51,570	NH $80,230	WA $70,220
IL $35,130	NJ $67,700	WI $54,770
IN $72,440	NM $61,740	WV .... no data
KS $44,590	NV .... more than $145,600	WY .... no data

Median Wages for the Largest Metropolitan Areas (Annual)

AZ: Phoenix $135,920	MI: Detroit $63,910
CA: Los Angeles $61,710	MN: Minneapolis $63,360
CA: Riverside $107,940	MO: Kansas City $87,640
CA: Sacramento $66,690	MO: St. Louis $47,240
CA: San Diego $83,910	NV: Las Vegas $84,650
CA: San Francisco .... no data	NY: New York $93,460
CO: Denver ....more than $145,600	OH: Cincinnati $70,440
DC: Washington $107,000	OH: Cleveland $68,290
FL: Miami $63,440	OH: Columbus $65,070
FL: Orlando $63,100	OR: Portland $61,320
FL: Tampa $63,310	PA: Philadelphia $57,870
GA: Atlanta $55,960	PA: Pittsburgh $46,010
IL: Chicago $37,200	TX: Dallas .... no data
MA: Boston $57,040	TX: Houston $69,080
MD: Baltimore $47,980	WA: Seattle $71,340

FACTORS THAT MAY AFFECT EARNINGS

Educational Attainment of Workers and Effect on Earnings

Figures are based on a group of occupations: Health Diagnosing and Treating Practitioners

	Percent at Level	Effect on Earnings
Less than High School	—	—
Some High School	0.5%	−51.9%
High School or Equivalent	3.7%	−35.9%
Some College but No Degree	6.1%	−22.2%
Associate Degree	25.7%	−14.6%
Bachelor's Degree	31.5%	1.4%
Master's Degree	14.5%	11.8%
Doctoral Degree	7.4%	30.3%
First Professional Degree	10.4%	22.8%

Flexibility of Earnings

Average Hours Worked: 30
Workers with a Varying Number of Hours: 17.0%
Workers Earning Some Overtime Pay, Tips, or Commissions: 13.6%
Earnings Benefit of Working Overtime: −11.4%

Gender

	Male	Female
Percent	38.2%	61.8%
Effect on Earnings	21.3%	−5.0%

Union Membership

Percentage Union Members: 14.1%
Earnings Benefit of Union Membership: 4.8%

Veteran Status

Percentage Who Have Been on Active Duty: 5.9%
Earnings Benefit of Veteran Status: 28.6%

29-2000 Health Technologists and Technicians

29-2011 Medical and Clinical Laboratory Technologists

Perform complex medical laboratory tests for diagnosis, treatment, and prevention of disease. May train or supervise staff.

- Education or Training Required: Bachelor's degree
- Job Growth: 20.5%
- Annual Openings: 14,000
- Self-Employed: 0.1%
- Part-Time: 27.8%

NATIONAL WAGE FIGURES (ANNUAL)

Beginning	25th Percentile	Median	Mean	75th Percentile	90th Percentile
$34,660	$41,680	$49,700	$50,550	$58,560	$69,260

Median Wages for Industries Employing Largest Numbers (Annual)

Industry	Median Income
Religious, Grantmaking, Civic, Professional, and Similar Organizations	$69,340
Management of Companies and Enterprises	$56,640
Federal, State, and Local Government	$55,900
Chemical Manufacturing	$53,220
Insurance Carriers and Related Activities	$52,720
Administrative and Support Services	$52,660
Merchant Wholesalers, Durable Goods	$52,400
Nursing and Residential Care Facilities	$50,480
Miscellaneous Manufacturing	$50,390
Professional, Scientific, and Technical Services	$50,010

Median Wages for States (Annual)

AK	$61,530	KY	$46,430	NY	$52,490
AL	$44,820	LA	$43,840	OH	$48,050
AR	$43,940	MA	$51,980	OK	$43,970
AZ	$48,550	MD	$55,100	OR	$55,790
CA	$67,300	ME	$46,210	PA	$47,300
CO	$50,310	MI	$50,040	RI	$57,350
CT	$58,390	MN	$50,870	SC	$41,050
DC	$47,800	MO	$48,940	SD	$43,620
DE	$50,890	MS	$44,700	TN	$48,710
FL	$47,620	MT	$48,090	TX	$45,770
GA	$48,600	NC	$46,100	UT	$48,290
HI	$47,920	ND	$42,710	VA	$47,000
IA	$46,310	NE	$45,200	VT	$47,550
ID	$41,690	NH	$48,350	WA	$55,200
IL	$47,530	NJ	$55,860	WI	$50,520
IN	$46,980	NM	$48,400	WV	$42,550
KS	$47,340	NV	$57,090	WY	$47,710

Median Wages for the Largest Metropolitan Areas (Annual)

AZ: Phoenix	$48,640	MI: Detroit	$51,250
CA: Los Angeles	$67,010	MN: Minneapolis	$52,870
CA: Riverside	$63,700	MO: Kansas City	$53,220
CA: Sacramento	$67,080	MO: St. Louis	$49,330
CA: San Diego	$62,770	NV: Las Vegas	$56,110
CA: San Francisco	$68,490	NY: New York	$55,870
CO: Denver	$50,640	OH: Cincinnati	$47,970
DC: Washington	$53,430	OH: Cleveland	$48,200
FL: Miami	$51,260	OH: Columbus	$45,590
FL: Orlando	$43,290	OR: Portland	$57,310
FL: Tampa	$46,650	PA: Philadelphia	$52,740
GA: Atlanta	$50,200	PA: Pittsburgh	$45,230
IL: Chicago	$48,760	TX: Dallas	$46,980
MA: Boston	$51,960	TX: Houston	$46,540
MD: Baltimore	$53,970	WA: Seattle	$55,380

FACTORS THAT MAY AFFECT EARNINGS

Educational Attainment of Workers and Effect on Earnings

Figures are based on a group of occupations: Health Technologists and Technicians

	Percent at Level	Effect on Earnings
Less than High School	—	—
Some High School	2.4%	−47.8%
High School or Equivalent	18.2%	−15.4%
Some College but No Degree	25.9%	−10.8%
Associate Degree	28.3%	1.4%
Bachelor's Degree	19.4%	23.8%
Master's Degree	3.7%	33.6%
Doctoral Degree	—	—
First Professional Degree	1.7%	18.2%

Flexibility of Earnings

Average Hours Worked: 33
Workers with a Varying Number of Hours: 6.5%
Workers Earning Some Overtime Pay, Tips, or Commissions: 15.4%
Earnings Benefit of Working Overtime: 1.7%

Gender

	Male	Female
Percent	21.9%	78.1%
Effect on Earnings	0.5%	−0.1%

Union Membership

Percentage Union Members: 9.5%
Earnings Benefit of Union Membership: 9.1%

Veteran Status

Percentage Who Have Been on Active Duty: 5.2%
Earnings Benefit of Veteran Status: 35.5%

29-2012 Medical and Clinical Laboratory Technicians

Perform routine medical laboratory tests for the diagnosis, treatment, and prevention of disease. May work under the supervision of a medical technologist.

- Education or Training Required: Associate degree
- Job Growth: 25.0%
- Annual Openings: 14,000
- Self-Employed: 0.1%
- Part-Time: 27.8%

NATIONAL WAGE FIGURES (ANNUAL)

Beginning	25th Percentile	Median	Mean	75th Percentile	90th Percentile
$21,830	$26,430	$32,840	$34,620	$41,020	$50,250

Median Wages for Industries Employing Largest Numbers (Annual)

Industry	Median Income
Wholesale Electronic Markets and Agents and Brokers	$44,320
Merchant Wholesalers, Durable Goods	$40,060
Miscellaneous Manufacturing	$39,260
Insurance Carriers and Related Activities	$36,850
Federal, State, and Local Government	$35,300
Professional, Scientific, and Technical Services	$35,170
Health and Personal Care Stores	$34,850
Hospitals	$34,190
Educational Services	$33,640
Chemical Manufacturing	$33,500

Median Wages for States (Annual)

AK	$42,990	KY	$31,950	NY	$36,980
AL	$27,200	LA	$26,970	OH	$33,420
AR	$29,580	MA	$34,200	OK	$27,000
AZ	$36,020	MD	$35,120	OR	$36,940
CA	$35,650	ME	$33,370	PA	$34,480
CO	$31,610	MI	$30,390	RI	$45,320
CT	$35,680	MN	$37,760	SC	$29,020
DC	$37,490	MO	$28,340	SD	$28,800
DE	$29,700	MS	$28,470	TN	$29,660
FL	$31,810	MT	$29,460	TX	$29,190
GA	$29,500	NC	$32,930	UT	$26,230
HI	$39,570	ND	$31,330	VA	$31,570
IA	$33,740	NE	$28,740	VT	$25,580
ID	$29,640	NH	$38,280	WA	$34,750
IL	$35,600	NJ	$38,900	WI	$35,840
IN	$31,950	NM	$33,500	WV	$31,230
KS	$27,210	NV	$33,400	WY	$28,520

Median Wages for the Largest Metropolitan Areas (Annual)

AZ: Phoenix	$34,200	MI: Detroit	$30,760
CA: Los Angeles	$34,740	MN: Minneapolis	$37,960
CA: Riverside	$37,500	MO: Kansas City	$28,910
CA: Sacramento	$34,400	MO: St. Louis	$29,620
CA: San Diego	$33,540	NV: Las Vegas	$33,350
CA: San Francisco	$42,850	NY: New York	$38,300
CO: Denver	$32,140	OH: Cincinnati	$30,130
DC: Washington	$35,750	OH: Cleveland	$33,620
FL: Miami	$31,450	OH: Columbus	$34,250
FL: Orlando	$34,350	OR: Portland	$36,950
FL: Tampa	$30,630	PA: Philadelphia	$37,230
GA: Atlanta	$32,020	PA: Pittsburgh	$31,270
IL: Chicago	$35,030	TX: Dallas	$29,120
MA: Boston	$34,340	TX: Houston	$29,640
MD: Baltimore	$32,750	WA: Seattle	$35,260

FACTORS THAT MAY AFFECT EARNINGS

Educational Attainment of Workers and Effect on Earnings

Figures are based on a group of occupations: Health Technologists and Technicians

	Percent at Level	Effect on Earnings
Less than High School	—	—
Some High School	2.4%	−47.8%
High School or Equivalent	18.2%	−15.4%
Some College but No Degree	25.9%	−10.8%
Associate Degree	28.3%	1.4%
Bachelor's Degree	19.4%	23.8%
Master's Degree	3.7%	33.6%
Doctoral Degree	—	—
First Professional Degree	1.7%	18.2%

Flexibility of Earnings

Average Hours Worked: 33
Workers with a Varying Number of Hours: 6.5%
Workers Earning Some Overtime Pay, Tips, or Commissions: 15.4%
Earnings Benefit of Working Overtime: 1.7%

Gender

	Male	Female
Percent	21.9%	78.1%
Effect on Earnings	0.5%	−0.1%

Union Membership

Percentage Union Members: 9.5%
Earnings Benefit of Union Membership: 9.1%

Veteran Status

Percentage Who Have Been on Active Duty: 5.2%
Earnings Benefit of Veteran Status: 35.5%

29-2021 Dental Hygienists

Clean teeth and examine oral areas, head, and neck for signs of oral disease. May educate patients on oral hygiene, take and develop X rays, or apply fluoride or sealants.

- Education or Training Required: Associate degree
- Job Growth: 43.3%
- Annual Openings: 17,000
- Self-Employed: 0.3%
- Part-Time: 44.4%

NATIONAL WAGE FIGURES (ANNUAL)

Beginning	25th Percentile	Median	Mean	75th Percentile	90th Percentile
$40,450	$51,240	$62,800	$62,430	$74,190	$86,530

Median Wages for Industries Employing Largest Numbers (Annual)

Industry	Median Income
Administrative and Support Services	$69,180
Professional, Scientific, and Technical Services	$66,540
Management of Companies and Enterprises	$65,780
Ambulatory Health Care Services	$62,930
Hospitals	$52,110
Educational Services	$50,910
Nursing and Residential Care Facilities	$50,820
Social Assistance	$48,370
Federal, State, and Local Government	$47,060

Median Wages for States (Annual)

AK $84,750	KY $51,870	NY $58,200
AL $38,340	LA $54,620	OH $58,970
AR $49,330	MA $70,230	OK $62,480
AZ $71,870	MD $64,510	OR $72,530
CA $76,600	ME $55,450	PA $50,320
CO $75,410	MI $58,450	RI.............. $63,960
CT $69,710	MN $65,290	SC.............. $48,370
DC $68,300	MO $63,860	SD $51,670
DE $61,210	MS $38,180	TN $53,400
FL $54,920	MT $59,860	TX $66,060
GA $61,780	NC $60,790	UT $62,710
HI $61,490	ND $52,410	VA $67,690
IA $60,490	NE $57,690	VT $56,560
ID $69,800	NH $70,140	WA $84,680
IL $63,120	NJ $71,080	WI $55,470
IN $62,090	NM $69,320	WV $46,260
KS $65,020	NV $68,490	WY $53,320

Median Wages for the Largest Metropolitan Areas (Annual)

AZ: Phoenix	$71,580	MI: Detroit	$62,460
CA: Los Angeles	$71,070	MN: Minneapolis	$68,340
CA: Riverside	$71,810	MO: Kansas City	$68,620
CA: Sacramento	$79,620	MO: St. Louis	$59,940
CA: San Diego	$84,290	NV: Las Vegas	$61,890
CA: San Francisco	$86,900	NY: New York	$69,300
CO: Denver	$80,010	OH: Cincinnati	$61,390
DC: Washington	$70,620	OH: Cleveland	$60,270
FL: Miami	$50,460	OH: Columbus	$65,690
FL: Orlando	$64,740	OR: Portland	$73,130
FL: Tampa	$51,960	PA: Philadelphia	$62,870
GA: Atlanta	$67,180	PA: Pittsburgh	$41,670
IL: Chicago	$68,380	TX: Dallas	$71,560
MA: Boston	$73,640	TX: Houston	$69,050
MD: Baltimore	$63,690	WA: Seattle	$86,670

FACTORS THAT MAY AFFECT EARNINGS

Educational Attainment of Workers and Effect on Earnings

	Percent at Level	Effect on Earnings
Less than High School	—	—
Some High School	—	—
High School or Equivalent	4.0%	−10.0%
Some College but No Degree	4.0%	−27.6%
Associate Degree	50.9%	−7.4%
Bachelor's Degree	38.9%	13.1%
Master's Degree	—	—
Doctoral Degree	—	—
First Professional Degree	—	—

Flexibility of Earnings

Average Hours Worked: 27
Workers with a Varying Number of Hours: 4.9%
Workers Earning Some Overtime Pay, Tips, or Commissions: 8.1%
Earnings Benefit of Working Overtime: 1.7%

Gender

	Male	Female
Percent	1.4%	98.6%
Effect on Earnings	—	−0.5%

Union Membership

Percentage Union Members: Insignificant
Earnings Benefit of Union Membership: No significant data available

Veteran Status

Percentage Who Have Been on Active Duty: 5.2%
Earnings Benefit of Veteran Status: 35.5%

29-2031 Cardiovascular Technologists and Technicians

Conduct tests on pulmonary or cardiovascular systems of patients for diagnostic purposes. May conduct or assist in electrocardiograms, cardiac catheterizations, pulmonary-functions, lung capacity, and similar tests.

- Education or Training Required: Associate degree
- Job Growth: 32.6%
- Annual Openings: 5,000
- Self-Employed: 0.4%
- Part-Time: 27.8%

NATIONAL WAGE FIGURES (ANNUAL)

Beginning	25th Percentile	Median	Mean	75th Percentile	90th Percentile
$23,670	$29,900	$42,300	$43,990	$55,670	$67,410

Median Wages for Industries Employing Largest Numbers (Annual)

Industry	Median Income
Management of Companies and Enterprises	$55,350
Educational Services	$48,560
Administrative and Support Services	$47,510
Federal, State, and Local Government	$43,770
Ambulatory Health Care Services	$42,880
Insurance Carriers and Related Activities	$42,110
Hospitals	$41,950
Professional, Scientific, and Technical Services	$32,140

Median Wages for States (Annual)

AK	$62,020	KY	$32,370	NY	$46,670
AL	$37,250	LA	$29,930	OH	$43,180
AR	$38,330	MA	$46,160	OK	$27,050
AZ	$36,270	MD	$47,490	OR	$52,050
CA	$51,500	ME	$50,620	PA	$40,150
CO	$41,520	MI	$45,790	RI	$49,710
CT	$45,100	MN	$45,580	SC	$40,860
DC	$45,260	MO	$35,930	SD	$39,750
DE	no data	MS	$39,230	TN	$32,600
FL	$31,940	MT	$39,810	TX	$41,280
GA	$36,920	NC	$45,270	UT	no data
HI	$57,590	ND	$33,590	VA	$45,670
IA	$37,070	NE	$45,580	VT	no data
ID	$47,920	NH	$51,200	WA	$55,720
IL	$40,820	NJ	$53,380	WI	$43,970
IN	$35,130	NM	$40,370	WV	$34,910
KS	$43,970	NV	$42,760	WY	no data

Median Wages for the Largest Metropolitan Areas (Annual)

AZ: Phoenix	$35,930	MI: Detroit	$45,600
CA: Los Angeles	$50,360	MN: Minneapolis	$47,610
CA: Riverside	$52,430	MO: Kansas City	$44,980
CA: Sacramento	$47,970	MO: St. Louis	$33,830
CA: San Diego	$54,160	NV: Las Vegas	$42,830
CA: San Francisco	$57,040	NY: New York	$50,620
CO: Denver	$37,540	OH: Cincinnati	$42,990
DC: Washington	$53,130	OH: Cleveland	$44,380
FL: Miami	$30,350	OH: Columbus	$45,400
FL: Orlando	no data	OR: Portland	$53,410
FL: Tampa	$37,200	PA: Philadelphia	$44,580
GA: Atlanta	$37,180	PA: Pittsburgh	$32,610
IL: Chicago	$41,000	TX: Dallas	$42,330
MA: Boston	$50,030	TX: Houston	$37,580
MD: Baltimore	$48,240	WA: Seattle	$60,410

FACTORS THAT MAY AFFECT EARNINGS

Educational Attainment of Workers and Effect on Earnings

Figures are based on a group of occupations: Health Technologists and Technicians

	Percent at Level	Effect on Earnings
Less than High School	—	—
Some High School	2.4%	−47.8%
High School or Equivalent	18.2%	−15.4%
Some College but No Degree	25.9%	−10.8%
Associate Degree	28.3%	1.4%
Bachelor's Degree	19.4%	23.8%
Master's Degree	3.7%	33.6%
Doctoral Degree	—	—
First Professional Degree	1.7%	18.2%

Flexibility of Earnings

Average Hours Worked: 33
Workers with a Varying Number of Hours: 6.5%
Workers Earning Some Overtime Pay, Tips, or Commissions: 15.4%
Earnings Benefit of Working Overtime: 30.5%

Gender

	Male	Female
Percent	27.1%	72.9%
Effect on Earnings	5.8%	−1.7%

Union Membership

Percentage Union Members: 9.5%
Earnings Benefit of Union Membership: 9.1%

Veteran Status

Percentage Who Have Been on Active Duty: 5.2%
Earnings Benefit of Veteran Status: 35.5%

29-2032 Diagnostic Medical Sonographers

Produce ultrasonic recordings of internal organs for use by physicians.

- Education or Training Required: Associate degree
- Job Growth: 34.8%
- Annual Openings: 5,000
- Self-Employed: 0.4%
- Part-Time: 27.8%

NATIONAL WAGE FIGURES (ANNUAL)

Beginning	25th Percentile	Median	Mean	75th Percentile	90th Percentile
$40,960	$48,890	$57,160	$58,110	$67,670	$77,520

Median Wages for Industries Employing Largest Numbers (Annual)

Industry	Median Income
Administrative and Support Services	$71,920
Federal, State, and Local Government	$70,360
Management of Companies and Enterprises	$67,010
Professional, Scientific, and Technical Services	$59,470
Educational Services	$57,290
Ambulatory Health Care Services	$57,240
Hospitals	$56,860
Nursing and Residential Care Facilities	$27,200

Median Wages for States (Annual)

State	Wage	State	Wage	State	Wage
AK	$75,740	KY	$51,890	NY	$57,270
AL	$46,630	LA	$52,770	OH	$54,480
AR	$42,600	MA	$66,140	OK	$56,550
AZ	$65,480	MD	$63,760	OR	$67,900
CA	$66,550	ME	$61,750	PA	$52,350
CO	$68,660	MI	$53,910	RI	$64,710
CT	$69,320	MN	$62,980	SC	$52,740
DC	$56,700	MO	$56,170	SD	$47,160
DE	$50,590	MS	$46,680	TN	$52,680
FL	$53,300	MT	$55,290	TX	$58,120
GA	$55,110	NC	$56,580	UT	$56,010
HI	$68,150	ND	$56,590	VA	$57,260
IA	$54,350	NE	$55,850	VT	$53,310
ID	$59,010	NH	$62,340	WA	$67,220
IL	$56,910	NJ	$59,180	WI	$68,200
IN	$53,120	NM	$56,120	WV	$48,220
KS	$58,580	NV	$59,980	WY	$51,650

Median Wages for the Largest Metropolitan Areas (Annual)

Area	Wage	Area	Wage
AZ: Phoenix	$65,740	MI: Detroit	$56,340
CA: Los Angeles	$59,980	MN: Minneapolis	$64,130
CA: Riverside	$67,360	MO: Kansas City	$63,280
CA: Sacramento	$72,610	MO: St. Louis	$55,350
CA: San Diego	$69,900	NV: Las Vegas	$58,720
CA: San Francisco	$77,370	NY: New York	$58,150
CO: Denver	no data	OH: Cincinnati	$56,900
DC: Washington	$65,560	OH: Cleveland	$49,700
FL: Miami	$55,120	OH: Columbus	$58,390
FL: Orlando	$47,920	OR: Portland	$69,720
FL: Tampa	$52,400	PA: Philadelphia	$55,930
GA: Atlanta	$56,450	PA: Pittsburgh	$46,660
IL: Chicago	$58,500	TX: Dallas	$61,920
MA: Boston	$67,020	TX: Houston	$55,490
MD: Baltimore	$61,070	WA: Seattle	$69,450

FACTORS THAT MAY AFFECT EARNINGS

Educational Attainment of Workers and Effect on Earnings

Figures are based on a group of occupations: Health Technologists and Technicians

	Percent at Level	Effect on Earnings
Less than High School	—	—
Some High School	2.4%	−47.8%
High School or Equivalent	18.2%	−15.4%
Some College but No Degree	25.9%	−10.8%
Associate Degree	28.3%	1.4%
Bachelor's Degree	19.4%	23.8%
Master's Degree	3.7%	33.6%
Doctoral Degree	—	—
First Professional Degree	1.7%	18.2%

Flexibility of Earnings

Average Hours Worked: 33
Workers with a Varying Number of Hours: 6.5%
Workers Earning Some Overtime Pay, Tips, or Commissions: 15.4%
Earnings Benefit of Working Overtime: 30.5%

Gender

	Male	Female
Percent	27.1%	72.9%
Effect on Earnings	5.8%	−1.7%

Union Membership

Percentage Union Members: 9.5%
Earnings Benefit of Union Membership: 9.1%

Veteran Status

Percentage Who Have Been on Active Duty: 5.2%
Earnings Benefit of Veteran Status: 35.5%

29-2033 Nuclear Medicine Technologists

Prepare, administer, and measure radioactive isotopes in therapeutic, diagnostic, and tracer studies, utilizing a variety of radioisotope equipment. Prepare stock solutions of radioactive materials and calculate doses to be administered by radiologists. Subject patients to radiation. Execute blood volume, red cell survival, and fat absorption studies, following standard laboratory techniques.

- Education or Training Required: Associate degree
- Job Growth: 21.5%
- Annual Openings: 2,000
- Self-Employed: 0.5%
- Part-Time: 27.8%

NATIONAL WAGE FIGURES (ANNUAL)

	25th Percentile	Median	Mean	75th Percentile	90th Percentile
Beginning					
$46,490	$53,530	$62,300	$63,000	$72,410	$82,310

Median Wages for Industries Employing Largest Numbers (Annual)

Industry	Median Income
Management of Companies and Enterprises	$74,650
Professional, Scientific, and Technical Services	$66,560
Ambulatory Health Care Services	$64,140
Educational Services	$62,110
Federal, State, and Local Government	$61,390
Hospitals	$61,310

Median Wages for States (Annual)

State	Wage	State	Wage	State	Wage
AK	no data	KY	$52,970	NY	$63,970
AL	$57,700	LA	$58,920	OH	$59,730
AR	$56,280	MA	$67,130	OK	$54,660
AZ	$67,220	MD	$73,750	OR	$68,510
CA	$72,770	ME	$59,630	PA	$55,070
CO	$62,670	MI	$60,700	RI	$71,500
CT	$69,240	MN	$67,520	SC	$56,780
DC	$54,510	MO	$58,580	SD	$52,430
DE	$63,510	MS	$55,340	TN	$60,250
FL	$62,740	MT	$58,490	TX	$61,710
GA	$59,450	NC	$58,340	UT	$54,270
HI	$63,730	ND	$52,260	VA	$57,810
IA	$59,820	NE	$60,600	VT	no data
ID	$56,230	NH	$65,680	WA	$71,310
IL	$60,540	NJ	$73,840	WI	$65,960
IN	$57,660	NM	$59,990	WV	$55,470
KS	$61,840	NV	$65,550	WY	$52,320

Median Wages for the Largest Metropolitan Areas (Annual)

Area	Wage	Area	Wage
AZ: Phoenix	$65,370	MI: Detroit	$64,920
CA: Los Angeles	$67,950	MN: Minneapolis	$67,170
CA: Riverside	$72,410	MO: Kansas City	$64,130
CA: Sacramento	$88,120	MO: St. Louis	$57,560
CA: San Diego	$70,800	NV: Las Vegas	$68,320
CA: San Francisco	$91,350	NY: New York	$71,150
CO: Denver	$63,920	OH: Cincinnati	$60,530
DC: Washington	$68,150	OH: Cleveland	$62,590
FL: Miami	$63,630	OH: Columbus	$62,300
FL: Orlando	$60,430	OR: Portland	$69,990
FL: Tampa	$61,500	PA: Philadelphia	$65,750
GA: Atlanta	$62,210	PA: Pittsburgh	$50,550
IL: Chicago	$62,790	TX: Dallas	$63,180
MA: Boston	$68,760	TX: Houston	$66,920
MD: Baltimore	$74,430	WA: Seattle	$73,610

FACTORS THAT MAY AFFECT EARNINGS

Educational Attainment of Workers and Effect on Earnings

Figures are based on a group of occupations: Health Technologists and Technicians

	Percent at Level	Effect on Earnings
Less than High School	—	—
Some High School	2.4%	−47.8%
High School or Equivalent	18.2%	−15.4%
Some College but No Degree	25.9%	−10.8%
Associate Degree	28.3%	1.4%
Bachelor's Degree	19.4%	23.8%
Master's Degree	3.7%	33.6%
Doctoral Degree	—	—
First Professional Degree	1.7%	18.2%

Flexibility of Earnings

Average Hours Worked: 33
Workers with a Varying Number of Hours: 6.5%
Workers Earning Some Overtime Pay, Tips, or Commissions: 15.4%
Earnings Benefit of Working Overtime: 30.5%

Gender

	Male	Female
Percent	27.1%	72.9%
Effect on Earnings	5.8%	−1.7%

Union Membership

Percentage Union Members: 9.5%
Earnings Benefit of Union Membership: 9.1%

Veteran Status

Percentage Who Have Been on Active Duty: 5.2%
Earnings Benefit of Veteran Status: 35.5%

29-2034 Radiologic Technologists and Technicians

Take X rays and Computerized Axial Tomography (CAT or CT) scans or administer nonradioactive materials into patient's bloodstream for diagnostic purposes. Includes technologists who specialize in other modalities, such as computed tomography, ultrasound, and magnetic resonance.

- Education or Training Required: Associate degree
- Job Growth: 23.2%
- Annual Openings: 17,000
- Self-Employed: 0.4%
- Part-Time: 27.8%

NATIONAL WAGE FIGURES (ANNUAL)

Beginning	25th Percentile	Median	Mean	75th Percentile	90th Percentile
$32,750	$39,840	$48,170	$49,320	$57,940	$68,920

Median Wages for Industries Employing Largest Numbers (Annual)

Industry	Median Income
Rental and Leasing Services	$63,650
Management of Companies and Enterprises	$55,740
Religious, Grantmaking, Civic, Professional, and Similar Organizations	$53,500
Administrative and Support Services	$52,990
Professional, Scientific, and Technical Services	$52,300
Insurance Carriers and Related Activities	$48,990
Hospitals	$48,830
Federal, State, and Local Government	$48,140
Educational Services	$46,800
Ambulatory Health Care Services	$46,690

Median Wages for States (Annual)

AK	$57,470	KY	$42,240	NY	$57,090
AL	$40,790	LA	$42,620	OH	$45,280
AR	$40,670	MA	$61,090	OK	$41,250
AZ	$47,860	MD	$57,460	OR	$53,480
CA	$58,310	ME	$47,580	PA	$44,710
CO	$49,230	MI	$46,240	RI	$54,470
CT	$54,070	MN	$51,810	SC	$44,280
DC	$51,500	MO	$45,180	SD	$40,150
DE	$46,970	MS	$42,010	TN	$44,740
FL	$45,930	MT	$43,970	TX	$45,870
GA	$45,130	NC	$46,460	UT	$43,870
HI	$55,930	ND	$39,620	VA	$47,290
IA	$41,210	NE	$42,810	VT	$46,210
ID	$42,060	NH	$51,020	WA	$56,120
IL	$48,440	NJ	$56,680	WI	$48,060
IN	$45,120	NM	$47,110	WV	$40,280
KS	$41,620	NV	$53,900	WY	$44,390

Median Wages for the Largest Metropolitan Areas (Annual)

AZ: Phoenix	$48,080	MI: Detroit	$49,880
CA: Los Angeles	$54,460	MN: Minneapolis	$53,580
CA: Riverside	$54,600	MO: Kansas City	$47,380
CA: Sacramento	$62,370	MO: St. Louis	$46,600
CA: San Diego	$59,080	NV: Las Vegas	$54,160
CA: San Francisco	$72,600	NY: New York	$60,630
CO: Denver	$50,490	OH: Cincinnati	$46,180
DC: Washington	$56,890	OH: Cleveland	$46,520
FL: Miami	$47,820	OH: Columbus	$46,670
FL: Orlando	$43,100	OR: Portland	$56,280
FL: Tampa	$46,880	PA: Philadelphia	$51,170
GA: Atlanta	$48,440	PA: Pittsburgh	$39,910
IL: Chicago	$51,260	TX: Dallas	$49,570
MA: Boston	$62,910	TX: Houston	$48,060
MD: Baltimore	$57,460	WA: Seattle	$60,580

FACTORS THAT MAY AFFECT EARNINGS

Educational Attainment of Workers and Effect on Earnings

Figures are based on a group of occupations: Health Technologists and Technicians

	Percent at Level	Effect on Earnings
Less than High School	—	—
Some High School	2.4%	−47.8%
High School or Equivalent	18.2%	−15.4%
Some College but No Degree	25.9%	−10.8%
Associate Degree	28.3%	1.4%
Bachelor's Degree	19.4%	23.8%
Master's Degree	3.7%	33.6%
Doctoral Degree	—	—
First Professional Degree	1.7%	18.2%

Flexibility of Earnings

Average Hours Worked: 33

Workers with a Varying Number of Hours: 6.5%

Workers Earning Some Overtime Pay, Tips, or Commissions: 15.4%

Earnings Benefit of Working Overtime: 30.5%

Gender

	Male	Female
Percent	27.1%	72.9%
Effect on Earnings	5.8%	−1.7%

Union Membership

Percentage Union Members: 9.5%

Earnings Benefit of Union Membership: 9.1%

Veteran Status

Percentage Who Have Been on Active Duty: 5.2%

Earnings Benefit of Veteran Status: 35.5%

29-2041 Emergency Medical Technicians and Paramedics

Assess injuries, administer emergency medical care, and extricate trapped individuals. Transport injured or sick persons to medical facilities.

- Education or Training Required: Postsecondary vocational training
- Job Growth: 27.3%
- Annual Openings: 21,000
- Self-Employed: 0.1%
- Part-Time: 5.6%

NATIONAL WAGE FIGURES (ANNUAL)

Beginning	25th Percentile	Median	Mean	75th Percentile	90th Percentile
$17,300	$21,290	$27,070	$29,390	$35,210	$45,280

Median Wages for Industries Employing Largest Numbers (Annual)

Industry	Median Income
Waste Management and Remediation Services	$40,600
Transportation Equipment Manufacturing	$38,100
Professional, Scientific, and Technical Services	$37,250
Primary Metal Manufacturing	$35,050
Educational Services	$33,080
Accommodation	$32,990
Management of Companies and Enterprises	$31,520
Federal, State, and Local Government	$29,390
Hospitals	$28,590
Transit and Ground Passenger Transportation	$27,520

Median Wages for States (Annual)

AK	$45,010	KY	$23,350	NY	$34,070
AL	$22,910	LA	$24,290	OH	$24,520
AR	$22,830	MA	$32,790	OK	$20,440
AZ	$23,360	MD	$37,090	OR	$32,630
CA	$25,360	ME	$26,170	PA	$25,020
CO	$32,250	MI	$27,550	RI	$31,190
CT	$33,450	MN	$27,430	SC	$26,600
DC	no data	MO	$26,690	SD	$23,230
DE	$32,940	MS	$23,890	TN	$25,580
FL	$27,540	MT	$20,010	TX	$26,510
GA	$27,400	NC	$26,840	UT	$24,650
HI	$37,620	ND	$26,820	VA	$28,120
IA	$25,920	NE	$26,680	VT	$26,920
ID	$30,870	NH	$29,940	WA	$36,860
IL	$26,750	NJ	$29,510	WI	$24,580
IN	$26,830	NM	$27,640	WV	$19,990
KS	$21,930	NV	$36,220	WY	$23,470

Median Wages for the Largest Metropolitan Areas (Annual)

AZ: Phoenix	$22,670	MI: Detroit	$31,370
CA: Los Angeles	$24,070	MN: Minneapolis	$33,080
CA: Riverside	$25,340	MO: Kansas City	$27,460
CA: Sacramento	$30,230	MO: St. Louis	$32,850
CA: San Diego	$30,310	NV: Las Vegas	no data
CA: San Francisco	$23,830	NY: New York	$36,130
CO: Denver	$32,060	OH: Cincinnati	$26,890
DC: Washington	$43,870	OH: Cleveland	$29,910
FL: Miami	$27,560	OH: Columbus	$20,320
FL: Orlando	$28,060	OR: Portland	no data
FL: Tampa	$27,440	PA: Philadelphia	$31,780
GA: Atlanta	$33,250	PA: Pittsburgh	$24,340
IL: Chicago	$28,380	TX: Dallas	$28,660
MA: Boston	$33,030	TX: Houston	$28,920
MD: Baltimore	$32,780	WA: Seattle	$36,010

FACTORS THAT MAY AFFECT EARNINGS

Educational Attainment of Workers and Effect on Earnings

	Percent at Level	Effect on Earnings
Less than High School	—	—
Some High School	—	—
High School or Equivalent	20.3%	−15.4%
Some College but No Degree	39.0%	−7.2%
Associate Degree	22.6%	18.0%
Bachelor's Degree	15.8%	8.8%
Master's Degree	—	—
Doctoral Degree	—	—
First Professional Degree	—	—

Flexibility of Earnings

Average Hours Worked: 38
Workers with a Varying Number of Hours: 10.5%
Workers Earning Some Overtime Pay, Tips, or Commissions: 28.6%
Earnings Benefit of Working Overtime: −8.4%

Gender

	Male	Female
Percent	68.1%	31.9%
Effect on Earnings	4.1%	—

Union Membership

Percentage Union Members: 27.1%
Earnings Benefit of Union Membership: 9.6%

Veteran Status

Percentage Who Have Been on Active Duty: 5.2%
Earnings Benefit of Veteran Status: 35.5%

29-2051 Dietetic Technicians

Assist dietitians in the provision of food service and nutritional programs. Under the supervision of dietitians, may plan and produce meals based on established guidelines, teach principles of food and nutrition, or counsel individuals.

- Education or Training Required: Moderate-term on-the-job training
- Job Growth: 19.1%
- Annual Openings: 3,000
- Self-Employed: 0.4%
- Part-Time: 27.8%

NATIONAL WAGE FIGURES (ANNUAL)

Beginning	25th Percentile	Median	Mean	75th Percentile	90th Percentile
$15,720	$18,750	$24,040	$26,090	$31,530	$38,520

Median Wages for Industries Employing Largest Numbers (Annual)

Industry	Median Income
Health and Personal Care Stores	$87,600
Management of Companies and Enterprises	$33,100
Federal, State, and Local Government	$27,630
Ambulatory Health Care Services	$27,050
Personal and Laundry Services	$26,990
Hospitals	$25,530
Social Assistance	$24,420
Educational Services	$22,900
Religious, Grantmaking, Civic, Professional, and Similar Organizations	$21,900
Real Estate	$21,600

Median Wages for States (Annual)

State	Wage	State	Wage	State	Wage
AK	no data	KY	$21,750	NY	$32,230
AL	$22,310	LA	$17,650	OH	$32,500
AR	$18,050	MA	$23,400	OK	$18,740
AZ	$18,200	MD	$30,530	OR	$32,940
CA	$30,720	ME	$26,450	PA	$23,230
CO	$25,250	MI	$24,760	RI	$25,210
CT	$31,500	MN	$33,480	SC	$22,640
DC	$25,280	MO	$23,760	SD	no data
DE	$19,320	MS	$18,160	TN	$21,940
FL	$24,530	MT	$20,410	TX	$20,910
GA	$19,630	NC	$21,400	UT	$22,510
HI	$27,070	ND	$26,880	VA	$21,630
IA	$21,120	NE	$24,830	VT	$24,430
ID	$21,580	NH	$25,990	WA	$34,130
IL	$20,520	NJ	$29,380	WI	$24,080
IN	$21,320	NM	$17,800	WV	no data
KS	$21,930	NV	$24,260	WY	no data

Median Wages for the Largest Metropolitan Areas (Annual)

Area	Wage	Area	Wage
AZ: Phoenix	$17,290	MI: Detroit	$31,190
CA: Los Angeles	$30,670	MN: Minneapolis	$34,700
CA: Riverside	$23,670	MO: Kansas City	$24,810
CA: Sacramento	$33,270	MO: St. Louis	$24,520
CA: San Diego	$23,430	NV: Las Vegas	$24,860
CA: San Francisco	$34,330	NY: New York	$33,900
CO: Denver	$25,690	OH: Cincinnati	$33,390
DC: Washington	$31,770	OH: Cleveland	$31,960
FL: Miami	$28,380	OH: Columbus	$33,880
FL: Orlando	$26,720	OR: Portland	$37,460
FL: Tampa	$25,050	PA: Philadelphia	$24,510
GA: Atlanta	$21,590	PA: Pittsburgh	$25,570
IL: Chicago	$20,840	TX: Dallas	$20,950
MA: Boston	$23,740	TX: Houston	$23,230
MD: Baltimore	$29,630	WA: Seattle	$34,700

FACTORS THAT MAY AFFECT EARNINGS

Educational Attainment of Workers and Effect on Earnings

Figures are based on a group of occupations: Health Technologists and Technicians

	Percent at Level	Effect on Earnings
Less than High School	—	—
Some High School	2.4%	−47.8%
High School or Equivalent	18.2%	−15.4%
Some College but No Degree	25.9%	−10.8%
Associate Degree	28.3%	1.4%
Bachelor's Degree	19.4%	23.8%
Master's Degree	3.7%	33.6%
Doctoral Degree	—	—
First Professional Degree	1.7%	18.2%

Flexibility of Earnings

Average Hours Worked: 33
Workers with a Varying Number of Hours: 6.5%
Workers Earning Some Overtime Pay, Tips, or Commissions: 15.4%
Earnings Benefit of Working Overtime: 1.7%

Gender

	Male	Female
Percent	19.9%	80.1%
Effect on Earnings	12.9%	−3.7%

Union Membership

Percentage Union Members: 9.5%
Earnings Benefit of Union Membership: 9.1%

Veteran Status

Percentage Who Have Been on Active Duty: 5.2%
Earnings Benefit of Veteran Status: 35.5%

29-2052 Pharmacy Technicians

Prepare medications under the direction of a pharmacist. May measure, mix, count out, label, and record amounts and dosages of medications.

- Education or Training Required: Moderate-term on-the-job training
- Job Growth: 28.6%
- Annual Openings: 35,000
- Self-Employed: 0.3%
- Part-Time: 27.8%

NATIONAL WAGE FIGURES (ANNUAL)

Beginning	25th Percentile	Median	Mean	75th Percentile	90th Percentile
$17,800	$21,010	$25,630	$26,510	$31,030	$36,720

Median Wages for Industries Employing Largest Numbers (Annual)

Industry	Median Income
Religious, Grantmaking, Civic, Professional, and Similar Organizations	$36,750
Federal, State, and Local Government	$34,780
Rental and Leasing Services	$32,150
Warehousing and Storage	$32,020
Wholesale Electronic Markets and Agents and Brokers	$31,090
Ambulatory Health Care Services	$30,860
Management of Companies and Enterprises	$30,570
Educational Services	$30,360
Hospitals	$28,860
Administrative and Support Services	$28,550

Median Wages for States (Annual)

AK	$33,760	KY	$22,190	NY	$26,690
AL	$21,830	LA	$23,050	OH	$23,460
AR	$21,640	MA	$26,630	OK	$22,020
AZ	$27,030	MD	$27,010	OR	$30,770
CA	$33,980	ME	$24,880	PA	$22,480
CO	$29,780	MI	$25,970	RI	$26,890
CT	$27,890	MN	$28,140	SC	$23,400
DC	$30,820	MO	$22,180	SD	$24,000
DE	$19,390	MS	$21,760	TN	$25,260
FL	$24,020	MT	$25,950	TX	$26,660
GA	$23,660	NC	$22,940	UT	$28,350
HI	$30,070	ND	$26,320	VA	$24,310
IA	$23,070	NE	$24,320	VT	$24,580
ID	$26,060	NH	$22,980	WA	$33,140
IL	$25,110	NJ	$24,850	WI	$25,020
IN	$24,200	NM	$26,580	WV	$21,250
KS	$24,340	NV	$30,020	WY	$27,380

Median Wages for the Largest Metropolitan Areas (Annual)

AZ: Phoenix	$27,450	MI: Detroit	$26,370
CA: Los Angeles	$33,410	MN: Minneapolis	$29,260
CA: Riverside	$31,830	MO: Kansas City	$23,310
CA: Sacramento	$35,490	MO: St. Louis	$22,760
CA: San Diego	$33,230	NV: Las Vegas	$29,890
CA: San Francisco	$36,640	NY: New York	$27,320
CO: Denver	$30,840	OH: Cincinnati	$23,840
DC: Washington	$28,280	OH: Cleveland	$23,840
FL: Miami	$25,060	OH: Columbus	$24,560
FL: Orlando	$24,160	OR: Portland	$32,180
FL: Tampa	$24,150	PA: Philadelphia	$23,390
GA: Atlanta	$24,120	PA: Pittsburgh	$22,440
IL: Chicago	$26,100	TX: Dallas	$28,260
MA: Boston	$26,710	TX: Houston	$27,790
MD: Baltimore	$27,360	WA: Seattle	$34,100

FACTORS THAT MAY AFFECT EARNINGS

Educational Attainment of Workers and Effect on Earnings

Figures are based on a group of occupations: Health Technologists and Technicians

	Percent at Level	Effect on Earnings
Less than High School	—	—
Some High School	2.4%	−47.8%
High School or Equivalent	18.2%	−15.4%
Some College but No Degree	25.9%	−10.8%
Associate Degree	28.3%	1.4%
Bachelor's Degree	19.4%	23.8%
Master's Degree	3.7%	33.6%
Doctoral Degree	—	—
First Professional Degree	1.7%	18.2%

Flexibility of Earnings

Average Hours Worked: 33
Workers with a Varying Number of Hours: 6.5%
Workers Earning Some Overtime Pay, Tips, or Commissions: 15.4%
Earnings Benefit of Working Overtime: 1.7%

Gender

	Male	Female
Percent	19.9%	80.1%
Effect on Earnings	12.9%	−3.7%

Union Membership

Percentage Union Members: 9.5%
Earnings Benefit of Union Membership: 9.1%

Veteran Status

Percentage Who Have Been on Active Duty: 5.2%
Earnings Benefit of Veteran Status: 35.5%

29-2053 Psychiatric Technicians

Care for mentally impaired or emotionally disturbed individuals, following physician instructions and hospital procedures. Monitor patients' physical and emotional well-being and report to medical staff. May participate in rehabilitation and treatment programs, help with personal hygiene, and administer oral medications and hypodermic injections.

- Education or Training Required: Moderate-term on-the-job training
- Job Growth: 3.2%
- Annual Openings: 6,000
- Self-Employed: 0.4%
- Part-Time: 27.8%

NATIONAL WAGE FIGURES (ANNUAL)

Beginning	25th Percentile	Median	Mean	75th Percentile	90th Percentile
$18,720	$21,960	$27,780	$30,450	$36,770	$47,210

Median Wages for Industries Employing Largest Numbers (Annual)

Industry	Median Income
Social Assistance	$31,240
Hospitals	$29,210
Administrative and Support Services	$29,150
Federal, State, and Local Government	$24,520
Ambulatory Health Care Services	$24,330
Nursing and Residential Care Facilities	$22,200

Median Wages for States (Annual)

State	Wage	State	Wage	State	Wage
AK	no data	KY	$21,900	NY	$33,560
AL	$21,840	LA	$18,610	OH	$29,690
AR	$20,960	MA	$32,730	OK	$22,840
AZ	$29,260	MD	$30,710	OR	no data
CA	$44,830	ME	$25,100	PA	$27,940
CO	$34,350	MI	$30,070	RI	$34,990
CT	$44,470	MN	$30,810	SC	$20,360
DC	$38,500	MO	$20,550	SD	$25,770
DE	no data	MS	$20,570	TN	no data
FL	$22,600	MT	$21,750	TX	$24,420
GA	no data	NC	$24,060	UT	$20,760
HI	no data	ND	$24,020	VA	$24,480
IA	$23,220	NE	no data	VT	$31,660
ID	$26,970	NH	$33,780	WA	$32,560
IL	$31,360	NJ	$38,620	WI	$29,140
IN	no data	NM	no data	WV	no data
KS	$25,100	NV	$25,590	WY	$25,010

Median Wages for the Largest Metropolitan Areas (Annual)

Area	Wage	Area	Wage
AZ: Phoenix	$29,790	MI: Detroit	$32,960
CA: Los Angeles	$44,560	MN: Minneapolis	no data
CA: Riverside	$45,550	MO: Kansas City	$21,110
CA: Sacramento	no data	MO: St. Louis	$20,570
CA: San Diego	$36,710	NV: Las Vegas	$25,710
CA: San Francisco	$52,710	NY: New York	$37,430
CO: Denver	$34,560	OH: Cincinnati	$27,470
DC: Washington	$33,180	OH: Cleveland	$33,340
FL: Miami	$23,480	OH: Columbus	no data
FL: Orlando	$21,150	OR: Portland	$36,020
FL: Tampa	$18,730	PA: Philadelphia	$28,510
GA: Atlanta	$18,110	PA: Pittsburgh	$27,660
IL: Chicago	$32,040	TX: Dallas	$26,140
MA: Boston	$33,130	TX: Houston	$25,050
MD: Baltimore	$32,780	WA: Seattle	$32,170

FACTORS THAT MAY AFFECT EARNINGS

Educational Attainment of Workers and Effect on Earnings

Figures are based on a group of occupations: Health Technologists and Technicians

	Percent at Level	Effect on Earnings
Less than High School	—	—
Some High School	2.4%	−47.8%
High School or Equivalent	18.2%	−15.4%
Some College but No Degree	25.9%	−10.8%
Associate Degree	28.3%	1.4%
Bachelor's Degree	19.4%	23.8%
Master's Degree	3.7%	33.6%
Doctoral Degree	—	—
First Professional Degree	1.7%	18.2%

Flexibility of Earnings

Average Hours Worked: 33

Workers with a Varying Number of Hours: 6.5%

Workers Earning Some Overtime Pay, Tips, or Commissions: 15.4%

Earnings Benefit of Working Overtime: 1.7%

Gender

	Male	Female
Percent	19.9%	80.1%
Effect on Earnings	12.9%	−3.7%

Union Membership

Percentage Union Members: 9.5%

Earnings Benefit of Union Membership: 9.1%

Veteran Status

Percentage Who Have Been on Active Duty: 5.2%

Earnings Benefit of Veteran Status: 35.5%

29-2054 Respiratory Therapy Technicians

Provide specific, well-defined respiratory care procedures under the direction of respiratory therapists and physicians.

- Education or Training Required: Associate degree
- Job Growth: 3.3%
- Annual Openings: 2,000
- Self-Employed: 0.3%
- Part-Time: 27.8%

NATIONAL WAGE FIGURES (ANNUAL)

Beginning	25th Percentile	Median	Mean	75th Percentile	90th Percentile
$25,940	$32,050	$39,120	$39,860	$46,930	$56,220

Median Wages for Industries Employing Largest Numbers (Annual)

Industry	Median Income
Health and Personal Care Stores	$56,100
Administrative and Support Services	$53,400
Insurance Carriers and Related Activities	$42,190
Educational Services	$41,520
Federal, State, and Local Government	$39,700
Hospitals	$39,500
Merchant Wholesalers, Durable Goods	$39,420
Nursing and Residential Care Facilities	$36,070
Ambulatory Health Care Services	$32,260
Rental and Leasing Services	$30,580

Median Wages for States (Annual)

AK	no data	KY	$34,320	NY	$47,730
AL	$32,150	LA	$39,100	OH	$37,350
AR	$32,340	MA	$49,710	OK	$35,550
AZ	$34,150	MD	$54,090	OR	$48,200
CA	$51,870	ME	$42,520	PA	$38,510
CO	$41,950	MI	$39,100	RI	no data
CT	$38,500	MN	$49,570	SC	$37,160
DC	$37,790	MO	$30,970	SD	no data
DE	$42,370	MS	$31,620	TN	$35,890
FL	$38,940	MT	$36,670	TX	$38,610
GA	$38,910	NC	$37,860	UT	$28,910
HI	$48,640	ND	no data	VA	$44,860
IA	$32,240	NE	$39,320	VT	no data
ID	no data	NH	no data	WA	$36,440
IL	$36,460	NJ	$51,660	WI	$40,250
IN	$40,420	NM	$41,610	WV	$31,960
KS	$30,810	NV	$54,590	WY	$32,720

Median Wages for the Largest Metropolitan Areas (Annual)

AZ: Phoenix	$33,670	MI: Detroit	$46,830
CA: Los Angeles	$50,950	MN: Minneapolis	$52,420
CA: Riverside	no data	MO: Kansas City	$28,290
CA: Sacramento	$42,290	MO: St. Louis	$33,250
CA: San Diego	$50,950	NV: Las Vegas	$50,200
CA: San Francisco	no data	NY: New York	$51,480
CO: Denver	no data	OH: Cincinnati	$37,820
DC: Washington	$47,640	OH: Cleveland	$37,590
FL: Miami	$38,930	OH: Columbus	$32,550
FL: Orlando	$40,550	OR: Portland	$46,850
FL: Tampa	$36,550	PA: Philadelphia	$39,680
GA: Atlanta	$43,860	PA: Pittsburgh	$37,810
IL: Chicago	$37,070	TX: Dallas	$40,240
MA: Boston	$53,990	TX: Houston	$35,950
MD: Baltimore	$54,520	WA: Seattle	no data

FACTORS THAT MAY AFFECT EARNINGS

Educational Attainment of Workers and Effect on Earnings

Figures are based on a group of occupations: Health Technologists and Technicians

	Percent at Level	Effect on Earnings
Less than High School	—	—
Some High School	2.4%	−47.8%
High School or Equivalent	18.2%	−15.4%
Some College but No Degree	25.9%	−10.8%
Associate Degree	28.3%	1.4%
Bachelor's Degree	19.4%	23.8%
Master's Degree	3.7%	33.6%
Doctoral Degree	—	—
First Professional Degree	1.7%	18.2%

Flexibility of Earnings

Average Hours Worked: 33
Workers with a Varying Number of Hours: 6.5%
Workers Earning Some Overtime Pay, Tips, or Commissions: 15.4%
Earnings Benefit of Working Overtime: 1.7%

Gender

	Male	Female
Percent	19.9%	80.1%
Effect on Earnings	12.9%	−3.7%

Union Membership

Percentage Union Members: 9.5%
Earnings Benefit of Union Membership: 9.1%

Veteran Status

Percentage Who Have Been on Active Duty: 5.2%
Earnings Benefit of Veteran Status: 35.5%

29-2055 Surgical Technologists

Assist in operations under the supervision of surgeons, registered nurses, or other surgical personnel. May help set up operating room; prepare and transport patients for surgery; adjust lights and equipment; pass instruments and other supplies to surgeons and surgeon's assistants; hold retractors; cut sutures; and help count sponges, needles, supplies, and instruments.

- Education or Training Required: Postsecondary vocational training
- Job Growth: 29.5%
- Annual Openings: 12,000
- Self-Employed: 0.3%
- Part-Time: 27.8%

NATIONAL WAGE FIGURES (ANNUAL)

Beginning	25th Percentile	Median	Mean	75th Percentile	90th Percentile
$25,490	$30,300	$36,080	$37,370	$43,560	$51,140

Median Wages for Industries Employing Largest Numbers (Annual)

Industry	Median Income
Management of Companies and Enterprises	$39,240
Administrative and Support Services	$38,790
Ambulatory Health Care Services	$36,640
Educational Services	$35,960
Hospitals	$35,880
Insurance Carriers and Related Activities	$33,640
Professional, Scientific, and Technical Services	$33,270

Median Wages for States (Annual)

State	Wage	State	Wage	State	Wage
AK	$46,230	KY	$33,110	NY	$36,110
AL	$28,630	LA	$30,980	OH	$35,110
AR	$29,260	MA	$42,390	OK	$29,510
AZ	$37,280	MD	$42,910	OR	$40,490
CA	$43,590	ME	$33,540	PA	$34,170
CO	$38,560	MI	$37,630	RI	$40,120
CT	$43,060	MN	$42,870	SC	$32,200
DC	$36,540	MO	$33,280	SD	$31,870
DE	$38,480	MS	$28,260	TN	$33,910
FL	$34,190	MT	$35,580	TX	$35,660
GA	$32,110	NC	$34,120	UT	$30,380
HI	$38,360	ND	$33,830	VA	$36,160
IA	$33,270	NE	$33,240	VT	$34,360
ID	$34,250	NH	$37,800	WA	$41,240
IL	$38,710	NJ	$42,200	WI	$41,000
IN	$35,860	NM	$30,350	WV	$29,270
KS	$33,280	NV	$41,370	WY	$32,570

Median Wages for the Largest Metropolitan Areas (Annual)

Area	Wage	Area	Wage
AZ: Phoenix	$38,700	MI: Detroit	$39,260
CA: Los Angeles	$42,770	MN: Minneapolis	$43,910
CA: Riverside	$39,580	MO: Kansas City	$41,550
CA: Sacramento	$44,490	MO: St. Louis	$33,720
CA: San Diego	$40,340	NV: Las Vegas	$41,180
CA: San Francisco	$54,580	NY: New York	$38,550
CO: Denver	$38,290	OH: Cincinnati	$35,150
DC: Washington	$43,600	OH: Cleveland	$37,120
FL: Miami	$35,310	OH: Columbus	$33,460
FL: Orlando	$32,290	OR: Portland	$42,050
FL: Tampa	$34,240	PA: Philadelphia	$37,070
GA: Atlanta	$35,020	PA: Pittsburgh	$31,710
IL: Chicago	$39,670	TX: Dallas	$36,930
MA: Boston	$42,190	TX: Houston	$37,560
MD: Baltimore	$41,430	WA: Seattle	$43,820

FACTORS THAT MAY AFFECT EARNINGS

Educational Attainment of Workers and Effect on Earnings

Figures are based on a group of occupations: Health Technologists and Technicians

	Percent at Level	Effect on Earnings
Less than High School	—	—
Some High School	2.4%	−47.8%
High School or Equivalent	18.2%	−15.4%
Some College but No Degree	25.9%	−10.8%
Associate Degree	28.3%	1.4%
Bachelor's Degree	19.4%	23.8%
Master's Degree	3.7%	33.6%
Doctoral Degree	—	—
First Professional Degree	1.7%	18.2%

Flexibility of Earnings

Average Hours Worked: 33
Workers with a Varying Number of Hours: 6.5%
Workers Earning Some Overtime Pay, Tips, or Commissions: 15.4%
Earnings Benefit of Working Overtime: 1.7%

Gender

	Male	Female
Percent	19.9%	80.1%
Effect on Earnings	12.9%	−3.7%

Union Membership

Percentage Union Members: 9.5%
Earnings Benefit of Union Membership: 9.1%

Veteran Status

Percentage Who Have Been on Active Duty: 5.2%
Earnings Benefit of Veteran Status: 35.5%

29-2056 Veterinary Technologists and Technicians

Perform medical tests in a laboratory environment for use in the treatment and diagnosis of diseases in animals. Prepare vaccines and serums for prevention of diseases. Prepare tissue samples; take blood samples; and execute laboratory tests, such as urinalysis and blood counts. Clean and sterilize instruments and materials and maintain equipment and machines.

- Education or Training Required: Associate degree
- Job Growth: 35.3%
- Annual Openings: 9,000
- Self-Employed: 0.3%
- Part-Time: 27.8%

NATIONAL WAGE FIGURES (ANNUAL)

Beginning	25th Percentile	Median	Mean	75th Percentile	90th Percentile
$18,280	$21,720	$26,780	$27,750	$32,800	$38,850

Median Wages for Industries Employing Largest Numbers (Annual)

Industry	Median Income
Federal, State, and Local Government	$39,100
Museums, Historical Sites, and Similar Institutions	$35,260
Merchant Wholesalers, Nondurable Goods	$34,440
Chemical Manufacturing	$33,540
Educational Services	$32,450
Hospitals	$32,010
Support Activities for Agriculture and Forestry	$28,860
Administrative and Support Services	$27,940
Religious, Grantmaking, Civic, Professional, and Similar Organizations	$26,700
Personal and Laundry Services	$26,500

Median Wages for States (Annual)

State	Wage	State	Wage	State	Wage
AK	$32,390	KY	$21,000	NY	$30,250
AL	$21,360	LA	$19,880	OH	$27,740
AR	$18,450	MA	$31,050	OK	$21,660
AZ	$25,310	MD	$25,910	OR	$29,590
CA	$30,540	ME	$27,950	PA	$26,970
CO	$27,210	MI	$32,270	RI	$29,660
CT	$33,750	MN	$28,100	SC	$25,420
DC	no data	MO	$25,020	SD	$22,430
DE	$28,520	MS	$22,860	TN	$22,790
FL	$23,970	MT	$22,740	TX	$22,450
GA	$24,670	NC	$24,470	UT	$24,050
HI	$24,150	ND	$25,740	VA	$28,590
IA	$24,290	NE	$22,930	VT	$26,700
ID	$25,120	NH	$28,020	WA	$30,170
IL	$31,450	NJ	$28,050	WI	$26,910
IN	$26,700	NM	$29,290	WV	$18,760
KS	$25,350	NV	$28,590	WY	$27,300

Median Wages for the Largest Metropolitan Areas (Annual)

Area	Wage	Area	Wage
AZ: Phoenix	$26,260	MI: Detroit	$32,530
CA: Los Angeles	$28,680	MN: Minneapolis	$29,470
CA: Riverside	$29,600	MO: Kansas City	$27,390
CA: Sacramento	$32,980	MO: St. Louis	$26,420
CA: San Diego	$32,570	NV: Las Vegas	$28,600
CA: San Francisco	$35,750	NY: New York	$30,600
CO: Denver	$25,730	OH: Cincinnati	$24,170
DC: Washington	$29,510	OH: Cleveland	$28,440
FL: Miami	$25,530	OH: Columbus	$29,240
FL: Orlando	$23,590	OR: Portland	$30,540
FL: Tampa	$25,490	PA: Philadelphia	$30,390
GA: Atlanta	$25,810	PA: Pittsburgh	$27,150
IL: Chicago	$33,150	TX: Dallas	$24,400
MA: Boston	$31,480	TX: Houston	$19,580
MD: Baltimore	$26,210	WA: Seattle	$32,520

FACTORS THAT MAY AFFECT EARNINGS

Educational Attainment of Workers and Effect on Earnings

Figures are based on a group of occupations: Health Technologists and Technicians

	Percent at Level	Effect on Earnings
Less than High School	—	—
Some High School	2.4%	−47.8%
High School or Equivalent	18.2%	−15.4%
Some College but No Degree	25.9%	−10.8%
Associate Degree	28.3%	1.4%
Bachelor's Degree	19.4%	23.8%
Master's Degree	3.7%	33.6%
Doctoral Degree	—	—
First Professional Degree	1.7%	18.2%

Flexibility of Earnings

Average Hours Worked: 33
Workers with a Varying Number of Hours: 6.5%
Workers Earning Some Overtime Pay, Tips, or Commissions: 15.4%
Earnings Benefit of Working Overtime: 1.7%

Gender

	Male	Female
Percent	19.9%	80.1%
Effect on Earnings	21.3%	−5.0%

Union Membership

Percentage Union Members: 9.5%
Earnings Benefit of Union Membership: 9.1%

Veteran Status

Percentage Who Have Been on Active Duty: 5.2%
Earnings Benefit of Veteran Status: 35.5%

29-2061 Licensed Practical and Licensed Vocational Nurses

Care for ill, injured, convalescent, or disabled persons in hospitals, nursing homes, clinics, private homes, group homes, and similar institutions. May work under the supervision of a registered nurse. Licensing required.

- Education or Training Required: Postsecondary vocational training
- Job Growth: 17.1%
- Annual Openings: 84,000
- Self-Employed: 0.6%
- Part-Time: 30.5%

NATIONAL WAGE FIGURES (ANNUAL)

Beginning	25th Percentile	Median	Mean	75th Percentile	90th Percentile
$26,380	$31,080	$36,550	$37,530	$43,640	$50,480

Median Wages for Industries Employing Largest Numbers (Annual)

Industry	Median Income
Administrative and Support Services	$41,910
Insurance Carriers and Related Activities	$41,860
Internet Service Providers, Web Search Portals, and Data-Processing Services	$41,390
Health and Personal Care Stores	$41,080
Real Estate	$39,870
Rental and Leasing Services	$39,820
Religious, Grantmaking, Civic, Professional, and Similar Organizations	$38,330
Nursing and Residential Care Facilities	$38,180
Federal, State, and Local Government	$36,900
Management of Companies and Enterprises	$36,580

Median Wages for States (Annual)

State	Wage	State	Wage	State	Wage
AK	$43,190	KY	$33,440	NY	$37,650
AL	$29,830	LA	$31,490	OH	$37,360
AR	$30,620	MA	$47,260	OK	$30,140
AZ	$41,030	MD	$45,530	OR	$41,220
CA	$44,070	ME	$35,240	PA	$37,280
CO	$37,500	MI	$38,800	RI	$45,390
CT	$50,730	MN	$36,280	SC	$33,920
DC	$45,460	MO	$31,980	SD	$29,890
DE	$44,090	MS	$29,430	TN	$32,100
FL	$36,700	MT	$30,900	TX	$35,600
GA	$32,580	NC	$36,220	UT	$34,810
HI	$38,640	ND	$32,050	VA	$34,870
IA	$32,850	NE	$33,360	VT	$35,680
ID	$34,480	NH	$39,590	WA	$40,530
IL	$37,230	NJ	$46,810	WI	$36,990
IN	$35,370	NM	$39,560	WV	$29,440
KS	$33,640	NV	$42,290	WY	$33,850

Median Wages for the Largest Metropolitan Areas (Annual)

Area	Wage	Area	Wage
AZ: Phoenix	$41,660	MI: Detroit	$42,630
CA: Los Angeles	$43,560	MN: Minneapolis	$39,570
CA: Riverside	$39,590	MO: Kansas City	$35,530
CA: Sacramento	$45,640	MO: St. Louis	$35,610
CA: San Diego	$40,870	NV: Las Vegas	$41,680
CA: San Francisco	$55,010	NY: New York	$45,520
CO: Denver	$40,740	OH: Cincinnati	$39,960
DC: Washington	$43,830	OH: Cleveland	$39,490
FL: Miami	$38,840	OH: Columbus	$40,220
FL: Orlando	$35,860	OR: Portland	$43,750
FL: Tampa	$36,940	PA: Philadelphia	$45,310
GA: Atlanta	$34,620	PA: Pittsburgh	$35,090
IL: Chicago	$40,270	TX: Dallas	$39,090
MA: Boston	$47,930	TX: Houston	$38,060
MD: Baltimore	$45,750	WA: Seattle	$42,800

FACTORS THAT MAY AFFECT EARNINGS

Educational Attainment of Workers and Effect on Earnings

	Percent at Level	Effect on Earnings
Less than High School	—	—
Some High School	—	—
High School or Equivalent	20.7%	−5.5%
Some College but No Degree	35.3%	−1.3%
Associate Degree	35.9%	−0.6%
Bachelor's Degree	5.1%	18.7%
Master's Degree	—	—
Doctoral Degree	—	—
First Professional Degree	1.6%	24.7%

Flexibility of Earnings

Average Hours Worked: 33
Workers with a Varying Number of Hours: 6.1%
Workers Earning Some Overtime Pay, Tips, or Commissions: 16.7%
Earnings Benefit of Working Overtime: 3.2%

Gender

	Male	Female
Percent	5.8%	94.2%
Effect on Earnings	—	−0.8%

Union Membership

Percentage Union Members: 9.9%
Earnings Benefit of Union Membership: 9.1%

Veteran Status

Percentage Who Have Been on Active Duty: 5.2%
Earnings Benefit of Veteran Status: 35.5%

29-2071 Medical Records and Health Information Technicians

Compile, process, and maintain medical records of hospital and clinic patients in a manner consistent with medical, administrative, ethical, legal, and regulatory requirements of the health-care system. Process, maintain, compile, and report patient information for health requirements and standards.

- Education or Training Required: Associate degree
- Job Growth: 28.9%
- Annual Openings: 14,000
- Self-Employed: 0.1%
- Part-Time: 22.6%

NATIONAL WAGE FIGURES (ANNUAL)

Beginning	25th Percentile	Median	Mean	75th Percentile	90th Percentile
$19,060	$22,420	$28,030	$30,140	$35,990	$45,260

Median Wages for Industries Employing Largest Numbers (Annual)

Industry	Median Income
Chemical Manufacturing	$40,220
Federal, State, and Local Government	$36,640
Insurance Carriers and Related Activities	$34,530
Educational Services	$34,330
Miscellaneous Manufacturing	$33,650
Religious, Grantmaking, Civic, Professional, and Similar Organizations	$33,030
Professional, Scientific, and Technical Services	$32,910
Merchant Wholesalers, Nondurable Goods	$31,640
Health and Personal Care Stores	$31,250
Management of Companies and Enterprises	$31,210

Median Wages for States (Annual)

AK	$31,780	KY	$26,720	NY	$33,430
AL	$22,130	LA	$21,520	OH	$27,860
AR	$24,440	MA	$29,620	OK	$24,640
AZ	$27,320	MD	$32,930	OR	$28,770
CA	$31,800	ME	$28,140	PA	$28,540
CO	$29,920	MI	$29,450	RI	$32,430
CT	$34,780	MN	$32,160	SC	$24,830
DC	$36,040	MO	$25,400	SD	$26,440
DE	$28,170	MS	$23,450	TN	$24,070
FL	$27,610	MT	$25,290	TX	$26,340
GA	$26,590	NC	$24,940	UT	$25,730
HI	$31,400	ND	$25,020	VA	$29,810
IA	$25,510	NE	$26,200	VT	$29,400
ID	$25,130	NH	$27,710	WA	$30,640
IL	$26,860	NJ	$38,540	WI	$29,020
IN	$25,900	NM	$24,740	WV	$22,680
KS	$24,550	NV	$29,650	WY	$28,160

Median Wages for the Largest Metropolitan Areas (Annual)

AZ: Phoenix	$27,510	MI: Detroit	$32,040
CA: Los Angeles	$31,140	MN: Minneapolis	$33,790
CA: Riverside	$31,440	MO: Kansas City	$27,810
CA: Sacramento	$35,650	MO: St. Louis	$25,280
CA: San Diego	$28,650	NV: Las Vegas	$30,060
CA: San Francisco	$38,250	NY: New York	$37,270
CO: Denver	$30,750	OH: Cincinnati	$29,230
DC: Washington	$35,710	OH: Cleveland	$33,120
FL: Miami	$27,990	OH: Columbus	$27,070
FL: Orlando	$26,190	OR: Portland	$32,580
FL: Tampa	$26,250	PA: Philadelphia	$29,570
GA: Atlanta	$28,430	PA: Pittsburgh	$29,050
IL: Chicago	$27,790	TX: Dallas	$26,840
MA: Boston	$29,790	TX: Houston	$29,800
MD: Baltimore	$33,420	WA: Seattle	$32,420

FACTORS THAT MAY AFFECT EARNINGS

Educational Attainment of Workers and Effect on Earnings

	Percent at Level	Effect on Earnings
Less than High School	—	—
Some High School	4.2%	−49.6%
High School or Equivalent	33.8%	−5.2%
Some College but No Degree	31.0%	−3.6%
Associate Degree	17.6%	−4.6%
Bachelor's Degree	11.3%	35.3%
Master's Degree	—	—
Doctoral Degree	—	—
First Professional Degree	—	—

Flexibility of Earnings

Average Hours Worked: 35
Workers with a Varying Number of Hours: 3.8%
Workers Earning Some Overtime Pay, Tips, or Commissions: 6.1%
Earnings Benefit of Working Overtime: 1.7%

Gender

	Male	Female
Percent	8.0%	92.0%
Effect on Earnings	—	−2.7%

Union Membership

Percentage Union Members: 10.9%
Earnings Benefit of Union Membership: 17.8%

Veteran Status

Percentage Who Have Been on Active Duty: 5.2%
Earnings Benefit of Veteran Status: 35.5%

29-2081 Opticians, Dispensing

Design, measure, fit, and adapt lenses and frames for client according to written optical prescription or specification. Assist client with selecting frames. Measure customer for size of eyeglasses and coordinate frames with facial and eye measurements and optical prescription. Prepare work order for optical laboratory containing instructions for grinding and mounting lenses in frames. Verify exactness of finished lens spectacles. Adjust frame and lens position to fit client. May shape or reshape frames.

- Education or Training Required: Long-term on-the-job training
- Job Growth: 13.6%
- Annual Openings: 6,000
- Self-Employed: 4.5%
- Part-Time: 30.0%

NATIONAL WAGE FIGURES (ANNUAL)

Beginning	25th Percentile	Median	Mean	75th Percentile	90th Percentile
$19,290	$23,560	$30,300	$32,220	$38,950	$47,630

Median Wages for Industries Employing Largest Numbers (Annual)

Industry	Median Income
Hospitals	$36,880
Educational Services	$35,830
Food and Beverage Stores	$32,680
Health and Personal Care Stores	$31,850
Miscellaneous Manufacturing	$30,230
Ambulatory Health Care Services	$30,090
Administrative and Support Services	$27,350
Merchant Wholesalers, Durable Goods	$23,930

Median Wages for States (Annual)

AK	$35,200	KY	$30,500	NY	$42,830
AL	$22,140	LA	$23,550	OH	$31,100
AR	$23,570	MA	$41,380	OK	$22,310
AZ	$28,630	MD	$30,960	OR	$29,380
CA	$33,980	ME	$29,590	PA	$29,100
CO	$31,000	MI	$29,770	RI	$43,930
CT	$43,870	MN	$32,060	SC	$26,790
DC	$30,130	MO	$26,150	SD	$23,660
DE	$32,680	MS	$25,370	TN	$31,280
FL	$35,900	MT	$23,920	TX	$26,160
GA	$29,720	NC	$32,210	UT	$26,510
HI	$34,260	ND	$23,010	VA	$40,740
IA	$24,290	NE	$23,860	VT	$32,430
ID	$23,840	NH	$32,910	WA	$34,700
IL	$28,070	NJ	$48,890	WI	$27,840
IN	$24,310	NM	$25,980	WV	$22,830
KS	$23,090	NV	$47,720	WY	$23,620

Median Wages for the Largest Metropolitan Areas (Annual)

AZ: Phoenix	$29,820	MI: Detroit	$31,030
CA: Los Angeles	$33,590	MN: Minneapolis	$33,270
CA: Riverside	$27,080	MO: Kansas City	$26,680
CA: Sacramento	$33,500	MO: St. Louis	$28,700
CA: San Diego	$37,500	NV: Las Vegas	$45,970
CA: San Francisco	$36,830	NY: New York	$47,100
CO: Denver	$34,580	OH: Cincinnati	$29,030
DC: Washington	$41,230	OH: Cleveland	$34,820
FL: Miami	$35,900	OH: Columbus	$30,290
FL: Orlando	$39,220	OR: Portland	$31,060
FL: Tampa	$33,660	PA: Philadelphia	$38,810
GA: Atlanta	$30,040	PA: Pittsburgh	$27,770
IL: Chicago	$29,010	TX: Dallas	$27,680
MA: Boston	$41,270	TX: Houston	$25,910
MD: Baltimore	$29,570	WA: Seattle	$32,210

FACTORS THAT MAY AFFECT EARNINGS

Educational Attainment of Workers and Effect on Earnings

	Percent at Level	Effect on Earnings
Less than High School	—	—
Some High School	—	—
High School or Equivalent	23.3%	−7.6%
Some College but No Degree	27.4%	3.7%
Associate Degree	15.1%	−43.4%
Bachelor's Degree	26.0%	19.0%
Master's Degree	—	—
Doctoral Degree	—	—
First Professional Degree	—	—

Figures do not total 100% because some levels have a very small sample size.

Flexibility of Earnings

Average Hours Worked: 33
Workers with a Varying Number of Hours: 9.0%
Workers Earning Some Overtime Pay, Tips, or Commissions: 17.8%
Earnings Benefit of Working Overtime: 1.7%

Gender

	Male	Female
Percent	36.2%	63.8%
Effect on Earnings	21.3%	−5.0%

Union Membership

Percentage Union Members: Insignificant
Earnings Benefit of Union Membership: No significant data available

Veteran Status

Percentage Who Have Been on Active Duty: 5.2%
Earnings Benefit of Veteran Status: 35.5%

29-2091 Orthotists and Prosthetists

Assist patients with disabling conditions of limbs and spine or with partial or total absence of limb by fitting and preparing orthopedic braces or prostheses.

- Education or Training Required: Bachelor's degree
- Job Growth: 18.0%
- Annual Openings: Fewer than 500
- Self-Employed: 14.4%
- Part-Time: 27.8%

NATIONAL WAGE FIGURES (ANNUAL)

Beginning	25th Percentile	Median	Mean	75th Percentile	90th Percentile
$31,060	$42,050	$58,980	$62,110	$75,730	$94,240

Median Wages for Industries Employing Largest Numbers (Annual)

Industry	Median Income
Merchant Wholesalers, Durable Goods	$70,870
Rental and Leasing Services	$69,170
Miscellaneous Manufacturing	$64,770
Health and Personal Care Stores	$61,830
Federal, State, and Local Government	$60,840
Educational Services	$55,740
Hospitals	$46,570
Ambulatory Health Care Services	$46,300

Median Wages for States (Annual)

State	Wage	State	Wage	State	Wage
AK	no data	KY	$46,260	NY	$67,280
AL	$53,530	LA	no data	OH	$55,410
AR	no data	MA	$45,520	OK	$41,030
AZ	$66,840	MD	$41,020	OR	$68,030
CA	$49,180	ME	no data	PA	$53,100
CO	$41,480	MI	$61,830	RI	no data
CT	$55,020	MN	$68,970	SC	$78,910
DC	no data	MO	$66,350	SD	no data
DE	no data	MS	$41,300	TN	$44,510
FL	$72,260	MT	no data	TX	$64,790
GA	$22,980	NC	no data	UT	no data
HI	no data	ND	no data	VA	$62,780
IA	no data	NE	no data	VT	no data
ID	no data	NH	$69,790	WA	$56,550
IL	$60,540	NJ	$55,710	WI	$61,460
IN	no data	NM	$37,300	WV	no data
KS	no data	NV	$84,640	WY	no data

Median Wages for the Largest Metropolitan Areas (Annual)

Area	Wage	Area	Wage
AZ: Phoenix	$67,460	MI: Detroit	$65,160
CA: Los Angeles	$54,300	MN: Minneapolis	$70,410
CA: Riverside	no data	MO: Kansas City	$78,390
CA: Sacramento	no data	MO: St. Louis	no data
CA: San Diego	$43,990	NV: Las Vegas	no data
CA: San Francisco	$43,190	NY: New York	$67,590
CO: Denver	no data	OH: Cincinnati	no data
DC: Washington	$64,030	OH: Cleveland	$50,020
FL: Miami	$71,810	OH: Columbus	no data
FL: Orlando	no data	OR: Portland	$68,470
FL: Tampa	$56,350	PA: Philadelphia	$57,960
GA: Atlanta	$22,180	PA: Pittsburgh	$50,330
IL: Chicago	$72,730	TX: Dallas	$68,900
MA: Boston	$44,750	TX: Houston	$78,090
MD: Baltimore	no data	WA: Seattle	$57,890

FACTORS THAT MAY AFFECT EARNINGS

Educational Attainment of Workers and Effect on Earnings

Figures are based on a group of occupations: Health Technologists and Technicians

	Percent at Level	Effect on Earnings
Less than High School	—	—
Some High School	2.4%	−47.8%
High School or Equivalent	18.2%	−15.4%
Some College but No Degree	25.9%	−10.8%
Associate Degree	28.3%	1.4%
Bachelor's Degree	19.4%	23.8%
Master's Degree	3.7%	33.6%
Doctoral Degree	—	—
First Professional Degree	1.7%	18.2%

Flexibility of Earnings

Average Hours Worked: 33
Workers with a Varying Number of Hours: 6.5%
Workers Earning Some Overtime Pay, Tips, or Commissions: 15.4%
Earnings Benefit of Working Overtime: 1.7%

Gender

	Male	Female
Percent	16.9%	83.1%
Effect on Earnings	21.3%	−5.0%

Union Membership

Percentage Union Members: 9.5%
Earnings Benefit of Union Membership: 9.1%

Veteran Status

Percentage Who Have Been on Active Duty: 5.2%
Earnings Benefit of Veteran Status: 35.5%

29-2099 Health Technologists and Technicians, All Other

All health technologists and technicians not listed separately.

- Education or Training Required: Postsecondary vocational training
- Job Growth: 22.9%
- Annual Openings: 8,000
- Self-Employed: 10.2%
- Part-Time: 27.8%

NATIONAL WAGE FIGURES (ANNUAL)

Beginning	25th Percentile	Median	Mean	75th Percentile	90th Percentile
$22,440	$27,620	$35,140	$38,260	$45,890	$59,020

Median Wages for Industries Employing Largest Numbers (Annual)

Industry	Median Income
Merchant Wholesalers, Durable Goods	$55,410
Religious, Grantmaking, Civic, Professional, and Similar Organizations	$47,070
Federal, State, and Local Government	$43,900
Management of Companies and Enterprises	$38,390
Insurance Carriers and Related Activities	$38,020
Merchant Wholesalers, Nondurable Goods	$37,480
Hospitals	$35,910
Administrative and Support Services	$35,890
Computer and Electronic Product Manufacturing	$35,750
Professional, Scientific, and Technical Services	$35,680

Median Wages for States (Annual)

AK	$41,870	KY	$36,960	NY	$40,500
AL	$26,680	LA	$28,260	OH	$32,790
AR	$23,680	MA	$41,210	OK	$27,970
AZ	$30,030	MD	$37,090	OR	$37,950
CA	$38,950	ME	$35,140	PA	$33,570
CO	$31,660	MI	$34,820	RI	$38,000
CT	$40,150	MN	$42,740	SC	$29,120
DC	$35,030	MO	$28,160	SD	no data
DE	$31,930	MS	$26,180	TN	$44,670
FL	$32,610	MT	$41,700	TX	$28,180
GA	$34,350	NC	$36,340	UT	$40,820
HI	$37,420	ND	$37,190	VA	$31,390
IA	$28,570	NE	$40,840	VT	$42,380
ID	$32,700	NH	$35,120	WA	$47,220
IL	$32,400	NJ	$41,160	WI	$36,220
IN	$28,540	NM	$39,260	WV	$31,350
KS	$29,250	NV	$32,640	WY	no data

Median Wages for the Largest Metropolitan Areas (Annual)

AZ: Phoenix	$31,900	MI: Detroit	$35,110
CA: Los Angeles	$36,780	MN: Minneapolis	$47,780
CA: Riverside	$38,310	MO: Kansas City	$34,180
CA: Sacramento	$38,250	MO: St. Louis	$27,320
CA: San Diego	$39,240	NV: Las Vegas	$33,440
CA: San Francisco	$41,860	NY: New York	$41,830
CO: Denver	$33,860	OH: Cincinnati	$31,850
DC: Washington	$39,290	OH: Cleveland	$35,710
FL: Miami	$32,060	OH: Columbus	$33,210
FL: Orlando	$32,800	OR: Portland	$41,560
FL: Tampa	$35,260	PA: Philadelphia	$32,950
GA: Atlanta	$35,300	PA: Pittsburgh	no data
IL: Chicago	$34,220	TX: Dallas	$30,230
MA: Boston	$42,250	TX: Houston	$27,980
MD: Baltimore	$34,930	WA: Seattle	$49,370

FACTORS THAT MAY AFFECT EARNINGS

Educational Attainment of Workers and Effect on Earnings

Figures are based on a group of occupations: Health Technologists and Technicians

	Percent at Level	Effect on Earnings
Less than High School	—	—
Some High School	2.4%	−47.8%
High School or Equivalent	18.2%	−15.4%
Some College but No Degree	25.9%	−10.8%
Associate Degree	28.3%	1.4%
Bachelor's Degree	19.4%	23.8%
Master's Degree	3.7%	33.6%
Doctoral Degree	—	—
First Professional Degree	1.7%	18.2%

Flexibility of Earnings

Average Hours Worked: 33
Workers with a Varying Number of Hours: 6.5%
Workers Earning Some Overtime Pay, Tips, or Commissions: 15.4%
Earnings Benefit of Working Overtime: 1.7%

Gender

	Male	Female
Percent	16.9%	83.1%
Effect on Earnings	21.3%	−5.0%

Union Membership

Percentage Union Members: 9.5%
Earnings Benefit of Union Membership: 9.1%

Veteran Status

Percentage Who Have Been on Active Duty: 5.2%
Earnings Benefit of Veteran Status: 35.5%

29-9000 Other Healthcare Practitioners and Technical Occupations

29-9011 Occupational Health and Safety Specialists

Review, evaluate, and analyze work environments and design programs and procedures to control, eliminate, and prevent disease or injury caused by chemical, physical, and biological agents or ergonomic factors. May conduct inspections and enforce adherence to laws and regulations governing the health and safety of individuals. May be employed in the public or private sector.

- Education or Training Required: Bachelor's degree
- Job Growth: 12.4%
- Annual Openings: 3,000
- Self-Employed: 5.0%
- Part-Time: 28.9%

NATIONAL WAGE FIGURES (ANNUAL)

Beginning	25th Percentile	Median	Mean	75th Percentile	90th Percentile
$35,250	$45,050	$58,030	$59,270	$72,660	$86,590

Median Wages for Industries Employing Largest Numbers (Annual)

Industry	Median Income
Oil and Gas Extraction	$69,240
Utilities	$69,170
Computer and Electronic Product Manufacturing	$66,470
Professional, Scientific, and Technical Services	$65,210
Insurance Carriers and Related Activities	$63,620
Waste Management and Remediation Services	$62,840
Transportation Equipment Manufacturing	$62,670
Chemical Manufacturing	$60,240
Management of Companies and Enterprises	$60,150
Ambulatory Health Care Services	$59,970

Median Wages for States (Annual)

AK	$78,220	KY	$52,100	NY	$58,000
AL	$56,800	LA	$50,350	OH	$60,220
AR	$49,390	MA	$64,300	OK	$51,100
AZ	$54,340	MD	$66,960	OR	$52,770
CA	$68,160	ME	$57,070	PA	$57,130
CO	$66,400	MI	$56,670	RI	$67,290
CT	$57,660	MN	$60,550	SC	$40,300
DC	$76,370	MO	$50,410	SD	$57,410
DE	$62,340	MS	$51,450	TN	$63,080
FL	$54,140	MT	$49,920	TX	$54,170
GA	$54,260	NC	$54,470	UT	$52,850
HI	$61,420	ND	$52,390	VA	$57,470
IA	$54,920	NE	$47,590	VT	$47,480
ID	$57,670	NH	$59,970	WA	$60,540
IL	$65,610	NJ	$66,100	WI	$55,440
IN	$46,350	NM	$53,200	WV	$63,200
KS	$48,090	NV	$59,530	WY	$60,980

Median Wages for the Largest Metropolitan Areas (Annual)

AZ: Phoenix	$57,270	MI: Detroit	$55,280
CA: Los Angeles	$65,750	MN: Minneapolis	$63,960
CA: Riverside	$66,460	MO: Kansas City	$57,990
CA: Sacramento	$65,880	MO: St. Louis	$55,650
CA: San Diego	$66,760	NV: Las Vegas	$59,760
CA: San Francisco	$75,330	NY: New York	$62,670
CO: Denver	$71,850	OH: Cincinnati	$65,460
DC: Washington	$69,840	OH: Cleveland	$64,510
FL: Miami	$50,440	OH: Columbus	$64,720
FL: Orlando	$55,310	OR: Portland	$55,340
FL: Tampa	$54,770	PA: Philadelphia	$63,410
GA: Atlanta	$49,530	PA: Pittsburgh	$58,310
IL: Chicago	$65,680	TX: Dallas	$56,580
MA: Boston	$65,770	TX: Houston	$59,810
MD: Baltimore	$64,110	WA: Seattle	$61,780

FACTORS THAT MAY AFFECT EARNINGS

Educational Attainment of Workers and Effect on Earnings

Figures are based on a group of occupations: Other Healthcare Practitioners and Technical Occupations

	Percent at Level	Effect on Earnings
Less than High School	—	—
Some High School	—	—
High School or Equivalent	16.3%	−20.7%
Some College but No Degree	15.0%	−14.2%
Associate Degree	—	—
Bachelor's Degree	33.8%	13.5%
Master's Degree	23.8%	10.3%
Doctoral Degree	—	—
First Professional Degree	—	—

Figures do not total 100% because some levels have a very small sample size.

Flexibility of Earnings

Average Hours Worked: 35
Workers with a Varying Number of Hours: 9.8%
Workers Earning Some Overtime Pay, Tips, or Commissions: 6.9%
Earnings Benefit of Working Overtime: −11.5%

Gender

	Male	Female
Percent	63.9%	36.1%
Effect on Earnings	21.3%	−5.0%

Union Membership

Percentage Union Members: 18.4%
Earnings Benefit of Union Membership: 7.6%

Veteran Status

Percentage Who Have Been on Active Duty: 13.8%
Earnings Benefit of Veteran Status: 6.9%

29-9012 Occupational Health and Safety Technicians

Collect data on work environments for analysis by occupational health and safety specialists. Implement and conduct evaluation of programs designed to limit chemical, physical, biological, and ergonomic risks to workers.

- Education or Training Required: Postsecondary vocational training
- Job Growth: 17.1%
- Annual Openings: 1,000
- Self-Employed: 0.0%
- Part-Time: 28.9%

NATIONAL WAGE FIGURES (ANNUAL)

Beginning	25th Percentile	Median	Mean	75th Percentile	90th Percentile
$25,240	$32,550	$42,160	$44,340	$53,840	$68,640

Median Wages for Industries Employing Largest Numbers (Annual)

Industry	Median Income
Insurance Carriers and Related Activities	$60,130
Chemical Manufacturing	$51,600
Utilities	$50,370
Computer and Electronic Product Manufacturing	$49,210
Support Activities for Mining	$48,750
Management of Companies and Enterprises	$47,240
Mining (Except Oil and Gas)	$47,240
Oil and Gas Extraction	$46,980
Ambulatory Health Care Services	$44,250
Nonmetallic Mineral Product Manufacturing	$44,070

Median Wages for States (Annual)

State		State		State	
AK	no data	KY	$42,980	NY	$42,890
AL	$40,290	LA	$43,730	OH	$43,900
AR	$28,640	MA	$44,100	OK	$38,280
AZ	$65,480	MD	$45,160	OR	$52,660
CA	$44,220	ME	no data	PA	no data
CO	$49,920	MI	$34,440	RI	no data
CT	$49,570	MN	$44,560	SC	no data
DC	no data	MO	no data	SD	no data
DE	no data	MS	$30,630	TN	$45,110
FL	$40,220	MT	$22,750	TX	$41,900
GA	$32,260	NC	$38,170	UT	$29,650
HI	no data	ND	no data	VA	$46,720
IA	$41,700	NE	$36,090	VT	no data
ID	no data	NH	no data	WA	$42,430
IL	$44,350	NJ	$38,360	WI	$43,010
IN	$38,070	NM	$51,050	WV	$62,820
KS	$41,900	NV	$42,390	WY	$34,860

Median Wages for the Largest Metropolitan Areas (Annual)

Area		Area	
AZ: Phoenix	no data	MI: Detroit	$35,340
CA: Los Angeles	$50,490	MN: Minneapolis	$47,590
CA: Riverside	$40,770	MO: Kansas City	$38,430
CA: Sacramento	no data	MO: St. Louis	no data
CA: San Diego	$44,780	NV: Las Vegas	$43,410
CA: San Francisco	$46,260	NY: New York	$42,460
CO: Denver	$57,520	OH: Cincinnati	$47,770
DC: Washington	$45,420	OH: Cleveland	$44,720
FL: Miami	$76,450	OH: Columbus	$46,990
FL: Orlando	$39,260	OR: Portland	$49,920
FL: Tampa	$38,480	PA: Philadelphia	$45,470
GA: Atlanta	no data	PA: Pittsburgh	$47,140
IL: Chicago	$44,970	TX: Dallas	$39,730
MA: Boston	$44,540	TX: Houston	$43,150
MD: Baltimore	$52,990	WA: Seattle	$42,970

FACTORS THAT MAY AFFECT EARNINGS

Educational Attainment of Workers and Effect on Earnings

Figures are based on a group of occupations: Other Healthcare Practitioners and Technical Occupations

	Percent at Level	Effect on Earnings
Less than High School	—	—
Some High School	—	—
High School or Equivalent	16.3%	−20.7%
Some College but No Degree	15.0%	−14.2%
Associate Degree	—	—
Bachelor's Degree	33.8%	13.5%
Master's Degree	23.8%	10.3%
Doctoral Degree	—	—
First Professional Degree	—	—

Figures do not total 100% because some levels have a very small sample size.

Flexibility of Earnings

Average Hours Worked: 35
Workers with a Varying Number of Hours: 9.8%
Workers Earning Some Overtime Pay, Tips, or Commissions: 6.9%
Earnings Benefit of Working Overtime: −11.5%

Gender

	Male	Female
Percent	63.9%	36.1%
Effect on Earnings	21.3%	−5.0%

Union Membership

Percentage Union Members: 18.4%
Earnings Benefit of Union Membership: 7.6%

Veteran Status

Percentage Who Have Been on Active Duty: 13.8%
Earnings Benefit of Veteran Status: 6.9%

29-9091 Athletic Trainers

Evaluate, advise, and treat athletes to assist recovery from injury, avoid injury, or maintain peak physical fitness.

- Education or Training Required: Bachelor's degree
- Job Growth: 29.3%
- Annual Openings: 1,000
- Self-Employed: 4.0%
- Part-Time: 28.9%

NATIONAL WAGE FIGURES (ANNUAL)

Beginning	25th Percentile	Median	Mean	75th Percentile	90th Percentile
$21,940	$28,920	$36,560	$38,860	$45,690	$57,580

Median Wages for Industries Employing Largest Numbers (Annual)

Industry	Median Income
Educational Services	$39,650
Hospitals	$38,110
Performing Arts, Spectator Sports, and Related Industries	$38,030
Ambulatory Health Care Services	$35,910
Administrative and Support Services	$35,760
Religious, Grantmaking, Civic, Professional, and Similar Organizations	$35,330
Nursing and Residential Care Facilities	$30,600
Amusement, Gambling, and Recreation Industries	$30,400

Median Wages for States (Annual)

AK	no data	KY	$37,460	NY	$33,890
AL	$33,400	LA	$37,530	OH	$40,080
AR	$42,480	MA	$38,410	OK	$27,460
AZ	$35,290	MD	no data	OR	$36,900
CA	$28,620	ME	$36,720	PA	$35,060
CO	$36,230	MI	$41,500	RI	$40,410
CT	$37,010	MN	$36,570	SC	no data
DC	$44,130	MO	$34,530	SD	$32,060
DE	$43,920	MS	$37,460	TN	$35,770
FL	$33,730	MT	$26,670	TX	$36,970
GA	$35,800	NC	$33,320	UT	no data
HI	no data	ND	$33,140	VA	$33,930
IA	$33,600	NE	$40,470	VT	$39,430
ID	no data	NH	$40,280	WA	$40,180
IL	$35,170	NJ	$46,800	WI	$41,820
IN	$34,960	NM	$32,690	WV	$31,300
KS	$38,590	NV	$32,120	WY	no data

Median Wages for the Largest Metropolitan Areas (Annual)

AZ: Phoenix	$35,100	MI: Detroit	$42,370
CA: Los Angeles	$22,860	MN: Minneapolis	$35,290
CA: Riverside	$28,610	MO: Kansas City	$35,870
CA: Sacramento	$41,050	MO: St. Louis	$35,390
CA: San Diego	$46,690	NV: Las Vegas	$37,470
CA: San Francisco	$41,960	NY: New York	$42,040
CO: Denver	$30,510	OH: Cincinnati	$41,690
DC: Washington	$42,740	OH: Cleveland	$39,150
FL: Miami	$39,370	OH: Columbus	$39,830
FL: Orlando	$39,740	OR: Portland	$34,560
FL: Tampa	$33,260	PA: Philadelphia	$36,410
GA: Atlanta	$37,160	PA: Pittsburgh	no data
IL: Chicago	$37,840	TX: Dallas	$33,500
MA: Boston	$38,290	TX: Houston	$42,070
MD: Baltimore	no data	WA: Seattle	$39,850

FACTORS THAT MAY AFFECT EARNINGS

Educational Attainment of Workers and Effect on Earnings

Figures are based on a group of occupations: Other Healthcare Practitioners and Technical Occupations

	Percent at Level	Effect on Earnings
Less than High School	—	—
Some High School	—	—
High School or Equivalent	16.3%	−20.7%
Some College but No Degree	15.0%	−14.2%
Associate Degree	—	—
Bachelor's Degree	33.8%	13.5%
Master's Degree	23.8%	10.3%
Doctoral Degree	—	—
First Professional Degree	—	—

Figures do not total 100% because some levels have a very small sample size.

Flexibility of Earnings

Average Hours Worked: 35
Workers with a Varying Number of Hours: 9.8%
Workers Earning Some Overtime Pay, Tips, or Commissions: 6.9%
Earnings Benefit of Working Overtime: −11.5%

Gender

	Male	Female
Percent	63.9%	36.1%
Effect on Earnings	21.3%	−5.0%

Union Membership

Percentage Union Members: 18.4%
Earnings Benefit of Union Membership: 7.6%

Veteran Status

Percentage Who Have Been on Active Duty: 13.8%
Earnings Benefit of Veteran Status: 6.9%

29-9099 Healthcare Practitioners and Technical Workers, All Other

All healthcare practitioners and technical workers not listed separately.

- Education or Training Required: Postsecondary vocational training
- Job Growth: 23.8%
- Annual Openings: 5,000
- Self-Employed: 0.0%
- Part-Time: 28.9%

NATIONAL WAGE FIGURES (ANNUAL)

Beginning	25th Percentile	Median	Mean	75th Percentile	90th Percentile
$21,720	$27,040	$37,200	$45,090	$56,890	$81,910

Note: The mean is significantly higher than the median because of the presence of a few star earners.

Median Wages for Industries Employing Largest Numbers (Annual)

Industry	Median Income
Utilities	$68,240
Federal, State, and Local Government	$56,450
Management of Companies and Enterprises	$51,980
Chemical Manufacturing	$48,410
Insurance Carriers and Related Activities	$48,320
Merchant Wholesalers, Durable Goods	$46,210
Professional, Scientific, and Technical Services	$45,390
Social Assistance	$44,560
Wholesale Electronic Markets and Agents and Brokers	$43,860
Miscellaneous Manufacturing	$43,410

Median Wages for States (Annual)

AK	$47,370	KY	$34,540	NY	$66,070
AL	$27,460	LA	$25,090	OH	$35,260
AR	$29,640	MA	$50,000	OK	$28,460
AZ	$30,130	MD	no data	OR	$36,280
CA	$54,610	ME	$34,020	PA	$38,090
CO	$42,110	MI	$40,950	RI	$42,380
CT	$69,390	MN	$45,970	SC	$35,950
DC	$45,660	MO	$32,540	SD	no data
DE	$29,860	MS	$28,110	TN	$35,280
FL	$31,850	MT	$27,250	TX	$39,530
GA	$29,050	NC	$35,090	UT	$35,790
HI	$65,720	ND	$47,450	VA	$47,060
IA	$29,740	NE	no data	VT	$40,820
ID	$44,710	NH	$48,850	WA	$46,450
IL	$31,310	NJ	$68,940	WI	$34,270
IN	$28,330	NM	$26,070	WV	$28,240
KS	$31,700	NV	$35,750	WY	$31,600

Median Wages for the Largest Metropolitan Areas (Annual)

AZ: Phoenix	$30,220	MI: Detroit	$48,390
CA: Los Angeles	$60,360	MN: Minneapolis	$45,760
CA: Riverside	$41,490	MO: Kansas City	$30,130
CA: Sacramento	no data	MO: St. Louis	$36,370
CA: San Diego	$48,820	NV: Las Vegas	$35,570
CA: San Francisco	$52,820	NY: New York	no data
CO: Denver	$47,420	OH: Cincinnati	$48,360
DC: Washington	no data	OH: Cleveland	$54,230
FL: Miami	$33,570	OH: Columbus	$33,690
FL: Orlando	$33,730	OR: Portland	$43,540
FL: Tampa	$28,620	PA: Philadelphia	$39,980
GA: Atlanta	$30,370	PA: Pittsburgh	$38,360
IL: Chicago	$32,390	TX: Dallas	no data
MA: Boston	$50,970	TX: Houston	$32,750
MD: Baltimore	$48,480	WA: Seattle	$48,180

FACTORS THAT MAY AFFECT EARNINGS

Educational Attainment of Workers and Effect on Earnings

Figures are based on a group of occupations: Other Healthcare Practitioners and Technical Occupations

	Percent at Level	Effect on Earnings
Less than High School	—	—
Some High School	—	—
High School or Equivalent	16.3%	−20.7%
Some College but No Degree	15.0%	−14.2%
Associate Degree	—	—
Bachelor's Degree	33.8%	13.5%
Master's Degree	23.8%	10.3%
Doctoral Degree	—	—
First Professional Degree	—	—

Figures do not total 100% because some levels have a very small sample size.

Flexibility of Earnings

Average Hours Worked: 35
Workers with a Varying Number of Hours: 9.8%
Workers Earning Some Overtime Pay, Tips, or Commissions: 6.9%
Earnings Benefit of Working Overtime: −11.5%

Gender

	Male	Female
Percent	63.9%	36.1%
Effect on Earnings	21.3%	−5.0%

Union Membership

Percentage Union Members: 18.4%
Earnings Benefit of Union Membership: 7.6%

Veteran Status

Percentage Who Have Been on Active Duty: 13.8%
Earnings Benefit of Veteran Status: 6.9%

31-0000: Healthcare Support Occupations

31-1000 Nursing, Psychiatric, and Home Health Aides

31-1011 Home Health Aides

Provide routine, personal health care, such as bathing, dressing, or grooming, to elderly, convalescent, or disabled persons in the home of patients or in a residential care facility.

- Education or Training Required: Short-term on-the-job training
- Job Growth: 56.0%
- Annual Openings: 170,000
- Self-Employed: 1.4%
- Part-Time: 32.7%

NATIONAL WAGE FIGURES (ANNUAL)

Beginning	25th Percentile	Median	Mean	75th Percentile	90th Percentile
$14,680	$16,610	$19,420	$20,100	$22,670	$27,030

Median Wages for Industries Employing Largest Numbers (Annual)

Industry	Median Income
Funds, Trusts, and Other Financial Vehicles	$34,360
Federal, State, and Local Government	$25,590
Educational Services	$23,490
Accommodation	$23,190
Heavy and Civil Engineering Construction	$22,320
Hospitals	$22,120
Health and Personal Care Stores	$21,930
Religious, Grantmaking, Civic, Professional, and Similar Organizations	$21,890
Administrative and Support Services	$20,930
Securities, Commodity Contracts, and Other Financial Investments and Related Activities	$20,530

Median Wages for States (Annual)

State	Wage	State	Wage	State	Wage
AK	$25,200	KY	$20,150	NY	$20,180
AL	$16,160	LA	$14,920	OH	$19,310
AR	$16,920	MA	$24,190	OK	$18,100
AZ	$19,820	MD	$21,120	OR	$18,970
CA	$19,510	ME	$20,770	PA	$19,150
CO	$21,720	MI	$19,170	RI	$24,340
CT	$25,030	MN	$21,980	SC	$17,620
DC	$18,960	MO	$17,450	SD	$20,430
DE	$21,680	MS	$16,810	TN	$17,660
FL	$19,630	MT	$17,790	TX	$14,910
GA	$17,430	NC	$18,150	UT	$18,550
HI	$24,450	ND	$19,810	VA	$18,010
IA	$19,580	NE	$21,460	VT	$20,610
ID	$18,350	NH	$22,080	WA	$20,510
IL	$20,140	NJ	$21,540	WI	$20,660
IN	$19,560	NM	$17,960	WV	$15,340
KS	$18,720	NV	$21,570	WY	$20,180

Median Wages for the Largest Metropolitan Areas (Annual)

Area	Wage	Area	Wage
AZ: Phoenix	$20,090	MI: Detroit	$19,330
CA: Los Angeles	$20,020	MN: Minneapolis	$23,190
CA: Riverside	$18,470	MO: Kansas City	$21,020
CA: Sacramento	$18,940	MO: St. Louis	$17,790
CA: San Diego	$20,770	NV: Las Vegas	$21,400
CA: San Francisco	$21,670	NY: New York	$20,120
CO: Denver	$23,690	OH: Cincinnati	$21,190
DC: Washington	$20,720	OH: Cleveland	$19,730
FL: Miami	$18,400	OH: Columbus	$20,390
FL: Orlando	$20,200	OR: Portland	$19,740
FL: Tampa	$21,770	PA: Philadelphia	$21,370
GA: Atlanta	$18,800	PA: Pittsburgh	$18,550
IL: Chicago	$20,330	TX: Dallas	$19,420
MA: Boston	$24,390	TX: Houston	$15,880
MD: Baltimore	$21,120	WA: Seattle	$22,050

FACTORS THAT MAY AFFECT EARNINGS

Educational Attainment of Workers and Effect on Earnings

Figures are based on a group of occupations: Nursing, Psychiatric, and Home Health Aides

	Percent at Level	Effect on Earnings
Less than High School	4.1%	−16.8%
Some High School	11.2%	−13.1%
High School or Equivalent	35.5%	−2.7%
Some College but No Degree	28.0%	−2.2%
Associate Degree	11.7%	−0.2%
Bachelor's Degree	7.5%	38.0%
Master's Degree	1.5%	44.2%
Doctoral Degree	—	—
First Professional Degree	—	—

Flexibility of Earnings

Average Hours Worked: 30
Workers with a Varying Number of Hours: 8.2%
Workers Earning Some Overtime Pay, Tips, or Commissions: 9.2%
Earnings Benefit of Working Overtime: 0.9%

Gender

	Male	Female
Percent	11.1%	88.9%
Effect on Earnings	17.8%	−1.3%

Union Membership

Percentage Union Members: 11.9%
Earnings Benefit of Union Membership: 22.6%

Veteran Status

Percentage Who Have Been on Active Duty: Insignificant
Earnings Benefit of Veteran Status: No significant data available

31-1012 Nursing Aides, Orderlies, and Attendants

Provide basic patient care under direction of nursing staff. Perform duties such as feeding, bathing, dressing, grooming, or moving patients or changing linens.

- Education or Training Required: Postsecondary vocational training
- Job Growth: 22.3%
- Annual Openings: 307,000
- Self-Employed: 1.9%
- Part-Time: 32.7%

NATIONAL WAGE FIGURES (ANNUAL)

Beginning	25th Percentile	Median	Mean	75th Percentile	90th Percentile
$16,190	$18,900	$22,180	$22,960	$26,630	$31,190

Median Wages for Industries Employing Largest Numbers (Annual)

Industry	Median Income
Federal, State, and Local Government	$26,630
Professional, Scientific, and Technical Services	$24,770
Educational Services	$24,080
Insurance Carriers and Related Activities	$24,020
Administrative and Support Services	$23,890
Religious, Grantmaking, Civic, Professional, and Similar Organizations	$23,710
Hospitals	$23,000
Ambulatory Health Care Services	$22,390
Management Companies and Enterprises	$21,630
Nursing and Residential Care Facilities	$21,420

Median Wages for States (Annual)

AK	$29,870	KY	$20,630	NY	$28,340
AL	$18,220	LA	$15,750	OH	$22,280
AR	$18,170	MA	$26,560	OK	$17,940
AZ	$22,020	MD	$25,890	OR	$23,030
CA	$23,590	ME	$21,720	PA	$23,320
CO	$24,110	MI	$24,140	RI	$25,250
CT	$28,150	MN	$25,080	SC	$19,180
DC	$25,940	MO	$19,560	SD	$19,920
DE	$25,630	MS	$16,970	TN	$20,300
FL	$21,500	MT	$19,770	TX	$19,620
GA	$18,890	NC	$21,130	UT	$19,890
HI	$26,070	ND	$21,430	VA	$21,150
IA	$21,860	NE	$21,600	VT	$22,180
ID	$19,200	NH	$25,460	WA	$23,910
IL	$21,010	NJ	$24,780	WI	$23,820
IN	$21,550	NM	$20,530	WV	$18,260
KS	$20,600	NV	$25,440	WY	$21,710

Median Wages for the Largest Metropolitan Areas (Annual)

AZ: Phoenix	$22,250	MI: Detroit	$24,980
CA: Los Angeles	$21,820	MN: Minneapolis	$27,970
CA: Riverside	$22,290	MO: Kansas City	$22,600
CA: Sacramento	$26,390	MO: St. Louis	$21,260
CA: San Diego	$23,260	NV: Las Vegas	$25,690
CA: San Francisco	$28,780	NY: New York	$29,470
CO: Denver	$26,100	OH: Cincinnati	$23,580
DC: Washington	$25,880	OH: Cleveland	$22,590
FL: Miami	$21,020	OH: Columbus	$23,470
FL: Orlando	$21,340	OR: Portland	$24,470
FL: Tampa	$22,120	PA: Philadelphia	$24,930
GA: Atlanta	$21,190	PA: Pittsburgh	$22,480
IL: Chicago	$21,830	TX: Dallas	$21,280
MA: Boston	$27,010	TX: Houston	$20,830
MD: Baltimore	$26,010	WA: Seattle	$26,370

FACTORS THAT MAY AFFECT EARNINGS

Educational Attainment of Workers and Effect on Earnings

Figures are based on a group of occupations: Nursing, Psychiatric, and Home Health Aides

	Percent at Level	Effect on Earnings
Less than High School	4.1%	−16.8%
Some High School	11.2%	−13.1%
High School or Equivalent	35.5%	−2.7%
Some College but No Degree	28.0%	−2.2%
Associate Degree	11.7%	−0.2%
Bachelor's Degree	7.5%	38.0%
Master's Degree	1.5%	44.2%
Doctoral Degree	—	—
First Professional Degree	—	—

Flexibility of Earnings

Average Hours Worked: 30
Workers with a Varying Number of Hours: 8.2%
Workers Earning Some Overtime Pay, Tips, or Commissions: 9.2%
Earnings Benefit of Working Overtime: 0.9%

Gender

	Male	Female
Percent	11.1%	88.9%
Effect on Earnings	17.8%	−1.3%

Union Membership

Percentage Union Members: 11.9%
Earnings Benefit of Union Membership: 22.6%

Veteran Status

Percentage Who Have Been on Active Duty: Insignificant
Earnings Benefit of Veteran Status: No significant data available

31-1013 Psychiatric Aides

Assist mentally impaired or emotionally disturbed patients, working under direction of nursing and medical staff.

- Education or Training Required: Short-term on-the-job training
- Job Growth: 2.3%
- Annual Openings: 10,000
- Self-Employed: 2.3%
- Part-Time: 32.7%

NATIONAL WAGE FIGURES (ANNUAL)

Beginning	25th Percentile	Median	Mean	75th Percentile	90th Percentile
$16,120	$19,130	$23,900	$24,990	$30,080	$36,020

Median Wages for Industries Employing Largest Numbers (Annual)

Industry	Median Income
Federal, State, and Local Government	$27,160
Hospitals	$24,650
Social Assistance	$22,910
Educational Services	$21,650
Ambulatory Health Care Services	$20,980
Nursing and Residential Care Facilities	$19,680

Median Wages for States (Annual)

State	Wage	State	Wage	State	Wage
AK	$33,840	KY	$18,220	NY	$31,830
AL	$20,140	LA	$19,120	OH	$18,820
AR	$16,780	MA	$28,270	OK	$19,620
AZ	$21,180	MD	$25,250	OR	no data
CA	$24,240	ME	$29,130	PA	$25,930
CO	$23,380	MI	no data	RI	no data
CT	$27,460	MN	$25,980	SC	no data
DC	$29,680	MO	$19,940	SD	$23,380
DE	no data	MS	$17,410	TN	no data
FL	$21,240	MT	$24,480	TX	$20,080
GA	$22,560	NC	$21,630	UT	$17,480
HI	$30,950	ND	no data	VA	$21,050
IA	$26,730	NE	no data	VT	no data
ID	$22,900	NH	$26,690	WA	no data
IL	$21,440	NJ	$30,170	WI	$21,050
IN	$22,830	NM	$25,320	WV	$15,760
KS	$21,640	NV	no data	WY	no data

Median Wages for the Largest Metropolitan Areas (Annual)

Area	Wage	Area	Wage
AZ: Phoenix	$21,180	MI: Detroit	no data
CA: Los Angeles	$23,920	MN: Minneapolis	$26,040
CA: Riverside	no data	MO: Kansas City	$21,930
CA: Sacramento	no data	MO: St. Louis	$19,800
CA: San Diego	$28,610	NV: Las Vegas	no data
CA: San Francisco	$23,720	NY: New York	$31,650
CO: Denver	$21,740	OH: Cincinnati	no data
DC: Washington	$28,580	OH: Cleveland	$17,250
FL: Miami	$20,930	OH: Columbus	$24,440
FL: Orlando	no data	OR: Portland	$29,360
FL: Tampa	$20,270	PA: Philadelphia	$26,620
GA: Atlanta	no data	PA: Pittsburgh	no data
IL: Chicago	$22,760	TX: Dallas	$20,870
MA: Boston	$28,660	TX: Houston	$20,620
MD: Baltimore	$26,040	WA: Seattle	no data

FACTORS THAT MAY AFFECT EARNINGS

Educational Attainment of Workers and Effect on Earnings

Figures are based on a group of occupations: Nursing, Psychiatric, and Home Health Aides

	Percent at Level	Effect on Earnings
Less than High School	4.1%	−16.8%
Some High School	11.2%	−13.1%
High School or Equivalent	35.5%	−2.7%
Some College but No Degree	28.0%	−2.2%
Associate Degree	11.7%	−0.2%
Bachelor's Degree	7.5%	38.0%
Master's Degree	1.5%	44.2%
Doctoral Degree	—	—
First Professional Degree	—	—

Flexibility of Earnings

Average Hours Worked: 30
Workers with a Varying Number of Hours: 8.2%
Workers Earning Some Overtime Pay, Tips, or Commissions: 9.2%
Earnings Benefit of Working Overtime: 0.9%

Gender

	Male	Female
Percent	11.1%	88.9%
Effect on Earnings	17.8%	−1.3%

Union Membership

Percentage Union Members: 11.9%
Earnings Benefit of Union Membership: 22.6%

Veteran Status

Percentage Who Have Been on Active Duty: Insignificant
Earnings Benefit of Veteran Status: No significant data available

31-2000 Occupational and Physical Therapist Assistants and Aides

31-2011 Occupational Therapist Assistants

Assist occupational therapists in providing occupational therapy treatments and procedures. May, in accordance with state laws, assist in development of treatment plans, carry out routine functions, direct activity programs, and document the progress of treatments. Generally requires formal training.

- Education or Training Required: Associate degree
- Job Growth: 34.1%
- Annual Openings: 2,000
- Self-Employed: 0.0%
- Part-Time: 34.3%

NATIONAL WAGE FIGURES (ANNUAL)

Beginning	25th Percentile	Median	Mean	75th Percentile	90th Percentile
$26,050	$34,130	$42,060	$42,110	$50,230	$58,270

Median Wages for Industries Employing Largest Numbers (Annual)

Industry	Median Income
Administrative and Support Services	$46,160
Ambulatory Health Care Services	$44,670
Nursing and Residential Care Facilities	$42,990
Management of Companies and Enterprises	$40,720
Hospitals	$40,260
Federal, State, and Local Government	$39,690
Professional, Scientific, and Technical Services	$38,860
Educational Services	$37,170
Social Assistance	$33,180

Median Wages for States (Annual)

State	Wage	State	Wage	State	Wage
AK	no data	KY	$44,430	NY	$39,130
AL	$44,110	LA	$42,040	OH	$44,220
AR	$39,700	MA	$41,290	OK	$42,160
AZ	$45,120	MD	$38,190	OR	$42,790
CA	$50,540	ME	$40,870	PA	$39,550
CO	$39,050	MI	$39,620	RI	$38,840
CT	$45,200	MN	$36,400	SC	$40,590
DC	$36,470	MO	$39,090	SD	$28,720
DE	$43,480	MS	$40,190	TN	$45,920
FL	$50,110	MT	$27,820	TX	$45,580
GA	$38,450	NC	$40,310	UT	$41,210
HI	$35,880	ND	$32,370	VA	$44,200
IA	$37,070	NE	$35,800	VT	$35,090
ID	$31,650	NH	$36,070	WA	$43,010
IL	$39,230	NJ	$45,600	WI	$36,740
IN	$41,060	NM	$38,800	WV	$41,080
KS	$41,170	NV	no data	WY	no data

Median Wages for the Largest Metropolitan Areas (Annual)

Area	Wage	Area	Wage
AZ: Phoenix	$46,230	MI: Detroit	$40,460
CA: Los Angeles	$50,900	MN: Minneapolis	$37,330
CA: Riverside	$53,140	MO: Kansas City	$40,520
CA: Sacramento	$53,950	MO: St. Louis	$39,440
CA: San Diego	$49,680	NV: Las Vegas	no data
CA: San Francisco	$49,650	NY: New York	$45,540
CO: Denver	$38,470	OH: Cincinnati	$43,840
DC: Washington	$42,460	OH: Cleveland	$46,260
FL: Miami	$52,330	OH: Columbus	$43,640
FL: Orlando	$44,480	OR: Portland	$43,340
FL: Tampa	$50,490	PA: Philadelphia	$45,010
GA: Atlanta	$40,010	PA: Pittsburgh	$39,320
IL: Chicago	$44,010	TX: Dallas	$48,520
MA: Boston	$42,520	TX: Houston	$40,890
MD: Baltimore	$39,760	WA: Seattle	$43,110

FACTORS THAT MAY AFFECT EARNINGS

Educational Attainment of Workers and Effect on Earnings

Figures are based on a group of occupations: Occupational and Physical Therapist Assistants and Aides

	Percent at Level	Effect on Earnings
Less than High School	—	—
Some High School	—	—
High School or Equivalent	15.1%	−26.4%
Some College but No Degree	14.2%	−36.9%
Associate Degree	46.2%	12.0%
Bachelor's Degree	18.9%	12.8%
Master's Degree	—	—
Doctoral Degree	—	—
First Professional Degree	—	—

Figures do not total 100% because some levels have a very small sample size.

Flexibility of Earnings

Average Hours Worked: 33
Workers with a Varying Number of Hours: 9.0%
Workers Earning Some Overtime Pay, Tips, or Commissions: 7.0%
Earnings Benefit of Working Overtime: 14.3%

Gender

	Male	Female
Percent	15.0%	85.0%
Effect on Earnings	18.7%	−1.4%

Union Membership

Percentage Union Members: Insignificant
Earnings Benefit of Union Membership: No significant data available

Veteran Status

Percentage Who Have Been on Active Duty: 4.3%
Earnings Benefit of Veteran Status: 61.3%

31-2012 Occupational Therapist Aides

Under close supervision of an occupational therapist or occupational therapy assistant, perform only delegated, selected, or routine tasks in specific situations. These duties include preparing patient and treatment room.

- Education or Training Required: Short-term on-the-job training
- Job Growth: 26.3%
- Annual Openings: Fewer than 500
- Self-Employed: 0.0%
- Part-Time: 34.3%

NATIONAL WAGE FIGURES (ANNUAL)

Beginning	25th Percentile	Median	Mean	75th Percentile	90th Percentile
$17,060	$20,460	$25,020	$27,760	$32,160	$44,130

Median Wages for Industries Employing Largest Numbers (Annual)

Industry	Median Income
Federal, State, and Local Government	$29,360
Ambulatory Health Care Services	$26,840
Hospitals	$25,890
Educational Services	$25,070
Nursing and Residential Care Facilities	$24,600
Social Assistance	$20,470

Median Wages for States (Annual)

State	Wage	State	Wage	State	Wage
AK	no data	KY	$25,670	NY	$28,880
AL	$20,770	LA	$22,700	OH	$25,460
AR	no data	MA	$26,610	OK	$19,460
AZ	$24,070	MD	$46,820	OR	no data
CA	$27,810	ME	$26,420	PA	$24,100
CO	$33,070	MI	$24,160	RI	no data
CT	$30,980	MN	$27,580	SC	$18,350
DC	$23,040	MO	$22,940	SD	no data
DE	no data	MS	$23,070	TN	$27,150
FL	$22,070	MT	no data	TX	$20,170
GA	$20,340	NC	$23,370	UT	$25,140
HI	$26,410	ND	no data	VA	$27,070
IA	$17,870	NE	$27,420	VT	no data
ID	no data	NH	no data	WA	$25,310
IL	$32,710	NJ	$25,920	WI	$21,970
IN	$22,850	NM	$19,340	WV	$22,750
KS	$23,020	NV	no data	WY	no data

Median Wages for the Largest Metropolitan Areas (Annual)

Area	Wage	Area	Wage
AZ: Phoenix	$23,350	MI: Detroit	$25,560
CA: Los Angeles	$26,140	MN: Minneapolis	$30,650
CA: Riverside	$25,580	MO: Kansas City	$21,990
CA: Sacramento	no data	MO: St. Louis	$25,810
CA: San Diego	$26,370	NV: Las Vegas	no data
CA: San Francisco	no data	NY: New York	$29,240
CO: Denver	no data	OH: Cincinnati	no data
DC: Washington	$23,880	OH: Cleveland	no data
FL: Miami	$21,460	OH: Columbus	no data
FL: Orlando	no data	OR: Portland	no data
FL: Tampa	no data	PA: Philadelphia	$28,470
GA: Atlanta	$19,570	PA: Pittsburgh	$23,520
IL: Chicago	$31,460	TX: Dallas	no data
MA: Boston	$28,090	TX: Houston	$18,750
MD: Baltimore	$49,410	WA: Seattle	$24,720

FACTORS THAT MAY AFFECT EARNINGS

Educational Attainment of Workers and Effect on Earnings

Figures are based on a group of occupations: Occupational and Physical Therapist Assistants and Aides

	Percent at Level	Effect on Earnings
Less than High School	—	—
Some High School	—	—
High School or Equivalent	15.1%	−26.4%
Some College but No Degree	14.2%	−36.9%
Associate Degree	46.2%	12.0%
Bachelor's Degree	18.9%	12.8%
Master's Degree	—	—
Doctoral Degree	—	—
First Professional Degree	—	—

Figures do not total 100% because some levels have a very small sample size.

Flexibility of Earnings

Average Hours Worked: 33
Workers with a Varying Number of Hours: 9.0%
Workers Earning Some Overtime Pay, Tips, or Commissions: 7.0%
Earnings Benefit of Working Overtime: 14.3%

Gender

	Male	Female
Percent	15.0%	85.0%
Effect on Earnings	18.7%	−1.4%

Union Membership

Percentage Union Members: Insignificant
Earnings Benefit of Union Membership: No significant data available

Veteran Status

Percentage Who Have Been on Active Duty: 4.3%
Earnings Benefit of Veteran Status: 61.3%

31-2021 *Physical Therapist Assistants*

Assist physical therapists in providing physical therapy treatments and procedures. May, in accordance with state laws, assist in the development of treatment plans, carry out routine functions, document the progress of treatment, and modify specific treatments in accordance with patient status and within the scope of treatment plans established by a physical therapist. Generally requires formal training.

- Education or Training Required: Associate degree
- Job Growth: 44.2%
- Annual Openings: 7,000
- Self-Employed: 0.2%
- Part-Time: 34.3%

NATIONAL WAGE FIGURES (ANNUAL)

Beginning	25th Percentile	Median	Mean	75th Percentile	90th Percentile
$26,190	$33,840	$41,360	$41,410	$49,010	$57,220

Median Wages for Industries Employing Largest Numbers (Annual)

Industry	Median Income
Administrative and Support Services	$45,760
Nursing and Residential Care Facilities	$44,400
Management of Companies and Enterprises	$44,100
Ambulatory Health Care Services	$41,070
Social Assistance	$40,720
Hospitals	$40,620
Insurance Carriers and Related Activities	$39,570
Educational Services	$39,310
Federal, State, and Local Government	$38,710
Amusement, Gambling, and Recreation Industries	$35,160

Median Wages for States (Annual)

AK	$39,490	KY	$40,070	NY	$40,550
AL	$42,780	LA	$40,080	OH	$42,820
AR	$38,680	MA	$44,060	OK	$38,280
AZ	$31,490	MD	$41,740	OR	$41,140
CA	$52,460	ME	$37,760	PA	$36,480
CO	$34,470	MI	$36,990	RI	$39,470
CT	$41,430	MN	$37,620	SC	$41,110
DC	$35,460	MO	$37,240	SD	$28,010
DE	$42,100	MS	$38,500	TN	$44,160
FL	$46,050	MT	$33,030	TX	$45,240
GA	$40,070	NC	$42,290	UT	$36,890
HI	$37,040	ND	$28,800	VA	$42,990
IA	$31,130	NE	$35,640	VT	$39,230
ID	$39,590	NH	$38,030	WA	$41,660
IL	$40,570	NJ	$41,430	WI	$38,910
IN	$44,180	NM	$35,940	WV	$35,470
KS	$40,090	NV	$43,790	WY	$35,490

Median Wages for the Largest Metropolitan Areas (Annual)

AZ: Phoenix	$30,000	MI: Detroit	$36,290
CA: Los Angeles	$54,810	MN: Minneapolis	$38,430
CA: Riverside	$51,560	MO: Kansas City	$40,220
CA: Sacramento	$47,790	MO: St. Louis	$39,600
CA: San Diego	$47,420	NV: Las Vegas	$44,050
CA: San Francisco	$56,630	NY: New York	$44,990
CO: Denver	$34,810	OH: Cincinnati	$44,530
DC: Washington	$37,400	OH: Cleveland	$43,330
FL: Miami	$49,070	OH: Columbus	$44,620
FL: Orlando	$44,830	OR: Portland	$40,500
FL: Tampa	$44,770	PA: Philadelphia	$39,870
GA: Atlanta	$45,150	PA: Pittsburgh	$36,020
IL: Chicago	$42,200	TX: Dallas	$47,370
MA: Boston	$43,690	TX: Houston	$42,630
MD: Baltimore	$49,800	WA: Seattle	$42,180

FACTORS THAT MAY AFFECT EARNINGS

Educational Attainment of Workers and Effect on Earnings

Figures are based on a group of occupations: Occupational and Physical Therapist Assistants and Aides

	Percent at Level	Effect on Earnings
Less than High School	—	—
Some High School	—	—
High School or Equivalent	15.1%	−26.4%
Some College but No Degree	14.2%	−36.9%
Associate Degree	46.2%	12.0%
Bachelor's Degree	18.9%	12.8%
Master's Degree	—	—
Doctoral Degree	—	—
First Professional Degree	—	—

Figures do not total 100% because some levels have a very small sample size.

Flexibility of Earnings

Average Hours Worked: 33
Workers with a Varying Number of Hours: 5.5%
Workers Earning Some Overtime Pay, Tips, or Commissions: 7.0%
Earnings Benefit of Working Overtime: 14.3%

Gender

	Male	Female
Percent	21.6%	78.4%
Effect on Earnings	18.7%	−1.4%

Union Membership

Percentage Union Members: Insignificant
Earnings Benefit of Union Membership: No significant data available

Veteran Status

Percentage Who Have Been on Active Duty: 4.3%
Earnings Benefit of Veteran Status: 61.3%

31-2022 Physical Therapist Aides

Under close supervision of a physical therapist or physical therapy assistant, perform only delegated, selected, or routine tasks in specific situations. These duties include preparing the patient and the treatment area.

- Education or Training Required: Short-term on-the-job training
- Job Growth: 34.4%
- Annual Openings: 5,000
- Self-Employed: 0.2%
- Part-Time: 34.3%

NATIONAL WAGE FIGURES (ANNUAL)

Beginning	25th Percentile	Median	Mean	75th Percentile	90th Percentile
$15,850	$18,550	$22,060	$23,290	$26,860	$32,600

Median Wages for Industries Employing Largest Numbers (Annual)

Industry	Median Income
Social Assistance	$25,240
Nursing and Residential Care Facilities	$24,130
Administrative and Support Services	$22,980
Hospitals	$22,900
Ambulatory Health Care Services	$21,470
Educational Services	$19,170
Amusement, Gambling, and Recreation Industries	$17,550

Median Wages for States (Annual)

State	Wage	State	Wage	State	Wage
AK	no data	KY	$19,730	NY	$24,070
AL	$18,670	LA	$18,050	OH	$22,440
AR	$18,610	MA	$26,620	OK	$18,310
AZ	$22,170	MD	$21,770	OR	$22,730
CA	$24,980	ME	$21,220	PA	$22,770
CO	$24,940	MI	$23,450	RI	$24,300
CT	$26,870	MN	$25,820	SC	$19,210
DC	$32,020	MO	$20,190	SD	$22,060
DE	$28,860	MS	$17,610	TN	$20,280
FL	$21,410	MT	$20,890	TX	$19,120
GA	$19,150	NC	$21,530	UT	$18,080
HI	$25,440	ND	$21,440	VA	$22,000
IA	$21,620	NE	$20,810	VT	$25,140
ID	$20,890	NH	$27,320	WA	$23,670
IL	$23,710	NJ	$22,020	WI	$24,140
IN	$21,530	NM	$23,800	WV	$21,340
KS	$21,200	NV	$23,620	WY	$20,770

Median Wages for the Largest Metropolitan Areas (Annual)

Area	Wage	Area	Wage
AZ: Phoenix	$22,160	MI: Detroit	$23,110
CA: Los Angeles	$25,540	MN: Minneapolis	$27,240
CA: Riverside	$23,870	MO: Kansas City	$22,740
CA: Sacramento	$23,340	MO: St. Louis	$21,860
CA: San Diego	$23,020	NV: Las Vegas	$24,200
CA: San Francisco	$30,170	NY: New York	$23,120
CO: Denver	$24,270	OH: Cincinnati	$23,120
DC: Washington	$23,260	OH: Cleveland	$23,310
FL: Miami	$22,290	OH: Columbus	$18,810
FL: Orlando	$19,600	OR: Portland	$24,170
FL: Tampa	$21,170	PA: Philadelphia	$22,780
GA: Atlanta	$21,510	PA: Pittsburgh	$22,890
IL: Chicago	$23,180	TX: Dallas	$21,490
MA: Boston	$26,150	TX: Houston	$20,960
MD: Baltimore	$20,210	WA: Seattle	$24,810

FACTORS THAT MAY AFFECT EARNINGS

Educational Attainment of Workers and Effect on Earnings

Figures are based on a group of occupations: Occupational and Physical Therapist Assistants and Aides

	Percent at Level	Effect on Earnings
Less than High School	—	—
Some High School	—	—
High School or Equivalent	15.1%	−26.4%
Some College but No Degree	14.2%	−36.9%
Associate Degree	46.2%	12.0%
Bachelor's Degree	18.9%	12.8%
Master's Degree	—	—
Doctoral Degree	—	—
First Professional Degree	—	—

Figures do not total 100% because some levels have a very small sample size.

Flexibility of Earnings

Average Hours Worked: 33
Workers with a Varying Number of Hours: 5.5%
Workers Earning Some Overtime Pay, Tips, or Commissions: 7.0%
Earnings Benefit of Working Overtime: 14.3%

Gender

	Male	Female
Percent	21.6%	78.4%
Effect on Earnings	18.7%	−1.4%

Union Membership

Percentage Union Members: Insignificant
Earnings Benefit of Union Membership: No significant data available

Veteran Status

Percentage Who Have Been on Active Duty: 4.3%
Earnings Benefit of Veteran Status: 61.3%

31-9000 Other Healthcare Support Occupations

31-9011 Massage Therapists

Massage customers for hygienic or remedial purposes.

- Education or Training Required: Postsecondary vocational training
- Job Growth: 23.6%
- Annual Openings: 12,000
- Self-Employed: 64.1%
- Part-Time: 48.3%

Note: A large fraction of the workforce for this occupation is self-employed and earns an average of $23,720. All other earnings figures for this occupation are based on workers who are paid a wage or salary.

NATIONAL WAGE FIGURES (ANNUAL)

Beginning	25th Percentile	Median	Mean	75th Percentile	90th Percentile
$15,550	$22,840	$33,400	$39,380	$50,370	$70,360

Median Wages for Industries Employing Largest Numbers (Annual)

Industry	Median Income
Management of Companies and Enterprises	$56,150
Performing Arts, Spectator Sports, and Related Industries	$45,570
Nursing and Residential Care Facilities	$45,150
Educational Services	$43,290
Hospitals	$39,400
Administrative and Support Services	$37,890
Ambulatory Health Care Services	$36,630
Religious, Grantmaking, Civic, Professional, and Similar Organizations	$35,490
Amusement, Gambling, and Recreation Industries	$35,280
Health and Personal Care Stores	$32,280

Median Wages for States (Annual)

AK	$51,130	KY	$25,840	NY	$44,150
AL	$32,620	LA	$30,490	OH	$35,310
AR	$38,070	MA	$45,380	OK	$25,810
AZ	$33,540	MD	$25,790	OR	$45,450
CA	$34,060	ME	$18,460	PA	$27,840
CO	$36,160	MI	no data	RI	$37,180
CT	$37,380	MN	$30,890	SC	$25,210
DC	$46,630	MO	$24,440	SD	$30,870
DE	$28,110	MS	$18,450	TN	$29,950
FL	$31,430	MT	$26,880	TX	$26,760
GA	$27,850	NC	$27,550	UT	$23,480
HI	$46,960	ND	$25,060	VA	$35,950
IA	$32,370	NE	$31,210	VT	$42,160
ID	$28,860	NH	$45,570	WA	$61,880
IL	$37,530	NJ	$42,310	WI	$32,090
IN	$28,810	NM	$26,250	WV	$28,810
KS	$29,560	NV	$17,620	WY	$24,290

Median Wages for the Largest Metropolitan Areas (Annual)

AZ: Phoenix	$36,030	MI: Detroit	$52,330
CA: Los Angeles	$28,970	MN: Minneapolis	$35,140
CA: Riverside	$29,610	MO: Kansas City	$24,180
CA: Sacramento	$45,100	MO: St. Louis	$22,310
CA: San Diego	$44,970	NV: Las Vegas	$17,900
CA: San Francisco	$46,930	NY: New York	$47,610
CO: Denver	$35,420	OH: Cincinnati	$25,640
DC: Washington	$28,640	OH: Cleveland	$80,700
FL: Miami	$34,100	OH: Columbus	$34,190
FL: Orlando	$32,200	OR: Portland	$52,110
FL: Tampa	$32,430	PA: Philadelphia	$38,520
GA: Atlanta	$30,490	PA: Pittsburgh	$26,740
IL: Chicago	$39,330	TX: Dallas	$28,510
MA: Boston	$46,230	TX: Houston	$26,380
MD: Baltimore	$29,360	WA: Seattle	$65,940

FACTORS THAT MAY AFFECT EARNINGS

Educational Attainment of Workers and Effect on Earnings

	Percent at Level	Effect on Earnings
Less than High School	—	—
Some High School	—	—
High School or Equivalent	21.3%	6.7%
Some College but No Degree	26.7%	−13.3%
Associate Degree	26.7%	−3.5%
Bachelor's Degree	21.3%	13.8%
Master's Degree	—	—
Doctoral Degree	—	—
First Professional Degree	—	—

Flexibility of Earnings

Average Hours Worked: 22
Workers with a Varying Number of Hours: 19.5%
Workers Earning Some Overtime Pay, Tips, or Commissions: 39.2%
Earnings Benefit of Working Overtime: 5.7%

Gender

	Male	Female
Percent	15.9%	84.1%
Effect on Earnings	18.7%	−1.4%

Union Membership

Percentage Union Members: Insignificant
Earnings Benefit of Union Membership: No significant data available

Veteran Status

Percentage Who Have Been on Active Duty: Insignificant
Earnings Benefit of Veteran Status: No significant data available

31-9091 Dental Assistants

Assist dentist, set up patient and equipment, and keep records.

- Education or Training Required: Moderate-term on-the-job training
- Job Growth: 42.7%
- Annual Openings: 45,000
- Self-Employed: 0.0%
- Part-Time: 41.9%

NATIONAL WAGE FIGURES (ANNUAL)

Beginning	25th Percentile	Median	Mean	75th Percentile	90th Percentile
$20,530	$24,820	$30,220	$30,850	$36,280	$43,040

Median Wages for Industries Employing Largest Numbers (Annual)

Industry	Median Income
Religious, Grantmaking, Civic, Professional, and Similar Organizations	$37,480
Administrative and Support Services	$33,930
Federal, State, and Local Government	$32,920
Professional, Scientific, and Technical Services	$32,670
Hospitals	$30,700
Ambulatory Health Care Services	$30,170
Educational Services	$28,790
Miscellaneous Manufacturing	$27,600
Social Assistance	$24,790
Management of Companies and Enterprises	$22,620

Median Wages for States (Annual)

State	Wage	State	Wage	State	Wage
AK	$36,730	KY	$27,540	NY	$30,370
AL	$23,920	LA	$24,690	OH	$29,380
AR	$24,120	MA	$35,620	OK	$26,240
AZ	$32,770	MD	$31,670	OR	$34,390
CA	$31,450	ME	$30,720	PA	$26,830
CO	$32,760	MI	$31,620	RI	$33,800
CT	$35,770	MN	$37,330	SC	$29,120
DC	$37,680	MO	$27,920	SD	$28,160
DE	$32,640	MS	$24,910	TN	$29,710
FL	$29,440	MT	$28,210	TX	$26,480
GA	$29,820	NC	$32,590	UT	$25,690
HI	$30,300	ND	$28,250	VA	$28,950
IA	$30,520	NE	$27,470	VT	$32,460
ID	$26,590	NH	$37,380	WA	$34,450
IL	$30,010	NJ	$34,980	WI	$29,170
IN	$31,100	NM	$28,650	WV	$23,470
KS	$27,830	NV	$34,080	WY	$22,930

Median Wages for the Largest Metropolitan Areas (Annual)

Metro Area	Wage	Metro Area	Wage
AZ: Phoenix	$33,250	MI: Detroit	$32,220
CA: Los Angeles	$29,910	MN: Minneapolis	$38,840
CA: Riverside	$28,190	MO: Kansas City	$29,530
CA: Sacramento	$35,110	MO: St. Louis	$28,410
CA: San Diego	$33,600	NV: Las Vegas	$33,420
CA: San Francisco	$34,730	NY: New York	$32,880
CO: Denver	$35,170	OH: Cincinnati	$32,050
DC: Washington	$33,520	OH: Cleveland	$28,180
FL: Miami	$28,800	OH: Columbus	$31,060
FL: Orlando	$32,810	OR: Portland	$35,370
FL: Tampa	$29,170	PA: Philadelphia	$30,400
GA: Atlanta	$32,160	PA: Pittsburgh	$25,930
IL: Chicago	$30,710	TX: Dallas	$28,940
MA: Boston	$36,390	TX: Houston	$23,240
MD: Baltimore	$32,110	WA: Seattle	$36,840

FACTORS THAT MAY AFFECT EARNINGS

Educational Attainment of Workers and Effect on Earnings

	Percent at Level	Effect on Earnings
Less than High School	—	—
Some High School	3.5%	−44.4%
High School or Equivalent	27.8%	−1.3%
Some College but No Degree	29.9%	−0.3%
Associate Degree	25.0%	3.5%
Bachelor's Degree	10.8%	7.8%
Master's Degree	—	—
Doctoral Degree	—	—
First Professional Degree	—	—

Flexibility of Earnings

Average Hours Worked: 31
Workers with a Varying Number of Hours: 6.8%
Workers Earning Some Overtime Pay, Tips, or Commissions: 6.0%
Earnings Benefit of Working Overtime: 5.7%

Gender

	Male	Female
Percent	4.6%	95.4%
Effect on Earnings	—	−0.2%

Union Membership

Percentage Union Members: Insignificant
Earnings Benefit of Union Membership: No significant data available

Veteran Status

Percentage Who Have Been on Active Duty: Insignificant
Earnings Benefit of Veteran Status: No significant data available

31-9092 Medical Assistants

Perform administrative and certain clinical duties under the direction of physician. Administrative duties may include scheduling appointments, maintaining medical records, billing, and coding for insurance purposes. Clinical duties may include taking and recording vital signs and medical histories, preparing patients for examination, drawing blood, and administering medications as directed by physician.

- Education or Training Required: Moderate-term on-the-job training
- Job Growth: 52.1%
- Annual Openings: 93,000
- Self-Employed: 0.0%
- Part-Time: 42.5%

NATIONAL WAGE FIGURES (ANNUAL)

Beginning	25th Percentile	Median	Mean	75th Percentile	90th Percentile
$18,860	$21,970	$26,290	$27,190	$31,210	$36,840

Median Wages for Industries Employing Largest Numbers (Annual)

Industry	Median Income
Insurance Carriers and Related Activities	$31,620
Professional, Scientific, and Technical Services	$29,160
Federal, State, and Local Government	$28,270
Hospitals	$27,330
Educational Services	$27,090
Social Assistance	$26,610
Health and Personal Care Stores	$26,570
Real Estate	$26,450
Administrative and Support Services	$26,370
Ambulatory Health Care Services	$26,170

Median Wages for States (Annual)

AK	$31,770	KY	$23,380	NY	$27,910
AL	$22,460	LA	$21,100	OH	$24,730
AR	$22,250	MA	$31,150	OK	$23,060
AZ	$26,830	MD	$27,180	OR	$29,580
CA	$28,720	ME	$26,880	PA	$24,950
CO	$28,330	MI	$26,470	RI	$27,070
CT	$31,040	MN	$29,410	SC	$25,110
DC	$33,540	MO	$24,390	SD	$22,760
DE	$28,180	MS	$21,900	TN	$24,010
FL	$25,410	MT	$24,130	TX	$22,720
GA	$26,680	NC	$25,850	UT	$23,230
HI	$29,400	ND	$24,810	VA	$25,080
IA	$25,620	NE	$24,170	VT	$26,810
ID	$27,320	NH	$28,490	WA	$30,440
IL	$27,420	NJ	$30,220	WI	$27,400
IN	$25,120	NM	$23,110	WV	$20,500
KS	$23,460	NV	$27,930	WY	$21,250

Median Wages for the Largest Metropolitan Areas (Annual)

AZ: Phoenix	$27,860	MI: Detroit	$26,930
CA: Los Angeles	$30,020	MN: Minneapolis	$30,770
CA: Riverside	$25,130	MO: Kansas City	$27,370
CA: Sacramento	$29,780	MO: St. Louis	$24,790
CA: San Diego	$26,680	NV: Las Vegas	$27,170
CA: San Francisco	$34,900	NY: New York	$29,650
CO: Denver	$30,380	OH: Cincinnati	$26,120
DC: Washington	$29,720	OH: Cleveland	$24,300
FL: Miami	$26,960	OH: Columbus	$25,970
FL: Orlando	$25,080	OR: Portland	$30,430
FL: Tampa	$25,090	PA: Philadelphia	$27,280
GA: Atlanta	$28,360	PA: Pittsburgh	$23,550
IL: Chicago	$27,940	TX: Dallas	$26,240
MA: Boston	$31,790	TX: Houston	$21,090
MD: Baltimore	$26,930	WA: Seattle	$32,860

FACTORS THAT MAY AFFECT EARNINGS

Educational Attainment of Workers and Effect on Earnings

Figures are based on a group of occupations: Medical Assistants and Other Healthcare Support Occupations

	Percent at Level	Effect on Earnings
Less than High School	1.0%	−8.6%
Some High School	9.2%	−33.3%
High School or Equivalent	24.5%	−6.5%
Some College but No Degree	28.1%	−5.0%
Associate Degree	22.6%	2.4%
Bachelor's Degree	10.8%	21.2%
Master's Degree	2.3%	67.0%
Doctoral Degree	—	—
First Professional Degree	1.3%	103.1%

Flexibility of Earnings

Average Hours Worked: 32
Workers with a Varying Number of Hours: 6.4%
Workers Earning Some Overtime Pay, Tips, or Commissions: 10.8%
Earnings Benefit of Working Overtime: 3.0%

Gender

	Male	Female
Percent	9.0%	91.0%
Effect on Earnings	18.7%	−1.4%

Union Membership

Percentage Union Members: 6.3%
Earnings Benefit of Union Membership: 16.0%

Veteran Status

Percentage Who Have Been on Active Duty: Insignificant
Earnings Benefit of Veteran Status: No significant data available

31-9093 Medical Equipment Preparers

Prepare, sterilize, install, or clean laboratory or health care equipment. May perform routine laboratory tasks and operate or inspect equipment.

- Education or Training Required: Short-term on-the-job training
- Job Growth: 20.0%
- Annual Openings: 8,000
- Self-Employed: 2.7%
- Part-Time: 42.5%

NATIONAL WAGE FIGURES (ANNUAL)

Beginning	25th Percentile	Median	Mean	75th Percentile	90th Percentile
$18,640	$21,550	$25,950	$26,980	$31,240	$37,140

Median Wages for Industries Employing Largest Numbers (Annual)

Industry	Median Income
Administrative and Support Services	$32,170
Miscellaneous Manufacturing	$31,350
Chemical Manufacturing	$30,330
Management of Companies and Enterprises	$30,000
Federal, State, and Local Government	$29,850
Rental and Leasing Services	$28,870
Health and Personal Care Stores	$26,710
Hospitals	$26,080
Nursing and Residential Care Facilities	$25,490
Professional, Scientific, and Technical Services	$25,390

Median Wages for States (Annual)

AK $32,360	KY $24,230	NY $32,020
AL $20,780	LA $20,120	OH $25,840
AR $21,010	MA $29,970	OK $21,520
AZ $25,070	MD $28,380	OR $26,350
CA $29,110	ME $27,220	PA $26,680
CO $26,600	MI $28,930	RI $28,690
CT $28,710	MN $30,690	SC $24,760
DC $27,390	MO $22,540	SD $25,070
DE $27,700	MS $18,690	TN $24,460
FL $22,290	MT $24,400	TX $23,940
GA $23,300	NC $24,810	UT no data
HI $28,970	ND $22,080	VA $25,310
IA $26,230	NE $25,890	VT no data
ID $24,550	NH $26,300	WA $28,660
IL $26,630	NJ $28,380	WI $27,600
IN $25,720	NM $22,820	WV $24,910
KS $25,640	NV $29,750	WY $22,820

Median Wages for the Largest Metropolitan Areas (Annual)

AZ: Phoenix $25,770	MI: Detroit $29,450
CA: Los Angeles $27,130	MN: Minneapolis $32,140
CA: Riverside $27,560	MO: Kansas City $27,390
CA: Sacramento $35,320	MO: St. Louis $22,410
CA: San Diego $29,200	NV: Las Vegas $32,310
CA: San Francisco $40,310	NY: New York $31,750
CO: Denver $27,040	OH: Cincinnati $25,830
DC: Washington $29,940	OH: Cleveland $27,120
FL: Miami $23,360	OH: Columbus $26,400
FL: Orlando $21,800	OR: Portland $29,110
FL: Tampa $21,730	PA: Philadelphia $28,870
GA: Atlanta $25,870	PA: Pittsburgh $24,910
IL: Chicago $27,050	TX: Dallas $25,430
MA: Boston $29,660	TX: Houston $25,540
MD: Baltimore $26,800	WA: Seattle $29,610

FACTORS THAT MAY AFFECT EARNINGS

Educational Attainment of Workers and Effect on Earnings

Figures are based on a group of occupations: Medical Assistants and Other Healthcare Support Occupations

	Percent at Level	Effect on Earnings
Less than High School	1.0%	−8.6%
Some High School	9.2%	−33.3%
High School or Equivalent	24.5%	−6.5%
Some College but No Degree	28.1%	−5.0%
Associate Degree	22.6%	2.4%
Bachelor's Degree	10.8%	21.2%
Master's Degree	2.3%	67.0%
Doctoral Degree	—	—
First Professional Degree	1.3%	103.1%

Flexibility of Earnings

Average Hours Worked: 32
Workers with a Varying Number of Hours: 6.4%
Workers Earning Some Overtime Pay, Tips, or Commissions: 10.8%
Earnings Benefit of Working Overtime: 3.0%

Gender

	Male	Female
Percent	9.0%	91.0%
Effect on Earnings	18.7%	−1.4%

Union Membership

Percentage Union Members: 6.3%
Earnings Benefit of Union Membership: 16.0%

Veteran Status

Percentage Who Have Been on Active Duty: Insignificant
Earnings Benefit of Veteran Status: No significant data available

© JIST Works

31-9094 Medical Transcriptionists

Use transcribing machines with headset and foot pedal to listen to recordings by physicians and other health-care professionals dictating a variety of medical reports, such as emergency room visits, diagnostic imaging studies, operations, chart reviews, and final summaries. Transcribe dictated reports and translate medical jargon and abbreviations into their expanded forms. Edit as necessary and return reports in either printed or electronic form to the dictator for review and signature or correction.

- Education or Training Required: Postsecondary vocational training
- Job Growth: 23.3%
- Annual Openings: 20,000
- Self-Employed: 9.7%
- Part-Time: 42.5%

NATIONAL WAGE FIGURES (ANNUAL)

Beginning	25th Percentile	Median	Mean	75th Percentile	90th Percentile
$21,260	$25,310	$29,950	$30,660	$35,490	$41,920

Median Wages for Industries Employing Largest Numbers (Annual)

Industry	Median Income
Social Assistance	$35,710
Insurance Carriers and Related Activities	$34,990
Federal, State, and Local Government	$34,090
Management of Companies and Enterprises	$33,040
Professional, Scientific, and Technical Services	$32,340
Educational Services	$30,670
Hospitals	$30,390
Administrative and Support Services	$29,950
Ambulatory Health Care Services	$29,190
Wholesale Electronic Markets and Agents and Brokers	$26,010

Median Wages for States (Annual)

AK	$37,770	KY	$28,430	NY	$31,450
AL	$25,460	LA	$26,390	OH	$28,650
AR	$25,360	MA	$33,990	OK	$25,660
AZ	$32,560	MD	$33,950	OR	$32,480
CA	$38,890	ME	$27,450	PA	$27,790
CO	$32,580	MI	$31,210	RI	$31,170
CT	$35,660	MN	$32,920	SC	$28,250
DC	$32,500	MO	$29,070	SD	$25,240
DE	$30,670	MS	$24,530	TN	$28,240
FL	$28,750	MT	$27,240	TX	$28,840
GA	$29,420	NC	$29,330	UT	$27,960
HI	$31,820	ND	$26,770	VA	$27,740
IA	$27,010	NE	$26,730	VT	$29,200
ID	$28,020	NH	$31,040	WA	$34,110
IL	$29,380	NJ	$35,080	WI	$30,560
IN	$27,600	NM	$26,540	WV	$24,130
KS	$26,690	NV	$33,620	WY	$23,540

Median Wages for the Largest Metropolitan Areas (Annual)

AZ: Phoenix	$32,910	MI: Detroit	$34,600
CA: Los Angeles	$41,600	MN: Minneapolis	$34,010
CA: Riverside	$37,620	MO: Kansas City	$30,050
CA: Sacramento	$38,340	MO: St. Louis	$31,140
CA: San Diego	$38,370	NV: Las Vegas	$33,810
CA: San Francisco	$40,750	NY: New York	$36,010
CO: Denver	$33,900	OH: Cincinnati	$32,500
DC: Washington	$38,100	OH: Cleveland	$29,950
FL: Miami	$31,740	OH: Columbus	$29,430
FL: Orlando	$28,970	OR: Portland	$36,420
FL: Tampa	$28,200	PA: Philadelphia	$31,080
GA: Atlanta	$31,990	PA: Pittsburgh	$27,850
IL: Chicago	$32,060	TX: Dallas	$34,810
MA: Boston	$34,420	TX: Houston	$33,360
MD: Baltimore	$34,210	WA: Seattle	$36,500

FACTORS THAT MAY AFFECT EARNINGS

Educational Attainment of Workers and Effect on Earnings

Figures are based on a group of occupations: Medical Assistants and Other Healthcare Support Occupations

	Percent at Level	Effect on Earnings
Less than High School	1.0%	−8.6%
Some High School	9.2%	−33.3%
High School or Equivalent	24.5%	−6.5%
Some College but No Degree	28.1%	−5.0%
Associate Degree	22.6%	2.4%
Bachelor's Degree	10.8%	21.2%
Master's Degree	2.3%	67.0%
Doctoral Degree	—	—
First Professional Degree	1.3%	103.1%

Flexibility of Earnings

Average Hours Worked: 32
Workers with a Varying Number of Hours: 6.4%
Workers Earning Some Overtime Pay, Tips, or Commissions: 10.8%
Earnings Benefit of Working Overtime: 3.0%

Gender

	Male	Female
Percent	9.0%	91.0%
Effect on Earnings	18.7%	−1.4%

Union Membership

Percentage Union Members: 6.3%
Earnings Benefit of Union Membership: 16.0%

Veteran Status

Percentage Who Have Been on Active Duty: Insignificant
Earnings Benefit of Veteran Status: No significant data available

31-9095 Pharmacy Aides

Record drugs delivered to the pharmacy, store incoming merchandise, and inform the supervisor of stock needs. May operate cash register and accept prescriptions for filling.

- Education or Training Required: Short-term on-the-job training
- Job Growth: 17.4%
- Annual Openings: 9,000
- Self-Employed: 3.9%
- Part-Time: 42.5%

NATIONAL WAGE FIGURES (ANNUAL)

Beginning	25th Percentile	Median	Mean	75th Percentile	90th Percentile
$14,390	$16,410	$19,440	$20,950	$24,090	$30,450

Median Wages for Industries Employing Largest Numbers (Annual)

Industry	Median Income
Educational Services	$31,580
Federal, State, and Local Government	$29,390
Nursing and Residential Care Facilities	$26,910
Administrative and Support Services	$26,700
Ambulatory Health Care Services	$25,570
Hospitals	$24,190
Management of Companies and Enterprises	$23,650
Merchant Wholesalers, Durable Goods	$23,490
Wholesale Electronic Markets and Agents and Brokers	$22,050
Professional, Scientific, and Technical Services	$20,750

Median Wages for States (Annual)

AK	no data	KY	$17,840	NY	$20,450
AL	$16,070	LA	$18,470	OH	$18,660
AR	$17,420	MA	$20,960	OK	$16,660
AZ	$22,450	MD	$19,780	OR	$21,680
CA	$21,450	ME	$18,590	PA	$16,620
CO	$23,600	MI	$19,020	RI	$20,950
CT	$21,560	MN	$20,240	SC	$17,380
DC	$24,810	MO	$20,840	SD	$17,820
DE	no data	MS	$16,040	TN	$18,080
FL	$17,700	MT	$19,830	TX	$19,370
GA	$18,150	NC	$17,200	UT	$21,430
HI	$22,210	ND	$19,180	VA	$18,100
IA	$20,870	NE	$19,130	VT	$20,670
ID	$22,450	NH	$21,080	WA	$22,320
IL	$25,000	NJ	$18,120	WI	$19,840
IN	$18,140	NM	$21,670	WV	$15,350
KS	$19,720	NV	$23,350	WY	$20,350

Median Wages for the Largest Metropolitan Areas (Annual)

AZ: Phoenix	$22,480	MI: Detroit	$19,540
CA: Los Angeles	$20,570	MN: Minneapolis	$20,060
CA: Riverside	$20,500	MO: Kansas City	$18,230
CA: Sacramento	$24,950	MO: St. Louis	$29,180
CA: San Diego	$20,960	NV: Las Vegas	$29,660
CA: San Francisco	$28,150	NY: New York	$21,010
CO: Denver	$24,160	OH: Cincinnati	$20,280
DC: Washington	$20,020	OH: Cleveland	$18,000
FL: Miami	$17,280	OH: Columbus	$21,190
FL: Orlando	$17,500	OR: Portland	$23,270
FL: Tampa	$17,950	PA: Philadelphia	$17,340
GA: Atlanta	$19,440	PA: Pittsburgh	$14,300
IL: Chicago	$27,160	TX: Dallas	$22,630
MA: Boston	$21,030	TX: Houston	$17,650
MD: Baltimore	$20,860	WA: Seattle	$22,740

FACTORS THAT MAY AFFECT EARNINGS

Educational Attainment of Workers and Effect on Earnings

Figures are based on a group of occupations: Medical Assistants and Other Healthcare Support Occupations

	Percent at Level	Effect on Earnings
Less than High School	1.0%	−8.6%
Some High School	9.2%	−33.3%
High School or Equivalent	24.5%	−6.5%
Some College but No Degree	28.1%	−5.0%
Associate Degree	22.6%	2.4%
Bachelor's Degree	10.8%	21.2%
Master's Degree	2.3%	67.0%
Doctoral Degree	—	—
First Professional Degree	1.3%	103.1%

Flexibility of Earnings

Average Hours Worked: 32

Workers with a Varying Number of Hours: 6.4%

Workers Earning Some Overtime Pay, Tips, or Commissions: 10.8%

Earnings Benefit of Working Overtime: 3.0%

Gender

	Male	Female
Percent	9.0%	91.0%
Effect on Earnings	18.7%	−1.4%

Union Membership

Percentage Union Members: 6.3%

Earnings Benefit of Union Membership: 16.0%

Veteran Status

Percentage Who Have Been on Active Duty: Insignificant

Earnings Benefit of Veteran Status: No significant data available

31-9096 *Veterinary Assistants and Laboratory Animal Caretakers*

Feed, water, and examine pets and other nonfarm animals for signs of illness, disease, or injury in laboratories and animal hospitals and clinics. Clean and disinfect cages and work areas and sterilize laboratory and surgical equipment. May provide routine post-operative care, administer medication orally or topically, or prepare samples for laboratory examination under the supervision of veterinary or laboratory animal technologists or technicians, veterinarians, or scientists.

- Education or Training Required: Short-term on-the-job training
- Job Growth: 21.0%
- Annual Openings: 14,000
- Self-Employed: 2.7%
- Part-Time: 42.5%

NATIONAL WAGE FIGURES (ANNUAL)

Beginning	25th Percentile	Median	Mean	75th Percentile	90th Percentile
$14,310	$16,610	$19,960	$21,060	$24,190	$29,510

Median Wages for Industries Employing Largest Numbers (Annual)

Industry	Median Income
Federal, State, and Local Government	$26,810
Hospitals	$26,070
Educational Services	$25,500
Chemical Manufacturing	$22,960
Museums, Historical Sites, and Similar Institutions	$22,120
Personal and Laundry Services	$21,610
Administrative and Support Services	$20,360
Religious, Grantmaking, Civic, Professional, and Similar Organizations	$20,250
Professional, Scientific, and Technical Services	$19,610

Median Wages for States (Annual)

AK	$22,520	KY	$19,540	NY	$22,270
AL	$16,870	LA	$17,360	OH	$20,540
AR	$17,090	MA	$26,520	OK	$17,570
AZ	$20,520	MD	$21,440	OR	$21,100
CA	$21,540	ME	$22,520	PA	$22,520
CO	$18,530	MI	$21,080	RI	$21,180
CT	$22,800	MN	$22,130	SC	$18,680
DC	$25,880	MO	$19,610	SD	$18,130
DE	$24,540	MS	$18,120	TN	$18,600
FL	$19,540	MT	$17,520	TX	$19,420
GA	$16,820	NC	$18,160	UT	$18,730
HI	$18,930	ND	$18,010	VA	$20,140
IA	$17,590	NE	$15,950	VT	$17,760
ID	$19,730	NH	$19,380	WA	$21,850
IL	$19,240	NJ	$19,580	WI	$20,400
IN	$19,030	NM	$19,980	WV	$17,190
KS	$16,450	NV	$18,760	WY	$17,110

Median Wages for the Largest Metropolitan Areas (Annual)

AZ: Phoenix	$22,120	MI: Detroit	$20,590
CA: Los Angeles	$19,780	MN: Minneapolis	$22,250
CA: Riverside	$22,680	MO: Kansas City	$18,760
CA: Sacramento	$21,230	MO: St. Louis	$19,570
CA: San Diego	$22,090	NV: Las Vegas	$19,150
CA: San Francisco	$25,670	NY: New York	$22,570
CO: Denver	$17,470	OH: Cincinnati	$20,290
DC: Washington	$22,470	OH: Cleveland	$22,360
FL: Miami	$21,700	OH: Columbus	$20,740
FL: Orlando	$18,270	OR: Portland	$21,690
FL: Tampa	$18,390	PA: Philadelphia	$21,680
GA: Atlanta	$16,520	PA: Pittsburgh	$24,340
IL: Chicago	$20,260	TX: Dallas	$20,920
MA: Boston	$26,630	TX: Houston	$20,180
MD: Baltimore	$21,060	WA: Seattle	$23,120

FACTORS THAT MAY AFFECT EARNINGS

Educational Attainment of Workers and Effect on Earnings

Figures are based on a group of occupations: Medical Assistants and Other Healthcare Support Occupations

	Percent at Level	Effect on Earnings
Less than High School	1.0%	−8.6%
Some High School	9.2%	−33.3%
High School or Equivalent	24.5%	−6.5%
Some College but No Degree	28.1%	−5.0%
Associate Degree	22.6%	2.4%
Bachelor's Degree	10.8%	21.2%
Master's Degree	2.3%	67.0%
Doctoral Degree	—	—
First Professional Degree	1.3%	103.1%

Flexibility of Earnings

Average Hours Worked: 32
Workers with a Varying Number of Hours: 6.4%
Workers Earning Some Overtime Pay, Tips, or Commissions: 10.8%
Earnings Benefit of Working Overtime: 3.0%

Gender

	Male	Female
Percent	9.0%	91.0%
Effect on Earnings	18.7%	−1.4%

Union Membership

Percentage Union Members: 6.3%
Earnings Benefit of Union Membership: 16.0%

Veteran Status

Percentage Who Have Been on Active Duty: Insignificant
Earnings Benefit of Veteran Status: No significant data available

31-9099 Healthcare Support Workers, All Other

All healthcare support workers not listed separately.

- Education or Training Required: Short-term on-the-job training
- Job Growth: 20.9%
- Annual Openings: 38,000
- Self-Employed: 6.1%
- Part-Time: 42.5%

NATIONAL WAGE FIGURES (ANNUAL)

Beginning	25th Percentile	Median	Mean	75th Percentile	90th Percentile
$18,040	$21,730	$26,990	$28,170	$33,530	$40,390

Median Wages for Industries Employing Largest Numbers (Annual)

Industry	Median Income
Federal, State, and Local Government	$35,070
Miscellaneous Manufacturing	$32,860
Rental and Leasing Services	$31,440
Health and Personal Care Stores	$31,370
Management of Companies and Enterprises	$30,120
Merchant Wholesalers, Durable Goods	$27,660
Educational Services	$27,410
Social Assistance	$27,210
Professional, Scientific, and Technical Services	$27,100
Amusement, Gambling, and Recreation Industries	$26,740

Median Wages for States (Annual)

State	Wage	State	Wage	State	Wage
AK	$33,360	KY	$23,710	NY	$31,670
AL	$20,780	LA	$21,160	OH	$24,650
AR	$20,330	MA	$31,790	OK	$22,770
AZ	$24,680	MD	$29,330	OR	$28,660
CA	$29,450	ME	$25,200	PA	$26,050
CO	$29,360	MI	$27,570	RI	$29,370
CT	$33,360	MN	$29,880	SC	$24,690
DC	$40,310	MO	$24,770	SD	$36,270
DE	$33,180	MS	$22,050	TN	$24,650
FL	$24,420	MT	$22,770	TX	$24,900
GA	$25,350	NC	$24,000	UT	$23,170
HI	$29,070	ND	$22,500	VA	$27,270
IA	$21,910	NE	$24,910	VT	$23,380
ID	$25,220	NH	$28,120	WA	$29,100
IL	$25,300	NJ	$29,040	WI	$25,670
IN	$24,530	NM	$23,980	WV	$25,190
KS	$22,000	NV	$29,030	WY	$28,510

Median Wages for the Largest Metropolitan Areas (Annual)

Area	Wage	Area	Wage
AZ: Phoenix	$24,320	MI: Detroit	$29,120
CA: Los Angeles	$27,310	MN: Minneapolis	$30,330
CA: Riverside	$27,680	MO: Kansas City	$25,820
CA: Sacramento	$30,050	MO: St. Louis	$27,340
CA: San Diego	$27,600	NV: Las Vegas	$29,170
CA: San Francisco	$37,720	NY: New York	$31,460
CO: Denver	$30,660	OH: Cincinnati	$25,200
DC: Washington	$30,630	OH: Cleveland	$24,980
FL: Miami	$23,770	OH: Columbus	$26,440
FL: Orlando	$26,410	OR: Portland	$30,750
FL: Tampa	$25,560	PA: Philadelphia	$28,560
GA: Atlanta	$26,610	PA: Pittsburgh	$25,330
IL: Chicago	$24,860	TX: Dallas	$27,010
MA: Boston	$32,000	TX: Houston	$26,750
MD: Baltimore	$28,920	WA: Seattle	$31,120

FACTORS THAT MAY AFFECT EARNINGS

Educational Attainment of Workers and Effect on Earnings

Figures are based on a group of occupations: Medical Assistants and Other Healthcare Support Occupations

	Percent at Level	Effect on Earnings
Less than High School	1.0%	−8.6%
Some High School	9.2%	−33.3%
High School or Equivalent	24.5%	−6.5%
Some College but No Degree	28.1%	−5.0%
Associate Degree	22.6%	2.4%
Bachelor's Degree	10.8%	21.2%
Master's Degree	2.3%	67.0%
Doctoral Degree	—	—
First Professional Degree	1.3%	103.1%

Flexibility of Earnings

Average Hours Worked: 32

Workers with a Varying Number of Hours: 6.2%

Workers Earning Some Overtime Pay, Tips, or Commissions: 10.8%

Earnings Benefit of Working Overtime: 3.0%

Gender

	Male	Female
Percent	9.6%	90.4%
Effect on Earnings	18.7%	−1.4%

Union Membership

Percentage Union Members: 6.3%

Earnings Benefit of Union Membership: 16.0%

Veteran Status

Percentage Who Have Been on Active Duty: Insignificant

Earnings Benefit of Veteran Status: No significant data available

33-0000: Protective Service Occupations

33-1000 First-Line Supervisors/Managers, Protective Service Workers

33-1011 First-Line Supervisors/Managers of Correctional Officers

Supervise and coordinate activities of correctional officers and jailers.

- Education or Training Required: Work experience in a related occupation
- Job Growth: 9.4%
- Annual Openings: 2,000
- Self-Employed: 0.0%
- Part-Time: 10.1%

NATIONAL WAGE FIGURES (ANNUAL)

Beginning	25th Percentile	Median	Mean	75th Percentile	90th Percentile
$33,270	$38,920	$52,580	$54,630	$67,820	$81,230

Median Wages for Industries Employing Largest Numbers (Annual)

Industry	Median Income
Hospitals	$53,050
Federal, State, and Local Government	$52,970
Nursing and Residential Care Facilities	$39,550
Administrative and Support Services	$37,430

Median Wages for States (Annual)

AK	$65,870	KY	no data	NY	$62,410
AL	$45,960	LA	$40,470	OH	no data
AR	$49,910	MA	no data	OK	$42,610
AZ	$40,420	MD	$49,070	OR	$50,340
CA	$77,730	ME	$44,720	PA	$52,010
CO	$60,480	MI	no data	RI	no data
CT	no data	MN	$60,700	SC	$41,940
DC	no data	MO	$37,950	SD	$52,200
DE	no data	MS	$32,040	TN	$42,120
FL	$49,470	MT	$42,060	TX	$36,770
GA	$41,930	NC	$38,770	UT	$46,750
HI	no data	ND	$43,270	VA	$47,810
IA	$55,770	NE	$38,750	VT	no data
ID	$37,110	NH	$50,530	WA	$61,430
IL	$60,490	NJ	$88,710	WI	$53,860
IN	no data	NM	$39,860	WV	$51,030
KS	$40,410	NV	$60,630	WY	$46,150

Median Wages for the Largest Metropolitan Areas (Annual)

AZ: Phoenix	$44,990	MI: Detroit	no data
CA: Los Angeles	$70,130	MN: Minneapolis	$64,870
CA: Riverside	$78,210	MO: Kansas City	$43,420
CA: Sacramento	no data	MO: St. Louis	$58,610
CA: San Diego	$75,710	NV: Las Vegas	no data
CA: San Francisco	$77,250	NY: New York	$71,070
CO: Denver	$68,260	OH: Cincinnati	$48,290
DC: Washington	$65,130	OH: Cleveland	$53,110
FL: Miami	$56,450	OH: Columbus	no data
FL: Orlando	$58,280	OR: Portland	$61,550
FL: Tampa	$64,810	PA: Philadelphia	$77,970
GA: Atlanta	$46,240	PA: Pittsburgh	$41,230
IL: Chicago	$61,440	TX: Dallas	$55,670
MA: Boston	$68,030	TX: Houston	$36,790
MD: Baltimore	no data	WA: Seattle	$66,230

FACTORS THAT MAY AFFECT EARNINGS

Educational Attainment of Workers and Effect on Earnings

	Percent at Level	Effect on Earnings
Less than High School	—	—
Some High School	—	—
High School or Equivalent	36.5%	−10.7%
Some College but No Degree	28.6%	−15.2%
Associate Degree	—	—
Bachelor's Degree	22.2%	29.3%
Master's Degree	—	—
Doctoral Degree	—	—
First Professional Degree	—	—

Figures do not total 100% because some levels have a very small sample size.

Flexibility of Earnings

Average Hours Worked: 39
Workers with a Varying Number of Hours: 4.3%
Workers Earning Some Overtime Pay, Tips, or Commissions: 13.4%
Earnings Benefit of Working Overtime: 0.9%

Gender

	Male	Female
Percent	84.5%	15.5%
Effect on Earnings	6.3%	−19.6%

Union Membership

Percentage Union Members: 35.8%
Earnings Benefit of Union Membership: 16.8%

Veteran Status

Percentage Who Have Been on Active Duty: 21.8%
Earnings Benefit of Veteran Status: 4.1%

33-1012 First-Line Supervisors/Managers of Police and Detectives

Supervise and coordinate activities of members of police force.

- Education or Training Required: Work experience in a related occupation
- Job Growth: 15.5%
- Annual Openings: 9,000
- Self-Employed: 0.0%
- Part-Time: 1.8%

NATIONAL WAGE FIGURES (ANNUAL)

Beginning	25th Percentile	Median	Mean	75th Percentile	90th Percentile
$41,260	$53,900	$69,310	$70,230	$83,940	$104,410

Median Wages for Industries Employing Largest Numbers (Annual)

Industry	Median Income
Federal, State, and Local Government	$69,510
Postal Service	$62,960
Educational Services	$56,900
Hospitals	$54,950

Median Wages for States (Annual)

AK $77,350	KY $54,760	NY .... no data
AL $48,000	LA $45,990	OH $62,690
AR $43,100	MA $73,810	OK $42,520
AZ $72,990	MD $69,870	OR $69,670
CA $92,850	ME $49,820	PA $71,350
CO $81,100	MI $66,860	RI $64,180
CT $72,540	MN $67,890	SC $44,030
DC $95,350	MO $55,310	SD $51,780
DE $83,960	MS $36,950	TN $50,700
FL $74,230	MT $55,720	TX $68,170
GA $50,800	NC $49,020	UT $58,640
HI $64,990	ND $55,800	VA $70,880
IA $56,410	NE $53,130	VT $64,120
ID $51,950	NH $60,040	WA $76,010
IL $80,100	NJ $99,780	WI $62,420
IN $55,520	NM $52,350	WV $47,620
KS $57,720	NV $84,020	WY $51,220

Median Wages for the Largest Metropolitan Areas (Annual)

AZ: Phoenix	$75,600	MI: Detroit	no data
CA: Los Angeles	no data	MN: Minneapolis	$72,790
CA: Riverside	$81,710	MO: Kansas City	$64,900
CA: Sacramento	$80,420	MO: St. Louis	$61,640
CA: San Diego	$79,290	NV: Las Vegas	no data
CA: San Francisco	$99,510	NY: New York	no data
CO: Denver	$87,460	OH: Cincinnati	$67,700
DC: Washington	$90,410	OH: Cleveland	$69,640
FL: Miami	$90,220	OH: Columbus	$68,580
FL: Orlando	$73,550	OR: Portland	$72,560
FL: Tampa	$76,420	PA: Philadelphia	$77,830
GA: Atlanta	$58,790	PA: Pittsburgh	$69,030
IL: Chicago	$82,800	TX: Dallas	$75,190
MA: Boston	$74,960	TX: Houston	$65,550
MD: Baltimore	$70,510	WA: Seattle	$81,360

FACTORS THAT MAY AFFECT EARNINGS

Educational Attainment of Workers and Effect on Earnings

	Percent at Level	Effect on Earnings
Less than High School	—	—
Some High School	—	—
High School or Equivalent	15.1%	−15.8%
Some College but No Degree	22.3%	−7.6%
Associate Degree	22.3%	−11.3%
Bachelor's Degree	33.1%	14.5%
Master's Degree	—	—
Doctoral Degree	—	—
First Professional Degree	—	—

Figures do not total 100% because some levels have a very small sample size.

Flexibility of Earnings

Average Hours Worked: 38
Workers with a Varying Number of Hours: 9.2%
Workers Earning Some Overtime Pay, Tips, or Commissions: 28.2%
Earnings Benefit of Working Overtime: 10.7%

Gender

	Male	Female
Percent	84.5%	15.5%
Effect on Earnings	2.7%	—

Union Membership

Percentage Union Members: 43.0%
Earnings Benefit of Union Membership: 0.0%

Veteran Status

Percentage Who Have Been on Active Duty: 21.8%
Earnings Benefit of Veteran Status: 4.1%

33-1021 First-Line Supervisors/Managers of Fire Fighting and Prevention Workers

Supervise and coordinate activities of workers engaged in fire fighting and fire prevention and control.

- Education or Training Required: Work experience in a related occupation
- Job Growth: 21.1%
- Annual Openings: 4,000
- Self-Employed: 0.0%
- Part-Time: 11.4%

NATIONAL WAGE FIGURES (ANNUAL)

Beginning	25th Percentile	Median	Mean	75th Percentile	90th Percentile
$36,820	$50,180	$62,900	$65,030	$79,060	$97,820

Median Wages for Industries Employing Largest Numbers (Annual)

Industry	Median Income
Federal, State, and Local Government	$63,050
Educational Services	$60,920
Professional, Scientific, and Technical Services	$59,030
Administrative and Support Services	$42,660

Median Wages for States (Annual)

AK	$63,060	KY	$46,620	NY	no data
AL	$48,850	LA	$45,150	OH	$57,190
AR	$53,080	MA	$64,300	OK	$55,300
AZ	$60,230	MD	$67,140	OR	$63,680
CA	$86,440	ME	$43,020	PA	$58,530
CO	$63,430	MI	$62,990	RI	$56,000
CT	$69,290	MN	$52,360	SC	$43,590
DC	no data	MO	$68,820	SD	no data
DE	no data	MS	$36,880	TN	$50,850
FL	$69,280	MT	$49,690	TX	$61,470
GA	$56,180	NC	$50,370	UT	$63,900
HI	$63,310	ND	$54,630	VA	$65,110
IA	$46,190	NE	no data	VT	no data
ID	$61,160	NH	$56,360	WA	$75,020
IL	$81,010	NJ	$87,940	WI	$60,420
IN	$54,780	NM	$43,900	WV	$42,700
KS	$51,960	NV	$61,970	WY	$51,610

Median Wages for the Largest Metropolitan Areas (Annual)

AZ: Phoenix	$73,480	MI: Detroit	no data
CA: Los Angeles	no data	MN: Minneapolis	$54,000
CA: Riverside	$60,440	MO: Kansas City	$61,060
CA: Sacramento	$83,710	MO: St. Louis	$85,290
CA: San Diego	$63,680	NV: Las Vegas	$75,640
CA: San Francisco	$108,380	NY: New York	no data
CO: Denver	$77,040	OH: Cincinnati	$58,310
DC: Washington	$79,730	OH: Cleveland	$61,410
FL: Miami	$85,140	OH: Columbus	no data
FL: Orlando	$64,670	OR: Portland	$72,450
FL: Tampa	$57,680	PA: Philadelphia	$64,050
GA: Atlanta	$61,020	PA: Pittsburgh	no data
IL: Chicago	$82,570	TX: Dallas	$74,280
MA: Boston	$67,740	TX: Houston	no data
MD: Baltimore	no data	WA: Seattle	$76,390

FACTORS THAT MAY AFFECT EARNINGS

Educational Attainment of Workers and Effect on Earnings

	Percent at Level	Effect on Earnings
Less than High School	—	—
Some High School	—	—
High School or Equivalent	32.7%	−6.6%
Some College but No Degree	27.3%	−3.9%
Associate Degree	30.9%	−5.9%
Bachelor's Degree	—	—
Master's Degree	—	—
Doctoral Degree	—	—
First Professional Degree	—	—

Figures do not total 100% because some levels have a very small sample size.

Flexibility of Earnings

Average Hours Worked: 41
Workers with a Varying Number of Hours: 13.7%
Workers Earning Some Overtime Pay, Tips, or Commissions: 30.4%
Earnings Benefit of Working Overtime: −18.1%

Gender

	Male	Female
Percent	84.5%	15.5%
Effect on Earnings	0.2%	−2.8%

Union Membership

Percentage Union Members: 51.8%
Earnings Benefit of Union Membership: 16.7%

Veteran Status

Percentage Who Have Been on Active Duty: 21.8%
Earnings Benefit of Veteran Status: 4.1%

33-1099 First-Line Supervisors/Managers, Protective Service Workers, All Other

All protective service supervisors not listed separately.

- Education or Training Required: Work experience in a related occupation
- Job Growth: 8.7%
- Annual Openings: 5,000
- Self-Employed: 1.4%
- Part-Time: 18.2%

NATIONAL WAGE FIGURES (ANNUAL)

Beginning	25th Percentile	Median	Mean	75th Percentile	90th Percentile
$24,900	$31,370	$41,570	$46,350	$56,580	$73,240

Median Wages for Industries Employing Largest Numbers (Annual)

Industry	Median Income
Utilities	$69,640
Transportation Equipment Manufacturing	$60,910
Fabricated Metal Product Manufacturing	$58,070
Federal, State, and Local Government	$55,840
Computer and Electronic Product Manufacturing	$54,320
Professional, Scientific, and Technical Services	$51,610
Insurance Carriers and Related Activities	$51,070
Credit Intermediation and Related Activities	$51,050
Management of Companies and Enterprises	$50,640
Educational Services	$47,250

Median Wages for States (Annual)

State	Wage	State	Wage	State	Wage
AK	$57,100	KY	$31,900	NY	$47,150
AL	$29,360	LA	$39,340	OH	$41,100
AR	$42,280	MA	$43,880	OK	$36,480
AZ	$43,700	MD	$44,070	OR	$34,130
CA	$40,770	ME	$42,040	PA	no data
CO	$40,360	MI	$44,180	RI	$51,120
CT	$46,260	MN	$44,370	SC	$37,460
DC	$44,290	MO	$41,950	SD	$36,100
DE	$39,730	MS	$31,690	TN	$34,040
FL	$38,850	MT	$50,660	TX	$38,790
GA	$37,070	NC	$37,130	UT	$37,560
HI	$42,110	ND	$39,230	VA	$45,780
IA	$44,380	NE	$42,960	VT	$38,910
ID	$44,410	NH	$42,530	WA	$46,620
IL	$50,010	NJ	$41,470	WI	$41,790
IN	$36,190	NM	$38,010	WV	$32,320
KS	$37,470	NV	$38,810	WY	$51,840

Median Wages for the Largest Metropolitan Areas (Annual)

Area	Wage	Area	Wage
AZ: Phoenix	$41,790	MI: Detroit	$44,500
CA: Los Angeles	$35,810	MN: Minneapolis	$44,130
CA: Riverside	$42,240	MO: Kansas City	$40,560
CA: Sacramento	$51,030	MO: St. Louis	$43,270
CA: San Diego	$35,540	NV: Las Vegas	$38,540
CA: San Francisco	$47,470	NY: New York	$45,840
CO: Denver	$39,960	OH: Cincinnati	$40,840
DC: Washington	$46,640	OH: Cleveland	$40,330
FL: Miami	$37,210	OH: Columbus	$40,170
FL: Orlando	$39,720	OR: Portland	$34,750
FL: Tampa	$38,090	PA: Philadelphia	$44,110
GA: Atlanta	$36,910	PA: Pittsburgh	no data
IL: Chicago	$40,970	TX: Dallas	$38,750
MA: Boston	$45,370	TX: Houston	$39,200
MD: Baltimore	$40,280	WA: Seattle	$45,320

FACTORS THAT MAY AFFECT EARNINGS

Educational Attainment of Workers and Effect on Earnings

	Percent at Level	Effect on Earnings
Less than High School	—	—
Some High School	—	—
High School or Equivalent	20.3%	−4.6%
Some College but No Degree	32.2%	−9.0%
Associate Degree	14.4%	−23.4%
Bachelor's Degree	23.7%	16.3%
Master's Degree	6.8%	29.1%
Doctoral Degree	—	—
First Professional Degree	—	—

Flexibility of Earnings

Average Hours Worked: 40
Workers with a Varying Number of Hours: 5.3%
Workers Earning Some Overtime Pay, Tips, or Commissions: 12.5%
Earnings Benefit of Working Overtime: 1.6%

Gender

	Male	Female
Percent	84.5%	15.5%
Effect on Earnings	6.3%	−19.6%

Union Membership

Percentage Union Members: 10.9%
Earnings Benefit of Union Membership: 22.4%

Veteran Status

Percentage Who Have Been on Active Duty: 21.8%
Earnings Benefit of Veteran Status: 4.1%

33-2000 Fire Fighting and Prevention Workers

33-2011 Fire Fighters

Control and extinguish fires or respond to emergency situations where life, property, or the environment is at risk. Duties may include fire prevention, emergency medical service, hazardous material response, search and rescue, and disaster management.

- Education or Training Required: Long-term on-the-job training
- Job Growth: 24.3%
- Annual Openings: 21,000
- Self-Employed: 0.1%
- Part-Time: 3.5%

NATIONAL WAGE FIGURES (ANNUAL)

Beginning	25th Percentile	Median	Mean	75th Percentile	90th Percentile
$20,660	$29,550	$41,190	$42,370	$54,120	$66,140

Median Wages for Industries Employing Largest Numbers (Annual)

Industry	Median Income
Petroleum and Coal Products Manufacturing	$56,380
Educational Services	$51,380
Chemical Manufacturing	$49,380
Performing Arts, Spectator Sports, and Related Industries	$46,400
Fabricated Metal Product Manufacturing	$46,040
Postal Service	$45,500
Ambulatory Health Care Services	$42,450
Federal, State, and Local Government	$41,480
Professional, Scientific, and Technical Services	$40,330
Transportation Equipment Manufacturing	$39,390

Median Wages for States (Annual)

AK	$29,460	KY	$29,730	NY	no data
AL	$32,660	LA	$24,980	OH	$36,570
AR	$31,820	MA	$45,970	OK	$33,700
AZ	$36,580	MD	$45,820	OR	$46,380
CA	$58,630	ME	$34,720	PA	$45,710
CO	$47,180	MI	$41,280	RI	$44,980
CT	$47,720	MN	$26,540	SC	$29,260
DC	no data	MO	$43,030	SD	$34,660
DE	no data	MS	$27,740	TN	$34,750
FL	$42,310	MT	$36,860	TX	$42,330
GA	$32,970	NC	$31,200	UT	$32,460
HI	$42,300	ND	$40,750	VA	$39,790
IA	$32,910	NE	$41,500	VT	$27,550
ID	$34,870	NH	$40,260	WA	$55,170
IL	$41,680	NJ	$60,050	WI	$30,580
IN	$38,860	NM	$29,430	WV	$32,600
KS	$32,430	NV	$45,390	WY	$37,010

Median Wages for the Largest Metropolitan Areas (Annual)

AZ: Phoenix	$41,270	MI: Detroit	$46,390
CA: Los Angeles	$69,760	MN: Minneapolis	$30,260
CA: Riverside	$43,110	MO: Kansas City	$44,680
CA: Sacramento	$42,350	MO: St. Louis	$48,030
CA: San Diego	$47,100	NV: Las Vegas	$50,510
CA: San Francisco	no data	NY: New York	no data
CO: Denver	$56,910	OH: Cincinnati	$34,910
DC: Washington	$50,040	OH: Cleveland	$42,390
FL: Miami	$55,890	OH: Columbus	$38,240
FL: Orlando	$33,450	OR: Portland	$53,620
FL: Tampa	$36,570	PA: Philadelphia	$53,750
GA: Atlanta	$37,530	PA: Pittsburgh	no data
IL: Chicago	$45,420	TX: Dallas	$48,660
MA: Boston	$48,930	TX: Houston	no data
MD: Baltimore	no data	WA: Seattle	$58,900

FACTORS THAT MAY AFFECT EARNINGS

Educational Attainment of Workers and Effect on Earnings

	Percent at Level	Effect on Earnings
Less than High School	—	—
Some High School	—	—
High School or Equivalent	24.4%	−11.5%
Some College but No Degree	31.3%	−1.7%
Associate Degree	21.3%	1.8%
Bachelor's Degree	19.2%	20.0%
Master's Degree	—	—
Doctoral Degree	—	—
First Professional Degree	—	—

Flexibility of Earnings

Average Hours Worked: 42
Workers with a Varying Number of Hours: 13.7%
Workers Earning Some Overtime Pay, Tips, or Commissions: 28.9%
Earnings Benefit of Working Overtime: −8.3%

Gender

	Male	Female
Percent	96.5%	3.5%
Effect on Earnings	0.7%	—

Union Membership

Percentage Union Members: 69.2%
Earnings Benefit of Union Membership: 4.8%

Veteran Status

Percentage Who Have Been on Active Duty: 19.5%
Earnings Benefit of Veteran Status: 6.2%

33-2021 Fire Inspectors and Investigators

Inspect buildings to detect fire hazards and enforce local ordinances and state laws. Investigate and gather facts to determine cause of fires and explosions.

- Education or Training Required: Work experience in a related occupation
- Job Growth: –5.5%
- Annual Openings: Fewer than 500
- Self-Employed: 0.0%
- Part-Time: 3.6%

NATIONAL WAGE FIGURES (ANNUAL)

Beginning	25th Percentile	Median	Mean	75th Percentile	90th Percentile
$29,840	$36,960	$48,050	$49,950	$61,160	$74,930

Median Wages for Industries Employing Largest Numbers (Annual)

Industry	Median Income
Insurance Carriers and Related Activities	$52,390
Professional, Scientific, and Technical Services	$51,930
Federal, State, and Local Government	$48,630
Merchant Wholesalers, Durable Goods	$44,970
Specialty Trade Contractors	$42,830
Hospitals	$39,900
Educational Services	$37,750
Administrative and Support Services	$37,230

Median Wages for States (Annual)

State	Wage	State	Wage	State	Wage
AK	no data	KY	$42,360	NY	$48,340
AL	$46,080	LA	$33,730	OH	$48,440
AR	no data	MA	$60,080	OK	$50,970
AZ	$56,230	MD	$48,770	OR	$65,390
CA	$75,190	ME	$35,110	PA	$42,870
CO	$57,510	MI	$48,460	RI	$43,950
CT	$53,720	MN	$55,900	SC	$34,620
DC	no data	MO	$49,730	SD	no data
DE	no data	MS	$36,060	TN	$42,720
FL	$49,130	MT	$35,200	TX	$46,890
GA	$37,400	NC	$42,060	UT	$47,040
HI	no data	ND	no data	VA	$44,320
IA	$56,760	NE	$42,710	VT	no data
ID	$53,100	NH	$41,220	WA	$64,820
IL	$52,940	NJ	$45,480	WI	$43,290
IN	$40,790	NM	$40,800	WV	$31,900
KS	$48,900	NV	$64,640	WY	$38,190

Median Wages for the Largest Metropolitan Areas (Annual)

Metro	Wage	Metro	Wage
AZ: Phoenix	$58,550	MI: Detroit	$62,840
CA: Los Angeles	no data	MN: Minneapolis	$56,110
CA: Riverside	$56,120	MO: Kansas City	$53,770
CA: Sacramento	no data	MO: St. Louis	$55,740
CA: San Diego	$67,050	NV: Las Vegas	$66,720
CA: San Francisco	$84,130	NY: New York	$47,150
CO: Denver	no data	OH: Cincinnati	$52,500
DC: Washington	$53,170	OH: Cleveland	$52,240
FL: Miami	$60,830	OH: Columbus	$57,360
FL: Orlando	$42,570	OR: Portland	no data
FL: Tampa	$44,810	PA: Philadelphia	$43,280
GA: Atlanta	$42,620	PA: Pittsburgh	no data
IL: Chicago	$49,770	TX: Dallas	$57,550
MA: Boston	$59,330	TX: Houston	no data
MD: Baltimore	$46,150	WA: Seattle	$67,740

FACTORS THAT MAY AFFECT EARNINGS

Educational Attainment of Workers and Effect on Earnings

Figures are based on a group of occupations: Fire Fighting and Prevention Workers

	Percent at Level	Effect on Earnings
Less than High School	—	—
Some High School	—	—
High School or Equivalent	25.1%	–9.7%
Some College but No Degree	30.9%	–2.5%
Associate Degree	20.6%	2.3%
Bachelor's Degree	19.3%	18.6%
Master's Degree	—	—
Doctoral Degree	—	—
First Professional Degree	—	—

Flexibility of Earnings

Average Hours Worked: 42

Workers with a Varying Number of Hours: 13.7%

Workers Earning Some Overtime Pay, Tips, or Commissions: 28.4%

Earnings Benefit of Working Overtime: –7.1%

Gender

	Male	Female
Percent	96.1%	3.9%
Effect on Earnings	6.3%	–19.6%

Union Membership

Percentage Union Members: 67.3%

Earnings Benefit of Union Membership: 4.9%

Veteran Status

Percentage Who Have Been on Active Duty: 19.5%

Earnings Benefit of Veteran Status: 6.2%

33-2022 Forest Fire Inspectors and Prevention Specialists

Enforce fire regulations and inspect for forest fire hazards. Report forest fires and weather conditions.

- Education or Training Required: Work experience in a related occupation
- Job Growth: –3.1%
- Annual Openings: Fewer than 500
- Self-Employed: 0.0%
- Part-Time: 3.6%

NATIONAL WAGE FIGURES (ANNUAL)

Beginning	25th Percentile	Median	Mean	75th Percentile	90th Percentile
$19,320	$23,170	$32,940	$35,810	$45,300	$59,050

Median Wages for Industries Employing Largest Numbers (Annual)

Industry	Median Income
Federal, State, and Local Government	$33,190

Median Wages for States (Annual)

State		State		State	
AK	no data	KY	no data	NY	$45,050
AL	$24,250	LA	no data	OH	no data
AR	$24,270	MA	no data	OK	$23,260
AZ	no data	MD	no data	OR	$34,940
CA	$54,720	ME	no data	PA	no data
CO	no data	MI	no data	RI	no data
CT	no data	MN	no data	SC	no data
DC	no data	MO	no data	SD	no data
DE	no data	MS	$21,460	TN	no data
FL	no data	MT	no data	TX	no data
GA	$40,200	NC	no data	UT	no data
HI	no data	ND	no data	VA	no data
IA	no data	NE	no data	VT	no data
ID	no data	NH	no data	WA	no data
IL	no data	NJ	$42,870	WI	no data
IN	no data	NM	no data	WV	no data
KS	no data	NV	no data	WY	no data

Median Wages for the Largest Metropolitan Areas (Annual)

Area		Area	
AZ: Phoenix	no data	MI: Detroit	no data
CA: Los Angeles	no data	MN: Minneapolis	no data
CA: Riverside	no data	MO: Kansas City	no data
CA: Sacramento	no data	MO: St. Louis	no data
CA: San Diego	no data	NV: Las Vegas	no data
CA: San Francisco	no data	NY: New York	$40,040
CO: Denver	no data	OH: Cincinnati	no data
DC: Washington	no data	OH: Cleveland	no data
FL: Miami	no data	OH: Columbus	no data
FL: Orlando	no data	OR: Portland	no data
FL: Tampa	no data	PA: Philadelphia	no data
GA: Atlanta	no data	PA: Pittsburgh	no data
IL: Chicago	no data	TX: Dallas	no data
MA: Boston	no data	TX: Houston	no data
MD: Baltimore	no data	WA: Seattle	no data

FACTORS THAT MAY AFFECT EARNINGS

Educational Attainment of Workers and Effect on Earnings

Figures are based on a group of occupations: Fire Fighting and Prevention Workers

	Percent at Level	Effect on Earnings
Less than High School	—	—
Some High School	—	—
High School or Equivalent	25.1%	–9.7%
Some College but No Degree	30.9%	–2.5%
Associate Degree	20.6%	2.3%
Bachelor's Degree	19.3%	18.6%
Master's Degree	—	—
Doctoral Degree	—	—
First Professional Degree	—	—

Flexibility of Earnings

Average Hours Worked: 42
Workers with a Varying Number of Hours: 13.7%
Workers Earning Some Overtime Pay, Tips, or Commissions: 28.4%
Earnings Benefit of Working Overtime: –7.1%

Gender

	Male	Female
Percent	96.1%	3.9%
Effect on Earnings	6.3%	–19.6%

Union Membership

Percentage Union Members: 67.3%
Earnings Benefit of Union Membership: 4.9%

Veteran Status

Percentage Who Have Been on Active Duty: 19.5%
Earnings Benefit of Veteran Status: 6.2%

33-3000 Law Enforcement Workers

33-3011 Bailiffs

Maintain order in courts of law.

- Education or Training Required: Moderate-term on-the-job training
- Job Growth: 13.2%
- Annual Openings: 2,000
- Self-Employed: 0.0%
- Part-Time: 3.8%

NATIONAL WAGE FIGURES (ANNUAL)

Beginning	25th Percentile	Median	Mean	75th Percentile	90th Percentile
$18,390	$25,130	$34,210	$36,260	$48,010	$58,270

Median Wages for Industries Employing Largest Numbers (Annual)

Industry	Median Income
Federal, State, and Local Government	$34,190

Median Wages for States (Annual)

AK	no data	KY	$19,600	NY	$51,760
AL	$30,330	LA	$25,240	OH	$34,760
AR	$27,860	MA	$51,110	OK	$28,270
AZ	$30,470	MD	$29,180	OR	$37,110
CA	$45,940	ME	$27,720	PA	no data
CO	$27,450	MI	$29,980	RI	no data
CT	no data	MN	$25,870	SC	$21,230
DC	no data	MO	$24,880	SD	no data
DE	$32,750	MS	$20,080	TN	$30,970
FL	$40,550	MT	no data	TX	$31,470
GA	$17,870	NC	$28,520	UT	$32,960
HI	no data	ND	no data	VA	$32,840
IA	no data	NE	$42,080	VT	no data
ID	$31,220	NH	$24,860	WA	$38,450
IL	no data	NJ	$28,670	WI	$22,170
IN	$27,510	NM	$24,570	WV	$25,050
KS	$32,910	NV	no data	WY	no data

Median Wages for the Largest Metropolitan Areas (Annual)

AZ: Phoenix	$30,540	MI: Detroit	$30,660
CA: Los Angeles	no data	MN: Minneapolis	$35,550
CA: Riverside	no data	MO: Kansas City	$27,780
CA: Sacramento	no data	MO: St. Louis	$28,340
CA: San Diego	no data	NV: Las Vegas	no data
CA: San Francisco	no data	NY: New York	no data
CO: Denver	$39,990	OH: Cincinnati	$34,640
DC: Washington	$27,010	OH: Cleveland	$33,720
FL: Miami	no data	OH: Columbus	no data
FL: Orlando	$46,290	OR: Portland	no data
FL: Tampa	no data	PA: Philadelphia	no data
GA: Atlanta	$21,200	PA: Pittsburgh	no data
IL: Chicago	no data	TX: Dallas	$35,810
MA: Boston	$50,490	TX: Houston	$33,010
MD: Baltimore	no data	WA: Seattle	no data

FACTORS THAT MAY AFFECT EARNINGS

Educational Attainment of Workers and Effect on Earnings

Figures are based on a group of occupations: Law Enforcement Workers

	Percent at Level	Effect on Earnings
Less than High School	—	—
Some High School	1.1%	−33.4%
High School or Equivalent	24.6%	−19.3%
Some College but No Degree	26.6%	−2.6%
Associate Degree	18.2%	−3.3%
Bachelor's Degree	23.7%	18.6%
Master's Degree	4.5%	36.6%
Doctoral Degree	—	—
First Professional Degree	1.0%	38.5%

Flexibility of Earnings

Average Hours Worked: 39

Workers with a Varying Number of Hours: 6.6%

Workers Earning Some Overtime Pay, Tips, or Commissions: 26.4%

Earnings Benefit of Working Overtime: −5.8%

Gender

	Male	Female
Percent	71.8%	28.2%
Effect on Earnings	6.9%	−11.1%

Union Membership

Percentage Union Members: 46.6%

Earnings Benefit of Union Membership: 9.2%

Veteran Status

Percentage Who Have Been on Active Duty: 25.4%

Earnings Benefit of Veteran Status: 1.2%

33-3012 Correctional Officers and Jailers

Guard inmates in penal or rehabilitative institution in accordance with established regulations and procedures. May guard prisoners in transit between jail, courtroom, prison, or other point. Includes deputy sheriffs and police who spend the majority of their time guarding prisoners in correctional institutions.

- Education or Training Required: Moderate-term on-the-job training
- Job Growth: 6.7%
- Annual Openings: 54,000
- Self-Employed: 0.0%
- Part-Time: 3.8%

NATIONAL WAGE FIGURES (ANNUAL)

Beginning	25th Percentile	Median	Mean	75th Percentile	90th Percentile
$23,600	$28,320	$35,760	$38,310	$46,500	$58,580

Median Wages for Industries Employing Largest Numbers (Annual)

Industry	Median Income
Hospitals	$44,830
Federal, State, and Local Government	$36,180
Administrative and Support Services	$25,040
Nursing and Residential Care Facilities	$25,020

Median Wages for States (Annual)

State	Wage	State	Wage	State	Wage
AK	$45,250	KY	$24,780	NY	$46,630
AL	$28,830	LA	$24,590	OH	no data
AR	$28,040	MA	$55,930	OK	$24,690
AZ	$32,950	MD	$38,790	OR	$43,060
CA	$64,090	ME	$29,120	PA	no data
CO	$41,010	MI	no data	RI	no data
CT	$44,650	MN	$38,340	SC	$27,760
DC	no data	MO	$24,620	SD	$28,200
DE	no data	MS	$22,290	TN	$26,040
FL	$34,990	MT	$28,880	TX	$29,530
GA	$28,800	NC	$28,590	UT	$34,510
HI	$38,940	ND	$29,200	VA	$34,240
IA	$39,340	NE	$29,440	VT	no data
ID	$28,830	NH	$34,960	WA	$38,200
IL	$45,310	NJ	$57,890	WI	$36,490
IN	no data	NM	$29,250	WV	$24,330
KS	$29,810	NV	$47,700	WY	$31,650

Median Wages for the Largest Metropolitan Areas (Annual)

Area	Wage	Area	Wage
AZ: Phoenix	$32,850	MI: Detroit	no data
CA: Los Angeles	no data	MN: Minneapolis	$39,960
CA: Riverside	$65,990	MO: Kansas City	$29,710
CA: Sacramento	no data	MO: St. Louis	$34,350
CA: San Diego	$53,290	NV: Las Vegas	$51,980
CA: San Francisco	$63,540	NY: New York	$55,140
CO: Denver	$44,910	OH: Cincinnati	no data
DC: Washington	$46,570	OH: Cleveland	no data
FL: Miami	$39,740	OH: Columbus	no data
FL: Orlando	$35,230	OR: Portland	$47,850
FL: Tampa	$41,790	PA: Philadelphia	$42,310
GA: Atlanta	$30,160	PA: Pittsburgh	$35,380
IL: Chicago	no data	TX: Dallas	$29,440
MA: Boston	$56,080	TX: Houston	$29,980
MD: Baltimore	$37,410	WA: Seattle	$39,810

FACTORS THAT MAY AFFECT EARNINGS

Educational Attainment of Workers and Effect on Earnings

Figures are based on a group of occupations: Law Enforcement Workers

	Percent at Level	Effect on Earnings
Less than High School	—	—
Some High School	1.1%	−33.4%
High School or Equivalent	24.6%	−19.3%
Some College but No Degree	26.6%	−2.6%
Associate Degree	18.2%	−3.3%
Bachelor's Degree	23.7%	18.6%
Master's Degree	4.5%	36.6%
Doctoral Degree	—	—
First Professional Degree	1.0%	38.5%

Flexibility of Earnings

Average Hours Worked: 39
Workers with a Varying Number of Hours: 6.6%
Workers Earning Some Overtime Pay, Tips, or Commissions: 26.4%
Earnings Benefit of Working Overtime: −5.8%

Gender

	Male	Female
Percent	71.8%	28.2%
Effect on Earnings	6.9%	−11.1%

Union Membership

Percentage Union Members: 46.6%
Earnings Benefit of Union Membership: 9.2%

Veteran Status

Percentage Who Have Been on Active Duty: 25.4%
Earnings Benefit of Veteran Status: 1.2%

33-3021 Detectives and Criminal Investigators

Conduct investigations related to suspected violations of federal, state, or local laws to prevent or solve crimes.

- Education or Training Required: Work experience in a related occupation
- Job Growth: 16.3%
- Annual Openings: 9,000
- Self-Employed: 0.0%
- Part-Time: 3.8%

NATIONAL WAGE FIGURES (ANNUAL)

Beginning	25th Percentile	Median	Mean	75th Percentile	90th Percentile
$34,480	$43,920	$58,260	$60,390	$76,350	$92,590

Median Wages for Industries Employing Largest Numbers (Annual)

Industry	Median Income
Postal Service	$76,920
Federal, State, and Local Government	$58,210
Educational Services	$51,370

Median Wages for States (Annual)

AK	$64,320	KY	$50,180	NY	$60,900
AL	$40,710	LA	$37,320	OH	$57,290
AR	$35,510	MA	$66,050	OK	$40,490
AZ	$54,240	MD	$72,060	OR	$60,810
CA	$73,960	ME	$50,000	PA	$60,100
CO	$68,580	MI	$60,710	RI	$56,720
CT	$63,190	MN	$60,290	SC	$40,150
DC	$83,550	MO	$44,300	SD	$48,280
DE	$60,050	MS	$37,570	TN	$47,770
FL	$54,220	MT	$54,550	TX	$54,740
GA	$45,520	NC	$40,060	UT	$48,900
HI	$64,780	ND	$51,640	VA	$65,540
IA	$54,010	NE	$52,360	VT	$59,220
ID	$50,290	NH	$48,470	WA	$68,730
IL	$76,030	NJ	$81,420	WI	$56,490
IN	$42,810	NM	$52,310	WV	$35,180
KS	$49,400	NV	$62,660	WY	$49,950

Median Wages for the Largest Metropolitan Areas (Annual)

AZ: Phoenix	$52,330	MI: Detroit	$65,050
CA: Los Angeles	$87,320	MN: Minneapolis	$62,610
CA: Riverside	$69,760	MO: Kansas City	$51,720
CA: Sacramento	$60,800	MO: St. Louis	$51,200
CA: San Diego	$61,270	NV: Las Vegas	$64,090
CA: San Francisco	$80,040	NY: New York	$72,570
CO: Denver	$70,730	OH: Cincinnati	$55,830
DC: Washington	$83,140	OH: Cleveland	$61,750
FL: Miami	$67,450	OH: Columbus	$59,690
FL: Orlando	$47,370	OR: Portland	$64,370
FL: Tampa	$55,850	PA: Philadelphia	$63,140
GA: Atlanta	$49,570	PA: Pittsburgh	$59,650
IL: Chicago	$77,970	TX: Dallas	$53,710
MA: Boston	$64,900	TX: Houston	$54,670
MD: Baltimore	$70,130	WA: Seattle	$71,650

FACTORS THAT MAY AFFECT EARNINGS

Educational Attainment of Workers and Effect on Earnings

	Percent at Level	Effect on Earnings
Less than High School	—	—
Some High School	—	—
High School or Equivalent	11.5%	−25.9%
Some College but No Degree	18.8%	−10.9%
Associate Degree	13.9%	−4.8%
Bachelor's Degree	41.8%	6.2%
Master's Degree	10.9%	33.7%
Doctoral Degree	—	—
First Professional Degree	—	—

Flexibility of Earnings

Average Hours Worked: 41
Workers with a Varying Number of Hours: 5.2%
Workers Earning Some Overtime Pay, Tips, or Commissions: 24.8%
Earnings Benefit of Working Overtime: 31.9%

Gender

	Male	Female
Percent	74.0%	26.0%
Effect on Earnings	9.5%	—

Union Membership

Percentage Union Members: 37.9%
Earnings Benefit of Union Membership: −1.7%

Veteran Status

Percentage Who Have Been on Active Duty: 25.4%
Earnings Benefit of Veteran Status: 1.2%

33-3031 Fish and Game Wardens

Patrol assigned area to prevent fish and game law violations. Investigate reports of damage to crops or property by wildlife. Compile biological data.

- Education or Training Required: Associate degree
- Job Growth: 10.5%
- Annual Openings: 1,000
- Self-Employed: 0.0%
- Part-Time: 3.8%

NATIONAL WAGE FIGURES (ANNUAL)

Beginning	25th Percentile	Median	Mean	75th Percentile	90th Percentile
$28,270	$34,380	$43,700	$44,200	$52,770	$62,270

Median Wages for Industries Employing Largest Numbers (Annual)

Industry	Median Income
Federal, State, and Local Government	$43,700

Median Wages for States (Annual)

State	Wage	State	Wage	State	Wage
AK	no data	KY	no data	NY	$59,870
AL	$42,450	LA	$45,550	OH	no data
AR	$36,740	MA	$51,590	OK	$40,350
AZ	$39,790	MD	no data	OR	no data
CA	$58,480	ME	$44,020	PA	no data
CO	$50,410	MI	no data	RI	no data
CT	$43,830	MN	no data	SC	no data
DC	no data	MO	no data	SD	$33,800
DE	no data	MS	$35,790	TN	no data
FL	no data	MT	$38,130	TX	$42,690
GA	$30,790	NC	$40,730	UT	no data
HI	no data	ND	$51,730	VA	$42,980
IA	$51,980	NE	$45,580	VT	no data
ID	$47,570	NH	no data	WA	$62,380
IL	no data	NJ	no data	WI	$43,330
IN	no data	NM	$30,470	WV	$36,840
KS	$46,780	NV	no data	WY	$42,540

Median Wages for the Largest Metropolitan Areas (Annual)

Area	Wage	Area	Wage
AZ: Phoenix	no data	MI: Detroit	no data
CA: Los Angeles	no data	MN: Minneapolis	no data
CA: Riverside	no data	MO: Kansas City	no data
CA: Sacramento	no data	MO: St. Louis	no data
CA: San Diego	no data	NV: Las Vegas	no data
CA: San Francisco	no data	NY: New York	no data
CO: Denver	no data	OH: Cincinnati	no data
DC: Washington	$48,810	OH: Cleveland	no data
FL: Miami	no data	OH: Columbus	no data
FL: Orlando	no data	OR: Portland	no data
FL: Tampa	no data	PA: Philadelphia	no data
GA: Atlanta	no data	PA: Pittsburgh	no data
IL: Chicago	no data	TX: Dallas	no data
MA: Boston	no data	TX: Houston	no data
MD: Baltimore	no data	WA: Seattle	no data

FACTORS THAT MAY AFFECT EARNINGS

Educational Attainment of Workers and Effect on Earnings

Figures are based on a group of occupations: Law Enforcement Workers

	Percent at Level	Effect on Earnings
Less than High School	—	—
Some High School	1.1%	−33.4%
High School or Equivalent	24.6%	−19.3%
Some College but No Degree	26.6%	−2.6%
Associate Degree	18.2%	−3.3%
Bachelor's Degree	23.7%	18.6%
Master's Degree	4.5%	36.6%
Doctoral Degree	—	—
First Professional Degree	1.0%	38.5%

Flexibility of Earnings

Average Hours Worked: 31
Workers with a Varying Number of Hours: 22.2%
Workers Earning Some Overtime Pay, Tips, or Commissions: 26.4%
Earnings Benefit of Working Overtime: 7.6%

Gender

	Male	Female
Percent	78.4%	21.6%
Effect on Earnings	6.3%	−19.6%

Union Membership

Percentage Union Members: 28.6%
Earnings Benefit of Union Membership: 9.2%

Veteran Status

Percentage Who Have Been on Active Duty: 25.4%
Earnings Benefit of Veteran Status: 1.2%

33-3041 Parking Enforcement Workers

Patrol assigned area, such as public parking lot or section of city, to issue tickets to overtime parking violators and illegally parked vehicles.

- Education or Training Required: Short-term on-the-job training
- Job Growth: 15.1%
- Annual Openings: 1,000
- Self-Employed: 1.5%
- Part-Time: 3.8%

NATIONAL WAGE FIGURES (ANNUAL)

Beginning	25th Percentile	Median	Mean	75th Percentile	90th Percentile
$18,440	$22,700	$30,160	$31,260	$38,900	$46,940

Median Wages for Industries Employing Largest Numbers (Annual)

Industry	Median Income
Federal, State, and Local Government	$31,010
Hospitals	$28,810
Personal and Laundry Services	$26,250
Administrative and Support Services	$22,860
Educational Services	$22,730

Median Wages for States (Annual)

AK	no data	KY	$21,930	NY	$29,840
AL	$26,130	LA	no data	OH	$29,440
AR	no data	MA	$32,580	OK	$27,590
AZ	$27,980	MD	$30,160	OR	$32,760
CA	$41,600	ME	$27,520	PA	$21,690
CO	no data	MI	$29,850	RI	no data
CT	$31,950	MN	$30,450	SC	$22,070
DC	no data	MO	$25,080	SD	no data
DE	no data	MS	$18,520	TN	$29,040
FL	$31,050	MT	no data	TX	$25,410
GA	$30,300	NC	$23,060	UT	$33,130
HI	no data	ND	no data	VA	$18,350
IA	$30,290	NE	no data	VT	no data
ID	no data	NH	$30,360	WA	no data
IL	$32,060	NJ	$24,960	WI	$33,700
IN	$24,150	NM	no data	WV	$19,000
KS	$26,120	NV	no data	WY	no data

Median Wages for the Largest Metropolitan Areas (Annual)

AZ: Phoenix	$25,040	MI: Detroit	no data
CA: Los Angeles	$36,240	MN: Minneapolis	no data
CA: Riverside	$38,400	MO: Kansas City	$29,500
CA: Sacramento	$36,830	MO: St. Louis	$25,500
CA: San Diego	$33,890	NV: Las Vegas	no data
CA: San Francisco	no data	NY: New York	$30,040
CO: Denver	no data	OH: Cincinnati	no data
DC: Washington	$29,300	OH: Cleveland	$33,360
FL: Miami	$33,270	OH: Columbus	no data
FL: Orlando	no data	OR: Portland	no data
FL: Tampa	$25,800	PA: Philadelphia	$29,360
GA: Atlanta	no data	PA: Pittsburgh	$16,510
IL: Chicago	$33,760	TX: Dallas	$26,490
MA: Boston	$33,190	TX: Houston	no data
MD: Baltimore	$26,890	WA: Seattle	no data

FACTORS THAT MAY AFFECT EARNINGS

Educational Attainment of Workers and Effect on Earnings

	Percent at Level	Effect on Earnings
Less than High School	—	—
Some High School	—	—
High School or Equivalent	53.8%	−27.7%
Some College but No Degree	—	—
Associate Degree	—	—
Bachelor's Degree	—	—
Master's Degree	—	—
Doctoral Degree	—	—
First Professional Degree	—	—

Figures do not total 100% because some levels have a very small sample size.

Flexibility of Earnings

Average Hours Worked: 38
Workers with a Varying Number of Hours: 6.6%
Workers Earning Some Overtime Pay, Tips, or Commissions: 15.4%
Earnings Benefit of Working Overtime: 7.6%

Gender

	Male	Female
Percent	45.8%	54.2%
Effect on Earnings	6.3%	−19.6%

Union Membership

Percentage Union Members: 30.8%
Earnings Benefit of Union Membership: 9.2%

Veteran Status

Percentage Who Have Been on Active Duty: 25.4%
Earnings Benefit of Veteran Status: 1.2%

33-3051 Police and Sheriff's Patrol Officers

Maintain order, enforce laws and ordinances, and protect life and property in an assigned patrol district. Perform combination of following duties: Patrol a specific area on foot or in a vehicle, direct traffic, issue traffic summonses, investigate accidents, apprehend and arrest suspects, or serve legal processes of courts.

- Education or Training Required: Long-term on-the-job training
- Job Growth: 15.5%
- Annual Openings: 47,000
- Self-Employed: 0.0%
- Part-Time: 4.7%

NATIONAL WAGE FIGURES (ANNUAL)

Beginning	25th Percentile	Median	Mean	75th Percentile	90th Percentile
$27,310	$35,600	$47,460	$48,410	$59,880	$72,450

Median Wages for Industries Employing Largest Numbers (Annual)

Industry	Median Income
Federal, State, and Local Government	$47,660
Hospitals	$45,640
Postal Service	$45,460
Educational Services	$40,340

Median Wages for States (Annual)

State	Wage	State	Wage	State	Wage
AK	$56,110	KY	$35,620	NY	no data
AL	$32,870	LA	$28,600	OH	$47,210
AR	$20,430	MA	$49,220	OK	$28,870
AZ	$49,390	MD	$49,720	OR	$51,510
CA	$68,890	ME	$35,270	PA	$53,580
CO	$53,190	MI	$49,940	RI	$46,890
CT	$55,580	MN	$49,040	SC	$34,120
DC	no data	MO	$32,010	SD	$33,420
DE	$48,590	MS	$28,260	TN	$31,730
FL	$46,060	MT	$37,610	TX	$44,270
GA	$35,590	NC	$36,060	UT	$40,100
HI	$45,990	ND	$39,120	VA	$42,850
IA	$41,850	NE	$38,930	VT	$32,520
ID	$41,140	NH	$40,130	WA	$59,240
IL	$59,930	NJ	$70,460	WI	$46,480
IN	$41,560	NM	$36,730	WV	$32,110
KS	$36,280	NV	$57,710	WY	$41,050

Median Wages for the Largest Metropolitan Areas (Annual)

Area	Wage	Area	Wage
AZ: Phoenix	$49,870	MI: Detroit	$52,700
CA: Los Angeles	$71,980	MN: Minneapolis	$55,490
CA: Riverside	$66,740	MO: Kansas City	$39,600
CA: Sacramento	$56,210	MO: St. Louis	$41,810
CA: San Diego	$67,150	NV: Las Vegas	no data
CA: San Francisco	$73,640	NY: New York	no data
CO: Denver	$57,660	OH: Cincinnati	$50,870
DC: Washington	$54,900	OH: Cleveland	$53,440
FL: Miami	$56,610	OH: Columbus	$50,090
FL: Orlando	$45,360	OR: Portland	$57,490
FL: Tampa	$46,790	PA: Philadelphia	$57,030
GA: Atlanta	$39,180	PA: Pittsburgh	$53,550
IL: Chicago	$62,000	TX: Dallas	$49,320
MA: Boston	$51,050	TX: Houston	$46,360
MD: Baltimore	$50,740	WA: Seattle	$62,060

FACTORS THAT MAY AFFECT EARNINGS

Educational Attainment of Workers and Effect on Earnings

	Percent at Level	Effect on Earnings
Less than High School	—	—
Some High School	—	—
High School or Equivalent	21.3%	−16.7%
Some College but No Degree	26.9%	−2.6%
Associate Degree	19.9%	−1.7%
Bachelor's Degree	26.8%	14.4%
Master's Degree	3.9%	16.4%
Doctoral Degree	—	—
First Professional Degree	—	—

Flexibility of Earnings

Average Hours Worked: 39
Workers with a Varying Number of Hours: 6.8%
Workers Earning Some Overtime Pay, Tips, or Commissions: 30.7%
Earnings Benefit of Working Overtime: −3.2%

Gender

	Male	Female
Percent	87.2%	12.8%
Effect on Earnings	2.1%	−12.5%

Union Membership

Percentage Union Members: 54.2%
Earnings Benefit of Union Membership: 11.2%

Veteran Status

Percentage Who Have Been on Active Duty: 25.4%
Earnings Benefit of Veteran Status: 1.2%

33-3052 Transit and Railroad Police

Protect and police railroad and transit property, employees, or passengers.

- Education or Training Required: Long-term on-the-job training
- Job Growth: 9.2%
- Annual Openings: Fewer than 500
- Self-Employed: 0.0%
- Part-Time: 3.8%

NATIONAL WAGE FIGURES (ANNUAL)

Beginning	25th Percentile	Median	Mean	75th Percentile	90th Percentile
$30,950	$37,200	$47,080	$49,620	$61,840	$73,430

Median Wages for Industries Employing Largest Numbers (Annual)

Industry	Median Income
Rail Transportation	$51,300
Federal, State, and Local Government	$46,330
Educational Services	$43,760
Transit and Ground Passenger Transportation	$30,440

Median Wages for States (Annual)

AK	no data	KY	no data	NY	$47,790
AL	no data	LA	no data	OH	$44,330
AR	no data	MA	no data	OK	no data
AZ	no data	MD	$46,630	OR	no data
CA	$41,360	ME	no data	PA	$42,260
CO	no data	MI	no data	RI	no data
CT	no data	MN	no data	SC	no data
DC	no data	MO	no data	SD	no data
DE	no data	MS	no data	TN	no data
FL	$42,700	MT	no data	TX	$51,990
GA	no data	NC	no data	UT	$49,800
HI	no data	ND	no data	VA	no data
IA	no data	NE	no data	VT	no data
ID	no data	NH	no data	WA	no data
IL	$39,950	NJ	no data	WI	no data
IN	$48,220	NM	no data	WV	no data
KS	no data	NV	no data	WY	no data

Median Wages for the Largest Metropolitan Areas (Annual)

AZ: Phoenix	no data	MI: Detroit	no data
CA: Los Angeles	$38,100	MN: Minneapolis	no data
CA: Riverside	no data	MO: Kansas City	no data
CA: Sacramento	no data	MO: St. Louis	no data
CA: San Diego	no data	NV: Las Vegas	no data
CA: San Francisco	no data	NY: New York	no data
CO: Denver	no data	OH: Cincinnati	no data
DC: Washington	no data	OH: Cleveland	no data
FL: Miami	no data	OH: Columbus	no data
FL: Orlando	no data	OR: Portland	no data
FL: Tampa	no data	PA: Philadelphia	no data
GA: Atlanta	no data	PA: Pittsburgh	no data
IL: Chicago	$40,260	TX: Dallas	no data
MA: Boston	no data	TX: Houston	no data
MD: Baltimore	no data	WA: Seattle	no data

FACTORS THAT MAY AFFECT EARNINGS

Educational Attainment of Workers and Effect on Earnings

Figures are based on a group of occupations: Law Enforcement Workers

	Percent at Level	Effect on Earnings
Less than High School	—	—
Some High School	1.1%	−33.4%
High School or Equivalent	24.6%	−19.3%
Some College but No Degree	26.6%	−2.6%
Associate Degree	18.2%	−3.3%
Bachelor's Degree	23.7%	18.6%
Master's Degree	4.5%	36.6%
Doctoral Degree	—	—
First Professional Degree	1.0%	38.5%

Flexibility of Earnings

Average Hours Worked: 27
Workers with a Varying Number of Hours: 28.6%
Workers Earning Some Overtime Pay, Tips, or Commissions: 50.0%
Earnings Benefit of Working Overtime: 7.6%

Gender

	Male	Female
Percent	66.7%	33.3%
Effect on Earnings	6.3%	−19.6%

Union Membership

Percentage Union Members: 46.6%
Earnings Benefit of Union Membership: 9.2%

Veteran Status

Percentage Who Have Been on Active Duty: 25.4%
Earnings Benefit of Veteran Status: 1.2%

33-9000 Other Protective Service Workers

33-9011 Animal Control Workers

Handle animals for the purpose of investigations of mistreatment or control of abandoned, dangerous, or unattended animals.

- Education or Training Required: Moderate-term on-the-job training
- Job Growth: 14.4%
- Annual Openings: 4,000
- Self-Employed: 4.9%
- Part-Time: 66.7%

NATIONAL WAGE FIGURES (ANNUAL)

Beginning	25th Percentile	Median	Mean	75th Percentile	90th Percentile
$17,160	$21,870	$27,910	$29,370	$35,690	$44,800

Median Wages for Industries Employing Largest Numbers (Annual)

Industry	Median Income
Educational Services	$34,640
Federal, State, and Local Government	$28,290
Religious, Grantmaking, Civic, Professional, and Similar Organizations	$24,620
Personal and Laundry Services	$21,460

Median Wages for States (Annual)

AK	no data	KY	$22,320	NY	$28,170
AL	$24,160	LA	$20,350	OH	$27,350
AR	$21,580	MA	$31,140	OK	$21,480
AZ	$28,860	MD	$30,800	OR	$38,060
CA	$41,830	ME	$18,440	PA	$22,800
CO	$34,680	MI	$33,340	RI	$31,200
CT	$26,860	MN	$30,010	SC	$25,450
DC	no data	MO	$25,550	SD	$20,530
DE	no data	MS	$20,870	TN	$25,920
FL	$27,740	MT	$26,570	TX	$26,240
GA	$26,090	NC	$26,080	UT	$28,390
HI	no data	ND	no data	VA	$29,940
IA	$29,350	NE	$27,870	VT	no data
ID	$22,200	NH	$25,400	WA	$35,100
IL	$27,580	NJ	$31,960	WI	$23,000
IN	$25,840	NM	$23,210	WV	$20,050
KS	$23,770	NV	$42,820	WY	$30,570

Median Wages for the Largest Metropolitan Areas (Annual)

AZ: Phoenix	$29,560	MI: Detroit	$35,280
CA: Los Angeles	no data	MN: Minneapolis	$29,220
CA: Riverside	$35,190	MO: Kansas City	$28,690
CA: Sacramento	no data	MO: St. Louis	$28,160
CA: San Diego	no data	NV: Las Vegas	no data
CA: San Francisco	no data	NY: New York	$32,820
CO: Denver	$37,990	OH: Cincinnati	$25,370
DC: Washington	$38,210	OH: Cleveland	$27,770
FL: Miami	$33,600	OH: Columbus	$31,710
FL: Orlando	$27,860	OR: Portland	$39,740
FL: Tampa	$32,860	PA: Philadelphia	$36,600
GA: Atlanta	$27,730	PA: Pittsburgh	$25,650
IL: Chicago	$34,230	TX: Dallas	$30,470
MA: Boston	$33,510	TX: Houston	$26,600
MD: Baltimore	$28,820	WA: Seattle	$42,990

FACTORS THAT MAY AFFECT EARNINGS

Educational Attainment of Workers and Effect on Earnings

Figures are based on a group of occupations: Other Protective Service Workers

	Percent at Level	Effect on Earnings
Less than High School	1.7%	−45.4%
Some High School	12.3%	−46.5%
High School or Equivalent	30.1%	−3.5%
Some College but No Degree	23.6%	−10.8%
Associate Degree	11.6%	7.9%
Bachelor's Degree	16.1%	39.7%
Master's Degree	4.0%	57.2%
Doctoral Degree	—	—
First Professional Degree	—	—

Flexibility of Earnings

Average Hours Worked: 28
Workers with a Varying Number of Hours: 18.6%
Workers Earning Some Overtime Pay, Tips, or Commissions: 30.8%
Earnings Benefit of Working Overtime: 21.3%

Gender

	Male	Female
Percent	39.1%	60.9%
Effect on Earnings	6.3%	−19.6%

Union Membership

Percentage Union Members: 38.5%
Earnings Benefit of Union Membership: 47.1%

Veteran Status

Percentage Who Have Been on Active Duty: 23.1%
Earnings Benefit of Veteran Status: 14.5%

33-9021 Private Detectives and Investigators

Detect occurrences of unlawful acts or infractions of rules in private establishment or seek, examine, and compile information for client.

- Education or Training Required: Work experience in a related occupation
- Job Growth: 17.7%
- Annual Openings: 7,000
- Self-Employed: 23.7%
- Part-Time: 33.3%

NATIONAL WAGE FIGURES (ANNUAL)

Beginning	25th Percentile	Median	Mean	75th Percentile	90th Percentile
$19,720	$24,180	$33,750	$38,290	$47,740	$64,380

Median Wages for Industries Employing Largest Numbers (Annual)

Industry	Median Income
Utilities	$60,830
Merchant Wholesalers, Durable Goods	$59,000
Transportation Equipment Manufacturing	$57,190
Hospitals	$56,310
Telecommunications	$55,400
Credit Intermediation and Related Activities	$53,220
Religious, Grantmaking, Civic, Professional, and Similar Organizations	$52,980
Educational Services	$50,260
Sporting Goods, Hobby, Book, and Music Stores	$49,780
Professional, Scientific, and Technical Services	$48,190

Median Wages for States (Annual)

AK	no data	KY	$26,030	NY	$41,020
AL	$33,080	LA	$27,760	OH	$26,710
AR	$28,830	MA	$34,920	OK	$40,950
AZ	$40,940	MD	$30,650	OR	$25,820
CA	$40,910	ME	$36,200	PA	$30,410
CO	$35,140	MI	$34,750	RI	$35,230
CT	$34,480	MN	$32,240	SC	$47,200
DC	no data	MO	$33,500	SD	no data
DE	$40,380	MS	$18,520	TN	$28,770
FL	$36,530	MT	$22,830	TX	$37,050
GA	no data	NC	$41,010	UT	$31,020
HI	no data	ND	no data	VA	$50,330
IA	$26,460	NE	no data	VT	no data
ID	$25,030	NH	no data	WA	$35,420
IL	$31,750	NJ	$47,290	WI	$30,160
IN	$28,580	NM	$23,240	WV	no data
KS	$25,060	NV	$35,120	WY	no data

Median Wages for the Largest Metropolitan Areas (Annual)

AZ: Phoenix	$45,600	MI: Detroit	$35,240
CA: Los Angeles	$43,470	MN: Minneapolis	$33,520
CA: Riverside	$25,060	MO: Kansas City	$31,640
CA: Sacramento	$27,670	MO: St. Louis	$45,030
CA: San Diego	$50,710	NV: Las Vegas	$34,140
CA: San Francisco	$56,230	NY: New York	$46,030
CO: Denver	$37,430	OH: Cincinnati	$24,990
DC: Washington	$33,310	OH: Cleveland	$27,040
FL: Miami	$39,000	OH: Columbus	$27,270
FL: Orlando	$35,660	OR: Portland	$33,980
FL: Tampa	$37,740	PA: Philadelphia	$32,350
GA: Atlanta	$22,820	PA: Pittsburgh	no data
IL: Chicago	$32,430	TX: Dallas	$36,160
MA: Boston	$35,210	TX: Houston	$39,860
MD: Baltimore	$31,570	WA: Seattle	$35,320

FACTORS THAT MAY AFFECT EARNINGS

Educational Attainment of Workers and Effect on Earnings

	Percent at Level	Effect on Earnings
Less than High School	—	—
Some High School	—	—
High School or Equivalent	20.2%	−16.0%
Some College but No Degree	23.6%	−14.5%
Associate Degree	11.2%	−33.1%
Bachelor's Degree	30.3%	8.3%
Master's Degree	13.5%	60.0%
Doctoral Degree	—	—
First Professional Degree	—	—

Flexibility of Earnings

Average Hours Worked: 33
Workers with a Varying Number of Hours: 12.5%
Workers Earning Some Overtime Pay, Tips, or Commissions: 10.4%
Earnings Benefit of Working Overtime: 21.3%

Gender

	Male	Female
Percent	61.8%	38.2%
Effect on Earnings	6.3%	−19.6%

Union Membership

Percentage Union Members: 21.9%
Earnings Benefit of Union Membership: 31.1%

Veteran Status

Percentage Who Have Been on Active Duty: 23.1%
Earnings Benefit of Veteran Status: 14.5%

33-9031 Gaming Surveillance Officers and Gaming Investigators

Act as oversight and security agent for management and customers. Observe casino or casino hotel operation for irregular activities such as cheating or theft by either employees or patrons. May utilize one-way mirrors above the casino floor and cashier's cage and from desk. Use of audio/video equipment is also common to observe operation of the business. Usually required to provide verbal and written reports of all violations and suspicious behavior to supervisor.

- Education or Training Required: Moderate-term on-the-job training
- Job Growth: 24.5%
- Annual Openings: 2,000
- Self-Employed: 0.8%
- Part-Time: 39.2%

NATIONAL WAGE FIGURES (ANNUAL)

Beginning	25th Percentile	Median	Mean	75th Percentile	90th Percentile
$18,720	$21,600	$27,130	$30,470	$35,970	$45,940

Median Wages for Industries Employing Largest Numbers (Annual)

Industry	Median Income
Accommodation	$32,080
Federal, State, and Local Government	$27,310
Amusement, Gambling, and Recreation Industries	$25,040
Performing Arts, Spectator Sports, and Related Industries	$22,900

Median Wages for States (Annual)

State	Wage	State	Wage	State	Wage
AK	no data	KY	no data	NY	$28,560
AL	$21,340	LA	$24,540	OH	no data
AR	no data	MA	no data	OK	$21,140
AZ	$25,090	MD	no data	OR	$25,700
CA	$28,870	ME	no data	PA	no data
CO	$30,220	MI	$31,390	RI	no data
CT	no data	MN	no data	SC	no data
DC	no data	MO	$28,090	SD	$20,580
DE	$24,830	MS	$30,750	TN	no data
FL	$22,850	MT	no data	TX	no data
GA	no data	NC	no data	UT	no data
HI	no data	ND	no data	VA	no data
IA	$25,200	NE	no data	VT	no data
ID	no data	NH	no data	WA	$24,880
IL	no data	NJ	no data	WI	no data
IN	$27,620	NM	$23,710	WV	no data
KS	no data	NV	$32,540	WY	no data

Median Wages for the Largest Metropolitan Areas (Annual)

Area	Wage	Area	Wage
AZ: Phoenix	$25,820	MI: Detroit	no data
CA: Los Angeles	no data	MN: Minneapolis	no data
CA: Riverside	no data	MO: Kansas City	$31,450
CA: Sacramento	no data	MO: St. Louis	$29,250
CA: San Diego	no data	NV: Las Vegas	$34,090
CA: San Francisco	no data	NY: New York	no data
CO: Denver	$31,640	OH: Cincinnati	no data
DC: Washington	no data	OH: Cleveland	no data
FL: Miami	no data	OH: Columbus	no data
FL: Orlando	no data	OR: Portland	no data
FL: Tampa	no data	PA: Philadelphia	no data
GA: Atlanta	no data	PA: Pittsburgh	no data
IL: Chicago	no data	TX: Dallas	no data
MA: Boston	no data	TX: Houston	no data
MD: Baltimore	no data	WA: Seattle	$27,220

FACTORS THAT MAY AFFECT EARNINGS

Educational Attainment of Workers and Effect on Earnings

Figures are based on a group of occupations: Other Protective Service Workers

	Percent at Level	Effect on Earnings
Less than High School	1.7%	−45.4%
Some High School	12.3%	−46.5%
High School or Equivalent	30.1%	−3.5%
Some College but No Degree	23.6%	−10.8%
Associate Degree	11.6%	7.9%
Bachelor's Degree	16.1%	39.7%
Master's Degree	4.0%	57.2%
Doctoral Degree	—	—
First Professional Degree	—	—

Flexibility of Earnings

Average Hours Worked: 30
Workers with a Varying Number of Hours: 12.9%
Workers Earning Some Overtime Pay, Tips, or Commissions: 13.2%
Earnings Benefit of Working Overtime: 19.7%

Gender

	Male	Female
Percent	77.0%	23.0%
Effect on Earnings	2.3%	−14.6%

Union Membership

Percentage Union Members: 11.1%
Earnings Benefit of Union Membership: 47.1%

Veteran Status

Percentage Who Have Been on Active Duty: 23.1%
Earnings Benefit of Veteran Status: 14.5%

33-9032 Security Guards

Guard, patrol, or monitor premises to prevent theft, violence, or infractions of rules.

- Education or Training Required: Short-term on-the-job training
- Job Growth: 12.6%
- Annual Openings: 230,000
- Self-Employed: 0.7%
- Part-Time: 39.2%

NATIONAL WAGE FIGURES (ANNUAL)

Beginning	25th Percentile	Median	Mean	75th Percentile	90th Percentile
$15,030	$17,620	$21,530	$23,620	$27,430	$35,840

Median Wages for Industries Employing Largest Numbers (Annual)

Industry	Median Income
Utilities	$39,110
Building Material and Garden Equipment and Supplies Dealers	$30,390
Credit Intermediation and Related Activities	$29,970
Transportation Equipment Manufacturing	$29,190
Professional, Scientific, and Technical Services	$29,180
Food and Beverage Stores	$28,640
Hospitals	$26,970
Federal, State, and Local Government	$26,570
Educational Services	$25,960
Warehousing and Storage	$25,860

Median Wages for States (Annual)

AK	$27,540	KY	$19,270	NY	$22,820
AL	$17,330	LA	$18,660	OH	$20,620
AR	$17,790	MA	$23,740	OK	$20,980
AZ	$20,950	MD	$23,970	OR	$20,880
CA	$21,730	ME	$21,300	PA	$21,070
CO	$23,550	MI	$22,490	RI	$23,520
CT	$24,280	MN	$24,990	SC	$20,180
DC	$27,730	MO	$21,880	SD	$20,780
DE	$21,780	MS	$17,290	TN	$18,640
FL	$19,620	MT	$18,950	TX	$20,540
GA	$20,650	NC	$20,600	UT	$21,940
HI	$22,650	ND	$20,520	VA	$22,940
IA	$21,620	NE	$21,970	VT	$23,790
ID	$22,920	NH	$25,320	WA	$24,890
IL	$21,980	NJ	$22,820	WI	$21,760
IN	$21,390	NM	$19,710	WV	$16,790
KS	$21,500	NV	$22,760	WY	$21,330

Median Wages for the Largest Metropolitan Areas (Annual)

AZ: Phoenix	$21,210	MI: Detroit	$23,370
CA: Los Angeles	$21,130	MN: Minneapolis	$25,360
CA: Riverside	$19,960	MO: Kansas City	$24,750
CA: Sacramento	$21,340	MO: St. Louis	$21,110
CA: San Diego	$20,640	NV: Las Vegas	$22,800
CA: San Francisco	$24,610	NY: New York	$23,220
CO: Denver	$23,810	OH: Cincinnati	$20,200
DC: Washington	$27,050	OH: Cleveland	$20,940
FL: Miami	$19,730	OH: Columbus	$21,540
FL: Orlando	$20,460	OR: Portland	$21,730
FL: Tampa	$18,740	PA: Philadelphia	$20,980
GA: Atlanta	$20,930	PA: Pittsburgh	$21,640
IL: Chicago	$22,140	TX: Dallas	$21,930
MA: Boston	$24,040	TX: Houston	$20,270
MD: Baltimore	$22,470	WA: Seattle	$25,280

FACTORS THAT MAY AFFECT EARNINGS

Educational Attainment of Workers and Effect on Earnings

Figures are based on a group of occupations: Other Protective Service Workers

	Percent at Level	Effect on Earnings
Less than High School	1.7%	−45.4%
Some High School	12.3%	−46.5%
High School or Equivalent	30.1%	−3.5%
Some College but No Degree	23.6%	−10.8%
Associate Degree	11.6%	7.9%
Bachelor's Degree	16.1%	39.7%
Master's Degree	4.0%	57.2%
Doctoral Degree	—	—
First Professional Degree	—	—

Flexibility of Earnings

Average Hours Worked: 30
Workers with a Varying Number of Hours: 12.9%
Workers Earning Some Overtime Pay, Tips, or Commissions: 13.2%
Earnings Benefit of Working Overtime: 19.7%

Gender

	Male	Female
Percent	77.0%	23.0%
Effect on Earnings	2.3%	−14.6%

Union Membership

Percentage Union Members: 11.1%
Earnings Benefit of Union Membership: 47.1%

Veteran Status

Percentage Who Have Been on Active Duty: 23.1%
Earnings Benefit of Veteran Status: 14.5%

33-9091 Crossing Guards

Guide or control vehicular or pedestrian traffic at such places as streets, schools, railroad crossings, or construction sites.

- Education or Training Required: Short-term on-the-job training
- Job Growth: 19.7%
- Annual Openings: 26,000
- Self-Employed: 0.0%
- Part-Time: 50.0%

NATIONAL WAGE FIGURES (ANNUAL)

Beginning	25th Percentile	Median	Mean	75th Percentile	90th Percentile
$13,870	$16,380	$21,060	$22,270	$26,630	$32,020

Median Wages for Industries Employing Largest Numbers (Annual)

Industry	Median Income
Heavy and Civil Engineering Construction	$27,080
Rental and Leasing Services	$24,720
Administrative and Support Services	$21,350
Federal, State, and Local Government	$21,300
Specialty Trade Contractors	$20,150
Educational Services	$19,070
Waste Management and Remediation Services	$17,940
Religious, Grantmaking, Civic, Professional, and Similar Organizations	$17,660
Motion Picture and Sound Recording Industries	$17,150

Median Wages for States (Annual)

State	Wage	State	Wage	State	Wage
AK	no data	KY	$19,440	NY	no data
AL	$15,290	LA	$14,950	OH	$18,980
AR	$14,370	MA	$22,410	OK	$14,860
AZ	$15,660	MD	$18,730	OR	$23,560
CA	$19,700	ME	$17,490	PA	$18,170
CO	$24,430	MI	$19,520	RI	$32,890
CT	$24,440	MN	$19,380	SC	$19,430
DC	no data	MO	$18,130	SD	$20,030
DE	$37,940	MS	$14,160	TN	$18,460
FL	$17,980	MT	$30,740	TX	$16,590
GA	$17,260	NC	$21,430	UT	$17,080
HI	$22,750	ND	no data	VA	$25,080
IA	$22,270	NE	$19,720	VT	$21,060
ID	$23,580	NH	$20,570	WA	$27,740
IL	$23,630	NJ	$25,100	WI	$21,680
IN	$18,710	NM	no data	WV	$16,240
KS	$17,050	NV	$19,680	WY	$24,160

Median Wages for the Largest Metropolitan Areas (Annual)

Area	Wage	Area	Wage
AZ: Phoenix	$15,370	MI: Detroit	$21,170
CA: Los Angeles	$17,880	MN: Minneapolis	$20,400
CA: Riverside	$20,210	MO: Kansas City	$17,530
CA: Sacramento	$23,570	MO: St. Louis	$19,370
CA: San Diego	$28,820	NV: Las Vegas	no data
CA: San Francisco	$23,090	NY: New York	no data
CO: Denver	$23,840	OH: Cincinnati	$16,810
DC: Washington	$25,760	OH: Cleveland	$19,010
FL: Miami	$19,900	OH: Columbus	$21,450
FL: Orlando	no data	OR: Portland	$22,660
FL: Tampa	$16,930	PA: Philadelphia	$18,650
GA: Atlanta	$21,320	PA: Pittsburgh	$20,130
IL: Chicago	$24,150	TX: Dallas	$18,530
MA: Boston	$25,040	TX: Houston	$19,400
MD: Baltimore	no data	WA: Seattle	$26,390

FACTORS THAT MAY AFFECT EARNINGS

Educational Attainment of Workers and Effect on Earnings

	Percent at Level	Effect on Earnings
Less than High School	—	—
Some High School	9.7%	−29.0%
High School or Equivalent	48.4%	15.0%
Some College but No Degree	22.6%	−9.3%
Associate Degree	12.9%	−13.7%
Bachelor's Degree	—	—
Master's Degree	—	—
Doctoral Degree	—	—
First Professional Degree	—	—

Figures do not total 100% because some levels have a very small sample size.

Flexibility of Earnings

Average Hours Worked: 16
Workers with a Varying Number of Hours: 10.7%
Workers Earning Some Overtime Pay, Tips, or Commissions: 9.5%
Earnings Benefit of Working Overtime: 21.3%

Gender

	Male	Female
Percent	39.4%	60.6%
Effect on Earnings	6.3%	−19.6%

Union Membership

Percentage Union Members: 19.0%
Earnings Benefit of Union Membership: −2.7%

Veteran Status

Percentage Who Have Been on Active Duty: 23.1%
Earnings Benefit of Veteran Status: 14.5%

33-9092 Lifeguards, Ski Patrol, and Other Recreational Protective Service Workers

Monitor recreational areas, such as pools, beaches, or ski slopes, to provide assistance and protection to participants.

- Education or Training Required: Short-term on-the-job training
- Job Growth: 20.4%
- Annual Openings: 49,000
- Self-Employed: 0.2%
- Part-Time: 61.3%

NATIONAL WAGE FIGURES (ANNUAL)

Beginning	25th Percentile	Median	Mean	75th Percentile	90th Percentile
$12,840	$14,700	$17,160	$18,410	$20,630	$25,440

Median Wages for Industries Employing Largest Numbers (Annual)

Industry	Median Income
Professional, Scientific, and Technical Services	$27,100
Hospitals	$18,890
Administrative and Support Services	$18,740
Real Estate	$18,590
Accommodation	$18,020
Heavy and Civil Engineering Construction	$17,980
Federal, State, and Local Government	$17,650
Educational Services	$17,460
Religious, Grantmaking, Civic, Professional, and Similar Organizations	$16,740
Ambulatory Health Care Services	$16,700

Median Wages for States (Annual)

AK	$24,130	KY	$15,160	NY	$19,550
AL	$14,700	LA	$13,990	OH	$15,010
AR	$13,370	MA	$21,330	OK	$14,330
AZ	$18,550	MD	$17,570	OR	$17,610
CA	$21,700	ME	$15,830	PA	$15,130
CO	$18,420	MI	$17,790	RI	$18,650
CT	$19,320	MN	$18,200	SC	$15,780
DC	$21,910	MO	$16,160	SD	$15,930
DE	$18,920	MS	$14,420	TN	$14,630
FL	$19,490	MT	$13,950	TX	$15,280
GA	$16,750	NC	$16,180	UT	$15,000
HI	$29,390	ND	$15,420	VA	$16,840
IA	$13,880	NE	$14,720	VT	$18,040
ID	$14,200	NH	$18,420	WA	$18,340
IL	$16,410	NJ	$17,510	WI	$16,790
IN	$15,020	NM	$15,400	WV	$13,430
KS	$14,970	NV	$18,380	WY	$13,810

Median Wages for the Largest Metropolitan Areas (Annual)

AZ: Phoenix	$19,260	MI: Detroit	$18,350
CA: Los Angeles	$22,470	MN: Minneapolis	$19,250
CA: Riverside	$19,920	MO: Kansas City	$16,770
CA: Sacramento	$18,230	MO: St. Louis	$16,250
CA: San Diego	$23,530	NV: Las Vegas	$18,430
CA: San Francisco	$23,580	NY: New York	$19,850
CO: Denver	$19,280	OH: Cincinnati	$14,130
DC: Washington	$17,620	OH: Cleveland	$16,760
FL: Miami	$24,730	OH: Columbus	$16,850
FL: Orlando	$17,890	OR: Portland	$17,850
FL: Tampa	$17,480	PA: Philadelphia	$16,410
GA: Atlanta	$17,020	PA: Pittsburgh	$14,410
IL: Chicago	$16,730	TX: Dallas	$16,190
MA: Boston	$21,820	TX: Houston	$16,130
MD: Baltimore	$18,090	WA: Seattle	$19,970

FACTORS THAT MAY AFFECT EARNINGS

Educational Attainment of Workers and Effect on Earnings

	Percent at Level	Effect on Earnings
Less than High School	—	—
Some High School	33.7%	−45.5%
High School or Equivalent	17.7%	4.6%
Some College but No Degree	30.3%	−3.0%
Associate Degree	—	—
Bachelor's Degree	12.6%	74.0%
Master's Degree	—	—
Doctoral Degree	—	—
First Professional Degree	—	—

Figures do not total 100% because some levels have a very small sample size.

Flexibility of Earnings

Average Hours Worked: 18
Workers with a Varying Number of Hours: 12.8%
Workers Earning Some Overtime Pay, Tips, or Commissions: 4.6%
Earnings Benefit of Working Overtime: 21.3%

Gender

	Male	Female
Percent	67.3%	32.7%
Effect on Earnings	6.3%	−19.6%

Union Membership

Percentage Union Members: 5.6%
Earnings Benefit of Union Membership: 86.3%

Veteran Status

Percentage Who Have Been on Active Duty: 23.1%
Earnings Benefit of Veteran Status: 14.5%

33-9099 Protective Service Workers, All Other

All protective service workers not listed separately.

- Education or Training Required: Short-term on-the-job training
- Job Growth: 9.6%
- Annual Openings: 53,000
- Self-Employed: 0.9%
- Part-Time: 61.3%

NATIONAL WAGE FIGURES (ANNUAL)

Beginning	25th Percentile	Median	Mean	75th Percentile	90th Percentile
$16,280	$20,090	$26,920	$30,420	$36,960	$50,460

Median Wages for Industries Employing Largest Numbers (Annual)

Industry	Median Income
Postal Service	$60,420
Utilities	$58,270
Wholesale Electronic Markets and Agents and Brokers	$48,480
Transportation Equipment Manufacturing	$39,980
Insurance Carriers and Related Activities	$35,860
Hospitals	$35,630
Computer and Electronic Product Manufacturing	$35,380
Professional, Scientific, and Technical Services	$35,030
Management of Companies and Enterprises	$33,230
Federal, State, and Local Government	$32,180

Median Wages for States (Annual)

State	Wage	State	Wage	State	Wage
AK	$29,950	KY	$26,510	NY	$29,390
AL	$21,010	LA	$23,030	OH	$31,690
AR	$23,830	MA	$24,860	OK	$26,880
AZ	$27,780	MD	$31,260	OR	$31,600
CA	$25,140	ME	$22,650	PA	$27,550
CO	$26,740	MI	$27,550	RI	$20,100
CT	$25,070	MN	$31,190	SC	$22,850
DC	no data	MO	$24,820	SD	$24,950
DE	$21,170	MS	no data	TN	$24,860
FL	$27,450	MT	$28,060	TX	no data
GA	$23,220	NC	$29,970	UT	$25,680
HI	$15,720	ND	$29,390	VA	$27,510
IA	$24,230	NE	$24,680	VT	$31,020
ID	$22,070	NH	$23,110	WA	$28,980
IL	$24,020	NJ	$39,350	WI	$29,410
IN	$22,980	NM	$24,970	WV	$20,040
KS	$25,260	NV	$34,330	WY	$30,160

Median Wages for the Largest Metropolitan Areas (Annual)

Area	Wage	Area	Wage
AZ: Phoenix	$25,250	MI: Detroit	$28,300
CA: Los Angeles	$23,430	MN: Minneapolis	$29,830
CA: Riverside	$22,960	MO: Kansas City	$24,780
CA: Sacramento	$22,120	MO: St. Louis	$24,750
CA: San Diego	$25,940	NV: Las Vegas	$34,050
CA: San Francisco	$31,890	NY: New York	$35,930
CO: Denver	$25,330	OH: Cincinnati	$29,410
DC: Washington	$33,310	OH: Cleveland	$33,630
FL: Miami	$27,710	OH: Columbus	no data
FL: Orlando	$25,730	OR: Portland	$28,980
FL: Tampa	$27,390	PA: Philadelphia	no data
GA: Atlanta	$24,800	PA: Pittsburgh	$29,400
IL: Chicago	$23,860	TX: Dallas	no data
MA: Boston	$26,710	TX: Houston	no data
MD: Baltimore	$30,970	WA: Seattle	$32,030

FACTORS THAT MAY AFFECT EARNINGS

Educational Attainment of Workers and Effect on Earnings

	Percent at Level	Effect on Earnings
Less than High School	—	—
Some High School	33.7%	−45.5%
High School or Equivalent	17.7%	4.6%
Some College but No Degree	30.3%	−3.0%
Associate Degree	—	—
Bachelor's Degree	12.6%	74.0%
Master's Degree	—	—
Doctoral Degree	—	—
First Professional Degree	—	—

Figures do not total 100% because some levels have a very small sample size.

Flexibility of Earnings

Average Hours Worked: 19
Workers with a Varying Number of Hours: 13.4%
Workers Earning Some Overtime Pay, Tips, or Commissions: 4.6%
Earnings Benefit of Working Overtime: 21.3%

Gender

	Male	Female
Percent	43.1%	56.9%
Effect on Earnings	6.3%	−19.6%

Union Membership

Percentage Union Members: 5.6%
Earnings Benefit of Union Membership: 86.3%

Veteran Status

Percentage Who Have Been on Active Duty: 23.1%
Earnings Benefit of Veteran Status: 14.5%

35-0000: Food Preparation and Serving Related Occupations

35-1000 Supervisors, Food Preparation and Serving Workers

35-1011 Chefs and Head Cooks

Direct the preparation, seasoning, and cooking of salads, soups, fish, meats, vegetables, desserts, or other foods. May plan and price menu items, order supplies, and keep records and accounts. May participate in cooking.

- Education or Training Required: Work experience in a related occupation
- Job Growth: 16.7%
- Annual Openings: 11,000
- Self-Employed: 4.4%
- Part-Time: 7.2%

NATIONAL WAGE FIGURES (ANNUAL)

Beginning	25th Percentile	Median	Mean	75th Percentile	90th Percentile
$20,160	$25,910	$34,370	$37,880	$46,040	$60,730

Median Wages for Industries Employing Largest Numbers (Annual)

Industry	Median Income
Federal, State, and Local Government	$53,260
Professional, Scientific, and Technical Services	$49,570
Publishing Industries (Except Internet)	$47,270
Credit Intermediation and Related Activities	$46,650
Beverage and Tobacco Product Manufacturing	$44,000
Performing Arts, Spectator Sports, and Related Industries	$42,990
Administrative and Support Services	$42,080
Amusement, Gambling, and Recreation Industries	$41,150
Hospitals	$40,970
General Merchandise Stores	$40,080

Median Wages for States (Annual)

AK	$29,830	KY	$29,330	NY	$42,130
AL	$26,310	LA	$29,560	OH	$35,150
AR	$28,610	MA	$39,200	OK	$20,750
AZ	$34,770	MD	$36,040	OR	$31,640
CA	$37,410	ME	$35,330	PA	$31,750
CO	$36,760	MI	$31,050	RI	$41,780
CT	$39,110	MN	$35,590	SC	$31,220
DC	$46,570	MO	$33,210	SD	$30,220
DE	$35,790	MS	$24,500	TN	$28,080
FL	$36,600	MT	$28,600	TX	$32,310
GA	$29,130	NC	$32,570	UT	$29,910
HI	$41,980	ND	$27,660	VA	$34,100
IA	$32,480	NE	$29,950	VT	$33,600
ID	$21,750	NH	$32,690	WA	$39,380
IL	$28,580	NJ	$44,480	WI	$28,860
IN	$31,030	NM	$28,030	WV	$25,810
KS	$24,530	NV	$39,850	WY	$30,060

Median Wages for the Largest Metropolitan Areas (Annual)

AZ: Phoenix	$37,690	MI: Detroit	$35,300
CA: Los Angeles	$37,130	MN: Minneapolis	$35,700
CA: Riverside	$34,510	MO: Kansas City	$31,650
CA: Sacramento	$37,550	MO: St. Louis	$36,530
CA: San Diego	$42,210	NV: Las Vegas	$40,500
CA: San Francisco	$39,940	NY: New York	$44,850
CO: Denver	$40,090	OH: Cincinnati	$38,510
DC: Washington	$40,000	OH: Cleveland	$37,900
FL: Miami	$37,280	OH: Columbus	$35,420
FL: Orlando	$37,870	OR: Portland	$32,800
FL: Tampa	$37,070	PA: Philadelphia	$36,480
GA: Atlanta	$35,000	PA: Pittsburgh	$29,020
IL: Chicago	$30,360	TX: Dallas	$35,610
MA: Boston	$39,230	TX: Houston	$36,450
MD: Baltimore	$36,400	WA: Seattle	$40,930

FACTORS THAT MAY AFFECT EARNINGS

Educational Attainment of Workers and Effect on Earnings

	Percent at Level	Effect on Earnings
Less than High School	7.7%	−26.6%
Some High School	9.4%	−35.3%
High School or Equivalent	33.2%	−6.8%
Some College but No Degree	17.7%	−1.3%
Associate Degree	18.4%	30.6%
Bachelor's Degree	12.3%	16.0%
Master's Degree	—	—
Doctoral Degree	—	—
First Professional Degree	—	—

Flexibility of Earnings

Average Hours Worked: 38
Workers with a Varying Number of Hours: 7.6%
Workers Earning Some Overtime Pay, Tips, or Commissions: 13.3%
Earnings Benefit of Working Overtime: 7.2%

Gender

	Male	Female
Percent	76.1%	23.9%
Effect on Earnings	2.6%	−12.1%

Union Membership

Percentage Union Members: 5.2%
Earnings Benefit of Union Membership: −3.7%

Veteran Status

Percentage Who Have Been on Active Duty: 5.0%
Earnings Benefit of Veteran Status: 25.3%

35-1012 First-Line Supervisors/Managers of Food Preparation and Serving Workers

Supervise workers engaged in preparing and serving food.

- Education or Training Required: Work experience in a related occupation
- Job Growth: 16.6%
- Annual Openings: 187,000
- Self-Employed: 3.7%
- Part-Time: 21.4%

NATIONAL WAGE FIGURES (ANNUAL)

Beginning	25th Percentile	Median	Mean	75th Percentile	90th Percentile
$17,340	$21,020	$26,980	$28,870	$34,950	$43,750

Median Wages for Industries Employing Largest Numbers (Annual)

Industry	Median Income
Water Transportation	$36,430
Management of Companies and Enterprises	$34,680
Federal, State, and Local Government	$34,490
Professional, Scientific, and Technical Services	$33,810
Administrative and Support Services	$33,150
Hospitals	$32,680
Accommodation	$31,410
Real Estate	$31,380
Amusement, Gambling, and Recreation Industries	$31,310
General Merchandise Stores	$31,150

Median Wages for States (Annual)

State	Wage	State	Wage	State	Wage
AK	$29,610	KY	$22,080	NY	$27,050
AL	$23,750	LA	$24,490	OH	$26,870
AR	$22,030	MA	$31,200	OK	$22,390
AZ	$27,480	MD	$30,990	OR	$28,030
CA	$25,280	ME	$25,670	PA	$29,790
CO	$28,590	MI	$27,970	RI	$32,400
CT	$31,360	MN	$25,320	SC	$26,720
DC	$34,180	MO	$31,560	SD	$25,180
DE	$31,320	MS	$23,420	TN	$23,490
FL	$30,770	MT	$24,620	TX	$23,130
GA	$26,910	NC	$25,630	UT	$27,800
HI	$29,750	ND	$25,060	VA	$29,850
IA	$25,870	NE	$25,200	VT	$32,620
ID	$20,460	NH	$31,540	WA	$35,320
IL	$29,940	NJ	$34,180	WI	$28,000
IN	$26,650	NM	$22,290	WV	$21,380
KS	$22,830	NV	$28,750	WY	$22,860

Median Wages for the Largest Metropolitan Areas (Annual)

Area	Wage	Area	Wage
AZ: Phoenix	$28,170	MI: Detroit	$30,580
CA: Los Angeles	$25,350	MN: Minneapolis	$26,730
CA: Riverside	$24,370	MO: Kansas City	$30,070
CA: Sacramento	$24,600	MO: St. Louis	$32,200
CA: San Diego	$24,790	NV: Las Vegas	$30,110
CA: San Francisco	$26,900	NY: New York	$31,480
CO: Denver	$29,810	OH: Cincinnati	$27,370
DC: Washington	$32,690	OH: Cleveland	$26,530
FL: Miami	$31,580	OH: Columbus	$28,560
FL: Orlando	$30,530	OR: Portland	$30,520
FL: Tampa	$32,090	PA: Philadelphia	$33,400
GA: Atlanta	$28,410	PA: Pittsburgh	$28,630
IL: Chicago	$31,170	TX: Dallas	$24,370
MA: Boston	$31,720	TX: Houston	$23,140
MD: Baltimore	$31,340	WA: Seattle	$37,230

FACTORS THAT MAY AFFECT EARNINGS

Educational Attainment of Workers and Effect on Earnings

	Percent at Level	Effect on Earnings
Less than High School	2.4%	−28.9%
Some High School	12.7%	−22.2%
High School or Equivalent	38.4%	−2.7%
Some College but No Degree	25.7%	−4.7%
Associate Degree	9.2%	16.1%
Bachelor's Degree	10.6%	35.3%
Master's Degree	—	—
Doctoral Degree	—	—
First Professional Degree	—	—

Flexibility of Earnings

Average Hours Worked: 35
Workers with a Varying Number of Hours: 9.6%
Workers Earning Some Overtime Pay, Tips, or Commissions: 15.3%
Earnings Benefit of Working Overtime: 10.2%

Gender

	Male	Female
Percent	41.3%	58.7%
Effect on Earnings	13.4%	−7.8%

Union Membership

Percentage Union Members: Insignificant
Earnings Benefit of Union Membership: No significant data available

Veteran Status

Percentage Who Have Been on Active Duty: 5.0%
Earnings Benefit of Veteran Status: 25.3%

35-2000 Cooks and Food Preparation Workers

35-2011 Cooks, Fast Food

Prepare and cook food in a fast food restaurant with a limited menu. Duties of the cooks are limited to preparation of a few basic items and normally involve operating large-volume single-purpose cooking equipment.

- Education or Training Required: Short-term on-the-job training
- Job Growth: 16.4%
- Annual Openings: 174,000
- Self-Employed: 0.8%
- Part-Time: 47.8%

NATIONAL WAGE FIGURES (ANNUAL)

Beginning	25th Percentile	Median	Mean	75th Percentile	90th Percentile
$12,170	$13,730	$15,410	$15,960	$17,700	$20,770

Median Wages for Industries Employing Largest Numbers (Annual)

Industry	Median Income
Hospitals	$21,550
Nursing and Residential Care Facilities	$21,060
General Merchandise Stores	$19,520
Accommodation	$18,680
Real Estate	$17,870
Nonstore Retailers	$17,390
Food and Beverage Stores	$17,050
Food Manufacturing	$16,920
Performing Arts, Spectator Sports, and Related Industries	$16,920
Amusement, Gambling, and Recreation Industries	$16,820

Median Wages for States (Annual)

AK	$17,590	KY	$14,030	NY	$16,010
AL	$13,490	LA	$13,470	OH	$14,870
AR	$13,510	MA	$19,200	OK	$14,220
AZ	$15,950	MD	$17,360	OR	$17,380
CA	$16,490	ME	$18,750	PA	$14,390
CO	$16,190	MI	$14,470	RI	$16,990
CT	$18,400	MN	$16,780	SC	$14,290
DC	$23,200	MO	$14,850	SD	$14,590
DE	$16,940	MS	$13,520	TN	$13,770
FL	$15,880	MT	$13,510	TX	$14,200
GA	$14,440	NC	$15,050	UT	$15,100
HI	$15,620	ND	$15,100	VA	$14,500
IA	$14,350	NE	$14,580	VT	$17,900
ID	$14,120	NH	$18,160	WA	$17,460
IL	$14,930	NJ	$16,890	WI	$16,320
IN	$14,250	NM	$14,250	WV	$13,260
KS	$13,810	NV	$14,400	WY	$13,580

Median Wages for the Largest Metropolitan Areas (Annual)

AZ: Phoenix	$16,530	MI: Detroit	$14,530
CA: Los Angeles	$16,540	MN: Minneapolis	$17,220
CA: Riverside	$16,160	MO: Kansas City	$15,930
CA: Sacramento	$16,400	MO: St. Louis	$15,690
CA: San Diego	$16,330	NV: Las Vegas	$14,330
CA: San Francisco	$17,180	NY: New York	$16,460
CO: Denver	$17,570	OH: Cincinnati	$16,500
DC: Washington	$17,110	OH: Cleveland	$14,820
FL: Miami	$16,050	OH: Columbus	$15,950
FL: Orlando	$15,960	OR: Portland	$17,310
FL: Tampa	$16,000	PA: Philadelphia	$15,730
GA: Atlanta	$15,330	PA: Pittsburgh	$14,950
IL: Chicago	$14,750	TX: Dallas	$14,280
MA: Boston	$19,740	TX: Houston	$14,670
MD: Baltimore	$17,690	WA: Seattle	$17,520

FACTORS THAT MAY AFFECT EARNINGS

Educational Attainment of Workers and Effect on Earnings

Figures are based on a group of occupations: Cooks and Food Preparation Workers

	Percent at Level	Effect on Earnings
Less than High School	10.5%	0.8%
Some High School	24.0%	−29.0%
High School or Equivalent	34.4%	8.1%
Some College but No Degree	18.2%	2.1%
Associate Degree	6.5%	18.1%
Bachelor's Degree	5.7%	39.6%
Master's Degree	—	—
Doctoral Degree	—	—
First Professional Degree	—	—

Flexibility of Earnings

Average Hours Worked: 26
Workers with a Varying Number of Hours: 10.8%
Workers Earning Some Overtime Pay, Tips, or Commissions: 11.3%
Earnings Benefit of Working Overtime: 7.8%

Gender

	Male	Female
Percent	56.6%	43.4%
Effect on Earnings	3.9%	−6.3%

Union Membership

Percentage Union Members: 5.7%
Earnings Benefit of Union Membership: 35.7%

Veteran Status

Percentage Who Have Been on Active Duty: Insignificant
Earnings Benefit of Veteran Status: No significant data available

35-2012 Cooks, Institution and Cafeteria

Prepare and cook large quantities of food for institutions, such as schools, hospitals, or cafeterias.

- Education or Training Required: Moderate-term on-the-job training
- Job Growth: 1.4%
- Annual Openings: 98,000
- Self-Employed: 1.0%
- Part-Time: 47.8%

NATIONAL WAGE FIGURES (ANNUAL)

Beginning	25th Percentile	Median	Mean	75th Percentile	90th Percentile
$13,450	$16,280	$20,410	$21,320	$25,280	$30,770

Median Wages for Industries Employing Largest Numbers (Annual)

Industry	Median Income
Support Activities for Transportation	$30,750
Support Activities for Mining	$30,470
Water Transportation	$28,510
Federal, State, and Local Government	$24,040
Museums, Historical Sites, and Similar Institutions	$23,320
Hospitals	$23,040
Insurance Carriers and Related Activities	$22,590
Nonstore Retailers	$22,450
Food Manufacturing	$22,400
Administrative and Support Services	$22,330

Median Wages for States (Annual)

State	Wage	State	Wage	State	Wage
AK	$31,270	KY	$19,140	NY	$26,090
AL	$14,870	LA	$14,290	OH	$23,230
AR	$14,820	MA	$27,800	OK	$15,860
AZ	$22,170	MD	$24,210	OR	$21,940
CA	$25,100	ME	$22,090	PA	$21,310
CO	$22,330	MI	$23,120	RI	$28,860
CT	$28,070	MN	$25,050	SC	$16,970
DC	$26,880	MO	$18,540	SD	$19,490
DE	$24,580	MS	$15,670	TN	$16,960
FL	$21,610	MT	$17,900	TX	$17,410
GA	$15,550	NC	$18,650	UT	$20,510
HI	$29,590	ND	$20,740	VA	$21,300
IA	$20,070	NE	$19,010	VT	$22,670
ID	$19,640	NH	$25,710	WA	$25,510
IL	$20,500	NJ	$26,460	WI	$22,360
IN	$19,990	NM	$17,620	WV	$18,100
KS	$18,140	NV	$24,440	WY	$19,070

Median Wages for the Largest Metropolitan Areas (Annual)

Area	Wage	Area	Wage
AZ: Phoenix	$22,750	MI: Detroit	$24,940
CA: Los Angeles	$23,430	MN: Minneapolis	$27,040
CA: Riverside	$23,340	MO: Kansas City	$19,640
CA: Sacramento	$25,970	MO: St. Louis	$19,870
CA: San Diego	$24,820	NV: Las Vegas	$25,340
CA: San Francisco	$32,110	NY: New York	$28,140
CO: Denver	$22,060	OH: Cincinnati	$23,780
DC: Washington	$25,930	OH: Cleveland	$23,460
FL: Miami	$22,830	OH: Columbus	$24,840
FL: Orlando	$20,400	OR: Portland	$22,150
FL: Tampa	$21,320	PA: Philadelphia	$22,480
GA: Atlanta	$15,750	PA: Pittsburgh	$20,210
IL: Chicago	$21,580	TX: Dallas	$17,700
MA: Boston	$28,180	TX: Houston	$18,710
MD: Baltimore	$24,240	WA: Seattle	$27,510

FACTORS THAT MAY AFFECT EARNINGS

Educational Attainment of Workers and Effect on Earnings

Figures are based on a group of occupations: Cooks and Food Preparation Workers

	Percent at Level	Effect on Earnings
Less than High School	10.5%	0.8%
Some High School	24.0%	−29.0%
High School or Equivalent	34.4%	8.1%
Some College but No Degree	18.2%	2.1%
Associate Degree	6.5%	18.1%
Bachelor's Degree	5.7%	39.6%
Master's Degree	—	—
Doctoral Degree	—	—
First Professional Degree	—	—

Flexibility of Earnings

Average Hours Worked: 26
Workers with a Varying Number of Hours: 10.8%
Workers Earning Some Overtime Pay, Tips, or Commissions: 11.3%
Earnings Benefit of Working Overtime: 7.8%

Gender

	Male	Female
Percent	56.6%	43.4%
Effect on Earnings	3.9%	−6.3%

Union Membership

Percentage Union Members: 5.7%
Earnings Benefit of Union Membership: 35.7%

Veteran Status

Percentage Who Have Been on Active Duty: Insignificant
Earnings Benefit of Veteran Status: No significant data available

35-2013 Cooks, Private Household

Prepare meals in private homes.

- Education or Training Required: Long-term on-the-job training
- Job Growth: −5.6%
- Annual Openings: 2,000
- Self-Employed: 0.9%
- Part-Time: 47.8%

NATIONAL WAGE FIGURES (ANNUAL)

Beginning	25th Percentile	Median	Mean	75th Percentile	90th Percentile
$14,690	$17,960	$22,870	$28,370	$31,050	$55,040

Note: The mean is significantly higher than the median because of the presence of a few star earners.

Median Wages for Industries Employing Largest Numbers (Annual)

Industry	Median Income
Religious, Grantmaking, Civic, Professional, and Similar Organizations	$22,830
Accommodation	$21,310
Real Estate	$21,180
Nursing and Residential Care Facilities	$21,010

Median Wages for States (Annual)

AK	no data	KY	no data	NY	$23,120
AL	no data	LA	$17,310	OH	$26,920
AR	no data	MA	no data	OK	no data
AZ	no data	MD	no data	OR	no data
CA	$36,410	ME	no data	PA	no data
CO	$22,370	MI	no data	RI	no data
CT	no data	MN	no data	SC	no data
DC	no data	MO	no data	SD	no data
DE	no data	MS	no data	TN	$21,370
FL	no data	MT	$13,410	TX	no data
GA	no data	NC	no data	UT	no data
HI	no data	ND	no data	VA	no data
IA	no data	NE	no data	VT	no data
ID	no data	NH	no data	WA	no data
IL	$20,610	NJ	no data	WI	no data
IN	$23,350	NM	no data	WV	no data
KS	no data	NV	no data	WY	no data

Median Wages for the Largest Metropolitan Areas (Annual)

AZ: Phoenix	no data	MI: Detroit	no data
CA: Los Angeles	no data	MN: Minneapolis	no data
CA: Riverside	no data	MO: Kansas City	no data
CA: Sacramento	no data	MO: St. Louis	no data
CA: San Diego	no data	NV: Las Vegas	no data
CA: San Francisco	$27,920	NY: New York	no data
CO: Denver	no data	OH: Cincinnati	no data
DC: Washington	no data	OH: Cleveland	no data
FL: Miami	no data	OH: Columbus	no data
FL: Orlando	no data	OR: Portland	no data
FL: Tampa	no data	PA: Philadelphia	no data
GA: Atlanta	no data	PA: Pittsburgh	no data
IL: Chicago	no data	TX: Dallas	no data
MA: Boston	no data	TX: Houston	no data
MD: Baltimore	no data	WA: Seattle	no data

FACTORS THAT MAY AFFECT EARNINGS

Educational Attainment of Workers and Effect on Earnings

Figures are based on a group of occupations: Cooks and Food Preparation Workers

	Percent at Level	Effect on Earnings
Less than High School	10.5%	0.8%
Some High School	24.0%	−29.0%
High School or Equivalent	34.4%	8.1%
Some College but No Degree	18.2%	2.1%
Associate Degree	6.5%	18.1%
Bachelor's Degree	5.7%	39.6%
Master's Degree	—	—
Doctoral Degree	—	—
First Professional Degree	—	—

Flexibility of Earnings

Average Hours Worked: 26
Workers with a Varying Number of Hours: 10.8%
Workers Earning Some Overtime Pay, Tips, or Commissions: 11.3%
Earnings Benefit of Working Overtime: 7.8%

Gender

	Male	Female
Percent	56.6%	43.4%
Effect on Earnings	3.9%	−6.3%

Union Membership

Percentage Union Members: 5.7%
Earnings Benefit of Union Membership: 35.7%

Veteran Status

Percentage Who Have Been on Active Duty: Insignificant
Earnings Benefit of Veteran Status: No significant data available

35-2014 Cooks, Restaurant

Prepare, season, and cook soups, meats, vegetables, desserts, or other foodstuffs in restaurants. May order supplies, keep records and accounts, price items on menu, or plan menu.

- Education or Training Required: Long-term on-the-job training
- Job Growth: 16.6%
- Annual Openings: 207,000
- Self-Employed: 0.8%
- Part-Time: 47.8%

NATIONAL WAGE FIGURES (ANNUAL)

Beginning	25th Percentile	Median	Mean	75th Percentile	90th Percentile
$14,370	$16,860	$20,340	$21,020	$24,260	$28,850

Median Wages for Industries Employing Largest Numbers (Annual)

Industry	Median Income
Clothing and Clothing Accessories Stores	$26,330
Accommodation	$23,380
Social Assistance	$22,680
Amusement, Gambling, and Recreation Industries	$22,670
General Merchandise Stores	$22,530
Scenic and Sightseeing Transportation	$21,870
Administrative and Support Services	$21,820
Museums, Historical Sites, and Similar Institutions	$21,820
Nursing and Residential Care Facilities	$21,640
Federal, State, and Local Government	$21,530

Median Wages for States (Annual)

State	Wage	State	Wage	State	Wage
AK	$23,910	KY	$18,010	NY	$23,240
AL	$17,860	LA	$18,080	OH	$19,500
AR	$16,840	MA	$25,570	OK	$16,850
AZ	$20,150	MD	$22,770	OR	$21,100
CA	$21,860	ME	$21,650	PA	$20,490
CO	$20,990	MI	$20,070	RI	$23,250
CT	$25,670	MN	$21,030	SC	$18,960
DC	$25,680	MO	$19,240	SD	$19,140
DE	$22,310	MS	$17,410	TN	$19,190
FL	$21,480	MT	$18,070	TX	$17,460
GA	$19,590	NC	$18,540	UT	$20,100
HI	$23,310	ND	$18,100	VA	$20,440
IA	$18,140	NE	$18,600	VT	$22,840
ID	$17,890	NH	$23,440	WA	$21,760
IL	$17,190	NJ	$23,170	WI	$19,210
IN	$19,010	NM	$17,730	WV	$16,230
KS	$17,970	NV	$24,930	WY	$18,440

Median Wages for the Largest Metropolitan Areas (Annual)

Area	Wage	Area	Wage
AZ: Phoenix	$21,180	MI: Detroit	$21,860
CA: Los Angeles	$21,550	MN: Minneapolis	$22,090
CA: Riverside	$21,300	MO: Kansas City	$20,850
CA: Sacramento	$22,440	MO: St. Louis	$20,520
CA: San Diego	$21,700	NV: Las Vegas	$26,720
CA: San Francisco	$24,020	NY: New York	$24,790
CO: Denver	$20,900	OH: Cincinnati	$20,410
DC: Washington	$23,360	OH: Cleveland	$20,910
FL: Miami	$22,150	OH: Columbus	$20,460
FL: Orlando	$21,550	OR: Portland	$21,590
FL: Tampa	$21,440	PA: Philadelphia	$22,970
GA: Atlanta	$20,750	PA: Pittsburgh	$20,120
IL: Chicago	$16,960	TX: Dallas	$18,210
MA: Boston	$25,700	TX: Houston	$17,440
MD: Baltimore	$23,400	WA: Seattle	$22,310

FACTORS THAT MAY AFFECT EARNINGS

Educational Attainment of Workers and Effect on Earnings

Figures are based on a group of occupations: Cooks and Food Preparation Workers

	Percent at Level	Effect on Earnings
Less than High School	10.5%	0.8%
Some High School	24.0%	−29.0%
High School or Equivalent	34.4%	8.1%
Some College but No Degree	18.2%	2.1%
Associate Degree	6.5%	18.1%
Bachelor's Degree	5.7%	39.6%
Master's Degree	—	—
Doctoral Degree	—	—
First Professional Degree	—	—

Flexibility of Earnings

Average Hours Worked: 26
Workers with a Varying Number of Hours: 10.8%
Workers Earning Some Overtime Pay, Tips, or Commissions: 11.3%
Earnings Benefit of Working Overtime: 7.8%

Gender

	Male	Female
Percent	56.6%	43.4%
Effect on Earnings	3.9%	−6.3%

Union Membership

Percentage Union Members: 5.7%
Earnings Benefit of Union Membership: 35.7%

Veteran Status

Percentage Who Have Been on Active Duty: Insignificant
Earnings Benefit of Veteran Status: No significant data available

35-2015 Cooks, Short Order

Prepare and cook to order a variety of foods that require only a short preparation time. May take orders from customers and serve patrons at counters or tables.

- Education or Training Required: Short-term on-the-job training
- Job Growth: 11.8%
- Annual Openings: 58,000
- Self-Employed: 0.9%
- Part-Time: 47.8%

NATIONAL WAGE FIGURES (ANNUAL)

Beginning	25th Percentile	Median	Mean	75th Percentile	90th Percentile
$12,930	$14,960	$17,880	$18,710	$21,820	$26,110

Median Wages for Industries Employing Largest Numbers (Annual)

Industry	Median Income
Management of Companies and Enterprises	$22,890
Hospitals	$22,260
Administrative and Support Services	$22,090
Heavy and Civil Engineering Construction	$22,090
Accommodation	$21,160
Water Transportation	$20,880
Motion Picture and Sound Recording Industries	$20,250
Educational Services	$20,210
Nursing and Residential Care Facilities	$20,150
Federal, State, and Local Government	$19,440

Median Wages for States (Annual)

State	Wage	State	Wage	State	Wage
AK	$25,050	KY	$15,880	NY	$20,120
AL	$14,080	LA	$15,390	OH	$17,920
AR	$16,130	MA	$22,720	OK	$15,450
AZ	$17,700	MD	$17,500	OR	$18,820
CA	$20,880	ME	$19,480	PA	$17,510
CO	$21,130	MI	$18,040	RI	$20,500
CT	$22,140	MN	$18,440	SC	$16,010
DC	$24,950	MO	$17,500	SD	$17,380
DE	$19,710	MS	$14,400	TN	$15,880
FL	$18,530	MT	$14,890	TX	$16,540
GA	$15,830	NC	$16,050	UT	$19,850
HI	$21,110	ND	$17,140	VA	$16,040
IA	$15,830	NE	$16,880	VT	$20,320
ID	$14,970	NH	$19,270	WA	$21,050
IL	$17,770	NJ	$20,440	WI	$17,240
IN	$16,310	NM	$16,930	WV	$15,470
KS	$15,100	NV	$22,140	WY	$16,660

Median Wages for the Largest Metropolitan Areas (Annual)

Area	Wage	Area	Wage
AZ: Phoenix	$18,870	MI: Detroit	$20,420
CA: Los Angeles	$21,020	MN: Minneapolis	$19,790
CA: Riverside	$19,440	MO: Kansas City	$18,460
CA: Sacramento	$20,510	MO: St. Louis	$18,220
CA: San Diego	$20,400	NV: Las Vegas	$22,500
CA: San Francisco	$23,480	NY: New York	$20,840
CO: Denver	$22,200	OH: Cincinnati	$16,850
DC: Washington	$17,260	OH: Cleveland	$20,540
FL: Miami	$20,080	OH: Columbus	$17,770
FL: Orlando	$18,570	OR: Portland	$18,730
FL: Tampa	$19,560	PA: Philadelphia	$19,030
GA: Atlanta	$16,320	PA: Pittsburgh	$16,670
IL: Chicago	$18,360	TX: Dallas	$18,070
MA: Boston	$22,760	TX: Houston	$17,750
MD: Baltimore	$19,400	WA: Seattle	$21,920

FACTORS THAT MAY AFFECT EARNINGS

Educational Attainment of Workers and Effect on Earnings

Figures are based on a group of occupations: Cooks and Food Preparation Workers

	Percent at Level	Effect on Earnings
Less than High School	10.5%	0.8%
Some High School	24.0%	−29.0%
High School or Equivalent	34.4%	8.1%
Some College but No Degree	18.2%	2.1%
Associate Degree	6.5%	18.1%
Bachelor's Degree	5.7%	39.6%
Master's Degree	—	—
Doctoral Degree	—	—
First Professional Degree	—	—

Flexibility of Earnings

Average Hours Worked: 26
Workers with a Varying Number of Hours: 10.8%
Workers Earning Some Overtime Pay, Tips, or Commissions: 11.3%
Earnings Benefit of Working Overtime: 7.8%

Gender

	Male	Female
Percent	56.6%	43.4%
Effect on Earnings	3.9%	−6.3%

Union Membership

Percentage Union Members: 5.7%
Earnings Benefit of Union Membership: 35.7%

Veteran Status

Percentage Who Have Been on Active Duty: Insignificant
Earnings Benefit of Veteran Status: No significant data available

35-2019 Cooks, All Other

All cooks not listed separately.

- Education or Training Required: Moderate-term on-the-job training
- Job Growth: 5.7%
- Annual Openings: 3,000
- Self-Employed: 0.6%
- Part-Time: 47.8%

NATIONAL WAGE FIGURES (ANNUAL)

Beginning	25th Percentile	Median	Mean	75th Percentile	90th Percentile
$15,200	$17,720	$21,610	$23,590	$27,880	$35,020

Median Wages for Industries Employing Largest Numbers (Annual)

Industry	Median Income
Water Transportation	$29,550
Health and Personal Care Stores	$28,490
Management of Companies and Enterprises	$28,380
Religious, Grantmaking, Civic, Professional, and Similar Organizations	$26,380
Food Manufacturing	$25,720
Food and Beverage Stores	$25,190
Amusement, Gambling, and Recreation Industries	$25,110
Federal, State, and Local Government	$24,120
Merchant Wholesalers, Nondurable Goods	$24,010
Support Activities for Transportation	$23,900

Median Wages for States (Annual)

State	Wage	State	Wage	State	Wage
AK	no data	KY	no data	NY	$24,590
AL	$17,380	LA	$19,530	OH	$18,910
AR	$17,380	MA	$26,580	OK	no data
AZ	no data	MD	$25,310	OR	$26,390
CA	$24,490	ME	no data	PA	$19,800
CO	$29,310	MI	$21,130	RI	no data
CT	$32,030	MN	$20,360	SC	$19,700
DC	no data	MO	$21,670	SD	no data
DE	no data	MS	no data	TN	$20,150
FL	$21,620	MT	no data	TX	$17,680
GA	$23,180	NC	$17,550	UT	no data
HI	$22,910	ND	no data	VA	$23,240
IA	$18,000	NE	no data	VT	no data
ID	$19,660	NH	$19,280	WA	$25,270
IL	$19,970	NJ	$25,520	WI	$21,660
IN	$26,580	NM	no data	WV	$13,690
KS	$25,540	NV	$25,920	WY	$21,360

Median Wages for the Largest Metropolitan Areas (Annual)

Metro	Wage	Metro	Wage
AZ: Phoenix	no data	MI: Detroit	$24,500
CA: Los Angeles	$22,040	MN: Minneapolis	no data
CA: Riverside	$17,380	MO: Kansas City	$21,780
CA: Sacramento	$31,530	MO: St. Louis	$22,580
CA: San Diego	$22,140	NV: Las Vegas	$26,860
CA: San Francisco	$28,130	NY: New York	$24,700
CO: Denver	no data	OH: Cincinnati	$19,660
DC: Washington	$24,350	OH: Cleveland	$18,080
FL: Miami	$22,310	OH: Columbus	$18,910
FL: Orlando	no data	OR: Portland	$20,630
FL: Tampa	$20,800	PA: Philadelphia	$21,310
GA: Atlanta	no data	PA: Pittsburgh	no data
IL: Chicago	$21,650	TX: Dallas	$17,630
MA: Boston	$25,590	TX: Houston	$17,450
MD: Baltimore	$24,140	WA: Seattle	$27,700

FACTORS THAT MAY AFFECT EARNINGS

Educational Attainment of Workers and Effect on Earnings

Figures are based on a group of occupations: Cooks and Food Preparation Workers

	Percent at Level	Effect on Earnings
Less than High School	10.5%	0.8%
Some High School	24.0%	−29.0%
High School or Equivalent	34.4%	8.1%
Some College but No Degree	18.2%	2.1%
Associate Degree	6.5%	18.1%
Bachelor's Degree	5.7%	39.6%
Master's Degree	—	—
Doctoral Degree	—	—
First Professional Degree	—	—

Flexibility of Earnings

Average Hours Worked: 26
Workers with a Varying Number of Hours: 10.8%
Workers Earning Some Overtime Pay, Tips, or Commissions: 11.3%
Earnings Benefit of Working Overtime: 7.8%

Gender

	Male	Female
Percent	56.6%	43.4%
Effect on Earnings	3.9%	−6.3%

Union Membership

Percentage Union Members: 5.7%
Earnings Benefit of Union Membership: 35.7%

Veteran Status

Percentage Who Have Been on Active Duty: Insignificant
Earnings Benefit of Veteran Status: No significant data available

35-2021 Food Preparation Workers

Perform a variety of food preparation duties other than cooking, such as preparing cold foods and shellfish, slicing meat, and brewing coffee or tea.

- Education or Training Required: Short-term on-the-job training
- Job Growth: 19.7%
- Annual Openings: 294,000
- Self-Employed: 0.7%
- Part-Time: 55.3%

NATIONAL WAGE FIGURES (ANNUAL)

Beginning	25th Percentile	Median	Mean	75th Percentile	90th Percentile
$13,190	$14,920	$17,410	$18,480	$21,230	$25,940

Median Wages for Industries Employing Largest Numbers (Annual)

Industry	Median Income
General Merchandise Stores	$20,530
Educational Services	$19,730
Ambulatory Health Care Services	$19,690
Hospitals	$19,290
Furniture and Home Furnishings Stores	$19,120
Accommodation	$18,980
Food and Beverage Stores	$18,750
Federal, State, and Local Government	$18,590
Amusement, Gambling, and Recreation Industries	$18,520
Sporting Goods, Hobby, Book, and Music Stores	$18,310

Median Wages for States (Annual)

State	Wage	State	Wage	State	Wage
AK	$22,830	KY	$17,680	NY	$18,350
AL	$14,920	LA	$13,700	OH	$16,880
AR	$14,140	MA	$20,330	OK	$14,790
AZ	$17,640	MD	$18,450	OR	$18,940
CA	$17,540	ME	$18,880	PA	$17,620
CO	$18,830	MI	$17,680	RI	$18,520
CT	$20,440	MN	$19,740	SC	$16,680
DC	$19,930	MO	$16,870	SD	$16,200
DE	$18,010	MS	$14,010	TN	$17,350
FL	$17,700	MT	$16,870	TX	$15,740
GA	$17,750	NC	$16,290	UT	$15,860
HI	$19,840	ND	$17,880	VA	$17,340
IA	$16,740	NE	$15,950	VT	$18,990
ID	$16,590	NH	$18,890	WA	$20,070
IL	$16,600	NJ	$18,400	WI	$17,810
IN	$16,940	NM	$16,190	WV	$15,340
KS	$16,170	NV	$20,370	WY	$16,960

Median Wages for the Largest Metropolitan Areas (Annual)

Area	Wage	Area	Wage
AZ: Phoenix	$17,580	MI: Detroit	$17,970
CA: Los Angeles	$17,110	MN: Minneapolis	$20,330
CA: Riverside	$17,700	MO: Kansas City	$17,440
CA: Sacramento	$18,260	MO: St. Louis	$16,900
CA: San Diego	$16,970	NV: Las Vegas	$22,330
CA: San Francisco	$20,280	NY: New York	$20,180
CO: Denver	$19,010	OH: Cincinnati	$17,910
DC: Washington	$19,280	OH: Cleveland	$17,340
FL: Miami	$17,800	OH: Columbus	$17,470
FL: Orlando	$16,870	OR: Portland	$19,860
FL: Tampa	$18,280	PA: Philadelphia	$18,390
GA: Atlanta	$18,720	PA: Pittsburgh	$17,310
IL: Chicago	$16,950	TX: Dallas	$17,080
MA: Boston	$20,190	TX: Houston	$16,310
MD: Baltimore	$18,880	WA: Seattle	$21,810

FACTORS THAT MAY AFFECT EARNINGS

Educational Attainment of Workers and Effect on Earnings

	Percent at Level	Effect on Earnings
Less than High School	9.8%	18.9%
Some High School	26.1%	−33.4%
High School or Equivalent	31.7%	6.4%
Some College but No Degree	20.0%	8.9%
Associate Degree	5.9%	9.7%
Bachelor's Degree	6.2%	35.8%
Master's Degree	—	—
Doctoral Degree	—	—
First Professional Degree	—	—

Flexibility of Earnings

Average Hours Worked: 24
Workers with a Varying Number of Hours: 10.8%
Workers Earning Some Overtime Pay, Tips, or Commissions: 13.5%
Earnings Benefit of Working Overtime: −20.7%

Gender

	Male	Female
Percent	40.8%	59.2%
Effect on Earnings	1.8%	−1.2%

Union Membership

Percentage Union Members: 6.6%
Earnings Benefit of Union Membership: 41.0%

Veteran Status

Percentage Who Have Been on Active Duty: Insignificant
Earnings Benefit of Veteran Status: No significant data available

35-3000 Food and Beverage Serving Workers

35-3011 Bartenders
Mix and serve drinks to patrons, directly or through waitstaff.

- Education or Training Required: Short-term on-the-job training
- Job Growth: 14.8%
- Annual Openings: 82,000
- Self-Employed: 1.3%
- Part-Time: 39.5%

NATIONAL WAGE FIGURES (ANNUAL)

Beginning	25th Percentile	Median	Mean	75th Percentile	90th Percentile
$12,480	$14,070	$16,350	$18,540	$21,010	$28,210

Median Wages for Industries Employing Largest Numbers (Annual)

Industry	Median Income
Museums, Historical Sites, and Similar Institutions	$26,980
Scenic and Sightseeing Transportation	$18,440
Performing Arts, Spectator Sports, and Related Industries	$18,320
Administrative and Support Services	$18,250
Accommodation	$18,230
Management of Companies and Enterprises	$18,000
Real Estate	$17,670
Motion Picture and Sound Recording Industries	$17,170
Miscellaneous Store Retailers	$17,010
Federal, State, and Local Government	$16,950

Median Wages for States (Annual)

State	Wage	State	Wage	State	Wage
AK	$21,410	KY	$14,040	NY	$19,420
AL	$14,380	LA	$13,880	OH	$13,950
AR	$14,510	MA	$21,090	OK	$13,970
AZ	$14,740	MD	$15,340	OR	$19,120
CA	$16,940	ME	$16,410	PA	$14,590
CO	$15,130	MI	$15,420	RI	$17,230
CT	$17,680	MN	$18,070	SC	$14,300
DC	$20,980	MO	$15,690	SD	$15,640
DE	$17,260	MS	$14,650	TN	$14,240
FL	$16,500	MT	$15,560	TX	$13,930
GA	$14,570	NC	$15,320	UT	$17,330
HI	$23,400	ND	$15,400	VA	$18,380
IA	$15,610	NE	$14,710	VT	$17,580
ID	$13,850	NH	$16,470	WA	$24,140
IL	$15,500	NJ	$22,960	WI	$16,820
IN	$15,710	NM	$13,830	WV	$13,970
KS	$15,260	NV	$18,400	WY	$14,120

Median Wages for the Largest Metropolitan Areas (Annual)

Area	Wage	Area	Wage
AZ: Phoenix	$15,380	MI: Detroit	$15,910
CA: Los Angeles	$16,360	MN: Minneapolis	$19,130
CA: Riverside	$16,630	MO: Kansas City	$15,160
CA: Sacramento	$17,310	MO: St. Louis	$16,220
CA: San Diego	$16,940	NV: Las Vegas	$21,180
CA: San Francisco	$18,600	NY: New York	$22,840
CO: Denver	$15,020	OH: Cincinnati	$14,250
DC: Washington	$19,310	OH: Cleveland	$13,820
FL: Miami	$17,360	OH: Columbus	$14,080
FL: Orlando	$17,640	OR: Portland	$19,130
FL: Tampa	$15,860	PA: Philadelphia	$16,750
GA: Atlanta	$14,220	PA: Pittsburgh	$13,970
IL: Chicago	$15,950	TX: Dallas	$14,080
MA: Boston	$22,430	TX: Houston	$13,930
MD: Baltimore	$14,790	WA: Seattle	$25,390

FACTORS THAT MAY AFFECT EARNINGS

Educational Attainment of Workers and Effect on Earnings

	Percent at Level	Effect on Earnings
Less than High School	—	—
Some High School	7.0%	−22.4%
High School or Equivalent	32.9%	−9.2%
Some College but No Degree	31.7%	2.0%
Associate Degree	12.2%	21.7%
Bachelor's Degree	13.5%	16.0%
Master's Degree	—	—
Doctoral Degree	—	—
First Professional Degree	—	—

Flexibility of Earnings
Average Hours Worked: 26
Workers with a Varying Number of Hours: 11.6%
Workers Earning Some Overtime Pay, Tips, or Commissions: 57.0%
Earnings Benefit of Working Overtime: −9.5%

Gender

	Male	Female
Percent	45.0%	55.0%
Effect on Earnings	14.6%	−8.5%

Union Membership
Percentage Union Members: Insignificant
Earnings Benefit of Union Membership: No significant data available

Veteran Status
Percentage Who Have Been on Active Duty: Insignificant
Earnings Benefit of Veteran Status: No significant data available

35-3021 Combined Food Preparation and Serving Workers, Including Fast Food

Perform duties that combine food preparation and food service.

- Education or Training Required: Short-term on-the-job training
- Job Growth: 17.1%
- Annual Openings: 751,000
- Self-Employed: 0.1%
- Part-Time: 57.3%

NATIONAL WAGE FIGURES (ANNUAL)

Beginning	25th Percentile	Median	Mean	75th Percentile	90th Percentile
$12,050	$13,450	$15,050	$15,930	$17,610	$21,130

Median Wages for Industries Employing Largest Numbers (Annual)

Industry	Median Income
Federal, State, and Local Government	$24,610
Hospitals	$20,200
Educational Services	$18,310
Food and Beverage Stores	$18,000
General Merchandise Stores	$17,880
Accommodation	$17,830
Nursing and Residential Care Facilities	$17,450
Sporting Goods, Hobby, Book, and Music Stores	$17,400
Nonstore Retailers	$16,950
Administrative and Support Services	$16,880

Median Wages for States (Annual)

State	Wage	State	Wage	State	Wage
AK	$17,330	KY	$13,610	NY	$14,750
AL	$13,410	LA	$13,610	OH	$14,130
AR	$13,240	MA	$17,500	OK	$13,620
AZ	$15,180	MD	$15,200	OR	$17,430
CA	$16,720	ME	$16,000	PA	$14,950
CO	$15,630	MI	$15,340	RI	$17,520
CT	$17,890	MN	$16,120	SC	$14,010
DC	$19,590	MO	$14,530	SD	$13,930
DE	$15,740	MS	$13,470	TN	$14,260
FL	$14,740	MT	$14,330	TX	$13,800
GA	$14,000	NC	$14,020	UT	$14,660
HI	$15,380	ND	$14,430	VA	$15,150
IA	$14,180	NE	$14,220	VT	$17,550
ID	$14,010	NH	$16,750	WA	$17,820
IL	$15,200	NJ	$15,790	WI	$15,390
IN	$14,530	NM	$13,560	WV	$13,370
KS	$13,910	NV	$15,820	WY	$14,810

Median Wages for the Largest Metropolitan Areas (Annual)

Area	Wage	Area	Wage
AZ: Phoenix	$15,930	MI: Detroit	$15,710
CA: Los Angeles	$16,490	MN: Minneapolis	$16,580
CA: Riverside	$16,220	MO: Kansas City	$15,360
CA: Sacramento	$16,530	MO: St. Louis	$14,830
CA: San Diego	$16,920	NV: Las Vegas	$15,740
CA: San Francisco	$17,910	NY: New York	$15,270
CO: Denver	$16,510	OH: Cincinnati	$14,760
DC: Washington	$16,380	OH: Cleveland	$14,100
FL: Miami	$14,730	OH: Columbus	$14,660
FL: Orlando	$15,130	OR: Portland	$17,460
FL: Tampa	$15,110	PA: Philadelphia	$15,610
GA: Atlanta	$14,620	PA: Pittsburgh	$14,740
IL: Chicago	$15,300	TX: Dallas	$14,090
MA: Boston	$17,530	TX: Houston	$13,780
MD: Baltimore	$15,500	WA: Seattle	$18,030

FACTORS THAT MAY AFFECT EARNINGS

Educational Attainment of Workers and Effect on Earnings

	Percent at Level	Effect on Earnings
Less than High School	3.0%	20.0%
Some High School	28.7%	−34.0%
High School or Equivalent	36.9%	13.7%
Some College but No Degree	19.1%	−0.1%
Associate Degree	4.6%	9.6%
Bachelor's Degree	6.6%	59.0%
Master's Degree	—	—
Doctoral Degree	—	—
First Professional Degree	—	—

Flexibility of Earnings

Average Hours Worked: 23
Workers with a Varying Number of Hours: 13.3%
Workers Earning Some Overtime Pay, Tips, or Commissions: 11.2%
Earnings Benefit of Working Overtime: 9.1%

Gender

	Male	Female
Percent	32.4%	67.6%
Effect on Earnings	−2.9%	0.9%

Union Membership

Percentage Union Members: 9.9%
Earnings Benefit of Union Membership: 21.6%

Veteran Status

Percentage Who Have Been on Active Duty: Insignificant
Earnings Benefit of Veteran Status: No significant data available

35-3022 Counter Attendants, Cafeteria, Food Concession, and Coffee Shop

Serve food to diners at counter or from a steam table.

- Education or Training Required: Short-term on-the-job training
- Job Growth: 17.5%
- Annual Openings: 199,000
- Self-Employed: 0.7%
- Part-Time: 66.2%

NATIONAL WAGE FIGURES (ANNUAL)

Beginning	25th Percentile	Median	Mean	75th Percentile	90th Percentile
$12,700	$14,240	$16,130	$16,950	$18,710	$22,590

Median Wages for Industries Employing Largest Numbers (Annual)

Industry	Median Income
General Merchandise Stores	$22,330
Hospitals	$20,650
Nonstore Retailers	$18,950
Accommodation	$18,730
Educational Services	$18,580
Beverage and Tobacco Product Manufacturing	$18,450
Nursing and Residential Care Facilities	$17,700
Museums, Historical Sites, and Similar Institutions	$17,550
Administrative and Support Services	$17,420
Sporting Goods, Hobby, Book, and Music Stores	$16,750

Median Wages for States (Annual)

State	Wage	State	Wage	State	Wage
AK	$17,820	KY	$15,470	NY	$15,650
AL	$14,470	LA	$14,030	OH	$13,800
AR	$13,540	MA	$18,020	OK	$14,100
AZ	$14,740	MD	$16,380	OR	$17,830
CA	$17,120	ME	$16,210	PA	$14,540
CO	$15,800	MI	$15,160	RI	$17,320
CT	$17,560	MN	$16,220	SC	$14,250
DC	$22,560	MO	$15,680	SD	$15,090
DE	$19,880	MS	$13,830	TN	$16,610
FL	$15,760	MT	$13,660	TX	$14,140
GA	$14,490	NC	$15,120	UT	$14,330
HI	$16,710	ND	$15,200	VA	$14,890
IA	$14,450	NE	$13,970	VT	$17,540
ID	$14,130	NH	$16,910	WA	$17,990
IL	$15,710	NJ	$16,380	WI	$15,430
IN	$14,270	NM	$13,710	WV	$13,470
KS	$13,650	NV	$16,940	WY	$13,240

Median Wages for the Largest Metropolitan Areas (Annual)

Area	Wage	Area	Wage
AZ: Phoenix	$14,860	MI: Detroit	$16,110
CA: Los Angeles	$16,840	MN: Minneapolis	$16,990
CA: Riverside	$16,590	MO: Kansas City	$14,640
CA: Sacramento	$16,630	MO: St. Louis	$16,150
CA: San Diego	$17,150	NV: Las Vegas	$16,640
CA: San Francisco	$18,410	NY: New York	$16,870
CO: Denver	$16,220	OH: Cincinnati	$14,550
DC: Washington	$17,150	OH: Cleveland	$13,360
FL: Miami	$15,800	OH: Columbus	$15,420
FL: Orlando	$15,650	OR: Portland	$18,420
FL: Tampa	$15,840	PA: Philadelphia	$16,220
GA: Atlanta	$14,730	PA: Pittsburgh	$13,730
IL: Chicago	$16,110	TX: Dallas	$15,010
MA: Boston	$17,860	TX: Houston	$13,900
MD: Baltimore	$15,930	WA: Seattle	$18,210

FACTORS THAT MAY AFFECT EARNINGS

Educational Attainment of Workers and Effect on Earnings

	Percent at Level	Effect on Earnings
Less than High School	4.3%	−26.9%
Some High School	47.3%	−35.0%
High School or Equivalent	21.6%	29.4%
Some College but No Degree	19.5%	25.7%
Associate Degree	3.4%	102.7%
Bachelor's Degree	3.7%	81.9%
Master's Degree	—	—
Doctoral Degree	—	—
First Professional Degree	—	—

Flexibility of Earnings

Average Hours Worked: 17
Workers with a Varying Number of Hours: 15.3%
Workers Earning Some Overtime Pay, Tips, or Commissions: 9.6%
Earnings Benefit of Working Overtime: 9.1%

Gender

	Male	Female
Percent	33.8%	66.2%
Effect on Earnings	—	2.4%

Union Membership

Percentage Union Members: Insignificant
Earnings Benefit of Union Membership: No significant data available

Veteran Status

Percentage Who Have Been on Active Duty: Insignificant
Earnings Benefit of Veteran Status: No significant data available

35-3031 Waiters and Waitresses

Take orders and serve food and beverages to patrons at tables in dining establishment.

- Education or Training Required: Short-term on-the-job training
- Job Growth: 16.7%
- Annual Openings: 800,000
- Self-Employed: 0.3%
- Part-Time: 54.0%

NATIONAL WAGE FIGURES (ANNUAL)

Beginning	25th Percentile	Median	Mean	75th Percentile	90th Percentile
$12,020	$13,360	$14,850	$17,190	$19,020	$25,910

Median Wages for Industries Employing Largest Numbers (Annual)

Industry	Median Income
Scenic and Sightseeing Transportation	$20,890
General Merchandise Stores	$19,750
Hospitals	$19,470
Museums, Historical Sites, and Similar Institutions	$17,820
Beverage and Tobacco Product Manufacturing	$17,730
Food Manufacturing	$16,900
Educational Services	$16,820
Nursing and Residential Care Facilities	$16,790
Real Estate	$16,740
Amusement, Gambling, and Recreation Industries	$16,620

Median Wages for States (Annual)

AK $16,890	KY $13,380	NY $19,960
AL $13,220	LA $13,590	OH $13,550
AR $13,530	MA $21,910	OK $13,680
AZ $13,870	MD $14,310	OR $18,990
CA $16,360	ME $14,870	PA $13,900
CO $14,040	MI $13,870	RI $16,830
CT $16,840	MN $15,130	SC $13,540
DC $16,700	MO $13,930	SD $13,460
DE $14,980	MS $13,300	TN $13,630
FL $16,240	MT $13,690	TX $13,520
GA $13,530	NC $13,850	UT $15,070
HI $18,330	ND $13,600	VA $14,350
IA $13,580	NE $13,610	VT $17,160
ID $13,650	NH $14,200	WA $23,730
IL $14,600	NJ $20,300	WI $14,250
IN $13,800	NM $13,570	WV $13,620
KS $13,640	NV $15,970	WY $13,610

Median Wages for the Largest Metropolitan Areas (Annual)

AZ: Phoenix $14,080	MI: Detroit $14,120
CA: Los Angeles $16,180	MN: Minneapolis $15,570
CA: Riverside $16,110	MO: Kansas City $13,750
CA: Sacramento $16,170	MO: St. Louis $14,490
CA: San Diego $16,320	NV: Las Vegas $18,060
CA: San Francisco $17,430	NY: New York $21,430
CO: Denver $14,350	OH: Cincinnati $13,780
DC: Washington $15,050	OH: Cleveland $13,570
FL: Miami $17,480	OH: Columbus $13,490
FL: Orlando $16,080	OR: Portland $19,490
FL: Tampa $17,100	PA: Philadelphia $15,260
GA: Atlanta $13,550	PA: Pittsburgh $13,730
IL: Chicago $14,650	TX: Dallas $13,610
MA: Boston $21,840	TX: Houston $13,780
MD: Baltimore $14,220	WA: Seattle $23,680

FACTORS THAT MAY AFFECT EARNINGS

Educational Attainment of Workers and Effect on Earnings

	Percent at Level	Effect on Earnings
Less than High School	3.1%	−20.9%
Some High School	18.3%	−37.7%
High School or Equivalent	28.1%	6.9%
Some College but No Degree	29.8%	2.1%
Associate Degree	8.7%	7.2%
Bachelor's Degree	10.3%	30.4%
Master's Degree	1.3%	50.4%
Doctoral Degree	—	—
First Professional Degree	—	—

Flexibility of Earnings

Average Hours Worked: 22
Workers with a Varying Number of Hours: 13.3%
Workers Earning Some Overtime Pay, Tips, or Commissions: 57.1%
Earnings Benefit of Working Overtime: 7.3%

Gender

	Male	Female
Percent	28.5%	71.5%
Effect on Earnings	10.5%	−4.1%

Union Membership

Percentage Union Members: Insignificant
Earnings Benefit of Union Membership: No significant data available

Veteran Status

Percentage Who Have Been on Active Duty: Insignificant
Earnings Benefit of Veteran Status: No significant data available

35-3041 Food Servers, Nonrestaurant

Serve food to patrons outside of a restaurant environment, such as in hotels, hospital rooms, or cars.

- Education or Training Required: Short-term on-the-job training
- Job Growth: 8.8%
- Annual Openings: 45,000
- Self-Employed: 0.2%
- Part-Time: 57.3%

NATIONAL WAGE FIGURES (ANNUAL)

Beginning	25th Percentile	Median	Mean	75th Percentile	90th Percentile
$13,240	$15,120	$18,090	$19,710	$22,610	$28,720

Median Wages for Industries Employing Largest Numbers (Annual)

Industry	Median Income
Professional, Scientific, and Technical Services	$25,500
Museums, Historical Sites, and Similar Institutions	$24,300
Scenic and Sightseeing Transportation	$21,640
Administrative and Support Services	$20,620
Federal, State, and Local Government	$20,520
Hospitals	$20,310
Religious, Grantmaking, Civic, Professional, and Similar Organizations	$19,870
Educational Services	$19,560
Insurance Carriers and Related Activities	$19,550
Ambulatory Health Care Services	$19,200

Median Wages for States (Annual)

State	Wage	State	Wage	State	Wage
AK	no data	KY	$14,910	NY	$26,870
AL	$15,880	LA	$14,680	OH	$18,110
AR	$13,640	MA	$20,250	OK	$14,000
AZ	$16,110	MD	$19,260	OR	$17,640
CA	$18,870	ME	$16,830	PA	$18,340
CO	$19,600	MI	$20,740	RI	$18,740
CT	$22,720	MN	$20,470	SC	$16,310
DC	$25,710	MO	$15,770	SD	$19,110
DE	$20,000	MS	$13,610	TN	$16,910
FL	$16,980	MT	$17,010	TX	$14,560
GA	$19,260	NC	$17,830	UT	$16,960
HI	$24,500	ND	$18,340	VA	$17,460
IA	$17,940	NE	$16,910	VT	$18,660
ID	$14,440	NH	$19,160	WA	$19,910
IL	$16,950	NJ	$19,910	WI	$19,440
IN	$17,700	NM	$13,900	WV	$16,710
KS	$14,090	NV	$18,030	WY	$16,170

Median Wages for the Largest Metropolitan Areas (Annual)

Area	Wage	Area	Wage
AZ: Phoenix	$15,530	MI: Detroit	$22,740
CA: Los Angeles	$18,160	MN: Minneapolis	$20,630
CA: Riverside	$19,310	MO: Kansas City	$16,260
CA: Sacramento	$18,110	MO: St. Louis	$16,090
CA: San Diego	$17,840	NV: Las Vegas	$19,030
CA: San Francisco	$24,650	NY: New York	$23,580
CO: Denver	$20,980	OH: Cincinnati	$19,230
DC: Washington	$20,820	OH: Cleveland	$19,690
FL: Miami	$17,370	OH: Columbus	$17,230
FL: Orlando	$15,960	OR: Portland	$17,690
FL: Tampa	$16,210	PA: Philadelphia	$19,630
GA: Atlanta	$21,170	PA: Pittsburgh	$16,720
IL: Chicago	$17,410	TX: Dallas	$15,870
MA: Boston	$20,850	TX: Houston	$14,450
MD: Baltimore	$19,410	WA: Seattle	$21,280

FACTORS THAT MAY AFFECT EARNINGS

Educational Attainment of Workers and Effect on Earnings

	Percent at Level	Effect on Earnings
Less than High School	4.2%	−9.0%
Some High School	24.1%	−37.3%
High School or Equivalent	40.3%	8.5%
Some College but No Degree	18.8%	4.3%
Associate Degree	6.3%	31.5%
Bachelor's Degree	6.3%	49.8%
Master's Degree	—	—
Doctoral Degree	—	—
First Professional Degree	—	—

Flexibility of Earnings

Average Hours Worked: 24
Workers with a Varying Number of Hours: 10.9%
Workers Earning Some Overtime Pay, Tips, or Commissions: 18.0%
Earnings Benefit of Working Overtime: 9.1%

Gender

	Male	Female
Percent	34.7%	65.3%
Effect on Earnings	—	−1.3%

Union Membership

Percentage Union Members: 12.2%
Earnings Benefit of Union Membership: 43.5%

Veteran Status

Percentage Who Have Been on Active Duty: Insignificant
Earnings Benefit of Veteran Status: No significant data available

35-9000 Other Food Preparation and Serving Related Workers

35-9011 Dining Room and Cafeteria Attendants and Bartender Helpers

Facilitate food service. Clean tables; carry dirty dishes; replace soiled table linens; set tables; replenish supply of clean linens, silverware, glassware, and dishes; supply service bar with food; and serve water, butter, and coffee to patrons.

- Education or Training Required: Short-term on-the-job training
- Job Growth: 15.6%
- Annual Openings: 174,000
- Self-Employed: 0.4%
- Part-Time: 65.5%

NATIONAL WAGE FIGURES (ANNUAL)

Beginning	25th Percentile	Median	Mean	75th Percentile	90th Percentile
$12,290	$13,780	$15,310	$16,320	$17,870	$22,050

Median Wages for Industries Employing Largest Numbers (Annual)

Industry	Median Income
Credit Intermediation and Related Activities	$20,420
Hospitals	$18,940
Insurance Carriers and Related Activities	$18,940
Beverage and Tobacco Product Manufacturing	$17,440
Food Manufacturing	$17,410
Educational Services	$17,380
Clothing and Clothing Accessories Stores	$17,040
Accommodation	$16,940
Federal, State, and Local Government	$16,800
Administrative and Support Services	$16,760

Median Wages for States (Annual)

AK	$18,000	KY	$14,720	NY	$15,790
AL	$14,260	LA	$13,840	OH	$13,930
AR	$13,840	MA	$18,330	OK	$13,600
AZ	$13,820	MD	$15,150	OR	$17,470
CA	$16,290	ME	$15,590	PA	$14,380
CO	$14,530	MI	$15,030	RI	$16,670
CT	$17,360	MN	$15,550	SC	$14,560
DC	$19,450	MO	$14,560	SD	$15,240
DE	$16,040	MS	$13,900	TN	$14,340
FL	$14,570	MT	$13,640	TX	$13,680
GA	$15,290	NC	$14,870	UT	$14,000
HI	$19,350	ND	$14,270	VA	$14,650
IA	$14,800	NE	$14,270	VT	$17,110
ID	$13,780	NH	$14,500	WA	$17,570
IL	$15,240	NJ	$15,680	WI	$14,420
IN	$14,090	NM	$13,500	WV	$13,580
KS	$13,920	NV	$17,620	WY	$13,810

Median Wages for the Largest Metropolitan Areas (Annual)

AZ: Phoenix	$13,990	MI: Detroit	$15,810
CA: Los Angeles	$16,010	MN: Minneapolis	$15,900
CA: Riverside	$16,240	MO: Kansas City	$14,470
CA: Sacramento	$16,500	MO: St. Louis	$14,970
CA: San Diego	$16,120	NV: Las Vegas	$19,150
CA: San Francisco	$17,390	NY: New York	$16,440
CO: Denver	$14,940	OH: Cincinnati	$14,460
DC: Washington	$16,630	OH: Cleveland	$13,560
FL: Miami	$14,500	OH: Columbus	$14,960
FL: Orlando	$14,790	OR: Portland	$17,660
FL: Tampa	$14,850	PA: Philadelphia	$15,180
GA: Atlanta	$15,330	PA: Pittsburgh	$14,410
IL: Chicago	$15,420	TX: Dallas	$13,860
MA: Boston	$18,940	TX: Houston	$13,530
MD: Baltimore	$14,580	WA: Seattle	$17,670

FACTORS THAT MAY AFFECT EARNINGS

Educational Attainment of Workers and Effect on Earnings

	Percent at Level	Effect on Earnings
Less than High School	13.9%	−4.4%
Some High School	27.2%	−32.2%
High School or Equivalent	32.7%	8.3%
Some College but No Degree	16.2%	−2.0%
Associate Degree	2.9%	57.7%
Bachelor's Degree	6.0%	64.1%
Master's Degree	—	—
Doctoral Degree	—	—
First Professional Degree	—	—

Flexibility of Earnings

Average Hours Worked: 22
Workers with a Varying Number of Hours: 11.0%
Workers Earning Some Overtime Pay, Tips, or Commissions: 22.0%
Earnings Benefit of Working Overtime: −11.5%

Gender

	Male	Female
Percent	51.5%	48.5%
Effect on Earnings	−1.3%	3.1%

Union Membership

Percentage Union Members: 9.1%
Earnings Benefit of Union Membership: 34.3%

Veteran Status

Percentage Who Have Been on Active Duty: Insignificant
Earnings Benefit of Veteran Status: No significant data available

35-9021 Dishwashers

Clean dishes, kitchen, food preparation equipment, or utensils.

- Education or Training Required: Short-term on-the-job training
- Job Growth: 15.8%
- Annual Openings: 164,000
- Self-Employed: 0.1%
- Part-Time: 54.3%

NATIONAL WAGE FIGURES (ANNUAL)

Beginning	25th Percentile	Median	Mean	75th Percentile	90th Percentile
$12,500	$14,090	$15,750	$16,190	$17,930	$20,800

Median Wages for Industries Employing Largest Numbers (Annual)

Industry	Median Income
Hospitals	$18,690
Furniture and Home Furnishings Stores	$18,130
Motion Picture and Sound Recording Industries	$17,440
Accommodation	$17,380
Water Transportation	$17,250
Rental and Leasing Services	$17,230
Beverage and Tobacco Product Manufacturing	$17,130
General Merchandise Stores	$16,810
Real Estate	$16,740
Federal, State, and Local Government	$16,730

Median Wages for States (Annual)

State	Wage	State	Wage	State	Wage
AK	$18,550	KY	$16,100	NY	$15,420
AL	$14,010	LA	$13,840	OH	$15,740
AR	$13,930	MA	$17,830	OK	$13,990
AZ	$15,080	MD	$16,260	OR	$17,470
CA	$16,610	ME	$15,930	PA	$14,660
CO	$16,610	MI	$14,900	RI	$17,000
CT	$18,330	MN	$16,230	SC	$14,990
DC	$19,310	MO	$15,160	SD	$14,030
DE	$16,680	MS	$14,500	TN	$16,200
FL	$15,370	MT	$13,810	TX	$13,960
GA	$14,940	NC	$15,290	UT	$15,390
HI	$17,390	ND	$14,600	VA	$15,380
IA	$14,390	NE	$14,490	VT	$17,090
ID	$14,300	NH	$17,320	WA	$17,840
IL	$15,140	NJ	$16,370	WI	$14,580
IN	$15,140	NM	$13,670	WV	$13,790
KS	$14,750	NV	$19,100	WY	$14,080

Median Wages for the Largest Metropolitan Areas (Annual)

Area	Wage	Area	Wage
AZ: Phoenix	$15,470	MI: Detroit	$15,840
CA: Los Angeles	$16,330	MN: Minneapolis	$17,420
CA: Riverside	$16,360	MO: Kansas City	$16,100
CA: Sacramento	$16,630	MO: St. Louis	$15,880
CA: San Diego	$16,880	NV: Las Vegas	$21,150
CA: San Francisco	$17,920	NY: New York	$16,360
CO: Denver	$16,940	OH: Cincinnati	$16,940
DC: Washington	$16,990	OH: Cleveland	$16,320
FL: Miami	$15,370	OH: Columbus	$17,050
FL: Orlando	$15,300	OR: Portland	$17,520
FL: Tampa	$15,560	PA: Philadelphia	$16,110
GA: Atlanta	$15,870	PA: Pittsburgh	$14,440
IL: Chicago	$15,210	TX: Dallas	$14,470
MA: Boston	$17,850	TX: Houston	$14,000
MD: Baltimore	$16,600	WA: Seattle	$18,570

FACTORS THAT MAY AFFECT EARNINGS

Educational Attainment of Workers and Effect on Earnings

	Percent at Level	Effect on Earnings
Less than High School	19.3%	1.8%
Some High School	35.7%	−31.6%
High School or Equivalent	30.2%	30.8%
Some College but No Degree	8.9%	−3.3%
Associate Degree	3.0%	−1.2%
Bachelor's Degree	2.6%	62.7%
Master's Degree	—	—
Doctoral Degree	—	—
First Professional Degree	—	—

Flexibility of Earnings

Average Hours Worked: 22
Workers with a Varying Number of Hours: 10.4%
Workers Earning Some Overtime Pay, Tips, or Commissions: 5.7%
Earnings Benefit of Working Overtime: −11.5%

Gender

	Male	Female
Percent	76.1%	23.9%
Effect on Earnings	0.3%	—

Union Membership

Percentage Union Members: Insignificant
Earnings Benefit of Union Membership: No significant data available

Veteran Status

Percentage Who Have Been on Active Duty: Insignificant
Earnings Benefit of Veteran Status: No significant data available

35-9031 Hosts and Hostesses, Restaurant, Lounge, and Coffee Shop

Welcome patrons, seat them at tables or in lounge, and help ensure quality of facilities and service.

- Education or Training Required: Short-term on-the-job training
- Job Growth: 16.3%
- Annual Openings: 116,000
- Self-Employed: 0.9%
- Part-Time: 65.8%

NATIONAL WAGE FIGURES (ANNUAL)

Beginning	25th Percentile	Median	Mean	75th Percentile	90th Percentile
$12,460	$14,130	$16,170	$16,860	$18,650	$22,470

Median Wages for Industries Employing Largest Numbers (Annual)

Industry	Median Income
Scenic and Sightseeing Transportation	$20,310
Hospitals	$19,830
Educational Services	$18,980
Real Estate	$18,600
Administrative and Support Services	$18,370
Accommodation	$18,080
Beverage and Tobacco Product Manufacturing	$17,980
Nursing and Residential Care Facilities	$17,890
General Merchandise Stores	$17,860
Federal, State, and Local Government	$17,850

Median Wages for States (Annual)

State		State		State	
AK	$18,240	KY	$15,240	NY	$18,110
AL	$14,440	LA	$14,490	OH	$15,190
AR	$14,870	MA	$19,650	OK	$13,980
AZ	$15,350	MD	$16,800	OR	$17,730
CA	$17,110	ME	$18,100	PA	$16,650
CO	$16,320	MI	$15,200	RI	$17,530
CT	$18,560	MN	$16,820	SC	$14,870
DC	$22,560	MO	$15,370	SD	$15,910
DE	$16,490	MS	$15,100	TN	$15,790
FL	$16,070	MT	$14,190	TX	$13,960
GA	$15,050	NC	$14,850	UT	$15,890
HI	$18,670	ND	$14,510	VA	$15,820
IA	$15,220	NE	$14,650	VT	$17,570
ID	$14,070	NH	$18,800	WA	$17,880
IL	$16,130	NJ	$17,190	WI	$16,050
IN	$15,290	NM	$13,900	WV	$14,340
KS	$15,170	NV	$18,650	WY	$13,710

Median Wages for the Largest Metropolitan Areas (Annual)

Area		Area	
AZ: Phoenix	$15,810	MI: Detroit	$15,910
CA: Los Angeles	$17,170	MN: Minneapolis	$17,380
CA: Riverside	$16,650	MO: Kansas City	$16,020
CA: Sacramento	$16,770	MO: St. Louis	$15,230
CA: San Diego	$17,320	NV: Las Vegas	$19,810
CA: San Francisco	$18,860	NY: New York	$19,360
CO: Denver	$16,650	OH: Cincinnati	$14,510
DC: Washington	$18,040	OH: Cleveland	$16,080
FL: Miami	$16,790	OH: Columbus	$15,860
FL: Orlando	$15,940	OR: Portland	$17,930
FL: Tampa	$15,670	PA: Philadelphia	$17,580
GA: Atlanta	$15,690	PA: Pittsburgh	$16,410
IL: Chicago	$16,590	TX: Dallas	$14,030
MA: Boston	$19,730	TX: Houston	$14,250
MD: Baltimore	$16,930	WA: Seattle	$18,120

FACTORS THAT MAY AFFECT EARNINGS

Educational Attainment of Workers and Effect on Earnings

	Percent at Level	Effect on Earnings
Less than High School	3.5%	−26.0%
Some High School	35.8%	−39.7%
High School or Equivalent	28.4%	22.1%
Some College but No Degree	21.6%	8.1%
Associate Degree	5.3%	63.9%
Bachelor's Degree	4.6%	69.9%
Master's Degree	—	—
Doctoral Degree	—	—
First Professional Degree	—	—

Flexibility of Earnings

Average Hours Worked: 18
Workers with a Varying Number of Hours: 11.6%
Workers Earning Some Overtime Pay, Tips, or Commissions: 26.9%
Earnings Benefit of Working Overtime: −11.5%

Gender

	Male	Female
Percent	13.6%	86.4%
Effect on Earnings	—	−1.1%

Union Membership

Percentage Union Members: Insignificant
Earnings Benefit of Union Membership: No significant data available

Veteran Status

Percentage Who Have Been on Active Duty: Insignificant
Earnings Benefit of Veteran Status: No significant data available

35-9099 *Food Preparation and Serving Related Workers, All Other*

All food preparation and serving related workers not listed separately.

- Education or Training Required: Short-term on-the-job training
- Job Growth: 16.7%
- Annual Openings: 28,000
- Self-Employed: 0.0%
- Part-Time: 50.0%

NATIONAL WAGE FIGURES (ANNUAL)

Beginning	25th Percentile	Median	Mean	75th Percentile	90th Percentile
$13,620	$15,150	$17,780	$19,360	$22,410	$27,970

Median Wages for Industries Employing Largest Numbers (Annual)

Industry	Median Income
Professional, Scientific, and Technical Services	$23,030
Merchant Wholesalers, Durable Goods	$21,060
Gasoline Stations	$20,260
General Merchandise Stores	$20,180
Nursing and Residential Care Facilities	$20,090
Hospitals	$20,020
Accommodation	$19,950
Religious, Grantmaking, Civic, Professional, and Similar Organizations	$19,710
Federal, State, and Local Government	$19,290
Food Manufacturing	$19,140

Median Wages for States (Annual)

State	Wage	State	Wage	State	Wage
AK	$18,210	KY	$18,360	NY	$17,940
AL	$18,510	LA	$14,770	OH	$15,740
AR	$12,880	MA	$17,020	OK	no data
AZ	$16,620	MD	$20,110	OR	no data
CA	$16,490	ME	no data	PA	$19,410
CO	$18,260	MI	$16,570	RI	$16,620
CT	$18,990	MN	$17,470	SC	$15,800
DC	$23,750	MO	no data	SD	no data
DE	no data	MS	$29,310	TN	$17,040
FL	$23,380	MT	no data	TX	$20,630
GA	$15,360	NC	$17,280	UT	$16,530
HI	$20,740	ND	no data	VA	$18,860
IA	$17,350	NE	$22,480	VT	no data
ID	$17,950	NH	$21,000	WA	$18,220
IL	$16,460	NJ	$19,420	WI	$17,430
IN	$15,900	NM	$14,040	WV	$16,080
KS	$16,200	NV	$20,600	WY	$14,250

Median Wages for the Largest Metropolitan Areas (Annual)

Area	Wage	Area	Wage
AZ: Phoenix	$18,650	MI: Detroit	no data
CA: Los Angeles	$16,040	MN: Minneapolis	$17,190
CA: Riverside	$16,160	MO: Kansas City	no data
CA: Sacramento	$17,260	MO: St. Louis	$19,630
CA: San Diego	$16,610	NV: Las Vegas	$21,260
CA: San Francisco	$17,950	NY: New York	$18,850
CO: Denver	$15,910	OH: Cincinnati	$15,950
DC: Washington	$21,020	OH: Cleveland	$17,370
FL: Miami	$26,280	OH: Columbus	$15,620
FL: Orlando	$19,630	OR: Portland	no data
FL: Tampa	$25,780	PA: Philadelphia	$20,450
GA: Atlanta	$15,680	PA: Pittsburgh	no data
IL: Chicago	$16,660	TX: Dallas	$19,750
MA: Boston	$16,930	TX: Houston	$20,040
MD: Baltimore	$20,910	WA: Seattle	$18,050

FACTORS THAT MAY AFFECT EARNINGS

Educational Attainment of Workers and Effect on Earnings

Figures are based on a group of occupations: Other Food Preparation and Serving Related Workers

	Percent at Level	Effect on Earnings
Less than High School	13.2%	−6.9%
Some High School	29.3%	−35.5%
High School or Equivalent	30.6%	17.3%
Some College but No Degree	16.3%	−0.7%
Associate Degree	4.4%	38.9%
Bachelor's Degree	5.3%	65.6%
Master's Degree	—	—
Doctoral Degree	—	—
First Professional Degree	—	—

Flexibility of Earnings

Average Hours Worked: 24
Workers with a Varying Number of Hours: 14.3%
Workers Earning Some Overtime Pay, Tips, or Commissions: 18.0%
Earnings Benefit of Working Overtime: −11.5%

Gender

	Male	Female
Percent	64.3%	35.7%
Effect on Earnings	4.9%	−4.3%

Union Membership

Percentage Union Members: 4.7%
Earnings Benefit of Union Membership: 48.1%

Veteran Status

Percentage Who Have Been on Active Duty: Insignificant
Earnings Benefit of Veteran Status: No significant data available

37-0000: Building and Grounds Cleaning and Maintenance Occupations

37-1000 Supervisors, Building and Grounds Cleaning and Maintenance Workers

37-1011 First-Line Supervisors/Managers of Housekeeping and Janitorial Workers

Supervise work activities of cleaning personnel in hotels, hospitals, offices, and other establishments.

- Education or Training Required: Work experience in a related occupation
- Job Growth: 19.0%
- Annual Openings: 21,000
- Self-Employed: 8.9%
- Part-Time: 20.0%

NATIONAL WAGE FIGURES (ANNUAL)

Beginning	25th Percentile	Median	Mean	75th Percentile	90th Percentile
$19,620	$24,230	$31,290	$33,610	$40,670	$51,490

Median Wages for Industries Employing Largest Numbers (Annual)

Industry	Median Income
Publishing Industries (Except Internet)	$40,590
Management of Companies and Enterprises	$39,000
Federal, State, and Local Government	$38,170
Credit Intermediation and Related Activities	$37,900
Warehousing and Storage	$37,710
Food Manufacturing	$36,540
Construction of Buildings	$36,210
Museums, Historical Sites, and Similar Institutions	$35,880
Professional, Scientific, and Technical Services	$35,750
Educational Services	$35,320

Median Wages for States (Annual)

AK	$35,480	KY	$25,760	NY	$40,010
AL	$26,180	LA	$24,390	OH	$30,580
AR	$24,090	MA	$36,880	OK	$26,360
AZ	$27,780	MD	$31,470	OR	$29,200
CA	$34,520	ME	$31,340	PA	$33,510
CO	$33,050	MI	$33,650	RI	$36,810
CT	$40,870	MN	$32,890	SC	$27,330
DC	$33,490	MO	$29,810	SD	$28,870
DE	$30,740	MS	$23,790	TN	$27,000
FL	$28,570	MT	$29,350	TX	$26,080
GA	$29,820	NC	$27,350	UT	$31,480
HI	$33,610	ND	$26,730	VA	$31,520
IA	$31,410	NE	$31,730	VT	$34,910
ID	$26,500	NH	$33,740	WA	$35,040
IL	$32,970	NJ	$39,110	WI	$33,270
IN	$31,500	NM	$23,210	WV	$23,430
KS	$28,550	NV	$29,340	WY	$27,020

Median Wages for the Largest Metropolitan Areas (Annual)

AZ: Phoenix	$29,120	MI: Detroit	$34,090
CA: Los Angeles	$34,340	MN: Minneapolis	$33,100
CA: Riverside	$36,240	MO: Kansas City	$29,910
CA: Sacramento	$34,710	MO: St. Louis	$33,950
CA: San Diego	$31,470	NV: Las Vegas	$29,520
CA: San Francisco	$39,270	NY: New York	$41,870
CO: Denver	$33,500	OH: Cincinnati	$30,400
DC: Washington	$33,360	OH: Cleveland	$30,500
FL: Miami	$26,420	OH: Columbus	$32,220
FL: Orlando	$28,770	OR: Portland	$31,510
FL: Tampa	$30,140	PA: Philadelphia	$36,110
GA: Atlanta	$31,910	PA: Pittsburgh	$32,980
IL: Chicago	$34,500	TX: Dallas	$29,850
MA: Boston	$37,220	TX: Houston	$24,510
MD: Baltimore	$30,330	WA: Seattle	$37,550

FACTORS THAT MAY AFFECT EARNINGS

Educational Attainment of Workers and Effect on Earnings

	Percent at Level	Effect on Earnings
Less than High School	2.7%	−30.1%
Some High School	15.2%	−27.1%
High School or Equivalent	40.6%	1.1%
Some College but No Degree	21.0%	15.2%
Associate Degree	7.6%	−3.0%
Bachelor's Degree	12.5%	13.2%
Master's Degree	—	—
Doctoral Degree	—	—
First Professional Degree	—	—

Flexibility of Earnings

Average Hours Worked: 34
Workers with a Varying Number of Hours: 11.0%
Workers Earning Some Overtime Pay, Tips, or Commissions: 13.0%
Earnings Benefit of Working Overtime: 16.6%

Gender

	Male	Female
Percent	67.4%	32.6%
Effect on Earnings	7.9%	−18.2%

Union Membership

Percentage Union Members: 13.0%
Earnings Benefit of Union Membership: 8.8%

Veteran Status

Percentage Who Have Been on Active Duty: 11.5%
Earnings Benefit of Veteran Status: 12.5%

37-1012 First-Line Supervisors/Managers of Land-scaping, Lawn Service, and Groundskeeping Workers

Plan, organize, direct, or coordinate activities of workers engaged in landscaping or groundskeeping activities, such as planting and maintaining ornamental trees, shrubs, flowers, and lawns and applying fertilizers, pesticides, and other chemicals, according to contract specifications. May also coordinate activities of workers engaged in terracing hillsides, building retaining walls, constructing pathways, installing patios, and similar activities in following a landscape design plan. Work may involve reviewing contracts to ascertain service, machine, and workforce requirements; answering inquiries from potential customers regarding methods, material, and price ranges; and preparing estimates according to labor, material, and machine costs.

- Education or Training Required: Work experience in a related occupation
- Job Growth: 17.8%
- Annual Openings: 14,000
- Self-Employed: 42.4%
- Part-Time: 10.8%

Note: Earnings figures do not reflect self-employed workers, who make up a large fraction of the workforce for this occupation.

NATIONAL WAGE FIGURES (ANNUAL)

Beginning	25th Percentile	Median	Mean	75th Percentile	90th Percentile
$23,940	$29,280	$37,300	$40,240	$48,130	$60,930

Median Wages for Industries Employing Largest Numbers (Annual)

Industry	Median Income
Federal, State, and Local Government	$43,630
Management of Companies and Enterprises	$42,900
Utilities	$42,600
Rental and Leasing Services	$41,600
Performing Arts, Spectator Sports, and Related Industries	$41,370
Amusement, Gambling, and Recreation Industries	$40,370
Heavy and Civil Engineering Construction	$40,370
Support Activities for Agriculture and Forestry	$40,120
Educational Services	$39,300
Religious, Grantmaking, Civic, Professional, and Similar Organizations	$39,100

Median Wages for States (Annual)

AK	no data	IA	$37,760	MO	$41,430
AL	$32,100	ID	$28,970	MS	$29,680
AR	$34,130	IL	$37,140	MT	$30,540
AZ	$34,360	IN	$35,140	NC	$34,210
CA	$41,380	KS	$32,690	ND	$34,830
CO	$44,730	KY	$29,220	NE	$39,750
CT	$45,480	LA	$29,470	NH	$39,380
DC	$45,410	MA	$46,480	NJ	$42,810
DE	$46,540	MD	$40,430	NM	$34,870
FL	$35,970	ME	$30,920	NV	$36,260
GA	$35,150	MI	$40,010	NY	$46,560
HI	$39,850	MN	$39,940	OH	$37,860

OK	$29,890	SD	$33,380	VT	$37,530
OR	$38,510	TN	$30,570	WA	$44,180
PA	$39,660	TX	$29,840	WI	$41,400
RI	$39,770	UT	$35,650	WV	$31,140
SC	$34,500	VA	$40,450	WY	$34,520

Median Wages for the Largest Metropolitan Areas (Annual)

AZ: Phoenix	$34,410	MI: Detroit	$43,400
CA: Los Angeles	$40,630	MN: Minneapolis	$40,570
CA: Riverside	$35,460	MO: Kansas City	$38,280
CA: Sacramento	$39,620	MO: St. Louis	$39,180
CA: San Diego	$39,270	NV: Las Vegas	$35,130
CA: San Francisco	$49,950	NY: New York	$49,590
CO: Denver	$47,680	OH: Cincinnati	$36,600
DC: Washington	$41,570	OH: Cleveland	$39,800
FL: Miami	$36,690	OH: Columbus	$41,810
FL: Orlando	$34,730	OR: Portland	$40,370
FL: Tampa	$34,400	PA: Philadelphia	$40,860
GA: Atlanta	$36,680	PA: Pittsburgh	$39,830
IL: Chicago	$38,040	TX: Dallas	$32,500
MA: Boston	$47,070	TX: Houston	$28,120
MD: Baltimore	$41,530	WA: Seattle	$45,100

FACTORS THAT MAY AFFECT EARNINGS

Educational Attainment of Workers and Effect on Earnings

	Percent at Level	Effect on Earnings
Less than High School	7.5%	−33.3%
Some High School	13.4%	−24.2%
High School or Equivalent	35.8%	5.7%
Some College but No Degree	17.2%	−3.7%
Associate Degree	11.9%	2.4%
Bachelor's Degree	13.4%	22.3%
Master's Degree	—	—
Doctoral Degree	—	—
First Professional Degree	—	—

Flexibility of Earnings

Average Hours Worked: 34
Workers with a Varying Number of Hours: 19.0%
Workers Earning Some Overtime Pay, Tips, or Commissions: 11.8%
Earnings Benefit of Working Overtime: −4.0%

Gender

	Male	Female
Percent	92.0%	8.0%
Effect on Earnings	1.3%	—

Union Membership

Percentage Union Members: 5.9%
Earnings Benefit of Union Membership: 2.8%

Veteran Status

Percentage Who Have Been on Active Duty: 11.5%
Earnings Benefit of Veteran Status: 12.5%

37-2000 Building Cleaning and Pest Control Workers

37-2011 Janitors and Cleaners, Except Maids and Housekeeping Cleaners

Keep buildings in clean and orderly condition. Perform heavy cleaning duties, such as cleaning floors, shampooing rugs, washing walls and glass, and removing rubbish. Duties may include tending furnace and boiler, performing routine maintenance activities, notifying management of need for repairs, and cleaning snow or debris from sidewalk.

- Education or Training Required: Short-term on-the-job training
- Job Growth: 18.5%
- Annual Openings: 528,000
- Self-Employed: 4.8%
- Part-Time: 41.4%

NATIONAL WAGE FIGURES (ANNUAL)

Beginning	25th Percentile	Median	Mean	75th Percentile	90th Percentile
$14,010	$16,220	$19,930	$21,730	$25,640	$33,060

Median Wages for Industries Employing Largest Numbers (Annual)

Industry	Median Income
Postal Service	$43,720
Federal, State, and Local Government	$24,550
Educational Services	$23,760
Construction of Buildings	$21,940
Hospitals	$21,750
Food Manufacturing	$21,640
Real Estate	$21,330
Management of Companies and Enterprises	$21,110
Fabricated Metal Product Manufacturing	$20,840
Merchant Wholesalers, Nondurable Goods	$20,790

Median Wages for States (Annual)

State	Wage	State	Wage	State	Wage
AK	$26,330	KY	$18,230	NY	$23,070
AL	$16,600	LA	$15,970	OH	$20,960
AR	$17,190	MA	$24,790	OK	$17,330
AZ	$17,720	MD	$19,220	OR	$21,310
CA	$20,750	ME	$22,070	PA	$21,020
CO	$21,420	MI	$23,020	RI	$23,700
CT	$22,730	MN	$22,110	SC	$16,820
DC	$22,450	MO	$18,680	SD	$19,110
DE	$19,150	MS	$16,650	TN	$17,830
FL	$18,120	MT	$19,430	TX	$16,470
GA	$17,670	NC	$18,090	UT	$18,030
HI	$20,840	ND	$19,660	VA	$18,130
IA	$20,510	NE	$19,700	VT	$21,580
ID	$19,640	NH	$22,390	WA	$24,080
IL	$21,140	NJ	$21,860	WI	$21,030
IN	$20,310	NM	$17,840	WV	$17,870
KS	$19,250	NV	$23,070	WY	$20,080

Median Wages for the Largest Metropolitan Areas (Annual)

Metro	Wage	Metro	Wage
AZ: Phoenix	$17,500	MI: Detroit	$23,760
CA: Los Angeles	$19,490	MN: Minneapolis	$22,700
CA: Riverside	$22,000	MO: Kansas City	$20,540
CA: Sacramento	$21,660	MO: St. Louis	$19,250
CA: San Diego	$19,860	NV: Las Vegas	$24,100
CA: San Francisco	$23,220	NY: New York	$23,890
CO: Denver	$21,240	OH: Cincinnati	$20,800
DC: Washington	$20,620	OH: Cleveland	$20,530
FL: Miami	$18,060	OH: Columbus	$21,440
FL: Orlando	$18,100	OR: Portland	$21,610
FL: Tampa	$17,970	PA: Philadelphia	$22,120
GA: Atlanta	$18,870	PA: Pittsburgh	$21,060
IL: Chicago	$21,450	TX: Dallas	$17,180
MA: Boston	$25,020	TX: Houston	$15,620
MD: Baltimore	$18,550	WA: Seattle	$25,570

FACTORS THAT MAY AFFECT EARNINGS

Educational Attainment of Workers and Effect on Earnings

	Percent at Level	Effect on Earnings
Less than High School	10.1%	−24.4%
Some High School	18.5%	−25.7%
High School or Equivalent	38.9%	10.2%
Some College but No Degree	17.1%	4.6%
Associate Degree	8.3%	14.2%
Bachelor's Degree	6.0%	23.8%
Master's Degree	0.9%	−16.5%
Doctoral Degree	—	—
First Professional Degree	—	—

Flexibility of Earnings

Average Hours Worked: 25
Workers with a Varying Number of Hours: 12.7%
Workers Earning Some Overtime Pay, Tips, or Commissions: 7.2%
Earnings Benefit of Working Overtime: 13.0%

Gender

	Male	Female
Percent	67.8%	32.2%
Effect on Earnings	7.7%	−9.6%

Union Membership

Percentage Union Members: 15.8%
Earnings Benefit of Union Membership: 43.4%

Veteran Status

Percentage Who Have Been on Active Duty: 7.0%
Earnings Benefit of Veteran Status: 26.4%

37-2012 Maids and Housekeeping Cleaners

Perform any combination of light cleaning duties to maintain private households or commercial establishments, such as hotels, restaurants, and hospitals, in a clean and orderly manner. Duties include making beds, replenishing linens, cleaning rooms and halls, and vacuuming.

- Education or Training Required: Short-term on-the-job training
- Job Growth: 11.6%
- Annual Openings: 314,000
- Self-Employed: 6.6%
- Part-Time: 45.4%

NATIONAL WAGE FIGURES (ANNUAL)

Beginning	25th Percentile	Median	Mean	75th Percentile	90th Percentile
$13,140	$15,060	$17,580	$18,700	$21,440	$26,390

Median Wages for Industries Employing Largest Numbers (Annual)

Industry	Median Income
Food and Beverage Stores	$20,510
Educational Services	$20,060
Hospitals	$20,030
General Merchandise Stores	$19,900
Religious, Grantmaking, Civic, Professional, and Similar Organizations	$19,760
Lessors of Nonfinancial Intangible Assets (Except Copyrighted Works)	$19,670
Federal, State, and Local Government	$19,600
Ambulatory Health Care Services	$19,450
Museums, Historical Sites, and Similar Institutions	$19,440
Professional, Scientific, and Technical Services	$18,870

Median Wages for States (Annual)

State	Wage	State	Wage	State	Wage
AK	$21,280	KY	$16,660	NY	$24,080
AL	$14,800	LA	$13,950	OH	$18,000
AR	$14,440	MA	$21,540	OK	$15,010
AZ	$16,890	MD	$18,750	OR	$17,910
CA	$18,590	ME	$18,070	PA	$17,930
CO	$18,400	MI	$19,270	RI	$20,560
CT	$21,690	MN	$19,540	SC	$16,120
DC	$26,830	MO	$16,990	SD	$16,100
DE	$17,860	MS	$14,460	TN	$16,070
FL	$16,700	MT	$15,890	TX	$15,140
GA	$16,220	NC	$16,440	UT	$16,580
HI	$26,390	ND	$16,080	VA	$17,250
IA	$17,540	NE	$16,810	VT	$20,180
ID	$15,060	NH	$20,230	WA	$19,270
IL	$17,620	NJ	$19,100	WI	$17,820
IN	$16,900	NM	$14,910	WV	$15,480
KS	$16,160	NV	$24,090	WY	$16,240

Median Wages for the Largest Metropolitan Areas (Annual)

Area	Wage	Area	Wage
AZ: Phoenix	$17,520	MI: Detroit	$21,070
CA: Los Angeles	$18,070	MN: Minneapolis	$20,740
CA: Riverside	$17,470	MO: Kansas City	$17,780
CA: Sacramento	$18,690	MO: St. Louis	$17,660
CA: San Diego	$18,100	NV: Las Vegas	$25,220
CA: San Francisco	$25,050	NY: New York	$25,990
CO: Denver	$17,980	OH: Cincinnati	$19,760
DC: Washington	$20,880	OH: Cleveland	$18,280
FL: Miami	$16,600	OH: Columbus	$18,000
FL: Orlando	$17,330	OR: Portland	$18,230
FL: Tampa	$16,510	PA: Philadelphia	$19,780
GA: Atlanta	$17,050	PA: Pittsburgh	$17,600
IL: Chicago	$18,290	TX: Dallas	$16,560
MA: Boston	$22,130	TX: Houston	$14,980
MD: Baltimore	$18,960	WA: Seattle	$20,650

FACTORS THAT MAY AFFECT EARNINGS

Educational Attainment of Workers and Effect on Earnings

	Percent at Level	Effect on Earnings
Less than High School	14.8%	−13.7%
Some High School	22.8%	−14.5%
High School or Equivalent	37.2%	8.4%
Some College but No Degree	12.9%	−1.5%
Associate Degree	5.7%	−2.9%
Bachelor's Degree	5.7%	39.2%
Master's Degree	0.7%	52.1%
Doctoral Degree	—	—
First Professional Degree	—	—

Flexibility of Earnings

Average Hours Worked: 25
Workers with a Varying Number of Hours: 12.7%
Workers Earning Some Overtime Pay, Tips, or Commissions: 5.2%
Earnings Benefit of Working Overtime: 6.0%

Gender

	Male	Female
Percent	9.7%	90.3%
Effect on Earnings	13.8%	−2.0%

Union Membership

Percentage Union Members: 8.2%
Earnings Benefit of Union Membership: 43.4%

Veteran Status

Percentage Who Have Been on Active Duty: 7.0%
Earnings Benefit of Veteran Status: 26.4%

37-2019 Building Cleaning Workers, All Other

All building cleaning workers not listed separately.

- Education or Training Required: Short-term on-the-job training
- Job Growth: 19.8%
- Annual Openings: 3,000
- Self-Employed: 3.2%
- Part-Time: 41.4%

NATIONAL WAGE FIGURES (ANNUAL)

Beginning	25th Percentile	Median	Mean	75th Percentile	90th Percentile
$15,750	$19,330	$25,090	$28,670	$34,950	$49,730

Median Wages for Industries Employing Largest Numbers (Annual)

Industry	Median Income
Chemical Manufacturing	$34,530
Support Activities for Transportation	$27,920
Miscellaneous Store Retailers	$27,480
Food Manufacturing	$26,960
Museums, Historical Sites, and Similar Institutions	$26,770
Administrative and Support Services	$25,730
Waste Management and Remediation Services	$24,920
Specialty Trade Contractors	$24,120
Construction of Buildings	$23,300
Repair and Maintenance	$22,270

Median Wages for States (Annual)

State	Wage	State	Wage	State	Wage
AK	$20,890	KY	$22,700	NY	$26,470
AL	$22,530	LA	no data	OH	$22,000
AR	no data	MA	$27,180	OK	no data
AZ	no data	MD	$19,960	OR	$22,810
CA	$27,730	ME	no data	PA	$25,250
CO	$23,160	MI	$21,330	RI	$25,250
CT	$15,600	MN	$29,460	SC	$13,360
DC	no data	MO	$26,400	SD	no data
DE	no data	MS	no data	TN	$20,710
FL	$23,460	MT	no data	TX	$18,600
GA	$21,290	NC	$23,050	UT	$21,990
HI	no data	ND	no data	VA	$14,770
IA	no data	NE	no data	VT	no data
ID	$22,740	NH	$17,810	WA	$25,210
IL	$47,530	NJ	$16,810	WI	$32,230
IN	$26,090	NM	$18,250	WV	$16,760
KS	no data	NV	no data	WY	no data

Median Wages for the Largest Metropolitan Areas (Annual)

Metro	Wage	Metro	Wage
AZ: Phoenix	no data	MI: Detroit	$23,700
CA: Los Angeles	$28,040	MN: Minneapolis	$30,330
CA: Riverside	no data	MO: Kansas City	$25,540
CA: Sacramento	no data	MO: St. Louis	$31,020
CA: San Diego	$29,730	NV: Las Vegas	no data
CA: San Francisco	no data	NY: New York	$24,850
CO: Denver	no data	OH: Cincinnati	$22,050
DC: Washington	$21,160	OH: Cleveland	no data
FL: Miami	$23,990	OH: Columbus	no data
FL: Orlando	$22,680	OR: Portland	$19,530
FL: Tampa	$24,420	PA: Philadelphia	$28,860
GA: Atlanta	no data	PA: Pittsburgh	$27,190
IL: Chicago	no data	TX: Dallas	$22,230
MA: Boston	$28,440	TX: Houston	no data
MD: Baltimore	$19,690	WA: Seattle	$25,600

FACTORS THAT MAY AFFECT EARNINGS

Educational Attainment of Workers and Effect on Earnings

	Percent at Level	Effect on Earnings
Less than High School	10.1%	−24.4%
Some High School	18.5%	−25.7%
High School or Equivalent	38.9%	10.2%
Some College but No Degree	17.1%	4.6%
Associate Degree	8.3%	14.2%
Bachelor's Degree	6.0%	23.8%
Master's Degree	0.9%	−16.5%
Doctoral Degree	—	—
First Professional Degree	—	—

Flexibility of Earnings

Average Hours Worked: 25
Workers with a Varying Number of Hours: 12.7%
Workers Earning Some Overtime Pay, Tips, or Commissions: 7.2%
Earnings Benefit of Working Overtime: 13.0%

Gender

	Male	Female
Percent	60.0%	40.0%
Effect on Earnings	7.7%	−9.6%

Union Membership

Percentage Union Members: 15.8%
Earnings Benefit of Union Membership: 43.4%

Veteran Status

Percentage Who Have Been on Active Duty: 7.0%
Earnings Benefit of Veteran Status: 26.4%

37-2021 Pest Control Workers

Spray or release chemical solutions or toxic gases and set traps to kill pests and vermin, such as mice, termites, and roaches, that infest buildings and surrounding areas.

- Education or Training Required: Moderate-term on-the-job training
- Job Growth: 18.4%
- Annual Openings: 4,000
- Self-Employed: 9.7%
- Part-Time: 20.0%

NATIONAL WAGE FIGURES (ANNUAL)

Beginning	25th Percentile	Median	Mean	75th Percentile	90th Percentile
$18,460	$22,440	$27,880	$29,350	$34,850	$43,370

Median Wages for Industries Employing Largest Numbers (Annual)

Industry	Median Income
Beverage and Tobacco Product Manufacturing	$37,780
Federal, State, and Local Government	$33,330
Educational Services	$31,370
Food Manufacturing	$30,390
Administrative and Support Services	$27,840
Food Services and Drinking Places	$22,170
Nursing and Residential Care Facilities	$17,290
Accommodation	$15,860

Median Wages for States (Annual)

State	Wage	State	Wage	State	Wage
AK	no data	KY	$24,390	NY	$30,580
AL	$27,840	LA	$23,530	OH	$28,470
AR	$23,080	MA	$30,610	OK	$25,590
AZ	$25,560	MD	$28,870	OR	$29,880
CA	$28,570	ME	$29,860	PA	$28,520
CO	$34,400	MI	$30,530	RI	$29,020
CT	$28,250	MN	$38,420	SC	$28,690
DC	no data	MO	$27,170	SD	$30,250
DE	$29,470	MS	$26,520	TN	$25,450
FL	$26,580	MT	$22,080	TX	$29,290
GA	$26,350	NC	$25,890	UT	$25,770
HI	$28,180	ND	$39,310	VA	$31,500
IA	$27,100	NE	$34,030	VT	no data
ID	$28,860	NH	$27,980	WA	$36,070
IL	$31,050	NJ	$31,510	WI	$36,150
IN	$25,730	NM	$32,050	WV	$23,520
KS	$30,680	NV	$35,730	WY	no data

Median Wages for the Largest Metropolitan Areas (Annual)

Area	Wage	Area	Wage
AZ: Phoenix	$25,980	MI: Detroit	$30,900
CA: Los Angeles	$27,870	MN: Minneapolis	$39,640
CA: Riverside	$26,350	MO: Kansas City	$35,180
CA: Sacramento	$31,630	MO: St. Louis	$26,190
CA: San Diego	$24,630	NV: Las Vegas	$36,320
CA: San Francisco	$29,930	NY: New York	$31,520
CO: Denver	$36,490	OH: Cincinnati	$30,050
DC: Washington	$30,740	OH: Cleveland	$28,870
FL: Miami	$26,930	OH: Columbus	$31,680
FL: Orlando	$28,090	OR: Portland	$34,980
FL: Tampa	$22,890	PA: Philadelphia	$28,560
GA: Atlanta	$26,430	PA: Pittsburgh	$24,630
IL: Chicago	$32,780	TX: Dallas	$35,480
MA: Boston	$29,970	TX: Houston	$30,060
MD: Baltimore	$32,990	WA: Seattle	$38,240

FACTORS THAT MAY AFFECT EARNINGS

Educational Attainment of Workers and Effect on Earnings

	Percent at Level	Effect on Earnings
Less than High School	—	—
Some High School	—	—
High School or Equivalent	48.4%	10.5%
Some College but No Degree	29.7%	−19.9%
Associate Degree	—	—
Bachelor's Degree	—	—
Master's Degree	—	—
Doctoral Degree	—	—
First Professional Degree	—	—

Figures do not total 100% because some levels have a very small sample size.

Flexibility of Earnings

Average Hours Worked: 35
Workers with a Varying Number of Hours: 13.2%
Workers Earning Some Overtime Pay, Tips, or Commissions: 28.8%
Earnings Benefit of Working Overtime: 15.4%

Gender

	Male	Female
Percent	97.8%	2.2%
Effect on Earnings	0.0%	—

Union Membership

Percentage Union Members: Insignificant
Earnings Benefit of Union Membership: No significant data available

Veteran Status

Percentage Who Have Been on Active Duty: 7.0%
Earnings Benefit of Veteran Status: 26.4%

37-3000 Grounds Maintenance Workers

37-3011 Landscaping and Groundskeeping Workers

Landscape or maintain grounds of property, using hand or power tools or equipment. Workers typically perform a variety of tasks, which may include any combination of the following: sod laying, mowing, trimming, planting, watering, fertilizing, digging, raking, sprinkler installation, and installation of mortarless segmental concrete masonry wall units.

- Education or Training Required: Short-term on-the-job training
- Job Growth: 19.5%
- Annual Openings: 243,000
- Self-Employed: 20.5%
- Part-Time: 32.8%

NATIONAL WAGE FIGURES (ANNUAL)

Beginning	25th Percentile	Median	Mean	75th Percentile	90th Percentile
$15,120	$17,430	$21,260	$23,010	$26,860	$34,240

Median Wages for Industries Employing Largest Numbers (Annual)

Industry	Median Income
Educational Services	$25,430
Federal, State, and Local Government	$24,750
Specialty Trade Contractors	$24,060
Rental and Leasing Services	$23,940
Hospitals	$23,630
Merchant Wholesalers, Nondurable Goods	$22,410
Museums, Historical Sites, and Similar Institutions	$22,190
Heavy and Civil Engineering Construction	$21,920
Construction of Buildings	$21,830
Management of Companies and Enterprises	$21,570

Median Wages for States (Annual)

AK	$25,560	KY	$20,240	NY	$23,700
AL	$18,890	LA	$17,870	OH	$20,660
AR	$17,850	MA	$27,850	OK	$18,680
AZ	$19,310	MD	$22,990	OR	$21,680
CA	$21,880	ME	$21,970	PA	$22,130
CO	$22,680	MI	$22,340	RI	$24,990
CT	$26,600	MN	$23,230	SC	$19,360
DC	$27,250	MO	$21,600	SD	$19,410
DE	$22,660	MS	$17,920	TN	$20,460
FL	$19,780	MT	$20,310	TX	$17,960
GA	$20,400	NC	$20,160	UT	$20,230
HI	$26,010	ND	$19,420	VA	$21,640
IA	$20,670	NE	$21,190	VT	$23,630
ID	$22,100	NH	$23,650	WA	$24,860
IL	$21,670	NJ	$24,020	WI	$22,350
IN	$20,230	NM	$17,940	WV	$16,710
KS	$19,510	NV	$21,650	WY	$20,860

Median Wages for the Largest Metropolitan Areas (Annual)

AZ: Phoenix	$19,050	MI: Detroit	$23,660
CA: Los Angeles	$20,930	MN: Minneapolis	$24,720
CA: Riverside	$19,670	MO: Kansas City	$22,700
CA: Sacramento	$20,750	MO: St. Louis	$22,040
CA: San Diego	$21,490	NV: Las Vegas	$21,070
CA: San Francisco	$24,760	NY: New York	$24,740
CO: Denver	$22,500	OH: Cincinnati	$21,600
DC: Washington	$22,880	OH: Cleveland	$21,110
FL: Miami	$19,320	OH: Columbus	$21,750
FL: Orlando	$20,250	OR: Portland	$21,820
FL: Tampa	$20,030	PA: Philadelphia	$23,700
GA: Atlanta	$21,050	PA: Pittsburgh	$20,990
IL: Chicago	$21,890	TX: Dallas	$19,200
MA: Boston	$28,120	TX: Houston	$17,300
MD: Baltimore	$23,510	WA: Seattle	$26,360

FACTORS THAT MAY AFFECT EARNINGS

Educational Attainment of Workers and Effect on Earnings

Figures are based on a group of occupations: Grounds Maintenance Workers

	Percent at Level	Effect on Earnings
Less than High School	12.6%	−14.0%
Some High School	20.4%	−29.1%
High School or Equivalent	33.2%	7.2%
Some College but No Degree	15.4%	−4.9%
Associate Degree	6.6%	24.2%
Bachelor's Degree	9.4%	43.3%
Master's Degree	—	—
Doctoral Degree	—	—
First Professional Degree	—	—

Flexibility of Earnings

Average Hours Worked: 28
Workers with a Varying Number of Hours: 13.7%
Workers Earning Some Overtime Pay, Tips, or Commissions: 6.7%
Earnings Benefit of Working Overtime: 10.9%

Gender

	Male	Female
Percent	93.8%	6.2%
Effect on Earnings	0.2%	—

Union Membership

Percentage Union Members: 4.9%
Earnings Benefit of Union Membership: 43.2%

Veteran Status

Percentage Who Have Been on Active Duty: 7.1%
Earnings Benefit of Veteran Status: 9.9%

37-3012 Pesticide Handlers, Sprayers, and Applicators, Vegetation

Mix or apply pesticides, herbicides, fungicides, or insecticides through sprays, dusts, vapors, soil incorporation, or chemical application on trees, shrubs, lawns, or botanical crops. Usually requires specific training and state or federal certification.

- Education or Training Required: Moderate-term on-the-job training
- Job Growth: 16.6%
- Annual Openings: 6,000
- Self-Employed: 19.6%
- Part-Time: 32.8%

NATIONAL WAGE FIGURES (ANNUAL)

Beginning	25th Percentile	Median	Mean	75th Percentile	90th Percentile
$18,180	$21,690	$26,700	$28,560	$33,580	$41,850

Median Wages for Industries Employing Largest Numbers (Annual)

Industry	Median Income
Educational Services	$32,820
Federal, State, and Local Government	$29,210
Religious, Grantmaking, Civic, Professional, and Similar Organizations	$27,490
Administrative and Support Services	$27,000
Building Material and Garden Equipment and Supplies Dealers	$24,690
Heavy and Civil Engineering Construction	$24,660
Merchant Wholesalers, Nondurable Goods	$24,520
Support Activities for Agriculture and Forestry	$24,430
Real Estate	$21,810
Hospitals	$18,760

Median Wages for States (Annual)

AK	no data	KY	$31,360	NY	$32,620
AL	$23,990	LA	$23,350	OH	$23,840
AR	$24,490	MA	$33,080	OK	$25,680
AZ	$20,060	MD	$28,310	OR	$34,790
CA	$29,780	ME	$20,710	PA	$27,980
CO	$27,840	MI	$28,320	RI	$28,420
CT	$32,400	MN	$27,130	SC	$26,150
DC	no data	MO	$25,710	SD	$23,490
DE	$30,510	MS	no data	TN	$22,380
FL	$24,400	MT	$18,720	TX	$25,710
GA	$26,640	NC	$26,150	UT	$23,520
HI	$33,810	ND	$25,850	VA	$28,860
IA	$25,760	NE	$21,130	VT	$26,970
ID	$22,550	NH	$31,370	WA	$29,050
IL	$31,890	NJ	$28,990	WI	$26,630
IN	$26,790	NM	$19,060	WV	no data
KS	$24,900	NV	$22,920	WY	$25,540

Median Wages for the Largest Metropolitan Areas (Annual)

AZ: Phoenix	$25,620	MI: Detroit	$28,770
CA: Los Angeles	$36,340	MN: Minneapolis	$27,720
CA: Riverside	$30,050	MO: Kansas City	$24,270
CA: Sacramento	$28,490	MO: St. Louis	$28,950
CA: San Diego	$23,630	NV: Las Vegas	no data
CA: San Francisco	$46,480	NY: New York	$33,510
CO: Denver	$26,680	OH: Cincinnati	$26,210
DC: Washington	$29,160	OH: Cleveland	$25,770
FL: Miami	$24,960	OH: Columbus	$21,520
FL: Orlando	$26,190	OR: Portland	$36,870
FL: Tampa	$22,880	PA: Philadelphia	$30,620
GA: Atlanta	$26,020	PA: Pittsburgh	$26,160
IL: Chicago	$36,220	TX: Dallas	$31,850
MA: Boston	$32,770	TX: Houston	$31,190
MD: Baltimore	$33,300	WA: Seattle	$30,880

FACTORS THAT MAY AFFECT EARNINGS

Educational Attainment of Workers and Effect on Earnings

Figures are based on a group of occupations: Grounds Maintenance Workers

	Percent at Level	Effect on Earnings
Less than High School	12.6%	−14.0%
Some High School	20.4%	−29.1%
High School or Equivalent	33.2%	7.2%
Some College but No Degree	15.4%	−4.9%
Associate Degree	6.6%	24.2%
Bachelor's Degree	9.4%	43.3%
Master's Degree	—	—
Doctoral Degree	—	—
First Professional Degree	—	—

Flexibility of Earnings

Average Hours Worked: 28
Workers with a Varying Number of Hours: 13.7%
Workers Earning Some Overtime Pay, Tips, or Commissions: 6.7%
Earnings Benefit of Working Overtime: 10.9%

Gender

	Male	Female
Percent	93.8%	6.2%
Effect on Earnings	0.2%	—

Union Membership

Percentage Union Members: 4.9%
Earnings Benefit of Union Membership: 43.2%

Veteran Status

Percentage Who Have Been on Active Duty: 7.1%
Earnings Benefit of Veteran Status: 9.9%

37-3013 Tree Trimmers and Pruners

Cut away dead or excess branches from trees or shrubs to maintain right-of-way for roads, sidewalks, or utilities or to improve appearance, health, and value of tree. Prune or treat trees or shrubs, using handsaws, pruning hooks, shears, and clippers. May use truck-mounted lifts and power pruners. May fill cavities in trees to promote healing and prevent deterioration.

- Education or Training Required: Short-term on-the-job training
- Job Growth: 16.5%
- Annual Openings: 11,000
- Self-Employed: 22.2%
- Part-Time: 32.8%

NATIONAL WAGE FIGURES (ANNUAL)

Beginning	25th Percentile	Median	Mean	75th Percentile	90th Percentile
$18,720	$22,300	$28,250	$29,910	$36,150	$44,350

Median Wages for Industries Employing Largest Numbers (Annual)

Industry	Median Income
Religious, Grantmaking, Civic, Professional, and Similar Organizations	$52,800
Educational Services	$37,300
Utilities	$35,310
Federal, State, and Local Government	$34,130
Professional, Scientific, and Technical Services	$28,670
Administrative and Support Services	$27,520
Forestry and Logging	$25,110
Waste Management and Remediation Services	$24,120
Heavy and Civil Engineering Construction	$23,860
Support Activities for Agriculture and Forestry	$22,650

Median Wages for States (Annual)

AK	no data	KY	$22,940	NY	$39,400
AL	$24,530	LA	$26,030	OH	$24,860
AR	no data	MA	$33,540	OK	$19,470
AZ	no data	MD	$32,600	OR	$29,750
CA	$35,680	ME	$28,050	PA	$28,610
CO	$30,430	MI	$28,750	RI	$36,580
CT	$38,620	MN	$36,910	SC	no data
DC	no data	MO	$30,230	SD	$22,170
DE	no data	MS	$21,970	TN	$26,790
FL	$27,510	MT	$36,470	TX	$22,490
GA	$22,530	NC	no data	UT	$26,520
HI	$33,890	ND	$23,790	VA	$41,280
IA	$29,950	NE	no data	VT	no data
ID	no data	NH	$34,440	WA	no data
IL	$29,190	NJ	$36,040	WI	$28,810
IN	$27,040	NM	$25,130	WV	$22,240
KS	$25,330	NV	$37,250	WY	$21,710

Median Wages for the Largest Metropolitan Areas (Annual)

AZ: Phoenix	no data	MI: Detroit	$29,020
CA: Los Angeles	$29,890	MN: Minneapolis	$37,710
CA: Riverside	$47,800	MO: Kansas City	$25,880
CA: Sacramento	$33,200	MO: St. Louis	$30,840
CA: San Diego	$30,700	NV: Las Vegas	no data
CA: San Francisco	$35,110	NY: New York	$39,470
CO: Denver	$32,280	OH: Cincinnati	$34,080
DC: Washington	$40,020	OH: Cleveland	$22,820
FL: Miami	$31,780	OH: Columbus	$32,740
FL: Orlando	$22,380	OR: Portland	$31,060
FL: Tampa	$30,900	PA: Philadelphia	$31,490
GA: Atlanta	$21,810	PA: Pittsburgh	$29,960
IL: Chicago	$33,050	TX: Dallas	$21,790
MA: Boston	$36,240	TX: Houston	$22,790
MD: Baltimore	$32,170	WA: Seattle	no data

FACTORS THAT MAY AFFECT EARNINGS

Educational Attainment of Workers and Effect on Earnings

Figures are based on a group of occupations: Grounds Maintenance Workers

	Percent at Level	Effect on Earnings
Less than High School	12.6%	−14.0%
Some High School	20.4%	−29.1%
High School or Equivalent	33.2%	7.2%
Some College but No Degree	15.4%	−4.9%
Associate Degree	6.6%	24.2%
Bachelor's Degree	9.4%	43.3%
Master's Degree	—	—
Doctoral Degree	—	—
First Professional Degree	—	—

Flexibility of Earnings

Average Hours Worked: 28
Workers with a Varying Number of Hours: 13.7%
Workers Earning Some Overtime Pay, Tips, or Commissions: 6.7%
Earnings Benefit of Working Overtime: 10.9%

Gender

	Male	Female
Percent	93.8%	6.2%
Effect on Earnings	0.2%	—

Union Membership

Percentage Union Members: 4.9%
Earnings Benefit of Union Membership: 43.2%

Veteran Status

Percentage Who Have Been on Active Duty: 7.1%
Earnings Benefit of Veteran Status: 9.9%

37-3019 Grounds Maintenance Workers, All Other

All grounds maintenance workers not listed separately.

- Education or Training Required: Short-term on-the-job training
- Job Growth: 26.3%
- Annual Openings: 5,000
- Self-Employed: 9.1%
- Part-Time: 32.8%

NATIONAL WAGE FIGURES (ANNUAL)

Beginning	25th Percentile	Median	Mean	75th Percentile	90th Percentile
$14,840	$17,160	$20,420	$24,490	$28,700	$41,830

Median Wages for Industries Employing Largest Numbers (Annual)

Industry	Median Income
Postal Service	$53,940
Performing Arts, Spectator Sports, and Related Industries	$43,290
Nonmetallic Mineral Product Manufacturing	$38,880
Heavy and Civil Engineering Construction	$30,760
Specialty Trade Contractors	$26,810
Utilities	$25,870
Food Manufacturing	$25,840
Professional, Scientific, and Technical Services	$24,590
Waste Management and Remediation Services	$23,020
Nursing and Residential Care Facilities	$22,810

Median Wages for States (Annual)

State	Wage	State	Wage	State	Wage
AK	$34,930	KY	$21,680	NY	no data
AL	$19,760	LA	$20,280	OH	$20,990
AR	$26,060	MA	$30,080	OK	no data
AZ	$26,760	MD	$20,740	OR	$24,420
CA	$24,170	ME	no data	PA	$32,440
CO	$30,610	MI	$21,670	RI	no data
CT	$28,860	MN	$23,490	SC	$18,930
DC	no data	MO	$20,590	SD	no data
DE	no data	MS	$22,450	TN	$18,160
FL	$21,200	MT	$21,670	TX	$26,520
GA	$20,250	NC	no data	UT	$19,510
HI	no data	ND	$17,860	VA	$19,750
IA	$18,440	NE	no data	VT	no data
ID	$26,280	NH	$20,700	WA	$27,290
IL	$17,470	NJ	$34,580	WI	$24,340
IN	$30,920	NM	$24,390	WV	no data
KS	$29,250	NV	$26,000	WY	$17,980

Median Wages for the Largest Metropolitan Areas (Annual)

Area	Wage	Area	Wage
AZ: Phoenix	$27,310	MI: Detroit	$21,370
CA: Los Angeles	$21,680	MN: Minneapolis	$23,730
CA: Riverside	$30,630	MO: Kansas City	$33,870
CA: Sacramento	$29,370	MO: St. Louis	$20,920
CA: San Diego	$26,530	NV: Las Vegas	no data
CA: San Francisco	$26,670	NY: New York	no data
CO: Denver	no data	OH: Cincinnati	$28,950
DC: Washington	$23,810	OH: Cleveland	$31,610
FL: Miami	$21,550	OH: Columbus	$25,310
FL: Orlando	no data	OR: Portland	$26,430
FL: Tampa	no data	PA: Philadelphia	$35,850
GA: Atlanta	$22,330	PA: Pittsburgh	no data
IL: Chicago	$17,540	TX: Dallas	no data
MA: Boston	$28,880	TX: Houston	$34,100
MD: Baltimore	$20,720	WA: Seattle	no data

FACTORS THAT MAY AFFECT EARNINGS

Educational Attainment of Workers and Effect on Earnings

Figures are based on a group of occupations: Grounds Maintenance Workers

	Percent at Level	Effect on Earnings
Less than High School	12.6%	−14.0%
Some High School	20.4%	−29.1%
High School or Equivalent	33.2%	7.2%
Some College but No Degree	15.4%	−4.9%
Associate Degree	6.6%	24.2%
Bachelor's Degree	9.4%	43.3%
Master's Degree	—	—
Doctoral Degree	—	—
First Professional Degree	—	—

Flexibility of Earnings

Average Hours Worked: 28
Workers with a Varying Number of Hours: 13.7%
Workers Earning Some Overtime Pay, Tips, or Commissions: 6.7%
Earnings Benefit of Working Overtime: 10.9%

Gender

	Male	Female
Percent	93.8%	6.2%
Effect on Earnings	0.2%	—

Union Membership

Percentage Union Members: 4.9%
Earnings Benefit of Union Membership: 43.2%

Veteran Status

Percentage Who Have Been on Active Duty: 7.1%
Earnings Benefit of Veteran Status: 9.9%

39-0000: Personal Care and Service Occupations

39-1000 Supervisors, Personal Care and Service Workers

39-1011 Gaming Supervisors

Supervise gaming operations and personnel in an assigned area. Circulate among tables and observe operations. Ensure that stations and games are covered for each shift. May explain and interpret operating rules of house to patrons. May plan and organize activities and create friendly atmosphere for guests in hotels/casinos. May adjust service complaints.

- Education or Training Required: Work experience in a related occupation
- Job Growth: 16.3%
- Annual Openings: 8,000
- Self-Employed: 29.6%
- Part-Time: 20.2%

NATIONAL WAGE FIGURES (ANNUAL)

Beginning	25th Percentile	Median	Mean	75th Percentile	90th Percentile
$25,110	$32,630	$41,160	$42,390	$51,150	$61,700

Median Wages for Industries Employing Largest Numbers (Annual)

Industry	Median Income
Accommodation	$43,450
Amusement, Gambling, and Recreation Industries	$41,260
Performing Arts, Spectator Sports, and Related Industries	$40,480
Federal, State, and Local Government	$38,670
Nursing and Residential Care Facilities	$27,140
Religious, Grantmaking, Civic, Professional, and Similar Organizations	$23,230

Median Wages for States (Annual)

AK	no data	KY	no data	NY	$40,310
AL	$31,930	LA	$41,840	OH	no data
AR	no data	MA	no data	OK	$32,720
AZ	$38,620	MD	no data	OR	$42,070
CA	$42,990	ME	no data	PA	no data
CO	$43,260	MI	$55,820	RI	no data
CT	no data	MN	$30,500	SC	$27,250
DC	no data	MO	$39,670	SD	$28,000
DE	no data	MS	$40,080	TN	$34,730
FL	$42,890	MT	$21,940	TX	$22,910
GA	no data	NC	no data	UT	no data
HI	no data	ND	$31,320	VA	no data
IA	$42,350	NE	$25,220	VT	no data
ID	no data	NH	no data	WA	$41,040
IL	$46,940	NJ	$44,070	WI	$33,210
IN	$43,750	NM	$33,290	WV	no data
KS	no data	NV	$42,980	WY	no data

Median Wages for the Largest Metropolitan Areas (Annual)

AZ: Phoenix	$38,330	MI: Detroit	no data
CA: Los Angeles	$41,900	MN: Minneapolis	$32,940
CA: Riverside	$44,210	MO: Kansas City	$41,160
CA: Sacramento	$42,250	MO: St. Louis	$41,310
CA: San Diego	$41,050	NV: Las Vegas	$44,430
CA: San Francisco	$57,170	NY: New York	$41,690
CO: Denver	$44,910	OH: Cincinnati	no data
DC: Washington	no data	OH: Cleveland	no data
FL: Miami	$44,890	OH: Columbus	no data
FL: Orlando	no data	OR: Portland	no data
FL: Tampa	no data	PA: Philadelphia	no data
GA: Atlanta	no data	PA: Pittsburgh	no data
IL: Chicago	$44,050	TX: Dallas	no data
MA: Boston	no data	TX: Houston	$18,890
MD: Baltimore	no data	WA: Seattle	$42,070

FACTORS THAT MAY AFFECT EARNINGS

Educational Attainment of Workers and Effect on Earnings

Figures are based on a group of occupations: Supervisors, Personal Care and Service Workers

	Percent at Level	Effect on Earnings
Less than High School	—	—
Some High School	—	—
High School or Equivalent	28.1%	–15.2%
Some College but No Degree	23.5%	–3.1%
Associate Degree	15.7%	–6.9%
Bachelor's Degree	23.5%	22.6%
Master's Degree	—	—
Doctoral Degree	—	—
First Professional Degree	—	—

Figures do not total 100% because some levels have a very small sample size.

Flexibility of Earnings

Average Hours Worked: 34
Workers with a Varying Number of Hours: 16.8%
Workers Earning Some Overtime Pay, Tips, or Commissions: 18.1%
Earnings Benefit of Working Overtime: 27.8%

Gender

	Male	Female
Percent	56.3%	43.7%
Effect on Earnings	11.8%	—

Union Membership

Percentage Union Members: Insignificant
Earnings Benefit of Union Membership: No significant data available

Veteran Status

Percentage Who Have Been on Active Duty: 8.9%
Earnings Benefit of Veteran Status: 15.8%

39-1012 Slot Key Persons

Coordinate/supervise functions of slot department workers to provide service to patrons. Handle and settle complaints of players. Verify and pay off jackpots. Reset slot machines after payoffs. Make minor repairs or adjustments to slot machines. Recommend removal of slot machines for repair. Report hazards and enforces safety rules.

- Education or Training Required: Postsecondary vocational training
- Job Growth: 23.0%
- Annual Openings: 5,000
- Self-Employed: 24.7%
- Part-Time: 20.2%

NATIONAL WAGE FIGURES (ANNUAL)

Beginning	25th Percentile	Median	Mean	75th Percentile	90th Percentile
$16,290	$19,240	$22,720	$25,300	$28,930	$38,510

Median Wages for Industries Employing Largest Numbers (Annual)

Industry	Median Income
Personal and Laundry Services	$33,040
Accommodation	$24,480
Amusement, Gambling, and Recreation Industries	$22,540
Federal, State, and Local Government	$21,820

Median Wages for States (Annual)

AK	no data	KY	no data	NY	$21,810
AL	no data	LA	$22,120	OH	no data
AR	no data	MA	no data	OK	$18,770
AZ	$24,410	MD	no data	OR	$24,700
CA	$21,240	ME	no data	PA	no data
CO	$29,640	MI	$21,260	RI	no data
CT	no data	MN	no data	SC	no data
DC	no data	MO	no data	SD	$32,160
DE	no data	MS	$22,410	TN	no data
FL	no data	MT	no data	TX	no data
GA	no data	NC	no data	UT	no data
HI	no data	ND	$21,900	VA	no data
IA	$25,380	NE	no data	VT	no data
ID	no data	NH	no data	WA	$22,110
IL	no data	NJ	$26,330	WI	$23,010
IN	$21,570	NM	no data	WV	no data
KS	no data	NV	$23,540	WY	no data

Median Wages for the Largest Metropolitan Areas (Annual)

AZ: Phoenix	$24,740	MI: Detroit	no data
CA: Los Angeles	no data	MN: Minneapolis	no data
CA: Riverside	$21,150	MO: Kansas City	no data
CA: Sacramento	no data	MO: St. Louis	$33,760
CA: San Diego	no data	NV: Las Vegas	$26,370
CA: San Francisco	no data	NY: New York	$31,720
CO: Denver	$29,750	OH: Cincinnati	no data
DC: Washington	no data	OH: Cleveland	no data
FL: Miami	no data	OH: Columbus	no data
FL: Orlando	no data	OR: Portland	no data
FL: Tampa	no data	PA: Philadelphia	no data
GA: Atlanta	no data	PA: Pittsburgh	no data
IL: Chicago	no data	TX: Dallas	no data
MA: Boston	no data	TX: Houston	no data
MD: Baltimore	no data	WA: Seattle	no data

FACTORS THAT MAY AFFECT EARNINGS

Educational Attainment of Workers and Effect on Earnings

Figures are based on a group of occupations: Supervisors, Personal Care and Service Workers

	Percent at Level	Effect on Earnings
Less than High School	—	—
Some High School	—	—
High School or Equivalent	28.1%	−15.2%
Some College but No Degree	23.5%	−3.1%
Associate Degree	15.7%	−6.9%
Bachelor's Degree	23.5%	22.6%
Master's Degree	—	—
Doctoral Degree	—	—
First Professional Degree	—	—

Figures do not total 100% because some levels have a very small sample size.

Flexibility of Earnings

Average Hours Worked: 34
Workers with a Varying Number of Hours: 16.8%
Workers Earning Some Overtime Pay, Tips, or Commissions: 18.1%
Earnings Benefit of Working Overtime: 27.8%

Gender

	Male	Female
Percent	37.3%	62.7%
Effect on Earnings	24.3%	−4.7%

Union Membership

Percentage Union Members: Insignificant
Earnings Benefit of Union Membership: No significant data available

Veteran Status

Percentage Who Have Been on Active Duty: 8.9%
Earnings Benefit of Veteran Status: 15.8%

39-1021 First-Line Supervisors/Managers of Personal Service Workers

Supervise and coordinate activities of personal service workers such as flight attendants, hairdressers, or caddies.

- Education or Training Required: Work experience in a related occupation
- Job Growth: 18.3%
- Annual Openings: 20,000
- Self-Employed: 33.8%
- Part-Time: 19.4%

Note: A large fraction of the workforce for this occupation is self-employed and earns an average of $29,590. All other earnings figures for this occupation are based on workers who are paid a wage or salary.

NATIONAL WAGE FIGURES (ANNUAL)

Beginning	25th Percentile	Median	Mean	75th Percentile	90th Percentile
$19,940	$25,240	$32,800	$36,090	$43,580	$56,960

Median Wages for Industries Employing Largest Numbers (Annual)

Industry	Median Income
Federal, State, and Local Government	$43,350
Air Transportation	$41,420
Professional, Scientific, and Technical Services	$38,920
Hospitals	$38,780
Administrative and Support Services	$38,130
Health and Personal Care Stores	$35,950
Transit and Ground Passenger Transportation	$35,600
Accommodation	$35,150
Educational Services	$34,960
Personal and Laundry Services	$34,420

Median Wages for States (Annual)

State	Wage	State	Wage	State	Wage
AK	$42,030	KY	$24,600	NY	$35,040
AL	$24,520	LA	$26,820	OH	$30,530
AR	$23,110	MA	$34,160	OK	$26,220
AZ	$31,830	MD	$34,650	OR	$31,580
CA	$34,720	ME	$28,290	PA	$35,630
CO	$31,340	MI	$33,780	RI	$36,760
CT	$40,060	MN	$30,330	SC	$29,190
DC	$49,800	MO	$32,250	SD	$29,290
DE	$34,630	MS	$24,730	TN	$30,290
FL	$38,460	MT	$26,070	TX	$26,210
GA	$28,500	NC	$29,930	UT	$30,670
HI	$33,110	ND	$30,520	VA	$35,330
IA	$28,210	NE	$31,300	VT	$34,170
ID	$25,460	NH	$31,230	WA	$39,640
IL	$34,610	NJ	$39,700	WI	$31,020
IN	$28,130	NM	$27,230	WV	$27,900
KS	$27,210	NV	$32,370	WY	$27,920

Median Wages for the Largest Metropolitan Areas (Annual)

Area	Wage	Area	Wage
AZ: Phoenix	$30,870	MI: Detroit	$34,920
CA: Los Angeles	$35,220	MN: Minneapolis	$32,210
CA: Riverside	$31,320	MO: Kansas City	$28,910
CA: Sacramento	$32,900	MO: St. Louis	$33,970
CA: San Diego	$34,960	NV: Las Vegas	$32,680
CA: San Francisco	$39,050	NY: New York	$38,040
CO: Denver	$31,250	OH: Cincinnati	$31,640
DC: Washington	$39,500	OH: Cleveland	$32,250
FL: Miami	$40,750	OH: Columbus	$32,500
FL: Orlando	$39,890	OR: Portland	$35,170
FL: Tampa	$33,530	PA: Philadelphia	$39,870
GA: Atlanta	$30,530	PA: Pittsburgh	$33,840
IL: Chicago	$35,760	TX: Dallas	$31,410
MA: Boston	$35,010	TX: Houston	$28,690
MD: Baltimore	$32,980	WA: Seattle	$42,600

FACTORS THAT MAY AFFECT EARNINGS

Educational Attainment of Workers and Effect on Earnings

	Percent at Level	Effect on Earnings
Less than High School	—	—
Some High School	—	—
High School or Equivalent	36.6%	−21.4%
Some College but No Degree	15.1%	1.5%
Associate Degree	18.3%	−8.0%
Bachelor's Degree	22.6%	33.1%
Master's Degree	—	—
Doctoral Degree	—	—
First Professional Degree	—	—

Figures do not total 100% because some levels have a very small sample size.

Flexibility of Earnings

Average Hours Worked: 33
Workers with a Varying Number of Hours: 16.8%
Workers Earning Some Overtime Pay, Tips, or Commissions: 19.4%
Earnings Benefit of Working Overtime: −3.5%

Gender

	Male	Female
Percent	33.3%	66.7%
Effect on Earnings	24.3%	−4.7%

Union Membership

Percentage Union Members: Insignificant
Earnings Benefit of Union Membership: No significant data available

Veteran Status

Percentage Who Have Been on Active Duty: 8.9%
Earnings Benefit of Veteran Status: 15.8%

39-2000 Animal Care and Service Workers

39-2011 Animal Trainers

Train animals for riding, harness, security, performance, or obedience or assisting persons with disabilities. Accustom animals to human voice and contact and condition animals to respond to commands. Train animals according to prescribed standards for show or competition. May train animals to carry pack loads or work as part of pack team.

- Education or Training Required: Moderate-term on-the-job training
- Job Growth: 20.3%
- Annual Openings: 3,000
- Self-Employed: 58.2%
- Part-Time: 23.6%

Note: A large fraction of the workforce for this occupation is self-employed and earns an average of $15,270. All other earnings figures for this occupation are based on workers who are paid a wage or salary.

NATIONAL WAGE FIGURES (ANNUAL)

Beginning	25th Percentile	Median	Mean	75th Percentile	90th Percentile
$15,930	$18,960	$26,310	$29,920	$36,170	$46,630

Median Wages for Industries Employing Largest Numbers (Annual)

Industry	Median Income
Educational Services	$41,780
Social Assistance	$35,420
Federal, State, and Local Government	$35,330
Personal and Laundry Services	$33,460
Religious, Grantmaking, Civic, Professional, and Similar Organizations	$32,350
Performing Arts, Spectator Sports, and Related Industries	$30,040
Amusement, Gambling, and Recreation Industries	$26,620
Support Activities for Agriculture and Forestry	$26,560
Museums, Historical Sites, and Similar Institutions	$24,730
Miscellaneous Store Retailers	$18,230

Median Wages for States (Annual)

AK	no data	KY	$27,280	NY	no data
AL	$31,460	LA	no data	OH	$18,320
AR	no data	MA	$24,590	OK	$25,190
AZ	no data	MD	$23,370	OR	$23,130
CA	$25,720	ME	no data	PA	$25,160
CO	$21,880	MI	$21,450	RI	no data
CT	$23,070	MN	$47,820	SC	$24,360
DC	no data	MO	$23,440	SD	no data
DE	$40,010	MS	no data	TN	$23,500
FL	$25,280	MT	no data	TX	$26,240
GA	$22,360	NC	$17,850	UT	$34,420
HI	no data	ND	no data	VA	$26,260
IA	$21,910	NE	no data	VT	no data
ID	$19,340	NH	no data	WA	$28,190
IL	$30,530	NJ	$35,440	WI	$30,390
IN	$19,850	NM	no data	WV	$20,830
KS	$16,630	NV	$22,180	WY	no data

Median Wages for the Largest Metropolitan Areas (Annual)

AZ: Phoenix	no data	MI: Detroit	no data
CA: Los Angeles	$26,260	MN: Minneapolis	$53,890
CA: Riverside	$21,230	MO: Kansas City	$30,950
CA: Sacramento	no data	MO: St. Louis	$23,030
CA: San Diego	no data	NV: Las Vegas	$18,270
CA: San Francisco	$32,900	NY: New York	$35,930
CO: Denver	$22,870	OH: Cincinnati	$33,410
DC: Washington	$27,600	OH: Cleveland	no data
FL: Miami	$26,600	OH: Columbus	$18,980
FL: Orlando	$24,140	OR: Portland	$30,180
FL: Tampa	no data	PA: Philadelphia	$32,470
GA: Atlanta	$21,850	PA: Pittsburgh	$31,510
IL: Chicago	$31,590	TX: Dallas	$31,910
MA: Boston	$23,970	TX: Houston	$23,070
MD: Baltimore	$22,710	WA: Seattle	no data

FACTORS THAT MAY AFFECT EARNINGS

Educational Attainment of Workers and Effect on Earnings

	Percent at Level	Effect on Earnings
Less than High School	—	—
Some High School	—	—
High School or Equivalent	23.1%	−52.1%
Some College but No Degree	26.9%	10.7%
Associate Degree	—	—
Bachelor's Degree	—	—
Master's Degree	—	—
Doctoral Degree	—	—
First Professional Degree	—	—

Figures do not total 100% because some levels have a very small sample size.

Flexibility of Earnings

Average Hours Worked: 30
Workers with a Varying Number of Hours: 23.9%
Workers Earning Some Overtime Pay, Tips, or Commissions: 11.5%
Earnings Benefit of Working Overtime: 34.7%

Gender

	Male	Female
Percent	27.9%	72.1%
Effect on Earnings	24.3%	−4.7%

Union Membership

Percentage Union Members: Insignificant
Earnings Benefit of Union Membership: No significant data available

Veteran Status

Percentage Who Have Been on Active Duty: Insignificant
Earnings Benefit of Veteran Status: No significant data available

39-2021 Nonfarm Animal Caretakers

Feed, water, groom, bathe, exercise, or otherwise care for pets and other nonfarm animals, such as dogs, cats, ornamental fish or birds, zoo animals, and mice. Work in settings such as kennels, animal shelters, zoos, circuses, and aquariums. May keep records of feedings, treatments, and animals received or discharged. May clean, disinfect, and repair cages, pens, or fish tanks.

- Education or Training Required: Short-term on-the-job training
- Job Growth: 25.6%
- Annual Openings: 31,000
- Self-Employed: 27.1%
- Part-Time: 40.5%

NATIONAL WAGE FIGURES (ANNUAL)

Beginning	25th Percentile	Median	Mean	75th Percentile	90th Percentile
$13,640	$15,590	$18,140	$20,230	$22,780	$30,460

Median Wages for Industries Employing Largest Numbers (Annual)

Industry	Median Income
Ambulatory Health Care Services	$32,950
Administrative and Support Services	$30,480
Chemical Manufacturing	$29,840
Management of Companies and Enterprises	$28,660
Accommodation	$27,320
Federal, State, and Local Government	$27,240
Social Assistance	$23,660
Museums, Historical Sites, and Similar Institutions	$22,360
Hospitals	$22,010
Educational Services	$21,590

Median Wages for States (Annual)

AK	$22,180	KY	$19,480	NY	$19,580
AL	$17,260	LA	$17,790	OH	$16,990
AR	$15,480	MA	$20,250	OK	$16,970
AZ	$17,190	MD	$21,220	OR	$19,200
CA	$19,010	ME	$18,630	PA	$16,640
CO	$18,750	MI	$18,090	RI	$22,330
CT	$19,350	MN	$17,200	SC	$17,320
DC	$26,170	MO	$16,750	SD	$17,910
DE	$19,390	MS	$16,780	TN	$17,440
FL	$18,390	MT	$17,080	TX	$17,120
GA	$17,360	NC	$17,830	UT	$17,750
HI	$31,160	ND	$14,900	VA	$18,880
IA	$16,540	NE	$17,520	VT	$19,840
ID	$24,030	NH	$17,900	WA	$18,840
IL	$17,550	NJ	$19,050	WI	$18,150
IN	$17,700	NM	$17,820	WV	$14,970
KS	$16,830	NV	$20,270	WY	$19,010

Median Wages for the Largest Metropolitan Areas (Annual)

AZ: Phoenix	$16,820	MI: Detroit	$19,330
CA: Los Angeles	$18,360	MN: Minneapolis	$17,590
CA: Riverside	$17,980	MO: Kansas City	$17,960
CA: Sacramento	$18,070	MO: St. Louis	$17,050
CA: San Diego	$18,960	NV: Las Vegas	$19,240
CA: San Francisco	$25,280	NY: New York	$19,520
CO: Denver	$19,270	OH: Cincinnati	$17,150
DC: Washington	$21,280	OH: Cleveland	$16,360
FL: Miami	$19,150	OH: Columbus	$17,660
FL: Orlando	$20,500	OR: Portland	$19,380
FL: Tampa	$18,100	PA: Philadelphia	$17,620
GA: Atlanta	$17,790	PA: Pittsburgh	$16,720
IL: Chicago	$17,780	TX: Dallas	$17,630
MA: Boston	$19,950	TX: Houston	$17,350
MD: Baltimore	$21,520	WA: Seattle	$19,110

FACTORS THAT MAY AFFECT EARNINGS

Educational Attainment of Workers and Effect on Earnings

	Percent at Level	Effect on Earnings
Less than High School	5.6%	−62.5%
Some High School	18.3%	−64.8%
High School or Equivalent	28.6%	26.8%
Some College but No Degree	24.6%	−25.9%
Associate Degree	9.5%	47.0%
Bachelor's Degree	10.3%	74.3%
Master's Degree	—	—
Doctoral Degree	—	—
First Professional Degree	—	—

Flexibility of Earnings

Average Hours Worked: 23
Workers with a Varying Number of Hours: 17.6%
Workers Earning Some Overtime Pay, Tips, or Commissions: 14.6%
Earnings Benefit of Working Overtime: 34.7%

Gender

	Male	Female
Percent	27.9%	72.1%
Effect on Earnings	24.3%	−4.7%

Union Membership

Percentage Union Members: Insignificant
Earnings Benefit of Union Membership: No significant data available

Veteran Status

Percentage Who Have Been on Active Duty: Insignificant
Earnings Benefit of Veteran Status: No significant data available

39-3000 Entertainment Attendants and Related Workers

39-3011 Gaming Dealers

Operate table games. Stand or sit behind table and operate games of chance by dispensing the appropriate number of cards or blocks to players or operating other gaming equipment. Compare the house's hand against players' hands and pay off or collect players' money or chips.

- Education or Training Required: Postsecondary vocational training
- Job Growth: 28.0%
- Annual Openings: 11,000
- Self-Employed: 0.6%
- Part-Time: 62.2%

NATIONAL WAGE FIGURES (ANNUAL)

Beginning	25th Percentile	Median	Mean	75th Percentile	90th Percentile
$11,910	$13,170	$14,730	$17,010	$17,530	$25,100

Median Wages for Industries Employing Largest Numbers (Annual)

Industry	Median Income
Food Services and Drinking Places	$18,470
Religious, Grantmaking, Civic, Professional, and Similar Organizations	$16,940
Federal, State, and Local Government	$16,550
Performing Arts, Spectator Sports, and Related Industries	$15,610
Amusement, Gambling, and Recreation Industries	$15,530
Accommodation	$13,720

Median Wages for States (Annual)

AK	no data	KY	no data	NY	$15,760
AL	no data	LA	$13,470	OH	no data
AR	no data	MA	no data	OK	$16,420
AZ	$13,800	MD	no data	OR	$24,880
CA	$17,580	ME	no data	PA	no data
CO	$13,560	MI	$16,630	RI	no data
CT	no data	MN	no data	SC	no data
DC	no data	MO	$13,670	SD	$20,880
DE	no data	MS	$13,590	TN	no data
FL	$14,560	MT	$17,530	TX	no data
GA	no data	NC	no data	UT	no data
HI	no data	ND	$16,400	VA	no data
IA	$16,010	NE	no data	VT	no data
ID	$16,240	NH	no data	WA	$23,100
IL	$14,570	NJ	no data	WI	$15,690
IN	$13,210	NM	$13,930	WV	no data
KS	no data	NV	$13,480	WY	no data

Median Wages for the Largest Metropolitan Areas (Annual)

AZ: Phoenix	$14,290	MI: Detroit	no data
CA: Los Angeles	$17,280	MN: Minneapolis	no data
CA: Riverside	$18,140	MO: Kansas City	$13,720
CA: Sacramento	$20,120	MO: St. Louis	$14,320
CA: San Diego	$17,060	NV: Las Vegas	$13,480
CA: San Francisco	no data	NY: New York	$50,850
CO: Denver	$13,020	OH: Cincinnati	no data
DC: Washington	no data	OH: Cleveland	no data
FL: Miami	$14,540	OH: Columbus	no data
FL: Orlando	no data	OR: Portland	no data
FL: Tampa	no data	PA: Philadelphia	no data
GA: Atlanta	no data	PA: Pittsburgh	no data
IL: Chicago	$14,260	TX: Dallas	no data
MA: Boston	no data	TX: Houston	no data
MD: Baltimore	no data	WA: Seattle	$23,550

FACTORS THAT MAY AFFECT EARNINGS

Educational Attainment of Workers and Effect on Earnings

Figures are based on a group of occupations: Entertainment Attendants and Related Workers

	Percent at Level	Effect on Earnings
Less than High School	—	—
Some High School	17.2%	−45.2%
High School or Equivalent	34.9%	7.9%
Some College but No Degree	29.3%	2.5%
Associate Degree	5.6%	−1.9%
Bachelor's Degree	7.3%	44.0%
Master's Degree	—	—
Doctoral Degree	—	—
First Professional Degree	—	—

Figures do not total 100% because some levels have a very small sample size.

Flexibility of Earnings

Average Hours Worked: 23
Workers with a Varying Number of Hours: 21.1%
Workers Earning Some Overtime Pay, Tips, or Commissions: 23.5%
Earnings Benefit of Working Overtime: −13.2%

Gender

	Male	Female
Percent	51.9%	48.1%
Effect on Earnings	24.3%	−4.7%

Union Membership

Percentage Union Members: 7.5%
Earnings Benefit of Union Membership: 59.7%

Veteran Status

Percentage Who Have Been on Active Duty: 10.4%
Earnings Benefit of Veteran Status: 1.5%

39-3012 Gaming and Sports Book Writers and Runners

Assist in the operation of games such as keno and bingo. Scan winning tickets presented by patrons, calculate amount of winnings, and pay patrons. May operate keno and bingo equipment. May start gaming equipment that randomly selects numbers. May announce number selected until total numbers specified for each game are selected. May pick up tickets from players; collect bets; and receive, verify, and record patrons' cash wagers.

- Education or Training Required: Short-term on-the-job training
- Job Growth: 22.1%
- Annual Openings: 2,000
- Self-Employed: 0.5%
- Part-Time: 62.2%

NATIONAL WAGE FIGURES (ANNUAL)

Beginning	25th Percentile	Median	Mean	75th Percentile	90th Percentile
$13,170	$15,410	$18,800	$20,850	$23,290	$33,030

Median Wages for Industries Employing Largest Numbers (Annual)

Industry	Median Income
Federal, State, and Local Government	$21,100
Accommodation	$20,660
Performing Arts, Spectator Sports, and Related Industries	$19,290
Social Assistance	$17,370
Religious, Grantmaking, Civic, Professional, and Similar Organizations	$17,250
Amusement, Gambling, and Recreation Industries	$16,820
Educational Services	$16,790
Food Services and Drinking Places	$15,290

Median Wages for States (Annual)

AK	$23,740	KY	no data	NY	$22,860
AL	$21,350	LA	$14,010	OH	no data
AR	no data	MA	no data	OK	$17,340
AZ	$17,680	MD	no data	OR	$21,230
CA	$21,360	ME	$15,350	PA	$14,130
CO	$21,730	MI	$29,890	RI	no data
CT	$21,220	MN	$19,200	SC	$16,710
DC	no data	MO	no data	SD	$17,030
DE	no data	MS	$15,630	TN	no data
FL	$19,680	MT	$14,400	TX	$16,030
GA	no data	NC	$13,610	UT	no data
HI	no data	ND	$18,940	VA	no data
IA	no data	NE	$16,620	VT	no data
ID	no data	NH	no data	WA	$19,400
IL	$34,870	NJ	no data	WI	$19,810
IN	$18,740	NM	$15,800	WV	$14,320
KS	no data	NV	$20,000	WY	no data

Median Wages for the Largest Metropolitan Areas (Annual)

AZ: Phoenix	$15,920	MI: Detroit	no data
CA: Los Angeles	no data	MN: Minneapolis	$18,950
CA: Riverside	$20,750	MO: Kansas City	no data
CA: Sacramento	no data	MO: St. Louis	no data
CA: San Diego	no data	NV: Las Vegas	$20,580
CA: San Francisco	no data	NY: New York	no data
CO: Denver	$20,760	OH: Cincinnati	no data
DC: Washington	no data	OH: Cleveland	no data
FL: Miami	no data	OH: Columbus	no data
FL: Orlando	no data	OR: Portland	$17,870
FL: Tampa	no data	PA: Philadelphia	no data
GA: Atlanta	no data	PA: Pittsburgh	no data
IL: Chicago	$34,180	TX: Dallas	no data
MA: Boston	no data	TX: Houston	$17,180
MD: Baltimore	no data	WA: Seattle	$19,850

FACTORS THAT MAY AFFECT EARNINGS

Educational Attainment of Workers and Effect on Earnings

Figures are based on a group of occupations: Entertainment Attendants and Related Workers

	Percent at Level	Effect on Earnings
Less than High School	—	—
Some High School	17.2%	−45.2%
High School or Equivalent	34.9%	7.9%
Some College but No Degree	29.3%	2.5%
Associate Degree	5.6%	−1.9%
Bachelor's Degree	7.3%	44.0%
Master's Degree	—	—
Doctoral Degree	—	—
First Professional Degree	—	—

Figures do not total 100% because some levels have a very small sample size.

Flexibility of Earnings

Average Hours Worked: 23
Workers with a Varying Number of Hours: 21.1%
Workers Earning Some Overtime Pay, Tips, or Commissions: 23.5%
Earnings Benefit of Working Overtime: −13.2%

Gender

	Male	Female
Percent	51.9%	48.1%
Effect on Earnings	24.3%	−4.7%

Union Membership

Percentage Union Members: 7.5%
Earnings Benefit of Union Membership: 59.7%

Veteran Status

Percentage Who Have Been on Active Duty: 10.4%
Earnings Benefit of Veteran Status: 1.5%

39-3019 Gaming Service Workers, All Other

All gaming service workers not listed separately.

- Education or Training Required: Moderate-term on-the-job training
- Job Growth: 24.2%
- Annual Openings: 2,000
- Self-Employed: 0.5%
- Part-Time: 62.2%

NATIONAL WAGE FIGURES (ANNUAL)

Beginning	25th Percentile	Median	Mean	75th Percentile	90th Percentile
$15,850	$18,090	$21,890	$24,110	$27,490	$36,360

Median Wages for Industries Employing Largest Numbers (Annual)

Industry	Median Income
Accommodation	$24,640
Amusement, Gambling, and Recreation Industries	$20,970
Federal, State, and Local Government	$20,690
Food Services and Drinking Places	$20,160
Administrative and Support Services	$19,240
Religious, Grantmaking, Civic, Professional, and Similar Organizations	$19,010

Median Wages for States (Annual)

State	Wage	State	Wage	State	Wage
AK	$20,510	KY	no data	NY	no data
AL	$22,580	LA	$21,690	OH	no data
AR	no data	MA	no data	OK	no data
AZ	$21,430	MD	no data	OR	$19,950
CA	$19,810	ME	no data	PA	no data
CO	$26,250	MI	no data	RI	no data
CT	no data	MN	$22,540	SC	$21,330
DC	no data	MO	no data	SD	no data
DE	no data	MS	no data	TN	no data
FL	$19,550	MT	no data	TX	$20,020
GA	no data	NC	no data	UT	no data
HI	no data	ND	no data	VA	no data
IA	no data	NE	no data	VT	no data
ID	no data	NH	no data	WA	$22,240
IL	$21,270	NJ	$24,980	WI	$20,300
IN	no data	NM	$20,470	WV	no data
KS	no data	NV	$24,600	WY	no data

Median Wages for the Largest Metropolitan Areas (Annual)

Area	Wage	Area	Wage
AZ: Phoenix	$21,610	MI: Detroit	no data
CA: Los Angeles	$19,770	MN: Minneapolis	no data
CA: Riverside	$21,930	MO: Kansas City	no data
CA: Sacramento	$20,220	MO: St. Louis	no data
CA: San Diego	$20,280	NV: Las Vegas	$25,230
CA: San Francisco	$22,560	NY: New York	no data
CO: Denver	$26,940	OH: Cincinnati	no data
DC: Washington	no data	OH: Cleveland	no data
FL: Miami	$19,570	OH: Columbus	no data
FL: Orlando	no data	OR: Portland	no data
FL: Tampa	no data	PA: Philadelphia	no data
GA: Atlanta	no data	PA: Pittsburgh	no data
IL: Chicago	no data	TX: Dallas	no data
MA: Boston	no data	TX: Houston	no data
MD: Baltimore	no data	WA: Seattle	$22,680

FACTORS THAT MAY AFFECT EARNINGS

Educational Attainment of Workers and Effect on Earnings

Figures are based on a group of occupations: Entertainment Attendants and Related Workers

	Percent at Level	Effect on Earnings
Less than High School	—	—
Some High School	17.2%	−45.2%
High School or Equivalent	34.9%	7.9%
Some College but No Degree	29.3%	2.5%
Associate Degree	5.6%	−1.9%
Bachelor's Degree	7.3%	44.0%
Master's Degree	—	—
Doctoral Degree	—	—
First Professional Degree	—	—

Figures do not total 100% because some levels have a very small sample size.

Flexibility of Earnings

Average Hours Worked: 23
Workers with a Varying Number of Hours: 21.1%
Workers Earning Some Overtime Pay, Tips, or Commissions: 23.5%
Earnings Benefit of Working Overtime: −13.2%

Gender

	Male	Female
Percent	51.9%	48.1%
Effect on Earnings	24.3%	−4.7%

Union Membership

Percentage Union Members: 7.5%
Earnings Benefit of Union Membership: 59.7%

Veteran Status

Percentage Who Have Been on Active Duty: 10.4%
Earnings Benefit of Veteran Status: 1.5%

39-3021 Motion Picture Projectionists

Set up and operate motion picture projection and related sound reproduction equipment.

- Education or Training Required: Short-term on-the-job training
- Job Growth: −9.9%
- Annual Openings: 4,000
- Self-Employed: 9.9%
- Part-Time: 30.0%

NATIONAL WAGE FIGURES (ANNUAL)

Beginning	25th Percentile	Median	Mean	75th Percentile	90th Percentile
$12,650	$14,500	$17,450	$20,180	$22,350	$29,650

Median Wages for Industries Employing Largest Numbers (Annual)

Industry	Median Income
Museums, Historical Sites, and Similar Institutions	$25,750
Performing Arts, Spectator Sports, and Related Industries	$20,260
Motion Picture and Sound Recording Industries	$17,330

Median Wages for States (Annual)

AK $17,800	KY $16,160	NY $27,190
AL $13,860	LA $16,290	OH $17,350
AR $14,490	MA $22,760	OK $13,980
AZ $15,550	MD $18,200	OR $17,640
CA $20,870	ME $16,980	PA $15,690
CO $18,310	MI $17,730	RI $20,770
CT $20,860	MN $16,000	SC $16,670
DC no data	MO $14,250	SD $17,240
DE no data	MS $16,570	TN $15,110
FL $17,730	MT $13,880	TX $14,290
GA $15,480	NC $16,140	UT $13,880
HI $20,120	ND $14,900	VA $17,320
IA $13,450	NE $16,780	VT no data
ID $14,130	NH $17,670	WA $20,160
IL $18,770	NJ $21,760	WI $16,820
IN $17,150	NM no data	WV no data
KS $13,720	NV $19,330	WY $17,700

Median Wages for the Largest Metropolitan Areas (Annual)

AZ: Phoenix $15,740	MI: Detroit $18,960
CA: Los Angeles $22,580	MN: Minneapolis $16,630
CA: Riverside $18,750	MO: Kansas City $15,250
CA: Sacramento $19,010	MO: St. Louis $14,590
CA: San Diego $21,120	NV: Las Vegas $20,420
CA: San Francisco $21,560	NY: New York $27,960
CO: Denver $18,610	OH: Cincinnati $19,200
DC: Washington $17,910	OH: Cleveland $16,930
FL: Miami $18,350	OH: Columbus no data
FL: Orlando $17,920	OR: Portland no data
FL: Tampa $17,140	PA: Philadelphia $16,960
GA: Atlanta $16,680	PA: Pittsburgh $13,670
IL: Chicago no data	TX: Dallas $14,360
MA: Boston $23,370	TX: Houston $13,280
MD: Baltimore $19,520	WA: Seattle $20,790

FACTORS THAT MAY AFFECT EARNINGS

Educational Attainment of Workers and Effect on Earnings

	Percent at Level	Effect on Earnings
Less than High School	—	—
Some High School	—	—
High School or Equivalent	60.0%	2.4%
Some College but No Degree	—	—
Associate Degree	—	—
Bachelor's Degree	—	—
Master's Degree	—	—
Doctoral Degree	—	—
First Professional Degree	—	—

Figures do not total 100% because some levels have a very small sample size.

Flexibility of Earnings

Average Hours Worked: 23
Workers with a Varying Number of Hours: 24.4%
Workers Earning Some Overtime Pay, Tips, or Commissions: 23.5%
Earnings Benefit of Working Overtime: −13.2%

Gender

	Male	Female
Percent	87.8%	12.2%
Effect on Earnings	24.3%	−4.7%

Union Membership

Percentage Union Members: 7.5%
Earnings Benefit of Union Membership: 59.7%

Veteran Status

Percentage Who Have Been on Active Duty: 10.4%
Earnings Benefit of Veteran Status: 1.5%

39-3031 Ushers, Lobby Attendants, and Ticket Takers

Assist patrons at entertainment events by performing duties such as collecting admission tickets and passes from patrons, assisting in finding seats, searching for lost articles, and locating such facilities as restrooms and telephones.

- Education or Training Required: Short-term on-the-job training
- Job Growth: 10.6%
- Annual Openings: 45,000
- Self-Employed: 0.0%
- Part-Time: 84.6%

NATIONAL WAGE FIGURES (ANNUAL)

Beginning	25th Percentile	Median	Mean	75th Percentile	90th Percentile
$12,380	$13,950	$15,880	$17,500	$18,800	$24,340

Median Wages for Industries Employing Largest Numbers (Annual)

Industry	Median Income
Real Estate	$22,490
Accommodation	$18,570
Scenic and Sightseeing Transportation	$18,240
Performing Arts, Spectator Sports, and Related Industries	$17,320
Museums, Historical Sites, and Similar Institutions	$17,310
Educational Services	$16,720
Federal, State, and Local Government	$16,460
Religious, Grantmaking, Civic, Professional, and Similar Organizations	$16,370
Food Services and Drinking Places	$16,000
Administrative and Support Services	$15,710

Median Wages for States (Annual)

State	Wage	State	Wage	State	Wage
AK	$17,840	KY	$15,300	NY	$21,620
AL	$13,070	LA	$13,700	OH	$14,190
AR	$14,630	MA	$17,750	OK	$14,040
AZ	$13,930	MD	$16,560	OR	$18,080
CA	$17,260	ME	$15,750	PA	$15,350
CO	$14,190	MI	$15,900	RI	$17,610
CT	$17,010	MN	$16,150	SC	$13,840
DC	$22,530	MO	$17,430	SD	$15,440
DE	$15,030	MS	$13,820	TN	$13,870
FL	$14,480	MT	$13,310	TX	$13,860
GA	$14,670	NC	$13,780	UT	$14,890
HI	$14,600	ND	$13,930	VA	$13,920
IA	$14,050	NE	no data	VT	$18,110
ID	$14,890	NH	$14,380	WA	$18,500
IL	$15,390	NJ	$14,920	WI	$14,170
IN	$15,680	NM	$15,110	WV	$13,560
KS	$14,490	NV	$17,630	WY	$13,520

Median Wages for the Largest Metropolitan Areas (Annual)

Area	Wage	Area	Wage
AZ: Phoenix	$13,860	MI: Detroit	$16,490
CA: Los Angeles	$17,040	MN: Minneapolis	$16,820
CA: Riverside	$15,990	MO: Kansas City	$14,900
CA: Sacramento	$16,820	MO: St. Louis	$17,840
CA: San Diego	$17,950	NV: Las Vegas	$18,610
CA: San Francisco	$18,960	NY: New York	$21,440
CO: Denver	$14,190	OH: Cincinnati	$15,630
DC: Washington	$17,430	OH: Cleveland	$14,330
FL: Miami	$14,690	OH: Columbus	$14,160
FL: Orlando	$14,540	OR: Portland	no data
FL: Tampa	$14,340	PA: Philadelphia	$16,010
GA: Atlanta	$16,450	PA: Pittsburgh	$17,440
IL: Chicago	$15,720	TX: Dallas	$14,690
MA: Boston	$17,750	TX: Houston	$13,500
MD: Baltimore	$15,430	WA: Seattle	$19,790

FACTORS THAT MAY AFFECT EARNINGS

Educational Attainment of Workers and Effect on Earnings

	Percent at Level	Effect on Earnings
Less than High School	—	—
Some High School	25.0%	−61.3%
High School or Equivalent	26.9%	25.4%
Some College but No Degree	25.0%	6.7%
Associate Degree	—	—
Bachelor's Degree	—	—
Master's Degree	—	—
Doctoral Degree	—	—
First Professional Degree	—	—

Figures do not total 100% because some levels have a very small sample size.

Flexibility of Earnings

Average Hours Worked: 16
Workers with a Varying Number of Hours: 20.6%
Workers Earning Some Overtime Pay, Tips, or Commissions: 7.3%
Earnings Benefit of Working Overtime: −13.2%

Gender

	Male	Female
Percent	59.2%	40.8%
Effect on Earnings	24.3%	−4.7%

Union Membership

Percentage Union Members: 9.1%
Earnings Benefit of Union Membership: 59.7%

Veteran Status

Percentage Who Have Been on Active Duty: 10.4%
Earnings Benefit of Veteran Status: 1.5%

39-3091 Amusement and Recreation Attendants

Perform variety of attending duties at amusement or recreation facility. May schedule use of recreation facilities, maintain and provide equipment to participants of sporting events or recreational pursuits, or operate amusement concessions and rides.

- Education or Training Required: Short-term on-the-job training
- Job Growth: 28.0%
- Annual Openings: 130,000
- Self-Employed: 0.8%
- Part-Time: 62.2%

NATIONAL WAGE FIGURES (ANNUAL)

Beginning	25th Percentile	Median	Mean	75th Percentile	90th Percentile
$12,650	$14,180	$16,290	$17,530	$19,270	$24,030

Median Wages for Industries Employing Largest Numbers (Annual)

Industry	Median Income
Heavy and Civil Engineering Construction	$19,120
Nursing and Residential Care Facilities	$19,000
Educational Services	$18,930
Federal, State, and Local Government	$17,620
Scenic and Sightseeing Transportation	$17,540
Social Assistance	$17,470
Rental and Leasing Services	$17,170
Food and Beverage Stores	$16,920
Accommodation	$16,910
Real Estate	$16,790

Median Wages for States (Annual)

State	Wage	State	Wage	State	Wage
AK	$20,040	KY	$14,970	NY	$16,850
AL	$13,940	LA	$13,420	OH	$14,730
AR	$14,520	MA	$18,190	OK	$14,130
AZ	$16,850	MD	no data	OR	$17,720
CA	$17,320	ME	$17,280	PA	$14,590
CO	$17,100	MI	$17,000	RI	$18,510
CT	$20,000	MN	$16,730	SC	$14,840
DC	$17,120	MO	$15,970	SD	$15,340
DE	$18,750	MS	$14,900	TN	$15,880
FL	$15,800	MT	$15,480	TX	$14,490
GA	$14,420	NC	$15,080	UT	$14,960
HI	$19,610	ND	$16,670	VA	$15,210
IA	$14,510	NE	$14,430	VT	$18,530
ID	$14,040	NH	$17,510	WA	$17,920
IL	$17,310	NJ	$16,810	WI	$16,320
IN	$15,210	NM	$17,930	WV	$14,240
KS	$14,450	NV	$15,640	WY	$16,520

Median Wages for the Largest Metropolitan Areas (Annual)

Area	Wage	Area	Wage
AZ: Phoenix	$17,220	MI: Detroit	$17,220
CA: Los Angeles	$17,420	MN: Minneapolis	$17,340
CA: Riverside	$16,920	MO: Kansas City	$15,820
CA: Sacramento	$17,040	MO: St. Louis	$15,940
CA: San Diego	$16,970	NV: Las Vegas	$15,470
CA: San Francisco	$18,520	NY: New York	$17,380
CO: Denver	$17,220	OH: Cincinnati	$14,100
DC: Washington	no data	OH: Cleveland	$15,180
FL: Miami	$17,260	OH: Columbus	$16,160
FL: Orlando	$16,020	OR: Portland	$17,740
FL: Tampa	$14,560	PA: Philadelphia	$17,090
GA: Atlanta	$14,190	PA: Pittsburgh	$13,890
IL: Chicago	$17,450	TX: Dallas	$15,290
MA: Boston	$18,630	TX: Houston	$14,250
MD: Baltimore	$15,140	WA: Seattle	$18,050

FACTORS THAT MAY AFFECT EARNINGS

Educational Attainment of Workers and Effect on Earnings

Figures are based on a group of occupations: Entertainment Attendants and Related Workers

	Percent at Level	Effect on Earnings
Less than High School	—	—
Some High School	17.2%	−45.2%
High School or Equivalent	34.9%	7.9%
Some College but No Degree	29.3%	2.5%
Associate Degree	5.6%	−1.9%
Bachelor's Degree	7.3%	44.0%
Master's Degree	—	—
Doctoral Degree	—	—
First Professional Degree	—	—

Figures do not total 100% because some levels have a very small sample size.

Flexibility of Earnings

Average Hours Worked: 23
Workers with a Varying Number of Hours: 21.1%
Workers Earning Some Overtime Pay, Tips, or Commissions: 23.5%
Earnings Benefit of Working Overtime: −13.2%

Gender

	Male	Female
Percent	57.3%	42.7%
Effect on Earnings	24.3%	−4.7%

Union Membership

Percentage Union Members: 7.5%
Earnings Benefit of Union Membership: 59.7%

Veteran Status

Percentage Who Have Been on Active Duty: 10.4%
Earnings Benefit of Veteran Status: 1.5%

39-3092 Costume Attendants

Select, fit, and take care of costumes for cast members and aid entertainers.

- Education or Training Required: Short-term on-the-job training
- Job Growth: 23.4%
- Annual Openings: 2,000
- Self-Employed: 0.9%
- Part-Time: 62.2%

NATIONAL WAGE FIGURES (ANNUAL)

Beginning	25th Percentile	Median	Mean	75th Percentile	90th Percentile
$14,950	$18,110	$25,740	$29,540	$36,180	$52,030

Median Wages for Industries Employing Largest Numbers (Annual)

Industry	Median Income
Motion Picture and Sound Recording Industries	$57,960
Performing Arts, Spectator Sports, and Related Industries	$29,550
Educational Services	$26,600
Accommodation	$26,020
Administrative and Support Services	$22,960
Federal, State, and Local Government	$21,410
Amusement, Gambling, and Recreation Industries	$17,400

Median Wages for States (Annual)

State	Wage	State	Wage	State	Wage
AK	no data	KY	no data	NY	$38,920
AL	$21,120	LA	no data	OH	$27,370
AR	no data	MA	$29,320	OK	no data
AZ	$30,560	MD	no data	OR	no data
CA	$31,640	ME	no data	PA	$29,650
CO	no data	MI	$22,580	RI	no data
CT	$34,490	MN	$28,750	SC	$16,180
DC	no data	MO	$23,780	SD	no data
DE	no data	MS	no data	TN	no data
FL	$21,850	MT	no data	TX	$21,300
GA	$18,690	NC	no data	UT	$21,070
HI	no data	ND	no data	VA	$15,440
IA	no data	NE	no data	VT	no data
ID	no data	NH	no data	WA	$34,360
IL	$21,330	NJ	$25,370	WI	$23,460
IN	$21,330	NM	no data	WV	no data
KS	no data	NV	$26,460	WY	no data

Median Wages for the Largest Metropolitan Areas (Annual)

Area	Wage	Area	Wage
AZ: Phoenix	no data	MI: Detroit	no data
CA: Los Angeles	$33,550	MN: Minneapolis	$31,710
CA: Riverside	no data	MO: Kansas City	no data
CA: Sacramento	no data	MO: St. Louis	no data
CA: San Diego	$28,560	NV: Las Vegas	$26,930
CA: San Francisco	$34,150	NY: New York	$38,980
CO: Denver	no data	OH: Cincinnati	no data
DC: Washington	no data	OH: Cleveland	no data
FL: Miami	no data	OH: Columbus	no data
FL: Orlando	$18,030	OR: Portland	no data
FL: Tampa	$17,680	PA: Philadelphia	$30,140
GA: Atlanta	no data	PA: Pittsburgh	no data
IL: Chicago	$21,980	TX: Dallas	no data
MA: Boston	$28,270	TX: Houston	no data
MD: Baltimore	no data	WA: Seattle	$34,590

FACTORS THAT MAY AFFECT EARNINGS

Educational Attainment of Workers and Effect on Earnings

Figures are based on a group of occupations: Entertainment Attendants and Related Workers

	Percent at Level	Effect on Earnings
Less than High School	—	—
Some High School	17.2%	−45.2%
High School or Equivalent	34.9%	7.9%
Some College but No Degree	29.3%	2.5%
Associate Degree	5.6%	−1.9%
Bachelor's Degree	7.3%	44.0%
Master's Degree	—	—
Doctoral Degree	—	—
First Professional Degree	—	—

Figures do not total 100% because some levels have a very small sample size.

Flexibility of Earnings

Average Hours Worked: 23
Workers with a Varying Number of Hours: 21.1%
Workers Earning Some Overtime Pay, Tips, or Commissions: 23.5%
Earnings Benefit of Working Overtime: −13.2%

Gender

	Male	Female
Percent	57.3%	42.7%
Effect on Earnings	24.3%	−4.7%

Union Membership

Percentage Union Members: 7.5%
Earnings Benefit of Union Membership: 59.7%

Veteran Status

Percentage Who Have Been on Active Duty: 10.4%
Earnings Benefit of Veteran Status: 1.5%

39-3093 Locker Room, Coatroom, and Dressing Room Attendants

Provide personal items to patrons or customers in locker rooms, dressing rooms, or coatrooms.

- Education or Training Required: Short-term on-the-job training
- Job Growth: 17.3%
- Annual Openings: 12,000
- Self-Employed: 0.8%
- Part-Time: 62.2%

NATIONAL WAGE FIGURES (ANNUAL)

Beginning	25th Percentile	Median	Mean	75th Percentile	90th Percentile
$14,030	$15,760	$18,610	$19,760	$22,410	$27,480

Median Wages for Industries Employing Largest Numbers (Annual)

Industry	Median Income
Educational Services	$22,340
Accommodation	$19,770
Religious, Grantmaking, Civic, Professional, and Similar Organizations	$19,190
Amusement, Gambling, and Recreation Industries	$18,650
Personal and Laundry Services	$18,490
General Merchandise Stores	$18,290
Performing Arts, Spectator Sports, and Related Industries	$18,050
Real Estate	$17,430
Hospitals	$17,380
Federal, State, and Local Government	$17,310

Median Wages for States (Annual)

State	Wage	State	Wage	State	Wage
AK	no data	KY	$18,160	NY	$20,720
AL	$17,850	LA	$16,610	OH	$17,200
AR	no data	MA	$18,580	OK	$17,110
AZ	$18,120	MD	$18,180	OR	$18,270
CA	$20,070	ME	no data	PA	$18,000
CO	$17,710	MI	$16,400	RI	$19,410
CT	$19,840	MN	$18,070	SC	$17,720
DC	$22,680	MO	$17,910	SD	no data
DE	$20,560	MS	no data	TN	$18,000
FL	$18,790	MT	$19,330	TX	$17,850
GA	$18,780	NC	$20,670	UT	$17,440
HI	$23,850	ND	$14,460	VA	$18,330
IA	$17,490	NE	$15,420	VT	no data
ID	$17,700	NH	no data	WA	$19,470
IL	$18,530	NJ	$19,440	WI	$20,010
IN	$17,430	NM	no data	WV	$15,900
KS	$15,430	NV	$21,720	WY	no data

Median Wages for the Largest Metropolitan Areas (Annual)

Area	Wage	Area	Wage
AZ: Phoenix	$18,250	MI: Detroit	$16,690
CA: Los Angeles	$19,920	MN: Minneapolis	$18,180
CA: Riverside	$20,250	MO: Kansas City	$15,380
CA: Sacramento	$19,760	MO: St. Louis	$17,550
CA: San Diego	$20,590	NV: Las Vegas	$23,320
CA: San Francisco	$20,560	NY: New York	$20,200
CO: Denver	$18,050	OH: Cincinnati	$19,160
DC: Washington	$19,020	OH: Cleveland	$17,090
FL: Miami	$19,310	OH: Columbus	$17,240
FL: Orlando	$17,900	OR: Portland	$18,270
FL: Tampa	$17,760	PA: Philadelphia	$20,810
GA: Atlanta	$18,730	PA: Pittsburgh	$16,290
IL: Chicago	$18,960	TX: Dallas	$17,800
MA: Boston	$20,420	TX: Houston	$17,670
MD: Baltimore	$17,890	WA: Seattle	$19,770

FACTORS THAT MAY AFFECT EARNINGS

Educational Attainment of Workers and Effect on Earnings

Figures are based on a group of occupations: Entertainment Attendants and Related Workers

	Percent at Level	Effect on Earnings
Less than High School	—	—
Some High School	17.2%	−45.2%
High School or Equivalent	34.9%	7.9%
Some College but No Degree	29.3%	2.5%
Associate Degree	5.6%	−1.9%
Bachelor's Degree	7.3%	44.0%
Master's Degree	—	—
Doctoral Degree	—	—
First Professional Degree	—	—

Figures do not total 100% because some levels have a very small sample size.

Flexibility of Earnings

Average Hours Worked: 23
Workers with a Varying Number of Hours: 21.1%
Workers Earning Some Overtime Pay, Tips, or Commissions: 23.5%
Earnings Benefit of Working Overtime: −13.2%

Gender

	Male	Female
Percent	57.3%	42.7%
Effect on Earnings	24.3%	−4.7%

Union Membership

Percentage Union Members: 7.5%
Earnings Benefit of Union Membership: 59.7%

Veteran Status

Percentage Who Have Been on Active Duty: 10.4%
Earnings Benefit of Veteran Status: 1.5%

39-3099 Entertainment Attendants and Related Workers, All Other

All entertainment attendants and related workers not listed separately.

- Education or Training Required: Moderate-term on-the-job training
- Job Growth: No data available
- Annual Openings: No data available
- Self-Employed: 0.6%
- Part-Time: 62.2%

NATIONAL WAGE FIGURES (ANNUAL)

Beginning	25th Percentile	Median	Mean	75th Percentile	90th Percentile
no data	no data	no data	no data	no data	no data

Median Wages for Industries Employing Largest Numbers (Annual)

Industry	Median Income
Museums, Historical Sites, and Similar Institutions	$23,450
Hospitals	$21,990
Accommodation	$21,260
Educational Services	$20,040
Performing Arts, Spectator Sports, and Related Industries	$19,640
Federal, State, and Local Government	$18,620
Administrative and Support Services	$17,860
Warehousing and Storage	$17,190
Broadcasting (Except Internet)	$17,070
Motion Picture and Sound Recording Industries	$17,000

Median Wages for States (Annual)

State		State		State	
AK	$22,020	KY	no data	NY	no data
AL	no data	LA	$18,190	OH	no data
AR	no data	MA	no data	OK	no data
AZ	no data	MD	no data	OR	$18,260
CA	$19,350	ME	no data	PA	no data
CO	no data	MI	$17,620	RI	no data
CT	no data	MN	$19,340	SC	no data
DC	no data	MO	no data	SD	no data
DE	no data	MS	no data	TN	no data
FL	no data	MT	no data	TX	$15,750
GA	no data	NC	no data	UT	no data
HI	no data	ND	no data	VA	no data
IA	$16,700	NE	no data	VT	no data
ID	$16,920	NH	no data	WA	$20,850
IL	no data	NJ	$20,710	WI	no data
IN	no data	NM	$15,500	WV	no data
KS	no data	NV	$21,250	WY	no data

Median Wages for the Largest Metropolitan Areas (Annual)

Area		Area	
AZ: Phoenix	no data	MI: Detroit	$18,220
CA: Los Angeles	$20,440	MN: Minneapolis	$19,670
CA: Riverside	$18,210	MO: Kansas City	no data
CA: Sacramento	$20,090	MO: St. Louis	no data
CA: San Diego	no data	NV: Las Vegas	$22,050
CA: San Francisco	$21,870	NY: New York	$20,800
CO: Denver	$19,890	OH: Cincinnati	$18,130
DC: Washington	no data	OH: Cleveland	$16,570
FL: Miami	no data	OH: Columbus	no data
FL: Orlando	no data	OR: Portland	$18,870
FL: Tampa	no data	PA: Philadelphia	no data
GA: Atlanta	no data	PA: Pittsburgh	no data
IL: Chicago	no data	TX: Dallas	$17,390
MA: Boston	no data	TX: Houston	$15,910
MD: Baltimore	no data	WA: Seattle	$21,580

FACTORS THAT MAY AFFECT EARNINGS

Educational Attainment of Workers and Effect on Earnings

Figures are based on a group of occupations: Entertainment Attendants and Related Workers

	Percent at Level	Effect on Earnings
Less than High School	—	—
Some High School	17.2%	−45.2%
High School or Equivalent	34.9%	7.9%
Some College but No Degree	29.3%	2.5%
Associate Degree	5.6%	−1.9%
Bachelor's Degree	7.3%	44.0%
Master's Degree	—	—
Doctoral Degree	—	—
First Professional Degree	—	—

Figures do not total 100% because some levels have a very small sample size.

Flexibility of Earnings

Average Hours Worked: 23
Workers with a Varying Number of Hours: 21.1%
Workers Earning Some Overtime Pay, Tips, or Commissions: 23.5%
Earnings Benefit of Working Overtime: −13.2%

Gender

	Male	Female
Percent	57.3%	42.7%
Effect on Earnings	24.3%	−4.7%

Union Membership

Percentage Union Members: 7.5%
Earnings Benefit of Union Membership: 59.7%

Veteran Status

Percentage Who Have Been on Active Duty: 10.4%
Earnings Benefit of Veteran Status: 1.5%

39-4000 Funeral Service Workers

39-4011 Embalmers

Prepare bodies for interment in conformity with legal requirements.

- Education or Training Required: Postsecondary vocational training
- Job Growth: 15.7%
- Annual Openings: 2,000
- Self-Employed: 0.0%
- Part-Time: 59.3%

NATIONAL WAGE FIGURES (ANNUAL)

Beginning	25th Percentile	Median	Mean	75th Percentile	90th Percentile
$23,290	$29,400	$37,840	$40,410	$47,450	$59,900

Median Wages for Industries Employing Largest Numbers (Annual)

Industry	Median Income
Personal and Laundry Services	$37,860

Median Wages for States (Annual)

AK .... no data	KY $31,740	NY $41,630
AL $35,420	LA $37,380	OH $35,040
AR $33,670	MA $49,000	OK $24,350
AZ $40,600	MD $45,490	OR .... no data
CA $38,710	ME .... no data	PA $32,700
CO $28,520	MI $41,070	RI............. $47,860
CT $49,850	MN .... no data	SC............. $37,010
DC .... no data	MO $41,080	SD .... no data
DE .... no data	MS $31,070	TN $38,890
FL $38,270	MT .... no data	TX $30,970
GA $35,410	NC $38,610	UT $37,970
HI .... no data	ND $33,830	VA $40,230
IA $52,390	NE .... no data	VT .... no data
ID .... no data	NH .... no data	WA $40,330
IL $42,010	NJ $53,570	WI $43,460
IN $44,270	NM .... no data	WV $38,410
KS $32,190	NV .... no data	WY .... no data

Median Wages for the Largest Metropolitan Areas (Annual)

AZ: Phoenix	no data	MI: Detroit	no data
CA: Los Angeles	$36,080	MN: Minneapolis	no data
CA: Riverside	$36,880	MO: Kansas City	$33,900
CA: Sacramento	$44,130	MO: St. Louis	$48,180
CA: San Diego	$39,250	NV: Las Vegas	no data
CA: San Francisco	$42,690	NY: New York	$44,800
CO: Denver	no data	OH: Cincinnati	$33,230
DC: Washington	$43,920	OH: Cleveland	$33,900
FL: Miami	$40,670	OH: Columbus	$37,310
FL: Orlando	$37,980	OR: Portland	no data
FL: Tampa	$39,060	PA: Philadelphia	$30,470
GA: Atlanta	$34,270	PA: Pittsburgh	$30,600
IL: Chicago	no data	TX: Dallas	$30,900
MA: Boston	$53,020	TX: Houston	$28,150
MD: Baltimore	no data	WA: Seattle	$37,980

FACTORS THAT MAY AFFECT EARNINGS

Educational Attainment of Workers and Effect on Earnings

Figures are based on a group of occupations: Funeral Service Workers

	Percent at Level	Effect on Earnings
Less than High School	—	—
Some High School	—	—
High School or Equivalent	—	—
Some College but No Degree	—	—
Associate Degree	—	—
Bachelor's Degree	—	—
Master's Degree	—	—
Doctoral Degree	—	—
First Professional Degree	—	—

Figures do not total 100% because some levels have a very small sample size.

Flexibility of Earnings

Average Hours Worked: 19
Workers with a Varying Number of Hours: 32.1%
Workers Earning Some Overtime Pay, Tips, or Commissions: 13.6%
Earnings Benefit of Working Overtime: 67.0%

Gender

	Male	Female
Percent	78.0%	22.0%
Effect on Earnings	24.3%	−4.7%

Union Membership

Percentage Union Members: 4.5%
Earnings Benefit of Union Membership: −57.0%

Veteran Status

Percentage Who Have Been on Active Duty: 27.3%
Earnings Benefit of Veteran Status: −43.0%

© JIST Works

39-4021 Funeral Attendants

Perform variety of tasks during funeral, such as placing casket in parlor or chapel prior to service, arranging floral offerings or lights around casket, directing or escorting mourners, closing casket, and issuing and storing funeral equipment.

- Education or Training Required: Short-term on-the-job training
- Job Growth: 20.8%
- Annual Openings: 8,000
- Self-Employed: 0.0%
- Part-Time: 59.3%

NATIONAL WAGE FIGURES (ANNUAL)

Beginning	25th Percentile	Median	Mean	75th Percentile	90th Percentile
$13,780	$16,480	$20,350	$21,970	$25,170	$32,390

Median Wages for Industries Employing Largest Numbers (Annual)

Industry	Median Income
Personal and Laundry Services	$20,340

Median Wages for States (Annual)

AK	no data	KY	$16,420	NY	$22,030
AL	$16,410	LA	$17,920	OH	$20,310
AR	$19,130	MA	$32,950	OK	$18,030
AZ	$22,830	MD	$20,520	OR	$21,950
CA	$24,610	ME	$23,050	PA	$19,410
CO	$21,250	MI	$21,780	RI	$23,760
CT	$23,570	MN	$21,420	SC	$18,340
DC	no data	MO	$18,680	SD	$18,080
DE	$22,030	MS	$21,060	TN	$19,060
FL	$18,070	MT	$22,820	TX	$16,950
GA	$20,900	NC	$20,180	UT	$26,130
HI	$22,670	ND	$17,330	VA	$19,530
IA	$19,620	NE	$18,400	VT	$28,990
ID	$18,250	NH	$24,290	WA	$26,380
IL	$21,530	NJ	$31,200	WI	$22,430
IN	$18,860	NM	$19,760	WV	$18,070
KS	$16,510	NV	$19,540	WY	$20,150

Median Wages for the Largest Metropolitan Areas (Annual)

AZ: Phoenix	$23,990	MI: Detroit	$23,940
CA: Los Angeles	$27,090	MN: Minneapolis	$20,060
CA: Riverside	$22,190	MO: Kansas City	$20,970
CA: Sacramento	$23,540	MO: St. Louis	$19,430
CA: San Diego	$22,310	NV: Las Vegas	$19,650
CA: San Francisco	$25,640	NY: New York	$25,180
CO: Denver	$24,110	OH: Cincinnati	$20,340
DC: Washington	$22,590	OH: Cleveland	$21,730
FL: Miami	$17,170	OH: Columbus	$21,880
FL: Orlando	$17,220	OR: Portland	$27,840
FL: Tampa	$18,720	PA: Philadelphia	$23,660
GA: Atlanta	$25,350	PA: Pittsburgh	$17,930
IL: Chicago	$21,640	TX: Dallas	$18,310
MA: Boston	$37,080	TX: Houston	$18,280
MD: Baltimore	$20,180	WA: Seattle	no data

FACTORS THAT MAY AFFECT EARNINGS

Educational Attainment of Workers and Effect on Earnings

Figures are based on a group of occupations: Funeral Service Workers

	Percent at Level	Effect on Earnings
Less than High School	—	—
Some High School	—	—
High School or Equivalent	—	—
Some College but No Degree	—	—
Associate Degree	—	—
Bachelor's Degree	—	—
Master's Degree	—	—
Doctoral Degree	—	—
First Professional Degree	—	—

Figures do not total 100% because some levels have a very small sample size.

Flexibility of Earnings

Average Hours Worked: 19
Workers with a Varying Number of Hours: 32.1%
Workers Earning Some Overtime Pay, Tips, or Commissions: 13.6%
Earnings Benefit of Working Overtime: 67.0%

Gender

	Male	Female
Percent	78.0%	22.0%
Effect on Earnings	24.3%	−4.7%

Union Membership

Percentage Union Members: 4.5%
Earnings Benefit of Union Membership: −57.0%

Veteran Status

Percentage Who Have Been on Active Duty: 27.3%
Earnings Benefit of Veteran Status: −43.0%

39-5000 Personal Appearance Workers

39-5011 Barbers

Provide barbering services, such as cutting, trimming, shampooing, and styling hair; trimming beards; or giving shaves.

- Education or Training Required: Postsecondary vocational training
- Job Growth: 8.2%
- Annual Openings: 5,000
- Self-Employed: 71.0%
- Part-Time: 28.1%

Note: A large fraction of the workforce for this occupation is self-employed and earns an average of $50,730. All other earnings figures for this occupation are based on workers who are paid a wage or salary.

NATIONAL WAGE FIGURES (ANNUAL)

Beginning	25th Percentile	Median	Mean	75th Percentile	90th Percentile
$14,810	$18,110	$23,150	$26,540	$29,640	$42,770

Median Wages for Industries Employing Largest Numbers (Annual)

Industry	Median Income
Federal, State, and Local Government	$33,940
Hospitals	$31,760
Educational Services	$28,860
Personal and Laundry Services	$22,970
Nursing and Residential Care Facilities	$19,780

Median Wages for States (Annual)

AK	no data	KY	$27,920	NY	$19,060
AL	$18,070	LA	$20,490	OH	$23,520
AR	no data	MA	no data	OK	$30,160
AZ	$17,810	MD	$27,220	OR	no data
CA	$21,440	ME	no data	PA	$26,170
CO	no data	MI	$25,610	RI	no data
CT	$23,180	MN	no data	SC	$27,800
DC	$20,380	MO	$21,450	SD	no data
DE	$26,140	MS	$17,510	TN	$22,070
FL	$18,140	MT	no data	TX	$21,890
GA	no data	NC	no data	UT	no data
HI	no data	ND	no data	VA	$17,410
IA	no data	NE	no data	VT	no data
ID	no data	NH	no data	WA	$24,400
IL	$24,120	NJ	$29,430	WI	$21,810
IN	no data	NM	no data	WV	$39,710
KS	$23,990	NV	no data	WY	no data

Median Wages for the Largest Metropolitan Areas (Annual)

AZ: Phoenix	no data	MI: Detroit	no data
CA: Los Angeles	$20,530	MN: Minneapolis	no data
CA: Riverside	no data	MO: Kansas City	no data
CA: Sacramento	no data	MO: St. Louis	$21,410
CA: San Diego	no data	NV: Las Vegas	no data
CA: San Francisco	$33,540	NY: New York	$21,010
CO: Denver	no data	OH: Cincinnati	no data
DC: Washington	$20,810	OH: Cleveland	$22,650
FL: Miami	$17,670	OH: Columbus	no data
FL: Orlando	no data	OR: Portland	no data
FL: Tampa	no data	PA: Philadelphia	$26,150
GA: Atlanta	no data	PA: Pittsburgh	no data
IL: Chicago	$24,820	TX: Dallas	no data
MA: Boston	no data	TX: Houston	$76,720
MD: Baltimore	no data	WA: Seattle	no data

FACTORS THAT MAY AFFECT EARNINGS

Educational Attainment of Workers and Effect on Earnings

	Percent at Level	Effect on Earnings
Less than High School	—	—
Some High School	—	—
High School or Equivalent	56.5%	9.7%
Some College but No Degree	21.7%	−21.7%
Associate Degree	13.0%	20.9%
Bachelor's Degree	—	—
Master's Degree	—	—
Doctoral Degree	—	—
First Professional Degree	—	—

Figures do not total 100% because some levels have a very small sample size.

Flexibility of Earnings

Average Hours Worked: 33
Workers with a Varying Number of Hours: 11.2%
Workers Earning Some Overtime Pay, Tips, or Commissions: 45.5%
Earnings Benefit of Working Overtime: −1.0%

Gender

	Male	Female
Percent	82.3%	17.7%
Effect on Earnings	—	−1.5%

Union Membership

Percentage Union Members: Insignificant
Earnings Benefit of Union Membership: No significant data available

Veteran Status

Percentage Who Have Been on Active Duty: Insignificant
Earnings Benefit of Veteran Status: No significant data available

39-5012 Hairdressers, Hairstylists, and Cosmetologists

Provide beauty services, such as shampooing, cutting, coloring, and styling hair and massaging and treating scalp. May also apply makeup, dress wigs, perform hair removal, and provide nail and skin care services.

- Education or Training Required: Postsecondary vocational training
- Job Growth: 16.1%
- Annual Openings: 59,000
- Self-Employed: 43.8%
- Part-Time: 32.0%

Note: A large fraction of the workforce for this occupation is self-employed and earns an average of $23,880. All other earnings figures for this occupation are based on workers who are paid a wage or salary.

NATIONAL WAGE FIGURES (ANNUAL)

Beginning	25th Percentile	Median	Mean	75th Percentile	90th Percentile
$13,880	$16,470	$21,320	$24,550	$28,600	$39,070

Median Wages for Industries Employing Largest Numbers (Annual)

Industry	Median Income
Motion Picture and Sound Recording Industries	$84,430
Broadcasting (Except Internet)	$27,100
Ambulatory Health Care Services	$25,720
Federal, State, and Local Government	$25,530
Hospitals	$25,090
Amusement, Gambling, and Recreation Industries	$24,460
Clothing and Clothing Accessories Stores	$24,090
Food and Beverage Stores	$23,960
Accommodation	$23,560
Nursing and Residential Care Facilities	$23,350

Median Wages for States (Annual)

State	Wage	State	Wage	State	Wage
AK	$27,900	KY	$18,420	NY	$21,550
AL	$18,490	LA	$19,120	OH	$20,190
AR	$16,330	MA	$26,930	OK	$18,660
AZ	$21,730	MD	$23,750	OR	$20,320
CA	$20,110	ME	$22,710	PA	$18,080
CO	$22,040	MI	$19,300	RI	$22,280
CT	$25,420	MN	$25,690	SC	$21,550
DC	no data	MO	$19,990	SD	$23,710
DE	$24,330	MS	$17,120	TN	$21,940
FL	$21,720	MT	$17,110	TX	$19,620
GA	$21,440	NC	$21,040	UT	$18,280
HI	$25,610	ND	$21,340	VA	$23,600
IA	$19,960	NE	$20,820	VT	$26,960
ID	$15,690	NH	$20,680	WA	$25,800
IL	$23,090	NJ	$26,170	WI	$20,700
IN	$20,270	NM	$15,440	WV	$18,490
KS	$19,650	NV	$19,930	WY	$22,060

Median Wages for the Largest Metropolitan Areas (Annual)

Area	Wage	Area	Wage
AZ: Phoenix	$21,270	MI: Detroit	$19,550
CA: Los Angeles	$20,640	MN: Minneapolis	$26,920
CA: Riverside	$18,070	MO: Kansas City	$20,070
CA: Sacramento	$20,320	MO: St. Louis	$21,910
CA: San Diego	$22,000	NV: Las Vegas	$18,230
CA: San Francisco	$21,270	NY: New York	$24,270
CO: Denver	$22,450	OH: Cincinnati	$20,960
DC: Washington	$28,520	OH: Cleveland	$23,290
FL: Miami	$21,580	OH: Columbus	$18,960
FL: Orlando	$19,960	OR: Portland	$20,260
FL: Tampa	$22,230	PA: Philadelphia	$22,390
GA: Atlanta	$23,100	PA: Pittsburgh	$16,460
IL: Chicago	$23,190	TX: Dallas	$19,740
MA: Boston	$27,420	TX: Houston	$20,540
MD: Baltimore	$23,360	WA: Seattle	$27,380

FACTORS THAT MAY AFFECT EARNINGS

Educational Attainment of Workers and Effect on Earnings

	Percent at Level	Effect on Earnings
Less than High School	2.3%	11.4%
Some High School	5.9%	−5.0%
High School or Equivalent	42.0%	−2.2%
Some College but No Degree	21.1%	−3.9%
Associate Degree	22.4%	3.5%
Bachelor's Degree	5.2%	19.6%
Master's Degree	—	—
Doctoral Degree	—	—
First Professional Degree	—	—

Flexibility of Earnings

Average Hours Worked: 27
Workers with a Varying Number of Hours: 15.7%
Workers Earning Some Overtime Pay, Tips, or Commissions: 49.4%
Earnings Benefit of Working Overtime: −1.1%

Gender

	Male	Female
Percent	6.6%	93.4%
Effect on Earnings	—	−1.5%

Union Membership

Percentage Union Members: Insignificant
Earnings Benefit of Union Membership: No significant data available

Veteran Status

Percentage Who Have Been on Active Duty: Insignificant
Earnings Benefit of Veteran Status: No significant data available

39-5091 Makeup Artists, Theatrical and Performance

Apply makeup to performers to reflect period, setting, and situation of their role.

- Education or Training Required: Postsecondary vocational training
- Job Growth: 13.2%
- Annual Openings: Fewer than 500
- Self-Employed: 35.8%
- Part-Time: 32.0%

Note: Earnings figures do not reflect self-employed workers, who make up a large fraction of the workforce for this occupation.

NATIONAL WAGE FIGURES (ANNUAL)

Beginning	25th Percentile	Median	Mean	75th Percentile	90th Percentile
$14,500	$18,070	$31,820	$36,730	$52,110	$70,750

Median Wages for Industries Employing Largest Numbers (Annual)

Industry	Median Income
Motion Picture and Sound Recording Industries	$56,310
Broadcasting (Except Internet)	$49,340
Performing Arts, Spectator Sports, and Related Industries	$39,630
Personal and Laundry Services	$23,360

Median Wages for States (Annual)

AK	no data	KY	no data	NY	$44,790
AL	no data	LA	no data	OH	$24,220
AR	no data	MA	no data	OK	no data
AZ	no data	MD	no data	OR	no data
CA	$34,970	ME	no data	PA	no data
CO	no data	MI	no data	RI	no data
CT	no data	MN	no data	SC	no data
DC	no data	MO	no data	SD	no data
DE	no data	MS	no data	TN	no data
FL	$36,460	MT	no data	TX	$22,280
GA	no data	NC	no data	UT	no data
HI	no data	ND	no data	VA	no data
IA	no data	NE	no data	VT	no data
ID	no data	NH	no data	WA	no data
IL	$18,790	NJ	no data	WI	no data
IN	no data	NM	no data	WV	no data
KS	no data	NV	no data	WY	no data

Median Wages for the Largest Metropolitan Areas (Annual)

AZ: Phoenix	no data	MI: Detroit	no data
CA: Los Angeles	$36,810	MN: Minneapolis	no data
CA: Riverside	no data	MO: Kansas City	no data
CA: Sacramento	no data	MO: St. Louis	no data
CA: San Diego	no data	NV: Las Vegas	no data
CA: San Francisco	no data	NY: New York	$44,220
CO: Denver	no data	OH: Cincinnati	no data
DC: Washington	no data	OH: Cleveland	no data
FL: Miami	$61,160	OH: Columbus	no data
FL: Orlando	no data	OR: Portland	no data
FL: Tampa	no data	PA: Philadelphia	no data
GA: Atlanta	no data	PA: Pittsburgh	no data
IL: Chicago	$25,540	TX: Dallas	$22,440
MA: Boston	no data	TX: Houston	$23,040
MD: Baltimore	no data	WA: Seattle	no data

FACTORS THAT MAY AFFECT EARNINGS

Educational Attainment of Workers and Effect on Earnings

Figures are based on a group of occupations: Personal Appearance Workers

	Percent at Level	Effect on Earnings
Less than High School	3.2%	−13.6%
Some High School	8.5%	−21.5%
High School or Equivalent	39.8%	1.5%
Some College but No Degree	21.0%	−2.5%
Associate Degree	19.8%	0.4%
Bachelor's Degree	6.9%	31.3%
Master's Degree	—	—
Doctoral Degree	—	—
First Professional Degree	—	—

Flexibility of Earnings

Average Hours Worked: 28
Workers with a Varying Number of Hours: 15.2%
Workers Earning Some Overtime Pay, Tips, or Commissions: 46.8%
Earnings Benefit of Working Overtime: −4.2%

Gender

	Male	Female
Percent	17.0%	83.0%
Effect on Earnings	—	−1.5%

Union Membership

Percentage Union Members: Insignificant
Earnings Benefit of Union Membership: No significant data available

Veteran Status

Percentage Who Have Been on Active Duty: Insignificant
Earnings Benefit of Veteran Status: No significant data available

39-5092 Manicurists and Pedicurists

Clean and shape customers' fingernails and toenails. May polish or decorate nails.

- Education or Training Required: Postsecondary vocational training
- Job Growth: 21.0%
- Annual Openings: 12,000
- Self-Employed: 30.5%
- Part-Time: 32.0%

Note: Earnings figures do not reflect self-employed workers, who make up a large fraction of the workforce for this occupation.

NATIONAL WAGE FIGURES (ANNUAL)

Beginning	25th Percentile	Median	Mean	75th Percentile	90th Percentile
$14,210	$15,870	$19,190	$21,280	$25,060	$31,910

Median Wages for Industries Employing Largest Numbers (Annual)

Industry	Median Income
Ambulatory Health Care Services	$30,290
Educational Services	$22,190
Amusement, Gambling, and Recreation Industries	$21,530
Accommodation	$20,790
Religious, Grantmaking, Civic, Professional, and Similar Organizations	$20,090
Personal and Laundry Services	$19,230
Health and Personal Care Stores	$17,980

Median Wages for States (Annual)

AK	$18,280	KY	$21,970	NY	$18,330
AL	$17,420	LA	$16,290	OH	$19,960
AR	$19,980	MA	$22,480	OK	$14,250
AZ	$17,660	MD	$20,830	OR	$19,010
CA	$17,030	ME	$16,560	PA	$17,650
CO	$23,530	MI	$15,480	RI	$19,110
CT	$21,130	MN	$19,730	SC	$18,900
DC	$27,910	MO	$17,540	SD	$19,070
DE	$18,400	MS	$17,550	TN	$18,170
FL	$23,680	MT	no data	TX	$17,130
GA	$17,670	NC	$23,000	UT	$17,850
HI	$22,170	ND	no data	VA	$19,850
IA	$20,790	NE	$16,090	VT	no data
ID	$27,850	NH	$20,580	WA	$16,880
IL	$25,370	NJ	$21,890	WI	$16,660
IN	$17,120	NM	$17,310	WV	$14,950
KS	$18,570	NV	$22,520	WY	no data

Median Wages for the Largest Metropolitan Areas (Annual)

AZ: Phoenix	$19,220	MI: Detroit	$15,370
CA: Los Angeles	$16,810	MN: Minneapolis	$19,530
CA: Riverside	$16,490	MO: Kansas City	$14,400
CA: Sacramento	$16,130	MO: St. Louis	$19,750
CA: San Diego	$17,060	NV: Las Vegas	$21,060
CA: San Francisco	$18,800	NY: New York	$19,030
CO: Denver	$23,190	OH: Cincinnati	$22,570
DC: Washington	$21,620	OH: Cleveland	$18,940
FL: Miami	$24,510	OH: Columbus	$19,690
FL: Orlando	$23,020	OR: Portland	$17,350
FL: Tampa	$20,660	PA: Philadelphia	$18,490
GA: Atlanta	$19,450	PA: Pittsburgh	$20,160
IL: Chicago	$25,420	TX: Dallas	$19,450
MA: Boston	$24,260	TX: Houston	$15,060
MD: Baltimore	$19,900	WA: Seattle	$16,200

FACTORS THAT MAY AFFECT EARNINGS

Educational Attainment of Workers and Effect on Earnings

Figures are based on a group of occupations: Personal Appearance Workers

	Percent at Level	Effect on Earnings
Less than High School	3.2%	−13.6%
Some High School	8.5%	−21.5%
High School or Equivalent	39.8%	1.5%
Some College but No Degree	21.0%	−2.5%
Associate Degree	19.8%	0.4%
Bachelor's Degree	6.9%	31.3%
Master's Degree	—	—
Doctoral Degree	—	—
First Professional Degree	—	—

Flexibility of Earnings

Average Hours Worked: 28
Workers with a Varying Number of Hours: 15.2%
Workers Earning Some Overtime Pay, Tips, or Commissions: 46.8%
Earnings Benefit of Working Overtime: −4.2%

Gender

	Male	Female
Percent	17.0%	83.0%
Effect on Earnings	—	−1.5%

Union Membership

Percentage Union Members: Insignificant
Earnings Benefit of Union Membership: No significant data available

Veteran Status

Percentage Who Have Been on Active Duty: Insignificant
Earnings Benefit of Veteran Status: No significant data available

39-5093 Shampooers

Shampoo and rinse customers' hair.

- Education or Training Required: Short-term on-the-job training
- Job Growth: 13.1%
- Annual Openings: 5,000
- Self-Employed: 35.8%
- Part-Time: 32.0%

Note: Earnings figures do not reflect self-employed workers, who make up a large fraction of the workforce for this occupation.

NATIONAL WAGE FIGURES (ANNUAL)

Beginning	25th Percentile	Median	Mean	75th Percentile	90th Percentile
$13,030	$14,190	$16,170	$17,050	$19,230	$22,630

Median Wages for Industries Employing Largest Numbers (Annual)

Industry	Median Income
Personal and Laundry Services	$16,170
Educational Services	$15,920

Median Wages for States (Annual)

AK	no data	KY	$14,020	NY	$16,810
AL	$15,480	LA	$15,930	OH	$15,510
AR	no data	MA	$18,860	OK	$14,500
AZ	$14,710	MD	$14,370	OR	no data
CA	$19,330	ME	no data	PA	$13,800
CO	$15,600	MI	$16,630	RI	no data
CT	$17,750	MN	$16,390	SC	$15,800
DC	$20,710	MO	$18,660	SD	no data
DE	$15,040	MS	no data	TN	$19,020
FL	$16,320	MT	no data	TX	$14,860
GA	$16,000	NC	$18,570	UT	no data
HI	$14,990	ND	no data	VA	$16,960
IA	no data	NE	no data	VT	no data
ID	no data	NH	no data	WA	no data
IL	$17,380	NJ	$16,310	WI	no data
IN	$16,040	NM	no data	WV	no data
KS	no data	NV	no data	WY	no data

Median Wages for the Largest Metropolitan Areas (Annual)

AZ: Phoenix	$15,470	MI: Detroit	$16,940
CA: Los Angeles	$19,450	MN: Minneapolis	$16,390
CA: Riverside	no data	MO: Kansas City	no data
CA: Sacramento	no data	MO: St. Louis	$18,900
CA: San Diego	$15,170	NV: Las Vegas	no data
CA: San Francisco	$21,000	NY: New York	$16,710
CO: Denver	$14,070	OH: Cincinnati	no data
DC: Washington	$17,770	OH: Cleveland	$16,050
FL: Miami	$16,220	OH: Columbus	no data
FL: Orlando	no data	OR: Portland	no data
FL: Tampa	$17,320	PA: Philadelphia	$14,860
GA: Atlanta	$17,180	PA: Pittsburgh	$13,390
IL: Chicago	$17,230	TX: Dallas	$14,380
MA: Boston	$19,210	TX: Houston	$15,180
MD: Baltimore	$14,170	WA: Seattle	no data

FACTORS THAT MAY AFFECT EARNINGS

Educational Attainment of Workers and Effect on Earnings

Figures are based on a group of occupations: Personal Appearance Workers

	Percent at Level	Effect on Earnings
Less than High School	3.2%	−13.6%
Some High School	8.5%	−21.5%
High School or Equivalent	39.8%	1.5%
Some College but No Degree	21.0%	−2.5%
Associate Degree	19.8%	0.4%
Bachelor's Degree	6.9%	31.3%
Master's Degree	—	—
Doctoral Degree	—	—
First Professional Degree	—	—

Flexibility of Earnings

Average Hours Worked: 28
Workers with a Varying Number of Hours: 15.2%
Workers Earning Some Overtime Pay, Tips, or Commissions: 46.8%
Earnings Benefit of Working Overtime: −4.2%

Gender

	Male	Female
Percent	17.0%	83.0%
Effect on Earnings	—	−1.5%

Union Membership

Percentage Union Members: Insignificant
Earnings Benefit of Union Membership: No significant data available

Veteran Status

Percentage Who Have Been on Active Duty: Insignificant
Earnings Benefit of Veteran Status: No significant data available

39-5094 Skin Care Specialists

Provide skin care treatments to face and body to enhance an individual's appearance.

- Education or Training Required: Postsecondary vocational training
- Job Growth: 20.4%
- Annual Openings: 6,000
- Self-Employed: 29.6%
- Part-Time: 32.0%

NATIONAL WAGE FIGURES (ANNUAL)

Beginning	25th Percentile	Median	Mean	75th Percentile	90th Percentile
$14,440	$18,240	$26,170	$29,550	$36,820	$51,040

Median Wages for Industries Employing Largest Numbers (Annual)

Industry	Median Income
Ambulatory Health Care Services	$33,100
Health and Personal Care Stores	$32,660
Amusement, Gambling, and Recreation Industries	$28,990
Personal and Laundry Services	$25,210
Accommodation	$23,300
Merchant Wholesalers, Nondurable Goods	$22,810
General Merchandise Stores	$21,780

Median Wages for States (Annual)

State	Wage	State	Wage	State	Wage
AK	no data	KY	$21,490	NY	$25,720
AL	$18,240	LA	$33,830	OH	$20,670
AR	$25,790	MA	$32,080	OK	$13,420
AZ	$30,320	MD	$21,370	OR	$37,770
CA	$29,110	ME	$18,890	PA	$17,500
CO	$31,430	MI	$26,850	RI	$34,350
CT	$33,020	MN	$27,410	SC	$28,410
DC	$40,020	MO	$27,390	SD	no data
DE	no data	MS	$14,570	TN	$28,280
FL	$26,510	MT	no data	TX	$28,180
GA	$23,780	NC	$22,880	UT	$30,220
HI	$21,410	ND	$26,590	VA	$23,340
IA	no data	NE	$35,270	VT	$27,930
ID	$30,790	NH	$24,630	WA	$35,650
IL	$28,440	NJ	$31,310	WI	$25,060
IN	$25,080	NM	no data	WV	no data
KS	$28,390	NV	$41,910	WY	no data

Median Wages for the Largest Metropolitan Areas (Annual)

Area	Wage	Area	Wage
AZ: Phoenix	$25,770	MI: Detroit	$26,650
CA: Los Angeles	$22,750	MN: Minneapolis	$27,900
CA: Riverside	$25,150	MO: Kansas City	$25,680
CA: Sacramento	$28,240	MO: St. Louis	$28,210
CA: San Diego	$23,830	NV: Las Vegas	$14,750
CA: San Francisco	$50,640	NY: New York	$27,220
CO: Denver	$32,420	OH: Cincinnati	$26,060
DC: Washington	$26,630	OH: Cleveland	$22,380
FL: Miami	$21,890	OH: Columbus	$23,350
FL: Orlando	$31,110	OR: Portland	$39,110
FL: Tampa	$23,310	PA: Philadelphia	$23,430
GA: Atlanta	$25,210	PA: Pittsburgh	$19,280
IL: Chicago	$29,850	TX: Dallas	$33,010
MA: Boston	$31,730	TX: Houston	$30,650
MD: Baltimore	$23,010	WA: Seattle	$42,590

FACTORS THAT MAY AFFECT EARNINGS

Educational Attainment of Workers and Effect on Earnings

Figures are based on a group of occupations: Personal Appearance Workers

	Percent at Level	Effect on Earnings
Less than High School	3.2%	−13.6%
Some High School	8.5%	−21.5%
High School or Equivalent	39.8%	1.5%
Some College but No Degree	21.0%	−2.5%
Associate Degree	19.8%	0.4%
Bachelor's Degree	6.9%	31.3%
Master's Degree	—	—
Doctoral Degree	—	—
First Professional Degree	—	—

Flexibility of Earnings

Average Hours Worked: 28
Workers with a Varying Number of Hours: 15.2%
Workers Earning Some Overtime Pay, Tips, or Commissions: 46.8%
Earnings Benefit of Working Overtime: −4.2%

Gender

	Male	Female
Percent	17.0%	83.0%
Effect on Earnings	—	−1.5%

Union Membership

Percentage Union Members: Insignificant
Earnings Benefit of Union Membership: No significant data available

Veteran Status

Percentage Who Have Been on Active Duty: Insignificant
Earnings Benefit of Veteran Status: No significant data available

39-6000 Transportation, Tourism, and Lodging Attendants

39-6011 Baggage Porters and Bellhops

Handle baggage for travelers at transportation terminals or for guests at hotels or similar establishments.

- Education or Training Required: Short-term on-the-job training
- Job Growth: 14.0%
- Annual Openings: 5,000
- Self-Employed: 0.0%
- Part-Time: 31.4%

NATIONAL WAGE FIGURES (ANNUAL)

Beginning	25th Percentile	Median	Mean	75th Percentile	90th Percentile
$13,410	$14,820	$18,360	$21,580	$25,940	$35,550

Median Wages for Industries Employing Largest Numbers (Annual)

Industry	Median Income
Rail Transportation	$32,800
Air Transportation	$32,530
Religious, Grantmaking, Civic, Professional, and Similar Organizations	$24,760
Real Estate	$24,270
Nursing and Residential Care Facilities	$21,260
Motor Vehicle and Parts Dealers	$20,920
Food Services and Drinking Places	$20,230
Hospitals	$20,180
Federal, State, and Local Government	$19,930
Personal and Laundry Services	$18,000

Median Wages for States (Annual)

AK	$18,000	KY	$16,890	NY	$25,880
AL	$13,450	LA	$14,740	OH	$16,810
AR	$15,210	MA	$21,480	OK	$14,260
AZ	$16,220	MD	$17,150	OR	$18,920
CA	$18,960	ME	$17,530	PA	no data
CO	$17,670	MI	no data	RI	$18,280
CT	$18,660	MN	$19,100	SC	$15,100
DC	$17,880	MO	$18,270	SD	$17,550
DE	$16,930	MS	$14,510	TN	$19,240
FL	$15,000	MT	$15,270	TX	$15,340
GA	$14,690	NC	no data	UT	$14,280
HI	$16,760	ND	$14,500	VA	$19,960
IA	$16,290	NE	$15,200	VT	$18,390
ID	$16,190	NH	$18,560	WA	$24,860
IL	$16,960	NJ	$18,930	WI	$15,180
IN	$18,350	NM	$14,800	WV	$15,640
KS	$14,730	NV	$20,630	WY	$15,930

Median Wages for the Largest Metropolitan Areas (Annual)

AZ: Phoenix	$16,200	MI: Detroit	no data
CA: Los Angeles	$17,610	MN: Minneapolis	$20,270
CA: Riverside	$19,530	MO: Kansas City	$20,400
CA: Sacramento	$18,040	MO: St. Louis	$17,340
CA: San Diego	$18,270	NV: Las Vegas	$21,050
CA: San Francisco	$23,640	NY: New York	$25,860
CO: Denver	$19,800	OH: Cincinnati	$15,490
DC: Washington	$19,690	OH: Cleveland	$18,200
FL: Miami	$15,420	OH: Columbus	$15,440
FL: Orlando	$15,540	OR: Portland	$19,240
FL: Tampa	$14,460	PA: Philadelphia	no data
GA: Atlanta	$14,430	PA: Pittsburgh	no data
IL: Chicago	$17,040	TX: Dallas	$15,780
MA: Boston	$20,310	TX: Houston	$15,590
MD: Baltimore	$29,590	WA: Seattle	$24,200

FACTORS THAT MAY AFFECT EARNINGS

Educational Attainment of Workers and Effect on Earnings

Figures are based on a group of occupations: Transportation, Tourism, and Lodging Attendants

	Percent at Level	Effect on Earnings
Less than High School	—	—
Some High School	7.5%	−50.7%
High School or Equivalent	24.4%	−18.8%
Some College but No Degree	29.3%	−1.2%
Associate Degree	9.0%	10.8%
Bachelor's Degree	24.4%	30.3%
Master's Degree	3.8%	18.3%
Doctoral Degree	—	—
First Professional Degree	—	—

Flexibility of Earnings

Average Hours Worked: 24
Workers with a Varying Number of Hours: 6.3%
Workers Earning Some Overtime Pay, Tips, or Commissions: 15.1%
Earnings Benefit of Working Overtime: 3.5%

Gender

	Male	Female
Percent	79.4%	20.6%
Effect on Earnings	1.0%	—

Union Membership

Percentage Union Members: 41.0%
Earnings Benefit of Union Membership: 25.0%

Veteran Status

Percentage Who Have Been on Active Duty: 7.7%
Earnings Benefit of Veteran Status: −0.1%

39-6012 Concierges

Assist patrons at hotel, apartment, or office building with personal services. May take messages; arrange or give·advice on transportation, business services, or entertainment; or monitor guest requests for housekeeping and maintenance.

- Education or Training Required: Moderate-term on-the-job training
- Job Growth: 16.0%
- Annual Openings: 2,000
- Self-Employed: 0.0%
- Part-Time: 31.4%

NATIONAL WAGE FIGURES (ANNUAL)

Beginning	25th Percentile	Median	Mean	75th Percentile	90th Percentile
$15,910	$19,580	$24,600	$26,000	$31,090	$38,210

Median Wages for Industries Employing Largest Numbers (Annual)

Industry	Median Income
Personal and Laundry Services	$29,870
Performing Arts, Spectator Sports, and Related Industries	$25,580
Real Estate	$25,280
Hospitals	$24,470
Accommodation	$23,880
Administrative and Support Services	$22,850
Religious, Grantmaking, Civic, Professional, and Similar Organizations	$22,740
Ambulatory Health Care Services	$22,150
Food Services and Drinking Places	$22,140
Amusement, Gambling, and Recreation Industries	$22,110

Median Wages for States (Annual)

AK	$23,600	KY	$19,290	NY	$35,840
AL	no data	LA	$19,920	OH	$22,690
AR	no data	MA	$27,340	OK	no data
AZ	$20,690	MD	$14,610	OR	$25,080
CA	$24,940	ME	no data	PA	$23,870
CO	$25,590	MI	$21,220	RI	$21,950
CT	$23,170	MN	$22,840	SC	$17,570
DC	$32,810	MO	$19,470	SD	no data
DE	no data	MS	$17,960	TN	$18,380
FL	$21,150	MT	no data	TX	$23,670
GA	$21,230	NC	$20,310	UT	$19,380
HI	$34,100	ND	no data	VA	$18,800
IA	no data	NE	no data	VT	no data
ID	$35,010	NH	$21,740	WA	$27,650
IL	$25,320	NJ	$21,340	WI	$21,440
IN	$18,680	NM	$21,650	WV	no data
KS	$17,580	NV	$28,570	WY	$21,970

Median Wages for the Largest Metropolitan Areas (Annual)

AZ: Phoenix	$20,780	MI: Detroit	$22,330
CA: Los Angeles	$21,190	MN: Minneapolis	$22,890
CA: Riverside	$24,790	MO: Kansas City	$19,270
CA: Sacramento	$26,210	MO: St. Louis	$19,400
CA: San Diego	$26,580	NV: Las Vegas	$30,620
CA: San Francisco	$31,270	NY: New York	$32,410
CO: Denver	$26,680	OH: Cincinnati	no data
DC: Washington	$32,160	OH: Cleveland	$24,450
FL: Miami	$22,390	OH: Columbus	$21,710
FL: Orlando	$19,340	OR: Portland	$28,530
FL: Tampa	$17,530	PA: Philadelphia	$25,010
GA: Atlanta	$21,930	PA: Pittsburgh	$21,930
IL: Chicago	$25,560	TX: Dallas	$24,310
MA: Boston	$27,660	TX: Houston	$23,200
MD: Baltimore	$14,220	WA: Seattle	$27,740

FACTORS THAT MAY AFFECT EARNINGS

Educational Attainment of Workers and Effect on Earnings

Figures are based on a group of occupations: Transportation, Tourism, and Lodging Attendants

	Percent at Level	Effect on Earnings
Less than High School	—	—
Some High School	7.5%	−50.7%
High School or Equivalent	24.4%	−18.8%
Some College but No Degree	29.3%	−1.2%
Associate Degree	9.0%	10.8%
Bachelor's Degree	24.4%	30.3%
Master's Degree	3.8%	18.3%
Doctoral Degree	—	—
First Professional Degree	—	—

Flexibility of Earnings

Average Hours Worked: 24
Workers with a Varying Number of Hours: 6.3%
Workers Earning Some Overtime Pay, Tips, or Commissions: 15.1%
Earnings Benefit of Working Overtime: 3.5%

Gender

	Male	Female
Percent	79.4%	20.6%
Effect on Earnings	1.0%	—

Union Membership

Percentage Union Members: 41.0%
Earnings Benefit of Union Membership: 25.0%

Veteran Status

Percentage Who Have Been on Active Duty: 7.7%
Earnings Benefit of Veteran Status: −0.1%

39-6021 Tour Guides and Escorts

Escort individuals or groups on sightseeing tours or through places of interest such as industrial establishments, public buildings, and art galleries.

- Education or Training Required: Moderate-term on-the-job training
- Job Growth: 16.6%
- Annual Openings: 5,000
- Self-Employed: 14.4%
- Part-Time: 31.4%

NATIONAL WAGE FIGURES (ANNUAL)

Beginning	25th Percentile	Median	Mean	75th Percentile	90th Percentile
$13,680	$15,810	$20,420	$22,310	$27,290	$34,630

Median Wages for Industries Employing Largest Numbers (Annual)

Industry	Median Income
Food Manufacturing	$31,380
Professional, Scientific, and Technical Services	$27,810
Federal, State, and Local Government	$27,490
Scenic and Sightseeing Transportation	$22,240
Administrative and Support Services	$22,090
Motion Picture and Sound Recording Industries	$21,660
Beverage and Tobacco Product Manufacturing	$21,550
Accommodation	$21,450
Performing Arts, Spectator Sports, and Related Industries	$21,370
Amusement, Gambling, and Recreation Industries	$20,920

Median Wages for States (Annual)

AK	$22,620	KY	$20,170	NY	$20,540
AL	$17,800	LA	$17,010	OH	$19,720
AR	$19,750	MA	$22,610	OK	$18,990
AZ	no data	MD	$15,280	OR	$22,500
CA	$21,930	ME	$20,950	PA	$22,350
CO	$23,380	MI	$22,560	RI	no data
CT	$18,620	MN	$23,720	SC	$16,100
DC	$26,020	MO	$17,460	SD	$18,100
DE	no data	MS	$13,920	TN	$16,410
FL	$16,840	MT	$14,850	TX	$18,840
GA	$21,160	NC	$17,270	UT	$21,340
HI	$22,240	ND	$16,880	VA	$20,310
IA	$17,700	NE	$17,270	VT	$22,910
ID	$28,420	NH	$19,600	WA	$26,330
IL	$18,650	NJ	$17,170	WI	$14,530
IN	$15,700	NM	$22,630	WV	$21,190
KS	$14,310	NV	$26,460	WY	no data

Median Wages for the Largest Metropolitan Areas (Annual)

AZ: Phoenix	$25,020	MI: Detroit	$23,980
CA: Los Angeles	$21,690	MN: Minneapolis	$27,580
CA: Riverside	$19,330	MO: Kansas City	$20,780
CA: Sacramento	$26,270	MO: St. Louis	$17,630
CA: San Diego	$22,360	NV: Las Vegas	$27,920
CA: San Francisco	$33,860	NY: New York	$20,970
CO: Denver	$22,490	OH: Cincinnati	no data
DC: Washington	$25,600	OH: Cleveland	$21,630
FL: Miami	$18,100	OH: Columbus	$21,720
FL: Orlando	$14,340	OR: Portland	no data
FL: Tampa	$17,120	PA: Philadelphia	$25,620
GA: Atlanta	$25,940	PA: Pittsburgh	$18,020
IL: Chicago	$18,290	TX: Dallas	$22,450
MA: Boston	$24,890	TX: Houston	$22,540
MD: Baltimore	$14,670	WA: Seattle	$25,890

FACTORS THAT MAY AFFECT EARNINGS

Educational Attainment of Workers and Effect on Earnings

Figures are based on a group of occupations: Transportation, Tourism, and Lodging Attendants

	Percent at Level	Effect on Earnings
Less than High School	—	—
Some High School	7.5%	−50.7%
High School or Equivalent	24.4%	−18.8%
Some College but No Degree	29.3%	−1.2%
Associate Degree	9.0%	10.8%
Bachelor's Degree	24.4%	30.3%
Master's Degree	3.8%	18.3%
Doctoral Degree	—	—
First Professional Degree	—	—

Flexibility of Earnings

Average Hours Worked: 24
Workers with a Varying Number of Hours: 25.3%
Workers Earning Some Overtime Pay, Tips, or Commissions: 15.1%
Earnings Benefit of Working Overtime: 3.5%

Gender

	Male	Female
Percent	25.8%	74.2%
Effect on Earnings	—	−6.3%

Union Membership

Percentage Union Members: 41.0%
Earnings Benefit of Union Membership: 25.0%

Veteran Status

Percentage Who Have Been on Active Duty: 7.7%
Earnings Benefit of Veteran Status: −0.1%

39-6022 Travel Guides

Plan, organize, and conduct long-distance cruises, tours, and expeditions for individuals and groups.

- Education or Training Required: Moderate-term on-the-job training
- Job Growth: 9.6%
- Annual Openings: 1,000
- Self-Employed: 18.0%
- Part-Time: 31.4%

NATIONAL WAGE FIGURES (ANNUAL)

Beginning	25th Percentile	Median	Mean	75th Percentile	90th Percentile
$17,060	$22,590	$28,460	$30,840	$36,180	$48,580

Median Wages for Industries Employing Largest Numbers (Annual)

Industry	Median Income
Transit and Ground Passenger Transportation	$41,700
Water Transportation	$30,990
Administrative and Support Services	$29,120
Scenic and Sightseeing Transportation	$26,680
Accommodation	$26,340
Amusement, Gambling, and Recreation Industries	$24,460
Federal, State, and Local Government	$19,060

Median Wages for States (Annual)

State	Wage	State	Wage	State	Wage
AK	no data	KY	no data	NY	$30,630
AL	no data	LA	no data	OH	$25,620
AR	no data	MA	$33,470	OK	no data
AZ	$40,640	MD	no data	OR	no data
CA	$27,870	ME	no data	PA	$26,510
CO	$22,120	MI	no data	RI	no data
CT	no data	MN	$19,460	SC	no data
DC	no data	MO	no data	SD	no data
DE	no data	MS	$18,830	TN	$25,350
FL	$30,570	MT	no data	TX	$42,330
GA	$30,060	NC	$28,000	UT	$27,490
HI	$28,380	ND	no data	VA	$29,790
IA	no data	NE	no data	VT	no data
ID	no data	NH	no data	WA	$35,750
IL	$38,470	NJ	$32,460	WI	$26,540
IN	$17,860	NM	no data	WV	no data
KS	no data	NV	no data	WY	no data

Median Wages for the Largest Metropolitan Areas (Annual)

Area	Wage	Area	Wage
AZ: Phoenix	no data	MI: Detroit	no data
CA: Los Angeles	$28,910	MN: Minneapolis	no data
CA: Riverside	no data	MO: Kansas City	no data
CA: Sacramento	no data	MO: St. Louis	no data
CA: San Diego	no data	NV: Las Vegas	no data
CA: San Francisco	$27,520	NY: New York	$31,890
CO: Denver	no data	OH: Cincinnati	no data
DC: Washington	$38,180	OH: Cleveland	no data
FL: Miami	$22,950	OH: Columbus	no data
FL: Orlando	$37,900	OR: Portland	no data
FL: Tampa	no data	PA: Philadelphia	no data
GA: Atlanta	$26,220	PA: Pittsburgh	no data
IL: Chicago	$38,680	TX: Dallas	no data
MA: Boston	$35,180	TX: Houston	$29,790
MD: Baltimore	no data	WA: Seattle	$35,980

FACTORS THAT MAY AFFECT EARNINGS

Educational Attainment of Workers and Effect on Earnings

Figures are based on a group of occupations: Transportation, Tourism, and Lodging Attendants

	Percent at Level	Effect on Earnings
Less than High School	—	—
Some High School	7.5%	−50.7%
High School or Equivalent	24.4%	−18.8%
Some College but No Degree	29.3%	−1.2%
Associate Degree	9.0%	10.8%
Bachelor's Degree	24.4%	30.3%
Master's Degree	3.8%	18.3%
Doctoral Degree	—	—
First Professional Degree	—	—

Flexibility of Earnings

Average Hours Worked: 24
Workers with a Varying Number of Hours: 25.3%
Workers Earning Some Overtime Pay, Tips, or Commissions: 15.1%
Earnings Benefit of Working Overtime: 3.5%

Gender

	Male	Female
Percent	25.8%	74.2%
Effect on Earnings	—	−6.3%

Union Membership

Percentage Union Members: 41.0%
Earnings Benefit of Union Membership: 25.0%

Veteran Status

Percentage Who Have Been on Active Duty: 7.7%
Earnings Benefit of Veteran Status: −0.1%

39-6031 Flight Attendants

Provide personal services to ensure the safety and comfort of airline passengers during flight. Greet passengers, verify tickets, explain use of safety equipment, and serve food or beverages.

- Education or Training Required: Long-term on-the-job training
- Job Growth: 16.3%
- Annual Openings: 7,000
- Self-Employed: 0.2%
- Part-Time: 31.4%

NATIONAL WAGE FIGURES (ANNUAL)

Beginning	25th Percentile	Median	Mean	75th Percentile	90th Percentile
$24,250	$33,320	$53,780	$56,150	$77,410	$99,300

Median Wages for Industries Employing Largest Numbers (Annual)

Industry	Median Income
Merchant Wholesalers, Durable Goods	$58,030
Air Transportation	$53,870

Median Wages for States (Annual)

AK	no data	KY	$62,400	NY	$58,020
AL	no data	LA	no data	OH	$47,430
AR	no data	MA	no data	OK	no data
AZ	no data	MD	no data	OR	$61,950
CA	$36,860	ME	no data	PA	no data
CO	no data	MI	no data	RI	no data
CT	no data	MN	no data	SC	no data
DC	no data	MO	no data	SD	no data
DE	no data	MS	no data	TN	$42,500
FL	no data	MT	no data	TX	$54,540
GA	no data	NC	no data	UT	no data
HI	$52,330	ND	no data	VA	no data
IA	no data	NE	no data	VT	no data
ID	no data	NH	no data	WA	no data
IL	$57,020	NJ	no data	WI	no data
IN	no data	NM	no data	WV	no data
KS	no data	NV	no data	WY	no data

Median Wages for the Largest Metropolitan Areas (Annual)

AZ: Phoenix	no data	MI: Detroit	no data
CA: Los Angeles	$43,990	MN: Minneapolis	no data
CA: Riverside	no data	MO: Kansas City	no data
CA: Sacramento	no data	MO: St. Louis	no data
CA: San Diego	no data	NV: Las Vegas	no data
CA: San Francisco	no data	NY: New York	$65,740
CO: Denver	no data	OH: Cincinnati	$62,570
DC: Washington	no data	OH: Cleveland	no data
FL: Miami	no data	OH: Columbus	no data
FL: Orlando	$52,170	OR: Portland	$63,680
FL: Tampa	no data	PA: Philadelphia	no data
GA: Atlanta	no data	PA: Pittsburgh	no data
IL: Chicago	$57,020	TX: Dallas	no data
MA: Boston	no data	TX: Houston	no data
MD: Baltimore	no data	WA: Seattle	no data

FACTORS THAT MAY AFFECT EARNINGS

Educational Attainment of Workers and Effect on Earnings

Figures are based on a group of occupations: Transportation, Tourism, and Lodging Attendants

	Percent at Level	Effect on Earnings
Less than High School	—	—
Some High School	7.5%	−50.7%
High School or Equivalent	24.4%	−18.8%
Some College but No Degree	29.3%	−1.2%
Associate Degree	9.0%	10.8%
Bachelor's Degree	24.4%	30.3%
Master's Degree	3.8%	18.3%
Doctoral Degree	—	—
First Professional Degree	—	—

Flexibility of Earnings

Average Hours Worked: 24
Workers with a Varying Number of Hours: 32.1%
Workers Earning Some Overtime Pay, Tips, or Commissions: 15.1%
Earnings Benefit of Working Overtime: 3.5%

Gender

	Male	Female
Percent	25.8%	74.2%
Effect on Earnings	—	−6.3%

Union Membership

Percentage Union Members: 41.0%
Earnings Benefit of Union Membership: 25.0%

Veteran Status

Percentage Who Have Been on Active Duty: 7.7%
Earnings Benefit of Veteran Status: −0.1%

39-6032 Transportation Attendants, Except Flight Attendants and Baggage Porters

Provide services to ensure the safety and comfort of passengers aboard ships, buses, or trains or within the station or terminal. Perform duties such as greeting passengers, explaining the use of safety equipment, serving meals or beverages, or answering questions related to travel.

- Education or Training Required: Short-term on-the-job training
- Job Growth: 15.9%
- Annual Openings: 2,000
- Self-Employed: 0.2%
- Part-Time: 31.4%

NATIONAL WAGE FIGURES (ANNUAL)

Beginning	25th Percentile	Median	Mean	75th Percentile	90th Percentile
$14,180	$16,360	$20,070	$21,140	$24,020	$30,580

Median Wages for Industries Employing Largest Numbers (Annual)

Industry	Median Income
Federal, State, and Local Government	$29,890
Water Transportation	$22,780
Air Transportation	$22,150
Rental and Leasing Services	$21,200
Scenic and Sightseeing Transportation	$21,130
Administrative and Support Services	$20,060
Educational Services	$19,580
Support Activities for Transportation	$19,570
Social Assistance	$19,420
Amusement, Gambling, and Recreation Industries	$19,350

Median Wages for States (Annual)

State	Wage	State	Wage	State	Wage
AK	$34,090	KY	no data	NY	$18,450
AL	no data	LA	$17,910	OH	$20,210
AR	no data	MA	$24,250	OK	$13,620
AZ	$17,550	MD	$18,860	OR	$21,480
CA	$21,010	ME	no data	PA	no data
CO	no data	MI	$19,700	RI	no data
CT	$21,700	MN	$20,700	SC	no data
DC	no data	MO	$17,170	SD	no data
DE	$24,390	MS	$13,290	TN	$19,210
FL	$19,960	MT	$14,600	TX	$21,550
GA	$18,410	NC	no data	UT	$23,970
HI	$22,290	ND	no data	VA	$23,060
IA	$16,740	NE	$20,660	VT	no data
ID	no data	NH	no data	WA	$20,870
IL	$18,820	NJ	$17,400	WI	$16,620
IN	$24,260	NM	$19,550	WV	no data
KS	no data	NV	$18,810	WY	$21,800

Median Wages for the Largest Metropolitan Areas (Annual)

Area	Wage	Area	Wage
AZ: Phoenix	$17,940	MI: Detroit	$22,670
CA: Los Angeles	$21,670	MN: Minneapolis	$20,630
CA: Riverside	$20,310	MO: Kansas City	no data
CA: Sacramento	no data	MO: St. Louis	$20,080
CA: San Diego	$17,480	NV: Las Vegas	$18,870
CA: San Francisco	$21,170	NY: New York	$17,380
CO: Denver	no data	OH: Cincinnati	$21,640
DC: Washington	$21,840	OH: Cleveland	$21,670
FL: Miami	$20,410	OH: Columbus	no data
FL: Orlando	no data	OR: Portland	$25,230
FL: Tampa	$18,790	PA: Philadelphia	no data
GA: Atlanta	$18,370	PA: Pittsburgh	$17,460
IL: Chicago	$18,730	TX: Dallas	$22,310
MA: Boston	$23,180	TX: Houston	$21,930
MD: Baltimore	$18,860	WA: Seattle	$20,560

FACTORS THAT MAY AFFECT EARNINGS

Educational Attainment of Workers and Effect on Earnings

Figures are based on a group of occupations: Transportation, Tourism, and Lodging Attendants

	Percent at Level	Effect on Earnings
Less than High School	—	—
Some High School	7.5%	−50.7%
High School or Equivalent	24.4%	−18.8%
Some College but No Degree	29.3%	−1.2%
Associate Degree	9.0%	10.8%
Bachelor's Degree	24.4%	30.3%
Master's Degree	3.8%	18.3%
Doctoral Degree	—	—
First Professional Degree	—	—

Flexibility of Earnings

Average Hours Worked: 24
Workers with a Varying Number of Hours: 32.1%
Workers Earning Some Overtime Pay, Tips, or Commissions: 15.1%
Earnings Benefit of Working Overtime: 3.5%

Gender

	Male	Female
Percent	25.8%	74.2%
Effect on Earnings	—	−6.3%

Union Membership

Percentage Union Members: 41.0%
Earnings Benefit of Union Membership: 25.0%

Veteran Status

Percentage Who Have Been on Active Duty: 7.7%
Earnings Benefit of Veteran Status: −0.1%

39-9000 Other Personal Care and Service Workers

39-9011 Child Care Workers

Attend to children at schools, businesses, private households, and child care institutions. Perform a variety of tasks, such as dressing, feeding, bathing, and overseeing play.

- Education or Training Required: Short-term on-the-job training
- Job Growth: 13.8%
- Annual Openings: 439,000
- Self-Employed: 31.9%
- Part-Time: 47.2%

Note: A large fraction of the workforce for this occupation is self-employed and earns an average of $23,540. All other earnings figures for this occupation are based on workers who are paid a wage or salary.

NATIONAL WAGE FIGURES (ANNUAL)

Beginning	25th Percentile	Median	Mean	75th Percentile	90th Percentile
$12,910	$14,790	$17,630	$18,820	$21,930	$27,050

Median Wages for Industries Employing Largest Numbers (Annual)

Industry	Median Income
Performing Arts, Spectator Sports, and Related Industries	$21,100
Nursing and Residential Care Facilities	$20,840
Motion Picture and Sound Recording Industries	$20,820
Furniture and Home Furnishings Stores	$20,390
Hospitals	$20,230
Educational Services	$20,170
Ambulatory Health Care Services	$19,660
Professional, Scientific, and Technical Services	$19,550
Federal, State, and Local Government	$19,380
Motor Vehicle and Parts Dealers	$18,420

Median Wages for States (Annual)

AK	$20,240	KY	$15,250	NY	$21,730
AL	$14,160	LA	$13,970	OH	$17,710
AR	$14,120	MA	$21,990	OK	$15,090
AZ	$15,520	MD	$20,250	OR	$17,840
CA	$20,540	ME	$20,680	PA	$17,290
CO	$18,750	MI	$18,760	RI	$19,420
CT	$20,340	MN	$18,270	SC	$15,230
DC	$22,760	MO	$16,610	SD	$15,940
DE	$19,400	MS	$14,090	TN	$15,220
FL	$17,290	MT	$16,390	TX	$14,540
GA	$15,680	NC	$17,260	UT	$16,090
HI	$16,410	ND	$16,270	VA	$16,840
IA	$15,300	NE	$16,480	VT	$18,530
ID	$16,920	NH	$18,170	WA	$18,300
IL	$18,550	NJ	$18,610	WI	$18,760
IN	$17,050	NM	$15,800	WV	$14,190
KS	$16,510	NV	$16,360	WY	$16,320

Median Wages for the Largest Metropolitan Areas (Annual)

AZ: Phoenix	$14,840	MI: Detroit	$19,450
CA: Los Angeles	$21,130	MN: Minneapolis	$19,170
CA: Riverside	$18,290	MO: Kansas City	$17,330
CA: Sacramento	$20,670	MO: St. Louis	$17,460
CA: San Diego	$20,610	NV: Las Vegas	$15,400
CA: San Francisco	$23,270	NY: New York	$22,380
CO: Denver	$19,440	OH: Cincinnati	$17,250
DC: Washington	$20,180	OH: Cleveland	$19,300
FL: Miami	$17,250	OH: Columbus	$18,090
FL: Orlando	$17,190	OR: Portland	$18,200
FL: Tampa	$17,950	PA: Philadelphia	$18,400
GA: Atlanta	$16,690	PA: Pittsburgh	$16,060
IL: Chicago	$18,920	TX: Dallas	$15,250
MA: Boston	$22,190	TX: Houston	$14,530
MD: Baltimore	$20,390	WA: Seattle	$18,810

FACTORS THAT MAY AFFECT EARNINGS

Educational Attainment of Workers and Effect on Earnings

	Percent at Level	Effect on Earnings
Less than High School	5.7%	−27.6%
Some High School	18.3%	−40.7%
High School or Equivalent	29.6%	6.2%
Some College but No Degree	23.4%	−3.3%
Associate Degree	8.0%	4.7%
Bachelor's Degree	12.7%	51.0%
Master's Degree	1.9%	40.8%
Doctoral Degree	—	—
First Professional Degree	—	—

Flexibility of Earnings

Average Hours Worked: 28
Workers with a Varying Number of Hours: 11.6%
Workers Earning Some Overtime Pay, Tips, or Commissions: 5.6%
Earnings Benefit of Working Overtime: −14.7%

Gender

	Male	Female
Percent	5.8%	94.2%
Effect on Earnings	—	−1.1%

Union Membership

Percentage Union Members: 5.9%
Earnings Benefit of Union Membership: 16.8%

Veteran Status

Percentage Who Have Been on Active Duty: Insignificant
Earnings Benefit of Veteran Status: No significant data available

39-9021 Personal and Home Care Aides

Assist elderly or disabled adults with daily living activities at the person's home or in a daytime non-residential facility. Duties performed at a place of residence may include keeping house (making beds, doing laundry, washing dishes) and preparing meals. May provide meals and supervised activities at non-residential care facilities. May advise families, the elderly, and disabled on such things as nutrition, cleanliness, and household utilities.

- Education or Training Required: Short-term on-the-job training
- Job Growth: 41.0%
- Annual Openings: 230,000
- Self-Employed: 4.5%
- Part-Time: 35.6%

NATIONAL WAGE FIGURES (ANNUAL)

Beginning	25th Percentile	Median	Mean	75th Percentile	90th Percentile
$12,590	$14,750	$17,770	$18,180	$21,200	$24,120

Median Wages for Industries Employing Largest Numbers (Annual)

Industry	Median Income
Securities, Commodity Contracts, and Other Financial Investments and Related Activities	$27,380
Educational Services	$20,880
Administrative and Support Services	$20,520
Amusement, Gambling, and Recreation Industries	$20,090
Management of Companies and Enterprises	$20,080
Federal, State, and Local Government	$19,770
Nursing and Residential Care Facilities	$19,460
Social Assistance	$19,120
Hospitals	$19,060
Real Estate	$18,640

Median Wages for States (Annual)

AK	$28,370	KY	$16,790	NY	$20,340
AL	$16,080	LA	$14,380	OH	$18,040
AR	$14,530	MA	$22,420	OK	$16,270
AZ	$19,830	MD	$20,370	OR	$21,060
CA	$19,850	ME	$18,430	PA	$19,320
CO	$17,850	MI	$18,150	RI	$21,780
CT	$20,120	MN	$21,890	SC	$17,200
DC	$17,770	MO	$17,140	SD	$17,700
DE	$20,850	MS	$13,930	TN	$17,040
FL	$17,910	MT	$17,520	TX	$13,340
GA	$17,890	NC	$17,370	UT	$18,900
HI	$17,370	ND	$18,070	VA	$16,070
IA	$19,490	NE	$19,310	VT	$21,240
ID	$17,170	NH	$20,000	WA	$20,970
IL	$17,090	NJ	$21,460	WI	$19,510
IN	$18,890	NM	$17,790	WV	$14,320
KS	$17,660	NV	$19,480	WY	$19,380

Median Wages for the Largest Metropolitan Areas (Annual)

AZ: Phoenix	$20,510	MI: Detroit	$18,790
CA: Los Angeles	$19,190	MN: Minneapolis	$22,100
CA: Riverside	$17,980	MO: Kansas City	$18,560
CA: Sacramento	$21,450	MO: St. Louis	$18,230
CA: San Diego	$18,990	NV: Las Vegas	$19,960
CA: San Francisco	$22,650	NY: New York	$20,580
CO: Denver	$18,210	OH: Cincinnati	$19,080
DC: Washington	$20,250	OH: Cleveland	$18,100
FL: Miami	$17,550	OH: Columbus	$20,300
FL: Orlando	$14,200	OR: Portland	$20,740
FL: Tampa	$17,920	PA: Philadelphia	$20,500
GA: Atlanta	$19,670	PA: Pittsburgh	$18,370
IL: Chicago	$17,460	TX: Dallas	$13,940
MA: Boston	$22,770	TX: Houston	$13,370
MD: Baltimore	$20,550	WA: Seattle	$21,390

FACTORS THAT MAY AFFECT EARNINGS

Educational Attainment of Workers and Effect on Earnings

	Percent at Level	Effect on Earnings
Less than High School	6.3%	−26.6%
Some High School	13.9%	−8.5%
High School or Equivalent	37.2%	4.4%
Some College but No Degree	21.4%	−5.2%
Associate Degree	12.1%	5.4%
Bachelor's Degree	7.3%	15.6%
Master's Degree	1.9%	29.2%
Doctoral Degree	—	—
First Professional Degree	—	—

Flexibility of Earnings

Average Hours Worked: 28
Workers with a Varying Number of Hours: 12.4%
Workers Earning Some Overtime Pay, Tips, or Commissions: 6.7%
Earnings Benefit of Working Overtime: −11.7%

Gender

	Male	Female
Percent	12.7%	87.3%
Effect on Earnings	10.6%	−1.9%

Union Membership

Percentage Union Members: 7.5%
Earnings Benefit of Union Membership: 14.0%

Veteran Status

Percentage Who Have Been on Active Duty: Insignificant
Earnings Benefit of Veteran Status: No significant data available

39-9031 Fitness Trainers and Aerobics Instructors

Instruct or coach groups or individuals in exercise activities and the fundamentals of sports. Demonstrate techniques and methods of participation. Observe participants and inform them of corrective measures necessary to improve their skills.

- Education or Training Required: Postsecondary vocational training
- Job Growth: 27.1%
- Annual Openings: 50,000
- Self-Employed: 6.6%
- Part-Time: 44.1%

NATIONAL WAGE FIGURES (ANNUAL)

Beginning	25th Percentile	Median	Mean	75th Percentile	90th Percentile
$14,880	$18,010	$25,910	$31,710	$41,040	$56,750

Note: The mean is significantly higher than the median because of the presence of a few star earners.

Median Wages for Industries Employing Largest Numbers (Annual)

Industry	Median Income
Professional, Scientific, and Technical Services	$43,420
Real Estate	$42,560
Hospitals	$29,570
Ambulatory Health Care Services	$29,230
Administrative and Support Services	$29,150
Repair and Maintenance	$29,050
Management of Companies and Enterprises	$28,380
Nursing and Residential Care Facilities	$27,850
Federal, State, and Local Government	$27,280
Amusement, Gambling, and Recreation Industries	$27,150

Median Wages for States (Annual)

AK	$30,090	KY	$18,990	NY	$36,350
AL	$19,530	LA	$23,950	OH	$20,270
AR	$18,680	MA	$29,410	OK	$20,950
AZ	$25,510	MD	$27,550	OR	$29,190
CA	$35,910	ME	$19,890	PA	$20,170
CO	$30,060	MI	$21,340	RI	$27,480
CT	$38,950	MN	$23,420	SC	$27,200
DC	$28,750	MO	$18,950	SD	$20,470
DE	$21,640	MS	$24,230	TN	$25,210
FL	$27,900	MT	$26,740	TX	$25,970
GA	$22,390	NC	$25,440	UT	$40,030
HI	$24,630	ND	$17,070	VA	$28,090
IA	$18,140	NE	$23,130	VT	$23,380
ID	$31,000	NH	$24,610	WA	$31,990
IL	$23,220	NJ	$37,260	WI	$18,880
IN	$18,890	NM	$21,420	WV	$16,470
KS	$20,730	NV	$31,330	WY	$18,750

Median Wages for the Largest Metropolitan Areas (Annual)

AZ: Phoenix	$26,940	MI: Detroit	$22,450
CA: Los Angeles	$37,240	MN: Minneapolis	$24,970
CA: Riverside	$22,780	MO: Kansas City	$24,490
CA: Sacramento	$41,860	MO: St. Louis	$19,560
CA: San Diego	$32,290	NV: Las Vegas	$29,190
CA: San Francisco	$41,990	NY: New York	$39,780
CO: Denver	$31,510	OH: Cincinnati	$21,810
DC: Washington	$32,860	OH: Cleveland	$21,680
FL: Miami	$27,440	OH: Columbus	$21,170
FL: Orlando	$31,650	OR: Portland	$37,150
FL: Tampa	$24,780	PA: Philadelphia	$21,970
GA: Atlanta	$23,180	PA: Pittsburgh	$17,630
IL: Chicago	$25,060	TX: Dallas	$34,170
MA: Boston	$36,200	TX: Houston	$25,390
MD: Baltimore	$28,170	WA: Seattle	$32,490

FACTORS THAT MAY AFFECT EARNINGS

Educational Attainment of Workers and Effect on Earnings

Figures are based on a group of occupations: Other Personal Care and Service Workers

	Percent at Level	Effect on Earnings
Less than High School	5.3%	−33.7%
Some High School	15.2%	−34.5%
High School or Equivalent	28.8%	1.6%
Some College but No Degree	23.3%	−0.2%
Associate Degree	10.4%	7.6%
Bachelor's Degree	12.9%	32.0%
Master's Degree	3.5%	40.9%
Doctoral Degree	—	—
First Professional Degree	—	—

Flexibility of Earnings

Average Hours Worked: 28
Workers with a Varying Number of Hours: 12.0%
Workers Earning Some Overtime Pay, Tips, or Commissions: 6.8%
Earnings Benefit of Working Overtime: 6.5%

Gender

	Male	Female
Percent	31.3%	68.7%
Effect on Earnings	7.0%	−2.2%

Union Membership

Percentage Union Members: 6.8%
Earnings Benefit of Union Membership: 30.3%

Veteran Status

Percentage Who Have Been on Active Duty: Insignificant
Earnings Benefit of Veteran Status: No significant data available

39-9032 Recreation Workers

Conduct recreation activities with groups in public, private, or volunteer agencies or recreation facilities. Organize and promote activities such as arts and crafts, sports, games, music, dramatics, social recreation, camping, and hobbies, taking into account the needs and interests of individual members.

- Education or Training Required: Short-term on-the-job training
- Job Growth: 17.3%
- Annual Openings: 69,000
- Self-Employed: 6.7%
- Part-Time: 44.1%

NATIONAL WAGE FIGURES (ANNUAL)

Beginning	25th Percentile	Median	Mean	75th Percentile	90th Percentile
$14,150	$16,360	$20,470	$22,950	$27,050	$35,780

Median Wages for Industries Employing Largest Numbers (Annual)

Industry	Median Income
Miscellaneous Store Retailers	$27,230
Hospitals	$23,710
Administrative and Support Services	$22,120
Real Estate	$22,120
Ambulatory Health Care Services	$21,870
Nursing and Residential Care Facilities	$21,780
Construction of Buildings	$21,380
Professional, Scientific, and Technical Services	$20,970
Federal, State, and Local Government	$20,870
Social Assistance	$20,610

Median Wages for States (Annual)

AK $29,300	KY $21,520	NY $21,660
AL $17,530	LA $17,290	OH $18,660
AR $17,330	MA $22,940	OK $16,270
AZ $19,570	MD .... no data	OR $24,120
CA $20,920	ME $22,190	PA $20,770
CO $21,480	MI $20,000	RI $19,040
CT $23,170	MN $21,730	SC $18,400
DC .... no data	MO $18,010	SD $21,490
DE $24,950	MS $18,090	TN $20,110
FL $20,470	MT $18,800	TX $18,830
GA $19,880	NC $21,070	UT $19,200
HI $25,700	ND $19,940	VA $21,390
IA $18,070	NE $19,060	VT $22,480
ID $20,540	NH $22,470	WA $21,180
IL $19,030	NJ $21,360	WI $19,920
IN $18,690	NM $17,110	WV $18,830
KS $20,640	NV $20,800	WY $20,350

Median Wages for the Largest Metropolitan Areas (Annual)

AZ: Phoenix $18,380	MI: Detroit $20,290
CA: Los Angeles $20,520	MN: Minneapolis $22,430
CA: Riverside $18,010	MO: Kansas City $22,590
CA: Sacramento $19,260	MO: St. Louis $17,940
CA: San Diego $21,480	NV: Las Vegas $23,110
CA: San Francisco $25,120	NY: New York $22,420
CO: Denver $22,290	OH: Cincinnati $18,210
DC: Washington ...... no data	OH: Cleveland $18,350
FL: Miami $20,630	OH: Columbus $19,110
FL: Orlando $20,350	OR: Portland $27,250
FL: Tampa $21,050	PA: Philadelphia $22,220
GA: Atlanta $20,490	PA: Pittsburgh $21,370
IL: Chicago $19,680	TX: Dallas $20,030
MA: Boston $23,780	TX: Houston $18,550
MD: Baltimore $25,660	WA: Seattle $21,950

FACTORS THAT MAY AFFECT EARNINGS

Educational Attainment of Workers and Effect on Earnings

Figures are based on a group of occupations: Other Personal Care and Service Workers

	Percent at Level	Effect on Earnings
Less than High School	5.3%	−33.7%
Some High School	15.2%	−34.5%
High School or Equivalent	28.8%	1.6%
Some College but No Degree	23.3%	−0.2%
Associate Degree	10.4%	7.6%
Bachelor's Degree	12.9%	32.0%
Master's Degree	3.5%	40.9%
Doctoral Degree	—	—
First Professional Degree	—	—

Flexibility of Earnings

Average Hours Worked: 28
Workers with a Varying Number of Hours: 12.0%
Workers Earning Some Overtime Pay, Tips, or Commissions: 6.8%
Earnings Benefit of Working Overtime: 6.5%

Gender

	Male	Female
Percent	31.3%	68.7%
Effect on Earnings	7.0%	−2.2%

Union Membership

Percentage Union Members: 6.8%
Earnings Benefit of Union Membership: 30.3%

Veteran Status

Percentage Who Have Been on Active Duty: Insignificant
Earnings Benefit of Veteran Status: No significant data available

39-9041 Residential Advisors

Coordinate activities for residents of boarding schools, college fraternities or sororities, college dormitories, or similar establishments. Order supplies and determine need for maintenance, repairs, and furnishings. May maintain household records and assign rooms. May refer residents to counseling resources if needed.

- Education or Training Required: Moderate-term on-the-job training
- Job Growth: 28.9%
- Annual Openings: 22,000
- Self-Employed: 0.0%
- Part-Time: 51.4%

NATIONAL WAGE FIGURES (ANNUAL)

Beginning	25th Percentile	Median	Mean	75th Percentile	90th Percentile
$15,230	$18,480	$22,670	$24,520	$28,700	$36,610

Median Wages for Industries Employing Largest Numbers (Annual)

Industry	Median Income
Hospitals	$27,730
Educational Services	$25,360
Federal, State, and Local Government	$24,110
Nursing and Residential Care Facilities	$21,730
Social Assistance	$21,680
Management of Companies and Enterprises	$21,290
Religious, Grantmaking, Civic, Professional, and Similar Organizations	$20,430
Accommodation	$19,900
Ambulatory Health Care Services	$19,550
Real Estate	$18,080

Median Wages for States (Annual)

AK	$33,820	KY	$19,720	NY	$28,100
AL	$20,820	LA	no data	OH	$25,700
AR	$20,180	MA	$25,310	OK	$17,210
AZ	$25,000	MD	$26,460	OR	$21,120
CA	$28,090	ME	$20,940	PA	$22,020
CO	$20,650	MI	$24,960	RI	$30,140
CT	$28,390	MN	$30,800	SC	$22,180
DC	$22,870	MO	$21,130	SD	$19,980
DE	$22,760	MS	$20,050	TN	$17,750
FL	$21,560	MT	$18,450	TX	$19,360
GA	$20,070	NC	$19,410	UT	$20,360
HI	$21,100	ND	$19,510	VA	$23,170
IA	$21,740	NE	$25,110	VT	$23,850
ID	$21,850	NH	$24,620	WA	$21,910
IL	$24,720	NJ	$31,450	WI	$25,810
IN	$23,930	NM	$20,660	WV	$19,220
KS	$19,510	NV	$25,120	WY	$25,710

Median Wages for the Largest Metropolitan Areas (Annual)

AZ: Phoenix	$25,250	MI: Detroit	$23,670
CA: Los Angeles	$29,680	MN: Minneapolis	$32,560
CA: Riverside	$26,900	MO: Kansas City	$23,240
CA: Sacramento	no data	MO: St. Louis	$21,810
CA: San Diego	$24,070	NV: Las Vegas	no data
CA: San Francisco	$27,950	NY: New York	$30,580
CO: Denver	$14,310	OH: Cincinnati	$22,510
DC: Washington	$24,210	OH: Cleveland	$20,820
FL: Miami	$21,210	OH: Columbus	$23,400
FL: Orlando	$21,420	OR: Portland	$24,050
FL: Tampa	$19,550	PA: Philadelphia	$21,970
GA: Atlanta	$22,950	PA: Pittsburgh	$21,710
IL: Chicago	$25,690	TX: Dallas	$20,490
MA: Boston	$25,300	TX: Houston	$21,100
MD: Baltimore	$26,050	WA: Seattle	$26,340

FACTORS THAT MAY AFFECT EARNINGS

Educational Attainment of Workers and Effect on Earnings

	Percent at Level	Effect on Earnings
Less than High School	—	—
Some High School	—	—
High School or Equivalent	15.9%	−0.9%
Some College but No Degree	40.2%	−12.8%
Associate Degree	13.4%	25.5%
Bachelor's Degree	15.9%	23.0%
Master's Degree	8.5%	9.7%
Doctoral Degree	—	—
First Professional Degree	—	—

Figures do not total 100% because some levels have a very small sample size.

Flexibility of Earnings

Average Hours Worked: 36
Workers with a Varying Number of Hours: 8.4%
Workers Earning Some Overtime Pay, Tips, or Commissions: 10.2%
Earnings Benefit of Working Overtime: −8.4%

Gender

	Male	Female
Percent	31.0%	69.0%
Effect on Earnings	24.3%	−4.7%

Union Membership

Percentage Union Members: 20.5%
Earnings Benefit of Union Membership: 41.8%

Veteran Status

Percentage Who Have Been on Active Duty: Insignificant
Earnings Benefit of Veteran Status: No significant data available

39-9099 Personal Care and Service Workers, All Other

All personal care and service workers not listed separately.

- Education or Training Required: Short-term on-the-job training
- Job Growth: 15.9%
- Annual Openings: 30,000
- Self-Employed: 18.4%
- Part-Time: 52.9%

NATIONAL WAGE FIGURES (ANNUAL)

Beginning	25th Percentile	Median	Mean	75th Percentile	90th Percentile
$13,540	$15,440	$18,970	$21,640	$24,550	$33,590

Median Wages for Industries Employing Largest Numbers (Annual)

Industry	Median Income
Real Estate	$27,170
Management of Companies and Enterprises	$23,940
Air Transportation	$22,560
Hospitals	$21,180
Support Activities for Transportation	$20,830
Educational Services	$20,620
Accommodation	$20,590
Building Material and Garden Equipment and Supplies Dealers	$20,510
Social Assistance	$20,250
Ambulatory Health Care Services	$20,140

Median Wages for States (Annual)

State	Wage	State	Wage	State	Wage
AK	$19,150	KY	no data	NY	$25,830
AL	$15,110	LA	$16,130	OH	$18,040
AR	$14,530	MA	$22,280	OK	$18,640
AZ	$18,100	MD	$15,650	OR	$18,120
CA	$21,750	ME	no data	PA	$20,370
CO	$21,110	MI	$19,960	RI	$18,900
CT	$15,800	MN	$22,000	SC	$19,870
DC	no data	MO	$17,950	SD	no data
DE	$37,800	MS	$16,400	TN	$17,160
FL	$18,250	MT	$15,590	TX	$14,820
GA	$17,020	NC	$15,280	UT	$18,090
HI	$17,740	ND	$17,540	VA	$18,390
IA	$15,960	NE	$16,930	VT	no data
ID	$14,260	NH	$18,800	WA	$17,890
IL	$21,180	NJ	$21,170	WI	$20,760
IN	$19,280	NM	$14,330	WV	no data
KS	$15,370	NV	$22,330	WY	$18,230

Median Wages for the Largest Metropolitan Areas (Annual)

Area	Wage	Area	Wage
AZ: Phoenix	$18,130	MI: Detroit	$19,390
CA: Los Angeles	no data	MN: Minneapolis	$20,810
CA: Riverside	$18,790	MO: Kansas City	no data
CA: Sacramento	$29,940	MO: St. Louis	$19,420
CA: San Diego	$21,200	NV: Las Vegas	$21,990
CA: San Francisco	$23,000	NY: New York	$21,500
CO: Denver	$18,880	OH: Cincinnati	$17,890
DC: Washington	$16,630	OH: Cleveland	$17,930
FL: Miami	$19,990	OH: Columbus	$17,720
FL: Orlando	$17,860	OR: Portland	$18,270
FL: Tampa	$18,810	PA: Philadelphia	no data
GA: Atlanta	$17,840	PA: Pittsburgh	$27,040
IL: Chicago	$23,970	TX: Dallas	$18,250
MA: Boston	$22,200	TX: Houston	$14,400
MD: Baltimore	$15,750	WA: Seattle	$21,040

FACTORS THAT MAY AFFECT EARNINGS

Educational Attainment of Workers and Effect on Earnings

	Percent at Level	Effect on Earnings
Less than High School	5.7%	−34.3%
Some High School	18.1%	−62.1%
High School or Equivalent	29.5%	−6.9%
Some College but No Degree	26.7%	27.8%
Associate Degree	—	—
Bachelor's Degree	11.4%	73.1%
Master's Degree	—	—
Doctoral Degree	—	—
First Professional Degree	—	—

Figures do not total 100% because some levels have a very small sample size.

Flexibility of Earnings

Average Hours Worked: 24
Workers with a Varying Number of Hours: 16.6%
Workers Earning Some Overtime Pay, Tips, or Commissions: 16.2%
Earnings Benefit of Working Overtime: −8.4%

Gender

	Male	Female
Percent	45.9%	54.1%
Effect on Earnings	24.3%	−4.7%

Union Membership

Percentage Union Members: Insignificant
Earnings Benefit of Union Membership: No significant data available

Veteran Status

Percentage Who Have Been on Active Duty: Insignificant
Earnings Benefit of Veteran Status: No significant data available

41-0000: Sales and Related Occupations

41-1000 Supervisors, Sales Workers

41-1011 First-Line Supervisors/Managers of Retail Sales Workers

Directly supervise sales workers in a retail establishment or department. Duties may include management functions, such as purchasing, budgeting, accounting, and personnel work, in addition to supervisory duties.

- Education or Training Required: Work experience in a related occupation
- Job Growth: 3.8%
- Annual Openings: 229,000
- Self-Employed: 31.9%
- Part-Time: 15.6%

Note: A large fraction of the workforce for this occupation is self-employed and earns an average of $48,370. All other earnings figures for this occupation are based on workers who are paid a wage or salary.

NATIONAL WAGE FIGURES (ANNUAL)

Beginning	25th Percentile	Median	Mean	75th Percentile	90th Percentile
$21,420	$26,490	$33,960	$38,830	$44,570	$59,710

Median Wages for Industries Employing Largest Numbers (Annual)

Industry	Median Income
Motor Vehicle and Parts Dealers......................................	$52,280
Merchant Wholesalers, Durable Goods	$46,000
Furniture and Home Furnishings Stores	$42,940
Telecommunications..	$39,680
Electronics and Appliance Stores	$39,120
Management of Companies and Enterprises......................	$38,870
Federal, State, and Local Government	$38,460
Merchant Wholesalers, Nondurable Goods	$37,880
Nonstore Retailers	$37,020
Professional, Scientific, and Technical Services	$36,430

Median Wages for States (Annual)

AK	$36,200	KY	$28,470	NY	$37,060
AL	$29,690	LA	$29,110	OH	$32,770
AR	$28,320	MA	$37,620	OK	$29,110
AZ	$34,350	MD	$36,370	OR	$34,480
CA	$35,830	ME	$30,350	PA	$35,420
CO	$36,310	MI	$35,660	RI	$35,280
CT	$38,260	MN	$32,720	SC	$33,080
DC	$38,080	MO	$34,420	SD	$33,740
DE	$36,270	MS	$28,240	TN	$31,270
FL	$37,000	MT	$28,150	TX	$32,690
GA	$30,420	NC	$30,240	UT	$31,890
HI	$35,460	ND	$30,220	VA	$34,140
IA	$31,930	NE	$32,190	VT	$36,730
ID	$30,980	NH	$34,290	WA	$40,950
IL	$35,140	NJ	$39,580	WI	$33,900
IN	$32,680	NM	$29,540	WV	$27,830
KS	$30,590	NV	$32,720	WY	$27,800

Median Wages for the Largest Metropolitan Areas (Annual)

AZ: Phoenix	$35,200	MI: Detroit	$36,960
CA: Los Angeles	$35,970	MN: Minneapolis	$34,610
CA: Riverside	$34,040	MO: Kansas City	$34,690
CA: Sacramento	$36,600	MO: St. Louis	$35,480
CA: San Diego	$35,970	NV: Las Vegas	$32,750
CA: San Francisco	$38,110	NY: New York	$40,240
CO: Denver	$38,460	OH: Cincinnati	$33,760
DC: Washington	$37,120	OH: Cleveland	$33,350
FL: Miami	$39,540	OH: Columbus	$34,130
FL: Orlando	$37,990	OR: Portland	$36,240
FL: Tampa	$35,340	PA: Philadelphia	$38,870
GA: Atlanta	$32,410	PA: Pittsburgh	$35,380
IL: Chicago	$37,080	TX: Dallas	$34,270
MA: Boston	$37,820	TX: Houston	$34,650
MD: Baltimore	$36,720	WA: Seattle	$42,730

FACTORS THAT MAY AFFECT EARNINGS

Educational Attainment of Workers and Effect on Earnings

	Percent at Level	Effect on Earnings
Less than High School	1.2%	−19.4%
Some High School	7.3%	−14.0%
High School or Equivalent	31.9%	−9.2%
Some College but No Degree	25.4%	−6.1%
Associate Degree	12.8%	−1.3%
Bachelor's Degree	16.8%	18.8%
Master's Degree	3.6%	57.8%
Doctoral Degree	0.4%	128.6%
First Professional Degree	0.6%	26.2%

Flexibility of Earnings

Average Hours Worked: 38
Workers with a Varying Number of Hours: 9.1%
Workers Earning Some Overtime Pay, Tips, or Commissions: 17.6%
Earnings Benefit of Working Overtime: 17.1%

Gender

	Male	Female
Percent	58.2%	41.8%
Effect on Earnings	14.6%	−16.1%

Union Membership

Percentage Union Members: Insignificant
Earnings Benefit of Union Membership: No significant data available

Veteran Status

Percentage Who Have Been on Active Duty: 8.7%
Earnings Benefit of Veteran Status: 7.2%

41-1012 First-Line Supervisors/Managers of Non-Retail Sales Workers

Directly supervise and coordinate activities of sales workers other than retail sales workers. May perform duties such as budgeting, accounting, and personnel work in addition to supervisory duties.

- Education or Training Required: Work experience in a related occupation
- Job Growth: 1.9%
- Annual Openings: 38,000
- Self-Employed: 37.1%
- Part-Time: 13.4%

Note: A large fraction of the workforce for this occupation is self-employed and earns an average of $55,680. All other earnings figures for this occupation are based on workers who are paid a wage or salary.

NATIONAL WAGE FIGURES (ANNUAL)

Beginning	25th Percentile	Median	Mean	75th Percentile	90th Percentile
$34,840	$48,900	$65,510	$76,840	$94,670	$135,270

Median Wages for Industries Employing Largest Numbers (Annual)

Industry	Median Income
Computer and Electronic Product Manufacturing	$85,520
Securities, Commodity Contracts, and Other Financial Investments and Related Activities	$84,530
Professional, Scientific, and Technical Services	$79,770
Telecommunications	$79,120
Wholesale Electronic Markets and Agents and Brokers	$78,260
Broadcasting (Except Internet)	$74,900
Chemical Manufacturing	$74,830
Miscellaneous Manufacturing	$74,680
Internet Service Providers, Web Search Portals, and Data-Processing Services	$74,630
Management of Companies and Enterprises	$73,640

Median Wages for States (Annual)

State	Wage	State	Wage	State	Wage
AK	$52,160	KY	$49,870	NY	$90,110
AL	$56,340	LA	$51,860	OH	$64,850
AR	$55,360	MA	$68,070	OK	$47,300
AZ	$54,900	MD	$68,550	OR	$61,030
CA	$66,340	ME	$49,900	PA	$70,860
CO	$66,390	MI	$68,560	RI	$67,250
CT	$69,340	MN	$74,690	SC	$53,650
DC	$62,480	MO	$63,270	SD	$64,480
DE	$70,010	MS	$54,580	TN	$60,880
FL	$63,780	MT	$48,930	TX	$62,470
GA	$56,130	NC	$60,300	UT	$55,020
HI	$56,250	ND	$45,280	VA	$75,550
IA	$60,240	NE	$58,690	VT	$57,330
ID	$53,320	NH	$67,120	WA	$67,460
IL	$72,000	NJ	$84,330	WI	$66,440
IN	$62,000	NM	$52,400	WV	$56,160
KS	$57,930	NV	$60,370	WY	$50,590

Median Wages for the Largest Metropolitan Areas (Annual)

Area	Wage	Area	Wage
AZ: Phoenix	$54,980	MI: Detroit	$75,290
CA: Los Angeles	$67,080	MN: Minneapolis	$79,520
CA: Riverside	$63,790	MO: Kansas City	$70,640
CA: Sacramento	$65,270	MO: St. Louis	$65,910
CA: San Diego	$63,480	NV: Las Vegas	$67,170
CA: San Francisco	$72,640	NY: New York	$93,850
CO: Denver	$69,930	OH: Cincinnati	$67,930
DC: Washington	$73,670	OH: Cleveland	$72,020
FL: Miami	$65,060	OH: Columbus	$65,730
FL: Orlando	$67,200	OR: Portland	$67,360
FL: Tampa	$66,320	PA: Philadelphia	$78,920
GA: Atlanta	$58,100	PA: Pittsburgh	$70,750
IL: Chicago	$76,270	TX: Dallas	$68,550
MA: Boston	$73,460	TX: Houston	$68,480
MD: Baltimore	$74,630	WA: Seattle	$72,120

FACTORS THAT MAY AFFECT EARNINGS

Educational Attainment of Workers and Effect on Earnings

	Percent at Level	Effect on Earnings
Less than High School	1.8%	−25.0%
Some High School	4.8%	−38.0%
High School or Equivalent	27.1%	−14.5%
Some College but No Degree	21.5%	−14.2%
Associate Degree	11.3%	−7.1%
Bachelor's Degree	23.3%	20.5%
Master's Degree	8.6%	45.1%
Doctoral Degree	—	—
First Professional Degree	1.2%	93.5%

Flexibility of Earnings

Average Hours Worked: 39
Workers with a Varying Number of Hours: 9.0%
Workers Earning Some Overtime Pay, Tips, or Commissions: 17.0%
Earnings Benefit of Working Overtime: 3.3%

Gender

	Male	Female
Percent	72.8%	27.2%
Effect on Earnings	8.1%	−17.5%

Union Membership

Percentage Union Members: Insignificant
Earnings Benefit of Union Membership: No significant data available

Veteran Status

Percentage Who Have Been on Active Duty: 8.7%
Earnings Benefit of Veteran Status: 7.2%

41-2000 Retail Sales Workers

41-2011 Cashiers

Receive and disburse money in establishments other than financial institutions. Usually involves use of electronic scanners, cash registers, or related equipment. Often involved in processing credit or debit card transactions and validating checks.

- Education or Training Required: Short-term on-the-job training
- Job Growth: 3.1%
- Annual Openings: 1,211,000
- Self-Employed: 0.9%
- Part-Time: 59.2%

NATIONAL WAGE FIGURES (ANNUAL)

Beginning	25th Percentile	Median	Mean	75th Percentile	90th Percentile
$12,850	$14,540	$16,810	$17,930	$19,640	$24,210

Median Wages for Industries Employing Largest Numbers (Annual)

Industry	Median Income
Federal, State, and Local Government	$23,390
Motor Vehicle and Parts Dealers	$19,670
Accommodation	$19,040
Educational Services	$19,010
Building Material and Garden Equipment and Supplies Dealers	$18,910
Credit Intermediation and Related Activities	$18,820
Performing Arts, Spectator Sports, and Related Industries	$18,570
Electronics and Appliance Stores	$17,920
Furniture and Home Furnishings Stores	$17,680
Administrative and Support Services	$17,510

Median Wages for States (Annual)

AK	$21,650	KY	$15,150	NY	$16,260
AL	$15,010	LA	$14,350	OH	$15,880
AR	$14,850	MA	$18,250	OK	$15,050
AZ	$17,920	MD	$17,470	OR	$18,600
CA	$18,440	ME	$17,120	PA	$15,820
CO	$18,920	MI	$17,100	RI	$17,780
CT	$18,510	MN	$17,520	SC	$14,940
DC	$20,330	MO	$16,230	SD	$16,130
DE	$17,440	MS	$14,770	TN	$15,700
FL	$16,530	MT	$15,980	TX	$16,080
GA	$15,990	NC	$16,010	UT	$16,700
HI	$18,400	ND	$15,330	VA	$16,350
IA	$15,730	NE	$15,880	VT	$18,050
ID	$16,360	NH	$18,000	WA	$20,460
IL	$16,820	NJ	$17,330	WI	$16,690
IN	$16,150	NM	$15,420	WV	$13,910
KS	$15,880	NV	$18,080	WY	$16,430

Median Wages for the Largest Metropolitan Areas (Annual)

AZ: Phoenix	$18,250	MI: Detroit	$17,860
CA: Los Angeles	$18,090	MN: Minneapolis	$18,390
CA: Riverside	$17,990	MO: Kansas City	$17,190
CA: Sacramento	$18,730	MO: St. Louis	$17,190
CA: San Diego	$18,350	NV: Las Vegas	$18,230
CA: San Francisco	$21,130	NY: New York	$17,030
CO: Denver	$19,510	OH: Cincinnati	$16,540
DC: Washington	$18,030	OH: Cleveland	$16,070
FL: Miami	$16,280	OH: Columbus	$17,050
FL: Orlando	$16,630	OR: Portland	$19,170
FL: Tampa	$16,490	PA: Philadelphia	$17,090
GA: Atlanta	$16,850	PA: Pittsburgh	$14,840
IL: Chicago	$17,270	TX: Dallas	$17,040
MA: Boston	$18,330	TX: Houston	$16,480
MD: Baltimore	$17,390	WA: Seattle	$21,550

FACTORS THAT MAY AFFECT EARNINGS

Educational Attainment of Workers and Effect on Earnings

	Percent at Level	Effect on Earnings
Less than High School	4.1%	−6.3%
Some High School	22.9%	−36.4%
High School or Equivalent	33.0%	9.8%
Some College but No Degree	22.7%	−1.8%
Associate Degree	7.3%	−5.0%
Bachelor's Degree	8.4%	59.3%
Master's Degree	1.2%	93.5%
Doctoral Degree	—	—
First Professional Degree	—	—

Flexibility of Earnings

Average Hours Worked: 27
Workers with a Varying Number of Hours: 9.5%
Workers Earning Some Overtime Pay, Tips, or Commissions: 6.6%
Earnings Benefit of Working Overtime: 18.0%

Gender

	Male	Female
Percent	25.2%	74.8%
Effect on Earnings	12.5%	−4.9%

Union Membership

Percentage Union Members: 5.7%
Earnings Benefit of Union Membership: 48.2%

Veteran Status

Percentage Who Have Been on Active Duty: 4.6%
Earnings Benefit of Veteran Status: 62.3%

41-2012 Gaming Change Persons and Booth Cashiers

Exchange coins and tokens for patrons' money. May issue payoffs and obtain customer's signature on receipt when winnings exceed the amount held in the slot machine. May operate a booth in the slot machine area and furnish change persons with money bank at the start of the shift or count and audit money in drawers.

- Education or Training Required: Short-term on-the-job training
- Job Growth: 18.5%
- Annual Openings: 11,000
- Self-Employed: 1.0%
- Part-Time: 51.0%

NATIONAL WAGE FIGURES (ANNUAL)

Beginning	25th Percentile	Median	Mean	75th Percentile	90th Percentile
$14,510	$16,970	$20,680	$21,470	$25,420	$30,150

Median Wages for Industries Employing Largest Numbers (Annual)

Industry	Median Income
Accommodation	$24,150
Religious, Grantmaking, Civic, Professional, and Similar Organizations	$20,570
Performing Arts, Spectator Sports, and Related Industries	$19,800
Federal, State, and Local Government	$19,750
Amusement, Gambling, and Recreation Industries	$19,400
Food Services and Drinking Places	$16,290

Median Wages for States (Annual)

AK	no data	KY	no data	NY	$18,140
AL	$18,420	LA	$20,070	OH	no data
AR	no data	MA	no data	OK	$16,890
AZ	$18,140	MD	no data	OR	no data
CA	$20,770	ME	no data	PA	no data
CO	$26,620	MI	$26,870	RI	no data
CT	no data	MN	$20,000	SC	no data
DC	no data	MO	$24,850	SD	$17,660
DE	$18,940	MS	$21,520	TN	no data
FL	$20,510	MT	$15,670	TX	$20,330
GA	no data	NC	no data	UT	no data
HI	no data	ND	$20,550	VA	no data
IA	$22,080	NE	no data	VT	no data
ID	no data	NH	$20,220	WA	$20,020
IL	$21,220	NJ	$24,950	WI	$18,400
IN	$21,260	NM	$17,830	WV	$14,760
KS	no data	NV	$22,810	WY	no data

Median Wages for the Largest Metropolitan Areas (Annual)

AZ: Phoenix	$17,610	MI: Detroit	no data
CA: Los Angeles	$22,390	MN: Minneapolis	$20,060
CA: Riverside	$19,800	MO: Kansas City	$25,510
CA: Sacramento	no data	MO: St. Louis	$22,230
CA: San Diego	$19,390	NV: Las Vegas	$24,910
CA: San Francisco	$23,380	NY: New York	no data
CO: Denver	$28,100	OH: Cincinnati	no data
DC: Washington	no data	OH: Cleveland	no data
FL: Miami	$20,790	OH: Columbus	no data
FL: Orlando	no data	OR: Portland	no data
FL: Tampa	no data	PA: Philadelphia	no data
GA: Atlanta	no data	PA: Pittsburgh	no data
IL: Chicago	$22,880	TX: Dallas	no data
MA: Boston	no data	TX: Houston	$21,720
MD: Baltimore	no data	WA: Seattle	$18,910

FACTORS THAT MAY AFFECT EARNINGS

Educational Attainment of Workers and Effect on Earnings

Figures are based on a group of occupations: Retail Sales Workers

	Percent at Level	Effect on Earnings
Less than High School	3.6%	−21.5%
Some High School	17.0%	−43.7%
High School or Equivalent	30.1%	3.0%
Some College but No Degree	24.2%	−6.9%
Associate Degree	8.9%	9.7%
Bachelor's Degree	12.4%	47.4%
Master's Degree	3.1%	57.6%
Doctoral Degree	0.4%	77.4%
First Professional Degree	0.4%	26.5%

Flexibility of Earnings

Average Hours Worked: 27
Workers with a Varying Number of Hours: 9.5%
Workers Earning Some Overtime Pay, Tips, or Commissions: 13.9%
Earnings Benefit of Working Overtime: 18.0%

Gender

	Male	Female
Percent	40.0%	60.0%
Effect on Earnings	21.2%	−22.5%

Union Membership

Percentage Union Members: Insignificant
Earnings Benefit of Union Membership: No significant data available

Veteran Status

Percentage Who Have Been on Active Duty: 4.6%
Earnings Benefit of Veteran Status: 62.3%

41-2021 Counter and Rental Clerks

Receive orders for repairs, rentals, and services. May describe available options, compute cost, and accept payment.

- Education or Training Required: Short-term on-the-job training
- Job Growth: 23.1%
- Annual Openings: 126,000
- Self-Employed: 0.8%
- Part-Time: 43.5%

NATIONAL WAGE FIGURES (ANNUAL)

Beginning	25th Percentile	Median	Mean	75th Percentile	90th Percentile
$13,650	$15,770	$19,570	$23,340	$27,150	$37,800

Median Wages for Industries Employing Largest Numbers (Annual)

Industry	Median Income
Motor Vehicle and Parts Dealers	$32,350
Merchant Wholesalers, Durable Goods	$28,120
Repair and Maintenance	$24,650
Building Material and Garden Equipment and Supplies Dealers	$24,350
Electronics and Appliance Stores	$23,970
Printing and Related Support Activities	$22,060
Clothing and Clothing Accessories Stores	$21,820
Credit Intermediation and Related Activities	$21,720
Real Estate	$21,590
Merchant Wholesalers, Nondurable Goods	$20,970

Median Wages for States (Annual)

State	Wage	State	Wage	State	Wage
AK	$20,840	KY	$15,190	NY	$19,110
AL	$16,570	LA	$18,240	OH	$18,190
AR	$16,420	MA	$20,730	OK	$18,310
AZ	$19,710	MD	$23,900	OR	$19,180
CA	$20,890	ME	$19,540	PA	$18,930
CO	$21,310	MI	$18,820	RI	$21,480
CT	$22,300	MN	$18,750	SC	$18,460
DC	$22,560	MO	$18,270	SD	$16,640
DE	$19,670	MS	$18,020	TN	$19,050
FL	$20,070	MT	$17,660	TX	$18,650
GA	$17,940	NC	$19,580	UT	$17,570
HI	$18,170	ND	$16,730	VA	$20,740
IA	$17,920	NE	$18,460	VT	$22,300
ID	$19,690	NH	$21,280	WA	$22,620
IL	$19,020	NJ	$21,900	WI	$18,980
IN	$18,780	NM	$20,460	WV	$16,150
KS	$19,380	NV	$20,280	WY	$14,490

Median Wages for the Largest Metropolitan Areas (Annual)

Area	Wage	Area	Wage
AZ: Phoenix	$20,130	MI: Detroit	$18,680
CA: Los Angeles	$21,590	MN: Minneapolis	$20,130
CA: Riverside	$20,060	MO: Kansas City	$20,050
CA: Sacramento	$20,900	MO: St. Louis	$19,460
CA: San Diego	$23,270	NV: Las Vegas	$20,060
CA: San Francisco	$21,150	NY: New York	$21,120
CO: Denver	$21,170	OH: Cincinnati	$18,860
DC: Washington	$22,750	OH: Cleveland	$18,540
FL: Miami	$21,730	OH: Columbus	$20,130
FL: Orlando	$20,850	OR: Portland	$20,890
FL: Tampa	$19,500	PA: Philadelphia	$21,090
GA: Atlanta	$20,490	PA: Pittsburgh	$19,310
IL: Chicago	$20,200	TX: Dallas	$19,290
MA: Boston	$21,370	TX: Houston	$21,270
MD: Baltimore	$25,890	WA: Seattle	$23,430

FACTORS THAT MAY AFFECT EARNINGS

Educational Attainment of Workers and Effect on Earnings

	Percent at Level	Effect on Earnings
Less than High School	4.1%	−46.2%
Some High School	21.5%	−41.7%
High School or Equivalent	29.7%	−7.6%
Some College but No Degree	24.4%	0.4%
Associate Degree	4.1%	−8.0%
Bachelor's Degree	13.4%	79.4%
Master's Degree	—	—
Doctoral Degree	—	—
First Professional Degree	—	—

Flexibility of Earnings

Average Hours Worked: 27
Workers with a Varying Number of Hours: 8.3%
Workers Earning Some Overtime Pay, Tips, or Commissions: 16.6%
Earnings Benefit of Working Overtime: 40.7%

Gender

	Male	Female
Percent	48.3%	51.7%
Effect on Earnings	21.2%	−22.5%

Union Membership

Percentage Union Members: Insignificant
Earnings Benefit of Union Membership: No significant data available

Veteran Status

Percentage Who Have Been on Active Duty: 4.6%
Earnings Benefit of Veteran Status: 62.3%

41-2022 Parts Salespersons

Sell spare and replacement parts and equipment in repair shop or parts store.

- Education or Training Required: Moderate-term on-the-job training
- Job Growth: –6.6%
- Annual Openings: 28,000
- Self-Employed: 0.5%
- Part-Time: 23.3%

NATIONAL WAGE FIGURES (ANNUAL)

Beginning	25th Percentile	Median	Mean	75th Percentile	90th Percentile
$16,810	$20,850	$27,430	$30,010	$36,510	$47,050

Median Wages for Industries Employing Largest Numbers (Annual)

Industry	Median Income
Furniture and Home Furnishings Stores	$38,380
Transportation Equipment Manufacturing	$33,190
Machinery Manufacturing	$32,770
Support Activities for Transportation	$31,340
Federal, State, and Local Government	$30,700
Merchant Wholesalers, Durable Goods	$30,210
Wholesale Electronic Markets and Agents and Brokers	$30,060
Specialty Trade Contractors	$29,520
Repair and Maintenance	$29,430
Fabricated Metal Product Manufacturing	$29,050

Median Wages for States (Annual)

State	Wage	State	Wage	State	Wage
AK	$30,690	KY	$24,130	NY	$29,280
AL	$23,230	LA	$25,200	OH	$24,160
AR	$23,510	MA	$31,860	OK	$23,350
AZ	$28,690	MD	$31,150	OR	$29,560
CA	$31,700	ME	$25,850	PA	$26,740
CO	$30,810	MI	$25,500	RI	$28,170
CT	$30,350	MN	$30,600	SC	$27,210
DC	$24,280	MO	$26,850	SD	$26,350
DE	$25,020	MS	$23,140	TN	$26,060
FL	$27,350	MT	$28,470	TX	$24,670
GA	$28,780	NC	$26,100	UT	$26,110
HI	$23,930	ND	$26,260	VA	$26,770
IA	$26,310	NE	$27,300	VT	$27,460
ID	$26,010	NH	$29,890	WA	$28,770
IL	$28,600	NJ	$30,900	WI	$30,020
IN	$26,620	NM	$25,570	WV	$23,820
KS	$25,500	NV	$30,040	WY	$26,740

Median Wages for the Largest Metropolitan Areas (Annual)

Area	Wage	Area	Wage
AZ: Phoenix	$31,570	MI: Detroit	$30,540
CA: Los Angeles	$33,050	MN: Minneapolis	$33,780
CA: Riverside	$32,190	MO: Kansas City	$27,620
CA: Sacramento	$31,180	MO: St. Louis	$30,660
CA: San Diego	$32,190	NV: Las Vegas	$29,710
CA: San Francisco	$39,400	NY: New York	$31,290
CO: Denver	$33,080	OH: Cincinnati	$26,060
DC: Washington	$31,190	OH: Cleveland	$24,990
FL: Miami	$27,630	OH: Columbus	$27,800
FL: Orlando	$27,130	OR: Portland	$31,700
FL: Tampa	$27,800	PA: Philadelphia	$30,330
GA: Atlanta	$31,490	PA: Pittsburgh	$26,420
IL: Chicago	$29,820	TX: Dallas	$24,240
MA: Boston	$33,010	TX: Houston	$29,040
MD: Baltimore	$30,010	WA: Seattle	$32,130

FACTORS THAT MAY AFFECT EARNINGS

Educational Attainment of Workers and Effect on Earnings

	Percent at Level	Effect on Earnings
Less than High School	—	—
Some High School	8.6%	–28.9%
High School or Equivalent	47.4%	1.2%
Some College but No Degree	23.0%	4.5%
Associate Degree	12.5%	–8.2%
Bachelor's Degree	7.9%	29.0%
Master's Degree	—	—
Doctoral Degree	—	—
First Professional Degree	—	—

Flexibility of Earnings

Average Hours Worked: 38

Workers with a Varying Number of Hours: 4.8%

Workers Earning Some Overtime Pay, Tips, or Commissions: 32.0%

Earnings Benefit of Working Overtime: 2.9%

Gender

	Male	Female
Percent	83.7%	16.3%
Effect on Earnings	5.3%	—

Union Membership

Percentage Union Members: Insignificant

Earnings Benefit of Union Membership: No significant data available

Veteran Status

Percentage Who Have Been on Active Duty: 4.6%

Earnings Benefit of Veteran Status: 62.3%

41-2031 Retail Salespersons

Sell merchandise, such as furniture, motor vehicles, appliances, or apparel, in a retail establishment.

- Education or Training Required: Short-term on-the-job training
- Job Growth: 17.3%
- Annual Openings: 1,350,000
- Self-Employed: 3.4%
- Part-Time: 43.3%

NATIONAL WAGE FIGURES (ANNUAL)

Beginning	25th Percentile	Median	Mean	75th Percentile	90th Percentile
$14,120	$16,250	$19,760	$23,940	$26,680	$38,430

Note: The mean is significantly higher than the median because of the presence of a few star earners.

Median Wages for Industries Employing Largest Numbers (Annual)

Industry	Median Income
Motor Vehicle and Parts Dealers	$34,910
Merchant Wholesalers, Durable Goods	$26,730
Repair and Maintenance	$26,180
Wholesale Electronic Markets and Agents and Brokers	$25,330
Furniture and Home Furnishings Stores	$24,420
Federal, State, and Local Government	$23,480
Building Material and Garden Equipment and Supplies Dealers	$23,470
Telecommunications	$23,090
Nonstore Retailers	$21,860
Merchant Wholesalers, Nondurable Goods	$21,840

Median Wages for States (Annual)

AK	$22,830	KY	$17,670	NY	$19,890
AL	$18,500	LA	$18,750	OH	$19,030
AR	$17,750	MA	$21,020	OK	$18,090
AZ	$21,160	MD	$19,140	OR	$21,540
CA	$20,680	ME	$21,500	PA	$19,280
CO	$21,120	MI	$19,470	RI	$21,290
CT	$22,810	MN	$19,640	SC	$19,600
DC	$21,450	MO	$19,250	SD	$18,260
DE	$19,560	MS	$18,810	TN	$19,530
FL	$21,170	MT	$18,590	TX	$18,620
GA	$18,940	NC	$19,230	UT	$19,680
HI	$19,850	ND	$18,130	VA	$19,340
IA	$18,550	NE	$18,370	VT	$21,600
ID	$19,430	NH	$21,040	WA	$23,270
IL	$19,790	NJ	$20,900	WI	$19,350
IN	$18,500	NM	$18,100	WV	$17,170
KS	$18,250	NV	$20,640	WY	$18,160

Median Wages for the Largest Metropolitan Areas (Annual)

AZ: Phoenix	$21,570	MI: Detroit	$19,540
CA: Los Angeles	$20,440	MN: Minneapolis	$20,340
CA: Riverside	$20,110	MO: Kansas City	$19,630
CA: Sacramento	$20,260	MO: St. Louis	$19,400
CA: San Diego	$20,600	NV: Las Vegas	$20,560
CA: San Francisco	$22,290	NY: New York	$20,590
CO: Denver	$21,170	OH: Cincinnati	$18,930
DC: Washington	$20,110	OH: Cleveland	$19,820
FL: Miami	$21,800	OH: Columbus	$19,290
FL: Orlando	$20,770	OR: Portland	$22,150
FL: Tampa	$20,510	PA: Philadelphia	$20,290
GA: Atlanta	$19,670	PA: Pittsburgh	$18,730
IL: Chicago	$20,250	TX: Dallas	$19,790
MA: Boston	$21,260	TX: Houston	$19,000
MD: Baltimore	$18,880	WA: Seattle	$24,160

FACTORS THAT MAY AFFECT EARNINGS

Educational Attainment of Workers and Effect on Earnings

	Percent at Level	Effect on Earnings
Less than High School	2.2%	−22.1%
Some High School	12.9%	−47.1%
High School or Equivalent	28.5%	1.0%
Some College but No Degree	26.2%	−11.1%
Associate Degree	9.3%	10.9%
Bachelor's Degree	15.9%	36.6%
Master's Degree	4.2%	44.4%
Doctoral Degree	0.5%	66.8%
First Professional Degree	0.3%	41.9%

Flexibility of Earnings

Average Hours Worked: 28
Workers with a Varying Number of Hours: 9.7%
Workers Earning Some Overtime Pay, Tips, or Commissions: 20.5%
Earnings Benefit of Working Overtime: 38.1%

Gender

	Male	Female
Percent	48.6%	51.4%
Effect on Earnings	20.9%	−18.0%

Union Membership

Percentage Union Members: Insignificant
Earnings Benefit of Union Membership: No significant data available

Veteran Status

Percentage Who Have Been on Active Duty: 4.6%
Earnings Benefit of Veteran Status: 62.3%

41-3000 Sales Representatives, Services

41-3011 Advertising Sales Agents

Sell or solicit advertising, including graphic art, advertising space in publications, custom-made signs, or TV and radio advertising time. May obtain leases for outdoor advertising sites or persuade retailer to use sales promotion display items.

- Education or Training Required: Moderate-term on-the-job training
- Job Growth: 16.3%
- Annual Openings: 24,000
- Self-Employed: 5.7%
- Part-Time: 28.8%

NATIONAL WAGE FIGURES (ANNUAL)

Beginning	25th Percentile	Median	Mean	75th Percentile	90th Percentile
$21,460	$29,450	$42,750	$51,370	$63,120	$91,280

Note: The mean is significantly higher than the median because of the presence of a few star earners.

Median Wages for Industries Employing Largest Numbers (Annual)

Industry	Median Income
Securities, Commodity Contracts, and Other Financial Investments and Related Activities	$62,080
Motion Picture and Sound Recording Industries	$55,110
Administrative and Support Services	$51,660
Printing and Related Support Activities	$51,250
Furniture and Home Furnishings Stores	$50,130
Wholesale Electronic Markets and Agents and Brokers	$49,360
Internet Service Providers, Web Search Portals, and Data-Processing Services	$47,980
Professional, Scientific, and Technical Services	$47,630
Performing Arts, Spectator Sports, and Related Industries	$46,780
Telecommunications	$46,330

Median Wages for States (Annual)

State	Wage	State	Wage	State	Wage
AK	$37,330	KY	$36,690	NY	$51,440
AL	no data	LA	$34,410	OH	$38,300
AR	$34,470	MA	$45,260	OK	$32,540
AZ	$40,910	MD	$42,130	OR	$42,940
CA	$49,330	ME	$32,320	PA	$40,920
CO	$41,680	MI	$50,500	RI	$31,570
CT	$52,960	MN	$42,320	SC	$35,620
DC	$56,750	MO	$36,560	SD	$29,930
DE	$57,250	MS	$31,280	TN	$35,840
FL	$40,470	MT	$29,340	TX	$35,840
GA	$38,840	NC	$39,410	UT	$38,260
HI	$49,510	ND	$36,620	VA	$37,800
IA	$30,210	NE	$34,060	VT	$30,090
ID	$39,860	NH	$40,470	WA	$45,600
IL	$40,930	NJ	$47,460	WI	$37,740
IN	$36,090	NM	$38,970	WV	$30,660
KS	$34,820	NV	$36,640	WY	$25,720

Median Wages for the Largest Metropolitan Areas (Annual)

Area	Wage	Area	Wage
AZ: Phoenix	$42,120	MI: Detroit	$62,600
CA: Los Angeles	$48,480	MN: Minneapolis	$48,400
CA: Riverside	$51,290	MO: Kansas City	$40,670
CA: Sacramento	$50,750	MO: St. Louis	$42,310
CA: San Diego	$49,170	NV: Las Vegas	$38,380
CA: San Francisco	$54,790	NY: New York	$53,280
CO: Denver	$44,980	OH: Cincinnati	$40,920
DC: Washington	$44,870	OH: Cleveland	$40,520
FL: Miami	$40,040	OH: Columbus	$39,330
FL: Orlando	$43,330	OR: Portland	$45,020
FL: Tampa	$41,050	PA: Philadelphia	$50,540
GA: Atlanta	$43,830	PA: Pittsburgh	$37,250
IL: Chicago	$43,660	TX: Dallas	$39,170
MA: Boston	$47,550	TX: Houston	$33,160
MD: Baltimore	$43,680	WA: Seattle	$52,740

FACTORS THAT MAY AFFECT EARNINGS

Educational Attainment of Workers and Effect on Earnings

	Percent at Level	Effect on Earnings
Less than High School	—	—
Some High School	2.9%	−40.7%
High School or Equivalent	18.1%	−29.1%
Some College but No Degree	19.1%	−8.4%
Associate Degree	11.8%	−1.1%
Bachelor's Degree	39.7%	14.2%
Master's Degree	7.4%	27.9%
Doctoral Degree	—	—
First Professional Degree	—	—

Flexibility of Earnings

Average Hours Worked: 35
Workers with a Varying Number of Hours: 8.0%
Workers Earning Some Overtime Pay, Tips, or Commissions: 36.3%
Earnings Benefit of Working Overtime: 29.5%

Gender

	Male	Female
Percent	46.1%	53.9%
Effect on Earnings	13.7%	−13.6%

Union Membership

Percentage Union Members: 5.2%
Earnings Benefit of Union Membership: 2.1%

Veteran Status

Percentage Who Have Been on Active Duty: 7.2%
Earnings Benefit of Veteran Status: −0.9%

41-3021 Insurance Sales Agents

Sell life, property, casualty, health, automotive, or other types of insurance. May refer clients to independent brokers, work as independent broker, or be employed by an insurance company.

- Education or Training Required: Bachelor's degree
- Job Growth: 6.6%
- Annual Openings: 44,000
- Self-Employed: 24.3%
- Part-Time: 15.5%

NATIONAL WAGE FIGURES (ANNUAL)

Beginning	25th Percentile	Median	Mean	75th Percentile	90th Percentile
$24,600	$31,640	$43,870	$58,450	$69,180	$115,090

Note: The mean is significantly higher than the median because of the presence of a few star earners.

Median Wages for Industries Employing Largest Numbers (Annual)

Industry	Median Income
Publishing Industries (Except Internet)	$54,650
Motor Vehicle and Parts Dealers	$49,490
Securities, Commodity Contracts, and Other Financial Investments and Related Activities	$47,190
Administrative and Support Services	$44,120
Insurance Carriers and Related Activities	$43,990
Real Estate	$43,750
Credit Intermediation and Related Activities	$42,690
Religious, Grantmaking, Civic, Professional, and Similar Organizations	$40,280
Management of Companies and Enterprises	$39,850
Professional, Scientific, and Technical Services	$39,600

Median Wages for States (Annual)

AK	$39,760	KY	$37,680	NY	$50,710
AL	$39,260	LA	$38,950	OH	$39,570
AR	$32,490	MA	$61,380	OK	$37,950
AZ	$42,390	MD	$45,190	OR	$41,670
CA	$55,220	ME	$42,120	PA	$43,730
CO	$41,400	MI	$46,580	RI	$57,220
CT	$58,430	MN	$51,360	SC	$36,980
DC	$48,810	MO	$37,010	SD	$35,770
DE	$39,690	MS	$35,070	TN	$35,850
FL	$42,230	MT	$30,350	TX	$38,750
GA	no data	NC	$37,240	UT	$42,390
HI	$42,320	ND	$46,050	VA	$41,400
IA	$35,910	NE	$36,120	VT	$45,310
ID	$31,940	NH	$47,480	WA	$49,620
IL	$43,970	NJ	$59,030	WI	$47,990
IN	$43,140	NM	$37,100	WV	$29,000
KS	$40,980	NV	$48,100	WY	$34,280

Median Wages for the Largest Metropolitan Areas (Annual)

AZ: Phoenix	$45,600	MI: Detroit	$55,710
CA: Los Angeles	$54,490	MN: Minneapolis	$61,590
CA: Riverside	$44,100	MO: Kansas City	$42,270
CA: Sacramento	$72,000	MO: St. Louis	$35,420
CA: San Diego	$56,140	NV: Las Vegas	$49,380
CA: San Francisco	$61,190	NY: New York	$55,510
CO: Denver	$41,730	OH: Cincinnati	$43,140
DC: Washington	$44,150	OH: Cleveland	$32,930
FL: Miami	$43,870	OH: Columbus	$51,050
FL: Orlando	$42,810	OR: Portland	$50,930
FL: Tampa	$41,740	PA: Philadelphia	$45,380
GA: Atlanta	$51,860	PA: Pittsburgh	$45,670
IL: Chicago	$46,500	TX: Dallas	$43,080
MA: Boston	$66,240	TX: Houston	$41,870
MD: Baltimore	$45,360	WA: Seattle	$56,970

FACTORS THAT MAY AFFECT EARNINGS

Educational Attainment of Workers and Effect on Earnings

	Percent at Level	Effect on Earnings
Less than High School	—	—
Some High School	—	—
High School or Equivalent	24.5%	−12.4%
Some College but No Degree	23.7%	−16.2%
Associate Degree	11.8%	−16.4%
Bachelor's Degree	32.0%	18.4%
Master's Degree	5.4%	54.9%
Doctoral Degree	—	—
First Professional Degree	—	—

Flexibility of Earnings

Average Hours Worked: 36
Workers with a Varying Number of Hours: 8.1%
Workers Earning Some Overtime Pay, Tips, or Commissions: 31.2%
Earnings Benefit of Working Overtime: 14.9%

Gender

	Male	Female
Percent	54.7%	45.3%
Effect on Earnings	18.4%	−13.2%

Union Membership

Percentage Union Members: Insignificant
Earnings Benefit of Union Membership: No significant data available

Veteran Status

Percentage Who Have Been on Active Duty: 7.2%
Earnings Benefit of Veteran Status: −0.9%

41-3031 Securities, Commodities, and Financial Services Sales Agents

Buy and sell securities in investment and trading firms or call upon businesses and individuals to sell financial services. Provide financial services, such as loan, tax, and securities counseling. May advise securities customers about such things as stocks, bonds, and market conditions.

- Education or Training Required: Bachelor's degree
- Job Growth: 11.5%
- Annual Openings: 37,000
- Self-Employed: 12.5%
- Part-Time: 12.5%

NATIONAL WAGE FIGURES (ANNUAL)

Beginning	25th Percentile	Median	Mean	75th Percentile	90th Percentile
$31,170	$42,630	$68,500	$90,380	$126,290	more than $145,600

Note: The mean is significantly higher than the median because of the presence of a few star earners.

Median Wages for Industries Employing Largest Numbers (Annual)

Industry	Median Income
Computer and Electronic Product Manufacturing	$101,270
Utilities	$94,950
Securities, Commodity Contracts, and Other Financial Investments and Related Activities	$83,710
Merchant Wholesalers, Nondurable Goods	$79,580
Monetary Authorities—Central Bank	$74,980
Professional, Scientific, and Technical Services	$71,990
Management of Companies and Enterprises	$70,620
Federal, State, and Local Government	$69,520
Internet Service Providers, Web Search Portals, and Data-Processing Services	$68,630
Funds, Trusts, and Other Financial Vehicles	$67,640

Median Wages for States (Annual)

AK	$55,800	KY	$77,120	NY	$90,050
AL	$55,680	LA	$66,210	OH	$51,670
AR	$47,370	MA	$106,070	OK	$49,860
AZ	$51,620	MD	$60,640	OR	$61,510
CA	$75,180	ME	$62,880	PA	$61,730
CO	$74,270	MI	$60,410	RI	$64,290
CT	$130,120	MN	$64,070	SC	$59,260
DC	$93,560	MO	$68,560	SD	$128,600
DE	$67,460	MS	no data	TN	$71,420
FL	$59,970	MT	no data	TX	no data
GA	$51,650	NC	$69,880	UT	$47,500
HI	no data	ND	$45,250	VA	$56,740
IA	no data	NE	$42,300	VT	$64,420
ID	no data	NH	$47,500	WA	$59,380
IL	$60,480	NJ	$84,410	WI	$47,830
IN	$57,470	NM	$63,890	WV	$40,990
KS	$61,710	NV	$36,650	WY	$47,070

Median Wages for the Largest Metropolitan Areas (Annual)

AZ: Phoenix	$52,210	MI: Detroit	$61,720
CA: Los Angeles	$70,900	MN: Minneapolis	$66,290
CA: Riverside	$60,530	MO: Kansas City	$78,380
CA: Sacramento	$55,790	MO: St. Louis	$63,980
CA: San Diego	$60,400	NV: Las Vegas	$49,990
CA: San Francisco	$114,590	NY: New York	$92,560
CO: Denver	$77,360	OH: Cincinnati	$58,040
DC: Washington	$61,780	OH: Cleveland	$64,920
FL: Miami	$67,250	OH: Columbus	$46,680
FL: Orlando	$48,610	OR: Portland	$58,770
FL: Tampa	$48,200	PA: Philadelphia	$68,820
GA: Atlanta	$52,260	PA: Pittsburgh	$58,260
IL: Chicago	$60,850	TX: Dallas	$66,080
MA: Boston	$84,730	TX: Houston	$102,510
MD: Baltimore	$63,500	WA: Seattle	$62,390

FACTORS THAT MAY AFFECT EARNINGS

Educational Attainment of Workers and Effect on Earnings

	Percent at Level	Effect on Earnings
Less than High School	—	—
Some High School	—	—
High School or Equivalent	18.4%	−22.2%
Some College but No Degree	16.9%	−20.8%
Associate Degree	9.8%	−15.4%
Bachelor's Degree	39.1%	15.7%
Master's Degree	13.9%	16.5%
Doctoral Degree	—	—
First Professional Degree	—	—

Flexibility of Earnings

Average Hours Worked: 38
Workers with a Varying Number of Hours: 7.2%
Workers Earning Some Overtime Pay, Tips, or Commissions: 36.6%
Earnings Benefit of Working Overtime: 2.4%

Gender

	Male	Female
Percent	70.7%	29.3%
Effect on Earnings	17.9%	−21.6%

Union Membership

Percentage Union Members: Insignificant
Earnings Benefit of Union Membership: No significant data available

Veteran Status

Percentage Who Have Been on Active Duty: 7.2%
Earnings Benefit of Veteran Status: −0.9%

41-3041 Travel Agents

Plan and sell transportation and accommodations for travel agency customers. Determine destination, modes of transportation, travel dates, costs, and accommodations required.

- Education or Training Required: Postsecondary vocational training
- Job Growth: –6.1%
- Annual Openings: 4,000
- Self-Employed: 14.2%
- Part-Time: 51.3%

NATIONAL WAGE FIGURES (ANNUAL)

Beginning	25th Percentile	Median	Mean	75th Percentile	90th Percentile
$18,100	$23,020	$29,210	$31,460	$36,920	$46,270

Median Wages for Industries Employing Largest Numbers (Annual)

Industry	Median Income
Performing Arts, Spectator Sports, and Related Industries	$41,000
Publishing Industries (Except Internet)	$39,130
Management of Companies and Enterprises	$35,300
Securities, Commodity Contracts, and Other Financial Investments and Related Activities	$34,760
Insurance Carriers and Related Activities	$31,540
Credit Intermediation and Related Activities	$30,500
Air Transportation	$29,490
Administrative and Support Services	$29,200
Water Transportation	$27,420
Professional, Scientific, and Technical Services	$26,450

Median Wages for States (Annual)

AK	$28,100	KY	$31,750	NY	$34,290
AL	$27,830	LA	$23,810	OH	$26,470
AR	$24,380	MA	$33,920	OK	$28,920
AZ	$29,590	MD	$30,020	OR	$23,750
CA	$29,890	ME	$29,940	PA	$29,630
CO	$29,340	MI	$30,340	RI	$29,660
CT	$32,960	MN	$33,430	SC	$26,840
DC	$30,490	MO	$28,360	SD	$22,610
DE	$31,270	MS	$29,040	TN	$32,260
FL	$28,120	MT	no data	TX	$27,940
GA	$31,180	NC	$30,410	UT	$28,270
HI	$27,110	ND	$22,810	VA	$31,220
IA	$26,500	NE	no data	VT	$30,910
ID	$27,810	NH	$32,990	WA	$32,530
IL	$25,820	NJ	$28,620	WI	$25,550
IN	$25,410	NM	$26,930	WV	no data
KS	$23,590	NV	$30,430	WY	$27,640

Median Wages for the Largest Metropolitan Areas (Annual)

AZ: Phoenix	$32,110	MI: Detroit	$33,540
CA: Los Angeles	$29,430	MN: Minneapolis	$34,700
CA: Riverside	$28,550	MO: Kansas City	$27,490
CA: Sacramento	$32,960	MO: St. Louis	$29,350
CA: San Diego	$30,880	NV: Las Vegas	$30,240
CA: San Francisco	$31,330	NY: New York	$33,570
CO: Denver	$30,760	OH: Cincinnati	$30,950
DC: Washington	$33,480	OH: Cleveland	$27,160
FL: Miami	$29,360	OH: Columbus	$31,880
FL: Orlando	$26,570	OR: Portland	$23,800
FL: Tampa	$27,360	PA: Philadelphia	$32,610
GA: Atlanta	$31,720	PA: Pittsburgh	$27,070
IL: Chicago	$26,020	TX: Dallas	no data
MA: Boston	$34,610	TX: Houston	$29,700
MD: Baltimore	$27,990	WA: Seattle	$34,650

FACTORS THAT MAY AFFECT EARNINGS

Educational Attainment of Workers and Effect on Earnings

	Percent at Level	Effect on Earnings
Less than High School	—	—
Some High School	—	—
High School or Equivalent	22.6%	–0.2%
Some College but No Degree	28.0%	–9.3%
Associate Degree	18.3%	–4.5%
Bachelor's Degree	22.6%	20.6%
Master's Degree	—	—
Doctoral Degree	—	—
First Professional Degree	—	—

Figures do not total 100% because some levels have a very small sample size.

Flexibility of Earnings

Average Hours Worked: 33
Workers with a Varying Number of Hours: 7.8%
Workers Earning Some Overtime Pay, Tips, or Commissions: 21.6%
Earnings Benefit of Working Overtime: 11.6%

Gender

	Male	Female
Percent	21.3%	78.7%
Effect on Earnings	21.2%	–22.5%

Union Membership

Percentage Union Members: Insignificant
Earnings Benefit of Union Membership: No significant data available

Veteran Status

Percentage Who Have Been on Active Duty: 7.2%
Earnings Benefit of Veteran Status: –0.9%

41-3099 Sales Representatives, Services, All Other

All services sales representatives not listed separately.

- Education or Training Required: Moderate-term on-the-job training
- Job Growth: 18.7%
- Annual Openings: 61,000
- Self-Employed: 5.4%
- Part-Time: 16.3%

NATIONAL WAGE FIGURES (ANNUAL)

Beginning	25th Percentile	Median	Mean	75th Percentile	90th Percentile
$24,340	$33,200	$48,100	$56,420	$70,300	$98,960

Median Wages for Industries Employing Largest Numbers (Annual)

Industry	Median Income
Internet Service Providers, Web Search Portals, and Data-Processing Services	$60,320
Professional, Scientific, and Technical Services	$57,300
Truck Transportation	$55,740
Construction of Buildings	$54,890
Support Activities for Transportation	$54,200
Wholesale Electronic Markets and Agents and Brokers	$54,050
Management of Companies and Enterprises	$52,860
Insurance Carriers and Related Activities	$52,560
Ambulatory Health Care Services	$51,570
Motor Vehicle and Parts Dealers	$51,530

Median Wages for States (Annual)

AK	$45,120	KY	$40,880	NY	$53,940
AL	$37,360	LA	no data	OH	$41,620
AR	$37,230	MA	$56,740	OK	$32,330
AZ	$41,100	MD	$55,350	OR	$41,940
CA	$52,890	ME	$43,780	PA	$50,370
CO	$46,340	MI	$47,470	RI	no data
CT	$58,070	MN	$50,080	SC	$37,520
DC	$58,250	MO	$45,780	SD	no data
DE	$47,540	MS	$34,520	TN	$42,160
FL	$44,400	MT	$40,920	TX	$47,000
GA	$43,470	NC	$45,750	UT	$40,600
HI	$46,430	ND	$40,390	VA	$52,560
IA	$40,470	NE	$38,960	VT	$39,940
ID	no data	NH	$48,420	WA	$47,800
IL	$47,630	NJ	$60,840	WI	$46,140
IN	$44,240	NM	$34,010	WV	$36,520
KS	$46,380	NV	$41,980	WY	$31,070

Median Wages for the Largest Metropolitan Areas (Annual)

AZ: Phoenix	$41,140	MI: Detroit	$48,420
CA: Los Angeles	$50,710	MN: Minneapolis	$51,260
CA: Riverside	$45,370	MO: Kansas City	$50,200
CA: Sacramento	$52,450	MO: St. Louis	$46,270
CA: San Diego	$52,840	NV: Las Vegas	$42,700
CA: San Francisco	$58,460	NY: New York	$57,920
CO: Denver	$47,290	OH: Cincinnati	$43,790
DC: Washington	$61,620	OH: Cleveland	$40,940
FL: Miami	$45,210	OH: Columbus	$50,550
FL: Orlando	$46,120	OR: Portland	$44,590
FL: Tampa	$44,500	PA: Philadelphia	$53,950
GA: Atlanta	$46,070	PA: Pittsburgh	$51,100
IL: Chicago	$51,080	TX: Dallas	$52,170
MA: Boston	$59,440	TX: Houston	$50,900
MD: Baltimore	$56,280	WA: Seattle	$50,270

FACTORS THAT MAY AFFECT EARNINGS

Educational Attainment of Workers and Effect on Earnings

	Percent at Level	Effect on Earnings
Less than High School	—	—
Some High School	3.5%	−51.8%
High School or Equivalent	22.6%	−16.3%
Some College but No Degree	24.5%	−14.0%
Associate Degree	12.1%	−4.2%
Bachelor's Degree	30.8%	23.3%
Master's Degree	4.7%	49.1%
Doctoral Degree	—	—
First Professional Degree	—	—

Flexibility of Earnings

Average Hours Worked: 37
Workers with a Varying Number of Hours: 5.9%
Workers Earning Some Overtime Pay, Tips, or Commissions: 30.7%
Earnings Benefit of Working Overtime: 16.4%

Gender

	Male	Female
Percent	67.2%	32.8%
Effect on Earnings	14.6%	−22.4%

Union Membership

Percentage Union Members: 4.3%
Earnings Benefit of Union Membership: −16.0%

Veteran Status

Percentage Who Have Been on Active Duty: 7.2%
Earnings Benefit of Veteran Status: −0.9%

41-4000 Sales Representatives, Wholesale and Manufacturing

41-4011 Sales Representatives, Wholesale and Manufacturing, Technical and Scientific Products

Sell goods for wholesalers or manufacturers where technical or scientific knowledge is required in such areas as biology, engineering, chemistry, and electronics, normally obtained from at least 2 years of postsecondary education.

- Education or Training Required: Moderate-term on-the-job training
- Job Growth: 14.4%
- Annual Openings: 47,000
- Self-Employed: 3.5%
- Part-Time: 14.9%

NATIONAL WAGE FIGURES (ANNUAL)

Beginning	25th Percentile	Median	Mean	75th Percentile	90th Percentile
$33,410	$45,630	$64,440	$72,700	$91,090	$121,850

Median Wages for Industries Employing Largest Numbers (Annual)

Industry	Median Income
Internet Service Providers, Web Search Portals, and Data-Processing Services	$73,980
Professional, Scientific, and Technical Services	$73,020
Computer and Electronic Product Manufacturing	$70,060
Wholesale Electronic Markets and Agents and Brokers	$69,510
Transportation Equipment Manufacturing	$69,420
Publishing Industries (Except Internet)	$69,350
Management of Companies and Enterprises	$69,270
Chemical Manufacturing	$67,450
Miscellaneous Manufacturing	$66,070
Merchant Wholesalers, Nondurable Goods	$64,600

Median Wages for States (Annual)

State	Wage	State	Wage	State	Wage
AK	$54,400	KY	$69,780	NY	$70,960
AL	$71,450	LA	$55,300	OH	$62,650
AR	$52,290	MA	$78,750	OK	$48,340
AZ	$46,640	MD	$69,610	OR	$70,980
CA	$69,140	ME	no data	PA	$65,720
CO	$76,140	MI	$67,590	RI	$68,690
CT	$72,490	MN	$73,370	SC	$54,710
DC	$60,140	MO	$64,930	SD	$51,560
DE	$91,300	MS	$53,850	TN	$60,220
FL	$58,750	MT	$43,060	TX	$64,220
GA	$70,500	NC	$54,120	UT	$55,760
HI	$54,990	ND	$53,240	VA	$66,590
IA	$55,580	NE	$58,470	VT	$56,620
ID	no data	NH	$62,830	WA	$67,980
IL	$62,540	NJ	$67,730	WI	$70,390
IN	$63,190	NM	$55,260	WV	$58,570
KS	$60,700	NV	$60,910	WY	$58,220

Median Wages for the Largest Metropolitan Areas (Annual)

Area	Wage	Area	Wage
AZ: Phoenix	$46,630	MI: Detroit	$72,210
CA: Los Angeles	$65,010	MN: Minneapolis	$74,170
CA: Riverside	$71,690	MO: Kansas City	$67,620
CA: Sacramento	$65,380	MO: St. Louis	$67,650
CA: San Diego	$70,190	NV: Las Vegas	$59,870
CA: San Francisco	$66,360	NY: New York	$71,110
CO: Denver	$77,550	OH: Cincinnati	$69,400
DC: Washington	$72,840	OH: Cleveland	$66,230
FL: Miami	$60,280	OH: Columbus	$68,380
FL: Orlando	$59,440	OR: Portland	$73,160
FL: Tampa	$57,800	PA: Philadelphia	$73,360
GA: Atlanta	$73,710	PA: Pittsburgh	$65,290
IL: Chicago	$66,030	TX: Dallas	$67,100
MA: Boston	$78,180	TX: Houston	$66,710
MD: Baltimore	$63,450	WA: Seattle	$71,120

FACTORS THAT MAY AFFECT EARNINGS

Educational Attainment of Workers and Effect on Earnings

Figures are based on a group of occupations: Supervisors, Sales Workers

	Percent at Level	Effect on Earnings
Less than High School	1.6%	−15.4%
Some High School	7.3%	−20.6%
High School or Equivalent	30.2%	−12.2%
Some College but No Degree	24.1%	−9.7%
Associate Degree	12.5%	−3.7%
Bachelor's Degree	17.9%	22.5%
Master's Degree	5.1%	59.8%
Doctoral Degree	—	—
First Professional Degree	0.9%	81.2%

Flexibility of Earnings

Average Hours Worked: 39
Workers with a Varying Number of Hours: 9.1%
Workers Earning Some Overtime Pay, Tips, or Commissions: 17.4%
Earnings Benefit of Working Overtime: −0.5%

Gender

	Male	Female
Percent	72.8%	27.2%
Effect on Earnings	6.3%	−21.2%

Union Membership

Percentage Union Members: Insignificant
Earnings Benefit of Union Membership: No significant data available

Veteran Status

Percentage Who Have Been on Active Duty: 8.7%
Earnings Benefit of Veteran Status: 7.2%

41-4012 Sales Representatives, Wholesale and Manufacturing, Except Technical and Scientific Products

Sell goods for wholesalers or manufacturers to businesses or groups of individuals. Work requires substantial knowledge of items sold.

- Education or Training Required: Moderate-term on-the-job training
- Job Growth: 12.9%
- Annual Openings: 169,000
- Self-Employed: 3.5%
- Part-Time: 14.9%

NATIONAL WAGE FIGURES (ANNUAL)

Beginning	25th Percentile	Median	Mean	75th Percentile	90th Percentile
$26,030	$35,460	$49,610	$58,540	$71,650	$101,030

Median Wages for Industries Employing Largest Numbers (Annual)

Industry	Median Income
Paper Manufacturing	$63,780
Computer and Electronic Product Manufacturing	$58,680
Chemical Manufacturing	$58,500
Professional, Scientific, and Technical Services	$58,180
Plastics and Rubber Products Manufacturing	$57,060
Management of Companies and Enterprises	$57,050
Machinery Manufacturing	$55,440
Wholesale Electronic Markets and Agents and Brokers	$54,900
Fabricated Metal Product Manufacturing	$54,480
Printing and Related Support Activities	$53,660

Median Wages for States (Annual)

AK	$46,670	KY	$45,000	NY	$55,160
AL	$42,890	LA	$44,590	OH	$53,460
AR	$42,550	MA	$58,860	OK	$42,410
AZ	$44,300	MD	$52,370	OR	$46,280
CA	$51,930	ME	$45,210	PA	$50,600
CO	$50,470	MI	$51,980	RI	$55,670
CT	$59,730	MN	$51,850	SC	$44,040
DC	$52,540	MO	$47,440	SD	$42,700
DE	$52,800	MS	$41,950	TN	$46,770
FL	$44,580	MT	$35,790	TX	$47,360
GA	$47,130	NC	$44,120	UT	$48,450
HI	$41,050	ND	$40,930	VA	$49,880
IA	$44,100	NE	$45,570	VT	$46,380
ID	$41,190	NH	$50,140	WA	$49,740
IL	$56,160	NJ	$59,910	WI	$51,570
IN	$48,480	NM	$37,890	WV	$41,850
KS	$50,980	NV	$44,850	WY	$33,820

Median Wages for the Largest Metropolitan Areas (Annual)

AZ: Phoenix	$44,820	MI: Detroit	$56,460
CA: Los Angeles	$49,960	MN: Minneapolis	$55,010
CA: Riverside	$52,230	MO: Kansas City	$54,900
CA: Sacramento	$49,810	MO: St. Louis	$52,050
CA: San Diego	$54,840	NV: Las Vegas	$46,360
CA: San Francisco	$55,670	NY: New York	$58,750
CO: Denver	$52,310	OH: Cincinnati	$57,040
DC: Washington	$55,430	OH: Cleveland	$53,710
FL: Miami	$41,530	OH: Columbus	$55,530
FL: Orlando	$48,840	OR: Portland	$49,690
FL: Tampa	$47,230	PA: Philadelphia	$55,830
GA: Atlanta	$48,770	PA: Pittsburgh	$52,290
IL: Chicago	$59,350	TX: Dallas	$51,250
MA: Boston	$61,450	TX: Houston	$51,200
MD: Baltimore	$54,480	WA: Seattle	$51,580

FACTORS THAT MAY AFFECT EARNINGS

Educational Attainment of Workers and Effect on Earnings

Figures are based on a group of occupations: Supervisors, Sales Workers

	Percent at Level	Effect on Earnings
Less than High School	1.6%	−15.4%
Some High School	7.3%	−20.6%
High School or Equivalent	30.2%	−12.2%
Some College but No Degree	24.1%	−9.7%
Associate Degree	12.5%	−3.7%
Bachelor's Degree	17.9%	22.5%
Master's Degree	5.1%	59.8%
Doctoral Degree	—	—
First Professional Degree	0.9%	81.2%

Flexibility of Earnings

Average Hours Worked: 39
Workers with a Varying Number of Hours: 9.1%
Workers Earning Some Overtime Pay, Tips, or Commissions: 17.4%
Earnings Benefit of Working Overtime: −0.5%

Gender

	Male	Female
Percent	72.8%	27.2%
Effect on Earnings	6.3%	−21.2%

Union Membership

Percentage Union Members: Insignificant
Earnings Benefit of Union Membership: No significant data available

Veteran Status

Percentage Who Have Been on Active Duty: 8.7%
Earnings Benefit of Veteran Status: 7.2%

41-9000 Other Sales and Related Workers

41-9011 Demonstrators and Product Promoters

Demonstrate merchandise and answer questions for the purpose of creating public interest in buying the product. May sell demonstrated merchandise.

- Education or Training Required: Moderate-term on-the-job training
- Job Growth: 16.5%
- Annual Openings: 32,000
- Self-Employed: 17.8%
- Part-Time: 31.8%

NATIONAL WAGE FIGURES (ANNUAL)

Beginning	25th Percentile	Median	Mean	75th Percentile	90th Percentile
$16,020	$18,230	$22,150	$25,770	$28,940	$40,090

Median Wages for Industries Employing Largest Numbers (Annual)

Industry	Median Income
Clothing and Clothing Accessories Stores	$34,900
Personal and Laundry Services	$29,240
Rental and Leasing Services	$28,150
Management of Companies and Enterprises	$27,300
Building Material and Garden Equipment and Supplies Dealers	$27,150
Furniture and Home Furnishings Stores	$26,380
Nonstore Retailers	$25,630
Real Estate	$25,380
Heavy and Civil Engineering Construction	$25,230
Merchant Wholesalers, Nondurable Goods	$24,900

Median Wages for States (Annual)

State	Wage	State	Wage	State	Wage
AK	$24,580	KY	$22,610	NY	$24,850
AL	$20,260	LA	$18,460	OH	$22,180
AR	$27,020	MA	$26,210	OK	$22,040
AZ	$22,340	MD	$22,780	OR	$18,560
CA	$23,700	ME	$20,860	PA	$21,020
CO	$24,340	MI	$20,810	RI	$23,700
CT	$22,700	MN	$21,770	SC	$22,790
DC	$23,090	MO	$22,550	SD	$18,430
DE	$23,860	MS	$21,620	TN	$24,550
FL	$21,530	MT	$17,590	TX	$22,570
GA	$20,270	NC	no data	UT	$23,700
HI	$18,220	ND	$18,380	VA	$21,770
IA	$18,000	NE	$20,080	VT	$22,210
ID	$18,230	NH	$21,800	WA	$20,120
IL	$21,710	NJ	$24,100	WI	$20,740
IN	$20,650	NM	$21,190	WV	$19,840
KS	$23,900	NV	$20,700	WY	$20,040

Median Wages for the Largest Metropolitan Areas (Annual)

Area	Wage	Area	Wage
AZ: Phoenix	no data	MI: Detroit	$22,140
CA: Los Angeles	$25,830	MN: Minneapolis	$22,850
CA: Riverside	$19,190	MO: Kansas City	$22,140
CA: Sacramento	$18,510	MO: St. Louis	$22,750
CA: San Diego	$21,910	NV: Las Vegas	$20,590
CA: San Francisco	$25,130	NY: New York	$26,400
CO: Denver	$27,350	OH: Cincinnati	$22,550
DC: Washington	$23,190	OH: Cleveland	$25,130
FL: Miami	$21,530	OH: Columbus	$16,210
FL: Orlando	$21,820	OR: Portland	$18,030
FL: Tampa	$19,750	PA: Philadelphia	$25,290
GA: Atlanta	$20,250	PA: Pittsburgh	no data
IL: Chicago	$21,550	TX: Dallas	$21,710
MA: Boston	$25,720	TX: Houston	$25,910
MD: Baltimore	$22,500	WA: Seattle	$20,710

FACTORS THAT MAY AFFECT EARNINGS

Educational Attainment of Workers and Effect on Earnings

Figures are based on a group of occupations: Other Sales and Related Workers

	Percent at Level	Effect on Earnings
Less than High School	2.1%	−67.5%
Some High School	8.5%	−54.4%
High School or Equivalent	24.0%	−24.9%
Some College but No Degree	22.6%	−5.3%
Associate Degree	11.1%	10.3%
Bachelor's Degree	21.9%	30.9%
Master's Degree	7.5%	54.8%
Doctoral Degree	—	—
First Professional Degree	1.6%	38.8%

Flexibility of Earnings

Average Hours Worked: 27
Workers with a Varying Number of Hours: 14.0%
Workers Earning Some Overtime Pay, Tips, or Commissions: 34.9%
Earnings Benefit of Working Overtime: 17.2%

Gender

	Male	Female
Percent	15.8%	84.2%
Effect on Earnings	6.3%	−21.2%

Union Membership

Percentage Union Members: Insignificant
Earnings Benefit of Union Membership: No significant data available

Veteran Status

Percentage Who Have Been on Active Duty: 8.3%
Earnings Benefit of Veteran Status: 20.9%

41-9012 Models

Model garments and other apparel to display clothing before prospective buyers at fashion shows, private showings, or retail establishments or before photographer. May pose for photos to be used for advertising purposes. May pose as subject for paintings, sculptures, and other types of artistic expression.

- Education or Training Required: Moderate-term on-the-job training
- Job Growth: 15.7%
- Annual Openings: 1,000
- Self-Employed: 26.3%
- Part-Time: 31.8%

NATIONAL WAGE FIGURES (ANNUAL)

Beginning	25th Percentile	Median	Mean	75th Percentile	90th Percentile
$15,960	$19,800	$23,340	$27,980	$29,990	$38,850

Median Wages for Industries Employing Largest Numbers (Annual)

Industry	Median Income
Management of Companies and Enterprises.....................	$52,160
Educational Services	$23,880

Median Wages for States (Annual)

AK............	no data	KY	no data	NY	no data
AL............	no data	LA	no data	OH	$18,580
AR............	no data	MA	no data	OK	no data
AZ............	no data	MD	$21,470	OR	$19,340
CA	$37,180	ME	no data	PA	no data
CO	no data	MI	no data	RI..............	no data
CT	no data	MN	no data	SC..............	no data
DC	no data	MO	no data	SD	no data
DE	no data	MS	no data	TN	no data
FL	no data	MT	no data	TX	$24,380
GA	no data	NC	$21,540	UT	no data
HI	no data	ND	no data	VA	$22,860
IA	no data	NE	no data	VT	no data
ID	no data	NH	no data	WA	$30,650
IL	no data	NJ	no data	WI	no data
IN	no data	NM	no data	WV	no data
KS	no data	NV	no data	WY	no data

Median Wages for the Largest Metropolitan Areas (Annual)

AZ: Phoenix............	no data	MI: Detroit	no data
CA: Los Angeles	no data	MN: Minneapolis	no data
CA: Riverside	no data	MO: Kansas City........	no data
CA: Sacramento	no data	MO: St. Louis............	no data
CA: San Diego	no data	NV: Las Vegas	no data
CA: San Francisco....	no data	NY: New York............	no data
CO: Denver	no data	OH: Cincinnati..........	no data
DC: Washington	no data	OH: Cleveland	no data
FL: Miami	no data	OH: Columbus	no data
FL: Orlando	no data	OR: Portland	no data
FL: Tampa	no data	PA: Philadelphia	no data
GA: Atlanta	no data	PA: Pittsburgh..........	no data
IL: Chicago	no data	TX: Dallas	no data
MA: Boston	no data	TX: Houston	no data
MD: Baltimore	$21,150	WA: Seattle	$29,340

FACTORS THAT MAY AFFECT EARNINGS

Educational Attainment of Workers and Effect on Earnings

Figures are based on a group of occupations: Other Sales and Related Workers

	Percent at Level	Effect on Earnings
Less than High School	2.1%	−67.5%
Some High School	8.5%	−54.4%
High School or Equivalent	24.0%	−24.9%
Some College but No Degree	22.6%	−5.3%
Associate Degree	11.1%	10.3%
Bachelor's Degree	21.9%	30.9%
Master's Degree	7.5%	54.8%
Doctoral Degree	—	—
First Professional Degree	1.6%	38.8%

Flexibility of Earnings

Average Hours Worked: 27
Workers with a Varying Number of Hours: 14.0%
Workers Earning Some Overtime Pay, Tips, or Commissions: 34.9%
Earnings Benefit of Working Overtime: 17.2%

Gender

	Male	Female
Percent	15.8%	84.2%
Effect on Earnings	6.3%	−21.2%

Union Membership

Percentage Union Members: Insignificant
Earnings Benefit of Union Membership: No significant data available

Veteran Status

Percentage Who Have Been on Active Duty: 8.3%
Earnings Benefit of Veteran Status: 20.9%

41-9021 Real Estate Brokers

Operate real estate office or work for commercial real estate firm, overseeing real estate transactions. Other duties usually include selling real estate or renting properties and arranging loans.

- Education or Training Required: Work experience in a related occupation
- Job Growth: 7.8%
- Annual Openings: 12,000
- Self-Employed: 59.9%
- Part-Time: 31.8%

Note: Earnings figures do not reflect self-employed workers, who make up a large fraction of the workforce for this occupation.

NATIONAL WAGE FIGURES (ANNUAL)

Beginning	25th Percentile	Median	Mean	75th Percentile	90th Percentile
$26,060	$37,800	$60,790	$80,230	$102,180	more than $145,600

Note: The mean is significantly higher than the median because of the presence of a few star earners.

Median Wages for Industries Employing Largest Numbers (Annual)

Industry	Median Income
Funds, Trusts, and Other Financial Vehicles	more than $145,600
Insurance Carriers and Related Activities	$83,750
Construction of Buildings	$71,260
Management of Companies and Enterprises	$65,640
Real Estate	$61,160
Religious, Grantmaking, Civic, Professional, and Similar Organizations	$60,940
Securities, Commodity Contracts, and Other Financial Investments and Related Activities	$56,170
Professional, Scientific, and Technical Services	$55,980
Heavy and Civil Engineering Construction	$52,960
Administrative and Support Services	$49,550

Median Wages for States (Annual)

AK	$57,870	KY	no data	NY	no data
AL	no data	LA	$53,820	OH	$45,490
AR	no data	MA	no data	OK	$60,210
AZ	$76,810	MD	no data	OR	$52,420
CA	$79,700	ME	$87,030	PA	$61,510
CO	$49,430	MI	no data	RI	no data
CT	$100,090	MN	no data	SC	$62,330
DC	$53,730	MO	$50,820	SD	$43,730
DE	$58,290	MS	$54,370	TN	no data
FL	$66,310	MT	no data	TX	$90,570
GA	$60,410	NC	$32,030	UT	$58,530
HI	no data	ND	no data	VA	no data
IA	$46,260	NE	$34,500	VT	no data
ID	no data	NH	$73,510	WA	$57,260
IL	$67,520	NJ	$85,020	WI	$62,270
IN	no data	NM	$58,410	WV	$48,800
KS	$98,120	NV	more than $145,600	WY	no data

Median Wages for the Largest Metropolitan Areas (Annual)

AZ: Phoenix	$106,630	MI: Detroit	no data
CA: Los Angeles	$58,100	MN: Minneapolis	$77,070
CA: Riverside	$81,360	MO: Kansas City	$97,940
CA: Sacramento	no data	MO: St. Louis	$74,690
CA: San Diego	no data	NV: Las Vegas	more than $145,600
CA: San Francisco	$132,620	NY: New York	$75,790
CO: Denver	$65,340	OH: Cincinnati	$55,210
DC: Washington	$59,920	OH: Cleveland	$47,880
FL: Miami	no data	OH: Columbus	no data
FL: Orlando	$80,410	OR: Portland	$73,000
FL: Tampa	$59,270	PA: Philadelphia	$63,320
GA: Atlanta	$64,250	PA: Pittsburgh	$55,010
IL: Chicago	$76,340	TX: Dallas	$97,580
MA: Boston	no data	TX: Houston	$91,250
MD: Baltimore	$57,380	WA: Seattle	$65,060

FACTORS THAT MAY AFFECT EARNINGS

Educational Attainment of Workers and Effect on Earnings

Figures are based on a group of occupations: Other Sales and Related Workers

	Percent at Level	Effect on Earnings
Less than High School	2.1%	−67.5%
Some High School	8.5%	−54.4%
High School or Equivalent	24.0%	−24.9%
Some College but No Degree	22.6%	−5.3%
Associate Degree	11.1%	10.3%
Bachelor's Degree	21.9%	30.9%
Master's Degree	7.5%	54.8%
Doctoral Degree	—	—
First Professional Degree	1.6%	38.8%

Flexibility of Earnings

Average Hours Worked: 27
Workers with a Varying Number of Hours: 14.0%
Workers Earning Some Overtime Pay, Tips, or Commissions: 34.9%
Earnings Benefit of Working Overtime: 7.2%

Gender

	Male	Female
Percent	40.1%	59.9%
Effect on Earnings	26.0%	−15.7%

Union Membership

Percentage Union Members: Insignificant
Earnings Benefit of Union Membership: No significant data available

Veteran Status

Percentage Who Have Been on Active Duty: 8.3%
Earnings Benefit of Veteran Status: 20.9%

41-9022 Real Estate Sales Agents

Rent, buy, or sell property for clients. Perform duties such as studying property listings, interviewing prospective clients, accompanying clients to property site, discussing conditions of sale, and drawing up real estate contracts. Includes agents who represent buyer.

- Education or Training Required: Postsecondary vocational training
- Job Growth: 14.7%
- Annual Openings: 41,000
- Self-Employed: 59.8%
- Part-Time: 31.8%

Note: Earnings figures do not reflect self-employed workers, who make up a large fraction of the workforce for this occupation.

NATIONAL WAGE FIGURES (ANNUAL)

Beginning	25th Percentile	Median	Mean	75th Percentile	90th Percentile
$20,170	$26,790	$39,760	$54,350	$65,270	$111,500

Note: The mean is significantly higher than the median because of the presence of a few star earners.

Median Wages for Industries Employing Largest Numbers (Annual)

Industry	Median Income
Utilities	$58,890
Federal, State, and Local Government	$58,380
Telecommunications	$57,570
Amusement, Gambling, and Recreation Industries	$55,890
Mining (Except Oil and Gas)	$55,540
Oil and Gas Extraction	$54,100
Securities, Commodity Contracts, and Other Financial Investments and Related Activities	$54,070
Construction of Buildings	$52,380
Management of Companies and Enterprises	$49,760
Heavy and Civil Engineering Construction	$49,320

Median Wages for States (Annual)

AK	$57,050	KY	$24,430	NY	$58,590
AL	$51,840	LA	$35,470	OH	$46,510
AR	$35,120	MA	$49,580	OK	$39,190
AZ	$46,190	MD	$54,510	OR	$52,000
CA	$55,460	ME	$29,560	PA	$39,680
CO	$45,970	MI	$38,570	RI	$34,750
CT	$57,450	MN	no data	SC	$32,640
DC	$56,690	MO	$40,110	SD	$45,590
DE	$37,830	MS	$33,370	TN	$28,770
FL	$34,900	MT	$45,060	TX	$32,520
GA	$28,200	NC	$43,770	UT	$41,140
HI	no data	ND	$42,730	VA	$36,980
IA	$36,370	NE	$39,070	VT	$56,810
ID	$34,740	NH	$30,270	WA	$45,450
IL	$40,970	NJ	$39,800	WI	$39,340
IN	$38,770	NM	$44,310	WV	$31,860
KS	$44,000	NV	$39,640	WY	$35,240

Median Wages for the Largest Metropolitan Areas (Annual)

AZ: Phoenix	$47,340	MI: Detroit	$37,090
CA: Los Angeles	no data	MN: Minneapolis	$31,730
CA: Riverside	$48,600	MO: Kansas City	$44,950
CA: Sacramento	$57,190	MO: St. Louis	$49,230
CA: San Diego	no data	NV: Las Vegas	$38,330
CA: San Francisco	$45,890	NY: New York	$60,320
CO: Denver	$56,300	OH: Cincinnati	$36,440
DC: Washington	$45,490	OH: Cleveland	$59,880
FL: Miami	$36,660	OH: Columbus	$47,940
FL: Orlando	$33,720	OR: Portland	$46,370
FL: Tampa	$38,820	PA: Philadelphia	$41,210
GA: Atlanta	$28,380	PA: Pittsburgh	$36,370
IL: Chicago	$42,260	TX: Dallas	$32,100
MA: Boston	no data	TX: Houston	$33,090
MD: Baltimore	$62,860	WA: Seattle	$49,330

FACTORS THAT MAY AFFECT EARNINGS

Educational Attainment of Workers and Effect on Earnings

Figures are based on a group of occupations: Other Sales and Related Workers

	Percent at Level	Effect on Earnings
Less than High School	2.1%	−67.5%
Some High School	8.5%	−54.4%
High School or Equivalent	24.0%	−24.9%
Some College but No Degree	22.6%	−5.3%
Associate Degree	11.1%	10.3%
Bachelor's Degree	21.9%	30.9%
Master's Degree	7.5%	54.8%
Doctoral Degree	—	—
First Professional Degree	1.6%	38.8%

Flexibility of Earnings

Average Hours Worked: 27
Workers with a Varying Number of Hours: 14.0%
Workers Earning Some Overtime Pay, Tips, or Commissions: 34.9%
Earnings Benefit of Working Overtime: 7.2%

Gender

	Male	Female
Percent	40.1%	59.9%
Effect on Earnings	26.0%	−15.7%

Union Membership

Percentage Union Members: Insignificant
Earnings Benefit of Union Membership: No significant data available

Veteran Status

Percentage Who Have Been on Active Duty: 8.3%
Earnings Benefit of Veteran Status: 20.9%

41-9031 Sales Engineers

Sell business goods or services, the selling of which requires a technical background equivalent to a baccalaureate degree in engineering.

- Education or Training Required: Bachelor's degree
- Job Growth: 14.0%
- Annual Openings: 8,000
- Self-Employed: 0.7%
- Part-Time: 31.8%

NATIONAL WAGE FIGURES (ANNUAL)

Beginning	25th Percentile	Median	Mean	75th Percentile	90th Percentile
$47,010	$59,490	$77,720	$83,080	$100,280	$127,680

Median Wages for Industries Employing Largest Numbers (Annual)

Industry	Median Income
Publishing Industries (Except Internet)	$99,440
Construction of Buildings	$92,210
Internet Service Providers, Web Search Portals, and Data-Processing Services	$89,180
Professional, Scientific, and Technical Services	$88,860
Utilities	$85,440
Telecommunications	$82,440
Wholesale Electronic Markets and Agents and Brokers	$81,580
Computer and Electronic Product Manufacturing	$81,540
Administrative and Support Services	$79,750
Electronics and Appliance Stores	$79,450

Median Wages for States (Annual)

AK	$86,440	KY	$68,910	NY	$84,270
AL	$69,810	LA	$64,580	OH	$71,190
AR	$60,810	MA	$78,850	OK	$56,860
AZ	$60,970	MD	$71,180	OR	no data
CA	$91,050	ME	$64,740	PA	$66,010
CO	$72,550	MI	$75,410	RI	$66,720
CT	$74,350	MN	$69,700	SC	no data
DC	no data	MO	$63,440	SD	$64,270
DE	no data	MS	$58,690	TN	no data
FL	$70,910	MT	$68,020	TX	$86,730
GA	$73,960	NC	$77,480	UT	$67,680
HI	no data	ND	no data	VA	$78,760
IA	$54,240	NE	$62,470	VT	$74,430
ID	$71,830	NH	$80,370	WA	$78,100
IL	$68,300	NJ	$83,070	WI	$74,090
IN	$66,620	NM	$53,130	WV	no data
KS	$62,420	NV	$60,240	WY	no data

Median Wages for the Largest Metropolitan Areas (Annual)

AZ: Phoenix	$63,310	MI: Detroit	$79,410
CA: Los Angeles	$85,840	MN: Minneapolis	$70,670
CA: Riverside	$83,750	MO: Kansas City	$64,750
CA: Sacramento	$80,730	MO: St. Louis	$66,280
CA: San Diego	$86,320	NV: Las Vegas	$56,560
CA: San Francisco	$95,490	NY: New York	$88,020
CO: Denver	$72,010	OH: Cincinnati	$77,510
DC: Washington	$82,520	OH: Cleveland	$67,770
FL: Miami	no data	OH: Columbus	$67,130
FL: Orlando	$70,750	OR: Portland	no data
FL: Tampa	$82,770	PA: Philadelphia	$66,960
GA: Atlanta	$74,960	PA: Pittsburgh	$66,210
IL: Chicago	$68,220	TX: Dallas	$88,710
MA: Boston	$79,800	TX: Houston	$91,870
MD: Baltimore	$69,050	WA: Seattle	$81,060

FACTORS THAT MAY AFFECT EARNINGS

Educational Attainment of Workers and Effect on Earnings

	Percent at Level	Effect on Earnings
Less than High School	—	—
Some High School	—	—
High School or Equivalent	—	—
Some College but No Degree	—	—
Associate Degree	14.3%	−8.1%
Bachelor's Degree	49.0%	6.6%
Master's Degree	16.3%	0.5%
Doctoral Degree	—	—
First Professional Degree	—	—

Figures do not total 100% because some levels have a very small sample size.

Flexibility of Earnings

Average Hours Worked: 42
Workers with a Varying Number of Hours: 6.2%
Workers Earning Some Overtime Pay, Tips, or Commissions: 38.6%
Earnings Benefit of Working Overtime: −14.1%

Gender

	Male	Female
Percent	86.5%	13.5%
Effect on Earnings	6.3%	−21.2%

Union Membership

Percentage Union Members: Insignificant
Earnings Benefit of Union Membership: No significant data available

Veteran Status

Percentage Who Have Been on Active Duty: 8.3%
Earnings Benefit of Veteran Status: 20.9%

41-9041 Telemarketers

Solicit orders for goods or services over the telephone.

- Education or Training Required: Short-term on-the-job training
- Job Growth: –10.0%
- Annual Openings: 156,000
- Self-Employed: 0.6%
- Part-Time: 46.2%

NATIONAL WAGE FIGURES (ANNUAL)

Beginning	25th Percentile	Median	Mean	75th Percentile	90th Percentile
$14,680	$16,980	$20,990	$24,190	$27,930	$38,430

Median Wages for Industries Employing Largest Numbers (Annual)

Industry	Median Income
Telecommunications	$33,620
Merchant Wholesalers, Durable Goods	$28,060
Securities, Commodity Contracts, and Other Financial Investments and Related Activities	$26,520
Merchant Wholesalers, Nondurable Goods	$26,490
Wholesale Electronic Markets and Agents and Brokers	$26,080
Credit Intermediation and Related Activities	$25,590
Internet Service Providers, Web Search Portals, and Data-Processing Services	$23,910
Broadcasting (Except Internet)	$23,810
Repair and Maintenance	$23,650
Insurance Carriers and Related Activities	$23,460

Median Wages for States (Annual)

State	Wage	State	Wage	State	Wage
AK	$18,390	KY	$17,910	NY	$25,200
AL	$18,780	LA	$24,010	OH	$19,140
AR	$18,580	MA	$28,890	OK	$16,180
AZ	$20,530	MD	$23,730	OR	$19,510
CA	$24,190	ME	$24,900	PA	$21,030
CO	$21,860	MI	$20,980	RI	$22,480
CT	$24,740	MN	$21,980	SC	$19,980
DC	$20,040	MO	$19,820	SD	$18,460
DE	$33,590	MS	no data	TN	$21,140
FL	$20,390	MT	no data	TX	$19,420
GA	$20,800	NC	$21,520	UT	$18,490
HI	$23,780	ND	$18,710	VA	$21,310
IA	$18,850	NE	$18,110	VT	$24,530
ID	$28,110	NH	$30,550	WA	$22,040
IL	$20,180	NJ	$26,530	WI	$19,240
IN	$22,700	NM	$22,960	WV	$19,660
KS	$20,960	NV	$21,090	WY	$18,280

Median Wages for the Largest Metropolitan Areas (Annual)

Area	Wage	Area	Wage
AZ: Phoenix	$21,240	MI: Detroit	$20,900
CA: Los Angeles	$23,500	MN: Minneapolis	$23,860
CA: Riverside	$22,020	MO: Kansas City	$21,530
CA: Sacramento	$24,820	MO: St. Louis	$19,220
CA: San Diego	$25,590	NV: Las Vegas	$19,840
CA: San Francisco	$26,110	NY: New York	$26,460
CO: Denver	$23,760	OH: Cincinnati	$22,870
DC: Washington	$23,650	OH: Cleveland	$21,660
FL: Miami	$22,500	OH: Columbus	$17,390
FL: Orlando	$19,930	OR: Portland	no data
FL: Tampa	$19,910	PA: Philadelphia	$23,790
GA: Atlanta	$21,650	PA: Pittsburgh	$23,430
IL: Chicago	$22,320	TX: Dallas	$23,580
MA: Boston	$29,820	TX: Houston	$18,680
MD: Baltimore	$23,190	WA: Seattle	$24,870

FACTORS THAT MAY AFFECT EARNINGS

Educational Attainment of Workers and Effect on Earnings

	Percent at Level	Effect on Earnings
Less than High School	—	—
Some High School	16.6%	–32.9%
High School or Equivalent	42.1%	–4.6%
Some College but No Degree	24.1%	–21.1%
Associate Degree	4.1%	35.2%
Bachelor's Degree	10.3%	77.7%
Master's Degree	—	—
Doctoral Degree	—	—
First Professional Degree	—	—

Flexibility of Earnings

Average Hours Worked: 23
Workers with a Varying Number of Hours: 9.1%
Workers Earning Some Overtime Pay, Tips, or Commissions: 23.1%
Earnings Benefit of Working Overtime: 17.2%

Gender

	Male	Female
Percent	34.7%	65.3%
Effect on Earnings	6.3%	–21.2%

Union Membership

Percentage Union Members: Insignificant
Earnings Benefit of Union Membership: No significant data available

Veteran Status

Percentage Who Have Been on Active Duty: 8.3%
Earnings Benefit of Veteran Status: 20.9%

41-9091 Door-To-Door Sales Workers, News and Street Vendors, and Related Workers

Sell goods or services door-to-door or on the street.

- Education or Training Required: Short-term on-the-job training
- Job Growth: -7.4%
- Annual Openings: 56,000
- Self-Employed: 91.8%
- Part-Time: 54.4%

Note: A large fraction of the workforce for this occupation is self-employed and earns an average of $37,270. All other earnings figures for this occupation are based on workers who are paid a wage or salary.

NATIONAL WAGE FIGURES (ANNUAL)

Beginning	25th Percentile	Median	Mean	75th Percentile	90th Percentile
$14,090	$15,530	$20,190	$26,880	$32,810	$50,740

Note: The mean is significantly higher than the median because of the presence of a few star earners.

Median Wages for Industries Employing Largest Numbers (Annual)

Industry	Median Income
Wholesale Electronic Markets and Agents and Brokers	$33,570
Merchant Wholesalers, Nondurable Goods	$31,850
Religious, Grantmaking, Civic, Professional, and Similar Organizations	$29,810
Miscellaneous Store Retailers	$27,640
Telecommunications..	$24,510
Administrative and Support Services	$24,380
Specialty Trade Contractors..	$22,530
Construction of Buildings	$22,490
Nonstore Retailers	$21,780
Merchant Wholesalers, Durable Goods	$19,040

Median Wages for States (Annual)

State	Wage	State	Wage	State	Wage
AK	no data	KY	$28,610	NY	$22,510
AL	no data	LA	no data	OH	$20,060
AR	no data	MA	no data	OK	$32,210
AZ	$16,540	MD	$14,360	OR	$21,150
CA	$18,110	ME	$20,520	PA	$23,580
CO	$26,970	MI	$28,440	RI	no data
CT	$57,160	MN	no data	SC	$26,030
DC	no data	MO	$14,730	SD	no data
DE	no data	MS	$33,510	TN	$19,850
FL	no data	MT	$22,860	TX	$21,480
GA	$20,730	NC	no data	UT	$20,780
HI	no data	ND	no data	VA	$19,690
IA	$24,160	NE	no data	VT	no data
ID	no data	NH	no data	WA	no data
IL	no data	NJ	$21,980	WI	$14,160
IN	$16,430	NM	no data	WV	no data
KS	$19,840	NV	$34,770	WY	$14,040

Median Wages for the Largest Metropolitan Areas (Annual)

Area	Wage	Area	Wage
AZ: Phoenix............	no data	MI: Detroit	no data
CA: Los Angeles	$18,350	MN: Minneapolis	no data
CA: Riverside	$15,180	MO: Kansas City........	no data
CA: Sacramento	no data	MO: St. Louis.............	no data
CA: San Diego	no data	NV: Las Vegas	$34,910
CA: San Francisco....	no data	NY: New York............	$25,580
CO: Denver	no data	OH: Cincinnati..........	no data
DC: Washington	no data	OH: Cleveland	no data
FL: Miami	no data	OH: Columbus	no data
FL: Orlando	no data	OR: Portland	no data
FL: Tampa	no data	PA: Philadelphia	$22,460
GA: Atlanta	$20,490	PA: Pittsburgh	no data
IL: Chicago	$20,070	TX: Dallas	$29,720
MA: Boston	no data	TX: Houston	no data
MD: Baltimore	$14,210	WA: Seattle	$17,890

FACTORS THAT MAY AFFECT EARNINGS

Educational Attainment of Workers and Effect on Earnings

	Percent at Level	Effect on Earnings
Less than High School	7.2%	-68.3%
Some High School	15.0%	-45.9%
High School or Equivalent	38.6%	8.3%
Some College but No Degree	22.9%	11.0%
Associate Degree	7.8%	-7.3%
Bachelor's Degree	6.5%	97.9%
Master's Degree	—	—
Doctoral Degree	—	—
First Professional Degree	—	—

Flexibility of Earnings

Average Hours Worked: 17
Workers with a Varying Number of Hours: 21.2%
Workers Earning Some Overtime Pay, Tips, or Commissions: 24.1%
Earnings Benefit of Working Overtime: 17.2%

Gender

	Male	Female
Percent	37.6%	62.4%
Effect on Earnings	6.3%	-21.2%

Union Membership

Percentage Union Members: Insignificant
Earnings Benefit of Union Membership: No significant data available

Veteran Status

Percentage Who Have Been on Active Duty: 8.3%
Earnings Benefit of Veteran Status: 20.9%

41-9099 Sales and Related Workers, All Other

All sales and related workers not listed separately.

- Education or Training Required: Moderate-term on-the-job training
- Job Growth: 18.4%
- Annual Openings: 53,000
- Self-Employed: 9.1%
- Part-Time: 35.7%

NATIONAL WAGE FIGURES (ANNUAL)

Beginning	25th Percentile	Median	Mean	75th Percentile	90th Percentile
$17,420	$23,490	$34,250	$40,820	$49,690	$72,450

Median Wages for Industries Employing Largest Numbers (Annual)

Industry	Median Income
Educational Services	$41,660
Motor Vehicle and Parts Dealers	$39,410
Religious, Grantmaking, Civic, Professional, and Similar Organizations	$38,300
Insurance Carriers and Related Activities	$38,110
Ambulatory Health Care Services	$38,010
Merchant Wholesalers, Durable Goods	$37,650
Rental and Leasing Services	$36,790
Publishing Industries (Except Internet)	$36,640
Social Assistance	$36,110
Specialty Trade Contractors	$35,840

Median Wages for States (Annual)

State	Wage	State	Wage	State	Wage
AK	$28,540	KY	$29,590	NY	$38,320
AL	$41,860	LA	$24,710	OH	$34,820
AR	$25,140	MA	$40,640	OK	$29,210
AZ	$28,160	MD	$31,690	OR	$29,980
CA	$35,500	ME	$36,520	PA	$37,810
CO	$34,270	MI	$34,520	RI	$28,270
CT	$41,020	MN	$40,550	SC	$35,580
DC	$50,770	MO	$36,380	SD	no data
DE	no data	MS	no data	TN	$27,520
FL	$30,500	MT	$29,720	TX	$27,100
GA	$34,120	NC	$32,580	UT	$31,540
HI	$39,960	ND	$27,850	VA	$46,960
IA	$33,180	NE	$39,310	VT	$29,680
ID	$27,520	NH	$35,620	WA	$39,020
IL	$33,110	NJ	$44,280	WI	$35,380
IN	$31,420	NM	$29,380	WV	no data
KS	$31,270	NV	$24,220	WY	$24,480

Median Wages for the Largest Metropolitan Areas (Annual)

Area	Wage	Area	Wage
AZ: Phoenix	$26,280	MI: Detroit	$38,290
CA: Los Angeles	$34,940	MN: Minneapolis	$43,310
CA: Riverside	$27,820	MO: Kansas City	$38,410
CA: Sacramento	$39,790	MO: St. Louis	$37,960
CA: San Diego	$31,210	NV: Las Vegas	$22,280
CA: San Francisco	$42,490	NY: New York	$43,090
CO: Denver	$38,050	OH: Cincinnati	$40,480
DC: Washington	no data	OH: Cleveland	$38,920
FL: Miami	$33,210	OH: Columbus	$34,720
FL: Orlando	$28,930	OR: Portland	$32,910
FL: Tampa	$30,390	PA: Philadelphia	$44,780
GA: Atlanta	$35,020	PA: Pittsburgh	$29,220
IL: Chicago	$33,240	TX: Dallas	$33,970
MA: Boston	$40,850	TX: Houston	$24,750
MD: Baltimore	$37,140	WA: Seattle	$38,970

FACTORS THAT MAY AFFECT EARNINGS

Educational Attainment of Workers and Effect on Earnings

	Percent at Level	Effect on Earnings
Less than High School	2.5%	−49.4%
Some High School	6.2%	−60.5%
High School or Equivalent	20.2%	−25.4%
Some College but No Degree	21.9%	−6.1%
Associate Degree	8.3%	−9.8%
Bachelor's Degree	29.3%	17.2%
Master's Degree	8.3%	77.7%
Doctoral Degree	—	—
First Professional Degree	—	—

Flexibility of Earnings

Average Hours Worked: 32
Workers with a Varying Number of Hours: 9.7%
Workers Earning Some Overtime Pay, Tips, or Commissions: 11.0%
Earnings Benefit of Working Overtime: 36.6%

Gender

	Male	Female
Percent	39.2%	60.8%
Effect on Earnings	6.3%	−21.2%

Union Membership

Percentage Union Members: Insignificant
Earnings Benefit of Union Membership: No significant data available

Veteran Status

Percentage Who Have Been on Active Duty: 8.3%
Earnings Benefit of Veteran Status: 20.9%

43-0000: Office and Administrative Support Occupations

43-1000 Supervisors, Office and Administrative Support Workers

43-1011 First-Line Supervisors/Managers of Office and Administrative Support Workers

Supervise and coordinate the activities of clerical and administrative support workers.

- Education or Training Required: Work experience in a related occupation
- Job Growth: 8.1%
- Annual Openings: 167,000
- Self-Employed: 1.5%
- Part-Time: 16.1%

NATIONAL WAGE FIGURES (ANNUAL)

Beginning	25th Percentile	Median	Mean	75th Percentile	90th Percentile
$26,530	$33,730	$43,510	$46,530	$56,130	$71,340

Median Wages for Industries Employing Largest Numbers (Annual)

Industry	Median Income
Telecommunications	$54,840
Securities, Commodity Contracts, and Other Financial Investments and Related Activities	$53,630
Insurance Carriers and Related Activities	$50,670
Support Activities for Transportation	$50,060
Management of Companies and Enterprises	$49,160
Publishing Industries (Except Internet)	$48,310
Professional, Scientific, and Technical Services	$48,080
Air Transportation	$47,920
Merchant Wholesalers, Durable Goods	$47,630
Construction of Buildings	$45,710

Median Wages for States (Annual)

AK	$45,010	KY	$36,970	NY	$48,840
AL	$37,470	LA	$32,780	OH	$41,880
AR	$34,600	MA	$49,370	OK	$35,880
AZ	$42,390	MD	$45,610	OR	$42,930
CA	$47,380	ME	$36,920	PA	$44,530
CO	$45,160	MI	$44,790	RI	$45,720
CT	$47,790	MN	$44,040	SC	$38,650
DC	$56,410	MO	$43,310	SD	$39,170
DE	$46,050	MS	$37,790	TN	$38,500
FL	$41,210	MT	$34,700	TX	$41,750
GA	$41,180	NC	$40,000	UT	$37,870
HI	$41,540	ND	$37,620	VA	$46,300
IA	$41,480	NE	$40,510	VT	$44,880
ID	$36,400	NH	$42,720	WA	$49,060
IL	$44,870	NJ	$48,730	WI	$42,660
IN	$40,680	NM	$36,010	WV	$33,940
KS	$37,610	NV	$39,760	WY	$35,990

Median Wages for the Largest Metropolitan Areas (Annual)

AZ: Phoenix	$43,780	MI: Detroit	$48,050
CA: Los Angeles	$47,720	MN: Minneapolis	$46,530
CA: Riverside	$43,730	MO: Kansas City	$43,890
CA: Sacramento	$51,860	MO: St. Louis	$45,510
CA: San Diego	$45,610	NV: Las Vegas	$39,410
CA: San Francisco	$51,850	NY: New York	$51,620
CO: Denver	$47,950	OH: Cincinnati	$42,050
DC: Washington	$51,750	OH: Cleveland	$43,810
FL: Miami	$43,530	OH: Columbus	$43,860
FL: Orlando	$40,200	OR: Portland	$45,660
FL: Tampa	$41,850	PA: Philadelphia	$47,500
GA: Atlanta	$43,110	PA: Pittsburgh	$43,990
IL: Chicago	$46,900	TX: Dallas	$44,410
MA: Boston	$51,150	TX: Houston	$44,490
MD: Baltimore	$45,860	WA: Seattle	$51,880

FACTORS THAT MAY AFFECT EARNINGS

Educational Attainment of Workers and Effect on Earnings

	Percent at Level	Effect on Earnings
Less than High School	0.6%	−16.7%
Some High School	3.4%	−22.2%
High School or Equivalent	28.7%	−8.7%
Some College but No Degree	24.9%	−4.6%
Associate Degree	15.0%	−7.1%
Bachelor's Degree	20.1%	16.4%
Master's Degree	5.6%	31.3%
Doctoral Degree	—	—
First Professional Degree	1.2%	29.0%

Flexibility of Earnings

Average Hours Worked: 37

Workers with a Varying Number of Hours: 4.2%

Workers Earning Some Overtime Pay, Tips, or Commissions: 11.1%

Earnings Benefit of Working Overtime: 7.5%

Gender

	Male	Female
Percent	27.8%	72.2%
Effect on Earnings	16.3%	−5.7%

Union Membership

Percentage Union Members: 6.3%

Earnings Benefit of Union Membership: 9.2%

Veteran Status

Percentage Who Have Been on Active Duty: 6.2%

Earnings Benefit of Veteran Status: 22.4%

43-2000 Communications Equipment Operators

43-2011 Switchboard Operators, Including Answering Service

Operate telephone business systems equipment or switchboards to relay incoming, outgoing, and interoffice calls. May supply information to callers and record messages.

- Education or Training Required: Short-term on-the-job training
- Job Growth: –8.8%
- Annual Openings: 34,000
- Self-Employed: 0.2%
- Part-Time: 42.9%

NATIONAL WAGE FIGURES (ANNUAL)

Beginning	25th Percentile	Median	Mean	75th Percentile	90th Percentile
$16,030	$19,020	$22,640	$23,640	$27,640	$33,140

Median Wages for Industries Employing Largest Numbers (Annual)

Industry	Median Income
Federal, State, and Local Government	$27,070
Securities, Commodity Contracts, and Other Financial Investments and Related Activities	$26,820
Professional, Scientific, and Technical Services	$26,420
Insurance Carriers and Related Activities	$25,580
Management of Companies and Enterprises	$24,660
Publishing Industries (Except Internet)	$24,450
Printing and Related Support Activities	$24,440
Telecommunications	$24,440
Educational Services	$24,260
Religious, Grantmaking, Civic, Professional, and Similar Organizations	$23,710

Median Wages for States (Annual)

AK $27,490	KY $21,380	NY $25,660
AL $19,380	LA $18,270	OH $22,580
AR $19,800	MA $25,110	OK $19,590
AZ $22,030	MD $23,600	OR $24,180
CA $24,430	ME $21,660	PA $22,560
CO $23,090	MI $24,020	RI $23,820
CT $26,350	MN $25,100	SC $21,470
DC $29,230	MO $21,580	SD $23,340
DE $22,830	MS $19,050	TN $21,700
FL $21,110	MT $19,250	TX $20,720
GA $21,980	NC $21,990	UT $22,660
HI $27,660	ND $21,230	VA $21,510
IA $22,120	NE $21,700	VT $22,920
ID $21,290	NH $24,850	WA $25,550
IL $22,690	NJ $24,750	WI $23,510
IN $22,030	NM $20,580	WV $18,930
KS $22,250	NV $26,280	WY $21,390

Median Wages for the Largest Metropolitan Areas (Annual)

AZ: Phoenix $22,260	MI: Detroit $25,060
CA: Los Angeles $24,390	MN: Minneapolis $25,950
CA: Riverside $22,260	MO: Kansas City $22,950
CA: Sacramento $24,040	MO: St. Louis $22,200
CA: San Diego $23,370	NV: Las Vegas $27,370
CA: San Francisco $31,350	NY: New York $27,500
CO: Denver $24,300	OH: Cincinnati $23,550
DC: Washington $26,320	OH: Cleveland $24,110
FL: Miami $21,500	OH: Columbus $22,880
FL: Orlando $20,600	OR: Portland $24,750
FL: Tampa $21,890	PA: Philadelphia $24,700
GA: Atlanta $23,710	PA: Pittsburgh $22,630
IL: Chicago $23,130	TX: Dallas $22,530
MA: Boston $25,810	TX: Houston $21,920
MD: Baltimore $23,100	WA: Seattle $26,720

FACTORS THAT MAY AFFECT EARNINGS

Educational Attainment of Workers and Effect on Earnings

	Percent at Level	Effect on Earnings
Less than High School	—	—
Some High School	—	—
High School or Equivalent	41.2%	7.7%
Some College but No Degree	32.4%	5.4%
Associate Degree	10.3%	11.0%
Bachelor's Degree	—	—
Master's Degree	—	—
Doctoral Degree	—	—
First Professional Degree	—	—

Figures do not total 100% because some levels have a very small sample size.

Flexibility of Earnings

Average Hours Worked: 31
Workers with a Varying Number of Hours: 3.5%
Workers Earning Some Overtime Pay, Tips, or Commissions: 9.6%
Earnings Benefit of Working Overtime: 18.7%

Gender

	Male	Female
Percent	11.9%	88.1%
Effect on Earnings	8.2%	−2.6%

Union Membership

Percentage Union Members: 8.2%
Earnings Benefit of Union Membership: 29.3%

Veteran Status

Percentage Who Have Been on Active Duty: 4.4%
Earnings Benefit of Veteran Status: 29.3%

43-2021 Telephone Operators

Provide information by accessing alphabetical and geographical directories. Assist customers with special billing requests, such as charges to a third party and credits or refunds for incorrectly dialed numbers or bad connections. May handle emergency calls and assist children or people with physical disabilities to make telephone calls.

- Education or Training Required: Short-term on-the-job training
- Job Growth: –35.7%
- Annual Openings: 3,000
- Self-Employed: 0.4%
- Part-Time: 12.5%

NATIONAL WAGE FIGURES (ANNUAL)

Beginning	25th Percentile	Median	Mean	75th Percentile	90th Percentile
$17,540	$22,180	$34,140	$32,710	$42,830	$46,670

Median Wages for Industries Employing Largest Numbers (Annual)

Industry	Median Income
Telecommunications	$39,010
Merchant Wholesalers, Durable Goods	$31,680
Federal, State, and Local Government	$30,420
Hospitals	$30,030
Insurance Carriers and Related Activities	$29,470
Educational Services	$27,190
Credit Intermediation and Related Activities	$27,150
Accommodation	$26,500
Religious, Grantmaking, Civic, Professional, and Similar Organizations	$25,940
Management of Companies and Enterprises	$24,230

Median Wages for States (Annual)

State	Wage	State	Wage	State	Wage
AK	$29,620	KY	no data	NY	$40,890
AL	$37,680	LA	$22,180	OH	no data
AR	no data	MA	no data	OK	$38,530
AZ	$28,120	MD	$27,520	OR	no data
CA	$38,780	ME	no data	PA	$30,730
CO	$22,440	MI	no data	RI	$38,690
CT	$28,300	MN	$40,360	SC	$21,370
DC	no data	MO	$27,550	SD	no data
DE	$29,210	MS	no data	TN	$18,770
FL	$22,550	MT	no data	TX	$39,300
GA	$23,240	NC	no data	UT	$28,760
HI	no data	ND	no data	VA	$38,950
IA	no data	NE	no data	VT	no data
ID	no data	NH	no data	WA	$24,840
IL	$41,530	NJ	$39,550	WI	no data
IN	$41,520	NM	no data	WV	no data
KS	no data	NV	no data	WY	no data

Median Wages for the Largest Metropolitan Areas (Annual)

Area	Wage	Area	Wage
AZ: Phoenix	no data	MI: Detroit	no data
CA: Los Angeles	$40,910	MN: Minneapolis	$40,810
CA: Riverside	no data	MO: Kansas City	no data
CA: Sacramento	no data	MO: St. Louis	$23,930
CA: San Diego	no data	NV: Las Vegas	no data
CA: San Francisco	$27,210	NY: New York	$40,120
CO: Denver	$21,610	OH: Cincinnati	no data
DC: Washington	$22,910	OH: Cleveland	no data
FL: Miami	$23,060	OH: Columbus	no data
FL: Orlando	$25,880	OR: Portland	no data
FL: Tampa	no data	PA: Philadelphia	$34,370
GA: Atlanta	$29,860	PA: Pittsburgh	$22,530
IL: Chicago	$42,200	TX: Dallas	no data
MA: Boston	$24,360	TX: Houston	no data
MD: Baltimore	$26,510	WA: Seattle	no data

FACTORS THAT MAY AFFECT EARNINGS

Educational Attainment of Workers and Effect on Earnings

	Percent at Level	Effect on Earnings
Less than High School	—	—
Some High School	—	—
High School or Equivalent	29.9%	2.5%
Some College but No Degree	38.8%	–9.0%
Associate Degree	14.9%	15.3%
Bachelor's Degree	10.4%	26.6%
Master's Degree	—	—
Doctoral Degree	—	—
First Professional Degree	—	—

Figures do not total 100% because some levels have a very small sample size.

Flexibility of Earnings

Average Hours Worked: 32
Workers with a Varying Number of Hours: 2.0%
Workers Earning Some Overtime Pay, Tips, or Commissions: 5.4%
Earnings Benefit of Working Overtime: 18.7%

Gender

	Male	Female
Percent	24.6%	75.4%
Effect on Earnings	8.2%	–2.6%

Union Membership

Percentage Union Members: 14.9%
Earnings Benefit of Union Membership: 35.1%

Veteran Status

Percentage Who Have Been on Active Duty: 4.4%
Earnings Benefit of Veteran Status: 29.3%

43-2099 Communications Equipment Operators, All Other

All communications equipment operators not listed separately.

- Education or Training Required: Short-term on-the-job training
- Job Growth: −10.8%
- Annual Openings: 1,000
- Self-Employed: 0.0%
- Part-Time: 28.0%

NATIONAL WAGE FIGURES (ANNUAL)

Beginning	25th Percentile	Median	Mean	75th Percentile	90th Percentile
$16,440	$20,880	$31,680	$33,130	$41,410	$51,120

Median Wages for Industries Employing Largest Numbers (Annual)

Industry	Median Income
Professional, Scientific, and Technical Services	$47,710
Insurance Carriers and Related Activities	$47,000
Management of Companies and Enterprises	$44,550
Credit Intermediation and Related Activities	$37,370
Federal, State, and Local Government	$36,900
Educational Services	$33,270
Accommodation	$32,050
Securities, Commodity Contracts, and Other Financial Investments and Related Activities	$30,780
Administrative and Support Services	$28,620
Hospitals	$28,470

Median Wages for States (Annual)

State		State		State	
AK	no data	KY	$33,750	NY	no data
AL	no data	LA	$29,380	OH	$36,380
AR	no data	MA	no data	OK	no data
AZ	$17,210	MD	$43,740	OR	no data
CA	$44,260	ME	no data	PA	$43,180
CO	$37,480	MI	no data	RI	no data
CT	$35,170	MN	no data	SC	$31,160
DC	no data	MO	$35,020	SD	no data
DE	no data	MS	no data	TN	$31,350
FL	$30,610	MT	no data	TX	$39,410
GA	$29,690	NC	$35,740	UT	no data
HI	no data	ND	no data	VA	$40,770
IA	$30,430	NE	$34,750	VT	no data
ID	no data	NH	no data	WA	$36,450
IL	$35,850	NJ	$35,090	WI	$31,490
IN	$32,690	NM	no data	WV	no data
KS	no data	NV	no data	WY	no data

Median Wages for the Largest Metropolitan Areas (Annual)

Area		Area	
AZ: Phoenix	$16,970	MI: Detroit	no data
CA: Los Angeles	$47,470	MN: Minneapolis	no data
CA: Riverside	no data	MO: Kansas City	no data
CA: Sacramento	no data	MO: St. Louis	$36,800
CA: San Diego	no data	NV: Las Vegas	no data
CA: San Francisco	no data	NY: New York	$40,590
CO: Denver	no data	OH: Cincinnati	no data
DC: Washington	$48,560	OH: Cleveland	no data
FL: Miami	$35,900	OH: Columbus	no data
FL: Orlando	no data	OR: Portland	no data
FL: Tampa	no data	PA: Philadelphia	$37,300
GA: Atlanta	$32,920	PA: Pittsburgh	no data
IL: Chicago	$36,900	TX: Dallas	no data
MA: Boston	no data	TX: Houston	no data
MD: Baltimore	no data	WA: Seattle	$37,540

FACTORS THAT MAY AFFECT EARNINGS

Educational Attainment of Workers and Effect on Earnings

Figures are based on a group of occupations: Communications Equipment Operators

	Percent at Level	Effect on Earnings
Less than High School	—	—
Some High School	7.1%	−45.0%
High School or Equivalent	32.9%	3.9%
Some College but No Degree	35.0%	−3.7%
Associate Degree	13.6%	5.2%
Bachelor's Degree	9.3%	28.3%
Master's Degree	—	—
Doctoral Degree	—	—
First Professional Degree	—	—

Flexibility of Earnings

Average Hours Worked: 34
Workers with a Varying Number of Hours: 6.1%
Workers Earning Some Overtime Pay, Tips, or Commissions: 25.0%
Earnings Benefit of Working Overtime: 18.7%

Gender

	Male	Female
Percent	33.3%	66.7%
Effect on Earnings	8.2%	−2.6%

Union Membership

Percentage Union Members: 25.0%
Earnings Benefit of Union Membership: 29.3%

Veteran Status

Percentage Who Have Been on Active Duty: 4.4%
Earnings Benefit of Veteran Status: 29.3%

43-3000 Financial Clerks

43-3011 Bill and Account Collectors

Locate and notify customers of delinquent accounts by mail, telephone, or personal visit to solicit payment. Duties include receiving payment and posting amount to customer's account, preparing statements to credit department if customer fails to respond, initiating repossession proceedings or service disconnection, and keeping records of collection and status of accounts.

- Education or Training Required: Short-term on-the-job training
- Job Growth: 21.4%
- Annual Openings: 85,000
- Self-Employed: 1.1%
- Part-Time: 20.4%

NATIONAL WAGE FIGURES (ANNUAL)

Beginning	25th Percentile	Median	Mean	75th Percentile	90th Percentile
$19,980	$23,900	$29,050	$30,640	$35,640	$43,930

Median Wages for Industries Employing Largest Numbers (Annual)

Industry	Median Income
Utilities	$36,200
Telecommunications	$34,370
Federal, State, and Local Government	$34,170
Wholesale Electronic Markets and Agents and Brokers	$32,230
Publishing Industries (Except Internet)	$32,000
Nursing and Residential Care Facilities	$31,980
Merchant Wholesalers, Durable Goods	$31,970
Insurance Carriers and Related Activities	$31,610
Educational Services	$31,490
Merchant Wholesalers, Nondurable Goods	$31,170

Median Wages for States (Annual)

AK	$35,610	KY	$27,040	NY	$30,260
AL	$23,690	LA	$24,960	OH	$27,470
AR	$23,830	MA	$34,650	OK	$26,010
AZ	$28,390	MD	$31,220	OR	$29,980
CA	$33,570	ME	$28,540	PA	$27,730
CO	$30,690	MI	$31,880	RI	$32,260
CT	$35,420	MN	$30,140	SC	$27,180
DC	$41,590	MO	$25,900	SD	$24,590
DE	$31,620	MS	$22,580	TN	$28,390
FL	$27,650	MT	$26,350	TX	$29,180
GA	$28,120	NC	$28,390	UT	$27,440
HI	$30,370	ND	$23,510	VA	$29,670
IA	$27,670	NE	$26,350	VT	$29,350
ID	$26,270	NH	$28,690	WA	$33,950
IL	$29,630	NJ	$33,290	WI	$28,280
IN	$28,020	NM	$25,210	WV	$23,870
KS	$25,090	NV	$29,060	WY	$23,210

Median Wages for the Largest Metropolitan Areas (Annual)

AZ: Phoenix	$29,500	MI: Detroit	$34,030
CA: Los Angeles	$33,600	MN: Minneapolis	$31,260
CA: Riverside	$29,960	MO: Kansas City	$26,420
CA: Sacramento	$34,050	MO: St. Louis	$26,820
CA: San Diego	$32,290	NV: Las Vegas	$28,870
CA: San Francisco	$40,190	NY: New York	$34,130
CO: Denver	$30,910	OH: Cincinnati	$28,830
DC: Washington	$36,320	OH: Cleveland	$26,850
FL: Miami	$28,540	OH: Columbus	$26,980
FL: Orlando	$27,840	OR: Portland	$30,770
FL: Tampa	$28,250	PA: Philadelphia	$31,100
GA: Atlanta	$29,000	PA: Pittsburgh	$27,300
IL: Chicago	$31,120	TX: Dallas	$30,880
MA: Boston	$34,710	TX: Houston	$30,830
MD: Baltimore	$30,720	WA: Seattle	$35,060

FACTORS THAT MAY AFFECT EARNINGS

Educational Attainment of Workers and Effect on Earnings

	Percent at Level	Effect on Earnings
Less than High School	—	—
Some High School	6.0%	−20.9%
High School or Equivalent	29.0%	−12.6%
Some College but No Degree	31.0%	−5.8%
Associate Degree	12.9%	12.5%
Bachelor's Degree	16.9%	16.7%
Master's Degree	3.6%	66.7%
Doctoral Degree	—	—
First Professional Degree	—	—

Flexibility of Earnings

Average Hours Worked: 35
Workers with a Varying Number of Hours: 3.9%
Workers Earning Some Overtime Pay, Tips, or Commissions: 18.4%
Earnings Benefit of Working Overtime: 11.9%

Gender

	Male	Female
Percent	37.8%	62.2%
Effect on Earnings	5.9%	−5.2%

Union Membership

Percentage Union Members: Insignificant
Earnings Benefit of Union Membership: No significant data available

Veteran Status

Percentage Who Have Been on Active Duty: Insignificant
Earnings Benefit of Veteran Status: No significant data available

43-3021 Billing and Posting Clerks and Machine Operators

Compile, compute, and record billing, accounting, statistical, and other numerical data for billing purposes. Prepare billing invoices for services rendered or for delivery or shipment of goods.

- Education or Training Required: Moderate-term on-the-job training
- Job Growth: 3.4%
- Annual Openings: 70,000
- Self-Employed: 2.6%
- Part-Time: 35.4%

NATIONAL WAGE FIGURES (ANNUAL)

Beginning	25th Percentile	Median	Mean	75th Percentile	90th Percentile
$20,140	$24,080	$28,850	$29,930	$34,970	$41,750

Median Wages for Industries Employing Largest Numbers (Annual)

Industry	Median Income
Utilities	$30,720
Insurance Carriers and Related Activities	$30,660
Management of Companies and Enterprises	$29,940
Professional, Scientific, and Technical Services	$29,890
Educational Services	$29,520
Nursing and Residential Care Facilities	$29,300
Support Activities for Transportation	$29,280
Credit Intermediation and Related Activities	$29,210
Fabricated Metal Product Manufacturing	$29,190
Miscellaneous Manufacturing	$29,170

Median Wages for States (Annual)

AK	$34,320	KY	$26,220	NY	$31,580
AL	$24,940	LA	$24,190	OH	$27,730
AR	$23,450	MA	$32,010	OK	$25,070
AZ	$28,780	MD	$31,980	OR	$30,290
CA	$31,360	ME	$26,380	PA	$27,600
CO	$31,190	MI	$30,620	RI	$30,210
CT	$34,270	MN	$31,470	SC	$26,460
DC	$36,200	MO	$26,820	SD	$22,020
DE	$31,060	MS	$23,940	TN	$26,670
FL	$27,640	MT	$23,010	TX	$27,420
GA	$28,480	NC	$28,060	UT	$26,700
HI	$30,490	ND	$25,590	VA	$28,870
IA	$27,350	NE	$26,800	VT	$27,930
ID	$26,240	NH	$29,740	WA	$31,860
IL	$30,430	NJ	$33,230	WI	$28,430
IN	$27,340	NM	$24,990	WV	$23,170
KS	$27,100	NV	$29,820	WY	$23,780

Median Wages for the Largest Metropolitan Areas (Annual)

AZ: Phoenix	$29,640	MI: Detroit	$32,550
CA: Los Angeles	$31,270	MN: Minneapolis	$32,770
CA: Riverside	$29,190	MO: Kansas City	$30,660
CA: Sacramento	$31,550	MO: St. Louis	$27,860
CA: San Diego	$30,360	NV: Las Vegas	$30,390
CA: San Francisco	$37,830	NY: New York	$34,270
CO: Denver	$33,240	OH: Cincinnati	$29,100
DC: Washington	$34,390	OH: Cleveland	$29,510
FL: Miami	$28,550	OH: Columbus	$28,580
FL: Orlando	$28,060	OR: Portland	$30,750
FL: Tampa	$27,850	PA: Philadelphia	$30,920
GA: Atlanta	$30,610	PA: Pittsburgh	$27,010
IL: Chicago	$31,900	TX: Dallas	$29,970
MA: Boston	$32,560	TX: Houston	$29,900
MD: Baltimore	$31,620	WA: Seattle	$34,310

FACTORS THAT MAY AFFECT EARNINGS

Educational Attainment of Workers and Effect on Earnings

	Percent at Level	Effect on Earnings
Less than High School	—	—
Some High School	3.0%	−19.3%
High School or Equivalent	37.2%	−5.7%
Some College but No Degree	25.2%	−9.8%
Associate Degree	16.5%	−6.1%
Bachelor's Degree	14.5%	23.5%
Master's Degree	2.5%	99.3%
Doctoral Degree	—	—
First Professional Degree	—	—

Flexibility of Earnings

Average Hours Worked: 34
Workers with a Varying Number of Hours: 3.4%
Workers Earning Some Overtime Pay, Tips, or Commissions: 9.4%
Earnings Benefit of Working Overtime: 28.0%

Gender

	Male	Female
Percent	11.9%	88.1%
Effect on Earnings	—	−1.3%

Union Membership

Percentage Union Members: 5.8%
Earnings Benefit of Union Membership: 6.0%

Veteran Status

Percentage Who Have Been on Active Duty: Insignificant
Earnings Benefit of Veteran Status: No significant data available

43-3031 Bookkeeping, Accounting, and Auditing Clerks

Compute, classify, and record numerical data to keep financial records complete. Perform any combination of routine calculating, posting, and verifying duties to obtain primary financial data for use in maintaining accounting records. May also check the accuracy of figures, calculations, and postings pertaining to business transactions recorded by other workers.

- Education or Training Required: Moderate-term on-the-job training
- Job Growth: 5.9%
- Annual Openings: 291,000
- Self-Employed: 7.0%
- Part-Time: 49.6%

NATIONAL WAGE FIGURES (ANNUAL)

Beginning	25th Percentile	Median	Mean	75th Percentile	90th Percentile
$19,760	$24,540	$30,560	$31,780	$37,780	$46,020

Median Wages for Industries Employing Largest Numbers (Annual)

Industry	Median Income
Securities, Commodity Contracts, and Other Financial Investments and Related Activities	$35,210
Federal, State, and Local Government	$33,380
Construction of Buildings	$32,400
Insurance Carriers and Related Activities	$32,340
Professional, Scientific, and Technical Services	$32,050
Real Estate	$31,710
Specialty Trade Contractors	$31,650
Fabricated Metal Product Manufacturing	$31,610
Ambulatory Health Care Services	$31,560
Merchant Wholesalers, Durable Goods	$31,490

Median Wages for States (Annual)

AK	$36,220	KY	$27,290	NY	$33,300
AL	$26,750	LA	$27,070	OH	$29,710
AR	$26,290	MA	$35,580	OK	$26,580
AZ	$30,020	MD	$34,710	OR	$30,580
CA	$34,810	ME	$28,810	PA	$29,120
CO	$32,290	MI	$31,050	RI	$33,600
CT	$37,230	MN	$32,010	SC	$27,760
DC	$39,390	MO	$28,300	SD	$23,690
DE	$32,610	MS	$27,820	TN	$28,040
FL	$29,000	MT	$26,060	TX	$28,810
GA	$29,120	NC	$28,920	UT	$27,720
HI	$31,140	ND	$25,670	VA	$32,170
IA	$27,350	NE	$26,680	VT	$29,970
ID	$26,910	NH	$31,710	WA	$33,020
IL	$30,800	NJ	$35,680	WI	$29,070
IN	$28,690	NM	$27,250	WV	$24,560
KS	$26,940	NV	$29,520	WY	$25,820

Median Wages for the Largest Metropolitan Areas (Annual)

AZ: Phoenix	$30,930	MI: Detroit	$33,290
CA: Los Angeles	$34,710	MN: Minneapolis	$34,230
CA: Riverside	$32,610	MO: Kansas City	$31,210
CA: Sacramento	$34,570	MO: St. Louis	$30,430
CA: San Diego	$34,650	NV: Las Vegas	$29,360
CA: San Francisco	$39,110	NY: New York	$36,130
CO: Denver	$33,970	OH: Cincinnati	$30,780
DC: Washington	$37,130	OH: Cleveland	$30,460
FL: Miami	$30,770	OH: Columbus	$32,660
FL: Orlando	$28,540	OR: Portland	$32,670
FL: Tampa	$28,380	PA: Philadelphia	$33,370
GA: Atlanta	$31,380	PA: Pittsburgh	$27,820
IL: Chicago	$32,260	TX: Dallas	$31,240
MA: Boston	$36,390	TX: Houston	$31,000
MD: Baltimore	$35,070	WA: Seattle	$34,880

FACTORS THAT MAY AFFECT EARNINGS

Educational Attainment of Workers and Effect on Earnings

	Percent at Level	Effect on Earnings
Less than High School	1.1%	−49.5%
Some High School	3.3%	−20.7%
High School or Equivalent	31.4%	−1.9%
Some College but No Degree	29.0%	6.5%
Associate Degree	16.4%	−6.4%
Bachelor's Degree	15.8%	4.0%
Master's Degree	2.2%	11.6%
Doctoral Degree	—	—
First Professional Degree	0.6%	18.9%

Flexibility of Earnings

Average Hours Worked: 30
Workers with a Varying Number of Hours: 8.2%
Workers Earning Some Overtime Pay, Tips, or Commissions: 10.4%
Earnings Benefit of Working Overtime: 3.4%

Gender

	Male	Female
Percent	9.7%	90.3%
Effect on Earnings	3.9%	−0.3%

Union Membership

Percentage Union Members: Insignificant
Earnings Benefit of Union Membership: No significant data available

Veteran Status

Percentage Who Have Been on Active Duty: Insignificant
Earnings Benefit of Veteran Status: No significant data available

43-3041 Gaming Cage Workers

In a gaming establishment, conduct financial transactions for patrons. May reconcile daily summaries of transactions to balance books. Accept patron's credit application and verify credit references to provide check-cashing authorization or to establish house credit accounts. May sell gambling chips, tokens, or tickets to patrons or to other workers for resale to patrons. May convert gaming chips, tokens, or tickets to currency upon patron's request. May use a cash register or computer to record transaction.

- Education or Training Required: Short-term on-the-job training
- Job Growth: 17.0%
- Annual Openings: 2,000
- Self-Employed: 0.0%
- Part-Time: 20.0%

NATIONAL WAGE FIGURES (ANNUAL)

Beginning	25th Percentile	Median	Mean	75th Percentile	90th Percentile
$17,030	$19,740	$23,150	$24,170	$28,120	$33,120

Median Wages for Industries Employing Largest Numbers (Annual)

Industry	Median Income
Accommodation	$24,860
Performing Arts, Spectator Sports, and Related Industries	$24,040
Amusement, Gambling, and Recreation Industries	$22,670
Federal, State, and Local Government	$22,390

Median Wages for States (Annual)

State	Wage	State	Wage	State	Wage
AK	no data	KY	no data	NY	$21,090
AL	no data	LA	$20,730	OH	no data
AR	no data	MA	no data	OK	$19,480
AZ	$22,470	MD	$27,280	OR	no data
CA	$24,350	ME	no data	PA	no data
CO	$26,890	MI	no data	RI	no data
CT	no data	MN	no data	SC	no data
DC	no data	MO	$22,560	SD	$18,010
DE	no data	MS	$22,420	TN	no data
FL	$21,370	MT	$16,890	TX	no data
GA	no data	NC	no data	UT	no data
HI	no data	ND	no data	VA	no data
IA	$21,440	NE	no data	VT	no data
ID	no data	NH	no data	WA	$22,360
IL	$25,550	NJ	no data	WI	$22,190
IN	$23,000	NM	$20,990	WV	no data
KS	no data	NV	$24,800	WY	no data

Median Wages for the Largest Metropolitan Areas (Annual)

Area	Wage	Area	Wage
AZ: Phoenix	$22,470	MI: Detroit	no data
CA: Los Angeles	no data	MN: Minneapolis	no data
CA: Riverside	$21,660	MO: Kansas City	$21,570
CA: Sacramento	$23,770	MO: St. Louis	no data
CA: San Diego	$26,540	NV: Las Vegas	$26,730
CA: San Francisco	$26,990	NY: New York	no data
CO: Denver	$28,500	OH: Cincinnati	no data
DC: Washington	no data	OH: Cleveland	no data
FL: Miami	no data	OH: Columbus	no data
FL: Orlando	no data	OR: Portland	no data
FL: Tampa	no data	PA: Philadelphia	no data
GA: Atlanta	no data	PA: Pittsburgh	no data
IL: Chicago	$23,730	TX: Dallas	no data
MA: Boston	no data	TX: Houston	no data
MD: Baltimore	no data	WA: Seattle	$23,180

FACTORS THAT MAY AFFECT EARNINGS

Educational Attainment of Workers and Effect on Earnings

	Percent at Level	Effect on Earnings
Less than High School	—	—
Some High School	—	—
High School or Equivalent	41.4%	14.8%
Some College but No Degree	37.9%	−13.5%
Associate Degree	—	—
Bachelor's Degree	—	—
Master's Degree	—	—
Doctoral Degree	—	—
First Professional Degree	—	—

Figures do not total 100% because some levels have a very small sample size.

Flexibility of Earnings

Average Hours Worked: 36
Workers with a Varying Number of Hours: 4.5%
Workers Earning Some Overtime Pay, Tips, or Commissions: 25.8%
Earnings Benefit of Working Overtime: 11.9%

Gender

	Male	Female
Percent	22.4%	77.6%
Effect on Earnings	8.2%	−2.6%

Union Membership

Percentage Union Members: 9.7%
Earnings Benefit of Union Membership: 24.2%

Veteran Status

Percentage Who Have Been on Active Duty: Insignificant
Earnings Benefit of Veteran Status: No significant data available

43-3051 Payroll and Timekeeping Clerks

Compile and post employee time and payroll data. May compute employees' time worked, production, and commission. May compute and post wages and deductions. May prepare paychecks.

- Education or Training Required: Moderate-term on-the-job training
- Job Growth: 17.3%
- Annual Openings: 36,000
- Self-Employed: 1.1%
- Part-Time: 25.6%

NATIONAL WAGE FIGURES (ANNUAL)

Beginning	25th Percentile	Median	Mean	75th Percentile	90th Percentile
$21,150	$26,190	$32,400	$33,140	$39,420	$46,500

Median Wages for Industries Employing Largest Numbers (Annual)

Industry	Median Income
Insurance Carriers and Related Activities	$35,460
Real Estate	$34,910
Federal, State, and Local Government	$34,650
Professional, Scientific, and Technical Services	$34,230
Management of Companies and Enterprises	$33,880
Educational Services	$33,570
Construction of Buildings	$33,400
Transportation Equipment Manufacturing	$33,360
Merchant Wholesalers, Nondurable Goods	$33,250
Hospitals	$33,010

Median Wages for States (Annual)

AK $39,100	KY $29,780	NY $34,220
AL $27,950	LA $27,040	OH $31,760
AR $25,530	MA $36,960	OK $27,610
AZ $31,400	MD $35,810	OR $33,500
CA $37,070	ME $29,090	PA $30,870
CO $35,630	MI $32,550	RI.............. $33,550
CT $38,610	MN $34,660	SC.............. $28,760
DC $42,630	MO $30,350	SD $25,970
DE $33,800	MS $27,160	TN $29,380
FL $30,700	MT $26,760	TX $30,030
GA $31,270	NC $30,020	UT $30,790
HI $35,170	ND $27,480	VA $33,850
IA $30,100	NE $30,880	VT $29,680
ID $27,870	NH $32,870	WA $37,260
IL $32,930	NJ $37,320	WI $32,310
IN $30,890	NM $26,500	WV $26,760
KS $29,670	NV $31,800	WY $28,180

Median Wages for the Largest Metropolitan Areas (Annual)

AZ: Phoenix $32,080	MI: Detroit $34,170
CA: Los Angeles $37,290	MN: Minneapolis $36,450
CA: Riverside $33,630	MO: Kansas City $33,600
CA: Sacramento $38,180	MO: St. Louis $32,940
CA: San Diego $36,890	NV: Las Vegas $31,630
CA: San Francisco $43,760	NY: New York $36,240
CO: Denver $37,160	OH: Cincinnati $32,190
DC: Washington $40,020	OH: Cleveland $34,620
FL: Miami $33,150	OH: Columbus $33,720
FL: Orlando $31,390	OR: Portland $35,560
FL: Tampa $28,920	PA: Philadelphia $34,670
GA: Atlanta $34,030	PA: Pittsburgh $31,240
IL: Chicago $34,250	TX: Dallas $32,670
MA: Boston $37,960	TX: Houston $32,390
MD: Baltimore $36,350	WA: Seattle $39,470

FACTORS THAT MAY AFFECT EARNINGS

Educational Attainment of Workers and Effect on Earnings

	Percent at Level	Effect on Earnings
Less than High School	—	—
Some High School	—	—
High School or Equivalent	33.7%	−13.0%
Some College but No Degree	30.8%	−5.8%
Associate Degree	17.8%	5.2%
Bachelor's Degree	14.4%	28.9%
Master's Degree	—	—
Doctoral Degree	—	—
First Professional Degree	—	—

Flexibility of Earnings

Average Hours Worked: 35
Workers with a Varying Number of Hours: 3.2%
Workers Earning Some Overtime Pay, Tips, or Commissions: 15.5%
Earnings Benefit of Working Overtime: 11.9%

Gender

	Male	Female
Percent	7.6%	92.4%
Effect on Earnings	—	−2.0%

Union Membership

Percentage Union Members: 10.3%
Earnings Benefit of Union Membership: 23.4%

Veteran Status

Percentage Who Have Been on Active Duty: Insignificant
Earnings Benefit of Veteran Status: No significant data available

43-3061 Procurement Clerks

Compile information and records to draw up purchase orders for procurement of materials and services.

- Education or Training Required: Short-term on-the-job training
- Job Growth: –2.7%
- Annual Openings: 10,000
- Self-Employed: 0.0%
- Part-Time: 22.2%

NATIONAL WAGE FIGURES (ANNUAL)

Beginning	25th Percentile	Median	Mean	75th Percentile	90th Percentile
$21,130	$26,320	$33,100	$33,540	$40,370	$47,180

Median Wages for Industries Employing Largest Numbers (Annual)

Industry	Median Income
Transportation Equipment Manufacturing	$38,150
Federal, State, and Local Government	$38,100
Professional, Scientific, and Technical Services	$37,230
Computer and Electronic Product Manufacturing	$35,610
Credit Intermediation and Related Activities	$35,570
Chemical Manufacturing	$35,510
Construction of Buildings	$34,570
Management of Companies and Enterprises	$33,860
Administrative and Support Services	$32,800
Electrical Equipment, Appliance, and Component Manufacturing	$31,910

Median Wages for States (Annual)

AK $41,650	KY $32,410	NY $33,690
AL $31,790	LA $29,010	OH $30,620
AR $30,550	MA $35,560	OK $32,970
AZ $33,080	MD $36,710	OR $33,880
CA $36,400	ME $34,610	PA $35,270
CO $35,100	MI $33,290	RI $31,660
CT $38,920	MN $30,870	SC.............. $29,030
DC $42,420	MO $27,730	SD $25,830
DE $38,380	MS $31,870	TN $30,370
FL $30,200	MT $30,090	TX $30,700
GA............ $32,670	NC $32,680	UT $30,910
HI $37,820	ND $31,750	VA $36,840
IA $31,010	NE $29,080	VT $32,860
ID $32,060	NH $29,690	WA $35,050
IL $34,310	NJ $36,560	WI $31,040
IN $29,440	NM $34,990	WV $30,330
KS $30,390	NV $32,560	WY $29,400

Median Wages for the Largest Metropolitan Areas (Annual)

AZ: Phoenix............ $33,270	MI: Detroit $34,360
CA: Los Angeles $34,950	MN: Minneapolis $32,780
CA: Riverside $34,170	MO: Kansas City........ $31,670
CA: Sacramento $34,900	MO: St. Louis............ $30,420
CA: San Diego $38,270	NV: Las Vegas $32,930
CA: San Francisco.... $42,670	NY: New York............ $36,120
CO: Denver $36,570	OH: Cincinnati........... $31,530
DC: Washington $40,360	OH: Cleveland $29,650
FL: Miami $29,500	OH: Columbus $36,550
FL: Orlando $30,680	OR: Portland $34,610
FL: Tampa $31,480	PA: Philadelphia $37,440
GA: Atlanta $32,730	PA: Pittsburgh $31,410
IL: Chicago $34,790	TX: Dallas $34,050
MA: Boston $38,270	TX: Houston $29,850
MD: Baltimore $37,310	WA: Seattle $35,000

FACTORS THAT MAY AFFECT EARNINGS

Educational Attainment of Workers and Effect on Earnings

	Percent at Level	Effect on Earnings
Less than High School	—	—
Some High School	—	—
High School or Equivalent	28.2%	–31.9%
Some College but No Degree	30.8%	2.3%
Associate Degree	—	—
Bachelor's Degree	25.6%	40.7%
Master's Degree	—	—
Doctoral Degree	—	—
First Professional Degree	—	—

Figures do not total 100% because some levels have a very small sample size.

Flexibility of Earnings

Average Hours Worked: 36
Workers with a Varying Number of Hours: 3.8%
Workers Earning Some Overtime Pay, Tips, or Commissions: 9.8%
Earnings Benefit of Working Overtime: 11.9%

Gender

	Male	Female
Percent	21.1%	78.9%
Effect on Earnings	8.2%	–2.6%

Union Membership

Percentage Union Members: 9.8%
Earnings Benefit of Union Membership: 24.2%

Veteran Status

Percentage Who Have Been on Active Duty: Insignificant
Earnings Benefit of Veteran Status: No significant data available

43-3071 Tellers

Receive and pay out money. Keep records of money and negotiable instruments involved in a financial institution's various transactions.

- Education or Training Required: Short-term on-the-job training
- Job Growth: 6.8%
- Annual Openings: 108,000
- Self-Employed: 0.0%
- Part-Time: 36.1%

NATIONAL WAGE FIGURES (ANNUAL)

Beginning	25th Percentile	Median	Mean	75th Percentile	90th Percentile
$16,770	$19,300	$22,140	$22,810	$25,880	$30,020

Median Wages for Industries Employing Largest Numbers (Annual)

Industry	Median Income
Religious, Grantmaking, Civic, Professional, and Similar Organizations	$29,450
Federal, State, and Local Government	$28,780
Air Transportation	$27,010
Monetary Authorities—Central Bank	$26,530
Educational Services	$26,470
Hospitals	$25,470
Insurance Carriers and Related Activities	$24,490
Real Estate	$23,720
Securities, Commodity Contracts, and Other Financial Investments and Related Activities	$23,270
Administrative and Support Services	$23,160

Median Wages for States (Annual)

AK	$24,970	KY	$20,210	NY	$22,380
AL	$19,640	LA	$19,860	OH	$21,820
AR	$19,550	MA	$25,780	OK	$19,670
AZ	$22,690	MD	$24,130	OR	$22,190
CA	$24,320	ME	$21,240	PA	$20,700
CO	$24,110	MI	$22,100	RI	$23,950
CT	$25,380	MN	$22,220	SC	$21,860
DC	$24,800	MO	$20,420	SD	$21,110
DE	$24,040	MS	$20,590	TN	$21,680
FL	$22,710	MT	$20,870	TX	$21,820
GA	$22,130	NC	$22,570	UT	$20,510
HI	$22,330	ND	$20,470	VA	$22,390
IA	$22,360	NE	$20,700	VT	$23,190
ID	$20,020	NH	$22,880	WA	$23,130
IL	$21,460	NJ	$22,550	WI	$21,580
IN	$21,040	NM	$20,040	WV	$18,170
KS	$20,320	NV	$22,130	WY	$20,260

Median Wages for the Largest Metropolitan Areas (Annual)

AZ: Phoenix	$22,990	MI: Detroit	$22,440
CA: Los Angeles	$24,320	MN: Minneapolis	$23,120
CA: Riverside	$23,390	MO: Kansas City	$21,450
CA: Sacramento	$23,920	MO: St. Louis	$21,970
CA: San Diego	$24,400	NV: Las Vegas	$21,960
CA: San Francisco	$26,850	NY: New York	$22,770
CO: Denver	$25,500	OH: Cincinnati	$21,730
DC: Washington	$24,750	OH: Cleveland	$24,750
FL: Miami	$23,020	OH: Columbus	$22,200
FL: Orlando	$22,220	OR: Portland	$22,750
FL: Tampa	$22,960	PA: Philadelphia	$21,410
GA: Atlanta	$23,280	PA: Pittsburgh	$20,400
IL: Chicago	$22,040	TX: Dallas	$22,970
MA: Boston	$26,070	TX: Houston	$23,490
MD: Baltimore	$23,290	WA: Seattle	$23,740

FACTORS THAT MAY AFFECT EARNINGS

Educational Attainment of Workers and Effect on Earnings

	Percent at Level	Effect on Earnings
Less than High School	—	—
Some High School	3.6%	−43.9%
High School or Equivalent	36.1%	8.1%
Some College but No Degree	34.1%	−11.5%
Associate Degree	12.4%	−4.5%
Bachelor's Degree	12.2%	23.6%
Master's Degree	1.4%	20.7%
Doctoral Degree	—	—
First Professional Degree	—	—

Flexibility of Earnings

Average Hours Worked: 33
Workers with a Varying Number of Hours: 3.8%
Workers Earning Some Overtime Pay, Tips, or Commissions: 6.4%
Earnings Benefit of Working Overtime: 11.9%

Gender

	Male	Female
Percent	15.2%	84.8%
Effect on Earnings	—	−1.9%

Union Membership

Percentage Union Members: Insignificant
Earnings Benefit of Union Membership: No significant data available

Veteran Status

Percentage Who Have Been on Active Duty: Insignificant
Earnings Benefit of Veteran Status: No significant data available

43-4000 Information and Record Clerks

43-4011 Brokerage Clerks

Perform clerical duties involving the purchase or sale of securities. Duties include writing orders for stock purchases and sales, computing transfer taxes, verifying stock transactions, accepting and delivering securities, tracking stock price fluctuations, computing equity, distributing dividends, and keeping records of daily transactions and holdings.

- Education or Training Required: Moderate-term on-the-job training
- Job Growth: 7.5%
- Annual Openings: 17,000
- Self-Employed: 0.0%
- Part-Time: 42.8%

NATIONAL WAGE FIGURES (ANNUAL)

Beginning	25th Percentile	Median	Mean	75th Percentile	90th Percentile
$24,590	$29,480	$36,390	$39,280	$46,030	$57,600

Median Wages for Industries Employing Largest Numbers (Annual)

Industry	Median Income
Federal, State, and Local Government	$45,780
Utilities	$37,520
Securities, Commodity Contracts, and Other Financial Investments and Related Activities	$37,240
Administrative and Support Services	$36,420
Credit Intermediation and Related Activities	$35,090
Insurance Carriers and Related Activities	$33,330
Management of Companies and Enterprises	$33,130
Real Estate	$31,820

Median Wages for States (Annual)

AK	$37,150	KY	$29,440	NY	$40,250
AL	$29,160	LA	$31,710	OH	$33,500
AR	$28,470	MA	no data	OK	$30,640
AZ	$32,460	MD	$36,910	OR	$34,720
CA	$43,410	ME	$33,630	PA	$33,420
CO	$32,970	MI	$35,880	RI	$36,690
CT	$39,060	MN	$39,980	SC	$28,140
DC	$40,010	MO	$30,940	SD	$28,480
DE	$35,820	MS	$28,020	TN	$32,720
FL	$30,810	MT	$30,080	TX	$36,990
GA	$32,810	NC	$33,840	UT	$29,270
HI	$32,070	ND	$28,770	VA	$34,490
IA	$29,400	NE	$31,570	VT	$31,380
ID	$37,800	NH	$35,910	WA	$37,980
IL	$39,220	NJ	$35,860	WI	$33,570
IN	$33,780	NM	$28,530	WV	no data
KS	$29,420	NV	$31,070	WY	no data

Median Wages for the Largest Metropolitan Areas (Annual)

AZ: Phoenix	$32,380	MI: Detroit	$36,130
CA: Los Angeles	$43,750	MN: Minneapolis	$40,820
CA: Riverside	$40,460	MO: Kansas City	$31,630
CA: Sacramento	$33,930	MO: St. Louis	$31,290
CA: San Diego	$40,240	NV: Las Vegas	$28,630
CA: San Francisco	$47,460	NY: New York	$39,930
CO: Denver	$33,140	OH: Cincinnati	$32,670
DC: Washington	$37,480	OH: Cleveland	$33,440
FL: Miami	$32,920	OH: Columbus	no data
FL: Orlando	$34,020	OR: Portland	$35,200
FL: Tampa	$30,300	PA: Philadelphia	$35,480
GA: Atlanta	$34,010	PA: Pittsburgh	$31,720
IL: Chicago	$39,260	TX: Dallas	$38,640
MA: Boston	$37,670	TX: Houston	$36,580
MD: Baltimore	$37,250	WA: Seattle	$39,860

FACTORS THAT MAY AFFECT EARNINGS

Educational Attainment of Workers and Effect on Earnings

Figures are based on a group of occupations: Information and Record Clerks

	Percent at Level	Effect on Earnings
Less than High School	1.3%	−43.7%
Some High School	7.9%	−42.4%
High School or Equivalent	28.5%	−2.5%
Some College but No Degree	27.1%	−5.8%
Associate Degree	15.1%	5.4%
Bachelor's Degree	15.7%	22.7%
Master's Degree	3.5%	39.5%
Doctoral Degree	0.4%	65.3%
First Professional Degree	0.4%	61.0%

Flexibility of Earnings

Average Hours Worked: 35
Workers with a Varying Number of Hours: 3.2%
Workers Earning Some Overtime Pay, Tips, or Commissions: 6.7%
Earnings Benefit of Working Overtime: 31.5%

Gender

	Male	Female
Percent	26.6%	73.4%
Effect on Earnings	8.2%	−2.6%

Union Membership

Percentage Union Members: 7.7%
Earnings Benefit of Union Membership: 30.9%

Veteran Status

Percentage Who Have Been on Active Duty: Insignificant
Earnings Benefit of Veteran Status: No significant data available

43-4021 Correspondence Clerks

Compose letters in reply to requests for merchandise, damage claims, credit and other information, delinquent accounts, incorrect billings, or unsatisfactory services. Duties may include gathering data to formulate reply and typing correspondence.

- Education or Training Required: Short-term on-the-job training
- Job Growth: −6.9%
- Annual Openings: 5,000
- Self-Employed: 0.0%
- Part-Time: 42.8%

NATIONAL WAGE FIGURES (ANNUAL)

Beginning	25th Percentile	Median	Mean	75th Percentile	90th Percentile
$19,700	$23,590	$28,700	$29,850	$35,350	$42,810

Median Wages for Industries Employing Largest Numbers (Annual)

Industry	Median Income
Funds, Trusts, and Other Financial Vehicles	$38,320
Publishing Industries (Except Internet)	$34,260
Support Activities for Transportation	$32,820
Securities, Commodity Contracts, and Other Financial Investments and Related Activities	$32,730
Management of Companies and Enterprises	$31,050
Nonstore Retailers	$29,900
Insurance Carriers and Related Activities	$29,630
Credit Intermediation and Related Activities	$29,540
Religious, Grantmaking, Civic, Professional, and Similar Organizations	$29,380
Truck Transportation	$28,570

Median Wages for States (Annual)

AK	no data	KY	$29,650	NY	$32,860
AL	$30,380	LA	$27,890	OH	$28,230
AR	$26,460	MA	$31,820	OK	$25,730
AZ	$29,400	MD	$38,390	OR	no data
CA	$32,490	ME	no data	PA	$26,240
CO	$27,000	MI	$31,100	RI	no data
CT	$33,570	MN	no data	SC	$21,730
DC	$42,450	MO	$25,330	SD	$25,470
DE	$31,620	MS	no data	TN	$30,020
FL	$26,720	MT	no data	TX	$30,560
GA	$34,790	NC	$29,100	UT	no data
HI	no data	ND	no data	VA	$31,370
IA	$27,440	NE	$26,310	VT	no data
ID	$33,220	NH	$28,670	WA	$36,380
IL	$31,470	NJ	$38,960	WI	$27,160
IN	$27,440	NM	$26,960	WV	$26,640
KS	no data	NV	no data	WY	no data

Median Wages for the Largest Metropolitan Areas (Annual)

AZ: Phoenix	$30,090	MI: Detroit	$30,270
CA: Los Angeles	$34,300	MN: Minneapolis	$31,160
CA: Riverside	$24,750	MO: Kansas City	$26,390
CA: Sacramento	$24,150	MO: St. Louis	$26,060
CA: San Diego	$33,210	NV: Las Vegas	no data
CA: San Francisco	$32,000	NY: New York	$36,370
CO: Denver	$27,890	OH: Cincinnati	$36,420
DC: Washington	$38,920	OH: Cleveland	$27,390
FL: Miami	$23,370	OH: Columbus	$27,910
FL: Orlando	$29,700	OR: Portland	no data
FL: Tampa	$31,100	PA: Philadelphia	$29,460
GA: Atlanta	$35,470	PA: Pittsburgh	no data
IL: Chicago	$33,350	TX: Dallas	$30,700
MA: Boston	$33,170	TX: Houston	$31,650
MD: Baltimore	$36,160	WA: Seattle	$36,480

FACTORS THAT MAY AFFECT EARNINGS

Educational Attainment of Workers and Effect on Earnings

Figures are based on a group of occupations: Information and Record Clerks

	Percent at Level	Effect on Earnings
Less than High School	1.3%	−43.7%
Some High School	7.9%	−42.4%
High School or Equivalent	28.5%	−2.5%
Some College but No Degree	27.1%	−5.8%
Associate Degree	15.1%	5.4%
Bachelor's Degree	15.7%	22.7%
Master's Degree	3.5%	39.5%
Doctoral Degree	0.4%	65.3%
First Professional Degree	0.4%	61.0%

Flexibility of Earnings

Average Hours Worked: 35
Workers with a Varying Number of Hours: 4.9%
Workers Earning Some Overtime Pay, Tips, or Commissions: 10.9%
Earnings Benefit of Working Overtime: 31.5%

Gender

	Male	Female
Percent	5.7%	94.3%
Effect on Earnings	8.2%	−2.6%

Union Membership

Percentage Union Members: 7.7%
Earnings Benefit of Union Membership: 30.9%

Veteran Status

Percentage Who Have Been on Active Duty: Insignificant
Earnings Benefit of Veteran Status: No significant data available

43-4031 Court, Municipal, and License Clerks

Perform clerical duties in courts of law, municipalities, and governmental licensing agencies and bureaus. May prepare docket of cases to be called, secure information for judges and court, prepare draft agendas or bylaws for town or city council, answer official correspondence, keep fiscal records and accounts, issue licenses or permits, record data, administer tests, or collect fees.

- Education or Training Required: Short-term on-the-job training
- Job Growth: 18.6%
- Annual Openings: 13,000
- Self-Employed: 2.9%
- Part-Time: 35.5%

NATIONAL WAGE FIGURES (ANNUAL)

Beginning	25th Percentile	Median	Mean	75th Percentile	90th Percentile
$20,090	$24,650	$30,980	$32,580	$38,500	$47,680

Median Wages for Industries Employing Largest Numbers (Annual)

Industry	Median Income
Credit Intermediation and Related Activities	$33,060
Federal, State, and Local Government	$31,210
Insurance Carriers and Related Activities	$28,760
Educational Services	$28,500
Religious, Grantmaking, Civic, Professional, and Similar Organizations	$26,230
Administrative and Support Services	$21,370

Median Wages for States (Annual)

AK	$35,520	KY	no data	NY	$39,170
AL	$26,020	LA	no data	OH	$30,840
AR	$22,410	MA	$39,000	OK	$21,820
AZ	$29,780	MD	no data	OR	$32,540
CA	$40,440	ME	$25,900	PA	$26,790
CO	$33,750	MI	$34,640	RI	$38,120
CT	$39,520	MN	$35,000	SC	$26,120
DC	no data	MO	$23,800	SD	$22,970
DE	$34,220	MS	$23,340	TN	$26,440
FL	$27,340	MT	$24,380	TX	$26,700
GA	$27,060	NC	$28,260	UT	$26,210
HI	$37,360	ND	$26,810	VA	$29,410
IA	$30,800	NE	$27,670	VT	$29,310
ID	$27,640	NH	$26,630	WA	$37,110
IL	no data	NJ	$34,710	WI	$33,380
IN	$25,330	NM	$29,810	WV	$25,800
KS	$28,830	NV	$37,830	WY	$27,400

Median Wages for the Largest Metropolitan Areas (Annual)

AZ: Phoenix	$31,340	MI: Detroit	$35,370
CA: Los Angeles	no data	MN: Minneapolis	$34,880
CA: Riverside	no data	MO: Kansas City	$29,380
CA: Sacramento	$37,330	MO: St. Louis	$29,800
CA: San Diego	$36,390	NV: Las Vegas	$39,360
CA: San Francisco	no data	NY: New York	$40,020
CO: Denver	$36,230	OH: Cincinnati	$29,040
DC: Washington	$35,910	OH: Cleveland	$31,850
FL: Miami	$29,350	OH: Columbus	$36,070
FL: Orlando	$27,050	OR: Portland	$33,200
FL: Tampa	$29,710	PA: Philadelphia	$34,400
GA: Atlanta	$29,840	PA: Pittsburgh	$25,810
IL: Chicago	$32,610	TX: Dallas	$29,720
MA: Boston	$40,380	TX: Houston	$27,700
MD: Baltimore	no data	WA: Seattle	$39,370

FACTORS THAT MAY AFFECT EARNINGS

Educational Attainment of Workers and Effect on Earnings

	Percent at Level	Effect on Earnings
Less than High School	—	—
Some High School	—	—
High School or Equivalent	34.5%	−4.2%
Some College but No Degree	27.5%	6.0%
Associate Degree	15.5%	−1.2%
Bachelor's Degree	19.0%	−2.1%
Master's Degree	—	—
Doctoral Degree	—	—
First Professional Degree	—	—

Flexibility of Earnings

Average Hours Worked: 36
Workers with a Varying Number of Hours: 4.5%
Workers Earning Some Overtime Pay, Tips, or Commissions: 7.1%
Earnings Benefit of Working Overtime: 31.5%

Gender

	Male	Female
Percent	19.3%	80.7%
Effect on Earnings	—	−4.4%

Union Membership

Percentage Union Members: 22.7%
Earnings Benefit of Union Membership: 9.3%

Veteran Status

Percentage Who Have Been on Active Duty: Insignificant
Earnings Benefit of Veteran Status: No significant data available

43-4041 Credit Authorizers, Checkers, and Clerks

Authorize credit charges against customers' accounts. Investigate history and credit standing of individuals or business establishments applying for credit. May interview applicants to obtain personal and financial data, determine creditworthiness, process applications, and notify customers of acceptance or rejection of credit.

- Education or Training Required: Short-term on-the-job training
- Job Growth: −41.2%
- Annual Openings: 5,000
- Self-Employed: 0.0%
- Part-Time: 11.1%

NATIONAL WAGE FIGURES (ANNUAL)

Beginning	25th Percentile	Median	Mean	75th Percentile	90th Percentile
$18,130	$23,390	$29,970	$31,710	$37,650	$46,390

Median Wages for Industries Employing Largest Numbers (Annual)

Industry	Median Income
Telecommunications	$40,500
Securities, Commodity Contracts, and Other Financial Investments and Related Activities	$34,940
Machinery Manufacturing	$34,740
Merchant Wholesalers, Durable Goods	$34,730
Chemical Manufacturing	$34,560
Hospitals	$34,140
Merchant Wholesalers, Nondurable Goods	$33,430
Federal, State, and Local Government	$32,940
Wholesale Electronic Markets and Agents and Brokers	$32,830
Management of Companies and Enterprises	$32,560

Median Wages for States (Annual)

State	Wage	State	Wage	State	Wage
AK	no data	KY	$28,650	NY	$34,230
AL	$24,780	LA	$24,020	OH	$28,920
AR	$27,940	MA	$34,430	OK	$28,180
AZ	no data	MD	$31,650	OR	$32,250
CA	$34,390	ME	no data	PA	$28,460
CO	$33,260	MI	$34,440	RI	no data
CT	$37,790	MN	$37,270	SC	$27,560
DC	$33,630	MO	$29,640	SD	$24,330
DE	no data	MS	$23,150	TN	$27,900
FL	$30,700	MT	no data	TX	$29,870
GA	$28,950	NC	$33,080	UT	$30,860
HI	$27,280	ND	$30,680	VA	$31,690
IA	$27,440	NE	$28,980	VT	$30,600
ID	$30,170	NH	$32,200	WA	$36,090
IL	$38,850	NJ	$32,600	WI	$29,700
IN	$28,490	NM	$24,680	WV	$27,730
KS	$31,660	NV	$30,330	WY	no data

Median Wages for the Largest Metropolitan Areas (Annual)

Area	Wage	Area	Wage
AZ: Phoenix	$18,630	MI: Detroit	$35,420
CA: Los Angeles	$34,460	MN: Minneapolis	$38,710
CA: Riverside	$29,820	MO: Kansas City	$35,840
CA: Sacramento	$36,050	MO: St. Louis	$29,310
CA: San Diego	$29,580	NV: Las Vegas	$31,840
CA: San Francisco	$37,020	NY: New York	$34,320
CO: Denver	$32,700	OH: Cincinnati	$32,170
DC: Washington	$33,070	OH: Cleveland	$28,340
FL: Miami	$34,060	OH: Columbus	$28,780
FL: Orlando	$29,010	OR: Portland	$34,960
FL: Tampa	$32,020	PA: Philadelphia	$33,130
GA: Atlanta	$29,720	PA: Pittsburgh	$26,850
IL: Chicago	$39,290	TX: Dallas	$33,070
MA: Boston	$35,050	TX: Houston	$29,230
MD: Baltimore	$35,530	WA: Seattle	$36,750

FACTORS THAT MAY AFFECT EARNINGS

Educational Attainment of Workers and Effect on Earnings

	Percent at Level	Effect on Earnings
Less than High School	—	—
Some High School	—	—
High School or Equivalent	36.1%	−26.7%
Some College but No Degree	31.9%	1.2%
Associate Degree	—	—
Bachelor's Degree	13.9%	−1.5%
Master's Degree	—	—
Doctoral Degree	—	—
First Professional Degree	—	—

Figures do not total 100% because some levels have a very small sample size.

Flexibility of Earnings

Average Hours Worked: 36
Workers with a Varying Number of Hours: 5.1%
Workers Earning Some Overtime Pay, Tips, or Commissions: 17.9%
Earnings Benefit of Working Overtime: 31.5%

Gender

	Male	Female
Percent	22.7%	77.3%
Effect on Earnings	8.2%	−2.6%

Union Membership

Percentage Union Members: 7.7%
Earnings Benefit of Union Membership: 30.9%

Veteran Status

Percentage Who Have Been on Active Duty: Insignificant
Earnings Benefit of Veteran Status: No significant data available

43-4051 Customer Service Representatives

Interact with customers to provide information in response to inquiries about products and services and to handle and resolve complaints.

- Education or Training Required: Moderate-term on-the-job training
- Job Growth: 22.8%
- Annual Openings: 510,000
- Self-Employed: 0.3%
- Part-Time: 36.3%

NATIONAL WAGE FIGURES (ANNUAL)

Beginning	25th Percentile	Median	Mean	75th Percentile	90th Percentile
$18,110	$22,310	$28,330	$30,400	$36,190	$45,990

Median Wages for Industries Employing Largest Numbers (Annual)

Industry	Median Income
Utilities	$35,120
Securities, Commodity Contracts, and Other Financial Investments and Related Activities	$34,620
Printing and Related Support Activities	$32,680
Telecommunications	$32,490
Merchant Wholesalers, Durable Goods	$31,930
Wholesale Electronic Markets and Agents and Brokers	$31,540
Insurance Carriers and Related Activities	$30,760
Professional, Scientific, and Technical Services	$30,380
Merchant Wholesalers, Nondurable Goods	$29,960
Management of Companies and Enterprises	$29,920

Median Wages for States (Annual)

State	Wage	State	Wage	State	Wage
AK	$32,220	KY	$26,130	NY	$30,940
AL	$25,240	LA	$22,890	OH	$28,380
AR	$24,970	MA	$34,660	OK	$23,630
AZ	$26,700	MD	$30,440	OR	$27,850
CA	$31,810	ME	$26,140	PA	$27,320
CO	$29,020	MI	$29,880	RI	$30,380
CT	$34,830	MN	$31,810	SC	$27,130
DC	$33,470	MO	$28,170	SD	$23,030
DE	$30,760	MS	$23,110	TN	$26,610
FL	$26,460	MT	$24,330	TX	$25,800
GA	$28,540	NC	$28,420	UT	$24,720
HI	$29,230	ND	$24,180	VA	$28,200
IA	$26,900	NE	$25,060	VT	$27,030
ID	$23,290	NH	$30,770	WA	$30,410
IL	$30,930	NJ	$31,600	WI	$29,410
IN	$27,580	NM	$24,590	WV	$21,860
KS	$26,240	NV	$28,810	WY	$22,510

Median Wages for the Largest Metropolitan Areas (Annual)

Area	Wage	Area	Wage
AZ: Phoenix	$28,080	MI: Detroit	$32,210
CA: Los Angeles	$31,210	MN: Minneapolis	$33,020
CA: Riverside	$29,500	MO: Kansas City	$29,070
CA: Sacramento	$31,290	MO: St. Louis	$29,250
CA: San Diego	$29,880	NV: Las Vegas	$29,000
CA: San Francisco	$36,220	NY: New York	$33,140
CO: Denver	$30,000	OH: Cincinnati	$29,450
DC: Washington	$32,150	OH: Cleveland	$29,630
FL: Miami	$26,970	OH: Columbus	$28,160
FL: Orlando	$25,980	OR: Portland	$30,030
FL: Tampa	$27,200	PA: Philadelphia	$29,830
GA: Atlanta	$30,300	PA: Pittsburgh	$26,850
IL: Chicago	$32,090	TX: Dallas	$29,010
MA: Boston	$35,780	TX: Houston	$27,550
MD: Baltimore	$30,610	WA: Seattle	$32,440

FACTORS THAT MAY AFFECT EARNINGS

Educational Attainment of Workers and Effect on Earnings

	Percent at Level	Effect on Earnings
Less than High School	1.5%	−42.6%
Some High School	8.4%	−50.2%
High School or Equivalent	28.2%	−4.8%
Some College but No Degree	28.8%	−6.3%
Associate Degree	13.0%	6.3%
Bachelor's Degree	17.2%	31.6%
Master's Degree	2.3%	68.7%
Doctoral Degree	—	—
First Professional Degree	—	—

Flexibility of Earnings

Average Hours Worked: 33
Workers with a Varying Number of Hours: 4.8%
Workers Earning Some Overtime Pay, Tips, or Commissions: 13.9%
Earnings Benefit of Working Overtime: 37.6%

Gender

	Male	Female
Percent	29.6%	70.4%
Effect on Earnings	11.0%	−3.8%

Union Membership

Percentage Union Members: 7.7%
Earnings Benefit of Union Membership: 25.3%

Veteran Status

Percentage Who Have Been on Active Duty: Insignificant
Earnings Benefit of Veteran Status: No significant data available

43-4061 Eligibility Interviewers, Government Programs

Determine eligibility of persons applying to receive assistance from government programs and agency resources, such as welfare, unemployment benefits, social security, and public housing.

- Education or Training Required: Moderate-term on-the-job training
- Job Growth: –9.4%
- Annual Openings: 10,000
- Self-Employed: 0.2%
- Part-Time: 42.8%

NATIONAL WAGE FIGURES (ANNUAL)

Beginning	25th Percentile	Median	Mean	75th Percentile	90th Percentile
$25,330	$29,950	$37,540	$37,770	$45,590	$50,550

Median Wages for Industries Employing Largest Numbers (Annual)

Industry	Median Income
Administrative and Support Services	$38,420
Federal, State, and Local Government	$38,070
Professional, Scientific, and Technical Services	$34,750
Internet Service Providers, Web Search Portals, and Data-Processing Services	$34,710
Nursing and Residential Care Facilities	$34,120
Hospitals	$34,100
Insurance Carriers and Related Activities	$34,100
Ambulatory Health Care Services	$29,370
Educational Services	$29,240
Real Estate	$28,660

Median Wages for States (Annual)

AK	$41,380	KY	$42,660	NY	$38,570
AL	$40,620	LA	$34,210	OH	$38,800
AR	$28,410	MA	$44,380	OK	$30,760
AZ	$33,220	MD	$42,010	OR	$31,720
CA	$42,650	ME	$32,140	PA	$41,930
CO	$40,410	MI	no data	RI	$44,170
CT	$56,580	MN	$39,570	SC	$36,220
DC	$41,330	MO	$29,930	SD	$28,910
DE	$36,290	MS	$23,980	TN	$30,330
FL	$33,150	MT	$30,050	TX	$37,790
GA	$43,280	NC	$29,140	UT	$40,050
HI	$37,950	ND	$31,340	VA	$34,730
IA	$41,510	NE	$27,940	VT	$37,130
ID	$33,210	NH	$32,690	WA	$43,370
IL	$40,720	NJ	$44,100	WI	$35,520
IN	$30,000	NM	$37,300	WV	$25,550
KS	$39,110	NV	$41,160	WY	$36,880

Median Wages for the Largest Metropolitan Areas (Annual)

AZ: Phoenix	$33,030	MI: Detroit	no data
CA: Los Angeles	no data	MN: Minneapolis	$41,380
CA: Riverside	$37,110	MO: Kansas City	$36,800
CA: Sacramento	$36,960	MO: St. Louis	$31,260
CA: San Diego	$40,110	NV: Las Vegas	$41,420
CA: San Francisco	$47,850	NY: New York	$40,740
CO: Denver	$43,430	OH: Cincinnati	$43,080
DC: Washington	$42,580	OH: Cleveland	$42,350
FL: Miami	$33,790	OH: Columbus	no data
FL: Orlando	$28,410	OR: Portland	$37,170
FL: Tampa	$34,610	PA: Philadelphia	$44,540
GA: Atlanta	$44,610	PA: Pittsburgh	$36,500
IL: Chicago	$40,670	TX: Dallas	$43,170
MA: Boston	$44,220	TX: Houston	$36,220
MD: Baltimore	$42,350	WA: Seattle	$43,340

FACTORS THAT MAY AFFECT EARNINGS

Educational Attainment of Workers and Effect on Earnings

	Percent at Level	Effect on Earnings
Less than High School	—	—
Some High School	—	—
High School or Equivalent	20.0%	–9.5%
Some College but No Degree	26.0%	–13.3%
Associate Degree	15.0%	0.2%
Bachelor's Degree	31.0%	14.4%
Master's Degree	7.0%	8.9%
Doctoral Degree	—	—
First Professional Degree	—	—

Flexibility of Earnings

Average Hours Worked: 37
Workers with a Varying Number of Hours: 1.0%
Workers Earning Some Overtime Pay, Tips, or Commissions: 10.2%
Earnings Benefit of Working Overtime: 31.5%

Gender

	Male	Female
Percent	13.7%	86.3%
Effect on Earnings	—	0.3%

Union Membership

Percentage Union Members: 39.8%
Earnings Benefit of Union Membership: 9.9%

Veteran Status

Percentage Who Have Been on Active Duty: Insignificant
Earnings Benefit of Veteran Status: No significant data available

43-4071 File Clerks

File correspondence, cards, invoices, receipts, and other records in alphabetical or numerical order or according to the filing system used. Locate and remove material from file when requested.

- Education or Training Required: Short-term on-the-job training
- Job Growth: −36.3%
- Annual Openings: 50,000
- Self-Employed: 2.1%
- Part-Time: 54.2%

NATIONAL WAGE FIGURES (ANNUAL)

Beginning	25th Percentile	Median	Mean	75th Percentile	90th Percentile
$15,130	$17,960	$22,090	$23,540	$27,690	$34,760

Median Wages for Industries Employing Largest Numbers (Annual)

Industry	Median Income
Telecommunications	$41,970
Motion Picture and Sound Recording Industries	$33,200
Food and Beverage Stores	$26,550
Warehousing and Storage	$26,510
Federal, State, and Local Government	$25,970
Management of Companies and Enterprises	$24,290
Securities, Commodity Contracts, and Other Financial Investments and Related Activities	$24,240
Internet Service Providers, Web Search Portals, and Data-Processing Services	$23,750
Credit Intermediation and Related Activities	$23,050
Professional, Scientific, and Technical Services	$23,010

Median Wages for States (Annual)

State	Wage	State	Wage	State	Wage
AK	$25,870	KY	$19,840	NY	$24,120
AL	$18,230	LA	$17,220	OH	$22,100
AR	$17,880	MA	$23,480	OK	$19,490
AZ	$20,280	MD	$25,680	OR	$22,250
CA	$23,460	ME	$21,200	PA	$21,680
CO	$24,990	MI	$21,630	RI	$24,940
CT	$22,790	MN	$24,610	SC	no data
DC	$30,980	MO	$21,570	SD	$19,130
DE	$24,570	MS	$17,350	TN	$21,190
FL	$21,680	MT	$17,850	TX	$21,840
GA	$20,970	NC	$21,740	UT	$22,830
HI	$20,390	ND	$20,630	VA	$22,370
IA	$21,410	NE	$20,580	VT	$21,460
ID	$24,870	NH	$21,830	WA	$23,880
IL	$22,150	NJ	$22,700	WI	$22,860
IN	$21,610	NM	$20,180	WV	$18,920
KS	$20,490	NV	$22,160	WY	$17,710

Median Wages for the Largest Metropolitan Areas (Annual)

Area	Wage	Area	Wage
AZ: Phoenix	$20,060	MI: Detroit	$22,380
CA: Los Angeles	$23,690	MN: Minneapolis	$25,150
CA: Riverside	$19,340	MO: Kansas City	$22,660
CA: Sacramento	$23,500	MO: St. Louis	$22,520
CA: San Diego	$22,610	NV: Las Vegas	$22,370
CA: San Francisco	$29,270	NY: New York	$24,530
CO: Denver	$26,740	OH: Cincinnati	$22,550
DC: Washington	$25,510	OH: Cleveland	$22,250
FL: Miami	$21,720	OH: Columbus	$25,210
FL: Orlando	$22,890	OR: Portland	$24,390
FL: Tampa	$22,360	PA: Philadelphia	$22,790
GA: Atlanta	$22,810	PA: Pittsburgh	$21,570
IL: Chicago	$23,350	TX: Dallas	$24,280
MA: Boston	$23,780	TX: Houston	$21,800
MD: Baltimore	$27,770	WA: Seattle	$26,180

FACTORS THAT MAY AFFECT EARNINGS

Educational Attainment of Workers and Effect on Earnings

	Percent at Level	Effect on Earnings
Less than High School	—	—
Some High School	10.1%	−56.8%
High School or Equivalent	30.7%	3.8%
Some College but No Degree	27.1%	1.2%
Associate Degree	12.7%	16.9%
Bachelor's Degree	15.5%	11.2%
Master's Degree	2.3%	48.6%
Doctoral Degree	—	—
First Professional Degree	—	—

Flexibility of Earnings

Average Hours Worked: 29
Workers with a Varying Number of Hours: 4.8%
Workers Earning Some Overtime Pay, Tips, or Commissions: 6.8%
Earnings Benefit of Working Overtime: 31.5%

Gender

	Male	Female
Percent	20.8%	79.2%
Effect on Earnings	−5.8%	1.9%

Union Membership

Percentage Union Members: 8.0%
Earnings Benefit of Union Membership: 54.0%

Veteran Status

Percentage Who Have Been on Active Duty: Insignificant
Earnings Benefit of Veteran Status: No significant data available

43-4081 Hotel, Motel, and Resort Desk Clerks

Accommodate hotel, motel, and resort patrons by registering and assigning rooms to guests, issuing room keys, transmitting and receiving messages, keeping records of occupied rooms and guests' accounts, making and confirming reservations, and presenting statements to and collecting payments from departing guests.

- Education or Training Required: Short-term on-the-job training
- Job Growth: 17.2%
- Annual Openings: 62,000
- Self-Employed: 0.4%
- Part-Time: 43.9%

NATIONAL WAGE FIGURES (ANNUAL)

Beginning	25th Percentile	Median	Mean	75th Percentile	90th Percentile
$13,690	$15,930	$18,460	$19,480	$22,220	$27,030

Median Wages for Industries Employing Largest Numbers (Annual)

Industry	Median Income
Hospitals	$25,550
Educational Services	$21,750
Religious, Grantmaking, Civic, Professional, and Similar Organizations	$21,200
Real Estate	$21,130
Administrative and Support Services	$20,540
Heavy and Civil Engineering Construction	$19,610
Federal, State, and Local Government	$19,230
Food Services and Drinking Places	$18,790
Accommodation	$18,390
Amusement, Gambling, and Recreation Industries	$18,350

Median Wages for States (Annual)

AK	$20,480	KY	$16,610	NY	$21,460
AL	$14,740	LA	$16,480	OH	$17,150
AR	$15,540	MA	$23,480	OK	$16,340
AZ	$18,290	MD	$20,010	OR	$18,670
CA	$20,890	ME	$20,600	PA	$18,710
CO	$19,730	MI	$17,770	RI	$21,420
CT	$21,960	MN	$18,310	SC	$18,020
DC	$27,020	MO	$17,270	SD	$16,470
DE	$19,650	MS	$16,360	TN	$17,090
FL	$19,700	MT	$16,470	TX	$16,320
GA	$17,580	NC	$18,530	UT	$17,780
HI	$30,790	ND	$16,300	VA	$18,300
IA	$16,690	NE	$16,530	VT	$21,330
ID	$15,850	NH	$20,760	WA	$19,420
IL	$18,950	NJ	$21,780	WI	$17,820
IN	$17,030	NM	$17,010	WV	$14,930
KS	$16,120	NV	$25,160	WY	$17,530

Median Wages for the Largest Metropolitan Areas (Annual)

AZ: Phoenix	$20,040	MI: Detroit	$19,010
CA: Los Angeles	$21,340	MN: Minneapolis	$20,840
CA: Riverside	$18,140	MO: Kansas City	$18,600
CA: Sacramento	$19,510	MO: St. Louis	$18,780
CA: San Diego	$20,380	NV: Las Vegas	$27,860
CA: San Francisco	$26,000	NY: New York	$24,620
CO: Denver	$19,560	OH: Cincinnati	$17,960
DC: Washington	$21,960	OH: Cleveland	$17,690
FL: Miami	$19,680	OH: Columbus	$17,760
FL: Orlando	$21,160	OR: Portland	$19,140
FL: Tampa	$18,810	PA: Philadelphia	$21,660
GA: Atlanta	$19,070	PA: Pittsburgh	$16,370
IL: Chicago	$19,690	TX: Dallas	$18,350
MA: Boston	$23,890	TX: Houston	$16,540
MD: Baltimore	$21,470	WA: Seattle	$20,800

FACTORS THAT MAY AFFECT EARNINGS

Educational Attainment of Workers and Effect on Earnings

	Percent at Level	Effect on Earnings
Less than High School	—	—
Some High School	—	—
High School or Equivalent	38.6%	2.8%
Some College but No Degree	28.8%	−8.6%
Associate Degree	11.4%	13.8%
Bachelor's Degree	12.9%	7.5%
Master's Degree	—	—
Doctoral Degree	—	—
First Professional Degree	—	—

Figures do not total 100% because some levels have a very small sample size.

Flexibility of Earnings

Average Hours Worked: 31
Workers with a Varying Number of Hours: 7.7%
Workers Earning Some Overtime Pay, Tips, or Commissions: 9.6%
Earnings Benefit of Working Overtime: 31.5%

Gender

	Male	Female
Percent	36.3%	63.7%
Effect on Earnings	—	−1.6%

Union Membership

Percentage Union Members: 4.8%
Earnings Benefit of Union Membership: 30.9%

Veteran Status

Percentage Who Have Been on Active Duty: Insignificant
Earnings Benefit of Veteran Status: No significant data available

43-4111 Interviewers, Except Eligibility and Loan

Interview persons by telephone, by mail, in person, or by other means for the purpose of completing forms, applications, or questionnaires. Ask specific questions, record answers, and assist persons with completing form. May sort, classify, and file forms.

- Education or Training Required: Short-term on-the-job training
- Job Growth: 26.0%
- Annual Openings: 43,000
- Self-Employed: 0.2%
- Part-Time: 50.6%

NATIONAL WAGE FIGURES (ANNUAL)

Beginning	25th Percentile	Median	Mean	75th Percentile	90th Percentile
$17,370	$21,060	$26,290	$27,190	$31,850	$38,620

Median Wages for Industries Employing Largest Numbers (Annual)

Industry	Median Income
Personal and Laundry Services	$33,470
Federal, State, and Local Government	$32,030
Real Estate	$31,850
Nursing and Residential Care Facilities	$31,700
Educational Services	$31,680
Insurance Carriers and Related Activities	$29,960
Securities, Commodity Contracts, and Other Financial Investments and Related Activities	$29,940
Funds, Trusts, and Other Financial Vehicles	$29,860
Management of Companies and Enterprises	$29,000
Credit Intermediation and Related Activities	$28,950

Median Wages for States (Annual)

AK	$31,180	KY	$22,660	NY	$29,140
AL	$23,500	LA	$21,220	OH	$26,570
AR	$20,490	MA	$30,620	OK	$21,600
AZ	$25,070	MD	$27,360	OR	$27,190
CA	$30,680	ME	$24,290	PA	$26,590
CO	$27,230	MI	$27,860	RI	$28,760
CT	$30,610	MN	$26,400	SC	$23,100
DC	$32,880	MO	$23,220	SD	$21,720
DE	$26,900	MS	$22,410	TN	$24,830
FL	$24,530	MT	$22,550	TX	$27,730
GA	$24,590	NC	$24,320	UT	$21,440
HI	$25,820	ND	$22,070	VA	$26,920
IA	$23,310	NE	$21,770	VT	$23,960
ID	$17,120	NH	$27,430	WA	$28,650
IL	$21,560	NJ	$28,430	WI	$25,730
IN	$23,490	NM	$25,670	WV	$20,390
KS	$24,210	NV	$26,550	WY	$20,370

Median Wages for the Largest Metropolitan Areas (Annual)

AZ: Phoenix	$25,190	MI: Detroit	$28,400
CA: Los Angeles	$27,970	MN: Minneapolis	$26,680
CA: Riverside	$40,760	MO: Kansas City	$25,700
CA: Sacramento	$32,380	MO: St. Louis	$24,960
CA: San Diego	$28,100	NV: Las Vegas	$27,130
CA: San Francisco	$37,490	NY: New York	$30,110
CO: Denver	$28,690	OH: Cincinnati	$25,620
DC: Washington	$28,680	OH: Cleveland	$28,420
FL: Miami	$27,320	OH: Columbus	$25,680
FL: Orlando	$24,500	OR: Portland	$29,350
FL: Tampa	$25,130	PA: Philadelphia	$27,180
GA: Atlanta	$26,370	PA: Pittsburgh	$26,140
IL: Chicago	$21,740	TX: Dallas	$27,510
MA: Boston	$30,800	TX: Houston	$28,750
MD: Baltimore	$28,130	WA: Seattle	$30,720

FACTORS THAT MAY AFFECT EARNINGS

Educational Attainment of Workers and Effect on Earnings

	Percent at Level	Effect on Earnings
Less than High School	—	—
Some High School	6.4%	−39.1%
High School or Equivalent	24.6%	−0.4%
Some College but No Degree	32.0%	−19.4%
Associate Degree	15.8%	12.7%
Bachelor's Degree	14.3%	28.6%
Master's Degree	4.9%	2.1%
Doctoral Degree	—	—
First Professional Degree	—	—

Flexibility of Earnings

Average Hours Worked: 29
Workers with a Varying Number of Hours: 7.9%
Workers Earning Some Overtime Pay, Tips, or Commissions: 9.2%
Earnings Benefit of Working Overtime: 31.5%

Gender

	Male	Female
Percent	17.9%	82.1%
Effect on Earnings	—	−0.9%

Union Membership

Percentage Union Members: 7.8%
Earnings Benefit of Union Membership: 36.3%

Veteran Status

Percentage Who Have Been on Active Duty: Insignificant
Earnings Benefit of Veteran Status: No significant data available

43-4121 Library Assistants, Clerical

Compile records; sort and shelve books; and issue and receive library materials such as pictures, cards, slides, and microfilm. Locate library materials for loan and replace material in shelving area, stacks, or files according to identification number and title. Register patrons to permit them to borrow books, periodicals, and other library materials.

- Education or Training Required: Short-term on-the-job training
- Job Growth: 12.5%
- Annual Openings: 26,000
- Self-Employed: 0.0%
- Part-Time: 70.0%

NATIONAL WAGE FIGURES (ANNUAL)

Beginning	25th Percentile	Median	Mean	75th Percentile	90th Percentile
$14,070	$16,780	$21,640	$22,940	$27,980	$34,810

Median Wages for Industries Employing Largest Numbers (Annual)

Industry	Median Income
Professional, Scientific, and Technical Services	$29,290
Ambulatory Health Care Services	$28,970
Publishing Industries (Except Internet)	$28,100
Hospitals	$26,350
Management of Companies and Enterprises	$26,100
Administrative and Support Services	$24,940
Educational Services	$23,700
Merchant Wholesalers, Nondurable Goods	$22,310
Social Assistance	$21,840
Religious, Grantmaking, Civic, Professional, and Similar Organizations	$20,790

Median Wages for States (Annual)

AK	$32,390	KY	$18,970	NY	$24,420
AL	$17,120	LA	$18,100	OH	$21,910
AR	$14,640	MA	$27,760	OK	$15,560
AZ	$23,320	MD	$21,600	OR	$26,590
CA	$27,860	ME	$20,530	PA	$20,110
CO	$19,930	MI	$19,940	RI	$22,660
CT	$23,140	MN	$21,680	SC	$20,710
DC	$25,910	MO	$18,790	SD	$17,580
DE	$25,780	MS	$16,670	TN	$21,020
FL	$21,830	MT	$18,340	TX	$19,910
GA	$19,670	NC	$20,200	UT	$19,320
HI	$26,470	ND	$15,110	VA	$22,990
IA	$18,070	NE	$16,150	VT	$24,900
ID	$21,100	NH	$21,320	WA	$23,970
IL	$21,960	NJ	$22,370	WI	$21,530
IN	$17,820	NM	$14,700	WV	$15,270
KS	$17,920	NV	$29,170	WY	$20,090

Median Wages for the Largest Metropolitan Areas (Annual)

AZ: Phoenix	$25,800	MI: Detroit	$17,760
CA: Los Angeles	$24,690	MN: Minneapolis	$25,270
CA: Riverside	$31,900	MO: Kansas City	$21,060
CA: Sacramento	$29,550	MO: St. Louis	$19,200
CA: San Diego	$24,320	NV: Las Vegas	$27,960
CA: San Francisco	$31,490	NY: New York	$26,160
CO: Denver	$19,650	OH: Cincinnati	$20,650
DC: Washington	$25,770	OH: Cleveland	$21,320
FL: Miami	$23,740	OH: Columbus	$22,330
FL: Orlando	$21,800	OR: Portland	$27,880
FL: Tampa	$20,380	PA: Philadelphia	$20,480
GA: Atlanta	$20,130	PA: Pittsburgh	$19,190
IL: Chicago	$22,960	TX: Dallas	$21,500
MA: Boston	$27,290	TX: Houston	$19,790
MD: Baltimore	$20,890	WA: Seattle	$23,930

FACTORS THAT MAY AFFECT EARNINGS

Educational Attainment of Workers and Effect on Earnings

	Percent at Level	Effect on Earnings
Less than High School	—	—
Some High School	4.7%	19.2%
High School or Equivalent	20.6%	−5.7%
Some College but No Degree	34.7%	−23.9%
Associate Degree	12.9%	7.9%
Bachelor's Degree	18.2%	8.0%
Master's Degree	7.1%	83.8%
Doctoral Degree	—	—
First Professional Degree	—	—

Flexibility of Earnings

Average Hours Worked: 23
Workers with a Varying Number of Hours: 5.7%
Workers Earning Some Overtime Pay, Tips, or Commissions: 1.1%
Earnings Benefit of Working Overtime: 31.5%

Gender

	Male	Female
Percent	12.1%	87.9%
Effect on Earnings	8.2%	−2.6%

Union Membership

Percentage Union Members: 18.8%
Earnings Benefit of Union Membership: 43.5%

Veteran Status

Percentage Who Have Been on Active Duty: Insignificant
Earnings Benefit of Veteran Status: No significant data available

43-4131 Loan Interviewers and Clerks

Interview loan applicants to elicit information; investigate applicants' backgrounds and verify references; prepare loan request papers; and forward findings, reports, and documents to appraisal department. Review loan papers to ensure completeness and complete transactions between loan establishment, borrowers, and sellers upon approval of loan.

- Education or Training Required: Short-term on-the-job training
- Job Growth: –0.6%
- Annual Openings: 36,000
- Self-Employed: 2.3%
- Part-Time: 14.7%

NATIONAL WAGE FIGURES (ANNUAL)

Beginning	25th Percentile	Median	Mean	75th Percentile	90th Percentile
$20,560	$25,100	$30,970	$32,680	$38,870	$47,140

Median Wages for Industries Employing Largest Numbers (Annual)

Industry	Median Income
Religious, Grantmaking, Civic, Professional, and Similar Organizations	$39,270
Construction of Buildings	$37,850
Rental and Leasing Services	$35,710
Motor Vehicle and Parts Dealers	$35,660
Heavy and Civil Engineering Construction	$35,640
Internet Service Providers, Web Search Portals, and Data-Processing Services	$34,650
Real Estate	$34,620
Insurance Carriers and Related Activities	$34,320
Wholesale Electronic Markets and Agents and Brokers	$33,480
Accommodation	$33,070

Median Wages for States (Annual)

State	Wage	State	Wage	State	Wage
AK	$33,640	KY	$26,740	NY	$34,490
AL	$25,850	LA	$23,330	OH	$29,170
AR	$25,800	MA	$34,400	OK	$25,640
AZ	$30,040	MD	$32,820	OR	$32,540
CA	$36,790	ME	$27,450	PA	$25,840
CO	$33,600	MI	$29,550	RI	$29,320
CT	$33,300	MN	$33,580	SC	$28,680
DC	$33,980	MO	$27,790	SD	$26,120
DE	$30,570	MS	$26,170	TN	$28,370
FL	$30,990	MT	$25,670	TX	$33,130
GA	$27,220	NC	$29,780	UT	no data
HI	$35,730	ND	$27,330	VA	$34,350
IA	$28,550	NE	$27,430	VT	$30,430
ID	$28,770	NH	$31,460	WA	$34,490
IL	$32,890	NJ	$34,600	WI	$28,560
IN	$27,260	NM	$23,900	WV	$23,230
KS	$28,840	NV	$33,140	WY	$24,320

Median Wages for the Largest Metropolitan Areas (Annual)

Area	Wage	Area	Wage
AZ: Phoenix	$30,070	MI: Detroit	$30,580
CA: Los Angeles	$36,520	MN: Minneapolis	$34,690
CA: Riverside	$36,150	MO: Kansas City	$31,430
CA: Sacramento	$39,850	MO: St. Louis	$29,560
CA: San Diego	$35,470	NV: Las Vegas	$32,740
CA: San Francisco	$39,560	NY: New York	$35,510
CO: Denver	$36,340	OH: Cincinnati	$30,920
DC: Washington	$35,750	OH: Cleveland	$29,650
FL: Miami	$31,830	OH: Columbus	$30,450
FL: Orlando	$30,820	OR: Portland	$33,600
FL: Tampa	$31,550	PA: Philadelphia	$28,920
GA: Atlanta	$27,760	PA: Pittsburgh	$26,390
IL: Chicago	$34,550	TX: Dallas	$35,210
MA: Boston	$35,380	TX: Houston	$38,470
MD: Baltimore	$31,720	WA: Seattle	$36,030

FACTORS THAT MAY AFFECT EARNINGS

Educational Attainment of Workers and Effect on Earnings

	Percent at Level	Effect on Earnings
Less than High School	—	—
Some High School	—	—
High School or Equivalent	39.0%	–6.1%
Some College but No Degree	28.1%	0.7%
Associate Degree	12.4%	0.8%
Bachelor's Degree	17.1%	16.7%
Master's Degree	—	—
Doctoral Degree	—	—
First Professional Degree	—	—

Flexibility of Earnings

Average Hours Worked: 36
Workers with a Varying Number of Hours: 3.3%
Workers Earning Some Overtime Pay, Tips, or Commissions: 19.1%
Earnings Benefit of Working Overtime: 14.8%

Gender

	Male	Female
Percent	23.3%	76.7%
Effect on Earnings	—	–0.3%

Union Membership

Percentage Union Members: Insignificant
Earnings Benefit of Union Membership: No significant data available

Veteran Status

Percentage Who Have Been on Active Duty: Insignificant
Earnings Benefit of Veteran Status: No significant data available

43-4141 New Accounts Clerks

Interview persons desiring to open bank accounts. Explain banking services available to prospective customers and assist them in preparing application form.

- Education or Training Required: Work experience in a related occupation
- Job Growth: 1.7%
- Annual Openings: 7,000
- Self-Employed: 0.0%
- Part-Time: 42.8%

NATIONAL WAGE FIGURES (ANNUAL)

Beginning	25th Percentile	Median	Mean	75th Percentile	90th Percentile
$20,650	$24,010	$28,390	$29,510	$34,150	$40,250

Median Wages for Industries Employing Largest Numbers (Annual)

Industry	Median Income
Securities, Commodity Contracts, and Other Financial Investments and Related Activities	$29,870
Management of Companies and Enterprises	$28,740
Credit Intermediation and Related Activities	$28,350
Insurance Carriers and Related Activities	$28,080
Professional, Scientific, and Technical Services	$28,040
Administrative and Support Services	$25,430

Median Wages for States (Annual)

AK	$30,160	KY	$26,730	NY	$29,480
AL	$23,790	LA	$23,650	OH	$28,050
AR	$23,980	MA	$33,170	OK	$24,940
AZ	$30,480	MD	$32,940	OR	$29,680
CA	$32,310	ME	$26,380	PA	$25,960
CO	$29,840	MI	$26,970	RI	no data
CT	$29,540	MN	$30,450	SC	$27,610
DC	$38,360	MO	$26,020	SD	$25,550
DE	$30,880	MS	$24,570	TN	$26,730
FL	$27,410	MT	$25,740	TX	$28,810
GA	$26,840	NC	$26,930	UT	$27,220
HI	$27,290	ND	$25,590	VA	$28,290
IA	$27,090	NE	$27,140	VT	$28,910
ID	$23,060	NH	$27,490	WA	$28,870
IL	$29,730	NJ	$28,760	WI	$28,260
IN	$26,250	NM	$26,150	WV	$25,900
KS	$26,230	NV	$29,860	WY	$24,450

Median Wages for the Largest Metropolitan Areas (Annual)

AZ: Phoenix	$31,520	MI: Detroit	$26,450
CA: Los Angeles	$32,670	MN: Minneapolis	$31,510
CA: Riverside	$30,590	MO: Kansas City	$27,160
CA: Sacramento	$32,510	MO: St. Louis	$26,460
CA: San Diego	$35,010	NV: Las Vegas	$30,430
CA: San Francisco	$32,170	NY: New York	$30,000
CO: Denver	$30,590	OH: Cincinnati	$28,450
DC: Washington	$34,400	OH: Cleveland	$29,750
FL: Miami	$29,650	OH: Columbus	$29,950
FL: Orlando	$26,160	OR: Portland	$30,460
FL: Tampa	$26,540	PA: Philadelphia	$27,370
GA: Atlanta	$27,530	PA: Pittsburgh	$25,350
IL: Chicago	$31,200	TX: Dallas	$31,490
MA: Boston	$33,960	TX: Houston	$30,360
MD: Baltimore	$32,500	WA: Seattle	$30,720

FACTORS THAT MAY AFFECT EARNINGS

Educational Attainment of Workers and Effect on Earnings

	Percent at Level	Effect on Earnings
Less than High School	—	—
Some High School	—	—
High School or Equivalent	23.1%	−22.3%
Some College but No Degree	50.0%	−16.2%
Associate Degree	—	—
Bachelor's Degree	23.1%	69.5%
Master's Degree	—	—
Doctoral Degree	—	—
First Professional Degree	—	—

Flexibility of Earnings

Average Hours Worked: 36
Workers with a Varying Number of Hours: 2.1%
Workers Earning Some Overtime Pay, Tips, or Commissions: 18.5%
Earnings Benefit of Working Overtime: 31.5%

Gender

	Male	Female
Percent	32.7%	67.3%
Effect on Earnings	50.2%	−24.4%

Union Membership

Percentage Union Members: 7.7%
Earnings Benefit of Union Membership: 30.9%

Veteran Status

Percentage Who Have Been on Active Duty: Insignificant
Earnings Benefit of Veteran Status: No significant data available

43-4151 Order Clerks

Receive and process incoming orders for materials; merchandise; classified ads; or services such as repairs, installations, or rental of facilities. Duties include informing customers of receipt, prices, shipping dates, and delays; preparing contracts; and handling complaints.

- Education or Training Required: Short-term on-the-job training
- Job Growth: –21.4%
- Annual Openings: 48,000
- Self-Employed: 0.7%
- Part-Time: 25.6%

NATIONAL WAGE FIGURES (ANNUAL)

Beginning	25th Percentile	Median	Mean	75th Percentile	90th Percentile
$17,010	$20,620	$26,340	$28,130	$33,740	$43,040

Median Wages for Industries Employing Largest Numbers (Annual)

Industry	Median Income
Telecommunications	$43,270
Computer and Electronic Product Manufacturing	$32,780
Management of Companies and Enterprises	$31,090
Machinery Manufacturing	$30,880
Chemical Manufacturing	$29,940
Fabricated Metal Product Manufacturing	$29,240
Merchant Wholesalers, Durable Goods	$28,450
Miscellaneous Manufacturing	$28,280
Motor Vehicle and Parts Dealers	$27,960
Wholesale Electronic Markets and Agents and Brokers	$27,790

Median Wages for States (Annual)

AK $28,970	KY $23,770	NY $27,470
AL $22,250	LA $22,200	OH $26,800
AR $21,380	MA $31,620	OK $22,480
AZ $25,150	MD $29,430	OR $27,420
CA $27,820	ME no data	PA $26,440
CO $27,630	MI $29,460	RI $27,220
CT $30,870	MN $30,380	SC $25,270
DC $33,040	MO $23,190	SD $21,850
DE $28,030	MS $22,630	TN $22,370
FL $23,310	MT $22,010	TX $24,700
GA $25,010	NC $27,250	UT $22,340
HI $26,160	ND $24,700	VA $25,210
IA $27,070	NE $19,490	VT $26,990
ID $30,180	NH $26,810	WA $28,860
IL $26,950	NJ $32,480	WI $27,440
IN $26,110	NM $22,300	WV $20,020
KS $22,560	NV $25,950	WY $20,730

Median Wages for the Largest Metropolitan Areas (Annual)

AZ: Phoenix	$25,390	MI: Detroit	$32,490
CA: Los Angeles	$27,380	MN: Minneapolis	$33,380
CA: Riverside	$26,950	MO: Kansas City	$25,240
CA: Sacramento	$29,690	MO: St. Louis	$27,220
CA: San Diego	$27,070	NV: Las Vegas	$26,750
CA: San Francisco	$30,370	NY: New York	$31,300
CO: Denver	$28,290	OH: Cincinnati	$27,810
DC: Washington	$29,410	OH: Cleveland	$26,240
FL: Miami	$23,390	OH: Columbus	$26,190
FL: Orlando	$24,380	OR: Portland	$29,830
FL: Tampa	$26,060	PA: Philadelphia	$30,470
GA: Atlanta	$29,060	PA: Pittsburgh	$25,650
IL: Chicago	$27,730	TX: Dallas	$24,940
MA: Boston	$32,810	TX: Houston	$26,400
MD: Baltimore	$31,790	WA: Seattle	$31,470

FACTORS THAT MAY AFFECT EARNINGS

Educational Attainment of Workers and Effect on Earnings

	Percent at Level	Effect on Earnings
Less than High School	—	—
Some High School	6.7%	–55.2%
High School or Equivalent	38.3%	9.2%
Some College but No Degree	28.9%	–9.0%
Associate Degree	9.4%	–23.4%
Bachelor's Degree	13.4%	46.2%
Master's Degree	—	—
Doctoral Degree	—	—
First Professional Degree	—	—

Flexibility of Earnings

Average Hours Worked: 32
Workers with a Varying Number of Hours: 5.5%
Workers Earning Some Overtime Pay, Tips, or Commissions: 11.8%
Earnings Benefit of Working Overtime: 31.5%

Gender

	Male	Female
Percent	30.6%	69.4%
Effect on Earnings	—	–1.7%

Union Membership

Percentage Union Members: 6.5%
Earnings Benefit of Union Membership: 28.7%

Veteran Status

Percentage Who Have Been on Active Duty: Insignificant
Earnings Benefit of Veteran Status: No significant data available

43-4161 Human Resources Assistants, Except Payroll and Timekeeping

Compile and keep personnel records. Record data for each employee, such as address, weekly earnings, absences, amount of sales or production, supervisory reports on ability, and date of and reason for termination. Compile and type reports from employment records. File employment records. Search employee files and furnish information to authorized persons.

- Education or Training Required: Short-term on-the-job training
- Job Growth: 16.7%
- Annual Openings: 28,000
- Self-Employed: 0.1%
- Part-Time: 21.4%

NATIONAL WAGE FIGURES (ANNUAL)

Beginning	25th Percentile	Median	Mean	75th Percentile	90th Percentile
$22,700	$27,430	$33,750	$34,740	$41,080	$48,670

Median Wages for Industries Employing Largest Numbers (Annual)

Industry	Median Income
Computer and Electronic Product Manufacturing	$37,540
Federal, State, and Local Government	$36,970
Professional, Scientific, and Technical Services	$36,350
Publishing Industries (Except Internet)	$35,690
Insurance Carriers and Related Activities	$34,890
Machinery Manufacturing	$34,510
Management of Companies and Enterprises	$34,260
Fabricated Metal Product Manufacturing	$34,180
Real Estate	$34,040
Religious, Grantmaking, Civic, Professional, and Similar Organizations	$33,960

Median Wages for States (Annual)

AK	$37,280	KY	$31,800	NY	$35,440
AL	$29,500	LA	$30,040	OH	$33,350
AR	$28,980	MA	$36,770	OK	$28,070
AZ	$34,050	MD	$37,190	OR	$34,230
CA	$38,840	ME	$28,460	PA	$33,830
CO	$35,880	MI	$35,530	RI	$32,520
CT	$39,500	MN	$34,710	SC	$30,740
DC	$41,440	MO	$33,080	SD	$25,850
DE	$35,320	MS	$30,070	TN	$31,900
FL	$29,580	MT	$28,920	TX	$31,310
GA	$31,870	NC	$30,400	UT	$29,730
HI	$34,550	ND	$29,760	VA	$35,740
IA	$31,820	NE	$29,920	VT	$31,970
ID	$31,420	NH	$33,060	WA	$35,250
IL	$34,700	NJ	$36,670	WI	$33,330
IN	$31,190	NM	$31,790	WV	$29,670
KS	$31,860	NV	$29,220	WY	$32,950

Median Wages for the Largest Metropolitan Areas (Annual)

AZ: Phoenix	$34,550	MI: Detroit	$36,040
CA: Los Angeles	$37,790	MN: Minneapolis	$36,160
CA: Riverside	$35,730	MO: Kansas City	$34,860
CA: Sacramento	$44,090	MO: St. Louis	$35,150
CA: San Diego	$35,310	NV: Las Vegas	$28,580
CA: San Francisco	$43,140	NY: New York	$37,360
CO: Denver	$37,750	OH: Cincinnati	$35,060
DC: Washington	$40,920	OH: Cleveland	$32,680
FL: Miami	$31,060	OH: Columbus	$34,690
FL: Orlando	$28,940	OR: Portland	$36,260
FL: Tampa	$28,810	PA: Philadelphia	$35,930
GA: Atlanta	$33,470	PA: Pittsburgh	$32,730
IL: Chicago	$35,650	TX: Dallas	$33,820
MA: Boston	$37,850	TX: Houston	$33,150
MD: Baltimore	$36,220	WA: Seattle	$36,410

FACTORS THAT MAY AFFECT EARNINGS

Educational Attainment of Workers and Effect on Earnings

	Percent at Level	Effect on Earnings
Less than High School	—	—
Some High School	—	—
High School or Equivalent	20.7%	−13.1%
Some College but No Degree	31.0%	−9.9%
Associate Degree	12.6%	4.4%
Bachelor's Degree	31.0%	18.2%
Master's Degree	—	—
Doctoral Degree	—	—
First Professional Degree	—	—

Flexibility of Earnings

Average Hours Worked: 34
Workers with a Varying Number of Hours: 3.5%
Workers Earning Some Overtime Pay, Tips, or Commissions: 4.3%
Earnings Benefit of Working Overtime: 31.5%

Gender

	Male	Female
Percent	8.1%	91.9%
Effect on Earnings	8.2%	−2.6%

Union Membership

Percentage Union Members: 9.6%
Earnings Benefit of Union Membership: 30.9%

Veteran Status

Percentage Who Have Been on Active Duty: Insignificant
Earnings Benefit of Veteran Status: No significant data available

43-4171 Receptionists and Information Clerks

Answer inquiries and obtain information for general public, customers, visitors, and other interested parties. Provide information regarding activities conducted at establishment and location of departments, offices, and employees within organization.

- Education or Training Required: Short-term on-the-job training
- Job Growth: 21.7%
- Annual Openings: 299,000
- Self-Employed: 0.8%
- Part-Time: 52.5%

NATIONAL WAGE FIGURES (ANNUAL)

Beginning	25th Percentile	Median	Mean	75th Percentile	90th Percentile
$15,670	$18,850	$22,900	$23,810	$28,100	$33,750

Median Wages for Industries Employing Largest Numbers (Annual)

Industry	Median Income
Securities, Commodity Contracts, and Other Financial Investments and Related Activities	$25,930
Management of Companies and Enterprises	$25,310
Federal, State, and Local Government	$24,930
Hospitals	$24,410
Merchant Wholesalers, Nondurable Goods	$24,350
Construction of Buildings	$24,330
Merchant Wholesalers, Durable Goods	$24,190
Ambulatory Health Care Services	$24,030
Specialty Trade Contractors	$23,970
Professional, Scientific, and Technical Services	$23,900

Median Wages for States (Annual)

State	Wage	State	Wage	State	Wage
AK	$28,100	KY	$20,920	NY	$25,830
AL	$19,810	LA	$19,100	OH	$21,740
AR	$19,630	MA	$25,310	OK	$20,520
AZ	$23,140	MD	$24,480	OR	$24,000
CA	$24,720	ME	$22,490	PA	$22,160
CO	$24,930	MI	$23,650	RI	$24,420
CT	$27,240	MN	$25,340	SC	$21,820
DC	$27,860	MO	$21,470	SD	$20,340
DE	$23,650	MS	$19,450	TN	$22,050
FL	$21,770	MT	$20,710	TX	$21,170
GA	$23,420	NC	$22,010	UT	$20,870
HI	$23,920	ND	$20,730	VA	$22,400
IA	$21,790	NE	$21,540	VT	$23,210
ID	$20,740	NH	$24,560	WA	$23,600
IL	$24,170	NJ	$24,490	WI	$23,640
IN	$21,650	NM	$20,160	WV	$19,120
KS	$21,630	NV	$23,330	WY	$20,350

Median Wages for the Largest Metropolitan Areas (Annual)

Area	Wage	Area	Wage
AZ: Phoenix	$24,180	MI: Detroit	$24,680
CA: Los Angeles	$24,910	MN: Minneapolis	$26,570
CA: Riverside	$22,360	MO: Kansas City	$24,200
CA: Sacramento	$24,750	MO: St. Louis	$22,080
CA: San Diego	$24,220	NV: Las Vegas	$23,340
CA: San Francisco	$28,640	NY: New York	$26,820
CO: Denver	$26,350	OH: Cincinnati	$22,420
DC: Washington	$26,400	OH: Cleveland	$22,910
FL: Miami	$22,370	OH: Columbus	$22,440
FL: Orlando	$21,440	OR: Portland	$25,270
FL: Tampa	$22,110	PA: Philadelphia	$25,000
GA: Atlanta	$25,530	PA: Pittsburgh	$20,300
IL: Chicago	$25,340	TX: Dallas	$24,250
MA: Boston	$25,790	TX: Houston	$21,940
MD: Baltimore	$24,090	WA: Seattle	$25,330

FACTORS THAT MAY AFFECT EARNINGS

Educational Attainment of Workers and Effect on Earnings

	Percent at Level	Effect on Earnings
Less than High School	1.1%	−42.4%
Some High School	9.7%	−41.8%
High School or Equivalent	31.6%	4.5%
Some College but No Degree	27.9%	−5.5%
Associate Degree	15.0%	7.2%
Bachelor's Degree	12.5%	20.5%
Master's Degree	1.7%	27.1%
Doctoral Degree	—	—
First Professional Degree	—	—

Flexibility of Earnings

Average Hours Worked: 29
Workers with a Varying Number of Hours: 4.9%
Workers Earning Some Overtime Pay, Tips, or Commissions: 7.1%
Earnings Benefit of Working Overtime: 13.0%

Gender

	Male	Female
Percent	7.3%	92.7%
Effect on Earnings	19.1%	−1.1%

Union Membership

Percentage Union Members: Insignificant
Earnings Benefit of Union Membership: No significant data available

Veteran Status

Percentage Who Have Been on Active Duty: Insignificant
Earnings Benefit of Veteran Status: No significant data available

43-4181 Reservation and Transportation Ticket Agents and Travel Clerks

Make and confirm reservations and sell tickets to passengers and for large hotel or motel chains. May check baggage and direct passengers to designated concourse, pier, or track; make reservations; deliver tickets; arrange for visas; contact individuals and groups to inform them of package tours; or provide tourists with travel information, such as points of interest, restaurants, rates, and emergency service.

- Education or Training Required: Short-term on-the-job training
- Job Growth: 2.4%
- Annual Openings: 30,000
- Self-Employed: 1.4%
- Part-Time: 21.4%

NATIONAL WAGE FIGURES (ANNUAL)

Beginning	25th Percentile	Median	Mean	75th Percentile	90th Percentile
$17,670	$21,640	$28,540	$30,120	$38,540	$45,400

Median Wages for Industries Employing Largest Numbers (Annual)

Industry	Median Income
Federal, State, and Local Government	$32,980
Air Transportation	$32,780
Rail Transportation	$32,650
Religious, Grantmaking, Civic, Professional, and Similar Organizations	$30,620
Performing Arts, Spectator Sports, and Related Industries	$26,980
Couriers and Messengers	$26,090
Water Transportation	$25,540
Scenic and Sightseeing Transportation	$24,800
Management of Companies and Enterprises	$24,370
Accommodation	$23,530

Median Wages for States (Annual)

AK	$32,220	KY	$27,270	NY	$30,910
AL	$27,030	LA	$23,520	OH	$29,390
AR	$21,000	MA	$34,850	OK	$27,510
AZ	$21,630	MD	$29,760	OR	$28,710
CA	$28,600	ME	$22,720	PA	$27,880
CO	$27,070	MI	$32,430	RI	no data
CT	no data	MN	no data	SC	$22,260
DC	$26,930	MO	$25,660	SD	no data
DE	no data	MS	$23,320	TN	$19,460
FL	$27,460	MT	$27,960	TX	$31,630
GA	no data	NC	$32,350	UT	$24,150
HI	$31,430	ND	no data	VA	$27,630
IA	$25,860	NE	$21,050	VT	$24,930
ID	$33,620	NH	$28,760	WA	$29,070
IL	$30,180	NJ	$31,690	WI	$22,130
IN	$23,730	NM	no data	WV	no data
KS	$27,620	NV	$28,140	WY	$23,200

Median Wages for the Largest Metropolitan Areas (Annual)

AZ: Phoenix	$21,890	MI: Detroit	$34,500
CA: Los Angeles	$29,570	MN: Minneapolis	no data
CA: Riverside	$22,000	MO: Kansas City	$29,580
CA: Sacramento	$24,650	MO: St. Louis	$26,640
CA: San Diego	$30,790	NV: Las Vegas	$29,420
CA: San Francisco	$29,330	NY: New York	$32,430
CO: Denver	$28,280	OH: Cincinnati	$28,720
DC: Washington	$27,500	OH: Cleveland	no data
FL: Miami	$27,340	OH: Columbus	$29,770
FL: Orlando	$23,830	OR: Portland	$31,090
FL: Tampa	$32,690	PA: Philadelphia	$33,680
GA: Atlanta	no data	PA: Pittsburgh	no data
IL: Chicago	$30,580	TX: Dallas	no data
MA: Boston	$37,550	TX: Houston	no data
MD: Baltimore	$31,380	WA: Seattle	$29,600

FACTORS THAT MAY AFFECT EARNINGS

Educational Attainment of Workers and Effect on Earnings

	Percent at Level	Effect on Earnings
Less than High School	—	—
Some High School	3.0%	−13.4%
High School or Equivalent	28.0%	−5.8%
Some College but No Degree	31.0%	−9.0%
Associate Degree	11.5%	10.9%
Bachelor's Degree	22.0%	13.7%
Master's Degree	4.0%	−13.2%
Doctoral Degree	—	—
First Professional Degree	—	—

Flexibility of Earnings

Average Hours Worked: 35
Workers with a Varying Number of Hours: 3.9%
Workers Earning Some Overtime Pay, Tips, or Commissions: 20.8%
Earnings Benefit of Working Overtime: 21.1%

Gender

	Male	Female
Percent	35.2%	64.8%
Effect on Earnings	—	−3.7%

Union Membership

Percentage Union Members: 19.0%
Earnings Benefit of Union Membership: 4.8%

Veteran Status

Percentage Who Have Been on Active Duty: Insignificant
Earnings Benefit of Veteran Status: No significant data available

43-4199 Information and Record Clerks, All Other

All information and record clerks not listed separately.

- Education or Training Required: Short-term on-the-job training
- Job Growth: –8.6%
- Annual Openings: 46,000
- Self-Employed: 0.3%
- Part-Time: 41.0%

NATIONAL WAGE FIGURES (ANNUAL)

Beginning	25th Percentile	Median	Mean	75th Percentile	90th Percentile
$19,600	$24,120	$31,150	$32,900	$39,620	$48,100

Median Wages for Industries Employing Largest Numbers (Annual)

Industry	Median Income
Postal Service	$45,510
Telecommunications	$38,110
Chemical Manufacturing	$36,890
Federal, State, and Local Government	$35,410
Securities, Commodity Contracts, and Other Financial Investments and Related Activities	$35,070
Performing Arts, Spectator Sports, and Related Industries	$34,640
Publishing Industries (Except Internet)	$34,190
Internet Service Providers, Web Search Portals, and Data-Processing Services	$33,090
Religious, Grantmaking, Civic, Professional, and Similar Organizations	$31,970
Support Activities for Transportation	$31,880

Median Wages for States (Annual)

AK	$36,200	KY	$27,520	NY	$32,720
AL	$28,820	LA	$26,680	OH	$29,100
AR	$27,160	MA	$34,330	OK	$30,150
AZ	$28,810	MD	$38,390	OR	$27,210
CA	$33,450	ME	$26,520	PA	$32,350
CO	$33,040	MI	$29,100	RI	$32,070
CT	$33,700	MN	$29,570	SC	$29,000
DC	$41,850	MO	$29,450	SD	$33,760
DE	$31,750	MS	$27,900	TN	$30,070
FL	$28,350	MT	$31,180	TX	$29,450
GA	$30,720	NC	$30,000	UT	$30,310
HI	$38,030	ND	$30,400	VA	$33,890
IA	$28,460	NE	$28,180	VT	$32,390
ID	$31,100	NH	$25,340	WA	$35,480
IL	$30,530	NJ	$35,930	WI	$29,700
IN	$28,000	NM	$30,640	WV	$32,630
KS	$29,370	NV	$30,470	WY	$29,650

Median Wages for the Largest Metropolitan Areas (Annual)

AZ: Phoenix	$28,650	MI: Detroit	$31,600
CA: Los Angeles	$32,800	MN: Minneapolis	$30,300
CA: Riverside	$31,660	MO: Kansas City	$31,680
CA: Sacramento	$32,550	MO: St. Louis	$30,360
CA: San Diego	$35,250	NV: Las Vegas	$31,530
CA: San Francisco	$40,780	NY: New York	$35,810
CO: Denver	$34,060	OH: Cincinnati	$28,660
DC: Washington	$41,450	OH: Cleveland	$28,480
FL: Miami	$29,750	OH: Columbus	$31,510
FL: Orlando	$28,100	OR: Portland	$27,400
FL: Tampa	$29,530	PA: Philadelphia	$33,500
GA: Atlanta	$31,490	PA: Pittsburgh	$32,020
IL: Chicago	$32,450	TX: Dallas	$31,860
MA: Boston	$34,030	TX: Houston	$29,330
MD: Baltimore	$35,280	WA: Seattle	$37,300

FACTORS THAT MAY AFFECT EARNINGS

Educational Attainment of Workers and Effect on Earnings

	Percent at Level	Effect on Earnings
Less than High School	—	—
Some High School	—	—
High School or Equivalent	32.5%	–5.5%
Some College but No Degree	18.7%	0.2%
Associate Degree	23.6%	–2.6%
Bachelor's Degree	16.3%	18.0%
Master's Degree	6.5%	16.7%
Doctoral Degree	—	—
First Professional Degree	—	—

Flexibility of Earnings

Average Hours Worked: 34
Workers with a Varying Number of Hours: 6.4%
Workers Earning Some Overtime Pay, Tips, or Commissions: 10.7%
Earnings Benefit of Working Overtime: 31.5%

Gender

	Male	Female
Percent	13.4%	86.6%
Effect on Earnings	8.2%	–2.6%

Union Membership

Percentage Union Members: 15.3%
Earnings Benefit of Union Membership: 18.8%

Veteran Status

Percentage Who Have Been on Active Duty: Insignificant
Earnings Benefit of Veteran Status: No significant data available

43-5000 Material Recording, Scheduling, Dispatching, and Distributing Workers

43-5011 Cargo and Freight Agents

Expedite and route movement of incoming and outgoing cargo and freight shipments in airline, train, and trucking terminals and shipping docks. Take orders from customers and arrange pickup of freight and cargo for delivery to loading platform. Prepare and examine bills of lading to determine shipping charges and tariffs.

- Education or Training Required: Moderate-term on-the-job training
- Job Growth: –5.6%
- Annual Openings: 12,000
- Self-Employed: 0.0%
- Part-Time: 11.1%

NATIONAL WAGE FIGURES (ANNUAL)

Beginning	25th Percentile	Median	Mean	75th Percentile	90th Percentile
$22,470	$27,750	$37,110	$38,560	$46,440	$57,440

Median Wages for Industries Employing Largest Numbers (Annual)

Industry	Median Income
Postal Service	$57,420
Rail Transportation	$45,860
Federal, State, and Local Government	$45,790
Merchant Wholesalers, Nondurable Goods	$44,180
Computer and Electronic Product Manufacturing	$42,510
Wholesale Electronic Markets and Agents and Brokers	$40,130
Professional, Scientific, and Technical Services	$39,690
Air Transportation	$38,130
Food Manufacturing	$37,970
Water Transportation	$37,860

Median Wages for States (Annual)

State	Wage	State	Wage	State	Wage
AK	$34,960	KY	$35,330	NY	$37,650
AL	$36,350	LA	no data	OH	$31,670
AR	$36,630	MA	$40,030	OK	$39,470
AZ	$34,450	MD	$32,470	OR	$28,720
CA	$42,750	ME	$38,180	PA	$29,460
CO	$35,150	MI	$34,770	RI	no data
CT	no data	MN	$41,330	SC	$37,640
DC	$42,090	MO	$41,440	SD	$38,670
DE	$35,380	MS	$32,530	TN	$37,160
FL	$35,640	MT	$33,750	TX	$32,920
GA	$35,370	NC	$38,100	UT	no data
HI	$24,410	ND	no data	VA	$37,750
IA	$40,060	NE	$44,640	VT	$27,210
ID	$34,860	NH	$42,180	WA	$46,200
IL	$38,440	NJ	$37,720	WI	$29,050
IN	$36,010	NM	$33,390	WV	$22,890
KS	no data	NV	$35,700	WY	no data

Median Wages for the Largest Metropolitan Areas (Annual)

Area	Wage	Area	Wage
AZ: Phoenix	$32,630	MI: Detroit	$32,030
CA: Los Angeles	$45,750	MN: Minneapolis	$38,300
CA: Riverside	$39,980	MO: Kansas City	$33,250
CA: Sacramento	$42,450	MO: St. Louis	$42,560
CA: San Diego	$34,080	NV: Las Vegas	$34,930
CA: San Francisco	$39,810	NY: New York	$38,490
CO: Denver	$34,130	OH: Cincinnati	$29,880
DC: Washington	$37,230	OH: Cleveland	$36,730
FL: Miami	$37,510	OH: Columbus	$32,980
FL: Orlando	$28,600	OR: Portland	$29,000
FL: Tampa	$30,050	PA: Philadelphia	$38,220
GA: Atlanta	$35,280	PA: Pittsburgh	$26,650
IL: Chicago	$38,700	TX: Dallas	$32,020
MA: Boston	$40,300	TX: Houston	$32,570
MD: Baltimore	no data	WA: Seattle	$45,480

FACTORS THAT MAY AFFECT EARNINGS

Educational Attainment of Workers and Effect on Earnings

	Percent at Level	Effect on Earnings
Less than High School	—	—
Some High School	—	—
High School or Equivalent	41.7%	9.8%
Some College but No Degree	29.2%	–2.5%
Associate Degree	—	—
Bachelor's Degree	—	—
Master's Degree	—	—
Doctoral Degree	—	—
First Professional Degree	—	—

Figures do not total 100% because some levels have a very small sample size.

Flexibility of Earnings

Average Hours Worked: 37
Workers with a Varying Number of Hours: 7.4%
Workers Earning Some Overtime Pay, Tips, or Commissions: 19.2%
Earnings Benefit of Working Overtime: 21.2%

Gender

	Male	Female
Percent	61.6%	38.4%
Effect on Earnings	8.2%	–2.6%

Union Membership

Percentage Union Members: 38.5%
Earnings Benefit of Union Membership: 20.7%

Veteran Status

Percentage Who Have Been on Active Duty: 12.5%
Earnings Benefit of Veteran Status: 28.7%

43-5021 Couriers and Messengers

Pick up and carry messages, documents, packages, and other items between offices or departments within an establishment or to other business concerns, traveling by foot, bicycle, motorcycle, automobile, or public conveyance.

- Education or Training Required: Short-term on-the-job training
- Job Growth: –8.6%
- Annual Openings: 24,000
- Self-Employed: 20.2%
- Part-Time: 29.3%

NATIONAL WAGE FIGURES (ANNUAL)

Beginning	25th Percentile	Median	Mean	75th Percentile	90th Percentile
$14,870	$17,430	$21,540	$23,170	$27,080	$34,510

Median Wages for Industries Employing Largest Numbers (Annual)

Industry	Median Income
Postal Service	$45,420
Warehousing and Storage	$28,210
Truck Transportation	$26,200
Educational Services	$24,690
Merchant Wholesalers, Nondurable Goods	$23,800
Federal, State, and Local Government	$23,790
Chemical Manufacturing	$23,180
Air Transportation	$23,150
Ambulatory Health Care Services	$22,950
Hospitals	$22,490

Median Wages for States (Annual)

AK $25,040	KY $19,220	NY $20,170
AL $16,530	LA $17,290	OH $22,130
AR $20,420	MA $24,890	OK $20,780
AZ $22,650	MD $25,180	OR $27,550
CA $20,740	ME $23,270	PA $20,820
CO $23,020	MI $22,180	RI .... no data
CT $26,820	MN .... no data	SC $17,720
DC $24,620	MO $22,790	SD $20,680
DE $23,260	MS $17,820	TN $20,630
FL $21,470	MT $17,170	TX $21,750
GA $21,060	NC $21,650	UT $20,720
HI $24,900	ND $18,730	VA $23,110
IA $18,870	NE $20,740	VT $23,700
ID $20,890	NH $22,530	WA $23,030
IL $20,870	NJ $25,830	WI $21,950
IN $21,420	NM $19,720	WV $17,900
KS $19,690	NV $21,600	WY $18,400

Median Wages for the Largest Metropolitan Areas (Annual)

AZ: Phoenix $22,830	MI: Detroit $23,610
CA: Los Angeles $18,910	MN: Minneapolis $36,840
CA: Riverside $19,680	MO: Kansas City $20,100
CA: Sacramento $23,050	MO: St. Louis $24,300
CA: San Diego $22,430	NV: Las Vegas $21,630
CA: San Francisco $24,070	NY: New York $20,930
CO: Denver $25,390	OH: Cincinnati $22,260
DC: Washington $27,260	OH: Cleveland $22,360
FL: Miami $22,200	OH: Columbus $24,140
FL: Orlando $20,080	OR: Portland $29,320
FL: Tampa $22,220	PA: Philadelphia $23,880
GA: Atlanta $22,210	PA: Pittsburgh $16,730
IL: Chicago $21,150	TX: Dallas $24,630
MA: Boston $24,640	TX: Houston $25,250
MD: Baltimore $27,120	WA: Seattle $25,410

FACTORS THAT MAY AFFECT EARNINGS

Educational Attainment of Workers and Effect on Earnings

	Percent at Level	Effect on Earnings
Less than High School	—	—
Some High School	8.1%	–51.0%
High School or Equivalent	33.3%	8.2%
Some College but No Degree	30.2%	–3.0%
Associate Degree	10.9%	–7.4%
Bachelor's Degree	14.0%	31.5%
Master's Degree	—	—
Doctoral Degree	—	—
First Professional Degree	—	—

Flexibility of Earnings

Average Hours Worked: 32
Workers with a Varying Number of Hours: 11.2%
Workers Earning Some Overtime Pay, Tips, or Commissions: 23.6%
Earnings Benefit of Working Overtime: 29.2%

Gender

	Male	Female
Percent	82.1%	17.9%
Effect on Earnings	3.2%	—

Union Membership

Percentage Union Members: 21.7%
Earnings Benefit of Union Membership: 56.5%

Veteran Status

Percentage Who Have Been on Active Duty: 12.5%
Earnings Benefit of Veteran Status: 28.7%

43-5031 Police, Fire, and Ambulance Dispatchers

Receive complaints from public concerning crimes and police emergencies. Broadcast orders to police patrol units in vicinity of complaint to investigate. Operate radio, telephone, or computer equipment to receive reports of fires and medical emergencies and relay information or orders to proper officials.

- Education or Training Required: Moderate-term on-the-job training
- Job Growth: 15.9%
- Annual Openings: 12,000
- Self-Employed: 1.3%
- Part-Time: 32.8%

NATIONAL WAGE FIGURES (ANNUAL)

Beginning	25th Percentile	Median	Mean	75th Percentile	90th Percentile
$20,010	$25,200	$31,470	$32,590	$39,040	$47,190

Median Wages for Industries Employing Largest Numbers (Annual)

Industry	Median Income
Fabricated Metal Product Manufacturing	$42,150
Telecommunications	$35,210
Professional, Scientific, and Technical Services	$35,000
Federal, State, and Local Government	$31,780
Administrative and Support Services	$31,240
Waste Management and Remediation Services	$30,110
Educational Services	$30,090
Hospitals	$28,490
Ambulatory Health Care Services	$27,590
Transit and Ground Passenger Transportation	$22,270

Median Wages for States (Annual)

AK $38,450	KY $24,440	NY $36,370
AL $24,050	LA $26,000	OH $35,370
AR $22,250	MA $35,150	OK $21,570
AZ $32,970	MD $34,630	OR $38,110
CA $46,370	ME $32,130	PA $30,760
CO $36,350	MI $35,630	RI $35,390
CT $35,510	MN $38,280	SC $25,920
DC .... no data	MO $25,890	SD $24,880
DE $33,910	MS $21,670	TN $26,760
FL $31,280	MT $26,990	TX $28,590
GA $26,760	NC $27,510	UT $30,120
HI $37,450	ND $28,870	VA $31,020
IA $29,880	NE $24,580	VT $33,570
ID $30,520	NH $31,560	WA $43,400
IL $36,250	NJ $35,240	WI $36,070
IN $27,410	NM $25,780	WV $19,930
KS $27,630	NV $47,220	WY $29,960

Median Wages for the Largest Metropolitan Areas (Annual)

AZ: Phoenix $35,660	MI: Detroit $38,240
CA: Los Angeles $49,960	MN: Minneapolis $42,960
CA: Riverside $40,220	MO: Kansas City $32,460
CA: Sacramento ...... no data	MO: St. Louis $32,730
CA: San Diego $45,970	NV: Las Vegas .... no data
CA: San Francisco $53,950	NY: New York $36,420
CO: Denver $37,130	OH: Cincinnati $36,300
DC: Washington $40,480	OH: Cleveland $36,030
FL: Miami $38,370	OH: Columbus $38,920
FL: Orlando $30,260	OR: Portland $45,950
FL: Tampa $31,300	PA: Philadelphia $35,170
GA: Atlanta $30,400	PA: Pittsburgh $27,780
IL: Chicago $38,420	TX: Dallas $33,650
MA: Boston $36,130	TX: Houston $30,620
MD: Baltimore $34,060	WA: Seattle $45,580

FACTORS THAT MAY AFFECT EARNINGS

Educational Attainment of Workers and Effect on Earnings

Figures are based on a group of occupations: Material Recording, Scheduling, Dispatching, and Distributing Workers

	Percent at Level	Effect on Earnings
Less than High School	2.8%	−35.8%
Some High School	11.5%	−42.9%
High School or Equivalent	35.9%	0.6%
Some College but No Degree	24.8%	4.8%
Associate Degree	11.3%	11.9%
Bachelor's Degree	11.1%	21.3%
Master's Degree	2.1%	21.3%
Doctoral Degree	—	—
First Professional Degree	—	—

Flexibility of Earnings

Average Hours Worked: 32
Workers with a Varying Number of Hours: 6.8%
Workers Earning Some Overtime Pay, Tips, or Commissions: 15.9%
Earnings Benefit of Working Overtime: 7.8%

Gender

	Male	Female
Percent	46.6%	53.4%
Effect on Earnings	10.9%	−8.4%

Union Membership

Percentage Union Members: 17.6%
Earnings Benefit of Union Membership: 42.6%

Veteran Status

Percentage Who Have Been on Active Duty: 12.5%
Earnings Benefit of Veteran Status: 28.7%

43-5032 Dispatchers, Except Police, Fire, and Ambulance

Schedule and dispatch workers, work crews, equipment, or service vehicles for conveyance of materials, freight, or passengers or for normal installation, service, or emergency repairs rendered outside the place of business. Duties may include using radio, telephone, or computer to transmit assignments and compiling statistics and reports on work progress.

- Education or Training Required: Moderate-term on-the-job training
- Job Growth: 5.7%
- Annual Openings: 19,000
- Self-Employed: 1.5%
- Part-Time: 32.8%

NATIONAL WAGE FIGURES (ANNUAL)

Beginning	25th Percentile	Median	Mean	75th Percentile	90th Percentile
$19,780	$24,860	$32,190	$34,450	$42,030	$53,250

Median Wages for Industries Employing Largest Numbers (Annual)

Industry	Median Income
Rail Transportation	$50,460
Utilities	$39,830
Motor Vehicle and Parts Dealers	$36,440
Truck Transportation	$36,060
Building Material and Garden Equipment and Supplies Dealers	$35,650
Nonmetallic Mineral Product Manufacturing	$35,370
Heavy and Civil Engineering Construction	$35,240
Couriers and Messengers	$35,220
Management of Companies and Enterprises	$34,930
Support Activities for Mining	$34,930

Median Wages for States (Annual)

State	Wage	State	Wage	State	Wage
AK	$39,150	KY	$30,520	NY	$30,280
AL	$29,470	LA	$28,940	OH	$32,910
AR	$30,850	MA	$36,370	OK	$28,910
AZ	$30,630	MD	$32,380	OR	$32,070
CA	$33,980	ME	$31,300	PA	$31,580
CO	$33,080	MI	$35,240	RI	$29,650
CT	$34,130	MN	$36,790	SC	$29,370
DC	$33,710	MO	$29,690	SD	$25,540
DE	$31,390	MS	$26,680	TN	$32,780
FL	$29,020	MT	$28,740	TX	$31,320
GA	$33,120	NC	$30,870	UT	$31,770
HI	$29,890	ND	$34,000	VA	$31,640
IA	$31,280	NE	$32,800	VT	$33,570
ID	$30,580	NH	$32,060	WA	$38,020
IL	$35,110	NJ	$37,260	WI	$33,480
IN	$31,690	NM	$30,070	WV	$26,520
KS	$31,330	NV	$29,020	WY	$33,670

Median Wages for the Largest Metropolitan Areas (Annual)

Area	Wage	Area	Wage
AZ: Phoenix	$31,450	MI: Detroit	$36,790
CA: Los Angeles	$32,920	MN: Minneapolis	$37,720
CA: Riverside	$32,840	MO: Kansas City	$34,330
CA: Sacramento	$35,630	MO: St. Louis	$30,620
CA: San Diego	$33,170	NV: Las Vegas	$28,360
CA: San Francisco	$36,850	NY: New York	$33,740
CO: Denver	$35,080	OH: Cincinnati	$33,520
DC: Washington	$32,060	OH: Cleveland	$28,990
FL: Miami	$29,610	OH: Columbus	$36,190
FL: Orlando	$29,440	OR: Portland	$33,510
FL: Tampa	$28,900	PA: Philadelphia	$33,220
GA: Atlanta	$33,900	PA: Pittsburgh	$29,880
IL: Chicago	$37,000	TX: Dallas	$32,150
MA: Boston	$35,700	TX: Houston	$34,260
MD: Baltimore	$31,940	WA: Seattle	$40,330

FACTORS THAT MAY AFFECT EARNINGS

Educational Attainment of Workers and Effect on Earnings

Figures are based on a group of occupations: Material Recording, Scheduling, Dispatching, and Distributing Workers

	Percent at Level	Effect on Earnings
Less than High School	2.8%	−35.8%
Some High School	11.5%	−42.9%
High School or Equivalent	35.9%	0.6%
Some College but No Degree	24.8%	4.8%
Associate Degree	11.3%	11.9%
Bachelor's Degree	11.1%	21.3%
Master's Degree	2.1%	21.3%
Doctoral Degree	—	—
First Professional Degree	—	—

Flexibility of Earnings

Average Hours Worked: 32
Workers with a Varying Number of Hours: 6.8%
Workers Earning Some Overtime Pay, Tips, or Commissions: 15.9%
Earnings Benefit of Working Overtime: 7.8%

Gender

	Male	Female
Percent	46.6%	53.4%
Effect on Earnings	10.9%	−8.4%

Union Membership

Percentage Union Members: 17.6%
Earnings Benefit of Union Membership: 42.6%

Veteran Status

Percentage Who Have Been on Active Duty: 12.5%
Earnings Benefit of Veteran Status: 28.7%

43-5041 Meter Readers, Utilities

Read meter and record consumption of electricity, gas, water, or steam.

- Education or Training Required: Short-term on-the-job training
- Job Growth: –44.9%
- Annual Openings: 8,000
- Self-Employed: 0.0%
- Part-Time: 32.8%

NATIONAL WAGE FIGURES (ANNUAL)

Beginning	25th Percentile	Median	Mean	75th Percentile	90th Percentile
$18,970	$23,580	$30,330	$32,040	$39,320	$49,150

Median Wages for Industries Employing Largest Numbers (Annual)

Industry	Median Income
Management of Companies and Enterprises	$37,190
Utilities	$33,970
Pipeline Transportation	$30,100
Federal, State, and Local Government	$28,310
Specialty Trade Contractors	$26,810
Administrative and Support Services	$25,890

Median Wages for States (Annual)

AK	$37,740	KY	$25,080	NY	$35,120
AL	$27,530	LA	$21,720	OH	$32,900
AR	$22,540	MA	$38,280	OK	$25,150
AZ	$35,420	MD	$40,930	OR	$34,320
CA	$37,150	ME	$34,470	PA	$36,550
CO	$36,690	MI	$34,120	RI	$42,630
CT	$45,100	MN	$39,870	SC	$26,420
DC	no data	MO	$29,050	SD	$26,270
DE	$42,990	MS	$23,200	TN	$29,600
FL	$28,130	MT	$28,780	TX	$26,490
GA	$26,530	NC	$26,700	UT	$28,350
HI	$42,630	ND	$21,080	VA	$29,710
IA	$31,640	NE	$38,340	VT	$33,400
ID	$30,880	NH	$36,420	WA	$43,210
IL	$29,860	NJ	$41,140	WI	$29,290
IN	$29,950	NM	$25,020	WV	$24,360
KS	$28,370	NV	$39,320	WY	$34,080

Median Wages for the Largest Metropolitan Areas (Annual)

AZ: Phoenix	$38,930	MI: Detroit	$35,720
CA: Los Angeles	no data	MN: Minneapolis	$38,420
CA: Riverside	$34,680	MO: Kansas City	$34,110
CA: Sacramento	$34,020	MO: St. Louis	$33,660
CA: San Diego	no data	NV: Las Vegas	$39,580
CA: San Francisco	$51,590	NY: New York	$41,500
CO: Denver	$37,170	OH: Cincinnati	$34,000
DC: Washington	$40,170	OH: Cleveland	$34,810
FL: Miami	$29,060	OH: Columbus	$29,000
FL: Orlando	$30,360	OR: Portland	$35,990
FL: Tampa	$26,540	PA: Philadelphia	$40,600
GA: Atlanta	$26,510	PA: Pittsburgh	$31,270
IL: Chicago	$28,290	TX: Dallas	$27,870
MA: Boston	$38,290	TX: Houston	$26,730
MD: Baltimore	$39,620	WA: Seattle	$39,480

FACTORS THAT MAY AFFECT EARNINGS

Educational Attainment of Workers and Effect on Earnings

	Percent at Level	Effect on Earnings
Less than High School	—	—
Some High School	—	—
High School or Equivalent	60.0%	–7.1%
Some College but No Degree	25.0%	21.9%
Associate Degree	—	—
Bachelor's Degree	—	—
Master's Degree	—	—
Doctoral Degree	—	—
First Professional Degree	—	—

Figures do not total 100% because some levels have a very small sample size.

Flexibility of Earnings

Average Hours Worked: 38
Workers with a Varying Number of Hours: 3.2%
Workers Earning Some Overtime Pay, Tips, or Commissions: 21.0%
Earnings Benefit of Working Overtime: 21.2%

Gender

	Male	Female
Percent	89.5%	10.5%
Effect on Earnings	1.2%	–10.1%

Union Membership

Percentage Union Members: 38.7%
Earnings Benefit of Union Membership: 24.2%

Veteran Status

Percentage Who Have Been on Active Duty: 12.5%
Earnings Benefit of Veteran Status: 28.7%

43-5051 Postal Service Clerks

Perform any combination of tasks in a post office, such as receiving letters and parcels; selling postage and revenue stamps, postal cards, and stamped envelopes; filling out and selling money orders; placing mail in pigeonholes of mail rack or in bags according to state, address, or other scheme; and examining mail for correct postage.

- Education or Training Required: Short-term on-the-job training
- Job Growth: 0.0%
- Annual Openings: 4,000
- Self-Employed: 0.0%
- Part-Time: 22.8%

NATIONAL WAGE FIGURES (ANNUAL)

Beginning	25th Percentile	Median	Mean	75th Percentile	90th Percentile
$38,980	$41,720	$44,800	$43,950	$47,890	$49,750

Median Wages for Industries Employing Largest Numbers (Annual)

Industry	Median Income
Postal Service	$44,810

Median Wages for States (Annual)

AK............ $44,470	KY $44,000	NY $45,070
AL $43,580	LA $44,780	OH $45,100
AR............ $43,610	MA.............. $45,120	OK $44,530
AZ $44,720	MD $45,230	OR $44,400
CA $44,540	ME $44,550	PA $44,910
CO $44,780	MI $45,050	RI.............. $45,100
CT $45,000	MN $44,500	SC.............. $44,910
DC $45,520	MO $44,650	SD $44,110
DE $44,390	MS $44,530	TN $44,390
FL $44,940	MT $44,940	TX $44,900
GA $44,910	NC $44,370	UT $44,200
HI $44,510	ND $44,480	VA $44,780
IA $45,200	NE $44,890	VT $44,390
ID $44,360	NH $44,750	WA $44,620
IL $45,230	NJ $45,170	WI $44,730
IN $44,890	NM $44,320	WV $44,130
KS $44,860	NV $44,530	WY $44,180

Median Wages for the Largest Metropolitan Areas (Annual)

AZ: Phoenix............ $44,720	MI: Detroit $45,320
CA: Los Angeles $45,020	MN: Minneapolis $44,910
CA: Riverside $43,540	MO: Kansas City........ $45,240
CA: Sacramento $44,020	MO: St. Louis............ $44,560
CA: San Diego $44,060	NV: Las Vegas $44,450
CA: San Francisco.... $45,030	NY: New York............ $45,280
CO: Denver $45,220	OH: Cincinnati.......... $45,230
DC: Washington $45,250	OH: Cleveland $45,290
FL: Miami $45,310	OH: Columbus $45,120
FL: Orlando $45,070	OR: Portland $44,460
FL: Tampa $44,650	PA: Philadelphia $45,080
GA: Atlanta $45,080	PA: Pittsburgh $44,540
IL: Chicago $45,340	TX: Dallas $45,250
MA: Boston $45,280	TX: Houston $45,160
MD: Baltimore $45,230	WA: Seattle $44,760

FACTORS THAT MAY AFFECT EARNINGS

Educational Attainment of Workers and Effect on Earnings

	Percent at Level	Effect on Earnings
Less than High School	—	—
Some High School	—	—
High School or Equivalent	34.7%	−0.2%
Some College but No Degree	27.3%	0.1%
Associate Degree	14.2%	3.0%
Bachelor's Degree	19.9%	−1.3%
Master's Degree	—	—
Doctoral Degree	—	—
First Professional Degree	—	—

Flexibility of Earnings

Average Hours Worked: 36
Workers with a Varying Number of Hours: 6.1%
Workers Earning Some Overtime Pay, Tips, or Commissions: 29.9%
Earnings Benefit of Working Overtime: −9.4%

Gender

	Male	Female
Percent	50.5%	49.5%
Effect on Earnings	0.0%	0.0%

Union Membership

Percentage Union Members: 63.4%
Earnings Benefit of Union Membership: 8.5%

Veteran Status

Percentage Who Have Been on Active Duty: 12.5%
Earnings Benefit of Veteran Status: 28.7%

43-5052 Postal Service Mail Carriers

Sort mail for delivery. Deliver mail on established route by vehicle or on foot.

- Education or Training Required: Short-term on-the-job training
- Job Growth: 0.0%
- Annual Openings: 19,000
- Self-Employed: 0.0%
- Part-Time: 25.2%

NATIONAL WAGE FIGURES (ANNUAL)

Beginning	25th Percentile	Median	Mean	75th Percentile	90th Percentile
$34,810	$40,290	$44,350	$43,750	$48,400	$50,830

Median Wages for Industries Employing Largest Numbers (Annual)

Industry	Median Income
Postal Service	$44,350

Median Wages for States (Annual)

AK $44,990	KY $43,730	NY $44,490
AL $43,510	LA $44,300	OH $44,550
AR $42,890	MA $44,790	OK $44,200
AZ $44,330	MD $44,440	OR $44,300
CA $44,780	ME $43,010	PA $44,750
CO $44,330	MI $44,170	RI.............. $44,820
CT $44,750	MN $44,020	SC.............. $43,430
DC $45,050	MO $43,950	SD $43,530
DE $44,030	MS $42,940	TN $43,960
FL $44,270	MT $43,630	TX $44,470
GA $43,590	NC $43,540	UT $44,430
HI $44,990	ND $43,470	VA $44,220
IA $44,230	NE $44,040	VT $42,290
ID $43,390	NH $43,750	WA $44,250
IL $44,550	NJ $44,700	WI $43,860
IN $43,920	NM $44,370	WV $43,680
KS $43,780	NV $44,250	WY $44,190

Median Wages for the Largest Metropolitan Areas (Annual)

AZ: Phoenix............	$44,320	MI: Detroit	$44,810
CA: Los Angeles	$45,010	MN: Minneapolis	$44,390
CA: Riverside	$44,370	MO: Kansas City........	$44,560
CA: Sacramento	$44,160	MO: St. Louis............	$44,400
CA: San Diego	$44,700	NV: Las Vegas	$44,310
CA: San Francisco....	$45,080	NY: New York............	$44,670
CO: Denver	$44,630	OH: Cincinnati..........	$44,630
DC: Washington	$44,760	OH: Cleveland	$45,080
FL: Miami	$44,610	OH: Columbus	$44,200
FL: Orlando	$44,380	OR: Portland	$44,480
FL: Tampa	$44,300	PA: Philadelphia	$44,970
GA: Atlanta	$43,960	PA: Pittsburgh	$44,820
IL: Chicago	$44,850	TX: Dallas	$44,600
MA: Boston	$44,780	TX: Houston	$44,670
MD: Baltimore	$44,360	WA: Seattle	$44,460

FACTORS THAT MAY AFFECT EARNINGS

Educational Attainment of Workers and Effect on Earnings

	Percent at Level	Effect on Earnings
Less than High School	—	—
Some High School	2.3%	−12.1%
High School or Equivalent	39.7%	−8.0%
Some College but No Degree	29.0%	3.6%
Associate Degree	12.4%	6.7%
Bachelor's Degree	13.2%	10.4%
Master's Degree	2.0%	15.4%
Doctoral Degree	—	—
First Professional Degree	—	—

Flexibility of Earnings

Average Hours Worked: 36
Workers with a Varying Number of Hours: 8.0%
Workers Earning Some Overtime Pay, Tips, or Commissions: 26.1%
Earnings Benefit of Working Overtime: −0.6%

Gender

	Male	Female
Percent	64.3%	35.7%
Effect on Earnings	4.4%	−9.1%

Union Membership

Percentage Union Members: 71.8%
Earnings Benefit of Union Membership: 8.4%

Veteran Status

Percentage Who Have Been on Active Duty: 12.5%
Earnings Benefit of Veteran Status: 28.7%

43-5053 Postal Service Mail Sorters, Processors, and Processing Machine Operators

Prepare incoming and outgoing mail for distribution. Examine, sort, and route mail by state, type of mail, or other scheme. Load, operate, and occasionally adjust and repair mail-processing, -sorting, and -canceling machinery. Keep records of shipments, pouches, and sacks and perform other duties related to mail handling within the postal service. Must complete a competitive exam.

- Education or Training Required: Short-term on-the-job training
- Job Growth: 0.0%
- Annual Openings: 11,000
- Self-Employed: 0.0%
- Part-Time: 16.7%

NATIONAL WAGE FIGURES (ANNUAL)

Beginning	25th Percentile	Median	Mean	75th Percentile	90th Percentile
$25,770	$40,350	$43,900	$41,070	$47,440	$49,570

Median Wages for Industries Employing Largest Numbers (Annual)

Industry	Median Income
Postal Service	$43,900

Median Wages for States (Annual)

AK $40,720	KY $42,040	NY $44,300
AL $43,440	LA $43,460	OH $44,100
AR $41,950	MA $44,210	OK $43,240
AZ $43,390	MD $44,130	OR $43,520
CA $43,760	ME $41,720	PA $44,060
CO $44,020	MI $44,430	RI $44,620
CT $44,530	MN $44,190	SC $43,150
DC $44,850	MO $43,470	SD $39,990
DE $44,300	MS $42,530	TN $44,130
FL $44,140	MT $39,370	TX $44,300
GA $44,360	NC $43,350	UT $41,570
HI $42,830	ND $38,730	VA $44,010
IA $43,170	NE $43,110	VT $40,800
ID $41,660	NH $42,040	WA $43,660
IL $44,460	NJ $44,280	WI $43,870
IN $43,850	NM $41,720	WV $39,230
KS $43,050	NV $42,670	WY $38,800

Median Wages for the Largest Metropolitan Areas (Annual)

AZ: Phoenix $43,690	MI: Detroit $44,930
CA: Los Angeles $43,960	MN: Minneapolis $44,830
CA: Riverside $43,300	MO: Kansas City $44,500
CA: Sacramento $42,270	MO: St. Louis $43,170
CA: San Diego $43,320	NV: Las Vegas $42,860
CA: San Francisco $44,350	NY: New York $44,560
CO: Denver $44,570	OH: Cincinnati $44,190
DC: Washington $44,590	OH: Cleveland $44,750
FL: Miami $44,100	OH: Columbus $44,170
FL: Orlando $44,110	OR: Portland $44,330
FL: Tampa $44,160	PA: Philadelphia $44,580
GA: Atlanta $44,730	PA: Pittsburgh $43,250
IL: Chicago $44,740	TX: Dallas $44,590
MA: Boston $44,280	TX: Houston $44,810
MD: Baltimore $44,130	WA: Seattle $44,110

FACTORS THAT MAY AFFECT EARNINGS

Educational Attainment of Workers and Effect on Earnings

	Percent at Level	Effect on Earnings
Less than High School	—	—
Some High School	—	—
High School or Equivalent	36.3%	2.1%
Some College but No Degree	29.0%	-4.0%
Associate Degree	16.1%	15.3%
Bachelor's Degree	12.1%	-11.5%
Master's Degree	—	—
Doctoral Degree	—	—
First Professional Degree	—	—

Figures do not total 100% because some levels have a very small sample size.

Flexibility of Earnings

Average Hours Worked: 36
Workers with a Varying Number of Hours: 5.0%
Workers Earning Some Overtime Pay, Tips, or Commissions: 25.4%
Earnings Benefit of Working Overtime: 6.1%

Gender

	Male	Female
Percent	52.5%	47.5%
Effect on Earnings	2.6%	—

Union Membership

Percentage Union Members: 69.6%
Earnings Benefit of Union Membership: 9.5%

Veteran Status

Percentage Who Have Been on Active Duty: 12.5%
Earnings Benefit of Veteran Status: 28.7%

43-5061 Production, Planning, and Expediting Clerks

Coordinate and expedite the flow of work and materials within or between departments of an establishment according to production schedule. Duties include reviewing and distributing production, work, and shipment schedules; conferring with department supervisors to determine progress of work and completion dates; and compiling reports on progress of work, inventory levels, costs, and production problems.

- Education or Training Required: Short-term on-the-job training
- Job Growth: 7.7%
- Annual Openings: 24,000
- Self-Employed: 1.2%
- Part-Time: 5.9%

NATIONAL WAGE FIGURES (ANNUAL)

Beginning	25th Percentile	Median	Mean	75th Percentile	90th Percentile
$23,470	$29,560	$38,620	$40,000	$48,900	$59,080

Median Wages for Industries Employing Largest Numbers (Annual)

Industry	Median Income
Telecommunications	$48,030
Federal, State, and Local Government	$46,900
Postal Service	$45,430
Chemical Manufacturing	$42,580
Transportation Equipment Manufacturing	$42,490
Paper Manufacturing	$41,820
Computer and Electronic Product Manufacturing	$41,810
Professional, Scientific, and Technical Services	$40,500
Primary Metal Manufacturing	$40,000
Printing and Related Support Activities	$39,820

Median Wages for States (Annual)

AK	$43,560	KY	$35,340	NY	$42,530
AL	$33,370	LA	$37,300	OH	$37,220
AR	$33,270	MA	$44,550	OK	$40,230
AZ	$38,060	MD	$41,550	OR	$39,330
CA	$41,810	ME	$37,470	PA	$36,040
CO	$41,330	MI	$41,800	RI	$37,180
CT	$43,160	MN	$40,380	SC	$35,690
DC	$45,100	MO	$35,410	SD	$28,660
DE	$41,660	MS	$32,120	TN	$34,740
FL	$34,310	MT	$32,960	TX	$36,330
GA	$36,920	NC	$34,680	UT	$28,110
HI	$38,610	ND	$36,760	VA	$40,690
IA	$34,000	NE	$32,780	VT	$35,910
ID	$34,260	NH	$38,900	WA	$42,010
IL	$40,070	NJ	$41,750	WI	$39,090
IN	$38,260	NM	$41,240	WV	$35,200
KS	$36,720	NV	$36,270	WY	$30,910

Median Wages for the Largest Metropolitan Areas (Annual)

AZ: Phoenix	$38,810	MI: Detroit	$44,130
CA: Los Angeles	$40,130	MN: Minneapolis	$41,630
CA: Riverside	$36,930	MO: Kansas City	$38,550
CA: Sacramento	$43,300	MO: St. Louis	$38,140
CA: San Diego	$44,520	NV: Las Vegas	$37,890
CA: San Francisco	$45,330	NY: New York	$43,320
CO: Denver	$41,390	OH: Cincinnati	$37,490
DC: Washington	$43,960	OH: Cleveland	$42,880
FL: Miami	$32,110	OH: Columbus	$38,480
FL: Orlando	$34,290	OR: Portland	$40,840
FL: Tampa	$34,990	PA: Philadelphia	$35,840
GA: Atlanta	$38,830	PA: Pittsburgh	$36,780
IL: Chicago	$41,230	TX: Dallas	$37,690
MA: Boston	$45,800	TX: Houston	$37,100
MD: Baltimore	$41,100	WA: Seattle	$41,740

FACTORS THAT MAY AFFECT EARNINGS

Educational Attainment of Workers and Effect on Earnings

	Percent at Level	Effect on Earnings
Less than High School	—	—
Some High School	4.0%	−31.6%
High School or Equivalent	29.0%	−6.7%
Some College but No Degree	25.5%	−4.3%
Associate Degree	12.5%	2.3%
Bachelor's Degree	23.1%	12.9%
Master's Degree	4.0%	11.2%
Doctoral Degree	—	—
First Professional Degree	—	—

Flexibility of Earnings

Average Hours Worked: 37

Workers with a Varying Number of Hours: 4.8%

Workers Earning Some Overtime Pay, Tips, or Commissions: 14.0%

Earnings Benefit of Working Overtime: 10.1%

Gender

	Male	Female
Percent	43.2%	56.8%
Effect on Earnings	20.4%	−9.1%

Union Membership

Percentage Union Members: 9.5%

Earnings Benefit of Union Membership: 2.9%

Veteran Status

Percentage Who Have Been on Active Duty: 12.5%

Earnings Benefit of Veteran Status: 28.7%

43-5071 Shipping, Receiving, and Traffic Clerks

Verify and keep records on incoming and outgoing shipments. Prepare items for shipment. Duties include assembling, addressing, stamping, and shipping merchandise or material; receiving, unpacking, verifying, and recording incoming merchandise or material; and arranging for the transportation of products.

- Education or Training Required: Short-term on-the-job training
- Job Growth: 3.7%
- Annual Openings: 121,000
- Self-Employed: 0.1%
- Part-Time: 22.0%

NATIONAL WAGE FIGURES (ANNUAL)

Beginning	25th Percentile	Median	Mean	75th Percentile	90th Percentile
$16,970	$20,670	$26,070	$27,480	$32,840	$40,590

Median Wages for Industries Employing Largest Numbers (Annual)

Industry	Median Income
Chemical Manufacturing	$29,430
Transportation Equipment Manufacturing	$29,220
Couriers and Messengers	$28,710
Machinery Manufacturing	$28,570
Warehousing and Storage	$28,200
Support Activities for Transportation	$27,920
Fabricated Metal Product Manufacturing	$27,840
Professional, Scientific, and Technical Services	$27,840
Computer and Electronic Product Manufacturing	$27,650
Plastics and Rubber Products Manufacturing	$27,530

Median Wages for States (Annual)

State	Wage	State	Wage	State	Wage
AK	$34,080	KY	$25,550	NY	$25,470
AL	$24,020	LA	$23,830	OH	$27,270
AR	$23,580	MA	$29,530	OK	$24,310
AZ	$19,470	MD	$26,860	OR	$27,350
CA	$26,840	ME	$26,060	PA	$26,720
CO	$26,730	MI	$28,300	RI	$28,190
CT	$29,940	MN	$29,080	SC	$25,220
DC	$35,340	MO	$24,790	SD	$24,360
DE	$24,210	MS	$22,580	TN	$25,620
FL	$24,310	MT	$23,370	TX	$23,830
GA	$25,500	NC	$25,270	UT	$23,380
HI	$25,140	ND	$24,620	VA	$26,380
IA	$25,470	NE	$25,970	VT	$27,020
ID	$23,550	NH	$27,970	WA	$28,650
IL	$26,550	NJ	$28,800	WI	$27,390
IN	$25,960	NM	$23,040	WV	$26,040
KS	$25,370	NV	$27,960	WY	$26,460

Median Wages for the Largest Metropolitan Areas (Annual)

Area	Wage	Area	Wage
AZ: Phoenix	$19,420	MI: Detroit	$29,300
CA: Los Angeles	$25,850	MN: Minneapolis	$30,440
CA: Riverside	$26,470	MO: Kansas City	$27,320
CA: Sacramento	$24,660	MO: St. Louis	$25,870
CA: San Diego	$26,400	NV: Las Vegas	$29,680
CA: San Francisco	$30,910	NY: New York	$27,040
CO: Denver	$27,590	OH: Cincinnati	$27,760
DC: Washington	$26,900	OH: Cleveland	$28,290
FL: Miami	$23,990	OH: Columbus	$28,050
FL: Orlando	$23,670	OR: Portland	$28,120
FL: Tampa	$24,470	PA: Philadelphia	$29,120
GA: Atlanta	$26,390	PA: Pittsburgh	$25,250
IL: Chicago	$27,150	TX: Dallas	$24,260
MA: Boston	$30,260	TX: Houston	$25,390
MD: Baltimore	$27,490	WA: Seattle	$29,720

FACTORS THAT MAY AFFECT EARNINGS

Educational Attainment of Workers and Effect on Earnings

	Percent at Level	Effect on Earnings
Less than High School	3.0%	−22.0%
Some High School	10.3%	−10.6%
High School or Equivalent	42.7%	0.5%
Some College but No Degree	27.6%	4.5%
Associate Degree	9.7%	−4.1%
Bachelor's Degree	6.2%	13.2%
Master's Degree	—	—
Doctoral Degree	—	—
First Professional Degree	—	—

Flexibility of Earnings

Average Hours Worked: 35
Workers with a Varying Number of Hours: 4.6%
Workers Earning Some Overtime Pay, Tips, or Commissions: 19.3%
Earnings Benefit of Working Overtime: 11.1%

Gender

	Male	Female
Percent	69.9%	30.1%
Effect on Earnings	3.5%	−6.4%

Union Membership

Percentage Union Members: 11.7%
Earnings Benefit of Union Membership: 24.4%

Veteran Status

Percentage Who Have Been on Active Duty: 12.5%
Earnings Benefit of Veteran Status: 28.7%

43-5081 Stock Clerks and Order Fillers

Receive, store, and issue sales floor merchandise, materials, equipment, and other items from stockroom, warehouse, or storage yard to fill shelves, racks, tables, or customers' orders. May mark prices on merchandise and set up sales displays.

- Education or Training Required: Short-term on-the-job training
- Job Growth: −7.3%
- Annual Openings: 351,000
- Self-Employed: 0.3%
- Part-Time: 44.2%

NATIONAL WAGE FIGURES (ANNUAL)

Beginning	25th Percentile	Median	Mean	75th Percentile	90th Percentile
$14,490	$16,670	$20,440	$22,440	$26,440	$34,200

Median Wages for Industries Employing Largest Numbers (Annual)

Industry	Median Income
Federal, State, and Local Government	$32,330
Transportation Equipment Manufacturing	$32,250
Machinery Manufacturing	$29,200
Warehousing and Storage	$27,590
Educational Services	$26,950
Computer and Electronic Product Manufacturing	$26,810
Hospitals	$25,880
Food Manufacturing	$25,590
Professional, Scientific, and Technical Services	$25,020
Wholesale Electronic Markets and Agents and Brokers	$23,790

Median Wages for States (Annual)

AK	$26,530	KY	$21,820	NY	$19,180
AL	$18,930	LA	$17,820	OH	$20,440
AR	$17,760	MA	$22,540	OK	$18,580
AZ	$18,970	MD	$21,280	OR	$23,330
CA	$21,560	ME	$19,650	PA	$19,400
CO	$23,450	MI	$21,690	RI	$21,410
CT	$22,620	MN	$21,340	SC	$19,890
DC	$22,260	MO	$20,210	SD	$17,500
DE	$20,170	MS	$18,370	TN	$19,760
FL	$19,570	MT	$19,670	TX	$19,990
GA	$20,610	NC	$20,620	UT	$21,180
HI	$22,270	ND	$19,310	VA	$20,650
IA	$18,870	NE	$20,660	VT	$20,680
ID	$20,320	NH	$22,010	WA	$23,810
IL	$19,900	NJ	$20,600	WI	$20,130
IN	$19,840	NM	$19,300	WV	$17,810
KS	$20,720	NV	$22,580	WY	$19,390

Median Wages for the Largest Metropolitan Areas (Annual)

AZ: Phoenix	$19,120	MI: Detroit	$22,620
CA: Los Angeles	$20,660	MN: Minneapolis	$22,510
CA: Riverside	$21,630	MO: Kansas City	$21,220
CA: Sacramento	$22,660	MO: St. Louis	$21,160
CA: San Diego	$21,940	NV: Las Vegas	$21,700
CA: San Francisco	$24,000	NY: New York	$19,680
CO: Denver	$24,260	OH: Cincinnati	$23,030
DC: Washington	$21,800	OH: Cleveland	$19,980
FL: Miami	$19,620	OH: Columbus	$21,620
FL: Orlando	$19,700	OR: Portland	$24,230
FL: Tampa	$19,170	PA: Philadelphia	$20,460
GA: Atlanta	$21,360	PA: Pittsburgh	$18,070
IL: Chicago	$20,140	TX: Dallas	$21,210
MA: Boston	$23,050	TX: Houston	$20,500
MD: Baltimore	$21,790	WA: Seattle	$25,060

FACTORS THAT MAY AFFECT EARNINGS

Educational Attainment of Workers and Effect on Earnings

	Percent at Level	Effect on Earnings
Less than High School	3.6%	−21.4%
Some High School	17.5%	−39.0%
High School or Equivalent	37.7%	4.8%
Some College but No Degree	22.9%	9.1%
Associate Degree	8.4%	7.2%
Bachelor's Degree	8.2%	28.0%
Master's Degree	1.5%	39.4%
Doctoral Degree	—	—
First Professional Degree	—	—

Flexibility of Earnings

Average Hours Worked: 29
Workers with a Varying Number of Hours: 7.2%
Workers Earning Some Overtime Pay, Tips, or Commissions: 10.6%
Earnings Benefit of Working Overtime: 35.3%

Gender

	Male	Female
Percent	60.9%	39.1%
Effect on Earnings	3.2%	−4.1%

Union Membership

Percentage Union Members: 9.3%
Earnings Benefit of Union Membership: 34.9%

Veteran Status

Percentage Who Have Been on Active Duty: 12.5%
Earnings Benefit of Veteran Status: 28.7%

43-5111 Weighers, Measurers, Checkers, and Samplers, Recordkeeping

Weigh, measure, and check materials, supplies, and equipment for the purpose of keeping relevant records. Duties are primarily clerical by nature.

- Education or Training Required: Short-term on-the-job training
- Job Growth: −11.3%
- Annual Openings: 7,000
- Self-Employed: 2.2%
- Part-Time: 36.8%

NATIONAL WAGE FIGURES (ANNUAL)

Beginning	25th Percentile	Median	Mean	75th Percentile	90th Percentile
$16,700	$20,100	$25,370	$27,330	$32,930	$41,150

Median Wages for Industries Employing Largest Numbers (Annual)

Industry	Median Income
Support Activities for Transportation	$39,970
Fabricated Metal Product Manufacturing	$31,840
Transportation Equipment Manufacturing	$30,900
Computer and Electronic Product Manufacturing	$30,340
Beverage and Tobacco Product Manufacturing	$30,330
Chemical Manufacturing	$29,550
Nonstore Retailers	$29,530
Management of Companies and Enterprises	$29,440
Federal, State, and Local Government	$28,700
Plastics and Rubber Products Manufacturing	$28,490

Median Wages for States (Annual)

State	Wage	State	Wage	State	Wage
AK	$27,620	KY	$24,060	NY	$24,380
AL	$23,530	LA	$25,430	OH	$26,760
AR	$21,750	MA	$30,740	OK	$23,110
AZ	$32,600	MD	no data	OR	$26,080
CA	$23,190	ME	$27,090	PA	$24,870
CO	$21,900	MI	$30,480	RI	$27,930
CT	$29,410	MN	$30,080	SC	$25,540
DC	no data	MO	$25,770	SD	$24,420
DE	$27,730	MS	$19,390	TN	$28,040
FL	$23,160	MT	$25,960	TX	$23,790
GA	$24,460	NC	$22,720	UT	$26,050
HI	$23,450	ND	$24,100	VA	$25,480
IA	$27,190	NE	$26,540	VT	$26,070
ID	$26,910	NH	$25,950	WA	$34,390
IL	$26,250	NJ	$29,050	WI	$28,590
IN	$23,740	NM	$27,750	WV	$26,970
KS	$24,570	NV	$28,610	WY	$23,080

Median Wages for the Largest Metropolitan Areas (Annual)

Area	Wage	Area	Wage
AZ: Phoenix	$32,550	MI: Detroit	$33,100
CA: Los Angeles	$22,480	MN: Minneapolis	$31,340
CA: Riverside	$25,510	MO: Kansas City	$29,720
CA: Sacramento	$24,030	MO: St. Louis	$28,210
CA: San Diego	$22,000	NV: Las Vegas	$27,700
CA: San Francisco	$28,490	NY: New York	$27,030
CO: Denver	$19,750	OH: Cincinnati	$27,040
DC: Washington	$28,550	OH: Cleveland	$25,590
FL: Miami	$22,450	OH: Columbus	$26,750
FL: Orlando	$24,080	OR: Portland	$28,110
FL: Tampa	$27,170	PA: Philadelphia	$28,510
GA: Atlanta	$25,540	PA: Pittsburgh	$30,720
IL: Chicago	$25,780	TX: Dallas	$27,730
MA: Boston	$30,790	TX: Houston	$24,690
MD: Baltimore	no data	WA: Seattle	$35,980

FACTORS THAT MAY AFFECT EARNINGS

Educational Attainment of Workers and Effect on Earnings

	Percent at Level	Effect on Earnings
Less than High School	—	—
Some High School	13.0%	−25.4%
High School or Equivalent	41.0%	−5.3%
Some College but No Degree	23.0%	8.0%
Associate Degree	7.0%	36.1%
Bachelor's Degree	11.0%	23.7%
Master's Degree	—	—
Doctoral Degree	—	—
First Professional Degree	—	—

Flexibility of Earnings

Average Hours Worked: 33
Workers with a Varying Number of Hours: 7.6%
Workers Earning Some Overtime Pay, Tips, or Commissions: 27.1%
Earnings Benefit of Working Overtime: 21.2%

Gender

	Male	Female
Percent	49.6%	50.4%
Effect on Earnings	8.2%	−2.6%

Union Membership

Percentage Union Members: 10.3%
Earnings Benefit of Union Membership: 1.8%

Veteran Status

Percentage Who Have Been on Active Duty: 12.5%
Earnings Benefit of Veteran Status: 28.7%

43-6000 Secretaries and Administrative Assistants

43-6011 Executive Secretaries and Administrative Assistants

Provide high-level administrative support by conducting research; preparing statistical reports; handling information requests; and performing clerical functions such as preparing correspondence, receiving visitors, arranging conference calls, and scheduling meetings. May also train and supervise lower-level clerical staff.

- Education or Training Required: Moderate-term on-the-job training
- Job Growth: 12.4%
- Annual Openings: 218,000
- Self-Employed: 1.2%
- Part-Time: 34.8%

NATIONAL WAGE FIGURES (ANNUAL)

Beginning	25th Percentile	Median	Mean	75th Percentile	90th Percentile
$25,190	$30,240	$37,240	$39,160	$46,160	$56,740

Median Wages for Industries Employing Largest Numbers (Annual)

Industry	Median Income
Computer and Electronic Product Manufacturing	$44,160
Securities, Commodity Contracts, and Other Financial Investments and Related Activities	$43,510
Management of Companies and Enterprises	$41,570
Transportation Equipment Manufacturing	$40,580
Wholesale Electronic Markets and Agents and Brokers	$40,400
Professional, Scientific, and Technical Services	$40,050
Chemical Manufacturing	$39,910
Publishing Industries (Except Internet)	$39,620
Insurance Carriers and Related Activities	$38,900
Heavy and Civil Engineering Construction	$38,500

Median Wages for States (Annual)

AK	$37,070	KY	$31,220	NY	$42,960
AL	$36,720	LA	$30,610	OH	$35,990
AR	$29,210	MA	$43,400	OK	$30,760
AZ	$32,860	MD	$40,740	OR	$35,910
CA	$41,840	ME	$37,280	PA	$35,450
CO	$39,960	MI	$38,720	RI	$40,110
CT	$42,170	MN	$38,930	SC	$33,830
DC	$45,430	MO	$36,670	SD	$28,260
DE	$38,150	MS	$29,530	TN	$31,620
FL	$34,130	MT	no data	TX	$35,420
GA	$36,210	NC	$33,640	UT	$35,070
HI	$39,670	ND	$31,330	VA	$41,310
IA	$32,970	NE	$31,030	VT	$36,520
ID	$30,100	NH	$36,290	WA	$42,520
IL	$37,560	NJ	$47,500	WI	$34,340
IN	$32,700	NM	$33,580	WV	$29,600
KS	$32,510	NV	$34,720	WY	$31,340

Median Wages for the Largest Metropolitan Areas (Annual)

AZ: Phoenix	$33,370	MI: Detroit	$40,480
CA: Los Angeles	$41,710	MN: Minneapolis	$40,010
CA: Riverside	$36,980	MO: Kansas City	$36,300
CA: Sacramento	$40,750	MO: St. Louis	$38,480
CA: San Diego	$39,910	NV: Las Vegas	$34,850
CA: San Francisco	$45,210	NY: New York	$45,850
CO: Denver	$41,220	OH: Cincinnati	$35,660
DC: Washington	$45,150	OH: Cleveland	$37,600
FL: Miami	$35,960	OH: Columbus	$37,440
FL: Orlando	$34,160	OR: Portland	$38,120
FL: Tampa	$33,980	PA: Philadelphia	$39,930
GA: Atlanta	$38,420	PA: Pittsburgh	$34,000
IL: Chicago	$38,890	TX: Dallas	$37,140
MA: Boston	$44,500	TX: Houston	$37,690
MD: Baltimore	$40,260	WA: Seattle	$43,120

FACTORS THAT MAY AFFECT EARNINGS

Educational Attainment of Workers and Effect on Earnings

Figures are based on a group of occupations: Secretaries and Administrative Assistants

	Percent at Level	Effect on Earnings
Less than High School	—	—
Some High School	4.1%	−29.4%
High School or Equivalent	28.7%	−4.5%
Some College but No Degree	27.6%	−2.0%
Associate Degree	18.4%	5.5%
Bachelor's Degree	17.2%	7.0%
Master's Degree	3.3%	18.7%
Doctoral Degree	—	—
First Professional Degree	—	—

Flexibility of Earnings

Average Hours Worked: 33
Workers with a Varying Number of Hours: 4.3%
Workers Earning Some Overtime Pay, Tips, or Commissions: 7.4%
Earnings Benefit of Working Overtime: 14.0%

Gender

	Male	Female
Percent	3.1%	96.9%
Effect on Earnings	−4.1%	0.2%

Union Membership

Percentage Union Members: 7.3%
Earnings Benefit of Union Membership: 15.5%

Veteran Status

Percentage Who Have Been on Active Duty: Insignificant
Earnings Benefit of Veteran Status: No significant data available

43-6012 Legal Secretaries

Perform secretarial duties, utilizing legal terminology, procedures, and documents. Prepare legal papers and correspondence, such as summonses, complaints, motions, and subpoenas. May also assist with legal research.

- Education or Training Required: Postsecondary vocational training
- Job Growth: 17.4%
- Annual Openings: 41,000
- Self-Employed: 1.2%
- Part-Time: 34.8%

NATIONAL WAGE FIGURES (ANNUAL)

Beginning	25th Percentile	Median	Mean	75th Percentile	90th Percentile
$23,870	$29,650	$38,190	$39,670	$48,520	$58,770

Median Wages for Industries Employing Largest Numbers (Annual)

Industry	Median Income
Publishing Industries (Except Internet)	$53,940
Miscellaneous Manufacturing	$53,740
Utilities	$50,970
Real Estate	$49,760
Chemical Manufacturing	$49,630
Rail Transportation	$48,770
Computer and Electronic Product Manufacturing	$47,990
Securities, Commodity Contracts, and Other Financial Investments and Related Activities	$47,740
Telecommunications	$47,240
Merchant Wholesalers, Durable Goods	$46,920

Median Wages for States (Annual)

AK	$41,440	KY	$33,760	NY	$41,590
AL	$29,140	LA	$33,390	OH	$35,060
AR	$26,170	MA	$42,220	OK	$30,800
AZ	$37,950	MD	$40,780	OR	$37,520
CA	$47,730	ME	$33,740	PA	$33,570
CO	$42,830	MI	$37,720	RI	$34,890
CT	$42,090	MN	$43,350	SC	$31,550
DC	$57,610	MO	$34,510	SD	$27,750
DE	$41,330	MS	$35,380	TN	$31,420
FL	$35,310	MT	$25,160	TX	$39,920
GA	$31,460	NC	$32,100	UT	$35,680
HI	$41,080	ND	$26,540	VA	$40,670
IA	$29,060	NE	$32,160	VT	$33,190
ID	$29,110	NH	$33,220	WA	$39,360
IL	$39,440	NJ	$41,750	WI	$32,670
IN	$30,160	NM	$30,670	WV	$28,780
KS	$29,050	NV	$41,320	WY	no data

Median Wages for the Largest Metropolitan Areas (Annual)

AZ: Phoenix	$39,880	MI: Detroit	$40,310
CA: Los Angeles	$48,280	MN: Minneapolis	$46,280
CA: Riverside	$39,950	MO: Kansas City	$36,620
CA: Sacramento	$43,250	MO: St. Louis	$35,900
CA: San Diego	$47,040	NV: Las Vegas	$40,340
CA: San Francisco	$54,480	NY: New York	$43,630
CO: Denver	$45,620	OH: Cincinnati	$36,110
DC: Washington	$54,560	OH: Cleveland	$39,230
FL: Miami	$36,900	OH: Columbus	$40,870
FL: Orlando	$38,530	OR: Portland	$42,010
FL: Tampa	$34,570	PA: Philadelphia	$39,430
GA: Atlanta	$35,700	PA: Pittsburgh	$33,150
IL: Chicago	$41,650	TX: Dallas	$46,810
MA: Boston	$44,320	TX: Houston	$48,370
MD: Baltimore	$42,070	WA: Seattle	$45,670

FACTORS THAT MAY AFFECT EARNINGS

Educational Attainment of Workers and Effect on Earnings

Figures are based on a group of occupations: Secretaries and Administrative Assistants

	Percent at Level	Effect on Earnings
Less than High School	—	—
Some High School	4.1%	−29.4%
High School or Equivalent	28.7%	−4.5%
Some College but No Degree	27.6%	−2.0%
Associate Degree	18.4%	5.5%
Bachelor's Degree	17.2%	7.0%
Master's Degree	3.3%	18.7%
Doctoral Degree	—	—
First Professional Degree	—	—

Flexibility of Earnings

Average Hours Worked: 33
Workers with a Varying Number of Hours: 4.3%
Workers Earning Some Overtime Pay, Tips, or Commissions: 7.4%
Earnings Benefit of Working Overtime: 14.0%

Gender

	Male	Female
Percent	3.1%	96.9%
Effect on Earnings	−4.1%	0.2%

Union Membership

Percentage Union Members: 7.3%
Earnings Benefit of Union Membership: 15.5%

Veteran Status

Percentage Who Have Been on Active Duty: Insignificant
Earnings Benefit of Veteran Status: No significant data available

43-6013 Medical Secretaries

Perform secretarial duties, utilizing specific knowledge of medical terminology and hospital, clinic, or laboratory procedures. Duties include scheduling appointments; billing patients; and compiling and recording medical charts, reports, and correspondence.

- Education or Training Required: Postsecondary vocational training
- Job Growth: 17.0%
- Annual Openings: 55,000
- Self-Employed: 1.1%
- Part-Time: 34.8%

NATIONAL WAGE FIGURES (ANNUAL)

Beginning	25th Percentile	Median	Mean	75th Percentile	90th Percentile
$19,750	$23,250	$28,090	$29,220	$34,210	$40,870

Median Wages for Industries Employing Largest Numbers (Annual)

Industry	Median Income
Insurance Carriers and Related Activities	$33,690
Management of Companies and Enterprises	$32,950
Educational Services	$30,570
Federal, State, and Local Government	$30,070
Ambulatory Health Care Services	$28,330
Religious, Grantmaking, Civic, Professional, and Similar Organizations	$28,000
Miscellaneous Manufacturing	$27,730
Hospitals	$27,660
Administrative and Support Services	$27,020
Health and Personal Care Stores	$26,840

Median Wages for States (Annual)

AK	$29,890	KY	$24,140	NY	$29,470
AL	$22,940	LA	$22,310	OH	$26,140
AR	$22,500	MA	$32,380	OK	$22,800
AZ	$28,440	MD	$29,000	OR	$31,470
CA	$29,380	ME	$27,320	PA	$26,600
CO	$29,850	MI	$28,820	RI	$30,310
CT	$33,400	MN	$31,940	SC	$24,850
DC	$32,270	MO	$26,960	SD	$27,580
DE	$29,020	MS	$23,920	TN	$24,520
FL	$25,490	MT	$25,900	TX	$26,280
GA	$26,130	NC	$25,680	UT	$24,610
HI	$31,710	ND	$23,890	VA	$27,350
IA	$26,210	NE	$26,950	VT	$27,130
ID	$25,050	NH	$30,440	WA	$32,760
IL	$30,200	NJ	$31,020	WI	$27,790
IN	$26,110	NM	$24,310	WV	$22,760
KS	$25,980	NV	$31,820	WY	$25,340

Median Wages for the Largest Metropolitan Areas (Annual)

AZ: Phoenix	$29,460	MI: Detroit	$30,460
CA: Los Angeles	$28,950	MN: Minneapolis	$32,730
CA: Riverside	$25,060	MO: Kansas City	$29,410
CA: Sacramento	$32,230	MO: St. Louis	$28,390
CA: San Diego	$27,770	NV: Las Vegas	$31,880
CA: San Francisco	$35,320	NY: New York	$32,150
CO: Denver	$32,510	OH: Cincinnati	$26,180
DC: Washington	$32,530	OH: Cleveland	$26,740
FL: Miami	$26,710	OH: Columbus	$28,010
FL: Orlando	$23,430	OR: Portland	$33,160
FL: Tampa	$25,430	PA: Philadelphia	$30,380
GA: Atlanta	$28,160	PA: Pittsburgh	$25,620
IL: Chicago	$31,590	TX: Dallas	$27,300
MA: Boston	$32,700	TX: Houston	$28,200
MD: Baltimore	$29,480	WA: Seattle	$34,990

FACTORS THAT MAY AFFECT EARNINGS

Educational Attainment of Workers and Effect on Earnings

Figures are based on a group of occupations: Secretaries and Administrative Assistants

	Percent at Level	Effect on Earnings
Less than High School	—	—
Some High School	4.1%	−29.4%
High School or Equivalent	28.7%	−4.5%
Some College but No Degree	27.6%	−2.0%
Associate Degree	18.4%	5.5%
Bachelor's Degree	17.2%	7.0%
Master's Degree	3.3%	18.7%
Doctoral Degree	—	—
First Professional Degree	—	—

Flexibility of Earnings

Average Hours Worked: 33
Workers with a Varying Number of Hours: 4.3%
Workers Earning Some Overtime Pay, Tips, or Commissions: 7.4%
Earnings Benefit of Working Overtime: 14.0%

Gender

	Male	Female
Percent	3.1%	96.9%
Effect on Earnings	−4.1%	0.2%

Union Membership

Percentage Union Members: 7.3%
Earnings Benefit of Union Membership: 15.5%

Veteran Status

Percentage Who Have Been on Active Duty: Insignificant
Earnings Benefit of Veteran Status: No significant data available

43-6014 Secretaries, Except Legal, Medical, and Executive

Perform routine clerical and administrative functions such as drafting correspondence, scheduling appointments, organizing and maintaining paper and electronic files, or providing information to callers.

- Education or Training Required: Moderate-term on-the-job training
- Job Growth: –2.5%
- Annual Openings: 231,000
- Self-Employed: 1.2%
- Part-Time: 34.8%

NATIONAL WAGE FIGURES (ANNUAL)

Beginning	25th Percentile	Median	Mean	75th Percentile	90th Percentile
$17,560	$21,830	$27,450	$28,460	$34,250	$41,550

Median Wages for Industries Employing Largest Numbers (Annual)

Industry	Median Income
Federal, State, and Local Government	$32,880
Management of Companies and Enterprises	$31,410
Securities, Commodity Contracts, and Other Financial Investments and Related Activities	$30,360
Hospitals	$28,830
Credit Intermediation and Related Activities	$28,460
Educational Services	$28,130
Ambulatory Health Care Services	$27,380
Professional, Scientific, and Technical Services	$27,280
Religious, Grantmaking, Civic, Professional, and Similar Organizations	$26,740
Wholesale Electronic Markets and Agents and Brokers	$26,720

Median Wages for States (Annual)

AK	$32,280	KY	$22,570	NY	$29,700
AL	$25,100	LA	$22,540	OH	$28,280
AR	$21,990	MA	$34,090	OK	$21,820
AZ	$25,880	MD	$31,770	OR	$28,080
CA	$32,060	ME	$27,110	PA	$26,880
CO	$29,740	MI	$30,290	RI	$32,880
CT	$33,540	MN	$33,920	SC	$26,010
DC	$39,580	MO	$26,790	SD	$21,660
DE	$29,930	MS	$22,790	TN	$23,820
FL	$25,230	MT	$21,440	TX	$24,550
GA	$24,940	NC	$26,270	UT	$25,970
HI	$32,060	ND	$25,950	VA	$32,850
IA	$24,510	NE	$25,160	VT	$26,720
ID	$23,090	NH	$27,130	WA	$33,000
IL	$26,910	NJ	$33,660	WI	$27,830
IN	$25,570	NM	$24,760	WV	$21,830
KS	$23,170	NV	$30,690	WY	$22,380

Median Wages for the Largest Metropolitan Areas (Annual)

AZ: Phoenix	$27,030	MI: Detroit	$32,800
CA: Los Angeles	$31,020	MN: Minneapolis	$34,530
CA: Riverside	$30,810	MO: Kansas City	$27,490
CA: Sacramento	$32,690	MO: St. Louis	$28,510
CA: San Diego	$31,820	NV: Las Vegas	$30,760
CA: San Francisco	$37,940	NY: New York	$32,110
CO: Denver	$31,530	OH: Cincinnati	$29,210
DC: Washington	$38,340	OH: Cleveland	$29,370
FL: Miami	$26,220	OH: Columbus	$30,710
FL: Orlando	$25,230	OR: Portland	$29,860
FL: Tampa	$24,660	PA: Philadelphia	$30,740
GA: Atlanta	$27,210	PA: Pittsburgh	$25,660
IL: Chicago	$28,400	TX: Dallas	$26,420
MA: Boston	$35,130	TX: Houston	$26,410
MD: Baltimore	$32,040	WA: Seattle	$34,560

FACTORS THAT MAY AFFECT EARNINGS

Educational Attainment of Workers and Effect on Earnings

Figures are based on a group of occupations: Secretaries and Administrative Assistants

	Percent at Level	Effect on Earnings
Less than High School	—	—
Some High School	4.1%	–29.4%
High School or Equivalent	28.7%	–4.5%
Some College but No Degree	27.6%	–2.0%
Associate Degree	18.4%	5.5%
Bachelor's Degree	17.2%	7.0%
Master's Degree	3.3%	18.7%
Doctoral Degree	—	—
First Professional Degree	—	—

Flexibility of Earnings

Average Hours Worked: 33
Workers with a Varying Number of Hours: 4.3%
Workers Earning Some Overtime Pay, Tips, or Commissions: 7.4%
Earnings Benefit of Working Overtime: 14.0%

Gender

	Male	Female
Percent	3.1%	96.9%
Effect on Earnings	–4.1%	0.2%

Union Membership

Percentage Union Members: 7.3%
Earnings Benefit of Union Membership: 15.5%

Veteran Status

Percentage Who Have Been on Active Duty: Insignificant
Earnings Benefit of Veteran Status: No significant data available

43-9000 Other Office and Administrative Support Workers

43-9011 Computer Operators

Monitor and control electronic computer and peripheral electronic data-processing equipment to process business, scientific, engineering, and other data according to operating instructions. May enter commands at a computer terminal and set controls on computer and peripheral devices. Monitor and respond to operating and error messages.

- Education or Training Required: Moderate-term on-the-job training
- Job Growth: –32.6%
- Annual Openings: 13,000
- Self-Employed: 1.9%
- Part-Time: 14.8%

NATIONAL WAGE FIGURES (ANNUAL)

Beginning	25th Percentile	Median	Mean	75th Percentile	90th Percentile
$20,510	$25,990	$33,560	$35,010	$43,060	$51,970

Median Wages for Industries Employing Largest Numbers (Annual)

Industry	Median Income
Postal Service	$45,600
Telecommunications	$41,530
Support Activities for Transportation	$38,560
Federal, State, and Local Government	$36,760
Securities, Commodity Contracts, and Other Financial Investments and Related Activities	$36,700
Merchant Wholesalers, Durable Goods	$36,290
Computer and Electronic Product Manufacturing	$35,690
Management of Companies and Enterprises	$35,260
Printing and Related Support Activities	$35,200
Warehousing and Storage	$34,870

Median Wages for States (Annual)

AK	$39,510	KY	$32,300	NY	$33,260
AL	$28,510	LA	$27,890	OH	$34,080
AR	$25,310	MA	$36,700	OK	$28,900
AZ	$27,740	MD	$37,030	OR	$32,520
CA	$37,150	ME	$28,850	PA	$33,710
CO	$37,620	MI	$35,840	RI	$34,920
CT	$39,110	MN	$34,270	SC	$31,230
DC	$47,080	MO	$36,750	SD	$26,300
DE	$35,650	MS	$26,020	TN	$29,900
FL	$33,810	MT	$25,320	TX	$31,420
GA	$29,390	NC	$33,590	UT	$27,440
HI	$33,220	ND	$28,010	VA	$35,180
IA	$27,530	NE	$27,610	VT	$31,290
ID	$29,720	NH	$37,370	WA	$37,090
IL	$35,730	NJ	$38,800	WI	$33,830
IN	$30,000	NM	$29,580	WV	$26,600
KS	$31,520	NV	$32,090	WY	$23,910

Median Wages for the Largest Metropolitan Areas (Annual)

AZ: Phoenix	$28,320	MI: Detroit	$38,410
CA: Los Angeles	$34,750	MN: Minneapolis	$35,150
CA: Riverside	$34,450	MO: Kansas City	$35,940
CA: Sacramento	$37,650	MO: St. Louis	$42,120
CA: San Diego	$35,270	NV: Las Vegas	$34,670
CA: San Francisco	$43,010	NY: New York	$37,340
CO: Denver	$37,840	OH: Cincinnati	$33,950
DC: Washington	$40,770	OH: Cleveland	$36,250
FL: Miami	$35,010	OH: Columbus	$37,180
FL: Orlando	$36,830	OR: Portland	$32,890
FL: Tampa	$32,850	PA: Philadelphia	$35,250
GA: Atlanta	$32,450	PA: Pittsburgh	$34,270
IL: Chicago	$37,160	TX: Dallas	$34,170
MA: Boston	$36,620	TX: Houston	$32,980
MD: Baltimore	$36,970	WA: Seattle	$39,020

FACTORS THAT MAY AFFECT EARNINGS

Educational Attainment of Workers and Effect on Earnings

	Percent at Level	Effect on Earnings
Less than High School	—	—
Some High School	2.7%	–71.3%
High School or Equivalent	29.7%	–21.0%
Some College but No Degree	26.5%	1.0%
Associate Degree	14.2%	2.9%
Bachelor's Degree	24.2%	27.6%
Master's Degree	—	—
Doctoral Degree	—	—
First Professional Degree	—	—

Flexibility of Earnings

Average Hours Worked: 35
Workers with a Varying Number of Hours: 5.0%
Workers Earning Some Overtime Pay, Tips, or Commissions: 10.1%
Earnings Benefit of Working Overtime: 20.8%

Gender

	Male	Female
Percent	50.4%	49.6%
Effect on Earnings	5.1%	–7.9%

Union Membership

Percentage Union Members: 8.6%
Earnings Benefit of Union Membership: 26.5%

Veteran Status

Percentage Who Have Been on Active Duty: 4.2%
Earnings Benefit of Veteran Status: 25.4%

43-9021 Data Entry Keyers

Operate data entry device, such as keyboard or photo-composing perforator. Duties may include verifying data and preparing materials for printing.

- Education or Training Required: Moderate-term on-the-job training
- Job Growth: –0.7%
- Annual Openings: 85,000
- Self-Employed: 1.0%
- Part-Time: 40.9%

NATIONAL WAGE FIGURES (ANNUAL)

Beginning	25th Percentile	Median	Mean	75th Percentile	90th Percentile
$17,050	$20,460	$24,690	$25,640	$29,700	$35,970

Median Wages for Industries Employing Largest Numbers (Annual)

Industry	Median Income
Postal Service	$29,630
Federal, State, and Local Government	$28,420
Securities, Commodity Contracts, and Other Financial Investments and Related Activities	$26,960
Religious, Grantmaking, Civic, Professional, and Similar Organizations	$26,700
Management of Companies and Enterprises	$25,950
Educational Services	$25,720
Nonstore Retailers	$25,720
Truck Transportation	$25,640
Hospitals	$25,580
Merchant Wholesalers, Durable Goods	$25,410

Median Wages for States (Annual)

State	Wage	State	Wage	State	Wage
AK	$27,750	KY	$22,230	NY	$26,090
AL	$22,310	LA	$21,530	OH	$23,290
AR	$21,160	MA	$28,680	OK	$20,670
AZ	$26,910	MD	$26,160	OR	$24,480
CA	$26,280	ME	$22,680	PA	$23,840
CO	$25,280	MI	$25,790	RI	$27,200
CT	$27,690	MN	$26,420	SC	$22,140
DC	$31,170	MO	$23,800	SD	$21,490
DE	$23,960	MS	$21,790	TN	$22,460
FL	$23,880	MT	$19,420	TX	$23,710
GA	$25,470	NC	$23,970	UT	$26,720
HI	$23,570	ND	$20,330	VA	$23,470
IA	$22,080	NE	$22,410	VT	$26,750
ID	$24,430	NH	$25,280	WA	$27,190
IL	$25,080	NJ	$27,150	WI	$23,350
IN	$24,180	NM	$19,450	WV	$22,760
KS	$25,510	NV	$23,150	WY	$22,220

Median Wages for the Largest Metropolitan Areas (Annual)

Area	Wage	Area	Wage
AZ: Phoenix	$27,180	MI: Detroit	$26,750
CA: Los Angeles	$25,330	MN: Minneapolis	$27,540
CA: Riverside	$23,500	MO: Kansas City	$25,320
CA: Sacramento	$30,170	MO: St. Louis	$23,710
CA: San Diego	$27,070	NV: Las Vegas	$23,250
CA: San Francisco	$29,300	NY: New York	$27,280
CO: Denver	$25,870	OH: Cincinnati	$24,710
DC: Washington	$27,950	OH: Cleveland	$24,090
FL: Miami	$24,050	OH: Columbus	$24,250
FL: Orlando	$21,330	OR: Portland	$25,630
FL: Tampa	$26,850	PA: Philadelphia	$26,090
GA: Atlanta	$26,300	PA: Pittsburgh	$23,050
IL: Chicago	$26,100	TX: Dallas	$25,120
MA: Boston	$28,820	TX: Houston	$23,650
MD: Baltimore	$27,180	WA: Seattle	$27,750

FACTORS THAT MAY AFFECT EARNINGS

Educational Attainment of Workers and Effect on Earnings

	Percent at Level	Effect on Earnings
Less than High School	—	—
Some High School	6.3%	–36.1%
High School or Equivalent	36.7%	–0.9%
Some College but No Degree	28.0%	3.3%
Associate Degree	13.4%	4.0%
Bachelor's Degree	11.9%	–0.5%
Master's Degree	3.1%	32.0%
Doctoral Degree	—	—
First Professional Degree	—	—

Flexibility of Earnings

Average Hours Worked: 32
Workers with a Varying Number of Hours: 4.0%
Workers Earning Some Overtime Pay, Tips, or Commissions: 9.0%
Earnings Benefit of Working Overtime: –1.4%

Gender

	Male	Female
Percent	18.4%	81.6%
Effect on Earnings	8.2%	–2.6%

Union Membership

Percentage Union Members: 7.4%
Earnings Benefit of Union Membership: 37.3%

Veteran Status

Percentage Who Have Been on Active Duty: 4.2%
Earnings Benefit of Veteran Status: 25.4%

43-9022 Word Processors and Typists

Use word processor/computer or typewriter to type letters, reports, forms, or other material from rough draft, corrected copy, or voice recording. May perform other clerical duties as assigned.

- Education or Training Required: Moderate-term on-the-job training
- Job Growth: –15.3%
- Annual Openings: 30,000
- Self-Employed: 7.5%
- Part-Time: 44.9%

NATIONAL WAGE FIGURES (ANNUAL)

Beginning	25th Percentile	Median	Mean	75th Percentile	90th Percentile
$20,200	$24,180	$29,430	$30,540	$35,950	$43,330

Median Wages for Industries Employing Largest Numbers (Annual)

Industry	Median Income
Transportation Equipment Manufacturing	$38,450
Securities, Commodity Contracts, and Other Financial Investments and Related Activities	$34,400
Professional, Scientific, and Technical Services	$33,890
Hospitals	$31,540
Real Estate	$31,400
Chemical Manufacturing	$30,780
Management of Companies and Enterprises	$30,640
Computer and Electronic Product Manufacturing	$30,330
Merchant Wholesalers, Nondurable Goods	$30,210
Internet Service Providers, Web Search Portals, and Data-Processing Services	$30,110

Median Wages for States (Annual)

State	Wage	State	Wage	State	Wage
AK	$32,180	KY	$25,410	NY	$30,240
AL	$26,330	LA	$22,690	OH	$30,310
AR	$22,770	MA	$32,520	OK	$26,130
AZ	$27,630	MD	$29,870	OR	$30,230
CA	$33,090	ME	$25,500	PA	$28,290
CO	$34,010	MI	$33,770	RI	$32,920
CT	$31,960	MN	$31,410	SC	$25,600
DC	$29,220	MO	$23,570	SD	no data
DE	$35,440	MS	$22,250	TN	$28,370
FL	$25,150	MT	$27,080	TX	$30,400
GA	no data	NC	$26,410	UT	$25,930
HI	$27,910	ND	$23,710	VA	$27,370
IA	$27,350	NE	$25,730	VT	$26,120
ID	$26,210	NH	$28,620	WA	$32,050
IL	$29,590	NJ	$31,410	WI	$29,120
IN	$25,400	NM	$27,640	WV	$28,340
KS	$26,090	NV	$26,140	WY	$26,960

Median Wages for the Largest Metropolitan Areas (Annual)

Area	Wage	Area	Wage
AZ: Phoenix	$28,290	MI: Detroit	$34,240
CA: Los Angeles	$34,460	MN: Minneapolis	$34,630
CA: Riverside	$31,520	MO: Kansas City	$24,990
CA: Sacramento	$30,460	MO: St. Louis	$24,800
CA: San Diego	$32,040	NV: Las Vegas	$25,630
CA: San Francisco	$34,630	NY: New York	$32,620
CO: Denver	$36,120	OH: Cincinnati	$31,000
DC: Washington	$28,630	OH: Cleveland	$31,050
FL: Miami	$26,670	OH: Columbus	$34,620
FL: Orlando	$25,960	OR: Portland	$32,410
FL: Tampa	$25,260	PA: Philadelphia	$29,940
GA: Atlanta	$18,150	PA: Pittsburgh	$26,020
IL: Chicago	$30,800	TX: Dallas	$33,750
MA: Boston	$33,400	TX: Houston	$33,040
MD: Baltimore	$31,300	WA: Seattle	$34,720

FACTORS THAT MAY AFFECT EARNINGS

Educational Attainment of Workers and Effect on Earnings

	Percent at Level	Effect on Earnings
Less than High School	—	—
Some High School	5.4%	–41.8%
High School or Equivalent	29.7%	2.9%
Some College but No Degree	33.3%	–8.1%
Associate Degree	14.9%	0.8%
Bachelor's Degree	14.5%	26.8%
Master's Degree	—	—
Doctoral Degree	—	—
First Professional Degree	—	—

Flexibility of Earnings

Average Hours Worked: 30
Workers with a Varying Number of Hours: 6.1%
Workers Earning Some Overtime Pay, Tips, or Commissions: 7.7%
Earnings Benefit of Working Overtime: 20.8%

Gender

	Male	Female
Percent	8.8%	91.2%
Effect on Earnings	—	–0.7%

Union Membership

Percentage Union Members: 14.3%
Earnings Benefit of Union Membership: 30.5%

Veteran Status

Percentage Who Have Been on Active Duty: 4.2%
Earnings Benefit of Veteran Status: 25.4%

43-9031 Desktop Publishers

Format typescript and graphic elements, using computer software to produce publication-ready material.

- Education or Training Required: Postsecondary vocational training
- Job Growth: 23.2%
- Annual Openings: 8,000
- Self-Employed: 1.1%
- Part-Time: 43.3%

NATIONAL WAGE FIGURES (ANNUAL)

Beginning	25th Percentile	Median	Mean	75th Percentile	90th Percentile
$20,550	$26,270	$34,130	$36,120	$44,360	$55,040

Median Wages for Industries Employing Largest Numbers (Annual)

Industry	Median Income
Transportation Equipment Manufacturing	$47,750
Funds, Trusts, and Other Financial Vehicles	$44,640
Computer and Electronic Product Manufacturing	$43,510
Securities, Commodity Contracts, and Other Financial Investments and Related Activities	$43,260
Machinery Manufacturing	$42,480
Internet Publishing and Broadcasting	$42,380
Credit Intermediation and Related Activities	$40,880
Management of Companies and Enterprises	$39,130
Hospitals	$38,070
Miscellaneous Manufacturing	$36,940

Median Wages for States (Annual)

AK $39,860	KY $34,080	NY $40,720
AL $28,070	LA $30,280	OH $30,630
AR $19,430	MA $43,830	OK $26,930
AZ $32,240	MD $40,850	OR $33,520
CA $35,520	ME $34,590	PA $38,550
CO $35,250	MI $33,000	RI $44,170
CT $39,870	MN $37,120	SC $30,840
DC $43,850	MO $34,290	SD $19,610
DE $34,650	MS $26,220	TN $28,510
FL $31,180	MT $28,180	TX $33,240
GA $32,580	NC $30,560	UT $30,470
HI $27,620	ND $22,940	VA $31,470
IA $25,020	NE $27,620	VT $34,260
ID $28,450	NH $34,380	WA $35,560
IL $35,810	NJ $40,500	WI $34,430
IN $28,090	NM $25,550	WV $29,720
KS $26,700	NV $28,150	WY $27,860

Median Wages for the Largest Metropolitan Areas (Annual)

AZ: Phoenix	$31,590	MI: Detroit	$34,140
CA: Los Angeles	$34,720	MN: Minneapolis	$41,530
CA: Riverside	$31,810	MO: Kansas City	$27,340
CA: Sacramento	$35,150	MO: St. Louis	$39,900
CA: San Diego	$34,910	NV: Las Vegas	$26,630
CA: San Francisco	$40,340	NY: New York	$44,350
CO: Denver	$43,480	OH: Cincinnati	$32,460
DC: Washington	$39,700	OH: Cleveland	$30,190
FL: Miami	$34,330	OH: Columbus	$32,110
FL: Orlando	$28,400	OR: Portland	$35,080
FL: Tampa	$30,230	PA: Philadelphia	$48,190
GA: Atlanta	$34,210	PA: Pittsburgh	$36,940
IL: Chicago	$37,580	TX: Dallas	$33,820
MA: Boston	$44,030	TX: Houston	$35,270
MD: Baltimore	$37,410	WA: Seattle	$38,630

FACTORS THAT MAY AFFECT EARNINGS

Educational Attainment of Workers and Effect on Earnings

Figures are based on a group of occupations: Other Office and Administrative Support Workers

	Percent at Level	Effect on Earnings
Less than High School	1.2%	−41.3%
Some High School	6.8%	−41.3%
High School or Equivalent	27.7%	−6.0%
Some College but No Degree	27.0%	−5.7%
Associate Degree	14.6%	4.8%
Bachelor's Degree	16.8%	17.5%
Master's Degree	5.0%	43.0%
Doctoral Degree	—	—
First Professional Degree	0.9%	63.1%

Flexibility of Earnings

Average Hours Worked: 35
Workers with a Varying Number of Hours: 5.4%
Workers Earning Some Overtime Pay, Tips, or Commissions: 10.0%
Earnings Benefit of Working Overtime: 20.8%

Gender

	Male	Female
Percent	32.4%	67.6%
Effect on Earnings	8.2%	−2.6%

Union Membership

Percentage Union Members: 8.2%
Earnings Benefit of Union Membership: 30.5%

Veteran Status

Percentage Who Have Been on Active Duty: 4.2%
Earnings Benefit of Veteran Status: 25.4%

43-9041 Insurance Claims and Policy Processing Clerks

Process new insurance policies, modifications to existing policies, and claims forms. Obtain information from policyholders to verify the accuracy and completeness of information on claims forms, applications and related documents, and company records. Update existing policies and company records to reflect changes requested by policyholders and insurance company representatives.

- Education or Training Required: Moderate-term on-the-job training
- Job Growth: 4.5%
- Annual Openings: 36,000
- Self-Employed: 0.1%
- Part-Time: 8.6%

NATIONAL WAGE FIGURES (ANNUAL)

Beginning	25th Percentile	Median	Mean	75th Percentile	90th Percentile
$21,390	$25,640	$31,120	$32,740	$38,020	$46,490

Median Wages for Industries Employing Largest Numbers (Annual)

Industry	Median Income
Postal Service	$45,500
Federal, State, and Local Government	$34,660
Religious, Grantmaking, Civic, Professional, and Similar Organizations	$33,580
Merchant Wholesalers, Durable Goods	$32,350
Management of Companies and Enterprises	$32,250
Securities, Commodity Contracts, and Other Financial Investments and Related Activities	$32,200
Insurance Carriers and Related Activities	$31,150
Real Estate	$31,000
Credit Intermediation and Related Activities	$30,780
Funds, Trusts, and Other Financial Vehicles	$30,720

Median Wages for States (Annual)

AK	$31,950	KY	$29,600	NY	$32,920
AL	$26,700	LA	$25,200	OH	$31,200
AR	$26,330	MA	$34,670	OK	$28,140
AZ	$27,830	MD	$33,230	OR	$33,090
CA	$35,100	ME	$28,330	PA	$29,780
CO	$35,220	MI	$32,890	RI	no data
CT	$37,110	MN	$32,270	SC	$26,650
DC	$34,510	MO	$27,810	SD	$23,680
DE	$30,810	MS	$27,700	TN	$31,560
FL	$29,840	MT	$25,780	TX	$27,870
GA	$30,580	NC	$31,590	UT	$26,560
HI	$32,140	ND	$25,680	VA	$30,030
IA	$27,270	NE	$27,910	VT	$30,550
ID	$27,540	NH	$30,050	WA	$32,800
IL	$33,090	NJ	$33,920	WI	$29,110
IN	$29,550	NM	$25,030	WV	$23,330
KS	$28,130	NV	$28,760	WY	$26,530

Median Wages for the Largest Metropolitan Areas (Annual)

AZ: Phoenix	$29,420	MI: Detroit	$34,710
CA: Los Angeles	$34,680	MN: Minneapolis	$33,450
CA: Riverside	$34,710	MO: Kansas City	$28,280
CA: Sacramento	$34,320	MO: St. Louis	$29,330
CA: San Diego	$34,770	NV: Las Vegas	$28,960
CA: San Francisco	$41,550	NY: New York	$34,760
CO: Denver	$35,580	OH: Cincinnati	$32,210
DC: Washington	$30,770	OH: Cleveland	$29,480
FL: Miami	$31,190	OH: Columbus	$33,020
FL: Orlando	$29,520	OR: Portland	$33,710
FL: Tampa	$29,270	PA: Philadelphia	$32,590
GA: Atlanta	$32,390	PA: Pittsburgh	$27,690
IL: Chicago	$33,820	TX: Dallas	$29,290
MA: Boston	$35,750	TX: Houston	$27,940
MD: Baltimore	$34,400	WA: Seattle	$34,920

FACTORS THAT MAY AFFECT EARNINGS

Educational Attainment of Workers and Effect on Earnings

	Percent at Level	Effect on Earnings
Less than High School	—	—
Some High School	2.1%	−35.4%
High School or Equivalent	30.5%	−7.5%
Some College but No Degree	30.1%	−8.1%
Associate Degree	15.2%	3.1%
Bachelor's Degree	19.1%	20.6%
Master's Degree	—	—
Doctoral Degree	—	—
First Professional Degree	—	—

Flexibility of Earnings

Average Hours Worked: 37
Workers with a Varying Number of Hours: 1.2%
Workers Earning Some Overtime Pay, Tips, or Commissions: 9.1%
Earnings Benefit of Working Overtime: 20.8%

Gender

	Male	Female
Percent	12.4%	87.6%
Effect on Earnings	—	−1.4%

Union Membership

Percentage Union Members: Insignificant
Earnings Benefit of Union Membership: No significant data available

Veteran Status

Percentage Who Have Been on Active Duty: 4.2%
Earnings Benefit of Veteran Status: 25.4%

43-9051 Mail Clerks and Mail Machine Operators, Except Postal Service

Prepare incoming and outgoing mail for distribution. Use hand or mail-handling machines to time-stamp, open, read, sort, and route incoming mail and address, seal, stamp, fold, stuff, and affix postage to outgoing mail or packages. Duties may also include keeping necessary records and completed forms.

- Education or Training Required: Short-term on-the-job training
- Job Growth: –37.1%
- Annual Openings: 33,000
- Self-Employed: 0.0%
- Part-Time: 39.4%

NATIONAL WAGE FIGURES (ANNUAL)

Beginning	25th Percentile	Median	Mean	75th Percentile	90th Percentile
$16,000	$19,330	$23,810	$25,060	$29,500	$36,100

Median Wages for Industries Employing Largest Numbers (Annual)

Industry	Median Income
Utilities	$33,100
Federal, State, and Local Government	$29,380
Funds, Trusts, and Other Financial Vehicles	$27,960
Securities, Commodity Contracts, and Other Financial Investments and Related Activities	$27,680
Real Estate	$27,390
Hospitals	$26,130
Merchant Wholesalers, Nondurable Goods	$26,070
Management of Companies and Enterprises	$25,360
Nonstore Retailers	$25,320
Merchant Wholesalers, Durable Goods	$25,300

Median Wages for States (Annual)

State	Wage	State	Wage	State	Wage
AK	$29,370	KY	$24,000	NY	$26,770
AL	$20,220	LA	$19,590	OH	$24,250
AR	$22,160	MA	$27,330	OK	$19,050
AZ	$21,540	MD	$25,250	OR	$23,880
CA	$23,900	ME	$23,070	PA	$22,490
CO	$26,600	MI	$24,820	RI	$24,510
CT	$26,270	MN	$25,520	SC	$22,800
DC	$33,430	MO	$23,020	SD	$20,280
DE	$24,220	MS	$20,350	TN	$23,870
FL	$22,070	MT	$18,850	TX	$23,550
GA	$23,170	NC	$22,290	UT	$22,320
HI	$25,610	ND	$20,850	VA	$25,270
IA	$22,400	NE	$22,030	VT	$24,000
ID	$23,660	NH	$23,200	WA	$28,530
IL	$21,780	NJ	$25,350	WI	$23,170
IN	$22,840	NM	$22,520	WV	$19,750
KS	$25,690	NV	$22,520	WY	$21,170

Median Wages for the Largest Metropolitan Areas (Annual)

Area	Wage	Area	Wage
AZ: Phoenix	$21,550	MI: Detroit	$24,590
CA: Los Angeles	$22,660	MN: Minneapolis	$25,550
CA: Riverside	$22,600	MO: Kansas City	$27,330
CA: Sacramento	$27,370	MO: St. Louis	$23,550
CA: San Diego	$23,580	NV: Las Vegas	$19,960
CA: San Francisco	$30,560	NY: New York	$26,460
CO: Denver	$27,510	OH: Cincinnati	$24,090
DC: Washington	$29,110	OH: Cleveland	$23,990
FL: Miami	$21,700	OH: Columbus	$25,750
FL: Orlando	$23,280	OR: Portland	$24,600
FL: Tampa	$22,860	PA: Philadelphia	$24,380
GA: Atlanta	$23,550	PA: Pittsburgh	$21,730
IL: Chicago	$21,970	TX: Dallas	$23,940
MA: Boston	$27,900	TX: Houston	$24,020
MD: Baltimore	$24,430	WA: Seattle	$29,560

FACTORS THAT MAY AFFECT EARNINGS

Educational Attainment of Workers and Effect on Earnings

	Percent at Level	Effect on Earnings
Less than High School	—	—
Some High School	12.3%	–31.9%
High School or Equivalent	37.7%	2.1%
Some College but No Degree	31.2%	11.6%
Associate Degree	7.1%	13.6%
Bachelor's Degree	7.1%	–7.2%
Master's Degree	—	—
Doctoral Degree	—	—
First Professional Degree	—	—

Flexibility of Earnings

Average Hours Worked: 32
Workers with a Varying Number of Hours: 4.6%
Workers Earning Some Overtime Pay, Tips, or Commissions: 13.3%
Earnings Benefit of Working Overtime: 20.8%

Gender

	Male	Female
Percent	45.8%	54.2%
Effect on Earnings	—	1.1%

Union Membership

Percentage Union Members: 15.0%
Earnings Benefit of Union Membership: 34.0%

Veteran Status

Percentage Who Have Been on Active Duty: 4.2%
Earnings Benefit of Veteran Status: 25.4%

43-9061 Office Clerks, General

Perform duties too varied and diverse to be classified in any specific office clerical occupation requiring limited knowledge of office management systems and procedures. Clerical duties may be assigned in accordance with the office procedures of individual establishments and may include a combination of answering telephones, bookkeeping, typing or word processing, stenography, office machine operation, and filing.

- Education or Training Required: Short-term on-the-job training
- Job Growth: 8.4%
- Annual Openings: 695,000
- Self-Employed: 0.4%
- Part-Time: 52.3%

NATIONAL WAGE FIGURES (ANNUAL)

Beginning	25th Percentile	Median	Mean	75th Percentile	90th Percentile
$14,850	$18,640	$23,710	$25,200	$30,240	$37,600

Median Wages for Industries Employing Largest Numbers (Annual)

Industry	Median Income
Federal, State, and Local Government	$27,110
Management of Companies and Enterprises	$26,500
Hospitals	$26,110
Publishing Industries (Except Internet)	$24,650
Credit Intermediation and Related Activities	$24,520
Merchant Wholesalers, Durable Goods	$24,520
Securities, Commodity Contracts, and Other Financial Investments and Related Activities	$23,890
Ambulatory Health Care Services	$23,860
Educational Services	$23,750
Insurance Carriers and Related Activities	$23,670

Median Wages for States (Annual)

AK $29,160	KY $22,080	NY $25,490
AL $20,080	LA $18,010	OH $22,570
AR $18,560	MA $27,950	OK $20,840
AZ $24,000	MD $26,880	OR $25,690
CA $25,890	ME $22,320	PA $23,690
CO $26,730	MI $24,530	RI $24,030
CT $28,290	MN $26,350	SC $22,270
DC $29,010	MO $22,410	SD $18,510
DE $25,500	MS $18,750	TN $23,560
FL $22,150	MT $20,440	TX $20,930
GA $22,160	NC $22,830	UT $21,540
HI $22,890	ND $20,710	VA $26,290
IA $22,900	NE $21,600	VT $23,360
ID $22,790	NH $27,040	WA $27,160
IL $23,780	NJ $25,580	WI $23,710
IN $22,140	NM $20,590	WV $20,600
KS $21,310	NV $23,800	WY $21,290

Median Wages for the Largest Metropolitan Areas (Annual)

AZ: Phoenix $24,810	MI: Detroit $25,270
CA: Los Angeles $24,780	MN: Minneapolis $28,020
CA: Riverside $24,020	MO: Kansas City $24,340
CA: Sacramento $28,200	MO: St. Louis $23,660
CA: San Diego $26,250	NV: Las Vegas $23,860
CA: San Francisco $30,250	NY: New York $26,510
CO: Denver $28,490	OH: Cincinnati $23,590
DC: Washington $30,030	OH: Cleveland $23,210
FL: Miami $22,470	OH: Columbus $24,720
FL: Orlando $22,640	OR: Portland $27,120
FL: Tampa $22,540	PA: Philadelphia $26,130
GA: Atlanta $23,580	PA: Pittsburgh $22,380
IL: Chicago $24,820	TX: Dallas $23,050
MA: Boston $28,540	TX: Houston $22,440
MD: Baltimore $27,160	WA: Seattle $28,520

FACTORS THAT MAY AFFECT EARNINGS

Educational Attainment of Workers and Effect on Earnings

	Percent at Level	Effect on Earnings
Less than High School	1.1%	−54.2%
Some High School	7.3%	−40.8%
High School or Equivalent	29.6%	1.6%
Some College but No Degree	28.3%	−11.4%
Associate Degree	13.0%	10.6%
Bachelor's Degree	15.9%	14.5%
Master's Degree	3.7%	46.7%
Doctoral Degree	—	—
First Professional Degree	0.9%	98.1%

Flexibility of Earnings

Average Hours Worked: 29
Workers with a Varying Number of Hours: 7.1%
Workers Earning Some Overtime Pay, Tips, or Commissions: 7.7%
Earnings Benefit of Working Overtime: 12.1%

Gender

	Male	Female
Percent	18.1%	81.9%
Effect on Earnings	5.0%	−0.6%

Union Membership

Percentage Union Members: 9.1%
Earnings Benefit of Union Membership: 38.3%

Veteran Status

Percentage Who Have Been on Active Duty: 4.2%
Earnings Benefit of Veteran Status: 25.4%

43-9071 Office Machine Operators, Except Computer

Operate one or more of a variety of office machines, such as photo-copying, photographic, and duplicating machines or other office machines.

- Education or Training Required: Short-term on-the-job training
- Job Growth: –21.9%
- Annual Openings: 19,000
- Self-Employed: 0.4%
- Part-Time: 46.2%

NATIONAL WAGE FIGURES (ANNUAL)

Beginning	25th Percentile	Median	Mean	75th Percentile	90th Percentile
$17,080	$20,190	$24,540	$26,010	$30,600	$37,330

Median Wages for Industries Employing Largest Numbers (Annual)

Industry	Median Income
Chemical Manufacturing	$41,850
Federal, State, and Local Government	$30,750
Monetary Authorities—Central Bank	$30,420
Securities, Commodity Contracts, and Other Financial Investments and Related Activities	$28,870
Religious, Grantmaking, Civic, Professional, and Similar Organizations	$28,400
Merchant Wholesalers, Durable Goods	$27,730
Educational Services	$27,460
Funds, Trusts, and Other Financial Vehicles	$26,760
Insurance Carriers and Related Activities	$26,550
Professional, Scientific, and Technical Services	$26,290

Median Wages for States (Annual)

State	Wage	State	Wage	State	Wage
AK	$31,680	KY	$22,650	NY	$24,570
AL	$19,190	LA	$24,090	OH	$25,730
AR	$22,470	MA	$25,810	OK	$23,770
AZ	$26,020	MD	$27,410	OR	$24,490
CA	$26,870	ME	$22,280	PA	$22,940
CO	$25,650	MI	$24,200	RI	$25,570
CT	$25,920	MN	$25,300	SC	$20,640
DC	$26,600	MO	$24,260	SD	$20,420
DE	$27,000	MS	$20,130	TN	$24,480
FL	$22,370	MT	$24,900	TX	$24,580
GA	$21,730	NC	$23,400	UT	$24,850
HI	$20,870	ND	$23,590	VA	$25,480
IA	$22,540	NE	$22,490	VT	$26,450
ID	no data	NH	$25,500	WA	$24,270
IL	$24,350	NJ	$24,670	WI	$25,470
IN	$23,490	NM	no data	WV	$22,040
KS	$24,310	NV	$23,970	WY	no data

Median Wages for the Largest Metropolitan Areas (Annual)

Area	Wage	Area	Wage
AZ: Phoenix	$26,590	MI: Detroit	$24,960
CA: Los Angeles	$26,920	MN: Minneapolis	$25,110
CA: Riverside	$22,410	MO: Kansas City	$29,190
CA: Sacramento	$30,100	MO: St. Louis	$22,180
CA: San Diego	$26,120	NV: Las Vegas	$23,080
CA: San Francisco	$28,560	NY: New York	$25,180
CO: Denver	$25,690	OH: Cincinnati	$28,100
DC: Washington	$26,890	OH: Cleveland	$25,190
FL: Miami	$22,220	OH: Columbus	$26,940
FL: Orlando	$23,210	OR: Portland	$26,210
FL: Tampa	$22,190	PA: Philadelphia	$25,780
GA: Atlanta	$21,920	PA: Pittsburgh	$21,660
IL: Chicago	$24,000	TX: Dallas	$26,530
MA: Boston	$25,970	TX: Houston	$23,490
MD: Baltimore	$29,290	WA: Seattle	$25,480

FACTORS THAT MAY AFFECT EARNINGS

Educational Attainment of Workers and Effect on Earnings

	Percent at Level	Effect on Earnings
Less than High School	—	—
Some High School	—	—
High School or Equivalent	45.0%	–2.2%
Some College but No Degree	32.5%	6.4%
Associate Degree	—	—
Bachelor's Degree	8.8%	–7.7%
Master's Degree	—	—
Doctoral Degree	—	—
First Professional Degree	—	—

Figures do not total 100% because some levels have a very small sample size.

Flexibility of Earnings

Average Hours Worked: 31
Workers with a Varying Number of Hours: 3.2%
Workers Earning Some Overtime Pay, Tips, or Commissions: 18.8%
Earnings Benefit of Working Overtime: 20.8%

Gender

	Male	Female
Percent	42.2%	57.8%
Effect on Earnings	8.2%	–2.6%

Union Membership

Percentage Union Members: 8.2%
Earnings Benefit of Union Membership: 30.5%

Veteran Status

Percentage Who Have Been on Active Duty: 4.2%
Earnings Benefit of Veteran Status: 25.4%

43-9081 Proofreaders and Copy Markers

Read transcript or proof type setup to detect and mark for correction any grammatical, typographical, or compositional errors.

- Education or Training Required: Short-term on-the-job training
- Job Growth: 1.7%
- Annual Openings: 5,000
- Self-Employed: 10.5%
- Part-Time: 62.5%

NATIONAL WAGE FIGURES (ANNUAL)

Beginning	25th Percentile	Median	Mean	75th Percentile	90th Percentile
$16,020	$20,900	$27,450	$29,380	$36,130	$45,410

Median Wages for Industries Employing Largest Numbers (Annual)

Industry	Median Income
Securities, Commodity Contracts, and Other Financial Investments and Related Activities	$37,320
Ambulatory Health Care Services	$35,860
Religious, Grantmaking, Civic, Professional, and Similar Organizations	$34,930
Internet Service Providers, Web Search Portals, and Data-Processing Services	$33,130
Administrative and Support Services	$33,080
Management of Companies and Enterprises	$32,630
Federal, State, and Local Government	$32,560
Professional, Scientific, and Technical Services	$32,180
Internet Publishing and Broadcasting	$31,740
Insurance Carriers and Related Activities	$31,500

Median Wages for States (Annual)

State	Wage	State	Wage	State	Wage
AK	no data	KY	$26,880	NY	$36,660
AL	$18,760	LA	$22,220	OH	$28,700
AR	$26,780	MA	$32,830	OK	no data
AZ	no data	MD	$30,850	OR	$34,600
CA	$30,360	ME	$25,560	PA	$27,490
CO	$23,810	MI	$31,800	RI	no data
CT	$29,570	MN	$30,670	SC	$22,710
DC	$34,850	MO	$24,490	SD	$20,170
DE	no data	MS	$22,830	TN	$26,030
FL	$26,420	MT	no data	TX	$28,280
GA	$25,980	NC	$23,300	UT	$22,690
HI	no data	ND	no data	VA	$24,630
IA	$22,710	NE	$23,770	VT	no data
ID	no data	NH	$26,370	WA	$31,800
IL	$28,630	NJ	$32,760	WI	$26,440
IN	$25,570	NM	$21,460	WV	$22,280
KS	no data	NV	$27,030	WY	no data

Median Wages for the Largest Metropolitan Areas (Annual)

Area	Wage	Area	Wage
AZ: Phoenix	$14,610	MI: Detroit	$32,640
CA: Los Angeles	$33,850	MN: Minneapolis	$37,340
CA: Riverside	no data	MO: Kansas City	$28,660
CA: Sacramento	$27,510	MO: St. Louis	no data
CA: San Diego	no data	NV: Las Vegas	no data
CA: San Francisco	no data	NY: New York	$36,850
CO: Denver	$22,670	OH: Cincinnati	$29,050
DC: Washington	$32,990	OH: Cleveland	$29,940
FL: Miami	$31,020	OH: Columbus	$32,020
FL: Orlando	no data	OR: Portland	$35,440
FL: Tampa	$25,880	PA: Philadelphia	$29,210
GA: Atlanta	$27,300	PA: Pittsburgh	$26,660
IL: Chicago	$29,350	TX: Dallas	$30,620
MA: Boston	$33,590	TX: Houston	$28,980
MD: Baltimore	$31,500	WA: Seattle	$34,570

FACTORS THAT MAY AFFECT EARNINGS

Educational Attainment of Workers and Effect on Earnings

	Percent at Level	Effect on Earnings
Less than High School	—	—
Some High School	—	—
High School or Equivalent	—	—
Some College but No Degree	—	—
Associate Degree	—	—
Bachelor's Degree	36.8%	15.8%
Master's Degree	—	—
Doctoral Degree	—	—
First Professional Degree	—	—

Figures do not total 100% because some levels have a very small sample size.

Flexibility of Earnings

Average Hours Worked: 30
Workers with a Varying Number of Hours: 7.5%
Workers Earning Some Overtime Pay, Tips, or Commissions: 5.3%
Earnings Benefit of Working Overtime: 20.8%

Gender

	Male	Female
Percent	21.2%	78.8%
Effect on Earnings	8.2%	−2.6%

Union Membership

Percentage Union Members: 10.5%
Earnings Benefit of Union Membership: 30.5%

Veteran Status

Percentage Who Have Been on Active Duty: 4.2%
Earnings Benefit of Veteran Status: 25.4%

43-9111 Statistical Assistants

Compile and compute data according to statistical formulas for use in statistical studies. May perform actuarial computations and compile charts and graphs for use by actuaries. Includes actuarial clerks.

- Education or Training Required: Moderate-term on-the-job training
- Job Growth: 5.7%
- Annual Openings: 1,000
- Self-Employed: 0.0%
- Part-Time: 57.1%

NATIONAL WAGE FIGURES (ANNUAL)

Beginning	25th Percentile	Median	Mean	75th Percentile	90th Percentile
$20,200	$25,020	$31,250	$32,950	$39,350	$48,690

Median Wages for Industries Employing Largest Numbers (Annual)

Industry	Median Income
Telecommunications	$43,970
Merchant Wholesalers, Nondurable Goods	$41,790
Publishing Industries (Except Internet)	$40,790
Utilities	$39,040
Chemical Manufacturing	$37,900
Computer and Electronic Product Manufacturing	$37,710
Air Transportation	$37,160
Insurance Carriers and Related Activities	$35,300
Professional, Scientific, and Technical Services	$34,450
Management of Companies and Enterprises	$33,940

Median Wages for States (Annual)

AK	$37,610	KY	$40,210	NY	$36,210
AL	$37,450	LA	$36,290	OH	$31,640
AR	$19,010	MA	$37,670	OK	no data
AZ	$28,700	MD	$39,440	OR	$38,100
CA	$36,410	ME	$30,690	PA	$28,740
CO	$41,500	MI	no data	RI	no data
CT	$34,940	MN	$34,940	SC	$28,590
DC	$43,170	MO	no data	SD	no data
DE	no data	MS	$30,480	TN	$32,360
FL	$29,740	MT	no data	TX	$36,590
GA	$25,160	NC	$28,870	UT	$28,800
HI	$29,370	ND	no data	VA	$41,790
IA	$40,450	NE	$31,010	VT	no data
ID	$29,600	NH	$35,250	WA	$36,130
IL	$32,040	NJ	$34,740	WI	$37,920
IN	$29,810	NM	no data	WV	no data
KS	no data	NV	no data	WY	no data

Median Wages for the Largest Metropolitan Areas (Annual)

AZ: Phoenix	$29,140	MI: Detroit	$41,930
CA: Los Angeles	$33,580	MN: Minneapolis	$36,010
CA: Riverside	no data	MO: Kansas City	no data
CA: Sacramento	$36,970	MO: St. Louis	$43,880
CA: San Diego	$40,070	NV: Las Vegas	no data
CA: San Francisco	$44,360	NY: New York	$37,560
CO: Denver	$44,030	OH: Cincinnati	no data
DC: Washington	$43,270	OH: Cleveland	$35,500
FL: Miami	$31,810	OH: Columbus	$34,460
FL: Orlando	$29,230	OR: Portland	$39,680
FL: Tampa	$30,260	PA: Philadelphia	$34,940
GA: Atlanta	$26,660	PA: Pittsburgh	$30,540
IL: Chicago	$32,780	TX: Dallas	no data
MA: Boston	$37,580	TX: Houston	$35,470
MD: Baltimore	$36,320	WA: Seattle	$37,390

FACTORS THAT MAY AFFECT EARNINGS

Educational Attainment of Workers and Effect on Earnings

	Percent at Level	Effect on Earnings
Less than High School	—	—
Some High School	—	—
High School or Equivalent	22.9%	−10.0%
Some College but No Degree	28.6%	−4.5%
Associate Degree	22.9%	17.4%
Bachelor's Degree	—	—
Master's Degree	—	—
Doctoral Degree	—	—
First Professional Degree	—	—

Figures do not total 100% because some levels have a very small sample size.

Flexibility of Earnings

Average Hours Worked: 36
Workers with a Varying Number of Hours: 5.1%
Workers Earning Some Overtime Pay, Tips, or Commissions: 10.5%
Earnings Benefit of Working Overtime: 20.8%

Gender

	Male	Female
Percent	28.7%	71.3%
Effect on Earnings	8.2%	−2.6%

Union Membership

Percentage Union Members: 10.5%
Earnings Benefit of Union Membership: 30.5%

Veteran Status

Percentage Who Have Been on Active Duty: 4.2%
Earnings Benefit of Veteran Status: 25.4%

43-9199 Office and Administrative Support Workers, All Other

All office and administrative support workers not listed separately.

- Education or Training Required: Short-term on-the-job training
- Job Growth: 10.0%
- Annual Openings: 63,000
- Self-Employed: 3.1%
- Part-Time: 38.0%

NATIONAL WAGE FIGURES (ANNUAL)

Beginning	25th Percentile	Median	Mean	75th Percentile	90th Percentile
$16,180	$20,510	$27,200	$29,260	$35,580	$45,260

Median Wages for Industries Employing Largest Numbers (Annual)

Industry	Median Income
Telecommunications	$43,530
Utilities	$42,400
Transportation Equipment Manufacturing	$39,560
Computer and Electronic Product Manufacturing	$34,900
Insurance Carriers and Related Activities	$31,790
Couriers and Messengers	$31,580
Management of Companies and Enterprises	$30,480
Credit Intermediation and Related Activities	$30,270
Merchant Wholesalers, Durable Goods	$30,260
Nursing and Residential Care Facilities	$29,940

Median Wages for States (Annual)

AK	$35,470	KY	$22,970	NY	$27,870
AL	$27,520	LA	$24,710	OH	$28,420
AR	$25,840	MA	$33,410	OK	no data
AZ	$29,740	MD	$30,430	OR	$25,890
CA	$24,730	ME	$27,170	PA	$30,780
CO	$31,100	MI	$30,820	RI	no data
CT	$27,570	MN	$29,620	SC	$27,470
DC	$34,520	MO	$27,410	SD	$32,820
DE	$33,750	MS	$33,920	TN	$31,530
FL	$23,060	MT	no data	TX	$30,620
GA	$27,320	NC	$28,970	UT	$24,310
HI	$27,300	ND	$29,490	VA	$33,320
IA	$24,070	NE	$24,880	VT	$27,030
ID	$28,080	NH	$21,920	WA	$29,550
IL	$27,520	NJ	$27,770	WI	$26,410
IN	$30,090	NM	$27,430	WV	$22,720
KS	$30,100	NV	$24,950	WY	$24,720

Median Wages for the Largest Metropolitan Areas (Annual)

AZ: Phoenix	$31,630	MI: Detroit	$34,220
CA: Los Angeles	$24,470	MN: Minneapolis	$30,560
CA: Riverside	$22,790	MO: Kansas City	$31,820
CA: Sacramento	$24,360	MO: St. Louis	$29,320
CA: San Diego	$27,500	NV: Las Vegas	$24,630
CA: San Francisco	$30,480	NY: New York	$24,860
CO: Denver	$31,440	OH: Cincinnati	$28,410
DC: Washington	$34,940	OH: Cleveland	$28,430
FL: Miami	$24,450	OH: Columbus	$30,820
FL: Orlando	$20,620	OR: Portland	$29,240
FL: Tampa	$21,900	PA: Philadelphia	$32,930
GA: Atlanta	$27,740	PA: Pittsburgh	$23,270
IL: Chicago	$28,280	TX: Dallas	$33,700
MA: Boston	$32,360	TX: Houston	$29,660
MD: Baltimore	$30,760	WA: Seattle	$30,700

FACTORS THAT MAY AFFECT EARNINGS

Educational Attainment of Workers and Effect on Earnings

	Percent at Level	Effect on Earnings
Less than High School	—	—
Some High School	3.3%	−31.1%
High School or Equivalent	23.9%	−12.0%
Some College but No Degree	26.1%	−7.0%
Associate Degree	16.3%	−8.0%
Bachelor's Degree	21.5%	14.8%
Master's Degree	7.2%	48.4%
Doctoral Degree	—	—
First Professional Degree	—	—

Flexibility of Earnings

Average Hours Worked: 34
Workers with a Varying Number of Hours: 5.8%
Workers Earning Some Overtime Pay, Tips, or Commissions: 9.7%
Earnings Benefit of Working Overtime: 23.8%

Gender

	Male	Female
Percent	21.5%	78.5%
Effect on Earnings	8.2%	−2.6%

Union Membership

Percentage Union Members: 7.2%
Earnings Benefit of Union Membership: 26.8%

Veteran Status

Percentage Who Have Been on Active Duty: 4.2%
Earnings Benefit of Veteran Status: 25.4%

45-0000: Farming, Fishing, and Forestry Occupations

45-1000 Supervisors, Farming, Fishing, and Forestry Workers

45-1011 First-Line Supervisors/Managers of Farming, Fishing, and Forestry Workers

Directly supervise and coordinate the activities of agricultural, forestry, aquacultural, and related workers.

- Education or Training Required: Work experience in a related occupation
- Job Growth: 3.6%
- Annual Openings: 11,000
- Self-Employed: 21.3%
- Part-Time: 8.7%

NATIONAL WAGE FIGURES (ANNUAL)

Beginning	25th Percentile	Median	Mean	75th Percentile	90th Percentile
$20,280	$27,280	$37,750	$40,210	$49,780	$64,310

Median Wages for Industries Employing Largest Numbers (Annual)

Industry	Median Income
Social Assistance	$60,790
Federal, State, and Local Government	$47,710
Forestry and Logging	$46,910
Truck Transportation	$44,940
Administrative and Support Services	$44,280
Wood Product Manufacturing	$43,090
Professional, Scientific, and Technical Services	$42,430
Beverage and Tobacco Product Manufacturing	$41,990
Food Manufacturing	$41,290
Religious, Grantmaking, Civic, Professional, and Similar Organizations	$40,600

Median Wages for States (Annual)

AK	no data	KY	$34,660	NY	$35,720
AL	$47,690	LA	$34,540	OH	$44,440
AR	$36,230	MA	no data	OK	no data
AZ	$38,160	MD	$43,610	OR	$39,310
CA	$28,400	ME	$44,980	PA	$51,160
CO	$35,520	MI	$48,790	RI	no data
CT	$44,010	MN	$42,780	SC	$46,180
DC	no data	MO	$40,020	SD	$31,640
DE	$46,420	MS	$38,500	TN	$34,130
FL	$39,520	MT	$40,240	TX	$34,720
GA	$40,440	NC	$38,660	UT	$37,860
HI	$37,030	ND	$44,350	VA	$43,410
IA	$47,230	NE	$38,430	VT	no data
ID	$41,620	NH	$40,010	WA	$42,380
IL	$52,680	NJ	$50,760	WI	$43,720
IN	$35,410	NM	$30,620	WV	$30,530
KS	$38,000	NV	$45,330	WY	no data

Median Wages for the Largest Metropolitan Areas (Annual)

AZ: Phoenix	$34,230	MI: Detroit	$40,620
CA: Los Angeles	$37,710	MN: Minneapolis	$37,290
CA: Riverside	$29,510	MO: Kansas City	no data
CA: Sacramento	$44,050	MO: St. Louis	no data
CA: San Diego	$32,040	NV: Las Vegas	no data
CA: San Francisco	$52,760	NY: New York	$52,630
CO: Denver	no data	OH: Cincinnati	$42,070
DC: Washington	$36,740	OH: Cleveland	$39,850
FL: Miami	$33,990	OH: Columbus	$41,570
FL: Orlando	$41,820	OR: Portland	$43,020
FL: Tampa	$36,960	PA: Philadelphia	$45,170
GA: Atlanta	$45,970	PA: Pittsburgh	$50,640
IL: Chicago	$40,480	TX: Dallas	$31,460
MA: Boston	no data	TX: Houston	$64,700
MD: Baltimore	$43,660	WA: Seattle	$39,010

FACTORS THAT MAY AFFECT EARNINGS

Educational Attainment of Workers and Effect on Earnings

	Percent at Level	Effect on Earnings
Less than High School	14.0%	−49.8%
Some High School	14.0%	−34.0%
High School or Equivalent	32.6%	5.7%
Some College but No Degree	18.6%	−8.2%
Associate Degree	—	—
Bachelor's Degree	—	—
Master's Degree	—	—
Doctoral Degree	—	—
First Professional Degree	—	—

Figures do not total 100% because some levels have a very small sample size.

Flexibility of Earnings

Average Hours Worked: 35
Workers with a Varying Number of Hours: 19.0%
Workers Earning Some Overtime Pay, Tips, or Commissions: 4.3%
Earnings Benefit of Working Overtime: −20.1%

Gender

	Male	Female
Percent	77.2%	22.8%
Effect on Earnings	3.6%	−11.6%

Union Membership

Percentage Union Members: 4.3%
Earnings Benefit of Union Membership: 59.6%

Veteran Status

Percentage Who Have Been on Active Duty: 15.6%
Earnings Benefit of Veteran Status: 73.4%

45-1012 Farm Labor Contractors

Recruit, hire, furnish, and supervise seasonal or temporary agricultural laborers for a fee. May transport, house, and provide meals for workers.

- Education or Training Required: Work experience in a related occupation
- Job Growth: No data available
- Annual Openings: No data available
- Self-Employed: 21.3%
- Part-Time: 8.7%

NATIONAL WAGE FIGURES (ANNUAL)

Beginning	25th Percentile	Median	Mean	75th Percentile	90th Percentile
$13,130	$16,020	$23,550	$28,850	$34,350	$48,320

Note: The mean is significantly higher than the median because of the presence of a few star earners.

Median Wages for Industries Employing Largest Numbers (Annual)

Industry	Median Income
Merchant Wholesalers, Nondurable Goods	$20,370

Median Wages for States (Annual)

AK	no data	KY	no data	NY	no data
AL	no data	LA	no data	OH	no data
AR	no data	MA	no data	OK	no data
AZ	$14,540	MD	no data	OR	no data
CA	$30,880	ME	no data	PA	no data
CO	no data	MI	no data	RI	no data
CT	no data	MN	no data	SC	no data
DC	no data	MO	no data	SD	no data
DE	no data	MS	no data	TN	no data
FL	$33,440	MT	no data	TX	$15,790
GA	$26,690	NC	no data	UT	no data
HI	no data	ND	no data	VA	no data
IA	$29,750	NE	no data	VT	no data
ID	no data	NH	no data	WA	no data
IL	no data	NJ	no data	WI	no data
IN	no data	NM	no data	WV	no data
KS	no data	NV	no data	WY	no data

Median Wages for the Largest Metropolitan Areas (Annual)

AZ: Phoenix	no data	MI: Detroit	no data
CA: Los Angeles	no data	MN: Minneapolis	no data
CA: Riverside	no data	MO: Kansas City	no data
CA: Sacramento	no data	MO: St. Louis	no data
CA: San Diego	no data	NV: Las Vegas	no data
CA: San Francisco	no data	NY: New York	no data
CO: Denver	no data	OH: Cincinnati	no data
DC: Washington	no data	OH: Cleveland	no data
FL: Miami	no data	OH: Columbus	no data
FL: Orlando	no data	OR: Portland	no data
FL: Tampa	no data	PA: Philadelphia	no data
GA: Atlanta	no data	PA: Pittsburgh	no data
IL: Chicago	no data	TX: Dallas	no data
MA: Boston	no data	TX: Houston	no data
MD: Baltimore	no data	WA: Seattle	no data

FACTORS THAT MAY AFFECT EARNINGS

Educational Attainment of Workers and Effect on Earnings

Figures are based on a group of occupations: First-Line Supervisors/Managers of Farming, Fishing, and Forestry Workers

	Percent at Level	Effect on Earnings
Less than High School	13.3%	−49.7%
Some High School	13.3%	−33.8%
High School or Equivalent	35.6%	4.3%
Some College but No Degree	17.8%	−7.9%
Associate Degree	—	—
Bachelor's Degree	—	—
Master's Degree	—	—
Doctoral Degree	—	—
First Professional Degree	—	—

Figures do not total 100% because some levels have a very small sample size.

Flexibility of Earnings

Average Hours Worked: 35
Workers with a Varying Number of Hours: 19.0%
Workers Earning Some Overtime Pay, Tips, or Commissions: 4.3%
Earnings Benefit of Working Overtime: −20.1%

Gender

	Male	Female
Percent	77.2%	22.8%
Effect on Earnings	3.6%	−11.6%

Union Membership

Percentage Union Members: 4.3%
Earnings Benefit of Union Membership: 59.6%

Veteran Status

Percentage Who Have Been on Active Duty: 15.6%
Earnings Benefit of Veteran Status: 73.4%

45-2000 Agricultural Workers

45-2011 Agricultural Inspectors

Inspect agricultural commodities, processing equipment, and facilities and fish and logging operations to ensure compliance with regulations and laws governing health, quality, and safety.

- Education or Training Required: Work experience in a related occupation
- Job Growth: 6.8%
- Annual Openings: 3,000
- Self-Employed: 0.0%
- Part-Time: 20.0%

NATIONAL WAGE FIGURES (ANNUAL)

Beginning	25th Percentile	Median	Mean	75th Percentile	90th Percentile
$23,930	$30,450	$38,100	$38,820	$46,910	$55,620

Median Wages for Industries Employing Largest Numbers (Annual)

Industry	Median Income
Administrative and Support Services	$43,920
Merchant Wholesalers, Nondurable Goods	$42,050
Federal, State, and Local Government	$39,320
Educational Services	$36,150
Professional, Scientific, and Technical Services	$33,490
Food Manufacturing	$27,140
Support Activities for Agriculture and Forestry	$24,900
Religious, Grantmaking, Civic, Professional, and Similar Organizations	$24,820

Median Wages for States (Annual)

AK	no data	KY	$34,290	NY	$45,390
AL	$37,520	LA	$41,220	OH	$46,560
AR	$38,280	MA	no data	OK	$32,080
AZ	$33,210	MD	no data	OR	$30,380
CA	$41,030	ME	$33,610	PA	$40,380
CO	$35,940	MI	no data	RI	no data
CT	$60,690	MN	$41,080	SC	$35,000
DC	no data	MO	$40,130	SD	$26,880
DE	$40,000	MS	$36,330	TN	$36,360
FL	$34,150	MT	$23,960	TX	$41,350
GA	$34,400	NC	$37,600	UT	$34,700
HI	$48,080	ND	$33,970	VA	$42,700
IA	$38,560	NE	$40,920	VT	no data
ID	$36,050	NH	no data	WA	$36,080
IL	$43,810	NJ	$43,560	WI	$37,210
IN	$38,070	NM	$32,270	WV	no data
KS	$37,480	NV	$24,120	WY	$35,870

Median Wages for the Largest Metropolitan Areas (Annual)

AZ: Phoenix	no data	MI: Detroit	no data
CA: Los Angeles	no data	MN: Minneapolis	$43,570
CA: Riverside	$48,000	MO: Kansas City	no data
CA: Sacramento	$36,200	MO: St. Louis	no data
CA: San Diego	no data	NV: Las Vegas	no data
CA: San Francisco	no data	NY: New York	$46,230
CO: Denver	$43,250	OH: Cincinnati	no data
DC: Washington	no data	OH: Cleveland	no data
FL: Miami	$33,040	OH: Columbus	no data
FL: Orlando	$39,460	OR: Portland	$44,510
FL: Tampa	$33,180	PA: Philadelphia	$42,350
GA: Atlanta	$32,500	PA: Pittsburgh	no data
IL: Chicago	$46,550	TX: Dallas	$42,580
MA: Boston	no data	TX: Houston	$48,260
MD: Baltimore	no data	WA: Seattle	$33,030

FACTORS THAT MAY AFFECT EARNINGS

Educational Attainment of Workers and Effect on Earnings

	Percent at Level	Effect on Earnings
Less than High School	—	—
Some High School	—	—
High School or Equivalent	36.0%	−22.6%
Some College but No Degree	—	—
Associate Degree	—	—
Bachelor's Degree	44.0%	13.2%
Master's Degree	—	—
Doctoral Degree	—	—
First Professional Degree	—	—

Figures do not total 100% because some levels have a very small sample size.

Flexibility of Earnings

Average Hours Worked: 36
Workers with a Varying Number of Hours: 6.6%
Workers Earning Some Overtime Pay, Tips, or Commissions: 12.0%
Earnings Benefit of Working Overtime: −6.7%

Gender

	Male	Female
Percent	77.2%	22.8%
Effect on Earnings	3.6%	−11.6%

Union Membership

Percentage Union Members: 20.0%
Earnings Benefit of Union Membership: 46.0%

Veteran Status

Percentage Who Have Been on Active Duty: 4.6%
Earnings Benefit of Veteran Status: 25.3%

45-2021 Animal Breeders

Breed animals, including cattle, goats, horses, sheep, swine, poultry, dogs, cats, or pet birds. Select and breed animals according to their genealogy, characteristics, and offspring. May require a knowledge of artificial insemination techniques and equipment use. May involve keeping records on heats, birth intervals, or pedigree.

- Education or Training Required: Short-term on-the-job training
- Job Growth: 5.6%
- Annual Openings: 1,000
- Self-Employed: 83.8%
- Part-Time: 28.7%

Note: Earnings figures do not reflect self-employed workers, who make up a large fraction of the workforce for this occupation.

NATIONAL WAGE FIGURES (ANNUAL)

Beginning	25th Percentile	Median	Mean	75th Percentile	90th Percentile
$16,360	$20,440	$27,090	$31,970	$39,260	$54,650

Median Wages for Industries Employing Largest Numbers (Annual)

Industry	Median Income
Support Activities for Agriculture and Forestry	$27,620
Performing Arts, Spectator Sports, and Related Industries	$27,080
Food Manufacturing	$23,510

Median Wages for States (Annual)

State		State		State	
AK	no data	KY	$20,600	NY	no data
AL	no data	LA	no data	OH	$29,850
AR	no data	MA	no data	OK	no data
AZ	no data	MD	no data	OR	no data
CA	$38,360	ME	no data	PA	no data
CO	no data	MI	no data	RI	no data
CT	no data	MN	no data	SC	no data
DC	no data	MO	$22,480	SD	no data
DE	no data	MS	no data	TN	no data
FL	$45,660	MT	no data	TX	no data
GA	$20,410	NC	no data	UT	no data
HI	no data	ND	no data	VA	$28,140
IA	$21,530	NE	no data	VT	no data
ID	no data	NH	no data	WA	no data
IL	$16,950	NJ	no data	WI	$31,250
IN	$21,570	NM	no data	WV	no data
KS	no data	NV	no data	WY	no data

Median Wages for the Largest Metropolitan Areas (Annual)

Area		Area	
AZ: Phoenix	no data	MI: Detroit	no data
CA: Los Angeles	no data	MN: Minneapolis	no data
CA: Riverside	no data	MO: Kansas City	no data
CA: Sacramento	no data	MO: St. Louis	no data
CA: San Diego	no data	NV: Las Vegas	no data
CA: San Francisco	no data	NY: New York	no data
CO: Denver	no data	OH: Cincinnati	no data
DC: Washington	no data	OH: Cleveland	no data
FL: Miami	no data	OH: Columbus	$28,550
FL: Orlando	no data	OR: Portland	no data
FL: Tampa	no data	PA: Philadelphia	no data
GA: Atlanta	no data	PA: Pittsburgh	no data
IL: Chicago	no data	TX: Dallas	no data
MA: Boston	no data	TX: Houston	no data
MD: Baltimore	no data	WA: Seattle	no data

FACTORS THAT MAY AFFECT EARNINGS

Educational Attainment of Workers and Effect on Earnings

Figures are based on a group of occupations: Agricultural Workers

	Percent at Level	Effect on Earnings
Less than High School	18.0%	−18.4%
Some High School	24.7%	−35.8%
High School or Equivalent	27.3%	13.5%
Some College but No Degree	12.0%	17.7%
Associate Degree	8.0%	23.4%
Bachelor's Degree	9.1%	36.8%
Master's Degree	—	—
Doctoral Degree	—	—
First Professional Degree	—	—

Flexibility of Earnings

Average Hours Worked: 27
Workers with a Varying Number of Hours: 27.3%
Workers Earning Some Overtime Pay, Tips, or Commissions: 8.6%
Earnings Benefit of Working Overtime: −6.7%

Gender

	Male	Female
Percent	77.2%	22.8%
Effect on Earnings	3.6%	−11.6%

Union Membership

Percentage Union Members: Insignificant
Earnings Benefit of Union Membership: No significant data available

Veteran Status

Percentage Who Have Been on Active Duty: 4.6%
Earnings Benefit of Veteran Status: 25.3%

45-2041 Graders and Sorters, Agricultural Products

Grade, sort, or classify unprocessed food and other agricultural products by size, weight, color, or condition.

- Education or Training Required: Work experience in a related occupation
- Job Growth: 7.9%
- Annual Openings: 4,000
- Self-Employed: 0.5%
- Part-Time: 34.1%

NATIONAL WAGE FIGURES (ANNUAL)

Beginning	25th Percentile	Median	Mean	75th Percentile	90th Percentile
$13,530	$14,910	$17,200	$18,610	$20,920	$25,650

Median Wages for Industries Employing Largest Numbers (Annual)

Industry	Median Income
Wood Product Manufacturing	$31,810
Merchant Wholesalers, Durable Goods	$28,850
Professional, Scientific, and Technical Services	$25,450
Federal, State, and Local Government	$23,680
Beverage and Tobacco Product Manufacturing	$20,360
Wholesale Electronic Markets and Agents and Brokers	$18,860
Food Manufacturing	$18,670
Food and Beverage Stores	$17,950
Merchant Wholesalers, Nondurable Goods	$17,180
Warehousing and Storage	$16,730

Median Wages for States (Annual)

State		State		State	
AK	no data	KY	$19,840	NY	$17,720
AL	$20,310	LA	$21,530	OH	$19,800
AR	$21,440	MA	$17,420	OK	$21,040
AZ	$16,710	MD	$17,510	OR	$17,940
CA	$17,350	ME	$18,260	PA	$18,090
CO	$14,780	MI	$14,520	RI	no data
CT	no data	MN	$28,530	SC	$18,910
DC	no data	MO	$21,710	SD	$21,760
DE	no data	MS	$15,860	TN	$22,490
FL	$14,610	MT	$21,410	TX	$14,760
GA	$14,190	NC	$14,120	UT	$18,610
HI	$19,970	ND	$18,550	VA	$21,270
IA	$18,480	NE	$21,050	VT	$18,520
ID	$14,130	NH	no data	WA	$17,970
IL	$20,490	NJ	$17,080	WI	no data
IN	$23,180	NM	$13,130	WV	no data
KS	$19,420	NV	no data	WY	no data

Median Wages for the Largest Metropolitan Areas (Annual)

Area		Area	
AZ: Phoenix	$19,030	MI: Detroit	no data
CA: Los Angeles	$16,680	MN: Minneapolis	$26,370
CA: Riverside	$16,560	MO: Kansas City	$21,540
CA: Sacramento	$21,760	MO: St. Louis	no data
CA: San Diego	$16,780	NV: Las Vegas	no data
CA: San Francisco	$17,270	NY: New York	$17,580
CO: Denver	no data	OH: Cincinnati	$17,780
DC: Washington	no data	OH: Cleveland	no data
FL: Miami	$14,890	OH: Columbus	no data
FL: Orlando	no data	OR: Portland	$17,730
FL: Tampa	$14,260	PA: Philadelphia	$16,590
GA: Atlanta	$17,810	PA: Pittsburgh	$17,130
IL: Chicago	$18,600	TX: Dallas	no data
MA: Boston	$17,370	TX: Houston	$15,640
MD: Baltimore	no data	WA: Seattle	no data

FACTORS THAT MAY AFFECT EARNINGS

Educational Attainment of Workers and Effect on Earnings

	Percent at Level	Effect on Earnings
Less than High School	14.9%	−33.8%
Some High School	21.3%	−9.1%
High School or Equivalent	33.0%	−7.2%
Some College but No Degree	13.8%	9.7%
Associate Degree	8.5%	19.3%
Bachelor's Degree	7.4%	81.3%
Master's Degree	—	—
Doctoral Degree	—	—
First Professional Degree	—	—

Flexibility of Earnings

Average Hours Worked: 32
Workers with a Varying Number of Hours: 10.1%
Workers Earning Some Overtime Pay, Tips, or Commissions: 25.5%
Earnings Benefit of Working Overtime: −6.7%

Gender

	Male	Female
Percent	35.1%	64.9%
Effect on Earnings	3.6%	−11.6%

Union Membership

Percentage Union Members: 8.8%
Earnings Benefit of Union Membership: 46.0%

Veteran Status

Percentage Who Have Been on Active Duty: 4.6%
Earnings Benefit of Veteran Status: 25.3%

45-2091 Agricultural Equipment Operators

Drive and control farm equipment to till soil and to plant, cultivate, and harvest crops. May perform tasks such as crop baling or hay bucking. May operate stationary equipment to perform post-harvest tasks, such as husking, shelling, threshing, and ginning.

- Education or Training Required: Moderate-term on-the-job training
- Job Growth: –0.1%
- Annual Openings: 12,000
- Self-Employed: 0.2%
- Part-Time: 28.7%

NATIONAL WAGE FIGURES (ANNUAL)

Beginning	25th Percentile	Median	Mean	75th Percentile	90th Percentile
$13,980	$16,420	$20,230	$21,950	$25,960	$32,100

Median Wages for Industries Employing Largest Numbers (Annual)

Industry	Median Income
Federal, State, and Local Government	$30,950
Beverage and Tobacco Product Manufacturing	$28,580
Waste Management and Remediation Services	$27,050
Educational Services	$26,770
Merchant Wholesalers, Durable Goods	$26,550
Merchant Wholesalers, Nondurable Goods	$25,510
Food Manufacturing	$25,350
Warehousing and Storage	$23,080
Building Material and Garden Equipment and Supplies Dealers	$22,730
Chemical Manufacturing	$22,540

Median Wages for States (Annual)

State	Wage	State	Wage	State	Wage
AK	no data	KY	$21,340	NY	$24,600
AL	$16,480	LA	$17,500	OH	$27,240
AR	$18,350	MA	no data	OK	$17,500
AZ	$16,860	MD	$30,130	OR	$23,450
CA	$19,190	ME	no data	PA	$33,720
CO	$32,860	MI	no data	RI	no data
CT	no data	MN	$26,960	SC	$24,400
DC	no data	MO	$17,970	SD	no data
DE	no data	MS	$17,630	TN	$21,350
FL	$21,860	MT	$24,910	TX	$14,790
GA	$19,670	NC	$16,630	UT	$21,520
HI	no data	ND	$25,360	VA	$21,340
IA	$25,670	NE	$22,410	VT	no data
ID	$18,450	NH	no data	WA	$22,500
IL	$27,660	NJ	no data	WI	$26,230
IN	$26,110	NM	$18,330	WV	no data
KS	$24,590	NV	no data	WY	no data

Median Wages for the Largest Metropolitan Areas (Annual)

Area	Wage	Area	Wage
AZ: Phoenix	$16,320	MI: Detroit	no data
CA: Los Angeles	no data	MN: Minneapolis	no data
CA: Riverside	$17,350	MO: Kansas City	$27,550
CA: Sacramento	$24,110	MO: St. Louis	no data
CA: San Diego	no data	NV: Las Vegas	no data
CA: San Francisco	no data	NY: New York	no data
CO: Denver	no data	OH: Cincinnati	no data
DC: Washington	no data	OH: Cleveland	no data
FL: Miami	$25,250	OH: Columbus	no data
FL: Orlando	no data	OR: Portland	$23,540
FL: Tampa	$16,260	PA: Philadelphia	$47,380
GA: Atlanta	$27,480	PA: Pittsburgh	no data
IL: Chicago	no data	TX: Dallas	$17,710
MA: Boston	no data	TX: Houston	no data
MD: Baltimore	$31,510	WA: Seattle	no data

FACTORS THAT MAY AFFECT EARNINGS

Educational Attainment of Workers and Effect on Earnings

Figures are based on a group of occupations: Agricultural Workers

	Percent at Level	Effect on Earnings
Less than High School	18.0%	–18.4%
Some High School	24.7%	–35.8%
High School or Equivalent	27.3%	13.5%
Some College but No Degree	12.0%	17.7%
Associate Degree	8.0%	23.4%
Bachelor's Degree	9.1%	36.8%
Master's Degree	—	—
Doctoral Degree	—	—
First Professional Degree	—	—

Flexibility of Earnings

Average Hours Worked: 28
Workers with a Varying Number of Hours: 10.5%
Workers Earning Some Overtime Pay, Tips, or Commissions: 8.6%
Earnings Benefit of Working Overtime: –5.0%

Gender

	Male	Female
Percent	70.1%	29.9%
Effect on Earnings	3.6%	–11.6%

Union Membership

Percentage Union Members: Insignificant
Earnings Benefit of Union Membership: No significant data available

Veteran Status

Percentage Who Have Been on Active Duty: 4.6%
Earnings Benefit of Veteran Status: 25.3%

45-2092 Farmworkers and Laborers, Crop, Nursery, and Greenhouse

Manually plant, cultivate, and harvest vegetables, fruits, nuts, horticultural specialties, and field crops. Use hand tools, such as shovels, trowels, hoes, tampers, pruning hooks, shears, and knives. Duties may include tilling soil and applying fertilizers; transplanting, weeding, thinning, or pruning crops; applying pesticides; and cleaning, grading, sorting, packing, and loading harvested products. May construct trellises, repair fences and farm buildings, or participate in irrigation activities.

- Education or Training Required: Short-term on-the-job training
- Job Growth: −2.7%
- Annual Openings: 121,000
- Self-Employed: 0.2%
- Part-Time: 28.7%

NATIONAL WAGE FIGURES (ANNUAL)

Beginning	25th Percentile	Median	Mean	75th Percentile	90th Percentile
$14,260	$15,110	$16,540	$17,630	$18,400	$23,110

Median Wages for Industries Employing Largest Numbers (Annual)

Industry	Median Income
Truck Transportation	$27,930
Federal, State, and Local Government	$25,880
Specialty Trade Contractors	$24,490
Educational Services	$24,270
Museums, Historical Sites, and Similar Institutions	$22,840
Rental and Leasing Services	$22,060
Beverage and Tobacco Product Manufacturing	$20,690
Social Assistance	$19,860
Heavy and Civil Engineering Construction	$19,550
Real Estate	$19,330

Median Wages for States (Annual)

State	Wage	State	Wage	State	Wage
AK	no data	KY	$17,600	NY	$20,140
AL	$17,470	LA	$17,970	OH	$18,880
AR	$17,390	MA	$22,240	OK	$16,560
AZ	$15,490	MD	$19,990	OR	$17,810
CA	$16,460	ME	$21,330	PA	$18,090
CO	$18,600	MI	$19,870	RI	$21,580
CT	$19,850	MN	$22,010	SC	$16,840
DC	no data	MO	$19,570	SD	$19,820
DE	$19,010	MS	$15,960	TN	$17,880
FL	$15,720	MT	$23,900	TX	$14,300
GA	$15,250	NC	$16,390	UT	$17,190
HI	$18,360	ND	$22,910	VA	$17,680
IA	$21,010	NE	$22,180	VT	no data
ID	$17,960	NH	$18,080	WA	$19,410
IL	$19,130	NJ	$19,770	WI	$18,170
IN	$20,940	NM	$13,370	WV	$19,850
KS	$18,660	NV	$18,760	WY	$16,650

Median Wages for the Largest Metropolitan Areas (Annual)

Area	Wage	Area	Wage
AZ: Phoenix	$14,290	MI: Detroit	$20,750
CA: Los Angeles	$17,940	MN: Minneapolis	$21,090
CA: Riverside	$17,060	MO: Kansas City	$17,010
CA: Sacramento	$16,500	MO: St. Louis	no data
CA: San Diego	$17,600	NV: Las Vegas	$19,690
CA: San Francisco	$20,310	NY: New York	$21,380
CO: Denver	$19,720	OH: Cincinnati	$17,570
DC: Washington	$22,220	OH: Cleveland	$19,560
FL: Miami	$15,080	OH: Columbus	$19,850
FL: Orlando	$17,930	OR: Portland	$17,850
FL: Tampa	$14,800	PA: Philadelphia	$17,950
GA: Atlanta	$15,440	PA: Pittsburgh	$15,850
IL: Chicago	$19,230	TX: Dallas	$16,140
MA: Boston	$21,380	TX: Houston	$16,080
MD: Baltimore	$20,300	WA: Seattle	$20,150

FACTORS THAT MAY AFFECT EARNINGS

Educational Attainment of Workers and Effect on Earnings

Figures are based on a group of occupations: Agricultural Workers

	Percent at Level	Effect on Earnings
Less than High School	18.0%	−18.4%
Some High School	24.7%	−35.8%
High School or Equivalent	27.3%	13.5%
Some College but No Degree	12.0%	17.7%
Associate Degree	8.0%	23.4%
Bachelor's Degree	9.1%	36.8%
Master's Degree	—	—
Doctoral Degree	—	—
First Professional Degree	—	—

Flexibility of Earnings

Average Hours Worked: 28
Workers with a Varying Number of Hours: 10.5%
Workers Earning Some Overtime Pay, Tips, or Commissions: 8.6%
Earnings Benefit of Working Overtime: −5.0%

Gender

	Male	Female
Percent	70.1%	29.9%
Effect on Earnings	3.6%	−11.6%

Union Membership

Percentage Union Members: Insignificant
Earnings Benefit of Union Membership: No significant data available

Veteran Status

Percentage Who Have Been on Active Duty: 4.6%
Earnings Benefit of Veteran Status: 25.3%

45-2093 Farmworkers, Farm and Ranch Animals

Attend to live farm, ranch, or aquacultural animals that may include cattle, sheep, swine, goats, horses and other equines, poultry, finfish, shellfish, and bees. Attend to animals produced for animal products, such as meat, fur, skins, feathers, eggs, milk, and honey. Duties may include feeding, watering, herding, grazing, castrating, branding, debeaking, weighing, catching, and loading animals. May maintain records on animals; examine animals to detect diseases and injuries; assist in birth deliveries; and administer medications, vaccinations, or insecticides as appropriate. May clean and maintain animal housing areas.

- Education or Training Required: Short-term on-the-job training
- Job Growth: 0.9%
- Annual Openings: 16,000
- Self-Employed: 0.1%
- Part-Time: 28.7%

NATIONAL WAGE FIGURES (ANNUAL)

Beginning	25th Percentile	Median	Mean	75th Percentile	90th Percentile
$13,510	$15,770	$19,060	$20,630	$23,830	$30,120

Median Wages for Industries Employing Largest Numbers (Annual)

Industry	Median Income
Federal, State, and Local Government	$29,930
Museums, Historical Sites, and Similar Institutions	$26,420
Securities, Commodity Contracts, and Other Financial Investments and Related Activities	$23,830
Educational Services	$23,060
Professional, Scientific, and Technical Services	$22,680
Religious, Grantmaking, Civic, Professional, and Similar Organizations	$22,010
Food and Beverage Stores	$21,400
Administrative and Support Services	$21,070
Funds, Trusts, and Other Financial Vehicles	$20,820
Fabricated Metal Product Manufacturing	$20,790

Median Wages for States (Annual)

AK	no data	KY	$18,380	NY	$19,230
AL	$18,750	LA	$16,800	OH	$19,970
AR	$17,460	MA	no data	OK	no data
AZ	$23,390	MD	$21,560	OR	$21,420
CA	$18,870	ME	no data	PA	$18,240
CO	$16,480	MI	$19,310	RI	no data
CT	$18,990	MN	$20,920	SC	$18,120
DC	no data	MO	$18,790	SD	$20,490
DE	$25,490	MS	$17,500	TN	$17,450
FL	$20,440	MT	$17,680	TX	$14,340
GA	$21,370	NC	$18,390	UT	$17,930
HI	$20,320	ND	no data	VA	$20,230
IA	$21,010	NE	$18,900	VT	no data
ID	$19,560	NH	$19,880	WA	$25,670
IL	$15,460	NJ	$23,550	WI	$21,550
IN	$21,850	NM	$16,330	WV	$16,400
KS	$21,220	NV	$14,300	WY	$29,050

Median Wages for the Largest Metropolitan Areas (Annual)

AZ: Phoenix	$23,670	MI: Detroit	no data
CA: Los Angeles	$20,830	MN: Minneapolis	$23,680
CA: Riverside	$19,810	MO: Kansas City	$14,430
CA: Sacramento	$20,430	MO: St. Louis	$15,080
CA: San Diego	$24,410	NV: Las Vegas	no data
CA: San Francisco	$26,160	NY: New York	$22,640
CO: Denver	$15,040	OH: Cincinnati	$21,480
DC: Washington	$22,630	OH: Cleveland	$20,670
FL: Miami	no data	OH: Columbus	no data
FL: Orlando	$17,530	OR: Portland	$22,090
FL: Tampa	$17,450	PA: Philadelphia	$20,000
GA: Atlanta	$23,420	PA: Pittsburgh	$18,030
IL: Chicago	$16,920	TX: Dallas	$16,450
MA: Boston	no data	TX: Houston	$14,170
MD: Baltimore	no data	WA: Seattle	no data

FACTORS THAT MAY AFFECT EARNINGS

Educational Attainment of Workers and Effect on Earnings

Figures are based on a group of occupations: Agricultural Workers

	Percent at Level	Effect on Earnings
Less than High School	18.0%	−18.4%
Some High School	24.7%	−35.8%
High School or Equivalent	27.3%	13.5%
Some College but No Degree	12.0%	17.7%
Associate Degree	8.0%	23.4%
Bachelor's Degree	9.1%	36.8%
Master's Degree	—	—
Doctoral Degree	—	—
First Professional Degree	—	—

Flexibility of Earnings

Average Hours Worked: 28
Workers with a Varying Number of Hours: 10.5%
Workers Earning Some Overtime Pay, Tips, or Commissions: 8.6%
Earnings Benefit of Working Overtime: −5.0%

Gender

	Male	Female
Percent	70.1%	29.9%
Effect on Earnings	3.6%	−11.6%

Union Membership

Percentage Union Members: Insignificant
Earnings Benefit of Union Membership: No significant data available

Veteran Status

Percentage Who Have Been on Active Duty: 4.6%
Earnings Benefit of Veteran Status: 25.3%

45-2099 Agricultural Workers, All Other

All agricultural workers not listed separately.

- Education or Training Required: Short-term on-the-job training
- Job Growth: 4.3%
- Annual Openings: 3,000
- Self-Employed: 0.1%
- Part-Time: 28.7%

NATIONAL WAGE FIGURES (ANNUAL)

Beginning	25th Percentile	Median	Mean	75th Percentile	90th Percentile
$14,730	$17,420	$22,470	$25,070	$29,480	$40,060

Median Wages for Industries Employing Largest Numbers (Annual)

Industry	Median Income
Forestry and Logging	$28,010
Federal, State, and Local Government	$27,170
Food Manufacturing	$24,900
Educational Services	$23,650
Wood Product Manufacturing	$21,610
Merchant Wholesalers, Durable Goods	$21,320
Professional, Scientific, and Technical Services	$21,090
Utilities	$20,140
Performing Arts, Spectator Sports, and Related Industries	$19,390
Merchant Wholesalers, Nondurable Goods	$19,100

Median Wages for States (Annual)

State	Wage	State	Wage	State	Wage
AK	$30,270	KY	no data	NY	$31,260
AL	$17,370	LA	$24,080	OH	$15,060
AR	$17,870	MA	no data	OK	$17,960
AZ	$27,880	MD	$30,480	OR	$15,870
CA	$24,190	ME	no data	PA	$21,460
CO	$22,910	MI	$22,270	RI	no data
CT	$19,770	MN	$18,700	SC	$19,440
DC	no data	MO	$21,260	SD	no data
DE	no data	MS	no data	TN	$20,910
FL	$14,860	MT	$17,430	TX	$13,930
GA	$18,820	NC	$18,740	UT	no data
HI	no data	ND	$22,100	VA	$20,210
IA	$21,760	NE	$22,920	VT	no data
ID	$24,020	NH	no data	WA	$26,650
IL	$31,230	NJ	no data	WI	$26,090
IN	no data	NM	$18,290	WV	no data
KS	$19,480	NV	$37,170	WY	$19,080

Median Wages for the Largest Metropolitan Areas (Annual)

Area	Wage	Area	Wage
AZ: Phoenix	no data	MI: Detroit	no data
CA: Los Angeles	$17,950	MN: Minneapolis	no data
CA: Riverside	$26,930	MO: Kansas City	no data
CA: Sacramento	$23,510	MO: St. Louis	no data
CA: San Diego	$24,680	NV: Las Vegas	no data
CA: San Francisco	$23,980	NY: New York	no data
CO: Denver	no data	OH: Cincinnati	no data
DC: Washington	no data	OH: Cleveland	no data
FL: Miami	no data	OH: Columbus	no data
FL: Orlando	no data	OR: Portland	no data
FL: Tampa	no data	PA: Philadelphia	no data
GA: Atlanta	no data	PA: Pittsburgh	no data
IL: Chicago	$23,840	TX: Dallas	no data
MA: Boston	no data	TX: Houston	no data
MD: Baltimore	no data	WA: Seattle	$28,510

FACTORS THAT MAY AFFECT EARNINGS

Educational Attainment of Workers and Effect on Earnings

Figures are based on a group of occupations: Agricultural Workers

	Percent at Level	Effect on Earnings
Less than High School	18.0%	−18.4%
Some High School	24.7%	−35.8%
High School or Equivalent	27.3%	13.5%
Some College but No Degree	12.0%	17.7%
Associate Degree	8.0%	23.4%
Bachelor's Degree	9.1%	36.8%
Master's Degree	—	—
Doctoral Degree	—	—
First Professional Degree	—	—

Flexibility of Earnings

Average Hours Worked: 28
Workers with a Varying Number of Hours: 10.5%
Workers Earning Some Overtime Pay, Tips, or Commissions: 8.6%
Earnings Benefit of Working Overtime: −5.0%

Gender

	Male	Female
Percent	70.1%	29.9%
Effect on Earnings	3.6%	−11.6%

Union Membership

Percentage Union Members: Insignificant
Earnings Benefit of Union Membership: No significant data available

Veteran Status

Percentage Who Have Been on Active Duty: 4.6%
Earnings Benefit of Veteran Status: 25.3%

45-3000 Fishing and Hunting Workers

45-3011 Fishers and Related Fishing Workers

Use nets, fishing rods, traps, or other equipment to catch and gather fish or other aquatic animals from rivers, lakes, or oceans for human consumption or other uses. May haul game onto ship.

- Education or Training Required: Moderate-term on-the-job training
- Job Growth: –17.2%
- Annual Openings: 6,000
- Self-Employed: 52.1%
- Part-Time: 10.9%

Note: A large fraction of the workforce for this occupation is self-employed and earns an average of $33,950. All other earnings figures for this occupation are based on workers who are paid a wage or salary.

NATIONAL WAGE FIGURES (ANNUAL)

Beginning	25th Percentile	Median	Mean	75th Percentile	90th Percentile
$15,280	$20,530	$27,250	$28,510	$32,480	$45,480

Median Wages for Industries Employing Largest Numbers (Annual)

Industry	Median Income
Federal, State, and Local Government	$35,510
Food Manufacturing	$27,380
Scenic and Sightseeing Transportation	$20,480

Median Wages for States (Annual)

AK	no data	KY	no data	NY	no data
AL	no data	LA	$27,500	OH	no data
AR	no data	MA	no data	OK	no data
AZ	no data	MD	no data	OR	no data
CA	$27,880	ME	no data	PA	no data
CO	no data	MI	no data	RI	no data
CT	no data	MN	no data	SC	no data
DC	no data	MO	no data	SD	no data
DE	no data	MS	no data	TN	no data
FL	no data	MT	no data	TX	no data
GA	no data	NC	no data	UT	no data
HI	no data	ND	no data	VA	no data
IA	no data	NE	no data	VT	no data
ID	no data	NH	no data	WA	$27,960
IL	no data	NJ	$20,950	WI	no data
IN	no data	NM	no data	WV	no data
KS	no data	NV	no data	WY	no data

Median Wages for the Largest Metropolitan Areas (Annual)

AZ: Phoenix	no data	MI: Detroit	no data
CA: Los Angeles	no data	MN: Minneapolis	no data
CA: Riverside	no data	MO: Kansas City	no data
CA: Sacramento	no data	MO: St. Louis	no data
CA: San Diego	no data	NV: Las Vegas	no data
CA: San Francisco	no data	NY: New York	$21,400
CO: Denver	no data	OH: Cincinnati	no data
DC: Washington	no data	OH: Cleveland	no data
FL: Miami	no data	OH: Columbus	no data
FL: Orlando	no data	OR: Portland	no data
FL: Tampa	no data	PA: Philadelphia	no data
GA: Atlanta	no data	PA: Pittsburgh	no data
IL: Chicago	no data	TX: Dallas	no data
MA: Boston	no data	TX: Houston	no data
MD: Baltimore	no data	WA: Seattle	no data

FACTORS THAT MAY AFFECT EARNINGS

Educational Attainment of Workers and Effect on Earnings

	Percent at Level	Effect on Earnings
Less than High School	—	—
Some High School	—	—
High School or Equivalent	45.5%	–19.3%
Some College but No Degree	—	—
Associate Degree	—	—
Bachelor's Degree	—	—
Master's Degree	—	—
Doctoral Degree	—	—
First Professional Degree	—	—

Figures do not total 100% because some levels have a very small sample size.

Flexibility of Earnings

Average Hours Worked: 22
Workers with a Varying Number of Hours: 38.3%
Workers Earning Some Overtime Pay, Tips, or Commissions: 4.5%
Earnings Benefit of Working Overtime: 1.7%

Gender

	Male	Female
Percent	90.9%	9.1%
Effect on Earnings	3.6%	–11.6%

Union Membership

Percentage Union Members: 4.5%
Earnings Benefit of Union Membership: 116.2%

Veteran Status

Percentage Who Have Been on Active Duty: 8.7%
Earnings Benefit of Veteran Status: –36.2%

45-4000 Forest, Conservation, and Logging Workers

45-4011 Forest and Conservation Workers

Under supervision, perform manual labor necessary to develop, maintain, or protect forest, forested areas, and woodlands through such activities as raising and transporting tree seedlings; combating insects, pests, and diseases harmful to trees; and building erosion and water control structures and leaching of forest soil. Includes forester aides, seedling pullers, and tree planters.

- Education or Training Required: Moderate-term on-the-job training
- Job Growth: 6.0%
- Annual Openings: 2,000
- Self-Employed: 25.2%
- Part-Time: 21.4%

NATIONAL WAGE FIGURES (ANNUAL)

Beginning	25th Percentile	Median	Mean	75th Percentile	90th Percentile
$15,650	$17,330	$20,810	$24,890	$31,540	$39,580

Median Wages for Industries Employing Largest Numbers (Annual)

Industry	Median Income
Wood Product Manufacturing	$32,210
Forestry and Logging	$28,090
Religious, Grantmaking, Civic, Professional, and Similar Organizations	$27,970
Professional, Scientific, and Technical Services	$26,960
Federal, State, and Local Government	$20,560
Educational Services	$18,540
Administrative and Support Services	$17,860
Social Assistance	$17,410

Median Wages for States (Annual)

State		State		State	
AK	no data	KY	no data	NY	no data
AL	no data	LA	$31,640	OH	no data
AR	$26,810	MA	$41,010	OK	no data
AZ	no data	MD	no data	OR	$22,590
CA	$18,700	ME	no data	PA	no data
CO	no data	MI	$25,020	RI	no data
CT	no data	MN	$17,950	SC	$22,690
DC	no data	MO	no data	SD	$21,260
DE	no data	MS	$21,890	TN	$22,490
FL	no data	MT	no data	TX	no data
GA	$14,460	NC	no data	UT	no data
HI	$30,140	ND	$21,910	VA	$29,650
IA	$21,370	NE	no data	VT	no data
ID	$30,620	NH	no data	WA	$17,470
IL	$40,570	NJ	$18,880	WI	$33,980
IN	no data	NM	$29,320	WV	no data
KS	no data	NV	no data	WY	no data

Median Wages for the Largest Metropolitan Areas (Annual)

Area		Area	
AZ: Phoenix	no data	MI: Detroit	no data
CA: Los Angeles	no data	MN: Minneapolis	no data
CA: Riverside	no data	MO: Kansas City	no data
CA: Sacramento	$18,580	MO: St. Louis	no data
CA: San Diego	$17,210	NV: Las Vegas	no data
CA: San Francisco	no data	NY: New York	no data
CO: Denver	no data	OH: Cincinnati	no data
DC: Washington	no data	OH: Cleveland	no data
FL: Miami	no data	OH: Columbus	no data
FL: Orlando	no data	OR: Portland	no data
FL: Tampa	no data	PA: Philadelphia	$16,710
GA: Atlanta	no data	PA: Pittsburgh	no data
IL: Chicago	$41,030	TX: Dallas	no data
MA: Boston	$41,350	TX: Houston	no data
MD: Baltimore	no data	WA: Seattle	$16,970

FACTORS THAT MAY AFFECT EARNINGS

Educational Attainment of Workers and Effect on Earnings

	Percent at Level	Effect on Earnings
Less than High School	—	—
Some High School	—	—
High School or Equivalent	35.3%	−3.3%
Some College but No Degree	—	—
Associate Degree	—	—
Bachelor's Degree	—	—
Master's Degree	—	—
Doctoral Degree	—	—
First Professional Degree	—	—

Figures do not total 100% because some levels have a very small sample size.

Flexibility of Earnings

Average Hours Worked: 28
Workers with a Varying Number of Hours: 14.4%
Workers Earning Some Overtime Pay, Tips, or Commissions: 5.3%
Earnings Benefit of Working Overtime: 21.4%

Gender

	Male	Female
Percent	83.3%	16.7%
Effect on Earnings	3.6%	−11.6%

Union Membership

Percentage Union Members: 5.3%
Earnings Benefit of Union Membership: 38.2%

Veteran Status

Percentage Who Have Been on Active Duty: 13.0%
Earnings Benefit of Veteran Status: 35.1%

45-4021 Fallers

Use axes or chain saws to fell trees, using knowledge of tree characteristics and cutting techniques to control direction of fall and minimize tree damage.

- Education or Training Required: Moderate-term on-the-job training
- Job Growth: –5.7%
- Annual Openings: 3,000
- Self-Employed: 34.6%
- Part-Time: 13.4%

Note: Earnings figures do not reflect self-employed workers, who make up a large fraction of the workforce for this occupation.

NATIONAL WAGE FIGURES (ANNUAL)

Beginning	25th Percentile	Median	Mean	75th Percentile	90th Percentile
$19,310	$23,160	$28,710	$32,960	$37,670	$55,040

Median Wages for Industries Employing Largest Numbers (Annual)

Industry	Median Income
Truck Transportation	$34,050
Forestry and Logging	$29,080
Administrative and Support Services	$26,670
Specialty Trade Contractors	$26,400
Wood Product Manufacturing	$24,700
Merchant Wholesalers, Durable Goods	$22,180

Median Wages for States (Annual)

State	Wage	State	Wage	State	Wage
AK	$72,100	KY	$23,950	NY	$30,550
AL	$26,220	LA	$27,620	OH	$21,840
AR	$26,370	MA	no data	OK	$32,320
AZ	$34,340	MD	no data	OR	$57,460
CA	no data	ME	$24,530	PA	$24,220
CO	$29,410	MI	$26,660	RI	no data
CT	$34,940	MN	$28,920	SC	$22,600
DC	no data	MO	$27,040	SD	no data
DE	no data	MS	$30,040	TN	$22,330
FL	$31,050	MT	no data	TX	$34,320
GA	$31,880	NC	$28,640	UT	no data
HI	no data	ND	no data	VA	$28,240
IA	no data	NE	no data	VT	no data
ID	$34,520	NH	no data	WA	$50,130
IL	no data	NJ	$24,970	WI	$26,780
IN	$32,690	NM	no data	WV	$20,270
KS	no data	NV	no data	WY	no data

Median Wages for the Largest Metropolitan Areas (Annual)

Area	Wage	Area	Wage
AZ: Phoenix	no data	MI: Detroit	no data
CA: Los Angeles	no data	MN: Minneapolis	no data
CA: Riverside	no data	MO: Kansas City	no data
CA: Sacramento	no data	MO: St. Louis	no data
CA: San Diego	no data	NV: Las Vegas	no data
CA: San Francisco	no data	NY: New York	$25,100
CO: Denver	no data	OH: Cincinnati	no data
DC: Washington	no data	OH: Cleveland	no data
FL: Miami	no data	OH: Columbus	no data
FL: Orlando	no data	OR: Portland	no data
FL: Tampa	no data	PA: Philadelphia	no data
GA: Atlanta	no data	PA: Pittsburgh	no data
IL: Chicago	no data	TX: Dallas	no data
MA: Boston	no data	TX: Houston	no data
MD: Baltimore	no data	WA: Seattle	$53,470

FACTORS THAT MAY AFFECT EARNINGS

Educational Attainment of Workers and Effect on Earnings

Figures are based on a group of occupations: Forest, Conservation, and Logging Workers

	Percent at Level	Effect on Earnings
Less than High School	—	—
Some High School	24.2%	–6.5%
High School or Equivalent	48.4%	–0.9%
Some College but No Degree	10.5%	14.8%
Associate Degree	—	—
Bachelor's Degree	—	—
Master's Degree	—	—
Doctoral Degree	—	—
First Professional Degree	—	—

Figures do not total 100% because some levels have a very small sample size.

Flexibility of Earnings

Average Hours Worked: 30
Workers with a Varying Number of Hours: 14.4%
Workers Earning Some Overtime Pay, Tips, or Commissions: 10.0%
Earnings Benefit of Working Overtime: 13.4%

Gender

	Male	Female
Percent	95.2%	4.8%
Effect on Earnings	0.0%	—

Union Membership

Percentage Union Members: 4.6%
Earnings Benefit of Union Membership: 38.2%

Veteran Status

Percentage Who Have Been on Active Duty: 13.0%
Earnings Benefit of Veteran Status: 35.1%

45-4022 Logging Equipment Operators

Drive logging tractor or wheeled vehicle equipped with one or more accessories, such as bulldozer blade, frontal shear, grapple, logging arch, cable winches, hoisting rack, or crane boom, to fell tree; to skid, load, unload, or stack logs; or to pull stumps or clear brush.

- Education or Training Required: Moderate-term on-the-job training
- Job Growth: 3.4%
- Annual Openings: 9,000
- Self-Employed: 31.7%
- Part-Time: 13.4%

Note: Earnings figures do not reflect self-employed workers, who make up a large fraction of the workforce for this occupation.

NATIONAL WAGE FIGURES (ANNUAL)

Beginning	25th Percentile	Median	Mean	75th Percentile	90th Percentile
$19,740	$23,860	$29,700	$30,880	$36,720	$44,490

Median Wages for Industries Employing Largest Numbers (Annual)

Industry	Median Income
Paper Manufacturing	$38,460
Truck Transportation	$35,980
Forestry and Logging	$30,240
Administrative and Support Services	$29,310
Wood Product Manufacturing	$26,320
Merchant Wholesalers, Durable Goods	$22,320

Median Wages for States (Annual)

State	Wage	State	Wage	State	Wage
AK	$36,710	KY	$21,640	NY	$29,390
AL	$25,470	LA	$31,050	OH	$24,270
AR	$30,190	MA	no data	OK	$29,540
AZ	$24,020	MD	$21,970	OR	$35,400
CA	$36,060	ME	$28,330	PA	$24,220
CO	$29,780	MI	$26,490	RI	no data
CT	no data	MN	$33,890	SC	$29,370
DC	no data	MO	$17,340	SD	$28,550
DE	no data	MS	$27,240	TN	$26,540
FL	$26,310	MT	$34,270	TX	$31,680
GA	$28,080	NC	$25,670	UT	no data
HI	no data	ND	no data	VA	$28,260
IA	no data	NE	no data	VT	$26,680
ID	$38,820	NH	$34,370	WA	$41,520
IL	$23,640	NJ	no data	WI	$24,380
IN	$23,430	NM	no data	WV	$23,700
KS	no data	NV	no data	WY	no data

Median Wages for the Largest Metropolitan Areas (Annual)

Area	Wage	Area	Wage
AZ: Phoenix	no data	MI: Detroit	no data
CA: Los Angeles	no data	MN: Minneapolis	no data
CA: Riverside	no data	MO: Kansas City	no data
CA: Sacramento	no data	MO: St. Louis	no data
CA: San Diego	no data	NV: Las Vegas	no data
CA: San Francisco	no data	NY: New York	no data
CO: Denver	no data	OH: Cincinnati	no data
DC: Washington	$25,980	OH: Cleveland	no data
FL: Miami	no data	OH: Columbus	no data
FL: Orlando	no data	OR: Portland	$38,910
FL: Tampa	no data	PA: Philadelphia	no data
GA: Atlanta	$30,930	PA: Pittsburgh	$25,960
IL: Chicago	no data	TX: Dallas	no data
MA: Boston	no data	TX: Houston	$32,820
MD: Baltimore	no data	WA: Seattle	$43,630

FACTORS THAT MAY AFFECT EARNINGS

Educational Attainment of Workers and Effect on Earnings

Figures are based on a group of occupations: Forest, Conservation, and Logging Workers

	Percent at Level	Effect on Earnings
Less than High School	—	—
Some High School	24.2%	−6.5%
High School or Equivalent	48.4%	−0.9%
Some College but No Degree	10.5%	14.8%
Associate Degree	—	—
Bachelor's Degree	—	—
Master's Degree	—	—
Doctoral Degree	—	—
First Professional Degree	—	—

Figures do not total 100% because some levels have a very small sample size.

Flexibility of Earnings

Average Hours Worked: 30
Workers with a Varying Number of Hours: 14.4%
Workers Earning Some Overtime Pay, Tips, or Commissions: 10.0%
Earnings Benefit of Working Overtime: 13.4%

Gender

	Male	Female
Percent	99.8%	0.2%
Effect on Earnings	0.0%	—

Union Membership

Percentage Union Members: 4.6%
Earnings Benefit of Union Membership: 38.2%

Veteran Status

Percentage Who Have Been on Active Duty: 13.0%
Earnings Benefit of Veteran Status: 35.1%

45-4023 Log Graders and Scalers

Grade logs or estimate the marketable content or value of logs or pulpwood in sorting yards, millpond, log deck, or similar locations. Inspect logs for defects or measure logs to determine volume.

- Education or Training Required: Moderate-term on-the-job training
- Job Growth: 1.7%
- Annual Openings: 2,000
- Self-Employed: 42.3%
- Part-Time: 13.4%

Note: Earnings figures do not reflect self-employed workers, who make up a large fraction of the workforce for this occupation.

NATIONAL WAGE FIGURES (ANNUAL)

Beginning	25th Percentile	Median	Mean	75th Percentile	90th Percentile
$19,290	$23,660	$29,240	$30,980	$36,510	$44,940

Median Wages for Industries Employing Largest Numbers (Annual)

Industry	Median Income
Administrative and Support Services	$36,750
Paper Manufacturing	$36,720
Merchant Wholesalers, Durable Goods	$32,520
Wood Product Manufacturing	$28,790
Forestry and Logging	$26,860

Median Wages for States (Annual)

AK	no data	KY	$26,410	NY	$31,960
AL	$24,410	LA	$26,810	OH	$29,500
AR	$25,830	MA	no data	OK	no data
AZ	no data	MD	no data	OR	$38,390
CA	$34,960	ME	$29,050	PA	$25,820
CO	no data	MI	$31,690	RI	no data
CT	no data	MN	no data	SC	$27,800
DC	no data	MO	$21,190	SD	no data
DE	no data	MS	$29,300	TN	$25,800
FL	no data	MT	no data	TX	no data
GA	$26,130	NC	$28,760	UT	no data
HI	no data	ND	no data	VA	$28,680
IA	no data	NE	no data	VT	$35,250
ID	$34,640	NH	$28,390	WA	$36,300
IL	no data	NJ	no data	WI	$29,380
IN	$28,960	NM	no data	WV	$26,420
KS	no data	NV	no data	WY	no data

Median Wages for the Largest Metropolitan Areas (Annual)

AZ: Phoenix	no data	MI: Detroit	no data
CA: Los Angeles	no data	MN: Minneapolis	no data
CA: Riverside	no data	MO: Kansas City	no data
CA: Sacramento	no data	MO: St. Louis	no data
CA: San Diego	no data	NV: Las Vegas	no data
CA: San Francisco	no data	NY: New York	no data
CO: Denver	no data	OH: Cincinnati	no data
DC: Washington	no data	OH: Cleveland	$32,860
FL: Miami	no data	OH: Columbus	no data
FL: Orlando	no data	OR: Portland	no data
FL: Tampa	no data	PA: Philadelphia	no data
GA: Atlanta	$19,300	PA: Pittsburgh	no data
IL: Chicago	no data	TX: Dallas	no data
MA: Boston	no data	TX: Houston	no data
MD: Baltimore	no data	WA: Seattle	$38,900

FACTORS THAT MAY AFFECT EARNINGS

Educational Attainment of Workers and Effect on Earnings

Figures are based on a group of occupations: Forest, Conservation, and Logging Workers

	Percent at Level	Effect on Earnings
Less than High School	—	—
Some High School	24.2%	−6.5%
High School or Equivalent	48.4%	−0.9%
Some College but No Degree	10.5%	14.8%
Associate Degree	—	—
Bachelor's Degree	—	—
Master's Degree	—	—
Doctoral Degree	—	—
First Professional Degree	—	—

Figures do not total 100% because some levels have a very small sample size.

Flexibility of Earnings

Average Hours Worked: 30
Workers with a Varying Number of Hours: 14.4%
Workers Earning Some Overtime Pay, Tips, or Commissions: 10.0%
Earnings Benefit of Working Overtime: 13.4%

Gender

	Male	Female
Percent	99.8%	0.2%
Effect on Earnings	0.0%	—

Union Membership

Percentage Union Members: 4.6%
Earnings Benefit of Union Membership: 38.2%

Veteran Status

Percentage Who Have Been on Active Duty: 13.0%
Earnings Benefit of Veteran Status: 35.1%

45-4029 Logging Workers, All Other

All logging workers not listed separately.

- Education or Training Required: Moderate-term on-the-job training
- Job Growth: –4.2%
- Annual Openings: 1,000
- Self-Employed: 19.9%
- Part-Time: 13.4%

NATIONAL WAGE FIGURES (ANNUAL)

Beginning	25th Percentile	Median	Mean	75th Percentile	90th Percentile
$18,150	$25,680	$31,870	$31,720	$38,300	$44,660

Median Wages for Industries Employing Largest Numbers (Annual)

Industry	Median Income
Paper Manufacturing	$37,280
Administrative and Support Services	$32,310
Forestry and Logging	$32,230
Wood Product Manufacturing	$25,570
Merchant Wholesalers, Durable Goods	$21,040

Median Wages for States (Annual)

State	Wage	State	Wage	State	Wage
AK	$31,320	KY	$20,220	NY	$20,770
AL	$18,710	LA	$19,440	OH	$25,890
AR	$14,390	MA	no data	OK	no data
AZ	no data	MD	no data	OR	$33,190
CA	$30,530	ME	no data	PA	no data
CO	no data	MI	$24,850	RI	no data
CT	no data	MN	no data	SC	no data
DC	no data	MO	no data	SD	no data
DE	no data	MS	$27,150	TN	$18,320
FL	$25,880	MT	$31,870	TX	no data
GA	$27,840	NC	no data	UT	no data
HI	no data	ND	no data	VA	no data
IA	no data	NE	no data	VT	no data
ID	no data	NH	$37,570	WA	$38,300
IL	no data	NJ	no data	WI	$31,890
IN	$13,100	NM	no data	WV	$18,560
KS	no data	NV	no data	WY	no data

Median Wages for the Largest Metropolitan Areas (Annual)

Area	Wage	Area	Wage
AZ: Phoenix	no data	MI: Detroit	no data
CA: Los Angeles	no data	MN: Minneapolis	no data
CA: Riverside	no data	MO: Kansas City	no data
CA: Sacramento	no data	MO: St. Louis	no data
CA: San Diego	no data	NV: Las Vegas	no data
CA: San Francisco	no data	NY: New York	no data
CO: Denver	no data	OH: Cincinnati	no data
DC: Washington	no data	OH: Cleveland	no data
FL: Miami	no data	OH: Columbus	no data
FL: Orlando	no data	OR: Portland	$32,070
FL: Tampa	no data	PA: Philadelphia	no data
GA: Atlanta	no data	PA: Pittsburgh	no data
IL: Chicago	no data	TX: Dallas	no data
MA: Boston	no data	TX: Houston	no data
MD: Baltimore	no data	WA: Seattle	$38,290

FACTORS THAT MAY AFFECT EARNINGS

Educational Attainment of Workers and Effect on Earnings

Figures are based on a group of occupations: Forest, Conservation, and Logging Workers

	Percent at Level	Effect on Earnings
Less than High School	—	—
Some High School	24.2%	–6.5%
High School or Equivalent	48.4%	–0.9%
Some College but No Degree	10.5%	14.8%
Associate Degree	—	—
Bachelor's Degree	—	—
Master's Degree	—	—
Doctoral Degree	—	—
First Professional Degree	—	—

Figures do not total 100% because some levels have a very small sample size.

Flexibility of Earnings

Average Hours Worked: 30
Workers with a Varying Number of Hours: 14.4%
Workers Earning Some Overtime Pay, Tips, or Commissions: 10.0%
Earnings Benefit of Working Overtime: 13.4%

Gender

	Male	Female
Percent	99.8%	0.2%
Effect on Earnings	0.0%	—

Union Membership

Percentage Union Members: 4.6%
Earnings Benefit of Union Membership: 38.2%

Veteran Status

Percentage Who Have Been on Active Duty: 13.0%
Earnings Benefit of Veteran Status: 35.1%

47-0000: Construction and Extraction Occupations

47-1000 Supervisors, Construction and Extraction Workers

47-1011 First-Line Supervisors/Managers of Construction Trades and Extraction Workers

Directly supervise and coordinate activities of construction or extraction workers.

- Education or Training Required: Work experience in a related occupation
- Job Growth: 10.9%
- Annual Openings: 57,000
- Self-Employed: 24.7%
- Part-Time: 5.9%

NATIONAL WAGE FIGURES (ANNUAL)

Beginning	25th Percentile	Median	Mean	75th Percentile	90th Percentile
$33,790	$41,990	$53,850	$57,500	$69,310	$87,270

Median Wages for Industries Employing Largest Numbers (Annual)

Industry	Median Income
Utilities	$64,050
Hospitals	$63,570
Mining (Except Oil and Gas)	$62,580
Management of Companies and Enterprises	$61,390
Oil and Gas Extraction	$61,130
Professional, Scientific, and Technical Services	$58,170
Rail Transportation	$58,020
Support Activities for Mining	$56,230
Real Estate	$55,700
Educational Services	$55,320

Median Wages for States (Annual)

State	Wage	State	Wage	State	Wage
AK	$72,810	KY	$46,640	NY	$65,950
AL	$43,710	LA	$44,560	OH	$55,550
AR	$43,610	MA	$63,910	OK	$48,630
AZ	$53,440	MD	$55,700	OR	$54,210
CA	$64,250	ME	$43,860	PA	$57,340
CO	$53,990	MI	$58,250	RI	$59,800
CT	$63,010	MN	$59,030	SC	$44,590
DC	$64,640	MO	$57,450	SD	$44,850
DE	$60,320	MS	$42,130	TN	$43,810
FL	$49,250	MT	$47,370	TX	$45,570
GA	$47,720	NC	$45,340	UT	$47,600
HI	$71,160	ND	$45,460	VA	$54,110
IA	$55,200	NE	$48,990	VT	$53,270
ID	$42,520	NH	$50,110	WA	$64,130
IL	$70,970	NJ	$69,620	WI	$56,320
IN	$53,180	NM	$46,660	WV	$60,750
KS	$47,200	NV	$57,780	WY	$50,250

Median Wages for the Largest Metropolitan Areas (Annual)

Area	Wage	Area	Wage
AZ: Phoenix	$55,450	MI: Detroit	$64,890
CA: Los Angeles	$61,740	MN: Minneapolis	$63,190
CA: Riverside	$59,780	MO: Kansas City	$59,070
CA: Sacramento	$67,930	MO: St. Louis	$63,640
CA: San Diego	$66,820	NV: Las Vegas	$57,180
CA: San Francisco	$75,460	NY: New York	$74,420
CO: Denver	$54,690	OH: Cincinnati	$55,250
DC: Washington	$59,220	OH: Cleveland	$60,060
FL: Miami	$53,810	OH: Columbus	$54,350
FL: Orlando	$50,490	OR: Portland	$56,880
FL: Tampa	$46,570	PA: Philadelphia	$62,450
GA: Atlanta	$51,280	PA: Pittsburgh	$62,130
IL: Chicago	$72,790	TX: Dallas	$49,440
MA: Boston	$65,210	TX: Houston	$47,110
MD: Baltimore	$54,500	WA: Seattle	$69,430

FACTORS THAT MAY AFFECT EARNINGS

Educational Attainment of Workers and Effect on Earnings

	Percent at Level	Effect on Earnings
Less than High School	4.1%	−5.6%
Some High School	11.9%	−13.7%
High School or Equivalent	42.8%	1.8%
Some College but No Degree	20.9%	5.7%
Associate Degree	11.8%	2.3%
Bachelor's Degree	7.3%	−2.4%
Master's Degree	1.1%	−15.6%
Doctoral Degree	—	—
First Professional Degree	—	—

Flexibility of Earnings

Average Hours Worked: 38
Workers with a Varying Number of Hours: 10.9%
Workers Earning Some Overtime Pay, Tips, or Commissions: 21.8%
Earnings Benefit of Working Overtime: 6.7%

Gender

	Male	Female
Percent	97.4%	2.6%
Effect on Earnings	0.7%	—

Union Membership

Percentage Union Members: 15.1%
Earnings Benefit of Union Membership: 16.2%

Veteran Status

Percentage Who Have Been on Active Duty: 14.3%
Earnings Benefit of Veteran Status: 5.2%

© JIST Works

47-2000 Construction Trades Workers

47-2011 Boilermakers

Construct, assemble, maintain, and repair stationary steam boilers and boiler house auxiliaries. Align structures or plate sections to assemble boiler frame tanks or vats, following blueprints. Work involves use of hand and power tools, plumb bobs, levels, wedges, dogs, or turnbuckles. Assist in testing assembled vessels. Direct cleaning of boilers and boiler furnaces. Inspect and repair boiler fittings, such as safety valves, regulators, automatic-control mechanisms, water columns, and auxiliary machines.

- Education or Training Required: Long-term on-the-job training
- Job Growth: 8.7%
- Annual Openings: 2,000
- Self-Employed: 0.0%
- Part-Time: 10.0%

NATIONAL WAGE FIGURES (ANNUAL)

Beginning	25th Percentile	Median	Mean	75th Percentile	90th Percentile
$30,410	$37,300	$46,960	$48,600	$59,710	$71,170

Median Wages for Industries Employing Largest Numbers (Annual)

Industry	Median Income
Chemical Manufacturing	$59,710
Management of Companies and Enterprises	$58,030
Petroleum and Coal Products Manufacturing	$53,100
Heavy and Civil Engineering Construction	$51,180
Primary Metal Manufacturing	$49,860
Construction of Buildings	$49,810
Specialty Trade Contractors	$49,400
Rail Transportation	$48,510
Professional, Scientific, and Technical Services	$48,190
Transportation Equipment Manufacturing	$47,070

Median Wages for States (Annual)

State	Wage	State	Wage	State	Wage
AK	no data	KY	$51,530	NY	no data
AL	$38,510	LA	$40,760	OH	$41,700
AR	no data	MA	$48,330	OK	$36,220
AZ	$39,610	MD	$59,300	OR	$59,900
CA	$52,870	ME	$42,530	PA	$46,820
CO	no data	MI	$50,100	RI	no data
CT	$54,350	MN	$50,630	SC	$39,750
DC	no data	MO	$59,960	SD	$43,800
DE	no data	MS	$36,100	TN	$52,230
FL	$41,800	MT	no data	TX	$41,550
GA	$44,200	NC	$45,050	UT	$52,320
HI	$50,010	ND	no data	VA	$41,240
IA	$44,530	NE	$37,940	VT	no data
ID	no data	NH	no data	WA	$47,000
IL	$58,550	NJ	$51,840	WI	$52,980
IN	$52,030	NM	$38,080	WV	$62,480
KS	no data	NV	no data	WY	no data

Median Wages for the Largest Metropolitan Areas (Annual)

Area	Wage	Area	Wage
AZ: Phoenix	$40,280	MI: Detroit	$45,830
CA: Los Angeles	$54,610	MN: Minneapolis	$51,950
CA: Riverside	$54,300	MO: Kansas City	no data
CA: Sacramento	no data	MO: St. Louis	$43,110
CA: San Diego	$37,910	NV: Las Vegas	no data
CA: San Francisco	$56,580	NY: New York	$69,940
CO: Denver	no data	OH: Cincinnati	$42,110
DC: Washington	$49,700	OH: Cleveland	$40,810
FL: Miami	no data	OH: Columbus	no data
FL: Orlando	no data	OR: Portland	no data
FL: Tampa	no data	PA: Philadelphia	$59,450
GA: Atlanta	$44,040	PA: Pittsburgh	$36,210
IL: Chicago	$59,050	TX: Dallas	$42,620
MA: Boston	$47,680	TX: Houston	$41,230
MD: Baltimore	$63,960	WA: Seattle	$42,930

FACTORS THAT MAY AFFECT EARNINGS

Educational Attainment of Workers and Effect on Earnings

	Percent at Level	Effect on Earnings
Less than High School	—	—
Some High School	—	—
High School or Equivalent	51.9%	1.1%
Some College but No Degree	22.2%	4.8%
Associate Degree	—	—
Bachelor's Degree	—	—
Master's Degree	—	—
Doctoral Degree	—	—
First Professional Degree	—	—

Figures do not total 100% because some levels have a very small sample size.

Flexibility of Earnings

Average Hours Worked: 31
Workers with a Varying Number of Hours: 10.6%
Workers Earning Some Overtime Pay, Tips, or Commissions: 29.6%
Earnings Benefit of Working Overtime: 10.1%

Gender

	Male	Female
Percent	92.7%	7.3%
Effect on Earnings	—	—

Union Membership

Percentage Union Members: 40.7%
Earnings Benefit of Union Membership: 35.1%

Veteran Status

Percentage Who Have Been on Active Duty: 10.2%
Earnings Benefit of Veteran Status: 19.5%

47-2021 Brickmasons and Blockmasons

Lay and bind building materials, such as brick, structural tile, concrete block, cinderblock, glass block, and terra-cotta block, with mortar and other substances to construct or repair walls, partitions, arches, sewers, and other structures.

- Education or Training Required: Long-term on-the-job training
- Job Growth: 12.0%
- Annual Openings: 17,000
- Self-Employed: 28.6%
- Part-Time: 16.8%

NATIONAL WAGE FIGURES (ANNUAL)

Beginning	25th Percentile	Median	Mean	75th Percentile	90th Percentile
$25,470	$33,190	$42,980	$44,370	$54,610	$67,450

Median Wages for Industries Employing Largest Numbers (Annual)

Industry	Median Income
Primary Metal Manufacturing	$55,400
Federal, State, and Local Government	$49,490
Merchant Wholesalers, Durable Goods	$46,620
Construction of Buildings	$43,910
Specialty Trade Contractors	$42,760
Mining (Except Oil and Gas)	$41,950
Administrative and Support Services	$41,870
Professional, Scientific, and Technical Services	$40,700
Educational Services	$40,390
Nonmetallic Mineral Product Manufacturing	$40,200

Median Wages for States (Annual)

State	Wage	State	Wage	State	Wage
AK	$66,940	KY	$39,250	NY	$49,280
AL	$37,280	LA	$39,450	OH	$49,110
AR	$37,920	MA	$76,540	OK	$41,660
AZ	$34,320	MD	$42,010	OR	$46,840
CA	$43,780	ME	$39,230	PA	$44,500
CO	$41,730	MI	$50,040	RI	$54,030
CT	$53,680	MN	$53,720	SC	$32,650
DC	$50,610	MO	$53,780	SD	$33,230
DE	$45,280	MS	$31,350	TN	$39,360
FL	$37,060	MT	$37,690	TX	$37,920
GA	$35,730	NC	$35,370	UT	$37,600
HI	$56,460	ND	$45,590	VA	$41,740
IA	$41,640	NE	$43,350	VT	$45,690
ID	$44,840	NH	$43,780	WA	$55,230
IL	$61,290	NJ	$60,090	WI	$49,970
IN	$49,790	NM	$31,540	WV	$38,120
KS	$40,870	NV	$44,530	WY	$34,170

Median Wages for the Largest Metropolitan Areas (Annual)

Metro	Wage	Metro	Wage
AZ: Phoenix	$35,770	MI: Detroit	$51,550
CA: Los Angeles	$29,770	MN: Minneapolis	$55,700
CA: Riverside	$41,510	MO: Kansas City	$55,960
CA: Sacramento	$56,750	MO: St. Louis	$54,020
CA: San Diego	$53,660	NV: Las Vegas	$44,240
CA: San Francisco	$66,660	NY: New York	$53,340
CO: Denver	$40,910	OH: Cincinnati	$50,320
DC: Washington	$45,070	OH: Cleveland	$53,320
FL: Miami	$40,270	OH: Columbus	$47,180
FL: Orlando	$37,720	OR: Portland	$48,330
FL: Tampa	$32,280	PA: Philadelphia	$50,410
GA: Atlanta	$36,210	PA: Pittsburgh	$47,980
IL: Chicago	$64,730	TX: Dallas	$37,980
MA: Boston	no data	TX: Houston	$38,550
MD: Baltimore	$35,860	WA: Seattle	$57,630

FACTORS THAT MAY AFFECT EARNINGS

Educational Attainment of Workers and Effect on Earnings

Figures are based on a group of occupations: Construction Trades Workers

	Percent at Level	Effect on Earnings
Less than High School	9.3%	−26.6%
Some High School	15.0%	−17.6%
High School or Equivalent	35.8%	5.7%
Some College but No Degree	19.0%	4.7%
Associate Degree	12.4%	12.3%
Bachelor's Degree	7.1%	9.0%
Master's Degree	0.9%	2.3%
Doctoral Degree	—	—
First Professional Degree	—	—

Flexibility of Earnings

Average Hours Worked: 32
Workers with a Varying Number of Hours: 12.4%
Workers Earning Some Overtime Pay, Tips, or Commissions: 15.4%
Earnings Benefit of Working Overtime: 10.1%

Gender

	Male	Female
Percent	98.4%	1.6%
Effect on Earnings	0.0%	—

Union Membership

Percentage Union Members: 17.8%
Earnings Benefit of Union Membership: 42.3%

Veteran Status

Percentage Who Have Been on Active Duty: 10.2%
Earnings Benefit of Veteran Status: 19.5%

47-2022 Stonemasons

Build stone structures, such as piers, walls, and abutments. Lay walks; curbstones; or special types of masonry for vats, tanks, and floors.

- Education or Training Required: Long-term on-the-job training
- Job Growth: 13.0%
- Annual Openings: 2,000
- Self-Employed: 23.1%
- Part-Time: 16.8%

NATIONAL WAGE FIGURES (ANNUAL)

Beginning	25th Percentile	Median	Mean	75th Percentile	90th Percentile
$21,540	$27,290	$35,960	$38,040	$45,850	$59,190

Median Wages for Industries Employing Largest Numbers (Annual)

Industry	Median Income
Professional, Scientific, and Technical Services	$52,210
Administrative and Support Services	$39,860
Specialty Trade Contractors	$36,710
Merchant Wholesalers, Durable Goods	$34,980
Construction of Buildings	$34,580
Mining (Except Oil and Gas)	$31,300
Nonmetallic Mineral Product Manufacturing	$30,150
Management of Companies and Enterprises	$27,070
Building Material and Garden Equipment and Supplies Dealers	$24,710
Miscellaneous Store Retailers	$21,140

Median Wages for States (Annual)

State	Wage	State	Wage	State	Wage
AK	no data	KY	$22,150	NY	$38,650
AL	$32,010	LA	$42,060	OH	$30,930
AR	$29,900	MA	$48,350	OK	$28,360
AZ	$29,220	MD	$36,340	OR	$29,960
CA	$40,890	ME	$28,160	PA	$36,670
CO	$42,080	MI	$34,280	RI	$41,800
CT	$45,480	MN	$42,590	SC	$31,950
DC	no data	MO	$28,170	SD	no data
DE	no data	MS	$27,930	TN	$29,000
FL	$29,540	MT	$37,550	TX	$27,680
GA	$27,780	NC	$31,800	UT	$30,740
HI	$47,680	ND	no data	VA	$33,910
IA	no data	NE	no data	VT	$38,480
ID	$33,370	NH	$35,720	WA	$41,290
IL	$66,790	NJ	$42,440	WI	$34,370
IN	$39,230	NM	$27,960	WV	$38,850
KS	$33,520	NV	$38,880	WY	$42,560

Median Wages for the Largest Metropolitan Areas (Annual)

Area	Wage	Area	Wage
AZ: Phoenix	$29,470	MI: Detroit	no data
CA: Los Angeles	$38,720	MN: Minneapolis	$51,170
CA: Riverside	$40,770	MO: Kansas City	$37,190
CA: Sacramento	$47,360	MO: St. Louis	$36,450
CA: San Diego	$40,500	NV: Las Vegas	$38,440
CA: San Francisco	$43,320	NY: New York	$43,110
CO: Denver	$31,250	OH: Cincinnati	no data
DC: Washington	$41,620	OH: Cleveland	$31,660
FL: Miami	$30,560	OH: Columbus	$30,860
FL: Orlando	no data	OR: Portland	$29,570
FL: Tampa	no data	PA: Philadelphia	$43,980
GA: Atlanta	$28,120	PA: Pittsburgh	$34,890
IL: Chicago	$66,470	TX: Dallas	$27,440
MA: Boston	$48,350	TX: Houston	no data
MD: Baltimore	$33,270	WA: Seattle	$43,270

FACTORS THAT MAY AFFECT EARNINGS

Educational Attainment of Workers and Effect on Earnings

Figures are based on a group of occupations: Construction Trades Workers

	Percent at Level	Effect on Earnings
Less than High School	9.3%	−26.6%
Some High School	15.0%	−17.6%
High School or Equivalent	35.8%	5.7%
Some College but No Degree	19.0%	4.7%
Associate Degree	12.4%	12.3%
Bachelor's Degree	7.1%	9.0%
Master's Degree	0.9%	2.3%
Doctoral Degree	—	—
First Professional Degree	—	—

Flexibility of Earnings

Average Hours Worked: 32
Workers with a Varying Number of Hours: 12.4%
Workers Earning Some Overtime Pay, Tips, or Commissions: 15.4%
Earnings Benefit of Working Overtime: 10.1%

Gender

	Male	Female
Percent	98.4%	1.6%
Effect on Earnings	0.0%	—

Union Membership

Percentage Union Members: 17.8%
Earnings Benefit of Union Membership: 42.3%

Veteran Status

Percentage Who Have Been on Active Duty: 10.2%
Earnings Benefit of Veteran Status: 19.5%

47-2031 Carpenters

Construct, erect, install, or repair structures and fixtures made of wood, such as concrete forms; building frameworks, including partitions, joists, studding, and rafters; wood stairways; window and door frames; and hardwood floors. May also install cabinets, siding, drywall, and batt or roll insulation. Includes brattice builders who build doors or brattices (ventilation walls or partitions) in underground passageways to control the proper circulation of air through the passageways and to the working places.

- Education or Training Required: Long-term on-the-job training
- Job Growth: 13.8%
- Annual Openings: 210,000
- Self-Employed: 32.4%
- Part-Time: 15.9%

Note: A large fraction of the workforce for this occupation is self-employed and earns an average of $37,110. All other earnings figures for this occupation are based on workers who are paid a wage or salary.

NATIONAL WAGE FIGURES (ANNUAL)

Beginning	25th Percentile	Median	Mean	75th Percentile	90th Percentile
$22,610	$28,190	$36,550	$39,930	$49,600	$63,330

Median Wages for Industries Employing Largest Numbers (Annual)

Industry	Median Income
Professional, Scientific, and Technical Services	$46,010
Accommodation	$44,950
Hospitals	$44,250
Performing Arts, Spectator Sports, and Related Industries	$42,720
Federal, State, and Local Government	$42,110
Waste Management and Remediation Services	$38,300
Repair and Maintenance	$37,810
Construction of Buildings	$37,590
Heavy and Civil Engineering Construction	$37,380
Real Estate	$37,230

Median Wages for States (Annual)

AK	$51,650	KY	$31,360	NY	$44,120
AL	$28,200	LA	$31,080	OH	$34,170
AR	$30,140	MA	$47,340	OK	$28,600
AZ	$33,140	MD	$37,700	OR	$35,220
CA	$48,880	ME	$31,570	PA	$36,340
CO	$37,350	MI	$39,640	RI	$38,670
CT	$46,470	MN	$41,060	SC	$29,920
DC	$49,000	MO	$39,890	SD	$26,880
DE	$42,130	MS	$27,520	TN	$29,500
FL	$31,220	MT	$31,880	TX	$28,600
GA	$30,710	NC	$29,190	UT	$32,010
HI	$56,930	ND	$29,600	VA	$34,090
IA	$31,900	NE	$30,060	VT	$35,440
ID	$29,940	NH	$35,950	WA	$44,390
IL	$52,430	NJ	$48,190	WI	$36,590
IN	$34,310	NM	$28,680	WV	$29,240
KS	$34,470	NV	$41,290	WY	$34,940

Median Wages for the Largest Metropolitan Areas (Annual)

AZ: Phoenix	$33,390	MI: Detroit	$47,470
CA: Los Angeles	$49,050	MN: Minneapolis	$44,820
CA: Riverside	$44,750	MO: Kansas City	$41,770
CA: Sacramento	$50,700	MO: St. Louis	$49,600
CA: San Diego	$44,980	NV: Las Vegas	$40,980
CA: San Francisco	$56,510	NY: New York	$50,850
CO: Denver	$37,930	OH: Cincinnati	$37,300
DC: Washington	$40,470	OH: Cleveland	$34,790
FL: Miami	$32,170	OH: Columbus	$35,180
FL: Orlando	$31,850	OR: Portland	$39,120
FL: Tampa	$29,980	PA: Philadelphia	$43,660
GA: Atlanta	$32,210	PA: Pittsburgh	$37,750
IL: Chicago	$56,520	TX: Dallas	$28,790
MA: Boston	$48,980	TX: Houston	$30,330
MD: Baltimore	$38,990	WA: Seattle	$48,400

FACTORS THAT MAY AFFECT EARNINGS

Educational Attainment of Workers and Effect on Earnings

	Percent at Level	Effect on Earnings
Less than High School	9.9%	−25.1%
Some High School	15.2%	−19.9%
High School or Equivalent	38.5%	6.5%
Some College but No Degree	18.2%	6.8%
Associate Degree	9.8%	9.8%
Bachelor's Degree	7.1%	12.9%
Master's Degree	1.1%	1.1%
Doctoral Degree	—	—
First Professional Degree	—	—

Flexibility of Earnings

Average Hours Worked: 32
Workers with a Varying Number of Hours: 13.0%
Workers Earning Some Overtime Pay, Tips, or Commissions: 12.7%
Earnings Benefit of Working Overtime: 1.4%

Gender

	Male	Female
Percent	97.6%	2.4%
Effect on Earnings	0.5%	—

Union Membership

Percentage Union Members: 13.0%
Earnings Benefit of Union Membership: 47.3%

Veteran Status

Percentage Who Have Been on Active Duty: 10.2%
Earnings Benefit of Veteran Status: 19.5%

47-2041 Carpet Installers

Lay and install carpet from rolls or blocks on floors. Install padding and trim flooring materials.

- Education or Training Required: Moderate-term on-the-job training
- Job Growth: 8.4%
- Annual Openings: 11,000
- Self-Employed: 46.4%
- Part-Time: 16.8%

Note: Earnings figures do not reflect self-employed workers, who make up a large fraction of the workforce for this occupation.

NATIONAL WAGE FIGURES (ANNUAL)

Beginning	25th Percentile	Median	Mean	75th Percentile	90th Percentile
$19,680	$25,080	$34,560	$38,280	$48,380	$64,710

Median Wages for Industries Employing Largest Numbers (Annual)

Industry	Median Income
Transportation Equipment Manufacturing	$62,640
Professional, Scientific, and Technical Services	$47,000
Federal, State, and Local Government	$44,760
Management of Companies and Enterprises	$42,290
Merchant Wholesalers, Durable Goods	$40,350
Construction of Buildings	$37,460
Educational Services	$35,700
Specialty Trade Contractors	$35,670
Accommodation	$33,110
Furniture and Home Furnishings Stores	$32,590

Median Wages for States (Annual)

AK	$35,240	KY	$29,680	NY	no data
AL	$26,390	LA	$33,380	OH	$40,350
AR	$31,390	MA	no data	OK	$28,920
AZ	$23,390	MD	$29,720	OR	$35,810
CA	$38,800	ME	$26,290	PA	$30,500
CO	$33,010	MI	$36,800	RI	$18,020
CT	$35,410	MN	$46,290	SC	$28,780
DC	no data	MO	$46,810	SD	no data
DE	$32,300	MS	$25,220	TN	$26,410
FL	$22,810	MT	no data	TX	$24,270
GA	$25,400	NC	$24,620	UT	$30,140
HI	$38,820	ND	$26,280	VA	$35,570
IA	$35,340	NE	$31,730	VT	$33,260
ID	$33,070	NH	$36,060	WA	$40,070
IL	$52,830	NJ	$34,320	WI	$36,480
IN	$34,770	NM	$23,250	WV	$26,780
KS	$32,830	NV	$40,670	WY	$27,800

Median Wages for the Largest Metropolitan Areas (Annual)

AZ: Phoenix	$22,910	MI: Detroit	$41,070
CA: Los Angeles	$33,880	MN: Minneapolis	$49,330
CA: Riverside	$38,730	MO: Kansas City	$48,350
CA: Sacramento	$45,910	MO: St. Louis	$39,870
CA: San Diego	$35,700	NV: Las Vegas	$44,520
CA: San Francisco	$48,790	NY: New York	no data
CO: Denver	$33,460	OH: Cincinnati	$32,950
DC: Washington	$31,630	OH: Cleveland	$46,950
FL: Miami	$39,420	OH: Columbus	$41,640
FL: Orlando	$23,550	OR: Portland	$41,410
FL: Tampa	no data	PA: Philadelphia	$31,970
GA: Atlanta	no data	PA: Pittsburgh	$31,360
IL: Chicago	$63,370	TX: Dallas	$23,440
MA: Boston	no data	TX: Houston	$26,680
MD: Baltimore	$34,920	WA: Seattle	$51,680

FACTORS THAT MAY AFFECT EARNINGS

Educational Attainment of Workers and Effect on Earnings

Figures are based on a group of occupations: Construction Trades Workers

	Percent at Level	Effect on Earnings
Less than High School	9.3%	−26.6%
Some High School	15.0%	−17.6%
High School or Equivalent	35.8%	5.7%
Some College but No Degree	19.0%	4.7%
Associate Degree	12.4%	12.3%
Bachelor's Degree	7.1%	9.0%
Master's Degree	0.9%	2.3%
Doctoral Degree	—	—
First Professional Degree	—	—

Flexibility of Earnings

Average Hours Worked: 32
Workers with a Varying Number of Hours: 12.4%
Workers Earning Some Overtime Pay, Tips, or Commissions: 15.4%
Earnings Benefit of Working Overtime: 10.1%

Gender

	Male	Female
Percent	97.6%	2.4%
Effect on Earnings	0.4%	—

Union Membership

Percentage Union Members: 17.8%
Earnings Benefit of Union Membership: 42.3%

Veteran Status

Percentage Who Have Been on Active Duty: 10.2%
Earnings Benefit of Veteran Status: 19.5%

47-2042 Floor Layers, Except Carpet, Wood, and Hard Tiles

Apply blocks, strips, or sheets of shock-absorbing, sound-deadening, or decorative coverings to floors.

- Education or Training Required: Moderate-term on-the-job training
- Job Growth: 10.2%
- Annual Openings: 4,000
- Self-Employed: 44.7%
- Part-Time: 16.8%

Note: Earnings figures do not reflect self-employed workers, who make up a large fraction of the workforce for this occupation.

NATIONAL WAGE FIGURES (ANNUAL)

Beginning	25th Percentile	Median	Mean	75th Percentile	90th Percentile
$20,330	$26,440	$34,190	$39,120	$49,450	$67,220

Median Wages for Industries Employing Largest Numbers (Annual)

Industry	Median Income
Educational Services	$40,780
Merchant Wholesalers, Durable Goods	$37,510
Specialty Trade Contractors	$35,700
Building Material and Garden Equipment and Supplies Dealers	$35,570
Furniture and Home Furnishings Stores	$30,850
Construction of Buildings	$30,100
Administrative and Support Services	$29,410
Wood Product Manufacturing	$24,460

Median Wages for States (Annual)

AK ... no data	KY ... $28,560	NY ... $35,270
AL ... $29,900	LA ... $33,770	OH ... $32,380
AR ... $25,630	MA ... $36,740	OK ... $34,520
AZ ... $26,390	MD ... $34,770	OR ... $51,650
CA ... $38,010	ME ... no data	PA ... $32,330
CO ... $42,250	MI ... $30,160	RI ... $27,160
CT ... $40,730	MN ... $50,640	SC ... $29,910
DC ... no data	MO ... $38,570	SD ... $28,020
DE ... $33,140	MS ... $26,600	TN ... $26,630
FL ... $30,240	MT ... no data	TX ... $27,550
GA ... $30,270	NC ... $26,310	UT ... $23,410
HI ... $63,640	ND ... no data	VA ... $30,700
IA ... $28,220	NE ... $40,450	VT ... $29,150
ID ... $29,510	NH ... no data	WA ... $40,030
IL ... $73,130	NJ ... $27,760	WI ... $34,990
IN ... $28,450	NM ... no data	WV ... $35,410
KS ... $38,110	NV ... no data	WY ... no data

Median Wages for the Largest Metropolitan Areas (Annual)

AZ: Phoenix ... $25,450	MI: Detroit ... no data
CA: Los Angeles ... $33,030	MN: Minneapolis ... no data
CA: Riverside ... $50,870	MO: Kansas City ... $45,340
CA: Sacramento ... $41,240	MO: St. Louis ... $38,440
CA: San Diego ... $37,250	NV: Las Vegas ... $42,750
CA: San Francisco ... $47,400	NY: New York ... $29,060
CO: Denver ... no data	OH: Cincinnati ... $43,460
DC: Washington ... $33,590	OH: Cleveland ... no data
FL: Miami ... $30,620	OH: Columbus ... no data
FL: Orlando ... no data	OR: Portland ... $40,000
FL: Tampa ... no data	PA: Philadelphia ... $41,490
GA: Atlanta ... no data	PA: Pittsburgh ... no data
IL: Chicago ... $73,090	TX: Dallas ... no data
MA: Boston ... $35,720	TX: Houston ... no data
MD: Baltimore ... $35,420	WA: Seattle ... $50,880

FACTORS THAT MAY AFFECT EARNINGS

Educational Attainment of Workers and Effect on Earnings

Figures are based on a group of occupations: Construction Trades Workers

	Percent at Level	Effect on Earnings
Less than High School	9.3%	−26.6%
Some High School	15.0%	−17.6%
High School or Equivalent	35.8%	5.7%
Some College but No Degree	19.0%	4.7%
Associate Degree	12.4%	12.3%
Bachelor's Degree	7.1%	9.0%
Master's Degree	0.9%	2.3%
Doctoral Degree	—	—
First Professional Degree	—	—

Flexibility of Earnings

Average Hours Worked: 32
Workers with a Varying Number of Hours: 12.4%
Workers Earning Some Overtime Pay, Tips, or Commissions: 15.4%
Earnings Benefit of Working Overtime: 10.1%

Gender

	Male	Female
Percent	97.6%	2.4%
Effect on Earnings	0.4%	—

Union Membership

Percentage Union Members: 17.8%
Earnings Benefit of Union Membership: 42.3%

Veteran Status

Percentage Who Have Been on Active Duty: 10.2%
Earnings Benefit of Veteran Status: 19.5%

47-2043 Floor Sanders and Finishers

Scrape and sand wooden floors to smooth surfaces, using floor scraper and floor sanding machine, and apply coats of finish.

- Education or Training Required: Moderate-term on-the-job training
- Job Growth: 8.2%
- Annual Openings: 2,000
- Self-Employed: 53.0%
- Part-Time: 16.8%

Note: Earnings figures do not reflect self-employed workers, who make up a large fraction of the workforce for this occupation.

NATIONAL WAGE FIGURES (ANNUAL)

Beginning	25th Percentile	Median	Mean	75th Percentile	90th Percentile
$18,890	$22,540	$28,890	$31,810	$38,420	$50,360

Median Wages for Industries Employing Largest Numbers (Annual)

Industry	Median Income
Building Material and Garden Equipment and Supplies Dealers	$37,500
Construction of Buildings	$35,840
Furniture and Home Furnishings Stores	$35,490
Specialty Trade Contractors	$29,200
Wood Product Manufacturing	$26,510
Furniture and Related Product Manufacturing	$21,660

Median Wages for States (Annual)

State	Wage	State	Wage	State	Wage
AK	no data	KY	$29,380	NY	no data
AL	$27,580	LA	$22,490	OH	$28,770
AR	$19,410	MA	no data	OK	$29,670
AZ	$20,530	MD	$28,880	OR	no data
CA	$38,940	ME	no data	PA	$26,630
CO	$34,210	MI	$28,950	RI	no data
CT	$33,200	MN	$39,780	SC	$24,180
DC	no data	MO	$43,120	SD	no data
DE	no data	MS	$19,280	TN	$27,210
FL	$23,630	MT	no data	TX	$24,600
GA	$26,320	NC	$24,630	UT	no data
HI	no data	ND	no data	VA	$28,070
IA	$38,470	NE	no data	VT	no data
ID	no data	NH	no data	WA	$32,460
IL	no data	NJ	$21,780	WI	$27,740
IN	$30,120	NM	no data	WV	$19,010
KS	$31,720	NV	$25,170	WY	no data

Median Wages for the Largest Metropolitan Areas (Annual)

Area	Wage	Area	Wage
AZ: Phoenix	$20,300	MI: Detroit	$29,230
CA: Los Angeles	$23,620	MN: Minneapolis	$44,640
CA: Riverside	no data	MO: Kansas City	$34,510
CA: Sacramento	no data	MO: St. Louis	$47,790
CA: San Diego	no data	NV: Las Vegas	no data
CA: San Francisco	$39,300	NY: New York	$21,450
CO: Denver	no data	OH: Cincinnati	$32,210
DC: Washington	$30,930	OH: Cleveland	$38,410
FL: Miami	no data	OH: Columbus	$28,070
FL: Orlando	no data	OR: Portland	no data
FL: Tampa	no data	PA: Philadelphia	$27,470
GA: Atlanta	$27,630	PA: Pittsburgh	no data
IL: Chicago	$43,600	TX: Dallas	no data
MA: Boston	no data	TX: Houston	no data
MD: Baltimore	no data	WA: Seattle	no data

FACTORS THAT MAY AFFECT EARNINGS

Educational Attainment of Workers and Effect on Earnings

Figures are based on a group of occupations: Construction Trades Workers

	Percent at Level	Effect on Earnings
Less than High School	9.3%	−26.6%
Some High School	15.0%	−17.6%
High School or Equivalent	35.8%	5.7%
Some College but No Degree	19.0%	4.7%
Associate Degree	12.4%	12.3%
Bachelor's Degree	7.1%	9.0%
Master's Degree	0.9%	2.3%
Doctoral Degree	—	—
First Professional Degree	—	—

Flexibility of Earnings

Average Hours Worked: 32
Workers with a Varying Number of Hours: 12.4%
Workers Earning Some Overtime Pay, Tips, or Commissions: 15.4%
Earnings Benefit of Working Overtime: 10.1%

Gender

	Male	Female
Percent	97.6%	2.4%
Effect on Earnings	0.4%	—

Union Membership

Percentage Union Members: 17.8%
Earnings Benefit of Union Membership: 42.3%

Veteran Status

Percentage Who Have Been on Active Duty: 10.2%
Earnings Benefit of Veteran Status: 19.5%

47-2044 Tile and Marble Setters

Apply hard tile, marble, and wood tile to walls, floors, ceilings, and roof decks.

- Education or Training Required: Long-term on-the-job training
- Job Growth: 22.9%
- Annual Openings: 9,000
- Self-Employed: 24.4%
- Part-Time: 16.8%

NATIONAL WAGE FIGURES (ANNUAL)

Beginning	25th Percentile	Median	Mean	75th Percentile	90th Percentile
$21,330	$27,360	$36,590	$39,360	$48,890	$62,290

Median Wages for Industries Employing Largest Numbers (Annual)

Industry	Median Income
Federal, State, and Local Government	$56,760
Specialty Trade Contractors	$37,620
Administrative and Support Services	$36,030
Merchant Wholesalers, Durable Goods	$35,690
Furniture and Home Furnishings Stores	$34,270
Building Material and Garden Equipment and Supplies Dealers	$33,500
Construction of Buildings	$31,100
Nonmetallic Mineral Product Manufacturing	$28,890
Plastics and Rubber Products Manufacturing	$23,590

Median Wages for States (Annual)

AK	$66,890	KY	$34,220	NY	$52,230
AL	$24,590	LA	$30,540	OH	$40,180
AR	$32,130	MA	$54,230	OK	$30,410
AZ	$28,940	MD	$41,740	OR	$31,330
CA	$40,620	ME	$30,920	PA	$41,720
CO	$38,040	MI	$40,380	RI	$43,850
CT	$51,700	MN	$44,050	SC	$27,670
DC	no data	MO	$37,280	SD	$27,110
DE	$58,900	MS	$26,320	TN	$27,940
FL	$31,660	MT	$36,930	TX	$27,930
GA	$33,650	NC	$28,140	UT	$32,130
HI	$54,680	ND	$22,040	VA	$34,890
IA	$42,150	NE	$35,840	VT	$32,860
ID	$28,740	NH	$34,960	WA	$50,230
IL	$46,060	NJ	$55,040	WI	$48,420
IN	$28,100	NM	$26,010	WV	no data
KS	$35,460	NV	$44,730	WY	$37,130

Median Wages for the Largest Metropolitan Areas (Annual)

AZ: Phoenix	$28,890	MI: Detroit	$39,740
CA: Los Angeles	$39,220	MN: Minneapolis	$44,340
CA: Riverside	$38,970	MO: Kansas City	$35,450
CA: Sacramento	$44,060	MO: St. Louis	$43,480
CA: San Diego	$42,260	NV: Las Vegas	$44,590
CA: San Francisco	$45,280	NY: New York	$56,140
CO: Denver	$42,510	OH: Cincinnati	$37,880
DC: Washington	$40,260	OH: Cleveland	$49,980
FL: Miami	$24,340	OH: Columbus	$36,570
FL: Orlando	$36,950	OR: Portland	$31,390
FL: Tampa	$35,730	PA: Philadelphia	$47,040
GA: Atlanta	$33,580	PA: Pittsburgh	$41,130
IL: Chicago	$47,180	TX: Dallas	$26,500
MA: Boston	$60,710	TX: Houston	$29,380
MD: Baltimore	$36,580	WA: Seattle	$50,750

FACTORS THAT MAY AFFECT EARNINGS

Educational Attainment of Workers and Effect on Earnings

Figures are based on a group of occupations: Construction Trades Workers

	Percent at Level	Effect on Earnings
Less than High School	9.3%	−26.6%
Some High School	15.0%	−17.6%
High School or Equivalent	35.8%	5.7%
Some College but No Degree	19.0%	4.7%
Associate Degree	12.4%	12.3%
Bachelor's Degree	7.1%	9.0%
Master's Degree	0.9%	2.3%
Doctoral Degree	—	—
First Professional Degree	—	—

Flexibility of Earnings

Average Hours Worked: 32
Workers with a Varying Number of Hours: 12.4%
Workers Earning Some Overtime Pay, Tips, or Commissions: 15.4%
Earnings Benefit of Working Overtime: 10.1%

Gender

	Male	Female
Percent	97.6%	2.4%
Effect on Earnings	0.4%	—

Union Membership

Percentage Union Members: 17.8%
Earnings Benefit of Union Membership: 42.3%

Veteran Status

Percentage Who Have Been on Active Duty: 10.2%
Earnings Benefit of Veteran Status: 19.5%

47-2051 Cement Masons and Concrete Finishers

Smooth and finish surfaces of poured concrete, such as floors, walks, sidewalks, roads, or curbs, using a variety of hand and power tools. Align forms for sidewalks, curbs, or gutters; patch voids; and use saws to cut expansion joints.

- Education or Training Required: Moderate-term on-the-job training
- Job Growth: 15.9%
- Annual Openings: 32,000
- Self-Employed: 3.1%
- Part-Time: 16.8%

NATIONAL WAGE FIGURES (ANNUAL)

Beginning	25th Percentile	Median	Mean	75th Percentile	90th Percentile
$20,840	$25,750	$32,650	$35,630	$43,060	$56,310

Median Wages for Industries Employing Largest Numbers (Annual)

Industry	Median Income
Hospitals	$50,630
Federal, State, and Local Government	$38,000
Educational Services	$37,550
Professional, Scientific, and Technical Services	$34,470
Construction of Buildings	$33,890
Miscellaneous Store Retailers	$33,720
Heavy and Civil Engineering Construction	$33,150
Specialty Trade Contractors	$32,760
Administrative and Support Services	$29,780
Merchant Wholesalers, Durable Goods	$29,530

Median Wages for States (Annual)

State	Wage	State	Wage	State	Wage
AK	$55,820	KY	$30,040	NY	$49,770
AL	$27,960	LA	$28,270	OH	$36,950
AR	$27,410	MA	$40,350	OK	$28,370
AZ	$33,670	MD	$35,610	OR	$35,780
CA	$40,550	ME	$27,520	PA	$36,270
CO	$31,800	MI	$39,660	RI	$46,170
CT	$42,800	MN	$45,590	SC	$26,390
DC	$40,910	MO	$32,450	SD	$25,590
DE	$38,480	MS	$25,990	TN	$29,050
FL	$28,760	MT	$31,780	TX	$25,440
GA	$28,380	NC	$26,740	UT	$31,990
HI	$56,030	ND	$29,220	VA	$31,260
IA	$29,390	NE	$29,360	VT	$35,070
ID	$26,180	NH	$33,070	WA	$44,750
IL	$45,850	NJ	$43,820	WI	$37,640
IN	$34,130	NM	$28,160	WV	$30,670
KS	$29,530	NV	$39,720	WY	$30,460

Median Wages for the Largest Metropolitan Areas (Annual)

Area	Wage	Area	Wage
AZ: Phoenix	$34,610	MI: Detroit	$47,370
CA: Los Angeles	$43,010	MN: Minneapolis	$47,750
CA: Riverside	$40,000	MO: Kansas City	$33,270
CA: Sacramento	$39,970	MO: St. Louis	$39,730
CA: San Diego	$49,230	NV: Las Vegas	$39,630
CA: San Francisco	$51,410	NY: New York	$52,710
CO: Denver	$32,520	OH: Cincinnati	$33,830
DC: Washington	$34,350	OH: Cleveland	$46,920
FL: Miami	$28,350	OH: Columbus	$36,130
FL: Orlando	$30,620	OR: Portland	$35,210
FL: Tampa	$27,640	PA: Philadelphia	$42,250
GA: Atlanta	$29,510	PA: Pittsburgh	$44,360
IL: Chicago	$48,250	TX: Dallas	$27,850
MA: Boston	$41,890	TX: Houston	$24,290
MD: Baltimore	$36,220	WA: Seattle	$53,060

FACTORS THAT MAY AFFECT EARNINGS

Educational Attainment of Workers and Effect on Earnings

Figures are based on a group of occupations: Construction Trades Workers

	Percent at Level	Effect on Earnings
Less than High School	9.3%	−26.6%
Some High School	15.0%	−17.6%
High School or Equivalent	35.8%	5.7%
Some College but No Degree	19.0%	4.7%
Associate Degree	12.4%	12.3%
Bachelor's Degree	7.1%	9.0%
Master's Degree	0.9%	2.3%
Doctoral Degree	—	—
First Professional Degree	—	—

Flexibility of Earnings

Average Hours Worked: 32
Workers with a Varying Number of Hours: 12.4%
Workers Earning Some Overtime Pay, Tips, or Commissions: 15.4%
Earnings Benefit of Working Overtime: 10.1%

Gender

	Male	Female
Percent	99.3%	0.7%
Effect on Earnings	1.7%	—

Union Membership

Percentage Union Members: 17.8%
Earnings Benefit of Union Membership: 42.3%

Veteran Status

Percentage Who Have Been on Active Duty: 10.2%
Earnings Benefit of Veteran Status: 19.5%

47-2053 Terrazzo Workers and Finishers

Apply a mixture of cement, sand, pigment, or marble chips to floors, stairways, and cabinet fixtures to fashion durable and decorative surfaces.

- Education or Training Required: Long-term on-the-job training
- Job Growth: 15.2%
- Annual Openings: 1,000
- Self-Employed: 3.4%
- Part-Time: 16.8%

NATIONAL WAGE FIGURES (ANNUAL)

Beginning	25th Percentile	Median	Mean	75th Percentile	90th Percentile
$19,360	$24,970	$31,630	$34,900	$42,640	$56,610

Median Wages for Industries Employing Largest Numbers (Annual)

Industry	Median Income
Specialty Trade Contractors	$33,730
Heavy and Civil Engineering Construction	$31,700
Construction of Buildings	$28,710
Nonmetallic Mineral Product Manufacturing	$23,170

Median Wages for States (Annual)

State	Wage	State	Wage	State	Wage
AK	no data	KY	$26,860	NY	no data
AL	$21,070	LA	no data	OH	$30,880
AR	no data	MA	no data	OK	no data
AZ	$22,880	MD	$42,650	OR	no data
CA	$33,710	ME	no data	PA	$47,940
CO	$30,580	MI	$35,750	RI	no data
CT	$44,890	MN	$48,310	SC	$27,810
DC	no data	MO	no data	SD	no data
DE	no data	MS	$25,720	TN	$27,220
FL	$27,000	MT	no data	TX	$28,550
GA	$27,530	NC	$28,750	UT	no data
HI	no data	ND	no data	VA	$31,890
IA	no data	NE	no data	VT	no data
ID	no data	NH	no data	WA	no data
IL	$49,690	NJ	$27,270	WI	no data
IN	no data	NM	no data	WV	no data
KS	no data	NV	$27,350	WY	no data

Median Wages for the Largest Metropolitan Areas (Annual)

Area	Wage	Area	Wage
AZ: Phoenix	no data	MI: Detroit	no data
CA: Los Angeles	$37,590	MN: Minneapolis	$54,050
CA: Riverside	$37,130	MO: Kansas City	no data
CA: Sacramento	no data	MO: St. Louis	no data
CA: San Diego	no data	NV: Las Vegas	$26,070
CA: San Francisco	$36,310	NY: New York	no data
CO: Denver	no data	OH: Cincinnati	$27,760
DC: Washington	$35,510	OH: Cleveland	no data
FL: Miami	$30,440	OH: Columbus	no data
FL: Orlando	no data	OR: Portland	no data
FL: Tampa	no data	PA: Philadelphia	$27,040
GA: Atlanta	no data	PA: Pittsburgh	no data
IL: Chicago	$51,340	TX: Dallas	$47,820
MA: Boston	no data	TX: Houston	$26,640
MD: Baltimore	no data	WA: Seattle	no data

FACTORS THAT MAY AFFECT EARNINGS

Educational Attainment of Workers and Effect on Earnings

Figures are based on a group of occupations: Construction Trades Workers

	Percent at Level	Effect on Earnings
Less than High School	9.3%	−26.6%
Some High School	15.0%	−17.6%
High School or Equivalent	35.8%	5.7%
Some College but No Degree	19.0%	4.7%
Associate Degree	12.4%	12.3%
Bachelor's Degree	7.1%	9.0%
Master's Degree	0.9%	2.3%
Doctoral Degree	—	—
First Professional Degree	—	—

Flexibility of Earnings

Average Hours Worked: 32
Workers with a Varying Number of Hours: 12.4%
Workers Earning Some Overtime Pay, Tips, or Commissions: 15.4%
Earnings Benefit of Working Overtime: 10.1%

Gender

	Male	Female
Percent	99.3%	0.7%
Effect on Earnings	1.7%	—

Union Membership

Percentage Union Members: 17.8%
Earnings Benefit of Union Membership: 42.3%

Veteran Status

Percentage Who Have Been on Active Duty: 10.2%
Earnings Benefit of Veteran Status: 19.5%

47-2061 Construction Laborers

Perform tasks involving physical labor at building, highway, and heavy construction projects; tunnel and shaft excavations; and demolition sites. May operate hand and power tools of all types: air hammers, earth tampers, cement mixers, small mechanical hoists, surveying and measuring equipment, and a variety of other equipment and instruments. May clean and prepare sites; dig trenches; set braces to support the sides of excavations; erect scaffolding; clean up rubble and debris; and remove asbestos, lead, and other hazardous waste materials. May assist other craft workers.

- Education or Training Required: Moderate-term on-the-job training
- Job Growth: 5.9%
- Annual Openings: 245,000
- Self-Employed: 12.9%
- Part-Time: 22.8%

NATIONAL WAGE FIGURES (ANNUAL)

Beginning	25th Percentile	Median	Mean	75th Percentile	90th Percentile
$16,970	$20,690	$26,320	$29,930	$36,010	$50,320

Median Wages for Industries Employing Largest Numbers (Annual)

Industry	Median Income
Hospitals	$42,210
Utilities	$34,100
Management of Companies and Enterprises	$31,670
Rental and Leasing Services	$30,210
Waste Management and Remediation Services	$30,180
Federal, State, and Local Government	$29,280
Merchant Wholesalers, Durable Goods	$29,220
Truck Transportation	$28,730
Miscellaneous Store Retailers	$28,470
Mining (Except Oil and Gas)	$28,410

Median Wages for States (Annual)

State	Wage	State	Wage	State	Wage
AK	$39,670	KY	$25,320	NY	$39,640
AL	$20,770	LA	$21,970	OH	$33,670
AR	$21,960	MA	$40,860	OK	$22,240
AZ	$25,280	MD	$27,470	OR	$29,080
CA	$30,850	ME	$24,870	PA	$29,200
CO	$25,830	MI	$32,370	RI	$38,960
CT	$34,980	MN	$38,450	SC	$21,670
DC	$28,690	MO	$33,390	SD	$21,890
DE	$26,640	MS	$20,280	TN	$23,720
FL	$22,540	MT	$26,050	TX	$20,060
GA	$22,510	NC	$22,510	UT	$22,880
HI	$39,760	ND	$24,900	VA	$23,910
IA	$29,060	NE	$22,960	VT	$25,830
ID	$25,500	NH	$27,480	WA	$30,420
IL	$45,190	NJ	$40,170	WI	$34,150
IN	$31,980	NM	$20,950	WV	$22,280
KS	$24,840	NV	$28,920	WY	$25,010

Median Wages for the Largest Metropolitan Areas (Annual)

Area	Wage	Area	Wage
AZ: Phoenix	$26,290	MI: Detroit	$34,170
CA: Los Angeles	$30,020	MN: Minneapolis	$47,210
CA: Riverside	$28,090	MO: Kansas City	$34,200
CA: Sacramento	$31,630	MO: St. Louis	$43,160
CA: San Diego	$29,910	NV: Las Vegas	$28,380
CA: San Francisco	$43,700	NY: New York	$45,900
CO: Denver	$26,510	OH: Cincinnati	$30,100
DC: Washington	$27,680	OH: Cleveland	$38,610
FL: Miami	$22,860	OH: Columbus	$32,140
FL: Orlando	$23,380	OR: Portland	$31,490
FL: Tampa	$22,670	PA: Philadelphia	$32,450
GA: Atlanta	$23,270	PA: Pittsburgh	$32,760
IL: Chicago	$51,320	TX: Dallas	$21,330
MA: Boston	$43,210	TX: Houston	$19,700
MD: Baltimore	$27,800	WA: Seattle	$31,640

FACTORS THAT MAY AFFECT EARNINGS

Educational Attainment of Workers and Effect on Earnings

	Percent at Level	Effect on Earnings
Less than High School	14.5%	−20.4%
Some High School	18.3%	−21.5%
High School or Equivalent	33.8%	9.9%
Some College but No Degree	17.5%	4.2%
Associate Degree	7.8%	13.3%
Bachelor's Degree	6.9%	19.0%
Master's Degree	1.0%	48.2%
Doctoral Degree	—	—
First Professional Degree	—	—

Flexibility of Earnings

Average Hours Worked: 29
Workers with a Varying Number of Hours: 14.2%
Workers Earning Some Overtime Pay, Tips, or Commissions: 12.4%
Earnings Benefit of Working Overtime: 14.6%

Gender

	Male	Female
Percent	96.3%	3.7%
Effect on Earnings	0.4%	—

Union Membership

Percentage Union Members: 11.3%
Earnings Benefit of Union Membership: 43.1%

Veteran Status

Percentage Who Have Been on Active Duty: 10.2%
Earnings Benefit of Veteran Status: 19.5%

47-2071 Paving, Surfacing, and Tamping Equipment Operators

Operate equipment used for applying concrete, asphalt, or other materials to roadbeds, parking lots, or airport runways and taxiways or equipment used for tamping gravel, dirt, or other materials. Includes concrete and asphalt paving machine operators, form tampers, tamping machine operators, and stone spreader operators.

- Education or Training Required: Moderate-term on-the-job training
- Job Growth: 15.6%
- Annual Openings: 7,000
- Self-Employed: 1.2%
- Part-Time: 14.3%

NATIONAL WAGE FIGURES (ANNUAL)

Beginning	25th Percentile	Median	Mean	75th Percentile	90th Percentile
$20,740	$24,920	$31,300	$34,210	$40,990	$52,620

Median Wages for Industries Employing Largest Numbers (Annual)

Industry	Median Income
Management of Companies and Enterprises	$40,000
Rail Transportation	$38,300
Petroleum and Coal Products Manufacturing	$34,710
Heavy and Civil Engineering Construction	$31,670
Specialty Trade Contractors	$31,210
Federal, State, and Local Government	$31,000
Professional, Scientific, and Technical Services	$29,290
Nonmetallic Mineral Product Manufacturing	$27,640
Waste Management and Remediation Services	$27,390
Construction of Buildings	$27,140

Median Wages for States (Annual)

AK	no data	KY	$33,600	NY	$47,970
AL	$26,340	LA	$25,120	OH	$40,720
AR	$27,630	MA	$38,860	OK	$27,290
AZ	$36,440	MD	$30,620	OR	$38,880
CA	$44,240	ME	$26,930	PA	$32,240
CO	$34,970	MI	$35,660	RI	$40,330
CT	$38,050	MN	$45,410	SC	$25,840
DC	$46,920	MO	$37,910	SD	$32,380
DE	$36,780	MS	$24,590	TN	$28,410
FL	$26,490	MT	$33,070	TX	$25,050
GA	$24,990	NC	$25,560	UT	$32,150
HI	$62,050	ND	$33,140	VA	$28,780
IA	$32,110	NE	$25,670	VT	$31,280
ID	$30,850	NH	$34,700	WA	$46,180
IL	$40,030	NJ	$42,790	WI	$42,300
IN	$34,730	NM	$27,550	WV	$29,840
KS	$28,780	NV	$37,770	WY	$31,670

Median Wages for the Largest Metropolitan Areas (Annual)

AZ: Phoenix	$38,510	MI: Detroit	$36,070
CA: Los Angeles	$43,820	MN: Minneapolis	$44,830
CA: Riverside	$41,370	MO: Kansas City	$39,380
CA: Sacramento	$42,780	MO: St. Louis	$42,950
CA: San Diego	$49,250	NV: Las Vegas	$35,610
CA: San Francisco	$63,600	NY: New York	$49,150
CO: Denver	$35,470	OH: Cincinnati	$40,180
DC: Washington	$31,920	OH: Cleveland	$40,480
FL: Miami	$30,270	OH: Columbus	$39,630
FL: Orlando	$23,870	OR: Portland	$41,020
FL: Tampa	$26,450	PA: Philadelphia	$36,020
GA: Atlanta	$27,610	PA: Pittsburgh	$37,040
IL: Chicago	$36,300	TX: Dallas	$28,030
MA: Boston	$38,380	TX: Houston	$24,860
MD: Baltimore	$30,760	WA: Seattle	$53,130

FACTORS THAT MAY AFFECT EARNINGS

Educational Attainment of Workers and Effect on Earnings

	Percent at Level	Effect on Earnings
Less than High School	—	—
Some High School	34.5%	−18.8%
High School or Equivalent	41.4%	14.2%
Some College but No Degree	—	—
Associate Degree	—	—
Bachelor's Degree	—	—
Master's Degree	—	—
Doctoral Degree	—	—
First Professional Degree	—	—

Figures do not total 100% because some levels have a very small sample size.

Flexibility of Earnings

Average Hours Worked: 27
Workers with a Varying Number of Hours: 14.6%
Workers Earning Some Overtime Pay, Tips, or Commissions: 16.7%
Earnings Benefit of Working Overtime: 10.1%

Gender

	Male	Female
Percent	98.3%	1.7%
Effect on Earnings	−0.5%	—

Union Membership

Percentage Union Members: 20.0%
Earnings Benefit of Union Membership: 42.3%

Veteran Status

Percentage Who Have Been on Active Duty: 10.2%
Earnings Benefit of Veteran Status: 19.5%

47-2072 Pile-Driver Operators

Operate pile drivers mounted on skids, barges, crawler treads, or locomotive cranes to drive pilings for retaining walls, bulkheads, and foundations of structures such as buildings, bridges, and piers.

- Education or Training Required: Moderate-term on-the-job training
- Job Growth: 11.9%
- Annual Openings: Fewer than 500
- Self-Employed: 0.0%
- Part-Time: 16.8%

NATIONAL WAGE FIGURES (ANNUAL)

Beginning	25th Percentile	Median	Mean	75th Percentile	90th Percentile
$26,690	$33,930	$46,180	$49,950	$65,820	$77,540

Median Wages for Industries Employing Largest Numbers (Annual)

Industry	Median Income
Heavy and Civil Engineering Construction	$52,900
Specialty Trade Contractors	$42,600
Federal, State, and Local Government	$42,400
Construction of Buildings	$36,330

Median Wages for States (Annual)

State	Wage	State	Wage	State	Wage
AK	$60,400	KY	$32,990	NY	no data
AL	$45,690	LA	$37,260	OH	no data
AR	no data	MA	$61,880	OK	no data
AZ	$48,330	MD	$35,280	OR	$61,640
CA	$68,030	ME	no data	PA	no data
CO	no data	MI	no data	RI	no data
CT	no data	MN	$59,700	SC	$39,000
DC	no data	MO	no data	SD	no data
DE	no data	MS	$28,960	TN	no data
FL	$35,120	MT	no data	TX	$34,540
GA	$24,740	NC	no data	UT	no data
HI	no data	ND	no data	VA	$38,220
IA	no data	NE	no data	VT	no data
ID	no data	NH	$58,520	WA	$62,170
IL	$72,730	NJ	$61,410	WI	no data
IN	$81,710	NM	no data	WV	no data
KS	$38,940	NV	no data	WY	no data

Median Wages for the Largest Metropolitan Areas (Annual)

Area	Wage	Area	Wage
AZ: Phoenix	$56,180	MI: Detroit	$41,050
CA: Los Angeles	$69,180	MN: Minneapolis	$60,240
CA: Riverside	no data	MO: Kansas City	$41,990
CA: Sacramento	$49,300	MO: St. Louis	no data
CA: San Diego	no data	NV: Las Vegas	no data
CA: San Francisco	$69,640	NY: New York	$65,700
CO: Denver	no data	OH: Cincinnati	no data
DC: Washington	$39,730	OH: Cleveland	no data
FL: Miami	$35,690	OH: Columbus	no data
FL: Orlando	no data	OR: Portland	$65,230
FL: Tampa	no data	PA: Philadelphia	$66,110
GA: Atlanta	no data	PA: Pittsburgh	no data
IL: Chicago	$81,520	TX: Dallas	no data
MA: Boston	$61,630	TX: Houston	$33,180
MD: Baltimore	no data	WA: Seattle	$64,670

FACTORS THAT MAY AFFECT EARNINGS

Educational Attainment of Workers and Effect on Earnings

Figures are based on a group of occupations: Construction Trades Workers

	Percent at Level	Effect on Earnings
Less than High School	9.3%	−26.6%
Some High School	15.0%	−17.6%
High School or Equivalent	35.8%	5.7%
Some College but No Degree	19.0%	4.7%
Associate Degree	12.4%	12.3%
Bachelor's Degree	7.1%	9.0%
Master's Degree	0.9%	2.3%
Doctoral Degree	—	—
First Professional Degree	—	—

Flexibility of Earnings

Average Hours Worked: 31
Workers with a Varying Number of Hours: 4.3%
Workers Earning Some Overtime Pay, Tips, or Commissions: 16.7%
Earnings Benefit of Working Overtime: 10.1%

Gender

	Male	Female
Percent	98.3%	1.7%
Effect on Earnings	−0.5%	—

Union Membership

Percentage Union Members: 16.7%
Earnings Benefit of Union Membership: 42.3%

Veteran Status

Percentage Who Have Been on Active Duty: 10.2%
Earnings Benefit of Veteran Status: 19.5%

47-2073 Operating Engineers and Other Construction Equipment Operators

Operate one or several types of power construction equipment, such as motor graders, bulldozers, scrapers, compressors, pumps, derricks, shovels, tractors, or front-end loaders, to excavate, move, and grade earth; erect structures; or pour concrete or other hard-surface pavement. May repair and maintain equipment in addition to other duties.

- Education or Training Required: Moderate-term on-the-job training
- Job Growth: 11.6%
- Annual Openings: 37,000
- Self-Employed: 5.4%
- Part-Time: 5.0%

NATIONAL WAGE FIGURES (ANNUAL)

Beginning	25th Percentile	Median	Mean	75th Percentile	90th Percentile
$24,010	$28,900	$36,890	$40,560	$49,890	$64,120

Median Wages for Industries Employing Largest Numbers (Annual)

Industry	Median Income
Rental and Leasing Services	$47,320
Utilities	$45,510
Chemical Manufacturing	$44,990
Personal and Laundry Services	$42,390
Rail Transportation	$42,270
Petroleum and Coal Products Manufacturing	$41,020
Heavy and Civil Engineering Construction	$39,310
Construction of Buildings	$38,050
Specialty Trade Contractors	$38,050
Professional, Scientific, and Technical Services	$37,050

Median Wages for States (Annual)

State	Wage	State	Wage	State	Wage
AK	$57,880	KY	$33,770	NY	$53,680
AL	$30,170	LA	$30,240	OH	$44,530
AR	$27,410	MA	$53,220	OK	$28,290
AZ	$39,260	MD	$38,510	OR	$41,510
CA	$57,670	ME	$30,630	PA	$40,910
CO	$39,510	MI	$43,910	RI	$53,660
CT	$49,250	MN	$48,280	SC	$28,990
DC	$42,370	MO	$41,570	SD	$30,360
DE	$39,540	MS	$26,650	TN	$29,210
FL	$30,220	MT	$38,840	TX	$28,280
GA	$29,580	NC	$29,730	UT	$34,980
HI	$63,370	ND	$35,700	VA	$32,830
IA	$36,570	NE	$31,560	VT	$31,550
ID	$34,860	NH	$38,660	WA	$50,630
IL	$60,270	NJ	$55,490	WI	$45,230
IN	$42,930	NM	$32,320	WV	$30,200
KS	$31,300	NV	$45,730	WY	$36,580

Median Wages for the Largest Metropolitan Areas (Annual)

Area	Wage	Area	Wage
AZ: Phoenix	$40,550	MI: Detroit	$48,870
CA: Los Angeles	$63,590	MN: Minneapolis	$54,740
CA: Riverside	$56,380	MO: Kansas City	$42,540
CA: Sacramento	$55,910	MO: St. Louis	$50,090
CA: San Diego	$56,510	NV: Las Vegas	$47,050
CA: San Francisco	$63,580	NY: New York	$65,040
CO: Denver	$41,090	OH: Cincinnati	$41,430
DC: Washington	$40,510	OH: Cleveland	$51,580
FL: Miami	$32,950	OH: Columbus	$40,820
FL: Orlando	$30,270	OR: Portland	$48,890
FL: Tampa	$28,250	PA: Philadelphia	$47,000
GA: Atlanta	$31,350	PA: Pittsburgh	$43,800
IL: Chicago	$68,010	TX: Dallas	$29,360
MA: Boston	$54,380	TX: Houston	$29,550
MD: Baltimore	$38,580	WA: Seattle	$56,030

FACTORS THAT MAY AFFECT EARNINGS

Educational Attainment of Workers and Effect on Earnings

	Percent at Level	Effect on Earnings
Less than High School	5.8%	−24.1%
Some High School	15.8%	−8.8%
High School or Equivalent	48.3%	2.0%
Some College but No Degree	17.3%	4.6%
Associate Degree	8.9%	11.3%
Bachelor's Degree	3.7%	3.3%
Master's Degree	—	—
Doctoral Degree	—	—
First Professional Degree	—	—

Flexibility of Earnings

Average Hours Worked: 35
Workers with a Varying Number of Hours: 9.7%
Workers Earning Some Overtime Pay, Tips, or Commissions: 32.3%
Earnings Benefit of Working Overtime: −4.5%

Gender

	Male	Female
Percent	98.3%	1.7%
Effect on Earnings	−0.5%	—

Union Membership

Percentage Union Members: 26.0%
Earnings Benefit of Union Membership: 23.8%

Veteran Status

Percentage Who Have Been on Active Duty: 10.2%
Earnings Benefit of Veteran Status: 19.5%

47-2081 Drywall and Ceiling Tile Installers

Apply plasterboard or other wallboard to ceilings or interior walls of buildings. Apply or mount acoustical tiles or blocks, strips, or sheets of shock-absorbing materials to ceilings and walls of buildings to reduce or reflect sound. Materials may be of decorative quality. Includes lathers who fasten wooden, metal, or rockboard lath to walls, ceilings, or partitions of buildings to provide support base for plaster, fireproofing, or acoustical material.

- Education or Training Required: Moderate-term on-the-job training
- Job Growth: 9.0%
- Annual Openings: 17,000
- Self-Employed: 23.4%
- Part-Time: 16.8%

NATIONAL WAGE FIGURES (ANNUAL)

Beginning	25th Percentile	Median	Mean	75th Percentile	90th Percentile
$22,680	$28,290	$36,140	$38,810	$46,960	$60,010

Median Wages for Industries Employing Largest Numbers (Annual)

Industry	Median Income
Educational Services	$36,470
Specialty Trade Contractors	$36,240
Construction of Buildings	$35,890
Administrative and Support Services	$33,730
Nonmetallic Mineral Product Manufacturing	$32,800
Merchant Wholesalers, Durable Goods	$31,810
Real Estate	$29,820
Wood Product Manufacturing	$28,470

Median Wages for States (Annual)

AK $49,010	KY $31,750	NY $46,140
AL $27,460	LA $32,740	OH $31,640
AR $29,820	MA $52,390	OK $29,610
AZ $29,720	MD $35,660	OR $41,000
CA $44,680	ME $36,880	PA $34,100
CO $33,100	MI $38,760	RI no data
CT $48,860	MN $61,090	SC $27,620
DC $36,770	MO $45,070	SD $29,540
DE $35,560	MS $30,280	TN $31,350
FL $32,100	MT $23,570	TX $28,370
GA $33,350	NC $28,060	UT $33,290
HI $51,290	ND $29,200	VA $34,070
IA $37,450	NE $30,840	VT $34,480
ID $32,940	NH $37,300	WA $50,660
IL $55,140	NJ $44,340	WI $40,550
IN $34,870	NM $31,400	WV $32,790
KS $33,490	NV $41,280	WY $31,820

Median Wages for the Largest Metropolitan Areas (Annual)

AZ: Phoenix $30,180	MI: Detroit $46,180
CA: Los Angeles $43,440	MN: Minneapolis $64,940
CA: Riverside $40,230	MO: Kansas City $40,850
CA: Sacramento $45,360	MO: St. Louis $49,810
CA: San Diego $41,310	NV: Las Vegas $42,310
CA: San Francisco $59,740	NY: New York no data
CO: Denver $33,260	OH: Cincinnati $38,150
DC: Washington $37,070	OH: Cleveland $29,980
FL: Miami $33,950	OH: Columbus $31,690
FL: Orlando $32,660	OR: Portland $45,620
FL: Tampa $32,120	PA: Philadelphia $41,900
GA: Atlanta $34,350	PA: Pittsburgh $31,880
IL: Chicago $62,980	TX: Dallas $28,600
MA: Boston $51,330	TX: Houston $28,530
MD: Baltimore $30,550	WA: Seattle $54,190

FACTORS THAT MAY AFFECT EARNINGS

Educational Attainment of Workers and Effect on Earnings

Figures are based on a group of occupations: Construction Trades Workers

	Percent at Level	Effect on Earnings
Less than High School	9.3%	−26.6%
Some High School	15.0%	−17.6%
High School or Equivalent	35.8%	5.7%
Some College but No Degree	19.0%	4.7%
Associate Degree	12.4%	12.3%
Bachelor's Degree	7.1%	9.0%
Master's Degree	0.9%	2.3%
Doctoral Degree	—	—
First Professional Degree	—	—

Flexibility of Earnings

Average Hours Worked: 32
Workers with a Varying Number of Hours: 12.4%
Workers Earning Some Overtime Pay, Tips, or Commissions: 15.4%
Earnings Benefit of Working Overtime: -0.6%

Gender

	Male	Female
Percent	97.1%	2.9%
Effect on Earnings	0.4%	—

Union Membership

Percentage Union Members: 17.8%
Earnings Benefit of Union Membership: 42.3%

Veteran Status

Percentage Who Have Been on Active Duty: 10.2%
Earnings Benefit of Veteran Status: 19.5%

47-2082 Tapers

Seal joints between plasterboard or other wallboard to prepare wall surface for painting or papering.

- Education or Training Required: Moderate-term on-the-job training
- Job Growth: 5.9%
- Annual Openings: 5,000
- Self-Employed: 21.0%
- Part-Time: 16.8%

NATIONAL WAGE FIGURES (ANNUAL)

Beginning	25th Percentile	Median	Mean	75th Percentile	90th Percentile
$24,110	$30,480	$41,280	$42,590	$53,450	$64,970

Median Wages for Industries Employing Largest Numbers (Annual)

Industry	Median Income
Construction of Buildings	$41,420
Specialty Trade Contractors	$41,260
Professional, Scientific, and Technical Services	$33,550

Median Wages for States (Annual)

AK	no data	KY	$34,920	NY	no data
AL	$28,610	LA	$36,370	OH	$31,280
AR	$27,480	MA	no data	OK	$35,450
AZ	$29,350	MD	$36,890	OR	$43,010
CA	$47,440	ME	$39,820	PA	$41,700
CO	$32,860	MI	$46,560	RI	$40,590
CT	$51,410	MN	$56,250	SC	$30,750
DC	no data	MO	$52,140	SD	$30,010
DE	no data	MS	$28,190	TN	$33,780
FL	$32,710	MT	no data	TX	$24,970
GA	$38,550	NC	$30,110	UT	$39,700
HI	$56,700	ND	$27,920	VA	$32,320
IA	$39,080	NE	$36,490	VT	$32,540
ID	$35,150	NH	$46,180	WA	$42,960
IL	$60,940	NJ	$61,710	WI	$47,090
IN	$41,740	NM	$32,250	WV	$37,850
KS	$40,460	NV	$43,070	WY	no data

Median Wages for the Largest Metropolitan Areas (Annual)

AZ: Phoenix	$29,460	MI: Detroit	$48,750
CA: Los Angeles	$44,140	MN: Minneapolis	$57,080
CA: Riverside	$48,700	MO: Kansas City	$51,340
CA: Sacramento	$44,760	MO: St. Louis	$52,280
CA: San Diego	$42,600	NV: Las Vegas	$43,880
CA: San Francisco	$60,970	NY: New York	$64,860
CO: Denver	$32,050	OH: Cincinnati	$29,590
DC: Washington	$36,010	OH: Cleveland	$38,540
FL: Miami	$28,810	OH: Columbus	$32,660
FL: Orlando	$36,370	OR: Portland	$43,620
FL: Tampa	$31,210	PA: Philadelphia	$47,710
GA: Atlanta	no data	PA: Pittsburgh	$39,660
IL: Chicago	$61,850	TX: Dallas	$25,970
MA: Boston	no data	TX: Houston	$27,350
MD: Baltimore	$32,290	WA: Seattle	$47,220

FACTORS THAT MAY AFFECT EARNINGS

Educational Attainment of Workers and Effect on Earnings

Figures are based on a group of occupations: Construction Trades Workers

	Percent at Level	Effect on Earnings
Less than High School	9.3%	−26.6%
Some High School	15.0%	−17.6%
High School or Equivalent	35.8%	5.7%
Some College but No Degree	19.0%	4.7%
Associate Degree	12.4%	12.3%
Bachelor's Degree	7.1%	9.0%
Master's Degree	0.9%	2.3%
Doctoral Degree	—	—
First Professional Degree	—	—

Flexibility of Earnings

Average Hours Worked: 32
Workers with a Varying Number of Hours: 12.4%
Workers Earning Some Overtime Pay, Tips, or Commissions: 15.4%
Earnings Benefit of Working Overtime: −0.6%

Gender

	Male	Female
Percent	97.1%	2.9%
Effect on Earnings	0.4%	—

Union Membership

Percentage Union Members: 17.8%
Earnings Benefit of Union Membership: 42.3%

Veteran Status

Percentage Who Have Been on Active Duty: 10.2%
Earnings Benefit of Veteran Status: 19.5%

47-2111 Electricians

Install, maintain, and repair electrical wiring, equipment, and fixtures. Ensure that work is in accordance with relevant codes. May install or service street lights, intercom systems, or electrical control systems.

- Education or Training Required: Long-term on-the-job training
- Job Growth: 11.8%
- Annual Openings: 68,000
- Self-Employed: 9.5%
- Part-Time: 9.5%

NATIONAL WAGE FIGURES (ANNUAL)

Beginning	25th Percentile	Median	Mean	75th Percentile	90th Percentile
$26,530	$33,420	$43,610	$46,620	$57,650	$72,700

Median Wages for Industries Employing Largest Numbers (Annual)

Industry	Median Income
Transportation Equipment Manufacturing	$61,510
Utilities	$55,810
Management of Companies and Enterprises	$55,690
Paper Manufacturing	$51,260
Chemical Manufacturing	$49,190
Professional, Scientific, and Technical Services	$48,330
Federal, State, and Local Government	$48,290
Primary Metal Manufacturing	$47,160
Hospitals	$46,980
Mining (Except Oil and Gas)	$45,610

Median Wages for States (Annual)

AK	$63,560	KY	$39,960	NY	$54,190
AL	$34,770	LA	$38,820	OH	$45,680
AR	$36,250	MA	$52,220	OK	$39,880
AZ	$36,710	MD	$46,010	OR	$56,810
CA	$49,180	ME	$43,450	PA	$48,120
CO	$43,770	MI	$58,780	RI	$48,860
CT	$50,400	MN	$59,490	SC	$34,890
DC	$55,740	MO	$48,720	SD	$36,020
DE	$46,350	MS	$35,690	TN	$39,640
FL	$34,280	MT	$46,700	TX	$37,240
GA	$37,590	NC	$34,160	UT	$39,780
HI	$56,170	ND	$41,610	VA	$40,640
IA	$42,390	NE	$36,220	VT	$38,540
ID	$40,990	NH	$41,850	WA	$50,150
IL	$61,470	NJ	$55,580	WI	$48,920
IN	$51,100	NM	$38,430	WV	$40,870
KS	$44,080	NV	$47,410	WY	$44,230

Median Wages for the Largest Metropolitan Areas (Annual)

AZ: Phoenix	$35,590	MI: Detroit	$66,210
CA: Los Angeles	$46,060	MN: Minneapolis	$65,990
CA: Riverside	$40,370	MO: Kansas City	$50,400
CA: Sacramento	$44,750	MO: St. Louis	$59,470
CA: San Diego	$43,520	NV: Las Vegas	$48,350
CA: San Francisco	$69,600	NY: New York	$59,250
CO: Denver	$45,540	OH: Cincinnati	$42,960
DC: Washington	$48,100	OH: Cleveland	$53,030
FL: Miami	$36,250	OH: Columbus	$44,250
FL: Orlando	$32,180	OR: Portland	$59,390
FL: Tampa	$33,570	PA: Philadelphia	$56,120
GA: Atlanta	$39,900	PA: Pittsburgh	$52,150
IL: Chicago	$64,080	TX: Dallas	$37,730
MA: Boston	$53,580	TX: Houston	$40,290
MD: Baltimore	$44,740	WA: Seattle	$51,290

FACTORS THAT MAY AFFECT EARNINGS

Educational Attainment of Workers and Effect on Earnings

	Percent at Level	Effect on Earnings
Less than High School	1.9%	−48.0%
Some High School	7.0%	−19.5%
High School or Equivalent	34.1%	−0.2%
Some College but No Degree	24.8%	4.5%
Associate Degree	23.2%	4.7%
Bachelor's Degree	8.6%	1.5%
Master's Degree	—	—
Doctoral Degree	—	—
First Professional Degree	—	—

Flexibility of Earnings

Average Hours Worked: 37
Workers with a Varying Number of Hours: 6.1%
Workers Earning Some Overtime Pay, Tips, or Commissions: 21.6%
Earnings Benefit of Working Overtime: 1.8%

Gender

	Male	Female
Percent	98.1%	1.9%
Effect on Earnings	0.4%	—

Union Membership

Percentage Union Members: 31.3%
Earnings Benefit of Union Membership: 22.8%

Veteran Status

Percentage Who Have Been on Active Duty: 10.2%
Earnings Benefit of Veteran Status: 19.5%

47-2121 Glaziers

Install glass in windows, skylights, storefronts, and display cases or on surfaces such as building fronts, interior walls, ceilings, and table-tops.

- Education or Training Required: Long-term on-the-job training
- Job Growth: 14.2%
- Annual Openings: 9,000
- Self-Employed: 11.0%
- Part-Time: 30.8%

NATIONAL WAGE FIGURES (ANNUAL)

Beginning	25th Percentile	Median	Mean	75th Percentile	90th Percentile
$21,190	$26,730	$34,610	$38,060	$46,140	$63,490

Median Wages for Industries Employing Largest Numbers (Annual)

Industry	Median Income
Federal, State, and Local Government	$50,800
Fabricated Metal Product Manufacturing	$49,120
Educational Services	$46,750
Management of Companies and Enterprises	$39,700
Construction of Buildings	$37,670
Specialty Trade Contractors	$35,540
Building Material and Garden Equipment and Supplies Dealers	$32,270
Merchant Wholesalers, Durable Goods	$32,130
Nonmetallic Mineral Product Manufacturing	$32,130
Repair and Maintenance	$31,620

Median Wages for States (Annual)

State	Wage	State	Wage	State	Wage
AK	no data	KY	$28,990	NY	$39,770
AL	$27,940	LA	$28,090	OH	$33,970
AR	$24,760	MA	$36,960	OK	$24,640
AZ	$29,850	MD	$37,640	OR	$35,180
CA	$44,590	ME	$33,350	PA	$34,260
CO	$39,230	MI	$37,390	RI	$29,190
CT	$47,130	MN	$40,630	SC	$26,490
DC	no data	MO	$48,160	SD	$27,020
DE	$29,640	MS	$28,970	TN	$27,050
FL	$30,020	MT	$31,220	TX	$29,810
GA	$32,900	NC	$28,470	UT	$33,650
HI	$47,090	ND	$28,990	VA	$34,910
IA	$34,850	NE	$33,250	VT	$33,110
ID	$34,920	NH	$37,480	WA	$42,950
IL	$65,340	NJ	$44,950	WI	$43,270
IN	$36,900	NM	$29,720	WV	$34,180
KS	$31,180	NV	$42,430	WY	$28,790

Median Wages for the Largest Metropolitan Areas (Annual)

Area	Wage	Area	Wage
AZ: Phoenix	$30,100	MI: Detroit	$40,020
CA: Los Angeles	$41,670	MN: Minneapolis	$43,540
CA: Riverside	$47,250	MO: Kansas City	$39,640
CA: Sacramento	$36,740	MO: St. Louis	$60,060
CA: San Diego	$53,830	NV: Las Vegas	$49,430
CA: San Francisco	$71,530	NY: New York	$44,310
CO: Denver	$41,760	OH: Cincinnati	$28,610
DC: Washington	$41,280	OH: Cleveland	$39,430
FL: Miami	$32,340	OH: Columbus	$38,400
FL: Orlando	$28,420	OR: Portland	$42,190
FL: Tampa	$32,060	PA: Philadelphia	$44,170
GA: Atlanta	$33,500	PA: Pittsburgh	no data
IL: Chicago	$66,120	TX: Dallas	$34,200
MA: Boston	$37,440	TX: Houston	$35,880
MD: Baltimore	$37,460	WA: Seattle	$45,770

FACTORS THAT MAY AFFECT EARNINGS

Educational Attainment of Workers and Effect on Earnings

	Percent at Level	Effect on Earnings
Less than High School	—	—
Some High School	—	—
High School or Equivalent	55.8%	−8.4%
Some College but No Degree	18.6%	3.1%
Associate Degree	—	—
Bachelor's Degree	—	—
Master's Degree	—	—
Doctoral Degree	—	—
First Professional Degree	—	—

Figures do not total 100% because some levels have a very small sample size.

Flexibility of Earnings

Average Hours Worked: 38
Workers with a Varying Number of Hours: 4.4%
Workers Earning Some Overtime Pay, Tips, or Commissions: 14.6%
Earnings Benefit of Working Overtime: 10.1%

Gender

	Male	Female
Percent	93.2%	6.8%
Effect on Earnings	0.3%	−13.9%

Union Membership

Percentage Union Members: 25.0%
Earnings Benefit of Union Membership: 45.4%

Veteran Status

Percentage Who Have Been on Active Duty: 10.2%
Earnings Benefit of Veteran Status: 19.5%

47-2131 Insulation Workers, Floor, Ceiling, and Wall

Line and cover structures with insulating materials. May work with batt, roll, or blown insulation materials.

- Education or Training Required: Moderate-term on-the-job training
- Job Growth: 3.0%
- Annual Openings: 4,000
- Self-Employed: 11.0%
- Part-Time: 16.8%

NATIONAL WAGE FIGURES (ANNUAL)

Beginning	25th Percentile	Median	Mean	75th Percentile	90th Percentile
$19,240	$23,420	$30,510	$34,280	$41,600	$57,730

Median Wages for Industries Employing Largest Numbers (Annual)

Industry	Median Income
Waste Management and Remediation Services	$62,910
Fabricated Metal Product Manufacturing	$51,800
Educational Services	$46,350
Utilities	$41,260
Management of Companies and Enterprises	$38,330
Heavy and Civil Engineering Construction	$37,380
Professional, Scientific, and Technical Services	$35,640
Transportation Equipment Manufacturing	$35,440
Administrative and Support Services	$35,430
Construction of Buildings	$33,780

Median Wages for States (Annual)

State	Wage	State	Wage	State	Wage
AK	no data	KY	$29,170	NY	$49,310
AL	$24,390	LA	no data	OH	$29,050
AR	$21,620	MA	$36,300	OK	$27,990
AZ	$24,340	MD	$37,930	OR	$31,210
CA	$34,010	ME	no data	PA	$33,570
CO	$28,430	MI	$30,510	RI	$43,170
CT	no data	MN	no data	SC	$26,520
DC	no data	MO	$30,510	SD	no data
DE	$31,900	MS	$25,240	TN	$29,130
FL	$38,100	MT	$22,970	TX	$24,270
GA	$25,070	NC	$28,730	UT	$25,690
HI	no data	ND	$26,320	VA	$29,310
IA	$24,300	NE	$32,910	VT	$25,970
ID	$23,680	NH	$27,740	WA	$38,580
IL	$64,270	NJ	$47,640	WI	$33,900
IN	$25,080	NM	$25,510	WV	$33,220
KS	$32,270	NV	$32,380	WY	$25,310

Median Wages for the Largest Metropolitan Areas (Annual)

Area	Wage	Area	Wage
AZ: Phoenix	$24,110	MI: Detroit	no data
CA: Los Angeles	$33,360	MN: Minneapolis	$41,610
CA: Riverside	$28,080	MO: Kansas City	$34,290
CA: Sacramento	no data	MO: St. Louis	$43,940
CA: San Diego	$31,980	NV: Las Vegas	$31,960
CA: San Francisco	$48,330	NY: New York	$51,230
CO: Denver	$28,510	OH: Cincinnati	$35,680
DC: Washington	$30,210	OH: Cleveland	$37,030
FL: Miami	$53,660	OH: Columbus	$24,300
FL: Orlando	$37,880	OR: Portland	$40,340
FL: Tampa	$29,640	PA: Philadelphia	no data
GA: Atlanta	$25,200	PA: Pittsburgh	$36,470
IL: Chicago	$66,820	TX: Dallas	$25,510
MA: Boston	$35,800	TX: Houston	$24,820
MD: Baltimore	$38,160	WA: Seattle	$40,070

FACTORS THAT MAY AFFECT EARNINGS

Educational Attainment of Workers and Effect on Earnings

Figures are based on a group of occupations: Construction Trades Workers

	Percent at Level	Effect on Earnings
Less than High School	9.3%	−26.6%
Some High School	15.0%	−17.6%
High School or Equivalent	35.8%	5.7%
Some College but No Degree	19.0%	4.7%
Associate Degree	12.4%	12.3%
Bachelor's Degree	7.1%	9.0%
Master's Degree	0.9%	2.3%
Doctoral Degree	—	—
First Professional Degree	—	—

Flexibility of Earnings

Average Hours Worked: 32
Workers with a Varying Number of Hours: 12.4%
Workers Earning Some Overtime Pay, Tips, or Commissions: 15.4%
Earnings Benefit of Working Overtime: 10.1%

Gender

	Male	Female
Percent	96.6%	3.4%
Effect on Earnings	3.0%	—

Union Membership

Percentage Union Members: 17.8%
Earnings Benefit of Union Membership: 42.3%

Veteran Status

Percentage Who Have Been on Active Duty: 10.2%
Earnings Benefit of Veteran Status: 19.5%

47-2132 Insulation Workers, Mechanical

Apply insulating materials to pipes or ductwork or other mechanical systems to help control and maintain temperature.

- Education or Training Required: Moderate-term on-the-job training
- Job Growth: 1.0%
- Annual Openings: 2,000
- Self-Employed: 6.8%
- Part-Time: 16.8%

NATIONAL WAGE FIGURES (ANNUAL)

Beginning	25th Percentile	Median	Mean	75th Percentile	90th Percentile
$21,870	$28,190	$36,900	$41,740	$52,250	$69,450

Median Wages for Industries Employing Largest Numbers (Annual)

Industry	Median Income
Utilities	$59,170
Petroleum and Coal Products Manufacturing	$53,860
Federal, State, and Local Government	$49,820
Repair and Maintenance	$41,740
Waste Management and Remediation Services	$39,520
Specialty Trade Contractors	$36,880
Professional, Scientific, and Technical Services	$35,620
Heavy and Civil Engineering Construction	$35,530
Support Activities for Mining	$35,430
Construction of Buildings	$33,400

Median Wages for States (Annual)

State	Wage	State	Wage	State	Wage
AK	$54,600	KY	$45,230	NY	$62,310
AL	$33,740	LA	$33,870	OH	$43,550
AR	$34,560	MA	no data	OK	$21,130
AZ	$30,890	MD	$34,070	OR	no data
CA	$43,170	ME	$33,380	PA	$66,490
CO	$32,640	MI	$38,570	RI	$49,580
CT	no data	MN	no data	SC	$29,060
DC	$39,630	MO	$55,480	SD	no data
DE	$40,960	MS	$25,980	TN	$36,050
FL	$33,200	MT	no data	TX	$32,600
GA	$29,940	NC	$29,490	UT	$30,370
HI	no data	ND	$32,990	VA	$31,930
IA	$32,300	NE	$31,940	VT	$35,270
ID	$36,000	NH	$29,560	WA	$52,250
IL	$50,920	NJ	no data	WI	$52,000
IN	$59,780	NM	$36,020	WV	$52,470
KS	$37,680	NV	$55,840	WY	$35,270

Median Wages for the Largest Metropolitan Areas (Annual)

Metro	Wage	Metro	Wage
AZ: Phoenix	$31,550	MI: Detroit	$61,430
CA: Los Angeles	$41,800	MN: Minneapolis	$72,140
CA: Riverside	no data	MO: Kansas City	$54,300
CA: Sacramento	$44,780	MO: St. Louis	$58,240
CA: San Diego	$67,090	NV: Las Vegas	$59,860
CA: San Francisco	no data	NY: New York	no data
CO: Denver	$34,430	OH: Cincinnati	$44,310
DC: Washington	$37,620	OH: Cleveland	no data
FL: Miami	$38,340	OH: Columbus	no data
FL: Orlando	$34,870	OR: Portland	no data
FL: Tampa	$33,020	PA: Philadelphia	$57,690
GA: Atlanta	$33,870	PA: Pittsburgh	no data
IL: Chicago	$52,480	TX: Dallas	$31,600
MA: Boston	no data	TX: Houston	$33,760
MD: Baltimore	$34,090	WA: Seattle	no data

FACTORS THAT MAY AFFECT EARNINGS

Educational Attainment of Workers and Effect on Earnings

Figures are based on a group of occupations: Construction Trades Workers

	Percent at Level	Effect on Earnings
Less than High School	9.3%	−26.6%
Some High School	15.0%	−17.6%
High School or Equivalent	35.8%	5.7%
Some College but No Degree	19.0%	4.7%
Associate Degree	12.4%	12.3%
Bachelor's Degree	7.1%	9.0%
Master's Degree	0.9%	2.3%
Doctoral Degree	—	—
First Professional Degree	—	—

Flexibility of Earnings

Average Hours Worked: 32
Workers with a Varying Number of Hours: 12.4%
Workers Earning Some Overtime Pay, Tips, or Commissions: 15.4%
Earnings Benefit of Working Overtime: 10.1%

Gender

	Male	Female
Percent	96.6%	3.4%
Effect on Earnings	3.0%	—

Union Membership

Percentage Union Members: 17.8%
Earnings Benefit of Union Membership: 42.3%

Veteran Status

Percentage Who Have Been on Active Duty: 10.2%
Earnings Benefit of Veteran Status: 19.5%

47-2141 Painters, Construction and Maintenance

Paint walls, equipment, buildings, bridges, and other structural surfaces, using brushes, rollers, and spray guns. May remove old paint to prepare surface prior to painting. May mix colors or oils to obtain desired color or consistency.

- Education or Training Required: Moderate-term on-the-job training
- Job Growth: 12.6%
- Annual Openings: 102,000
- Self-Employed: 44.6%
- Part-Time: 21.9%

Note: A large fraction of the workforce for this occupation is self-employed and earns an average of $35,420. All other earnings figures for this occupation are based on workers who are paid a wage or salary.

NATIONAL WAGE FIGURES (ANNUAL)

Beginning	25th Percentile	Median	Mean	75th Percentile	90th Percentile
$20,740	$25,340	$31,190	$34,220	$40,580	$53,280

Median Wages for Industries Employing Largest Numbers (Annual)

Industry	Median Income
Utilities	$61,030
Primary Metal Manufacturing	$43,520
Federal, State, and Local Government	$42,830
Hospitals	$40,300
Management of Companies and Enterprises	$39,820
Waste Management and Remediation Services	$38,100
Educational Services	$37,440
Accommodation	$37,370
Transportation Equipment Manufacturing	$35,090
Miscellaneous Manufacturing	$32,660

Median Wages for States (Annual)

State	Wage	State	Wage	State	Wage
AK	$41,140	KY	$28,040	NY	$38,620
AL	$26,080	LA	$29,110	OH	$32,790
AR	$26,780	MA	$38,950	OK	$27,970
AZ	$28,410	MD	$33,290	OR	$31,490
CA	$35,550	ME	$32,710	PA	$36,100
CO	$32,950	MI	$37,950	RI	$31,150
CT	$36,790	MN	$36,640	SC	$27,970
DC	$39,530	MO	$35,070	SD	$24,680
DE	$34,460	MS	$27,670	TN	$27,260
FL	$27,520	MT	$28,370	TX	$26,330
GA	$28,190	NC	$27,120	UT	$29,520
HI	$43,210	ND	$28,060	VA	$30,270
IA	$31,220	NE	$27,450	VT	$30,150
ID	$24,450	NH	$29,960	WA	$34,220
IL	$39,550	NJ	$35,060	WI	$33,550
IN	$31,220	NM	$28,250	WV	$30,210
KS	$28,750	NV	$38,330	WY	$27,780

Median Wages for the Largest Metropolitan Areas (Annual)

Area	Wage	Area	Wage
AZ: Phoenix	$28,780	MI: Detroit	$44,250
CA: Los Angeles	$34,930	MN: Minneapolis	$38,050
CA: Riverside	$28,400	MO: Kansas City	$29,550
CA: Sacramento	$41,170	MO: St. Louis	$46,930
CA: San Diego	$34,040	NV: Las Vegas	$39,580
CA: San Francisco	$43,190	NY: New York	$38,480
CO: Denver	$33,930	OH: Cincinnati	$34,310
DC: Washington	$33,190	OH: Cleveland	$34,080
FL: Miami	$28,140	OH: Columbus	$29,300
FL: Orlando	$27,030	OR: Portland	$33,760
FL: Tampa	$26,940	PA: Philadelphia	$38,430
GA: Atlanta	$28,720	PA: Pittsburgh	$48,530
IL: Chicago	$40,490	TX: Dallas	$27,430
MA: Boston	$40,420	TX: Houston	$26,650
MD: Baltimore	$33,850	WA: Seattle	$35,740

FACTORS THAT MAY AFFECT EARNINGS

Educational Attainment of Workers and Effect on Earnings

	Percent at Level	Effect on Earnings
Less than High School	11.1%	−23.0%
Some High School	20.7%	−26.2%
High School or Equivalent	37.5%	17.5%
Some College but No Degree	17.3%	9.8%
Associate Degree	7.1%	−16.2%
Bachelor's Degree	5.3%	17.0%
Master's Degree	—	—
Doctoral Degree	—	—
First Professional Degree	—	—

Flexibility of Earnings

Average Hours Worked: 29
Workers with a Varying Number of Hours: 16.1%
Workers Earning Some Overtime Pay, Tips, or Commissions: 7.9%
Earnings Benefit of Working Overtime: 11.3%

Gender

	Male	Female
Percent	92.3%	7.7%
Effect on Earnings	0.2%	—

Union Membership

Percentage Union Members: 9.1%
Earnings Benefit of Union Membership: 43.6%

Veteran Status

Percentage Who Have Been on Active Duty: 10.2%
Earnings Benefit of Veteran Status: 19.5%

47-2142 Paperhangers

Cover interior walls and ceilings of rooms with decorative wallpaper or fabric or attach advertising posters on surfaces such as walls and billboards. Duties include removing old materials from surface to be papered.

- Education or Training Required: Moderate-term on-the-job training
- Job Growth: 3.2%
- Annual Openings: 3,000
- Self-Employed: 43.9%
- Part-Time: 40.0%

Note: Earnings figures do not reflect self-employed workers, who make up a large fraction of the workforce for this occupation.

NATIONAL WAGE FIGURES (ANNUAL)

Beginning	25th Percentile	Median	Mean	75th Percentile	90th Percentile
$21,500	$27,280	$33,710	$36,230	$42,880	$55,680

Median Wages for Industries Employing Largest Numbers (Annual)

Industry	Median Income
Construction of Buildings	$50,840
Specialty Trade Contractors	$34,550
Administrative and Support Services	$33,700
Professional, Scientific, and Technical Services	$30,860
Miscellaneous Manufacturing	$30,030

Median Wages for States (Annual)

State		State		State	
AK	no data	KY	$35,010	NY	$38,200
AL	$23,030	LA	no data	OH	$35,690
AR	no data	MA	$38,760	OK	$33,050
AZ	$46,530	MD	$31,220	OR	$33,770
CA	$40,050	ME	$28,510	PA	$32,620
CO	$32,370	MI	$26,920	RI	no data
CT	$41,440	MN	$37,370	SC	$27,620
DC	no data	MO	$39,420	SD	no data
DE	no data	MS	no data	TN	no data
FL	$31,680	MT	$22,860	TX	$24,540
GA	$34,880	NC	$27,830	UT	no data
HI	no data	ND	no data	VA	$36,630
IA	no data	NE	no data	VT	no data
ID	no data	NH	no data	WA	$44,970
IL	$31,920	NJ	$49,460	WI	$33,830
IN	$41,080	NM	no data	WV	$26,540
KS	no data	NV	$50,750	WY	no data

Median Wages for the Largest Metropolitan Areas (Annual)

Area		Area	
AZ: Phoenix	$46,530	MI: Detroit	$33,490
CA: Los Angeles	no data	MN: Minneapolis	no data
CA: Riverside	no data	MO: Kansas City	$37,290
CA: Sacramento	no data	MO: St. Louis	no data
CA: San Diego	no data	NV: Las Vegas	$53,810
CA: San Francisco	$69,590	NY: New York	$41,200
CO: Denver	no data	OH: Cincinnati	$42,360
DC: Washington	$40,180	OH: Cleveland	$47,930
FL: Miami	no data	OH: Columbus	no data
FL: Orlando	no data	OR: Portland	$33,700
FL: Tampa	no data	PA: Philadelphia	$43,830
GA: Atlanta	$35,130	PA: Pittsburgh	no data
IL: Chicago	$32,810	TX: Dallas	$31,990
MA: Boston	no data	TX: Houston	$29,120
MD: Baltimore	$31,470	WA: Seattle	no data

FACTORS THAT MAY AFFECT EARNINGS

Educational Attainment of Workers and Effect on Earnings

Figures are based on a group of occupations: Construction Trades Workers

	Percent at Level	Effect on Earnings
Less than High School	9.3%	−26.6%
Some High School	15.0%	−17.6%
High School or Equivalent	35.8%	5.7%
Some College but No Degree	19.0%	4.7%
Associate Degree	12.4%	12.3%
Bachelor's Degree	7.1%	9.0%
Master's Degree	0.9%	2.3%
Doctoral Degree	—	—
First Professional Degree	—	—

Flexibility of Earnings

Average Hours Worked: 36
Workers with a Varying Number of Hours: 16.1%
Workers Earning Some Overtime Pay, Tips, or Commissions: 15.4%
Earnings Benefit of Working Overtime: 10.1%

Gender

	Male	Female
Percent	78.1%	21.9%
Effect on Earnings	0.3%	−13.9%

Union Membership

Percentage Union Members: 17.8%
Earnings Benefit of Union Membership: 42.3%

Veteran Status

Percentage Who Have Been on Active Duty: 10.2%
Earnings Benefit of Veteran Status: 19.5%

47-2151 Pipelayers

Lay pipe for storm or sanitation sewers, drains, and water mains. Perform any combination of the following tasks: Grade trenches or culverts, position pipe, or seal joints.

- Education or Training Required: Moderate-term on-the-job training
- Job Growth: 9.9%
- Annual Openings: 7,000
- Self-Employed: 11.9%
- Part-Time: 16.8%

NATIONAL WAGE FIGURES (ANNUAL)

Beginning	25th Percentile	Median	Mean	75th Percentile	90th Percentile
$20,240	$24,440	$30,330	$33,710	$41,100	$53,510

Median Wages for Industries Employing Largest Numbers (Annual)

Industry	Median Income
Computer and Electronic Product Manufacturing	$48,450
Utilities	$36,950
Professional, Scientific, and Technical Services	$35,640
Nonmetallic Mineral Product Manufacturing	$32,230
Support Activities for Mining	$32,070
Specialty Trade Contractors	$31,220
Federal, State, and Local Government	$30,370
Construction of Buildings	$29,620
Heavy and Civil Engineering Construction	$29,620
Administrative and Support Services	$28,040

Median Wages for States (Annual)

State	Wage	State	Wage	State	Wage
AK	$63,610	KY	$32,410	NY	$42,170
AL	$27,220	LA	$26,910	OH	$38,600
AR	$25,700	MA	$45,370	OK	$23,360
AZ	$29,750	MD	$31,850	OR	$40,840
CA	$42,710	ME	$29,230	PA	$34,570
CO	$32,210	MI	$35,200	RI	$52,190
CT	$45,090	MN	$49,830	SC	$28,470
DC	$32,410	MO	$37,380	SD	$28,350
DE	$35,060	MS	$22,890	TN	$27,730
FL	$27,590	MT	$28,700	TX	$24,210
GA	$26,480	NC	$25,440	UT	$28,260
HI	$38,450	ND	$27,360	VA	$30,650
IA	$30,150	NE	$31,370	VT	$35,020
ID	$33,960	NH	$37,930	WA	$48,480
IL	$59,050	NJ	$51,460	WI	$48,510
IN	$40,630	NM	$28,360	WV	$36,060
KS	$34,240	NV	$37,710	WY	$27,860

Median Wages for the Largest Metropolitan Areas (Annual)

Area	Wage	Area	Wage
AZ: Phoenix	$29,570	MI: Detroit	$38,150
CA: Los Angeles	$42,710	MN: Minneapolis	$51,100
CA: Riverside	$41,950	MO: Kansas City	$45,720
CA: Sacramento	$43,350	MO: St. Louis	$47,080
CA: San Diego	$43,780	NV: Las Vegas	$36,070
CA: San Francisco	$50,160	NY: New York	$49,960
CO: Denver	$32,890	OH: Cincinnati	$39,720
DC: Washington	$33,960	OH: Cleveland	$42,470
FL: Miami	$29,040	OH: Columbus	$35,070
FL: Orlando	$25,500	OR: Portland	$44,240
FL: Tampa	$27,830	PA: Philadelphia	$34,400
GA: Atlanta	$27,960	PA: Pittsburgh	$44,020
IL: Chicago	$61,470	TX: Dallas	$24,660
MA: Boston	$46,920	TX: Houston	$24,710
MD: Baltimore	$29,250	WA: Seattle	$49,120

FACTORS THAT MAY AFFECT EARNINGS

Educational Attainment of Workers and Effect on Earnings

Figures are based on a group of occupations: Construction Trades Workers

	Percent at Level	Effect on Earnings
Less than High School	9.3%	−26.6%
Some High School	15.0%	−17.6%
High School or Equivalent	35.8%	5.7%
Some College but No Degree	19.0%	4.7%
Associate Degree	12.4%	12.3%
Bachelor's Degree	7.1%	9.0%
Master's Degree	0.9%	2.3%
Doctoral Degree	—	—
First Professional Degree	—	—

Flexibility of Earnings

Average Hours Worked: 32
Workers with a Varying Number of Hours: 12.4%
Workers Earning Some Overtime Pay, Tips, or Commissions: 15.4%
Earnings Benefit of Working Overtime: −0.4%

Gender

	Male	Female
Percent	98.2%	1.8%
Effect on Earnings	0.3%	−13.9%

Union Membership

Percentage Union Members: 17.8%
Earnings Benefit of Union Membership: 42.3%

Veteran Status

Percentage Who Have Been on Active Duty: 10.2%
Earnings Benefit of Veteran Status: 19.5%

47-2152 Plumbers, Pipefitters, and Steamfitters

Assemble, install, alter, and repair pipelines or pipe systems that carry water, steam, air, or other liquids or gases. May install heating and cooling equipment and mechanical control systems.

- Education or Training Required: Long-term on-the-job training
- Job Growth: 15.7%
- Annual Openings: 61,000
- Self-Employed: 13.3%
- Part-Time: 16.8%

NATIONAL WAGE FIGURES (ANNUAL)

	25th			75th	90th
Beginning	Percentile	Median	Mean	Percentile	Percentile
$25,580	$32,490	$42,770	$45,830	$57,280	$72,360

Median Wages for Industries Employing Largest Numbers (Annual)

Industry	Median Income
Management of Companies and Enterprises.....................	$55,040
Transportation Equipment Manufacturing.......................	$53,970
Primary Metal Manufacturing	$52,530
Paper Manufacturing	$52,510
Chemical Manufacturing..	$52,010
Utilities	$51,550
Pipeline Transportation	$49,800
Petroleum and Coal Products Manufacturing	$48,940
Hospitals	$47,010
Educational Services	$45,580

Median Wages for States (Annual)

AK............	$59,290	KY	$42,310	NY	$52,980
AL	$33,170	LA	$39,250	OH	$45,890
AR	$33,240	MA..............	$53,420	OK	$34,620
AZ	$35,920	MD	$47,000	OR	$56,940
CA	$44,730	ME	$40,530	PA	$47,080
CO	$42,610	MI	$54,220	RI..............	$45,540
CT	$53,270	MN	$58,120	SC..............	$33,260
DC	$52,970	MO	$49,750	SD	$34,300
DE	$44,850	MS	$29,670	TN	$36,150
FL	$33,940	MT	$45,980	TX	$36,880
GA	$35,950	NC	$33,430	UT	$43,330
HI	$46,180	ND	$40,550	VA	$37,600
IA	$41,600	NE	$47,210	VT	$37,250
ID	$40,470	NH	$41,870	WA	$51,740
IL	$66,710	NJ	$53,260	WI	$56,120
IN	$51,230	NM	$35,410	WV	$39,240
KS	$43,990	NV	$40,890	WY	$41,800

Median Wages for the Largest Metropolitan Areas (Annual)

AZ: Phoenix............	$35,950	MI: Detroit	$60,160
CA: Los Angeles	$41,440	MN: Minneapolis	$62,930
CA: Riverside	$35,720	MO: Kansas City........	$49,280
CA: Sacramento	$45,770	MO: St. Louis............	$61,180
CA: San Diego	$44,960	NV: Las Vegas	$39,860
CA: San Francisco....	$60,340	NY: New York............	$55,530
CO: Denver	$41,620	OH: Cincinnati..........	$40,750
DC: Washington	$46,000	OH: Cleveland	$58,200
FL: Miami	$35,900	OH: Columbus	$43,500
FL: Orlando	$33,980	OR: Portland	$59,870
FL: Tampa	$33,380	PA: Philadelphia	$48,850
GA: Atlanta	$38,620	PA: Pittsburgh	$54,050
IL: Chicago	$68,840	TX: Dallas	$39,030
MA: Boston	$55,620	TX: Houston	$39,710
MD: Baltimore	$45,910	WA: Seattle	$54,010

FACTORS THAT MAY AFFECT EARNINGS

Educational Attainment of Workers and Effect on Earnings

Figures are based on a group of occupations: Construction Trades Workers

	Percent at Level	Effect on Earnings
Less than High School	9.3%	−26.6%
Some High School	15.0%	−17.6%
High School or Equivalent	35.8%	5.7%
Some College but No Degree	19.0%	4.7%
Associate Degree	12.4%	12.3%
Bachelor's Degree	7.1%	9.0%
Master's Degree	0.9%	2.3%
Doctoral Degree	—	—
First Professional Degree	—	—

Flexibility of Earnings

Average Hours Worked: 32
Workers with a Varying Number of Hours: 12.4%
Workers Earning Some Overtime Pay, Tips, or Commissions: 15.4%
Earnings Benefit of Working Overtime: −0.4%

Gender

	Male	Female
Percent	98.2%	1.8%
Effect on Earnings	0.3%	−13.9%

Union Membership

Percentage Union Members: 17.8%
Earnings Benefit of Union Membership: 42.3%

Veteran Status

Percentage Who Have Been on Active Duty: 10.2%
Earnings Benefit of Veteran Status: 19.5%

47-2161 Plasterers and Stucco Masons

Apply interior or exterior plaster, cement, stucco, or similar materials. May also set ornamental plaster.

- Education or Training Required: Long-term on-the-job training
- Job Growth: 8.2%
- Annual Openings: 6,000
- Self-Employed: 5.0%
- Part-Time: 17.8%

NATIONAL WAGE FIGURES (ANNUAL)

Beginning	25th Percentile	Median	Mean	75th Percentile	90th Percentile
$22,540	$28,130	$34,700	$37,260	$44,200	$56,810

Median Wages for Industries Employing Largest Numbers (Annual)

Industry	Median Income
Federal, State, and Local Government	$54,090
Hospitals	$43,230
Educational Services	$36,690
Construction of Buildings	$35,200
Administrative and Support Services	$35,100
Specialty Trade Contractors	$34,540
Nonmetallic Mineral Product Manufacturing	$29,140

Median Wages for States (Annual)

State	Wage	State	Wage	State	Wage
AK	no data	KY	$36,320	NY	$45,900
AL	$32,840	LA	$32,040	OH	$41,060
AR	$35,070	MA	$45,860	OK	$36,020
AZ	$26,450	MD	$31,760	OR	$35,630
CA	$37,060	ME	no data	PA	$40,620
CO	$30,440	MI	$52,180	RI	$37,100
CT	$48,340	MN	$56,680	SC	$32,340
DC	$39,270	MO	$40,490	SD	$21,280
DE	$38,170	MS	$27,200	TN	$31,550
FL	$34,270	MT	$35,500	TX	$28,790
GA	$28,850	NC	$28,190	UT	$29,270
HI	$54,450	ND	$38,870	VA	$32,510
IA	$31,910	NE	$37,790	VT	no data
ID	$28,050	NH	$41,680	WA	$52,210
IL	$54,420	NJ	$38,920	WI	$36,910
IN	$47,620	NM	$30,880	WV	no data
KS	$35,190	NV	$34,770	WY	no data

Median Wages for the Largest Metropolitan Areas (Annual)

Area	Wage	Area	Wage
AZ: Phoenix	$26,250	MI: Detroit	$59,980
CA: Los Angeles	$34,680	MN: Minneapolis	$57,920
CA: Riverside	$37,740	MO: Kansas City	$40,570
CA: Sacramento	$33,480	MO: St. Louis	$52,430
CA: San Diego	$41,490	NV: Las Vegas	$35,700
CA: San Francisco	$49,140	NY: New York	$46,260
CO: Denver	$31,070	OH: Cincinnati	$37,710
DC: Washington	$32,440	OH: Cleveland	$41,080
FL: Miami	$35,700	OH: Columbus	no data
FL: Orlando	$33,000	OR: Portland	$36,120
FL: Tampa	$33,760	PA: Philadelphia	$40,100
GA: Atlanta	no data	PA: Pittsburgh	$42,690
IL: Chicago	no data	TX: Dallas	$33,570
MA: Boston	$47,100	TX: Houston	$27,200
MD: Baltimore	$36,690	WA: Seattle	$56,180

FACTORS THAT MAY AFFECT EARNINGS

Educational Attainment of Workers and Effect on Earnings

	Percent at Level	Effect on Earnings
Less than High School	28.1%	−18.7%
Some High School	26.3%	−5.0%
High School or Equivalent	29.8%	24.7%
Some College but No Degree	—	—
Associate Degree	—	—
Bachelor's Degree	—	—
Master's Degree	—	—
Doctoral Degree	—	—
First Professional Degree	—	—

Figures do not total 100% because some levels have a very small sample size.

Flexibility of Earnings

Average Hours Worked: 32
Workers with a Varying Number of Hours: 12.3%
Workers Earning Some Overtime Pay, Tips, or Commissions: 5.3%
Earnings Benefit of Working Overtime: 10.1%

Gender

	Male	Female
Percent	98.0%	2.0%
Effect on Earnings	0.6%	—

Union Membership

Percentage Union Members: 13.2%
Earnings Benefit of Union Membership: 82.1%

Veteran Status

Percentage Who Have Been on Active Duty: 10.2%
Earnings Benefit of Veteran Status: 19.5%

47-2171 Reinforcing Iron and Rebar Workers

Position and secure steel bars or mesh in concrete forms to reinforce concrete. Use a variety of fasteners, rod-bending machines, blowtorches, and hand tools.

- Education or Training Required: Long-term on-the-job training
- Job Growth: 14.1%
- Annual Openings: 6,000
- Self-Employed: 2.3%
- Part-Time: 16.7%

NATIONAL WAGE FIGURES (ANNUAL)

Beginning	25th Percentile	Median	Mean	75th Percentile	90th Percentile
$21,310	$27,350	$38,220	$42,330	$56,230	$71,030

Median Wages for Industries Employing Largest Numbers (Annual)

Industry	Median Income
Administrative and Support Services	$39,710
Specialty Trade Contractors	$39,320
Construction of Buildings	$38,640
Merchant Wholesalers, Durable Goods	$36,470
Fabricated Metal Product Manufacturing	$35,650
Heavy and Civil Engineering Construction	$32,860
Primary Metal Manufacturing	$28,470
Nonmetallic Mineral Product Manufacturing	$24,010

Median Wages for States (Annual)

AK .... no data	KY $37,270	NY $60,870
AL $29,480	LA $41,580	OH $53,150
AR $30,950	MA .... no data	OK $30,240
AZ $29,250	MD $39,130	OR $69,440
CA $50,040	ME .... no data	PA $54,410
CO $29,980	MI $51,110	RI .... no data
CT .... no data	MN $56,200	SC $28,290
DC .... no data	MO $47,340	SD $30,090
DE $36,540	MS $29,690	TN $32,990
FL $30,900	MT $32,670	TX $26,620
GA $30,810	NC $27,820	UT $36,950
HI $59,390	ND .... no data	VA $39,000
IA $44,360	NE .... no data	VT $22,940
ID $45,340	NH $33,730	WA $62,180
IL $71,290	NJ $71,470	WI $45,500
IN $40,320	NM $23,240	WV $52,720
KS $34,630	NV .... no data	WY .... no data

Median Wages for the Largest Metropolitan Areas (Annual)

AZ: Phoenix	$30,020	MI: Detroit	$48,880
CA: Los Angeles	$40,350	MN: Minneapolis	$58,450
CA: Riverside	$55,470	MO: Kansas City	$38,170
CA: Sacramento	$36,140	MO: St. Louis	$58,400
CA: San Diego	$39,200	NV: Las Vegas	no data
CA: San Francisco	$62,210	NY: New York	$68,880
CO: Denver	$27,310	OH: Cincinnati	$52,630
DC: Washington	$43,570	OH: Cleveland	$54,350
FL: Miami	$31,730	OH: Columbus	no data
FL: Orlando	$32,830	OR: Portland	$70,060
FL: Tampa	$31,020	PA: Philadelphia	$60,160
GA: Atlanta	$31,480	PA: Pittsburgh	$58,550
IL: Chicago	$71,410	TX: Dallas	$25,400
MA: Boston	no data	TX: Houston	$27,150
MD: Baltimore	$39,400	WA: Seattle	no data

FACTORS THAT MAY AFFECT EARNINGS

Educational Attainment of Workers and Effect on Earnings

Figures are based on a group of occupations: Construction Trades Workers

	Percent at Level	Effect on Earnings
Less than High School	9.3%	−26.6%
Some High School	15.0%	−17.6%
High School or Equivalent	35.8%	5.7%
Some College but No Degree	19.0%	4.7%
Associate Degree	12.4%	12.3%
Bachelor's Degree	7.1%	9.0%
Master's Degree	0.9%	2.3%
Doctoral Degree	—	—
First Professional Degree	—	—

Flexibility of Earnings

Average Hours Worked: 29
Workers with a Varying Number of Hours: 12.5%
Workers Earning Some Overtime Pay, Tips, or Commissions: 15.4%
Earnings Benefit of Working Overtime: 10.1%

Gender

	Male	Female
Percent	96.6%	3.4%
Effect on Earnings	0.3%	−13.9%

Union Membership

Percentage Union Members: 28.6%
Earnings Benefit of Union Membership: 42.3%

Veteran Status

Percentage Who Have Been on Active Duty: 10.2%
Earnings Benefit of Veteran Status: 19.5%

47-2181 Roofers

Cover roofs of structures with shingles, slate, asphalt, aluminum, wood, and related materials. May spray roofs, sidings, and walls with material to bind, seal, insulate, or soundproof sections of structures.

- Education or Training Required: Moderate-term on-the-job training
- Job Growth: 16.8%
- Annual Openings: 38,000
- Self-Employed: 23.8%
- Part-Time: 11.7%

NATIONAL WAGE FIGURES (ANNUAL)

Beginning	25th Percentile	Median	Mean	75th Percentile	90th Percentile
$20,390	$25,210	$32,260	$35,340	$43,250	$55,720

Median Wages for Industries Employing Largest Numbers (Annual)

Industry	Median Income
Professional, Scientific, and Technical Services	$66,540
Federal, State, and Local Government	$47,300
Merchant Wholesalers, Durable Goods	$40,240
Educational Services	$40,090
Administrative and Support Services	$39,050
Specialty Trade Contractors	$32,250
Construction of Buildings	$29,330
Petroleum and Coal Products Manufacturing	$28,720
Wood Product Manufacturing	$28,190
Real Estate	$27,950

Median Wages for States (Annual)

AK	$45,580	KY	$28,760	NY	$36,420
AL	$25,190	LA	$28,020	OH	$32,780
AR	$29,170	MA	$44,960	OK	$27,080
AZ	$28,770	MD	$36,470	OR	$30,360
CA	$41,400	ME	$28,430	PA	$34,300
CO	$28,350	MI	$35,630	RI	$33,610
CT	$37,420	MN	$48,110	SC	$24,700
DC	no data	MO	$36,430	SD	$22,630
DE	$32,690	MS	$25,230	TN	$28,460
FL	$29,130	MT	$29,140	TX	$25,370
GA	$28,740	NC	$26,410	UT	$30,770
HI	$43,790	ND	$30,020	VA	$30,090
IA	$28,850	NE	$28,520	VT	$28,830
ID	$31,870	NH	$31,090	WA	$39,700
IL	$51,970	NJ	$40,200	WI	$33,260
IN	$31,550	NM	$24,440	WV	$22,910
KS	$25,630	NV	$34,920	WY	$27,720

Median Wages for the Largest Metropolitan Areas (Annual)

AZ: Phoenix	$28,250	MI: Detroit	$46,170
CA: Los Angeles	$41,040	MN: Minneapolis	$54,580
CA: Riverside	$38,100	MO: Kansas City	$41,480
CA: Sacramento	$43,410	MO: St. Louis	$39,900
CA: San Diego	$41,850	NV: Las Vegas	$35,870
CA: San Francisco	$41,490	NY: New York	$39,060
CO: Denver	$27,280	OH: Cincinnati	$31,910
DC: Washington	$34,320	OH: Cleveland	$31,910
FL: Miami	$31,170	OH: Columbus	$33,820
FL: Orlando	$27,690	OR: Portland	$34,600
FL: Tampa	$27,700	PA: Philadelphia	$39,860
GA: Atlanta	$30,280	PA: Pittsburgh	$32,190
IL: Chicago	$57,110	TX: Dallas	$27,040
MA: Boston	no data	TX: Houston	$28,710
MD: Baltimore	$38,840	WA: Seattle	$46,540

FACTORS THAT MAY AFFECT EARNINGS

Educational Attainment of Workers and Effect on Earnings

	Percent at Level	Effect on Earnings
Less than High School	21.0%	−21.1%
Some High School	17.3%	−12.5%
High School or Equivalent	40.7%	14.4%
Some College but No Degree	14.2%	−5.1%
Associate Degree	—	—
Bachelor's Degree	—	—
Master's Degree	—	—
Doctoral Degree	—	—
First Professional Degree	—	—

Figures do not total 100% because some levels have a very small sample size.

Flexibility of Earnings

Average Hours Worked: 28
Workers with a Varying Number of Hours: 18.3%
Workers Earning Some Overtime Pay, Tips, or Commissions: 10.0%
Earnings Benefit of Working Overtime: 6.8%

Gender

	Male	Female
Percent	98.9%	1.1%
Effect on Earnings	0.2%	—

Union Membership

Percentage Union Members: 8.0%
Earnings Benefit of Union Membership: 43.1%

Veteran Status

Percentage Who Have Been on Active Duty: 10.2%
Earnings Benefit of Veteran Status: 19.5%

47-2211 Sheet Metal Workers

Fabricate, assemble, install, and repair sheet metal products and equipment, such as ducts, control boxes, drainpipes, and furnace casings. Work may involve any of the following: setting up and operating fabricating machines to cut, bend, and straighten sheet metal; shaping metal over anvils, blocks, or forms, using hammer; operating soldering and welding equipment to join sheet metal parts; and inspecting, assembling, and smoothing seams and joints of burred surfaces.

- Education or Training Required: Long-term on-the-job training
- Job Growth: 12.2%
- Annual Openings: 50,000
- Self-Employed: 4.9%
- Part-Time: 3.0%

NATIONAL WAGE FIGURES (ANNUAL)

Beginning	25th Percentile	Median	Mean	75th Percentile	90th Percentile
$21,540	$27,660	$37,360	$40,780	$51,760	$67,180

Median Wages for Industries Employing Largest Numbers (Annual)

Industry	Median Income
Hospitals	$59,250
Educational Services	$51,600
Food Manufacturing	$49,810
Chemical Manufacturing	$47,410
Rail Transportation	$46,760
Federal, State, and Local Government	$46,560
Heavy and Civil Engineering Construction	$43,080
Transportation Equipment Manufacturing	$41,010
Professional, Scientific, and Technical Services	$40,940
Waste Management and Remediation Services	$40,570

Median Wages for States (Annual)

State	Wage	State	Wage	State	Wage
AK	$47,790	KY	$30,030	NY	$54,360
AL	$29,850	LA	$31,680	OH	$47,560
AR	$27,090	MA	$45,750	OK	$41,930
AZ	$32,320	MD	$37,030	OR	$41,760
CA	$43,530	ME	$36,340	PA	$44,300
CO	$33,430	MI	$49,880	RI	$40,390
CT	$44,540	MN	$51,840	SC	$28,470
DC	$51,500	MO	$40,130	SD	$27,020
DE	$40,670	MS	$25,880	TN	$31,680
FL	$31,390	MT	$35,760	TX	$30,860
GA	$32,310	NC	$29,040	UT	$39,930
HI	$61,940	ND	$35,180	VA	$34,080
IA	$37,210	NE	$44,700	VT	$33,850
ID	$33,850	NH	$35,080	WA	$49,350
IL	$55,530	NJ	$50,810	WI	$48,770
IN	$39,900	NM	$34,630	WV	$36,590
KS	$43,210	NV	$48,910	WY	$37,200

Median Wages for the Largest Metropolitan Areas (Annual)

Area	Wage	Area	Wage
AZ: Phoenix	$33,200	MI: Detroit	$51,900
CA: Los Angeles	$40,300	MN: Minneapolis	$57,460
CA: Riverside	$36,790	MO: Kansas City	$52,090
CA: Sacramento	$57,640	MO: St. Louis	$54,170
CA: San Diego	$44,620	NV: Las Vegas	$53,530
CA: San Francisco	$55,000	NY: New York	$60,540
CO: Denver	$32,800	OH: Cincinnati	$39,480
DC: Washington	$39,440	OH: Cleveland	$54,300
FL: Miami	$33,540	OH: Columbus	$44,480
FL: Orlando	$29,750	OR: Portland	$42,760
FL: Tampa	$32,190	PA: Philadelphia	$47,610
GA: Atlanta	$32,250	PA: Pittsburgh	$48,100
IL: Chicago	$62,350	TX: Dallas	$26,750
MA: Boston	$45,720	TX: Houston	$32,500
MD: Baltimore	$38,760	WA: Seattle	$47,490

FACTORS THAT MAY AFFECT EARNINGS

Educational Attainment of Workers and Effect on Earnings

	Percent at Level	Effect on Earnings
Less than High School	—	—
Some High School	8.6%	−6.4%
High School or Equivalent	49.7%	−0.6%
Some College but No Degree	20.5%	−8.0%
Associate Degree	12.6%	29.4%
Bachelor's Degree	4.6%	9.1%
Master's Degree	—	—
Doctoral Degree	—	—
First Professional Degree	—	—

Flexibility of Earnings

Average Hours Worked: 34
Workers with a Varying Number of Hours: 8.3%
Workers Earning Some Overtime Pay, Tips, or Commissions: 24.4%
Earnings Benefit of Working Overtime: −10.1%

Gender

	Male	Female
Percent	96.9%	3.1%
Effect on Earnings	−0.6%	—

Union Membership

Percentage Union Members: 32.4%
Earnings Benefit of Union Membership: 21.0%

Veteran Status

Percentage Who Have Been on Active Duty: 10.2%
Earnings Benefit of Veteran Status: 19.5%

47-2221 Structural Iron and Steel Workers

Raise, place, and unite iron or steel girders, columns, and other structural members to form completed structures or structural frameworks. May erect metal storage tanks and assemble prefabricated metal buildings.

- Education or Training Required: Long-term on-the-job training
- Job Growth: 15.0%
- Annual Openings: 13,000
- Self-Employed: 2.3%
- Part-Time: 14.3%

NATIONAL WAGE FIGURES (ANNUAL)

Beginning	25th Percentile	Median	Mean	75th Percentile	90th Percentile
$22,760	$29,350	$40,480	$43,950	$56,320	$72,340

Median Wages for Industries Employing Largest Numbers (Annual)

Industry	Median Income
Utilities	$58,390
Rental and Leasing Services	$55,810
Primary Metal Manufacturing	$48,760
Machinery Manufacturing	$47,330
Heavy and Civil Engineering Construction	$43,890
Wholesale Electronic Markets and Agents and Brokers	$42,710
Specialty Trade Contractors	$42,640
Rail Transportation	$41,450
Support Activities for Mining	$39,690
Professional, Scientific, and Technical Services	$39,280

Median Wages for States (Annual)

State	Wage	State	Wage	State	Wage
AK	$58,910	KY	$38,050	NY	$72,030
AL	$33,900	LA	$34,550	OH	$51,540
AR	$29,400	MA	$64,340	OK	$39,460
AZ	$31,690	MD	$51,240	OR	$45,800
CA	$52,340	ME	$38,880	PA	$48,790
CO	$39,640	MI	$48,780	RI	$57,990
CT	$61,000	MN	$60,590	SC	$34,770
DC	no data	MO	$48,030	SD	$25,800
DE	$41,430	MS	$29,070	TN	$37,070
FL	$34,690	MT	$39,550	TX	$28,100
GA	$27,690	NC	$31,750	UT	$37,120
HI	$54,130	ND	$37,300	VA	$34,210
IA	$43,480	NE	$37,990	VT	$30,790
ID	$26,960	NH	$38,270	WA	$55,060
IL	$69,590	NJ	$64,910	WI	$49,820
IN	$49,200	NM	$34,880	WV	$30,350
KS	$27,230	NV	$64,230	WY	$28,120

Median Wages for the Largest Metropolitan Areas (Annual)

Area	Wage	Area	Wage
AZ: Phoenix	$31,330	MI: Detroit	$53,550
CA: Los Angeles	$58,110	MN: Minneapolis	$66,630
CA: Riverside	$38,910	MO: Kansas City	$50,630
CA: Sacramento	no data	MO: St. Louis	$53,920
CA: San Diego	$39,090	NV: Las Vegas	$64,970
CA: San Francisco	$63,060	NY: New York	$77,120
CO: Denver	$42,350	OH: Cincinnati	$49,770
DC: Washington	$38,290	OH: Cleveland	$53,900
FL: Miami	$36,870	OH: Columbus	$50,880
FL: Orlando	$35,390	OR: Portland	$64,750
FL: Tampa	$32,050	PA: Philadelphia	$51,290
GA: Atlanta	$28,330	PA: Pittsburgh	$56,310
IL: Chicago	$69,660	TX: Dallas	$26,810
MA: Boston	$64,220	TX: Houston	$32,830
MD: Baltimore	$51,980	WA: Seattle	$57,010

FACTORS THAT MAY AFFECT EARNINGS

Educational Attainment of Workers and Effect on Earnings

	Percent at Level	Effect on Earnings
Less than High School	—	—
Some High School	12.3%	−23.6%
High School or Equivalent	50.8%	13.0%
Some College but No Degree	21.5%	−12.8%
Associate Degree	—	—
Bachelor's Degree	—	—
Master's Degree	—	—
Doctoral Degree	—	—
First Professional Degree	—	—

Figures do not total 100% because some levels have a very small sample size.

Flexibility of Earnings

Average Hours Worked: 33
Workers with a Varying Number of Hours: 12.8%
Workers Earning Some Overtime Pay, Tips, or Commissions: 16.7%
Earnings Benefit of Working Overtime: 10.1%

Gender

	Male	Female
Percent	97.8%	2.2%
Effect on Earnings	0.3%	−13.9%

Union Membership

Percentage Union Members: 34.6%
Earnings Benefit of Union Membership: 14.1%

Veteran Status

Percentage Who Have Been on Active Duty: 10.2%
Earnings Benefit of Veteran Status: 19.5%

47-3000 Helpers, Construction Trades

47-3011 Helpers—Brickmasons, Blockmasons, Stone-masons, and Tile and Marble Setters

Help brickmasons, blockmasons, stonemasons, or tile and marble setters by performing duties of lesser skill. Duties include using, supplying, or holding materials or tools and cleaning work area and equipment.

- Education or Training Required: Short-term on-the-job training
- Job Growth: 14.9%
- Annual Openings: 14,000
- Self-Employed: 0.8%
- Part-Time: 32.2%

NATIONAL WAGE FIGURES (ANNUAL)

Beginning	25th Percentile	Median	Mean	75th Percentile	90th Percentile
$18,000	$20,980	$25,350	$27,850	$31,460	$42,220

Median Wages for Industries Employing Largest Numbers (Annual)

Industry	Median Income
Administrative and Support Services	$29,240
Miscellaneous Store Retailers	$28,200
Construction of Buildings	$26,680
Specialty Trade Contractors	$25,280
Merchant Wholesalers, Durable Goods	$23,560
Heavy and Civil Engineering Construction	$22,640
Building Material and Garden Equipment and Supplies Dealers	$22,110
Furniture and Home Furnishings Stores	$21,270
Nonmetallic Mineral Product Manufacturing	$20,760

Median Wages for States (Annual)

AK	no data	KY	$25,780	NY	$39,160
AL	$20,170	LA	$21,630	OH	$30,820
AR	$20,910	MA	$45,780	OK	$24,660
AZ	$22,310	MD	$26,510	OR	$27,870
CA	$27,370	ME	$28,030	PA	$27,740
CO	$27,160	MI	$30,160	RI	$35,750
CT	$34,830	MN	$30,930	SC	$21,390
DC	no data	MO	$31,680	SD	$21,200
DE	$27,090	MS	$20,150	TN	$22,250
FL	$23,420	MT	$28,670	TX	$21,450
GA	$22,230	NC	$21,880	UT	$21,810
HI	$27,990	ND	$26,280	VA	$24,920
IA	$29,140	NE	$27,580	VT	$29,380
ID	$27,190	NH	$32,120	WA	$35,420
IL	$35,060	NJ	$27,530	WI	$29,020
IN	$28,780	NM	$18,880	WV	$18,920
KS	$26,200	NV	$26,100	WY	$26,900

Median Wages for the Largest Metropolitan Areas (Annual)

AZ: Phoenix	$23,450	MI: Detroit	$30,560
CA: Los Angeles	$24,140	MN: Minneapolis	$33,130
CA: Riverside	$30,570	MO: Kansas City	$28,510
CA: Sacramento	$31,530	MO: St. Louis	$41,100
CA: San Diego	$26,480	NV: Las Vegas	$25,970
CA: San Francisco	$29,930	NY: New York	$28,390
CO: Denver	$28,790	OH: Cincinnati	$28,950
DC: Washington	$26,710	OH: Cleveland	$30,730
FL: Miami	$23,770	OH: Columbus	$29,820
FL: Orlando	$22,650	OR: Portland	$29,440
FL: Tampa	$22,380	PA: Philadelphia	$30,910
GA: Atlanta	$23,730	PA: Pittsburgh	$23,740
IL: Chicago	$36,560	TX: Dallas	$21,240
MA: Boston	$45,990	TX: Houston	$21,740
MD: Baltimore	$28,080	WA: Seattle	$37,120

FACTORS THAT MAY AFFECT EARNINGS

Educational Attainment of Workers and Effect on Earnings

Figures are based on a group of occupations: Helpers, Construction Trades

	Percent at Level	Effect on Earnings
Less than High School	13.2%	−28.1%
Some High School	21.7%	−12.9%
High School or Equivalent	34.0%	7.1%
Some College but No Degree	20.8%	20.1%
Associate Degree	—	—
Bachelor's Degree	—	—
Master's Degree	—	—
Doctoral Degree	—	—
First Professional Degree	—	—

Figures do not total 100% because some levels have a very small sample size.

Flexibility of Earnings

Average Hours Worked: 28
Workers with a Varying Number of Hours: 12.9%
Workers Earning Some Overtime Pay, Tips, or Commissions: 12.2%
Earnings Benefit of Working Overtime: 3.2%

Gender

	Male	Female
Percent	93.8%	6.2%
Effect on Earnings	0.0%	—

Union Membership

Percentage Union Members: 4.7%
Earnings Benefit of Union Membership: 46.4%

Veteran Status

Percentage Who Have Been on Active Duty: 4.2%
Earnings Benefit of Veteran Status: 104.8%

47-3012 Helpers—Carpenters

Help carpenters by performing duties of lesser skill. Duties include using, supplying, or holding materials or tools and cleaning work area and equipment.

- Education or Training Required: Short-term on-the-job training
- Job Growth: 14.5%
- Annual Openings: 24,000
- Self-Employed: 0.7%
- Part-Time: 32.2%

NATIONAL WAGE FIGURES (ANNUAL)

Beginning	25th Percentile	Median	Mean	75th Percentile	90th Percentile
$16,120	$19,390	$23,060	$24,190	$28,020	$33,630

Median Wages for Industries Employing Largest Numbers (Annual)

Industry	Median Income
Professional, Scientific, and Technical Services	$28,840
Merchant Wholesalers, Durable Goods	$26,750
Hospitals	$25,310
Federal, State, and Local Government	$25,190
Performing Arts, Spectator Sports, and Related Industries	$24,840
Construction of Buildings	$23,540
Heavy and Civil Engineering Construction	$23,240
Specialty Trade Contractors	$22,780
Fabricated Metal Product Manufacturing	$22,710
Nonmetallic Mineral Product Manufacturing	$22,450

Median Wages for States (Annual)

State	Wage	State	Wage	State	Wage
AK	$33,290	KY	$18,430	NY	$24,880
AL	$20,680	LA	$20,530	OH	$21,780
AR	$22,580	MA	$29,990	OK	$20,410
AZ	$22,100	MD	$25,790	OR	$23,400
CA	$24,960	ME	$21,860	PA	$23,790
CO	$25,350	MI	$22,050	RI	$27,940
CT	$29,050	MN	$22,590	SC	$21,650
DC	$30,530	MO	$25,360	SD	$18,910
DE	$22,990	MS	$21,070	TN	$22,230
FL	$21,840	MT	$23,790	TX	$22,150
GA	$22,810	NC	$21,420	UT	$22,220
HI	$31,120	ND	$21,790	VA	$24,020
IA	$22,290	NE	$21,980	VT	$26,200
ID	$29,280	NH	$22,760	WA	$26,530
IL	$25,730	NJ	$26,340	WI	$25,060
IN	$23,050	NM	$18,330	WV	$19,500
KS	$22,040	NV	$24,420	WY	$24,580

Median Wages for the Largest Metropolitan Areas (Annual)

Area	Wage	Area	Wage
AZ: Phoenix	$21,950	MI: Detroit	$21,510
CA: Los Angeles	$25,880	MN: Minneapolis	$25,790
CA: Riverside	$25,690	MO: Kansas City	$23,820
CA: Sacramento	$23,270	MO: St. Louis	$27,620
CA: San Diego	$24,140	NV: Las Vegas	$24,940
CA: San Francisco	$26,600	NY: New York	$25,160
CO: Denver	$23,630	OH: Cincinnati	$21,790
DC: Washington	$27,090	OH: Cleveland	$15,090
FL: Miami	$22,750	OH: Columbus	$24,230
FL: Orlando	$22,180	OR: Portland	$23,970
FL: Tampa	$20,830	PA: Philadelphia	$25,250
GA: Atlanta	$25,470	PA: Pittsburgh	$25,320
IL: Chicago	$27,900	TX: Dallas	$23,150
MA: Boston	$33,560	TX: Houston	$23,050
MD: Baltimore	$25,960	WA: Seattle	$25,110

FACTORS THAT MAY AFFECT EARNINGS

Educational Attainment of Workers and Effect on Earnings

Figures are based on a group of occupations: Helpers, Construction Trades

	Percent at Level	Effect on Earnings
Less than High School	13.2%	−28.1%
Some High School	21.7%	−12.9%
High School or Equivalent	34.0%	7.1%
Some College but No Degree	20.8%	20.1%
Associate Degree	—	—
Bachelor's Degree	—	—
Master's Degree	—	—
Doctoral Degree	—	—
First Professional Degree	—	—

Figures do not total 100% because some levels have a very small sample size.

Flexibility of Earnings

Average Hours Worked: 28
Workers with a Varying Number of Hours: 12.9%
Workers Earning Some Overtime Pay, Tips, or Commissions: 12.2%
Earnings Benefit of Working Overtime: 3.2%

Gender

	Male	Female
Percent	93.8%	6.2%
Effect on Earnings	0.0%	—

Union Membership

Percentage Union Members: 4.7%
Earnings Benefit of Union Membership: 46.4%

Veteran Status

Percentage Who Have Been on Active Duty: 4.2%
Earnings Benefit of Veteran Status: 104.8%

47-3013 Helpers—Electricians

Help electricians by performing duties of lesser skill. Duties include using, supplying, or holding materials or tools and cleaning work area and equipment.

- Education or Training Required: Short-term on-the-job training
- Job Growth: 4.0%
- Annual Openings: 19,000
- Self-Employed: 0.9%
- Part-Time: 32.2%

NATIONAL WAGE FIGURES (ANNUAL)

Beginning	25th Percentile	Median	Mean	75th Percentile	90th Percentile
$16,730	$19,800	$23,760	$25,050	$29,120	$35,500

Median Wages for Industries Employing Largest Numbers (Annual)

Industry	Median Income
Hospitals	$47,360
Federal, State, and Local Government	$41,030
Mining (Except Oil and Gas)	$37,000
Performing Arts, Spectator Sports, and Related Industries	$36,540
Utilities	$34,530
Professional, Scientific, and Technical Services	$32,860
Management of Companies and Enterprises	$31,980
Food Manufacturing	$29,650
Miscellaneous Manufacturing	$28,720
Electrical Equipment, Appliance, and Component Manufacturing	$28,670

Median Wages for States (Annual)

AK	$31,360	KY	$22,430	NY	$30,460
AL	$20,000	LA	$21,800	OH	$23,810
AR	$23,070	MA	$29,110	OK	$23,210
AZ	$19,330	MD	$27,330	OR	$29,440
CA	$27,150	ME	$29,530	PA	$25,980
CO	$28,170	MI	$25,770	RI	$26,310
CT	$28,620	MN	$22,630	SC	$22,540
DC	$30,590	MO	$26,740	SD	$21,420
DE	$25,100	MS	$21,720	TN	$23,660
FL	$21,600	MT	no data	TX	$23,390
GA	$23,100	NC	$22,940	UT	$20,340
HI	$33,180	ND	$20,190	VA	$24,060
IA	$22,530	NE	$22,840	VT	$25,080
ID	$23,600	NH	$28,900	WA	$27,670
IL	$32,230	NJ	$28,920	WI	$23,850
IN	$23,240	NM	$23,970	WV	$23,180
KS	$23,990	NV	$22,110	WY	$24,550

Median Wages for the Largest Metropolitan Areas (Annual)

AZ: Phoenix	$19,920	MI: Detroit	$15,580
CA: Los Angeles	$26,780	MN: Minneapolis	$27,450
CA: Riverside	$25,550	MO: Kansas City	$28,460
CA: Sacramento	$25,840	MO: St. Louis	$36,530
CA: San Diego	$27,380	NV: Las Vegas	$21,640
CA: San Francisco	$36,680	NY: New York	$30,640
CO: Denver	$28,690	OH: Cincinnati	$22,850
DC: Washington	$28,370	OH: Cleveland	$23,610
FL: Miami	$22,910	OH: Columbus	$24,860
FL: Orlando	$19,940	OR: Portland	$30,670
FL: Tampa	$23,530	PA: Philadelphia	$27,600
GA: Atlanta	$24,340	PA: Pittsburgh	$26,810
IL: Chicago	$35,070	TX: Dallas	$25,130
MA: Boston	$28,920	TX: Houston	$24,230
MD: Baltimore	$26,780	WA: Seattle	$26,860

FACTORS THAT MAY AFFECT EARNINGS

Educational Attainment of Workers and Effect on Earnings

Figures are based on a group of occupations: Helpers, Construction Trades

	Percent at Level	Effect on Earnings
Less than High School	13.2%	−28.1%
Some High School	21.7%	−12.9%
High School or Equivalent	34.0%	7.1%
Some College but No Degree	20.8%	20.1%
Associate Degree	—	—
Bachelor's Degree	—	—
Master's Degree	—	—
Doctoral Degree	—	—
First Professional Degree	—	—

Figures do not total 100% because some levels have a very small sample size.

Flexibility of Earnings

Average Hours Worked: 28
Workers with a Varying Number of Hours: 12.9%
Workers Earning Some Overtime Pay, Tips, or Commissions: 12.2%
Earnings Benefit of Working Overtime: 3.2%

Gender

	Male	Female
Percent	93.8%	6.2%
Effect on Earnings	0.0%	—

Union Membership

Percentage Union Members: 4.7%
Earnings Benefit of Union Membership: 46.4%

Veteran Status

Percentage Who Have Been on Active Duty: 4.2%
Earnings Benefit of Veteran Status: 104.8%

47-3014 Helpers—Painters, Paperhangers, Plasterers, and Stucco Masons

Help painters, paperhangers, plasterers, or stucco masons by performing duties of lesser skill. Duties include using, supplying, or holding materials or tools and cleaning work area and equipment.

- Education or Training Required: Short-term on-the-job training
- Job Growth: 11.5%
- Annual Openings: 6,000
- Self-Employed: 0.9%
- Part-Time: 32.2%

NATIONAL WAGE FIGURES (ANNUAL)

Beginning	25th Percentile	Median	Mean	75th Percentile	90th Percentile
$15,860	$17,970	$21,330	$22,620	$25,490	$30,820

Median Wages for Industries Employing Largest Numbers (Annual)

Industry	Median Income
Federal, State, and Local Government	$37,820
Educational Services	$29,220
Real Estate	$22,770
Heavy and Civil Engineering Construction	$21,610
Specialty Trade Contractors	$21,330
Fabricated Metal Product Manufacturing	$21,300
Construction of Buildings	$21,140
Administrative and Support Services	$20,740
Professional, Scientific, and Technical Services	$20,610
Transportation Equipment Manufacturing	$20,440

Median Wages for States (Annual)

AK	no data	KY	$19,900	NY	$20,860
AL	$18,600	LA	$21,120	OH	$26,600
AR	$19,330	MA	$23,430	OK	$21,580
AZ	$20,680	MD	$19,850	OR	$21,960
CA	$22,360	ME	no data	PA	$23,250
CO	$25,340	MI	$25,740	RI	$21,420
CT	no data	MN	$24,560	SC	$20,500
DC	no data	MO	$31,690	SD	$18,660
DE	$27,920	MS	$21,600	TN	$21,970
FL	$20,810	MT	$20,510	TX	$18,330
GA	$18,390	NC	$19,520	UT	$20,360
HI	$20,660	ND	no data	VA	$18,630
IA	no data	NE	$17,650	VT	$20,610
ID	no data	NH	$23,040	WA	$26,350
IL	$28,590	NJ	$21,400	WI	$25,200
IN	$20,710	NM	$18,900	WV	$22,560
KS	$18,530	NV	$21,870	WY	no data

Median Wages for the Largest Metropolitan Areas (Annual)

AZ: Phoenix	$20,190	MI: Detroit	$26,230
CA: Los Angeles	$22,470	MN: Minneapolis	$29,060
CA: Riverside	$22,720	MO: Kansas City	$19,100
CA: Sacramento	$22,100	MO: St. Louis	$49,590
CA: San Diego	$23,310	NV: Las Vegas	$22,530
CA: San Francisco	$22,240	NY: New York	$23,070
CO: Denver	$26,250	OH: Cincinnati	$28,620
DC: Washington	$19,590	OH: Cleveland	no data
FL: Miami	$20,550	OH: Columbus	no data
FL: Orlando	$19,390	OR: Portland	$22,680
FL: Tampa	$20,280	PA: Philadelphia	$23,050
GA: Atlanta	$17,490	PA: Pittsburgh	$24,980
IL: Chicago	$29,230	TX: Dallas	$19,940
MA: Boston	$21,930	TX: Houston	$18,530
MD: Baltimore	$21,990	WA: Seattle	$26,630

FACTORS THAT MAY AFFECT EARNINGS

Educational Attainment of Workers and Effect on Earnings

Figures are based on a group of occupations: Helpers, Construction Trades

	Percent at Level	Effect on Earnings
Less than High School	13.2%	−28.1%
Some High School	21.7%	−12.9%
High School or Equivalent	34.0%	7.1%
Some College but No Degree	20.8%	20.1%
Associate Degree	—	—
Bachelor's Degree	—	—
Master's Degree	—	—
Doctoral Degree	—	—
First Professional Degree	—	—

Figures do not total 100% because some levels have a very small sample size.

Flexibility of Earnings

Average Hours Worked: 28
Workers with a Varying Number of Hours: 12.9%
Workers Earning Some Overtime Pay, Tips, or Commissions: 12.2%
Earnings Benefit of Working Overtime: 3.2%

Gender

	Male	Female
Percent	93.8%	6.2%
Effect on Earnings	0.0%	—

Union Membership

Percentage Union Members: 4.7%
Earnings Benefit of Union Membership: 46.4%

Veteran Status

Percentage Who Have Been on Active Duty: 4.2%
Earnings Benefit of Veteran Status: 104.8%

47-3015 Helpers—Pipelayers, Plumbers, Pipefitters, and Steamfitters

Help plumbers, pipefitters, steamfitters, or pipelayers by performing duties of lesser skill. Duties include using, supplying, or holding materials or tools and cleaning work area and equipment.

- Education or Training Required: Short-term on-the-job training
- Job Growth: 16.6%
- Annual Openings: 17,000
- Self-Employed: 0.8%
- Part-Time: 32.2%

NATIONAL WAGE FIGURES (ANNUAL)

Beginning	25th Percentile	Median	Mean	75th Percentile	90th Percentile
$17,020	$20,190	$23,910	$25,430	$29,270	$35,800

Median Wages for Industries Employing Largest Numbers (Annual)

Industry	Median Income
Hospitals	$43,130
Utilities	$40,930
Educational Services	$32,780
Pipeline Transportation	$30,630
Professional, Scientific, and Technical Services	$28,950
Transportation Equipment Manufacturing	$26,860
Merchant Wholesalers, Durable Goods	$26,360
Repair and Maintenance	$25,300
Construction of Buildings	$25,180
Support Activities for Mining	$24,580

Median Wages for States (Annual)

State	Wage	State	Wage	State	Wage
AK	no data	KY	$23,320	NY	$27,490
AL	$19,720	LA	$22,610	OH	$22,710
AR	$21,840	MA	$29,560	OK	$21,040
AZ	$22,500	MD	$26,950	OR	$33,960
CA	$26,580	ME	$24,990	PA	$23,570
CO	$26,350	MI	$27,100	RI	$26,790
CT	$30,350	MN	$27,730	SC	$22,330
DC	$26,070	MO	$24,360	SD	$20,990
DE	$25,290	MS	$21,890	TN	$22,610
FL	$21,680	MT	$29,660	TX	$22,760
GA	$23,830	NC	$23,340	UT	$23,240
HI	$28,790	ND	$23,430	VA	$22,570
IA	$24,150	NE	$25,820	VT	$26,000
ID	$28,210	NH	$27,260	WA	$27,240
IL	$33,390	NJ	$28,580	WI	$24,520
IN	$26,410	NM	$25,340	WV	$20,750
KS	$24,220	NV	$27,870	WY	$21,570

Median Wages for the Largest Metropolitan Areas (Annual)

Metro Area	Wage	Metro Area	Wage
AZ: Phoenix	$23,030	MI: Detroit	$26,600
CA: Los Angeles	$24,960	MN: Minneapolis	$29,210
CA: Riverside	$26,320	MO: Kansas City	$25,610
CA: Sacramento	$24,210	MO: St. Louis	$42,300
CA: San Diego	$28,900	NV: Las Vegas	$27,470
CA: San Francisco	$36,120	NY: New York	$27,960
CO: Denver	$28,800	OH: Cincinnati	$24,210
DC: Washington	$27,590	OH: Cleveland	$23,330
FL: Miami	$21,670	OH: Columbus	$21,760
FL: Orlando	$20,850	OR: Portland	$34,460
FL: Tampa	$21,800	PA: Philadelphia	$22,880
GA: Atlanta	$24,970	PA: Pittsburgh	$29,790
IL: Chicago	$36,280	TX: Dallas	$24,200
MA: Boston	$27,450	TX: Houston	$24,530
MD: Baltimore	$27,350	WA: Seattle	$27,180

FACTORS THAT MAY AFFECT EARNINGS

Educational Attainment of Workers and Effect on Earnings

Figures are based on a group of occupations: Helpers, Construction Trades

	Percent at Level	Effect on Earnings
Less than High School	13.2%	−28.1%
Some High School	21.7%	−12.9%
High School or Equivalent	34.0%	7.1%
Some College but No Degree	20.8%	20.1%
Associate Degree	—	—
Bachelor's Degree	—	—
Master's Degree	—	—
Doctoral Degree	—	—
First Professional Degree	—	—

Figures do not total 100% because some levels have a very small sample size.

Flexibility of Earnings

Average Hours Worked: 28
Workers with a Varying Number of Hours: 12.9%
Workers Earning Some Overtime Pay, Tips, or Commissions: 12.2%
Earnings Benefit of Working Overtime: 3.2%

Gender

	Male	Female
Percent	93.8%	6.2%
Effect on Earnings	0.0%	—

Union Membership

Percentage Union Members: 4.7%
Earnings Benefit of Union Membership: 46.4%

Veteran Status

Percentage Who Have Been on Active Duty: 4.2%
Earnings Benefit of Veteran Status: 104.8%

47-3016 Helpers—Roofers

Help roofers by performing duties of lesser skill. Duties include using, supplying, or holding materials or tools and cleaning work area and equipment.

- Education or Training Required: Short-term on-the-job training
- Job Growth: 16.5%
- Annual Openings: 5,000
- Self-Employed: 0.7%
- Part-Time: 32.2%

NATIONAL WAGE FIGURES (ANNUAL)

Beginning	25th Percentile	Median	Mean	75th Percentile	90th Percentile
$16,020	$18,590	$21,760	$22,740	$26,060	$31,340

Median Wages for Industries Employing Largest Numbers (Annual)

Industry	Median Income
Specialty Trade Contractors	$21,770
Construction of Buildings	$21,540
Administrative and Support Services	$19,590

Median Wages for States (Annual)

State	Wage	State	Wage	State	Wage
AK	no data	KY	$21,560	NY	$20,550
AL	$19,340	LA	$18,570	OH	$23,190
AR	$20,250	MA	$31,600	OK	$20,310
AZ	$18,340	MD	$27,750	OR	$21,220
CA	$23,360	ME	$22,560	PA	$23,600
CO	$22,410	MI	$24,350	RI	$27,690
CT	$23,670	MN	$31,460	SC	$18,820
DC	no data	MO	$24,900	SD	$21,750
DE	$24,080	MS	$20,520	TN	$21,650
FL	$20,970	MT	$25,890	TX	$19,390
GA	$20,490	NC	$20,320	UT	$21,240
HI	$23,190	ND	$22,000	VA	$23,040
IA	$22,970	NE	$19,620	VT	$21,040
ID	$19,340	NH	$25,510	WA	$27,670
IL	$23,860	NJ	$25,910	WI	$25,960
IN	$25,100	NM	$19,180	WV	$17,380
KS	$17,260	NV	$21,820	WY	$20,470

Median Wages for the Largest Metropolitan Areas (Annual)

Area	Wage	Area	Wage
AZ: Phoenix	$18,590	MI: Detroit	$22,730
CA: Los Angeles	$23,100	MN: Minneapolis	$34,670
CA: Riverside	$24,880	MO: Kansas City	$26,970
CA: Sacramento	$31,920	MO: St. Louis	$25,650
CA: San Diego	no data	NV: Las Vegas	$21,350
CA: San Francisco	$23,310	NY: New York	$22,560
CO: Denver	$21,730	OH: Cincinnati	$23,760
DC: Washington	$28,990	OH: Cleveland	$25,380
FL: Miami	$20,370	OH: Columbus	$23,770
FL: Orlando	$20,360	OR: Portland	$22,960
FL: Tampa	$23,090	PA: Philadelphia	$26,010
GA: Atlanta	$20,360	PA: Pittsburgh	$23,080
IL: Chicago	$23,980	TX: Dallas	$18,810
MA: Boston	$32,680	TX: Houston	$22,750
MD: Baltimore	$27,750	WA: Seattle	$28,220

FACTORS THAT MAY AFFECT EARNINGS

Educational Attainment of Workers and Effect on Earnings

Figures are based on a group of occupations: Helpers, Construction Trades

	Percent at Level	Effect on Earnings
Less than High School	13.2%	−28.1%
Some High School	21.7%	−12.9%
High School or Equivalent	34.0%	7.1%
Some College but No Degree	20.8%	20.1%
Associate Degree	—	—
Bachelor's Degree	—	—
Master's Degree	—	—
Doctoral Degree	—	—
First Professional Degree	—	—

Figures do not total 100% because some levels have a very small sample size.

Flexibility of Earnings

Average Hours Worked: 28
Workers with a Varying Number of Hours: 12.9%
Workers Earning Some Overtime Pay, Tips, or Commissions: 12.2%
Earnings Benefit of Working Overtime: 3.2%

Gender

	Male	Female
Percent	93.8%	6.2%
Effect on Earnings	0.0%	—

Union Membership

Percentage Union Members: 4.7%
Earnings Benefit of Union Membership: 46.4%

Veteran Status

Percentage Who Have Been on Active Duty: 4.2%
Earnings Benefit of Veteran Status: 104.8%

47-3019 Helpers, Construction Trades, All Other

All construction trades helpers not listed separately.

- Education or Training Required: Short-term on-the-job training
- Job Growth: 1.8%
- Annual Openings: 8,000
- Self-Employed: 0.8%
- Part-Time: 32.2%

NATIONAL WAGE FIGURES (ANNUAL)

Beginning	25th Percentile	Median	Mean	75th Percentile	90th Percentile
$15,650	$18,930	$22,760	$24,820	$28,540	$36,460

Median Wages for Industries Employing Largest Numbers (Annual)

Industry	Median Income
Utilities	$42,160
Rental and Leasing Services	$30,850
Machinery Manufacturing	$26,380
Real Estate	$26,380
Professional, Scientific, and Technical Services	$26,140
Waste Management and Remediation Services	$25,920
Rail Transportation	$25,690
Transportation Equipment Manufacturing	$24,650
Educational Services	$24,000
Heavy and Civil Engineering Construction	$23,370

Median Wages for States (Annual)

State	Wage	State	Wage	State	Wage
AK	no data	KY	$21,400	NY	$24,450
AL	$19,300	LA	$22,060	OH	$23,310
AR	$19,660	MA	$25,470	OK	$20,440
AZ	$22,080	MD	$27,240	OR	$23,530
CA	$25,790	ME	$22,140	PA	$22,970
CO	$22,710	MI	$29,670	RI	$25,270
CT	$22,950	MN	$21,360	SC	$19,010
DC	no data	MO	$23,420	SD	no data
DE	$21,470	MS	$18,830	TN	$18,870
FL	$22,010	MT	$25,560	TX	$22,170
GA	$18,500	NC	$20,960	UT	$21,850
HI	$26,110	ND	$24,210	VA	$23,980
IA	$24,110	NE	$22,310	VT	no data
ID	$30,330	NH	$25,030	WA	$27,280
IL	$26,120	NJ	$24,280	WI	$26,960
IN	$22,260	NM	$22,570	WV	$23,140
KS	$18,570	NV	$27,630	WY	$22,760

Median Wages for the Largest Metropolitan Areas (Annual)

Area	Wage	Area	Wage
AZ: Phoenix	$22,930	MI: Detroit	$30,700
CA: Los Angeles	$19,280	MN: Minneapolis	$18,400
CA: Riverside	$23,990	MO: Kansas City	$19,140
CA: Sacramento	$29,640	MO: St. Louis	$26,200
CA: San Diego	$29,030	NV: Las Vegas	$29,450
CA: San Francisco	$25,220	NY: New York	$27,110
CO: Denver	$22,130	OH: Cincinnati	$21,780
DC: Washington	$30,090	OH: Cleveland	$49,910
FL: Miami	$21,800	OH: Columbus	$22,920
FL: Orlando	$26,820	OR: Portland	$23,570
FL: Tampa	$22,240	PA: Philadelphia	$21,830
GA: Atlanta	$19,620	PA: Pittsburgh	$22,950
IL: Chicago	$37,880	TX: Dallas	$22,250
MA: Boston	$28,210	TX: Houston	$22,730
MD: Baltimore	$27,190	WA: Seattle	$29,240

FACTORS THAT MAY AFFECT EARNINGS

Educational Attainment of Workers and Effect on Earnings

Figures are based on a group of occupations: Helpers, Construction Trades

	Percent at Level	Effect on Earnings
Less than High School	13.2%	−28.1%
Some High School	21.7%	−12.9%
High School or Equivalent	34.0%	7.1%
Some College but No Degree	20.8%	20.1%
Associate Degree	—	—
Bachelor's Degree	—	—
Master's Degree	—	—
Doctoral Degree	—	—
First Professional Degree	—	—

Figures do not total 100% because some levels have a very small sample size.

Flexibility of Earnings

Average Hours Worked: 28
Workers with a Varying Number of Hours: 12.9%
Workers Earning Some Overtime Pay, Tips, or Commissions: 12.2%
Earnings Benefit of Working Overtime: 3.2%

Gender

	Male	Female
Percent	93.8%	6.2%
Effect on Earnings	0.0%	—

Union Membership

Percentage Union Members: 4.7%
Earnings Benefit of Union Membership: 46.4%

Veteran Status

Percentage Who Have Been on Active Duty: 4.2%
Earnings Benefit of Veteran Status: 104.8%

47-4000 Other Construction and Related Workers

47-4011 Construction and Building Inspectors

Inspect structures, using engineering skills to determine structural soundness and compliance with specifications, building codes, and other regulations. Inspections may be general in nature or may be limited to a specific area, such as electrical systems or plumbing.

- Education or Training Required: Work experience in a related occupation
- Job Growth: 22.3%
- Annual Openings: 6,000
- Self-Employed: 10.2%
- Part-Time: 11.9%

NATIONAL WAGE FIGURES (ANNUAL)

Beginning	25th Percentile	Median	Mean	75th Percentile	90th Percentile
$29,210	$36,610	$46,570	$48,620	$58,780	$72,590

Median Wages for Industries Employing Largest Numbers (Annual)

Industry	Median Income
Pipeline Transportation	$86,140
Management of Companies and Enterprises	$58,540
Support Activities for Mining	$58,480
Utilities	$57,130
Construction of Buildings	$51,920
Educational Services	$50,420
Real Estate	$49,450
Heavy and Civil Engineering Construction	$49,120
Specialty Trade Contractors	$46,920
Professional, Scientific, and Technical Services	$46,680

Median Wages for States (Annual)

AK	no data	KY	$39,840	NY	$48,160
AL	$40,370	LA	$41,330	OH	$45,420
AR	$38,180	MA	$46,430	OK	$36,090
AZ	$45,100	MD	$44,380	OR	$52,130
CA	$61,130	ME	$40,230	PA	$40,600
CO	$49,890	MI	$49,880	RI	$43,050
CT	$55,980	MN	$54,350	SC	$39,160
DC	$57,660	MO	$42,660	SD	$41,190
DE	$43,980	MS	$33,730	TN	$39,020
FL	$45,400	MT	$35,930	TX	$40,750
GA	$42,370	NC	$43,120	UT	$38,810
HI	$51,010	ND	$49,010	VA	$47,360
IA	$45,640	NE	$39,770	VT	$41,980
ID	$42,790	NH	$42,070	WA	$57,860
IL	$52,640	NJ	$53,610	WI	$46,840
IN	$36,520	NM	$39,580	WV	$39,000
KS	$42,610	NV	$56,700	WY	$41,340

Median Wages for the Largest Metropolitan Areas (Annual)

AZ: Phoenix	$45,880	MI: Detroit	$51,580
CA: Los Angeles	$67,610	MN: Minneapolis	$56,680
CA: Riverside	$52,190	MO: Kansas City	$42,710
CA: Sacramento	$54,440	MO: St. Louis	$43,800
CA: San Diego	$63,250	NV: Las Vegas	$57,530
CA: San Francisco	$68,350	NY: New York	$52,570
CO: Denver	$49,440	OH: Cincinnati	$47,340
DC: Washington	$53,250	OH: Cleveland	$44,420
FL: Miami	$52,150	OH: Columbus	$47,300
FL: Orlando	$44,840	OR: Portland	$53,490
FL: Tampa	$45,090	PA: Philadelphia	$45,440
GA: Atlanta	$44,770	PA: Pittsburgh	$40,620
IL: Chicago	$53,610	TX: Dallas	$45,790
MA: Boston	$47,810	TX: Houston	$43,180
MD: Baltimore	$42,400	WA: Seattle	$60,710

FACTORS THAT MAY AFFECT EARNINGS

Educational Attainment of Workers and Effect on Earnings

	Percent at Level	Effect on Earnings
Less than High School	—	—
Some High School	—	—
High School or Equivalent	30.7%	2.7%
Some College but No Degree	24.8%	−0.3%
Associate Degree	13.9%	6.6%
Bachelor's Degree	21.8%	−0.1%
Master's Degree	—	—
Doctoral Degree	—	—
First Professional Degree	—	—

Figures do not total 100% because some levels have a very small sample size.

Flexibility of Earnings

Average Hours Worked: 36
Workers with a Varying Number of Hours: 8.0%
Workers Earning Some Overtime Pay, Tips, or Commissions: 18.6%
Earnings Benefit of Working Overtime: 8.3%

Gender

	Male	Female
Percent	91.2%	8.8%
Effect on Earnings	−1.8%	—

Union Membership

Percentage Union Members: 24.8%
Earnings Benefit of Union Membership: 9.2%

Veteran Status

Percentage Who Have Been on Active Duty: 14.3%
Earnings Benefit of Veteran Status: −2.6%

47-4021 Elevator Installers and Repairers

Assemble, install, repair, or maintain electric or hydraulic freight or passenger elevators, escalators, or dumbwaiters.

- Education or Training Required: Long-term on-the-job training
- Job Growth: 14.8%
- Annual Openings: 3,000
- Self-Employed: 0.4%
- Part-Time: 11.5%

NATIONAL WAGE FIGURES (ANNUAL)

Beginning	25th Percentile	Median	Mean	75th Percentile	90th Percentile
$36,990	$49,710	$63,620	$61,930	$74,390	$87,660

Median Wages for Industries Employing Largest Numbers (Annual)

Industry	Median Income
Professional, Scientific, and Technical Services	$74,290
Merchant Wholesalers, Durable Goods	$65,920
Wholesale Electronic Markets and Agents and Brokers	$65,180
Specialty Trade Contractors	$63,870
Educational Services	$59,600
Federal, State, and Local Government	$58,810
Machinery Manufacturing	$49,030

Median Wages for States (Annual)

AK	no data	KY	$65,870	NY	$66,990
AL	no data	LA	no data	OH	$67,950
AR	no data	MA	$72,520	OK	no data
AZ	$64,290	MD	$67,670	OR	no data
CA	$72,810	ME	$63,010	PA	$63,100
CO	no data	MI	$62,540	RI	no data
CT	$68,970	MN	$66,060	SC	$47,190
DC	$64,990	MO	$68,210	SD	no data
DE	no data	MS	no data	TN	$49,230
FL	$58,020	MT	no data	TX	$50,020
GA	$55,690	NC	$57,270	UT	no data
HI	$77,360	ND	no data	VA	$54,930
IA	$68,340	NE	$64,190	VT	no data
ID	no data	NH	no data	WA	no data
IL	$59,650	NJ	$64,830	WI	$52,850
IN	$70,110	NM	no data	WV	$64,920
KS	no data	NV	no data	WY	no data

Median Wages for the Largest Metropolitan Areas (Annual)

AZ: Phoenix	no data	MI: Detroit	$59,650
CA: Los Angeles	$68,660	MN: Minneapolis	$66,420
CA: Riverside	no data	MO: Kansas City	$64,860
CA: Sacramento	no data	MO: St. Louis	$69,290
CA: San Diego	no data	NV: Las Vegas	no data
CA: San Francisco	$84,010	NY: New York	$66,660
CO: Denver	no data	OH: Cincinnati	$66,480
DC: Washington	$66,600	OH: Cleveland	$72,620
FL: Miami	$54,160	OH: Columbus	no data
FL: Orlando	$59,010	OR: Portland	no data
FL: Tampa	no data	PA: Philadelphia	$58,170
GA: Atlanta	$59,600	PA: Pittsburgh	$52,690
IL: Chicago	$78,750	TX: Dallas	$60,170
MA: Boston	$72,990	TX: Houston	$43,320
MD: Baltimore	$67,940	WA: Seattle	no data

FACTORS THAT MAY AFFECT EARNINGS

Educational Attainment of Workers and Effect on Earnings

	Percent at Level	Effect on Earnings
Less than High School	—	—
Some High School	—	—
High School or Equivalent	41.7%	-0.7%
Some College but No Degree	16.7%	-3.5%
Associate Degree	16.7%	28.7%
Bachelor's Degree	—	—
Master's Degree	—	—
Doctoral Degree	—	—
First Professional Degree	—	—

Figures do not total 100% because some levels have a very small sample size.

Flexibility of Earnings

Average Hours Worked: 39
Workers with a Varying Number of Hours: 3.4%
Workers Earning Some Overtime Pay, Tips, or Commissions: 20.0%
Earnings Benefit of Working Overtime: 8.3%

Gender

	Male	Female
Percent	97.3%	2.7%
Effect on Earnings	0.3%	-13.9%

Union Membership

Percentage Union Members: 67.5%
Earnings Benefit of Union Membership: 16.1%

Veteran Status

Percentage Who Have Been on Active Duty: 14.3%
Earnings Benefit of Veteran Status: -2.6%

47-4031 Fence Erectors

Erect and repair metal and wooden fences and fence gates around highways, industrial establishments, residences, or farms, using hand and power tools.

- Education or Training Required: Moderate-term on-the-job training
- Job Growth: 9.9%
- Annual Openings: 5,000
- Self-Employed: 34.6%
- Part-Time: 15.0%

Note: A large fraction of the workforce for this occupation is self-employed and earns an average of $27,800. All other earnings figures for this occupation are based on workers who are paid a wage or salary.

NATIONAL WAGE FIGURES (ANNUAL)

Beginning	25th Percentile	Median	Mean	75th Percentile	90th Percentile
$17,690	$21,270	$26,400	$28,130	$32,430	$40,830

Median Wages for Industries Employing Largest Numbers (Annual)

Industry	Median Income
Rental and Leasing Services	$35,160
Heavy and Civil Engineering Construction	$31,230
Fabricated Metal Product Manufacturing	$26,920
Specialty Trade Contractors	$26,320
Building Material and Garden Equipment and Supplies Dealers	$25,680
Merchant Wholesalers, Durable Goods	$23,240
Administrative and Support Services	$19,500

Median Wages for States (Annual)

AK	no data	KY	$22,950	NY	$27,680
AL	$21,380	LA	$21,720	OH	$25,670
AR	$25,000	MA	$34,900	OK	$20,890
AZ	$24,150	MD	$32,000	OR	$27,400
CA	$30,060	ME	no data	PA	$28,220
CO	$28,050	MI	$33,570	RI	$29,120
CT	$29,360	MN	$28,560	SC	$24,130
DC	no data	MO	$25,820	SD	$28,080
DE	no data	MS	$18,770	TN	$28,310
FL	$26,730	MT	$22,620	TX	$22,220
GA	$19,240	NC	no data	UT	$21,320
HI	$21,920	ND	$24,510	VA	$26,380
IA	$27,230	NE	$26,570	VT	$26,990
ID	$20,920	NH	$26,220	WA	$30,320
IL	$31,660	NJ	$27,100	WI	$30,960
IN	$24,260	NM	$16,790	WV	$27,090
KS	$26,220	NV	$26,330	WY	$27,640

Median Wages for the Largest Metropolitan Areas (Annual)

AZ: Phoenix	$24,290	MI: Detroit	no data
CA: Los Angeles	$30,720	MN: Minneapolis	$32,270
CA: Riverside	$31,210	MO: Kansas City	$29,340
CA: Sacramento	$28,900	MO: St. Louis	$27,590
CA: San Diego	no data	NV: Las Vegas	$27,080
CA: San Francisco	$30,300	NY: New York	$27,900
CO: Denver	$27,960	OH: Cincinnati	no data
DC: Washington	$30,320	OH: Cleveland	no data
FL: Miami	$30,640	OH: Columbus	no data
FL: Orlando	no data	OR: Portland	no data
FL: Tampa	no data	PA: Philadelphia	$28,760
GA: Atlanta	no data	PA: Pittsburgh	no data
IL: Chicago	no data	TX: Dallas	$23,560
MA: Boston	$33,300	TX: Houston	$22,410
MD: Baltimore	no data	WA: Seattle	$34,280

FACTORS THAT MAY AFFECT EARNINGS

Educational Attainment of Workers and Effect on Earnings

	Percent at Level	Effect on Earnings
Less than High School	20.7%	1.4%
Some High School	20.7%	−13.5%
High School or Equivalent	48.3%	−4.7%
Some College but No Degree	—	—
Associate Degree	—	—
Bachelor's Degree	—	—
Master's Degree	—	—
Doctoral Degree	—	—
First Professional Degree	—	—

Figures do not total 100% because some levels have a very small sample size.

Flexibility of Earnings

Average Hours Worked: 33
Workers with a Varying Number of Hours: 10.5%
Workers Earning Some Overtime Pay, Tips, or Commissions: 3.0%
Earnings Benefit of Working Overtime: 8.3%

Gender

	Male	Female
Percent	98.5%	1.5%
Effect on Earnings	0.3%	−13.9%

Union Membership

Percentage Union Members: 6.1%
Earnings Benefit of Union Membership: 24.2%

Veteran Status

Percentage Who Have Been on Active Duty: 14.3%
Earnings Benefit of Veteran Status: −2.6%

47-4041 Hazardous Materials Removal Workers

Identify, remove, pack, transport, or dispose of hazardous materials, including asbestos, lead-based paint, waste oil, fuel, transmission fluid, radioactive materials, contaminated soil, and so on. Specialized training and certification in hazardous materials handling or a confined entry permit are generally required. May operate earth-moving equipment or trucks.

- Education or Training Required: Moderate-term on-the-job training
- Job Growth: 31.2%
- Annual Openings: 11,000
- Self-Employed: 0.0%
- Part-Time: 16.7%

NATIONAL WAGE FIGURES (ANNUAL)

Beginning	25th Percentile	Median	Mean	75th Percentile	90th Percentile
$22,910	$27,680	$35,450	$38,340	$47,320	$59,180

Median Wages for Industries Employing Largest Numbers (Annual)

Industry	Median Income
Transportation Equipment Manufacturing	$50,180
Fabricated Metal Product Manufacturing	$46,890
Professional, Scientific, and Technical Services	$43,170
Educational Services	$42,860
Federal, State, and Local Government	$42,470
Utilities	$41,620
Chemical Manufacturing	$36,810
Computer and Electronic Product Manufacturing	$35,460
Waste Management and Remediation Services	$35,020
Construction of Buildings	$33,470

Median Wages for States (Annual)

AK	no data	KY	$31,830	NY	$46,850
AL	$26,340	LA	$28,810	OH	$33,630
AR	$28,720	MA	$36,460	OK	$28,400
AZ	$27,390	MD	$30,070	OR	$33,970
CA	$35,430	ME	$32,470	PA	$36,840
CO	$35,290	MI	$38,890	RI	$51,160
CT	$38,270	MN	$53,610	SC	$42,860
DC	$38,990	MO	$41,580	SD	no data
DE	no data	MS	$30,930	TN	$29,450
FL	$29,650	MT	$30,820	TX	$27,610
GA	$35,820	NC	$23,020	UT	$36,880
HI	$30,830	ND	$33,830	VA	$30,900
IA	$33,940	NE	$32,590	VT	$34,310
ID	$28,970	NH	$34,510	WA	$58,480
IL	$46,070	NJ	$46,880	WI	no data
IN	$34,220	NM	no data	WV	$36,890
KS	$29,830	NV	no data	WY	no data

Median Wages for the Largest Metropolitan Areas (Annual)

AZ: Phoenix	$27,160	MI: Detroit	$36,360
CA: Los Angeles	$35,830	MN: Minneapolis	$54,520
CA: Riverside	$42,620	MO: Kansas City	$42,000
CA: Sacramento	$35,400	MO: St. Louis	$43,330
CA: San Diego	$38,610	NV: Las Vegas	$63,600
CA: San Francisco	$35,350	NY: New York	$47,890
CO: Denver	$35,070	OH: Cincinnati	$33,190
DC: Washington	$34,890	OH: Cleveland	$33,500
FL: Miami	$26,540	OH: Columbus	$38,430
FL: Orlando	$27,150	OR: Portland	$34,630
FL: Tampa	$33,280	PA: Philadelphia	$35,850
GA: Atlanta	$36,020	PA: Pittsburgh	$36,320
IL: Chicago	$46,050	TX: Dallas	$26,970
MA: Boston	$34,990	TX: Houston	$28,240
MD: Baltimore	$29,480	WA: Seattle	$52,660

FACTORS THAT MAY AFFECT EARNINGS

Educational Attainment of Workers and Effect on Earnings

	Percent at Level	Effect on Earnings
Less than High School	—	—
Some High School	—	—
High School or Equivalent	40.5%	−17.6%
Some College but No Degree	16.2%	52.6%
Associate Degree	—	—
Bachelor's Degree	27.0%	10.9%
Master's Degree	—	—
Doctoral Degree	—	—
First Professional Degree	—	—

Figures do not total 100% because some levels have a very small sample size.

Flexibility of Earnings

Average Hours Worked: 32
Workers with a Varying Number of Hours: 6.3%
Workers Earning Some Overtime Pay, Tips, or Commissions: 7.9%
Earnings Benefit of Working Overtime: 8.3%

Gender

	Male	Female
Percent	90.8%	9.2%
Effect on Earnings	0.3%	−13.9%

Union Membership

Percentage Union Members: 26.3%
Earnings Benefit of Union Membership: 18.0%

Veteran Status

Percentage Who Have Been on Active Duty: 14.3%
Earnings Benefit of Veteran Status: −2.6%

47-4051 Highway Maintenance Workers

Maintain highways, municipal and rural roads, airport runways, and rights-of-way. Duties include patching broken or eroded pavement and repairing guardrails, highway markers, and snow fences. May also mow or clear brush from along road or plow snow from roadway.

- Education or Training Required: Moderate-term on-the-job training
- Job Growth: 23.3%
- Annual Openings: 27,000
- Self-Employed: 1.2%
- Part-Time: 14.6%

NATIONAL WAGE FIGURES (ANNUAL)

Beginning	25th Percentile	Median	Mean	75th Percentile	90th Percentile
$19,940	$24,890	$31,540	$32,370	$38,960	$46,890

Median Wages for Industries Employing Largest Numbers (Annual)

Industry	Median Income
Waste Management and Remediation Services	$37,160
Support Activities for Transportation	$33,220
Federal, State, and Local Government	$31,590
Administrative and Support Services	$30,890
Heavy and Civil Engineering Construction	$29,990
Educational Services	$27,700
Miscellaneous Manufacturing	$24,830
Specialty Trade Contractors	$23,450

Median Wages for States (Annual)

State	Wage	State	Wage	State	Wage
AK	$50,920	KY	$24,120	NY	$33,480
AL	$22,980	LA	$21,510	OH	$33,800
AR	$24,780	MA	$38,140	OK	$23,660
AZ	$28,110	MD	$32,320	OR	$35,380
CA	$43,850	ME	$26,980	PA	$29,820
CO	$35,370	MI	$36,370	RI	$34,270
CT	$44,920	MN	$39,510	SC	$25,460
DC	no data	MO	$27,770	SD	$25,750
DE	$30,860	MS	$21,470	TN	$22,670
FL	$26,490	MT	$32,310	TX	$25,570
GA	$22,570	NC	$25,110	UT	$35,810
HI	no data	ND	$29,060	VA	$34,770
IA	$34,350	NE	$28,390	VT	$30,330
ID	$32,990	NH	$27,620	WA	$40,410
IL	$43,030	NJ	$41,060	WI	$33,650
IN	$27,470	NM	$28,720	WV	$23,050
KS	$26,590	NV	$37,390	WY	$33,090

Median Wages for the Largest Metropolitan Areas (Annual)

Area	Wage	Area	Wage
AZ: Phoenix	$28,970	MI: Detroit	$40,000
CA: Los Angeles	no data	MN: Minneapolis	$42,800
CA: Riverside	$43,930	MO: Kansas City	$29,700
CA: Sacramento	$42,850	MO: St. Louis	$36,210
CA: San Diego	$43,340	NV: Las Vegas	$37,700
CA: San Francisco	$48,230	NY: New York	$40,720
CO: Denver	$37,110	OH: Cincinnati	$33,430
DC: Washington	$39,050	OH: Cleveland	$38,950
FL: Miami	$27,150	OH: Columbus	$35,870
FL: Orlando	$28,830	OR: Portland	$38,220
FL: Tampa	$26,400	PA: Philadelphia	$38,080
GA: Atlanta	$26,000	PA: Pittsburgh	$27,600
IL: Chicago	$40,910	TX: Dallas	$28,650
MA: Boston	$38,760	TX: Houston	$27,140
MD: Baltimore	$32,730	WA: Seattle	$44,980

FACTORS THAT MAY AFFECT EARNINGS

Educational Attainment of Workers and Effect on Earnings

	Percent at Level	Effect on Earnings
Less than High School	4.7%	−5.1%
Some High School	17.1%	−17.9%
High School or Equivalent	47.3%	4.6%
Some College but No Degree	16.3%	−0.4%
Associate Degree	7.0%	0.2%
Bachelor's Degree	7.8%	14.9%
Master's Degree	—	—
Doctoral Degree	—	—
First Professional Degree	—	—

Flexibility of Earnings

Average Hours Worked: 36
Workers with a Varying Number of Hours: 5.1%
Workers Earning Some Overtime Pay, Tips, or Commissions: 16.8%
Earnings Benefit of Working Overtime: 8.3%

Gender

	Male	Female
Percent	96.2%	3.8%
Effect on Earnings	0.2%	—

Union Membership

Percentage Union Members: 30.3%
Earnings Benefit of Union Membership: 17.6%

Veteran Status

Percentage Who Have Been on Active Duty: 14.3%
Earnings Benefit of Veteran Status: −2.6%

47-4061 Rail-Track Laying and Maintenance Equipment Operators

Lay, repair, and maintain track for standard or narrow-gauge railroad equipment used in regular railroad service or in plant yards, quarries, sand and gravel pits, and mines. Includes ballast-cleaning-machine operators and roadbed-tamping-machine operators.

- Education or Training Required: Moderate-term on-the-job training
- Job Growth: –10.8%
- Annual Openings: 1,000
- Self-Employed: 0.0%
- Part-Time: 11.5%

NATIONAL WAGE FIGURES (ANNUAL)

Beginning	25th Percentile	Median	Mean	75th Percentile	90th Percentile
$25,530	$32,590	$40,000	$39,640	$45,780	$53,860

Median Wages for Industries Employing Largest Numbers (Annual)

Industry	Median Income
Federal, State, and Local Government	$47,440
Mining (Except Oil and Gas)	$41,680
Rail Transportation	$40,680
Heavy and Civil Engineering Construction	$31,520
Construction of Buildings	$25,520
Support Activities for Transportation	$24,020

Median Wages for States (Annual)

State	Wage	State	Wage	State	Wage
AK	no data	KY	no data	NY	$41,950
AL	$35,910	LA	$39,740	OH	$41,820
AR	$39,750	MA	no data	OK	$38,410
AZ	no data	MD	$41,990	OR	$40,670
CA	$40,710	ME	no data	PA	$41,110
CO	$43,670	MI	$38,920	RI	no data
CT	no data	MN	$35,140	SC	$23,780
DC	no data	MO	$40,310	SD	no data
DE	no data	MS	$35,630	TN	$41,250
FL	$34,890	MT	no data	TX	$38,970
GA	$36,170	NC	$35,460	UT	no data
HI	no data	ND	no data	VA	$41,090
IA	$40,480	NE	$39,070	VT	no data
ID	$42,990	NH	no data	WA	no data
IL	$41,730	NJ	no data	WI	$41,250
IN	$46,400	NM	no data	WV	no data
KS	no data	NV	no data	WY	no data

Median Wages for the Largest Metropolitan Areas (Annual)

Metro	Wage	Metro	Wage
AZ: Phoenix	no data	MI: Detroit	no data
CA: Los Angeles	$31,740	MN: Minneapolis	no data
CA: Riverside	no data	MO: Kansas City	no data
CA: Sacramento	no data	MO: St. Louis	$40,260
CA: San Diego	no data	NV: Las Vegas	no data
CA: San Francisco	no data	NY: New York	$43,470
CO: Denver	no data	OH: Cincinnati	no data
DC: Washington	no data	OH: Cleveland	no data
FL: Miami	no data	OH: Columbus	no data
FL: Orlando	no data	OR: Portland	no data
FL: Tampa	no data	PA: Philadelphia	no data
GA: Atlanta	no data	PA: Pittsburgh	no data
IL: Chicago	no data	TX: Dallas	no data
MA: Boston	no data	TX: Houston	$24,350
MD: Baltimore	no data	WA: Seattle	$39,080

FACTORS THAT MAY AFFECT EARNINGS

Educational Attainment of Workers and Effect on Earnings

	Percent at Level	Effect on Earnings
Less than High School	—	—
Some High School	—	—
High School or Equivalent	38.9%	–20.7%
Some College but No Degree	—	—
Associate Degree	—	—
Bachelor's Degree	—	—
Master's Degree	—	—
Doctoral Degree	—	—
First Professional Degree	—	—

Figures do not total 100% because some levels have a very small sample size.

Flexibility of Earnings

Average Hours Worked: 37
Workers with a Varying Number of Hours: 9.9%
Workers Earning Some Overtime Pay, Tips, or Commissions: 27.8%
Earnings Benefit of Working Overtime: 8.3%

Gender

	Male	Female
Percent	94.2%	5.8%
Effect on Earnings	0.3%	–13.9%

Union Membership

Percentage Union Members: 77.8%
Earnings Benefit of Union Membership: 0.5%

Veteran Status

Percentage Who Have Been on Active Duty: 14.3%
Earnings Benefit of Veteran Status: –2.6%

47-4071 Septic Tank Servicers and Sewer Pipe Cleaners

Clean and repair septic tanks, sewer lines, or drains. May patch walls and partitions of tank, replace damaged drain tile, or repair breaks in underground piping.

- Education or Training Required: Moderate-term on-the-job training
- Job Growth: 21.8%
- Annual Openings: 3,000
- Self-Employed: 12.9%
- Part-Time: 11.5%

NATIONAL WAGE FIGURES (ANNUAL)

Beginning	25th Percentile	Median	Mean	75th Percentile	90th Percentile
$19,310	$24,420	$31,430	$32,560	$39,060	$47,870

Median Wages for Industries Employing Largest Numbers (Annual)

Industry	Median Income
Federal, State, and Local Government	$35,450
Administrative and Support Services	$33,950
Rental and Leasing Services	$33,850
Heavy and Civil Engineering Construction	$33,760
Construction of Buildings	$33,080
Merchant Wholesalers, Durable Goods	$32,400
Utilities	$30,310
Waste Management and Remediation Services	$29,690
Specialty Trade Contractors	$29,490
Nonmetallic Mineral Product Manufacturing	$29,380

Median Wages for States (Annual)

State	Wage	State	Wage	State	Wage
AK	$34,050	KY	$19,220	NY	$35,960
AL	$23,540	LA	$29,830	OH	$30,190
AR	$24,420	MA	$35,390	OK	$28,120
AZ	$24,940	MD	$33,100	OR	$35,520
CA	$35,890	ME	$30,290	PA	$33,100
CO	$36,580	MI	$32,370	RI	$37,710
CT	$40,730	MN	$39,070	SC	$23,280
DC	no data	MO	$24,700	SD	$20,720
DE	$30,760	MS	$20,030	TN	$25,920
FL	$25,980	MT	$26,690	TX	$25,890
GA	$25,160	NC	$27,250	UT	$36,620
HI	no data	ND	$23,900	VA	$28,120
IA	$29,720	NE	$26,850	VT	$29,750
ID	$26,220	NH	$30,470	WA	$36,390
IL	$38,890	NJ	$39,560	WI	$34,870
IN	$31,160	NM	$23,500	WV	$28,280
KS	$36,890	NV	$31,100	WY	$34,890

Median Wages for the Largest Metropolitan Areas (Annual)

Area	Wage	Area	Wage
AZ: Phoenix	$24,530	MI: Detroit	$33,220
CA: Los Angeles	$47,510	MN: Minneapolis	$37,510
CA: Riverside	$37,340	MO: Kansas City	$19,700
CA: Sacramento	no data	MO: St. Louis	$31,900
CA: San Diego	$34,220	NV: Las Vegas	no data
CA: San Francisco	$49,960	NY: New York	$38,770
CO: Denver	$44,030	OH: Cincinnati	$27,730
DC: Washington	$33,900	OH: Cleveland	$37,090
FL: Miami	$31,390	OH: Columbus	no data
FL: Orlando	$27,310	OR: Portland	$36,100
FL: Tampa	$28,970	PA: Philadelphia	$34,820
GA: Atlanta	$29,680	PA: Pittsburgh	$33,840
IL: Chicago	$40,280	TX: Dallas	$31,590
MA: Boston	$35,350	TX: Houston	$31,710
MD: Baltimore	$33,980	WA: Seattle	$45,510

FACTORS THAT MAY AFFECT EARNINGS

Educational Attainment of Workers and Effect on Earnings

	Percent at Level	Effect on Earnings
Less than High School	—	—
Some High School	—	—
High School or Equivalent	50.0%	10.9%
Some College but No Degree	—	—
Associate Degree	—	—
Bachelor's Degree	—	—
Master's Degree	—	—
Doctoral Degree	—	—
First Professional Degree	—	—

Figures do not total 100% because some levels have a very small sample size.

Flexibility of Earnings

Average Hours Worked: 36
Workers with a Varying Number of Hours: 11.3%
Workers Earning Some Overtime Pay, Tips, or Commissions: 15.4%
Earnings Benefit of Working Overtime: 8.3%

Gender

	Male	Female
Percent	98.5%	1.5%
Effect on Earnings	0.3%	−13.9%

Union Membership

Percentage Union Members: 30.8%
Earnings Benefit of Union Membership: 24.2%

Veteran Status

Percentage Who Have Been on Active Duty: 14.3%
Earnings Benefit of Veteran Status: −2.6%

47-4091 Segmental Pavers

Lay out, cut, and paste segmental paving units. Includes installers of bedding and restraining materials for the paving units.

- Education or Training Required: Moderate-term on-the-job training
- Job Growth: 12.6%
- Annual Openings: Fewer than 500
- Self-Employed: 31.4%
- Part-Time: 11.5%

Note: Earnings figures do not reflect self-employed workers, who make up a large fraction of the workforce for this occupation.

NATIONAL WAGE FIGURES (ANNUAL)

Beginning	25th Percentile	Median	Mean	75th Percentile	90th Percentile
$17,480	$21,780	$28,700	$28,600	$35,450	$39,740

Median Wages for Industries Employing Largest Numbers (Annual)

Industry	Median Income
Heavy and Civil Engineering Construction	$30,320
Specialty Trade Contractors	$29,110

Median Wages for States (Annual)

AK	no data	KY	no data	NY	no data
AL	no data	LA	no data	OH	no data
AR	no data	MA	no data	OK	no data
AZ	$25,620	MD	no data	OR	no data
CA	$33,860	ME	no data	PA	no data
CO	no data	MI	no data	RI	no data
CT	no data	MN	no data	SC	$19,200
DC	no data	MO	no data	SD	no data
DE	no data	MS	no data	TN	no data
FL	no data	MT	no data	TX	$21,070
GA	no data	NC	no data	UT	no data
HI	no data	ND	no data	VA	no data
IA	no data	NE	no data	VT	no data
ID	no data	NH	no data	WA	no data
IL	no data	NJ	no data	WI	no data
IN	no data	NM	no data	WV	no data
KS	no data	NV	no data	WY	no data

Median Wages for the Largest Metropolitan Areas (Annual)

AZ: Phoenix	$25,620	MI: Detroit	no data
CA: Los Angeles	no data	MN: Minneapolis	no data
CA: Riverside	no data	MO: Kansas City	no data
CA: Sacramento	no data	MO: St. Louis	no data
CA: San Diego	no data	NV: Las Vegas	no data
CA: San Francisco	no data	NY: New York	no data
CO: Denver	no data	OH: Cincinnati	no data
DC: Washington	$34,510	OH: Cleveland	no data
FL: Miami	no data	OH: Columbus	no data
FL: Orlando	no data	OR: Portland	no data
FL: Tampa	no data	PA: Philadelphia	no data
GA: Atlanta	no data	PA: Pittsburgh	no data
IL: Chicago	no data	TX: Dallas	no data
MA: Boston	no data	TX: Houston	$18,680
MD: Baltimore	no data	WA: Seattle	no data

FACTORS THAT MAY AFFECT EARNINGS

Educational Attainment of Workers and Effect on Earnings

Figures are based on a group of occupations: Other Construction and Related Workers

	Percent at Level	Effect on Earnings
Less than High School	3.9%	−14.7%
Some High School	12.3%	−24.2%
High School or Equivalent	38.0%	−1.2%
Some College but No Degree	20.1%	2.3%
Associate Degree	11.1%	8.7%
Bachelor's Degree	13.5%	15.7%
Master's Degree	—	—
Doctoral Degree	—	—
First Professional Degree	—	—

Flexibility of Earnings

Average Hours Worked: 35
Workers with a Varying Number of Hours: 7.0%
Workers Earning Some Overtime Pay, Tips, or Commissions: 16.4%
Earnings Benefit of Working Overtime: 8.3%

Gender

	Male	Female
Percent	94.2%	5.8%
Effect on Earnings	0.3%	−13.9%

Union Membership

Percentage Union Members: 31.1%
Earnings Benefit of Union Membership: 24.2%

Veteran Status

Percentage Who Have Been on Active Duty: 14.3%
Earnings Benefit of Veteran Status: −2.6%

47-4099 Construction and Related Workers, All Other

All construction and related workers not listed separately.

- Education or Training Required: Moderate-term on-the-job training
- Job Growth: 27.5%
- Annual Openings: 9,000
- Self-Employed: 9.3%
- Part-Time: 11.5%

NATIONAL WAGE FIGURES (ANNUAL)

Beginning	25th Percentile	Median	Mean	75th Percentile	90th Percentile
$18,340	$23,240	$30,470	$32,880	$39,420	$51,550

Median Wages for Industries Employing Largest Numbers (Annual)

Industry	Median Income
Oil and Gas Extraction	$80,630
Utilities	$54,940
Hospitals	$38,690
Management of Companies and Enterprises	$38,370
Telecommunications	$38,180
Rail Transportation	$36,450
Rental and Leasing Services	$35,460
Educational Services	$33,790
Real Estate	$33,660
Construction of Buildings	$31,710

Median Wages for States (Annual)

State	Wage	State	Wage	State	Wage
AK	$43,160	KY	$23,050	NY	$35,460
AL	$21,610	LA	$24,820	OH	$30,280
AR	$24,050	MA	no data	OK	$28,480
AZ	$30,860	MD	$28,960	OR	$36,130
CA	$37,910	ME	$31,570	PA	$36,050
CO	$32,460	MI	$32,940	RI	$35,100
CT	$31,820	MN	$30,340	SC	$20,800
DC	no data	MO	$28,130	SD	no data
DE	$30,140	MS	no data	TN	$30,900
FL	$27,080	MT	no data	TX	$29,370
GA	$26,330	NC	$27,970	UT	$18,550
HI	$19,720	ND	$29,720	VA	no data
IA	$27,530	NE	$30,290	VT	$24,230
ID	$28,000	NH	$33,910	WA	$34,650
IL	no data	NJ	$33,960	WI	$28,240
IN	$32,650	NM	$20,000	WV	$39,910
KS	$21,920	NV	$38,580	WY	$24,560

Median Wages for the Largest Metropolitan Areas (Annual)

Area	Wage	Area	Wage
AZ: Phoenix	$30,440	MI: Detroit	$37,110
CA: Los Angeles	$38,560	MN: Minneapolis	$35,550
CA: Riverside	$40,830	MO: Kansas City	$29,000
CA: Sacramento	$38,940	MO: St. Louis	$37,330
CA: San Diego	$35,840	NV: Las Vegas	$38,100
CA: San Francisco	$40,420	NY: New York	$34,810
CO: Denver	$37,240	OH: Cincinnati	$33,100
DC: Washington	$32,040	OH: Cleveland	$32,190
FL: Miami	$27,810	OH: Columbus	$30,100
FL: Orlando	$30,040	OR: Portland	$32,630
FL: Tampa	$28,470	PA: Philadelphia	no data
GA: Atlanta	$24,580	PA: Pittsburgh	$30,070
IL: Chicago	no data	TX: Dallas	$26,580
MA: Boston	no data	TX: Houston	$30,810
MD: Baltimore	$29,970	WA: Seattle	$31,350

FACTORS THAT MAY AFFECT EARNINGS

Educational Attainment of Workers and Effect on Earnings

Figures are based on a group of occupations: Other Construction and Related Workers

	Percent at Level	Effect on Earnings
Less than High School	3.9%	−14.7%
Some High School	12.3%	−24.2%
High School or Equivalent	38.0%	−1.2%
Some College but No Degree	20.1%	2.3%
Associate Degree	11.1%	8.7%
Bachelor's Degree	13.5%	15.7%
Master's Degree	—	—
Doctoral Degree	—	—
First Professional Degree	—	—

Flexibility of Earnings

Average Hours Worked: 35
Workers with a Varying Number of Hours: 7.0%
Workers Earning Some Overtime Pay, Tips, or Commissions: 16.4%
Earnings Benefit of Working Overtime: 8.3%

Gender

	Male	Female
Percent	94.2%	5.8%
Effect on Earnings	0.3%	−13.9%

Union Membership

Percentage Union Members: 31.1%
Earnings Benefit of Union Membership: 24.2%

Veteran Status

Percentage Who Have Been on Active Duty: 14.3%
Earnings Benefit of Veteran Status: −2.6%

47-5000 Extraction Workers

47-5011 Derrick Operators, Oil and Gas

Rig derrick equipment and operate pumps to circulate mud through drill hole.

- Education or Training Required: Moderate-term on-the-job training
- Job Growth: -0.5%
- Annual Openings: 1,000
- Self-Employed: 3.0%
- Part-Time: 4.9%

NATIONAL WAGE FIGURES (ANNUAL)

Beginning	25th Percentile	Median	Mean	75th Percentile	90th Percentile
$24,390	$28,870	$36,240	$37,930	$46,000	$55,100

Median Wages for Industries Employing Largest Numbers (Annual)

Industry	Median Income
Utilities	$41,890
Support Activities for Mining	$36,470
Oil and Gas Extraction	$32,720

Median Wages for States (Annual)

AK	$42,460	KY	no data	NY	no data
AL	no data	LA	$39,100	OH	$34,340
AR	$30,090	MA	no data	OK	$43,140
AZ	no data	MD	no data	OR	no data
CA	$37,580	ME	no data	PA	$31,610
CO	$36,010	MI	$31,490	RI	no data
CT	no data	MN	no data	SC	no data
DC	no data	MO	no data	SD	no data
DE	no data	MS	$31,020	TN	no data
FL	no data	MT	$51,680	TX	$32,650
GA	no data	NC	no data	UT	$36,370
HI	no data	ND	$45,140	VA	no data
IA	no data	NE	no data	VT	no data
ID	no data	NH	no data	WA	no data
IL	$26,060	NJ	no data	WI	no data
IN	no data	NM	$38,010	WV	$27,920
KS	$29,560	NV	no data	WY	$40,570

Median Wages for the Largest Metropolitan Areas (Annual)

AZ: Phoenix	no data	MI: Detroit	no data
CA: Los Angeles	no data	MN: Minneapolis	no data
CA: Riverside	no data	MO: Kansas City	no data
CA: Sacramento	no data	MO: St. Louis	no data
CA: San Diego	no data	NV: Las Vegas	no data
CA: San Francisco	no data	NY: New York	no data
CO: Denver	no data	OH: Cincinnati	no data
DC: Washington	no data	OH: Cleveland	no data
FL: Miami	no data	OH: Columbus	no data
FL: Orlando	no data	OR: Portland	no data
FL: Tampa	no data	PA: Philadelphia	no data
GA: Atlanta	no data	PA: Pittsburgh	no data
IL: Chicago	no data	TX: Dallas	$32,900
MA: Boston	no data	TX: Houston	$33,800
MD: Baltimore	no data	WA: Seattle	no data

FACTORS THAT MAY AFFECT EARNINGS

Educational Attainment of Workers and Effect on Earnings

Figures are based on a group of occupations: Extraction Workers

	Percent at Level	Effect on Earnings
Less than High School	4.1%	-42.9%
Some High School	17.8%	-12.0%
High School or Equivalent	46.1%	3.3%
Some College but No Degree	20.1%	2.3%
Associate Degree	8.9%	14.7%
Bachelor's Degree	—	—
Master's Degree	—	—
Doctoral Degree	—	—
First Professional Degree	—	—

Flexibility of Earnings

Average Hours Worked: 40
Workers with a Varying Number of Hours: 15.0%
Workers Earning Some Overtime Pay, Tips, or Commissions: 39.1%
Earnings Benefit of Working Overtime: -4.8%

Gender

	Male	Female
Percent	97.2%	2.8%
Effect on Earnings	0.3%	-13.9%

Union Membership

Percentage Union Members: 10.1%
Earnings Benefit of Union Membership: 5.4%

Veteran Status

Percentage Who Have Been on Active Duty: 13.2%
Earnings Benefit of Veteran Status: 3.5%

47-5012 Rotary Drill Operators, Oil and Gas

Set up or operate a variety of drills to remove petroleum products from the earth and to find and remove core samples for testing during oil and gas exploration.

- Education or Training Required: Moderate-term on-the-job training
- Job Growth: 0.1%
- Annual Openings: 1,000
- Self-Employed: 2.8%
- Part-Time: 4.9%

NATIONAL WAGE FIGURES (ANNUAL)

Beginning	25th Percentile	Median	Mean	75th Percentile	90th Percentile
$25,190	$30,860	$38,460	$42,350	$53,520	$65,140

Median Wages for Industries Employing Largest Numbers (Annual)

Industry	Median Income
Oil and Gas Extraction	$40,550
Heavy and Civil Engineering Construction	$40,410
Rental and Leasing Services	$39,810
Support Activities for Mining	$38,340
Specialty Trade Contractors	$37,730
Machinery Manufacturing	$32,500
Professional, Scientific, and Technical Services	$31,920

Median Wages for States (Annual)

State	Wage	State	Wage	State	Wage
AK	$61,440	KY	$22,670	NY	no data
AL	no data	LA	$40,710	OH	$30,640
AR	$33,230	MA	no data	OK	$51,430
AZ	no data	MD	$31,720	OR	no data
CA	$49,360	ME	no data	PA	$36,030
CO	$40,600	MI	$35,290	RI	no data
CT	no data	MN	no data	SC	no data
DC	no data	MO	no data	SD	no data
DE	no data	MS	$34,060	TN	no data
FL	no data	MT	$38,950	TX	$36,390
GA	no data	NC	no data	UT	$41,580
HI	no data	ND	$44,460	VA	$37,010
IA	no data	NE	no data	VT	no data
ID	no data	NH	no data	WA	$37,730
IL	$31,320	NJ	no data	WI	no data
IN	no data	NM	$36,990	WV	$35,230
KS	$33,220	NV	no data	WY	$49,760

Median Wages for the Largest Metropolitan Areas (Annual)

Area	Wage	Area	Wage
AZ: Phoenix	no data	MI: Detroit	no data
CA: Los Angeles	$53,770	MN: Minneapolis	no data
CA: Riverside	no data	MO: Kansas City	no data
CA: Sacramento	no data	MO: St. Louis	no data
CA: San Diego	no data	NV: Las Vegas	no data
CA: San Francisco	no data	NY: New York	no data
CO: Denver	no data	OH: Cincinnati	no data
DC: Washington	$39,660	OH: Cleveland	no data
FL: Miami	no data	OH: Columbus	no data
FL: Orlando	no data	OR: Portland	no data
FL: Tampa	no data	PA: Philadelphia	no data
GA: Atlanta	no data	PA: Pittsburgh	$49,580
IL: Chicago	no data	TX: Dallas	$34,760
MA: Boston	no data	TX: Houston	$36,600
MD: Baltimore	no data	WA: Seattle	no data

FACTORS THAT MAY AFFECT EARNINGS

Educational Attainment of Workers and Effect on Earnings

Figures are based on a group of occupations: Extraction Workers

	Percent at Level	Effect on Earnings
Less than High School	4.1%	−42.9%
Some High School	17.8%	−12.0%
High School or Equivalent	46.1%	3.3%
Some College but No Degree	20.1%	2.3%
Associate Degree	8.9%	14.7%
Bachelor's Degree	—	—
Master's Degree	—	—
Doctoral Degree	—	—
First Professional Degree	—	—

Flexibility of Earnings

Average Hours Worked: 40
Workers with a Varying Number of Hours: 15.0%
Workers Earning Some Overtime Pay, Tips, or Commissions: 39.1%
Earnings Benefit of Working Overtime: −4.8%

Gender

	Male	Female
Percent	97.2%	2.8%
Effect on Earnings	0.3%	−13.9%

Union Membership

Percentage Union Members: 10.1%
Earnings Benefit of Union Membership: 5.4%

Veteran Status

Percentage Who Have Been on Active Duty: 13.2%
Earnings Benefit of Veteran Status: 3.5%

47-5013 Service Unit Operators, Oil, Gas, and Mining

Operate equipment to increase oil flow from producing wells or to remove stuck pipe, casing, tools, or other obstructions from drilling wells. May also perform similar services in mining exploration operations.

- Education or Training Required: Moderate-term on-the-job training
- Job Growth: –0.6%
- Annual Openings: 1,000
- Self-Employed: 2.3%
- Part-Time: 4.9%

NATIONAL WAGE FIGURES (ANNUAL)

Beginning	25th Percentile	Median	Mean	75th Percentile	90th Percentile
$21,330	$25,810	$32,910	$36,120	$43,200	$55,370

Median Wages for Industries Employing Largest Numbers (Annual)

Industry	Median Income
Pipeline Transportation	$60,930
Rental and Leasing Services	$40,840
Oil and Gas Extraction	$36,710
Machinery Manufacturing	$35,900
Specialty Trade Contractors	$34,140
Merchant Wholesalers, Durable Goods	$32,580
Support Activities for Mining	$32,380
Utilities	$32,270
Heavy and Civil Engineering Construction	$30,620

Median Wages for States (Annual)

AK $42,750	KY $24,200	NY no data
AL $31,310	LA $35,600	OH $24,840
AR $28,110	MA no data	OK $33,240
AZ no data	MD no data	OR no data
CA $39,140	ME no data	PA $26,290
CO no data	MI $32,490	RI no data
CT no data	MN no data	SC no data
DC no data	MO no data	SD no data
DE no data	MS $36,150	TN no data
FL no data	MT no data	TX $31,400
GA no data	NC no data	UT $34,550
HI no data	ND $40,240	VA no data
IA no data	NE no data	VT no data
ID no data	NH no data	WA no data
IL $27,160	NJ no data	WI no data
IN no data	NM $37,410	WV $28,590
KS $30,590	NV no data	WY $43,300

Median Wages for the Largest Metropolitan Areas (Annual)

AZ: Phoenix	no data	MI: Detroit	no data
CA: Los Angeles	$39,500	MN: Minneapolis	no data
CA: Riverside	no data	MO: Kansas City	no data
CA: Sacramento	$37,680	MO: St. Louis	no data
CA: San Diego	no data	NV: Las Vegas	no data
CA: San Francisco	no data	NY: New York	no data
CO: Denver	no data	OH: Cincinnati	no data
DC: Washington	no data	OH: Cleveland	no data
FL: Miami	no data	OH: Columbus	no data
FL: Orlando	no data	OR: Portland	no data
FL: Tampa	no data	PA: Philadelphia	no data
GA: Atlanta	no data	PA: Pittsburgh	$25,050
IL: Chicago	no data	TX: Dallas	no data
MA: Boston	no data	TX: Houston	$33,700
MD: Baltimore	no data	WA: Seattle	no data

FACTORS THAT MAY AFFECT EARNINGS

Educational Attainment of Workers and Effect on Earnings

Figures are based on a group of occupations: Extraction Workers

	Percent at Level	Effect on Earnings
Less than High School	4.1%	–42.9%
Some High School	17.8%	–12.0%
High School or Equivalent	46.1%	3.3%
Some College but No Degree	20.1%	2.3%
Associate Degree	8.9%	14.7%
Bachelor's Degree	—	—
Master's Degree	—	—
Doctoral Degree	—	—
First Professional Degree	—	—

Flexibility of Earnings

Average Hours Worked: 40
Workers with a Varying Number of Hours: 15.0%
Workers Earning Some Overtime Pay, Tips, or Commissions: 39.1%
Earnings Benefit of Working Overtime: –4.8%

Gender

	Male	Female
Percent	97.2%	2.8%
Effect on Earnings	0.3%	–13.9%

Union Membership

Percentage Union Members: 10.1%
Earnings Benefit of Union Membership: 5.4%

Veteran Status

Percentage Who Have Been on Active Duty: 13.2%
Earnings Benefit of Veteran Status: 3.5%

47-5021 Earth Drillers, Except Oil and Gas

Operate a variety of drills—such as rotary, churn, and pneumatic—to tap sub-surface water and salt deposits, to remove core samples during mineral exploration or soil testing, and to facilitate the use of explosives in mining or construction. May use explosives. Includes horizontal and earth-boring machine operators.

- Education or Training Required: Moderate-term on-the-job training
- Job Growth: 7.9%
- Annual Openings: 4,000
- Self-Employed: 10.5%
- Part-Time: 5.7%

NATIONAL WAGE FIGURES (ANNUAL)

Beginning	25th Percentile	Median	Mean	75th Percentile	90th Percentile
$22,310	$27,500	$34,500	$37,030	$43,670	$54,750

Median Wages for Industries Employing Largest Numbers (Annual)

Industry	Median Income
Utilities	$47,990
Federal, State, and Local Government	$38,610
Mining (Except Oil and Gas)	$37,210
Specialty Trade Contractors	$35,440
Administrative and Support Services	$35,210
Heavy and Civil Engineering Construction	$33,890
Professional, Scientific, and Technical Services	$33,100
Support Activities for Mining	$32,280
Merchant Wholesalers, Nondurable Goods	$31,060
Waste Management and Remediation Services	$30,230

Median Wages for States (Annual)

State	Wage	State	Wage	State	Wage
AK	no data	KY	$30,460	NY	$37,820
AL	$29,950	LA	$41,500	OH	$32,220
AR	$34,950	MA	$39,620	OK	$27,460
AZ	$33,490	MD	$41,940	OR	$42,500
CA	$47,240	ME	$34,210	PA	$32,790
CO	$31,390	MI	$33,770	RI	$41,400
CT	$43,360	MN	$40,110	SC	no data
DC	no data	MO	$32,530	SD	$29,610
DE	no data	MS	$32,630	TN	$29,370
FL	$33,650	MT	$39,820	TX	$28,790
GA	$29,370	NC	$30,950	UT	$24,590
HI	no data	ND	$34,370	VA	$33,550
IA	$34,880	NE	$26,250	VT	$30,400
ID	$32,550	NH	$36,020	WA	$49,820
IL	$37,630	NJ	$44,920	WI	$35,650
IN	$31,430	NM	$39,450	WV	$36,560
KS	$36,210	NV	$44,910	WY	$31,090

Median Wages for the Largest Metropolitan Areas (Annual)

Area	Wage	Area	Wage
AZ: Phoenix	$23,660	MI: Detroit	no data
CA: Los Angeles	$44,750	MN: Minneapolis	$36,020
CA: Riverside	$82,780	MO: Kansas City	$46,170
CA: Sacramento	$42,840	MO: St. Louis	$34,910
CA: San Diego	$54,690	NV: Las Vegas	$43,880
CA: San Francisco	$35,330	NY: New York	$44,180
CO: Denver	no data	OH: Cincinnati	no data
DC: Washington	$36,720	OH: Cleveland	no data
FL: Miami	$32,930	OH: Columbus	$34,780
FL: Orlando	$30,290	OR: Portland	no data
FL: Tampa	$32,070	PA: Philadelphia	$40,770
GA: Atlanta	$34,100	PA: Pittsburgh	$35,620
IL: Chicago	$43,230	TX: Dallas	$29,620
MA: Boston	$38,140	TX: Houston	$31,110
MD: Baltimore	no data	WA: Seattle	$66,810

FACTORS THAT MAY AFFECT EARNINGS

Educational Attainment of Workers and Effect on Earnings

	Percent at Level	Effect on Earnings
Less than High School	—	—
Some High School	22.0%	1.8%
High School or Equivalent	56.1%	−9.3%
Some College but No Degree	—	—
Associate Degree	—	—
Bachelor's Degree	—	—
Master's Degree	—	—
Doctoral Degree	—	—
First Professional Degree	—	—

Figures do not total 100% because some levels have a very small sample size.

Flexibility of Earnings

Average Hours Worked: 39
Workers with a Varying Number of Hours: 13.6%
Workers Earning Some Overtime Pay, Tips, or Commissions: 37.8%
Earnings Benefit of Working Overtime: −4.8%

Gender

	Male	Female
Percent	97.6%	2.4%
Effect on Earnings	0.3%	−13.9%

Union Membership

Percentage Union Members: 11.1%
Earnings Benefit of Union Membership: 5.4%

Veteran Status

Percentage Who Have Been on Active Duty: 13.2%
Earnings Benefit of Veteran Status: 3.5%

47-5031 Explosives Workers, Ordnance Handling Experts, and Blasters

Place and detonate explosives to demolish structures or to loosen, remove, or displace earth, rock, or other materials. May perform specialized handling, storage, and accounting procedures. Includes seismograph shooters.

- Education or Training Required: Moderate-term on-the-job training
- Job Growth: 2.2%
- Annual Openings: 1,000
- Self-Employed: 0.0%
- Part-Time: 4.9%

NATIONAL WAGE FIGURES (ANNUAL)

Beginning	25th Percentile	Median	Mean	75th Percentile	90th Percentile
$28,660	$33,700	$39,890	$41,240	$47,740	$56,190

Median Wages for Industries Employing Largest Numbers (Annual)

Industry	Median Income
Fabricated Metal Product Manufacturing	$48,700
Specialty Trade Contractors	$43,290
Chemical Manufacturing	$43,120
Merchant Wholesalers, Nondurable Goods	$42,890
Mining (Except Oil and Gas)	$40,310
Federal, State, and Local Government	$38,200
Support Activities for Mining	$35,340
Nonmetallic Mineral Product Manufacturing	$34,050

Median Wages for States (Annual)

AK	no data	KY	$35,470	NY	$44,200
AL	$42,070	LA	no data	OH	$42,650
AR	$36,260	MA	no data	OK	$35,650
AZ	$42,040	MD	$44,830	OR	$44,680
CA	$46,320	ME	$38,030	PA	$35,930
CO	$42,770	MI	$39,750	RI	no data
CT	$55,650	MN	$45,240	SC	no data
DC	no data	MO	$48,280	SD	$44,330
DE	no data	MS	no data	TN	$44,040
FL	$43,260	MT	no data	TX	$34,820
GA	$28,970	NC	$43,360	UT	$40,160
HI	$49,990	ND	no data	VA	$40,410
IA	no data	NE	no data	VT	no data
ID	no data	NH	no data	WA	$43,120
IL	$43,070	NJ	no data	WI	$52,900
IN	$36,260	NM	$51,820	WV	$38,340
KS	$35,540	NV	$44,540	WY	$50,580

Median Wages for the Largest Metropolitan Areas (Annual)

AZ: Phoenix	no data	MI: Detroit	no data
CA: Los Angeles	no data	MN: Minneapolis	no data
CA: Riverside	no data	MO: Kansas City	$47,050
CA: Sacramento	no data	MO: St. Louis	no data
CA: San Diego	no data	NV: Las Vegas	no data
CA: San Francisco	no data	NY: New York	no data
CO: Denver	no data	OH: Cincinnati	no data
DC: Washington	$41,570	OH: Cleveland	no data
FL: Miami	no data	OH: Columbus	no data
FL: Orlando	no data	OR: Portland	no data
FL: Tampa	no data	PA: Philadelphia	$42,490
GA: Atlanta	no data	PA: Pittsburgh	$34,300
IL: Chicago	no data	TX: Dallas	no data
MA: Boston	no data	TX: Houston	no data
MD: Baltimore	no data	WA: Seattle	no data

FACTORS THAT MAY AFFECT EARNINGS

Educational Attainment of Workers and Effect on Earnings

	Percent at Level	Effect on Earnings
Less than High School	—	—
Some High School	—	—
High School or Equivalent	40.0%	−9.7%
Some College but No Degree	—	—
Associate Degree	—	—
Bachelor's Degree	—	—
Master's Degree	—	—
Doctoral Degree	—	—
First Professional Degree	—	—

Figures do not total 100% because some levels have a very small sample size.

Flexibility of Earnings

Average Hours Worked: 42
Workers with a Varying Number of Hours: 3.5%
Workers Earning Some Overtime Pay, Tips, or Commissions: 26.7%
Earnings Benefit of Working Overtime: −4.8%

Gender

	Male	Female
Percent	98.3%	1.7%
Effect on Earnings	0.3%	−13.9%

Union Membership

Percentage Union Members: 6.7%
Earnings Benefit of Union Membership: 5.4%

Veteran Status

Percentage Who Have Been on Active Duty: 13.2%
Earnings Benefit of Veteran Status: 3.5%

47-5041 Continuous Mining Machine Operators

Operate self-propelled mining machines that rip coal, metal and nonmetal ores, rock, stone, or sand from the face and load it onto conveyors or into shuttle cars in a continuous operation.

- Education or Training Required: Moderate-term on-the-job training
- Job Growth: –12.4%
- Annual Openings: 1,000
- Self-Employed: 0.5%
- Part-Time: 4.9%

NATIONAL WAGE FIGURES (ANNUAL)

Beginning	25th Percentile	Median	Mean	75th Percentile	90th Percentile
$26,690	$33,540	$40,430	$40,310	$46,290	$54,520

Median Wages for Industries Employing Largest Numbers (Annual)

Industry	Median Income
Mining (Except Oil and Gas)	$40,940
Support Activities for Mining	$33,100
Nonmetallic Mineral Product Manufacturing	$30,440
Merchant Wholesalers, Durable Goods	$27,560

Median Wages for States (Annual)

AK	no data	KY	$39,090	NY	$28,270
AL	$38,960	LA	no data	OH	$38,120
AR	no data	MA	no data	OK	no data
AZ	$36,550	MD	no data	OR	no data
CA	$39,200	ME	no data	PA	$32,780
CO	$41,700	MI	$39,120	RI	no data
CT	no data	MN	no data	SC	$32,190
DC	no data	MO	$30,770	SD	no data
DE	no data	MS	no data	TN	$28,950
FL	no data	MT	$45,970	TX	$22,330
GA	$28,720	NC	$35,690	UT	$43,520
HI	no data	ND	no data	VA	$32,150
IA	no data	NE	no data	VT	no data
ID	$41,000	NH	no data	WA	$44,770
IL	$42,260	NJ	no data	WI	$38,090
IN	$31,190	NM	$41,090	WV	$41,380
KS	$28,410	NV	$48,630	WY	$35,530

Median Wages for the Largest Metropolitan Areas (Annual)

AZ: Phoenix	$33,810	MI: Detroit	no data
CA: Los Angeles	no data	MN: Minneapolis	no data
CA: Riverside	no data	MO: Kansas City	no data
CA: Sacramento	no data	MO: St. Louis	$37,500
CA: San Diego	no data	NV: Las Vegas	no data
CA: San Francisco	no data	NY: New York	no data
CO: Denver	no data	OH: Cincinnati	no data
DC: Washington	no data	OH: Cleveland	no data
FL: Miami	no data	OH: Columbus	no data
FL: Orlando	no data	OR: Portland	no data
FL: Tampa	no data	PA: Philadelphia	no data
GA: Atlanta	$27,570	PA: Pittsburgh	$34,790
IL: Chicago	no data	TX: Dallas	no data
MA: Boston	no data	TX: Houston	no data
MD: Baltimore	no data	WA: Seattle	no data

FACTORS THAT MAY AFFECT EARNINGS

Educational Attainment of Workers and Effect on Earnings

Figures are based on a group of occupations: Extraction Workers

	Percent at Level	Effect on Earnings
Less than High School	4.1%	–42.9%
Some High School	17.8%	–12.0%
High School or Equivalent	46.1%	3.3%
Some College but No Degree	20.1%	2.3%
Associate Degree	8.9%	14.7%
Bachelor's Degree	—	—
Master's Degree	—	—
Doctoral Degree	—	—
First Professional Degree	—	—

Flexibility of Earnings

Average Hours Worked: 40
Workers with a Varying Number of Hours: 15.0%
Workers Earning Some Overtime Pay, Tips, or Commissions: 39.1%
Earnings Benefit of Working Overtime: –6.9%

Gender

	Male	Female
Percent	97.2%	2.8%
Effect on Earnings	0.3%	–13.9%

Union Membership

Percentage Union Members: 10.1%
Earnings Benefit of Union Membership: 5.4%

Veteran Status

Percentage Who Have Been on Active Duty: 13.2%
Earnings Benefit of Veteran Status: 3.5%

47-5042 Mine Cutting and Channeling Machine Operators

Operate machinery—such as longwall shears, plows, and cutting machines—to cut or channel along the face or seams of coal mines, stone quarries, or other mining surfaces to facilitate blasting, separating, or removing minerals or materials from mines or from the earth's surface.

- Education or Training Required: Moderate-term on-the-job training
- Job Growth: –11.1%
- Annual Openings: Fewer than 500
- Self-Employed: 0.7%
- Part-Time: 4.9%

NATIONAL WAGE FIGURES (ANNUAL)

Beginning	25th Percentile	Median	Mean	75th Percentile	90th Percentile
$24,480	$31,190	$39,990	$38,930	$45,450	$50,990

Median Wages for Industries Employing Largest Numbers (Annual)

Industry	Median Income
Chemical Manufacturing	$43,930
Mining (Except Oil and Gas)	$40,320
Support Activities for Mining	$38,640
Specialty Trade Contractors	$29,290
Nonmetallic Mineral Product Manufacturing	$21,840

Median Wages for States (Annual)

AK	no data	KY	$38,580	NY	$32,430
AL	$38,610	LA	no data	OH	$33,920
AR	no data	MA	no data	OK	no data
AZ	$22,490	MD	$28,090	OR	no data
CA	$27,810	ME	no data	PA	$46,230
CO	$47,990	MI	$26,400	RI	no data
CT	no data	MN	no data	SC	no data
DC	no data	MO	$25,810	SD	no data
DE	no data	MS	no data	TN	$32,900
FL	no data	MT	no data	TX	$21,300
GA	$35,370	NC	no data	UT	no data
HI	no data	ND	no data	VA	$36,100
IA	no data	NE	no data	VT	no data
ID	no data	NH	no data	WA	no data
IL	$38,740	NJ	no data	WI	no data
IN	$38,490	NM	no data	WV	$40,190
KS	no data	NV	$47,050	WY	$60,810

Median Wages for the Largest Metropolitan Areas (Annual)

AZ: Phoenix	no data	MI: Detroit	no data
CA: Los Angeles	no data	MN: Minneapolis	no data
CA: Riverside	no data	MO: Kansas City	no data
CA: Sacramento	no data	MO: St. Louis	no data
CA: San Diego	no data	NV: Las Vegas	no data
CA: San Francisco	no data	NY: New York	no data
CO: Denver	no data	OH: Cincinnati	no data
DC: Washington	no data	OH: Cleveland	no data
FL: Miami	no data	OH: Columbus	no data
FL: Orlando	no data	OR: Portland	no data
FL: Tampa	no data	PA: Philadelphia	no data
GA: Atlanta	no data	PA: Pittsburgh	$32,900
IL: Chicago	$31,670	TX: Dallas	no data
MA: Boston	no data	TX: Houston	no data
MD: Baltimore	no data	WA: Seattle	no data

FACTORS THAT MAY AFFECT EARNINGS

Educational Attainment of Workers and Effect on Earnings

Figures are based on a group of occupations: Extraction Workers

	Percent at Level	Effect on Earnings
Less than High School	4.1%	–42.9%
Some High School	17.8%	–12.0%
High School or Equivalent	46.1%	3.3%
Some College but No Degree	20.1%	2.3%
Associate Degree	8.9%	14.7%
Bachelor's Degree	—	—
Master's Degree	—	—
Doctoral Degree	—	—
First Professional Degree	—	—

Flexibility of Earnings

Average Hours Worked: 40
Workers with a Varying Number of Hours: 15.0%
Workers Earning Some Overtime Pay, Tips, or Commissions: 39.1%
Earnings Benefit of Working Overtime: –6.9%

Gender

	Male	Female
Percent	97.2%	2.8%
Effect on Earnings	0.3%	–13.9%

Union Membership

Percentage Union Members: 10.1%
Earnings Benefit of Union Membership: 5.4%

Veteran Status

Percentage Who Have Been on Active Duty: 13.2%
Earnings Benefit of Veteran Status: 3.5%

47-5049 Mining Machine Operators, All Other

All mining machine operators not listed separately.

- Education or Training Required: Moderate-term on-the-job training
- Job Growth: 0.9%
- Annual Openings: Fewer than 500
- Self-Employed: 0.7%
- Part-Time: 4.9%

NATIONAL WAGE FIGURES (ANNUAL)

Beginning	25th Percentile	Median	Mean	75th Percentile	90th Percentile
$23,060	$30,080	$37,370	$38,490	$44,730	$57,660

Median Wages for Industries Employing Largest Numbers (Annual)

Industry	Median Income
Specialty Trade Contractors	$47,980
Support Activities for Mining	$42,480
Mining (Except Oil and Gas)	$37,070
Nonmetallic Mineral Product Manufacturing	$32,390

Median Wages for States (Annual)

State		State		State	
AK	no data	KY	no data	NY	no data
AL	$38,700	LA	no data	OH	no data
AR	$33,860	MA	no data	OK	no data
AZ	no data	MD	no data	OR	no data
CA	$42,260	ME	no data	PA	no data
CO	$41,760	MI	no data	RI	no data
CT	no data	MN	no data	SC	$27,780
DC	no data	MO	no data	SD	no data
DE	no data	MS	no data	TN	no data
FL	no data	MT	$38,220	TX	no data
GA	$36,340	NC	no data	UT	no data
HI	no data	ND	no data	VA	$28,940
IA	no data	NE	no data	VT	no data
ID	$35,930	NH	no data	WA	no data
IL	$34,830	NJ	no data	WI	no data
IN	no data	NM	$40,820	WV	no data
KS	no data	NV	no data	WY	no data

Median Wages for the Largest Metropolitan Areas (Annual)

Area		Area	
AZ: Phoenix	no data	MI: Detroit	no data
CA: Los Angeles	no data	MN: Minneapolis	no data
CA: Riverside	no data	MO: Kansas City	no data
CA: Sacramento	no data	MO: St. Louis	no data
CA: San Diego	no data	NV: Las Vegas	no data
CA: San Francisco	no data	NY: New York	no data
CO: Denver	no data	OH: Cincinnati	no data
DC: Washington	no data	OH: Cleveland	no data
FL: Miami	no data	OH: Columbus	no data
FL: Orlando	no data	OR: Portland	no data
FL: Tampa	no data	PA: Philadelphia	no data
GA: Atlanta	no data	PA: Pittsburgh	no data
IL: Chicago	no data	TX: Dallas	no data
MA: Boston	no data	TX: Houston	no data
MD: Baltimore	no data	WA: Seattle	no data

FACTORS THAT MAY AFFECT EARNINGS

Educational Attainment of Workers and Effect on Earnings

Figures are based on a group of occupations: Extraction Workers

	Percent at Level	Effect on Earnings
Less than High School	4.1%	−42.9%
Some High School	17.8%	−12.0%
High School or Equivalent	46.1%	3.3%
Some College but No Degree	20.1%	2.3%
Associate Degree	8.9%	14.7%
Bachelor's Degree	—	—
Master's Degree	—	—
Doctoral Degree	—	—
First Professional Degree	—	—

Flexibility of Earnings

Average Hours Worked: 40
Workers with a Varying Number of Hours: 15.0%
Workers Earning Some Overtime Pay, Tips, or Commissions: 39.1%
Earnings Benefit of Working Overtime: −6.9%

Gender

	Male	Female
Percent	97.2%	2.8%
Effect on Earnings	0.3%	−13.9%

Union Membership

Percentage Union Members: 10.1%
Earnings Benefit of Union Membership: 5.4%

Veteran Status

Percentage Who Have Been on Active Duty: 13.2%
Earnings Benefit of Veteran Status: 3.5%

47-5051 Rock Splitters, Quarry

Separate blocks of rough-dimension stone from quarry mass, using jackhammer and wedges.

- Education or Training Required: Moderate-term on-the-job training
- Job Growth: 4.1%
- Annual Openings: 1,000
- Self-Employed: 5.8%
- Part-Time: 6.1%

NATIONAL WAGE FIGURES (ANNUAL)

Beginning	25th Percentile	Median	Mean	75th Percentile	90th Percentile
$17,780	$21,270	$27,130	$28,940	$34,430	$43,540

Median Wages for Industries Employing Largest Numbers (Annual)

Industry	Median Income
Nonmetallic Mineral Product Manufacturing	$31,340
Mining (Except Oil and Gas)	$27,330

Median Wages for States (Annual)

State	Wage	State	Wage	State	Wage
AK	no data	KY	no data	NY	no data
AL	no data	LA	no data	OH	$30,090
AR	$23,810	MA	no data	OK	$19,560
AZ	no data	MD	no data	OR	no data
CA	$17,960	ME	$20,900	PA	$32,500
CO	$24,930	MI	no data	RI	no data
CT	no data	MN	no data	SC	$31,110
DC	no data	MO	$26,290	SD	no data
DE	no data	MS	no data	TN	$28,650
FL	no data	MT	no data	TX	$29,750
GA	$27,120	NC	$24,030	UT	no data
HI	no data	ND	no data	VA	$27,350
IA	$29,870	NE	no data	VT	no data
ID	no data	NH	no data	WA	$23,650
IL	$38,490	NJ	no data	WI	$23,760
IN	$36,250	NM	no data	WV	no data
KS	$26,220	NV	$19,150	WY	no data

Median Wages for the Largest Metropolitan Areas (Annual)

Area	Wage	Area	Wage
AZ: Phoenix	no data	MI: Detroit	no data
CA: Los Angeles	no data	MN: Minneapolis	no data
CA: Riverside	no data	MO: Kansas City	no data
CA: Sacramento	no data	MO: St. Louis	no data
CA: San Diego	no data	NV: Las Vegas	no data
CA: San Francisco	no data	NY: New York	no data
CO: Denver	no data	OH: Cincinnati	no data
DC: Washington	no data	OH: Cleveland	no data
FL: Miami	no data	OH: Columbus	no data
FL: Orlando	no data	OR: Portland	no data
FL: Tampa	no data	PA: Philadelphia	$40,650
GA: Atlanta	$26,940	PA: Pittsburgh	$33,930
IL: Chicago	no data	TX: Dallas	no data
MA: Boston	no data	TX: Houston	no data
MD: Baltimore	no data	WA: Seattle	no data

FACTORS THAT MAY AFFECT EARNINGS

Educational Attainment of Workers and Effect on Earnings

	Percent at Level	Effect on Earnings
Less than High School	—	—
Some High School	19.4%	−21.7%
High School or Equivalent	49.3%	24.9%
Some College but No Degree	17.9%	−20.4%
Associate Degree	—	—
Bachelor's Degree	—	—
Master's Degree	—	—
Doctoral Degree	—	—
First Professional Degree	—	—

Figures do not total 100% because some levels have a very small sample size.

Flexibility of Earnings

Average Hours Worked: 40
Workers with a Varying Number of Hours: 15.0%
Workers Earning Some Overtime Pay, Tips, or Commissions: 34.2%
Earnings Benefit of Working Overtime: −5.5%

Gender

	Male	Female
Percent	97.2%	2.8%
Effect on Earnings	0.3%	−13.9%

Union Membership

Percentage Union Members: 9.2%
Earnings Benefit of Union Membership: 5.4%

Veteran Status

Percentage Who Have Been on Active Duty: 13.2%
Earnings Benefit of Veteran Status: 3.5%

47-5061 Roof Bolters, Mining

Operate machinery to install roof support bolts in underground mine.

- Education or Training Required: Moderate-term on-the-job training
- Job Growth: −29.5%
- Annual Openings: 1,000
- Self-Employed: 0.0%
- Part-Time: 4.9%

NATIONAL WAGE FIGURES (ANNUAL)

Beginning	25th Percentile	Median	Mean	75th Percentile	90th Percentile
$33,040	$36,820	$41,250	$42,200	$45,950	$52,930

Median Wages for Industries Employing Largest Numbers (Annual)

Industry	Median Income
Support Activities for Mining	$41,500
Mining (Except Oil and Gas)	$41,260

Median Wages for States (Annual)

AK	no data	KY	$37,150	NY	no data
AL	no data	LA	no data	OH	no data
AR	no data	MA	no data	OK	no data
AZ	no data	MD	no data	OR	no data
CA	no data	ME	no data	PA	$45,290
CO	$47,240	MI	no data	RI	no data
CT	no data	MN	no data	SC	no data
DC	no data	MO	no data	SD	no data
DE	no data	MS	no data	TN	no data
FL	no data	MT	no data	TX	no data
GA	no data	NC	no data	UT	$42,150
HI	no data	ND	no data	VA	$40,300
IA	no data	NE	no data	VT	no data
ID	no data	NH	no data	WA	no data
IL	$42,120	NJ	no data	WI	no data
IN	no data	NM	no data	WV	$42,570
KS	no data	NV	no data	WY	$62,230

Median Wages for the Largest Metropolitan Areas (Annual)

AZ: Phoenix	no data	MI: Detroit	no data
CA: Los Angeles	no data	MN: Minneapolis	no data
CA: Riverside	no data	MO: Kansas City	no data
CA: Sacramento	no data	MO: St. Louis	no data
CA: San Diego	no data	NV: Las Vegas	no data
CA: San Francisco	no data	NY: New York	no data
CO: Denver	no data	OH: Cincinnati	no data
DC: Washington	no data	OH: Cleveland	no data
FL: Miami	no data	OH: Columbus	no data
FL: Orlando	no data	OR: Portland	no data
FL: Tampa	no data	PA: Philadelphia	no data
GA: Atlanta	no data	PA: Pittsburgh	no data
IL: Chicago	no data	TX: Dallas	no data
MA: Boston	no data	TX: Houston	no data
MD: Baltimore	no data	WA: Seattle	no data

FACTORS THAT MAY AFFECT EARNINGS

Educational Attainment of Workers and Effect on Earnings

Figures are based on a group of occupations: Extraction Workers

	Percent at Level	Effect on Earnings
Less than High School	4.1%	−42.9%
Some High School	17.8%	−12.0%
High School or Equivalent	46.1%	3.3%
Some College but No Degree	20.1%	2.3%
Associate Degree	8.9%	14.7%
Bachelor's Degree	—	—
Master's Degree	—	—
Doctoral Degree	—	—
First Professional Degree	—	—

Flexibility of Earnings

Average Hours Worked: 32
Workers with a Varying Number of Hours: 12.5%
Workers Earning Some Overtime Pay, Tips, or Commissions: 71.4%
Earnings Benefit of Working Overtime: −4.8%

Gender

	Male	Female
Percent	97.2%	2.8%
Effect on Earnings	0.3%	−13.9%

Union Membership

Percentage Union Members: 10.1%
Earnings Benefit of Union Membership: 5.4%

Veteran Status

Percentage Who Have Been on Active Duty: 13.2%
Earnings Benefit of Veteran Status: 3.5%

47-5071 Roustabouts, Oil and Gas

Assemble or repair oil field equipment, using hand and power tools. Perform other tasks as needed.

- Education or Training Required: Moderate-term on-the-job training
- Job Growth: 1.0%
- Annual Openings: 6,000
- Self-Employed: 0.0%
- Part-Time: 4.9%

NATIONAL WAGE FIGURES (ANNUAL)

Beginning	25th Percentile	Median	Mean	75th Percentile	90th Percentile
$17,490	$20,750	$25,700	$26,890	$31,620	$38,430

Median Wages for Industries Employing Largest Numbers (Annual)

Industry	Median Income
Pipeline Transportation	$42,000
Utilities	$29,110
Professional, Scientific, and Technical Services	$28,640
Merchant Wholesalers, Durable Goods	$28,490
Rental and Leasing Services	$26,680
Oil and Gas Extraction	$26,310
Support Activities for Mining	$25,950
Heavy and Civil Engineering Construction	$23,090
Repair and Maintenance	$22,510
Waste Management and Remediation Services	$22,240

Median Wages for States (Annual)

AK	$34,860	KY	$30,450	NY	no data
AL	$35,620	LA	$27,080	OH	$24,310
AR	$26,310	MA	no data	OK	no data
AZ	no data	MD	no data	OR	no data
CA	$34,380	ME	no data	PA	$25,530
CO	$28,970	MI	$30,700	RI	no data
CT	no data	MN	no data	SC	no data
DC	no data	MO	no data	SD	no data
DE	no data	MS	$24,830	TN	no data
FL	no data	MT	$42,290	TX	$23,950
GA	no data	NC	no data	UT	$26,950
HI	no data	ND	$31,820	VA	$21,920
IA	no data	NE	$29,920	VT	no data
ID	no data	NH	no data	WA	no data
IL	$25,830	NJ	no data	WI	no data
IN	$22,390	NM	$24,190	WV	$26,930
KS	$25,250	NV	no data	WY	$28,750

Median Wages for the Largest Metropolitan Areas (Annual)

AZ: Phoenix	no data	MI: Detroit	no data
CA: Los Angeles	$31,030	MN: Minneapolis	no data
CA: Riverside	no data	MO: Kansas City	no data
CA: Sacramento	no data	MO: St. Louis	no data
CA: San Diego	no data	NV: Las Vegas	no data
CA: San Francisco	no data	NY: New York	no data
CO: Denver	no data	OH: Cincinnati	no data
DC: Washington	no data	OH: Cleveland	no data
FL: Miami	no data	OH: Columbus	no data
FL: Orlando	no data	OR: Portland	no data
FL: Tampa	no data	PA: Philadelphia	no data
GA: Atlanta	no data	PA: Pittsburgh	$24,990
IL: Chicago	no data	TX: Dallas	$27,580
MA: Boston	no data	TX: Houston	$26,360
MD: Baltimore	no data	WA: Seattle	no data

FACTORS THAT MAY AFFECT EARNINGS

Educational Attainment of Workers and Effect on Earnings

Figures are based on a group of occupations: Extraction Workers

	Percent at Level	Effect on Earnings
Less than High School	4.1%	−42.9%
Some High School	17.8%	−12.0%
High School or Equivalent	46.1%	3.3%
Some College but No Degree	20.1%	2.3%
Associate Degree	8.9%	14.7%
Bachelor's Degree	—	—
Master's Degree	—	—
Doctoral Degree	—	—
First Professional Degree	—	—

Flexibility of Earnings

Average Hours Worked: 43
Workers with a Varying Number of Hours: 14.3%
Workers Earning Some Overtime Pay, Tips, or Commissions: 42.9%
Earnings Benefit of Working Overtime: −4.8%

Gender

	Male	Female
Percent	97.2%	2.8%
Effect on Earnings	0.3%	−13.9%

Union Membership

Percentage Union Members: 10.1%
Earnings Benefit of Union Membership: 5.4%

Veteran Status

Percentage Who Have Been on Active Duty: 13.2%
Earnings Benefit of Veteran Status: 3.5%

47-5081 Helpers—Extraction Workers

Help extraction craft workers, such as earth drillers, blasters and explosives workers, derrick operators, and mining machine operators, by performing duties of lesser skill. Duties include supplying equipment or cleaning work area.

- Education or Training Required: Short-term on-the-job training
- Job Growth: –0.1%
- Annual Openings: 4,000
- Self-Employed: 0.0%
- Part-Time: 4.9%

NATIONAL WAGE FIGURES (ANNUAL)

Beginning	25th Percentile	Median	Mean	75th Percentile	90th Percentile
$18,980	$22,740	$28,680	$30,460	$37,760	$44,860

Median Wages for Industries Employing Largest Numbers (Annual)

Industry	Median Income
Mining (Except Oil and Gas)	$35,770
Support Activities for Mining	$28,850
Nonmetallic Mineral Product Manufacturing	$28,510
Oil and Gas Extraction	$25,220
Professional, Scientific, and Technical Services	$24,790
Specialty Trade Contractors	$24,280
Heavy and Civil Engineering Construction	$24,210
Waste Management and Remediation Services	$24,160
Merchant Wholesalers, Nondurable Goods	$23,870
Administrative and Support Services	$21,950

Median Wages for States (Annual)

State	Wage	State	Wage	State	Wage
AK	$52,200	KY	$29,100	NY	$28,770
AL	no data	LA	$32,500	OH	$27,420
AR	$26,370	MA	$24,830	OK	$30,010
AZ	$23,970	MD	$27,580	OR	$25,870
CA	$33,420	ME	no data	PA	$30,500
CO	$31,260	MI	$27,790	RI	no data
CT	$23,520	MN	$23,420	SC	$21,880
DC	no data	MO	$21,070	SD	no data
DE	no data	MS	$22,130	TN	$25,830
FL	$23,710	MT	$29,350	TX	$22,540
GA	$26,800	NC	$21,410	UT	$27,480
HI	no data	ND	$23,890	VA	$27,750
IA	no data	NE	no data	VT	no data
ID	$28,130	NH	$27,760	WA	$28,410
IL	$37,020	NJ	$29,940	WI	$22,030
IN	$24,690	NM	$29,130	WV	$38,710
KS	$25,690	NV	$28,120	WY	$39,150

Median Wages for the Largest Metropolitan Areas (Annual)

Area	Wage	Area	Wage
AZ: Phoenix	$22,410	MI: Detroit	$23,490
CA: Los Angeles	$37,120	MN: Minneapolis	no data
CA: Riverside	no data	MO: Kansas City	no data
CA: Sacramento	$29,390	MO: St. Louis	$43,340
CA: San Diego	$29,620	NV: Las Vegas	no data
CA: San Francisco	no data	NY: New York	$33,660
CO: Denver	$28,450	OH: Cincinnati	no data
DC: Washington	$28,770	OH: Cleveland	no data
FL: Miami	$23,600	OH: Columbus	no data
FL: Orlando	no data	OR: Portland	$27,020
FL: Tampa	no data	PA: Philadelphia	$25,760
GA: Atlanta	$23,850	PA: Pittsburgh	$32,290
IL: Chicago	$38,600	TX: Dallas	$21,800
MA: Boston	$26,100	TX: Houston	$23,610
MD: Baltimore	no data	WA: Seattle	no data

FACTORS THAT MAY AFFECT EARNINGS

Educational Attainment of Workers and Effect on Earnings

	Percent at Level	Effect on Earnings
Less than High School	—	—
Some High School	—	—
High School or Equivalent	60.0%	12.2%
Some College but No Degree	—	—
Associate Degree	—	—
Bachelor's Degree	—	—
Master's Degree	—	—
Doctoral Degree	—	—
First Professional Degree	—	—

Figures do not total 100% because some levels have a very small sample size.

Flexibility of Earnings

Average Hours Worked: 34
Workers with a Varying Number of Hours: 38.5%
Workers Earning Some Overtime Pay, Tips, or Commissions: 60.0%
Earnings Benefit of Working Overtime: –4.8%

Gender

	Male	Female
Percent	97.2%	2.8%
Effect on Earnings	0.3%	–13.9%

Union Membership

Percentage Union Members: 10.1%
Earnings Benefit of Union Membership: 5.4%

Veteran Status

Percentage Who Have Been on Active Duty: 13.2%
Earnings Benefit of Veteran Status: 3.5%

47-5099 Extraction Workers, All Other

All extraction workers not listed separately.

- Education or Training Required: Moderate-term on-the-job training
- Job Growth: –0.7%
- Annual Openings: 3,000
- Self-Employed: 7.7%
- Part-Time: 6.1%

NATIONAL WAGE FIGURES (ANNUAL)

Beginning	25th Percentile	Median	Mean	75th Percentile	90th Percentile
$20,900	$26,690	$35,450	$38,470	$45,880	$64,550

Median Wages for Industries Employing Largest Numbers (Annual)

Industry	Median Income
Federal, State, and Local Government	$43,780
Professional, Scientific, and Technical Services	$38,260
Support Activities for Mining	$37,420
Mining (Except Oil and Gas)	$35,430
Nonmetallic Mineral Product Manufacturing	$35,190
Oil and Gas Extraction	$35,150
Specialty Trade Contractors	$33,300
Heavy and Civil Engineering Construction	$32,540
Pipeline Transportation	$31,420
Repair and Maintenance	$29,320

Median Wages for States (Annual)

State		State		State	
AK	no data	KY	$34,290	NY	no data
AL	$45,240	LA	$42,700	OH	$34,110
AR	no data	MA	no data	OK	$35,970
AZ	no data	MD	$41,590	OR	no data
CA	$35,090	ME	no data	PA	$31,020
CO	$36,990	MI	$35,360	RI	no data
CT	no data	MN	no data	SC	no data
DC	no data	MO	$34,990	SD	no data
DE	no data	MS	no data	TN	$20,630
FL	no data	MT	$35,590	TX	$29,580
GA	$28,180	NC	no data	UT	$40,700
HI	no data	ND	no data	VA	$28,210
IA	$28,210	NE	no data	VT	no data
ID	$39,200	NH	no data	WA	no data
IL	$32,250	NJ	no data	WI	$27,160
IN	$36,500	NM	$32,930	WV	no data
KS	$30,200	NV	$45,040	WY	$42,750

Median Wages for the Largest Metropolitan Areas (Annual)

Area		Area	
AZ: Phoenix	no data	MI: Detroit	$40,650
CA: Los Angeles	$24,530	MN: Minneapolis	no data
CA: Riverside	$48,060	MO: Kansas City	$32,820
CA: Sacramento	no data	MO: St. Louis	$37,580
CA: San Diego	no data	NV: Las Vegas	no data
CA: San Francisco	no data	NY: New York	no data
CO: Denver	no data	OH: Cincinnati	no data
DC: Washington	$27,160	OH: Cleveland	$31,570
FL: Miami	no data	OH: Columbus	no data
FL: Orlando	no data	OR: Portland	no data
FL: Tampa	no data	PA: Philadelphia	no data
GA: Atlanta	$27,870	PA: Pittsburgh	no data
IL: Chicago	no data	TX: Dallas	no data
MA: Boston	no data	TX: Houston	no data
MD: Baltimore	$41,950	WA: Seattle	no data

FACTORS THAT MAY AFFECT EARNINGS

Educational Attainment of Workers and Effect on Earnings

	Percent at Level	Effect on Earnings
Less than High School	—	—
Some High School	19.4%	–21.7%
High School or Equivalent	49.3%	24.9%
Some College but No Degree	17.9%	–20.4%
Associate Degree	—	—
Bachelor's Degree	—	—
Master's Degree	—	—
Doctoral Degree	—	—
First Professional Degree	—	—

Figures do not total 100% because some levels have a very small sample size.

Flexibility of Earnings

Average Hours Worked: 42
Workers with a Varying Number of Hours: 14.5%
Workers Earning Some Overtime Pay, Tips, or Commissions: 34.2%
Earnings Benefit of Working Overtime: –5.5%

Gender

	Male	Female
Percent	98.0%	2.0%
Effect on Earnings	0.3%	–13.9%

Union Membership

Percentage Union Members: 9.2%
Earnings Benefit of Union Membership: 5.4%

Veteran Status

Percentage Who Have Been on Active Duty: 13.2%
Earnings Benefit of Veteran Status: 3.5%

49-0000: Installation, Maintenance, and Repair Occupations

49-1000 Supervisors of Installation, Maintenance, and Repair Workers

49-1011 First-Line Supervisors/Managers of Mechanics, Installers, and Repairers

Supervise and coordinate the activities of mechanics, installers, and repairers.

- Education or Training Required: Work experience in a related occupation
- Job Growth: 12.4%
- Annual Openings: 33,000
- Self-Employed: 0.3%
- Part-Time: 2.4%

NATIONAL WAGE FIGURES (ANNUAL)

Beginning	25th Percentile	Median	Mean	75th Percentile	90th Percentile
$32,820	$41,530	$53,890	$56,110	$68,520	$83,670

Median Wages for Industries Employing Largest Numbers (Annual)

Industry	Median Income
Utilities	$67,750
Telecommunications	$67,200
Transportation Equipment Manufacturing	$64,410
Chemical Manufacturing	$63,490
Air Transportation	$59,020
Rail Transportation	$58,410
Management of Companies and Enterprises	$57,510
Machinery Manufacturing	$57,150
Federal, State, and Local Government	$55,550
Food Manufacturing	$55,080

Median Wages for States (Annual)

AK	$64,740	KY	$46,820	NY	$60,860
AL	$46,070	LA	$47,190	OH	$52,600
AR	$44,170	MA	$59,800	OK	$52,480
AZ	$53,920	MD	$56,840	OR	$53,440
CA	$58,070	ME	$45,690	PA	$56,090
CO	$54,860	MI	$58,620	RI	$55,710
CT	$61,660	MN	$54,460	SC	$47,460
DC	$60,430	MO	$54,720	SD	$51,870
DE	$58,490	MS	$45,120	TN	$46,690
FL	$50,680	MT	$48,970	TX	$49,300
GA	$51,090	NC	$49,960	UT	$52,660
HI	$56,640	ND	$50,500	VA	$57,440
IA	$52,080	NE	$52,030	VT	$52,260
ID	$44,110	NH	$54,700	WA	$62,950
IL	$60,020	NJ	$62,700	WI	$54,450
IN	$51,730	NM	$47,530	WV	$49,490
KS	$50,300	NV	$53,970	WY	$53,010

Median Wages for the Largest Metropolitan Areas (Annual)

AZ: Phoenix	$55,940	MI: Detroit	$65,750
CA: Los Angeles	$57,170	MN: Minneapolis	$56,590
CA: Riverside	$55,850	MO: Kansas City	$57,380
CA: Sacramento	$56,630	MO: St. Louis	$55,860
CA: San Diego	$60,040	NV: Las Vegas	$53,450
CA: San Francisco	$63,740	NY: New York	$66,700
CO: Denver	$56,040	OH: Cincinnati	$51,570
DC: Washington	$61,660	OH: Cleveland	$55,320
FL: Miami	$52,230	OH: Columbus	$53,300
FL: Orlando	$52,100	OR: Portland	$55,960
FL: Tampa	$47,320	PA: Philadelphia	$61,230
GA: Atlanta	$54,450	PA: Pittsburgh	$55,750
IL: Chicago	$63,060	TX: Dallas	$51,270
MA: Boston	$62,660	TX: Houston	$53,490
MD: Baltimore	$58,520	WA: Seattle	$66,130

FACTORS THAT MAY AFFECT EARNINGS

Educational Attainment of Workers and Effect on Earnings

	Percent at Level	Effect on Earnings
Less than High School	—	—
Some High School	5.6%	−31.3%
High School or Equivalent	39.9%	−7.2%
Some College but No Degree	24.0%	2.7%
Associate Degree	17.3%	4.4%
Bachelor's Degree	9.8%	20.2%
Master's Degree	3.1%	43.1%
Doctoral Degree	—	—
First Professional Degree	—	—

Flexibility of Earnings

Average Hours Worked: 41
Workers with a Varying Number of Hours: 5.4%
Workers Earning Some Overtime Pay, Tips, or Commissions: 23.7%
Earnings Benefit of Working Overtime: 0.6%

Gender

	Male	Female
Percent	91.5%	8.5%
Effect on Earnings	1.3%	—

Union Membership

Percentage Union Members: 9.7%
Earnings Benefit of Union Membership: 8.7%

Veteran Status

Percentage Who Have Been on Active Duty: 23.3%
Earnings Benefit of Veteran Status: 1.0%

49-2000 Electrical and Electronic Equipment Mechanics, Installers, and Repairers

49-2011 Computer, Automated Teller, and Office Machine Repairers

Repair, maintain, or install computers; word-processing systems; automated teller machines; and electronic office machines, such as duplicating and fax machines.

- Education or Training Required: Postsecondary vocational training
- Job Growth: 3.8%
- Annual Openings: 31,000
- Self-Employed: 13.7%
- Part-Time: 21.1%

NATIONAL WAGE FIGURES (ANNUAL)

Beginning	25th Percentile	Median	Mean	75th Percentile	90th Percentile
$22,150	$28,210	$36,480	$38,050	$46,670	$56,910

Median Wages for Industries Employing Largest Numbers (Annual)

Industry	Median Income
Warehousing and Storage	$49,590
Broadcasting (Except Internet)	$49,580
Postal Service	$45,490
Internet Service Providers, Web Search Portals, and Data-Processing Services	$42,730
Telecommunications	$41,570
Management of Companies and Enterprises	$41,190
Insurance Carriers and Related Activities	$40,680
Professional, Scientific, and Technical Services	$40,480
Federal, State, and Local Government	$40,440
Merchant Wholesalers, Durable Goods	$39,640

Median Wages for States (Annual)

State	Wage	State	Wage	State	Wage
AK	$41,320	KY	$30,550	NY	$40,570
AL	$36,330	LA	$29,680	OH	$37,200
AR	$29,660	MA	$40,290	OK	$29,090
AZ	$37,590	MD	$45,260	OR	$35,880
CA	$37,870	ME	$30,010	PA	$39,650
CO	$37,340	MI	$40,680	RI	$35,680
CT	$44,570	MN	$36,900	SC	$35,800
DC	$47,520	MO	$33,550	SD	$32,780
DE	$36,400	MS	$28,290	TN	$31,970
FL	$35,690	MT	$31,510	TX	$29,300
GA	$35,840	NC	$36,620	UT	$39,900
HI	$35,140	ND	$33,590	VA	$38,860
IA	$32,310	NE	$34,670	VT	$37,740
ID	$29,580	NH	$39,720	WA	$38,270
IL	$38,620	NJ	$43,390	WI	$35,550
IN	$33,570	NM	$36,870	WV	$33,320
KS	$35,400	NV	$34,920	WY	$24,140

Median Wages for the Largest Metropolitan Areas (Annual)

Area	Wage	Area	Wage
AZ: Phoenix	$38,300	MI: Detroit	$42,610
CA: Los Angeles	$37,280	MN: Minneapolis	$39,440
CA: Riverside	$33,270	MO: Kansas City	$37,900
CA: Sacramento	$34,330	MO: St. Louis	$34,930
CA: San Diego	$37,110	NV: Las Vegas	$34,860
CA: San Francisco	$43,320	NY: New York	$43,270
CO: Denver	$38,510	OH: Cincinnati	$38,140
DC: Washington	$44,430	OH: Cleveland	$36,290
FL: Miami	$37,040	OH: Columbus	$38,710
FL: Orlando	$34,610	OR: Portland	$37,780
FL: Tampa	$38,080	PA: Philadelphia	$41,320
GA: Atlanta	$36,690	PA: Pittsburgh	$36,560
IL: Chicago	$40,470	TX: Dallas	$27,250
MA: Boston	$41,550	TX: Houston	$27,250
MD: Baltimore	$42,790	WA: Seattle	$39,250

FACTORS THAT MAY AFFECT EARNINGS

Educational Attainment of Workers and Effect on Earnings

	Percent at Level	Effect on Earnings
Less than High School	—	—
Some High School	—	—
High School or Equivalent	19.0%	−0.1%
Some College but No Degree	31.0%	−13.0%
Associate Degree	23.9%	6.7%
Bachelor's Degree	21.8%	15.6%
Master's Degree	2.1%	4.9%
Doctoral Degree	—	—
First Professional Degree	—	—

Flexibility of Earnings

Average Hours Worked: 36
Workers with a Varying Number of Hours: 5.2%
Workers Earning Some Overtime Pay, Tips, or Commissions: 13.5%
Earnings Benefit of Working Overtime: −5.0%

Gender

	Male	Female
Percent	90.3%	9.7%
Effect on Earnings	0.8%	—

Union Membership

Percentage Union Members: 6.6%
Earnings Benefit of Union Membership: 15.6%

Veteran Status

Percentage Who Have Been on Active Duty: 21.6%
Earnings Benefit of Veteran Status: 14.6%

49-2021 Radio Mechanics

Test or repair mobile or stationary radio transmitting and receiving equipment and two-way radio communications systems used in ship-to-shore communications and found in service and emergency vehicles.

- Education or Training Required: Postsecondary vocational training
- Job Growth: –1.1%
- Annual Openings: 1,000
- Self-Employed: 6.2%
- Part-Time: 15.2%

NATIONAL WAGE FIGURES (ANNUAL)

Beginning	25th Percentile	Median	Mean	75th Percentile	90th Percentile
$22,760	$29,200	$37,690	$39,880	$47,880	$59,360

Median Wages for Industries Employing Largest Numbers (Annual)

Industry	Median Income
Utilities	$62,270
Specialty Trade Contractors	$54,720
Federal, State, and Local Government	$46,630
Internet Service Providers, Web Search Portals, and Data-Processing Services	$43,240
Broadcasting (Except Internet)	$43,030
Telecommunications	$39,160
Management of Companies and Enterprises	$36,270
Merchant Wholesalers, Durable Goods	$35,780
Repair and Maintenance	$33,850
Electronics and Appliance Stores	$32,500

Median Wages for States (Annual)

State	Wage	State	Wage	State	Wage
AK	no data	KY	$35,350	NY	$52,130
AL	$38,190	LA	$36,050	OH	$33,280
AR	$31,510	MA	$43,440	OK	$34,990
AZ	no data	MD	$53,550	OR	$34,870
CA	$48,010	ME	no data	PA	$23,130
CO	$50,250	MI	$39,700	RI	no data
CT	$44,300	MN	no data	SC	$30,740
DC	no data	MO	$33,890	SD	no data
DE	no data	MS	no data	TN	$42,510
FL	$39,220	MT	no data	TX	$36,100
GA	$35,190	NC	$32,640	UT	$33,690
HI	no data	ND	no data	VA	$42,020
IA	$31,600	NE	$37,640	VT	no data
ID	no data	NH	$18,030	WA	$52,740
IL	$27,510	NJ	$45,360	WI	$37,980
IN	$40,620	NM	no data	WV	no data
KS	no data	NV	no data	WY	$33,570

Median Wages for the Largest Metropolitan Areas (Annual)

Area	Wage	Area	Wage
AZ: Phoenix	no data	MI: Detroit	$39,590
CA: Los Angeles	$33,020	MN: Minneapolis	$58,860
CA: Riverside	no data	MO: Kansas City	no data
CA: Sacramento	no data	MO: St. Louis	$30,900
CA: San Diego	$48,800	NV: Las Vegas	no data
CA: San Francisco	no data	NY: New York	$58,080
CO: Denver	$49,320	OH: Cincinnati	no data
DC: Washington	no data	OH: Cleveland	no data
FL: Miami	$46,770	OH: Columbus	no data
FL: Orlando	$40,220	OR: Portland	no data
FL: Tampa	$46,120	PA: Philadelphia	no data
GA: Atlanta	$35,980	PA: Pittsburgh	no data
IL: Chicago	$28,640	TX: Dallas	no data
MA: Boston	no data	TX: Houston	$37,160
MD: Baltimore	$48,600	WA: Seattle	$55,700

FACTORS THAT MAY AFFECT EARNINGS

Educational Attainment of Workers and Effect on Earnings

Figures are based on a group of occupations: Electrical and Electronic Equipment Mechanics, Installers, and Repairers

	Percent at Level	Effect on Earnings
Less than High School	—	—
Some High School	3.5%	–44.7%
High School or Equivalent	25.0%	3.3%
Some College but No Degree	29.4%	–6.1%
Associate Degree	22.2%	4.1%
Bachelor's Degree	16.4%	13.0%
Master's Degree	2.2%	7.5%
Doctoral Degree	—	—
First Professional Degree	—	—

Flexibility of Earnings

Average Hours Worked: 36
Workers with a Varying Number of Hours: 6.0%
Workers Earning Some Overtime Pay, Tips, or Commissions: 17.9%
Earnings Benefit of Working Overtime: –11.6%

Gender

	Male	Female
Percent	84.8%	15.2%
Effect on Earnings	1.0%	—

Union Membership

Percentage Union Members: 12.9%
Earnings Benefit of Union Membership: 26.3%

Veteran Status

Percentage Who Have Been on Active Duty: 21.6%
Earnings Benefit of Veteran Status: 14.6%

49-2022 Telecommunications Equipment Installers and Repairers, Except Line Installers

Set up, rearrange, or remove switching and dialing equipment used in central offices. Service or repair telephones and other communication equipment on customers' property. May install equipment in new locations or install wiring and telephone jacks in buildings under construction.

- Education or Training Required: Long-term on-the-job training
- Job Growth: –4.9%
- Annual Openings: 21,000
- Self-Employed: 6.6%
- Part-Time: 15.2%

NATIONAL WAGE FIGURES (ANNUAL)

Beginning	25th Percentile	Median	Mean	75th Percentile	90th Percentile
$31,110	$42,490	$52,430	$50,610	$59,610	$68,310

Median Wages for Industries Employing Largest Numbers (Annual)

Industry	Median Income
Utilities	$64,040
Computer and Electronic Product Manufacturing	$60,890
Waste Management and Remediation Services	$58,120
Management of Companies and Enterprises	$55,220
Telecommunications	$54,220
Professional, Scientific, and Technical Services	$53,050
Internet Service Providers, Web Search Portals, and Data-Processing Services	$51,280
Merchant Wholesalers, Durable Goods	$50,620
Administrative and Support Services	$49,370
Real Estate	$49,300

Median Wages for States (Annual)

State	Wage	State	Wage	State	Wage
AK	$57,980	KY	$50,300	NY	$60,850
AL	$47,440	LA	$43,890	OH	$51,310
AR	$42,110	MA	$59,450	OK	$45,230
AZ	$50,790	MD	$51,620	OR	$51,720
CA	$54,790	ME	$44,090	PA	$50,420
CO	$53,710	MI	$55,030	RI	no data
CT	$46,950	MN	$51,960	SC	$45,330
DC	no data	MO	$51,170	SD	$51,520
DE	$55,810	MS	$49,300	TN	$48,050
FL	$48,680	MT	$50,010	TX	$51,130
GA	$46,110	NC	$50,370	UT	$53,390
HI	$58,340	ND	$51,180	VA	$55,700
IA	$49,280	NE	$48,490	VT	no data
ID	$52,010	NH	$60,380	WA	$53,310
IL	$59,940	NJ	$59,040	WI	$48,480
IN	$50,490	NM	$54,240	WV	$50,490
KS	$49,090	NV	$46,080	WY	$51,090

Median Wages for the Largest Metropolitan Areas (Annual)

Area	Wage	Area	Wage
AZ: Phoenix	$49,430	MI: Detroit	no data
CA: Los Angeles	$56,570	MN: Minneapolis	$52,690
CA: Riverside	$52,650	MO: Kansas City	$49,120
CA: Sacramento	no data	MO: St. Louis	$52,500
CA: San Diego	no data	NV: Las Vegas	$44,280
CA: San Francisco	$58,160	NY: New York	$62,010
CO: Denver	$54,740	OH: Cincinnati	$39,260
DC: Washington	$59,840	OH: Cleveland	no data
FL: Miami	$52,050	OH: Columbus	$52,750
FL: Orlando	$43,490	OR: Portland	$52,670
FL: Tampa	$42,570	PA: Philadelphia	$55,820
GA: Atlanta	$45,610	PA: Pittsburgh	$49,250
IL: Chicago	$60,560	TX: Dallas	$51,210
MA: Boston	$59,500	TX: Houston	no data
MD: Baltimore	$44,320	WA: Seattle	$53,280

FACTORS THAT MAY AFFECT EARNINGS

Educational Attainment of Workers and Effect on Earnings

Figures are based on a group of occupations: Electrical and Electronic Equipment Mechanics, Installers, and Repairers

	Percent at Level	Effect on Earnings
Less than High School	—	—
Some High School	3.5%	–44.7%
High School or Equivalent	25.0%	3.3%
Some College but No Degree	29.4%	–6.1%
Associate Degree	22.2%	4.1%
Bachelor's Degree	16.4%	13.0%
Master's Degree	2.2%	7.5%
Doctoral Degree	—	—
First Professional Degree	—	—

Flexibility of Earnings

Average Hours Worked: 36
Workers with a Varying Number of Hours: 6.0%
Workers Earning Some Overtime Pay, Tips, or Commissions: 17.9%
Earnings Benefit of Working Overtime: –11.6%

Gender

	Male	Female
Percent	84.8%	15.2%
Effect on Earnings	1.0%	—

Union Membership

Percentage Union Members: 12.9%
Earnings Benefit of Union Membership: 26.3%

Veteran Status

Percentage Who Have Been on Active Duty: 21.6%
Earnings Benefit of Veteran Status: 14.6%

49-2091 Avionics Technicians

Install, inspect, test, adjust, or repair avionics equipment, such as radar, radio, navigation, and missile control systems in aircraft or space vehicles.

- Education or Training Required: Postsecondary vocational training
- Job Growth: 9.1%
- Annual Openings: 2,000
- Self-Employed: 0.0%
- Part-Time: 15.2%

NATIONAL WAGE FIGURES (ANNUAL)

Beginning	25th Percentile	Median	Mean	75th Percentile	90th Percentile
$32,540	$39,570	$46,950	$47,380	$55,420	$63,090

Median Wages for Industries Employing Largest Numbers (Annual)

Industry	Median Income
Air Transportation	$55,670
Merchant Wholesalers, Durable Goods	$51,950
Professional, Scientific, and Technical Services	$51,080
Administrative and Support Services	$50,460
Educational Services	$48,890
Computer and Electronic Product Manufacturing	$47,710
Federal, State, and Local Government	$46,700
Motor Vehicle and Parts Dealers	$46,270
Transportation Equipment Manufacturing	$46,180
Repair and Maintenance	$46,150

Median Wages for States (Annual)

AK	$53,240	KY	$45,330	NY	$53,430
AL	$37,890	LA	$45,080	OH	$53,000
AR	$43,300	MA	$56,900	OK	no data
AZ	$41,940	MD	$46,900	OR	$42,120
CA	$51,600	ME	no data	PA	$52,840
CO	$49,940	MI	$37,640	RI	no data
CT	$48,790	MN	$45,980	SC	$42,970
DC	no data	MO	no data	SD	no data
DE	$44,090	MS	$45,280	TN	$43,410
FL	$42,650	MT	$41,910	TX	$46,480
GA	$43,970	NC	$45,770	UT	$44,320
HI	$59,900	ND	no data	VA	$43,720
IA	$43,880	NE	$53,570	VT	no data
ID	$34,120	NH	$38,720	WA	$44,340
IL	$52,040	NJ	$51,860	WI	$43,430
IN	$53,580	NM	$40,560	WV	no data
KS	$47,240	NV	$39,210	WY	no data

Median Wages for the Largest Metropolitan Areas (Annual)

AZ: Phoenix	$43,360	MI: Detroit	$36,160
CA: Los Angeles	$50,080	MN: Minneapolis	$51,670
CA: Riverside	$45,480	MO: Kansas City	no data
CA: Sacramento	$49,380	MO: St. Louis	no data
CA: San Diego	no data	NV: Las Vegas	$36,230
CA: San Francisco	no data	NY: New York	$52,570
CO: Denver	$53,600	OH: Cincinnati	no data
DC: Washington	no data	OH: Cleveland	$45,370
FL: Miami	$41,860	OH: Columbus	no data
FL: Orlando	$45,750	OR: Portland	$43,480
FL: Tampa	no data	PA: Philadelphia	$59,280
GA: Atlanta	$57,070	PA: Pittsburgh	$45,830
IL: Chicago	$53,320	TX: Dallas	$48,420
MA: Boston	$56,770	TX: Houston	$38,930
MD: Baltimore	$49,710	WA: Seattle	$47,190

FACTORS THAT MAY AFFECT EARNINGS

Educational Attainment of Workers and Effect on Earnings

	Percent at Level	Effect on Earnings
Less than High School	—	—
Some High School	—	—
High School or Equivalent	25.0%	−4.1%
Some College but No Degree	29.2%	7.0%
Associate Degree	25.0%	−11.7%
Bachelor's Degree	—	—
Master's Degree	—	—
Doctoral Degree	—	—
First Professional Degree	—	—

Figures do not total 100% because some levels have a very small sample size.

Flexibility of Earnings

Average Hours Worked: 38
Workers with a Varying Number of Hours: 4.3%
Workers Earning Some Overtime Pay, Tips, or Commissions: 25.0%
Earnings Benefit of Working Overtime: −1.2%

Gender

	Male	Female
Percent	88.7%	11.3%
Effect on Earnings	1.0%	—

Union Membership

Percentage Union Members: 20.8%
Earnings Benefit of Union Membership: 26.3%

Veteran Status

Percentage Who Have Been on Active Duty: 21.6%
Earnings Benefit of Veteran Status: 14.6%

49-2092 Electric Motor, Power Tool, and Related Repairers

Repair, maintain, or install electric motors, wiring, or switches.

- Education or Training Required: Postsecondary vocational training
- Job Growth: 4.1%
- Annual Openings: 3,000
- Self-Employed: 21.2%
- Part-Time: 13.3%

NATIONAL WAGE FIGURES (ANNUAL)

Beginning	25th Percentile	Median	Mean	75th Percentile	90th Percentile
$20,750	$26,120	$32,860	$34,810	$42,100	$52,760

Median Wages for Industries Employing Largest Numbers (Annual)

Industry	Median Income
Support Activities for Mining	$50,800
Management of Companies and Enterprises	$45,020
Educational Services	$44,890
Chemical Manufacturing	$42,730
Food Manufacturing	$42,350
Paper Manufacturing	$41,630
Health and Personal Care Stores	$39,490
Federal, State, and Local Government	$39,460
Utilities	$37,370
Wholesale Electronic Markets and Agents and Brokers	$35,180

Median Wages for States (Annual)

State	Wage	State	Wage	State	Wage
AK	no data	KY	$24,390	NY	$36,200
AL	$31,000	LA	$35,240	OH	$34,560
AR	$28,590	MA	$38,940	OK	$31,650
AZ	no data	MD	$29,110	OR	$30,600
CA	$34,090	ME	$31,380	PA	$36,940
CO	$29,540	MI	$37,100	RI	$34,520
CT	$42,700	MN	$37,060	SC	$28,740
DC	no data	MO	$29,750	SD	$19,720
DE	no data	MS	$28,940	TN	$29,420
FL	$29,360	MT	$26,750	TX	$30,490
GA	$36,730	NC	$29,360	UT	$36,930
HI	$33,960	ND	$27,290	VA	$35,350
IA	$32,710	NE	$33,850	VT	$33,200
ID	$29,020	NH	$35,780	WA	$39,560
IL	$39,680	NJ	$37,240	WI	$37,120
IN	$30,740	NM	no data	WV	$32,840
KS	$32,230	NV	$35,490	WY	no data

Median Wages for the Largest Metropolitan Areas (Annual)

Area	Wage	Area	Wage
AZ: Phoenix	$25,070	MI: Detroit	$40,240
CA: Los Angeles	$28,560	MN: Minneapolis	$40,380
CA: Riverside	$41,740	MO: Kansas City	$39,160
CA: Sacramento	$25,980	MO: St. Louis	$37,880
CA: San Diego	no data	NV: Las Vegas	$36,100
CA: San Francisco	$48,040	NY: New York	$40,060
CO: Denver	$29,700	OH: Cincinnati	$37,540
DC: Washington	$28,630	OH: Cleveland	$29,000
FL: Miami	$33,870	OH: Columbus	$32,210
FL: Orlando	$27,100	OR: Portland	$38,490
FL: Tampa	$30,670	PA: Philadelphia	$37,580
GA: Atlanta	$39,600	PA: Pittsburgh	$33,060
IL: Chicago	$40,500	TX: Dallas	$33,900
MA: Boston	$42,590	TX: Houston	$31,930
MD: Baltimore	$31,440	WA: Seattle	$41,360

FACTORS THAT MAY AFFECT EARNINGS

Educational Attainment of Workers and Effect on Earnings

	Percent at Level	Effect on Earnings
Less than High School	—	—
Some High School	—	—
High School or Equivalent	33.3%	–5.7%
Some College but No Degree	22.9%	14.4%
Associate Degree	29.2%	6.5%
Bachelor's Degree	—	—
Master's Degree	—	—
Doctoral Degree	—	—
First Professional Degree	—	—

Figures do not total 100% because some levels have a very small sample size.

Flexibility of Earnings

Average Hours Worked: 37
Workers with a Varying Number of Hours: 6.0%
Workers Earning Some Overtime Pay, Tips, or Commissions: 33.3%
Earnings Benefit of Working Overtime: –1.2%

Gender

	Male	Female
Percent	97.8%	2.2%
Effect on Earnings	0.3%	–6.1%

Union Membership

Percentage Union Members: 17.6%
Earnings Benefit of Union Membership: 26.3%

Veteran Status

Percentage Who Have Been on Active Duty: 21.6%
Earnings Benefit of Veteran Status: 14.6%

49-2093 Electrical and Electronics Installers and Repairers, Transportation Equipment

Install, adjust, or maintain mobile electronics communication equipment, including sound, sonar, security, navigation, and surveillance systems on trains, watercraft, or other mobile equipment.

- Education or Training Required: Postsecondary vocational training
- Job Growth: 6.6%
- Annual Openings: 2,000
- Self-Employed: 0.0%
- Part-Time: 15.2%

NATIONAL WAGE FIGURES (ANNUAL)

Beginning	25th Percentile	Median	Mean	75th Percentile	90th Percentile
$27,550	$34,930	$43,110	$43,650	$52,200	$59,870

Median Wages for Industries Employing Largest Numbers (Annual)

Industry	Median Income
Administrative and Support Services	$51,820
Educational Services	$49,050
Professional, Scientific, and Technical Services	$48,040
Rail Transportation	$46,530
Transit and Ground Passenger Transportation	$46,280
Support Activities for Transportation	$45,540
Machinery Manufacturing	$42,050
Transportation Equipment Manufacturing	$40,290
Motor Vehicle and Parts Dealers	$39,650
Merchant Wholesalers, Durable Goods	$39,070

Median Wages for States (Annual)

AK	no data	KY	no data	NY	no data
AL	no data	LA	$37,060	OH	$35,550
AR	no data	MA	$41,440	OK	$32,240
AZ	$33,870	MD	$54,160	OR	$45,100
CA	$49,100	ME	$36,310	PA	$42,670
CO	$48,180	MI	$43,740	RI	no data
CT	$49,490	MN	no data	SC	$35,800
DC	no data	MO	$42,410	SD	no data
DE	$39,960	MS	$48,140	TN	$44,260
FL	$38,500	MT	no data	TX	$39,070
GA	$34,670	NC	$38,930	UT	$40,070
HI	$43,400	ND	no data	VA	$51,230
IA	$38,320	NE	$47,340	VT	no data
ID	$65,080	NH	no data	WA	$55,750
IL	$43,930	NJ	$41,260	WI	$41,250
IN	$40,490	NM	$47,380	WV	$35,360
KS	no data	NV	$40,630	WY	no data

Median Wages for the Largest Metropolitan Areas (Annual)

AZ: Phoenix	$33,360	MI: Detroit	$43,190
CA: Los Angeles	$49,580	MN: Minneapolis	no data
CA: Riverside	$45,410	MO: Kansas City	$36,110
CA: Sacramento	$41,490	MO: St. Louis	$43,340
CA: San Diego	$40,710	NV: Las Vegas	$21,960
CA: San Francisco	$58,080	NY: New York	no data
CO: Denver	$40,830	OH: Cincinnati	$45,200
DC: Washington	no data	OH: Cleveland	$35,260
FL: Miami	$39,880	OH: Columbus	$35,580
FL: Orlando	$37,070	OR: Portland	$37,200
FL: Tampa	$31,170	PA: Philadelphia	$39,330
GA: Atlanta	$41,000	PA: Pittsburgh	no data
IL: Chicago	$40,750	TX: Dallas	$36,890
MA: Boston	$42,670	TX: Houston	$38,390
MD: Baltimore	$46,260	WA: Seattle	$61,790

FACTORS THAT MAY AFFECT EARNINGS

Educational Attainment of Workers and Effect on Earnings

Figures are based on a group of occupations: Electrical and Electronic Equipment Mechanics, Installers, and Repairers

	Percent at Level	Effect on Earnings
Less than High School	—	—
Some High School	3.5%	−44.7%
High School or Equivalent	25.0%	3.3%
Some College but No Degree	29.4%	−6.1%
Associate Degree	22.2%	4.1%
Bachelor's Degree	16.4%	13.0%
Master's Degree	2.2%	7.5%
Doctoral Degree	—	—
First Professional Degree	—	—

Flexibility of Earnings

Average Hours Worked: 33
Workers with a Varying Number of Hours: 10.5%
Workers Earning Some Overtime Pay, Tips, or Commissions: 25.0%
Earnings Benefit of Working Overtime: −1.2%

Gender

	Male	Female
Percent	94.7%	5.3%
Effect on Earnings	0.3%	−6.1%

Union Membership

Percentage Union Members: 25.0%
Earnings Benefit of Union Membership: 26.3%

Veteran Status

Percentage Who Have Been on Active Duty: 21.6%
Earnings Benefit of Veteran Status: 14.6%

49-2094 Electrical and Electronics Repairers, Commercial and Industrial Equipment

Repair, test, adjust, or install electronic equipment, such as industrial controls, transmitters, and antennas.

- Education or Training Required: Postsecondary vocational training
- Job Growth: 9.7%
- Annual Openings: 8,000
- Self-Employed: 0.0%
- Part-Time: 8.3%

NATIONAL WAGE FIGURES (ANNUAL)

Beginning	25th Percentile	Median	Mean	75th Percentile	90th Percentile
$27,940	$35,740	$45,180	$45,670	$55,310	$64,270

Median Wages for Industries Employing Largest Numbers (Annual)

Industry	Median Income
Utilities	$55,610
Transportation Equipment Manufacturing	$54,760
Paper Manufacturing	$50,180
Chemical Manufacturing	$49,290
Fabricated Metal Product Manufacturing	$48,910
Federal, State, and Local Government	$48,760
Professional, Scientific, and Technical Services	$47,700
Telecommunications	$46,610
Broadcasting (Except Internet)	$45,750
Management of Companies and Enterprises	$45,260

Median Wages for States (Annual)

State	Wage	State	Wage	State	Wage
AK	$61,640	KY	$44,530	NY	$35,800
AL	$42,340	LA	$52,240	OH	$43,960
AR	$41,760	MA	$49,920	OK	$45,190
AZ	$52,170	MD	$46,230	OR	$51,100
CA	$51,200	ME	$45,420	PA	$44,220
CO	$45,000	MI	$46,280	RI	no data
CT	$47,190	MN	$46,140	SC	$40,180
DC	$59,550	MO	$49,440	SD	$39,760
DE	$47,160	MS	$40,680	TN	$42,110
FL	$39,870	MT	$51,470	TX	$44,210
GA	$47,250	NC	$43,460	UT	$47,400
HI	$55,540	ND	$45,980	VA	$45,280
IA	$42,050	NE	$42,390	VT	$41,320
ID	$41,410	NH	$45,220	WA	$58,920
IL	$48,000	NJ	$45,850	WI	$44,380
IN	$34,910	NM	$55,370	WV	$45,950
KS	$42,890	NV	$45,890	WY	$46,390

Median Wages for the Largest Metropolitan Areas (Annual)

Area	Wage	Area	Wage
AZ: Phoenix	$53,170	MI: Detroit	$47,050
CA: Los Angeles	$48,230	MN: Minneapolis	$46,320
CA: Riverside	$52,000	MO: Kansas City	$43,590
CA: Sacramento	no data	MO: St. Louis	$53,850
CA: San Diego	$47,980	NV: Las Vegas	$47,630
CA: San Francisco	$54,450	NY: New York	$42,040
CO: Denver	$43,550	OH: Cincinnati	$46,750
DC: Washington	$49,530	OH: Cleveland	$44,000
FL: Miami	$35,200	OH: Columbus	$37,430
FL: Orlando	$38,130	OR: Portland	$52,270
FL: Tampa	$36,490	PA: Philadelphia	$51,530
GA: Atlanta	$50,880	PA: Pittsburgh	$44,940
IL: Chicago	$50,610	TX: Dallas	$44,550
MA: Boston	$50,460	TX: Houston	$48,370
MD: Baltimore	$45,380	WA: Seattle	$61,180

FACTORS THAT MAY AFFECT EARNINGS

Educational Attainment of Workers and Effect on Earnings

	Percent at Level	Effect on Earnings
Less than High School	—	—
Some High School	—	—
High School or Equivalent	35.3%	0.3%
Some College but No Degree	—	—
Associate Degree	47.1%	2.8%
Bachelor's Degree	—	—
Master's Degree	—	—
Doctoral Degree	—	—
First Professional Degree	—	—

Figures do not total 100% because some levels have a very small sample size.

Flexibility of Earnings

Average Hours Worked: 36
Workers with a Varying Number of Hours: 7.7%
Workers Earning Some Overtime Pay, Tips, or Commissions: 11.1%
Earnings Benefit of Working Overtime: –1.2%

Gender

	Male	Female
Percent	89.5%	10.5%
Effect on Earnings	0.3%	–6.1%

Union Membership

Percentage Union Members: 27.8%
Earnings Benefit of Union Membership: 26.3%

Veteran Status

Percentage Who Have Been on Active Duty: 21.6%
Earnings Benefit of Veteran Status: 14.6%

49-2095 Electrical and Electronics Repairers, Powerhouse, Substation, and Relay

Inspect, test, repair, or maintain electrical equipment in generating stations, substations, and in-service relays.

- Education or Training Required: Postsecondary vocational training
- Job Growth: –0.4%
- Annual Openings: 2,000
- Self-Employed: 0.0%
- Part-Time: 8.3%

NATIONAL WAGE FIGURES (ANNUAL)

Beginning	25th Percentile	Median	Mean	75th Percentile	90th Percentile
$40,390	$49,130	$57,400	$56,870	$66,700	$73,830

Median Wages for Industries Employing Largest Numbers (Annual)

Industry	Median Income
Broadcasting (Except Internet)	$64,140
Utilities	$58,780
Professional, Scientific, and Technical Services	$56,530
Federal, State, and Local Government	$54,600
Heavy and Civil Engineering Construction	$54,190
Management of Companies and Enterprises	$52,790
Pipeline Transportation	$52,630
Telecommunications	$51,820
Merchant Wholesalers, Durable Goods	$51,730
Administrative and Support Services	$45,740

Median Wages for States (Annual)

State	Wage	State	Wage	State	Wage
AK	$63,880	KY	$56,330	NY	$64,660
AL	$53,810	LA	$59,280	OH	$55,110
AR	$51,210	MA	no data	OK	$46,200
AZ	$60,200	MD	$65,670	OR	$64,860
CA	$56,660	ME	$59,060	PA	$56,820
CO	$58,930	MI	$61,380	RI	no data
CT	$60,010	MN	$58,950	SC	no data
DC	no data	MO	$61,440	SD	$51,760
DE	no data	MS	$51,800	TN	$43,490
FL	$55,790	MT	$60,960	TX	$56,800
GA	$50,470	NC	no data	UT	$65,580
HI	$64,720	ND	$62,960	VA	no data
IA	no data	NE	$62,690	VT	$55,940
ID	$63,960	NH	$54,540	WA	$61,530
IL	$64,280	NJ	$58,360	WI	$66,970
IN	$54,880	NM	$53,370	WV	$53,300
KS	$61,170	NV	no data	WY	$59,710

Median Wages for the Largest Metropolitan Areas (Annual)

Metro	Wage	Metro	Wage
AZ: Phoenix	$60,750	MI: Detroit	no data
CA: Los Angeles	$63,640	MN: Minneapolis	no data
CA: Riverside	$37,710	MO: Kansas City	$59,150
CA: Sacramento	$68,420	MO: St. Louis	$64,610
CA: San Diego	no data	NV: Las Vegas	no data
CA: San Francisco	no data	NY: New York	$59,510
CO: Denver	no data	OH: Cincinnati	$57,360
DC: Washington	$59,830	OH: Cleveland	$54,870
FL: Miami	$55,560	OH: Columbus	$57,730
FL: Orlando	no data	OR: Portland	$64,460
FL: Tampa	$56,820	PA: Philadelphia	$58,370
GA: Atlanta	$51,110	PA: Pittsburgh	$56,570
IL: Chicago	$62,630	TX: Dallas	$55,710
MA: Boston	no data	TX: Houston	$79,330
MD: Baltimore	$68,250	WA: Seattle	$58,680

FACTORS THAT MAY AFFECT EARNINGS

Educational Attainment of Workers and Effect on Earnings

	Percent at Level	Effect on Earnings
Less than High School	—	—
Some High School	—	—
High School or Equivalent	35.3%	0.3%
Some College but No Degree	—	—
Associate Degree	47.1%	2.8%
Bachelor's Degree	—	—
Master's Degree	—	—
Doctoral Degree	—	—
First Professional Degree	—	—

Figures do not total 100% because some levels have a very small sample size.

Flexibility of Earnings

Average Hours Worked: 36
Workers with a Varying Number of Hours: 7.7%
Workers Earning Some Overtime Pay, Tips, or Commissions: 11.1%
Earnings Benefit of Working Overtime: –1.2%

Gender

	Male	Female
Percent	89.5%	10.5%
Effect on Earnings	0.3%	–6.1%

Union Membership

Percentage Union Members: 27.8%
Earnings Benefit of Union Membership: 26.3%

Veteran Status

Percentage Who Have Been on Active Duty: 21.6%
Earnings Benefit of Veteran Status: 14.6%

49-2096 Electronic Equipment Installers and Repairers, Motor Vehicles

Install, diagnose, or repair communications, sound, security, or navigation equipment in motor vehicles.

- Education or Training Required: Postsecondary vocational training
- Job Growth: 13.6%
- Annual Openings: 1,000
- Self-Employed: 16.5%
- Part-Time: 50.0%

NATIONAL WAGE FIGURES (ANNUAL)

Beginning	25th Percentile	Median	Mean	75th Percentile	90th Percentile
$18,990	$22,410	$28,220	$31,190	$36,210	$48,770

Median Wages for Industries Employing Largest Numbers (Annual)

Industry	Median Income
Federal, State, and Local Government	$52,710
Specialty Trade Contractors	$39,460
Professional, Scientific, and Technical Services	$39,200
Computer and Electronic Product Manufacturing	$33,870
Transportation Equipment Manufacturing	$33,700
Miscellaneous Store Retailers	$33,060
Repair and Maintenance	$32,770
Merchant Wholesalers, Durable Goods	$30,880
Administrative and Support Services	$30,610
Sporting Goods, Hobby, Book, and Music Stores	$28,600

Median Wages for States (Annual)

AK	$28,280	KY	$31,520	NY	$27,780
AL	$27,260	LA	$34,670	OH	$31,410
AR	no data	MA	$30,200	OK	$31,480
AZ	$28,460	MD	$36,220	OR	$24,600
CA	$27,140	ME	$24,270	PA	$33,190
CO	$28,030	MI	$32,220	RI	no data
CT	$32,020	MN	$29,120	SC	$23,690
DC	no data	MO	$27,280	SD	$23,510
DE	$30,000	MS	$24,220	TN	$23,440
FL	$24,820	MT	$31,170	TX	$29,080
GA	$26,960	NC	$27,810	UT	$27,180
HI	no data	ND	$21,370	VA	$29,930
IA	$30,700	NE	$23,750	VT	no data
ID	$27,710	NH	$28,930	WA	$25,760
IL	$35,050	NJ	$31,140	WI	$28,790
IN	$31,790	NM	no data	WV	$13,790
KS	$24,240	NV	$22,870	WY	no data

Median Wages for the Largest Metropolitan Areas (Annual)

AZ: Phoenix	$32,200	MI: Detroit	$27,060
CA: Los Angeles	$26,450	MN: Minneapolis	$29,930
CA: Riverside	$27,190	MO: Kansas City	$33,420
CA: Sacramento	$26,080	MO: St. Louis	$25,770
CA: San Diego	$35,470	NV: Las Vegas	$23,810
CA: San Francisco	$30,250	NY: New York	$30,970
CO: Denver	$30,070	OH: Cincinnati	$25,820
DC: Washington	$32,580	OH: Cleveland	$30,900
FL: Miami	$27,440	OH: Columbus	no data
FL: Orlando	$24,880	OR: Portland	$24,650
FL: Tampa	$20,880	PA: Philadelphia	$37,100
GA: Atlanta	$29,570	PA: Pittsburgh	no data
IL: Chicago	$39,660	TX: Dallas	$34,510
MA: Boston	$31,250	TX: Houston	$25,060
MD: Baltimore	$37,420	WA: Seattle	$24,390

FACTORS THAT MAY AFFECT EARNINGS

Educational Attainment of Workers and Effect on Earnings

	Percent at Level	Effect on Earnings
Less than High School	—	—
Some High School	—	—
High School or Equivalent	29.2%	−28.6%
Some College but No Degree	37.5%	5.9%
Associate Degree	—	—
Bachelor's Degree	—	—
Master's Degree	—	—
Doctoral Degree	—	—
First Professional Degree	—	—

Figures do not total 100% because some levels have a very small sample size.

Flexibility of Earnings

Average Hours Worked: 39
Workers with a Varying Number of Hours: 1.9%
Workers Earning Some Overtime Pay, Tips, or Commissions: 25.0%
Earnings Benefit of Working Overtime: −1.2%

Gender

	Male	Female
Percent	89.5%	10.5%
Effect on Earnings	0.3%	−6.1%

Union Membership

Percentage Union Members: 37.5%
Earnings Benefit of Union Membership: 26.3%

Veteran Status

Percentage Who Have Been on Active Duty: 21.6%
Earnings Benefit of Veteran Status: 14.6%

49-2097 Electronic Home Entertainment Equipment Installers and Repairers

Repair, adjust, or install audio or television receivers, stereo systems, camcorders, video systems, or other electronic home entertainment equipment.

- Education or Training Required: Postsecondary vocational training
- Job Growth: 4.7%
- Annual Openings: 6,000
- Self-Employed: 30.7%
- Part-Time: 8.7%

Note: Earnings figures do not reflect self-employed workers, who make up a large fraction of the workforce for this occupation.

NATIONAL WAGE FIGURES (ANNUAL)

Beginning	25th Percentile	Median	Mean	75th Percentile	90th Percentile
$18,650	$23,960	$29,980	$31,710	$37,940	$46,640

Median Wages for Industries Employing Largest Numbers (Annual)

Industry	Median Income
Federal, State, and Local Government	$40,460
Miscellaneous Manufacturing	$39,340
Management of Companies and Enterprises	$37,830
Merchant Wholesalers, Durable Goods	$35,350
Computer and Electronic Product Manufacturing	$34,670
Broadcasting (Except Internet)	$33,340
Heavy and Civil Engineering Construction	$32,150
Internet Service Providers, Web Search Portals, and Data-Processing Services	$32,140
Amusement, Gambling, and Recreation Industries	$32,030
Educational Services	$31,760

Median Wages for States (Annual)

State	Wage	State	Wage	State	Wage
AK	$38,630	KY	$26,990	NY	$30,380
AL	no data	LA	$33,980	OH	$30,100
AR	$28,130	MA	$34,780	OK	$31,450
AZ	$22,920	MD	$35,700	OR	$34,150
CA	$32,130	ME	$29,440	PA	$27,570
CO	$37,120	MI	$26,400	RI	no data
CT	$38,800	MN	$33,660	SC	$28,160
DC	no data	MO	$33,580	SD	$26,920
DE	$37,490	MS	$27,680	TN	$27,830
FL	$30,950	MT	$27,680	TX	$26,170
GA	$28,370	NC	$28,330	UT	$30,550
HI	no data	ND	$27,460	VA	$29,970
IA	$28,080	NE	$31,540	VT	$30,310
ID	$27,790	NH	$32,430	WA	$35,370
IL	$35,120	NJ	$31,930	WI	$31,210
IN	$32,880	NM	$30,930	WV	$28,940
KS	$26,710	NV	$31,500	WY	no data

Median Wages for the Largest Metropolitan Areas (Annual)

Area	Wage	Area	Wage
AZ: Phoenix	$23,220	MI: Detroit	no data
CA: Los Angeles	$31,460	MN: Minneapolis	$34,940
CA: Riverside	no data	MO: Kansas City	$26,600
CA: Sacramento	$27,770	MO: St. Louis	$35,060
CA: San Diego	$33,950	NV: Las Vegas	$30,920
CA: San Francisco	$34,220	NY: New York	$30,280
CO: Denver	$38,320	OH: Cincinnati	no data
DC: Washington	$30,400	OH: Cleveland	$29,620
FL: Miami	$33,340	OH: Columbus	$21,210
FL: Orlando	$32,610	OR: Portland	$34,670
FL: Tampa	$28,920	PA: Philadelphia	$29,330
GA: Atlanta	$30,200	PA: Pittsburgh	$29,900
IL: Chicago	$43,770	TX: Dallas	$27,900
MA: Boston	$37,230	TX: Houston	$26,360
MD: Baltimore	$39,530	WA: Seattle	$36,910

FACTORS THAT MAY AFFECT EARNINGS

Educational Attainment of Workers and Effect on Earnings

	Percent at Level	Effect on Earnings
Less than High School	—	—
Some High School	—	—
High School or Equivalent	40.8%	−5.9%
Some College but No Degree	32.7%	6.4%
Associate Degree	12.2%	23.2%
Bachelor's Degree	—	—
Master's Degree	—	—
Doctoral Degree	—	—
First Professional Degree	—	—

Figures do not total 100% because some levels have a very small sample size.

Flexibility of Earnings

Average Hours Worked: 36
Workers with a Varying Number of Hours: 9.2%
Workers Earning Some Overtime Pay, Tips, or Commissions: 19.6%
Earnings Benefit of Working Overtime: −1.2%

Gender

	Male	Female
Percent	98.8%	1.2%
Effect on Earnings	0.3%	−6.1%

Union Membership

Percentage Union Members: 5.9%
Earnings Benefit of Union Membership: 26.3%

Veteran Status

Percentage Who Have Been on Active Duty: 21.6%
Earnings Benefit of Veteran Status: 14.6%

49-2098 Security and Fire Alarm Systems Installers

Install, program, maintain, and repair security and fire alarm wiring and equipment. Ensure that work is in accordance with relevant codes.

- Education or Training Required: Postsecondary vocational training
- Job Growth: 21.7%
- Annual Openings: 15,000
- Self-Employed: 1.5%
- Part-Time: 2.6%

NATIONAL WAGE FIGURES (ANNUAL)

Beginning	25th Percentile	Median	Mean	75th Percentile	90th Percentile
$22,030	$27,330	$34,810	$36,410	$43,940	$53,830

Median Wages for Industries Employing Largest Numbers (Annual)

Industry	Median Income
Federal, State, and Local Government	$42,350
Utilities	$42,250
Repair and Maintenance	$41,130
Wholesale Electronic Markets and Agents and Brokers	$40,510
Educational Services	$38,170
Specialty Trade Contractors	$36,090
Computer and Electronic Product Manufacturing	$36,060
Professional, Scientific, and Technical Services	$34,370
Merchant Wholesalers, Durable Goods	$34,040
Administrative and Support Services	$33,870

Median Wages for States (Annual)

AK	$44,340	KY	$29,110	NY	$35,310
AL	$27,170	LA	$28,200	OH	$34,640
AR	$29,710	MA	$44,750	OK	$32,480
AZ	$40,660	MD	$34,520	OR	$45,130
CA	$37,640	ME	$40,840	PA	$37,640
CO	$38,480	MI	$38,550	RI	$41,110
CT	$41,820	MN	$38,400	SC	$30,690
DC	no data	MO	$30,500	SD	$31,440
DE	$36,450	MS	$33,520	TN	$29,570
FL	$31,260	MT	$30,130	TX	$30,670
GA	$31,130	NC	$34,650	UT	$34,810
HI	$33,960	ND	no data	VA	$34,770
IA	$35,690	NE	$36,880	VT	$33,000
ID	$29,590	NH	$39,970	WA	$40,000
IL	$49,880	NJ	$39,070	WI	$34,130
IN	$33,840	NM	$30,300	WV	$23,540
KS	$27,860	NV	$38,130	WY	no data

Median Wages for the Largest Metropolitan Areas (Annual)

AZ: Phoenix	$42,560	MI: Detroit	$40,710
CA: Los Angeles	$37,640	MN: Minneapolis	$42,940
CA: Riverside	$37,890	MO: Kansas City	$29,970
CA: Sacramento	$35,940	MO: St. Louis	$37,520
CA: San Diego	$34,360	NV: Las Vegas	$39,470
CA: San Francisco	$42,080	NY: New York	$37,290
CO: Denver	$37,520	OH: Cincinnati	$34,660
DC: Washington	$36,270	OH: Cleveland	$35,800
FL: Miami	$30,730	OH: Columbus	$39,400
FL: Orlando	$32,840	OR: Portland	$42,840
FL: Tampa	$33,060	PA: Philadelphia	$42,800
GA: Atlanta	$31,650	PA: Pittsburgh	$41,210
IL: Chicago	$51,410	TX: Dallas	$34,560
MA: Boston	$46,260	TX: Houston	$29,390
MD: Baltimore	$34,440	WA: Seattle	$41,220

FACTORS THAT MAY AFFECT EARNINGS

Educational Attainment of Workers and Effect on Earnings

	Percent at Level	Effect on Earnings
Less than High School	—	—
Some High School	—	—
High School or Equivalent	23.3%	4.4%
Some College but No Degree	42.5%	−5.2%
Associate Degree	12.3%	8.2%
Bachelor's Degree	13.7%	13.1%
Master's Degree	—	—
Doctoral Degree	—	—
First Professional Degree	—	—

Figures do not total 100% because some levels have a very small sample size.

Flexibility of Earnings

Average Hours Worked: 35
Workers with a Varying Number of Hours: 10.5%
Workers Earning Some Overtime Pay, Tips, or Commissions: 21.5%
Earnings Benefit of Working Overtime: −1.2%

Gender

	Male	Female
Percent	97.6%	2.4%
Effect on Earnings	−0.4%	—

Union Membership

Percentage Union Members: 10.1%
Earnings Benefit of Union Membership: 26.3%

Veteran Status

Percentage Who Have Been on Active Duty: 21.6%
Earnings Benefit of Veteran Status: 14.6%

49-3000 Vehicle and Mobile Equipment Mechanics, Installers, and Repairers

49-3011 Aircraft Mechanics and Service Technicians

Diagnose, adjust, repair, or overhaul aircraft engines and assemblies, such as hydraulic and pneumatic systems.

- Education or Training Required: Postsecondary vocational training
- Job Growth: 13.4%
- Annual Openings: 11,000
- Self-Employed: 3.0%
- Part-Time: 18.2%

NATIONAL WAGE FIGURES (ANNUAL)

Beginning	25th Percentile	Median	Mean	75th Percentile	90th Percentile
$31,080	$39,440	$47,740	$49,300	$58,480	$71,780

Median Wages for Industries Employing Largest Numbers (Annual)

Industry	Median Income
Couriers and Messengers	$67,430
Oil and Gas Extraction	$60,750
Performing Arts, Spectator Sports, and Related Industries	$60,180
Securities, Commodity Contracts, and Other Financial Investments and Related Activities	$57,900
Air Transportation	$55,760
Insurance Carriers and Related Activities	$55,070
Hospitals	$50,930
Computer and Electronic Product Manufacturing	$50,700
Rental and Leasing Services	$50,140
Forestry and Logging	$48,590

Median Wages for States (Annual)

State	Wage	State	Wage	State	Wage
AK	$49,200	KY	$46,570	NY	$50,800
AL	$38,780	LA	$46,720	OH	$46,890
AR	$36,580	MA	$51,290	OK	no data
AZ	$46,040	MD	no data	OR	$51,240
CA	$55,850	ME	$39,000	PA	$49,310
CO	$49,060	MI	$46,630	RI	$46,500
CT	$45,080	MN	no data	SC	$41,340
DC	no data	MO	$49,170	SD	$42,030
DE	$47,970	MS	$43,880	TN	$55,520
FL	$44,250	MT	$43,210	TX	$45,730
GA	$53,190	NC	$41,010	UT	$46,050
HI	$54,530	ND	$42,130	VA	$45,630
IA	$42,990	NE	$41,800	VT	$43,450
ID	$42,980	NH	$41,940	WA	$55,250
IL	$52,640	NJ	$59,930	WI	$47,080
IN	$52,420	NM	$43,290	WV	$46,450
KS	$46,250	NV	$53,170	WY	$44,070

Median Wages for the Largest Metropolitan Areas (Annual)

Metro	Wage	Metro	Wage
AZ: Phoenix	$48,070	MI: Detroit	$52,640
CA: Los Angeles	$56,170	MN: Minneapolis	no data
CA: Riverside	$47,700	MO: Kansas City	$48,090
CA: Sacramento	$50,300	MO: St. Louis	$48,400
CA: San Diego	$48,020	NV: Las Vegas	$52,710
CA: San Francisco	no data	NY: New York	$53,810
CO: Denver	$57,050	OH: Cincinnati	$52,770
DC: Washington	$46,120	OH: Cleveland	$35,520
FL: Miami	$43,990	OH: Columbus	$45,270
FL: Orlando	$46,850	OR: Portland	$54,230
FL: Tampa	$44,010	PA: Philadelphia	$53,910
GA: Atlanta	no data	PA: Pittsburgh	no data
IL: Chicago	$54,860	TX: Dallas	$49,670
MA: Boston	$53,170	TX: Houston	$52,170
MD: Baltimore	$43,460	WA: Seattle	$58,370

FACTORS THAT MAY AFFECT EARNINGS

Educational Attainment of Workers and Effect on Earnings

	Percent at Level	Effect on Earnings
Less than High School	—	—
Some High School	—	—
High School or Equivalent	32.1%	−1.7%
Some College but No Degree	24.5%	2.9%
Associate Degree	30.8%	3.6%
Bachelor's Degree	9.4%	−8.7%
Master's Degree	—	—
Doctoral Degree	—	—
First Professional Degree	—	—

Flexibility of Earnings

Average Hours Worked: 38
Workers with a Varying Number of Hours: 3.8%
Workers Earning Some Overtime Pay, Tips, or Commissions: 15.4%
Earnings Benefit of Working Overtime: 12.4%

Gender

	Male	Female
Percent	94.7%	5.3%
Effect on Earnings	−0.8%	—

Union Membership

Percentage Union Members: 31.3%
Earnings Benefit of Union Membership: 8.9%

Veteran Status

Percentage Who Have Been on Active Duty: 16.3%
Earnings Benefit of Veteran Status: 12.6%

49-3021 Automotive Body and Related Repairers

Repair and refinish automotive vehicle bodies and straighten vehicle frames.

- Education or Training Required: Long-term on-the-job training
- Job Growth: 10.3%
- Annual Openings: 18,000
- Self-Employed: 17.6%
- Part-Time: 13.1%

NATIONAL WAGE FIGURES (ANNUAL)

Beginning	25th Percentile	Median	Mean	75th Percentile	90th Percentile
$21,000	$27,040	$35,180	$38,230	$46,450	$59,720

Median Wages for Industries Employing Largest Numbers (Annual)

Industry	Median Income
Postal Service	$56,420
Utilities	$47,380
Transportation Equipment Manufacturing	$44,720
Federal, State, and Local Government	$43,220
Professional, Scientific, and Technical Services	$38,500
Educational Services	$38,340
Administrative and Support Services	$37,490
Motor Vehicle and Parts Dealers	$36,560
Warehousing and Storage	$36,450
Nonstore Retailers	$35,470

Median Wages for States (Annual)

State	Wage	State	Wage	State	Wage
AK	$48,590	KY	$32,860	NY	$30,760
AL	$33,870	LA	$33,200	OH	$33,830
AR	$32,340	MA	$40,870	OK	$28,250
AZ	$34,740	MD	$40,180	OR	$35,980
CA	$39,720	ME	$29,470	PA	$32,270
CO	$44,980	MI	$39,140	RI	$37,600
CT	$37,920	MN	$40,300	SC	$34,290
DC	$33,150	MO	$38,110	SD	$31,400
DE	$36,830	MS	$30,130	TN	$30,250
FL	$34,260	MT	$29,080	TX	$31,690
GA	$39,180	NC	$36,830	UT	$33,630
HI	$32,330	ND	$36,070	VA	$37,430
IA	$31,460	NE	$32,200	VT	$30,580
ID	$31,090	NH	$35,180	WA	$38,090
IL	$39,850	NJ	$39,450	WI	$34,910
IN	$35,510	NM	$32,070	WV	$26,720
KS	$31,900	NV	$39,370	WY	$33,870

Median Wages for the Largest Metropolitan Areas (Annual)

Area	Wage	Area	Wage
AZ: Phoenix	$34,930	MI: Detroit	$43,170
CA: Los Angeles	$36,850	MN: Minneapolis	$45,270
CA: Riverside	$28,140	MO: Kansas City	$35,120
CA: Sacramento	$45,750	MO: St. Louis	$45,910
CA: San Diego	$42,470	NV: Las Vegas	$43,830
CA: San Francisco	$49,100	NY: New York	$35,410
CO: Denver	$48,360	OH: Cincinnati	$36,870
DC: Washington	$45,210	OH: Cleveland	$39,260
FL: Miami	$31,850	OH: Columbus	$36,510
FL: Orlando	$35,760	OR: Portland	$35,650
FL: Tampa	$39,870	PA: Philadelphia	$37,610
GA: Atlanta	$44,700	PA: Pittsburgh	$31,360
IL: Chicago	$41,140	TX: Dallas	$29,360
MA: Boston	$42,410	TX: Houston	$33,000
MD: Baltimore	$39,880	WA: Seattle	$38,930

FACTORS THAT MAY AFFECT EARNINGS

Educational Attainment of Workers and Effect on Earnings

	Percent at Level	Effect on Earnings
Less than High School	5.1%	−7.8%
Some High School	16.2%	−26.3%
High School or Equivalent	55.1%	9.2%
Some College but No Degree	11.8%	−4.9%
Associate Degree	10.3%	3.9%
Bachelor's Degree	—	—
Master's Degree	—	—
Doctoral Degree	—	—
First Professional Degree	—	—

Flexibility of Earnings

Average Hours Worked: 35
Workers with a Varying Number of Hours: 9.0%
Workers Earning Some Overtime Pay, Tips, or Commissions: 19.1%
Earnings Benefit of Working Overtime: 8.3%

Gender

	Male	Female
Percent	99.4%	0.6%
Effect on Earnings	0.4%	—

Union Membership

Percentage Union Members: Insignificant
Earnings Benefit of Union Membership: No significant data available

Veteran Status

Percentage Who Have Been on Active Duty: 16.3%
Earnings Benefit of Veteran Status: 12.6%

49-3022 Automotive Glass Installers and Repairers

Replace or repair broken windshields and window glass in motor vehicles.

- Education or Training Required: Long-term on-the-job training
- Job Growth: 15.1%
- Annual Openings: 2,000
- Self-Employed: 16.6%
- Part-Time: 42.1%

NATIONAL WAGE FIGURES (ANNUAL)

Beginning	25th Percentile	Median	Mean	75th Percentile	90th Percentile
$19,120	$23,790	$30,720	$32,050	$38,310	$46,220

Median Wages for Industries Employing Largest Numbers (Annual)

Industry	Median Income
Nonmetallic Mineral Product Manufacturing	$40,120
Transportation Equipment Manufacturing	$38,240
Building Material and Garden Equipment and Supplies Dealers	$34,100
Merchant Wholesalers, Durable Goods	$31,680
Rental and Leasing Services	$31,230
Repair and Maintenance	$30,790
Motor Vehicle and Parts Dealers	$30,220
Management of Companies and Enterprises	$30,030
Specialty Trade Contractors	$28,010

Median Wages for States (Annual)

State	Wage	State	Wage	State	Wage
AK	$35,770	KY	$31,960	NY	$28,760
AL	$28,800	LA	$22,470	OH	$31,090
AR	$25,490	MA	$34,660	OK	$33,960
AZ	$30,890	MD	$31,370	OR	$40,720
CA	$27,380	ME	$26,320	PA	$31,850
CO	$27,460	MI	$38,500	RI	$27,090
CT	$37,170	MN	$41,800	SC	$31,490
DC	no data	MO	$30,120	SD	$23,530
DE	no data	MS	$27,480	TN	$34,020
FL	$28,940	MT	$31,980	TX	$26,170
GA	$39,360	NC	$31,640	UT	$33,080
HI	no data	ND	$23,290	VA	$33,760
IA	$25,830	NE	$25,890	VT	$47,180
ID	$28,660	NH	$33,730	WA	$36,580
IL	$30,630	NJ	$22,680	WI	$37,510
IN	$29,920	NM	$17,930	WV	$30,110
KS	$37,410	NV	$34,350	WY	$29,500

Median Wages for the Largest Metropolitan Areas (Annual)

Area	Wage	Area	Wage
AZ: Phoenix	$33,050	MI: Detroit	$43,850
CA: Los Angeles	$20,740	MN: Minneapolis	$43,230
CA: Riverside	$32,790	MO: Kansas City	$32,060
CA: Sacramento	$37,000	MO: St. Louis	$31,090
CA: San Diego	no data	NV: Las Vegas	$34,350
CA: San Francisco	$34,220	NY: New York	$28,060
CO: Denver	$29,660	OH: Cincinnati	$32,680
DC: Washington	$33,840	OH: Cleveland	no data
FL: Miami	$31,200	OH: Columbus	$33,600
FL: Orlando	$31,790	OR: Portland	no data
FL: Tampa	no data	PA: Philadelphia	$27,450
GA: Atlanta	$40,100	PA: Pittsburgh	$33,240
IL: Chicago	$29,950	TX: Dallas	$26,040
MA: Boston	$35,430	TX: Houston	$28,140
MD: Baltimore	no data	WA: Seattle	$37,950

FACTORS THAT MAY AFFECT EARNINGS

Educational Attainment of Workers and Effect on Earnings

	Percent at Level	Effect on Earnings
Less than High School	—	—
Some High School	—	—
High School or Equivalent	57.1%	14.3%
Some College but No Degree	—	—
Associate Degree	—	—
Bachelor's Degree	—	—
Master's Degree	—	—
Doctoral Degree	—	—
First Professional Degree	—	—

Figures do not total 100% because some levels have a very small sample size.

Flexibility of Earnings

Average Hours Worked: 31
Workers with a Varying Number of Hours: 18.1%
Workers Earning Some Overtime Pay, Tips, or Commissions: 23.8%
Earnings Benefit of Working Overtime: –0.6%

Gender

	Male	Female
Percent	99.4%	0.6%
Effect on Earnings	0.4%	—

Union Membership

Percentage Union Members: 16.3%
Earnings Benefit of Union Membership: 24.4%

Veteran Status

Percentage Who Have Been on Active Duty: 16.3%
Earnings Benefit of Veteran Status: 12.6%

49-3023 Automotive Service Technicians and Mechanics

Diagnose, adjust, repair, or overhaul automotive vehicles.

- Education or Training Required: Postsecondary vocational training
- Job Growth: 15.7%
- Annual Openings: 93,000
- Self-Employed: 14.8%
- Part-Time: 13.8%

NATIONAL WAGE FIGURES (ANNUAL)

Beginning	25th Percentile	Median	Mean	75th Percentile	90th Percentile
$19,070	$24,880	$33,780	$36,070	$44,840	$56,620

Median Wages for Industries Employing Largest Numbers (Annual)

Industry	Median Income
Telecommunications	$53,630
Couriers and Messengers	$51,980
Utilities	$49,630
Performing Arts, Spectator Sports, and Related Industries	$48,810
Postal Service	$46,180
Professional, Scientific, and Technical Services	$45,420
Federal, State, and Local Government	$40,210
Educational Services	$38,370
Management of Companies and Enterprises	$38,340
Warehousing and Storage	$38,040

Median Wages for States (Annual)

AK	$47,450	KY	$28,460	NY	$33,440
AL	$28,890	LA	$29,220	OH	$33,370
AR	$27,510	MA	$37,180	OK	$28,900
AZ	$38,010	MD	$37,100	OR	$35,420
CA	$37,580	ME	$29,830	PA	$32,990
CO	$36,170	MI	$38,200	RI	$34,130
CT	$38,920	MN	$34,740	SC	$31,030
DC	$37,330	MO	$33,930	SD	$30,990
DE	$32,950	MS	$27,370	TN	$29,620
FL	$32,320	MT	$32,430	TX	$30,800
GA	$32,150	NC	$33,640	UT	$31,630
HI	$33,740	ND	$30,730	VA	$34,630
IA	$31,270	NE	$30,150	VT	$31,830
ID	$32,050	NH	$35,670	WA	$39,800
IL	$34,610	NJ	$37,230	WI	$34,140
IN	$32,900	NM	$31,470	WV	$22,610
KS	$33,810	NV	$35,940	WY	$31,400

Median Wages for the Largest Metropolitan Areas (Annual)

AZ: Phoenix	$39,620	MI: Detroit	$43,830
CA: Los Angeles	$33,480	MN: Minneapolis	$36,970
CA: Riverside	$36,390	MO: Kansas City	$37,640
CA: Sacramento	$36,790	MO: St. Louis	$38,090
CA: San Diego	$40,970	NV: Las Vegas	$34,960
CA: San Francisco	$48,920	NY: New York	$36,290
CO: Denver	$37,370	OH: Cincinnati	$33,250
DC: Washington	$42,070	OH: Cleveland	$37,360
FL: Miami	$32,250	OH: Columbus	$34,390
FL: Orlando	$35,300	OR: Portland	$35,070
FL: Tampa	$33,140	PA: Philadelphia	$37,550
GA: Atlanta	$35,370	PA: Pittsburgh	$32,160
IL: Chicago	$36,280	TX: Dallas	$32,210
MA: Boston	$39,030	TX: Houston	$31,920
MD: Baltimore	$33,730	WA: Seattle	$44,320

FACTORS THAT MAY AFFECT EARNINGS

Educational Attainment of Workers and Effect on Earnings

	Percent at Level	Effect on Earnings
Less than High School	4.4%	−32.0%
Some High School	13.5%	−27.1%
High School or Equivalent	37.1%	7.2%
Some College but No Degree	18.8%	−1.7%
Associate Degree	20.6%	8.0%
Bachelor's Degree	5.2%	19.3%
Master's Degree	—	—
Doctoral Degree	—	—
First Professional Degree	—	—

Flexibility of Earnings

Average Hours Worked: 36
Workers with a Varying Number of Hours: 9.2%
Workers Earning Some Overtime Pay, Tips, or Commissions: 19.8%
Earnings Benefit of Working Overtime: −2.1%

Gender

	Male	Female
Percent	98.4%	1.6%
Effect on Earnings	0.2%	—

Union Membership

Percentage Union Members: 6.7%
Earnings Benefit of Union Membership: 23.0%

Veteran Status

Percentage Who Have Been on Active Duty: 16.3%
Earnings Benefit of Veteran Status: 12.6%

49-3031 Bus and Truck Mechanics and Diesel Engine Specialists

Diagnose, adjust, repair, or overhaul trucks, buses, and all types of diesel engines. Includes mechanics working primarily with automobile diesel engines.

- Education or Training Required: Postsecondary vocational training
- Job Growth: 14.4%
- Annual Openings: 32,000
- Self-Employed: 5.3%
- Part-Time: 7.3%

NATIONAL WAGE FIGURES (ANNUAL)

Beginning	25th Percentile	Median	Mean	75th Percentile	90th Percentile
$24,370	$30,110	$37,660	$38,440	$45,900	$55,120

Median Wages for Industries Employing Largest Numbers (Annual)

Industry	Median Income
Utilities	$53,440
Couriers and Messengers	$50,480
Rail Transportation	$46,440
Federal, State, and Local Government	$43,090
Transportation Equipment Manufacturing	$40,620
Mining (Except Oil and Gas)	$40,280
Wholesale Electronic Markets and Agents and Brokers	$38,680
Motor Vehicle and Parts Dealers	$38,650
Merchant Wholesalers, Durable Goods	$38,320
Warehousing and Storage	$38,300

Median Wages for States (Annual)

State		State		State	
AK	$49,020	KY	$32,730	NY	$44,670
AL	$32,370	LA	$32,150	OH	$36,150
AR	$32,550	MA	$43,570	OK	$32,400
AZ	$35,760	MD	$42,220	OR	$39,390
CA	$42,550	ME	$32,970	PA	$36,200
CO	$40,540	MI	$40,010	RI	$41,630
CT	$43,940	MN	$39,400	SC	$32,560
DC	$43,660	MO	$36,460	SD	$31,420
DE	$42,010	MS	$30,020	TN	$34,610
FL	$35,950	MT	$33,500	TX	$33,580
GA	$37,970	NC	$35,590	UT	$39,220
HI	$42,830	ND	$34,670	VA	$36,640
IA	$33,660	NE	$38,990	VT	$34,330
ID	$33,810	NH	$39,260	WA	$42,550
IL	$41,270	NJ	$43,960	WI	$37,670
IN	$36,290	NM	$33,220	WV	$28,310
KS	$34,260	NV	$42,450	WY	$41,260

Median Wages for the Largest Metropolitan Areas (Annual)

Area		Area	
AZ: Phoenix	$36,230	MI: Detroit	$44,380
CA: Los Angeles	$45,050	MN: Minneapolis	$41,430
CA: Riverside	$39,770	MO: Kansas City	$35,410
CA: Sacramento	$46,510	MO: St. Louis	$39,730
CA: San Diego	$37,930	NV: Las Vegas	$41,150
CA: San Francisco	$49,470	NY: New York	$48,960
CO: Denver	$41,860	OH: Cincinnati	$38,260
DC: Washington	$41,830	OH: Cleveland	$40,460
FL: Miami	$38,820	OH: Columbus	$37,500
FL: Orlando	$36,680	OR: Portland	$41,170
FL: Tampa	$33,480	PA: Philadelphia	$41,820
GA: Atlanta	$41,810	PA: Pittsburgh	$34,270
IL: Chicago	$44,360	TX: Dallas	$38,160
MA: Boston	$44,880	TX: Houston	$34,470
MD: Baltimore	$43,710	WA: Seattle	$47,400

FACTORS THAT MAY AFFECT EARNINGS

Educational Attainment of Workers and Effect on Earnings

	Percent at Level	Effect on Earnings
Less than High School	3.1%	−18.3%
Some High School	12.3%	−24.1%
High School or Equivalent	39.4%	−1.4%
Some College but No Degree	20.9%	4.4%
Associate Degree	18.7%	7.9%
Bachelor's Degree	4.2%	21.6%
Master's Degree	—	—
Doctoral Degree	—	—
First Professional Degree	—	—

Flexibility of Earnings

Average Hours Worked: 39
Workers with a Varying Number of Hours: 4.7%
Workers Earning Some Overtime Pay, Tips, or Commissions: 25.1%
Earnings Benefit of Working Overtime: 6.1%

Gender

	Male	Female
Percent	99.1%	0.9%
Effect on Earnings	0.0%	—

Union Membership

Percentage Union Members: 21.8%
Earnings Benefit of Union Membership: 18.6%

Veteran Status

Percentage Who Have Been on Active Duty: 16.3%
Earnings Benefit of Veteran Status: 12.6%

49-3041 Farm Equipment Mechanics

Diagnose, adjust, repair, or overhaul farm machinery and vehicles, such as tractors, harvesters, dairy equipment, and irrigation systems.

- Education or Training Required: Postsecondary vocational training
- Job Growth: 3.3%
- Annual Openings: 3,000
- Self-Employed: 3.2%
- Part-Time: 12.7%

NATIONAL WAGE FIGURES (ANNUAL)

Beginning	25th Percentile	Median	Mean	75th Percentile	90th Percentile
$19,340	$23,580	$29,460	$30,320	$36,090	$43,210

Median Wages for Industries Employing Largest Numbers (Annual)

Industry	Median Income
Federal, State, and Local Government	$35,900
Specialty Trade Contractors	$34,290
Rental and Leasing Services	$33,460
Food Manufacturing	$32,430
Wholesale Electronic Markets and Agents and Brokers	$32,000
Educational Services	$30,270
Merchant Wholesalers, Durable Goods	$29,910
Motor Vehicle and Parts Dealers	$29,350
Machinery Manufacturing	$29,330
Building Material and Garden Equipment and Supplies Dealers	$28,930

Median Wages for States (Annual)

AK	no data	KY	$23,570	NY	$29,960
AL	$27,950	LA	$28,680	OH	$29,470
AR	$25,610	MA	$28,490	OK	$26,680
AZ	$27,290	MD	$32,370	OR	$34,600
CA	$32,050	ME	$28,590	PA	$30,430
CO	$28,600	MI	$29,560	RI	no data
CT	$24,690	MN	$33,960	SC	$28,800
DC	no data	MO	$29,360	SD	$28,280
DE	no data	MS	$26,480	TN	$25,590
FL	$23,250	MT	$28,600	TX	$27,520
GA	$28,840	NC	$30,470	UT	$28,920
HI	no data	ND	$29,420	VA	$30,680
IA	$29,790	NE	$26,990	VT	$32,410
ID	$27,600	NH	$33,180	WA	$33,050
IL	$30,580	NJ	$33,150	WI	$30,440
IN	$30,130	NM	$27,810	WV	$22,520
KS	$31,180	NV	$35,010	WY	$30,430

Median Wages for the Largest Metropolitan Areas (Annual)

AZ: Phoenix	$26,370	MI: Detroit	$25,090
CA: Los Angeles	$31,650	MN: Minneapolis	$36,650
CA: Riverside	$30,110	MO: Kansas City	$31,250
CA: Sacramento	$35,330	MO: St. Louis	$31,320
CA: San Diego	no data	NV: Las Vegas	no data
CA: San Francisco	no data	NY: New York	$33,360
CO: Denver	no data	OH: Cincinnati	$26,100
DC: Washington	$35,100	OH: Cleveland	no data
FL: Miami	$19,380	OH: Columbus	$30,260
FL: Orlando	no data	OR: Portland	$33,420
FL: Tampa	no data	PA: Philadelphia	$37,260
GA: Atlanta	$25,620	PA: Pittsburgh	$29,450
IL: Chicago	$36,970	TX: Dallas	$29,360
MA: Boston	$40,980	TX: Houston	$27,070
MD: Baltimore	$33,390	WA: Seattle	$40,310

FACTORS THAT MAY AFFECT EARNINGS

Educational Attainment of Workers and Effect on Earnings

Figures are based on a group of occupations: Vehicle and Mobile Equipment Mechanics, Installers, and Repairers

	Percent at Level	Effect on Earnings
Less than High School	4.8%	−28.2%
Some High School	11.7%	−27.4%
High School or Equivalent	36.8%	3.4%
Some College but No Degree	21.4%	2.4%
Associate Degree	18.0%	9.1%
Bachelor's Degree	5.7%	14.5%
Master's Degree	—	—
Doctoral Degree	—	—
First Professional Degree	—	—

Flexibility of Earnings

Average Hours Worked: 37
Workers with a Varying Number of Hours: 7.8%
Workers Earning Some Overtime Pay, Tips, or Commissions: 22.2%
Earnings Benefit of Working Overtime: −6.4%

Gender

	Male	Female
Percent	98.6%	1.4%
Effect on Earnings	0.0%	—

Union Membership

Percentage Union Members: 16.3%
Earnings Benefit of Union Membership: 24.4%

Veteran Status

Percentage Who Have Been on Active Duty: 16.3%
Earnings Benefit of Veteran Status: 12.6%

49-3042 Mobile Heavy Equipment Mechanics, Except Engines

Diagnose, adjust, repair, or overhaul mobile mechanical, hydraulic, and pneumatic equipment, such as cranes, bulldozers, graders, and conveyors, used in construction, logging, and surface mining.

- Education or Training Required: Postsecondary vocational training
- Job Growth: 8.8%
- Annual Openings: 14,000
- Self-Employed: 2.9%
- Part-Time: 12.7%

NATIONAL WAGE FIGURES (ANNUAL)

Beginning	25th Percentile	Median	Mean	75th Percentile	90th Percentile
$26,280	$32,550	$40,440	$41,390	$48,770	$58,620

Median Wages for Industries Employing Largest Numbers (Annual)

Industry	Median Income
Support Activities for Transportation	$55,280
Utilities	$49,020
Primary Metal Manufacturing	$46,650
Federal, State, and Local Government	$43,970
Oil and Gas Extraction	$43,880
Wholesale Electronic Markets and Agents and Brokers	$43,470
Mining (Except Oil and Gas)	$41,960
Professional, Scientific, and Technical Services	$40,890
Heavy and Civil Engineering Construction	$39,990
Administrative and Support Services	$39,960

Median Wages for States (Annual)

State	Wage	State	Wage	State	Wage
AK	$57,290	KY	$36,560	NY	$43,430
AL	$37,760	LA	$35,630	OH	$40,230
AR	$35,480	MA	$44,320	OK	$35,130
AZ	$42,300	MD	$42,200	OR	$42,300
CA	$49,140	ME	$36,890	PA	$41,160
CO	$42,660	MI	$45,030	RI	$42,940
CT	$45,950	MN	$45,360	SC	$36,790
DC	no data	MO	$39,350	SD	$37,750
DE	$45,080	MS	$33,170	TN	$33,430
FL	$35,270	MT	$38,310	TX	$34,480
GA	$38,320	NC	$36,850	UT	$43,490
HI	$53,810	ND	$39,850	VA	$38,270
IA	$40,050	NE	$37,370	VT	$37,830
ID	$36,080	NH	$38,960	WA	$45,670
IL	$47,680	NJ	$48,210	WI	$41,850
IN	$39,570	NM	$39,640	WV	$34,710
KS	$40,510	NV	$48,890	WY	$44,930

Median Wages for the Largest Metropolitan Areas (Annual)

Area	Wage	Area	Wage
AZ: Phoenix	$43,270	MI: Detroit	$56,000
CA: Los Angeles	$53,300	MN: Minneapolis	$48,160
CA: Riverside	$45,940	MO: Kansas City	$41,580
CA: Sacramento	$46,460	MO: St. Louis	$43,530
CA: San Diego	$57,090	NV: Las Vegas	$45,540
CA: San Francisco	$59,020	NY: New York	$51,220
CO: Denver	$43,780	OH: Cincinnati	$41,470
DC: Washington	$42,550	OH: Cleveland	$43,130
FL: Miami	$36,050	OH: Columbus	$42,480
FL: Orlando	$36,060	OR: Portland	$45,680
FL: Tampa	$36,540	PA: Philadelphia	$43,740
GA: Atlanta	$40,480	PA: Pittsburgh	$39,610
IL: Chicago	$50,310	TX: Dallas	$35,530
MA: Boston	$44,690	TX: Houston	$33,700
MD: Baltimore	$42,140	WA: Seattle	$48,610

FACTORS THAT MAY AFFECT EARNINGS

Educational Attainment of Workers and Effect on Earnings

Figures are based on a group of occupations: Vehicle and Mobile Equipment Mechanics, Installers, and Repairers

	Percent at Level	Effect on Earnings
Less than High School	4.8%	−28.2%
Some High School	11.7%	−27.4%
High School or Equivalent	36.8%	3.4%
Some College but No Degree	21.4%	2.4%
Associate Degree	18.0%	9.1%
Bachelor's Degree	5.7%	14.5%
Master's Degree	—	—
Doctoral Degree	—	—
First Professional Degree	—	—

Flexibility of Earnings

Average Hours Worked: 37
Workers with a Varying Number of Hours: 7.8%
Workers Earning Some Overtime Pay, Tips, or Commissions: 22.2%
Earnings Benefit of Working Overtime: −6.4%

Gender

	Male	Female
Percent	98.6%	1.4%
Effect on Earnings	0.0%	—

Union Membership

Percentage Union Members: 16.3%
Earnings Benefit of Union Membership: 24.4%

Veteran Status

Percentage Who Have Been on Active Duty: 16.3%
Earnings Benefit of Veteran Status: 12.6%

49-3043 Rail Car Repairers

Diagnose, adjust, repair, or overhaul railroad rolling stock, mine cars, or mass-transit rail cars.

- Education or Training Required: Long-term on-the-job training
- Job Growth: –1.2%
- Annual Openings: 2,000
- Self-Employed: 2.1%
- Part-Time: 12.7%

NATIONAL WAGE FIGURES (ANNUAL)

Beginning	25th Percentile	Median	Mean	75th Percentile	90th Percentile
$25,960	$34,840	$43,320	$43,010	$51,400	$58,270

Median Wages for Industries Employing Largest Numbers (Annual)

Industry	Median Income
Rail Transportation	$44,990
Rental and Leasing Services	$36,150
Repair and Maintenance	$32,710
Support Activities for Transportation	$32,390
Transportation Equipment Manufacturing	$28,230

Median Wages for States (Annual)

State	Wage	State	Wage	State	Wage
AK	no data	KY	$33,530	NY	no data
AL	$29,900	LA	$39,440	OH	$40,720
AR	no data	MA	no data	OK	no data
AZ	$33,510	MD	$41,130	OR	no data
CA	$47,630	ME	no data	PA	$41,030
CO	$42,930	MI	$41,300	RI	no data
CT	no data	MN	$45,660	SC	$41,700
DC	no data	MO	$36,960	SD	no data
DE	$40,840	MS	$39,950	TN	$43,630
FL	$42,900	MT	no data	TX	$35,170
GA	$43,090	NC	$31,600	UT	$67,440
HI	no data	ND	$47,110	VA	$44,480
IA	$32,350	NE	$46,520	VT	no data
ID	$30,850	NH	no data	WA	no data
IL	$42,830	NJ	$48,490	WI	$44,980
IN	$37,550	NM	no data	WV	$42,750
KS	$38,790	NV	$34,790	WY	$35,200

Median Wages for the Largest Metropolitan Areas (Annual)

Area	Wage	Area	Wage
AZ: Phoenix	no data	MI: Detroit	$26,040
CA: Los Angeles	$35,960	MN: Minneapolis	$29,970
CA: Riverside	no data	MO: Kansas City	$30,330
CA: Sacramento	no data	MO: St. Louis	$39,800
CA: San Diego	no data	NV: Las Vegas	no data
CA: San Francisco	no data	NY: New York	no data
CO: Denver	$33,530	OH: Cincinnati	no data
DC: Washington	$40,520	OH: Cleveland	no data
FL: Miami	no data	OH: Columbus	no data
FL: Orlando	no data	OR: Portland	no data
FL: Tampa	$25,580	PA: Philadelphia	$32,590
GA: Atlanta	no data	PA: Pittsburgh	$27,690
IL: Chicago	$40,970	TX: Dallas	$34,800
MA: Boston	no data	TX: Houston	$29,610
MD: Baltimore	no data	WA: Seattle	$33,280

FACTORS THAT MAY AFFECT EARNINGS

Educational Attainment of Workers and Effect on Earnings

Figures are based on a group of occupations: Vehicle and Mobile Equipment Mechanics, Installers, and Repairers

	Percent at Level	Effect on Earnings
Less than High School	4.8%	–28.2%
Some High School	11.7%	–27.4%
High School or Equivalent	36.8%	3.4%
Some College but No Degree	21.4%	2.4%
Associate Degree	18.0%	9.1%
Bachelor's Degree	5.7%	14.5%
Master's Degree	—	—
Doctoral Degree	—	—
First Professional Degree	—	—

Flexibility of Earnings

Average Hours Worked: 37
Workers with a Varying Number of Hours: 7.8%
Workers Earning Some Overtime Pay, Tips, or Commissions: 22.2%
Earnings Benefit of Working Overtime: –6.4%

Gender

	Male	Female
Percent	98.6%	1.4%
Effect on Earnings	0.0%	—

Union Membership

Percentage Union Members: 16.3%
Earnings Benefit of Union Membership: 24.4%

Veteran Status

Percentage Who Have Been on Active Duty: 16.3%
Earnings Benefit of Veteran Status: 12.6%

49-3051 Motorboat Mechanics

Repair and adjust electrical and mechanical equipment of gasoline or diesel-powered inboard or inboard-outboard boat engines.

- Education or Training Required: Long-term on-the-job training
- Job Growth: 15.1%
- Annual Openings: 7,000
- Self-Employed: 18.9%
- Part-Time: 12.7%

NATIONAL WAGE FIGURES (ANNUAL)

Beginning	25th Percentile	Median	Mean	75th Percentile	90th Percentile
$20,680	$26,330	$33,210	$34,430	$41,610	$50,750

Median Wages for Industries Employing Largest Numbers (Annual)

Industry	Median Income
Water Transportation	$47,160
Federal, State, and Local Government	$38,420
Educational Services	$34,840
Amusement, Gambling, and Recreation Industries	$34,770
Transportation Equipment Manufacturing	$33,580
Repair and Maintenance	$33,420
Motor Vehicle and Parts Dealers	$32,590
Administrative and Support Services	$32,160
Support Activities for Transportation	$32,130
Rental and Leasing Services	$31,910

Median Wages for States (Annual)

State	Wage	State	Wage	State	Wage
AK	$40,540	KY	$22,730	NY	$33,450
AL	$31,030	LA	$30,580	OH	$26,700
AR	$25,150	MA	$39,730	OK	$26,690
AZ	$28,040	MD	$36,740	OR	$31,800
CA	$35,540	ME	$33,800	PA	$26,740
CO	$33,820	MI	$30,900	RI	$37,930
CT	$43,610	MN	$34,090	SC	$30,710
DC	no data	MO	$33,150	SD	$23,200
DE	$26,050	MS	$29,130	TN	$26,200
FL	$33,130	MT	$17,780	TX	$29,790
GA	$34,560	NC	$33,950	UT	$32,260
HI	$32,880	ND	$29,990	VA	$37,390
IA	$28,670	NE	$34,730	VT	$33,950
ID	$29,680	NH	$41,120	WA	$35,370
IL	$34,540	NJ	$38,300	WI	$31,160
IN	$32,300	NM	no data	WV	$27,960
KS	$23,140	NV	$32,280	WY	no data

Median Wages for the Largest Metropolitan Areas (Annual)

Area	Wage	Area	Wage
AZ: Phoenix	$18,740	MI: Detroit	$35,000
CA: Los Angeles	$33,470	MN: Minneapolis	$34,180
CA: Riverside	$35,590	MO: Kansas City	no data
CA: Sacramento	$37,460	MO: St. Louis	$38,200
CA: San Diego	$29,170	NV: Las Vegas	$31,600
CA: San Francisco	$58,760	NY: New York	$42,490
CO: Denver	$39,680	OH: Cincinnati	$31,090
DC: Washington	$42,020	OH: Cleveland	$29,660
FL: Miami	$34,460	OH: Columbus	no data
FL: Orlando	$25,250	OR: Portland	$35,690
FL: Tampa	$47,640	PA: Philadelphia	$35,440
GA: Atlanta	$35,690	PA: Pittsburgh	$20,640
IL: Chicago	$35,100	TX: Dallas	$29,470
MA: Boston	$42,380	TX: Houston	$27,790
MD: Baltimore	$38,730	WA: Seattle	$40,620

FACTORS THAT MAY AFFECT EARNINGS

Educational Attainment of Workers and Effect on Earnings

Figures are based on a group of occupations: Vehicle and Mobile Equipment Mechanics, Installers, and Repairers

	Percent at Level	Effect on Earnings
Less than High School	4.8%	−28.2%
Some High School	11.7%	−27.4%
High School or Equivalent	36.8%	3.4%
Some College but No Degree	21.4%	2.4%
Associate Degree	18.0%	9.1%
Bachelor's Degree	5.7%	14.5%
Master's Degree	—	—
Doctoral Degree	—	—
First Professional Degree	—	—

Flexibility of Earnings

Average Hours Worked: 37
Workers with a Varying Number of Hours: 7.8%
Workers Earning Some Overtime Pay, Tips, or Commissions: 22.2%
Earnings Benefit of Working Overtime: −0.6%

Gender

	Male	Female
Percent	96.6%	3.4%
Effect on Earnings	0.3%	−6.1%

Union Membership

Percentage Union Members: 16.3%
Earnings Benefit of Union Membership: 24.4%

Veteran Status

Percentage Who Have Been on Active Duty: 16.3%
Earnings Benefit of Veteran Status: 12.6%

49-3052 Motorcycle Mechanics

Diagnose, adjust, repair, or overhaul motorcycles, scooters, mopeds, dirt bikes, or similar motorized vehicles.

- Education or Training Required: Long-term on-the-job training
- Job Growth: 13.7%
- Annual Openings: 6,000
- Self-Employed: 15.7%
- Part-Time: 12.7%

NATIONAL WAGE FIGURES (ANNUAL)

Beginning	25th Percentile	Median	Mean	75th Percentile	90th Percentile
$18,640	$23,530	$30,050	$32,000	$38,290	$48,480

Median Wages for Industries Employing Largest Numbers (Annual)

Industry	Median Income
Merchant Wholesalers, Durable Goods	$38,210
Transportation Equipment Manufacturing	$34,010
Building Material and Garden Equipment and Supplies Dealers	$30,850
Motor Vehicle and Parts Dealers	$30,040
Repair and Maintenance	$28,500
Sporting Goods, Hobby, Book, and Music Stores	$28,410
Rental and Leasing Services	$28,260

Median Wages for States (Annual)

AK	no data	KY	$27,010	NY	$26,440
AL	$26,890	LA	$25,410	OH	$27,330
AR	$26,260	MA	$32,150	OK	$31,230
AZ	$26,250	MD	$32,340	OR	$29,090
CA	$38,060	ME	$28,180	PA	$30,000
CO	$32,690	MI	$30,740	RI	no data
CT	$32,030	MN	$31,880	SC	$27,510
DC	no data	MO	$30,120	SD	$27,610
DE	$32,550	MS	$27,510	TN	$28,080
FL	$32,880	MT	$27,120	TX	$31,840
GA	$31,960	NC	$27,400	UT	$28,860
HI	$33,600	ND	$27,450	VA	$29,040
IA	$24,860	NE	$21,460	VT	$29,330
ID	$28,220	NH	$33,710	WA	$35,340
IL	$31,800	NJ	$30,800	WI	$32,290
IN	$26,840	NM	$31,350	WV	$20,490
KS	$27,760	NV	$36,080	WY	$26,770

Median Wages for the Largest Metropolitan Areas (Annual)

AZ: Phoenix	$27,180	MI: Detroit	$32,910
CA: Los Angeles	$34,510	MN: Minneapolis	$35,580
CA: Riverside	$43,130	MO: Kansas City	$29,670
CA: Sacramento	$39,300	MO: St. Louis	$32,340
CA: San Diego	$44,230	NV: Las Vegas	$38,070
CA: San Francisco	$43,240	NY: New York	$28,330
CO: Denver	$37,090	OH: Cincinnati	$30,270
DC: Washington	$32,050	OH: Cleveland	no data
FL: Miami	$46,630	OH: Columbus	$27,930
FL: Orlando	$35,830	OR: Portland	$34,430
FL: Tampa	$34,330	PA: Philadelphia	$36,420
GA: Atlanta	$36,100	PA: Pittsburgh	$28,650
IL: Chicago	$31,380	TX: Dallas	$37,420
MA: Boston	$34,590	TX: Houston	$36,200
MD: Baltimore	$37,670	WA: Seattle	$35,920

FACTORS THAT MAY AFFECT EARNINGS

Educational Attainment of Workers and Effect on Earnings

Figures are based on a group of occupations: Vehicle and Mobile Equipment Mechanics, Installers, and Repairers

	Percent at Level	Effect on Earnings
Less than High School	4.8%	−28.2%
Some High School	11.7%	−27.4%
High School or Equivalent	36.8%	3.4%
Some College but No Degree	21.4%	2.4%
Associate Degree	18.0%	9.1%
Bachelor's Degree	5.7%	14.5%
Master's Degree	—	—
Doctoral Degree	—	—
First Professional Degree	—	—

Flexibility of Earnings

Average Hours Worked: 37
Workers with a Varying Number of Hours: 7.8%
Workers Earning Some Overtime Pay, Tips, or Commissions: 22.2%
Earnings Benefit of Working Overtime: −0.6%

Gender

	Male	Female
Percent	96.6%	3.4%
Effect on Earnings	0.3%	−6.1%

Union Membership

Percentage Union Members: 16.3%
Earnings Benefit of Union Membership: 24.4%

Veteran Status

Percentage Who Have Been on Active Duty: 16.3%
Earnings Benefit of Veteran Status: 12.6%

49-3053 Outdoor Power Equipment and Other Small Engine Mechanics

Diagnose, adjust, repair, or overhaul small engines used to power lawn mowers, chain saws, and related equipment.

- Education or Training Required: Moderate-term on-the-job training
- Job Growth: 14.0%
- Annual Openings: 10,000
- Self-Employed: 19.2%
- Part-Time: 12.7%

NATIONAL WAGE FIGURES (ANNUAL)

Beginning	25th Percentile	Median	Mean	75th Percentile	90th Percentile
$17,280	$21,540	$26,910	$27,950	$33,390	$40,170

Median Wages for Industries Employing Largest Numbers (Annual)

Industry	Median Income
Machinery Manufacturing	$40,200
Federal, State, and Local Government	$37,330
Educational Services	$33,120
Religious, Grantmaking, Civic, Professional, and Similar Organizations	$32,000
Wholesale Electronic Markets and Agents and Brokers	$30,530
Management of Companies and Enterprises	$29,810
Accommodation	$29,180
Administrative and Support Services	$29,150
Merchant Wholesalers, Nondurable Goods	$28,900
Amusement, Gambling, and Recreation Industries	$28,330

Median Wages for States (Annual)

AK	$32,360	KY	$23,740	NY	$30,340
AL	$21,690	LA	$26,170	OH	$24,440
AR	$25,320	MA	$33,160	OK	$21,890
AZ	$26,950	MD	$31,520	OR	$26,810
CA	$27,680	ME	$24,100	PA	$26,300
CO	$31,690	MI	$26,250	RI	no data
CT	$33,310	MN	$26,950	SC	$27,590
DC	no data	MO	$27,800	SD	$22,980
DE	$32,270	MS	$21,410	TN	$22,690
FL	$28,330	MT	$19,900	TX	$24,030
GA	$28,530	NC	$26,460	UT	$25,860
HI	$38,930	ND	$22,740	VA	$26,940
IA	$26,130	NE	$26,120	VT	$26,730
ID	$22,470	NH	$28,470	WA	$28,860
IL	$27,280	NJ	$32,410	WI	$25,950
IN	$25,900	NM	$23,810	WV	$18,680
KS	$20,580	NV	$31,250	WY	$25,640

Median Wages for the Largest Metropolitan Areas (Annual)

AZ: Phoenix	$27,780	MI: Detroit	$33,450
CA: Los Angeles	$28,270	MN: Minneapolis	$29,420
CA: Riverside	$26,260	MO: Kansas City	$35,680
CA: Sacramento	$37,580	MO: St. Louis	$27,950
CA: San Diego	no data	NV: Las Vegas	$32,740
CA: San Francisco	$33,680	NY: New York	$34,660
CO: Denver	$32,070	OH: Cincinnati	$26,360
DC: Washington	$32,150	OH: Cleveland	$26,120
FL: Miami	$28,830	OH: Columbus	$30,240
FL: Orlando	$25,390	OR: Portland	$32,910
FL: Tampa	$28,900	PA: Philadelphia	$32,090
GA: Atlanta	$32,160	PA: Pittsburgh	$27,100
IL: Chicago	$27,050	TX: Dallas	$25,180
MA: Boston	$34,050	TX: Houston	$25,640
MD: Baltimore	$26,130	WA: Seattle	$32,350

FACTORS THAT MAY AFFECT EARNINGS

Educational Attainment of Workers and Effect on Earnings

Figures are based on a group of occupations: Vehicle and Mobile Equipment Mechanics, Installers, and Repairers

	Percent at Level	Effect on Earnings
Less than High School	4.8%	−28.2%
Some High School	11.7%	−27.4%
High School or Equivalent	36.8%	3.4%
Some College but No Degree	21.4%	2.4%
Associate Degree	18.0%	9.1%
Bachelor's Degree	5.7%	14.5%
Master's Degree	—	—
Doctoral Degree	—	—
First Professional Degree	—	—

Flexibility of Earnings

Average Hours Worked: 37
Workers with a Varying Number of Hours: 7.8%
Workers Earning Some Overtime Pay, Tips, or Commissions: 22.2%
Earnings Benefit of Working Overtime: −0.6%

Gender

	Male	Female
Percent	96.6%	3.4%
Effect on Earnings	0.3%	−6.1%

Union Membership

Percentage Union Members: 16.3%
Earnings Benefit of Union Membership: 24.4%

Veteran Status

Percentage Who Have Been on Active Duty: 16.3%
Earnings Benefit of Veteran Status: 12.6%

49-3091 Bicycle Repairers

Repair and service bicycles.

- Education or Training Required: Moderate-term on-the-job training
- Job Growth: 14.3%
- Annual Openings: 2,000
- Self-Employed: 3.4%
- Part-Time: 12.7%

NATIONAL WAGE FIGURES (ANNUAL)

Beginning	25th Percentile	Median	Mean	75th Percentile	90th Percentile
$15,550	$18,280	$21,790	$22,610	$26,350	$31,090

Median Wages for Industries Employing Largest Numbers (Annual)

Industry	Median Income
Clothing and Clothing Accessories Stores	$23,240
Rental and Leasing Services	$23,050
Sporting Goods, Hobby, Book, and Music Stores	$21,710
Motor Vehicle and Parts Dealers	$21,460
Miscellaneous Store Retailers	$20,940

Median Wages for States (Annual)

State	Wage	State	Wage	State	Wage
AK	no data	KY	$33,150	NY	$20,100
AL	no data	LA	no data	OH	$21,490
AR	no data	MA	no data	OK	no data
AZ	$18,880	MD	$17,250	OR	$22,080
CA	$23,400	ME	$16,860	PA	$18,320
CO	$22,780	MI	$18,460	RI	no data
CT	$25,440	MN	$24,820	SC	no data
DC	no data	MO	$21,000	SD	$18,950
DE	no data	MS	no data	TN	no data
FL	$24,010	MT	no data	TX	$21,240
GA	$21,260	NC	$25,260	UT	$20,100
HI	no data	ND	$21,880	VA	$22,350
IA	$20,030	NE	$16,640	VT	$21,670
ID	$25,040	NH	$22,070	WA	$21,850
IL	$22,760	NJ	$24,550	WI	$20,930
IN	$21,360	NM	$19,270	WV	no data
KS	$22,070	NV	$17,120	WY	no data

Median Wages for the Largest Metropolitan Areas (Annual)

Metro	Wage	Metro	Wage
AZ: Phoenix	$18,830	MI: Detroit	no data
CA: Los Angeles	$23,240	MN: Minneapolis	$28,810
CA: Riverside	no data	MO: Kansas City	$25,910
CA: Sacramento	$20,170	MO: St. Louis	$22,350
CA: San Diego	$24,970	NV: Las Vegas	no data
CA: San Francisco	$22,340	NY: New York	$20,570
CO: Denver	no data	OH: Cincinnati	$20,870
DC: Washington	$21,970	OH: Cleveland	no data
FL: Miami	$25,080	OH: Columbus	no data
FL: Orlando	no data	OR: Portland	$23,720
FL: Tampa	no data	PA: Philadelphia	$24,490
GA: Atlanta	$22,830	PA: Pittsburgh	$23,500
IL: Chicago	$19,260	TX: Dallas	no data
MA: Boston	no data	TX: Houston	$22,060
MD: Baltimore	no data	WA: Seattle	$22,190

FACTORS THAT MAY AFFECT EARNINGS

Educational Attainment of Workers and Effect on Earnings

Figures are based on a group of occupations: Vehicle and Mobile Equipment Mechanics, Installers, and Repairers

	Percent at Level	Effect on Earnings
Less than High School	4.8%	−28.2%
Some High School	11.7%	−27.4%
High School or Equivalent	36.8%	3.4%
Some College but No Degree	21.4%	2.4%
Associate Degree	18.0%	9.1%
Bachelor's Degree	5.7%	14.5%
Master's Degree	—	—
Doctoral Degree	—	—
First Professional Degree	—	—

Flexibility of Earnings

Average Hours Worked: 37
Workers with a Varying Number of Hours: 7.8%
Workers Earning Some Overtime Pay, Tips, or Commissions: 22.2%
Earnings Benefit of Working Overtime: −0.6%

Gender

	Male	Female
Percent	97.9%	2.1%
Effect on Earnings	0.3%	−6.1%

Union Membership

Percentage Union Members: 16.3%
Earnings Benefit of Union Membership: 24.4%

Veteran Status

Percentage Who Have Been on Active Duty: 16.3%
Earnings Benefit of Veteran Status: 12.6%

49-3092 Recreational Vehicle Service Technicians

Diagnose, inspect, adjust, repair, or overhaul recreational vehicles, including travel trailers. May specialize in maintaining gas, electrical, hydraulic, plumbing, or chassis/towing systems as well as repairing generators, appliances, and interior components.

- Education or Training Required: Long-term on-the-job training
- Job Growth: 19.5%
- Annual Openings: 3,000
- Self-Employed: 3.6%
- Part-Time: 12.7%

NATIONAL WAGE FIGURES (ANNUAL)

Beginning	25th Percentile	Median	Mean	75th Percentile	90th Percentile
$19,910	$24,950	$31,510	$33,280	$40,270	$48,300

Median Wages for Industries Employing Largest Numbers (Annual)

Industry	Median Income
Transportation Equipment Manufacturing	$34,630
Rental and Leasing Services	$34,600
Motor Vehicle and Parts Dealers	$31,940
Accommodation	$31,100
Repair and Maintenance	$29,740
Miscellaneous Store Retailers	$28,870
Merchant Wholesalers, Durable Goods	$24,600
Amusement, Gambling, and Recreation Industries	$21,660

Median Wages for States (Annual)

State	Wage	State	Wage	State	Wage
AK	no data	KY	$28,460	NY	$27,850
AL	$30,630	LA	$29,170	OH	$29,240
AR	$23,490	MA	$30,740	OK	$28,560
AZ	$38,380	MD	$24,780	OR	$39,340
CA	$34,260	ME	$28,590	PA	$31,450
CO	$33,050	MI	$29,170	RI	$30,150
CT	$33,230	MN	$34,050	SC	$32,050
DC	no data	MO	$24,870	SD	$25,420
DE	$31,120	MS	$30,060	TN	$28,610
FL	$35,050	MT	$27,670	TX	$30,840
GA	$29,750	NC	$32,950	UT	$34,860
HI	no data	ND	$31,410	VA	$31,460
IA	$29,810	NE	$22,730	VT	no data
ID	$29,340	NH	$32,580	WA	$35,450
IL	$27,940	NJ	$34,420	WI	$31,080
IN	$30,870	NM	no data	WV	$24,770
KS	$24,260	NV	$35,980	WY	$26,630

Median Wages for the Largest Metropolitan Areas (Annual)

Area	Wage	Area	Wage
AZ: Phoenix	$41,060	MI: Detroit	$30,100
CA: Los Angeles	$40,060	MN: Minneapolis	$43,150
CA: Riverside	$33,840	MO: Kansas City	$27,890
CA: Sacramento	$37,410	MO: St. Louis	$25,690
CA: San Diego	$25,770	NV: Las Vegas	$41,090
CA: San Francisco	no data	NY: New York	$35,900
CO: Denver	$35,250	OH: Cincinnati	$32,200
DC: Washington	no data	OH: Cleveland	$30,900
FL: Miami	$36,440	OH: Columbus	no data
FL: Orlando	$28,770	OR: Portland	$42,880
FL: Tampa	no data	PA: Philadelphia	$35,360
GA: Atlanta	$37,900	PA: Pittsburgh	$18,640
IL: Chicago	no data	TX: Dallas	$37,130
MA: Boston	$31,150	TX: Houston	$36,120
MD: Baltimore	$22,890	WA: Seattle	$37,820

FACTORS THAT MAY AFFECT EARNINGS

Educational Attainment of Workers and Effect on Earnings

Figures are based on a group of occupations: Vehicle and Mobile Equipment Mechanics, Installers, and Repairers

	Percent at Level	Effect on Earnings
Less than High School	4.8%	−28.2%
Some High School	11.7%	−27.4%
High School or Equivalent	36.8%	3.4%
Some College but No Degree	21.4%	2.4%
Associate Degree	18.0%	9.1%
Bachelor's Degree	5.7%	14.5%
Master's Degree	—	—
Doctoral Degree	—	—
First Professional Degree	—	—

Flexibility of Earnings

Average Hours Worked: 37
Workers with a Varying Number of Hours: 7.8%
Workers Earning Some Overtime Pay, Tips, or Commissions: 22.2%
Earnings Benefit of Working Overtime: −0.6%

Gender

	Male	Female
Percent	97.9%	2.1%
Effect on Earnings	0.3%	−6.1%

Union Membership

Percentage Union Members: 16.3%
Earnings Benefit of Union Membership: 24.4%

Veteran Status

Percentage Who Have Been on Active Duty: 16.3%
Earnings Benefit of Veteran Status: 12.6%

49-3093 Tire Repairers and Changers

Repair and replace tires.

- Education or Training Required: Short-term on-the-job training
- Job Growth: 4.5%
- Annual Openings: 17,000
- Self-Employed: 3.4%
- Part-Time: 12.7%

NATIONAL WAGE FIGURES (ANNUAL)

Beginning	25th Percentile	Median	Mean	75th Percentile	90th Percentile
$15,330	$17,780	$21,340	$22,790	$26,130	$32,890

Median Wages for Industries Employing Largest Numbers (Annual)

Industry	Median Income
Mining (Except Oil and Gas)	$50,810
Postal Service	$45,320
Wholesale Electronic Markets and Agents and Brokers	$31,470
Warehousing and Storage	$30,980
Educational Services	$30,430
Federal, State, and Local Government	$29,220
Waste Management and Remediation Services	$28,190
Food and Beverage Stores	$26,040
Management of Companies and Enterprises	$25,660
Merchant Wholesalers, Durable Goods	$25,190

Median Wages for States (Annual)

AK	$22,000	KY	$19,720	NY	$20,580
AL	$20,320	LA	$18,070	OH	$21,060
AR	$19,130	MA	$20,150	OK	$18,630
AZ	$21,200	MD	$21,260	OR	$23,530
CA	$21,790	ME	$19,130	PA	$21,830
CO	$21,570	MI	$21,880	RI	$28,080
CT	$21,710	MN	$23,100	SC	$21,880
DC	$21,590	MO	$21,230	SD	$20,690
DE	$19,540	MS	$20,690	TN	$20,210
FL	$21,370	MT	$20,610	TX	$20,870
GA	$21,860	NC	$21,170	UT	$19,930
HI	no data	ND	$22,390	VA	$22,080
IA	$21,530	NE	$21,150	VT	$21,690
ID	$22,880	NH	$21,180	WA	$24,310
IL	$21,740	NJ	$21,410	WI	$21,200
IN	$22,090	NM	$20,570	WV	$18,270
KS	$20,990	NV	$26,800	WY	$19,140

Median Wages for the Largest Metropolitan Areas (Annual)

AZ: Phoenix	$22,390	MI: Detroit	$21,300
CA: Los Angeles	$21,660	MN: Minneapolis	$23,090
CA: Riverside	$21,230	MO: Kansas City	$22,040
CA: Sacramento	$20,950	MO: St. Louis	$23,250
CA: San Diego	$22,250	NV: Las Vegas	$26,240
CA: San Francisco	$22,400	NY: New York	$21,300
CO: Denver	$22,380	OH: Cincinnati	$22,820
DC: Washington	$22,090	OH: Cleveland	$20,690
FL: Miami	$20,850	OH: Columbus	$23,500
FL: Orlando	$21,860	OR: Portland	$23,570
FL: Tampa	$21,520	PA: Philadelphia	$21,300
GA: Atlanta	$24,040	PA: Pittsburgh	$21,680
IL: Chicago	$21,640	TX: Dallas	$22,560
MA: Boston	$21,610	TX: Houston	$21,910
MD: Baltimore	$22,580	WA: Seattle	$23,000

FACTORS THAT MAY AFFECT EARNINGS

Educational Attainment of Workers and Effect on Earnings

Figures are based on a group of occupations: Vehicle and Mobile Equipment Mechanics, Installers, and Repairers

	Percent at Level	Effect on Earnings
Less than High School	4.8%	−28.2%
Some High School	11.7%	−27.4%
High School or Equivalent	36.8%	3.4%
Some College but No Degree	21.4%	2.4%
Associate Degree	18.0%	9.1%
Bachelor's Degree	5.7%	14.5%
Master's Degree	—	—
Doctoral Degree	—	—
First Professional Degree	—	—

Flexibility of Earnings

Average Hours Worked: 37

Workers with a Varying Number of Hours: 7.8%

Workers Earning Some Overtime Pay, Tips, or Commissions: 22.2%

Earnings Benefit of Working Overtime: −0.6%

Gender

	Male	Female
Percent	97.9%	2.1%
Effect on Earnings	0.3%	−6.1%

Union Membership

Percentage Union Members: 16.3%

Earnings Benefit of Union Membership: 24.4%

Veteran Status

Percentage Who Have Been on Active Duty: 16.3%

Earnings Benefit of Veteran Status: 12.6%

49-9000 Other Installation, Maintenance, and Repair Occupations

49-9011 Mechanical Door Repairers

Install, service, or repair opening and closing mechanisms of automatic doors and hydraulic door closers. Includes garage door mechanics.

- Education or Training Required: Moderate-term on-the-job training
- Job Growth: 15.8%
- Annual Openings: 1,000
- Self-Employed: 0.0%
- Part-Time: 11.1%

NATIONAL WAGE FIGURES (ANNUAL)

Beginning	25th Percentile	Median	Mean	75th Percentile	90th Percentile
$21,660	$25,940	$31,610	$34,060	$40,320	$50,520

Median Wages for Industries Employing Largest Numbers (Annual)

Industry	Median Income
Repair and Maintenance	$40,240
Educational Services	$36,170
Merchant Wholesalers, Durable Goods	$33,570
Specialty Trade Contractors	$31,850
Building Material and Garden Equipment and Supplies Dealers	$30,040
Federal, State, and Local Government	$28,900
Fabricated Metal Product Manufacturing	$28,530

Median Wages for States (Annual)

State	Wage	State	Wage	State	Wage
AK	no data	KY	$35,810	NY	$29,940
AL	$25,470	LA	$31,920	OH	$30,810
AR	$23,240	MA	$41,840	OK	$27,340
AZ	$32,340	MD	$29,790	OR	$34,680
CA	$34,650	ME	$27,560	PA	$37,750
CO	$28,790	MI	$34,580	RI	no data
CT	$37,810	MN	$35,030	SC	$30,240
DC	no data	MO	$28,420	SD	$29,360
DE	$25,160	MS	$23,510	TN	no data
FL	$32,950	MT	$27,210	TX	$29,530
GA	$33,580	NC	$34,980	UT	$35,240
HI	no data	ND	$27,120	VA	$31,660
IA	$33,280	NE	$26,900	VT	no data
ID	no data	NH	no data	WA	$31,630
IL	$27,560	NJ	$32,890	WI	$36,000
IN	$29,960	NM	no data	WV	no data
KS	$28,890	NV	$38,310	WY	no data

Median Wages for the Largest Metropolitan Areas (Annual)

Area	Wage	Area	Wage
AZ: Phoenix	$32,410	MI: Detroit	$37,700
CA: Los Angeles	$43,310	MN: Minneapolis	$39,060
CA: Riverside	$36,670	MO: Kansas City	$27,850
CA: Sacramento	no data	MO: St. Louis	no data
CA: San Diego	$32,450	NV: Las Vegas	no data
CA: San Francisco	$43,100	NY: New York	$31,030
CO: Denver	no data	OH: Cincinnati	$37,290
DC: Washington	$33,790	OH: Cleveland	$28,760
FL: Miami	$58,110	OH: Columbus	no data
FL: Orlando	$44,960	OR: Portland	no data
FL: Tampa	no data	PA: Philadelphia	$34,900
GA: Atlanta	$34,320	PA: Pittsburgh	no data
IL: Chicago	$27,290	TX: Dallas	$30,280
MA: Boston	no data	TX: Houston	$31,070
MD: Baltimore	$26,690	WA: Seattle	$34,530

FACTORS THAT MAY AFFECT EARNINGS

Educational Attainment of Workers and Effect on Earnings

Figures are based on a group of occupations: Other Installation, Maintenance, and Repair Occupations

	Percent at Level	Effect on Earnings
Less than High School	3.5%	−30.0%
Some High School	9.5%	−32.6%
High School or Equivalent	37.7%	0.3%
Some College but No Degree	21.1%	7.0%
Associate Degree	18.3%	8.7%
Bachelor's Degree	8.8%	11.1%
Master's Degree	0.9%	−6.2%
Doctoral Degree	—	—
First Professional Degree	—	—

Flexibility of Earnings

Average Hours Worked: 36
Workers with a Varying Number of Hours: 7.6%
Workers Earning Some Overtime Pay, Tips, or Commissions: 27.7%
Earnings Benefit of Working Overtime: 2.3%

Gender

	Male	Female
Percent	95.4%	4.6%
Effect on Earnings	0.3%	−6.1%

Union Membership

Percentage Union Members: 18.7%
Earnings Benefit of Union Membership: 21.4%

Veteran Status

Percentage Who Have Been on Active Duty: 18.7%
Earnings Benefit of Veteran Status: 11.0%

49-9012 Control and Valve Installers and Repairers, Except Mechanical Door

Install, repair, and maintain mechanical regulating and controlling devices, such as electric meters, gas regulators, thermostats, safety and flow valves, and other mechanical governors.

- Education or Training Required: Moderate-term on-the-job training
- Job Growth: 4.9%
- Annual Openings: 4,000
- Self-Employed: 0.0%
- Part-Time: 11.1%

NATIONAL WAGE FIGURES (ANNUAL)

Beginning	25th Percentile	Median	Mean	75th Percentile	90th Percentile
$25,050	$32,970	$45,440	$45,290	$56,370	$66,380

Median Wages for Industries Employing Largest Numbers (Annual)

Industry	Median Income
Oil and Gas Extraction	$52,710
Utilities	$52,460
Paper Manufacturing	$51,590
Pipeline Transportation	$50,900
Petroleum and Coal Products Manufacturing	$49,860
Management of Companies and Enterprises	$49,620
Educational Services	$46,840
Chemical Manufacturing	$46,830
Warehousing and Storage	$46,740
Construction of Buildings	$46,700

Median Wages for States (Annual)

AK	$52,870	KY	$29,190	NY	$58,970
AL	$36,180	LA	$39,570	OH	$51,860
AR	$30,060	MA	$43,670	OK	$45,290
AZ	$52,930	MD	$50,210	OR	$47,360
CA	no data	ME	$51,250	PA	$47,410
CO	$52,900	MI	no data	RI	$48,040
CT	$55,710	MN	$49,290	SC	$45,050
DC	no data	MO	$50,630	SD	$39,500
DE	no data	MS	$33,630	TN	$34,030
FL	$33,700	MT	$27,800	TX	$35,900
GA	$33,670	NC	$38,200	UT	$44,610
HI	$46,840	ND	$49,930	VA	$39,440
IA	$41,890	NE	$49,510	VT	$39,250
ID	$44,590	NH	$33,630	WA	$46,140
IL	$49,950	NJ	$49,670	WI	$47,800
IN	$45,810	NM	$37,670	WV	$45,620
KS	$44,380	NV	$43,770	WY	$42,670

Median Wages for the Largest Metropolitan Areas (Annual)

AZ: Phoenix	$64,180	MI: Detroit	no data
CA: Los Angeles	no data	MN: Minneapolis	$47,100
CA: Riverside	$58,720	MO: Kansas City	$53,090
CA: Sacramento	$39,740	MO: St. Louis	no data
CA: San Diego	no data	NV: Las Vegas	$27,770
CA: San Francisco	$65,220	NY: New York	$57,840
CO: Denver	no data	OH: Cincinnati	$52,040
DC: Washington	$48,900	OH: Cleveland	$53,960
FL: Miami	$31,850	OH: Columbus	$44,310
FL: Orlando	$33,400	OR: Portland	$49,950
FL: Tampa	$35,000	PA: Philadelphia	$55,610
GA: Atlanta	$39,560	PA: Pittsburgh	$46,140
IL: Chicago	$43,200	TX: Dallas	$37,040
MA: Boston	$46,650	TX: Houston	$35,530
MD: Baltimore	$53,000	WA: Seattle	no data

FACTORS THAT MAY AFFECT EARNINGS

Educational Attainment of Workers and Effect on Earnings

Figures are based on a group of occupations: Other Installation, Maintenance, and Repair Occupations

	Percent at Level	Effect on Earnings
Less than High School	3.5%	−30.0%
Some High School	9.5%	−32.6%
High School or Equivalent	37.7%	0.3%
Some College but No Degree	21.1%	7.0%
Associate Degree	18.3%	8.7%
Bachelor's Degree	8.8%	11.1%
Master's Degree	0.9%	−6.2%
Doctoral Degree	—	—
First Professional Degree	—	—

Flexibility of Earnings

Average Hours Worked: 36
Workers with a Varying Number of Hours: 7.6%
Workers Earning Some Overtime Pay, Tips, or Commissions: 27.7%
Earnings Benefit of Working Overtime: 2.3%

Gender

	Male	Female
Percent	95.4%	4.6%
Effect on Earnings	0.3%	−6.1%

Union Membership

Percentage Union Members: 18.7%
Earnings Benefit of Union Membership: 21.4%

Veteran Status

Percentage Who Have Been on Active Duty: 18.7%
Earnings Benefit of Veteran Status: 11.0%

49-9021 Heating, Air Conditioning, and Refrigeration Mechanics and Installers

Install or repair heating, central air conditioning, or refrigeration systems, including oil burners, hot-air furnaces, and heating stoves.

- Education or Training Required: Long-term on-the-job training
- Job Growth: 19.0%
- Annual Openings: 33,000
- Self-Employed: 13.1%
- Part-Time: 8.7%

NATIONAL WAGE FIGURES (ANNUAL)

Beginning	25th Percentile	Median	Mean	75th Percentile	90th Percentile
$23,680	$29,370	$37,660	$39,710	$48,510	$59,430

Median Wages for Industries Employing Largest Numbers (Annual)

Industry	Median Income
Transportation Equipment Manufacturing	$59,480
Postal Service	$55,190
Telecommunications	$53,690
Management of Companies and Enterprises	$45,630
Utilities	$45,560
Chemical Manufacturing	$44,360
Federal, State, and Local Government	$43,140
Hospitals	$42,890
Merchant Wholesalers, Durable Goods	$42,030
Wholesale Electronic Markets and Agents and Brokers	$41,950

Median Wages for States (Annual)

State	Wage	State	Wage	State	Wage
AK	$54,740	KY	$32,090	NY	$44,640
AL	$29,500	LA	$29,140	OH	$37,340
AR	$30,150	MA	$46,610	OK	$33,130
AZ	$36,010	MD	$42,620	OR	$38,750
CA	$44,330	ME	$36,130	PA	$39,390
CO	$39,110	MI	$44,690	RI	$43,480
CT	$48,310	MN	$46,740	SC	$33,580
DC	$51,270	MO	$38,560	SD	$34,510
DE	$38,830	MS	$29,250	TN	$28,640
FL	$33,390	MT	$31,690	TX	$35,270
GA	$34,410	NC	$34,220	UT	$35,940
HI	$47,050	ND	$32,390	VA	$35,450
IA	$31,720	NE	$33,730	VT	$37,440
ID	$35,650	NH	$38,520	WA	$46,230
IL	$42,450	NJ	$46,970	WI	$40,240
IN	$36,840	NM	$33,830	WV	$26,900
KS	$36,300	NV	$42,530	WY	$33,850

Median Wages for the Largest Metropolitan Areas (Annual)

Area	Wage	Area	Wage
AZ: Phoenix	$36,340	MI: Detroit	$46,510
CA: Los Angeles	$44,680	MN: Minneapolis	$47,890
CA: Riverside	$41,330	MO: Kansas City	$43,340
CA: Sacramento	$43,100	MO: St. Louis	$43,380
CA: San Diego	$47,840	NV: Las Vegas	$43,270
CA: San Francisco	$49,480	NY: New York	$50,340
CO: Denver	$44,720	OH: Cincinnati	$41,110
DC: Washington	$45,410	OH: Cleveland	$40,670
FL: Miami	$33,490	OH: Columbus	$37,850
FL: Orlando	$32,960	OR: Portland	$42,970
FL: Tampa	$35,110	PA: Philadelphia	$43,540
GA: Atlanta	$38,070	PA: Pittsburgh	$33,600
IL: Chicago	$44,330	TX: Dallas	$38,270
MA: Boston	$46,530	TX: Houston	$36,010
MD: Baltimore	$42,500	WA: Seattle	$52,790

FACTORS THAT MAY AFFECT EARNINGS

Educational Attainment of Workers and Effect on Earnings

	Percent at Level	Effect on Earnings
Less than High School	2.4%	−24.7%
Some High School	10.3%	−30.8%
High School or Equivalent	36.3%	1.5%
Some College but No Degree	22.7%	7.2%
Associate Degree	19.6%	1.1%
Bachelor's Degree	7.9%	17.3%
Master's Degree	—	—
Doctoral Degree	—	—
First Professional Degree	—	—

Flexibility of Earnings

Average Hours Worked: 37
Workers with a Varying Number of Hours: 7.6%
Workers Earning Some Overtime Pay, Tips, or Commissions: 25.9%
Earnings Benefit of Working Overtime: −1.0%

Gender

	Male	Female
Percent	97.3%	2.7%
Effect on Earnings	0.7%	—

Union Membership

Percentage Union Members: 14.1%
Earnings Benefit of Union Membership: 17.3%

Veteran Status

Percentage Who Have Been on Active Duty: 18.7%
Earnings Benefit of Veteran Status: 11.0%

49-9031 Home Appliance Repairers

Repair, adjust, or install all types of electric or gas household appliances, such as refrigerators, washers, dryers, and ovens.

- Education or Training Required: Long-term on-the-job training
- Job Growth: 2.6%
- Annual Openings: 3,000
- Self-Employed: 18.0%
- Part-Time: 17.5%

NATIONAL WAGE FIGURES (ANNUAL)

Beginning	25th Percentile	Median	Mean	75th Percentile	90th Percentile
$19,490	$25,730	$33,860	$35,350	$43,250	$53,750

Median Wages for Industries Employing Largest Numbers (Annual)

Industry	Median Income
Utilities	$54,740
Construction of Buildings	$50,720
Social Assistance	$45,740
Educational Services	$36,560
Administrative and Support Services	$36,380
Repair and Maintenance	$35,130
Furniture and Related Product Manufacturing	$35,000
Management of Companies and Enterprises	$34,960
Support Activities for Transportation	$34,820
Food and Beverage Stores	$34,210

Median Wages for States (Annual)

AK	$45,460	KY	$34,250	NY	$34,880
AL	$27,730	LA	$26,790	OH	$35,210
AR	$23,040	MA	$34,710	OK	$31,680
AZ	$37,310	MD	$43,420	OR	$27,090
CA	$36,240	ME	$34,110	PA	$31,420
CO	$34,930	MI	$33,970	RI	$39,430
CT	$38,530	MN	$44,930	SC	$25,800
DC	no data	MO	$36,120	SD	$29,210
DE	$29,830	MS	$26,830	TN	$32,820
FL	$34,290	MT	$26,600	TX	$28,320
GA	$33,910	NC	$29,710	UT	$32,270
HI	$40,410	ND	$25,810	VA	$26,930
IA	$34,330	NE	$27,660	VT	$29,950
ID	$32,040	NH	$40,820	WA	$39,940
IL	$38,030	NJ	$44,110	WI	$32,400
IN	$30,720	NM	$32,850	WV	$23,990
KS	$29,990	NV	$41,730	WY	$29,260

Median Wages for the Largest Metropolitan Areas (Annual)

AZ: Phoenix	$37,770	MI: Detroit	$40,480
CA: Los Angeles	$34,770	MN: Minneapolis	$48,360
CA: Riverside	no data	MO: Kansas City	$30,870
CA: Sacramento	$50,270	MO: St. Louis	$41,910
CA: San Diego	$32,700	NV: Las Vegas	no data
CA: San Francisco	$39,480	NY: New York	$38,160
CO: Denver	$43,870	OH: Cincinnati	$34,580
DC: Washington	$43,860	OH: Cleveland	$51,980
FL: Miami	$38,040	OH: Columbus	$41,980
FL: Orlando	$23,300	OR: Portland	$27,920
FL: Tampa	$35,380	PA: Philadelphia	$39,340
GA: Atlanta	$33,980	PA: Pittsburgh	no data
IL: Chicago	$39,870	TX: Dallas	$29,690
MA: Boston	$36,720	TX: Houston	$27,440
MD: Baltimore	$37,670	WA: Seattle	$50,540

FACTORS THAT MAY AFFECT EARNINGS

Educational Attainment of Workers and Effect on Earnings

	Percent at Level	Effect on Earnings
Less than High School	—	—
Some High School	—	—
High School or Equivalent	59.6%	3.0%
Some College but No Degree	—	—
Associate Degree	17.0%	25.7%
Bachelor's Degree	—	—
Master's Degree	—	—
Doctoral Degree	—	—
First Professional Degree	—	—

Figures do not total 100% because some levels have a very small sample size.

Flexibility of Earnings

Average Hours Worked: 32
Workers with a Varying Number of Hours: 14.1%
Workers Earning Some Overtime Pay, Tips, or Commissions: 34.0%
Earnings Benefit of Working Overtime: 2.3%

Gender

	Male	Female
Percent	98.5%	1.5%
Effect on Earnings	0.3%	−6.1%

Union Membership

Percentage Union Members: 12.8%
Earnings Benefit of Union Membership: 21.4%

Veteran Status

Percentage Who Have Been on Active Duty: 18.7%
Earnings Benefit of Veteran Status: 11.0%

49-9041 Industrial Machinery Mechanics

Repair, install, adjust, or maintain industrial production and processing machinery or refinery and pipeline distribution systems.

- Education or Training Required: Long-term on-the-job training
- Job Growth: –0.2%
- Annual Openings: 13,000
- Self-Employed: 2.3%
- Part-Time: 2.4%

NATIONAL WAGE FIGURES (ANNUAL)

Beginning	25th Percentile	Median	Mean	75th Percentile	90th Percentile
$26,710	$33,010	$41,050	$42,570	$50,880	$62,080

Median Wages for Industries Employing Largest Numbers (Annual)

Industry	Median Income
Petroleum and Coal Products Manufacturing	$54,870
Utilities	$52,720
Transportation Equipment Manufacturing	$51,760
Federal, State, and Local Government	$47,190
Chemical Manufacturing	$45,470
Paper Manufacturing	$44,870
Professional, Scientific, and Technical Services	$44,220
Electrical Equipment, Appliance, and Component Manufacturing	$43,490
Computer and Electronic Product Manufacturing	$43,060
Beverage and Tobacco Product Manufacturing	$42,100

Median Wages for States (Annual)

State	Wage	State	Wage	State	Wage
AK	$60,390	KY	$39,990	NY	$41,840
AL	$34,870	LA	$39,630	OH	$44,110
AR	$35,310	MA	$44,530	OK	$38,810
AZ	$43,930	MD	$43,260	OR	$42,860
CA	$45,880	ME	$39,130	PA	$39,700
CO	$43,740	MI	$50,280	RI	$40,270
CT	$43,910	MN	$43,530	SC	$38,470
DC	$55,340	MO	$40,550	SD	$34,690
DE	$50,050	MS	$37,260	TN	$36,150
FL	$39,080	MT	$43,270	TX	$38,080
GA	$37,040	NC	$35,990	UT	$41,850
HI	$46,260	ND	$41,940	VA	$41,360
IA	$36,360	NE	$35,550	VT	$36,250
ID	$41,650	NH	$40,780	WA	$47,380
IL	$42,690	NJ	$44,800	WI	$42,890
IN	$46,120	NM	$36,120	WV	$39,980
KS	$36,640	NV	$45,790	WY	$42,390

Median Wages for the Largest Metropolitan Areas (Annual)

Area	Wage	Area	Wage
AZ: Phoenix	$47,600	MI: Detroit	$57,660
CA: Los Angeles	$43,980	MN: Minneapolis	$45,330
CA: Riverside	$44,710	MO: Kansas City	$39,570
CA: Sacramento	$46,590	MO: St. Louis	$49,220
CA: San Diego	$44,680	NV: Las Vegas	$49,630
CA: San Francisco	$56,260	NY: New York	$45,020
CO: Denver	$45,350	OH: Cincinnati	$47,740
DC: Washington	$46,820	OH: Cleveland	$41,800
FL: Miami	$38,240	OH: Columbus	$42,620
FL: Orlando	$38,270	OR: Portland	$45,460
FL: Tampa	$39,720	PA: Philadelphia	$44,740
GA: Atlanta	$40,000	PA: Pittsburgh	$41,160
IL: Chicago	$46,780	TX: Dallas	$40,520
MA: Boston	$47,130	TX: Houston	$41,650
MD: Baltimore	$43,460	WA: Seattle	$51,770

FACTORS THAT MAY AFFECT EARNINGS

Educational Attainment of Workers and Effect on Earnings

	Percent at Level	Effect on Earnings
Less than High School	2.5%	–23.0%
Some High School	10.3%	–25.6%
High School or Equivalent	40.3%	0.4%
Some College but No Degree	20.7%	8.1%
Associate Degree	17.8%	7.5%
Bachelor's Degree	8.0%	2.9%
Master's Degree	—	—
Doctoral Degree	—	—
First Professional Degree	—	—

Flexibility of Earnings

Average Hours Worked: 36
Workers with a Varying Number of Hours: 6.3%
Workers Earning Some Overtime Pay, Tips, or Commissions: 33.5%
Earnings Benefit of Working Overtime: –3.4%

Gender

	Male	Female
Percent	96.2%	3.8%
Effect on Earnings	0.1%	—

Union Membership

Percentage Union Members: 18.7%
Earnings Benefit of Union Membership: 10.0%

Veteran Status

Percentage Who Have Been on Active Duty: 18.7%
Earnings Benefit of Veteran Status: 11.0%

49-9042 Maintenance and Repair Workers, General

Perform work involving the skills of two or more maintenance or craft occupations to keep machines, mechanical equipment, or the structure of an establishment in repair. Duties may involve pipe fitting; boiler making; insulating; welding; machining; carpentry; repairing electrical or mechanical equipment; installing, aligning, and balancing new equipment; and repairing buildings, floors, or stairs.

- Education or Training Required: Moderate-term on-the-job training
- Job Growth: 15.2%
- Annual Openings: 154,000
- Self-Employed: 0.6%
- Part-Time: 14.1%

NATIONAL WAGE FIGURES (ANNUAL)

Beginning	25th Percentile	Median	Mean	75th Percentile	90th Percentile
$19,140	$24,250	$31,910	$33,510	$41,390	$50,840

Median Wages for Industries Employing Largest Numbers (Annual)

Industry	Median Income
Paper Manufacturing	$43,430
Chemical Manufacturing	$42,020
Transportation Equipment Manufacturing	$41,840
Plastics and Rubber Products Manufacturing	$38,290
Primary Metal Manufacturing	$37,910
Professional, Scientific, and Technical Services	$37,830
Machinery Manufacturing	$37,340
Nonmetallic Mineral Product Manufacturing	$36,730
Fabricated Metal Product Manufacturing	$36,440
Food Manufacturing	$35,160

Median Wages for States (Annual)

AK $40,960	KY $29,240	NY $33,840
AL $30,620	LA $28,040	OH $33,660
AR $27,810	MA $38,190	OK $29,010
AZ $29,210	MD $32,880	OR $32,500
CA $34,580	ME $30,440	PA $32,690
CO $32,220	MI $36,640	RI $33,970
CT $38,710	MN $36,110	SC $30,200
DC $37,260	MO $31,020	SD $25,570
DE $33,960	MS $24,700	TN $31,320
FL $27,650	MT $30,870	TX $25,960
GA $31,210	NC $32,010	UT $29,490
HI $33,770	ND $29,970	VA $32,370
IA $31,960	NE $29,470	VT $30,980
ID $30,380	NH $32,590	WA $36,100
IL $36,710	NJ $36,090	WI $34,940
IN $32,070	NM $25,670	WV $24,710
KS $29,610	NV $35,320	WY $34,550

Median Wages for the Largest Metropolitan Areas (Annual)

AZ: Phoenix $30,070	MI: Detroit $39,890
CA: Los Angeles $32,790	MN: Minneapolis $39,040
CA: Riverside $33,570	MO: Kansas City $33,260
CA: Sacramento $34,390	MO: St. Louis $34,400
CA: San Diego $33,320	NV: Las Vegas $37,310
CA: San Francisco $41,290	NY: New York $36,000
CO: Denver $33,550	OH: Cincinnati $34,700
DC: Washington $35,300	OH: Cleveland $35,070
FL: Miami $27,910	OH: Columbus $33,790
FL: Orlando $26,780	OR: Portland $34,730
FL: Tampa $26,890	PA: Philadelphia $35,460
GA: Atlanta $33,270	PA: Pittsburgh $32,770
IL: Chicago $38,030	TX: Dallas $29,610
MA: Boston $39,280	TX: Houston $27,530
MD: Baltimore $33,230	WA: Seattle $38,330

FACTORS THAT MAY AFFECT EARNINGS

Educational Attainment of Workers and Effect on Earnings

	Percent at Level	Effect on Earnings
Less than High School	5.6%	−20.5%
Some High School	10.2%	−32.3%
High School or Equivalent	38.6%	0.4%
Some College but No Degree	20.1%	4.0%
Associate Degree	16.3%	13.4%
Bachelor's Degree	8.5%	15.3%
Master's Degree	—	—
Doctoral Degree	—	—
First Professional Degree	—	—

Flexibility of Earnings

Average Hours Worked: 36
Workers with a Varying Number of Hours: 6.2%
Workers Earning Some Overtime Pay, Tips, or Commissions: 17.2%
Earnings Benefit of Working Overtime: 5.9%

Gender

	Male	Female
Percent	96.0%	4.0%
Effect on Earnings	0.9%	—

Union Membership

Percentage Union Members: 14.6%
Earnings Benefit of Union Membership: 24.6%

Veteran Status

Percentage Who Have Been on Active Duty: 18.7%
Earnings Benefit of Veteran Status: 11.0%

49-9043 Maintenance Workers, Machinery

Lubricate machinery, change parts, or perform other routine machinery maintenance.

- Education or Training Required: Short-term on-the-job training
- Job Growth: 2.8%
- Annual Openings: 6,000
- Self-Employed: 0.0%
- Part-Time: 12.5%

NATIONAL WAGE FIGURES (ANNUAL)

Beginning	25th Percentile	Median	Mean	75th Percentile	90th Percentile
$21,400	$26,840	$34,550	$36,390	$44,780	$55,030

Median Wages for Industries Employing Largest Numbers (Annual)

Industry	Median Income
Beverage and Tobacco Product Manufacturing	$43,620
Heavy and Civil Engineering Construction	$42,970
Paper Manufacturing	$41,740
Utilities	$41,670
Electrical Equipment, Appliance, and Component Manufacturing	$41,340
Chemical Manufacturing	$40,250
Mining (Except Oil and Gas)	$39,170
Federal, State, and Local Government	$38,850
Machinery Manufacturing	$38,100
Transportation Equipment Manufacturing	$37,150

Median Wages for States (Annual)

State	Wage	State	Wage	State	Wage
AK	$30,730	KY	$33,890	NY	$40,720
AL	$31,130	LA	$33,640	OH	$37,240
AR	$27,780	MA	$38,880	OK	$31,660
AZ	$30,880	MD	$33,580	OR	$31,080
CA	$39,240	ME	$33,630	PA	$36,130
CO	$29,060	MI	$39,560	RI	$34,500
CT	$41,220	MN	$32,640	SC	$33,430
DC	$34,280	MO	$32,420	SD	$21,720
DE	$36,980	MS	$32,720	TN	$30,240
FL	$33,450	MT	$31,090	TX	$28,060
GA	$27,960	NC	$31,620	UT	$34,190
HI	$35,700	ND	$29,250	VA	$35,710
IA	$35,080	NE	$30,650	VT	$29,900
ID	$35,220	NH	$46,070	WA	$35,420
IL	$40,770	NJ	$37,860	WI	$37,020
IN	$40,180	NM	$30,830	WV	$33,060
KS	$29,620	NV	$37,720	WY	$59,670

Median Wages for the Largest Metropolitan Areas (Annual)

Metro	Wage	Metro	Wage
AZ: Phoenix	$30,510	MI: Detroit	$41,370
CA: Los Angeles	$29,680	MN: Minneapolis	$36,760
CA: Riverside	$38,000	MO: Kansas City	$30,750
CA: Sacramento	$45,630	MO: St. Louis	$35,410
CA: San Diego	$47,940	NV: Las Vegas	$37,830
CA: San Francisco	$41,970	NY: New York	$40,120
CO: Denver	$26,270	OH: Cincinnati	$42,400
DC: Washington	$31,780	OH: Cleveland	$36,640
FL: Miami	$35,560	OH: Columbus	$41,020
FL: Orlando	$36,510	OR: Portland	$28,790
FL: Tampa	$30,300	PA: Philadelphia	$37,110
GA: Atlanta	$26,400	PA: Pittsburgh	$43,150
IL: Chicago	$40,870	TX: Dallas	$31,760
MA: Boston	$43,910	TX: Houston	$28,420
MD: Baltimore	$34,170	WA: Seattle	$35,390

FACTORS THAT MAY AFFECT EARNINGS

Educational Attainment of Workers and Effect on Earnings

	Percent at Level	Effect on Earnings
Less than High School	—	—
Some High School	7.3%	−38.7%
High School or Equivalent	52.4%	3.1%
Some College but No Degree	20.7%	14.8%
Associate Degree	11.0%	11.6%
Bachelor's Degree	—	—
Master's Degree	—	—
Doctoral Degree	—	—
First Professional Degree	—	—

Figures do not total 100% because some levels have a very small sample size.

Flexibility of Earnings

Average Hours Worked: 37
Workers with a Varying Number of Hours: 6.4%
Workers Earning Some Overtime Pay, Tips, or Commissions: 32.3%
Earnings Benefit of Working Overtime: 17.5%

Gender

	Male	Female
Percent	95.3%	4.7%
Effect on Earnings	0.3%	—

Union Membership

Percentage Union Members: 16.1%
Earnings Benefit of Union Membership: 15.7%

Veteran Status

Percentage Who Have Been on Active Duty: 18.7%
Earnings Benefit of Veteran Status: 11.0%

49-9044 Millwrights

Install, dismantle, or move machinery and heavy equipment according to layout plans, blueprints, or other drawings.

- Education or Training Required: Long-term on-the-job training
- Job Growth: 5.9%
- Annual Openings: 5,000
- Self-Employed: 1.1%
- Part-Time: 11.1%

NATIONAL WAGE FIGURES (ANNUAL)

Beginning	25th Percentile	Median	Mean	75th Percentile	90th Percentile
$28,790	$35,640	$45,630	$47,820	$61,200	$71,540

Median Wages for Industries Employing Largest Numbers (Annual)

Industry	Median Income
Transportation Equipment Manufacturing	$65,310
Warehousing and Storage	$65,000
Management of Companies and Enterprises	$57,140
Wholesale Electronic Markets and Agents and Brokers	$56,890
Paper Manufacturing	$52,190
Chemical Manufacturing	$51,590
Food Manufacturing	$50,280
Machinery Manufacturing	$47,560
Federal, State, and Local Government	$46,770
Plastics and Rubber Products Manufacturing	$46,240

Median Wages for States (Annual)

AK	$56,370	KY	$48,830	NY	$51,660
AL	$37,260	LA	$37,970	OH	$60,990
AR	$39,300	MA	$44,520	OK	$36,630
AZ	$36,520	MD	$50,790	OR	$42,810
CA	$50,150	ME	$41,600	PA	$38,690
CO	$38,640	MI	$62,900	RI	$65,360
CT	$38,310	MN	$52,060	SC	$38,450
DC	no data	MO	$51,210	SD	$33,570
DE	$58,350	MS	$34,450	TN	$42,530
FL	$33,020	MT	$39,830	TX	$38,500
GA	$39,730	NC	$36,510	UT	no data
HI	no data	ND	$45,310	VA	$42,280
IA	$41,460	NE	$33,030	VT	$36,580
ID	$36,900	NH	$43,230	WA	$48,290
IL	$54,670	NJ	$58,690	WI	$52,410
IN	$54,580	NM	$36,220	WV	$37,810
KS	$37,950	NV	$33,370	WY	$47,290

Median Wages for the Largest Metropolitan Areas (Annual)

AZ: Phoenix	$36,680	MI: Detroit	no data
CA: Los Angeles	$53,830	MN: Minneapolis	$55,550
CA: Riverside	$39,500	MO: Kansas City	$44,950
CA: Sacramento	$49,770	MO: St. Louis	$53,140
CA: San Diego	$35,800	NV: Las Vegas	$31,710
CA: San Francisco	$67,710	NY: New York	$67,750
CO: Denver	$39,850	OH: Cincinnati	$64,520
DC: Washington	$56,900	OH: Cleveland	$45,420
FL: Miami	$30,770	OH: Columbus	$60,660
FL: Orlando	no data	OR: Portland	$49,200
FL: Tampa	$31,510	PA: Philadelphia	$42,180
GA: Atlanta	$41,520	PA: Pittsburgh	$44,740
IL: Chicago	$59,770	TX: Dallas	$39,880
MA: Boston	$45,580	TX: Houston	$44,640
MD: Baltimore	$47,730	WA: Seattle	$54,220

FACTORS THAT MAY AFFECT EARNINGS

Educational Attainment of Workers and Effect on Earnings

	Percent at Level	Effect on Earnings
Less than High School	—	—
Some High School	—	—
High School or Equivalent	48.2%	–3.5%
Some College but No Degree	23.5%	0.2%
Associate Degree	16.5%	20.4%
Bachelor's Degree	—	—
Master's Degree	—	—
Doctoral Degree	—	—
First Professional Degree	—	—

Figures do not total 100% because some levels have a very small sample size.

Flexibility of Earnings

Average Hours Worked: 37
Workers with a Varying Number of Hours: 6.7%
Workers Earning Some Overtime Pay, Tips, or Commissions: 44.9%
Earnings Benefit of Working Overtime: –15.1%

Gender

	Male	Female
Percent	97.1%	2.9%
Effect on Earnings	–0.3%	—

Union Membership

Percentage Union Members: 49.4%
Earnings Benefit of Union Membership: 9.2%

Veteran Status

Percentage Who Have Been on Active Duty: 18.7%
Earnings Benefit of Veteran Status: 11.0%

49-9045 Refractory Materials Repairers, Except Brickmasons

Build or repair furnaces, kilns, cupolas, boilers, converters, ladles, soaking pits, ovens, etc., using refractory materials.

- Education or Training Required: Moderate-term on-the-job training
- Job Growth: –5.2%
- Annual Openings: Fewer than 500
- Self-Employed: 2.7%
- Part-Time: 2.4%

NATIONAL WAGE FIGURES (ANNUAL)

Beginning	25th Percentile	Median	Mean	75th Percentile	90th Percentile
$25,720	$32,790	$40,780	$40,790	$46,530	$57,910

Median Wages for Industries Employing Largest Numbers (Annual)

Industry	Median Income
Merchant Wholesalers, Durable Goods	$47,360
Repair and Maintenance	$44,270
Specialty Trade Contractors	$43,370
Primary Metal Manufacturing	$39,810
Heavy and Civil Engineering Construction	$39,060
Nonmetallic Mineral Product Manufacturing	$38,770
Fabricated Metal Product Manufacturing	$36,340

Median Wages for States (Annual)

State	Wage	State	Wage	State	Wage
AK	no data	KY	no data	NY	$39,240
AL	$34,980	LA	$38,210	OH	$42,450
AR	$40,510	MA	no data	OK	$32,910
AZ	no data	MD	no data	OR	no data
CA	$39,390	ME	no data	PA	$40,860
CO	no data	MI	$47,100	RI	no data
CT	no data	MN	no data	SC	$40,410
DC	no data	MO	no data	SD	no data
DE	no data	MS	no data	TN	$41,190
FL	no data	MT	no data	TX	$34,910
GA	$30,410	NC	$42,140	UT	no data
HI	no data	ND	no data	VA	$41,450
IA	$45,750	NE	no data	VT	no data
ID	no data	NH	no data	WA	no data
IL	no data	NJ	no data	WI	$45,060
IN	$40,640	NM	no data	WV	$34,710
KS	no data	NV	no data	WY	no data

Median Wages for the Largest Metropolitan Areas (Annual)

Area	Wage	Area	Wage
AZ: Phoenix	no data	MI: Detroit	$55,890
CA: Los Angeles	$38,910	MN: Minneapolis	no data
CA: Riverside	no data	MO: Kansas City	no data
CA: Sacramento	no data	MO: St. Louis	no data
CA: San Diego	no data	NV: Las Vegas	no data
CA: San Francisco	no data	NY: New York	$44,610
CO: Denver	no data	OH: Cincinnati	no data
DC: Washington	$43,490	OH: Cleveland	no data
FL: Miami	no data	OH: Columbus	$42,600
FL: Orlando	no data	OR: Portland	no data
FL: Tampa	no data	PA: Philadelphia	no data
GA: Atlanta	$29,080	PA: Pittsburgh	$35,950
IL: Chicago	$40,620	TX: Dallas	no data
MA: Boston	no data	TX: Houston	no data
MD: Baltimore	no data	WA: Seattle	no data

FACTORS THAT MAY AFFECT EARNINGS

Educational Attainment of Workers and Effect on Earnings

	Percent at Level	Effect on Earnings
Less than High School	2.5%	–23.0%
Some High School	10.3%	–25.6%
High School or Equivalent	40.3%	0.4%
Some College but No Degree	20.7%	8.1%
Associate Degree	17.8%	7.5%
Bachelor's Degree	8.0%	2.9%
Master's Degree	—	—
Doctoral Degree	—	—
First Professional Degree	—	—

Flexibility of Earnings

Average Hours Worked: 36
Workers with a Varying Number of Hours: 6.3%
Workers Earning Some Overtime Pay, Tips, or Commissions: 33.5%
Earnings Benefit of Working Overtime: –3.4%

Gender

	Male	Female
Percent	95.4%	4.6%
Effect on Earnings	0.1%	—

Union Membership

Percentage Union Members: 18.7%
Earnings Benefit of Union Membership: 10.0%

Veteran Status

Percentage Who Have Been on Active Duty: 18.7%
Earnings Benefit of Veteran Status: 11.0%

49-9051 Electrical Power-Line Installers and Repairers

Install or repair cables or wires used in electrical power or distribution systems. May erect poles and light- or heavy-duty transmission towers.

- Education or Training Required: Long-term on-the-job training
- Job Growth: 2.5%
- Annual Openings: 11,000
- Self-Employed: 2.3%
- Part-Time: 4.8%

NATIONAL WAGE FIGURES (ANNUAL)

Beginning	25th Percentile	Median	Mean	75th Percentile	90th Percentile
$29,040	$38,960	$50,780	$49,900	$60,120	$71,130

Median Wages for Industries Employing Largest Numbers (Annual)

Industry	Median Income
Repair and Maintenance	$56,220
Utilities	$54,190
Pipeline Transportation	$51,040
Telecommunications	$50,550
Federal, State, and Local Government	$49,510
Administrative and Support Services	$49,420
Specialty Trade Contractors	$45,270
Management of Companies and Enterprises	$44,960
Educational Services	$41,730
Heavy and Civil Engineering Construction	$40,120

Median Wages for States (Annual)

AK	$66,820	KY	$45,650	NY	$64,390
AL	$51,890	LA	$39,780	OH	$51,110
AR	$39,610	MA	$56,340	OK	$40,640
AZ	$60,930	MD	$54,610	OR	$68,270
CA	$62,620	ME	$46,770	PA	$52,100
CO	$57,170	MI	$56,830	RI	no data
CT	no data	MN	$58,190	SC	$43,830
DC	no data	MO	$50,220	SD	$48,040
DE	$57,470	MS	$40,620	TN	$49,500
FL	$51,170	MT	$57,740	TX	$40,370
GA	$45,130	NC	$43,620	UT	$49,520
HI	$65,590	ND	$53,570	VA	$47,090
IA	$50,830	NE	$46,860	VT	$50,750
ID	$60,560	NH	$51,390	WA	$65,760
IL	$54,940	NJ	$52,560	WI	$54,390
IN	$52,400	NM	$40,330	WV	$50,150
KS	$49,200	NV	$64,190	WY	$49,540

Median Wages for the Largest Metropolitan Areas (Annual)

AZ: Phoenix	$62,520	MI: Detroit	$59,040
CA: Los Angeles	no data	MN: Minneapolis	$65,900
CA: Riverside	$54,080	MO: Kansas City	$55,060
CA: Sacramento	no data	MO: St. Louis	$41,890
CA: San Diego	no data	NV: Las Vegas	$63,750
CA: San Francisco	no data	NY: New York	$61,420
CO: Denver	$60,310	OH: Cincinnati	no data
DC: Washington	$49,530	OH: Cleveland	$52,160
FL: Miami	$51,980	OH: Columbus	$50,180
FL: Orlando	$50,950	OR: Portland	$70,630
FL: Tampa	$50,300	PA: Philadelphia	$50,400
GA: Atlanta	$43,180	PA: Pittsburgh	$48,580
IL: Chicago	$55,510	TX: Dallas	$37,770
MA: Boston	$58,070	TX: Houston	$51,870
MD: Baltimore	$55,980	WA: Seattle	$60,720

FACTORS THAT MAY AFFECT EARNINGS

Educational Attainment of Workers and Effect on Earnings

	Percent at Level	Effect on Earnings
Less than High School	—	—
Some High School	—	—
High School or Equivalent	45.4%	6.6%
Some College but No Degree	26.2%	3.9%
Associate Degree	20.8%	−6.2%
Bachelor's Degree	—	—
Master's Degree	—	—
Doctoral Degree	—	—
First Professional Degree	—	—

Figures do not total 100% because some levels have a very small sample size.

Flexibility of Earnings

Average Hours Worked: 39
Workers with a Varying Number of Hours: 4.8%
Workers Earning Some Overtime Pay, Tips, or Commissions: 33.1%
Earnings Benefit of Working Overtime: 6.4%

Gender

	Male	Female
Percent	99.1%	0.9%
Effect on Earnings	0.0%	—

Union Membership

Percentage Union Members: 48.8%
Earnings Benefit of Union Membership: 17.1%

Veteran Status

Percentage Who Have Been on Active Duty: 18.7%
Earnings Benefit of Veteran Status: 11.0%

© JIST Works

49-9052 Telecommunications Line Installers and Repairers

String and repair telephone and television cable, including fiber optics and other equipment for transmitting messages or television programming.

- Education or Training Required: Long-term on-the-job training
- Job Growth: 10.8%
- Annual Openings: 23,000
- Self-Employed: 1.5%
- Part-Time: 15.0%

NATIONAL WAGE FIGURES (ANNUAL)

Beginning	25th Percentile	Median	Mean	75th Percentile	90th Percentile
$24,700	$32,370	$46,280	$45,740	$59,070	$68,220

Median Wages for Industries Employing Largest Numbers (Annual)

Industry	Median Income
Management of Companies and Enterprises	$65,290
Utilities	$54,660
Wholesale Electronic Markets and Agents and Brokers	$53,250
Telecommunications	$52,890
Warehousing and Storage	$52,360
Internet Service Providers, Web Search Portals, and Data-Processing Services	$49,520
Federal, State, and Local Government	$47,410
Professional, Scientific, and Technical Services	$42,450
Fabricated Metal Product Manufacturing	$42,000
Administrative and Support Services	$41,030

Median Wages for States (Annual)

State	Wage	State	Wage	State	Wage
AK	$60,180	KY	$29,570	NY	$66,640
AL	$33,470	LA	$31,260	OH	$41,170
AR	$40,400	MA	$61,450	OK	$38,150
AZ	$32,930	MD	$53,350	OR	$37,720
CA	$50,670	ME	$62,360	PA	$53,260
CO	$39,290	MI	$42,250	RI	no data
CT	$38,390	MN	$39,450	SC	$32,590
DC	no data	MO	$44,110	SD	$32,690
DE	$56,650	MS	$27,520	TN	$39,470
FL	$40,620	MT	$42,800	TX	$42,210
GA	$34,910	NC	$34,530	UT	$39,860
HI	$49,070	ND	$37,130	VA	$44,980
IA	$37,370	NE	$34,820	VT	$59,680
ID	$38,940	NH	$57,410	WA	$43,950
IL	$56,140	NJ	$60,010	WI	$41,930
IN	$40,840	NM	$28,980	WV	$51,930
KS	$43,780	NV	$47,840	WY	$29,800

Median Wages for the Largest Metropolitan Areas (Annual)

Area	Wage	Area	Wage
AZ: Phoenix	$34,730	MI: Detroit	$36,610
CA: Los Angeles	$51,290	MN: Minneapolis	$40,430
CA: Riverside	$53,390	MO: Kansas City	$49,780
CA: Sacramento	$47,930	MO: St. Louis	$47,580
CA: San Diego	$58,920	NV: Las Vegas	$48,950
CA: San Francisco	$42,970	NY: New York	$65,780
CO: Denver	$42,550	OH: Cincinnati	$49,590
DC: Washington	$44,020	OH: Cleveland	$38,570
FL: Miami	$36,620	OH: Columbus	$44,610
FL: Orlando	$37,580	OR: Portland	$39,720
FL: Tampa	$47,720	PA: Philadelphia	$58,530
GA: Atlanta	$37,020	PA: Pittsburgh	$49,940
IL: Chicago	$61,940	TX: Dallas	$43,440
MA: Boston	$61,660	TX: Houston	$44,490
MD: Baltimore	$50,230	WA: Seattle	$44,190

FACTORS THAT MAY AFFECT EARNINGS

Educational Attainment of Workers and Effect on Earnings

	Percent at Level	Effect on Earnings
Less than High School	—	—
Some High School	5.3%	−36.3%
High School or Equivalent	40.4%	−3.1%
Some College but No Degree	27.9%	4.5%
Associate Degree	15.9%	−1.4%
Bachelor's Degree	9.1%	21.3%
Master's Degree	—	—
Doctoral Degree	—	—
First Professional Degree	—	—

Flexibility of Earnings

Average Hours Worked: 38
Workers with a Varying Number of Hours: 4.7%
Workers Earning Some Overtime Pay, Tips, or Commissions: 30.5%
Earnings Benefit of Working Overtime: 3.6%

Gender

	Male	Female
Percent	91.4%	8.6%
Effect on Earnings	1.0%	—

Union Membership

Percentage Union Members: 30.9%
Earnings Benefit of Union Membership: 22.1%

Veteran Status

Percentage Who Have Been on Active Duty: 18.7%
Earnings Benefit of Veteran Status: 11.0%.

49-9061 Camera and Photographic Equipment Repairers

Repair and adjust cameras and photographic equipment, including commercial video and motion picture camera equipment.

- Education or Training Required: Moderate-term on-the-job training
- Job Growth: –9.1%
- Annual Openings: Fewer than 500
- Self-Employed: 22.6%
- Part-Time: 11.1%

NATIONAL WAGE FIGURES (ANNUAL)

Beginning	25th Percentile	Median	Mean	75th Percentile	90th Percentile
$19,020	$26,750	$34,850	$36,600	$43,760	$54,860

Median Wages for Industries Employing Largest Numbers (Annual)

Industry	Median Income
Rental and Leasing Services	$77,960
Motion Picture and Sound Recording Industries	$45,180
Wholesale Electronic Markets and Agents and Brokers	$42,430
Broadcasting (Except Internet)	$39,920
Personal and Laundry Services	$38,150
Machinery Manufacturing	$37,980
Merchant Wholesalers, Durable Goods	$36,900
Repair and Maintenance	$36,810
Administrative and Support Services	$32,890
Professional, Scientific, and Technical Services	$32,270

Median Wages for States (Annual)

AK	no data	KY	no data	NY	no data
AL	$26,500	LA	$26,670	OH	$32,850
AR	no data	MA	$34,730	OK	$44,320
AZ	$27,970	MD	$38,510	OR	$31,550
CA	$37,420	ME	$41,130	PA	$41,750
CO	$39,200	MI	$33,530	RI	no data
CT	no data	MN	$36,290	SC	no data
DC	no data	MO	$25,860	SD	no data
DE	no data	MS	no data	TN	$34,420
FL	$39,150	MT	no data	TX	$28,230
GA	$27,560	NC	$29,820	UT	no data
HI	no data	ND	no data	VA	$29,190
IA	no data	NE	no data	VT	no data
ID	no data	NH	no data	WA	$35,160
IL	$33,380	NJ	$32,060	WI	no data
IN	no data	NM	no data	WV	no data
KS	no data	NV	no data	WY	no data

Median Wages for the Largest Metropolitan Areas (Annual)

AZ: Phoenix	no data	MI: Detroit	$33,830
CA: Los Angeles	$55,960	MN: Minneapolis	no data
CA: Riverside	$31,920	MO: Kansas City	no data
CA: Sacramento	no data	MO: St. Louis	$24,130
CA: San Diego	$34,660	NV: Las Vegas	no data
CA: San Francisco	$36,040	NY: New York	$37,250
CO: Denver	$40,230	OH: Cincinnati	$33,000
DC: Washington	$32,030	OH: Cleveland	$40,940
FL: Miami	no data	OH: Columbus	no data
FL: Orlando	$41,530	OR: Portland	no data
FL: Tampa	no data	PA: Philadelphia	no data
GA: Atlanta	$28,460	PA: Pittsburgh	no data
IL: Chicago	$39,070	TX: Dallas	no data
MA: Boston	$38,680	TX: Houston	no data
MD: Baltimore	no data	WA: Seattle	$33,570

FACTORS THAT MAY AFFECT EARNINGS

Educational Attainment of Workers and Effect on Earnings

Figures are based on a group of occupations: Other Installation, Maintenance, and Repair Occupations

	Percent at Level	Effect on Earnings
Less than High School	3.5%	–30.0%
Some High School	9.5%	–32.6%
High School or Equivalent	37.7%	0.3%
Some College but No Degree	21.1%	7.0%
Associate Degree	18.3%	8.7%
Bachelor's Degree	8.8%	11.1%
Master's Degree	0.9%	–6.2%
Doctoral Degree	—	—
First Professional Degree	—	—

Flexibility of Earnings

Average Hours Worked: 36
Workers with a Varying Number of Hours: 7.6%
Workers Earning Some Overtime Pay, Tips, or Commissions: 27.7%
Earnings Benefit of Working Overtime: 2.3%

Gender

	Male	Female
Percent	86.1%	13.9%
Effect on Earnings	0.3%	–6.1%

Union Membership

Percentage Union Members: 18.7%
Earnings Benefit of Union Membership: 21.4%

Veteran Status

Percentage Who Have Been on Active Duty: 18.7%
Earnings Benefit of Veteran Status: 11.0%

49-9062 Medical Equipment Repairers

Test, adjust, or repair biomedical or electromedical equipment.

- Education or Training Required: Associate degree
- Job Growth: 14.8%
- Annual Openings: 4,000
- Self-Employed: 16.2%
- Part-Time: 11.1%

NATIONAL WAGE FIGURES (ANNUAL)

Beginning	25th Percentile	Median	Mean	75th Percentile	90th Percentile
$23,700	$30,260	$40,580	$43,040	$52,860	$66,160

Median Wages for Industries Employing Largest Numbers (Annual)

Industry	Median Income
Federal, State, and Local Government	$48,970
Administrative and Support Services	$47,570
Chemical Manufacturing	$47,540
Educational Services	$46,240
Merchant Wholesalers, Durable Goods	$43,870
Hospitals	$43,360
Computer and Electronic Product Manufacturing	$43,280
Merchant Wholesalers, Nondurable Goods	$42,560
Repair and Maintenance	$42,280
Professional, Scientific, and Technical Services	$41,320

Median Wages for States (Annual)

State	Wage	State	Wage	State	Wage
AK	no data	KY	$34,170	NY	$42,570
AL	$34,570	LA	$41,560	OH	$40,450
AR	$33,580	MA	$36,490	OK	$38,850
AZ	$31,760	MD	$41,260	OR	$46,900
CA	$50,410	ME	$46,920	PA	$44,060
CO	$46,840	MI	$39,720	RI	$39,890
CT	$44,170	MN	$49,530	SC	$32,230
DC	$44,510	MO	$39,920	SD	$50,060
DE	$28,530	MS	$30,520	TN	$40,000
FL	$35,120	MT	$52,060	TX	$34,950
GA	$33,860	NC	$43,920	UT	$54,540
HI	no data	ND	$38,370	VA	$41,360
IA	$47,650	NE	$45,520	VT	$49,200
ID	$44,710	NH	$40,980	WA	$39,040
IL	$37,230	NJ	$43,120	WI	$46,150
IN	$37,080	NM	$21,390	WV	$28,080
KS	$33,750	NV	no data	WY	$29,030

Median Wages for the Largest Metropolitan Areas (Annual)

Area	Wage	Area	Wage
AZ: Phoenix	$34,290	MI: Detroit	$41,700
CA: Los Angeles	$59,830	MN: Minneapolis	$49,800
CA: Riverside	$41,920	MO: Kansas City	$33,530
CA: Sacramento	$49,090	MO: St. Louis	$41,050
CA: San Diego	$66,850	NV: Las Vegas	no data
CA: San Francisco	$40,810	NY: New York	$44,860
CO: Denver	$47,800	OH: Cincinnati	$41,470
DC: Washington	$39,940	OH: Cleveland	$41,840
FL: Miami	$34,540	OH: Columbus	$38,990
FL: Orlando	$39,590	OR: Portland	$49,950
FL: Tampa	$34,020	PA: Philadelphia	$44,960
GA: Atlanta	$32,740	PA: Pittsburgh	$38,740
IL: Chicago	$36,110	TX: Dallas	$43,660
MA: Boston	$38,740	TX: Houston	$42,550
MD: Baltimore	$43,390	WA: Seattle	$39,130

FACTORS THAT MAY AFFECT EARNINGS

Educational Attainment of Workers and Effect on Earnings

Figures are based on a group of occupations: Other Installation, Maintenance, and Repair Occupations

	Percent at Level	Effect on Earnings
Less than High School	3.5%	−30.0%
Some High School	9.5%	−32.6%
High School or Equivalent	37.7%	0.3%
Some College but No Degree	21.1%	7.0%
Associate Degree	18.3%	8.7%
Bachelor's Degree	8.8%	11.1%
Master's Degree	0.9%	−6.2%
Doctoral Degree	—	—
First Professional Degree	—	—

Flexibility of Earnings

Average Hours Worked: 36
Workers with a Varying Number of Hours: 7.6%
Workers Earning Some Overtime Pay, Tips, or Commissions: 27.7%
Earnings Benefit of Working Overtime: 2.3%

Gender

	Male	Female
Percent	86.1%	13.9%
Effect on Earnings	0.3%	−6.1%

Union Membership

Percentage Union Members: 18.7%
Earnings Benefit of Union Membership: 21.4%

Veteran Status

Percentage Who Have Been on Active Duty: 18.7%
Earnings Benefit of Veteran Status: 11.0%

49-9063 Musical Instrument Repairers and Tuners

Repair percussion, stringed, reed, or wind instruments. May specialize in one area, such as piano tuning.

- Education or Training Required: Long-term on-the-job training
- Job Growth: 2.8%
- Annual Openings: 1,000
- Self-Employed: 16.8%
- Part-Time: 11.1%

NATIONAL WAGE FIGURES (ANNUAL)

Beginning	25th Percentile	Median	Mean	75th Percentile	90th Percentile
$16,230	$22,190	$29,200	$31,850	$39,600	$50,580

Median Wages for Industries Employing Largest Numbers (Annual)

Industry	Median Income
Educational Services	$43,350
Rental and Leasing Services	$39,720
Nonstore Retailers	$32,380
Miscellaneous Manufacturing	$32,220
Sporting Goods, Hobby, Book, and Music Stores	$28,490
Repair and Maintenance	$28,190

Median Wages for States (Annual)

State	Wage	State	Wage	State	Wage
AK	no data	KY	$29,220	NY	$24,850
AL	$26,700	LA	no data	OH	$24,870
AR	no data	MA	$37,310	OK	$25,780
AZ	$34,720	MD	no data	OR	no data
CA	$34,700	ME	no data	PA	$24,960
CO	$28,000	MI	$38,590	RI	no data
CT	$35,140	MN	$31,780	SC	$23,900
DC	no data	MO	$28,280	SD	no data
DE	$24,930	MS	no data	TN	$25,170
FL	$29,180	MT	no data	TX	$28,080
GA	$26,510	NC	$33,280	UT	$28,480
HI	no data	ND	no data	VA	no data
IA	$28,030	NE	$22,210	VT	no data
ID	no data	NH	$28,910	WA	$25,280
IL	$34,750	NJ	$36,030	WI	$24,370
IN	$25,660	NM	no data	WV	no data
KS	$36,730	NV	no data	WY	no data

Median Wages for the Largest Metropolitan Areas (Annual)

Area	Wage	Area	Wage
AZ: Phoenix	no data	MI: Detroit	$48,950
CA: Los Angeles	$30,710	MN: Minneapolis	$33,190
CA: Riverside	no data	MO: Kansas City	$25,650
CA: Sacramento	no data	MO: St. Louis	$30,100
CA: San Diego	no data	NV: Las Vegas	no data
CA: San Francisco	no data	NY: New York	$31,340
CO: Denver	no data	OH: Cincinnati	no data
DC: Washington	$42,070	OH: Cleveland	$18,720
FL: Miami	no data	OH: Columbus	no data
FL: Orlando	no data	OR: Portland	$26,370
FL: Tampa	no data	PA: Philadelphia	$27,390
GA: Atlanta	$25,900	PA: Pittsburgh	$25,020
IL: Chicago	$34,540	TX: Dallas	$25,950
MA: Boston	$37,640	TX: Houston	$31,410
MD: Baltimore	no data	WA: Seattle	no data

FACTORS THAT MAY AFFECT EARNINGS

Educational Attainment of Workers and Effect on Earnings

Figures are based on a group of occupations: Other Installation, Maintenance, and Repair Occupations

	Percent at Level	Effect on Earnings
Less than High School	3.5%	−30.0%
Some High School	9.5%	−32.6%
High School or Equivalent	37.7%	0.3%
Some College but No Degree	21.1%	7.0%
Associate Degree	18.3%	8.7%
Bachelor's Degree	8.8%	11.1%
Master's Degree	0.9%	−6.2%
Doctoral Degree	—	—
First Professional Degree	—	—

Flexibility of Earnings

Average Hours Worked: 36
Workers with a Varying Number of Hours: 7.6%
Workers Earning Some Overtime Pay, Tips, or Commissions: 27.7%
Earnings Benefit of Working Overtime: 2.3%

Gender

	Male	Female
Percent	86.1%	13.9%
Effect on Earnings	0.3%	−6.1%

Union Membership

Percentage Union Members: 18.7%
Earnings Benefit of Union Membership: 21.4%

Veteran Status

Percentage Who Have Been on Active Duty: 18.7%
Earnings Benefit of Veteran Status: 11.0%

49-9064 Watch Repairers

Repair, clean, and adjust mechanisms of timing instruments, such as watches and clocks.

- Education or Training Required: Long-term on-the-job training
- Job Growth: 0.6%
- Annual Openings: Fewer than 500
- Self-Employed: 19.5%
- Part-Time: 11.1%

NATIONAL WAGE FIGURES (ANNUAL)

Beginning	25th Percentile	Median	Mean	75th Percentile	90th Percentile
$17,020	$23,070	$30,900	$32,760	$40,480	$52,160

Median Wages for Industries Employing Largest Numbers (Annual)

Industry	Median Income
Miscellaneous Manufacturing	$34,550
Clothing and Clothing Accessories Stores	$30,610
Repair and Maintenance	$30,290
Merchant Wholesalers, Durable Goods	$30,280
General Merchandise Stores	$21,920

Median Wages for States (Annual)

State		State		State	
AK	no data	KY	no data	NY	$40,280
AL	no data	LA	no data	OH	$30,680
AR	no data	MA	$52,290	OK	no data
AZ	$23,480	MD	no data	OR	no data
CA	$29,000	ME	no data	PA	$26,430
CO	no data	MI	$33,590	RI	no data
CT	no data	MN	$38,150	SC	no data
DC	no data	MO	no data	SD	no data
DE	no data	MS	no data	TN	no data
FL	$30,380	MT	no data	TX	$25,650
GA	$15,520	NC	no data	UT	no data
HI	no data	ND	no data	VA	no data
IA	$23,590	NE	$32,820	VT	no data
ID	no data	NH	$18,840	WA	no data
IL	$33,650	NJ	$45,870	WI	no data
IN	$36,220	NM	no data	WV	no data
KS	no data	NV	no data	WY	no data

Median Wages for the Largest Metropolitan Areas (Annual)

Area		Area	
AZ: Phoenix	$17,840	MI: Detroit	no data
CA: Los Angeles	$29,070	MN: Minneapolis	$38,450
CA: Riverside	no data	MO: Kansas City	no data
CA: Sacramento	no data	MO: St. Louis	no data
CA: San Diego	no data	NV: Las Vegas	no data
CA: San Francisco	$27,520	NY: New York	$44,230
CO: Denver	no data	OH: Cincinnati	no data
DC: Washington	no data	OH: Cleveland	$30,420
FL: Miami	$32,390	OH: Columbus	no data
FL: Orlando	no data	OR: Portland	no data
FL: Tampa	$22,790	PA: Philadelphia	$43,110
GA: Atlanta	no data	PA: Pittsburgh	no data
IL: Chicago	$34,130	TX: Dallas	no data
MA: Boston	$52,290	TX: Houston	no data
MD: Baltimore	no data	WA: Seattle	no data

FACTORS THAT MAY AFFECT EARNINGS

Educational Attainment of Workers and Effect on Earnings

Figures are based on a group of occupations: Other Installation, Maintenance, and Repair Occupations

	Percent at Level	Effect on Earnings
Less than High School	3.5%	−30.0%
Some High School	9.5%	−32.6%
High School or Equivalent	37.7%	0.3%
Some College but No Degree	21.1%	7.0%
Associate Degree	18.3%	8.7%
Bachelor's Degree	8.8%	11.1%
Master's Degree	0.9%	−6.2%
Doctoral Degree	—	—
First Professional Degree	—	—

Flexibility of Earnings

Average Hours Worked: 36
Workers with a Varying Number of Hours: 7.6%
Workers Earning Some Overtime Pay, Tips, or Commissions: 27.7%
Earnings Benefit of Working Overtime: 2.3%

Gender

	Male	Female
Percent	86.1%	13.9%
Effect on Earnings	0.3%	−6.1%

Union Membership

Percentage Union Members: 18.7%
Earnings Benefit of Union Membership: 21.4%

Veteran Status

Percentage Who Have Been on Active Duty: 18.7%
Earnings Benefit of Veteran Status: 11.0%

49-9069 Precision Instrument and Equipment Repairers, All Other

All precision instrument and equipment repairers not listed separately.

- Education or Training Required: Moderate-term on-the-job training
- Job Growth: 7.7%
- Annual Openings: 2,000
- Self-Employed: 17.8%
- Part-Time: 11.1%

NATIONAL WAGE FIGURES (ANNUAL)

Beginning	25th Percentile	Median	Mean	75th Percentile	90th Percentile
$27,350	$36,010	$46,250	$47,230	$57,510	$69,280

Median Wages for Industries Employing Largest Numbers (Annual)

Industry	Median Income
Utilities	$61,520
Paper Manufacturing	$60,350
Pipeline Transportation	$54,830
Chemical Manufacturing	$53,900
Repair and Maintenance	$49,060
Management of Companies and Enterprises	$48,820
Federal, State, and Local Government	$48,480
Waste Management and Remediation Services	$48,000
Merchant Wholesalers, Nondurable Goods	$47,090
Food Manufacturing	$45,520

Median Wages for States (Annual)

State	Wage	State	Wage	State	Wage
AK	$57,080	KY	$47,250	NY	$50,430
AL	$42,220	LA	$39,040	OH	$49,370
AR	$28,200	MA	$44,420	OK	$47,280
AZ	$48,790	MD	$48,740	OR	$42,250
CA	$52,760	ME	$42,460	PA	$43,710
CO	$50,990	MI	$46,800	RI	no data
CT	$45,230	MN	$45,070	SC	$38,800
DC	no data	MO	$37,200	SD	no data
DE	no data	MS	$35,070	TN	$46,880
FL	$38,400	MT	no data	TX	$51,290
GA	$50,010	NC	$50,130	UT	$46,230
HI	$61,060	ND	$46,730	VA	$43,530
IA	$40,120	NE	$41,940	VT	no data
ID	$32,840	NH	$40,760	WA	$59,920
IL	$40,070	NJ	$53,120	WI	$42,360
IN	$30,980	NM	$42,530	WV	$52,070
KS	$39,130	NV	$51,480	WY	$66,500

Median Wages for the Largest Metropolitan Areas (Annual)

Area	Wage	Area	Wage
AZ: Phoenix	$50,020	MI: Detroit	$52,750
CA: Los Angeles	$36,470	MN: Minneapolis	$45,000
CA: Riverside	$51,680	MO: Kansas City	$34,860
CA: Sacramento	$60,150	MO: St. Louis	$39,670
CA: San Diego	$47,500	NV: Las Vegas	$49,290
CA: San Francisco	$64,410	NY: New York	$55,710
CO: Denver	$58,650	OH: Cincinnati	no data
DC: Washington	$46,330	OH: Cleveland	$46,480
FL: Miami	$27,340	OH: Columbus	$50,480
FL: Orlando	$29,650	OR: Portland	$50,380
FL: Tampa	$42,280	PA: Philadelphia	$46,410
GA: Atlanta	$52,550	PA: Pittsburgh	$34,150
IL: Chicago	$37,570	TX: Dallas	$44,000
MA: Boston	$41,760	TX: Houston	$66,510
MD: Baltimore	no data	WA: Seattle	$58,230

FACTORS THAT MAY AFFECT EARNINGS

Educational Attainment of Workers and Effect on Earnings

Figures are based on a group of occupations: Other Installation, Maintenance, and Repair Occupations

	Percent at Level	Effect on Earnings
Less than High School	3.5%	−30.0%
Some High School	9.5%	−32.6%
High School or Equivalent	37.7%	0.3%
Some College but No Degree	21.1%	7.0%
Associate Degree	18.3%	8.7%
Bachelor's Degree	8.8%	11.1%
Master's Degree	0.9%	−6.2%
Doctoral Degree	—	—
First Professional Degree	—	—

Flexibility of Earnings

Average Hours Worked: 36
Workers with a Varying Number of Hours: 7.6%
Workers Earning Some Overtime Pay, Tips, or Commissions: 27.7%
Earnings Benefit of Working Overtime: 2.3%

Gender

	Male	Female
Percent	86.1%	13.9%
Effect on Earnings	0.3%	−6.1%

Union Membership

Percentage Union Members: 18.7%
Earnings Benefit of Union Membership: 21.4%

Veteran Status

Percentage Who Have Been on Active Duty: 18.7%
Earnings Benefit of Veteran Status: 11.0%

49-9091 Coin, Vending, and Amusement Machine Servicers and Repairers

Install, service, adjust, or repair coin, vending, or amusement machines, including video games, jukeboxes, pinball machines, or slot machines.

- Education or Training Required: Moderate-term on-the-job training
- Job Growth: 2.4%
- Annual Openings: 7,000
- Self-Employed: 17.5%
- Part-Time: 23.5%

NATIONAL WAGE FIGURES (ANNUAL)

Beginning	25th Percentile	Median	Mean	75th Percentile	90th Percentile
$18,240	$22,540	$28,710	$29,820	$35,840	$44,410

Median Wages for Industries Employing Largest Numbers (Annual)

Industry	Median Income
Telecommunications	$52,000
Real Estate	$48,580
Wholesale Electronic Markets and Agents and Brokers	$41,060
Accommodation	$35,350
Warehousing and Storage	$34,500
Specialty Trade Contractors	$33,840
Beverage and Tobacco Product Manufacturing	$31,760
Repair and Maintenance	$31,450
Merchant Wholesalers, Nondurable Goods	$31,320
Federal, State, and Local Government	$31,300

Median Wages for States (Annual)

State	Wage	State	Wage	State	Wage
AK	$31,390	KY	$26,620	NY	$30,690
AL	$26,120	LA	$26,010	OH	$27,450
AR	$21,560	MA	$32,880	OK	$25,880
AZ	$29,390	MD	$32,460	OR	$37,450
CA	$30,210	ME	$27,470	PA	$31,100
CO	$31,920	MI	$29,920	RI	$29,000
CT	$31,910	MN	$33,800	SC	$26,370
DC	no data	MO	$27,530	SD	$25,510
DE	$30,280	MS	$27,230	TN	$27,050
FL	$24,340	MT	$26,680	TX	$25,470
GA	$25,640	NC	$29,550	UT	$31,870
HI	$26,900	ND	$27,180	VA	$27,770
IA	$28,660	NE	$26,920	VT	no data
ID	$25,540	NH	$29,040	WA	$35,010
IL	$26,300	NJ	$32,590	WI	$31,020
IN	$28,250	NM	$27,430	WV	$23,070
KS	$29,950	NV	$34,470	WY	$24,900

Median Wages for the Largest Metropolitan Areas (Annual)

Area	Wage	Area	Wage
AZ: Phoenix	$31,560	MI: Detroit	$37,890
CA: Los Angeles	$24,870	MN: Minneapolis	$35,820
CA: Riverside	$28,650	MO: Kansas City	$27,760
CA: Sacramento	$32,580	MO: St. Louis	$29,020
CA: San Diego	$31,880	NV: Las Vegas	$36,720
CA: San Francisco	$32,980	NY: New York	$29,810
CO: Denver	$33,390	OH: Cincinnati	$31,710
DC: Washington	$34,770	OH: Cleveland	$30,540
FL: Miami	$23,370	OH: Columbus	$25,920
FL: Orlando	$18,510	OR: Portland	$42,240
FL: Tampa	$27,950	PA: Philadelphia	$34,090
GA: Atlanta	$26,520	PA: Pittsburgh	$26,960
IL: Chicago	$26,750	TX: Dallas	$26,850
MA: Boston	$32,950	TX: Houston	$26,840
MD: Baltimore	$31,010	WA: Seattle	$35,070

FACTORS THAT MAY AFFECT EARNINGS

Educational Attainment of Workers and Effect on Earnings

	Percent at Level	Effect on Earnings
Less than High School	—	—
Some High School	13.0%	−14.7%
High School or Equivalent	42.0%	−8.9%
Some College but No Degree	24.6%	−9.3%
Associate Degree	13.0%	63.2%
Bachelor's Degree	—	—
Master's Degree	—	—
Doctoral Degree	—	—
First Professional Degree	—	—

Figures do not total 100% because some levels have a very small sample size.

Flexibility of Earnings

Average Hours Worked: 34
Workers with a Varying Number of Hours: 8.4%
Workers Earning Some Overtime Pay, Tips, or Commissions: 18.7%
Earnings Benefit of Working Overtime: 3.3%

Gender

	Male	Female
Percent	85.7%	14.3%
Effect on Earnings	0.3%	−6.1%

Union Membership

Percentage Union Members: 14.7%
Earnings Benefit of Union Membership: 25.0%

Veteran Status

Percentage Who Have Been on Active Duty: 18.7%
Earnings Benefit of Veteran Status: 11.0%

49-9092 Commercial Divers

Work below surface of water, using scuba gear to inspect, repair, remove, or install equipment and structures. May use a variety of power and hand tools, such as drills, sledgehammers, torches, and welding equipment. May conduct tests or experiments, rig explosives, or photograph structures or marine life.

- Education or Training Required: Moderate-term on-the-job training
- Job Growth: 9.4%
- Annual Openings: Fewer than 500
- Self-Employed: 6.6%
- Part-Time: 11.1%

NATIONAL WAGE FIGURES (ANNUAL)

Beginning	25th Percentile	Median	Mean	75th Percentile	90th Percentile
$26,600	$32,890	$39,590	$45,410	$51,210	$75,770

Median Wages for Industries Employing Largest Numbers (Annual)

Industry	Median Income
Support Activities for Transportation	$46,390
Administrative and Support Services	$40,840
Amusement, Gambling, and Recreation Industries	$37,370
Heavy and Civil Engineering Construction	$35,390
Professional, Scientific, and Technical Services	$35,190
Federal, State, and Local Government	$28,160
Accommodation	$27,850

Median Wages for States (Annual)

AK	no data	KY	no data	NY	$49,980
AL	no data	LA	no data	OH	no data
AR	no data	MA	$42,670	OK	no data
AZ	no data	MD	$35,190	OR	no data
CA	$59,930	ME	no data	PA	no data
CO	no data	MI	no data	RI	no data
CT	no data	MN	no data	SC	$38,720
DC	no data	MO	$36,270	SD	no data
DE	no data	MS	$36,570	TN	no data
FL	$39,990	MT	no data	TX	$36,640
GA	no data	NC	$30,080	UT	no data
HI	no data	ND	no data	VA	$47,290
IA	no data	NE	no data	VT	no data
ID	no data	NH	no data	WA	$44,510
IL	no data	NJ	no data	WI	no data
IN	no data	NM	no data	WV	no data
KS	no data	NV	no data	WY	no data

Median Wages for the Largest Metropolitan Areas (Annual)

AZ: Phoenix	no data	MI: Detroit	no data
CA: Los Angeles	no data	MN: Minneapolis	no data
CA: Riverside	no data	MO: Kansas City	no data
CA: Sacramento	no data	MO: St. Louis	$35,810
CA: San Diego	no data	NV: Las Vegas	no data
CA: San Francisco	no data	NY: New York	$84,240
CO: Denver	no data	OH: Cincinnati	no data
DC: Washington	$35,030	OH: Cleveland	no data
FL: Miami	$44,290	OH: Columbus	no data
FL: Orlando	$36,280	OR: Portland	no data
FL: Tampa	no data	PA: Philadelphia	no data
GA: Atlanta	no data	PA: Pittsburgh	no data
IL: Chicago	no data	TX: Dallas	no data
MA: Boston	no data	TX: Houston	no data
MD: Baltimore	no data	WA: Seattle	no data

FACTORS THAT MAY AFFECT EARNINGS

Educational Attainment of Workers and Effect on Earnings

Figures are based on a group of occupations: Other Installation, Maintenance, and Repair Occupations

	Percent at Level	Effect on Earnings
Less than High School	3.5%	−30.0%
Some High School	9.5%	−32.6%
High School or Equivalent	37.7%	0.3%
Some College but No Degree	21.1%	7.0%
Associate Degree	18.3%	8.7%
Bachelor's Degree	8.8%	11.1%
Master's Degree	0.9%	−6.2%
Doctoral Degree	—	—
First Professional Degree	—	—

Flexibility of Earnings

Average Hours Worked: 26
Workers with a Varying Number of Hours: 40.9%
Workers Earning Some Overtime Pay, Tips, or Commissions: 40.0%
Earnings Benefit of Working Overtime: 2.3%

Gender

	Male	Female
Percent	95.4%	4.6%
Effect on Earnings	0.3%	−6.1%

Union Membership

Percentage Union Members: 20.0%
Earnings Benefit of Union Membership: 21.4%

Veteran Status

Percentage Who Have Been on Active Duty: 18.7%
Earnings Benefit of Veteran Status: 11.0%

49-9093 Fabric Menders, Except Garment

Repair tears, holes, and other defects in fabrics, such as draperies, linens, parachutes, and tents.

- Education or Training Required: Moderate-term on-the-job training
- Job Growth: –0.5%
- Annual Openings: Fewer than 500
- Self-Employed: 18.5%
- Part-Time: 20.5%

NATIONAL WAGE FIGURES (ANNUAL)

Beginning	25th Percentile	Median	Mean	75th Percentile	90th Percentile
$17,620	$22,240	$28,370	$30,260	$37,630	$46,400

Median Wages for Industries Employing Largest Numbers (Annual)

Industry	Median Income
Repair and Maintenance	$42,250
Textile Product Mills	$26,170
Textile Mills	$25,200

Median Wages for States (Annual)

State	Wage	State	Wage	State	Wage
AK	no data	KY	no data	NY	$31,290
AL	$31,020	LA	no data	OH	no data
AR	no data	MA	$29,010	OK	no data
AZ	no data	MD	no data	OR	no data
CA	$26,300	ME	no data	PA	no data
CO	no data	MI	no data	RI	no data
CT	$28,860	MN	no data	SC	$27,320
DC	no data	MO	no data	SD	no data
DE	no data	MS	no data	TN	no data
FL	no data	MT	no data	TX	no data
GA	$27,680	NC	$17,390	UT	no data
HI	no data	ND	no data	VA	no data
IA	no data	NE	no data	VT	no data
ID	no data	NH	no data	WA	no data
IL	no data	NJ	no data	WI	no data
IN	no data	NM	no data	WV	no data
KS	no data	NV	no data	WY	no data

Median Wages for the Largest Metropolitan Areas (Annual)

Area	Wage	Area	Wage
AZ: Phoenix	no data	MI: Detroit	no data
CA: Los Angeles	$30,000	MN: Minneapolis	no data
CA: Riverside	no data	MO: Kansas City	no data
CA: Sacramento	no data	MO: St. Louis	no data
CA: San Diego	no data	NV: Las Vegas	no data
CA: San Francisco	no data	NY: New York	$27,450
CO: Denver	no data	OH: Cincinnati	no data
DC: Washington	no data	OH: Cleveland	no data
FL: Miami	no data	OH: Columbus	no data
FL: Orlando	no data	OR: Portland	no data
FL: Tampa	no data	PA: Philadelphia	no data
GA: Atlanta	no data	PA: Pittsburgh	no data
IL: Chicago	no data	TX: Dallas	no data
MA: Boston	no data	TX: Houston	no data
MD: Baltimore	no data	WA: Seattle	no data

FACTORS THAT MAY AFFECT EARNINGS

Educational Attainment of Workers and Effect on Earnings

	Percent at Level	Effect on Earnings
Less than High School	4.8%	–31.1%
Some High School	13.2%	–28.4%
High School or Equivalent	39.0%	–0.9%
Some College but No Degree	20.6%	11.7%
Associate Degree	11.8%	–2.6%
Bachelor's Degree	9.6%	27.4%
Master's Degree	—	—
Doctoral Degree	—	—
First Professional Degree	—	—

Flexibility of Earnings

Average Hours Worked: 33
Workers with a Varying Number of Hours: 11.2%
Workers Earning Some Overtime Pay, Tips, or Commissions: 18.4%
Earnings Benefit of Working Overtime: 4.3%

Gender

	Male	Female
Percent	93.6%	6.4%
Effect on Earnings	0.3%	–6.1%

Union Membership

Percentage Union Members: 8.7%
Earnings Benefit of Union Membership: 32.2%

Veteran Status

Percentage Who Have Been on Active Duty: 18.7%
Earnings Benefit of Veteran Status: 11.0%

49-9094 Locksmiths and Safe Repairers

Repair and open locks, make keys, change locks and safe combinations, and install and repair safes.

- Education or Training Required: Moderate-term on-the-job training
- Job Growth: 16.1%
- Annual Openings: 5,000
- Self-Employed: 37.6%
- Part-Time: 50.0%

Note: Earnings figures do not reflect self-employed workers, who make up a large fraction of the workforce for this occupation.

NATIONAL WAGE FIGURES (ANNUAL)

Beginning	25th Percentile	Median	Mean	75th Percentile	90th Percentile
$18,320	$23,760	$32,020	$33,560	$42,180	$51,170

Median Wages for Industries Employing Largest Numbers (Annual)

Industry	Median Income
Professional, Scientific, and Technical Services	$51,580
Transportation Equipment Manufacturing	$47,470
Accommodation	$44,830
Federal, State, and Local Government	$44,450
Hospitals	$43,600
Educational Services	$41,020
Fabricated Metal Product Manufacturing	$39,790
Specialty Trade Contractors	$34,470
Merchant Wholesalers, Durable Goods	$30,780
Administrative and Support Services	$29,700

Median Wages for States (Annual)

State	Wage	State	Wage	State	Wage
AK	$37,170	KY	$22,700	NY	$35,070
AL	$19,680	LA	$22,310	OH	$31,610
AR	$22,440	MA	$37,380	OK	$32,130
AZ	$35,010	MD	$40,910	OR	$30,640
CA	$37,170	ME	$32,340	PA	$36,930
CO	$34,480	MI	$31,820	RI	$38,920
CT	$46,360	MN	$31,370	SC	$29,260
DC	$44,300	MO	$30,430	SD	no data
DE	no data	MS	$27,360	TN	$31,510
FL	$23,600	MT	$30,240	TX	$31,070
GA	$31,290	NC	$29,260	UT	$26,650
HI	$35,030	ND	$22,940	VA	$37,030
IA	$29,600	NE	$13,820	VT	no data
ID	$23,420	NH	$32,720	WA	$32,580
IL	$31,120	NJ	$41,740	WI	$33,200
IN	$26,440	NM	$22,420	WV	$27,180
KS	$26,820	NV	$36,680	WY	no data

Median Wages for the Largest Metropolitan Areas (Annual)

Area	Wage	Area	Wage
AZ: Phoenix	$35,860	MI: Detroit	$30,180
CA: Los Angeles	$33,620	MN: Minneapolis	$31,450
CA: Riverside	$42,450	MO: Kansas City	$40,970
CA: Sacramento	$33,820	MO: St. Louis	$29,620
CA: San Diego	$36,630	NV: Las Vegas	$32,400
CA: San Francisco	$38,730	NY: New York	$40,390
CO: Denver	$39,470	OH: Cincinnati	$36,340
DC: Washington	$41,810	OH: Cleveland	$41,760
FL: Miami	$22,120	OH: Columbus	$34,320
FL: Orlando	$23,640	OR: Portland	$32,700
FL: Tampa	$21,590	PA: Philadelphia	$42,280
GA: Atlanta	$31,050	PA: Pittsburgh	$30,890
IL: Chicago	$24,750	TX: Dallas	$34,910
MA: Boston	$36,990	TX: Houston	$32,620
MD: Baltimore	$40,440	WA: Seattle	$41,430

FACTORS THAT MAY AFFECT EARNINGS

Educational Attainment of Workers and Effect on Earnings

	Percent at Level	Effect on Earnings
Less than High School	—	—
Some High School	—	—
High School or Equivalent	54.2%	−6.7%
Some College but No Degree	—	—
Associate Degree	—	—
Bachelor's Degree	—	—
Master's Degree	—	—
Doctoral Degree	—	—
First Professional Degree	—	—

Figures do not total 100% because some levels have a very small sample size.

Flexibility of Earnings

Average Hours Worked: 34
Workers with a Varying Number of Hours: 11.7%
Workers Earning Some Overtime Pay, Tips, or Commissions: 12.5%
Earnings Benefit of Working Overtime: 2.3%

Gender

	Male	Female
Percent	94.2%	5.8%
Effect on Earnings	0.3%	−6.1%

Union Membership

Percentage Union Members: 12.5%
Earnings Benefit of Union Membership: 21.4%

Veteran Status

Percentage Who Have Been on Active Duty: 18.7%
Earnings Benefit of Veteran Status: 11.0%

49-9095 Manufactured Building and Mobile Home Installers

Move or install mobile homes or prefabricated buildings.

- Education or Training Required: Moderate-term on-the-job training
- Job Growth: 7.9%
- Annual Openings: 2,000
- Self-Employed: 17.1%
- Part-Time: 16.7%

NATIONAL WAGE FIGURES (ANNUAL)

Beginning	25th Percentile	Median	Mean	75th Percentile	90th Percentile
$17,850	$20,790	$25,080	$26,600	$30,620	$37,770

Median Wages for Industries Employing Largest Numbers (Annual)

Industry	Median Income
Merchant Wholesalers, Durable Goods	$28,120
Construction of Buildings	$27,230
Wood Product Manufacturing	$27,070
Miscellaneous Store Retailers	$25,960
Truck Transportation	$24,080
Rental and Leasing Services	$24,050
Real Estate	$23,350
Motor Vehicle and Parts Dealers	$23,010
Specialty Trade Contractors	$21,810
Fabricated Metal Product Manufacturing	$21,400

Median Wages for States (Annual)

State	Wage	State	Wage	State	Wage
AK	no data	KY	$27,450	NY	$21,000
AL	$25,370	LA	$28,630	OH	$23,020
AR	$20,680	MA	no data	OK	$23,150
AZ	$19,460	MD	$23,260	OR	$35,080
CA	$27,760	ME	$27,010	PA	$25,020
CO	$29,980	MI	$28,320	RI	no data
CT	no data	MN	$28,710	SC	$26,790
DC	no data	MO	$25,200	SD	$25,510
DE	$25,500	MS	$22,110	TN	$28,430
FL	$26,250	MT	$27,240	TX	$22,310
GA	$23,500	NC	$23,450	UT	no data
HI	no data	ND	$25,120	VA	$21,860
IA	$25,540	NE	no data	VT	$30,290
ID	no data	NH	$30,800	WA	$25,620
IL	$30,690	NJ	no data	WI	$28,420
IN	$27,360	NM	$21,210	WV	$18,040
KS	$24,060	NV	no data	WY	$27,980

Median Wages for the Largest Metropolitan Areas (Annual)

Area	Wage	Area	Wage
AZ: Phoenix	no data	MI: Detroit	no data
CA: Los Angeles	no data	MN: Minneapolis	$29,190
CA: Riverside	no data	MO: Kansas City	no data
CA: Sacramento	no data	MO: St. Louis	$29,970
CA: San Diego	no data	NV: Las Vegas	no data
CA: San Francisco	no data	NY: New York	no data
CO: Denver	no data	OH: Cincinnati	no data
DC: Washington	no data	OH: Cleveland	no data
FL: Miami	no data	OH: Columbus	no data
FL: Orlando	no data	OR: Portland	no data
FL: Tampa	no data	PA: Philadelphia	no data
GA: Atlanta	$22,440	PA: Pittsburgh	no data
IL: Chicago	no data	TX: Dallas	$27,570
MA: Boston	no data	TX: Houston	no data
MD: Baltimore	no data	WA: Seattle	no data

FACTORS THAT MAY AFFECT EARNINGS

Educational Attainment of Workers and Effect on Earnings

Figures are based on a group of occupations: Other Installation, Maintenance, and Repair Occupations

	Percent at Level	Effect on Earnings
Less than High School	3.5%	−30.0%
Some High School	9.5%	−32.6%
High School or Equivalent	37.7%	0.3%
Some College but No Degree	21.1%	7.0%
Associate Degree	18.3%	8.7%
Bachelor's Degree	8.8%	11.1%
Master's Degree	0.9%	−6.2%
Doctoral Degree	—	—
First Professional Degree	—	—

Flexibility of Earnings

Average Hours Worked: 30
Workers with a Varying Number of Hours: 20.3%
Workers Earning Some Overtime Pay, Tips, or Commissions: 14.3%
Earnings Benefit of Working Overtime: 2.3%

Gender

	Male	Female
Percent	95.0%	5.0%
Effect on Earnings	0.3%	−6.1%

Union Membership

Percentage Union Members: 7.1%
Earnings Benefit of Union Membership: 21.4%

Veteran Status

Percentage Who Have Been on Active Duty: 18.7%
Earnings Benefit of Veteran Status: 11.0%

49-9096 Riggers

Set up or repair rigging for construction projects, manufacturing plants, logging yards, ships and shipyards, or for the entertainment industry.

- Education or Training Required: Short-term on-the-job training
- Job Growth: 13.9%
- Annual Openings: 2,000
- Self-Employed: 0.0%
- Part-Time: 11.1%

NATIONAL WAGE FIGURES (ANNUAL)

Beginning	25th Percentile	Median	Mean	75th Percentile	90th Percentile
$21,450	$28,790	$39,220	$39,670	$48,960	$58,700

Median Wages for Industries Employing Largest Numbers (Annual)

Industry	Median Income
Accommodation	$54,940
Federal, State, and Local Government	$48,740
Professional, Scientific, and Technical Services	$45,340
Performing Arts, Spectator Sports, and Related Industries	$43,660
Administrative and Support Services	$42,470
Construction of Buildings	$41,400
Truck Transportation	$39,760
Forestry and Logging	$38,700
Support Activities for Transportation	$38,210
Heavy and Civil Engineering Construction	$37,750

Median Wages for States (Annual)

AK .... no data	KY .... no data	NY $45,060
AL $39,130	LA $27,820	OH $41,120
AR $18,570	MA $43,900	OK $43,810
AZ .... no data	MD $50,390	OR $35,930
CA $47,530	ME $39,020	PA $42,390
CO $44,900	MI $29,540	RI $37,170
CT $36,860	MN $43,550	SC $37,730
DC .... no data	MO .... no data	SD .... no data
DE .... no data	MS $24,200	TN .... no data
FL $34,840	MT .... no data	TX $40,070
GA $43,830	NC $29,940	UT $28,320
HI .... no data	ND .... no data	VA $40,090
IA $29,080	NE $28,160	VT .... no data
ID $28,450	NH .... no data	WA $52,700
IL $35,630	NJ $32,540	WI $30,330
IN $26,160	NM .... no data	WV $23,650
KS .... no data	NV .... no data	WY .... no data

Median Wages for the Largest Metropolitan Areas (Annual)

AZ: Phoenix	no data	MI: Detroit	no data
CA: Los Angeles	$53,530	MN: Minneapolis	$43,610
CA: Riverside	no data	MO: Kansas City	no data
CA: Sacramento	no data	MO: St. Louis	no data
CA: San Diego	$43,780	NV: Las Vegas	$51,440
CA: San Francisco	$43,010	NY: New York	$44,040
CO: Denver	$40,710	OH: Cincinnati	$34,750
DC: Washington	$37,670	OH: Cleveland	no data
FL: Miami	$24,670	OH: Columbus	no data
FL: Orlando	$45,250	OR: Portland	$33,990
FL: Tampa	$27,870	PA: Philadelphia	$48,870
GA: Atlanta	no data	PA: Pittsburgh	no data
IL: Chicago	$52,110	TX: Dallas	$38,690
MA: Boston	$44,740	TX: Houston	$40,440
MD: Baltimore	$51,030	WA: Seattle	$41,030

FACTORS THAT MAY AFFECT EARNINGS

Educational Attainment of Workers and Effect on Earnings

	Percent at Level	Effect on Earnings
Less than High School	—	—
Some High School	—	—
High School or Equivalent	53.3%	2.6%
Some College but No Degree	—	—
Associate Degree	—	—
Bachelor's Degree	—	—
Master's Degree	—	—
Doctoral Degree	—	—
First Professional Degree	—	—

Figures do not total 100% because some levels have a very small sample size.

Flexibility of Earnings

Average Hours Worked: 41
Workers with a Varying Number of Hours: 3.6%
Workers Earning Some Overtime Pay, Tips, or Commissions: 43.8%
Earnings Benefit of Working Overtime: 2.3%

Gender

	Male	Female
Percent	95.4%	4.6%
Effect on Earnings	0.3%	−6.1%

Union Membership

Percentage Union Members: 31.3%
Earnings Benefit of Union Membership: 21.4%

Veteran Status

Percentage Who Have Been on Active Duty: 18.7%
Earnings Benefit of Veteran Status: 11.0%

49-9097 Signal and Track Switch Repairers

Install, inspect, test, maintain, or repair electric gate crossings, signals, signal equipment, track switches, section lines, or intercommunications systems within a railroad system.

- Education or Training Required: Moderate-term on-the-job training
- Job Growth: 2.3%
- Annual Openings: 1,000
- Self-Employed: 0.0%
- Part-Time: 11.1%

NATIONAL WAGE FIGURES (ANNUAL)

Beginning	25th Percentile	Median	Mean	75th Percentile	90th Percentile
$37,910	$44,050	$50,150	$49,870	$56,100	$62,840

Median Wages for Industries Employing Largest Numbers (Annual)

Industry	Median Income
Rail Transportation	$49,860
Specialty Trade Contractors	$37,000
Support Activities for Transportation	$32,260

Median Wages for States (Annual)

AK	no data	KY	no data	NY	no data
AL	$47,010	LA	$50,230	OH	$47,290
AR	no data	MA	$47,310	OK	no data
AZ	$38,780	MD	$49,970	OR	no data
CA	no data	ME	no data	PA	$51,050
CO	no data	MI	no data	RI	no data
CT	no data	MN	$51,420	SC	no data
DC	no data	MO	no data	SD	no data
DE	no data	MS	no data	TN	$52,270
FL	$39,570	MT	no data	TX	no data
GA	$45,660	NC	no data	UT	no data
HI	no data	ND	no data	VA	$52,720
IA	no data	NE	no data	VT	no data
ID	no data	NH	no data	WA	no data
IL	$53,960	NJ	$53,310	WI	$52,480
IN	$52,110	NM	no data	WV	no data
KS	$47,900	NV	no data	WY	no data

Median Wages for the Largest Metropolitan Areas (Annual)

AZ: Phoenix	no data	MI: Detroit	no data
CA: Los Angeles	no data	MN: Minneapolis	no data
CA: Riverside	no data	MO: Kansas City	no data
CA: Sacramento	no data	MO: St. Louis	no data
CA: San Diego	no data	NV: Las Vegas	no data
CA: San Francisco	no data	NY: New York	no data
CO: Denver	no data	OH: Cincinnati	no data
DC: Washington	no data	OH: Cleveland	no data
DE: Miami	no data	OH: Columbus	no data
FL: Miami	no data	OR: Portland	no data
FL: Orlando	no data	PA: Philadelphia	no data
FL: Tampa	no data	PA: Pittsburgh	no data
GA: Atlanta	no data	TX: Dallas	no data
IL: Chicago	no data	TX: Houston	$34,210
MA: Boston	no data	WA: Seattle	no data
MD: Baltimore	no data		

FACTORS THAT MAY AFFECT EARNINGS

Educational Attainment of Workers and Effect on Earnings

Figures are based on a group of occupations: Other Installation, Maintenance, and Repair Occupations

	Percent at Level	Effect on Earnings
Less than High School	3.5%	−30.0%
Some High School	9.5%	−32.6%
High School or Equivalent	37.7%	0.3%
Some College but No Degree	21.1%	7.0%
Associate Degree	18.3%	8.7%
Bachelor's Degree	8.8%	11.1%
Master's Degree	0.9%	−6.2%
Doctoral Degree	—	—
First Professional Degree	—	—

Flexibility of Earnings

Average Hours Worked: 34
Workers with a Varying Number of Hours: 14.7%
Workers Earning Some Overtime Pay, Tips, or Commissions: 28.6%
Earnings Benefit of Working Overtime: 2.3%

Gender

	Male	Female
Percent	88.2%	11.8%
Effect on Earnings	0.3%	−6.1%

Union Membership

Percentage Union Members: 18.7%
Earnings Benefit of Union Membership: 21.4%

Veteran Status

Percentage Who Have Been on Active Duty: 18.7%
Earnings Benefit of Veteran Status: 11.0%

49-9098 Helpers—Installation, Maintenance, and Repair Workers

Help installation, maintenance, and repair workers in maintenance, parts replacement, and repair of vehicles, industrial machinery, and electrical and electronic equipment. Perform duties such as furnishing tools, materials, and supplies to other workers; cleaning work area, machines, and tools; and holding materials or tools for other workers.

- Education or Training Required: Short-term on-the-job training
- Job Growth: 16.4%
- Annual Openings: 41,000
- Self-Employed: 0.9%
- Part-Time: 46.2%

NATIONAL WAGE FIGURES (ANNUAL)

Beginning	25th Percentile	Median	Mean	75th Percentile	90th Percentile
$14,860	$17,800	$22,270	$24,210	$28,770	$36,720

Median Wages for Industries Employing Largest Numbers (Annual)

Industry	Median Income
Utilities	$30,780
Hospitals	$28,690
Federal, State, and Local Government	$27,850
Telecommunications	$26,760
Waste Management and Remediation Services	$26,220
Educational Services	$25,900
Fabricated Metal Product Manufacturing	$25,380
Professional, Scientific, and Technical Services	$24,280
Support Activities for Mining	$23,810
Merchant Wholesalers, Durable Goods	$23,740

Median Wages for States (Annual)

AK	$26,900	KY	$20,930	NY	$27,450
AL	$18,220	LA	$20,830	OH	$22,000
AR	$19,910	MA	$26,170	OK	$21,100
AZ	$22,820	MD	$24,060	OR	$24,100
CA	$22,350	ME	$21,790	PA	$22,880
CO	$24,110	MI	$24,090	RI	$22,910
CT	$26,980	MN	$23,090	SC	$20,780
DC	$35,250	MO	$23,650	SD	$17,170
DE	$25,430	MS	$20,710	TN	$24,750
FL	$20,140	MT	$21,840	TX	$20,690
GA	$21,820	NC	$21,860	UT	$21,100
HI	$26,040	ND	$19,930	VA	$23,680
IA	$22,950	NE	$21,320	VT	$22,290
ID	$24,930	NH	$22,130	WA	$22,680
IL	$25,760	NJ	$22,890	WI	$22,350
IN	$23,360	NM	$19,920	WV	$16,920
KS	$21,820	NV	$24,110	WY	$19,440

Median Wages for the Largest Metropolitan Areas (Annual)

AZ: Phoenix	$23,200	MI: Detroit	$24,820
CA: Los Angeles	$21,790	MN: Minneapolis	$25,980
CA: Riverside	$21,170	MO: Kansas City	$26,100
CA: Sacramento	$22,200	MO: St. Louis	$25,820
CA: San Diego	$21,910	NV: Las Vegas	$25,370
CA: San Francisco	$27,520	NY: New York	$27,230
CO: Denver	$25,140	OH: Cincinnati	$22,710
DC: Washington	$27,600	OH: Cleveland	$23,580
FL: Miami	$19,050	OH: Columbus	$23,060
FL: Orlando	$21,350	OR: Portland	$25,220
FL: Tampa	$21,980	PA: Philadelphia	$23,100
GA: Atlanta	$23,550	PA: Pittsburgh	$23,160
IL: Chicago	$27,930	TX: Dallas	$21,490
MA: Boston	$26,590	TX: Houston	$22,290
MD: Baltimore	$22,940	WA: Seattle	$24,580

FACTORS THAT MAY AFFECT EARNINGS

Educational Attainment of Workers and Effect on Earnings

	Percent at Level	Effect on Earnings
Less than High School	—	—
Some High School	34.2%	−12.1%
High School or Equivalent	39.5%	26.7%
Some College but No Degree	—	—
Associate Degree	—	—
Bachelor's Degree	—	—
Master's Degree	—	—
Doctoral Degree	—	—
First Professional Degree	—	—

Figures do not total 100% because some levels have a very small sample size.

Flexibility of Earnings

Average Hours Worked: 30
Workers with a Varying Number of Hours: 7.4%
Workers Earning Some Overtime Pay, Tips, or Commissions: 28.6%
Earnings Benefit of Working Overtime: 2.3%

Gender

	Male	Female
Percent	90.9%	9.1%
Effect on Earnings	0.3%	−6.1%

Union Membership

Percentage Union Members: 7.1%
Earnings Benefit of Union Membership: 21.4%

Veteran Status

Percentage Who Have Been on Active Duty: 18.7%
Earnings Benefit of Veteran Status: 11.0%

49-9099 Installation, Maintenance, and Repair Workers, All Other

All mechanical, installation, and repair workers and helpers not listed separately.

- Education or Training Required: Moderate-term on-the-job training
- Job Growth: 11.0%
- Annual Openings: 22,000
- Self-Employed: 19.5%
- Part-Time: 11.1%

NATIONAL WAGE FIGURES (ANNUAL)

Beginning	25th Percentile	Median	Mean	75th Percentile	90th Percentile
$19,220	$24,430	$32,940	$35,560	$44,870	$56,370

Median Wages for Industries Employing Largest Numbers (Annual)

Industry	Median Income
Utilities	$53,470
Computer and Electronic Product Manufacturing	$46,810
Transportation Equipment Manufacturing	$46,810
Federal, State, and Local Government	$44,000
Machinery Manufacturing	$40,080
Educational Services	$39,470
Miscellaneous Manufacturing	$35,280
Management of Companies and Enterprises	$34,830
Furniture and Related Product Manufacturing	$34,030
Fabricated Metal Product Manufacturing	$32,510

Median Wages for States (Annual)

State	Wage	State	Wage	State	Wage
AK	$56,410	KY	$32,350	NY	$32,380
AL	$29,650	LA	$27,760	OH	$31,920
AR	$30,140	MA	$40,710	OK	no data
AZ	$29,720	MD	$36,270	OR	$28,580
CA	$35,090	ME	$35,270	PA	$37,170
CO	$31,240	MI	$40,670	RI	$31,310
CT	$32,700	MN	$37,520	SC	$33,110
DC	$47,840	MO	$28,190	SD	$26,070
DE	$33,950	MS	$40,880	TN	$27,520
FL	$27,230	MT	$46,380	TX	$27,910
GA	$29,000	NC	$29,610	UT	$26,640
HI	$53,110	ND	$36,460	VA	$33,280
IA	$30,710	NE	$32,860	VT	$27,510
ID	$30,250	NH	$29,410	WA	$38,940
IL	$34,030	NJ	$38,480	WI	$34,160
IN	$32,720	NM	$33,940	WV	$29,830
KS	$28,400	NV	$43,280	WY	$30,300

Median Wages for the Largest Metropolitan Areas (Annual)

Metro Area	Wage	Metro Area	Wage
AZ: Phoenix	$28,880	MI: Detroit	$44,690
CA: Los Angeles	$32,440	MN: Minneapolis	$39,410
CA: Riverside	$33,740	MO: Kansas City	$34,490
CA: Sacramento	$33,760	MO: St. Louis	$29,270
CA: San Diego	$36,790	NV: Las Vegas	$42,660
CA: San Francisco	$42,910	NY: New York	$36,490
CO: Denver	$30,660	OH: Cincinnati	$32,120
DC: Washington	$35,980	OH: Cleveland	$36,300
FL: Miami	$28,580	OH: Columbus	$30,360
FL: Orlando	$27,230	OR: Portland	$29,390
FL: Tampa	$27,610	PA: Philadelphia	$39,840
GA: Atlanta	$29,230	PA: Pittsburgh	$40,590
IL: Chicago	$32,870	TX: Dallas	$30,830
MA: Boston	$43,080	TX: Houston	$23,100
MD: Baltimore	$38,180	WA: Seattle	$37,650

FACTORS THAT MAY AFFECT EARNINGS

Educational Attainment of Workers and Effect on Earnings

Figures are based on a group of occupations: Other Installation, Maintenance, and Repair Occupations

	Percent at Level	Effect on Earnings
Less than High School	3.5%	−30.0%
Some High School	9.5%	−32.6%
High School or Equivalent	37.7%	0.3%
Some College but No Degree	21.1%	7.0%
Associate Degree	18.3%	8.7%
Bachelor's Degree	8.8%	11.1%
Master's Degree	0.9%	−6.2%
Doctoral Degree	—	—
First Professional Degree	—	—

Flexibility of Earnings

Average Hours Worked: 33
Workers with a Varying Number of Hours: 10.9%
Workers Earning Some Overtime Pay, Tips, or Commissions: 27.7%
Earnings Benefit of Working Overtime: 4.3%

Gender

	Male	Female
Percent	95.4%	4.6%
Effect on Earnings	0.3%	−6.1%

Union Membership

Percentage Union Members: 18.7%
Earnings Benefit of Union Membership: 21.4%

Veteran Status

Percentage Who Have Been on Active Duty: 18.7%
Earnings Benefit of Veteran Status: 11.0%

51-0000: Production Occupations

51-1000 Supervisors, Production Workers

51-1011 First-Line Supervisors/Managers of Production and Operating Workers

Supervise and coordinate the activities of production and operating workers, such as inspectors, precision workers, machine setters and operators, assemblers, fabricators, and plant and system operators.

- Education or Training Required: Work experience in a related occupation
- Job Growth: 2.7%
- Annual Openings: 89,000
- Self-Employed: 3.9%
- Part-Time: 4.3%

NATIONAL WAGE FIGURES (ANNUAL)

Beginning	25th Percentile	Median	Mean	75th Percentile	90th Percentile
$29,300	$36,770	$47,300	$50,480	$60,770	$76,820

Median Wages for Industries Employing Largest Numbers (Annual)

Industry	Median Income
Utilities	$69,260
Chemical Manufacturing	$55,430
Federal, State, and Local Government	$53,820
Paper Manufacturing	$53,570
Professional, Scientific, and Technical Services	$52,550
Computer and Electronic Product Manufacturing	$52,490
Transportation Equipment Manufacturing	$51,610
Machinery Manufacturing	$50,770
Primary Metal Manufacturing	$50,010
Printing and Related Support Activities	$49,580

Median Wages for States (Annual)

AK	$57,960	KY	$45,040	NY	$49,570
AL	$43,560	LA	$44,140	OH	$47,280
AR	$41,100	MA	$52,070	OK	$43,420
AZ	$44,300	MD	$51,070	OR	$45,990
CA	$47,790	ME	$44,050	PA	$49,500
CO	$48,390	MI	$54,590	RI	$50,170
CT	$54,850	MN	$47,580	SC	$46,960
DC	$59,730	MO	$46,450	SD	$42,590
DE	$57,520	MS	$40,210	TN	$42,230
FL	$48,550	MT	$40,820	TX	$46,040
GA	$44,030	NC	$44,500	UT	$44,550
HI	$45,950	ND	$44,220	VA	$48,000
IA	$45,280	NE	$44,600	VT	$48,360
ID	$40,980	NH	$49,020	WA	$54,900
IL	$50,330	NJ	$52,840	WI	$48,300
IN	$45,560	NM	$43,610	WV	$46,750
KS	$44,640	NV	$45,310	WY	$49,480

Median Wages for the Largest Metropolitan Areas (Annual)

AZ: Phoenix	$44,720	MI: Detroit	$60,640
CA: Los Angeles	$45,400	MN: Minneapolis	$51,720
CA: Riverside	$43,860	MO: Kansas City	$50,230
CA: Sacramento	$48,910	MO: St. Louis	$51,470
CA: San Diego	$50,860	NV: Las Vegas	$44,430
CA: San Francisco	$53,900	NY: New York	$53,050
CO: Denver	$47,900	OH: Cincinnati	$49,660
DC: Washington	$53,500	OH: Cleveland	$50,370
FL: Miami	$48,670	OH: Columbus	$45,480
FL: Orlando	$46,900	OR: Portland	$50,280
FL: Tampa	$48,710	PA: Philadelphia	$55,930
GA: Atlanta	$45,910	PA: Pittsburgh	$49,810
IL: Chicago	$51,810	TX: Dallas	$46,830
MA: Boston	$54,350	TX: Houston	$50,590
MD: Baltimore	$52,570	WA: Seattle	$57,350

FACTORS THAT MAY AFFECT EARNINGS

Educational Attainment of Workers and Effect on Earnings

	Percent at Level	Effect on Earnings
Less than High School	1.7%	−38.5%
Some High School	8.4%	−18.7%
High School or Equivalent	42.0%	−9.4%
Some College but No Degree	21.9%	0.1%
Associate Degree	11.4%	14.2%
Bachelor's Degree	11.8%	26.6%
Master's Degree	2.4%	56.9%
Doctoral Degree	—	—
First Professional Degree	—	—

Flexibility of Earnings

Average Hours Worked: 40
Workers with a Varying Number of Hours: 6.3%
Workers Earning Some Overtime Pay, Tips, or Commissions: 26.5%
Earnings Benefit of Working Overtime: 7.7%

Gender

	Male	Female
Percent	80.6%	19.4%
Effect on Earnings	7.5%	−24.2%

Union Membership

Percentage Union Members: 8.5%
Earnings Benefit of Union Membership: 9.2%

Veteran Status

Percentage Who Have Been on Active Duty: 13.2%
Earnings Benefit of Veteran Status: 6.2%

51-2000 Assemblers and Fabricators

51-2011 Aircraft Structure, Surfaces, Rigging, and Systems Assemblers

Assemble, fit, fasten, and install parts of airplanes, space vehicles, or missiles, such as tails, wings, fuselage, bulkheads, stabilizers, landing gear, rigging and control equipment, or heating and ventilating systems.

- Education or Training Required: Long-term on-the-job training
- Job Growth: 7.8%
- Annual Openings: 4,000
- Self-Employed: 0.0%
- Part-Time: 16.2%

NATIONAL WAGE FIGURES (ANNUAL)

Beginning	25th Percentile	Median	Mean	75th Percentile	90th Percentile
$25,430	$34,260	$45,410	$43,860	$54,070	$59,540

Median Wages for Industries Employing Largest Numbers (Annual)

Industry	Median Income
Computer and Electronic Product Manufacturing	$49,740
Transportation Equipment Manufacturing	$46,090
Professional, Scientific, and Technical Services	$34,610
Machinery Manufacturing	$32,460

Median Wages for States (Annual)

State		State		State	
AK	no data	KY	no data	NY	$43,650
AL	$35,890	LA	no data	OH	$36,670
AR	no data	MA	no data	OK	no data
AZ	$37,600	MD	no data	OR	no data
CA	$51,880	ME	no data	PA	no data
CO	$49,590	MI	$34,170	RI	no data
CT	$39,110	MN	no data	SC	no data
DC	no data	MO	no data	SD	no data
DE	no data	MS	no data	TN	$36,050
FL	$43,290	MT	no data	TX	$42,180
GA	$35,020	NC	no data	UT	no data
HI	no data	ND	no data	VA	no data
IA	no data	NE	no data	VT	no data
ID	no data	NH	no data	WA	no data
IL	no data	NJ	$30,480	WI	$34,600
IN	no data	NM	no data	WV	$35,460
KS	no data	NV	no data	WY	no data

Median Wages for the Largest Metropolitan Areas (Annual)

Area		Area	
AZ: Phoenix	$37,880	MI: Detroit	no data
CA: Los Angeles	no data	MN: Minneapolis	no data
CA: Riverside	no data	MO: Kansas City	no data
CA: Sacramento	no data	MO: St. Louis	no data
CA: San Diego	no data	NV: Las Vegas	no data
CA: San Francisco	no data	NY: New York	$36,260
CO: Denver	$52,380	OH: Cincinnati	no data
DC: Washington	$33,950	OH: Cleveland	$33,190
FL: Miami	$38,690	OH: Columbus	no data
FL: Orlando	no data	OR: Portland	no data
FL: Tampa	$43,430	PA: Philadelphia	no data
GA: Atlanta	no data	PA: Pittsburgh	no data
IL: Chicago	no data	TX: Dallas	no data
MA: Boston	no data	TX: Houston	no data
MD: Baltimore	no data	WA: Seattle	no data

FACTORS THAT MAY AFFECT EARNINGS

Educational Attainment of Workers and Effect on Earnings

	Percent at Level	Effect on Earnings
Less than High School	—	—
Some High School	—	—
High School or Equivalent	37.5%	−31.9%
Some College but No Degree	37.5%	41.0%
Associate Degree	—	—
Bachelor's Degree	—	—
Master's Degree	—	—
Doctoral Degree	—	—
First Professional Degree	—	—

Figures do not total 100% because some levels have a very small sample size.

Flexibility of Earnings

Average Hours Worked: 40
Workers with a Varying Number of Hours: 1.8%
Workers Earning Some Overtime Pay, Tips, or Commissions: 12.5%
Earnings Benefit of Working Overtime: 21.1%

Gender

	Male	Female
Percent	82.1%	17.9%
Effect on Earnings	11.1%	−22.7%

Union Membership

Percentage Union Members: 25.0%
Earnings Benefit of Union Membership: 39.2%

Veteran Status

Percentage Who Have Been on Active Duty: 8.4%
Earnings Benefit of Veteran Status: 27.5%

51-2021 Coil Winders, Tapers, and Finishers

Wind wire coils used in electrical components such as resistors and transformers and in electrical equipment and instruments such as field cores, bobbins, armature cores, electrical motors, generators, and control equipment.

- Education or Training Required: Short-term on-the-job training
- Job Growth: –28.5%
- Annual Openings: 4,000
- Self-Employed: 1.7%
- Part-Time: 16.2%

NATIONAL WAGE FIGURES (ANNUAL)

Beginning	25th Percentile	Median	Mean	75th Percentile	90th Percentile
$16,890	$20,700	$26,300	$26,910	$32,240	$37,450

Median Wages for Industries Employing Largest Numbers (Annual)

Industry	Median Income
Primary Metal Manufacturing	$30,270
Machinery Manufacturing	$29,900
Repair and Maintenance	$28,550
Plastics and Rubber Products Manufacturing	$28,090
Electrical Equipment, Appliance, and Component Manufacturing	$27,770
Transportation Equipment Manufacturing	$26,640
Fabricated Metal Product Manufacturing	$26,240
Computer and Electronic Product Manufacturing	$22,820
Administrative and Support Services	$22,570
Merchant Wholesalers, Durable Goods	$21,010

Median Wages for States (Annual)

AK	no data	KY	$29,230	NY	$19,810
AL	$28,370	LA	$29,760	OH	$30,150
AR	$24,530	MA	$27,730	OK	$26,440
AZ	$20,670	MD	$23,710	OR	no data
CA	$25,440	ME	$29,340	PA	$28,920
CO	no data	MI	$31,270	RI	no data
CT	$22,700	MN	no data	SC	$28,400
DC	no data	MO	$29,520	SD	$21,230
DE	no data	MS	no data	TN	$26,730
FL	$21,040	MT	no data	TX	$25,190
GA	$30,300	NC	$28,200	UT	$24,270
HI	no data	ND	no data	VA	$26,850
IA	$23,270	NE	$22,600	VT	no data
ID	no data	NH	$28,300	WA	$22,630
IL	$20,750	NJ	$25,840	WI	$24,030
IN	$30,840	NM	no data	WV	no data
KS	$26,130	NV	$23,170	WY	no data

Median Wages for the Largest Metropolitan Areas (Annual)

AZ: Phoenix	$19,750	MI: Detroit	$30,940
CA: Los Angeles	$24,410	MN: Minneapolis	no data
CA: Riverside	$26,570	MO: Kansas City	no data
CA: Sacramento	no data	MO: St. Louis	$29,140
CA: San Diego	$21,720	NV: Las Vegas	no data
CA: San Francisco	no data	NY: New York	$24,320
CO: Denver	no data	OH: Cincinnati	$28,140
DC: Washington	no data	OH: Cleveland	$29,300
FL: Miami	$23,590	OH: Columbus	$31,480
FL: Orlando	no data	OR: Portland	no data
FL: Tampa	$19,170	PA: Philadelphia	$25,420
GA: Atlanta	$31,540	PA: Pittsburgh	$32,410
IL: Chicago	$20,700	TX: Dallas	$30,120
MA: Boston	$31,300	TX: Houston	$26,620
MD: Baltimore	no data	WA: Seattle	$18,340

FACTORS THAT MAY AFFECT EARNINGS

Educational Attainment of Workers and Effect on Earnings

Figures are based on a group of occupations: Assemblers and Fabricators

	Percent at Level	Effect on Earnings
Less than High School	7.7%	–29.3%
Some High School	12.1%	–27.8%
High School or Equivalent	45.2%	6.9%
Some College but No Degree	18.8%	6.6%
Associate Degree	8.9%	7.8%
Bachelor's Degree	6.2%	8.8%
Master's Degree	—	—
Doctoral Degree	—	—
First Professional Degree	—	—

Flexibility of Earnings

Average Hours Worked: 35
Workers with a Varying Number of Hours: 4.5%
Workers Earning Some Overtime Pay, Tips, or Commissions: 19.4%
Earnings Benefit of Working Overtime: 5.4%

Gender

	Male	Female
Percent	48.3%	51.7%
Effect on Earnings	11.1%	–22.7%

Union Membership

Percentage Union Members: 15.0%
Earnings Benefit of Union Membership: 39.2%

Veteran Status

Percentage Who Have Been on Active Duty: 8.4%
Earnings Benefit of Veteran Status: 27.5%

51-2022 Electrical and Electronic Equipment Assemblers

Assemble or modify electrical or electronic equipment, such as computers, test equipment telemetering systems, electric motors, and batteries.

- Education or Training Required: Short-term on-the-job training
- Job Growth: –6.4%
- Annual Openings: 33,000
- Self-Employed: 1.5%
- Part-Time: 16.2%

NATIONAL WAGE FIGURES (ANNUAL)

Beginning	25th Percentile	Median	Mean	75th Percentile	90th Percentile
$17,160	$20,470	$25,560	$27,510	$32,870	$41,210

Median Wages for Industries Employing Largest Numbers (Annual)

Industry	Median Income
Educational Services	$32,590
Publishing Industries (Except Internet)	$31,100
Professional, Scientific, and Technical Services	$29,850
Machinery Manufacturing	$28,760
Transportation Equipment Manufacturing	$27,560
Printing and Related Support Activities	$27,290
Nonmetallic Mineral Product Manufacturing	$27,240
Fabricated Metal Product Manufacturing	$26,520
Miscellaneous Manufacturing	$25,810
Electrical Equipment, Appliance, and Component Manufacturing	$25,790

Median Wages for States (Annual)

State	Wage	State	Wage	State	Wage
AK	no data	KY	$26,070	NY	$26,190
AL	$29,530	LA	$26,920	OH	$27,650
AR	$28,680	MA	$31,430	OK	$27,010
AZ	$26,260	MD	$27,850	OR	$26,500
CA	$25,390	ME	$20,690	PA	$25,240
CO	$24,750	MI	$27,220	RI	$22,920
CT	$25,630	MN	$26,800	SC	$30,360
DC	no data	MO	$24,610	SD	$22,260
DE	$23,450	MS	$26,660	TN	$23,100
FL	$22,500	MT	$22,220	TX	$24,540
GA	$25,090	NC	$26,530	UT	$21,300
HI	no data	ND	$22,280	VA	$25,990
IA	$23,020	NE	$25,510	VT	no data
ID	$22,650	NH	$27,280	WA	$28,680
IL	$23,370	NJ	$26,200	WI	$26,910
IN	$21,720	NM	$21,810	WV	$21,120
KS	$25,000	NV	$23,190	WY	no data

Median Wages for the Largest Metropolitan Areas (Annual)

Area	Wage	Area	Wage
AZ: Phoenix	$26,460	MI: Detroit	$28,020
CA: Los Angeles	$21,840	MN: Minneapolis	$28,940
CA: Riverside	$20,670	MO: Kansas City	$22,560
CA: Sacramento	$26,480	MO: St. Louis	$24,770
CA: San Diego	$27,030	NV: Las Vegas	$23,420
CA: San Francisco	$30,800	NY: New York	$26,850
CO: Denver	$26,460	OH: Cincinnati	$27,510
DC: Washington	$30,580	OH: Cleveland	$28,630
FL: Miami	$21,650	OH: Columbus	$27,920
FL: Orlando	$22,580	OR: Portland	$26,650
FL: Tampa	$23,310	PA: Philadelphia	$26,870
GA: Atlanta	$26,800	PA: Pittsburgh	$24,380
IL: Chicago	$22,600	TX: Dallas	$28,880
MA: Boston	$32,310	TX: Houston	$22,110
MD: Baltimore	$31,830	WA: Seattle	$30,960

FACTORS THAT MAY AFFECT EARNINGS

Educational Attainment of Workers and Effect on Earnings

Figures are based on a group of occupations: Assemblers and Fabricators

	Percent at Level	Effect on Earnings
Less than High School	7.7%	–29.3%
Some High School	12.1%	–27.8%
High School or Equivalent	45.2%	6.9%
Some College but No Degree	18.8%	6.6%
Associate Degree	8.9%	7.8%
Bachelor's Degree	6.2%	8.8%
Master's Degree	—	—
Doctoral Degree	—	—
First Professional Degree	—	—

Flexibility of Earnings

Average Hours Worked: 35
Workers with a Varying Number of Hours: 4.5%
Workers Earning Some Overtime Pay, Tips, or Commissions: 19.4%
Earnings Benefit of Working Overtime: 5.4%

Gender

	Male	Female
Percent	48.3%	51.7%
Effect on Earnings	13.6%	–14.4%

Union Membership

Percentage Union Members: 15.0%
Earnings Benefit of Union Membership: 39.2%

Veteran Status

Percentage Who Have Been on Active Duty: 8.4%
Earnings Benefit of Veteran Status: 27.5%

51-2023 Electromechanical Equipment Assemblers

Assemble or modify electromechanical equipment or devices, such as servomechanisms, gyros, dynamometers, magnetic drums, tape drives, brakes, control linkages, actuators, and appliances.

- Education or Training Required: Short-term on-the-job training
- Job Growth: –13.9%
- Annual Openings: 8,000
- Self-Employed: 1.3%
- Part-Time: 16.2%

NATIONAL WAGE FIGURES (ANNUAL)

Beginning	25th Percentile	Median	Mean	75th Percentile	90th Percentile
$18,090	$21,810	$27,560	$28,930	$34,920	$42,600

Median Wages for Industries Employing Largest Numbers (Annual)

Industry	Median Income
Wholesale Electronic Markets and Agents and Brokers	$34,200
Professional, Scientific, and Technical Services	$32,100
Machinery Manufacturing	$30,520
Merchant Wholesalers, Durable Goods	$28,990
Transportation Equipment Manufacturing	$28,620
Miscellaneous Manufacturing	$28,110
Fabricated Metal Product Manufacturing	$26,940
Computer and Electronic Product Manufacturing	$26,720
Electrical Equipment, Appliance, and Component Manufacturing	$26,530
Administrative and Support Services	$23,800

Median Wages for States (Annual)

State	Wage	State	Wage	State	Wage
AK	no data	KY	$27,040	NY	$32,060
AL	$24,720	LA	$31,340	OH	$31,730
AR	no data	MA	$29,670	OK	$27,110
AZ	$29,800	MD	$29,870	OR	$30,410
CA	$27,310	ME	$21,010	PA	$32,250
CO	$28,490	MI	$27,540	RI	$27,490
CT	$29,790	MN	$29,440	SC	$31,520
DC	no data	MO	$30,670	SD	no data
DE	no data	MS	$26,450	TN	$25,100
FL	$23,770	MT	$25,920	TX	$24,310
GA	$25,360	NC	$24,980	UT	no data
HI	no data	ND	no data	VA	$32,050
IA	$20,620	NE	$28,150	VT	$29,840
ID	$26,270	NH	$28,670	WA	$29,420
IL	$27,840	NJ	$30,030	WI	$26,770
IN	$26,530	NM	$24,950	WV	$26,020
KS	$24,550	NV	$26,140	WY	no data

Median Wages for the Largest Metropolitan Areas (Annual)

Area	Wage	Area	Wage
AZ: Phoenix	$30,660	MI: Detroit	$28,450
CA: Los Angeles	$22,890	MN: Minneapolis	$30,230
CA: Riverside	$27,630	MO: Kansas City	$22,850
CA: Sacramento	$30,280	MO: St. Louis	$22,120
CA: San Diego	$30,610	NV: Las Vegas	$27,190
CA: San Francisco	$32,140	NY: New York	$29,890
CO: Denver	$31,070	OH: Cincinnati	$33,380
DC: Washington	no data	OH: Cleveland	$33,590
FL: Miami	$23,380	OH: Columbus	no data
FL: Orlando	$28,900	OR: Portland	$31,180
FL: Tampa	$24,920	PA: Philadelphia	$31,420
GA: Atlanta	$24,620	PA: Pittsburgh	$32,770
IL: Chicago	$28,660	TX: Dallas	$23,750
MA: Boston	$29,980	TX: Houston	$23,950
MD: Baltimore	$33,250	WA: Seattle	$28,940

FACTORS THAT MAY AFFECT EARNINGS

Educational Attainment of Workers and Effect on Earnings

Figures are based on a group of occupations: Assemblers and Fabricators

	Percent at Level	Effect on Earnings
Less than High School	7.7%	–29.3%
Some High School	12.1%	–27.8%
High School or Equivalent	45.2%	6.9%
Some College but No Degree	18.8%	6.6%
Associate Degree	8.9%	7.8%
Bachelor's Degree	6.2%	8.8%
Master's Degree	—	—
Doctoral Degree	—	—
First Professional Degree	—	—

Flexibility of Earnings

Average Hours Worked: 35
Workers with a Varying Number of Hours: 4.5%
Workers Earning Some Overtime Pay, Tips, or Commissions: 19.4%
Earnings Benefit of Working Overtime: 5.4%

Gender

	Male	Female
Percent	48.3%	51.7%
Effect on Earnings	13.6%	–14.4%

Union Membership

Percentage Union Members: 15.0%
Earnings Benefit of Union Membership: 39.2%

Veteran Status

Percentage Who Have Been on Active Duty: 8.4%
Earnings Benefit of Veteran Status: 27.5%

51-2031 Engine and Other Machine Assemblers

Construct, assemble, or rebuild machines such as engines, turbines, and similar equipment used in such industries as construction, extraction, textiles, and paper manufacturing.

- Education or Training Required: Short-term on-the-job training
- Job Growth: 0.2%
- Annual Openings: 2,000
- Self-Employed: 0.0%
- Part-Time: 16.2%

NATIONAL WAGE FIGURES (ANNUAL)

Beginning	25th Percentile	Median	Mean	75th Percentile	90th Percentile
$20,080	$24,950	$33,250	$35,400	$45,720	$55,530

Median Wages for Industries Employing Largest Numbers (Annual)

Industry	Median Income
Repair and Maintenance	$50,720
Fabricated Metal Product Manufacturing	$43,140
Transportation Equipment Manufacturing	$42,740
Machinery Manufacturing	$31,600
Merchant Wholesalers, Durable Goods	$28,710
Rental and Leasing Services	$28,320
Electrical Equipment, Appliance, and Component Manufacturing	$27,860
Miscellaneous Manufacturing	$27,780
Professional, Scientific, and Technical Services	$25,270
Motor Vehicle and Parts Dealers	$24,850

Median Wages for States (Annual)

AK	no data	KY	no data	NY	$36,260
AL	no data	LA	$24,410	OH	$34,440
AR	$26,150	MA	$30,830	OK	$29,590
AZ	$39,590	MD	$39,280	OR	$27,160
CA	$32,710	ME	no data	PA	$32,860
CO	$48,990	MI	$40,450	RI	no data
CT	$51,790	MN	$34,970	SC	$28,310
DC	no data	MO	$24,490	SD	$24,500
DE	no data	MS	$27,280	TN	$24,420
FL	$25,960	MT	no data	TX	$40,150
GA	$28,930	NC	$30,440	UT	$27,540
HI	no data	ND	no data	VA	no data
IA	$32,230	NE	$23,520	VT	no data
ID	no data	NH	$25,170	WA	no data
IL	$23,300	NJ	$34,770	WI	$37,430
IN	$33,550	NM	$29,450	WV	no data
KS	$51,940	NV	$49,740	WY	no data

Median Wages for the Largest Metropolitan Areas (Annual)

AZ: Phoenix	$43,520	MI: Detroit	$53,360
CA: Los Angeles	$36,910	MN: Minneapolis	$36,500
CA: Riverside	$18,510	MO: Kansas City	$52,990
CA: Sacramento	no data	MO: St. Louis	no data
CA: San Diego	$33,760	NV: Las Vegas	no data
CA: San Francisco	$49,180	NY: New York	$31,530
CO: Denver	$50,890	OH: Cincinnati	$54,860
DC: Washington	$32,120	OH: Cleveland	no data
FL: Miami	$24,300	OH: Columbus	$29,090
FL: Orlando	no data	OR: Portland	$26,170
FL: Tampa	no data	PA: Philadelphia	$39,330
GA: Atlanta	$34,310	PA: Pittsburgh	$32,030
IL: Chicago	$21,970	TX: Dallas	$44,550
MA: Boston	no data	TX: Houston	$22,740
MD: Baltimore	$36,190	WA: Seattle	no data

FACTORS THAT MAY AFFECT EARNINGS

Educational Attainment of Workers and Effect on Earnings

	Percent at Level	Effect on Earnings
Less than High School	—	—
Some High School	—	—
High School or Equivalent	55.6%	−0.8%
Some College but No Degree	—	—
Associate Degree	—	—
Bachelor's Degree	—	—
Master's Degree	—	—
Doctoral Degree	—	—
First Professional Degree	—	—

Figures do not total 100% because some levels have a very small sample size.

Flexibility of Earnings

Average Hours Worked: 33
Workers with a Varying Number of Hours: 7.9%
Workers Earning Some Overtime Pay, Tips, or Commissions: 5.3%
Earnings Benefit of Working Overtime: 21.1%

Gender

	Male	Female
Percent	70.0%	30.0%
Effect on Earnings	11.1%	−22.7%

Union Membership

Percentage Union Members: 10.5%
Earnings Benefit of Union Membership: 39.2%

Veteran Status

Percentage Who Have Been on Active Duty: 8.4%
Earnings Benefit of Veteran Status: 27.5%

51-2041 Structural Metal Fabricators and Fitters

Fabricate, lay out, position, align, and fit parts of structural metal products.

- Education or Training Required: Moderate-term on-the-job training
- Job Growth: 2.9%
- Annual Openings: 18,000
- Self-Employed: 3.1%
- Part-Time: 16.2%

NATIONAL WAGE FIGURES (ANNUAL)

Beginning	25th Percentile	Median	Mean	75th Percentile	90th Percentile
$19,960	$24,380	$30,290	$31,440	$36,680	$44,850

Median Wages for Industries Employing Largest Numbers (Annual)

Industry	Median Income
Federal, State, and Local Government	$37,020
Wood Product Manufacturing	$36,290
Professional, Scientific, and Technical Services	$34,300
Heavy and Civil Engineering Construction	$33,780
Construction of Buildings	$32,280
Repair and Maintenance	$31,880
Specialty Trade Contractors	$31,760
Machinery Manufacturing	$31,500
Nonmetallic Mineral Product Manufacturing	$31,420
Electrical Equipment, Appliance, and Component Manufacturing	$31,240

Median Wages for States (Annual)

AK	$39,670	KY	$31,880	NY	$29,840
AL	$28,060	LA	$31,800	OH	$31,040
AR	$25,460	MA	$37,450	OK	$29,050
AZ	$27,470	MD	$33,240	OR	$33,550
CA	$33,310	ME	no data	PA	$32,030
CO	$33,400	MI	$32,710	RI	no data
CT	$31,260	MN	$34,790	SC	$30,970
DC	no data	MO	$29,380	SD	$25,080
DE	$33,180	MS	$28,510	TN	$31,480
FL	$27,900	MT	$27,570	TX	$26,710
GA	$26,540	NC	$30,820	UT	$26,810
HI	no data	ND	$29,180	VA	$29,600
IA	$29,730	NE	$26,400	VT	$27,490
ID	$29,890	NH	$31,630	WA	$33,950
IL	$32,550	NJ	$34,190	WI	$33,890
IN	$29,850	NM	$25,110	WV	$29,200
KS	$27,890	NV	$31,190	WY	$32,570

Median Wages for the Largest Metropolitan Areas (Annual)

AZ: Phoenix	$28,230	MI: Detroit	$35,680
CA: Los Angeles	$30,780	MN: Minneapolis	$37,840
CA: Riverside	$29,670	MO: Kansas City	$32,570
CA: Sacramento	$37,830	MO: St. Louis	$32,910
CA: San Diego	$39,440	NV: Las Vegas	$30,130
CA: San Francisco	$39,980	NY: New York	$32,660
CO: Denver	$33,000	OH: Cincinnati	$34,620
DC: Washington	$32,110	OH: Cleveland	$34,540
FL: Miami	$27,350	OH: Columbus	no data
FL: Orlando	$26,700	OR: Portland	$38,900
FL: Tampa	$29,110	PA: Philadelphia	$35,760
GA: Atlanta	$27,950	PA: Pittsburgh	$31,000
IL: Chicago	$33,600	TX: Dallas	$25,550
MA: Boston	$38,890	TX: Houston	$27,620
MD: Baltimore	$35,750	WA: Seattle	$34,150

FACTORS THAT MAY AFFECT EARNINGS

Educational Attainment of Workers and Effect on Earnings

	Percent at Level	Effect on Earnings
Less than High School	—	—
Some High School	—	—
High School or Equivalent	54.8%	1.0%
Some College but No Degree	—	—
Associate Degree	16.7%	−0.2%
Bachelor's Degree	—	—
Master's Degree	—	—
Doctoral Degree	—	—
First Professional Degree	—	—

Figures do not total 100% because some levels have a very small sample size.

Flexibility of Earnings

Average Hours Worked: 40
Workers with a Varying Number of Hours: 3.8%
Workers Earning Some Overtime Pay, Tips, or Commissions: 35.7%
Earnings Benefit of Working Overtime: 21.1%

Gender

	Male	Female
Percent	94.4%	5.6%
Effect on Earnings	11.1%	−22.7%

Union Membership

Percentage Union Members: 19.0%
Earnings Benefit of Union Membership: 39.2%

Veteran Status

Percentage Who Have Been on Active Duty: 8.4%
Earnings Benefit of Veteran Status: 27.5%

51-2091 Fiberglass Laminators and Fabricators

Laminate layers of fiberglass on molds to form boat decks and hulls, bodies for golf carts or automobiles, or other products.

- Education or Training Required: Moderate-term on-the-job training
- Job Growth: 4.0%
- Annual Openings: 6,000
- Self-Employed: 2.3%
- Part-Time: 16.2%

NATIONAL WAGE FIGURES (ANNUAL)

Beginning	25th Percentile	Median	Mean	75th Percentile	90th Percentile
$17,820	$21,230	$25,980	$26,960	$31,470	$37,510

Median Wages for Industries Employing Largest Numbers (Annual)

Industry	Median Income
Paper Manufacturing	$42,610
Specialty Trade Contractors	$34,040
Management of Companies and Enterprises	$33,160
Primary Metal Manufacturing	$32,440
Motor Vehicle and Parts Dealers	$31,370
Amusement, Gambling, and Recreation Industries	$30,160
Computer and Electronic Product Manufacturing	$27,550
Professional, Scientific, and Technical Services	$27,460
Electrical Equipment, Appliance, and Component Manufacturing	$27,030
Transportation Equipment Manufacturing	$26,860

Median Wages for States (Annual)

State	Wage	State	Wage	State	Wage
AK	no data	KY	$24,750	NY	$22,720
AL	$21,280	LA	$24,630	OH	$26,510
AR	$22,800	MA	$29,270	OK	$18,690
AZ	$27,680	MD	$28,880	OR	$24,670
CA	$26,820	ME	$33,970	PA	$26,060
CO	$18,490	MI	$27,360	RI	$32,090
CT	$27,070	MN	$26,410	SC	$25,780
DC	no data	MO	$22,660	SD	no data
DE	no data	MS	$21,880	TN	$25,730
FL	$27,530	MT	no data	TX	$23,440
GA	$24,260	NC	$24,540	UT	$22,450
HI	no data	ND	$24,730	VA	$22,110
IA	$25,040	NE	$23,330	VT	no data
ID	$21,090	NH	no data	WA	$30,470
IL	$30,800	NJ	$31,370	WI	$26,650
IN	$27,250	NM	$25,940	WV	no data
KS	$25,150	NV	$31,460	WY	no data

Median Wages for the Largest Metropolitan Areas (Annual)

Area	Wage	Area	Wage
AZ: Phoenix	$27,070	MI: Detroit	$31,790
CA: Los Angeles	$27,390	MN: Minneapolis	$25,750
CA: Riverside	$22,110	MO: Kansas City	$25,480
CA: Sacramento	$26,850	MO: St. Louis	$26,990
CA: San Diego	$31,380	NV: Las Vegas	no data
CA: San Francisco	$31,440	NY: New York	$26,630
CO: Denver	no data	OH: Cincinnati	$28,490
DC: Washington	$33,260	OH: Cleveland	$25,520
FL: Miami	$27,360	OH: Columbus	no data
FL: Orlando	$28,370	OR: Portland	no data
FL: Tampa	$26,410	PA: Philadelphia	no data
GA: Atlanta	$29,420	PA: Pittsburgh	no data
IL: Chicago	no data	TX: Dallas	$32,710
MA: Boston	$34,260	TX: Houston	$23,440
MD: Baltimore	$27,440	WA: Seattle	$30,760

FACTORS THAT MAY AFFECT EARNINGS

Educational Attainment of Workers and Effect on Earnings

Figures are based on a group of occupations: Assemblers and Fabricators

	Percent at Level	Effect on Earnings
Less than High School	7.7%	−29.3%
Some High School	12.1%	−27.8%
High School or Equivalent	45.2%	6.9%
Some College but No Degree	18.8%	6.6%
Associate Degree	8.9%	7.8%
Bachelor's Degree	6.2%	8.8%
Master's Degree	—	—
Doctoral Degree	—	—
First Professional Degree	—	—

Flexibility of Earnings

Average Hours Worked: 35
Workers with a Varying Number of Hours: 4.5%
Workers Earning Some Overtime Pay, Tips, or Commissions: 19.4%
Earnings Benefit of Working Overtime: 22.7%

Gender

	Male	Female
Percent	58.9%	41.1%
Effect on Earnings	11.1%	−22.7%

Union Membership

Percentage Union Members: 15.0%
Earnings Benefit of Union Membership: 39.2%

Veteran Status

Percentage Who Have Been on Active Duty: 8.4%
Earnings Benefit of Veteran Status: 27.5%

51-2092 Team Assemblers

Work as part of a team having responsibility for assembling an entire product or component of a product. Team assemblers can perform all tasks conducted by the team in the assembly process and rotate through all or most of them rather than being assigned to a specific task on a permanent basis. May participate in making management decisions affecting the work. Team leaders who work as part of the team should be included.

- Education or Training Required: Moderate-term on-the-job training
- Job Growth: 7.3%
- Annual Openings: 262,000
- Self-Employed: 1.8%
- Part-Time: 16.2%

NATIONAL WAGE FIGURES (ANNUAL)

Beginning	25th Percentile	Median	Mean	75th Percentile	90th Percentile
$16,000	$19,180	$24,190	$26,180	$31,050	$39,810

Median Wages for Industries Employing Largest Numbers (Annual)

Industry	Median Income
Transportation Equipment Manufacturing	$29,040
Primary Metal Manufacturing	$28,330
Paper Manufacturing	$27,040
Machinery Manufacturing	$26,600
Electrical Equipment, Appliance, and Component Manufacturing	$26,200
Professional, Scientific, and Technical Services	$25,450
Nonmetallic Mineral Product Manufacturing	$25,120
Warehousing and Storage	$24,810
Chemical Manufacturing	$24,490
Fabricated Metal Product Manufacturing	$24,480

Median Wages for States (Annual)

State	Wage	State	Wage	State	Wage
AK	no data	KY	$26,960	NY	$21,660
AL	$22,790	LA	$24,060	OH	$27,060
AR	$23,640	MA	$26,140	OK	$22,300
AZ	$21,800	MD	$24,930	OR	$25,470
CA	$22,220	ME	$22,750	PA	$26,040
CO	$23,000	MI	$27,520	RI	$21,050
CT	$27,270	MN	$25,760	SC	$26,350
DC	no data	MO	$24,360	SD	$21,770
DE	$35,540	MS	$23,300	TN	$25,410
FL	$21,590	MT	$21,800	TX	$20,490
GA	$23,820	NC	$23,380	UT	$21,880
HI	$23,990	ND	$25,310	VA	$23,350
IA	$25,970	NE	$25,740	VT	$26,590
ID	$23,120	NH	$25,950	WA	$25,780
IL	$21,480	NJ	$24,630	WI	$25,260
IN	$27,560	NM	$20,820	WV	$23,030
KS	$24,980	NV	$24,450	WY	$21,230

Median Wages for the Largest Metropolitan Areas (Annual)

Area	Wage	Area	Wage
AZ: Phoenix	$21,690	MI: Detroit	$28,180
CA: Los Angeles	$20,780	MN: Minneapolis	$25,860
CA: Riverside	$22,400	MO: Kansas City	$31,520
CA: Sacramento	$23,660	MO: St. Louis	$25,290
CA: San Diego	$21,480	NV: Las Vegas	$24,880
CA: San Francisco	$26,430	NY: New York	$21,510
CO: Denver	$23,120	OH: Cincinnati	$26,100
DC: Washington	$25,340	OH: Cleveland	$25,710
FL: Miami	$20,590	OH: Columbus	$25,950
FL: Orlando	$21,400	OR: Portland	$24,350
FL: Tampa	$22,500	PA: Philadelphia	$27,780
GA: Atlanta	$23,170	PA: Pittsburgh	$24,190
IL: Chicago	$19,730	TX: Dallas	$20,810
MA: Boston	$27,060	TX: Houston	$21,160
MD: Baltimore	$23,080	WA: Seattle	$27,040

FACTORS THAT MAY AFFECT EARNINGS

Educational Attainment of Workers and Effect on Earnings

Figures are based on a group of occupations: Assemblers and Fabricators

	Percent at Level	Effect on Earnings
Less than High School	7.7%	−29.3%
Some High School	12.1%	−27.8%
High School or Equivalent	45.2%	6.9%
Some College but No Degree	18.8%	6.6%
Associate Degree	8.9%	7.8%
Bachelor's Degree	6.2%	8.8%
Master's Degree	—	—
Doctoral Degree	—	—
First Professional Degree	—	—

Flexibility of Earnings

Average Hours Worked: 35
Workers with a Varying Number of Hours: 4.5%
Workers Earning Some Overtime Pay, Tips, or Commissions: 19.4%
Earnings Benefit of Working Overtime: 22.7%

Gender

	Male	Female
Percent	58.9%	41.1%
Effect on Earnings	11.1%	−22.7%

Union Membership

Percentage Union Members: 15.0%
Earnings Benefit of Union Membership: 39.2%

Veteran Status

Percentage Who Have Been on Active Duty: 8.4%
Earnings Benefit of Veteran Status: 27.5%

51-2093 Timing Device Assemblers, Adjusters, and Calibrators

Perform precision assembling or adjusting, within narrow tolerances, of timing devices, such as watches, clocks, or chronometers.

- Education or Training Required: Moderate-term on-the-job training
- Job Growth: –1.5%
- Annual Openings: 1,000
- Self-Employed: 4.1%
- Part-Time: 16.2%

NATIONAL WAGE FIGURES (ANNUAL)

Beginning	25th Percentile	Median	Mean	75th Percentile	90th Percentile
$18,080	$23,550	$28,830	$30,530	$35,590	$46,760

Median Wages for Industries Employing Largest Numbers (Annual)

Industry	Median Income
Professional, Scientific, and Technical Services	$46,790
Machinery Manufacturing	$35,580
Repair and Maintenance	$32,520
Fabricated Metal Product Manufacturing	$32,340
Transportation Equipment Manufacturing	$31,720
Computer and Electronic Product Manufacturing	$26,990
Electrical Equipment, Appliance, and Component Manufacturing	$26,880

Median Wages for States (Annual)

State		State		State	
AK	no data	KY	no data	NY	$30,010
AL	no data	LA	no data	OH	no data
AR	no data	MA	$33,750	OK	no data
AZ	no data	MD	no data	OR	no data
CA	$30,930	ME	no data	PA	$30,660
CO	no data	MI	$34,380	RI	no data
CT	$26,270	MN	$29,420	SC	no data
DC	no data	MO	no data	SD	no data
DE	no data	MS	no data	TN	$30,260
FL	no data	MT	no data	TX	$34,830
GA	no data	NC	no data	UT	no data
HI	no data	ND	no data	VA	no data
IA	$20,560	NE	no data	VT	no data
ID	no data	NH	no data	WA	no data
IL	$25,760	NJ	no data	WI	no data
IN	no data	NM	no data	WV	no data
KS	no data	NV	no data	WY	no data

Median Wages for the Largest Metropolitan Areas (Annual)

Area		Area	
AZ: Phoenix	no data	MI: Detroit	no data
CA: Los Angeles	$27,730	MN: Minneapolis	$29,450
CA: Riverside	no data	MO: Kansas City	no data
CA: Sacramento	$41,590	MO: St. Louis	no data
CA: San Diego	no data	NV: Las Vegas	no data
CA: San Francisco	$22,930	NY: New York	$30,100
CO: Denver	no data	OH: Cincinnati	no data
DC: Washington	no data	OH: Cleveland	no data
FL: Miami	no data	OH: Columbus	no data
FL: Orlando	no data	OR: Portland	no data
FL: Tampa	no data	PA: Philadelphia	$26,950
GA: Atlanta	no data	PA: Pittsburgh	no data
IL: Chicago	$25,720	TX: Dallas	no data
MA: Boston	$33,930	TX: Houston	$29,950
MD: Baltimore	no data	WA: Seattle	no data

FACTORS THAT MAY AFFECT EARNINGS

Educational Attainment of Workers and Effect on Earnings

Figures are based on a group of occupations: Assemblers and Fabricators

	Percent at Level	Effect on Earnings
Less than High School	7.7%	–29.3%
Some High School	12.1%	–27.8%
High School or Equivalent	45.2%	6.9%
Some College but No Degree	18.8%	6.6%
Associate Degree	8.9%	7.8%
Bachelor's Degree	6.2%	8.8%
Master's Degree	—	—
Doctoral Degree	—	—
First Professional Degree	—	—

Flexibility of Earnings

Average Hours Worked: 35
Workers with a Varying Number of Hours: 4.5%
Workers Earning Some Overtime Pay, Tips, or Commissions: 19.4%
Earnings Benefit of Working Overtime: 22.7%

Gender

	Male	Female
Percent	58.9%	41.1%
Effect on Earnings	11.1%	–22.7%

Union Membership

Percentage Union Members: 15.0%
Earnings Benefit of Union Membership: 39.2%

Veteran Status

Percentage Who Have Been on Active Duty: 8.4%
Earnings Benefit of Veteran Status: 27.5%

51-2099 Assemblers and Fabricators, All Other

All assemblers and fabricators not listed separately.

- Education or Training Required: Moderate-term on-the-job training
- Job Growth: 4.5%
- Annual Openings: 55,000
- Self-Employed: 2.4%
- Part-Time: 16.2%

NATIONAL WAGE FIGURES (ANNUAL)

Beginning	25th Percentile	Median	Mean	75th Percentile	90th Percentile
$16,080	$19,580	$26,730	$31,000	$39,820	$55,130

Median Wages for Industries Employing Largest Numbers (Annual)

Industry	Median Income
Primary Metal Manufacturing	$52,240
Transportation Equipment Manufacturing	$48,560
Electrical Equipment, Appliance, and Component Manufacturing	$31,830
Professional, Scientific, and Technical Services	$27,900
Machinery Manufacturing	$27,570
Management of Companies and Enterprises	$26,980
Merchant Wholesalers, Durable Goods	$25,990
Computer and Electronic Product Manufacturing	$25,690
Fabricated Metal Product Manufacturing	$25,060
Specialty Trade Contractors	$25,020

Median Wages for States (Annual)

State	Wage	State	Wage	State	Wage
AK	$25,540	KY	no data	NY	$29,700
AL	$21,720	LA	no data	OH	$34,440
AR	$20,190	MA	$22,650	OK	$20,700
AZ	$23,660	MD	$26,240	OR	$26,680
CA	$22,070	ME	$21,830	PA	$27,490
CO	$23,930	MI	$50,320	RI	$24,740
CT	$27,760	MN	$26,190	SC	$23,960
DC	no data	MO	no data	SD	no data
DE	no data	MS	$18,040	TN	$24,170
FL	$20,300	MT	$20,370	TX	$19,170
GA	$31,440	NC	$24,130	UT	$21,610
HI	$23,480	ND	$19,670	VA	$22,880
IA	$24,260	NE	$24,090	VT	$20,830
ID	no data	NH	$26,440	WA	$27,440
IL	$26,550	NJ	$26,630	WI	$30,160
IN	$28,970	NM	$19,840	WV	$22,680
KS	$20,510	NV	$22,510	WY	$25,430

Median Wages for the Largest Metropolitan Areas (Annual)

Area	Wage	Area	Wage
AZ: Phoenix	$24,310	MI: Detroit	no data
CA: Los Angeles	$20,390	MN: Minneapolis	$27,660
CA: Riverside	$19,150	MO: Kansas City	$21,270
CA: Sacramento	$23,700	MO: St. Louis	no data
CA: San Diego	$22,510	NV: Las Vegas	$22,570
CA: San Francisco	$25,370	NY: New York	$25,870
CO: Denver	$24,500	OH: Cincinnati	$25,600
DC: Washington	$23,320	OH: Cleveland	no data
FL: Miami	$19,000	OH: Columbus	$31,220
FL: Orlando	$23,420	OR: Portland	$30,860
FL: Tampa	$19,820	PA: Philadelphia	$37,220
GA: Atlanta	$52,640	PA: Pittsburgh	$22,780
IL: Chicago	$27,010	TX: Dallas	$22,610
MA: Boston	$26,820	TX: Houston	$15,600
MD: Baltimore	$26,420	WA: Seattle	$29,040

FACTORS THAT MAY AFFECT EARNINGS

Educational Attainment of Workers and Effect on Earnings

Figures are based on a group of occupations: Assemblers and Fabricators

	Percent at Level	Effect on Earnings
Less than High School	7.7%	−29.3%
Some High School	12.1%	−27.8%
High School or Equivalent	45.2%	6.9%
Some College but No Degree	18.8%	6.6%
Associate Degree	8.9%	7.8%
Bachelor's Degree	6.2%	8.8%
Master's Degree	—	—
Doctoral Degree	—	—
First Professional Degree	—	—

Flexibility of Earnings

Average Hours Worked: 35
Workers with a Varying Number of Hours: 4.5%
Workers Earning Some Overtime Pay, Tips, or Commissions: 19.4%
Earnings Benefit of Working Overtime: 22.7%

Gender

	Male	Female
Percent	58.9%	41.1%
Effect on Earnings	11.1%	−22.7%

Union Membership

Percentage Union Members: 15.0%
Earnings Benefit of Union Membership: 39.2%

Veteran Status

Percentage Who Have Been on Active Duty: 8.4%
Earnings Benefit of Veteran Status: 27.5%

51-3000 Food Processing Workers

51-3011 Bakers

Mix and bake ingredients according to recipes to produce breads, rolls, cookies, cakes, pies, pastries, or other baked goods.

- Education or Training Required: Long-term on-the-job training
- Job Growth: 15.2%
- Annual Openings: 37,000
- Self-Employed: 8.1%
- Part-Time: 38.7%

NATIONAL WAGE FIGURES (ANNUAL)

Beginning	25th Percentile	Median	Mean	75th Percentile	90th Percentile
$15,180	$17,720	$22,030	$23,710	$28,190	$35,380

Median Wages for Industries Employing Largest Numbers (Annual)

Industry	Median Income
Management of Companies and Enterprises	$28,310
Federal, State, and Local Government	$27,370
Accommodation	$26,240
Hospitals	$26,100
Educational Services	$25,490
Performing Arts, Spectator Sports, and Related Industries	$24,210
Amusement, Gambling, and Recreation Industries	$23,840
General Merchandise Stores	$23,620
Personal and Laundry Services	$23,570
Nursing and Residential Care Facilities	$23,510

Median Wages for States (Annual)

AK	$32,520	KY	$18,320	NY	$22,940
AL	$17,770	LA	$18,690	OH	$21,890
AR	$16,860	MA	$24,800	OK	$17,980
AZ	$22,330	MD	$25,840	OR	$23,380
CA	$22,720	ME	$21,480	PA	$21,930
CO	$26,400	MI	$21,780	RI	$26,330
CT	$22,560	MN	$24,930	SC	$18,450
DC	$25,430	MO	$20,900	SD	$19,960
DE	$20,410	MS	$19,540	TN	$18,260
FL	$22,030	MT	$21,120	TX	$20,200
GA	$19,920	NC	$20,280	UT	$22,670
HI	$22,310	ND	$19,490	VA	$21,610
IA	$21,400	NE	$21,120	VT	$23,120
ID	$21,490	NH	$23,920	WA	$28,130
IL	$21,200	NJ	$24,270	WI	$22,130
IN	$21,660	NM	$21,330	WV	$17,370
KS	$19,810	NV	$28,800	WY	$19,740

Median Wages for the Largest Metropolitan Areas (Annual)

AZ: Phoenix	$22,380	MI: Detroit	$24,940
CA: Los Angeles	$21,100	MN: Minneapolis	$27,690
CA: Riverside	$21,040	MO: Kansas City	$21,320
CA: Sacramento	$29,160	MO: St. Louis	$24,050
CA: San Diego	$19,700	NV: Las Vegas	$30,160
CA: San Francisco	$25,520	NY: New York	$24,270
CO: Denver	$29,810	OH: Cincinnati	$24,150
DC: Washington	$24,650	OH: Cleveland	$23,770
FL: Miami	$22,890	OH: Columbus	$20,520
FL: Orlando	$19,140	OR: Portland	$26,380
FL: Tampa	$22,990	PA: Philadelphia	$24,020
GA: Atlanta	$21,100	PA: Pittsburgh	$20,170
IL: Chicago	$21,380	TX: Dallas	$21,640
MA: Boston	$24,980	TX: Houston	$20,400
MD: Baltimore	$24,810	WA: Seattle	$28,310

FACTORS THAT MAY AFFECT EARNINGS

Educational Attainment of Workers and Effect on Earnings

	Percent at Level	Effect on Earnings
Less than High School	9.2%	−14.5%
Some High School	18.8%	−15.5%
High School or Equivalent	39.9%	−0.1%
Some College but No Degree	20.2%	−2.8%
Associate Degree	5.0%	8.8%
Bachelor's Degree	6.9%	64.0%
Master's Degree	—	—
Doctoral Degree	—	—
First Professional Degree	—	—

Flexibility of Earnings

Average Hours Worked: 32
Workers with a Varying Number of Hours: 7.7%
Workers Earning Some Overtime Pay, Tips, or Commissions: 6.9%
Earnings Benefit of Working Overtime: 17.0%

Gender

	Male	Female
Percent	42.1%	57.9%
Effect on Earnings	12.9%	−14.5%

Union Membership

Percentage Union Members: 13.4%
Earnings Benefit of Union Membership: 18.6%

Veteran Status

Percentage Who Have Been on Active Duty: 4.5%
Earnings Benefit of Veteran Status: 27.4%

51-3021 Butchers and Meat Cutters

Cut, trim, or prepare consumer-sized portions of meat for use or sale in retail establishments.

- Education or Training Required: Long-term on-the-job training
- Job Growth: 7.9%
- Annual Openings: 20,000
- Self-Employed: 1.4%
- Part-Time: 32.8%

NATIONAL WAGE FIGURES (ANNUAL)

Beginning	25th Percentile	Median	Mean	75th Percentile	90th Percentile
$16,520	$20,630	$26,930	$28,310	$35,240	$43,260

Median Wages for Industries Employing Largest Numbers (Annual)

Industry	Median Income
Federal, State, and Local Government	$39,060
General Merchandise Stores	$34,320
Nonstore Retailers	$33,280
Accommodation	$33,150
Management of Companies and Enterprises	$32,920
Administrative and Support Services	$30,760
Food and Beverage Stores	$27,320
Merchant Wholesalers, Nondurable Goods	$25,660
Warehousing and Storage	$25,380
Food Manufacturing	$23,110

Median Wages for States (Annual)

AK	$39,960	KY	$23,170	NY	$32,500
AL	$23,390	LA	$22,020	OH	$28,440
AR	$21,380	MA	$39,400	OK	$22,460
AZ	$34,550	MD	$32,540	OR	$33,510
CA	$27,550	ME	$29,250	PA	$26,830
CO	$29,500	MI	$26,370	RI	$30,870
CT	$39,960	MN	$34,960	SC	$25,650
DC	$25,100	MO	$25,010	SD	$23,770
DE	$33,590	MS	$22,180	TN	$25,700
FL	$26,640	MT	$23,970	TX	$24,670
GA	$23,360	NC	$24,280	UT	$27,720
HI	$37,650	ND	$22,540	VA	$29,450
IA	$22,730	NE	$24,220	VT	$33,390
ID	$27,220	NH	$34,500	WA	$38,830
IL	$24,360	NJ	$41,090	WI	$29,480
IN	$25,780	NM	$27,800	WV	$21,890
KS	$27,700	NV	$30,640	WY	$25,250

Median Wages for the Largest Metropolitan Areas (Annual)

AZ: Phoenix	$34,920	MI: Detroit	$28,670
CA: Los Angeles	$22,790	MN: Minneapolis	$40,830
CA: Riverside	$27,340	MO: Kansas City	$32,520
CA: Sacramento	$40,150	MO: St. Louis	$29,150
CA: San Diego	$26,400	NV: Las Vegas	$28,740
CA: San Francisco	$35,870	NY: New York	$38,680
CO: Denver	$29,750	OH: Cincinnati	$28,820
DC: Washington	$33,680	OH: Cleveland	$28,860
FL: Miami	$26,410	OH: Columbus	$32,030
FL: Orlando	$26,060	OR: Portland	$36,040
FL: Tampa	$27,310	PA: Philadelphia	$31,980
GA: Atlanta	$24,750	PA: Pittsburgh	$24,210
IL: Chicago	$24,250	TX: Dallas	$26,080
MA: Boston	$37,830	TX: Houston	$25,730
MD: Baltimore	$32,400	WA: Seattle	$41,520

FACTORS THAT MAY AFFECT EARNINGS

Educational Attainment of Workers and Effect on Earnings

Figures are based on a group of occupations: Food Processing Workers

	Percent at Level	Effect on Earnings
Less than High School	14.3%	−6.8%
Some High School	18.8%	−19.8%
High School or Equivalent	36.2%	6.0%
Some College but No Degree	18.8%	3.1%
Associate Degree	5.9%	6.2%
Bachelor's Degree	5.4%	23.0%
Master's Degree	—	—
Doctoral Degree	—	—
First Professional Degree	—	—

Flexibility of Earnings

Average Hours Worked: 33
Workers with a Varying Number of Hours: 8.1%
Workers Earning Some Overtime Pay, Tips, or Commissions: 10.3%
Earnings Benefit of Working Overtime: 26.6%

Gender

	Male	Female
Percent	70.1%	29.9%
Effect on Earnings	8.9%	−13.7%

Union Membership

Percentage Union Members: 18.6%
Earnings Benefit of Union Membership: 24.9%

Veteran Status

Percentage Who Have Been on Active Duty: 4.5%
Earnings Benefit of Veteran Status: 27.4%

51-3022 Meat, Poultry, and Fish Cutters and Trimmers

Use hand tools to perform routine cutting and trimming of meat, poultry, and fish.

- Education or Training Required: Short-term on-the-job training
- Job Growth: 15.8%
- Annual Openings: 23,000
- Self-Employed: 1.6%
- Part-Time: 32.8%

NATIONAL WAGE FIGURES (ANNUAL)

Beginning	25th Percentile	Median	Mean	75th Percentile	90th Percentile
$14,960	$17,100	$20,370	$21,260	$24,120	$29,070

Median Wages for Industries Employing Largest Numbers (Annual)

Industry	Median Income
General Merchandise Stores	$25,170
Merchant Wholesalers, Nondurable Goods	$21,630
Food and Beverage Stores	$20,560
Food Manufacturing	$20,350
Professional, Scientific, and Technical Services	$20,100
Wholesale Electronic Markets and Agents and Brokers	$19,410
Food Services and Drinking Places	$18,500
Warehousing and Storage	$18,410

Median Wages for States (Annual)

AK $19,730	KY $21,690	NY $19,490
AL $18,780	LA $17,400	OH $18,930
AR $19,540	MA $26,060	OK $18,640
AZ $21,460	MD $27,920	OR $20,670
CA $19,070	ME $22,050	PA $22,080
CO $22,920	MI $21,770	RI $22,360
CT $21,560	MN $22,690	SC $16,880
DC $31,080	MO $20,100	SD .... no data
DE $17,850	MS $18,720	TN $19,300
FL $19,830	MT $16,750	TX $18,150
GA $19,390	NC $18,930	UT $23,210
HI $21,480	ND $21,510	VA $19,810
IA $24,230	NE $24,980	VT $20,640
ID .... no data	NH $23,460	WA $22,800
IL $23,020	NJ $23,110	WI $22,500
IN $18,740	NM $19,280	WV $19,780
KS $25,850	NV $26,930	WY .... no data

Median Wages for the Largest Metropolitan Areas (Annual)

AZ: Phoenix $19,780	MI: Detroit $22,960
CA: Los Angeles $17,720	MN: Minneapolis $26,800
CA: Riverside $18,010	MO: Kansas City $23,060
CA: Sacramento $27,510	MO: St. Louis $19,540
CA: San Diego $20,150	NV: Las Vegas $26,210
CA: San Francisco $25,610	NY: New York $22,050
CO: Denver .... no data	OH: Cincinnati $17,830
DC: Washington $24,970	OH: Cleveland $20,930
FL: Miami $19,900	OH: Columbus $20,680
FL: Orlando $24,450	OR: Portland $24,220
FL: Tampa $19,490	PA: Philadelphia $22,800
GA: Atlanta $17,690	PA: Pittsburgh .... no data
IL: Chicago $21,690	TX: Dallas .... no data
MA: Boston $27,510	TX: Houston $16,670
MD: Baltimore $29,650	WA: Seattle $26,450

FACTORS THAT MAY AFFECT EARNINGS

Educational Attainment of Workers and Effect on Earnings

Figures are based on a group of occupations: Food Processing Workers

	Percent at Level	Effect on Earnings
Less than High School	14.3%	−6.8%
Some High School	18.8%	−19.8%
High School or Equivalent	36.2%	6.0%
Some College but No Degree	18.8%	3.1%
Associate Degree	5.9%	6.2%
Bachelor's Degree	5.4%	23.0%
Master's Degree	—	—
Doctoral Degree	—	—
First Professional Degree	—	—

Flexibility of Earnings

Average Hours Worked: 33
Workers with a Varying Number of Hours: 8.1%
Workers Earning Some Overtime Pay, Tips, or Commissions: 10.3%
Earnings Benefit of Working Overtime: 26.6%

Gender

	Male	Female
Percent	70.1%	29.9%
Effect on Earnings	8.9%	−13.7%

Union Membership

Percentage Union Members: 18.6%
Earnings Benefit of Union Membership: 24.9%

Veteran Status

Percentage Who Have Been on Active Duty: 4.5%
Earnings Benefit of Veteran Status: 27.4%

51-3023 Slaughterers and Meat Packers

Work in slaughtering, meat packing, or wholesale establishments performing precision functions involving the preparation of meat. Work may include specialized slaughtering tasks, cutting standard or premium cuts of meat for marketing, making sausage, or wrapping meats.

- Education or Training Required: Moderate-term on-the-job training
- Job Growth: 13.8%
- Annual Openings: 22,000
- Self-Employed: 1.3%
- Part-Time: 32.8%

NATIONAL WAGE FIGURES (ANNUAL)

Beginning	25th Percentile	Median	Mean	75th Percentile	90th Percentile
$15,950	$18,290	$21,690	$21,940	$25,440	$28,570

Median Wages for Industries Employing Largest Numbers (Annual)

Industry	Median Income
Merchant Wholesalers, Nondurable Goods	$23,330
Food Manufacturing	$21,700
Food and Beverage Stores	$20,690
Administrative and Support Services	$20,040

Median Wages for States (Annual)

AK	no data	KY	$19,590	NY	$25,030
AL	$19,370	LA	$17,420	OH	$24,220
AR	$19,850	MA	$31,790	OK	no data
AZ	$21,380	MD	$20,480	OR	$21,650
CA	$18,460	ME	no data	PA	$22,330
CO	$23,860	MI	$30,380	RI	no data
CT	$19,080	MN	$24,900	SC	$17,270
DC	no data	MO	$21,670	SD	no data
DE	no data	MS	$23,310	TN	$19,710
FL	no data	MT	$21,540	TX	$18,340
GA	$20,020	NC	$18,960	UT	$21,470
HI	no data	ND	no data	VA	$22,630
IA	$24,410	NE	$25,200	VT	no data
ID	$21,760	NH	no data	WA	$21,490
IL	$18,310	NJ	$23,130	WI	$23,000
IN	$25,780	NM	$21,550	WV	$21,450
KS	$25,260	NV	no data	WY	no data

Median Wages for the Largest Metropolitan Areas (Annual)

AZ: Phoenix	$21,350	MI: Detroit	no data
CA: Los Angeles	$17,610	MN: Minneapolis	no data
CA: Riverside	$17,020	MO: Kansas City	$19,100
CA: Sacramento	no data	MO: St. Louis	$21,620
CA: San Diego	no data	NV: Las Vegas	no data
CA: San Francisco	$19,890	NY: New York	$25,460
CO: Denver	$23,910	OH: Cincinnati	$24,700
DC: Washington	no data	OH: Cleveland	no data
FL: Miami	$16,480	OH: Columbus	$20,690
FL: Orlando	no data	OR: Portland	$23,160
FL: Tampa	no data	PA: Philadelphia	no data
GA: Atlanta	$17,630	PA: Pittsburgh	$20,310
IL: Chicago	$18,400	TX: Dallas	$17,120
MA: Boston	$23,920	TX: Houston	no data
MD: Baltimore	no data	WA: Seattle	$23,630

FACTORS THAT MAY AFFECT EARNINGS

Educational Attainment of Workers and Effect on Earnings

Figures are based on a group of occupations: Food Processing Workers

	Percent at Level	Effect on Earnings
Less than High School	14.3%	−6.8%
Some High School	18.8%	−19.8%
High School or Equivalent	36.2%	6.0%
Some College but No Degree	18.8%	3.1%
Associate Degree	5.9%	6.2%
Bachelor's Degree	5.4%	23.0%
Master's Degree	—	—
Doctoral Degree	—	—
First Professional Degree	—	—

Flexibility of Earnings

Average Hours Worked: 33
Workers with a Varying Number of Hours: 8.1%
Workers Earning Some Overtime Pay, Tips, or Commissions: 10.3%
Earnings Benefit of Working Overtime: 26.6%

Gender

	Male	Female
Percent	70.1%	29.9%
Effect on Earnings	8.9%	−13.7%

Union Membership

Percentage Union Members: 18.6%
Earnings Benefit of Union Membership: 24.9%

Veteran Status

Percentage Who Have Been on Active Duty: 4.5%
Earnings Benefit of Veteran Status: 27.4%

51-3091 Food and Tobacco Roasting, Baking, and Drying Machine Operators and Tenders

Operate or tend food or tobacco roasting, baking, or drying equipment, including hearth ovens, kiln driers, roasters, char kilns, and vacuum-drying equipment.

- Education or Training Required: Short-term on-the-job training
- Job Growth: 4.7%
- Annual Openings: 2,000
- Self-Employed: 0.6%
- Part-Time: 32.8%

NATIONAL WAGE FIGURES (ANNUAL)

Beginning	25th Percentile	Median	Mean	75th Percentile	90th Percentile
$15,910	$18,820	$23,510	$25,710	$31,540	$38,740

Median Wages for Industries Employing Largest Numbers (Annual)

Industry	Median Income
Beverage and Tobacco Product Manufacturing	$29,760
Warehousing and Storage	$26,870
Food Manufacturing	$24,240
Machinery Manufacturing	$23,540
Management of Companies and Enterprises	$22,910
Merchant Wholesalers, Nondurable Goods	$22,840
Food Services and Drinking Places	$21,280
Support Activities for Agriculture and Forestry	$19,670
Food and Beverage Stores	$19,020
Administrative and Support Services	$17,540

Median Wages for States (Annual)

AK	no data	KY	$26,310	NY	$20,980
AL	$26,890	LA	$15,470	OH	$22,310
AR	$26,300	MA	$30,330	OK	no data
AZ	$25,200	MD	$22,900	OR	$20,650
CA	$19,390	ME	$28,800	PA	$24,660
CO	$23,140	MI	$22,660	RI	no data
CT	no data	MN	$25,370	SC	$19,940
DC	no data	MO	$25,140	SD	$24,540
DE	no data	MS	no data	TN	$18,990
FL	$22,980	MT	no data	TX	$21,360
GA	$23,920	NC	$41,200	UT	$22,060
HI	$24,390	ND	$35,360	VA	$24,710
IA	$24,730	NE	$24,030	VT	no data
ID	$29,300	NH	no data	WA	$32,260
IL	$25,200	NJ	$17,590	WI	$24,790
IN	$24,790	NM	$20,860	WV	$18,720
KS	$24,310	NV	no data	WY	no data

Median Wages for the Largest Metropolitan Areas (Annual)

AZ: Phoenix	$25,240	MI: Detroit	no data
CA: Los Angeles	$17,890	MN: Minneapolis	$30,900
CA: Riverside	$21,780	MO: Kansas City	no data
CA: Sacramento	$17,470	MO: St. Louis	$22,540
CA: San Diego	$17,480	NV: Las Vegas	no data
CA: San Francisco	$22,700	NY: New York	$17,480
CO: Denver	$22,230	OH: Cincinnati	$24,240
DC: Washington	$32,460	OH: Cleveland	$22,720
FL: Miami	$21,460	OH: Columbus	$21,370
FL: Orlando	no data	OR: Portland	$20,020
FL: Tampa	$21,500	PA: Philadelphia	$24,900
GA: Atlanta	$22,090	PA: Pittsburgh	$18,270
IL: Chicago	$25,990	TX: Dallas	$24,030
MA: Boston	$29,600	TX: Houston	$21,290
MD: Baltimore	$23,240	WA: Seattle	$27,420

FACTORS THAT MAY AFFECT EARNINGS

Educational Attainment of Workers and Effect on Earnings

	Percent at Level	Effect on Earnings
Less than High School	—	—
Some High School	—	—
High School or Equivalent	66.7%	1.3%
Some College but No Degree	—	—
Associate Degree	—	—
Bachelor's Degree	—	—
Master's Degree	—	—
Doctoral Degree	—	—
First Professional Degree	—	—

Figures do not total 100% because some levels have a very small sample size.

Flexibility of Earnings

Average Hours Worked: 40
Workers with a Varying Number of Hours: 8.9%
Workers Earning Some Overtime Pay, Tips, or Commissions: 36.8%
Earnings Benefit of Working Overtime: 17.0%

Gender

	Male	Female
Percent	74.3%	25.7%
Effect on Earnings	11.1%	−22.7%

Union Membership

Percentage Union Members: 31.6%
Earnings Benefit of Union Membership: 24.9%

Veteran Status

Percentage Who Have Been on Active Duty: 4.5%
Earnings Benefit of Veteran Status: 27.4%

51-3092 Food Batchmakers

Set up and operate equipment that mixes or blends ingredients used in the manufacturing of food products. Includes candy makers and cheese makers.

- Education or Training Required: Short-term on-the-job training
- Job Growth: 7.9%
- Annual Openings: 16,000
- Self-Employed: 2.1%
- Part-Time: 41.2%

NATIONAL WAGE FIGURES (ANNUAL)

Beginning	25th Percentile	Median	Mean	75th Percentile	90th Percentile
$15,060	$17,730	$23,100	$24,790	$30,120	$37,930

Median Wages for Industries Employing Largest Numbers (Annual)

Industry	Median Income
Professional, Scientific, and Technical Services	$29,030
Plastics and Rubber Products Manufacturing	$28,890
Beverage and Tobacco Product Manufacturing	$27,590
General Merchandise Stores	$26,750
Management of Companies and Enterprises	$26,740
Wholesale Electronic Markets and Agents and Brokers	$25,780
Food Manufacturing	$24,020
Chemical Manufacturing	$21,530
Machinery Manufacturing	$20,600
Merchant Wholesalers, Nondurable Goods	$19,690

Median Wages for States (Annual)

State	Wage	State	Wage	State	Wage
AK	$22,510	KY	$25,820	NY	$18,160
AL	$20,050	LA	$16,690	OH	$26,180
AR	$24,420	MA	$25,360	OK	$23,080
AZ	$17,740	MD	$26,660	OR	$23,390
CA	$22,210	ME	$25,960	PA	$26,430
CO	$22,210	MI	$26,970	RI	$21,280
CT	$23,070	MN	$29,440	SC	$22,010
DC	no data	MO	$25,230	SD	$24,240
DE	$24,110	MS	$19,970	TN	$34,530
FL	$23,340	MT	$22,420	TX	$16,920
GA	$21,900	NC	$20,920	UT	$21,120
HI	$18,520	ND	$18,850	VA	$26,130
IA	$25,340	NE	$22,680	VT	$24,590
ID	$22,230	NH	$23,820	WA	$21,820
IL	$25,870	NJ	$24,520	WI	$28,470
IN	$27,010	NM	$19,920	WV	$21,370
KS	$21,320	NV	$19,120	WY	$24,200

Median Wages for the Largest Metropolitan Areas (Annual)

Area	Wage	Area	Wage
AZ: Phoenix	$17,460	MI: Detroit	$25,340
CA: Los Angeles	$19,130	MN: Minneapolis	$31,320
CA: Riverside	$24,760	MO: Kansas City	$26,920
CA: Sacramento	$26,100	MO: St. Louis	$26,660
CA: San Diego	$19,120	NV: Las Vegas	$22,610
CA: San Francisco	$23,540	NY: New York	$18,360
CO: Denver	$23,470	OH: Cincinnati	$28,910
DC: Washington	$25,650	OH: Cleveland	$22,250
FL: Miami	$22,070	OH: Columbus	$28,220
FL: Orlando	$24,250	OR: Portland	$24,640
FL: Tampa	$20,600	PA: Philadelphia	$25,500
GA: Atlanta	$22,190	PA: Pittsburgh	$22,100
IL: Chicago	$26,070	TX: Dallas	$17,930
MA: Boston	$24,660	TX: Houston	$16,110
MD: Baltimore	$26,840	WA: Seattle	$21,000

FACTORS THAT MAY AFFECT EARNINGS

Educational Attainment of Workers and Effect on Earnings

	Percent at Level	Effect on Earnings
Less than High School	10.7%	−18.9%
Some High School	17.0%	−30.0%
High School or Equivalent	40.2%	23.6%
Some College but No Degree	18.8%	−18.3%
Associate Degree	8.9%	3.3%
Bachelor's Degree	—	—
Master's Degree	—	—
Doctoral Degree	—	—
First Professional Degree	—	—

Flexibility of Earnings

Average Hours Worked: 30
Workers with a Varying Number of Hours: 9.6%
Workers Earning Some Overtime Pay, Tips, or Commissions: 18.7%
Earnings Benefit of Working Overtime: 17.0%

Gender

	Male	Female
Percent	41.4%	58.6%
Effect on Earnings	11.1%	−22.7%

Union Membership

Percentage Union Members: 17.1%
Earnings Benefit of Union Membership: 26.2%

Veteran Status

Percentage Who Have Been on Active Duty: 4.5%
Earnings Benefit of Veteran Status: 27.4%

51-3093 Food Cooking Machine Operators and Tenders

Operate or tend cooking equipment, such as steam cooking vats, deep-fry cookers, pressure cookers, kettles, and boilers, to prepare food products.

- Education or Training Required: Short-term on-the-job training
- Job Growth: 2.9%
- Annual Openings: 3,000
- Self-Employed: 0.0%
- Part-Time: 12.5%

NATIONAL WAGE FIGURES (ANNUAL)

Beginning	25th Percentile	Median	Mean	75th Percentile	90th Percentile
$14,600	$17,160	$21,280	$22,750	$27,140	$34,350

Median Wages for Industries Employing Largest Numbers (Annual)

Industry	Median Income
Accommodation	$31,020
Management of Companies and Enterprises	$24,280
Machinery Manufacturing	$23,830
Food Manufacturing	$23,800
Merchant Wholesalers, Nondurable Goods	$22,990
Food and Beverage Stores	$19,290
Administrative and Support Services	$18,230
Food Services and Drinking Places	$17,100

Median Wages for States (Annual)

State	Wage	State	Wage	State	Wage
AK	$24,090	KY	$22,820	NY	$22,140
AL	$21,170	LA	$18,490	OH	$23,390
AR	$20,160	MA	$25,120	OK	$16,890
AZ	$21,820	MD	$17,640	OR	$24,350
CA	$20,220	ME	$19,370	PA	$22,980
CO	$21,490	MI	$24,790	RI	$21,720
CT	$26,550	MN	$24,010	SC	$23,080
DC	no data	MO	$20,090	SD	$23,770
DE	$17,750	MS	$18,770	TN	$20,900
FL	no data	MT	$20,890	TX	$18,890
GA	$16,170	NC	$20,740	UT	$28,320
HI	$18,090	ND	$27,260	VA	$23,790
IA	$24,850	NE	$21,590	VT	$19,870
ID	$25,020	NH	$20,530	WA	$26,030
IL	$24,030	NJ	$26,550	WI	$23,760
IN	$18,660	NM	$19,040	WV	no data
KS	$19,030	NV	$19,870	WY	no data

Median Wages for the Largest Metropolitan Areas (Annual)

Area	Wage	Area	Wage
AZ: Phoenix	$21,450	MI: Detroit	$28,060
CA: Los Angeles	$18,880	MN: Minneapolis	$22,820
CA: Riverside	$19,290	MO: Kansas City	$21,170
CA: Sacramento	$30,190	MO: St. Louis	$21,930
CA: San Diego	$17,580	NV: Las Vegas	$19,240
CA: San Francisco	$20,400	NY: New York	$21,750
CO: Denver	$22,310	OH: Cincinnati	$25,820
DC: Washington	$20,620	OH: Cleveland	$20,790
FL: Miami	no data	OH: Columbus	$24,150
FL: Orlando	no data	OR: Portland	$24,090
FL: Tampa	$20,420	PA: Philadelphia	$26,580
GA: Atlanta	$14,010	PA: Pittsburgh	$17,070
IL: Chicago	$24,260	TX: Dallas	$21,860
MA: Boston	$25,450	TX: Houston	$16,450
MD: Baltimore	$17,570	WA: Seattle	$22,150

FACTORS THAT MAY AFFECT EARNINGS

Educational Attainment of Workers and Effect on Earnings

Figures are based on a group of occupations: Food Processing Workers

	Percent at Level	Effect on Earnings
Less than High School	14.3%	−6.8%
Some High School	18.8%	−19.8%
High School or Equivalent	36.2%	6.0%
Some College but No Degree	18.8%	3.1%
Associate Degree	5.9%	6.2%
Bachelor's Degree	5.4%	23.0%
Master's Degree	—	—
Doctoral Degree	—	—
First Professional Degree	—	—

Flexibility of Earnings

Average Hours Worked: 25
Workers with a Varying Number of Hours: 14.3%
Workers Earning Some Overtime Pay, Tips, or Commissions: 9.1%
Earnings Benefit of Working Overtime: 17.0%

Gender

	Male	Female
Percent	40.3%	59.7%
Effect on Earnings	11.1%	−22.7%

Union Membership

Percentage Union Members: 9.1%
Earnings Benefit of Union Membership: 24.9%

Veteran Status

Percentage Who Have Been on Active Duty: 4.5%
Earnings Benefit of Veteran Status: 27.4%

51-4000 Metal Workers and Plastic Workers

51-4011 Computer-Controlled Machine Tool Operators, Metal and Plastic

Operate computer-controlled machines or robots to perform one or more machine functions on metal or plastic workpieces.

- Education or Training Required: Moderate-term on-the-job training
- Job Growth: –1.2%
- Annual Openings: 13,000
- Self-Employed: 0.0%
- Part-Time: 7.2%

NATIONAL WAGE FIGURES (ANNUAL)

Beginning	25th Percentile	Median	Mean	75th Percentile	90th Percentile
$20,600	$25,170	$31,670	$32,820	$39,190	$46,690

Median Wages for Industries Employing Largest Numbers (Annual)

Industry	Median Income
Specialty Trade Contractors	$34,800
Machinery Manufacturing	$34,500
Merchant Wholesalers, Nondurable Goods	$33,870
Support Activities for Transportation	$33,210
Miscellaneous Manufacturing	$32,970
Electrical Equipment, Appliance, and Component Manufacturing	$32,080
Professional, Scientific, and Technical Services	$31,870
Transportation Equipment Manufacturing	$31,500
Fabricated Metal Product Manufacturing	$31,250
Merchant Wholesalers, Durable Goods	$30,680

Median Wages for States (Annual)

AK	no data	KY	$29,090	NY	$29,830
AL	$23,870	LA	$32,170	OH	$31,530
AR	$29,330	MA	$36,220	OK	$29,340
AZ	$32,450	MD	$34,700	OR	$33,940
CA	$30,380	ME	$33,630	PA	$31,560
CO	$29,990	MI	$31,900	RI	$31,640
CT	$38,890	MN	$34,390	SC	$28,750
DC	no data	MO	$27,780	SD	$27,890
DE	$37,750	MS	$24,200	TN	$30,080
FL	$28,100	MT	$29,270	TX	$30,310
GA	$29,190	NC	$30,950	UT	$30,300
HI	no data	ND	$32,170	VA	$33,190
IA	$30,750	NE	$32,100	VT	$30,640
ID	$23,270	NH	$31,660	WA	$42,770
IL	$34,230	NJ	$37,560	WI	$33,930
IN	$31,350	NM	$33,390	WV	$28,270
KS	$33,520	NV	$29,010	WY	no data

Median Wages for the Largest Metropolitan Areas (Annual)

AZ: Phoenix	$32,720	MI: Detroit	$34,270
CA: Los Angeles	$29,750	MN: Minneapolis	$37,850
CA: Riverside	$28,550	MO: Kansas City	$38,010
CA: Sacramento	$36,070	MO: St. Louis	$33,390
CA: San Diego	$30,750	NV: Las Vegas	$31,150
CA: San Francisco	$35,520	NY: New York	$33,530
CO: Denver	no data	OH: Cincinnati	$33,660
DC: Washington	$36,120	OH: Cleveland	$34,230
FL: Miami	$26,490	OH: Columbus	$29,130
FL: Orlando	$23,450	OR: Portland	$33,870
FL: Tampa	$29,280	PA: Philadelphia	$36,390
GA: Atlanta	$32,170	PA: Pittsburgh	$31,370
IL: Chicago	$34,820	TX: Dallas	$28,010
MA: Boston	$35,730	TX: Houston	$32,280
MD: Baltimore	$35,330	WA: Seattle	$46,920

FACTORS THAT MAY AFFECT EARNINGS

Educational Attainment of Workers and Effect on Earnings

Figures are based on a group of occupations: Metal Workers and Plastic Workers

	Percent at Level	Effect on Earnings
Less than High School	5.6%	–31.1%
Some High School	11.6%	–16.7%
High School or Equivalent	42.1%	0.8%
Some College but No Degree	21.4%	4.0%
Associate Degree	12.4%	13.3%
Bachelor's Degree	5.8%	12.6%
Master's Degree	0.8%	–0.6%
Doctoral Degree	—	—
First Professional Degree	—	—

Flexibility of Earnings

Average Hours Worked: 38
Workers with a Varying Number of Hours: 4.8%
Workers Earning Some Overtime Pay, Tips, or Commissions: 28.1%
Earnings Benefit of Working Overtime: 3.3%

Gender

	Male	Female
Percent	91.8%	8.2%
Effect on Earnings	11.1%	–22.7%

Union Membership

Percentage Union Members: 18.5%
Earnings Benefit of Union Membership: 19.3%

Veteran Status

Percentage Who Have Been on Active Duty: 14.2%
Earnings Benefit of Veteran Status: 7.6%

51-4012 Numerical Tool and Process Control Programmers

Develop programs to control machining or processing of parts by automatic machine tools, equipment, or systems.

- Education or Training Required: Long-term on-the-job training
- Job Growth: −1.1%
- Annual Openings: 2,000
- Self-Employed: 0.0%
- Part-Time: 7.2%

NATIONAL WAGE FIGURES (ANNUAL)

Beginning	25th Percentile	Median	Mean	75th Percentile	90th Percentile
$27,260	$33,560	$42,480	$44,810	$53,270	$66,260

Median Wages for Industries Employing Largest Numbers (Annual)

Industry	Median Income
Professional, Scientific, and Technical Services	$53,970
Repair and Maintenance	$48,930
Merchant Wholesalers, Durable Goods	$48,700
Administrative and Support Services	$46,710
Transportation Equipment Manufacturing	$45,270
Machinery Manufacturing	$43,750
Primary Metal Manufacturing	$43,300
Chemical Manufacturing	$41,990
Fabricated Metal Product Manufacturing	$41,420
Electrical Equipment, Appliance, and Component Manufacturing	$40,900

Median Wages for States (Annual)

AK	no data	KY	$40,640	NY	$38,720
AL	$33,790	LA	$41,020	OH	$41,520
AR	$35,450	MA	$46,360	OK	$40,070
AZ	$47,670	MD	$45,020	OR	$50,890
CA	$51,850	ME	$41,650	PA	$41,860
CO	$49,010	MI	$43,640	RI	$37,620
CT	$44,670	MN	$45,530	SC	$33,700
DC	no data	MO	$42,300	SD	$31,620
DE	no data	MS	$36,290	TN	$36,070
FL	$40,880	MT	no data	TX	$35,690
GA	$35,230	NC	$37,630	UT	$42,820
HI	no data	ND	no data	VA	$49,810
IA	$37,070	NE	$35,080	VT	$36,830
ID	$35,410	NH	$33,530	WA	$61,220
IL	$48,240	NJ	$45,210	WI	$43,080
IN	$37,250	NM	no data	WV	no data
KS	$41,930	NV	$44,790	WY	no data

Median Wages for the Largest Metropolitan Areas (Annual)

AZ: Phoenix	$55,890	MI: Detroit	$47,710
CA: Los Angeles	$53,760	MN: Minneapolis	$48,780
CA: Riverside	$46,070	MO: Kansas City	$44,150
CA: Sacramento	$45,870	MO: St. Louis	$46,320
CA: San Diego	$42,160	NV: Las Vegas	no data
CA: San Francisco	$57,700	NY: New York	$42,370
CO: Denver	$53,310	OH: Cincinnati	$46,220
DC: Washington	$52,900	OH: Cleveland	$46,730
FL: Miami	$37,850	OH: Columbus	$30,640
FL: Orlando	no data	OR: Portland	$52,260
FL: Tampa	$43,470	PA: Philadelphia	$44,900
GA: Atlanta	$38,490	PA: Pittsburgh	$44,380
IL: Chicago	$46,930	TX: Dallas	$30,360
MA: Boston	$44,850	TX: Houston	$37,220
MD: Baltimore	$46,270	WA: Seattle	$63,490

FACTORS THAT MAY AFFECT EARNINGS

Educational Attainment of Workers and Effect on Earnings

Figures are based on a group of occupations: Metal Workers and Plastic Workers

	Percent at Level	Effect on Earnings
Less than High School	5.6%	−31.1%
Some High School	11.6%	−16.7%
High School or Equivalent	42.1%	0.8%
Some College but No Degree	21.4%	4.0%
Associate Degree	12.4%	13.3%
Bachelor's Degree	5.8%	12.6%
Master's Degree	0.8%	−0.6%
Doctoral Degree	—	—
First Professional Degree	—	—

Flexibility of Earnings

Average Hours Worked: 38
Workers with a Varying Number of Hours: 4.8%
Workers Earning Some Overtime Pay, Tips, or Commissions: 28.1%
Earnings Benefit of Working Overtime: 3.3%

Gender

	Male	Female
Percent	91.8%	8.2%
Effect on Earnings	11.1%	−22.7%

Union Membership

Percentage Union Members: 18.5%
Earnings Benefit of Union Membership: 19.3%

Veteran Status

Percentage Who Have Been on Active Duty: 14.2%
Earnings Benefit of Veteran Status: 7.6%

51-4021 Extruding and Drawing Machine Setters, Operators, and Tenders, Metal and Plastic

Set up, operate, or tend machines to extrude or draw thermoplastic or metal materials into tubes, rods, hoses, wire, bars, or structural shapes.

- Education or Training Required: Moderate-term on-the-job training
- Job Growth: –21.3%
- Annual Openings: 9,000
- Self-Employed: 0.0%
- Part-Time: 7.2%

NATIONAL WAGE FIGURES (ANNUAL)

Beginning	25th Percentile	Median	Mean	75th Percentile	90th Percentile
$19,030	$22,710	$28,250	$29,330	$34,630	$41,920

Median Wages for Industries Employing Largest Numbers (Annual)

Industry	Median Income
Federal, State, and Local Government	$46,600
Specialty Trade Contractors	$36,940
Transportation Equipment Manufacturing	$35,300
Primary Metal Manufacturing	$30,980
Management of Companies and Enterprises	$30,390
Electrical Equipment, Appliance, and Component Manufacturing	$30,140
Nonmetallic Mineral Product Manufacturing	$29,530
Fabricated Metal Product Manufacturing	$29,040
Paper Manufacturing	$28,620
Chemical Manufacturing	$28,560

Median Wages for States (Annual)

AK .... no data	KY $32,290	NY $30,270
AL $27,080	LA $25,760	OH $27,550
AR $28,060	MA $31,540	OK $28,070
AZ $29,540	MD $30,120	OR $27,160
CA $23,830	ME $29,000	PA $31,770
CO $29,570	MI $25,740	RI $34,120
CT $31,160	MN $30,740	SC $28,350
DC .... no data	MO $31,780	SD $24,460
DE $32,810	MS $26,820	TN $27,530
FL $26,340	MT .... no data	TX $26,320
GA $28,410	NC $28,500	UT $27,220
HI .... no data	ND .... no data	VA $29,060
IA $28,060	NE $27,140	VT $30,550
ID $30,660	NH $27,910	WA $34,220
IL $27,310	NJ $25,380	WI $28,690
IN $31,480	NM $21,720	WV $27,580
KS $23,700	NV $26,210	WY .... no data

Median Wages for the Largest Metropolitan Areas (Annual)

AZ: Phoenix	$32,060	MI: Detroit	$23,870
CA: Los Angeles	$22,890	MN: Minneapolis	$29,860
CA: Riverside	$25,870	MO: Kansas City	$23,370
CA: Sacramento	no data	MO: St. Louis	$34,940
CA: San Diego	$24,270	NV: Las Vegas	$23,550
CA: San Francisco	$30,360	NY: New York	$25,690
CO: Denver	$30,330	OH: Cincinnati	$30,360
DC: Washington	$31,230	OH: Cleveland	$36,820
FL: Miami	$25,840	OH: Columbus	$24,220
FL: Orlando	$29,840	OR: Portland	$28,400
FL: Tampa	$27,120	PA: Philadelphia	$31,340
GA: Atlanta	$30,170	PA: Pittsburgh	$30,460
IL: Chicago	$27,890	TX: Dallas	$27,080
MA: Boston	$31,710	TX: Houston	$26,910
MD: Baltimore	no data	WA: Seattle	$34,340

FACTORS THAT MAY AFFECT EARNINGS

Educational Attainment of Workers and Effect on Earnings

	Percent at Level	Effect on Earnings
Less than High School	—	—
Some High School	—	—
High School or Equivalent	72.7%	9.9%
Some College but No Degree	—	—
Associate Degree	—	—
Bachelor's Degree	—	—
Master's Degree	—	—
Doctoral Degree	—	—
First Professional Degree	—	—

Figures do not total 100% because some levels have a very small sample size.

Flexibility of Earnings

Average Hours Worked: 37
Workers with a Varying Number of Hours: 8.1%
Workers Earning Some Overtime Pay, Tips, or Commissions: 31.8%
Earnings Benefit of Working Overtime: 14.8%

Gender

	Male	Female
Percent	83.9%	16.1%
Effect on Earnings	11.1%	–22.7%

Union Membership

Percentage Union Members: 22.7%
Earnings Benefit of Union Membership: 19.3%

Veteran Status

Percentage Who Have Been on Active Duty: 14.2%
Earnings Benefit of Veteran Status: 7.6%

51-4022 Forging Machine Setters, Operators, and Tenders, Metal and Plastic

Set up, operate, or tend forging machines to taper, shape, or form metal or plastic parts.

- Education or Training Required: Moderate-term on-the-job training
- Job Growth: –4.6%
- Annual Openings: 4,000
- Self-Employed: 0.7%
- Part-Time: 7.2%

NATIONAL WAGE FIGURES (ANNUAL)

Beginning	25th Percentile	Median	Mean	75th Percentile	90th Percentile
$18,430	$23,230	$28,980	$29,980	$35,600	$43,560

Median Wages for Industries Employing Largest Numbers (Annual)

Industry	Median Income
Federal, State, and Local Government	$45,520
Fabricated Metal Product Manufacturing	$31,900
Computer and Electronic Product Manufacturing	$31,220
Primary Metal Manufacturing	$31,050
Transportation Equipment Manufacturing	$29,030
Machinery Manufacturing	$27,380
Specialty Trade Contractors	$25,760
Furniture and Related Product Manufacturing	$25,310
Electrical Equipment, Appliance, and Component Manufacturing	$25,100
Miscellaneous Manufacturing	$25,010

Median Wages for States (Annual)

State	Wage	State	Wage	State	Wage
AK	no data	KY	$23,300	NY	$31,180
AL	$26,070	LA	$24,950	OH	$33,830
AR	$25,880	MA	$36,580	OK	$20,410
AZ	$26,340	MD	$31,070	OR	$42,120
CA	$29,940	ME	no data	PA	$31,600
CO	$40,540	MI	$29,450	RI	$33,210
CT	$30,510	MN	$30,940	SC	$29,480
DC	no data	MO	$28,500	SD	$28,990
DE	no data	MS	$27,780	TN	$29,940
FL	$23,070	MT	$21,540	TX	$24,320
GA	$26,010	NC	$28,070	UT	$28,160
HI	no data	ND	no data	VA	$26,250
IA	$27,950	NE	$28,590	VT	no data
ID	no data	NH	no data	WA	$30,150
IL	$29,480	NJ	$23,230	WI	$31,790
IN	$28,590	NM	$31,450	WV	$24,260
KS	$27,050	NV	$28,960	WY	no data

Median Wages for the Largest Metropolitan Areas (Annual)

Area	Wage	Area	Wage
AZ: Phoenix	$26,670	MI: Detroit	$31,520
CA: Los Angeles	$29,470	MN: Minneapolis	$31,550
CA: Riverside	$26,240	MO: Kansas City	no data
CA: Sacramento	no data	MO: St. Louis	$38,880
CA: San Diego	$35,790	NV: Las Vegas	no data
CA: San Francisco	$38,050	NY: New York	$26,180
CO: Denver	$42,810	OH: Cincinnati	$28,440
DC: Washington	no data	OH: Cleveland	$39,520
FL: Miami	$20,220	OH: Columbus	no data
FL: Orlando	no data	OR: Portland	$38,840
FL: Tampa	$24,660	PA: Philadelphia	$33,380
GA: Atlanta	$26,900	PA: Pittsburgh	$31,070
IL: Chicago	$32,760	TX: Dallas	$27,930
MA: Boston	no data	TX: Houston	$19,950
MD: Baltimore	$34,500	WA: Seattle	$33,820

FACTORS THAT MAY AFFECT EARNINGS

Educational Attainment of Workers and Effect on Earnings

	Percent at Level	Effect on Earnings
Less than High School	—	—
Some High School	—	—
High School or Equivalent	50.0%	–2.7%
Some College but No Degree	—	—
Associate Degree	—	—
Bachelor's Degree	—	—
Master's Degree	—	—
Doctoral Degree	—	—
First Professional Degree	—	—

Figures do not total 100% because some levels have a very small sample size.

Flexibility of Earnings

Average Hours Worked: 35
Workers with a Varying Number of Hours: 6.8%
Workers Earning Some Overtime Pay, Tips, or Commissions: 15.4%
Earnings Benefit of Working Overtime: 14.8%

Gender

	Male	Female
Percent	93.5%	6.5%
Effect on Earnings	11.1%	–22.7%

Union Membership

Percentage Union Members: 23.1%
Earnings Benefit of Union Membership: 19.3%

Veteran Status

Percentage Who Have Been on Active Duty: 14.2%
Earnings Benefit of Veteran Status: 7.6%

51-4023 Rolling Machine Setters, Operators, and Tenders, Metal and Plastic

Set up, operate, or tend machines to roll steel or plastic, forming bends, beads, knurls, rolls, or plate, or to flatten, temper, or reduce gauge of material.

- Education or Training Required: Moderate-term on-the-job training
- Job Growth: –3.9%
- Annual Openings: 4,000
- Self-Employed: 0.0%
- Part-Time: 40.0%

NATIONAL WAGE FIGURES (ANNUAL)

Beginning	25th Percentile	Median	Mean	75th Percentile	90th Percentile
$19,830	$24,560	$31,050	$32,080	$38,520	$45,970

Median Wages for Industries Employing Largest Numbers (Annual)

Industry	Median Income
Primary Metal Manufacturing	$35,180
Transportation Equipment Manufacturing	$34,730
Food Manufacturing	$33,710
Wood Product Manufacturing	$31,260
Electrical Equipment, Appliance, and Component Manufacturing	$29,830
Merchant Wholesalers, Nondurable Goods	$29,720
Management of Companies and Enterprises	$29,320
Fabricated Metal Product Manufacturing	$29,260
Machinery Manufacturing	$28,280
Nonmetallic Mineral Product Manufacturing	$28,190

Median Wages for States (Annual)

AK	no data	KY	$36,860	NY	$29,740
AL	$31,890	LA	$28,850	OH	$33,160
AR	$29,640	MA	$32,490	OK	$27,790
AZ	$24,730	MD	no data	OR	$36,830
CA	$28,230	ME	no data	PA	$31,660
CO	$34,930	MI	$34,170	RI	$30,150
CT	$34,630	MN	$31,120	SC	$34,210
DC	no data	MO	$30,070	SD	$24,120
DE	$40,970	MS	$27,150	TN	$27,840
FL	$23,590	MT	no data	TX	$25,970
GA	$27,490	NC	$31,190	UT	$28,210
HI	no data	ND	no data	VA	$28,050
IA	$32,990	NE	$27,610	VT	no data
ID	$19,350	NH	$27,780	WA	$35,670
IL	$30,860	NJ	$27,950	WI	$33,580
IN	$35,400	NM	no data	WV	$32,770
KS	$31,330	NV	$22,340	WY	no data

Median Wages for the Largest Metropolitan Areas (Annual)

AZ: Phoenix	$24,280	MI: Detroit	$37,450
CA: Los Angeles	$25,210	MN: Minneapolis	$31,650
CA: Riverside	$29,450	MO: Kansas City	no data
CA: Sacramento	$28,020	MO: St. Louis	$33,540
CA: San Diego	$35,120	NV: Las Vegas	no data
CA: San Francisco	$38,400	NY: New York	$25,640
CO: Denver	$32,660	OH: Cincinnati	$31,170
DC: Washington	$26,550	OH: Cleveland	$36,870
FL: Miami	$21,580	OH: Columbus	$30,990
FL: Orlando	no data	OR: Portland	no data
FL: Tampa	$21,220	PA: Philadelphia	$30,520
GA: Atlanta	$27,520	PA: Pittsburgh	$32,870
IL: Chicago	$33,730	TX: Dallas	$25,270
MA: Boston	$30,300	TX: Houston	$23,790
MD: Baltimore	no data	WA: Seattle	$34,030

FACTORS THAT MAY AFFECT EARNINGS

Educational Attainment of Workers and Effect on Earnings

	Percent at Level	Effect on Earnings
Less than High School	—	—
Some High School	—	—
High School or Equivalent	72.7%	–1.6%
Some College but No Degree	—	—
Associate Degree	—	—
Bachelor's Degree	—	—
Master's Degree	—	—
Doctoral Degree	—	—
First Professional Degree	—	—

Figures do not total 100% because some levels have a very small sample size.

Flexibility of Earnings

Average Hours Worked: 36
Workers with a Varying Number of Hours: 6.2%
Workers Earning Some Overtime Pay, Tips, or Commissions: 21.7%
Earnings Benefit of Working Overtime: 14.8%

Gender

	Male	Female
Percent	83.5%	16.5%
Effect on Earnings	11.1%	–22.7%

Union Membership

Percentage Union Members: 13.0%
Earnings Benefit of Union Membership: 19.3%

Veteran Status

Percentage Who Have Been on Active Duty: 14.2%
Earnings Benefit of Veteran Status: 7.6%

51-4031 Cutting, Punching, and Press Machine Setters, Operators, and Tenders, Metal and Plastic

Set up, operate, or tend machines to saw, cut, shear, slit, punch, crimp, notch, bend, or straighten metal or plastic material.

- Education or Training Required: Moderate-term on-the-job training
- Job Growth: –17.2%
- Annual Openings: 13,000
- Self-Employed: 0.4%
- Part-Time: 6.3%

NATIONAL WAGE FIGURES (ANNUAL)

Beginning	25th Percentile	Median	Mean	75th Percentile	90th Percentile
$17,510	$21,050	$26,340	$27,730	$32,980	$40,400

Median Wages for Industries Employing Largest Numbers (Annual)

Industry	Median Income
Chemical Manufacturing	$30,130
Repair and Maintenance	$29,510
Specialty Trade Contractors	$29,390
Paper Manufacturing	$28,890
Primary Metal Manufacturing	$28,450
Electrical Equipment, Appliance, and Component Manufacturing	$28,400
Transportation Equipment Manufacturing	$28,220
Wholesale Electronic Markets and Agents and Brokers	$27,840
Machinery Manufacturing	$27,830
Merchant Wholesalers, Durable Goods	$27,420

Median Wages for States (Annual)

State	Wage	State	Wage	State	Wage
AK	$28,860	KY	$27,010	NY	$24,740
AL	$25,130	LA	$24,230	OH	$27,210
AR	$24,520	MA	$29,890	OK	$23,850
AZ	$24,260	MD	$31,170	OR	$25,890
CA	$24,980	ME	$25,860	PA	$27,970
CO	$28,500	MI	$28,940	RI	$20,040
CT	$28,820	MN	$30,420	SC	$25,650
DC	no data	MO	$25,360	SD	$26,680
DE	$28,820	MS	$23,440	TN	$25,610
FL	$23,590	MT	$23,480	TX	$22,470
GA	$25,890	NC	$25,040	UT	$25,360
HI	$19,870	ND	$28,470	VA	$27,180
IA	$27,710	NE	$26,750	VT	$24,900
ID	$23,870	NH	$26,740	WA	$28,740
IL	$25,840	NJ	$24,600	WI	$28,870
IN	$26,620	NM	$21,570	WV	$29,520
KS	$23,170	NV	$27,760	WY	$29,400

Median Wages for the Largest Metropolitan Areas (Annual)

Area	Wage	Area	Wage
AZ: Phoenix	$24,000	MI: Detroit	$29,440
CA: Los Angeles	$23,760	MN: Minneapolis	$30,970
CA: Riverside	$22,920	MO: Kansas City	$24,620
CA: Sacramento	$26,910	MO: St. Louis	$26,670
CA: San Diego	$25,310	NV: Las Vegas	$25,940
CA: San Francisco	$30,890	NY: New York	$23,930
CO: Denver	$28,910	OH: Cincinnati	$26,400
DC: Washington	$25,400	OH: Cleveland	$28,190
FL: Miami	$23,990	OH: Columbus	$26,380
FL: Orlando	$21,910	OR: Portland	$26,360
FL: Tampa	$23,590	PA: Philadelphia	$28,540
GA: Atlanta	$26,420	PA: Pittsburgh	$27,430
IL: Chicago	$25,740	TX: Dallas	$21,530
MA: Boston	$31,360	TX: Houston	$24,870
MD: Baltimore	$34,000	WA: Seattle	$30,250

FACTORS THAT MAY AFFECT EARNINGS

Educational Attainment of Workers and Effect on Earnings

	Percent at Level	Effect on Earnings
Less than High School	8.1%	–29.6%
Some High School	11.3%	–22.8%
High School or Equivalent	56.5%	2.5%
Some College but No Degree	16.1%	11.9%
Associate Degree	5.6%	28.5%
Bachelor's Degree	—	—
Master's Degree	—	—
Doctoral Degree	—	—
First Professional Degree	—	—

Flexibility of Earnings

Average Hours Worked: 35
Workers with a Varying Number of Hours: 4.6%
Workers Earning Some Overtime Pay, Tips, or Commissions: 17.6%
Earnings Benefit of Working Overtime: 14.8%

Gender

	Male	Female
Percent	82.1%	17.9%
Effect on Earnings	1.9%	—

Union Membership

Percentage Union Members: 18.3%
Earnings Benefit of Union Membership: 18.5%

Veteran Status

Percentage Who Have Been on Active Duty: 14.2%
Earnings Benefit of Veteran Status: 7.6%

51-4032 Drilling and Boring Machine Tool Setters, Operators, and Tenders, Metal and Plastic

Set up, operate, or tend drilling machines to drill, bore, ream, mill, or countersink metal or plastic workpieces.

- Education or Training Required: Moderate-term on-the-job training
- Job Growth: –8.4%
- Annual Openings: 2,000
- Self-Employed: 0.0%
- Part-Time: 7.2%

NATIONAL WAGE FIGURES (ANNUAL)

Beginning	25th Percentile	Median	Mean	75th Percentile	90th Percentile
$19,750	$23,960	$29,870	$31,640	$37,590	$47,370

Median Wages for Industries Employing Largest Numbers (Annual)

Industry	Median Income
Management of Companies and Enterprises	$35,170
Heavy and Civil Engineering Construction	$33,580
Transportation Equipment Manufacturing	$33,420
Machinery Manufacturing	$32,330
Electrical Equipment, Appliance, and Component Manufacturing	$29,600
Miscellaneous Manufacturing	$28,540
Nonmetallic Mineral Product Manufacturing	$28,480
Fabricated Metal Product Manufacturing	$28,310
Furniture and Related Product Manufacturing	$27,480
Support Activities for Mining	$27,060

Median Wages for States (Annual)

AK	no data	KY	$31,160	NY	$31,630
AL	$28,460	LA	$25,770	OH	$36,200
AR	$27,250	MA	$40,830	OK	$29,890
AZ	$26,520	MD	$39,780	OR	$32,920
CA	$26,290	ME	$31,470	PA	$31,690
CO	$22,590	MI	$32,960	RI	$28,200
CT	$28,680	MN	$34,080	SC	$30,790
DC	no data	MO	$26,570	SD	$25,950
DE	no data	MS	no data	TN	$26,410
FL	$24,250	MT	no data	TX	$24,020
GA	$26,890	NC	$29,100	UT	$26,970
HI	no data	ND	no data	VA	$28,080
IA	$29,660	NE	$29,530	VT	$27,900
ID	$34,900	NH	$29,870	WA	$28,790
IL	$29,600	NJ	$23,930	WI	$31,100
IN	$33,310	NM	no data	WV	$25,610
KS	$30,190	NV	$25,740	WY	no data

Median Wages for the Largest Metropolitan Areas (Annual)

AZ: Phoenix	$26,180	MI: Detroit	$36,410
CA: Los Angeles	$26,350	MN: Minneapolis	$37,230
CA: Riverside	$24,140	MO: Kansas City	$30,300
CA: Sacramento	$21,260	MO: St. Louis	$30,790
CA: San Diego	$28,860	NV: Las Vegas	no data
CA: San Francisco	$28,310	NY: New York	$25,940
CO: Denver	$22,590	OH: Cincinnati	$32,190
DC: Washington	$24,920	OH: Cleveland	$32,910
FL: Miami	$26,680	OH: Columbus	$26,380
FL: Orlando	$24,980	OR: Portland	$33,620
FL: Tampa	$25,230	PA: Philadelphia	$34,750
GA: Atlanta	$27,600	PA: Pittsburgh	$31,660
IL: Chicago	$29,980	TX: Dallas	$23,490
MA: Boston	$40,010	TX: Houston	$25,290
MD: Baltimore	$33,320	WA: Seattle	$29,120

FACTORS THAT MAY AFFECT EARNINGS

Educational Attainment of Workers and Effect on Earnings

Figures are based on a group of occupations: Metal Workers and Plastic Workers

	Percent at Level	Effect on Earnings
Less than High School	5.6%	–31.1%
Some High School	11.6%	–16.7%
High School or Equivalent	42.1%	0.8%
Some College but No Degree	21.4%	4.0%
Associate Degree	12.4%	13.3%
Bachelor's Degree	5.8%	12.6%
Master's Degree	0.8%	–0.6%
Doctoral Degree	—	—
First Professional Degree	—	—

Flexibility of Earnings

Average Hours Worked: 40
Workers with a Varying Number of Hours: 3.4%
Workers Earning Some Overtime Pay, Tips, or Commissions: 16.7%
Earnings Benefit of Working Overtime: 14.8%

Gender

	Male	Female
Percent	80.0%	20.0%
Effect on Earnings	11.1%	–22.7%

Union Membership

Percentage Union Members: 8.3%
Earnings Benefit of Union Membership: 19.3%

Veteran Status

Percentage Who Have Been on Active Duty: 14.2%
Earnings Benefit of Veteran Status: 7.6%

51-4033 Grinding, Lapping, Polishing, and Buffing Machine Tool Setters, Operators, and Tenders, Metal and Plastic

Set up, operate, or tend grinding and related tools that remove excess material or burrs from surfaces; sharpen edges or corners; or buff, hone, or polish metal or plastic workpieces.

- Education or Training Required: Moderate-term on-the-job training
- Job Growth: –10.0%
- Annual Openings: 5,000
- Self-Employed: 1.2%
- Part-Time: 7.2%

NATIONAL WAGE FIGURES (ANNUAL)

Beginning	25th Percentile	Median	Mean	75th Percentile	90th Percentile
$18,200	$22,100	$28,080	$29,780	$35,510	$44,560

Median Wages for Industries Employing Largest Numbers (Annual)

Industry	Median Income
Management of Companies and Enterprises	$41,050
Wholesale Electronic Markets and Agents and Brokers	$33,350
Transportation Equipment Manufacturing	$32,110
Paper Manufacturing	$31,750
Machinery Manufacturing	$30,350
Electrical Equipment, Appliance, and Component Manufacturing	$28,360
Primary Metal Manufacturing	$27,900
Miscellaneous Manufacturing	$27,410
Fabricated Metal Product Manufacturing	$27,220
Wood Product Manufacturing	$27,100

Median Wages for States (Annual)

State	Wage	State	Wage	State	Wage
AK	no data	KY	$25,780	NY	$29,680
AL	$24,520	LA	$21,940	OH	$29,610
AR	$25,220	MA	$33,020	OK	$25,890
AZ	$27,650	MD	$27,470	OR	$30,280
CA	$24,410	ME	$31,420	PA	$30,090
CO	$24,910	MI	$33,940	RI	$26,170
CT	$29,350	MN	$32,850	SC	$29,200
DC	no data	MO	$29,740	SD	$22,350
DE	$29,130	MS	$22,910	TN	$27,480
FL	$23,410	MT	$23,400	TX	$22,440
GA	$28,530	NC	$28,360	UT	$25,060
HI	no data	ND	$24,840	VA	$26,110
IA	$30,850	NE	$26,830	VT	$29,340
ID	$24,160	NH	$29,450	WA	$27,480
IL	$28,790	NJ	$27,590	WI	$31,050
IN	$32,390	NM	$26,700	WV	$25,080
KS	$26,530	NV	$24,800	WY	no data

Median Wages for the Largest Metropolitan Areas (Annual)

Area	Wage	Area	Wage
AZ: Phoenix	$28,250	MI: Detroit	$40,830
CA: Los Angeles	$24,200	MN: Minneapolis	$35,390
CA: Riverside	$22,440	MO: Kansas City	$27,130
CA: Sacramento	$24,030	MO: St. Louis	$34,220
CA: San Diego	$24,090	NV: Las Vegas	$25,090
CA: San Francisco	$27,690	NY: New York	$27,040
CO: Denver	$25,430	OH: Cincinnati	$32,810
DC: Washington	$23,320	OH: Cleveland	$27,620
FL: Miami	$23,150	OH: Columbus	$34,330
FL: Orlando	$22,980	OR: Portland	$29,760
FL: Tampa	$23,300	PA: Philadelphia	$30,260
GA: Atlanta	$31,170	PA: Pittsburgh	$30,450
IL: Chicago	$29,160	TX: Dallas	$23,130
MA: Boston	$34,650	TX: Houston	$21,910
MD: Baltimore	$27,770	WA: Seattle	$28,810

FACTORS THAT MAY AFFECT EARNINGS

Educational Attainment of Workers and Effect on Earnings

	Percent at Level	Effect on Earnings
Less than High School	—	—
Some High School	14.1%	−26.4%
High School or Equivalent	39.4%	6.2%
Some College but No Degree	25.4%	0.4%
Associate Degree	—	—
Bachelor's Degree	8.5%	−6.2%
Master's Degree	—	—
Doctoral Degree	—	—
First Professional Degree	—	—

Figures do not total 100% because some levels have a very small sample size.

Flexibility of Earnings

Average Hours Worked: 37
Workers with a Varying Number of Hours: 3.4%
Workers Earning Some Overtime Pay, Tips, or Commissions: 26.6%
Earnings Benefit of Working Overtime: 14.8%

Gender

	Male	Female
Percent	94.4%	5.6%
Effect on Earnings	0.9%	—

Union Membership

Percentage Union Members: 12.7%
Earnings Benefit of Union Membership: 9.9%

Veteran Status

Percentage Who Have Been on Active Duty: 14.2%
Earnings Benefit of Veteran Status: 7.6%

51-4034 Lathe and Turning Machine Tool Setters, Operators, and Tenders, Metal and Plastic

Set up, operate, or tend lathe and turning machines to turn, bore, thread, form, or face metal or plastic materials, such as wire, rod, or bar stock.

- Education or Training Required: Moderate-term on-the-job training
- Job Growth: –9.0%
- Annual Openings: 7,000
- Self-Employed: 0.0%
- Part-Time: 7.2%

NATIONAL WAGE FIGURES (ANNUAL)

Beginning	25th Percentile	Median	Mean	75th Percentile	90th Percentile
$20,770	$25,660	$32,160	$33,250	$39,730	$48,190

Median Wages for Industries Employing Largest Numbers (Annual)

Industry	Median Income
Professional, Scientific, and Technical Services	$42,120
Management of Companies and Enterprises	$38,910
Nonmetallic Mineral Product Manufacturing	$36,760
Repair and Maintenance	$35,290
Machinery Manufacturing	$33,920
Transportation Equipment Manufacturing	$33,840
Electrical Equipment, Appliance, and Component Manufacturing	$31,520
Fabricated Metal Product Manufacturing	$31,170
Primary Metal Manufacturing	$30,980
Miscellaneous Manufacturing	$30,970

Median Wages for States (Annual)

AK	no data	KY	$30,400	NY	$32,330
AL	$29,250	LA	$32,740	OH	$32,510
AR	$27,190	MA	$38,080	OK	$27,670
AZ	$34,300	MD	$39,560	OR	$42,150
CA	$30,400	ME	$32,130	PA	$34,000
CO	$38,350	MI	$39,710	RI	$33,020
CT	$36,280	MN	$35,180	SC	$30,900
DC	no data	MO	$31,510	SD	$26,790
DE	no data	MS	$26,370	TN	$30,570
FL	$29,110	MT	$28,590	TX	$27,220
GA	$30,450	NC	$32,480	UT	$32,210
HI	no data	ND	no data	VA	$29,980
IA	$32,570	NE	no data	VT	$26,990
ID	$25,820	NH	$29,860	WA	$39,570
IL	$35,070	NJ	$33,290	WI	$32,170
IN	$31,590	NM	no data	WV	$23,940
KS	$29,100	NV	$30,930	WY	no data

Median Wages for the Largest Metropolitan Areas (Annual)

AZ: Phoenix	$36,220	MI: Detroit	$42,070
CA: Los Angeles	$29,610	MN: Minneapolis	$36,120
CA: Riverside	$28,590	MO: Kansas City	$32,500
CA: Sacramento	no data	MO: St. Louis	$32,120
CA: San Diego	$34,340	NV: Las Vegas	no data
CA: San Francisco	$31,940	NY: New York	$33,320
CO: Denver	$39,950	OH: Cincinnati	$30,260
DC: Washington	no data	OH: Cleveland	$33,320
FL: Miami	$31,630	OH: Columbus	$34,660
FL: Orlando	$29,300	OR: Portland	$42,100
FL: Tampa	no data	PA: Philadelphia	$36,180
GA: Atlanta	$29,870	PA: Pittsburgh	$33,930
IL: Chicago	$36,420	TX: Dallas	$27,650
MA: Boston	$40,010	TX: Houston	$27,310
MD: Baltimore	$37,120	WA: Seattle	$41,590

FACTORS THAT MAY AFFECT EARNINGS

Educational Attainment of Workers and Effect on Earnings

	Percent at Level	Effect on Earnings
Less than High School	—	—
Some High School	—	—
High School or Equivalent	50.0%	14.4%
Some College but No Degree	20.6%	7.8%
Associate Degree	—	—
Bachelor's Degree	—	—
Master's Degree	—	—
Doctoral Degree	—	—
First Professional Degree	—	—

Figures do not total 100% because some levels have a very small sample size.

Flexibility of Earnings

Average Hours Worked: 36
Workers with a Varying Number of Hours: 7.6%
Workers Earning Some Overtime Pay, Tips, or Commissions: 15.0%
Earnings Benefit of Working Overtime: 14.8%

Gender

	Male	Female
Percent	89.5%	10.5%
Effect on Earnings	11.1%	−22.7%

Union Membership

Percentage Union Members: 7.5%
Earnings Benefit of Union Membership: 19.3%

Veteran Status

Percentage Who Have Been on Active Duty: 14.2%
Earnings Benefit of Veteran Status: 7.6%

51-4035 Milling and Planing Machine Setters, Operators, and Tenders, Metal and Plastic

Set up, operate, or tend milling or planing machines to mill, plane, shape, groove, or profile metal or plastic workpieces.

- Education or Training Required: Moderate-term on-the-job training
- Job Growth: −5.3%
- Annual Openings: 2,000
- Self-Employed: 0.0%
- Part-Time: 7.2%

NATIONAL WAGE FIGURES (ANNUAL)

Beginning	25th Percentile	Median	Mean	75th Percentile	90th Percentile
$19,960	$24,760	$31,570	$32,280	$38,700	$46,170

Median Wages for Industries Employing Largest Numbers (Annual)

Industry	Median Income
Professional, Scientific, and Technical Services	$35,960
Transportation Equipment Manufacturing	$35,090
Computer and Electronic Product Manufacturing	$33,620
Machinery Manufacturing	$33,610
Primary Metal Manufacturing	$32,730
Food Manufacturing	$32,460
Nonmetallic Mineral Product Manufacturing	$31,590
Fabricated Metal Product Manufacturing	$30,200
Miscellaneous Manufacturing	$29,020
Chemical Manufacturing	$28,510

Median Wages for States (Annual)

State	Wage	State	Wage	State	Wage
AK	no data	KY	$29,390	NY	$31,660
AL	$35,480	LA	$28,630	OH	$28,640
AR	$27,090	MA	$36,800	OK	$24,470
AZ	$33,310	MD	$39,630	OR	$35,330
CA	$29,850	ME	$26,600	PA	$33,460
CO	$29,500	MI	$35,200	RI	$30,280
CT	$35,690	MN	$34,890	SC	$32,770
DC	no data	MO	$32,710	SD	no data
DE	no data	MS	$22,790	TN	$26,880
FL	$29,220	MT	$26,460	TX	$28,150
GA	$25,000	NC	$26,560	UT	$33,260
HI	no data	ND	no data	VA	$28,160
IA	$33,310	NE	$26,610	VT	$23,200
ID	$18,910	NH	$34,060	WA	$41,310
IL	$33,210	NJ	$32,470	WI	$32,020
IN	$36,260	NM	$24,150	WV	no data
KS	$30,560	NV	$36,000	WY	no data

Median Wages for the Largest Metropolitan Areas (Annual)

Area	Wage	Area	Wage
AZ: Phoenix	$33,980	MI: Detroit	$38,540
CA: Los Angeles	$27,150	MN: Minneapolis	$37,900
CA: Riverside	$30,080	MO: Kansas City	$30,760
CA: Sacramento	$36,690	MO: St. Louis	$30,940
CA: San Diego	$35,750	NV: Las Vegas	no data
CA: San Francisco	$35,520	NY: New York	$32,190
CO: Denver	$31,240	OH: Cincinnati	$31,010
DC: Washington	no data	OH: Cleveland	$29,680
FL: Miami	$32,470	OH: Columbus	$29,030
FL: Orlando	no data	OR: Portland	$34,750
FL: Tampa	$30,690	PA: Philadelphia	$33,020
GA: Atlanta	$31,680	PA: Pittsburgh	$35,040
IL: Chicago	$33,260	TX: Dallas	$26,890
MA: Boston	$40,050	TX: Houston	$30,140
MD: Baltimore	$28,210	WA: Seattle	$41,600

FACTORS THAT MAY AFFECT EARNINGS

Educational Attainment of Workers and Effect on Earnings

Figures are based on a group of occupations: Metal Workers and Plastic Workers

	Percent at Level	Effect on Earnings
Less than High School	5.6%	−31.1%
Some High School	11.6%	−16.7%
High School or Equivalent	42.1%	0.8%
Some College but No Degree	21.4%	4.0%
Associate Degree	12.4%	13.3%
Bachelor's Degree	5.8%	12.6%
Master's Degree	0.8%	−0.6%
Doctoral Degree	—	—
First Professional Degree	—	—

Flexibility of Earnings

Average Hours Worked: 39
Workers with a Varying Number of Hours: 3.7%
Workers Earning Some Overtime Pay, Tips, or Commissions: 16.7%
Earnings Benefit of Working Overtime: 14.8%

Gender

	Male	Female
Percent	85.2%	14.8%
Effect on Earnings	11.1%	−22.7%

Union Membership

Percentage Union Members: 16.7%
Earnings Benefit of Union Membership: 19.3%

Veteran Status

Percentage Who Have Been on Active Duty: 14.2%
Earnings Benefit of Veteran Status: 7.6%

51-4041 Machinists

Set up and operate a variety of machine tools to produce precision parts and instruments. Includes precision instrument makers who fabricate, modify, or repair mechanical instruments. May also fabricate and modify parts to make or repair machine tools or maintain industrial machines, applying knowledge of mechanics, shop mathematics, metal properties, layout, and machining procedures.

- Education or Training Required: Long-term on-the-job training
- Job Growth: 4.3%
- Annual Openings: 33,000
- Self-Employed: 1.0%
- Part-Time: 9.8%

NATIONAL WAGE FIGURES (ANNUAL)

Beginning	25th Percentile	Median	Mean	75th Percentile	90th Percentile
$21,400	$27,330	$34,770	$35,810	$43,300	$52,640

Median Wages for Industries Employing Largest Numbers (Annual)

Industry	Median Income
Utilities	$53,450
Federal, State, and Local Government	$48,490
Petroleum and Coal Products Manufacturing	$42,890
Educational Services	$42,030
Air Transportation	$41,140
Professional, Scientific, and Technical Services	$40,810
Rail Transportation	$40,240
Management of Companies and Enterprises	$39,620
Paper Manufacturing	$38,500
Transportation Equipment Manufacturing	$38,080

Median Wages for States (Annual)

AK	$49,250	KY	$30,930	NY	$35,650
AL	$32,810	LA	$35,910	OH	$33,890
AR	$31,840	MA	$39,300	OK	$32,180
AZ	$34,920	MD	$39,990	OR	$39,110
CA	$36,770	ME	$38,850	PA	$34,140
CO	$37,140	MI	$39,280	RI	$38,880
CT	$37,360	MN	$38,990	SC	$31,760
DC	$66,950	MO	$30,610	SD	$28,630
DE	$44,210	MS	$29,220	TN	$32,880
FL	$32,620	MT	$31,730	TX	$31,470
GA	$31,470	NC	$32,040	UT	$37,500
HI	$50,280	ND	$34,060	VA	$35,800
IA	$33,160	NE	$30,940	VT	$35,100
ID	$32,470	NH	$36,830	WA	$41,790
IL	$34,070	NJ	$39,170	WI	$36,440
IN	$35,780	NM	$45,240	WV	$33,130
KS	$30,520	NV	$37,340	WY	$38,330

Median Wages for the Largest Metropolitan Areas (Annual)

AZ: Phoenix	$34,840	MI: Detroit	$40,820
CA: Los Angeles	$35,220	MN: Minneapolis	$41,090
CA: Riverside	$31,380	MO: Kansas City	$35,120
CA: Sacramento	$37,560	MO: St. Louis	$36,680
CA: San Diego	$38,960	NV: Las Vegas	$35,410
CA: San Francisco	$43,900	NY: New York	$37,310
CO: Denver	$38,120	OH: Cincinnati	$33,030
DC: Washington	$39,130	OH: Cleveland	$32,400
FL: Miami	$30,030	OH: Columbus	$35,000
FL: Orlando	$29,410	OR: Portland	$39,850
FL: Tampa	$33,830	PA: Philadelphia	$39,130
GA: Atlanta	$34,370	PA: Pittsburgh	$32,720
IL: Chicago	$33,950	TX: Dallas	$31,420
MA: Boston	$40,380	TX: Houston	$32,770
MD: Baltimore	$40,780	WA: Seattle	$43,080

FACTORS THAT MAY AFFECT EARNINGS

Educational Attainment of Workers and Effect on Earnings

	Percent at Level	Effect on Earnings
Less than High School	4.0%	−42.8%
Some High School	11.5%	−13.0%
High School or Equivalent	41.1%	−2.6%
Some College but No Degree	21.7%	5.3%
Associate Degree	14.7%	11.8%
Bachelor's Degree	5.7%	15.3%
Master's Degree	—	—
Doctoral Degree	—	—
First Professional Degree	—	—

Flexibility of Earnings

Average Hours Worked: 39
Workers with a Varying Number of Hours: 4.5%
Workers Earning Some Overtime Pay, Tips, or Commissions: 29.0%
Earnings Benefit of Working Overtime: 12.4%

Gender

	Male	Female
Percent	93.3%	6.7%
Effect on Earnings	1.8%	—

Union Membership

Percentage Union Members: 17.6%
Earnings Benefit of Union Membership: 15.5%

Veteran Status

Percentage Who Have Been on Active Duty: 14.2%
Earnings Benefit of Veteran Status: 7.6%

51-4051 Metal-Refining Furnace Operators and Tenders

Operate or tend furnaces, such as gas, oil, coal, electric-arc or electric induction, open-hearth, or oxygen furnaces, to melt and refine metal before casting or to produce specified types of steel.

- Education or Training Required: Moderate-term on-the-job training
- Job Growth: –13.5%
- Annual Openings: 2,000
- Self-Employed: 0.2%
- Part-Time: 7.2%

NATIONAL WAGE FIGURES (ANNUAL)

Beginning	25th Percentile	Median	Mean	75th Percentile	90th Percentile
$21,600	$26,260	$32,640	$33,560	$39,650	$46,860

Median Wages for Industries Employing Largest Numbers (Annual)

Industry	Median Income
Mining (Except Oil and Gas)	$43,870
Nonmetallic Mineral Product Manufacturing	$33,790
Primary Metal Manufacturing	$33,300
Computer and Electronic Product Manufacturing	$31,550
Machinery Manufacturing	$31,360
Transportation Equipment Manufacturing	$31,040
Merchant Wholesalers, Durable Goods	$27,840
Fabricated Metal Product Manufacturing	$27,270
Chemical Manufacturing	$26,960

Median Wages for States (Annual)

AK	no data	KY	$37,120	NY	$35,340
AL	$28,120	LA	$29,850	OH	$31,650
AR	$36,490	MA	$36,580	OK	$32,900
AZ	$35,910	MD	no data	OR	no data
CA	$26,140	ME	no data	PA	$33,180
CO	$33,670	MI	$33,510	RI	$31,010
CT	$33,940	MN	$33,750	SC	$29,420
DC	no data	MO	no data	SD	no data
DE	no data	MS	$25,930	TN	$31,170
FL	$27,520	MT	no data	TX	$25,060
GA	$27,260	NC	$39,280	UT	$33,550
HI	no data	ND	no data	VA	$31,130
IA	$33,630	NE	no data	VT	no data
ID	no data	NH	no data	WA	$35,580
IL	$27,040	NJ	$28,200	WI	$33,100
IN	$36,420	NM	no data	WV	$36,200
KS	$28,000	NV	$49,120	WY	no data

Median Wages for the Largest Metropolitan Areas (Annual)

AZ: Phoenix	$33,150	MI: Detroit	$32,060
CA: Los Angeles	$24,700	MN: Minneapolis	$35,890
CA: Riverside	no data	MO: Kansas City	no data
CA: Sacramento	no data	MO: St. Louis	$34,540
CA: San Diego	no data	NV: Las Vegas	no data
CA: San Francisco	$33,220	NY: New York	$29,860
CO: Denver	no data	OH: Cincinnati	$40,800
DC: Washington	no data	OH: Cleveland	$33,120
FL: Miami	no data	OH: Columbus	no data
FL: Orlando	no data	OR: Portland	no data
FL: Tampa	$24,590	PA: Philadelphia	$35,150
GA: Atlanta	$29,540	PA: Pittsburgh	$34,900
IL: Chicago	$28,840	TX: Dallas	$24,930
MA: Boston	no data	TX: Houston	$22,090
MD: Baltimore	no data	WA: Seattle	no data

FACTORS THAT MAY AFFECT EARNINGS

Educational Attainment of Workers and Effect on Earnings

Figures are based on a group of occupations: Metal Workers and Plastic Workers

	Percent at Level	Effect on Earnings
Less than High School	5.6%	–31.1%
Some High School	11.6%	–16.7%
High School or Equivalent	42.1%	0.8%
Some College but No Degree	21.4%	4.0%
Associate Degree	12.4%	13.3%
Bachelor's Degree	5.8%	12.6%
Master's Degree	0.8%	–0.6%
Doctoral Degree	—	—
First Professional Degree	—	—

Flexibility of Earnings

Average Hours Worked: 38
Workers with a Varying Number of Hours: 4.8%
Workers Earning Some Overtime Pay, Tips, or Commissions: 28.1%
Earnings Benefit of Working Overtime: 14.8%

Gender

	Male	Female
Percent	88.4%	11.6%
Effect on Earnings	11.1%	–22.7%

Union Membership

Percentage Union Members: 18.5%
Earnings Benefit of Union Membership: 19.3%

Veteran Status

Percentage Who Have Been on Active Duty: 14.2%
Earnings Benefit of Veteran Status: 7.6%

51-4052 Pourers and Casters, Metal

Operate hand-controlled mechanisms to pour and regulate the flow of molten metal into molds to produce castings or ingots.

- Education or Training Required: Moderate-term on-the-job training
- Job Growth: –16.1%
- Annual Openings: 1,000
- Self-Employed: 0.2%
- Part-Time: 7.2%

NATIONAL WAGE FIGURES (ANNUAL)

Beginning	25th Percentile	Median	Mean	75th Percentile	90th Percentile
$20,060	$24,350	$29,570	$30,930	$35,850	$43,660

Median Wages for Industries Employing Largest Numbers (Annual)

Industry	Median Income
Machinery Manufacturing	$34,070
Primary Metal Manufacturing	$29,580
Transportation Equipment Manufacturing	$28,020
Miscellaneous Manufacturing	$23,080

Median Wages for States (Annual)

State	Wage	State	Wage	State	Wage
AK	no data	KY	$27,870	NY	$26,380
AL	$25,950	LA	no data	OH	$29,720
AR	$33,270	MA	$33,170	OK	$26,530
AZ	$27,540	MD	no data	OR	$28,770
CA	$24,730	ME	no data	PA	$30,460
CO	$20,580	MI	$27,780	RI	$22,440
CT	$33,530	MN	$33,300	SC	$36,680
DC	no data	MO	$27,230	SD	$22,750
DE	no data	MS	no data	TN	$34,310
FL	$26,250	MT	$39,710	TX	$31,200
GA	$26,980	NC	$31,640	UT	$23,940
HI	no data	ND	no data	VA	$28,920
IA	$30,910	NE	$29,180	VT	no data
ID	$25,420	NH	$33,440	WA	$29,920
IL	$30,100	NJ	$26,290	WI	$30,800
IN	$33,280	NM	no data	WV	no data
KS	$22,540	NV	no data	WY	no data

Median Wages for the Largest Metropolitan Areas (Annual)

Area	Wage	Area	Wage
AZ: Phoenix	$28,270	MI: Detroit	$28,290
CA: Los Angeles	$22,170	MN: Minneapolis	$35,140
CA: Riverside	$40,760	MO: Kansas City	no data
CA: Sacramento	no data	MO: St. Louis	$47,960
CA: San Diego	$21,930	NV: Las Vegas	no data
CA: San Francisco	$31,030	NY: New York	$26,140
CO: Denver	$19,290	OH: Cincinnati	$28,660
DC: Washington	no data	OH: Cleveland	$29,730
FL: Miami	no data	OH: Columbus	$32,730
FL: Orlando	no data	OR: Portland	$28,990
FL: Tampa	no data	PA: Philadelphia	$36,500
GA: Atlanta	$27,200	PA: Pittsburgh	$30,000
IL: Chicago	$30,370	TX: Dallas	$27,300
MA: Boston	$33,470	TX: Houston	$20,680
MD: Baltimore	no data	WA: Seattle	$29,700

FACTORS THAT MAY AFFECT EARNINGS

Educational Attainment of Workers and Effect on Earnings

Figures are based on a group of occupations: Metal Workers and Plastic Workers

	Percent at Level	Effect on Earnings
Less than High School	5.6%	–31.1%
Some High School	11.6%	–16.7%
High School or Equivalent	42.1%	0.8%
Some College but No Degree	21.4%	4.0%
Associate Degree	12.4%	13.3%
Bachelor's Degree	5.8%	12.6%
Master's Degree	0.8%	–0.6%
Doctoral Degree	—	—
First Professional Degree	—	—

Flexibility of Earnings

Average Hours Worked: 38
Workers with a Varying Number of Hours: 4.8%
Workers Earning Some Overtime Pay, Tips, or Commissions: 28.1%
Earnings Benefit of Working Overtime: 14.8%

Gender

	Male	Female
Percent	88.4%	11.6%
Effect on Earnings	11.1%	–22.7%

Union Membership

Percentage Union Members: 18.5%
Earnings Benefit of Union Membership: 19.3%

Veteran Status

Percentage Who Have Been on Active Duty: 14.2%
Earnings Benefit of Veteran Status: 7.6%

51-4061 Model Makers, Metal and Plastic

Set up and operate machines, such as lathes, milling and engraving machines, and jig borers, to make working models of metal or plastic objects.

- Education or Training Required: Moderate-term on-the-job training
- Job Growth: –4.0%
- Annual Openings: 1,000
- Self-Employed: 0.0%
- Part-Time: 7.2%

NATIONAL WAGE FIGURES (ANNUAL)

Beginning	25th Percentile	Median	Mean	75th Percentile	90th Percentile
$22,800	$30,650	$42,050	$44,130	$57,270	$71,590

Median Wages for Industries Employing Largest Numbers (Annual)

Industry	Median Income
Computer and Electronic Product Manufacturing	$49,080
Management of Companies and Enterprises	$47,350
Federal, State, and Local Government	$45,720
Electrical Equipment, Appliance, and Component Manufacturing	$43,650
Machinery Manufacturing	$40,170
Furniture and Related Product Manufacturing	$39,870
Professional, Scientific, and Technical Services	$39,760
Miscellaneous Manufacturing	$36,040
Fabricated Metal Product Manufacturing	$35,510
Primary Metal Manufacturing	$32,320

Median Wages for States (Annual)

State	Wage	State	Wage	State	Wage
AK	no data	KY	$35,640	NY	$41,690
AL	$22,840	LA	$29,660	OH	$38,910
AR	$45,750	MA	$47,190	OK	$28,640
AZ	$30,060	MD	$36,580	OR	$57,050
CA	$39,330	ME	no data	PA	$32,720
CO	$36,180	MI	no data	RI	no data
CT	$48,870	MN	$48,420	SC	$41,060
DC	no data	MO	$32,040	SD	no data
DE	no data	MS	no data	TN	$31,370
FL	$33,950	MT	no data	TX	$29,360
GA	no data	NC	$33,870	UT	$38,210
HI	no data	ND	no data	VA	$28,870
IA	$38,120	NE	no data	VT	$36,980
ID	$21,890	NH	no data	WA	no data
IL	$37,730	NJ	$34,970	WI	$44,270
IN	$44,230	NM	no data	WV	no data
KS	$27,790	NV	no data	WY	no data

Median Wages for the Largest Metropolitan Areas (Annual)

Area	Wage	Area	Wage
AZ: Phoenix	$29,320	MI: Detroit	no data
CA: Los Angeles	$40,300	MN: Minneapolis	$51,080
CA: Riverside	no data	MO: Kansas City	no data
CA: Sacramento	no data	MO: St. Louis	no data
CA: San Diego	no data	NV: Las Vegas	no data
CA: San Francisco	no data	NY: New York	$38,260
CO: Denver	$31,270	OH: Cincinnati	no data
DC: Washington	no data	OH: Cleveland	no data
FL: Miami	$27,320	OH: Columbus	$39,280
FL: Orlando	no data	OR: Portland	$57,680
FL: Tampa	no data	PA: Philadelphia	$36,810
GA: Atlanta	no data	PA: Pittsburgh	$34,530
IL: Chicago	$37,700	TX: Dallas	no data
MA: Boston	$50,170	TX: Houston	$30,520
MD: Baltimore	$34,590	WA: Seattle	no data

FACTORS THAT MAY AFFECT EARNINGS

Educational Attainment of Workers and Effect on Earnings

Figures are based on a group of occupations: Metal Workers and Plastic Workers

	Percent at Level	Effect on Earnings
Less than High School	5.6%	–31.1%
Some High School	11.6%	–16.7%
High School or Equivalent	42.1%	0.8%
Some College but No Degree	21.4%	4.0%
Associate Degree	12.4%	13.3%
Bachelor's Degree	5.8%	12.6%
Master's Degree	0.8%	–0.6%
Doctoral Degree	—	—
First Professional Degree	—	—

Flexibility of Earnings

Average Hours Worked: 38
Workers with a Varying Number of Hours: 4.8%
Workers Earning Some Overtime Pay, Tips, or Commissions: 28.1%
Earnings Benefit of Working Overtime: 14.8%

Gender

	Male	Female
Percent	88.4%	11.6%
Effect on Earnings	11.1%	–22.7%

Union Membership

Percentage Union Members: 18.5%
Earnings Benefit of Union Membership: 19.3%

Veteran Status

Percentage Who Have Been on Active Duty: 14.2%
Earnings Benefit of Veteran Status: 7.6%

51-4062 Patternmakers, Metal and Plastic

Lay out, machine, fit, and assemble castings and parts to metal or plastic foundry patterns, core boxes, or match plates.

- Education or Training Required: Moderate-term on-the-job training
- Job Growth: –7.5%
- Annual Openings: 1,000
- Self-Employed: 0.0%
- Part-Time: 7.2%

NATIONAL WAGE FIGURES (ANNUAL)

Beginning	25th Percentile	Median	Mean	75th Percentile	90th Percentile
$21,340	$27,140	$35,380	$38,090	$48,160	$59,260

Median Wages for Industries Employing Largest Numbers (Annual)

Industry	Median Income
Transportation Equipment Manufacturing	$46,390
Fabricated Metal Product Manufacturing	$38,770
Machinery Manufacturing	$36,500
Primary Metal Manufacturing	$34,500
Plastics and Rubber Products Manufacturing	$26,020
Merchant Wholesalers, Durable Goods	$23,790
Miscellaneous Manufacturing	$22,590

Median Wages for States (Annual)

State		State		State	
AK	no data	KY	no data	NY	$33,190
AL	$30,740	LA	no data	OH	$41,870
AR	no data	MA	$35,480	OK	$23,840
AZ	$26,380	MD	no data	OR	$32,750
CA	$45,480	ME	no data	PA	$33,880
CO	no data	MI	$51,130	RI	no data
CT	no data	MN	$38,640	SC	$27,940
DC	no data	MO	$40,910	SD	no data
DE	no data	MS	no data	TN	$38,260
FL	$30,980	MT	no data	TX	$23,870
GA	no data	NC	$34,740	UT	no data
HI	no data	ND	no data	VA	$33,830
IA	$40,690	NE	no data	VT	no data
ID	no data	NH	no data	WA	no data
IL	$32,670	NJ	no data	WI	$36,240
IN	$43,850	NM	no data	WV	no data
KS	$47,500	NV	no data	WY	no data

Median Wages for the Largest Metropolitan Areas (Annual)

Area		Area	
AZ: Phoenix	$26,510	MI: Detroit	$43,290
CA: Los Angeles	$48,430	MN: Minneapolis	no data
CA: Riverside	no data	MO: Kansas City	no data
CA: Sacramento	no data	MO: St. Louis	$53,520
CA: San Diego	$29,880	NV: Las Vegas	no data
CA: San Francisco	$53,340	NY: New York	$30,700
CO: Denver	no data	OH: Cincinnati	$41,350
DC: Washington	no data	OH: Cleveland	no data
FL: Miami	no data	OH: Columbus	no data
FL: Orlando	no data	OR: Portland	no data
FL: Tampa	$21,680	PA: Philadelphia	no data
GA: Atlanta	$51,720	PA: Pittsburgh	no data
IL: Chicago	$32,050	TX: Dallas	$30,500
MA: Boston	no data	TX: Houston	$24,040
MD: Baltimore	no data	WA: Seattle	$55,730

FACTORS THAT MAY AFFECT EARNINGS

Educational Attainment of Workers and Effect on Earnings

Figures are based on a group of occupations: Metal Workers and Plastic Workers

	Percent at Level	Effect on Earnings
Less than High School	5.6%	–31.1%
Some High School	11.6%	–16.7%
High School or Equivalent	42.1%	0.8%
Some College but No Degree	21.4%	4.0%
Associate Degree	12.4%	13.3%
Bachelor's Degree	5.8%	12.6%
Master's Degree	0.8%	–0.6%
Doctoral Degree	—	—
First Professional Degree	—	—

Flexibility of Earnings

Average Hours Worked: 38
Workers with a Varying Number of Hours: 4.8%
Workers Earning Some Overtime Pay, Tips, or Commissions: 28.1%
Earnings Benefit of Working Overtime: 14.8%

Gender

	Male	Female
Percent	88.4%	11.6%
Effect on Earnings	11.1%	–22.7%

Union Membership

Percentage Union Members: 18.5%
Earnings Benefit of Union Membership: 19.3%

Veteran Status

Percentage Who Have Been on Active Duty: 14.2%
Earnings Benefit of Veteran Status: 7.6%

51-4071 Foundry Mold and Coremakers

Make or form wax or sand cores or molds used in the production of metal castings in foundries.

- Education or Training Required: Moderate-term on-the-job training
- Job Growth: −13.3%
- Annual Openings: 2,000
- Self-Employed: 0.4%
- Part-Time: 7.2%

NATIONAL WAGE FIGURES (ANNUAL)

Beginning	25th Percentile	Median	Mean	75th Percentile	90th Percentile
$19,390	$23,330	$28,740	$29,950	$35,120	$42,630

Median Wages for Industries Employing Largest Numbers (Annual)

Industry	Median Income
Machinery Manufacturing	$39,340
Electrical Equipment, Appliance, and Component Manufacturing	$32,080
Plastics and Rubber Products Manufacturing	$31,250
Administrative and Support Services	$28,780
Nonmetallic Mineral Product Manufacturing	$28,560
Transportation Equipment Manufacturing	$28,430
Primary Metal Manufacturing	$28,250
Fabricated Metal Product Manufacturing	$26,320

Median Wages for States (Annual)

State	Wage	State	Wage	State	Wage
AK	no data	KY	no data	NY	$32,180
AL	$26,990	LA	no data	OH	$27,460
AR	no data	MA	$36,300	OK	$24,930
AZ	$29,360	MD	no data	OR	no data
CA	$24,200	ME	no data	PA	$27,470
CO	$23,890	MI	$33,480	RI	$46,400
CT	$27,860	MN	$32,330	SC	$31,640
DC	no data	MO	$31,130	SD	no data
DE	no data	MS	$27,020	TN	no data
FL	$27,090	MT	no data	TX	$22,350
GA	$28,040	NC	$22,880	UT	$24,350
HI	no data	ND	no data	VA	$26,570
IA	$28,760	NE	$29,540	VT	$29,260
ID	$22,630	NH	$28,880	WA	$27,880
IL	$31,800	NJ	$27,640	WI	$29,670
IN	$31,570	NM	$24,320	WV	$26,530
KS	$26,840	NV	no data	WY	no data

Median Wages for the Largest Metropolitan Areas (Annual)

Area	Wage	Area	Wage
AZ: Phoenix	$29,850	MI: Detroit	$40,110
CA: Los Angeles	$22,940	MN: Minneapolis	$34,900
CA: Riverside	$25,470	MO: Kansas City	$33,330
CA: Sacramento	no data	MO: St. Louis	$31,730
CA: San Diego	$24,450	NV: Las Vegas	no data
CA: San Francisco	$32,750	NY: New York	$29,150
CO: Denver	$21,230	OH: Cincinnati	$28,140
DC: Washington	no data	OH: Cleveland	$28,380
FL: Miami	$29,520	OH: Columbus	$24,740
FL: Orlando	no data	OR: Portland	no data
FL: Tampa	$26,190	PA: Philadelphia	$35,490
GA: Atlanta	$25,040	PA: Pittsburgh	$29,530
IL: Chicago	$27,160	TX: Dallas	$20,410
MA: Boston	$36,350	TX: Houston	$24,760
MD: Baltimore	no data	WA: Seattle	$29,010

FACTORS THAT MAY AFFECT EARNINGS

Educational Attainment of Workers and Effect on Earnings

Figures are based on a group of occupations: Metal Workers and Plastic Workers

	Percent at Level	Effect on Earnings
Less than High School	5.6%	−31.1%
Some High School	11.6%	−16.7%
High School or Equivalent	42.1%	0.8%
Some College but No Degree	21.4%	4.0%
Associate Degree	12.4%	13.3%
Bachelor's Degree	5.8%	12.6%
Master's Degree	0.8%	−0.6%
Doctoral Degree	—	—
First Professional Degree	—	—

Flexibility of Earnings

Average Hours Worked: 38
Workers with a Varying Number of Hours: 4.8%
Workers Earning Some Overtime Pay, Tips, or Commissions: 28.1%
Earnings Benefit of Working Overtime: 14.8%

Gender

	Male	Female
Percent	88.4%	11.6%
Effect on Earnings	11.1%	−22.7%

Union Membership

Percentage Union Members: 18.5%
Earnings Benefit of Union Membership: 19.3%

Veteran Status

Percentage Who Have Been on Active Duty: 14.2%
Earnings Benefit of Veteran Status: 7.6%

51-4072 Molding, Coremaking, and Casting Machine Setters, Operators, and Tenders, Metal and Plastic

Set up, operate, or tend metal or plastic molding, casting, or coremaking machines to mold or cast metal or thermoplastic parts or products.

- Education or Training Required: Moderate-term on-the-job training
- Job Growth: −9.5%
- Annual Openings: 17,000
- Self-Employed: 0.3%
- Part-Time: 7.2%

NATIONAL WAGE FIGURES (ANNUAL)

Beginning	25th Percentile	Median	Mean	75th Percentile	90th Percentile
$16,890	$20,320	$25,560	$27,330	$32,400	$40,270

Median Wages for Industries Employing Largest Numbers (Annual)

Industry	Median Income
Federal, State, and Local Government	$46,920
Paper Manufacturing	$32,600
Professional, Scientific, and Technical Services	$32,100
Primary Metal Manufacturing	$28,510
Food Manufacturing	$28,090
Electrical Equipment, Appliance, and Component Manufacturing	$28,060
Transportation Equipment Manufacturing	$27,940
Management of Companies and Enterprises	$27,860
Machinery Manufacturing	$27,650
Miscellaneous Manufacturing	$27,320

Median Wages for States (Annual)

AK	no data	KY	$24,380	NY	$25,080
AL	$24,020	LA	$21,020	OH	$24,630
AR	$23,050	MA	$27,610	OK	$23,370
AZ	$26,090	MD	$25,730	OR	$26,040
CA	$21,850	ME	$29,840	PA	$27,430
CO	$23,770	MI	$27,220	RI	$23,670
CT	$26,500	MN	$28,230	SC	$26,040
DC	no data	MO	$22,190	SD	$22,580
DE	no data	MS	$23,670	TN	$25,800
FL	$23,470	MT	$20,560	TX	$22,390
GA	$29,100	NC	$25,780	UT	$23,080
HI	$52,260	ND	$20,880	VA	$26,930
IA	$25,270	NE	$25,860	VT	$24,230
ID	$21,980	NH	$27,830	WA	$26,610
IL	$26,670	NJ	$22,980	WI	$28,020
IN	$28,250	NM	$20,970	WV	$21,750
KS	$24,200	NV	$18,440	WY	$19,490

Median Wages for the Largest Metropolitan Areas (Annual)

AZ: Phoenix	$26,430	MI: Detroit	no data
CA: Los Angeles	$20,650	MN: Minneapolis	$28,760
CA: Riverside	$20,530	MO: Kansas City	$23,730
CA: Sacramento	$26,920	MO: St. Louis	$22,810
CA: San Diego	$20,980	NV: Las Vegas	$21,320
CA: San Francisco	$25,980	NY: New York	$21,880
CO: Denver	$22,890	OH: Cincinnati	$23,480
DC: Washington	$25,450	OH: Cleveland	$26,230
FL: Miami	$19,940	OH: Columbus	$23,130
FL: Orlando	$25,530	OR: Portland	$27,320
FL: Tampa	$23,220	PA: Philadelphia	$27,660
GA: Atlanta	$30,390	PA: Pittsburgh	$32,270
IL: Chicago	$26,120	TX: Dallas	$23,210
MA: Boston	$29,150	TX: Houston	$22,190
MD: Baltimore	$26,100	WA: Seattle	$26,950

FACTORS THAT MAY AFFECT EARNINGS

Educational Attainment of Workers and Effect on Earnings

Figures are based on a group of occupations: Metal Workers and Plastic Workers

	Percent at Level	Effect on Earnings
Less than High School	5.6%	−31.1%
Some High School	11.6%	−16.7%
High School or Equivalent	42.1%	0.8%
Some College but No Degree	21.4%	4.0%
Associate Degree	12.4%	13.3%
Bachelor's Degree	5.8%	12.6%
Master's Degree	0.8%	−0.6%
Doctoral Degree	—	—
First Professional Degree	—	—

Flexibility of Earnings

Average Hours Worked: 38
Workers with a Varying Number of Hours: 4.8%
Workers Earning Some Overtime Pay, Tips, or Commissions: 28.1%
Earnings Benefit of Working Overtime: 14.8%

Gender

	Male	Female
Percent	82.9%	17.1%
Effect on Earnings	1.4%	—

Union Membership

Percentage Union Members: 18.5%
Earnings Benefit of Union Membership: 19.3%

Veteran Status

Percentage Who Have Been on Active Duty: 14.2%
Earnings Benefit of Veteran Status: 7.6%

51-4081 Multiple Machine Tool Setters, Operators, and Tenders, Metal and Plastic

Set up, operate, or tend more than one type of cutting or forming machine tool or robot.

- Education or Training Required: Moderate-term on-the-job training
- Job Growth: 0.3%
- Annual Openings: 6,000
- Self-Employed: 0.0%
- Part-Time: 25.0%

NATIONAL WAGE FIGURES (ANNUAL)

Beginning	25th Percentile	Median	Mean	75th Percentile	90th Percentile
$19,120	$23,630	$30,530	$32,140	$38,710	$49,890

Median Wages for Industries Employing Largest Numbers (Annual)

Industry	Median Income
Transportation Equipment Manufacturing	$37,650
Computer and Electronic Product Manufacturing	$34,030
Paper Manufacturing	$33,600
Machinery Manufacturing	$31,890
Electrical Equipment, Appliance, and Component Manufacturing	$30,940
Food Manufacturing	$30,330
Professional, Scientific, and Technical Services	$29,970
Primary Metal Manufacturing	$29,860
Fabricated Metal Product Manufacturing	$29,000
Merchant Wholesalers, Durable Goods	$28,640

Median Wages for States (Annual)

State	Wage	State	Wage	State	Wage
AK	no data	KY	$28,190	NY	$28,490
AL	$25,060	LA	$36,650	OH	$34,810
AR	$27,780	MA	$33,210	OK	$31,830
AZ	$23,940	MD	$30,020	OR	$29,140
CA	$27,590	ME	no data	PA	$31,030
CO	$28,030	MI	$37,060	RI	$28,490
CT	$34,150	MN	$35,880	SC	$29,620
DC	no data	MO	$28,820	SD	$22,110
DE	no data	MS	$21,870	TN	$26,970
FL	$24,680	MT	no data	TX	$21,430
GA	$26,740	NC	$32,540	UT	$24,020
HI	no data	ND	$23,540	VA	$28,040
IA	$31,290	NE	$31,910	VT	no data
ID	no data	NH	$36,960	WA	$32,330
IL	$27,980	NJ	$29,980	WI	$34,120
IN	$34,420	NM	no data	WV	$25,820
KS	$26,780	NV	$31,690	WY	no data

Median Wages for the Largest Metropolitan Areas (Annual)

Area	Wage	Area	Wage
AZ: Phoenix	$22,760	MI: Detroit	$34,360
CA: Los Angeles	$26,620	MN: Minneapolis	$38,860
CA: Riverside	$26,560	MO: Kansas City	$27,590
CA: Sacramento	$32,440	MO: St. Louis	$33,470
CA: San Diego	$27,220	NV: Las Vegas	no data
CA: San Francisco	$29,140	NY: New York	$30,040
CO: Denver	$29,360	OH: Cincinnati	$38,140
DC: Washington	$22,950	OH: Cleveland	$32,490
FL: Miami	$21,600	OH: Columbus	$32,440
FL: Orlando	$20,840	OR: Portland	$30,410
FL: Tampa	$26,910	PA: Philadelphia	$31,400
GA: Atlanta	$26,060	PA: Pittsburgh	$31,560
IL: Chicago	$27,210	TX: Dallas	$23,240
MA: Boston	$33,360	TX: Houston	$21,430
MD: Baltimore	$29,940	WA: Seattle	$32,790

FACTORS THAT MAY AFFECT EARNINGS

Educational Attainment of Workers and Effect on Earnings

Figures are based on a group of occupations: Metal Workers and Plastic Workers

	Percent at Level	Effect on Earnings
Less than High School	5.6%	−31.1%
Some High School	11.6%	−16.7%
High School or Equivalent	42.1%	0.8%
Some College but No Degree	21.4%	4.0%
Associate Degree	12.4%	13.3%
Bachelor's Degree	5.8%	12.6%
Master's Degree	0.8%	−0.6%
Doctoral Degree	—	—
First Professional Degree	—	—

Flexibility of Earnings

Average Hours Worked: 39
Workers with a Varying Number of Hours: 9.3%
Workers Earning Some Overtime Pay, Tips, or Commissions: 20.0%
Earnings Benefit of Working Overtime: 14.8%

Gender

	Male	Female
Percent	57.8%	42.2%
Effect on Earnings	11.1%	−22.7%

Union Membership

Percentage Union Members: 30.0%
Earnings Benefit of Union Membership: 19.3%

Veteran Status

Percentage Who Have Been on Active Duty: 14.2%
Earnings Benefit of Veteran Status: 7.6%

51-4111 Tool and Die Makers

Analyze specifications; lay out metal stock; set up and operate machine tools; and fit and assemble parts to make and repair dies, cutting tools, jigs, fixtures, gauges, and machinists' hand tools.

- Education or Training Required: Long-term on-the-job training
- Job Growth: –2.6%
- Annual Openings: 7,000
- Self-Employed: 2.7%
- Part-Time: 9.7%

NATIONAL WAGE FIGURES (ANNUAL)

Beginning	25th Percentile	Median	Mean	75th Percentile	90th Percentile
$28,810	$35,970	$44,290	$45,650	$55,670	$67,420

Median Wages for Industries Employing Largest Numbers (Annual)

Industry	Median Income
Transportation Equipment Manufacturing	$56,720
Federal, State, and Local Government	$55,640
Computer and Electronic Product Manufacturing	$47,080
Management of Companies and Enterprises	$46,280
Chemical Manufacturing	$45,740
Professional, Scientific, and Technical Services	$45,280
Furniture and Related Product Manufacturing	$44,740
Electrical Equipment, Appliance, and Component Manufacturing	$43,970
Administrative and Support Services	$43,560
Miscellaneous Manufacturing	$43,430

Median Wages for States (Annual)

AK	no data	KY	$42,740	NY	$42,880
AL	$40,470	LA	$47,870	OH	$43,510
AR	$35,700	MA	$42,840	OK	$43,260
AZ	$43,130	MD	$43,700	OR	$47,120
CA	$45,710	ME	$43,180	PA	$39,520
CO	$44,900	MI	$51,350	RI	$43,090
CT	$50,080	MN	$46,370	SC	$41,740
DC	no data	MO	$43,960	SD	$35,650
DE	no data	MS	$36,800	TN	$41,720
FL	$37,090	MT	$41,830	TX	$36,730
GA	$39,690	NC	$39,800	UT	$43,620
HI	no data	ND	$35,860	VA	$42,160
IA	$39,620	NE	$40,810	VT	$45,120
ID	$36,640	NH	$41,650	WA	$61,400
IL	$47,370	NJ	$46,210	WI	$45,110
IN	$45,260	NM	$51,080	WV	$34,090
KS	$47,430	NV	$45,300	WY	no data

Median Wages for the Largest Metropolitan Areas (Annual)

AZ: Phoenix	$42,900	MI: Detroit	$53,580
CA: Los Angeles	$46,190	MN: Minneapolis	$47,990
CA: Riverside	$42,090	MO: Kansas City	$44,880
CA: Sacramento	$42,990	MO: St. Louis	$50,560
CA: San Diego	$43,960	NV: Las Vegas	$41,830
CA: San Francisco	$58,370	NY: New York	$45,270
CO: Denver	$43,490	OH: Cincinnati	$44,260
DC: Washington	$43,980	OH: Cleveland	$42,960
FL: Miami	$37,740	OH: Columbus	$40,410
FL: Orlando	$39,320	OR: Portland	$50,380
FL: Tampa	$33,050	PA: Philadelphia	$45,270
GA: Atlanta	$42,230	PA: Pittsburgh	$37,060
IL: Chicago	$48,900	TX: Dallas	$37,990
MA: Boston	$45,340	TX: Houston	$37,260
MD: Baltimore	$44,640	WA: Seattle	no data

FACTORS THAT MAY AFFECT EARNINGS

Educational Attainment of Workers and Effect on Earnings

	Percent at Level	Effect on Earnings
Less than High School	—	—
Some High School	—	—
High School or Equivalent	42.6%	–1.7%
Some College but No Degree	25.9%	5.3%
Associate Degree	22.2%	7.6%
Bachelor's Degree	—	—
Master's Degree	—	—
Doctoral Degree	—	—
First Professional Degree	—	—

Figures do not total 100% because some levels have a very small sample size.

Flexibility of Earnings

Average Hours Worked: 39
Workers with a Varying Number of Hours: 5.5%
Workers Earning Some Overtime Pay, Tips, or Commissions: 28.6%
Earnings Benefit of Working Overtime: 10.4%

Gender

	Male	Female
Percent	99.1%	0.9%
Effect on Earnings	–0.4%	—

Union Membership

Percentage Union Members: 24.4%
Earnings Benefit of Union Membership: 17.0%

Veteran Status

Percentage Who Have Been on Active Duty: 14.2%
Earnings Benefit of Veteran Status: 7.6%

51-4121 Welders, Cutters, Solderers, and Brazers

Use hand-welding, flame-cutting, hand soldering, or brazing equipment to weld or join metal components or to fill holes, indentations, or seams of fabricated metal products.

- Education or Training Required: Long-term on-the-job training
- Job Growth: 5.0%
- Annual Openings: 52,000
- Self-Employed: 6.3%
- Part-Time: 7.2%

NATIONAL WAGE FIGURES (ANNUAL)

Beginning	25th Percentile	Median	Mean	75th Percentile	90th Percentile
$20,970	$25,590	$31,400	$32,880	$38,410	$46,800

Median Wages for Industries Employing Largest Numbers (Annual)

Industry	Median Income
Federal, State, and Local Government	$45,340
Utilities	$44,320
Rail Transportation	$41,140
Professional, Scientific, and Technical Services	$37,220
Mining (Except Oil and Gas)	$36,340
Heavy and Civil Engineering Construction	$35,730
Support Activities for Mining	$35,460
Construction of Buildings	$34,740
Waste Management and Remediation Services	$33,830
Specialty Trade Contractors	$33,350

Median Wages for States (Annual)

State	Wage	State	Wage	State	Wage
AK	$48,730	KY	$29,950	NY	$32,830
AL	$29,160	LA	$34,980	OH	$31,540
AR	$26,740	MA	$36,150	OK	$29,030
AZ	$29,200	MD	$34,220	OR	$32,110
CA	$31,530	ME	$32,900	PA	$32,900
CO	$32,640	MI	$35,610	RI	$36,070
CT	$37,010	MN	$34,510	SC	$31,080
DC	$54,930	MO	$29,310	SD	$26,460
DE	$33,800	MS	$30,570	TN	$30,120
FL	$30,150	MT	no data	TX	$28,880
GA	$28,690	NC	$31,450	UT	$30,920
HI	$49,160	ND	$32,000	VA	$33,720
IA	$30,060	NE	$28,190	VT	$29,660
ID	$30,360	NH	$36,450	WA	$39,290
IL	$31,380	NJ	$36,580	WI	$33,450
IN	$31,960	NM	$29,540	WV	$28,970
KS	$27,150	NV	$37,960	WY	$36,070

Median Wages for the Largest Metropolitan Areas (Annual)

Area	Wage	Area	Wage
AZ: Phoenix	$28,850	MI: Detroit	$45,540
CA: Los Angeles	$28,330	MN: Minneapolis	$39,120
CA: Riverside	$30,100	MO: Kansas City	$31,710
CA: Sacramento	$33,860	MO: St. Louis	$31,020
CA: San Diego	$33,710	NV: Las Vegas	$37,830
CA: San Francisco	$42,250	NY: New York	$34,260
CO: Denver	$32,110	OH: Cincinnati	$34,290
DC: Washington	$37,140	OH: Cleveland	$32,340
FL: Miami	$30,670	OH: Columbus	$30,470
FL: Orlando	$31,470	OR: Portland	$34,390
FL: Tampa	$31,250	PA: Philadelphia	$36,840
GA: Atlanta	$28,670	PA: Pittsburgh	$33,150
IL: Chicago	$34,040	TX: Dallas	$28,270
MA: Boston	$36,930	TX: Houston	$31,990
MD: Baltimore	$34,010	WA: Seattle	$41,060

FACTORS THAT MAY AFFECT EARNINGS

Educational Attainment of Workers and Effect on Earnings

Figures are based on a group of occupations: Metal Workers and Plastic Workers

	Percent at Level	Effect on Earnings
Less than High School	5.6%	−31.1%
Some High School	11.6%	−16.7%
High School or Equivalent	42.1%	0.8%
Some College but No Degree	21.4%	4.0%
Associate Degree	12.4%	13.3%
Bachelor's Degree	5.8%	12.6%
Master's Degree	0.8%	−0.6%
Doctoral Degree	—	—
First Professional Degree	—	—

Flexibility of Earnings

Average Hours Worked: 38
Workers with a Varying Number of Hours: 4.8%
Workers Earning Some Overtime Pay, Tips, or Commissions: 28.1%
Earnings Benefit of Working Overtime: 10.0%

Gender

	Male	Female
Percent	94.1%	5.9%
Effect on Earnings	3.9%	—

Union Membership

Percentage Union Members: 18.5%
Earnings Benefit of Union Membership: 19.3%

Veteran Status

Percentage Who Have Been on Active Duty: 14.2%
Earnings Benefit of Veteran Status: 7.6%

51-4122 Welding, Soldering, and Brazing Machine Setters, Operators, and Tenders

Set up, operate, or tend welding, soldering, or brazing machines or robots that weld, braze, solder, or heat-treat metal products, components, or assemblies.

- Education or Training Required: Moderate-term on-the-job training
- Job Growth: 0.4%
- Annual Openings: 7,000
- Self-Employed: 7.4%
- Part-Time: 7.2%

NATIONAL WAGE FIGURES (ANNUAL)

Beginning	25th Percentile	Median	Mean	75th Percentile	90th Percentile
$20,700	$25,010	$30,980	$33,440	$39,310	$52,920

Median Wages for Industries Employing Largest Numbers (Annual)

Industry	Median Income
Federal, State, and Local Government	$43,260
Food Manufacturing	$42,270
Mining (Except Oil and Gas)	$36,780
Professional, Scientific, and Technical Services	$35,110
Heavy and Civil Engineering Construction	$34,940
Transportation Equipment Manufacturing	$34,550
Nonmetallic Mineral Product Manufacturing	$33,120
Electrical Equipment, Appliance, and Component Manufacturing	$31,480
Specialty Trade Contractors	$31,250
Machinery Manufacturing	$31,180

Median Wages for States (Annual)

AK	no data	KY	$29,470	NY	$39,680
AL	$52,030	LA	$35,170	OH	$30,660
AR	$27,800	MA	$36,590	OK	$30,530
AZ	$29,620	MD	$32,260	OR	$30,570
CA	$28,500	ME	no data	PA	$29,980
CO	$37,140	MI	$49,320	RI	$25,270
CT	$33,190	MN	$34,120	SC	$30,870
DC	no data	MO	$26,630	SD	$28,730
DE	$43,810	MS	$29,380	TN	$26,610
FL	$25,890	MT	$29,620	TX	$24,820
GA	$28,520	NC	$29,060	UT	$28,930
HI	no data	ND	no data	VA	$32,760
IA	$31,870	NE	$28,240	VT	$26,810
ID	$28,000	NH	$30,560	WA	$36,070
IL	$32,010	NJ	$31,970	WI	$31,770
IN	$28,140	NM	$30,150	WV	$30,330
KS	$27,390	NV	$32,670	WY	$23,720

Median Wages for the Largest Metropolitan Areas (Annual)

AZ: Phoenix	$29,600	MI: Detroit	no data
CA: Los Angeles	$29,970	MN: Minneapolis	$39,590
CA: Riverside	$23,860	MO: Kansas City	$28,860
CA: Sacramento	$25,470	MO: St. Louis	$29,350
CA: San Diego	$29,780	NV: Las Vegas	$30,240
CA: San Francisco	$28,370	NY: New York	$32,390
CO: Denver	no data	OH: Cincinnati	$28,530
DC: Washington	$30,560	OH: Cleveland	$31,050
FL: Miami	$31,420	OH: Columbus	$28,700
FL: Orlando	$25,280	OR: Portland	$28,630
FL: Tampa	$24,670	PA: Philadelphia	$31,510
GA: Atlanta	$28,800	PA: Pittsburgh	$30,460
IL: Chicago	$30,190	TX: Dallas	$26,150
MA: Boston	$35,510	TX: Houston	$23,800
MD: Baltimore	$32,040	WA: Seattle	$37,210

FACTORS THAT MAY AFFECT EARNINGS

Educational Attainment of Workers and Effect on Earnings

Figures are based on a group of occupations: Metal Workers and Plastic Workers

	Percent at Level	Effect on Earnings
Less than High School	5.6%	−31.1%
Some High School	11.6%	−16.7%
High School or Equivalent	42.1%	0.8%
Some College but No Degree	21.4%	4.0%
Associate Degree	12.4%	13.3%
Bachelor's Degree	5.8%	12.6%
Master's Degree	0.8%	−0.6%
Doctoral Degree	—	—
First Professional Degree	—	—

Flexibility of Earnings

Average Hours Worked: 38
Workers with a Varying Number of Hours: 4.8%
Workers Earning Some Overtime Pay, Tips, or Commissions: 28.1%
Earnings Benefit of Working Overtime: 10.0%

Gender

	Male	Female
Percent	94.1%	5.9%
Effect on Earnings	3.9%	—

Union Membership

Percentage Union Members: 18.5%
Earnings Benefit of Union Membership: 19.3%

Veteran Status

Percentage Who Have Been on Active Duty: 14.2%
Earnings Benefit of Veteran Status: 7.6%

51-4191 Heat Treating Equipment Setters, Operators, and Tenders, Metal and Plastic

Set up, operate, or tend heating equipment, such as heat-treating furnaces, flame-hardening machines, induction machines, soaking pits, or vacuum equipment to temper, harden, anneal, or heat-treat metal or plastic objects.

- Education or Training Required: Moderate-term on-the-job training
- Job Growth: –0.4%
- Annual Openings: 3,000
- Self-Employed: 2.4%
- Part-Time: 7.2%

NATIONAL WAGE FIGURES (ANNUAL)

Beginning	25th Percentile	Median	Mean	75th Percentile	90th Percentile
$20,270	$24,840	$30,850	$31,750	$37,340	$45,330

Median Wages for Industries Employing Largest Numbers (Annual)

Industry	Median Income
Federal, State, and Local Government	$45,850
Primary Metal Manufacturing	$33,740
Transportation Equipment Manufacturing	$33,270
Nonmetallic Mineral Product Manufacturing	$32,920
Machinery Manufacturing	$32,890
Electrical Equipment, Appliance, and Component Manufacturing	$31,680
Miscellaneous Manufacturing	$30,880
Administrative and Support Services	$29,950
Fabricated Metal Product Manufacturing	$29,290
Plastics and Rubber Products Manufacturing	$28,660

Median Wages for States (Annual)

State	Wage	State	Wage	State	Wage
AK	no data	KY	$34,550	NY	$34,550
AL	$28,900	LA	$29,900	OH	$29,900
AR	$35,620	MA	$31,950	OK	$32,230
AZ	$27,050	MD	no data	OR	$32,560
CA	$31,210	ME	$25,530	PA	$32,130
CO	$29,530	MI	$32,240	RI	$30,580
CT	$32,640	MN	$30,440	SC	$31,330
DC	no data	MO	$26,710	SD	no data
DE	no data	MS	$21,050	TN	$30,520
FL	$28,720	MT	no data	TX	$25,830
GA	$27,290	NC	$28,410	UT	$33,450
HI	no data	ND	no data	VA	$28,010
IA	$34,020	NE	$27,830	VT	no data
ID	$32,210	NH	$32,880	WA	$34,820
IL	$30,920	NJ	$28,310	WI	$29,590
IN	$33,880	NM	no data	WV	$30,670
KS	$40,440	NV	no data	WY	no data

Median Wages for the Largest Metropolitan Areas (Annual)

Area	Wage	Area	Wage
AZ: Phoenix	$31,280	MI: Detroit	$33,540
CA: Los Angeles	$29,370	MN: Minneapolis	$32,480
CA: Riverside	$38,480	MO: Kansas City	$26,240
CA: Sacramento	no data	MO: St. Louis	$32,270
CA: San Diego	$32,170	NV: Las Vegas	no data
CA: San Francisco	$36,300	NY: New York	$28,740
CO: Denver	$26,830	OH: Cincinnati	$32,610
DC: Washington	$31,650	OH: Cleveland	$26,680
FL: Miami	no data	OH: Columbus	$32,220
FL: Orlando	no data	OR: Portland	$32,000
FL: Tampa	no data	PA: Philadelphia	$33,080
GA: Atlanta	$29,950	PA: Pittsburgh	$31,170
IL: Chicago	$33,170	TX: Dallas	$22,600
MA: Boston	$34,500	TX: Houston	$30,250
MD: Baltimore	no data	WA: Seattle	$34,270

FACTORS THAT MAY AFFECT EARNINGS

Educational Attainment of Workers and Effect on Earnings

	Percent at Level	Effect on Earnings
Less than High School	—	—
Some High School	—	—
High School or Equivalent	68.8%	–4.1%
Some College but No Degree	—	—
Associate Degree	—	—
Bachelor's Degree	—	—
Master's Degree	—	—
Doctoral Degree	—	—
First Professional Degree	—	—

Figures do not total 100% because some levels have a very small sample size.

Flexibility of Earnings

Average Hours Worked: 41
Workers with a Varying Number of Hours: 3.4%
Workers Earning Some Overtime Pay, Tips, or Commissions: 43.8%
Earnings Benefit of Working Overtime: 14.8%

Gender

	Male	Female
Percent	82.8%	17.2%
Effect on Earnings	11.1%	–22.7%

Union Membership

Percentage Union Members: 18.8%
Earnings Benefit of Union Membership: 19.3%

Veteran Status

Percentage Who Have Been on Active Duty: 14.2%
Earnings Benefit of Veteran Status: 7.6%

51-4192 Lay-Out Workers, Metal and Plastic

Lay out reference points and dimensions on metal or plastic stock or workpieces, such as sheets, plates, tubes, structural shapes, castings, or machine parts, for further processing. Includes shipfitters.

- Education or Training Required: Moderate-term on-the-job training
- Job Growth: –4.6%
- Annual Openings: 1,000
- Self-Employed: 0.0%
- Part-Time: 7.2%

NATIONAL WAGE FIGURES (ANNUAL)

Beginning	25th Percentile	Median	Mean	75th Percentile	90th Percentile
$19,800	$26,140	$33,600	$35,080	$42,460	$53,890

Median Wages for Industries Employing Largest Numbers (Annual)

Industry	Median Income
Federal, State, and Local Government	$47,550
Primary Metal Manufacturing	$39,420
Specialty Trade Contractors	$36,190
Transportation Equipment Manufacturing	$34,270
Electrical Equipment, Appliance, and Component Manufacturing	$33,740
Machinery Manufacturing	$32,930
Fabricated Metal Product Manufacturing	$32,450
Merchant Wholesalers, Durable Goods	$31,210
Furniture and Related Product Manufacturing	$28,530
Computer and Electronic Product Manufacturing	$26,080

Median Wages for States (Annual)

AK	no data	KY	$29,390	NY	$34,040
AL	$28,300	LA	no data	OH	$35,960
AR	$31,080	MA	no data	OK	$29,320
AZ	$32,910	MD	$41,820	OR	$39,000
CA	$30,320	ME	$40,870	PA	$32,960
CO	$40,320	MI	$51,560	RI	no data
CT	$42,970	MN	$31,290	SC	$29,240
DC	no data	MO	$31,220	SD	$23,490
DE	no data	MS	$21,680	TN	$32,710
FL	$26,530	MT	no data	TX	$26,220
GA	$31,170	NC	$32,440	UT	$31,130
HI	no data	ND	no data	VA	$39,950
IA	$32,620	NE	no data	VT	no data
ID	no data	NH	$35,690	WA	$45,750
IL	$38,400	NJ	$40,380	WI	$36,470
IN	$36,430	NM	$33,310	WV	$31,480
KS	$33,380	NV	$48,800	WY	no data

Median Wages for the Largest Metropolitan Areas (Annual)

AZ: Phoenix	no data	MI: Detroit	$58,630
CA: Los Angeles	$22,550	MN: Minneapolis	$36,420
CA: Riverside	$24,990	MO: Kansas City	no data
CA: Sacramento	no data	MO: St. Louis	$29,150
CA: San Diego	$32,550	NV: Las Vegas	$56,720
CA: San Francisco	no data	NY: New York	$33,360
CO: Denver	$44,020	OH: Cincinnati	$35,630
DC: Washington	no data	OH: Cleveland	$63,980
FL: Miami	no data	OH: Columbus	$39,780
FL: Orlando	no data	OR: Portland	no data
FL: Tampa	$26,180	PA: Philadelphia	$34,570
GA: Atlanta	$31,860	PA: Pittsburgh	$33,210
IL: Chicago	$38,460	TX: Dallas	$26,880
MA: Boston	$39,750	TX: Houston	$25,550
MD: Baltimore	$43,500	WA: Seattle	$41,630

FACTORS THAT MAY AFFECT EARNINGS

Educational Attainment of Workers and Effect on Earnings

Figures are based on a group of occupations: Metal Workers and Plastic Workers

	Percent at Level	Effect on Earnings
Less than High School	5.6%	–31.1%
Some High School	11.6%	–16.7%
High School or Equivalent	42.1%	0.8%
Some College but No Degree	21.4%	4.0%
Associate Degree	12.4%	13.3%
Bachelor's Degree	5.8%	12.6%
Master's Degree	0.8%	–0.6%
Doctoral Degree	—	—
First Professional Degree	—	—

Flexibility of Earnings

Average Hours Worked: 46
Workers with a Varying Number of Hours: 4.6%
Workers Earning Some Overtime Pay, Tips, or Commissions: 75.0%
Earnings Benefit of Working Overtime: 14.8%

Gender

	Male	Female
Percent	88.4%	11.6%
Effect on Earnings	11.1%	–22.7%

Union Membership

Percentage Union Members: 12.5%
Earnings Benefit of Union Membership: 19.3%

Veteran Status

Percentage Who Have Been on Active Duty: 14.2%
Earnings Benefit of Veteran Status: 7.6%

51-4193 Plating and Coating Machine Setters, Operators, and Tenders, Metal and Plastic

Set up, operate, or tend plating or coating machines to coat metal or plastic products with chromium, zinc, copper, cadmium, nickel, or other metal to protect or decorate surfaces. Includes electrolytic processes.

- Education or Training Required: Moderate-term on-the-job training
- Job Growth: −4.0%
- Annual Openings: 9,000
- Self-Employed: 2.8%
- Part-Time: 7.2%

NATIONAL WAGE FIGURES (ANNUAL)

Beginning	25th Percentile	Median	Mean	75th Percentile	90th Percentile
$17,900	$21,600	$27,470	$29,280	$35,200	$43,970

Median Wages for Industries Employing Largest Numbers (Annual)

Industry	Median Income
Transportation Equipment Manufacturing	$45,790
Federal, State, and Local Government	$44,690
Repair and Maintenance	$36,720
Paper Manufacturing	$36,570
Primary Metal Manufacturing	$33,540
Furniture and Related Product Manufacturing	$33,420
Electrical Equipment, Appliance, and Component Manufacturing	$32,610
Nonmetallic Mineral Product Manufacturing	$31,280
Petroleum and Coal Products Manufacturing	$28,580
Machinery Manufacturing	$27,730

Median Wages for States (Annual)

AK	no data	KY	$27,550	NY	$28,180
AL	$30,510	LA	$27,150	OH	$28,260
AR	$29,430	MA	$32,200	OK	$28,580
AZ	$23,270	MD	$28,710	OR	$28,800
CA	$23,000	ME	$30,490	PA	$31,830
CO	$25,330	MI	$26,750	RI	$27,730
CT	$26,860	MN	$31,560	SC	$26,200
DC	no data	MO	$26,820	SD	$23,990
DE	no data	MS	$31,290	TN	$24,010
FL	$24,090	MT	no data	TX	$23,930
GA	$26,610	NC	$26,510	UT	$29,360
HI	no data	ND	$24,020	VA	$27,540
IA	$31,690	NE	$27,930	VT	$25,130
ID	$20,170	NH	$28,930	WA	$29,410
IL	$27,150	NJ	$27,120	WI	$27,420
IN	$34,000	NM	no data	WV	$39,590
KS	$26,570	NV	$21,230	WY	no data

Median Wages for the Largest Metropolitan Areas (Annual)

AZ: Phoenix	$23,510	MI: Detroit	$26,250
CA: Los Angeles	$22,030	MN: Minneapolis	$32,620
CA: Riverside	$24,200	MO: Kansas City	$27,340
CA: Sacramento	$23,080	MO: St. Louis	$31,580
CA: San Diego	$18,960	NV: Las Vegas	no data
CA: San Francisco	$26,610	NY: New York	$29,100
CO: Denver	$24,270	OH: Cincinnati	$27,550
DC: Washington	$32,150	OH: Cleveland	$27,870
FL: Miami	$23,240	OH: Columbus	$42,380
FL: Orlando	no data	OR: Portland	$31,080
FL: Tampa	$24,890	PA: Philadelphia	$29,360
GA: Atlanta	$22,190	PA: Pittsburgh	$30,400
IL: Chicago	$27,060	TX: Dallas	$21,830
MA: Boston	$32,170	TX: Houston	$26,060
MD: Baltimore	$29,470	WA: Seattle	$29,950

FACTORS THAT MAY AFFECT EARNINGS

Educational Attainment of Workers and Effect on Earnings

	Percent at Level	Effect on Earnings
Less than High School	—	—
Some High School	—	—
High School or Equivalent	50.0%	−7.7%
Some College but No Degree	—	—
Associate Degree	—	—
Bachelor's Degree	—	—
Master's Degree	—	—
Doctoral Degree	—	—
First Professional Degree	—	—

Figures do not total 100% because some levels have a very small sample size.

Flexibility of Earnings

Average Hours Worked: 38
Workers with a Varying Number of Hours: 2.0%
Workers Earning Some Overtime Pay, Tips, or Commissions: 25.7%
Earnings Benefit of Working Overtime: 14.8%

Gender

	Male	Female
Percent	95.7%	4.3%
Effect on Earnings	11.1%	−24.9%

Union Membership

Percentage Union Members: 14.3%
Earnings Benefit of Union Membership: 19.3%

Veteran Status

Percentage Who Have Been on Active Duty: 14.2%
Earnings Benefit of Veteran Status: 7.6%

51-4194 Tool Grinders, Filers, and Sharpeners

Perform precision smoothing, sharpening, polishing, or grinding of metal objects.

- Education or Training Required: Moderate-term on-the-job training
- Job Growth: –7.7%
- Annual Openings: 2,000
- Self-Employed: 3.7%
- Part-Time: 33.3%

NATIONAL WAGE FIGURES (ANNUAL)

Beginning	25th Percentile	Median	Mean	75th Percentile	90th Percentile
$19,770	$24,340	$30,640	$32,210	$38,740	$46,240

Median Wages for Industries Employing Largest Numbers (Annual)

Industry	Median Income
Transportation Equipment Manufacturing	$44,620
Chemical Manufacturing	$39,430
Computer and Electronic Product Manufacturing	$33,660
Wood Product Manufacturing	$33,400
Machinery Manufacturing	$31,830
Miscellaneous Manufacturing	$31,490
Fabricated Metal Product Manufacturing	$29,080
Primary Metal Manufacturing	$28,710
Electrical Equipment, Appliance, and Component Manufacturing	$27,830
Merchant Wholesalers, Durable Goods	$27,220

Median Wages for States (Annual)

State	Wage	State	Wage	State	Wage
AK	no data	KY	$24,930	NY	$35,360
AL	$22,560	LA	$24,570	OH	$30,780
AR	$31,220	MA	$29,450	OK	$27,970
AZ	$30,390	MD	$36,830	OR	$37,450
CA	$27,390	ME	$30,530	PA	$30,910
CO	$29,220	MI	$36,430	RI	no data
CT	$35,540	MN	$32,780	SC	$29,150
DC	no data	MO	$28,560	SD	$23,490
DE	no data	MS	$26,960	TN	$35,120
FL	$26,320	MT	$37,640	TX	$28,260
GA	$27,660	NC	$27,900	UT	$24,620
HI	no data	ND	$26,680	VA	$22,610
IA	$32,410	NE	$26,350	VT	$30,310
ID	$29,700	NH	$29,800	WA	$40,390
IL	$31,340	NJ	$34,550	WI	$34,820
IN	$29,590	NM	$27,000	WV	$26,770
KS	$38,650	NV	$26,240	WY	no data

Median Wages for the Largest Metropolitan Areas (Annual)

Area	Wage	Area	Wage
AZ: Phoenix	$30,260	MI: Detroit	$37,880
CA: Los Angeles	$25,740	MN: Minneapolis	$36,500
CA: Riverside	$26,670	MO: Kansas City	$27,930
CA: Sacramento	$30,350	MO: St. Louis	$33,800
CA: San Diego	$30,290	NV: Las Vegas	no data
CA: San Francisco	$28,590	NY: New York	$28,250
CO: Denver	$35,260	OH: Cincinnati	$29,650
DC: Washington	no data	OH: Cleveland	$33,820
FL: Miami	no data	OH: Columbus	$31,970
FL: Orlando	$23,770	OR: Portland	$39,330
FL: Tampa	$24,570	PA: Philadelphia	$36,050
GA: Atlanta	$28,800	PA: Pittsburgh	$35,430
IL: Chicago	$31,810	TX: Dallas	$25,820
MA: Boston	$28,740	TX: Houston	$29,490
MD: Baltimore	$38,140	WA: Seattle	$46,400

FACTORS THAT MAY AFFECT EARNINGS

Educational Attainment of Workers and Effect on Earnings

	Percent at Level	Effect on Earnings
Less than High School	—	—
Some High School	—	—
High School or Equivalent	63.6%	6.3%
Some College but No Degree	—	—
Associate Degree	—	—
Bachelor's Degree	—	—
Master's Degree	—	—
Doctoral Degree	—	—
First Professional Degree	—	—

Figures do not total 100% because some levels have a very small sample size.

Flexibility of Earnings

Average Hours Worked: 38
Workers with a Varying Number of Hours: 4.8%
Workers Earning Some Overtime Pay, Tips, or Commissions: 45.5%
Earnings Benefit of Working Overtime: 14.8%

Gender

	Male	Female
Percent	93.8%	6.2%
Effect on Earnings	11.1%	–24.9%

Union Membership

Percentage Union Members: 18.5%
Earnings Benefit of Union Membership: 19.3%

Veteran Status

Percentage Who Have Been on Active Duty: 14.2%
Earnings Benefit of Veteran Status: 7.6%

51-4199 Metal Workers and Plastic Workers, All Other

All metalworkers and plastic workers not listed separately.

- Education or Training Required: Moderate-term on-the-job training
- Job Growth: –13.6%
- Annual Openings: 5,000
- Self-Employed: 2.4%
- Part-Time: 4.4%

NATIONAL WAGE FIGURES (ANNUAL)

Beginning	25th Percentile	Median	Mean	75th Percentile	90th Percentile
$19,420	$24,920	$34,710	$37,730	$51,460	$59,850

Median Wages for Industries Employing Largest Numbers (Annual)

Industry	Median Income
Utilities	$45,540
Federal, State, and Local Government	$42,880
Primary Metal Manufacturing	$34,940
Management of Companies and Enterprises	$33,960
Professional, Scientific, and Technical Services	$33,390
Heavy and Civil Engineering Construction	$32,160
Furniture and Related Product Manufacturing	$30,310
Machinery Manufacturing	$29,910
Merchant Wholesalers, Nondurable Goods	$29,430
Fabricated Metal Product Manufacturing	$28,870

Median Wages for States (Annual)

AK	no data	KY	$39,950	NY	$55,720
AL	$31,250	LA	$35,910	OH	$32,710
AR	no data	MA	$32,580	OK	no data
AZ	$23,190	MD	$32,510	OR	$33,420
CA	$28,520	ME	$40,340	PA	$36,700
CO	$28,760	MI	$52,870	RI	$29,820
CT	$32,790	MN	$26,780	SC	$25,730
DC	no data	MO	$44,200	SD	no data
DE	no data	MS	no data	TN	$25,680
FL	$32,530	MT	no data	TX	$48,040
GA	$30,060	NC	$33,460	UT	$25,460
HI	no data	ND	no data	VA	$34,190
IA	$24,790	NE	$18,370	VT	no data
ID	$18,920	NH	$29,120	WA	$40,590
IL	$25,110	NJ	$24,990	WI	$45,590
IN	$52,140	NM	$37,020	WV	$34,040
KS	$26,300	NV	$31,610	WY	no data

Median Wages for the Largest Metropolitan Areas (Annual)

AZ: Phoenix	$23,380	MI: Detroit	no data
CA: Los Angeles	$27,480	MN: Minneapolis	$27,850
CA: Riverside	$31,070	MO: Kansas City	$27,760
CA: Sacramento	$17,160	MO: St. Louis	no data
CA: San Diego	$23,070	NV: Las Vegas	$32,030
CA: San Francisco	$35,600	NY: New York	$25,370
CO: Denver	$28,360	OH: Cincinnati	$29,740
DC: Washington	no data	OH: Cleveland	$31,570
FL: Miami	$34,820	OH: Columbus	$33,050
FL: Orlando	$25,020	OR: Portland	$32,970
FL: Tampa	$24,480	PA: Philadelphia	$37,530
GA: Atlanta	$22,670	PA: Pittsburgh	no data
IL: Chicago	$25,340	TX: Dallas	no data
MA: Boston	$30,310	TX: Houston	$42,790
MD: Baltimore	$34,180	WA: Seattle	$46,560

FACTORS THAT MAY AFFECT EARNINGS

Educational Attainment of Workers and Effect on Earnings

	Percent at Level	Effect on Earnings
Less than High School	8.4%	–30.3%
Some High School	15.3%	–21.8%
High School or Equivalent	45.4%	7.4%
Some College but No Degree	18.0%	2.3%
Associate Degree	6.4%	6.0%
Bachelor's Degree	5.4%	27.0%
Master's Degree	—	—
Doctoral Degree	—	—
First Professional Degree	—	—

Flexibility of Earnings

Average Hours Worked: 36
Workers with a Varying Number of Hours: 4.9%
Workers Earning Some Overtime Pay, Tips, or Commissions: 24.2%
Earnings Benefit of Working Overtime: 14.3%

Gender

	Male	Female
Percent	71.2%	28.8%
Effect on Earnings	11.1%	–16.4%

Union Membership

Percentage Union Members: 18.1%
Earnings Benefit of Union Membership: 18.2%

Veteran Status

Percentage Who Have Been on Active Duty: 14.2%
Earnings Benefit of Veteran Status: 7.6%

51-5000 Printing Workers

51-5011 Bindery Workers

Set up or operate binding machines that produce books and other printed materials.

- Education or Training Required: Short-term on-the-job training
- Job Growth: –10.4%
- Annual Openings: 8,000
- Self-Employed: 0.4%
- Part-Time: 20.5%

NATIONAL WAGE FIGURES (ANNUAL)

Beginning	25th Percentile	Median	Mean	75th Percentile	90th Percentile
$16,500	$20,120	$25,570	$27,370	$33,320	$41,880

Median Wages for Industries Employing Largest Numbers (Annual)

Industry	Median Income
Federal, State, and Local Government	$43,990
Miscellaneous Manufacturing	$37,730
Religious, Grantmaking, Civic, Professional, and Similar Organizations	$31,340
Insurance Carriers and Related Activities	$29,260
Educational Services	$26,990
Printing and Related Support Activities	$26,070
Machinery Manufacturing	$25,980
Publishing Industries (Except Internet)	$25,950
Computer and Electronic Product Manufacturing	$25,290
Social Assistance	$25,210

Median Wages for States (Annual)

AK	$27,340	KY	$28,790	NY	$26,190
AL	$21,970	LA	$23,460	OH	$27,580
AR	$22,900	MA	$29,470	OK	$23,760
AZ	$22,140	MD	$27,740	OR	$28,960
CA	$23,390	ME	$25,720	PA	$28,560
CO	$27,280	MI	$28,810	RI	$22,140
CT	$26,470	MN	$28,850	SC	$19,880
DC	$42,660	MO	$25,690	SD	$21,690
DE	$25,550	MS	$26,450	TN	$23,640
FL	$24,370	MT	$21,270	TX	$22,150
GA	$23,590	NC	$18,390	UT	$26,150
HI	$18,250	ND	$19,520	VA	$26,880
IA	$24,840	NE	$26,870	VT	$26,920
ID	$23,110	NH	$27,300	WA	$25,370
IL	$26,650	NJ	$23,520	WI	$25,670
IN	$27,510	NM	$25,270	WV	$20,710
KS	$21,560	NV	$22,380	WY	$19,550

Median Wages for the Largest Metropolitan Areas (Annual)

AZ: Phoenix	$22,800	MI: Detroit	$30,280
CA: Los Angeles	$23,230	MN: Minneapolis	$29,660
CA: Riverside	$19,930	MO: Kansas City	$24,900
CA: Sacramento	$23,270	MO: St. Louis	$28,280
CA: San Diego	$20,330	NV: Las Vegas	$21,640
CA: San Francisco	$27,010	NY: New York	$26,170
CO: Denver	$27,390	OH: Cincinnati	$27,250
DC: Washington	$31,050	OH: Cleveland	$32,730
FL: Miami	$25,930	OH: Columbus	$29,080
FL: Orlando	$25,270	OR: Portland	$28,850
FL: Tampa	$27,040	PA: Philadelphia	$25,210
GA: Atlanta	$25,170	PA: Pittsburgh	$23,990
IL: Chicago	$26,810	TX: Dallas	$22,780
MA: Boston	$32,830	TX: Houston	$24,000
MD: Baltimore	$26,740	WA: Seattle	$25,920

FACTORS THAT MAY AFFECT EARNINGS

Educational Attainment of Workers and Effect on Earnings

Figures are based on a group of occupations: Printing Workers

	Percent at Level	Effect on Earnings
Less than High School	—	—
Some High School	11.9%	–28.7%
High School or Equivalent	43.5%	6.3%
Some College but No Degree	20.8%	–2.3%
Associate Degree	8.6%	0.1%
Bachelor's Degree	11.6%	9.9%
Master's Degree	—	—
Doctoral Degree	—	—
First Professional Degree	—	—

Flexibility of Earnings

Average Hours Worked: 35
Workers with a Varying Number of Hours: 4.7%
Workers Earning Some Overtime Pay, Tips, or Commissions: 18.5%
Earnings Benefit of Working Overtime: 7.0%

Gender

	Male	Female
Percent	69.7%	30.3%
Effect on Earnings	11.1%	–32.0%

Union Membership

Percentage Union Members: 11.1%
Earnings Benefit of Union Membership: 31.8%

Veteran Status

Percentage Who Have Been on Active Duty: 9.2%
Earnings Benefit of Veteran Status: 21.0%

51-5012 Bookbinders

Perform highly skilled hand-finishing operations, such as grooving and lettering, to bind books.

- Education or Training Required: Moderate-term on-the-job training
- Job Growth: −4.5%
- Annual Openings: 1,000
- Self-Employed: 0.3%
- Part-Time: 20.5%

NATIONAL WAGE FIGURES (ANNUAL)

Beginning	25th Percentile	Median	Mean	75th Percentile	90th Percentile
$17,250	$21,800	$30,260	$32,210	$40,220	$47,200

Median Wages for Industries Employing Largest Numbers (Annual)

Industry	Median Income
Federal, State, and Local Government	$51,550
Educational Services	$33,530
Printing and Related Support Activities	$30,610
Publishing Industries (Except Internet)	$25,530
Merchant Wholesalers, Nondurable Goods	$24,160
Professional, Scientific, and Technical Services	$21,730

Median Wages for States (Annual)

AK	no data	KY	$19,190	NY	no data
AL	$38,490	LA	no data	OH	$25,970
AR	no data	MA	$22,430	OK	no data
AZ	no data	MD	$41,860	OR	no data
CA	$33,350	ME	no data	PA	$34,290
CO	no data	MI	no data	RI	no data
CT	$27,140	MN	no data	SC	$31,790
DC	no data	MO	$27,890	SD	no data
DE	no data	MS	no data	TN	$26,750
FL	$33,970	MT	no data	TX	$25,730
GA	$17,590	NC	$22,320	UT	$20,470
HI	no data	ND	no data	VA	no data
IA	$40,700	NE	no data	VT	$28,280
ID	no data	NH	no data	WA	$51,820
IL	$38,320	NJ	no data	WI	$34,340
IN	no data	NM	no data	WV	no data
KS	$33,720	NV	no data	WY	no data

Median Wages for the Largest Metropolitan Areas (Annual)

AZ: Phoenix	no data	MI: Detroit	no data
CA: Los Angeles	$31,760	MN: Minneapolis	no data
CA: Riverside	no data	MO: Kansas City	$37,870
CA: Sacramento	no data	MO: St. Louis	$25,860
CA: San Diego	no data	NV: Las Vegas	no data
CA: San Francisco	no data	NY: New York	$29,770
CO: Denver	no data	OH: Cincinnati	$18,950
DC: Washington	$47,310	OH: Cleveland	no data
FL: Miami	$30,450	OH: Columbus	$34,910
FL: Orlando	no data	OR: Portland	no data
FL: Tampa	no data	PA: Philadelphia	$35,080
GA: Atlanta	$22,320	PA: Pittsburgh	no data
IL: Chicago	$38,540	TX: Dallas	$33,440
MA: Boston	no data	TX: Houston	$20,280
MD: Baltimore	$42,690	WA: Seattle	$53,230

FACTORS THAT MAY AFFECT EARNINGS

Educational Attainment of Workers and Effect on Earnings

Figures are based on a group of occupations: Printing Workers

	Percent at Level	Effect on Earnings
Less than High School	—	—
Some High School	11.9%	−28.7%
High School or Equivalent	43.5%	6.3%
Some College but No Degree	20.8%	−2.3%
Associate Degree	8.6%	0.1%
Bachelor's Degree	11.6%	9.9%
Master's Degree	—	—
Doctoral Degree	—	—
First Professional Degree	—	—

Flexibility of Earnings

Average Hours Worked: 35
Workers with a Varying Number of Hours: 4.7%
Workers Earning Some Overtime Pay, Tips, or Commissions: 18.5%
Earnings Benefit of Working Overtime: 7.0%

Gender

	Male	Female
Percent	69.7%	30.3%
Effect on Earnings	11.1%	−32.0%

Union Membership

Percentage Union Members: 11.1%
Earnings Benefit of Union Membership: 31.8%

Veteran Status

Percentage Who Have Been on Active Duty: 9.2%
Earnings Benefit of Veteran Status: 21.0%

51-5021 Job Printers

Set type according to copy, operate press to print job order, read proof for errors and clarity of impression, and correct imperfections. Job printers are often found in small establishments where work combines several job skills.

- Education or Training Required: Long-term on-the-job training
- Job Growth: 1.8%
- Annual Openings: 8,000
- Self-Employed: 8.0%
- Part-Time: 28.6%

NATIONAL WAGE FIGURES (ANNUAL)

Beginning	25th Percentile	Median	Mean	75th Percentile	90th Percentile
$19,880	$25,260	$32,410	$34,020	$41,250	$51,370

Median Wages for Industries Employing Largest Numbers (Annual)

Industry	Median Income
Management of Companies and Enterprises	$35,430
Insurance Carriers and Related Activities	$35,080
Federal, State, and Local Government	$34,320
Religious, Grantmaking, Civic, Professional, and Similar Organizations	$34,270
Hospitals	$33,840
Publishing Industries (Except Internet)	$33,670
Educational Services	$33,620
Printing and Related Support Activities	$32,770
Merchant Wholesalers, Durable Goods	$32,700
Credit Intermediation and Related Activities	$32,220

Median Wages for States (Annual)

AK	$32,620	KY	$27,720	NY	$34,030
AL	$26,680	LA	$26,770	OH	$31,960
AR	$26,900	MA	$31,730	OK	$28,310
AZ	$33,640	MD	$34,400	OR	$31,430
CA	$38,060	ME	$29,590	PA	$31,010
CO	$37,020	MI	$33,280	RI	$38,140
CT	$33,300	MN	$38,390	SC	$27,230
DC	$31,050	MO	$34,810	SD	no data
DE	$38,230	MS	$31,430	TN	$35,800
FL	$27,280	MT	$26,080	TX	$29,420
GA	$30,530	NC	$30,120	UT	$28,830
HI	$30,260	ND	$26,170	VA	$38,060
IA	$34,440	NE	$32,450	VT	$34,960
ID	$32,200	NH	$38,010	WA	$34,900
IL	$35,320	NJ	$40,120	WI	$32,540
IN	$33,000	NM	$21,450	WV	$26,840
KS	$31,440	NV	$35,040	WY	no data

Median Wages for the Largest Metropolitan Areas (Annual)

AZ: Phoenix	$35,020	MI: Detroit	$36,600
CA: Los Angeles	$35,660	MN: Minneapolis	$44,160
CA: Riverside	$28,990	MO: Kansas City	$33,700
CA: Sacramento	$42,560	MO: St. Louis	$40,460
CA: San Diego	$40,530	NV: Las Vegas	$36,550
CA: San Francisco	$48,560	NY: New York	$36,390
CO: Denver	$39,420	OH: Cincinnati	$35,160
DC: Washington	$39,070	OH: Cleveland	$39,350
FL: Miami	$27,080	OH: Columbus	$30,750
FL: Orlando	$26,850	OR: Portland	$35,220
FL: Tampa	$28,690	PA: Philadelphia	$33,060
GA: Atlanta	$31,390	PA: Pittsburgh	$29,430
IL: Chicago	$36,810	TX: Dallas	$29,840
MA: Boston	$32,200	TX: Houston	$31,810
MD: Baltimore	$36,410	WA: Seattle	$40,050

FACTORS THAT MAY AFFECT EARNINGS

Educational Attainment of Workers and Effect on Earnings

	Percent at Level	Effect on Earnings
Less than High School	—	—
Some High School	10.3%	−2.6%
High School or Equivalent	48.3%	−5.8%
Some College but No Degree	15.5%	−4.8%
Associate Degree	10.3%	−8.6%
Bachelor's Degree	12.1%	40.3%
Master's Degree	—	—
Doctoral Degree	—	—
First Professional Degree	—	—

Flexibility of Earnings

Average Hours Worked: 35
Workers with a Varying Number of Hours: 2.0%
Workers Earning Some Overtime Pay, Tips, or Commissions: 16.4%
Earnings Benefit of Working Overtime: 7.0%

Gender

	Male	Female
Percent	72.1%	27.9%
Effect on Earnings	11.1%	−32.0%

Union Membership

Percentage Union Members: 18.0%
Earnings Benefit of Union Membership: 58.4%

Veteran Status

Percentage Who Have Been on Active Duty: 9.2%
Earnings Benefit of Veteran Status: 21.0%

51-5022 Prepress Technicians and Workers

Set up and prepare material for printing presses.

- Education or Training Required: Postsecondary vocational training
- Job Growth: −8.4%
- Annual Openings: 10,000
- Self-Employed: 2.1%
- Part-Time: 33.3%

NATIONAL WAGE FIGURES (ANNUAL)

Beginning	25th Percentile	Median	Mean	75th Percentile	90th Percentile
$19,480	$24,910	$33,310	$34,730	$43,040	$53,480

Median Wages for Industries Employing Largest Numbers (Annual)

Industry	Median Income
Federal, State, and Local Government	$47,750
Nonstore Retailers	$39,430
Transportation Equipment Manufacturing	$37,410
Machinery Manufacturing	$36,950
Primary Metal Manufacturing	$36,900
Management of Companies and Enterprises	$36,660
Paper Manufacturing	$34,460
Printing and Related Support Activities	$34,190
Electrical Equipment, Appliance, and Component Manufacturing	$33,780
Professional, Scientific, and Technical Services	$33,760

Median Wages for States (Annual)

AK	$29,370	KY	$32,370	NY	$38,300
AL	$28,610	LA	$28,950	OH	$32,580
AR	$27,630	MA	$37,530	OK	$24,980
AZ	$27,360	MD	$38,100	OR	$33,890
CA	$37,070	ME	$31,970	PA	$32,870
CO	$39,710	MI	$35,410	RI	$33,740
CT	$38,540	MN	$38,500	SC	$28,250
DC	$56,120	MO	$30,890	SD	$23,080
DE	$33,170	MS	$26,510	TN	$33,310
FL	$29,790	MT	$31,850	TX	$26,900
GA	$30,910	NC	$32,800	UT	$27,500
HI	$33,460	ND	$22,690	VA	$33,480
IA	$31,340	NE	$31,700	VT	$34,660
ID	no data	NH	$28,160	WA	$38,710
IL	$35,890	NJ	$42,390	WI	$36,030
IN	$34,020	NM	$26,770	WV	$24,620
KS	$28,560	NV	$35,980	WY	$19,570

Median Wages for the Largest Metropolitan Areas (Annual)

AZ: Phoenix	$27,150	MI: Detroit	$36,450
CA: Los Angeles	$35,530	MN: Minneapolis	$44,180
CA: Riverside	$37,800	MO: Kansas City	$30,800
CA: Sacramento	$38,450	MO: St. Louis	$41,150
CA: San Diego	$35,770	NV: Las Vegas	$32,720
CA: San Francisco	$43,460	NY: New York	$43,530
CO: Denver	$46,890	OH: Cincinnati	$30,280
DC: Washington	$41,020	OH: Cleveland	$39,790
FL: Miami	$32,060	OH: Columbus	$34,980
FL: Orlando	$30,110	OR: Portland	$35,880
FL: Tampa	$29,050	PA: Philadelphia	$35,810
GA: Atlanta	$34,890	PA: Pittsburgh	$33,840
IL: Chicago	$37,070	TX: Dallas	$29,570
MA: Boston	$36,810	TX: Houston	$27,330
MD: Baltimore	$39,000	WA: Seattle	$40,540

FACTORS THAT MAY AFFECT EARNINGS

Educational Attainment of Workers and Effect on Earnings

	Percent at Level	Effect on Earnings
Less than High School	—	—
Some High School	—	—
High School or Equivalent	30.2%	−7.4%
Some College but No Degree	30.2%	−7.7%
Associate Degree	—	—
Bachelor's Degree	28.3%	13.5%
Master's Degree	—	—
Doctoral Degree	—	—
First Professional Degree	—	—

Figures do not total 100% because some levels have a very small sample size.

Flexibility of Earnings

Average Hours Worked: 32
Workers with a Varying Number of Hours: 7.2%
Workers Earning Some Overtime Pay, Tips, or Commissions: 16.1%
Earnings Benefit of Working Overtime: 7.0%

Gender

	Male	Female
Percent	48.1%	51.9%
Effect on Earnings	11.1%	−32.0%

Union Membership

Percentage Union Members: 7.1%
Earnings Benefit of Union Membership: 31.8%

Veteran Status

Percentage Who Have Been on Active Duty: 9.2%
Earnings Benefit of Veteran Status: 21.0%

51-5023 *Printing Machine Operators*

Set up or operate various types of printing machines, such as offset, letterset, intaglio, or gravure presses or screen printers, to produce print on paper or other materials.

- Education or Training Required: Moderate-term on-the-job training
- Job Growth: 2.9%
- Annual Openings: 26,000
- Self-Employed: 3.2%
- Part-Time: 10.4%

NATIONAL WAGE FIGURES (ANNUAL)

Beginning	25th Percentile	Median	Mean	75th Percentile	90th Percentile
$18,390	$23,110	$30,990	$32,840	$40,540	$50,400

Median Wages for Industries Employing Largest Numbers (Annual)

Industry	Median Income
Federal, State, and Local Government	$40,150
Publishing Industries (Except Internet)	$35,910
Wholesale Electronic Markets and Agents and Brokers	$34,990
Paper Manufacturing	$34,330
Insurance Carriers and Related Activities	$32,370
Printing and Related Support Activities	$32,340
Educational Services	$32,030
Chemical Manufacturing	$31,900
Management of Companies and Enterprises	$29,490
Fabricated Metal Product Manufacturing	$29,350

Median Wages for States (Annual)

AK $41,270	KY $32,140	NY $30,670
AL $25,650	LA $24,920	OH $31,660
AR $25,970	MA $36,130	OK $26,400
AZ $29,950	MD $34,790	OR $33,160
CA $31,700	ME $28,980	PA $32,440
CO $33,760	MI $32,030	RI $31,150
CT $34,550	MN $37,350	SC $27,290
DC $54,950	MO $27,860	SD $25,790
DE $27,920	MS $26,120	TN $25,740
FL $29,490	MT $22,730	TX $27,590
GA $33,430	NC $29,400	UT $21,650
HI $29,680	ND $22,940	VA $30,280
IA $29,740	NE $26,440	VT $29,110
ID $26,440	NH $31,990	WA $35,080
IL $30,470	NJ $36,400	WI $34,590
IN $31,410	NM $26,390	WV $23,540
KS $29,280	NV $33,280	WY $25,220

Median Wages for the Largest Metropolitan Areas (Annual)

AZ: Phoenix	$30,970	MI: Detroit	$30,390
CA: Los Angeles	$29,250	MN: Minneapolis	$39,910
CA: Riverside	$36,460	MO: Kansas City	$32,460
CA: Sacramento	$34,650	MO: St. Louis	$27,040
CA: San Diego	$27,210	NV: Las Vegas	$30,220
CA: San Francisco	$40,920	NY: New York	$31,820
CO: Denver	$35,880	OH: Cincinnati	$33,430
DC: Washington	$41,440	OH: Cleveland	$29,270
FL: Miami	$29,080	OH: Columbus	$34,600
FL: Orlando	$29,390	OR: Portland	$34,980
FL: Tampa	$30,860	PA: Philadelphia	$36,560
GA: Atlanta	$34,420	PA: Pittsburgh	$27,580
IL: Chicago	$31,500	TX: Dallas	$32,580
MA: Boston	$37,030	TX: Houston	$28,060
MD: Baltimore	$31,550	WA: Seattle	$34,310

FACTORS THAT MAY AFFECT EARNINGS

Educational Attainment of Workers and Effect on Earnings

	Percent at Level	Effect on Earnings
Less than High School	3.1%	−38.0%
Some High School	12.0%	−30.7%
High School or Equivalent	47.6%	8.0%
Some College but No Degree	21.8%	3.3%
Associate Degree	7.6%	−13.8%
Bachelor's Degree	7.1%	−2.4%
Master's Degree	—	—
Doctoral Degree	—	—
First Professional Degree	—	—

Flexibility of Earnings

Average Hours Worked: 36
Workers with a Varying Number of Hours: 4.8%
Workers Earning Some Overtime Pay, Tips, or Commissions: 18.5%
Earnings Benefit of Working Overtime: 9.2%

Gender

	Male	Female
Percent	77.8%	22.2%
Effect on Earnings	6.7%	—

Union Membership

Percentage Union Members: 9.8%
Earnings Benefit of Union Membership: 18.3%

Veteran Status

Percentage Who Have Been on Active Duty: 9.2%
Earnings Benefit of Veteran Status: 21.0%

51-6000 Textile, Apparel, and Furnishings Workers

51-6011 Laundry and Dry-Cleaning Workers

Operate or tend washing or dry-cleaning machines to wash or dry clean industrial or household articles, such as cloth garments, suede, leather, furs, blankets, draperies, fine linens, rugs, and carpets.

- Education or Training Required: Moderate-term on-the-job training
- Job Growth: 12.7%
- Annual Openings: 44,000
- Self-Employed: 5.2%
- Part-Time: 39.5%

NATIONAL WAGE FIGURES (ANNUAL)

Beginning	25th Percentile	Median	Mean	75th Percentile	90th Percentile
$13,530	$15,330	$17,850	$18,890	$21,610	$26,210

Median Wages for Industries Employing Largest Numbers (Annual)

Industry	Median Income
Specialty Trade Contractors	$25,860
Federal, State, and Local Government	$24,430
Food Manufacturing	$23,730
Warehousing and Storage	$22,940
Professional, Scientific, and Technical Services	$21,560
Textile Product Mills	$21,490
Administrative and Support Services	$20,960
Religious, Grantmaking, Civic, Professional, and Similar Organizations	$20,910
Merchant Wholesalers, Durable Goods	$20,650
Management of Companies and Enterprises	$20,200

Median Wages for States (Annual)

State	Wage	State	Wage	State	Wage
AK	$21,470	KY	$16,780	NY	$18,710
AL	$16,720	LA	$14,860	OH	$18,380
AR	$15,850	MA	$19,860	OK	$15,900
AZ	$16,990	MD	$18,360	OR	$18,570
CA	$18,500	ME	$19,200	PA	$19,300
CO	$18,920	MI	$20,460	RI	$19,160
CT	$21,650	MN	$23,410	SC	$17,020
DC	$22,030	MO	$17,710	SD	$17,950
DE	$18,330	MS	$15,750	TN	$17,060
FL	$17,300	MT	$17,410	TX	$15,620
GA	$16,380	NC	$17,140	UT	$17,760
HI	$24,270	ND	$18,850	VA	$17,820
IA	$19,810	NE	$17,730	VT	$18,610
ID	$17,900	NH	$20,340	WA	$20,200
IL	$16,780	NJ	$18,650	WI	$19,270
IN	$18,080	NM	$15,160	WV	$17,010
KS	$17,370	NV	$20,890	WY	$17,260

Median Wages for the Largest Metropolitan Areas (Annual)

Area	Wage	Area	Wage
AZ: Phoenix	$17,290	MI: Detroit	$21,240
CA: Los Angeles	$18,060	MN: Minneapolis	$25,210
CA: Riverside	$17,450	MO: Kansas City	$18,620
CA: Sacramento	$19,380	MO: St. Louis	$18,140
CA: San Diego	$17,940	NV: Las Vegas	$21,780
CA: San Francisco	$21,430	NY: New York	$18,940
CO: Denver	$19,820	OH: Cincinnati	$19,790
DC: Washington	$19,460	OH: Cleveland	$18,980
FL: Miami	$17,180	OH: Columbus	$18,800
FL: Orlando	$17,070	OR: Portland	$20,180
FL: Tampa	$17,370	PA: Philadelphia	$19,800
GA: Atlanta	$16,600	PA: Pittsburgh	$18,480
IL: Chicago	$16,770	TX: Dallas	$16,690
MA: Boston	$20,240	TX: Houston	$15,440
MD: Baltimore	$18,240	WA: Seattle	$21,060

FACTORS THAT MAY AFFECT EARNINGS

Educational Attainment of Workers and Effect on Earnings

	Percent at Level	Effect on Earnings
Less than High School	17.6%	−13.3%
Some High School	21.6%	−16.7%
High School or Equivalent	40.7%	11.8%
Some College but No Degree	12.1%	7.8%
Associate Degree	3.0%	−8.6%
Bachelor's Degree	4.0%	13.9%
Master's Degree	—	—
Doctoral Degree	—	—
First Professional Degree	—	—

Flexibility of Earnings

Average Hours Worked: 29
Workers with a Varying Number of Hours: 10.4%
Workers Earning Some Overtime Pay, Tips, or Commissions: 9.8%
Earnings Benefit of Working Overtime: 18.7%

Gender

	Male	Female
Percent	37.6%	62.4%
Effect on Earnings	—	−6.9%

Union Membership

Percentage Union Members: 7.3%
Earnings Benefit of Union Membership: −3.3%

Veteran Status

Percentage Who Have Been on Active Duty: Insignificant
Earnings Benefit of Veteran Status: No significant data available

51-6021 Pressers, Textile, Garment, and Related Materials

Press or shape articles by hand or machine.

- Education or Training Required: Short-term on-the-job training
- Job Growth: 2.9%
- Annual Openings: 14,000
- Self-Employed: 0.1%
- Part-Time: 41.7%

NATIONAL WAGE FIGURES (ANNUAL)

Beginning	25th Percentile	Median	Mean	75th Percentile	90th Percentile
$13,540	$15,490	$17,800	$18,470	$21,070	$24,350

Median Wages for Industries Employing Largest Numbers (Annual)

Industry	Median Income
Federal, State, and Local Government	$29,350
General Merchandise Stores	$25,830
Textile Product Mills	$22,730
Hospitals	$21,850
Repair and Maintenance	$20,820
Accommodation	$19,710
Transportation Equipment Manufacturing	$19,700
Textile Mills	$19,110
Nonstore Retailers	$19,070
Sporting Goods, Hobby, Book, and Music Stores	$18,470

Median Wages for States (Annual)

AK	$18,210	KY	$17,290	NY	$17,340
AL	$15,850	LA	$15,620	OH	$18,540
AR	$16,490	MA	$20,790	OK	$18,650
AZ	$14,670	MD	$19,670	OR	$18,860
CA	$18,140	ME	$20,520	PA	$18,840
CO	$19,790	MI	$18,140	RI	$20,250
CT	$20,790	MN	$22,190	SC	$17,020
DC	$20,340	MO	$19,270	SD	$17,950
DE	$22,920	MS	$15,320	TN	$17,720
FL	$18,220	MT	$17,850	TX	$15,190
GA	$17,300	NC	$17,790	UT	$18,280
HI	$18,190	ND	$17,500	VA	$17,840
IA	$20,090	NE	$16,640	VT	$17,800
ID	$18,060	NH	$21,740	WA	$19,720
IL	$17,790	NJ	$19,870	WI	$19,370
IN	$18,430	NM	$15,720	WV	$16,380
KS	$16,240	NV	$20,650	WY	$17,600

Median Wages for the Largest Metropolitan Areas (Annual)

AZ: Phoenix	$14,700	MI: Detroit	$20,050
CA: Los Angeles	$17,520	MN: Minneapolis	$22,960
CA: Riverside	$17,900	MO: Kansas City	$18,620
CA: Sacramento	$19,680	MO: St. Louis	$20,500
CA: San Diego	$19,060	NV: Las Vegas	$20,490
CA: San Francisco	$20,040	NY: New York	$17,380
CO: Denver	$20,220	OH: Cincinnati	$18,650
DC: Washington	$19,540	OH: Cleveland	$18,930
FL: Miami	$19,810	OH: Columbus	$20,260
FL: Orlando	$19,540	OR: Portland	$19,770
FL: Tampa	$17,830	PA: Philadelphia	$21,520
GA: Atlanta	$17,880	PA: Pittsburgh	$16,290
IL: Chicago	$17,660	TX: Dallas	$15,780
MA: Boston	no data	TX: Houston	$14,610
MD: Baltimore	$21,840	WA: Seattle	$20,760

FACTORS THAT MAY AFFECT EARNINGS

Educational Attainment of Workers and Effect on Earnings

	Percent at Level	Effect on Earnings
Less than High School	27.9%	2.4%
Some High School	29.4%	−15.7%
High School or Equivalent	35.3%	16.4%
Some College but No Degree	—	—
Associate Degree	—	—
Bachelor's Degree	—	—
Master's Degree	—	—
Doctoral Degree	—	—
First Professional Degree	—	—

Figures do not total 100% because some levels have a very small sample size.

Flexibility of Earnings

Average Hours Worked: 32
Workers with a Varying Number of Hours: 7.2%
Workers Earning Some Overtime Pay, Tips, or Commissions: 8.3%
Earnings Benefit of Working Overtime: 18.7%

Gender

	Male	Female
Percent	29.2%	70.8%
Effect on Earnings	11.1%	−32.0%

Union Membership

Percentage Union Members: Insignificant
Earnings Benefit of Union Membership: No significant data available

Veteran Status

Percentage Who Have Been on Active Duty: Insignificant
Earnings Benefit of Veteran Status: No significant data available

51-6031 Sewing Machine Operators

Operate or tend sewing machines to join, reinforce, decorate, or perform related sewing operations in the manufacture of garment or nongarment products.

- Education or Training Required: Moderate-term on-the-job training
- Job Growth: –36.5%
- Annual Openings: 20,000
- Self-Employed: 6.7%
- Part-Time: 29.5%

NATIONAL WAGE FIGURES (ANNUAL)

Beginning	25th Percentile	Median	Mean	75th Percentile	90th Percentile
$14,320	$15,970	$18,810	$20,340	$23,300	$28,850

Median Wages for Industries Employing Largest Numbers (Annual)

Industry	Median Income
Furniture and Related Product Manufacturing	$22,710
Transportation Equipment Manufacturing	$22,320
Warehousing and Storage	$22,100
Miscellaneous Store Retailers	$21,630
Merchant Wholesalers, Nondurable Goods	$21,620
Nonstore Retailers	$21,450
Management of Companies and Enterprises	$21,150
Repair and Maintenance	$20,810
Clothing and Clothing Accessories Stores	$20,530
Machinery Manufacturing	$20,430

Median Wages for States (Annual)

State	Wage	State	Wage	State	Wage
AK	$22,900	KY	$17,910	NY	$17,830
AL	$17,790	LA	$16,700	OH	$21,890
AR	$16,680	MA	$22,060	OK	$18,620
AZ	$20,810	MD	$21,520	OR	$20,840
CA	$17,570	ME	$23,530	PA	$18,970
CO	$21,720	MI	$21,930	RI	$23,400
CT	$23,120	MN	$23,220	SC	$20,410
DC	no data	MO	$19,510	SD	$18,660
DE	$20,970	MS	$19,990	TN	$18,850
FL	$19,360	MT	$16,870	TX	$17,870
GA	$19,960	NC	$20,630	UT	$17,310
HI	$15,860	ND	$20,140	VA	$18,940
IA	$19,580	NE	$19,250	VT	$21,020
ID	$18,520	NH	$23,590	WA	$21,570
IL	$18,420	NJ	$22,110	WI	$22,340
IN	$21,570	NM	$17,520	WV	$16,930
KS	$17,970	NV	$21,120	WY	$17,290

Median Wages for the Largest Metropolitan Areas (Annual)

Area	Wage	Area	Wage
AZ: Phoenix	$21,220	MI: Detroit	$22,920
CA: Los Angeles	$17,320	MN: Minneapolis	$24,080
CA: Riverside	$20,810	MO: Kansas City	$21,560
CA: Sacramento	$20,070	MO: St. Louis	$20,070
CA: San Diego	$19,500	NV: Las Vegas	$20,690
CA: San Francisco	$18,280	NY: New York	$18,200
CO: Denver	$21,680	OH: Cincinnati	$21,550
DC: Washington	$21,970	OH: Cleveland	$27,340
FL: Miami	$16,910	OH: Columbus	$21,650
FL: Orlando	$20,730	OR: Portland	$21,600
FL: Tampa	$20,240	PA: Philadelphia	$18,830
GA: Atlanta	$20,140	PA: Pittsburgh	$19,530
IL: Chicago	$18,300	TX: Dallas	$19,280
MA: Boston	$23,050	TX: Houston	$19,870
MD: Baltimore	$21,520	WA: Seattle	$21,860

FACTORS THAT MAY AFFECT EARNINGS

Educational Attainment of Workers and Effect on Earnings

	Percent at Level	Effect on Earnings
Less than High School	23.0%	–11.3%
Some High School	19.2%	–7.7%
High School or Equivalent	34.7%	3.9%
Some College but No Degree	12.2%	14.2%
Associate Degree	4.7%	–9.9%
Bachelor's Degree	4.7%	36.3%
Master's Degree	—	—
Doctoral Degree	—	—
First Professional Degree	—	—

Flexibility of Earnings

Average Hours Worked: 32
Workers with a Varying Number of Hours: 7.8%
Workers Earning Some Overtime Pay, Tips, or Commissions: 10.1%
Earnings Benefit of Working Overtime: 8.7%

Gender

	Male	Female
Percent	22.1%	77.9%
Effect on Earnings	6.3%	–1.7%

Union Membership

Percentage Union Members: Insignificant
Earnings Benefit of Union Membership: No significant data available

Veteran Status

Percentage Who Have Been on Active Duty: Insignificant
Earnings Benefit of Veteran Status: No significant data available

51-6041 Shoe and Leather Workers and Repairers

Construct, decorate, or repair leather and leather-like products, such as luggage, shoes, and saddles.

- Education or Training Required: Long-term on-the-job training
- Job Growth: –16.0%
- Annual Openings: 2,000
- Self-Employed: 28.2%
- Part-Time: 11.1%

NATIONAL WAGE FIGURES (ANNUAL)

Beginning	25th Percentile	Median	Mean	75th Percentile	90th Percentile
$14,690	$16,890	$20,450	$21,660	$24,820	$30,710

Median Wages for Industries Employing Largest Numbers (Annual)

Industry	Median Income
Clothing and Clothing Accessories Stores	$22,120
Leather and Allied Product Manufacturing	$20,340
Repair and Maintenance	$20,100
Apparel Manufacturing	$19,230
Sporting Goods, Hobby, Book, and Music Stores	$16,830

Median Wages for States (Annual)

AK	no data	KY	no data	NY	$20,090
AL	$19,150	LA	no data	OH	$21,320
AR	$17,030	MA	$19,560	OK	$15,980
AZ	no data	MD	no data	OR	$24,430
CA	$19,590	ME	$26,380	PA	$20,730
CO	$29,120	MI	no data	RI	no data
CT	$21,730	MN	no data	SC	$20,060
DC	no data	MO	no data	SD	no data
DE	no data	MS	no data	TN	$20,760
FL	$14,660	MT	no data	TX	$19,200
GA	$21,300	NC	$18,850	UT	no data
HI	no data	ND	$14,080	VA	$21,100
IA	no data	NE	no data	VT	no data
ID	no data	NH	no data	WA	no data
IL	no data	NJ	$19,450	WI	$22,730
IN	$23,170	NM	$26,820	WV	no data
KS	no data	NV	no data	WY	no data

Median Wages for the Largest Metropolitan Areas (Annual)

AZ: Phoenix	$25,700	MI: Detroit	no data
CA: Los Angeles	$19,460	MN: Minneapolis	$22,200
CA: Riverside	no data	MO: Kansas City	no data
CA: Sacramento	no data	MO: St. Louis	no data
CA: San Diego	no data	NV: Las Vegas	no data
CA: San Francisco	no data	NY: New York	$19,590
CO: Denver	no data	OH: Cincinnati	no data
DC: Washington	$21,720	OH: Cleveland	no data
FL: Miami	$14,280	OH: Columbus	no data
FL: Orlando	no data	OR: Portland	$24,840
FL: Tampa	no data	PA: Philadelphia	$18,570
GA: Atlanta	no data	PA: Pittsburgh	no data
IL: Chicago	no data	TX: Dallas	$18,600
MA: Boston	$18,870	TX: Houston	$20,860
MD: Baltimore	no data	WA: Seattle	no data

FACTORS THAT MAY AFFECT EARNINGS

Educational Attainment of Workers and Effect on Earnings

Figures are based on a group of occupations: Textile, Apparel, and Furnishings Workers

	Percent at Level	Effect on Earnings
Less than High School	17.3%	–9.8%
Some High School	19.2%	–13.9%
High School or Equivalent	38.7%	10.1%
Some College but No Degree	12.0%	–2.2%
Associate Degree	5.5%	13.9%
Bachelor's Degree	5.9%	5.9%
Master's Degree	—	—
Doctoral Degree	—	—
First Professional Degree	—	—

Flexibility of Earnings

Average Hours Worked: 38
Workers with a Varying Number of Hours: 9.9%
Workers Earning Some Overtime Pay, Tips, or Commissions: 20.0%
Earnings Benefit of Working Overtime: 18.7%

Gender

	Male	Female
Percent	86.8%	13.2%
Effect on Earnings	11.1%	–32.0%

Union Membership

Percentage Union Members: 10.0%
Earnings Benefit of Union Membership: 4.0%

Veteran Status

Percentage Who Have Been on Active Duty: Insignificant
Earnings Benefit of Veteran Status: No significant data available

51-6042 Shoe Machine Operators and Tenders

Operate or tend a variety of machines to join, decorate, reinforce, or finish shoes and shoe parts.

- Education or Training Required: Moderate-term on-the-job training
- Job Growth: –27.3%
- Annual Openings: Fewer than 500
- Self-Employed: 0.0%
- Part-Time: 36.1%

NATIONAL WAGE FIGURES (ANNUAL)

Beginning	25th Percentile	Median	Mean	75th Percentile	90th Percentile
$15,100	$17,570	$21,910	$22,710	$27,170	$31,810

Median Wages for Industries Employing Largest Numbers (Annual)

Industry	Median Income
Leather and Allied Product Manufacturing	$21,890

Median Wages for States (Annual)

AK	no data	KY	no data	NY	no data
AL	no data	LA	no data	OH	no data
AR	$18,550	MA	$21,290	OK	no data
AZ	no data	MD	no data	OR	no data
CA	$20,240	ME	$26,000	PA	no data
CO	no data	MI	no data	RI	no data
CT	no data	MN	no data	SC	no data
DC	no data	MO	$22,350	SD	no data
DE	no data	MS	no data	TN	no data
FL	$30,390	MT	no data	TX	$20,030
GA	no data	NC	no data	UT	no data
HI	no data	ND	no data	VA	no data
IA	no data	NE	no data	VT	no data
ID	no data	NH	no data	WA	no data
IL	no data	NJ	no data	WI	no data
IN	no data	NM	no data	WV	no data
KS	no data	NV	no data	WY	no data

Median Wages for the Largest Metropolitan Areas (Annual)

AZ: Phoenix	no data	MI: Detroit	no data
CA: Los Angeles	$19,950	MN: Minneapolis	no data
CA: Riverside	no data	MO: Kansas City	no data
CA: Sacramento	no data	MO: St. Louis	no data
CA: San Diego	no data	NV: Las Vegas	no data
CA: San Francisco	no data	NY: New York	$19,210
CO: Denver	no data	OH: Cincinnati	no data
DC: Washington	no data	OH: Cleveland	no data
FL: Miami	no data	OH: Columbus	no data
FL: Orlando	no data	OR: Portland	no data
FL: Tampa	no data	PA: Philadelphia	no data
GA: Atlanta	no data	PA: Pittsburgh	no data
IL: Chicago	$17,970	TX: Dallas	no data
MA: Boston	$20,670	TX: Houston	no data
MD: Baltimore	no data	WA: Seattle	no data

FACTORS THAT MAY AFFECT EARNINGS

Educational Attainment of Workers and Effect on Earnings

Figures are based on a group of occupations: Textile, Apparel, and Furnishings Workers

	Percent at Level	Effect on Earnings
Less than High School	17.3%	–9.8%
Some High School	19.2%	–13.9%
High School or Equivalent	38.7%	10.1%
Some College but No Degree	12.0%	–2.2%
Associate Degree	5.5%	13.9%
Bachelor's Degree	5.9%	5.9%
Master's Degree	—	—
Doctoral Degree	—	—
First Professional Degree	—	—

Flexibility of Earnings

Average Hours Worked: 37
Workers with a Varying Number of Hours: 5.8%
Workers Earning Some Overtime Pay, Tips, or Commissions: 9.1%
Earnings Benefit of Working Overtime: 18.7%

Gender

	Male	Female
Percent	43.4%	56.6%
Effect on Earnings	11.1%	–32.0%

Union Membership

Percentage Union Members: 18.2%
Earnings Benefit of Union Membership: 4.0%

Veteran Status

Percentage Who Have Been on Active Duty: Insignificant
Earnings Benefit of Veteran Status: No significant data available

51-6051 Sewers, Hand

Sew, join, reinforce, or finish, usually with needle and thread, a variety of manufactured items. Includes weavers and stitchers.

- Education or Training Required: Short-term on-the-job training
- Job Growth: –19.7%
- Annual Openings: 2,000
- Self-Employed: 59.2%
- Part-Time: 36.1%

Note: Earnings figures do not reflect self-employed workers, who make up a large fraction of the workforce for this occupation.

NATIONAL WAGE FIGURES (ANNUAL)

Beginning	25th Percentile	Median	Mean	75th Percentile	90th Percentile
$14,190	$16,520	$20,370	$21,680	$24,790	$31,730

Median Wages for Industries Employing Largest Numbers (Annual)

Industry	Median Income
Performing Arts, Spectator Sports, and Related Industries	$30,710
Printing and Related Support Activities	$25,340
Accommodation	$23,830
Administrative and Support Services	$22,500
Professional, Scientific, and Technical Services	$22,250
Clothing and Clothing Accessories Stores	$21,960
Merchant Wholesalers, Nondurable Goods	$21,640
Transportation Equipment Manufacturing	$21,410
Repair and Maintenance	$21,130
Furniture and Related Product Manufacturing	$20,710

Median Wages for States (Annual)

AK	no data	KY	no data	NY	$22,140
AL	$21,140	LA	$17,660	OH	$21,600
AR	$18,300	MA	$20,840	OK	$19,450
AZ	no data	MD	$20,890	OR	$24,000
CA	$19,900	ME	$25,150	PA	$15,140
CO	$21,160	MI	$18,830	RI	$20,780
CT	$21,710	MN	$19,020	SC	$19,710
DC	no data	MO	$18,470	SD	no data
DE	no data	MS	$16,320	TN	$17,400
FL	$20,470	MT	no data	TX	$15,650
GA	$21,700	NC	$19,920	UT	$14,750
HI	no data	ND	no data	VA	$19,080
IA	no data	NE	no data	VT	$23,210
ID	no data	NH	no data	WA	$24,610
IL	$21,230	NJ	$22,720	WI	$20,560
IN	$22,030	NM	no data	WV	$23,070
KS	no data	NV	$23,630	WY	no data

Median Wages for the Largest Metropolitan Areas (Annual)

AZ: Phoenix	no data	MI: Detroit	$20,700
CA: Los Angeles	$19,820	MN: Minneapolis	no data
CA: Riverside	no data	MO: Kansas City	no data
CA: Sacramento	no data	MO: St. Louis	$19,440
CA: San Diego	$20,620	NV: Las Vegas	$24,730
CA: San Francisco	$18,530	NY: New York	$22,100
CO: Denver	no data	OH: Cincinnati	$21,540
DC: Washington	no data	OH: Cleveland	no data
FL: Miami	$21,120	OH: Columbus	$21,470
FL: Orlando	$18,780	OR: Portland	$27,860
FL: Tampa	$20,940	PA: Philadelphia	$24,280
GA: Atlanta	$22,520	PA: Pittsburgh	no data
IL: Chicago	$21,500	TX: Dallas	no data
MA: Boston	$20,560	TX: Houston	$14,670
MD: Baltimore	no data	WA: Seattle	$25,550

FACTORS THAT MAY AFFECT EARNINGS

Educational Attainment of Workers and Effect on Earnings

Figures are based on a group of occupations: Textile, Apparel, and Furnishings Workers

	Percent at Level	Effect on Earnings
Less than High School	17.3%	–9.8%
Some High School	19.2%	–13.9%
High School or Equivalent	38.7%	10.1%
Some College but No Degree	12.0%	–2.2%
Associate Degree	5.5%	13.9%
Bachelor's Degree	5.9%	5.9%
Master's Degree	—	—
Doctoral Degree	—	—
First Professional Degree	—	—

Flexibility of Earnings

Average Hours Worked: 31
Workers with a Varying Number of Hours: 9.2%
Workers Earning Some Overtime Pay, Tips, or Commissions: 10.8%
Earnings Benefit of Working Overtime: 18.7%

Gender

	Male	Female
Percent	31.1%	68.9%
Effect on Earnings	11.1%	–32.0%

Union Membership

Percentage Union Members: 4.7%
Earnings Benefit of Union Membership: 4.0%

Veteran Status

Percentage Who Have Been on Active Duty: Insignificant
Earnings Benefit of Veteran Status: No significant data available

51-6052 Tailors, Dressmakers, and Custom Sewers

Design, make, alter, repair, or fit garments.

- Education or Training Required: Long-term on-the-job training
- Job Growth: 0.3%
- Annual Openings: 4,000
- Self-Employed: 48.8%
- Part-Time: 36.1%

Note: Earnings figures do not reflect self-employed workers, who make up a large fraction of the workforce for this occupation.

NATIONAL WAGE FIGURES (ANNUAL)

Beginning	25th Percentile	Median	Mean	75th Percentile	90th Percentile
$15,230	$18,430	$22,910	$24,770	$29,200	$36,680

Median Wages for Industries Employing Largest Numbers (Annual)

Industry	Median Income
Performing Arts, Spectator Sports, and Related Industries	$31,060
Merchant Wholesalers, Nondurable Goods	$30,670
General Merchandise Stores	$28,280
Accommodation	$26,520
Federal, State, and Local Government	$26,120
Nonstore Retailers	$26,020
Museums, Historical Sites, and Similar Institutions	$25,580
Miscellaneous Store Retailers	$24,680
Clothing and Clothing Accessories Stores	$24,580
Hospitals	$23,640

Median Wages for States (Annual)

State	Wage	State	Wage	State	Wage
AK	$26,910	KY	$24,360	NY	$28,140
AL	$19,080	LA	$19,280	OH	$22,860
AR	$16,470	MA	$21,410	OK	$23,370
AZ	$24,920	MD	$23,060	OR	$25,340
CA	$24,920	ME	$21,420	PA	$24,250
CO	$22,690	MI	$24,790	RI	$26,350
CT	$25,170	MN	$27,930	SC	$18,760
DC	$39,830	MO	$20,320	SD	no data
DE	$30,150	MS	$20,060	TN	$20,090
FL	$22,230	MT	$20,580	TX	$21,500
GA	$19,550	NC	$21,250	UT	$19,440
HI	$23,860	ND	$20,090	VA	$22,720
IA	$20,570	NE	$20,760	VT	no data
ID	$18,240	NH	$24,800	WA	$28,260
IL	$23,690	NJ	$20,420	WI	$25,950
IN	$19,370	NM	$17,780	WV	$19,920
KS	$18,610	NV	$26,010	WY	no data

Median Wages for the Largest Metropolitan Areas (Annual)

Area	Wage	Area	Wage
AZ: Phoenix	$25,020	MI: Detroit	$25,400
CA: Los Angeles	$25,650	MN: Minneapolis	$32,680
CA: Riverside	$24,280	MO: Kansas City	$27,060
CA: Sacramento	$24,490	MO: St. Louis	$21,820
CA: San Diego	$19,120	NV: Las Vegas	$26,960
CA: San Francisco	$30,290	NY: New York	$25,820
CO: Denver	$22,260	OH: Cincinnati	$23,700
DC: Washington	$23,060	OH: Cleveland	$23,810
FL: Miami	$23,380	OH: Columbus	$23,510
FL: Orlando	$22,570	OR: Portland	$26,060
FL: Tampa	$18,150	PA: Philadelphia	$26,440
GA: Atlanta	$22,360	PA: Pittsburgh	$26,000
IL: Chicago	$25,230	TX: Dallas	$23,080
MA: Boston	no data	TX: Houston	$22,600
MD: Baltimore	$25,160	WA: Seattle	$30,170

FACTORS THAT MAY AFFECT EARNINGS

Educational Attainment of Workers and Effect on Earnings

Figures are based on a group of occupations: Textile, Apparel, and Furnishings Workers

	Percent at Level	Effect on Earnings
Less than High School	17.3%	−9.8%
Some High School	19.2%	−13.9%
High School or Equivalent	38.7%	10.1%
Some College but No Degree	12.0%	−2.2%
Associate Degree	5.5%	13.9%
Bachelor's Degree	5.9%	5.9%
Master's Degree	—	—
Doctoral Degree	—	—
First Professional Degree	—	—

Flexibility of Earnings

Average Hours Worked: 31
Workers with a Varying Number of Hours: 9.2%
Workers Earning Some Overtime Pay, Tips, or Commissions: 10.8%
Earnings Benefit of Working Overtime: 18.7%

Gender

	Male	Female
Percent	25.3%	74.7%
Effect on Earnings	11.1%	−32.0%

Union Membership

Percentage Union Members: 4.7%
Earnings Benefit of Union Membership: 4.0%

Veteran Status

Percentage Who Have Been on Active Duty: Insignificant
Earnings Benefit of Veteran Status: No significant data available

51-6061 Textile Bleaching and Dyeing Machine Operators and Tenders

Operate or tend machines to bleach, shrink, wash, dye, or finish textiles or synthetic or glass fibers.

- Education or Training Required: Moderate-term on-the-job training
- Job Growth: –45.3%
- Annual Openings: 4,000
- Self-Employed: 0.0%
- Part-Time: 36.1%

NATIONAL WAGE FIGURES (ANNUAL)

Beginning	25th Percentile	Median	Mean	75th Percentile	90th Percentile
$16,420	$19,340	$23,290	$23,920	$27,800	$32,720

Median Wages for Industries Employing Largest Numbers (Annual)

Industry	Median Income
Paper Manufacturing	$40,730
Nonmetallic Mineral Product Manufacturing	$35,990
Leather and Allied Product Manufacturing	$27,810
Textile Product Mills	$26,060
Textile Mills	$23,230
Wholesale Electronic Markets and Agents and Brokers	$23,070
Merchant Wholesalers, Nondurable Goods	$22,470
Apparel Manufacturing	$21,270
Administrative and Support Services	$18,680

Median Wages for States (Annual)

State	Wage	State	Wage	State	Wage
AK	no data	KY	no data	NY	no data
AL	$21,860	LA	no data	OH	$21,470
AR	no data	MA	$27,310	OK	no data
AZ	no data	MD	$27,180	OR	no data
CA	$18,540	ME	$27,100	PA	$25,490
CO	no data	MI	$27,690	RI	$29,240
CT	$21,370	MN	$24,180	SC	$24,540
DC	no data	MO	$28,780	SD	no data
DE	no data	MS	$25,440	TN	$26,370
FL	$20,630	MT	no data	TX	$28,760
GA	$23,170	NC	$23,760	UT	no data
HI	no data	ND	no data	VA	$22,910
IA	no data	NE	no data	VT	no data
ID	no data	NH	$26,820	WA	no data
IL	no data	NJ	$26,550	WI	$25,970
IN	no data	NM	no data	WV	no data
KS	no data	NV	no data	WY	no data

Median Wages for the Largest Metropolitan Areas (Annual)

Area	Wage	Area	Wage
AZ: Phoenix	no data	MI: Detroit	no data
CA: Los Angeles	$18,520	MN: Minneapolis	no data
CA: Riverside	no data	MO: Kansas City	no data
CA: Sacramento	no data	MO: St. Louis	no data
CA: San Diego	no data	NV: Las Vegas	no data
CA: San Francisco	$18,620	NY: New York	$29,110
CO: Denver	no data	OH: Cincinnati	$22,990
DC: Washington	no data	OH: Cleveland	no data
FL: Miami	$19,670	OH: Columbus	no data
FL: Orlando	no data	OR: Portland	no data
FL: Tampa	no data	PA: Philadelphia	$25,050
GA: Atlanta	$24,830	PA: Pittsburgh	no data
IL: Chicago	no data	TX: Dallas	$23,400
MA: Boston	$24,220	TX: Houston	no data
MD: Baltimore	no data	WA: Seattle	no data

FACTORS THAT MAY AFFECT EARNINGS

Educational Attainment of Workers and Effect on Earnings

	Percent at Level	Effect on Earnings
Less than High School	—	—
Some High School	—	—
High School or Equivalent	77.8%	–0.3%
Some College but No Degree	—	—
Associate Degree	—	—
Bachelor's Degree	—	—
Master's Degree	—	—
Doctoral Degree	—	—
First Professional Degree	—	—

Figures do not total 100% because some levels have a very small sample size.

Flexibility of Earnings

Average Hours Worked: 32
Workers with a Varying Number of Hours: 3.2%
Workers Earning Some Overtime Pay, Tips, or Commissions: 44.4%
Earnings Benefit of Working Overtime: 18.7%

Gender

	Male	Female
Percent	82.1%	17.9%
Effect on Earnings	11.1%	–32.0%

Union Membership

Percentage Union Members: 22.2%
Earnings Benefit of Union Membership: 4.0%

Veteran Status

Percentage Who Have Been on Active Duty: Insignificant
Earnings Benefit of Veteran Status: No significant data available

51-6062 Textile Cutting Machine Setters, Operators, and Tenders

Set up, operate, or tend machines that cut textiles.

- Education or Training Required: Moderate-term on-the-job training
- Job Growth: –25.0%
- Annual Openings: 1,000
- Self-Employed: 10.8%
- Part-Time: 36.1%

NATIONAL WAGE FIGURES (ANNUAL)

Beginning	25th Percentile	Median	Mean	75th Percentile	90th Percentile
$15,240	$17,720	$21,620	$22,740	$26,770	$32,620

Median Wages for Industries Employing Largest Numbers (Annual)

Industry	Median Income
Furniture and Related Product Manufacturing	$25,070
Clothing and Clothing Accessories Stores	$24,970
Nonstore Retailers	$23,560
Professional, Scientific, and Technical Services	$23,290
Transportation Equipment Manufacturing	$22,920
Printing and Related Support Activities	$22,510
Chemical Manufacturing	$22,380
Machinery Manufacturing	$22,300
Merchant Wholesalers, Nondurable Goods	$22,300
Miscellaneous Manufacturing	$22,100

Median Wages for States (Annual)

State	Wage	State	Wage	State	Wage
AK	no data	KY	$22,250	NY	$20,140
AL	$20,950	LA	no data	OH	$30,340
AR	$22,500	MA	$21,630	OK	$19,030
AZ	$23,040	MD	$18,880	OR	$21,450
CA	$19,290	ME	$22,270	PA	$20,460
CO	no data	MI	$29,300	RI	$22,240
CT	$22,340	MN	$25,070	SC	$23,200
DC	no data	MO	$23,460	SD	no data
DE	no data	MS	$21,010	TN	$23,560
FL	$21,130	MT	no data	TX	$21,400
GA	$21,890	NC	$23,850	UT	$18,480
HI	no data	ND	no data	VA	$20,500
IA	$21,890	NE	no data	VT	no data
ID	no data	NH	$21,620	WA	$23,970
IL	$20,270	NJ	$23,450	WI	$23,180
IN	$23,550	NM	no data	WV	no data
KS	$18,890	NV	no data	WY	no data

Median Wages for the Largest Metropolitan Areas (Annual)

Area	Wage	Area	Wage
AZ: Phoenix	no data	MI: Detroit	no data
CA: Los Angeles	$18,590	MN: Minneapolis	$27,810
CA: Riverside	$23,720	MO: Kansas City	$21,680
CA: Sacramento	no data	MO: St. Louis	$21,720
CA: San Diego	$25,400	NV: Las Vegas	no data
CA: San Francisco	$24,380	NY: New York	$20,720
CO: Denver	no data	OH: Cincinnati	$31,540
DC: Washington	$27,570	OH: Cleveland	$17,540
FL: Miami	$20,440	OH: Columbus	$24,240
FL: Orlando	no data	OR: Portland	$23,340
FL: Tampa	$22,940	PA: Philadelphia	$23,640
GA: Atlanta	$19,630	PA: Pittsburgh	$18,570
IL: Chicago	$21,340	TX: Dallas	$24,720
MA: Boston	no data	TX: Houston	$22,970
MD: Baltimore	no data	WA: Seattle	$24,010

FACTORS THAT MAY AFFECT EARNINGS

Educational Attainment of Workers and Effect on Earnings

	Percent at Level	Effect on Earnings
Less than High School	—	—
Some High School	—	—
High School or Equivalent	40.0%	–27.6%
Some College but No Degree	—	—
Associate Degree	—	—
Bachelor's Degree	—	—
Master's Degree	—	—
Doctoral Degree	—	—
First Professional Degree	—	—

Figures do not total 100% because some levels have a very small sample size.

Flexibility of Earnings

Average Hours Worked: 34
Workers with a Varying Number of Hours: 3.4%
Workers Earning Some Overtime Pay, Tips, or Commissions: 10.8%
Earnings Benefit of Working Overtime: 18.7%

Gender

	Male	Female
Percent	64.5%	35.5%
Effect on Earnings	11.1%	–32.0%

Union Membership

Percentage Union Members: 4.7%
Earnings Benefit of Union Membership: 4.0%

Veteran Status

Percentage Who Have Been on Active Duty: Insignificant
Earnings Benefit of Veteran Status: No significant data available

51-6063 Textile Knitting and Weaving Machine Setters, Operators, and Tenders

Set up, operate, or tend machines that knit, loop, weave, or draw in textiles.

- Education or Training Required: Long-term on-the-job training
- Job Growth: –56.2%
- Annual Openings: 6,000
- Self-Employed: 4.9%
- Part-Time: 23.5%

NATIONAL WAGE FIGURES (ANNUAL)

Beginning	25th Percentile	Median	Mean	75th Percentile	90th Percentile
$17,040	$20,270	$24,290	$24,530	$28,310	$32,800

Median Wages for Industries Employing Largest Numbers (Annual)

Industry	Median Income
Chemical Manufacturing	$31,600
Plastics and Rubber Products Manufacturing	$29,310
Professional, Scientific, and Technical Services	$27,660
Textile Product Mills	$25,700
Textile Mills	$24,880
Transportation Equipment Manufacturing	$22,550
Apparel Manufacturing	$21,260
Miscellaneous Manufacturing	$19,080
Administrative and Support Services	$17,850
Merchant Wholesalers, Durable Goods	$15,260

Median Wages for States (Annual)

State		State		State	
AK	no data	KY	no data	NY	$25,210
AL	$21,740	LA	$17,230	OH	$20,220
AR	no data	MA	$26,090	OK	no data
AZ	no data	MD	$26,130	OR	no data
CA	$19,110	ME	no data	PA	$22,930
CO	no data	MI	$21,870	RI	$21,840
CT	$27,840	MN	$26,560	SC	$26,180
DC	no data	MO	$21,110	SD	no data
DE	no data	MS	$23,140	TN	$20,680
FL	$15,420	MT	no data	TX	$24,330
GA	$25,880	NC	$24,190	UT	no data
HI	no data	ND	no data	VA	$24,500
IA	no data	NE	no data	VT	$23,330
ID	no data	NH	$31,620	WA	$22,390
IL	$26,470	NJ	$23,910	WI	no data
IN	$25,570	NM	no data	WV	no data
KS	no data	NV	no data	WY	no data

Median Wages for the Largest Metropolitan Areas (Annual)

Area		Area	
AZ: Phoenix	no data	MI: Detroit	$19,380
CA: Los Angeles	$18,550	MN: Minneapolis	no data
CA: Riverside	no data	MO: Kansas City	no data
CA: Sacramento	no data	MO: St. Louis	no data
CA: San Diego	$20,910	NV: Las Vegas	no data
CA: San Francisco	no data	NY: New York	$24,270
CO: Denver	no data	OH: Cincinnati	no data
DC: Washington	no data	OH: Cleveland	no data
FL: Miami	$15,240	OH: Columbus	no data
FL: Orlando	no data	OR: Portland	no data
FL: Tampa	no data	PA: Philadelphia	$23,750
GA: Atlanta	$26,720	PA: Pittsburgh	$20,760
IL: Chicago	$25,960	TX: Dallas	$24,760
MA: Boston	$26,960	TX: Houston	no data
MD: Baltimore	no data	WA: Seattle	$21,190

FACTORS THAT MAY AFFECT EARNINGS

Educational Attainment of Workers and Effect on Earnings

	Percent at Level	Effect on Earnings
Less than High School	—	—
Some High School	—	—
High School or Equivalent	36.8%	–18.8%
Some College but No Degree	—	—
Associate Degree	—	—
Bachelor's Degree	—	—
Master's Degree	—	—
Doctoral Degree	—	—
First Professional Degree	—	—

Figures do not total 100% because some levels have a very small sample size.

Flexibility of Earnings

Average Hours Worked: 27
Workers with a Varying Number of Hours: 18.4%
Workers Earning Some Overtime Pay, Tips, or Commissions: 26.3%
Earnings Benefit of Working Overtime: 18.7%

Gender

	Male	Female
Percent	42.3%	57.7%
Effect on Earnings	11.1%	–32.0%

Union Membership

Percentage Union Members: 5.3%
Earnings Benefit of Union Membership: 4.0%

Veteran Status

Percentage Who Have Been on Active Duty: Insignificant
Earnings Benefit of Veteran Status: No significant data available

51-6064 Textile Winding, Twisting, and Drawing Out Machine Setters, Operators, and Tenders

Set up, operate, or tend machines that wind or twist textiles or draw out and combine sliver, such as wool, hemp, or synthetic fibers.

- Education or Training Required: Moderate-term on-the-job training
- Job Growth: –45.5%
- Annual Openings: 9,000
- Self-Employed: 0.0%
- Part-Time: 36.1%

NATIONAL WAGE FIGURES (ANNUAL)

Beginning	25th Percentile	Median	Mean	75th Percentile	90th Percentile
$17,800	$20,260	$23,050	$23,550	$26,740	$30,150

Median Wages for Industries Employing Largest Numbers (Annual)

Industry	Median Income
Paper Manufacturing	$42,970
Nonmetallic Mineral Product Manufacturing	$31,480
Primary Metal Manufacturing	$28,630
Chemical Manufacturing	$28,350
Fabricated Metal Product Manufacturing	$27,410
Textile Product Mills	$24,920
Management of Companies and Enterprises	$24,820
Textile Mills	$22,430
Apparel Manufacturing	$21,190
Machinery Manufacturing	$19,280

Median Wages for States (Annual)

State		State		State	
AK	no data	KY	no data	NY	$25,370
AL	$22,320	LA	$20,960	OH	$28,070
AR	$22,590	MA	$23,340	OK	no data
AZ	no data	MD	$23,110	OR	$21,740
CA	$17,460	ME	$24,480	PA	$23,000
CO	no data	MI	$34,370	RI	$19,120
CT	$25,520	MN	no data	SC	$22,130
DC	no data	MO	$22,550	SD	no data
DE	no data	MS	$22,150	TN	$24,760
FL	$25,560	MT	no data	TX	$23,150
GA	$24,630	NC	$21,760	UT	no data
HI	no data	ND	no data	VA	$22,420
IA	no data	NE	no data	VT	$21,500
ID	no data	NH	no data	WA	$24,030
IL	$19,520	NJ	$22,880	WI	$22,500
IN	no data	NM	no data	WV	no data
KS	$23,920	NV	no data	WY	no data

Median Wages for the Largest Metropolitan Areas (Annual)

Area		Area	
AZ: Phoenix	no data	MI: Detroit	no data
CA: Los Angeles	$17,310	MN: Minneapolis	no data
CA: Riverside	no data	MO: Kansas City	no data
CA: Sacramento	no data	MO: St. Louis	$22,910
CA: San Diego	no data	NV: Las Vegas	no data
CA: San Francisco	no data	NY: New York	$23,840
CO: Denver	no data	OH: Cincinnati	$27,110
DC: Washington	no data	OH: Cleveland	no data
FL: Miami	$20,090	OH: Columbus	no data
FL: Orlando	no data	OR: Portland	no data
FL: Tampa	no data	PA: Philadelphia	$23,390
GA: Atlanta	$29,070	PA: Pittsburgh	no data
IL: Chicago	no data	TX: Dallas	$28,680
MA: Boston	$22,760	TX: Houston	no data
MD: Baltimore	no data	WA: Seattle	no data

FACTORS THAT MAY AFFECT EARNINGS

Educational Attainment of Workers and Effect on Earnings

	Percent at Level	Effect on Earnings
Less than High School	—	—
Some High School	—	—
High School or Equivalent	52.6%	–0.1%
Some College but No Degree	—	—
Associate Degree	—	—
Bachelor's Degree	—	—
Master's Degree	—	—
Doctoral Degree	—	—
First Professional Degree	—	—

Figures do not total 100% because some levels have a very small sample size.

Flexibility of Earnings

Average Hours Worked: 34
Workers with a Varying Number of Hours: 4.4%
Workers Earning Some Overtime Pay, Tips, or Commissions: 26.3%
Earnings Benefit of Working Overtime: 18.7%

Gender

	Male	Female
Percent	48.5%	51.5%
Effect on Earnings	11.1%	–32.0%

Union Membership

Percentage Union Members: 4.7%
Earnings Benefit of Union Membership: 4.0%

Veteran Status

Percentage Who Have Been on Active Duty: Insignificant
Earnings Benefit of Veteran Status: No significant data available

51-6091 Extruding and Forming Machine Setters, Operators, and Tenders, Synthetic and Glass Fibers

Set up, operate, or tend machines that extrude and form continuous filaments from synthetic materials, such as liquid polymer, rayon, and fiberglass.

- Education or Training Required: Moderate-term on-the-job training
- Job Growth: –25.3%
- Annual Openings: 2,000
- Self-Employed: 0.0%
- Part-Time: 36.1%

NATIONAL WAGE FIGURES (ANNUAL)

Beginning	25th Percentile	Median	Mean	75th Percentile	90th Percentile
$19,330	$23,310	$28,670	$29,910	$35,710	$43,390

Median Wages for Industries Employing Largest Numbers (Annual)

Industry	Median Income
Chemical Manufacturing	$32,660
Miscellaneous Manufacturing	$31,700
Electrical Equipment, Appliance, and Component Manufacturing	$30,980
Paper Manufacturing	$29,050
Textile Product Mills	$28,600
Plastics and Rubber Products Manufacturing	$28,390
Nonmetallic Mineral Product Manufacturing	$28,340
Management of Companies and Enterprises	$28,330
Furniture and Related Product Manufacturing	$28,290
Textile Mills	$27,530

Median Wages for States (Annual)

AK	no data	KY	$33,070	NY	$25,420
AL	$27,030	LA	no data	OH	$27,480
AR	$28,920	MA	$28,150	OK	$31,530
AZ	no data	MD	no data	OR	no data
CA	$22,290	ME	no data	PA	$27,190
CO	no data	MI	$31,230	RI	no data
CT	no data	MN	$23,910	SC	$29,820
DC	no data	MO	$39,160	SD	no data
DE	$27,060	MS	$39,110	TN	$33,790
FL	$20,310	MT	no data	TX	$22,750
GA	$27,840	NC	$28,750	UT	$25,190
HI	no data	ND	no data	VA	$26,840
IA	no data	NE	no data	VT	no data
ID	no data	NH	no data	WA	no data
IL	$29,600	NJ	$27,510	WI	$33,640
IN	$32,090	NM	no data	WV	$30,470
KS	$32,320	NV	no data	WY	no data

Median Wages for the Largest Metropolitan Areas (Annual)

AZ: Phoenix	no data	MI: Detroit	no data
CA: Los Angeles	$22,600	MN: Minneapolis	$23,800
CA: Riverside	no data	MO: Kansas City	$35,500
CA: Sacramento	no data	MO: St. Louis	$32,380
CA: San Diego	no data	NV: Las Vegas	no data
CA: San Francisco	$31,740	NY: New York	$23,750
CO: Denver	no data	OH: Cincinnati	no data
DC: Washington	no data	OH: Cleveland	$29,420
FL: Miami	no data	OH: Columbus	$23,720
FL: Orlando	no data	OR: Portland	no data
FL: Tampa	no data	PA: Philadelphia	$31,350
GA: Atlanta	$26,690	PA: Pittsburgh	no data
IL: Chicago	$28,620	TX: Dallas	$23,380
MA: Boston	$27,700	TX: Houston	$22,000
MD: Baltimore	no data	WA: Seattle	no data

FACTORS THAT MAY AFFECT EARNINGS

Educational Attainment of Workers and Effect on Earnings

Figures are based on a group of occupations: Textile, Apparel, and Furnishings Workers

	Percent at Level	Effect on Earnings
Less than High School	17.3%	–9.8%
Some High School	19.2%	–13.9%
High School or Equivalent	38.7%	10.1%
Some College but No Degree	12.0%	–2.2%
Associate Degree	5.5%	13.9%
Bachelor's Degree	5.9%	5.9%
Master's Degree	—	—
Doctoral Degree	—	—
First Professional Degree	—	—

Flexibility of Earnings

Average Hours Worked: 38
Workers with a Varying Number of Hours: 13.1%
Workers Earning Some Overtime Pay, Tips, or Commissions: 16.7%
Earnings Benefit of Working Overtime: 18.7%

Gender

	Male	Female
Percent	69.6%	30.4%
Effect on Earnings	11.1%	–32.0%

Union Membership

Percentage Union Members: 16.7%
Earnings Benefit of Union Membership: 4.0%

Veteran Status

Percentage Who Have Been on Active Duty: Insignificant
Earnings Benefit of Veteran Status: No significant data available

51-6092 Fabric and Apparel Patternmakers

Draw and construct sets of precision master fabric patterns or layouts. May also mark and cut fabrics and apparel.

- Education or Training Required: Long-term on-the-job training
- Job Growth: –30.5%
- Annual Openings: 1,000
- Self-Employed: 0.0%
- Part-Time: 36.1%

NATIONAL WAGE FIGURES (ANNUAL)

Beginning	25th Percentile	Median	Mean	75th Percentile	90th Percentile
$18,480	$23,970	$32,730	$38,380	$50,780	$69,110

Median Wages for Industries Employing Largest Numbers (Annual)

Industry	Median Income
Apparel Manufacturing	$45,080
Merchant Wholesalers, Nondurable Goods	$43,550
Professional, Scientific, and Technical Services	$39,410
Management of Companies and Enterprises	$35,810
Repair and Maintenance	$32,620
Furniture and Related Product Manufacturing	$28,070
Leather and Allied Product Manufacturing	$26,890
Textile Mills	$26,520
Textile Product Mills	$26,430
Transportation Equipment Manufacturing	$20,750

Median Wages for States (Annual)

State		State		State	
AK	no data	KY	no data	NY	$53,780
AL	$21,940	LA	no data	OH	no data
AR	no data	MA	$46,250	OK	no data
AZ	$19,490	MD	$24,070	OR	$35,380
CA	$46,740	ME	no data	PA	$29,000
CO	no data	MI	$28,620	RI	$26,280
CT	no data	MN	$28,940	SC	$25,480
DC	no data	MO	$27,080	SD	no data
DE	no data	MS	$27,310	TN	$26,690
FL	$29,740	MT	no data	TX	$21,410
GA	$26,630	NC	$30,960	UT	no data
HI	no data	ND	no data	VA	$22,420
IA	$22,540	NE	no data	VT	no data
ID	no data	NH	no data	WA	$30,010
IL	$21,190	NJ	$41,430	WI	$32,910
IN	$30,400	NM	no data	WV	no data
KS	$26,200	NV	no data	WY	no data

Median Wages for the Largest Metropolitan Areas (Annual)

Area		Area	
AZ: Phoenix	$19,420	MI: Detroit	$30,080
CA: Los Angeles	$48,250	MN: Minneapolis	no data
CA: Riverside	no data	MO: Kansas City	no data
CA: Sacramento	no data	MO: St. Louis	$29,980
CA: San Diego	no data	NV: Las Vegas	no data
CA: San Francisco	$39,500	NY: New York	$53,690
CO: Denver	no data	OH: Cincinnati	no data
DC: Washington	no data	OH: Cleveland	no data
FL: Miami	$31,720	OH: Columbus	no data
FL: Orlando	no data	OR: Portland	$34,120
FL: Tampa	no data	PA: Philadelphia	$29,900
GA: Atlanta	$27,870	PA: Pittsburgh	no data
IL: Chicago	$19,070	TX: Dallas	$24,910
MA: Boston	$50,950	TX: Houston	no data
MD: Baltimore	no data	WA: Seattle	$31,550

FACTORS THAT MAY AFFECT EARNINGS

Educational Attainment of Workers and Effect on Earnings

Figures are based on a group of occupations: Textile, Apparel, and Furnishings Workers

	Percent at Level	Effect on Earnings
Less than High School	17.3%	–9.8%
Some High School	19.2%	–13.9%
High School or Equivalent	38.7%	10.1%
Some College but No Degree	12.0%	–2.2%
Associate Degree	5.5%	13.9%
Bachelor's Degree	5.9%	5.9%
Master's Degree	—	—
Doctoral Degree	—	—
First Professional Degree	—	—

Flexibility of Earnings

Average Hours Worked: 31
Workers with a Varying Number of Hours: 5.9%
Workers Earning Some Overtime Pay, Tips, or Commissions: 10.8%
Earnings Benefit of Working Overtime: 18.7%

Gender

	Male	Female
Percent	11.1%	88.9%
Effect on Earnings	11.1%	–32.0%

Union Membership

Percentage Union Members: 4.7%
Earnings Benefit of Union Membership: 4.0%

Veteran Status

Percentage Who Have Been on Active Duty: Insignificant
Earnings Benefit of Veteran Status: No significant data available

51-6093 *Upholsterers*

Make, repair, or replace upholstery for household furniture or transportation vehicles.

- Education or Training Required: Long-term on-the-job training
- Job Growth: –16.5%
- Annual Openings: 4,000
- Self-Employed: 27.5%
- Part-Time: 32.4%

NATIONAL WAGE FIGURES (ANNUAL)

Beginning	25th Percentile	Median	Mean	75th Percentile	90th Percentile
$17,280	$21,330	$27,230	$28,500	$34,400	$41,950

Median Wages for Industries Employing Largest Numbers (Annual)

Industry	Median Income
Accommodation	$41,610
Federal, State, and Local Government	$41,270
Educational Services	$34,870
Miscellaneous Manufacturing	$31,380
Merchant Wholesalers, Durable Goods	$27,940
Furniture and Related Product Manufacturing	$27,670
Furniture and Home Furnishings Stores	$27,640
Textile Product Mills	$27,280
Transportation Equipment Manufacturing	$26,560
Repair and Maintenance	$26,220

Median Wages for States (Annual)

AK	no data	KY	$27,640
AL	$20,890	LA	$23,060
AR	$18,720	MA	$32,280
AZ	$24,500	MD	$30,630
CA	$25,960	ME	$31,940
CO	$28,720	MI	$26,540
CT	$30,880	MN	$24,260
DC	no data	MO	$20,350
DE	$31,960	MS	$28,380
FL	$24,480	MT	$25,190
GA	$25,540	NC	$32,050
HI	$27,620	ND	$18,930
IA	$29,230	NE	no data
ID	$22,480	NH	no data
IL	$30,080	NJ	$29,630
IN	$26,640	NM	$24,110
KS	$24,700	NV	$31,260

NY	$32,640
OH	$27,010
OK	$23,600
OR	$25,420
PA	$27,620
RI	$27,000
SC	$31,440
SD	$21,760
TN	$27,170
TX	$22,120
UT	no data
VA	$27,480
VT	no data
WA	$33,260
WI	$27,570
WV	$21,530
WY	no data

Median Wages for the Largest Metropolitan Areas (Annual)

AZ: Phoenix	$24,590	MI: Detroit	$24,970
CA: Los Angeles	$24,400	MN: Minneapolis	$31,420
CA: Riverside	$24,510	MO: Kansas City	$25,260
CA: Sacramento	$32,740	MO: St. Louis	$31,420
CA: San Diego	$31,110	NV: Las Vegas	$36,310
CA: San Francisco	$35,320	NY: New York	$33,790
CO: Denver	$30,150	OH: Cincinnati	$27,630
DC: Washington	$29,210	OH: Cleveland	$30,100
FL: Miami	$23,360	OH: Columbus	$27,630
FL: Orlando	$25,340	OR: Portland	$27,250
FL: Tampa	$20,220	PA: Philadelphia	$24,980
GA: Atlanta	$26,410	PA: Pittsburgh	$27,370
IL: Chicago	$30,530	TX: Dallas	$23,300
MA: Boston	$34,500	TX: Houston	$24,000
MD: Baltimore	$31,690	WA: Seattle	$34,370

FACTORS THAT MAY AFFECT EARNINGS

Educational Attainment of Workers and Effect on Earnings

	Percent at Level	Effect on Earnings
Less than High School	—	—
Some High School	17.5%	–15.6%
High School or Equivalent	52.5%	3.6%
Some College but No Degree	—	—
Associate Degree	—	—
Bachelor's Degree	—	—
Master's Degree	—	—
Doctoral Degree	—	—
First Professional Degree	—	—

Figures do not total 100% because some levels have a very small sample size.

Flexibility of Earnings

Average Hours Worked: 32
Workers with a Varying Number of Hours: 12.6%
Workers Earning Some Overtime Pay, Tips, or Commissions: 20.0%
Earnings Benefit of Working Overtime: 18.7%

Gender

	Male	Female
Percent	86.0%	14.0%
Effect on Earnings	11.1%	–32.0%

Union Membership

Percentage Union Members: 4.4%
Earnings Benefit of Union Membership: 4.0%

Veteran Status

Percentage Who Have Been on Active Duty: Insignificant
Earnings Benefit of Veteran Status: No significant data available

51-6099 Textile, Apparel, and Furnishings Workers, All Other

All textile, apparel, and furnishings workers not listed separately.

- Education or Training Required: Short-term on-the-job training
- Job Growth: –29.8%
- Annual Openings: 3,000
- Self-Employed: 6.8%
- Part-Time: 26.1%

NATIONAL WAGE FIGURES (ANNUAL)

Beginning	25th Percentile	Median	Mean	75th Percentile	90th Percentile
$15,420	$18,220	$22,950	$24,770	$29,080	$36,600

Median Wages for Industries Employing Largest Numbers (Annual)

Industry	Median Income
Federal, State, and Local Government	$44,300
Clothing and Clothing Accessories Stores	$30,200
Repair and Maintenance	$26,580
Leather and Allied Product Manufacturing	$25,570
Textile Product Mills	$24,430
Construction of Buildings	$24,410
Miscellaneous Manufacturing	$24,390
Textile Mills	$23,680
Management of Companies and Enterprises	$23,370
Furniture and Related Product Manufacturing	$23,320

Median Wages for States (Annual)

State	Wage	State	Wage	State	Wage
AK	no data	KY	no data	NY	$24,000
AL	$19,730	LA	$31,640	OH	$19,240
AR	$17,170	MA	$25,800	OK	$17,780
AZ	$24,530	MD	$31,970	OR	$23,740
CA	$17,860	ME	$27,150	PA	$23,840
CO	$19,320	MI	$27,570	RI	$27,580
CT	$27,210	MN	$19,430	SC	$25,350
DC	no data	MO	$25,710	SD	no data
DE	$31,410	MS	$24,390	TN	$23,790
FL	$22,700	MT	$15,710	TX	$19,250
GA	$24,560	NC	$21,390	UT	$26,500
HI	$30,200	ND	$24,100	VA	$24,920
IA	$20,830	NE	$22,190	VT	no data
ID	$22,780	NH	$24,610	WA	$32,270
IL	$20,450	NJ	$23,170	WI	$29,020
IN	$21,580	NM	$24,630	WV	$33,500
KS	$26,600	NV	$19,240	WY	$22,150

Median Wages for the Largest Metropolitan Areas (Annual)

Area	Wage	Area	Wage
AZ: Phoenix	$22,850	MI: Detroit	$25,880
CA: Los Angeles	$17,240	MN: Minneapolis	$21,130
CA: Riverside	$25,060	MO: Kansas City	$23,450
CA: Sacramento	$28,840	MO: St. Louis	no data
CA: San Diego	no data	NV: Las Vegas	$19,060
CA: San Francisco	$16,910	NY: New York	$25,500
CO: Denver	$24,450	OH: Cincinnati	$22,370
DC: Washington	$37,010	OH: Cleveland	$32,810
FL: Miami	$30,020	OH: Columbus	$19,960
FL: Orlando	$20,840	OR: Portland	$22,830
FL: Tampa	$21,850	PA: Philadelphia	$29,730
GA: Atlanta	$19,480	PA: Pittsburgh	no data
IL: Chicago	$20,280	TX: Dallas	no data
MA: Boston	$25,900	TX: Houston	no data
MD: Baltimore	$25,470	WA: Seattle	$31,570

FACTORS THAT MAY AFFECT EARNINGS

Educational Attainment of Workers and Effect on Earnings

	Percent at Level	Effect on Earnings
Less than High School	—	—
Some High School	—	—
High School or Equivalent	55.6%	19.7%
Some College but No Degree	—	—
Associate Degree	—	—
Bachelor's Degree	—	—
Master's Degree	—	—
Doctoral Degree	—	—
First Professional Degree	—	—

Figures do not total 100% because some levels have a very small sample size.

Flexibility of Earnings

Average Hours Worked: 27
Workers with a Varying Number of Hours: 17.0%
Workers Earning Some Overtime Pay, Tips, or Commissions: 25.9%
Earnings Benefit of Working Overtime: 18.7%

Gender

	Male	Female
Percent	47.5%	52.5%
Effect on Earnings	11.1%	–32.0%

Union Membership

Percentage Union Members: 4.7%
Earnings Benefit of Union Membership: 4.0%

Veteran Status

Percentage Who Have Been on Active Duty: Insignificant
Earnings Benefit of Veteran Status: No significant data available

51-7000 Woodworkers

51-7011 Cabinetmakers and Bench Carpenters

Cut, shape, and assemble wooden articles or set up and operate a variety of woodworking machines such as power saws, jointers, and mortisers to surface, cut, or shape lumber or to fabricate parts for wood products.

- Education or Training Required: Long-term on-the-job training
- Job Growth: 4.1%
- Annual Openings: 12,000
- Self-Employed: 15.7%
- Part-Time: 17.5%

NATIONAL WAGE FIGURES (ANNUAL)

Beginning	25th Percentile	Median	Mean	75th Percentile	90th Percentile
$17,660	$21,350	$27,010	$28,760	$34,290	$43,060

Median Wages for Industries Employing Largest Numbers (Annual)

Industry	Median Income
Federal, State, and Local Government	$48,310
Hospitals	$37,930
Support Activities for Transportation	$36,770
Performing Arts, Spectator Sports, and Related Industries	$34,990
Educational Services	$33,940
Construction of Buildings	$30,800
Fabricated Metal Product Manufacturing	$30,300
Furniture and Home Furnishings Stores	$29,900
Merchant Wholesalers, Nondurable Goods	$28,800
Miscellaneous Manufacturing	$28,760

Median Wages for States (Annual)

AK	$30,340	KY	$25,330	NY	$30,810
AL	$21,820	LA	$22,490	OH	$27,480
AR	$23,560	MA	$35,670	OK	$22,260
AZ	$27,100	MD	$32,420	OR	$27,590
CA	$26,940	ME	$26,830	PA	$28,640
CO	$30,340	MI	$31,060	RI	$36,820
CT	$35,230	MN	$31,920	SC	$23,100
DC	no data	MO	$24,960	SD	$23,300
DE	$28,200	MS	$22,010	TN	$24,770
FL	$27,920	MT	$26,720	TX	$23,430
GA	$26,070	NC	$25,440	UT	$22,690
HI	$29,990	ND	$26,820	VA	$27,700
IA	$25,950	NE	$26,970	VT	$28,260
ID	$23,190	NH	$29,190	WA	$29,440
IL	$33,920	NJ	$36,720	WI	$29,480
IN	$26,830	NM	$24,460	WV	no data
KS	$24,040	NV	$30,490	WY	$25,430

Median Wages for the Largest Metropolitan Areas (Annual)

AZ: Phoenix	$27,070	MI: Detroit	$33,830
CA: Los Angeles	$23,380	MN: Minneapolis	$34,650
CA: Riverside	$26,520	MO: Kansas City	$26,180
CA: Sacramento	$26,220	MO: St. Louis	$31,740
CA: San Diego	$28,890	NV: Las Vegas	$32,800
CA: San Francisco	$37,010	NY: New York	$34,830
CO: Denver	$28,750	OH: Cincinnati	$30,550
DC: Washington	$33,100	OH: Cleveland	$29,370
FL: Miami	$29,140	OH: Columbus	$29,460
FL: Orlando	$29,960	OR: Portland	$28,890
FL: Tampa	$25,810	PA: Philadelphia	$39,060
GA: Atlanta	$27,260	PA: Pittsburgh	$29,910
IL: Chicago	$37,070	TX: Dallas	$23,740
MA: Boston	$36,940	TX: Houston	$24,540
MD: Baltimore	$32,010	WA: Seattle	$29,200

FACTORS THAT MAY AFFECT EARNINGS

Educational Attainment of Workers and Effect on Earnings

	Percent at Level	Effect on Earnings
Less than High School	10.2%	−18.8%
Some High School	15.3%	−18.5%
High School or Equivalent	48.0%	12.3%
Some College but No Degree	13.3%	2.8%
Associate Degree	6.1%	5.7%
Bachelor's Degree	—	—
Master's Degree	—	—
Doctoral Degree	—	—
First Professional Degree	—	—

Figures do not total 100% because some levels have a very small sample size.

Flexibility of Earnings

Average Hours Worked: 36
Workers with a Varying Number of Hours: 8.9%
Workers Earning Some Overtime Pay, Tips, or Commissions: 14.9%
Earnings Benefit of Working Overtime: 30.3%

Gender

	Male	Female
Percent	95.6%	4.4%
Effect on Earnings	0.0%	—

Union Membership

Percentage Union Members: 5.8%
Earnings Benefit of Union Membership: 16.0%

Veteran Status

Percentage Who Have Been on Active Duty: 9.1%
Earnings Benefit of Veteran Status: −8.8%

51-7021 Furniture Finishers

Shape, finish, and refinish damaged, worn, or used furniture or new high-grade furniture to specified color or finish.

- Education or Training Required: Long-term on-the-job training
- Job Growth: –13.3%
- Annual Openings: 2,000
- Self-Employed: 28.5%
- Part-Time: 17.6%

NATIONAL WAGE FIGURES (ANNUAL)

Beginning	25th Percentile	Median	Mean	75th Percentile	90th Percentile
$16,850	$20,090	$25,010	$26,680	$31,260	$39,500

Median Wages for Industries Employing Largest Numbers (Annual)

Industry	Median Income
Transportation Equipment Manufacturing	$39,490
Construction of Buildings	$38,180
Specialty Trade Contractors	$33,570
Truck Transportation	$33,370
Furniture and Home Furnishings Stores	$29,580
Warehousing and Storage	$29,480
Management of Companies and Enterprises	$29,060
Merchant Wholesalers, Durable Goods	$27,280
Performing Arts, Spectator Sports, and Related Industries	$27,050
Furniture and Related Product Manufacturing	$24,460

Median Wages for States (Annual)

AK	no data	KY	$26,930	NY	$28,030
AL	$20,000	LA	$25,690	OH	$23,020
AR	$21,040	MA	$27,060	OK	$23,780
AZ	$26,350	MD	$27,700	OR	$27,460
CA	$21,660	ME	$22,500	PA	$26,240
CO	$31,830	MI	$30,680	RI	$24,000
CT	$33,690	MN	$27,890	SC	$24,480
DC	no data	MO	$23,060	SD	$21,310
DE	no data	MS	$21,800	TN	$22,860
FL	$26,040	MT	no data	TX	$21,420
GA	$20,470	NC	$24,500	UT	$25,800
HI	no data	ND	$23,980	VA	$25,490
IA	$24,980	NE	$25,920	VT	$26,540
ID	$24,380	NH	$28,570	WA	$28,360
IL	$31,360	NJ	$28,290	WI	$26,000
IN	$24,620	NM	$21,620	WV	no data
KS	$27,010	NV	$29,830	WY	no data

Median Wages for the Largest Metropolitan Areas (Annual)

AZ: Phoenix	$26,820	MI: Detroit	$36,510
CA: Los Angeles	$20,530	MN: Minneapolis	$30,750
CA: Riverside	$19,100	MO: Kansas City	$24,810
CA: Sacramento	$30,440	MO: St. Louis	$34,270
CA: San Diego	$28,520	NV: Las Vegas	no data
CA: San Francisco	$26,200	NY: New York	$32,420
CO: Denver	$30,980	OH: Cincinnati	$24,460
DC: Washington	$36,140	OH: Cleveland	$22,300
FL: Miami	$30,170	OH: Columbus	$31,210
FL: Orlando	$27,090	OR: Portland	$34,420
FL: Tampa	$23,930	PA: Philadelphia	$39,710
GA: Atlanta	$20,650	PA: Pittsburgh	$23,980
IL: Chicago	$34,270	TX: Dallas	$21,240
MA: Boston	$30,800	TX: Houston	$25,570
MD: Baltimore	$25,330	WA: Seattle	$29,670

FACTORS THAT MAY AFFECT EARNINGS

Educational Attainment of Workers and Effect on Earnings

	Percent at Level	Effect on Earnings
Less than High School	—	—
Some High School	—	—
High School or Equivalent	61.3%	9.1%
Some College but No Degree	—	—
Associate Degree	—	—
Bachelor's Degree	—	—
Master's Degree	—	—
Doctoral Degree	—	—
First Professional Degree	—	—

Figures do not total 100% because some levels have a very small sample size.

Flexibility of Earnings

Average Hours Worked: 33
Workers with a Varying Number of Hours: 8.4%
Workers Earning Some Overtime Pay, Tips, or Commissions: 21.2%
Earnings Benefit of Working Overtime: 24.7%

Gender

	Male	Female
Percent	68.3%	31.7%
Effect on Earnings	11.1%	–32.0%

Union Membership

Percentage Union Members: 9.1%
Earnings Benefit of Union Membership: 16.0%

Veteran Status

Percentage Who Have Been on Active Duty: 9.1%
Earnings Benefit of Veteran Status: –8.8%

51-7031 Model Makers, Wood

Construct full-size and scale wooden precision models of products. Includes wood jig builders and loft workers.

- Education or Training Required: Long-term on-the-job training
- Job Growth: 9.0%
- Annual Openings: 1,000
- Self-Employed: 0.0%
- Part-Time: 22.6%

NATIONAL WAGE FIGURES (ANNUAL)

Beginning	25th Percentile	Median	Mean	75th Percentile	90th Percentile
$18,520	$21,710	$28,470	$33,000	$37,660	$63,240

Median Wages for Industries Employing Largest Numbers (Annual)

Industry	Median Income
Federal, State, and Local Government	$55,410
Professional, Scientific, and Technical Services	$46,380
Miscellaneous Manufacturing	$28,250
Wood Product Manufacturing	$27,120
Machinery Manufacturing	$26,240
Furniture and Related Product Manufacturing	$25,980

Median Wages for States (Annual)

State		State		State	
AK	no data	KY	no data	NY	$27,350
AL	no data	LA	no data	OH	$32,500
AR	$24,300	MA	no data	OK	no data
AZ	no data	MD	no data	OR	no data
CA	$21,860	ME	no data	PA	$35,870
CO	no data	MI	no data	RI	no data
CT	no data	MN	no data	SC	no data
DC	no data	MO	no data	SD	no data
DE	no data	MS	$30,000	TN	$32,770
FL	no data	MT	no data	TX	$21,700
GA	no data	NC	$25,980	UT	no data
HI	no data	ND	no data	VA	$27,100
IA	no data	NE	no data	VT	no data
ID	no data	NH	no data	WA	no data
IL	$32,250	NJ	no data	WI	no data
IN	$26,240	NM	no data	WV	no data
KS	no data	NV	no data	WY	no data

Median Wages for the Largest Metropolitan Areas (Annual)

Area		Area	
AZ: Phoenix	no data	MI: Detroit	no data
CA: Los Angeles	$21,460	MN: Minneapolis	no data
CA: Riverside	no data	MO: Kansas City	no data
CA: Sacramento	no data	MO: St. Louis	no data
CA: San Diego	no data	NV: Las Vegas	no data
CA: San Francisco	no data	NY: New York	no data
CO: Denver	no data	OH: Cincinnati	no data
DC: Washington	no data	OH: Cleveland	no data
FL: Miami	no data	OH: Columbus	no data
FL: Orlando	no data	OR: Portland	no data
FL: Tampa	no data	PA: Philadelphia	no data
GA: Atlanta	no data	PA: Pittsburgh	no data
IL: Chicago	no data	TX: Dallas	$21,700
MA: Boston	no data	TX: Houston	no data
MD: Baltimore	no data	WA: Seattle	no data

FACTORS THAT MAY AFFECT EARNINGS

Educational Attainment of Workers and Effect on Earnings

Figures are based on a group of occupations: Woodworkers

	Percent at Level	Effect on Earnings
Less than High School	10.2%	−24.9%
Some High School	15.7%	−21.2%
High School or Equivalent	47.7%	8.3%
Some College but No Degree	13.4%	3.9%
Associate Degree	5.6%	34.3%
Bachelor's Degree	—	—
Master's Degree	—	—
Doctoral Degree	—	—
First Professional Degree	—	—

Figures do not total 100% because some levels have a very small sample size.

Flexibility of Earnings

Average Hours Worked: 34
Workers with a Varying Number of Hours: 8.8%
Workers Earning Some Overtime Pay, Tips, or Commissions: 18.3%
Earnings Benefit of Working Overtime: 24.7%

Gender

	Male	Female
Percent	86.4%	13.6%
Effect on Earnings	11.1%	−32.0%

Union Membership

Percentage Union Members: 7.2%
Earnings Benefit of Union Membership: 16.0%

Veteran Status

Percentage Who Have Been on Active Duty: 9.1%
Earnings Benefit of Veteran Status: −8.8%

51-7032 Patternmakers, Wood

Plan, lay out, and construct wooden unit or sectional patterns used in forming sand molds for castings.

- Education or Training Required: Long-term on-the-job training
- Job Growth: 3.2%
- Annual Openings: Fewer than 500
- Self-Employed: 0.0%
- Part-Time: 22.6%

NATIONAL WAGE FIGURES (ANNUAL)

Beginning	25th Percentile	Median	Mean	75th Percentile	90th Percentile
$19,500	$23,770	$31,510	$33,690	$39,660	$55,090

Median Wages for Industries Employing Largest Numbers (Annual)

Industry	Median Income
Federal, State, and Local Government	$55,120
Primary Metal Manufacturing	$36,890
Machinery Manufacturing	$35,410
Fabricated Metal Product Manufacturing	$34,620
Furniture and Related Product Manufacturing	$27,690
Nonmetallic Mineral Product Manufacturing	$26,520
Wood Product Manufacturing	$24,090

Median Wages for States (Annual)

State		State		State	
AK	no data	KY	no data	NY	$32,020
AL	no data	LA	no data	OH	$35,300
AR	no data	MA	no data	OK	no data
AZ	$28,930	MD	no data	OR	$49,610
CA	$32,130	ME	no data	PA	$32,750
CO	no data	MI	$48,220	RI	no data
CT	no data	MN	no data	SC	no data
DC	no data	MO	$20,890	SD	no data
DE	no data	MS	no data	TN	$26,140
FL	no data	MT	no data	TX	$20,610
GA	$42,410	NC	$28,430	UT	no data
HI	no data	ND	no data	VA	no data
IA	$32,650	NE	no data	VT	no data
ID	no data	NH	no data	WA	no data
IL	$26,840	NJ	no data	WI	$34,940
IN	$35,130	NM	no data	WV	no data
KS	no data	NV	no data	WY	no data

Median Wages for the Largest Metropolitan Areas (Annual)

Area		Area	
AZ: Phoenix	$28,930	MI: Detroit	$47,220
CA: Los Angeles	$21,230	MN: Minneapolis	no data
CA: Riverside	no data	MO: Kansas City	no data
CA: Sacramento	no data	MO: St. Louis	no data
CA: San Diego	no data	NV: Las Vegas	no data
CA: San Francisco	no data	NY: New York	$38,350
CO: Denver	no data	OH: Cincinnati	no data
DC: Washington	no data	OH: Cleveland	no data
FL: Miami	no data	OH: Columbus	no data
FL: Orlando	no data	OR: Portland	$53,320
FL: Tampa	no data	PA: Philadelphia	no data
GA: Atlanta	$34,620	PA: Pittsburgh	no data
IL: Chicago	$23,870	TX: Dallas	$20,050
MA: Boston	no data	TX: Houston	no data
MD: Baltimore	no data	WA: Seattle	no data

FACTORS THAT MAY AFFECT EARNINGS

Educational Attainment of Workers and Effect on Earnings

Figures are based on a group of occupations: Woodworkers

	Percent at Level	Effect on Earnings
Less than High School	10.2%	−24.9%
Some High School	15.7%	−21.2%
High School or Equivalent	47.7%	8.3%
Some College but No Degree	13.4%	3.9%
Associate Degree	5.6%	34.3%
Bachelor's Degree	—	—
Master's Degree	—	—
Doctoral Degree	—	—
First Professional Degree	—	—

Figures do not total 100% because some levels have a very small sample size.

Flexibility of Earnings

Average Hours Worked: 34
Workers with a Varying Number of Hours: 8.8%
Workers Earning Some Overtime Pay, Tips, or Commissions: 18.3%
Earnings Benefit of Working Overtime: 24.7%

Gender

	Male	Female
Percent	86.4%	13.6%
Effect on Earnings	11.1%	−32.0%

Union Membership

Percentage Union Members: 7.2%
Earnings Benefit of Union Membership: 16.0%

Veteran Status

Percentage Who Have Been on Active Duty: 9.1%
Earnings Benefit of Veteran Status: −8.8%

51-7041 Sawing Machine Setters, Operators, and Tenders, Wood

Set up, operate, or tend wood sawing machines. Includes head sawyers.

- Education or Training Required: Moderate-term on-the-job training
- Job Growth: –11.3%
- Annual Openings: 11,000
- Self-Employed: 1.0%
- Part-Time: 28.6%

NATIONAL WAGE FIGURES (ANNUAL)

Beginning	25th Percentile	Median	Mean	75th Percentile	90th Percentile
$16,290	$19,620	$24,280	$25,380	$29,930	$36,220

Median Wages for Industries Employing Largest Numbers (Annual)

Industry	Median Income
Management of Companies and Enterprises	$30,900
Warehousing and Storage	$30,220
Miscellaneous Manufacturing	$27,240
Merchant Wholesalers, Durable Goods	$26,000
Truck Transportation	$25,700
Specialty Trade Contractors	$25,350
Building Material and Garden Equipment and Supplies Dealers	$25,030
Transportation Equipment Manufacturing	$24,910
Machinery Manufacturing	$24,530
Primary Metal Manufacturing	$24,530

Median Wages for States (Annual)

AK	$32,280	KY	$21,610	NY	$23,950
AL	$20,730	LA	$25,230	OH	$26,300
AR	$23,090	MA	$27,910	OK	$21,390
AZ	$19,910	MD	$23,200	OR	$29,830
CA	$25,760	ME	$24,160	PA	$24,650
CO	$24,920	MI	$26,260	RI	$21,800
CT	$27,140	MN	$27,970	SC	$24,710
DC	no data	MO	$20,790	SD	$23,150
DE	$28,680	MS	$22,000	TN	$22,350
FL	$23,900	MT	$30,510	TX	$19,780
GA	$21,910	NC	$24,270	UT	$23,860
HI	$24,210	ND	$21,920	VA	$25,960
IA	no data	NE	$20,400	VT	$26,750
ID	$26,730	NH	$27,270	WA	$32,120
IL	$26,150	NJ	no data	WI	$26,440
IN	$25,090	NM	$25,110	WV	$19,850
KS	$21,500	NV	$25,520	WY	$20,030

Median Wages for the Largest Metropolitan Areas (Annual)

AZ: Phoenix	$22,770	MI: Detroit	$29,120
CA: Los Angeles	$22,700	MN: Minneapolis	$30,770
CA: Riverside	$22,930	MO: Kansas City	$22,850
CA: Sacramento	$26,270	MO: St. Louis	$22,350
CA: San Diego	$23,590	NV: Las Vegas	$27,270
CA: San Francisco	$31,670	NY: New York	$26,800
CO: Denver	$26,340	OH: Cincinnati	$31,050
DC: Washington	$26,650	OH: Cleveland	$31,090
FL: Miami	$22,600	OH: Columbus	$23,190
FL: Orlando	$27,680	OR: Portland	$29,410
FL: Tampa	$26,500	PA: Philadelphia	$26,740
GA: Atlanta	$23,020	PA: Pittsburgh	$21,320
IL: Chicago	$26,440	TX: Dallas	$18,350
MA: Boston	$35,540	TX: Houston	$20,350
MD: Baltimore	$23,890	WA: Seattle	$31,800

FACTORS THAT MAY AFFECT EARNINGS

Educational Attainment of Workers and Effect on Earnings

	Percent at Level	Effect on Earnings
Less than High School	14.0%	–30.3%
Some High School	26.0%	–6.5%
High School or Equivalent	44.0%	9.4%
Some College but No Degree	12.0%	22.2%
Associate Degree	—	—
Bachelor's Degree	—	—
Master's Degree	—	—
Doctoral Degree	—	—
First Professional Degree	—	—

Flexibility of Earnings

Average Hours Worked: 35
Workers with a Varying Number of Hours: 5.6%
Workers Earning Some Overtime Pay, Tips, or Commissions: 29.3%
Earnings Benefit of Working Overtime: 24.7%

Gender

	Male	Female
Percent	89.5%	10.5%
Effect on Earnings	11.1%	–32.0%

Union Membership

Percentage Union Members: 15.5%
Earnings Benefit of Union Membership: 16.0%

Veteran Status

Percentage Who Have Been on Active Duty: 9.1%
Earnings Benefit of Veteran Status: –8.8%

51-7042 Woodworking Machine Setters, Operators, and Tenders, Except Sawing

Set up, operate, or tend woodworking machines, such as drill presses, lathes, shapers, routers, sanders, planers, and wood-nailing machines.

- Education or Training Required: Moderate-term on-the-job training
- Job Growth: −11.0%
- Annual Openings: 13,000
- Self-Employed: 2.4%
- Part-Time: 26.3%

NATIONAL WAGE FIGURES (ANNUAL)

Beginning	25th Percentile	Median	Mean	75th Percentile	90th Percentile
$16,410	$19,460	$23,940	$25,110	$29,480	$35,950

Median Wages for Industries Employing Largest Numbers (Annual)

Industry	Median Income
Paper Manufacturing	$40,680
Construction of Buildings	$38,650
Specialty Trade Contractors	$32,090
Miscellaneous Store Retailers	$31,770
Management of Companies and Enterprises	$30,240
Warehousing and Storage	$29,290
Federal, State, and Local Government	$29,210
Support Activities for Transportation	$29,180
Transportation Equipment Manufacturing	$27,290
Primary Metal Manufacturing	$26,110

Median Wages for States (Annual)

State	Wage	State	Wage	State	Wage
AK	no data	KY	$22,610	NY	$24,370
AL	$21,020	LA	$25,510	OH	$24,950
AR	$23,400	MA	$32,150	OK	$21,070
AZ	$21,890	MD	$23,220	OR	$30,900
CA	$22,450	ME	$22,310	PA	$25,470
CO	$26,130	MI	$28,710	RI	$26,400
CT	$28,890	MN	$27,820	SC	$23,210
DC	no data	MO	$22,290	SD	$23,260
DE	$26,190	MS	$21,260	TN	$21,400
FL	$22,220	MT	$25,080	TX	$20,010
GA	$20,610	NC	$24,270	UT	$24,280
HI	$28,440	ND	$23,730	VA	$25,080
IA	$24,060	NE	$24,990	VT	$25,820
ID	$26,310	NH	$26,300	WA	$29,310
IL	$25,890	NJ	$28,530	WI	$26,590
IN	$24,040	NM	$21,070	WV	$19,900
KS	$22,260	NV	$22,770	WY	$21,330

Median Wages for the Largest Metropolitan Areas (Annual)

Area	Wage	Area	Wage
AZ: Phoenix	$21,280	MI: Detroit	no data
CA: Los Angeles	$21,530	MN: Minneapolis	$28,070
CA: Riverside	$20,280	MO: Kansas City	$23,870
CA: Sacramento	$24,630	MO: St. Louis	$25,290
CA: San Diego	$24,080	NV: Las Vegas	$22,280
CA: San Francisco	$24,690	NY: New York	$25,610
CO: Denver	$25,900	OH: Cincinnati	$25,470
DC: Washington	$23,290	OH: Cleveland	$27,630
FL: Miami	$18,970	OH: Columbus	$26,890
FL: Orlando	$23,060	OR: Portland	$27,620
FL: Tampa	$21,180	PA: Philadelphia	$37,520
GA: Atlanta	$21,100	PA: Pittsburgh	$21,380
IL: Chicago	$28,410	TX: Dallas	$20,420
MA: Boston	$31,130	TX: Houston	$21,270
MD: Baltimore	$23,790	WA: Seattle	$27,750

FACTORS THAT MAY AFFECT EARNINGS

Educational Attainment of Workers and Effect on Earnings

	Percent at Level	Effect on Earnings
Less than High School	12.7%	−23.4%
Some High School	14.5%	−35.0%
High School or Equivalent	54.5%	−6.9%
Some College but No Degree	—	—
Associate Degree	—	—
Bachelor's Degree	—	—
Master's Degree	—	—
Doctoral Degree	—	—
First Professional Degree	—	—

Figures do not total 100% because some levels have a very small sample size.

Flexibility of Earnings

Average Hours Worked: 35
Workers with a Varying Number of Hours: 6.8%
Workers Earning Some Overtime Pay, Tips, or Commissions: 19.7%
Earnings Benefit of Working Overtime: 24.7%

Gender

	Male	Female
Percent	68.0%	32.0%
Effect on Earnings	11.1%	−32.0%

Union Membership

Percentage Union Members: 9.8%
Earnings Benefit of Union Membership: 16.0%

Veteran Status

Percentage Who Have Been on Active Duty: 9.1%
Earnings Benefit of Veteran Status: −8.8%

51-7099 Woodworkers, All Other

All woodworkers not listed separately.

- Education or Training Required: Moderate-term on-the-job training
- Job Growth: –13.9%
- Annual Openings: 5,000
- Self-Employed: 50.1%
- Part-Time: 31.3%

Note: A large fraction of the workforce for this occupation is self-employed and earns an average of $28,750. All other earnings figures for this occupation are based on workers who are paid a wage or salary.

NATIONAL WAGE FIGURES (ANNUAL)

Beginning	25th Percentile	Median	Mean	75th Percentile	90th Percentile
$15,770	$18,210	$22,580	$25,030	$29,380	$39,250

Median Wages for Industries Employing Largest Numbers (Annual)

Industry	Median Income
Federal, State, and Local Government	$43,670
Merchant Wholesalers, Nondurable Goods	$32,480
Professional, Scientific, and Technical Services	$31,430
Transportation Equipment Manufacturing	$26,520
Repair and Maintenance	$25,440
Fabricated Metal Product Manufacturing	$24,880
Building Material and Garden Equipment and Supplies Dealers	$24,300
Specialty Trade Contractors	$24,110
Miscellaneous Manufacturing	$22,760
Furniture and Home Furnishings Stores	$22,490

Median Wages for States (Annual)

State	Wage	State	Wage	State	Wage
AK	no data	KY	$19,850	NY	$24,440
AL	$24,440	LA	$20,500	OH	$22,720
AR	$21,260	MA	no data	OK	no data
AZ	$40,080	MD	$35,360	OR	$30,570
CA	$20,490	ME	$25,650	PA	$24,730
CO	$21,130	MI	$23,810	RI	$27,430
CT	$24,720	MN	$21,420	SC	$20,840
DC	no data	MO	no data	SD	no data
DE	no data	MS	no data	TN	$19,490
FL	$20,020	MT	$27,960	TX	$19,390
GA	$22,810	NC	$27,470	UT	no data
HI	no data	ND	$16,720	VA	$25,910
IA	$18,590	NE	no data	VT	no data
ID	no data	NH	$19,850	WA	$24,910
IL	$22,120	NJ	$23,070	WI	$20,260
IN	$21,420	NM	$25,070	WV	no data
KS	$17,500	NV	$19,640	WY	no data

Median Wages for the Largest Metropolitan Areas (Annual)

Area	Wage	Area	Wage
AZ: Phoenix	no data	MI: Detroit	no data
CA: Los Angeles	$19,540	MN: Minneapolis	$22,420
CA: Riverside	$18,640	MO: Kansas City	no data
CA: Sacramento	$18,470	MO: St. Louis	$21,280
CA: San Diego	$26,010	NV: Las Vegas	no data
CA: San Francisco	$23,470	NY: New York	$23,320
CO: Denver	no data	OH: Cincinnati	$33,850
DC: Washington	$23,370	OH: Cleveland	no data
FL: Miami	$28,360	OH: Columbus	no data
FL: Orlando	no data	OR: Portland	no data
FL: Tampa	$16,630	PA: Philadelphia	$22,990
GA: Atlanta	no data	PA: Pittsburgh	no data
IL: Chicago	$21,650	TX: Dallas	no data
MA: Boston	$20,870	TX: Houston	no data
MD: Baltimore	no data	WA: Seattle	$24,650

FACTORS THAT MAY AFFECT EARNINGS

Educational Attainment of Workers and Effect on Earnings

	Percent at Level	Effect on Earnings
Less than High School	—	—
Some High School	—	—
High School or Equivalent	63.0%	5.0%
Some College but No Degree	—	—
Associate Degree	—	—
Bachelor's Degree	—	—
Master's Degree	—	—
Doctoral Degree	—	—
First Professional Degree	—	—

Figures do not total 100% because some levels have a very small sample size.

Flexibility of Earnings

Average Hours Worked: 30
Workers with a Varying Number of Hours: 17.5%
Workers Earning Some Overtime Pay, Tips, or Commissions: 16.7%
Earnings Benefit of Working Overtime: 24.7%

Gender

	Male	Female
Percent	86.8%	13.2%
Effect on Earnings	11.1%	–32.0%

Union Membership

Percentage Union Members: 7.2%
Earnings Benefit of Union Membership: 16.0%

Veteran Status

Percentage Who Have Been on Active Duty: 9.1%
Earnings Benefit of Veteran Status: –8.8%

51-8000 Plant and System Operators

51-8011 Nuclear Power Reactor Operators

Control nuclear reactors.

- Education or Training Required: Long-term on-the-job training
- Job Growth: –0.5%
- Annual Openings: 1,000
- Self-Employed: 0.0%
- Part-Time: 1.3%

NATIONAL WAGE FIGURES (ANNUAL)

Beginning	25th Percentile	Median	Mean	75th Percentile	90th Percentile
$54,180	$61,590	$69,370	$70,800	$78,150	$92,240

Median Wages for Industries Employing Largest Numbers (Annual)

Industry	Median Income
Utilities	$69,590

Median Wages for States (Annual)

AK	no data	KY	no data	NY	no data
AL	no data	LA	no data	OH	$69,410
AR	no data	MA	no data	OK	no data
AZ	no data	MD	no data	OR	no data
CA	no data	ME	no data	PA	$64,980
CO	no data	MI	no data	RI	no data
CT	no data	MN	no data	SC	no data
DC	no data	MO	no data	SD	no data
DE	no data	MS	no data	TN	no data
FL	no data	MT	no data	TX	no data
GA	no data	NC	no data	UT	no data
HI	no data	ND	no data	VA	no data
IA	no data	NE	no data	VT	no data
ID	no data	NH	no data	WA	no data
IL	$79,180	NJ	no data	WI	no data
IN	no data	NM	no data	WV	no data
KS	no data	NV	no data	WY	no data

Median Wages for the Largest Metropolitan Areas (Annual)

AZ: Phoenix	no data	MI: Detroit	no data
CA: Los Angeles	no data	MN: Minneapolis	no data
CA: Riverside	no data	MO: Kansas City	no data
CA: Sacramento	no data	MO: St. Louis	no data
CA: San Diego	no data	NV: Las Vegas	no data
CA: San Francisco	no data	NY: New York	no data
CO: Denver	no data	OH: Cincinnati	no data
DC: Washington	no data	OH: Cleveland	no data
FL: Miami	no data	OH: Columbus	no data
FL: Orlando	no data	OR: Portland	no data
FL: Tampa	no data	PA: Philadelphia	no data
GA: Atlanta	no data	PA: Pittsburgh	no data
IL: Chicago	no data	TX: Dallas	no data
MA: Boston	no data	TX: Houston	no data
MD: Baltimore	no data	WA: Seattle	no data

FACTORS THAT MAY AFFECT EARNINGS

Educational Attainment of Workers and Effect on Earnings

Figures are based on a group of occupations: Plant and System Operators

	Percent at Level	Effect on Earnings
Less than High School	—	—
Some High School	4.6%	–25.0%
High School or Equivalent	43.9%	–3.4%
Some College but No Degree	22.8%	0.5%
Associate Degree	15.3%	4.8%
Bachelor's Degree	9.5%	10.4%
Master's Degree	—	—
Doctoral Degree	—	—
First Professional Degree	—	—

Flexibility of Earnings

Average Hours Worked: 38

Workers with a Varying Number of Hours: 3.7%

Workers Earning Some Overtime Pay, Tips, or Commissions: 25.9%

Earnings Benefit of Working Overtime: 1.5%

Gender

	Male	Female
Percent	97.7%	2.3%
Effect on Earnings	11.1%	–32.0%

Union Membership

Percentage Union Members: 33.5%

Earnings Benefit of Union Membership: 15.7%

Veteran Status

Percentage Who Have Been on Active Duty: 20.9%

Earnings Benefit of Veteran Status: 8.5%

51-8012 Power Distributors and Dispatchers

Coordinate, regulate, or distribute electricity or steam.

- Education or Training Required: Long-term on-the-job training
- Job Growth: 0.0%
- Annual Openings: 1,000
- Self-Employed: 0.0%
- Part-Time: 1.3%

NATIONAL WAGE FIGURES (ANNUAL)

Beginning	25th Percentile	Median	Mean	75th Percentile	90th Percentile
$42,370	$52,510	$62,590	$62,640	$73,920	$85,740

Median Wages for Industries Employing Largest Numbers (Annual)

Industry	Median Income
Management of Companies and Enterprises	$67,590
Federal, State, and Local Government	$66,210
Utilities	$62,150
Heavy and Civil Engineering Construction	$59,360
Primary Metal Manufacturing	$54,210
Electrical Equipment, Appliance, and Component Manufacturing	$32,270
Hospitals	$27,950

Median Wages for States (Annual)

AK	$73,280	KY	$63,170	NY	$47,000
AL	no data	LA	$63,010	OH	$47,470
AR	$58,820	MA	$63,730	OK	no data
AZ	$53,200	MD	$68,820	OR	$75,090
CA	$75,420	ME	no data	PA	$60,950
CO	$67,000	MI	$64,550	RI	no data
CT	$69,790	MN	$67,310	SC	$66,960
DC	no data	MO	$56,890	SD	$66,440
DE	$69,650	MS	no data	TN	no data
FL	$60,570	MT	$67,620	TX	$53,820
GA	no data	NC	$40,950	UT	$71,770
HI	no data	ND	$70,380	VA	$52,920
IA	$55,830	NE	$61,640	VT	no data
ID	no data	NH	no data	WA	$76,470
IL	$65,340	NJ	$58,380	WI	$60,530
IN	$61,080	NM	no data	WV	no data
KS	$54,270	NV	$75,200	WY	no data

Median Wages for the Largest Metropolitan Areas (Annual)

AZ: Phoenix	no data	MI: Detroit	no data
CA: Los Angeles	$59,550	MN: Minneapolis	$77,110
CA: Riverside	no data	MO: Kansas City	$64,990
CA: Sacramento	$85,650	MO: St. Louis	no data
CA: San Diego	no data	NV: Las Vegas	no data
CA: San Francisco	no data	NY: New York	$61,150
CO: Denver	no data	OH: Cincinnati	no data
DC: Washington	$56,600	OH: Cleveland	$53,240
FL: Miami	$59,070	OH: Columbus	$46,010
FL: Orlando	no data	OR: Portland	$79,490
FL: Tampa	$60,630	PA: Philadelphia	$62,520
GA: Atlanta	no data	PA: Pittsburgh	no data
IL: Chicago	$59,850	TX: Dallas	no data
MA: Boston	$63,920	TX: Houston	$59,070
MD: Baltimore	no data	WA: Seattle	$75,290

FACTORS THAT MAY AFFECT EARNINGS

Educational Attainment of Workers and Effect on Earnings

Figures are based on a group of occupations: Plant and System Operators

	Percent at Level	Effect on Earnings
Less than High School	—	—
Some High School	4.6%	−25.0%
High School or Equivalent	43.9%	−3.4%
Some College but No Degree	22.8%	0.5%
Associate Degree	15.3%	4.8%
Bachelor's Degree	9.5%	10.4%
Master's Degree	—	—
Doctoral Degree	—	—
First Professional Degree	—	—

Flexibility of Earnings

Average Hours Worked: 38
Workers with a Varying Number of Hours: 3.7%
Workers Earning Some Overtime Pay, Tips, or Commissions: 25.9%
Earnings Benefit of Working Overtime: 1.5%

Gender

	Male	Female
Percent	97.7%	2.3%
Effect on Earnings	11.1%	−32.0%

Union Membership

Percentage Union Members: 33.5%
Earnings Benefit of Union Membership: 15.7%

Veteran Status

Percentage Who Have Been on Active Duty: 20.9%
Earnings Benefit of Veteran Status: 8.5%

51-8013 Power Plant Operators

Control, operate, or maintain machinery to generate electric power. Includes auxiliary equipment operators.

- Education or Training Required: Long-term on-the-job training
- Job Growth: –0.4%
- Annual Openings: 5,000
- Self-Employed: 0.0%
- Part-Time: 1.3%

NATIONAL WAGE FIGURES (ANNUAL)

Beginning	25th Percentile	Median	Mean	75th Percentile	90th Percentile
$35,590	$45,110	$55,000	$55,340	$65,460	$75,240

Median Wages for Industries Employing Largest Numbers (Annual)

Industry	Median Income
Heavy and Civil Engineering Construction	$58,890
Management of Companies and Enterprises	$58,460
Pipeline Transportation	$56,780
Utilities	$56,650
Paper Manufacturing	$56,200
Primary Metal Manufacturing	$52,690
Mining (Except Oil and Gas)	$51,470
Professional, Scientific, and Technical Services	$48,570
Administrative and Support Services	$46,800
Federal, State, and Local Government	$46,030

Median Wages for States (Annual)

State	Wage	State	Wage	State	Wage
AK	no data	KY	$51,780	NY	$66,790
AL	$50,320	LA	$45,450	OH	$53,730
AR	$54,230	MA	no data	OK	$54,870
AZ	$52,270	MD	$54,630	OR	no data
CA	$63,850	ME	$57,530	PA	$50,520
CO	$51,660	MI	$53,100	RI	$56,740
CT	$58,170	MN	$58,820	SC	$61,800
DC	no data	MO	$50,470	SD	no data
DE	$61,860	MS	$49,680	TN	$37,410
FL	$56,670	MT	no data	TX	$53,750
GA	no data	NC	$52,350	UT	$52,200
HI	$60,930	ND	$58,920	VA	$44,210
IA	$48,060	NE	$49,450	VT	$32,760
ID	$65,130	NH	$47,580	WA	$65,620
IL	$54,040	NJ	$60,910	WI	$47,090
IN	$56,320	NM	no data	WV	$53,680
KS	$44,230	NV	$60,960	WY	$55,180

Median Wages for the Largest Metropolitan Areas (Annual)

Area	Wage	Area	Wage
AZ: Phoenix	no data	MI: Detroit	$55,570
CA: Los Angeles	$63,970	MN: Minneapolis	$61,510
CA: Riverside	$64,120	MO: Kansas City	no data
CA: Sacramento	$59,920	MO: St. Louis	$47,480
CA: San Diego	no data	NV: Las Vegas	no data
CA: San Francisco	$65,600	NY: New York	$65,930
CO: Denver	no data	OH: Cincinnati	no data
DC: Washington	$53,770	OH: Cleveland	$52,990
FL: Miami	$56,580	OH: Columbus	$42,340
FL: Orlando	$51,390	OR: Portland	no data
FL: Tampa	$57,110	PA: Philadelphia	$58,630
GA: Atlanta	no data	PA: Pittsburgh	$48,320
IL: Chicago	$54,770	TX: Dallas	$50,560
MA: Boston	no data	TX: Houston	$58,320
MD: Baltimore	$53,590	WA: Seattle	$69,440

FACTORS THAT MAY AFFECT EARNINGS

Educational Attainment of Workers and Effect on Earnings

Figures are based on a group of occupations: Plant and System Operators

	Percent at Level	Effect on Earnings
Less than High School	—	—
Some High School	4.6%	−25.0%
High School or Equivalent	43.9%	−3.4%
Some College but No Degree	22.8%	0.5%
Associate Degree	15.3%	4.8%
Bachelor's Degree	9.5%	10.4%
Master's Degree	—	—
Doctoral Degree	—	—
First Professional Degree	—	—

Flexibility of Earnings

Average Hours Worked: 38
Workers with a Varying Number of Hours: 3.7%
Workers Earning Some Overtime Pay, Tips, or Commissions: 25.9%
Earnings Benefit of Working Overtime: 1.5%

Gender

	Male	Female
Percent	97.7%	2.3%
Effect on Earnings	11.1%	−32.0%

Union Membership

Percentage Union Members: 33.5%
Earnings Benefit of Union Membership: 15.7%

Veteran Status

Percentage Who Have Been on Active Duty: 20.9%
Earnings Benefit of Veteran Status: 8.5%

51-8021 Stationary Engineers and Boiler Operators

Operate or maintain stationary engines, boilers, or other mechanical equipment to provide utilities for buildings or industrial processes. Operate equipment such as steam engines, generators, motors, turbines, and steam boilers.

- Education or Training Required: Long-term on-the-job training
- Job Growth: 3.4%
- Annual Openings: 5,000
- Self-Employed: 1.0%
- Part-Time: 1.3%

NATIONAL WAGE FIGURES (ANNUAL)

Beginning	25th Percentile	Median	Mean	75th Percentile	90th Percentile
$28,370	$36,490	$46,040	$46,990	$57,380	$68,690

Median Wages for Industries Employing Largest Numbers (Annual)

Industry	Median Income
Postal Service	$66,730
Transportation Equipment Manufacturing	$65,950
Professional, Scientific, and Technical Services	$54,570
Ambulatory Health Care Services	$54,460
Utilities	$50,210
Federal, State, and Local Government	$50,000
Fabricated Metal Product Manufacturing	$49,260
Specialty Trade Contractors	$49,160
Machinery Manufacturing	$48,580
Management of Companies and Enterprises	$47,700

Median Wages for States (Annual)

State	Wage	State	Wage	State	Wage
AK	$54,760	KY	$39,460	NY	$51,530
AL	$40,460	LA	$32,840	OH	$44,020
AR	$33,340	MA	$45,230	OK	$35,100
AZ	$43,380	MD	$43,280	OR	$44,570
CA	$57,670	ME	$39,470	PA	$45,050
CO	$48,500	MI	$48,750	RI	$46,370
CT	$48,490	MN	$47,190	SC	$40,280
DC	$55,380	MO	$38,450	SD	$32,200
DE	$58,380	MS	$38,990	TN	$50,430
FL	$33,700	MT	$39,990	TX	$38,850
GA	$35,180	NC	$37,690	UT	$50,290
HI	$50,850	ND	$32,190	VA	$40,220
IA	$38,210	NE	$36,780	VT	$33,880
ID	$39,250	NH	$41,560	WA	$49,800
IL	$64,950	NJ	$45,090	WI	$43,200
IN	$38,620	NM	$39,690	WV	$41,180
KS	$43,340	NV	$51,470	WY	$52,960

Median Wages for the Largest Metropolitan Areas (Annual)

Area	Wage	Area	Wage
AZ: Phoenix	$40,300	MI: Detroit	$51,230
CA: Los Angeles	$55,200	MN: Minneapolis	$50,110
CA: Riverside	$55,190	MO: Kansas City	$45,240
CA: Sacramento	$54,740	MO: St. Louis	$50,030
CA: San Diego	$53,310	NV: Las Vegas	no data
CA: San Francisco	$64,260	NY: New York	$57,210
CO: Denver	$48,450	OH: Cincinnati	$46,660
DC: Washington	$53,990	OH: Cleveland	$46,590
FL: Miami	$33,230	OH: Columbus	$44,220
FL: Orlando	$26,940	OR: Portland	$47,370
FL: Tampa	$35,940	PA: Philadelphia	$45,350
GA: Atlanta	$38,000	PA: Pittsburgh	$49,770
IL: Chicago	$63,480	TX: Dallas	$40,060
MA: Boston	$45,630	TX: Houston	$39,480
MD: Baltimore	$41,510	WA: Seattle	$51,990

FACTORS THAT MAY AFFECT EARNINGS

Educational Attainment of Workers and Effect on Earnings

	Percent at Level	Effect on Earnings
Less than High School	—	—
Some High School	—	—
High School or Equivalent	48.1%	0.1%
Some College but No Degree	19.8%	−2.4%
Associate Degree	16.8%	4.4%
Bachelor's Degree	6.9%	−8.0%
Master's Degree	—	—
Doctoral Degree	—	—
First Professional Degree	—	—

Figures do not total 100% because some levels have a very small sample size.

Flexibility of Earnings

Average Hours Worked: 38
Workers with a Varying Number of Hours: 3.3%
Workers Earning Some Overtime Pay, Tips, or Commissions: 24.3%
Earnings Benefit of Working Overtime: 15.1%

Gender

	Male	Female
Percent	97.7%	2.3%
Effect on Earnings	0.6%	—

Union Membership

Percentage Union Members: 34.7%
Earnings Benefit of Union Membership: 12.8%

Veteran Status

Percentage Who Have Been on Active Duty: 20.9%
Earnings Benefit of Veteran Status: 8.5%

51-8031 Water and Liquid Waste Treatment Plant and System Operators

Operate or control an entire process or system of machines, often through the use of control boards, to transfer or treat water or liquid waste.

- Education or Training Required: Long-term on-the-job training
- Job Growth: 16.2%
- Annual Openings: 6,000
- Self-Employed: 0.0%
- Part-Time: 3.8%

NATIONAL WAGE FIGURES (ANNUAL)

Beginning	25th Percentile	Median	Mean	75th Percentile	90th Percentile
$21,860	$28,120	$36,070	$37,180	$45,190	$55,120

Median Wages for Industries Employing Largest Numbers (Annual)

Industry	Median Income
Transportation Equipment Manufacturing	$49,780
Plastics and Rubber Products Manufacturing	$43,950
Paper Manufacturing	$43,880
Administrative and Support Services	$42,380
Chemical Manufacturing	$39,980
Management of Companies and Enterprises	$39,390
Professional, Scientific, and Technical Services	$37,990
Electrical Equipment, Appliance, and Component Manufacturing	$37,700
Federal, State, and Local Government	$36,330
Waste Management and Remediation Services	$36,130

Median Wages for States (Annual)

State	Wage	State	Wage	State	Wage
AK	$41,060	KY	$29,250	NY	$42,480
AL	$32,660	LA	$25,080	OH	$38,800
AR	$29,200	MA	$42,100	OK	$24,030
AZ	$40,750	MD	$41,070	OR	$41,400
CA	$50,560	ME	$34,080	PA	$36,110
CO	$40,510	MI	$37,980	RI	$39,990
CT	$41,060	MN	$42,180	SC	$32,770
DC	no data	MO	$31,150	SD	$32,660
DE	$37,730	MS	$27,660	TN	$30,430
FL	$38,140	MT	$33,190	TX	$29,400
GA	$30,120	NC	$31,530	UT	$36,890
HI	$42,590	ND	$35,540	VA	$34,860
IA	$34,960	NE	$33,350	VT	$31,900
ID	$30,700	NH	$39,270	WA	$49,040
IL	$45,210	NJ	$48,290	WI	$37,970
IN	$33,220	NM	$27,330	WV	$26,670
KS	$30,030	NV	$52,740	WY	$40,700

Median Wages for the Largest Metropolitan Areas (Annual)

Area	Wage	Area	Wage
AZ: Phoenix	$44,430	MI: Detroit	no data
CA: Los Angeles	$51,830	MN: Minneapolis	$45,570
CA: Riverside	$49,710	MO: Kansas City	$30,830
CA: Sacramento	$48,570	MO: St. Louis	$39,810
CA: San Diego	$51,180	NV: Las Vegas	$57,930
CA: San Francisco	$63,540	NY: New York	$47,730
CO: Denver	$47,030	OH: Cincinnati	$40,780
DC: Washington	$41,160	OH: Cleveland	$42,040
FL: Miami	$44,570	OH: Columbus	$36,610
FL: Orlando	$36,700	OR: Portland	$44,480
FL: Tampa	$37,670	PA: Philadelphia	$41,030
GA: Atlanta	$33,920	PA: Pittsburgh	$30,290
IL: Chicago	$46,360	TX: Dallas	$33,370
MA: Boston	$43,000	TX: Houston	$31,600
MD: Baltimore	$40,810	WA: Seattle	$54,970

FACTORS THAT MAY AFFECT EARNINGS

Educational Attainment of Workers and Effect on Earnings

	Percent at Level	Effect on Earnings
Less than High School	—	—
Some High School	7.4%	−14.4%
High School or Equivalent	45.1%	−5.6%
Some College but No Degree	21.3%	0.3%
Associate Degree	13.1%	5.0%
Bachelor's Degree	9.8%	18.7%
Master's Degree	—	—
Doctoral Degree	—	—
First Professional Degree	—	—

Flexibility of Earnings

Average Hours Worked: 38
Workers with a Varying Number of Hours: 4.2%
Workers Earning Some Overtime Pay, Tips, or Commissions: 20.4%
Earnings Benefit of Working Overtime: 1.5%

Gender

	Male	Female
Percent	96.0%	4.0%
Effect on Earnings	1.8%	—

Union Membership

Percentage Union Members: 32.8%
Earnings Benefit of Union Membership: 18.3%

Veteran Status

Percentage Who Have Been on Active Duty: 20.9%
Earnings Benefit of Veteran Status: 8.5%

51-8091 Chemical Plant and System Operators

Control or operate an entire chemical process or system of machines.

- Education or Training Required: Long-term on-the-job training
- Job Growth: −17.7%
- Annual Openings: 8,000
- Self-Employed: 0.1%
- Part-Time: 1.3%

NATIONAL WAGE FIGURES (ANNUAL)

Beginning	25th Percentile	Median	Mean	75th Percentile	90th Percentile
$32,640	$39,910	$49,080	$48,930	$57,560	$66,820

Median Wages for Industries Employing Largest Numbers (Annual)

Industry	Median Income
Pipeline Transportation	$55,400
Utilities	$53,230
Food Manufacturing	$51,460
Machinery Manufacturing	$50,400
Petroleum and Coal Products Manufacturing	$49,780
Chemical Manufacturing	$49,240
Paper Manufacturing	$47,980
Mining (Except Oil and Gas)	$45,800
Oil and Gas Extraction	$45,120
Merchant Wholesalers, Nondurable Goods	$44,190

Median Wages for States (Annual)

State		State		State	
AK	no data	KY	$49,240	NY	$50,520
AL	$50,600	LA	$54,490	OH	$45,930
AR	$44,060	MA	$43,990	OK	$41,230
AZ	$34,210	MD	$44,230	OR	$50,170
CA	$54,740	ME	no data	PA	$43,800
CO	$38,810	MI	$48,160	RI	no data
CT	$51,970	MN	$41,460	SC	$41,140
DC	no data	MO	$38,930	SD	no data
DE	no data	MS	$42,590	TN	$43,650
FL	$43,900	MT	no data	TX	$55,960
GA	$45,010	NC	$40,160	UT	no data
HI	no data	ND	no data	VA	$47,280
IA	$42,730	NE	$40,510	VT	no data
ID	$43,230	NH	$35,030	WA	$52,990
IL	$44,050	NJ	$49,190	WI	$42,480
IN	$40,840	NM	no data	WV	$53,720
KS	$46,180	NV	no data	WY	$56,300

Median Wages for the Largest Metropolitan Areas (Annual)

AZ: Phoenix	$35,060	MI: Detroit	$53,230
CA: Los Angeles	$52,620	MN: Minneapolis	$41,500
CA: Riverside	$53,700	MO: Kansas City	$39,200
CA: Sacramento	no data	MO: St. Louis	$35,410
CA: San Diego	no data	NV: Las Vegas	no data
CA: San Francisco	$50,400	NY: New York	$44,690
CO: Denver	$33,040	OH: Cincinnati	$47,840
DC: Washington	$44,660	OH: Cleveland	$49,860
FL: Miami	no data	OH: Columbus	$49,740
FL: Orlando	no data	OR: Portland	$49,230
FL: Tampa	no data	PA: Philadelphia	$54,670
GA: Atlanta	$37,820	PA: Pittsburgh	$47,570
IL: Chicago	$42,470	TX: Dallas	$50,160
MA: Boston	$41,720	TX: Houston	$57,780
MD: Baltimore	$43,830	WA: Seattle	$51,840

FACTORS THAT MAY AFFECT EARNINGS

Educational Attainment of Workers and Effect on Earnings

Figures are based on a group of occupations: Plant and System Operators

	Percent at Level	Effect on Earnings
Less than High School	—	—
Some High School	4.6%	−25.0%
High School or Equivalent	43.9%	−3.4%
Some College but No Degree	22.8%	0.5%
Associate Degree	15.3%	4.8%
Bachelor's Degree	9.5%	10.4%
Master's Degree	—	—
Doctoral Degree	—	—
First Professional Degree	—	—

Flexibility of Earnings

Average Hours Worked: 38
Workers with a Varying Number of Hours: 3.7%
Workers Earning Some Overtime Pay, Tips, or Commissions: 25.9%
Earnings Benefit of Working Overtime: 1.5%

Gender

	Male	Female
Percent	87.0%	13.0%
Effect on Earnings	11.1%	−32.0%

Union Membership

Percentage Union Members: 33.5%
Earnings Benefit of Union Membership: 15.7%

Veteran Status

Percentage Who Have Been on Active Duty: 20.9%
Earnings Benefit of Veteran Status: 8.5%

51-8092 Gas Plant Operators

Distribute or process gas for utility companies and others by controlling compressors to maintain specified pressures on main pipelines.

- Education or Training Required: Long-term on-the-job training
- Job Growth: 7.7%
- Annual Openings: 2,000
- Self-Employed: 0.1%
- Part-Time: 1.3%

NATIONAL WAGE FIGURES (ANNUAL)

Beginning	25th Percentile	Median	Mean	75th Percentile	90th Percentile
$38,020	$45,710	$53,670	$53,870	$62,430	$72,200

Median Wages for Industries Employing Largest Numbers (Annual)

Industry	Median Income
Waste Management and Remediation Services	$65,570
Management of Companies and Enterprises	$58,350
Utilities	$56,730
Petroleum and Coal Products Manufacturing	$51,810
Oil and Gas Extraction	$51,230
Pipeline Transportation	$50,990
Chemical Manufacturing	$50,510
Federal, State, and Local Government	$38,620
Nonstore Retailers	$33,690

Median Wages for States (Annual)

State	Wage	State	Wage	State	Wage
AK	no data	KY	$51,850	NY	$70,810
AL	$43,820	LA	$43,530	OH	$54,460
AR	$50,570	MA	$56,360	OK	$49,100
AZ	no data	MD	$55,780	OR	no data
CA	$67,750	ME	no data	PA	$47,260
CO	$51,840	MI	no data	RI	no data
CT	$53,910	MN	$45,770	SC	$46,280
DC	no data	MO	$49,620	SD	no data
DE	no data	MS	$51,090	TN	$41,720
FL	$53,510	MT	$59,360	TX	$52,120
GA	no data	NC	$41,560	UT	$53,740
HI	no data	ND	no data	VA	$56,070
IA	$60,570	NE	no data	VT	no data
ID	no data	NH	no data	WA	no data
IL	$56,030	NJ	$60,990	WI	$63,440
IN	$45,980	NM	$48,150	WV	$49,820
KS	$54,310	NV	no data	WY	$53,090

Median Wages for the Largest Metropolitan Areas (Annual)

Metro	Wage	Metro	Wage
AZ: Phoenix	no data	MI: Detroit	$53,020
CA: Los Angeles	$64,250	MN: Minneapolis	$50,550
CA: Riverside	$73,220	MO: Kansas City	no data
CA: Sacramento	no data	MO: St. Louis	$52,550
CA: San Diego	no data	NV: Las Vegas	no data
CA: San Francisco	no data	NY: New York	$71,620
CO: Denver	no data	OH: Cincinnati	no data
DC: Washington	$54,870	OH: Cleveland	$54,420
FL: Miami	no data	OH: Columbus	no data
FL: Orlando	no data	OR: Portland	no data
FL: Tampa	no data	PA: Philadelphia	no data
GA: Atlanta	no data	PA: Pittsburgh	$46,990
IL: Chicago	$55,090	TX: Dallas	$53,230
MA: Boston	$59,350	TX: Houston	$52,050
MD: Baltimore	$56,590	WA: Seattle	no data

FACTORS THAT MAY AFFECT EARNINGS

Educational Attainment of Workers and Effect on Earnings

Figures are based on a group of occupations: Plant and System Operators

	Percent at Level	Effect on Earnings
Less than High School	—	—
Some High School	4.6%	−25.0%
High School or Equivalent	43.9%	−3.4%
Some College but No Degree	22.8%	0.5%
Associate Degree	15.3%	4.8%
Bachelor's Degree	9.5%	10.4%
Master's Degree	—	—
Doctoral Degree	—	—
First Professional Degree	—	—

Flexibility of Earnings

Average Hours Worked: 38
Workers with a Varying Number of Hours: 3.7%
Workers Earning Some Overtime Pay, Tips, or Commissions: 25.9%
Earnings Benefit of Working Overtime: 1.5%

Gender

	Male	Female
Percent	94.4%	5.6%
Effect on Earnings	11.1%	−32.0%

Union Membership

Percentage Union Members: 33.5%
Earnings Benefit of Union Membership: 15.7%

Veteran Status

Percentage Who Have Been on Active Duty: 20.9%
Earnings Benefit of Veteran Status: 8.5%

51-8093 Petroleum Pump System Operators, Refinery Operators, and Gaugers

Control the operation of petroleum-refining or -processing units. May specialize in controlling manifold and pumping systems, gauging or testing oil in storage tanks, or regulating the flow of oil into pipelines.

- Education or Training Required: Long-term on-the-job training
- Job Growth: –8.6%
- Annual Openings: 6,000
- Self-Employed: 0.1%
- Part-Time: 1.3%

NATIONAL WAGE FIGURES (ANNUAL)

Beginning	25th Percentile	Median	Mean	75th Percentile	90th Percentile
$33,650	$43,230	$52,380	$52,410	$61,500	$72,050

Median Wages for Industries Employing Largest Numbers (Annual)

Industry	Median Income
Utilities	$65,550
Merchant Wholesalers, Durable Goods	$61,710
Oil and Gas Extraction	$54,980
Petroleum and Coal Products Manufacturing	$53,380
Pipeline Transportation	$52,120
Management of Companies and Enterprises	$51,050
Professional, Scientific, and Technical Services	$50,040
Merchant Wholesalers, Nondurable Goods	$48,070
Warehousing and Storage	$46,080
Federal, State, and Local Government	$44,710

Median Wages for States (Annual)

State	Wage	State	Wage	State	Wage
AK	no data	KY	$42,580	NY	$47,240
AL	$43,780	LA	$53,900	OH	$55,250
AR	$43,390	MA	no data	OK	$52,330
AZ	$44,950	MD	$43,420	OR	$49,080
CA	$57,120	ME	no data	PA	$46,740
CO	$53,130	MI	$45,510	RI	no data
CT	$42,530	MN	$45,600	SC	no data
DC	no data	MO	$50,970	SD	no data
DE	no data	MS	$62,650	TN	$42,470
FL	$42,710	MT	$56,380	TX	$53,800
GA	$46,840	NC	$42,940	UT	$45,000
HI	$54,150	ND	$49,400	VA	$50,270
IA	$54,380	NE	$48,320	VT	no data
ID	no data	NH	no data	WA	$61,040
IL	$41,260	NJ	$53,710	WI	$43,280
IN	$48,660	NM	$44,150	WV	$43,170
KS	$49,110	NV	$41,890	WY	$44,630

Median Wages for the Largest Metropolitan Areas (Annual)

Area	Wage	Area	Wage
AZ: Phoenix	$46,030	MI: Detroit	$46,860
CA: Los Angeles	$61,600	MN: Minneapolis	no data
CA: Riverside	$47,060	MO: Kansas City	no data
CA: Sacramento	no data	MO: St. Louis	$44,130
CA: San Diego	$55,130	NV: Las Vegas	no data
CA: San Francisco	$55,640	NY: New York	$50,190
CO: Denver	$56,120	OH: Cincinnati	$40,260
DC: Washington	no data	OH: Cleveland	no data
FL: Miami	$41,230	OH: Columbus	no data
FL: Orlando	no data	OR: Portland	$49,210
FL: Tampa	no data	PA: Philadelphia	$45,580
GA: Atlanta	no data	PA: Pittsburgh	$54,080
IL: Chicago	$41,880	TX: Dallas	$45,490
MA: Boston	no data	TX: Houston	$54,340
MD: Baltimore	$42,690	WA: Seattle	$54,390

FACTORS THAT MAY AFFECT EARNINGS

Educational Attainment of Workers and Effect on Earnings

Figures are based on a group of occupations: Plant and System Operators

	Percent at Level	Effect on Earnings
Less than High School	—	—
Some High School	4.6%	–25.0%
High School or Equivalent	43.9%	–3.4%
Some College but No Degree	22.8%	0.5%
Associate Degree	15.3%	4.8%
Bachelor's Degree	9.5%	10.4%
Master's Degree	—	—
Doctoral Degree	—	—
First Professional Degree	—	—

Flexibility of Earnings

Average Hours Worked: 38
Workers with a Varying Number of Hours: 3.7%
Workers Earning Some Overtime Pay, Tips, or Commissions: 25.9%
Earnings Benefit of Working Overtime: 1.5%

Gender

	Male	Female
Percent	94.4%	5.6%
Effect on Earnings	11.1%	–32.0%

Union Membership

Percentage Union Members: 33.5%
Earnings Benefit of Union Membership: 15.7%

Veteran Status

Percentage Who Have Been on Active Duty: 20.9%
Earnings Benefit of Veteran Status: 8.5%

51-8099 Plant and System Operators, All Other

All plant and system operators not listed separately.

- Education or Training Required: Long-term on-the-job training
- Job Growth: 7.1%
- Annual Openings: 2,000
- Self-Employed: 0.2%
- Part-Time: 1.3%

NATIONAL WAGE FIGURES (ANNUAL)

Beginning	25th Percentile	Median	Mean	75th Percentile	90th Percentile
$26,140	$35,620	$46,270	$46,450	$56,700	$65,840

Median Wages for Industries Employing Largest Numbers (Annual)

Industry	Median Income
Utilities	$55,900
Transportation Equipment Manufacturing	$55,380
Pipeline Transportation	$51,730
Federal, State, and Local Government	$48,680
Paper Manufacturing	$46,720
Administrative and Support Services	$45,890
Chemical Manufacturing	$45,430
Management of Companies and Enterprises	$44,090
Credit Intermediation and Related Activities	$43,040
Waste Management and Remediation Services	$42,660

Median Wages for States (Annual)

State	Wage	State	Wage	State	Wage
AK	no data	KY	$41,630	NY	$47,390
AL	$46,340	LA	$36,730	OH	$32,940
AR	$28,190	MA	$47,860	OK	$43,300
AZ	$45,290	MD	$54,250	OR	no data
CA	$57,250	ME	$33,600	PA	$40,750
CO	$45,100	MI	$52,110	RI	no data
CT	$38,960	MN	$42,910	SC	$37,960
DC	no data	MO	$49,880	SD	no data
DE	$36,440	MS	$45,350	TN	$42,780
FL	$39,600	MT	no data	TX	$42,360
GA	$45,010	NC	no data	UT	$37,630
HI	$43,570	ND	no data	VA	$48,120
IA	$43,750	NE	$46,310	VT	no data
ID	$34,410	NH	$51,040	WA	$55,860
IL	$39,600	NJ	$46,510	WI	$50,640
IN	$39,480	NM	$37,320	WV	$49,790
KS	$41,630	NV	$42,820	WY	$36,700

Median Wages for the Largest Metropolitan Areas (Annual)

Area	Wage	Area	Wage
AZ: Phoenix	$41,920	MI: Detroit	$53,400
CA: Los Angeles	$46,020	MN: Minneapolis	$43,640
CA: Riverside	$53,510	MO: Kansas City	$45,750
CA: Sacramento	no data	MO: St. Louis	$48,080
CA: San Diego	$51,710	NV: Las Vegas	no data
CA: San Francisco	no data	NY: New York	$53,560
CO: Denver	$48,720	OH: Cincinnati	$41,850
DC: Washington	$55,490	OH: Cleveland	$28,420
FL: Miami	$40,110	OH: Columbus	no data
FL: Orlando	$39,710	OR: Portland	$54,250
FL: Tampa	no data	PA: Philadelphia	$49,610
GA: Atlanta	$51,480	PA: Pittsburgh	$40,660
IL: Chicago	$43,080	TX: Dallas	$51,880
MA: Boston	$54,590	TX: Houston	$42,840
MD: Baltimore	$53,090	WA: Seattle	$55,110

FACTORS THAT MAY AFFECT EARNINGS

Educational Attainment of Workers and Effect on Earnings

Figures are based on a group of occupations: Plant and System Operators

	Percent at Level	Effect on Earnings
Less than High School	—	—
Some High School	4.6%	−25.0%
High School or Equivalent	43.9%	−3.4%
Some College but No Degree	22.8%	0.5%
Associate Degree	15.3%	4.8%
Bachelor's Degree	9.5%	10.4%
Master's Degree	—	—
Doctoral Degree	—	—
First Professional Degree	—	—

Flexibility of Earnings

Average Hours Worked: 38
Workers with a Varying Number of Hours: 3.7%
Workers Earning Some Overtime Pay, Tips, or Commissions: 25.9%
Earnings Benefit of Working Overtime: 1.5%

Gender

	Male	Female
Percent	94.4%	5.6%
Effect on Earnings	11.1%	−32.0%

Union Membership

Percentage Union Members: 33.5%
Earnings Benefit of Union Membership: 15.7%

Veteran Status

Percentage Who Have Been on Active Duty: 20.9%
Earnings Benefit of Veteran Status: 8.5%

51-9000 Other Production Occupations

51-9011 Chemical Equipment Operators and Tenders

Operate or tend equipment to control chemical changes or reactions in the processing of industrial or consumer products. Equipment used includes devulcanizers, steam-jacketed kettles, and reactor vessels.

- Education or Training Required: Moderate-term on-the-job training
- Job Growth: –4.5%
- Annual Openings: 6,000
- Self-Employed: 0.8%
- Part-Time: 15.8%

NATIONAL WAGE FIGURES (ANNUAL)

Beginning	25th Percentile	Median	Mean	75th Percentile	90th Percentile
$25,280	$31,960	$40,290	$41,300	$50,150	$58,440

Median Wages for Industries Employing Largest Numbers (Annual)

Industry	Median Income
Mining (Except Oil and Gas)	$47,180
Petroleum and Coal Products Manufacturing	$43,270
Paper Manufacturing	$42,700
Food Manufacturing	$41,730
Plastics and Rubber Products Manufacturing	$41,710
Professional, Scientific, and Technical Services	$40,620
Chemical Manufacturing	$40,050
Merchant Wholesalers, Nondurable Goods	$39,600
Machinery Manufacturing	$39,200
Wood Product Manufacturing	$39,000

Median Wages for States (Annual)

State	Wage	State	Wage	State	Wage
AK	no data	KY	$49,970	NY	$43,160
AL	$46,360	LA	$46,820	OH	$33,380
AR	no data	MA	$38,040	OK	$40,690
AZ	$31,030	MD	$38,090	OR	$43,610
CA	$43,030	ME	$37,040	PA	$38,260
CO	$34,650	MI	$42,940	RI	$35,740
CT	$36,280	MN	$32,380	SC	$47,000
DC	no data	MO	$37,840	SD	$27,470
DE	$43,830	MS	$40,550	TN	$40,280
FL	$39,900	MT	no data	TX	$52,680
GA	$34,640	NC	$41,190	UT	$37,850
HI	no data	ND	no data	VA	$41,430
IA	$34,510	NE	$28,730	VT	no data
ID	$46,930	NH	$34,740	WA	$37,800
IL	$37,410	NJ	$41,450	WI	$38,370
IN	$33,390	NM	no data	WV	$42,780
KS	no data	NV	$42,550	WY	no data

Median Wages for the Largest Metropolitan Areas (Annual)

Area	Wage	Area	Wage
AZ: Phoenix	$26,630	MI: Detroit	$47,470
CA: Los Angeles	$42,060	MN: Minneapolis	$31,740
CA: Riverside	$38,140	MO: Kansas City	$34,030
CA: Sacramento	no data	MO: St. Louis	$43,060
CA: San Diego	$44,330	NV: Las Vegas	no data
CA: San Francisco	$36,640	NY: New York	$41,740
CO: Denver	no data	OH: Cincinnati	$43,860
DC: Washington	$34,700	OH: Cleveland	$30,500
FL: Miami	$27,640	OH: Columbus	no data
FL: Orlando	no data	OR: Portland	no data
FL: Tampa	$37,060	PA: Philadelphia	$41,670
GA: Atlanta	$34,180	PA: Pittsburgh	$37,960
IL: Chicago	$36,820	TX: Dallas	$43,490
MA: Boston	$37,560	TX: Houston	$55,300
MD: Baltimore	$38,220	WA: Seattle	$43,550

FACTORS THAT MAY AFFECT EARNINGS

Educational Attainment of Workers and Effect on Earnings

Figures are based on a group of occupations: Other Production Occupations

	Percent at Level	Effect on Earnings
Less than High School	7.0%	–35.1%
Some High School	12.3%	–28.6%
High School or Equivalent	40.7%	3.9%
Some College but No Degree	19.3%	4.8%
Associate Degree	10.8%	9.0%
Bachelor's Degree	8.0%	25.5%
Master's Degree	1.6%	23.4%
Doctoral Degree	—	—
First Professional Degree	—	—

Flexibility of Earnings

Average Hours Worked: 35
Workers with a Varying Number of Hours: 7.2%
Workers Earning Some Overtime Pay, Tips, or Commissions: 22.3%
Earnings Benefit of Working Overtime: 17.2%

Gender

	Male	Female
Percent	61.4%	38.6%
Effect on Earnings	11.1%	–32.0%

Union Membership

Percentage Union Members: 15.3%
Earnings Benefit of Union Membership: 26.5%

Veteran Status

Percentage Who Have Been on Active Duty: 10.3%
Earnings Benefit of Veteran Status: 25.8%

51-9012 Separating, Filtering, Clarifying, Precipitating, and Still Machine Setters, Operators, and Tenders

Set up, operate, or tend continuous flow or vat-type equipment; filter presses; shaker screens; centrifuges; condenser tubes; precipitating, fermenting, or evaporating tanks; scrubbing towers; or batch stills. These machines extract, sort, or separate liquids, gases, or solids from other materials to recover a refined product. Includes dairy processing equipment operators.

- Education or Training Required: Moderate-term on-the-job training
- Job Growth: 1.6%
- Annual Openings: 5,000
- Self-Employed: 0.6%
- Part-Time: 15.8%

NATIONAL WAGE FIGURES (ANNUAL)

Beginning	25th Percentile	Median	Mean	75th Percentile	90th Percentile
$20,520	$26,980	$34,970	$36,130	$44,220	$53,620

Median Wages for Industries Employing Largest Numbers (Annual)

Industry	Median Income
Paper Manufacturing	$39,450
Beverage and Tobacco Product Manufacturing	$39,270
Mining (Except Oil and Gas)	$39,240
Professional, Scientific, and Technical Services	$39,110
Federal, State, and Local Government	$38,300
Chemical Manufacturing	$36,970
Petroleum and Coal Products Manufacturing	$36,620
Nonmetallic Mineral Product Manufacturing	$34,670
Food Manufacturing	$32,600
Food Services and Drinking Places	$31,960

Median Wages for States (Annual)

State	Wage	State	Wage	State	Wage
AK	$42,460	KY	$33,780	NY	$32,940
AL	$30,310	LA	$29,170	OH	$41,840
AR	$31,480	MA	$39,630	OK	$23,680
AZ	$33,980	MD	$31,510	OR	$36,170
CA	$40,850	ME	$35,500	PA	$36,610
CO	$33,520	MI	$29,330	RI	no data
CT	$35,400	MN	$30,220	SC	$35,690
DC	no data	MO	$30,290	SD	$22,730
DE	no data	MS	$23,250	TN	$37,920
FL	$32,790	MT	$34,110	TX	$30,240
GA	$36,960	NC	$40,260	UT	$34,720
HI	no data	ND	$27,580	VA	$29,740
IA	$30,790	NE	$25,900	VT	$27,960
ID	$31,900	NH	$39,130	WA	$35,950
IL	$37,100	NJ	$48,030	WI	$32,210
IN	$39,040	NM	$16,850	WV	$43,350
KS	$31,060	NV	$36,710	WY	$53,210

Median Wages for the Largest Metropolitan Areas (Annual)

Area	Wage	Area	Wage
AZ: Phoenix	$27,780	MI: Detroit	$28,430
CA: Los Angeles	$43,980	MN: Minneapolis	$34,420
CA: Riverside	$45,980	MO: Kansas City	$31,410
CA: Sacramento	$41,610	MO: St. Louis	$31,140
CA: San Diego	$39,550	NV: Las Vegas	$31,580
CA: San Francisco	$37,910	NY: New York	$41,110
CO: Denver	$32,750	OH: Cincinnati	$48,900
DC: Washington	$27,630	OH: Cleveland	$40,930
FL: Miami	$25,310	OH: Columbus	$44,260
FL: Orlando	$19,750	OR: Portland	$38,800
FL: Tampa	$23,830	PA: Philadelphia	$40,560
GA: Atlanta	$44,250	PA: Pittsburgh	$35,280
IL: Chicago	$37,920	TX: Dallas	$32,780
MA: Boston	$42,780	TX: Houston	$30,060
MD: Baltimore	$34,950	WA: Seattle	$37,910

FACTORS THAT MAY AFFECT EARNINGS

Educational Attainment of Workers and Effect on Earnings

Figures are based on a group of occupations: Other Production Occupations

	Percent at Level	Effect on Earnings
Less than High School	7.0%	−35.1%
Some High School	12.3%	−28.6%
High School or Equivalent	40.7%	3.9%
Some College but No Degree	19.3%	4.8%
Associate Degree	10.8%	9.0%
Bachelor's Degree	8.0%	25.5%
Master's Degree	1.6%	23.4%
Doctoral Degree	—	—
First Professional Degree	—	—

Flexibility of Earnings

Average Hours Worked: 35
Workers with a Varying Number of Hours: 7.2%
Workers Earning Some Overtime Pay, Tips, or Commissions: 22.3%
Earnings Benefit of Working Overtime: 17.2%

Gender

	Male	Female
Percent	61.4%	38.6%
Effect on Earnings	11.1%	−32.0%

Union Membership

Percentage Union Members: 15.3%
Earnings Benefit of Union Membership: 26.5%

Veteran Status

Percentage Who Have Been on Active Duty: 10.3%
Earnings Benefit of Veteran Status: 25.8%

51-9021 Crushing, Grinding, and Polishing Machine Setters, Operators, and Tenders

Set up, operate, or tend machines to crush, grind, or polish materials such as coal, glass, grain, stone, food, or rubber.

- Education or Training Required: Moderate-term on-the-job training
- Job Growth: 0.8%
- Annual Openings: 6,000
- Self-Employed: 1.0%
- Part-Time: 15.8%

NATIONAL WAGE FIGURES (ANNUAL)

Beginning	25th Percentile	Median	Mean	75th Percentile	90th Percentile
$17,810	$21,870	$28,080	$29,570	$35,790	$44,140

Median Wages for Industries Employing Largest Numbers (Annual)

Industry	Median Income
Paper Manufacturing	$41,800
Support Activities for Mining	$38,640
Federal, State, and Local Government	$38,120
Petroleum and Coal Products Manufacturing	$36,410
Mining (Except Oil and Gas)	$33,070
Professional, Scientific, and Technical Services	$32,320
Machinery Manufacturing	$31,560
Electrical Equipment, Appliance, and Component Manufacturing	$31,110
Transportation Equipment Manufacturing	$29,740
Primary Metal Manufacturing	$29,530

Median Wages for States (Annual)

AK	$46,270	KY	$32,590	NY	$29,470
AL	$24,500	LA	$25,730	OH	$28,970
AR	$26,950	MA	$31,500	OK	$22,940
AZ	$29,940	MD	$25,330	OR	$33,290
CA	$30,490	ME	$38,600	PA	$31,400
CO	$24,580	MI	$27,380	RI	no data
CT	$30,940	MN	$28,690	SC	$33,930
DC	no data	MO	$29,400	SD	$26,480
DE	$32,840	MS	$23,050	TN	$26,510
FL	$26,680	MT	$28,610	TX	$22,330
GA	$30,430	NC	$22,960	UT	$28,010
HI	$34,010	ND	$35,780	VA	$28,260
IA	$25,970	NE	$23,330	VT	$33,890
ID	$30,890	NH	$30,950	WA	$30,760
IL	$29,220	NJ	$31,940	WI	$28,780
IN	$36,380	NM	$26,400	WV	$33,820
KS	$26,210	NV	$27,680	WY	$42,020

Median Wages for the Largest Metropolitan Areas (Annual)

AZ: Phoenix	$25,430	MI: Detroit	$32,860
CA: Los Angeles	$27,530	MN: Minneapolis	$45,660
CA: Riverside	$33,320	MO: Kansas City	$28,500
CA: Sacramento	$32,920	MO: St. Louis	$29,540
CA: San Diego	$17,500	NV: Las Vegas	$24,930
CA: San Francisco	$42,480	NY: New York	$30,370
CO: Denver	$23,340	OH: Cincinnati	no data
DC: Washington	$29,350	OH: Cleveland	$29,750
FL: Miami	$24,430	OH: Columbus	$31,590
FL: Orlando	$26,270	OR: Portland	$35,680
FL: Tampa	$26,150	PA: Philadelphia	$29,550
GA: Atlanta	$31,980	PA: Pittsburgh	$31,030
IL: Chicago	$33,000	TX: Dallas	$21,820
MA: Boston	$32,550	TX: Houston	$24,080
MD: Baltimore	$25,280	WA: Seattle	$27,730

FACTORS THAT MAY AFFECT EARNINGS

Educational Attainment of Workers and Effect on Earnings

Figures are based on a group of occupations: Other Production Occupations

	Percent at Level	Effect on Earnings
Less than High School	7.0%	−35.1%
Some High School	12.3%	−28.6%
High School or Equivalent	40.7%	3.9%
Some College but No Degree	19.3%	4.8%
Associate Degree	10.8%	9.0%
Bachelor's Degree	8.0%	25.5%
Master's Degree	1.6%	23.4%
Doctoral Degree	—	—
First Professional Degree	—	—

Flexibility of Earnings

Average Hours Worked: 35
Workers with a Varying Number of Hours: 7.2%
Workers Earning Some Overtime Pay, Tips, or Commissions: 22.3%
Earnings Benefit of Working Overtime: 17.1%

Gender

	Male	Female
Percent	88.8%	11.2%
Effect on Earnings	3.4%	—

Union Membership

Percentage Union Members: 15.3%
Earnings Benefit of Union Membership: 26.5%

Veteran Status

Percentage Who Have Been on Active Duty: 10.3%
Earnings Benefit of Veteran Status: 25.8%

51-9022 *Grinding and Polishing Workers, Hand*

Grind, sand, or polish, using hand tools or hand-held power tools, a variety of metal, wood, stone, clay, plastic, or glass objects.

- Education or Training Required: Moderate-term on-the-job training
- Job Growth: –8.7%
- Annual Openings: 6,000
- Self-Employed: 0.9%
- Part-Time: 15.8%

NATIONAL WAGE FIGURES (ANNUAL)

Beginning	25th Percentile	Median	Mean	75th Percentile	90th Percentile
$16,740	$19,730	$23,880	$25,460	$29,820	$36,180

Median Wages for Industries Employing Largest Numbers (Annual)

Industry	Median Income
Electrical Equipment, Appliance, and Component Manufacturing	$31,060
Specialty Trade Contractors	$28,430
Building Material and Garden Equipment and Supplies Dealers	$27,560
Transportation Equipment Manufacturing	$26,260
Primary Metal Manufacturing	$25,990
Nonmetallic Mineral Product Manufacturing	$25,020
Machinery Manufacturing	$24,850
Fabricated Metal Product Manufacturing	$23,790
Miscellaneous Manufacturing	$23,340
Computer and Electronic Product Manufacturing	$23,120

Median Wages for States (Annual)

AK	no data	KY	$24,560	NY	$22,380
AL	$20,780	LA	$23,290	OH	$27,050
AR	$21,520	MA	$28,150	OK	$21,960
AZ	$23,190	MD	$25,000	OR	$22,280
CA	$21,380	ME	$26,360	PA	$28,220
CO	$25,240	MI	$23,870	RI	$25,120
CT	$27,910	MN	$28,820	SC	$24,220
DC	no data	MO	$25,200	SD	$21,750
DE	no data	MS	$22,410	TN	$26,780
FL	$25,020	MT	$20,930	TX	$21,190
GA	$23,620	NC	$23,620	UT	$23,620
HI	no data	ND	$21,260	VA	$24,960
IA	$24,650	NE	no data	VT	$29,310
ID	$18,240	NH	$23,220	WA	$27,440
IL	$22,970	NJ	$29,480	WI	$27,560
IN	$24,530	NM	$20,430	WV	$20,460
KS	$22,600	NV	$24,990	WY	no data

Median Wages for the Largest Metropolitan Areas (Annual)

AZ: Phoenix	$23,390	MI: Detroit	$22,740
CA: Los Angeles	$19,560	MN: Minneapolis	$30,870
CA: Riverside	$22,390	MO: Kansas City	$25,170
CA: Sacramento	$28,330	MO: St. Louis	$27,550
CA: San Diego	$22,910	NV: Las Vegas	no data
CA: San Francisco	$25,040	NY: New York	$25,980
CO: Denver	$25,880	OH: Cincinnati	$26,660
DC: Washington	$23,140	OH: Cleveland	$28,630
FL: Miami	$22,490	OH: Columbus	$23,810
FL: Orlando	$25,660	OR: Portland	$22,460
FL: Tampa	$24,140	PA: Philadelphia	$30,590
GA: Atlanta	$23,200	PA: Pittsburgh	$28,990
IL: Chicago	$23,410	TX: Dallas	$19,710
MA: Boston	$28,390	TX: Houston	$22,160
MD: Baltimore	$25,860	WA: Seattle	$27,620

FACTORS THAT MAY AFFECT EARNINGS

Educational Attainment of Workers and Effect on Earnings

Figures are based on a group of occupations: Other Production Occupations

	Percent at Level	Effect on Earnings
Less than High School	7.0%	–35.1%
Some High School	12.3%	–28.6%
High School or Equivalent	40.7%	3.9%
Some College but No Degree	19.3%	4.8%
Associate Degree	10.8%	9.0%
Bachelor's Degree	8.0%	25.5%
Master's Degree	1.6%	23.4%
Doctoral Degree	—	—
First Professional Degree	—	—

Flexibility of Earnings

Average Hours Worked: 35
Workers with a Varying Number of Hours: 7.2%
Workers Earning Some Overtime Pay, Tips, or Commissions: 22.3%
Earnings Benefit of Working Overtime: 17.1%

Gender

	Male	Female
Percent	88.8%	11.2%
Effect on Earnings	11.1%	–32.0%

Union Membership

Percentage Union Members: 15.3%
Earnings Benefit of Union Membership: 26.5%

Veteran Status

Percentage Who Have Been on Active Duty: 10.3%
Earnings Benefit of Veteran Status: 25.8%

51-9023 Mixing and Blending Machine Setters, Operators, and Tenders

Set up, operate, or tend machines to mix or blend materials such as chemicals, tobacco, liquids, color pigments, or explosive ingredients.

- Education or Training Required: Moderate-term on-the-job training
- Job Growth: 2.0%
- Annual Openings: 16,000
- Self-Employed: 0.8%
- Part-Time: 15.8%

NATIONAL WAGE FIGURES (ANNUAL)

Beginning	25th Percentile	Median	Mean	75th Percentile	90th Percentile
$18,890	$22,950	$29,330	$30,790	$37,020	$45,550

Median Wages for Industries Employing Largest Numbers (Annual)

Industry	Median Income
Paper Manufacturing	$37,960
Primary Metal Manufacturing	$35,700
Machinery Manufacturing	$35,250
Specialty Trade Contractors	$32,160
Mining (Except Oil and Gas)	$31,930
Printing and Related Support Activities	$31,690
Electrical Equipment, Appliance, and Component Manufacturing	$31,400
Merchant Wholesalers, Durable Goods	$31,190
Computer and Electronic Product Manufacturing	$31,100
Management of Companies and Enterprises	$30,780

Median Wages for States (Annual)

AK	no data	KY	$28,680	NY	$33,590
AL	$26,800	LA	$29,080	OH	$32,490
AR	$25,390	MA	$32,630	OK	$27,810
AZ	$24,340	MD	$36,850	OR	$29,120
CA	$27,350	ME	$35,640	PA	$33,530
CO	$30,360	MI	$31,600	RI	$28,680
CT	$34,510	MN	$32,480	SC	$30,880
DC	no data	MO	$31,290	SD	$26,590
DE	$39,680	MS	$26,650	TN	$29,910
FL	$26,650	MT	no data	TX	$23,410
GA	$27,760	NC	$27,930	UT	$27,000
HI	$28,130	ND	$24,040	VA	$30,110
IA	$28,450	NE	$26,540	VT	$28,230
ID	$30,940	NH	$29,900	WA	$33,480
IL	$28,050	NJ	$29,040	WI	$32,480
IN	$31,530	NM	$24,990	WV	$28,120
KS	$28,790	NV	$30,540	WY	$28,150

Median Wages for the Largest Metropolitan Areas (Annual)

AZ: Phoenix	$24,250	MI: Detroit	$33,520
CA: Los Angeles	$25,820	MN: Minneapolis	$35,930
CA: Riverside	$27,190	MO: Kansas City	$33,540
CA: Sacramento	$31,400	MO: St. Louis	$34,300
CA: San Diego	$25,990	NV: Las Vegas	$28,000
CA: San Francisco	$31,050	NY: New York	$29,460
CO: Denver	$31,250	OH: Cincinnati	$38,560
DC: Washington	$34,200	OH: Cleveland	$30,910
FL: Miami	$25,810	OH: Columbus	$37,990
FL: Orlando	$27,570	OR: Portland	$30,420
FL: Tampa	$26,890	PA: Philadelphia	$34,360
GA: Atlanta	$28,220	PA: Pittsburgh	$33,410
IL: Chicago	$27,180	TX: Dallas	$24,750
MA: Boston	$33,730	TX: Houston	$23,160
MD: Baltimore	$38,270	WA: Seattle	$34,500

FACTORS THAT MAY AFFECT EARNINGS

Educational Attainment of Workers and Effect on Earnings

Figures are based on a group of occupations: Other Production Occupations

	Percent at Level	Effect on Earnings
Less than High School	7.0%	−35.1%
Some High School	12.3%	−28.6%
High School or Equivalent	40.7%	3.9%
Some College but No Degree	19.3%	4.8%
Associate Degree	10.8%	9.0%
Bachelor's Degree	8.0%	25.5%
Master's Degree	1.6%	23.4%
Doctoral Degree	—	—
First Professional Degree	—	—

Flexibility of Earnings

Average Hours Worked: 35
Workers with a Varying Number of Hours: 7.2%
Workers Earning Some Overtime Pay, Tips, or Commissions: 22.3%
Earnings Benefit of Working Overtime: 17.1%

Gender

	Male	Female
Percent	88.8%	11.2%
Effect on Earnings	11.1%	−32.0%

Union Membership

Percentage Union Members: 15.3%
Earnings Benefit of Union Membership: 26.5%

Veteran Status

Percentage Who Have Been on Active Duty: 10.3%
Earnings Benefit of Veteran Status: 25.8%

51-9031 Cutters and Trimmers, Hand

Use hand tools or hand-held power tools to cut and trim a variety of manufactured items, such as carpet, fabric, stone, glass, or rubber.

- Education or Training Required: Short-term on-the-job training
- Job Growth: 2.4%
- Annual Openings: 3,000
- Self-Employed: 1.9%
- Part-Time: 15.8%

NATIONAL WAGE FIGURES (ANNUAL)

Beginning	25th Percentile	Median	Mean	75th Percentile	90th Percentile
$15,710	$17,960	$22,330	$24,370	$28,930	$36,300

Median Wages for Industries Employing Largest Numbers (Annual)

Industry	Median Income
Transportation Equipment Manufacturing	$30,100
Administrative and Support Services	$27,480
Professional, Scientific, and Technical Services	$26,550
Furniture and Related Product Manufacturing	$26,430
Specialty Trade Contractors	$26,260
Primary Metal Manufacturing	$25,700
Nonmetallic Mineral Product Manufacturing	$25,030
Building Material and Garden Equipment and Supplies Dealers	$24,910
Machinery Manufacturing	$24,280
Wood Product Manufacturing	$24,250

Median Wages for States (Annual)

AK	no data	KY	$22,550	NY	$27,830
AL	$23,920	LA	$19,700	OH	$23,830
AR	$22,610	MA	$24,410	OK	$20,130
AZ	$24,540	MD	$24,420	OR	$21,430
CA	$19,230	ME	$23,990	PA	$21,660
CO	$22,890	MI	$21,790	RI	$22,840
CT	$23,390	MN	$25,390	SC	$23,900
DC	no data	MO	$23,080	SD	$20,440
DE	$25,420	MS	$23,740	TN	$23,420
FL	$25,220	MT	$23,750	TX	$19,060
GA	$21,120	NC	$27,330	UT	$21,560
HI	$21,180	ND	$21,240	VA	$20,990
IA	$25,900	NE	$22,170	VT	$30,050
ID	$19,350	NH	$19,030	WA	$22,740
IL	$24,830	NJ	$20,560	WI	$26,370
IN	$23,650	NM	no data	WV	$19,030
KS	$21,480	NV	$18,200	WY	no data

Median Wages for the Largest Metropolitan Areas (Annual)

AZ: Phoenix	$25,730	MI: Detroit	$21,940
CA: Los Angeles	$18,310	MN: Minneapolis	$28,320
CA: Riverside	$19,830	MO: Kansas City	$23,730
CA: Sacramento	$34,940	MO: St. Louis	$25,090
CA: San Diego	$21,530	NV: Las Vegas	no data
CA: San Francisco	$24,480	NY: New York	$22,680
CO: Denver	$23,840	OH: Cincinnati	$21,690
DC: Washington	$18,240	OH: Cleveland	$22,990
FL: Miami	$27,790	OH: Columbus	$22,690
FL: Orlando	no data	OR: Portland	$21,070
FL: Tampa	$17,950	PA: Philadelphia	$21,330
GA: Atlanta	$23,090	PA: Pittsburgh	$27,410
IL: Chicago	$25,480	TX: Dallas	$21,520
MA: Boston	$25,040	TX: Houston	$18,780
MD: Baltimore	$24,260	WA: Seattle	$22,250

FACTORS THAT MAY AFFECT EARNINGS

Educational Attainment of Workers and Effect on Earnings

Figures are based on a group of occupations: Other Production Occupations

	Percent at Level	Effect on Earnings
Less than High School	7.0%	−35.1%
Some High School	12.3%	−28.6%
High School or Equivalent	40.7%	3.9%
Some College but No Degree	19.3%	4.8%
Associate Degree	10.8%	9.0%
Bachelor's Degree	8.0%	25.5%
Master's Degree	1.6%	23.4%
Doctoral Degree	—	—
First Professional Degree	—	—

Flexibility of Earnings

Average Hours Worked: 35
Workers with a Varying Number of Hours: 7.2%
Workers Earning Some Overtime Pay, Tips, or Commissions: 22.3%
Earnings Benefit of Working Overtime: 17.2%

Gender

	Male	Female
Percent	75.2%	24.8%
Effect on Earnings	12.5%	—

Union Membership

Percentage Union Members: 15.3%
Earnings Benefit of Union Membership: 26.5%

Veteran Status

Percentage Who Have Been on Active Duty: 10.3%
Earnings Benefit of Veteran Status: 25.8%

51-9032 Cutting and Slicing Machine Setters, Operators, and Tenders

Set up, operate, or tend machines that cut or slice materials, such as glass, stone, cork, rubber, tobacco, food, paper, or insulating material.

- Education or Training Required: Moderate-term on-the-job training
- Job Growth: –2.7%
- Annual Openings: 6,000
- Self-Employed: 1.8%
- Part-Time: 15.8%

NATIONAL WAGE FIGURES (ANNUAL)

Beginning	25th Percentile	Median	Mean	75th Percentile	90th Percentile
$17,810	$21,790	$27,930	$29,610	$35,830	$44,310

Median Wages for Industries Employing Largest Numbers (Annual)

Industry	Median Income
Construction of Buildings	$34,000
Paper Manufacturing	$32,040
Transportation Equipment Manufacturing	$31,030
Petroleum and Coal Products Manufacturing	$29,980
Chemical Manufacturing	$29,480
Nonmetallic Mineral Product Manufacturing	$29,380
Mining (Except Oil and Gas)	$29,230
Printing and Related Support Activities	$28,930
Specialty Trade Contractors	$28,880
Merchant Wholesalers, Nondurable Goods	$28,250

Median Wages for States (Annual)

State	Wage	State	Wage	State	Wage
AK	no data	KY	$26,200	NY	$29,860
AL	$34,230	LA	$28,390	OH	$28,480
AR	$27,650	MA	$30,240	OK	$21,770
AZ	$26,550	MD	$32,290	OR	$32,690
CA	$25,130	ME	$28,560	PA	$29,420
CO	$24,040	MI	$28,430	RI	$20,490
CT	$30,890	MN	$31,860	SC	$23,230
DC	no data	MO	$27,350	SD	$24,650
DE	$27,990	MS	$23,780	TN	$30,000
FL	$25,900	MT	$32,630	TX	$21,760
GA	$27,100	NC	$32,580	UT	$23,810
HI	no data	ND	$25,540	VA	$27,540
IA	$27,220	NE	$25,290	VT	$25,330
ID	$29,740	NH	$28,120	WA	$26,540
IL	$28,530	NJ	$32,350	WI	$32,370
IN	$29,980	NM	$22,960	WV	$25,120
KS	$25,390	NV	$27,310	WY	no data

Median Wages for the Largest Metropolitan Areas (Annual)

Area	Wage	Area	Wage
AZ: Phoenix	$26,230	MI: Detroit	$26,200
CA: Los Angeles	$23,610	MN: Minneapolis	$35,050
CA: Riverside	$30,150	MO: Kansas City	$26,730
CA: Sacramento	$27,790	MO: St. Louis	$29,850
CA: San Diego	$27,760	NV: Las Vegas	$28,010
CA: San Francisco	$27,720	NY: New York	$30,340
CO: Denver	$23,320	OH: Cincinnati	$31,320
DC: Washington	$34,900	OH: Cleveland	$24,510
FL: Miami	$25,120	OH: Columbus	$27,860
FL: Orlando	$26,510	OR: Portland	$31,720
FL: Tampa	$26,170	PA: Philadelphia	$31,580
GA: Atlanta	$28,830	PA: Pittsburgh	$24,780
IL: Chicago	$28,890	TX: Dallas	$22,230
MA: Boston	$28,850	TX: Houston	$21,280
MD: Baltimore	$30,700	WA: Seattle	$33,100

FACTORS THAT MAY AFFECT EARNINGS

Educational Attainment of Workers and Effect on Earnings

Figures are based on a group of occupations: Other Production Occupations

	Percent at Level	Effect on Earnings
Less than High School	7.0%	–35.1%
Some High School	12.3%	–28.6%
High School or Equivalent	40.7%	3.9%
Some College but No Degree	19.3%	4.8%
Associate Degree	10.8%	9.0%
Bachelor's Degree	8.0%	25.5%
Master's Degree	1.6%	23.4%
Doctoral Degree	—	—
First Professional Degree	—	—

Flexibility of Earnings

Average Hours Worked: 35
Workers with a Varying Number of Hours: 7.2%
Workers Earning Some Overtime Pay, Tips, or Commissions: 22.3%
Earnings Benefit of Working Overtime: 17.2%

Gender

	Male	Female
Percent	75.2%	24.8%
Effect on Earnings	12.5%	—

Union Membership

Percentage Union Members: 15.3%
Earnings Benefit of Union Membership: 26.5%

Veteran Status

Percentage Who Have Been on Active Duty: 10.3%
Earnings Benefit of Veteran Status: 25.8%

51-9041 Extruding, Forming, Pressing, and Compacting Machine Setters, Operators, and Tenders

Set up, operate, or tend machines, such as glass-forming machines, plodder machines, and tuber machines, to shape and form products such as glassware, food, rubber, soap, brick, tile, clay, wax, tobacco, or cosmetics.

- Education or Training Required: Moderate-term on-the-job training
- Job Growth: –2.2%
- Annual Openings: 8,000
- Self-Employed: 0.0%
- Part-Time: 15.8%

NATIONAL WAGE FIGURES (ANNUAL)

Beginning	25th Percentile	Median	Mean	75th Percentile	90th Percentile
$18,450	$22,210	$27,710	$29,230	$34,830	$43,380

Median Wages for Industries Employing Largest Numbers (Annual)

Industry	Median Income
Petroleum and Coal Products Manufacturing	$35,660
Paper Manufacturing	$33,420
Primary Metal Manufacturing	$31,120
Mining (Except Oil and Gas)	$31,060
Electrical Equipment, Appliance, and Component Manufacturing	$30,250
Chemical Manufacturing	$30,010
Furniture and Related Product Manufacturing	$29,910
Beverage and Tobacco Product Manufacturing	$29,570
Computer and Electronic Product Manufacturing	$28,910
Printing and Related Support Activities	$28,500

Median Wages for States (Annual)

State	Wage	State	Wage	State	Wage
AK	no data	KY	$28,040	NY	$30,420
AL	$31,780	LA	$22,270	OH	$27,290
AR	$28,250	MA	$28,110	OK	$26,990
AZ	$26,800	MD	$24,640	OR	$29,580
CA	$23,570	ME	$28,480	PA	$32,930
CO	$27,930	MI	$27,020	RI	$30,260
CT	$26,750	MN	$32,890	SC	$31,750
DC	no data	MO	$27,680	SD	$28,090
DE	$27,500	MS	$24,090	TN	$27,390
FL	$26,590	MT	$22,570	TX	$22,660
GA	$27,070	NC	$29,050	UT	$22,420
HI	$23,520	ND	$26,830	VA	$32,850
IA	$26,980	NE	$29,510	VT	$26,300
ID	$25,710	NH	$28,230	WA	$29,910
IL	$29,820	NJ	$27,640	WI	$28,490
IN	$29,430	NM	$22,380	WV	$23,100
KS	$31,340	NV	$28,360	WY	$24,220

Median Wages for the Largest Metropolitan Areas (Annual)

Area	Wage	Area	Wage
AZ: Phoenix	$27,120	MI: Detroit	$24,810
CA: Los Angeles	$23,160	MN: Minneapolis	$34,280
CA: Riverside	no data	MO: Kansas City	$25,560
CA: Sacramento	$29,000	MO: St. Louis	$29,720
CA: San Diego	$28,230	NV: Las Vegas	$28,770
CA: San Francisco	$29,640	NY: New York	$24,630
CO: Denver	$27,310	OH: Cincinnati	$27,250
DC: Washington	$30,240	OH: Cleveland	$24,620
FL: Miami	$22,800	OH: Columbus	$35,160
FL: Orlando	$19,730	OR: Portland	$29,350
FL: Tampa	$24,040	PA: Philadelphia	$33,660
GA: Atlanta	$28,150	PA: Pittsburgh	$33,370
IL: Chicago	$30,140	TX: Dallas	$23,410
MA: Boston	$29,590	TX: Houston	$21,310
MD: Baltimore	$26,250	WA: Seattle	$30,260

FACTORS THAT MAY AFFECT EARNINGS

Educational Attainment of Workers and Effect on Earnings

	Percent at Level	Effect on Earnings
Less than High School	—	—
Some High School	—	—
High School or Equivalent	69.1%	2.5%
Some College but No Degree	—	—
Associate Degree	—	—
Bachelor's Degree	—	—
Master's Degree	—	—
Doctoral Degree	—	—
First Professional Degree	—	—

Figures do not total 100% because some levels have a very small sample size.

Flexibility of Earnings

Average Hours Worked: 36
Workers with a Varying Number of Hours: 7.1%
Workers Earning Some Overtime Pay, Tips, or Commissions: 31.0%
Earnings Benefit of Working Overtime: 17.2%

Gender

	Male	Female
Percent	69.2%	30.8%
Effect on Earnings	11.1%	–32.0%

Union Membership

Percentage Union Members: 27.6%
Earnings Benefit of Union Membership: 24.9%

Veteran Status

Percentage Who Have Been on Active Duty: 10.3%
Earnings Benefit of Veteran Status: 25.8%

51-9051 Furnace, Kiln, Oven, Drier, and Kettle Operators and Tenders

Operate or tend heating equipment other than basic metal, plastic, or food-processing equipment. Includes activities such as annealing glass, drying lumber, curing rubber, removing moisture from materials, or boiling soap.

- Education or Training Required: Moderate-term on-the-job training
- Job Growth: –4.2%
- Annual Openings: 3,000
- Self-Employed: 0.4%
- Part-Time: 5.9%

NATIONAL WAGE FIGURES (ANNUAL)

Beginning	25th Percentile	Median	Mean	75th Percentile	90th Percentile
$19,940	$24,370	$30,320	$31,720	$37,960	$46,180

Median Wages for Industries Employing Largest Numbers (Annual)

Industry	Median Income
Paper Manufacturing	$38,950
Federal, State, and Local Government	$37,620
Mining (Except Oil and Gas)	$35,470
Hospitals	$34,770
Primary Metal Manufacturing	$33,820
Petroleum and Coal Products Manufacturing	$32,720
Furniture and Related Product Manufacturing	$32,660
Plastics and Rubber Products Manufacturing	$31,140
Nonmetallic Mineral Product Manufacturing	$30,850
Food Manufacturing	$30,130

Median Wages for States (Annual)

AK	no data	KY	$31,730
AL	$30,580	LA	$33,680
AR	$31,260	MA	$33,700
AZ	$26,080	MD	$38,700
CA	$28,560	ME	$33,490
CO	$35,460	MI	$32,570
CT	$35,140	MN	$38,710
DC	no data	MO	$25,580
DE	$27,320	MS	$28,570
FL	$27,650	MT	$31,590
GA	$28,070	NC	$29,530
HI	no data	ND	$32,030
IA	$30,570	NE	$33,830
ID	$33,080	NH	$30,360
IL	$27,260	NJ	$32,000
IN	$30,370	NM	no data
KS	$28,640	NV	$41,420

NY	$31,720
OH	$29,100
OK	$31,980
OR	$35,320
PA	$32,830
RI	$28,590
SC	$29,630
SD	$31,030
TN	$28,360
TX	$26,920
UT	$24,750
VA	$26,790
VT	$25,120
WA	$38,510
WI	$33,600
WV	$24,410
WY	$43,620

Median Wages for the Largest Metropolitan Areas (Annual)

AZ: Phoenix	$26,460	MI: Detroit	$34,530
CA: Los Angeles	$25,880	MN: Minneapolis	no data
CA: Riverside	$26,340	MO: Kansas City	$25,820
CA: Sacramento	no data	MO: St. Louis	$30,590
CA: San Diego	no data	NV: Las Vegas	$41,780
CA: San Francisco	$34,510	NY: New York	$23,990
CO: Denver	$33,280	OH: Cincinnati	$26,630
DC: Washington	$31,680	OH: Cleveland	$25,480
FL: Miami	$25,580	OH: Columbus	no data
FL: Orlando	no data	OR: Portland	$31,250
FL: Tampa	$25,540	PA: Philadelphia	$31,630
GA: Atlanta	$29,820	PA: Pittsburgh	$33,290
IL: Chicago	$32,000	TX: Dallas	$23,180
MA: Boston	$34,180	TX: Houston	$22,550
MD: Baltimore	$40,060	WA: Seattle	$41,530

FACTORS THAT MAY AFFECT EARNINGS

Educational Attainment of Workers and Effect on Earnings

	Percent at Level	Effect on Earnings
Less than High School	—	—
Some High School	—	—
High School or Equivalent	35.3%	–9.7%
Some College but No Degree	—	—
Associate Degree	—	—
Bachelor's Degree	—	—
Master's Degree	—	—
Doctoral Degree	—	—
First Professional Degree	—	—

Figures do not total 100% because some levels have a very small sample size.

Flexibility of Earnings

Average Hours Worked: 31
Workers with a Varying Number of Hours: 15.9%
Workers Earning Some Overtime Pay, Tips, or Commissions: 38.9%
Earnings Benefit of Working Overtime: 17.2%

Gender

	Male	Female
Percent	69.2%	30.8%
Effect on Earnings	11.1%	–32.0%

Union Membership

Percentage Union Members: 16.7%
Earnings Benefit of Union Membership: 26.5%

Veteran Status

Percentage Who Have Been on Active Duty: 10.3%
Earnings Benefit of Veteran Status: 25.8%

51-9061 Inspectors, Testers, Sorters, Samplers, and Weighers

Inspect, test, sort, sample, or weigh nonagricultural raw materials or processed, machined, fabricated, or assembled parts or products for defects, wear, and deviations from specifications. May use precision measuring instruments and complex test equipment.

- Education or Training Required: Moderate-term on-the-job training
- Job Growth: –2.6%
- Annual Openings: 85,000
- Self-Employed: 1.9%
- Part-Time: 12.0%

NATIONAL WAGE FIGURES (ANNUAL)

Beginning	25th Percentile	Median	Mean	75th Percentile	90th Percentile
$17,990	$22,540	$29,420	$32,190	$39,080	$51,690

Median Wages for Industries Employing Largest Numbers (Annual)

Industry	Median Income
Federal, State, and Local Government	$42,390
Transportation Equipment Manufacturing	$39,120
Machinery Manufacturing	$33,300
Primary Metal Manufacturing	$32,190
Chemical Manufacturing	$32,030
Electrical Equipment, Appliance, and Component Manufacturing	$31,350
Fabricated Metal Product Manufacturing	$31,320
Professional, Scientific, and Technical Services	$30,920
Paper Manufacturing	$30,860
Nonmetallic Mineral Product Manufacturing	$30,430

Median Wages for States (Annual)

State	Wage	State	Wage	State	Wage
AK	$58,020	KY	$28,940	NY	$30,410
AL	$23,760	LA	$31,290	OH	$31,670
AR	$26,650	MA	$34,450	OK	$30,330
AZ	$28,290	MD	$34,890	OR	$30,420
CA	$29,640	ME	$27,000	PA	$31,080
CO	$31,070	MI	$33,890	RI	$30,000
CT	$35,610	MN	$31,880	SC	$27,000
DC	$45,880	MO	$30,180	SD	$26,040
DE	$31,330	MS	$25,130	TN	$26,970
FL	$25,790	MT	$29,800	TX	$27,610
GA	$26,810	NC	$26,200	UT	$28,500
HI	$31,650	ND	$29,900	VA	$29,810
IA	$30,930	NE	$29,700	VT	$28,700
ID	$25,160	NH	$31,870	WA	$37,670
IL	$29,460	NJ	$29,610	WI	$29,080
IN	$30,100	NM	$34,680	WV	$29,960
KS	$31,140	NV	$27,180	WY	$26,950

Median Wages for the Largest Metropolitan Areas (Annual)

Area	Wage	Area	Wage
AZ: Phoenix	$27,360	MI: Detroit	$36,720
CA: Los Angeles	$27,090	MN: Minneapolis	$34,020
CA: Riverside	$28,540	MO: Kansas City	$32,050
CA: Sacramento	$29,050	MO: St. Louis	$34,700
CA: San Diego	$33,580	NV: Las Vegas	$23,710
CA: San Francisco	$32,790	NY: New York	$29,480
CO: Denver	$32,280	OH: Cincinnati	$32,710
DC: Washington	$39,300	OH: Cleveland	$33,010
FL: Miami	$21,050	OH: Columbus	$30,770
FL: Orlando	$24,700	OR: Portland	$31,590
FL: Tampa	$26,200	PA: Philadelphia	$34,110
GA: Atlanta	$28,050	PA: Pittsburgh	$34,930
IL: Chicago	$29,190	TX: Dallas	$27,430
MA: Boston	$36,590	TX: Houston	$29,850
MD: Baltimore	$34,330	WA: Seattle	$45,020

FACTORS THAT MAY AFFECT EARNINGS

Educational Attainment of Workers and Effect on Earnings

	Percent at Level	Effect on Earnings
Less than High School	3.7%	–39.1%
Some High School	8.7%	–33.5%
High School or Equivalent	37.6%	–1.5%
Some College but No Degree	22.9%	0.8%
Associate Degree	13.1%	5.4%
Bachelor's Degree	11.7%	29.3%
Master's Degree	2.2%	16.4%
Doctoral Degree	—	—
First Professional Degree	—	—

Flexibility of Earnings

Average Hours Worked: 37
Workers with a Varying Number of Hours: 5.6%
Workers Earning Some Overtime Pay, Tips, or Commissions: 25.1%
Earnings Benefit of Working Overtime: 10.1%

Gender

	Male	Female
Percent	61.2%	38.8%
Effect on Earnings	19.8%	–17.6%

Union Membership

Percentage Union Members: 13.3%
Earnings Benefit of Union Membership: 17.9%

Veteran Status

Percentage Who Have Been on Active Duty: 10.3%
Earnings Benefit of Veteran Status: 25.8%

51-9071 Jewelers and Precious Stone and Metal Workers

Design, fabricate, adjust, repair, or appraise jewelry, gold, silver, other precious metals, or gems. Includes diamond polishers and gem cutters and persons who perform precision casting and modeling of molds, casting metal in molds, or setting precious and semi-precious stones for jewelry and related products.

- Education or Training Required: Postsecondary vocational training
- Job Growth: 0.0%
- Annual Openings: 6,000
- Self-Employed: 38.0%
- Part-Time: 27.6%

Note: Earnings figures do not reflect self-employed workers, who make up a large fraction of the workforce for this occupation.

NATIONAL WAGE FIGURES (ANNUAL)

Beginning	25th Percentile	Median	Mean	75th Percentile	90th Percentile
$17,760	$22,390	$29,750	$33,300	$40,160	$54,940

Median Wages for Industries Employing Largest Numbers (Annual)

Industry	Median Income
Nonstore Retailers	$48,710
Management of Companies and Enterprises	$35,490
Primary Metal Manufacturing	$35,160
Warehousing and Storage	$32,540
Clothing and Clothing Accessories Stores	$32,440
General Merchandise Stores	$32,220
Merchant Wholesalers, Durable Goods	$32,160
Miscellaneous Store Retailers	$31,200
Credit Intermediation and Related Activities	$29,770
Repair and Maintenance	$28,550

Median Wages for States (Annual)

State	Wage	State	Wage	State	Wage
AK	$28,950	KY	$36,520	NY	$33,120
AL	$28,960	LA	no data	OH	$26,690
AR	$31,460	MA	$33,670	OK	$32,070
AZ	$27,540	MD	$28,440	OR	$26,020
CA	$26,580	ME	$32,520	PA	$35,600
CO	$28,610	MI	$34,020	RI	$24,210
CT	$44,260	MN	$36,750	SC	$35,420
DC	no data	MO	$37,420	SD	$24,130
DE	$29,060	MS	$29,110	TN	$31,950
FL	$30,780	MT	$24,980	TX	$27,120
GA	$36,470	NC	$31,600	UT	$22,920
HI	$23,550	ND	no data	VA	$28,160
IA	$35,530	NE	$28,830	VT	$33,350
ID	$32,720	NH	$45,910	WA	$35,250
IL	$27,170	NJ	$38,340	WI	$35,940
IN	$33,870	NM	$20,480	WV	$25,790
KS	$37,310	NV	$33,810	WY	no data

Median Wages for the Largest Metropolitan Areas (Annual)

Area	Wage	Area	Wage
AZ: Phoenix	$28,360	MI: Detroit	$37,820
CA: Los Angeles	$22,920	MN: Minneapolis	$39,520
CA: Riverside	$26,290	MO: Kansas City	$36,130
CA: Sacramento	$30,700	MO: St. Louis	$38,120
CA: San Diego	$30,200	NV: Las Vegas	$34,840
CA: San Francisco	$40,800	NY: New York	$34,380
CO: Denver	$28,670	OH: Cincinnati	$33,290
DC: Washington	no data	OH: Cleveland	$23,470
FL: Miami	$30,190	OH: Columbus	$27,350
FL: Orlando	$33,490	OR: Portland	$36,170
FL: Tampa	$32,710	PA: Philadelphia	$22,590
GA: Atlanta	$49,140	PA: Pittsburgh	$41,130
IL: Chicago	$27,200	TX: Dallas	$32,330
MA: Boston	no data	TX: Houston	$23,040
MD: Baltimore	$31,640	WA: Seattle	$38,540

FACTORS THAT MAY AFFECT EARNINGS

Educational Attainment of Workers and Effect on Earnings

	Percent at Level	Effect on Earnings
Less than High School	—	—
Some High School	—	—
High School or Equivalent	37.8%	−6.2%
Some College but No Degree	18.9%	−1.3%
Associate Degree	—	—
Bachelor's Degree	—	—
Master's Degree	—	—
Doctoral Degree	—	—
First Professional Degree	—	—

Figures do not total 100% because some levels have a very small sample size.

Flexibility of Earnings

Average Hours Worked: 26
Workers with a Varying Number of Hours: 22.2%
Workers Earning Some Overtime Pay, Tips, or Commissions: 13.2%
Earnings Benefit of Working Overtime: 17.2%

Gender

	Male	Female
Percent	45.0%	55.0%
Effect on Earnings	11.1%	−32.0%

Union Membership

Percentage Union Members: 5.3%
Earnings Benefit of Union Membership: 26.5%

Veteran Status

Percentage Who Have Been on Active Duty: 10.3%
Earnings Benefit of Veteran Status: 25.8%

51-9081 Dental Laboratory Technicians

Construct and repair full or partial dentures or dental appliances.

- Education or Training Required: Long-term on-the-job training
- Job Growth: 7.6%
- Annual Openings: 3,000
- Self-Employed: 10.2%
- Part-Time: 15.8%

NATIONAL WAGE FIGURES (ANNUAL)

Beginning	25th Percentile	Median	Mean	75th Percentile	90th Percentile
$19,050	$24,140	$32,580	$34,910	$42,790	$54,350

Median Wages for Industries Employing Largest Numbers (Annual)

Industry	Median Income
Federal, State, and Local Government	$48,220
Educational Services	$41,440
Merchant Wholesalers, Durable Goods	$38,200
Administrative and Support Services	$37,560
Ambulatory Health Care Services	$36,630
Miscellaneous Manufacturing	$31,400

Median Wages for States (Annual)

State	Wage	State	Wage	State	Wage
AK	$39,320	KY	$31,570	NY	$37,150
AL	$27,190	LA	$26,750	OH	$32,920
AR	$34,810	MA	$39,320	OK	$25,370
AZ	$30,430	MD	$35,040	OR	$34,900
CA	$33,710	ME	$27,550	PA	$30,620
CO	$40,520	MI	$31,080	RI	$35,160
CT	$33,180	MN	$39,650	SC	$29,030
DC	$61,320	MO	$31,730	SD	$22,460
DE	$33,120	MS	$26,860	TN	$29,560
FL	$32,150	MT	no data	TX	$27,890
GA	$31,860	NC	$31,850	UT	$23,030
HI	$27,540	ND	$27,230	VA	$32,000
IA	$27,810	NE	$29,180	VT	$27,610
ID	$27,150	NH	$33,030	WA	$37,540
IL	$29,000	NJ	$35,470	WI	$33,460
IN	$32,450	NM	$32,880	WV	$27,380
KS	$29,320	NV	$33,700	WY	no data

Median Wages for the Largest Metropolitan Areas (Annual)

Area	Wage	Area	Wage
AZ: Phoenix	$32,880	MI: Detroit	$32,050
CA: Los Angeles	$32,580	MN: Minneapolis	$39,000
CA: Riverside	$42,550	MO: Kansas City	$31,540
CA: Sacramento	$34,400	MO: St. Louis	$30,930
CA: San Diego	$28,180	NV: Las Vegas	$31,910
CA: San Francisco	$35,920	NY: New York	$37,720
CO: Denver	$41,180	OH: Cincinnati	$33,200
DC: Washington	$37,280	OH: Cleveland	$32,950
FL: Miami	$30,920	OH: Columbus	$34,300
FL: Orlando	$29,420	OR: Portland	$36,420
FL: Tampa	$34,160	PA: Philadelphia	$37,770
GA: Atlanta	$33,210	PA: Pittsburgh	$22,660
IL: Chicago	$30,550	TX: Dallas	$28,810
MA: Boston	$39,620	TX: Houston	$26,090
MD: Baltimore	$27,040	WA: Seattle	$38,180

FACTORS THAT MAY AFFECT EARNINGS

Educational Attainment of Workers and Effect on Earnings

Figures are based on a group of occupations: Other Production Occupations

	Percent at Level	Effect on Earnings
Less than High School	7.0%	−35.1%
Some High School	12.3%	−28.6%
High School or Equivalent	40.7%	3.9%
Some College but No Degree	19.3%	4.8%
Associate Degree	10.8%	9.0%
Bachelor's Degree	8.0%	25.5%
Master's Degree	1.6%	23.4%
Doctoral Degree	—	—
First Professional Degree	—	—

Flexibility of Earnings

Average Hours Worked: 35
Workers with a Varying Number of Hours: 7.2%
Workers Earning Some Overtime Pay, Tips, or Commissions: 22.3%
Earnings Benefit of Working Overtime: 17.2%

Gender

	Male	Female
Percent	49.2%	50.8%
Effect on Earnings	11.1%	−32.0%

Union Membership

Percentage Union Members: 15.3%
Earnings Benefit of Union Membership: 26.5%

Veteran Status

Percentage Who Have Been on Active Duty: 10.3%
Earnings Benefit of Veteran Status: 25.8%

51-9082 Medical Appliance Technicians

Construct, fit, maintain, or repair medical supportive devices, such as braces, artificial limbs, joints, arch supports, and other surgical and medical appliances.

- Education or Training Required: Long-term on-the-job training
- Job Growth: 13.3%
- Annual Openings: 1,000
- Self-Employed: 9.7%
- Part-Time: 15.8%

NATIONAL WAGE FIGURES (ANNUAL)

Beginning	25th Percentile	Median	Mean	75th Percentile	90th Percentile
$18,580	$23,590	$31,180	$34,450	$40,870	$56,160

Median Wages for Industries Employing Largest Numbers (Annual)

Industry	Median Income
Educational Services	$44,680
Federal, State, and Local Government	$40,080
Computer and Electronic Product Manufacturing	$36,590
Merchant Wholesalers, Durable Goods	$35,870
Hospitals	$32,010
Miscellaneous Manufacturing	$31,060
Ambulatory Health Care Services	$30,700
Health and Personal Care Stores	$29,030
Rental and Leasing Services	$24,980

Median Wages for States (Annual)

State	Wage	State	Wage	State	Wage
AK	no data	KY	$29,430	NY	$28,680
AL	$32,720	LA	$32,360	OH	$32,040
AR	$23,580	MA	$38,850	OK	no data
AZ	$27,260	MD	$40,000	OR	$33,250
CA	$35,180	ME	no data	PA	$27,900
CO	$33,640	MI	$32,930	RI	$16,780
CT	$36,420	MN	$40,430	SC	$28,520
DC	no data	MO	$29,580	SD	no data
DE	$32,860	MS	$23,100	TN	$30,460
FL	$25,640	MT	no data	TX	$30,010
GA	$30,170	NC	$35,980	UT	$30,330
HI	no data	ND	no data	VA	$32,840
IA	$34,870	NE	no data	VT	no data
ID	$56,880	NH	$36,200	WA	$31,010
IL	$27,350	NJ	$30,880	WI	$28,890
IN	$35,310	NM	$34,740	WV	$32,600
KS	$26,040	NV	$34,940	WY	no data

Median Wages for the Largest Metropolitan Areas (Annual)

Area	Wage	Area	Wage
AZ: Phoenix	$30,970	MI: Detroit	$34,610
CA: Los Angeles	$36,510	MN: Minneapolis	$38,860
CA: Riverside	$24,440	MO: Kansas City	no data
CA: Sacramento	no data	MO: St. Louis	$37,660
CA: San Diego	no data	NV: Las Vegas	no data
CA: San Francisco	$42,350	NY: New York	$34,100
CO: Denver	$44,510	OH: Cincinnati	no data
DC: Washington	$45,910	OH: Cleveland	$33,970
FL: Miami	$24,600	OH: Columbus	$32,470
FL: Orlando	$24,440	OR: Portland	$30,550
FL: Tampa	$19,180	PA: Philadelphia	$24,170
GA: Atlanta	$32,650	PA: Pittsburgh	$23,200
IL: Chicago	$27,660	TX: Dallas	$24,890
MA: Boston	no data	TX: Houston	$35,930
MD: Baltimore	$35,330	WA: Seattle	$42,790

FACTORS THAT MAY AFFECT EARNINGS

Educational Attainment of Workers and Effect on Earnings

Figures are based on a group of occupations: Other Production Occupations

	Percent at Level	Effect on Earnings
Less than High School	7.0%	−35.1%
Some High School	12.3%	−28.6%
High School or Equivalent	40.7%	3.9%
Some College but No Degree	19.3%	4.8%
Associate Degree	10.8%	9.0%
Bachelor's Degree	8.0%	25.5%
Master's Degree	1.6%	23.4%
Doctoral Degree	—	—
First Professional Degree	—	—

Flexibility of Earnings

Average Hours Worked: 35
Workers with a Varying Number of Hours: 7.2%
Workers Earning Some Overtime Pay, Tips, or Commissions: 22.3%
Earnings Benefit of Working Overtime: 17.2%

Gender

	Male	Female
Percent	49.2%	50.8%
Effect on Earnings	11.1%	−32.0%

Union Membership

Percentage Union Members: 15.3%
Earnings Benefit of Union Membership: 26.5%

Veteran Status

Percentage Who Have Been on Active Duty: 10.3%
Earnings Benefit of Veteran Status: 25.8%

51-9083 Ophthalmic Laboratory Technicians

Cut, grind, and polish eyeglasses, contact lenses, or other precision optical elements. Assemble and mount lenses into frames or process other optical elements.

- Education or Training Required: Moderate-term on-the-job training
- Job Growth: 7.8%
- Annual Openings: 2,000
- Self-Employed: 0.0%
- Part-Time: 15.8%

NATIONAL WAGE FIGURES (ANNUAL)

Beginning	25th Percentile	Median	Mean	75th Percentile	90th Percentile
$17,440	$20,520	$25,460	$27,770	$32,910	$41,560

Median Wages for Industries Employing Largest Numbers (Annual)

Industry	Median Income
Federal, State, and Local Government	$42,270
Educational Services	$39,240
Computer and Electronic Product Manufacturing	$37,990
Hospitals	$37,500
Machinery Manufacturing	$31,720
Ambulatory Health Care Services	$28,500
Miscellaneous Manufacturing	$24,160
Health and Personal Care Stores	$23,900
Merchant Wholesalers, Durable Goods	$23,380
Management of Companies and Enterprises	$20,980

Median Wages for States (Annual)

State	Wage	State	Wage	State	Wage
AK	no data	KY	$24,160	NY	$27,180
AL	$22,790	LA	$22,040	OH	$24,940
AR	$22,700	MA	$28,280	OK	$22,340
AZ	$30,450	MD	no data	OR	$26,950
CA	$28,770	ME	$26,070	PA	$25,140
CO	$33,320	MI	$33,530	RI	$23,590
CT	$33,000	MN	$26,670	SC	$22,100
DC	no data	MO	$26,520	SD	$22,540
DE	$23,490	MS	$24,610	TN	$23,140
FL	$24,640	MT	$23,930	TX	$22,610
GA	$23,920	NC	$24,320	UT	no data
HI	$23,740	ND	$22,320	VA	$24,960
IA	$22,280	NE	$23,530	VT	no data
ID	$23,180	NH	$19,500	WA	$28,410
IL	$28,230	NJ	$26,390	WI	$27,170
IN	$23,310	NM	$25,250	WV	$21,740
KS	$26,980	NV	$23,250	WY	no data

Median Wages for the Largest Metropolitan Areas (Annual)

Area	Wage	Area	Wage
AZ: Phoenix	$29,570	MI: Detroit	$34,000
CA: Los Angeles	$21,150	MN: Minneapolis	$27,490
CA: Riverside	$28,330	MO: Kansas City	$26,680
CA: Sacramento	$29,640	MO: St. Louis	$31,200
CA: San Diego	$29,310	NV: Las Vegas	$23,010
CA: San Francisco	$37,820	NY: New York	$29,330
CO: Denver	$36,940	OH: Cincinnati	$24,830
DC: Washington	$25,600	OH: Cleveland	$23,390
FL: Miami	$28,310	OH: Columbus	no data
FL: Orlando	$29,070	OR: Portland	$27,380
FL: Tampa	$23,680	PA: Philadelphia	$27,520
GA: Atlanta	$24,400	PA: Pittsburgh	$21,090
IL: Chicago	$28,410	TX: Dallas	$22,010
MA: Boston	$27,080	TX: Houston	$20,940
MD: Baltimore	$27,200	WA: Seattle	no data

FACTORS THAT MAY AFFECT EARNINGS

Educational Attainment of Workers and Effect on Earnings

Figures are based on a group of occupations: Other Production Occupations

	Percent at Level	Effect on Earnings
Less than High School	7.0%	−35.1%
Some High School	12.3%	−28.6%
High School or Equivalent	40.7%	3.9%
Some College but No Degree	19.3%	4.8%
Associate Degree	10.8%	9.0%
Bachelor's Degree	8.0%	25.5%
Master's Degree	1.6%	23.4%
Doctoral Degree	—	—
First Professional Degree	—	—

Flexibility of Earnings

Average Hours Worked: 35
Workers with a Varying Number of Hours: 7.2%
Workers Earning Some Overtime Pay, Tips, or Commissions: 22.3%
Earnings Benefit of Working Overtime: 17.2%

Gender

	Male	Female
Percent	49.2%	50.8%
Effect on Earnings	11.1%	−32.0%

Union Membership

Percentage Union Members: 15.3%
Earnings Benefit of Union Membership: 26.5%

Veteran Status

Percentage Who Have Been on Active Duty: 10.3%
Earnings Benefit of Veteran Status: 25.8%

51-9111 Packaging and Filling Machine Operators and Tenders

Operate or tend machines to prepare industrial or consumer products for storage or shipment. Includes cannery workers who pack food products.

- Education or Training Required: Short-term on-the-job training
- Job Growth: 2.3%
- Annual Openings: 80,000
- Self-Employed: 0.1%
- Part-Time: 16.2%

NATIONAL WAGE FIGURES (ANNUAL)

Beginning	25th Percentile	Median	Mean	75th Percentile	90th Percentile
$15,340	$18,130	$22,990	$25,000	$30,190	$37,930

Median Wages for Industries Employing Largest Numbers (Annual)

Industry	Median Income
Mining (Except Oil and Gas)	$29,510
Beverage and Tobacco Product Manufacturing	$28,050
Primary Metal Manufacturing	$27,640
Nonmetallic Mineral Product Manufacturing	$27,030
Electrical Equipment, Appliance, and Component Manufacturing	$26,970
Petroleum and Coal Products Manufacturing	$25,520
Chemical Manufacturing	$25,450
Warehousing and Storage	$24,740
Miscellaneous Manufacturing	$24,690
Food Manufacturing	$24,440

Median Wages for States (Annual)

AK	$16,620	KY	$25,020	NY	$22,830
AL	$20,220	LA	$20,000	OH	$26,320
AR	$21,930	MA	$24,550	OK	$21,630
AZ	$21,320	MD	$23,430	OR	$23,120
CA	$21,550	ME	$24,300	PA	$26,300
CO	$26,470	MI	$24,280	RI	$22,070
CT	$28,730	MN	$25,180	SC	$22,050
DC	$15,890	MO	$24,120	SD	$23,270
DE	$27,270	MS	$19,980	TN	$23,890
FL	$20,780	MT	$23,270	TX	$20,520
GA	$21,530	NC	$22,560	UT	$22,280
HI	$20,760	ND	$23,110	VA	$23,550
IA	$23,850	NE	$25,020	VT	$24,320
ID	$25,080	NH	$21,580	WA	$24,640
IL	$23,670	NJ	$21,400	WI	$25,480
IN	$25,910	NM	$18,300	WV	$23,810
KS	$24,930	NV	$27,260	WY	$30,080

Median Wages for the Largest Metropolitan Areas (Annual)

AZ: Phoenix	$22,720	MI: Detroit	$24,800
CA: Los Angeles	$19,580	MN: Minneapolis	$24,560
CA: Riverside	$21,830	MO: Kansas City	$26,070
CA: Sacramento	$23,730	MO: St. Louis	$23,450
CA: San Diego	$20,800	NV: Las Vegas	$27,960
CA: San Francisco	$27,240	NY: New York	$20,890
CO: Denver	$26,540	OH: Cincinnati	$24,260
DC: Washington	$24,760	OH: Cleveland	$27,020
FL: Miami	$20,020	OH: Columbus	$36,450
FL: Orlando	$21,340	OR: Portland	$22,760
FL: Tampa	$17,920	PA: Philadelphia	$27,010
GA: Atlanta	$20,700	PA: Pittsburgh	$29,890
IL: Chicago	$24,140	TX: Dallas	$20,700
MA: Boston	$24,870	TX: Houston	$21,820
MD: Baltimore	$22,220	WA: Seattle	$25,900

FACTORS THAT MAY AFFECT EARNINGS

Educational Attainment of Workers and Effect on Earnings

	Percent at Level	Effect on Earnings
Less than High School	14.0%	−20.6%
Some High School	19.4%	−24.5%
High School or Equivalent	47.1%	13.8%
Some College but No Degree	13.7%	1.4%
Associate Degree	2.9%	21.1%
Bachelor's Degree	—	—
Master's Degree	—	—
Doctoral Degree	—	—
First Professional Degree	—	—

Flexibility of Earnings

Average Hours Worked: 34
Workers with a Varying Number of Hours: 4.7%
Workers Earning Some Overtime Pay, Tips, or Commissions: 17.0%
Earnings Benefit of Working Overtime: 26.1%

Gender

	Male	Female
Percent	44.5%	55.5%
Effect on Earnings	9.9%	−6.3%

Union Membership

Percentage Union Members: 15.2%
Earnings Benefit of Union Membership: 35.1%

Veteran Status

Percentage Who Have Been on Active Duty: 10.3%
Earnings Benefit of Veteran Status: 25.8%

51-9121 Coating, Painting, and Spraying Machine Setters, Operators, and Tenders

Set up, operate, or tend machines to coat or paint any of a wide variety of products, including food, glassware, cloth, ceramics, metal, plastic, paper, or wood, with lacquer, silver, copper, rubber, varnish, glaze, enamel, oil, or rustproofing materials.

- Education or Training Required: Moderate-term on-the-job training
- Job Growth: –3.4%
- Annual Openings: 16,000
- Self-Employed: 6.5%
- Part-Time: 15.8%

NATIONAL WAGE FIGURES (ANNUAL)

Beginning	25th Percentile	Median	Mean	75th Percentile	90th Percentile
$18,030	$21,510	$26,830	$28,230	$33,860	$41,320

Median Wages for Industries Employing Largest Numbers (Annual)

Industry	Median Income
Paper Manufacturing	$33,660
Federal, State, and Local Government	$33,140
Printing and Related Support Activities	$32,790
Repair and Maintenance	$29,550
Transportation Equipment Manufacturing	$28,780
Primary Metal Manufacturing	$28,710
Machinery Manufacturing	$28,140
Electrical Equipment, Appliance, and Component Manufacturing	$27,810
Computer and Electronic Product Manufacturing	$27,680
Plastics and Rubber Products Manufacturing	$27,400

Median Wages for States (Annual)

State	Wage	State	Wage	State	Wage
AK	no data	KY	$27,140	NY	$28,350
AL	$23,440	LA	$25,460	OH	$27,500
AR	$26,070	MA	$30,110	OK	$25,800
AZ	$24,350	MD	$31,700	OR	$27,580
CA	$24,430	ME	$34,480	PA	$31,000
CO	$26,640	MI	$28,800	RI	$23,780
CT	$29,300	MN	$33,010	SC	$28,900
DC	no data	MO	$27,060	SD	$24,050
DE	$32,710	MS	$24,410	TN	$25,090
FL	$24,020	MT	$22,770	TX	$21,960
GA	$27,060	NC	$26,490	UT	$22,640
HI	no data	ND	$30,150	VA	$26,740
IA	$29,280	NE	$24,420	VT	$25,550
D	$25,700	NH	$30,800	WA	$27,590
IL	$27,680	NJ	$27,880	WI	$30,610
IN	$27,060	NM	$25,720	WV	$26,150
KS	$25,730	NV	$25,710	WY	no data

Median Wages for the Largest Metropolitan Areas (Annual)

Area	Wage	Area	Wage
AZ: Phoenix	$24,180	MI: Detroit	$28,030
CA: Los Angeles	$22,920	MN: Minneapolis	$34,870
CA: Riverside	$24,210	MO: Kansas City	$28,840
CA: Sacramento	$23,790	MO: St. Louis	$27,590
CA: San Diego	$25,860	NV: Las Vegas	$23,920
CA: San Francisco	$26,330	NY: New York	$30,130
CO: Denver	$26,350	OH: Cincinnati	$26,260
DC: Washington	$28,240	OH: Cleveland	$29,020
FL: Miami	$21,960	OH: Columbus	$29,150
FL: Orlando	$22,740	OR: Portland	$30,340
FL: Tampa	$25,910	PA: Philadelphia	$30,470
GA: Atlanta	$28,850	PA: Pittsburgh	$30,090
IL: Chicago	$27,470	TX: Dallas	$22,790
MA: Boston	$29,500	TX: Houston	$20,460
MD: Baltimore	$34,020	WA: Seattle	$27,420

FACTORS THAT MAY AFFECT EARNINGS

Educational Attainment of Workers and Effect on Earnings

Figures are based on a group of occupations: Other Production Occupations

	Percent at Level	Effect on Earnings
Less than High School	7.0%	−35.1%
Some High School	12.3%	−28.6%
High School or Equivalent	40.7%	3.9%
Some College but No Degree	19.3%	4.8%
Associate Degree	10.8%	9.0%
Bachelor's Degree	8.0%	25.5%
Master's Degree	1.6%	23.4%
Doctoral Degree	—	—
First Professional Degree	—	—

Flexibility of Earnings

Average Hours Worked: 35
Workers with a Varying Number of Hours: 7.2%
Workers Earning Some Overtime Pay, Tips, or Commissions: 22.3%
Earnings Benefit of Working Overtime: 0.6%

Gender

	Male	Female
Percent	61.4%	38.6%
Effect on Earnings	7.9%	—

Union Membership

Percentage Union Members: 15.3%
Earnings Benefit of Union Membership: 26.5%

Veteran Status

Percentage Who Have Been on Active Duty: 10.3%
Earnings Benefit of Veteran Status: 25.8%

51-9122 Painters, Transportation Equipment

Operate or tend painting machines to paint surfaces of transportation equipment, such as automobiles, buses, trucks, trains, boats, and airplanes.

- Education or Training Required: Long-term on-the-job training
- Job Growth: 14.1%
- Annual Openings: 10,000
- Self-Employed: 5.4%
- Part-Time: 15.8%

NATIONAL WAGE FIGURES (ANNUAL)

Beginning	25th Percentile	Median	Mean	75th Percentile	90th Percentile
$22,510	$27,650	$35,680	$38,630	$48,010	$58,450

Median Wages for Industries Employing Largest Numbers (Annual)

Industry	Median Income
Professional, Scientific, and Technical Services	$50,460
Performing Arts, Spectator Sports, and Related Industries	$48,020
Federal, State, and Local Government	$45,040
Rail Transportation	$41,110
Motor Vehicle and Parts Dealers	$36,640
Transportation Equipment Manufacturing	$36,630
Repair and Maintenance	$35,370
Rental and Leasing Services	$34,820
Merchant Wholesalers, Durable Goods	$32,880
Specialty Trade Contractors	$32,850

Median Wages for States (Annual)

AK	$48,960	KY	no data	NY	$30,250
AL	$29,660	LA	$32,450	OH	$36,330
AR	$29,180	MA	$37,250	OK	$30,510
AZ	$33,480	MD	$40,560	OR	$36,040
CA	$38,540	ME	$30,060	PA	$36,020
CO	$40,220	MI	$50,890	RI	$33,820
CT	$31,300	MN	$36,570	SC	$31,310
DC	no data	MO	$36,790	SD	$26,640
DE	$40,780	MS	$31,110	TN	$42,600
FL	$31,410	MT	$28,830	TX	$32,640
GA	$35,950	NC	$40,140	UT	$35,790
HI	$33,840	ND	$29,100	VA	$35,590
IA	$28,740	NE	$32,200	VT	no data
ID	$30,260	NH	$34,060	WA	$47,760
IL	$40,790	NJ	$39,550	WI	$37,600
IN	$31,420	NM	no data	WV	$27,620
KS	$34,230	NV	$41,830	WY	$36,420

Median Wages for the Largest Metropolitan Areas (Annual)

AZ: Phoenix	$32,810	MI: Detroit	$53,880
CA: Los Angeles	$39,640	MN: Minneapolis	$49,580
CA: Riverside	$28,910	MO: Kansas City	$34,970
CA: Sacramento	$47,570	MO: St. Louis	$40,430
CA: San Diego	$36,930	NV: Las Vegas	$41,010
CA: San Francisco	$47,450	NY: New York	$37,540
CO: Denver	$42,970	OH: Cincinnati	$40,000
DC: Washington	$48,470	OH: Cleveland	no data
FL: Miami	$31,030	OH: Columbus	$32,600
FL: Orlando	$29,540	OR: Portland	$43,740
FL: Tampa	$29,230	PA: Philadelphia	$39,520
GA: Atlanta	$36,540	PA: Pittsburgh	$33,620
IL: Chicago	$40,610	TX: Dallas	$37,900
MA: Boston	$41,660	TX: Houston	$30,790
MD: Baltimore	$41,350	WA: Seattle	$54,250

FACTORS THAT MAY AFFECT EARNINGS

Educational Attainment of Workers and Effect on Earnings

Figures are based on a group of occupations: Other Production Occupations

	Percent at Level	Effect on Earnings
Less than High School	7.0%	−35.1%
Some High School	12.3%	−28.6%
High School or Equivalent	40.7%	3.9%
Some College but No Degree	19.3%	4.8%
Associate Degree	10.8%	9.0%
Bachelor's Degree	8.0%	25.5%
Master's Degree	1.6%	23.4%
Doctoral Degree	—	—
First Professional Degree	—	—

Flexibility of Earnings

Average Hours Worked: 35
Workers with a Varying Number of Hours: 7.2%
Workers Earning Some Overtime Pay, Tips, or Commissions: 22.3%
Earnings Benefit of Working Overtime: 0.6%

Gender

	Male	Female
Percent	83.4%	16.6%
Effect on Earnings	7.9%	—

Union Membership

Percentage Union Members: 15.3%
Earnings Benefit of Union Membership: 26.5%

Veteran Status

Percentage Who Have Been on Active Duty: 10.3%
Earnings Benefit of Veteran Status: 25.8%

51-9123 Painting, Coating, and Decorating Workers

Paint, coat, or decorate articles such as furniture, glass, plateware, pottery, jewelry, cakes, toys, books, or leather.

- Education or Training Required: Short-term on-the-job training
- Job Growth: 7.9%
- Annual Openings: 5,000
- Self-Employed: 7.0%
- Part-Time: 15.8%

NATIONAL WAGE FIGURES (ANNUAL)

Beginning	25th Percentile	Median	Mean	75th Percentile	90th Percentile
$15,700	$18,730	$22,970	$25,260	$29,310	$37,910

Median Wages for Industries Employing Largest Numbers (Annual)

Industry	Median Income
Federal, State, and Local Government	$42,780
Paper Manufacturing	$30,850
Professional, Scientific, and Technical Services	$29,850
Chemical Manufacturing	$28,960
Transportation Equipment Manufacturing	$28,540
Computer and Electronic Product Manufacturing	$26,980
Machinery Manufacturing	$26,400
Food and Beverage Stores	$25,790
Leather and Allied Product Manufacturing	$24,710
Furniture and Related Product Manufacturing	$24,000

Median Wages for States (Annual)

AK	no data	KY	$21,420	NY	$23,990
AL	$21,790	LA	$23,480	OH	$21,470
AR	$17,320	MA	$30,210	OK	$20,970
AZ	$22,480	MD	$25,070	OR	$26,300
CA	$21,050	ME	$20,060	PA	$26,030
CO	$25,640	MI	$22,370	RI	$24,550
CT	$29,340	MN	$23,070	SC	$23,020
DC	no data	MO	$20,260	SD	$21,490
DE	$23,900	MS	no data	TN	$21,980
FL	$21,940	MT	$24,400	TX	$20,810
GA	$23,810	NC	$22,870	UT	$23,430
HI	no data	ND	no data	VA	$22,070
IA	$25,250	NE	$20,990	VT	$24,660
ID	$24,320	NH	$20,010	WA	$32,860
IL	$24,890	NJ	$24,760	WI	$22,690
IN	$21,310	NM	$20,580	WV	$21,520
KS	$20,540	NV	$27,460	WY	$20,830

Median Wages for the Largest Metropolitan Areas (Annual)

AZ: Phoenix	$21,850	MI: Detroit	$20,320
CA: Los Angeles	$20,000	MN: Minneapolis	$23,010
CA: Riverside	$22,470	MO: Kansas City	$22,600
CA: Sacramento	$17,740	MO: St. Louis	$26,780
CA: San Diego	$26,350	NV: Las Vegas	$30,000
CA: San Francisco	$23,360	NY: New York	$25,250
CO: Denver	$26,080	OH: Cincinnati	$21,990
DC: Washington	$27,670	OH: Cleveland	$26,690
FL: Miami	$23,050	OH: Columbus	$22,850
FL: Orlando	$19,480	OR: Portland	$27,080
FL: Tampa	$24,860	PA: Philadelphia	$27,780
GA: Atlanta	$23,720	PA: Pittsburgh	$20,280
IL: Chicago	$24,880	TX: Dallas	$22,380
MA: Boston	$27,860	TX: Houston	$21,060
MD: Baltimore	$25,700	WA: Seattle	$36,500

FACTORS THAT MAY AFFECT EARNINGS

Educational Attainment of Workers and Effect on Earnings

Figures are based on a group of occupations: Other Production Occupations

	Percent at Level	Effect on Earnings
Less than High School	7.0%	−35.1%
Some High School	12.3%	−28.6%
High School or Equivalent	40.7%	3.9%
Some College but No Degree	19.3%	4.8%
Associate Degree	10.8%	9.0%
Bachelor's Degree	8.0%	25.5%
Master's Degree	1.6%	23.4%
Doctoral Degree	—	—
First Professional Degree	—	—

Flexibility of Earnings

Average Hours Worked: 35
Workers with a Varying Number of Hours: 7.2%
Workers Earning Some Overtime Pay, Tips, or Commissions: 22.3%
Earnings Benefit of Working Overtime: 0.6%

Gender

	Male	Female
Percent	83.4%	16.6%
Effect on Earnings	7.9%	—

Union Membership

Percentage Union Members: 15.3%
Earnings Benefit of Union Membership: 26.5%

Veteran Status

Percentage Who Have Been on Active Duty: 10.3%
Earnings Benefit of Veteran Status: 25.8%

51-9131 Photographic Process Workers

Perform precision work involved in photographic processing, such as editing photographic negatives and prints, using photo-mechanical, chemical, or computerized methods.

- Education or Training Required: Moderate-term on-the-job training
- Job Growth: –11.4%
- Annual Openings: 7,000
- Self-Employed: 1.9%
- Part-Time: 15.8%

NATIONAL WAGE FIGURES (ANNUAL)

Beginning	25th Percentile	Median	Mean	75th Percentile	90th Percentile
$15,230	$17,910	$23,280	$26,710	$31,450	$44,580

Median Wages for Industries Employing Largest Numbers (Annual)

Industry	Median Income
Motion Picture and Sound Recording Industries	$49,030
Transportation Equipment Manufacturing	$45,240
Federal, State, and Local Government	$33,560
Printing and Related Support Activities	$31,620
Merchant Wholesalers, Durable Goods	$30,450
Management of Companies and Enterprises	$30,260
Educational Services	$29,890
Publishing Industries (Except Internet)	$29,290
Performing Arts, Spectator Sports, and Related Industries	$26,030
Computer and Electronic Product Manufacturing	$25,360

Median Wages for States (Annual)

State	Wage	State	Wage	State	Wage
AK	no data	KY	$19,080	NY	no data
AL	$21,650	LA	no data	OH	$26,000
AR	$20,700	MA	$25,950	OK	$18,400
AZ	$25,010	MD	no data	OR	$25,560
CA	$25,990	ME	$27,770	PA	$20,440
CO	$21,820	MI	$24,110	RI	$22,140
CT	$22,960	MN	$27,140	SC	$23,330
DC	no data	MO	$21,170	SD	$22,070
DE	$22,400	MS	$23,250	TN	$21,930
FL	$21,370	MT	$25,170	TX	$18,480
GA	$24,850	NC	$19,000	UT	$26,980
HI	$20,680	ND	no data	VA	$17,610
IA	$20,340	NE	$18,970	VT	$27,210
ID	no data	NH	$27,160	WA	$23,490
IL	$28,440	NJ	$30,370	WI	$24,350
IN	$22,880	NM	$21,630	WV	$17,180
KS	$22,120	NV	$29,590	WY	$23,100

Median Wages for the Largest Metropolitan Areas (Annual)

Area	Wage	Area	Wage
AZ: Phoenix	$24,570	MI: Detroit	$25,020
CA: Los Angeles	$25,380	MN: Minneapolis	$31,660
CA: Riverside	no data	MO: Kansas City	$18,420
CA: Sacramento	$26,780	MO: St. Louis	$24,910
CA: San Diego	$28,060	NV: Las Vegas	$35,620
CA: San Francisco	$27,730	NY: New York	$34,660
CO: Denver	$20,500	OH: Cincinnati	$18,550
DC: Washington	$20,980	OH: Cleveland	$27,220
FL: Miami	$23,140	OH: Columbus	$26,490
FL: Orlando	$20,690	OR: Portland	$25,670
FL: Tampa	$18,520	PA: Philadelphia	$23,140
GA: Atlanta	$28,280	PA: Pittsburgh	$17,220
IL: Chicago	$28,360	TX: Dallas	$17,650
MA: Boston	$26,010	TX: Houston	$19,850
MD: Baltimore	$21,000	WA: Seattle	$22,670

FACTORS THAT MAY AFFECT EARNINGS

Educational Attainment of Workers and Effect on Earnings

Figures are based on a group of occupations: Other Production Occupations

	Percent at Level	Effect on Earnings
Less than High School	7.0%	–35.1%
Some High School	12.3%	–28.6%
High School or Equivalent	40.7%	3.9%
Some College but No Degree	19.3%	4.8%
Associate Degree	10.8%	9.0%
Bachelor's Degree	8.0%	25.5%
Master's Degree	1.6%	23.4%
Doctoral Degree	—	—
First Professional Degree	—	—

Flexibility of Earnings

Average Hours Worked: 35
Workers with a Varying Number of Hours: 7.2%
Workers Earning Some Overtime Pay, Tips, or Commissions: 22.3%
Earnings Benefit of Working Overtime: 17.2%

Gender

	Male	Female
Percent	48.2%	51.8%
Effect on Earnings	11.1%	–32.0%

Union Membership

Percentage Union Members: 15.3%
Earnings Benefit of Union Membership: 26.5%

Veteran Status

Percentage Who Have Been on Active Duty: 10.3%
Earnings Benefit of Veteran Status: 25.8%

51-9132 *Photographic Processing Machine Operators*

Operate photographic processing machines, such as photographic printing machines, film-developing machines, and mounting presses.

- Education or Training Required: Short-term on-the-job training
- Job Growth: –30.7%
- Annual Openings: 10,000
- Self-Employed: 1.9%
- Part-Time: 15.8%

NATIONAL WAGE FIGURES (ANNUAL)

Beginning	25th Percentile	Median	Mean	75th Percentile	90th Percentile
$14,890	$16,660	$19,500	$21,540	$23,800	$31,030

Median Wages for Industries Employing Largest Numbers (Annual)

Industry	Median Income
Motion Picture and Sound Recording Industries	$59,870
Federal, State, and Local Government	$34,430
Educational Services	$27,010
Printing and Related Support Activities	$25,930
Administrative and Support Services	$23,170
Miscellaneous Store Retailers	$22,430
Personal and Laundry Services	$21,950
Computer and Electronic Product Manufacturing	$20,380
Food and Beverage Stores	$20,370
Publishing Industries (Except Internet)	$20,330

Median Wages for States (Annual)

AK	$22,780	KY	no data	NY	$18,560
AL	no data	LA	no data	OH	$18,380
AR	no data	MA	$19,880	OK	no data
AZ	$18,580	MD	$19,480	OR	$21,370
CA	$22,500	ME	no data	PA	$17,640
CO	$21,800	MI	$20,820	RI	$19,630
CT	$21,450	MN	$21,500	SC	$18,640
DC	$25,980	MO	$19,500	SD	$18,400
DE	$21,840	MS	no data	TN	$19,100
FL	$18,850	MT	no data	TX	$18,530
GA	$20,070	NC	$19,220	UT	$21,620
HI	$23,880	ND	no data	VA	$19,290
IA	no data	NE	no data	VT	$18,970
ID	no data	NH	$19,200	WA	$21,600
IL	$19,970	NJ	$18,710	WI	$19,360
IN	$19,450	NM	no data	WV	no data
KS	no data	NV	$22,570	WY	no data

Median Wages for the Largest Metropolitan Areas (Annual)

AZ: Phoenix	$18,550	MI: Detroit	$21,050
CA: Los Angeles	$26,550	MN: Minneapolis	$22,290
CA: Riverside	$20,240	MO: Kansas City	$23,620
CA: Sacramento	$21,540	MO: St. Louis	$20,240
CA: San Diego	$22,740	NV: Las Vegas	$23,180
CA: San Francisco	$22,180	NY: New York	$19,130
CO: Denver	$22,810	OH: Cincinnati	$20,630
DC: Washington	$21,200	OH: Cleveland	$18,260
FL: Miami	$18,960	OH: Columbus	$19,180
FL: Orlando	$19,600	OR: Portland	$23,550
FL: Tampa	$18,920	PA: Philadelphia	$18,010
GA: Atlanta	$22,270	PA: Pittsburgh	no data
IL: Chicago	$20,900	TX: Dallas	$21,200
MA: Boston	$20,200	TX: Houston	$17,710
MD: Baltimore	$18,230	WA: Seattle	$21,330

FACTORS THAT MAY AFFECT EARNINGS

Educational Attainment of Workers and Effect on Earnings

Figures are based on a group of occupations: Other Production Occupations

	Percent at Level	Effect on Earnings
Less than High School	7.0%	–35.1%
Some High School	12.3%	–28.6%
High School or Equivalent	40.7%	3.9%
Some College but No Degree	19.3%	4.8%
Associate Degree	10.8%	9.0%
Bachelor's Degree	8.0%	25.5%
Master's Degree	1.6%	23.4%
Doctoral Degree	—	—
First Professional Degree	—	—

Flexibility of Earnings

Average Hours Worked: 35
Workers with a Varying Number of Hours: 7.2%
Workers Earning Some Overtime Pay, Tips, or Commissions: 22.3%
Earnings Benefit of Working Overtime: 17.2%

Gender

	Male	Female
Percent	48.2%	51.8%
Effect on Earnings	11.1%	–32.0%

Union Membership

Percentage Union Members: 15.3%
Earnings Benefit of Union Membership: 26.5%

Veteran Status

Percentage Who Have Been on Active Duty: 10.3%
Earnings Benefit of Veteran Status: 25.8%

51-9141 Semiconductor Processors

Perform any or all of the following functions in the manufacture of electronic semiconductors: Load semiconductor material into furnace; saw formed ingots into segments; load individual segment into crystal-growing chamber and monitor controls; locate crystal axis in ingot, using X-ray equipment, and saw ingots into wafers; and clean, polish, and load wafers into series of special-purpose furnaces, chemical baths, and equipment used to form circuitry and change conductive properties.

- Education or Training Required: Associate degree
- Job Growth: –7.5%
- Annual Openings: 7,000
- Self-Employed: 0.0%
- Part-Time: 15.8%

NATIONAL WAGE FIGURES (ANNUAL)

Beginning	25th Percentile	Median	Mean	75th Percentile	90th Percentile
$21,700	$26,680	$32,860	$34,730	$40,620	$49,470

Median Wages for Industries Employing Largest Numbers (Annual)

Industry	Median Income
Administrative and Support Services	$34,800
Computer and Electronic Product Manufacturing	$32,770
Professional, Scientific, and Technical Services	$31,780

Median Wages for States (Annual)

State		State		State	
AK	no data	KY	no data	NY	$32,410
AL	no data	LA	no data	OH	no data
AR	no data	MA	$31,070	OK	no data
AZ	$36,180	MD	no data	OR	$30,800
CA	$34,380	ME	no data	PA	$32,300
CO	no data	MI	$36,640	RI	no data
CT	$30,680	MN	$33,240	SC	no data
DC	no data	MO	no data	SD	no data
DE	no data	MS	no data	TN	no data
FL	no data	MT	no data	TX	$32,040
GA	no data	NC	no data	UT	no data
HI	no data	ND	no data	VA	$31,770
IA	no data	NE	no data	VT	no data
ID	no data	NH	$24,770	WA	$26,890
IL	no data	NJ	$33,790	WI	no data
IN	$28,100	NM	no data	WV	no data
KS	no data	NV	no data	WY	no data

Median Wages for the Largest Metropolitan Areas (Annual)

Metro	Wage	Metro	Wage
AZ: Phoenix	no data	MI: Detroit	no data
CA: Los Angeles	$34,110	MN: Minneapolis	$33,050
CA: Riverside	no data	MO: Kansas City	no data
CA: Sacramento	$32,230	MO: St. Louis	no data
CA: San Diego	$26,400	NV: Las Vegas	no data
CA: San Francisco	$29,310	NY: New York	$33,430
CO: Denver	no data	OH: Cincinnati	no data
DC: Washington	$27,770	OH: Cleveland	no data
FL: Miami	no data	OH: Columbus	no data
FL: Orlando	no data	OR: Portland	no data
FL: Tampa	no data	PA: Philadelphia	$30,240
GA: Atlanta	no data	PA: Pittsburgh	$21,780
IL: Chicago	no data	TX: Dallas	$29,330
MA: Boston	$30,760	TX: Houston	no data
MD: Baltimore	no data	WA: Seattle	$37,120

FACTORS THAT MAY AFFECT EARNINGS

Educational Attainment of Workers and Effect on Earnings

Figures are based on a group of occupations: Other Production Occupations

	Percent at Level	Effect on Earnings
Less than High School	7.0%	–35.1%
Some High School	12.3%	–28.6%
High School or Equivalent	40.7%	3.9%
Some College but No Degree	19.3%	4.8%
Associate Degree	10.8%	9.0%
Bachelor's Degree	8.0%	25.5%
Master's Degree	1.6%	23.4%
Doctoral Degree	—	—
First Professional Degree	—	—

Flexibility of Earnings

Average Hours Worked: 32
Workers with a Varying Number of Hours: 16.0%
Workers Earning Some Overtime Pay, Tips, or Commissions: 16.7%
Earnings Benefit of Working Overtime: 17.2%

Gender

	Male	Female
Percent	48.2%	51.8%
Effect on Earnings	11.1%	–32.0%

Union Membership

Percentage Union Members: 15.3%
Earnings Benefit of Union Membership: 26.5%

Veteran Status

Percentage Who Have Been on Active Duty: 10.3%
Earnings Benefit of Veteran Status: 25.8%

51-9191 Cementing and Gluing Machine Operators and Tenders

Operate or tend cementing and gluing machines to join items for further processing or to form a completed product. Processes include joining veneer sheets into plywood; gluing paper; and joining rubber and rubberized fabric parts, plastic, simulated leather, or other materials.

- Education or Training Required: Moderate-term on-the-job training
- Job Growth: 1.9%
- Annual Openings: 4,000
- Self-Employed: 0.0%
- Part-Time: 13.3%

NATIONAL WAGE FIGURES (ANNUAL)

Beginning	25th Percentile	Median	Mean	75th Percentile	90th Percentile
$16,360	$19,810	$25,170	$26,840	$32,470	$39,810

Median Wages for Industries Employing Largest Numbers (Annual)

Industry	Median Income
Paper Manufacturing	$29,640
Electrical Equipment, Appliance, and Component Manufacturing	$29,210
Chemical Manufacturing	$28,170
Merchant Wholesalers, Nondurable Goods	$28,090
Wood Product Manufacturing	$25,430
Administrative and Support Services	$25,240
Transportation Equipment Manufacturing	$24,870
Computer and Electronic Product Manufacturing	$24,670
Machinery Manufacturing	$24,460
Textile Mills	$23,360

Median Wages for States (Annual)

State	Wage	State	Wage	State	Wage
AK	no data	KY	$22,930	NY	$23,410
AL	$22,960	LA	$27,730	OH	$29,030
AR	$22,340	MA	$31,440	OK	no data
AZ	$25,130	MD	$25,020	OR	$30,440
CA	$22,780	ME	$26,240	PA	$26,040
CO	$30,810	MI	$25,990	RI	$21,850
CT	$27,720	MN	$28,850	SC	$24,880
DC	no data	MO	$20,610	SD	$24,070
DE	no data	MS	$22,530	TN	$27,490
FL	$26,350	MT	no data	TX	$20,620
GA	$25,020	NC	$24,840	UT	$23,740
HI	no data	ND	$18,410	VA	$25,790
IA	$25,110	NE	$41,400	VT	no data
ID	$33,320	NH	$19,040	WA	$28,350
IL	$27,030	NJ	$25,240	WI	$30,680
IN	$25,800	NM	no data	WV	no data
KS	$32,400	NV	no data	WY	no data

Median Wages for the Largest Metropolitan Areas (Annual)

Area	Wage	Area	Wage
AZ: Phoenix	$25,070	MI: Detroit	$24,540
CA: Los Angeles	$19,810	MN: Minneapolis	$28,940
CA: Riverside	$36,010	MO: Kansas City	$21,980
CA: Sacramento	$19,870	MO: St. Louis	$22,550
CA: San Diego	no data	NV: Las Vegas	no data
CA: San Francisco	$23,740	NY: New York	$22,820
CO: Denver	$31,050	OH: Cincinnati	$27,140
DC: Washington	no data	OH: Cleveland	$28,410
FL: Miami	$20,100	OH: Columbus	$24,740
FL: Orlando	$30,700	OR: Portland	no data
FL: Tampa	$33,080	PA: Philadelphia	$28,900
GA: Atlanta	$28,110	PA: Pittsburgh	$22,530
IL: Chicago	$26,050	TX: Dallas	$20,330
MA: Boston	$32,470	TX: Houston	$20,070
MD: Baltimore	$36,180	WA: Seattle	$32,910

FACTORS THAT MAY AFFECT EARNINGS

Educational Attainment of Workers and Effect on Earnings

	Percent at Level	Effect on Earnings
Less than High School	—	—
Some High School	—	—
High School or Equivalent	65.2%	−12.8%
Some College but No Degree	—	—
Associate Degree	—	—
Bachelor's Degree	—	—
Master's Degree	—	—
Doctoral Degree	—	—
First Professional Degree	—	—

Figures do not total 100% because some levels have a very small sample size.

Flexibility of Earnings

Average Hours Worked: 31
Workers with a Varying Number of Hours: 11.6%
Workers Earning Some Overtime Pay, Tips, or Commissions: 16.7%
Earnings Benefit of Working Overtime: 17.2%

Gender

	Male	Female
Percent	42.9%	57.1%
Effect on Earnings	11.1%	−32.0%

Union Membership

Percentage Union Members: 4.2%
Earnings Benefit of Union Membership: 26.5%

Veteran Status

Percentage Who Have Been on Active Duty: 10.3%
Earnings Benefit of Veteran Status: 25.8%

51-9192 Cleaning, Washing, and Metal Pickling Equipment Operators and Tenders

Operate or tend machines to wash or clean products such as barrels or kegs, glass items, tin plate, food, pulp, coal, plastic, or rubber to remove impurities.

- Education or Training Required: Moderate-term on-the-job training
- Job Growth: 1.0%
- Annual Openings: 3,000
- Self-Employed: 4.9%
- Part-Time: 50.0%

NATIONAL WAGE FIGURES (ANNUAL)

Beginning	25th Percentile	Median	Mean	75th Percentile	90th Percentile
$15,900	$18,450	$22,850	$25,420	$30,780	$39,410

Median Wages for Industries Employing Largest Numbers (Annual)

Industry	Median Income
Paper Manufacturing	$42,530
Petroleum and Coal Products Manufacturing	$39,250
Primary Metal Manufacturing	$38,510
Mining (Except Oil and Gas)	$34,260
Electrical Equipment, Appliance, and Component Manufacturing	$28,780
Beverage and Tobacco Product Manufacturing	$27,440
Fabricated Metal Product Manufacturing	$26,830
Machinery Manufacturing	$25,300
Nonmetallic Mineral Product Manufacturing	$25,280
Transportation Equipment Manufacturing	$24,820

Median Wages for States (Annual)

State	Wage	State	Wage	State	Wage
AK	no data	KY	$28,910	NY	$28,700
AL	$22,780	LA	$21,850	OH	$28,160
AR	$20,650	MA	$26,630	OK	$19,840
AZ	$19,520	MD	no data	OR	$22,310
CA	$19,900	ME	no data	PA	$22,670
CO	$26,600	MI	$23,600	RI	$31,480
CT	$29,050	MN	$31,420	SC	$19,900
DC	no data	MO	$24,330	SD	$25,090
DE	no data	MS	$25,540	TN	$25,230
FL	$20,310	MT	no data	TX	$19,620
GA	$22,000	NC	$20,400	UT	$23,960
HI	no data	ND	no data	VA	$22,520
IA	$22,380	NE	$24,870	VT	$26,330
ID	$19,270	NH	$30,270	WA	$32,360
IL	$22,060	NJ	$22,320	WI	$30,890
IN	$28,410	NM	$18,020	WV	$20,320
KS	$22,420	NV	no data	WY	no data

Median Wages for the Largest Metropolitan Areas (Annual)

Area	Wage	Area	Wage
AZ: Phoenix	$18,310	MI: Detroit	$26,170
CA: Los Angeles	$17,960	MN: Minneapolis	$32,690
CA: Riverside	$22,410	MO: Kansas City	$23,230
CA: Sacramento	no data	MO: St. Louis	$29,970
CA: San Diego	$35,530	NV: Las Vegas	$21,800
CA: San Francisco	$20,100	NY: New York	$22,730
CO: Denver	no data	OH: Cincinnati	$27,940
DC: Washington	$27,030	OH: Cleveland	$25,970
FL: Miami	$18,850	OH: Columbus	$26,110
FL: Orlando	no data	OR: Portland	no data
FL: Tampa	$19,000	PA: Philadelphia	$28,830
GA: Atlanta	$20,910	PA: Pittsburgh	no data
IL: Chicago	$22,930	TX: Dallas	$18,480
MA: Boston	$27,690	TX: Houston	$18,830
MD: Baltimore	no data	WA: Seattle	no data

FACTORS THAT MAY AFFECT EARNINGS

Educational Attainment of Workers and Effect on Earnings

Figures are based on a group of occupations: Other Production Occupations

	Percent at Level	Effect on Earnings
Less than High School	7.0%	−35.1%
Some High School	12.3%	−28.6%
High School or Equivalent	40.7%	3.9%
Some College but No Degree	19.3%	4.8%
Associate Degree	10.8%	9.0%
Bachelor's Degree	8.0%	25.5%
Master's Degree	1.6%	23.4%
Doctoral Degree	—	—
First Professional Degree	—	—

Flexibility of Earnings

Average Hours Worked: 34
Workers with a Varying Number of Hours: 6.9%
Workers Earning Some Overtime Pay, Tips, or Commissions: 21.4%
Earnings Benefit of Working Overtime: 17.2%

Gender

	Male	Female
Percent	71.9%	28.1%
Effect on Earnings	11.1%	−32.0%

Union Membership

Percentage Union Members: 7.1%
Earnings Benefit of Union Membership: 26.5%

Veteran Status

Percentage Who Have Been on Active Duty: 10.3%
Earnings Benefit of Veteran Status: 25.8%

51-9193 Cooling and Freezing Equipment Operators and Tenders

Operate or tend equipment, such as cooling and freezing units, refrigerators, batch freezers, and freezing tunnels, to cool or freeze products, food, blood plasma, and chemicals.

- Education or Training Required: Moderate-term on-the-job training
- Job Growth: 0.8%
- Annual Openings: 1,000
- Self-Employed: 0.0%
- Part-Time: 50.0%

NATIONAL WAGE FIGURES (ANNUAL)

Beginning	25th Percentile	Median	Mean	75th Percentile	90th Percentile
$16,510	$19,810	$23,880	$25,970	$31,620	$39,160

Median Wages for Industries Employing Largest Numbers (Annual)

Industry	Median Income
Machinery Manufacturing	$32,760
Food Services and Drinking Places	$31,210
Warehousing and Storage	$28,160
Merchant Wholesalers, Nondurable Goods	$28,060
Support Activities for Agriculture and Forestry	$27,510
Petroleum and Coal Products Manufacturing	$25,160
Fabricated Metal Product Manufacturing	$24,490
Food Manufacturing	$23,930
Beverage and Tobacco Product Manufacturing	$22,410
Chemical Manufacturing	$21,940

Median Wages for States (Annual)

AK	$23,130	KY	$36,260	NY	$30,290
AL	$20,970	LA	$20,080	OH	$33,720
AR	$21,510	MA	$27,140	OK	$22,140
AZ	$22,850	MD	$24,380	OR	$28,320
CA	$31,840	ME	no data	PA	$28,130
CO	$27,050	MI	$31,030	RI	no data
CT	no data	MN	$26,290	SC	$27,180
DC	no data	MO	$27,520	SD	no data
DE	no data	MS	$19,860	TN	$22,660
FL	$21,660	MT	no data	TX	$19,300
GA	$22,120	NC	$23,630	UT	$25,110
HI	no data	ND	no data	VA	$19,520
IA	$30,240	NE	$28,980	VT	$22,700
ID	$22,730	NH	no data	WA	$31,940
IL	$21,880	NJ	$25,890	WI	$22,410
IN	$31,900	NM	no data	WV	no data
KS	$23,000	NV	no data	WY	no data

Median Wages for the Largest Metropolitan Areas (Annual)

AZ: Phoenix	no data	MI: Detroit	$36,350
CA: Los Angeles	$37,770	MN: Minneapolis	$21,830
CA: Riverside	no data	MO: Kansas City	$22,450
CA: Sacramento	no data	MO: St. Louis	$34,160
CA: San Diego	no data	NV: Las Vegas	no data
CA: San Francisco	no data	NY: New York	$25,150
CO: Denver	$33,560	OH: Cincinnati	$27,130
DC: Washington	no data	OH: Cleveland	no data
FL: Miami	$23,510	OH: Columbus	no data
FL: Orlando	$24,560	OR: Portland	no data
FL: Tampa	$21,310	PA: Philadelphia	$26,060
GA: Atlanta	$23,140	PA: Pittsburgh	no data
IL: Chicago	$20,900	TX: Dallas	$18,050
MA: Boston	$27,730	TX: Houston	no data
MD: Baltimore	no data	WA: Seattle	$27,850

FACTORS THAT MAY AFFECT EARNINGS

Educational Attainment of Workers and Effect on Earnings

Figures are based on a group of occupations: Other Production Occupations

	Percent at Level	Effect on Earnings
Less than High School	7.0%	−35.1%
Some High School	12.3%	−28.6%
High School or Equivalent	40.7%	3.9%
Some College but No Degree	19.3%	4.8%
Associate Degree	10.8%	9.0%
Bachelor's Degree	8.0%	25.5%
Master's Degree	1.6%	23.4%
Doctoral Degree	—	—
First Professional Degree	—	—

Flexibility of Earnings

Average Hours Worked: 43
Workers with a Varying Number of Hours: 9.5%
Workers Earning Some Overtime Pay, Tips, or Commissions: 50.0%
Earnings Benefit of Working Overtime: 17.2%

Gender

	Male	Female
Percent	61.4%	38.6%
Effect on Earnings	11.1%	−32.0%

Union Membership

Percentage Union Members: 25.0%
Earnings Benefit of Union Membership: 26.5%

Veteran Status

Percentage Who Have Been on Active Duty: 10.3%
Earnings Benefit of Veteran Status: 25.8%

51-9194 Etchers and Engravers

Engrave or etch metal, wood, rubber, or other materials for identification or decorative purposes. Includes such workers as etcher-circuit processors, pantograph engravers, and silk screen etchers.

- Education or Training Required: Long-term on-the-job training
- Job Growth: 2.1%
- Annual Openings: 2,000
- Self-Employed: 18.5%
- Part-Time: 25.0%

NATIONAL WAGE FIGURES (ANNUAL)

Beginning	25th Percentile	Median	Mean	75th Percentile	90th Percentile
$16,320	$20,180	$25,590	$27,750	$32,580	$42,320

Median Wages for Industries Employing Largest Numbers (Annual)

Industry	Median Income
Federal, State, and Local Government	$55,570
Management of Companies and Enterprises	$44,670
Transportation Equipment Manufacturing	$34,250
Printing and Related Support Activities	$29,080
Primary Metal Manufacturing	$28,630
Merchant Wholesalers, Durable Goods	$27,510
Plastics and Rubber Products Manufacturing	$26,940
Fabricated Metal Product Manufacturing	$26,840
Merchant Wholesalers, Nondurable Goods	$26,520
Electrical Equipment, Appliance, and Component Manufacturing	$26,350

Median Wages for States (Annual)

AK	no data	KY	$22,120	NY	$27,770
AL	$21,630	LA	$25,970	OH	$26,360
AR	$23,830	MA	$31,740	OK	$19,930
AZ	$23,100	MD	$27,690	OR	$30,490
CA	$26,750	ME	$25,100	PA	$23,990
CO	$25,520	MI	$30,330	RI	$28,260
CT	$42,380	MN	$26,920	SC	$23,200
DC	no data	MO	$21,480	SD	$19,000
DE	no data	MS	no data	TN	$24,010
FL	$18,350	MT	no data	TX	$23,260
GA	no data	NC	$24,100	UT	$22,360
HI	$22,720	ND	no data	VA	$31,380
IA	$24,940	NE	$23,200	VT	no data
ID	$20,790	NH	no data	WA	$27,420
IL	$28,110	NJ	$27,520	WI	$31,640
IN	$27,060	NM	no data	WV	$19,090
KS	$32,330	NV	no data	WY	no data

Median Wages for the Largest Metropolitan Areas (Annual)

AZ: Phoenix	no data	MI: Detroit	$35,130
CA: Los Angeles	$25,900	MN: Minneapolis	$27,710
CA: Riverside	no data	MO: Kansas City	$35,580
CA: Sacramento	$25,960	MO: St. Louis	$27,470
CA: San Diego	$24,250	NV: Las Vegas	no data
CA: San Francisco	$34,030	NY: New York	$28,070
CO: Denver	no data	OH: Cincinnati	no data
DC: Washington	$27,960	OH: Cleveland	$34,860
FL: Miami	$17,160	OH: Columbus	$21,190
FL: Orlando	$22,030	OR: Portland	no data
FL: Tampa	$33,430	PA: Philadelphia	$23,070
GA: Atlanta	$18,140	PA: Pittsburgh	$26,720
IL: Chicago	$33,550	TX: Dallas	$32,250
MA: Boston	$32,810	TX: Houston	$24,780
MD: Baltimore	$27,320	WA: Seattle	$27,110

FACTORS THAT MAY AFFECT EARNINGS

Educational Attainment of Workers and Effect on Earnings

	Percent at Level	Effect on Earnings
Less than High School	—	—
Some High School	—	—
High School or Equivalent	53.3%	–5.8%
Some College but No Degree	—	—
Associate Degree	—	—
Bachelor's Degree	—	—
Master's Degree	—	—
Doctoral Degree	—	—
First Professional Degree	—	—

Figures do not total 100% because some levels have a very small sample size.

Flexibility of Earnings

Average Hours Worked: 35
Workers with a Varying Number of Hours: 8.5%
Workers Earning Some Overtime Pay, Tips, or Commissions: 6.7%
Earnings Benefit of Working Overtime: 17.2%

Gender

	Male	Female
Percent	52.5%	47.5%
Effect on Earnings	11.1%	–32.0%

Union Membership

Percentage Union Members: 15.3%
Earnings Benefit of Union Membership: 26.5%

Veteran Status

Percentage Who Have Been on Active Duty: 10.3%
Earnings Benefit of Veteran Status: 25.8%

51-9195 Molders, Shapers, and Casters, Except Metal and Plastic

Mold, shape, form, cast, or carve products, such as food products, figurines, tile, pipes, and candles, consisting of clay, glass, plaster, concrete, stone, or combinations of materials.

- Education or Training Required: Moderate-term on-the-job training
- Job Growth: –7.0%
- Annual Openings: 7,000
- Self-Employed: 18.1%
- Part-Time: 19.0%

NATIONAL WAGE FIGURES (ANNUAL)

Beginning	25th Percentile	Median	Mean	75th Percentile	90th Percentile
$16,250	$19,640	$25,010	$26,730	$32,150	$39,400

Median Wages for Industries Employing Largest Numbers (Annual)

Industry	Median Income
Federal, State, and Local Government	$42,840
Transportation Equipment Manufacturing	$34,630
Performing Arts, Spectator Sports, and Related Industries	$34,400
Educational Services	$34,030
Machinery Manufacturing	$33,490
Paper Manufacturing	$33,140
Computer and Electronic Product Manufacturing	$31,360
Chemical Manufacturing	$30,330
Personal and Laundry Services	$29,820
Electrical Equipment, Appliance, and Component Manufacturing	$29,630

Median Wages for States (Annual)

State	Wage	State	Wage	State	Wage
AK	no data	KY	$23,740	NY	$27,340
AL	$23,580	LA	$22,930	OH	$24,400
AR	$22,560	MA	$31,460	OK	$24,620
AZ	$17,760	MD	$24,620	OR	$27,190
CA	$21,950	ME	$25,350	PA	$30,210
CO	$23,010	MI	$29,820	RI	$29,650
CT	$28,520	MN	$32,150	SC	$31,340
DC	no data	MO	$29,340	SD	no data
DE	$22,990	MS	no data	TN	$24,650
FL	$24,320	MT	$19,370	TX	$20,770
GA	$27,170	NC	$23,460	UT	$28,600
HI	$32,350	ND	$22,500	VA	$23,900
IA	$29,880	NE	$24,080	VT	$25,670
ID	$22,940	NH	$31,790	WA	$30,330
IL	$25,840	NJ	$30,430	WI	$29,520
IN	$28,400	NM	$16,610	WV	$19,630
KS	$23,700	NV	$27,180	WY	no data

Median Wages for the Largest Metropolitan Areas (Annual)

Area	Wage	Area	Wage
AZ: Phoenix	$16,900	MI: Detroit	no data
CA: Los Angeles	$20,370	MN: Minneapolis	$30,190
CA: Riverside	$21,350	MO: Kansas City	$22,960
CA: Sacramento	$25,590	MO: St. Louis	$26,470
CA: San Diego	$21,410	NV: Las Vegas	$26,460
CA: San Francisco	$27,620	NY: New York	$26,730
CO: Denver	$22,450	OH: Cincinnati	$22,140
DC: Washington	$25,160	OH: Cleveland	$25,490
FL: Miami	$25,810	OH: Columbus	$23,180
FL: Orlando	$22,490	OR: Portland	$27,900
FL: Tampa	$22,770	PA: Philadelphia	$31,280
GA: Atlanta	$28,270	PA: Pittsburgh	$31,020
IL: Chicago	$27,340	TX: Dallas	$21,040
MA: Boston	$31,560	TX: Houston	$22,200
MD: Baltimore	$23,790	WA: Seattle	$34,500

FACTORS THAT MAY AFFECT EARNINGS

Educational Attainment of Workers and Effect on Earnings

	Percent at Level	Effect on Earnings
Less than High School	—	—
Some High School	—	—
High School or Equivalent	56.3%	3.5%
Some College but No Degree	—	—
Associate Degree	—	—
Bachelor's Degree	—	—
Master's Degree	—	—
Doctoral Degree	—	—
First Professional Degree	—	—

Figures do not total 100% because some levels have a very small sample size.

Flexibility of Earnings

Average Hours Worked: 34
Workers with a Varying Number of Hours: 13.6%
Workers Earning Some Overtime Pay, Tips, or Commissions: 20.0%
Earnings Benefit of Working Overtime: 17.2%

Gender

	Male	Female
Percent	80.1%	19.9%
Effect on Earnings	11.1%	–32.0%

Union Membership

Percentage Union Members: 14.3%
Earnings Benefit of Union Membership: 26.5%

Veteran Status

Percentage Who Have Been on Active Duty: 10.3%
Earnings Benefit of Veteran Status: 25.8%

51-9196 Paper Goods Machine Setters, Operators, and Tenders

Set up, operate, or tend paper goods machines that perform a variety of functions, such as converting, sawing, corrugating, banding, wrapping, boxing, stitching, forming, or sealing paper or paperboard sheets into products.

- Education or Training Required: Moderate-term on-the-job training
- Job Growth: 2.4%
- Annual Openings: 15,000
- Self-Employed: 0.7%
- Part-Time: 13.0%

NATIONAL WAGE FIGURES (ANNUAL)

Beginning	25th Percentile	Median	Mean	75th Percentile	90th Percentile
$19,730	$24,960	$31,490	$32,610	$39,090	$47,850

Median Wages for Industries Employing Largest Numbers (Annual)

Industry	Median Income
Wholesale Electronic Markets and Agents and Brokers	$47,120
Wood Product Manufacturing	$34,950
Warehousing and Storage	$34,560
Paper Manufacturing	$32,090
Plastics and Rubber Products Manufacturing...................	$28,670
Printing and Related Support Activities	$28,560
Merchant Wholesalers, Nondurable Goods	$27,960
Merchant Wholesalers, Durable Goods	$27,480
Publishing Industries (Except Internet)	$27,400
Chemical Manufacturing...	$27,280

Median Wages for States (Annual)

AK............	no data	KY	$33,730	NY	$29,010
AL............	$41,100	LA	$40,540	OH	$30,480
AR............	$33,530	MA	$32,990	OK	$34,270
AZ	$30,190	MD	$30,150	OR	$42,400
CA	$30,760	ME	$39,010	PA	$32,780
CO	$35,110	MI	$33,590	RI	$26,360
CT	$31,070	MN	$33,330	SC.............	$33,780
DC	no data	MO	$28,960	SD	$26,260
DE	no data	MS	$28,760	TN	$28,280
FL	$26,230	MT	$20,110	TX	$26,830
GA	$32,160	NC	$31,130	UT	$27,500
HI	$32,340	ND	no data	VA	$27,280
IA	$30,070	NE	$27,390	VT	$27,530
ID	$38,290	NH	$30,930	WA	$42,890
IL	$30,780	NJ	$27,100	WI	$35,490
IN	$29,810	NM	$20,990	WV	$24,680
KS	$30,410	NV	$27,870	WY	no data

Median Wages for the Largest Metropolitan Areas (Annual)

AZ: Phoenix............	$27,640	MI: Detroit	$33,370
CA: Los Angeles	$29,140	MN: Minneapolis	$33,800
CA: Riverside	$32,950	MO: Kansas City	$29,960
CA: Sacramento	$29,500	MO: St. Louis............	$30,180
CA: San Diego	$27,610	NV: Las Vegas	no data
CA: San Francisco....	$29,590	NY: New York............	$27,450
CO: Denver	$34,480	OH: Cincinnati...........	$30,250
DC: Washington	$28,270	OH: Cleveland	$31,370
FL: Miami	$26,990	OH: Columbus	$30,820
FL: Orlando	$25,310	OR: Portland	$42,750
FL: Tampa	$22,100	PA: Philadelphia	$34,130
GA: Atlanta	$31,250	PA: Pittsburgh	$30,620
IL: Chicago	$31,410	TX: Dallas	$28,030
MA: Boston	$29,990	TX: Houston	$26,320
MD: Baltimore	$26,990	WA: Seattle	$44,110

FACTORS THAT MAY AFFECT EARNINGS

Educational Attainment of Workers and Effect on Earnings

	Percent at Level	Effect on Earnings
Less than High School	10.0%	−32.3%
Some High School	16.7%	−37.4%
High School or Equivalent	51.7%	1.4%
Some College but No Degree	15.0%	42.6%
Associate Degree	—	—
Bachelor's Degree	—	—
Master's Degree	—	—
Doctoral Degree	—	—
First Professional Degree	—	—

Figures do not total 100% because some levels have a very small sample size.

Flexibility of Earnings

Average Hours Worked: 35
Workers with a Varying Number of Hours: 7.3%
Workers Earning Some Overtime Pay, Tips, or Commissions: 23.8%
Earnings Benefit of Working Overtime: 17.2%

Gender

	Male	Female
Percent	69.4%	30.6%
Effect on Earnings	11.1%	−32.0%

Union Membership

Percentage Union Members: 47.6%
Earnings Benefit of Union Membership: 25.7%

Veteran Status

Percentage Who Have Been on Active Duty: 10.3%
Earnings Benefit of Veteran Status: 25.8%

51-9197 Tire Builders

Operate machines to build tires from rubber components.

- Education or Training Required: Moderate-term on-the-job training
- Job Growth: −16.6%
- Annual Openings: 4,000
- Self-Employed: 0.0%
- Part-Time: 15.8%

NATIONAL WAGE FIGURES (ANNUAL)

Beginning	25th Percentile	Median	Mean	75th Percentile	90th Percentile
$20,520	$26,290	$38,120	$38,220	$50,010	$56,940

Median Wages for Industries Employing Largest Numbers (Annual)

Industry	Median Income
Plastics and Rubber Products Manufacturing	$39,690
Motor Vehicle and Parts Dealers	$25,090

Median Wages for States (Annual)

State	Wage	State	Wage	State	Wage
AK	no data	KY	$30,220	NY	no data
AL	no data	LA	no data	OH	$36,660
AR	no data	MA	no data	OK	$46,500
AZ	no data	MD	no data	OR	$23,730
CA	$27,630	ME	$24,570	PA	$29,490
CO	no data	MI	$23,390	RI	no data
CT	no data	MN	no data	SC	no data
DC	no data	MO	$28,410	SD	no data
DE	no data	MS	no data	TN	no data
FL	$21,260	MT	no data	TX	$22,770
GA	$23,590	NC	$43,160	UT	no data
HI	no data	ND	no data	VA	$27,590
IA	no data	NE	$18,710	VT	no data
ID	no data	NH	no data	WA	$28,640
IL	$36,370	NJ	no data	WI	no data
IN	no data	NM	no data	WV	$23,550
KS	$45,890	NV	no data	WY	no data

Median Wages for the Largest Metropolitan Areas (Annual)

Area	Wage	Area	Wage
AZ: Phoenix	no data	MI: Detroit	no data
CA: Los Angeles	no data	MN: Minneapolis	no data
CA: Riverside	no data	MO: Kansas City	$38,760
CA: Sacramento	no data	MO: St. Louis	$26,080
CA: San Diego	no data	NV: Las Vegas	no data
CA: San Francisco	no data	NY: New York	$26,560
CO: Denver	no data	OH: Cincinnati	$29,420
DC: Washington	no data	OH: Cleveland	no data
FL: Miami	$17,150	OH: Columbus	no data
FL: Orlando	no data	OR: Portland	no data
FL: Tampa	no data	PA: Philadelphia	$27,420
GA: Atlanta	$25,140	PA: Pittsburgh	no data
IL: Chicago	$30,890	TX: Dallas	no data
MA: Boston	no data	TX: Houston	no data
MD: Baltimore	no data	WA: Seattle	$23,640

FACTORS THAT MAY AFFECT EARNINGS

Educational Attainment of Workers and Effect on Earnings

	Percent at Level	Effect on Earnings
Less than High School	—	—
Some High School	—	—
High School or Equivalent	56.7%	−12.0%
Some College but No Degree	—	—
Associate Degree	—	—
Bachelor's Degree	—	—
Master's Degree	—	—
Doctoral Degree	—	—
First Professional Degree	—	—

Figures do not total 100% because some levels have a very small sample size.

Flexibility of Earnings

Average Hours Worked: 36
Workers with a Varying Number of Hours: 10.8%
Workers Earning Some Overtime Pay, Tips, or Commissions: 40.0%
Earnings Benefit of Working Overtime: 17.2%

Gender

	Male	Female
Percent	92.8%	7.2%
Effect on Earnings	11.1%	−32.0%

Union Membership

Percentage Union Members: 40.0%
Earnings Benefit of Union Membership: 31.0%

Veteran Status

Percentage Who Have Been on Active Duty: 10.3%
Earnings Benefit of Veteran Status: 25.8%

51-9198 Helpers—Production Workers

Help production workers by performing duties of lesser skill. Duties include supplying or holding materials or tools and cleaning work area and equipment.

- Education or Training Required: Short-term on-the-job training
- Job Growth: 7.9%
- Annual Openings: 107,000
- Self-Employed: 0.1%
- Part-Time: 36.8%

NATIONAL WAGE FIGURES (ANNUAL)

Beginning	25th Percentile	Median	Mean	75th Percentile	90th Percentile
$14,870	$17,040	$20,740	$22,120	$25,960	$32,340

Median Wages for Industries Employing Largest Numbers (Annual)

Industry	Median Income
Paper Manufacturing	$25,920
Electrical Equipment, Appliance, and Component Manufacturing	$25,220
Primary Metal Manufacturing	$24,980
Nonmetallic Mineral Product Manufacturing	$22,830
Plastics and Rubber Products Manufacturing	$22,800
Transportation Equipment Manufacturing	$22,800
Chemical Manufacturing	$22,720
Beverage and Tobacco Product Manufacturing	$22,660
Machinery Manufacturing	$22,650
Computer and Electronic Product Manufacturing	$21,440

Median Wages for States (Annual)

AK	$21,740	KY	$21,380	NY	$19,050
AL	$20,140	LA	$20,590	OH	$22,770
AR	$21,180	MA	$22,800	OK	$18,820
AZ	$20,950	MD	$21,600	OR	$23,540
CA	$19,220	ME	$22,160	PA	$23,190
CO	$21,240	MI	$22,130	RI	$19,650
CT	$21,290	MN	$23,290	SC	$19,880
DC	$26,020	MO	$20,360	SD	$18,920
DE	$17,080	MS	$20,780	TN	$20,800
FL	$18,910	MT	$21,770	TX	$17,790
GA	$19,970	NC	$21,150	UT	$18,560
HI	$17,910	ND	$20,720	VA	$21,080
IA	$23,570	NE	$22,940	VT	$22,980
ID	$18,550	NH	$22,130	WA	$22,120
IL	$19,930	NJ	$19,940	WI	$23,650
IN	$21,780	NM	$18,380	WV	$20,980
KS	$20,900	NV	$19,580	WY	$21,800

Median Wages for the Largest Metropolitan Areas (Annual)

AZ: Phoenix	$21,300	MI: Detroit	$22,540
CA: Los Angeles	$18,370	MN: Minneapolis	$23,170
CA: Riverside	$18,300	MO: Kansas City	$21,720
CA: Sacramento	$19,910	MO: St. Louis	$23,150
CA: San Diego	$20,730	NV: Las Vegas	$17,770
CA: San Francisco	$23,200	NY: New York	$19,060
CO: Denver	$20,290	OH: Cincinnati	$22,470
DC: Washington	$22,410	OH: Cleveland	$22,050
FL: Miami	$17,310	OH: Columbus	$21,800
FL: Orlando	$18,380	OR: Portland	$24,060
FL: Tampa	$19,670	PA: Philadelphia	$22,390
GA: Atlanta	$19,920	PA: Pittsburgh	$24,530
IL: Chicago	$19,370	TX: Dallas	$17,240
MA: Boston	$23,000	TX: Houston	$18,840
MD: Baltimore	$20,890	WA: Seattle	$22,750

FACTORS THAT MAY AFFECT EARNINGS

Educational Attainment of Workers and Effect on Earnings

	Percent at Level	Effect on Earnings
Less than High School	13.0%	−22.9%
Some High School	27.5%	−34.4%
High School or Equivalent	47.8%	29.3%
Some College but No Degree	8.7%	−16.4%
Associate Degree	—	—
Bachelor's Degree	—	—
Master's Degree	—	—
Doctoral Degree	—	—
First Professional Degree	—	—

Flexibility of Earnings

Average Hours Worked: 29
Workers with a Varying Number of Hours: 14.0%
Workers Earning Some Overtime Pay, Tips, or Commissions: 23.3%
Earnings Benefit of Working Overtime: 17.2%

Gender

	Male	Female
Percent	74.8%	25.2%
Effect on Earnings	11.1%	−32.0%

Union Membership

Percentage Union Members: 9.6%
Earnings Benefit of Union Membership: 26.5%

Veteran Status

Percentage Who Have Been on Active Duty: 10.3%
Earnings Benefit of Veteran Status: 25.8%

51-9199 Production Workers, All Other

All production workers not listed separately.

- Education or Training Required: Moderate-term on-the-job training
- Job Growth: –1.3%
- Annual Openings: 45,000
- Self-Employed: 2.9%
- Part-Time: 13.3%

NATIONAL WAGE FIGURES (ANNUAL)

Beginning	25th Percentile	Median	Mean	75th Percentile	90th Percentile
$15,640	$18,420	$24,890	$28,740	$35,380	$50,610

Median Wages for Industries Employing Largest Numbers (Annual)

Industry	Median Income
Transportation Equipment Manufacturing	$48,520
Primary Metal Manufacturing	$36,800
Federal, State, and Local Government	$36,650
Paper Manufacturing	$35,690
Chemical Manufacturing	$32,290
Nonmetallic Mineral Product Manufacturing	$31,260
Machinery Manufacturing	$29,200
Computer and Electronic Product Manufacturing	$28,030
Fabricated Metal Product Manufacturing	$27,750
Professional, Scientific, and Technical Services	$27,430

Median Wages for States (Annual)

AK	no data	KY	$25,820	NY	$24,640
AL	$25,210	LA	$23,270	OH	$27,540
AR	$24,160	MA	$31,280	OK	$21,880
AZ	$22,940	MD	$29,050	OR	$24,570
CA	$19,240	ME	$19,420	PA	$29,370
CO	$25,010	MI	$30,560	RI	$27,960
CT	$29,880	MN	$27,530	SC	$21,990
DC	$39,000	MO	$19,620	SD	no data
DE	$26,120	MS	$17,290	TN	$25,320
FL	$22,660	MT	$29,800	TX	$24,990
GA	$26,210	NC	$23,360	UT	$17,330
HI	$28,610	ND	$24,030	VA	$21,870
IA	$26,290	NE	$28,480	VT	no data
ID	$24,900	NH	$24,940	WA	$28,630
IL	$23,170	NJ	$32,420	WI	$28,610
IN	$32,510	NM	$16,890	WV	$24,820
KS	$25,600	NV	$32,440	WY	$21,810

Median Wages for the Largest Metropolitan Areas (Annual)

AZ: Phoenix	$24,330	MI: Detroit	no data
CA: Los Angeles	$18,320	MN: Minneapolis	$29,440
CA: Riverside	$18,110	MO: Kansas City	$21,230
CA: Sacramento	$19,280	MO: St. Louis	$19,800
CA: San Diego	$19,400	NV: Las Vegas	$30,730
CA: San Francisco	$21,540	NY: New York	$31,260
CO: Denver	$25,240	OH: Cincinnati	$29,050
DC: Washington	$26,200	OH: Cleveland	$48,000
FL: Miami	$22,100	OH: Columbus	$27,250
FL: Orlando	$20,970	OR: Portland	$23,930
FL: Tampa	$25,040	PA: Philadelphia	$31,120
GA: Atlanta	$27,300	PA: Pittsburgh	$27,020
IL: Chicago	$22,770	TX: Dallas	$27,600
MA: Boston	$30,710	TX: Houston	$22,910
MD: Baltimore	$30,340	WA: Seattle	$32,660

FACTORS THAT MAY AFFECT EARNINGS

Educational Attainment of Workers and Effect on Earnings

	Percent at Level	Effect on Earnings
Less than High School	7.0%	–36.8%
Some High School	13.4%	–20.2%
High School or Equivalent	45.5%	5.8%
Some College but No Degree	18.5%	2.9%
Associate Degree	8.4%	8.1%
Bachelor's Degree	6.1%	16.3%
Master's Degree	1.0%	44.0%
Doctoral Degree	—	—
First Professional Degree	—	—

Flexibility of Earnings

Average Hours Worked: 34
Workers with a Varying Number of Hours: 7.0%
Workers Earning Some Overtime Pay, Tips, or Commissions: 21.9%
Earnings Benefit of Working Overtime: 16.5%

Gender

	Male	Female
Percent	67.7%	32.3%
Effect on Earnings	11.1%	–32.0%

Union Membership

Percentage Union Members: 18.5%
Earnings Benefit of Union Membership: 29.0%

Veteran Status

Percentage Who Have Been on Active Duty: 10.3%
Earnings Benefit of Veteran Status: 25.8%

53-0000: Transportation and Material Moving Occupations

53-1000 Supervisors, Transportation and Material Moving Workers

53-1011 Aircraft Cargo Handling Supervisors

Direct ground crew in the loading, unloading, securing, and staging of aircraft cargo or baggage. Determine the quantity and orientation of cargo and compute aircraft center of gravity. May accompany aircraft as member of flight crew, monitor and handle cargo in flight, and assist and brief passengers on safety and emergency procedures.

- Education or Training Required: Work experience in a related occupation
- Job Growth: 17.4%
- Annual Openings: 1,000
- Self-Employed: 1.5%
- Part-Time: 4.1%

NATIONAL WAGE FIGURES (ANNUAL)

Beginning	25th Percentile	Median	Mean	75th Percentile	90th Percentile
$23,500	$28,750	$39,840	$45,440	$59,780	$75,040

Median Wages for Industries Employing Largest Numbers (Annual)

Industry	Median Income
Postal Service	$76,330
Motor Vehicle and Parts Dealers	$63,300
Waste Management and Remediation Services	$59,560
Management of Companies and Enterprises	$54,990
Federal, State, and Local Government	$54,950
Couriers and Messengers	$51,010
Merchant Wholesalers, Nondurable Goods	$46,740
Truck Transportation	$46,710
Transportation Equipment Manufacturing	$45,330
Air Transportation	$43,460

Median Wages for States (Annual)

State		State		State	
AK	$44,960	KY	no data	NY	$53,460
AL	no data	LA	$39,520	OH	$52,020
AR	$36,980	MA	no data	OK	no data
AZ	$33,680	MD	$47,360	OR	$48,360
CA	$47,810	ME	no data	PA	$28,900
CO	$35,320	MI	$49,080	RI	no data
CT	$30,280	MN	no data	SC	no data
DC	no data	MO	$39,110	SD	no data
DE	no data	MS	no data	TN	$29,040
FL	$35,920	MT	no data	TX	$31,820
GA	no data	NC	$43,580	UT	$27,520
HI	no data	ND	no data	VA	$39,630
IA	no data	NE	no data	VT	no data
ID	$27,060	NH	no data	WA	$40,230
IL	$50,080	NJ	no data	WI	$32,130
IN	$33,360	NM	$30,060	WV	no data
KS	$27,520	NV	$32,090	WY	no data

Median Wages for the Largest Metropolitan Areas (Annual)

Area		Area	
AZ: Phoenix	no data	MI: Detroit	no data
CA: Los Angeles	$52,100	MN: Minneapolis	no data
CA: Riverside	no data	MO: Kansas City	$32,730
CA: Sacramento	no data	MO: St. Louis	no data
CA: San Diego	$38,520	NV: Las Vegas	$31,530
CA: San Francisco	$40,960	NY: New York	$53,510
CO: Denver	$34,940	OH: Cincinnati	$44,720
DC: Washington	$37,620	OH: Cleveland	no data
FL: Miami	$34,350	OH: Columbus	$70,010
FL: Orlando	$29,440	OR: Portland	$48,690
FL: Tampa	no data	PA: Philadelphia	$35,170
GA: Atlanta	no data	PA: Pittsburgh	no data
IL: Chicago	$47,170	TX: Dallas	$48,220
MA: Boston	$44,210	TX: Houston	no data
MD: Baltimore	$49,310	WA: Seattle	$39,020

FACTORS THAT MAY AFFECT EARNINGS

Educational Attainment of Workers and Effect on Earnings

Figures are based on a group of occupations: Supervisors, Transportation and Material Moving Workers

	Percent at Level	Effect on Earnings
Less than High School	—	—
Some High School	5.1%	−35.7%
High School or Equivalent	38.5%	−3.1%
Some College but No Degree	28.2%	−0.2%
Associate Degree	11.5%	−6.3%
Bachelor's Degree	14.1%	23.2%
Master's Degree	—	—
Doctoral Degree	—	—
First Professional Degree	—	—

Flexibility of Earnings

Average Hours Worked: 40
Workers with a Varying Number of Hours: 7.0%
Workers Earning Some Overtime Pay, Tips, or Commissions: 18.8%
Earnings Benefit of Working Overtime: −7.8%

Gender

	Male	Female
Percent	81.8%	18.2%
Effect on Earnings	5.1%	—

Union Membership

Percentage Union Members: 18.2%
Earnings Benefit of Union Membership: 5.5%

Veteran Status

Percentage Who Have Been on Active Duty: 16.8%
Earnings Benefit of Veteran Status: 11.3%

53-1021 First-Line Supervisors/Managers of Helpers, Laborers, and Material Movers, Hand

Supervise and coordinate the activities of helpers, laborers, or material movers.

- Education or Training Required: Work experience in a related occupation
- Job Growth: 8.1%
- Annual Openings: 15,000
- Self-Employed: 1.3%
- Part-Time: 4.1%

NATIONAL WAGE FIGURES (ANNUAL)

Beginning	25th Percentile	Median	Mean	75th Percentile	90th Percentile
$24,420	$30,660	$39,570	$41,940	$50,660	$63,490

Median Wages for Industries Employing Largest Numbers (Annual)

Industry	Median Income
Transportation Equipment Manufacturing	$46,760
Truck Transportation	$43,940
Chemical Manufacturing	$43,140
Federal, State, and Local Government	$43,060
Management of Companies and Enterprises	$42,970
Waste Management and Remediation Services	$42,560
Merchant Wholesalers, Nondurable Goods	$41,750
Merchant Wholesalers, Durable Goods	$41,330
Nonmetallic Mineral Product Manufacturing	$41,090
Warehousing and Storage	$40,190

Median Wages for States (Annual)

State	Wage	State	Wage	State	Wage
AK	$40,490	KY	$34,880	NY	$45,160
AL	$34,830	LA	$34,280	OH	$40,270
AR	$37,690	MA	$42,620	OK	$35,960
AZ	$37,490	MD	$42,230	OR	$36,540
CA	$39,690	ME	$33,390	PA	$41,960
CO	$41,450	MI	$45,560	RI	$38,810
CT	$42,090	MN	$41,490	SC	$40,690
DC	$51,170	MO	$40,480	SD	$35,920
DE	$46,620	MS	$35,390	TN	$39,420
FL	$35,940	MT	$34,480	TX	$36,430
GA	$38,010	NC	$35,820	UT	$35,550
HI	$35,900	ND	$35,550	VA	$41,490
IA	$40,150	NE	$40,750	VT	$39,530
ID	$31,770	NH	$39,180	WA	$43,990
IL	$39,940	NJ	$44,230	WI	$42,280
IN	$40,720	NM	$35,020	WV	$37,670
KS	$36,730	NV	$39,370	WY	$34,660

Median Wages for the Largest Metropolitan Areas (Annual)

Area	Wage	Area	Wage
AZ: Phoenix	$37,690	MI: Detroit	$52,160
CA: Los Angeles	$39,440	MN: Minneapolis	$44,380
CA: Riverside	$40,610	MO: Kansas City	$40,140
CA: Sacramento	$39,940	MO: St. Louis	$45,380
CA: San Diego	$36,610	NV: Las Vegas	$39,110
CA: San Francisco	$42,050	NY: New York	$46,060
CO: Denver	$42,280	OH: Cincinnati	$43,900
DC: Washington	$44,620	OH: Cleveland	$42,840
FL: Miami	$36,840	OH: Columbus	$38,590
FL: Orlando	$35,800	OR: Portland	$38,890
FL: Tampa	$35,360	PA: Philadelphia	$43,540
GA: Atlanta	$38,490	PA: Pittsburgh	$40,050
IL: Chicago	$40,190	TX: Dallas	$39,160
MA: Boston	$42,500	TX: Houston	$39,130
MD: Baltimore	$41,320	WA: Seattle	$46,590

FACTORS THAT MAY AFFECT EARNINGS

Educational Attainment of Workers and Effect on Earnings

Figures are based on a group of occupations: Supervisors, Transportation and Material Moving Workers

	Percent at Level	Effect on Earnings
Less than High School	—	—
Some High School	5.1%	−35.7%
High School or Equivalent	38.5%	−3.1%
Some College but No Degree	28.2%	−0.2%
Associate Degree	11.5%	−6.3%
Bachelor's Degree	14.1%	23.2%
Master's Degree	—	—
Doctoral Degree	—	—
First Professional Degree	—	—

Flexibility of Earnings

Average Hours Worked: 40
Workers with a Varying Number of Hours: 7.0%
Workers Earning Some Overtime Pay, Tips, or Commissions: 18.8%
Earnings Benefit of Working Overtime: −7.8%

Gender

	Male	Female
Percent	83.3%	16.7%
Effect on Earnings	5.1%	—

Union Membership

Percentage Union Members: 18.2%
Earnings Benefit of Union Membership: 5.5%

Veteran Status

Percentage Who Have Been on Active Duty: 16.8%
Earnings Benefit of Veteran Status: 11.3%

53-1031 First-Line Supervisors/Managers of Transportation and Material-Moving Machine and Vehicle Operators

Directly supervise and coordinate activities of transportation and material-moving machine and vehicle operators and helpers.

- Education or Training Required: Work experience in a related occupation
- Job Growth: 15.3%
- Annual Openings: 22,000
- Self-Employed: 1.3%
- Part-Time: 4.1%

NATIONAL WAGE FIGURES (ANNUAL)

Beginning	25th Percentile	Median	Mean	75th Percentile	90th Percentile
$28,860	$36,910	$48,330	$50,990	$61,220	$76,270

Median Wages for Industries Employing Largest Numbers (Annual)

Industry	Median Income
Postal Service	$61,580
Rail Transportation	$60,640
Couriers and Messengers	$55,960
Federal, State, and Local Government	$52,790
Support Activities for Transportation	$52,370
Management of Companies and Enterprises	$52,240
Waste Management and Remediation Services	$50,610
Food Manufacturing	$50,270
Truck Transportation	$49,840
Heavy and Civil Engineering Construction	$49,550

Median Wages for States (Annual)

AK	$60,230	KY	$42,700	NY	$54,870
AL	$44,160	LA	$45,070	OH	$48,140
AR	$42,130	MA	$53,200	OK	$42,160
AZ	$48,440	MD	$48,800	OR	$46,450
CA	$51,270	ME	$44,030	PA	$47,690
CO	$48,410	MI	$50,250	RI	$49,780
CT	$52,050	MN	$45,850	SC	$44,490
DC	$31,280	MO	$50,310	SD	$45,780
DE	$50,400	MS	$39,720	TN	$43,270
FL	$47,580	MT	$42,790	TX	$46,380
GA	$45,170	NC	$43,460	UT	$48,170
HI	$49,710	ND	$45,130	VA	$50,210
IA	$45,110	NE	$50,350	VT	$50,950
ID	$38,940	NH	$46,830	WA	$55,740
IL	$52,930	NJ	$54,700	WI	$48,520
IN	$46,860	NM	$46,540	WV	$42,100
KS	$43,340	NV	$46,520	WY	$45,090

Median Wages for the Largest Metropolitan Areas (Annual)

AZ: Phoenix	$51,100	MI: Detroit	$52,980
CA: Los Angeles	$50,270	MN: Minneapolis	$48,840
CA: Riverside	$49,750	MO: Kansas City	$50,750
CA: Sacramento	$52,770	MO: St. Louis	$53,010
CA: San Diego	$48,470	NV: Las Vegas	$44,870
CA: San Francisco	$56,950	NY: New York	$58,000
CO: Denver	$49,500	OH: Cincinnati	$50,470
DC: Washington	$51,940	OH: Cleveland	$51,600
FL: Miami	$50,310	OH: Columbus	$49,350
FL: Orlando	$45,790	OR: Portland	$52,110
FL: Tampa	$45,780	PA: Philadelphia	$49,160
GA: Atlanta	$48,900	PA: Pittsburgh	$48,790
IL: Chicago	$54,240	TX: Dallas	$48,700
MA: Boston	$53,170	TX: Houston	$47,240
MD: Baltimore	$47,420	WA: Seattle	$58,040

FACTORS THAT MAY AFFECT EARNINGS

Educational Attainment of Workers and Effect on Earnings

Figures are based on a group of occupations: Supervisors, Transportation and Material Moving Workers

	Percent at Level	Effect on Earnings
Less than High School	—	—
Some High School	5.1%	−35.7%
High School or Equivalent	38.5%	−3.1%
Some College but No Degree	28.2%	−0.2%
Associate Degree	11.5%	−6.3%
Bachelor's Degree	14.1%	23.2%
Master's Degree	—	—
Doctoral Degree	—	—
First Professional Degree	—	—

Flexibility of Earnings

Average Hours Worked: 40
Workers with a Varying Number of Hours: 7.0%
Workers Earning Some Overtime Pay, Tips, or Commissions: 18.8%
Earnings Benefit of Working Overtime: −7.8%

Gender

	Male	Female
Percent	83.3%	16.7%
Effect on Earnings	5.1%	—

Union Membership

Percentage Union Members: 18.2%
Earnings Benefit of Union Membership: 5.5%

Veteran Status

Percentage Who Have Been on Active Duty: 16.8%
Earnings Benefit of Veteran Status: 11.3%

53-2000 Air Transportation Workers

53-2011 Airline Pilots, Copilots, and Flight Engineers

Pilot and navigate the flight of multi-engine aircraft in regularly scheduled service for the transport of passengers and cargo. Requires Federal Air Transport rating and certification in specific aircraft type used.

- Education or Training Required: Bachelor's degree
- Job Growth: 17.2%
- Annual Openings: 7,000
- Self-Employed: 2.4%
- Part-Time: 10.1%

NATIONAL WAGE FIGURES (ANNUAL)

Beginning	25th Percentile	Median	Mean	75th Percentile	90th Percentile
$50,470	$81,080	$141,090	$140,380	more than $145,600	more than $145,600

Median Wages for Industries Employing Largest Numbers (Annual)

Industry	Median Income
Air Transportation	more than $145,600
Securities, Commodity Contracts, and Other Financial Investments and Related Activities	$118,290
Insurance Carriers and Related Activities	$101,290
Transportation Equipment Manufacturing	$99,970
Utilities	$95,570
Professional, Scientific, and Technical Services	$91,640
Credit Intermediation and Related Activities	$91,060
Federal, State, and Local Government	$88,470
Administrative and Support Services	$85,360
Management of Companies and Enterprises	$83,140

Median Wages for States (Annual)

AK $141,780	KY .... no data	NY .. more than $145,600
AL $81,520	LA .... no data	OH $77,470
AR $69,270	MA .... more than $145,600	OK $91,050
AZ .... no data	MD .... no data	OR .. more than $145,600
CA .. more than $145,600	ME .... no data	PA .... no data
CO $111,640	MI .... no data	RI $84,320
CT $107,510	MN .... no data	SC $77,450
DC .... no data	MO .... no data	SD $51,180
DE $92,080	MS $82,670	TN $84,770
FL .. more than $145,600	MT $40,110	TX $144,980
GA $118,500	NC .... no data	UT .... no data
HI $77,380	ND $71,230	VA .... more than $145,600
IA $79,820	NE .... no data	VT .... no data
ID $45,220	NH $64,300	WA .... no data
IL .. more than $145,600	NJ .... no data	WI .... no data
IN $74,010	NM $74,410	WV .... no data
KS $85,130	NV $71,370	WY .... no data

Median Wages for the Largest Metropolitan Areas (Annual)

AZ: Phoenix	no data	MI: Detroit	no data
CA: Los Angeles	more than $145,600	MN: Minneapolis	no data
CA: Riverside	$89,380	MO: Kansas City	no data
CA: Sacramento	$84,070	MO: St. Louis	no data
CA: San Diego	no data	NV: Las Vegas	$81,950
CA: San Francisco	no data	NY: New York	more than $145,600
CO: Denver	no data	OH: Cincinnati	no data
DC: Washington	more than $145,600	OH: Cleveland	$58,310
FL: Miami	no data	OH: Columbus	$90,890
FL: Orlando	$96,770	OR: Portland	no data
FL: Tampa	no data	PA: Philadelphia	no data
GA: Atlanta	no data	PA: Pittsburgh	no data
IL: Chicago	more than $145,600	TX: Dallas	no data
MA: Boston	no data	TX: Houston	no data
MD: Baltimore	no data	WA: Seattle	no data

FACTORS THAT MAY AFFECT EARNINGS

Educational Attainment of Workers and Effect on Earnings

Figures are based on a group of occupations: Air Transportation Workers

	Percent at Level	Effect on Earnings
Less than High School	—	—
Some High School	—	—
High School or Equivalent	11.6%	−11.7%
Some College but No Degree	19.7%	−6.3%
Associate Degree	15.0%	−8.4%
Bachelor's Degree	40.5%	6.3%
Master's Degree	12.1%	7.7%
Doctoral Degree	—	—
First Professional Degree	—	—

Flexibility of Earnings

Average Hours Worked: 28
Workers with a Varying Number of Hours: 35.1%
Workers Earning Some Overtime Pay, Tips, or Commissions: 12.6%
Earnings Benefit of Working Overtime: −26.5%

Gender

	Male	Female
Percent	97.8%	2.2%
Effect on Earnings	0.9%	—

Union Membership

Percentage Union Members: 52.7%
Earnings Benefit of Union Membership: 10.9%

Veteran Status

Percentage Who Have Been on Active Duty: 35.3%
Earnings Benefit of Veteran Status: 11.6%

53-2012 Commercial Pilots

Pilot and navigate the flight of small fixed or rotary-winged aircraft primarily for the transport of cargo and passengers. Requires Commercial Rating.

- Education or Training Required: Postsecondary vocational training
- Job Growth: 16.8%
- Annual Openings: 2,000
- Self-Employed: 2.5%
- Part-Time: 10.1%

NATIONAL WAGE FIGURES (ANNUAL)

Beginning	25th Percentile	Median	Mean	75th Percentile	90th Percentile
$28,450	$40,780	$57,480	$66,720	$83,760	$115,220

Median Wages for Industries Employing Largest Numbers (Annual)

Industry	Median Income
Merchant Wholesalers, Durable Goods	$93,460
Transportation Equipment Manufacturing	$87,650
Utilities	$80,130
Securities, Commodity Contracts, and Other Financial Investments and Related Activities	$79,380
Computer and Electronic Product Manufacturing	$76,850
Management of Companies and Enterprises	$76,560
Performing Arts, Spectator Sports, and Related Industries	$71,860
Oil and Gas Extraction	$68,860
Motor Vehicle and Parts Dealers	$67,610
Insurance Carriers and Related Activities	$63,770

Median Wages for States (Annual)

AK	$57,200	KY	$51,500	NY	$82,120
AL	$62,770	LA	$56,440	OH	$105,760
AR	$56,010	MA	no data	OK	$54,470
AZ	$52,600	MD	$52,010	OR	$44,830
CA	$62,710	ME	$41,000	PA	$55,300
CO	$52,150	MI	$53,930	RI	no data
CT	$64,670	MN	$41,540	SC	$54,930
DC	no data	MO	$50,500	SD	$44,270
DE	$59,540	MS	$54,070	TN	$52,270
FL	$48,180	MT	$56,530	TX	$59,370
GA	$59,800	NC	$57,940	UT	no data
HI	$68,030	ND	$53,850	VA	$53,950
IA	$60,980	NE	$54,890	VT	no data
ID	$66,230	NH	$76,090	WA	$53,080
IL	$73,880	NJ	$57,720	WI	$47,450
IN	$52,120	NM	$39,990	WV	$54,950
KS	$61,420	NV	$52,910	WY	$65,310

Median Wages for the Largest Metropolitan Areas (Annual)

AZ: Phoenix	$43,490	MI: Detroit	$51,090
CA: Los Angeles	$56,330	MN: Minneapolis	$41,230
CA: Riverside	$47,800	MO: Kansas City	$48,720
CA: Sacramento	$59,240	MO: St. Louis	$49,260
CA: San Diego	$73,310	NV: Las Vegas	$62,260
CA: San Francisco	$82,860	NY: New York	$68,200
CO: Denver	$54,480	OH: Cincinnati	$74,380
DC: Washington	$40,800	OH: Cleveland	$53,540
FL: Miami	$72,170	OH: Columbus	$68,910
FL: Orlando	$32,650	OR: Portland	$36,490
FL: Tampa	no data	PA: Philadelphia	$56,990
GA: Atlanta	$59,790	PA: Pittsburgh	$52,440
IL: Chicago	$82,480	TX: Dallas	$87,530
MA: Boston	no data	TX: Houston	$52,400
MD: Baltimore	no data	WA: Seattle	$62,560

FACTORS THAT MAY AFFECT EARNINGS

Educational Attainment of Workers and Effect on Earnings

Figures are based on a group of occupations: Air Transportation Workers

	Percent at Level	Effect on Earnings
Less than High School	—	—
Some High School	—	—
High School or Equivalent	11.6%	−11.7%
Some College but No Degree	19.7%	−6.3%
Associate Degree	15.0%	−8.4%
Bachelor's Degree	40.5%	6.3%
Master's Degree	12.1%	7.7%
Doctoral Degree	—	—
First Professional Degree	—	—

Flexibility of Earnings

Average Hours Worked: 28
Workers with a Varying Number of Hours: 35.1%
Workers Earning Some Overtime Pay, Tips, or Commissions: 12.6%
Earnings Benefit of Working Overtime: −26.5%

Gender

	Male	Female
Percent	97.8%	2.2%
Effect on Earnings	0.9%	—

Union Membership

Percentage Union Members: 52.7%
Earnings Benefit of Union Membership: 10.9%

Veteran Status

Percentage Who Have Been on Active Duty: 35.3%
Earnings Benefit of Veteran Status: 11.6%

53-2021 Air Traffic Controllers

Control air traffic on and within vicinity of airport and movement of air traffic between altitude sectors and control centers according to established procedures and policies. Authorize, regulate, and control commercial airline flights according to government or company regulations to expedite and ensure flight safety.

- Education or Training Required: Long-term on-the-job training
- Job Growth: 14.3%
- Annual Openings: 2,000
- Self-Employed: 1.8%
- Part-Time: 10.1%

NATIONAL WAGE FIGURES (ANNUAL)

Beginning	25th Percentile	Median	Mean	75th Percentile	90th Percentile
$59,410	$86,860	$117,240	$110,270	$142,210	more than $145,600

Median Wages for Industries Employing Largest Numbers (Annual)

Industry	Median Income
Federal, State, and Local Government	$121,590
Administrative and Support Services	$75,900
Air Transportation	$71,160
Support Activities for Transportation	$53,500
Professional, Scientific, and Technical Services	$51,650

Median Wages for States (Annual)

AK $78,730	KY $115,450	NY $133,350
AL $92,840	LA $76,590	OH $128,800
AR $89,820	MA $103,620	OK $101,090
AZ $94,070	MD $114,500	OR $104,210
CA $123,310	ME .... no data	PA $104,710
CO $127,880	MI $103,160	RI $111,250
CT $60,590	MN $137,220	SC $83,850
DC .... no data	MO $116,390	SD .... no data
DE .... no data	MS $73,960	TN $121,230
FL $122,900	MT $92,900	TX $115,830
GA $133,030	NC $101,930	UT .... no data
HI $99,320	ND $78,150	VA $134,970
IA $87,380	NE $93,400	VT .... no data
ID $74,630	NH $140,950	WA $104,040
IL $134,650	NJ $109,580	WI $101,750
IN $127,340	NM $117,870	WV $85,650
KS $126,210	NV $92,950	WY $65,750

Median Wages for the Largest Metropolitan Areas (Annual)

AZ: Phoenix $103,860	MI: Detroit $120,300
CA: Los Angeles $122,220	MN: Minneapolis $138,760
CA: Riverside $89,410	MO: Kansas City $128,510
CA: Sacramento $133,670	MO: St. Louis $120,910
CA: San Diego $135,380	NV: Las Vegas $95,210
CA: San Francisco $136,810	NY: New York $138,170
CO: Denver $136,410	OH: Cincinnati .... no data
DC: Washington $135,040	OH: Cleveland .... no data
FL: Miami $134,500	OH: Columbus .... no data
FL: Orlando .... no data	OR: Portland $113,720
FL: Tampa $135,100	PA: Philadelphia $127,600
GA: Atlanta $137,470	PA: Pittsburgh $145,600
IL: Chicago $139,340	TX: Dallas $122,970
MA: Boston $141,430	TX: Houston $134,480
MD: Baltimore .... no data	WA: Seattle $112,220

FACTORS THAT MAY AFFECT EARNINGS

Educational Attainment of Workers and Effect on Earnings

Figures are based on a group of occupations: Air Transportation Workers

	Percent at Level	Effect on Earnings
Less than High School	—	—
Some High School	—	—
High School or Equivalent	11.6%	−11.7%
Some College but No Degree	19.7%	−6.3%
Associate Degree	15.0%	−8.4%
Bachelor's Degree	40.5%	6.3%
Master's Degree	12.1%	7.7%
Doctoral Degree	—	—
First Professional Degree	—	—

Flexibility of Earnings

Average Hours Worked: 28
Workers with a Varying Number of Hours: 2.0%
Workers Earning Some Overtime Pay, Tips, or Commissions: 12.6%
Earnings Benefit of Working Overtime: −23.4%

Gender

	Male	Female
Percent	91.3%	8.7%
Effect on Earnings	4.5%	−25.5%

Union Membership

Percentage Union Members: 52.7%
Earnings Benefit of Union Membership: 10.9%

Veteran Status

Percentage Who Have Been on Active Duty: 35.3%
Earnings Benefit of Veteran Status: 11.6%

53-2022 Airfield Operations Specialists

Ensure the safe takeoff and landing of commercial and military aircraft. Duties include coordination between air traffic control and maintenance personnel; dispatching; using airfield landing and navigational aids; implementing airfield safety procedures; monitoring and maintaining flight records; and applying knowledge of weather information.

- Education or Training Required: Long-term on-the-job training
- Job Growth: 15.0%
- Annual Openings: Fewer than 500
- Self-Employed: 2.1%
- Part-Time: 10.1%

NATIONAL WAGE FIGURES (ANNUAL)

Beginning	25th Percentile	Median	Mean	75th Percentile	90th Percentile
$19,050	$26,340	$37,630	$41,400	$51,790	$70,860

Median Wages for Industries Employing Largest Numbers (Annual)

Industry	Median Income
Transportation Equipment Manufacturing	$65,110
Federal, State, and Local Government	$46,320
Professional, Scientific, and Technical Services	$45,020
Air Transportation	$35,250
Couriers and Messengers	$33,340
Support Activities for Transportation	$26,310

Median Wages for States (Annual)

AK	$47,790	KY	no data	NY	$43,890
AL	$40,670	LA	$46,850	OH	$24,800
AR	no data	MA	no data	OK	$44,240
AZ	$40,470	MD	no data	OR	$33,410
CA	$58,560	ME	no data	PA	$40,130
CO	$42,540	MI	$44,660	RI	no data
CT	no data	MN	$23,860	SC	$30,870
DC	no data	MO	no data	SD	no data
DE	no data	MS	no data	TN	$21,620
FL	$37,150	MT	no data	TX	$35,310
GA	$56,370	NC	$31,400	UT	$26,350
HI	no data	ND	no data	VA	$35,390
IA	no data	NE	no data	VT	no data
ID	$42,560	NH	no data	WA	$61,800
IL	$35,290	NJ	no data	WI	$37,830
IN	no data	NM	no data	WV	no data
KS	$47,480	NV	$52,130	WY	no data

Median Wages for the Largest Metropolitan Areas (Annual)

AZ: Phoenix	no data	MI: Detroit	$46,280
CA: Los Angeles	$50,370	MN: Minneapolis	$23,820
CA: Riverside	$54,320	MO: Kansas City	no data
CA: Sacramento	no data	MO: St. Louis	no data
CA: San Diego	no data	NV: Las Vegas	no data
CA: San Francisco	no data	NY: New York	$44,590
CO: Denver	no data	OH: Cincinnati	no data
DC: Washington	$35,520	OH: Cleveland	no data
FL: Miami	$39,960	OH: Columbus	no data
FL: Orlando	$31,450	OR: Portland	$35,640
FL: Tampa	no data	PA: Philadelphia	$31,840
GA: Atlanta	$50,660	PA: Pittsburgh	no data
IL: Chicago	$44,890	TX: Dallas	$48,870
MA: Boston	no data	TX: Houston	$32,140
MD: Baltimore	no data	WA: Seattle	$64,890

FACTORS THAT MAY AFFECT EARNINGS

Educational Attainment of Workers and Effect on Earnings

Figures are based on a group of occupations: Air Transportation Workers

	Percent at Level	Effect on Earnings
Less than High School	—	—
Some High School	—	—
High School or Equivalent	11.6%	−11.7%
Some College but No Degree	19.7%	−6.3%
Associate Degree	15.0%	−8.4%
Bachelor's Degree	40.5%	6.3%
Master's Degree	12.1%	7.7%
Doctoral Degree	—	—
First Professional Degree	—	—

Flexibility of Earnings

Average Hours Worked: 28
Workers with a Varying Number of Hours: 2.0%
Workers Earning Some Overtime Pay, Tips, or Commissions: 12.6%
Earnings Benefit of Working Overtime: −23.4%

Gender

	Male	Female
Percent	91.3%	8.7%
Effect on Earnings	4.5%	−25.5%

Union Membership

Percentage Union Members: 52.7%
Earnings Benefit of Union Membership: 10.9%

Veteran Status

Percentage Who Have Been on Active Duty: 35.3%
Earnings Benefit of Veteran Status: 11.6%

53-3000 Motor Vehicle Operators

53-3011 Ambulance Drivers and Attendants, Except Emergency Medical Technicians

Drive ambulance or assist ambulance driver in transporting sick, injured, or convalescent persons. Assist in lifting patients.

- Education or Training Required: Moderate-term on-the-job training
- Job Growth: 28.0%
- Annual Openings: 5,000
- Self-Employed: 11.0%
- Part-Time: 36.4%

NATIONAL WAGE FIGURES (ANNUAL)

Beginning	25th Percentile	Median	Mean	75th Percentile	90th Percentile
$14,140	$16,340	$20,370	$21,930	$25,140	$31,800

Median Wages for Industries Employing Largest Numbers (Annual)

Industry	Median Income
Food and Beverage Stores	$23,080
Federal, State, and Local Government	$21,860
Hospitals	$21,550
Ambulatory Health Care Services	$19,810
Transit and Ground Passenger Transportation	$19,760
Nursing and Residential Care Facilities	$18,930
Social Assistance	$17,160

Median Wages for States (Annual)

State	Wage	State	Wage	State	Wage
AK	no data	KY	no data	NY	$21,610
AL	$15,940	LA	$25,180	OH	$17,430
AR	$14,280	MA	$26,450	OK	$19,770
AZ	$22,720	MD	$27,970	OR	$22,310
CA	$25,140	ME	$18,590	PA	$19,240
CO	$21,530	MI	$20,960	RI	$23,570
CT	$22,760	MN	$20,390	SC	$17,640
DC	no data	MO	no data	SD	no data
DE	$21,840	MS	$15,980	TN	$22,580
FL	$17,020	MT	$19,080	TX	$21,020
GA	$16,200	NC	$22,400	UT	no data
HI	no data	ND	$17,160	VA	$16,890
IA	$20,210	NE	$20,290	VT	no data
ID	$34,730	NH	$22,560	WA	$22,620
IL	$16,580	NJ	$23,660	WI	$19,550
IN	$19,150	NM	$16,760	WV	$14,290
KS	$17,420	NV	$25,720	WY	$13,740

Median Wages for the Largest Metropolitan Areas (Annual)

Area	Wage	Area	Wage
AZ: Phoenix	$24,780	MI: Detroit	$21,240
CA: Los Angeles	$26,710	MN: Minneapolis	no data
CA: Riverside	$24,370	MO: Kansas City	no data
CA: Sacramento	$34,950	MO: St. Louis	$20,370
CA: San Diego	no data	NV: Las Vegas	no data
CA: San Francisco	$25,240	NY: New York	$22,680
CO: Denver	$21,360	OH: Cincinnati	$18,900
DC: Washington	$24,700	OH: Cleveland	$18,050
FL: Miami	$16,980	OH: Columbus	$18,720
FL: Orlando	no data	OR: Portland	no data
FL: Tampa	$16,990	PA: Philadelphia	$23,300
GA: Atlanta	$16,630	PA: Pittsburgh	$18,720
IL: Chicago	$16,700	TX: Dallas	$27,960
MA: Boston	$27,250	TX: Houston	$19,990
MD: Baltimore	$28,650	WA: Seattle	$24,460

FACTORS THAT MAY AFFECT EARNINGS

Educational Attainment of Workers and Effect on Earnings

	Percent at Level	Effect on Earnings
Less than High School	—	—
Some High School	—	—
High School or Equivalent	36.8%	−10.4%
Some College but No Degree	42.1%	23.3%
Associate Degree	—	—
Bachelor's Degree	—	—
Master's Degree	—	—
Doctoral Degree	—	—
First Professional Degree	—	—

Figures do not total 100% because some levels have a very small sample size.

Flexibility of Earnings

Average Hours Worked: 30

Workers with a Varying Number of Hours: 13.8%

Workers Earning Some Overtime Pay, Tips, or Commissions: 21.1%

Earnings Benefit of Working Overtime: 14.7%

Gender

	Male	Female
Percent	72.0%	28.0%
Effect on Earnings	4.5%	−25.5%

Union Membership

Percentage Union Members: 15.8%

Earnings Benefit of Union Membership: 25.0%

Veteran Status

Percentage Who Have Been on Active Duty: 19.0%

Earnings Benefit of Veteran Status: 2.8%

53-3021 Bus Drivers, Transit and Intercity

Drive bus or motor coach, including regular route operations, charters, and private carriage. May assist passengers with baggage. May collect fares or tickets.

- Education or Training Required: Moderate-term on-the-job training
- Job Growth: 21.7%
- Annual Openings: 34,000
- Self-Employed: 0.5%
- Part-Time: 17.7%

NATIONAL WAGE FIGURES (ANNUAL)

Beginning	25th Percentile	Median	Mean	75th Percentile	90th Percentile
$19,270	$24,050	$32,090	$33,050	$41,310	$50,090

Median Wages for Industries Employing Largest Numbers (Annual)

Industry	Median Income
Federal, State, and Local Government	$36,270
Performing Arts, Spectator Sports, and Related Industries	$29,730
Museums, Historical Sites, and Similar Institutions	$28,850
Food and Beverage Stores	$27,460
Truck Transportation	$27,280
Educational Services	$27,100
Transit and Ground Passenger Transportation	$26,790
Rental and Leasing Services	$25,150
Support Activities for Transportation	$25,030
Scenic and Sightseeing Transportation	$24,370

Median Wages for States (Annual)

AK	$29,080	KY	$31,290	NY	$43,840
AL	$16,140	LA	no data	OH	$38,340
AR	$21,200	MA	$29,330	OK	$24,060
AZ	$26,420	MD	$34,320	OR	no data
CA	$35,100	ME	$30,120	PA	$27,070
CO	$29,330	MI	$29,230	RI	$32,220
CT	$26,880	MN	$32,100	SC	$18,290
DC	no data	MO	no data	SD	$22,050
DE	no data	MS	$18,110	TN	$22,840
FL	$23,810	MT	$25,280	TX	$31,880
GA	$28,000	NC	$25,050	UT	$30,850
HI	$33,920	ND	$21,640	VA	$26,030
IA	$22,220	NE	$25,600	VT	$27,010
ID	$22,790	NH	$31,540	WA	$40,890
IL	no data	NJ	$30,910	WI	$34,700
IN	$26,050	NM	$24,390	WV	$22,130
KS	$21,990	NV	$27,900	WY	$23,820

Median Wages for the Largest Metropolitan Areas (Annual)

AZ: Phoenix	$26,200	MI: Detroit	$31,430
CA: Los Angeles	$33,690	MN: Minneapolis	no data
CA: Riverside	$31,460	MO: Kansas City	no data
CA: Sacramento	$32,190	MO: St. Louis	no data
CA: San Diego	$26,200	NV: Las Vegas	$27,730
CA: San Francisco	$48,860	NY: New York	$42,790
CO: Denver	$29,070	OH: Cincinnati	$37,020
DC: Washington	$32,970	OH: Cleveland	no data
FL: Miami	$22,850	OH: Columbus	no data
FL: Orlando	$26,170	OR: Portland	no data
FL: Tampa	$30,370	PA: Philadelphia	no data
GA: Atlanta	no data	PA: Pittsburgh	no data
IL: Chicago	no data	TX: Dallas	no data
MA: Boston	$29,230	TX: Houston	$33,460
MD: Baltimore	$32,320	WA: Seattle	no data

FACTORS THAT MAY AFFECT EARNINGS

Educational Attainment of Workers and Effect on Earnings

Figures are based on a group of occupations: Motor Vehicle Operators

	Percent at Level	Effect on Earnings
Less than High School	5.1%	−17.6%
Some High School	12.7%	−12.1%
High School or Equivalent	39.5%	8.3%
Some College but No Degree	21.9%	−0.4%
Associate Degree	10.3%	−6.0%
Bachelor's Degree	8.7%	0.1%
Master's Degree	1.4%	−18.0%
Doctoral Degree	—	—
First Professional Degree	—	—

Flexibility of Earnings

Average Hours Worked: 34
Workers with a Varying Number of Hours: 17.6%
Workers Earning Some Overtime Pay, Tips, or Commissions: 21.3%
Earnings Benefit of Working Overtime: 9.5%

Gender

	Male	Female
Percent	50.4%	49.6%
Effect on Earnings	11.6%	−10.2%

Union Membership

Percentage Union Members: 16.6%
Earnings Benefit of Union Membership: 25.0%

Veteran Status

Percentage Who Have Been on Active Duty: 19.0%
Earnings Benefit of Veteran Status: 2.8%

53-3022 Bus Drivers, School

Transport students or special clients, such as the elderly or persons with disabilities. Ensure adherence to safety rules. May assist passengers in boarding or exiting.

- Education or Training Required: Short-term on-the-job training
- Job Growth: 13.6%
- Annual Openings: 76,000
- Self-Employed: 0.5%
- Part-Time: 17.7%

NATIONAL WAGE FIGURES (ANNUAL)

Beginning	25th Percentile	Median	Mean	75th Percentile	90th Percentile
$13,690	$18,700	$24,820	$25,130	$30,820	$36,630

Median Wages for Industries Employing Largest Numbers (Annual)

Industry	Median Income
Waste Management and Remediation Services	$30,150
Truck Transportation	$29,230
Repair and Maintenance	$29,060
Federal, State, and Local Government	$28,690
Support Activities for Transportation	$27,480
Transit and Ground Passenger Transportation	$25,910
Merchant Wholesalers, Nondurable Goods	$25,110
Educational Services	$24,100
Administrative and Support Services	$23,870
Management of Companies and Enterprises	$22,980

Median Wages for States (Annual)

State	Wage	State	Wage	State	Wage
AK	$29,580	KY	$26,350	NY	$30,580
AL	$13,360	LA	$14,350	OH	$27,490
AR	$18,220	MA	$29,840	OK	$16,210
AZ	$22,630	MD	$26,460	OR	$26,090
CA	$29,860	ME	$26,280	PA	$22,560
CO	$28,030	MI	$30,560	RI	$26,150
CT	$26,820	MN	$28,630	SC	$16,800
DC	no data	MO	$23,840	SD	$23,330
DE	$25,510	MS	$13,890	TN	$15,120
FL	$23,810	MT	$24,560	TX	$19,740
GA	$14,650	NC	$22,360	UT	$27,940
HI	$29,970	ND	$27,310	VA	$24,070
IA	$26,090	NE	$24,180	VT	$26,630
ID	$23,910	NH	$24,520	WA	$32,150
IL	$25,730	NJ	$27,190	WI	$23,970
IN	$26,070	NM	$19,310	WV	$21,080
KS	$22,540	NV	$29,710	WY	$21,120

Median Wages for the Largest Metropolitan Areas (Annual)

Area	Wage	Area	Wage
AZ: Phoenix	$23,600	MI: Detroit	$31,630
CA: Los Angeles	$29,270	MN: Minneapolis	$29,270
CA: Riverside	$30,520	MO: Kansas City	$24,160
CA: Sacramento	$26,080	MO: St. Louis	$25,710
CA: San Diego	$31,360	NV: Las Vegas	$31,160
CA: San Francisco	$30,520	NY: New York	$30,570
CO: Denver	$29,770	OH: Cincinnati	$27,220
DC: Washington	$31,630	OH: Cleveland	$27,490
FL: Miami	$24,790	OH: Columbus	$26,820
FL: Orlando	$24,950	OR: Portland	$27,440
FL: Tampa	$24,370	PA: Philadelphia	$27,090
GA: Atlanta	$18,970	PA: Pittsburgh	$22,430
IL: Chicago	$26,580	TX: Dallas	$23,000
MA: Boston	$30,620	TX: Houston	$20,330
MD: Baltimore	$24,490	WA: Seattle	$32,870

FACTORS THAT MAY AFFECT EARNINGS

Educational Attainment of Workers and Effect on Earnings

Figures are based on a group of occupations: Motor Vehicle Operators

	Percent at Level	Effect on Earnings
Less than High School	5.1%	−17.6%
Some High School	12.7%	−12.1%
High School or Equivalent	39.5%	8.3%
Some College but No Degree	21.9%	−0.4%
Associate Degree	10.3%	−6.0%
Bachelor's Degree	8.7%	0.1%
Master's Degree	1.4%	−18.0%
Doctoral Degree	—	—
First Professional Degree	—	—

Flexibility of Earnings

Average Hours Worked: 34
Workers with a Varying Number of Hours: 17.6%
Workers Earning Some Overtime Pay, Tips, or Commissions: 21.3%
Earnings Benefit of Working Overtime: 9.5%

Gender

	Male	Female
Percent	50.4%	49.6%
Effect on Earnings	11.6%	−10.2%

Union Membership

Percentage Union Members: 16.6%
Earnings Benefit of Union Membership: 25.0%

Veteran Status

Percentage Who Have Been on Active Duty: 19.0%
Earnings Benefit of Veteran Status: 2.8%

53-3031 Driver/Sales Workers

Drive truck or other vehicle over established routes or within an established territory and sell goods, such as food products, including restaurant take-out items, or pick up and deliver items such as laundry. May also take orders and collect payments. Includes newspaper delivery drivers.

- Education or Training Required: Short-term on-the-job training
- Job Growth: 13.8%
- Annual Openings: 72,000
- Self-Employed: 8.8%
- Part-Time: 17.7%

NATIONAL WAGE FIGURES (ANNUAL)

Beginning	25th Percentile	Median	Mean	75th Percentile	90th Percentile
$12,880	$14,800	$20,770	$24,380	$31,190	$42,230

Median Wages for Industries Employing Largest Numbers (Annual)

Industry	Median Income
Couriers and Messengers	$40,680
Management of Companies and Enterprises	$32,430
Food and Beverage Stores	$31,410
Food Manufacturing	$31,150
Personal and Laundry Services	$30,680
Truck Transportation	$30,680
Beverage and Tobacco Product Manufacturing	$30,030
Warehousing and Storage	$29,590
Nonstore Retailers	$27,330
Merchant Wholesalers, Nondurable Goods	$27,060

Median Wages for States (Annual)

AK	$20,080	KY	$21,760	NY	$25,410
AL	$21,410	LA	$22,480	OH	$16,940
AR	$22,520	MA	$28,740	OK	$20,230
AZ	$15,480	MD	$25,460	OR	$21,470
CA	$18,140	ME	$22,200	PA	$20,890
CO	$16,350	MI	$21,630	RI	$18,770
CT	$29,020	MN	$21,790	SC	$20,910
DC	$18,850	MO	$17,610	SD	$23,940
DE	$25,770	MS	$23,470	TN	$22,670
FL	$21,350	MT	$22,840	TX	$15,820
GA	$20,300	NC	$20,660	UT	$20,310
HI	$24,310	ND	$19,580	VA	$22,010
IA	$22,460	NE	$19,550	VT	$23,640
ID	$22,600	NH	$19,140	WA	$25,410
IL	$21,810	NJ	$23,890	WI	$21,000
IN	$20,900	NM	$25,420	WV	$14,390
KS	$21,340	NV	$24,240	WY	$20,670

Median Wages for the Largest Metropolitan Areas (Annual)

AZ: Phoenix	$16,810	MI: Detroit	$24,280
CA: Los Angeles	$18,310	MN: Minneapolis	$21,730
CA: Riverside	$17,380	MO: Kansas City	$22,830
CA: Sacramento	$18,080	MO: St. Louis	$15,760
CA: San Diego	$20,440	NV: Las Vegas	$23,060
CA: San Francisco	$21,920	NY: New York	$27,770
CO: Denver	$17,330	OH: Cincinnati	$20,950
DC: Washington	$22,040	OH: Cleveland	$17,070
FL: Miami	$21,030	OH: Columbus	$16,350
FL: Orlando	$19,460	OR: Portland	$23,650
FL: Tampa	$21,520	PA: Philadelphia	$24,120
GA: Atlanta	$19,450	PA: Pittsburgh	$16,830
IL: Chicago	$28,190	TX: Dallas	$14,320
MA: Boston	$27,610	TX: Houston	$17,850
MD: Baltimore	$26,770	WA: Seattle	$25,970

FACTORS THAT MAY AFFECT EARNINGS

Educational Attainment of Workers and Effect on Earnings

Figures are based on a group of occupations: Motor Vehicle Operators

	Percent at Level	Effect on Earnings
Less than High School	5.1%	−17.6%
Some High School	12.7%	−12.1%
High School or Equivalent	39.5%	8.3%
Some College but No Degree	21.9%	−0.4%
Associate Degree	10.3%	−6.0%
Bachelor's Degree	8.7%	0.1%
Master's Degree	1.4%	−18.0%
Doctoral Degree	—	—
First Professional Degree	—	—

Flexibility of Earnings

Average Hours Worked: 34
Workers with a Varying Number of Hours: 17.6%
Workers Earning Some Overtime Pay, Tips, or Commissions: 21.3%
Earnings Benefit of Working Overtime: 13.2%

Gender

	Male	Female
Percent	94.8%	5.2%
Effect on Earnings	1.4%	−32.1%

Union Membership

Percentage Union Members: 16.6%
Earnings Benefit of Union Membership: 25.0%

Veteran Status

Percentage Who Have Been on Active Duty: 19.0%
Earnings Benefit of Veteran Status: 2.8%

53-3032 Truck Drivers, Heavy and Tractor-Trailer

Drive a tractor-trailer combination or a truck with a capacity of at least 26,000 GVW to transport and deliver goods, livestock, or materials in liquid, loose, or packaged form. May be required to unload truck. May require use of automated routing equipment. Requires commercial drivers' license.

- Education or Training Required: Moderate-term on-the-job training
- Job Growth: 12.9%
- Annual Openings: 274,000
- Self-Employed: 9.3%
- Part-Time: 17.7%

NATIONAL WAGE FIGURES (ANNUAL)

Beginning	25th Percentile	Median	Mean	75th Percentile	90th Percentile
$22,460	$27,720	$35,040	$36,320	$43,770	$52,820

Median Wages for Industries Employing Largest Numbers (Annual)

Industry	Median Income
Couriers and Messengers	$44,740
Warehousing and Storage	$38,280
Truck Transportation	$37,090
Management of Companies and Enterprises	$35,870
Merchant Wholesalers, Nondurable Goods	$35,300
Rental and Leasing Services	$34,550
Food Manufacturing	$33,900
Mining (Except Oil and Gas)	$33,350
Wholesale Electronic Markets and Agents and Brokers	$33,350
Fabricated Metal Product Manufacturing	$33,270

Median Wages for States (Annual)

State	Wage	State	Wage	State	Wage
AK	$42,850	KY	$32,280	NY	$37,730
AL	$32,310	LA	$29,080	OH	$35,380
AR	$36,570	MA	$40,010	OK	$30,690
AZ	$34,860	MD	$36,280	OR	$33,680
CA	$37,540	ME	$30,890	PA	$35,530
CO	$35,750	MI	$37,190	RI	$36,880
CT	$38,550	MN	$37,370	SC	$31,970
DC	$35,100	MO	$35,130	SD	$29,430
DE	$34,090	MS	$32,380	TN	$34,960
FL	$30,440	MT	$31,920	TX	$31,560
GA	$35,040	NC	$34,550	UT	$35,300
HI	$36,020	ND	$33,100	VA	$33,210
IA	$31,010	NE	$34,340	VT	$31,100
ID	$30,180	NH	$35,490	WA	$36,950
IL	$38,540	NJ	$39,270	WI	$36,360
IN	$37,290	NM	$30,590	WV	$26,880
KS	$33,620	NV	$37,960	WY	$34,130

Median Wages for the Largest Metropolitan Areas (Annual)

Area	Wage	Area	Wage
AZ: Phoenix	$36,030	MI: Detroit	$40,440
CA: Los Angeles	$36,610	MN: Minneapolis	$40,210
CA: Riverside	$39,500	MO: Kansas City	$36,140
CA: Sacramento	$38,010	MO: St. Louis	$37,000
CA: San Diego	$40,120	NV: Las Vegas	$37,100
CA: San Francisco	$40,150	NY: New York	$40,550
CO: Denver	$37,170	OH: Cincinnati	$35,290
DC: Washington	$36,450	OH: Cleveland	$37,240
FL: Miami	$31,570	OH: Columbus	$35,680
FL: Orlando	$29,680	OR: Portland	$35,670
FL: Tampa	$31,330	PA: Philadelphia	$39,320
GA: Atlanta	$37,460	PA: Pittsburgh	$34,080
IL: Chicago	$41,280	TX: Dallas	$35,470
MA: Boston	$41,220	TX: Houston	$31,510
MD: Baltimore	$37,280	WA: Seattle	$38,740

FACTORS THAT MAY AFFECT EARNINGS

Educational Attainment of Workers and Effect on Earnings

Figures are based on a group of occupations: Motor Vehicle Operators

	Percent at Level	Effect on Earnings
Less than High School	5.1%	−17.6%
Some High School	12.7%	−12.1%
High School or Equivalent	39.5%	8.3%
Some College but No Degree	21.9%	−0.4%
Associate Degree	10.3%	−6.0%
Bachelor's Degree	8.7%	0.1%
Master's Degree	1.4%	−18.0%
Doctoral Degree	—	—
First Professional Degree	—	—

Flexibility of Earnings

Average Hours Worked: 34
Workers with a Varying Number of Hours: 17.6%
Workers Earning Some Overtime Pay, Tips, or Commissions: 21.3%
Earnings Benefit of Working Overtime: 13.2%

Gender

	Male	Female
Percent	94.8%	5.2%
Effect on Earnings	1.4%	−32.1%

Union Membership

Percentage Union Members: 16.6%
Earnings Benefit of Union Membership: 25.0%

Veteran Status

Percentage Who Have Been on Active Duty: 19.0%
Earnings Benefit of Veteran Status: 2.8%

53-3033 Truck Drivers, Light or Delivery Services

Drive a truck or van with a capacity of under 26,000 GVW primarily to deliver or pick up merchandise or to deliver packages within a specified area. May require use of automatic routing or location software. May load and unload truck.

- Education or Training Required: Short-term on-the-job training
- Job Growth: 15.7%
- Annual Openings: 169,000
- Self-Employed: 8.9%
- Part-Time: 17.7%

NATIONAL WAGE FIGURES (ANNUAL)

Beginning	25th Percentile	Median	Mean	75th Percentile	90th Percentile
$15,540	$19,370	$25,300	$27,520	$33,620	$44,160

Median Wages for Industries Employing Largest Numbers (Annual)

Industry	Median Income
Couriers and Messengers	$36,070
Truck Transportation	$30,010
Warehousing and Storage	$28,360
Specialty Trade Contractors	$27,770
Support Activities for Transportation	$27,760
Nonstore Retailers	$27,040
Federal, State, and Local Government	$26,540
Fabricated Metal Product Manufacturing	$25,820
Merchant Wholesalers, Nondurable Goods	$25,680
Food Manufacturing	$25,500

Median Wages for States (Annual)

State		State		State	
AK	$28,590	KY	$23,420	NY	$27,630
AL	$22,530	LA	$20,930	OH	$25,480
AR	$20,320	MA	$30,090	OK	$21,010
AZ	$25,980	MD	$26,790	OR	$26,600
CA	$25,780	ME	$23,480	PA	$24,890
CO	$28,350	MI	$28,420	RI	$27,350
CT	$29,230	MN	$26,770	SC	$23,700
DC	$30,600	MO	$25,590	SD	$22,700
DE	$26,320	MS	$23,410	TN	$24,130
FL	$24,550	MT	$21,050	TX	$23,370
GA	$25,320	NC	$25,410	UT	$22,800
HI	$23,960	ND	$22,990	VA	$22,730
IA	$22,660	NE	$25,230	VT	$25,500
ID	$24,740	NH	$26,710	WA	$27,520
IL	$27,900	NJ	$28,640	WI	$23,760
IN	$24,970	NM	$23,690	WV	$19,840
KS	$23,030	NV	$27,110	WY	$24,960

Median Wages for the Largest Metropolitan Areas (Annual)

Area		Area	
AZ: Phoenix	$26,420	MI: Detroit	$30,380
CA: Los Angeles	$24,980	MN: Minneapolis	$28,300
CA: Riverside	$24,330	MO: Kansas City	$24,450
CA: Sacramento	$28,790	MO: St. Louis	$30,030
CA: San Diego	$23,650	NV: Las Vegas	$26,340
CA: San Francisco	$29,170	NY: New York	$30,540
CO: Denver	$29,480	OH: Cincinnati	$25,160
DC: Washington	$26,930	OH: Cleveland	$27,500
FL: Miami	$26,480	OH: Columbus	$27,410
FL: Orlando	$26,540	OR: Portland	$27,650
FL: Tampa	$22,680	PA: Philadelphia	$26,990
GA: Atlanta	$28,060	PA: Pittsburgh	$23,940
IL: Chicago	$28,860	TX: Dallas	$25,540
MA: Boston	$30,450	TX: Houston	$24,200
MD: Baltimore	$27,240	WA: Seattle	$28,990

FACTORS THAT MAY AFFECT EARNINGS

Educational Attainment of Workers and Effect on Earnings

Figures are based on a group of occupations: Motor Vehicle Operators

	Percent at Level	Effect on Earnings
Less than High School	5.1%	−17.6%
Some High School	12.7%	−12.1%
High School or Equivalent	39.5%	8.3%
Some College but No Degree	21.9%	−0.4%
Associate Degree	10.3%	−6.0%
Bachelor's Degree	8.7%	0.1%
Master's Degree	1.4%	−18.0%
Doctoral Degree	—	—
First Professional Degree	—	—

Flexibility of Earnings

Average Hours Worked: 34
Workers with a Varying Number of Hours: 17.6%
Workers Earning Some Overtime Pay, Tips, or Commissions: 21.3%
Earnings Benefit of Working Overtime: 13.2%

Gender

	Male	Female
Percent	94.8%	5.2%
Effect on Earnings	1.4%	−32.1%

Union Membership

Percentage Union Members: 16.6%
Earnings Benefit of Union Membership: 25.0%

Veteran Status

Percentage Who Have Been on Active Duty: 19.0%
Earnings Benefit of Veteran Status: 2.8%

53-3041 Taxi Drivers and Chauffeurs

Drive automobiles, vans, or limousines to transport passengers. May occasionally carry cargo.

- Education or Training Required: Short-term on-the-job training
- Job Growth: 24.8%
- Annual Openings: 43,000
- Self-Employed: 25.7%
- Part-Time: 27.7%

NATIONAL WAGE FIGURES (ANNUAL)

Beginning	25th Percentile	Median	Mean	75th Percentile	90th Percentile
$14,250	$16,640	$20,350	$22,080	$25,360	$32,860

Median Wages for Industries Employing Largest Numbers (Annual)

Industry	Median Income
Securities, Commodity Contracts, and Other Financial Investments and Related Activities	$34,770
Professional, Scientific, and Technical Services	$33,920
Insurance Carriers and Related Activities	$28,090
Educational Services	$23,040
Hospitals	$22,890
Federal, State, and Local Government	$22,790
Truck Transportation	$22,750
Management of Companies and Enterprises	$22,380
Transit and Ground Passenger Transportation	$20,990
Scenic and Sightseeing Transportation	$20,980

Median Wages for States (Annual)

State	Wage	State	Wage	State	Wage
AK	$21,770	KY	$17,900	NY	$23,870
AL	$15,560	LA	$16,320	OH	$19,720
AR	$15,150	MA	$22,350	OK	$17,250
AZ	$20,660	MD	$21,050	OR	$18,500
CA	$21,640	ME	$18,980	PA	$19,160
CO	$21,110	MI	$19,690	RI	$22,300
CT	$25,710	MN	$21,970	SC	$17,520
DC	$27,930	MO	$19,520	SD	$19,110
DE	$23,900	MS	$18,030	TN	$17,800
FL	$18,320	MT	$14,740	TX	$17,480
GA	$17,950	NC	$19,010	UT	$20,560
HI	$19,810	ND	$16,300	VA	$20,320
IA	$18,150	NE	$18,980	VT	$19,180
ID	$17,570	NH	$20,750	WA	$24,370
IL	$19,970	NJ	$22,860	WI	$18,980
IN	$17,130	NM	$16,990	WV	$15,040
KS	$17,160	NV	$24,050	WY	$17,000

Median Wages for the Largest Metropolitan Areas (Annual)

Area	Wage	Area	Wage
AZ: Phoenix	$19,250	MI: Detroit	$20,380
CA: Los Angeles	$21,550	MN: Minneapolis	$22,770
CA: Riverside	$20,240	MO: Kansas City	$19,610
CA: Sacramento	$21,140	MO: St. Louis	$20,770
CA: San Diego	$19,240	NV: Las Vegas	$24,450
CA: San Francisco	$25,360	NY: New York	$25,620
CO: Denver	$22,150	OH: Cincinnati	$20,950
DC: Washington	$23,440	OH: Cleveland	$21,550
FL: Miami	$18,540	OH: Columbus	$20,150
FL: Orlando	$18,610	OR: Portland	$19,910
FL: Tampa	$18,100	PA: Philadelphia	$20,740
GA: Atlanta	$19,130	PA: Pittsburgh	$19,850
IL: Chicago	$21,240	TX: Dallas	$19,060
MA: Boston	$22,640	TX: Houston	$19,030
MD: Baltimore	$20,570	WA: Seattle	$26,290

FACTORS THAT MAY AFFECT EARNINGS

Educational Attainment of Workers and Effect on Earnings

	Percent at Level	Effect on Earnings
Less than High School	4.5%	−19.4%
Some High School	10.8%	−20.1%
High School or Equivalent	40.1%	5.6%
Some College but No Degree	19.4%	−23.3%
Associate Degree	8.1%	−13.2%
Bachelor's Degree	14.0%	60.5%
Master's Degree	—	—
Doctoral Degree	—	—
First Professional Degree	—	—

Flexibility of Earnings

Average Hours Worked: 31
Workers with a Varying Number of Hours: 15.2%
Workers Earning Some Overtime Pay, Tips, or Commissions: 21.5%
Earnings Benefit of Working Overtime: 9.6%

Gender

	Male	Female
Percent	84.0%	16.0%
Effect on Earnings	6.7%	—

Union Membership

Percentage Union Members: 8.1%
Earnings Benefit of Union Membership: 29.8%

Veteran Status

Percentage Who Have Been on Active Duty: 19.0%
Earnings Benefit of Veteran Status: 2.8%

53-3099 Motor Vehicle Operators, All Other

All motor vehicle operators not listed separately.

- Education or Training Required: Short-term on-the-job training
- Job Growth: 25.7%
- Annual Openings: 23,000
- Self-Employed: 1.0%
- Part-Time: 69.2%

NATIONAL WAGE FIGURES (ANNUAL)

Beginning	25th Percentile	Median	Mean	75th Percentile	90th Percentile
$14,040	$16,570	$22,710	$26,550	$34,410	$45,000

Median Wages for Industries Employing Largest Numbers (Annual)

Industry	Median Income
Rail Transportation	$41,580
Professional, Scientific, and Technical Services	$41,520
Transportation Equipment Manufacturing	$35,280
Federal, State, and Local Government	$34,700
Merchant Wholesalers, Nondurable Goods	$32,910
Educational Services	$31,310
Specialty Trade Contractors	$30,960
Hospitals	$30,190
Couriers and Messengers	$28,870
Support Activities for Transportation	$23,860

Median Wages for States (Annual)

AK $49,480	KY $22,450	NY $30,620
AL $17,790	LA $17,220	OH $18,400
AR $22,810	MA $22,930	OK $40,440
AZ $25,270	MD $36,530	OR $21,730
CA $21,800	ME $16,310	PA $18,660
CO $21,180	MI $21,960	RI.............. $35,880
CT $20,870	MN $19,530	SC.............. $35,920
DC $43,980	MO $17,350	SD $31,440
DE $32,660	MS $30,430	TN $22,380
FL $21,080	MT $37,020	TX $19,090
GA $20,920	NC $26,580	UT $23,100
HI $41,180	ND $22,240	VA $28,230
IA $20,730	NE $40,310	VT $16,320
ID $17,260	NH $17,370	WA $32,830
IL $33,120	NJ $21,480	WI $15,550
IN $14,100	NM $30,870	WV $17,300
KS $17,150	NV $36,090	WY $43,150

Median Wages for the Largest Metropolitan Areas (Annual)

AZ: Phoenix	$21,210	MI: Detroit	$23,700
CA: Los Angeles	$20,650	MN: Minneapolis	$19,180
CA: Riverside	$19,640	MO: Kansas City	$19,450
CA: Sacramento	$22,850	MO: St. Louis	no data
CA: San Diego	$20,220	NV: Las Vegas	$38,780
CA: San Francisco	$21,030	NY: New York	$29,480
CO: Denver	$19,550	OH: Cincinnati	$20,120
DC: Washington	$41,120	OH: Cleveland	$18,290
FL: Miami	$22,390	OH: Columbus	$32,430
FL: Orlando	$21,530	OR: Portland	$24,920
FL: Tampa	$22,010	PA: Philadelphia	$24,980
GA: Atlanta	$22,430	PA: Pittsburgh	$19,740
IL: Chicago	$30,590	TX: Dallas	$15,550
MA: Boston	$21,040	TX: Houston	$16,710
MD: Baltimore	$39,810	WA: Seattle	$30,040

FACTORS THAT MAY AFFECT EARNINGS

Educational Attainment of Workers and Effect on Earnings

	Percent at Level	Effect on Earnings
Less than High School	—	—
Some High School	11.0%	−9.3%
High School or Equivalent	43.9%	−3.4%
Some College but No Degree	18.3%	11.1%
Associate Degree	7.3%	34.4%
Bachelor's Degree	12.2%	−15.8%
Master's Degree	—	—
Doctoral Degree	—	—
First Professional Degree	—	—

Figures do not total 100% because some levels have a very small sample size.

Flexibility of Earnings

Average Hours Worked: 20
Workers with a Varying Number of Hours: 27.3%
Workers Earning Some Overtime Pay, Tips, or Commissions: 2.3%
Earnings Benefit of Working Overtime: 14.7%

Gender

	Male	Female
Percent	88.0%	12.0%
Effect on Earnings	4.5%	−25.5%

Union Membership

Percentage Union Members: 11.4%
Earnings Benefit of Union Membership: 92.8%

Veteran Status

Percentage Who Have Been on Active Duty: 19.0%
Earnings Benefit of Veteran Status: 2.8%

53-4000 Rail Transportation Workers

53-4011 Locomotive Engineers

Drive electric, diesel-electric, steam, or gas-turbine-electric locomotives to transport passengers or freight. Interpret train orders, electronic or manual signals, and railroad rules and regulations.

- Education or Training Required: Moderate-term on-the-job training
- Job Growth: –2.5%
- Annual Openings: 2,000
- Self-Employed: 0.0%
- Part-Time: 18.1%

NATIONAL WAGE FIGURES (ANNUAL)

Beginning	25th Percentile	Median	Mean	75th Percentile	90th Percentile
$36,060	$44,180	$57,990	$61,850	$78,860	$93,720

Median Wages for Industries Employing Largest Numbers (Annual)

Industry	Median Income
Rail Transportation	$58,740
Federal, State, and Local Government	$54,260
Primary Metal Manufacturing	$42,860
Support Activities for Transportation	$34,970
Transportation Equipment Manufacturing	$34,710
Scenic and Sightseeing Transportation	$27,300

Median Wages for States (Annual)

State	Wage	State	Wage	State	Wage
AK	no data	KY	$42,040	NY	$47,060
AL	$37,380	LA	no data	OH	$41,180
AR	no data	MA	$52,730	OK	no data
AZ	no data	MD	$59,140	OR	no data
CA	$54,200	ME	$58,140	PA	$57,070
CO	$72,470	MI	$52,120	RI	no data
CT	no data	MN	$61,190	SC	no data
DC	no data	MO	no data	SD	no data
DE	no data	MS	$72,830	TN	no data
FL	$34,020	MT	no data	TX	no data
GA	no data	NC	no data	UT	$68,700
HI	no data	ND	no data	VA	$63,200
IA	no data	NE	$70,240	VT	$42,510
ID	no data	NH	no data	WA	no data
IL	$66,750	NJ	no data	WI	$59,080
IN	$46,040	NM	no data	WV	no data
KS	no data	NV	no data	WY	no data

Median Wages for the Largest Metropolitan Areas (Annual)

Metro	Wage	Metro	Wage
AZ: Phoenix	no data	MI: Detroit	no data
CA: Los Angeles	$45,310	MN: Minneapolis	no data
CA: Riverside	no data	MO: Kansas City	no data
CA: Sacramento	no data	MO: St. Louis	no data
CA: San Diego	no data	NV: Las Vegas	no data
CA: San Francisco	no data	NY: New York	no data
CO: Denver	no data	OH: Cincinnati	no data
DC: Washington	no data	OH: Cleveland	no data
FL: Miami	no data	OH: Columbus	no data
FL: Orlando	no data	OR: Portland	no data
FL: Tampa	no data	PA: Philadelphia	no data
GA: Atlanta	no data	PA: Pittsburgh	no data
IL: Chicago	no data	TX: Dallas	no data
MA: Boston	no data	TX: Houston	no data
MD: Baltimore	no data	WA: Seattle	no data

FACTORS THAT MAY AFFECT EARNINGS

Educational Attainment of Workers and Effect on Earnings

Figures are based on a group of occupations: Rail Transportation Workers

	Percent at Level	Effect on Earnings
Less than High School	—	—
Some High School	—	—
High School or Equivalent	45.2%	–3.7%
Some College but No Degree	27.4%	4.6%
Associate Degree	13.7%	5.8%
Bachelor's Degree	11.0%	7.8%
Master's Degree	—	—
Doctoral Degree	—	—
First Professional Degree	—	—

Flexibility of Earnings

Average Hours Worked: 38
Workers with a Varying Number of Hours: 16.6%
Workers Earning Some Overtime Pay, Tips, or Commissions: 28.0%
Earnings Benefit of Working Overtime: –5.2%

Gender

	Male	Female
Percent	95.4%	4.6%
Effect on Earnings	4.5%	–25.5%

Union Membership

Percentage Union Members: 75.0%
Earnings Benefit of Union Membership: 8.6%

Veteran Status

Percentage Who Have Been on Active Duty: 26.0%
Earnings Benefit of Veteran Status: 17.3%

53-4012 Locomotive Firers

Monitor locomotive instruments and watch for dragging equipment, obstacles on rights-of-way, and train signals during run. Watch for and relay traffic signals from yard workers to yard engineer in railroad yard.

- Education or Training Required: Moderate-term on-the-job training
- Job Growth: –2.5%
- Annual Openings: 2,000
- Self-Employed: 0.0%
- Part-Time: 18.1%

NATIONAL WAGE FIGURES (ANNUAL)

Beginning	25th Percentile	Median	Mean	75th Percentile	90th Percentile
$30,020	$33,990	$41,290	$45,680	$50,730	$78,210

Median Wages for Industries Employing Largest Numbers (Annual)

Industry	Median Income
Rail Transportation	$40,990

Median Wages for States (Annual)

AK............	no data	KY	no data	NY	no data
AL	no data	LA	no data	OH	no data
AR............	no data	MA	no data	OK	no data
AZ	no data	MD	no data	OR	no data
CA	$34,900	ME	no data	PA	$39,500
CO	no data	MI	no data	RI..............	no data
CT	no data	MN	no data	SC..............	no data
DC	no data	MO	no data	SD	no data
DE	no data	MS	no data	TN	no data
FL	no data	MT	no data	TX	no data
GA	no data	NC	no data	UT	no data
HI	no data	ND	no data	VA	no data
IA	no data	NE	no data	VT	no data
ID	no data	NH	no data	WA	no data
IL	no data	NJ	no data	WI	no data
IN	no data	NM	no data	WV	no data
KS	no data	NV	no data	WY	no data

Median Wages for the Largest Metropolitan Areas (Annual)

AZ: Phoenix............	no data	MI: Detroit	no data
CA: Los Angeles	no data	MN: Minneapolis	no data
CA: Riverside	no data	MO: Kansas City	no data
CA: Sacramento	no data	MO: St. Louis............	no data
CA: San Diego	no data	NV: Las Vegas	no data
CA: San Francisco....	no data	NY: New York............	no data
CO: Denver	no data	OH: Cincinnati..........	no data
DC: Washington	no data	OH: Cleveland	no data
FL: Miami	no data	OH: Columbus	no data
FL: Orlando	no data	OR: Portland	no data
FL: Tampa	no data	PA: Philadelphia	no data
GA: Atlanta	no data	PA: Pittsburgh	no data
IL: Chicago	no data	TX: Dallas	no data
MA: Boston	no data	TX: Houston	no data
MD: Baltimore	no data	WA: Seattle	no data

FACTORS THAT MAY AFFECT EARNINGS

Educational Attainment of Workers and Effect on Earnings

Figures are based on a group of occupations: Rail Transportation Workers

	Percent at Level	Effect on Earnings
Less than High School	—	—
Some High School	—	—
High School or Equivalent	45.2%	–3.7%
Some College but No Degree	27.4%	4.6%
Associate Degree	13.7%	5.8%
Bachelor's Degree	11.0%	7.8%
Master's Degree	—	—
Doctoral Degree	—	—
First Professional Degree	—	—

Flexibility of Earnings

Average Hours Worked: 38
Workers with a Varying Number of Hours: 16.6%
Workers Earning Some Overtime Pay, Tips, or Commissions: 28.0%
Earnings Benefit of Working Overtime: –5.2%

Gender

	Male	Female
Percent	95.4%	4.6%
Effect on Earnings	4.5%	–25.5%

Union Membership

Percentage Union Members: 75.0%
Earnings Benefit of Union Membership: 8.6%

Veteran Status

Percentage Who Have Been on Active Duty: 26.0%
Earnings Benefit of Veteran Status: 17.3%

53-4013 Rail Yard Engineers, Dinkey Operators, and Hostlers

Drive switching or other locomotive or dinkey engines within railroad yard, industrial plant, quarry, construction project, or similar location.

- Education or Training Required: Moderate-term on-the-job training
- Job Growth: –2.5%
- Annual Openings: 2,000
- Self-Employed: 0.0%
- Part-Time: 18.1%

NATIONAL WAGE FIGURES (ANNUAL)

Beginning	25th Percentile	Median	Mean	75th Percentile	90th Percentile
$24,470	$29,770	$37,880	$40,020	$47,180	$56,670

Median Wages for Industries Employing Largest Numbers (Annual)

Industry	Median Income
Federal, State, and Local Government	$45,410
Rail Transportation	$43,660
Primary Metal Manufacturing	$39,030
Mining (Except Oil and Gas)	$38,320
Support Activities for Transportation	$28,930

Median Wages for States (Annual)

State	Wage	State	Wage	State	Wage
AK	no data	KY	$33,370	NY	no data
AL	$32,720	LA	$29,480	OH	$27,900
AR	no data	MA	no data	OK	no data
AZ	no data	MD	no data	OR	$31,580
CA	no data	ME	no data	PA	$48,820
CO	no data	MI	$33,870	RI	no data
CT	no data	MN	$40,650	SC	no data
DC	no data	MO	no data	SD	no data
DE	no data	MS	$47,320	TN	no data
FL	$43,510	MT	no data	TX	$29,560
GA	$40,190	NC	no data	UT	no data
HI	no data	ND	no data	VA	$32,430
IA	no data	NE	no data	VT	no data
ID	no data	NH	no data	WA	no data
IL	$32,040	NJ	no data	WI	no data
IN	$38,140	NM	no data	WV	$40,470
KS	no data	NV	no data	WY	no data

Median Wages for the Largest Metropolitan Areas (Annual)

Metro	Wage	Metro	Wage
AZ: Phoenix	no data	MI: Detroit	no data
CA: Los Angeles	no data	MN: Minneapolis	no data
CA: Riverside	no data	MO: Kansas City	no data
CA: Sacramento	no data	MO: St. Louis	no data
CA: San Diego	no data	NV: Las Vegas	no data
CA: San Francisco	no data	NY: New York	no data
CO: Denver	no data	OH: Cincinnati	no data
DC: Washington	no data	OH: Cleveland	no data
FL: Miami	no data	OH: Columbus	no data
FL: Orlando	no data	OR: Portland	$31,040
FL: Tampa	no data	PA: Philadelphia	no data
GA: Atlanta	no data	PA: Pittsburgh	no data
IL: Chicago	$32,560	TX: Dallas	$33,230
MA: Boston	no data	TX: Houston	no data
MD: Baltimore	no data	WA: Seattle	no data

FACTORS THAT MAY AFFECT EARNINGS

Educational Attainment of Workers and Effect on Earnings

Figures are based on a group of occupations: Rail Transportation Workers

	Percent at Level	Effect on Earnings
Less than High School	—	—
Some High School	—	—
High School or Equivalent	45.2%	–3.7%
Some College but No Degree	27.4%	4.6%
Associate Degree	13.7%	5.8%
Bachelor's Degree	11.0%	7.8%
Master's Degree	—	—
Doctoral Degree	—	—
First Professional Degree	—	—

Flexibility of Earnings

Average Hours Worked: 38
Workers with a Varying Number of Hours: 16.6%
Workers Earning Some Overtime Pay, Tips, or Commissions: 28.0%
Earnings Benefit of Working Overtime: –5.2%

Gender

	Male	Female
Percent	95.4%	4.6%
Effect on Earnings	4.5%	–25.5%

Union Membership

Percentage Union Members: 75.0%
Earnings Benefit of Union Membership: 8.6%

Veteran Status

Percentage Who Have Been on Active Duty: 26.0%
Earnings Benefit of Veteran Status: 17.3%

53-4021 Railroad Brake, Signal, and Switch Operators

Operate railroad track switches. Couple or uncouple rolling stock to make up or break up trains. Signal engineers by hand or by flagging. May inspect couplings, air hoses, journal boxes, and hand brakes.

- Education or Training Required: Moderate-term on-the-job training
- Job Growth: –38.5%
- Annual Openings: 1,000
- Self-Employed: 0.0%
- Part-Time: 18.1%

NATIONAL WAGE FIGURES (ANNUAL)

Beginning	25th Percentile	Median	Mean	75th Percentile	90th Percentile
$31,150	$39,660	$48,860	$52,110	$65,030	$77,160

Median Wages for Industries Employing Largest Numbers (Annual)

Industry	Median Income
Rail Transportation	$50,180
Support Activities for Transportation	$27,380

Median Wages for States (Annual)

AK	no data	KY	no data	NY	no data
AL	$37,980	LA	$45,140	OH	$39,820
AR	no data	MA	$50,540	OK	no data
AZ	no data	MD	no data	OR	no data
CA	$42,390	ME	no data	PA	no data
CO	$57,810	MI	$54,390	RI	no data
CT	no data	MN	no data	SC	no data
DC	no data	MO	no data	SD	no data
DE	no data	MS	$63,030	TN	$59,790
FL	$26,880	MT	no data	TX	$53,080
GA	no data	NC	$41,270	UT	no data
HI	no data	ND	no data	VA	$32,580
IA	$44,270	NE	$58,130	VT	no data
ID	no data	NH	no data	WA	no data
IL	$56,340	NJ	no data	WI	$48,500
IN	$43,060	NM	no data	WV	no data
KS	no data	NV	no data	WY	no data

Median Wages for the Largest Metropolitan Areas (Annual)

AZ: Phoenix	no data	MI: Detroit	no data
CA: Los Angeles	$24,730	MN: Minneapolis	no data
CA: Riverside	$42,320	MO: Kansas City	no data
CA: Sacramento	no data	MO: St. Louis	no data
CA: San Diego	no data	NV: Las Vegas	no data
CA: San Francisco	no data	NY: New York	no data
CO: Denver	no data	OH: Cincinnati	no data
DC: Washington	no data	OH: Cleveland	no data
FL: Miami	no data	OH: Columbus	no data
FL: Orlando	no data	OR: Portland	no data
FL: Tampa	no data	PA: Philadelphia	no data
GA: Atlanta	no data	PA: Pittsburgh	no data
IL: Chicago	no data	TX: Dallas	no data
MA: Boston	no data	TX: Houston	$25,670
MD: Baltimore	no data	WA: Seattle	no data

FACTORS THAT MAY AFFECT EARNINGS

Educational Attainment of Workers and Effect on Earnings

	Percent at Level	Effect on Earnings
Less than High School	—	—
Some High School	—	—
High School or Equivalent	66.7%	8.5%
Some College but No Degree	—	—
Associate Degree	—	—
Bachelor's Degree	—	—
Master's Degree	—	—
Doctoral Degree	—	—
First Professional Degree	—	—

Figures do not total 100% because some levels have a very small sample size.

Flexibility of Earnings

Average Hours Worked: 36
Workers with a Varying Number of Hours: 23.1%
Workers Earning Some Overtime Pay, Tips, or Commissions: 38.9%
Earnings Benefit of Working Overtime: –5.2%

Gender

	Male	Female
Percent	87.7%	12.3%
Effect on Earnings	4.5%	–25.5%

Union Membership

Percentage Union Members: 66.7%
Earnings Benefit of Union Membership: 18.5%

Veteran Status

Percentage Who Have Been on Active Duty: 26.0%
Earnings Benefit of Veteran Status: 17.3%

53-4031 Railroad Conductors and Yardmasters

Conductors coordinate activities of train crew on passenger or freight train. Coordinate activities of switch-engine crew within yard of railroad, industrial plant, or similar location. Yardmasters coordinate activities of workers engaged in railroad traffic operations, such as the makeup or breakup of trains and yard switching, and review train schedules and switching orders.

- Education or Training Required: Moderate-term on-the-job training
- Job Growth: 20.2%
- Annual Openings: 3,000
- Self-Employed: 0.0%
- Part-Time: 18.1%

NATIONAL WAGE FIGURES (ANNUAL)

Beginning	25th Percentile	Median	Mean	75th Percentile	90th Percentile
$35,960	$42,870	$55,530	$58,880	$74,440	$89,460

Median Wages for Industries Employing Largest Numbers (Annual)

Industry	Median Income
Rail Transportation	$55,610
Chemical Manufacturing	$41,360
Support Activities for Transportation	$36,850

Median Wages for States (Annual)

AK	no data	KY	$67,550	NY	$51,340
AL	no data	LA	no data	OH	$40,080
AR	no data	MA	no data	OK	no data
AZ	no data	MD	no data	OR	no data
CA	$45,000	ME	$58,290	PA	$45,570
CO	$65,970	MI	$47,860	RI	no data
CT	no data	MN	$52,030	SC	no data
DC	no data	MO	no data	SD	no data
DE	no data	MS	$67,000	TN	no data
FL	$43,870	MT	no data	TX	no data
GA	no data	NC	no data	UT	no data
HI	no data	ND	no data	VA	$57,740
IA	no data	NE	$69,430	VT	no data
ID	no data	NH	no data	WA	no data
IL	$61,840	NJ	$50,530	WI	$55,820
IN	$55,820	NM	no data	WV	no data
KS	no data	NV	no data	WY	no data

Median Wages for the Largest Metropolitan Areas (Annual)

AZ: Phoenix	no data	MI: Detroit	no data
CA: Los Angeles	no data	MN: Minneapolis	no data
CA: Riverside	no data	MO: Kansas City	no data
CA: Sacramento	no data	MO: St. Louis	no data
CA: San Diego	no data	NV: Las Vegas	no data
CA: San Francisco	no data	NY: New York	$57,030
CO: Denver	no data	OH: Cincinnati	no data
DC: Washington	no data	OH: Cleveland	no data
FL: Miami	no data	OH: Columbus	no data
FL: Orlando	no data	OR: Portland	no data
FL: Tampa	no data	PA: Philadelphia	no data
GA: Atlanta	no data	PA: Pittsburgh	no data
IL: Chicago	no data	TX: Dallas	no data
MA: Boston	no data	TX: Houston	$39,850
MD: Baltimore	no data	WA: Seattle	no data

FACTORS THAT MAY AFFECT EARNINGS

Educational Attainment of Workers and Effect on Earnings

	Percent at Level	Effect on Earnings
Less than High School	—	—
Some High School	—	—
High School or Equivalent	40.3%	−8.3%
Some College but No Degree	31.3%	6.4%
Associate Degree	10.4%	−16.4%
Bachelor's Degree	17.9%	17.0%
Master's Degree	—	—
Doctoral Degree	—	—
First Professional Degree	—	—

Flexibility of Earnings

Average Hours Worked: 39
Workers with a Varying Number of Hours: 16.6%
Workers Earning Some Overtime Pay, Tips, or Commissions: 31.1%
Earnings Benefit of Working Overtime: −2.3%

Gender

	Male	Female
Percent	93.5%	6.5%
Effect on Earnings	0.1%	—

Union Membership

Percentage Union Members: 79.7%
Earnings Benefit of Union Membership: 7.0%

Veteran Status

Percentage Who Have Been on Active Duty: 26.0%
Earnings Benefit of Veteran Status: 17.3%

53-4041 Subway and Streetcar Operators

Operate subway or elevated suburban train with no separate locomotive or electric-powered streetcar to transport passengers. May handle fares.

- Education or Training Required: Moderate-term on-the-job training
- Job Growth: 13.7%
- Annual Openings: 1,000
- Self-Employed: 0.0%
- Part-Time: 18.1%

NATIONAL WAGE FIGURES (ANNUAL)

Beginning	25th Percentile	Median	Mean	75th Percentile	90th Percentile
$31,160	$39,820	$48,980	$46,180	$53,960	$57,150

Median Wages for Industries Employing Largest Numbers (Annual)

Industry	Median Income
Federal, State, and Local Government	$49,130

Median Wages for States (Annual)

AK	no data	KY	no data	NY	no data
AL	no data	LA	no data	OH	no data
AR	no data	MA	no data	OK	no data
AZ	no data	MD	no data	OR	no data
CA	$52,950	ME	no data	PA	no data
CO	no data	MI	no data	RI	no data
CT	no data	MN	no data	SC	no data
DC	no data	MO	no data	SD	no data
DE	no data	MS	no data	TN	no data
FL	no data	MT	no data	TX	$37,430
GA	no data	NC	no data	UT	no data
HI	no data	ND	no data	VA	no data
IA	no data	NE	no data	VT	no data
ID	no data	NH	no data	WA	no data
IL	no data	NJ	no data	WI	no data
IN	no data	NM	no data	WV	no data
KS	no data	NV	no data	WY	no data

Median Wages for the Largest Metropolitan Areas (Annual)

AZ: Phoenix	no data	MI: Detroit	no data
CA: Los Angeles	no data	MN: Minneapolis	no data
CA: Riverside	no data	MO: Kansas City	no data
CA: Sacramento	no data	MO: St. Louis	no data
CA: San Diego	no data	NV: Las Vegas	no data
CA: San Francisco	no data	NY: New York	no data
CO: Denver	no data	OH: Cincinnati	no data
DC: Washington	no data	OH: Cleveland	no data
FL: Miami	no data	OH: Columbus	no data
FL: Orlando	no data	OR: Portland	no data
FL: Tampa	no data	PA: Philadelphia	no data
GA: Atlanta	no data	PA: Pittsburgh	no data
IL: Chicago	no data	TX: Dallas	$39,120
MA: Boston	no data	TX: Houston	no data
MD: Baltimore	no data	WA: Seattle	no data

FACTORS THAT MAY AFFECT EARNINGS

Educational Attainment of Workers and Effect on Earnings

	Percent at Level	Effect on Earnings
Less than High School	—	—
Some High School	—	—
High School or Equivalent	57.1%	–3.4%
Some College but No Degree	—	—
Associate Degree	—	—
Bachelor's Degree	—	—
Master's Degree	—	—
Doctoral Degree	—	—
First Professional Degree	—	—

Figures do not total 100% because some levels have a very small sample size.

Flexibility of Earnings

Average Hours Worked: 38
Workers with a Varying Number of Hours: 16.6%
Workers Earning Some Overtime Pay, Tips, or Commissions: 14.3%
Earnings Benefit of Working Overtime: –5.2%

Gender

	Male	Female
Percent	95.4%	4.6%
Effect on Earnings	4.5%	–25.5%

Union Membership

Percentage Union Members: 66.7%
Earnings Benefit of Union Membership: 1.8%

Veteran Status

Percentage Who Have Been on Active Duty: 26.0%
Earnings Benefit of Veteran Status: 17.3%

53-4099 Rail Transportation Workers, All Other

All rail transportation workers not listed separately.

- Education or Training Required: Moderate-term on-the-job training
- Job Growth: −30.8%
- Annual Openings: Fewer than 500
- Self-Employed: 0.0%
- Part-Time: 18.1%

NATIONAL WAGE FIGURES (ANNUAL)

Beginning	25th Percentile	Median	Mean	75th Percentile	90th Percentile
$24,400	$31,470	$39,150	$38,330	$44,560	$51,570

Median Wages for Industries Employing Largest Numbers (Annual)

Industry	Median Income
Federal, State, and Local Government	$44,180
Primary Metal Manufacturing	$43,630
Rail Transportation	$39,410
Administrative and Support Services	$39,100
Support Activities for Transportation	$28,350

Median Wages for States (Annual)

AK	no data	KY	$40,640	NY	no data
AL	no data	LA	$40,520	OH	$39,140
AR	$42,220	MA	no data	OK	no data
AZ	no data	MD	no data	OR	no data
CA	no data	ME	no data	PA	$39,280
CO	no data	MI	$26,220	RI	no data
CT	no data	MN	$41,020	SC	no data
DC	no data	MO	no data	SD	no data
DE	no data	MS	no data	TN	no data
FL	no data	MT	no data	TX	$33,590
GA	$31,180	NC	$36,890	UT	no data
HI	no data	ND	no data	VA	no data
IA	$33,430	NE	no data	VT	no data
ID	no data	NH	no data	WA	no data
IL	$42,520	NJ	no data	WI	$39,200
IN	no data	NM	no data	WV	$26,280
KS	no data	NV	no data	WY	no data

Median Wages for the Largest Metropolitan Areas (Annual)

AZ: Phoenix	no data	MI: Detroit	no data
CA: Los Angeles	no data	MN: Minneapolis	no data
CA: Riverside	no data	MO: Kansas City	no data
CA: Sacramento	no data	MO: St. Louis	no data
CA: San Diego	no data	NV: Las Vegas	no data
CA: San Francisco	no data	NY: New York	no data
CO: Denver	no data	OH: Cincinnati	no data
DC: Washington	no data	OH: Cleveland	no data
FL: Miami	no data	OH: Columbus	no data
FL: Orlando	no data	OR: Portland	no data
FL: Tampa	no data	PA: Philadelphia	no data
GA: Atlanta	no data	PA: Pittsburgh	no data
IL: Chicago	no data	TX: Dallas	no data
MA: Boston	no data	TX: Houston	no data
MD: Baltimore	no data	WA: Seattle	no data

FACTORS THAT MAY AFFECT EARNINGS

Educational Attainment of Workers and Effect on Earnings

	Percent at Level	Effect on Earnings
Less than High School	—	—
Some High School	—	—
High School or Equivalent	57.1%	−3.4%
Some College but No Degree	—	—
Associate Degree	—	—
Bachelor's Degree	—	—
Master's Degree	—	—
Doctoral Degree	—	—
First Professional Degree	—	—

Figures do not total 100% because some levels have a very small sample size.

Flexibility of Earnings

Average Hours Worked: 34
Workers with a Varying Number of Hours: 11.6%
Workers Earning Some Overtime Pay, Tips, or Commissions: 14.3%
Earnings Benefit of Working Overtime: −5.2%

Gender

	Male	Female
Percent	98.9%	1.1%
Effect on Earnings	4.5%	−25.5%

Union Membership

Percentage Union Members: 66.7%
Earnings Benefit of Union Membership: 1.8%

Veteran Status

Percentage Who Have Been on Active Duty: 26.0%
Earnings Benefit of Veteran Status: 17.3%

53-5000 Water Transportation Workers

53-5011 Sailors and Marine Oilers

Stand watch to look for obstructions in path of vessel; measure water depth; turn wheel on bridge; or use emergency equipment as directed by captain, mate, or pilot. Break out, rig, overhaul, and store cargo-handling gear, stationary rigging, and running gear. Perform a variety of maintenance tasks to preserve the painted surface of the ship and to maintain line and ship equipment. Must hold government-issued certification and tankerman certification when working aboard liquid-carrying vessels.

- Education or Training Required: Short-term on-the-job training
- Job Growth: 5.2%
- Annual Openings: 4,000
- Self-Employed: 0.0%
- Part-Time: 3.4%

NATIONAL WAGE FIGURES (ANNUAL)

Beginning	25th Percentile	Median	Mean	75th Percentile	90th Percentile
$19,220	$23,790	$30,630	$32,710	$39,830	$49,650

Median Wages for Industries Employing Largest Numbers (Annual)

Industry	Median Income
Accommodation	$41,400
Federal, State, and Local Government	$35,980
Food Manufacturing	$34,700
Professional, Scientific, and Technical Services	$32,420
Support Activities for Transportation	$30,980
Water Transportation	$30,350
Heavy and Civil Engineering Construction	$29,870
Administrative and Support Services	$29,620
Educational Services	$29,030
Mining (Except Oil and Gas)	$28,310

Median Wages for States (Annual)

AK	$39,240	KY	$31,250	NY	$33,920
AL	$26,170	LA	$28,900	OH	$32,600
AR	$24,550	MA	$33,120	OK	no data
AZ	no data	MD	$24,290	OR	$32,920
CA	$30,240	ME	$26,920	PA	$25,630
CO	no data	MI	$31,180	RI	$22,760
CT	no data	MN	$44,320	SC	$23,510
DC	no data	MO	$27,640	SD	no data
DE	no data	MS	$31,920	TN	$30,390
FL	$32,500	MT	no data	TX	$24,860
GA	$22,820	NC	$35,380	UT	no data
HI	$27,230	ND	no data	VA	$35,260
IA	$22,280	NE	no data	VT	no data
ID	no data	NH	no data	WA	$42,490
IL	$32,280	NJ	$27,930	WI	$25,980
IN	$28,500	NM	no data	WV	$22,300
KS	no data	NV	no data	WY	no data

Median Wages for the Largest Metropolitan Areas (Annual)

AZ: Phoenix	no data	MI: Detroit	$14,540
CA: Los Angeles	$28,800	MN: Minneapolis	no data
CA: Riverside	no data	MO: Kansas City	no data
CA: Sacramento	$34,540	MO: St. Louis	$28,210
CA: San Diego	$28,560	NV: Las Vegas	no data
CA: San Francisco	$33,300	NY: New York	$33,600
CO: Denver	no data	OH: Cincinnati	$22,850
DC: Washington	$27,810	OH: Cleveland	no data
FL: Miami	no data	OH: Columbus	no data
FL: Orlando	no data	OR: Portland	$42,770
FL: Tampa	$42,010	PA: Philadelphia	no data
GA: Atlanta	no data	PA: Pittsburgh	$32,440
IL: Chicago	$31,600	TX: Dallas	no data
MA: Boston	no data	TX: Houston	$24,190
MD: Baltimore	$25,300	WA: Seattle	$42,500

FACTORS THAT MAY AFFECT EARNINGS

Educational Attainment of Workers and Effect on Earnings

	Percent at Level	Effect on Earnings
Less than High School	—	—
Some High School	—	—
High School or Equivalent	26.1%	−1.0%
Some College but No Degree	34.8%	−25.0%
Associate Degree	—	—
Bachelor's Degree	—	—
Master's Degree	—	—
Doctoral Degree	—	—
First Professional Degree	—	—

Figures do not total 100% because some levels have a very small sample size.

Flexibility of Earnings

Average Hours Worked: 41

Workers with a Varying Number of Hours: 21.8%

Workers Earning Some Overtime Pay, Tips, or Commissions: 19.2%

Earnings Benefit of Working Overtime: −11.4%

Gender

	Male	Female
Percent	88.9%	11.1%
Effect on Earnings	4.5%	−25.5%

Union Membership

Percentage Union Members: 15.4%

Earnings Benefit of Union Membership: 49.3%

Veteran Status

Percentage Who Have Been on Active Duty: 18.3%

Earnings Benefit of Veteran Status: 38.8%

53-5021 Captains, Mates, and Pilots of Water Vessels

Command or supervise operations of ships and water vessels, such as tugboats and ferryboats, that travel into and out of harbors, estuaries, straits, and sounds and on rivers, lakes, bays, and oceans. Required to hold license issued by U.S. Coast Guard.

- Education or Training Required: Work experience in a related occupation
- Job Growth: 4.8%
- Annual Openings: 2,000
- Self-Employed: 5.4%
- Part-Time: 6.4%

NATIONAL WAGE FIGURES (ANNUAL)

Beginning	25th Percentile	Median	Mean	75th Percentile	90th Percentile
$29,360	$38,880	$53,430	$57,060	$69,570	$89,230

Median Wages for Industries Employing Largest Numbers (Annual)

Industry	Median Income
Motor Vehicle and Parts Dealers	$63,380
Food Manufacturing	$60,430
Support Activities for Transportation	$57,140
Water Transportation	$56,300
Museums, Historical Sites, and Similar Institutions	$55,340
Federal, State, and Local Government	$54,870
Rental and Leasing Services	$52,480
Support Activities for Mining	$51,670
Merchant Wholesalers, Nondurable Goods	$51,340
Real Estate	$50,510

Median Wages for States (Annual)

AK	$52,530	KY	$54,080	NY	$62,850
AL	$53,960	LA	$57,930	OH	$55,290
AR	$45,720	MA	$40,550	OK	$44,860
AZ	no data	MD	$38,630	OR	$62,850
CA	$49,390	ME	$43,620	PA	$55,330
CO	no data	MI	$51,950	RI	$39,220
CT	$57,700	MN	$53,810	SC	$41,960
DC	no data	MO	$59,600	SD	no data
DE	$38,960	MS	$56,220	TN	$44,560
FL	$52,240	MT	no data	TX	$55,500
GA	$51,080	NC	no data	UT	no data
HI	$38,440	ND	no data	VA	$57,770
IA	$54,060	NE	no data	VT	no data
ID	no data	NH	no data	WA	$61,370
IL	$45,920	NJ	$49,340	WI	$44,470
IN	no data	NM	no data	WV	$50,090
KS	no data	NV	no data	WY	no data

Median Wages for the Largest Metropolitan Areas (Annual)

AZ: Phoenix	no data	MI: Detroit	more than $145,600
CA: Los Angeles	$44,020	MN: Minneapolis	$45,640
CA: Riverside	no data	MO: Kansas City	no data
CA: Sacramento	no data	MO: St. Louis	$51,940
CA: San Diego	$39,560	NV: Las Vegas	no data
CA: San Francisco	$56,360	NY: New York	$60,910
CO: Denver	no data	OH: Cincinnati	$53,160
DC: Washington	$62,440	OH: Cleveland	no data
FL: Miami	$54,720	OH: Columbus	no data
FL: Orlando	no data	OR: Portland	$64,430
FL: Tampa	$56,470	PA: Philadelphia	$54,100
GA: Atlanta	no data	PA: Pittsburgh	$51,340
IL: Chicago	$48,120	TX: Dallas	no data
MA: Boston	$37,740	TX: Houston	$53,760
MD: Baltimore	$38,450	WA: Seattle	$61,640

FACTORS THAT MAY AFFECT EARNINGS

Educational Attainment of Workers and Effect on Earnings

Figures are based on a group of occupations: Water Transportation Workers

	Percent at Level	Effect on Earnings
Less than High School	—	—
Some High School	—	—
High School or Equivalent	39.7%	−7.8%
Some College but No Degree	23.3%	−3.2%
Associate Degree	—	—
Bachelor's Degree	15.1%	37.3%
Master's Degree	—	—
Doctoral Degree	—	—
First Professional Degree	—	—

Figures do not total 100% because some levels have a very small sample size.

Flexibility of Earnings

Average Hours Worked: 39
Workers with a Varying Number of Hours: 20.4%
Workers Earning Some Overtime Pay, Tips, or Commissions: 17.9%
Earnings Benefit of Working Overtime: −11.4%

Gender

	Male	Female
Percent	92.5%	7.5%
Effect on Earnings	4.5%	−25.5%

Union Membership

Percentage Union Members: 17.1%
Earnings Benefit of Union Membership: 49.3%

Veteran Status

Percentage Who Have Been on Active Duty: 18.3%
Earnings Benefit of Veteran Status: 38.8%

53-5022 Motorboat Operators

Operate small motor-driven boats to carry passengers and freight between ships or between ship and shore. May patrol harbors and beach areas. May assist in navigational activities.

- Education or Training Required: Moderate-term on-the-job training
- Job Growth: 4.4%
- Annual Openings: Fewer than 500
- Self-Employed: 7.0%
- Part-Time: 6.4%

NATIONAL WAGE FIGURES (ANNUAL)

Beginning	25th Percentile	Median	Mean	75th Percentile	90th Percentile
$17,270	$23,340	$32,350	$34,810	$45,850	$55,170

Median Wages for Industries Employing Largest Numbers (Annual)

Industry	Median Income
Federal, State, and Local Government	$47,030
Support Activities for Transportation	$36,230
Water Transportation	$35,920
Administrative and Support Services	$30,710
Amusement, Gambling, and Recreation Industries	$28,260
Scenic and Sightseeing Transportation	$25,790

Median Wages for States (Annual)

AK	no data	KY	no data	NY	$28,660
AL	no data	LA	$44,360	OH	$40,410
AR	no data	MA	no data	OK	no data
AZ	no data	MD	$42,410	OR	$41,580
CA	$46,270	ME	$34,870	PA	$29,200
CO	no data	MI	no data	RI	no data
CT	no data	MN	no data	SC	no data
DC	no data	MO	no data	SD	no data
DE	no data	MS	no data	TN	no data
FL	$25,790	MT	no data	TX	$15,530
GA	no data	NC	no data	UT	no data
HI	$25,090	ND	no data	VA	no data
IA	no data	NE	no data	VT	no data
ID	no data	NH	no data	WA	$41,340
IL	$25,840	NJ	$27,260	WI	$26,510
IN	no data	NM	no data	WV	no data
KS	no data	NV	no data	WY	no data

Median Wages for the Largest Metropolitan Areas (Annual)

AZ: Phoenix	no data	MI: Detroit	no data
CA: Los Angeles	no data	MN: Minneapolis	no data
CA: Riverside	no data	MO: Kansas City	no data
CA: Sacramento	$47,510	MO: St. Louis	no data
CA: San Diego	no data	NV: Las Vegas	no data
CA: San Francisco	$51,280	NY: New York	$27,470
CO: Denver	no data	OH: Cincinnati	no data
DC: Washington	no data	OH: Cleveland	no data
FL: Miami	$25,510	OH: Columbus	no data
FL: Orlando	$14,500	OR: Portland	$41,670
FL: Tampa	$29,420	PA: Philadelphia	no data
GA: Atlanta	no data	PA: Pittsburgh	no data
IL: Chicago	$24,030	TX: Dallas	no data
MA: Boston	no data	TX: Houston	no data
MD: Baltimore	no data	WA: Seattle	no data

FACTORS THAT MAY AFFECT EARNINGS

Educational Attainment of Workers and Effect on Earnings

Figures are based on a group of occupations: Water Transportation Workers

	Percent at Level	Effect on Earnings
Less than High School	—	—
Some High School	—	—
High School or Equivalent	39.7%	−7.8%
Some College but No Degree	23.3%	−3.2%
Associate Degree	—	—
Bachelor's Degree	15.1%	37.3%
Master's Degree	—	—
Doctoral Degree	—	—
First Professional Degree	—	—

Figures do not total 100% because some levels have a very small sample size.

Flexibility of Earnings

Average Hours Worked: 39
Workers with a Varying Number of Hours: 20.4%
Workers Earning Some Overtime Pay, Tips, or Commissions: 17.9%
Earnings Benefit of Working Overtime: −11.4%

Gender

	Male	Female
Percent	92.5%	7.5%
Effect on Earnings	4.5%	−25.5%

Union Membership

Percentage Union Members: 17.1%
Earnings Benefit of Union Membership: 49.3%

Veteran Status

Percentage Who Have Been on Active Duty: 18.3%
Earnings Benefit of Veteran Status: 38.8%

53-5031 Ship Engineers

Supervise and coordinate activities of crew engaged in operating and maintaining engines; boilers; deck machinery; and electrical, sanitary, and refrigeration equipment aboard ship.

- Education or Training Required: Postsecondary vocational training
- Job Growth: 12.7%
- Annual Openings: 1,000
- Self-Employed: 3.7%
- Part-Time: 6.4%

NATIONAL WAGE FIGURES (ANNUAL)

Beginning	25th Percentile	Median	Mean	75th Percentile	90th Percentile
$34,140	$41,190	$54,820	$59,340	$74,360	$92,860

Median Wages for Industries Employing Largest Numbers (Annual)

Industry	Median Income
Support Activities for Transportation	$57,870
Support Activities for Mining	$57,070
Water Transportation	$54,490
Federal, State, and Local Government	$53,330
Food Manufacturing	$51,570
Professional, Scientific, and Technical Services	$51,440
Rental and Leasing Services	$47,880
Amusement, Gambling, and Recreation Industries	$44,920
Scenic and Sightseeing Transportation	$39,330

Median Wages for States (Annual)

AK	$55,480	KY	$58,110	NY	$65,110
AL	$43,130	LA	$57,180	OH	$56,040
AR	no data	MA	$44,790	OK	no data
AZ	no data	MD	$59,550	OR	no data
CA	$53,200	ME	$35,440	PA	$53,420
CO	no data	MI	$54,660	RI	no data
CT	no data	MN	no data	SC	$49,400
DC	no data	MO	no data	SD	no data
DE	no data	MS	$39,030	TN	no data
FL	$58,910	MT	no data	TX	$52,970
GA	no data	NC	$35,510	UT	no data
HI	$39,860	ND	no data	VA	$55,000
IA	no data	NE	no data	VT	no data
ID	no data	NH	no data	WA	$62,830
IL	no data	NJ	$61,450	WI	no data
IN	$56,640	NM	no data	WV	$46,270
KS	no data	NV	no data	WY	no data

Median Wages for the Largest Metropolitan Areas (Annual)

AZ: Phoenix	no data	MI: Detroit	no data
CA: Los Angeles	$54,120	MN: Minneapolis	no data
CA: Riverside	no data	MO: Kansas City	no data
CA: Sacramento	no data	MO: St. Louis	no data
CA: San Diego	no data	NV: Las Vegas	no data
CA: San Francisco	no data	NY: New York	$62,700
CO: Denver	no data	OH: Cincinnati	$42,780
DC: Washington	$55,620	OH: Cleveland	no data
FL: Miami	no data	OH: Columbus	no data
FL: Orlando	no data	OR: Portland	no data
FL: Tampa	$61,230	PA: Philadelphia	no data
GA: Atlanta	no data	PA: Pittsburgh	$55,920
IL: Chicago	no data	TX: Dallas	no data
MA: Boston	no data	TX: Houston	no data
MD: Baltimore	no data	WA: Seattle	$62,490

FACTORS THAT MAY AFFECT EARNINGS

Educational Attainment of Workers and Effect on Earnings

Figures are based on a group of occupations: Water Transportation Workers

	Percent at Level	Effect on Earnings
Less than High School	—	—
Some High School	—	—
High School or Equivalent	39.7%	−7.8%
Some College but No Degree	23.3%	−3.2%
Associate Degree	—	—
Bachelor's Degree	15.1%	37.3%
Master's Degree	—	—
Doctoral Degree	—	—
First Professional Degree	—	—

Figures do not total 100% because some levels have a very small sample size.

Flexibility of Earnings

Average Hours Worked: 37
Workers with a Varying Number of Hours: 15.8%
Workers Earning Some Overtime Pay, Tips, or Commissions: 12.5%
Earnings Benefit of Working Overtime: −11.4%

Gender

	Male	Female
Percent	87.8%	12.2%
Effect on Earnings	4.5%	−25.5%

Union Membership

Percentage Union Members: 12.5%
Earnings Benefit of Union Membership: 49.3%

Veteran Status

Percentage Who Have Been on Active Duty: 18.3%
Earnings Benefit of Veteran Status: 38.8%

53-6000 Other Transportation Workers

53-6011 Bridge and Lock Tenders

Operate and tend bridges, canal locks, and lighthouses to permit marine passage on inland waterways, near shores, and at danger points in waterway passages. May supervise such operations. Includes drawbridge operators, lock tenders and operators, and slip bridge operators.

- Education or Training Required: Short-term on-the-job training
- Job Growth: 7.2%
- Annual Openings: Fewer than 500
- Self-Employed: 0.0%
- Part-Time: 40.4%

NATIONAL WAGE FIGURES (ANNUAL)

Beginning	25th Percentile	Median	Mean	75th Percentile	90th Percentile
$17,090	$25,060	$39,010	$35,930	$46,010	$50,360

Median Wages for Industries Employing Largest Numbers (Annual)

Industry	Median Income
Rail Transportation	$43,160
Federal, State, and Local Government	$40,340

Median Wages for States (Annual)

State		State		State	
AK	no data	KY	$44,970	NY	$36,680
AL	$44,550	LA	$26,300	OH	$44,350
AR	$42,450	MA	$31,700	OK	no data
AZ	no data	MD	$14,150	OR	no data
CA	$41,370	ME	no data	PA	$44,120
CO	no data	MI	$34,360	RI	no data
CT	no data	MN	$46,210	SC	no data
DC	no data	MO	$31,200	SD	no data
DE	no data	MS	$38,580	TN	$44,660
FL	$22,350	MT	no data	TX	$42,960
GA	no data	NC	$14,090	UT	no data
HI	no data	ND	no data	VA	no data
IA	$44,810	NE	no data	VT	no data
ID	no data	NH	no data	WA	$44,190
IL	$46,110	NJ	$40,520	WI	$40,020
IN	$42,430	NM	no data	WV	$45,050
KS	no data	NV	no data	WY	no data

Median Wages for the Largest Metropolitan Areas (Annual)

Area		Area	
AZ: Phoenix	no data	MI: Detroit	$18,030
CA: Los Angeles	no data	MN: Minneapolis	no data
CA: Riverside	no data	MO: Kansas City	no data
CA: Sacramento	no data	MO: St. Louis	$50,050
CA: San Diego	no data	NV: Las Vegas	no data
CA: San Francisco	no data	NY: New York	$36,930
CO: Denver	no data	OH: Cincinnati	no data
DC: Washington	no data	OH: Cleveland	no data
FL: Miami	no data	OH: Columbus	no data
FL: Orlando	no data	OR: Portland	no data
FL: Tampa	no data	PA: Philadelphia	$37,170
GA: Atlanta	no data	PA: Pittsburgh	$45,200
IL: Chicago	$45,550	TX: Dallas	no data
MA: Boston	$31,140	TX: Houston	no data
MD: Baltimore	no data	WA: Seattle	$44,720

FACTORS THAT MAY AFFECT EARNINGS

Educational Attainment of Workers and Effect on Earnings

Figures are based on a group of occupations: Other Transportation Workers

	Percent at Level	Effect on Earnings
Less than High School	—	—
Some High School	12.6%	−46.9%
High School or Equivalent	35.2%	10.7%
Some College but No Degree	25.7%	−10.7%
Associate Degree	9.5%	3.1%
Bachelor's Degree	12.3%	41.3%
Master's Degree	—	—
Doctoral Degree	—	—
First Professional Degree	—	—

Flexibility of Earnings

Average Hours Worked: 39
Workers with a Varying Number of Hours: 8.2%
Workers Earning Some Overtime Pay, Tips, or Commissions: 12.5%
Earnings Benefit of Working Overtime: 5.6%

Gender

	Male	Female
Percent	86.3%	13.7%
Effect on Earnings	4.5%	−25.5%

Union Membership

Percentage Union Members: 37.5%
Earnings Benefit of Union Membership: 46.3%

Veteran Status

Percentage Who Have Been on Active Duty: 17.4%
Earnings Benefit of Veteran Status: 56.5%

53-6021 Parking Lot Attendants

Park automobiles or issue tickets for customers in a parking lot or garage. May collect fee.

- Education or Training Required: Short-term on-the-job training
- Job Growth: –8.7%
- Annual Openings: 28,000
- Self-Employed: 0.0%
- Part-Time: 56.8%

NATIONAL WAGE FIGURES (ANNUAL)

Beginning	25th Percentile	Median	Mean	75th Percentile	90th Percentile
$13,540	$14,850	$17,320	$18,450	$20,960	$25,500

Median Wages for Industries Employing Largest Numbers (Annual)

Industry	Median Income
Repair and Maintenance	$21,030
Merchant Wholesalers, Durable Goods	$20,660
Hospitals	$20,430
Ambulatory Health Care Services	$20,380
Transit and Ground Passenger Transportation	$20,230
Religious, Grantmaking, Civic, Professional, and Similar Organizations	$20,210
Wholesale Electronic Markets and Agents and Brokers	$19,760
Real Estate	$19,630
Food and Beverage Stores	$19,520
Federal, State, and Local Government	$19,450

Median Wages for States (Annual)

State	Wage	State	Wage	State	Wage
AK	$21,380	KY	$17,530	NY	$17,500
AL	$15,830	LA	$14,870	OH	$16,690
AR	$16,770	MA	$20,370	OK	$16,420
AZ	$17,730	MD	$17,750	OR	$18,740
CA	$17,580	ME	$15,160	PA	$17,010
CO	$19,020	MI	$16,840	RI	$18,330
CT	$19,630	MN	$19,380	SC	$14,240
DC	$20,080	MO	$16,760	SD	$18,250
DE	$18,010	MS	$13,740	TN	$16,840
FL	$14,980	MT	$14,440	TX	$16,520
GA	$16,420	NC	$16,920	UT	$16,730
HI	$15,440	ND	$14,270	VA	$17,270
IA	$16,030	NE	$17,330	VT	$18,000
ID	$15,680	NH	$20,790	WA	$18,480
IL	$18,060	NJ	$18,130	WI	$18,730
IN	$18,210	NM	$16,750	WV	$14,630
KS	$15,980	NV	$17,390	WY	no data

Median Wages for the Largest Metropolitan Areas (Annual)

Area	Wage	Area	Wage
AZ: Phoenix	$17,780	MI: Detroit	$17,190
CA: Los Angeles	$16,880	MN: Minneapolis	$19,490
CA: Riverside	$17,080	MO: Kansas City	$16,470
CA: Sacramento	$17,190	MO: St. Louis	$16,730
CA: San Diego	no data	NV: Las Vegas	$18,260
CA: San Francisco	$21,710	NY: New York	$17,820
CO: Denver	$18,780	OH: Cincinnati	$15,960
DC: Washington	$19,300	OH: Cleveland	$14,910
FL: Miami	$15,100	OH: Columbus	$19,970
FL: Orlando	$14,550	OR: Portland	$18,980
FL: Tampa	$14,680	PA: Philadelphia	$17,290
GA: Atlanta	$17,270	PA: Pittsburgh	$16,440
IL: Chicago	$18,710	TX: Dallas	$16,910
MA: Boston	$20,430	TX: Houston	$16,190
MD: Baltimore	$17,360	WA: Seattle	$18,490

FACTORS THAT MAY AFFECT EARNINGS

Educational Attainment of Workers and Effect on Earnings

	Percent at Level	Effect on Earnings
Less than High School	—	—
Some High School	14.9%	–30.2%
High School or Equivalent	28.4%	9.5%
Some College but No Degree	29.7%	–12.0%
Associate Degree	—	—
Bachelor's Degree	12.2%	55.2%
Master's Degree	—	—
Doctoral Degree	—	—
First Professional Degree	—	—

Figures do not total 100% because some levels have a very small sample size.

Flexibility of Earnings

Average Hours Worked: 27

Workers with a Varying Number of Hours: 10.1%

Workers Earning Some Overtime Pay, Tips, or Commissions: 25.9%

Earnings Benefit of Working Overtime: 5.6%

Gender

	Male	Female
Percent	80.5%	19.5%
Effect on Earnings	4.5%	–25.5%

Union Membership

Percentage Union Members: 6.2%

Earnings Benefit of Union Membership: 46.3%

Veteran Status

Percentage Who Have Been on Active Duty: 17.4%

Earnings Benefit of Veteran Status: 56.5%

53-6031 Service Station Attendants

Service automobiles, buses, trucks, boats, and other automotive or marine vehicles with fuel, lubricants, and accessories. Collect payment for services and supplies. May lubricate vehicle; change motor oil; install antifreeze; or replace lights or other accessories, such as windshield wiper blades or fan belts. May repair or replace tires.

- Education or Training Required: Short-term on-the-job training
- Job Growth: 7.5%
- Annual Openings: 26,000
- Self-Employed: 0.3%
- Part-Time: 44.9%

NATIONAL WAGE FIGURES (ANNUAL)

Beginning	25th Percentile	Median	Mean	75th Percentile	90th Percentile
$13,700	$15,600	$17,750	$19,150	$21,600	$27,290

Median Wages for Industries Employing Largest Numbers (Annual)

Industry	Median Income
Federal, State, and Local Government	$32,830
Utilities	$28,660
General Merchandise Stores	$27,540
Educational Services	$25,250
Merchant Wholesalers, Durable Goods	$22,560
Rental and Leasing Services	$21,840
Transit and Ground Passenger Transportation	$21,310
Religious, Grantmaking, Civic, Professional, and Similar Organizations	$20,250
Motor Vehicle and Parts Dealers	$20,070
Management of Companies and Enterprises	$19,920

Median Wages for States (Annual)

State	Wage	State	Wage	State	Wage
AK	$21,120	KY	$17,720	NY	$17,160
AL	$16,820	LA	$15,670	OH	$16,500
AR	$17,750	MA	$19,260	OK	$16,730
AZ	$18,420	MD	$20,630	OR	$17,350
CA	$20,260	ME	$16,030	PA	$17,190
CO	$18,820	MI	$19,450	RI	$20,420
CT	$18,300	MN	$20,490	SC	$16,790
DC	no data	MO	$17,270	SD	$17,710
DE	$17,560	MS	$16,710	TN	$17,060
FL	$19,820	MT	$16,490	TX	$17,400
GA	$17,230	NC	$17,470	UT	$18,030
HI	$17,400	ND	$18,040	VA	$18,080
IA	$15,800	NE	$16,980	VT	$17,300
ID	$18,710	NH	$18,880	WA	$20,010
IL	$15,740	NJ	$16,500	WI	$18,740
IN	$16,590	NM	$17,910	WV	$14,020
KS	$18,280	NV	$17,990	WY	$17,160

Median Wages for the Largest Metropolitan Areas (Annual)

AZ: Phoenix	$18,200	MI: Detroit	$21,070
CA: Los Angeles	$21,080	MN: Minneapolis	$21,270
CA: Riverside	$19,710	MO: Kansas City	$19,220
CA: Sacramento	$21,320	MO: St. Louis	$17,990
CA: San Diego	$21,710	NV: Las Vegas	$17,450
CA: San Francisco	$19,450	NY: New York	$16,440
CO: Denver	$18,250	OH: Cincinnati	$20,890
DC: Washington	$19,080	OH: Cleveland	$15,790
FL: Miami	$18,420	OH: Columbus	$17,220
FL: Orlando	$22,840	OR: Portland	$17,580
FL: Tampa	$21,610	PA: Philadelphia	$17,910
GA: Atlanta	$18,260	PA: Pittsburgh	$17,580
IL: Chicago	$16,490	TX: Dallas	$17,990
MA: Boston	$19,320	TX: Houston	$18,050
MD: Baltimore	$23,950	WA: Seattle	$20,620

FACTORS THAT MAY AFFECT EARNINGS

Educational Attainment of Workers and Effect on Earnings

	Percent at Level	Effect on Earnings
Less than High School	—	—
Some High School	17.9%	−31.0%
High School or Equivalent	41.1%	23.2%
Some College but No Degree	24.1%	−25.5%
Associate Degree	6.3%	−2.6%
Bachelor's Degree	6.3%	53.7%
Master's Degree	—	—
Doctoral Degree	—	—
First Professional Degree	—	—

Flexibility of Earnings

Average Hours Worked: 30
Workers with a Varying Number of Hours: 8.6%
Workers Earning Some Overtime Pay, Tips, or Commissions: 9.4%
Earnings Benefit of Working Overtime: 19.5%

Gender

	Male	Female
Percent	90.2%	9.8%
Effect on Earnings	1.9%	—

Union Membership

Percentage Union Members: 5.8%
Earnings Benefit of Union Membership: 46.3%

Veteran Status

Percentage Who Have Been on Active Duty: 17.4%
Earnings Benefit of Veteran Status: 56.5%

53-6041 Traffic Technicians

Conduct field studies to determine traffic volume, speed, effectiveness of signals, adequacy of lighting, and other factors influencing traffic conditions under direction of traffic engineer.

- Education or Training Required: Short-term on-the-job training
- Job Growth: 14.1%
- Annual Openings: 1,000
- Self-Employed: 0.0%
- Part-Time: 40.4%

NATIONAL WAGE FIGURES (ANNUAL)

Beginning	25th Percentile	Median	Mean	75th Percentile	90th Percentile
$23,490	$27,620	$37,140	$38,840	$48,560	$57,250

Median Wages for Industries Employing Largest Numbers (Annual)

Industry	Median Income
Federal, State, and Local Government	$38,180
Professional, Scientific, and Technical Services	$25,950

Median Wages for States (Annual)

AK	no data	KY	no data	NY	no data
AL	$33,610	LA	$24,090	OH	$44,450
AR	$38,660	MA	$43,960	OK	$30,470
AZ	$58,330	MD	$42,830	OR	$48,780
CA	no data	ME	no data	PA	$43,850
CO	$44,650	MI	$43,080	RI	no data
CT	$47,520	MN	no data	SC	no data
DC	no data	MO	$34,400	SD	no data
DE	no data	MS	no data	TN	$29,430
FL	$31,870	MT	no data	TX	$33,040
GA	$29,130	NC	$32,750	UT	$34,550
HI	no data	ND	no data	VA	$39,790
IA	no data	NE	no data	VT	no data
ID	$27,940	NH	no data	WA	$43,930
IL	$43,760	NJ	$42,190	WI	no data
IN	no data	NM	$31,170	WV	no data
KS	$43,660	NV	no data	WY	no data

Median Wages for the Largest Metropolitan Areas (Annual)

AZ: Phoenix	no data	MI: Detroit	no data
CA: Los Angeles	no data	MN: Minneapolis	no data
CA: Riverside	$24,670	MO: Kansas City	$37,950
CA: Sacramento	$28,410	MO: St. Louis	no data
CA: San Diego	no data	NV: Las Vegas	no data
CA: San Francisco	$56,400	NY: New York	no data
CO: Denver	no data	OH: Cincinnati	no data
DC: Washington	$47,860	OH: Cleveland	no data
FL: Miami	no data	OH: Columbus	no data
FL: Orlando	$33,090	OR: Portland	$48,760
FL: Tampa	$30,190	PA: Philadelphia	no data
GA: Atlanta	$29,140	PA: Pittsburgh	no data
IL: Chicago	no data	TX: Dallas	$38,290
MA: Boston	$44,080	TX: Houston	$35,740
MD: Baltimore	$37,530	WA: Seattle	no data

FACTORS THAT MAY AFFECT EARNINGS

Educational Attainment of Workers and Effect on Earnings

Figures are based on a group of occupations: Other Transportation Workers

	Percent at Level	Effect on Earnings
Less than High School	—	—
Some High School	12.6%	−46.9%
High School or Equivalent	35.2%	10.7%
Some College but No Degree	25.7%	−10.7%
Associate Degree	9.5%	3.1%
Bachelor's Degree	12.3%	41.3%
Master's Degree	—	—
Doctoral Degree	—	—
First Professional Degree	—	—

Flexibility of Earnings

Average Hours Worked: 32
Workers with a Varying Number of Hours: 8.2%
Workers Earning Some Overtime Pay, Tips, or Commissions: 17.8%
Earnings Benefit of Working Overtime: 5.6%

Gender

	Male	Female
Percent	86.3%	13.7%
Effect on Earnings	4.5%	−25.5%

Union Membership

Percentage Union Members: 17.4%
Earnings Benefit of Union Membership: 46.3%

Veteran Status

Percentage Who Have Been on Active Duty: 17.4%
Earnings Benefit of Veteran Status: 56.5%

53-6051 Transportation Inspectors

Inspect equipment or goods in connection with the safe transport of cargo or people. Includes rail transport inspectors, such as freight inspectors, car inspectors, rail inspectors, and other nonprecision inspectors of other types of transportation vehicles.

- Education or Training Required: Work experience in a related occupation
- Job Growth: 11.4%
- Annual Openings: 2,000
- Self-Employed: 1.9%
- Part-Time: 5.3%

NATIONAL WAGE FIGURES (ANNUAL)

Beginning	25th Percentile	Median	Mean	75th Percentile	90th Percentile
$25,550	$37,520	$50,390	$55,370	$71,210	$95,310

Median Wages for Industries Employing Largest Numbers (Annual)

Industry	Median Income
Air Transportation	$67,170
Federal, State, and Local Government	$55,690
Transportation Equipment Manufacturing	$55,360
Educational Services	$49,820
Rail Transportation	$47,930
Support Activities for Transportation	$42,480
Transit and Ground Passenger Transportation	$42,230
Warehousing and Storage	$41,580
Professional, Scientific, and Technical Services	$40,610
Rental and Leasing Services	$38,920

Median Wages for States (Annual)

State	Wage	State	Wage	State	Wage
AK	$73,050	KY	$47,380	NY	no data
AL	$39,690	LA	$40,490	OH	$43,880
AR	no data	MA	$34,920	OK	$42,520
AZ	$61,270	MD	$40,950	OR	$39,270
CA	$63,190	ME	$65,800	PA	$52,300
CO	no data	MI	$47,830	RI	no data
CT	$60,310	MN	$66,330	SC	$64,020
DC	$104,220	MO	$41,910	SD	$32,970
DE	$42,570	MS	$44,820	TN	$56,430
FL	$67,610	MT	$43,020	TX	$42,780
GA	$54,420	NC	$49,670	UT	$43,130
HI	$48,860	ND	$56,530	VA	$39,030
IA	$46,510	NE	$49,730	VT	$46,110
ID	$47,500	NH	no data	WA	$59,440
IL	$44,920	NJ	$60,960	WI	$43,240
IN	$50,940	NM	$40,520	WV	$76,090
KS	$44,570	NV	$47,130	WY	$43,330

Median Wages for the Largest Metropolitan Areas (Annual)

Area	Wage	Area	Wage
AZ: Phoenix	$68,580	MI: Detroit	$49,010
CA: Los Angeles	$57,120	MN: Minneapolis	$83,860
CA: Riverside	$74,770	MO: Kansas City	$34,330
CA: Sacramento	$66,500	MO: St. Louis	$40,140
CA: San Diego	$85,740	NV: Las Vegas	$43,240
CA: San Francisco	no data	NY: New York	no data
CO: Denver	$84,990	OH: Cincinnati	$37,750
DC: Washington	$75,600	OH: Cleveland	$49,610
FL: Miami	$86,680	OH: Columbus	$53,340
FL: Orlando	$84,410	OR: Portland	$52,430
FL: Tampa	$21,710	PA: Philadelphia	$45,970
GA: Atlanta	$76,660	PA: Pittsburgh	$46,850
IL: Chicago	$53,780	TX: Dallas	$40,050
MA: Boston	$46,600	TX: Houston	$45,440
MD: Baltimore	$35,160	WA: Seattle	$63,120

FACTORS THAT MAY AFFECT EARNINGS

Educational Attainment of Workers and Effect on Earnings

	Percent at Level	Effect on Earnings
Less than High School	—	—
Some High School	—	—
High School or Equivalent	27.0%	5.8%
Some College but No Degree	28.6%	−7.5%
Associate Degree	12.7%	5.4%
Bachelor's Degree	22.2%	5.0%
Master's Degree	—	—
Doctoral Degree	—	—
First Professional Degree	—	—

Figures do not total 100% because some levels have a very small sample size.

Flexibility of Earnings

Average Hours Worked: 37
Workers with a Varying Number of Hours: 6.9%
Workers Earning Some Overtime Pay, Tips, or Commissions: 22.1%
Earnings Benefit of Working Overtime: 5.6%

Gender

	Male	Female
Percent	80.8%	19.2%
Effect on Earnings	4.5%	−25.5%

Union Membership

Percentage Union Members: 42.6%
Earnings Benefit of Union Membership: −0.5%

Veteran Status

Percentage Who Have Been on Active Duty: 17.4%
Earnings Benefit of Veteran Status: 56.5%

© JIST Works

53-6099 Transportation Workers, All Other

All transportation workers not listed separately.

- Education or Training Required: Short-term on-the-job training
- Job Growth: 13.9%
- Annual Openings: 4,000
- Self-Employed: 0.0%
- Part-Time: 33.3%

NATIONAL WAGE FIGURES (ANNUAL)

Beginning	25th Percentile	Median	Mean	75th Percentile	90th Percentile
$17,070	$21,230	$30,180	$32,350	$42,040	$49,590

Median Wages for Industries Employing Largest Numbers (Annual)

Industry	Median Income
Air Transportation	$40,070
Management of Companies and Enterprises	$37,830
Water Transportation	$37,430
Rail Transportation	$37,070
Federal, State, and Local Government	$35,080
Couriers and Messengers	$34,430
Professional, Scientific, and Technical Services	$34,220
Truck Transportation	$32,530
Merchant Wholesalers, Nondurable Goods	$28,640
Scenic and Sightseeing Transportation	$27,390

Median Wages for States (Annual)

State	Wage	State	Wage	State	Wage
AK	no data	KY	$21,630	NY	$35,850
AL	$26,070	LA	$32,630	OH	$36,470
AR	$22,340	MA	$41,440	OK	$28,590
AZ	no data	MD	$27,380	OR	$24,140
CA	$38,480	ME	$14,050	PA	$36,560
CO	no data	MI	$28,510	RI	$34,450
CT	$26,010	MN	$29,800	SC	$17,930
DC	$27,230	MO	$28,470	SD	no data
DE	no data	MS	$21,550	TN	$27,870
FL	$26,020	MT	no data	TX	$26,420
GA	no data	NC	$29,390	UT	no data
HI	$32,110	ND	$22,290	VA	no data
IA	$18,010	NE	$24,090	VT	no data
ID	no data	NH	$19,220	WA	$37,110
IL	no data	NJ	$32,620	WI	$15,220
IN	no data	NM	$22,890	WV	$20,540
KS	$21,190	NV	$22,970	WY	$22,080

Median Wages for the Largest Metropolitan Areas (Annual)

Area	Wage	Area	Wage
AZ: Phoenix	$22,070	MI: Detroit	$33,080
CA: Los Angeles	$38,680	MN: Minneapolis	$30,880
CA: Riverside	$18,780	MO: Kansas City	no data
CA: Sacramento	$55,030	MO: St. Louis	$30,660
CA: San Diego	$40,730	NV: Las Vegas	$23,150
CA: San Francisco	no data	NY: New York	$36,250
CO: Denver	no data	OH: Cincinnati	no data
DC: Washington	no data	OH: Cleveland	$41,780
FL: Miami	$25,160	OH: Columbus	no data
FL: Orlando	$37,780	OR: Portland	$32,180
FL: Tampa	$21,090	PA: Philadelphia	$38,870
GA: Atlanta	no data	PA: Pittsburgh	$33,670
IL: Chicago	no data	TX: Dallas	$24,930
MA: Boston	no data	TX: Houston	$31,200
MD: Baltimore	$28,230	WA: Seattle	$24,520

FACTORS THAT MAY AFFECT EARNINGS

Educational Attainment of Workers and Effect on Earnings

	Percent at Level	Effect on Earnings
Less than High School	—	—
Some High School	—	—
High School or Equivalent	58.3%	5.8%
Some College but No Degree	—	—
Associate Degree	—	—
Bachelor's Degree	—	—
Master's Degree	—	—
Doctoral Degree	—	—
First Professional Degree	—	—

Figures do not total 100% because some levels have a very small sample size.

Flexibility of Earnings

Average Hours Worked: 38
Workers with a Varying Number of Hours: 5.5%
Workers Earning Some Overtime Pay, Tips, or Commissions: 28.0%
Earnings Benefit of Working Overtime: 5.6%

Gender

	Male	Female
Percent	99.1%	0.9%
Effect on Earnings	4.5%	−25.5%

Union Membership

Percentage Union Members: 44.0%
Earnings Benefit of Union Membership: −7.0%

Veteran Status

Percentage Who Have Been on Active Duty: 17.4%
Earnings Benefit of Veteran Status: 56.5%

53-7000 Material Moving Workers

53-7011 Conveyor Operators and Tenders

Control or tend conveyors or conveyor systems that move materials or products to and from stockpiles, processing stations, departments, or vehicles. May control speed and routing of materials or products.

- Education or Training Required: Short-term on-the-job training
- Job Growth: 7.7%
- Annual Openings: 3,000
- Self-Employed: 0.0%
- Part-Time: 29.5%

NATIONAL WAGE FIGURES (ANNUAL)

Beginning	25th Percentile	Median	Mean	75th Percentile	90th Percentile
$17,170	$21,490	$27,220	$27,970	$33,460	$40,030

Median Wages for Industries Employing Largest Numbers (Annual)

Industry	Median Income
Mining (Except Oil and Gas)	$35,060
Paper Manufacturing	$32,350
Primary Metal Manufacturing	$32,030
Waste Management and Remediation Services	$29,530
Nonmetallic Mineral Product Manufacturing	$29,370
Plastics and Rubber Products Manufacturing	$29,250
Couriers and Messengers	$28,940
Chemical Manufacturing	$28,190
Petroleum and Coal Products Manufacturing	$28,020
Warehousing and Storage	$27,880

Median Wages for States (Annual)

State	Wage	State	Wage	State	Wage
AK	no data	KY	$27,960	NY	$27,520
AL	$23,250	LA	$22,730	OH	$31,710
AR	$23,880	MA	$30,180	OK	$21,580
AZ	$25,630	MD	$27,790	OR	$28,850
CA	$30,340	ME	$27,860	PA	$28,340
CO	$24,080	MI	$26,920	RI	no data
CT	$24,050	MN	$27,970	SC	no data
DC	no data	MO	$27,380	SD	$23,270
DE	$31,220	MS	$22,210	TN	no data
FL	$26,450	MT	$29,720	TX	$23,400
GA	$26,070	NC	$23,130	UT	$25,150
HI	$32,030	ND	$25,360	VA	$26,000
IA	$23,820	NE	$23,710	VT	no data
ID	$24,920	NH	$27,830	WA	$27,380
IL	$26,700	NJ	$32,280	WI	$30,610
IN	$27,400	NM	$27,750	WV	$40,820
KS	$28,350	NV	$27,270	WY	$50,050

Median Wages for the Largest Metropolitan Areas (Annual)

Area	Wage	Area	Wage
AZ: Phoenix	$24,380	MI: Detroit	$28,510
CA: Los Angeles	$29,600	MN: Minneapolis	$28,190
CA: Riverside	$30,970	MO: Kansas City	$31,920
CA: Sacramento	$31,680	MO: St. Louis	$26,950
CA: San Diego	$29,830	NV: Las Vegas	no data
CA: San Francisco	$29,220	NY: New York	$31,510
CO: Denver	$24,500	OH: Cincinnati	$31,500
DC: Washington	$29,270	OH: Cleveland	$29,170
FL: Miami	$24,030	OH: Columbus	$28,500
FL: Orlando	$27,490	OR: Portland	$27,960
FL: Tampa	$26,050	PA: Philadelphia	$28,630
GA: Atlanta	$27,090	PA: Pittsburgh	$36,380
IL: Chicago	$28,000	TX: Dallas	$26,870
MA: Boston	$28,440	TX: Houston	$26,980
MD: Baltimore	$27,150	WA: Seattle	$27,510

FACTORS THAT MAY AFFECT EARNINGS

Educational Attainment of Workers and Effect on Earnings

Figures are based on a group of occupations: Material Moving Workers

	Percent at Level	Effect on Earnings
Less than High School	8.5%	−26.1%
Some High School	19.4%	−27.0%
High School or Equivalent	39.6%	11.1%
Some College but No Degree	19.0%	6.9%
Associate Degree	6.5%	8.9%
Bachelor's Degree	6.2%	17.4%
Master's Degree	0.7%	10.7%
Doctoral Degree	—	—
First Professional Degree	—	—

Flexibility of Earnings

Average Hours Worked: 38
Workers with a Varying Number of Hours: 8.5%
Workers Earning Some Overtime Pay, Tips, or Commissions: 50.0%
Earnings Benefit of Working Overtime: 20.1%

Gender

	Male	Female
Percent	81.4%	18.6%
Effect on Earnings	4.5%	−25.5%

Union Membership

Percentage Union Members: 62.5%
Earnings Benefit of Union Membership: 35.7%

Veteran Status

Percentage Who Have Been on Active Duty: 8.8%
Earnings Benefit of Veteran Status: 22.1%

53-7021 Crane and Tower Operators

Operate mechanical boom and cable or tower and cable equipment to lift and move materials, machines, or products in many directions.

- Education or Training Required: Long-term on-the-job training
- Job Growth: 8.2%
- Annual Openings: 4,000
- Self-Employed: 0.0%
- Part-Time: 6.9%

NATIONAL WAGE FIGURES (ANNUAL)

Beginning	25th Percentile	Median	Mean	75th Percentile	90th Percentile
$24,240	$30,080	$39,040	$41,450	$50,890	$63,210

Median Wages for Industries Employing Largest Numbers (Annual)

Industry	Median Income
Support Activities for Transportation	$58,440
Utilities	$48,560
Paper Manufacturing	$46,640
Transportation Equipment Manufacturing	$45,240
Federal, State, and Local Government	$45,030
Water Transportation	$44,250
Specialty Trade Contractors	$44,180
Administrative and Support Services	$44,110
Rental and Leasing Services	$41,780
Rail Transportation	$41,640

Median Wages for States (Annual)

State	Wage	State	Wage	State	Wage
AK	no data	KY	$38,530	NY	$42,960
AL	$30,120	LA	$35,080	OH	$34,170
AR	$31,190	MA	$56,240	OK	$39,920
AZ	$39,470	MD	$47,060	OR	$36,350
CA	$57,950	ME	$37,320	PA	$36,610
CO	$44,560	MI	$49,410	RI	no data
CT	$62,180	MN	$46,850	SC	$41,420
DC	no data	MO	$44,440	SD	$34,590
DE	$38,770	MS	$31,740	TN	$35,840
FL	$39,790	MT	$47,090	TX	$32,170
GA	$41,350	NC	$37,420	UT	$46,830
HI	$62,480	ND	$43,390	VA	$40,190
IA	$40,250	NE	$34,760	VT	$33,800
ID	$33,350	NH	$48,820	WA	$57,110
IL	$51,210	NJ	$52,740	WI	$40,750
IN	$36,600	NM	$47,850	WV	$27,870
KS	$33,040	NV	$68,910	WY	$39,630

Median Wages for the Largest Metropolitan Areas (Annual)

Area	Wage	Area	Wage
AZ: Phoenix	$40,530	MI: Detroit	$47,030
CA: Los Angeles	no data	MN: Minneapolis	$48,830
CA: Riverside	$41,190	MO: Kansas City	$48,930
CA: Sacramento	$45,410	MO: St. Louis	$50,550
CA: San Diego	$60,740	NV: Las Vegas	$76,000
CA: San Francisco	$60,560	NY: New York	$55,160
CO: Denver	$51,390	OH: Cincinnati	$28,590
DC: Washington	$52,430	OH: Cleveland	$34,260
FL: Miami	$43,410	OH: Columbus	$35,440
FL: Orlando	$45,780	OR: Portland	$38,720
FL: Tampa	$36,580	PA: Philadelphia	$37,710
GA: Atlanta	$42,750	PA: Pittsburgh	$37,830
IL: Chicago	$38,550	TX: Dallas	$31,450
MA: Boston	$57,150	TX: Houston	$34,400
MD: Baltimore	$43,000	WA: Seattle	$56,930

FACTORS THAT MAY AFFECT EARNINGS

Educational Attainment of Workers and Effect on Earnings

	Percent at Level	Effect on Earnings
Less than High School	—	—
Some High School	11.1%	9.3%
High School or Equivalent	60.3%	0.3%
Some College but No Degree	19.0%	8.3%
Associate Degree	—	—
Bachelor's Degree	—	—
Master's Degree	—	—
Doctoral Degree	—	—
First Professional Degree	—	—

Figures do not total 100% because some levels have a very small sample size.

Flexibility of Earnings

Average Hours Worked: 38
Workers with a Varying Number of Hours: 9.5%
Workers Earning Some Overtime Pay, Tips, or Commissions: 37.3%
Earnings Benefit of Working Overtime: 20.1%

Gender

	Male	Female
Percent	98.5%	1.5%
Effect on Earnings	4.5%	−25.5%

Union Membership

Percentage Union Members: 37.3%
Earnings Benefit of Union Membership: 36.8%

Veteran Status

Percentage Who Have Been on Active Duty: 8.8%
Earnings Benefit of Veteran Status: 22.1%

53-7031 Dredge Operators

Operate dredge to remove sand, gravel, or other materials from lakes, rivers, or streams and to excavate and maintain navigable channels in waterways.

- Education or Training Required: Moderate-term on-the-job training
- Job Growth: 3.7%
- Annual Openings: Fewer than 500
- Self-Employed: 29.6%
- Part-Time: 29.5%

NATIONAL WAGE FIGURES (ANNUAL)

Beginning	25th Percentile	Median	Mean	75th Percentile	90th Percentile
$22,320	$27,630	$33,820	$37,050	$44,130	$57,930

Median Wages for Industries Employing Largest Numbers (Annual)

Industry	Median Income
Heavy and Civil Engineering Construction	$40,400
Federal, State, and Local Government	$40,120
Specialty Trade Contractors	$39,020
Nonmetallic Mineral Product Manufacturing	$32,990
Mining (Except Oil and Gas)	$31,500

Median Wages for States (Annual)

AK	no data	KY	no data	NY	no data
AL	$22,230	LA	$27,210	OH	$34,450
AR	no data	MA	no data	OK	no data
AZ	no data	MD	no data	OR	no data
CA	$55,660	ME	no data	PA	no data
CO	no data	MI	$39,900	RI	no data
CT	no data	MN	$53,950	SC	no data
DC	no data	MO	$37,890	SD	no data
DE	no data	MS	$25,240	TN	$28,730
FL	$30,910	MT	no data	TX	$38,760
GA	$40,140	NC	no data	UT	no data
HI	no data	ND	no data	VA	$41,010
IA	$32,500	NE	$26,830	VT	no data
ID	no data	NH	no data	WA	no data
IL	$34,440	NJ	$54,450	WI	no data
IN	$30,100	NM	no data	WV	no data
KS	$32,870	NV	no data	WY	no data

Median Wages for the Largest Metropolitan Areas (Annual)

AZ: Phoenix	no data	MI: Detroit	no data
CA: Los Angeles	no data	MN: Minneapolis	no data
CA: Riverside	no data	MO: Kansas City	no data
CA: Sacramento	no data	MO: St. Louis	no data
CA: San Diego	no data	NV: Las Vegas	no data
CA: San Francisco	no data	NY: New York	no data
CO: Denver	no data	OH: Cincinnati	$32,510
DC: Washington	no data	OH: Cleveland	no data
FL: Miami	no data	OH: Columbus	no data
FL: Orlando	$30,980	OR: Portland	no data
FL: Tampa	$30,830	PA: Philadelphia	no data
GA: Atlanta	no data	PA: Pittsburgh	no data
IL: Chicago	$33,430	TX: Dallas	no data
MA: Boston	no data	TX: Houston	$38,190
MD: Baltimore	no data	WA: Seattle	no data

FACTORS THAT MAY AFFECT EARNINGS

Educational Attainment of Workers and Effect on Earnings

Figures are based on a group of occupations: Material Moving Workers

	Percent at Level	Effect on Earnings
Less than High School	8.5%	−26.1%
Some High School	19.4%	−27.0%
High School or Equivalent	39.6%	11.1%
Some College but No Degree	19.0%	6.9%
Associate Degree	6.5%	8.9%
Bachelor's Degree	6.2%	17.4%
Master's Degree	0.7%	10.7%
Doctoral Degree	—	—
First Professional Degree	—	—

Flexibility of Earnings

Average Hours Worked: 31
Workers with a Varying Number of Hours: 8.5%
Workers Earning Some Overtime Pay, Tips, or Commissions: 18.7%
Earnings Benefit of Working Overtime: −2.9%

Gender

	Male	Female
Percent	98.5%	1.5%
Effect on Earnings	4.5%	−25.5%

Union Membership

Percentage Union Members: 17.7%
Earnings Benefit of Union Membership: 35.7%

Veteran Status

Percentage Who Have Been on Active Duty: 8.8%
Earnings Benefit of Veteran Status: 22.1%

53-7032 *Excavating and Loading Machine and Dragline Operators*

Operate or tend machinery equipped with scoops, shovels, or buckets to excavate and load loose materials.

- Education or Training Required: Moderate-term on-the-job training
- Job Growth: 8.0%
- Annual Openings: 11,000
- Self-Employed: 19.1%
- Part-Time: 29.5%

NATIONAL WAGE FIGURES (ANNUAL)

Beginning	25th Percentile	Median	Mean	75th Percentile	90th Percentile
$22,150	$26,690	$32,930	$35,740	$42,270	$54,460

Median Wages for Industries Employing Largest Numbers (Annual)

Industry	Median Income
Pipeline Transportation	$49,530
Chemical Manufacturing	$48,870
Rail Transportation	$38,540
Primary Metal Manufacturing	$37,260
Rental and Leasing Services	$36,900
Construction of Buildings	$36,710
Fabricated Metal Product Manufacturing	$35,880
Administrative and Support Services	$35,140
Petroleum and Coal Products Manufacturing	$33,730
Mining (Except Oil and Gas)	$33,310

Median Wages for States (Annual)

AK	no data	KY	$32,890	NY	$37,550
AL	$28,050	LA	$27,190	OH	$33,510
AR	$26,880	MA	$47,250	OK	$29,100
AZ	$37,050	MD	$36,550	OR	$32,750
CA	$52,050	ME	$31,790	PA	$29,870
CO	$37,300	MI	$41,620	RI	$43,580
CT	$42,650	MN	$45,340	SC	$28,570
DC	no data	MO	$41,770	SD	$31,100
DE	$35,970	MS	$25,580	TN	$27,850
FL	$28,220	MT	$33,260	TX	$27,280
GA	$31,320	NC	$28,400	UT	$34,080
HI	$44,780	ND	$37,300	VA	$31,400
IA	$29,670	NE	$29,440	VT	$31,410
ID	$34,810	NH	$35,100	WA	$48,410
IL	$50,540	NJ	$43,630	WI	$35,150
IN	$34,640	NM	$34,810	WV	$40,690
KS	$31,570	NV	$34,130	WY	$37,840

Median Wages for the Largest Metropolitan Areas (Annual)

AZ: Phoenix	$37,910	MI: Detroit	$48,470
CA: Los Angeles	$47,820	MN: Minneapolis	$52,370
CA: Riverside	$61,380	MO: Kansas City	$41,240
CA: Sacramento	$50,160	MO: St. Louis	$52,100
CA: San Diego	$33,300	NV: Las Vegas	$33,730
CA: San Francisco	no data	NY: New York	$43,540
CO: Denver	$41,270	OH: Cincinnati	$34,540
DC: Washington	$35,990	OH: Cleveland	$51,170
FL: Miami	$31,030	OH: Columbus	$34,770
FL: Orlando	$27,710	OR: Portland	$40,410
FL: Tampa	$27,180	PA: Philadelphia	$33,180
GA: Atlanta	$32,760	PA: Pittsburgh	$31,420
IL: Chicago	$53,570	TX: Dallas	$28,860
MA: Boston	$44,590	TX: Houston	$26,640
MD: Baltimore	$40,160	WA: Seattle	$49,910

FACTORS THAT MAY AFFECT EARNINGS

Educational Attainment of Workers and Effect on Earnings

Figures are based on a group of occupations: Material Moving Workers

	Percent at Level	Effect on Earnings
Less than High School	8.5%	−26.1%
Some High School	19.4%	−27.0%
High School or Equivalent	39.6%	11.1%
Some College but No Degree	19.0%	6.9%
Associate Degree	6.5%	8.9%
Bachelor's Degree	6.2%	17.4%
Master's Degree	0.7%	10.7%
Doctoral Degree	—	—
First Professional Degree	—	—

Flexibility of Earnings

Average Hours Worked: 31
Workers with a Varying Number of Hours: 8.5%
Workers Earning Some Overtime Pay, Tips, or Commissions: 18.7%
Earnings Benefit of Working Overtime: −2.9%

Gender

	Male	Female
Percent	98.5%	1.5%
Effect on Earnings	4.5%	−25.5%

Union Membership

Percentage Union Members: 17.7%
Earnings Benefit of Union Membership: 35.7%

Veteran Status

Percentage Who Have Been on Active Duty: 8.8%
Earnings Benefit of Veteran Status: 22.1%

53-7033 Loading Machine Operators, Underground Mining

Operate underground loading machine to load coal, ore, or rock into shuttle or mine car or onto conveyors. Loading equipment may include power shovels, hoisting engines equipped with cable-drawn scraper or scoop, or machines equipped with gathering arms and conveyor.

- Education or Training Required: Moderate-term on-the-job training
- Job Growth: −8.3%
- Annual Openings: Fewer than 500
- Self-Employed: 22.4%
- Part-Time: 29.5%

NATIONAL WAGE FIGURES (ANNUAL)

Beginning	25th Percentile	Median	Mean	75th Percentile	90th Percentile
$26,530	$31,770	$37,250	$40,290	$44,210	$54,930

Median Wages for Industries Employing Largest Numbers (Annual)

Industry	Median Income
Mining (Except Oil and Gas)	$37,610
Merchant Wholesalers, Durable Goods	$34,030
Nonmetallic Mineral Product Manufacturing	$33,470

Median Wages for States (Annual)

AK	no data	KY	$37,170	NY	$34,340
AL	no data	LA	no data	OH	no data
AR	no data	MA	no data	OK	$35,410
AZ	$33,170	MD	no data	OR	no data
CA	$35,870	ME	no data	PA	$38,390
CO	no data	MI	no data	RI	no data
CT	no data	MN	no data	SC..............	no data
DC	no data	MO	$28,600	SD	no data
DE	no data	MS	no data	TN	$30,590
FL	no data	MT	no data	TX	no data
GA	$33,270	NC	$32,890	UT	no data
HI	no data	ND	no data	VA	no data
IA	no data	NE	no data	VT	no data
ID	no data	NH	no data	WA	no data
IL	$36,030	NJ	no data	WI	no data
IN	no data	NM	no data	WV	$38,850
KS	no data	NV	no data	WY	no data

Median Wages for the Largest Metropolitan Areas (Annual)

AZ: Phoenix............	no data	MI: Detroit	no data
CA: Los Angeles	no data	MN: Minneapolis	no data
CA: Riverside	no data	MO: Kansas City........	no data
CA: Sacramento	no data	MO: St. Louis.............	no data
CA: San Diego	no data	NV: Las Vegas	no data
CA: San Francisco....	no data	NY: New York............	no data
CO: Denver	no data	OH: Cincinnati.........	no data
DC: Washington	no data	OH: Cleveland	no data
FL: Miami	no data	OH: Columbus	no data
FL: Orlando	no data	OR: Portland	no data
FL: Tampa	no data	PA: Philadelphia	no data
GA: Atlanta	$29,420	PA: Pittsburgh	$48,500
IL: Chicago	$37,860	TX: Dallas	no data
MA: Boston	no data	TX: Houston	no data
MD: Baltimore	no data	WA: Seattle	no data

FACTORS THAT MAY AFFECT EARNINGS

Educational Attainment of Workers and Effect on Earnings

Figures are based on a group of occupations: Material Moving Workers

	Percent at Level	Effect on Earnings
Less than High School	8.5%	−26.1%
Some High School	19.4%	−27.0%
High School or Equivalent	39.6%	11.1%
Some College but No Degree	19.0%	6.9%
Associate Degree	6.5%	8.9%
Bachelor's Degree	6.2%	17.4%
Master's Degree	0.7%	10.7%
Doctoral Degree	—	—
First Professional Degree	—	—

Flexibility of Earnings

Average Hours Worked: 31
Workers with a Varying Number of Hours: 8.5%
Workers Earning Some Overtime Pay, Tips, or Commissions: 18.7%
Earnings Benefit of Working Overtime: −2.9%

Gender

	Male	Female
Percent	98.5%	1.5%
Effect on Earnings	4.5%	−25.5%

Union Membership

Percentage Union Members: 17.7%
Earnings Benefit of Union Membership: 35.7%

Veteran Status

Percentage Who Have Been on Active Duty: 8.8%
Earnings Benefit of Veteran Status: 22.1%

53-7041 Hoist and Winch Operators

Operate or tend hoists or winches to lift and pull loads, using power-operated cable equipment.

- Education or Training Required: Moderate-term on-the-job training
- Job Growth: 7.0%
- Annual Openings: 1,000
- Self-Employed: 0.0%
- Part-Time: 29.5%

NATIONAL WAGE FIGURES (ANNUAL)

Beginning	25th Percentile	Median	Mean	75th Percentile	90th Percentile
$22,280	$26,470	$33,620	$36,530	$44,080	$59,640

Median Wages for Industries Employing Largest Numbers (Annual)

Industry	Median Income
Primary Metal Manufacturing	$48,840
Utilities	$45,760
Federal, State, and Local Government	$42,270
Mining (Except Oil and Gas)	$41,330
Support Activities for Transportation	$37,560
Forestry and Logging	$36,910
Support Activities for Mining	$36,190
Specialty Trade Contractors	$35,970
Transportation Equipment Manufacturing	$34,080
Heavy and Civil Engineering Construction	$29,410

Median Wages for States (Annual)

State		State		State	
AK	no data	KY	no data	NY	no data
AL	no data	LA	$25,630	OH	$50,400
AR	$30,750	MA	no data	OK	no data
AZ	no data	MD	$37,490	OR	$38,300
CA	$63,070	ME	no data	PA	$41,820
CO	$34,070	MI	$28,180	RI	no data
CT	no data	MN	no data	SC	no data
DC	no data	MO	no data	SD	no data
DE	no data	MS	$26,550	TN	no data
FL	$26,380	MT	no data	TX	$27,440
GA	$39,830	NC	no data	UT	no data
HI	no data	ND	no data	VA	$29,650
IA	no data	NE	no data	VT	no data
ID	no data	NH	no data	WA	$44,390
IL	$38,840	NJ	$45,870	WI	no data
IN	$41,990	NM	no data	WV	no data
KS	$25,900	NV	no data	WY	no data

Median Wages for the Largest Metropolitan Areas (Annual)

Area		Area	
AZ: Phoenix	no data	MI: Detroit	no data
CA: Los Angeles	$65,810	MN: Minneapolis	no data
CA: Riverside	no data	MO: Kansas City	no data
CA: Sacramento	no data	MO: St. Louis	no data
CA: San Diego	no data	NV: Las Vegas	no data
CA: San Francisco	no data	NY: New York	$35,280
CO: Denver	no data	OH: Cincinnati	no data
DC: Washington	no data	OH: Cleveland	no data
FL: Miami	no data	OH: Columbus	no data
FL: Orlando	no data	OR: Portland	$39,980
FL: Tampa	no data	PA: Philadelphia	no data
GA: Atlanta	$42,870	PA: Pittsburgh	no data
IL: Chicago	no data	TX: Dallas	no data
MA: Boston	no data	TX: Houston	$23,990
MD: Baltimore	no data	WA: Seattle	no data

FACTORS THAT MAY AFFECT EARNINGS

Educational Attainment of Workers and Effect on Earnings

Figures are based on a group of occupations: Material Moving Workers

	Percent at Level	Effect on Earnings
Less than High School	8.5%	−26.1%
Some High School	19.4%	−27.0%
High School or Equivalent	39.6%	11.1%
Some College but No Degree	19.0%	6.9%
Associate Degree	6.5%	8.9%
Bachelor's Degree	6.2%	17.4%
Master's Degree	0.7%	10.7%
Doctoral Degree	—	—
First Professional Degree	—	—

Flexibility of Earnings

Average Hours Worked: 29
Workers with a Varying Number of Hours: 25.7%
Workers Earning Some Overtime Pay, Tips, or Commissions: 37.5%
Earnings Benefit of Working Overtime: 20.1%

Gender

	Male	Female
Percent	98.5%	1.5%
Effect on Earnings	4.5%	−25.5%

Union Membership

Percentage Union Members: 12.5%
Earnings Benefit of Union Membership: 35.7%

Veteran Status

Percentage Who Have Been on Active Duty: 8.8%
Earnings Benefit of Veteran Status: 22.1%

53-7051 Industrial Truck and Tractor Operators

Operate industrial trucks or tractors equipped to move materials around a warehouse, storage yard, factory, construction site, or similar location.

- Education or Training Required: Short-term on-the-job training
- Job Growth: 7.9%
- Annual Openings: 114,000
- Self-Employed: 0.2%
- Part-Time: 8.2%

NATIONAL WAGE FIGURES (ANNUAL)

Beginning	25th Percentile	Median	Mean	75th Percentile	90th Percentile
$18,980	$22,320	$27,270	$29,090	$34,000	$42,900

Median Wages for Industries Employing Largest Numbers (Annual)

Industry	Median Income
Federal, State, and Local Government	$40,840
General Merchandise Stores	$39,150
Support Activities for Transportation	$35,450
Transportation Equipment Manufacturing	$33,330
Paper Manufacturing	$30,430
Truck Transportation	$30,130
Primary Metal Manufacturing	$29,870
Wholesale Electronic Markets and Agents and Brokers	$29,780
Beverage and Tobacco Product Manufacturing	$29,280
Chemical Manufacturing	$28,970

Median Wages for States (Annual)

AK	$33,890	KY	$26,900	NY	$29,460
AL	$24,680	LA	$25,180	OH	$28,040
AR	$24,590	MA	$30,500	OK	$24,250
AZ	$25,700	MD	$28,740	OR	$29,490
CA	$29,730	ME	$26,850	PA	$28,560
CO	$28,250	MI	$33,460	RI	$29,790
CT	$29,770	MN	$31,900	SC	$25,690
DC	$28,000	MO	$26,420	SD	$25,620
DE	$27,670	MS	$23,420	TN	$26,690
FL	$24,560	MT	$28,700	TX	$23,310
GA	$25,270	NC	$25,670	UT	$25,950
HI	$29,440	ND	$28,530	VA	$26,370
IA	$27,060	NE	$26,680	VT	$26,520
ID	$24,440	NH	$27,620	WA	$31,410
IL	$28,570	NJ	$30,070	WI	$29,390
IN	$28,170	NM	$23,780	WV	$24,990
KS	$26,640	NV	$27,640	WY	$30,330

Median Wages for the Largest Metropolitan Areas (Annual)

AZ: Phoenix	$25,670	MI: Detroit	$38,430
CA: Los Angeles	$30,790	MN: Minneapolis	$34,150
CA: Riverside	$27,230	MO: Kansas City	$28,110
CA: Sacramento	$28,600	MO: St. Louis	$28,690
CA: San Diego	$27,780	NV: Las Vegas	$27,910
CA: San Francisco	$34,790	NY: New York	$30,000
CO: Denver	$28,980	OH: Cincinnati	$28,600
DC: Washington	$29,010	OH: Cleveland	$29,600
FL: Miami	$24,630	OH: Columbus	$27,200
FL: Orlando	$25,020	OR: Portland	$30,890
FL: Tampa	$23,640	PA: Philadelphia	$30,400
GA: Atlanta	$25,740	PA: Pittsburgh	$28,200
IL: Chicago	$28,630	TX: Dallas	$24,570
MA: Boston	$30,550	TX: Houston	$24,250
MD: Baltimore	$29,940	WA: Seattle	$34,720

FACTORS THAT MAY AFFECT EARNINGS

Educational Attainment of Workers and Effect on Earnings

	Percent at Level	Effect on Earnings
Less than High School	8.5%	−20.1%
Some High School	14.9%	−7.2%
High School or Equivalent	48.5%	0.4%
Some College but No Degree	17.8%	13.4%
Associate Degree	5.9%	14.1%
Bachelor's Degree	3.2%	−17.3%
Master's Degree	—	—
Doctoral Degree	—	—
First Professional Degree	—	—

Flexibility of Earnings

Average Hours Worked: 36
Workers with a Varying Number of Hours: 5.5%
Workers Earning Some Overtime Pay, Tips, or Commissions: 26.2%
Earnings Benefit of Working Overtime: 8.5%

Gender

	Male	Female
Percent	92.8%	7.2%
Effect on Earnings	0.2%	—

Union Membership

Percentage Union Members: 20.8%
Earnings Benefit of Union Membership: 24.2%

Veteran Status

Percentage Who Have Been on Active Duty: 8.8%
Earnings Benefit of Veteran Status: 22.1%

53-7061 Cleaners of Vehicles and Equipment

Wash or otherwise clean vehicles, machinery, and other equipment. Use such materials as water, cleaning agents, brushes, cloths, and hoses.

- Education or Training Required: Short-term on-the-job training
- Job Growth: 8.3%
- Annual Openings: 111,000
- Self-Employed: 3.3%
- Part-Time: 30.4%

NATIONAL WAGE FIGURES (ANNUAL)

Beginning	25th Percentile	Median	Mean	75th Percentile	90th Percentile
$13,330	$15,210	$18,060	$20,130	$22,740	$29,820

Median Wages for Industries Employing Largest Numbers (Annual)

Industry	Median Income
Transportation Equipment Manufacturing	$50,210
Rail Transportation	$28,140
Air Transportation	$26,830
Couriers and Messengers	$25,910
Warehousing and Storage	$25,110
Waste Management and Remediation Services	$23,510
Food Manufacturing	$21,840
Textile Mills	$20,850
Wholesale Electronic Markets and Agents and Brokers	$20,680
Fabricated Metal Product Manufacturing	$20,590

Median Wages for States (Annual)

State	Wage	State	Wage	State	Wage
AK	$22,110	KY	$17,280	NY	$20,600
AL	$17,490	LA	$16,550	OH	$18,440
AR	$18,100	MA	$22,000	OK	$17,990
AZ	$16,820	MD	$19,140	OR	$18,990
CA	$17,710	ME	$20,070	PA	$17,870
CO	$19,170	MI	$20,030	RI	$21,400
CT	$21,420	MN	$20,860	SC	$16,970
DC	$18,330	MO	$17,790	SD	$16,180
DE	$18,140	MS	$17,590	TN	$17,030
FL	$17,830	MT	$15,520	TX	$16,970
GA	$17,530	NC	$17,200	UT	$17,370
HI	$18,810	ND	$16,050	VA	$18,820
IA	$17,800	NE	$18,850	VT	$22,810
ID	$17,730	NH	$23,020	WA	$19,520
IL	$17,550	NJ	$19,260	WI	$18,650
IN	$17,210	NM	$16,070	WV	$14,630
KS	$18,090	NV	$17,210	WY	$17,070

Median Wages for the Largest Metropolitan Areas (Annual)

Area	Wage	Area	Wage
AZ: Phoenix	$16,650	MI: Detroit	$22,920
CA: Los Angeles	$17,370	MN: Minneapolis	$21,650
CA: Riverside	$17,520	MO: Kansas City	$20,030
CA: Sacramento	$18,970	MO: St. Louis	$17,210
CA: San Diego	$17,390	NV: Las Vegas	$16,810
CA: San Francisco	$19,100	NY: New York	$21,820
CO: Denver	$20,390	OH: Cincinnati	$18,400
DC: Washington	$19,090	OH: Cleveland	$20,590
FL: Miami	$17,590	OH: Columbus	$19,360
FL: Orlando	$18,580	OR: Portland	$19,080
FL: Tampa	$17,420	PA: Philadelphia	$17,370
GA: Atlanta	$17,350	PA: Pittsburgh	$16,490
IL: Chicago	$17,650	TX: Dallas	$17,980
MA: Boston	$22,110	TX: Houston	$17,560
MD: Baltimore	$19,740	WA: Seattle	$20,020

FACTORS THAT MAY AFFECT EARNINGS

Educational Attainment of Workers and Effect on Earnings

	Percent at Level	Effect on Earnings
Less than High School	15.0%	−8.2%
Some High School	25.9%	−33.1%
High School or Equivalent	35.6%	22.3%
Some College but No Degree	16.9%	7.1%
Associate Degree	3.8%	13.7%
Bachelor's Degree	2.5%	7.7%
Master's Degree	—	—
Doctoral Degree	—	—
First Professional Degree	—	—

Flexibility of Earnings

Average Hours Worked: 29
Workers with a Varying Number of Hours: 9.0%
Workers Earning Some Overtime Pay, Tips, or Commissions: 11.5%
Earnings Benefit of Working Overtime: 7.8%

Gender

	Male	Female
Percent	85.0%	15.0%
Effect on Earnings	0.0%	—

Union Membership

Percentage Union Members: 8.4%
Earnings Benefit of Union Membership: 42.3%

Veteran Status

Percentage Who Have Been on Active Duty: 8.8%
Earnings Benefit of Veteran Status: 22.1%

53-7062 Laborers and Freight, Stock, and Material Movers, Hand

Manually move freight, stock, or other materials or perform other unskilled general labor. Includes all unskilled manual laborers not elsewhere classified.

- Education or Training Required: Short-term on-the-job training
- Job Growth: 10.2%
- Annual Openings: 671,000
- Self-Employed: 0.6%
- Part-Time: 39.4%

NATIONAL WAGE FIGURES (ANNUAL)

Beginning	25th Percentile	Median	Mean	75th Percentile	90th Percentile
$14,660	$17,090	$21,220	$23,050	$27,230	$34,780

Median Wages for Industries Employing Largest Numbers (Annual)

Industry	Median Income
Transportation Equipment Manufacturing	$28,480
Truck Transportation	$25,380
Warehousing and Storage	$24,560
Federal, State, and Local Government	$24,270
Couriers and Messengers	$23,810
Support Activities for Transportation	$23,370
Specialty Trade Contractors	$23,300
Plastics and Rubber Products Manufacturing	$22,850
Fabricated Metal Product Manufacturing	$22,540
Merchant Wholesalers, Durable Goods	$22,230

Median Wages for States (Annual)

AK	$28,800	KY	$21,330	NY	$22,060
AL	$19,450	LA	$19,210	OH	$21,810
AR	$18,470	MA	$24,700	OK	$19,190
AZ	$20,940	MD	$21,800	OR	$22,580
CA	$20,490	ME	$20,970	PA	$22,610
CO	$22,820	MI	$23,580	RI	$23,460
CT	$24,940	MN	$24,090	SC	$19,950
DC	$23,600	MO	$21,500	SD	$19,530
DE	$23,110	MS	$19,480	TN	$21,000
FL	$19,450	MT	$20,700	TX	$19,470
GA	$20,100	NC	$20,770	UT	$20,800
HI	$24,600	ND	$20,930	VA	$21,280
IA	$21,350	NE	$21,500	VT	$22,250
ID	$19,790	NH	$23,520	WA	$23,090
IL	$21,510	NJ	$22,390	WI	$23,420
IN	$22,310	NM	$17,800	WV	$18,110
KS	$21,120	NV	$22,570	WY	$21,730

Median Wages for the Largest Metropolitan Areas (Annual)

AZ: Phoenix	$21,470	MI: Detroit	$24,370
CA: Los Angeles	$19,360	MN: Minneapolis	$25,170
CA: Riverside	$19,610	MO: Kansas City	$23,510
CA: Sacramento	$22,640	MO: St. Louis	$23,030
CA: San Diego	$21,160	NV: Las Vegas	$22,700
CA: San Francisco	$24,830	NY: New York	$22,140
CO: Denver	$23,330	OH: Cincinnati	$21,990
DC: Washington	$23,100	OH: Cleveland	$20,110
FL: Miami	$19,130	OH: Columbus	$22,450
FL: Orlando	$19,080	OR: Portland	$23,470
FL: Tampa	$20,870	PA: Philadelphia	$23,840
GA: Atlanta	$20,940	PA: Pittsburgh	$21,920
IL: Chicago	$21,590	TX: Dallas	$20,840
MA: Boston	$25,370	TX: Houston	$19,880
MD: Baltimore	$21,770	WA: Seattle	$23,440

FACTORS THAT MAY AFFECT EARNINGS

Educational Attainment of Workers and Effect on Earnings

	Percent at Level	Effect on Earnings
Less than High School	5.9%	−28.0%
Some High School	19.9%	−38.8%
High School or Equivalent	40.7%	13.3%
Some College but No Degree	20.0%	3.1%
Associate Degree	6.0%	10.9%
Bachelor's Degree	6.7%	41.1%
Master's Degree	0.7%	−3.0%
Doctoral Degree	—	—
First Professional Degree	—	—

Flexibility of Earnings

Average Hours Worked: 29
Workers with a Varying Number of Hours: 9.2%
Workers Earning Some Overtime Pay, Tips, or Commissions: 15.1%
Earnings Benefit of Working Overtime: 20.2%

Gender

	Male	Female
Percent	83.1%	16.9%
Effect on Earnings	2.1%	−13.1%

Union Membership

Percentage Union Members: 17.5%
Earnings Benefit of Union Membership: 29.3%

Veteran Status

Percentage Who Have Been on Active Duty: 8.8%
Earnings Benefit of Veteran Status: 22.1%

53-7063 Machine Feeders and Offbearers

Feed materials into or remove materials from machines or equipment that is automatic or tended by other workers.

- Education or Training Required: Short-term on-the-job training
- Job Growth: –18.0%
- Annual Openings: 20,000
- Self-Employed: 0.0%
- Part-Time: 47.6%

NATIONAL WAGE FIGURES (ANNUAL)

Beginning	25th Percentile	Median	Mean	75th Percentile	90th Percentile
$15,670	$18,380	$22,640	$24,080	$28,370	$35,100

Median Wages for Industries Employing Largest Numbers (Annual)

Industry	Median Income
Electrical Equipment, Appliance, and Component Manufacturing	$28,960
Beverage and Tobacco Product Manufacturing	$28,630
Paper Manufacturing	$26,580
Primary Metal Manufacturing	$25,250
Nonmetallic Mineral Product Manufacturing	$25,070
Leather and Allied Product Manufacturing	$24,270
Printing and Related Support Activities	$24,040
Computer and Electronic Product Manufacturing	$23,690
Textile Product Mills	$23,390
Fabricated Metal Product Manufacturing	$23,080

Median Wages for States (Annual)

State	Wage	State	Wage	State	Wage
AK	no data	KY	$22,290	NY	$22,210
AL	$22,270	LA	$24,630	OH	$24,730
AR	$22,980	MA	$27,180	OK	$22,630
AZ	$18,880	MD	$25,060	OR	$23,910
CA	$19,380	ME	$24,760	PA	$25,410
CO	$19,880	MI	$25,500	RI	$21,990
CT	$22,180	MN	$27,820	SC	$23,910
DC	no data	MO	$24,330	SD	$20,450
DE	$38,410	MS	$23,110	TN	$20,520
FL	$21,740	MT	$31,060	TX	$22,570
GA	$22,570	NC	$22,120	UT	$19,430
HI	$24,810	ND	$24,710	VA	$20,250
IA	$25,660	NE	$24,350	VT	$21,200
ID	$24,180	NH	$23,380	WA	$24,390
IL	$23,590	NJ	$19,520	WI	$24,700
IN	$23,480	NM	$23,530	WV	$17,910
KS	$28,030	NV	$20,510	WY	$49,160

Median Wages for the Largest Metropolitan Areas (Annual)

Area	Wage	Area	Wage
AZ: Phoenix	$19,170	MI: Detroit	$25,910
CA: Los Angeles	$19,650	MN: Minneapolis	$28,440
CA: Riverside	$20,450	MO: Kansas City	$27,530
CA: Sacramento	$20,150	MO: St. Louis	$23,300
CA: San Diego	$18,790	NV: Las Vegas	$18,460
CA: San Francisco	$22,690	NY: New York	$19,730
CO: Denver	$20,450	OH: Cincinnati	$25,530
DC: Washington	$20,270	OH: Cleveland	$26,660
FL: Miami	$20,850	OH: Columbus	$27,040
FL: Orlando	$20,920	OR: Portland	$21,700
FL: Tampa	$20,640	PA: Philadelphia	$22,080
GA: Atlanta	$24,310	PA: Pittsburgh	$23,570
IL: Chicago	$23,300	TX: Dallas	$22,590
MA: Boston	$26,510	TX: Houston	$22,870
MD: Baltimore	$26,970	WA: Seattle	$25,720

FACTORS THAT MAY AFFECT EARNINGS

Educational Attainment of Workers and Effect on Earnings

	Percent at Level	Effect on Earnings
Less than High School	—	—
Some High School	16.1%	–18.1%
High School or Equivalent	57.1%	–0.9%
Some College but No Degree	12.5%	8.5%
Associate Degree	—	—
Bachelor's Degree	—	—
Master's Degree	—	—
Doctoral Degree	—	—
First Professional Degree	—	—

Figures do not total 100% because some levels have a very small sample size.

Flexibility of Earnings

Average Hours Worked: 31
Workers with a Varying Number of Hours: 9.0%
Workers Earning Some Overtime Pay, Tips, or Commissions: 25.0%
Earnings Benefit of Working Overtime: 20.1%

Gender

	Male	Female
Percent	45.4%	54.6%
Effect on Earnings	2.1%	–13.1%

Union Membership

Percentage Union Members: 20.0%
Earnings Benefit of Union Membership: 8.2%

Veteran Status

Percentage Who Have Been on Active Duty: 8.8%
Earnings Benefit of Veteran Status: 22.1%

53-7064 Packers and Packagers, Hand

Pack or package by hand a wide variety of products and materials.

- Education or Training Required: Short-term on-the-job training
- Job Growth: 10.1%
- Annual Openings: 194,000
- Self-Employed: 0.4%
- Part-Time: 32.0%

NATIONAL WAGE FIGURES (ANNUAL)

Beginning	25th Percentile	Median	Mean	75th Percentile	90th Percentile
$13,260	$14,930	$17,650	$19,340	$22,240	$28,330

Median Wages for Industries Employing Largest Numbers (Annual)

Industry	Median Income
Transportation Equipment Manufacturing	$24,080
Nonmetallic Mineral Product Manufacturing	$23,670
Machinery Manufacturing	$22,310
Furniture and Related Product Manufacturing	$21,910
Warehousing and Storage	$21,390
Fabricated Metal Product Manufacturing	$21,260
Computer and Electronic Product Manufacturing	$20,940
Paper Manufacturing	$20,940
Truck Transportation	$20,580
Merchant Wholesalers, Durable Goods	$20,550

Median Wages for States (Annual)

AK	$20,900	KY	$19,230	NY	$17,820
AL	$16,750	LA	$14,440	OH	$18,940
AR	$19,820	MA	$19,330	OK	$15,330
AZ	$14,510	MD	$19,750	OR	$17,570
CA	$17,180	ME	$17,190	PA	$19,600
CO	$16,720	MI	$17,850	RI	$18,760
CT	$19,500	MN	$20,330	SC	$16,880
DC	$17,830	MO	$17,770	SD	$17,970
DE	no data	MS	$17,440	TN	$18,630
FL	$16,050	MT	$14,410	TX	$15,660
GA	$17,040	NC	$17,720	UT	$14,970
HI	$16,700	ND	$15,820	VA	$17,630
IA	$17,110	NE	$18,460	VT	$20,230
ID	$14,490	NH	$18,260	WA	$18,300
IL	$18,100	NJ	$16,810	WI	$20,570
IN	$19,810	NM	$14,110	WV	$16,210
KS	$17,570	NV	$17,830	WY	$14,370

Median Wages for the Largest Metropolitan Areas (Annual)

AZ: Phoenix	$14,460	MI: Detroit	$18,340
CA: Los Angeles	$16,940	MN: Minneapolis	$21,580
CA: Riverside	$17,310	MO: Kansas City	$17,210
CA: Sacramento	$17,640	MO: St. Louis	$19,150
CA: San Diego	$17,230	NV: Las Vegas	$14,850
CA: San Francisco	$18,090	NY: New York	$16,850
CO: Denver	$16,550	OH: Cincinnati	$17,420
DC: Washington	$17,810	OH: Cleveland	$19,840
FL: Miami	$15,950	OH: Columbus	$17,960
FL: Orlando	$17,190	OR: Portland	$17,670
FL: Tampa	$16,380	PA: Philadelphia	$19,940
GA: Atlanta	$17,500	PA: Pittsburgh	$19,500
IL: Chicago	$17,910	TX: Dallas	$17,030
MA: Boston	$19,230	TX: Houston	$14,900
MD: Baltimore	$20,150	WA: Seattle	$18,230

FACTORS THAT MAY AFFECT EARNINGS

Educational Attainment of Workers and Effect on Earnings

	Percent at Level	Effect on Earnings
Less than High School	15.7%	−15.9%
Some High School	19.8%	−11.9%
High School or Equivalent	37.3%	6.8%
Some College but No Degree	14.4%	16.9%
Associate Degree	5.7%	12.4%
Bachelor's Degree	6.9%	−20.0%
Master's Degree	—	—
Doctoral Degree	—	—
First Professional Degree	—	—

Flexibility of Earnings

Average Hours Worked: 30
Workers with a Varying Number of Hours: 7.3%
Workers Earning Some Overtime Pay, Tips, or Commissions: 12.3%
Earnings Benefit of Working Overtime: 33.4%

Gender

	Male	Female
Percent	42.5%	57.5%
Effect on Earnings	4.5%	−25.5%

Union Membership

Percentage Union Members: 10.3%
Earnings Benefit of Union Membership: 26.9%

Veteran Status

Percentage Who Have Been on Active Duty: 8.8%
Earnings Benefit of Veteran Status: 22.1%

53-7071 Gas Compressor and Gas Pumping Station Operators

Operate steam, gas, electric motor, or internal combustion engine-driven compressors. Transmit, compress, or recover gases such as butane, nitrogen, hydrogen, and natural gas.

- Education or Training Required: Moderate-term on-the-job training
- Job Growth: –21.3%
- Annual Openings: 1,000
- Self-Employed: 7.8%
- Part-Time: 29.5%

NATIONAL WAGE FIGURES (ANNUAL)

Beginning	25th Percentile	Median	Mean	75th Percentile	90th Percentile
$27,760	$35,330	$45,400	$44,760	$54,120	$61,190

Median Wages for Industries Employing Largest Numbers (Annual)

Industry	Median Income
Pipeline Transportation	$49,560
Support Activities for Mining	$45,530
Utilities	$45,060
Management of Companies and Enterprises	$44,000
Oil and Gas Extraction	$37,190
Merchant Wholesalers, Nondurable Goods	$30,660
Nonstore Retailers	$28,020

Median Wages for States (Annual)

AK	no data	KY	no data	NY	no data
AL	$47,270	LA	$51,880	OH	$49,410
AR	$49,460	MA	no data	OK	$38,050
AZ	$47,990	MD	no data	OR	no data
CA	$49,440	ME	no data	PA	$46,850
CO	no data	MI	$37,190	RI	no data
CT	no data	MN	$31,280	SC	no data
DC	no data	MO	no data	SD	no data
DE	no data	MS	no data	TN	no data
FL	no data	MT	$44,330	TX	$41,420
GA	no data	NC	no data	UT	$53,590
HI	no data	ND	no data	VA	$34,940
IA	no data	NE	$51,540	VT	no data
ID	no data	NH	no data	WA	no data
IL	no data	NJ	no data	WI	no data
IN	no data	NM	$52,390	WV	$36,170
KS	$48,680	NV	no data	WY	$47,820

Median Wages for the Largest Metropolitan Areas (Annual)

AZ: Phoenix	no data	MI: Detroit	no data
CA: Los Angeles	no data	MN: Minneapolis	$30,740
CA: Riverside	no data	MO: Kansas City	no data
CA: Sacramento	no data	MO: St. Louis	no data
CA: San Diego	no data	NV: Las Vegas	no data
CA: San Francisco	no data	NY: New York	no data
CO: Denver	no data	OH: Cincinnati	$51,900
DC: Washington	$31,810	OH: Cleveland	no data
FL: Miami	no data	OH: Columbus	no data
FL: Orlando	no data	OR: Portland	no data
FL: Tampa	no data	PA: Philadelphia	no data
GA: Atlanta	no data	PA: Pittsburgh	no data
IL: Chicago	no data	TX: Dallas	no data
MA: Boston	no data	TX: Houston	$38,260
MD: Baltimore	no data	WA: Seattle	no data

FACTORS THAT MAY AFFECT EARNINGS

Educational Attainment of Workers and Effect on Earnings

Figures are based on a group of occupations: Material Moving Workers

	Percent at Level	Effect on Earnings
Less than High School	8.5%	–26.1%
Some High School	19.4%	–27.0%
High School or Equivalent	39.6%	11.1%
Some College but No Degree	19.0%	6.9%
Associate Degree	6.5%	8.9%
Bachelor's Degree	6.2%	17.4%
Master's Degree	0.7%	10.7%
Doctoral Degree	—	—
First Professional Degree	—	—

Flexibility of Earnings

Average Hours Worked: 31
Workers with a Varying Number of Hours: 8.5%
Workers Earning Some Overtime Pay, Tips, or Commissions: 18.7%
Earnings Benefit of Working Overtime: 20.1%

Gender

	Male	Female
Percent	81.4%	18.6%
Effect on Earnings	4.5%	–25.5%

Union Membership

Percentage Union Members: 17.7%
Earnings Benefit of Union Membership: 35.7%

Veteran Status

Percentage Who Have Been on Active Duty: 8.8%
Earnings Benefit of Veteran Status: 22.1%

53-7072 Pump Operators, Except Wellhead Pumpers

Tend, control, or operate power-driven, stationary, or portable pumps and manifold systems to transfer gases, oil, other liquids, slurries, or powdered materials to and from various vessels and processes.

- Education or Training Required: Moderate-term on-the-job training
- Job Growth: –22.2%
- Annual Openings: 2,000
- Self-Employed: 6.8%
- Part-Time: 29.5%

NATIONAL WAGE FIGURES (ANNUAL)

Beginning	25th Percentile	Median	Mean	75th Percentile	90th Percentile
$23,000	$30,510	$39,800	$40,670	$50,940	$59,880

Median Wages for Industries Employing Largest Numbers (Annual)

Industry	Median Income
Professional, Scientific, and Technical Services	$51,300
Warehousing and Storage	$48,170
Pipeline Transportation	$47,990
Machinery Manufacturing	$46,200
Petroleum and Coal Products Manufacturing	$45,830
Mining (Except Oil and Gas)	$45,250
Management of Companies and Enterprises	$44,940
Chemical Manufacturing	$42,320
Specialty Trade Contractors	$40,060
Federal, State, and Local Government	$38,620

Median Wages for States (Annual)

State	Wage	State	Wage	State	Wage
AK	$53,490	KY	$32,750	NY	$35,890
AL	$34,500	LA	$40,500	OH	$46,240
AR	$26,850	MA	$44,700	OK	$41,770
AZ	no data	MD	no data	OR	$42,550
CA	$45,020	ME	no data	PA	$42,630
CO	$32,370	MI	$43,510	RI	no data
CT	no data	MN	no data	SC	$36,880
DC	no data	MO	no data	SD	no data
DE	no data	MS	no data	TN	$32,690
FL	$28,980	MT	$36,390	TX	$43,320
GA	$33,580	NC	$40,550	UT	no data
HI	$47,520	ND	no data	VA	no data
IA	$27,490	NE	$19,990	VT	no data
ID	$29,270	NH	no data	WA	$41,150
IL	no data	NJ	$34,250	WI	no data
IN	$50,520	NM	$28,880	WV	no data
KS	no data	NV	no data	WY	$43,240

Median Wages for the Largest Metropolitan Areas (Annual)

Area	Wage	Area	Wage
AZ: Phoenix	no data	MI: Detroit	no data
CA: Los Angeles	$46,910	MN: Minneapolis	no data
CA: Riverside	no data	MO: Kansas City	no data
CA: Sacramento	no data	MO: St. Louis	no data
CA: San Diego	no data	NV: Las Vegas	no data
CA: San Francisco	$50,580	NY: New York	$34,510
CO: Denver	$39,980	OH: Cincinnati	no data
DC: Washington	no data	OH: Cleveland	no data
FL: Miami	$30,490	OH: Columbus	no data
FL: Orlando	no data	OR: Portland	no data
FL: Tampa	no data	PA: Philadelphia	$34,750
GA: Atlanta	no data	PA: Pittsburgh	no data
IL: Chicago	$46,840	TX: Dallas	no data
MA: Boston	$51,780	TX: Houston	$48,250
MD: Baltimore	no data	WA: Seattle	no data

FACTORS THAT MAY AFFECT EARNINGS

Educational Attainment of Workers and Effect on Earnings

Figures are based on a group of occupations: Material Moving Workers

	Percent at Level	Effect on Earnings
Less than High School	8.5%	–26.1%
Some High School	19.4%	–27.0%
High School or Equivalent	39.6%	11.1%
Some College but No Degree	19.0%	6.9%
Associate Degree	6.5%	8.9%
Bachelor's Degree	6.2%	17.4%
Master's Degree	0.7%	10.7%
Doctoral Degree	—	—
First Professional Degree	—	—

Flexibility of Earnings

Average Hours Worked: 31
Workers with a Varying Number of Hours: 8.5%
Workers Earning Some Overtime Pay, Tips, or Commissions: 18.7%
Earnings Benefit of Working Overtime: 20.1%

Gender

	Male	Female
Percent	81.4%	18.6%
Effect on Earnings	4.5%	–25.5%

Union Membership

Percentage Union Members: 17.7%
Earnings Benefit of Union Membership: 35.7%

Veteran Status

Percentage Who Have Been on Active Duty: 8.8%
Earnings Benefit of Veteran Status: 22.1%

53-7073 Wellhead Pumpers

Operate power pumps and auxiliary equipment to produce flow of oil or gas from wells in oil field.

- Education or Training Required: Moderate-term on-the-job training
- Job Growth: –23.6%
- Annual Openings: 2,000
- Self-Employed: 5.6%
- Part-Time: 29.5%

NATIONAL WAGE FIGURES (ANNUAL)

Beginning	25th Percentile	Median	Mean	75th Percentile	90th Percentile
$22,120	$27,980	$36,150	$36,760	$45,760	$53,950

Median Wages for Industries Employing Largest Numbers (Annual)

Industry	Median Income
Heavy and Civil Engineering Construction	$39,740
Oil and Gas Extraction	$39,470
Pipeline Transportation	$39,300
Support Activities for Mining	$32,150

Median Wages for States (Annual)

AK	no data	KY	$33,700	NY	$27,280
AL	$30,780	LA	no data	OH	$32,200
AR	$29,870	MA	no data	OK	$45,640
AZ	no data	MD	no data	OR	no data
CA	$47,610	ME	no data	PA	$28,390
CO	$38,040	MI	$29,910	RI	no data
CT	no data	MN	no data	SC	no data
DC	no data	MO	no data	SD	no data
DE	no data	MS	$38,440	TN	no data
FL	no data	MT	$36,840	TX	$36,550
GA	no data	NC	no data	UT	no data
HI	no data	ND	$35,380	VA	$30,510
IA	no data	NE	$29,300	VT	no data
ID	no data	NH	no data	WA	no data
IL	$32,020	NJ	no data	WI	no data
IN	no data	NM	$39,290	WV	$23,170
KS	$34,170	NV	no data	WY	$41,880

Median Wages for the Largest Metropolitan Areas (Annual)

AZ: Phoenix	no data	MI: Detroit	no data
CA: Los Angeles	$41,310	MN: Minneapolis	no data
CA: Riverside	no data	MO: Kansas City	$22,700
CA: Sacramento	no data	MO: St. Louis	no data
CA: San Diego	no data	NV: Las Vegas	no data
CA: San Francisco	no data	NY: New York	no data
CO: Denver	$42,200	OH: Cincinnati	no data
DC: Washington	no data	OH: Cleveland	no data
FL: Miami	no data	OH: Columbus	$33,720
FL: Orlando	no data	OR: Portland	no data
FL: Tampa	no data	PA: Philadelphia	no data
GA: Atlanta	no data	PA: Pittsburgh	$31,660
IL: Chicago	no data	TX: Dallas	no data
MA: Boston	no data	TX: Houston	$32,490
MD: Baltimore	no data	WA: Seattle	no data

FACTORS THAT MAY AFFECT EARNINGS

Educational Attainment of Workers and Effect on Earnings

Figures are based on a group of occupations: Material Moving Workers

	Percent at Level	Effect on Earnings
Less than High School	8.5%	–26.1%
Some High School	19.4%	–27.0%
High School or Equivalent	39.6%	11.1%
Some College but No Degree	19.0%	6.9%
Associate Degree	6.5%	8.9%
Bachelor's Degree	6.2%	17.4%
Master's Degree	0.7%	10.7%
Doctoral Degree	—	—
First Professional Degree	—	—

Flexibility of Earnings

Average Hours Worked: 31
Workers with a Varying Number of Hours: 8.5%
Workers Earning Some Overtime Pay, Tips, or Commissions: 18.7%
Earnings Benefit of Working Overtime: 20.1%

Gender

	Male	Female
Percent	81.4%	18.6%
Effect on Earnings	4.5%	–25.5%

Union Membership

Percentage Union Members: 17.7%
Earnings Benefit of Union Membership: 35.7%

Veteran Status

Percentage Who Have Been on Active Duty: 8.8%
Earnings Benefit of Veteran Status: 22.1%

53-7081 Refuse and Recyclable Material Collectors

Collect and dump refuse or recyclable materials from containers into truck. May drive truck.

- Education or Training Required: Short-term on-the-job training
- Job Growth: 8.9%
- Annual Openings: 31,000
- Self-Employed: 4.2%
- Part-Time: 36.0%

NATIONAL WAGE FIGURES (ANNUAL)

Beginning	25th Percentile	Median	Mean	75th Percentile	90th Percentile
$16,600	$21,550	$28,970	$31,110	$38,490	$50,790

Median Wages for Industries Employing Largest Numbers (Annual)

Industry	Median Income
Specialty Trade Contractors	$51,250
Postal Service	$45,350
Religious, Grantmaking, Civic, Professional, and Similar Organizations	$38,910
Truck Transportation	$36,590
Chemical Manufacturing	$32,360
Waste Management and Remediation Services	$29,680
Educational Services	$29,200
Warehousing and Storage	$28,720
Federal, State, and Local Government	$28,350
Wholesale Electronic Markets and Agents and Brokers	$26,560

Median Wages for States (Annual)

State	Wage	State	Wage	State	Wage
AK	$36,510	KY	$20,340	NY	no data
AL	$21,510	LA	$21,230	OH	$30,710
AR	$21,390	MA	$34,890	OK	$23,280
AZ	$33,090	MD	$27,970	OR	$35,280
CA	$36,050	ME	$22,020	PA	$26,820
CO	$29,370	MI	$32,730	RI	$35,720
CT	$30,350	MN	$32,270	SC	$20,120
DC	no data	MO	$25,050	SD	$22,290
DE	$32,460	MS	$21,590	TN	$20,940
FL	$25,200	MT	$28,790	TX	$24,330
GA	$22,570	NC	$21,960	UT	$26,730
HI	$33,720	ND	$24,920	VA	$23,950
IA	$25,640	NE	$22,550	VT	$25,130
ID	$25,600	NH	$27,190	WA	$38,250
IL	$41,780	NJ	$38,010	WI	$36,940
IN	$29,010	NM	$26,780	WV	$21,610
KS	$23,870	NV	no data	WY	$30,000

Median Wages for the Largest Metropolitan Areas (Annual)

Area	Wage	Area	Wage
AZ: Phoenix	$33,840	MI: Detroit	$31,460
CA: Los Angeles	$34,290	MN: Minneapolis	$35,590
CA: Riverside	$32,960	MO: Kansas City	no data
CA: Sacramento	$35,300	MO: St. Louis	$30,510
CA: San Diego	$34,750	NV: Las Vegas	no data
CA: San Francisco	$47,020	NY: New York	$45,230
CO: Denver	$29,740	OH: Cincinnati	$29,620
DC: Washington	$29,720	OH: Cleveland	$31,660
FL: Miami	$25,030	OH: Columbus	$32,040
FL: Orlando	$27,360	OR: Portland	$37,810
FL: Tampa	$27,140	PA: Philadelphia	$32,770
GA: Atlanta	$24,930	PA: Pittsburgh	$30,790
IL: Chicago	$44,390	TX: Dallas	$30,270
MA: Boston	$37,150	TX: Houston	$24,270
MD: Baltimore	$26,490	WA: Seattle	$41,960

FACTORS THAT MAY AFFECT EARNINGS

Educational Attainment of Workers and Effect on Earnings

	Percent at Level	Effect on Earnings
Less than High School	9.8%	−26.7%
Some High School	17.4%	−12.3%
High School or Equivalent	45.7%	11.0%
Some College but No Degree	19.6%	−8.1%
Associate Degree	—	—
Bachelor's Degree	—	—
Master's Degree	—	—
Doctoral Degree	—	—
First Professional Degree	—	—

Figures do not total 100% because some levels have a very small sample size.

Flexibility of Earnings

Average Hours Worked: 30
Workers with a Varying Number of Hours: 10.0%
Workers Earning Some Overtime Pay, Tips, or Commissions: 13.2%
Earnings Benefit of Working Overtime: 20.1%

Gender

	Male	Female
Percent	93.9%	6.1%
Effect on Earnings	2.5%	—

Union Membership

Percentage Union Members: 22.6%
Earnings Benefit of Union Membership: 56.8%

Veteran Status

Percentage Who Have Been on Active Duty: 8.8%
Earnings Benefit of Veteran Status: 22.1%

53-7111 Shuttle Car Operators

Operate diesel or electric-powered shuttle car in underground mine to transport materials from working face to mine cars or conveyor.

- Education or Training Required: Short-term on-the-job training
- Job Growth: –42.4%
- Annual Openings: Fewer than 500
- Self-Employed: 0.0%
- Part-Time: 29.5%

NATIONAL WAGE FIGURES (ANNUAL)

Beginning	25th Percentile	Median	Mean	75th Percentile	90th Percentile
$31,020	$34,510	$39,060	$39,350	$43,930	$48,320

Median Wages for Industries Employing Largest Numbers (Annual)

Industry	Median Income
Mining (Except Oil and Gas)	$39,370
Amusement, Gambling, and Recreation Industries	$37,790
Rental and Leasing Services	$27,970

Median Wages for States (Annual)

AK	no data	KY	$36,430	NY	no data
AL	$38,220	LA	no data	OH	$40,440
AR	no data	MA	no data	OK	no data
AZ	$30,700	MD	no data	OR	no data
CA	no data	ME	no data	PA	$43,230
CO	$49,580	MI	no data	RI	no data
CT	no data	MN	no data	SC	no data
DC	no data	MO	no data	SD	no data
DE	no data	MS	no data	TN	no data
FL	no data	MT	no data	TX	no data
GA	no data	NC	no data	UT	$42,220
HI	no data	ND	no data	VA	$33,330
IA	no data	NE	no data	VT	no data
ID	no data	NH	no data	WA	no data
IL	$39,870	NJ	no data	WI	no data
IN	no data	NM	no data	WV	$40,310
KS	no data	NV	no data	WY	$58,470

Median Wages for the Largest Metropolitan Areas (Annual)

AZ: Phoenix	no data	MI: Detroit	no data
CA: Los Angeles	no data	MN: Minneapolis	no data
CA: Riverside	no data	MO: Kansas City	no data
CA: Sacramento	no data	MO: St. Louis	no data
CA: San Diego	no data	NV: Las Vegas	no data
CA: San Francisco	no data	NY: New York	no data
CO: Denver	no data	OH: Cincinnati	no data
DC: Washington	no data	OH: Cleveland	no data
FL: Miami	no data	OH: Columbus	no data
FL: Orlando	no data	OR: Portland	no data
FL: Tampa	no data	PA: Philadelphia	no data
GA: Atlanta	no data	PA: Pittsburgh	no data
IL: Chicago	no data	TX: Dallas	no data
MA: Boston	no data	TX: Houston	no data
MD: Baltimore	no data	WA: Seattle	no data

FACTORS THAT MAY AFFECT EARNINGS

Educational Attainment of Workers and Effect on Earnings

Figures are based on a group of occupations: Material Moving Workers

	Percent at Level	Effect on Earnings
Less than High School	8.5%	–26.1%
Some High School	19.4%	–27.0%
High School or Equivalent	39.6%	11.1%
Some College but No Degree	19.0%	6.9%
Associate Degree	6.5%	8.9%
Bachelor's Degree	6.2%	17.4%
Master's Degree	0.7%	10.7%
Doctoral Degree	—	—
First Professional Degree	—	—

Flexibility of Earnings

Average Hours Worked: 35
Workers with a Varying Number of Hours: 5.3%
Workers Earning Some Overtime Pay, Tips, or Commissions: 40.0%
Earnings Benefit of Working Overtime: 20.1%

Gender

	Male	Female
Percent	81.4%	18.6%
Effect on Earnings	4.5%	–25.5%

Union Membership

Percentage Union Members: 40.0%
Earnings Benefit of Union Membership: 35.7%

Veteran Status

Percentage Who Have Been on Active Duty: 8.8%
Earnings Benefit of Veteran Status: 22.1%

53-7121 Tank Car, Truck, and Ship Loaders

Load and unload chemicals and bulk solids such as coal, sand, and grain into or from tank cars, trucks, or ships, using material moving equipment. May perform a variety of other tasks relating to shipment of products. May gauge or sample shipping tanks and test them for leaks.

- Education or Training Required: Moderate-term on-the-job training
- Job Growth: −11.0%
- Annual Openings: 2,000
- Self-Employed: 0.0%
- Part-Time: 29.5%

NATIONAL WAGE FIGURES (ANNUAL)

Beginning	25th Percentile	Median	Mean	75th Percentile	90th Percentile
$19,850	$25,050	$31,970	$34,200	$41,090	$53,330

Median Wages for Industries Employing Largest Numbers (Annual)

Industry	Median Income
Utilities	$46,270
Primary Metal Manufacturing	$40,960
Chemical Manufacturing	$36,850
Support Activities for Transportation	$35,110
Warehousing and Storage	$34,560
Pipeline Transportation	$34,500
Petroleum and Coal Products Manufacturing	$33,630
Water Transportation	$32,860
Mining (Except Oil and Gas)	$31,390
Merchant Wholesalers, Nondurable Goods	$29,740

Median Wages for States (Annual)

AK	no data	KY	$27,960	NY	no data
AL	$28,120	LA	$27,960	OH	$31,650
AR	$21,140	MA	$28,040	OK	$26,510
AZ	no data	MD	no data	OR	$39,740
CA	$33,440	ME	no data	PA	$28,860
CO	no data	MI	$24,350	RI	no data
CT	no data	MN	$32,650	SC	$29,870
DC	no data	MO	$28,140	SD	no data
DE	$48,550	MS	no data	TN	$26,950
FL	$30,870	MT	no data	TX	$32,630
GA	$31,460	NC	$32,470	UT	no data
HI	no data	ND	no data	VA	$41,160
IA	$28,270	NE	$19,930	VT	no data
ID	no data	NH	no data	WA	$44,920
IL	$33,580	NJ	$35,030	WI	$33,380
IN	$36,240	NM	$26,730	WV	$29,300
KS	no data	NV	$30,700	WY	no data

Median Wages for the Largest Metropolitan Areas (Annual)

AZ: Phoenix	no data	MI: Detroit	no data
CA: Los Angeles	$37,110	MN: Minneapolis	$49,640
CA: Riverside	$34,920	MO: Kansas City	no data
CA: Sacramento	no data	MO: St. Louis	$37,160
CA: San Diego	$31,240	NV: Las Vegas	$30,640
CA: San Francisco	$33,940	NY: New York	$42,230
CO: Denver	no data	OH: Cincinnati	$32,340
DC: Washington	no data	OH: Cleveland	$40,090
FL: Miami	no data	OH: Columbus	no data
FL: Orlando	$21,960	OR: Portland	$42,690
FL: Tampa	no data	PA: Philadelphia	$34,860
GA: Atlanta	no data	PA: Pittsburgh	$25,130
IL: Chicago	$34,220	TX: Dallas	$29,570
MA: Boston	no data	TX: Houston	$33,330
MD: Baltimore	no data	WA: Seattle	$40,800

FACTORS THAT MAY AFFECT EARNINGS

Educational Attainment of Workers and Effect on Earnings

Figures are based on a group of occupations: Material Moving Workers

	Percent at Level	Effect on Earnings
Less than High School	8.5%	−26.1%
Some High School	19.4%	−27.0%
High School or Equivalent	39.6%	11.1%
Some College but No Degree	19.0%	6.9%
Associate Degree	6.5%	8.9%
Bachelor's Degree	6.2%	17.4%
Master's Degree	0.7%	10.7%
Doctoral Degree	—	—
First Professional Degree	—	—

Flexibility of Earnings

Average Hours Worked: 35
Workers with a Varying Number of Hours: 12.9%
Workers Earning Some Overtime Pay, Tips, or Commissions: 37.5%
Earnings Benefit of Working Overtime: 20.1%

Gender

	Male	Female
Percent	81.4%	18.6%
Effect on Earnings	4.5%	−25.5%

Union Membership

Percentage Union Members: 17.7%
Earnings Benefit of Union Membership: 35.7%

Veteran Status

Percentage Who Have Been on Active Duty: 8.8%
Earnings Benefit of Veteran Status: 22.1%

53-7199 Material Moving Workers, All Other

All material moving workers not listed separately.

- Education or Training Required: Moderate-term on-the-job training
- Job Growth: –5.3%
- Annual Openings: 8,000
- Self-Employed: 0.0%
- Part-Time: 23.1%

NATIONAL WAGE FIGURES (ANNUAL)

Beginning	25th Percentile	Median	Mean	75th Percentile	90th Percentile
$16,920	$21,290	$30,270	$33,000	$42,450	$52,670

Median Wages for Industries Employing Largest Numbers (Annual)

Industry	Median Income
Utilities	$53,930
Couriers and Messengers	$35,130
Primary Metal Manufacturing	$33,270
Truck Transportation	$32,330
Federal, State, and Local Government	$31,640
Transportation Equipment Manufacturing	$30,920
Merchant Wholesalers, Durable Goods	$29,500
Waste Management and Remediation Services	$28,580
Warehousing and Storage	$27,990
Chemical Manufacturing	$27,530

Median Wages for States (Annual)

State	Wage	State	Wage	State	Wage
AK	$31,940	KY	$30,500	NY	$22,900
AL	$24,070	LA	$22,340	OH	$32,500
AR	$21,960	MA	no data	OK	$18,820
AZ	$32,650	MD	no data	OR	$31,210
CA	$33,550	ME	$22,050	PA	$28,260
CO	$21,720	MI	$35,610	RI	$27,910
CT	$18,370	MN	no data	SC	$23,600
DC	no data	MO	$35,780	SD	no data
DE	no data	MS	$23,820	TN	$28,500
FL	$34,510	MT	$33,550	TX	$34,270
GA	$30,860	NC	$18,780	UT	$37,770
HI	$45,370	ND	no data	VA	$33,680
IA	$32,390	NE	no data	VT	no data
ID	$21,400	NH	$18,830	WA	$25,360
IL	$25,800	NJ	$38,010	WI	$21,550
IN	$38,340	NM	$16,730	WV	$27,390
KS	$17,140	NV	$22,460	WY	$17,840

Median Wages for the Largest Metropolitan Areas (Annual)

Area	Wage	Area	Wage
AZ: Phoenix	$48,140	MI: Detroit	$36,490
CA: Los Angeles	$22,810	MN: Minneapolis	no data
CA: Riverside	$29,030	MO: Kansas City	no data
CA: Sacramento	$41,780	MO: St. Louis	no data
CA: San Diego	$27,740	NV: Las Vegas	$21,220
CA: San Francisco	$60,620	NY: New York	$27,540
CO: Denver	no data	OH: Cincinnati	$40,190
DC: Washington	$30,280	OH: Cleveland	$29,100
FL: Miami	no data	OH: Columbus	$33,800
FL: Orlando	no data	OR: Portland	$31,140
FL: Tampa	$29,960	PA: Philadelphia	no data
GA: Atlanta	$36,210	PA: Pittsburgh	$27,720
IL: Chicago	$26,660	TX: Dallas	$38,000
MA: Boston	$34,670	TX: Houston	$39,770
MD: Baltimore	no data	WA: Seattle	$27,550

FACTORS THAT MAY AFFECT EARNINGS

Educational Attainment of Workers and Effect on Earnings

	Percent at Level	Effect on Earnings
Less than High School	—	—
Some High School	14.1%	–6.7%
High School or Equivalent	51.6%	–10.2%
Some College but No Degree	15.6%	19.7%
Associate Degree	9.4%	34.0%
Bachelor's Degree	—	—
Master's Degree	—	—
Doctoral Degree	—	—
First Professional Degree	—	—

Figures do not total 100% because some levels have a very small sample size.

Flexibility of Earnings

Average Hours Worked: 33
Workers with a Varying Number of Hours: 11.7%
Workers Earning Some Overtime Pay, Tips, or Commissions: 25.4%
Earnings Benefit of Working Overtime: 20.1%

Gender

	Male	Female
Percent	88.1%	11.9%
Effect on Earnings	4.5%	–25.5%

Union Membership

Percentage Union Members: 26.9%
Earnings Benefit of Union Membership: 29.2%

Veteran Status

Percentage Who Have Been on Active Duty: 8.8%
Earnings Benefit of Veteran Status: 22.1%

PART IV

Frequently Asked Questions About Salary

Salary is a complicated subject with some legal implications. If you are planning to negotiate your salary with your current boss or with a possible employer, you may need answers to some of the questions in this section.

All of the answers that follow are derived from the United States Department of Labor and describe federal law. In some cases state laws may differ, so go to www.dol.gov/dol/location.htm and find the link to the appropriate state Web site to learn whether different laws apply in your state.

What Is the Minimum Wage, and Who Qualifies for It?

The federal minimum wage applies to businesses that engage in interstate commerce. It also applies to hospitals, businesses providing medical or nursing care for residents, schools and preschools, government agencies, and any other business with at least two employees and an annual dollar volume of sales or business done of at least $500,000. The employees it applies to are those called "nonexempt," which means they are the same workers who normally receive overtime pay when they work more than the normal number of hours per week. ("Exempt" workers tend to be in managerial or professional roles and are usually paid well above the minimum wage.)

In the summer of 2007, the federal minimum wage was raised to $5.85 per hour; it will increase to $6.55 in the summer of 2008 and $7.25 in the summer of 2009. Workers under age 20 can be paid at a lower rate until they have worked 90 consecutive days or reach age 20, at which time they must be paid the minimum wage. Lower wages also can be paid to full-time students working a limited work week and to high school students in vocational education programs.

Many states set a minimum wage for their workers, and this wage level applies when it is higher than the federal minimum wage. You can find your state's minimum wage at www.dol.gov/esa/minwage/america.htm.

Some employers avoid minimum-wage requirements and other labor laws by classifying some workers as independent contractors rather than as employees. If the job is one that normally is at or near the minimum wage, you should try to avoid this kind of work arrangement if possible because it limits your legal protections.

Part IV

If I Receive Some Income from Tips, Can My Employer Pay Me Less Than the Minimum Wage?

You are a tipped employee if you work in a job where you customarily and regularly receive more than $30 per month in tips. If that is your situation, your employer is required by federal law to pay at least $2.13 per hour in direct wages if that amount combined with the tips received at least equals the federal minimum wage. If the combination of the tips and the employer's direct wages do not equal the federal minimum hourly wage, your employer must make up the difference.

Many states, however, require higher direct wage amounts for tipped employees, so check your state's minimum wages for tipped employees at www.dol.gov/esa/programs/whd/state/tipped.htm.

What Is Overtime Pay?

Federal law requires that employees who work more than 40 hours per week be paid for those extra hours at 50 percent more than their normal hourly rate (also called time-and-a-half). Note that overtime is defined only by the number of hours in the work week, so weekend or evening work does not count as overtime work unless it makes the work week exceed 40 hours. Nevertheless, some employees have arrangements to be paid at the overtime rate for weekend, night, or holiday work hours.

Many employees are considered "exempt" from this overtime-pay requirement. Included are managerial and professional workers, many commissioned sales workers, auto mechanics, farmworkers, and some others. For a complete list, see www.dol.gov/elaws/esa/flsa/screen75.asp.

Does My Employer Have to Pay Me for Holidays?

The federal Fair Labor Standards Act does not require employers to pay you for time when you're not working. However, holiday pay is a very common fringe benefit. It also is required for some jobs that are being done under federal contracts.

What Can I Do If My Pay Is Lower Because of Discrimination?

The right of employees to be free from discrimination in their compensation is protected under several federal laws, including the following, enforced by the U.S. Equal Employment Opportunity Commission (EEOC): the Equal Pay Act of 1963, Title VII of the Civil Rights Act of 1964, the Age Discrimination in Employment Act of 1967, and Title I of the Americans with Disabilities Act of 1990.

The Equal Pay Act (EPA) requires that men and women be given equal pay for equal work in the same establishment. The jobs need not be identical, but they must be substantially equal. It is job content, not job titles, that determines whether jobs are substantially equal. Specifically, the jobs must require substantially equal skill, effort, and responsibility and must be performed under similar working conditions within the same establishment. Pay differentials are permitted when they are based on seniority, merit, quantity or quality of production, or a factor other than sex.

Title VII of the Civil Rights Act, the Age Discrimination in Employment Act (ADEA), and the Americans with Disabilities Act (ADA) prohibit compensation discrimination on the basis of race, color, religion, sex, national origin, age, or disability. Unlike the EPA, there is no requirement under Title VII, the ADEA, or the ADA that the claimant's job be substantially equal to that of a higher-paid person outside the claimant's protected class, nor do these statutes require the claimant to work in the same establishment as the higher-paid worker. Note that under some of these laws you have a limited amount of time in which to file a discrimination suit; for example, under Title VII you have 180 days after an incident of discrimination.

Many states and municipalities have enacted protections against discrimination based on sexual orientation, status as a parent, marital status, and political affiliation. For information, contact the EEOC District Office nearest you.

You can find your local EEOC District Office in the section of your phone book that lists government agencies or on the Web at www.eeoc.gov/offices.html.

Can My Pay Consist *Entirely* of Commissions (with No Base Pay)?

Yes. Many sales workers receive a combination of base pay and commissions. The base pay guarantees you a certain amount of income even during periods when sales are slow, and the commissions reward you when you are more productive. Employers are not required to offer commissions, but neither are they required to offer base pay when they do offer commissions.

For detailed explanation of the federal laws relating to commissions, see www.dol.gov/dol/topic/wages/commissions.htm.

What Is Merit Pay?

Merit pay, also known as pay-for-performance, is defined as a raise in pay based on a set of criteria determined by the employer. If it is available to you, usually your employer conducts a review meeting with you to discuss your work performance during a certain time period. These review

870 *Salary Facts Handbook* © JIST Works

meetings can be helpful because they can help you learn what you have been doing right and wrong on the job. Merit pay is a matter between your employer and you (or your representative) and is not covered by federal law.

Do I Qualify for Hazard Pay?

Hazard pay means additional pay for performing hazardous duty or work involving physical hardship. Work duty that causes extreme physical discomfort and distress that is not adequately alleviated by protective devices is deemed to impose a physical hardship. The federal Fair Labor Standards Act does not address the subject of hazard pay, except to require that it be included as part of a federal employee's regular rate of pay in computing the employee's overtime pay.

What Is Severance Pay?

Severance pay is often granted to employees upon termination of employment, but it is not required by federal law. It is usually based on the worker's length of employment and sometimes is accompanied by other benefits, such as medical coverage that continues for a limited time period. To accept severance pay, terminated employees often have to sign an agreement that they will make no additional claims against the employer.

If I Quit or Get Fired, Can My Employer Delay Giving Me My Final Paycheck?

Employers are not required by federal law to give former employees their final paycheck immediately. Some states, however, may require immediate payment. If the regular payday for your last pay period has passed and you have not been paid, contact your state department of labor.

Some of My Pay Is Being Garnished Because of a Debt I Owe. Can My Employer Fire Me for This?

Wage garnishment is a legal procedure in which a person's earnings are required by court order to be withheld by an employer for the payment of a debt such as child support. Title III of the Consumer Credit Protection Act protects employees from being discharged by their employers because their wages have been garnished for any *one* debt and limits the amount of employees' earnings that may be garnished in any one week. It does not, however, protect an employee from discharge if the employee's earnings have been subject to garnishment for a second or subsequent debts.

APPENDIX A

Resources for Further Exploration

The facts and pointers in this book provide a good introduction to salary and occupations. If you want additional details, we suggest you consult some of the resources listed here. All of the books are published by JIST and are available at www.jist.com.

Salary Information at the State and Regional Levels

You can get information about state and regional salaries at the CareerOneStop. Go to www.careeronestop .org/, click Salary + Benefits, and then click Compare Metro Wages. Choose an occupation and up to 10 metropolitan areas to compare.

Another way to access this information is to go to the Web site of your state's workforce agency. For links to these sites, see www.bls.gov/bls/ofolist.htm.

Facts (Other Than Salaries) About Careers

Occupational Outlook Handbook (or the *OOH*): Updated every two years by the U.S. Department of Labor, this book provides descriptions for almost 270 major jobs covering more than 85 percent of the workforce. For a quick-reading version of the *OOH*, consult the *EZ Occupational Outlook Handbook* from JIST.

Enhanced Occupational Outlook Handbook: Includes all descriptions in the *OOH* plus descriptions of more than 6,300 more-specialized jobs related to them.

O*NET Dictionary of Occupational Titles: The only printed source of the more than 900 jobs described in the U.S. Department of Labor's Occupational Information Network database. (The O*NET taxonomy of jobs has more jobs than the 800 used in this book because it takes some jobs to a finer level of detail.) It offers more information topics than we were able to fit here.

New Guide for Occupational Exploration: An important career reference that allows you to explore all major O*NET jobs based on your interests. The 16 Interest Areas in the book are based on the career clusters developed by the U.S. Department of Education.

Career Decision Making and Planning

Overnight Career Choice, by Michael Farr: This book can help you choose a career goal based on a variety of criteria, including skills, interests, and values. It is part of the *Help in a Hurry* series, so it is designed to produce quick results.

50 Best Jobs for Your Personality, by Michael Farr and Laurence Shatkin, Ph.D.: Built around the six Holland personality types, this book includes an assessment to help you identify your dominant and secondary personality types, plus lists and descriptions of high-paying and high-growth jobs linked to those personality types. Other books in the *Best Jobs* series are targeted to help college graduates, people without four-year degrees, baby boomers, transitioning military service members, introverts, apprentices, and others.

Today's Hot Job Targets, by Michael Farr and Laurence Shatkin, Ph.D.: Quickly identify the 100 careers with fast hiring, sizzling growth, and security through 2014. This brief book features an express checklist for matching yourself to the hottest jobs, plus job snapshots with the number of openings, pay, and education needed.

Job Hunting

Same-Day Resume, by Michael Farr: Learn how to write an effective resume in an hour. This book includes dozens of sample resumes from professional writers and even offers advice on cover letters, online resumes, and more.

The Ultimate Job Search, by Richard Beatty: Million-selling career author and consultant Richard H. Beatty shares the inside scoop on self-assessment and job objectives, powerful resumes and cover letters, working with search firms and employment agencies, want ads, the Internet, direct-mail job search campaigns, networking, interviewing, negotiating job offers, and succeeding on the new job.

Job Banks by Occupation. This is a set of links offered by America's Career InfoNet. At www.acinet.org, find the Career Tools box. Click Career Resource Library and then click Job & Resume Banks. The Job Banks by Occupation link leads you to groups of jobs such as "Healthcare Practitioners and Technical Occupations" and "Legal Occupations," which in turn lead you to more-specific job titles and occupation-specific job-listing sites maintained by various organizations.

APPENDIX B

Salary Adjustment Percentages for All Metropolitan Areas

Metropolitan areas are listed alphabetically by primary state and, within the state, by area name. Use the percentage figure to adjust national averages upward or downward to match salary trends in the metro area where you live—or the metro area closest to you.

Here's the formula to plug into your pocket calculator: [national average] **+** [percentage figure] **%**. (Don't forget to press the minus key if the percentage is negative.)

Note that these percentages are based on trends for *all* occupations. For a *specific* occupation, the actual percentage difference from the national average for that occupation may be somewhat different.

Metro Area	Percentage Figure for Adjusting National Averages	Metro Area	Percentage Figure for Adjusting National Averages
Anchorage, AK	21.8%	Fort Smith, AR–OK	−18.3%
Anchorage, AK	21.8%	Hot Springs, AR	−26.2%
Fairbanks, AK	23.3%	Jonesboro, AR	−23.8%
Anniston–Oxford, AL	−15.0%	Little Rock–North Little Rock, AR	−11.4%
Auburn–Opelika, AL	−22.4%	Pine Bluff, AR	−14.0%
Birmingham–Hoover, AL	−6.2%	Flagstaff, AZ	−15.2%
Decatur, AL	−15.4%	Prescott, AZ	−13.8%
Dothan, AL	−21.3%	Tucson, AZ	−6.4%
Florence–Muscle Shoals, AL	−25.3%	Yuma, AZ	−25.3%
Gadsden, AL	−22.8%	Bakersfield, CA	−8.2%
Huntsville, AL	2.0%	Chico, CA	−7.6%
Mobile, AL	−15.3%	El Centro, CA	−18.0%
Montgomery, AL	−13.7%	Fresno, CA	−7.1%
Tuscaloosa, AL	−14.6%	Hanford–Corcoran, CA	−2.3%
Fayetteville–Springdale–Rogers, AR–MO	−12.7%	Madera, CA	−11.6%

(continued)

Appendix B

(continued)

Metro Area	Percentage Figure for Adjusting National Averages
Merced, CA	−10.3%
Modesto, CA	−2.8%
Napa, CA	14.4%
Oxnard–Thousand Oaks–Ventura, CA	7.2%
Redding, CA	−3.1%
Salinas, CA	−7.2%
San Jose–Sunnyvale–Santa Clara, CA	54.3%
San Luis Obispo–Paso Robles, CA	−2.4%
Santa Barbara–Santa Maria, CA	3.6%
Santa Cruz–Watsonville, CA	11.3%
Santa Rosa–Petaluma, CA	16.2%
Stockton, CA	1.0%
Vallejo–Fairfield, CA	11.6%
Visalia–Porterville, CA	−20.1%
Yuba City, CA	−5.0%
Boulder, CO	23.9%
Colorado Springs, CO	1.7%
Fort Collins–Loveland, CO	1.6%
Grand Junction, CO	−8.5%
Greeley, CO	−3.1%
Pueblo, CO	−11.2%
Bridgeport–Stamford–Norwalk, CT	30.0%
Danbury, CT	15.9%
Hartford–West Hartford–East Hartford, CT	27.4%
New Haven, CT	19.5%
Norwich–New London, CT–RI	5.8%
Waterbury, CT	5.9%
Dover, DE	−5.2%
Cape Coral–Fort Myers, FL	−9.0%
Deltona–Daytona Beach–Ormond Beach, FL	−16.7%
Fort Walton Beach–Crestview–Destin, FL	−15.2%
Gainesville, FL	−8.3%
Jacksonville, FL	−4.9%
Lakeland, FL	−11.8%
Naples–Marco Island, FL	−7.1%
Ocala, FL	−16.6%
Palm Bay–Melbourne–Titusville, FL	−4.9%
Panama City–Lynn Haven, FL	−15.3%
Pensacola–Ferry Pass–Brent, FL	−12.9%
Port St. Lucie–Fort Pierce, FL	−11.2%
Punta Gorda, FL	−14.8%
Sarasota–Bradenton–Venice, FL	−10.7%
Sebastian–Vero Beach, FL	−9.8%
Tallahassee, FL	−4.0%
Albany, GA	−16.7%
Athens–Clarke County, GA	−12.5%
Augusta–Richmond County, GA–SC	−12.2%
Brunswick, GA	−16.3%
Columbus, GA–AL	−17.4%
Dalton, GA	−11.6%
Gainesville, GA	−9.2%
Hinesville–Fort Stewart, GA	−13.1%
Macon, GA	−11.3%
Rome, GA	−13.4%
Savannah, GA	−8.9%
Valdosta, GA	−23.9%
Warner Robins, GA	5.6%
Honolulu, HI	4.6%
Ames, IA	−0.6%
Cedar Rapids, IA	−1.4%
Davenport–Moline–Rock Island, IA–IL	−8.9%
Des Moines–West Des Moines, IA	4.1%
Dubuque, IA	−14.0%
Iowa City, IA	−2.9%
Sioux City, IA–NE–SD	−14.5%
Waterloo–Cedar Falls, IA	−12.5%
Boise City–Nampa, ID	−3.4%
Coeur d'Alene, ID	−10.4%
Idaho Falls, ID	−14.6%
Lewiston, ID–WA	−4.6%
Pocatello, ID	−13.9%
Bloomington–Normal, IL	−0.3%
Champaign–Urbana, IL	−9.3%
Danville, IL	−9.0%
Decatur, IL	−8.0%
Kankakee–Bradley, IL	−10.1%
Peoria, IL	−6.1%
Rockford, IL	−2.5%
Springfield, IL	3.0%
Anderson, IN	−14.1%
Bloomington, IN	−14.0%
Columbus, IN	−5.8%
Elkhart–Goshen, IN	−5.9%
Evansville, IN–KY	−6.8%
Fort Wayne, IN	−4.4%
Indianapolis–Carmel, IN	0.5%
Kokomo, IN	13.5%
Lafayette, IN	−1.4%
Michigan City–La Porte, IN	−12.1%
Muncie, IN	−15.7%
South Bend–Mishawaka, IN–MI	−7.5%
Terre Haute, IN	−12.2%
Lawrence, KS	−15.3%
Topeka, KS	−3.3%
Wichita, KS	−4.9%
Bowling Green, KY	−18.4%
Elizabethtown, KY	−12.7%
Lexington–Fayette, KY	−4.1%
Louisville–Jefferson County, KY–IN	−4.7%
Owensboro, KY	−14.3%
Alexandria, LA	−21.5%
Baton Rouge, LA	−6.5%
Houma–Bayou Cane–Thibodaux, LA	−11.8%
Lafayette, LA	−16.5%
Lake Charles, LA	−17.2%
Monroe, LA	−20.3%
New Orleans–Metairie–Kenner, LA	−6.2%
Shreveport–Bossier City, LA	−15.6%
Barnstable Town, MA	4.9%

© JIST Works

Metro Area	Percentage Figure for Adjusting National Averages	Metro Area	Percentage Figure for Adjusting National Averages
Leominster–Fitchburg–Gardner, MA	3.0%	Grand Forks, ND–MN	–13.2%
New Bedford, MA	–5.7%	Lincoln, NE	–4.3%
Pittsfield, MA	–0.5%	Omaha–Council Bluffs, NE–IA	–2.6%
Springfield, MA–CT	8.3%	Manchester, NH	10.1%
Worcester, MA–CT	11.6%	Portsmouth, NH–ME	15.0%
Cumberland, MD–WV	–17.6%	Rochester–Dover, NH–ME	–2.9%
Hagerstown–Martinsburg, MD–WV	–8.0%	Atlantic City, NJ	–8.4%
Salisbury, MD	–7.2%	Ocean City, NJ	–7.2%
Bangor, ME	–9.3%	Trenton–Ewing, NJ	32.8%
Lewiston–Auburn, ME	–9.8%	Vineland–Millville–Bridgeton, NJ	4.0%
Portland–South Portland–Biddeford, ME	0.5%	Albuquerque, NM	–7.8%
Ann Arbor, MI	24.9%	Farmington, NM	–12.4%
Battle Creek, MI	0.8%	Las Cruces, NM	–23.4%
Bay City, MI	–6.7%	Santa Fe, NM	–3.4%
Flint, MI	3.4%	Carson City, NV	7.3%
Grand Rapids–Wyoming, MI	2.8%	Reno–Sparks, NV	–0.6%
Holland–Grand Haven, MI	4.1%	Albany–Schenectady–Troy, NY	10.4%
Jackson, MI	3.0%	Binghamton, NY	–6.5%
Kalamazoo–Portage, MI	–2.7%	Buffalo–Niagara Falls, NY	–1.0%
Lansing–East Lansing, MI	13.4%	Elmira, NY	–6.3%
Monroe, MI	2.8%	Glens Falls, NY	–9.1%
Muskegon–Norton Shores, MI	–7.6%	Ithaca, NY	–2.3%
Niles–Benton Harbor, MI	–5.5%	Kingston, NY	–2.2%
Saginaw–Saginaw Township North, MI	1.1%	Poughkeepsie–Newburgh–Middletown, NY	7.9%
Duluth, MN–WI	–0.5%	Rochester, NY	2.5%
Rochester, MN	14.7%	Syracuse, NY	–0.8%
St. Cloud, MN	–5.5%	Utica–Rome, NY	–6.8%
Columbia, MO	–12.0%	Akron, OH	–0.8%
Jefferson City, MO	–9.4%	Canton–Massillon, OH	–10.9%
Joplin, MO	–24.1%	Dayton, OH	2.1%
Springfield, MO	–19.0%	Lima, OH	–6.6%
St. Joseph, MO–KS	–15.2%	Mansfield, OH	–9.5%
Gulfport–Biloxi, MS	–16.5%	Sandusky, OH	–8.5%
Hattiesburg, MS	–23.3%	Springfield, OH	–10.9%
Jackson, MS	–11.6%	Toledo, OH	–2.4%
Pascagoula, MS	–2.8%	Youngstown–Warren–Boardman, OH–PA	–10.5%
Billings, MT	–14.8%	Lawton, OK	–22.3%
Great Falls, MT	–19.7%	Oklahoma City, OK	–9.7%
Missoula, MT	–14.3%	Tulsa, OK	–9.7%
Asheville, NC	–12.5%	Bend, OR	–4.1%
Burlington, NC	–15.6%	Corvallis, OR	–1.9%
Charlotte–Gastonia–Concord, NC–SC	2.6%	Eugene–Springfield, OR	–3.8%
Durham, NC	14.4%	Medford, OR	–9.3%
Fayetteville, NC	–14.2%	Salem, OR	–4.3%
Goldsboro, NC	–17.9%	Allentown–Bethlehem–Easton, PA–NJ	–2.1%
Greensboro–High Point, NC	–7.0%	Altoona, PA	–19.4%
Greenville, NC	–15.5%	Erie, PA	–12.4%
Hickory–Lenior–Morgantown, NC	–13.1%	Harrisburg–Carlisle, PA	2.4%
Jacksonville, NC	–26.8%	Johnstown, PA	–20.2%
Raleigh–Cary, NC	1.6%	Lancaster, PA	–6.1%
Rocky Mount, NC	–16.5%	Lebanon, PA	–11.0%
Wilmington, NC	–14.4%	Reading, PA	–5.0%
Winston–Salem, NC	–5.5%	Scranton–Wilkes-Barre, PA	–12.4%
Bismarck, ND	–10.5%	State College, PA	–8.1%
Fargo, ND–MN	–8.8%	Williamsport, PA	–14.4%

(continued)

(continued)

Metro Area	Percentage Figure for Adjusting National Averages
York–Hanover, PA	–5.1%
Aguadilla–Isabela–San Sebastián, PR	–52.3%
Fajardo, PR	–47.9%
Guayama, PR	–42.3%
Mayaguez, PR	–51.4%
Ponce, PR	–49.1%
San German–Cabo Rojo, PR	–50.3%
San Juan–Caguas–Guaynabo, PR	–39.7%
Yauco, PR	–52.5%
Providence–Fall River–Warwick, RI–MA	4.1%
Anderson, SC	–16.4%
Charleston–North Charleston, SC	–8.7%
Columbia, SC	–7.5%
Florence, SC	–15.4%
Greenville, SC	–9.8%
Myrtle Beach–Conway–North Myrtle Beach, SC	–25.9%
Spartanburg, SC	–6.7%
Sumter, SC	–20.9%
Rapid City, SD	–19.1%
Sioux Falls, SD	–12.6%
Chattanooga, TN–GA	–11.0%
Clarksville, TN–KY	–16.8%
Cleveland, TN	–18.2%
Jackson, TN	–13.2%
Johnson City, TN	–18.8%
Kingsport–Bristol–Bristol, TN–VA	–18.2%
Knoxville, TN	–10.3%
Memphis, TN–MS–AR	–7.3%
Morristown, TN	–17.7%
Nashville–Davidson–Murfreesboro, TN	–2.7%
Abilene, TX	–26.5%
Amarillo, TX	–18.9%
Austin–Round Rock, TX	0.6%
Beaumont–Port Arthur, TX	–11.5%
Brownsville–Harlingen, TX	–38.2%
College Station–Bryan, TX	–12.9%
Corpus Christi, TX	–20.3%
El Paso, TX	–25.6%
Killeen–Temple–Fort Hood, TX	–17.8%
Laredo, TX	–31.8%
Longview, TX	–18.7%
Lubbock, TX	–21.6%
McAllen–Edinburg–Mission, TX	–35.4%
Midland, TX	–15.6%
Odessa, TX	–15.0%
San Angelo, TX	–24.8%
San Antonio, TX	–15.8%
Sherman–Denison, TX	–16.1%

Metro Area	Percentage Figure for Adjusting National Averages
Texarkana–Texarkana, TX–AR	–15.7%
Tyler, TX	–17.0%
Victoria, TX	–17.2%
Waco, TX	–18.5%
Wichita Falls, TX	–18.4%
Logan, UT–ID	–20.3%
Ogden–Clearfield, UT	–8.6%
Provo–Orem, UT	–14.0%
Salt Lake City, UT	–3.1%
St. George, UT	–14.4%
Blacksburg–Christiansburg–Radford, VA	–14.1%
Charlottesville, VA	2.3%
Danville, VA	–21.9%
Harrisonburg, VA	–14.5%
Lynchburg, VA	–14.4%
Richmond, VA	4.4%
Roanoke, VA	–10.4%
Virginia Beach–Norfolk–Newport News, VA–NC	–5.3%
Winchester, VA–WV	–7.7%
Burlington–South Burlington, VT	3.2%
Bellingham, WA	–0.9%
Bremerton–Silverdale, WA	14.8%
Kennewick–Richland–Pasco, WA	11.2%
Longview, WA	4.8%
Mount Vernon–Anacortes, WA	2.7%
Olympia, WA	15.5%
Spokane, WA	–2.1%
Wenatchee, WA	–6.9%
Yakima, WA	–6.5%
Appleton, WI	–2.5%
Eau Claire, WI	–8.5%
Fond du Lac, WI	–1.7%
Green Bay, WI	–0.3%
Janesville, WI	–4.3%
La Crosse, WI–MN	–7.6%
Madison, WI	8.4%
Milwaukee–Waukesha–West Allis, WI	5.9%
Oshkosh–Neenah, WI	6.3%
Racine, WI	–3.9%
Sheboygan, WI	2.7%
Wausau, WI	–1.2%
Charleston, WV	–8.7%
Huntington–Ashland, WV–KY–OH	–19.0%
Morgantown, WV	–20.3%
Parkersburg–Marietta–Vienna, WV–OH	–18.4%
Weirton–Steubenville, WV–OH	–19.6%
Wheeling, WV–OH	–21.1%
Casper, WY	–5.4%
Cheyenne, WY	–10.8%

Metropolitan Areas Used in This Book

The table in Part III that lists median wages for 30 metropolitan areas identifies each area by the name of the principal city. However, most of these metropolitan areas include an additional city or cities, sometimes in a bordering state. You may not live within the principal city or even in the same state, yet you may still be within the metropolitan area.

This appendix can help you determine whether or not you live in one of the 30 metro areas surrounding the principal cities. It lists the official names that the government uses for these areas.

Note that if you live in a metro area that is *not* one of these 30, you can estimate your expected wage by using the percentage figure listed in Appendix B.

Metro Area Name in Book	Official Metro Area Name
AZ: Phoenix	Phoenix-Mesa-Scottsdale, AZ
CA: Los Angeles	Los Angeles-Long Beach-Santa Ana, CA
CA: Riverside	Riverside-San Bernardino-Ontario, CA
CA: Sacramento	Sacramento-Arden-Arcade-Roseville, CA
CA: San Diego	San Diego-Carlsbad-San Marcos, CA
CA: San Francisco	San Francisco-Oakland-Fremont, CA
CO: Denver	Denver-Aurora, CO
DC: Washington	Washington-Arlington-Alexandria, DC-VA-MD-WV
FL: Miami	Miami-Fort Lauderdale-Miami Beach, FL
FL: Orlando	Orlando-Kissimmee, FL
FL: Tampa	Tampa-St. Petersburg-Clearwater, FL
GA: Atlanta	Atlanta-Sandy Springs-Marietta, GA
IL: Chicago	Chicago-Naperville-Joliet, IL-IN-WI
MA: Boston	Boston-Cambridge-Quincy, MA-NH
MD: Baltimore	Baltimore-Towson, MD

Metro Area Name in Book	Official Metro Area Name
MI: Detroit	Detroit-Warren-Livonia, MI
MN: Minneapolis	Minneapolis-St. Paul-Bloomington, MN-WI
MO: Kansas City	Kansas City, MO-KS
MO: St. Louis	St. Louis, MO-IL
NV: Las Vegas	Las Vegas-Paradise, NV
NY: New York	New York-Northern New Jersey-Long Island, NY-NJ-PA
OH: Cincinnati	Cincinnati-Middletown, OH-KY-IN
OH: Cleveland	Cleveland-Elyria-Mentor, OH
OH: Columbus	Columbus, OH
OR: Portland	Portland-Vancouver-Beaverton, OR-WA
PA: Philadelphia	Philadelphia-Camden-Wilmington, PA-NJ-DE-MD
PA: Pittsburgh	Pittsburgh, PA
TX: Dallas	Dallas-Fort Worth-Arlington, TX
TX: Houston	Houston-Sugar Land-Baytown, TX
WA: Seattle	Seattle-Tacoma-Bellevue, WA

Index

A

E

G

V

W

X–Z